October 29 - November 2, 2012
Nara, Japan

Association for
Computing Machinery

Advancing Computing as a Science & Profession

MM'12 Vol. 1 of 2

The Proceedings of the 20th ACM International Conference on Multimedia

Co-located with:
ACM Multimedia 2012

Sponsored by:
ACM SIGMM

Association for
Computing Machinery

Advancing Computing as a Science & Profession

The Association for Computing Machinery
2 Penn Plaza, Suite 701
New York, New York 10121-0701

ISBN: 978-1-4503-1089-5 (Digital)

ISBN: 978-1-4503-2008-5 (Print)

Additional copies may be ordered prepaid from:

ACM Order Department
PO Box 30777
New York, NY 10087-0777, USA

Phone: 1-800-342-6626 (USA and Canada)
+1-212-626-0500 (Global)
Fax: +1-212-944-1318
E-mail: acmhelp@acm.org
Hours of Operation: 8:30 am – 4:30 pm ET

ACM Order Number: 433127

Printed in the USA

Message from the General Chairs

We are delighted to welcome you to 20th ACM International Conference on Multimedia, ACM Multimedia 2012, which is held from October 29th to November 2nd, 2012 in Nara, Japan. Welcome to Japan's ancient capital, the cradle of Japanese culture and final destination of the Silk Road.

Like the Silk Road of ancient times, multimedia today provides a medium allowing the diverse exchange of ideas across many fields including signal processing, information retrieval, machine learning, content analysis, networking, applications, human-centered systems, art and education and many more. Because of this confluence, multimedia has become one of the fastest growing and most interesting areas in Computer Science. It is again in 2012 that Nara, Japan is a final destination, this time for sharing ideas in multimedia.

ACM Multimedia is the premier conference and worldwide event bringing together multimedia experts and practitioners across academia and industry. The central feature of the conference, which continues this year as in every year since its inception, is the outstanding Technical Program. This year's conference features both oral and poster presentations covering all aspects of the multimedia field chosen through a highly selective review process. Notably, this year's conference includes special Technical Program activities recognizing the 20th anniversary of ACM Multimedia.

In addition to the Technical Program, this year's conference features a diverse range of activities including Panels, Demonstrations and Tutorials. Additionally, a wide array of Workshops brings focus on new topics for investigation. The conference features also special sessions on Brave New Ideas, a Grand Challenge contest and Open Source Software Competition and includes a Doctoral Symposium for mentoring graduate students. Finally, the conference provides a rich Multimedia Art Exhibition to stimulate artists and researchers alike to meet and discover the frontiers of multimedia artistic communication!

The 20th Anniversary Keynote Talk and 20th Anniversary Panel

This year celebrates the 20th Anniversary of ACM Multimedia, which was first initiated by the ACM SIGMM in 1993. To mark this auspicious occasion, the conference features a 20th Anniversary Keynote Talk and a 20th Anniversary Panel. These two events reflect on major milestones and achievements in multimedia as well as discuss promising ideas and directions for the future.

Innovations for this Year's Conference:

In attempt to continuously improve ACM Multimedia and ensure its vibrant role for the multimedia community, we have made a number of enhancements for this year's conference:

- The Technical Program Committee defined eleven Technical Areas for major focus for this year's conference, including introducing new Technical Areas for Multimedia Activity and Event Understanding and Social Media to reflect their growing interest and promise.
- Technical Short Papers are presented as plenary posters to make them more visible at this year's conference, which reflects the growing quality of short papers.
- Plenary sessions bring singular focus to conference activities in the morning sessions each day, and afternoon sessions are held in parallel to allow pursuit of more specialized interests at the conference.
- Workshops and Tutorials are held on separate days from the main conference in order to reduce conflict with the regular Technical Program.

- Since Workshops are important seeds for the next generation of multimedia, two complementary workshop registrations are provided for invited talks of each workshop to encourage participation of notable speakers.
- The Multimedia Art Exhibition features both invited and selected artists and is open for two weeks in the satellite venue close to the main conference with good public access, which allows stimulation broadly to visitors to Nara.
- Following the last year's precedent, Tutorials are made free for all participants.
- Recognizing that students are the lifeblood of our next generation of multimedia thinkers, this year's Student Travel Grant is greatly expanded.

We hope these innovations make for a special conference this year.

We greatly acknowledge those who have contributed to the success of ACM Multimedia 2012. We thank the many paper authors and proposal contributors for the various technical and program components. We thank the large number of volunteers, including the Organizing Committee members and Technical Program Committee members who worked very hard to create this year's outstanding conference. Every aspect of the conference was also aided by local committee members, mainly from the Kansai area in Japan, to whom we are very grateful. We thank also ACM staff and Sheridan Printing Company for their constant support.

Finally, we thank our many supporters from Japan and around the world who generously supported ACM Multimedia 2012. They include FXPAL, Google, HUAWEI, IBM Research, NTT DOCOMO, Technicolor, DeNA, HP, KDDI R&D Labs, Microsoft Research, Mitsubishi Electric, OMRON, Panasonic, SHARP, YAHOO! LABS, Facebook, foo.log, Fuji Xerox, GREE, IBM Japan, NETCOMPASS, Nikon, NTT DATA, TOSHIBA, YAHOO! JAPAN, ARUBA and CTC. Other generous support was kindly provided by JSPS, KDDI Foundation, Nara Visitors Bureau, Springer, Telecommunication Advancement Foundation.

Enjoy ACM Multimedia 2012!

ACM Multimedia 2012 General Chairs

Kiyoharu Aizawa
The University of Tokyo

Noboru Babaguchi
Osaka Univeristy

John R. Smith
IBM T. J. Watson Research Center

Message from the Technical Program Chairs

We are very pleased to be able to present an exciting technical program at ACM Multimedia 2012 in Nara, Japan. The outcome of the work of the Technical Program Committee (TPC) is of course entirely depending on the quantity and quality of submitted papers, which was excellent in 2012. Following the guidelines of the ACM Multimedia Review Committee, the conference is structured into 11 Areas, with a two-tier TPC, a double-blind review process, and a target acceptance rate of 20% for long papers and 30% for short papers.

Based on the experience from last year's ACM Multimedia and the responses to our "Call for Areas" that we issued to the community, we selected the following Areas for ACM Multimedia 2012: (1) Media Content Analysis and Processing, (2) Multimedia Activity and Event Understanding, (3) Multimedia Search and Retrieval, (4) Mobile and Location-Based Media, (5) Social Media, (6) Multimedia Systems and Middleware, (7) Media Transport and Sharing, (8) Multimedia Security and Forensics, (9) Multimedia Authoring, Production and Consumption, (10) Multimedia Interaction and Applications, (11) Multimedia Art, Entertainment and Culture.

The two-tier TPC was staffed in a two stage process: first we invited for each area in between two to four Area Chairs, and together with the Area Chairs we invited for the 11 Areas the TPC members. The number of Area Chairs and TPC members per Area was related to the estimated numbers of submissions to the Areas. The response to the Call for Papers in form of long and short papers was overwhelming. Out of all received papers, 331 and 407 papers went through review process for full and short paper track, respectively. The distribution to the different Areas was as expected unbalanced, ranging from the most popular Areas 1 and 10 with 78 and 54 long paper submissions, to the least popular Areas 8 and 9 with 11 and 14 long paper submissions respectively. The following figure gives a full overview on the number of submission and acceptance rate per Area and per paper type.

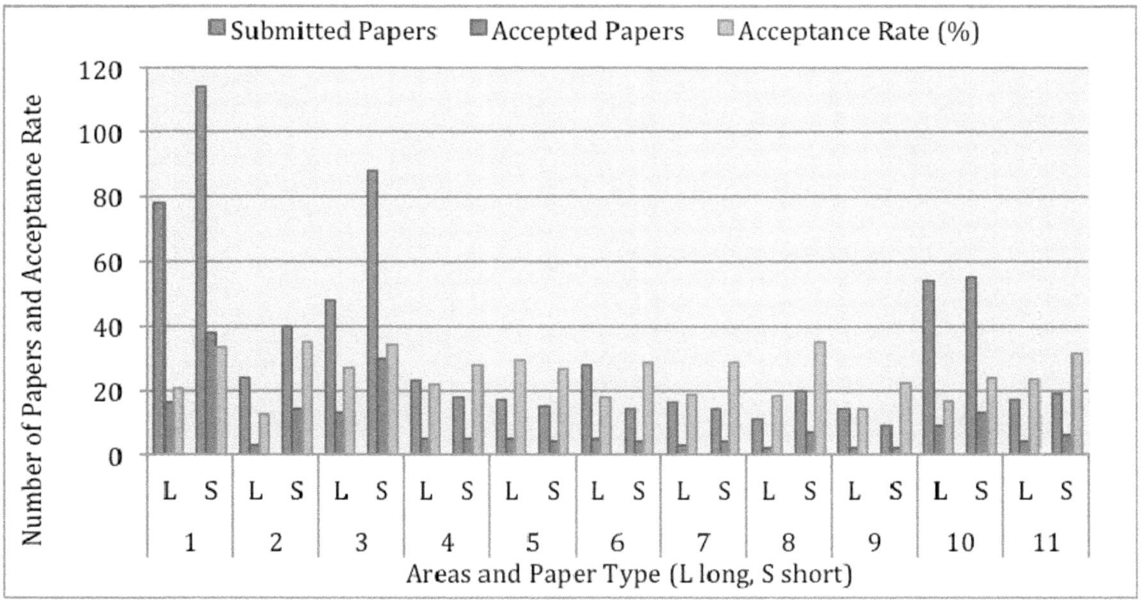

Each submission was reviewed by at least three TPC members with very few exceptions. The authors of long papers received the reviews and wrote a rebuttal. The reviewers had an on-line discussion of the submissions, their reviews, and the rebuttal comments from the authors. Based on this on-line process, the

Area Chairs wrote a meta-review for each paper before the physical TPC meeting at IBM T. J. Watson Research Center Hawthorn on June 16 and 17.

On the first day of the TPC meeting, the Area Chairs, Technical Program Chairs, and General Chairs worked in breakout sessions and plenary sessions to select the papers to be accepted – except conflict-of-interest papers that were co-authored by Area Chairs. To seek for the fairness, no submissions were made by the General Chairs and Technical Program Chairs. For the selection process, the papers themselves, (meta-) reviews, on-line discussions and authors' rebuttal comments were considered. On the second day, the General Chairs and the TP Chairs finalized the technical program. One important part of this task was discussions and decisions for conflict-of-interest papers. The set of accepted papers results in an overall acceptance rate for long papers of 20.2% and for short papers of 31.2%. Finally, the set of 67 accepted long papers were structured into 17 oral sessions, including the Best Paper session. The Best Paper session comprises four papers from four different areas which compete for the Best Paper Award of ACM Multimedia 2012. The quality of these papers and their diversity promises that this session will be one of the highlights at the conference.

All accepted long papers were shepherded by Area Chairs or TPC members to achieve the highest possible quality for the camera-ready version of the papers. As such, we are now able to present this high quality Technical Program and want to thank all authors, TPC members, and Area Chairs for their dedication and hard work.

We hope to see you in Nara!

Shin'ichi Satoh
National Institute of Informatics, Japan

Thomas Plagemann
University of Oslo, Norway

Xian-Sheng Hua
Microsoft, USA

Rong Yan
Facebook, USA

Message from the ACM SIGMM Chair

ACM Multimedia 2012 is a continuation of an outstanding tradition to present best innovative work in the area of multimedia systems, content, applications, and interfaces, taking a very broad view of what is happening in the multimedia area. This year's ACM Multimedia 2012 is held in Nara, Japan, October 29–November 2, and it represents a very special occasion, since it marks the 20th anniversary of the ACM International Conference Multimedia (ACM Multimedia) venue. The first ACM Multimedia conference was presented in Anaheim, California, USA, August 1–6, 1993. Since then the ACM Special Interest Group in Multimedia (SIGMM) has been a leader in the international multimedia community, annually sponsoring the worldwide premier event in the field. The ACM Multimedia Conference consistently presents the most original, intriguing and important work in its discipline.

During the ACM Multimedia 2012 conference, we celebrate the 20th anniversary of the conference with an exciting program, but especially in this 'Message from the SIGMM chair' I want to stress two important events that are specifically designed to look back, reflect and consider new multimedia opportunities:

- The Panel "**Coulda, Woulda, Shoulda: 20 Years of Multimedia Opportunities**" is moderated by Klara Nahrstedt and Malcolm Slaney, and hosts four distinguished panelists, Lawrence Rowe, Ramesh Jain, Ralf Steinmetz, and Dick Bulterman. These pioneers discuss the exciting opportunities and accomplishments they have witnessed within the multimedia community during their 20 years in the field. They also take note of opportunities missed and express their enthusiasm about those still to come (http://www.acmmm12.org/panel-sessions/).
- The Special Issue on the "**20th Anniversary of ACM SIGMM Multimedia**" appears in the leading multimedia journal, the ACM Transactions on Multimedia Computing, Communications and Applications (TOMMCAP) in 2013, where historical views of multimedia technologies are to be presented together with the impact of past inventions on current and future multimedia technologies. The special issue is led by the Guest Editors, Klara Nahrstedt, Rainer Lienhart and Malcolm Slaney, with extensive support from the TOMCCAP Editor-in-Chief Ralf Steinmetz (http://tomccap.acm.org/TOMCCAP-CFP-2012-v2.pdf).

I wish to thank many members of the SIGMM community for the interesting and innovative ideas to celebrate the ACM Multimedia 20th anniversary, but special thanks goes to Malcolm Slaney, Kiyo Aizawa, Nobory Babaguchi, John Smith, Rainer Lienhart, Mohan Kankanhalli, Ramesh Jain, Ralf Steinmetz, Lawrence Rowe, Dick Bulterman, and our ACM SIGMM coordinator, Fran Spinola.

Klara Nahrstedt
ACM SIGMM Chair

Table of Contents

Full Paper Session 1: Content-Based Image Retrieval

Session Chair: Benoit Huet *(EURECOM)*

Full Paper Session 2: Audio and Music

Session Chair: Gerald Friedland *(ICSI and University of California, Berkeley)*

Full Paper Session 3: Video Applications

Session Chair: Alexander G. Hauptmann *(Carnegie Mellon University)*

Full Paper Session 4: Large Scale Search

Session Chair: Chong-Wah Ngo *(City University of Hong Kong)*

Full Paper Session 5: Person and Face Analysis

Session Chair: Nicu Sebe *(University of Trento)*

Full Paper Session 6: Video Distribution

Session Chair: Nalini Venkatasubrahanian *(University of California, Irvine)*

Full Paper Session 7: Visual Search

Session Chair: Qi Tian *(University of Texas at San Antonio)*

Full Paper Session 8: Human-centric Media

Session Chair: Frank Nack *(University of Amsterdam)*

Full Paper Session 10: Haptics

Session Chair: Yuichi Nakamura *(Kyoto University)*

Full Paper Session 11: Event Recognition

Session Chair: Ansgar Scherp *(University of Koblenz-Landau)*

Full Paper Session 12: Semantic Tagging

Session Chair: Lexing Xie *(Australian National University)*

Full Paper Session 13: Image Analysis

Session Chair: Shuicheng Yan *(National University of Singapore)*

Full Paper Session 14: Mobile Systems

Session Chair: Tao Mei *(Microsoft Research Asia)*

Poster Session 2

Session Chair: Liangliang Cao *(IBM T. J. Watson Research Center)*

Poster Session 3

Session Chair: Sethuraman Panchanathan *(Arizona State University)*

Brave New Ideas Program

Session Chairs: Alejandro Jaimes *(Yahoo! Research)* and Tat-seng Chua *(National University of Singapore)*

Technical Demo Session 1

Session Chair: Hirokazu Kato *(NAIST)*

Technical Demo Session 2

Session Chair: Qi Tian *(University of Texas at San Antonio)*

Technical Demo Session 3

Session Chair: Hirokazu Kato *(NAIST)*

Multimedia Grand Challenge

Session Chairs: Marcel Worring *(University of Amsterdam)* and Yushi Jing *(Google Research)*

Doctoral Symposium Session 1: Best Paper Session

Session Chairs: Chong-Wah Ngo *(City University of Hong Kong)* and Keiji Yanai *(University of Electro-Communication)*

Doctoral Symposium 2: Oral Paper Session

Session Chairs: Chong-Wah Ngo *(City University of Hong Kong)* and Keiji Yanai *(University of Electro-Communication)*

Doctoral Symposium 3: Poster Session

Session Chairs: Chong-Wah Ngo *(City University of Hong Kong)* and Keiji Yanai *(University of Electro-Communication)*

Video Program

Multimedia Art Exhibition

Workshops

Session Chairs: Jiebo Luo *(University of Rochester)* and Svetha Venkatesh *(Deakin University)*

Tutorials

Session Chairs: Susanne Boll *(University of Oldenburg)* and Changsheng Xu *(Chinese Academy of Sciences)*

MM 2012 Conference Organization

General Chairs: Noboru Babaguchi (Osaka University, Japan)
Kiyoharu Aizawa (The University of Tokyo, Japan)
John Smith (IBM, USA)

Technical Program Chairs: Shin'ichi Satoh (National Institute of Informatics, Japan)
Thomas Plagemann (University of Oslo, Norway)
Xian-Sheng Hua (Microsoft, USA)
Rong Yan (Facebook, USA)

Local Arrangements Chairs: Tomio Echigo (Osaka Electro-Communication University, Japan)
Naoko Nitta (Osaka University, Japan)

Twentieth Anniversary Liaison: Ramesh Jain (University of California at Irvine, USA)
Malcolm Slaney (Yahoo! Research, USA)

Panels Chairs: Yong Rui (Microsoft Research, China)
Shih-Fu Chang (Columbia University, USA)

Brave New Ideas Program Chairs: Alejandro Jaimes (Yahoo! Research, Spain)
Tat-Seng Chua (National University of Singapore, Singapore)

Multimedia Grand Challenge Chairs: Marcel Worring (University of Amsterdam, The Netherlands)
Yushi Jing (Google Research, USA)
Go Irie (Nippon Telegraph & Telephone Corporation, Japan)

Multimedia Art Program Chairs: Tomoe Moriyama (Tokyo Museum of Contemporary Art, Japan)
Hideyuki Ando (Osaka University, Japan)
Aisling Kelliher (Arizona State University, USA)
David A. Shamma (Yahoo! Research, USA)

Technical Demonstration Chairs: Qi Tian (University of Texas at San Antonio, USA)
Hirokazu Kato (Nara Institute of Science & Technology, Japan)

Open Source Software Competition Chairs: Daniel Gatica Perez (IDIAP Research Institute, Switzerland)
Masanori Sano (Japan Broadcasting Corporation, Japan)

Video Program Chairs: Tao Mei (Microsoft Research Asia, China)
Koichi Shinoda (Tokyo Institute of Technology, Japan)

Doctoral Symposium Chairs: Chong-Wah Ngo (City University of Hong Kong, Hong Kong)
Keiji Yanai (The University of Electro-Communications, Japan)

Tutorials Chairs: Susanne Boll (University of Oldenburg, Germany)
Changsheng Xu (Chinese Academy of Sciences, China)

Workshop Chairs: Jiebo Luo (University of Rochester, USA)
Svetha Venkatesh (Deakin University, Australia)

Industrial Liaison: Minoru Etoh (NTT Docomo, Japan)
Yoichiro Miyake (Square Enix, Japan)

Web & Social Media Chairs: Ichiro Ide (Nagoya University, Japan)
Ikki Ohmukai (National Institute of Informatics, Japan)
Duy-Dinh Le (National Institute of Informatics, Japan)
Takatsugu Hirayama (Nagoya University, Japan)

Publicity Chairs: K. Selcuk Candan (Arizona State University, USA)
Michael S. Lew (Leiden University, The Netherlands)
Mark Liao (Academia Sinica, Taiwan)
Yong Man Ro (Korea Advanced Institute of Science & Technology, Korea)

Finance Chair: Shigeyuki Sakazawa (KDDI R&D Labs, Japan)

History Preservation Chairs: Alberto del Bimbo (Univ. of Firenze, Italy)
Sethuraman Panchanathan (Arizona State University, USA)

Publication Chairs: Hiroshi Mo (National Institute of Informatics, Japan)
Chamin Morikawa (The University of Tokyo, Japan)

SIGMM Chair: Klara Nahrstedt (University of Illinois at Urbana-Champaign, USA)

SIGMM Director of Conferences: Mohan S. Kankanhalli (National University of Singapore, Singapore)

Local Arrangements Committee: Hitoshi Habe (Kinki University, Japan)
Sei Ikeda (Osaka University, Japan)
Yoshimichi Ito (Osaka University, Japan)
Norihiko Kawai (Nara Institute of Science & Technology, Japan)
Kazuaki Kondo (Kyoto University, Japan)
Yuta Nakashima (Nara Institute of Science & Technology, Japan)
Atsushi Nakazawa (Osaka University, Japan)
Takafumi Taketomi (Nara Institute of Science & Technology, Japan)
Yuki Uranishi (Osaka University, Japan)

MM 2012 Technical Program Area Chairs

Liangliang Cao *(IBM, USA)*
Scott Craver *(SUNY Binghamton, USA)*
Gerald Friedland *(University of California at Berkeley, USA)*
Alex Hauptmann *(Carnegie Mellon University, USA)*
Steven Hoi *(Nanyang Technological University, Singapore)*
Winston Hsu *(National Taiwan University, Taiwan)*
Gang Hua *(Steven's Institute of Technology, USA)*
Benoit Huet *(Eurecom, France)*
Hirokazu Kato *(Nara Institute of Science and Technology, Japan)*
Yiannis Kompatsiaris *(Informatics and Telematics Institute (CERTH-ITI), Greece)*
Baochun Li *(University of Toronto, Canada)*
Jiebo Luo *(University of Rochester, USA)*
Tao Mei *(Microsoft Research Asia, China)*
Frank Nack *(University of Amsterdam, The Netherlands)*
Yuichi Nakamura *(Kyoto University, Japan)*
Chong-Wah Ngo *(City University of Hong Kong, Hong Kong)*
Ansgar Scherp *(University of Koblenz-Landau, Germany)*
Nicu Sebe *(University of Trento, Italy)*
Doree Seligmann *(Avaya, USA)*
David Shamma *(Yahoo! Research, USA)*
Heng T Shen *(The University of Queensland, Australia)*
Cees Snoek *(University of Amsterdam, USA)*
Qi Tian *(University of Texas at San Antonio, USA)*
Nalini Venkatasubrahanian *(University of California at Irvine, USA)*
Zhen Wen *(IBM T. J. Watson Research Center, USA)*
Marcel Worring *(Universiteit van Amsterdam, The Netherlands)*
Lexing Xie *(The Australian National University, Australia)*
Shuicheng Yan *(National University of Singapore, Singapore)*
Wenjun Zeng *(University of Missouri, USA)*
Lei Zhang *(Microsoft Research Asia, China)*

MM 2012 Technical Program Committee

Brett Adams *(Curtin University, Australia)*
John Adcock *(FXPAL, USA)*
Kevin Almeroth *(University of California, Santa Barbara, USA)*
Xavier Anguera *(Telefonica Research, Spain)*
Pradeep K Atrey *(University of Winnipeg, Canada)*
Yannis Avrithis *(National Technical University of Athens, Greece)*
Ivan V Bajic *(Simon Fraser University, USA)*
Lamberto Ballan *(University of Florence, Italy)*
Hichem Bannour *(Ecole Centrale Paris, France)*
Frank Bentley *(Motorola, USA)*
Marco Bertini *(University of Florence, Italy)*
Mark Billinghurst *(University of Canterbury, New Zealand)*
Susanne Boll *(University of Oldenburg, Germany)*
Anders Bouwer *(Universiteit van Amsterdam, Netherlands)*
John Buford *(Avaya Labs Research, USA)*
Dick Bulterman *(CWI, The Netherlands)*
Daragh Byrne *(ASU, USA)*
Yang Cai *(Carnegie Mellon University, USA)*
K. Selcuk Candan *(Arizona State University, USA)*
Liangliang Cao *(IBM Research, USA)*
Marc O Cavazza *(Teesside University, USA)*
Pablo Cesar *(CWI, The Netherlands)*
Antoni Chan *(City University of Hong Kong, Hong Kong)*
Surendar Chandra *(FXPAL, USA)*
Krishna Chandramouli *(Vellore Institute of Technology University, India)*
Mainak Chatterjee *(University of Central Florida, USA)*
Lei Chen *(Hong Kong University of Science and Technology, Hong Kong)*
Longbin Chen *(Twitter, USA)*
Qiang Chen *(National University of Singapore, Singapore)*
Songqing Chen *(George Mason University, USA)*
Jian Cheng *(Chinese Academy of Sciences, China)*
Tim Cheng *(University of California, Santa Barbara, USA)*
Wen-Huang Cheng *(Academia Sinica, Taiwan)*
Wei-Ta Chu *(National Chung Cheng University, China)*
Elizabeth F Churchill *(Yahoo! Research, USA)*
Noel C Codella *(IBM, USA)*
Filipe Coelho *(INESC TEC, Portugal)*
Matthew Cooper *(FXPAL, USA)*
Nuno Correia *(Universidade Nova de Lisboa, Portugal)*
Peng Cui *(Tsinghua University, China)*
Ivan Damnjanovic *(Queen Mary, University of London, United Kingdom)*
Ritendra Datta *(Google, USA)*
Fernando de la Torre *(Carnegie Mellon University, USA)*
Alberto Del Bimbo *(University of Florence, Italy)*
Lei Ding *(PayPal, USA)*
Jana Dittmann *(University Magdeburg, USA)*
Gwenaël Doërr *(Technicolor, USA)*
Ling-Yu Duan *(Peking University, China)*
Carlos Duarte *(Universidade de Lisboa, Portugal)*
Henry B Duh *(National University of Singapore, Singapore)*
Touradj Ebrahimi *(EPFL, Switzerland)*
Venkatesan Ekambaram *(University of California, Berkeley, USA)*
Sabu Emmanuel *(Nanyang Technological University, Singapore)*
Gwenn Englebienne *(Universiteit van Amsterdam, The Netherlands)*
Minoru Etoh *(NTT Docomo, Japan)*
Jianping Fan *(University of North Carolina at Charlotte, USA)*
Jiashi Feng *(National University of Singapore, Singapore)*
Wu-Chi Feng *(Portland State University, USA)*
Gerald Friedland *(ICSI and UC Berkeley, USA)*
Yun Fu *(SUNY at Buffalo, USA)*
Andrew Gallagher *(Cornell University, USA)*
Zeno Geradts *(Netherlands Forensics Institute, Netherlands)*
Andreas Girgensohn *(FXPAL, USA)*
Fausto Giunchiglia *(University of Trento, Italy)*
Vera Goebel *(University of Oslo, Norway)*
Marcin Grzegorzek *(University of Siegen, Germany)*
Radek Grzeszczuk *(Nokia Research Center, Finland)*

Yang Guo *(Bell Labs, USA)*
Amarnath Gupta *(University of California, San Diego, USA)*
Hakim Hacid *(Alcatel-Lucent Bell Labs, USA)*
Paal Halvorsen *(University of Oslo, Norway)*
Mei Han *(Google Research, USA)*
Allan Hanbury *(Vienna University of Technology, Austria)*
Alan Hanjalic *(Delft University of Technology, The Netherlands)*
Mohamed Hefeeda *(Qatar Computing Research Institute, Qatar)*
Nils Henze *(OFFIS, Germany)*
Keiichiro Hoashi *(KDDI Labs, Japan)*
Richang Hong *(Hefei University of Technology, China)*
Cheng-Hsin Hsu *(National Tsing Hua University, Taiwan)*
Winston Hsu *(National Taiwan University, Taiwan)*
Yu-Feng J Hsu *(Industrial Technology Research Institute, Taiwan)*
Cheng Huang *(Microsoft Research Redmond, USA)*
Jiwu Huang *(Sun Yat-Sen University, China)*
Zi Huang *(University of Queensland, Australia)*
Wolfgang Hürst *(Utrecht University, Netherlands)*
Ichiro Ide *(Nagoya University, Japan)*
Rosa Iglesias *(Ikerlan Technology Research Center, Spain)*
Masataka Imura *(Osaka University, Japan)*
Bogdan Ionescu *(University Politehnica of Bucharest, Romania)*
Michal Jacovi *(IBM Research, USA)*
Christian Jacquemin *(LIMSI-CNRS and University Paris-Sud, France)*
Alejandro Jaimes *(Yahoo! Research, Spain)*
Rongrong Ji *(Columbia University, USA)*
Shuqiang Jiang *(Chinese Academy of Sciences, China)*
Wei Jiang *(Kodak Research, USA)*
Yu-Gang Jiang *(Fudan University, China)*
Ajita John *(Avaya Labs, USA)*
Dhiraj Joshi *(Eastman Kodak Company, USA)*
Yasuaki Kakehi *(Keio University, Japan)*
Ton Kalker *(DTS Inc., USA)*
Vana Kalogeraki *(Athens University of Economics and Business, Greece)*
Jayashree Kalpathy-Cramer *(Oregon Health and Science University, USA)*
Ichiroh Kanaya *(Osaka University, Japan)*
Mohan Kankanhalli *(National University of Singapore, Singapore)*
Qifa Ke *(Microsoft Research, China)*
Aisling Kelliher *(Arizona State University, USA)*
Lyndon Kennedy *(Yahoo! Research, USA)*
Andruid Kerne *(Texas A&M University, USA)*
Kyungbaek Kim *(Chonnam National University, Korea)*
Irwin King *(Chinese University of Hong Kong, Hong Kong)*
Matthias Kirchner *(ICSI Berkeley, USA)*
Yoshifumi Kitamura *(Tohoku University, Japan)*
Peter Knees *(Johannes Kepler University Linz, Austria)*
Lars Knipping *(Berlin Institute of Technology, Germany)*
Hiroki Kobayashi *(University of Tokyo, Japan)*
Kazuaki Kondo *(Kyoto University, Japan)*
Stephan Kopf *(University of Mannheim, Germany)*
Karen Johanne Kortbek *(Alexandra Institute, Denmark)*
Jay C.-C. Kuo *(University of Southern California, USA)*
Takeshi Kurata *(National Institute of Advanced Industrial Science and Technology, Japan)*
Gregorij Kurillo *(University of California, Berkeley, USA)*
Rodrigo Laiola Guimarães *(CWI, Netherlands)*
Martha Larson *(Delft University of Technology, The Netherlands)*
Kyoungwoo Lee *(Yonsei University, Korea)*
Chengqing Li *(Xiangtan University, China)*
Hongbing Li *(Huawei Technologies, China)*
Hong-Yuan M Liao *(Academia Sinica, Taiwan)*
Rainer Lienhart *(Augsburg University, Germany)*
Joo Hwee Lim *(Institute for Infocomm Research, Singapore)*
Chia-Wen Lin *(National Tsing Hua University, Taiwan)*
Wei-Hao Lin *(Carnegie Mellon University, USA)*
Christopher Lindinger *(Ars Electronica Futurelab, Austria)*
Dong Liu *(Columbia University, USA)*
Jiangchuan Liu *(Simon Fraser University, USA)*
Kang Liu *(University of Missouri, USA)*

Xiaobai Liu *(University of California, Los Angeles, USA)*
Xueliang Liu *(EUERCOM, France)*
Zhu Liu *(AT&T Labs Research, USA)*
Zicheng Liu *(Microsoft Research Asia, China)*
Alex Loui *(Kodak Research, USA)*
Yijuan Lu *(Texas State University, USA)*
Artur Lugmayr *(University of Tampere, Finland)*
R. Manmatha *(University of Massachusetts, Amherst, USA)*
Andreas Mauthe *(Lancaster University, United Kingdom)*
Kevin McGee *(National University of Singapore, Singapore)*
Sharad Mehrotra *(University of California, Irvine, USA)*
Gregoris Mentzas *(National Technical University of Athens, Greece)*
Bernard Merialdo *(EURECOM, France)*
Vasileios Mezaris *(CERTH-ITI, Greece)*
Jun Miyazaki *(Nara Institute of Science and Technology, Japan)*
Shivajit Mohapatra *(Motorola Mobility, USA)*
Ann Morrison *(Aalborg University, USA)*
Phivos Mylonas *(National Technical University of Athens, Greece)*
Frank Nack *(Universiteit van Amsterdam, The Netherlands)*
Klara Nahrstedt *(University of Illinois at Urbana-Champaign, USA)*
Vidhya Navalpakkam *(Google, USA)*
Tian-Tsong Ng *(Institute for Infocomm Research, Singapore)*
Bingbing Ni *(ADSC, Singapore)*
Spiros Nikolopoulos *(CERTH-ITI, Greece)*
Noel O'Connor *(Dublin City University, Ireland)*
Timo Ojala *(University of Oulu, Finland)*
Nuria Oliver *(Telefonica Research, Spain)*
Wei Tsang Ooi *(National University of Singapore, Singapore)*
Symeon Papadopoulos *(CERTH-ITI, Greece)*
Minwoo Park *(Eastman Kodak Company, USA)*
Philippe Pasquier *(Simon Fraser University, USA)*
Yuxin Peng *(Peking University, China)*
Georgios Petkos *(CERTH-ITI, Greece)*
Chen Qiang *(National University of Singapore, Singapore)*
Cecile Roisin *(Grenoble University-Inria, France)*
Daisuke Sakamoto *(University of Tokyo, Japan)*
Mike Sammon *(Avaya Labs, USA)*
Jurgen Scheible *(Stuttgart Media University, Germany)*
Ansgar Scherp *(University of Koblenz-Landau, Germany)*
Karsten Schwan *(Georgia Institute of Technology, USA)*
Vidya Setlur *(Nokia Research Center, Finland)*
Behzad Shahraray *(AT&T Labs Research, USA)*
Ling Shao *(The University of Sheffield, United Kingdom)*
Jialie Shen *(Singapore Management University, Singapore)*
Renata Sheppard *(Independent Artist and Researcher, USA)*
Shantanu Singh *(Broad Institute of MIT and Harvard, USA)*
Alan Smeaton *(Dublin City University, Ireland)*
Eckehard Steinbach *(Technische Universitaet Muenchen, Germany)*
Julian Stöttinger *(University of Trento, Italy)*
Ramanathan Subramanian *(University of Trento, Italy)*
Maki Sugimoto *(Keio University, Japan)*
Masanori Sugimoto *(University of Tokyo, Japan)*
Yasuyuki Sumi *(Future University-Hakodate, Japan)*
Aixin Sun *(Nanyang Technological University, Singapore)*
Qibin Sun *(Cisco Systems, USA)*
Hari Sundaram *(Arizona State University, USA)*
Hung-Khoon Tan *(University Tunku Abdul Rahman, Malaysia)*
Jinhui Tang *(Nanjing University of Science and Technology, China)*
Dacheng Tao *(University of Technology Sydney, Australia)*
Murat A Tekalp *(Koc University, Turkey)*
George K Thiruvathukal *(Loyola University Chicago, USA)*
Bruce Thomas *(University of South Australia, Australia)*
Xinmei Tian *(University of Science and Technology of China, China)*

Christian Timmerer *(Alpen-Adria-Universität Klagenfurt, Austria)*
Dian Tjondronegoro *(Queensland University of Technology, Australia)*
Wei Tong *(Carnegie Mellon University, USA)*
Raphaël Troncy *(EURECOM, France)*
Konstantinos Tserpes *(Harokopio University of Athens, Greece)*
Jasper Uijlings *(University of Trento, Italy)*
Marian F Ursu *(Goldsmiths, University of London, United Kingdom)*
Roelof Van Zwol *(Netflix, USA)*
Michael Vernick *(Avaya Labs, USA)*
Catherine Vuong *(Arizona State University, USA)*
Feng Wang *(East China Normal University, China)*
Jingdong Wang *(Microsoft Research Asia, China)*
Jun Wang *(IBM, USA)*
Meng Wang *(National University of Singapore, Singapore)*
Xin-Jing Wang *(Microsoft Research Asia, China)*
Xiao-Yong Wei *(Sichuan University of China, China)*
Lynn Wilcox *(FXPAL, USA)*
Chuan Wu *(University of Hong Kong, Hong Kong)*
Fei Wu *(Zhejiang University, China)*
Ja-Ling Wu *(National Taiwan University, Taiwan)*
Lei Wu *(University of Pittsburgh, USA)*
Min Wu *(Maryland University, USA)*
Mingquan Wu *(Huawei Technologies, China)*
Xiao Wu *(Southwest Jiaotong University, China)*
YongDong Wu *(Institute for Infocomm Research, Singapore)*
Zhong Wu *(Microsoft, USA)*
Xing Xie *(Microsoft Research Asia, China)*
Changsheng Xu *(National Laboratory of Pattern Recognition, China)*
Min Xu *(University of Technology Sydney, Australia)*
Xinshun Xu *(Shandong University, China)*
Goshiro Yamamoto *(Nara Institute of Science and Technology, Japan)*
Toshihiko Yamasaki *(University of Tokyo, Japan)*
Keiji Yanai *(University of Electro-Communication, Japan)*
Linjun Yang *(Microsoft Research Asia, China)*
Ming Yang *(NEC Laboratories America, USA)*
Yi Yang *(Carnegie Mellon University, USA)*
Yi-Hsuan Yang *(Academia Sinica, Taiwan)*
Jude Yew *(University of Michigan, USA)*
Hiromasa Yoshimoto *(Kyoto University, Japan)*
Felix X Yu *(Columbia University, USA)*
Qian Yu *(SRI Sarnoff, USA)*
Zhiwen Yu *(Northwestern Polytechnical University, USA)*
Junsong Yuan *(Nanyang Technological University, Singapore)*
Zheng-Jun Zha *(National University of Singapore, Singapore)*
Dong-Qing Zhang *(Huawei Technologies, China)*
Xiao-Ping Zhang *(Ryerson University, Canada)*
Wengang Zhou *(University of Texas at San Antonio, USA)*
Xiangdong Zhou *(Fudan University, China)*
You Zhou *(Microsoft, USA)*
Wenwu Zhu *(Tsinghua University, China)*
Jinfeng Zhuang *(Microsoft, USA)*
Roger Zimmermann *(National University of Singapore, Singapore)*

MM 2012 Additional Reviewers

Timo Ahonen *(Nokia Research Center, USA)*
Andreas Arzt *(Johannes Kepler University, Linz, Austria)*
Andrew Bagdanov *(University of Florence, Italy)*
Jerome Berclaz *(Nokia Research Center, USA)*
Sebastian Böck *(Johannes Kepler University, Linz, Austria)*
Yang Cai *(Carnegie Mellon University, USA)*
Janko Calic *(Surrey University, United Kingdom)*
Ethem F. Can *(University of Massachusetts, Amherst, USA)*
Chen Cao *(Hong Kong University of Science and Technology, Hong Kong)*
Ching-Ting Chen *(Columbia University, USA)*
Uros Damnjanovic *(Cyprus Institute, Cyprus)*
Saptarshi Debroy *(University of Central Florida, USA)*
Cem Direkoglu *(Dublin City University, Ireland)*
Keisuke Doman *(Nagoya University, Japan)*
Bo Geng *(Microsoft, USA)*
Xin Guo *(Beijing University of Posts and Telecom, China)*
Varsha Hedau *(Nokia Research Center, Finland)*
Mark Hughes *(Dublin City University, Ireland)*
I-Hong Jhuo *(National Taiwan University, Taiwan)*
Jau-Hong Kao *(Industrial Technology Research Institute, Taiwan)*
Svebor Karaman *(University of Florence, Italy)*
Paulo Vinicius Koerich Borges *(CSIRO, Australia)*
Hongzhi Li *(Columbia University, USA)*
Jianguo Li *(Ohio State University, USA)*
Xiang Lian *(University of Texas - Pan American, USA)*
Suzanne Little *(Dublin City University, Ireland)*
Bo Liu *(The State University of New Jersey, USA)*
Xianglong Liu *(Beihang University, China)*
Zhengzheng Lou *(Zhengzhou University, China)*
Hong Lu *(Fudan University, China)*
Wenjun Lu *(University of Maryland, USA)*
Kohei Matsumura *(Future University-Hakodate, Japan)*
Kevin A McGuinness *(Dublin City University, Ireland)*
Thanh D Ngo *(The Graduate University for Advanced Studies, Japan)*
Tam V Nguyen *(National University of Singapore, Singapore)*
Federico Pernici *(University of Florence, Italy)*
Timo Pylvanainen *(Nokia Research Center, Finland)*
Behzad Sajadi *(University of California, Irvine, USA)*
Markus Schedl *(Johannes Kepler University, Linz, Austria)*
Jan Schlüter *(Austrian Research Institute for Artificial Intelligence, Austria)*
Lorenzo Seidenari *(University of Florence, Italy)*
Giuseppe Serra *(University of Florence, Italy)*
Lifeng Shang *(The University of Hong Kong, Hong Kong)*
Jianping Shi *(Chinese University of Hong Kong, Hong Kong)*
Piotr Srebrny *(University of Oslo, Norway)*
Tomokazu Takahashi *(Gifu Shotoku Gakuen University, Japan)*
Ming-Hen Tsai *(Columbia University, USA)*
Sam Tsai *(Stanford University, USA)*
Avinash Varna *(Intel, USA)*
Mukundan Venkataraman *(Stevens Institute of Technology, USA)*
Oriol Vinyals *(University of California, Berkeley, USA)*
Yan Wang *(Columbia University, USA)*
Mingliang Xu *(Zhengzhou University, China)*
Ismet Z Yalniz *(University of Massachusetts, Amherst, USA)*
Kuiyuan Yang *(University of Science and Technology of China, China)*
Guangnan Ye *(Columbia University, USA)*
Mingxuan Yuan *(Hong Kong University of Science and Technology, Hong Kong)*
Dan Zhang *(Purdue University, USA)*
Xiaofei Zhang *(Hong Kong University of Science and Technology, Hong Kong)*
Yuqian Zhang *(Columbia University, USA)*
Xiangmin Zhou *(CSIRO, Australia)*
Zhenfeng Zhu *(Zhengzhou University, China)*

MM 2012 Technical Demo Program Committee

Junjie Cai *(University of Texas at San Antonio, USA)*
Tomio Echigo *(Osaka Electro-Communication University, Japan)*
Yue Gao *(National University of Singapore, Singapore)*
Raphael Grasset *(Graz University of Technology, Austria)*
Pål Halvorsen *(University of Oslo, Norway)*
Mei Han *(Google Research, USA)*
Richang Hong *(Hefei University of Technology, China)*
Qingming Huang *(Graduate University of Chinese Academy of Sciences, China)*
Sei Ikeda *(Osaka University, Japan)*
Masataka Imura *(Osaka University, Japan)*
Rongrong Ji *(Columbia University, USA)*
Hiroyuki Kajimoto *(University of Electro-Communications, Japan)*
Norihiko Kawai *(Nara Institute of Science and Technology, Japan)*
Kazuaki Kondo *(Kyoto University, Japan)*
Duy-Dinh Le *(National Institute of Informatics, Japan)*
Dong Liu *(Columbia University, USA)*
Yijuan Lu *(Texas State University, USA)*
Tao Mei *(Microsoft Research Asia, China)*
Yuta Nakashima *(Nara Institute of Science and Technology, Japan)*
Atsushi Nakazawa *(Osaka University, Japan)*
Chong-Wah Ngo *(City University of Hong Kong, Hong Kong)*
Wei-Tsang Ooi *(National University of Singapore, Singapore)*
Nobuchika Sakata *(Osaka University, Japan)*
Shin'Ichi Satoh *(National Institute of Informatics, Japan)*
Takafumi Taketomi *(Nara Institute of Science and Technology, Japan)*
Jinhui Tang *(Nanjing University of Science and Technology, China)*
Xinmei Tian *(University of Science and Technology of China, China)*
Yuki Uranishi *(Nara Institute of Science and Technology, Japan)*
Changhu Wang *(Microsoft Research Asia, China)*
Jingdong Wang *(Microsoft Research Asia, China)*
Meng Wang *(Hefei University of Technology, China)*
Feng Wu *(Microsoft Research Asia, China)*
Changsheng Xu *(Chinese Academy of Sciences, China)*
Shuicheng Yan *(National University of Singapore, Singapore)*
Ming Yang *(NEC Laboratories America, USA)*
Junsong Yuan *(Nanyang Technological University, Singapore)*
Zheng-Jun Zha *(National University of Singapore, Singapore)*
Lei Zhang *(Microsoft Research Asia, China)*
Wengang Zhou *(University of Texas at San Antonio, USA)*
Roger Zimmermann *(National University of Singapore, Singapore)*

MM 2012 Brave New Ideas Program Committee

Dick Bulterman *(CWI Amsterdam, The Netherlands)*
K. Selçuk Candan *(Arizona State University, USA)*
Shih-Fu Chang *(Columbia University, USA)*
Wu-Chi Feng *(Portland State University, USA)*
Stefan Göbel *(Technische Universität Darmstadt, Germany)*
Mohan Kankanhalli *(National University of Singapore, Singapore)*
Wei-Tsang Ooi *(National University of Singapore, Singapore)*
Larry Rowe *(FXPAL, USA)*
Ye Wang *(National University of Singapore, Singapore)*
Lynn Wilcox *(FXPAL, USA)*
Marcel Worring *(University of Amsterdam, The Netherlands)*
Shuicheng Yan *(National University of Singapore, Singapore)*

MM 2012 Doctoral Symposium Program Committee

Alexander Eichhorn *(Simula Research Laboratory, Norway)*
Benoit Huet *(EURECOM, France)*
Gerald Friedland *(ICSI /University of California, Berkeley, USA)*
Ichiro Ide *(Nagoya University, Japan)*
Isao Echizen *(National Institute of Informatics, Japan)*
K. Selçuk Candan *(Arizona State University, USA)*
Maria L Sapino *(University of Turin, Italy)*
Michel Crucianu *(CNAM, France)*
Shervin Shirmohammadi *(University of Ottawa, Canada)*
Surendar Chandra *(FXPAL Inc., USA)*
Thomas Haenselmann *(University of Mannheim, Germany)*
Valerie G Brunet *(CNAM, France)*
Vincent Oria *(NJIT, USA)*
Yu-Gang Jiang *(Fudan University, China)*

MM 2012 Sponsors & Supporters

Sponsors: ACM SIGMM

Corporate Supporters:

FX PAL
PALO ALTO LABORATORY

Google™

HUAWEI

IBM Research

NTT docomo

technicolor

DeNA

hp

KDDI
KDDI R&D LABS

Microsoft Research

MITSUBISHI ELECTRIC
Changes for the Better

OMRON

Panasonic

SHARP

WiFi Providers:

Institution Supporters:

EiC

一般社団法人 情報処理学会
Information Processing Society of Japan

ITE 映像情報メディア学会
The Institute of Image Information and Television Engineers

JSPS 独立行政法人 日本学術振興会
Japan Society for the Promotion of Science

KDDI
KDDI Foundation

一般財団法人 奈良県ビジターズビューロー
Nara Visitors Bureau

Springer

財団法人 電気通信普及財団
The Telecommunications Advancement Foundation

Future Direction of Digital Content

20th Anniversary Keynote Talk

Masahiro Fujita
Sony Corporation
Japan
masahirof@jp.sony.com

ABSTRACT

We review the history and trends of multimedia technologies, especially focusing on audio & video products. Our lifestyles have been changing according to the developments of these technologies. We forecast the direction of multimedia technologies and our lifestyles in future.

We can guess that the future direction of audio & video is going to higher and higher fidelity. Display devices will be larger and flexible. In addition, wearable devices will be popular as consumer products. It will be achieved by printing manufacture technologies. These devices and high fidelity content will realize immersive super reality.

While we will enjoy the traditional audio & video content with the immersive super reality, we will use more social media by which realtime & global human-human interaction will be realized. We will be able to utilize other people's knowledge and decisions in realtime using the interactive & immersive super reality.

In addition to the social networks with humans, sensor & actuator networks will also be globally established. This will extend our perception and decision abilities. We will find new problems with the distributed sensor & actuator networks, which we did not find with our ordinary perceptions. Using interactive & immersive super reality, we will collaboratively solve personal daily problems as well as global problems.

Thus, in future we will realize collaborative community with interactive & immersive super reality. In the community we will enjoy entertainment content and will solve many problems collaboratively. This community itself will be the content in the future.

Categories and Subject Descriptors

H.4 [**Information Systems Applications**]: Miscellaneous; H.5.1 Information Systems Applications [**Multimedia Information Systems**]: Video

General Terms

Human Factors

MM'12, October 29–November 2, 2012, Nara, Japan.
ACM 978-1-4503-1089-5/12/10.

Keywords

Digital content, Display devices, Printing manufacture, Interactive & Immersive Super reality, Social media, Collaborative community

Bio

Masahiro Fujita is currently Vice President of System and Software Technology Platform at Sony Corporation, Tokyo, Japan. He received a B.A. in Electronics and Communications from Waseda University, Tokyo, in 1981, and an M.S.in Electrical Engineering from University of California Irvine, in 1989.

He joined Sony Corporation in 1981, and worked for development of a spread spectrum communication system, which was used in a receiver of global positioning system for a car navigation, and for VLBI (Very Long Baseline Interferometetry) for a earth quake forecast system. From 1988, he became a graduate student of University of California, Irvine, and studied artificial neural networks for visual perception. After he returned to Sony, he started the Robot Entertainment project from 1993, and developed the entertainment robot AIBO, which started to sell in 1999. After the AIBO project, he has been in charge of development for cognitive part of a small humanoid robot QRIO. In 1998 he proposed to establish RoboCup four-legged robot league using AIBO as platform, which was one of 4 official physical robot leagues in RoboCup until 2007.

In 2008 he became a president of System Technologies Laboratories, Sony Corporation, where he led incorporating intelligent functions for Sony products and services, such as personalized recommendation, augmented reality (SmartAR), and so on.

Coulda, Woulda, Shoulda: 20 Years of Multimedia Opportunities (20th Anniversary Panel)

Klara Nahrstedt
University of Illinois at Urbana-Champaign
klara@illinois.edu

Malcolm Slaney
Microsoft, Mountain View, CA
malcolm@ieee.org

ABSTRACT

The ACM Special Interest Group on Multimedia (SIGMM) is celebrating the 20th anniversary of establishing its premier conference, the ACM International Conference on Multimedia (ACM Multimedia). The panel "Coulda, Woulda, Shoulda" is part of the celebration at the ACM Multimedia 2012. The panelists and the audience will discuss the 20 years of multimedia opportunities that our community has seen, took upon and pushed forward to advance the state of the art.

Categories and Subject Descriptors

C.2 [Computer-Communication Networks],H.2 [Database Management], H.4. [Information Systems Applications], H.5 [Information Interfaces and Presentation], I.4 [Image Processing and Computer Vision], J. [Computer Applications], K.8 [Personal Computing]

General Terms

Algorithms, Experimentation, Human Factors, Measurement, Performance, Standardization.

1. PANEL OVERVIEW

In August 1-6, 1993, the ACM Special Interest Group in Multimedia (SIGMM) came together in Anaheim, California, to talk about challenges, solutions, and results related to digital images, audio, video, graphics, and multimedia. The initial Anaheim conference, chaired by the General Chair J.J. Garcia-Luna-Aceves, started a strong tradition of annual conference meetings for the SIGMM community and this became the SIGMM's premier multimedia conference event, the ACM International Conference on Multimedia (ACM Multimedia).

The last 20 years has seen numerous interesting, innovative, engineering multimedia challenges, solutions, results, opportunities, failures and successes. The agenda of the annual meetings include problems in multimedia synchronization, multicasting, streaming, peer-to-peer, storage, multimedia scheduling, quality of service, content analysis, human interfaces quality of experiences, applications such as video conferencing, authoring, tele-presence, video-on-demand, games, and many others.

We have seen many generations of multimedia researchers, from industry and academia, bring to the conference new and different insights to problems of the time. We have seen new multimedia companies start and grow in the multimedia area, including Google, Yahoo!, YouTube, Akamai and Facebook. We have seen existing companies — such as Sony, Toshiba, Philips, IBM, Microsoft, HP, Apple — change their focus to include digital media including. We have seen multimedia companies merge including AltaVista, Inktomi and others. The bottom line is that the ACM Multimedia conference venue has seen many multimedia opportunities over the 20 years.

The aim of this panel is to look back at the various multimedia opportunities over the 20 years, and encourage a discussion what **did** we do, what **could** we have done, and what **should** we have done with the multimedia opportunities.

The Panel consists of four outstanding researchers who have been in the field over the last 20th years.

- Dr. Dick Bulterman has been an integral part of the multimedia authoring and document processing area, tackling problems of multimedia specifications and tools, and especially introducing and pressing for standardization of SMIL (Synchronized Multimedia Integration Language).
- Dr. Ramesh Jain has been part of the excitement around multimedia content analysis, addressing problems ranging from computer vision, multimedia databases to multimedia context and quality of experience.
- Dr. Lawrence Rowe has been part of the multimedia system community, working on fundamental system challenges, such as enabling the community to work with the MPEG1-encoder/decoder and player, and experiment with MBone multicast system.
- Dr. Ralf Steinmetz has been part of the multimedia networking community, working especially on challenging issues of synchronization, multimedia transport, and quality of services.

The Panel will start the discussion with reflections on multimedia opportunities from their areas of expertise, and then, together with the audience, will discuss the following issues and questions:

Q1: Nowadays, the multimedia industry is booming and represents a successful and important market. What do you think were the game changing contributions over the last 20 years to enable the prospering markets?

Q2: What were some of the missed opportunities that we as a research community did not see coming?

Q3: What results were you surprised to see get overwhelming attention, resources, and mind-share from academic and industrial

MM'12, October 29–November 2, 2012, Nara, Japan.
ACM 978-1-4503-1089-5/12/10.

community? What results, do you think, would gain attention, but did not get any from the academic/industry community?

Q4: What could and should the SIGMM/ACM Multimedia community do better to impact and increase development, deployment and acceptance of new multimedia results by the multimedia industry?

2. PANELISTS BIOS

Dick Bulterman is a senior researcher at CWI in Amsterdam, where since 2004 he heads the Distributed and Interactive Systems group. He holds the professorship of Distributed Multimedia Languages and Interfaces with the Department of Computer science at the Vrije Universiteit in Amsterdam. Previously, he led CWI's Department of Computer Systems and Telematics and he was head of the Multimedia and Human Computer theme at CWI. Prior to CWI, he was on the faculty of the Division of Engineering at Brown, where he was part of the Laboratory for Engineering Man/Machine Systems.

In 1999, he started Oratrix Development BV that transferred the group's SMIL-based GR*i*NS software to many parts of the civilized world. Dr. Bulterman received a Ph.D. in computer science from Brown University (USA). He also holds a Sc.M. in applied mathematics and computer science from Brown and a B.A. in political economics (with a minor in mathematics) from Hope College. He is on the editorial board of Springer Multimedia Systems Journal and Multimedia Tools and Applications. He is co-chair of the W3C Synchronized Multimedia working group and is a member of various conference steering committees. He is a member of Sigma Xi, the ACM and the IEEE.

Ramesh Jain is a Donald Bren Professor in Information & Computer Sciences at University of California, Irvine where he is doing research in *EventWeb* and *Experiential Computing* for developing and building *Social Life Networks*. Earlier he served on faculty of Georgia Tech, University of California at San Diego, The university of Michigan, Ann Arbor, Wayne State University, and Indian Institute of Technology, Kharagpur. He has published over 350 research papers. He is the recipient of several awards including the ACM SIGMM Technical Achievement Award 2010. He is a Fellow of ACM, IEEE, AAAI, IAPR, and SPIE.

Ramesh co-founded several companies, managed them in initial stages, and then turned them over to professional management. These included PRAJA in event-based business activity monitoring (acquired by Tibco); Virage for visual information management (a NASDAQ company acquired by Autonomy); and ImageWare for surface modeling (acquired by SDRC).

Dr. Lawrence A. Rowe has been President of FX Palo Alto Laboratory (FXPAL) since April 2007. Prior to that, he was a Professor of Electrical Engineering and Computer Science at the University of California, Berkeley (1976-2003). Dr. Rowe's research interests are in multimedia systems and applications, application development tools, and database management systems. He has been involved with several start-up companies as an angel investor, advisor, or active participant including the original Ingres Corporation, Inktomi, Dust, and NCast.

Dr. Rowe is an ACM Fellow, recipient of the SIGMM Technical Achievement Award in 2009, past chair of ACM SIG Multimedia (1998-2003), recipient of the 2002 U.C. Technology Leadership Council Award for his development of the Berkeley Lecture Webcasting System, and U.C. Irvine Donald Bren School of Information and Computer Science Distinguished Alumni Award in 2007.

Ralf Steinmetz is a Professor in the Department of Electrical Engineering at the Technical University, Darmstadt, Germany. He worked for over nine years in industrial research and development of distributed multimedia systems and applications. He has been head, since 1996, of the Multimedia Communications lab (KOM) at Darmstadt University of Technology, Germany. From 1997 to 2001 he directed the Fraunhofer (former GMD) Integrated Publishing Systems Institute IPSI in Darmstadt. In 1999 he founded the Hessian Telemedia Technology Competence Center (httc e.V.). His thematic focus in research and teaching is on multimedia communications with his vision of real "seamless multimedia communications". With over 200 refereed publications he has become ICCC Governor in 1999; was awarded the ranking of Fellow of both, the IEEE in 1999 and the ACM in 2002.

3. MODERATORS BIOS

Klara Nahrstedt is a Ralf and Catherine Fisher Professor in the Department of Computer Science at the University of Illinois at Urbana-Champaign. Her research interests are directed toward multimedia systems. She is the co-author of `Multimedia: Computing, Communications and Applications' published by Prentice Hall 1995, 'Multimedia Systems' published by Springer Verlag 2004, and the author of 'QoS in Wireless Networks over Unlicensed Spectrum', published by Morgan & Claypool Publisher 2012. She is the recipient of the IEEE Communication Society Leonard Abraham Award for Research Achievements, University Scholar, Humboldt Awardee, IEEE Technical Achievement Award, and the current Chair of SIG Multimedia.

Klara Nahrstedt received her Diploma in Mathematics from Humboldt University, Berlin, Germany in numerical analysis, her PhD from the University of Pennsylvania in the Department of Computer and Information Science. She is the member of ACM and an IEEE Fellow.

Malcolm Slaney is a principal scientist in the Conversational Systems Laboratory at Microsoft in Mountain View, CA. He is interested in building computational models of users, sounds, images, and video in order to better connect users and signals. For the last 20 years he has organized the Stanford CCRMA Hearing Seminar, where he is a (Consulting) Professor. Before joining Microsoft he was a researcher at Yahoo and IBM's Almaden Research Center, working on multimedia analysis and user models. He has also been employed by Interval Research, Apple's Advanced Technology Group, Schlumberger's Palo Alto Research Laboratory, and Bell Labs.

He is the coauthor of the book "Principles of Computerized Tomographic Imaging," which was recently republished by SIAM as a "Classics in Applied Mathematics." He is coeditor of the book "Computational Models of Auditory Function." He has served as an associate editor for IEEE Transactions on Audio, Speech and Language Processing, IEEE Multimedia Magazine, and the Proceedings of the IEEE. He is a Fellow of the IEEE.

Decoding Visual Experience from the Human Brain

Plenary Talk

Yukiyasu Kamitani
ATR Computational Neuroscience Laboratories
Japan
kmtn@atr.jp

ABSTRACT

Brain activity can be seen as "codes" that encode mental states. Recent advances in human neuroimaging such as functional magnetic resonance imaging (fMRI) have revealed brain regions that encode specific behavior and cognition. Despite the wide-spread use of human neuroimaging, its potential to read out, or "decode", mental contents from brain activity has not been fully explored. In this talk, I present methods for decoding visual representations from fMRI activity patterns based on machine learning techniques. I show how early visual features represented in "subvoxel" neural structures could be decoded from ensemble fMRI responses. Decoding of stimulus features is extended to the method for neural mind-reading, which attempts to predict a person's subjective state using a decoder trained with unambiguous stimulus presentation. We then discuss a modular decoding approach, in which a wide variety of percepts can be decoded by combining the outputs of multiple decoder modules. On the basis of this approach, we were able to reconstruct arbitrary visual images using the decoder trained on fMRI responses to only several hundred random images. Finally, I discuss potential applications of neural decoding to brain-based communications.

Categories and Subject Descriptors

H.4 [**Information Systems Applications**]: Miscellaneous; I.2 [**Artificial Intelligence**]: Cognitive Simulation

Keywords

fMRI, neural decoding, machine learning, vision

Bio

Yukiyasu Kamitani is currently the head of Department of Neuroinformatics at ATR Computational Neuroscience Laboratories, Kyoto, Japan, and a professor at Nara Institute of Science and Technology (NAIST). He received B.A. in Cognitive Science from University of Tokyo in 1993, M.S. in Philosophy of Science from University of Tokyo in 1995, and Ph.D. in Computation and Neural Systems from California Institute of Technology in 2001. He continued his research in cognitive and computational neuroscience as a research fellow at Beth Israel Deaconess Medical Center (Harvard Medical School), and as a research staff member at Princeton University. In 2004, he joined ATR Computational Neuroscience Laboratories, where he currently works on neural decoding of human brain signals. He was named Research Leader in Neural Imaging on the 2005 "Scientific American 50."

MM'12, October 29–November 2, 2012, Nara, Japan.
ACM 978-1-4503-1089-5/12/10.

Content is Dead; Long-live Content!

Panel Organizers:

Lexing Xie
Australian National University
lexing.xie@anu.edu.au

David Ayman Shamma
Yahoo! Research
aymans@acm.org

Cees Snoek
University of Amsterdam
cgmsnoek@uva.nl

Categories and Subject Descriptors: H.3.1 [Information Storage and Retrieval]: Content Analysis and Indexing; I.5.0 [Pattern Recognition]: General—*multimedia*

General Terms: Design, Implementation

Keywords: multimedia content, context, social

Panel Overview

Multimedia content analysis has always held a major research role in the ACM Multimedia research community. Ten years ago, at ACM MM 2002, a panel debated on "Media Semantics: Who Needs It and Why?" [2] Today, the answer is obvious. Multimedia content analysis has burgeoned on a foundation of machine learning and data-intensive algorithms, and has influenced many recent applications, from finding faces to augmenting reality.

The past decade has brought new paradigms in media semantics such as tagging, social networks, location-based services and mobility or SoLoMo as it is often abbreviated. This is the time to ask how much, and in what ways do these changes shift the foundations of content analysis – how is having such rich metadata narrowing the well-known *sensory gap* [3] between media capture and real-world experience, or does it narrow the *semantic gap* [3] between automatic understanding and user interpretation? What do emerging approaches and paradigms – search and annotation in social information networks, crowd-sourced content tagging – mean for the future of content analysis in general? Is multimedia content analysis in its traditional legacy still a valid area of inquiry? Does the use and analysis of media need to be cast in new lights in order to maintain relevant for emerging modes of media sharing?

This panel hosts senior experts from academia and the major industry Internet principals to debate whether content can continue to play a role in multimedia research and address utility and direction of content analysis in the age of social media. The title of this panel is inspired by a debate in the world-wide-web community in 2010 [1].

A list of questions that will be posed to the panel include:

- What has been the biggest change in multimedia content analysis over the past ten years?
- Is multimedia content analysis in its traditional legacy still a valid area of inquiry?
- Should emerging modes of media creation, use and sharing change how content analysis problems are posed and solved?
- What are the two most important and fundamental multimedia questions for the next ten years?
- How does the tool (Twitter vs Instagram vs Email vs etc) change the perceived semantics of the multimedia?
- Content ... really? Do we still need it at all or is SoLoMo sufficient?
- What changes does content analysis need, if any? Should we now bifurcate into content semantics and context semantics?
- What other signals, aside from content and SoLoMo, should be added into multimedia research in the next 5 years?

References

[1] A. Broder, E. F. Churchill, M. Hearst, B. Pell, P. Raghavan, and A. Tomkins. Search is dead!: long live search. WWW '10, pages 1337–1338, 2010.

[2] C. Dorai, A. Mauthe, F. Nack, L. Rutledge, T. Sikora, and H. Zettl. Media semantics: who needs it and why? ACM Multimedia, pages 580–583, 2002.

[3] A. Smeulders, M. Worring, S. Santini, A. Gupta, and R. Jain. Content-based image retrieval at the end of the early years. *Pattern Analysis and Machine Intelligence, IEEE Transactions on*, 22(12):1349–1380, 2000.

MM'12, October 29–November 2, 2012, Nara, Japan.
ACM 978-1-4503-1089-5/12/10.

Finding Perfect Rendezvous On the Go: Accurate Mobile Visual Localization and Its Applications to Routing *

Heng Liu [1], Tao Mei [2], Jiebo Luo [3], Houqiang Li [1], Shipeng Li [2]
[1] University of Science and Technology of China, Hefei 230027, P. R. China
[2] Microsoft Research Asia, Beijing 100080, P. R. China
[3] University of Rochester, Rochester, NY 14627, USA
{sorcerer@mail., lihq@}ustc.edu.cn; {tmei, spli}@microsoft.com; jluo@cs.rochester.edu

ABSTRACT

While on the go, more and more people are using their phones to enjoy ubiquitous location-based services (LBS). One of the fundamental problems of LBS is localization. Researchers are now investigating ways to use a phone-captured image for localization as it contains more scene context information than the embedded sensors. In this paper, we present a novel approach to mobile visual localization that accurately senses geographic scene context according to the current image (typically associated with a rough GPS position). Unlike most existing visual localization methods, the proposed approach is capable of providing a complete set of more accurate parameters about the scene geo—including the actual locations of both the mobile user and perhaps more importantly the captured scene along with the viewing direction. Our approach takes advantage of advanced techniques for large-scale image retrieval and 3D model reconstruction from photos. Specifically, we first perform joint geo-visual clustering in the cloud to generate scene clusters, with each scene represented by a 3D model. The 3D scene models are then indexed using a visual vocabulary tree structure. The phone-captured image is used to retrieve the relevant scene models, then aligned with the models, and further registered to the real-world map. Our approach achieves an estimation accuracy of user location within 14 meters, viewing direction within 9 degrees, and scene location within 21 meters. Such a complete set of accurate geo-parameters can lead to various LBS applications for routing that cannot be achieved with most existing methods. In particular, we showcase three novel applications: 1) accurate self-localization, 2) collaborative localization for rendezvous routing, and 3) routing for photographing. The evaluations through user studies indicate these applications are effective for facilitating the perfect rendezvous for mobile users.

Categories and Subject Descriptors

H.3.3 [**Information Storage and Retrieval**]: Information Search and Retrieval—*search process*; I.4.8 [**Computing Methodologies**]: Image Processing and Computer Vision—*scene analysis*

* This work was performed at Microsoft Research Asia.

MM'12, October 29–November 2, 2012, Nara, Japan.

General Terms

Algorithms, Performance, Design, Experimentation.

Keywords

Mobile Visual Localization, Geo-tagging, Scene Reconstruction, Location-based Services.

1. INTRODUCTION

Location-based services (LBS) are becoming ubiquitous. People are using their mobile phones to enjoy the many LBS applications on the move. For example, 18% of U.S. smartphone users accessed at least one LBS application per month in 2011, and 10% of mobile applications in the market are LBS-oriented. One of the fundamental problems in these applications is localization—How to automatically obtain the accurate location context of mobile users still remains a challenge.

Traditional approaches for mobile localization employ inertial hardware such as embedded GPS or cellular tower proximity to determine location in outdoor environments, or WiFi/GSM-based alternatives for indoor operation. Unfortunately, the embedded GPS modules rely on a satellite navigation system and need a clear view of at least four satellites to provide sufficient positioning accuracy. As a result, the estimated GPS location in a crowded urban scene or on a cloudy day is error prone, usually leading to an error of 50$\sim$100 meters [5], [29]. Moreover, in a multimedia-oriented application, when users annotate their photos or videos using these records, they are actually labeling according to the camera location rather than the true scene location, which can cause significant deviations in many LBS applications. Similar problems exist in positioning with other sensors such as Cell-IDs or WiFi.

Precise geographic information about location plays a key role in LBS, especially in multimedia-oriented applications (e.g., augmented reality) that have a high expectation of location accuracy in meters or less. Researchers are now investigating ways to use the phone-captured images for localization as a complement or an alternative, as it contains more context information than embedded sensors, leading to a more precise location description. A typical approach is to match the captured image against a database with geo-referenced images, and use the geo-tag from the (near-) duplicate images to determine location [2], [32]. However, this approach relies heavily on the "ill-posed" geo-referenced image database, where images are associated with the geo-locations by the mobile devices (since the geo-locations are usually obtained from the embedded GPS devices) rather than the scenes themselves. This could result in incorrect geo-tagging because the distance between the mobile user and the scene is undetermined.

We are investigating in this paper if we can provide a complete

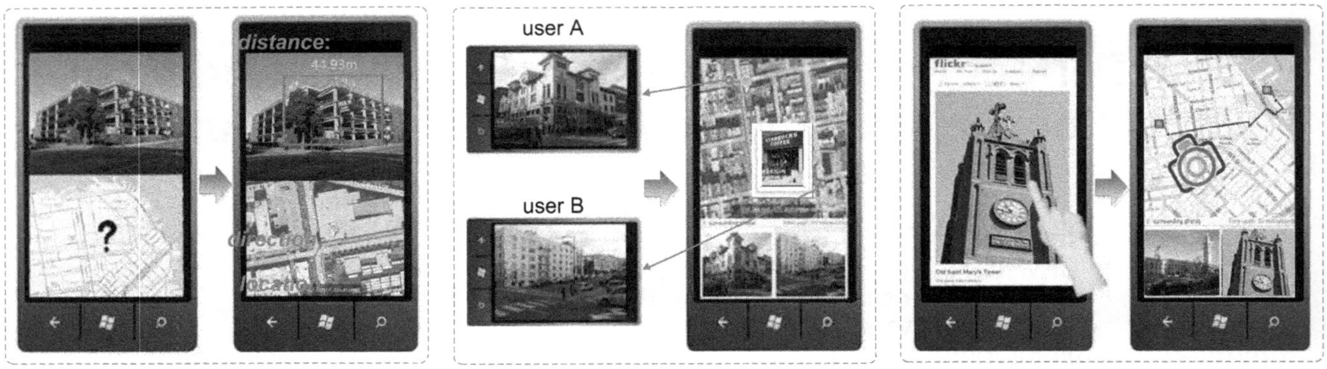

(a) accurate self-localization (b) collaborative localization for routing (c) routing for photographing suggestion

Figure 1: LBS applications based on accurate mobile visual location: (a) accurate self-localization: a mobile user wants to determine the accurate location of himself and the building, as well as his viewing direction, (b) collaborative localization for routing: two users are finding a perfect rendezvous point collaboratively by taking pictures, and (c) routing for photography suggestions: a tourist is finding the best place to photograph a landmark appearing in a shared picture.

set of more accurate parameters for the geo-context of a scene. The geo-context parameters include the actual location of a mobile user, the viewing direction, as well as the location of the scene. This is quite different from most existing approaches that only focus on one or part of these attributes [2], [5], [11], [25], [28], [32]. The comprehensive set of geo-context attributes can lead to a wide variety of LBS applications that cannot be achieved by any existing system. Figure 1 shows three novel applications of this kind:

- Accurate self-localization for a single user. A mobile user takes a picture of a landmark to determine his location, viewing direction, and the distance from the landmark.
- Collaborative localization for finding the perfect rendezvous. Two users or a group of users are looking for a place in a crowded area to gather. They all take pictures of nearby buildings through their phones independently. They can then determine each other's location, , as well as a suggested rendezvous point and its route.
- Routing for photography suggestions. A tourist is interested in a photo of a church shared by his friend. He then wants to know where to take a similar picture of this church (i.e., the route to this church, and the location and viewing direction for photographing this church).

Our approach takes advantage of the advanced techniques for large-scale image retrieval and 3D model reconstruction from photos. Specifically, we first perform joint geo-visual clustering in the cloud to generate scene clusters, with each scene represented by a 3D model reconstructed from the images in this cluster. The 3D scene models are then indexed using a visual vocabulary tree structure. The phone-captured image is used to retrieve relevant scene models, aligned with the models, and further registered to the real-world map. As a result, we are able to achieve an estimation accuracy of user location within 14 meters, viewing direction within 9 degrees, and scene location within 21 meters.

In summary, our contributions are two-fold. First, we propose an approach for accurate image localization for mobile users, by taking advantage of the the geo-referenced images on the web and reconstructed 3D scene models. Our approach can provide a more comprehensive set of accurate parameters of a scene's context. Second, we present a wide variety of LBS applications based on accurate location context, including 1) accurate self-location, 2) collaborative localization for rendezvous routing, and 3) routing for photographing.

The remainder of this paper is organized as follows. Section 2 reviews the related work for image-based localization and mobile location recognition. Section 3 describes our proposed approach to accurate mobile visual localization. Section 4 showcases various applications derived from our system. Experiments are presented in Section 5, followed by the conclusions in Section 6.

2. RELATED WORK

2.1 Image-based Localization

With the growth of geo-referenced data, image-based location recognition has drawn extensive interest from multimedia and vision communities [20]. Zhang and Kosecka propose a framework that searches the closest reference views for an image and provide a coarse method for location recognition in an urban environment [33]. However, their scheme cannot scale up for large datasets. Schindler *et al.* use an inverted file indexed with a vocabulary tree for city-scale location recognition [28]. Their dataset contains 30,000 images. Zamir *et al.* propose a method to exploit repetitive features discovered in large urban environments to achieve higher accuracy for image search and GPS estimation [32]. The authors combine the features from similar images to form "scene maps" to compress the data and achieve considerable improvement for retrieval [2].

Some researchers have moved a step further—they are more concerned about how to estimate the view directions of photos. Kroepfl *et al.* locate photos by registering on street view panoramas [15]. Similarly, Park *et al.* utilize both Google Street View [9] and Google Earth Map [8] to estimate the view direction of a geo-referenced image [25]. In [21], given a query image, a set of matched photos of the underlying scene is found ind the database using the Scale-Invariant Feature Transform (SIFT) Flow [18]. The photos with view directions pointing to the user-indicated region are returned by the system. However, these systems cannot deal with the estimation of location and do not work without an initial GPS position.

In some recent works [12], [16], [17], [27], the structure-form-motion (SfM) technique is exploited to reconstruct a 3D scene from a collection of images. The images are then localized by matching the feature points to the 3D models. This could produce more precise localization results. However, the scene models are usually reconstructed from the datasets at the scale of 10^3 to 10^5 photos,

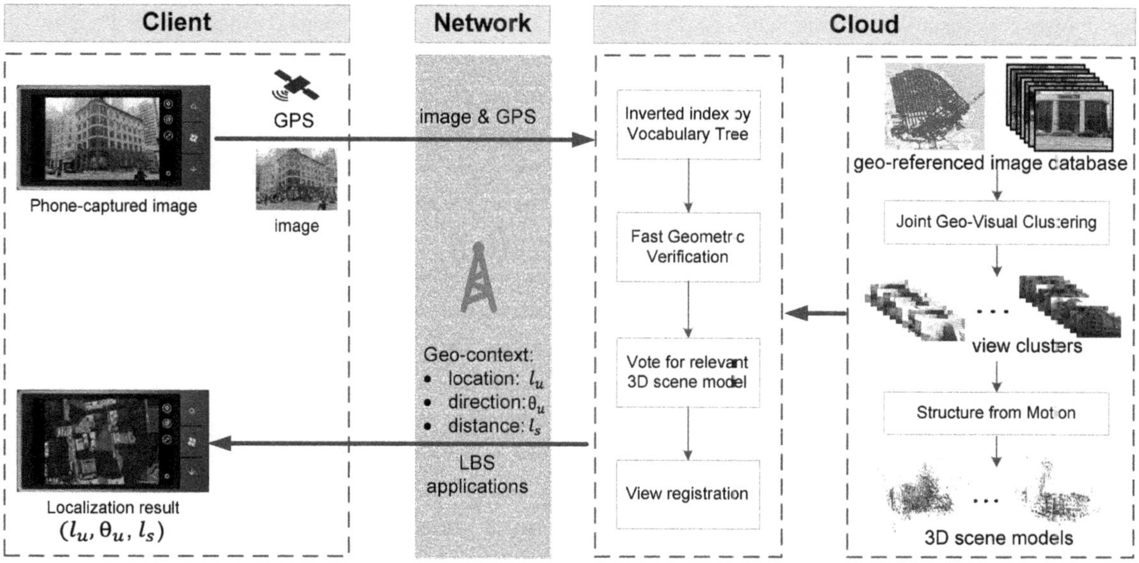

Figure 2: The proposed framework for accurate mobile visual localization and its applications.

acquired by text-based search from the Web or artificially captured. As a result, the models usually cover a small fraction of the whole city. Furthermore, in these works the reconstruction treats all the images as a whole while ignoring context such as geo-information, which could be used to guide the reconstruction for a better performance.

2.2 Mobile Location Recognition

Schroth *et al.* is concerned about the latency and the limited storage of the mobile device [29]. Chen *et al.* build a million-scale street view dataset and conducted comprehensive experiments to evaluate their retrieval scheme [5]. Ji *et al.* propose a discriminative vocabulary coding scheme to achieve a low latency query delivery and discriminative description [13]. In particular, the authors in [31] present a mobile application that can teach mobile users to capture pictures that can distinctively represent the surrounding scenes.

In contrast to the above systems, our proposed framework aims to provide the complete information of a scene's geo-context: location, view direction, and distance to the captured scene with a higher accuracy than the GPS-level. Accurately estimating geo-context can lead to better LBS services for mobile users.

3. ACCURATE MOBILE VISUAL LOCALIZATION

Figure 2 shows the proposed system architecture for accurate mobile localization, including: clients, network, and the cloud. The localization is considered a combination of retrieval and registration problems in a geo-referenced database. To better utilize geometric constraints and derive a more accurate estimation of query image, we build up the geo-reference database that not only has images but also 3D scene models. Given a photo captured by a user with a mobile device, an image (with a rough GPS location from the sensor) is transmitted through a wireless network to the cloud for more accurate localization. First, we extract the SIFT descriptors from the query image. Then, we retrieve the related 3D scene models in the database using the Bag-of-Word (BoW) representation indexed with a vocabulary tree structure [23]. If we have the GPS information associated with the query image, then we use this information to filter unrelated images. The query image will finally be aligned to 3D models on a real-world map. In this way, we can obtain the complete scene context $(\mathbf{l}_u, \theta_u, \mathbf{l}_s)$, with the location of the mobile user $\mathbf{l}_u$, the view direction θ_u, and location of the captured scene $\mathbf{l}_s$. In the following section we will describe the major components of our system in details.

3.1 Building 3D Scene Models

To localize the query images, searching should be conducted in a geo-referenced dataset. The most commonly seen type of dataset is a collection of images with GPS information. Luckily, with the increasingly popularity and accessibility of online photo-sharing services, such as Flickr [6] and Panoramio [24], more and more people are sharing their photos, a portion of which are geo-tagged. This abundant resource of geo-referenced images has proven very useful in many multimedia and visualization applications. However, the contents is diverse and noisy. One way to build a better-structured database is harnessing street view images that are obtained by vehicles equipped with cameras and other sensors (like GPS) [5]. Existing visual location recognition systems are mainly based on these collected datasets. However, they can only estimate limited parameters as the search results from these datasets consist only of the images with GPS information. To predict the geographic information of a query image, we need more accurate information or models from these datasets, e.g., the epipolar geometry among the images [33].

To accurate localize image in a million-scale database, we take advantage of both geo-information and visual content to support 3D scene reconstruction and retrieval. Images which are geographically and visually close to each other should be clustered into the same group. Then, we can reconstruct 3D models using the structure-from-motion (SfM) technique in these groups. To achieve this, we present a joint geo-visual clustering strategyto do the preprocessing.

3.1.1 *Geo-clustering of database images*

First, *geo-clustering* is performed using the location information $(latitude, longitude)$ to ensure that only geographically-nearby image are able to depict the same scene. This will significantly reduce the computational costs of the succeeding visual-clustering. For simplicity, images far away from each other are disconnected by leveraging an open-ball operation with the radius r_g, thus the geographical similarity matrix is computed as follows:

$$Sim_g(i,j) = \begin{cases} g_{i,j}, & d_{geo}(i,j) < r_g \\ 0, & d_{geo}(i,j) \geq r_g \end{cases}, \quad (1)$$

where $g_{i,j} = exp\{\frac{-d_{geo}(i,j)}{\sigma_g}\}$ denotes the geo-proximity of two images, $d_{geo}(i,j)$ is the distance from the location of image i to image j, and σ_g is the scale factor. Then, the affinity propagation (AP) algorithm is adopted to find the geo-clusters [7]. AP is widely used to group data into a number of groups according to the similarity between pairs of data points. The total number of groups is automatically inferred from the data.

3.1.2 *Visual-clustering of database images*

After we determine the geo-clusters, we further conduct clustering based on the visual similarity of images. Similar with the geo-clustering, we also need to compute a matrix Sim_v for each geo-cluster that represents the pairwise visual similarity between images. Unlike geo-clustering, computing pairwise similarity of images is the most computational procedure. Typically this is done by matching local visual features, followed by checking the consistency in the geometry using RANSAC and other forms of spatial matching [26]. To speed up this procedure, we use the inverted-indexing technique. For each image in the cluster, its features are quantized as visual words, as described in Sec 3.2. Then, each image is represented by a histogram of visual words. Matching this image to others in the cluster is followed by fast geometric verification. This matching is conducted in a small subset rather than the whole database, thus allowing one query per image in each cluster. Furthermore, we restrict the process to ensure that only the image pairs with the number of inlier matched features more than r_v are connected in the visual graph. The visual similarity matrix is:

$$Sim_v(i,j) = \begin{cases} v_{i,j}, & v_{i,j} \geq r_v \\ 0, & v_{i,j} < v_g \end{cases}, \quad (2)$$

where $v_{i,j}$ is the number of inlier matches between image i and j, representing their visual similarity.

Finally the visual-clusters are obtained using AP with the visual similarity matrix. The results of geo-clustering in a city and an example of visual-clusters of a geo-cluster are given in Figure 3, where each row in 3(b) depicts the images in the same visual cluster. The reconstructed 3D models are shown at the end of each row.

3.1.3 *3D Reconstruction via SfM*

After the geo-visual clustering, we have a set of N image clusters $\{C_i\}_{i=1}^N$. Each cluster $C_i = \{I_i^m\}_{m=1}^{M_i}$ consists of images depicting the same scene. Instead of representing the scenes with sets of images, a better choice is using 3D models that contain stronger geometric constraints. These geometric constraints can deliver the pose of images directly compared to the 2D image matches.

A 3D model can be created using multiple-view vision methods from image clusters $\mathcal{C} = \{I^m\}_{m=1}^M$. In our system, the reconstruction of 3D scenes from images in the same cluster is mainly based on the state of the art **SfM** algorithm [30]. We briefly summarize the related steps for 3D scene reconstruction as follows. First, for each pair of images, the key point descriptors are matched using the approximate nearest neighbors (ANN) KD-tree algorithm [1]. We next reconstruct the set of cameras and 3D points. We start the reconstruction from a initial selected image pair which has a large number of matches and a wide baseline. The five point algorithm is used to estimate camera parameters for this initial pair [22]. The matched image points are triangulated. Then, by adding a few images to the model at a time, we can build the scene model incrementally. The reconstructed model $\mathcal{S}(\mathcal{C}) \triangleq (\mathcal{X}, \mathcal{A}, \mathcal{W})$ of a cluster $\mathcal{C}$ is represented with the following structure: 1) a set of 3D points $\mathcal{X} = \{X^n\}_{n=1}^N$ in 3D Euclid coordinate (U, V, Z), 2) a set of camera $\mathcal{A} = \{A^m\}_{m=1}^M$, where each camera A^m consists of an image I^m, a rotation matrix $\mathbf{R}^m$, a translation $\mathbf{t}^m$, and a focal length l^m, and 3) a set of Binary mappings $\mathcal{W} = \{w_{n,m}\}_{n,m=1}^{n=N,m=M}$ between the points and cameras indicates whether X^n can be observed from camera A^m. If $X^n = (X_U^n, X_V^n, X_Z^n)$ is observable in A^m, then there exists an 2D feature point $x^{n,m} = (x_u^{n,m}, x_v^{n,m})$ represented in 2D image coordinate (u, v). At each iteration, the reconstructed model is further refined using a bundle adjustment. It is equivalent to the following optimization problem that minimize the reprojection errors:

$$\arg \min_{X,\mathbf{R},t,l} \sum_{X^n,\mathbf{R}^m,t^m,l^m} w_{n,m} \parallel x^{n,m} - \widehat{x}^{n,m} \parallel^2, \quad (3)$$

where $\widehat{x}^{n,m} = (\widehat{x}_u^{n,m}, \widehat{x}_v^{n,m})$ is the reprojection of X^n into image I^m, the reprojection is computed as:

$$\lambda \begin{pmatrix} \widehat{x}_u^{n,m} \\ \widehat{x}_v^{n,m} \\ 1 \end{pmatrix} = l^m(\mathbf{R}^m\mathbf{X}^n + \mathbf{t}^m), \quad (4)$$

where λ is an arbitrary homogeneous scaling factor. Thus bundle adjustment jointly refines the estimated camera parameters and 3D points. Finally, when the reconstruction has been completed, we convert the coordinate into a real world coordinate. With the labeled GPS information of the images, a similar transformation can register the 3D model into real world coordinate. Finally, the query image can be localized by searching for and registering the 3D scenes in the geo-referenced database.

3.2 Searching 3D Scene Models

To efficiently find the relevant images and scenes for the query image, a visual vocabulary tree structure is adopted for indexing. We will describe these steps in the following sections.

3.2.1 *Image Representation*

A SIFT descriptor is exploited for image representation because of its strong capacity for description and discrimination [19]. For each image, a set of interest points are detected, each with a 128-dimensional descriptor, the orientation, and the scale of the key point. We use the BoW scheme to quantize the local descriptors. Each descriptor is mapped to an integer visual word ID. The visual words are typically trained from a sampled SIFT descriptor set by clustering, while the clustering centroids are defined as visual words. For efficient clustering and quantization, a hierarchical tree based structure is adopted and the resulting leaf nodes are considered visual words [23]. The hierarchical tree has two basic parameters: branching factor B and hierarchical layer H, where B controls the number of clusters in each layer of the tree and H determines the depth of the tree. In general, the number of visual words is approximately B^H. The total number of comparison operations is $B \times H$. In our implementation, we set the parameters as $B = 10$, $H = 6$, yielding a codebook with one million visual words. Finally, the inverted file system is exploited to index the images with the trained vocabulary tree.

3.2.2 *Searching with GPS*

Our system can deal with a situation where no initial GPS information is available in addition to the image. However, a rough GPS initiation can be very beneficial for guiding a search that is limited

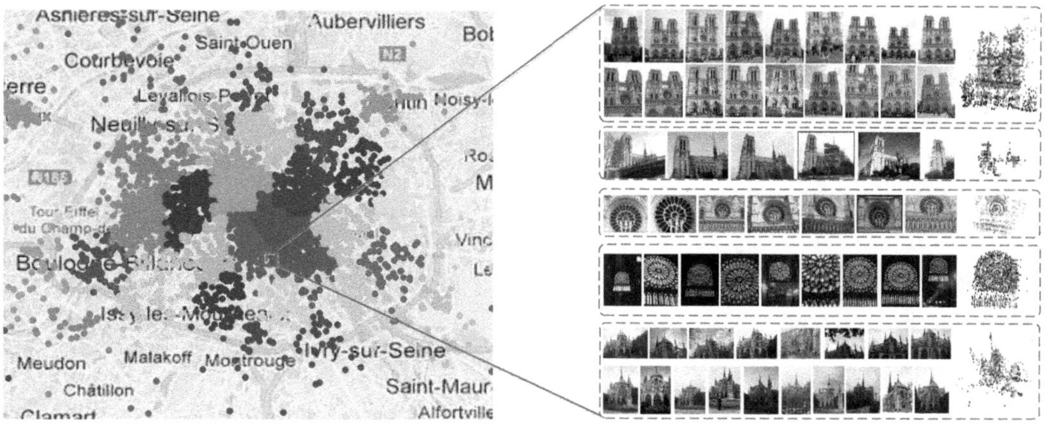

(a) (b)

Figure 3: An example of geo-visual clustering in the city of Paris. (a) The geographical regions are generated by employing Affinity Propagation clustering. Different clusters are denoted by different colors. (b) Part of the visual clusters in one geo-cluster near Norte Dame de Paris. Each row represents images in the same visual cluster along with the reconstructed 3D scene model.

in scope compared to the whole database. This could be helpful both in accelerating the retrieval speed and enhancing the retrieval precision. When a GPS context is available for the query image, only those images in the vicinity of the current GPS record are scored in the inverted index matching. Given $\mathbf{G} = (G_{lat}, G_{long})$ as the GPS coordinate for a query image, we define the area within R meters as the vicinity. We choose $R = 300$ in our experiments according to the report in [5] that it would be appropriate in most cases.

3.2.3 Fast Geometric Verification

A subsequent geometric verification (GV) considering the spatial consistency of local features is needed to reject the false-positive matches. Especially, this verification is useful and indispensable in landmark or street view image retrieval where repetitive structures are common and local patches like windows are similar so that multiple descriptors might be mapped to the same visual word. Usually, RANSAC-based methods with an affine or epipolar geometry model are applied. But the full verification with RANSAC is time consuming thus can only be performed on a small set in the top results. Moreover, images of landmarks or street views are usually captured with known gravity orientation. This gravity-aligned property has been analyzed and utilized for more precise feature matching in previous works [5]. In our work we also noticed this characteristic of the landmark images. So we choose to use a relaxed but efficient GV strategy proposed in [34]. First, each descriptor is quantized in both descriptor and orientation spaces to enhance the matching accuracy. A soft quantization strategy is employed to mitigate the quantization error. Then, the concise binary matrices named spatial maps that encode the relative feature positions in each image are generated. By comparing the spatial maps we can find and remove the false matches effectively. This achieves performance comparable to RANSAC and the computational time is greatly reduced, thus enabling retrieval in a large-scale database. If the number of inliers after the geometric verification is higher than threshold T_{GV}, the retrieved image is accepted as a true match, otherwise the image is rejected.

3.3 Localization by View Registration

The retrieval process returns a short list of candidate images, along with the filtered feature matches between the query image and these candidates. At the same time, all the 3D scene models in the database that have related candidate images ($\{\mathcal{S}(\mathcal{C}_i) | q \cap \mathcal{C}_i \neq \oslash\}$) can be evaluated using the image retrieval results. We use a majority voting scheme to select the 3D scene model with which the query image q has the most overlap. For each 3D scene model $\mathcal{S}(\mathcal{C}_i)$, a voting score $V(\mathcal{S}(\mathcal{C}_i), q)$ is computed by

$$V(\mathcal{S}(\mathcal{C}_i), q) = \sum\nolimits_{f^q \in q} \delta(f^q, \mathcal{S}(\mathcal{C}_i)), \tag{5}$$

where $\delta(f^q, \mathcal{S}(\mathcal{C}_i)) \rightarrow \{0, 1\}$ indicates whether a feature point f^q in the query image q can find a match in the candidate images belonging to the scene model $\mathcal{C}_i$. Thus, $V(\mathcal{S}(\mathcal{C}_i), q)$ denotes the approximate strength of the link between the query image and $\mathcal{S}(\mathcal{C}_i)$ by measuring how many feature points in the query image are covered by the scene model. The scene model with the highest number of hits is chosen to further align the query image for an accurate localization.

From the previous voting procedure, the most related scene model can be determined. Figure 4 illustrates the registration procedure. The camera pose can be estimated by registering the query image to 3D points. For each 3D model, a KD-tree is established. Features extracted from the query image can search the nearest neighbor in this tree to find 2D-to-3D matches. When there is sufficient correspondences between image features x and 3D points X, the 3×4 projection matrix $\mathbf{P}$ can be estimated.

$$\lambda \begin{bmatrix} x_u \\ x_v \\ 1 \end{bmatrix} = \mathbf{P} \begin{bmatrix} X_U \\ X_V \\ X_Z \\ 1 \end{bmatrix}, \tag{6}$$

where λ is an arbitrary homogeneous scaling factor that is the same as in section 3.1.3, There are 11 degrees of freedom (DOF) in $\mathbf{P}$ and the 6-point DLT algorithm is usually adopted [10]. $\mathbf{P}$ can be decomposed into a 3×3 intrinsic matrix $\mathbf{K}$, a 3×3 rotation matrix $\mathbf{R}$, and a translation vector $\mathbf{t}$. where

$$\mathbf{P} = \mathbf{K}[\mathbf{R}|\mathbf{t}], \tag{7}$$

$$\mathbf{K} = \begin{bmatrix} l & \gamma & u_0 \\ 0 & l & v_0 \\ 0 & 0 & 1 \end{bmatrix}, \tag{8}$$

where l is the focal length of the camera, γ is the skew of the camera which is often 0, and u_0 and v_0 define the principal point of the

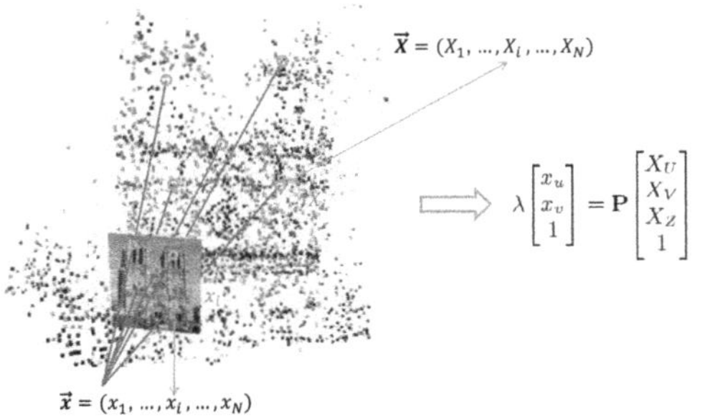

Figure 4: Localization by view registration, the feature points in the image are matched to the 3D points to estimate the camera pose.

image, usually in the center. With these assumptions, only l need to be considered in $\mathbf{K}$. Notice that $\mathbf{R}$ is actually determined by three constituent Euler angles and t is a 3-vector, so that the total DOF is reduced to 7 and only 4-points are needed.

There are methods that can estimate the focal length and other parameters such as the 4-point-solver recently proposed in [14]. When focal length is given, e.g., in the EXIF, the 3-point perspective pose estimation method can be used. According to the report in [16] and [27], using the focal length recorded in the EXIF can reduce the estimation errors and is beneficial for real-time estimation. Thus, in our system we assume the focal length is always available. For a query image in which the EXIF is not available, we transfer the focal lengths from the top candidate images. So the query image is aligned using the 3-point method. With the estimated parameters R and t, the camera position of the image is given by $-\mathbf{R}'\mathbf{t}$ and view direction is $-\mathbf{R}'\begin{bmatrix}0 & 0 & 1\end{bmatrix}'$. The scene position is estimated using the 3D points that can be observed from the query image and we use their mean as the scene location of the image. Finally we register the image to the real world map. We estimate a similar transform from 3D model's horizontal axis to the GPS coordinate. Then we can get $(\mathbf{l}_u, \theta_u, \mathbf{l}_s)$ denoting the camera location, the camera view direction, and the scene location respectively from this similar transform.

3.4 Collaborative Localization with Multiple Images

We are also concerned about the collaboration in the localization using a group of K images $\mathcal{Q} = \{q_k\}_{k=1}^{K}$, with the assumption that the images are taken in nearby areas. First, features are extracted from the query images. A set of candidate images are returned for each query image. Then we check whether there are overlaps in the retrieval results. If the images have any overlap, then we combine the feature vector of the images to search again in the database. The voting score for each scene model $\mathcal{S}(\mathcal{C}_i)$ in this situation is:

$$V_m(\mathcal{S}(\mathcal{C}_i), \mathcal{Q}) = \sum\nolimits_k \frac{V(\mathcal{S}(\mathcal{C}_i), q_k)}{K}, \tag{9}$$

- If these images are capturing the same scene, they will share features. Thus, by combining the feature vectors the shared features will have a higher weight in the search.

- Using this combined feature vector, the scenes in the database that cover more query images will have higher match score and thus are more likely to be retrieved. So, we can localize these images in the same scene to get their relative distance and directions.

If the images have no overlap, each image is localized individually.

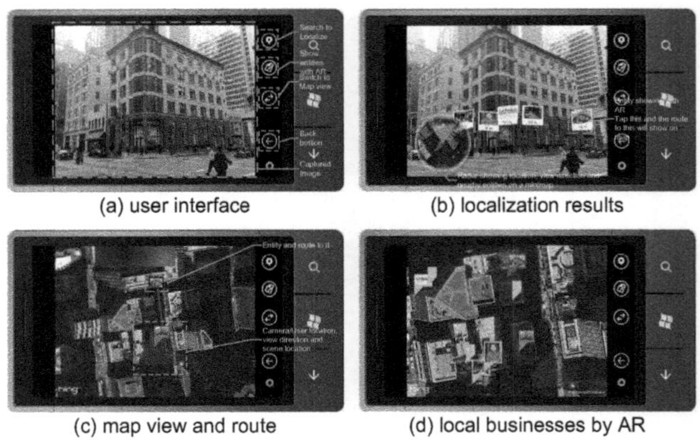

(a) user interface (b) localization results

(c) map view and route (d) local businesses by AR

Figure 5: The user interface for mobile visual localization. (a) shows that the user captures the scene with the phone camera. (b) Then the location and view direction are estimated by the proposed framework. Nearby businesses are shown on the screen to augment reality. (c) The map view of the localization results and the route to the selected destination. (d) The map view with nearby local businesses.

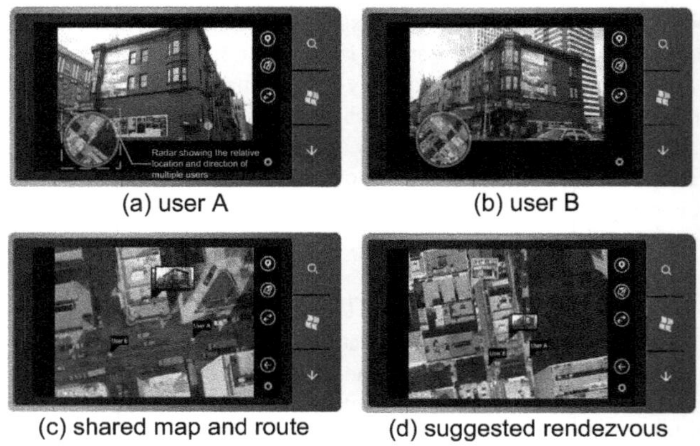

(a) user A (b) user B

(c) shared map and route (d) suggested rendezvous

Figure 6: User interface for collaborative user location. (a)(b) Two users are located in collaboration. (c) Their relative locations, view directions and suggested rendezvous points shared on the same map. (d) The suggested rendezvous and route.

4. APPLICATIONS WITH ACCURATE GEO-CONTEXT

In this section, we will show how the proposed accurate mobile visual localization framework can be integrated into a variety of practical applications for mobile users.

Application I: Accurate self-localization As its core functionality, our framework can supply accurate localization and mapping service for a mobile user. Consequently, the user can obtain accurate geographic information and other information such as local business. This can help the user better explore his/her surroundings. The user interface for this application is shown in Figure 5. First, the user uses the camera to capture a photo as a fingerprint of the scene. Then by pressing the "localization" button the image and rough GPS will be transmitted to the cloud. Our service will return to the user the location $\mathbf{l}_u$, view direction θ_u, and the location of user captured scene $\mathbf{l}_s$. With the rich and accurate information, we can supply better mapping services to help the user better explore the area. In addition, we can recommend nearby businesses to the user and show related entities along the view direction θ_u using augmented reality techniques. In Figure 5 (b), the radar shows the surrounding area of the user within one kilometer.

Figure 7: When a user is browsing a photo online, we can calculate the location and view direction so that the user can take a similar photo and suggest route from the user's current location to photography spot.

Application II: Collaborative localization for finding rendezvous points. The proposed framework can also be used to serve multiple users. A useful application for multiple users is guiding them to a rendezvous point—the perfect place for gathering and meeting. Another scenario is that friends in a crowded area may get separated from each other, especially in an unfamiliar location. To locate themselves and quickly find their way back together, each of them can take a photo of a landmark at his/her location and upload the photos to the cloud. With the multiple image localization service, they will receive accurate geographic information for themselves and their friends. Let $(\mathbf{l}_{u1}, \theta_{u1}, \mathbf{l}_{s1})$ and $(\mathbf{l}_{u2}, \theta_{u2}, \mathbf{l}_{s2})$ denote their localized context respectively. This information is shown with a radar on the screen as a guideline for the users—whether they have been to the same location ($\mathbf{l}_{u1}$ close to $\mathbf{l}_{u2}$), and which direction they should turn ($\theta_{u1} \leftrightarrow \theta_{u2}$). Moreover, we will recommend the rendezvous point for them according to their intended activity (e.g., dining together) and the geo-context, and suggest a route.

Application III: Rendezvous point for photographing. This is an application useful for tourists. When visiting a city, people may turn to websites such as Flickr [6] or Panoramio [24] to browse for scenic spots, since there is substantial information shared by other tourists (e.g., photos, ratings, and comments). While browsing these photos, people may be attracted to some of them. They will think about where these pictures were taken and plan to visit the same spot to take a similar photo. Our system could help the user to find a the specific "rendezvous" point based on the scenery in a photograph. When the user is attracted by an online photo (e.g., when the user is browsing Flickr), he or she could use this mobile application to search for the location where this photo was taken. As described in Section 3.3, we can return the $\mathbf{R}, \mathbf{t}, \mathbf{K}$ of the photo to the user, which can be further translated to $(\mathbf{l}_p, \theta_p, \mathbf{l}_s)$. Other parameters can also be suggested to the user for photographing. Through this application, we can suggest the user: where to go ($\mathbf{l}_p$), what to photograph ($\mathbf{l}_s$), and the best camera pose (θ_p could further be decomposed to heading, tilt, and roll of the camera) and parameters (e.g, focal length) to capture a satisfying photo [4].

5. EXPERIMENTS

In this section, we first introduce the datasets and queries used for evaluation, and then show a series of experimental results of geo-visual clustering, scene reconstruction, single image localization, and multiple localization. Finally, we conduct user studies to evaluate the usability of our proposed accurate mobile visual localization system (AMVL).

5.1 Datasets

To evaluate the performance of AMVL, we conducted experiments on several challenging real-world datasets. We collected two types of datasets, which consist of images with geo-context information such as GPS, but have some differences in their modalities.

- San Francisco street view dataset (**SF street view**). This is a public dataset provided by Stanford and NAVTEQ[1]. It consists of street view photos in San Francisco captured by a vehicle with adequate cameras and other equipment like GPS [5]. There are about 1.06 million images in this database. A set of 803 queries collected by mobile phones with GPS is also provided. There are no other ground truth data, such as view direction, location of the scene available for the queries. However these are essential to evaluate the performance of our AMVL. We have therefore selected a subset of 100 images from the given queries and manually labeled these images with the help of Bing Street Side [3] and Google Street Views [9].

- Images of five cities crawled from Flickr (**Flickr five cities**): This dataset consists of images crawled from the most popular photo-sharing site Flickr [6], which covers the urban area of five cities: Beijing, New York, Paris, San Francisco, and Seattle (Figure 8). Images in **Flickr five cities** contain diverse visual content. They are dense near some popular landmarks. Moreover, the GPS tags are much noisier than those in the **SF street view** dataset. To collect queries, we select the images from the 10 densest regions in the city, so that there are 50 queries in total. Similar to **SF street view**, these selected queries are also manually labeled with camera location, view direction, and scene location.

5.2 Objective Evaluation

Evaluation of joint geo-visual clustering. As mentioned in Section 3.1, we should cluster the images in the database into small clusters using geo-visual clustering. (1) For **SF street view** dataset, image locations are uniformly distributed so that it is much easier to get image clusters. For simplicity we quantize locations into small rectangular tiles with a radius of 50 meters leading to about 150 images per geo-cluster. Then, visual clustering is performed to each small geo-cluster to generate 5$\sim$10 visual clusters with 15$\sim$40 images in each. (2) For **Flickr five cities** dataset, as the images are more diverse in both geographical and visual space, in geo-clustering, we choose a radius $r_g = 700m$ to get larger geo-clusters. While for fast clustering a spatial tile with size $50m \times 50m$ is used instead of single image locations as the basic unit for geo-clustering. We build inverted index files in every geo-clusters so the visual similarity matrix can be computed quickly. Even with large geo-clusters(up to thousands of images in the largest geo-cluster), we can achieve very fast visual clustering. Finally we can get visual clusters, but there are many clusters that are single images due to the diversity of Flickr images. Once the clustering is finished, we can get the index of images to the cluster.

Evaluation of 3D scene model reconstruction. Images in the same visual cluster represent the same scene or similar views of the same scene. We build a 3D scene model for each visual cluster from these images. The scene models are 3D point clouds and camera parameters reconstructed using SfM. In our experiments, the bundler toolbox [30] is adopted to compute the reconstruction. As we have clustered the images into small groups, the reconstruction are conducted with around dozens of images, which is small compared to those used in the Photo Tourism system [30]. Thus the reconstruction requires low computational power and can be performed on a single PC. The average time for constructing a scene

[1] `http://www.stanford.edu/~dmchen/mvs.html`

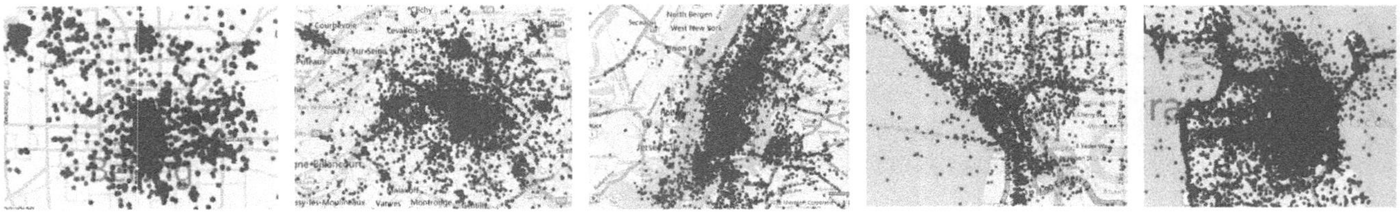

Figure 8: Geographical distribution of images of five cities crawled from Flickr are shown on the map. The five cities from left to right are: Beijing, Paris, New York, Seattle and San Francisco.

(a) A query image and it's retrieved 3D scene built from one geo-visual cluster in "SF street view" dataset.

(b) Query image and retrieved 3D scene of a landmark(Norte Dame de Paris) in "Flickr 5 cities" dataset.

Figure 9: The query image and retrieved 3D scene models built from images in geo-visual cluster.

is 2∼10 min since the clusters' size are usually 15∼40. We can reconstruct several scenes in parallel to further speed up the reconstruction. Figure 9 shows two 3D scenes for example.

Evaluation of self-localization using single image. We follow the procedure introduced in Section 3.2 to estimate the accurate geographic context of an image. First, SIFT features are extracted from the images. Then the features are quantized to visual words using the vocabulary tree method. As $B = 10, H = 6$ in our experiments, we use a tree with $1M$ leaf nodes. Inverted file and fast geometric verification are used to retrieve and filter candidate images. The filtered top 20 candidate images are used to vote for the most related scene. Then the query image is aligned to the 3D scene. We have evaluated the image retrieval and localization performance. We use mean Average Precision (mAP) as the evaluation criterion of our image retrieval system. Given $\mathcal{Q} = \{q_i\}$ denoting the query image set, the mAP at rank N is defined by:

$$mAP@N = \frac{1}{|\mathcal{Q}|}\sum_{i=1}^{|\mathcal{Q}|}\Big(\frac{\sum_{r=1}^{N} P_i(r)}{N}\Big), \qquad (10)$$

where $|\mathcal{Q}|$ is the number of queries and $P_i(r)$ is the precision of $i\text{-}th$ query image at rank r. We have evaluate the precision of several image retrieval strategies. 1) *BoW*: state of the art Bag-of-Words method with TF-IDF weighting. 2) BoW+GPS: excluding faraway (> 300m) candidates by coarse GPS of the query image. 3) BoW+GV: BoW with feature orientation quantization and spatial verification. Orientation quantization also embeds geometric information, so we relegate it into GV. 4) BoW+GV+GPS. The retrieval performance can be seen in Figure 10. It can be observed from the results that the BoW method, which merely considering the matched feature weight leads to the worst performance. Feature orientation and geometric verification are important in image retrieval, because the structure information provides additional knowledge. This is especially useful in the dataset of street views and landmark images, where the image content is highly structured and mostly gravity-aligned. GPS coordinates associated with the query image to constrain the search range could further enhance the retrieval precision.

After image retrieval, we can use the obtained candidate scenes

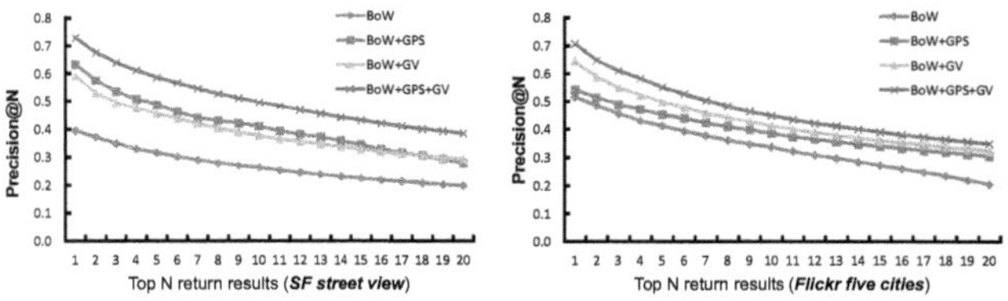

Figure 10: The retrieval performance on SF street view and Flickr five cities datasets with several retrieve strategies.

Table 1: The error statistics of estimated geographical information of queries in SF street view. AMVL is the proposed system in this paper. Comparison results implementing two other localization approaches are also shown in this table.

Errors		Camera location	View direction	Scene location	Phone GPS
AMVL	Mean	13.787m	8.963°	20.675m	30.344m
	Std.	25.844m	11.708°	26.089m	44.330m
VPS [27]	Mean	15.218m	9.531°	22.758m	-
	Std.	25.793m	12.967°	26.647m	-
BGPS-I [25]	Mean	-	19.864°	-	-
	Std.	-	22.836°	-	-
BGPS-II [25]	Mean	-	12.774°	-	-
	Std.	-	12.179°	-	-

models to perform view registration with the query images. The estimation errors of camera location, view direction and scene location are listed in Table 1 for **SF street view** and Table 2 for **Flickr five cities**. As there are images that cannot find the proper scenes or fail to align to the scene models, these results are calculated using the subset that successfully aligned to a scene model. In **SF street view**, 60 out of the total 100 query images are successfully aligned to a scene model. From the statistics we can see the proposed mobile visual localization system could reduce the mean localization error to 13.787 meters compared to the GPS data collected by mobile phone sensors, and the view direction estimation has an average mean error of 8.963 degrees. It can be seen from Figure 11 that most images achieve a high accuracy of localization. Notice that the estimated scene locations have a larger mean error than camera locations. That is probably because we estimate the scene location using the matched 3D points, while there may be 3D points from other buildings making the estimated scene align to further locations. The efficiency of the proposed system is evaluated and shown in Table 3. The total time cost for successfully localizing a 640 × 480 photo is 3.5∼6 seconds. Similar results of **Flickr five cities** can be seen in Table 2, where 37 out of 50 query images are successfully localized, but with greater mean errors and deviations. This was caused by the noisy GPS labels of Flickr images, which affected the estimation accuracy of similar transforms that map the camera to real-world coordinates.

We compared the localization performance with two other methods on the **SF street view** dataset. The first is the Vocabulary-

Table 2: **The error statistics of estimated geographical information of queries in Flickr five cities**

Errors	**Camera location**	**View direction**	**Scene location**	**Labeled GPS**
Mean	25.457m	14.547°	32.654m	50.487m
Std.	28.766m	13.876°	37.205m	66.325m

Table 3: Time complexity of the system (sec).

Operation	Uploading	Extract SIFT	Vocabulary tree search
Time	<0.2	0.7∼1.2	<0.3
Operation	Vote for 3D	Align to 3D	Register to map
Time	<0.02	2∼4	<0.1

based Prioritized Search (VPS) [27] which performs direct 2D-to-3D matching, while the second is Beyond GPS (BGPS) [25] where an approximation algorithm estimates the view direction of a geotagged photo using nearby street view images as references. For VPS, since it needs time to load descriptors, only the models within a certain radius (300m) of each query image are considered to conduct the 2D-to-3D matching. For BGPS, it requires the input image with given camera GPS and only estimates the view directions. We have evaluated the performance of BGPS for two settings: 1) with the noisy phone GPS as the input camera location (BGPS-I), 2) with groundtruth camera location (BGPS-II). Street view images within a certain peripheral area are used as references (the radius is 100m in our implementation). The experimental results are also shown in Table 1. From the results we can observe that the BGPS performance is good with the accurate camera location. However, it degenerates quickly when using noisy GPS coordinates. Our performance (13.787m) is comparable to VPS (15.218m), with even smaller mean error. This is probably because the accuracy of VPS is sensitive to some badly localized 3D points. However, we should point out that our system requires lower memory cost compared to VPS. The main memory cost of our system is the inverted table of quantized image features. Then a small 3D scene model voted on by image retrieval results is loaded into the memory for localization by view registration. For a database with about one million images the memory cost of our system is about 4 Gigabytes (Inverted Index) plus 10 megabytes (voted 3D model). Meanwhile, VPS needs to keep the 128-bytes descriptors for all 3D points in the memory. For a database with about 16K cameras, VPS requires more than 2 gigabytes. Thus, our system has better scalability than VPS.

Evaluation of collaborative localization. To examine the performance of localization of multiple images in collaboration, we use images in groups for evaluation. Images in the same group are taken within the same area of radius 300m. As discussed in Section 3.4, we use the combined feature vector to search whether the images have any overlap. We found this achieves a better localization for a group of images than and individual image. Figure 12 shows some group localization examples:

5.3 Usability Evaluation

We invited 12 subjects to use our AMVL system on Windows Phone 7 devices. The subjects include three female and nine male college students, with the ages ranging from 22 to 28. Half of them were undergraduates and the rest were graduate. Most of them had 1∼3 years of experience of using smart mobile phones and localization applications such as Google Maps [8], while two had a longer experience of 3∼5 years and two had never used such applications on mobile phones. After a 5-min orientation and demonstration, all of them knew how to use this application. Some of

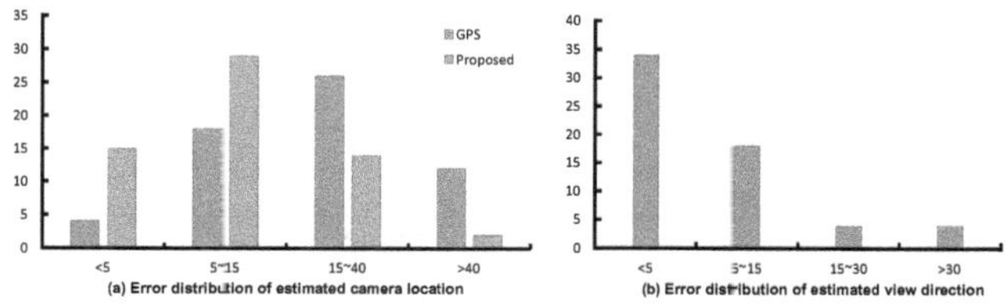

Figure 11: The error distributions of SF street view queries. (a) the error of estimated camera locations using propose framework compared to data collected from mobile phone sensors, (b) the estimated view direction errors.

(a) (b) (c)

Figure 12: Examples of multi-image co-localization: (a) pair of query images; (b) images of the retrieved scene; (c) collaborative localization results, on a shared map.

them liked the augmented reality of showing local business along their viewing direction on the screen. Compared with having only their location and nearby local business shown on the map, they agreed that their intent can be expressed more clearly with our system.

After learning to use the system, the users were asked to use the application to accomplish the following tasks:

- The user is in the street and lost his/her way. Given a street view photo captured by the phone and the GPS data from the sensor, the user should try to obtain his/her location and orientation. Then the user is encouraged to find a way to the restaurant/café/bar in front of him/her.
- The user and his/her friends each capture a photo in front of them then log in to our system, share their locations, directions, and pictures with their friends on the same map. They can find a way to meet in the crowded area.

As our system has not been released to the public yet, the subjects were unable to conduct the tasks under actual circumstances. Thus we simulated 100 locations in San Francisco.. Meanwhile, the street view images queried with the estimated geo-context were shown to the user to check the localization accuracy. The users felt it was easy to fulfill these tasks and found AMVL successfully facilitates their intent. A questionnaire was also filled out by each

Table 4: **A summary of the user study. Each metric is rated from 1 to 5 indicating the worst to the best level.**

ID	Questions	Satisfaction
1	Attractiveness&Naturalness	3.7
2	Efficiency	3.3
3	Clarity of intent	3.8
4	Practicality	3.8
5	Ease to use	4.2
6	Finding Rendezvous point with friends	4.4
7	Preference/Recommendation	4.3

participant to evaluate the usability, user friendliness, and experience. The quantitative evaluation of users' satisfaction with the mobile visual localization system is shown in Table 4. As can be seen from the results, the users found our application attractive and easy to use with a friendly user interface. Some subjects were satisfied with the relevant local businesses shown on the screen. They agreed that this can assist them to sense their surroundings better. 91.7% of the subjects thought the multi-user system where one can share photo and geo-context with friends was quite useful, especially when they were going to meet in an unfamiliar place or were separated by a crowd. Most of them gave a positive response when asked whether they will install this application and recommend it to their friends. Moreover, they were asked about new features from our system. Some of them were concerned about the latency in the 3G wireless network environment, as it takes 3.5∼6 sec in our WiFi-based system. Some of them noticed that when the direction estimation was incorrect, it could mislead the user. They thought this could be used together with GPS and other sensors for better results.

6. DISCUSSION AND CONCLUSIONS

This paper presents a mobile visual localization system that achieve a comprehensive set of geo-context information. Compared to existing visual localization approaches, the proposed system combines advanced techniques of large-scale image retrieval, 3D model reconstruction, and localization by 2D-to-3D matching. It can achieve high localization accuracy and good scalability. The experiments show that the proposed system can provide more accurate and complete geo-context to the user. A variety of applications show the improved user experience in location-based services. However, it may fail when the query image is not able to find accurate candidate images, or the related images are unable to reconstruct a 3D scene model with enough points.

Our future works include: 1) helping the user to find distinctive views, which will enhance the accuracy of visual-based retrieval to make our system more robust and reliable, and 2) leveraging compressed representation of images to reduce the system latency to enable real-time localization.

7. ACKNOWLEDGEMENT

This work is partly supported by NSFC general project fund "Intelligent Video Processing and Coding Based on Cloud Computing."

8. REFERENCES

[1] S. Arya, D. Mount, N. Netanyahu, R. Silverman, and A. Wu. An optimal algorithm for approximate nearest neighbor searching fixed dimensions. *JACM*, 1998.

[2] Y. Avrithis, Y. Kalantidis, G. Tolias, and E. Spyrou. Retrieving landmark and non-landmark images from community photo collections. In *ACM Multimedia*, 2010.

[3] Bing street side. `http://www.microsoft.com/maps/streetside.aspx`.

[4] S. Bourke, K. McCarthy, and B. Smyth. The social camera: a case-study in contextual image recommendation. In *IUI*, 2011.

[5] D. Chen, G. Baatz, K. Koser, S. Tsai, R. Vedantham, T. Pylvanainen, K. Roimela, X. Chen, J. Bach, M. Pollefeys, et al. City-scale landmark identification on mobile devices. In *CVPR*, 2011.

[6] Flickr. `http://www.flickr.com/`.

[7] B. J. Frey and D. Dueck. Clustering by passing messages between data points. *Science*, 2007.

[8] Google Earth. `http://earth.google.com/`.

[9] Google street view. `http://www.google.com/streetview`.

[10] R. I. Hartley and A. Zisserman. *Multiple View Geometry in Computer Vision*. Second edition, 2004.

[11] J. Hays and A. Efros. Im2gps: estimating geographic information from a single image. In *CVPR*, 2008.

[12] A. Irschara, C. Zach, J. Frahm, and H. Bischof. From structure-from-motion point clouds to fast location recognition. In *CVPR*, 2009.

[13] R. Ji, L. Duan, J. Chen, H. Yao, Y. Rui, S. Chang, and W. Gao. Towards low bit rate mobile visual search with multiple-channel coding. In *ACM Multimedia*, 2011.

[14] K. Josephson and M. Byrod. Pose estimation with radial distortion and unknown focal length. In *CVPR*, 2009.

[15] M. Kroepfl, Y. Wexler, and E. Ofek. Efficiently locating photographs in many panoramas. In *GIS*, 2010.

[16] X. Li, C. Wu, C. Zach, S. Lazebnik, and J. Frahm. Modeling and recognition of landmark image collections using iconic scene graphs. In *ECCV*, 2008.

[17] Y. Li, N. Snavely, and D. Huttenlocher. Location recognition using prioritized feature matching. In *ECCV*, 2010.

[18] C. Liu, J. Yuen, A. Torralba, J. Sivic, and W. Freeman. Sift flow: Dense correspondence across different scenes. In *ECCV*, 2008.

[19] D. Lowe. Distinctive image features from scale-invariant keypoints. *IJCV*, 2004.

[20] J. Luo, D. Joshi, J. Yu, and A. Gallagher. Geotagging in multimedia and computer vision: a survey. *MTA*, 2011.

[21] Z. Luo, H. Li, J. Tang, R. Hong, and T. Chua. Viewfocus: explore places of interests on google maps using photos with view direction filtering. In *ACM Multimedia*, 2009.

[22] D. Nistér. An efficient solution to the five-point relative pose problem. *PAMI*, 2004.

[23] D. Nister and H. Stewenius. Scalable recognition with a vocabulary tree. In *CVPR*, 2006.

[24] Panoramio. `http://www.panoramio.com/`.

[25] M. Park, J. Luo, R. Collins, and Y. Liu. Beyond gps: determining the camera viewing direction of a geotagged image. In *ACM Multimedia*, 2010.

[26] J. Philbin, O. Chum, M. Isard, J. Sivic, and A. Zisserman. Object retrieval with large vocabularies and fast spatial matching. In *CVPR*, 2007.

[27] T. Sattler, B. Leibe, and L. Kobbelt. Fast image-based localization using direct 2d-to-3d matching. In *ICCV*, 2011.

[28] G. Schindler, M. Brown, and R. Szeliski. City-scale location recognition. In *CVPR*, 2007.

[29] G. Schroth, R. Huitl, D. Chen, M. Abu-Alqumsan, A. Al-Nuaimi, and E. Steinbach. Mobile visual location recognition. *Signal Processing Magazine*, 2011.

[30] N. Snavely, S. Seitz, and R. Szeliski. Photo tourism: exploring photo collections in 3d. In *TOG*, 2006.

[31] F. Yu, R. Ji, and S. Chang. Active query sensing for mobile location search. In *ACM Multimedia*, 2011.

[32] A. Zamir and M. Shah. Accurate image localization based on google maps street view. In *ECCV*, 2010.

[33] W. Zhang and J. Kosecka. Image based localization in urban environments. In *3DPVT*, 2006.

[34] W. Zhou, Y. Lu, H. Li, Y. Song, and Q. Tian. Spatial coding for large scale partial-duplicate web image search. In *ACM Multimedia*, 2010.

Right Buddy Makes the Difference: an Early Exploration of Social Relation Analysis in Multimedia Applications

Jitao Sang[1,2], Changsheng Xu[1,2]
[1]National Lab of Pattern Recognition, Institute of Automation, CAS, Beijing 100190, China
[2]China-Singapore Institute of Digital Media, Singapore, 119613, Singapore
{jtsang, csxu}@nlpr.ia.ac.cn

ABSTRACT

Social media is becoming popular these days, where user necessarily interacts with each other to form social networks. Influence network, as one special case of social network, has been recognized as significantly impacting social activities and user decisions. We emphasize in this paper that the inter-user influence is essentially topic-sensitive, as for different tasks users tend to trust different influencers and be influenced most by them. While existing research focuses on global influence modeling and applies to text-based networks, this work investigates the problem of topic-sensitive influence modeling in the multimedia domain.

We propose a multi-modal probabilistic model, considering both users' textual annotation and uploaded visual image. This model is capable of simultaneously extracting user topic distributions and topic-sensitive influence strengths. By identifying the topic-sensitive influencer, we are able to conduct applications like collective search and collaborative recommendation. A risk minimization-based general framework for personalized image search is further presented, where the image search task is transferred to measure the distance of image and personalized query language models. The framework considers the noisy tag issue and enables easy incorporation of social influence. We have conducted experiments on a large-scale Flickr dataset. Qualitative as well as quantitative evaluation results have validated the effectiveness of the topic-sensitive influencer mining model, and demonstrated the advantage of incorporating topic-sensitive influence in personalized image search and topic-based image recommendation.

Categories and Subject Descriptors

H.3.3 [**Information Storage and Retrieval**]: Information Search and Retrieval; H.4.m [**Information Systems**]: Miscellaneous

General Terms

Algorithms, Experimentation, Performance

Keywords

social relation analysis, multimedia application

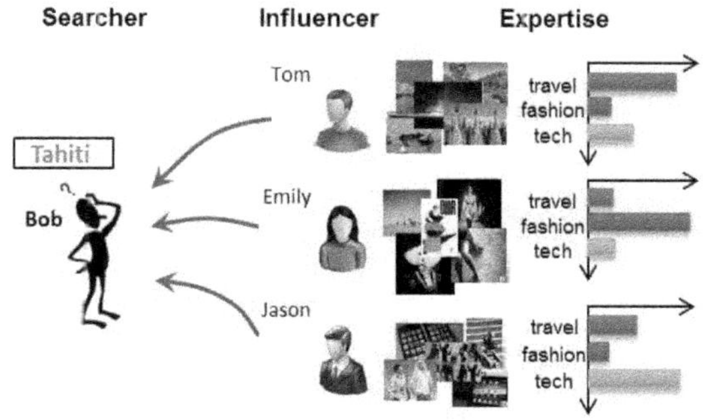

Figure 1: The toy example for topic-sensitive influencer.

1. INTRODUCTION

Social media has revolutionized the way people share and access information. In social media services, users necessarily interact with each other into communities, i.e., social networks. The social interactions include two-way links like "connect" in LinkedIn and "add friend" in Facebook, and one-way links like "follow" in Twitter, "contact" in Flickr and "subscribe" in Youtube. The social links are well recognized forces that govern the behaviors of involved users as well as the dynamics of social networks. For example, the colleagues on LinkedIn will largely impact one's choices in work, while the friends from Facebook have strong influence on one's preferences in daily life. Therefore, understanding social links can benefit various applications such as viral marketing [1], collaborative recommendation [2] and collective information retrieval [3]. In this work, we first focus on modeling the one-way social link, or influence [4], in photo sharing websites, and then exploit it for the application of personalized image search.

Social influence analysis has attracted extensive research interests, such as investigating the existence of influence [5, 6], maximizing influence propagation [7, 8] and identifying the evolved influencer [9]. For social influence-based retrieval, the basic premise behind is that the preferences of other users, who are the influencers to the searcher, provide a good indication for the searcher's preference. The influence link between influencers and searcher has two intrinsic characteristics: (1) The influence is continuous. This is easy to understand, as binary influence link (i.e., influencer or not) is too coarse to model the relationship strength. Recently, continuous influence modeling has been addressed in [10, 11]. (2) The influence is topic-sensitive. Given a one-way influence network, the actual influencer is task-dependent. We use a toy example to elaborate this. Fig. 1 shows the contact network of user Bob in Flickr which includes three influencers: Tom, Emily and Jason. On the right we illustrate the expertise of each influencer regarding topics on *travel*, *fashion* and *technology*. Assuming Bob

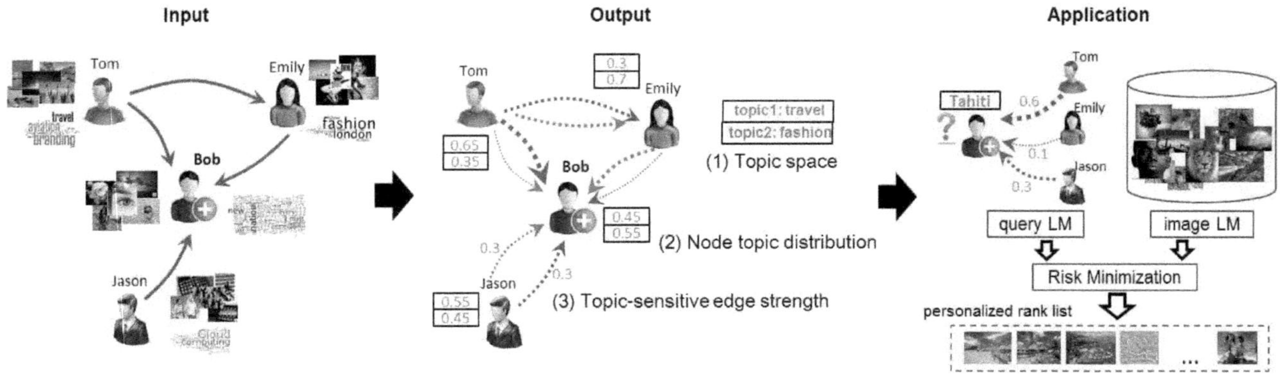

(a) Topic-sensitive Influencer Mining

(b) Personalized Image Search

Figure 2: Problem illustration (best viewed in color).

is searching photos of "Tahiti" for his honeymoon trip, obviously Tom's preference will influence him most. While, when Bob searches photos of "D&G fashion show", the advice from Emily will be most appreciated. This demonstrates that some influencers in certain topics might be more trustworthy than others and the influence value is topic-sensitive. However, little work has investigated the problem of topic-level influence modeling, especially in multimedia domain.

In this paper, we investigate the problem of topic-sensitive influencer mining in social media communities. In particular, we take Flickr, one of the most popular photo sharing websites, as the social media platform in our study. In Flickr, users are allowed to add others as their contacts, which is analogous to the influencers. Besides the explicit one-way influence link between users, the uploaded images and associated tags can also be leveraged. The multi-modal information available on photo sharing websites provide challenges as well as opportunities to the problem of topic-sensitive influencer mining. As shown in Fig.2(a), we formulate the *multi-modal Topic-sensitive Influence Modeling* (mmTIM) problem as follows: The input is users' contact networks, annotation sets and uploaded image sets. We propose a probabilistic generative model to infer the output, which inverses the generation process of image content as well as the associated tags. With users as nodes, user-influencer social links as edges, the output includes (1) the learned topic space, (2) the topic distribution of each node and (3) the topic-sensitive edge strength [1]. The edge strengths correspond to the topic-sensitive influence values, while the node topic distribution indicates the topic expertise of corresponding user. After mining the topic-sensitive influencer in the contact network, we apply it to the application of personalized search. Following the risk minimization-based information retrieval scheme, we present a general framework for personalized image search. The new framework benefits from the consideration of influencer preference and annotation confidence in the modeling process. Topic-sensitive influence and user expertise can be readily integrated in the expansion of the language models (LM) for queries and image documents. Therefore, the main contributions of this paper can be summarized as follows:

- We address the topic-sensitive influencer mining problem for applications of collaborative recommendation and collective search in multimedia domain.
- A multi-modal topic-sensitive influence model is presented, which enables simultaneous extraction of node topic distribution, topic-sensitive edge strength and the topic space.
- We propose a risk minimization-based theoretical framework for personalized image search. Topic-sensitive influence and annotation confidence can be seamlessly incorporated.

[1] The solid line indicates the explicit social link, and the dashed line indicates the implicit topic-sensitive influence strength.

2. RELATED WORK

Our work is closely related to two research topics: (1) social influence modeling and (2) personalized information retrieval.

2.1 Social Influence Modeling

One research line in social influence modeling is to investigate the influence spread patterns, such as influence propagation maximization [7, 8], influence diffusion over social networks [12, 13] and influence network evolution [9]. Several works focus on another research line by analyzing influence for social activity understanding. For example, in [14] the authors demonstrated from results of questionnaire that influencer behavior subjects to influence and impacts influence network evolution. [5] studied the correlation between influence and social activities, and concluded that social influence plays an important role in dictating user behaviors. Ronald et al. [15] proposed an agent-based model to describe social activities between users in influence network. They found influence network has an significant effect on the number and type of the social activities.

The influence networks used in above works are either binary or continuous. For binary influence modeling, a number of efforts have been made to identify the existence of social influence in online social networks. Anagnustogpolos et al. [5] provided a theoretical justification to identify influence as a source of social correlation. In the same year, Crandall et al. [6] analyzed the binary influence link by investigating the correlation between social similarity and influence. Compared with binary influence, continuous influence leads to more precise description of the social relation. The study in [10] developed a link-based latent variable model to estimate influence strength from user similarity and interaction activities (e.g., communication, collaborative tagging). Zhuang et al. [11] further addressed this problem by exploring the heterogeneous data in photo sharing websites and proposing a multiple kernel-based learning-to-rank method to combine them.

As discussed in the previous section, in many cases, the influence strength is actually topic-sensitive. Topic-sensitive influence modeling, which provides more delicate and informative descriptions of social relations between people, is necessary to applications like collaborative recommendation and collective search. So far as we know, only two papers have addressed this problem, which are focused on text-based citation alike networks. Tang et al. [16] introduced topic-sensitive social influence modeling and proposed a Topical Affinity Propagation (TAP) approach to tackle the problem. In their formulation, the topic space and topic distribution for each user node are assumed available and employed as inputs. In [17], the authors moved one step further and presented a graphical probabilistic model to learn the node topic distributions and topic-sensitive influence jointly. The information they utilized include the heterogeneous link and the textual content associated with each node. Our work is different from them in that we are investigating the topic-sensitive influence in the multimedia context. Besides the explicit influence link and the textual annotation, we provide a multi-modal framework simultaneously modeling visual content.

2.2 Personalized Information Retrieval

Extensive efforts have been focusing on personalized information retrieval these days. The resources being leveraged include explicit user profile, relevance feedback, click-through data, context information, social annotation and social network. Chirita *et al.* [18] conducted an early work by re-ranking search results according to the cosine distance between each URL and explicit user interest profiles. Kraft *et al.* [19] utilized the search context information collected from users' feedback to refine the raw query for second search. In [20], the authors utilized user's click-through history to construct user preference vector and extended Topic-Sensitive PageRank for personalized search. [21] introduces a local search system by considering context information (e.g., time, location, weather) as well as user query log for search result personalization. [22] demonstrates that user-generated metadata indicates user's interest and can be used to personalize information. They extracted latent topics from tagging data and used the latent user interest profile for personalized image search. In similar spirits, Lu et al. [23] utilized user activities of tagging and joining interest group to extract latent interest profile and re-rank the returned images by combining latent interest-based user preference and query relevance. Recently, an interesting work is performed in [24], where the authors proposed to extract user-specific topic spaces by expanding the raw annotation set for each user. Queries are mapped to the derived user-specific topics spaces and the personalized relevance score over images are calculated.

Several approaches have directly or indirectly employed user's social relations for personalized search. Bender et al. [25] proposed a PageRank-like algorithm to exploit the utilization of social relations. They assumed that a document receives an extra "friendship" score when tagged by the searcher's friends. Carmel et al. [3] explicitly defined familiar and similar scores to model relations between users. With familiar score estimated from explicit social link and similar score calculated from collaborative activities, personalization is conducted according to the searcher's relationship strength with users in the social network. Similarly, in [26], a multilevel actor similarity method is proposed to first measure the social affinity between users. The personalized ranking score is then calculated by combining the query-video relevance and the affinity score between the searcher and the video's owner. Lin et al. [27] leveraged the output of community discovery and proposed a community-oriented re-ranking scheme to aggregate query-video relevance and user-community-video preference.

Our work differentiates from existing social network-based approaches in that, we exploit the topic-sensitive social relations between users and integrate query-dependent social strength into personalized ranking score calculation. Moreover, for the first time, we present a theoretical personalized image search framework by jointly modeling social influence preference and annotation confidence.

Table 1: List of key notations

Notations	Description
$\mathcal{U}$	Flickr user set
$\mathcal{C}_u, \mathcal{D}_u, \mathcal{T}_u$	a collection of contact users, images and tags for user u
Φ^w, Φ^v	word and visual descriptor distributions for topics
Ω	topic mixture matrix
$\Psi(t)$	the influencing strength matrix for t-th topic
$\mathbf{w}, \mathbf{v}$	tag word and visual descriptor vectors
z^w, z^v	topic assignments for tag word and visual descriptor
s^w, s^v	binary labels denoting whether the generation of word and visual descriptor is influenced or not
c^w, c^v	the sampled influencer during the generation of tag word and visual descriptor
λ	the parameter to draw the label s^w and s^v
γ	the parameter to sample influencer
α	Dirichlet prior for hidden variables
$N(\cdot)$	the number of samples during Gibbs sampling
$\lvert\cdot\rvert$	the cardinality of set
$\mathbf{I}(\cdot)$	indicator function

3. TOPIC-SENSITIVE INFLUENCER MINING

This section introduces the topic-sensitive influencer mining problem. Table 1 lists the key notations. First, we formally define the problem:

DEFINITION 1 (TOPIC-SENSITIVE INFLUENCER MINING). *Given a collection of Flickr users $\mathcal{U}$, each user $u \in \mathcal{U}$ corresponds to a three-dimensional tuple $[\mathcal{C}_u, \mathcal{D}_u, \mathcal{T}_u]$. The goal of topic-sensitive influencer mining is to learn (1) Topic space $\Phi^w \subset \mathbb{R}^{T\times|\mathcal{W}|}$ and $\Phi^v \subset \mathbb{R}^{T\times|\mathcal{V}|}$ [2]; (2) Node topic distribution $\Omega_u \subset \mathbb{R}^{T\times 1}$ for each user u; and (3) Topic-sensitive edge strength $\Psi(t) \subset \mathbb{R}^{|\mathcal{U}|\times|\mathcal{U}|}$, $t = \{1, \cdots, T\}$* [3].

We propose a probabilistic generative model for topic-sensitive influencer mining. Since the model specifies the generation process of the visual image content as well as the textual tag words for each user, we call it multi-modal Topic-sensitive Influence Model (mmTIM).

3.1 Multi-Modal Topic-sensitive Influence Model

It is well recognized that users' online activity is impacted a lot by their influencers [5, 15]. The uploaded images and annotated tags can be viewed as observations of users' activities. Inspired by this, for each user, we assume that his/her tag words and uploaded images are generated in two ways, either *innovative*–mainly depending on his/her own interest or *influenced*–being more influenced by the influencers. For example, when Bob uploads an image, the theme of the image may match his own original interest, or follow one of his influencers. Another example, the tag Bob choos-

[2] We use topic distributions over tag words and visual descriptors to represent the topic space: T is the number of topics, $|\mathcal{W}|$ is the size of tag vocabulary, $|\mathcal{V}|$ is the size of visual-descriptor vocabulary.

[3] $\Psi_{u_1,u_2}(t)$, $u_2 \in \mathcal{C}_{u_1}$ measures the influence strength from user u_2 to u_1 in t-th topic.

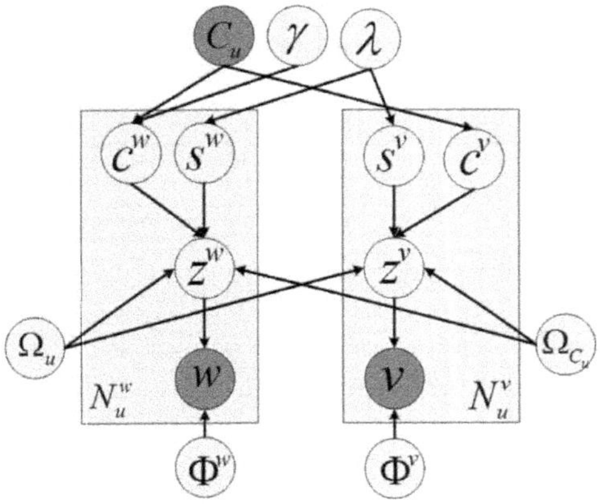

Figure 3: Probabilistic generative model of mmTIM.

es for annotation can be viewed as either generated innovatively or borrowed from his contact users.

Fig. 3 illustrates our understanding of the generation process as graphical structure. For image visual content, we first construct a visual vocabulary and represent each user by the visual descriptor responses **v** of his/her uploaded images. In the model, we use binary variables s^w and s^v to control whether the tag words and visual descriptors are generated by the users themselves or according to one of the influencers. When $s^w = 1$, the tag word is generated based on user's own interest Ω_u. When $s^w = 0$, the tag word is influenced by one of users in the contact list $\mathcal{C}_u$, and it is generated based on the interest Ω_{c^w} of the sampled influencer c^w. The details of the generative process for tag words of user u are as follows:

For each tag word $w_{u,i} \in \mathbf{w}_u$,

(1) Draw a switch variable from a bernoulli distribution: $s^w_{u,i} \sim Bernoulli(\lambda)$;

(2) If $s^w_{u,i} = 0$, then

i. Draw a influencer from u's contact list, which follows multinominal distribution parametered by γ: $c^w_{u,i} \sim Multi(\gamma)$;

ii. Draw a topic from influencer $c^w_{u,i}$'s topic distribution: $z^w_{u,i} \sim Multi(\Omega_{c^w_{u,i}})$;

(3) If $s^w_{u,i} = 1$, then

i. Draw a topic from u's own topic distribution: $z^w_{u,i} \sim Multi(\Omega_u)$;

(4) Draw a word $w_{u,i}$ from the topic-word distribution: $w_{u,i} \sim Multi(\Phi^w_{z^w_{u,i}})$.

The generative process of visual descriptors is similar other than that the visual descriptor $v_{u,i}$ is sampled from topic-visual descriptor distribution $\Phi^v_{z^v_{u,i}}$. Actually, during the model learning process, we assume the prior distributions follow symmetric Dirichlet, which are conjugate priors for multinomial (or Beta for Bernoulli). For simplification, we do not draw the hyperparameters in the graphical model.

Note that the proposed mmTIM is much inspired by the model presented in [17], but with two important differences: (1) [17] focuses on social network based on textual information, while we present its multimodal version to explore the multimedia social network, by considering both textual annotation and visual image information; (2) Instead of building influencer set at document-level as in [17], we build the influencer set at user-level, which is more intuitive for user-oriented applications like personalized search and collaborative recommendation.

3.2 Learning mmTIM by Gibbs Sampling

The mmTIM model includes three sets of latent variables, the binary switch labels s^w, s^v, the influencer c^w, c^v and the topic assignments z^w, z^v. We use Gibbs sampling [28] for model learning. When using Gibbs sampling to train a generative model, a Markov chain is formed. The joint distribution is approximated by drawing a sequence of samples and each latent variable is iteratively updated by fixing other variables. The derivation of update rules is detailed in the appendix. We list the update rules for latent variables concerning tag words as follows.

$$p(s_i^w = 0|\mathbf{s}^w_{-i}, u_i^w, c_i^w, z_i^w, \cdot) \propto \frac{N^w_{U,S}(u_i^w, 0) + \alpha_\lambda - 1}{N^w_U(u_i^w) + 2\alpha_\lambda - 1} \cdot \frac{N^w_{U,Z}(c_i^w, z_i^w) + \alpha_\Omega - 1}{N^w_U(c_i^w) + T\alpha_\Omega - 1} \quad (1)$$

$$p(s_i^w = 1|\mathbf{s}^w_{-i}, u_i^w, z_i^w, \cdot) \propto \frac{N^w_{U,S}(u_i^w, 1) + \alpha_\lambda - 1}{N^w_U(u_i^w) + 2\alpha_\lambda - 1} \cdot \frac{N^w_{U,S,Z}(u_i^w, 1, z_i^w) + \alpha_\Omega - 1}{N^w_{U,S}(u_i^w, 1) + T\alpha_\Omega - 1} \quad (2)$$

$$p(c_i^w|\mathbf{c}^w_{-i}, s_i^w = 0, u_i^w, z_i^w, \mathcal{C}_{u_i^w}, \cdot) \propto \frac{N^w_{U,C,S,Z}(u_i^w, c_i^w, 0, z_i^w) + \alpha_\gamma}{N^w_{U,S,Z}(u_i^w, 0, z_i^w) + |\mathcal{C}_{u_i^w}|} \cdot \frac{N^w_{U,Z}(c_i^w, z_i^w) + \alpha_\Omega - 1}{N^w_U(c_i^w) + T\alpha_\Omega - 1} \quad (3)$$

$$p(z_i^w|\mathbf{z}^w_{-i}, s_i^w = 0, w_i, \cdot) \propto \frac{N^w_{U,Z}(c_i^w, z_i^w) + \alpha_\Omega - 1}{N^w_U(c_i^w) + T\alpha_\Omega - 1} \cdot \frac{N^w_{Z,W}(z_i^w, w_i) + \alpha_{\Phi^w}}{N^w_Z(z_i^w) + |\mathcal{W}|\alpha_{\Phi^w}} \quad (4)$$

$$p(z_i^w|\mathbf{z}^w_{-i}, s_i^w = 1, w_i, \cdot) \propto \frac{N^w_{U,S,Z}(u_i^w, 1, z_i^w) + \alpha_\Omega - 1}{N^w_{U,S}(u_i^w, 1) + T\alpha_\Omega - 1} \cdot \frac{N^w_{Z,W}(z_i^w, w_i) + \alpha_{\Phi^w}}{N^w_Z(z_i^w) + |\mathcal{W}|\alpha_{\Phi^w}} \quad (5)$$

where u_i^w denotes the user to which the i-th word belongs, z_i^w denotes the topic assignment of the i-th word, $\alpha_\Omega, \alpha_{\Phi^w}, \alpha_{\Phi^v}, \alpha_\lambda, \alpha_\gamma$ are symmetric hyperparameters controlling the corresponding Dirichlet prior distributions. $N(\cdot)$ stores the number of samples satisfying certain requirements during the iterative sampling process. For example, $N^w_{U,C,S,Z}(u_i^w, c_i^w, 0, z_i^w)$ represents the number of tag words for user u_i^w which are supposed to be influenced by contact user c_i^w and generated from topic z_i^w. The update rules for variables concerning visual descriptors are similar and omitted here for the space reason.

3.3 Parameter Estimation

After Gibbs sampling, we can obtain the sampled latent variables of $s_i^w, s_i^v, c_i^w, c_i^v, z_i^w, z_i^v$. Topic-word and topic-visual descriptor distributions Φ^w, Φ^v, which represent the learned topic space, can be easily computed from sampled topic assignments z_i^w, z_i^v. Since $\Phi^w_{t,j}$ actually measures the probability of the j-th tag word in the t-th topic, it can be estimated by normalizing the counter $N_{Z,W}(\cdot)$. It is similar to Φ^v. Therefore, we have:

$$\Phi^w_{t,j} = \frac{N^w_{Z,W}(Z_t, w_j) + \alpha_{\Phi^w}}{N^w_Z(Z_t) + |\mathcal{W}|\alpha_{\Phi^w}} \quad (6)$$

$$\Phi^v_{t,j} = \frac{N^v_{Z,V}(Z_t, v_j) + \alpha_{\Phi^v}}{N^v_Z(Z_t) + |\mathcal{W}|\alpha_{\Phi^v}} \quad (7)$$

where Z_t denotes the t-th topic, which is different from the topic assignment variables z_i^w and z_i^v. The node topic distribution for m-th user U_m can be computed by:

$$\Omega_{m,t} = \frac{N^w_{U,S,Z}(U_m, 1, Z_t) + N^v_{U,S,Z}(U_m, 1, Z_t) + \alpha_\Omega}{N^w_{U,S}(U_m, 1) + N^v_{U,S}(U_m, 1) + T\alpha_\Omega} \quad (8)$$

The t-th topical influence strength $\Psi_{m1,m2}(t)$ from user U_{m1} to user U_{m2}, can be estimated by the number of words/visual descriptors for user U_{m2} which are influenced by U_{m1} in t-th topic, i.e., $N_{U,C,S,Z}(U_{m2}, U_{m1}, 0, Z_t)$:

$$\Psi_{m1,m2}(t) = \frac{N^w_{U,C,S,Z}(U_{m2}, U_{m1}, 0, Z_t) + N^v_{U,C,S,Z}(U_{m2}, U_{m1}, 0, Z_t) + \alpha_\gamma}{N^w_{U,S,Z}(U_{m2}, 0, Z_t) + N^v_{U,S,Z}(U_{m2}, 0, Z_t) + |C_{U_{m2}}|\alpha_\gamma} \quad (9)$$

This equation is quite intuitive in that if one user U_{m2} has more tag words or visual images from topic Z_t likely to be influenced from the contact user U_{m1}, then U_{m1} is supposed to influence U_{m2} strongly in t-th topic.

4. PERSONALIZED IMAGE SEARCH UNDER RISK MINIMIZATION

In this section, we propose a risk minimization-based framework to incorporate the derived topic-sensitive influences for multimedia application of personalized image search. Risk minimization is a popular information retrieval framework with solid theoretical foundation [29]. It formulates query and document by language models (LM [30]), where queries and documents are modeled respectively from a generative process. Risk minimization views the retrieval of relevant documents from the perspective of Bayesian decision theory, and the goal is equivalent to minimizing the expected loss.

4.1 Risk Minimization Framework

In the context of personalized image search, we view the query as generated from a probabilistic process associated with searcher u, and each image as generated from a probabilistic process associated with the candidate image set. Specifically, query is the result of first choosing a language model, and then generating the query from that model. The generative process of each image is similar. Note that the query and image language models provide entrance to the incorporation of rich information. For example, the query model can encode detailed user information and searching context when issuing the query (time, location, searcher's mood, etc.); the image model can encode information of uploader, annotator and comments of the candidate images. In this paper, we incorporate user interest into the query model and annotator information into the image model.

We assume each candidate image d is associated with visual content $\mathbf{v}_d$ and annotation $\mathbf{w}_d$. The generative process of query q and image d is illustrated in Fig. 4. θ^u_Q denotes the parameter of the query model by user u, θ^v_D, θ^w_D denote the parameters of the image model for generating the visual content and textual annotation. For each image d, there are two hidden relevance variable $r(q, u, \mathbf{v}_d)$ and $r(q, u, \mathbf{w}_d)$, which depends on $[\theta^u_Q, \theta^v_D]$ and $[\theta^u_Q, \theta^w_D]$, respectively. User u generates the query q by first selecting θ^u_q and then choose a query from the selected model. Similar hierarchical process happens to image visual content $\mathbf{v}_d$ and textual annotation $\mathbf{w}_d$. Therefore, the generative process in Fig. 4 can be summarized by: $u \rightarrow \theta^u_Q \rightarrow q, \mathcal{V} \rightarrow \theta^v_D \rightarrow \mathbf{v}_D$ and $\mathcal{W} \rightarrow \theta^w_D \rightarrow \mathbf{w}_D$.

We consider the task of personalized image search as returning a list of images to the issued query q according to preference of searcher u. In the context of Bayesian decision theory, to each action, there is an associated loss L, which, in our case, is the loss for returning an individual image to the searcher. Under this framework, the expected risk of returning individual image d is decomposed into two components:

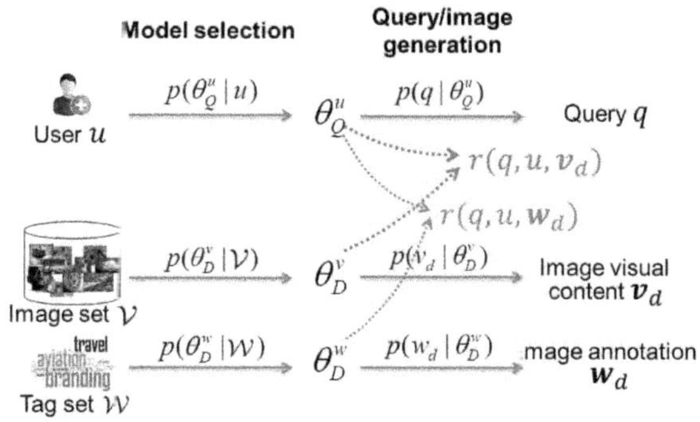

Figure 4: Generative process of query q and image d in personalized image search.

$$\begin{aligned} R(q, u, d) =& \mu R(q, u, \mathbf{v}_d) + (1-\mu) R(q, u, \mathbf{w}_d) \\ =& \mu \int_{\Theta^u_Q} \int_{\Theta^{\mathcal{V}}_D} p(\theta^u_Q | q, u) p(\theta^v_D | \mathbf{v}_d) p(r(q, u, \mathbf{v}_d) | \theta^u_Q, \theta^v_D) \times \\ & L(\theta^u_Q, \theta^v_D, r(q, u, \mathbf{v}_d)) d\theta^v_D d\theta^u_Q + (1-\mu) \int_{\Theta^u_Q} \int_{\Theta^{\mathcal{W}}_D} \\ & p(\theta^u_Q | q, u) p(\theta^w_D | \mathbf{w}_d) p(r(q, u, \mathbf{w}_d) | \theta^u_Q, \theta^v_D) \times \\ & L(\theta^u_Q, \theta^w_D, r(q, u, \mathbf{w}_d)) d\theta^w_D d\theta^u_Q \end{aligned} \quad (10)$$

where μ is weight parameter controlling the strength of visual content and tag words, $p(r|\theta^u_Q, \theta_D)$ is the probability of generating relevance r given the query and image model parameters θ^u_Q and θ_D. Following the derivation operation from [29], we consider the case that the loss function L depends only on model parameters θ^u_Q and θ_D. Formally, let L be proportional to a distance measure $\Delta(\cdot)$ between model parameters, i.e.,

$$L(\theta^u_Q, \theta_D, r) \propto \Delta(\theta^u_Q, \theta_D)$$

Intuitively, if the models θ^u_Q, θ_D are similar, $\Delta(\theta^u_Q, \theta_D)$ should be small. With this assumption, we can have

$$\begin{aligned} R(q, u, d) \propto& \mu \int_{\Theta^u_Q} \int_{\Theta^{\mathcal{V}}_D} p(\theta^u_Q | q, u) p(\theta^v_D | \mathbf{v}_d) \Delta(\theta^u_Q, \theta^v_D) d\theta^v_D d\theta^u_Q + \\ & (1-\mu) \int_{\Theta^u_Q} \int_{\Theta^{\mathcal{W}}_D} p(\theta^u_Q | q, u) \times p(\theta^w_D | \mathbf{w}_d) \Delta(\theta^u_Q, \theta^w_D) d\theta^w_D d\theta^u_Q \\ \propto& \mu\, p(\theta^u_Q | q, u) p(\theta^v_D | \mathbf{v}_d) \Delta(\hat{\theta}^u_Q, \hat{\theta}^v_D) + (1-\mu) p(\theta^u_Q | q, u) \times \\ & p(\theta^w_D | \mathbf{w}_d) \Delta(\hat{\theta}^u_Q, \hat{\theta}^w_D), \end{aligned}$$

$\hat{\theta}^u_Q, \hat{\theta}^v_D, \hat{\theta}^w_D$ are posterior point estimate of the model parameters:

$$\begin{aligned} \hat{\theta}^u_Q &= \arg\max p(\theta^u_Q | q, u) \\ \hat{\theta}^v_D &= \arg\max p(\theta^v_D | \mathbf{v}_d) \\ \hat{\theta}^w_D &= \arg\max p(\theta^w_D | \mathbf{w}_d), \end{aligned}$$

Since $p(\theta^u_Q|q, u)$ does not depend on d and we further assume $p(\theta^v_D|\mathbf{v}_d)$ and $p(\theta^v_D|\mathbf{v}_d)$ are the same for all d for ranking. The risk minimization framework finally reduces to measurement of the similarity between LMs. We employ the Kullback-Leibler divergence to measure $\Delta(\cdot)$:

$$\begin{aligned} R(q, u, d) \propto& \mu \Delta(\hat{\theta}^u_Q, \hat{\theta}^v_D) + (1-\mu) \Delta(\hat{\theta}^u_Q, \hat{\theta}^w_D) \\ \propto& \mu \sum_t p(Z_t | \hat{\theta}^u_Q) log \frac{p(Z_t | \hat{\theta}^u_Q)}{p(Z_t | \hat{\theta}^v_D)} + (1-\mu) \times \\ & \sum_t p(Z_t | \hat{\theta}^u_Q) log \frac{p(Z_t | \hat{\theta}^u_Q)}{p(Z_t | \hat{\theta}^w_D)} \end{aligned} \quad (11)$$

With the expected risk for returning individual image $R(q, u, d)$, we make simplification by further assuming the risk of returning each image is independent of returning others. It can be easily derived that, the final rank of each image $rank(q, u, d)$ which minimizes the overall risk is inversely proportional to its individual risk:

$$rank(q, u, d) \propto \frac{1}{R(q, u, d)} \tag{12}$$

In the following subsection, we will instantiate the query and image LMs by incorporating annotation confidence and topic-sensitive influences.

4.2 Query and Image Language Models

In personalized search, the query model should consider both the query and user information. Following the topic-sensitive influence modeling discussed in previous sections, we define query model θ_Q^u as the distribution over the learned topics given query q and user u:

$$\theta_Q^u \triangleq p(z|q, u) = \frac{p(z|u)p(q|z, u)}{p(q|u)} \tag{13}$$

Since the denominator $p(q|u)$ does not affect ranking, and q has no direct relation with u, we have

$$\theta_Q^u \propto p(z|u)p(q|z) \propto p(z|u) \prod_{w_i \in q} p(w_i|z) \tag{14}$$

where query $q =< w_1, \cdots, w_{n_q} >$, $p(z|u)$ and $p(w_i|z)$ can be directly obtained from user topic distribution Ω_u and topic-word distribution Φ^w. Note that we actually utilize the unigram language model in this paper.

From the standard language model-based information retrieval in [29], image model θ_D^v can be directly represented as the topic distribution of the image visual content $\mathbf{v}_d =< v_{d1}, \cdots, v_{dn_d^v} >$:

$$\theta_D^v \triangleq p(z|\mathbf{v}_d) = \frac{1}{n_d^v} \sum_{i=1}^{n_d^v} p(z|v_{di}) = \frac{p(z)}{n_d^v} \sum_{i=1}^{n_d^v} \frac{p(v_{di}|z)}{p(v_{di})} \tag{15}$$

where n_d^v indicates the number of visual descriptors in image d, $p(v_{di}|z)$ is the topic-visual descriptor distribution, $p(z)$ is the topic prior distribution and $p(v_{di})$ is visual descriptor prior distribution [4].

We consider noisy issue of user-generated annotations when representing image model θ_D^w. Besides aggregating each tag's topic-word distribution, we incorporate the annotator authority as annotation confidence as weight for the corresponding tag word. Formally, we have:

$$\theta_D^w \triangleq p(z|\mathbf{w}_d) = \frac{p(z)}{n_d^w} \sum_{i=1}^{n_d^w} \frac{p(z|u_{w_{di}})p(w_{di}|z)}{p(w_{di})} \tag{16}$$

where n_d^w indicates the number of tag word in annotation of image d, $u_{w_{di}}$ is the annotator for tag w_{di}. Since user's dominant topic distribution can be viewed as his/her expertise, we employ the annotator's topic distribution $p(z|u_{w_{di}})$ to represent the authority on topic z, which determines the trust we place on each tag. Now we have introduced the basic personalized image search framework which is based on risk minimization. As discussed at the beginning of this section, one important advantage of language model is its expansibility. We have successfully encoded annotation confidence to tackle with noisy user-generated social tags by Eq. (16). In the following, we will discuss how to incorporate the topic-sensitive influence analysis between users into the proposed framework.

Based on the above formulation, we can compute a personalized risk value for each individual image when searching by u as $R(q, u, d)$. In the context of influence network, searcher's influencer will impact the personalized rank by modifying the risk as follows:

$$\hat{R}(q, u, d) = \rho R(q, u, d) + \frac{1-\rho}{|\mathcal{C}_u|} \sum_{c \in \mathcal{C}_u} \Big(\sum_t p(Z_t|u, c)p(Z_t|q)\Big) R(q, c, d) \tag{17}$$

where $R(q, c, d)$ is the risk value when searching by user c, ρ is weight term balancing contributions from the searcher and his/her influencers, $p(Z_t|u, c)$ is the topic-sensitive influence strength between user u and c on topic Z_t. The intuition here is that, if one influencer has high influence to the searcher on the query-concerning topic ($\sum_t p(Z_t|u, c)p(Z_t|q)$), his/her preference to each candidate images ($R(q, c, d)$) should be emphasized and attached larger weight. Recall the toy example in Fig. 1, since word "Tahiti" closely relates to the *travel* topic, when Bob searches "Tahiti", Tom's suggestion will be highly valued and contribute most to the final decision.

5. EXPERIMENTS

5.1 Dataset

The data are collected from a large-scale Flickr dataset NUS-WIDE [31], which consists of 269,648 images. We crawled the image's uploader information and obtained 50,120 unique users. Since the focus in this paper is social influence analysis from user perspective, we remove the users uploading less than 15 images and conduct experiments on the remaining users and their images. For each user, we collected his/her annotation set and contact list. If there exists contact relation between two users, we refer to it as one contact edge. The statistic of resulted dataset is shown in Table 2.

Table 2: The statistics of the collected Flickr data.

#user	#contact edge	#image	#tag token	#unique tag
3,372	53,952	124,099	623,254	30,108

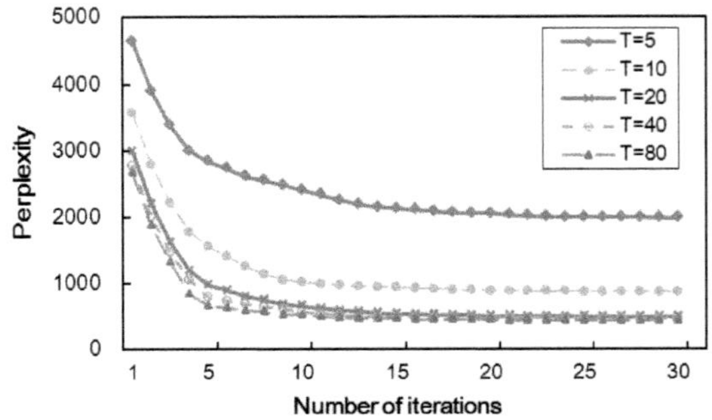

Figure 5: The perplexities over iterations for different topic number T.

In this work, we choose to represent the image visual content by region-level Maximally Stable Extremal Region (MSER) feature. Compared with key-point based descriptor, MSER regions indicate local homogeneous parts in objects and shown higher distinctness [32]. In our implementation, each detected elliptical region from MSER is normalized into a circular region, from which a

[4] We assume that visual descriptor prior and tag word prior all follow Uniform distribution, i.e., $p(v_{di}) = \frac{1}{|\mathcal{V}|}$, $p(w_{di}) = \frac{1}{|\mathcal{W}|}$

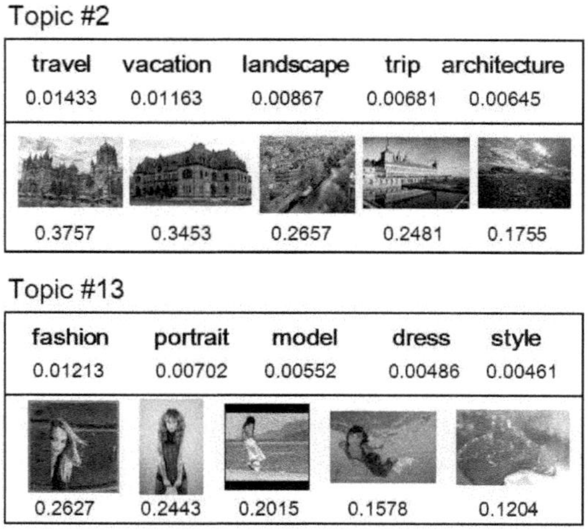

Figure 6: Illustration of discovered topics by mmTIM.

SIFT descriptor is computed. About 6M MSER descriptors are extracted from sampled 50,000 images, which are further quantized to constitute a dictionary of 5,000 visual words. In the following, we will show the experimental results for topic-sensitive influencer mining and personalized image search, respectively.

5.2 Topic-sensitive Influencer Mining Evaluation

5.2.1 *Topic Number T Selection*

In topic modeling, the selection of topic number T is not trivial. We resort to the perplexity measure in this paper, which is a standard measure for estimating how well one generative model fits the data. The lower the perplexity score is, the better the performance. The perplexity of a set of tag-visual descriptor test pairs $(\mathbf{w}_d, \mathbf{v}_d)$, for all $d \in \mathcal{D}_{test}$ images, is defined as the exponential of the negative normalized predictive log-likelihood using the trained model. Formally,

$$\text{Perplexity}(\mathcal{D}_{test}) = \exp\left\{-\frac{\sum_{d\in\mathcal{D}_{test}} \ln p(\mathbf{w}_d|\mathbf{v}_d)}{\sum_{d\in\mathcal{D}_{test}} n_d^v + n_d^w}\right\} \quad (18)$$

where

$$p(\mathbf{w}_d|\mathbf{v}_d) = \prod_{(w_d,v_d)\in\{\mathbf{w}_d,\mathbf{v}_d\}} \sum_{t=1}^{T} p(w_d|Z_t)p(Z_t|v_d)$$

We first test the perplexity of model on a held-out set of 2,000 images for different settings of topic number T. The perplexity scores of the proposed mmTIM over iterations are shown in Fig. 5. We can see that the perplexity scores decreases dramatically during the first several iterations and converges to a stable level within 20 iterations. Since larger topic number requires more computation cost and captures weak semantics, we prefer the smallest T that yields small perplexity and fast convergence. It is clear that the perplexity decreases much slower when $T > 20$ and we choose the desired topic number T to be 20 for mmTIM in the following experiments.

5.2.2 *Illustration of Discovered Topics*

In order to interpret the derived latent topic space, we visualize two of the discovered 20 topics by providing five top-ranked tag words and the most five related images. As represented in Fig.6, the tag words are sorted by their probability of being generated from the corresponding topic $p(w_i|Z_t)$, while images are sorted by counting the topic indicator variables of visual descriptors and tag words $p(Z_t|\mathbf{w}_d, \mathbf{v}_d)$:

$$p(Z_t|\mathbf{w}_d, \mathbf{v}_d) = \frac{\sum_{i=1}^{n_d^v} \mathbf{I}(z_{d,i}^v = t) + \sum_{i=1}^{n_d^w} \mathbf{I}(z_{d,i}^w = t)}{n_d^v + n_d^w},$$

where $z_{d,i}^v$ and $z_{d,i}^w$ are the topic assignments for the i-th tag word and visual descriptor for image d, and $\mathbf{I}(\cdot)$ is indicator function returning 1 is it is true and 0 otherwise.

By providing a combination of representative words and image, it becomes very easy to interpret the domain knowledge associated with each topic. We can see that, by considering both textual tag words and visual image content, the discovered latent topics show high consistency between semantic concepts and visual themes.

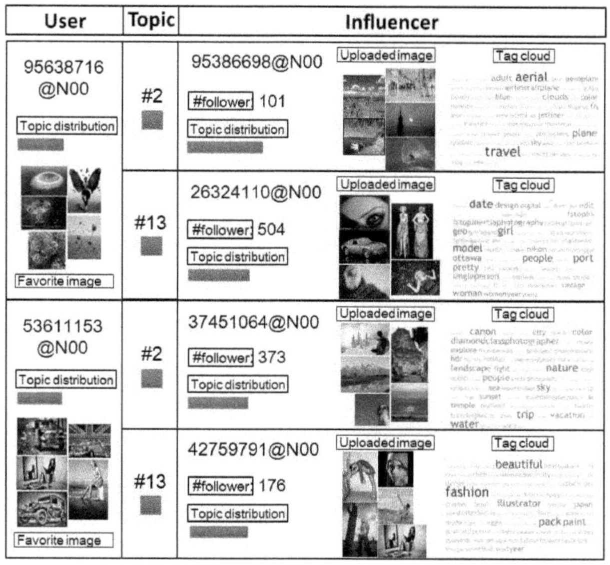

Figure 7: Topic-sensitive influencer mining case study.

5.2.3 *Qualitative Case Study*

We demonstrate the effectiveness of mmTIM on topic-sensitive influencer identification of sampled users. Fig 7 shows two test users and influencers who impact them most on discovered Topic #2 and #13. We show the node topic distribution by lengthy color bars, which indicate users' interest proportion on the corresponding topics. Since users explicitly express their preferences by adding *Favorite* marks to images, the exemplary favorite images are displayed below the two test users for user preference illustration. For each influencer, we provide the number of their followers, five exemplary images from their uploaded image set and the tag clouds. While #follower indicates the general influence strength, the uploaded images and annotations offer knowledge about the influencers' topic-related expertise.

We can see that, mmTIM shows its capability in identifying the most influential contact users on topic level. The identified influencers have high #follower and show strong expertise on the corresponding topics. For example, user "95386698@N00" has major interest in topic #2 from his/her topic distribution. From the uploaded exemplary images and tag cloud, we can see he/she has conducted extensive activities related to topic #2. Combining the large #follower and the decent design and fashion images uploaded by user "26324110@N00", we may roughly conclude that he/she is an expert on fashion topics, i.e., topic #13.

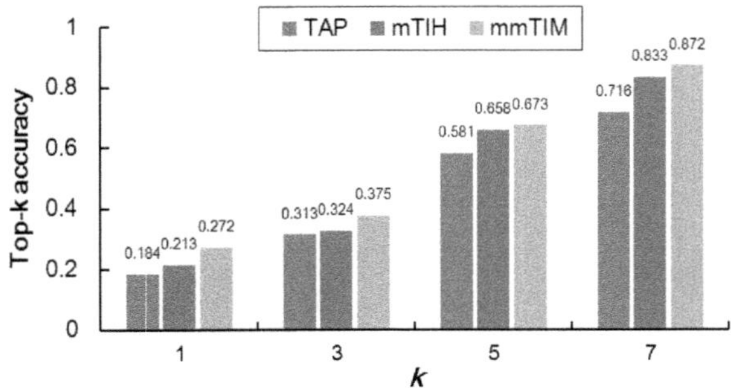

Figure 8: Topic-sensitive influencer identification performance comparison.

5.2.4 Quantitative Evaluation

Now we conduct quantitative evaluation of topic-sensitive influencer mining. Recall that the goal is to identify contact users with the most influence to the target user on specific topic. Observing that many of the images to which user add *Favorite* marks are uploaded by his/her contact users, we leverage user's *Favorite* images to generate ground-truth information for the evaluation. Specifically, for each *Favorite* image d of test user U_i, we calculate its topic proportion and assume the image belongs to the dominant topic, which is denoted as z_d. On each topic, the contact user U_j owning the top #images *Favorited* by U_i is considered most influential to U_i on this topic. Formally, the most influential contact user to user U_i on the t-th topic is defined as:

$$I^t_{U_i} = \arg\max \sum_{U_j \in \mathcal{C}_{U_i};\, d \in \mathcal{F}_{U_i}} \mathbf{I}(z_d = t, u_d = U_j)$$

where u_d is uploader of image d, $\mathcal{F}_{U_i}$ is *Favorite* image set of U_i.

We consider the following two topic-sensitive influence modeling methods for comparison:

- Topical Affinity Propagation (TAP [16]): a method learning topic space and topic-sensitive influences separately by inputting the nodes' topic mixtures;
- Mining Topic-level Influence on Heterogeneous networks (mTIH [17]): a probabilistic model exploiting the heterogeneous link and textual content information, which targets at text-based citation networks.

Note that the topic space of TAP is pre-extracted by running a standard LDA on the user-annotation corpus with each user's annotation set as one document and specific tag as word, and the citation link between users in [16, 17] is replaced by the contact relation in our implementation.

We utilize top-k accuracy as the evaluation metric. For each test user U_i, we rank the contact users by their influence values on the t-th topic. Denoting the rank of ground-truth influencer $I^t_{U_i}$ in contact list $\mathcal{C}_{U_i}$ as $\pi(I^t_{U_i})$, the top-k accuracy is calculated as

$$\text{Accuracy}(k) = \frac{\sum_{t,U_i} \mathbf{I}(\pi(I^t_{U_i}) \le k)}{T \cdot |\mathcal{U}|} \tag{19}$$

The results are shown in Fig.8. We can see that the proposed mmTIM consistently outperforms the two baselines. Note that the average #contact user is around 15. The top-1 accuracy of mmTIM is about 25%, which indicates that one out of four trials, mmTIM succeeds to identify the real topic-sensitive influencer at the first rank. The problem of TAP can be summarized in two-fold: First, TAP assumes that topic space and node topic distribution are available before social influence modeling. However, the pre-defined topic space extracted from user-annotation may be insufficient to capture the semantics in social influence links. Second, when modeling topic-sensitive influence, TAP only utilizes the link information of user-contact user, which loses information of relations between users and images. mTIH obtains better performance than TAP by addressing the above two problems. However, mTIH is proposed for text-based citation networks and does not address the multi-modality issue, which results in the inferior performance to mmTIM. Moreover, compared with mmTIM, mTIH is more focused on the document-level (i.e., image or paper) instead of user-level, by explicitly building the influencer set from user-document relations. While, under social media settings, the influencer set of specific user is actually available by follow or friend list.

5.3 Personalized Image Search Evaluation

The derived topic-sensitive influence values can be applied to applications like social search, friend recommendation, group suggestion, etc. Based on the proposed risk minimization-based theoretical framework, we evaluate the effectiveness of mmTIM on personalized image search and topic-based image recommendation.

In the query and image language models, according to Eq. (17), there is a weight parameter ρ controlling the strength of searcher and influencer. We choose ρ based on the assumption that the searcher himself/herself should be more trustworthy if he/she has much annotation activities, otherwise the influencer should be more trusted. Formally, for searcher U_i, ρ is set as:

$$\rho = \frac{|\mathcal{T}_{U_i}|}{|\mathcal{T}_{U_i}| + \frac{1}{|\mathcal{C}_{U_i}|}\sum_{U_j \in \mathcal{C}_{U_i}} |\mathcal{T}_{U_j}|}$$

By this setting, if the searcher owns more #tag than the average #tag of his/her influencers, $\rho > 0.5$, and $R(q, u, d)$ will contribute more the final rank list. Otherwise, the influencer's preference $R(q, c, d)$ will be emphasized more.

5.3.1 Personalized Image Search

Since users' tagging activities indicate their personal relevance judgement, we employ social annotations for personalized search evaluation. The main assumption is that the images tagged by user U_i with tag w_j will be considered relevant if U_i issues w_j as a query. The random selected 100 users who tagged $50-100$ images constitute the test user set $\mathcal{U}_{test}$. The overlapping 21 tags the 100 users used constitute test query set $\mathcal{T}_{test}$. In order to reduce the dependency between user annotation and evaluation, for the training process, we remove the tagging data related to the test queries.

Based on the proposed personalized image search framework, we consider the following four settings:

- *Basic*: basic personalized image search based on Eq. (12), which computes θ^w_D without considering annotation confidence;
- Basic + annotation confidence (*Basic_AC*): basic personalized image search leveraging annotator authority as annotation confidence in Eq. (16);
- Social network with global influence (*Social_global*): social-based personalized image search by considering global influence from contact users, which modified Eq. (17) as:

$$\hat{R}(q, u, d) = \rho R(q, u, d) + \frac{1-\rho}{|\mathcal{C}_u|} \sum_{c \in \mathcal{C}_u} \Big(\sum_t p(Z_t|u, c)\Big) R(q, c, d)$$

  We estimate the global influence by simply aggregating influences over topics which is irrelevant to queries;
- Social network with topic-sensitive influence (*Social_topic*): social-based personalized image search by considering topic-sensitive influences computed from mmTIM.

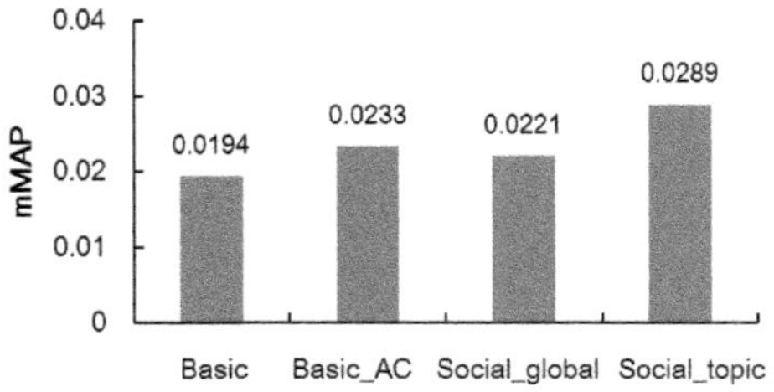

(a) personalized image search

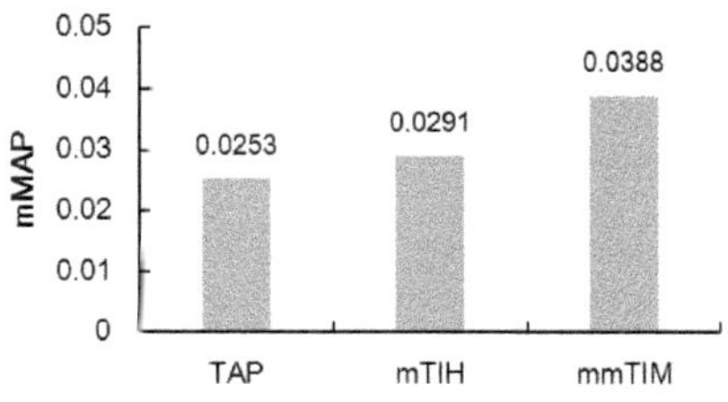

(b) topic-based image recommendation

Figure 9: The mMAP for the examined methods.

We use mMAP as the evaluation metric, which is the mean of the Mean Average Precisions (MAP) for all test users. mMAP is defined as:

$$\text{mMAP} = \frac{\sum_{i=1}^{|\mathcal{U}_{test}|} \frac{\sum_{j=1}^{|\mathcal{T}_{test}|} \text{AP}(i,j)}{|\mathcal{T}_{test}|}}{|\mathcal{U}_{test}|} \tag{20}$$

where $\text{AP}(i, j)$ denotes the Average Precision value of the j-th test query for the i-th user. The results are shown in Fig. 9(a). It is shown that *Basic_AC* outperforms *Basic* by 20%, which demonstrates the effectiveness of addressing the noisy annotation issue by incorporating annotator authority. By further considering the influence from contact users, it is weird that the performance of *Social_global* is inferior to that of *Basic_AC*. The reason may be that *Social_global* ignores the relation to the query and treats the social influence as constant for all topics. This result coincides with the motivation illustrated by the toy example we introduce at the beginning of the paper. By considering the topic-sensitive influence values for different queries, *Social_topic* obtain better performance than both *Basic_AC* and *Social_global*, which validates the advantage of the proposed framework to incorporate topic-sensitive influence modeling for personalized search.

5.3.2 Topic-based Image Recommendation

In social media websites, users will explicitly fill in interest profile or express their interests by following certain themes, e.g., sport, music, travel, etc. In this case, users will appreciate if resources based on the expressed user preferences are recommended. In this paper, we simulate the process of expressing interests by assuming user selecting one extracted topic and evaluate the performance of topic-based image recommendation.

The *Favorite* images are again employed as ground-truth for evaluation. The intuition is that, if image d_j is marked *Favorite* by user U_i and its dominant topic is Z_t, then d_j is treated as relevant when U_i selects topic Z_t. In our experiments, 100 randomly selected users who marked *Favorite* to $50 - 100$ images constitute the test set and a total of $7,725$ *Favorite* images constitute the relevant image set for the topic-based test queries. Following the proposed risk minimization-based framework in Eq. (11) (12) (17), query q is replaced by the selected topic Z_t and we can compare between the three topic-sensitive influence modeling methods: TAP, mTIH and mmTIM. mMAP is utilized for evaluation and the results are demonstrated in Fig. 9(b). It is shown that the proposed mmTIM obtains better performance than the other two methods, which is consistent with the results shown in Fig. 8. This further validates the effectiveness of incorporating multi-modal information for image-related tasks. The fact that mmTIM and mTIH outperform TAP coincides with out motivation that more accurate topic-sensitive influence modeling contributes to better recommendation and search results.

6. CONCLUSIONS

In this paper, a multi-modal probabilistic model is proposed to deal with the problem of topic-sensitive influencer mining in social sharing websites. The proposed model is delicate and informative, which provides better representation of the influence network and social annotation activity. The derived topic-sensitive influence has demonstrated its effectiveness through our introduced LM-based general framework in applications of personalized image search and topic-based image recommendation. We hope this paper could serve as a good chance to further the agenda of social relation analysis in this community.

This work can be extended in the following four directions: (1) We exploit social annotation for the influence modeling in this paper. How the social influence correlates with other social activities, like *Favorite*, share, comment, rate, is not clear and remains an interesting question. (2) Since the semantic tag and low-level visual feature account for different-level descriptions of the image, it is arbitrary to mix them in the same topic. To develop models allowing for more flexible sampling of word topics and visual topics will be another future direction. (3) We have demonstrated the potential of topic-sensitive influence modeling by two simple applications. Based on the proposed generative model, more real applications can be designed, such as friend suggestion, user behavior prediction, and so on. (4) The proposed personalized image search framework provides one of the first theoretical attempts to address this challenging problem. It is important to find the correlations with other personalized search methods in the future.

7. ACKNOWLEDGEMENT

This work was supported in part by National Program on Key Basic Research Project (973 Program, Project No. 2012CB316304) and the National Natural Science Foundation of China (Grant No. 90920303, 61003161).

8. REFERENCES

[1] David Arthur, Rajeev Motwani, Aneesh Sharma, and Ying Xu. Pricing strategies for viral marketing on social networks. *CoRR*, abs/0902.3485, 2009.

[2] Ioannis Konstas, Vassilios Stathopoulos, and Joemon M. Jose. On social networks and collaborative recommendation. In *SIGIR*, pages 195–202, 2009.

[3] David Carmel, Naama Zwerdling, Ido Guy, Shila Ofek-Koifman, Nadav Har'El, Inbal Ronen, Erel Uziel, Sivan Yogev, and Sergey Chernov. Personalized social search based on the user's social network. In *CIKM*, pages 1227–1236, 2009.

[4] Lindzey Gardner and Aronson Elliot. *Handbook of Social Psychology, Third Edition (Set)*. Lawrence Erlbaum Assoc Inc, 2006.

[5] Aris Anagnostopoulos, Ravi Kumar, and Mohammad Mahdian. Influence and correlation in social networks. In *KDD*, pages 7–15, 2008.

[6] David J. Crandall, Dan Cosley, Daniel P. Huttenlocher, Jon M. Kleinberg, and Siddharth Suri. Feedback effects between similarity

and social influence in online communities. In *KDD*, pages 160–168, 2008.

[7] David Kempe, Jon M. Kleinberg, and Éva Tardos. Maximizing the spread of influence through a social network. In *KDD*, pages 137–146, 2003.

[8] Wei Chen, Chi Wang, and Yajun Wang. Scalable influence maximization for prevalent viral marketing in large-scale social networks. In *KDD*, pages 1029–1038, 2010.

[9] Dongyuan Lu, Qiudan Li, and Stephen Liao. A graph-based action network framework to identify prestigious members through member's prestige evolution. *Decision Support Systems*, 53(1):44–54, 2012.

[10] Rongjing Xiang, Jennifer Neville, and Monica Rogati. Modeling relationship strength in online social networks. In *WWW*, pages 981–990, 2010.

[11] Jinfeng Zhuang, Tao Mei, Steven C. H. Hoi, Xian-Sheng Hua, and Shipeng Li. Modeling social strength in social media community via kernel-based learning. In *ACM Multimedia*, pages 113–122, 2011.

[12] Eytan Bakshy, Brian Karrer, and Lada A. Adamic. Social influence and the diffusion of user-created content. In *ACM Conference on Electronic Commerce*, pages 325–334, 2009.

[13] Manuel Gomez-Rodriguez, Jure Leskovec, and Andreas Krause. Inferring networks of diffusion and influence. *TKDD*, 5(4):21, 2012.

[14] Naohiro Matsumura and Yoshihiro Sasaki. Human influence network for understanding leadership behavior. *KES Journal*, 11(5):291–300, 2007.

[15] Nicole Ronald, Virginia Dignum, and Catholijn M. Jonker. When will i see you again: Modelling the influence of social networks on social activities. In *MALLOW*, 2010.

[16] Jie Tang, Jimeng Sun, Chi Wang, and Zi Yang. Social influence analysis in large-scale networks. In *KDD*, pages 807–816, 2009.

[17] Lu Liu, Jie Tang, Jiawei Han, Meng Jiang, and Shiqiang Yang. Mining topic-level influence in heterogeneous networks. In *CIKM*, pages 199–208, 2010.

[18] Paul-Alexandru Chirita, Wolfgang Nejdl, Raluca Paiu, and Christian Kohlschütter. Using odp metadata to personalize search. In *SIGIR*, pages 178–185, 2005.

[19] Reiner Kraft, Farzin Maghoul, and Chi-Chao Chang. Y!q: contextual search at the point of inspiration. In *CIKM*, pages 816–823, 2005.

[20] Feng Qiu and Junghoo Cho. Automatic identification of user interest for personalized search. In *WWW*, pages 727–736, 2006.

[21] Nicholas D. Lane, Dimitrios Lymberopoulos, Feng Zhao, and Andrew T. Campbell. Hapori: context-based local search for mobile phones using community behavioral modeling and similarity. In *UbiComp*, pages 109–118, 2010.

[22] Kristina Lerman. *Handbook of Research on Web 2.0, 3.0, and X.0: Technologies, Business, and Social Applications*, chapter Leveraging User-specified Metadata to Personalize Image Search. IGI Global, 2009.

[23] Dongyuan Lu and Qiudan Li. Personalized search on flickr based on searcher's preference prediction. In *WWW (Companion Volume)*, pages 81–82, 2011.

[24] Jitao Sang, Changsheng Xu, and Dongyuan Lu. Learn to personalized image search from the photo sharing websites. *IEEE Trans. Multimedia*, 14(4), 2012.

[25] Matthias Bender, Tom Crecelius, Mouna Kacimi, Sebastian Michel, Thomas Neumann, Josiane Xavier Parreira, Ralf Schenkel, and Gerhard Weikum. Exploiting social relations for query expansion and result ranking. In *ICDE Workshops*, pages 501–506, 2008.

[26] Liang Gou, Hung-Hsuan Chen, Jung-Hyun Kim, Xiaolong Zhang, and C. Lee Giles. Sndocrank: a social network-based video search ranking framework. In *Multimedia Information Retrieval*, pages 367–376, 2010.

[27] Lin Pang, Juan Cao, Yongdong Zhang, and Shouxun Lin. Leveraging collective wisdom for web video retrieval through heterogeneous community discovery. In *ACM Multimedia*, pages 1485–1488, 2011.

[28] Christian P. Robert and George Casella. *Monte Carlo Statistical Methods*. Springer-Verlag, 1999.

[29] John D. Lafferty and ChengXiang Zhai. Document language models, query models, and risk minimization for information retrieval. In *SIGIR*, pages 111–119, 2001.

[30] Jay M. Ponte and W. Bruce Croft. A language modeling approach to information retrieval. In *Proceedings of the 21st annual international ACM SIGIR conference on Research and development in information retrieval*, pages 275–281, 1998.

[31] Tat-Seng Chua, Jinhui Tang, Richang Hong, Haojie Li, Zhiping Luo, and Yantao Zheng. Nus-wide: a real-world web image database from national university of singapore. In *CIVR*, 2009.

[32] Krystian Mikolajczyk and Cordelia Schmid. A performance evaluation of local descriptors. *IEEE Trans. Pattern Anal. Mach. Intell.*, 27(10):1615–1630, 2005.

APPENDIX

We start from deriving the joint distribution. According to the generative process, the posterior joint distribution of the whole dataset is:

$$
\begin{aligned}
&p(\mathbf{w},\mathbf{v},\mathbf{z}^w,\mathbf{z}^v,\mathbf{s}^w,\mathbf{s}^v,\mathbf{c}^w,\mathbf{c}^v|\alpha_\Omega,\alpha_{\Phi^w},\alpha_{\Phi^v},\alpha_\lambda,\alpha_\gamma)\\
&\propto \int p(\mathbf{s}^w,\mathbf{s}^v|\lambda)p(\lambda|\alpha_\lambda)d\lambda \int p(\mathbf{c}^w,\mathbf{c}^v|\gamma)p(\gamma|\alpha_\gamma)d\gamma\\
&\quad \int p(\mathbf{z}^w|\mathbf{c}^w,\mathbf{s}^w,\mathbf{\Omega})p(\mathbf{z}^v|\mathbf{c}^v,\mathbf{s}^v,\mathbf{\Omega})p(\mathbf{\Omega}|\alpha_\Omega)d\mathbf{\Omega}\\
&\quad \int p(\mathbf{w}|\mathbf{z}^w,\Phi^w)p(\Phi^w|\alpha_{\Phi^w})d\Phi^w \int p(\mathbf{v}|\mathbf{z}^v,\Phi^v)p(\Phi^v|\alpha_{\Phi^v})d\Phi^v
\end{aligned} \tag{21}
$$

In order to sample from the joint distribution using Gibbs sampling, we need the full conditional posterior distribution $p(\Theta_i|\Theta_{-i},\cdot)$, where Θ_{-i} denotes all sampled latent variables Θ_j's with $j \neq i$. In the following, we exemplify the derivation of the update rule for $\mathbf{s}^w$, and the other latent variables can be derived analogously.

Canceling factors that do not depend on $\mathbf{s}^w_{-i}$, and following the definition of conditional probability, we have

$$
\begin{aligned}
&p(s^w_i|\mathbf{s}^w_{-i},u^w_i,z^w_i,\cdot)\\
&=\frac{p(\mathbf{w},\mathbf{v},\mathbf{z}^w,\mathbf{z}^v,\mathbf{s}^w,\mathbf{s}^v,\mathbf{c}^w,\mathbf{c}^v|\alpha_\Omega,\alpha_{\Phi^w},\alpha_{\Phi^v},\alpha_\lambda,\alpha_\gamma)}{p(\mathbf{w},\mathbf{v},\mathbf{z}^w,\mathbf{z}^v,\mathbf{s}^w_{-i},\mathbf{s}^v,\mathbf{c}^w,\mathbf{c}^v|\alpha_\Omega,\alpha_{\Phi^w},\alpha_{\Phi^v},\alpha_\lambda,\alpha_\gamma)}\\
&=\frac{\int p(\mathbf{s}^w|\lambda)p(\lambda|\alpha_\lambda)d\lambda}{\int p(\mathbf{s}^w_{-i}|\lambda)p(\lambda|\alpha_\lambda)d\lambda}\cdot\frac{\int p(\mathbf{z}^w|\mathbf{c}^w,\mathbf{s}^w,\mathbf{\Omega})p(\mathbf{\Omega}|\alpha_\Omega)d\mathbf{\Omega}}{\int p(\mathbf{z}^w|\mathbf{c}^w,\mathbf{s}^w_{-i},\mathbf{\Omega})p(\mathbf{\Omega}|\alpha_\Omega)d\mathbf{\Omega}}
\end{aligned} \tag{22}
$$

We derive the first component of Eq. (22). For the numerator, since $p(\mathbf{s}^w|\lambda)$ has multinomial distribution and $p(\lambda|\alpha_\lambda)$ has conjugate Dirichlet distribution:

$$
\begin{aligned}
&\int p(\mathbf{s}^w|\lambda)p(\lambda|\alpha_\lambda)d\lambda\\
&=\prod_{m=1}^{|\mathcal{U}|}\frac{1}{B(\alpha_\lambda)}\int\prod_{n=0}^{1}\lambda_{U_m,n}^{N^w_{U,S}(U_m,n)+\alpha_\lambda-1}d\lambda\\
&=\prod_{m=1}^{|\mathcal{U}|}\frac{B(\alpha_\lambda+\mathbf{N}^w_U(U_m))}{B(\alpha_\lambda)}
\end{aligned} \tag{23}
$$

where $B(\alpha)$ is gamma function paramtered with α, $N^w_{U,S}(U_m,n)$ denotes the number of words in the tag set of user U_m which are supposed to be innovationally generated (if $n=1$) or influenced by others (if $n=0$). The denominator has a similar form, and we can get when $s^w_i=0$:

$$
\begin{aligned}
\frac{\int p(\mathbf{s}^w|\lambda)p(\lambda|\alpha_\lambda)d\lambda}{\int p(\mathbf{s}^w_{-i}|\lambda)p(\lambda|\alpha_\lambda)d\lambda}&=\prod_{m=1}^{|\mathcal{U}|}\frac{B(\alpha_\lambda+\mathbf{N}^w_U(U_m))}{B(\alpha_\lambda+\mathbf{N}^w_{U,-i}(U_m))}\\
&=\frac{N^w_{U,S}(u^w_i,0)+\alpha_\lambda-1}{N^w_U(u^w_i)+2\alpha_\lambda-1}
\end{aligned} \tag{24}
$$

and when $s^w_i=1$:

$$
\frac{\int p(\mathbf{s}^w|\lambda)p(\lambda|\alpha_\lambda)d\lambda}{\int p(\mathbf{s}^w_{-i}|\lambda)p(\lambda|\alpha_\lambda)d\lambda}=\frac{N^w_{U,S}(u^w_i,1)+\alpha_\lambda-1}{N^w_U(u^w_i)+2\alpha_\lambda-1} \tag{25}
$$

The second component of Eq. (22) can be derived analogously.

Propagation-Based Social-Aware Replication for Social Video Contents

Zhi Wang[1], Lifeng Sun[1], Xiangwen Chen[2], Wenwu Zhu[1],
Jiangchuan Liu[3], Minghua Chen[2] and Shiqiang Yang[1]

[1]Tsinghua National Laboratory for Information Science and Technology
Department of Computer Science and Technology, Tsinghua University
[2]Department of Information Engineering, The Chinese University of Hong Kong
[3]School of Computing Science, Simon Fraser University

ABSTRACT

Online social network has reshaped the way how video contents are generated, distributed and consumed on today's Internet. Given the massive number of videos generated and shared in online social networks, it has been popular for users to directly access video contents in their preferred social network services. It is intriguing to study the service provision of social video contents for global users with satisfactory quality-of-experience. In this paper, we conduct large-scale measurement of a real-world online social network system to study the propagation of the social video contents. We have summarized important characteristics from the video propagation patterns, including social locality, geographical locality and temporal locality. Motivated by the measurement insights, we propose a propagation-based social-aware replication framework using a hybrid edge-cloud and peer-assisted architecture, namely PSAR, to serve the social video contents. Our replication strategies in PSAR are based on the design of three propagation-based replication indices, including a geographic influence index and a content propagation index to guide how the edge-cloud servers backup the videos, and a social influence index to guide how peers cache the videos for their friends. By incorporating these replication indices into our system design, PSAR has significantly improved the replication performance and the video service quality. Our trace-driven experiments further demonstrate the effectiveness and superiority of PSAR, which improves the local download ratio in the edge-cloud replication by 30%, and the local cache hit ratio in the peer-assisted replication by 40%, against traditional approaches.

Categories and Subject Descriptors

C.2.4 [**Distributed System**]: Distributed Applications; H.4 [**Information Retrieval**]: Social Network

MM'12, October 29–November 2, 2012, Nara, Japan.

General Terms

Measurement, Design

Keywords

Social network, video replication, hybrid edge-cloud and P2P

1. INTRODUCTION

Recent years have witnessed the blossom of online social network service (*e.g.*, Facebook, Twitter) and online video service (*e.g.*, YouTube, Youku), as well as the rapid convergence of the two services [28]. *Social video contents*, or *social videos* in short that are *generated* and *shared* by users in online social networks are becoming increasingly popular on today's Internet. ForeSee has reported that more than 18% users are influenced by the social network when accessing video contents [3]. It is fascinating to study how the social video contents can be served to users with satisfactory Quality-of-Experience (QoE).

In the online social network, users create and maintain different social connections, *e.g.*, *friending* their friends in real life, *following* celebrities or even *liking* virtual social entities. Such social connections determine which videos can reach a user in the online social network [16]. The unique *propagation* properties make the video access pattern in the online social network quite different from that in the traditional centralized video service systems, in that (1) video contents are no longer produced by a few centralized content providers, but by all individual users; and (2) social connections and social activities determine the propagation of the videos among the users.

We are facing the following challenges in distributing the social video contents with satisfactory QoE: (1) A huge number of user-generated videos require a large amount of storage and network resource, *e.g.*, YouTube has hit a new record of 60 hours' worth of videos uploaded by users per minute [4]; (2) Newly generated videos are the ones that tend to attract most of the users, but it is difficult to estimate their popularity for the video service allocation, which are dynamically affected by the social network [9]; (3) Social video contents have close-to-uniform and highly-volatile popularity profiles, because a large portion of the videos are shared among small social groups (*e.g.*, family members).

Challenge (1) makes traditional service paradigms (*e.g.*, C/S) not suitable, and a common practice to provision these video services is to replicate videos in severs at different geographic regions [5] by allocating resource from the CDN (Content Devilry Network) or cloud, where videos can be dynamically placed to serve users all over the world. Challenges (2) and (3) make the traditional replication approaches, which work well only for videos with skewed and stable popularity profiles, not suitable in the context of online social network. Mislove *et al.* [21] have observed a large deduction of cache hit ratio when traditional caching schemes are used to replicate social contents. In this paper, we reveal a key observation that the social videos, unlike regular videos, do not propagate among users randomly. Instead, they propagate along the social-network topology according to several rules determined by the social propagation. Exploiting the new design space enabled by this observation, we develop a social-aware replication system — PSAR, to effectively distribute social videos with superb QoE.

First, we demonstrate that the statistic information obtained from the online social network can guide the video replication. We conduct large-scale measurement to explore the connection between the social propagation and the replication, and discover the propagation characteristics of social video contents, including social locality that videos are generally shared among users who are socially connected, geographical locality that most of the videos are shared between users that are geographically close to each other, and temporal locality that most of the activities are issued to videos that are recently generated or shared.

Second, based on the measurement, we propose a hybrid edge-cloud and peer-assisted video replication framework, where videos are replicated by both the edge-cloud servers and peers at different geographic locations. In this framework, we are facing the following problems: (a) which videos should be replicated to which edge-cloud servers? (b) how much bandwidth should be reserved for each video by the edge-cloud? and (c) which videos should be served by which peers? We address these questions in the design of PSAR as follows. (1) We summarize three replication indices from the propagation patterns; (2) We design the edge-cloud replication strategies based on the geographic influence index and content propagation index, determining the region selection and bandwidth reservation for each video; (3) We further design the peer-assisted replication based on the social influence index, performing social-aware cache replacement at each peer.

The remainder of this paper is organized as follows. In Sec. 2, we discuss related work. In Sec. 3, we motivate our design by a measurement study on social video propagation. We present the architecture of PSAR in Sec. 4, and the detailed design in Sec. 5. In Sec. 6, we evaluate the performance of PSAR by trace-driven simulations. Finally, we conclude the paper in Sec. 7.

2. RELATED WORK

Propagation in Online Social Network. Online social network has become a popular Internet service. Based on traces from Flickr, YouTube, LiveJournal and Orkut, Mislove *et al.* [20] study the topology of the social graph, and confirm the power-law, small-world, and scale-free properties of the online social network. Krishnamurthy *et al.* [7] investigate Twitter, and identify the distinct classes of Twitter users and their behaviors, as well as the geographic growth patterns of the social network.

In an online social network, contents spread among users by their social activities. A number of research efforts have been devoted to studying the propagation of information in online social networks. Kwak *et al.* [16] investigate the impact of users' retweets on information diffusion in Twitter. Dodds *et al.* [12] use the epidemic model to study the information propagation, where a piece of information is regarded as an infective disease that spreads via the social connections. Kempe *et al.* [15] investigate how to maximize the spread of influence in an online social network, and Hartline *et al.* [13] utilize such maximum spread to achieve revenue maximization.

In this paper, we will study how to connect the social propagation and the social video replication, *i.e.*, how statistic information about the video propagation can be utilized to guide the video content replication in a joint edge-cloud and peer-assisted architecture.

Social Video Replication. Many architectures have been proposed in large-scale video service systems, including (1) the server-based architecture, *e.g.*, CDN and cloud-based approaches [23], (2) the client-based architecture, *e.g.*, the P2P content distribution [18], and (3) the hybrid architecture, *e.g.*, a hybrid CDN and P2P distribution framework [30]. For Internet-scale social video service, replicating the videos at different geographic regions is a promising approach to provide good service quality to users [6].

However, online social network has greatly changed the assumptions in traditional replication algorithms [8], *e.g.*, the distribution of video contents is shifted from a "central-edge" manner to an "edge-edge" manner, resulting in the close-to-uniform popularity distribution. Li *et al.* [17] study the video sharing in the online social network, and observed the skewed popularity distribution of contents and the power-law activity of users. To better serve such social video contents, some social-aware video replications have been proposed. Pujol *et al.* [24] investigate the difficulties of scaling online social networks, and designed a social partition and replication middle-ware where users' friends' data can be co-located in the same server. Tran *et al.* [26] study the partition of contents in the online social network by taking social relationships into consideration. Nguyen *et al.* [22] study how to improve the system efficiency in case of server failures by taking social locality into consideration. Wang *et al.* [27] observe that a social network can be used to help predict the video access pattern in a standalone video-on-demand system. Wu *et al.* [29] study how to minimize the cost in social media migration among servers at different regions. Cheng *et al.* [11] study the social media partition to balance the server load and preserve the social relationship.

This paper focuses on effectively distributing videos generated and propagated inside the social network. We will study how to improve the user experience of watching social videos by exploring a joint edge-cloud and P2P design based on the propagation characteristics of social videos extracted from real-world measurement.

3. MEASUREMENT OF PROPAGATION

In this section, we investigate how videos are generated and distributed among users in the online social network.

3.1 Measurement Setup

In our measurement, we have collected traces from Tencent Weibo [2], which is a microblogging website, where users can broadcast a message including at most 140 characters

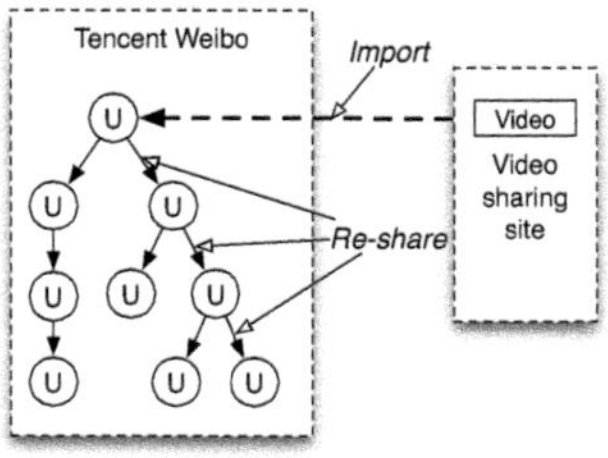

Figure 1: Connection between Weibo and video sharing systems.

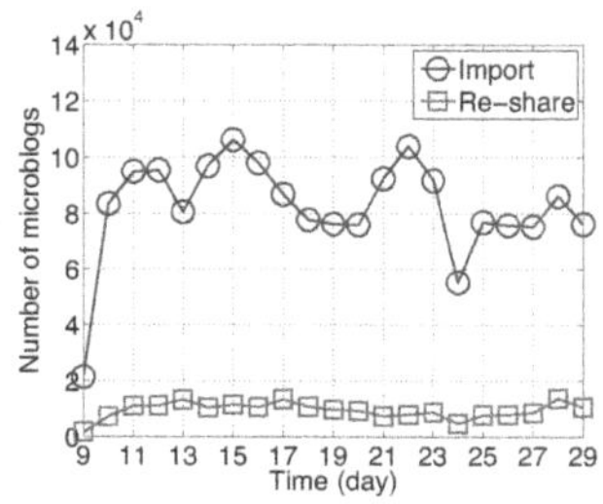

Figure 2: Imports and re-shares over time.

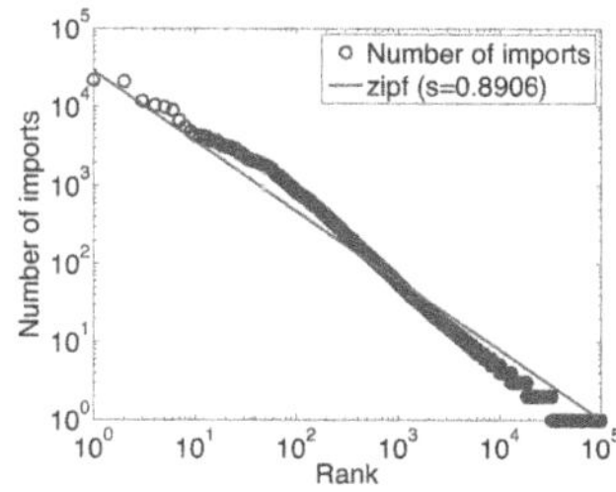

Figure 3: Number of imports of a video versus its rank.

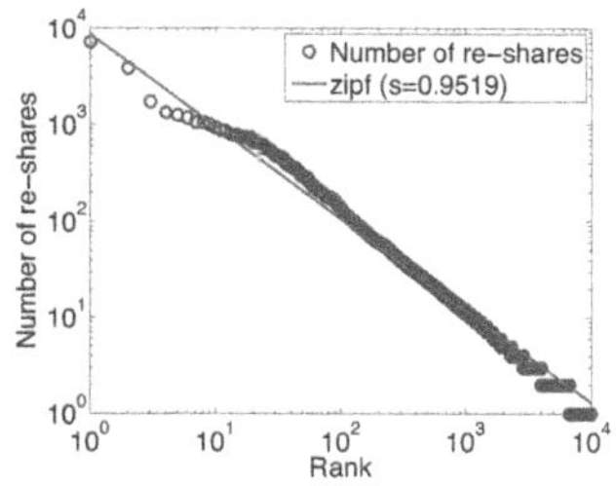

Figure 4: Number of re-shares of a video versus its rank.

to their friends. Tencent Weibo features several social activities in the system, *e.g.*, online chatting with friends who mutually follow each other. We obtained Weibo traces from the technical team of Tencent, containing valuable runtime data of the system in 20 days (October 9 – October 29) in 2011. Each entry in the traces corresponds to one microblog posted, including ID, name, IP address, geographic location of the publisher, time stamp when the microblog was posted, IDs of the parent and root microbloggers if it is a re-post, and contents of the microblog. The traces were recorded on an hourly basis.

We are focused on microblogs with video links which are imported from external video sharing websites. In particular, we have collected 350, 860 video links from 5 popular video sharing sites: Youku, Ku6, Tudou, Xunlei and Tencent Video. We then retrieve the microblogs which are related to these video links, *i.e.*, the microblogs either include the video links to these videos in the contents or they are re-shares of the ones that include the links. These video links cover 1, 923, 507 microblogs in the time span. Besides, we also retrieve the profiles of users who have posted these microblogs, *e.g.*, their friend lists. In our measurement, we use the number of microblog posts to estimate the number of video views, in a sense that the microblog publishers can represent a sample of users who have watched the videos.

Fig. 1 illustrates how Tencent Weibo are connected with the video sharing sites. After a video is published on a video sharing site, the link to that video can be imported by users to Weibo. We will regard the import as the video generation by that user. Then users who are socially connected to that user can be reached by the imported video and further re-share the video.

3.2 Generation, Distribution and Popularity of Social Video Contents

Video Generation and Distribution. On Tencent Weibo, users generate videos by importing the links to the videos from the external video sharing sites, and distribute the videos by re-sharing the microblogs containing the links. Import and re-share are the most important activities that determine how videos reach users in the online social network. Fig. 2 illustrates the number of imports and re-shares of the targeted videos over time. We observe that (1) more users are generating videos instead of distributing them in the online social network, and (2) the number of imports shows more obvious weekly pattern than the number of re-shares, indicating more randomness in users' re-sharing of social video contents.

Popularity Profiles. Videos can reach many people in the online social network by users' importing and re-sharing, which determine the video propagation range. We observe that different videos attract quite different levels of imports and re-shares, resulting in a skewed popularity distribution of videos in the online social network. We study the popularity distribution of the social video contents, in terms of their imports and re-shares in a given time period of 1 day. In Fig. 3, videos are ranked in their import number's descending order. Each sample illustrates the number of imports of a video versus the rank of that video. We observe that the video import popularity is highly skewed, following a zipf-like distribution with a shape parameter of $s = 0.8906$. Similarly, Fig. 4 illustrates the number of re-shares versus the rank of the video, and we observe the video re-share popularity also follows a zipf-like distribution with a shape parameter of $s = 0.9519$. The popularity distributions of the import and re-share indicate that there are a dominate fraction of unpopular videos in the online social network — it is of great challenge to serve all the videos to users locally, with limited storage and network resources.

We further investigate in which types of social groups are these unpopular videos propagating. By randomly collecting 50 videos with different propagation size (the number of users involved in a video's propagation), we explore the correlation between the propagation size and the clustering coefficient of the social group formed by the users involved in the propagation. In Fig. 5, each sample illustrates the video propagation size versus the clustering coefficient of the corresponding social group [1]. We observe a relatively strong correlation between the propagation size and the clustering coefficient. The reason is that the unpopular videos tend to be shared among small social groups that are relatively closely connected (socially). The trend of many unpopular videos to be shared among small social groups results in a close-to-uniform popularity distribution, which makes the replication extremely challenging.

3.3 Characteristics of Social Video Propagation

The above measurement has demonstrated the challenges in the replication of social video contents. Next, we study the characteristics of the social video propagation to guide the replication design.

3.3.1 Social Locality in Propagation

The generation and re-share of a video on Weibo form a propagation tree which is rooted by the user who generates the video. Any user who re-shares the video will become

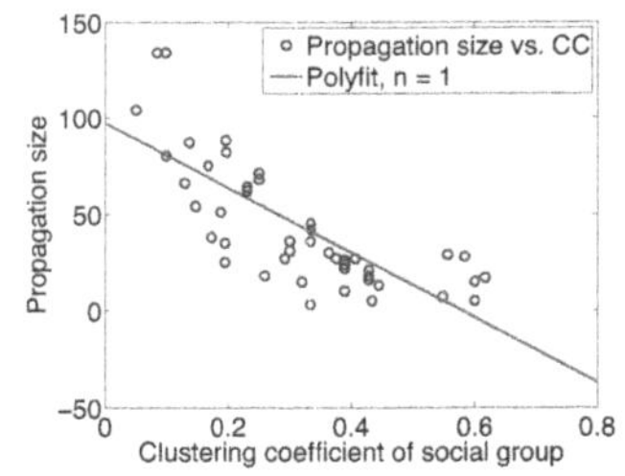

Figure 5: Propagation size versus the clustering coefficient of social group.

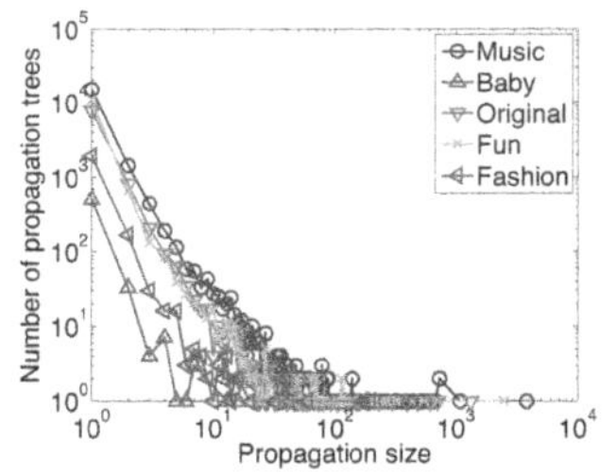

Figure 6: The number of propagation trees versus the propagation size.

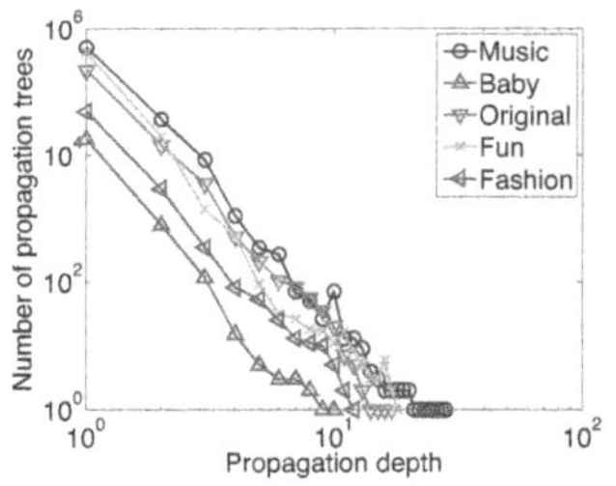

Figure 7: The number of propagation trees versus the propagation depth.

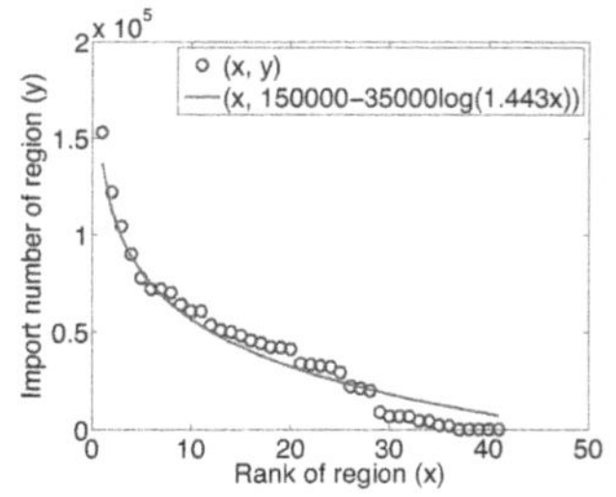

Figure 8: The import number of a region versus the rank of the region.

a new leaf node in the propagation tree. Fig. 6 shows the propagation size of videos in 5 different categories. Each sample illustrates the number of propagation trees (with the same propagation size) versus the size of these propagation trees. We observe that the size of most propagation trees is very small, *e.g.*, about 90% of the propagation trees are smaller than 100. Next, we study the propagation depth, which is defined as the average number of social hops between users in the propagation tree and the root user. Fig. 7 illustrates the propagation depth of videos in the same 5 categories. Each sample represents the number of propagation trees (with the same propagation depth) versus their propagation depth. We observe that in most of the propagation trees, the depth does not exceed 10, *i.e.*, users who re-share the video are socially close to the root user (with a small number of social hops between them).

The limited propagation size and propagation depth indicate that in each propagation tree, only users within a *limited social range* will be reached by the video. This observation motivates us to design the peer-assisted replication so that users who are both socially and geographically close to each other, can help distribute the video contents among themselves effectively.

3.3.2 Geographical Locality in Propagation

Users who generate, re-share and view the social videos are located in a variety of regions over the world. For Internet-scale video service providers, when performing replication for the social video contents, they need to strategically determine the regions (where datacenters are deployed) where the videos should be stored and served. To this end, we investigate how a social video content propagates among different geographic regions.

First, we observe that the popularity of different regions is quite different. We define the import number of a region as the number of total imports issued by users in the region. In Fig. 8, we rank 41 regions in their import number's descending order. Each sample in this figure illustrates the import number of a region versus the rank of the region. We observe that the popularity distribution of regions with respect to their import numbers follows a logarithm function $y = 150000 - 35000\log(1.443x)$. This observation indicates that it is not necessary to replicate each video to all the regions. A video should be replicated to a region only when the region is in the video's propagation range.

Next, we explore how to utilize the propagation information to estimate the geographical range of the video propagation. We observe that the propagation size can be used

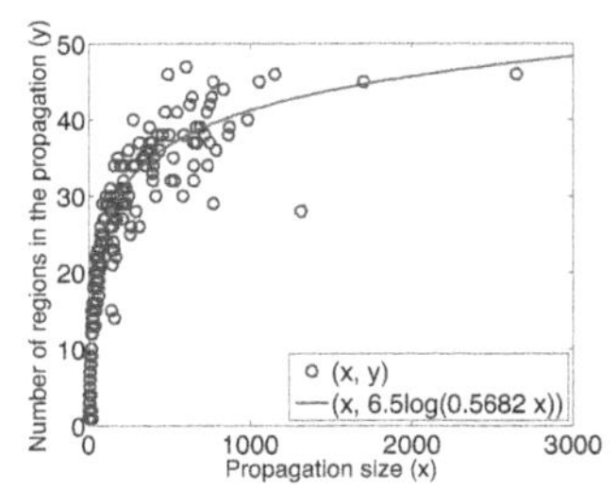

Figure 9: Number of regions in the propagation versus the size of the propagation.

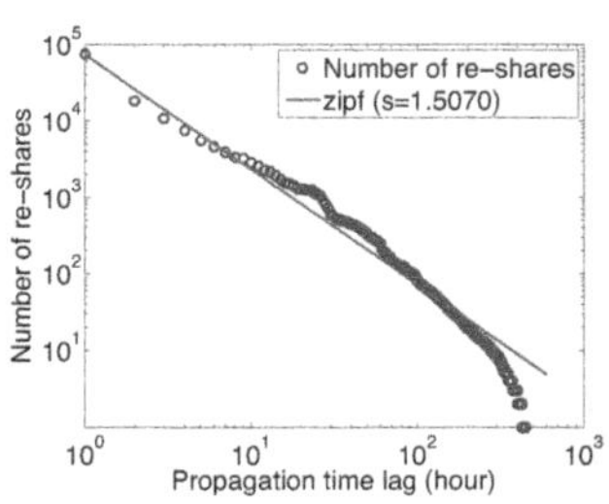

Figure 10: Number of re-shares versus the time lag.

to predict the geographical propagation range. Fig. 9 illustrates the correlation between the number of regions involved in the video propagation and the propagation size for different videos. We observe that a large propagation size generally results in more regions involved in the propagation. The relationship follows a logarithm function $y = 6.5\log(0.5682x)$. In PSAR, the propagation size is utilized to determine whether a video will be replicated to more regions. Intuitively, a video should be replicated to more regions when the predicted number of regions involved in the propagation is larger than the number of regions it has already been replicated to.

3.3.3 Temporal Locality in Propagation

In the online social network, we observe that users are more likely to re-share new video contents, *i.e.*, videos that are recently imported or re-shared. Fig. 10 illustrates the number of re-shares of a video in a time slot (1 hour) versus the time lag since it is generated. We observe that most of the re-shares happen in the recent hours, and the re-share number against the time lag follows a zipf-like distribution with a shape parameter $s = 1.5070$. This observation indicates that new videos in the online social network can attract more re-shares, leading to more viewers of the videos. We will also incorporate the temporal locality into the design of PSAR.

4. ARCHITECTURE OF PSAR

Based on the characteristics of the social video propagation, in this section, we present the conceptual architecture of PSAR and its key components, respectively.

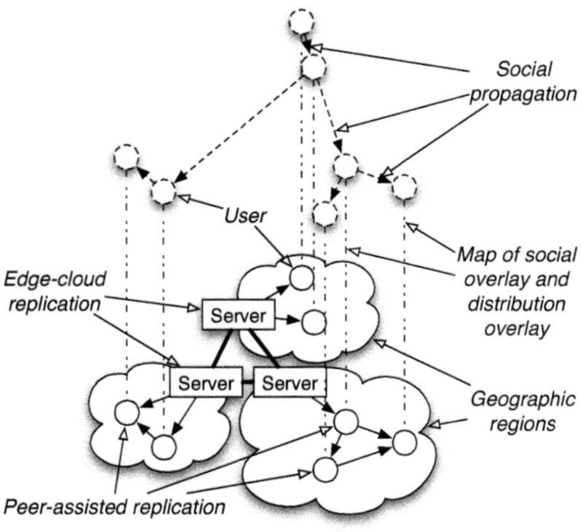

Figure 11: Conceptual architecture of PSAR.

4.1 Conceptual Architecture

We employ a joint edge-cloud and P2P architecture to replicate the social video contents, where the edge-cloud can support the time-varying bandwidth and storage allocations requested by different regions, while the peers are able to help contribute to each other in similar social groups. Fig. 11 illustrates the conceptual architecture of our design. In this figure, two overlays are presented as follows: (1) *social propagation overlay* based on the social graph, which determines the video propagation among friends, *i.e.*, users after generating a video, can share the video with their direct friends, who will further re-share the video to more people, and (2) *delivery overlay* which determines how video contents are delivered from edge-cloud servers to users or among themselves in a P2P paradigm. In this architecture, on one hand, we make use of the edge-cloud servers distributed at different geographic regions, to serve the social videos to users from different regions; on the other hand, we let peers cache the video contents in their local storage, so that they can help each other to download the videos. In the design of PSAR, we will study the edge-cloud replication on how videos are replicated to edge-cloud servers, as well as the peer-assisted replication on how videos are cached at a peer.

4.2 Framework and Key Components

In our measurement, we have shown that the social video propagation demonstrates social locality, geographical locality and temporal locality. In PSAR, we design three indices based on the social propagation to guide the replication: the geographic influence index which represents a video's propagation range among different regions, the content propagation index which represents the video's ability to attract new users in the online social network, and the social influence index which represents the possibility for a video to be requested by a peer's local friends. Based on the three replication indices, we design the edge-cloud replication and the peer-assisted replication, respectively.

4.2.1 Edge-Cloud Replication

Purpose. In the edge-cloud video replication, video contents are generally replicated to servers located in different geographic regions. The main purpose of the edge-cloud replication is for users at different locations to download the wanted videos from their local servers, which are located in the same regions with the users, to improve the video service quality [6].

Redesign. We redesign the edge-cloud replication by taking the social propagation into account. We first select the videos that are the most likely to propagate across geographic regions, by evaluating the videos' geographic influence index we design. Since the selected videos are more likely to attract users from more regions in the future, we replicate them to more regions so that users can be better served by the local servers. After that, based on the social influence index, which reflect their popularity in the near future, we determine which regions to replicate these videos to and how much bandwidths to allocate for the videos. We will present the detailed design in Sec. 5.2.

4.2.2 Peer-Assisted Replication

Purpose. The reason we propose a joint edge-cloud and peer-assisted paradigm in the social video replication lies two-folds. (1) Social videos are generally shared in small social groups, resulting in the close-to-uniform popularity distribution of the videos, which cost a huge amount of server resource to be distributed to users. To scale the delivery system, peers' resource is in demand. (2) Users typically share videos with their friends, who are observed geographically close to each other [25] — these socially connected users tend to have good Internet connectivity between each other to perform the peer-assisted video download [14].

Redesign. In traditional peer-assisted video distribution, LRU and LFU-based cache replacement algorithms are widely used. Such algorithms only depend on the static popularity of the video contents, which cannot achieve good performance when the access patterns of videos are affected by the social activities in the online social network. Based on the social influence index summarized from the propagation pattern, we redesign the peer cache replacement algorithm. In particular, we let peers cache videos that not only improve the general peer contribution (*i.e.*, the fraction of video contents upload by peers over all videos uploaded), but also improve the possibility for peers to serve the unpopular videos to their local friends. These friend users can benefit from the good Internet connectivity to the local peers. We will present the detailed design in Sec. 5.3.

5. SYSTEM DESIGN OF PSAR

In this section, we first present the design challenges in PSAR. Then, we establish the connection between the social video propagation and the video replication. After that, we present the detailed design of PSAR based on the connection.

5.1 Challenges in the Design of PSAR

In PSAR, the replication of social video contents is facing great resource-allocation challenges in the presence of multiple video propagations. Fig. 12 illustrates an example when there are only two videos. In this figure, the circles represent users in the online social network, which are located in different geographic regions, *e.g.*, region 1 and region 2. User A generates and shares video a in time slot T, then the video is re-shared by his friends C and D in time slot $T+1$. At the same time, another user B generates a different video b. Video a and video b will propagate across the social connections, and the two propagation trees may intersect in

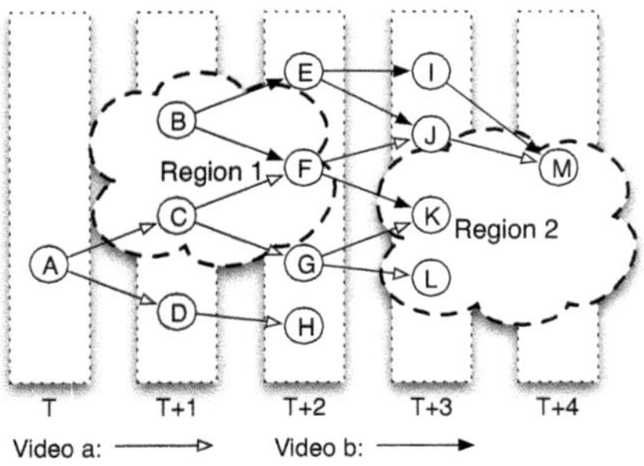

Figure 12: Example of two propagation trees.

the same region or at the same peer, *e.g.*, both region 1 and region 2 are involved in the two propagation trees, and both videos can reach user K in time slot $T+3$. The resource allocation has to determine (1) how to serve video a and b by the edge-cloud servers in region 1 and 2, and (2) how to cache video a and b at the peers to help others. It is of great challenge when many videos are propagating at the same time. The two problems will be discussed in the edge-cloud replication and the peer-assisted replication, respectively.

5.2 Edge-Cloud Replication

The edge-cloud provides the backup servers when peers are not able to download videos from the neighboring peers. We design two replication indices to guide the edge-cloud replication. When performing the edge-cloud replication, we first select the videos to be replicated and determine regions they should be replicated to, then we reserve upload bandwidth at edge-cloud servers for them.

5.2.1 Social-Aware Edge-Cloud Replication Indices

To perform social-aware replication at the edge-cloud servers, we design two replication indices based on the social propagation.

Geographic Influence Index. When performing video replication, we need to find out the videos that may propagate to more regions in the future. We deign the geographic influence index for that. In our measurement study, we observe that the number of propagation regions can be predicted from the propagation size of the video. Based on our measurement, we design the geographic influence index, which is calculated as follows:

$$g_v^{(T)} = c_1 \log(c_2 s_v^{(T)}),$$

where $s_v^{(T)}$ is the propagation size of the propagation tree of video v in time slot T. Large $g_v^{(T)}$ indicates that more regions will be involved in the propagation of the video. To achieve a better video download quality, a video with a larger $g_v^{(T)}$ should be replicated to more regions to serve users locally. In our experiments, we use $c_1 = 6.5, c_2 = 0.5682$ which are consistent with our measurement results. Based on the geographic influence index, we can predict whether the regions where the video has been replicated are enough.

Content Propagation Index. We design a content propagation index to evaluate the strength of a video's propagation in time slot T based on the propagation information as follows: (1) the current propagation size ($s_v^{(T)}$); (2) the current propagation depth ($h_v^{(T)}$); and (3) the time lag since the propagation tree is formed ($\tau_v^{(T)}$). The content propagation index is defined as follows:

$$e_v^{(T)} = z_s(\tau_v^{(T)})(s_v^{(T)}/h_v^{(T)}),$$

where $z_s(\tau_v^{(T)})$ is a decreasing function to make use of the temporal locality, which can adjust the content propagation index according to $\tau_v^{(T)}$ so that more recently generated or shared videos will have larger content propagation index. Based on our observation in Sec. 3.3.3, $z_s(t)$ is defined as follows:

$$z_s(t) = 1/(t^s \sum_{k=1}^{N} \frac{1}{k^s}),$$

where s is the zipf shape parameter and N is the number of hours between the initial time of the earliest video and the latest video. In our experiments, we let $s = 1.507$ and $N = 600$, which are the same as used in our measurement of Tencent Weibo's traces. In our design, $e_v^{(T)}$ will be used to guide the replication. Larger $e_v^{(T)}$ indicates that more users can join the propagation tree in time slot T. The rationale of $e_v^{(T)}$ lies as follows: (1) Larger $s_v^{(T)}$ indicates that more users can be reached by the video, and these users are the potential viewers (downloaders) of video v; (2) According to the social locality, small $h_v^{(T)}$ indicates that users in the propagation tree are still socially close to the root user and the video can propagate more; (3) According to the temporal locality, large $\tau_v^{(T)}$ slows down the propagation. Based on the content propagation index, we will determine how much bandwidth we will reserve for a video in the future time slot in PSAR.

5.2.2 Video and Region Selection

Initial Replication. After video v is first generated by a user in the online social network, it will be stored by a server which is closest to the user's friends. Let $d_{r,i}, i \in \mathcal{F}_v$ denote the geographic distance between region r and user i, where $\mathcal{F}_v$ is the set of friends of the root user of video v ("distance" based on Internet connectivity measurement can also be used, *e.g.*, bandwidth or RTT). The initial region is then selected by solving the problem as follows:

$$r_v = \arg\min_{r \in \mathcal{R}} \sum_{i \in \mathcal{F}_v} d_{r,i},$$

where $\mathcal{R}$ is the set of regions that can be used for the replication, and r_v is the region selected for the replication.

Selecting Existing Videos for Replication. According to our measurement study, we observe that although there are a massive number of videos in the online social network, in each time slot, only limited videos are shared among users. In particular, we observe that among 350,860 videos that we study in our measurement, only 1919 of them are re-shared in one time slot (1 hour) on average. Thus, in each time slot, only a little fraction of existing videos need to be replicated to improve the service quality. How should we select the candidate videos for replication? We observe that the overlapped fraction of the common videos that are re-shared in time slot T and $T-1$ over all videos re-shared in time slot T can be as large as 49%. In our design, the replication video set $\mathcal{V}^{(T)}$ is constructed as follows. (1) We build a candidate video set $\mathcal{W}^{(T)}$ by selecting videos that are imported or re-shared in the previous time slot. In particular, we randomly choose 80% of the videos that have been imported or re-shared in the previous time slot and 20% of the videos among the most popular ones in history. (2) We choose the videos in $\mathcal{W}^{(T)}$ that have the geographic influence index $g_v^{(T)}$ larger than $\theta_v^{(T)}$, which is a control parameter depending on the current replication status of video v, to form the video replication set $\mathcal{V}^{(T)}$. In our experiments, we let $\theta_v^{(T)} = 0.8|\mathcal{R}_v^{(T)}|$, where $\mathcal{R}_v^{(T)}$ is the set of regions that v has been replicated to. The rationale is that a video should be replicated to more regions if its current replication is under the requirement estimated from the geographic influence index.

Selecting Replication Regions for Videos in $\mathcal{V}^{(T)}$. After $\mathcal{V}^{(T)}$ has been constructed, the videos in $\mathcal{V}^{(T)}$ need to be replicated to more regions. Since these videos are the candidates that can attract users from more regions, we have to determine which videos need to be replicated to which regions. In our design, we extend the replication of a video to one more region each time. The selection of the region is similar to the approach used in the initial region selection. We minimize the geographic distance between the region and the potential users who may join the propagation tree. Let $\mathcal{L}_v^{(T)}$ denote the set of users who join the propagation tree in the previous time slot. The selection is as follows:

$$r_v = \arg \min_{r \in \mathcal{R} - \mathcal{R}_v^{(T)}} \sum_{i \in \bigcup_{k \in \mathcal{L}_v^{(T)}} \mathcal{F}_k} d_{r,i},$$

where $\mathcal{F}_k$ is the friend set of user k. The rationale is that users in $\mathcal{L}_v^{(T)}$ are the ones who join the propagation tree in the previous time slot, and it is likely for them to attract new users of the video, due to the temporal locality of the propagation. We utilize these users' friends' locations as a sample of all the users that can join the propagation tree, and select the region that is closest to all the users. The benefit of always extending a video to a new region in the replication (*i.e.*, r_v is selected from $\mathcal{R} - \mathcal{R}_v^{(T)}$) is that users in a popular propagation tree can choose more regions to download the video contents from, and our scheme improves the possibility for them to select the preferred regions.

5.2.3 *Bandwidth Reservation*

In each schedule round, we need to allocate upload bandwidths at the edge-cloud servers for the videos replicated. In our design, the bandwidth reservation depends on the social propagation strength, which can be evaluated by the content propagation index $e_v^{(T)}$. Let $\mathcal{V}_r$ denote the set of videos that are replicated in region r, the bandwidth reservation is then performed as follows:

$$b_{v,r_v} = B_{r_v} e_v^{(T)} / \sum_{v \in \mathcal{V}_{r_v}} e_v^{(T)}, \forall v \in \mathcal{V}^{(T)},$$

where b_{v,r_v} is the amount of bandwidth to be reserved for video v in the selected replication region r_v when the region is fully requested by users of different videos; and a video can extend to use more than b_{v,r_v} when the region is not fully loaded. B_r is the upload capacity of region r. The rationale of the bandwidth reservation is that videos with larger $e_v^{(T)}$ tend to attract more users in the propagation in the near future, and more upload bandwidth should be allocated for these videos' propagation to benefit the potential downloaders. Our edge-cloud replication algorithm is illustrated in Algorithm 1.

Algorithm 1 Edge-Cloud Replication Algorithm.

procedure VIDEO AND REGION SELECTION
    $\mathcal{V}^{(T)} \leftarrow \Phi$
    if v is newly published **then**
        $\mathcal{V}^{(T)} \leftarrow \mathcal{V}^{(T)} \cup \{v\}$
        $r_v \leftarrow \arg\min_{r \in \mathcal{R}} \sum_{i \in \mathcal{F}_v} d_{r,i}$
    else
        if $v \in \mathcal{W}^{(T)}$ **and** $g_v^{(T)} > \theta_v^{(T)}$ **then**
            $\mathcal{V}^{(T)} \leftarrow \mathcal{V}^{(T)} \cup \{v\}$
            $r_v \leftarrow \arg\min_{r \in \mathcal{R} - \mathcal{R}_v^{(T)}} \sum_{i \in \bigcup_{k \in \mathcal{L}_v^{(T)}} \mathcal{F}_k} d_{r,i}$
        end if
    end if
end procedure
procedure BANDWIDTH RESERVATION
    for all $v \in \mathcal{V}^{(T)}$ **do**
        if v is replicated at region r_v **then**
            $b_{v,r_v} \leftarrow B_{r_v} e_v^{(T)} / \sum_{v \in \mathcal{V}_{r_v}} e_v^{(T)}$
        end if
    end for
end procedure

5.2.4 *Reduction of Replications*

In our measurement study, we have shown the temporal locality of the social video propagation, *i.e.*, after a period of time since its publication, a video content will not be able to attract as many users as before. Though the bandwidth reservation can adapt to reduce the upload capacity allocated for a video that becomes less popular, the replications of the video still occupy the storage at edge-cloud servers. Thus, we need to reduce a video's replications on the edge-cloud servers to make room for new videos generated by users in the system. We let each edge-cloud server determine the replication reduction as follows: (1) the region of a video's initial replication acts as a permanent backup of the video; (2) other regions of a video's extended replications locally dump the video contents according to their geographic influence index, *i.e.*, videos with a smaller geographic influence index are more likely to be removed from an edge-cloud server to make room for new ones.

5.3 Peer-Assisted Replication

In Sec. 4, we have justified that the unique propagation pattern makes it very promising to utilized the peer-assisted paradigm to allocate certain amount of resource from the users to replicate the video contents, and peers (users) can serve their social neighbors with good Internet connectivity. In our peer-assisted replication, we assume users download video contents according to their own demands, and we design the social-aware cache replacement strategy for peers to determine which videos are cached to help other users, since peers' cache strategy can greatly affect the performance of a P2P system [19].

5.3.1 *Social-Aware Cache Replacement*

In PSAR, a peer locally performs the cache replacement using not only the perceived video popularity, but also the local social factors. In particular, the following information is used at peer i: (1) the local popularity which is the number of requests for video v received by peer i, denoted as p_i^v; (2) the fraction of peer i's friends that can join the propagation tree of video v, denoted as f_i^v. f_i^v is calculated by historical records for different video categories, *i.e.*, peer i keeps a record of the fraction of friends that have been attracted in each category in the history; and (3) the time lag between the propagation tree is constructed and the time when the peer re-shares the video, *i.e.*, $\tau_v^{(T)}$.

Social Influence Index. Based on the social propagation, we design a social influence index as follows:

$$q_v = z_s(\tau_v^{(T)})(p_i^v f_i^v).$$

In the peer-assisted replication, videos with smaller social influence index are more likely to be dumped by the peer. The rationale of the social influence index is that larger $p_i^v f_i^v$ indicates that peer i can potentially attract more users to re-share video v from its friends in the future, and $\tau_v^{(T)}$ is utilized to reflect the temporal locality. Large social influence index indicates that the video can be potentially downloaded by more local friends, and the peer should keep it to serve these friends. Thus, in our cache replacement algorithm, the peer will try to dump videos with the smallest q_v's until the capacity is enough for new videos.

5.3.2 Collaboration with Edge-Cloud Servers

In the distribution of social video contents, edge-cloud servers compensate the upload capacities when peers are not able to fully serve all the requests. The collaboration between the edge-cloud servers and the peers in PSAR is based on the replication indices as follows: (1) for the popular videos with large geographic influence and content propagation indices, they can be replicated to many regions to serve different users, who can download the contents from either the neighboring peers or the local edge-cloud servers; (2) for the unpopular videos, they are usually not widely replicated by the edge-cloud servers because their geographic influence index is small. However, a large fraction of such videos are shared in small social groups according to our measurement results, in which users can download the videos from their local friends, according to the social influence index. In both cases, users can achieve a good local download quality.

6. PERFORMANCE EVALUATION

6.1 Experiment Setup

Based on the same traces used in our measurement, we select 9318 videos from the original traces in the last 10 days for our experiments. These videos propagate among the regions captured by Tencent Weibo. Peers are located in the regions according to their profiles, and an edge-cloud server is deployed in each region. In our experiments, we assume the records of imports and re-shares indicate users' downloads of these videos. Thus, these records are used to drive users' downloads in the simulation. We also assume the user-generated videos have the same short duration [10], and we let the replication unit be a whole video for both servers and peers. We normalize the geographic distance between peers and servers in the evaluation. In the peer-assisted replication, peers exchange their cache states with socially connected neighbors periodically, so that they are aware of what can be downloaded from these social neighbors. When downloading from other peers, a tracker server is employed to help peers find each other. A peer downloads a video according to the following rules: (1) It first tries to download the video from neighboring peers, where peers that are socially connected in the same region are prioritized; (2) If no peer is able to serve the video, it will resort to the edge-cloud servers in the same region; (3) If the local servers are not able to serve it, it will try other servers with the smallest geographic distances.

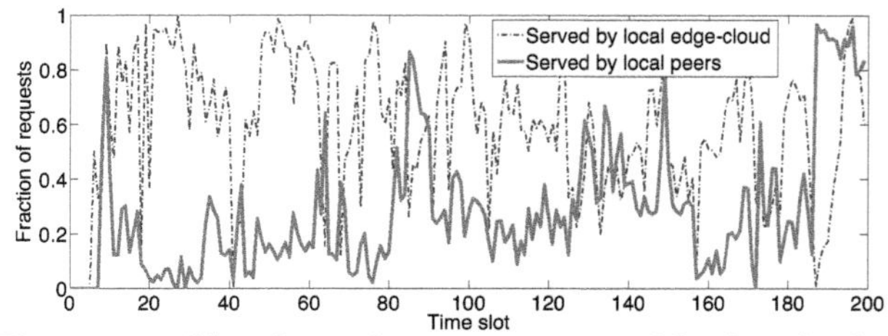

Figure 13: Number of requests served by local edge-cloud servers and local peers.

We first show the performance of PSAR over time. Fig. 13 illustrates the fraction of requests served by their local edge-cloud servers over all server-served requests and the fraction of requests served by local peers over all peer-served requests, respectively. We observe that our replication can reach relatively high levels of requests that are served by local edge-cloud servers and local peers (58.7% and 28.5%, respectively). Meanwhile, in PSAR, we observe that the local edge-cloud servers and peers can compensate each other to serve the users over time. Next, we will evaluate the detailed performance of PSAR.

6.2 Efficiency of Edge-Cloud Replication

In the edge-cloud replication, we compare PSAR with the following algorithms that are widely used in real-world video service systems. (1) A popularity-based replication, where videos are prioritized to be replicated or removed according to the videos' historical popularity, *i.e.*, the number of total imports and re-shares in the recent period. The videos selected for replication are assigned to regions so that the load (overall popularity of videos) can be balanced among the regions. In each region, the edge-cloud server allocates upload bandwidth for a video proportionally to its recent popularity. (2) A random approach where videos are replicated randomly in different regions and reserved with a random amount of upload bandwidth. Note that these two algorithms are also executed periodically in each time slot.

Fraction of Locally Served Requests. We first evaluate how many requests of videos can be served by local servers using different replication algorithms. We define a local download ratio as the fraction of requests that are served by users' local servers, *i.e.*, servers in the same geographic region with the users issuing the requests. Fig. 14 illustrates the local download ratio versus the average upload capacity allocated at an edge-cloud server. We observe that our edge-cloud replication in PSAR can greatly improve the local download ratio, and as the available server bandwidth capacity grows, the local download ratio in PSAR increases faster than the popularity-based and random algorithms, indicating that users can benefit more from increased server resources in PSAR.

Normalized Download Geo-Distance from Servers. We also evaluate the normalized download distance, which is define as the average normalized geographic distance between the users and the servers from which they download the videos. Fig. 15 illustrates the normalized download distance versus the average server capacity. We observe that PSAR

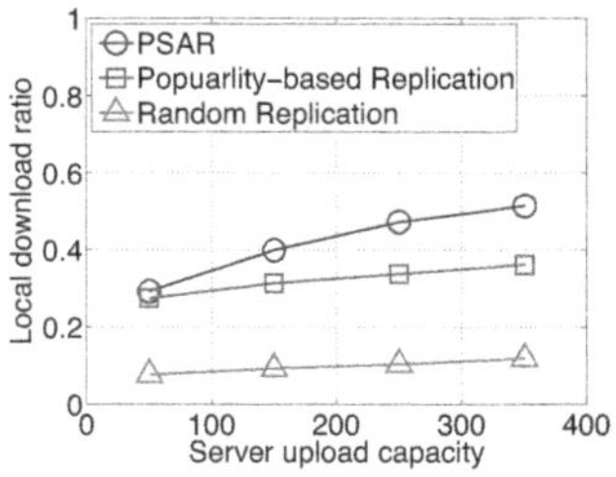

Figure 14: Local download ratio versus the server capacity.

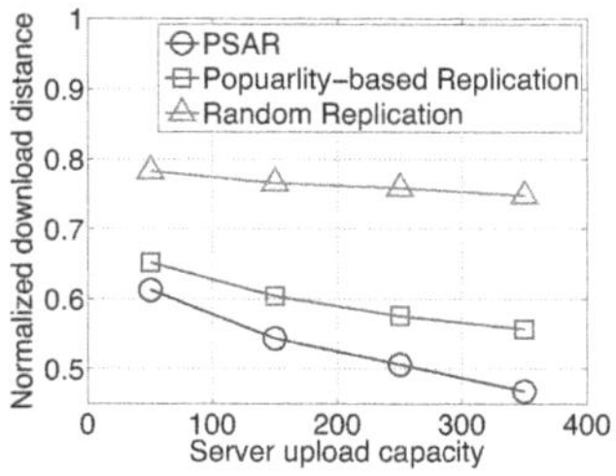

Figure 15: Normalized download distance versus the server capacity.

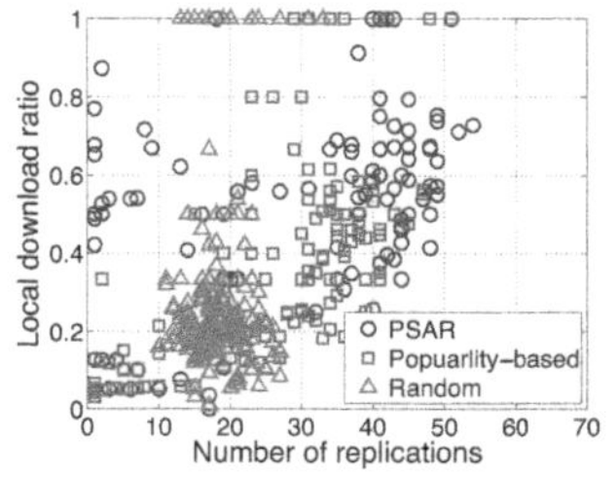

Figure 16: Local download ratio of a video versus the number of its replications.

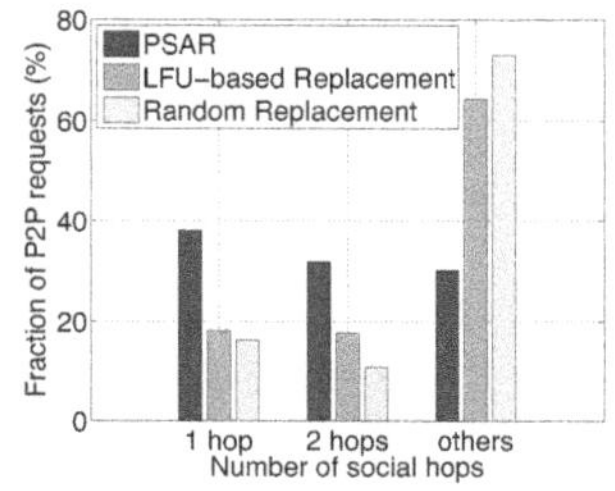

Figure 17: Peer contribution versus the number of social hops between the pair of peers.

achieves a smaller download distance than the other two algorithms. The reason is that by inferring the geographic influence index, the content propagation index and users' social connections, better prediction of a video's propagation range can be utilized to perform the region selection. Similarly, we observe that the normalized download distance in PSAR decreases faster than other algorithms when server capacity increases.

Number of Replications. We further study the impact of the number of replications of a video on the service quality. Fig. 16 compares the local download ratio of a video in the three strategies in terms of different numbers of video replications. We observe that in the random replication, all the videos have the similar number of replications — this is the reason for its inefficiency for contents that are either very popular or only propagated among small social groups. The replication number in the popularity-based replication is similar to that in PSAR; however, PSAR is more effective to replicate videos that are propagated in small social groups and the ones that are highly propagating across many regions.

6.3 Efficiency of Peer-Assisted Replication

We also evaluate the efficiency of the peer-assisted replication. We compare PSAR with (1) an LFU-based peer cache replacement algorithm where videos least requested recently (a reference time window of 24 hours) are dumped to make room for new ones, (2) an LRU-based cache replacement algorithm where videos that have not been recently requested are dumped, and (3) a random replacement algorithm where randomly selected videos are dumped.

Local Cache Hit Ratio. We first evaluate the local cache hit ratio, which is defined as the fraction of videos that can be directly downloaded from the socially connected peers. Higher local cache hit ratio indicates better local download performance, since we have already justified that peers which are socially connected to each other are also geographically close to each other, resulting in a better Internet connectivity. Fig. 18 illustrates the local cache hit ratio versus the storage capacity at each peer (the number of videos that can be stored). We observe that our design significantly outperforms other strategies. As the cache capacity increases, the cache hit ratio in our design improves much faster than other algorithms. The reason for the inefficiency of LFU and LRU is that many unpopular videos cannot be efficiently cached according to users' historical requests; while they can be addressed in our design where peers actively cache them for their friends based on the social influence index. We also observe that LFU and LRU have achieved the similar ratio, because LFU with a small reference time window acts similar to LRU, since requests are distributed close to the time when the user generates the content in the online social network.

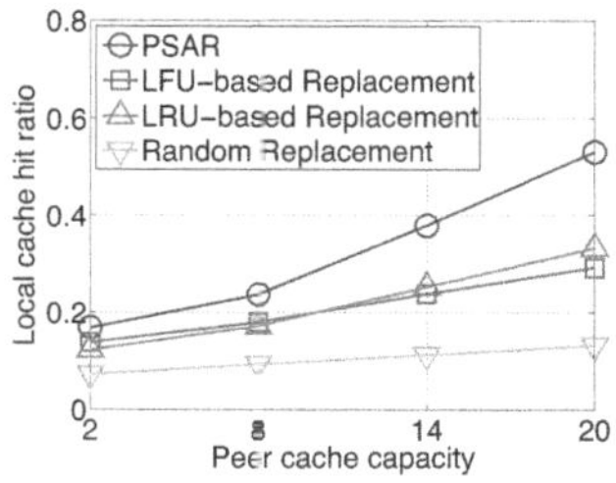

Figure 18: Local cache hit ratio versus peer's capacity.

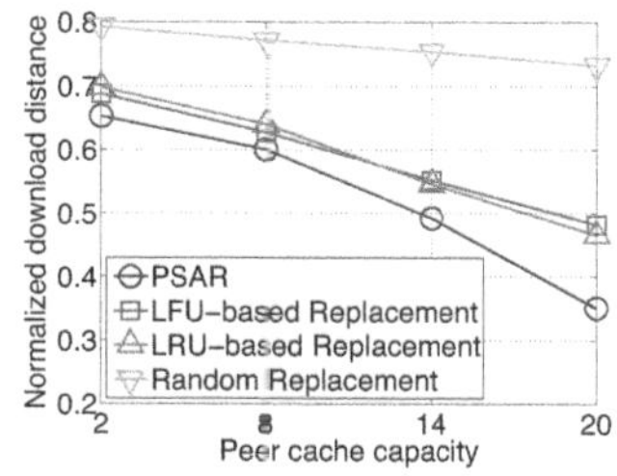

Figure 19: Normalized download distance versus peer's capacity.

Normalized Download Geo-Distance from Peers. We also evaluate the normalized geographic distance between the neighboring peers. Fig. 19 illustrates the average normalized download distance between peers who upload videos to each other versus the cache storage capacity at each peer. We observe that our social-aware cache replacement achieves a much smaller geographic download distance than the other algorithms, meaning that a peer is more likely to find a close neighbor to download the videos from, thereby achieving a better Internet connectivity for both sides. We also observe that when a large cache capacity is allocated at a peer, our design benefits more than other algorithms.

Social-Aware Contribution. We further investigate the P2P networks by studying which type of peers upload contents to the users. Fig. 17 illustrates the fraction of requests served by peers versus the number of social hops between the pair of peers. We observe that in our design, much more requests are served by their direct friends or two-hop friends in the social network, so that more local peers can be used to upload the contents. The reason is that in PSAR, videos are cached according to not only the requests of users, but also the level of friends that can be influenced by the video in the future.

7. CONCLUDING REMARKS

This paper addresses the challenges in the replication of social video contents, resulting from the massive number of the videos generated by users and the close-to-uniform popularity distribution. By conducting extensive measurement of traces obtained from a representative online social network system, we observe unique characteristics, which demonstrate social, geographical and temporal localities in the propagation. Based on the social propagation characteristics in the propagation, we propose a propagation-based social-aware replication strategy to serve such social video contents to users. Specifically, we design three replication indices: a geographic influence index, a content propagation index and a social influence index, which can guide the region selection, bandwidth reservation and cache replacement in the joint edge-cloud and peer-assisted replication. Extensive experiments driven by the real-world traces further demonstrate the effectiveness and superiority of our design.

Acknowledgment

We would like to thank Chong Yuan from Tsinghua University to conduct the experiments on the peer-assisted replication, and the Tsinghua-Tencent Joint Lab to provide the traces used in our research. This work is supported by the National Basic Research Program (973) under Grant No. 2011CB302206, the National Natural Science Foundation of China under Grant No. 60833009 and 60933013, and the Tsinghua National Laboratory for Information Science and Technology under Grant No. 916-042003091.

8. REFERENCES

[1] http://en.wikipedia.org/wiki/clustering_coefficient.

[2] http://t.qq.com.

[3] http://www.foreseeresults.com.

[4] http://www.youtube.com.

[5] V. Adhikari, S. Jain, Y. Chen, and Z. Zhang. Reverse Engineering the YouTube Video Delivery Cloud. In *Proc. of IEEE Hot Topics in Media Delivery Workshop*, 2011.

[6] V. Adhikari, S. Jain, and Z. Zhang. Where Do You Tube? Uncovering YouTube Server Selection Strategy. In *Proc. of IEEE International Conference on Computer Communications and Networks (ICCCN)*, 2011.

[7] M. A. Balachander Krishnamurthy, Phillipa Gill. A Few Chirps About Twitter. In *Proc. of ACM WOSN*, 2008.

[8] F. Benevenuto, T. Rodrigues, M. Cha, and V. Almeida. Characterizing User Behavior in Online Social Networks. In *Proc. of ACM IMC*, 2009.

[9] M. Cha, A. Mislove, and K. P. Gummadi. A Measurement-driven Analysis of Information Propagation in the Flickr Social Network. In *Proc. of ACM WWW*, 2009.

[10] X. Cheng, C. Dale, and J. Liu. Statistics and Social Network of YouTube Videos. In *Proc. of IEEE IWQoS*, 2008.

[11] X. Cheng and J. Liu. Load-Balanced Migration of Social Media to Content Clouds. In *Proc. of ACM NOSSDAV*, 2011.

[12] P. Dodds and D. Watts. A Generalized Model of Social and Biological Contagion. *Journal of Theoretical Biology*, 232(4):587–604, 2005.

[13] J. Hartline, V. Mirrokni, and M. Sundararajan. Optimal Marketing Strategies over Social Networks. In *Proc. of ACM WWW*, 2008.

[14] B. Huffaker, M. Fomenkov, D. Plummer, D. Moore, and K. Claffy. Distance Metrics in the Internet. In *Proc. of IEEE International Telecommunications Symposium (ITS)*, 2002.

[15] D. Kempe, J. Kleinberg, and É. Tardos. Maximizing the Spread of Influence Through a Social Network. In *Proc. of ACM SIGKDD*, 2003.

[16] H. Kwak, C. Lee, H. Park, and S. Moon. What Is Twitter, a Social Network or a News Media? In *Proc. of ACM WWW*, 2010.

[17] H. Li, H. Wang, and J. Liu. Video Sharing in Online Social Network: Measurement and Analysis. In *Proc. of ACM NOSSDAV*, 2012.

[18] Y. Liu, Y. Guo, and C. Liang. A Survey on Peer-To-Peer Video Streaming Systems. *Peer-to-peer Networking and Applications*, 1(1):18–28, 2008.

[19] J. Luo, Q. Zhang, Y. Tang, and S. Yang. A Trace-Driven Approach to Evaluate the Scalability of P2P-Based Video-On-Demand Service. *IEEE Transactions on Parallel and Distributed Systems*, 20(1):59–70, 2009.

[20] A. Mislove, M. Marcon, K. Gummadi, P. Druschel, and B. Bhattacharjee. Measurement and Analysis of Online Social Networks. In *Proc. of ACM IMC*, 2007.

[21] A. Mislove, B. Viswanath, K. Gummadi, and P. Druschel. You Are Who You Know: Inferring User Profiles in Online Social Networks. In *Proc. of ACM WSDM*, 2010.

[22] K. Nguyen, C. Pham, D. Tran, and F. Zhang. Preserving Social Locality in Data Replication for Social Networks. In *Proc. of IEEE ICDCS Workshop on Simplifying Complex Networks for Practitioners*, 2011.

[23] G. Peng. CDN: Content Distribution Network. *Arxiv preprint cs/0411069*, 2004.

[24] J. M. Pujol, V. Erramilli, G. Siganos, X. Yang, N. Laoutaris, P. Chhabra, and P. Rodriguez. The Little Engine(s) That Could: Scaling Online Social Networks. *SIGCOMM Comput. Commun. Rev.*, 40:375–386, Aug. 2010.

[25] S. Scellato, C. Mascolo, M. Musolesi, and V. Latora. Distance Matters: Geo-Social Metrics for Online Social Networks. In *Proc. of Conference on Online Social Networks*. USENIX Association, 2010.

[26] D. Tran, K. Nguyen, and C. Pham. S-CLONE: Socially-Aware Data Replication for Social Networks. *Computer Networks*, 2012.

[27] Z. Wang, L. Sun, C. Wu, and S. Yang. Guiding Internet-Scale Video Service Deployment Using Microblog-Based Prediction. In *Proc. of IEEE INFOCOM Mini-Conference*, 2012.

[28] Z. Wang, L. Sun, S. Yang, and W. Zhu. Prefetching Strategy in Peer-assisted Social Video Streaming. In *Proc. of ACM Multimedia*, 2011.

[29] Y. Wu, C. Wu, B. Li, L. Zhang, Z. Li, and F. C. Lau. Scaling Social Media Applications into Geo-Distributed Clouds. In *Proc. of IEEE INFOCOM*, 2012.

[30] D. Xu, S. Kulkarni, C. Rosenberg, and H. Chai. Analysis of a CDN–P2P Hybrid Architecture for Cost-Effective Streaming Media Distribution. *Multimedia Systems*, 11(4):383–399, 2006.

Action Recognition for Human-Marionette Interaction

Shih-Yao Lin
Graduate Institute of Networking and Multimedia,
National Taiwan University, Taiwan, ROC
d00944001@csie.ntu.edu.tw

Chuen-Kai Shie
Graduate Institute of Networking and Multimedia,
National Taiwan University, Taiwan, ROC
sunvictor777@hotmail.com

Shen-Chi Chen
Dept. of Computer Science and Information Engineering,
National Taiwan University, Taiwan, ROC
d98922030@csie.ntu.edu.tw

Yi-Ping Hung
Graduate Institute of Networking and Multimedia,
National Taiwan University, Taiwan, ROC
hung@csie.ntu.edu.tw

ABSTRACT
In this paper, we propose a human-marionette interaction system based on a human action recognition approach for applications to **interactive artistic puppetry** and a **mimicking-marionette game**. We developed an intelligent marionette called "*i*-marionette" that is controlled by a sophisticated control device to achieve various human actions. Moreover, we utilized an action recognition approach to enable the *i*-marionette to learn and recognize complex dance movements. The idea of artistic puppetry is to present a conflict scenario between two different cultural worlds: the **performer** is active and represents the culture of modern technology based in the real world. In contrast, the ***i*-marionette** represents traditional culture and is passive and based in a virtual world. The active performer guides the passive *i*-marionette to form a space-time connection between the real world and the virtual world. The *i*-marionette mimics the performer's action, while the performer also mimics the *i*-marionette's action. The performance represents an artistic conception in which humans invent technology and the *i*-marionette is manipulated by human control. However, in this interactive circle, the human is implicitly affected by the *i*-marionette. In our mimicking-marionette game, a player mimics the *i*-marionette's action. Subsequently, our human action recognition system measures the action similarity between the player and the *i*-marionette, and our system provides a similarity score.

Categories and Subject Descriptors
I.2.1 [Computing Methodologies]: Artificial Intelligence-*Applications and Expert Systems*; I.5.4 [Computing Methodologies]: Pattern Recognition-*Applications*; J.5 [Computer Applications]: Arts and Humanities

Keywords
Human action recognition, interactive art, interactive game.

Figure 1. Interactive Artistic Puppetry: Performer was guiding the *i*-marionette from the virtual world to the real world.

1. INTRODUCTION
In the past, a typical marionette (or "string puppet") was manipulated by a puppeteer. There is an implicit conflict between the marionette and the puppeteer. In puppetry, the puppeteer acts as a guide who compels the marionette to perform in the way the puppeteer wants. In this respect, the marionette is a follower who is passively dominated by the puppeteer. In contrast with the marionette, the puppeteer represents an active manipulator who controls the marionette's actions. With no puppeteer, the marionette is merely an inanimate object. Our artistic motivation is to exploit a scenario in which the marionette becomes fully automatic. What if the marionette becomes an active manipulator and guides the puppeteer? Is the puppeteer influenced by the marionette?

To create this artwork, we propose a human-marionette interaction system based on human action recognition technology. Through our action recognition approach, the proposed *i*-marionette is capable of human behavior understanding. In addition, we propose two applications of our human-marionette system to perform interactive artistic puppetry and an entertaining mimicking-marionette game. Unlike a typical marionette, in our proposed interactive puppetry, the *i*-marionette is capable of controlling itself. This artwork attempts to explore the peculiar relationship between the puppeteer and the marionette. The performer (puppeteer) implies modern technology, and the *i*-marionette implies traditional culture. Through the interactions between the *i*-marionette and the puppeteer, puppetry represents an interactive circle: humans invent technology, the technology controls the marionette, and the marionette influences humans as well. Figure 1 shows an interaction between the performer (puppeteer) and our *i*-marionette. Although the outer appearance is that the *i*-marionette is manipulated by the performer, the performer is implicitly affected by the *i*-marionette.

In our mimicking-marionette game, the *i*-marionette performs a contemporary dance for the player to mimic by following its actions. Our action recognition system measures the action similarity between the player and the *i*-marionette. At the end of the game, the system demonstrates the measured similarity as a score. If the score is high, the actions of the player and the marionette are similar. If the score is low, the actions of the player and the marionette are not similar. The mimicking-marionette game is not only for entertainment purposes. The major motivation is to make the player experience being affected by the marionette. When the player obtains a high similarity score, the player appears to win this game. However, the player has been influenced by the marionette as well. That is to say, humans develop the mimicking-marionette game, a human plays the game, and the game influences the human. In the end, the human was manipulated by the game.

Figure 2. Chinese Liyuan Dance

To recognize and learn complex and sophisticated human actions, we present an approach called the Action Trait Code (ATC) [15] for human action classification. Our approach involves a Microsoft Kinect sensor and derived 3D body joints obtained with the Kinect SDK. ATC represents an action with a set of velocity types derived from the average velocity of each body part. An effective graph model based on ATC classification is employed for learning and recognizing human actions. To examine the recognition accuracy, we evaluate our approach on a self-collected database containing six dance videos. Each dance video is composed of several Chinese Liyuan basic dance steps (Figure 2). The experimental results show that the proposed approach not only achieves high recognition accuracy but also operates in real time.

The rest of this paper is organized as follows: Section 2 briefly introduces the related works. Section 3 specifies the proposed action recognition approach. The *i*-marionette and its control device are described in Section 4. Section 5 describes the interactive artistic puppetry and its artistic motivation. The mimicking-marionette game is presented in Section 6. Conclusions are drawn in Section 7.

(a) (b)

Figure 3. Robot dance: (a) Honda Asimo is capable of learning and mimicking human actions; (b) HRP-2 reproduced the Japanese folk dance with a geisha. Although these robots can perform human actions, they are limited by a predefined program.

2. RELATED WORK

The marionette is a sophisticated mechanical system, often containing more than 40 degrees of freedom. Some researchers have attempted to create an automatic marionette for puppetry art. Murphey et al. [1][2] propose a motion description language (MDLp) for specifying and encoding autonomous puppetry plays. Sillam and Luciani [14] create puppetry art by building a physical puppet model and connecting the strings to handles connected to piano keys. The puppet is triggered by pressing a piano key.

In addition to studies attempting to create electronic marionettes, we are also interested in the study of human-robot interaction. Many researchers have studied human-robot interaction in the context of dance. The Honda humanoid robot called Aismo [12] has been developed to learn and mimic a person's movement (Figure 3a). HRP-2 [9] is a humanoid dancing robot designed by Japanese researchers that is programmed to reproduce the Japanese folk dance with a geisha (Figure 3b). HRP-4C [10], fembot (female robot), moves like a human, mimics human facial movements, and executes dance steps. However, HRP-4C is also programmed by a choreographed program. In the above studies, even if the robots successfully performed the complex movements, such as dancing, they are limited by the predefined program.

Human action recognition and categorization have been attracting much attention over the past few decades due to their applicability to many areas, including human-computer interaction and game design. However, the recognition task involves many challenging problems. According to a comprehensive survey [5], many previous studies on action recognition have concentrated on using 2D videos [3][5] or still images [7]. However, those approaches are limited to expressing lateral motion only. Recently, 3D body joint locations have been widely used in human action recognition tasks [4][6][8] because they provide more explicit information for describing human movement. Sung et al. [6] propose a hierarchical maximum entropy Markov model (MEMM) using 3D skeleton data to perform human detection and recognition of unstructured human activity in an unstructured environment. Raptis et al. [8] propose a real-time dance gestures classification system, which is composed of an angular representation of the skeleton designed, a cascaded correlation-based classifier, and a

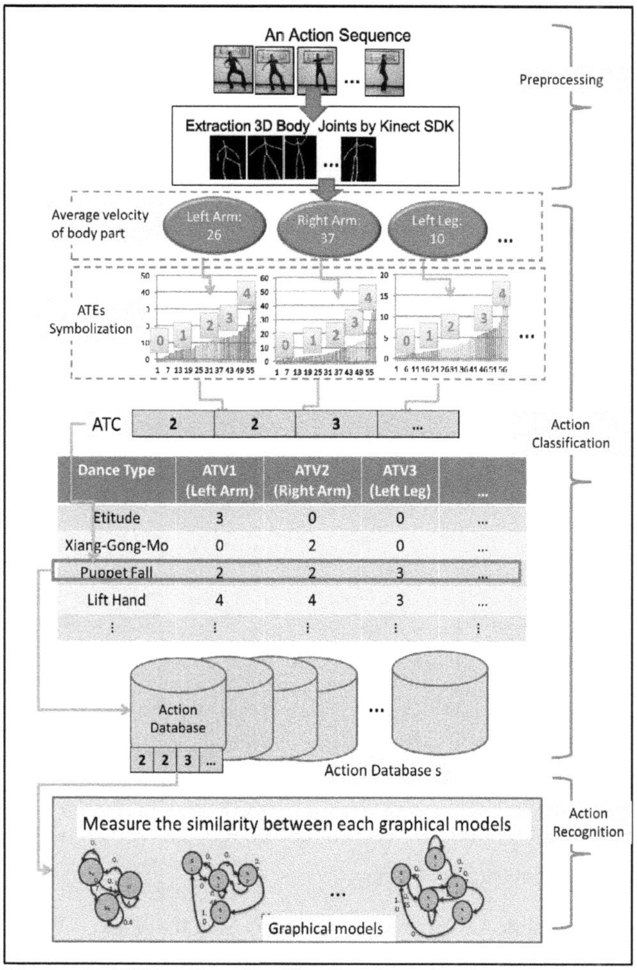

Figure 4. ATC action classification flow chart.

distance metric based on dynamic time-warping. To successfully allow robots to realize human behaviors, many studies have focused on robot vision for human behavior understanding. Jenkins et al. [11] present a method for kinematic pose estimation and action recognition from monocular robot vision using dynamic human motion vocabularies. Theodoridis et al. [13] employ activity recognition to discern aggressive human action in robotic systems.

3. Human Action Recognition

To recognize complex human activity, such as contemporary dance, we propose a robust action recognition approach to address this problem. In this paper, we divide the human action understanding task into two processes. One process is a classical action recognition task in which we employ a probabilistic model for learning and recognizing human actions. The second process is an action categorization task in which we classify actions based on quantized human movement.

3.1 Action Recognition Overview

Our proposed action recognition system comprises three major parts, including preprocessing, action classification, and action recognition. A detailed flowchart is shown in Figure 4.

During preprocessing, our system extracts the 3D body joint sequence from a human action. For classifying human action, we employ an approach called Action Trait Code (ATC) [15] for human action classification in the action classification step. ATC represents an action with a set of velocity types derived by the average velocity of each body part.

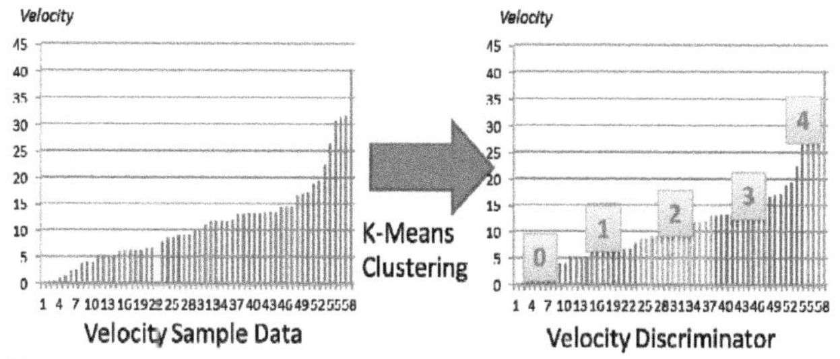

Figure 5. Velocity Discriminator Generation.

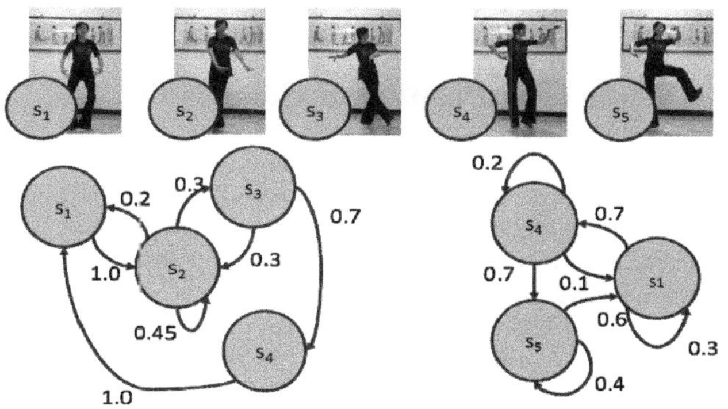
Figure 6. Action learning by graphical models: each node of the graph representing a salient pose.

The action recognition part introduces an effective graph model based on an ATC classification, which is then employed for learning and recognizing human actions.

3.2 Action Trait Code

An Action Trait Element represents the average velocity of a specific body part using the mean distance of corresponding joints of the 3D skeleton in a pose sequence (a human action).

We divide the human body into N body parts. Let $\Psi = \{\varphi_1, \varphi_2, ..., \varphi_N\}$ be a velocity detector set, where φ_i denotes the ith velocity detector. Given a body part J^i with a set of corresponding L joints, $\{j^i_1, ..., j^i_L\}$. The average velocity of J^i can be obtained by

$$\varphi_i(J^i) = \sum_{t=0}^{T-1} \sum_{k=1}^{L} dist(j^i_{k,t}, j^i_{k,t-1}) / T \qquad (1)$$

where T denotes the length of the input action sequence and *dist*(.) is a distance function that is formulated with the Euclidean distance.

A velocity discriminator is employed for quantifying each body part's average velocity. If the number of action training data is q, then the velocity discriminator uses the k-means algorithm (Figure 5) to divide the q average velocity values into k clusters. In other words, the range of ATE is from 0 to k. Therefore, each average velocity of J^i is tagged with a number as a symbol for the Action Trait Element.

3.3 ATC Encoding based on ATC

An ATC is like a specific body movement describer of an action. An ATC is constructed by a combination of ATEs. Each ATE is represented by values ranging from 0 to k. Therefore, each action can be encoded to an individual ATC.

If we use a length N for the ATC (using N body parts) and each ATE is divided into k levels, then the ATC codebook represents k^N action types. Thus, the action retrieval process using ATC classification reduces the computational cost by k^N times. Furthermore, to prevent the over-fitting problem, we employ the k-means algorithm to cluster similar ATCs by calculating the L2 distance between two ATCs.

3.4 Action Classification based on ATC

In our system, we precategorize actions by ATCs. In other words, an action database is grouped into several small action databases. Thus, the recognition process reduces much of the computational burden by measuring the similarity in a small action database only. Our action classification task comprises two steps. First, we calculate an ATC from the input action sequence. Second, we search the specific action dataset for the matched ATC. However, because ATC is encoded using each body part's movement, various types of actions might be categorized in the same database. Therefore, we use a graphical model for dealing with the recognition process.

3.5 Graphical Modeling based on ATC

The Action Graph [3][4] is a useful graphic model approach to represent a dynamic human motion with a set of salient poses (Figure 6). The salient poses are shared among the various actions. The proposed modified action graph G_{c_i} from the database of action class c_i that encodes L actions with M salient postures $\Omega_{c_i} = \{ \omega_{c_i,1}, \omega_{c_i,2}, \ldots, \omega_{c_i,M} \}$ can be represented as

$$G_{c_i} = \left\{ \Omega_{c_i}, A_{c_i,1} \ldots, A_{c_i,L} \right\} \quad (2)$$

where each pose represents a node and $A_{c_i,l} = \left\{ p(\omega_{c_i,j} | \omega_{c_i,i}, \lambda_{c_i,l}) \right\}_{i,j=1:M}^{l=1:L}$ denotes the transitional probability matrix of the lth action $\lambda_{c_i,l}$ in an action dataset c_i.

According to the graphical interpretation, we describe the recognition system using a quadruplet:

$$\Phi_{c_i} = (\Lambda_{c_i}, \Omega_{c_i}, \Upsilon_{c_i}, G_{c_i}) \quad (3)$$

where $\Upsilon = \{ p(x_{c_i} | \omega_{c_i,1}),\ p(x_{c_i} | \omega_{c_i,2}), \ldots, p(x_{c_i} | \omega_{c_i,M}) \}$. In the action modeling process, Φ_{c_i} involves three major steps: (1) extract salient postures Ω_{c_i} from the training data, (2) model each posture by likelihood functions Υ, and (3) construct the action graph G_{c_i}. Each salient pose is a set of similar poses, which is obtained by clustering the sample poses into M clusters. We cluster these poses into M salient postures by the k-means algorithm. We assume that the distribution of the points for a posture can be approximated by statistically independent. The posture model can be represented as the joint distribution of the points.

$$p(p_{\omega_{c_i}} | \omega_{c_i}) = \prod_{i=1}^{n} \sum_{j=1}^{c} \pi_{j,\omega_{c_i}} N(p_i | \mu_{j,\omega_{c_i}}, \Sigma_{j,\omega_{c_i}}) \quad (4)$$

where $N(.)$ is a Gaussian function In the recognition task, we present a modified action graph based on ATC to recognize human action.

The action recognition process is to seek the most likely action λ^* from a set of action models $\Lambda = \{\lambda_1, \lambda_2, \ldots, \lambda_L\}$. Let $X = \{x_1, x_2, \ldots, x_T\}$ be a set of pose sequences derived by the input action sequence with T frames. The action recognition process can be formulated as

$$\begin{aligned} \lambda^* &= \arg\max_{\lambda} p(c_i, X, \lambda) \\ &= \arg \max_{\lambda_{c_i} \in \Lambda_{c_i}, S_{c_i} \subset \Omega_{c_i}} p(X_{c_i}, S_{c_i}, \lambda_{c_i} | c_i) p(c_i) \\ &= \arg \max_{\lambda_{c_i} \in \Lambda_{c_i}, S_{c_i} \subset \Omega_{c_i}} p(x_{c_i,1}, \ldots, x_{c_i,n} | s_{c_i,1}, \ldots, s_{c_i,n}, \lambda_{c_i}, c_i) \\ &\qquad \times p(s_{c_i,1}, \ldots, s_{c_i,n} | \lambda_{c_i}, c_i) p(\lambda_{c_i}, c_i) \end{aligned} \quad (5)$$

where $S_{c_i} = \left\{ s_{c_i,1}, \ldots, s_{c_i,n} \right\}$ represents the corresponding posture sequence derived from X and $p(c_i)$ is a prior value based on the confidence of ATC classification. We here assume $p(c_i) = 1$. Assume that $x_{c_i,t}$ statistically depends only on $s_{c_i,t}$, $x_{c_i,t}$ is statistically independent of λ_{c_i} given by S_{c_i}, and $s_{c_i,t}$ only depends on its previous state $s_{c_i,t-1}$.

Table 1. Chinese Liyuan Basic Step database.

Type 1	 Walk Step+ Hand Lift+ Arrange Hat
Type 2	 Hand Lift + Foot Stamp + Field Across
Type 3	 Wave Over Elbow+ Lift hand+ Seven Step Jolt
Type 4	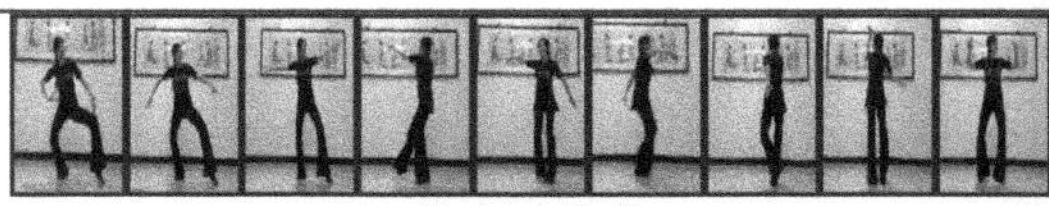 Puppet Fall
Type 5	 Xiang-Gong-Mo + Hand Swing + Bolting Pose
Type 6	 Etitude + Hop

Table 2. Computational time of each dance step.

Dance Type	Length of Video (Second)	Frame Number	Computational Time (Second)
Type 1	7.2	218	1.14
Type 2	10.1	304	1.20
Type 3	11.0	332	1.33
Type 4	10.3	310	1.25
Type 5	9.3	281	0.80
Type 6	9.5	285	1.20

Thus, we can reformulate Eq. (2) as

$$\lambda^* = \arg \max_{\lambda_{c_i} \in \Lambda_{c_i}, S_{c_i} \subset \Omega_{c_i}} \prod_{t=1}^{N} p(x_{c_i,t} \mid s_{c_i,t}, c_i) \times p(\lambda_{c_i}, c_i) \times p(s_{c_i,1}, \ldots, s_{c_i,n} \mid \lambda_{c_i}, c_i) \quad (6)$$

where $p(x_{c_i,t} \mid s_{c_i,t}, c_i)$ expresses the probability of observation $x_{c_i,t}$, which is derived from salient posture $s_{c_i,t}$.

3.6 Evaluation of Chinese Liyuan Basic Steps

We evaluate our approach on a self-collected action database: the "Chinese Liyuan Basic Step dataset." It is derived from the "Pear Orchard opera," a mixture of songs, dances, and Chinese Nanyin music. It was performed at the imperial court during the Tang Dynasty. The dance step of the Chinese Liyuan dance involves complex movements. We use six dance types for evaluating our action recognition approach. Each dance type is a combination of 1~3 basic dance steps, and each basic dance step is a series of complex movements. Table 1 shows the details of each collected dance data type. The experimental result shows that our approach achieves 100% recognition accuracy. In addition, Table 2 demonstrates the computational time for each dance type. As shown in the table 2, even though the length of each action in our database is longer than 9 seconds, our system successfully achieves the recognition task very quick which enable the *i*-marionette to interact with humans.

The reason that our approach achieves 100% recognition accuracy is because the discrepancy of each dance data is highly dissimilar, even if the dance movement is complex. The video of each self-collected dance data is shown in the attached webpage: http://www.csie.ntu.edu.tw/~d97944010/research/mm2012/ Moreover, we had also evaluated our approach on a more complex action database, e.g., street dance database. As shown in http://www.csie.ntu.edu.tw/~d97944010/research/icpr2012/, the proposed approach not only successfully achieves high recognition accuracy (97%) but also performs in nearly real-time.

4. *I*-MARIONETTE

The marionette is a sophisticated and challenging mechanical system. We aimed at the creation of a fully automated marionette, which is capable of performing various human actions. In this section, we introduce our performance stage, our intelligent marionette called the "*i*-marionette," and its control equipment.

4.1 *i*-Marionette

Our *i*-marionette has a humanoid body shape (Figure 7a) and a realistic female face (Figure 7b). The entire body of the marionette is composed of fifty body parts, consisting of a head, a torso, a pelvis, two upper arms, two lower arms, two hands, two

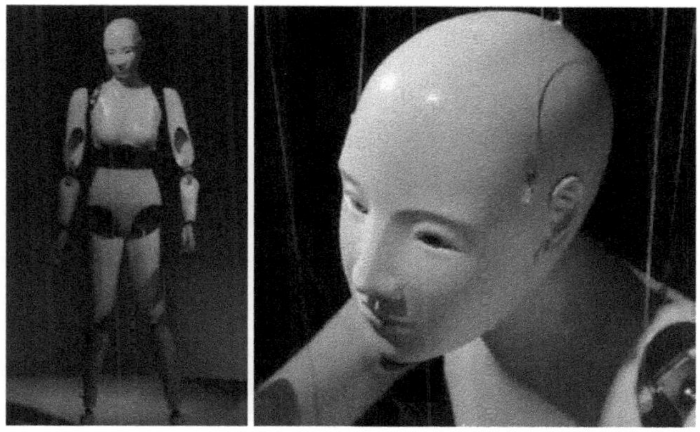

(a) (b)

Figure 7. *i*-Marionette: (a) Full body of the *i*-marionette; (b) The *i*-marionette has a realistic female face.

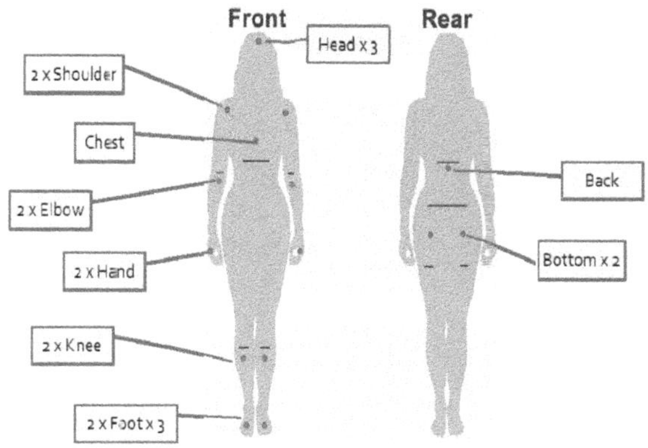

Figure 8. Each hook position as it relates to the *i*-marionette's body parts.

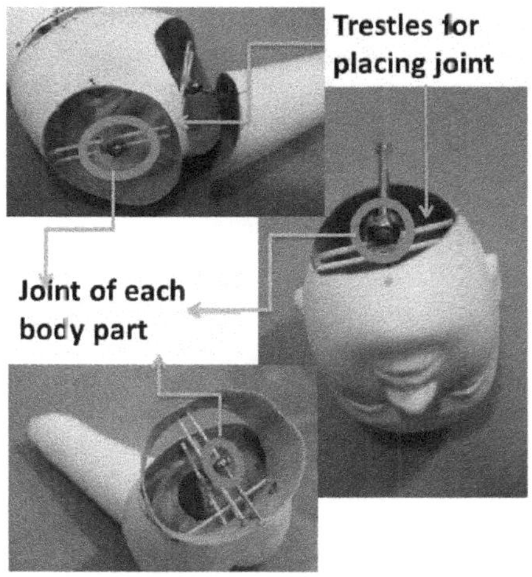

Figure 9. Joint setting in each hollow body part.

thighs, two legs, and two feet. To construct the appearance of our i-marionette, we use a commercial mannequin for the basis of the *i*-marionette's body shape and set the hook in each body part. Each hook position is used to truss the string for suspending each body part. Figure 8 illustrates the hook positions of the *i*-marionette. In addition, because each body part is hollow, we employ trestles for placing the joints in hollow body parts. We

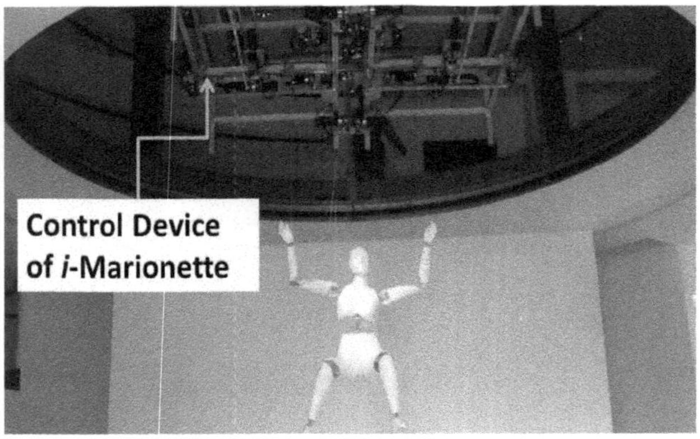

Figure 10. Performance stage with the *i*-marionette and its control device.

Figure 11. Control device of the *i*-marionette.

also limit each joint's movement by referring to the joint's kinematic limitation. Figure 9 shows the joint setting in the hollow body parts. To construct humanoid movement for the *i*-marionette, we recorded an enormous human motion database including a huge number of 3D human motion data derived by the Kinect SDK and captured by a Kinect sensor. The 3D human motion data drives the *i*-marionette to perform various human actions.

4.2 Performance Stage and Control Device

Figure 10 shows the performance stage with the *i*-marionette and its control device. Along the stage, we placed three Kinect sensors to form a triangle area to sense the triggered action from the performer.

In the control device (Figure 11), we use a set of trusses to sustain 29 motors and the *i*-marionette. These motors control the *i*-marionette by dragging strings suspended on the *i*-marionette's body. We divide human body motion into two parts: global motion and local motion. Global motion refers to the translation and the rotation of the entire body. In addition, the local motion denotes the body joint angle for each limb. For the above reasons, the architecture of our control device is designed by two layers of motor equipment (Figure 12). The first layer controls the global motion of the *i*-marionette, and the second layer manipulates the local motion. To send a package of commands to all of the motors,

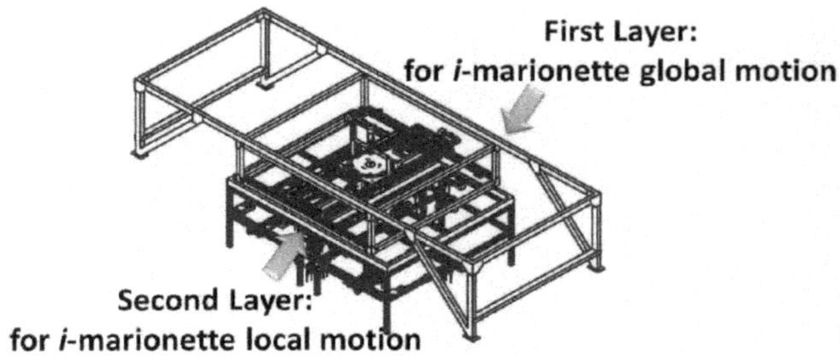

Figure 12. Our two-layer control device.

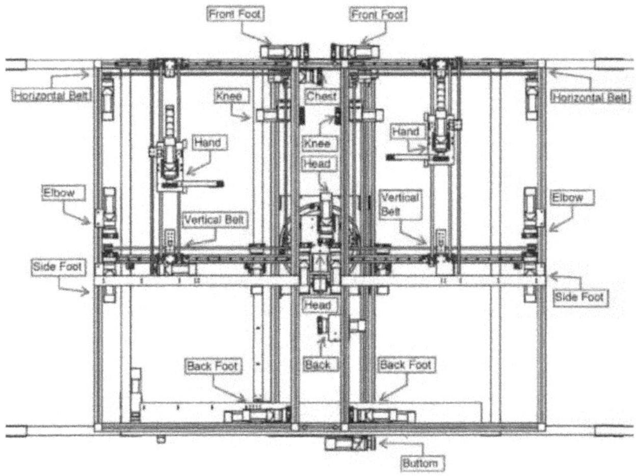

Figure 13. Bird's eye view of the control device with the layout of the motor controllers.

(a) (b)

Figure 14. A conflicting relation between a marionette and puppeteer: (a) traditional puppetry in which a marionette is manipulated by a puppeteer; (b) the puppeteer is a "human marionette" who is influenced by the marionette.

the motors are connected through RS485 wire. The layout of the motor controllers is shown in Figure 13.

5. INTERACTIVE ARTISTIC PUPPETRY

In traditional puppetry, the marionette is manipulated by a puppeteer. As shown in Figure 14a[1][16], there has been a conflicting relation between the marionette and puppeteer.

---

[1]http://en.wikipedia.org/wiki/File:Prague-Marionette.jpg by Chmouel under Creative Commons Attribution-ShareAlike 3.0 Unported (CC BY-SA 3.0)

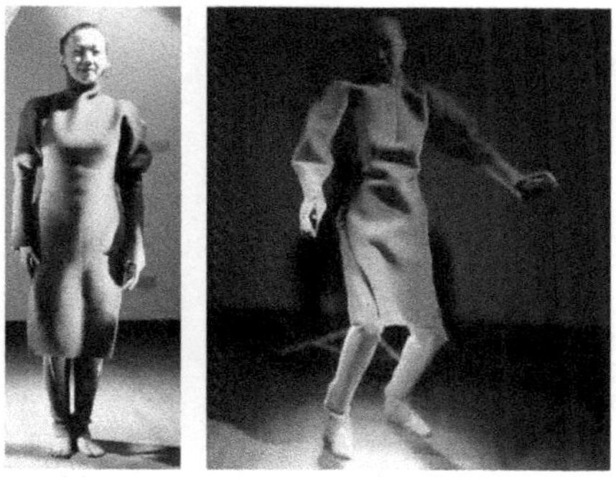

(a) (b)

Figure 15. The two roles in our interactive artistic puppetry: (a) a puppeteer who implies modern technology; (b) a marionette that implies traditional culture.

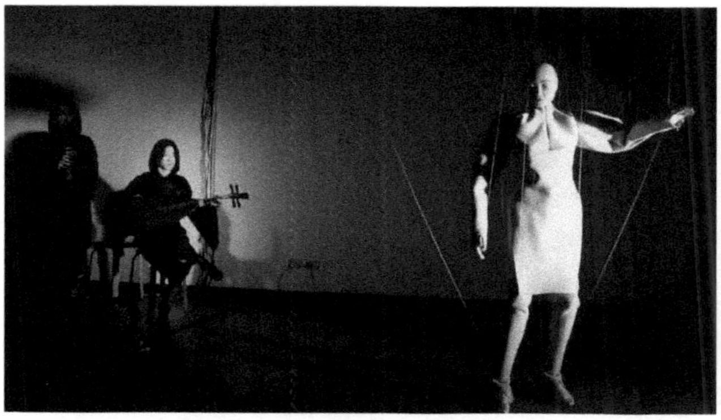

Figure 16. The marionette, implying traditional culture, arrives from a virtual world.

The marionette is like a follower who is passively dominated by the puppeteer. In this respect, the puppeteer is an active guide who controls the marionette to act the way the puppeteer wants. While the puppeteer manipulates the marionette, he looks like a dominator. However, the puppeteer is also influenced by the marionette. When the puppeteer tries to manipulate the marionette well, the marionette causes the puppeteer to pay more attention to it. Therefore, the puppeteer becomes a "human marionette," (Figure 14b) who is influenced by a "marionette puppeteer". We were inspired by the above observations, and we started to think about the following issues: what if the marionette becomes fully automatic? What if the marionette becomes an active manipulator and guides the puppeteer? Is the puppeteer influenced by the marionette?

This artwork attempts to explore the conflict relationship between the puppeteer and the marionette. Our interactive artistic puppetry is performed by two characters. The first one is a performer (puppeteer), implying modern technology in the real world (Figure 15 a), and the second one is the *i*-marionette (Figure 15 b), implying traditional culture in a virtual world. As shown in Figure 15, the performer wears a modern technology dress, and the *i*-marionette wears traditional clothing. Through the proposed action recognition approach, the marionette can recognize human behavior in real time. In the beginning, the *i*-marionette, which is coming from the virtual world (traditional culture), arrives in the real world (modern technology), see Figure 16. The background music is a traditional opera (the Chinese Liyuan opera), which is represented by the marionette. Subsequently, the puppeteer (performer) arrives, and then she walks up to the marionette and puts a spell on the marionette, see Figure 17a.

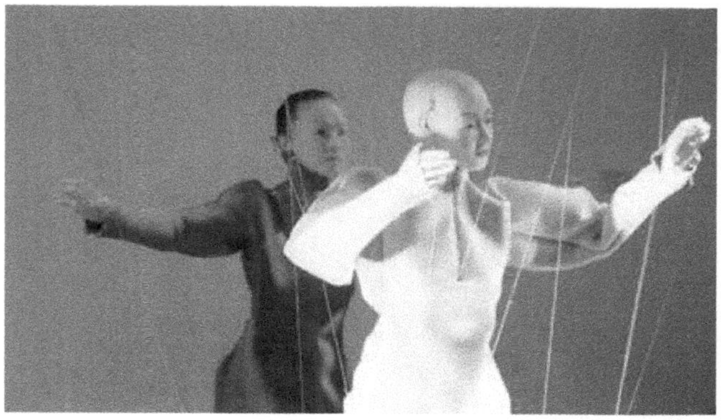

(a)

(b)

Figure 17. The marionette was dominated by the puppeteer: (a) the marionette was gradually losing its consciousness; (b) the marionette begins to follow the puppeteer's action.

Figure 18. The puppeteer is mimicking the marionette' s action

The marionette gradually loses its consciousness. Then, the puppeteer attempts to force the marionette to mimic her actions, see Figure 17b. Surprisingly, the marionette unconsciously follows the puppeteer's action. After a while, the marionette wakes up and shakes off the puppeteer's control. Meanwhile, as a role-swap, the puppeteer begins to mimic the marionette's action (Figure 18), which means that the puppeteer is affected by the marionette. Through the interactions between the marionette and the puppeteer, puppetry represents an interactive circle: humans invent technology, the technology controls the marionette, and the marionette influences the human.

Figure 19. At the end of the puppetry show, the puppeteer sends the marionette back to the virtual world.

Figure 21. Mimicking-marionette game: a player was mimicking the *i*-marionette's action.

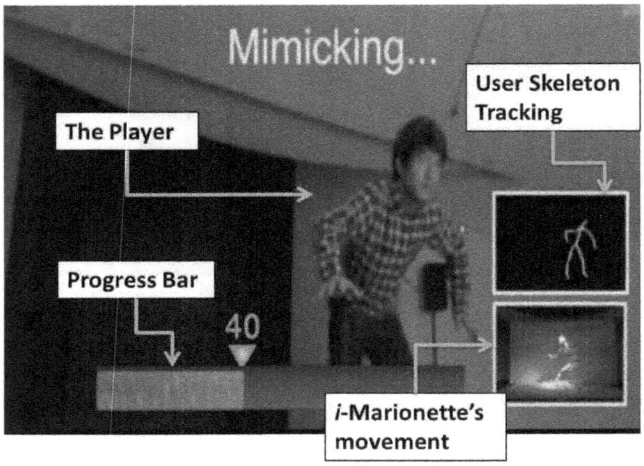

Figure 20. Interface of the mimicking-marionette game.

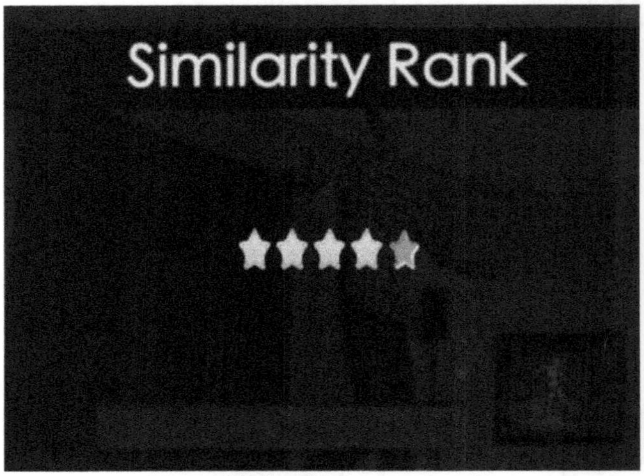

Figure 22. Similarity score result.

Figure 19 shows that the puppeteer sending the marionette back to the virtual world at the end of the puppetry show.

6. MIMICKING-MARIONETTE GAME

The mimicking-marionette is a role swap game (Figure 20) that transforms the *i*-marionette into a puppeteer and the player into a marionette. In the game, the *i*-marionette performs a contemporary dance for the player to mimic and follow its actions. The game interface is shown in Figure 21. The i-marionette in the small window is used to help the players modify their postures. Figure 22 shows the window of the measured result of the action similarity. The similarity result is represented as a score in the game. The system demonstrates the measured similarity as a score. A high score indicates that the actions of the player and the *i*-marionette are similar. In contrast, a lower score indicates that the actions of the player and the *i*-marionette are not similar. The major motivation of the mimicking-marionette game is not only entertainment but also to allow the player to experience the sensation of being affected by the marionette. As the player earns a high similarity score, the player appears to be the winner of the game. However, the player has been affected by the marionette. That is to say, humans develop the mimicking-marionette game, humans play the game, and the game influences the humans. In the end, the human was manipulated by the game.

7. CONCLUSION

This paper presents a human-marionette interaction system based on human action recognition. We applied our human-marionette interactive system for two applications: interactive artistic puppetry and a mimicking-marionette game. The main idea behind these two applications is to explore the peculiar relationship between the puppeteer and the marionette. The interactive artistic puppetry presents a conflict scenario between two different cultural worlds: The performer implies modern technology based in the real world. In contrast, the *i*-marionette implies traditional culture based in a virtual world. Through the interactions between the marionette and the puppeteer, puppetry represents an interactive circle: humans invent technology, the technology controls the marionette, and the marionette affects the human. In the other application, the mimicking-marionette game, which is similar to a role-swap game, the player pretends to be a marionette and experiences the sensation of being affected by the marionette. As the player gains a high similarity score, the player appears to be the winner of the game. However, the player has been manipulated by the marionette. That is to say, humans develop the mimicking-marionette game, a human plays the game, and the game influences the human. In the end, the human was manipulated by the game. To recognize and learn complex and sophisticated human actions, we present an approach, Action Trait Code, for human action classification and employ an effective graph model based on ATC classification for learning and recognizing human actions.

8. ACKNOWLEDGEMENTS

This work was supported in part by the National Science Council, Taiwan, under grant NSC 101-2622-E-002-005-CC2. We would like to thank the colleagues in the Digital Art Center, Taipei, including Wen-Hao Huang and Ruey-Ning Shih, for their technical supports in this work. Special thanks go to the dancer Ho-Wen Hsiao, for her outstanding performance.

9. REFERENCES

[1] M. Egerstedt, T.D. Murphey, and Jon Ludwig, "Motion Programs for Puppet Choreography and Control," In *HSCC*, 2007.

[2] T.D. Murphey, and M. Egerstedt, "Choreography for Marionettes: Imitation, Planning, and Control." In Proc. of IEEE Int. Conf. on Intelligent and Robotic (IROS) Workshop on Art and Robotics, 2008.

[3] W. Li, Z. Zhang, and Z. Liu. Expandable data-driven graphical modeling of human actions based on salient postures. In IEEE Trans. on Circuits and Systems for Video Technology, 18(11):1499–1510, 2008

[4] W. Li, Z. Zhang, and Z. Liu. Action Recognition Based on A Bag of 3D Points, In *IEEE International Workshop on CVPR for Human Communicative Behavior Analysis*, 2010.

[5] J. K. Aggarwal, M. S. Ryoo, " Human Activity Analysis: A Review," *ACM Computing Survey*, 2011

[6] J. Sung, C. Ponce, B. Selman, A. Saxena, "Unstructured Human Activity Detection from RGBD Images," In *ICRA*, 2012.

[7] B. Yao, X. Jiang, A. Khosla, "Classifying Actions and Measuring Action Similarity by Modeling the Mutual Context of Objects and Human Poses," In *ICML*, 2011

[8] M. Raptis, D. Kirovski, H. Hoppe, "Real-Time Classification of Dance Gestures from Skeleton Animation," *Symposium on Computer Animation*, 2011.

[9] Kawada Industries, Inc, "Humanoid Robot HRP-2Promet," 2010.

[10] A description of "HRP-4C" from Wikipedia: http://en.wikipedia.org/wiki/HRP-4C

[11] O. Jenkins, G. González, and M. Loper, "Tracking human motion and actions for interactive robots," In *HRI,* 2007.

[12] Honda Asimo: http://asimo.honda.com/.

[13] T. Theodoridis, A. Agapitos, H. Hu, and S. M. Lucas, "Ubiquitous robotics in physical human action regression: A comparison between dynamic ANNs and GP," In *ICRA*, 2008.

[14] K. Sillam, A. Luciani, "Somnambule, " *ACM MM*, 2009.

[15] Shih-Yao Lin, Chuen-Kai Shie, Shen-Chi Chen, Ming-Sui Lee, and Yi-Ping Hung, "Human Action Recognition Using Action Trait Code," In *ICPR*, 2012.

[16] Creative Commons Attribution-ShareAlike 3.0 Unported (CC BY-SA 3.0).

A Bag-of-Objects Retrieval Model for Web Image Search*

Yang Yang†‡, Linjun Yang‡, Gangshan Wu†, Shipeng Li‡

† State Key Laboratory for Novel Software Technology, Nanjing 210046, P.R. China
‡ Microsoft Research Asia, Beijing 100190, P.R. China
charlie.yang.nju@gmail.com, {linjuny,spli}@microsoft.com, gswu@nju.edu.cn

ABSTRACT

Image search reranking has been an active research topic in recent years to boost the performance of the existing web image search engine which is mostly based on textual metadata of images. Various approaches have been proposed to rerank images for general queries and argue that, they may not necessarily be optimal for queries in specific domain, e.g., object queries, since the reranking algorithms are operated on whole images, instead of the relevant parts of images. In this paper, we propose a novel bag-of-objects retrieval model for image search reranking of object queries. Firstly, we employ a common object discovery algorithm to discover query-relevant objects from the search results returned by text-based image search engine. Then, the query and its result images are represented as a language model on the query-relevant object vocabulary, based on which the ranking function can be derived. As the common object discovery is unreliable and may introduce noises, we propose to incorporate the attributes of the discovered objects, e.g., size, position, etc., into the ranking function through a linear model, and the weights on the object attributes can be learned. The experiments on two subsets of Web Queries dataset comprising object queries demonstrate that our approach can significantly outperform the existing reranking methods on object queries.

Categories and Subject Descriptors

H.3.3 [**Information Systems Applications**]: Retrieval models

General Terms

Algorithms, Performance, Experimentation

*This work was performed when Yang Yang was visiting Microsoft Research Asia as a research intern.

MM'12, October 29–November 2, 2012, Nara, Japan.

Figure 1: A reranking example for query "Eiffel Tower". The first row is the result by text based search and the second row is the result after reranking based on PRF assumption.

Keywords

Image search reranking, supervised reranking, bag-of-objects model, retrieval model

1. INTRODUCTION

As the major image search engines index and rank images mainly based on the surrounding text information, it usually leads to unsatisfactory results being returned to users. This is due to the mismatch between image content and the textual description. Image search reranking has been an active research topic in multimedia retrieval, aiming to refine the text-based search results based on cues from images' visual content.

The existing reranking approaches [6, 7, 28, 10, 11, 30, 31] are mostly based on the cluster assumption and PRF (Pseudo Relevance Feedback) assumption. The cluster assumption suggests that the relevant images are visually similar while irrelevant images have different appearances. This has been extensively adopted in various graph-based reranking algorithms based on the visual similarity graph [10, 11, 30, 31]. In the PRF assumption, the images ranked in the top of the text-based search result are regarded as pseudo-relevant, which can then be employed to learn a classifier [17] or multiple classifiers [36]. While these assumptions have been demonstrated as generally effective in the previous works [6, 7, 28], we can see that they are not sufficiently appropriate for object queries, for which users are likely to find images containing an object such as car. For such queries, the images which users are interested in may be partially related to the query. In other words, only some parts of these images are relevant to the query while the rest may not. Then, the cluster assumption or PRF assumption which operates on the whole image cannot sufficiently capture useful information from the initial text-based search result.

Figure 1 shows an example for the query "Eiffel Tower". The upper row is the result from a text-based search engine. The lower row is the reranking result by PRF assumption where the first image is regarded as positive sample. In this case, two irrelevant images are boosted to the top, because image **F** and **D** have high visual similarity to image **A**.

We argue that the problem is mainly caused by the fact that the existing reranking approaches based on above assumptions usually employ the visual features on the whole image, such as histogram of visual words [3, 37]. However, for the object queries, i.e., the queries by which the user intends to search for images containing desired objects, including people/faces, logos, animals, buildings and industrial productions, images can be said relevant if only part of the image is about the query object. Hence, the assumptions operating on the whole image may be too rigid. For the above example, we may achieve a better performance if the reranking algorithm is performed on object level, so that images such as **B**, **C** and **E** containing the Eiffel Tower but with distinct viewpoints (or with different backgrounds) can still have a fair chance to be promoted.

Hence, we propose a bag-of-objects retrieval model to represent the query and its result images as a language model based on the containing object appearances. To make the models focus more on the query-relevant objects but be insensitive to noises or backgrounds, we represent the image and query language models on a query-relevant object vocabulary.

To construct such a query-relevant object vocabulary. we extend the iterative link analysis approach proposed in [15], which tries to mine the common objects in a set of images by a *PageRank*-like algorithm [15] on image regions. Since the text-based intial ranking can provide useful information on which image is more relevant than the others, we utilize this to improve the algorithm in [15] by considering the text-based ranking as a prior in *PageRank* to differentiate the images at different rank positions. Although the query-specific object discovery is generally effective, it may not be sufficiently reliable in complex circumstances and leads to irrelevant objects being discovered.

To estimate the relevance and confidence of discovered objects to the query, we compute a set of attribute scores based on the the position, size, and visual density of objects in containing images, etc. Then these attributes are integrated into the retrieval model so that a linear weighted ranking function is derived. The weights can be learned through RankSVM [13] from a human labeled training set.

The proposed approaches are evaluated on two subsets of the publicly available Web Queries dataset [17]. One comprises named person queries and the other comprises the other object queries. The results show that the bag-of-objects retrieval model outperform all the other reranking methods. It improves the result from the search engine by 39.52% in the term of Mean Average Precision (MAP) and the result from the state-of-the-art reranking method [36] by 6.84%.

The rest of this paper is organized as follows. After reviewing the related work on image search reranking, object-based image retrieval and common object discovery in Section 2, we describe the proposed bag-of-objects retrieval model with an illustrative example in Section 3. Section 4 presents the experimental results and analysis of our approach. In Section 5, we complete this paper with remarkable conclusions and a summary of future works.

2. RELATED WORK

In this section, we will review the related work on image search reranking, object-based image retrieval and common object detection and position the contribution of our paper with regard to these existing work.

Image Search Reranking. The existing image search reranking methods can generally be classified into unsupervised and supervised ones. The unsupervised reranking approaches are mostly based on assumptions on the structure of the initial text-based search result, among which the most well-known are cluster assumption and PRF (Pseudo-Relevance Feedback) assumption. The cluster assumption suggests that the relevant images are mostly visually similar while irrelevant images are not [30]. As the assumption can be naturally represented in a graph structure, various graph-based reranking methods are proposed to interpret this assumption from different viewpoints [30, 31, 11, 10]. Specifically, in these methods, a graph is firstly constructed with images as nodes and the edges are based on the visual similarity. Then image search reranking can be achieved by the propagation of ranking scores or positions on the graph. The main drawback of such approaches is that the visual similarity is difficult to estimate, and most of the approaches are based on the global visual features, which cannot handle object queries well, since the image similarity should be computed with regard to the relevant objects. The second is the PRF assumption, which rigidly assumes that the top-ranked images in text-based search result are relevant to the query. Based on this assumption a number of reranking models [33, 6, 7, 28, 21] are proposed, which learn a classifier by taking the top-ranked images as positive and then use this classifier to rank images. As the learned classifiers are mostly on the whole image without regard to objects in the image, these approaches will not perform sufficiently well for object queries.

Supervised reranking methods are proposed to introduce human labeling to train a reranking model which can better accord with users' perception. The different approaches differ mostly on how to derive the relevance features between the textual query and images which are in different modalities. In [35] and [17] the reranking features are usually manually designed, based on the domain knowledge of the authors on image search problem. While, in [36], the reranking features are automatically extracted by learning multiple classifiers, assuming the different importance for images with different text-based ranks. Our proposed approach follows the supervised reranking fashion, but with two major contributions to extend the existing work. First, instead of operating on the whole image as in the existing approaches, we build an object-based model so that the reranking process can be aware of the query-relevant objects. Second, in our work, we are not attempting to learn models to combine different reranking features, but targeting to learn parameters in the bag-of-objects retrieval model, where the parameters indicate the usefulness of different object attributes.

Object-based Image Retrieval. Object-based image retrieval is a well studied problem, for which the user usually provides a query image with the object of interest being specified through e.g., a bounding box. Different approaches were proposed in the past years. In [26, 27, 23], objects on database images are manually labeled and then indexed by visual features such as color, texture and shape. In [9] images are firstly segmented into small regions and the query object is modeled based on the regions using Latent Semantic Analysis (LSA). In [34], images are represented as a bag of visual words, and then the language modeling approach to information retrieval is employed for ranking images. The authors argue that the object context is important, and thus visual words locating outside the object region should also be taken into consideration in the retrieval process, but with a discounted weight. The problem studied in our paper is different from object-based image retrieval, in which the query is specified by a keyword, instead of an example image with object of interest. Hence, our problem is more challenging because we need to infer the representation of the object of interest based on the user provided keyword query.

Common Object Discovery. Common object discovery is a recently investigated topic which aims to find the frequent objects in a group of images. The different approaches of common object discovery can be divided into two classes: segmentation based methods [16, 14, 8, 32] and bounding box based methods [15, 19, 4].

Segmentation based common object discovery, which is also known as co-segmentation, segments the frequent objects of each image simultaneously. Rother et al. [25], formulate the problem as minimizing an energy function consists of the Markov Random Field (MRF) smoothness for separating foreground and background and a histogram matching term guarantees foreground of images to be similar. In [16], the authors first segment each image into a group of super pixels and then segment the common foreground by a greedy expansion algorithm. The main drawbacks of these method are two-fold, limiting their application in out work: First, most of the co-segmentation methods are designed for images with clear foreground, which may not be effective on the web images with complicated background. Second, co-segmentation methods are very time consuming, which usually take hours when applied on hundreds of images.

Bounding box based methods aim to find the common object in the form of bounding box. These methods usually build a set of hypotheses regions of interest (ROI) based on the saliency map. In [4] a conditional random field (CRF) is built for all the candidate ROIs and the common object discovery problem is transformed as finding an optimal configuration in the CRF. In [15] a link analysis algorithm is iteratively applied on all the ROIs to find the centrality as the common objects. For image search reranking, since the initial image ranking from the text-based search engine can provide useful information on the usefulness of images to the query, we extend [15] by incorporating such prior ranking information to build the query-relevant object vocabulary.

3. APPROACH

Our approach starts with the construction of query-relevant object vocabulary by mining the query-relevant objects from the images returned by the text-based search engine. Then, a bag-of-objects retrieval model is proposed to formulate the reranking problem based on the language modeling approach for information retrieval. To compute the ranking scores for each image based on the bag-of-objects retrieval model, we estimate the image and query models based on the results of query-relevant object discovery. Finally, we present the approach which learns the parameters in the retrieval model.

3.1 Query-relevant object vocabulary construction

The query-relevant objects are those different objects instances or different appearances of one object which are relevant to the query. For example, for the query "Eiffel Tower", the query-relevant objects may include the appearances of Eiffel Tower from different viewpoints or with different lighting conditions. For the query "Car", the query-relevant objects may comprise the different car instances such as "Audi A6" ad "BMW Q5".

The query-relevant object vocabulary is critical to our approach to serve as the foundation of the later processing. In this paper, we propose an algorithm based on link analysis [15] to discover those objects.

3.1.1 Algorithm overview

We first detect 30 ROIs with the highest saliency on each image using saliency object detection method proposed in [5], which are regarded as the hypotheses for query-relevant objects.

Our method is composed of two steps. In the first step, we select the qualified hypotheses that are highly confident to be query-relevant objects. The second step is to cluster the selected ROIs and use the clusters as query-relevant object vocabulary.

In the ROI selection step, the algorithm iteratively refines query-relevant ROI set until it becomes stable. In each iteration, the algorithm first recommends several representative ROIs which are considered to be the most query-relevant. These ROIs are called "hubs". Then, an ROI refinement procedure is applied on each image, where those ROIs with the highest similarity to the hubs are taken as query-relevant ROIs. The query-relevant ROIs selected by the second procedure is taken as the input of the next iteration.

3.1.2 ROI selection

In iteration t, the "hubs" are obtained using link analysis technique of *PageRank* [2]. Different from the hub-seeking procedure adopted in [15], the hubs selected in our method should not only be representative to an object, but also relevant enough to the query.

To achieve this, we construct an augmented bipartite graph $\boldsymbol{G}^{(t)}$ between $\boldsymbol{\mathcal{S}}^{(t-1)}$ and $\boldsymbol{\mathcal{C}}$, where $\boldsymbol{\mathcal{S}}^{(t-1)} = \{s_i^{(t-1)}\}$ denotes the ROIs selected in the last iteration, and $\boldsymbol{\mathcal{C}}$ is the image ranking list of the current query returned by the search engine. The *Page Rank* algorithm calculates the ranking score for each vertex in $\boldsymbol{G}^{(t)}$, where the ranking score on the vertex of an ROI intuitively shows the object confidence and query relevance. The augmented bipartite graph $\boldsymbol{G}^{(t)}$ is written as follows:

$$\boldsymbol{G}^{(t)} = \begin{bmatrix} \alpha \boldsymbol{G}_s & (1-\alpha)\boldsymbol{G}_d \\ \boldsymbol{G}_d^T & 0 \end{bmatrix}, \quad (1)$$

where $\boldsymbol{G}_s$ is a k-nearest neighbour (k-NN) self-similarity graph constructed on $\boldsymbol{\mathcal{S}}^{(t-1)}$. $\boldsymbol{G}_d$ is a bipartite graph constructed between $\boldsymbol{\mathcal{S}}^{(t-1)}$ and the ranking list $\boldsymbol{\mathcal{C}}$, where each image document is linked to all its containing ROIs appeared in $\boldsymbol{\mathcal{S}}^{(t-1)}$ with edge weight set to 1. In our experiment we set $\alpha = 0.8$.

For *PageRank* algorithm, the score vector $\boldsymbol{p}$ is updated as follows:

$$\tilde{\boldsymbol{p}} = \beta \boldsymbol{G}\boldsymbol{p} + (1-\beta)\boldsymbol{I}. \tag{2}$$

Here, $\boldsymbol{I}$ is the vector for priori probabilities and $\boldsymbol{I} = [\boldsymbol{I}^k\ \boldsymbol{I}^d]$, where $\boldsymbol{I}^k_i = \frac{1}{|\boldsymbol{S}^{(t-1)}|}$ and $\boldsymbol{I}^d_i = \frac{1}{\log(i+1)M}$ with the normalization term $M = \sum_i^{|\boldsymbol{C}|} \frac{1}{\log(i+1)}$. The variable i indicates the ranking position of the image. Vector $\boldsymbol{I}^d$ is set in this way because we assume images with higher ranking from text-based search engine are more likely to be relevant to the query. In each iteration, the text-based ranking score of each image is propagated to all its linked ROIs through the bipartite graph $\boldsymbol{G}_d$.

After *PageRank* converges, we follow the hub-seeking method in [15] to find the ROIs which are diverse and also representative to the query by choosing the ROI vertices with local maxima of *PageRank* score.

The procedure of ROI refinement on each image is achieved by applying the *PageRank* on an augmented bipartite graph between the image's belonging ROIs and the hubs. From these ROIs, we selected the ones with the highest ranking score as potential object instances and use them as the input of the next iteration.

3.1.3 ROI Clustering

Since the "hubs" are regarded as typical for query-relevant objects, we treat each selected hub in the last iteration as the representation of a query-relevant object. Then, each selected ROI is assigned to its nearest hub if the distance is less than a threshold γ as the instance of the query-relevant object.

We argue that the ROI's distance to the hub is not accurate enough in measuring its confidence of belonging to a query-relevant object. Thus, we re-estimate this confidence by *PageRank*. We first construct a k-NN self-similarity graph among the ROIs within the cluster and apply the *PageRank* procedure. For an instance k_i of the object $\boldsymbol{k}$, we denote the score as $S(k_i, \boldsymbol{k})$. We call the set of discovered objects as the *object vocabulary*, and denote it as $\boldsymbol{\mathcal{K}}$.

3.1.4 An illustrative example

Figure 2 (a) shows an example process of query-relevant object discovery on the query "Arc de triumph". From each image, a group of ROI hypotheses is detected by the saliency object detection approach in [5]. We can see from the figure that the building of Arc de triumph is perfectly bounded by a certain ROI among the hypotheses. After applying iterative link analysis, these bounding boxes are selected due to similar visual appearance. On the contrary, the image of a leaf on the right has no selected ROI because it is not similar to any of the extracted hubs thus regarded as an outlier.

Figure 2 (b) shows the 4 object clusters extracted with respect to the selected hubs, where the ROI list is sorted by belonging confidence $S(k_i, \boldsymbol{k})$ in descending order. According to definition in the beginning of Section 3.1, query-relevant objects can be different object appearances as well as different objects. Due to the different view points and illuminating conditions, ROIs of "Arc de triumph" are clustered into 3 different categories. In Figure 2 (b), images of object 2 show the exact front of the arch but object 1 is taken from a different viewpoint. Object 3 comprises the images of query object in the night, and object 4 is irrelevant and showing another famous landmark "Arc de ceil". The reasons that the object 4 is detected as a hub are two-fold. First, several images of this arch exist in the search result, thus the appearance of this arc is regarded as frequent. Second, "Arc de ceil" is also an arch, and visually very similar to the query object, thus some images of "Arc de triumph" would also vote for this hub.

We can see that although above query-relevant object discovery is effective, it will also fail in some cases. Besides object 4, several ROIs not relevant to the query are also selected as instances of query-relevant objects, as shown in Figure 2 (b). Hence, we propose the bag-of-objects retrieval model to resolve this problem in the following.

3.2 Bag-of-objects retrieval model

Given the discovered query-relevant object vocabulary in the above, we can represent the images and the query as a bag-of-objects. Then the reranking problem can be formulated as a risk minimization following [18].

The ranking objective of an image $\boldsymbol{d}$ is related to the risk of returning it for a given query $\boldsymbol{q}$, which can be defined on the query and document language models:

$$\begin{aligned} R(\boldsymbol{d};\boldsymbol{q}) &= R(a=\boldsymbol{d}|\boldsymbol{q},\boldsymbol{G}) \\ &= \sum_{r\in 0,1} \int_{\theta_Q}\int_{\theta_D} L(\theta_Q,\theta_D,r) \times p(\theta_Q|\boldsymbol{q}) \\ & p(\theta_D|\boldsymbol{d}) p(r|\theta_Q,\theta_D) d\theta_Q d\theta_D. \end{aligned} \tag{3}$$

Here, $a = \boldsymbol{d}$ means the action of returning the document $\boldsymbol{d}$ for the query $\boldsymbol{q}$, and $\boldsymbol{G}$ is the document collection in the database, r is the query-document relevance. θ_Q and θ_D are the language models for the query and the document, which are also called *query model* and *document model* respectively. L is the loss function which can usually be modeled by Kullback-Leibler divergence (KL divergence) between the query model and document model, written as follows:

$$\Delta(\theta_Q,\theta_D) = \sum_{i=1}^{M_{\mathcal{K}}} p(k_i|\theta_Q)\log\frac{p(k_i|\theta_Q)}{p(k_i|\theta_D)}. \tag{4}$$

Then, based on some derivations we can obtain the following ranking function:

$$R(\boldsymbol{d};\boldsymbol{q}) \propto -\sum_{i=1}^{M_{\mathcal{K}}} p(k_i|\hat{\theta}_Q)\log p(k_i|\hat{\theta}_D) + \xi_q, \tag{5}$$

where $\hat{\theta}_Q$ and $\hat{\theta}_D$ are the *the maximum a posteriori estimation* of the query and document models, and ξ_q is a constant which can be ignored for ranking. By sorting the image list with respect to the ranking function in Equation (5), we can get the reranked results.

In the following section, we are going to show how to estimate the *document model* in Section 3.3.1 and the *query model* in Section 3.3.2.

3.3 Document and query modeling

3.3.1 Document Model

In this paper, we assume our document model follows the following distribution

$$p(\boldsymbol{d}|\theta_D) \propto \prod_{i=1}^{M_d} p(d_i|\theta_D), \tag{6}$$

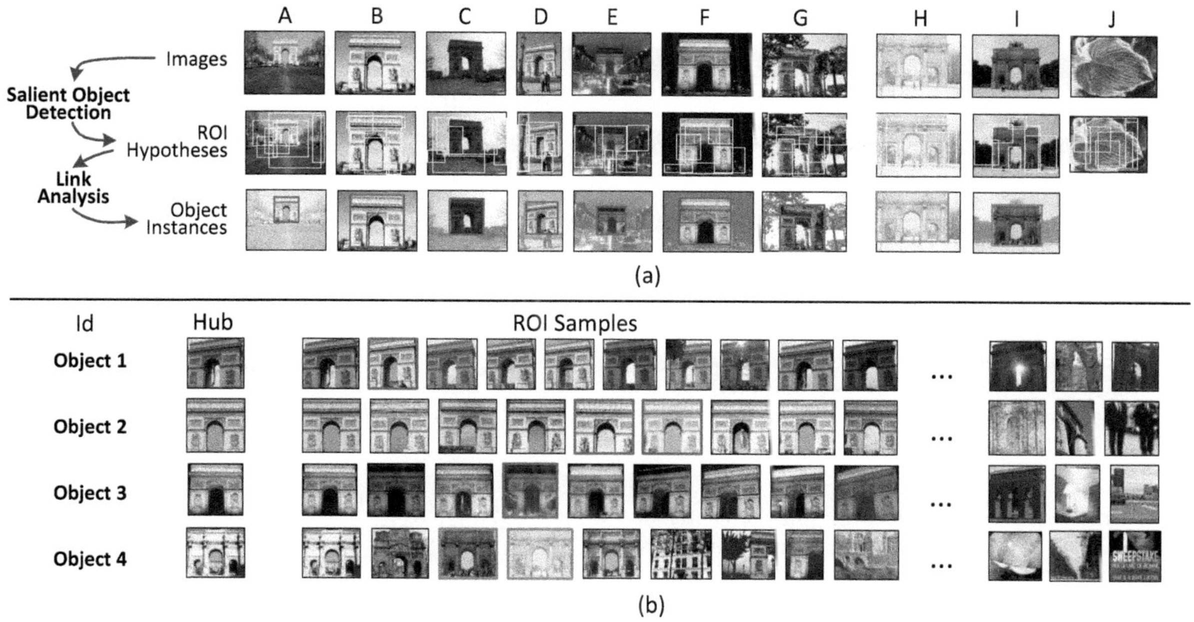

Figure 2: An example of Query dominant object extraction on the query "Arc de Triumph".

where d_i stands for the i_{th} object instance in image $\boldsymbol{d}$. We define

$$p(d_i|\theta_D) = \prod_{j=1}^{M_{\mathcal{K}}} p(\boldsymbol{k}_j|\boldsymbol{d})^{S(d_i,\boldsymbol{k}_i)\delta(d_i,\boldsymbol{k}_j)}, \tag{7}$$

where function $\delta(d_i, \boldsymbol{k}_j)$ indicates whether d_i is associated as an instance of object $\boldsymbol{k}_j$ in the query-relevant discovery and $S(d_i, \boldsymbol{k}_j)$ is a score obtained by the *PageRank* applied in Section 3.1.3, showing the confidence that the instance d_i belongs to object $\boldsymbol{k}_j$.

Then, the maximum-likehood estimation (MLE) of the *document model* is derived as follows:

$$p(\boldsymbol{k}_i|\theta_D) = \frac{\sum_{j=1}^{M_d} S(d_j, \boldsymbol{k}_i)\delta(d_j, \boldsymbol{k}_i)}{\sum_{j=1}^{M_d} S(d_j, \boldsymbol{k}_i)}. \tag{8}$$

3.3.2 *Query Model*

In this paper, the query is also modeled as a bag of objects. Since the text query itself does not have any visual information, we estimate the query language model θ_Q with respect to the query-relevant object vocabulary $\boldsymbol{\mathcal{K}}$ and the ranked image list $\boldsymbol{\mathcal{C}}$ from text-based search. The distribution of each query-relevant object for query $\boldsymbol{q}$ is denoted as $p(\boldsymbol{k}_i|\theta_Q)$, which we assume follows the following distribution:

$$\begin{aligned} p(\boldsymbol{q}|\theta_Q) &= p(\boldsymbol{\mathcal{K}}, \boldsymbol{\mathcal{C}}|\theta_Q) \\ &\propto \prod_{i=1}^{M_q} p(\boldsymbol{k}_i, \boldsymbol{\mathcal{C}}|\theta_Q), \end{aligned} \tag{9}$$

with

$$p(\boldsymbol{k}_i, \boldsymbol{\mathcal{C}}|\theta_Q) = p(\boldsymbol{k}_i|\theta_Q)^{S(\boldsymbol{k}_i,\boldsymbol{\mathcal{C}})}. \tag{10}$$

The function $S(\boldsymbol{k}_i, \boldsymbol{\mathcal{C}})$ computes the object relevance with respect to the initial rank list $\boldsymbol{\mathcal{C}}$. With the distribution described in Equation (9), the maximum likehood estimation of the query's object model θ_Q is then derived as follows:

$$p(\boldsymbol{k}_i|\hat{\theta}_Q) = \frac{S(\boldsymbol{k}_i, \boldsymbol{\mathcal{C}})}{\sum_{j=1}^{M_q} S(\boldsymbol{k}_j, \boldsymbol{\mathcal{C}})}. \tag{11}$$

In this paper, we calculate the object relevance $S(\boldsymbol{k}_i, \boldsymbol{\mathcal{C}})$ based on the attributes from each object. These attributes are proposed below to indicate the object relevance to the query. As the below attributes are extracted on each containing instance of the object, we calculate the score of each object based on the expectation and variance of the comprising instances' attribute scores, such that each attribute can capture not only the average information but also the variance of the instances. To reduce the impact of noisy ROIs, the score of each instance is weighted by its belonging confidence $S(k_i, \boldsymbol{k})$ calculated in Section 3.1.3.

- **Initial ranking:** As stated in PRF based methods, the initial ranking of each image is critical to its relevance. Motivated by this, we assume that if an object has a set of instance whose parent images are all highly ranked by text-based search engine, the object can be regarded as query-relevant with a high probability. On the contrary, if all the instance of the object are ranked at the bottom of the ranking list, the object is probably irrelevant to the query. In this paper, we calculate the ranking score of each image with respect to its ranking position as follows:

$$IR(x) = \frac{1}{\log(R(x) + 1)}, \tag{12}$$

  where $R(x)$ stands for the ranking position of image x.

- **Initial ranking of neighborhood:** The information from the visual neighborhood can be propagated to improve the robustness of the estimation. Hence, we propose to use the initial ranking of neighborhood of each instance. Which is calculated as follows:

$$NR(x_i) = \frac{1}{|nn(x_i;k)|} \sum_{x_j \in nn(x_i;k)} IR(x_j), \quad (13)$$

where $nn(x_i;k)$ stands for the k-nearest neighborhood of object instance x_i.

- **Object size:** Intuitively, if an ROI region occupies a big part of an image, it is probably the topic of the image. On the contrary, if an ROI is small, it is likely to be a background object which is irrelevant to the topic of the image and so to the query. Also, a small ROI may not have reliable visual features to compute the distance correctly, which misleads the ROI to belong to the query-relevant object category. To avoid the influence of image size, we normalize the area of bounding box by it.

- **Object location:** An ROI locating on the center of the image intuitively tells that the photographer is taking a shot directly towards the object. Therefore, the distance from the ROI to the image center indicates the confidence that the object is representing the image. In this paper, we adopt the shift of the ROI to the image center along X and Y axis, as well as the euclidean distance of the ROI to the center.

- **Saliency:** We assume ROI with high saliency is more likely to be an object while low saliency suggests a probability to be an scene. Hence, we use the average saliency scores of an ROI as one dimensional attribute score to reflect the relevance of the ROI to be relevant to the object query.

- **Visual density:** We follow the assumption in [29] that relevant images have higher density than irrelevant images. Thus, we argue that relevant object instances may have higher density on visual appearance. For each instance, its density is calculated by the Kernel Density Estimation (KDE) [24] follows

$$p(x_i) = \frac{1}{|nn(x_i;k)|} \sum_{x_j \in nn(x_i;k)} \chi(x_i - x_j), \quad (14)$$

where $nn(x_i;k)$ suggests the k-nearest neighborhood of region x_i, and $\chi(x)$ is a kernel function with $\chi(x) > 0$ and $\int \chi(x)dx = 1$.

The attributes scores computed using the above approaches are formed into a feature vector $\boldsymbol{L}_i^q$. Then, the function $S(\boldsymbol{k}_i, \boldsymbol{\mathcal{C}})$ can be written as follows:

$$S(\boldsymbol{k}_i, \boldsymbol{\mathcal{C}}) = \boldsymbol{W}^T \boldsymbol{L}_i^q, \quad (15)$$

where W^T is the weight vector of the combination model.

We then substitute the Equation (15) into Equation (11), then $p(\boldsymbol{k}_i|\hat{\theta}_Q)$ becomes

$$\begin{aligned} p(\boldsymbol{k}_i|\hat{\theta}_Q) &= \frac{S(\boldsymbol{k}_i, \boldsymbol{\mathcal{C}})}{\sum_{j=1}^{|\mathcal{K}|} S(\boldsymbol{k}_j, \boldsymbol{\mathcal{C}})} \\ &= \frac{\boldsymbol{W}^T \boldsymbol{L}_i^q}{\sum_{j=1}^{|\mathcal{K}|} \boldsymbol{W}^T \boldsymbol{L}_j^q}. \end{aligned} \quad (16)$$

Since the denominator of Equation (16) is mainly for normalization, it can be ignored for ranking. By integrating Equation (16) into the ranking function (5), we can get the final ranking function for the bag-of-objects retrieval model.

3.4 Learning

As the ranking function is a linear function we can naturally employ Ranking SVM to learn the parameters. Ranking SVM [13] is an adaptation of the classification SVM to the ranking problem. It decomposes the rankings into a set of pair-wise preferences and then reduces the ranking learning problem into the classification of pairs. The optimization problem of Ranking SVM is

$$\begin{aligned} \min_{\boldsymbol{W}} \quad & \frac{1}{2}\boldsymbol{W}^T\boldsymbol{W} + C\sum \varepsilon_{x,y}^i \\ \text{s.t.} \quad & \forall q_i, k_x \succ k_y : R(x;q_i) - R(y;q_i) \geq 1 - \varepsilon_{x,y}^i \\ & \forall x, y, i : \varepsilon_{x,y}^i \geq 0. \end{aligned} \quad (17)$$

The problem can be efficiently solved using SMO (Sequential Minimal Optimization) or cutting-plane algorithm. In this paper, we particularly employ the software provided in [12] for the learning process.

4. EXPERIMENTS

To demonstrate the effectiveness of our proposed approach, we perform an experimental study on two subsets of a publicly available dataset, comprising the queries of objects and the queries for people. Various baseline approaches including the result from the search engine, the existing unsupervised and supervised reranking methods are compared to show the superiority of our proposed approach.

4.1 Experimental Steps

4.1.1 Dataset

To make our experiment as reproducible as possible, we employ a publicly available Web Queries dataset[1] for evaluating our approach and comparing with the baseline approaches. The dataset contains totally 353 representative image search queries, covering a wide range of topics including products, celebrities, animals etc. Then, these queries are issued to an image search engine to collect top ranked image results. Finally 71478 images are obtained in total. A binary relevance between label each query and the retrieved images is provided by human as the ground-truth.

As proposed approach is designed for object queries, we construct two subsets of the Web Queries dataset by selecting those object queries. The WEB_QRY_OBJECTS dataset comprises object queries including landmarks, products, flags and logos. To more comprehensively evaluate our approach, the WEB_QRY_HUMAN dataset is constructed by selecting those named person queries. Finally, the WEB_QRY_OBJECTS dataset is consisted of 101 queries with 19586 images, while WEB_QRY_HUMAN dataset contains 103 queries and 20398 images.

4.1.2 Experimental Settings

To demonstrate the effectiveness of our method, we compare it with different baseline approaches, including text-based search engine (*"Text-baseline"*) and the Bayesian reranking(*"Bayesian"*) [30], pseudo relevance feedback rerank-

[1]`http://lear.inrialpes.fr/~krapac/webqueries/webqueries.html`

Table 1: The performance comparison of various reranking methods WEB_QRY_OBJECTS.

Methods	MAP	NDCG@10	NDCG@25	NDCG@40
Text-baseline	0.582	0.674	0.649	0.667
Bayesian	0.647 (+11.17%)	0.739 (+9.64%)	0.717 (+10.48%)	0.698 (+4.65%)
PRF	0.743 (+27.66%)	0.850 (+26.11%)	0.830 (+27.89%)	0.809 (+21.29%)
Letorr	0.746 (+28.18%)	0.809 (+20.03%)	0.833 (+28.35%)	0.812 (+21.74%)
Query-relative	0.750 (+28.87%)	0.859 (+27.45%)	0.839 (+29.28%)	0.817 (+22.49%)
L^2	0.760 (+30.58%)	0.856 (+27.00%)	0.838 (+29.12%)	0.830 (+24.44%)
Proposed method	0.812 (+39.52%)	0.847 (+25.67%)	0.844 (+30.05%)	0.848 (+27.14%)

Table 2: The performance comparison of various reranking methods on WEB_QRY_HUMAN.

Methods	MAP	NDCG@10	NDCG@25	NDCG@40
Text-baseline	0.603	0.762	0.725	0.688
PRF	0.620(+2.89%)	0.761(-0.16%)	0.713(-1.18%)	0.682(-0.92%)
Bayesian	0.675(+11.94%)	0.876(+14.96%)	0.819(+12.97%)	0.772(+12.21%)
Letorr	0.680(+12.84%)	0.819(+7.57%)	0.784(+8.19%)	0.755(+9.70%)
Query-relative	0.640(+6.23%)	0.761(-0.04%)	0.737(+1.71%)	0.714(+3.78%)
L^2	0.721(+19.69%)	0.888(+16.62%)	0.848(+17.01%)	0.813(+18.13%)
Proposed method	0.764(+26.70%)	0.861(+12.99%)	0.853(+17.66%)	0.827(+20.20%)

ing(*"PRF"*) [33], supervised-reranking(*"Loterr"*) [35], the query-relative classifier (*"Query-relative"*) [17] and the L^2 reranking (*"L^2"*) [36]. For PRF reranking, top ranked images are selected as positive samples while the negative samples are sampled following [36]. When evaluating Bayesian reranking, the pair-wise ranking distance and the best performing local learning consistency is adopted.

For the supervised reranking approaches including L^2 reranking, superived-reranking, query-relative classifier, and ours, ranking models are trained by RankSVM[13]. To better evaluate these approaches, we randomly split the dataset into 10 folds and employ the cross validation strategy to train and evaluate different queries in a round robin way. In each round, 8 of 10 folds are used for training, one for parameter validation, and the rest one is used for evaluation.

For each image in our dataset, we extract the Pyramid Histogram Of visual Words (PHOW) described in [1] as the visual feature representation of images. Firstly, SIFT[22] descriptors are extracted on the points based on dense sampling in different image pyramids. Specifically, 4 SIFT descriptors on 4 different scale levels are computed on each sampled point. Then, descriptors are quantized into visual words based on the k-means quantization. Finally, each image is represented by a spatial pyramid histogram of the quantized visual words. We adopt the histogram intersection kernel on PHOW feature for the computation of image similarity, which has shown generally good performance for object recognition. As a special case, we adopt linear kernel for SVM in L^2 reranking and query-relative classifier, as suggested in the papers.

To better deal with the images in "WEB_QRY_HUMAN" dataset, we employ a face detector embedded in OpenCV[2] to obtain facial ROIs as a supplement to ROIs sampled from saliency map.

4.1.3 Evaluation Measure

The ranking performance is measured by Averrage Precision (AP) and Normalized Discounted Cumulative Gain (NDCG), which are widely used to evaluate search and ranking methods. AP is defined as average of precisions at various recall levels, and MAP is the average of APs among all queries. NDCG is defined as follows:

$$\text{NDCG@}k = \frac{\text{DCG@}k}{\text{IDCG@}k}, \tag{18}$$

where

$$\text{DCG@}k = \sum_{i=1}^{k} \frac{2^{r_i} - 1}{\log_2(i+1)}. \tag{19}$$

In Equation (19), r_i is the ground truth labeling of relevance for the i_{th} image, while k is the truncation level.

[2] `http://opencv.willowgarage.com`

4.2 Experimental Results

4.2.1 Performance Comparison

Table 1 shows the performance comparison of the different reranking on the WEB_QRY_OBJECT dataset, in terms of MAP, NDCG@10, NDCG@25 and NDCG@40. It is obvious that all reranking methods can outperform the text-baseline in the term of MAP, for example L^2 reranking improves the text-baseline by 30.58%, and our method improves it by 39.52%. This demonstrates that the reranking approaches are generally effective to boost the image search ranking performance. Among all the evaluated reranking methods, our method outperforms the other 5 reranking methods. Specifically, it can improve the Superived-reranking, query-relative classifier and L^2 reranking by 19.41%, 26.88% and 6.84%. This suggests the general effectiveness of our approach on object queries.

Table 2 compares all the evaluated methods on the dataset WEB_QRY_HUMAN. We can see that the baseline reranking methods are much less effective on this dataset comparing to WEB_QRY_OBJECT, because of the specification of human images. For example, the state-of-the-art method L^2 reranking can only achieve an improvement of 19.69% on MAP, while it can increase the performance on WEB_QRY_OBJECT dataset by 30.58%. This is because

Table 3: **The performance of each individual object attribute.**

Attribute mean	Initial ranking	Initial ranking of neighborhood	Saliency	Size	Location	Visual density
MAP	0.730	0.764	0.733	0.711	0.749	0.763
Attribute var.	Initial ranking	Initial ranking of neighborhood	Saliency	Size	Location	Visual density.
MAP	0.716	0.749	0.721	0.713	0.740	0.754

Table 4: **The performance by leaving one attribute out.**

Attribute mean	Initial ranking	Initial ranking of neighborhood	Saliency	Size	Location	Visual density
MAP	0.780	0.764	0.780	0.778	0.771	0.760
Attribute var.	Initial ranking	Initial ranking of neighborhood	Saliency	Size	Location	Visual density.
MAP	0.787	0.772	0.779	0.789	0.777	0.768

global features extracted from the whole image have a limited ability in identifying people. Our method achieves an improvement of 26.70% in the term of MAP, with the help of query-relevant objects and face detector. The proposed method improves the Superived-reranking by 12.35% and L^2 reranking by 5.96%. This experiment shows that our method is able to address the limitation of existing methods on human queries.

We can see from both Table 1 and Table 2 that our method has no improvement compared to L^2 reranking in terms of NDCG@10. One of the reasons is that in the training process, we select the optimal parameter C for Ranking SVM by validating MAP on the validation set.

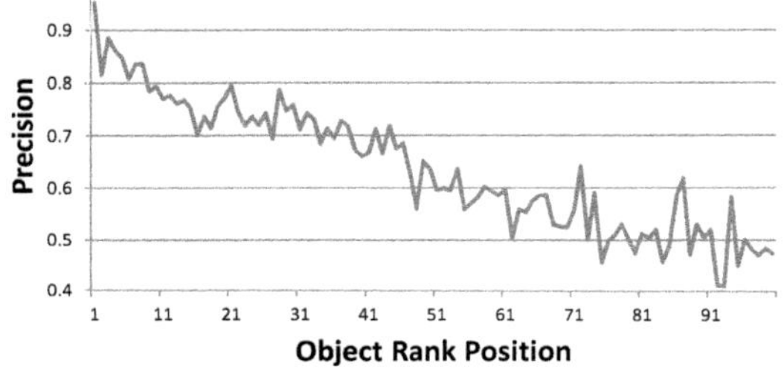

Figure 3: The average quality of objects on different rank positions.

4.2.2 *Object Ranking Analysis*

In this section, we evaluate the performance of object relevance prediction in our approach. To study the correlation between the prediction sore and the object relevance, we first calculate the precision of each object's containing images, which roughly indicates the object relevance. Then, the precisions of objects on the same ranking position from different queries are averaged. From Figure 3, we can see that the precisions on top positions are higher than those of bottom positions. This suggests that highly relevant objects are boosted by the proposed prediction model in Equation (15), while irrelevant objects are suppressed by a low score.

4.2.3 *Object Attribute Analysis*

In this section, we will analyse the usefulness of the 6 proposed object attributes individually. We measure the importance of each attribute using two strategies. One is to evaluate the performance of each attribute feature individually. The other is to evaluate the performance of the proposed approach by leaving each attribute feature out from the model once a time. We can observe from Table 3 and 4 that the attribute "Visual density" and "Initial ranking of neighborhood" are the two most important features. The importance of "Initial ranking of neighborhood" suggests that the ranking voted by visual neighbors is more reliable than the ranking of the image itself. Besides, attribute "Object Location" plays a very important role due to its high performance. It is because human tends to locate the important objects at the center of an image.

4.2.4 *Performance Analysis over Different Queries*

By comparing our result with that of L^2 reranking, 74% of queries in WEB_QRY_OBJECTS and 71% of queries in WEB_QRY_HUMAN is improved in terms of MAP. Figure 4 shows several examples of the search result by L^2 reranking and our method. The query "Champions League" improves because most of the "UEFA" logos lie on a small region of images. L^2 reranking with global PHOW feature cannot deal with such case. But in our method, this logo can be easily detected by query-relevant object discovery. The query "Aircraft Carrier" shows a failure case of our method. It is because the images for this query show too much different postures of the aircraft carrier, and our query-relevant object discovery method fails to detect any ROIs in common.

5. CONCLUSION AND FUTURE WORK

Image search reranking has been studied for several years and various approaches have been developed recently to boost the performance of text-based image search engine for general queries. In this paper we argue that there is no single method which can fit well all queries and the research on image search reranking requires a new methodology developing specific models for queries in different domains.

This paper serves as a first attempt on this direction. We observe that the existing reranking methods which operate on the whole image may not perform sufficiently well for object queries where only part of an image is required to be relevant. Motivated by that, we propose a novel bag-of-objects retrieval model for reranking images for object queries. The retrieval model is developed based on language modeling techniques for information retrieval. By discovering common objects relevant to the query from the search results returned by the text-based search engine, we can build object language models for the query and images on this query-relevant object vocabulary. The attributes of discovered objects are computed to represent how relevant and confident the objects are to the query, which are incorporated with weights into the ranking function, to address the possible unreliability and noises in the query-relevant objects. Finally, a learning to rank approach is employed to learn the weights on object attributes from human labeled data. The experimental results on two subsets of Web Queries dataset demonstrate that the proposed approach can improve 6.84% compared to the state-of-the-art reranking approaches.

We believe that this is a right and promising direction for further advancing image search reranking. Regarding this general direction as well as the specific work in this paper, we envision the following future works. First, we will systematically classify queries into different domains regarding the possibility of image search reranking, and then develop algorithms to solve them respectively. Second, motivated by the object bank image representation [20], we may combine the object vocabulary discovered for the query and the objects from the collection to seek a more comprehensive representation of images and queries. Third, we hope to identify and address the system challenges so as to most efficiently integrate this algorithm into a real-world image search engine.

6. REFERENCES

[1] A. Bosch, A. Zisserman, and X. Muoz. Image classification using random forests and ferns. In *CVPR*, pages 1–8, 2007.

[2] S. Brin and L. Page. The anatomy of a large-scale hypertextual web search engine. *Computer networks and ISDN systems*, 30(1-7):107–117, 1998.

[3] G. Csurka, C. Dance, L. Fan, J. Willamowski, and C. Bray. Visual categorization with bags of keypoints. In *Workshop on statistical learning in computer vision, ECCV*, volume 1, page 22, 2004.

[4] T. Deselaers, B. Alexe, and V. Ferrari. Localizing objects while learning their appearance. *ECCV*, pages 452–466, 2010.

[5] J. Feng, Y. Wei, L. Tao, C. Zhang, and J. Sun. Salient object detection by composition. In *ICCV*, pages 1028–1035, 2011.

[6] R. Fergus, L. Fei-Fei, P. Perona, and A. Zisserman. Learning object categories from google's image search. In *ICCV*, volume 2, pages 1816–1823, 2005.

[7] M. Fritz and B. Schiele. Decomposition, discovery and detection of visual categories using topic models. In *CVPR*, pages 1–8, 2008.

[8] D. Hochbaum and V. Singh. An efficient algorithm for co-segmentation. In *ICCV*, pages 269–276, 2009.

[9] L. Hohl, F. Souvannavong, B. Merialdo, and B. Huet. Enhancing latent semantic analysis video object retrieval with structural information. In *ICIP*, volume 3, pages 1609–1612, 2004.

[10] W. Hsu, L. Kennedy, and S. Chang. Video search reranking through random walk over document-level context graph. In *ACM Multimedia*, pages 971–980, 2007.

[11] Y. Jing and S. Baluja. Visualrank: Applying pagerank to large-scale image search. *IEEE Trans. on PAMI*, 30(11):1877–1890, 2008.

[12] T. Joachims. Making large-scale svm learning practical. *Advances in Kernel Methods Support Vector Learning*, pages 169–184, 1999.

[13] T. Joachims. Training linear svms in linear time. In *ACM SIGKDD*, pages 217–226, 2006.

[14] A. Joulin, F. Bach, and J. Ponce. Discriminative clustering for image co-segmentation. In *CVPR*, pages 1943–1950, 2010.

[15] G. Kim and A. Torralba. Unsupervised Detection of Regions of Interest using Iterative Link Analysis. In *NIPS*, 2009.

[16] G. Kim, E. Xing, L. Fei-Fei, and T. Kanade. Distributed cosegmentation via submodular optimization on anisotropic diffusion. In *Computer Vision (ICCV), 2011 IEEE International Conference on*, pages 169–176, 2011.

[17] J. Krapac, M. Allan, J. Verbeek, and F. Juried. Improving web image search results using query-relative classifiers. In *CVPR*, pages 1094–1101, 2010.

[18] J. Lafferty and C. Zhai. Document language models, query models, and risk minimization for information retrieval. In *ACM SIGIR*, pages 111–119, 2001.

[19] Y. Lee and K. Grauman. Object-graphs for context-aware category discovery. In *CVPR*, pages 1–8, 2010.

[20] L. Li, H. Su, E. Xing, and L. Fei-Fei. Object bank: A high-level image representation for scene classification and semantic feature sparsification. *NIPS*, 2010.

[21] Y. Liu, T. Mei, X. Hua, J. Tang, X. Wu, and S. Li. Learning to video search rerank via pseudo preference feedback. In *ICME*, pages 297–300, 2008.

[22] D. Lowe. Distinctive image features from scale-invariant keypoints. *IJCV*, 60(2):91–110, 2004.

[23] E. Oomoto and K. Tanaka. Ovid: Design and implementation of a video-object database system. *IEEE Trans. on KDE*, 5(4):629–643, 1993.

[24] E. Parzen. On estimation of a probability density function and mode. *The annals of mathematical statistics*, 33(3):1065–1076, 1962.

[25] C. Rother, T. Minka, A. Blake, and V. Kolmogorov. Cosegmentation of image pairs by histogram matching-incorporating a global constraint into mrfs. In *CVPR*, volume 1, pages 993–1000, 2006.

[26] S. Sav, G. Jones, H. Lee, N. O'Connor, and A. Smeaton. Interactive experiments in object-based retrieval. *Image and Video Retrieval*, pages 1–10, 2006.

[27] S. Sav, H. Lee, A. Smeaton, N. O'Connor, and N. Murphy. Using video objects and relevance feedback in video retrieval. 6015:353–364, 2005.

[28] F. Schroff, A. Criminisi, and A. Zisserman. Harvesting image databases from the web. In *ICCV*, pages 1–8, 2007.

[29] X. Tian, Y. Lu, L. Yang, and Q. Tian. Learning to judge image search results. In *ACM Multimedia*, pages 363–372, 2011.

[30] X. Tian, L. Yang, J. Wang, Y. Yang, X. Wu, and X. Hua. Bayesian video search reranking. In *ACM Multimedia*, pages 131–140, 2008.

[31] X. Tian, L. Yang, X. Wu, and X. Hua. Visual reranking with local learning consistency. *Advances in Multimedia Modeling*, pages 163–173, 2010.

[32] S. Vicente, V. Kolmogorov, and C. Rother. Cosegmentation revisited: Models and optimization. *ECCV*, pages 465–479, 2010.

[33] R. Yan, A. Hauptmann, and R. Jin. Multimedia

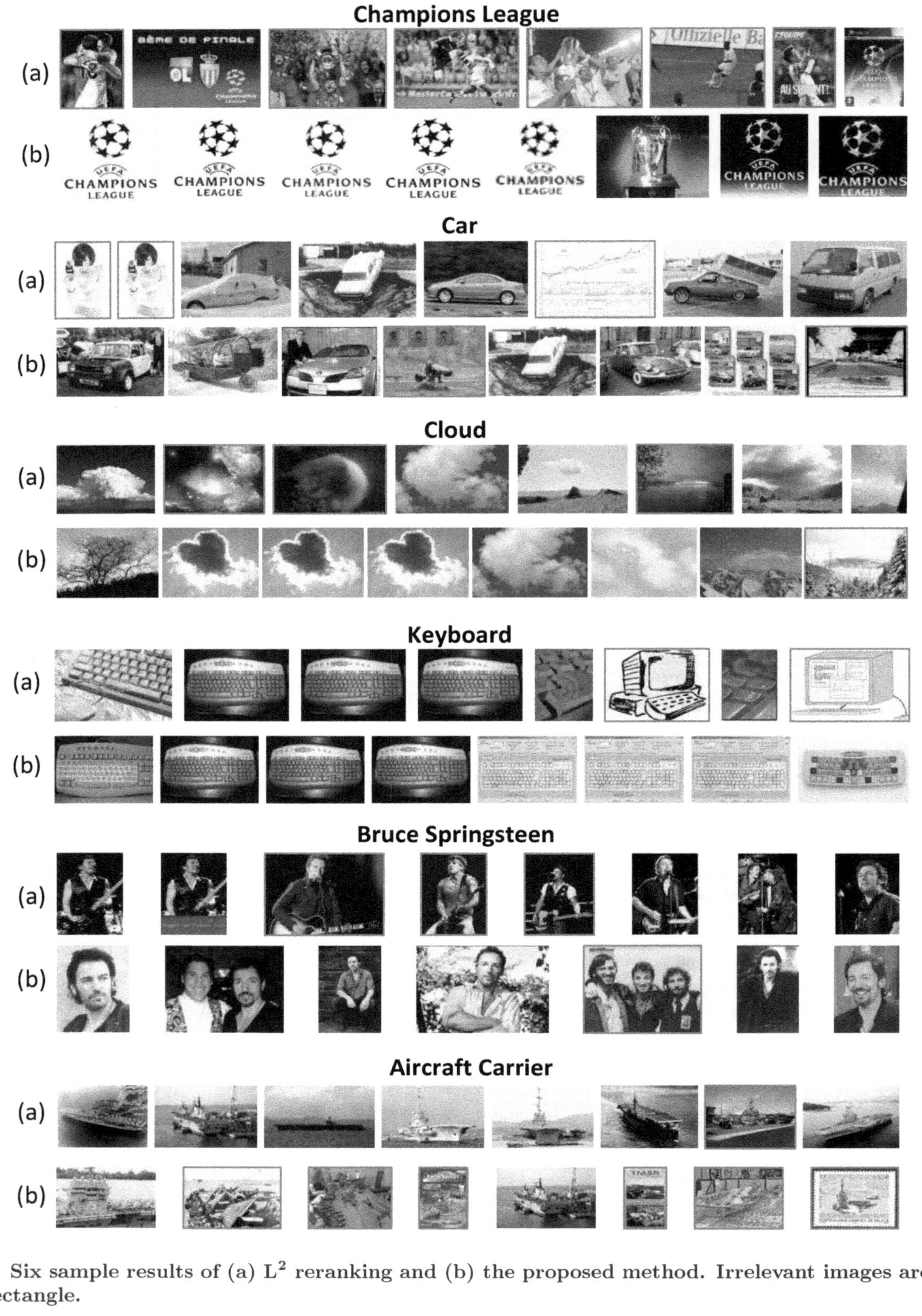

Figure 4: Six sample results of (a) L^2 reranking and (b) the proposed method. Irrelevant images are marked by red rectangle.

search with pseudo-relevance feedback. *Image and Video Retrieval*, pages 649–654, 2003.

[34] L. Yang, B. Geng, Y. Cai, A. Hanjalic, and X. Hua. Object retrieval using visual query context. *IEEE Trans. on Multimedia*, (99):1–1, 2011.

[35] L. Yang and A. Hanjalic. Supervised reranking for web image search. In *ACM Multimedia*, pages 183–192, 2010.

[36] L. Yang and A. Hanjalic. learning from search engine and human supervision web image search. In *ACM Multimedia*, pages 1365–1368, 2011.

[37] S. Zhang, Q. Tian, G. Hua, Q. Huang, and S. Li. Descriptive visual words and visual phrases for image applications. In *ACM Multimedia*, pages 75–84, 2009.

Harvesting Visual Concepts for Image Search with Complex Queries

Liqiang Nie†, Shuicheng Yan†, Meng Wang§, Richang Hong§ and Tat-Seng Chua†
† National University of Singapore
§ Hefei University of Technology
{nieliqiang, eric.mengwang, hongrc.hfut}@gmail.com
{eleyans, chuats}@nus.edu.sg

ABSTRACT

The use of image reranking to boost retrieval performance has been found to be successful for simple queries. It is, however, less effective for complex queries due to the widened semantic gap. This paper presents a scheme to enhance web image reranking for complex queries by fully exploring the information from simple visual concepts. Given a complex query, our scheme first detects the noun-phrase based visual concepts and crawls their top ranked images from popular image search engines. Next, it constructs a heterogeneous probabilistic network to model the relatedness between the complex query and each of its crawled images. The network seamlessly integrates three layers of relationships, i.e., the semantic-level, cross-modality level as well as visual-level. These mutually reinforced layers are established among the complex query and its involved visual concepts, by harnessing the contents of images and their associated textual cues. Based on the derived relevance scores, a new ranking list is generated. Extensive evaluations on a real-world dataset demonstrate that our model is able to characterize the complex queries well and achieve promising performance as compared to the state-of-the-art methods. Based on the proposed scheme, we introduce two applications: photo-based question answering and textual news visualization. Comprehensive experiments well validate the proposed scheme.

Categories and Subject Descriptors

H.3.3 [**Information Search and Retrieval**]: Retrieval models; H.3.5 [**Information Systems**]: Information Storage and Retrieval

Keywords

Complex Image Query, Photo-based QA, News Visualization

1. INTRODUCTION

With the exponential growth of image contents available online, searching for images is becoming an indispensable activity in people's daily lives. Meanwhile, web image retrieval has attracted world-wide research attentions and achieved great success for simple textual queries [25, 13, 20, 31]. As the web surfers get increasingly savvy and specific with their search behaviors, the queries tend to be more complex and sophisticated. This phenomenon is consistent with the report from Hitwise [1] in late *2009*: the average query length is getting longer from *2007*. In addition, long queries are becoming more and more popular in various media search applications, such as multimedia question answering [24], text illustration [17, 11], and known item search [8].

A complex image query is defined as a natural language query comprising several inter-related concepts. One example is the query "a baby with an apple lying on the bed". Here there are three concepts: baby, apple and bed. These concepts are linked by internal relationships: baby with an apple, both baby and apple are on the bed. It is obvious that complex queries can express specific information needs more precisely than the shorter ones. However, current commercial web search engines do not, in general, perform well with verbose queries, especially for image retrieval[1]. This is due to the following reasons. First, compared to simple queries, long ones frequently consist of more concepts, which further widen the semantic gap between the textual queries and the visual contents. Second, a complex query usually depicts the intrinsic semantic relationships among its constituent visual concepts. These kind images have loose coupled relationships with the surrounding textual descriptions, causing poor text-based search performance. Third, while there are abundant positive samples and query logs for simple queries, the positive samples are rare for complex queries. This makes learning based model less effective. Therefore, it is not surprising that the returned images are often incorrectly ranked for complex queries.

Visual reranking techniques can drastically improve the traditional text-based image search results. The existing approaches generally fall into two categories. One is pseudo relevance feedback (PRF) based [23, 34, 20]. They treat a significant fraction of the top images as pseudo-positive examples and collect some bottom images as pseudo-negative examples. They then either learn a classifier or cluster the images to perform reranking. But, for complex queries, relevant samples are usually rare or not ranked at the top of the

[1] A study in [28] shows that a failed image query tends to be longer than the average successful query, which indicates longer queries' higher specificity of contents and also reveals the limitations of current web image search engines for complex queries.

Figure 1: Image retrieval results comparison. The search results of a complex query are less visually consistent than those retrieved by its constituent visual concepts.

result list. This severely limits the ability to select pseudo positive and negative training samples. The other category is graph based [32, 12, 30] that propagates the initial ranking information over the whole graph until convergence. However, for complex query, many irrelevant images are frequently distributed in high ranked positions initially. These irrelevant images can hardly be pushed down by the graph-based methods, since they often have low similarities with other irrelevant images in the lower ranked positions [22]. Consequently new approaches towards image reranking for complex queries are highly desired.

To tackle this problem, we hypothesize that the search results of a complex query are less visually consistent and coherent than those retrieved by each of its constituent visual concept; and the latter characterize the former's partial features in terms of both semantics and visual exemplars. An example illustrating the assumption is intuitively demonstrated in Figure 1. Based on this assumption, we explore the information cues from visual concepts to enhance Web image reranking for complex queries. Specifically, we propose a scheme, which contains two main components as shown in Figure 2. The first component identifies the involved visual concepts by leveraging lexical and corpus-dependent knowledge, and collects the top relevant datapoints from popular image search engines. The second component constructs a heterogeneous probabilistic network to model the relevance between the complex query and each of its retrieved images. This network comprises three sub-networks, each representing a layer of relationship, including: (a) the underlying relationship among image pairs, (b) the cross-modality relationship between the image and the visual concept[2], and (c) the high-level semantic relationship between visual concept and the complex query[3]. The three layers are strongly connected by a probabilistic model. The layers mutually reinforce each other to facilitate the estimation of relevance scores for new reanking list generation. Most importantly, the whole process is unsupervised and can be extended to handle large-scale data.

Based on the proposed scheme, we introduce two potential application scenarios of web image reranking for complex queries: photo-based question answering (PQA) and textual news visualization (TNV) [17]. PQA is a sub-branch of multimedia question answering [24], aiming to answer questions with precise image information, which provides answer seekers with better multimedia experience. TNV is to complement the textual news with context associated images, which may better draw the readers' attention or help them grasp the textual information quickly. By conducting experiments on the real-world datasets, we demonstrate that our proposed scheme yields significant gains in reranking performance for complex queries, and achieves fairly satisfactory results for these two applications.

The main contributions of this research are:

1. To the best of our knowledge, this is the first that targets web images reranking for complex queries from the probabilistic perspective. This work unravels the unreliable initial ranking list problem of the existing image reranking approaches for complex queries.
2. It proposes a heuristic approach to detect noun-phrase based visual concepts from complex query, instead of just treating individual terms as possible concepts.
3. It proposes a heterogeneous probabilistic network to automatically estimate the relevance score of each image, which jointly couples three layer relationships, spanning from semantic level to visual level. This is different from the conventional complex query modelling approaches [35, 16, 36, 2] that either require human interactions or consider the query terms independently and neglect the connections among them.

The remainder is organized as follows. Sections 2 and 3 respectively review the related work and briefly introduce the reranking scheme. Sections 4 and 5 introduce visual concept detection and the proposed heterogeneous probabilistic network, respectively. Experimental results and analysis are presented in Section 6, followed by the applications in Section 7. Finally, Section 8 contains our remarks.

2. RELATED WORK

2.1 Complex Queries in Text Search

Several recent research efforts have been conducted for improving long query performance in text-based information retrieval. These efforts can be broadly categorized into automatic query term re-weighting [6, 5, 15, 7] and query reduction [13, 14, 4] approaches.

It has been found that assigning appropriate weights to query concepts has significant positive effects on retrieval performance [6]. Bendersky and Croft [5] developed and evaluated a technique that assigns weights to the identified key concepts in the verbose query, and observed improved retrieval effectiveness. Lease et al. [15] presented a regression framework to estimate term weights based on knowledge from past queries. A novel method beyond unsupervised estimation of concept importance was proposed in [7], which weights the query concept using a parameterized combination of diverse importance features.

Pruning the complex query to retain only the important terms is also recognized as one crucial dimension to improve search performance. Kumaran and Allan [13, 14] proposed an interactive query induction approach, by presenting the users with the top 10 ranked sub-queries along with corresponding top ranking snippets. The tabbed interface allows the user to click on each sub-query to view the associated snippet, and select the most promising one as their new query. A more practical approach was proposed in [4], utilizing efficient query quality prediction techniques to evaluate

[2]The underlying visual associations among visual concepts are also integrated.

[3]The semantic associations among visual concepts are also considered in this layer.

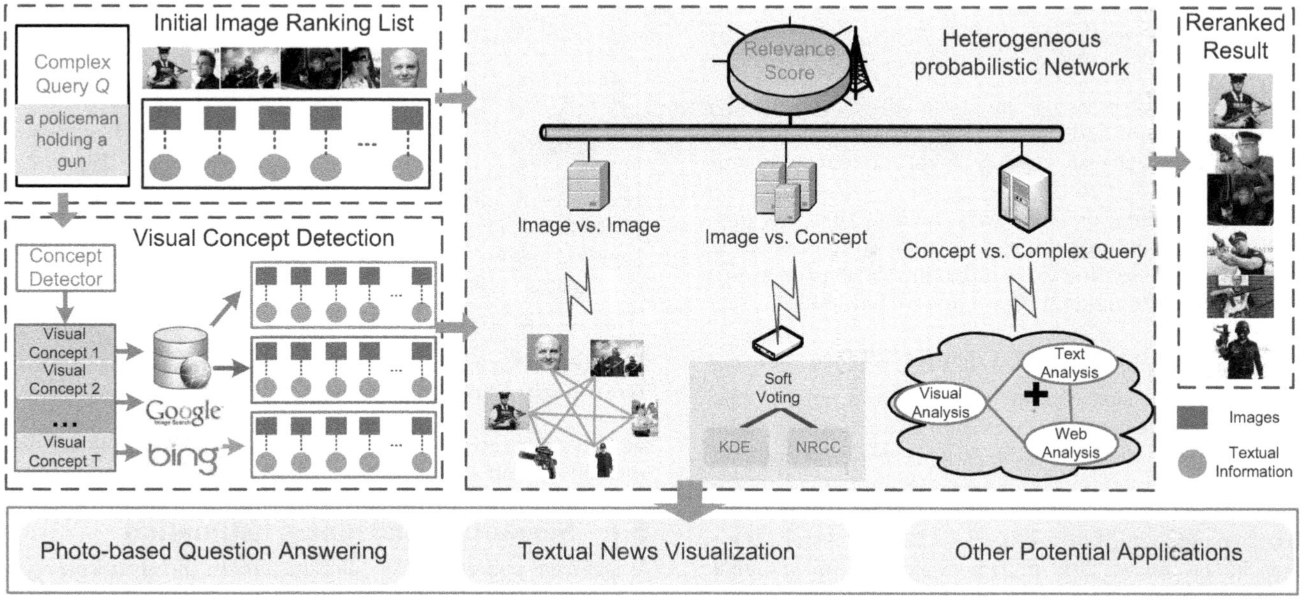

Figure 2: Illustration of the proposed web image reranking scheme for complex queries. It contains two components, i.e., visual concept detection and relevance estimation. This scheme facilitates many applications, including photo-based question answering, textual news visualization and others.

the reduced versions of the original query that were obtained by dropping one single term at a time. It can be incorporated into existing web search engines' architectures without requiring modifications to the underlying search algorithms.

Though great success has been achieved for complex query processing in text search domain, these techniques cannot be directly applied to the general media domain due to the different modalities between the query and search results.

2.2 Complex Queries in Media Search

Some research efforts have been conducted on modelling complex queries in media search. For example, Aly et al. [2] proposed fusion strategies to model combined semantic concepts by simply aggregating the search results from their constituent primitive concepts. However, such approach fails to characterize complex queries as it overlooks the mutual relationships among different aspects of complex queries. Image search by concept map was proposed in [33]. It presents a novel interface to enable users to indicate the spatial distribution among semantic concepts. However, the input model is not consistent with the current popular search engines and the concept-relationship is not limited to spacial arrangement. Yuan et al. [35] explored how to utilize the plentiful but partially related samples, as well as the users' feedbacks, to learn complex queries in interactive concept-based video search. This work gracefully compensates the insufficient relevant samples. Further, Yuan [36] moved one step beyond primitive concepts and proposed a higher-level semantic descriptor named "concept bundle" to enhance video search of complex queries. But these two works are supervised. Recently, harvesting social images for bi-concept search was proposed in [16] to retrieve images in which two concepts are co-occurring. However, it is unable to handle multiple concepts.

Overall, literature regarding complex queries in media search is still relatively sparse, and the existing approaches either view the query terms independently or require intensive human interactions. Differing from the existing works, our approach models the complex queries automatically, and jointly considers the relationships between concepts and the complex queries from high-level to low-level.

3. WEB IMAGE RERANKING SCHEME

As aforementioned, a complex query Q comprises several visual and abstract concepts as well as their intrinsic relations. As shown in the left part of Figure 2, we first perform visual concepts selection, since they have strong description in images. Supposing T visual concepts $\mathcal{C} = \{q_1, q_2, \ldots, q_T\}$ are detected. The T visual concepts are then regarded as simple queries to a commercial search engine and retrieve a collection of images $\mathcal{D} = \{(\mathbf{x}_1, y_1), (\mathbf{x}_2, y_2), \ldots, (\mathbf{x}_L, y_L)\}$. Here the image $\mathbf{x}_i$ ($\mathbf{x}_i \in R^d$) is crawled using simple visual concept y_i ($y_i \in \mathcal{C}$). Complex query Q has an ordered image list $\mathcal{X} = \{(\mathbf{x}_{L+1}, \mathbf{x}_{L+2}, \ldots, \mathbf{x}_{L+N}\}$. Our target is to explore the visual concepts and their partial relations to enhance the image relevance estimation with respect to the given complex query, i.e., $Score(Q, \mathbf{x}_u)$, $u = L+1, \ldots, L+N$. Based on these relevance scores, a new refined ranking list will be generated.

To estimate the relevance score, we propose a heterogeneous probabilistic network as displayed in the middle part of Figure 2, which is inspired by the KL-divergence measure [3]. It is composed of several dissimilar sub-networks, which provide probabilistic estimations from different angles. But the constituents are of a conglomerate mass, strongly connected by a probabilistic model. It is formally formulated as,

$$Score(Q, \mathbf{x}_u) = -\sum_{q_c \in Q} P(q_c|Q) \times \log P(q_c|\mathbf{x}_u) \quad (1)$$

where $P(q_c|Q)$ measures the importance of a visual concept q_c given the complex query Q, i.e., the high level semantic relatedness between a visual concept and the complex query. The second term in Eq.(1) can be further decomposed as,

$$P(q_c|\mathbf{x}_u) = \sum_{i=1}^{L} P(q_c|\mathbf{x}_i) \times P(\mathbf{x}_i|\mathbf{x}_u) \quad (2)$$

where $P(q_c|\mathbf{x}_i)$ involves two different modalities, specifically, the high level concept and the low level visual content; while $P(\mathbf{x}_i|\mathbf{x}_u)$ measures the underlying visual relatedness of image pairs.

The above formulation intuitively reflects that our proposed heterogeneous probabilistic network comprises three sub-networks, representing three different relationship layers: semantic level, cross-modality level and visual level.

4. VISUAL CONCEPT DETECTION

In this paper, a visual concept is defined as a noun phrase depicting a concrete entity with a visual form. Beyond visual concepts, complex queries tend to contain several redundant chunks. These redundant chunks have grammatical meaning for communication between humans to help understand the key concepts [26], but are hard to model visually. One example is the query, "find images describing the moment the astronaut getting out of the cabin". In this query, only "the astronaut" and "the cabin" have high correspondence with the visual contents, while the use of other chunks may bring unpredictable noise to the image reranking method. Therefore, to differentiate the visual content related chunks from unrelated ones, we propose a heuristic framework for visual concept detection as illustrated in Figure 3. A central resource in this framework is an automatically constructed visual vocabulary. Now given a complex query, we extract its constituent visual concepts as follows:

1. We segment a given complex query Q into several chunks using the openNLP[4] tool.
2. For each chunk, we match it against our constructed visual vocabulary. If any of its terms matches a term in our visual vocabulary, the chuck is classified as a visual concept. This detected visual concept is used as a simple query to retrieve the top ranked images and their surrounding texts for reranking purpose.
3. We construct a flexible vocabulary containing visual related words, by leveraging the lexical and corpus-dependent knowledge. Specifically, we collect all the noun terms from our dataset utilizing the Part-Of-Speech Tagger[5], and remove stop words from the noun set. For each selected noun word, we traverse along its hypernyms path in the WordNet, until one of the five predefined high-level categories is reached. They are "color", "thing", "artifact", "organism", and "natural phenomenon". These 5 categories cover almost all the key concepts in our dataset. The noun words that match to these 5 categories are recognized as visual related. This approach is analogous to [18].

Compared to the conventional single-word based visual concept definition [18, 31], the noun-phrase based definition is able to incorporate a lot of adjunct terms, such as "a red apple", which carries additional color cue for "apple".

5. HETEROGENEOUS NETWORK

In this section, we will discuss in greater detail each component of our proposed heterogeneous probabilistic network, namely, semantic relatedness estimation, visual relatedness estimation and cross-modality relatedness estimation.

[4]http://incubator.apache.org/opennlp/

[5]http://nlp.stanford.edu/software/tagger.shtml

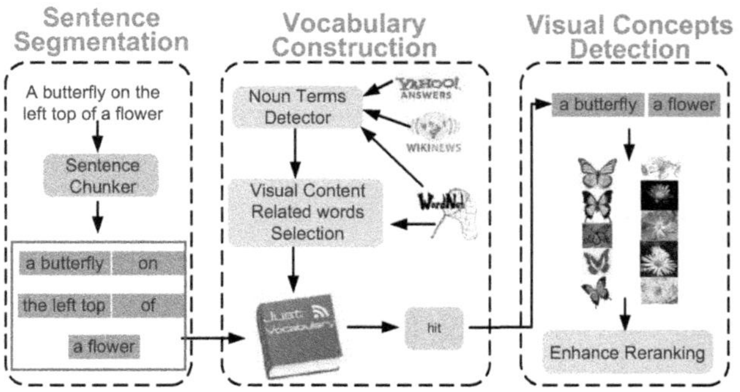

Figure 3: An illustration of visual concepts detection from a given complex query.

5.1 Semantic Relatedness Estimation

Different concepts play different roles in the given complex query, and concept weighting [5, 15, 7] has been studied for decades to quantify their importances. However, these conventional methods are developed for long query in text search domain; few of them take the visual information into consideration. Instead, our approach estimates the semantic relatedness in image search by linearly integrating multi-faceted cues, i.e., visual analysis, external resource analysis as well as surrounding text analysis.

First, from the perspective of underlying visual analysis, we respectively denote $\mathcal{X}_c$ and $\mathcal{X}$ to be the set of images retrieved by the visual concept q_c and complex query Q. Their relatedness can be defined as,

$$V(q_c, Q) = \frac{1}{|\mathcal{X}_c| \times |\mathcal{X}|} \sum_{\mathbf{x}_i \in X_c, \mathbf{x}_j \in X} K(\mathbf{x}_i, \mathbf{x}_j) \quad (3)$$

$K(\cdot,\cdot)$ is the Gaussian similarity function, defined as,

$$K(\mathbf{x}_i, \mathbf{x}_j) = exp(-\frac{||\mathbf{x}_i - \mathbf{x}_j||^2}{\sigma^2}) \quad (4)$$

where the radius parameter, σ, is simply set as the median of the Euclidean distances of all related image pairs.

Second, actually the visual concepts detected from the same complex query are usually not independent. For example, for the complex image query "a lady driving a red car on the road", the semantical relationship between "a red car" and "the road" is relatively high. Inspired by Google distance [10], we estimate the inter-concepts relatedness based on the frequency of their co-occurrence by exploring the Flickr image resource as the largest publicly available multimedia corpus,

$$NGD(q_c, q_j) = \frac{\max(\log f(q_c), \log f(q_j)) - \log f(q_c, q_j)}{\log M - \min(\log f(q_c), \log f(q_j))} \quad (5)$$

where M is the total number of images retrieved from Flickr, roughly estimated as 5 billion. $f(q_c)$ and $f(q_j)$ are respectively the numbers of hits for search concepts q_c and q_j, and $f(q_c, q_j)$ is the number of web images on which both q_c and q_j co-occur. Note that we define $NGD(q_c, q_j) = 0$, if $q_c = q_j$. Then the relatedness between q_c and the given complex query Q is:

$$G(q_c, Q) = \frac{1}{T}\sum_{q_j \in \mathcal{C}} NGD(q_c, q_j) \tag{6}$$

where T is the number of visual concepts detected from Q. This estimation can be viewed as exploring the external web image knowledge to weight the visual concepts.

Third, we estimate the semantic relatedness by using the surrounding text-matching score. For each complex query Q, we first merge all surrounding textual information of its retrieved images, such as tag, title, description, etc, into a single document. The same operation is then conducted for all the T detected visual concepts, resulting in T documents. We then parse the $T+1$ documents using the OpenNLP tool. All nouns and adjectives are selected as salient words, since they are observed to be more descriptive and informative than verbs or adverbs. Based on these salient words, the tf-idf scores [36] are computed to represent the semantic relatedness between a visual concept q_c and the given complex query Q, denoted as $T(q_c, Q)$.

Finally, we linearly combine these three measures as,

$$P(q_c|Q) = \alpha_1 V(q_c, Q) + \alpha_2 G(q_c, Q) + \alpha_3 T(q_c, Q) \tag{7}$$

where α_i is the fusing weight with sum being 1. They are selected based on a training set comprising 20 complex queries, which are randomly sampled from our constructed complex query collection. We tune the weights to the values that optimize the average NDCG@50 with grid search.

5.2 Visual Relatedness Estimation

To explore the visual relationship between images, we perform Markov random walk over a K nearest neighbour graph to propagate the relatedness among images. The vertices of the graph are the $L+N$ images and the undirected edges are weighted with pair-wise similarity. We use $\mathbf{W}$ to denote the similarity matrix and W_{ij}, its (i,j)-th element, indicates the similarity between $\mathbf{x}_i$ and $\mathbf{x}_j$. Typically, it is estimated as

$$W_{ij} = \begin{cases} K(\mathbf{x}_i, \mathbf{x}_j) & \text{if } \mathbf{x}_j \in N_K(\mathbf{x}_i) \text{ or } \mathbf{x}_i \in N_K(\mathbf{x}_j) \\ 0 & \text{otherwise} \end{cases} \tag{8}$$

where $N_K(\mathbf{x}_i)$ denotes the index set for the K nearest neighbours of image x_i computed by Euclidean distance. Noting that W_{ii} is set as 1, so that self-loop is included.

Denoting $\mathbf{A}$ as the one step transition matrix. Its element A_{iu} indicates the probability of the transition from node i to node u and is computed directly from the related weights,

$$A_{iu} = \frac{W_{iu}}{\sum_j W_{ij}} \tag{9}$$

The L_1 normalization of each row turns $\mathbf{A}$ into a stochastic transition matrix. Then the probability of a random walk, which initially starts from node i, and stops at node u after t steps, can be denoted as

$$P(\mathbf{x}_u(t)|\mathbf{x}_i(0)) = [\mathbf{A}^t]_{iu} \tag{10}$$

Based on Eq.(10), we can simply evaluate the probability that the walker starts from $\mathbf{x}_i$ at time 0 given that it ends at $\mathbf{x}_u$ at time t, with the reasonable assumption that the starting node is uniformly chosen,

$$\begin{aligned} P(\mathbf{x}_i(0)|\mathbf{x}_u(t)) &= \frac{P(\mathbf{x}_u(t)|\mathbf{x}_i(0)) \times P(\mathbf{x}_i(0))}{P(\mathbf{x}_u(t))} \\ &= \frac{P(\mathbf{x}_u(t)|\mathbf{x}_i(0))}{\sum_j P(\mathbf{x}_u(t)|\mathbf{x}_j(0))} \\ &= \frac{[\mathbf{A}^t]_{iu}}{\sum_j [\mathbf{A}^t]_{ju}} \end{aligned} \tag{11}$$

Since visual concepts and complex query are associated with the starting and ending images, respectively, Eq.(2) can be rewritten as

$$P(q_c|\mathbf{x}_u) = \sum_{i=1}^{L} P(q_c|\mathbf{x}_i) \times P(\mathbf{x}_i(0)|\mathbf{x}_u(t)) \tag{12}$$

5.3 Cross-Modality Relatedness Estimation

As mentioned above, $P(q_c|\mathbf{x}_i)$ in Eq.(2) measures the relatedness between two different modalities, the high-level concept and the low-level visual information. We now present two techniques to link these two modalities: kernel density estimation approach (KDE) [19] and normalizing relatedness cross concepts (NRCC) [29].

5.3.1 KDE Approach

For each image $\mathbf{x}_u$ retrieved by Q, $P(q_c)$ is identical and $P(\mathbf{x}_i)$ is assumed to be uniform. Therefore Eq.(12) can be restated as,

$$P(q_c|\mathbf{x}_u) \propto \sum_{i=1}^{L} P(\mathbf{x}_i|q_c) \times P(\mathbf{x}_i(0)|\mathbf{x}_u(t)) \tag{13}$$

where $P(\mathbf{x}_i|q_c)$ is the probability density function, representing the relevance of an image to the given visual concept. KDE approach is utilized to perform the estimation.

We use $\mathcal{X}_c$ to denote the set of images retrieved by the visual concept q_c, the KDE approach measures $P(\mathbf{x}_i|q_c)$ as

$$P(\mathbf{x}_i|q_c) = \frac{1}{|\mathcal{X}_c|}\sum_{\mathbf{x}_j \in \mathcal{X}_c} K(\mathbf{x}_i, \mathbf{x}_j) \tag{14}$$

The above equation can be intuitively interpreted as follows: q_c and each of its retrieved images in $\mathcal{X}_c$ can respectively be viewed as a family and family members. Then the closeness of an unknown image to this family is estimated by averaging the soft voting from all family members.

5.3.2 NRCC Approach

The drawback of the KDE approach is that it does not take the underlying associations among visual concepts belonging to the same complex query into consideration. To compensate for this limitation, we formally define $P(q_c|\mathbf{x}_i)$ as,

$$P(q_c|\mathbf{x}_i) = \frac{1}{Z_i}\sum_{\mathbf{x}_j \in \mathcal{X}_c} P(\mathbf{x}_j(0)|\mathbf{x}_i(t)) \tag{15}$$

where Z_u is a normalizing factor, and formulated as,

$$Z_i = \sum_{q_c \in \mathcal{C}}\sum_{\mathbf{x}_j \in \mathcal{X}_c} P(\mathbf{x}_j(0)|\mathbf{x}_i(t)) \tag{16}$$

As its formulation implies, this approach is named as normalizing relatedness cross concepts (NRCC), which has been preliminarily studied in [29].

Compared to the KDE approach, by regarding $\mathcal{C}$ as a community with several families, the relatedness between the given image $\mathbf{x}_i$ and a family q_c, is determined not only by the family members $\mathbf{x}_j$ in q_c, but also other community families in $\mathcal{C}$.

5.4 Discussions

To further study the impact of the number of transitions t on visual relatedness, we first define the stationary probability vector $\boldsymbol{\pi}$ of the stochastic transition matrix $\mathbf{A}$ that does not change under the power of $\mathbf{A}$. Mathematically, it is expressed as,

$$\boldsymbol{\pi}\mathbf{A} = \boldsymbol{\pi} \tag{17}$$

The Perron-Frobenius theorem [27] ensures every stochastic matrix has such vectors; and for a matrix with strictly positive entries, this vector is unique. It can be computed by observing that for any i,

$$\lim_{t\to\infty} [\mathbf{A}^t]_{iu} = \pi_u \tag{18}$$

where π_u is the u-th element of the row vector $\boldsymbol{\pi}$. It implies that when $t \to \infty$, the probability of being in a state u is independent of the initial state i. Namely, all the starting points become indistinguishable. In the other limiting case, when $t = 1$, we utilize only the neighbourhood graph, which will be totally influenced by K.

The local neighbourhood size K should be large enough to guarantee a singly connected graph. Meanwhile, K should be sufficiently small to avoid introducing more edges between the relevant and irrelevant samples, which may degrade the reranking performance drastically. However, too small a K will miss the "correct" edges between the relevant samples, resulting in the weakening of the key consistency.

The computational complexity of our approach mainly comes from two parts: feature extraction and transition matrix iteration. The former is the most computationally expensive step, but can be handled off-line. The cost of the latter scales as $O(d(L+N)^2 + t(L+N)^2)$, where d is the 1428-dimension features, and t is the number of transitions in dozens level. Since we only use the top results, $L+N$ is usually in the order of thousands. Thus the computational cost is very low. In our experiments, the process can be completed in less than 1 second if we do not take the feature extraction part into account (3.4GHz and 8G memory).

It is worthy emphasizing that our proposed scheme can also be applied for other image repositories, even for those images without surrounding texts by simply ignoring the last term in Eq.(7).

6. EXPERIMENTS

6.1 Experimental Settings

We collected a large real-world dataset from WikiAnswers, which contains $1,944,492$ unique QA pairs and covers a wide range of topics, including entertainment, life, education, etc. Based on this dataset, we constructed a visual word vocabulary, from which 100 most frequent visual words are selected. We then issued these terms into Google Image and selected 50 suggested complex queries according to our definition. Some representative samples are listed in Table 1. For each complex query and its embedded visual concepts, the top 500 images are crawled from Google Image.

Table 1: The representative complex queries generated based on our corpus and Google Image suggestion. Here we do not illustrate all the queries due to limited space.

ID	Complex Query
1	President Obama and troops
2	Women swimming in pool
3	Soldiers holding American flag on the mountain
4	Baby with an apple lying in the bed
5	A lady driving a red car on the street
6	A cowboy riding a horse at sundown
7	Lions attacking zebras on the grassland
8	A man walking his dog in the park
9	A lady wears sunglasses on the sea beach
10	Comparison between white iphone and black iphone

To obtain the relevance ground truth of each image, we conduct a manual labelling procedure. Five human annotators were involved in the process. Each image was labelled to be very relevant (score 2), relevant (score 1) or irrelevant (score 0) with respect to the given query. We performed a voting to establish the final relevance level of each image. For the cases that there were two classes having the same number of ballots, a discussion was carried out among the labelers to decide the final ground truths.

To represent the content of each image, we extracted the following features:

1. We used the difference of Gaussians to detect keypoints in each image and extracted their SIFT descriptors. By building a visual codebook of size 1000 based on K-means, we obtained a 1000-dimensional bag-of-visual-words histogram for each image.
2. We further extracted 428-dimensional global visual features, including 225-dimensional block-wise color moments based on 5-by-5 fixed partition of the image; 128-dimensional wavelet texture; and 75-D edge direction histogram.

When it comes to reranking performance evaluation, we adopted NDCG@n as our metric,

$$NDCG@n = \frac{rel_1 + \sum_{i=2}^{n} \frac{rel_i}{\log_2 i}}{IDCG} \tag{19}$$

where rel_i is the relevance score of the i-th image in the ranked list, $IDCG$ is the normalizing factor that makes NDCG@n being 1 for a perfect ranking.

6.2 On Visual Concept Detection

Following our heuristic rules stated in Section 3, we first selected all the noun terms from WikiAnswers dataset the by Stanford Log-linear Part-Of-Speech Tagger. We filtered out the stop words from the noun set. We then went through the WordNet 3.0[6] hypernym hierarch within 10 steps, from bottom to top, to identify each selected word's hypernyms, until one of the five predefined high-level categories are matched: "color", "thing", "artifact", "organism", and "natural phenomenon". As shown in [18], these 5 categories cover a substantial part of many frequently used concepts in computer vision and multimedia domains. In this way, we constructed a visual word vocabulary containing $12,812$ noun entries. Table 2 illustrates their distribution statistics over the 5 categories in our vocabulary.

[6]http://wordnet.princeton.edu/

Table 2: The distribution of visual words over five predefined high-level categories.

Visual Category	Visual Words #	Percentage
Color	159	1.24%
Thing	919	7.17%
Artifact	4219	32.93%
Organism	7214	56.31%
Natural phenomenon	301	2.35%

Table 3: The confusion matrix of visual concept detection results. The prediction accuracy is 89.27%.

Prediction \ Class	Visual Concepts	Non Visual Concepts
Visual Concepts	102	5
Non Visual Concepts	17	81

From the selected 50 complex queries, 205 chucks are detected by OpenNLP, among which 119 chucks are manually voted as visual concepts by 5 volunteers. As mentioned previously, for each term in a given chuck, we search it in our constructed visual vocabulary, and this chuck will be categorized as a visual concept if at least one term is matched. Table 3 illustrates the confusion matrix obtained by our proposed visual concept detection. We can see that our approach achieves fairly good performance, i.e., 89.27%. The misclassification results mainly come from some chunks that are product names not archived in the WordNet, such as "iphone", "ipad", etc, and also from some verb chunks that have visual content descriptive attribute, such as "wear", etc. In our further work, we will broaden our visual word dictionary by incorporating product name list to boost our classification performance.

6.3 On Query Performance Analysis

We first conducted experiment to evaluate the retrieval effectiveness of the current dominant image search engines for simple and complex queries, respectively.

The selected 50 queries and their 119 involved visual concepts are regarded as complex queries and simple queries, respectively. Figure 4 displays the average search performance comparison. From the figure we can see that the search results of simple queries remarkably outperform those based on complex queries. And along with the increase of NDCG-depth n, the average performance of complex queries drops at a faster rate. This observation partially verifies our hypothesis that: compared to complex queries, the search results of simple queries are more visually consistent and

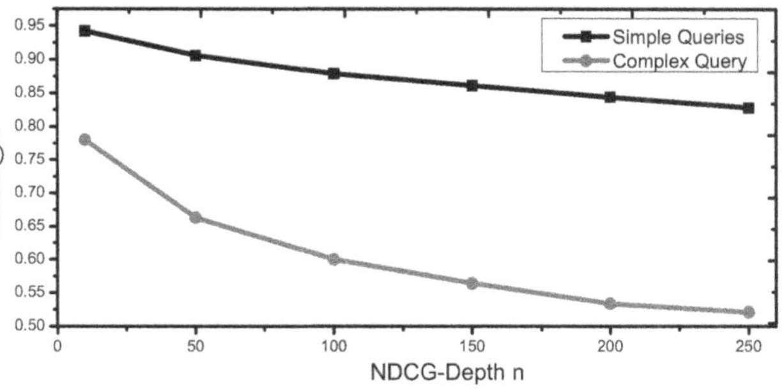

Figure 4: Retrieval performance comparison between complex queries and their belonging primitive visual concepts.

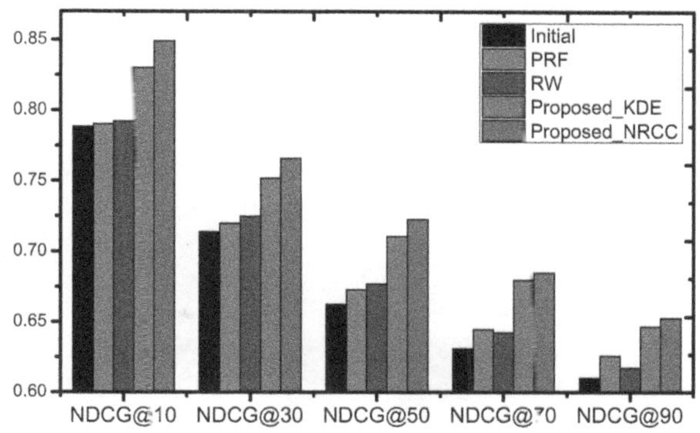

Figure 5: Performance comparison of different reranking approaches in terms of NDCGs.

coherent. Also, it reveals the fact that the current search engines, especially the image search engine, do not perform well for complex queries, even though great success has been achieved for simple queries. So effective image reranking for complex queries is highly desirable.

6.4 On Reranking Performance Comparison

To demonstrate the effectiveness of our proposed approach, we comparatively evaluate the following unsupervised reranking methods:

- **RW**: Random walk reranking [12] is a typical graph-based reranking method jointly exploiting both initial ranking result and visual similarity between images. The stationary probability of random walk is used to compute the final relevance scores. (Baseline 1)
- **PRF**: Pseudo-Relevance Feedback [34]. A support vector machine (SVM) classifier is trained to perform the reranking based on the assumption that the top-ranked images for each query are more relevant than the low-ranked results in general. (Baseline 2)
- **Proposed_KDE**: Our proposed probabilistic reranking approach with cross-modalities relatedness estimation by KDE method.
- **Proposed_NRCC**: Our proposed probabilistic reranking approach with cross-modalities relatedness estimation by NRCC method.

For each method mentioned above, the involved parameters are carefully tuned, and the parameters with the best performances are used to report the final comparison results.

The experimental results are illustrated in Figure 5. It can be observed that our proposed approaches are consistently and substantially better than the current publicly disclosed state-of-the-art web image reranking algorithms across all evaluated NDCGs. From this figure, we can also observe that the improvements over the initial ranking result from RW and PRF are much slighter, especially for NDCGs with smaller n. The main reason is that they both have problems of unreliable initial ranking list, which frequently exists in complex query search. In contrast, our proposed scheme for complex queries is more robust, since it tends not to be affected too much by the initial ordering of images.

Further, it is observed that the proposed_NRCC stably outperforms the proposed_KDE approach. This is due to the fact that NRCC takes the relationship between visual concepts in the same complex query into consideration, while

Figure 6: Illustrative results for complex query "soldiers holding American flag on the mountain" based on different reranking approaches. Our proposed approaches obtain the most satisfying results.

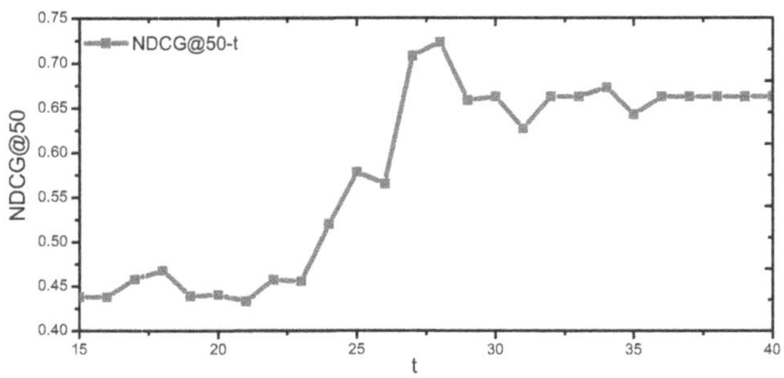

Figure 7: The performance with different t when K is fixed as 304.

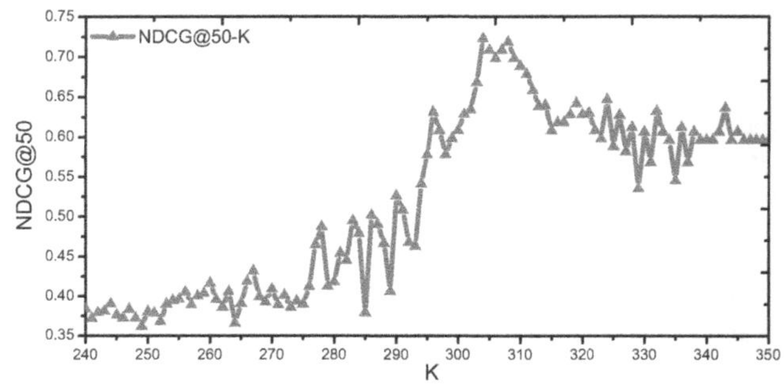

Figure 8: The performance with different K when t is fixed as 28.

KDE assumes that these visual concepts are independent, when estimating the relatedness between a visual concept and a given image.

Figure 6 illustrates the top 10 images before and after reranking for different reranking approaches for the complex query "soldiers holding American flag on the mountain". Obviously, our proposed approaches obtain the most satisfying results.

However, after examining the performance of each query, it is observed that our scheme fails to handle some queries that have explicit spatial or action relationship constraints between visual concepts. Examples include "a butterfly on the left top of the flower" and "a man listening to a mobile phone". We will integrate this kind information into our scheme for general complex queries in our future work.

6.5 On the Sensitivity of Parameters

As discussed above, both the number of transitions t and local neighbour size K are important parameters in our method. In this section, we further conduct experiments to investigate the effect of these parameters based on the proposed_NRCC. We first perform grid search with step size 1, to seek the t and K with optimal reranking performance. 28 and 304 are located for t and K, respectively.

The NDCG@50-t curve is presented in Figure 7 with K fixed as 304. As illustrated, the performance increases with t growing and arrives at a peak at a certain t, then the performance sharply decreases, and finally becomes relatively constant. This result is consistent with our previous analysis that when t tends towards infinite, all the starting points become indistinguishable.

Similarly, Figure 8 shows the NDCG@50-K curve with t fixed as 28, where the performance varies according to different K. With the gradual increase of K, more relevant samples are connected to each other, and "incorrect" edges between the relevant samples and irrelevant samples are potentially introduced. From Figure 8, it can be observed that NDCG@50 obtains the peak performance at $K = 304$, which is a trade-off value.

7. APPLICATIONS

In this section, we introduce two potential application scenarios of image reranking for complex queries: photo-based question answering and textual news visualization.

7.1 Photo-based Question Answering

7.1.1 *Application Scenario*

Community question answering (cQA) services have gained great popularity over the past decades [24, 21, 9], which encourage askers to post their specific questions on any topic and obtain answers provided by other participants. It also facilitates general users to seek information from the large repository of well-answered questions. However, existing cQA forums, such as Yahoo!Answers, Answerbag, MetaFilter, usually support only textual answers, which are not in-

Table 4: The distribution of visual concepts embedded in the generated queries for photo-based QA.

One Visual Concepts	Two Visual Concepts	More Than Two Visual Concepts
46.15%	38.85%	15.0%

tuitive for many questions, such as the question "what is the difference between alligators and crocodiles". Even when the answer is described by several very long sentences in Yahoo!Answers, it is still hard for users to grasp the appearance differences. Here it reflects the fact that a picture is worth a thousand words. However, noting that not all the QA pairs prefer image answers. Textual answer is sufficient when it comes to the quantity-type questions, such as "what is the population in China". Also video answers will be much more lively and interesting for procedure-oriented questions, such as "how to assemble a computer". Actually this is the so-called multimedia question answering [9], a rising topic in media search domain.

In this paper, we only focus on the QA pairs which may be better explained with images. However, as stated in [24], the queries generated from the textual QA pairs are usually very verbose and complex, not supported well by the current commercial image search engines. Based on our proposed approach, we develop a photo-based QA system, which automatically complements the original textual answers with relevant web images.

7.1.2 *Experiments*

To demonstrate the effectiveness of the PQA system, we conducted the experiment on 1000 non-conversational QA pairs, selected from Yahoo!Answers dataset [21], which contains 4,483,032 QA pairs. For each QA pair, five volunteers were invited to vote whether it can provide users with better experience by adding images instead of using purely texture descriptions. Around 260 QA pairs were selected. We then directly employed the method in [24] to generate a most informative query from each QA pair. Our statistics are shown in Table 4, which show that more than 53% of queries contain two or more visual concepts.

Accordingly, a query-aware reranking approach is proposed to select the top 10 relevant images. To be specific, if the query is simple, i.e., containing only one visual concept, then the RW [12] will be used directly. On the other hand, if the query is complex, we employ the proposed_NRCC. We compare our proposed approach with the following methods.

- **Naive Search**: Simply perform image search with each query on Google Image without reranking.
- **Naive Fusion**: Simply perform image search with each visual concept in the generated complex query, and then fuse the results.

Figure 9 shows the comparison of these three methods. It can be observed that our query-aware reranking approach outperforms the other two methods remarkably.

7.2 Textual News Visualization

7.2.1 *Application Scenario*

"Every picture tells a story" suggests to us the essence of visual communication via pictures. This phrase is also consistent with our common sense, i.e., pictures in textual news always facilitate and expedite our understanding, especially for elderly and juvenile. Meanwhile, searching the image database in order to provide several meaningful and illustrative pictures to their textual news is a routine task for news writers.

However, the pictures contained in news documents are usually very few as shown in Table 5. which shows that more than 46% news documents do not contain any pictures. The statistical result is based on the experimental dataset. To assist news readers and news writers, we propose a scheme to automatically seek relevant web images that best contextualize the content of news.

Table 5: The distribution of the number of pictures involved in news documents.

Without Any Picture	One Pictures	Two Pictures	> Two Pictures
46.15%	38.85%	15.0%	38.85%

7.2.2 *Experiments*

We directly used the news dataset in [17], crawled from ABCNews.com, BBS.co.uk, CNN.com and GoogleNews; it contains up to 48,429 unique documents after duplicate removal. To save manual labelling efforts, we randomly select 100 news documents from the whole data set for evaluation. It is observed that most of the news articles are fairly long, and it is not an easy task to extract descriptive queries. So we simply regard the expert generated titles of the news documents as complex queries due to their obvious summarizing attribute.

Further, it is observed that more than 43% of titles contain at least one person-related visual concept. So we propose to employ query dependent image representations for reranking. Specifically, let $\mathcal{X}_c$ and $\mathcal{X}$ the set of images retrieved by the visual concept q_c and complex query Q, respectively; and q_c is predicted as person related query by the method in [11]. Then for each image in $\mathcal{X}_c$ and $\mathcal{X}$, we performed face detection. We extracted the 256-dimensional Local Binary Pattern (LBP) features [28] from the largest face region for any $\mathbf{x}_i$ in $\mathcal{X}_c$; and the same features are extracted for all the detected faces for any $\mathbf{x}_u$ in $\mathcal{X}$. The similarity between $\mathbf{x}_i$ and $\mathbf{x}_u$ is then computed as,

$$W_{iu} = \max_{x \in \mathcal{O}_u} K(\mathbf{x}_i, \mathbf{x}) \quad (20)$$

where $\mathcal{O}_u$ is the set of LBP features extracted from the faces in image $\mathbf{x}_u$. Other image pair similarity is the same as previously introduced. We call this the query-aware presentation method.

To demonstrate the effectiveness of our proposed query-aware image presentation method, we compare it with the query independent unified image presentation method as described earlier, i.e., all the images are presented by the combination of bag-of-visual-words and global features. The result is presented in Figure 10, which shows that our query-aware image presentation is better than query-independent image presentation approach, even though both of them are based on our same reranking principles. The inial ranking performance reflects lower search performance. This is because the news titles generally contain some redundant terms, which overwhelm the key concepts and potentially confuse the search engines.

8. CONCLUSIONS AND FUTURE WORK

In this paper, we proposed a scheme to rerank web images for complex queries, which is robust to the unreliable

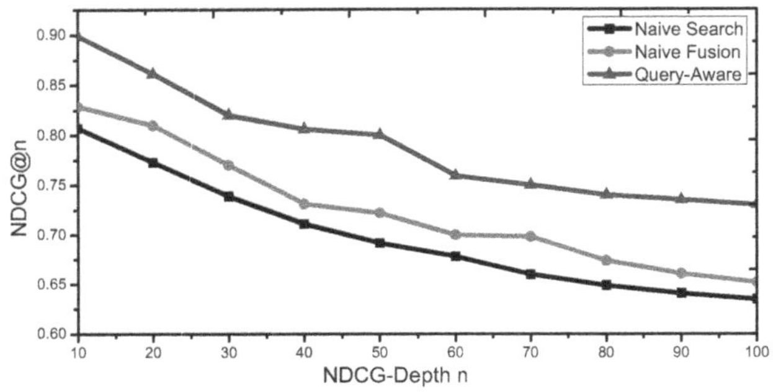

Figure 9: The average performance comparison of Photo-based QA System.

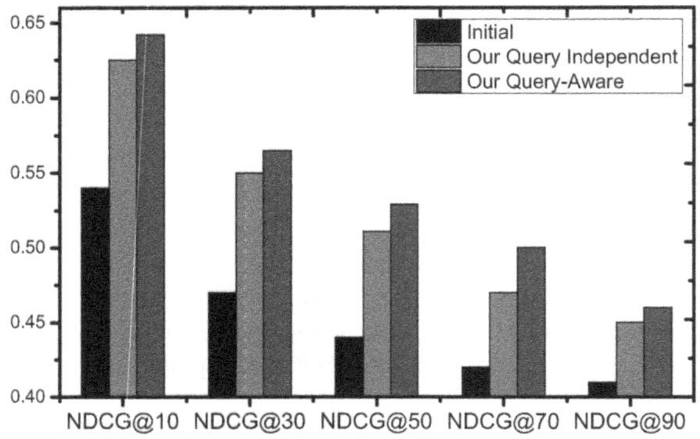

Figure 10: Performance comparison among different methods for textual news visualization.

initial ranking list. For a given complex query, it first detects the noun-phrase based visual concepts and collects their relevant images simultaneously. It then constructs a heterogeneous probabilistic network to estimate the image relevance score, which consists of three mutual reinforced sub-networks. These sub-networks represent different relationship layers, spanning from semantic level to visual level, which are established among the complex query and its detected visual concepts, by harnessing the content of images and their associated textual information. Based on these relevance scores, a new ranking list is generated. The experimental results showed that our scheme is significantly better than the other existing state-of-the-art approaches. We also introduced two application scenarios, which can benefit from our scheme, namely photo-based question answering and textual news visualization.

A limitation of current work is that it ignores the relationships explicitly described by the complex query, which have no uniform patterns and are notoriously hard to model. We will integrate this kind information into our scheme for general complex queries in our future work.

9. ACKNOWLEDGEMENTS

This work was supported by NUS-Tsinghua Extreme Search project under the grant number: R-252-300-001-490.

10. REFERENCES

[1] Hitwise. see `http://weblogs.hitwise.com/alan-long/2009/11/searches_getting_longer.html`.
[2] R. Aly, D. Hiemstra, and R. Ordelman. Building detectors to support searches on combined semantic concepts. In *MIR Workshop*, 2007.
[3] J. Bai, D. Song, P. Bruza, J.-Y. Nie, and G. Cao. Query expansion using term relationships in language models for information retrieval. In *CIKM*, 2005.
[4] N. Balasubramanian, G. Kumaran, and V. Carvalho. Exploring reductions for long web queries. In *SIGIR*, 2010.
[5] M. Bendersky and W. B. Croft. Discovering key concepts in verbose queries. In *SIGIR*, 2008.
[6] M. Bendersky, D. Metzler, and W. B. Croft. Learning concept importance using a weighted dependence model. In *WSDM*, 2010.
[7] M. Bendersky, D. Metzler, and W. B. Croft. Parameterized concept weighting in verbose queries. In *SIGIR*, 2011.
[8] X. Chen, J. Yuan, L. Nie, Z.-j. Zha, S. Yan, and T.-s. Chua. Known-item search by nus. In *NIST TRECVID*, 2010.
[9] T.-S. Chua, R. Hong, G. Li, and J. Tang. From text question-answering to multimedia qa on web-scale media resources. In *LS-MMRM*, 2009.
[10] R. L. Cilibrasi and P. M. B. Vitanyi. The google similarity distance. *TKDE*, 2007.
[11] D. Delgado, J. Magalhaes, and N. Correia. Assisted news reading with automated illustration. In *MM*, 2010.
[12] W. H. Hsu, L. S. Kennedy, and S.-F. Chang. Video search reranking through random walk over document-level context graph. In *MM*, 2007.
[13] G. Kumaran and J. Allan. A case for shorter queries, and helping users create them. In *NAACL-HLT*, 2007.
[14] G. Kumaran and J. Allan. Effective and efficient user interaction for long queries. In *SIGIR*, 2008.
[15] M. Lease, J. Allan, and W. B. Croft. Regression rank: Learning to meet the opportunity of descriptive queries. In *ECIR*, 2009.
[16] X. Li, C. G. M. Snoek, M. Worring, and A. W. M. Smeulders. Harvesting social images for bi-concept search. *TMM*, 2012.
[17] Z. Li, M. Wang, J. Liu, C. Xu, and H. Lu. News contextualization with geographic and visual information. In *MM*, 2011.
[18] D. Liu, X.-S. Hua, M. Wang, and H.-J. Zhang. Image retagging. In *MM*, 2010.
[19] D. Liu, X.-S. Hua, L. Yang, M. Wang, and H.-J. Zhang. Tag ranking. In *WWW*, 2009.
[20] Y. Liu, T. Mei, X.-S. Hua, J. Tang, X. Wu, and S. Li. Learning to video search rerank via pseudo preference feedback. In *ICME*, 2008.
[21] M. C. Mihai Surdeanu and H. Zaragoza. Learning to rank answers on large online qa collections. In *ACL*, 2008.
[22] N. Morioka and J. Wang. Robust visual reranking via sparsity and ranking constraints. In *MM*, 2011.
[23] A. P. Natsev, M. R. Naphade, and J. TešiĆ. Learning the semantics of multimedia queries and concepts from a small number of examples. In *MM*, 2005.
[24] L. Nie, M. Wang, Z.-j. Zha, G. Li, and T.-S. Chua. Multimedia answering: enriching text qa with media information. In *SIGIR*, 2011.
[25] L. N. Nie, M. Wang, Z. Zha, and T.-S. Chua. Oracle in image search: A content-based approach to performance prediction. *TOIS*, 2012.
[26] J. H. Park and W. B. Croft. Query term ranking based on dependency parsing of verbose queries. In *SIGIR*, 2010.
[27] S. U. Pillai, T. Suel, and S. Cha. The Perron-Frobenius theorem: some of its applications. *Signal Processing Magazine, IEEE*, 2005.
[28] H.-T. Pu. An analysis of failed queries for web image retrieval. *Journal of Information Science*, 2008.
[29] M. Szummer and T. Jaakkola. Partially labeled classification with markov random walks. *NIPS*, 2002.
[30] X. Tian, L. Yang, J. Wang, Y. Yang, X. Wu, and X.-S. Hua. Bayesian video search reranking. In *MM*, 2008.
[31] A. Torralba, R. Fergus, and W. Freeman. 80 million tiny images: A large data set for nonparametric object and scene recognition. *TPAMI*, 2008.
[32] M. Wang, K. Yang, X.-S. Hua, and H.-J. Zhang. Towards a relevant and diverse search of social images. *TMM*, 2010.
[33] H. Xu, J. Wang, X.-S. Hua, and S. Li. Image search by concept map. In *SIGIR*, 2010.
[34] R. Yan, E. Hauptmann, and R. Jin. Multimedia search with pseudo-relevance feedback. In *ICVR*, 2003.
[35] J. Yuan, Z.-J. Zha, Y.-T. Zheng, W. Meng, X. Zhou, and T.-S. Chua. Utilizing related samples to enhance interactive concept-based video search. *TMM*, 2011.
[36] J. Yuan, Z.-J. Zha, Y.-T. Zheng, M. Wang, X. Zhou, and T.-S. Chua. Learning concept bundles for video search with complex queries. In *MM*, 2011.

Exploiting Visual Word Co-occurrence for Image Retrieval *

Miaojing Shi ‡, Xinghai Sun ‡, Dacheng Tao #, Chao Xu ‡

‡ Key Laboratory of Machine Perception (Ministry of Education), Peking University, Beijing, P.R.China †
# Centre for Quantum Computation and Intelligent Systems, University of Technology, Sydney, Australia
{shimj,sunxh,xuchao}@cis.pku.edu.cn, Dacheng.Tao@uts.edu.au

ABSTRACT

Bag-of-visual-words (BOVW) based image representation has received intense attention in recent years and has improved content based image retrieval (CBIR) significantly. BOVW does not consider the spatial correlation between visual words in natural images and thus biases the generated visual words towards noise when the corresponding visual features are not stable. In this paper, we construct a visual word co-occurrence table by exploring visual word co-occurrence extracted from small affine-invariant regions in a large collection of natural images. Based on this visual word co-occurrence table, we first present a novel high-order predictor to accelerate the generation of neighboring visual words. A co-occurrence matrix is introduced to refine the similarity measure for image ranking. Like the inverse document frequency (idf), it down-weights the contribution of the words that are less discriminative because of frequent co-occurrence. We conduct experiments on *Oxford* and *Paris Building* datasets, in which the *ImageNet* dataset is used to implement a large scale evaluation. Thorough experimental results suggest that our method outperforms the state-of-the-art, especially when the vocabulary size is comparatively small. In addition, our method is not much more costly than the BOVW model.

Categories and Subject Descriptors

H.3.3 [**Information Search and Retrieval**]: Retrieval models

General Terms

Algorithms, Experimentation, Performance.

Keywords

BOVW, high-order predictor, co-occurrence matrix

1. INTRODUCTION

Bag-of-visual-words (BOVW) based image representation has received intense attention in recent years and has improved content based image retrieval (CBIR) significantly [23]. BOVW represents an image as a visual document composed of distinctive visual words, which is very important for both the effectiveness and efficiency of image retrieval, especially in a large scale database. The visual document is in the same format as a text document, and image retrieval can therefore be improved by many mature text retrieval techniques, and run as fast as text retrieval. It has been demonstrated that BOVW is one of the most promising approaches for large scale image retrieval [17, 18, 19].

The visual words are derived from clustering and quantization of local features. The scale-invariant feature transform (SIFT) [14] is adopted as the local feature. SIFT features are clustered and quantized into visual words with the K-means algorithm [17]. The tf-idf weight [2] is widely used, which up-weights the contribution of a word that occurs frequently in an image with the tf (term frequency), while it down-weights the contribution of a word that commonly occurs in many images with the idf (inverse document frequency), and is regarded as being less discriminative to the relevance score. Image similarity is measured with the cosine similarity between the query image and an image in the collection. The ranked list is determined according to the values of similarity scores.

Two important issues need to be addressed for the BOVW representation: 1) how to quickly map the local feature to the visual word via the correlation between visual words; 2) how to refine the cosine similarity by reducing the correlation between visual words. Regarding the first issue, as is known from the state-of-the-art methods, each feature is independently mapped to a word, which causes the word generation to be the most time-consuming step in BOVW. Regarding the second issue, the tf-idf weight does not take into account the correlation between visual words, which is important for similarity measure. Like the idf, a word co-occurring with many words is also regarded as being less discriminative and should be down-weighted.

In this paper, we present two approaches for the two issues: the fast visual word generation method and the refined cosine similarity measure, both based on the spatial co-occurrence of visual words. Spatial co-occurrence means

*Area Chair: Gang Hua

†This paper is supported by NBRPC 2011CB302400, NSFC 60975014, 61121002 and NSFB 4102024.

MM'12, October 29–November 2, 2012, Nara, Japan.

(a) radcliffe_camera (b) vw pattern (17998, 10363) (c) vw pattern (43393, 65762)

Figure 1: An illustration of different co-occurring patterns from a $100K$ vocabulary constructed on *Oxford Building* dataset: (a) one of the selected landmarks: radcliffe_camera, two pairs of visual words (the red dot and the green dot inside the red frames) are selected with their ID (17998, 10363), and (43393, 65762); (b) nine images share a visual word (vw) pair (17998, 10363), but although they are related, the locations of the pair are not fully matched; (c) 9 other images share another pair (43393, 65762), although they are irrelevant.

that visual words co-occur in a small spatial region of an image, instead of in the entire image.

We find that the features of natural images correlate substantially, as illustrated in Fig. 1. One local feature's existence can semantically indicate the presence or absence of certain other features in its neighborhood. This is what we unconsciously do in human vision: a local feature or structure spotted by the human eyes can intuitively hint to our brain that certain other features or structures in the vicinity are possible or impossible. In mathematical language, we build a visual word co-occurrence table to record the co-occurring number of any two visual words in the vocabulary, to indicate the semantic correlation of any two visual words.

Our first perspective is inspired by *predictive coding*, in which random variables can be predicted from previously observed random variables. As shown in Fig .1, some visual word pairs, e.g., (43393, 65762), (17998, 10363), selected from the $100K$ vocabulary on *Oxford Building* dataset [18] frequently co-occur in many images, both relevant and irrelevant. In this context, visual word can be predicted by its co-occurring visual words. The co-occurring visual words are collected from the image database. We develop a high-order predictor to accelerate the generation of visual words. Here the high-order predictor refers to the prediction based on multiple co-occurring words. The information from multiple co-occurring words is used to estimate posterior probability for the purpose of choosing a few candidate words. The prediction can significantly decrease the number of words to search, with a consequent saving in computation.

Our second contribution is to embed the co-occurring information into the cosine similarity. We believe that if a visual word co-occurs with many words, its uniqueness and distinctiveness decline, such as a word occurring in many irrelevant images, as shown in Fig. 1(c). We design a co-occurrence matrix to refine the cosine similarity measure for image ranking, and this co-occurrence matrix helps to increase the discriminative capability of visual words by subtracting the co-occurring redundancies from other visual words.

The rest of the paper is organized as follows. In Section 2, related works are introduced. We present the fast visual word generation algorithm in Section 3. In Section 4 we propose the refined cosine similarity measure for image ranking. Section 5 presents the experimental results. The conclusion is discussed in Section 6.

2. RELATED WORK

This section reviews the state-of-the-art methods in two related aspects: 1) visual word generation for local features; 2) image ranking by exploiting spatial correlation.

Visual word generation. The common method of visual word generation is to index the visual words through a multi-branch tree. Representative tree based algorithms include KD-tree [3] [1] [22] and K-means tree [28] [13] [17]. Arya et al. [1] utilized a priority queue to the tree to speed up the search; Anan et al. [22] utilized multiple random KD-trees (RKD) simultaneously to search words; Uhlmann [28] proposed a "RkNN" tree, which evaluated an efficient approximative search in arbitrary metric spaces; Nister et al. [17] presented a new K-means tree by accessing a single leaf hierarchically; that is, the hierarchical K-means (HKM) tree; Muja et al. [16] selected two best tree structures(RKD and HKM), and utilized a fast library for approximate nearest neighbors (FLANN) to automatically determine the best algorithm and parameters for a given dataset.

Typical algorithms search words for each feature in an image independently of other features, and some researchers have already tried to exploit the nearest neighbor information for certain word generation [8] [31]. In this paper, we endeavor to exploit the correlation information to predict the likely words for each feature, thus the number of words to be searched is reduced significantly. To enhance the precision of the prediction, we design the predictor with high-order posterior probability containing the co-occurring information of multiple words.

Image ranking. Spatial correlation is extensively explored in image retrieval [18, 30, 36, 32, 35, 25, 34, 12, 10]. General approaches come from bundling features in concrete structures and segments; for example, bounding box was manually initialized in [18] and different weighing terms were added to the visual words inside and outside the bounding box [32]. In [30, 36, 35, 10] features are bundled in maximally stable extremal region (MSER) [15] or a feature's affine-invariant region and taken as contextual visual phrases; these phrases are leveraged to provide more information for the indexing and retrieval processes. Furthermore, spatial correlation has been embedded in building a dictionary of contextual synonyms in [19] and [25].

The spatial co-occurrence used in this paper seems to resemble the visual phrase [33, 35]. But in fact they are utilized in totally different ways. A visual phrase can be considered as a kind of feature expansion to provide better image representation [37]. By contrast, our spatial co-occurrence is used to down-weight a single word: in other words, it removes the correlated noise to refine each local feature. Researches that share a similar motivation in down-weighting the tf-idf of visual words in consideration of their correlations can be found in [7, 29, 26]. Other important papers striving to increase the discriminative capability of visual words include the contextual dissimilarity measure [9] and reciprocal neighborhoods [8].

3. FAST VISUAL WORD GENERATION

Our image retrieval scheme is based on the BOVW model. An image is represented by a vector descriptor, and an entry of the vector is a tf-idf weight for a visual word. The visual words are derived from the clustering and quantization of local SIFT features. As many features co-occur in images, we construct a spatial co-occurrence table to speed up the word generation of the query image and refine the similarity measure in image ranking.

3.1 Co-occurrence Table

Given two visual words w_m and w_n co-occurring in an affine-invariant region, where w_n is located at the center of the region, $N^i(w_m, w_n)$ is their co-occurring number in the i-th image, $N(w_m, w_n)$ is their total co-occurring number over the entire database,

$$N(w_m, w_n) = \sum_i N^i(w_m, w_n) \tag{1}$$

visual word w_m can be regarded as co-occurring with w_n, if its feature is located inside the feature's affine region of w_n. Considering the relatively small size of a feature's affine-invariant region, we magnify the region five times to incorporate more features. We record the co-occurring number of any two visual words and thereby construct a visual word co-occurrence table. Apart from the co-occurring number, the occurrence $N(w_m)$ of every single visual word over the entire database is also recorded.

3.2 Prediction Based on Approximate Posterior Probability

Inspired by *predictive coding*, if we have one letter I, we can claim that the next letter is in a decreased letter set less than 26 letters, furthermore, if we already have four letters $I - m - a - g$, then the next letter is highly likely to be e, for the known word *Image*. We propose a high-order predictor to predict the corresponding word of a feature depending on the multi-words of its neighboring features.

Given a number of visual words $S = \{w_0, w_1 ... w_{s-1}\}$, where s is the set size, we plan to predict the word of their neighboring feature on the basis of S. The co-occurring words and numbers for each visual word collected from the

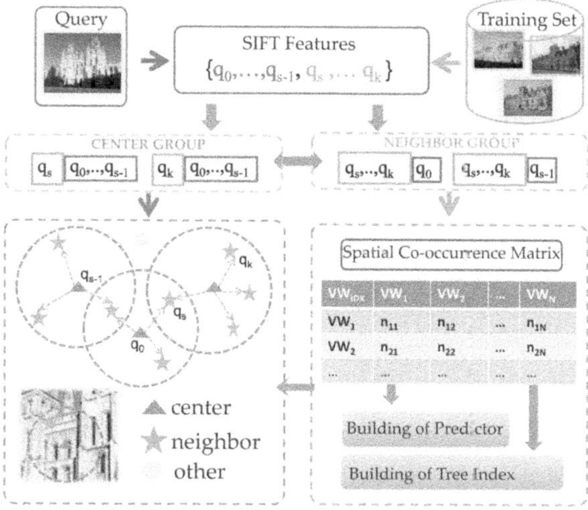

Figure 2: visual word generation with high-order prediction. For the training set, neighboring features are grouped in their affine-invariant regions; in the right block, a co-occurrence table is constructed off-line after mapping *Neighbor Group* to that of the visual words; the high-order predictor is then built for visual word prediction; the tree index is necessary for precise search. For the test images, grouped features are in the inverse form, called *Center Group*, and the left block indicates the prediction modes of the high-order predictor.

entire database, have been recorded in the co-occurrence table. Since the table is sparse and the size of each list is small, we bundle all the co-occurring visual words of the sample set S as the candidate visual word set $W = \{w_{S0}, w_{S1} ... w_{Sv}\}$ of their neighboring features, v is the size of W.

We adopt a Bayesian criterion to predict the optimal visual word $\overset{*}{w}_s$ of the neighboring feature from W that is most likely to co-occur with these w_0, w_1,...,w_{s-1}. This likelihood is calculated in terms of the posterior possibility $p(\hat{w}_s | w_0, ..., w_{s-1})$, and the feature in W with the largest conditional probability of occurring is predicted,

$$\overset{*}{w}_s = \arg\max_{\hat{w}_s \in W} p(\hat{w}_s | w_0, ..., w_{s-1}) \tag{2}$$

this conditional probability can be computed from the joint probability,

$$p(\hat{w}_s | w_0, ..., w_{s-1}) = \frac{p(\hat{w}_s, w_0, ..., w_{s-1})}{p(w_0, ..., w_{s-1})} \tag{3}$$

where $p(\hat{w}_s, w_0, ..., w_{s-1})$ is the joint probability of $\hat{w}_s$, w_0, ..., w_{s-1} in the neighborhood over the entire database, they can be obtained after normalizing their total co-occurring number $N(\hat{w}_s, w_0, ..., w_{s-1})$ by the number of all the visual word occurrences N_T. We decompose $p(\hat{w}_s, w_0, ..., w_{s-1})$:

$$\begin{aligned} & p(\hat{w}_s, w_0, ..., w_{s-1}) \\ & = p(w_{s-1} | \hat{w}_s, w_{s-2}, ..., w_0) ... p(w_1 | \hat{w}_s, w_0) p(w_0 | \hat{w}_s) p(\hat{w}_s) \end{aligned} \tag{4}$$

where the prior $p(w_{s-1} | \hat{w}_s, w_{s-2}, ..., w_0) ... p(w_0 \; \hat{w}_s)$ measure the possibility that certain word may co-occur with its nearby words $\hat{w}_s,..,w_0$. The prior $p(\hat{w}_s)$ can be estimated from $N(\hat{w}_s)$. To formulate this equation, we assume the sampled words $w_0, w_1...w_{s-1}$ are conditionally independent, because they have already been generated. In this manner $p(w_0, ..., w_{s-1})$ can be approximated as $\prod_{w_i} p(w_i)$, while $p(w_{s-1}|\hat{w}_s, w_{s-2}, ..., w_0)... \ p(w_0|\hat{w}_s)$ are only dependent on the unknown word $\hat{w}_s$, so they can be approximated by the first-order probabilities on $\hat{w}_s$,

$$\begin{array}{l} p(\hat{w}_s, w_0, ..., w_{s-1}) \approx p(\hat{w}_s) \prod_{w_i \in S} p(w_i|\hat{w}_s) \\ p(w_0, ..., w_{s-1}) \approx \prod_{w_i \in S} p(w_i) \end{array} \tag{5}$$

where $p(w_i|\hat{w}_s)$ can be estimated from the prior co-occurring number of $N(w_i, \hat{w}_s)$ collected by the co-occurrence table. The posterior probability of Eqn. 2 corresponds to the following decomposition:

$$\begin{aligned} \overset{*}{w}_s &= \arg\max_{\hat{w}_s \in W} p(\hat{w}_s | w_0, ..., w_{s-1}) \\ &\approx \arg\max_{\hat{w}_s \in W} \frac{p(\hat{w}_s) \prod_{w_i \in S} p(w_i|\hat{w}_s)}{\prod_{w_i \in S} p(w_i)} \\ &= \arg\max_{\hat{w}_s \in W} \frac{N(\hat{w}_s) \prod_{w_i \in S} \frac{N(w_i, \hat{w}_s)}{N(\hat{w}_s)}}{\prod_{w_i \in S} N(w_i)} \end{aligned} \tag{6}$$

the approximation indicates that the cascade co-occurring possibilities of $w_0, w_1, ..., w_{s-1}$ on the condition of current optimal visual word $\overset{*}{w}_s$ should be the largest, which means the small region composing the words $w_0, w_1, ..., w_{s-1}, w_s$ is the most probable co-occurring pattern at the current location.

Since the co-occurrence table is sparse, zero terms in the table will affect the calculation in Eqn. 6, which makes the probability zero. To solve the problem, we group $\hat{w}_s$ based on its number of zero items in $N(w_i, \hat{w}_s)$. In the same group, we can compare two $p(\hat{w}_s|w_0, ..., w_{s-1})$ by simply removing the zero items. For those $\hat{w}_s$ with different numbers of zeros terms in $N(w_i, \hat{w}_s)$, we regard the one $p(\hat{w}_s|w_0, ..., w_{s-1})$ with less zero items $N(w_i, \hat{w}_s)$ in its decomposition is larger than that with more zero items.

3.3 Grouping of Neighbors and Centers

Because the affine invariant region of one feature is too small to contain more neighbors, we attempt to access more co-occurring neighbors for the generation of visual words by enlarging the region five times.

Our proposed scheme is shown in Fig. 2. Instead of looking for neighboring features $q_s, .., q_k$ around the center q_0, we record all the centers whose regions include a certain feature, i.e., q_s. In this manner, more neighboring centers of q_s are incorporated in the inverse form. The observation of the inverse form is because of the asymmetry between the center q_0 and its neighbor q_s, that is, when q_s is taken as a center, its region might not include q_0.

In summary, the co-occurrence table is constructed and utilized in the usual way; every center feature is grouped with its neighbors in the affine-invariant region, called *Neighbor Group* in Fig. 2. After mapping *Neighbor Groups* of features into those of visual words, the co-occurrence table is constructed. In contrast, the prediction of a word is carried out in an inverse way. We record the centers that one feature belongs to, as shown in Fig. 2, the *Center Group*. After generating all the center words $(w_0, ..., w_{s-1})$ from their corresponding features $(q_0, ..., q_{s-1})$, the next step is to determine the candidate visual word set of features, i.e., q_s. Since the sizes of *Center Group* and *Neighbor Group* are small and the computation of the approximate posterior probability is easy, all the neighboring words collected from the co-occurrence table of q_s's center lists are regarded as its candidate visual word set. Thus a number of approximate posterior probabilities are calculated from Eqn. 6, and the optimal $\overset{*}{w}_s$ is discovered through comparison. The center independence assumption in Eqn. 6 is an approximation to simplify the calculation of the high-order probability. Empirically, the number of co-occurring center words is not large and usually no more than 4 for predicting each single word, so the center independence assumption is reasonable and performs well. This manner of prediction is easy but not precise, because it only indicates higher likelihood. To generate the precise word, Euclidean distance is necessary. We select K-candidates with the top K-maximal probabilities to compute their Euclidean distances to the feature q_s. The word with the minimal Euclidean distance is the selected word.

3.4 Procedure of Visual Word Generation

We have presented key techniques for fast word generation based on spatial co-occurrence information, and we now detail the procedure.

1. Given a query image, extract the local features.
2. Randomly select 20% features as centers (as illustrated in Fig. 2, the left block, the red triangles) determine their neighboring features (the green stars) in their magnified affine-invariant regions (the red circles).
3. Map the 20% center features to their words through FLANN.
4. Predict those neighboring features of centers whose *Center Groups* contain the words of the quantized centers. Provide the K-candidate words by Eqn. 6 and generate the words for the features by their Euclidean distances.
5. If any features (the yellow dot) do not belong to any centers, or the Euclidean distance from the current optimal visual word to the corresponding feature is still large, apply FLANN to action further search.

The proportion of the initial center features is set to 20%. This setting maintains a good balance between a wide coverage of the whole image and the small time cost of an exact nearest neighbor search for the center features. Random selection offers a simple yet effective treatment for every feature in an image. The word generation algorithm runs fast because it utilizes correlation information between features instead of generating each feature independently. The prediction based on approximate posterior probabilities provides fewer candidates that are more likely to occur than the widely used tree structure, so computation complexity is reduced.

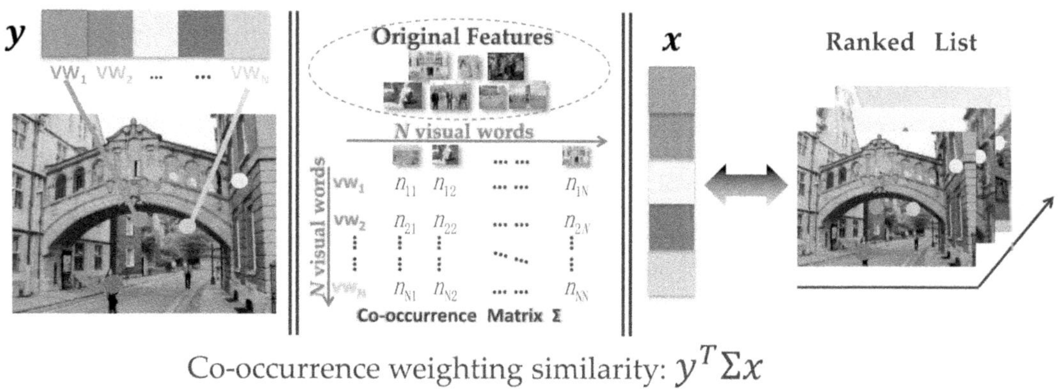

Figure 3: Overview of similarity measure by co-occurrence weighting scheme.

4. IMAGE RANKING

In the BOVW model, once a query image is given, the images in the database are ranked in the order of their similarity scores to query. The general similarity measure is the cosine distance. As previously noted, the BOVW model does not take the correlation between visual words into account, so the spatial information is ignored in the cosine similarity. We embed the spatial co-occurrence information in a refined cosine similarity to improve the ranking performance, instead of adding a re-ranking stage to conduct spatial verification generally.

4.1 Cosine Similarity

In the BOVW representation, an image is represented by a N-dimensional vector (N is the vocabulary size), and an element of the vector is the tf-idf value of a word. The tf-idf weight [2] is a commonly used scheme in image ranking. It down-weights the contribution that commonly occurs and and less discriminative, words are therefore included in the relevance score. The simplest ranking function is by the normalized cosine measure:

$$Sim(x,y) = \frac{x^T y}{||x||||y||} \tag{7}$$

where y is query vector, x is the vector of an image in database. The larger $Sim(x,y)$ is, the more relevant x is to the query image, thus, the higher it is ranked in the returned list.

We embed the co-occurrence information into the cosine similarity measure. Mathematically, the cosine similarity is equivalent to using a unit diagonal matrix I to measure the similarity between two vectors, $Sim(x,y) = \frac{x^T I y}{||x||||y||}$. In the following, we utilize a co-occurrence matrix $\sum$ to refine the similarity measure for image ranking $Sim(x,y) = \frac{x^T \sum y}{||x||||y||}$, as shown in Fig. 3.

4.2 Co-occurrence Weighting Similarity

As is known, idf is a measure of whether a word is common or rare across entire database. If a word is common, it is less discriminative to the relevance score and its contribution will be down-weighted through idf. In this section we manage to further exploit the importance of a visual word from its co-occurring attribute with other words. As mentioned in the Introduction and Fig. 1: 1) the images containing the same co-occurring pairs might be totally different; 2) the locations of co-occurring pairs for the related images could be different; 3) if a visual word co-occurs with a large number of words, its uniqueness and distinctiveness decline. Thus, although a visual word associated with high occurrence or co-occurrence can be regarded as having a high probability of occurring in the word generation process, it performs a less discriminative role in retrieving a visual object. Like idf, we claim that if a visual word commonly co-occurs with other words, and is therefore less discriminative to the relevance score, we should down-weight its contribution in the similarity measure.

Since our approach focuses on near duplicated image retrieval, the number of relevant images for a given query should be small in large scale dataset. All irrelevant images in the database can be taken as noises that produces negative information in image ranking [27]. We build a co-occurrence matrix $\mathbf{\Sigma} = \{n_{ij}\}$ on the noisy set, referred to Section 3.1, Fig.3; its element $n_{ij} = N(w_i, w_j)$ denotes the co-occurring number of visual word w_j with visual word w_i. We propose a new similarity measure, called the co-occurrence weighting similarity measure (Co-Sim):

$$\begin{aligned} Sim(x,y) &= \frac{x^T(I - \frac{1}{\beta}\Sigma)y}{||x||||y||} \\ &= \frac{x^T y}{||x||||y||} - \frac{1}{\beta}\frac{x^T \Sigma y}{||x||||y||} \end{aligned} \tag{8}$$

where $\frac{x^T y}{||x||||y||}$ is the basic cosine similarity and $\frac{x^T \Sigma y}{||x||||y||}$ is the new term introduced to encode the correlation between two any visual words. The linear combination coefficient $\frac{1}{\beta}$ allows a continuum of the model between the cosine form and the Σ form. Σ describes the co-occurring distribution of the noisy images, if $\frac{x^T \Sigma y}{||x||||y||}$ is comparative large, it means that the visual words of the current image are more likely to be drawn from the noisy distribution. To indicate this negative effect, a subtraction is operated. This idea is similar to the contextual dissimilarity measure [9] and cross-category knowledge [6, 20]. In fact, because the number of images relevant to a query is so small compared to the large scale database, the negative effect of the entire corpus obviously overwhelms the trivial positive effect of the relevant images. In practice, we do not need the labels of the images, likewise [5], because the co-occurrence matrix is constructed on the entire database and naturally reflects the statistical distribution of the database.

In fact, β indicates a normalization of the matrix. Empirically, if we normalize the co-occurrence matrix Σ by rows ($\sum_j N(w_i, w_j) = 1$), only slight adjustment by β is then needed to overcome the statistical uncertainty of the matrix when applied to a different database. In general $\beta \in (1.2, 1.5)$, the performance stays stable in this case.

Our proposed similarity (Eqn.8) can be considered as an inner product of a query vector y and vector $x^T(I - \frac{1}{\beta}\Sigma)$, where $x^T(I - \frac{1}{\beta}\Sigma)$ is a linear transformation performed on the vector x (or the same transformation from the query viewpoint, $(I - \frac{1}{\beta}\Sigma)y$ and x). Such a linear transformation acts a down-weighting role on the tf-idf of each visual word. The transformed vector is denoted as $x' = x^T(I - \frac{1}{\beta}\Sigma)$ (or $y' = (I - \frac{1}{\beta}\Sigma)y$), where each element of x' can be rewritten as:

$$x_i' = x_i - \frac{1}{\beta}\sum_j N(w_i, w_j)x_j, \quad (9)$$

here, x_i and x_j denote the corresponding tf-idf values of the i-th and j-th visual words for the image and $N(w_i, w_j)$ is the co-occurring number as a weighting term. As previously mentioned, if a visual word co-occurs with a large number of words, its uniqueness and distinctiveness decline.

The proposed method appears to be similar to query expansion [19] [10]. In fact, we do not add any new visual words for retrieval; on the contrary, we down-weight the contribution of each visual word in the similarity measure. Moreover, we do not require any knowledge of the matched visual words, our observation is focused on the considerable unmatched words. They are penalized in scoring by subtracting the co-occurring redundancies from other visual words. We admit that mis-scores may exist as a result of building the co-occurrence matrix on the entire database, but the general elimination of redundant information always outweighs the mistakes we have made, which means that in spite of decline of score on each visual word, the relative scores of importance for distinctive words is comparatively enhanced.

4.3 Algorithm Flow

We describe the image retrieval method based on the co-occurrence of visual words, as shown in Algorithm 1. In the offline process, the co-occurrence table is built on the entire image database. The predictor and the co-occurrence matrix are learned for visual word generation and image ranking, respectively. In the online phase, given a query image, we first generate image representation through the visual word high-order predictor. The co-occurrence weighting similarity measure is then adopted to evaluate the candidate images in the database. The ranked list is returned according to the similarity scores.

5. EXPERIMENTAL RESULTS

5.1 Dataset and Evaluation

The *Oxford* dataset. This dataset [18] of 5062 images is a standard image retrieval test set, which we name *Ox* for short. 55 images comprising 11 *Oxford* landmarks are selected as query images, and their ground truth retrieval results are provided.

Algorithm 1 Exploiting visual word co-occurrence for image retrieval

build co-occurrence table (matrix Σ);
input: query image y, max-check
output: ranked list S
visual word generation
randomly select 20% features as centers
group features with their centers in the neighborhood
for center feature q_c **do**
  accurate generate w_c by FLANN
end for
for neighboring features q_s **do**
  while current check $K <$ length $(W) <$ max-check **do**
    provide K candidate words with
    $K - \arg\max_{\hat{w}_s \in W} p(\hat{w}_s | w_0, ..., w_{s-1})$
    compute $\overset{*}{w}_s$ with minimal Euclidean distance to q_s
  end while
  while length $(W) <$ current check $K <$ max-check **do**
    search $\overset{*}{w}_s$ by FLANN
  end while
end for
image ranking
for each image x **in** database **do**
  similarity measure $Sim(x, y)$ to query
  $Sim(x, y) = \{x | \forall y : x^T(I - \frac{1}{\beta}\Sigma)y\}$
end for
return the ranked list S : $S - \arg\max Sim(x, y)$.

The *ImageNet* dataset. Approximately $100K$ and $500K$ images are sampled from $10M$ images in *ImageNet* [4], which we respectively call *I1* and *I2* for short.

The *Paris* dataset. This dataset contains 6300 images by querying the associated text tags for famous *Paris* landmarks such as "*Paris Eiffel Tower*" or "*Paris Arc de Triomphe*" [21].

Four databases are constructed for conducting the experiments: the first experiment is on the *Oxford* (*Ox*, 5062 images) and the second is on *Paris* (6390 images) dataset. To implement the proposed method on a large scale dataset, we construct two new databases by combining the *Oxford* dataset with *ImageNet* $100K$ and $500K$ datasets, *Ox+I1*, *Ox+I2*. The new collections are composed of approximately $105K$ and $505K$ images. Since the images from $100K$ and $500K$ *ImageNet* are not relevant to the 55 queries in *Oxford* dataset, they are noisy images that disturb the image retrieval process. Evaluations are still carried out on the 55 *Oxford* queries.

According to our two contributions, the experiment results are presented in two parts: the visual word generation results and the similarity measure in image ranking results. Average precision (AP) is evaluated to measure retrieval performance, which is defined as the area under the precision-recall curve. The AP score is computed for each query and averaged to obtain a mean average precision (mAP). Comparisons on hard- and soft-assignment, with or without bounding box, demonstrate a superior performance to the state-of-the-art presented in [19] [32] [35] [10].

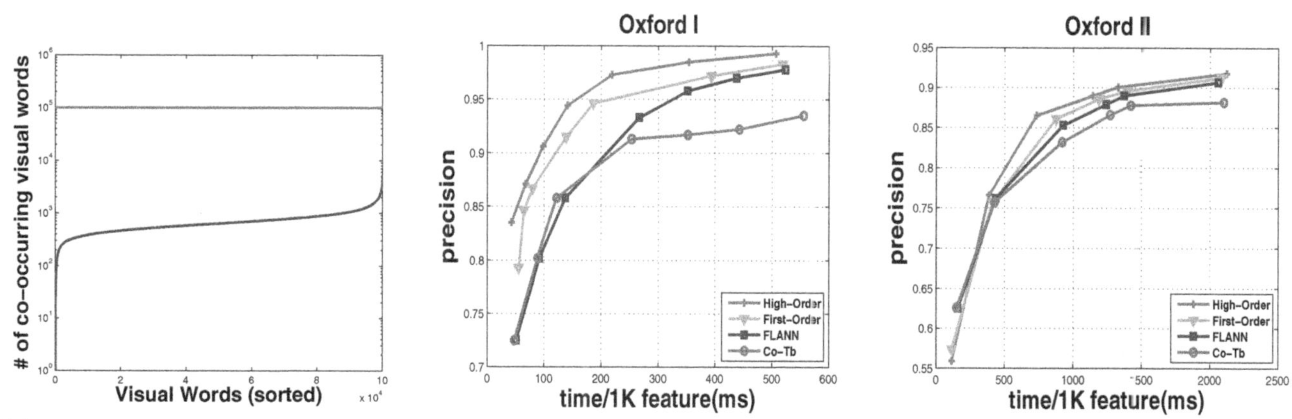

(a) statistics of the co-occurrence table; (b) vocabulary size is $100K$; (c) vocabulary size is $1M$;

Figure 4: (a)The corresponding co-occurring visual word numbers for every visual word, they are sorted in ascending order and shown in the blue line. It can be intuitively compared with the total visual word number (the red line, $100K$); (b) (c) the visual word generation results of *Oxford* dataset.

5.2 Visual Word Generation

The experiments are tested on the *Oxford* dataset. The entire database is split into two parts: one part containing 90% images is used to build the co-occurrence table, while the other 10% is retained for query evaluation. We randomly split the dateset 10 times and report the average visual word generation time per $1K$ feature. The precision of the approximate nearest neighbor search is defined as the proportion of the number of exact nearest neighbors to the total. We set different max-checks and compare the corresponding precision and time. Since the generation results are used to represent the image, we need to guarantee the level of precision. Once the max-check is larger than the number of co-occurring visual words to be searched, the tree index FLANN [16] is adopted to continue the search; those nodes that have been checked in the predictor will not be checked again. In this manner, the high-order predictor will not affect retrieval effectiveness but will significantly improve the overall retrieval efficiency.

Note that the quantization time we provide is tested on our computer using the public FLANN code on the UBC website. For different datasets and computer configurations, the time costs might be different.

***Oxford* dataset.** Vocabularies are clustered by the hierarchical K-means tree [17]. An average of 3,228 local SIFT descriptors are extracted from each image in the *Oxford* dataset. Corresponding average generation time per image on the *Oxford* dataset are shown in Fig. 4. Comparative tests are mainly carried out on the representative fast library approximate nearest neighbor (FLANN) algorithm [16], indicated by the blue line, which is a combination library of two best tree structures of random KD-trees (RKD)[22] and hierarchal K-means tree (HKM)[17]. The magenta line shows the performance of the co-occurrence table (Co-Tb) method [31], which is superior to FLANN when the approximate nearest neighbor precision is comparatively low, although limited to a certain value with an increase in the number of predefined checks. To demonstrate the effectiveness of the high-order predictor, we also give the generation performance of first-order predictor (green line). We select its nearest center for each feature as its co-occurring center and build the predictor on first-order conditional probabilities, which are easily obtained from the visual word co-occurrence table.

From the results in Fig. 4 we conclude that, in general, the high-order predictor (red line) is clearly superior to FLANN (blue line), especially when the max-check is small. This is because the high-order co-occurring information contributes to the generation during this stage, which holds a nearly constant time complexity. By comparing the first-order predictor with high-order predictor, we see that the high-order predictor exhibits a more appealing performance as a result of incorporating more co-occurring information.

The experimental performance on the $100K$ vocabulary is better than that of the $1M$ vocabulary. With increasing in vocabulary size, data bias is introduced to the conditional probability. Moreover, the co-occurrence is more stochastic when vocabulary size is large, which leads to a situation, for any given center, where the number for many of its co-occurring visual words is 1. Their conditional probabilities can therefore hardly be distinguished, nor can they be indexed in the predictor. Notwithstanding, this does not mean that the smaller the vocabulary is, the better the performance will be. A certain degree of sparsity is necessary to predict the visual word in a nearly constant time. On the other hand, with a decrease in vocabulary size, the performance of the tree index is closer to its theoretically optimal time complexity [1].

5.3 Image Ranking

We report the image ranking results with our proposed co-occurrence weighting similarity in *Oxford*, *Paris* and *ImageNet* datasets. Parameter sensitivity is analyzed and we then carefully test our proposed similarity measure in multi-scenarios: with hard-assignment or soft-assignment, with or without query bounding box, The performance in each case proves that our method achieves a considerable improvement over other methods.

Parameter sensitivity. Table 1 shows the retrieval performances with different parameter β settings on the *Oxford* and *Paris* datasets. Here we normalize the co-occurrence matrix Σ by rows ($\sum_j N(w_i, w_j) = 1$). It can be seen from

(a) Oxford (100K);

(b) Paris (500K);

Figure 5: An illustration of retrieval results for three query images on *Oxford* and *Paris* datasets. The two rows of search results correspond respectively hard-assignment and our proposed method. False alarms are marked with red boxes.

Table 1: Comparison of different parameter settings on the *Oxford* and *Paris* datasets. Corresponding numbers are their mAP values.

β	Oxford(100K)	Oxford(1M)	Paris
1.5	0.5827	0.6590	0.7034
1.4	**0.5844**	0.6596	**0.7037**
1.3	0.5830	**0.6598**	0.7035
1.2	0.5803	0.6597	0.7025
baseline	0.514[18]	0.613[18]	0.666[21]

the table that the retrieval performances vary little with changing β. In particular, $\beta \in (1.2, 1.5)$, the ranking results stay stable. We also find that the parameter β stays stable across different vocabulary sizes (as shown in the table, the best parameter does not change greatly in the 100K vocabulary vs. the 1M vocabulary), and across different datasets (*Oxford* vs. *Paris*). Therefore, in real implementation, regardless of vocabulary size and dataset to retrieval, β in our proposed similarity measure can simply set to 1.35 for satisfactory performance. A small adjustment (± 0.15) might be added to refine the final performance, as shown in Fig. 5.

Effect of vocabulary size. We evaluate the effectiveness of our co-occurrence weighting similarity measure (Co-Sim) on the *Oxford* dataset for different hard-assigned (HA) vocabularies, as shown in Fig. 6. The mAP of baselines and the corresponding improvements by Co-Sim are shown by the red line and blue line, respectively.

One visual word is too coarse to distinguish descriptors extracted from semantically different objects. This polysemic phenomenon is particularly prominent when the visual vocabulary is small. Our method, however, is of greater benefit on smaller vocabularies. We attribute this to its ability to overcome the uncertainty of visual word co-occurrence when

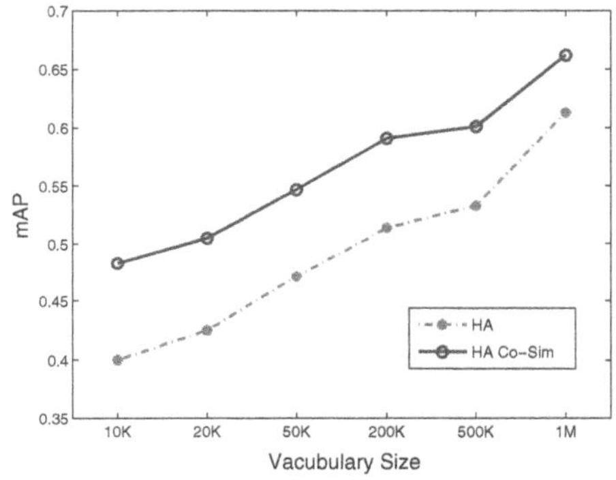

Figure 6: Comparisons of two approaches with different sizes of hard-assigned vocabulary

the smaller vocabularies are adopted. With an increase in vocabulary size, the improvement produced by our scheme declines due to the bias of the matrix.

Hard assignment vs. soft assignment. The proposed Co-Sim is simply a novel similarity measure, which can be embedded into any ranking or re-ranking method. In Table 2 we test its performance with both hard- and soft-assigned vocabularies [19] on the *Oxford* dataset. It can be seen that the increases in mAP on different vocabularies are considerable (14.8% and 13.8% improvements for the hard- and soft-assigned 100K vocabulary, 8.0% and 11.4% improvements for the 1M vocabulary).

Though soft-assignment achieved an apparent improvement by assigning a weighted combination of visual words to each descriptor, our Co-Sim measure on the hard-assigned vocabulary (Hard + Co-Sim) has already clearly outperformed it.

Table 2: **Performance of Co-Sim embedded on hard- and soft-assigned vocabularies with or without bounding box (BB) on the *Oxford* dataset. These results are the corresponding mAP values for $100K$ and $1M$ vocabularies.**

	BB	Co-Sim	Ox ($100K$)	Ox ($1M$)
Hard			0.514	0.613
Hard		+	**0.584**	**0.660**
Hard	+		0.514	0.613
Hard	+	+	**0.577**	**0.648**
Soft			0.529	0.640
Soft		+	**0.602**	**0.719**
Soft	+		0.554	0.673
Soft	+	+	**0.611***	**0.730***

With vs. without query bounding box. In real implementation, visual bounding boxes are often manually labeled for query images to get rid of the nonsensical parts of images. We compare the results of our Co-Sim with and without query bounding box. Table 2 shows that the new scheme without bounding box apparently outperforms the results of hard- and soft-assignment even with bounding box. We suggest that this is because, the proposed similarity, while it does not need a manually labeled bounding box, functions intrinsically as a virtual bounding box, with the contribution of nonsensical words being smoothed down to trivia. Such a virtual bounding effect can work better than a manually labeled bounding box, because the elimination of redundant information is carried out in the feature space rather than the image geometric space.

We also note that if we add a real hard bounding box to our scheme, the performance improves little, and even in some cases it declines. This is due to the penalty effect implemented on all the visual words as mentioned at the end of Section 4. If we add a real bounding box, the general elimination of the redundancy effect might not always outweighs the mistakes we have made on the matched points, although in general mis-matched points are in the majority.

By embedding the Co-Sim into soft-assignment with query bounding box, the final mAP for $1M$ vocabulary reaches 0.73, and for the $100K$ vocabulary it reaches 0.611. Note that even without spatial verification techniques, our method has already outperformed the retrieval results in [30] [11].

Comparison with the state-of-the-art. Detailed comparisons are evaluated on the *Oxford* dataset with $100K$ and $1M$ hard-assigned vocabularies. Representative approaches include the baseline (Philbin07) [18], Soft Assignment (SA) [19], Contextual Model (CM) [32] constructed from the language model [24], Contextual Visual Vocabulary (CVV) [35] and Spatial Co-occurrence Query Expansion (SCQE) [10].

Results are summarized in Table 3. In general, our Co-Sim method is superior than the state-of-the-art. The mAP for the $100K$ vocabulary is 0.584, and achieves the best performance of 0.611 on soft-assignment (Co-Sim (Soft)); for the $1M$ vocabulary, Co-Sim is a little lower than soft-assignment [19] due to the increased bias of the co-occurrence matrix. Nevertheless, because of the scalability of our Co-Sim measure, it can be evaluated on the soft-assigned vocabulary, and the mAP reaches the highest value of 0.73.

Large scale evaluation. To validate the effectiveness of our proposed similarity measure on a large scale dataset, *ImageNet* dataset is introduced to carry out large scale evaluation[1]. Comparisons with Soft Assignment (SA) [19], Contextual Visual Vocabulary (CVV) [35], and SCQE [10] on the *Ox+I1* and *Ox+I2* datasets are given in Table 4. For [35] and [10], they exhibit inferior performances on the large scale dataset as a result of the noise introduced by the *ImageNet*. In contrast, our similarity measure is robust enough to denoise the irrelevant images on a large scale. Overall, we show that it is always beneficial for us to embed Co-Sim in image retrieval.

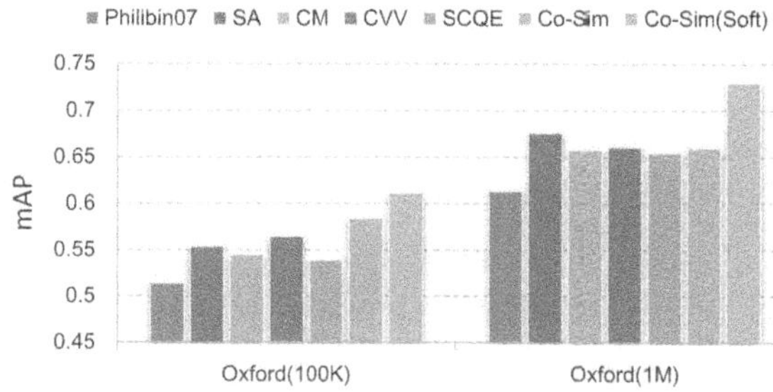

Figure 7: Bar graph of the results in comparison with representative approaches.

Table 3: Detailed experimental mAPs in comparisons with representative approaches.

Vocabulary	*Ox(100K)*	*Ox(1M)*
Philbin(07)[18]	0.514	0.613
SA[19]	0.554	0.676
CM[32]	0.545	0.658
CVV[35]	0.565	0.661
SCQE[10]	0.539	0.655
Co-Sim	0.584	0.660
Co-Sim(Soft)	**0.611**	**0.730**

Table 4: Large scale retrieval results in comparison with state-of-the-art models. Corresponding numbers are their mAP values.

Vocabulary	*Ox+I1(1M)*	*Ox+I2(1M)*
Philbin(07)[18]	0.566	0.499
SA[19]	0.603	0.534
CVV[35]	0.610	0.549
SCQE[10]	0.616	0.574
Co-Sim	**0.630**	**0.615**

5.4 Computational Complexity

The co-occurrence matrix is sparse since the local regions are small and the number of co-occurrence patterns is also small. Thus, 1) the storage overheads for $100K$ and $1M$ vocabularies (it is mainly dependent on the method for extracting the local regions and the sizes of the extracted regions) are roughly identical, around $500MB$ and is ac-

[1]We have also evaluated the cross-dataset performance by obtaining the co-occurrence table from the *ImageNet* dataset and testing it on the *Oxford* dataset. The mAP is mildly improved from 0.613 (baseline) to 0.625, instead of 0.66 on its own co-occurrence table.

ceptable for practical systems, and 2) the average computational time for the *Oxford* dataset ($100K$ vocabulary) is around $245ms$ per query for the improved cosine distance and around $28ms$ for the cosine distance. However, this time increment is compensated for by the time decrement in word prediction (i.e., at the 0.95 precision, the cost of time per image (around $3K$ features) drops from $1100ms$ by FLANN [16] to $500ms$ by the proposed high-order predictor shown in Fig. 4). Notwithstanding, for large scale image retrieval, the calculation of the similarity between image pairs will dominate the retrieval time, i.e., for the *Ox+I2* test with $1M$ vocabulary, the calculation time of the proposed Co-Sim can reach $3.2s$ per query compared to that of $0.98s$ for single *Ox* test.

6. CONCLUSIONS

This paper has proposed a novel image retrieval approach that exploits the spatial co-occurrence of visual words. It improves the retrieval performance on standard datasets by presenting two novel methods: fast word generation via candidate prediction and refined cosine similarity measure via down-weighting. By exploiting the visual word co-occurrence information, a high-order predictor and co-occurrence weighting cosine distance are developed and embedded into our scheme for visual word generation and similarity measure in image ranking, respectively. The word generation is faster than approaches using tree index, and the refined similarity measure is more precise than the original cosine similarity measure, thus the entire image ranking performance is improved. The theoretical analysis presented in this paper also proves the superiority of our method. The two novel techniques can be used independently and can be embedded in most image retrieval algorithms, as shown in our experiments. They can also be applied to other applications, such image classification, object recognition and video surveillance.

7. REFERENCES

[1] S. Arya, D. Mount, N. Netanyahu, R. Silverman, and A. Wu. An optimal algorithm for approximate nearest neighbor searching fixed dimensions. *JACM*, 1998.

[2] R. Baeza-Yates and B. Ribeiro-Neto. *Modern information retrieval.* 1999.

[3] J. Beis and D. Lowe. Shape indexing using approximate nearest-neighbour search in high-dimensional spaces. In *CVPR*, 1997.

[4] J. Deng, W. Dong, R. Socher, L. Li, K. Li, and L. Fei-Fei. Imagenet: A large-scale hierarchical image database. In *CVPR*, 2009.

[5] B. Geng, Y. Li, D. Tao, M. Wang, Z. Zha, and C. Xu. Parallel lasso for large scale video concept detection. *IEEE TMM*, 2012.

[6] B. Geng, D. Tao, and C. Xu. Daml: Domain adaptation metric learning. *IEEE TIP*, 2010.

[7] H. Jegou, M. Douze, and C. Schmid. On the burstiness of visual elements. In *CVPR*, 2009.

[8] H. Jegou, M. Douze, and C. Schmid. Exploiting descriptor distances for precise image search. *Research Report*, 2011.

[9] H. Jegou, C. Schmid, H. Harzallah, and J. Verbeek. Accurate image search using the contextual dissimilarity measure. *TPAMI*, 2010.

[10] Y. Li, B. Geng, Z. Zha, Y. Li, D. Tao, and C. Xu. Query expansion by spatial co-occurrence for image retrieval. In *ACM MM*, 2011.

[11] Y. Li, B. Geng, Z. Zha, D. Tao, L. Yang, and C. Xu. Difficulty guided image retrieval using linear multiview embedding. In *ACM MM*, 2011.

[12] L. Liu and L. Wang. Exploring latent class information for image retrieval using the bag-of-feature model. In *ACM MM*, 2011.

[13] T. Liu, A. Moore, A. Gray, and K. Yang. An investigation of practical approximate nearest neighbor algorithms. *NIPS*, 2004.

[14] D. Lowe. Distinctive image features from scale-invariant keypoints. *IJCV*, 2004.

[15] J. Matas, O. Chum, M. Urban, and T. Pajdla. Robust wide-baseline stereo from maximally stable extremal regions. In *BMVC*, 2004.

[16] M. Muja and D. Lowe. Fast approximate nearest neighbors with automatic algorithm configuration. In *VISAPP*, 2009.

[17] D. Nister and H. Stewenius. Scalable recognition with a vocabulary tree. In *CVPR*, 2006.

[18] J. Philbin, O. Chum, M. Isard, J. Sivic, and A. Zisserman. Object retrieval with large vocabularies and fast spatial matching. In *CVPR*, 2007.

[19] J. Philbin, O. Chum, M. Isard, J. Sivic, and A. Zisserman. Lost in quantization: Improving particular object retrieval in large scale image databases. In *CVPR*, 2008.

[20] G. Qi, C. Aggarwal, Y. Rui, Q. Tian, S. Chang, and T. Huang. Towards cross-category knowledge propagation for learning visual concepts. In *CVPR*, 2011.

[21] D. Qin, S. Gammeter, L. Bossard, T. Quack, and L. van Gool. Hello neighbor: accurate object retrieval with k-reciprocal nearest neighbors. In *CVPR*, 2011.

[22] C. Silpa-Anan and R. Hartley. Optimised kd-trees for fast image descriptor matching. In *CVPR*, 2008.

[23] J. Sivic and A. Zisserman. Video google: A text retrieval approach to object matching in videos. In *CVPR*, 2003.

[24] F. Song and W. Croft. A general language model for information retrieval. In *ACM CIKM*.

[25] W. Tang, R. Cai, Z. Li, and L. Zhang. Contextual synonym dictionary for visual object retrieval. In *ACM MM*, 2011.

[26] Q. Tian, S. Zhang, W. Zhou, R. Ji, B. Ni, and N. Sebe. Building descriptive and discriminative visual codebook for large-scale image applications. *Multimedia Tools and Applications*, 2011.

[27] X. Tian, D. Tao, and Y. Rui. Sparse transfer learning for interactive video search reranking. *ACM TMCCA*, 2011.

[28] J. Uhlmann. Satisfying general proximity/similarity queries with metric trees. *IPL*, 1991.

[29] X. Wang, M. Yang, T. Cour, S. Zhu, K. Yu, and T. Han. Contextual weighting for vocabulary tree based image retrieval. In *ICCV*, 2011.

[30] Z. Wu, Q. Ke, M. Isard, and J. Sun. Bundling features for large scale partial-duplicate web image search. In *CVPR*, 2009.

[31] R. Xu, M. Shi, B. Geng, and C. Xu. Fast visual word assignment via spatial neighborhood boosting. In *ICME*, 2011.

[32] L. Yang, B. Geng, A. Hanjalic, and X. Hua. Contextual image retrieval model. In *ACM CIVR*, 2010.

[33] J. Yuan, Y. Wu, and M. Yang. Discovery of collocation patterns: from visual words to visual phrases. In *CVPR*, 2007.

[34] J. Yuan, Z. Zha, Y. Zheng, M. Wang, X. Zhou, and T. Chua. Learning concept bundles for video search with complex queries. In *ACM MM*, 2011.

[35] S. Zhang, Q. Huang, G. Hua, S. Jiang, W. Gao, and Q. Tian. Building contextual visual vocabulary for large-scale image applications. In *ACM MM*, 2010.

[36] S. Zhang, Q. Tian, G. Hua, Q. Huang, and S. Li. Descriptive visual words and visual phrases for image applications. In *ACM MM*, 2009.

[37] Y. Zhang, Z. Jia, and T. Chen. Image retrieval with geometry-preserving visual phrases. In *CVPR*, 2011.

Attribute Feedback

Hanwang Zhang†, Zheng-Jun Zha†, Shuicheng Yan§, Jingwen Bian† and Tat-Seng Chua†
† School of Computing, National University of Singapore
§ Dept. of Electrical and Computer Engineering, National University of Singapore
†{hanwang, zhazj, bian_jingwen, chuats}@comp.nus.edu.sg
§eleyans@nus.edu.sg

ABSTRACT

This work presents a new interactive Content Based Image Retrieval (CBIR) scheme, termed Attribute Feedback (AF). Unlike traditional relevance feedback purely founded on low-level visual features, the Attribute Feedback system shapes users' information needs more precisely and quickly by collecting feedbacks on intermediate level semantic attributes. At each interactive iteration, AF first determines the most informative binary attributes for feedbacks, preferring the attributes that frequently (rarely) appear in current search results but are unlikely (likely) to be users' interest. The binary attribute feedbacks are then augmented by a new type of attributes, "affinity attributes", each of which is off-line learnt to describe the distance between user's envisioned image(s) and a retrieved image with respect to the corresponding affinity attribute. Based on the feedbacks on binary and affinity attributes, the images in corpus are further re-ranked towards better fitting the users' information needs. Extensive experiments on two real-world image datasets well demonstrate the superiority of the proposed scheme over other state-of-the-art relevance feedback based CBIR solutions.

Categories and Subject Descriptors

H.3.3 [**Information Search and Retrieval**]: Retrieval Model

General Terms

Algorithms, Experimentation, Performance

Keywords

Image Search, Attribute Feedback, Relevance Feedback

1. INTRODUCTION

With the growing volume of on-line images as well as the increasing requirements in many multimedia applications, Content Based Image Retrieval (CBIR) has attracted significant attention in both academia and industry [19, 26, 33]. Most CBIR systems allow users to specify their information needs by means of uploading an example image as query, called Query by Example (QBE). CBIR systems retrieve images based on their visual similarities to the query example. A major challenge in CBIR is the well-known "*semantic gap*" [9] between the low-level visual features and high-level semantic meanings that interpret users' search intent.

To address this problem, relevance feedback has been introduced into CBIR [35]. Relevance feedback involves users in the search loop. Typically, users are asked to label the top images returned by the search model as "relevant" or "irrelevant". The feedbacks are then used to refine the search model. Through iterative feedback and model refinement, relevance feedback attempts to capture users' information needs and improve search results gradually. Although relevance feedback has shown encouraging potential in CBIR, its performance is usually unsatisfactory due to the following problems. First, relevance feedback relies on the search system to infer users' search intent from their "relevant" and/or "irrelevant" feedbacks, essentially based on the low-level visual features of the relevant or irrelevant images. It suffers from the "semantic gap" between users' intent and low-level visual cues and thus it is usually ineffective in narrowing down the search to target [24]. Second, the retrieval results are usually unsatisfactory, where the top results may contain rare or even no relevant samples. With no/rare relevant samples, most relevance feedback approaches are not able to perform well or even no longer applicable [32, 21].

In this paper, we move beyond the conventional relevance feedback (RF), and propose a novel interactive search scheme, named Attribute Feedback (AF), for content based image retrieval. Attribute refers to the **visual properties** (e.g., "round" as shape, "metallic" as texture), **components** (e.g., "has wheel", "has leg") and **functionalities** (e.g., "can fly", "man-made") of objects. As illustrated in Figure 1, AF allows users to deliver search intent by providing feedbacks on binary attributes to state which attributes are in their search intent and which are not. For example, when users are searching for "dog" images, they may give positive feedbacks on attributes "snout" and "leg" as well as negative feedbacks on "cloth" and "wheel". Here, attributes act as the bridge connecting user intent and visual features. The binary feedbacks compose a clear semantic description of users' search intent, such as "*has snout and leg, has no wheel and cloth*". However, the binary feedbacks on some attributes, which are shared by many categories, are not discriminative enough. For example, the feedback "*has snout*" is not discriminative enough to distinguish users' target (e.g., "dog") from other animals, since "snout" is shared by many animal categories (e.g., "dog" and "crocodile"). Hence, we propose a new type of attributes, termed Affinity Attribute. *Affinity attributes refer to attributes that are shared by many categories and have large variance in appearances.* For each affinity attribute of interest, AF allows users to give affinity judgments on the images containing this attribute to indicate which images are similar

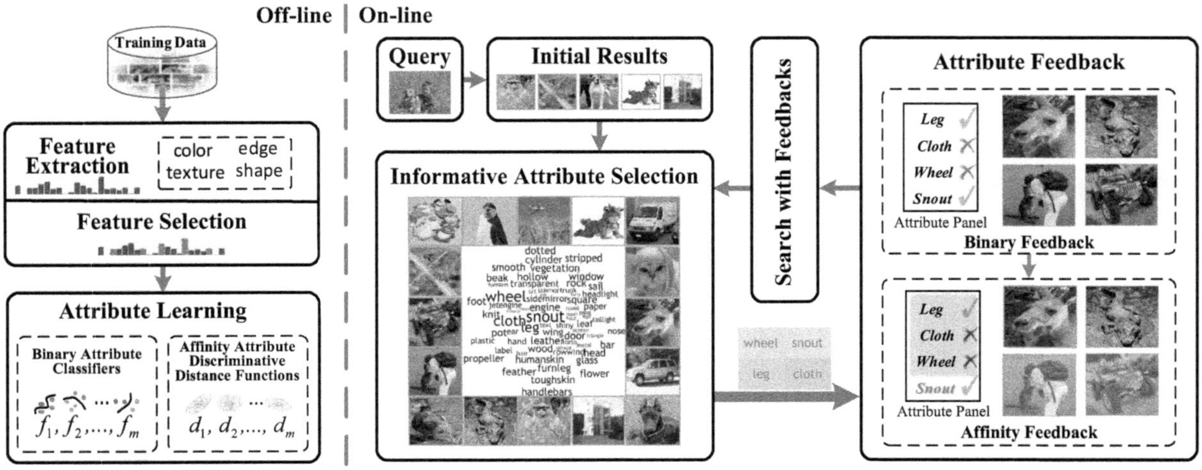

Figure 1: The flowchart of the proposed Attribute Feedback (AF) framework. The user's intent is "*find me dogs*" though the query image at hand is "*a boy and a dog*". ✓ and × denote "yes/no" feedbacks on the binary attributes. Users may further give affinity feedbacks for a binary attribute (e.g., "snout"). By that time, images without such binary attribute will be shadowed. $\sim$ and $\nsim$ denote the "similar/dissimiar" feedbacks on affinity attributes with the context of the referenced attributes (e.g., "snout"). By collecting user's binary and affinity attribute feedbacks iteratively, AF shapes user's intent precisely and quickly, leading to search results that well fit user's intent.

or dissimilar to their envisioned target images with respect to this attribute. As shown in Figure 1, for the attribute "snout", user can make affinity feedbacks to state that the "snout" in their envisioned images is similar to that in the retrieved "alpaca" image but dissimilar to that in the "crocodile" image. Such affinity feedbacks further reveal users' search intent. Different from traditional relevance feedback that simply states which images are relevant or irrelevant, AF helps users to specify their search intent more precisely through the binary and affinity attribute judgements. Therefore, AF permits the search system to quickly narrow down the search to users' information needs with less interaction efforts. Moreover, even when the top search results contain no relevant sample, some of the results might be partially similar to users' envisioned images on certain attribute(s). For example, the retrieved "alpaca" image is irrelevant to users' target, i.e., "dog", but is similar to "alpaca" on the attribute "snout". By accumulating users' feedbacks on such attribute(s), AF can push the search closer to users' target gradually. Hence, AF is expected to be able to overcome the no/rare relevant sample problem.

The flowchart of the proposed Attribute Feedback framework is illustrated in Figure 1. In the off-line part, we learn a set of binary classifiers, each of which predicts the presence of an attribute in an image. For each affinity attribute, we learn a discriminative distance function, which computes the distance between two images with respect to the corresponding affinity attribute. At each on-line feedback iteration, a set of informative attributes are selected and presented for feedbacks. In particular, the informative attributes refers to the attributes on which users' feedbacks can drastically enhance the subsequent search results. An attribute is considered as informative if it frequently (rarely) appears in current search results but is unlikely (likely) to be the users' interests. We propose a statistical attribute selection approach to select the most informative attributes. The approach simultaneously exploits both the search results at the current and previous iterations (see Section 4.1). In particular, we maintain a set of probabilistic models, each of which infers the candidacy of an attribute being selected. At the beginning of every feedback iteration, the posterior probabilities of these models are up-to-date based on the current search results and previous informative posteriors. The attributes with high posterior probabilities are then selected as informative attributes. After obtaining users' binary and affinity attribute feedbacks, a search model is then executed to update the search results.

To the best of our knowledge, this work presents the first attempt towards exploring attribute feedbacks for content based image retrieval. The main contributions of this paper are summarized as follows:

- We propose a novel interactive search scheme named Attribute Feedback for content based image retrieval. AF enables the search system to quickly narrow down the search to users' target based on their binary and affinity feedbacks. Moreover, AF performs well in case of the no/rare relevant sample problem that often exists in real-world CBIR.
- We develop an informative attribute selection approach, which simultaneously takes into account the current and previous search results.
- We define a new type of attribute, named affinity attribute. A discriminative distance function is learnt for each attribute to make effective use of users' affinity feedbacks.

The rest of this paper is organized as follows. Section 2 reviews the related works. Section 3 describes the attribute learning technologies, including classifier learning for binary attributes and discriminative distance function learning for affinity attributes. Section 3 elaborates the proposed AF framework, including informative attribute selection and image search with attribute feedbacks. Experimental results and analysis are given in Section 4, followed by the conclusions and future works in Section 5.

2. RELATED WORK

2.1 Attributes

Attributes are human-nameable *intermediate* semantic descriptors, refer to the visual properties (e.g., "round" as shape, "metallic" as texture), components (e.g., "has wheel", "has leg") and functionalities (e.g., "can fly", "man-made") of objects [6, 7, 13, 12]. As opposed to low-level visual features, e.g., the bag of visual words representation, an attribute has a semantic meaning and it is relatively easier than full objects (e.g., "car", "dog") to recognize for a machine [6, 7]. A popular attribute learning method is to train a binary classifier (e.g., SVM) for each attribute by training samples with and without such attribute. Then, the presence (confidence) of the attribute in an image can be predicted by the binary (probabilistic) output of the classifier. Attributes learned by such method are well-known as binary attributes [6, 13, 12]. Binary attributes form a general semantic base for various object categories [12, 27] and enable knowledge transfer across object categories [5], or even from known-categories to unknown-categories [13]. However, when objects share almost the same attribute vocabulary, using merely binary attributes are not sufficient to discriminate and describe the objects precisely.

There are several works on extending the discriminative and descriptive ability of attributes [6, 12, 16]. As a pioneering work, Farhadi et.al [6] exhaustively trained thousands of classifiers by random splitting the training data and choosing some of them which were good at distinguishing objects (e.g., attributes that "cat" and "dog" have but "sheep" and "horse" do not) as *discriminative* attributes. Kumar et al. [12] defined a new set of binary attributes called *similes* for face verifications. Similes are exclusive classifiers specialized for one category, e.g., "the Angelina Jolie's mouth". However, such category-dependent attributes are contrary to the spirit of attributes, i.e., knowledge that is generalizable and transferrable. Recently, Parikh and Grauman [16] proposed a new idea in describing and naming attributes called *relative* attributes, which describe the strength of the attribute presence in a relative way, e.g., "while A and B are both *shiny*, A is *shinier* than B". Instead of trained by binary classifiers, relative attributes are learned by ranking functions (i.e., the ranking SVM). The output of a ranking function indicates the relative presence of the corresponding attribute.

Attributes are also revealing the power in image search [12, 4, 18, 27]. The works in [12, 4, 27] focused on composing semantic feature (index) vectors by the confidence scores of binary attribute classifiers. Images are then retrieved by such features (index) instead of low-level features (index). In a different approach, Siddiquie et al. [18] proposed a structural SVM based approach for image search using multi-attribute text-based queries specified by users. Their approach explicitly models the correlations of attributes that are or not parts of the query. The output of the structural SVM is then considered as the ranking results of retrieved images.

2.2 Relevance Feedback

Relevance Feedback (RF) is the key technique to narrow down the *semantic gap* in CBIR by exploiting user interactions [35, 3]. Users are encouraged to label the retrieved images as being either "relevant" or "irrelevant". Users' feedbacks are then exploited by a relevance feedback algorithm to refine the search model. Through iterative feedbacks and refinement, relevance feedback attempts to capture users' search intent and improve the search results gradually. A wealth of methods has been proposed to learn a relevance feedback model based on users' feedbacks [17, 34, 8, 20, 10, 23]. At each feedback iteration, the model is updated using the labeled images as training samples. For example, Query Point Movement (QPM) [17] method gradually modifies the low-level visual features of the query image to make them more similar to "relevant" feedbacks and more dissimilar to "irrelevant" ones. Hence, the query feature is moving towards the search region of users' intent. Guo et al. [8] proposed to use SVM as the RF model. In each feedback loop, a SVM classifier is trained by the labeled samples and images in the database are further ranked according to the response from the classifiers. Zhou and Huang [34] developed Biased Discriminant Analysis (BDA) to learn a low-dimensional subspace from feedbacks in each loop. Then, all the images in the database are embedded into the subspace and ranked according to their Euclidean distance to the mean feature vector of the "relevant" images. Different from the above RF methods that present top retrieved images for user labeling, SVMactive [20] method actively selects images with high uncertainty for labeling in each feedback iterations. Please refer to [35, 3, 15] for more comprehensive reviews on RF. As aforementioned, the traditional relevance feedback suffers from the gap between users' search intent and low-level visual features and thus it is usually ineffective in narrowing down the search to users' target.

Recently, Kovashka et al. [11] proposed to collect user feedbacks like *"show me shoes more formal than these and shinier than those"* in terms of relative attributes [16]. A ranking SVM score function learned in relative attribute training can be used to whittle away images not meeting users' descriptions. Compared to our work, their approach aims to improve text-based image search with query-by-word by collecting text feedbacks while our work is targeting at CBIR with query-by-example. Moreover, binary and affinity attribute feedbacks proposed in this paper offer more general attribute descriptions of users' intent. For example, relative attributes are capable of describing adjectives like "shiny" ("shinier") but unable to describe nouns like "eye". However, we can always use binary and affinity attributes to describe precisely what we do and do not want (e.g., "A should have *ear* but should not have *feather*") and what are similar or not (e.g., "A is *shiny* like B" or "A's *eye* is dissimilar to B's").

3. ATTRIBUTE LEARNING

We refer attributes to the visual properties (e.g., "round" as shape, "metallic" as texture), components (e.g., "has wheel", "has leg") and functionalities (e.g., "can fly", "man-made") of objects [6, 13, 12]. In this work, we exploit the visual property and component attributes. The presence of the attributes can be predicted by the output of binary classifiers, e.g., a binary classifier for "wheel" can be used to predict whether an object has "wheel". Thus, we call such attributes the *binary attributes*. Binary attributes are good at in describing objects, especially unseen ones. For example, even we have no training samples of "cat" (unseen category), we can still describe "cat" as an animal that has "ear", "eye" and "furry" by using those binary attribute classifiers trained by seen categories. Although binary attributes offer users a way to describe their desired objects across categories, some attributes are not discriminative enough in distinguishing users' target with other objects. For example "ear" is not discriminative enough to distinguish different animals because it is shared by many animals.

To this end, we introduce a new kind of attributes called *affinity attributes*, which refer to the attributes that are shared by many categories and have large variance in appearances. We learn a distance function for each affinity attribute in order to quantitatively describe how close the affinity of two images for the referenced affinity attribute. As illustrated in Figure 2, given three images of, say, two "sheep" and one "monkey". The "sheep" images are more similar than the "monkey" and "sheep" images with respect to the affinity attribute "ear". The distance function will presumably judge the "ear" of two "sheep" closer while that of the "sheep" and the "monkey" farther. Therefore, affinity attributes enable further comparisons between images who share common binary attributes and thus endow more discriminative information than binary attributes. Besides, the introduction of affinity attributes remains the size of attribute vocabulary unchanged.

Figure 2: Motivation of Affinity Attributes. The two *sheep* images are similar on the affinity attribute "ear", while the *monkey* image is dissimilar to them on "ear".

Next, we will describe the details in learning binary and affinity attributes.

3.1 Binary Attribute Learning

Suppose we have an image collection $\mathcal{X} = \{x_1, x_2, ..., x_N\}$, where $x_i \in \mathbb{R}^n$ is a n-dimensional feature representation of image i. Moreover, we have defined a vocabulary of m binary attributes $\mathcal{A} = \{a_1, a_2, ..., a_m\}$, where $a_i \in \{0, 1\}$ denotes the presence of the i-th attribute. The binary classifier of attribute a_i predicts the presence of this attribute in an image x_j, with the probability $P(a_i = 1|x_j)$.

Given a training set of images which are labeled with attributes, one can easily train the binary classifiers such as SVM in [13]. However, due to the large visual variance of some attributes (e.g., the "wing" of a plane looks much differently from the "wing" of a bird), standard training methods cannot be directly applied because they may be trained by irrelevant feature dimensions. For example, the "wing" classifier may be unfortunately trained based on the feature dimensions related to "sky". Therefore, we need to select feature dimensions that are mostly informative and effective for the target attribute.

In this paper, we apply the feature selection method as described in [6]. The selected feature dimensions $\phi_a(x_i)$ of attribute a for image x_i are the union of feature dimensions that are most discriminative for sub-categories. For example, in order to train the "wing" classifier, we first collect "bird" with and without "wing" as training samples, and train a preliminary *linear* classifier (e.g., $\langle w_{bird}, x_i \rangle$), called "bird wing". Then, we may train another preliminary classifier called "plane wing" and so on. By doing so, we finally obtain a set of parameters (e.g., w_{bird}, w_{plane}) of such preliminary classifiers. Particularly, due to the success of ℓ_1-norm in signal representation [28] and image annotation [30, 31], we use the ℓ_1-norm regression model as the preliminary classifiers to learn sparse parameters. The features are then selected by pooling the union of indices of the sparse non-zeros entries in those parameters. Formally, for attribute a, we denote I_a as the union of the non-zero parameter indices and then the selected feature dimensions of attribute a for x_i is $\phi_a(x_i) = x_j(I_{a_i})$, where $x(I_a)$ returns the selected dimensions of x_i according to I_a. Once we have selected the feature dimensions, we can apply the standard training methods to learn an overall binary attribute classifier (e.g., SVM) of a, i.e., $P(a = 1|\phi_a(x_i))$. For the sake of simplicity, from now on and throughout this paper, we always denote $x_i \leftarrow \phi_a(x_i)$ when the context is clear.

3.2 Affinity Attribute Learning

For each affinity attribute a, we learn a distance function which computes the affinity between two images with respect to the referenced attribute. In particular, we define the distance function as a Mahalanobis distance metric as:

$$d_a(x_i, x_j) = \sqrt{(x_i - x_j)^T \mathbf{M}_a (x_i - x_j)}, \tag{1}$$

where the $\mathbf{M}_a$ is a semi-definite symmetric matrix, i.e., $\mathbf{M}_a \succeq \mathbf{0}$. Denote $x_i \sim_a x_j$ (or $x_i \nsim_a x_j$) as "image x_i is similar (or dissimilar) to image x_j with respect to attribute a". In order to characterize the affinity of two images with respect to attribute a, the distance metric $d_a(\cdot)$ should measure the distance of x_i and x_j closer than the distance of x_k and x_j if $x_i \sim_a x_j$ and $x_k \nsim_a x_j$, i.e.,

$$\begin{aligned} & d_a(x_j, x_k) - d_a(x_i, x_j) \geq c, \\ & s.t.\ x_i \sim_a x_j,\ x_k \nsim_a x_j, \end{aligned} \tag{2}$$

where $c > 0$ is a margin constant.

Given the training sample pairs $\tilde{\mathcal{S}}_a = \{(x_i, x_j)|x_i \sim_a x_j\}$ as the similar set and $\tilde{\mathcal{D}}_a = \{(x_j, x_k)|x_j \nsim_a x_k\}$ as the dissimilar set, we want to learn $\mathbf{M}_a$ in a discriminative way by favoring similar images to be closer while penalizing the distance of dissimilar ones that are not sufficiently farther than the distance of similar ones. Therefore, we have the following semi-definite programming (SDP) problem:

$$\begin{aligned} \min_{\mathbf{M}_a} & \sum_{i,j} d_a(x_i, x_j) + \lambda \sum_{i,j,k} \xi_{ijk}, \\ s.t.\ & d_a(x_j, x_k) - d_a(x_i, x_j) \geq 1 - \xi_{ijk}, \\ & \xi_{ijk} \geq 0,\ \mathbf{M} \succeq \mathbf{0}, \\ & (x_i, x_j) \in \tilde{\mathcal{S}}_a,\ (x_j, x_k) \in \tilde{\mathcal{D}}_a. \end{aligned} \tag{3}$$

where $\lambda > 0$ is a trade-off parameter and ξ_{ijk} is the slack variable. In order to avoid over-fitting and to shorten the training time, we first reduce the dimensions of the attribute feature vectors to d (e.g., $d = 200$) using PCA and then learn the distance matrix of size $d \times d$. Since it is expensive to label the attribute-level training pairs, in our implementation, $\tilde{\mathcal{S}}_a$ and $\tilde{\mathcal{D}}_a$ can be easily collected by randomly sampling image pairs with positive attribute labels from the same and distinct categories.

4. ATTRIBUTE FEEDBACK

In this section, our goal is to assist the user to find more target images via interactive feedbacks on attributes. With users in the loop, the system will learn how to describe the target images precisely using both binary and affinity attributes. The attribute descriptions will then serve as semantic cues for the system to find relevant results.

Without loss of generality, suppose we are at the t-th feedback iteration. The system displays the image set $\mathcal{R}_t$ (e.g., top 100 results) to the user and a binary attribute set $\mathcal{C}_t$ on the attribute panel (as illustrated in Figure 1). Then, through $\mathcal{C}_t$, the user will response to the system which attributes are positive (expected to appear) or negative (expected to disappear) in $\mathcal{R}_t$. Furthermore, when a positive binary attribute coincides with the name of an affinity attribute, the user may also give affinity feedbacks on images by telling the system whether an image in $\mathcal{R}_t$ is similar or dissimilar to her target image with respect to the referenced attribute.

Meanwhile, from the system's perspective, it maintains the sets $\mathcal{A}_t^+$ and $\mathcal{A}_t^-$ that record all the positive and negative binary attribute feedbacks accumulated from the $(t-1)$-th iteration, respectively. For the affinity attribute feedbacks, the system records $\mathcal{S}_t^l = \{x_i|x_i \sim_{a_l} x^*\}$ that accumulates the images similar to the user's envisioned image x^* with respect to the affinity attribute a_l. Correspondingly, the set $\mathcal{D}_t^l = \{x_i|x_i \nsim_{a_l} x^*\}$ accumulates the dissimilar images. Let the sets $\{\mathcal{S}_t^l\}_{l=1}^m$ and $\{\mathcal{D}_t^l\}_{l=1}^m$ be the feedbacks of similar and dissimilar images collected through all the attributes. We denote $\mathcal{T}_t = \{\mathcal{A}_t^+, \mathcal{A}_t^-, \{\mathcal{S}_t^l\}, \{\mathcal{D}_t^l\}\}$ as the attribute descriptions of the target image in terms of attribute feedbacks collected thus far. The system will then exploit such descriptions $\mathcal{T}_t$ to refine the search results.

The attribute feedback system has two key components as follows:

- *Informative Attribute Selection.* This component focuses on selecting attributes from the attribute vocabulary to form $\mathcal{C}_t$. The selected attributes should be informative for users to give feedbacks.

- *Search with Feedbacks.* Given the gathered user's attribute feedbacks $\mathcal{T}_t$, this component is targeted at retrieving images to form $\mathcal{R}_{t+1}$.

Next, we introduce the use of a Bayesian framework to select the most informative attributes for the first component. For the second one, we propose a discriminative model as the score function to search images with feedbacks.

4.1 Informative Attribute Selection

A straightforward approach is to let $\mathcal{C}_t = \mathcal{A}$, i.e., forcing the user to label all the attributes. However, it is unreasonable for users to complete such tedious task. Another method is to use only the most "apparent" attributes in the query image. However, using only the attributes extracted from one query cannot comprehensively describe the user's information needs. For example, although the attribute "wheel" is missing from a query image "car", the "wheel" is still highly informative for a user to find a "car".

We argue that an attribute is informative if it frequently (rarely) appears in search results $\mathcal{R}_t$ but is unlikely (likely) to be the users' interests. Such cases suggest there is a big difference between retrieved results at present and the user's search intent. Therefore, if an attribute frequently (rarely) appears in the results, a negative (positive) feedback on this attribute will drastically improve the subsequent results. We should also note that some trivially missing attributes should not be counted as informative. For example, it is absurd to let the user give feedback on the attribute "engine" when she is looking for "monkey" since "engine" hardly appears in "monkey" albeit it rarely appears in retrieved results.

We propose a Bayesian framework based on the currently and previously retrieved results gathered by $\mathcal{Y}_t = \{\mathcal{R}_s\}_{s=1}^t$. Suppose a binary random variable c_i is associated to each attribute $a_i \in \mathcal{A}$: $c_i = 1$ if $a_i \in \mathcal{C}_t$ and $c_i = 0$ otherwise. Our framework maintains m parallel Bayesian systems $p_t(c_i) = P(c_i = 1|\mathcal{Y}_t)$ which is the posterior probability of the informativeness of a_i based on $\mathcal{Y}_t$. Ordered by such probabilities in $p_t(c_i)$, the system will select up to K attributes to form $\mathcal{C}_t$.

Applying the Bayes' rule, we obtain the updating rule for model $p_t(c_i)$ as:

$$p_t(c_i) = \frac{P(\mathcal{R}_t|c_i = 1)p_{t-1}(c_i)}{P(\mathcal{R}_t|c_i=1)p_{t-1}(c_i) + P(\mathcal{R}_t|c_i=0)(1-p_{t-1}(c_i))}. \quad (4)$$

For initialization, given the initial query image x_q, we set $p_0(c_i)$ to the output of classifier $P(a_i|x_q)$ and $\mathcal{R}_1$ be the initial retrieved results by any search model (e.g., low-level feature matching).

The above derivation makes use of the basic statistical assumption:

$$P(\mathcal{R}_t|c_i, \mathcal{Y}_{t-1}) = P(\mathcal{R}_t|c_i), \quad (5)$$

which means that given c_i, the current search results $\mathcal{R}_t$ is independent of the history $\mathcal{Y}_{t-1}$. In other word, we say that c_i is a sufficient statistic for $\mathcal{Y}_{t-1}$ since $\mathcal{Y}_{t-1}$ only affects the distribution of $\mathcal{R}_t$ through c_i. This assumption stems from the intuition that the inference of c_i is evident from $\mathcal{Y}_t$ and thus it is evident from $\mathcal{Y}_{t-1}$.

Now we show how to compute $P(\mathcal{R}_t|c_i)$. We assume the images in $\mathcal{R}_t$ contain users' intent and use conditional entropy of a_i given the images in $\mathcal{R}_t$ to delineate frequency (or rarity) of a_i. Formally, we define the probabilities $P(\mathcal{R}_t|c_i = 1)$ and $P(\mathcal{R}_t|c_i = 0)$ of the form:

$$P(\mathcal{R}_t|c_i = 1) = \frac{\psi^-(H(a_i|\mathcal{R}_t))P(a_i = 1|\mathcal{R}_t)}{\sum_i \psi^-(H(a_i|\mathcal{R}_t))P(a_i = 1|\mathcal{R}_t)}, \quad (6a)$$

$$P(\mathcal{R}_t|c_i = 0) = \frac{\psi^+(H(a_i|\mathcal{R}_t))P(a_i = 0|\mathcal{R}_t)}{\sum_i \psi^+(H(a_i|\mathcal{R}_t))P(a_i = 0|\mathcal{R}_t)}, \quad (6b)$$

where $\psi^-(\cdot)$ and $\psi^+(\cdot)$ are monotonically decreasing and increasing functions, which will be defined later (in Eq. (8)). Here, $P(a_i|\mathcal{R}_t)$ is used as a regularization term to prevent trivial results that attributes are unlikely to appear in the $\mathcal{R}_t$ albeit the entropy of them is also very large. The probability $P(a_i = 1|\mathcal{R}_t) = 1 - P(a_i = 0|\mathcal{R}_t)$ is the average of the probabilistic outputs of the classifier of a_i, i.e., $P(a_i = 1|\mathcal{R}_t) = \sum_{x_j \in \mathcal{R}_t} P(a_i = 1|x_j)/|\mathcal{R}_t|$.

We compute the conditional entropy $H(a_i|\mathcal{R}_t)$ as:

$$\begin{aligned} H(a_i|\mathcal{R}_t) &= -\sum_{x_j \in \mathcal{R}_t} P(x_j)H(a_i|x_j) \\ &= -\frac{1}{|\mathcal{R}_t|}\sum_{x_j \in \mathcal{R}_t}\sum_{b\in\{0,1\}} P(a_i = b|x_j)\log P(a_i = b|x_j), \end{aligned} \quad (7)$$

where we assume the prior $P(x_j) = 1/|\mathcal{R}_t|$.

Note the maximum and minimum of $H(a_i|\mathcal{R}_t)$ is 1 and 0, respectively. Therefore, typical definitions of $\psi^-(\cdot)$ and $\psi^+(\cdot)$ can be:

$$\psi^-(H(a_i|\mathcal{R}_t)) = 1 - H(a_i|\mathcal{R}_t),\ \psi^+(H(a_i|\mathcal{R}_t)) = H(a_i|\mathcal{R}_t). \quad (8)$$

The intuition of these definitions is consistent with our argument on attribute informativeness. Frequently (rarely) appeared attributes (small $H(a_i|\mathcal{R}_t)$) and low users' interests (small normalization value in Eq. (6a)) result in large $P(\mathcal{R}_t|c_i = 1)$ and small $P(\mathcal{R}_t|c_i = 0)$, i.e., large informativeness $p(c_i)$.

The time complexity of updating all the Bayesian systems is $\mathcal{O}(m)$, where m is the size of the attribute vocabulary. Hence, the informative attribute selection can be applied in real-time systems. Next, we will introduce how to retrieve images based on the user's attribute feedbacks.

4.2 Search with Feedbacks

The search model aims to score an image x in the image collection by its relevance to the user's intent in terms of the attribute feedbacks, $\mathcal{T}_t = \{\mathcal{A}_t^+, \mathcal{A}_t^-, \{\mathcal{S}_t^i\}, \{\mathcal{D}_t^i\}\}$. The score function is a discriminative model of $\mathcal{T}_t$ given x:

$$P(\mathcal{T}_t|x) \propto P(\mathcal{B}_t|x)\Psi^+(\{\mathcal{S}_t^i\}, x)\Psi^-(\{\mathcal{D}_t^i\}, x), \quad (9)$$

where $\mathcal{B}_t = \{a_i | a_i \in \mathcal{A}_t^+ \cup \mathcal{A}_t^-,\ s.t.\ \mathcal{S}_t^i = \phi,\ \mathcal{D}_t^i = \phi\}$ is the set of attributes without any affinity feedbacks (i.e., pure binary feedbacks).

The first term $P(\mathcal{B}_t|x)$ in Eq. (9) measures the relevance of image x to the user's target image with respect to binary feedbacks. By assuming that the attributes in $\mathcal{B}_t$ to be conditionally independent of x, we have:

$$P(\mathcal{B}_t|x) = \prod_{a_i \in \mathcal{B}_t \cap \mathcal{A}_t^+} P(a_i = 1|x) \prod_{a_i \in \mathcal{B}_t \cap \mathcal{A}_t^-} P(a_i = 0|x), \tag{10}$$

The second and third terms in Eq. (9) are positive and negative potential functions that jointly model the relevance of image x with respect to the affinity attribute feedbacks. If $x_j \in \mathcal{S}_t^i$ (or $x_j \in \mathcal{D}_t^i$), the presence of a_i in x, i.e., $P(a_i = 1|x)$, should be enhanced if the affinity of x_j and x is close (or far) with respect to a_i. Thus, we define the two potential functions as:

$$\begin{cases} \Psi^+(\{\mathcal{S}_t^i\}, x) = \prod_i P(a_i = 1|x)^{1-\psi(\mathcal{S}_t^i, x)}, \\ \Psi^-(\{\mathcal{D}_t^i\}, x) = \prod_i P(a_i = 1|x)^{\psi(\mathcal{D}_t^i, x)}, \end{cases} \tag{11}$$

where $\psi(\mathcal{S}_t^i, x)$ is defined as:

$$\psi(\mathcal{S}_t^i, x) = exp\left(-\frac{\sum_{x_j \in \mathcal{S}_t^i} d_{a_i}(x, x_j)}{2\sigma^2}\right). \tag{12}$$

Here, σ is the Gaussian normalization parameter, $d_{a_i}(x, x_j)$ is the distance function of affinity attribute a_i in Eq. (1) and $\psi(\mathcal{D}_t^i, x)$ can be defined similarly. We should force $d_{a_i}(x, x_j) = 0$ if a_i is absent in x. The absence of a_i can be determined if $P(a_i = 1|x)$ is smaller than $\sum_j P(a_i = 1|x_j)/(|\mathcal{S}_t^i| + |\mathcal{D}_t^i|)$, where $x_j \in \mathcal{S}_t^i \cup \mathcal{D}_t^i$. Note that this threshold is reasonable because users will always give affinity feedbacks on images (gathered by $\mathcal{S}_t^i \cup \mathcal{D}_t^i$) where the reference attribute a_i is present.

The search complexity with attribute feedbacks is $\mathcal{O}(Nm)$, which is linear with the size N of the image corpus. For large-scale databases, the time complexity of the model $P(\mathcal{B}_t|x)$, $\psi(\mathcal{S}_t^i, x)$ and $\psi(\mathcal{D}_t^i, x)$ can be reduced using any advanced CBIR search or indexing technologies [29, 25].

5. EXPERIMENTS

In this section, we systematically evaluate the proposed Attribute Feedback framework. We first investigate the attribute learning accuracy and then evaluate the performance of CBIR with attribute feedbacks.

5.1 Data and Methodology

5.1.1 Dataset Description

We conducted experiments over two real-world image datasets: the Pascal-Yahoo! image corpus [6] and the Web Image collection downloaded from the Microsoft Bing image search engine.

Pascal-Yahoo!. This dataset was used in [6]. It contains 15,339 images collected from Pascal VOC 2008 (12,695 images) and Yahoo! image search engine (2,644 images). The images are from 32 object categories (20 in Pascal and 12 in Yahoo!) and all of them were annotated with 64 pre-defined attributes, such as shapes "round", materials "wool" and parts "wheel", among which 39 attributes are considered as affinity attributes, such as "eye", "leg", etc. All the images were split into two subsets [6]. In particular, 6,340 images from Pascal were used to train the classifiers for all the 64 binary attribute and learn the discriminative distance functions for the 39 affinity attributes. The rest of 6,355 images in Pascal together with the 2,644 images in Yahoo! were used for image retrieval. We randomly selected 10 images from each category as experimental queries. This gives rise to 320 queries in total.

Web Image[1]. We collected another web image corpus from the Microsoft Bing image search engine with 120 popular text queries in *Animal* and *Object* domains. For the ambiguous queries, we were interested in only one of its multiple facets. Take the query "apple" as example, we only downloaded the images of "apple, the fruit" by using "apple fruit" as the query. In total, 102,657 images were collected. We invited 21 annotators to manually remove the irrelevant images. 76,303 relevant images were eventually kept as our experimental data. There are around 300-800 images within one query category. We defined 67 semantic attributes by referring to the 64 attributes in the Pascal-Yahoo! dataset. In particular, we followed the naming protocol of attributes in [6], except that we remove "2D_Boxy" and "3D_Boxy" since they were very ambiguous to our annotators. Moreover, we added 5 more attributes, such as "Transparent" and "ToughSkin". Among the 67 binary attributes, 39 attributes were considered as affinity attributes. We randomly selected 50 categories with 25,203 images as the development set for attribute learning, and the remaining 70 categories with 51,100 images as the test set for retrieval. Due to the high cost of manual labeling, we only manually annotated the 67 attributes on the development set. The annotation followed the same criteria as in [6]. 80% of images in the development set were used as training samples in attribute learning, and the remaining 20% of images were used for testing. For retrieval, we randomly selected 10 images from each of the 70 categories as the experimental queries, and obtained 700 queries in total.

5.1.2 Visual Features

We used four types of features, including color and texture, which are good for material attributes; edge, which is useful for shape attributes; and scale-invariant feature transform (SIFT) descriptor, which is useful for part attributes. We used a bag-of-words style representation for each of these four features.

Color descriptors were densely extracted from each pixel as the 3-channel LAB values. The color descriptors of each image were then quantized into a 128-bin histogram. Texture descriptors were computed for each pixel as the 48-dimensional responses of texton filter banks [14]. The texture descriptors of each image were then quantized into a 256-bin histogram. Edges were found using the standard canny edge detector and their orientations were quantized into 8 unsigned bins. This gives rise to a 8-bin edge histogram for each image. SIFT descriptors [22] were densely extracted from the 8×8 neighboring block of each pixel with 4-pixel step size. The descriptors were quantized into a 1,000-dimensional bag-of-words feature. Afterward, for each image, we concatenated these four type of features into a 1,392-dimensional vector, which was used in image retrieval. Since attributes usually appear in one or more regions in an image, we further split each image into 2×3 grids and extracted the above four kinds of features from each grid respectively. Finally, we obtained a 9,744-dimensional feature for each image, consisting of a $1{,}392 \times 6$-dimensional feature from the grids and a 1,392-dimensional feature from the whole image. The 9,744-dimensional feature was used in attribute learning.

5.1.3 Experimental Setting

In our implementation, we employed the publicly available toolbox L1_LOGREG[2] to learn the ℓ_1-norm regression functions for feature selection and adopted LIBSVM [1] for training the binary attribute classifiers. The regularization parameter of ℓ_1-norm regression was set to 0.01 empirically and the parameters of SVM classifiers were determined through five-fold cross validation. For

[1]http://www.comp.nus.edu.sg/~hanwang/data.html
[2]http://stanford.edu/~boyd/l1_logreg/index.html

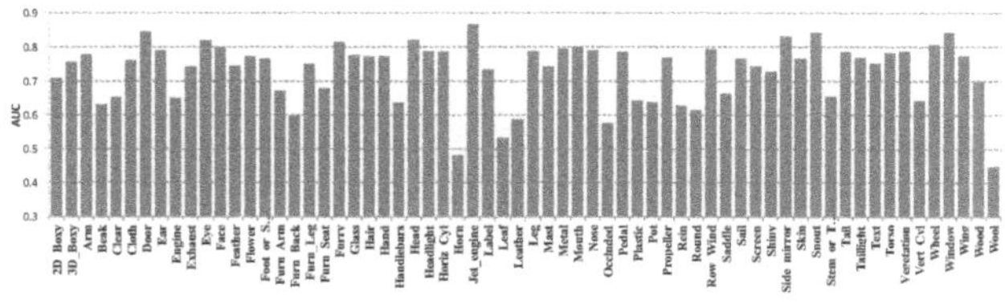

(a) Pascal-Yahoo!

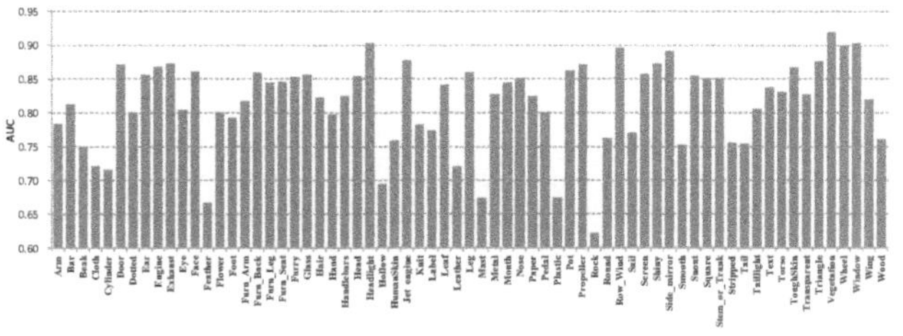

(b) Web Image

Figure 3: Classification performance of (a) the 64 attributes on the Pascal-Yahoo! dataset and (b) the 67 binary attributes on the Web Image dataset.

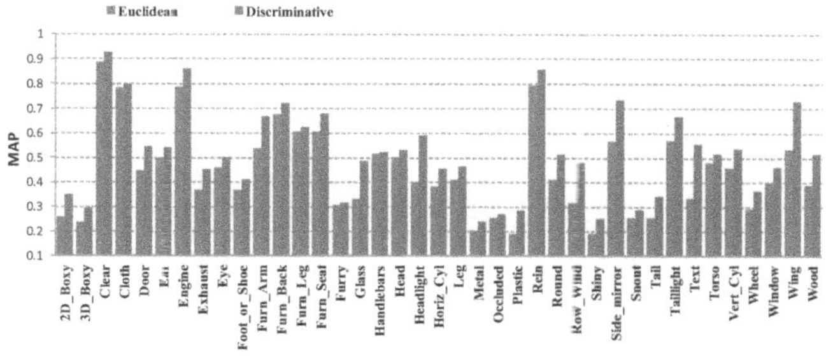

(a) Pascal-Yahoo!

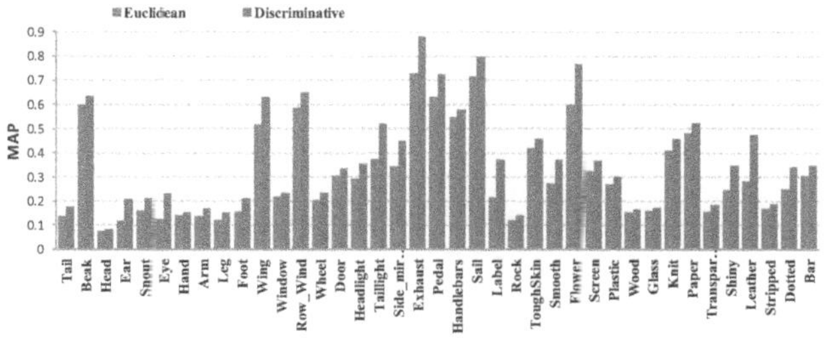

(b) Web Image

Figure 4: Performance of the discriminative distance functions for the 39 affinity attributes on (a) the Pascal-Yahoo! dataset and (b) the Web Image dataset.

learning the discriminative distance functions of affinity attributes, we used the SDPLIB[3], where the tradeoff parameter λ was set by five-fold cross validation.

To evaluate the effectiveness of the proposed Attribute Feedback (**AF**) approach, we compared it against four popular relevance feedback methods and one active learning approach: (a) **QPM** [17]. Query Point Movement method gradually refines the query point based on user's "relevance" and "irrelevance" feedbacks in each feedback iteration. The images in database are ranked according to their Euclidean distances to the refined query. (b) **SVM** [8]. This approach learns a SVM classifier from user's "relevance" and "irrelevance" feedbacks and ranks images according to SVM's outputs on them; (c) **BDA** [34]. Biased Discriminant Analysis algorithm learns a low-dimensional subspace from user's feedbacks. All the images in database are embedded into this subspace and ranked according to their Euclidean distance to the mean feature vector of the "relevant" images; and (d) **SVMactive** [20]. Different from the above relevance feedbacks methods that present top retrieved images for user labeling, SVMactive method actively selects images with high uncertainty for labeling in each feedback iteration. The labeled images are then utilized to learn a SVM classifier, which is in turn used to rank the images in the database. The parameter settings of these baseline methods were identical to those in the corresponding papers.

We conducted the retrieval process for each query as follows. For each submitted query, the search system generated initial search results based on low-level visual features. The number of feedbacks per round is widely set as 10-20 in leteratures [35]. We set it to 20 as in [20, 34]. For QPM, SVM and BDA baseline methods, the top 20 returned images were presented for users to label at each feedback iteration. For the SVMactive approach, 20 images were selected by this approach and presented to users for labeling. The label information was then used to update the search results. In the proposed attribute feedback (AF) method, ten informative attributes, including binary and affinity attributes, were presented for user feedback at each iteration. For each affinity attribute with positive feedback, user further made comparative judgements on some images from the top 20 ones to state which images are similar or dissimilar to their intent with respect to the referenced attribute. For the sake of fair comparison, we constrained the number of attribute feedbacks in each iteration to be the same in the baseline methods. That is, the total number of feedbacks on binary attributes and comparative judgments on affinity attribute was limited to 20.

5.1.4 Performance Metric

We adopted the widely used metric AUC (area under ROC curve) value for evaluating the accuracies of attribute classifiers. AUC describes the probability that a randomly chosen positive sample will be ranked higher than a randomly chosen negative sample. We used the mean Average Precision (MAP) for evaluating the distance functions of affinity attributes. In particular, we collected all the testing and training images containing a certain affinity attribute. For each testing image, all the training images were ranked according to their distances to the testing image. We used the Average Precision (AP) to evaluate the ranking list for each testing image and averaged the APs over all the testing images to obtain the MAP. The distances were computed using the distance function learned for this attribute. We used precision in the top K results as the basic evaluation metric for all the feedback methods. When the top K images are considered and there are R relevant images, the precision within the top K images is defined to be R/K.

5.2 Experimental Results

5.2.1 Evaluations on Attribute Learning

Figure 3 shows the AUC values of the 64 and 67 binary attribute classifiers on the Pascal-Yahoo! and the Web Image datasets, respectively. The detection accuracy is comparable to the state-of-the-art methods. The average AUC on the Pascal-Yahoo! dataset is 0.76 comparable to 0.73 in [6]. On the Web Image dataset, the average AUC is 0.82 and can be also considered reliable. Moreover, AF is flexible to use any binary attribute learning method.

Figure 4 details the MAP of all the 39 affinity attributes com-

[3]http://euler.nmt.edu/~brian/sdplib/sdplib.html

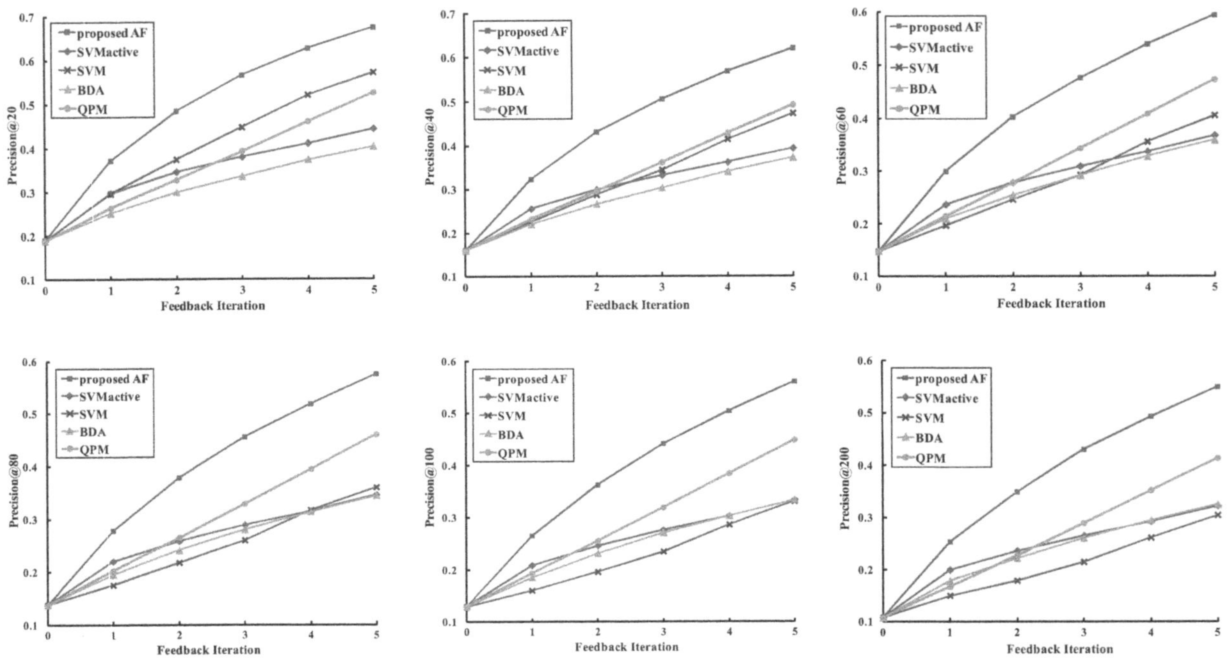

Figure 5: Precision@20, 40, 60, 80, 100, 200 over 320 queries with AF and the four baseline methods at five feedback iterations on the Pascal-Yahoo! dataset.

pared using the original Euclidean distance and the learned discriminative Mahalanobis distance. As we can see from the results, the discriminative ability of the affinity attributes is significantly improved across query categories. More specifically, affinity attributes improve the discriminative ability of attributes which are even ambiguous to human beings. For example, on the Web Image dataset, the "Taillight" can be correctly classified into different vehicles with over 0.5 MAP while only 0.37 is achieved when directly using Euclidean distance. Unfortunately, the "Head" attribute on the Web Image is not well improved. This may due to the large within-attribute variance of "Head".

5.2.2 *Evaluations on Attribute Feedback*

Figure 5 illustrates the retrieval performance on the Pascal-Yahoo! dataset by the proposed AF approach and the four state-of-the art relevance feedback methods, i.e., SVMactive, SVM, BDA and QPM. In particular, the average precision over 320 experimental queries at top 20, 40, 60, 80, 100, and 200 search results in five feedback iterations are reported here. Figure 6 shows the retrieval performance over 700 queries on the Web Image dataset. From the results, we can derive the following key observations.

- The proposed AF approach outperforms the other four methods at every iteration and on the entire scope (i.e., top 20, 40, 60, 80, 100, 200 results) on both datasets. For example, consider the precision@20 on the Pascal-Yahoo! dataset. At the first feedback iteration, AF achieves 25.2%, 25.6%, 47.8% and 41.1% relative improvements over SVMactive, SVM, BDA and QPM, respectively. The relative improvements at the last iteration are 51.7%, 17.9%, 66.8%, 28.0%, respectively. On the Web Image dataset, AF achieves 39.6%, 22.9%, 33.2%, 45.4% relative improvements at the first iteration and 181.4%, 67.0%, 154.0%, 99.0% relative improvements at the last iteration.
- On both datasets, AF significantly reduces the interaction efforts while it achieves comparable performance to the other four methods. For example, consider the precision at top 20 results on the Pascal-Yahoo! dataset, AF obtains a comparable performance at the 2nd, 3rd, 1st, 3rd iteration compared to SVMactive, SVM, BDA, QPM at the last round, respectively. That is to say, AF can reduce labeling efforts by about 60%, 40%, 80%, 40% as compared to the four methods. For the top 20 results on the Web Image dataset, AF achieves a better performance at the 1st, 3rd, 1st, 2nd iteration as compared to the four methods at the last iteration.

The above results demonstrate the superiority of AF over the traditional relevance feedback methods. The reasons behind this are three folds. First, feedbacks on binary attributes empower users to specify search intent more precisely than traditional "relevant" and "irrelevant" feedbacks on images. Second, the informative attribute selection aids the users to feedback on attributes of their interests efficiently. Third, feedbacks on affinity attributes offer the users to feedback on the more fine-grained and discriminative semantics. Therefore, AF can shape users' intent more precisely and quickly.

Figure 8 presents the detailed results over all the query categories on the Web Image dataset at the first iteration. Due to page limitation, we here only report the precision@20 performance at the first iteration on the Web Image dataset. We can see that AF outperforms the other four methods on most of the query categories. While the traditional RF methods purely based on low-level visual features may suffer from the large within-category variance especially on the Web Image dataset, the proposed AF exploits intermediate-level semantic attributes and thus can well model users' intent by collecting feedbacks on attributes.

At last, we investigate the performance of AF in the case of no relevant samples in the initial search results. Since the Pascal-Yahoo! dataset is of small within-class variance, there is no such case happened in the experiments on the Pascal-Yahoo! dataset. However, on the Web Image dataset, this situation is fairly common. In particular, among the 70 query categories, there are 127 queries from 23 categories suffered from this problem. Figure 7

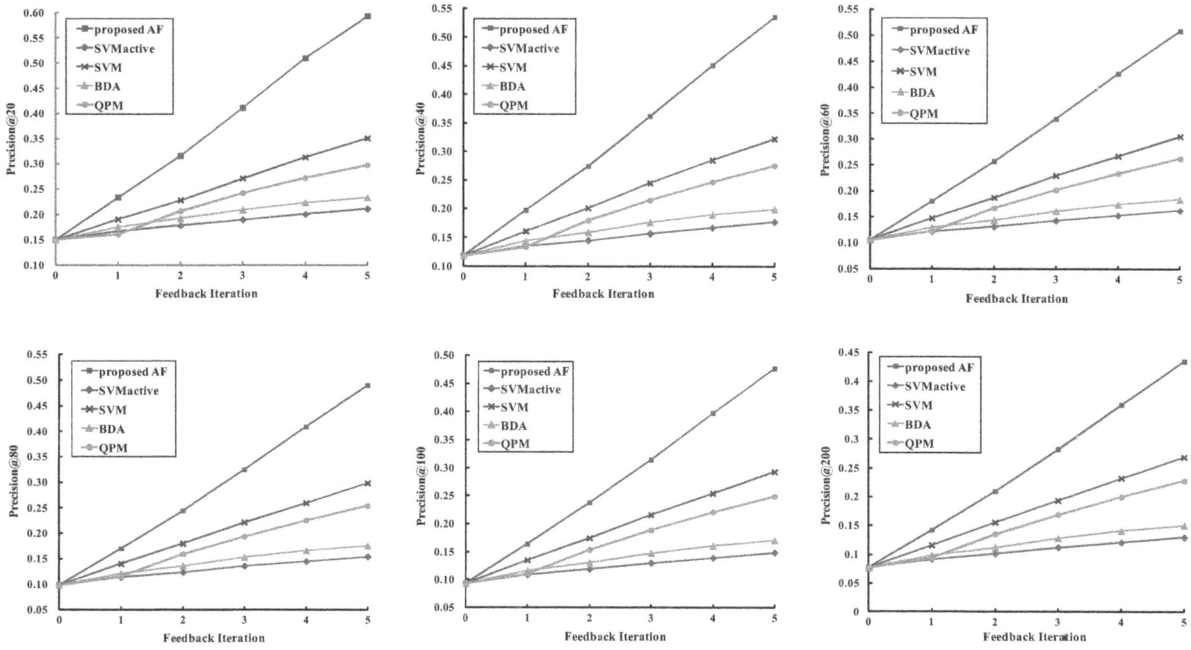

Figure 6: Precision@20, 40, 60, 80, 100, 200 over 700 queries with AF and the four baseline methods at five feedback iterations on the Web Image dataset.

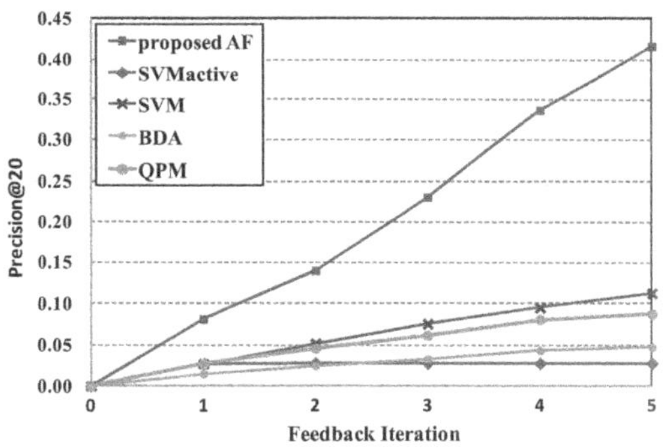

Figure 7: Average Precision@20 by the proposed AF and the four baseline methods with queries that have no relevant samples in the initial search results on the Web Image dataset.

illustrates the performance of the five feedback algorithms with the 127 queries that have no relevant samples in the initial search results on the Web Image dataset. When faced with such situation, the only positive example that the traditional RF methods can use is the query image. Such insufficient cues severely degrade the performance. We can see that AF significantly outperforms the other four methods. This demonstrates the capability of AF in handling no relevant sample problem in CBIR.

6. CONCLUSION AND FUTURE WORK

In this paper, we proposed a new interactive CBIR scheme, named Attribute Feedback. Unlike traditional relevance feedback that purely based on low-level features, AF allows user to provide feedbacks on intermediate-level semantic attributes and thus can shape user's search intent more precisely and quickly. At each interactive iteration, a set of informative attributes are selected and presented for user feedbacks. A statistical informative attribute selection approach has been proposed. In order to offer more discriminative attribute feedbacks, we proposed a new type of attributes, called "affinity attributes", each of which is learnt off-line to describe the distance between user's envisioned image(s) and a retrieved image with respect to the corresponding affinity attribute. Based on users' feedbacks on binary and affinity attributes, a discriminative search model is then updated towards better fitting users' search intent. We have conducted extensive experiments on two real-world image datasets: the Pascal-Yahoo! corpus containing 15,339 images within 32 categories; and the Web Image collection with 76,303 images of 120 categories. The experimental results demonstrated that the proposed AF scheme outperforms other state-of-the-art relevance feedback based CBIR approaches.

Our future work focuses on the algorithmic and systematic aspects of AF. First, we will incorporate inter-attribute dependencies such as inclusive and exclusive attribute co-occurrence [2] for informative attribute selection. Second, for the robustness of the binary attribute detections, we will refine the attribute classifiers based on the user feedback logs. Last but not the least, we will conduct a comprehensive user study on the practical usefulness of AF in large-scale Web images search.

Acknowledgments

This work was supported by NUS-Tsinghua Extreme Search (NExT) project under the grant number: R-252-300-001-490.

7. REFERENCES

[1] C. Chang and C. Lin. LIBSVM: A library for support vector machines. *ACM TIST*, 2011.

[2] X. Chen, X. Yuan, S. Yan, Y. Rui, and T. Chua. Towards multi-semantic image annotation with graph regularized exclusive group lasso. In *MM*, 2011.

[3] R. Datta, D. Joshi, J. Li, and J. Wang. Image retrieval: Ideas,

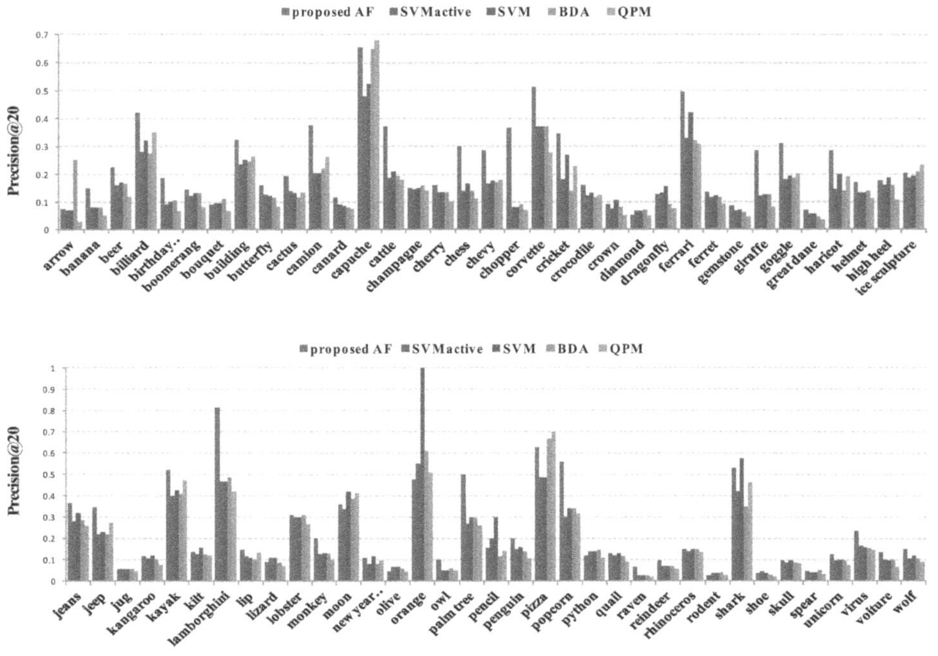

Figure 8: Detailed retrieval performance over the 70 testing query categories at the first iteration on the Web Image dataset.

influences, and trends of the new age. *ACM Computing Surveys*, 2008.

[4] M. Douze, A. Ramisa, and C. Schmid. Combining attributes and fisher vectors for efficient image retrieval. In *CVPR*, 2011.

[5] A. Farhadi, I. Endres, and D. Hoiem. Attribute-centric recognition for cross-category generalization. In *CVPR*, 2010.

[6] A. Farhadi, I. Endres, D. Hoiem, and D. Forsyth. Describing objects by their attributes. In *CVPR*, 2009.

[7] V. Ferrari and A. Zisserman. Learning visual attributes. In *NIPS*, 2008.

[8] G. Guo, A. Jain, W. Ma, and H. Zhang. Learning similarity measure for natural image retrieval with relevance feedback. *TNN*, 2002.

[9] J. Hare, P. Lewis, P. Enser, and C. Sandom. Mind the gap: Another look at the problem of the semantic gap in image retrieval. *Multimedia Content Analysis, Management, and Retrieval*, 2006.

[10] T. Huang and X. Zhou. Image retrieval with relevance feedback: From heuristic weight adjustment to optimal learning methods. In *ICIP*, 2001.

[11] A. Kovashka, D. Parikh, and K. Grauman. Whittlesearch: Image search with relative attribute feedback. In *CVPR*, 2012.

[12] N. Kumar, A. Berg, P. Belhumeur, and S. Nayar. Describable visual attributes for face verification and image search. *TPAMI*, 2011.

[13] C. Lampert, H. Nickisch, and S. Harmeling. Learning to detect unseen object classes by between-class attribute transfer. In *CVPR*, 2009.

[14] T. Leung and J. Malik. Representing and recognizing the visual appearance of materials using three-dimensional textons. *IJCV*, 2001.

[15] M. Lew, N. Sebe, C. Djeraba, and R. Jain. Content-based multimedia information retrieval: State of the art and challenges. *TOMCCAP*, 2006.

[16] D. Parikh and K. Grauman. Relative attributes. In *ICCV*, 2011.

[17] Y. Rui, T. Huang, and S. Mehrotra. Content-based image retrieval with relevance feedback in mars. In *ICIP*, 1997.

[18] B. Siddiquie, R. Feris, and L. Davis. Image ranking and retrieval based on multi-attribute queries. In *CVPR*, 2011.

[19] A. Smeulders, M. Worring, S. Santini, A. Gupta, and R. Jain. Content-based image retrieval at the end of the early years. *TPAMI*, 2000.

[20] S. Tong and E. Chang. Support vector machine active learning for image retrieval. In *MM*, 2001.

[21] S. Uchihashi and T. Kanade. Content-free image retrieval based on relations exploited from user feedbacks. In *ICME*, 2005.

[22] A. Vedaldi and B. Fulkerson. Vlfeat: An open and portable library of computer vision algorithms. In *MM*, 2010.

[23] M. Wang and X. Hua. Active learning in multimedia annotation and retrieval: A survey. *TIST*, 2011.

[24] Z.-J. Zha., L. Yang, T. Mei, M. Wang, and Z.-F. Wang. Visual query suggestion. In *MM*, 2009.

[25] W. Zhou., Y. LU, H. Li, Y. Song, and Q. Tian. Spatial Coding for Large Scale Partial-Duplicate Web Image Search. In *MM*, 2010.

[26] M. Wang, K. Yang, X.-S. Hua, and H. Zhang. Towards a relevant and diverse search of social images. *TMM*, 2010.

[27] X. Wang, K. Liu, and X. Tang. Query-specific visual semantic spaces for web image re-ranking. In *CVPR*, 2011.

[28] J. Wright, Y. Ma, J. Mairal, G. Sapiro, T. Huang, and S. Yan. Sparse representation for computer vision and pattern recognition. *PIEEE*, 2010.

[29] Z.-J. Zha, M. Wang, Y.-T. Zheng, Y. Yang, R. Hong, and T.-S. Chua. Interactive video indexing with statistical active learning. *TMM*, 2012.

[30] F. Wu, Y. Han, Q. Tian, and Y. Zhuang. Multi-label boosting for image annotation by structural grouping sparsity. In *MM*, 2010.

[31] Y. Yang, Y. Yang, Z. Huang, H. Shen, and F. Nie. Tag localization with spatial correlations and joint group sparsity. In *CVPR*, 2011.

[32] J. Yuan, Z.-J. Zha, Y. Zheng, M. Wang, X. Zhou, and T.-S. Chua. Utilizing related samples to enhance interactive concept-based video search. *TMM*, 2011.

[33] Z.-J. Zha., L. Yang, T. Mei, M. Wang, Z.-F. Wang, T.-S. Chua, and X.-S. Hua. Visual query suggestion: Towards capturing user intent in internet image search. *TOMCCAP*, 2010.

[34] X. Zhou and T. Huang. Small sample learning during multimedia retrieval using biasmap. In *CVPR*, 2001.

[35] X. Zhou and T. Huang. Relevance feedback in image retrieval: A comprehensive review. *Multimedia Systems*, 2003.

The Acoustic Emotion Gaussians Model for Emotion-based Music Annotation and Retrieval

Ju-Chiang Wang[1,2], Yi-Hsuan Yang[2,3], Hsin-Min Wang[2,3] and Shyh-Kang Jeng[1]
[1] Department of Electrical Engineering, National Taiwan University, Taipei, Taiwan
[2] Institute of Information Science, Academia Sinica, Taipei, Taiwan
[3] Research Center for Information Technology Innovation, Academia Sinica, Taipei, Taiwan
{asriver, yang, whm}@iis.sinica.edu.tw; skjeng@cc.ee.ntu.edu.tw

ABSTRACT

One of the most exciting but challenging endeavors in music research is to develop a computational model that comprehends the affective content of music signals and organizes a music collection according to emotion. In this paper, we propose a novel *acoustic emotion Gaussians* (AEG) model that defines a proper generative process of emotion perception in music. As a generative model, AEG permits easy and straightforward interpretations of the model learning processes. To bridge the acoustic feature space and music emotion space, a set of *latent feature classes*, which are learned from data, is introduced to perform the end-to-end semantic mappings between the two spaces. Based on the space of latent feature classes, the AEG model is applicable to both automatic music emotion annotation and emotion-based music retrieval. To gain insights into the AEG model, we also provide illustrations of the model learning process. A comprehensive performance study is conducted to demonstrate the superior accuracy of AEG over its predecessors, using two emotion annotated music corpora MER60 and MTurk. Our results show that the AEG model outperforms the state-of-the-art methods in automatic music emotion annotation. Moreover, for the first time a quantitative evaluation of emotion-based music retrieval is reported.

Categories and Subject Descriptors

H.5.5 [**Sound and Music Computing**]: Methodologies and Techniques, Systems

General Terms

Algorithms, Experimentation, Performance

Keywords

Computational emotion model, automatic music emotion recognition, music retrieval, Gaussian mixture model, EM algorithm.

1. INTRODUCTION

One of the most exciting but challenging endeavors in music research is to develop a computational model that comprehends the affective content of music signals and organizes a music collection according to emotion [12, 29]. Such a model is desirable as the pursuit of emotional experience is the primary motivation for music listening [11]. Behavioral studies have also identified emotion as one of the most important attributes used by people for music retrieval [25].

Automatic annotation of music emotion is challenging because the perception of emotion is in nature subjective.[1] Oftentimes people perceive differently when listening to the same song [5]. Consequently, one cannot assume that there is an objective, single ground truth label that applies equally well to every listener. Instead, one needs to learn directly from multiple labels provided by different annotators [17] and present as the final result a *soft* (probabilistic) emotion assignment instead of a *hard* (deterministic) one.

Modeling the time-varying dynamics of music emotion poses another challenge. A music piece can express different emotions as time unfolds, and it has been argued that music's most expressive qualities are related to its structural changes across time [6]. To capture the continuous changes of emotional expression, the *dimensional* representation of emotion is found superior to its *categorical* counterpart [5, 23]. In this representation, emotions are considered as numerical values (instead of discrete labels) over a number of emotion dimensions, such as *valence* (positive/negative affective states) and *activation* (or arousal; energy level) – the two most fundamental dimensions found by psychologists [18].[2] In this way, music emotion recognition becomes the prediction of the moment-to-moment valence and activation (VA) values of a music piece corresponding to a series of points in the emotion space [29].

While early approaches to emotion recognition neglected the above two properties and represented the emotion of a song by a single, song-level discrete emotion label [9, 15, 24], recent years have witnessed a growing number of attempts that modeled the emotion of a song or a segment as a probabilistic *distribution* in the emotion space [26, 30], as shown in Figure 1, to better account for the subjective nature of

[1] We define music emotion as the emotion human *perceives* as being expressed in a piece of music, rather than the emotion *feels* in response to the piece. This distinction is made as we may not feel sorrow when listening to a sad tune [5].

[2] For example, happiness is an emotion associated with a positive valence and a high activation, while sadness is an emotion associated with a negative valence and a low activation.

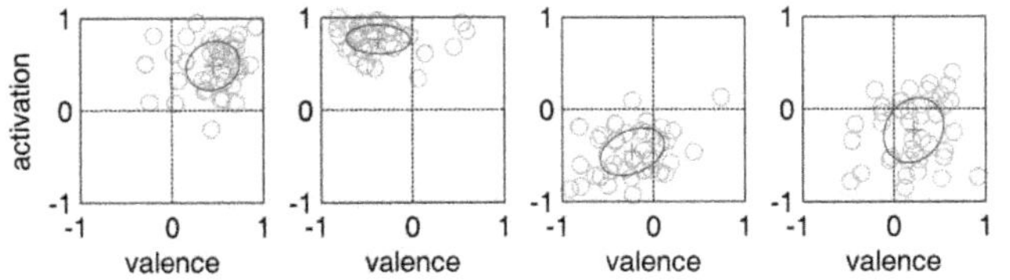

Figure 1: Subjects' annotations in the emotion space [18] for four 30-second clips.[4] Each circle corresponds to a subject's annotation for a clip, and the overall annotations for a clip can be modeled by a 2-D Gaussian distribution (i.e., the blue ellipse) [30].

emotion perception [30]. This can be approached by modeling the emotion distribution of each temporal segment as a bivariate Gaussian distribution and using regression algorithms to predict the mean, variance, and covariance of valence and activation directly from the acoustic features [30]. In this way, developers of an emotion-based music retrieval system can better understand how likely a specific emotional expression (defined in terms of VA values) would be perceived at each temporal moment. For a music piece whose perceived emotion is more listener-dependent, its emotion distribution in the emotion space would be sparser.

From the application point of view, this approach also creates a simple user interface for music retrieval through the specification of a point or a trajectory in the emotion space [29]. With this interface, users can easily retrieve music pieces of certain emotions without specifying the titles and can discover new pieces whose emotion is similar to that of a favorite piece. Users can also draw a trajectory in the display of a mobile device to indicate the desired emotion variation within a music piece or a playlist (e.g., changing from aggressive to tender).

From the theoretical point of view, the shift of music emotion modeling from a fixed label towards a time-varying, stochastic distribution is significant as a functional music retrieval system cannot be dissociated from the underlying psychological implications [2].

In this paper, we propose a novel *acoustic emotion Gaussians* (AEG) model that realizes a proper generative process of music emotion perception in a probabilistic and parametric framework. The AEG model learns from data two sets of Gaussian mixture models (GMMs), namely *acoustic GMM* and *VA GMM*, to describe the low-level acoustic feature space and high-level emotion space, respectively. A set of *latent feature classes* is introduced to play the end-to-end linkage between the two spaces and aligns the two GMMs. As a principled probabilistic model, AEG is applicable to both automatic music emotion annotation and emotion-based music retrieval.

The proposed AEG framework has three additional advantages. First, as a generative model, AEG permits easy and straightforward interpretation of the model learning and semantic mapping processes. Second, as AEG mainly involves light-weight computations of emotion prediction, it can track the moment-to-moment emotion distributions of a music piece in real-time. Third, due to its parametric and probabilistic nature, AEG provides great flexibility to future extension, such as personalizing the AEG model via model adaptation techniques or incorporating music tags for advanced music browsing and retrieval purposes.

A comprehensive performance study is conducted to demonstrate the superior accuracy of AEG over its predecessors, using two emotion annotated music corpora MER60 [30] and MTurk [26]. Moreover, for the first time a quantitative evaluation of emotion-based music retrieval is reported.

The remainder of this paper is organized as follows: First, we briefly review related work in Section 2. Next, we provide an overview of the AEG model in Section 3. The details of model learning, emotion annotation, and emotion-based retrieval are described in Sections 4 and 5. We then offer insights into the model learning process of AEG with empirical data in Section 6. Section 7 presents and discusses the evaluation results on both emotion-based music annotation and retrieval. Finally, we conclude the paper in Section 8.

2. RELATED WORK

A great amount of effort has been made by psychologists to study the relationship between music and emotion [7]. To identify the internal human representations of emotion, psychologists have applied factor analysis techniques such as multidimensional scaling to the emotion ratings of music stimuli. Although differ in names, existing studies give very similar interpretations of the resulting fundamental factors, most of which correspond to valence and activation [18].

Early approaches to automatic music emotion recognition [4, 16, 31] usually assumed that the perceived emotion of a music clip can be represented as a *single point* in the emotion space, in which VA values are considered as numerical values. The pair of ground truth VA values of a music clip is obtained by averaging the annotations of a number of subjects, without considering the variance of the annotations. Then, a regression algorithm, such as multiple linear regression (MLR) or support vector regression (SVR) [22], can be applied to train regression models for predicting the VA values. To exploit the temporal continuity of emotion variation within a clip, techniques such as Kalman filtering [20] or system identification [13] have also been used. Associated with the VA values, a music clip is visualized as a point in the VA space, and the similarity between clips are measured by the Euclidean distance in the emotion space.

However, because emotion perception is inherently subjective, simply representing a clip as a point according to the mean VA values is not enough to capture the nuance of human perception, as illustrated in Figure 1. Moreover, it has been argued that the VA space may not be an Euclidean space [27] and that it is better to measure the similarity of two songs according to the divergence between the corresponding two emotion distributions [30].

To better account for the subjective nature of emotion perception, algorithms for predicting the emotion distribution of a music clip from acoustic features have been proposed recently. Existing approaches can be divided into two categories. The *heatmap* approach [21, 30] quantizes each emotion dimension by G equally spaced discrete samples, leading to a $G \times G$ grid representation of the emotion space, and trains G^2 regression models for predicting the *emotion intensity* of each emotion point. Higher emotion intensity at an emotion sample indicates higher probability for a listener to perceive that emotion when listening to the music segment. The emotion intensity over the VA space cre-

[4]The four clips from left to right are *Dancing Queen* by ABBA, *Civil War* by Guns N' Roses, *Suzanne* by Leonard Cohen, and *All I Have To Do Is Dream* by the Everly Brothers, respectively.

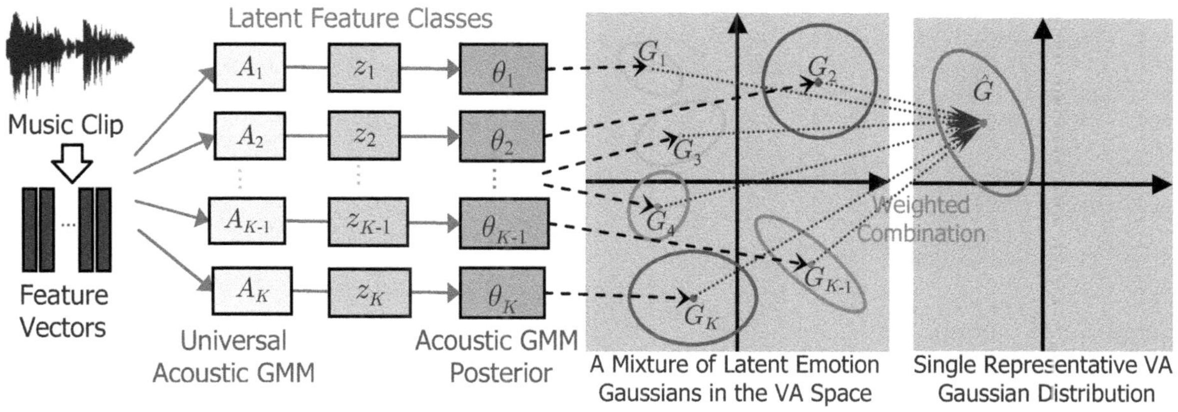

Figure 2: Illustration of AEG. Music emotion distribution can be generated from the acoustic features.

ates a heatmap like representation of emotion distribution. The drawback of this approach is that heatmap is a discrete rather than continuous representation of the VA space, and that emotion intensity cannot be regarded as a probability estimate in a strict sense.

The *Gaussian-parameter* approach [19,26,30] directly learns five regression models to predict the mean, variance, and covariance of valence and activation, respectively. This approach allows easier performance analysis; one can analyze the impact of separate acoustic features for the prediction of each Gaussian parameter. In addition, the modeling of mean VA values has been studied for years [4,16,31]. However, neither this approach nor the heatmap approach renders a strict probabilistic foundation. Moreover, the correlation among the mean and variance of valence and activation is not exploited, as the regression models are trained independently.

3. FRAMEWORK OVERVIEW

This section introduces AEG from a high-level point of view and outlines the system architecture. The details of each system component are described in Sections 4 and 5.

3.1 The Acoustic Emotion Gaussians Model

There are two basic assumptions underlying AEG. First, we assume that the emotion annotations of a music clip can be parameterized by a *bivariate Gaussian distribution.*[5] Second, we assume that music clips similar in acoustic features (e.g., loudness, timbre, rhythm, and harmony) also result in similar emotion distributions in the VA space.

As shown in Figure 2, the AEG model realizes the generation of music emotion in the emotion space. At the most abstract level, the relationship between the acoustic feature space and music emotion space can be observed from an annotated music corpus. However, such a relationship may be sometimes complicated and difficult to identify directly. Therefore, we introduce a set of *latent feature classes*, $\{z_k\}_{k=1}^K$, which functions as a linkage between the two spaces, into the generative process of music emotion.

Suppose that each z_k, which is defined by a latent acoustic classifier A_k, can map a specific pattern of acoustic features to a specific area G_k in the VA space. The set of latent acoustic classifiers, $\{A_k\}_{k=1}^K$, can be implemented by a universal acoustic Gaussian mixture model (GMM), denoted as the *acoustic GMM*, in which each component Gaussian A_k represents a specific acoustic pattern discovered by the GMM learning in the frame-based acoustic feature space. In the meanwhile, G_k can be modeled by a bivariate Gaussian distribution, denoted as a latent VA Gaussian. The mixture of latent VA Gaussians is called the *VA GMM* hereafter.

3.2 Generation of Music Emotion

As shown in the left hand side of Figure 2, the acoustic features of a music clip can be represented by computing the posterior probabilities over the acoustic GMM (i.e., each component Gaussian A_k leads to a posterior probability θ_k) based on its frame-based feature vectors. We denote this clip-level acoustic feature representation as the *acoustic GMM posterior*, $\{\theta_k\}_{k=1}^K$, subject to $\sum_k \theta_k = 1$. Therefore, the acoustic GMM posterior is able to capture the acoustic characteristics of every music clip in a K-dimensional probabilistic space. In the right hand side of Figure 2, the emotion distribution of a music clip in the VA space can be generated by the weighted combination of all latent VA Gaussians as $\sum_k \theta_k G_k$ using $\{\theta_k\}_{k=1}^K$ as weights. Consequently, the generative process of emotion of a music clip can be interpreted as that, for example, if human has perceived only the acoustic pattern of z_1 from a music clip's acoustic features (this will lead to $\theta_1 = 1$, and $\theta_k = 0$, $\forall k \neq 1$), then his/her emotion perception would exactly follow G_1.

Since it is more intuitive to interpret the final emotion prediction of a music clip to the users with only a set of mean (center) and covariance (uncertainty) rather than a complicated VA GMM, the $\boldsymbol{\theta}$-weighted VA GMM is finally combined into a single 2-D VA Gaussian $\hat{G}$ in the emotion prediction phase, as shown in the rightmost of Figure 2.

3.3 Emotion-based Music Retrieval

As shown in Figure 3, the proposed emotion-based music retrieval system can be divided into two phases: the *feature indexing phase* and the *music retrieval phase*. In the indexing phase, each music clip in the un-labeled music database is indexed with two indexing approaches based on the music clip's acoustic features: indexing with the *acoustic GMM posterior* (a fixed-dimensional vector) of a clip using the acoustic GMM, or indexing with the *predicted emotion distribution* (a single 2-D Gaussian) of a clip given by automatic

[5]The assumptions that the VA space can be considered as Euclidean and that the VA values can be modeled as a Gaussian distribution are made in prior work (cf. Section 2). We will not discuss this issue further but instead empirically validate the effectiveness of emotion-based music information systems built upon these assumptions for practical uses.

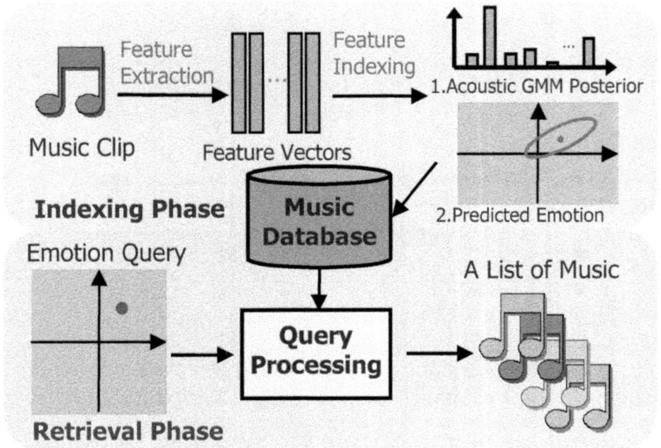

Figure 3: The flowchart of the content-based music search system using a VA-based emotion query.

Table 1: The two implementations of the emotion-based music search system.

Approach	Indexing	Retrieval
Fold-In	Acoustic GMM Posterior (K-dim Vector $\{\theta_k\}_{k=1}^K$)	Pseudo Song $\{\lambda_k\}_{k=1}^K$
Emotion Prediction	Predicted Emotion Distribution (2-D Gaussian $\hat{G}$)	Distribution Likelihood

emotion prediction. In the retrieval phase, given a point query from the emotion (VA) space, the system will return a ranked list of relevant music clips. We apply two matching methods, namely *pseudo song-based matching* and *distribution likelihood-based matching*; each corresponding to one of the two indexing approaches. In pseudo song-based matching, the point query is first transformed into a pseudo song (i.e., the estimated acoustic GMM posterior for the point query), and then matched with clips in an unlabeled music database. In distribution likelihood-based matching, a point query is fed into the predicted emotion distribution of each clip in an unlabeled music database, and the system ranks all the clips according to the estimated likelihoods. Table 1 summarizes the two implementations of the emotion-based music retrieval system.

3.3.1 Pseudo Song Estimation

In the Fold-In method, a given query point is transformed into probabilities $\{\lambda_k\}_{k=1}^K$, s.t. $\sum_k \lambda_k = 1$, as shown in Figure 4. The resulted λ_k represents the importance of the k-th latent VA Gaussian for the input query point. Suppose that the estimated $\{\lambda_k\}_{k=1}^K$ have a similar property with the acoustic GMM posterior $\{\theta_k\}_{k=1}^K$ that are used to index music clips in the music database. For instance, in the case shown in Figure 4, the 2-nd latent VA Gaussian is extremely likely to generate the input query point, the Fold-In process will assign a dominative weight λ_2 to z_2, e.g., $\lambda_2 = 1$, and $\lambda_k = 0$, $\forall k \neq 2$, which means that the query point is extremely relevant to the song whose acoustic GMM posterior is dominated by θ_2. Therefore, the pseudo song can be used to match with the clips in the un-labeled music database.

4. LEARNING THE AEG MODEL

This section will first present the mathematical generative process of the AEG model, i.e., introducing the learning

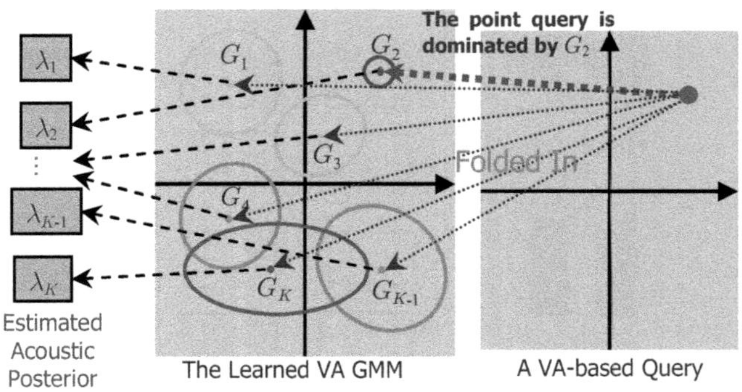

Figure 4: The Fold-In process. A point query is projected into the space of acoustic GMM posterior.

from the acoustic GMM to the VA GMM, and then coming up with a summarized learning algorithm of the VA GMM.

4.1 Acoustic GMM Posterior Representation

To start the generative process of the AEG model, we utilize a universal acoustic GMM, which is pre-learned using the expectation-maximization (EM) algorithm on a universal set of frame vectors $\mathcal{F}$, to span a probabilistic space with a set of diverse acoustic Gaussians. The learned acoustic GMM is expressed as follows,

$$p(\mathbf{x}) = \sum_{k=1}^{K} \pi_k \mathcal{N}(\mathbf{x}|z_k, \mathbf{m}_k, \mathbf{S}_k), \quad (1)$$

where $\mathbf{x}$ is a frame-based feature vector; π_k, $\mathbf{m}_k$, and $\mathbf{S}_k$ are the prior weight, mean vector, and covariance matrix of the k-th component Gaussian A_k, respectively.

Suppose that we have an annotated music corpus $\mathcal{X}$ with N clips, each is denoted as s_i, and its t-th frame vector is denoted as $\{\mathbf{x}_{it}\}_{t=1}^{T_i}$, where T_i is the number of frames. The acoustic posterior probability of z_k for $\mathbf{x}_{it}$ is computed by,

$$p(z_k|\mathbf{x}_{it}) = \frac{\mathcal{N}(\mathbf{x}_{it}|z_k, \mathbf{m}_k, \mathbf{S}_k)}{\sum_{h=1}^{K} \mathcal{N}(\mathbf{x}_{it}|z_h, \mathbf{m}_h, \mathbf{S}_h)}. \quad (2)$$

In our implementation, the mixture prior (i.e., π_k and π_h) in Eq. 2 is replaced by $\frac{1}{K}$, because it is not useful in the previous work [28].

The clip-level acoustic GMM posterior probability θ_{ik} can be summarized by averaging the frame-level ones,

$$\theta_{ik} \leftarrow p(z_k|s_i) = \frac{1}{T_i} \sum_{t=1}^{T_i} p(z_k|\mathbf{x}_{it}). \quad (3)$$

Finally, the acoustic GMM posterior of s_i is represented by vector $\boldsymbol{\theta}_i$, whose k-th component is θ_{ik}.

4.2 Prior Model for Emotion Annotation

To cover the emotion perception of different subjects, typically a clip in $\mathcal{X}$ is annotated by multiple subjects. However, as some annotations may be unreliable, we introduce a user prior model to express the contribution of each individual subject. Given the emotion annotations $\{\mathbf{e}_{ij}\}_{j=1}^{U_i}$ of s_i, where $\mathbf{e}_{ij}$ denotes the annotation by the j-th subject u_{ij} and U_i denotes the number of subjects who have annotated s_i, we build a label confidence model γ with the following Gaussian distribution,

$$\gamma(\mathbf{e}_{ij}|u_{ij}, s_i) \equiv \mathcal{N}(\mathbf{e}_{ij}|s_i, \mathbf{a}_i, \mathbf{B}_i), \quad (4)$$

where $\mathbf{a}_i = \frac{1}{U_i}\sum_j \mathbf{e}_{ij}$ and $\mathbf{B}_i = \frac{1}{U_i}\sum_j (\mathbf{e}_{ij} - \mathbf{a}_i)(\mathbf{e}_{ij} - \mathbf{a}_i)^T$. The confidence of $\mathbf{e}_{ij}$ can be estimated based on the likelihood calculated by Eq. 4. Therefore, if an annotation is far away from other annotations for the same song, it would be considered less reliable. Note that any criterion that is able to reflect the importance of a user's subjective annotation of a clip can be applied to model γ. In our preliminary study, we found that a single Gaussian empirically performs better than a GMM in describing γ.

Then, the posterior probability of user u_{ij} can be calculated by normalizing the confidence likelihood of $\mathbf{e}_{ij}$ over the cumulative confidence likelihood of all users for s_i,

$$p(u_{ij}|s_i) \equiv \frac{\gamma(\mathbf{e}_{ij}|u_{ij}, s_i)}{\sum_{r=1}^{U_i} \gamma(\mathbf{e}_{ir}|u_{ir}, s_i)}. \quad (5)$$

$p(u_{ij}|s_i)$ is referred to as the *clip-level user prior*, as it indicates the confidence of each annotation for the clip. Based on the clip-level user prior, we further define the *corpus-level clip prior* to describe the importance of each clip as follows,

$$p(s_i|\mathcal{X}) \equiv \frac{\sum_{j=1}^{U_i} \gamma(\mathbf{e}_{ij}|u_{ij}, s_i)}{\sum_{q=1}^{N}\sum_{r=1}^{U_q} \gamma(\mathbf{e}_{qr}|u_{qr}, s_q)}. \quad (6)$$

If the annotations of a clip are more consistent (i.e., the covariance values in $\mathbf{B}_i$ are small), the song is considered less subjective. If a song is annotated by more subjects, the corresponding γ model should be more reliable. The above two cases both lead to larger cumulative annotation confidence likelihoods.

With the two priors $p(u_{ij}|s_i)$ and $p(s_i|\mathcal{X})$, we define the *annotation prior* γ_{ij} by multiplying Eqs. 5 and 6,

$$\gamma_{ij} \leftarrow p(u_{ij}, s_i|\mathcal{X}) = \frac{\gamma(\mathbf{e}_{ij}|u_{ij}, s_i)}{\sum_{q=1}^{N}\sum_{r=1}^{U_q} \gamma(\mathbf{e}_{qr}|u_{qr}, s_q)}. \quad (7)$$

The probabilities derived from Eqs. 5–7 are computed beforehand and then fixed in the learning process of AEG.

4.3 Learning the VA GMM

As described in the model overview, we assume that $\mathbf{e}_{ij}$ of s_i for u_{ij} in $\mathcal{X}$ can be generated from a weighted VA GMM governed by the acoustic GMM posterior $\boldsymbol{\theta}_i$ of s_i,

$$p(\mathbf{e}_{ij}|u_{ij}, s_i, \boldsymbol{\theta}_i) = \sum_{k=1}^{K} \theta_{ik}\mathcal{N}(\mathbf{e}_{ij}|\boldsymbol{\mu}_k, \boldsymbol{\Sigma}_k), \quad (8)$$

where $\boldsymbol{\mu}_k$ and $\boldsymbol{\Sigma}_k$ denote the mean vector and covariance matrix of the k-th latent VA Gaussian G_k shown in Figure 2 to be learned by means of the following algorithm.

First, for each clip s_i, we derive its acoustic prior $\boldsymbol{\theta}_i$, which is the acoustic GMM posterior vector, and the annotation prior γ_{ij} for each annotator u_{ij} of s_i. These two priors are computed beforehand and stay fixed in the learning process. Using $\mathbf{E}$ to denote the whole set of annotations in $\mathcal{X}$, the total likelihood can be derived by,

$$\begin{aligned} p(\mathbf{E}|\mathcal{X}) &= \textstyle\sum_i p(\mathbf{E}_i, s_i|\mathcal{X}) = \sum_i p(s_i|\mathcal{X})p(\mathbf{E}_i|s_i, \mathcal{X}) \\ &= \textstyle\sum_i p(s_i|\mathcal{X}) \sum_j p(\mathbf{e}_{ij}, u_{ij}|s_i, \mathcal{X}) \\ &= \textstyle\sum_i p(s_i|\mathcal{X}) \sum_j p(u_{ij}|s_i, \mathcal{X})p(\mathbf{e}_{ij}|u_{ij}, s_i, \mathcal{X}) \\ &= \textstyle\sum_i \sum_j p(u_{ij}, s_i|\mathcal{X}) \sum_k \theta_{ik}\mathcal{N}(\mathbf{e}_{ij}|\boldsymbol{\mu}_k, \boldsymbol{\Sigma}_k). \end{aligned} \quad (9)$$

Taking the logarithm of Eq. 9 and replacing $p(u_{ij}, s_i|\mathcal{X})$ by γ_{ij} leads to,

$$L = \log \sum_i \sum_j \gamma_{ij} \sum_k \theta_{ik}\mathcal{N}(\mathbf{e}_{ij}|\boldsymbol{\mu}_k, \boldsymbol{\Sigma}_k), \quad (10)$$

where $\sum_i\sum_j \gamma_{ij} = 1$. To learn the VA GMM, we can maximize the log-likelihood in Eq. 10 with respect to the parameters of VA GMM. However, direct maximization of L is intractable as two-layer summation over the latent variables z_k appears inside the logarithm [1]. We therefore first derive a lower bound of L according to Jensen's inequality,

$$L \geq L_{\text{bound}} = \sum_{i,j} \gamma_{ij} \log \sum_k \theta_{ik}\mathcal{N}(\mathbf{e}_{ij}|\boldsymbol{\mu}_k, \boldsymbol{\Sigma}_k). \quad (11)$$

Then, we treat L_{bound} as a surrogate of L. Although maximizing L_{bound} is still intractable, the logarithm now acts only on one-layer summation over the latent variables z_k. Therefore, we can maximize it with the EM algorithm [1].

In the E-step, we derive the expectation over the posterior probability of z_k given a user's annotation $\mathbf{e}_{ij}$ for s_i,

$$Q = \sum_{i,j} \gamma_{ij} \sum_k p(z_k|\mathbf{e}_{ij}, s_i) \left(\log \theta_{ik} + \log \mathcal{N}(\mathbf{e}_{ij}|\hat{\boldsymbol{\mu}}_k, \hat{\boldsymbol{\Sigma}}_k)\right), \quad (12)$$

where

$$p(z_k|\mathbf{e}_{ij}, s_i) = \frac{\theta_{ik}\mathcal{N}(\mathbf{e}_{ij}|\boldsymbol{\mu}_k, \boldsymbol{\Sigma}_k)}{\sum_{h=1}^{K} \theta_{ih}\mathcal{N}(\mathbf{e}_{ij}|\boldsymbol{\mu}_h, \boldsymbol{\Sigma}_h)}. \quad (13)$$

In the M-step, we maximize Eq. 12 and derive the following update rules:

$$\hat{\boldsymbol{\mu}}_k' \leftarrow \frac{\sum_i \sum_j \gamma_{ij} p(z_k|\mathbf{e}_{ij}, s_i)\mathbf{e}_{ij}}{\sum_i \sum_j \gamma_{ij} p(z_k|\mathbf{e}_{ij}, s_i)}, \quad (14)$$

$$\boldsymbol{\Sigma}_k' \leftarrow \frac{\sum_i \sum_j \gamma_{ij} p(z_k|\mathbf{e}_{ij}, s_i)(\mathbf{e}_{ij} - \boldsymbol{\mu}_k')(\mathbf{e}_{ij} - \boldsymbol{\mu}_k')^T}{\sum_i \sum_j \gamma_{ij} p(z_k|\mathbf{e}_{ij}, s_i)}. \quad (15)$$

At the last iteration of the EM learning process, we keep the prior model of the VA GMM,

$$\rho_k \leftarrow p(z_k) = \frac{1}{N} \sum_{i=1}^{N} \sum_{j=1}^{U_i} \gamma_{ij} p(z_k|\mathbf{e}_{ij}, s_i), \quad (16)$$

for the Fold-In method in the later retrieval work. The prior ρ_k of the VA GMM involves all the prior information of $\mathcal{X}$ over the set of latent feature classes. The learning process of the VA GMM is summarized in Algorithm 1.

Algorithm 1: The learning process of the VA GMM

Input: Initial model $\{\boldsymbol{\mu}_k^{(0)}, \boldsymbol{\Sigma}_k^{(0)}\}_{k=1}^{K}$; acoustic prior $\{\boldsymbol{\theta}_i\}_{i=1}^{N}$; annotation prior $\{\gamma_{ij}\}_{i=1,j=1}^{N,U_i}$;
Output: Model parameters $\{\rho_k, \boldsymbol{\mu}_k', \boldsymbol{\Sigma}_k'\}_{k=1}^{K}$;
1 Iteration index $t \leftarrow 0$;
2 **while** $t \leq ITER$ **do**
3 Compute the posterior probability using Eq. 13 with $\boldsymbol{\mu}_k^{(t)}$ and $\boldsymbol{\Sigma}_k^{(t)}$;
4 $t \leftarrow t + 1$;
5 Update $\boldsymbol{\mu}_k^{(t)}$ and $\boldsymbol{\Sigma}_k^{(t)}$ using Eqs. 14 and 15;
6 **if** $\boldsymbol{\Sigma}_k^{(t)}$ is *non-positive definite* **then break**;
7 **end**
8 Compute the prior model ρ_k using Eq. 16;
9 Let $\boldsymbol{\mu}_k' \leftarrow \boldsymbol{\mu}_k^{(t)}$ and $\boldsymbol{\Sigma}_k' \leftarrow \boldsymbol{\Sigma}_k^{(t)}$;

4.3.1 Discussion

As shown in Eqs. 14 and 15, the parameters $\boldsymbol{\mu}_k'$ and $\boldsymbol{\Sigma}_k'$ of each Gaussian component in the learned VA GMM are softly contributed by all annotations $\mathbf{e}_{ij}$, and the responsibility is governed by the product of γ_{ij} and $p(z_k|\mathbf{e}_{ij}, s_i)$. As a result, the learning process seamlessly takes the annotation prior, acoustic prior, and likelihood over the current VA

GMM into consideration. As the VA GMM is getting fitted to the data, it may appear that two far-separate groups of annotations jointly have fairly large responsibilities on the covariance of a component VA Gaussian. This would make the covariance matrix non-positive definite (non-PD), which means the covariance shape of the VA Gaussian will become a straight line. The learning process will stop if the non-PD case occurs, as shown in line 6 in Algorithm 1.

5. EMOTION-BASED ANNOTATION AND RETRIEVAL USING AEG

In this section, we first explain how to use the AEG model for distribution-based emotion prediction and analyze the complexity of prediction. Then, we introduce how the model effects content-based music retrieval from the Emotion Prediction and the Fold-In perspectives, respectively.

5.1 Automatic Emotion Prediction

As described in Section 3.2, the VA GMM can generate the emotion annotation of an unseen music clip $\hat{s}$ given the clip's acoustic GMM posterior $\hat{\boldsymbol{\theta}}$ as follows,

$$p(\mathbf{e}|\hat{\boldsymbol{\theta}}) = \sum\nolimits_{k=1}^{K} \hat{\theta}_k \mathcal{N}(\mathbf{e}|\boldsymbol{\mu}_k, \boldsymbol{\Sigma}_k), \tag{17}$$

where $\{\boldsymbol{\mu}_k, \boldsymbol{\Sigma}_k\}_{k=1}^{K}$ are the learned VA GMM. The predicted emotion distribution of an unseen clip shown in Eq. 17 may be unnecessarily complicated, and presenting the result as a mixture of Gaussians also makes it difficult for a user to interpret the result of emotion prediction. Instead, a single and representative VA Gaussian $\mathcal{N}(\mathbf{e}|\hat{\boldsymbol{\mu}}, \hat{\boldsymbol{\Sigma}})$ is practically more useful as explained in Section 3.2. This can be resorted to the information theory to calculate the mean and covariance of the representative VA Gaussian by solving the following optimization problem,

$$\mathcal{N}(\mathbf{e}|\hat{\boldsymbol{\mu}}, \hat{\boldsymbol{\Sigma}}) = \underset{\{\boldsymbol{\mu}, \boldsymbol{\Sigma}\}}{\operatorname{argmin}} \sum\nolimits_{k} \hat{\theta}_k D_{\mathrm{KL}}(\mathcal{N}(\mathbf{e}|\boldsymbol{\mu}_k, \boldsymbol{\Sigma}_k) \| \mathcal{N}(\mathbf{e}|\boldsymbol{\mu}, \boldsymbol{\Sigma})), \tag{18}$$

where $D_{\mathrm{KL}}(\mathcal{N}_A \| \mathcal{N}_B)$ denotes the one-way KL divergence from $\mathcal{N}(\mathbf{e}|\boldsymbol{\mu}_A, \boldsymbol{\Sigma}_A)$ to $\mathcal{N}(\mathbf{e}|\boldsymbol{\mu}_B, \boldsymbol{\Sigma}_B)$:

$$\begin{aligned} D_{\mathrm{KL}}(\mathcal{N}_A \| \mathcal{N}_B) =& \frac{1}{2}\left(\operatorname{tr}(\boldsymbol{\Sigma}_A \boldsymbol{\Sigma}_B^{-1}) - \log|\boldsymbol{\Sigma}_A \boldsymbol{\Sigma}_B^{-1}|\right) \\ &+ \frac{1}{2}(\boldsymbol{\mu}_A - \boldsymbol{\mu}_B)^T \boldsymbol{\Sigma}_B^{-1}(\boldsymbol{\mu}_A - \boldsymbol{\mu}_B) - 1, \end{aligned} \tag{19}$$

The optimal mean vector and covariance matrix for Eq. 18 are obtained by [3]:

$$\hat{\boldsymbol{\mu}} = \sum\nolimits_{k=1}^{K} \hat{\theta}_k \boldsymbol{\mu}_k, \tag{20}$$

$$\hat{\boldsymbol{\Sigma}} = \sum\nolimits_{k=1}^{K} \hat{\theta}_k \left(\boldsymbol{\Sigma}_k + (\boldsymbol{\mu}_k - \hat{\boldsymbol{\mu}})(\boldsymbol{\mu}_k - \hat{\boldsymbol{\mu}})^T\right). \tag{21}$$

The AEG-based emotion prediction is very efficient. The complexity mainly depends on the size of latent feature classes K. One only needs to compute the acoustic GMM posterior representation of a music clip and use it to generate a bivariate Gaussian distribution by using Eqs. 20 and 21. The method is efficient enough to be applied to real-time music emotion tracking on a sequence of short music segments on a mobile device. The application can also be incorporated into a music player to create a real-time visualization of music content to enrich the experience of music listening.

5.2 Emotion-based Music Retrieval

As described in Section 3.3, two methods with the AEG model can be used for music retrieval from an un-labeled database given a point query in the VA space. In the Emotion Prediction method, each music clip is indexed as a single bivariate Gaussian distribution estimated by automatic emotion prediction. Given a point query, the music clips in the database are ranked according to the likelihoods of their automatically predicted Gaussian PDFs.

As for the Fold-In method, given a query point $\hat{\mathbf{e}}$, the system has to fold in the point into the AEG model and estimate a pseudo song $\hat{\boldsymbol{\lambda}}$ in an online fashion. This is achieved by maximizing the $\boldsymbol{\lambda}$-weighted VA GMM as follows:

$$\hat{\boldsymbol{\lambda}} = \underset{\boldsymbol{\lambda}}{\operatorname{argmax}} \log \sum\nolimits_{k} \lambda_k \mathcal{N}(\hat{\mathbf{e}}|\boldsymbol{\mu}_k, \boldsymbol{\Sigma}_k). \tag{22}$$

That is to say, $\hat{\boldsymbol{\lambda}}$ corresponds to the most likely weighted combination of VA GMM for generating $\hat{\mathbf{e}}$. Eq. 22 can also be solved by the EM algorithm. In the E-step, the posterior probability of z_k given the query is computed by

$$p(z_k|\hat{\mathbf{e}}) = \frac{\lambda_k \mathcal{N}(\hat{\mathbf{e}}|\boldsymbol{\mu}_k, \boldsymbol{\Sigma}_k)}{\sum_h \lambda_h \mathcal{N}(\hat{\mathbf{e}}|\boldsymbol{\mu}_h, \boldsymbol{\Sigma}_h)}. \tag{23}$$

Then, in the M-step, we only update λ_k by $\hat{\lambda}_k \leftarrow p(z_k|\hat{\mathbf{e}})$. Note that in estimating the pseudo song, the prior model of the VA GMM $\{\rho_k\}_{k=1}^{K}$ can be used for initialization. In our preliminary study, initializing with $\{\rho_k\}_{k=1}^{K}$ exhibits the best performance among other settings, such as uniform or random initialization.

Since each music clip in the un-labeled database has been indexed by an acoustic GMM posterior vector and the estimated pseudo song $\hat{\boldsymbol{\lambda}}$ of a query lies in the same vector space, the retrieval system ranks all the clips in descending order of cosine similarity in response to the query.

5.2.1 Remark

The Emotion Prediction method for retrieval is intuitive since we developed the system from the emotion prediction perspective. The Fold-In method goes one step further and leverages the learned relationship between audio patterns and emotions to represent a music clip and an emotion query in the same latent class space. Although the Fold-In method needs an additional step for pseudo song estimation, it is actually more flexible and efficient for incorporating external information. For example, when user feedback is available, online personalization is possible by performing adaptation on the learned VA GMM without retraining the model and re-annotating the songs in the database.

6. INTERPRETATION OF AEG

This section describes the annotated music corpora and the frame-based acoustic features utilized in this work. An in-depth analysis of the model learning process of AEG is conducted using the annotated corpora to offer insights to the VA GMM.

6.1 Music Corpora

Two corpora are employed in this work.[6] The first corpus MER60 consists of 60 clips (each is 30-second long) collected

[6] The datasets are available at `http://mac.iis.sinica.edu.tw/~yang/MER/NTUMIR-60/` and `http://music.ece.drexel.edu/research/emotion/moodswingsturk`.

from the chorus parts of English pop songs [30]. A total of 99 subjects were recruited for emotion annotation, making each clip annotated by 40 subjects. The subjects were asked to rate the VA values that best describe their general (instead of moment-to-moment) emotion perception of each clip in a silent computer lab. The VA values are entered by clicking on the emotion space on a computer display.

The second corpus, MTurk, is composed of 240 clips (each is 15-second long) drawn from the well-known uspop2002 database [26]. The emotion annotation is collected via Amazon's Mechanical Turk,[7] an online crowdscourcing engine. Each subject was asked to rate the per-second VA values for 11 randomly-selected clips using a graphical interface. After an automatic verification step that removes unreliable annotations, each clip is annotated by 7 to 23 subjects.

6.2 Frame-based Acoustic Features

In this work, we adopt the bag-of-frames modeling and extract frame-based musical features for acoustic modeling [28]. A frame that captures detailed temporal features can facilitate the ability of clip-level acoustic modeling of the acoustic GMM posterior representation. Instead of analyzing the emotion of a specific frame, we aggregate all the frames in a clip into the acoustic GMM posterior vector $\boldsymbol{\theta}$ (cf. Eq. 3) and perform our analysis of emotion at the clip level. Although it may be interesting to extract long-term mid-level features such as melody, rhythm, chord, or structural segments that directly characterizes the musical information, such features are not used because the extraction of them is still not perfect and they may introduce noises to the system. We leave this issue in our future work.

We use MIRToolbox 1.3 [14] to extract the following four types of frame-based acoustic features: *dynamic* (root-mean-squared energy), *spectral* (centroid, spread, skewness, kurtosis, entropy, flatness, rolloff 85%, rolloff 95%, brightness, roughness, and irregularity), *timbre* (zero crossing rate, spectral flux, 13 MFCCs, 13 delta MFCCs, and 13 delta-delta MFCCs), and *tonal* (key clarity, key mode possibility, HCDF, 12-bin chroma, chroma peak, and chroma centroid). All of the frame-based features are extracted with the same frame size of 50ms and 50% hop size to ensure easy alignment. Each dimension in all extracted frame vectors is normalized to have zero mean and one standard deviation. Two frame vector representations are considered in the performance evaluation: a 39-D vector that consists of MFCC-related features only and a 70-D vector that concatenates all the features.

For the MTurk corpus, since the audio waveforms are not available, we use the following four types of features that are kindly provided by the authors of [19, 26].

- **MFCCs** (20-D): Low-dimensional representation of the spectrum warped according to Mel-scale.
- **Chroma** (12-D): Autocorrelation of chroma is used, providing an indication of modality.
- **Spectrum descriptors** (4-D): Spectral centroid, flux, rolloff and flatness. Often related to timbral texture.
- **Spectral contrast** (14-D): Rough representation of the harmonic content in the frequency domain.

In the experiments, the individual feature sets are either used separately or concatenated into a 50-D vector.

[7] http://www.mturk.com

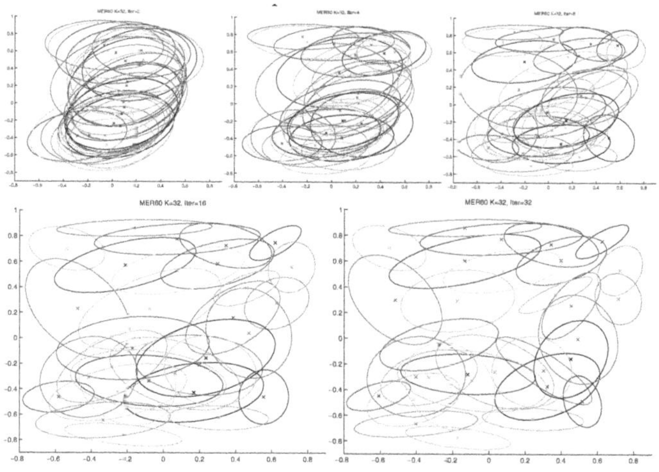

Figure 5: The learned VA GMMs (K=32) at different iterations (Iter=2, 4, 8, 16, and 32). Each component Gaussian is represented by an ellipse with a unique color. The horizontal and vertical axes correspond to valence and activation, respectively.

6.3 Interpretation of the Learned VA GMM on the MER60 Corpus

To observe the learning of AEG and interpret the resulting VA GMM we fit the AEG model on MER60 and examine the learned VA GMM at each iteration of Algorithm 1. We first use an external music collection to form the global frame vector set $\mathcal{F}$ containing 235K 70-D frame vectors. Then, the acoustic GMMs are learned with several K values using the EM algorithm. We initialize all the Gaussian components of the VA GMM with the sample mean vector and covariance matrix of the emotion annotations of the whole training set.

Figure 5 illustrates the VA GMM learned at a number of iterations, from which one can observe that, while being tied together in the beginning, the VA Gaussians gradually separate one from the others as the learning process progresses. The ellipse of each VA Gaussian gets smaller and smaller after each iteration until convergence. As shown in the last sub-figure in Figure 5, in the end, different Gaussians cover different areas in the emotion space, and the learned VA GMM appears to be able to approximate all kinds of emotion distributions by using different sets of acoustic GMM posterior probabilities. Since our preliminary study indicates that over-small VA Gaussians may not help for emotion prediction, early stop is required.

The specific area covered by a VA Gaussian actually gives a semantic meaning to the corresponding latent feature class defined by the acoustic GMM. That is, the mapping from the acoustic space to the emotion space can be easily observed and interpreted. We also notice that there are many Gaussians with horizontally elongated ellipses, suggesting that the annotations along the valence dimension are more difficult to model from acoustic features. This is not surprising as much previous work has pointed out that valence perception is in nature much more subjective than activation perception and, thus, is more difficult to model [29].

Recall the definition of latent feature classes, the mapped VA Gaussians can show us the discriminability of each latent acoustic Gaussian. We could take away those ill-conditioned VA Gaussians as well as their mapped acoustic Gaussians either manually or via a stacked discriminative learning, e.g., by minimizing the prediction error with respect to Gaussian selection or adaptation on the VA GMM. In addition, the current latent acoustic Gaussian classifiers can also be replaced by kernel-based classifiers that map the frame vector space to a higher dimensional feature space, so that they may help generate a set of more discriminative VA Gaussians. We plan to leverage these insights to further improve the proposed framework in the future.

7. EVALUATION AND RESULTS

In this section, we first describe the evaluation setups for the emotion-based annotation and retrieval tasks, respectively. We then present the evaluation results of AEG with different settings of acoustic features and parameters, and compare them with that of two state-of-the-art methods.

7.1 Evaluation Setting and Metric

In Section 6.3, we have described the training setup for MER60. As for the MTurk corpus, the frame-based feature vectors of a song are provided by the authors of [26]. Since each piece has 15 second-by-second annotation sets (each annotation set is aligned with a specific second), we extract the frames corresponding to each one-second segment of each song. The resulting corpus contains 240×15=3,600 segments with corresponding annotations, which were normalized to $[-0.5, 0.5]$[8]. In addition, we select 300K frames at random from the remaining frames (excluding those annotated frames) of all songs to form the global frame set $\mathcal{F}$. The VA GMM is initialized with the global sample mean vector and covariance matrix of the emotion annotations of the whole training set.

The AEG model can predict the emotion of an input music piece as a mixture of VA Gaussians (i.e., a VA GMM) as well as a single VA Gaussian. Since measuring the distance between two GMMs is complicated and sometimes inaccurate [8],[9] we finally chose to evaluate the accuracy of emotion prediction based on a single Gaussian rather than a GMM. To evaluate the emotion annotation task, each set of ground truth annotations of a song is summarized by a ground truth Gaussian. The performance can be evaluated by two evaluation metrics, namely, the one-way KL divergence (cf. Eq. 19) and the Euclidean distance of mean vectors between the predicted and ground truth VA Gaussians for a clip.

For the emotion-based music retrieval task, we follow the music retrieval scenario described in Section 3, i.e., a user inputs a point query on the VA plane and receives a ranked list of pieces from an un-labeled music database. We randomly generate 500 2-D points uniformly covering the available VA space to form a test query set. To evaluate the retrieval performance using the test query set, we first derive the ground truth relevance $R(i)$ between a query point and the i-th piece in the database by feeding the query point into the ground truth Gaussian PDF of the i-th piece. For each test query point, the ground truth relevances is incorporated into the normalized discounted cumulative gain (NDCG) [10] to evaluate the ranking of pieces. The NDCG@P, which represents the quality of ranking of the top P retrieved music pieces for the query, is formulated as follows:

$$\text{NDCG@}P = \frac{1}{Q_P}\left\{R(1) + \sum_{j=2}^{P}\frac{R(j)}{\log_2 j}\right\}, \tag{24}$$

where $R(j)$ is the ground truth relevance of the j-th piece on the ranked list, and Q_P is the normalization term that guarantees the ideal NDCG@P to be 1.

In the train/test evaluation scenario, we perform different settings for MER60 and MTurk. For MER60, we only execute the leave-one-out setting for the annotation task due to its limited number of songs [30]. That is, each song is taken as a test song in turn to predict its emotion annotation, and the remaining songs are used for training the models. For Mturk, in order to follow the work in [26], we randomly select 70% of songs (168 songs) for training and 30% (72 songs) for testing. The test set with 72×15=1,080 segments is used for emotion prediction and serves as the unseen music database for emotion-based retrieval. Since each segment has its unique audio content and the corresponding ground truth VA Gaussian, we treat each segment as an individual music piece for retrieval evaluation.

7.2 Results of Automatic Emotion Prediction

We evaluate the performance of emotion annotation in terms of average KL divergence (AKL) and average mean Euclidean distance (AMD) over the test set. Smaller AKL and AMD correspond to better performance. For MER60, the following factors in AEG are considered: the frame-level feature representation (either 39-D MFCCs or 70-D concatenated features), the number of latent feature classes K, and whether to use the annotation prior described in Section 4.2 or not. For example, "AEG-APrior-70DConcat" means using the annotation prior with the 70-D concatenated features. We test the AEG model with K ranging from 8 to 512. When the annotation prior is not used, we simply replace all γ_{ij} by 1 in the learning process. We compare the AEG method with support vector regression (SVR) [22] with different acoustic features. The SVR-Melody method using the melody features was the best performed setting reported in [30]. We also investigate the performance of SVR using the acoustic features used in our method.

From Figures 6 (a) and (b), we observe that the AEG method consistently outperforms the SVR method in almost all cases. Particularly, AEG-APrior-70DConcat (K=32) significantly outperforms SVR-Melody in terms of both AKL and AMD (p-value< 1% under the two-tailed t-test). The AKL shows a consistent tendency in performance difference for different AEG settings. In general, the annotation prior model improves the performance, and the 70-D concatenated features outperform the 39-D MFCCs when K is small. As for AMD, a general tendency is not observed. Interestingly, it seems that the performance of AEG-APrior-39DMFCC straightly improves as K increases, and that the performance does not saturate when K is 512. AEG obtains the lowest AKL when K=32. Such a result demonstrates its superior efficiency.

For MTurk, the annotation prior is adopted because of its superior performance on MER60. For each setting, we repeat the one-second prediction experiment 20 times and compute the average performance. We compare the AEG method with the systems in [26], including the multiple lin-

[8]The valence and activation of raw annotations derived from MTurk are both in the range of $[-200, 200]$.

[9]A single Gaussian representation is practically useful as explained in Secion 3.2.

Table 2: **The comparison of automatic emotion annotation methods, each with the optimal setting.**

Corpus	Method	AKL	AMD
MER60	SVR	1.894 ± 1.697	0.391 ± 0.177
	AEG	$\mathbf{1.230 \pm 1.421}$	$\mathbf{0.344 \pm 0.168}$
MTurk	MLR	0.654 ± 0.066	0.130 ± 0.006
	AEG	$\mathbf{0.577 \pm 0.031}$	0.128 ± 0.002

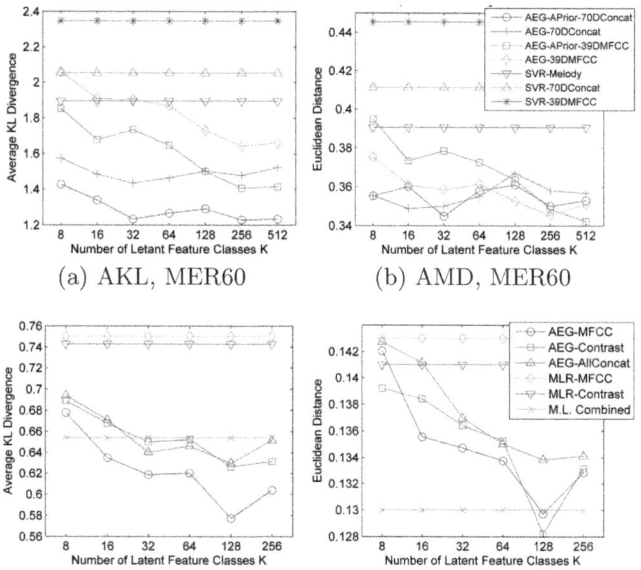

(a) AKL, MER60 (b) AMD, MER60

(c) AKL, MTurk (d) AMD, MTurk

Figure 6: Results of automatic emotion annotation.

ear regression (MLR) method and the multi-layer combined (M.L. Combined) method, which employs multiple acoustic feature regressors and two layer prediction. M.L. Combined is considered as the ultimate fusion system in [19].

The results in Figures 6 (c) and (d) indicate that the AEG method significantly outperforms the MLR method using either MFCCs or Contrast features alone in almost all cases.[10] In many cases, AEG-MFCC and AEG-Contrast even outperform the M.L. Combined method in terms of AKL. We find that AEG does not benefit from the concatenated features on MTurk. On the contrary, AEG-MFCC performs consistently better than almost all other settings, except for AEG-Contrast in terms of AMD. The performance of AEG is observed to saturate when K is 128.

In general, the performance of AEG grows along with K when K is small, and then saturates after K is sufficiently large. This is reasonable as the value of K is closely related to the resolution in acoustic modeling and the model complexity. Nevertheless, the results suggest that the optimal value of K is corpus dependent, and it seems to be helpful to use a large K when the scale of the training corpus is large.

We summarize the comparison of best performance of AEG versus SVR and MLR fusion in Table 2. We also demonstrate the results of short-time emotion tracking in Figure 7. Empirically we found that it is easy to obtain better average performance and lower standard deviation for MTurk than for MER60 since the ground truth annotation

[10]Comparing to the standard formulation of KL divergence, the one used in [26] is two times larger. We therefore divided the KL divergences listed in [26] by two for fairness.

Table 3: The retrieval performance of different methods in terms of NDCG@5, 10, and 20.

Method (best K)	P=5	P=10	P=20
Predict MFCC (K=256)	0.886	0.825	0.785
Predict Contrast (K=256)	0.894	0.841	0.811
Predict AllConcat (K=128)	0.892	0.839	0.805
Fold-In MFCC (K=32)	0.874	0.814	0.767
Fold-In Contrast (K=32)	0.902	0.831	0.781
Fold-In AllConcat (K=64)	0.898	0.832	0.786

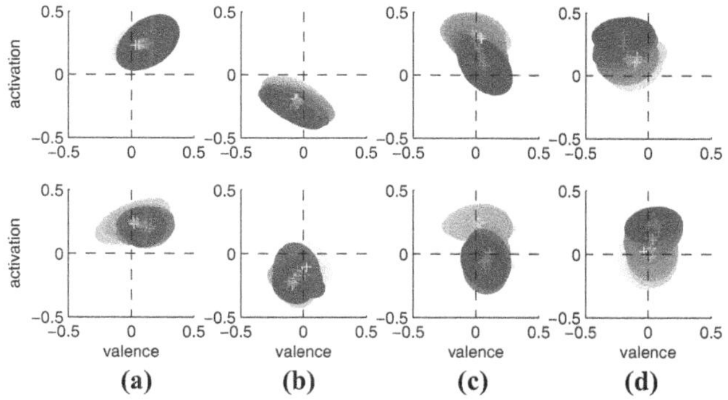

Figure 7: Demonstration for automatic emotion tracking of four 15-second clips on MTurk.[12] The top row shows the second-by-second ground truth 2-D annotation Gaussians (blue ellipse with a red cross representing the center), and the bottom row presents the corresponding predicted ones. The color gets darker as time unfolds.

Gaussians of MTurk are less diverse. This is evident from the fact that, when we measure the pair-wise KL divergence (PWKL) between the ground truth annotation Gaussians of each pair of clips in a corpus, the average PWKL for MTurk (1.985) is much smaller than that for MER60 (5.095). We also found that the annotation Gaussians of many clips in MTurk can be simply approximated by a Gaussian centered at the origin. But this is not the case for MER60, which consists of many clips whose annotation Gaussians are centered far away from the origin. Therefore, the evaluation results of MER60 should be considered more important and representative. In summary, the evaluation results demonstrate the effectiveness of the AEG model, and suggest that the proposed method indeed offers a potential solution for automatic VA-based emotion annotation.

7.3 Results of Emotion-Based Music Retrieval

The retrieval performance over the test query set of the pre-generated 500 points is given in Table 3. Each retrieval method with a type of acoustic features is evaluated with K ranging from 8 and 256, as done in the annotation task. Due to the space limit, we only show the best performance in Table 3 among different settings of K.

In general, the two retrieval methods exhibit similar performance. Interestingly, the Emotion Prediction method favors a larger K while Fold-In favors a smaller one. This makes sense since a larger K leads to better annotation performance, which would in turn benefit the Emotion Prediction based retrieval strategy. As for the Fold-In method, a

[12]The four clips are (a) *Same Old Song and Dance* by Aerosmith, (b) *Save Me* by Queen, (c) *Waitress* by Live, and (d) *Microphone Fiend* by Rage Against the Machine.

larger K might introduce randomness to the estimation of the corresponding pseudo song and, therefore, degrade the retrieval performance. When K is large, there will be multiple overlapping VA Gaussians in Figure 5. When a query point is located in an area with multiple overlapping VA Gaussians, the pseudo song estimated by Eq. 22 would be highly sensitive to the initialization of the model parameters. This would reduce the discriminative power in transforming a proper mapped pseudo song. We also notice that Fold-In achieves better performance when P (i.e., the number of retrieved pieces) in NDCG is small.

8. CONCLUSION AND FUTURE WORK

This paper has presented the novel acoustic emotion Gaussians model, which provides a principled probabilistic framework for music emotion analysis. We have interpreted the learning of AEG and provided insights. A comprehensive evaluation of automatic music emotion annotation on two emotion annotated music corpora has demonstrated the effectiveness of AEG over state-of-the-art methods. Moreover, we have also demonstrated the potential application of AEG for emotion-based music retrieval.

Our future work is four-fold. First, the probabilistic framework provides a blueprint for multi-modal music emotion modeling. The latent feature classes can not only be defined from music signals, but also from other relevant modalities such as lyrics, tags, and music video. Second, with a set of learned latent feature classes, multi-modal features can be aligned to one another. For example, if we have a *tagged* corpus and a *VA-annotated* corpus, we can automatically position the mood tags in the VA space by means of the fixed acoustic GMM. Third, we will investigate personalized music emotion recommendation. The AEG model can be used as a background model for general users. A collection of personal feedback data can then be used to adapt either acoustic GMM or VA GMM of the background model to create a personalized one. Finally, it would be interesting to study non-parametric Bayesian methods for the modeling of music emotion, and to investigate whether we can get better results without assuming that the VA space is Euclidean.

9. ACKNOWLEDGMENTS

This work was supported by the National Science Council of Taiwan under Grants: NSC-101-2221-E-001-019, NSC-101-2631-H-001-007, and NSC-100-2218-E-001-009. We thank the reviewers for their helpful comments.

10. REFERENCES

[1] C. M. Bishop. *Pattern Recognition and Machine Learning*. Springer-Verlag New York, Inc., 2006.

[2] R. A. Calvo and S. D'Mello. Affect detection: An interdisciplinary review of models, methods, and their applications. *IEEE Trans. Affective Computing*, 1(1):18–37, 2010.

[3] J. V. Davis and I. S. Dhillon. Differential entropic clustering of multivariate Gaussians. In *NIPS*, 2006.

[4] T. Eerola, O. Lartillot, and P. Toiviainen. Prediction of multidimensional emotional ratings in music from audio using multivariate regression models. In *ISMIR*, 2009.

[5] A. Gabrielsson. Emotion perceived and emotion felt: Same or different? *Musicae Scientiae*, pages 123–147, 2002.

[6] P. Gomez and B. Danuser. Relationships between musical structure and psychophysiological measures of emotion. *Emotion*, 7(2):377–87, 2007.

[7] S. Hallam, I. Cross, and M. Thaut. *The Oxford Handbook of Music Psychology*. Oxford University Press, 2008.

[8] J. Hershey and P. Olsen. Approximating the Kullback Leibler divergence between Gaussian mixture models. In *ICASSP*, pages 317–320, 2007.

[9] X. Hu, J. S. Downie, C. Laurier, M. Bay, and A. F. Ehmann. The 2007 MIREX audio mood classification task: Lessons learned. In *ISMIR*, 2008.

[10] K. Jarvelin and J. Kekalainen. Cumulated gain-based evaluation of IR techniques. *ACM Trans. on Info. Syst.*, 20(4):422–446, 2002.

[11] P. N. Juslin and P. Laukka. Expression, perception, and induction of musical emotions: A review and a questionnaire study of everyday listening. *J. New Music Res.*, 33(3):217–238, 2004.

[12] Y. E. Kim and et al. Music emotion recognition: A state of the art review. In *ISMIR*, 2010.

[13] M. D. Korhonen, D. A. Clausi, and M. E. Jernigan. Modeling emotional content of music using system identification. *IEEE Trans. System, Man and Cybernetics*, 36(3):588–599, 2006.

[14] O. Lartillot and P. Toiviainen. A Matlab toolbox for musical feature extraction from audio. In *DAFx*, 2007.

[15] L. Lu, D. Liu, and H. Zhang. Automatic mood detection and tracking of music audio signals. *IEEE Trans. Audio, Speech and Lang. Proc.*, 14(1):5–18, 2006.

[16] K. F. MacDorman, S. Ough, and C.-C. Ho. Automatic emotion prediction of song excerpts: Index construction, algorithm design, and empirical comparison. *J. New Music Res.*, 36(4):281–299, 2007.

[17] V. C. Raykar, S. Yu, L. H. Zhao, G. H. Valadez, C. Florin, L. Bogoni, and L. Moy. Learning from crowds. *J. Machine Learning Res.*, 11:1297–1322, 2010.

[18] J. A. Russell. A circumplex model of affect. *J. Personality and Social Science*, 39(6):1161–1178, 1980.

[19] E. M. Schmidt and Y. E. Kim. Prediction of time-varying musical mood distributions from audio. In *ISMIR*, 2010.

[20] E. M. Schmidt and Y. E. Kim. Prediction of time-varying musical mood distributions using Kalman filtering. In *ICMLA*, 2010.

[21] E. M. Schmidt and Y. E. Kim. Modeling musical emotion dynamics with conditional random fields. In *ISMIR*, 2011.

[22] B. Schölkopf, A. J. Smola, R. C. Williamson, and P. L. Bartlett. New support vector algorithms. *Neural Computation*, 12:1207–1245, 2000.

[23] E. Schubert. Modeling perceived emotion with continuous musical features. *Music Perception*, 21(4):561–585, 2004.

[24] B. Schuller, C. Hage, D. Schuller, and G. Rigoll. "Mister D.J., Cheer Me Up!": Musical and textual features for automatic mood classification. *J. New Music Res.*, 39(1):13–34, 2010.

[25] R. Sease and D. W. McDonald. The organization of home media. *ACM Trans. Com.-Hum. Interact.*, 18:1–20, 2011.

[26] J. A. Speck, E. M. Schmidt, B. G. Morton, and Y. E. Kim. A comparative study of collaborative vs. traditional musical mood annotation. In *ISMIR*, 2011.

[27] W. Trost, T. Ethofer, M. Zentner, and P. Vuilleumier. Mapping aesthetic musical emotions in the brain. *Cerebral Cortex*, 2011.

[28] J.-C. Wang, H.-S. Lee, H.-M. Wang, and S.-K. Jeng. Learning the similarity of audio music in bag-of-frames representation from tagged music data. In *ISMIR*, 2011.

[29] Y.-H. Yang and H. H. Chen. *Music Emotion Recognition*. CRC Press, Feb. 2011.

[30] Y.-H. Yang and H. H. Chen. Predicting the distribution of perceived emotions of a music signal for content retrieval. *IEEE Trans. Audio, Speech and Lang. Proc.*, 19(7):2184–2196, 2011.

[31] Y.-H. Yang, Y.-C. Lin, Y.-F. Su, and H. H. Chen. A regression approach to music emotion recognition. *IEEE Trans. Audio, Speech and Lang. Proc.*, 16(2):448–457, 2008.

Context-Aware Mobile Music Recommendation for Daily Activities

Xinxi Wang, David Rosenblum, Ye Wang
School of Computing, National University of Singapore
{wangxinxi,david,wangye}@comp.nus.edu.sg

ABSTRACT

Existing music recommendation systems rely on collaborative filtering or content-based technologies to satisfy users' long-term music playing needs. Given the popularity of mobile music devices with rich sensing and wireless communication capabilities, we present in this paper a novel approach to employ contextual information collected with mobile devices for satisfying users' short-term music playing needs. We present a probabilistic model to integrate contextual information with music content analysis to offer music recommendation for daily activities, and we present a prototype implementation of the model. Finally, we present evaluation results demonstrating good accuracy and usability of the model and prototype.

Categories and Subject Descriptors

H.3.3 [**Information Search and Retrieval**]: Retrieval models; H.5.5 [**Sound and Music Computing**]: [Modeling, Signal analysis, synthesis and processing]

General Terms

Algorithms, Design, Experimentation

Keywords

activity classification, context awareness, mobile computing, music recommendation, sensors

1. INTRODUCTION

Music recommendation systems help users find music from large music databases, and an effective system is one that consistently matches a user's preference. Most of the existing music recommendation systems that model users' long-term preferences provide an elegant solution to satisfying long-term music information needs [1]. However, according to some studies of the psychology and sociology of music, users' short-term needs are usually influenced by the users' *context*, such as their emotional states, activities, or external environment [2–4]. For instance, a user who is running generally will prefer loud, energizing music. Existing commercial music recommendation systems such as Last.fm and Pandora cannot satisfy these short-term needs very well. However, the advent of smart mobile phones with rich sensing capabilities makes real-time context information collection and exploitation a possibility [5–10]. Considerable attention has focused recently on *context-aware music recommender systems* (CAMRSs) in order to utilize contextual information and better satisfy users' short-term needs [11–28].

Existing CAMRSs have explored many kinds of context information, such as location [13, 19, 21, 24, 28], time [12, 19, 25, 26, 29, 30], emotional state [4, 12, 16, 18, 23, 27], physiological state [13, 17, 22, 25], running pace [11, 14, 17], weather [12, 25], and low-level activities [16]. To the best of our knowledge, none of the existing systems can recommend suitable music *explicitly* for *daily activities* such as working, sleeping, running, and studying. It is known that people prefer different music for different daily activities [2, 3]. But with current technology, people must create playlists manually for different activities and then switch to an appropriate playlist upon changing activities, which is time-consuming and inconvenient. A music system that can detect users' daily activities in real-time and play suitable music automatically thus could save time and effort.

Most existing collaborative filtering-based systems, content-based systems and CAMRSs require explicit user ratings or other manual annotations [1]. These systems cannot handle new users or new songs, because without annotations and ratings, these systems are not aware of anything about the particular user or song. This is the so-called *cold-start* problem [31]. However, as we demonstrate in this paper, with automated *music audio content analysis* (or, simply, music content analysis), it is possible to judge computationally whether or not a song is suitable for some daily activity. Moreover, with data from sensors on mobile phones such as acceleration, ambient noise, time of day, and so on, it is possible to infer automatically a user's current activity. Therefore, we expect that a system that *combines* activity inference with music content analysis can outperform existing systems when no rating or annotation exists, thus providing a solution to the cold-start problem.

Motivated by these observations, this paper presents a ubiquitous system built using off-the-shelf mobile phones that infers automatically a user's activity from low-level, real-time sensor data and then recommends songs matching

MM'12, October 29–November 2, 2012, Nara, Japan.

the inferred activity based on music content analysis. More specifically, we make the following contributions:

- *Automated activity classification:* We present the first system we are aware of that recommends songs explicitly for everyday user activities including *working*, *studying*, *running*, *sleeping*, *walking* and *shopping*. We present algorithms for classifying these contexts in real time from low-level data gathered from the sensors of users' mobile phones.
- *Automated music content analysis:* We present the results of a feasibility study demonstrating strong agreement among different people regarding songs that are suitable for particular daily activities. We then describe how we use music content analysis to train a statistical model for predicting the activities for which a song is suitable. This analysis can operate offline since the predictions they produce are independent of individual user activities or listening behaviors.
- *Solution to the cold-start problem:* We present an efficient probabilistic model for *Adaptive Context-Aware Content Filtering* (ACACF) that seamlessly unifies the activity classification and music content analysis results. This model can be updated *on-the-fly* for each user to adapt to their ongoing listening behavior.
- *Implementation and evaluation:* We present a prototype mobile application that implements all parts of the ACACF model except music content analysis entirely on a mobile phone, and we present evaluation results demonstrating its accuracy and usability.

This paper is organized as follows. Section 2 presents an overview of traditional music recommender systems. Section 3 formulates the probabilistic model used to do context-aware recommendation based on context inference and music content analysis. Section 4 describes the system design and implementation. Section 5 describes evaluations of our model and system. Section 6 discusses previous research that is most closely related to our own. Section 7 concludes the paper with a discussion of plans for future work.

2. BACKGROUND

Traditional music recommender systems can be classified according to three categories of recommendation methods: *collaborative filtering* (CF), *content-based* methods, and *hybrid* methods [1]. The main idea behind CF is that if user A and user B have similar music preferences, then songs liked by A but not yet considered by B will be recommended to B. CF-based systems suffer from the cold-start problem since they cannot recommend songs to new users whose preferences are unknown (the *new-user* problem) or recommend new songs to users (the *new-song* problem) [31]. In contrast to CF, content-based systems work as follows: If user A likes song S, then songs having content (i.e., musical features) similar to S will be recommended to A. Content-based systems help solve the new-song problem, but they still suffer from the new-user problem. Hybrid methods combine CF and content-based methods.

Traditional music recommender systems model only users' long-term preferences. CAMRSs, which take advantage of users' short-term context information, have been explored by some researchers. We next present our own CAMRS so that we may later discuss related work on CAMRSs.

3. UNIFIED PROBABILISTIC MODEL

In this section we present our Adaptive Context-Aware Content Filtering model, ACACF. The model uses a Bayesian framework to seamlessly integrate context-aware *activity classification* and *music content analysis*.

3.1 Problem Formulation

Let $\mathcal{S}$ be a set of songs and $\mathcal{C}$ a set of context categories.[1] For our model, the contexts are daily activities, with $\mathcal{C}$ ={*running*, *walking*, *sleeping*, *studying*, *working*, *shopping*}, but we can extend the model to other activities. A user is assumed to be in exactly one context category $c \in \mathcal{C}$ at any time. We also assume the user always carries his/her mobile phone, and that a sensor data stream can be recorded continuously from the phone. For our model, the sensor data includes time of day, accelerometer data, and audio from a microphone. The sensor data stream is divided into a sequence of frames, possibly with overlap between adjacent frames. For each frame, a vector $\mathbf{f}$ of *features* of the sensed data is extracted. The recommendation problem is then formulated as a two-step process: (1) infer the user's current context category $c \in \mathcal{C}$ from $\mathbf{f}$, and (2) find a song $s \in \mathcal{S}$ matching c the best. We call the first step *context inference* and the second step *music content analysis*.

3.2 Probability Models

Inferring a user's current context category c from the feature vector $\mathbf{f}$ is not an easy task. In our early experience we found it difficult sometimes to differentiate working and studying by a mobile phone; as sensed activities they appear to be similar, but they need to be differentiated because people have different music preferences when working versus studying. In order to capture such uncertainty, instead of obtaining exactly one context category from $\mathbf{f}$, we obtain a probability distribution $p(c_i|\mathbf{f})$ over all categories. For instance, if there is complete uncertainty about whether a user is working or studying, then we can assign the probability 0.5 to both working and studying. Using Bayes's rule, $p(c|\mathbf{f})$ can be as in Equation (1):[2]

$$p(c|\mathbf{f}) = \frac{p(\mathbf{f}|c)p(c)}{p(\mathbf{f})} \propto p(\mathbf{f}|c)p(c) \tag{1}$$

We call this part of our model the *sensor-context* model, and we elaborate it further in Section 3.4.

To model whether a song s is suitable for a context category c, we introduce a random variable $R \in \{0, 1\}$. $R = 1$ means s is suitable for c, and $R = 0$ otherwise. Then we use the probability $p(R = 1|c, s)$ to indicate the user satisfaction degree of song s when he/she is in context c. We call this part of our model the *music-context* model, and we elaborate it further in Section 3.3.

Combining $p(\mathbf{f}|c)p(c)$ with $p(R = 1|c, s)$, we obtain the joint probability shown in Equation (2):

$$p(c, \mathbf{f}, R, s) \propto p(\mathbf{f}|c)p(R|c, s)p(c) \tag{2}$$

[1]In the notation we present, bold letters represent vectors, calligraphic upper case letters represent sets, and random variables and their values are indicated by italicized upper-case and lower-case letters respectively.

[2]In this and subsequent formulas, we indicate proportional equivalents where normalizing constants can be omitted, thereby improving computation efficiency.

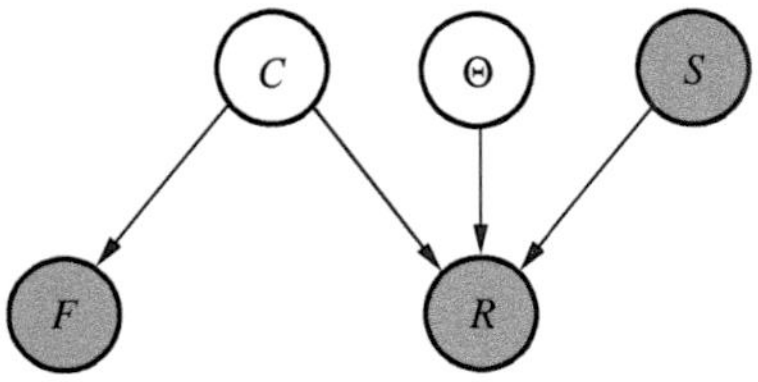

Figure 1: Graphical representation of the ACACF Model. Shaded and unshaded nodes represent observed and unobserved variables, respectively.

We assume that all songs share the same prior probability, so $p(s)$ can be omitted. The combined model can be represented by the graph depicted in Figure 1. The combined model is our ACACF model. Random variable Θ is a probability prior and will be explained in Section 3.3.1. The model is adaptive in that the component probabilities are updated dynamically as a result of evolving user behavior; the adaptive features of ACACF are presented in Sections 3.3.1 and 3.4.

With this model, the recommendation task is defined as follows: Given the feature vector $\mathbf{f}$ calculated from sensor data, find a song s that maximizes the user satisfaction $p(R=1|s,\mathbf{f})$, which is calculated in Equation (3) as the sum of the joint probabilities for all possible context categories:

$$\begin{aligned} p(R=1|s,\mathbf{f}) &\propto p(R=1,s,\mathbf{f}) \\ &= \sum_{i=1}^{|C|} p(R=1,s,\mathbf{f},c_i) \end{aligned} \quad (3)$$

To calculate the joint probabilities of Equation (2), we compute estimates for the probabilities of the music-context model and the sensor-context model, as explained in Sections 3.3 and 3.4, respectively.

3.3 Music-Context Model

3.3.1 Modeling and Adaptation

As described later in Section 5.2, we have found that users agree on the *features* of music they prefer when they are doing a particular activity. However, in general, different users like different songs. Thus, to provide a more personalized recommendation, ACACF incorporates implicit user feedback. For example, if a user listened to a song completely, the user probably likes the song; we call this *positive feedback*. If the user skipped a song after listening for only a few seconds, then the user probably dislikes the song; we call this *negative feedback*. Implicit feedback has been exploited by some researchers [32], and we integrate it seamlessly and efficiently in our own ACACF model.

To model implicit feedback, for each user we assign a *probability prior* (or simply a *prior*) $\Theta_{c,s} \sim beta(\theta_{c,s}; a_{c,s}, b_{c,s})$ to $p(R|c,s)$ for every pair (c,s). $beta(\theta,a,b)$ indicates the beta distribution with shape parameters a, b. Here a,b can be interpreted as the total number of occurrences of negative and positive feedback, respectively, when the user is in context c and is recommended song s. Therefore, the prior captures the personal history of preferences of the user. The probability $p(R=1|c,s)$ can be expressed as in Equation (4):

$$p(R=1|c,s) = \frac{b}{a+b} \quad (4)$$

User feedback can be described as a triple $\mathbf{x} = (\mathbf{f}, s, r)$, where $\mathbf{f}$ is a feature vector extracted from mobile phone sensors during the play of a recommended song, s is the recommended song, and r is the observed value of R, which is the user feedback. The value $r=0$ indicates negative feedback, while $r=1$ indicates positive feedback.

The user's true context category is unknown, and thus c is a *latent variable* during adaptation. In this situation, updating the beta prior by exact Bayesian learning is computation-intensive, and thus not suitable for mobile phones. Here approximate inference is used to reduce the computation. First the MAP estimation $\hat{c}$ of c is given by Equation (5):

$$\hat{c} = \arg\max_c p(c|\mathbf{f}) \quad (5)$$

Then the corresponding beta prior $\hat{\theta}$ for pair $(\hat{c}, s)$ is updated as in Equation (6):

$$p(\hat{\theta}|\mathbf{x}) \approx \begin{cases} beta(\hat{\theta}; a+1, b) & \text{if } r=0 \\ beta(\hat{\theta}; a, b+1) & \text{if } r=1 \end{cases} \quad (6)$$

Finally, the corresponding $p(R=1|\hat{c}, s.\mathbf{x})$ representing the user's preference is updated as in Equation (7):

$$p(R=1|\hat{c},s,\mathbf{x}) \approx \begin{cases} \frac{b}{a+b+1} & \text{if } r=0 \\ \frac{b+1}{a+b+1} & \text{if } r=1 \end{cases} \quad (7)$$

Comparing Equation (7) with Equation (4), we can see that when a user skips song s in context $\hat{c}$, $r=0$ and the probability of that song $p(R=1|\hat{c},s)$ decreases. Thus, s will have a smaller chance of being recommended next time. Otherwise, if the user listened completely ($r=1$), then the probability $p(R=1|\hat{c},s)$ increases, and thus s will be more likely to be recommended next time.

The whole updating process is very efficient: We first obtain the MAP estimation $\hat{c}$, and then the counters a,b and $p(R=1|\hat{c},s)$ are updated. The adaptation can be done directly on a mobile phone without the use of backend servers.

We next describe the use of music content analysis results to initialize the beta priors.

3.3.2 Initialization

We model the relationship between music and context by examining the music audio content. There are many existing works on music content classification, such as genre classification, mood classification, and so on. Classification usually assumes that the classes are mutually exclusive. The problem here is different, since one song can be suitable for many context categories. Thus, our problem is similar to the tagging problem: Given a song, we want to know the probability that a tag is suitable for the song. Therefore, we use a state-of-the-art music tagging method called Autotagger [33].

Autotagger estimates the probability $\pi_{c,s}$ that a song s is suitable for context c for *all* users. We use $\pi_{c,s}$ in our model to initialize the prior $beta(\theta; a, b)$ described in Section 3.3.1. First, the ratio of a and b is determined by Equation (8):

$$p(R=1|c,s) = \frac{b}{a+b} = \pi_{c,s} \quad (8)$$

To further determine a and b, the equivalent sample size β is needed:

$$a+b=\beta$$

	Prediction	Incremental training
AdaBoost	Fast	Slow and Non-trivial
C4.5	Fast	Slow and Non-trivial
LR	Fast	Not supported
NB	Fast	Fast
SVM	Fast	Slow and Non-trivial
KNN	Slow	Fast

Table 1: Comparison of Classifiers

β is a free parameter of the system, balancing user feedback against music content analysis results. A large β indicates a belief that music content analysis results are good enough to provide a good recommendation, and that the adaptation (Equation (7)) will change $p(R = 1|c, s)$ very slowly. On the other hand, a small β indicates that music content analysis is relatively inaccurate, requiring more reliance on user feedback to perform recommendation. From our subjects' experiences, $\beta = 5$ is a reasonable setting.

After initialization, $p(R = 1|c, s)$ is adapted dynamically to the particular user according to Equation (7).

3.4 Sensor-Context Model

There are many ways to infer context categories from sensor data. Choosing a proper model is very important and requires careful consideration. First, since much of the computation is to be done on a mobile phone, energy consumption is critically important. Second, the model needs be accurate. Third, in order to adapt the model to a user on the fly as he/she is using the system, the model should support efficient incremental training.

We considered six popular methods used in activity recognition—AdaBoost, C4.5 decision trees, logistic regression (LR), Naive Bayes (NB), support vector machine (SVM) and K-nearest neighbors (KNN). We compared them from three perspectives: prediction accuracy, overhead of prediction computation, and incremental training. Table 1 compares the methods qualitatively in terms of prediction overhead and incremental training, and we present results on prediction accuracy in Section 5.3.3. We chose Naive Bayes because it offers very good incremental training and prediction overhead with just a small relative loss in accuracy.

Feature vectors extracted from sensor data are usually real-valued vectors. Since Naive Bayes cannot handle real-valued feature attributes directly, we first discretize the attributes using the well known *equal frequency discretization* method. As a result, every feature vector $\mathbf{f}$ becomes a vector of integers: $(f_1, f_2, \ldots, f_v)$, and $1 \leq f_l \leq d_l$, where d_l is the number of bins of the l-th attribute. Using the Naive Bayes assumption (that the features are conditionally independent), the sensor-context model $p(\mathbf{f}|c)p(c)$ can be decomposed as follows:

$$p(\mathbf{f}|c)p(c) = \prod_{l=1}^{v} p(f_l|c)p(c) \tag{9}$$

To estimate the parameters $p(c)$ and $p(f_l|c)$ in Equation (9), training samples need to be collected, which are tuples of the form $(\mathbf{f}^k, c^k)$, where $\mathbf{f}^k$ is the k-th observed feature vector, and c^k is the corresponding context category. Then, based on Maximum Likelihood Estimation, parameters are learned using Equations (10) and (11), where $n(c)$ indicates the number of times that category c occurs in the training samples, and $n(F_l = f, c)$ indicates the number of times that the l-th attribute of $\mathbf{f}$ is f and the context category is c:

$$p(c) = \frac{n(c)}{\sum_{i=1}^{|C|} n(c_i)} \tag{10}$$

$$p(f_l|c) = \frac{n(F_l = f_l, c)}{\sum_{f=1}^{d_l} n(F_l = f, c)} \tag{11}$$

An alternative to incremental training for adaptation is to store all old training data in the mobile phone, and then newly arriving training data is combined with the old data and a new model trained again on the combined dataset. We argue that this is not suitable for a mobile application. First, storing all the training data in the mobile phone is too expensive due to the limited storage space. Second, retraining the model on the complete data after each update would be too expensive computationally.

For these reasons we opt for incremental training. First, it trains a model on some training data and then discards that training data. When new data arrives, instead of training a completely new model, it uses the new training data to update the model *incrementally* and then again discards the new training data. In this way, no training data needs to be stored, and the model can be updated efficiently.

Incremental training in Naive Bayes is straightforward. According to Equation (10) and (11), the parameters are estimated using counters $n(c)$ and $n(F_l = f, c)$, which are the sufficient statistics of the sensor-context model. When new training data arrives, these counters are updated, and then parameters $p(c)$, $p(F_l = f|c)$ are updated via Equations (10) and (11). In this way, the sensor-context model can be efficiently updated to adapt to the user.

4. SYSTEM IMPLEMENTATION

We have implemented the ACACF model in a prototype system, which comprises two components: (1) music audio content analysis on a remote server, and (2) a context-aware music recommender application on a mobile phone.

Music content analysis is done on a server since it is compute-intensive and needs to be performed just once per song. Doing it on a mobile phone would quickly drain the battery.

The mobile application is implemented on the Android SDK, and its interface is depicted in Figure 2. To stream music, the application connects to the server via a wireless connection (3G or WiFi). The application also can run without connecting to the server, but then songs and music content analysis results must be cached beforehand.

At the top of the user interface is a list of activities. Users can let the system infer his/her current activity automatically, which is called the *auto mode* and is shown as Figure 2a. The background intensity of the activity labels is adjusted according to the inferred probabilities. The whiter the background is, the higher the activity's probability is. Users also can select a single category manually, which is called *manual mode* and is shown as Figure 2b. When an activity is selected manually, its background becomes yellow. To switch back to auto mode from manual model, the user just needs to tap the yellow label once.

When the application is in manual mode, the selected activity and sensor data are used to update the sensor-context model described in Section 3.4, which makes context inference increasingly accurate. Ideally, manual mode will not

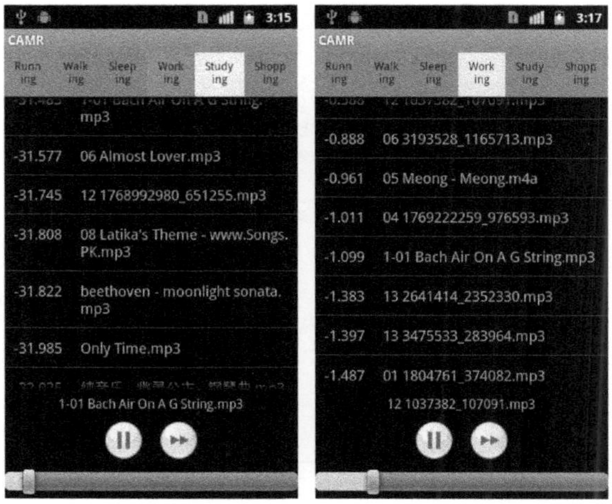

(a) auto mode (b) manual mode

Figure 2: Context-aware mobile music recommender.

be needed after several days since auto mode should be accurate enough by then.

The list in the middle of the user interface contains the recommended songs ranked by the probabilities described in Equation (3); logarithms of these probabilities are shown on the left side of the songs. At the bottom of the user interface are play/pause and skip buttons.

The adaptation described in Section 3.3.1 is performed whenever the user finishes listening to a song or skips a song. After adaptation, the probability of the song just listened to or skipped will be updated, and all songs will be re-ranked. This makes the list of recommended songs increasingly accurate, thereby adapting to the user's personal preferences.

5. EXPERIMENTS

In this section we describe results from our evaluation of the ACACF model and its prototype implementation. We have conducted extensive experimental evaluations of both model accuracy and system usability, and the results demonstrate significant promise from both perspectives.

5.1 Datasets

5.1.1 Playlists Crawled from the Web

To build and evaluate the music-context model, we require a large number of songs with context labels, which we use as ground truth for activity prediction. One dataset we considered is the publicly available CAL500 dataset, which incorporates some usage annotations such as *driving* and *sleeping* [34]. However, those annotations only partially cover our six categories. Furthermore, although the annotations were made by a large number of subjects (66 undergraduates), each subject annotated only a small portion of the dataset, and each song was annotated only by around three subjects, which is too few to obtain reliable results.

For these reasons, we constructed a new, larger dataset of 24224 songs crawled from Grooveshark[3] and YouTube[4]. Grooveshark has numerous playlists created by users , titled with context information such as *Studying*, *running songs*, etc. From Grooveshark we therefore collected playlists that match our context categories. The audio tracks for the songs were then crawled from YouTube through YouTube's open data API. Details of the dataset are presented in Table 2; the total number of 22108 distinct songs shown in the table is less than 24224, since latter number includes songs not associated with any of our six context categories.

Context	Playlists	Distinct Songs	Observations
Running	393	3430	7810
Walking	197	3601	4123
Sleeping	195	3941	5318
Working	194	4533	4988
Studying	195	3405	4363
Shopping	77	3786	3847
Total	1251	22108	30449

Table 2: Summary of the Grooveshark Dataset. *Distinct Songs* indicates the number of distinct songs from the playlists for the specified context, while *Observations* indicates the total number of songs including duplicates.

5.1.2 Context Annotation of 1200 Songs

From the 22108 distinct songs shown in Table 2, we selected 1200 for annotation. It was necessary to consider fewer songs for two reasons. First, data crawled from the Web is inevitably noisy, since some users may be careless in their creation of playlists. Second, in order to verify agreement between different users, we require songs labeled by multiple users. In the Grooveshark dataset, most songs exist in only a single playlist. For these reasons, it was necessary to carry out an additional phase of annotation in which *all* songs were annotated by *multiple* subjects to produce the ground truth classification for our study. 1200 songs provides a large sample size but not so large as to make the annotation effort unreasonable for our subjects. We randomly chose the 1200 songs so that there would be roughly an equal number of songs from each context category (as classified by the Grooveshark playlist titles).

We recruited 10 students to annotate all 1200 songs. There were equal numbers of males and females. All of them listen to music at least one hour a day, and exercise regularly (at least 3 hour-long sessions per week). They have different culture background and are from India, Malaysia, Singapore, Indonesia, China, and Vietnam. Every participant was rewarded with a small token payment for their time and effort. Participants were chosen with the requirement that they listen to music regularly for at least one hour per day. Annotation was performed through a Web site we set up that simply required clicking checkboxes. Because different parts of the same song can have very different styles, we required the subjects to listen to each song for at least 45 seconds. Subjects were allowed to advance or rewind the music playback. For each song, each subject selected one or more suitable context categories.

The resulting dataset thus contains 1200 songs, with each song annotated by all 10 subjects, and with each subject having selected one or more context categories per song.

5.1.3 Sensor Data Collection

To build and evaluate the sensor-context model, we had the same 10 subjects collect data from onboard sensors on

[3]http://grooveshark.com
[4]http://www.youtube.com

Activity	Kappa Agreement	Percent Agreement
Running	**0.27**	0.35
Working	0.03	0.02
Sleeping	**0.29**	0.28
Walking	0.03	0.03
Shopping	0.07	0.17
Studying	0.09	0.11

Table 3: Inter-Subject Agreement on Music Preferences for Different Activities

their mobile phones. The sensors we used were gyroscopes, accelerometers, GPS receivers, microphones and ambient light sensors.

Sensor data was collected by a mobile application we designed, which will be offered to other interested researchers in the future. All the mobile phones used are based on Android OS. To make the trained model robust to different phone models, we provided our subjects with five different phone models we purchased from Samsung and HTC. The quality of these phones is also different. Some are expensive and have all the sensors mentioned above, while some are cheaper models having only accelerometer, a GPS receiver and a microphone. We imposed no restrictions on how the subjects held or carried or used their phones. To record a data session, a subject first selected their current context category from the application interface and then recorded 30 minutes of data. Each subject was required to record one session for every context category. The recorded sensor data and selected context category were stored together in a SQLite database on the mobile phone's SD card. The resulting 30-hour dataset contains 6 context categories, and every category has 0.5 hour sensor data collected by every of the 10 subjects.

5.2 Music-Context Model Evaluation

Demonstrating agreement on suitable songs for an activity is a very important foundation for music content analysis, because if there is no agreement among people, then a trained music-context model will work only for the users in the training set but will not reliably generalize to other users. Therefore, we first studied inter-subject agreement. Fleiss's Kappa [35] and percent agreement were calculated among the 10 subjects for every context category, and the results are presented as Table 3. We observe that all Kappa values are significantly higher than 0 (p-value < 0.0001) and are and especially high for *running* and *sleeping*. The results therefore indicate that subjects have statistically significant agreement on context categories, indicating the feasibility of training generalizable statistical models.

Next, the music-context model was trained. The videos we crawled from YouTube were first converted by *ffmpeg*[5] into mono channel WAV files with a 16KHz sampling rate. Then feature vectors were extracted using a program we developed based on the MARSYAS library[6], in which a window size of 512 was used without overlapping. The features we used and their dimensionalities are ZeroCrossing (1), Centroid (1), Rolloff (1), Flux (1), MFCC (13), Chroma (14), SCF (24) and SFM (24). To reduce the training set size, we used the mean and standard deviation of feature vectors computed from every 30-second period. Finally, the we

[5]`http://ffmpeg.org`

[6]`http://marsyas.sourceforge.net`

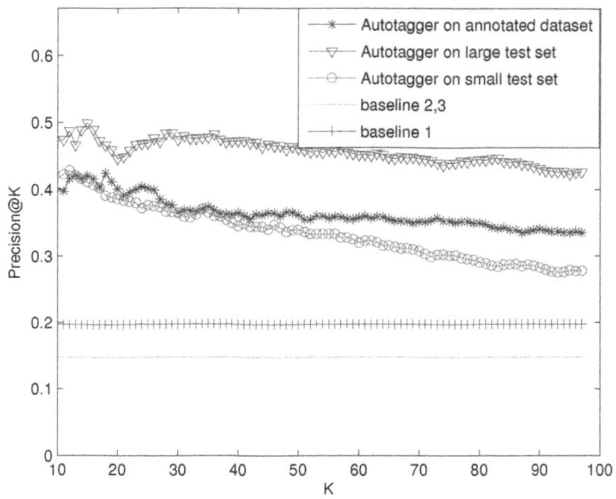

Figure 3: Retrieval performance of the music-context model.

added the 1-dimensional feature *tempo* to the summarized feature vectors. So the resulting combined feature vector is $79 \times 2 + 1 = 159$-dimensional.

We split the Grooveshark dataset into three disjoint subsets: a training set of 16281 songs, a large test set of 6943 songs, and our annotated dataset of 1200 songs, which we also used as a test set. We used the Autotagger method for the training: Using the training set, one binary AdaBoost classifier was trained for every context category. The classifier for context c_i estimates the probability that a song s_j is suitable for context c_i, which is $p(R = 1|c_i, s_j)$.

To measure the accuracy of these classifiers, we simulated the following retrieval process: Given context c as the query, we use its corresponding classifier to compute the probability $p(R = 1|c, s_j)$ for every song s_j and then rank all songs in descending order according to the estimated probabilities. Then the top-K songs are returned. Suppose there are only L songs of the top-K are labeled with context c in our dataset. Then L/K is the Precision@K for context c. The final Precision@K is the average of all Precision@K for the six categories.

We tested the classifiers on the three datasets. For our dataset of 1200 annotated songs, we used majority voting to determine the context for every song. For instance, if at least six of the 10 subjects annotated a song as being suitable for context c, then the song was labeled with c. The retrieval performance measured by Precision@K depends on the test set size, because the more songs we have, the more likely that we can find good songs for a context category, and thus the Precision@K will be higher. Therefore, in order to produce results that are comparable between our annotated song set and the large test set of 6943 songs, a set of 1200 songs was randomly sampled from the large test set; we refer to this as the *small test set* below.

We used a random estimator as our baseline, which ranks all songs randomly. The random estimator was also tested on the annotated dataset (baseline 1), the large test set (baseline 2) and the small test set (baseline 3). All results are presented in Figure 3. We observe that our trained models significantly outperformed the random estimator. Therefore, the models are able to associate a song accurately with daily activities by examining the song's audio content.

	AdaBoost	C4.5	LR	NB	SVM	KNN
Running	0.974	0.976	0.975	0.841	0.974	0.97
Working	0.933	0.932	0.921	0.876	0.929	0.922
Sleeping	0.999	0.999	0.999	0.994	0.999	0.993
Walking	0.961	0.960	0.955	0.909	0.960	0.953
Shopping	0.972	0.972	0.948	0.953	0.965	0.955
Studying	0.854	0.867	0.835	0.694	0.860	0.855
overall	0.951	0.952	0.941	0.893	0.950	0.943

Table 4: Activity Classification Accuracy

5.3 Sensor-Context Model Evaluation

5.3.1 Sensor Selection

Time data were used with data from accelerometers and microphones in our sensor-context model. Although GPS data are used by much of the previous work in human activity recognition, we did not use it for our own work because our activity set is different from other work, plus GPS appears not to increase classification accuracy even though it consumes a great deal of power. Additionally, we did not use the ambient light sensors and gyroscopes, for two reasons: First, gyroscopes do not improve accuracy very much since accelerometers already provide good motion data. Second, both kinds of sensors reside only in a small number of relatively expensive phones, while our aim is to build a model suitable for most available Android phones.

5.3.2 Feature Extraction from Sensor Data

Performing feature extraction from sensor data involves computing feature vectors from the sensor data stream.

Human daily activities have very strong time regularity. Most of us sleep at night and work during the day. Therefore, time is a very important feature for daily activity recognition, and we use the hour of the day in our feature set.

Window size in feature extraction is important. Generally, a larger window size can make inference more accurate because it captures more information. However, a larger window size also reduces system responsiveness, thus degrading the user experience. From our experience, a window size of five seconds appears to be a reasonable setting.

Each accelerometer data sample has three axes, x, y and z. From this data we use the magnitude $m = \sqrt{x^2 + y^2 + z^2}$, which is robust to the direction of the phone. Then the mean, standard deviation, minimum and maximum of all five-second samples of m are used in the final feature vectors.

For audio data from a microphone, we calculate the average amplitude of all samples as a measure of how noisy the environment of the phone is is. The final feature vector therefore has $1 + 4 + 1 = 6$ dimensions.

5.3.3 Context Classification Accuracy

We evaluated AdaBoost, C4.5, LR, NB, SVM and KNN for context classification, and we used 10-fold cross-validation to compare their accuracy. The results are presented in Table 4, with a value of 1.0 representing perfect accuracy. We observe that while NB is not as accurate as other methods, it still produces very good results. The categories *studying* and *working* are not distinguished well by any of the methods, because the context information sensed during those two activities is very similar. In fact, sometimes even human beings cannot distinguish the two.

	Questions	Mean	Stdev
Q1	I prefer different music (different genre, tempo, pitch, dynamics etc.) when I'm in different context (In different contexts means doing different things e.g. running, sleeping, or at different places e.g. school, home).	3.7	0.95
Q2	I usually listen to different sets of music when I'm in different context .	3.5	1.18
Q3	It is time consuming to create different lists of songs for different contexts with existing technologies.	4.4	0.97
Q4	It is not convenient to change music when I'm doing other things with existing technologies.	4.0	0.94
Q5	I want to have a mobile application that can accurately play suitable music to me according to my context automatically.	4.4	0.52

Table 5: Questionnaire 1

5.4 User Study

5.4.1 User Needs Study

To understand user needs for music recommendation, we conducted a survey (Questionnaire 1) with our 10 subjects. The questionnaire and survey results are presented in Table 5. All questions were answered on a 5-point Likert scale from "strongly disagree" (1) to "strongly agree" (5). *Q*1 helps in understanding user needs for a context-aware music experience; the results demonstrate that subjects generally prefer different music in different contexts. The results for *Q*2, *Q*3 and *Q*4 demonstrate that their requirements cannot be satisfied very well with the existing technologies. Finally, the results for *Q*5 demonstrate that a context-aware mobile music recommender potentially can satisfy their needs better.

5.4.2 Evaluation of Recommendation Quality

Most existing music recommender systems, including context-aware ones, require user ratings or annotations. During the cold-start stage, these systems are able only to recommend songs randomly. Comparison with existing CAMRSs is impossible, for three reasons: First, we focus on daily activities, and none of the reported literature has used these before. Second, most existing CAMRSs do not infer context categories from mobile phone sensor data. Third, most existing CAMRSs do not use music content analysis. Therefore, for our evaluation we undertook a comparison between the following three kinds of recommendations:

(R1) recommending songs completely randomly. This simulates traditional recommender systems during the cold-start stage.

(R2) recommending songs with context category inferred by the system automatically. This is the auto mode of our application.

(R3) recommending songs with context category selected by subjects manually. This is the manual mode of our application.

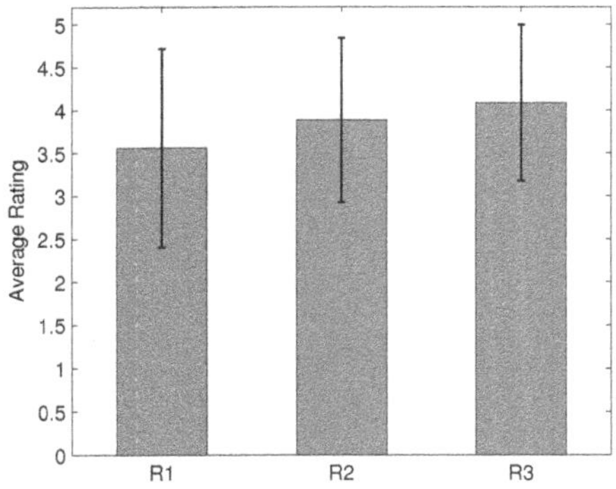

Figure 4: Average recommendation ratings. The error bars show the standard deviation of the ratings.

The same 10 subjects participated in this evaluation. The subjects were divided into an experimental group and a control group of five subjects each. The experimental group tested R2 and R3, and the control group tested R1. The subjects did not know which group they were in. All phones were supplied with the music content analysis results and with an identical set of 800 songs chosen randomly from the large test set of 6943 songs described in Section 5.2. During evaluation, each subject did each of the six activities for about 20 minutes while listening to the activity's top recommended songs. Each song was played for about a minute and then rated with the above 5-point Likert scale. Thus, the higher the rating for a song, the more the subject liked the song. Adaptation of both the music-context model and sensor-context model was turned off during this evaluation.

The average and standard deviation of the resulting ratings are presented in Figure 4. We observe that R2 performs significantly better than R1 (p-value = 0.0478), and R3 is much better than R1 (p-value = 0.0001). These results indicate that context-awareness combined with music content analysis can produce significantly better results than random recommendation. Therefore, our system provides a promising solution to the cold-start problem. R3 is better than R2 but not significantly better (p-value=0.1374), demonstrating that auto mode is almost as good as manual mode, and further demonstrating the accuracy of automated context inference.

5.4.3 Adaptation Evaluation

Two of our 10 subjects participated in a one-week adaptation evaluation. The subjects used the application continuously every day for a week. Most of the time the application was used in auto mode. If a subject found that the recommended songs did not match his/her activity, he/she could switch the application to manual mode or skip the recommended song. The whole system was updated continuously and became more and more accurate over the one-week period with respect to the subject's preferences. We compared the accuracy of both context inference and recommendation quality, both before the one-week adaptation period and after the one-week adaptation period.

Context inference: The trained Naive Bayes model described in Section 5.3.3 was used as the initial sensor-context model. Before and after adaptation, each subject's sensor-context model was evaluated on sensor data collected by that subject. The average classification accuracy for the two subjects is presented in Table 6.

	Before Adaptation	After Adaptation
Context Inference	0.87	0.96
Recommendation	0.68	0.93

Table 6: Context Inference and Recommendation Accuracy Before and After Adaptation

	Questions	Mean	Stdev
Q6	I can fully understand the functionalities of the mobile application and it's easy to use.	4.6	0.51
Q7	I'm willing to use the application if I have a copy.	4.4	0.84

Table 7: Questionnaire 2

Recommendation: Each subject rated the top-20 recommended songs with "like", and "dislike" for every context category, both before and after adaptation. Recommendation accuracy is defined as the proportion of liked songs. The results are presented as Table 6.

We observe that the accuracy of both context inference and recommendation increased significantly after one week of adaptation. Therefore, our model is able to adapt accurately to individual user preferences.

5.4.4 User Experience

All 10 subjects completed a second survey at the end of the study (Questionnaire 2). Two of the questions and the survey results are presented in Table 7. All questions were answered with a 5-point Likert scale as before. We observe that most of the subjects agree that the application is easy to use and are willing to use it. One subject commented, "I really like the idea, hope you can improve on it and sell it". However, some of the subjects thought that more context categories should be added, such as: *entertaining* (playing games, surfing the Web), *cooking*, *traveling* (bicycle/bus/subway), *partying* and *just relaxing and enjoying music* (no work, no study). Two of the subjects thought the interface could be made more appealing.

6. RELATED WORK

6.1 Existing CAMRSs

XPod is a mobile music player that selects songs matching a users' emotional and activity states [16]. The player uses an external physiological data collection device called BodyMedia SensorWear. Compared to the activities we consider, the activities considered in XPod are very coarse-grained, namely *resting*, *passive* and *active*. User ratings and metadata are used to associate songs with these activities, but recommendation quality is not evaluated.

In addition to XPod, many other CAMRs exploit user emotional states as a context factor. Park *et al.* were probably the first to propose the concept of context-aware music recommendation [12]. They used a fuzzy Bayesian network to infer a user's mood (*depressed*, *content*, *exuberant*, or *anxious/frantic*) from context information including weather, noise, time, gender and age. Music is then recommended to match the inferred mood using mood labels manually annotated on each available song. In the work of Cunningham *et al.*, user emotional states are deduced from user movements, temperature, weather and lighting of the surroundings based on reasoning with a manually built knowledge base [18]. Rho *et al.* built an ontology to infer a user's mood from context information including time, location, event, and demographic information, and then the inferred mood is matched with the mood of songs predicted from music content [23,27]. However, we believe that with current mobile phones, it is too difficult to infer a user's mood automatically.

Some work tries to incorporate context information into CF. Lee *et al.* proposed a context-aware music recommendation system based on case-based reasoning [21]. In this work, in order to recommend music to a target user, other users who have similar context as the target user are selected, and then CF is performed among the selected users and the target user. This work considers time, region and weather as the context information. Similarly, Su *et al.* use context information that includes physiological signal, weather, noise, light condition, motion, time and location to pre-filter users and items [25]. Both context and content information are used to calculate similarities and are incorporated into CF.

SuperMusic [19], developed at Nokia, is a streaming context-aware mobile service. Location (GPS and cell ID) and time are considered as the context information. Since that application cannot show a user's current context categories explicitly, many users get confused about the application's "situation" concept: "If I'm being honest, I didn't understand the concept of situation. ... I don't know if there is music for my situation at all?" [19]. This inspired us to design our system recommending music explicitly for understandable context categories such as *working*, *sleeping*, etc.

Resa *et al.* studied the relationship between temporal information (e.g., day of week, hour of day) and music listening preferences such as genre and artist [26]. Baltrunas *et al.* described similar work that aims to predict a user's music preference based on the current time [30]. Several other works exploit physiological signals to generate music playlists automatically for exercising [11,14,17]. Only the tempo attribute of music was considered in those works, whereas in our work, several music audio features including timbre, pitch and tempo are considered. Kaminskas *et al.* recommend music for places of interest by matching tags of places with tags on songs [28]. In other work by Baltrunas *et al.*, a song's most suitable context is predicted from user ratings [36], and a CAMRS was built specifically for the context of riding in a car [37].

Reddy *et al.* proposed a context-aware mobile music player but did not describe how they infer context categories from sensor data or how they combine context information with music recommendation [15]. In addition, they provide no evaluation of their system. Seppänen *et al.* argue that mobile music experiences in the future should be both personalized and situationalized (i.e., context-aware) [20]. In this work, no CAMRS is implemented. Bostrom *et al.* also tried to build a context-aware mobile music recommender system, but the recommendation part was not implemented, and no evaluation is presented [38].

6.2 Content Analysis in CAMRSs

Only a relatively small number of CAMRSs described in the literature use music content information. To associate songs with context categories such as emotional states, most of them use manually supplied metadata or annotation labels or ratings [12,16–19,21,28,36], or implicit feedback [16]. In other cases, content is not directly associated with context, but is used instead to measure the similarity between two songs in order to support content-based recommendation [19,25].

The method of Rho, Han *et al.* is similar to ours [23,27]: Emotion classifiers are first trained, and then every song is classified into a single emotional state. But there are also differences: First, we associate music content with daily activities instead of mood. Second, in our models, a song can belong to multiple categories simultaneously. The method that we use to associate music content with daily activities is called Autotagger [33]. Similar methods have been proposed by others [34], but Autotagger is the only one evaluated on a large dataset. All these methods were used originally to annotate songs with multiple semantic tags, including genre, mood and usage. Although their tags include some of our context categories such as *sleeping*, the training dataset used in these studies (the CAL500 dataset discussed in Section 5.1.1) is too small (500 songs with around 3 annotations per song), and evaluations were done together with other tags. From their reported results, it is difficult to know whether or not the trained models capture the relationship between daily activities and music content.

6.3 Context Inference in CAMRSs

None of the existing CAMRSs tries to infer user activities using a mobile phone. XPod uses an external device for classification—the classified activities are very low-level, and classification is performed on a laptop [16]. While activity recognition using mobile phones is itself not a new idea, none of the systems that have been studied can be updated incrementally to adapt to a particular user [5–10]. In one remarkable work, Berchtold *et al.* proposed an activity recognition service supporting online personalized optimization [7]. However, their model needs to search in a large space using a genetic algorithm, which requires significant computation. And to update the model to adapt to a particular user, all of that user's sensor data history is needed, thus requiring significant storage.

7. CONCLUSION

In this paper we have described a novel probabilistic model for music recommendation that combines automated activity classification with automated music content analysis, with support for a rich set of activities and music content features. We collected three datasets—a set of playlists from the Web, a set of 1200 cleanly annotated songs, and a set of sensor data recorded from daily activities. These datasets will be offered eventually to researchers who want to carry out related research on context-aware music recommendation. Based on the set of 1200 annotated songs, we found that although context annotation can be subjective, people nevertheless often do agree on their annotations. Using the datasets, both the sensor-context model and the music-context model were evaluated, and the results are very promising. Based on the probabilistic model, we implemented a CAMRS for off-the-shelf mobile phones. The results from our user study demonstrate that the system is easy to use and can provide good recommendations even in the absence of pre-existing user ratings or annotations, a situation in which traditional systems only can recommend songs randomly. Therefore, our system satisfies users' short-term needs better because of context-awareness, and also provides a solution to the cold-start problem. Evaluation results demonstrate that our system can update itself in real-time to adapt to a particular user.

We are currently improving the user experience of the system and will eventually publish it in the Google Android Market. We also are exploring the integration of context-awareness with collaborative filtering to provide even more accurate recommendations.

8. ACKNOWLEDGMENTS

This work is supported by grant R-252-000-473-133 and R-252-000-428-290 from the School of Computing at the National University of Singapore.

9. REFERENCES

[1] G. Adomavicius and A. Tuzhilin, "Toward the next generation of recommender systems: A survey of the State-of-the-Art and possible extensions," *IEEE Trans. on Knowl. and Data Eng.*, vol. 17, pp. 734–749, June 2005.

[2] A. C. North, D. J. Hargreaves, and J. J. Hargreaves, "Uses of Music in Everyday Life," *Music Perception: An Interdisciplinary Journal*, vol. 22, no. 1, 2004.

[3] D. J. Levitin and J. McGill, "Life Soundtracks: The uses of music in everyday life." 2007.

[4] G. Reynolds, D. Barry, T. Burke, and E. Coyle, "Interacting with large music collections: Towards the use of environmental metadata," in *ICME*, June 2008.

[5] T. S. Saponas, J. Lester, J. Froehlich, J. Fogarty, and J. Landay, "iLearn on the iPhone: Real-Time Human Activity Classification on Commodity Mobile Phones," in *UW CSE Tech Report*, 2008.

[6] T. Brezmes, J.-L. Gorricho, and J. Cotrina, "Activity Recognition from Accelerometer Data on a Mobile Phone," in *IWANN*, 2009.

[7] M. Berchtold, M. Budde, D. Gordon, H. R. Schmidtke, and M. Beigl, "ActiServ: Activity Recognition Service for mobile phones," in *ISWC*, pp. 1–8, Oct. 2010.

[8] M. Khan, S. I. Ahamed, M. Rahman, and R. O. Smith, "A Feature Extraction Method for Real time Human Activity Recognition on Cell Phones," in *isQoLT*, 2011.

[9] J. R. Kwapisz, G. M. Weiss, and S. A. Moore, "Activity recognition using cell phone accelerometers," *SIGKDD Explor. Newsl.*, vol. 12, pp. 74–82, Mar. 2011.

[10] Y. S. Lee and S. B. Cho, "Activity recognition using hierarchical hidden markov models on a smartphone with 3D accelerometer," in *HAIS*, pp. 460–467, 2011.

[11] G. Wijnalda, S. Pauws, F. Vignoli, and H. Stuckenschmidt, "A Personalized Music System for Motivation in Sport Performance," *IEEE Pervasive Computing*, vol. 4, pp. 26–32, July 2005.

[12] H.-S. Park, J.-O. Yoo, and S.-B. Cho, "A Context-Aware Music Recommendation System Using Fuzzy Bayesian Networks with Utility Theory," in *FSKD*, 2006.

[13] J.-H. Kim, C.-W. Song, K.-W. Lim, and J.-H. Lee, "Design of Music Recommendation System Using Context Information," in *LNCS*, vol. 4088, ch. 83, pp. 708–713, 2006.

[14] G. T. Elliott and B. Tomlinson, "PersonalSoundtrack: context-aware playlists that adapt to user pace," in *SIGCHI*, 2006.

[15] S. Reddy and J. Mascia, "Lifetrak: music in tune with your life," in *HCM*, 2006.

[16] S. Dornbush, A. Joshi, Z. Segall, and T. Oates, "A Human Activity Aware Learning Mobile Music Player," in *Proc. of the 2007 conference on Advances in Ambient Intelligence*, 2007.

[17] R. D. Oliveira and N. Oliver, "TripleBeat: enhancing exercise performance with persuasion," in *MobileHCI*, 2008.

[18] S. Cunningham, S. Caulder, and V. Grout, "Saturday Night or Fever? Context-Aware Music Playlists," in *AM '08*, 2008.

[19] A. Lehtiniemi, "Evaluating SuperMusic: streaming context-aware mobile music service," in *ACE*, 2008.

[20] J. Seppänen and J. Huopaniemi, "Interactive and context-aware mobile music experiences," in *DAFx-08*, Sept. 2008.

[21] J. Lee and J. Lee, "Context Awareness by Case-Based Reasoning in a Music Recommendation System," *Ubiquitous Computing Systems*, pp. 45–58, 2008.

[22] H. Liu, J. Hu, and M. Rauterberg, "Music Playlist Recommendation Based on User Heartbeat and Music Preference," in *ICCTD*, 2009.

[23] S. Rho, B. J. Han, and E. Hwang, "SVR-based music mood classification and context-based music recommendation," in *ACM MM*, 2009.

[24] A. Camurri, G. Volpe, H. Vinet, R. Bresin, M. Fabiani, G. Dubus, E. Maestre, J. Llop, J. Kleimola, S. Oksanen, V. Välimäki, and J. Seppanen, "User-Centric Context-Aware Mobile Applications for Embodied Music Listening User Centric Media," in *LNICST*, pp. 21–30, 2010.

[25] J.-H. Su, H.-H. Yeh, P. S. Yu, and V. S. Tseng, "Music Recommendation Using Content and Context Information Mining," *Intelligent Systems, IEEE*, vol. 25, pp. 16–26, Jan. 2010.

[26] Z. Resa, "Towards Time-aware Contextual Music Recommendation: An Exploration of Temporal Patterns of Music Listening Using Circular Statistics," Master's thesis, 2010.

[27] B. J. Han, S. Rho, S. Jun, and E. Hwang, "Music emotion classification and context-based music recommendation," *Multimedia Tools Appl.*, vol. 47, pp. 433–460, May 2010.

[28] M. Kaminskas and F. Ricci, "Location-Adapted Music Recommendation Using Tags.," in *UMAP*, 2011.

[29] D. Leake, A. Maguitman, and T. Reichherzer, "Cases, Context, and Comfort: Opportunities for Case-Based Reasoning in Smart Homes," in *Designing Smart Homes*, LNCS, 2006.

[30] L. Baltrunas and X. Amatriain, "Towards Time-Dependant Recommendation based on Implicit Feedback," in *CARS*, 2009.

[31] A. I. Schein, A. Popescul, L. H. Ungar, and D. M. Pennock, "Methods and metrics for cold-start recommendations," in *SIGIR*, 2002.

[32] Y. Hu and M. Ogihara, "Nextone player: A music recommendation system based on user behavior," in *ISMIR*, 2011.

[33] T. Bertin-Mahieux, D. Eck, F. Maillet, and P. Lamere, "Autotagger: A Model for Predicting Social Tags from Acoustic Features on Large Music Databases," *JNMR*, vol. 37, pp. 115–135, June 2008.

[34] D. Turnbull, L. Barrington, D. Torres, and G. Lanckriet, "Towards musical query-by-semantic-description using the CAL500 data set," in *SIGIR*, 2007.

[35] J. R. Landis and G. G. Koch, "The measurement of observer agreement for categorical data.," *Biometrics*, vol. 33, pp. 159–174, Mar. 1977.

[36] L. Baltrunas, M. Kaminskas, F. Ricci, L. Rokach, B. Shapira, and K. H. Luke, "Best Usage Context Prediction for Music Tracks," in *CARS*, Sept. 2010.

[37] L. Baltrunas, M. Kaminskas, B. Ludwig, O. Moling, F. Ricci, A. Aydin, K.-H. Lüke, and R. Schwaiger, "InCarMusic: Context-Aware Music Recommendations in a Car E-Commerce and Web Technologies," in *LNBIP*, 2011.

[38] F. Boström, "AndroMedia - Towards a Context-aware Mobile Music Recommender," Master's thesis, 2008.

MusicScore: Mobile Music Composition for Practice and Fun

Zimu Liu, Yuan Feng, Baochun Li
Department of Electrical and Computer Engineering
University of Toronto

ABSTRACT

In this paper, we present our design of *MusicScore*, a professional grade application on the iOS platform for music composition and live performance tracking, used by composers and amateurs alike. As its foundation, we have designed and implemented a high-quality music engraver, capable of real-time interactive rendering on mobile devices, as well as an intuitive user interface based on multi-touch, both built from scratch using Objective-C and Cocoa Touch. To make *MusicScore* appealing to the general population for their practice and fun, we have introduced a unique auditory capability to *MusicScore*, so that it can "listen" to and analyze live instrument performance in real time. In order to compensate for the imperfect audio sensing system on mobile devices, we have proposed a collaborative sensing solution to better capture music signals in real time. To maximize the accuracy of live progress tracking and performance evaluation using a mobile device, we have designed a collection of note detection and tempo-based note matching algorithms, using a combination of microphone and accelerometer sensors. Based on our real-world implementation of MusicScore, extensive evaluation results show that *MusicScore* can achieve acceptably low error ratios, even for music pieces performed by highly inexperienced players.

Categories and Subject Descriptors

H.5 [**Information Interfaces and Presentation**]: User Interfaces and Presentation; H.5.5 [**Information Interfaces and Presentation**]: Sound and Music Computing—*Signal Analysis, Synthesis, and Processing*

Keywords

Music Composition, Mobile Application, Signal Processing

1. INTRODUCTION

Since the advent of the iPad, there has been a steady trend of new professional-grade applications (or "apps") released for multi-touch mobile devices with a large display, such as Adobe Photoshop Touch for image processing, as well as GarageBand for soundtrack editing. Such professional applications have made it possible for creative professionals to work on their projects effectively with a mobile device.

With a burgeoning repository of mobile apps for professionals, it may be a surprise that no mobile apps exist for interactive music composition, score editing, and live performance tracking. Table 1 lists a few representative mobile apps, related to music composition and practice. For music composition, Symphony is the only existing mobile app supporting music editing, in comparison to NoteStar and forScore, which only provide simple annotation in downloaded images of music sheets. However, we notice that Symphony suffers from a poorly designed music typesetting system that violates basic score layout guidelines, an inferior user interface that is hard to learn and use, and an incomplete music symbol support. With respect to live performance tracking, Tonara claims that automatic page-turning is supported using sensed live piano performance. However, in reality, Tonara can only track simple music pieces at moderate tempo, and it fails to work as a slightly complicated piece is played or a piece is played in a fast manner. Such a lack of high-quality apps in this category reflects the inherent complexity of developing professional-grade music apps. Hence, we firmly believe that a well designed, interactive, high-performance and feature-complete music composition app should be designed and built. This paper presents design challenges and our proposed solutions in *MusicScore*, a professional-grade music app on iOS mobile devices, such as the iPad.

Table 1: Representative mobile apps related to music composition and practice.

Mobile App	Features
Symphony	Music composition; Real-time score rendering; Music synthesis
NoteStar	Music sheet display; Key transposition; Demo play with progress indication
forScore	Music sheet display; Simple annotation
Etude	Music sheet display; Demo play with progress indication
Tonara	Music sheet display; Auto page-turning

First, *MusicScore* is designed for professional composers. We developed a high-quality music engraver from scratch in Objective-C, achieving artistic and pleasing engraving results by strictly conforming to traditional engraving rules. Our music engraver is optimized for real-time interactive score editing on a resource-limited mobile device, based on intuitive multi-touch gestures. *Second*, *MusicScore* is also designed for the general population who love music, such as piano learners and amateur musicians. An iPad with *MusicScore* can be used on the music stand to display a music score digitally, and to keep track of the progress of a live performance by

MM'12, October 29–November 2, 2012, Nara, Japan.

automatically highlighting the notes and measures being played, as well as turning pages. Thanks to such live progress tracking, *MusicScore* is also able to evaluate the quality of live performance, and point out mistakes and imperfections along the way (*e.g.*, an inconsistent tempo and a missed note).

In order to make it possible for *MusicScore* to accurately "listen" to a live music performance and keep track of its progress, a number of important challenges needs to be addressed. *First*, due to limitations of built-in sensors in mobile devices and inherent constraints of audio signal processing, we discover that it is a non-trivial task to capture high-quality signals and conduct accurate performance tracking. In *MusicScore*, we take full advantage of available sensors on mobile device to sense signals from the instrument. After carefully integrating signals from the microphone and the accelerometer sensor, *MusicScore* uses a set of carefully designed algorithms to identify the notes played, and compare them with the music score for live performance tracking and evaluation. Due to the complexity of instrument signals, we present a note matching algorithm using tempo estimation to minimize errors when identifying notes, typically due to mistakes made by inexperienced players.

To objectively assess the quality of *MusicScore*, we present a thorough evaluation of the performance on our implementation. Individual functional components are carefully tested and measured, so that all design and implementation details are examined.

The remainder of this paper is organized as follows. In Sec. 2, we first introduce *MusicScore*'s music engraver and user interface, designed for professional composers using a mobile device. In Sec. 3, we discuss limitations and challenges on mobile devices as we are trying to support the auditory capability in *MusicScore*. Sec. 4 presents in detail how audio and vibration signals are processed in *MusicScore* to achieve accurate and efficient tracking of live instrument performance. In Sec. 5, we thoroughly evaluate *MusicScore* to understand its quality as a professional music composition application, and its accuracy as an automated performance evaluator. We conclude the paper with a discussion of related work and final remarks in Sec. 6 and Sec. 7, respectively.

2. *MUSICSCORE* FOR PROFESSIONAL COMPOSERS

The primary design objective of *MusicScore* is to provide professional composers with a well designed, interactive, high-performance and feature-complete mobile app for composing and editing music scores. *MusicScore* is designed and built from scratch to work on mobile devices with limited capabilities, rather than as a desktop application, where alternatives have been available for a long time. To the best of our knowledge, no such mobile apps exist to fulfill the need of professional composers to compose music, perhaps due to the inherent complexity of designing and building it.

2.1 A Professional Music Engraver

To make composing music on mobile devices possible, the most critical component is a typesetting engine that supports dynamic music notation layout and rendering, commonly referred to as an *engraver*. We believe that a professional-quality engraver on mobile devices must exhibit two important properties. *First*, correctness of engraving layout. As an app used by professional composers, the music sheet produced by the app must conform to strict artistic rules of music engraving (with its legacy spanning centuries), so that the result of engraving is intuitive and artistically pleasing to sightread. *Second*, efficiency. The engraver must respond swiftly to user input in real time, so that a smooth and satisfactory user experience is guaranteed. Unfortunately, after an extensive investigation on existing works, it is discovered that neither of the two top-of-the-line open-source engravers, libmscore (from the MuseScore project on the desktop) and LilyPond [10], satisfies our demanding needs, as shown in Table 2. Therefore, in *MusicScore*, we have designed and built a new mobile music engraver entirely from scratch, making design decisions that are tailored to offer the best user experience on mobile devices.

Table 2: Two open-source engravers: a comparison.

	libmscore	LilyPond
Correctness	○ Some major layout errors	● Almost perfect
Efficiency	● Suitable for interactive score editing	○ Complex layout decision making suitable for batch processing only
Suitability for mobile OS	◐ Based on Qt (in immature α-stage on iOS)	● Based on pure C++ and Scheme

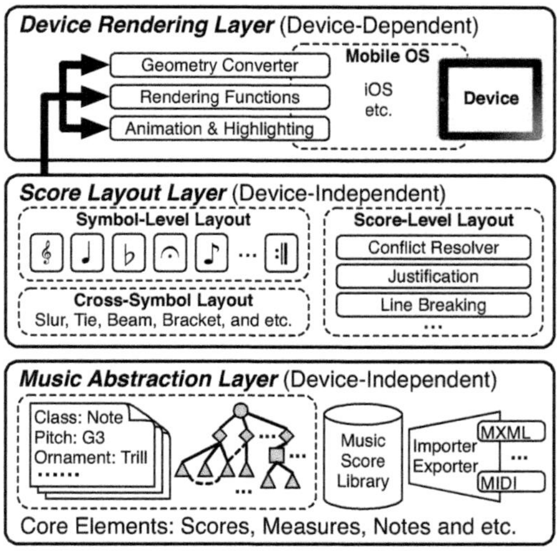

Figure 1: An architectural overview of *MusicScore* engraver.

To guarantee the engraving quality and to maximize the efficiency of our new engraver on mobile systems, we adopt a layering design pattern as illustrated in Fig. 1. The device rendering layer is closely tied to the mobile OS and device hardware, while the score layout layer and the music abstraction layer are *device independent*, in that the core data structures storing score elements and the core algorithms used to compute the score layout are not tied to a particular type of mobile OS or device hardware.

The Music Abstraction Layer contains the metadata of all musical elements, from the score at the highest level, to notes and rests at the lowest. These elements are organized using a tree-like hierarchical data structure, with some special links between nodes, *e.g.*, two tied notes. Such a core data structure essentially captures and presents the complex structure of a music score. Scores are indexed and stored in the `sqlite`-powered Music Score Library, and can be imported or exported through various public score-exchange formats, such as `MusicXML` and MIDI. To improve its flexibility, additional formats can be supported using external import/export plug-ins.

The Score Layout Layer is in charge of the layout placement of musical elements in a score, by strictly following guidelines of traditional music engraving [12]. Within this layer, we further partition layout components into three levels: symbol level, cross-symbol level (such as the placement of a bracket over a group of notes), and score level, as shown in the figure. Each component is decoupled from others using the *delegate* mechanism. All engraving algorithms inside the score layout layer are fully optimized so that results can be computed swiftly on mobile devices. In addition, the produced layout results are expressed in an abstracted score coordination system, using the quarter note head as its unit of size, which can be easily converted to any device-specific coordination system at the rendering stage.

The Device Rendering Layer retrieves the detailed layout results from the score layout layer, and renders them in the actual device through the OS drawing API. Since every mobile device has its own geometric properties, conversions from device-independent coordinates to device-specific coordinates should be conducted accordingly. To make it possible for users to interact with musical symbols, each musical symbol is encapsulated by a graphic container in the OS, so that touches on that symbol can be easily detected.

2.2 A Score Composition User Interface

Taking full advantage of multi-touch capabilities on the iPad, we have designed an intuitive user interface to compose music scores using a combination of simple touch operations and multi-touch gestures. For example, the pitch of a note can be changed by dragging a note vertically, a group of musical symbols can be selected by dragging a selection box, and a chord can be selected using a two-finger touch. As demonstrated in Fig. 2, all properties of musical elements can be edited "in-place" using popover controls, with minimal finger movement. Users may also enter a score using a multi-touch virtual keyboard, as if they are composing on an actual piano keyboard.

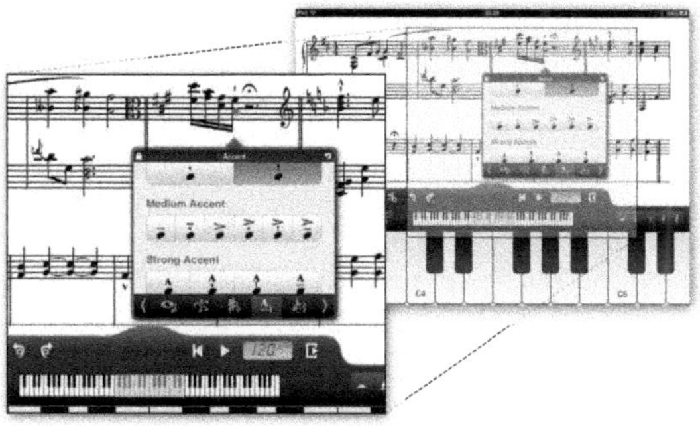

Figure 2: A screenshot of running *MusicScore* on the iPad.

When composing music, it is critical to provide users with audio feedback in real time. In order to achieve this goal, we have implemented a real-time audio engine with a 256-channel synthesizer, as shown in Fig. 3, supporting music score playback as well as interactive user operations, *e.g.*, when playing on the virtual piano keyboard and when modifying the pitch of a note. Using both the `vDSP` framework and the `AudioUnit` framework at the lowest level, the *MusicScore* audio engine is carefully tuned to achieve the highest possible performance on the iPad, with respect to both processing delays and the sound quality. To support sounds from multiple instruments as in an electronic keyboard, sound libraries can be dynamically loaded or unloaded in the audio engine, so that users may enjoy the same piece played back with different musical instruments.

3. *MUSICSCORE* FOR PRACTICE AND FUN

MusicScore is designed from the ground up to allow professionals to create music using a user-friendly composition interface and

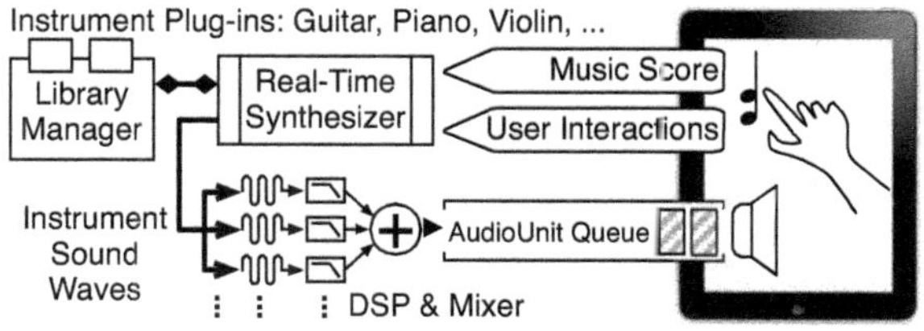

Figure 3: The real-time audio engine in *MusicScore*.

a powerful engraving backend. In addition, we are firm believers that a high-quality mobile app should be exciting and fun for everyone, and we strive to make *MusicScore* useful to piano learners and amateur musicians alike. A casual *MusicScore* user may not be interested in composing music, yet she may find *MusicScore* useful and fun if it is capable of performing the following tasks:

- ▷ Displaying music scores on the iPad placed on a music stand, and allowing her to change the score to suit her own tastes (*e.g.*, adding ornaments and fingering). Since *MusicScore* is designed to support complex engraving and interactive editing, this can be achieved without difficulty.
- ▷ "Listening" to her live piano performance, keeping track of the progress of her play in the music score, and automatically turn pages for her as needed.
- ▷ Dynamically evaluating her live piano performance, by identifying possible errors in real time as the performance progresses, including incorrect or missed notes, incorrect note timing, and inconsistent tempo. As errors are being highlighted in the score, she can focus more on her weaknesses. As such, *MusicScore* acts as a private music tutor when she is practicing.

Clearly, to achieve these goals, we must enable the auditory capability in *MusicScore*, *i.e.*, audio and other signals from a piano must be captured and analyzed on mobile devices in real time. In this section, we describe the characteristics of signals to be sensed by devices, and discuss the challenges to support high-quality music signal sensing on mobile devices in real time.

3.1 Characteristics of Sound from the Piano

To be able to "listen" to a live piano performance, the first step is to thoroughly understand signals from the piano. Different from the unpleasant pure tones defined by note pitches, which have sinusoidal and periodic waveforms with certain frequencies, the sound generated from a piano has a complicated waveform. Though musical sounds vary from a piano to another piano, they share a set of characteristics that can be utilized for real-time analysis.

Fundamental frequency. The fundamental frequency, often denoted as f_0, represents the lowest of frequency of a periodic waveform. In a modern Western music system with twelve-tone equal temperament, each note pitch is assigned to a unique fundamental frequency, so that all instruments can be tuned for a performance. By international standard, the `A4` is set at 440 Hz, and other notes' fundamental frequencies can be derived using the logarithmic rule—the frequency ratio between two adjacent notes is the twelfth root of two, $2^{1/12} \approx 1.0595$. Furthermore, notes are grouped by octaves, where an octave corresponds to a doubling in frequency, *i.e.*, $f_0^{\mathtt{A5}} = 2f_0^{\mathtt{A4}} = 880$ Hz. Naturally, to evaluate a player's performance, we should compare frequency characteristics of sound, against the expected fundamental frequencies of notes in the score. Note that a few notes of a piano might be slightly out of tune due to temperature or humidity changes. *MusicScore* can be calibrated with the player's piano and learn its sound characteristics, so that notes slightly out of tune can be correctly recognized.

Harmonic series. Musical instruments are often based on acoustic resonators, such as strings in a piano. Due to the inherent spacing of the resonances, frequencies of waves are mostly at integer multiples, or *harmonics*, of the fundamental frequency f_0, and a harmonic series is hereby formed. Take note A0 as an example, the power is ideally concentrated at frequency points around $f_0^{\text{A0}} = 28$ Hz, $2f_0^{\text{A0}} = 56$ Hz, $3f_0^{\text{A0}} = 84$ Hz, and etc., and the higher orders of harmonics have decreasing levels of energy. However, because of the stiffness of real strings in the piano, the frequencies are not exactly harmonic and can be modeled by $f_n = nf_0\sqrt{1 + Bn^2}$, where B is the inharmonicity coefficient of an instrument [5]. Since the order of magnitude of B is usually between 10^{-4} and 10^{-5} for the piano, only lower harmonics ($n \leq 4$) can be used to accurately infer f_0.

Amplitude envelope. When an acoustic musical instrument produces sound, the loudness of the sound changes over time. To quantify the loudness, we can measure the instantaneous amplitude of the wave, as illustrated in Fig. 4. Though the changes of amplitude vary significantly across players and instruments, the sound of a single-note play can be, in general, partitioned into the following four stages [11]: (1) *Attack*: the initial rise of energy from zero to peak after the key is pressed; (2) *Decay*: the subsequent slight drop of energy from the attack level to an almost constant level; (3) *Sustain*: the period when the loudness is nearly constant after the decay, until the key is released; and (4) *Release*: the time taken for the sound to fade away after the key is released. Although there is only one global peak, we observe that there exist several local peaks in the attack, decay, and sustain stages, where energy level is higher in general. Clearly, when multiple notes are played sequentially or simultaneously, as instructed in a music score, the overlapping sound waves would produce a series of peaks: some represent real note attacks, but others do not. In order to keep track of the progress of live piano play and to identify the timing of each note, we would need to correctly detect true attacks of notes when they are mixed together.

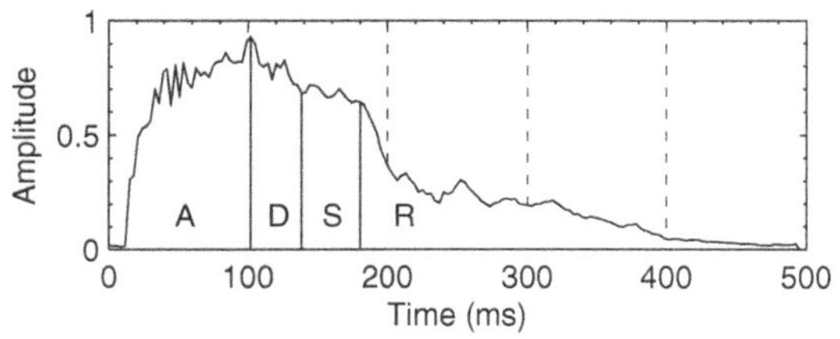

Figure 4: The instantaneous amplitude of note G4, played on a grand piano, with four stages labeled.

3.2 Imperfect Audio Sensors on Mobile Devices

Modern mobile devices have been equipped with various sensors, including the microphone, accelerometer, proximity sensor, ambient light sensor, and gyro, serving as "input" sources of mobile apps. Though mobile sensors have empowered mobile apps, they do have their limitations. In the application scenario of *MusicScore*, the built-in microphone is naturally the major signal source of *MusicScore*. In order to accurately and effectively track and analyze the player's live performance, we must identify constraints of the audio sensing system on mobile devices.

Frequency response. In contrast to professional grade audio recording systems, most audio recording systems on mobile devices have a limited frequency response, due to inferior microphone sensors, analog-to-digital converters, and software limiters. As shown in Fig. 5, it can be observed that there exists a clear drop of frequency response below 150 Hz on mobile devices. Therefore, to some extent, mobile devices would experience "listening" problems for notes below D3, whose fundamental frequencies are below 150 Hz.

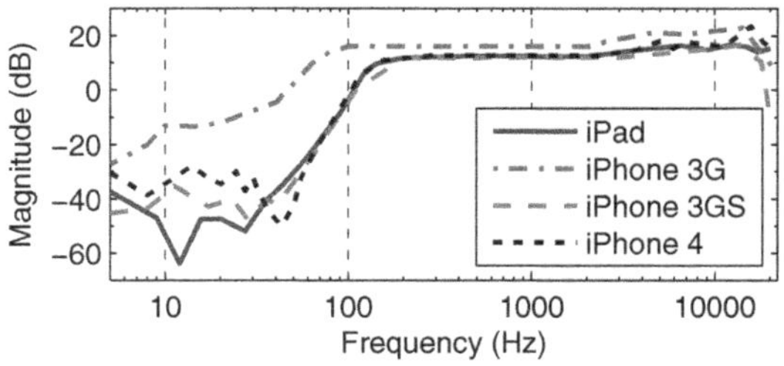

Figure 5: The frequency response of built-in microphones on iOS mobile devices.

To address the issue of the inferior frequency response below 150 Hz, we take advantage of the harmonic effect in a piano, and in particular lower orders of harmonics ($k \cdot f_0, k = 2, 3, 4$), to help us identify notes with low f_0s. For example, a weak peak of B0 at $f_0 = 31$ Hz can be confirmed by a growing energy peaks at 62 Hz, 124 Hz, and 247 Hz. It should be noted that higher orders of harmonics are not used in *MusicScore* due to the aforementioned inharmonicity.

Directional characteristics. Although most microphones on mobile devices are omnidirectional, they are usually embedded into the body of the device for a better external look, and sound waves can only reach the internal microphone through a hole or cone carved on the body frame. Such a design leads to a unidirectional-like sound perception, *i.e.*, the microphone picks up sound mostly from the direction that the hole faces, and to a lesser extent, the sides as well. To evaluate the effect of directionality of built-in microphones on mobile devices, we have recorded a grand piano playing in a $4 \times 4 \times 2.5$ m^3 room, using an iPad is placed on the music stand with microphone facing the ceiling (portrait mode). As shown in Fig. 6, even though notes are played in the same key-press velocity, some notes cannot be clearly "heard."

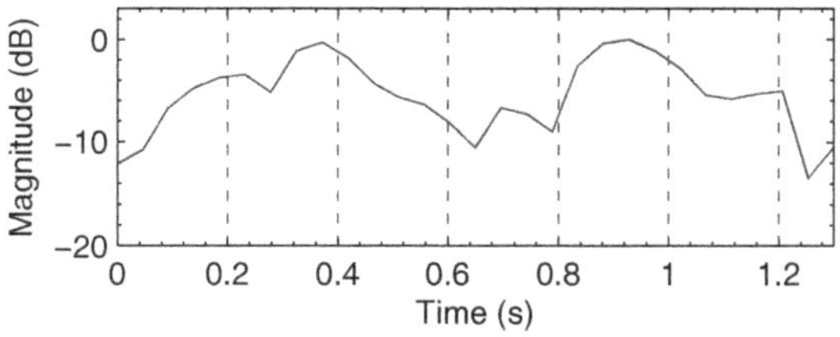

Figure 6: The normalized magnitude envelope of FFT on signals from the iPad on the music stand.

Although the note pitch can still be identified, the amplitude envelope cannot accurately reflect the exact timing of the note attack, due to the directionality of the built-in microphone. Such a deficiency of the audio sensor on mobile devices suggests that we may consider other sensing sources to evaluate the piano player's live performance.

3.3 Collaborative Sensing for Real-Time Music Capture

Since we need to judge whether a piano performer plays the *correct note pitches* at *righting times*, we need to conduct spectral analysis on the audio signal, after slicing the stream of audio samples into "frames" using a sliding window. By examining the sound's frequency spectrum within a specific time frame, against the expected fundamental frequencies of one or more notes at the corresponding time in the score, the player's performance can then be evaluated in real time. In *MusicScore*, the zero-padded Quadratically Interpolated Fast Fourier Transform (QIFFT) is adopted, due to its simplicity and accuracy. However, as stated by the Heisenberg-Gabor limit, one cannot achieve a high temporal resolution (in the time domain) and a high frequency resolution (in the frequency domain after the Fourier transform) at the same time, *i.e.*, simply applying QIFFT on the audio signal cannot achieve satisfactory spectral and temporal accuracies, which are required in *MusicScore*. Hence, we must carefully design special techniques, taking into account the application scenario of real-time performance evaluation.

Intuitively, QIFFT is sufficient to identify a single note attack or notes played far apart. However, in music pieces, chords, which consist of a set of two or more "nearby" notes sounding simultaneously (*e.g.*, `C2-E2-G2` in `C` major), are often seen. In order to correctly identify a chord, we must be able to distinguish individual note pitches of the chord within a single frame. In the context of the spectral analysis for *MusicScore*, this implies that the minimum frequency separation of QIFFT should be no greater than than frequency difference between two notes in an arbitrary chord. As we have previously mentioned, the f_0 spacing between adjacent notes is logarithmic rather than linear, *i.e.*, the frequency difference between two adjacent notes of low pitches will be much smaller than that of high pitches. For piano, the required minimum frequency separation should be less than the frequency difference between its two lowest notes, *i.e.*, $\Delta f_{\min} = (2^{\frac{1}{12}} - 1) \cdot f_0^{\text{lowest}} = 1.6$ Hz. To achieve such a frequency separation, each frame must be longer than $\text{MAFS}/\Delta f_{\min}$ seconds long [1], where MAFS is the minimum allowable frequency separation coefficient given by a set of QIFFT parameters, and MAFS is greater than 1. For a zero-padding factor of 5 (*i.e.*, the QIFFT input size is 5 times the frame size with zeros padded) with the widely used Hann window function, MAFS is 2.28 in practice, implying that each frame would be at least 1.4 seconds long, which will clearly hurt the temporal resolution of our signal analysis. In addition, a one-second lag is noticeable to users, and intolerable for real-time interaction. Aiming to improve the temporal resolution and reducing the processing delay, we propose to take advantage of the effect of harmonics in the piano discussed in Sec. 3.1, and use the fourth-order harmonic to distinguish adjacent notes, so that $\Delta f_{\min}$ can be relaxed to 12.8 Hz and the each frame can thus be reduced to 178 ms long.

However, in the time domain, a 178-ms resolution is still not enough for live play progress tracking. For example, in a typical performance with *Allegro* tempo (a quarter note = 140 beats per minute (BPM) = 428 ms), each eighth note lasts for around 214 ms. To accurately identify a consecutive sequence of eighth notes at the same pitch, which are often seen in a score, we should achieve a temporal resolution of 100 ms, or even shorter, so that peaks and valleys of power can be observed. Note that by allowing two consecutive frames overlapping with each other 50%, we may reduce the interval between frames by a half. However, a shorter interval does not result in a better temporal resolution, since overlapping will also blur the changes of power in the time domain.

To overcome the shortcoming of audio signal processing with respect to the temporal resolution, in *MusicScore*, the built-in high-sensitivity accelerometer is used to work *in collaboration* with the audio recording system. When a mobile device is in contact with a piano, vibrations of the sounding board can be passed to the device body, and then be sensed by the internal high-sensitivity accelerometer (*e.g.*, iOS devices can achieve a sensitivity of 1 mg). Using the maximum accelerometer sampling rate of 100 Hz, we may be able to achieve a detection interval of 10 ms, which would help to significantly improve the accuracy of note attack identification and shorten its response delay.

To justify the feasibility of vibration sensing, we have conducted a few preliminary experiments using the built-in accelerometer. Fig. 7 shows that, when the device is placed on the music stand of the piano, all 15 note attacks can be identified from the accelerometer readings. Another advantage of such a collaborative sensing solution is that the directionality problem of internal microphones is resolved naturally, as the the hammer striking the string gives an abrupt beginning of a note.

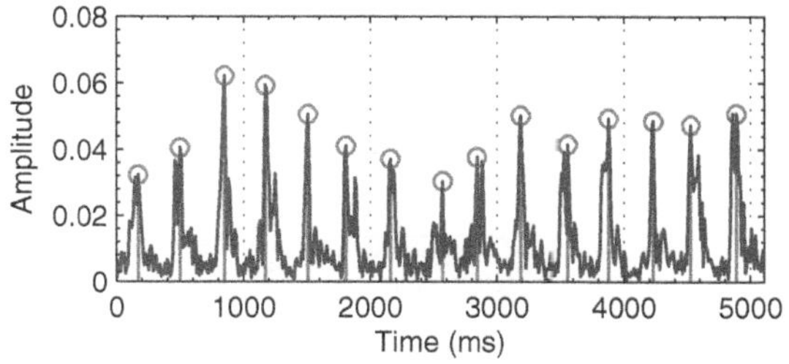

Figure 7: The instantaneous amplitude of accelerometer readings when a `C5` → `C6` → `C5` scale is practiced at a fast tempo of 180 BPM.

4. EVALUATING LIVE PERFORMANCE IN *MUSICSCORE*

In this section, we present our complete solution for evaluating live music performance, using innovative signal processing algorithms within our collaborative sensing solution.

4.1 Evaluating Live Performance with Progress Tracking: an Overview

In order to evaluate a live piano performance, both the sensed note pitches and the timing of the attack should be compared against the original music score. Hence, we first analyze the score to prepare the expected note attack sequence as *a priori* knowledge for real-time performance evaluation. Such a note attack sequence reflects the expected structures of input signals, including fundamental frequencies and timing information, as demonstrated in Table 3. This sequence will then be fed into signal processing modules running on mobile devices, as illustrated in Fig. 8, to conduct progress tracking and performance evaluation. Note that, though cloud-based signal processing is widely adopted in recent years, it does not satisfy the stringent delay requirements enforced by our real-time interactive music application. Our measurements on residential Internet connections have shown that the average round-trip time to popular cloud service providers is around 103 ms, with delay jitters up to 400 − 600 ms. Clearly, this would lead to a very uncomfortable experience during real-time progress tracking, automated page turning, as well as music performance evaluation. Hence, all signal processing procedures are running on local mobile devices, rather than in the cloud.

4.2 Note Pitch-Attack Analyzer on Audio Signals

To sense the note pitch and timing, we first need to analyze the piano sound using QIFFT, as discussed in Sec. 3. In *MusicScore*, the captured audio stream is partitioned into overlapped frames (with frame size $n = 8192$ and overlapping coefficient $\alpha = 75\%$),

Table 3: An example of the expected note attack sequence produced in *MusicScore*.

#	Relative Duration Since Last Attack	Note	f_0 (Hz)	Relative Duration
1	-	C5 C4	523 262	1/8 1/4
2	1/8	D5	587	1/8
3	1/8	E5 G4	659 392	1/8 1/4
⋮	⋮	⋮	⋮	⋮

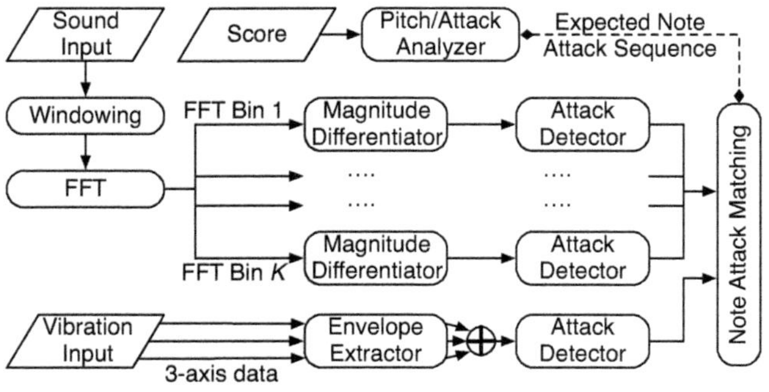

Figure 8: The signal processing flow chart in *MusicScore*.

and each frame of data is multiplied by a Hanning window function. Since the fundamental frequencies of notes in logarithmic scale while FFT bins are in linear scale, applying the Hanning window function can effectively minimize the effect of spectral leakage due to unaligned frequencies. After conducting FFT on the windowed data, we can easily derive the power in each FFT bin, *i.e.*, the magnitude of sinusoid with f_k^{bin}, as shown in the upper panel of Fig. 9. As we mainly focus on the frequency points covering Octave $0-8$, only FFT bins below 10 kHz are processed.

To identify note attacks from magnitude signals at any given f_0, we first use a high-pass filter to cut off the magnitude values below the human-audible note attack threshold, so that magnitude peaks of irrelevant background noise are excluded, and those representing potential note attacks are preserved. It must be noted that the computed magnitude values only represent the relative energy measured by the microphone, and we empirically choose 35 dB for the iOS audio system. Afterwards, the first-order different function is calculated and half-wave rectified, as demonstrated in the lower panel of Fig. 9, to unveil peaks in the processed magnitude curve after high-pass filtering. To efficiently extract peaks in real time, we choose the rectified first-order differentiation, since it can be conducted by simply storing magnitude values from previous FFT frame and subtracting current and previous values in a vectorized manner, which not only conserves memory usage on mobile devices but also reduces computational complexity.

Thanks to the smoothing effect of overlapped frames, magnitude series are smoothed over time and contain much fewer local sub-peaks around major peaks. Thus, the corresponding rectified difference series $\mathcal{D}(t)$ are able to reveal major peaks evidently. We identify the note attacks in audio signal by picking all local maxima in $\mathcal{D}(t)$ satisfying a threshold:

$$\mathrm{Attack}(t) = (\mathcal{D}_t >= \mathcal{D}_{t-1}) \wedge (\mathcal{D}_t > \mathcal{D}_{t+1}) \wedge (\mathcal{D}_t >= \mathcal{D}_{\mathrm{th}}).$$

By studying magnitude series of very "soft" piano play with the *una corda* pedal, we discover that $\mathcal{D}_{\mathrm{th}}$ should be set to as low as

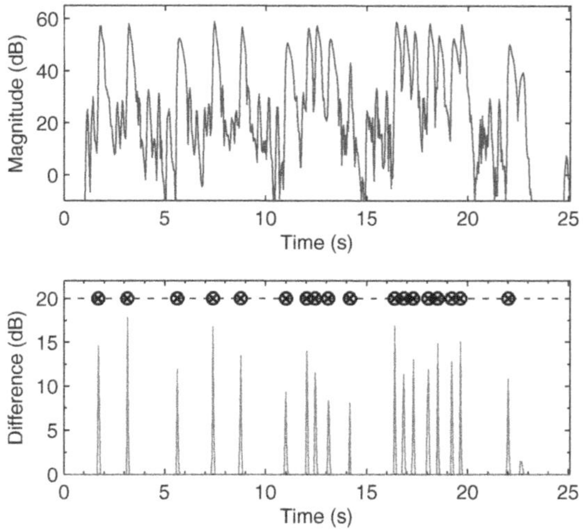

Figure 9: An example of audio signal processing for a performance with 16 measures. The upper panel shows the magnitude curve of FFT bin of 657 Hz (the bin closest to C5 = 659 Hz); and the lower one shows the half-wave rectified difference of magnitude signal after high-pass filtering, with identified note attacks marked on the top.

4.7 dB (*i.e.*, around three times of energy increase for a valid attack) to capture soft note attacks, which are often heard in a performance. Note that this threshold can be automatically adjusted by calibrating *MusicScore* with a user's own instrument.

4.3 High-Resolution Attack Detection using Vibration Signals

Due to the temporal resolution issue that we have previously discussed in Sec. 3, vibration signals from the accelerometer should also be properly processed to improve the accuracy of note attack analysis. For each signal sequence from 3 axes, the envelope of the vibration amplitude is first extracted by convolving with a 40-ms half Hanning window, which keeps the sharp attacks in the amplitude curve. After the envelope is extracted, envelope curves of all axes are summed for note attack detection. Fig. 7 has revealed that peaks in vibration signals generally rise much faster than they fall, which is very similar to an ADSR-shape curve of a note attack in audio signals. In order to extract note attacks from the vibration signal, we have designed a simple, yet sufficiently efficient, adaptive threshold algorithm for *MusicScore*, which is able to achieve a reasonable accuracy at its inherent temporal resolution.

To be specific, two criteria are used to detect a potential note attack: (1) The current amplitude envelope rises above the mean of the last few values, *i.e.*, $\mathcal{V}(t) \geq \beta \sum_{i=1}^{L} \mathcal{V}(t-i)/L$, where β represents the threshold coefficient and L is the number of historical values to be considered. This criterion is mainly based on our observations of the fast-rise and slow-drop phenomena in the signal. (2) No note attack has been identified yet, since the time t_v of the last valley in signal $\mathcal{V}$ received so far ($t_v = \sup\{t' : t' < t, \nabla\mathcal{V}(t') \leq 0\}$). This criterion effectively merges subsequent ("back-to-back") rises of amplitude into the first rise of a note attack.

In reality, for a sensitive note attack, we have chosen $\beta = 1.2$ to accommodate some slower rises of the amplitude envelope, which appear occasionally in our experiments due to "soft" notes; and, L is set to 4 (*i.e.*, 40 ms) to ensure a swift and accurate response to a passage of consecutive short note attacks. Fig. 10 demonstrates an

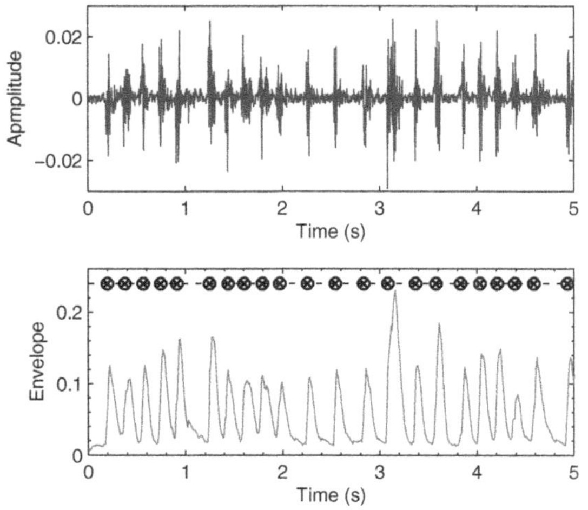

Figure 10: An example of vibration signal processing showing the first 5 measures in a performance. The upper panel shows the waveform of x-axis accelerometer data; the lower one shows the aggregated envelope with identified note attacks marked on the top.

example of vibration analysis using our proposed algorithm. Similar to $\mathcal{D}_{\text{th}}$, β can be learned by *MusicScore* during calibration. Note that, the attack detection criteria we have chosen can be easily implemented without logging the entire history of $\mathcal{V}$. Fortunately, with the `vDSP`-accelerated convolutional envelope extraction, the process of vibration signal analysis can be fully optimized for mobile devices.

Once both audio and vibration signals are processed, the potential attacks are merged to obtain accurate pitch and timing information, and then compared against notes in the expected play sequence from the score. As notes are matched progressively, *MusicScore* will automatically advance the play progress indicator, turning to the next page if necessary, and highlighting any detected mistakes (*e.g.*, pressing a wrong key) on the music score.

4.4 Intelligent Note Matching with Tempo Estimation

To achieve a better understanding of our proposed signal processing algorithms in real-world scenarios, we have invited two groups of piano players (5 people in each group), one with over 5 years of experience and another with less than one year of experience, to play two pieces of music with different tempos, and use *MusicScore* to track their performance. Although preliminary experiments show that our algorithm successfully handled the music piece performed by more experienced players at a moderate speed, the accuracy dropped significantly when notes were played in a very fast tempo, *e.g.*, a sequence of sixteenth notes at the tempo of *Vivace*, or when inexperienced players made some unexpected mistakes, *e.g.*, a key was accidentally pressed twice. As *MusicScore* is designed to serve the general population with a wide range of music background, it is a must to further improve its accuracy so that it is sufficiently robust to handle various performing speeds and human errors.

To achieve this goal, we need to identify possible cases that we may face in real-world performances. By analyzing collected sound tracks of musical performances, we believe that the accuracy is mainly affected by two categories of mismatching between sensed note attacks and actual notes in the score: (1) *Missed note attacks (false negatives)* usually happen when a very weak attack appears in-between a sequence of strong attacks of the same note or notes in different octaves, or in the worst case, when a player forgets to play a note. (2) *False note attacks (false positives)* occur as two or more adjacent peaks exist on a single note, or, some unexpected "attacks" from background noise. As demonstrated in Fig. 11, both cases will result in incorrect matching of note attacks.

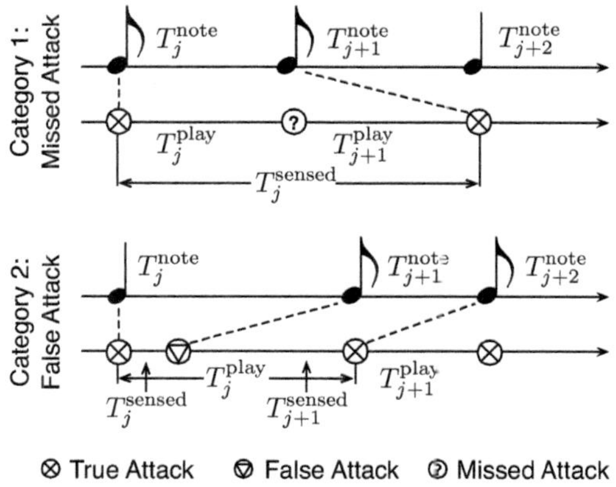

Figure 11: Two examples of tempo estimation when some note attacks are not identified accurately.

Since a piece of music is expected to be played in a near-steady tempo for a pleasant audition, we propose to use tempo tracking and prediction to minimize mismatching and further improve our algorithms. Before presenting our robust note matching algorithm, we first describe the mathematical terms used. Let T_i^{note} be the relative duration of the i-th note (*e.g.*, half note, quarter note, and etc.), T_i^{play} be the actual played duration for the i-th note (regardless whether or not the note is detected), and T_i^{sensed} be the sensed duration. In the ideal case, the corresponding true tempo is computed by $S_i = T_i^{\text{note}}/T_i^{\text{play}}$. As illustrated in Fig. 11, for the first category of mismatching, when p note attacks are missed after the j-th note, the system would compute the tempo as

$$\tilde{S}_j = \frac{T_j^{\text{note}}}{T_j^{\text{sensed}}} = \frac{T_j^{\text{note}}}{\sum_{i=j}^{j+p} T_i^{\text{play}}} = \frac{T_j^{\text{play}}}{\sum_{i=j}^{j+p} T_i^{\text{play}}} \cdot S_j.$$

For the second category, when q false attacks are detected after the j-th note, the system would calculate the tempo as

$$\begin{aligned}
\tilde{S}_j &= \frac{T_j^{\text{note}}}{T_j^{\text{sensed}}} = \frac{T_j^{\text{note}}}{\gamma_0 T_j^{\text{play}}} = \frac{1}{\gamma_0} \cdot S_j, \\
\tilde{S}_{j+1} &= \frac{T_{j+1}^{\text{note}}}{T_{j+1}^{\text{sensed}}} = \frac{T_{j+1}^{\text{note}}}{\gamma_1 T_j^{\text{play}}} = \frac{T_{j+1}^{\text{play}}}{\gamma_1 T_j^{\text{play}}} \cdot S_{j+1}, \\
\tilde{S}_{j+2} &= \ldots,
\end{aligned}$$

where $\sum_{k=0}^{q} \gamma_k = 1$. Note that it is safe to assume that γ_0 is not close 1, because when $\gamma_0 \to 1^-$ the case is equivalent to $q-1$ attacks are falsely detected after the $(j+1)$-th note. Since nearby T_i^{play} and T_i^{note} are mostly comparable due to the rhythmic structure of a performance, the relative error $\eta = |(\tilde{S}_j - S_j)/S_j|$ would be outstanding if either missed or false attacks occur. Observing that tempo tends to be relatively steady for a short passage, we could infer an expected tempo $\hat{S}_j$ from the history of played notes, and then compare it against $\tilde{S}_j$ to detect any significant error.

In order to derive the expected tempo from historical data, we need a valid prediction model for $\hat{S}$. Although many generic prediction models, such as ARMA, have been widely used for prediction, the model parameter training usually involves complex computational procedures based on historical tempo data, and complicated data pre-processing has to be conducted to fulfill special requirements of these models [3]. Instead, we propose a simple but effective adaptive moving average model, which directly takes the sensed tempo history, and fully considers special characteristics of music performance. In a nutshell, our algorithm calculates $\hat{S}$ as the arithmetic mean of previous M values, where M is a varying window size determined by the structure of the music score. Since our empirical studies reveal that notes in adjacent beats are played with a more consistent tempo, M is automatically adjusted so that the averaging window always covers all the notes from the previous beat to the current one.

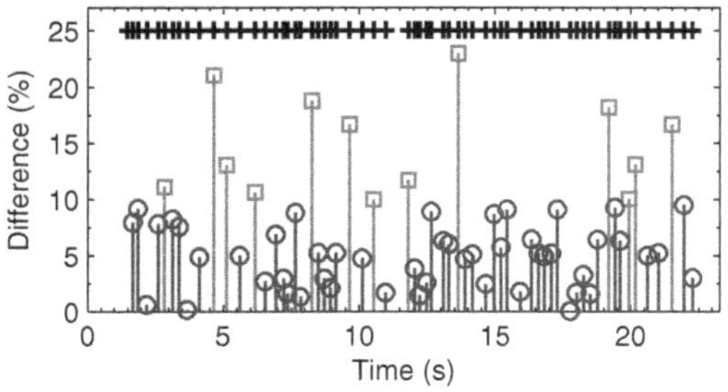

Figure 12: The normalized difference of true tempo series of a music piece performed by a typical inexperienced player, with note series marked on the top. Red stems with a square head indicate significant changes of tempo ($\geq 10\%$).

With the tempo $\hat{S}$ predicted, we also need to determine the relative error threshold η_{th} for comparing against $\tilde{S}$. Instead of using a constant for η_{th}, we have discovered that η_{th} would be best chosen according to the context of the current note being processed. As shown in Fig. 12, it is evident that the inexperienced player performs at a tempo that varies significantly as the note density changes, *i.e.*, when the relative note duration T_i^{note} of close-by notes changes notably. Such a observation implies that η_{th} should be a function of T_i^{note} to better deal with human errors. Consistent with the $\hat{S}$ prediction algorithm, we adopt the same adaptive windowing strategy. Then, within the window-covered range, the geometric mean is computed over the relative note duration ratios in logarithmic scale, since T_i^{note} is usually in the power of 2. Finally, using the Weber-Fechner logarithmic law [13], η_{th} is calculated as

$$\eta_{\text{base}} + \eta_{\text{flex}} \log_{10} \left(\prod_{i \in \text{Window}} \left| \log_2 \frac{T_i^{\text{note}}}{T_{i+1}^{\text{note}}} \right| \right)^{\frac{1}{M}},$$

where $\eta_{\text{base}} = 10\%$ and $\eta_{\text{flex}} = 20\%$, considering that the logarithmic ratio seldom exceeds 5 in music pieces. Note that the equation above can be further simplified to a form of arithmetic mean over $\log_{10} \left| \log_2 T_i^{\text{note}} - \log_2 T_{i+1}^{\text{note}} \right|$, which is easier to compute in a vectorized manner.

With carefully chosen models of $\hat{S}$ and η_{th}, we can then detect missed and false attacks using our intelligent note detection algorithm with tempo estimation. Our proposed algorithm, summarized in Algorithm 1, is executed every time when a newly sensed attack is going to be matched with the $(j+1)$-th note (*i.e.*, all previous j notes have matched with valid sensed attacks). Any false attacks can be detected if $\tilde{S}$ is alarmingly high as shown in Line $3-5$, while missed attacks can be detected iteratively when $\tilde{S}$ is significantly lower than $\hat{S}$ as shown in Line $6-14$.

Algorithm 1 *Intelligent Note Matching with Tempo Estimation*, triggered when a sensed note attack is going to be matched with the $(j+1)$-th note.

Input: The sensed note duration T_j^{sensed}, *i.e.*, the time since j-th note attack.
Output: If the sensed attack is valid
1: Obtain the expected tempo $\hat{S}_j$ using adaptive moving average prediction and derive the relative error threshold η_{th}.
2: Use the sensed note duration to compute the tempo $\tilde{S}_j = T_j^{\text{note}} / T_j^{\text{sensed}}$.
3: **if** $\tilde{S}_j > \hat{S}_j$ **and** $|(\tilde{S}_j - \hat{S}_j)/\hat{S}_j| \geq \eta_{\text{th}}$ **then**
4: **return** The sensed attack is invalid (a false attack).
5: **end if**
6: Set the counter of missed notes $p = 0$.
7: Set $T^{\text{left}} = T_j^{\text{sensed}}$ for iterative missed note detection.
8: **while** $\tilde{S}_{j+p} < \hat{S}_{j+p}$ **and** $|(\tilde{S}_{j+p} - \hat{S}_{j+p})/\hat{S}_{j+p}| \geq \eta_{\text{th}}$ **do**
9: Mark the $(j+p)$-th note as detected (missed note attack).
10: Estimate the play duration of the missed note $\hat{T}_{j+p}^{\text{play}} = T_{j+p}^{\text{note}} / \hat{S}_{j+p}$, and add $\hat{S}_{j+p}$ into the tempo series.
11: Update $T^{\text{left}} = T^{\text{left}} - \hat{T}_{j+p}^{\text{play}}$.
12: Increase p to consider the next note.
13: Compute the tempo $\tilde{S}_{j+p} = T_{j+p}^{\text{note}} / T^{\text{left}}$.
14: Predict the expected tempo $\hat{S}_{j+p}$, and update η_{th}.
15: **end while**
16: **return** The sensed attack, which matches with the $(j+p)$-th note, is valid.

5. *MUSICSCORE*: EXPERIMENTAL EVALUATION

In this section, we conduct a thorough evaluation of *MusicScore*, developed on the iOS platform in Objective-C.

5.1 Professional Music Composition

As a professional music composition app for mobile devices, we first evaluate the quality of our music engraver, which serves as the cornerstone of *MusicScore*. The *MusicScore* engraver is designed to produce artistically pleasing music sheets, by strictly following traditional guidelines of music engraving. To examine its engraving quality, we carefully compare engraving outputs of *MusicScore* with hand-tuned engraving results [12]. In addition, we conduct a set of regression tests from LilyPond [10], which include a large number of scenarios a professional engraver needs to solve. For comparisons, regression tests are also run in Symphony for iOS, LilyPond, and libmscore. We discover that the *MusicScore* engraver produces a satisfying engraving output on mobile devices. For example, in the accidental and beaming tests, as shown in Fig. 13, *MusicScore* produces almost identical output as compared to LilyPond, while both Symphony and libmscore have severely violated basic engraving rules (marked by red rectangles): (1) accidentals are too far away from notes; (2) the ledger line is unreadable; (3) the slope of the beam is incorrect; (4) the partial beam is in a wrong direction. Clearly, these engraving errors may lead to a lack of comfort as professional musicians are composing or playing.

Since *MusicScore* targets mobile devices with limited computational capabilities, the efficiency of the engraver is also critically important. Using powerful instrumentation tools from Xcode, we evaluate in detail the performance of the *MusicScore* engraver on-the-fly in terms of its CPU usage, in both static and dynamic engraving scenarios. As summarized in Table 4, when *MusicScore* is

Figure 13: A comparison of engraver output among *MusicScore*, Symphony, LilyPond, and libmscore. Red rectangles indicate incorrect engraving results.

running on a less powerful first generation iPad, the average CPU load is no more than 25% for typical usage, such as digital music sheet display and music composition routines. The CPU load exceeds 50% only during engraving preparation (usually no more 2 – 3 seconds at the loading stage), or when the score is being edited intensively. Considering the inherent complexity of professional engraving, we believe *MusicScore* has successfully achieved a satisfactory level of performance on mobile devices.

Table 4: Average CPU load of the *MusicScore* engraver.

Workload	Description	CPU (%)
Engraving preparation	One-time engraving preparation when loading a score	68.5 ± 10.3
Music sheet page turning	Rendering a full page of the music sheet	5.5 ± 3.9
Moderate interactive editing	Using multi-touch gestures to add notes, change properties, and organize the score	13.9 ± 7.1
Intensive interactive editing	Adding a large number of complicated chords with the virtual keyboard, and etc.	53.2 ± 9.3

5.2 Assessment of Play Progress Tracking and Music Performance Evaluation

In addition to features designed for professional users, we strive to provide casual users with the best possible features in *MusicScore*, such as play progress tracking, automated page turning, and live performance evaluation. To evaluate the accuracy of algorithms in *MusicScore*, we conduct our evaluations in a progressive manner, with aforementioned two groups of piano players.

First, we focus on our proposed note detection algorithms based on audio signals. Given digital music scores from the Canadian Royal Conservatory of Music Grade 3 syllabus, by using QIFFT based spectrum analysis to sense notes played in live performance, it is shown that *MusicScore* can achieve an overall detection accuracy of 98.6%, in terms of the note pitch. In Fig. 14, we further summarize the identification accuracy along with the 95% CI, in different octaves. The results reveal that notes in low octaves with low f_0 may be mistakenly identified as wrong notes, due to the limited input frequency response on iOS devices.

When note attack timing is considered, we measure the accuracy of our algorithm using two metrics: the ratio of missed attacks (R_{m}) and the ratio of false attacks (R_{f}), both over the total number of true note attacks. As shown in Table 5, the accuracy is reasonably high when the tempo of the music is slow, but R_{m} and R_{f} increase remarkably as the tempo becomes faster, particularly for

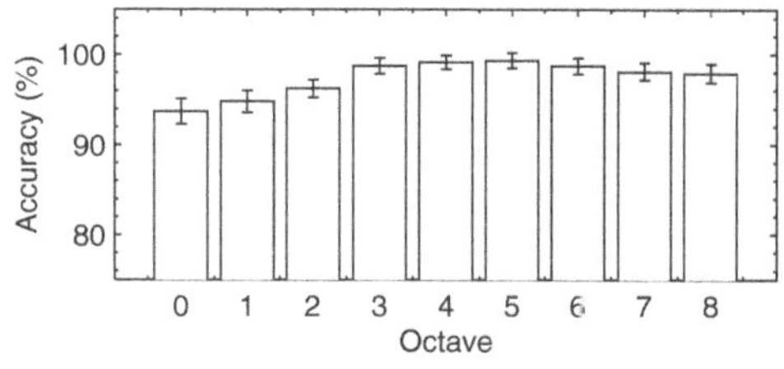

Figure 14: The accuracy of note pitch detection.

inexperienced players. This confirms the need for an intelligent note matching mechanism — to be later evaluated — to identify both false and missed attacks.

As the music sound analysis lacks sufficient temporal resolution for accurate performance evaluation, vibration signals are analyzed in *MusicScore*. We evaluate the improvement of temporal resolution by comparing the note attack timing detected by audio and vibration signals, respectively. As listed in Table 6, with the assistance of vibration signals, 46.4% of note attacks can be detected 100 – 200 ms ahead of audio-based attack detection. Given that the temporal resolution of QIFFT in *MusicScore* is around 200 ms, the accuracy of note timing has been significantly improved.

Table 5: The accuracy of audio-based note detection, evaluated by a pair of metrics ($R_{\mathrm{m}}, R_{\mathrm{f}}$). Both experienced and inexperienced players are invited to play music pieces at different tempos.

Music Tempo	Players	
	Experienced	Inexperienced
Slow	(0.5%, 0.3%)	(2.8%, 3.2%)
Moderate	(3.2%, 5.6%)	(10.4%, 8.7%)
Fast	(12.3%, 8.9%)	(17.9%, 14.6%)

Table 6: Statistics of attack timing difference between a note detected from vibration signals and the same note from audio signals. A positive value implies that a note is first detected by vibration signals.

Time Diff. Range	%	Time Diff. Range	%
Note not detected by vibration signals	1.5	[100 ms, 150 ms)	24.8
< 0 ms	0.8	[150 ms, 200 ms)	17.8
[0 ms, 50 ms)	15.1	$\geq$ 200 ms	10.7
[50 ms, 100 ms)	21.6	Note not detected by audio signals	7.7

By integrating audio and vibration processing modules with intelligent note matching using tempo estimation, we can then assess the accuracy of the performance evaluation feature in *MusicScore*. Compared to Table 5, we measure the accuracy using R_{m} and R_{f} after intelligent note matching. As shown in Table 7, a significant degree of accuracy improvement is observed after missed note attacks and false attacks have been carefully handled by our proposed algorithm based on tempo estimation. We observe that, for experienced players who have a better control of tempo, error ratios have no strong correlation with the music tempo; and the total error ratio is lower than 10% in general, even for inexperienced players.

Since all play progress tracking and performance evaluation algorithms are running in real time, it is critical to evaluate their per-

Table 7: The accuracy of performance evaluation, evaluated by a pair of metrics (R_m, R_f).

Music Tempo	Players	
	Experienced	Inexperienced
Slow	$(< 0.1\%, < 0.1\%)$	$(0.3\%, 0.7\%)$
Moderate	$(0.9\%, 1.1\%)$	$(2.4\%, 2.5\%)$
Fast	$(1.3\%, 1.0\%)$	$(4.2\%, 3.7\%)$

formance when running on mobile devices. All our proposed algorithms must meet the deadline for timely signal processing, such that users experience no uncomfortable lags when using *MusicScore* to track a live performance. As shown in Fig. 15, we measure the average CPU times consumed in every iteration of our algorithms. With respect to audio signals, one iteration takes a frame of the audio stream as input, while one iteration of vibration signal processing reads 3 values from the 3-axis accelerometer. Our measurement results show that both iPhone 4S with a faster CPU and iPad (first generation) with a slower CPU can finish our signal processing tasks within 1 ms, which can be attributed to the simplicity of our algorithms, as well as the fully optimized implementation using the iOS `vDSP` framework.

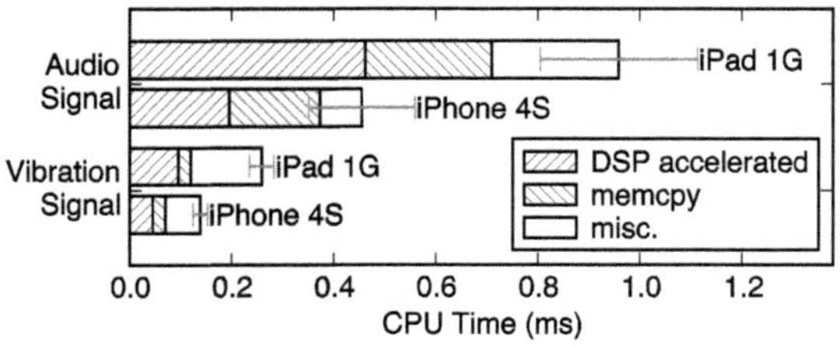

Figure 15: CPU times consumed for signal processing.

6. RELATED WORK

In the existing literature, pitch analysis and note attack detection algorithms have been widely studied. Harmonic product spectrum based algorithms proposed to extract the note pitch by finding the maximum coincidence of harmonics among Fourier transform outputs [7], while Master proposed to extract the pitch using Cepstrum along with the harmonic product spectrum [8]. In addition, an autocorrelation function is applied in the time domain to identify the fundamental frequency, which reveals a strong autocorrelation pattern [4]. With respect to note attack detection, Scheirer proposed a tempo analysis algorithm using bandpass filters and banks of parallel comb filters [13]. Goto used a simple peak-picking algorithm to roughly detect note attacks for music beat tracking [6]. Different from these algorithms which have no *a priori* knowledge about the signals to be analyzed, *MusicScore* is targeting a different scenario, where algorithms are carefully designed to analyze signals with the knowledge of the score being played. As we have made full use of available information, detection errors have been greatly reduced, so that users can enjoy a smooth experience with *MusicScore*. Another closely related research area is real-time score following, which aims to synchronize positions between the audio and the digital score. Arzt and Widmer proposed to use online dynamic time warping with simple tempo models to follow the music [2], while Montecchio and Cont modeled the system as a state tracking problem with various probabilities carefully trained [9]. Distinguished from these works, *MusicScore* can not only track the live performance, but also identify wrongly played notes or tempo. Furthermore, these existing score following algorithms require either time-consuming searching or complicated training, *i.e.*, they are not suitable for mobile devices with limited computational power.

7. CONCLUDING REMARKS

This paper presents the design and implementation of *MusicScore*, the first professional grade music composition application on the iOS platform. *MusicScore* is designed for both professional and casual users, as music scores can not only be composed and edited, but also be used for live performance tracking and evaluation, all taking place in real time. Our design in *MusicScore* features a number of salient highlights: a professional-grade interactive engraver, a collaborative sensor solution that mitigates the limitations of the audio recording system on mobile devices, new attack detection algorithms that use both audio and vibration signals, as well as a note matching algorithm with tempo estimation. All combined, *MusicScore* is shown to perform well as it tracks live performance of both experienced and inexperienced players, while staying comfortably within the limits of the computational power on mobile devices.

8. REFERENCES

[1] M. Abe and J. O. Smith, III. Design Criteria for Simple Sinusoidal Parameter Estimation Based on Quadratic Interpolation of FFT Magnitude Peaks. In *Audio Engineering Society Convention*, 2004.

[2] A. Arzt and G. Widmer. Simple Tempo Models for Real-Time Music Tracking. In *Proc. Sound and Music Computing Conference (SMC)*, 2010.

[3] G. E. P. Box, G. M. Jenkins, and G. C. Reinsel. *Time Series Analysis: Forecasting and Control*. Wiley, 4 edition, 2008.

[4] A. de Cheveigne and H. Kawahara. YIN, A Fundamental Frequency Estimator for Speech and Music. *J. Acoust. Soc. Am.*, 111(4):1917–1930, 2002.

[5] H. Fletcher, E. D. Blackham, and R. Stratton. Quality of Piano Tones. *J. Acoust. Soc. Am.*, 34(6):749–761, 1962.

[6] M. Goto. An Audio-based Real-Time Beat Tracking System for Music with or without Drum-Sounds. *Journal of New Music Research*, 30(2):159–171, 2001.

[7] Y. Li and D. Wang. Pitch Detection in Polyphonic Music Using Instrument Tone Models. In *Proc. IEEE Int'l Conf. on Acoustics, Speech and Signal Processing (ICASSP)*, volume 2, pages 481–484, 2007.

[8] A. S. Master. Speech Spectrum Modelling from Multiple Sources. Master's thesis, University of Cambridge, 2000.

[9] N. Montecchio and A. Cont. A Unified Approach to Real Time Audio-To-Score and Audio-To-Audio Alignment using Sequential Montecarlo Inference Techniques. In *Proc. IEEE Int'l Conf. on Acoustics, Speech and Signal Processing (ICASSP)*, pages 193–196, 2011.

[10] H. W. Nienhuys and J. Nieuwenhuizen. LilyPond, A System for Automated Music Engraving. In *Proc. Colloquium on Musical Informatics*, 2003.

[11] T. Pinch and F. Trocco. *Analog Days: The Invention and Impact of the Moog Synthesizer*. Harvard University Press, 2004.

[12] T. Ross. *The Art of Music Engraving and Processing*. Hansen Books, 1970.

[13] E. D. Scheirer. Tempo and Beat Analysis of Acoustic Musical Signals. *J. Acoust. Soc. Am.*, 103(1):588–601, 1998.

Modeling the QoE of Rate Changes in SKYPE/SILK VoIP Calls

Chien-nan Chen*, Cing-yu Chu†, Su-ling Yeh‡, Hao-hua Chu*, Polly Huang*†
* Graduate Institute of Networking and Multimedia, National Taiwan University, Taipei, Taiwan
† Graduate Institute of Electrical Engineering, National Taiwan University, Taipei, Taiwan
‡ Department of Psychology, National Taiwan University, Taipei, Taiwan
*†‡ {r99944043, r99921035, suling, haochu, pollyhuang}@ntu.edu.tw

ABSTRACT
The effective end-to-end transport of delay-sensitive voice data has long been a problem in multimedia networking. One of the major issues is determining the sending rate of real-time VoIP streams such that the user experience is maximized per unit network resource consumed. A particularly interesting complication that remains to be addressed is that the available bandwidth is often dynamic. Thus, it is unclear whether a marginal increase warrants better user experience. If a user naively tunes the sending rate to the optimum at any given opportunity, the user experience could fluctuate.

To investigate the effects of magnitude and frequency of rate changes on user experience, we recruited 127 human participants to systematically score emulated Skype calls with different combinations of rate changes, including varying magnitude and frequency of rate changes. Results show that 1) the rate change frequency affects the user experience on a logarithmic scale, echoing Weber-Fechner's Law [1], 2) the effect of rate change magnitude depends on how users perceive the quality difference, and 3) this study derives a closed-form model of user perception for rate changes for Skype calls.

Categories and Subject Descriptors
H.1.2 [**Models and Principles**]: User/Machine Systems – *human factors.* H.5.1 [**Information Interfaces and Presentation**]: Multimedia Information Systems – *evaluation/methodology.*

General Terms
Performance, Design, Experimentation, Human Factors.

Keywords
VoIP, Rate Adaptation, User Perception, QoE, Psychophysics.

1. INTRODUCTION
The effective end-to-end transport of delay-sensitive voice data has long been a subject of study in multimedia networking. In recent years, researchers have proposed a number of methods approaching this issue from a user-centric view (i.e., adapting the sending rate of voice calls based on user satisfaction [2][3]). Rate adaptation mechanisms ramp up the sending rate quickly when the available bandwidth is sufficient, and carefully tune up or down the sending rate when the network becomes congested. Although users prefer calls with a higher bit rate, sending voice data with an unnecessarily high bit rate could waste network resources or result in congestion. This in turn could compromise the quality of the user's experience.

The user-centric approach is a promising approach [4]. However, most studies on this topic focus on identifying a sending rate to optimize the user experience. An issue that has largely been overlooked is how users perceive rate changes. The bandwidth available during an end-to-end connection is often dynamic. Thus, a (naive) increase in the sending rate might not always result in better user experience because 1) the change might not be detectable by the user, and 2) the change might be disturbing if the available bandwidth fluctuates. In addition, increasing the sending rate costs the system more network resources.

What we are advocating is that designing the rate adaptation mechanism is a significantly more subtle task. It is not just to determine the optimal sending rate, but to determine, for what it is worth, the optimal magnitude and frequency of changes in the sending rate.

How humans perceive the quality of voice, images, or motion pictures has long been a subject of study in psychophysics. Weber and Fechner proposed in 1834 [1] that the human "notice-ability" of a change is relative to the current experience (i.e., the degree of noticeability depends on the log of the stimulus's intensity). To place the subject of our interest, VoIP calls, in context, this study investigates 1) whether user experience is logarithmic to the sending rate, and 2) whether user experience is logarithmic to the time interval and/or the rate change magnitude. In short, does Weber-Fechner's Law apply to streaming VoIP calls?

The objective of the study is twofold. First, we address the above-raised questions. Second, we address a fundamental problem in user-centric rate adaptation mechanisms: modeling the relationship of user perception and the magnitude/frequency of rate changes in VoIP calls. This relationship is codec- and environment-sensitive. This study uses Skype, the most popular VoIP service, as the first research target. The experiments in this study are geared to emulate the specifics of Skype conversations.

The methodology is based on ITU-T P.830 [5]. First, we recorded various human speech samples. These raw audio tracks were encoded at different rates using the SILK codec [6], an open source toolkit made available by Skype. A wide range of test tracks, with varying degrees and frequency of rate changes, were synthesized. In total, 127 human participants were invited to score the synthesized tracks. Three data sets, each containing different speech contents and different sets of human participants, were compiled independently. These data sets were first examined by ANOVA [7] tests and then used to model and verify the relationship of user perception and rate changes.

This study 1) confirms that the user experience-sending rate exhibits log-like behavior, echoing Weber's theory; 2) shows that the experience-frequency of rate change relationship also exhibits log-like behavior; 3) shows that the experience-magnitude of rate change relationship is determined by how users perceive the quality difference; and 4) derives a closed form model of user experience to rate changes has an average error ratio and R-square of 9.8% and 0.85, respectively. These findings provide a foundation for voice quality assessment and voice data delivery. For example, Skype's rate adaptation mechanism can be redesigned to optimize the user experience under dynamic network conditions.

The rest of the paper is organized as follows: Section 2 presents related work on multimedia networking and psychophysics; Section 3 presents findings from the preliminary experiments, forming the basis for modeling the relationship of user experience and rate changes in Section 4; using large-scale experiments, Section 5 derives the specifics for the models; Section 6 presents an evaluation of models; and finally, this paper concludes with a description of future work.

2. BACKGROUND AND FUNDAMENTALS

2.1 Quality of Service

Whether a network application is providing a "good enough" service is traditionally measured by throughput, loss rate, delay, and delay jitter [8]. These measurements are referred to as Quality of Service (QoS) measurements. For years, measured QoS represented the performance of a network application. The quality of the best-effort data, transported through TCP [9], is typically measured primarily by throughput, whereas the quality of real-time streaming media, transported through UDP [10], is typically measured by additional metrics such as loss rate, delay, and delay jitter.

Early rate control mechanisms attempted to improve QoS for the data delivered [11]. For example, TCP employs an additive-increase-multiplicative-decrease (AIMD) policy to control the send-window size. This allows the exploration of maximum available bandwidth and avoids data loss during network congestion. AVoIP [12], designed to transport voice data, employs a similar AIMD policy to control the sending rates of VoIP calls.

2.2 Quality of Experience

An increasing trend in this area is to measure network services using the Quality of Experience (QoE). As defined by the International Telecommunication Union (ITU), QoE is "the overall acceptability of an application or service, as perceived subjectively by the end-user," and "includes the complete end-to-end system effect" and "may be influenced by user expectations and context" [13]. The metrics of QoE, such as responsiveness [14] and the mean opinion score (MOS) [15], directly reflect the user's perception of the network services.

However, QoE measurements are difficult to acquire without application-level support [14][15]. Responsiveness might require data content analysis, and MOS requires user feedback. Rate adaption mechanisms based on these measurements are inherently difficult to implement. Furthermore, the delay of acquiring these measurements might exceed the granularity of network dynamics, rendering the approach impractical.

2.3 QoS-QoE Synergy

Despite their differences, QoS and QoE are not in competition to each other. Rather, they are complementary pieces in the long-standing puzzle of assessing the quality of multimedia services in real time. Recent research dedicated to map the objective, network-centric QoS to the direct, user-centric QoE has enabled the practical implementation of service quality assessment in real time. The authors of [14] proposed a formula mapping bit rate, loss, delay, and jitter to user satisfaction in Skype calls. [16] and [17] investigated the QoS and QoE of a wide range of network services, including Web page browsing, photo sharing, file downloading, and VoIP. These QoS-to-QoE mappings exhibit logarithmic relationships.

Previous QoS and QoE mapping techniques have provided insights on how users perceive multimedia streams in steady states. However, they are insufficient to derive adaptation strategies that deliver real-time multimedia streams, which are under the influence of frequent network dynamics. Thus, this study derives the relationship between rate changes and human perception. This is an essential issue that has not yet been thoroughly investigated.

2.4 QoE-Based Adaptation

Similar to the ultimate goal of this study, previous researchers have proposed a number of adaptation schemes using QoE metrics as the criteria. For a 3D tele-immersive video service, the authors of [18] identified two metrics, "Just Noticeable Degradation" and "Just Unacceptable Degradation," and proposed a quality adaptor based on these two metrics to reduce resource usage while enhancing perceived visual quality. For a mobile video service, the authors of [19] defined a QoE metric, "Acceptability," to indicate whether users are pleased with the service under different content types and codec settings. These QoE metrics are binary in that their assessment results are acceptable or unacceptable. To facilitate fine-grained quality assessment, and therefore, to enable more sophisticated adaptation, this study investigates the effect of rate changes on user experience and derives a user experience model in the continuous space.

2.5 Psychophysics

Weber-Fechner's Law [1] provides a plausible explanation of the logarithmic relationships between various QoS and QoE metrics. Studies on the relationships between stimulus and human perception date back to 1834, when Ernst Heinrich Weber published his insights into the human sensory system. Quantitatively, Weber showed that the ratio of the noticeable threshold of stimulus intensity change to the intensity of original stimulus is a constant:

$$\frac{\Delta I}{I} = K$$

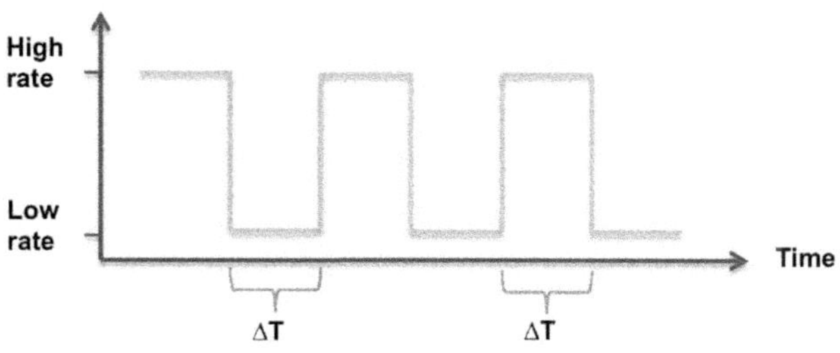

Figure 1. The quality fluctuation.

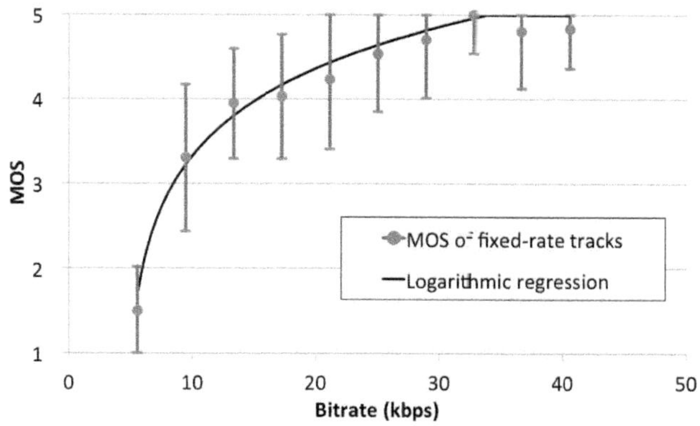

Figure 2. MOS-bitrate plot of fixed rate tests.

where ΔI is the amount of intensity difference being just noticeable, I is the original intensity, and the constant K is called the Weber fraction. Take weight lifting as an example. Assume that one starts with a 25 kg object, and the carrier does not notice the difference until it increases by 5 kg. Here, K for weight lifting is 1/5, and the just-noticeable increment is 1 kg if the carrier starts from 5 kg.

Shortly after the publication of Weber's Law, Gustav Theodor Fechner presented a mathematic model known as Weber-Fechner's Law. Given a stimulus S and its responding quantitative perception P, the relationship between S and P is as follows:

$$dP = k \times \frac{dS}{S}$$

where dS and dP are the differences of stimulus and perception, respectively, and k is a constant scale factor. Integrating both sides of the equation produces the following:

$$P = k \times \ln S + c$$

where c is the constant introduced by integration. Weber-Fechner's Law is applicable to a wide range of human perceptions [20][21][22][23], including hearing, vision, taste, sense of touch and heat, and even in temporal, spatial, and numerical cognitions.

3. PRELIMINARY EXPERIMENT

The purpose of the preliminary experiment in this study was to examine, through user tests, whether changes in sending rates decreases the user experience, and at what scale the mean opinion score (MOS) is influenced by the magnitude and frequency of changes. For clarity, we define magnitude and frequency, the two key aspects of a rate change, as follows. As shown in Fig. 1, magnitude is determined by a pair of bitrates, namely the high rate (hr) and the low rate (lr), whereas frequency is defined as the time interval (ΔT) between two adjacent rate changes.

3.1 Methodology

Audio Source: Following the recommendations of ITU-T P.830 [5], the source material consisted of a number of simple, short, meaningful sentences with no obvious contextual connections. Two female and two male speakers were recruited to produce the audio samples to avoid bias caused by contextual and speaker characteristics. Each audio sample lasted 30 s, and the sampling rate of each recording was a standard 44.1 kHz.

Fixed-Rate Tracks: This study used Skype, a state-of-the-art commercial VoIP application, as the experimental environment. The latest version of Skype [24] uses the SILK [6] audio codec for its PC-to-PC service. Thus, the audio source was encoded by SILK for all the experiments. Based on the limitations of the SILK freeware's functionality, the audio sources were encoded in 10 different bitrates, uniformly from 40.6 to 5.6 kbps, as shown in Fig. 2.

Variable-Rate Tracks: We synthesized test tracks with varying qualities by combining two audio tracks with different bitrates into one with different time intervals. The high and low bitrates were chosen from 40.6, 28.9, 17.2, or 5.6 kbps. This pairing produced 6 pairs of high-low rate changes, indicated as (hr, lr). The time interval between rate changes was chosen from 1, 2, 3, 5, and 10 s. Thirty test tracks were generated to form the variable-rate test group for the experiment. For most video codecs capable of generating fixed-rate and variable-rate video streams, a video stream of variable bitrates is very likely different from composition of fixed-rate streams. However, SILK works in such a manner that, given a bandwidth limit, it generates an audio stream at the given limit. Skype sends a variable bitrate stream by feeding SILK a sequence of available bandwidths measured from the network. The manner in which the variable-rate tracks are synthesized in the study utilizes this Skype characteristic.

Number of Participants: Each test track was rated by 14 non-expert participants [25] using a 5-point MOS, where 5 representing the best quality, and 1 representing the worst [15]. Among all the participants, there were 10 males and 4 females whose ages ranged from 23 to 31 years, with a mean age of 25.6 years. All of them are graduate students. The original audio source of the 44.1 kbps bitrate was presented to participants at the beginning of the experiment for two reasons: to provide a reference of the most desirable case, and to allow the participants to focus on experiencing the quality of the audio for subsequent samples, instead of focusing on the content of the conversation. Other than the reference track, the remaining 40 test tracks were randomly ordered to avoid time-dependent bias. Each participant rated 41 audio tracks, taking slightly longer than 20 min to complete.

3.2 Fixed-Rate Results

Increasing the sending rate does not produce a proportional improvement in user experience. Fig 2 shows the MOS of the fixed-rate tracks. The x-axis indicates the sending rate, and the

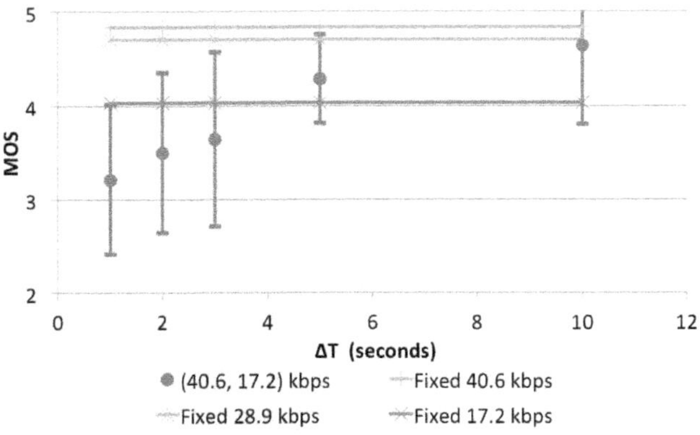

Figure 3. MOS-ΔT plot of (40.6, 17.2) kbps set.

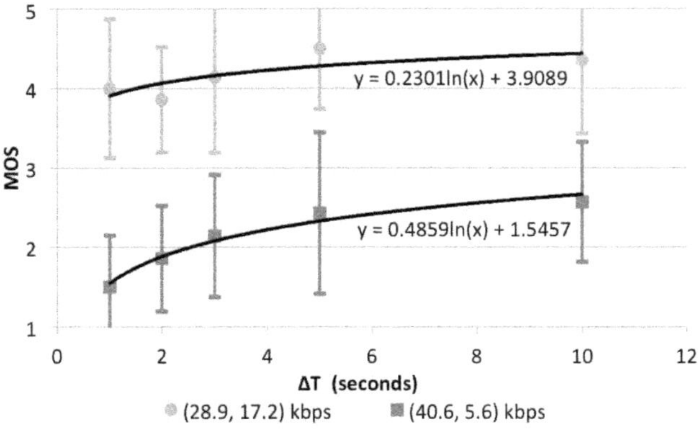

Figure 4. MOS-ΔT plot of (28.9, 17.2) kbps and (40.6, 5.6) kbps tests.

y-axis indicates the corresponding MOS. The opinion score increases as the sending rate increases. In particular, the degree of MOS increase is not proportional to that of the rate increase (i.e., the MOS-bitrate relationship is sub-linear). Applying a regression test to the data set shows a logarithmic fit to the convexity with a substantially high R-square value: 0.9607. This is a strong indication that the MOS (P) and sending rate (S) relationship exhibit Weber-Fechner's Law.

In the preliminary experiments, the sending rates tested were evenly distributed, approximately 11 kbps apart. This is a shortcoming in support of Weber-Fechner's Law in the MOS-bitrate relationship. The region between 7 and 10 kbps is where the regression suggests a rapid increase in the MOS. However, data points are insufficient to confirm that the relationship is logarithmic. The large-scale experiments described in Section 5 consider this shortcoming and address this issue.

3.3 Variable-Rate Results

Fluctuation in sending rates significantly affects the user experience. Thus, keeping the rate low and steady might be significantly better than maximizing it. Fig. 3 plots the MOS of variable-rate tracks, where (hr, lr) = (40.6, 17.2) kbps. The MOSs of the fixed-rate 17.2, 28.9, and 40.6 kbps tracks are 4.0, 4.7, and 4.8, respectively, and are indicated in the figure to highlight the following findings: 1) User experience at the fixed low rate (17.2 kbps) can be better than that of a dynamic one that runs no lower than the low rate throughout the track (i.e., those in the (40.6, 17.2) kbps set). This phenomenon is particularly distinct when the change frequency is high. 2) The MOS of the fixed average-rate track, the 28.9 kbps test, exceeds that of the variable-rate track (40.6, 17.2) kbps. This suggests that the average scores of the two steady tracks cannot quantitatively represent the user experience of a dynamic audio track. Thus, modeling the user experience of the fixed-rate audio streams is insufficient to derive values as measured under variable rates.

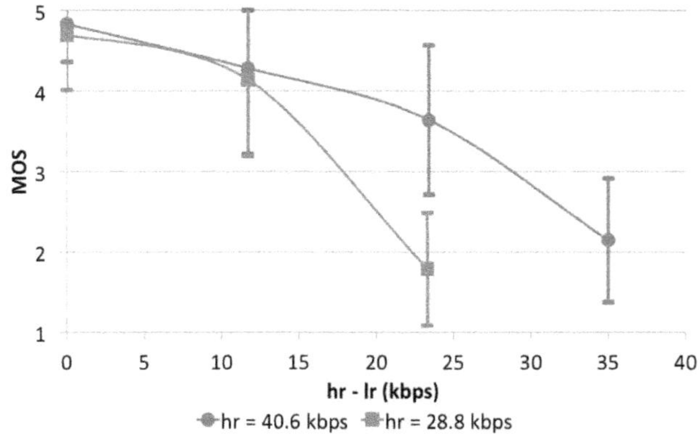

Figure 5. MOS-(hr − lr) plot of hr = 40.6 and hr = 28.9 kbps tests.

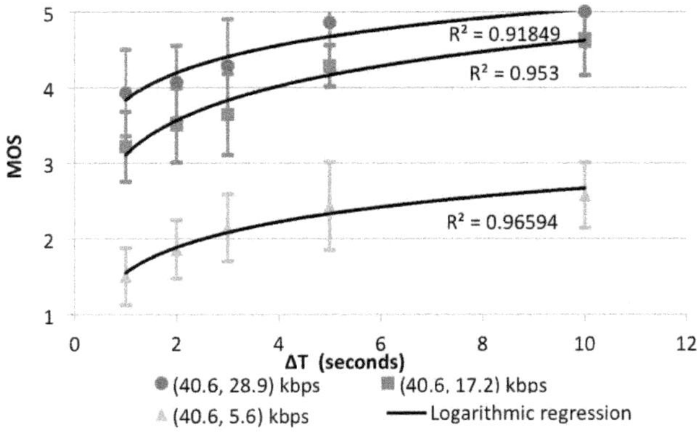

Figure 6. MOS-ΔT plot of (40.6, 28.9) kbps, (40.6, 17.2) kbps, (40.6, 5.6) kbps tests.

3.4 Effects of Rate Change Magnitude

Variable-rate tracks with the same average rate do not produce the same level of user experience. For variable-rate tracks with the same average sending rate, participants prefer the one with a smaller rate change magnitude. Fig. 4 shows the MOSs of two variable-rate tracks, where (hr, lr) = (28.9, 17.2) kbps and (40.6, 5.6) kbps. The two tracks share the same 20.6 kbps average rate. However, they have relatively different MOSs. Regardless of ΔT, tracks that are smaller in change magnitude, (28.9, 17.2) kbps, are consistently better than those that are large in change of magnitude, (40.6, 5.6) kbps. This observation suggests that the MOS depends on the rate change magnitude.

The rate change magnitude does not directly determine the user experience, which instead depends on the specifics of hr and lr. Fig. 5 shows the MOS (y-axis) across rate change magnitudes (x-axis). The data points labeled 40.6 kbps are the variable-rate tracks with hr = 40.6 kbps, and those labeled 28.9 kbps are hr = 28.9 kbps. The MOS generally declines as the magnitude increases, echoing the results above. Particularly, the MOS of the tracks with hr = 40.6 kbps declines slower than that of the

hr = 28.9 kbps tracks. This indicates that the MOS is a function of hr and lr, and not only the change magnitude ($hr - lr$). This finding sets the stage for the modeling task in Section 4.

3.5 Effects of Rate Change Frequency

Frequent changes in sending rate frustrate users. The results of the variable-rate track tests indicate a negative correlation between rate change frequency and MOS. Fig. 6 shows the resulting MOS-ΔT plot for three of the variable-rate cases, where (hr, lr) = (40.6, 28.9) kbps, (40.6, 17.2) kbps, and (40.6, 5.6) kbps. As the frequency of change decreases, the MOS increases. Furthermore, the logarithmic trend indicates that the MOS-ΔT relationship likely obeys Weber-Fechner's Law.

Regression tests were conducted on each of the variable-rate track results. The R-square values are all higher than 0.9, except for the (28.9, 17.2) kbps case. This may be attributed to the similarity of the two bitrates. According to the post-experiment feedbacks, participants were indifferent to, or did not notice, the quality changes between two similar rates. Although the MOS-ΔT relationship generally exhibits logarithmic behavior, it is subtler and depends on the specific hr and lr of a rate change.

4. PROPOSED MODEL

Based on the findings of Section 3, this section proceeds one step further and proposes models that quantify the user experience for fixed-rate and variable-rate Skype calls.

4.1 Fixed-Rate Model

The fixed-rate model is straightforward. Based on the logarithmic relationship observed in MOS-bitrate, as described in Section 3.2, this study proposes a closed-form formula to predict the MOS from the sending rate as follows:

$$f_{FIX}(br) = \gamma \times \ln(br - \alpha) + \beta$$

where br is the bitrate, and α, β, and γ are coefficients to be determined by SILK characteristics. The bitrate shift (α) is caused by the limit of human perception. According to the formula, the $br - \alpha$ term, being inside the ln operator, can only be positive. When the quality drops below α, users are unable to notice any difference. Based on a large-scale experiment, Section 5 presents the specifics of the coefficients.

4.2 Variable-Rate Model

The variable-rate model is based on the finding outlined in Section 3.4 that the MOS of variable-rate tracks depends on hr and lr, and the finding of Section 3.5 that the MOS is logarithmic to ΔT. To capture these effects, this study proposes the following closed-form formula for rate-changing SILK streams:

$$f_{FLUC}(hr, lr, \Delta T) = SCALE(hr, lr) \times \ln(\Delta T) + SHIFT(hr, lr)$$

where the effect of change frequency is distributed to the logarithm term, and the effect of hr and lr is distributed to the two subroutines, $SCALE()$ and $SHIFT()$.

- $\ln(\Delta T)$ represents the MOS-ΔT relationship, in which the MOS increases logarithmically to ΔT.

- $SCALE()$ represents the influence of hr and lr of the rate change on $\ln(\Delta T)$. This helps rescale the logarithmic effect introduced by ΔT and control the degree of quality change when ΔT varies. Hence, we can interpret $SCALE()$ as the sensitivity to the rate change frequency. A (hr, lr) pair is more sensitive to the rate change frequency if it has a larger value of $SCALE()$. The finding in Section 3.4 suggests that a larger difference between hr and lr indicates higher sensitivity. Thus, $SCALE()$ is a function that increases with the rate difference. Another caution to take with $SCALE()$ is that, according to Section 3.4, the sensitivity to rate change frequency is not solely determined by the rate change magnitude. Instead, it is lower when the corresponding hr and lr are high. Fig. 5 shows that the decline of MOS to $hr - lr$ is slower in the $hr = 40.6$ kbps case, but faster in the $hr = 28.9$ kbps case. Thus, the $SCALE()$ term captures this dimension of interaction between the rate change frequency and the level of sending rates as well.

- $SHIFT()$ is the remaining portion of MOS that is not influenced by ΔT. This value can be derived by projecting the value of MOS when ΔT approaches the duration of the audio track. As ΔT grows, the effect of fluctuation decreases and the variable-rate case becomes indistinguishable from a fixed-rate version. The quality of this fixed rate equivalent is called the *dominant quality of the fluctuation*. As mentioned in Section 3.3, this dominant quality is not the average quality of the high and low rates. The dominant quality is the quality a user expects when the effect of fluctuation decreases. For the modeling task, the resulting MOS serves as an anchor point of the formula. Although the term does not depend on ΔT, its value varies by case in the preliminary results. Therefore, the $SHIFT()$ subroutine is formulated with an association to hr and lr.

5. LARGE-SCALE EXPERIMENT

This section reports a large-scale experiment conducted for two purposes: to re-examine the MOS-bitrate and MOS-ΔT relationships using ANOVA tests to verify the proposed models, and to derive the unknown coefficients and the exact forms of $SCALE()$ and $SHIFT()$ in the proposed formulas.

5.1 Methodology

Audio Source: The audio source is the same as that used in the preliminary experiments.

Fixed-Rate Tracks: Nine rates were selected in this set of experiments. Unlike the preliminary experiments, the chosen rates were separated evenly by their expected MOS, and not by the bitrates. The expected MOSs were estimated by the logarithmic fit obtained from the preliminary experiments to address the shortcoming mentioned in Section 3.2. The sending rates were (r1, r2, r3, r4, r5, r6, r7, r8, r9) = (40.6, 27.7, 19.4, 14.1, 10.7, 8.5, 7.1, 6.1, 5.6) kbps.

Variable-Rate Tracks: Each variable-rate track contains a high rate and a low rate selected from the nine bitrates used in the fixed-rate group. This pairing produced 36 (hr, lr) combinations. The frequencies used here are the same as those in the preliminary experiments: 1, 2, 3, 5, and 10 s.

Number of Participants: The participants in this study rated 189 thirty-second tracks, of which 180 were variable-rate tracks and 9 were fixed-rate tracks. Based on the recommendation of ITU-T P.911 [25], which states that each track should be rated by 6 to 40 participants and each experiment should not exceed 30 min, we recruited 127 human participants, and each of them rated 45 randomly chosen tracks (5760 scores acquired). Among all the participants, there were 96 males and 31 females. Their age ranged from 18 to 29 years, with an average of 22.8 years. All of them had received undergraduate level education, and 61 of them had also received graduate level education. Besides, none of them had participated in the preliminary experiment. The experiment duration, including the time spent listening to the reference track

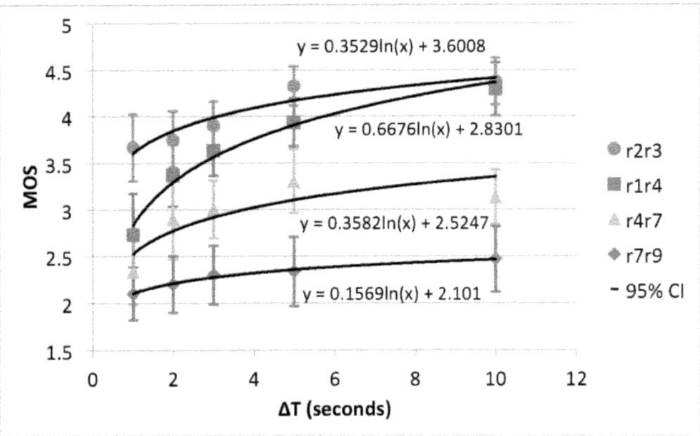

Figure 7. Non-parallel MOS-ΔT relationships indicate interaction.

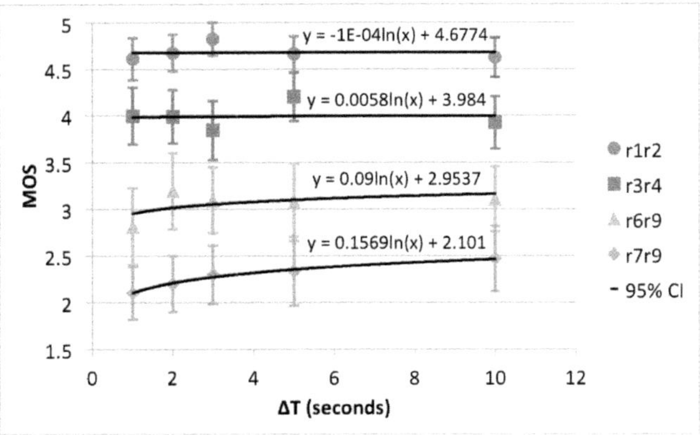

Figure 8. MOS-ΔT plots of indiscernible tests.

presented at the beginning and inserted in the experiment for score calibration, was approximately 25 min. Each track was rated by at least 30 participants.

Score Calibration: Forty-five tracks are quite a few to rate. This study uses a modified Absolute Category Rating with the Hidden Reference (ACR-HR) approach to calibrate scores that might be biased because of fatigue [26]. The main idea of ACR-HR is to play a reference track before each test track, so that the participants can adjust the MOS of each track based on the corresponding reference. ACR-HR provides a good approach to compare the scores of different tracks, but also prolongs the test duration. As a compromise to the original ACR-HR, which essentially doubles the experimentation time, we modified ACR-HR to insert one high-quality (44.1 kbps) reference track for every nine test tracks.

For data processing, a differential quality score (DMOS) [26] was computed between each track and its corresponding reference using the following formula:

$$DMOS = MOS_{TEST} - MOS_{REF} + 5$$

Because DMOS might exceed 5, we applied a 2-point crushing function [26] to prevent DMOS from unduly influencing the overall MOS:

$$DMOS_{crushed} = \frac{7 \times DMOS}{2 + DMOS}, when\ DMOS > 5$$

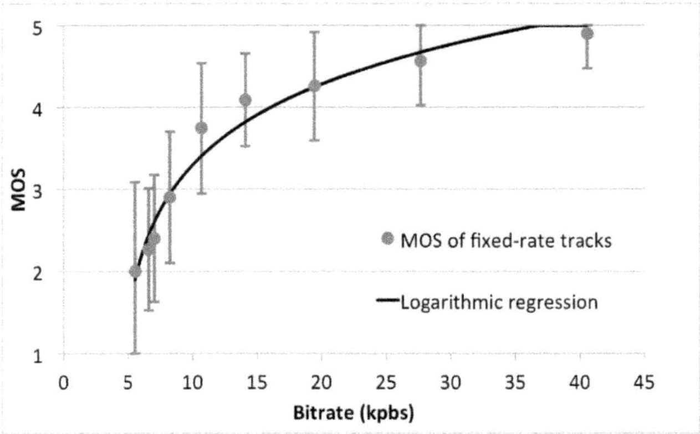

Figure 9. MOS-bitrate plot of fixed-rate tests in large-scale experiments.

5.2 ANOVA Tests

MOS-bitrate: The one-way ANOVA test was performed to determine the significance of the bitrate's influence to MOS. The p value for the MOS-bitrate test is 1.38e-58, indicating a significant influence. The R-square value of a logarithmic fit to MOS-bitrate relationship is 0.9645, confirming Weber-Fechner's Law observed in the preliminary experiment.

Interaction between ΔT *and* (hr, lr): To confirm that an interaction exists between these two factors, a two-way ANOVA was conducted on ΔT and the difference of hr and lr. The p value of interaction is 7.94e-14, which strongly supports the significance of an interactive term. This confirms the multiplication of $SCALE(hr, lr)$ and $\ln(\Delta T)$ in the proposed variable-rate model. Fig. 7 depicts the MOS-ΔT relationships of a number of variable-rate tracks. The regression fits are not parallel to each other, suggesting an interaction between ΔT and (hr, lr).

MOS-ΔT: For each given pair of hr and lr, one-way ANOVA was conducted with respect to ΔT of the rate changes. A p value less than .05 indicates that ΔT has a significant influence on MOS. Otherwise, it suggests that participants are unable to notice the change of bitrates with varying ΔT.

Table 1. Indiscernible variable-rate data sets

Test	p value	Test	p value	Test	p value
r1r2	.31	r6r7	.31	r7r8	.26
r3r4	.42	r6r8	.11	r7r9	.34
r4r5	.31	r6r9	.09	r8r9	.32

Table 1 shows the variable-rate data sets with p values exceeding .05. The hr and lr pairs are all similar to each other in these data sets. This echoes the odd case identified in Section 3.5, in which ΔT would be irrelevant if the rate change is indiscernible. Fig. 8 shows the MOS-ΔT relationships for some of the variable-rate tracks in Table I. The MOS does not vary significantly across ΔT in these data sets. This effect is captured by the $SCALE()$ subroutine, which tends to give a small value when the difference between the two bitrates is small.

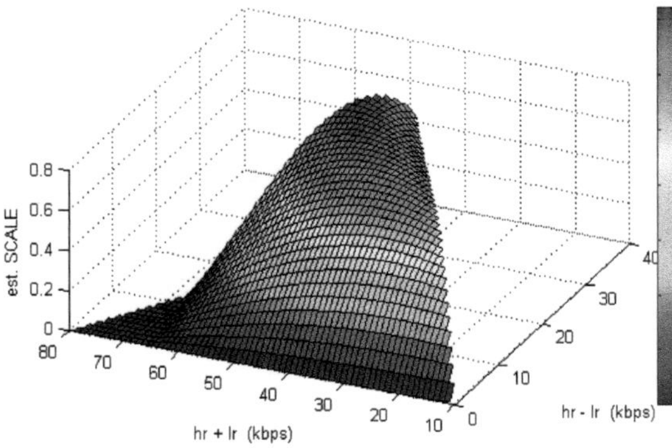

Figure 10. 3D plot of SCALE().

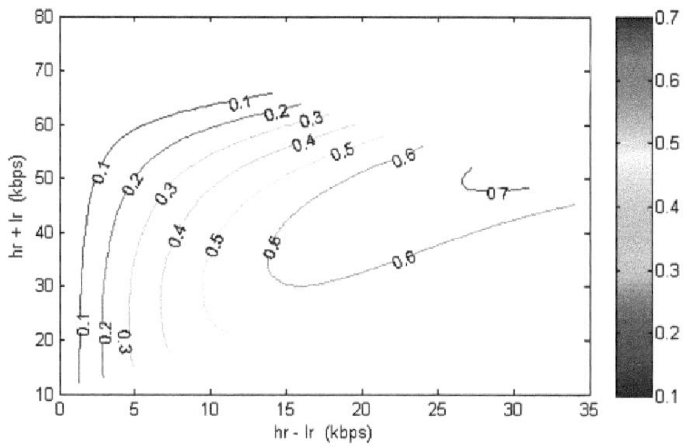

Figure 11. Contour of SCALE().

5.3 Model Specifics

1) Coefficients of Fixed-rate Formula: As Fig. 9 shows, the data are fitted by the proposed fixed-rate formula with $\alpha = 4.091$, $\beta = 1.515$, and $\gamma = 1.000$. Thus, the relationship between QoS(bitrate) and QoE(MOS) for a fixed-rate Skype VoIP service can be described using the following formula:

$$f_{FIX}(br) = \gamma \times \ln(br - 4.091) + 1.515$$

where *br* is the bitrate of the service. The lower bound of user perception can be further inferred by:

$$1(MOS) = f_{FIX}(br') = \ln(br' - 4.091) + 1.515$$

$$\rightarrow br' = 4.091 + e^{-0.515} \approx 5.0(kbps)$$

where br' is the bitrate that provides the baseline user satisfaction (MOS=1). In other words, any bitrate lower than br' does not affect the QoE. The resulting $br' = 5.0$ kbps is close to the lower bound of SILK's encoding capability (5.6 kbps), suggesting that SILK is likely designed with insights to the limits of human perception, e.g., the one indicated by α in Section 4.1.

2) SCALE() Subroutine of Variable-rate Formula: The $SCALE()$ term is named as such because it is the scaling coefficient of the $\ln(\Delta T)$ fit and it represents the sensitivity of users to the rate change frequencies. The preliminary experiments in this study show that the MOS and the magnitude of rate changes are positively correlated, meaning that $SCALE()$ in the formula is an increasing function of $hr - lr$. However, as discussed in Section 4.2, $SCALE()$ returns a small value when the levels of sending rates are high. To identify the exact relationship of $SCALE()$ to (hr, lr), we logarithmically fit the MOS-ΔT relationship to each (hr, lr) pair. The coefficient of the $\ln(\Delta T)$ component serves as the value of $SCALE()$ for the rate pair.

Given that the $SCALE()$ term is not simply decided by $hr - lr$, but also the level of hr and lr, we take the analysis to another space, where x is $hr - lr$ and y is $hr + lr$. The two variables proposed here are designed to capture the complexity of perceptual sensitivity to rate change frequency. The term $hr - lr$ allows a large $SCALE()$ when the rate difference is large, whereas the term $hr + lr$ allows a small $SCALE()$ when both hr and lr are large. After applying polynomial regression to the new variables, the resulting polynomial form of $SCALE()$ can be expressed as:

$$SCALE(hr, lr) = f(x, y)$$
$$= p_{00} + p_{10}x + p_{01}y + p_{20}x^2 + p_{11}xy + p_{02}y^2 + \cdots$$

where $x = hr - lr$ and $y = hr + lr$.

The wider variety of fluctuations tested in the large-scale experiment enables polynomial regression to a higher degree. After exploring different degrees, we find that the cubic polynomial function fits sufficiently well (i.e., the fit is not significantly better taken to a degree higher than 3). Table 2 presents the corresponding coefficients of the polynomial.

Table 2. Coefficient of Polynomial Fit to SCALE()

p_{00}	p_{10}	p_{01}	p_{20}
0.02122	0.06465	-0.001637	-0.004956
p_{11}	p_{02}	p_{30}	p_{21}
0.001538	3.488e-005	-9.562e-007	8.639e-005
p_{12}	p_{03}		
-3.903e005	-2.21e-007		

To gain a complete picture of how hr and lr influence $SCALE()$, this study plots the derived polynomial and depicts the resulting 3D surface in Fig. 10. To facilitate the discussion, Fig. 11 shows the contour of $SCALE()$.

As shown in these figures, the relationship between $SCALE()$ and (hr, lr) is as follows: 1) With the same $hr + lr$, $SCALE()$ generally increases as $hr - lr$ increases. This confirms the findings in the previous sections that the rate change becomes more disturbing when users are more aware of the quality difference. 2) Along each contour line, $SCALE()$ tends to be smaller when $hr + lr$ becomes large. A larger $hr + lr$ means that both hr and lr are high. Based on the fixed-rate model, the quality differences between two high rates are relatively smaller. Consequently, users are less aware of the difference. Thus, the case leads to a smaller $SCALE()$, or a lower sensitivity to ΔT. 3) After $hr - lr$ exceeds a certain level, such as 15 kbps, $SCALE()$ declines when $hr + lr$ decreases. This means that if the quality difference is large while both hr and lr are low, the sensitivity to ΔT decreases with the sending rates. This indicates that, despite users being able to perceive a rate change, reducing the frequency of rate change does not improve the quality of experience because the effect of rate change frequency is bounded by users' perceptual limit to low-rate audio tracks.

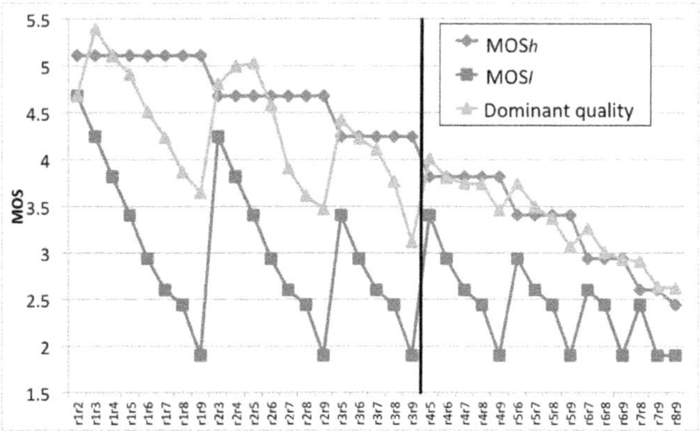

Figure 12. Dominant quality.

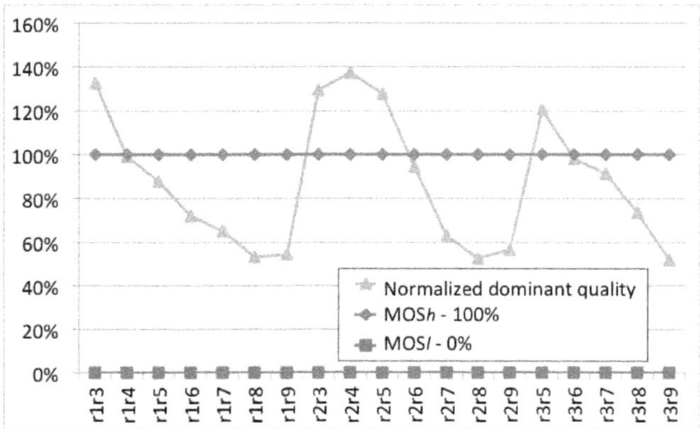

Figure 13. Normalized dominant quality.

3) SHIFT() Subroutine of Variable-rate Formula: This term is derived by projecting MOS when ΔT approaches the length of the audio track (i.e., 30 s). The MOS at $\Delta T = 30$ is called the dominant quality of the variable-rate track, and denoted as $D()$. For each (hr, lr) pair, this study identifies the regression fit of the MOS-ΔT relationship and then projects the MOS value for $\Delta T = 30$. These values are plotted in Fig. 12 and indicated as the Dominant Quality data set. This figure also plots the MOS of the hr and lr based on the $f_{FIX}(br)$ formula. The MOS of hr and lr are denoted as MOS_h and MOS_l, respectively.

The findings are 1) the dominant quality is generally bounded by MOS_h and MOS_l. It can be slightly better than MOS_h when the hr is high and the rate change magnitude is relatively small (e.g., r1r3 and r2r4). 2) For cases before r3r9, the dominant quality decreases as the rate change magnitude increases. This suggests that when the variation increases, the changes become disturbing. 3) The behavior of the dominant quality diverges as both hr and lr drop below 14.1 kbps (i.e., the cases from r4r5 and on). According to the analysis mentioned earlier, users cannot easily perceive the changes when both rates of the fluctuation are low. For these cases, the curves of the dominant quality and MOS_h are intertwined.

The results presented here show that $D()$ equals MOS_h for cases where $hr \leq 14.1$ kbps. For the remaining cases, this study examines if a closer relationship exists between the dominant quality and the rate change magnitude. Fig. 13 shows the MOS of dominant quality normalized by MOS_h and MOS_l, where they are 100% and 0%, respectively. Fig. 14 shows the MOS of dominant

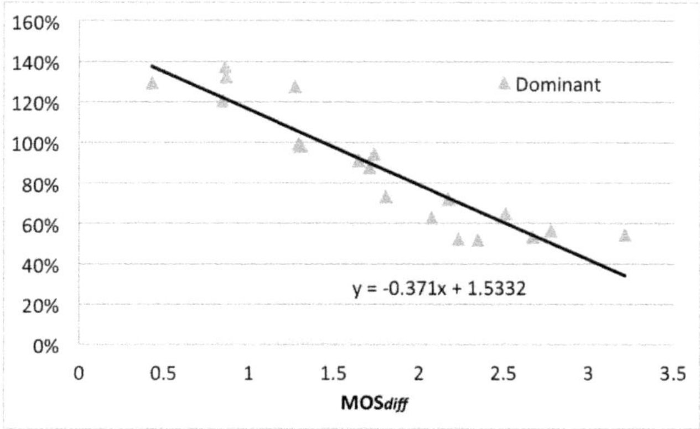

Figure 14. Normalized dominant quality-MOS_{diff} plot.

quality with the difference between MOS_h and MOS_l, denoted as MOS_{diff}, as its x-axis. A significant linear relationship exists between the normalized dominant quality and MOS_{diff}. A linear regression fit to the relationship in Fig. 14 produces $D()$ for cases in which $hr > 14.1$ kbps. Thus, the $SHIFT()$ subroutine can be formulated as follows:

$$SHIFT(hr, lr) = D(hr, lr) - SCALE(hr, lr) \times \ln(30)$$

$$D(hr, lr) = \begin{cases} MOS_h, & if\ hr \leq 14.1, \\ \max(0.55, 1.5332 - 0.371 \times MOS_{diff}) \times MOS_{diff} + MOS_l, & else \end{cases}$$

The term "$max(0.55, \bullet)$" in the formula indicates that the relationship between MOS_{diff} and $D()$ for $hr > 14.1$ kbps is more complex than simply linear. This term is based on the bounded decrease of the plot in Fig. 14. This figure shows that the degradation of the normalized dominant MOS is limited. A bound near 50% is apparent, indicating that the lower bound of dominant quality is approximately the average MOS value of hr and lr.

6. EVALUATION AND DISCUSSION

The evaluation of the proposed model is twofold. First, we evaluate the goodness of fit [7] of the mathematic form of the model with respect to the training data by examining its R-square value. A high R-square value confirms the robustness of model derivation, including the establishment of subroutines $SCALE()$ and $SHIFT()$. Second, the model is tested using two sets of data that are independent of the model construction. The purpose of this phase is to evaluate the prediction accuracy of the model by showing its average error ratio for the two data sets. In summary, the purpose of presenting the R-square and average error ratio is to examine whether the proposed model is capable of capturing the average human perception. To this end, both metrics are computed based on the average score of each track from the three data sets.

The resulting R-square of the proposed model on the training data is 0.8504, which indicates that the data do not deviate significantly from the statistical fit. Thus, the proposed $SCALE()$ and $SHIFT()$ functions and the logarithmic approximation do capture the characteristics of the data. The scatter plot in Fig. 15 shows the fitted score (as the x-axis) and the user score (as the y-axis) for each rate pair and time interval test set. The proposed model closely follows the measured data as the points fall densely around the 45° line, indicating the goodness of fit and supporting the robustness of model derivation.

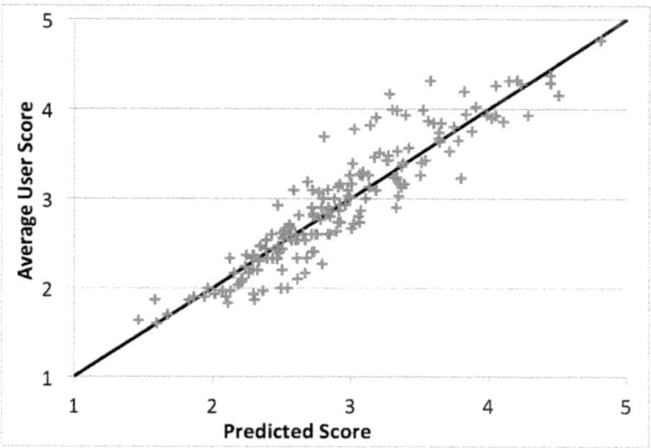

Figure 15. Goodness of fit of training data.

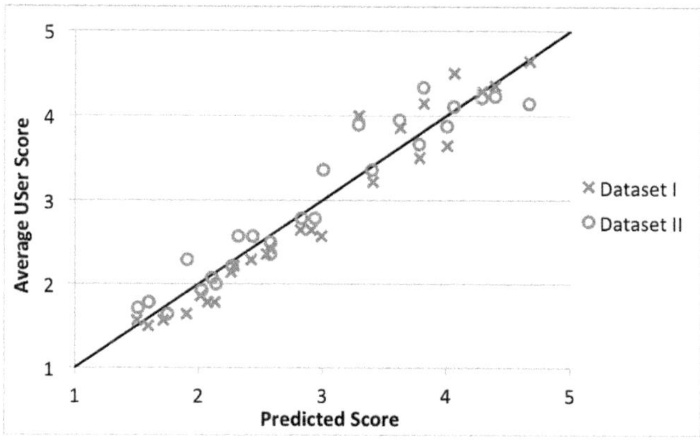

Figure 16. Accuracy of prediction.

This study uses two additional data sets to evaluate prediction accuracy. The first data set is the result of the preliminary experiment in Section 3, where data is collected independently of those used for model construction. The other data set is taken from an additional set of a subjective experiment, in which the audio content, speakers, and participants are all different from the prior experiments. In this additional experiment, 11 male and 3 female participants were recruited. Their ages ranged from 21 to 28 with an average of 24.8 years. 4 of them were undergraduate students and the rest are graduate students. For simplicity, the results of the preliminary and this new experiment are labeled as data sets I and II, respectively.

The resulting average error ratios of the two data sets are 9.8% and 9.7%, respectively, indicating that the proposed model is able to capture the average user experience. In addition to the numerical result, Fig. 16 shows the accuracy of the proposed model. In this figure, the predictions of both data sets closely track the measured data, regardless of the difference in audio content and speaker. The average error ratios of the two data sets are similar, confirming that ITU guidelines for subjective study can operatively minimize the contextual and speaker bias.

Three major issues to address next include 1) in-depth exploration of the terms shown after numerical fit, 2) whether Weber-Fechner's Law exists in other VoIP services, and 3) a model that produces distribution as its output instead of a single average value. First, the relationship between the rate change magnitude and $SCALE()$ in the preliminary experiments is unclear. The term $D()$ has a relatively complex structure. Furthermore, there could be a certain connection between the fixed-rate and variable-rate models, which might lead to one concise model. Second, although the good average error ratio and R-square over three sets of experiments support the proposed models, it is unclear whether the relationships of MOS to magnitude/frequency of rate changes will remain the same for a different codec or experimental setting (e.g., mobile or lossy VoIP calls). Third, the current model has the ability to handle average user perception and provide suggestions for designing rate adaptation mechanisms. However, the variance among each user has not been fully explored. Adding probabilistic components might produce a model that can better describe user variance and provide more realistic predictions. These are subjects for future research.

7. CONCLUSION

The findings of this study provide a foundation for rate adaptation mechanism design in real-time voice data delivery. This study 1) confirms that user experience versus the bitrate relationship exhibits a log-like behavior, echoing Weber's theory; 2) shows that the experience versus frequency of the rate change relationship also exhibits a log-like behavior; 3) shows that the experience versus magnitude of the rate change relationship is determined by how users perceive the quality difference; and 4) derives a closed form model of user experience to rate changes with an average error ratio and R-square of 9.8% and 0.85, respectively.

Although this study was motivated by a networking problem (i.e., how to better provide multimedia services over the Internet), the work itself is content-centric in that it focuses on how users perceive the quality of the multimedia content delivered. In addition to its technical findings, this study indicates the need for interdisciplinary research that considers both content and network. A solid understanding of multimedia content is fundamental to better engineering of the network applications. For example, knowing that, given the same amount of increase in bitrate, user experience improves marginally when the call quality is already good, a rate adaptation mechanism should allocate network bandwidth to calls of lower quality. This approach can maximize the overall QoE. This study also shows that frequent changes in the sending rate decrease the perceived quality. Thus, a rate adaptation mechanism should not increase the sending rate at any given opportunity, but instead, dynamically adapt adjustment sensitivity based on network stability.

8. REFERENCES

[1] K. R. Boff, L. Kaufman, and J. P. Thomas, "Handbook of Perception and Human Performance", Wiley-Interscience, ISBN 0-47-182957-9, 1986.

[2] J. Matta, C. Pépin, K. Lashkari, and R. Jain, "A Source and Channel Rate Adaptation Algorithm for AMR in VoIP Using the E-model," in Proceedings of ACM Network and Operating System Support for Digital Audio and Video, NOSSDAV, 2003.

[3] Z. Qiao, L. Sun, N. Heilemann, and E. Ifeachor, "A New Method for VoIP Quality of Service Control Use Combined Adaptive Sender Rate and Priority Marking," in Proceedings of IEEE International Communications Conference, ICC, 2004.

[4] T.-Y. Huang, P. Huang, K.-T. Chen, and P.-J. Wang, "Can Skype be More Satisfying? A QoE-Centric Study of the FEC Mechanism in the Internet-Scale VoIP System," IEEE Network, Vol. 24(2), pp.42–48, 2010.

[5] ITU-T Recommendation P.830, "Subjective Performance Assessment of Telephone-band and Wideband Digital Codecs" 1996.

[6] Skype Developer, http://developer.skype.com/silk.

[7] R. A. Fisher, "Statistical Methods for Research Workers", Oliver and Boyd, ISBN 0-05-002170-2, 1925.

[8] R. Beuran, M. Ivanovici, and B. Dobinson, "Network Quality of Service Measurement System for Application Requirements Evaluation", in Proceedings of IEEE International Symposium on Performance Evaluation of Computer and Telecommunication Systems, SPECTS, 2003.

[9] RFC 793, "Transmission Control Protocol," 1981.

[10] RFC 768, "User Datagram Protocol," 1980.

[11] J. Bolot and T. Turletti, "A Rate Control Mechanism for Packet Video in the Internet", in Proceedings of IEEE International Conference on Computer Communications, INFOCOM, 1994.

[12] A. Barberis, C. Casetti, J.C. De Martin, and M. Meo, "A Simulation Study of Adaptive Voice Communications on IP Networks." Computer Communications, Vol. 24(9), pp.757–767, 2001.

[13] ITU-T Recommendation P.10/G.100, "Vocabulary for Performance and Quality of Service", 2008.

[14] K.-T. Chen, C.-Y. Huang, P. Huang, and C.-L. Lei, "Quantifying Skype User Satisfaction", in Proceedings of ACM Communications and Computer Networks, SIGCOMM, 2006.

[15] ITU-T Recommendation P.800, "Methods for Subjective Determination of Transmission Quality," 1996.

[16] M. Fiedler, T. Hossfeld, and P. Tran-Gia, "A Generic Quantitative Relationship between Quality of Experience and Quality of Service" IEEE Network, vol. 24(2), pp.36-41, 2010.

[17] P. Reichl, S. Egger, R. Schatz, and A. D'Alconzo, "The Logarithmic Nature of QoE and the Role of the Weber-Fechner Law in QoE Assessment," in Proceedings of IEEE International Communications Conference, ICC, 2010.

[18] W. Wu, A. Arefin, G. Kurillo, P. Agarwal, K. Nahrstedt, and R. Bajcsy, "Color-plus-Depth Level-of-Detail in 3D Tele-immersive Video: A Psychophysical Approach", in Proceedings of ACM Multimedia, MM, 2011.

[19] W. Song, D. W. Tjondronegoro, and M. Docherty, "Saving Bitrate vs. Pleasing Users: Where is the Break-Even Point in Mobile Video Quality", in Proceedings of ACM Multimedia, MM, 2011.

[20] J. Shen, "On the Foundations of Vision Modeling: I. Weber's law and Weberized TV restoration," Physica D: Nonlinear Phenomena, vol. 175(3-4), pp.241–251, 2003.

[21] E. D. Scheirer, "Tempo and Beat Analysis of Acoustic Musical Signals," Journal of the Acoustical Society of America, vol. 103(1), pp.588–601, 1998.

[22] R. S. Moyer and T. K. Landauer, "Time Required for Judgments of Numerical Inequality," Nature, vol. 215(5109), pp.1519–20, 1967.

[23] M. R. Longo and S. F. Lourenco, "Spatial Attention and the Mental Number Line: Evidence for Characteristic Biases and Compression," Neuropsychologia, vol.45, pp.1400-1406, 2007.

[24] Skype for Windows - v5.10.1.115, released on July 5, 2012, http://www.skype.com /get-skype/.

[25] ITU-T Recommendation P.911, "Subjective Audiovisual Quality Assessment Methods for Multimedia Applications," 1998.

[26] ITU-T Recommendation P.910, "Subjective Video Quality Assessment Methods for Multimedia Applications," 2008.

PaperVideo: Interacting with Videos on Multiple Paper-like Displays

Roman Lissermann[1], Simon Olberding[2], Benjamin Petry[1], Max Mühlhäuser[1], Jürgen Steimle[2]

[1]Technische Universität Darmstadt
64289 Darmstadt, Germany
{lissermann,benjaminpetry,max}@tk.informatik.tu-darmstadt.de

[2]MIT Media Lab
Cambridge, MA, USA
{simon_o, steimle}@media.mit.edu

ABSTRACT
Sifting and sense-making of video collections are important tasks in many professions. In contrast to sense-making of paper documents, where physical structuring of many documents has proven to be key to effective work, interaction with video is still restricted to the traditional "one video at a time" paradigm. This paper investigates how interaction with video can benefit from paper-like displays that allow for working with multiple videos simultaneously in physical space. We present a corresponding approach and system called PaperVideo, including novel interaction concepts for both video and audio. These include spatial techniques for temporal navigation, arranging, grouping and linking of videos, as well as for managing video contents and simultaneous audio playback on multiple displays. An evaluation with users provides insights into how paper-based navigation with videos improves active video work.

Categories and Subject Descriptors
H.5.2 [**Information Interfaces and Presentation**]: User Interface

General Terms: Design, Human Factor

Keywords: Tangible user interface, electronic paper, flexible display, thin-film display, multiple displays, video, pile.

1. INTRODUCTION
People from a variety of professional backgrounds are confronted daily with large amounts of video footage that they must sift trough and make sense of: TV news editors have to deal with approximately 30 hours of video material offered per news agency and day (such as Reuters). A Hollywood movie director must distill hundreds of hours of footage into a blockbuster movie. Analysts and researchers must make sense of information that is contained within many videos, such as CCTV recordings or recordings of scientific experiments. The Youtube era extends these tasks of sifting and making sense out of many videos to the general population, for hobby and scholarly activities. These examples show that *active video work* with large amounts of video material (as opposed to passive watching of a single video) is a daily routine of many people. As such it is obvious that better usability for active video work is a research topic of primary importance.

In contrast to active video work, sifting and sense-making of *paper-based* information is a well-researched field. Research shows that the key is using not only one, but multiple documents or sheets of paper simultaneously, in order to manipulate and organize information in physical space. Amongst others, this has proven to effectively support comparison, generating an overview and better orientation [11,28]. All these activities are also of paramount importance when working with videos.

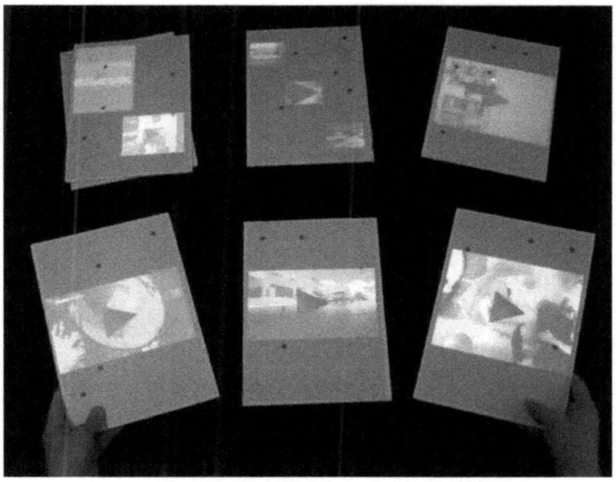

Figure 1: PaperVideo: A system for interacting with multiple videos in physical space

Compared to these paper-based practices, today's user interfaces for active video work are characterized by two main shortcomings: (1) While standard navigation techniques for videos have their obvious benefits, they lack the effectiveness of physical interaction [11,13,28] for spatially structuring videos. (2) The traditional "one video at a time" paradigm does not leverage the whole spectrum of human perception. While humans are able to focus only on limited information, they are able to grasp a much higher amount of information in the periphery, which is helpful for getting an overview and structuring tasks.

We argue that these affordances of working with multiple documents in physical space can be beneficially transferred to the domain of video. We advocate a paradigm for videos which consists of using many videos simultaneously, similarly to how we lay out multiple printed documents on our desk. In this paper, we investigate how interactions known from physical documents can be transferred to the world of videos and fitted to a computing device that offers multiple electronic displays, which are very similar to paper. Note that we do not aim to replace existing practices of watching a movie for entertainment purposes. We aim at supporting three widespread scenarios that all involve actively working with multiple videos:

1. *Systematic analysis* of videos, e.g. for learning or research, similar to active reading of text documents [1]. Thereby the main activities are sorting, comparing and (re)structuring.

2. *Playful exploration* of video contents, e.g. at installations in museums or shops, by providing an intuitive way of interaction and
3. *Lightweight video editing,* where people select and combine video clips, e.g. to create a personal excerpt.

In this paper we present PaperVideo, a coherent system that allows users to play back and navigate through videos and collections of videos with multiple physical displays (Fig. 1). It enables users to create an overview of multiple videos as well as structure and organize video contents by leveraging physical arrangements. We contribute a set of interaction techniques for video content that takes advantage of the characteristics of dynamic displays. These techniques go beyond established physical interactions such as arranging and piling of paper. Furthermore, we introduce interaction techniques supporting the management of contents on multiple displays. Addressing the possibility of viewing multiple videos in parallel, we finally contribute several novel sound concepts that allow the user to mentally grasp multiple audio sources of videos simultaneously. Results from a qualitative user study show that the system effectively supports active video work.

To technically realize displays that can be manipulated like paper, the system makes use of a projection-tracking setup. Passive cardboards are tracked in real-time. Visual content is automatically projected onto them, correcting for perspective distortions. We envision such systems to be installed at offices, schools, libraries, museums, and stores. Moreover, given the rapid advances in mobile devices, future tablet devices are very likely to be much thinner and more lightweight than nowadays. This will eventually render projection-tracking obsolete and also allow for mobile use cases of our system.

The remainder of the paper is organized as follows. First, we discuss related work then describe the underlying requirements of our design. Next, we present the system design, starting with interactions for spatial arrangements of video, followed by interactions for managing multiple physical displays and ending with sound concepts for multiple videos. Later we present the implementation of our system. Finally, we discuss the results of a user study.

2. RELATED WORK

Prior research on video navigation investigated interaction on PCs [3,10,18,26] and mobile devices [7,8,33]. Manske introduced a concept for browsing a video on a large display by visualizing the video as a 3D content tree [16]. Schoeffmann has concentrated on hierarchical video browsing, with 3D graphics support, and provided an intuitive way of content navigation within a video [25]. Nevertheless, all of these systems provide only one single screen. In contrast, CThru [9] combined multimedia content (images, videos and text) with a storytelling educational video on an interactive tabletop and duplicated the view onto a wall size display. None of these works have focused on digital spatial management and spatial cues while handling video content.

A large body of empirical work [11,28,34] shows that physical space management is important for overview and organization of information and that physical interactions with paper have different qualities than physically-inspired interactions on touch screens. The usage of multiple physical displays has been investigated for several purposes. Rekimoto [20] presented a system where multiple transparent tiles were transformed into interactive controls by placing them onto a flat panel display. Siftables [17] demonstrated the technical feasibility of a system with tiny, wirelessly interconnected color displays, introducing multi-display interactions for gaming and educational purposes. Other work presented examples of how several tiny bezel-less screens can be used for interactive board games [22] and studied gestures for linking multiple displays [5]. These works inspired us to provide dynamic visual contents on multiple displays.

Several systems support tangible interaction with video contents: Video Mosaic offers a tangible interface for editing video [13]. A snippet of normal paper can be used as a physical token that represents a video. By holding the snippet in front of a camera, the video is played back on a PC screen. A similar approach, using RFID tokens, is presented in [29]. However, these systems do not display the video on the paper snippet, but on a nearby screen. This creates an indirection that is overcome in our work. Video mosaic targets video editing whereas our focus is on sifting, exploration and sense-making of video collections. Finally, Tangible Video Editor [36] presented a set of small active displays that can each host a video snippet. By physically arranging displays in a linear sequence, the temporal sequence of clips can be edited. The full video can then be displayed on a computer screen. This work influenced our approach of physically arranging video displays. In contrast, our work supports large video displays, a wider range of activities and introduces novel tangible interactions.

Ongoing advances in OLED display technology allow for displaying full color video on very thin and lightweight displays. Interaction with lightweight and thin displays has been a focus of various research projects since the seminal DigitalDesk [35] introduced first user interfaces such as a projected virtual calculator. Within this stream of research, PaperWindows [6] is very influential work. It was the first to present a user interface that is distributed over a set of very thin and lightweight paper-like displays. PaperWindows further contributed a set of interaction techniques for basic windowing tasks, however, it did not address interaction with videos. PaperLens [30] demonstrated how the space above the tabletop can be used for interactions with single paper-like displays. Our conceptual model (cf. section 4) was inspired by previous works [6,31] that have investigated gestures and an interaction vocabulary of paper-like displays. We improve upon these works by addressing paper-based interaction with both visual and audio contents, by introducing a set of interactions for managing multiple displays and by providing first empirical insights into how people use systems with multiple paper-like displays.

Our system setup allows users to play back multiple videos simultaneously. Multiple parallel audio outputs located in space produce the well-known cocktail party effect [2]. Our sound concepts are inspired by Audiosteamer [23] and Audio Hallway [24]. These works presented interaction techniques for browsing multiple audio sources by creating an audio-only environment and virtually placing the audio sources around the user's head. By simply turning the head, the user could select his sound of interest. In our work, we refine this research for audiovisual contents and tangible interaction while introducing further spatial audio concepts.

3. DESIGN REQUIREMENTS

3.1 Video-based Activities

With PaperVideo we aim at supporting three main scenarios of active video work, which benefit from multiple video displays:

1. Systematic video analysis: *Active reading* [1] is a well-studied domain. Active reading involves intensely engaging with documents, for instance by following references, annotating, and comparing documents. People often work with multiple documents simultaneously and by effectively arranging them in a physical space to support their reading. Analogously, we propose systematic video analysis as a way of actively working with video material: people explore a set of videos, prioritize the content, study related content and compare and (re)structure the content. As outlined in the introduction, these activities are of crucial importance in a wide range of professions.

Different areas like film (post)production by novice/professional users or analysts of a huge amount of multiperspective camera recordings from a catastrophe are in need of prioritizing, comparing and (re)structuring video snippets. Based on the mentioned needs of actively working with videos, we are convinced that also in the case of videos, the use of space provides effective support for such highly creative and dynamic activities.

2. Playful video exploration: Multiple displays can be beneficial for exploring collections of videos, for instance at installations in places like stores, museums, or exhibition booths. We envision videos spread on booths or tables, where visitors can stop by and playfully explore new topics or products individually or collaboratively. The focus of such systems is not only on functionality, but also on high user experience as well as ease of access. Further, it enables users to serendipitously discover content. The system should be intuitively usable to allow a playful exploration and a positive experience to people of all ages and professional backgrounds.

3. Video editing: Simple video editing is a common part of using videos as a consumer. For instance, people trim video snippets or they order and align several snippets in a personal excerpt. PaperVideo supports such simple editing tasks. They are conceptually similar to highlighting or excerpting passages in active reading of text documents, which serve for better understanding and condensing the contents. This is opposed to advanced video editing that focuses on production of videos, including specific functions like time-stamping or synchronizing footage from multiple cameras over time, for sorting the recordings, annotating and augmenting video snippets or position in a video with additional information.

All of these scenarios have a set of functionality in common: users require functionality for quickly getting an overview of a single or multiple videos, for prioritizing content, finding related content, comparing content, and (re)structuring content. The system should support quick temporal navigation, cross-video use for overview, comparison and linking, as well as flexible means for prioritizing, grouping, and structuring.

3.2 Technical Requirements

Today's PCs and mobile devices usually have only one or two displays. Our system should support a significantly higher number of displays to support physical interactions that are known from the world of paper. These displays should be very thin and lightweight such that they can be easily moved and arranged in physical structures, such as piles. The displays should provide color output, high resolution and high update rate to play back video. Each display should also support direct input for navigation purposes as well as sound output. To allow for physical interactions that span multiple displays, each display should have knowledge about its relative position in space with respect to its neighbors.

While large tabletop displays would allow for laying out multiple videos in space, interaction on tabletops is inherently limited compared to using multiple physical displays: First, while tabletop interfaces mimic basic interactions with physical objects, the resulting interaction styles have been shown to be fundamentally different [34]. In particular, while people make ample use of both hands in physical setups, they mostly restrict interaction to only one hand at a time on tabletops. Physicality also offers a number of advantages such as cues for implicitly assessing the quantity of objects. It is also more difficult for users to arrange objects in a way that can be ergonomically read or viewed on a tabletop than with physical displays (this aspect was called micro-mobility [12] in the literature). Finally, tabletops require a static, immobile setup. In contrast, several small physical displays can be used in nomadic setups. While currently available technology does not yet allow us to realize our system without a static setup, nomadic uses can be supported in the near future.

To technically realize a system with multiple paper-like displays, our prototype uses a tracking-projection setup. Details about our prototype are provided in the implementation section below. The setup is well-suited for installations at fixed places, e.g. at work, in museums, stores and schools. The tracking-projection approach allows us to realize paper-like displays already today, even though currently available tablets are still too heavy and too thick for our interactions. This is very likely to change in the near future when thin-film OLED technology will further slims down the form factor of tablet devices. Our proposed interaction techniques can be fully transferred to such devices and will then allow for use in mobile settings in addition to the settings that can be supported currently.

4. INPUT DESIGN SPACE OF MULTIPLE DISPLAYS

For a systematic design of our interaction techniques, we investigated the design space of how input is performed with multiple location-aware displays. This allowed us to identify several interaction primitives, grouped along three different basic forms of input (see Fig. 2):

Spatial location input: Moving the display in space is translated into input. Thereby the absolute position of a display in physical space is captured.

Display proximity input: Changes in the relative positioning among two or more displays are translated into input. Interaction primitives include piling of displays and using one display as a pointer for selecting content on another display.

Gestures with and input on the display: The user can perform physical gestures with one display or with a set of displays, e.g. by shaking. Moreover, the user can directly interact with contents on a display using direct touch or pen input (our prototype currently supports only pen input).

5. INTERACTING WITH VIDEOS IN PHYSICAL SPACE

In this section, we present interaction techniques that support a set of base activities for individual videos and collections of videos. These techniques leverage the manipulation and arrangement of one or several displays in physical space.

5.1 Temporal Navigation

Temporal navigation within a video is one of the most basic functionalities. It is required to get an overview of the video as well as for quickly accessing specific passages. Similarly to

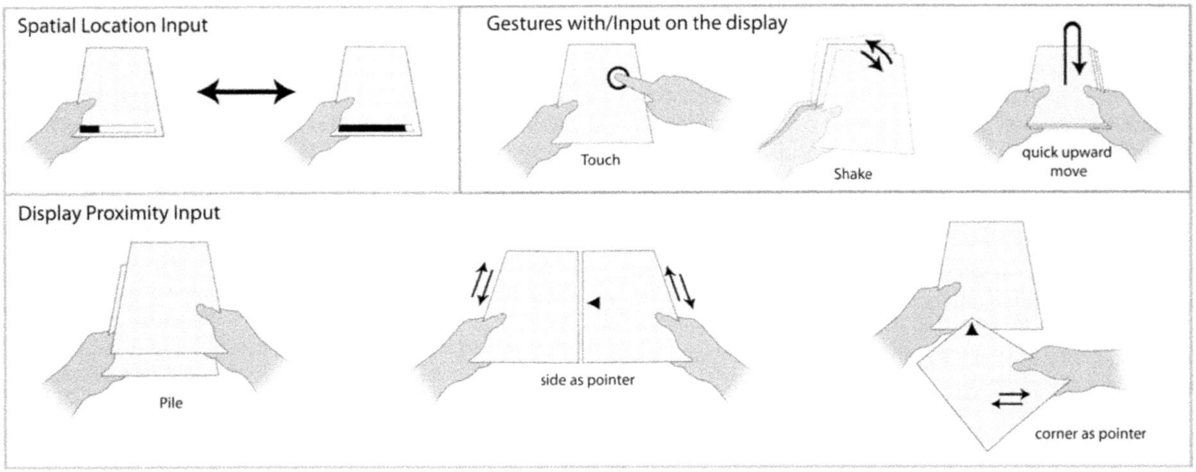

Figure 2: Input design space of multiple location aware displays

existing user interfaces for desktop computers and mobile devices, our design allows users to start, pause, and skim a video by directly interacting with widgets on the display using a stylus (see Fig. 3a, 3b). In contrast to most existing interfaces, it is possible to play multiple videos simultaneously.

Space is a strong cue for encoding information, for instance sequences [11]. This motivated us to design a technique in which the physical workspace encodes temporal positions. The timeline of the video is virtually spread out in physical space, extending from left to right within the user's arm reach (Fig. 3c). Each spatial position is mapped to a temporal position within the video. By moving a display through space (simultaneously moving several displays is also possible), the user navigates through the video. This technique allows for quickly skimming as well as for jumping back and forth between several passages of a video. To avoid interfering with free arrangements of multiple displays (see next subsection), temporal navigation is activated when the user lifts the display up to a higher level above the table surface, the "temporal layer".

5.2 Arranging

Similar to arranging objects in the real world, the thin and lightweight displays can be freely arranged on the table surface. To state only a couple examples, two videos can be compared by placing them side-by-side while multiple videos can be ordered in a spatially-encoded sequence. Videos can be prioritized by placing them closer or more distant to the user. Such arrangements enable powerful ways of organizing information in space [11].

5.3 See-through Pile

A large body of research shows the relevance of piling for managing information [14,15]. Users can place multiple displays on top of one another to form a pile of videos. Our pile is more advanced in comparison to piles of ordinary physical objects. Since the system is aware of which displays are occluded, the content of the *entire* pile is visualized on the topmost display, resulting in an "x-ray style" view (see Fig. 4). All of the content on the topmost display is fully interactive. So the user can view, play or skim any video in the pile easily.

Piling or unpiling does not interrupt playback; the video continues to play inside or outside a pile.

5.4 Accessing Related Videos

Many videos are organized in collections, in which they are linked to related videos. This is the case for influential video platforms such as YouTube, iTunes U [37], and OpenCourseWare [38]. We present a spatial technique for navigating video relations using multiple displays. By bringing an empty display near to a display with a video (see Fig. 5), the mode for selecting related videos is entered. A list of related videos visualizes on the video. By moving the empty display or the video display up or down, a related video can be selected from the list. While doing so, a preview of the currently selected video is shown on the empty display. By slightly removing one display from the other, the list shows categories or groups of videos instead of individual videos, allowing for a selection at a higher level. By moving one display apart, the related video (or group of videos) is eventually selected and displayed on the previously empty display (see Fig. 5).

There are two main advantages in this gesture while working with multiple displays. First, the original video is not replaced by the related one, as in most current solutions, but remains visible. Hence a spatial overview can be easily generated by leaving a trace of "where we came from". Second, multiple related videos can be opened by using multiple displays. These videos can then be spatially arranged and also viewed in parallel, if desired.

5.5 Linking Videos

The user can create his own hyperlinks between any two videos. This is done by taking two displays with different videos and bumping them against each other (see Fig. 6). From now on, the videos appear in the respective lists of linked videos.

5.6 Lightweight Video Editing

When people actively work with text documents, they highlight passages that are of high interest, write excerpts, and create text collages by copying and pasting relevant passages into a new document. In contrast, video documents are usually consumed as-is, without personalizing them. We propose a lightweight interaction technique for cutting videos. We do not aim for professional video editing, but on providing a simple interaction technique. This can be used for focusing on specific passages of a video and for composing a "video excerpt".

For cutting out a section of an existing video, an additional empty display is needed. By placing one corner of the empty display onto the timeline of the video, the corners are used as a video

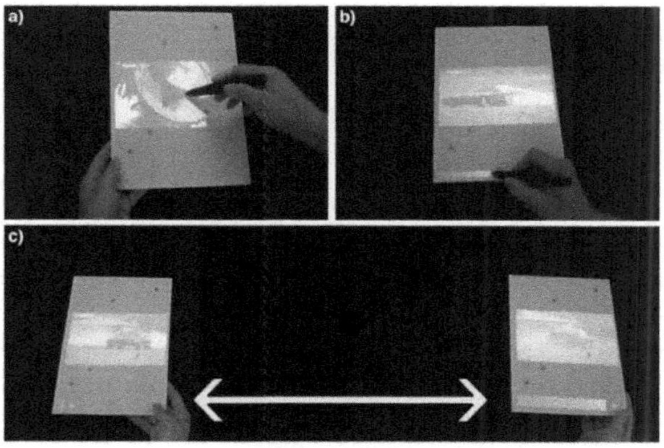

Figure 3: a) Playback, b) skimming, c) temporal navigation in space

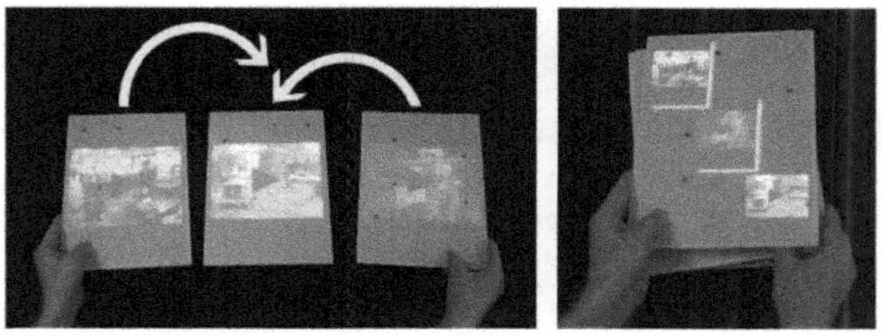

Figure 4: Physical piling of videos. The topmost display allows for interacting with all videos.

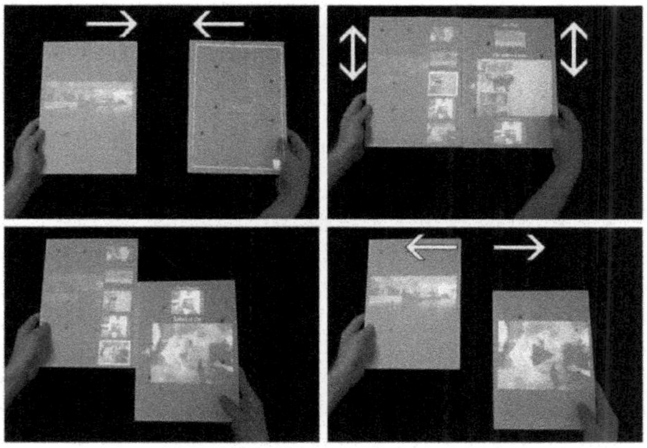

Figure 5: Accessing related videos by bringing displays side by side, selecting a related video and moving the displays apart

cutting tool. The start and end positions of the cut are selected with the upper-left and upper-right corners, respectively. While selecting, the start and end frames are visualized on the previously empty display and the entire passage is highlighted in the video timeline (see Fig. 7). By moving the display apart, the cut is executed and the newly created video snippet is made available on this display. From now on, the user can interact with this snippet as with any ordinary video. The next section discusses how several physical video snippets can be combined to one video.

6. MANAGING MULTIPLE DISPLAYS: VIRTUALIZING AND MATERIALIZING CONTENTS

Paper documents have a static mapping between contents and the physical carrier medium. One page of content is permanently bound to one page of the carrier medium: this is a one-to-one mapping. Most computing devices have only one screen. Here, in contrast, the content is dynamic. Potentially, an infinite number of content can be displayed on one physical screen: here we have a many-to-one mapping. Both types of content mappings are well-understood.

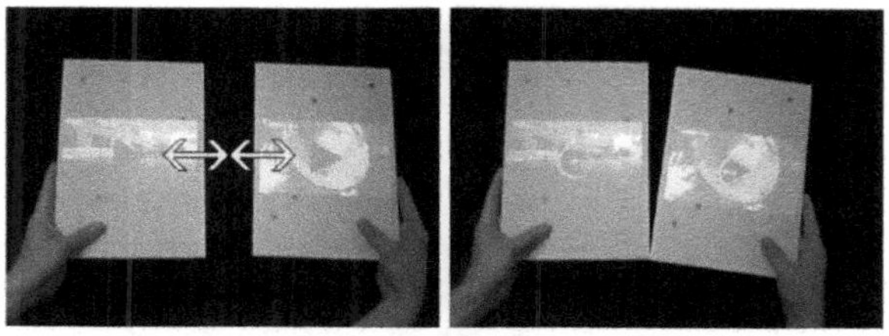

Figure 6: Linking two videos by bumping them against each other

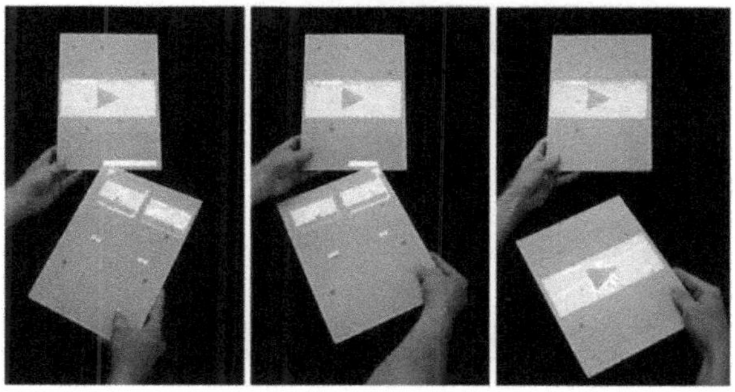

Figure 7: Playful video cutting with multiple displays

Given the expectation that future displays will be low-priced and lightweight, we imagine that users will have a number of displays which combined are much smaller than the number of sheets of paper that we typically use with printed documents today. Hence we are not limited to tight one-to-one mapping of content to displays. This would also not be desirable, as it would limit the display's capability of dynamically changing its content.

Therefore systems that offer many paper-like displays have a many-to-many mapping. Such systems mimic the physical interactions of paper, however with a smaller number of carrier media. Previous work has shown how contents can be easily transferred from one display to another [6,21]. However, it is not clear how the handling and association of content on many displays should work. How can content be temporarily disassociated from displays to generate free carriers for displaying additional contents? How can such "virtualized" contents be "materialized" again and bound to physical carriers? We present interaction techniques that allow the user to combine contents onto one single display, distribute content over multiple displays and to clear and to restore content.

6.1 Combine and Distribute Content

By combining videos that are currently bound to a physical display, physical displays can be freed from contents. Thereafter they can serve as physical carriers for additional videos. To combine one or several videos, the user creates a pile out of the respective displays. Quickly moving the entire pile upwards combines all videos into the topmost display. The remaining displays inside the pile become empty. The metaphor of this interaction is to push all videos up, which are caught by the topmost display.

The reverse direction, distributing videos from a video collection, is done by placing one or several empty displays underneath a display containing a video collection. By quickly moving the pile

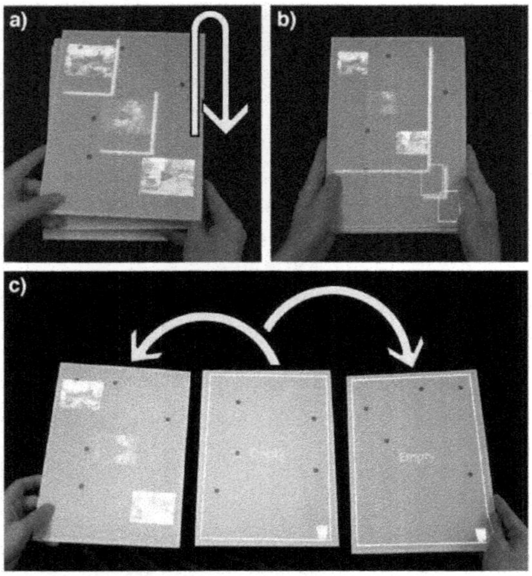

Figure 8: Virtualizing a physical pile (a), onto one single display (b). This clears the remaining displays (c).

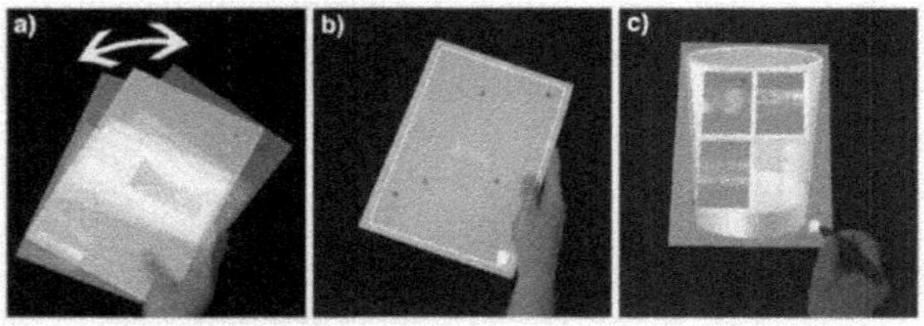

Figure 9: Clear content by shaking the display (a and b). Restore content from the recycle bin (c).

downwards, the videos from the collection are distributed onto the empty displays in the pile (see Fig. 8).

6.2 Clear and Restore Content

Contents can also be virtualized by clearing a display. Clearing is performed by shaking the display, as if one shook contents off. Cleared contents are available in the recycle bin, which can be accessed by tapping on an icon that is available on all empty displays (see Fig. 9).

7. SOUND CONCEPTS FOR PARALLEL VIDEOS

Since multiple videos can be laid out in physical space and played back simultaneously, multiple audio sources can be active at the same time. This produces the well-known cocktail party effect [2], which might make it difficult to perceive information conveyed on the audio channel.

The standard case with multiple display devices is that each display has a built-in speaker to generate the audio of the video that is displayed on this device. This makes sure that both visual contents and audio track of one video are located at the same position in space. The sound is perceived in space at a position relative to the user's position and head orientation. Moving the sound source away from the user reduces its volume slightly. We call this sound concept Real-World Behavior (see Fig. 10a) and implemented it as our baseline.

In this section we introduce three additional sound concepts that will allow users to more effectively mentally grasp (focus) on one or multiple sound sources that are located in space, reducing the cocktail party effect.

7.1 Distance-based Focusing

In work with paper documents, it is a well-established practice to focus on documents by placing them directly in front of the user. Documents are brought out of focus by placing them farther away, but still within an arm's reach [28]. Inspired by this behavior, we propose a sound concept for focusing on sound sources based on their distance.

Moving a display closer to or more distant from the user increases or decreases its volume (see Fig. 10b). In contrast to the Real-World Behavior, where distance has only a barely noticeable effect on the volume, the Euclidean distance between the user and the display is mapped inverse exponentially to the volume. As a result, volume can be finely adjusted, somewhat similar to a slider of an audio mixer. Placing the display an arm's length away is distant enough to reduce the volume to zero.

7.2 Orientation-based Focusing

When people focus their attention on a person or on object, they usually look at it. We propose a concept that leverages head orientation of the user for focusing on sound sources.

A virtual line originates from the user's head in the head's orientation. The volume of each display is mapped inverse exponentially to its relative distance from the virtual line. Hence sound originating from displays that are directly within the user's orientation has the highest volume and is located in the center. Sound originating from displays to the left or right side of the line has a lower volume and is located to the left or right of the user. Sound from displays at the extreme outer sides is muted (see Fig. 10d). By reorienting his head, the user can easily and quickly change his focus to different videos.

7.3 Pick-up-based Focusing

It is common practice to pick up an object to focus on it. Inspired by this behavior, we introduce a further sound concept. Sound from displays that are lying down on the table is set to mute. By lifting up one or multiple displays, the sound of these displays is played back (see Fig. 10c). While picked up, sound sources expose a Real-World Behavior, being correctly located in space.

8. TECHNICAL REALIZATION

Our prototype system realizes paper-like displays by tracking passive cardboards in real-time and projecting contents onto them. An overview of the system is shown in Fig. 11. Our system consists of an optical tracking system with 6 infrared cameras, two full HD projectors mounted on the ceiling, and a set of cardboards, each augmented with infrared retro-reflective markers. The high-resolution projection frustum measures approximately 200 * 120 * 40 cm^3. The information which is provided by the tracking system (position, orientation of the cardboards), is used to warp the projected images onto the cardboards in real-time. In our software toolkit, we simulate the environment by constructing a Direct3D world model. In an initial calibration step, the two Direct3D cameras are set to the positions and orientations of the two projectors, thus the camera "sees" the multiple cardboards and renders their contents from the correct perspective. The projectors display the camera views, which are generated by Direct3D, while the world model is continuously updated by the tracker data. For recognizing the different gestures, we implemented a gesture recognizer that analyzes positional information of each of the displays.

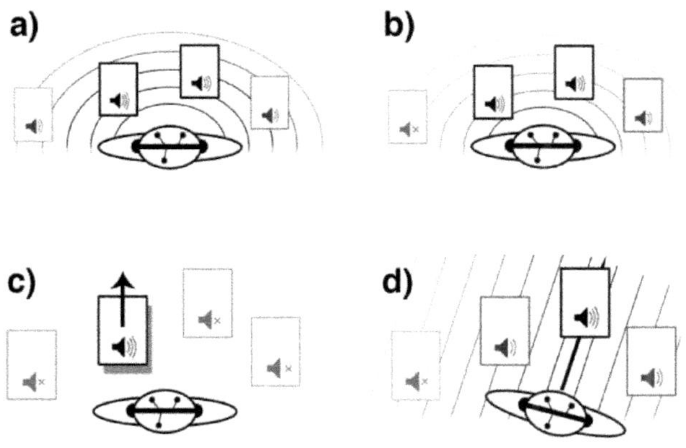

Figure 10: Sound concepts a) Real-World Behavior b) Distance-based Focusing c)Pick-up based Focusing d)Orientation-based Focusing

The application is implemented in C# and WPF. Each display owns its own WPF window that is screen captured and rendered onto the display on demand. Our prototype currently supports seven different cardboard displays, but could be easily modified to support more.

Stylus input is realized using an Anoto Digital Pen ADP-301 and the Letras software framework [4]. Each cardboard is therefore augmented with the Anoto pattern.

We added a layer of Anoto pattern on each cardboard. By using Letras Framework the pen could send pen coordinates, which we then converted to mouse events in the WPF application. We refrained from supporting touch input for the following reasons. Pressure sensitive or capacitive touch foils either require tethering or too bulky of electronic components. While optical touch tracking would be a suitable approach with a single display or a small number of displays, it is too unreliable with the large number of displays supported by our system and the corresponding large number of markers which is required for tracking of displays.

For generating a 3D perception of sound, we used the OpenAL Framework [39]. The user was equipped with headphones which where augmented with markers to track the user's head position and orientation so that the sound sources could be positioned accurately in space.

This system setup is suitable for stationary installations, e.g. in schools, libraries, museums, or stores. In the near future, an alternative system setup can be created which consists of multiple thin-film OLED displays that are connected wirelessly instead of the stationary tracking-projection system. This will make the system easily portable and will allow to it to be used in at various places.

9. EVALUATION

PaperVideo introduces a novel way of tangible interaction while actively working with videos. It allows for a broad range of new styles of working with videos. Rather than focusing onto single variables (like time efficiency) and thereby limiting our view to a subset of scenarios, it is of primary importance to understand the broad range of new styles of working with videos that are enabled by our system. In particular, an evaluation must provide first insights into how users treat and use multiple displays simultaneously and how this affects the interaction with videos. Hence, answering the 'why' and 'how' is very important; this requires a qualitative research methodology, rather than a

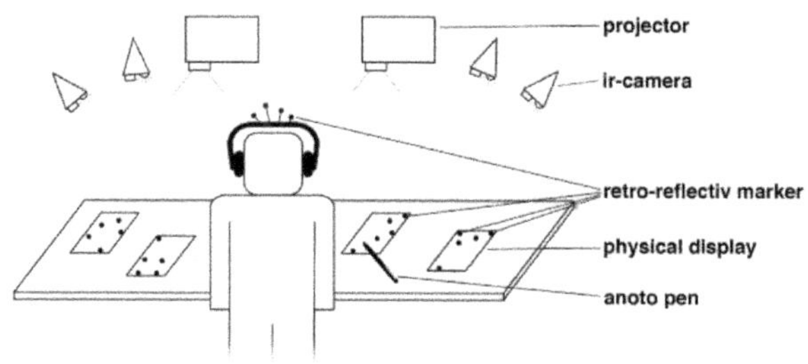

Figure 11: Technical setup

quantitative one, and a detailed analysis of a small, but focused sample. The in-depth analysis of users' practices and mental models which is presented in this section provides the foundation for future quantitative analyses of specific questions that are beyond the scope of this paper.

9.1 Study Design

Six experts participated in single-user sessions, each of approximately 3 hours length. All of them are video power users, spending a large amount of time on watching videos (avg=13 hours a week, SD=4.2), and having extensive recording and video authoring experience. To ensure a wide range of viewpoints, we recruited participants with different professional backgrounds: medicine, computer science, philosophy, cultural science and product design. All participants were male. Their median age was 24. All of them were familiar with modern computing devices, all owning a smart phone and two of them owning an iPad.

Each session was organized as follows. After 10 minutes of guided introduction to the system and its basic interaction techniques, the participant was given ample time to get familiar with the devices. Then the participant was asked to perform the following tasks using a think-aloud protocol:

1. The first task consisted of navigating within one video on a single display. The participant was asked to give a short oral summary about two different scenes of the video, one situated near the beginning, the other near the end of the video. He was free to decide which interaction technique to use (pen or timeline in space).
2. The participant was given all 7 displays. His task was to explore a collection of 6 related videos, to group them in two meaningful groups, to explain his grouping, and to regroup all videos following another criterion.
3. Before the third task, we introduced the interaction techniques for combining and distributing content. The task consisted of exploring a collection of 14 related videos and grouping it into two given topics, followed by giving an overview of all videos in the collection. This task was performed twice with different contents: once using all 7 displays, once using only 3 displays (the order was counterbalanced).
4. Before the next task we introduced the lightweight video editing technique to the participant. He had to provide a summarized video of soccer goals by creating a video excerpt which contained the goal sequences from 3 soccer videos.
5. Before the last task, the participant was introduced to the four sound concepts. Then he had to perform four sub-tasks, each with a different sound concept. The order was randomized. In each sub-task he was given a set of 5 videos on 5 displays and had to explore and decide which of the videos he liked.

These tasks allowed us to study a range of phenomena: how users leverage space to interact with multiple videos on multiple displays (tasks 1–3), how they combine and distribute content over different amount of displays (task 3), how they perform lightweight video editing (task 4), as well how they were able to manipulate and focus on multiple parallel sound sources (task 5).

9.2 Data Gathering and Analysis

As methodologies, we used semi-structured interviews (at the end of each task and after the whole session) and observation. The entire session was videotaped. Interviews and observations were transcribed and analyzed using an open coding approach [32].

10. RESULTS AND DISCUSSION

10.1 Task Support

The system itself was positively received by all participants. For instance P5 mentioned: *"I have the video with the page really in my hands (...) that's great."* All participants explicitly mentioned that they could easily gain an overview of the videos and could easily structure them by having multiple displays that could be rearranged in space. To more quickly get an overview of a video collection, one participant (P1) watched two videos in parallel on two adjacent displays. This allowed him to decide whether he liked the video and sort the video into the appropriate category.

Four participants emphasized that they would use the system for working purposes, such as learning, ordering and organizing videos as well as video editing. However, these participants were skeptical in using the system to just watch videos, such as watching a theater movie or YouTube video. P4 stated that the system is *"good for teaching video navigation to PC novices"*. P5 envisioned that the system be used at an exhibition booth in order to attract people via promotional videos.

10.2 Functional Zones

In the tasks where participants could use all seven displays, table space was used similarly to how it is reported in the literature about traditional paper documents [19,27]. In the video recordings, we clearly identified two different functional zones: The area situated directly in front of the participants, in the center of attention, can be characterized as the working area. Less important videos were moved to the periphery of attention, at the outer, more distant zones of the table surface. Following Scott et al., we call this the storage area.

Most intense interaction with video displays (such as playback, seeking, accessing related videos, clearing contents, video cutting) was done in the working area. Only one single participant navigated videos in the storage space. In contrast, all participants moved displays that were currently not needed (whether they were filled with content or be they empty) out of their attention into the storage space. These displays were placed on a free spot or piled onto other displays. 3 participants loosely arranged displays in the storage area, without piling. P6 explained: *"I have not piled because I'm not a person who orders things directly"*. In contrast, other participants preferred less cluttered arrangements and piled the displays as soon as they placed them in the storage area.

In contrast to the above findings for seven displays, participants behaved differently in tasks where they disposed only of three displays. 2 participants kept all displays inside the working area. Four participants placed only one single display in the storage area, which contained a virtualized pile. These findings show that the number of available displays directly influences the spatial practices of how the system is used. While with only three displays the system is used very much like an enhanced computing device with only very limited spatial interaction, already a relatively small number of additional displays is sufficient for unleashing the power of paper-based interactions.

10.3 Functional Roles of Displays

As long as the number of videos did not exceed the number of available displays, all participants realized a fixed one-to-one mapping of videos to displays. The display has thereby one single functional role: being a physical carrier of the video content.

In cases where the number of videos exceeded the number of displays, we observed two general strategies of participants to cope with the fewer number of displays. One group (3 of 6) can be characterized as "materializers". These participants preferred having as many videos as possible available in tangible form. They filled as many empty displays with content as possible. Only once all displays were full, they combined videos onto one carrier display to get free displays. In turn all of these displays were filled before virtualizing again. In contrast, the other group (3 of 6) can be characterized as "virtualizers". They filled just one (or at most two empty displays) and directly grouped the videos onto a virtual pile.

Participants assigned stable functional roles to physical displays. We identified three different roles of display usage that all participants assigned to displays in tasks 2-4: (a) information source, (b) working display, (c) information container. The information source was a display that contained all the related videos. The working display was used to iteratively open, watch and assess a related video before moving it into an information container. An information container display was used to group and store several videos that represented a topic. Both "materializers" and "virtualizers" attributed these roles to displays, with the only difference being that virtualizers had only one working display, whereas materializers had several.

Despite the possibility of using many displays, P6 and P4, both "virtualizers", used only 3 or 4 of them. P6 stated: *"Oh yes that goes well with 3, with 3 I have a better overview of the displays."* P4 even felt three displays to be more efficient than with more of them and was amazed how easily the tasks could be performed. In contrast, P1 and P5, both "materializers" found it inconvenient to work with only 3 displays.

We conclude from the results that depending on their strategy, users prefer more or less working displays. The system should provide enough displays to leave the choice to the user.

10.4 Dynamic vs. Static Content

In this section we focus on how dynamic content on paper displays was perceived in contrast to traditional static content on paper. Five participants found that dynamic content was easy and intuitive to use. P1 stated: *"It is better that videos can be detached from the medium whereas content on paper is bound to paper."* Furthermore the *"x-ray view"* (P5) through the pile was found to be beneficial to paper by all participants: *"I can see through the pile and still interact with it."* (P2). P5 mentioned: *"It saves me from flipping through pages. That's convenient; I can directly continue to work."*

All participants positively perceived that contents of the displays within a pile change dynamically when a pile is virtualized. P6 commented: *"This allows me to work with less displays."* However, comments about how specifically display contents should change in this case revealed two different mental models of the participants. This is best made clear by an example given by P5: The participant wanted to add a video to an existing virtual pile of videos. To do so he placed the display with the single video on top of the virtual pile and then performed the up gesture for virtualizing the pile. This automatically "pushed" all contents to the topmost display, which now contained the virtual pile. The remaining displays were empty. Thereby, the former working display changed its role to an information container and vice versa. This participant had a mental model that focused on the roles of the *physical* displays. He disliked their changing roles, which he described as "computer logic" (P5). In contrast the remaining 5 participants had a mental model that focused rather on the dynamic contents. They did not even notice that the physical carrier medium changed its role.

From these results we conclude that dynamic content on physical displays is appreciated and does not need high rethinking or high cognitive effort in contrast to the known behavior of traditional paper. However, to account for the mental model that focuses on the physical carrier medium, systems should equally support interactions that keep the roles of the physical displays steady. For instance, videos can be added to an existing pile by dragging and dropping them from the working display onto the information container.

10.5 Physical vs. Touch Input

We were interested to find out which interactions should be delegated to physical input (manipulating displays in space) and which ones to surface-based input (direct touch or pen input).

We observed that interactions like arranging and piling videos in space as well as combining and distributing contents were performed intuitively by physical input. In contrast, all participants intuitively used surface-based input for playback and skimming in videos. The interaction for temporal navigation in space was rarely used. Participants stated that skimming with the pen requires less effort and less space and moreover is more precise than moving the display in space. Furthermore, two participants (P2, P4) proposed a function for reordering videos within a pile by dragging & dropping their small representations on the topmost display. P3 suggested that the list of related videos be accessed by touch and that related videos be opened by dragging & dropping them from the list onto an empty display. However, P2 appreciated the physical gesture and mentioned browsing relations, by bringing displays near to each other, is intuitive and easy to use.

From these results we conclude that interactions that naturally anchor information in physical space would rather be done using physical interactions. For instance, if users arrange displays or pile them they expect the physical arrangements to change. On the other hand, interactions that have no spatial anchor and are without spatial consequences are performed using surface-based input. This particularly concerns interactions that apply to only one single display, such as temporal navigation within a video. Future work should explore spatial temporal navigation with multiple displays that are linked to only one video. By moving and arranging displays in space, the user could sneak-peak into different temporal locations of the video simultaneously and easily compare contents within one video. We assume that in this case, users prefer physical over touch input.

10.6 Sound Concepts for Multiple Videos

In this section, we evaluate and contrast the four sound concepts.

10.6.1 Real World Behavior

The evaluation showed that the sound concept which realizes real world behavior is not suitable for viewing multiple videos on multiple displays at the same time. Three participants watched the videos one after another. P5 who tried to view the videos in parallel stated: *"It feels better when only one video is playing."* All other sound concepts where judged to be better than this one.

10.6.2 Distance-based focusing

Our observations and comments from the users clearly showed that the distance-based focusing concept is much better suited for watching multiple videos. With this technique, five of six participants watched videos in parallel. Four of six participants rated this to be the best of all concepts, since it allowed for the most flexible sound manipulation with a very intuitive mapping. For instance, P2 stated that *"It is easy to manipulate the volume"*. The remaining participant did not watch videos in parallel with any of the concepts.

10.6.3 Orientation-based focusing

Three of the five participants who watched videos in parallel criticized this concept because of too much noise coming from displays at the outer sides. Two other participants mentioned that this concept is good for only focusing on audio without visual feedback, but not both combined.

10.6.4 Pick-up-based focusing

The pick-up-based focusing had the advantage that many videos can be played back in parallel without generating sound disturbance. Two participants, P1 and P5, started all the videos right at the start: *"I do not miss anything, I can still see everything.*" One participant (P6) mentioned: *"I can focus on one video more clearly.*" However, two participants (P1, P4) stressed that they *"have just two hands"* so that they can only hold and listen to two videos at a time. Moreover, one of them (P4) feared that holding the display for a long period could be tiring. P4 proposed as an improvement that *"shortly picking up a video could toggle between active and deactivated sound"*.

We conclude that with our sound concepts, in contrast to the real-world behavior, it is possible to watch videos in parallel and be able to explicitly and easily change the sound focus. The results show that distance-based focusing, preferred for its high flexibility and intuitiveness, was the best technique. Pick-up-based focusing also has its strengths in situations where users focus only on one or two videos at a time from a set of many videos that are simultaneously played back. A video installation at an exhibition booth is one example.

11. CONCLUSION

In this paper we proposed a novel paradigm for spatial interaction with video. We introduced a set of interaction techniques and spatial sound concepts that support playback, flexible navigation and spatial organization of videos on multiple physical displays. Results from a qualitative evaluation shed light on how people use multiple interactive displays simultaneously and how this affects the interaction with video contents. The results show that users can flexibly organize and structure videos in physical space while generating a good overview of multiple videos. They thereby flexibly attribute three different functional roles to paper-like displays: information source, working display and information container. The study further showed that advanced spatial sound concepts effectively support a user in simultaneously viewing multiple videos which contain audio tracks. Finally, we have characterized different mental models and strategies of users ("materializers" vs. "virtualizers") to cope with a restricted number of displays.

In future work, we plan to explore the use of the system in a collaborative environment.

12. REFERENCES

[1] Adler, M.J. and Van Doren, C.L. *How to read a book*. Simon and Schuster, 1972.

[2] Arons, B. A review of the cocktail party effect. *Journal of the American Voice IO Society 12*, 7 (1992).

[3] Glass, J., Hazen, T.J., Cyphers, S., Malioutov, I., Huynh, D., and Barzilay, R. Recent Progress in the MIT Spoken Lecture Processing Project. *Artificial Intelligence*, (2007).

[4] Heinrichs, F., Steimle, J., Schreiber, D., and Mühlhäuser, M. Letras: an architecture and framework for ubiquitous pen-and-paper interaction. *Proc. EICS '10*, (2010).

[5] Hinckley, K. Synchronous gestures for multiple persons and computers. *Proc. UIST 03*, (2003).

[6] Holman, D., Vertegaal, R., Altosaar, M., Kl, C., Troje, N., and Johns, D. PaperWindows□: Interaction Techniques for Digital Paper. *Interfaces*, (2005).

[7] Huber, J., Steimle, J., and Mühlhäuser, M. Toward more efficient user interfaces for mobile video browsing. *Proc. MM '10*, (2010).

[8] Hürst, W., Götz, G., and Welte, M. Interactive video browsing on mobile devices. *Proc. MM '07*, (2007).

[9] Jiang, H., Viel, A., Bajaj, M., Lue, R.A., and Shen, C. CThru: exploration in a video-centered information space for educational purposes. *Proc. CHI '09*, (2009).

[10] Karrer, T., Weiss, M., Lee, E., and Borchers, J. DRAGON□: A Direct Manipulation Interface for Frame-Accurate In-Scene Video Navigation. *Evaluation*, (2008).

[11] Kirsh, D. The intelligent use of space. *Artificial Intelligence 73*, (1995)

[12] Luff, P. and Heath, C. Mobility in collaboration. *Proc. CSCW '98*, (1998).

[13] Mackay, W.E. and Pagani, D.S. Video Mosaic: Laying Out Time in a Physical Space. *Proc. MM '94*, (1994).

[14] Malone, T.W. How do people organize their desks?: Implications for the design of office information systems. *ACM Transactions on Information Systems 1*, (1983).

[15] Mander, R., Salomon, G., and Wong, Y.Y. A "pile" metaphor for supporting casual organization of information. *Proc. CHI '92*, ACM Press (1992).

[16] Manske, K. and Mühlhäuser, M. OBVI: Hierarchical 3D Video-Browsing. *Proceedings of ACM Multimedia*, (1998).

[17] Merrill, D., Kalanithi, J., and Maes, P. Siftables: towards sensor network user interfaces. *Proc. TEI '07*, (2007).

[18] Mertens, R. and Vornberger, O. Hypermedia Navigation Concepts for Lecture Recordings Navigation in Hypermedia. *World Conference on ELearning in Corporate Government Healthcare Higher Education*, (2004), 2480-2487.

[19] O'Hara, K. and Sellen, A. A comparison of reading paper and on-line documents. *Proc. CHI '97*, ACM Press (1997).

[20] Rekimoto, J., Ullmer, B., and Oba, H. DataTiles: a modular platform for mixed physical and graphical interactions. *Proc. CHI '01*, ACM Press (2001).

[21] Rekimoto, J. Pick-and-drop: a direct manipulation technique for multiple computer environments. *Symposium on User Interface Software and Technology*, (1997).

[22] Rooke, M. and Vertegaal, R. Physics on display: tangible graphics on hexagonal bezel-less screens. *TEI '10*, (2010).

[23] Schmandt, C. and Mullins, A. AudioStreamer: Exploting Simultaneity for Listening. *Proceedings of CHI 95*, (1995).

[24] Schmandt, C. Audio hallway: a virtual acoustic environment for browsing. *Proc. UIST 98*, (1998).

[25] Schoeffmann, K. and Fabro, M. del. Hierarchical video browsing with a 3D carousel. *Proc. MM '11*, (2011).

[26] Schoeffmann, K., Hopfgartner, F., Marques, O., Boeszoermenyi, L., and Jose, J. Video browsing interfaces and applications: a review. *SPIE Reviews 1*, 1 (2010).

[27] Scott, S.D., Sheelagh, M., Carpendale, T., and Inkpen, K.M. Territoriality in collaborative tabletop workspaces. *Proc. CSCW 04 04pages*, (2004).

[28] Sellen, A.J. and Harper, R.H.R. *The Myth of the Paperless Office*. The MIT Press, 2001.

[29] Sokoler, T. and Edeholt, H. Physically embodied video snippets supporting collaborative exploration of video material during design sessions. *Proc. NordiCHI '02*, (2002).

[30] Spindler, M., Stellmach, S., and Dachselt, R. PaperLens: advanced magic lens interaction above the tabletop. *Proc. ITS '09*, ACM (2009).

[31] Spindler, M., Tominski, C., Schumann, H., and Dachselt, R. *Tangible views for information visualization*. ACM Press, New York, New York, USA, 2010.

[32] Strauss, A. and Corbin, J. *Basics of Qualitative Research: Techniques and Procedures for Developing Grounded Theory*. Sage, 2008.

[33] Sun, Q. and Hürst, W. Video Browsing on Handheld Devices - Interface Designs for the Next Generation of Mobile Video Players. *IEEE Multimedia 15*, 3 (2008).

[34] Terrenghi, L., Kirk, D., Sellen, A., and Izadi, S. Affordances for manipulation of physical versus digital media on interactive surfaces. *Proc. CHI 07 8*, September (2007).

[35] Wellner, P. The DigitalDesk calculator: tangible manipulation on a desk top display. *Communications of the ACM 36*, 7 (1993).

[36] Zigelbaum, J., Horn, M.S., and Jacob, R.J.K. The Tangible Video Editor□: Collaborative Video Editing with Active Tokens. *Design*, (2007).

[37] iTunes U. http://www.apple.com/education/mobile-learning/.

[38] MIT OpenCourseWare. http://ocw.mit.edu/.

[39] OpenAL. http://connect.creativelabs.com/openal/default.aspx.

MoViMash: Online Mobile Video Mashup

Mukesh Saini
Dept. of Computer Science
National University of Singapore
mksaini@comp.nus.edu.sg

Raghudeep Gadde
Dept. of ECE
National University of Singapore
elerdg@nus.edu.sg

Shuicheng Yan
Dept. of ECE
National University of Singapore
eleyans@nus.edu.sg

Wei Tsang Ooi
Dept. of Computer Science
National University of Singapore
ooiwt@comp.nus.edu.sg

ABSTRACT

With the proliferation of mobile video cameras, it is becoming easier for users to capture videos of live performances and socially share them with friends and public. As an attendee of such live performances typically has limited mobility, each video camera is able to capture only from a range of restricted viewing angles and distance, producing a rather monotonous video clip. At such performances, however, multiple video clips can be captured by different users, likely from different angles and distances. These videos can be combined to produce a more interesting and representative mashup of the live performances for broadcasting and sharing. The earlier works select video shots merely based on the quality of currently available videos. In real video editing process, however, recent selection history plays an important role in choosing future shots. In this work, we present MoViMash, a framework for automatic online video mashup that makes smooth shot transitions to cover the performance from diverse perspectives. Shot transition and shot length distributions are learned from professionally edited videos. Further, we introduce view quality assessment in the framework to filter out shaky, occluded, and tilted videos. To the best of our knowledge, this is the first attempt to incorporate history-based diversity measurement, state-based video editing rules, and view quality in automated video mashup generations. Experimental results have been provided to demonstrate the effectiveness of MoViMash framework.

Categories and Subject Descriptors: I.2.10 [Vision and Scene Understanding]: Video Analysis

General Terms: Algorithms, Design.

Keywords: Mobile Video, Virtual Director, Video Mashup.

1. INTRODUCTION

Worldwide shipment of camera phones were estimated to reach 1.14 billion in the year 2011 alone [1]. Furthermore, a survey of over 2,500 respondents by Photobucket reveals that 45% of the respondents use mobile devices to shoot video at least once weekly during the summer of 2011, validating the significant increase in the amount of mobile video uploaded to Photobucket's video sharing website (14× in Summer 2011 compared to December 2010) [2].

Proliferation of such mobile devices with video capture capability has enabled users to capture video of their life events such as concerts, parades, outdoor performances, etc, and socially share them with friends and public as it happens. Videos recorded by a single user at such events are shot from a limited range of angles and distances from the performance stage, as an attendee typically has limited mobility (e.g., constraint by seating arrangement). The recorded video can be monotonous and uninteresting. Furthermore, videos recorded are typically short (in the order of minutes or tens of minutes), due to tired arms or power constraint of mobile devices. There are, however, likely to have more than one users recording the same performance from different angles at the same time, especially at a well-attended performance.

These recorded and shared video clips of the same performance can be cut and joined together to produce a new *mashup* video, similar to how a TV director of a live TV show would switch between different cameras to produce the show. Generation of a video mashup can be cast as a video selection problem: given a set of video clips capturing the same performance event, automatically select one of the video clips at any one time instance to be included in the output mashup video.

In this paper, we introduce MoViMash, our approach to solve the above video selection problem. MoViMash aims to produce mashup video from a set of mobile devices that is interesting and pleasing to watch, and uses a combinations of content-analysis, state-based transitions, history-based diversity, and learning from human editors to achieve this goal.

We now provide an overview of how MoViMash works in the usual setting of live performances, shown in Figure 1. There is generally a staging area and an audience area where the audiences either sit or stand to watch the performance, and record the performance with a mobile device. This setting poses a few challenges to video mashup.

Since the videos are recorded with a hand-held mobile device, from the audience area, and likely by non-professional, there is no guarantee on the view quality. The videos can be shaky or tilted. Furthermore, it is common to include the back of the head of other audiences in the view. As other audiences move, the view can be temporarily occluded. When MoViMash needs to decide which video to select, it first filters out the videos with bad views currently from further consideration for selection. To achieve this, MoViMash analyzes the video to determine the current shakiness, the tilt angle, and the level of occlusion in the video. Note that shakiness

MM'12, October 29–November 2, 2012, Nara, Japan.

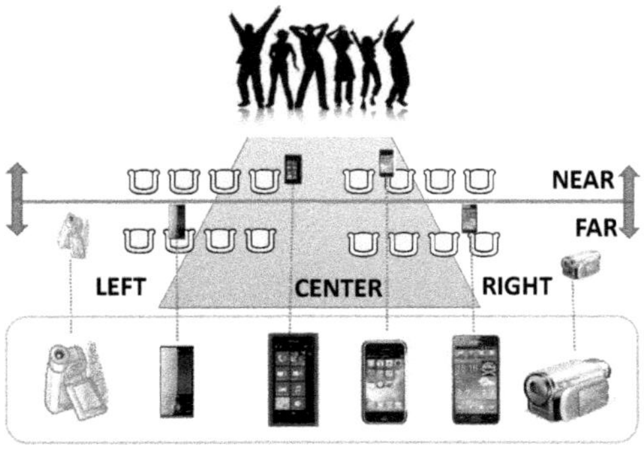

Figure 1: A general performance scenario

and tilt angle can be obtained from easily sensory data of mobile device when available.

The shooting angle of the remaining videos are then classified as either center, left, and right; and distance from the stage as near and far as shown in Figure 1. This classification is done every time we perform video selection because mobile users may change their position over time. MoViMash now decides which shooting angle and distance should be used; and for how long the selected class should persist. To this end, MoViMash tries to imitate a professional video editor, by using a finite state machine, whose transition probabilities are learned from analyzing professionally edited videos of the same type of event. The rationale behind the inclusion of learning is that, we have observed that there are no generic editing rules that can be precisely defined to work with all types of events. The video editors make fine decisions such as shot lengths and transitions based on their experience which is hard to enumerate.

The videos from the selected class are further ranked based on the video quality and diversity values to make the final selection. To consider video quality, MoViMash favors video with low blurriness, low blockiness (good compression), good contrast, and good illumination in each video. To consider diversity, MoViMash stores a history of recent video selections and favors videos with dissimilar views with recent selections.

We have developed MoViMash's algorithm such that it is online and only depends on history information. As such, even though it is not our main goal in this paper, MoViMash can be applied to mashup of live video feeds from mobile devices.

We now briefly compare MoViMash to existing work to highlight the contribution of this paper. There has been few works on video selection in a lecture broadcast and video streaming [21] [6] and video conferencing [3]. In these works the camera is mainly selected based on speaker detection. Live performances are not speaker centric. In fact, the speech signals are generally noise from the crowd. In one recent work, Shrestha et al. [15] propose a method to create a video mashup from a given set of concert recordings. In that work, the authors select the shots based on mainly video quality, mostly ignoring view quality. Also, the diversity is only calculated based on the comparison of the last image of the current shot and first image of the next shot. It does not consider the history of video selection and the time for which a particular camera is selected. Further, video editing rules, which are subtle in the case of live performances, are not considered.

Contributions. We now summarize our contributions in this paper as follows:

- We propose a state-based approach for shot selection that incorporates the selection history in the decision process. Earlier methods select shots based on only currently available videos.
- We include view quality in the framework to filter out the bad views that are occluded, tilted, or shaky. Earlier methods only considered video quality.
- We build a comprehensive model to calculate diversity that considers both previously selected videos and shot lengths.
- We propose a learning-based approach where the shot transition probabilities and shot lengths are learned from professionally edited videos.

Organization. The rest of the paper is organized as follows. We provide a review of earlier work in Section 2. In Section 3 we describe proposed mashup framework. We evaluate our system in Section 4. The conclusions are provided in Section 5.

2. PREVIOUS WORK

There has been only few works on online camera selection. In most of these works, videos are mainly selected to show the speakers. In the work by Machnicki and Rowe [9], an online lecture webcast system is presented in which the cameras that are focusing on speaker and the presentation (the screen) are selected iteratively until anybody from audience asks question. When audience ask question, the camera that is focusing the person asking question is selected. The automatic selection of cameras in a lecture webcast is extended by Zhang et al. [21] to include audio based localization and speaker tracking. Similar approach is taken by Cutler et al. [6] in a meeting scenario where camera that shows the current speaker is selected. Ranjan et al. [12] use face tracking and audio analysis to show the close-up of the person talking. Since performers play more important role than speakers in live concerts, a speaker based selection is not appropriate. Further, the faces are generally far from the camera which cannot be detected. Therefore, face detection is not a reliable basis to select videos.

Al-Hames et al. [3] extends the camera selection work to include the motion features. We do not use motion features in our framework because both performers and audience generate continuous motion. Also, the movement of the mobile camera can inject erroneous motion in the video, which is aesthetically appealing. Yu et al. [20] propose to customize the camera selection and shot lengths based on user preferences. At every lecture webcast receiving site, the user can give score to the videos and specify rules for shot lengths. While such an interactive selection of cameras is useful for educational scenarios, people may find it annoying and stressful for performances, particularly when the number of videos is large.

A camera selection method for sports video broadcast is proposed by Wang et al. [16]. The authors assume one main camera and other sub cameras. The empirical main camera duration is found to be from 4 to 24 seconds, and sub camera duration is found to be 1.5 to 8 seconds. They select a sub camera based on the clarity of the view, determined using motion features. In our work, along with shakiness of the videos, we also calculate view quality in terms of occlusion and rotation; and video quality in terms of contrast, blur, illumination, and blockiness. We also include explicit measurement of diversity in the framework. Engstrom et al. [8] discuss automatic camera selection for broadcast in a sports event capture scenario. The work mainly promotes collaborative video production, i.e., video recorded by production team as well as the consumers.

In other media production applications, the shots are selected to convey the story to the audience. For instance, de Lima et al. [7]

Table 1: A Comparison of Previous Work

Work	Online	Diversity	Learning	Video Quality	View Quality	Scenario
Machnicki et al. [9]	Yes	No	No	No	No	Lecture webcast
Cutler et al. [6]	No	No	No	No	No	Meeting
Al-Hames et al. [3]	Yes	No	No	No	No	Meeting
Yu et al. [20]	Yes	No	No	No	No	Lecture webcast
Zhang et al. [21]	Yes	No	No	No	No	Lecture Webcast
Wang et al. [16]	Yes	No	No	Yes	No	Sports Broadcast
Engstrom et al. [8]	Yes	No	No	No	No	Sports Broadcast
Lima et al. [7]	No	No	No	No	No	Storyline
Ranjan et al. [12]	Yes	No	No	No	No	Meeting
Shrestha et al. [15]	No	No	No	Yes	No	Live Performances
Proposed	Yes	Yes	Yes	Yes	Yes	Live Performances

propose a method to automatically select shots from multiple cameras for storytelling, according to the rules provided by the director. These methods are not useful for us as live performances generally do not have any story.

Recently, there has been works on creating video mashups from given set of videos. In one of the most recent works [15], Shrestha et al. select the cameras based on video quality. Although the authors refer to term 'diversity' in the paper, it is merely a comparison of current frame and the next frame of the corresponding camera. The authors completely ignore the selection history and the time for which each view is selected. The authors also ignore editing rules corresponding to different views, which we incorporate through learning based classification and selection. Furthermore, unlike the method proposed in this paper, the authors rely on the future video for current shot selection. While this approach is fine for combining stored videos, it is not suitable for live applications such as broadcasting and live sharing.

We have provided a comparison of the related work in Table 1. The works have been compared with respect to the following aspects: (1) can the method be applied online (a method that uses future information cannot be applied online)? (2) is selection history-based diversity considered? (3) is learning incorporated? (4) is video quality (clarity, contrast etc.) considered? (5) is view quality (view occlusion, tilted view etc.) considered? and (6) what is the underlying application scenario? It can be easily seen that the proposed method is the first attempt to consider history based diversity through learning for online video selection for live performances.

3. MOVIMASH FRAMEWORK

In this section, we first enumerate the design principles that we have followed in the development of MoViMash and then describe the framework. After an overview of MoViMash, we focus on individual components.

3.1 Design Principles

The end goal of the MoViMash is to produce a mashup that users like. To achieve this goal, we have followed a set of design principles as follows:

- **Video Quality**: In our discussion, video quality includes sharpness, contrast, illumination, and blockiness (due to video compression). A good image quality gives pleasing experience to the viewers [10]. Therefore, in our framework we give priority to good quality videos.

- **View Quality**: A video that is captured by a tilted camera (rotated around horizontal axis) may have very good video quality, yet, users generally do not like tilted views. Similarly, a view in which a person or object is occluding stage area (blocking performance view) may be annoying to the user. Therefore view quality is also important. We measure view quality in terms of occlusion, tilt, and shakiness.

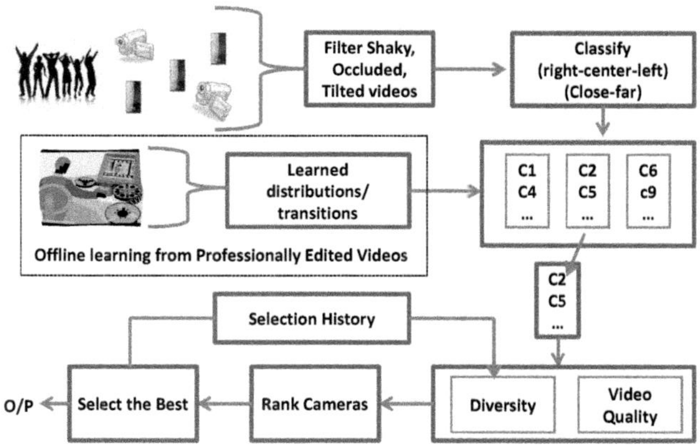

Figure 2: The virtual director framework

- **Diversity**: While static cameras always record videos from same perspective, mobile users generally shoot videos from a number of views and diverse perspectives. We take this opportunity to include more diversified views in the mashup. Both temporal and spatial aspects of diversity are considered in the proposed framework.

- **Learning**: When professionals edit the videos, they make many decisions based on their experience. Such decisions include shooting angle, distance from the stage, and shot length. It is, however, difficult to precisely state this experience in terms of hard-coded rules. Therefore, in this work, we learn the shot transitions and lengths from professionally edited videos.

The above mentioned design principles are met in our framework through various quality metrics and video selection/filtering phases, as described in the following section.

3.2 Framework

At every time instant, we have a number of videos to choose from. Once we have chosen the video, we also need to decide when to switch to another video. Hence, there are two main questions involved here that need to be answered for combining videos: (1) which video to select? (2) when to switch to another video? We use a three-phase method to select the video while the length is determined based on learned editing rules and overall quality score of the selected video.

Figure 2 shows the block diagram of overall framework. The proposed framework consists of one offline learning phase and three online selection phases namely filtering, classification, and selection. At any given time, the following steps are taken to select the most suitable video at current instant:

1. **Filtering**: In the filtering step, we determine videos that are unusable by comparing occlusion, shakiness, and tilt scores against empirically determined thresholds. The remaining videos are passed to the classification stage.

2. **Classification**: The selected cameras are classified as one of right, center, and left according to the capturing angle. Further, according to the viewing distance from the stage, they are classified as near or far.

3. **Class Prediction**: According to the class of currently selected video, and class transition probabilities learned from professionally edited videos, a most suitable class is predicted and videos from that class are selected for further consideration.

4. **Video Selection**: The classified cameras are further ranked with respect to a combined score of video quality, diversity, and shakiness. The video with highest score is selected.

5. **Shot Length**: The length of the video is selected based on learned distributions and video quality. A higher quality video is generally selected for longer time.

While filtering and selection phase ensure view and video quality, the classification and diversity ensure that we select videos recorded with different angles and viewing distances to provide a complete and interesting coverage of the performance. We now describe each component of the framework in detail.

3.3 View Quality

The view quality is measured in terms of three characteristics: occlusion, shakiness, and camera tilt. The details of measurement of each of these quantities is given below.

3.3.1 Occlusion

For both a stand mounted camera and a mobile camera, there is always a chance of view occlusion. At crowded places, people sometime do not notice the cameras recording the video and occlude the performance view. Even if people notice the cameras, they stand in front of or walk across the cameras, because the main purpose of the performances is to entertain the audience who are present at the venue rather than video recording. Therefore, we detect the videos which are recorded by occluded cameras and filter them out.

Occlusion detection methods are popular in the field of object tracking [13, 19]. There methods employ various appearance models to seamlessly track multiple objects. In this case, the occlusion occurs when an object is hidden behind another. In live performances, this could be intentionally done by the performers, i.e., one performer coming in front of other. We are more interested in detecting the audience blocking the view. Therefore, those works are not applicable here.

We have developed an edge density based method to detect videos with occluded views. The method is based on the assumption that the objects that occlude the performance area will result in lower edge density than the performance area. Therefore, the non-occluded area of the image, which is far from the camera, will result in more dense edge points than the occluded area. To differentiate between homogeneous regions of the stage area, which could also have less edge density, and occluded area; we perform connected components on the edge image. Following are the steps of the occlusion detection in a given image I:

- Edge Detection: In the first step, we calculate the presence of an edge at each pixel location. Let I^e be the resulting binary edge image:

$$I^e(x,y) = \begin{cases} 1 & \text{if edge is detected at pixel } I(x,y) \\ 0 & \text{otherwise} \end{cases} \tag{1}$$

- Edge Density: We convolve the edge image with a square matrix W with all of its elements unity:

$$I^d = I^e \odot W \tag{2}$$

  The output of the operation gives the density of edges around each pixel.

- Labeling the Patches: The image is now divided into patches of block size $b \times b$. Each patch is labeled as 1 if the sum of edge densities is less that a threshold, else it is labeled as 0.

$$I^p(x',y') = \begin{cases} 1 & \text{if the sum of edge densities in the} \\ & \text{patch } (x',y') \text{ is greater than threshold} \\ 0 & \text{otherwise.} \end{cases} \tag{3}$$

  The 1's in the patch image shows potentially occluded regions.

- Connected Components: There can be homogeneous regions in the non-occluded area as well. These regions, however, are generally small. Therefore, connected components operation is performed to find the size of largest group of connected patches with label 1, which corresponds to occluded region.

- Occlusion Score: To calculate the final occlusion score S^o, we first calculate the fractional occluded region f in the connected components output image, i.e.,

$$f = \frac{\text{No of 1 patches}}{\text{Total number of patches}} \tag{4}$$

We also observed that generally the dynamic range of f is very small. Therefore, we expand its range with an exponential function to calculate the final score S^o:

$$S^o = 1 - e^{-f} \tag{5}$$

The resulting occlusion scores for an example video sequence are shown in the Figure 3. The sequence shows a person walking across a camera, which is recording an outdoor performance. We can see that as the person enters the camera view, the occlusion score starts increasing. We obtained similar results for night videos also, which are not shown due to space limitation. We found that for a patch size of 20*15 pixels, videos with occlusion score more than 0.2 are very bad, so these are filtered in the framework.

3.3.2 Tilt

In this work, we define tilt as the rotation of the camera around horizontal axis. User's generally do not like the videos recorded by tilted cameras. Therefore, we detect the tilted camera views and filter them. Here we use the heuristic that for a horizontally placed camera, most of the lines in the view are horizontal, while an inclined view generally has non-horizontal lines. The following steps are taken to calculation tilt:

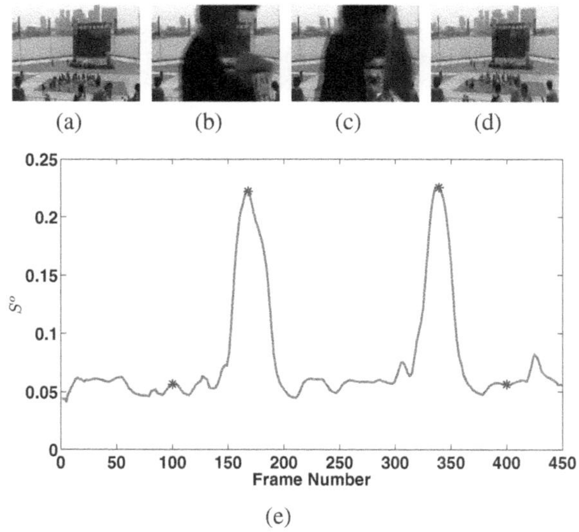

Figure 3: Occlusion detection. Figures (a)-(d) show the frames 100, 168, 339, and 400 of the test video respectively. Figure (e) shows the corresponding occlusion score

- Line Detection: We use Hough transform to detect the straight line in the image. Let l'_i be the length of the ith line and o'_i the angle with respect to the horizontal line.
- Angle Restriction: We assume that the maximum tilt a camera can have is less than $\pm\pi/4$ and any line with the inclination above this angle is noise and not considered in calculation. Let the resulting orientation of l'_i line be o_i.
- The final tilt score S^t is calculated as absolute of the mean weighted orientation and normalized by $\pi/4$:

$$S^t = \frac{abs\left(\frac{1}{N^l}\sum_{i=1}^{N^l} o_i * l_i\right)}{\pi/4} \tag{6}$$

where N^l is the total number of lines in the image.

An example of tilt calculation is shown in Figure 4; the upper row shows frames from the video and the figure in lower row shows occlusion scores. The video clip is recorded by a mobile phone camera. In between, the mobile user gets engaged in some other activity, and the mobile phone gets tilted. We can observe in the frames itself the straight lines getting tilted. It gets reflected in the tilt score as shown in Figure 4 for frames 200 and 216. The videos with a tilt score of 0.4 are found unusable and they are filtered.

3.3.3 *Shakiness*

Shakiness is calculated based on the method described in [4]. In this method, the pixel values are projected on horizontal and vertical axes. The horizontal and vertical projections are matched across the frames for calculating camera motion. A median filtered is finally applied on the motion vectors to differentiate the shakiness from the smooth camera motion. The final value of shakiness score, S^s, is calculated by summing the absolute difference of original motion vector and median filtered motion vector. The score is normalized by calculating maximum difference empirically. For a shakiness window of 100 frames, the normalization value is 300; for any value above 300, S^s is saturated to 1.

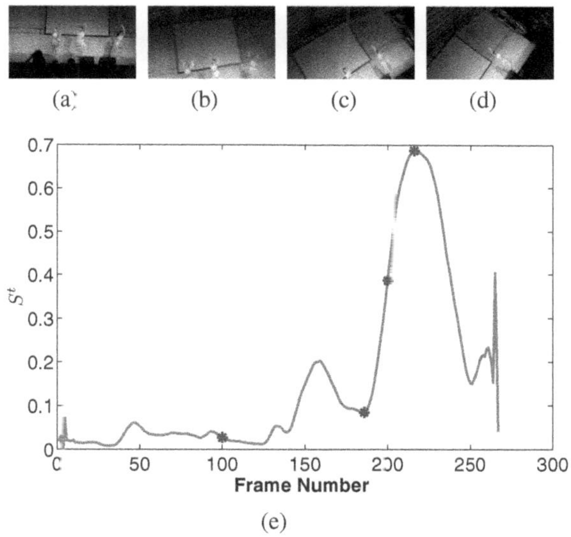

Figure 4: Tilt results. Figures (a)-(d) show the frames 100, 186, 200, and 286 of the test video respectively. Figure (e) shows the corresponding tilt score

3.4 Learning

As mentioned earlier in Section 1, it is difficult to precisely enumerate all the rules which professional editors follow in selecting a video and its corresponding shot length. In MoViMash, we propose to learn the behavior of professional editor statistically for use in creating mashup. We use professionally edited videos for this purpose. The rules are learned in terms of shooting angle, shooting distance, and shot length. Following are the steps taken in the process of learning:

- At first, we divide the video into a sequence of shots and record shot length.
- Each shot is classified as right ($\mathcal{R}$), left ($\mathcal{L}$), or center ($\mathcal{C}$) based on shooting angle (Figure 1).
- Depending on the distance of the recording device from the stage, the videos are further classified as near ($\mathcal{N}$) or far ($\mathcal{F}$) (Figure 1).
- Based on both classifications, we define six states (also referred as classes in the paper) in which a video can be at any time instant, i.e., $\mathcal{CN}$, $\mathcal{CF}$, $\mathcal{RN}$, $\mathcal{RF}$, $\mathcal{LN}$, and $\mathcal{LF}$.
- From the sequence of the shots, we calculate the state transition probabilities for the above described six states.
- We now feed the transition probabilities (transition matrix) along with shot lengths (emission matrix) to an hidden Markov model (HMM). The HMM generates a sequence of shot states and their corresponding lengths.

$$\begin{array}{c c} & \begin{array}{cccccc} \mathcal{CN} & \mathcal{CF} & \mathcal{RN} & \mathcal{RF} & \mathcal{LN} & \mathcal{LF} \end{array} \\ \begin{array}{c} \mathcal{CN} \\ \mathcal{CF} \\ \mathcal{RN} \\ \mathcal{RF} \\ \mathcal{LN} \\ \mathcal{LF} \end{array} & \left(\begin{array}{cccccc} 0 & 0.4 & 0.2 & 0.1 & 0.2 & 0.1 \\ 0.6 & 0 & 0.1 & 0.1 & 0.1 & 0.1 \\ 0.5 & 0.1 & 0 & 0.1 & 0.2 & 0.1 \\ 0.2 & 0.2 & 0.4 & 0 & 0.1 & 0.1 \\ 0.4 & 0.2 & 0.2 & 0.1 & 0 & 0.1 \\ 0.2 & 0.2 & 0.1 & 0.1 & 0.4 & 0 \end{array} \right) \end{array} \tag{7}$$

$$\begin{array}{c} \\ \mathcal{CN} \\ \mathcal{CF} \\ \mathcal{RN} \\ \mathcal{RF} \\ \mathcal{LN} \\ \mathcal{LF} \end{array} \begin{array}{c} \begin{array}{ccccccc} 1 & 2 & 3 & 4 & 5 & 6 & 7 \end{array} \\ \begin{pmatrix} 1/31 & 2/31 & 4/31 & 7/31 & 7/31 & 6/31 & 4/31 \\ 3/12 & 4/12 & 2/12 & 1/12 & 1/12 & 1/12 & 0 \\ 2/15 & 3/15 & 4/15 & 3/15 & 2/15 & 1/15 & 0 \\ 3/10 & 4/10 & 2/10 & 1/10 & 0 & 0 & 0 \\ 2/15 & 3/15 & 4/15 & 3/15 & 2/15 & 1/15 & 0 \\ 3/10 & 4/10 & 2/10 & 1/10 & 0 & 0 & 0 \end{pmatrix} \end{array} \quad (8)$$

We use affine transformation to classify the video, giving an accuracy of $\approx 77\%$ on our dataset. However, since learning is one time job, we performed manual classification of shots during the learning phase to get accurate statistics. Equation 7 shows the learned transition matrix while Equation 8 emission matrix. We have carefully selected five videos (live group dances with length of videos ranging from 210 to 300 seconds), which are professionally edited and aired on television. We downloaded these videos from YouTube.

These videos include concerts by professional bands and performance at the Academy Awards ceremony. We observed that in dance videos, the shot lengths are relatively smaller (average around 2.3 seconds) compared to solo singing videos (average around 3.5 seconds). This finding implies that the learning dataset should comply with the type of performance for mashup. We also observed that the average shot lengths for all five dance videos ranged between 2.2 seconds to 2.4 seconds, showing little variations, which shows that a particular type of events have similar pattern of transitions and shot lengths which can be learned and applied to create online mashup.

3.5 Video Quality

We can have different quality videos because of the limitation of recording devices, varied camera positioning, lighting conditions, camera angle, and video recording skills of the person. To produce aesthetically beautiful video, it is important to consider the quality of the videos.We are considering the following aspects to obtain video quality score:

- **Blockiness**: The blocking effect mainly comes due to poor quality of data compression. To measure blockiness, we take current image as sample and calculate its compression quality using the method described in [18]. The method generates a score that takes a value between 1 and 10 (10 represents the best quality, 1 the worst). We normalize the score between 0 and 1. Let S^b be the blockiness score.

- **Blur**: The video can be blurred due to many reasons such as out-of-focus recording, camera movement etc. We are calculating blur based on the method described in [5]. Let S^{br} be the blur score which varies between 0 to 1 (0 represents blurred and 1 sharp).

- **Illumination**: There can be videos that are recorded in poor lighting conditions. The purpose of including this metric in quality measurement is to avoid selecting dark videos. The illumination score for the image S^{im} (with width N_w and height N_h) is calculated as average gray value, normalized by 255.

$$S^{im} = \frac{1}{255} \frac{1}{N^w * N^h} \sum_{x=0,}^{N_w} \sum_{y=0}^{N_h} I(x, y) \quad (9)$$

- **Contrast**: It has also been found in the literature that an image with good contrast is appreciated by the viewers [10]. Therefore, contrast is also chosen as one of the metrics. The contrast score S^c is calculated as standard deviation of the pixel intensities.

$$S^c = \frac{1}{255} \sqrt{\frac{1}{N^w * N^h} \sum_{x=0,}^{N_w} \sum_{y=0}^{N_h} (I(x, y) - \overline{I})^2} \quad (10)$$

Its value varies from 0 to 1 where 1 is the desired value corresponding to high contrast.

- **Burned Pixels**: It has been identified that pixels that are close to 255 or 0 are generally not informative [15]. If N^b is the number of such pixels, the quality score representing burnt pixels is calculated as follows:

$$S^{bp} = \begin{cases} 1 - N^b/(0.25 * N^i) & \text{if } N^b/(0.25 * N^i) < 1 \\ 0 & \text{otherwise} \end{cases} \quad (11)$$

where N^i is the total number of pixels in the image. In this case, a value of 1 represents best quality, i.e., no burnt pixels; while a value of 0 means at least 25% pixels are burnt.

The individual quality scores are multiplied to calculate overall video quality score S^q, i.e.,

$$S^q = S^b \times S^{br} \times S^{im} \times S^c \times S^{bp} \quad (12)$$

We have chosen to multiply the individual scores because we want to give priority to the videos that are good in all aspects.

3.6 Diversity

The aspect of diversity is included in the framework by calculating the similarity of the views of the videos selected in the recent past. Let $\mathcal{H}$ be the history of the cameras that have been selected so far. The history is stored as set of chronologically order tuples, i.e.,

$$\mathcal{H} = \{(I_j^h, \Delta_j) | 1 \leq j \leq N^v\} \quad (13)$$

where N^v is the number videos selected in the recent past. Each tuple has the following two entries:

- I^h - Snapshot from the selected cameras at the time of selection.

- Δ - The time for which the particular camera is selected. It is normalized between 0 to 1 by dividing each video duration by the total time over which history is stored.

Let VS be the view similarity matrix:

$$VS = \{v_{ij} | 1 \leq i \leq n; 1 \leq j \leq N^v; \forall i = j, v_{ij} = 1\} \quad (14)$$

where n is number of cameras, and v_{ij} is the view similarity measure between current frame from the ith video and j^{th} frame of the history. The motivation of defining the view similarity VS is to select video with different views. The overall steps of diversity calculation are as follows:

1. Determine the view similarity matrix VS by comparing current frame with the frames stored in the history, i.e.,

$$v_{ij} = Diff(I_i^c, I_j^h) \quad (15)$$

where I_i^c is the current frame of ith camera, I_j^h is the jth frame of the history, and $Diff$ can be any function to calculate view similarity. We are using SSIM [17] for this purpose.

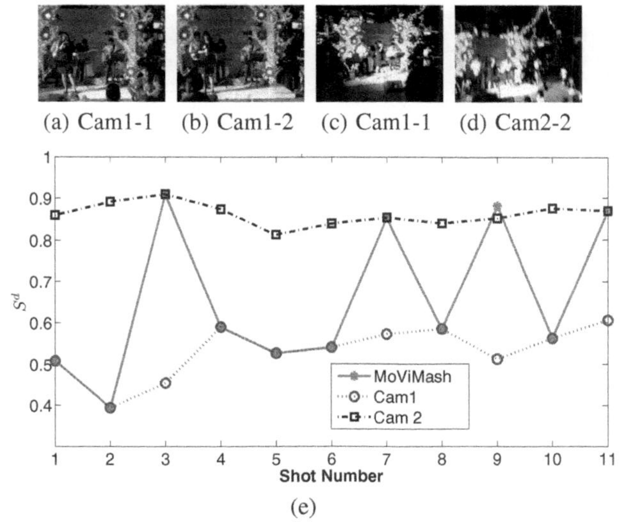

Figure 5: Diversity value for two candidate videos and final mashup

2. For the given content, the user interest decreases with time over which the user watches same or similar content. Hence, the diversity score of the ith video, i.e., S^d is calculated for each of the current videos as follows:

$$S^d = \sum_{j=1}^{N^v} v_{ij} * \Delta_j \qquad (16)$$

3. Store the viewing time of the previous video and the current frame of the selected video in $\mathcal{H}$. If we choose a scheme where each camera is selected only for fixed amount of time, we may just store the current frame of the selected video.

The diversity scores for two candidate videos (Cam 1, Cam 2) and final mashup created using MoViMash for a performance (P3 in Table 2) are shown in the Figure 5. Although we are showing diversity for only two videos for clarity, there were five candidate videos in total. We can see that whenever a video gets selected, its diversity generally reduces, e.g., diversity of Cam 1 after Shot 8 and diversity of Cam 2 after Shot 3. At Shot 4, Cam 1 gets selected despite low diversity because its video quality is much better than others (Figure 5.a-b) with a stable view. Sometimes the diversity increases even when the video is currently selected (Shot 2, Cam 1) due to change in camera view, or when one of previous selections of the video moves out of history window. The diversity of Cam 2 decreases even though it is not selected. It is because during this time, its view is similar to Cam 1, resulting in large (near 1) value of v_{12} (Equation 15). At Shot 9, a third (other than Cam 1 and Cam 2) video gets selected until Cam 1's diversity increases enough so that it gets selected again. In summary, the metric S^d is able to capture and spatial and temporal diversity of videos.

3.7 Final Ranking

For all the videos of the selected class, we have three metrics: video quality score, diversity score, and shakiness score. We calculated weighted sum of these values to calculate final score S^f:

$$S^f = \alpha_1 S^q + \alpha_2 S^d + \alpha_3(1 - S^s) \qquad (17)$$

where α_1, α_2, and α_3 are weighting coefficients and $\alpha_1 + \alpha_2 + \alpha_3 = 1$. In the experiments, we are using $\alpha_1 = \alpha_2 = \alpha_3$, which gives equal weightage to the quality, diversity, and stability of the videos. Nevertheless, these coefficients should be determined based on the type of performance. For instance, in a hip-hop video mashup we can give less weightage to shakiness for better diversity and quality. A shaky video, however, can be annoying if the performance has smooth movements such as a tango performance. We therefore need to keep α_3 higher in this case. Furthermore, if the videos are generally bad in the quality, we can give set high value for α_1. The shot from the video with the highest score is selected at the current time instant.

Table 2: Details of the dataset

Performance	Type	Recordings	Duration (m)	Frame rate	Resolution
P1	Group Dance	12	4'	30	720*480
P2	Group Dance	12	3'50"	30	720*480
P3	Solo Singing	5	2'5"	25	640*480

3.8 Length Selection

To determine the switching instant, we are using a method which combines the learning based prediction to obey the editing rules and the superiority (in terms of overall quality) of the currently selected video. As discussed in the learning section (Section 3.4), every class of the videos follows a length distribution. For example the center videos are generally selected for longer duration while the left and right videos for relatively smaller duration.

Suppose the length predicted for the current class of the videos is L^e. To accommodate the quality of the selected video in length calculation, we define bonus length L^b. The purpose of the bonus length is to reward the high quality videos by extending their length. Suppose S_1^f is the final combined score of the best camera and S_2^f of the second best camera. Now the length for the currently selected video, L^s, is determined as follows:

$$L^s = (1 - \varsigma)L^e + \varsigma L^b \upsilon \qquad (18)$$

where υ is the difference of the scores, i.e., $\upsilon = S_1^f - S_2^f$ and ς is weighting coefficient. In our experiments, we found the empirical values of $L^b = 25$ and $\varsigma = 0.1$ works well. A higher value of ς will increase impact of the bonus length L^b on the selected shot length. In this way, ς can be manipulated to override the prediction made by learned statistics to select longer or shorter shots of given quality score S^f.

In general cases, camera switching only takes place after the selected length of time. MoViMash, however, performs continuous check on occlusion and shakiness every second, and whenever the value goes above threshold (same as the one used in the filtering step), video selection is triggered. We added this optimization to take care of the situations where the view gets occluded after it is selection. While a lower video quality can still be acceptable, an occluded or shaky video annoys the viewers.

4. EVALUATION

The main goal of the experiments is to show that the proposed framework produces a mashup with better view quality and diversity than earlier works. In addition, we also compare our result with human-edited versions of mashups. The dataset consists of video recordings of four performances. For each performance, we create three mashups: (1) using proposed framework (MoViMash) (2) based on ranking average of shakiness, diversity, and video quality

Figure 6: Selected frames from the recordings: (a-d) P1, (e-h) P2, (i-l) P3

only (VQ-Only) (3) by human editor with editing experience (H-Edited). Users are asked to rate the quality of all three versions of mashup.

4.1 Dataset

The main application of the proposed framework is to combine the videos recorded by mobile phone users. Therefore, we went to three public performances and handed over smart phones to the audiences for recording. The audience were given a scenario where they were recording the video for sharing with their friends who were not present at the performance. All the performances happened during the night time. The video clips are converted to a common resolution and synchronized before generating the mashups. In this work, we synchronized the videos manually as our main focus is on video selection. The issue of automatic synchronization is being researched separately [14]. The details of the performances and video recordings are given in the Table 2. Figure 6 shows selected frames for each performance.

4.2 User Study

In the user study, we ask the users to watch the mashups created by the three methods and rate them accordingly. A total of seventeen users participated in the study, with age range from 20 to 30. The users were mainly graduate students, males and females. The three methods used to create the mashups were not disclosed to the users. Further, the order of the videos produced by the different methods was randomized for different performances to reduce the bias the users may have due to particular presentation order.

The user study was conducted online with relevant instructions explained beforehand. It is told to the users that "the main purpose of this user study is to evaluate quality of video editing". Users were asked to rate three distinct performance (P1, P2 and P3). The three mashups (generated by MoViMash, VQ-Only and H-Edited) are juxtaposed on a website with questions below them. The users were allowed to replay the videos while answering the questions. The users rate the videos with a rating ranged between 1 to 5, where 1 represent worst and 5 being the best. The list of questions asked are given in Table 3.

Table 3: User study questions

A	Quality of video editing
B	Visual quality of video
C	Camera positioning in the video
D	Interestingness (does video editing makes an interesting overview of the performance?)
E	Overall quality (how likely you will recommend the video to a friend?)

4.3 Result Analysis

The average responses of the users, along with their standard deviations, are plotted in Figure 7 and Figure 8. We observed responses of the users for Questions A,B,C,D to be similar and with slight variation for Question E.

4.3.1 Analysis of Questions A, B, C, and D

We observed that majority of users responded homogeneously for all four of them. The responses indicated that the ratings were based on some distinct characteristics of the video. Based on additional comments provided by the users, we infer that most of user ratings were based on the quality of the selected video and coverage of stage areas.

For P2 and P3, the users preferred the MoViMash created mashup. For both the performances, user's found the shot transitions to be smooth and pleasing. We relate this response of the user's to our class-based learning for predicting the shot transitions. The users also remarked that MoViMash produced videos had less occlusions in comparison with VQ-Only based mashup.

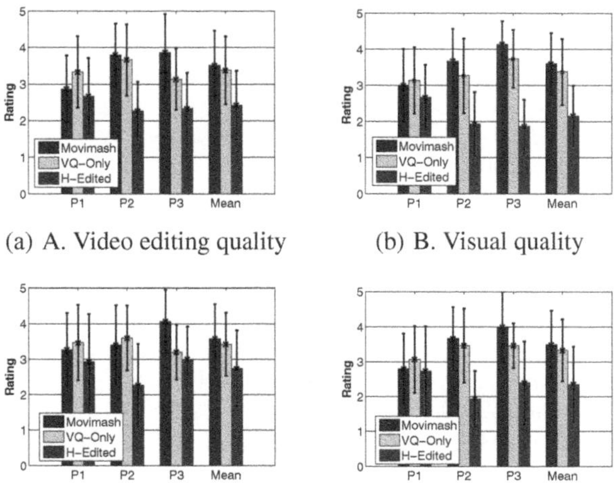

(a) A. Video editing quality (b) B. Visual quality

(c) C. Camera positioning (d) D. Interestingness

Figure 7: User responses for questions A, B, C, and D

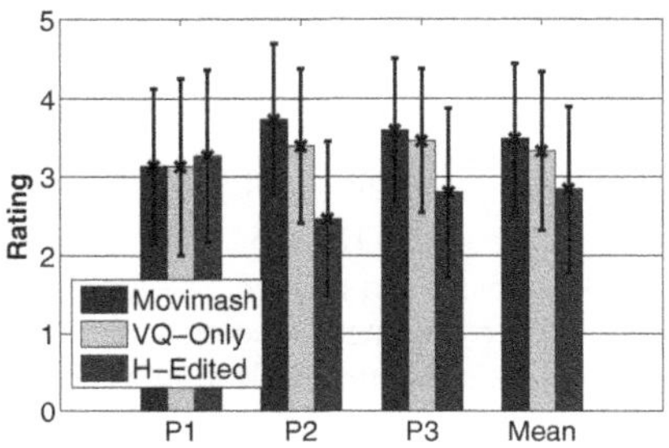

Figure 8: User response on overall quality of video

While users liked MoViMash created mashups of P2 and P3, they preferred VQ-Only mashup for P1. By analyzing the recordings and user comments, we found that P1 differs from P2 and P3 in a common aspect. While P2 and P3 had a large number of similar quality videos to select from at each time instant, the videos recordings of P1 were skewed with respect to quality. There were 2 to 3 videos which were stable and had very high video quality, whereas all other videos were relatively bad in quality. Since MoViMash attempts to maximize diversity along with video quality through class-based shot selection, sometimes poor quality videos are selected.

On the other hand, P2 and P3 had many similar quality videos to choose from, which allowed MoViMash to select videos of different classes with smooth transitions. Therefore, in the scenarios where the quality of videos is skewed with only few good quality videos, our MoViMash should be tuned to give more priority to the quality rather than smooth transitions. The further tuning can be done by selecting video from multiple future classes. However, with proliferation of mobile camera, we envision that in future the number of video recording will increase. An increased number of recordings will ensure that there are sufficient number of reasonably good quality videos to ensure diversity of shots and smooth transitions.

The human-edited version received lowest ratings for all three performances. After discussing with the human editor, we found that most of video editing techniques they learn assume availability of high quality videos. The video artifacts such as small camera shake, illumination variation etc. are generally negligible in these high quality videos. Therefore, they are generally not comfortable with the videos captured by mobile devices. Further, it would be very difficult for a human editor to evaluate and precisely compare quality of videos, particularly when the number of videos is large. The performance of video editors can get even worse when they have to make video selection in real-time. This finding makes a strong case for automated mashup creation for live applications of video sharing and broadcasting.

4.3.2 Overall Video Quality

User ratings for overall video quality are shown in the Figure 8. We can see that on average, MoViMash outperforms other methods in overall video quality. Users generally liked the quality of videos created by MoViMash for all three performances. Further, the user ratings related to MoViMash had the least standard deviation among all three mashups. This result implies that the users had highly correlated opinion about the superiority of MoViMash. According to the comments users provided to justify their overall video quality ratings, they liked following things about MoViMash: complete coverage (from many angles), smooth shot transitions, less occlusion, and balanced camera selection. Yet, there might be instances where the semantics of the video govern the video selection, e.g., celebrity appearance, funny behavior by crowd, interesting gestures and expressions by audiences, etc. It is hard for the proposed automatic system to identify these instances; and a human can be introduced in the selection to improve the mashup quality in such scenarios.

It is important to note that although many users liked VQ-Only created videos more than MoViMash, they did not specify any concrete aspect they liked about the video except selection of less shaky videos. Thus, for the given dataset, even though VQ-Only method is also able to produce videos with reasonable good quality, it will fail in many real scenarios as it does not have any provision for view quality and smooth shot transitions

4.4 Discussion

The MoViMash framework takes automatic mashup creation methods closer to the human editors. It, however, adds to the processing cost. The enhanced diversity model requires more memory for storing the history and more number of comparisons. Similarly, occlusion and tilt also require data processing that would have quadratic complexity in terms of the number of pixels in the image. Therefore, individual components of the framework could be enabled or disabled depending on the quality of the candidate videos. For example, if the videos are taken from the stand-mounted cameras, shakiness calculation can be omitted. Furthermore, to make the system scalable, we can process downscaled images as the video resolution is not critical for the current system components.

5. CONCLUSIONS & FUTURE WORK

In this paper, we have proposed and validated an online video mashup creation framework, MoViMash, for videos recorded by mobile devices. Based on the experiments and user study, we make following conclusions:

- MoViMash creates better quality mashups in comparison to human editor, and other methods that are mainly based on video quality.

- Proposed learning framework is able to imitate professional editor's experience to have smooth shot transitions in the final mashup. The proposed framework is most effective when there are a number of similar visual quality videos to chose from.

- The proposed framework is able to filter occluded and tilted views providing better viewing experience to the users.
- Human editors are not comfortable in editing videos that are recorded by mobile devices, particularly when there are large number of videos with varying quality.
- Proposed diversity model is able to incorporate both temporal and spatial aspects of the selection history.

In the future, we want to extensively evaluate individual components of the system with respect to end-to-end system delay and output mashup quality. As current mobiles are capable of recording full HD video, we want to insert artificial zoom and pan in the mashup using zoomable video techniques [11]. Further, a human director can only compare a limited number of videos at a time. A powerful computer, however, can process and compare a large number of videos simultaneously. Therefore, in the future we want to study the impact of the number of videos on the quality of the final mashup.

Acknowledgment

This research is conducted under the NExT Search Center, supported by the Singapore National Research Foundation and the Interactive Digital Media R&D Program Office of Media Development Authority under research grant WBS:R-252-300-001-490.

6. REFERENCES

[1] http://www.bloomberg.com/news/2011-04-07/high-resolution-cameras-will-drive-mobile-phone-shipments-above-1-billion.html.

[2] http://www.businesswire.com/news/home/20110829005068/en/photobucket-survey-video-uploads-mobile-devices-rise.

[3] M. Al-Hames, B. Hörnler, C. Scheuermann, and G. Rigoll. Using audio, visual, and lexical features in a multi-modal virtual meeting director. In *Proc. of Machine Learning for Multimodal Interaction*, pages 63–74. Springer, Bethesda, MD, USA, May 2006.

[4] M. Campanella, H. Weda, and M. Barbieri. Edit while watching: home video editing made easy. In *Proc. of SPIE 19th Ann. Symp. Electronic Imaging, Multimedia Content Access: Algorithms and Systems*, volume 6506, page 21, San Jose, CA, USA, January 2007.

[5] F. Crete, T. Dolmiere, P. Ladret, and M. Nicolas. The blur effect: perception and estimation with a new no-reference perceptual blur metric. In *Proc. of SPIE Human Vision and Electronic Imaging XII*, volume 6492, San Jose, CA, USA, January 2007.

[6] R. Cutler, Y. Rui, A. Gupta, J. Cadiz, I. Tashev, L. He, A. Colburn, Z. Zhang, Z. Liu, and S. Silverberg. Distributed meetings: A meeting capture and broadcasting system. In *Proc. of ACM International Conference on Multimedia*, pages 503–512. ACM, Juan Les Pins, France, December 2002.

[7] E. de Lima, C. Pozzer, M. d'Ornellas, A. Ciarlini, B. Feijó, and A. Furtado. Virtual cinematography director for interactive storytelling. In *Proc. of International Conference on Advances in Computer Enterntainment Technology*, pages 263–270, Athens, Greece, October 2009.

[8] A. Engstrom, M. Esbjornsson, O. Juhlin, and M. Perry. Producing collaborative video: developing an interactive user experience for mobile tv. In *Proc. of the International Conference on Designing Interactive User Experiences for TV and Video*, pages 115–124, Silicon Valley, CA, USA, October 2008.

[9] E. Machnicki and L. Rowe. Virtual director: Automating a webcast. In *Proc. of the SPIE Multimedia Computing and Networking*, volume 4673, 2002.

[10] A. K. Moorthy, P. Obrador, and N. Oliver. Towards computational models of the visual aesthetic appeal of consumer videos. In *Proc. of the 11th European conference on Computer vision: Part V*, pages 1–14, Crete, Greece, September 2010.

[11] N. Quang Minh Khiem, G. Ravindra, A. Carlier, and W. Ooi. Supporting zoomable video streams with dynamic region-of-interest cropping. In *Proc. of the first annual ACM SIGMM Conference on Multimedia Systems*, pages 259–270. ACM, 2010.

[12] A. Ranjan, R. Henrikson, J. Birnholtz, R. Balakrishnan, and D. Lee. Automatic camera control using unobtrusive vision and audio tracking. In *Proc. of Graphics Interface*, pages 47–54. Canadian Information Processing Society, Ottawa, Ontario, Canada, May 2010.

[13] A. Senior, A. Hampapur, Y. Tian, L. Brown, S. Pankanti, and R. Bolle. Appearance models for occlusion handling. *Image and Vision Computing*, 24(11):1233–1243, 2006.

[14] P. Shrestha, M. Barbieri, and H. Weda. Synchronization of multi-camera video recordings based on audio. In *Proc of ACM International Conference on Multimedia*, pages 545–548, Augsburg, Germany, September 2007.

[15] P. Shrestha, H. de With Peter, H. Weda, M. Barbieri, and E. Aarts. Automatic mashup generation from multiple-camera concert recordings. In *Proc. of ACM International Conference on Multimedia*, pages 541–550, Firenze, Italy, October 2010.

[16] J. Wang, C. Xu, E. Chng, H. Lu, and Q. Tian. Automatic composition of broadcast sports video. *Multimedia Systems*, 14(4):179–193, 2008.

[17] Z. Wang, A. C. Bovik, H. R. Sheikh, and E. P. Simoncelli. Image quality assessment: From error visibility to structural similarity. *IEEE Trans. on Image Processing*, 13(4):600–612, 2004.

[18] Z. Wang, H. Sheikh, and A. Bovik. No-reference perceptual quality assessment of jpeg compressed images. In *Proc. of IEEE International Conference on Image Processing*, pages 477–480, Rochester, NY, USA, September 2002.

[19] T. Yang, Q. Pan, J. Li, and S. Li. Real-time multiple objects tracking with occlusion handling in dynamic scenes. In *Proc. of IEEE Conference on Computer Vision and Pattern Recognition*, pages 970–975, San Diego, CA, USA, June 2005.

[20] B. Yu, C. Zhang, Y. Rai, and K. Nahrstedt. A three-layer virtual director model for supporting automated multi-site distributed education. In *IEEE International Conference on Multimedia and Expo*, pages 637–640, Toronto, Ontario, Canada, July 2006.

[21] C. Zhang, Y. Rui, J. Crawford, and L. He. An automated end-to-end lecture capture and broadcasting system. *ACM Tran. on Multimedia Computing, Communications, and Applications*, 4(1):6:1–6:23, 2008.

An Interactive System of Stereoscopic Video Conversion

Zhebin Zhang[†] Chen Zhou[†] Bo Xin[†] Yizhou Wang[†‡] Wen Gao[†‡]
[†]National Engineering Lab. for Video Technology,
[‡]Key Lab. of Machine Perception (MoE),
School of EECS, Peking University, Beijing, 100871, China
{zbzhang, zhouch, boxin, yizhou.wang, wgao}@pku.edu.cn

ABSTRACT

With the recent booming of 3DTV industry, more and more stereoscopic videos are demanded by the market. This paper presents a system of converting conventional monocular videos to stereoscopic ones. In this system, an input video is firstly segmented into shots to reduce operations on similar frames. Then, automatic depth estimation and interactive image segmentation are integrated to obtain depth maps and foreground/background segments on selected key frames. Within each video shot, such results are propagated from key frames to non-key frames. Combined with a depth-to-disparity conversion method, the system synthesizes the counterpart (either left or right) view for stereoscopic display by warping the original frame according to disparity maps. For evaluation, we use human labeled depth map as the reference and compute both the mean opinion score (MOS) and Peak signal-to-noise ratio (PSNR) to evaluate the converted video quality. Experiment results demonstrate that the proposed conversion system and methods achieves encouraging performance.

Categories and Subject Descriptors

H.4 [**Information Systems Applications**]: Miscellaneous; I.4.8 [**Image Processing and Computer Vision**]: Scene Analysis—*Sensor fusion, Depth cues*

Keywords

3DTV, 2D-to-3D conversion, depth estimation, depth to disparity, foreground segmentation

1. INTRODUCTION

Due to the amazing development speed of 3DTV industry, e.g. broadcasting of many 3D channels, the number of available stereoscopic videos is largely inadequate to satisfy the great demand of the market even with the new-make of such videos using stereoscopic cameras. Converting conventional monocular videos into stereoscopic ones is definitely a complimentary solution.

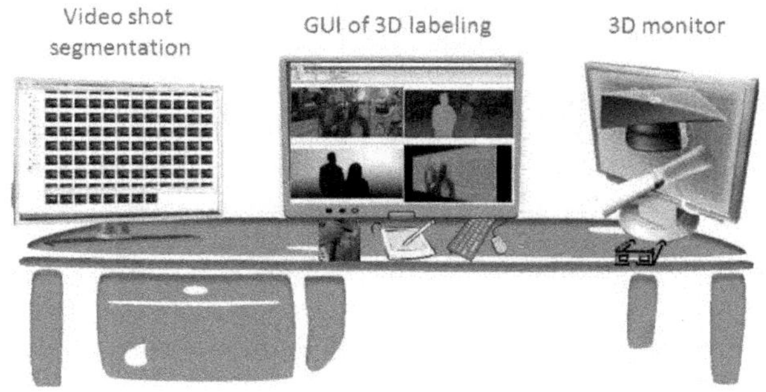

Figure 1: The interfaces of the stereoscopic conversion system.

However, automatic 2D-to-3D video conversion still remains a challenging problem. This is mainly because that the core problem – depth from monocular view – has not been solved. Although there exist techniques to estimate depth from monocular image sequences, such as structure from motion (SfM) [28], it requires such a constrained camera motion and foreground stillness and rigidity assumptions that a large proportion of real videos falls beyond its regime. In addition, in order to obtain good estimate, these algorithms always require high quality intermediate results such as good correspondence matching and motion estimation. Whereas, in real videos, such requirement may be too demanding due to all kinds of variations and occlusions.

In this paper, an interactive system is proposed to convert monocular videos into stereoscopic ones (shown in Figure 1). We introduce human in the loop only to rescue the deficiency of the state-of-the-art algorithms. In the system, advanced video processing techniques are embedded so as to increase the conversion efficiency. Specifically, before the conversion, the system segments an input monocular video into shots so that the labeled information such as foreground object contours and depths can be propagated efficiently and reliably within each shot. We propose a new multi-cue depth estimation method by integrating a few robust monocular depth perception cues adopted by human beings, such as depth from defocus, depth from aerial perspective, depth from motion. These cues largely improve the depth estimation performance by freeing the constraints of the structure from motion (SfM) method and its extensions (e.g. [16],[28]). Using the proposed method, the estimated depth is continuous and its range is much wider than SfM based methods. To improve the stereoscopic visual quality, we adopt interactive methods to segment foreground objects, and estimate their shape and depth position in particular. We propose to integrate depth information in tracking algorithms so as to improve the foreground object tracking accuracy within each shot. Moreover, a depth-to-disparity conversion model based on supervised learning is proposed, which predicts foreground disparity according to its motion, screen location and the background motion. The disparities of the rest pixels are computed according the their relative depth w.r.t. the foreground object. This method automatic generates inside/on/outside screen visual effect learned from stereoscopic movies.

In summary the proposed interactive 2D-to-3D conversion system is easy to operate, and the conversion is robust and efficient, it adapts to a wide range of depth estimation from monocular videos.

Another contribution of the paper is that, due to the lack of evaluation methods in this field (especially on conventional movies), we propose one using human labeled depth maps as reference so as to assess the visual quality of converted stereoscopic videos both subjectively and objectively. Specifically, we compute both the mean opinion score (MOS) and Peak signal-to-noise ratio (PSNR) to evaluate the converted video quality. The experiment results demonstrate the advantage of the proposed system.

The rest of the paper is organized as follows: some closely related work is introduced in Section 2. In Section 3, we describe the work flow and architecture of the system, followed by expatiations of important functions and methods in Section 4. In section 5, evaluation and experimental results are provided. Finally, Section 6 concludes the paper.

2. RELATED WORK

In the literature, the 2D-to-3D conversion methods can be roughly categorized into two classes, the automatic conversion and interactive conversion. Automatic conversion methods (e.g. [12][13][20][22]) exploit motion cues to predict the depth/disparity of pixels. Some commercial softwares, such as DDD's TriDef 3D player and Samsung's 3DTV, leverage both motion and image location priors to generate stereoscopic views from monocular videos. However, the motion cues, e.g. optical flows, can be unreliable to extract in real image sequences, and motion parallax can be ambiguous in estimating relative depth between objects in a complex dynamic system (i.e. multiple objects moving with different velocities at different depths). In addition, specific image location assumptions can be too strong to be true, e.g. the bottom region of an image is closer to view point compared to the upper part. In conclusion, fully automatic conversion methods usually are incompetent to give an accurate estimation of depth/disparities of a scene given the current state of the art computer vision algorithms.

The other category of conversion methods exploit user interactions. For example, in [6] and [16], at key frames, user scribbles are used to initialize depth values and depth layers of objects in a scene respectively, and then the depth information is automatically propagated to non-key-frames. Compared with these methods, the proposed model integrates more monocular cues in depth estimation, so that it adapts to more variety real videos and generate a wider estimation of continuous depth range. IMAX developed a

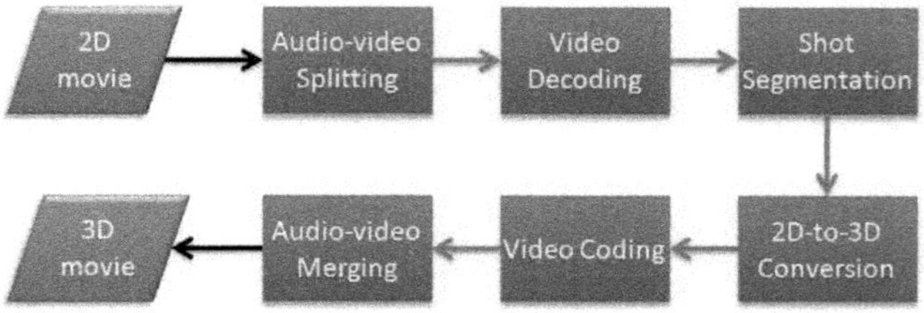

Figure 2: The work flow of the conversion system.

sophisticated interactive conversion commercial system [11], which requires intensive manual work and can generate impressive stereoscopic visual effect.

Estimating pixel disparities/depth from monocular videos is the key step in 2D-to-3D video conversion and it is an active yet challenging research topic in computer vision. Researchers took advantage of various cues for this task, such as photometry cues, e.g. [8][21][29], geometry cues, e.g. [4][5], motion cues, e.g. [12][13][20][22] and appearance cues, e.g. [6][24]. In the following we review these work even though some of them has not been applied to stereoscopic video conversion yet.

Photometry cues Objects in an image usually are not all in focus [21]. Valencia *et. al.* [29] used wavelet analysis and edge de-focus estimation to obtain relative depth. Besides, scene atmospheric light also facilitates depth perception. Atmospheric radiance images of outdoor scenes are usually degraded by the turbid medium in the atmosphere. Irradiance received by a camera from a scene point is attenuated along the line of sight. He *et. al.* [8] proposed a dark channel prior to remove haze and also provided estimated depth map of a scene.

Geometry cues Parallel edge lines converging at infinity due to perspective projection provide us a convenient geometry formulation to reconstruct the relative distance between objects [4][5][7].

Motion cues Under the condition of constrained camera motion and assuming that scenes are static, there are two ways to estimate disparity maps, using (i) Structure from Motion (SfM), e.g. [28], and (ii) motion parallax [12]. However, in real scenario such as movies, the constrained camera motion condition and static scene assumption are often violated, which leads to the failure of applying the two methods in disparity estimation.

Appearance cues By using appearance features from superpixels (e.g. color, texture and shape), Hoiem *et. al.* [9] casted the depth estimation from single images to a multilabel classification problem. Saxena *et. al.* [24] employed Markov random field (MRF) to model the unstructured scene and directly learned the relation between the planar 3D structures and the superpixel's texture and color features. Both methods adopted supervised learning strategy, which requires training data to learn the model; this makes them difficult to be generalized to real data beyond the distribution of the training data sets.

3. SYSTEM OVERVIEW

As shown in Figure 2, the whole system starts with splitting video and audio apart, followed by video decoding, and then it converts the video into a stereoscopic one. After this, it compresses the video by the same codec, and finally the

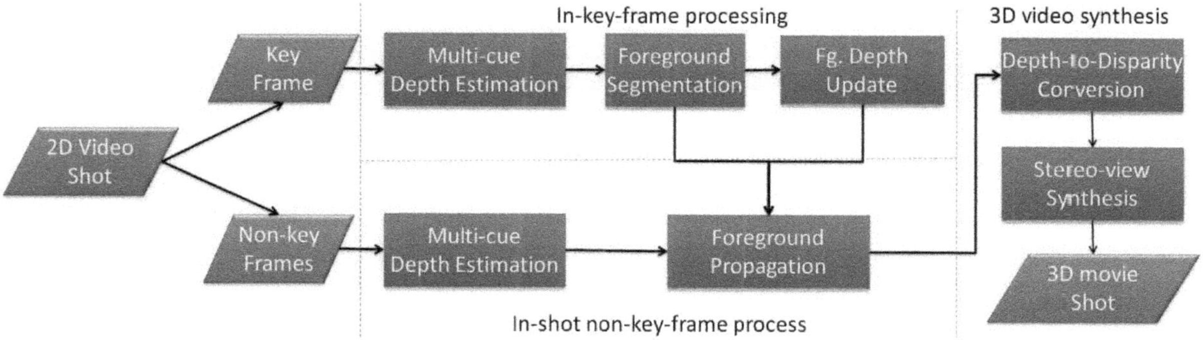

Figure 3: The flowchart of the *2D-to-3D conversion module* in Figure 2.

system merges the coded video with the original audio into a required video file format. The system is designed to reduce interactive operations as far as possible. Hence, before a video is sent to the 2D-to-3D conversion module, the whole video is segmented into shots so that the labeled information can be reliably propagated within a shot (Figure 5).

3.1 The interfaces and interactions

The proposed system interacts with users through the following three interfaces (shown in Figure 1).

A shot segmentation interface (shown in Figure 5), where users can select certain shots to process.

A 3D labeling interface consists of four windows as shown in Figure 4 (a). In window 1, user scribbles on foreground objects and their vicinity regions of background in a video frame, so that foreground objects are segmented semiautomatically. Window 2 displays estimated depth map of a frame. In window 3, both foreground objects and background are displayed in a 3D grid so that the user can clearly see their relative depth in 3D space. In addition, a virtual screen (the green plane) is provided to demonstrate their relative position w.r.t to the display (i.e. whether an object is inside, on or outside the screen). The depth value of every pixel of a scene as well as the virtual screen are manually adjustable, so the user can easily correct depth estimation errors, and acquire desired rendering effect w.r.t. the screen. Window 4 shows a color map demonstrating the inside/on/outside screen distribution of the objects in a scene. Red areas indicate that the regions are outside of the screen, green is on the screen, and blue is inside the screen.

A stereoscopic monitor, where users can examine the rendered stereoscopic effect of converted key frames and videos. If the results are not satisfying, users can refine it by adjusting the labels through the 3D labeling interface.

4. 2D-TO-3D CONVERSION METHODS

The proposed system first segments an input video into shots, then converts each shot into stereoscopic one with in following steps (shown in Figure 3): (i) An initial depth map for each frame is automatically predicted by a proposed multi-cue depth estimation method. (ii) In order to refine the initial depth map, for key frames, foreground objects are interactively labeled and segmented out from background. Consequently, the depth values in the foreground regions are updated. (iii) The foreground/ background labels are propagated to other frames and their initial depth maps are

(a) Object segmentation interaction

(b) Interactive object segmentation

(c) Contour refinement

Figure 4: Segmentation of foreground objects.

also updated in the foreground regions; (iv) A disparity map for each frame is predicted using trained models. (v) The stereo view of the frame is synthesized based on the original frame and the disparity map.

In the rest of the section, we introduce the details of each step.

4.1 Shot segmentation

Video shots are defined as a set of meaningful and manageable segments which share the same background setting [15]. Consequently, information can be easily propagated within a shot. Our video segmentation algorithm follows the following steps: (i) feature extraction, (ii) dissimilarity computation between frames and (iii) shot boundary detection.

Feature extraction Both color histogram and tiny image [27] are used as features. In detail, a color histogram in RGB space with 16 bins for each channel is computed from a frame. To better preserve structural information, a frame is down-sampled by 16 times resulting in a 24×12 pixel tiny image.

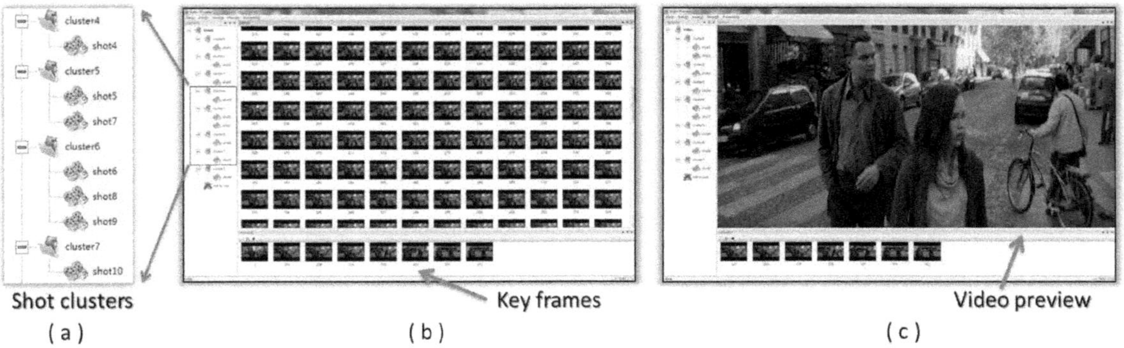

Figure 5: Video shot segmentation interface.

Dissimilarity computation In [17], Liu *et. al.* defined a dissimilarity metric of two images as a combination of L_1 norm distance between their color histograms and mutual information between them. A similar definition of dissimilarity metric is proposed in this paper, except that the contribution of tiny image is taken into consideration.

Let $C_i(k)$ and $T_i(k)$ denote the color histogram and tiny image pixel value for the ith frame respectively, where k is one of the K_* possible values ($K_C = 48$ for color histogram and $K_T = 24 \times 12$ for tiny image in our case). Then the L_1 norm distances between two color histograms and two tiny images are defined as $\Gamma_C(i,j) = \sum_{k=1}^{K_C} |C_i(k) - C_j(k)|$ and $\Gamma_T(i,j) = \sum_{k=1}^{K_T} |T_i(k) - T_j(k)|$, respectively. The mutual information between the ith and the jth frame is computed based on color, $MI(C_i, C_j) = H(C_i) + H(C_j) - H(C_i, C_j)$.

Finally, the dissimilarity between two frames is

$$\Gamma(i,j) = w_C * \frac{\Gamma_C(i,j)}{MI(C_i, C_j)} + w_T * \Gamma_T(i,j), \qquad (1)$$

where $w_C = w_T = 0.5$ in our implementation.

Shot boundary detection To decide shot boundaries, an adaptive segmentation threshold at frame t is proposed as,

$$T(t) = \eta * \frac{\sum_{i=2}^{t} \Gamma(i, i-1)}{t-1}, \qquad (2)$$

where i indexes the ith frame of one shot. It is an averaged dissimilarly up to frame t multiplying with a factor η, which is introduced to avoid under-segmentation ($\eta = 4.0$ in our implementation). A shot boundary is marked at t, when $\Gamma(t, t-1) > T(t)$.

4.2 Depth estimation by multi-cue fusion

In this paper, we deliberately select three depth perception cues to estimate the initial depth map of video frames, *i.e. motion cue, defocus cue and aerial perspective cue*, because each of them governs a different range of depth estimation. Using SfM method is able to accurately estimation scene depth at near distance; defocus cue is good to predict mid-range depth; and aerial perspective cue can give reasonable estimate of scene depth at a far distance. Although each cue alone cannot reliably recover the depth of a scene due to its algorithmic flaws (for example, motion cue is not applicable to textureless regions, a bright or gray colored object in front will be labeled as a distant object if using the aerial perspective cue, and the depth ambiguity in defocus cue), the combination of the three usually is able to robustly estimate scene depth by compensating the weakness of each other.

Denote the depth map of a frame I predicted by each cue as $\alpha_m(I)$, $\alpha_d(I)$, $\alpha_a(I)$, respectively. Let x be the coordinates of a pixel on I, Then, its depth value is fused by

$$\alpha(x) = w_m \alpha_m(x) + w_d \alpha_d(x) + w_a \alpha_a(x), \qquad (3)$$

where w_m, w_d, w_h are the fusing weights for each cue. In this paper, $w_m = w_d = w_a = 1/3$. Fig.6(b) shows an example depth map by the multi-cue estimation.

Next we introduce depth estimation from each cue.

Depth from aerial perspective cue. As described in [8], the irradiance attenuates along the sight in a scene. Here we use it as one depth cue.

$$\alpha_h(x) = -\epsilon \ln t(x), \qquad (4)$$

where ϵ is the scattering coefficient of the atmosphere and $t(x)$ is the medium transmission, which is estimated using the dark-channel prior proposed in [8],

$$t(x) = 1 - \omega \min_c(\min_{y \in \Omega} \frac{I^c(y)}{A^c}), \qquad (5)$$

where ω is a constant parameter $0 < \omega < 1$, y is a pixel in a local patch centered at x, $I^c(y)$ is the intensity value in the color channel c (in RGB color space), and A^c is the atmospheric light intensity (please refer to [8] for the details of estimating A^c).

Pseudo-depth from motion. Here we make very simple assumptions that object with smaller motion is further away from the viewing point,

$$\alpha_m(x) = 1 - \frac{m(x)}{\max_{x \in I} m(x)}, \qquad (6)$$

where $m(x)$ is the optical flow magnitude at pixel x.

Although the assumption is simple, it is generally true especially for background, as the foreground objects are treated particularly in the system at a later stage (see Section 4.3).

Depth from defocus. In movies, cameramen often take advantage of focus/defocus skills to enhance visual effect, e.g. closeups. Thus depth from defocus can be applied to many video shots. In our system, we estimate depth from defocus as follow,

1. 2D wavelet transform is applied to a frame at three scales.

2. The degree factor is defined as

$$\varepsilon(x) = \frac{1}{|\partial x|} \sum_{y \in \partial x} \omega(y)/F(y), \tag{7}$$

where y is a pixel in the neighbor ∂x of x, $F(x)$ is the maximum spectral energies of the wavelets at the three scales. $\omega(y)$ is the weight on pixel y's focus degree. $\omega(y)$ is computed as

$$\omega(y) = e^{-\frac{||x-y||}{s(f(x),f(y))}} \tag{8}$$

where $||\cdot||$ is the Euclidean norm, $f(x)$ is color feature vector in RGB, $s(f(x), f(y))$ is the Cosine distance function between the two color vectors at pixel x and y.

3. Then, the depth estimated by defocus cue is computed as

$$\alpha_d(x) = \frac{\varepsilon(x)}{\max_{x \in I} \varepsilon(x)}. \tag{9}$$

4.3 Foreground depth refinement

It is important to get accurate depth maps for key frames; Not only does it ensure the quality of stereo visual effect, but also provide seeds for depth propagation to the other frames in a video shot. Although the above multi-cue fusion method can provide a good depth estimation for background, the depth values of foreground pixels can be inaccurate if the foreground is in motion. Moreover, cognitive studies [14] suggested that human visual system is more sensitive to the quality of foreground objects. With such concern, we add an interactive step for foreground depth refinement. The refinement takes the following steps, (i) interactive segmentation of foreground objects, followed by (ii) foreground depth re-estimation and interactive adjustment.

4.3.1 Foreground segmentation

The interaction for foreground segmentation is shown in Fig.4 (b), where scribbles are drawn to indicate the foreground region (in red) or background region (in yellow). To segment an object, we modify the GrabCut method [23] by adding depth information to the model. In the original GrabCut method, the segmentation label $\ell_n \in \{0,1\}$ for each pixel is obtained by iteratively minimizing an energy function

$$E(\ell, k, \theta, I) = U(\ell, k, \theta, I) + V(\ell, I), \tag{10}$$

where $U(\cdot)$ is the data term modeled by a Gaussian Mixture Model(GMM) of color with model parameter θ and k components, $V(\cdot)$ is the smoothness term, I is pixel color intensity. (Please refer to [23] for the details of the GrabCut method.) In our system, besides color, the depth values $\alpha(I)$ obtained from the multi-cue depth estimation module (described in Section 4.2) are also considered in both the data term and smoothness term. Hence, we modify the original GrabCut data term as

$$U(\ell, k, \theta, I, \alpha(I)) = \sum_{x} D(\ell_x, k_x, \theta, I(x), \alpha(x)), \tag{11}$$

where $D(\cdot) = -\lambda_c \log p(I(x)) - \lambda_\alpha \log p(\alpha(x))$, λ_c and λ_α are weights for the log probability of color and depth of GMM, respectively.

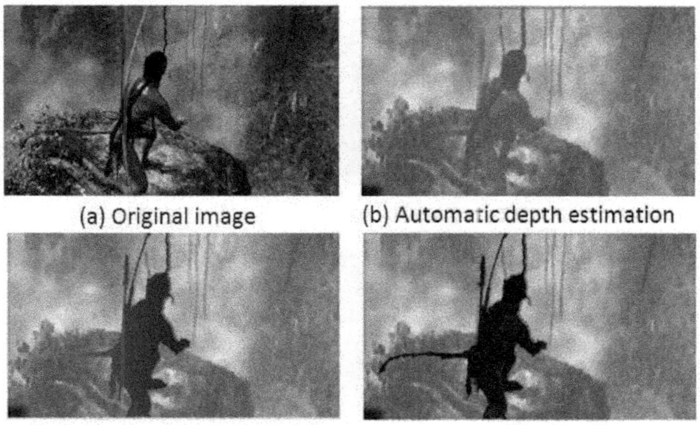

(a) Original image (b) Automatic depth estimation (c) Updating by plane model (d) Updating by defocus cue

Figure 6: Depth estimation and foreground depth re-estimate.

The modified smoothness term is

$$V(\ell, I, \alpha(I)) = \sum_{x_m \in \partial x_n} S(x_m, x_n) \tag{12}$$

where $S(\cdot) = [\ell_m \neq \ell_n] e^{-\gamma_1 ||x_m - x_n|| - \gamma_2 |\alpha(x_m) - \alpha(x_n)|}$, and $[\ell_m \neq \ell_n]$ is 1 if $\ell_m \neq \ell_n$; otherwise 0. $||x_m - x_n||$ is Euclidean distance between two pixel coordinates. $|\alpha(x_m) - \alpha(x_n)|$ is the absolute difference of the depth, which penalizes neighboring pixels of different depth values.

If the GrabCut doesn't give an accurate segmentation, the system provide users with interactive interface to adjust object contours. We adopt Intelligent Scissors [19] to facilitate users to refine the segmentation contours efficiently. Figure 4 (c) shows the refinement of the hat contour by just dragging the three blue control points using Intelligent Scissors.

4.3.2 Foreground depth re-estimate

Foreground object depth and structure estimation can be inaccurate if the objects are in motion or no defocus cue can be leveraged. If the multi-cue depth estimation result is not satisfying for an foreground object, the system provides users to choose different methods to re-estimate the structure of an foreground object, i.e. (i) If the defocus cue is strong, user can select to use depth from defocus. An example is shown in Fig.6(d). (ii) If the object is static and the camera motion satisfies SfM constraint, user can use SfM. (iii) If no good cue to use at all, user can just adopt a plane surface model to represent the object structure as shown in Fig.6 (c).

Besides the structure of foreground objects, their locations in the scene may also need adjustment. Although the foreground depth by multi-cue fusion may be noisy, we assume that the majority of pixels are accurate; Hence, we can decide the object location/depth by majority voting the foreground pixels. Or user can manually adjust foreground object locations using the 3D labeling interface (shown in Figure 4 (a) window 4, and Figure 9).

4.4 Foreground propagation

After the foreground depth is updated, the whole depth map for a key frame is completely generated. In this section, we introduce a method which propagates the key frame

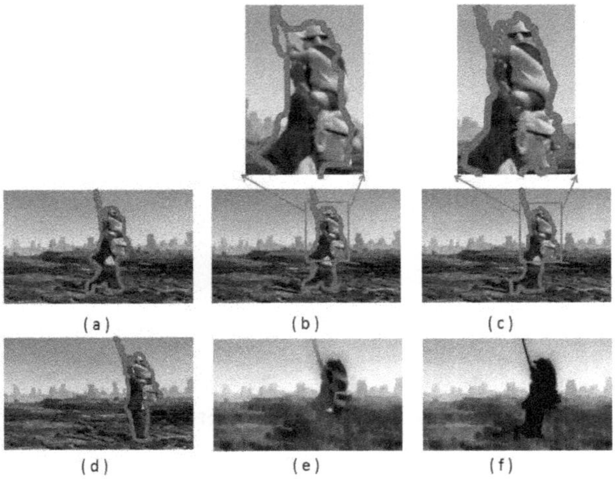

Figure 7: Foreground object tracking and depth update. (a) Labeled foreground object (red curve denotes its boundary) at a key frame $t-1$. (b) Warped foreground object contour from frame $t-1$ to frame t using KLT [18]. (c) Object boundary refinement by proposed level set method. (d) Tracked object at frame $t+1$. (e) Initial depth map estimated by multi-cue fusion at frame t. (f) The updated depth of foreground object after boundary refinement.

depth to the non-key-frames in the same shot based on object tracking and segmentation.

Given an foreground object and the depth map of a key frame, we first directly warp the object contours to the non-key-frames according to the object motion, and use the warped curve as initialization of the object location, and then evolve the warped contour to the object boundary at the non-key-frames using an adapted Level set method based on [3]. We introduce the details in the following.

Let $\phi : \Omega \rightarrow \Re^2$ be a level set function defined on a domain Ω. Then the proposed energy functional $\xi(\phi)$ is defined as

$$\xi(\phi) = \mu R_p(\phi) + E_{img}(\phi) \tag{13}$$

where μ is a constant and the level set regularization term $R_p(\phi)$ can be written as:

$$R_p(\phi) = \int_\Omega p(|\nabla\phi|)dx, \tag{14}$$

where p is a potential function $p : [0, \infty) \rightarrow \Re$

$$p(\phi) = \frac{1}{2}\int_\Omega (|\nabla\phi| - 1)^2 dx. \tag{15}$$

It is a metric to characterize how close a function $|\nabla\phi|$ is to a signed distance function which must satisfy a desirable property of $|\nabla\phi| = 1$ in $\Omega \rightarrow \Re^2$.

$E_{img}(\phi)$ is the adapted term of the external energy in [3]. It depends upon the image data and depth map:

$$E_{img}(\phi) = aL_g(\phi) + bA_g(\phi) + c\Delta_\kappa(\phi) \tag{16}$$

where a, b and c are the coefficients of the energy functionals $L_g(\phi)$, $A_g(\phi)$ and $D_d(\phi)$, respectively.

$$L_g(\phi) = \int_\Omega g\delta(\phi)(|\nabla\phi|)dx \tag{17}$$

Figure 8: Results for depth propagation in a video shot.

$$A_g(\phi) = \int_\Omega gH(-\phi)dx \tag{18}$$

and

$$\Delta_\kappa(\phi) = \int_\Omega \kappa H(-\phi)dx \tag{19}$$

where δ and H are the Dirac delta function and the Heaviside function, respectively. Function g is defined as an edge indicator by

$$g = \frac{1}{1 + |\nabla G_\sigma * I|^2} \tag{20}$$

where I denotes for the frame on the domain Ω, and G_σ is a Gaussian kernel with a standard deviation σ. $L_g(\phi)$ relates to the length of the zero level curve ϕ and $A_g(\phi)$ is introduced to accelerate the process of curve evolution.

In the proposed propagation method, we integrate depth map into the level set data term, the function κ is defined as

$$\kappa = \frac{1}{1 + \sum_{x,y \in N} |\alpha(x) - \alpha(y)|} \tag{21}$$

where N is a set of neighborhood pixels x and y in the domain Ω; $\alpha(x)$ is the depth value of pixel x.

The energy functional $\Delta_\kappa(\phi)$ is a new added term to the original formulation proposed in [3]. Assuming that pixels on an object share similar depths, it is proposed to estimate accurate contours of foreground objects according to the gradient field of a depth map in addition to the intensity map. $\Delta_\kappa(\phi)$ is introduced to penalize the case when the depth values inside the segmented object are quite different with each other. In experiments, it confirms that the final

Figure 9: Depth labeling interface for evaluation.

Figure 10: (a) Original frame (b) Depth map in our system (c) Difference between human labeled depth and the estimated one (d) the converted stereo frame

segmentation result is improved greatly by adding this term and the object's depth is more reliable after updated based on the refined segment, as shown in Fig. 7.

To speed up the evolution process and to obtain more refined result, we initialize the level set function based on the segmentation result of its previous frame. Given the segmented foreground object, we extract SURF(Speeded Up Robust Features) [2] as feature points for feature tracking and warp contour using KLT tracking [18] method, which is a fast, efficient, scale- and rotation-invariant interest point detector. The approximate contour of the foreground object is propagated from its previous frame and can be used as a good initialization, which reduces the number of iterations to move the zero level set to the desired object boundary compared the general initialization. We apply a standard method to minimize the energy functional by finding the steady state of its gradient flow as [1].

More propagation results are shown in Figure 8. The first row shows the labeling result at frame $t-1$. The warping results using KLT [18] are shown in the second row. The direct warping seems inaccurate, especially when the displacement of the foreground objects is large, e.g. Figure 8(b). The third row displays the refined segmentation results by the proposed method. We can see the contours of the objects are localized very well. The fourth row shows the depth map estimated by the multi-cue fusion method described in section 4.2). In the fifth row, updated/re-estimated foreground depth of the objects are presented. The improvement is evident. The objects at frame $T+1$ can be reliably tracked from T using the same method.

4.5 Stereo view frame synthesis

Before stereo view synthesis, it is necessary to convert a depth map $\alpha(I)$ to a disparity map $d(I)$. The disparity value $d(x)$ at pixel x is the horizontal coordinate difference between the corresponding pixel in the left view and the right view of a stereo frame pair. When display, a pixel with negative disparity value is perceived as a point outside screen by viewers, and vice versa. A larger absolute value of $d(x)$ indicates a longer distance between the screen and the point.

In the system, a depth map $\alpha(I)$ is converted to a disparity map $d(I)$ by

$$d(x) = s \cdot W_I \cdot (\frac{\alpha(x) - \alpha_{min}(I)}{\alpha_{max}(I) - \alpha_{min}(I)} - \tau) \qquad (22)$$

where W_I is the image width, $\alpha_{max}(I)$ is the maxima of depth values. s is a control factor to restrict the maxima of absolute disparity, which makes the system adaptive to different screen sizes. Generally speaking, for devices whose screens are larger than 70 inches, s should be less than 1%. $\tau (0 \leq \tau < 1)$ is a parameter that shifts the disparity to negative value and produce inside/outside screen effects. In our system, τ is determined by the stereo effect of a reference foreground object in the scene. Let x_{ref} be the reference point on a foreground object, and $\alpha(x_{ref})$ be its depth value. τ is computed as

$$\tau = \frac{\alpha(x_{ref}) - \alpha_{min}(I)}{\alpha_{max}(I) - \alpha_{min}(I)} - \frac{d(x_{ref})}{s \cdot W_I} \qquad (23)$$

$d(x_{ref})$ is the disparity of the reference point/object, which is automatically predicted by a trained disparity estimation model - a multi-label SVM .

We use motion and position of a segmented object as the features to predict its disparity value. The feature vector is composed of four components: (i) object motion magnitude and orientation histograms, (ii) pixel location histogram of the object region ,(iii) mean and variance of the depth values (by multi-cue estimation in Section 4.2) of the object points, and (iv) the motion magnitude and orientation histograms of the background region, which is an indication of camera motion.

In the learning phase, given a pair of training stereoscopic video sequences sampled from commercial 3D movies, disparity maps are first directly computed by state-of-the-art stereo matching method [25]. Notice that we do not perform parallel view rectification before the stereo matching, hence, the disparity has signed value. Since the disparity values computed by stereo matching are always quantized into several disparity layers, we can use them as the labels in the multi-label Support Vector Machines (SVM). After extracted the motion and position features, the SVM is trained in one-vs-all manner. It is expected that the trained model can capture the correlation between the motion and the **signed disparity**. In the testing phase, features are first extracted from the test 2D video, then object disparity values are predicted.

During stereo view synthesis, an original 2D frame I is considered as the middle view between the synthesized left view I_l and right view I_r of the stereo image pair. So, I_l and I_r can be synthesized by warping I according to the predicted disparity map d(I).

$$I_r(x) = I(x + 0.5 \times d(x)) \quad (24)$$

$$I_l(x) = I(x - 0.5 \times d(x)) \quad (25)$$

After warping, there appear some "holes" due to the discontinuity of the disparity values. An inpainting method [26] is utilized to fill these holes, and the system generates the final stereo views.

5. EVALUATION AND EXPERIMENTS

In experiments, we convert several well-known films into stereoscopic ones. Figure 11 shows the conversion results of key frames from six movie. Some propagation results are shown in Figure 7 and 8.

5.1 Evaluation method

The proposed depth estimation method is particularly suitable for professional movie, because in such high quality videos the three monocular cues are prevalent and can be fully exploited in estimating scene depth. Although he inexpensive cameras with depth sensors (such as Kinect) and the Make3D dataset [24] provide videos with corresponding depth maps, neither of them provides high quality videos. For this reason, we did not test the proposed depth estimation method using these videos and the corresponding depth maps as the ground truth data. Since there is lack of depth data from conventional movies, we propose to use human labeled depth maps as reference to assess the visual quality of converted stereoscopic video as follows.

1. Generating human labeled depth maps.
Given an input video, we first use the proposed system to get the initial estimation of depth maps for every frame of the video, denoted as $\alpha_0(t)$. Then both the depth maps and the original frames $I(t)$ are given to a user. With the help of the interactive 3D labeling interface (Figure 9 shows the interface of the depth modifier.) and some guidelines, the user is asked to revise the depth maps according to his/her sense of depth and produce a refined depth map $\alpha_1(t)$, which is considered as the reference data.

2. *Objective evaluation* on depth maps.
We use three objective criteria to evaluate the accuracy of estimated depth maps, i.e. the Mean Square Error (MSE), Peak Signal Noise Ratio (PSNR) and the percentage of pixels been modified.

$$MSE = \frac{1}{mnt} \sum_t \sum_{i=0}^{m-1} \sum_{j=0}^{n-1} (\alpha_0(t,i,j) - \alpha_1(t,i,j))^2, \quad (26)$$

where m and n are image height and width in pixels, respectively.

$$PSNR = 10 \log \frac{255^2}{MSE} \quad (27)$$

3. *Subjective evaluation* on stereoscopic videos.
We adopt the Mean Opinion Score (MOS) in the Double Stimulus Impairment Scale (DISI) method to evaluate the visual effect of converted stereoscopic videos generated from the depth maps. Let the stereoscopic video produced by $\alpha_1(t)$ and $I(t)$ be the unimpaired reference and stereoscopic video produced by $\alpha_0(t)$ and $I(t)$ be the impaired one.

Table 1: Mean Opinion Score (MOS)

MOS	Quality	Impairment
5	Excellent	Imperceptible
4	Good	Perceptible but not annoying
3	Fair	Slightly annoying
2	Poor	Annoying
1	Bad	Very annoying

5.2 Evaluation setup and results

We use 6 clips from 6 different movies in evaluation. Figure 10 shows some of the key frames we use.

For the *objective evaluation* we use a 4% soft margin to simulate the depth of field (Dof) effect and the final results show that on average 24.5% pixels on the estimated depth maps are different from the reference data. And on average the MSE value between α_0 and α_1 is 1403.29 at 256 depth scales, and the average PSNR is 21.57dB. From figure 10 we can see that most of the difference takes place in textureless regions or on boundaries.

For the *subjective evaluation* we ask 13 subjects (trained experts) to report their subjective impression on the stereoscopic key frames shown to them. The subjects are presented with the stereoscopic key frame generated by system and the one by the human labeled reference depth map side by side. Then he/she is asked to vote on the first image using a 5-level impairment scale (from "impairments are imperceptible" to "impairments are very annoying"). Table 1 is a list of 5 level scores.

Our experiments report an average of 4.28 score of impairment. High score demonstrates the competence of our system of producing visually pleasing stereoscopic contents. Also notice that most of the time people could not perceive the difference in the background even some amount of pixels are different from the reference one. This implies that while watch stereoscopic view, people pay much more attention on the foreground objects and their depth order than that of the background, which attests our assumption that a better foreground will greatly improve visual impression. We also test these experts with a video shot in the same way and the average score increases to 4.58. This indicates that while watching image sequences, the artifacts can be even less noticeable.

5.3 Efficiency

The system is efficient in both interactive operations and the automatic modules. For a video with 1280×720 frames, the average time consumption of video is about $7s$ to $9s$ per frame, among which user interaction costs about $3 - 5s$ on a key-frame, and the automatic computation takes about 4s per frame. We list the details of the time consumption in Table2.

The IMAX system is a commercial system, its data are unavailable for us to compare. However, from media reports on the internet, the IMAX system takes about 6 to 10 weeks to convert a 2-hour 2D film into a stereo one; James Cameron used about 300 computer artists,60 weeks and 750,000 man

Table 2: Time consumption table

Item	Time(per frame)
Shot segmentation	$10ms$
Depth propagation	$3s$
Automatic depth estimation	$0.5s$
Depth to disparity conversion	$0.1s$
Foreground segmentation	$3s$ to $5s$
Total	$7s$ to $9s$

hours to convert the Titanic[10], while our system only takes about 10 days of PC-hours for automatic computation and 20-50 man-hours for user interaction.

Comparing to fully manual conversion systems, the proposed system is much more efficient due to the following reasons: (1) There are a number of automatic algorithms used in the system to reduce the labor of user interaction, e.g. the automatic background depth estimation, label propagation from key-frames to non-key frames, and disparity estimation; (2) The major user interaction is the foreground object segmentation on only key frames, but the segmentation algorithms are semi-automatic facilitated by a convenient U.I., i.e. the adapted Graph cut and intelligent scissors.

6. CONCLUSIONS

In this paper, we presented an interactive system of 2D-to-3D video converting. The system is comprehensive and it consists of a number of modules ranging from depth estimation, depth-to-disparity conversion, stereo view synthesis, video coding/decoding to audio-video splitting/merging. We also proposed a new evaluation method to assess visual quality of converted stereoscopic video. Experiment results demonstrate the advantage of the proposed system.

However, there are still some limitations in this method, e.g. the integrated monocular cues are still limited, they prefer high quality videos; and the fusion of depth estimation from different cues is simple (it is using a linear model). In the future, we shall extend the current system by incorporating more monocular cues for depth estimation and study advanced models of multi-cue fusion, so that it is able to robustly estimate scene depth from regular or even low quality videos as well. Then we can evaluate the performance of the proposed system using collected range data, i.e. by Kinect.

7. ACKNOWLEDGEMENT

We'd like to thank for the support from the following research grants 973-2009CB320904, NSFC-61121002 and NSFC-90920012. And thanks Yanhui Liang's help in part of the system implementation.

8. REFERENCES

[1] G. Aubert and P. Kornprobst. *Mathematical Problems in Image Processing: Partial Differential Equations and the Calculus of Variations.* New York: Springer-Verlag, 2002.

[2] H. Bay, T. Tuytelaars, and L. V. Gool. Surf: Speeded up robust features. In *ECCV*, 2006.

[3] L. Chunming, X. Chenyang, G. Changfeng, and F. M. D. Distance regularized level set evolution and its application to image segmentation. *IEEE Transactions on Image Processing*, 2010.

[4] A. Criminisi, I. Reid, and A. Zisserman. Single view metrology. *IJCV*, 2000.

[5] G. Guo, L. Liu, Z. Zhang, Y. Wang, and W. Gao. An interactive method for curve extraction. In *ICIP*, 2010.

[6] M. Guttmann, L. Wolf, and D. Cohen-Or. Semi-automatic stereo extraction from video footage. In *ICCV*, 2009.

[7] R. I. Hartley and A. Zisserman. *Multiple View Geometry in Computer Vision.* Cambridge University Press, 2000.

[8] K. He, J. Sun, and X. Tang. Single image haze removal using dark channel prior. In *CVPR*, 2009.

[9] D. Hoiem, A. A. Efros, and M. Hebert. Closing the loop on scene interpretation. In *CVPR*, 2008.

[10] IEEE. Ieee and the titanic: A century of technological heritage and innovation, $http://www.ieee.org/about/news/2012/12april_2012.html$.

[11] IMAX. Imax 2d to 3d conversion, http://www.imax.com/corporate/technology/2d-to-3d-conversion/.

[12] D. Kim, D. Min, and K. Sohn. A stereoscopic video generation method using stereoscopic display characterization and motion analysis. *IEEE Trans. on Broadcasting*, 2008.

[13] S. Knorr and T. Sikora. An image-based rendering IBR approach for realistic stereo view synthesis of tv broadcast based on structure from motion. In *ICIP*, 2007.

[14] J. J. Koenderink, A. J. van Doorn, A M. Kappers, and J. T. Todd. Ambiguity and the 'mental eye' in pictorial relief. *Perception*, 2001.

[15] I. Koprinska and S. Carrato. Temporal video segmentation: A survey. *Signal Processing: Image Communication*, 2001.

[16] M. Liao, J. Gao, R. Yang, and M. Gong. Video stereolization: Combining motion analysis with user interaction. *IEEE. Trans. on Visualization and Computer Graphics*, 2011.

[17] C. Liu, H. Liu, S. Jiang, Q. Huang, Y. Zheng, and W. Zhang. Jdl at trecvid 2006 shot boundary detection. In *TRECVID*, 2006.

[18] B. D. Lucas and T. Kanade. An iterative image registration technique with an application to stereo vision. In *International Joint Conference on Artificial Intelligence*, 1981.

[19] E. Mortensen and W. Barrett. Intelligent scissors for image composition. In *Siggraph*, 1995.

[20] K. Moustakas, D. Tzovaras, and M. Strintzis. Stereoscopic video generation based on efficient layered structure and motion estimation from a monoscopic image sequence. *IEEE Trans. on Circuits and Systems for Video Technology*, 2005.

[21] A. P. Pentland. A new sense for depth of field. *IEEE Trans. on PAMI*, 1987.

[22] E. Rotem, K. Wolowelsky, and D. Pelz. Automatic video to stereoscopic video conversion. In *SPIE*, 2005.

[23] C. Rother, V. Kolmogorov, and A. Blake. "grabcut.

[24] A. Saxena, M. Sun, and A. Y. Ng. Make3D: Learning 3-D scene structure from a single still image. *IEEE Trans. on PAMI*, 2008.

[25] D. Scharstein and R. Szeliski. A taxonomy and evaluation of dense two-frame stereo correspondence algorithm. *IJCV*, 2002.

[26] A. Telea. An image inpainting technique based on the fast marching method. *Journal of Graphics, GPU, and Game Tools*, 2006.

[27] J. Tighe and S. Lazebnik. Superparsing: Scalable nonparametric image parsing with superpixels. In *ECCV*, 2010.

[28] C. Tomasi. Shape and motion from image streams under orthography: a factorization method. *IJCV*, 1992.

[29] S. A. Valencia and R. M. Rodriguez-Dagnino. Synthesizing stereo 3d views from focus cues in monoscopic 2d images. In *Proc. SPIE*, 2003.

Figure 11: Some results. (a) Original frames. (b) System generated depth maps. (c) Stereoscopic effects illustration wrt virtual screen. Red, green and blue colors indicate outside, on and inside screen respectively. (d)Red-cyan anaglyphs.

Enabling 'Togetherness' in High-Quality Domestic Video Conferencing

[1] Ian Kegel, [2] Pablo Cesar, [2] Jack Jansen, [2] Dick Bulterman, [1] Tim Stevens, [3] Joke Kort, [4] Nikolaus Färber

[1]BT Research & Technology
Adastral Park
Martlesham Heath
Ipswich IP5 3RE, UK

[2]CWI: Centrum Wiskunde & Informatica
Science Park 123
1098 XG Amsterdam
Netherlands

[3]TNO ICT
PO Box 15000
9700 CD Groningen
Netherlands

[4]Fraunhofer IIS
Am Wolfsmantel 33
91058 Erlangen
Germany

ian.c.kegel@bt.com, p.s.cesar@cwi.nl, jack.jansen@cwi.nl, dick.bulterman@cwi.nl, tim.s.stevens@bt.com, joke.kort@tno.nl, nikolaus.faerber@iis.fraunhofer.de

ABSTRACT
Low-cost video conferencing systems have provided an existence proof for the value of video communication in a home setting. At the same time, current systems have a number of fundamental limitations that inhibit more general social interactions among multiple groups of participants. In our work, we describe the development, implementation and evaluation of a domestic video conferencing system that is geared to providing true 'togetherness' among conference participants. We show that such interactions require sophisticated support for high-quality audiovisual presentation, and processing support for person identification and localisation. In this paper, we describe user requirements for effective interpersonal interaction. We then report on a system that implements these requirements. We conclude with a systems and user evaluation of this work. We present results that show that participants in a video conference can be made feel as 'together' as collocated players of a board game.

Categories and Subject Descriptors
H.1.2 [**Models and Principles**]: User/Machine Systems – *Human factors*. H.5.1 [**Information Interfaces and Presentation**]: Multimedia Information Systems – *Audio, Video*.

Keywords
video conferencing, social communication, interaction, visual composition, togetherness

1. INTRODUCTION
In 1910, the artist Villemard created a series of 24 postcards that illustrated how technology would influence life 90 years later, in 2000. Most postcards show flying bicycles and other intricate forms of public transport. In one picture, however, it is not the public at large being transported from one place to another, but a single person (see Figure 1). Sitting in the comfort of his own home, a gentleman is able to interact remotely with his wife (or mistress). A large, lifelike display helps give a feeling of remote presence. Judging from the microphone and the phonograph-like loudspeaker, it is clear that both audio and visual information play important roles in this inter-personal communication.

Figure 1: Remote interpersonal communication, as envisioned by Villemard

There is a lot of familiar technology in this picture: we see a network infrastructure, active content filtering (evidenced by the fact that the woman's background context has been removed) and even appropriate furniture. All of this technology is important, but so is the faithful assistant of the couple who is orchestrating the communication between them. Even in 1910, it was clear that microphones, cameras and networks alone were not enough to support intimate interactions.

Figure 2: Remote interpersonal communication, as instantiated by Skype

Part of Villemard's vision has become reality. Although a full 10 years later than Villemard thought, it is now fairly commonplace to have remote audio and visual conferences between people in home settings. The cameras are smaller and the microphones more subtle, but - as we can see in the image of a Skype-style desktop (see Figure 2) - the naturalness of the communication among the parties still has a way to go before reaching the ideal of Villemard's drawing. With Skype, nobody seems to know where to look, and nobody appears to be 'together'.This paper reports our efforts in supporting high-quality interpersonal communication for domestic videoconferences involving multiple participants at each end. Our goal is to better understand how a multi-camera home environment can help to make communication and engagement easier between groups of people separated in space – a concept we call *togetherness*. We particularly focus on the processes of data capture, encoding and composition, since they play a key role in supporting social communications. These processes make it possible for content originating from multiple sources to be presented at each location in a dynamic and flexible way using embedded control within a system (much like the faithful assistant would do in Villemard's vision).

The specific contributions discussed in this paper are:

- The evaluation of a prototype which supports social video conferencing based around a shared activity, carried out between multiple people at each location by using multiple cameras and dynamic multimedia composition.
- A technical implementation which uniquely combines low-delay, high quality audiovisual communication (including high definition video and multi-channel audio) with dynamic content from a shared application.
- An interaction architecture which provides the ability to dynamically modify audiovisual streams so that the movements of participants, verbal and non-verbal interactions and changes in a shared activity can be presented effectively.
- Application-level support for aesthetically integrating content streams and end-user interaction (such as game play)

This paper describes a system that was used for a series of interactive gaming experiments. It contains an evaluation of technical aspects of our work and the results of a user study on the impact of this technology on a feeling of togetherness among participants. Using objective and subjective measurements, we conclude that high-quality communication not only depends on the technology, but as well on how well social interactions are supported.

The paper begins by summarising related work in Section 2. Section 3 discusses requirements for supporting interaction rituals in remote interpersonal communication. Section 4 describes our technical implementation, focusing on the key data capture, encoding and composition features of the system. Sections 5 and 6 report the results of a number of trials evaluating the system from both a technology and a human perspective. Finally, Section 7 discusses the lessons learned during the process of implementing the system.

2. RELATED WORK

Domestic video conferencing is becoming commonplace, with Skype providing a convincing existence proof on the viability of home video communication. Still, users encounter many limitations with existing technology. Recent studies on human factors have identified common restrictions when using Skype at home. Some of them relate to performance: "Families frequently encounter technical difficulties even after the call is established: unreliable Internet connections, microphones with feedback, video lag or visual artifacts, frozen screens, and crashed applications were all common" [1]. Other restrictions refer to functionality: "The systems used in the homes we observed were often used by multiple people... This suggests a need to develop a home appliance for multiparty viewing and use" [14]. These results corroborate our own research into user requirements [23].

A key assumption within our research is the need to bound social video conferencing with a shared activity. Kirk et al. concluded that "... there were also times when it was clearly important that video could be meshed with other activities as necessary" [14]. Social games such as Mafia [2] provide another example, in which users value the ability to perform a shared activity together with remote parties. It has been shown that *interaction rituals* are important for maintaining social relationships and for building social cohesion and social identity [8]. It has been noted [5][11] that an important part of these rituals is performing mutual activities. It has also been suggested [5] that interaction rituals which make use of the full expressive capacity of human beings will make a stronger impact than those only based on language.

We are seeking to achieve a form of communication that is much less limited, in terms of its embodied interaction, than forms of mediated communication that are popularised today [7], especially by providing a focus on groups and not individuals as actors [17].

Our prototype introduces the dynamic composition of audiovisual streams and content. This functionality has been identified (although not implemented) in other works, highlighting the importance of manipulating and managing components within a set of video streams [10]. Studies on video-mediated free play between children found that different kinds of views led to different types of play [22], while other experiments demonstrate that good framing techniques improve social communication [18], and provide more vivid recorded lectures [16]. More recently, evaluations of remote game playing have shown that framing techniques can improve the effectiveness of the participants [12].

Visual Composition is an architectural block which is not usually present in video chat applications. In video chat, content stream manipulations happen after capture (e.g. effects in Apple's iChat application), while more immersive systems require complex content stream manipulations and camera control [4][19] [21]. In our research, we have applied the latter techniques for improving social video conferencing. Unlike previous research and commercial systems (e.g. from Cisco, Polycom or Lifesize), our composition component is reactive to the social interactions of the participants (e.g. non-verbal cues) and the shared activity (e.g. turn taking in a shared game).

In previous work [13], we reported on experiments to determine the approximate end-to-end delay of both commercial video conferencing systems and video chat applications. These experiments suggest delay figures around 300ms for commercial systems and also for Skype, and less than 200ms for Apple's iChat application – although both video chat applications were using 4CIF video resolution rather than 720p HD. In Section 5, this paper reports on more rigorous experiments which verify that delay figures for typical commercial systems are significantly higher than measured on our prototype system at comparable video resolutions.

3. SUPPORTING INTERACTION RITUALS

Traditionally, user requirements for domestic video conferencing have been defined based on performance measures such as video quality and latency. The requirements have typically focused on the low-level transfer of communication bits. In contrast, our work has focused on a broader understanding of high-level interpersonal communication.

In order to better understand these requirements, we conducted interviews within 16 families across four countries (U.K., Sweden, Netherlands, and Germany) [13][23]. The families consisted of adults, as well as children aged between about 6 and 25. Based on the interviews, we concluded that the use of video communication (particularly Skype) was not found compelling because of the technology. Users complained about the quality of the video and about the de-synchronisation between audio and video. Results of the interviews allowed us to identify a number of performance requirements: multiple cameras to support the framing of people, high definition video for fitting groups of people in front of the camera(s), high quality multi-channel audio that allows for speaker identification, and low delay audiovisual transmission.

More interestingly, in the interviews playful activities and games were considered as the common way families interacted in person. Some of the interviewees agreed that they did not see the games as an end in themselves, but tended to play them rather as a convenient excuse for getting together physically. This finding imposed a functional requirement for enabling high-quality communications: video communication should be bounded and reactive to social activities.

Based on these results, we designed and implemented a system that supported playful activities between multiple people at remote locations. In particular, we focused on a shared game, *Space Alert*, as a typical activity for a family gathering. Since our goal was in gaining insights into participant togetherness, we wanted to mimic a relatively common living room environment at each location where the game was to be played.

In the first iteration of our system we designed the shared game to closely replicate the physical board game by which it was inspired. The participants used a conventional TV screen predominantly for video communication, while at the same time a touchscreen provided an interactive representation of the game board which was synchronised between locations. This first prototype worked well and enabled us to obtain and report early results on the architecture for dynamic composition of audiovisual streams [13]. But it also showed that the two separate screen presentations (TV and touchscreen) did not support communication very well. Participants tended to focus most of their time on the game board to the detriment of the composed video presentation.

In the second iteration of our system, the focus of this paper, the Space Alert game was adapted away from the traditional board game metaphor with the aim of providing a single focus for participants' attention, less complex game rules, and most importantly to enable subjective evaluation of a new concept: the tight integration of both audiovisual communication, game content and interaction. In this new design, the participants use only the TV screen both for social communication and playing the game. Playing cards embedded with RFID tags are used to control chance aspects of the game, while the participants use their own bodies (via a Microsoft Kinect 3D motion sensor) as the interface to completing a series of mini-games. The game is intrinsically cooperative: players in different locations must collaborate to achieve a common goal in each mini-game – for example collectively steering a ship through an asteroid field – by taking different individual roles which require communication. Figure 3 shows example screenshots and photos of this shared game in practice. Playing a game together like this is a valuable way of fostering strong ties. This is typically an immersive and emotional experience (a ritual) that creates shared memories and thus enhances togetherness in the long term.

(a) Choosing a planet to explore (view of room A)

(b) Choosing a planet to explore (view of room B)

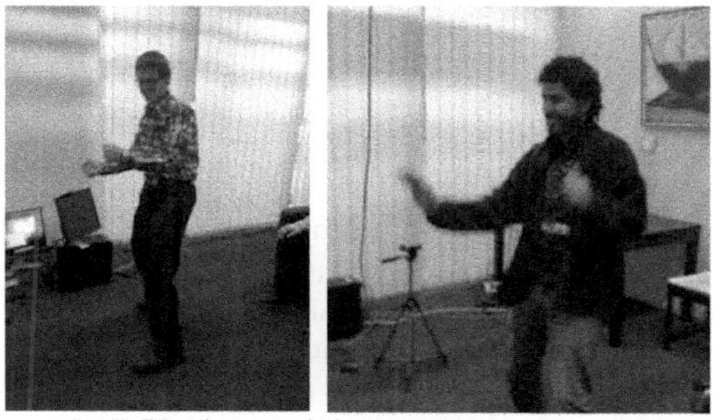

(c) (d) Playing a mini-game (rooms A and B)

Figure 3: Playing the Space Alert shared game. Images (a) and (b) show different presentations of the game at the same time in two locations. Images (c) and (d) show players interacting co-operatively during the game.

A critical component of this shared game is the presentation of the game's features and the effective display of interactions among participants. Composition in togetherness-based applications is inherently dynamic: the content will need to change as the focus of the activity (and the roles of the participants) develops. For example, positioning cameras to allow people to address the TV screen, and hence their friends, from different parts of the room is more useful than a camera that covers the whole space of the room. For collaborative, cooperative games, the game and visual elements should be composited on the same screen to encourage eye contact and to enhance the value derived from the communication. Seeing your partner in a natural, non-monotonic manner seems essential for this activity.

4. SYSTEM DESIGN AND IMPLEMENTATION

In Section 2 we explained how existing video conferencing and video chat systems are limited in their ability to effectively

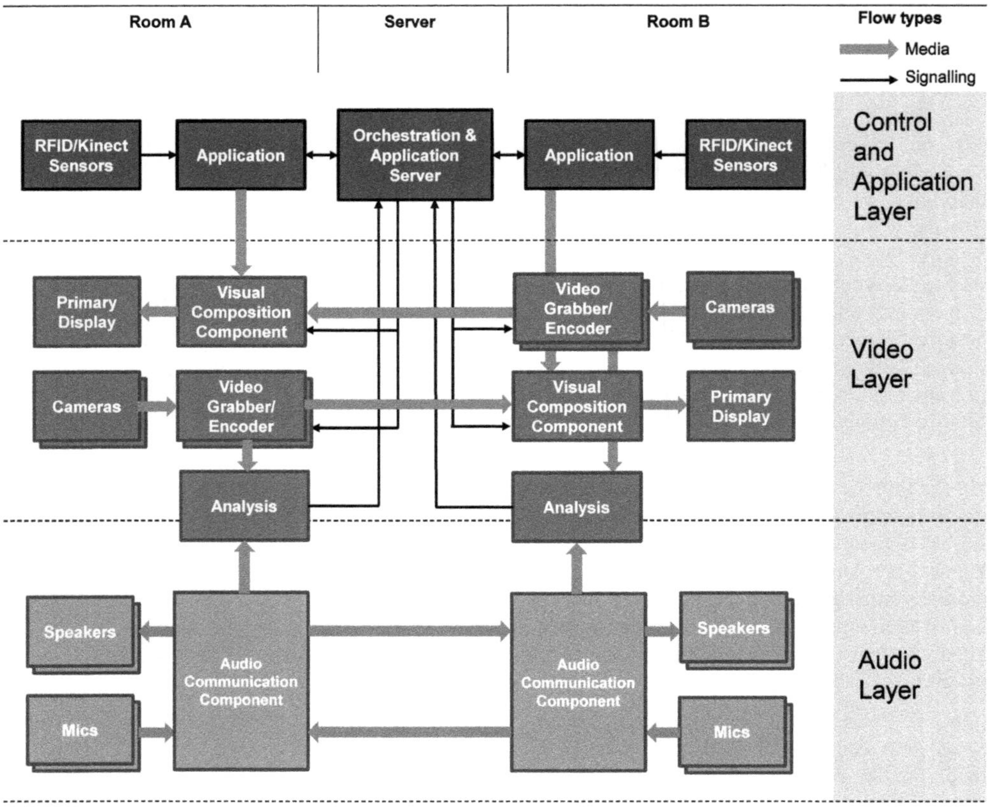

Figure 4: Overall system architecture

address groups and to provide flexible, dynamic composition of both live streams and content related to a shared application. In Section 3 we described how these limitations were reflected by interviews with typical families, and how through two iterations we have created a shared game which is tightly integrated with audiovisual communication. We therefore needed to develop a technical system support the Space Alert experience and to help us gain insights into togetherness in social interactions between groups. This section describes that system, highlighting why its features are important to the achievement of togetherness.

As discussed in Section 3, the system is designed to support a game shared between different locations. This involves rich communication (video and speech), together with a shared application (the game), which can be enjoyed by multiple people, at multiple ends, captured by multiple cameras. The design must be capable of handling both real time and recorded streams of both audio and video at each location independently. In addition the system must be able to intelligently decide how to compose the video and audio outputs at each location. This intelligent decision-making process, which we call *orchestration*, is partly based on analysis of audio and video signals captured in each location.

Figure 4 shows the overall architecture that spans three abstraction layers. The Control and Application layer contains components that could be proprietary (e.g. the games) and those responsible for instructing video composition (*orchestration*). The Video Layer contains all the video processing components. Its key inputs are video streams from one or more cameras at each location, as well as repositories of generic or application-specific resources (for example images, graphics, pre-recorded video, or interactive components such as Flash movies). Repositories can exist on the server side to provide input of pre-recorded video streams for multiple clients. The layer's key output is the primary screen – in our case the living room TV on which video compositions will be rendered. The Audio Layer contains all the audio processing components. Its key inputs are audio streams from multiple microphones at each client, and its key outputs are speakers through which sound is reproduced – usually in a domestic living room. Finally, the analysis components take both audio and video streams to generate cues relating to the activity that is taking place at each client location – and hence sit between the Video and Audio Layers.

The following sub-sections focus on the key data capture, encoding and composition features of the system and explain how they provide functionality beyond the state of the art, moving from personal software focused on single users (such as Skype and Google+ Hangouts) to a system which is shared by groups at each location. Analysis and orchestration are beyond the scope of this paper, but further information about their functionality and performance can be found elsewhere [9][15].

4.1 Audio Communication

The goal of audio communication should be to enable the same user experience *as if speaking to someone in the same room*. This is especially challenging for communication between groups in a family living room, where clip-on microphones and headsets cannot be practically used, and the environment may be noisy and reverberant. The quality of phone calls today is still generally limited to mono at less than 4 kHz audio bandwidth, but user experience evaluations between groups have shown the importance of audio quality for the effective communication.

We obtained the results shown in Figure 5 from video conferencing tests in which two different audio systems were compared during social interaction between groups of people. Each group was exposed to "high" and "low" audio quality for a duration of about 5 minutes each and then asked to express their agreement to the statement *"The communication was natural and without problems"* on a 5-point rating scale ranging from 1 (strongly agree) to 5 (strongly disagree). The difference in subjective evaluation between high and low audio quality is striking.

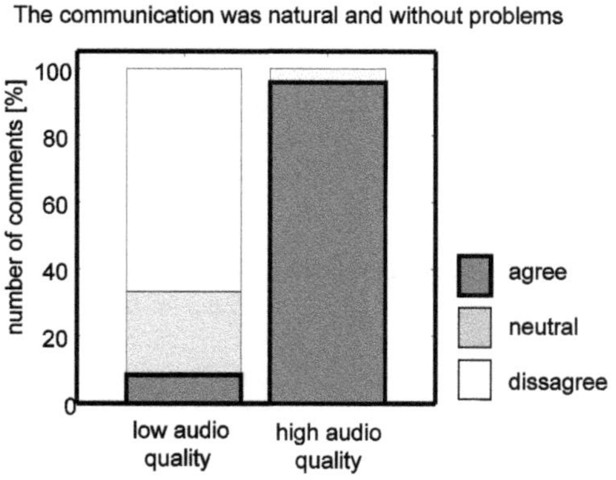

Figure 5: User experience during interactive group activity for low and high audio quality

The "high" audio quality used in the above tests - and in our Audio Layer - is a super-wideband Voice over IP (VoIP) system providing multi-channel audio at low delay and full audio bandwidth (24 kHz). The Audio Communication Component captures audio from an array of between two and four high quality microphones. It encodes and transmits the audio signals as two or three distinct channels (left, right, and optionally centre) using the MPEG AAC Enhanced Low Delay (AAC-ELD) audio codec – the same codec also employed in Apple's Facetime application. It performs echo control on the audio it captures and renders, and also allows external audio signals to be mixed with real-time audio signals, via stereo analogue inputs on the sound card to provide, for example, sound effects from a shared application. For transmission over IP, it incorporates Error Concealment (EC) and sophisticated Jitter Buffer Management (JBM) to handle packet loss and delay variations. By adaptively changing the playout time using Time Scale Modification (TCM) it achieves an optimal trade-off between late-loss and buffering-delay.

4.2 Video Communication

To provide effective coverage of social communication between groups, a higher quality video experience must be provided. A higher video resolution is necessary to provide both peripheral awareness of other participants and, when appropriate, eye contact plus the ability to transmit and interpret gestures and body language. Low delay is particularly important for the coherence of conversations, especially if they involve multiple participants. The use of multiple cameras also provides the flexibility to capture different views of each location, again improving the ability for the system to ensure that the activities of a group are effectively conveyed on the remote screen. While some commercial video telepresence systems do offer high resolution, low delay and even multiple cameras, they are designed for controlled room environments and optimised private networks – neither of which can be assumed in a domestic context.

The Video Grabber/Encoder in our Video Layer is a high performance component designed to capture images from an HD video camera, encode them and transmit them to the remote location with minimal added delay (below 100ms for an ideal end-to-end system). The Video Grabber captures digital or analogue video from a single camera using a hardware capture card. The SDI (Serial Digital Interface) standard is the preferred form of camera output, although signals can also be captured from low-cost HD webcam devices over USB. The Video Encoder is an H.264 encoder which is optimised for low-delay video transmission by using a number of techniques from the H.264 standard, including: not using B frames (bi-predictive pictures), using Constant Bit Rate (CBR) transmission, and minimising buffering throughout the system. A separate Video Grabber/Encoder is required for each HD video camera.

4.3 Audiovisual Composition

As previously mentioned, a critical aspect of combining a shared activity with audiovisual communication is the presentation of the game's features and the effective display of interactions among participants. This composition must be dynamic because the content will need to change as the focus of the activity and participants' roles develop.

The Visual Composition component enables our system to dynamically and seamlessly compose visual images at each location. It provides decoding and rendering to screen of real-time video at the lowest possible delay. It is capable of compositing the real-time video streams with pre-recorded media from a local repository. It can also incorporate other forms of content, such as Flash, from applications running locally. This enables a wide variety of visual presentations to be configured. It supports composition effects such as alpha blending for increased flexibility in presentation design. This component receives control and composition instructions from an orchestration module (or a faithful assistant). Composition information is expressed using the Synchronized Media Integration Language (SMIL) [3], which has been extended to define how real-time and pre-recorded media can be composited spatially and temporally.

Video feeds into the Visual Composition component are initially set up using RTSP (Real Time Streaming Protocol). Because live video is treated just as any other media renderer there is no architectural limitation on the number of simultaneous incoming video streams: the available hardware is the only factor determining how many video feeds can be displayed simultaneously. Video streams can also be decoded without display, in a form of 'standby mode'. This offers the significant advantage that, if control instructions decide to switch the currently displayed video to a stream that is in standby mode, the switch can happen instantaneously because the new video data has already been received and decoded. Setting up a new stream using RTSP would delay the switching time by least a few hundred milliseconds, and possibly significantly longer in practice in the case of aggressively optimised H.264 streams.

5. EVALUATING THE TECHNOLOGY

Following implementation of the prototype system described in Section 4, we carried out experiments to evaluate specific aspects of the data capture, encoding and composition components. As explained in Section 3, low-delay audiovisual communication and the dynamic composition of different camera views with game content were key requirements. We therefore chose to focus our technology evaluation on these requirements, and to provide comparisons with the state of the art where possible.

We have taken care to incorporate all components (e.g. from camera through to screen, or 'glass-to-glass') in our evaluations. This means that we have measured true end-to-end delays, and not isolated algorithmic or networking delays. For this reason, the results presented here are not always directly comparable to data published by other sources.

5.1 Video Transmission Chain

We measured the user-perceived round-trip delay of the video transmission chain as follows. Our experimental system comprised one endpoint in Amsterdam, The Netherlands, and another in Ipswich, England, both connected via the public Internet. These systems were equipped with the Video Grabber/Encoder and Visual Composition components described in Section 4.

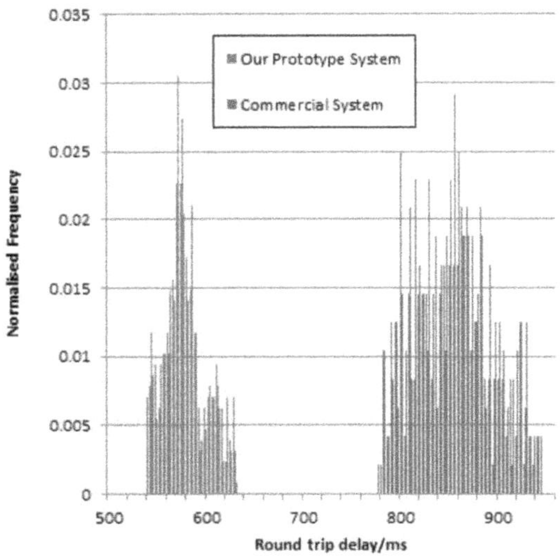

Figure 6: Round-trip video delay measurements

The network delay between the systems was 11ms. We took 500 measurements and measured an average delay of 580ms (with a standard deviation of 22ms); the distribution plot is presented in Figure 6. These are round-trip measurements including capture, encoding, transmission and display, and also the delays introduced by the measurement system itself. As the measurement system was measured to have a delay of 97ms (standard deviation 15ms) the actual end-to-end delay of our video chain is 242ms (standard deviation 37ms).

For comparison, we measured an equivalent commercial video conferencing system (using equipment from Polycom and Lifesize) connected through a conferencing bridge also via the Internet. This was the closest emulation of our prototype we could achieve using commercially-available equipment. The network delay between the systems was again 11ms. The measured round trip delay was 855ms (standard deviation 40ms); the distribution plot is provided for comparison in Figure 6. After correction for the measurement system delay, the actual end-to-end delay of the commercial system was 379ms (standard deviation 55ms). For this measurement we took care to use the similar codecs, bitrates and video sizes as we used for our own prototype.

While these results clearly show a significant improvement over a typical commercial system available today, the challenge remains to reduce the end-to-end delay as far as possible. In a laboratory environment, additional experiments were carried out to reduce delay times further, although these could not be incorporated in our prototype system.

A rolling shutter on the camera allows an image to be transmitted before a whole frame has been captured, and can reduce the delay by a fraction of the time it takes to capture one frame (25fps 40ms; 30fps 33ms, 60fps, 16.7ms). In addition, the Gradual Decoder Refresh (GDR) scheme enables I-frame information to be staggered over several frames, which reduces the bandwidth requirement and/or decreases the requirement for buffering and hence reduces the delay.

To effectively employ these techniques we developed an HD camera with a rolling shutter, and a capture card employing the above techniques and capable of handling the output from the rolling shutter camera. The glass-to-glass delay on the optimised video chain was measured at 85ms [13], a significant reduction on our prototype system.

5.2 Audio Transmission Chain

A different approach was required to perform measurements on the audio transmission chain, partly because the echo control in our prototype system meant that round-trip measurements could not be made. Instead, a PC-based oscilloscope was used to automatically measure the time difference between plots of a reference pulse which was passed into one Audio Communication Component, over a local network and out of a second such component. Several test runs of 1000 samples were carried out by repeating the reference pulse over long periods of time. The minimum delay end-to-end delay measured using this approach was about 52ms. It can be seen from Figure 7 that the distribution of delay values follows a repetitive sawtooth pattern. This is an interesting side-effect due to unsynchronised clocks at each Audio Communication Component. The resulting slight difference in sampling frequency produced an excess or deficit number of samples at the opposing sound card causing buffers to fill or empty respectively. The buffer control then dropped or created a frame when the latency grew too large.

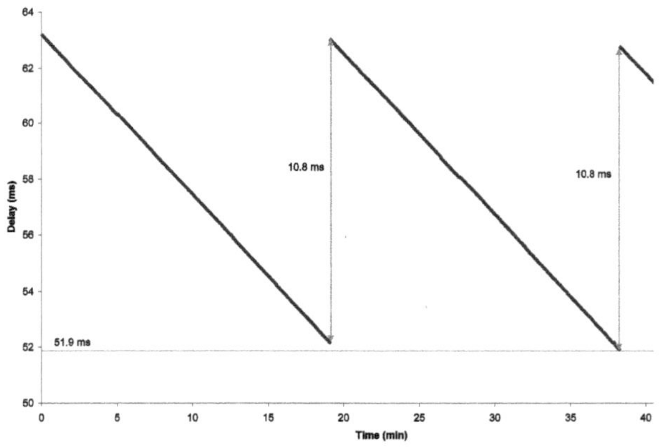

Figure 7: End-to-end audio delay measurements

If the measured network delay of 11ms for the Internet-connected systems used in the video delay tests is added to the delay observed here, the average end-to-end audio delay is approximately 70ms. While this could be reduced slightly by better clock synchronisation, it is still significantly smaller than the equivalent video delay. During subjective evaluation of our prototype system, it was necessary to artificially delay the audio transmission chain in order to achieve lip synchronisation between the audio and the video streams.

5.3 Audiovisual Composition

The Visual Composition Component is responsible for the seamless blending of visual streams, creating an immersive experience for the user where social communication and activities (e.g. gaming) become integrated. Because this functionality is very different to any other video communication system, no appropriate comparative performance metrics could be determined experimentally for the Visual Composition Component in isolation. Therefore, this subsection lists the component's features which were required to support effective integration of a shared activity, and which extend the implementation of visual composition which we have previously reported [13]:

- Aesthetic composition of real-time audiovisual streams and other pre-recorded media (text, graphics, video, Adobe Flash content)
- Both temporal (when to render) and spatial (where to render) composition
- Graphic overlays via an alpha channel with varying transparency
- Dynamic manipulation of visual elements, for example enabling external functions such as 'cut to camera'

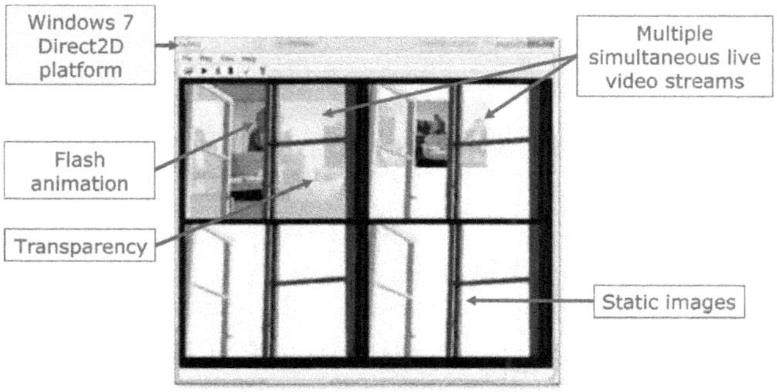

(a) Composition of real-time audiovisual streams and other pre-recorded media

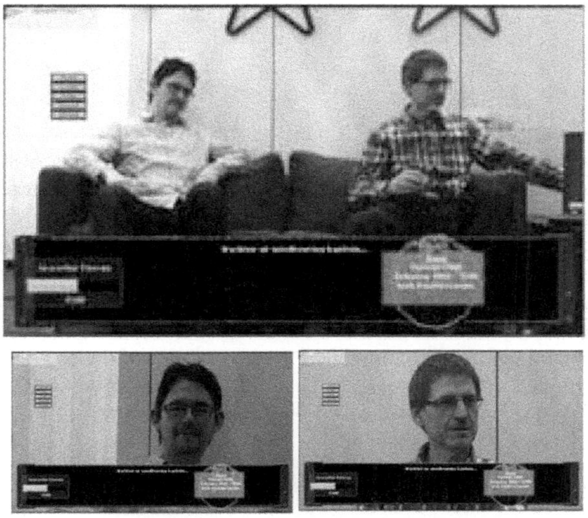

(b) Dynamic composition of visual elements during gameplay (e.g. cut to camera)

Figure 8: Visual Composition tests. The images above show key features of the Visual Composition Component, including the representation of different camera shots combined with game graphics.

Figure 8 shows some results obtained from tests of the Visual Composition Component, including the composition of real-time audiovisual streams and other pre-recorded media, and the dynamic composition of visual elements during game play (illustrating how camera sources can be switched within the same graphic composition).

6. EVALUATING SOCIAL INTERACTION

In addition to the technology evaluation described in Section 5, we carefully evaluated our system with real users in a representative social setting. This section describes the design of that evaluation and our findings.

Directly measuring togetherness is a difficult task: we wanted the users of our prototype system to be able to freely participate in social activities (without being wired with a dozen sensors), but we still wanted to obtain a number of objective results that would help us determine the added value of our technological choices. We felt that a comparison with existing conferencing technology was unfair (the use of better audio and video would highly skew the results in our favour, but say little about our approach in an abstract sense). We decided to compare interaction via our prototype with a more ground-truth-like togetherness experience: playing a board game in a physically co-located setting.

As discussed in Section 3, the basic interactive game model that we used was based on an outer space metaphor. Instead of developing one long game, we devised three short games, or *mini-games*. The mini games tested during the evaluation we: *Space Cruiser*, *Meteorite Girl* and *Pitch Matching*. The mini-game approach meant that a feeling of togetherness would be less dependent on the game logic: each mini-game was intentionally a short, focused and directed interactive experience. Collectively, we refer to this suite of mini-games as The Family Game.

The board game we selected was, like the Family Game suite, a turn-based cooperative game. The final goal was to evaluate how our system would compare to face-to-face game playing. We are aware of the differences between these two situations of game playing. The underlying game mechanics and in the interaction itself are different. The board game is played on a board, with playing cards and other game pieces and people communicate directly with each other (not-mediated), whereas Family Game is played through interaction with the Microsoft Kinect sensor and RFID playing cards - and people communicate through audio/video communication (mediated). Figure 9 illustrates some of the room infrastructure we used for running the Family Game evaluations.

6.1 Approach

The evaluation consisted of two parts: the evaluation of the *remote* Family Game, and the evaluation of the *co-located* board game. In order to perform the evaluations we used the Social User Experience Framework (SUX). This framework is intended for better understanding how people use and experience mediated social communication. The framework studies, among other issues, *interactics* (referring to people's experiences of interacting with the system and with others) and *aesthetics* (referring to the sensorial qualities of the system that enable social communication). *Interactic* experiences are based on human cognition (shortly) before, during, and (shortly) after interaction, and include the following constructs: *Quality of Communication*; *Social Connectedness*; *Challenge*; *Group Attraction*; *Inclusion of Other in Self*; *Overlap of Self, Ingroup and Outgroup*; and *Emotion*. *Aesthetics* are closely related to human perception, and include the following constructs: *Social Presence and Presence*,

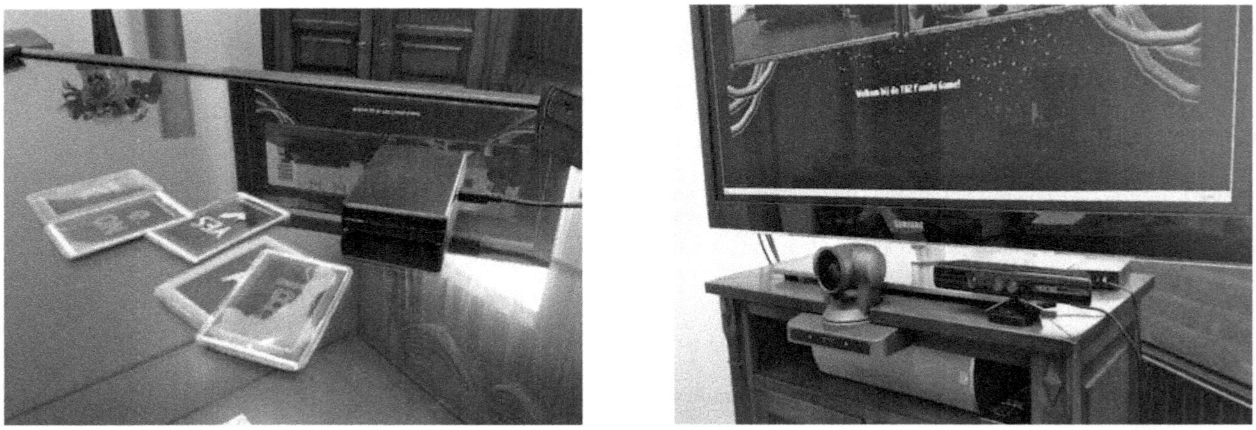

RFID readers for interacting with the game (left), and main capture camera and Kinect sensor (right).

Figure 9: Room infrastructure for running the subjective evaluations

Naturalness, and *Immersion/Engagement*. Further information about this framework and the questionnaires used in our study are beyond the scope of this paper, but can be found elsewhere [20].

During the evaluation we used multiple methods for data collection, including several questionnaires:

- A general questionnaire beforehand (asking for information about the relationship of a specific person towards others in the group playing the game and to the group as a whole.
- Questionnaires after each condition (playing the Family Game or playing the board game).

Group interviews were used after playing both games to obtain qualitative information about people's experiences. Furthermore video recordings were made throughout the evaluations (in both conditions). All of our participants were paid a modest sum (€30) to take part in our experiments.

Each evaluation group consisted of four people who knew each other well (families or groups of friends). In total 36 people participated in the experiments. Half of the groups started with the Family Game (45 minutes) and then played the board game (45 minutes). The other half of the groups started with the board game and then played the Family Game. The youngest participant was 9 years old, the eldest 59. The mean age of the 36 participants was 22.5 years old. We realise that these 36 people represent only a modest sample group, but we feel that the results they provided are sufficiently instructive to warrant use.

Participants were invited to fill out several questionnaires:

- Characteristics of their personal relationship with the others and with the others as a group.
- Characteristics of their personal relationship as experienced at that moment (immediately after playing).
- *Aesthetic* experiences: Social Presence and Presence, Naturalness and Immersion/Engagement.
- *Interactic* experiences: Quality of Communication, Social Connectedness, Challenge and Emotion: affect (positive versus negative), arousal (relaxed versus aroused), and dominance (being in control versus being controlled).

The sessions closed with group interviews in which the focus was on how people experienced both conditions in terms of social connectedness and a feeling of togetherness.

6.2 Findings

Cronbach's Alpha [6] is widely used as a statistic to estimate the reliability of results from a sequence of experiments. Table 1 summarises the Cronbach's Alphas for the *aesthetic* constructs: SPP, N, and I/E. From this table we can conclude that the Cronbach's Alphas are consistent enough over different measures/evaluations. In reading the tables, it can be generally assumed that similar scores for the board game and the online, interactive Family Game means that the 'togetherness experience' is reasonable similar. This means that the infrastructure and the remoteness does not degrade the feeling of togetherness.

Table 1: Cronbach's Alpha for SPP, N, and I/E

	Family Game	Board game
Social presence/Presence	.899	.640
Naturalness	.851	.877
Immersion/Engagement	.897	.635

The use of Cronbach's Alphas means that constructs show 'internal validity' across measures for the aesthetic constructs. The Social Presence and Presence (SPP) for the board game is somewhat different from the other Cronbach's Alphas. This is due to the fact that one item (measuring the feeling of presence in the virtual situation) was lacking. Immersion/engagement (I/E) in the board game has a lower Cronbach's Alpha as well. We assign this result to the fact that in real life situations, or in this case playing the board game, the item related to 'feeling part of the activity' is interpreted differently than it is in a 'virtual situation' as is the case in the other measures. When this item is left out of I/E, the Cronbach's Alpha goes up and is .660, a little higher.

Table 2: Cronbach's Alpha for QC, SC, Ch

	Family Game	Board game
Quality of Communication (QC)	.866	.861
Social Quality (SC) (2 items remaining)	.889	.824
Challenge (Ch)	.785	.851

When we compare the Cronbach's Alphas for the *interactic* experiences, we see that the Alphas are very similar across playing the board game and playing Family Game — see Table 2.

This indicates that these constructs have sufficient 'internal validity' over both tested situations.

When we look at the aspects playing a role in long term relationships and how these are experienced over time (e.g. personal effort, thinking about each other, sharing experiences, staying in touch, recognition, and group attraction) we see that only the Cronbach's Alphas for thinking about each other and for group attraction carry sufficient internal validity — see Table 3.

Table 3: Cronbach's Alpha for thinking about each other and group attraction

	Before start of experiment	After Family Game	After board game
Thinking about each other	.700	.545	.603
Group attraction	.858	.903	.851

The reason why these two constructs are interpreted in the same way when asked in the context of one's relationship or after playing the game (Family Game or board game) is that they ask about an experience on a specific moment in time (e.g. a contact moment in the past and what happens after that in terms of experiences). The other constructs carry items that more generally ask a participant about their experiences of a social relationship over time, not a specific moment therein. When asked in the context of your relationship to the others, the items are therefore differently interpreted than when asked about your experience of a specific contact moment.

Table 4: Paired Sample Tests: Family Game versus Board Game

	Dif. Mean	S. Dev.	Sign.
Social presence/ Presence	-.714	.921	.000
Naturalness	-.676	.921	.000
Immersion/ Engagement	-.509	.845	.001
Challenge	-.396	.768	.004
Social Connectedness	-.287	.643	.011
Quality of Communication	-.456	.661	.000
Affect	.444	.909	.006
Arousal	.139	.990	.406*

If we look at the other constructs, we see differences in means between the Family Game and the board game, but most of these differences are not statistically significant — see Table 4. For most measures, the board game scores on average a little bit better. For the emotional arousal, the Family Game scores best and this difference is statistically significant. The emotional affect is also higher, but this difference is not statistically significant.

Related to the fun people had during both games, people often reported a preference for the board game, but they sometimes had more fun during playing the Family Game. We think this is largely related to the fact that the Family Game was more thrilling, and there was more tension in short periods of time than was the case during the board game. In the board game fun was often related to the social communication and a feeling of connectedness and direct contact. In the Family Game fun was often related to the thrill of playing the mini games.

The experience of the Family Game was more positive compared to the board game (though not statistically significant). Arousal was higher in the Family Game (statistically significant). Overall, it can be concluded that the Family Game did very well compared to the board game in these tests since there are only few significant differences. Though people tended to find a real life situation better and socially more enjoyable, the Family Game is a very good alternative to have high quality social interaction with others when no other means are available.

7. DISCUSSION

Current-generation video conferencing has provided a powerful communication tool for people and (to a more limited extent) families who wish to stay in touch while apart. In our work, we have looked at a next generation of domestic video conferencing, in which fluid interactions and higher quality audio and visual content - some of which is generated and composed dynamically - provide a sounder basis for a greater feeling of togetherness. Our work has consisted of doing a significant analysis of user requirements, followed by the development of a research prototype that has been deployed and tested in an international setting. We conducted a systems-level evaluation of the user interaction requirements for domestic multi-person, multi-party conferences. Finally, we conducted an analysis of the social aspects of perceived 'togetherness' compared with a baseline situation of intimate family interactions.

We can conclude that the original performance and functional requirements developed in Section 2 for domestic video communication were met. Our solutions advance not only the state of the art for home conferencing, but also provide advances over 'conventional' video conferencing in a business environment. In Section 5 we have shown advances in terms of audiovisual transmission and composition, while in Section 6 we have reported on a comparative study between of our system and a collocated board game. In general the results are encouraging, indicating that our system is a good alternative for family gatherings when apart.

During our work, we have gathered a number of lessons learned that we believe will be useful for other researchers attempting to follow our lead.

A key result, we feel, is that interaction in video conferencing requires more support than the efficient end-to-end transport of bits. Multiple information sources need to be gathered, selected and composed to support effective interaction. Our Visual Composition Component was designed to enable the separation of composition mechanisms and composition policies. This way, external components (manual or automatic) could be used to signal composition instructions, while reusing the core system. This allows for reusability in different contexts (e.g. supporting other activities) and conditions (e.g. reacting to other low-level cues).

Effective interaction will always be related to the underlying performance of the overall system. Calculating end-to-end delays is typically done at the network level. Unfortunately, this level alone does not measure perceived quality, since delays in processing and rendering the media are not considered. Typically, manual solutions (cameras and high-precision clocks) can be used for measuring, but these are tedious and prone to errors. In our research, we have determined the necessity to develop a standalone tool to obtain computable measurements of round trip delay times (glass-to-glass delay) for a complete end-to-end system. Further research in this area is still required.

The combination of the AAC-ELD audio codec with low-delay streaming and multi-channel echo control provided an extremely effective Audio Communication Component. The use of a 4-microphone array proved to be essential in providing directional audio. This support is essential if participants are to have the freedom of movement required to support interaction in an unencumbered manner.

While we are encouraged by the results of this work, it is clear that there are many nuances to supporting interaction that could be further developed. The context of the activity (a game, a birthday party, a shared remote dinner) could be used to influence the types of shots selected from the multiple cameras that are available in each location. This process could be manual (as in Villemard's vision in Figure 1), or it could be automatic. We suspect that some hybrid form will need to be developed first.

There is also scope to explore the applicability of our results for domestic multi-party video conferencing to very different contexts. One such example is the teaching of skills which require embodied learning, such as playing a musical instrument. The use of multiple cameras and dynamic composition could significantly improve the experience of a remote lesson conducted through a video conferencing system. We also anticipate that our approach could be applied to other domains including remote healthcare and semi-structured business environments.

Regardless of its type, not only will the context of the activity influence the selection of individual shots, it may also help influence graceful degradation of network connections between parties. More work is required to really understand how social togetherness can be maintained in the face of transient resource situations.

Finally, at the highest level, an in-home system should be responsive to the privacy needs of parties who are incidental to the shared interaction taking place. Unlike a managed office setting, the home often has multiple parallel activities taking place. These need to be protected and potentially exploited.

The advent of a new generation of super-fast broadband access networks, with increased speeds upstream as well as downstream, is making high quality domestic video conferencing viable in many countries for the first time. We feel that we have demonstrated the requirements and a solution for supporting increased 'togetherness' for domestic video conferencing – and shown that network speed alone is not enough to provide support for fine-grained home interaction. Our approach provides a valuable model for the development of future conferencing systems for both consumer and business applications.

8. ACKNOWLEDGEMENTS

The authors would like to acknowledge the support of Orlando Verde and Wolfgang Van Raemdonck at Alcatel-Lucent, Rene Kaiser and his team at Joanneum Research and Dr. Marian Ursu and his team at Goldsmiths, University of London. This work was supported in part by funding from the European Community's Seventh Framework Programme (FP7/2007-2013) under grant agreement no. ICT-2011-287760.

REFERENCES

[1] Ames, M. G., Go, J., Kaye, J., and Spasojevic, M. 2010. Making love in the network closet: the benefits and work of family videochat. In *Proceedings of ACM CSCW*, 145-154.

[2] Batcheller, A. L., Hilligoss, B., Nam, K., Rader, E., Rey-Babarro, M., and Zhou, X. 2007. Testing the technology: playing games with video conferencing. In *Proceedings of ACM CHI*, 849-852.

[3] Bulterman, D.C.A., Jansen, J., Cesar, P., et al. 2008. Synchronized Multimedia Integration Language (SMIL 3.0). *W3C Recommendation*. URL=http://www.w3.org/TR/SMIL/

[4] Chen, M. 2001. Design of a virtual auditorium. In *Proceedings of the ACM International Conference on Multimedia*, 19-28.

[5] Collins, R. 2005. *Interaction Ritual Chains*. Princeton University Press.

[6] Cortina. J. M. 1993. What is coefficient alpha? An examination of theory and applications. *Journal of Applied Psychology*, 78, 98-1

[7] Dourish, P. 2001. *Where the action is: The Foundations of Embodied interaction*. Cambridge Massachusetts: MIT Press.

[8] Durkheim, E. 1971. *The elementary forms of the religious life*. Allen and Unwin.

[9] Falelakis M., Kaiser R., Weiss W., Ursu M.F. Reasoning for video-mediated group communication. 2011. *Proceedings of IEEE ICME*, pp 1526-1530.

[10] Gaver, W., Sellen, A., Heath, C., and Luff, P. 1993. One is not enough: multiple views in a media space. In *Proceedings of ACM CHI*, 335-341.

[11] Goffman, E. 1967. *Interaction Ritual: Essays on Face-to-Face Behavior*. Anchor Books.

[12] Groen, M., Ursu, M.F., Falelakis, M., Michalakopoulos, S., and Gasparis, E. 2012. Improving Video-Mediated Communication with Orchestration. *Journal of Computers in Human Behaviour*, 28(5): 1575–1579.

[13] Jansen, J., Cesar, P., Bulterman, D.C.A., Stevens, T., Kegel, I., and Issing, J. 2011. Enabling Composition-Based Video-Conferencing for the Home. *IEEE Transactions on Multimedia*, 13(5): 869-881.

[14] Kirk, D. S., Sellen, A., and Cao, X. 2010. Home video communication: mediating 'closeness'. In *Proceedings of ACM CSCW*, 135-144.

[15] Korchagin, D., Motlicek, P., Duffner, S. and Bourlard, H. 2011. Just-in-time multi- modal association and fusion from home entertainment. *Proceedings of IEEE ICME*.

[16] Lampi, F., Kopf, S., and Effelsberg, W. 2008. Automatic lecture recording. In Proceeding of the ACM international Conference on Multimedia, 1103-1104.

[17] Ljungstrand, P., and Björk S. 2008. Supporting group relationships in mediated domestic environments. *Proceedings of Mindtrek*, pp. 59-63.

[18] Nguyen, D.T. and Canny, J. 2009. More than face-to-face: empathy effects of video framing. In *Proceedings of ACM CHI*, 423-432.

[19] Ott, D.E., and Mayer-Patel, K. 2004. Coordinated multi-streaming for 3D tele-immersion. In *Proceedings of the ACM International Conference on Multimedia*, 596–603.

[20] Steen, M. (ed.). 2012. D8.8: User Evaluations of TA2 Concepts. *TA2 Project Public Deliverable*.

[21] Yang, Z., Wu, W., Nahrstedt, K., Kurillo, G., and Bajcsy, R. 2010. Enabling multi-party 3D tele-immersive environments with ViewCast. *ACM TOMCCAP*, 6(2): article number 7.

[22] Yarosh, S., Inkpen, K.M., and Brush, A.J.B. 2010. Video playdate: toward free play across distance. In *Proceeding of ACM CHI*, 1251-1260.

[23] Williams, D., Ursu, M.F., Meenowa, J., Cesar, P., Kegel, I., and Bergström, K. 2011. Video mediated social interaction between groups: System requirements and technology challenges. *Telematics and Informatics*, 28(4): 251-270.

Scalar Quantization for Large Scale Image Search

Wengang Zhou[1], Yijuan Lu[2], Houqiang Li[3], Qi Tian[1]
Dept. of Computer Science, University of Texas at San Antonio[1], Texas, TX 78249
Dept. of Computer Science, Texas State University[2], Texas, TX 78666
Dept. of EEIS, University of Science and Technology of China[3], Hefei, P.R. China
wengang.zhou@utsa.edu[1], yl12@txstate.edu[2], lihq@ustc.edu.cn[3], qitian@cs.utsa.edu[1]

ABSTRACT
Bag-of-Words (BoW) model based on SIFT has been widely used in large scale image retrieval applications. Feature quantization plays a crucial role in BoW model, which generates visual words from the high dimensional SIFT features, so as to adapt to the inverted file structure for indexing. Traditional feature quantization approaches suffer several problems: 1) high computational cost—visual words generation (codebook construction) is time consuming especially with large amount of features; 2) limited reliability—different collections of images may produce totally different codebooks and quantization error is hard to be controlled; 3) update inefficiency—once the codebook is constructed, it is not easy to be updated. In this paper, a novel feature quantization algorithm, *scalar quantization*, is proposed. With scalar quantization, a SIFT feature is quantized to a descriptive and discriminative bit-vector, of which the first tens of bits are taken out as *code word*. Our quantizer is independent of collections of images. In addition, the result of scalar quantization naturally lends itself to adapt to the classic inverted file structure for image indexing. Moreover, the quantization error can be flexibly reduced and controlled by efficiently enumerating nearest neighbors of code words.

The performance of scalar quantization has been evaluated in partial-duplicate Web image search on a database of one million images. Experiments reveal that the proposed scalar quantization achieves a relatively 42% improvement in mean average precision over the baseline (hierarchical visual vocabulary tree approach), and also outperforms the state-of-the-art Hamming Embedding approach and soft assignment method.

Categories and Subject Descriptors
I.2.10 [**Vision and Scene Understanding**]: VISION

General Terms
Algorithms, Experimentation, Verification

Keywords
Large-scale image retrieval, scalar quantization, SIFT.

1. INTRODUCTION
The last decade has witnessed the great advance in content-based image retrieval on large-scale database. Most state-of-the-art approaches utilize SIFT features [1] to represent images and leverage the BoW model [2] to index large-scale image dataset for scalable retrieval. Some post-processing techniques, such as spatial verification [3] [4] and query expansion [5] [24], are also explored to further boost the retrieval accuracy. Of them, one of the key steps is feature quantization, which first generates visual words from the high dimensional SIFT features, and then quantize features to the corresponding visual words for indexing.

The most popular feature quantization method is vector quantization. Originally used in lossy data compression, vector quantization divides a large set of training SIFT features into groups. Each group corresponds to a sub-space in the feature space, and is represented by its center, which is called visual word [2]. All visual words constitute a visual codebook. Then, given a novel feature, vector quantization assigns it the visual word ID of the sub-space where the feature falls in. The most popular visual codebook generation approach is k-means [2] clustering. When the visual codebook size becomes very large (e.g. 1 million), it is infeasible to train the codebook with k-means, and hierarchical k-means [6] is more preferred to improve codebook generation speed and enhance feature quantization efficiency.

Traditional vector quantization suffers several problems. 1) **High computational cost**: visual codebook generation is computationally expensive especially with a large amount of features. For example, in order to train a large visual codebook containing 1 million visual words, usually about 50 million SIFT features may need, considering both feature coverage and affordable memory size. However, for the SIFT descriptor space with as large as 128 dimensions, it is still unknown whether 50 million SIFT features are enough to capture the feature distribution. Even if the memory would afford several orders of magnitude more training features, it would take intolerable time cost to finish the clustering for codebook generation. 2) **Limited reliability**: codebook construction in vector quantization relies on the collection of image features and codebook generation methods. Different collections of image features may produce totally different codebooks. Even with the same collection of images and the same clustering methods, generated codebook may be still different due to the variability of k-means. Therefore, quantization error is hard to be controlled. 3) **Update inefficiency**: with many new features collected, the codebook/quantizer should be updated accordingly. However, the codebook updating needs lots of effort. The huge amount of features have to be re-clustered, which is computationally inefficient.

To address the above problems, in this paper, a novel quantization strategy, *scalar quantization*, is proposed. Distinguished from the traditional vector quantization methods, the proposed scalar quantization approach does not involve any form of visual codebook training or clustering. Instead, it transforms each feature to a bit-vector with a quantizer, which is independent of collections of image features. Our quantization operation is very simple and requires low computational cost. The bit-vector generated by scalar quantization achieves more compact representation of the original SIFT descriptors, but still keeps the discriminative power of SIFT feature. Since our quantization method is independent of collections of images, even with new collected features, there is no need to update our quantizer.

Moreover, scalar quantization can index features to the classic inverted file structure easily by extracting the first tens of bits from the quantized bit-vector to generate code word. And the remaining bits of the quantized bit-vector are stored in the inverted file list for matching verification. Furthermore, a novel soft quantization strategy is applied in scalar quantization to address the quantization loss by enumerating the nearest neighbors of the code word. Consequently, more candidate matches are included for matching verification, which greatly boost the retrieval accuracy in large-scale image database.

In this paper, we only focus on the feature quantization step. To further improve the image retrieval performance, our approach can also be flexibly integrated with many other algorithms, such as weak geometric consistency [15], fast spatial matching [3], geometric verification [4] [17], and query expansion [5], *etc.*

To summarize, the main contributions of this paper lie in three aspects:

(1) We propose a new scalar quantization method to quantize the SIFT descriptor to a compact bit-vector, with the discriminative power kept. No visual codebook is needed to be trained in our quantization scheme.

(2) We adapt the quantized bit-vectors to the popular inverted index file structure for scalable image search.

(3) We propose a soft quantization scheme based on our indexing structure to reduce the quantization error.

The rest of the paper is organized as follows. Section 2 reviews related work in large-scale image search. Section 3 discusses the proposed algorithm in details. Experimental results are given in Section 4. Section 5 makes discussions on three issues. Finally, the conclusion is provided in Section 6.

2. RELATED WORK

In large-scale content-based image search applications, Bag-of-Words (BoW) model based on local features has been widely adopted. Generally, in those BoW-based approaches, there are four major key components: local feature representation, feature quantization, index strategy, and post-processing. In this section, we make a review of related work in each component.

Local Feature Representation Extraction of local feature usually involves two steps, *i.e.* interest point detection and feature description. The detected interest points are expected to have high repeatability over various changes. Popular detectors include Difference of Gaussian (DoG) [1], MSER [7], and Hessian affine [8]. After interest point detection, a descriptor is extracted to represent the visual appearance of the local region centered at the interest point. Usually, the descriptor should be invariant to rotation and scale, and also robust to affine distortion, addition of noise, and illumination changes, *etc.* The most popular choice with the above merits is SFIT feature [1]. As a variation, SURF [9] demonstrates good performance but achieves better efficiency. Recently, a binary feature BRIEF [10] and its variation ORB [11] have been proposed and attracted lots of attention.

Feature Quantization Usually, several hundred or thousand local features are extracted from a single image. To achieve a compact representation, high-dimensional local features are quantized to visual words, and an image can be represented as a "bag" of visual words. Therefore, a visual codebook containing visual words needs to be generated first. The most intuitive visual codebook generation method is k-means [2] or hierarchical k-means [6] for large size visual codebook generation.

With visual codebook defined, feature quantization is to assign a visual word ID to each feature. The most naive choice is finding the closest (the most similar) visual word of a given feature by linear scan, which, however, suffers expensive computational cost. Usually, approximate nearest neighbor (ANN) search methods are adopted to speed up the searching process, with sacrifice of accuracy to some extent. In [1], a k-d tree [21] is utilized with a best-bin-first modification to find approximate nearest neighbors to the descriptor vector of the query. In [6], based on hierarchical vocabulary tree, an efficient approximate nearest neighbor search is achieved by propagating the query feature vector from the root node down the tree by comparing the corresponding child nodes and choosing the closest one. In [12], a k-d forest approximation algorithm is proposed with reduced time complexity. To reduce the quantization loss, a descriptor-dependent soft assignment scheme [13] is proposed to map a feature vector to a weighted combination of several visual words. In [14], the high dimensional SIFT descriptor space is partitioned into regular lattices. Although demonstrated to work well in image classification, in [13], regular lattice quantization is reported working significant worse than [6][13] in large-scale image search. In [27], a novel scheme is proposed to jointly optimize the dimension reduction and indexing. In [28], a compact image signature, called Residual Enhanced Visual Vector, is designed via quantization residue aggregation and classification-aware dimensionality reduction. In [29] and [30], descriptive and contextual visual vocabularies are generated respectively for large-scale image applications, such as image search.

In [15], for each feature quantized to a visual word, feature dimension is further performed and a binary signature is generated with a pre-trained median vector. Such binary signature will be used for feature matching verification in on-line retrieval. In [26], a variation of Hamming Embedding [15], *i.e.*, the Asymmetric Hamming Embedding scheme, is proposed to better exploit the information conveyed by the binary signature.

Index Strategy Inspired by the success of text search engines, inverted file structure [23] has been successfully used for large-scale image search [2][3][4][5][6][13][15][16]. In essence, inverted file structure is a compact representation of a sparse matrix, whose row and column denote visual word and image, respectively. In on-line retrieval, only those images sharing common visual words with the query image need to be checked. Therefore, the number of candidate images to be compared is greatly reduced, achieving efficient response.

In inverted file structure, each visual word is followed by an inverted file list of entries. Each entry stores the ID of image where the visual word appears, and some other clues for verification or similarity measurement. For instance, Hamming Embedding [15] generates a 64-bit Hamming code for each feature to verify descriptor matching. Bundled Feature [16] stores the x-order and y-order of each SIFT feature located in the bundled area. The geometric clues, such as feature position, scale, and orientation, are also stored in inverted file list for verification of geometric consistency [3][4][15][16][17].

To further reduce the memory cost of inverted file structure, a visual word vector is mapped to a low-dimensional representation by a group of min-hash functions [18] [19]. Consequently, only a small constant amount of data per image needs to be stored.

Post Processing The initially returned result list can be further refined by exploring the spatial context or enhancing the original query. Spatial verification [3] [4] [15] [17] [19] and query expansion [5] [24] are two of the most successful post-processing techniques to boost the accuracy of large-scale image search.

Spatial context is an important clue to remove false positive visual matches. Lots of work has been done on spatial verification. In [2], locally spatial consistency is imposed to filter visual-word matches with low support. In [15], weak geometric consistency on scale and orientation is imposed to quickly filter potential false matches. In [3], global spatial verification is performed based on a variation of RANSAC [20]. An affine model is estimated to filter local matches that fail to fit the model. In [4] [17], the geometric context among local features is encoded into binary maps. And then it recursively removes geometrically inconsistent matches by analyzing those coding maps.

Query expansion, leveraged from text retrieval, reissues the initial highly-ranked results to generate new queries. Some relevant features, which are not present in the original query, can be used to enrich the original query to further improve the recall performance. Several strategies, such as average query expansion, transitive closure expansion, recursive expansion, intra-expansion, and inter-expansion, *etc.* have been discussed in [5] [24].

3. METHOD

In this paper, we focus on feature quantization, which plays a key role of BoW model. We first introduce our scalar quantization strategy in Section 3.1. Then, in Section 3.2, we discuss how to adapt the scalar quantization result to the classic inverted file structure for scalable image search. In Section 3.3, we discuss a soft quantization scheme to further reduce the quantization error in on-line query stage. Finally, a summary of our quantization algorithm is given in Section 3.4.

3.1 Scalar Quantization

High dimensional SIFT descriptors (L_2-normalized 128-D vectors [1]) are extracted from images for discrimination. Each dimension of the descriptor vector corresponds to a bin of concatenated orientation histograms. Generally, similar SIFT features have relatively smaller distances than different features. Features from the same source, e.g. image patch, may not be exactly same due to image noise. But their values on the 128 bins usually share some common patterns, e.g., the pair-wise differences between most of bins are similar and stable. Therefore, it can be easily extended that the differences between bins and a predefined threshold are stable for most bins. Based on such observation, we propose a scalar quantization strategy.

Given a high dimensional feature vector $f = (f_1, f_2, \cdots, f_d)^T \in R^d$, where $f_i \in R, (i = 1,2,\cdots,d)$, and d denotes the feature dimension size. For SIFT descriptor, $d = 128$. We define a quantization function $q(\cdot)$ to transform f to a bit vector $b = (b_1, b_2, \cdots, b_d)^T$, as follows:

$$b_i = \begin{cases} 1 & \text{if } f_i > \hat{f} \\ 0 & \text{if } f_i \leq \hat{f} \end{cases} \qquad (i = 1,2,\cdots,d) \qquad (1)$$

where $\hat{f}$ is a threshold determined by vector f.

The threshold $\hat{f}$ is an important parameter, which determines the discriminative power of the quantization results. If the discriminative power of SIFT is well kept in scalar quantization, the Hamming distance between scalar vectors b should be consistent with the L_2 distance between original feature vectors f. There are many methods to choose the threshold $\hat{f}$. In this paper, we choose $\hat{f}$ as the median value of vector f. The philosophy behind it is that, the median value is relatively stable to changes in some bins of a long vector. The quantization function $q(\cdot)$ is a kind of hashing. Unlike classic LSH methods involving many hashing tables and functions [8] [19], our scheme needs only one hash function and therefore is much simpler and more efficient.

With each high dimension feature quantized to a bit-stream vector, the feature comparison is transformed to the comparison of binary vectors, which can be efficiently accomplished by exclusive-OR operation and measured by Hamming distance.

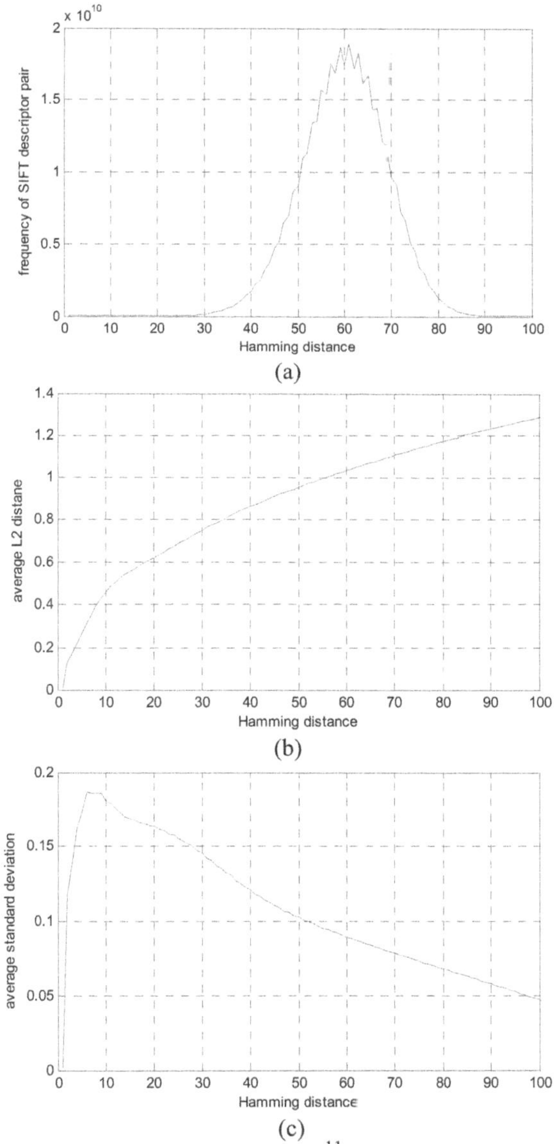

Figure 1. The statistics on 4.08×10^{11} pairs of SIFT descriptors. (a) Descriptor pair frequency vs. Hamming distance; (b) The average L_2-distance vs. Hamming distance; (c) The average standard deviation vs. Hamming distance.

To demonstrate the discriminative power of SIFT descriptors is well kept in our scalar quantization, we have made a statistical study on 4.08×10^{11} SIFT descriptor pairs, which include every SIFT pair extracted from image pairs randomly sampled from a large image dataset. For each descriptor pair, its L_2 distance before scalar quantization and Hamming distance after scalar quantization are calculated. As shown in Fig. 1(a), the distribution of Hamming distances between these descriptors exhibits a Gaussian-like distribution. From Fig. 1 (b) and Fig. 1(c), it is observed that the Hamming distance between our quantized bit-vectors is consistent with the average L_2-distance, with relatively small standard deviation (computed on the unit-normalized descriptors). To further reduce the deviation, we use a variation of Eq. (1) and transform the descriptor vector to a 256-bit vector, which will be discussed at the end of this section.

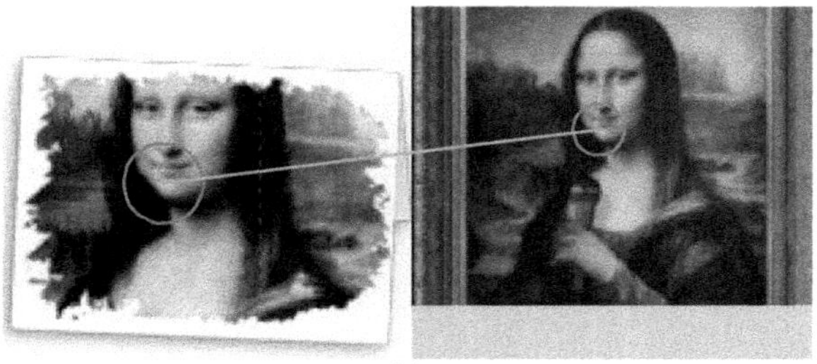

(a)

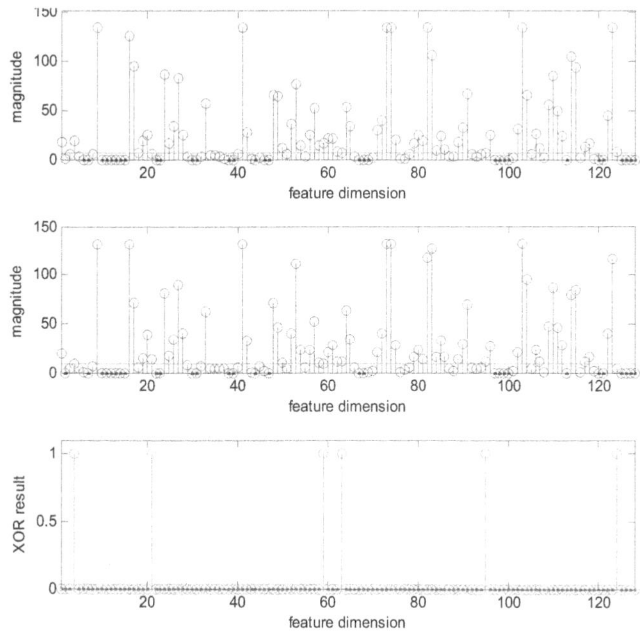

(b)

Figure 2. Example of feature matches. (a) A local match between two images. The endpoints of the green line denote the key point positions of two SIFT features. The radius of the red circle centered at the key points is proportional to the SIFT feature's characteristic scale. (b) top: the 128-D descriptor of the matched SIFT feature in the left image; middle: the 128-D descriptor of the matched SIFT feature in the right image; bottom: the XOR result of the binary SIFT features from the two matched SIFT features. The red horizontal lines in the "top" and "bottom" figure denote the median values of the two SIFT descriptors, respectively.

It should be noted that our approach is different from the SIFT quantization methods proposed in lattice quantization [14] and Hamming Embedding [15]. In [14], the descriptor space is arbitrarily split along dimension axes into regular lattice. In [15], for each bin/dimension, a median value of all training features on that bin in the reduced dimensional space is computed for binarizing the corresponding dimension. Both two approaches ignore the unique property of every individual SIFT descriptor.

As shown in Fig. 1, the original features' difference in Euclidean distance can be well captured by their Hamming distance after scalar quantization. Fig. 2 shows a real instance of local descriptor match across two images with scalar quantization. From Fig. 2(b), it can be observed that these two SIFT descriptors have similar magnitude in the corresponding bins with some small variations before quantization. After scalar quantization, they differ from each other in six bins. With a proper threshold, it can be easily determined whether the local match is true or false just by the exclusive-OR (XOR) operation between the quantized bit-vectors. Obviously, the error in the exclusive-OR result is likely to occur in those bins with magnitude around the median value. Intuitively, the median threshold could be increased to some upper level, which can make the Hamming distance between similar SIFT descriptors smaller. However, such modification will also reduce the Hamming distance between irrelevant descriptors and cause false descriptor matches.

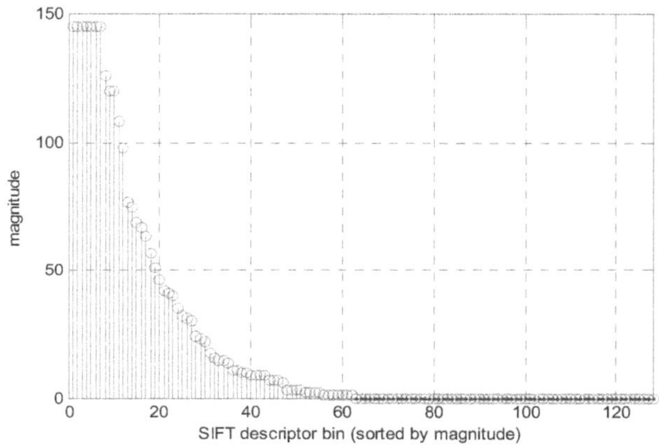

(a)

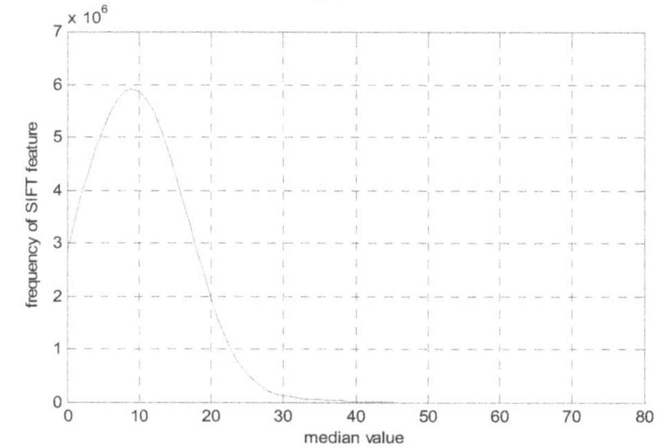

(b)

Figure 3. Statistics of SIFT descriptors. (a) A typical SIFT descriptor with bins sorted by magnitude in each dimension; (b) The frequency distribution of median value of the descriptor vector among 100 million SIFT descriptors.

Another statistical study on the distribution of median value of SIFT descriptor is also performed. 100 million SIFT descriptors are sampled from a large dataset, and the median value of each 128-D descriptor vector is computed. As shown in Fig. 3, the median value of most SIFT descriptors is relatively small, around 10, but the maximum magnitude in some bins still can reach more than 140. This may incur potential quantization loss since those bins with magnitude above the median are not well distinguished. To address this issue, the same scalar quantization strategy could be conducted again on those bins with magnitude above the median. Intuitively, such operation can be performed recursively. However, it will cause additional storage cost. In our implementation, we only perform the scalar quantization twice, *i.e.*, first on the whole 128 elements, and second on those elements with magnitude above the median value. Consequently, a SIFT descriptor $f = (f_1, f_2, \cdots, f_{128})^T \in R^{128}$ is quantized to a 256-bit vector $\tilde{b} = (b_1, b_2, \cdots, b_{256})^T$, as follows:

$$(b_i, b_{i+128}) = \begin{cases} (1,\ 1) & \text{if } f_i > \hat{f}_2 \\ (1,\ 0) & \text{if } \hat{f}_1 < f_i \le \hat{f}_2 \\ (0, 0) & \text{if } f_i \le \hat{f}_1 \end{cases} \quad (i = 1, 2, \cdots, 128) \qquad (2)$$

where $\hat{f}_1 = \frac{g_{64} + g_{65}}{2}$, $\hat{f}_2 = \frac{g_{32} + g_{33}}{2}$, $(g_1, g_2, \cdots, g_{128})$ is the sorted vector from $(f_1, f_2, \cdots, f_{128})$ in descending order. With Eq. (2), each dimension of SIFT descriptor is divided into three parts, and two bits are used to encode each part.

With scalar quantization by Eq. (2), the comparison of SIFT descriptors in L_2-distance is captured by the Hamming distance of the corresponding 256-bit vectors. Since our target is large-scale image search, how to adapt our scalar quantization result to the classic inverted file structure for scalable image search needs to be explored.

3.2 Indexing with Inverted File Structure

In image search, the problem of feature matching between images can be regarded as finding feature's nearest or approximate-nearest neighbors. When the feature amount becomes very large, say, over one billion, it is too computationally expensive to find the nearest neighbors by linearly comparing all features' binary vectors. To address this problem, leveraged from text retrieval, inverted file structure can be used for scalable indexing of large-scale image dataset.

In traditional inverted file structure for image search, a group of visual words are pre-trained. And each visual word is followed with an entry list of image features, which are quantized to this followed visual word. Each indexed feature in the list records its image ID and some other clues.

To adapt to the classic inverted file structure to index image features, we define *code word*[1] by the first t bits of the binary code generated by scalar quantization result. Then, the rest bits of features are recorded in the entry list of the corresponding code word. In fact, any other t bits of the binary code are expected to be equivalent. A toy example is shown in Fig. 4. Intuitively, if a code word is represented with t bits, the total number of code words could be amounted up to 2^t. However, it is found from experiments that, when t increases above 20, the amount of non-empty code words becomes much smaller than 2^t, as shown in Fig. 5. For example, when t increases to 32, the total number of code words could be up to $2^{32} \approx 4 \times 10^9$ (4 billion). However, the number of unique code words generated by scalar quantization (on one million image database) is even much less than 10^8.

Generally, the more code words are generated, the shorter the average length of indexed feature list becomes, and the less the time cost is needed to query a new feature. However, in our method, we will introduce a soft quantization scheme (Section 3.3) to expand more code words for each query feature. And the number of expanded indexed feature lists is polynomial to t. To make a tradeoff, in our experiments, we select $t = 32$, and 46.5 million "code words" are obtained.

Fig. 6 shows the distribution of code word occurrence on one million image database. It can be observed that, of the 46.5 million code words, only the top few thousand code words have very high frequency. Those code words are prevalent in many images, and their distinctive power is weak. As suggested by [2], we apply a stop-list to ignore those high frequency code words that occur in more than 0.11% of the total image dataset. Experiments reveal that a proper stop-list may not affect the search accuracy, but does avoid checking many code word lists and achieves gain in efficiency.

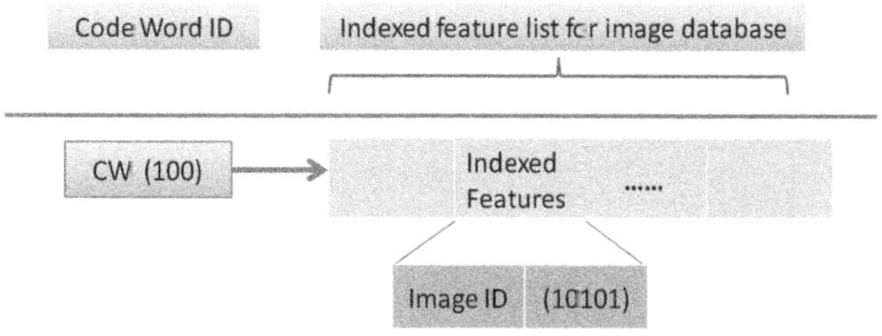

Figure 4. A toy example of image feature indexed with inverted file structure. The scalar quantization result of the indexed feature is an 8-bit vector (1001 0101). The first three bits denote its code word ID (100), and the remaining 5 bits (10101) are stored in the inverted file list.

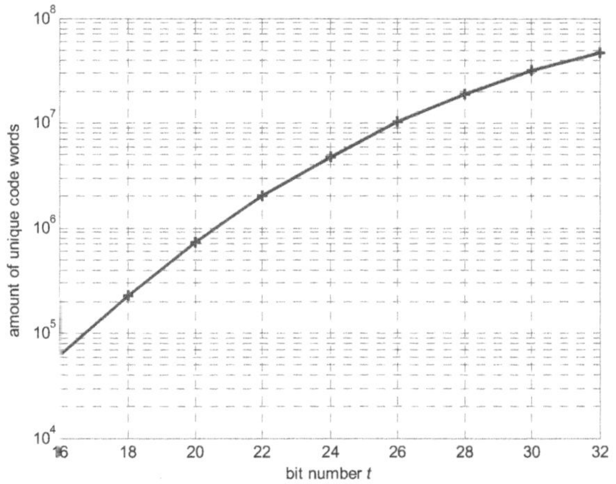

Figure 5. The amount of unique code words (top t bits from 256-bit vector) for different t on 1-million image database.

[1] It should be noted that our code word is different from the traditional visual word [2] [6].

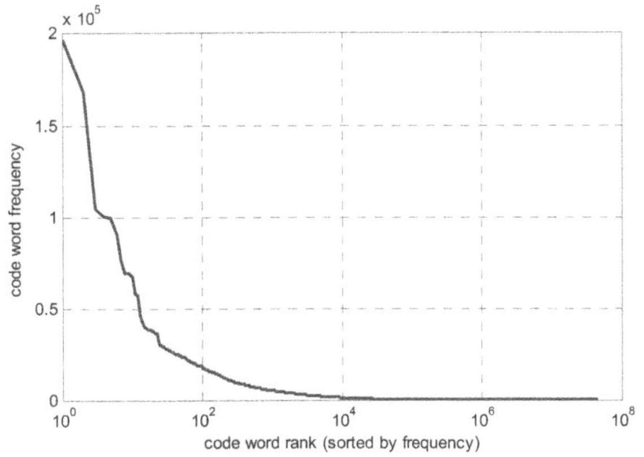

Figure 6. Frequency of code words among one million images.

Once all features of an image dataset have been indexed with the inverted file structure, given a new SIFT descriptor, it will be first quantized to a 256-bit vector with scalar quantization. Then through the top 32 bits, the corresponding code word can be located. And only the indexed features following the matched code word will be checked. Therefore, the searching space is greatly reduced. Finally, the exclusive-OR operation is performed on the remained 224 bits of the query vector and those of indexed features recorded in the entry list of the matched code word. A threshold κ on the Hamming distance between 256-bit vectors needs to be set for true-match judgment, such that those matches with Hamming distance no larger than κ will be accepted as true matches. The impact of κ will be studied in Section 4.1.

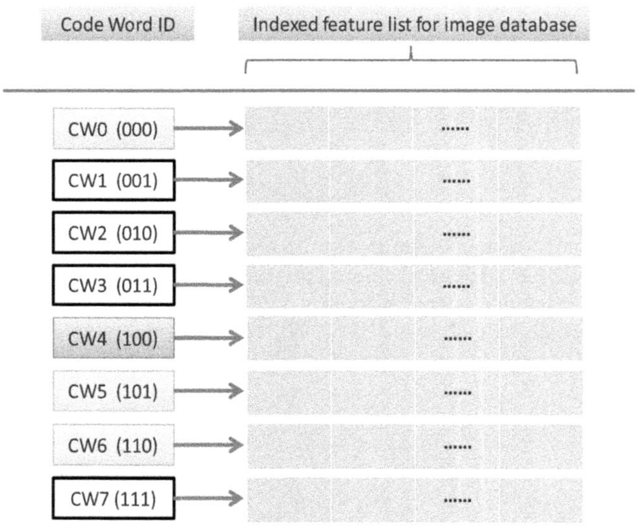

Figure 7. A toy example of soft quantization with bit-stream code words. There are eight code words, each represented with a three-bit vector. Each code word is followed by an indexed image feature list. (Best viewed in color PDF)

3.3 Reduction of Quantization Error

In Section 3.2, we define code word by the top 32 bits of the bit vector from scalar quantization. However, such simple processing will exclude some candidate features that have some flipping bits among the top 32 bits (e.g., 0 changes to 1) due to noise. To address this issue, we propose a soft strategy to reduce the quantization error. Assuming such flipping happens only to very few dimensions, features before and after the flipping should be still very similar, *i.e.*, small Hamming distance. To identify these candidate features, it is desired to quickly enumerate all of its possible nearest neighbors within a predefined Hamming distance d, just by alternatively flipping some bits. This is equivalent to a tolerant expansion of the original code word. The impact of expansion-bit number d will be studied in Section 4.1.

As shown in the toy example in Fig. 7, the code word of a new query feature is a bit-vector 100, *i.e.*, CW4 in pink color. To identify all of candidate features, its possible nearest neighbors (e.g., Hamming distance d=1) will be obtained by flipping one bit in turn, which generates three additional code words (in green color): CW0 (000), CW5 (101) and CW6 (110). These code words are nearest neighbors of CW4 in the Hamming space. Then, besides CW4, the indexed feature lists of these three expanded code words will be also considered as candidate true matches, and all features in these expanded lists will be further compared on their rest bit-codes.

Off-line Indexing with Scalar Quantization

1) Given a 128-D SIFT descriptor from an index image, convert it to a 256-bit vector by Eq. (2);
2) Identify code word ID V_d by the first 32 bits of the 256-bit vector.
3) In the inverted image list of V_d, store both the ID of the image where the feature appears, and the remaining 224 bits of the quantized 256-bit vector.

Figure 8. The general steps of off-line indexing with scalar quantization.

On-line Querying with Scalar Quantization

1) Given a 128-D SIFT descriptor in a query image, convert it to a 256-bit vector by Eq. (2);
2) Identify its code word ID V_q by the first 32 bits of the 256-bit vector.
3) For each feature in the inverted image list linked to V_q, compare its indexed 224-bit vector with the query feature. If the total Hamming distance in 256-bit is not greater than κ, accept the indexed feature as true match.
4) Expand the V_q to include its nearest code words $\{V_q^i,\ i=1,2,\cdots\}$ with Hamming distance no greater than d.
5) For each V_q^i, repeat step (3).

Figure 9. The general steps of on-line querying with scalar quantization.

3.4 Algorithm Summary

Overall, the proposed scalar quantization consists of two stages: offline indexing and on-line querying. In this section, we summarize the general steps of these two stages in Fig. 8 and Fig. 9, respectively. Given a query image, after looking up the index file with the proposed on-line querying steps, we can obtain the matching results between the query image and target images. Finally, we formulate image retrieval as a voting problem and define the similarity between two images by the cardinality of matched feature set.

4. EXPERIMENTS

Our basic dataset is built by crawling one million images from the Web. We take the partial-duplicate image dataset released in [17] as the ground-truth dataset, which contains 1104 images from 33 groups, including "Mona Lisa", "KFC logo", "American Gothic Painting", "Seven-eleven logo", *etc.* To evaluate the performance with respect to the size of dataset, we construct three smaller datasets (50K, 200K, and 500K) by sampling the basic dataset. From the ground truth dataset, 108 representative query images are randomly selected for evaluation comparison. Similar to [3][14][16], mean average precision (mAP) is selected to evaluate the accuracy performance of all methods.

We use the standard SIFT feature [1] for image representation. Key points are detected with the Difference-of-Gaussian (DoG) detector. A 128-D orientation histogram (SIFT descriptor) is extracted to capture the visual appearance of local patch centered at each key point. Before feature extraction, large images are scaled to have a maximum axis size of 400.

4.1 Parameter Analysis

There are two parameters in our approach: Hamming distance threshold κ and expansion-bit number d. To study the impact of these two parameters on search performance and computational cost, we compare the mAP performance and average time cost per query under different parameter settings of κ and d on the 1-M image dataset. The results are shown in Fig. 10.

From Fig. 10(a), it can be observed that when the Hamming distance threshold κ increases, the mAP performance first increases and then keeps stable and gradually drops a little after it reaches the peak, where $\kappa = 24$. This is intuitive, since increasing κ always includes more candidate true matches, but when κ is too large, many noisy matches are also included and pollute the results. On the other hand, when expansion-bit number d increases, the mAP gradually increases. This is due to the fact that more candidate code word lists are involved in matching verification, and more true matches will be kept.

In terms of efficiency, as shown in Fig. 10(b), the average time cost per query increases when κ increases. This is due to that, when κ is larger, we have to make more exclusive-OR operations, until the Hamming distance between two 224-bit vectors is above a threshold. As d increases, the querying time cost rises significantly. This is because the expanded code word list number is exponential to the expansion-bit number d.

Considering the tradeoff between mAP performance and time cost, κ is set as 24 and d is set as 2 in the rest experiments.

4.2 Evaluation

Comparison Algorithms: We compare our approach with three state-of-the-art feature quantization algorithms in large-scale image search. The BoW approach with visual vocabulary tree [6] is selected as the "baseline" method. We test various sizes of visual word vocabulary, and the 1-million vocabulary gives the best overall performance. As suggested in [2][6], the stop-list strategy is also adopted to improve efficiency. To enhance the baseline, two other algorithms, *i.e.*, soft assignment [13] and Hamming embedding [15], are also compared.

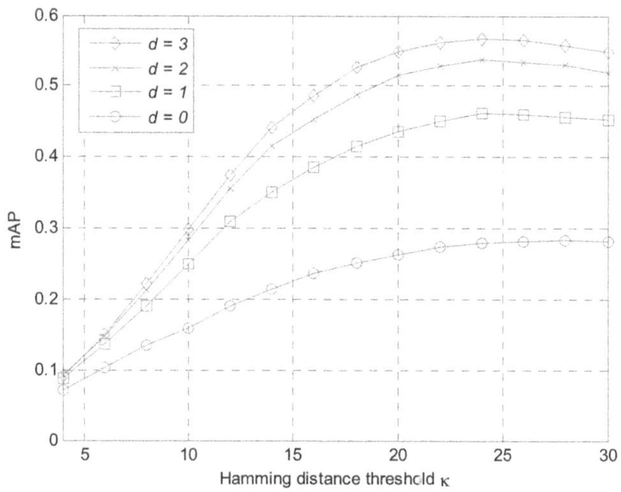

(a)

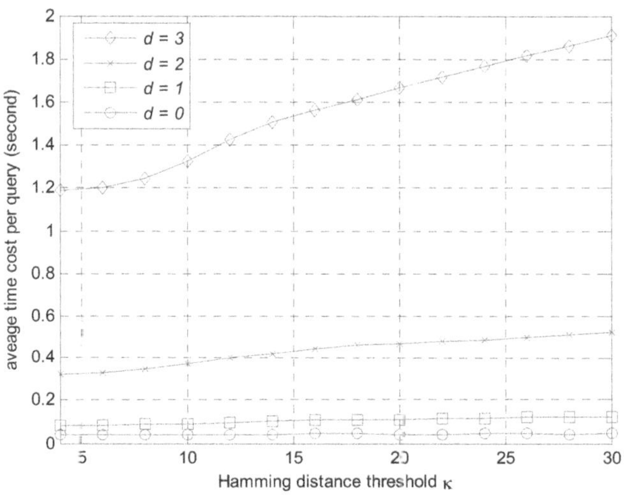

(b)

Figure 10. (a)The mAP performance and (b) average time cost per query under different parameter settings of κ and d on the 1-million image dataset.

Soft assignment [13] identifies a local feature with a weighted combination of three nearby visual words. We use the default parameters as set in [13]. The "nearby" visual words for a given feature are found by the approximate nearest neighbor search algorithm *k*-d tree [21][25]. A public library for approximate nearest neighbor (ANN) searching [22] is used in our experiments. To make a tradeoff between accuracy and efficiency, we select the error bound parameter [22] as five.

Hamming embedding [15] generates additional Hamming codes (64 bits) to filter more candidate features which are quantized to the same visual word but have large hamming distance to the query feature. We denote this method as "HE". We have tested different thresholds for the Hamming distance in HE, and the best performance is achieved when the threshold is selected as 12. Since the focus of this paper is feature quantization, the weak geometric consistency scheme proposed in the Hamming embedding approach is not added in the experiments.

Accuracy: From Fig. 11, it can be observed that our approach outperforms all the other three methods on large image databases. On the 1-million dataset, The mAP of the baseline is 0.38. Our approach hits 0.54, a relatively 42.1% improvement. Since Hamming codes can effectively filter false featurs, the Hamming Embdding approach achieves a mAP of 0.43, but still 11% lower than our approach. The mAP improvement of soft assignment approach is higher than HE. It reaches a mAP of 0.48. Compared with soft assignment, our approach still enjoys a relatively 12.5% improvement. Such improvement stems from the distance based thresholding for matching verification of our approach. It is interesting to note that, when the database size decreases to 50 K, our approach is worse than the soft assignment. This is due to our tradeoff selection on the expansion bit number and efficiency.

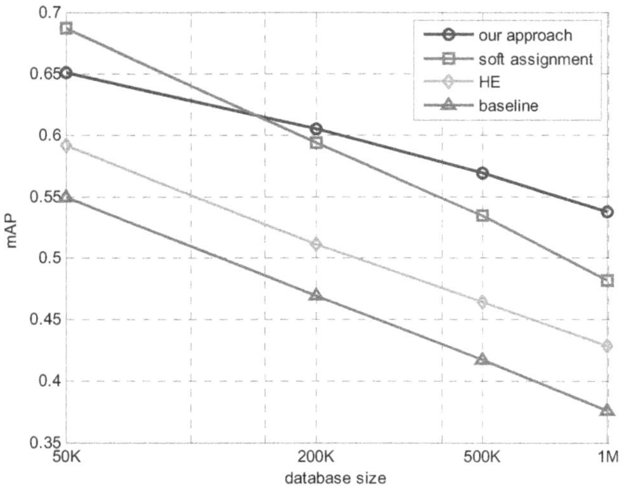

Figure 11. Performance (mAP) comparison of different methods with different database sizes.

Efficiency: The experiments are performed on a server with 3.4 GHz CPU and 16 GB memory. We compare efficiency in both off-line indexing and on-line query. From Table 1, it can be observed that our approach is the most efficient one in indexing image features. It takes our approach 18.86 seconds to index one million SIFT features, which is 2 times, 2.5 times, and 40 times faster than the baseline, HE and soft assignment approach, respectively. Fig. 12 shows the average time cost per query of all four approaches. It should be noted that the time cost of SIFT feature extraction is not included for all approaches. It takes the baseline 0.12 second in average to perform one query. HE is the most time-efficient one and costs only 0.05 second to finish one query in average. Soft assignment is the most time-consuming approach, consuming 0.52 second in average per query. Although our approach costs more time than the baseline approach, it may still meet user's expectation of fast response time (average 0.48 second per query) but with much higher search accuracy. It is slightly more efficient than the soft assignment approach, with 0.04 second less in average per query.

It should be noted that a distinctive characteristic of our approach from other three comparison methods is that, no visual codebook needed to be trained before feature quantization, which could save a lot of computational time. As a contrast, all three comparison algorithms have to train a large visual codebook containing as many as one million visual words, which usually costs days of time. In order to train a visual codebook of one million in size, usually about 100 million SFIT descriptors are needed as training samples. However, even with so many training samples, it is still unclear whether these training samples are enough to generate desired visual words to capture the sample distribution in the so large 128-D descriptor space. Moreover, when more new features are indexed, it may be necessary to update the visual codebook accordingly (*e.g.*, re-cluster all the features), which is always time consuming and computationally expensive. On the contrary, our scalar quantization just needs to incrementally add new code words to the existing visual codebook (code word set).

Table 1. Time cost to index 1 million SIFT features for four approaches in off-line stage.

Method	baseline	HE	soft assignment	our approach
Time cost (second)	53.72	64.82	771.09	18.86

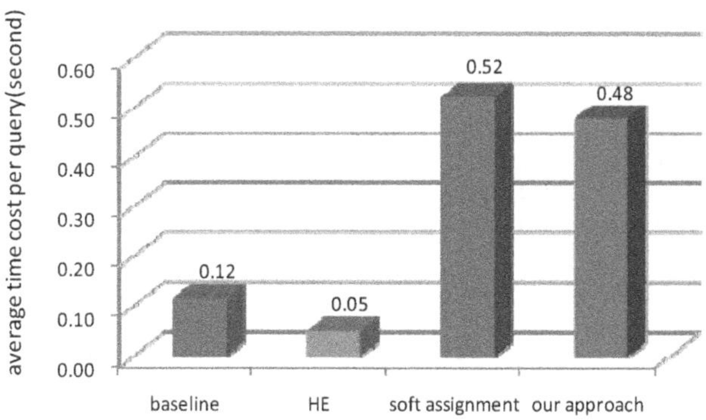

Figure 12. Comparison of average query time cost of different methods on the 1M database. (Not including the time cost for SIFT feature extraction)

Table 2. Memory cost for four approaches.

	Memory cost per indexed feature (byte)	Memory cost for quantizer (byte)
baseline	8	142M
HE	12	398M
soft assignment	24	506M
our approach	32	0

Memory Cost: We compare memory cost of all approaches on both indexed feature and quantizer, as listed in Table 2. In terms of memory cost per indexed feature, for each feature, the baseline approach needs 4 bytes to store image ID and another 4 bytes to store the *tf-idf* weight. The soft assignment has to store each indexed features in three visual word lists, therefore it costs 24 bytes, three times the memory cost of the baseline approach. In Hamming Embedding approach, it allocates 4 bytes on image ID and 8 bytes on the 64-bit Hamming code. Compared with the above three methods, our approach consumes more memory. It takes 4 bytes to store image ID and additional 28 bytes to store another 224 bits from quantization results.

Besides indexed feature, all the three comparison methods have to load a large quantizer into main memory. A hierarchical visual vocabulary tree (about 142M bytes) is required for both the baseline and HE. Besides, HE has to store a 64-D median vector (floating point values) for each leaf node. As for soft assignment approach, besides the visual words (leaf nodes of the vocabulary tree, 128M bytes), it also needs to generate a *k*-d tree (about 378M bytes)to quantize features. As a contrast, our approach needs no memory cost on quantizer.

4.3 Sample Results

In Fig. 13, a sample edited image "Apollo" is selected as a query to demonstrate the search performance of all four approaches on the 1-million dataset. For this query, compared with the baseline approach, our approach improves the mAP from 0.36 to 0.846, with relatively 135% improvement. Fig. 13 (c) and (d) show the top images returned by the baseline approach and our approach, respectively. Due to the poor quality of the query image, the returned results of the baseline are polluted by irrelevant images. As for our approach, more relevant images are ranked to the top.

Fig. 14 shows a difficult image sample on which our method works poorly. The query image is the first image with label rank-1 in Fig. 14(a). Since the query contains a large portion of patches containing rich text, the returned results are polluted by many screenshot images of documents or web pages. The matching result between the query and the fifth returned image is shown in Fig. 14(b). Although irrelevant in visual content, they still share many local similar patterns. Such query is also very challenging for the other three comparison methods. To filter such false positives, spatial verification algorithms [3] [17] could be combined with our scalar quantization to re-rank the results.

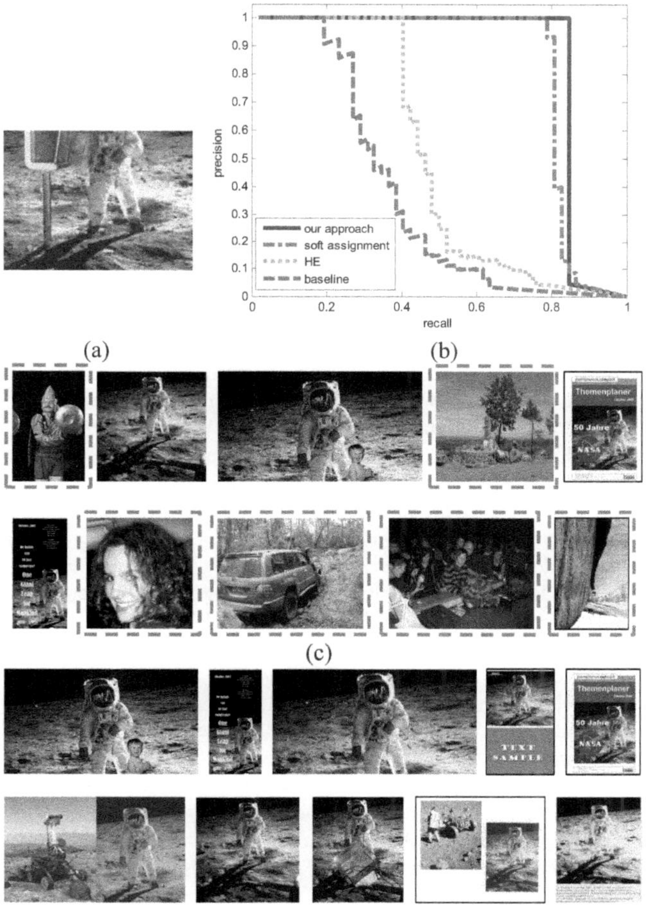

Figure 13. Sample results comparing the baseline and our approach. (a) Query image; (b) Comparison of the precision-recall curves of all four approaches; (c) The top images (rank 11 to rank 20) returned by the baseline; (d) The top images returned by our approach (rank 11 to rank 20). The first 10 images are true positive for both baseline and our approach and therefore are not shown. The false positives are shown with red dashed bounding boxes. (Best viewed in color PDF)

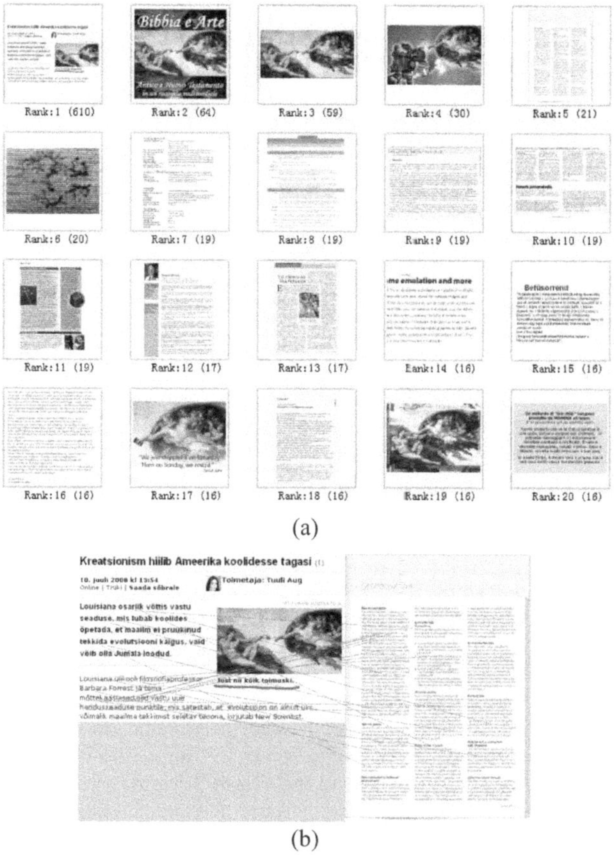

Figure 14. Retrieval examples. (a) Retrieval results of the query (Rank 1). The number of local matches is shown in the bracket below each image. (b) Feature matching between the query and the rank 5 result. (Best viewed in color PDF)

5. DISCUSSION

5.1 Threshold in Quantization

In our scalar quantization, the threshold $\hat{f}$ in Eq. (1) is selected as the median value of the feature descriptor, so as in Eq. (2). However, it is still an open question whether the median value is the best choice. There are many alternatives for it, such as mean value of vector f . Alternatively, we can also cluster the 128 elements of a SIFT descriptor into two clusters and choose the cluster boundary as the threshold $\hat{f}$. For some specific applications, $\hat{f}$ can also be learned by training. For example, some positive and negative matching pairs are manually labeled beforehand. Then, the threshold $\hat{f}$ can be learned to yield the best classification performance for discrimination.

5.2 Dimension Reduction

Our approach consumes more memory to index each feature (28 bytes) than other three approaches. It is desired that the memory cost can be further reduced without much sacrifice of search accuracy. As discussed in Section 3.1, it can be inferred that the size of scalar quantization result is proportional to the dimension of SIFT descriptors. If SIFT descriptors can be reduced in dimension, the quantization result will be more compact. There are two possible ways to achieve this goal. One method is to project SIFT descriptors to a low dimensional space by PCA. The dimension-reduced features are expected to keep the characteristics of the original SIFT descriptors, so that our scalar quantization can be applied in the new feature space as well.

The second possible method is to change the formulation of SIFT descriptors, instead of performing dimension reduction. The original SIFT descriptor is designed as a combination of 8-D orientation histogram on 16 (4×4) patches. It is possible to reformulate it in a simple way, such as dividing the local region into 3×3 patches instead of 4×4, and extracting an 8-D orientation histogram on each patch. And SIFT descriptor dimension will be reduced from 128 to 72. It is demonstrated by Lowe [1] that, such a design only causes a small drop on the closest neighbor matching. Its impact on large-scale image search still needs to be further studied.

5.3 Extension to General Features

In this paper, we present our scalar quantization based on SIFT descriptors. An intuitive question "can the proposed scalar quantization algorithm be extended to general feature vectors?" may be interesting. SIFT descriptors are very distinctive, with most energy concentrated on relatively few bins, as shown by a typical example in Fig. 3(a). Besides, it captures the local visual appearance with very strict representation. Such property makes our approach work well on SIFT descriptors. Therefore, our scalar quantization can be generally extended to other features with similar property as SIFT feature.

6. CONCLUSION

In this paper, a novel quantization scheme "scalar quantization" is proposed on SIFT descriptors for large-scale image search. Scalar quantization quantizes a SIFT descriptor to a 256-bit vector, which can be easily adapted to the classic inverted file structure for indexing. Distinguished from the traditional vector quantization approaches, the proposed scalar quantization approach does not involve any kind of visual codebook training or clustering. The quantizer is defined by an individual feature itself and is independent of collections of images. Further, soft quantization is proposed to efficiently enumerate the nearest code words for quantization error reduction. Experiments on large-scale image search demonstrate the superiority of scalar quantization on retrieval accuracy over other state-of-the-art methods

In the future, investigation will be performed on developing more compact bit-vector representation in scalar quantization. Moreover, the flipping behavior of bit-vectors of similar SIFT descriptors will be explored. Some insights are expected to be obtained from this study, which may be beneficial for searching space reduction in soft quantization step and consequently improve retrieval efficiency. Further, various choices for threshold selection in scalar quantization will be studied.

7. ACKNOWLEDGMENTS

This work was supported in part to Dr. Lu by Research Enhancement Program (REP), start-up funding from the Texas State University and DoD HBCU/MI grant W911NF-12-1-0057, in part to Dr. Li by NSFC general project "Intelligent Video Processing and Coding Based on Cloud Computing", and in part to Dr. Tian by ARO grant W911NF-12-1-0057, NSF IIS 1052851, Faculty Research Awards by Google, NEC Laboratories of America and FXPAL, UTSA START-R award, respectively.

8. REFERENCES

[1] D. Lowe. Distinctive image features form scale-invariant keypoints. *IJCV*, 20(2): 91-110, 2004.

[2] J. Sivic and A. Zisserman. Video Google: a text retrieval approach to object matching in videos. In *Proc. ICCV*, 2003.

[3] J. Philbin, et al. Object retrieval with large vocabularies and fast spatial matching. In *Proc. CVPR*, 2007.

[4] W. Zhou, Y. Lu, H. Li, Y. Song, and Q. Tian. Spatial coding for large scale partial-duplicate Web image search. In *Proc. ACM Multimedia*, 2010.

[5] O. Chum, J. Philbin, J. Sivic, M. Isard, and A. Zisserman. Total recall: Automatic query expansion with a generative feature model for object retrieval. In *Proc. ICCV*, 2007.

[6] D. Nister and H. Stewenius. Scalable recognition with a vocabulary tree. In *Proc. CVPR*, 2006.

[7] J. Matas, et al. Robust wide baseline stereo from maximally stable extremal regions. In *Proc. BMVC*, 2002.

[8] K. Mikolajczyk and C. Schmid. Scale & affine invariant interest point detectors. *IJCV*, 1(60):63–86, 2004.

[9] H. Bay, T. Tuytelaars, L. V. Gool. SURF: Speeded up robust features. In *Proc. ECCV*, 2006.

[10] M. Calonder, et al. BRIEF: binary robust independent elementary features. In *Proc. ECCV*, 2010.

[11] Ethan Rublee, et al. ORB: an efficient alternative to SIFT or SURF. In *Proc. ICCV*, 2011.

[12] C. Silpa-Anan and R. Hartley. Localization using an image map. In *Australasian Conf. on Robo. and Auto.*, 2004.

[13] J. Philbin, O. Chum, M. Isard, J. Sivic and A. Zisserman. Lost in quantization: Improving particular object retrieval in large scale image databases. In *Proc. CVPR*, 2008.

[14] T. Tuytelaars, C. Schmid. Vector quantizing feature space with a regular lattice. In *Proc. ICCV*, 2010.

[15] H. Jegou, M. Douze, and C. Schmid. Hamming embedding and weak geometric consistency for large scale image search. In *Proc. ECCV*, 2008.

[16] Z. Wu, Q. Ke, et al. Bundling features for large scale partial-duplicate Web image search. In *Proc. CVPR*, 2009.

[17] W. Zhou, H. Li, Y. Lu, Q. Tian, Large scale image search with geometric coding. In *Proc. ACM Multimedia*, 2011.

[18] O. Chum, J. Philbin, et al. Near duplicate image detection: min-Hash and tf-idf weighting. In *Proc. BMVC*, 2008.

[19] O. Chum, M. Perdoch, and J. Matas. Geometric min-Hashing: finding a (thick) needle in a haystack. In *Proc. CVPR*, 2009.

[20] M. A. Fischler, et al. Random Sample Consensus: A paradigm for model fitting with applications to image analysis and automated cartography. *Comm. of the ACM*, 24: 381–395, 1981.

[21] J. L. Bentley. K-d trees for semidynamic point sets. In Proc. 6th Ann. *ACM Sympos. Comput. Geom.*, pp. 187-197, 1990.

[22] S. Arya and D. Mount. Ann: Library for approximate nearest neighbor searching. *Available at* http://www.cs.umd.edu/~mount/ANN/.

[23] R. Baeza-Yates and B. Ribeiro-Neto. Modern information retrieval. *ACM Press*, ISBN: 020139829, 1999.

[24] Y. Kuo, K. Chen, et al. Query expansion for hash-based image object retrieval. In *Proc. ACM Multimedia*, 2009.

[25] J. H. Friedman, J. L. Bentley, and R. A. Finkel. An algorithm for finding best matches in logarithmic expected time. *ACM Transactions on Mathematical Software*, 3(3):209-226, 1977.

[26] M. Jain, H. Jégou and P. Gros. Asymmetric Hamming embedding: taking the best of our bits for large scale image search. In *Proc. ACM Multimedia*, 2011.

[27] H. Jégou, et al. Aggregating local descriptors into a compact image representation. In *Proc. CVPR*, 2010.

[28] D. Chen, S. Tsai, et al. Residual enhanced visual vectors for on-device image matching. In *Asilomar Conference on Signals, Systems, and Computers*, 2011.

[29] S. Zhang, Q. Tian, G. Hua, Q. Huang, and W. Gao. Generating descriptive visual words and visual phrases for large-scale image applications. *TIP*, 20(9): 2664-2677, 2011.

[30] S. Zhang, et al. Building contextual visual vocabulary for large-scale image applications. In *Proc. ACM Multimedia*, 2010.

Query-Driven Iterated Neighborhood Graph Search for Large Scale Indexing

Jingdong Wang   Shipeng Li
Microsoft Research Asia, Beijing, P. R. China
{jingdw, spli}@microsoft.com

ABSTRACT

In this paper, we address the approximate nearest neighbor (ANN) search problem over large scale visual descriptors. We investigate a simple but very effective approach, neighborhood graph search, which constructs a neighborhood graph to index the data points and conducts a local search, expanding neighborhoods with a best-first manner, for ANN search. Our empirical analysis shows that neighborhood expansion is very efficient, with $O(1)$ cost, for a new NN candidate location, and has high chances to locate true NNs and hence it usually performs well. However, it often gets sub-optimal solutions since local search only checks the neighborhood of the current solution, or conducts exhaustive and continuous neighborhood expansions to find better solutions, which deteriorates the query efficiency.

In this paper, we propose a query-driven iterated neighborhood graph search approach to improve the performance. We follow the iterated local search (ILS) strategy, widely-used in combinatorial optimization, to find a solution beyond a local optimum. We handle the key challenge in making neighborhood graph search adapt to ILS, Perturbation, which generates a new pivot to restart a local search. To this end, we present a criterion to check if the local search over a neighborhood graph arrives at the local solution. Moreover, we exploit the query and search history to design the perturbation scheme, resulting in a more effective search. The major benefit is avoiding unnecessary neighborhood expansions and hence more efficiently finding true NNs. Experimental results on large scale SIFT matching, similar image search, and shape retrieval with non-metric distance measures, show that our approach performs much better than previous state-of-the-art ANN search approaches.

Categories and Subject Descriptors

H.3.1 [**Information Storage and Retrieval**]: Content Analysis and Indexing—*Indexing methods*; H.3.1 [**Information Storage and Retrieval**]: Information Search and Retrieval—*Search process*

General Terms

Algorithms, Experimentation

Keywords

Local neighborhood graph search, iterated, query-driven, ANN search

1. INTRODUCTION

Large scale indexing has been attracting more and more interest in multimedia search. Efficient and effective approximate nearest neighbor search plays an important role in this field. For instance, the state-of-the-art duplicate image search [49, 50] depends on the bag-of-words descriptor, which usually exploits ANN search techniques to group large scale local features into visual words using k-means or similar algorithms [36] and map visual features to visual words. Other examples include finding the best matches for local image features in large data sets [37] and large scale similar image search [22].

In the communities of multimedia and computer vision, two main categories of ANN search schemes, partitioning trees and hashing, are studies. Partitioning trees, including kd-trees [6, 13] and its variants [4, 5, 19, 35], metric trees (e.g., ball trees [24], vantage point trees (vp-tree) [48], spill-trees [23]), and hierarchical k-means trees [29], organize data points using tree structures by recursively partitioning the space into subspaces, and each subspace, associated with a subset of data points, corresponds to a subtree. The query procedure is to traverse the tree by expanding the subtrees (subspaces) down to the leaf nodes to obtain NN candidates, in some order, e.g., depth-first or best-first. Such a scheme takes too much *time overhead*, which is defined as the time cost of discovering new NN candidates in this paper. In partitioning trees, the time overhead is the cost of locating a leaf node. Moreover, the *search order*, which means the order of accessing NN candidates, is not good enough to make the searching path quickly move towards the true NNs. Note that time overhead and search order are the key factors determining the ANN search performance.

Hashing based approaches include locality sensitive hashing (LSH) [8], spectral hashing [45], and other variants [16, 22, 46]. The query procedure has to check a large number of NN candidates from the buckets that correspond to the same (or similar) hash codes with the query point, to guarantee the accuracy. However, it does not discriminate the points in the buckets and has no optimized search order to access them, which leads to high time cost on checking the points with low probabilities to be true NNs. The paper [8] suggests a sub-optimal search order, increasing gradually the radius R in R-NN search, to access NN candidates, which is shown to be much slower than partitioning trees [27].

In this paper, we propose to exploit the neighborhood graph structure for large scale visual descriptor indexing. The intuition of its workability is that the points, near a point that is close to the query, have high probabilities to be also close to the query. The search procedure, early presented in [3] and reproposed in [15], named as a local neighborhood graph search, starts from one or several data points and conducts a best-first strategy to discover new NN candidates, by first checking the points in the neighborhood of the best one among the previously-discovered NN candidates whose neighborhoods are not expanded yet. The advantages include that the time overhead to access a new NN candidate is significantly reduced, only $O(1)$, and particularly the search order to access the candidates determined from the neighborhoods is better than partitioning trees and hashing based methods. Fig. 1 presents the comparisons over $1M$ GIST descriptors of tiny images between the neighborhood graph and partitioning trees to demonstrate such advantages. It can be observed (1) that the time overhead with the NG search is only a half of that with kd-trees and is about $\frac{2}{5}$ of the time cost of computing the distances between the query and the accessed points when accessing 6000 points and (2) that the accuracy of the NG search is larger than that of kd-trees. However, the local neighborhood graph search often gets sub-optimal solutions, or conducts exhaustive and continuous neighborhood expansions to find better solutions, which deteriorates the query efficiency.

We propose a query-driven iterated neighborhood graph search approach for searching ANNs beyond local optima. In order to make the local neighborhood graph search adapt to the widely-used iterated local search strategy in operation research, we resolve the key challenge, i.e., designing Perturbation to generate a new pivot to restart a local search, by introducing a criterion to check if the ANN search over a neighborhood graph reaches a local optimum. Moreover, we propose to utilize the query and search history to drive the perturbation scheme to make the search more effective. The major benefit from them is avoiding unnecessary neighborhood expansions and more efficiently finding true NNs. Experimental results of ANN search for visual descriptors (e.g., 128-dimensional SIFT descriptors) demonstrate that our approach gets the superior performance. Particularly, when searching higher-dimensional visual descriptors (e..g, 384-dimensional GIST descriptors) and requiring higher search accuracy, the superiority of our approach over existing ANN search algorithms is more significant.

2. RELATED WORK

In the literature of multimedia search, ANN search methods include two main categories, partitioning tree and hashing, as well as other methods, e.g., low dimensional embedding. In the following, we will present a short review on ANN search methods that are widely investigated in multimedia. More could be found from [31].

Partitioning trees. The partitioning tree based approaches recursively split the space into subspaces, and organize the subspaces using a tree (called space partitioning tree). Most space-partitioning systems use hyperplanes or

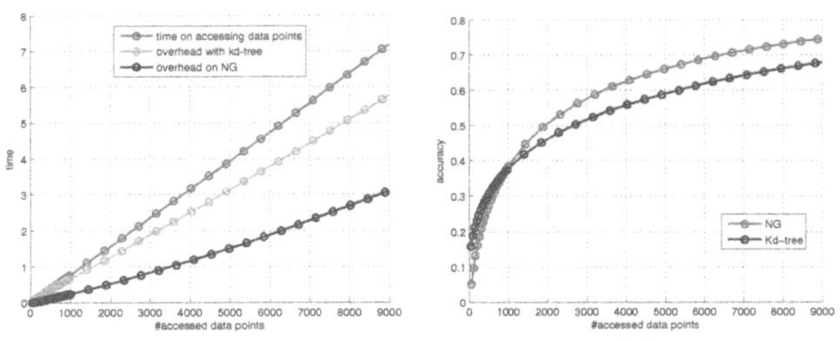

(a) (b)

Figure 1: Illustrating the superiority of ANN search with a neighborhood graph over with multiple randomized kd-trees. (a) comparison in terms of #accessed data points vs. average search time, and (b) comparison in terms of #accessed data points vs. average search accuracy.

hyperspheres to divide the space, and data points are accordingly partitioned into two subsets, with each lying in one side. Points exactly on the plane are usually arbitrarily assigned to either side. Recursively partitioning space in this way produces a binary partitioning tree, for example, kd-trees [6, 13] and its variants [4, 5, 19, 35], and metric trees (e.g., ball trees [24], vantage point trees (vp-tree) [48], and spill-trees [23]). Using other criteria to split the space may yield multi-way partitioning trees, such as Quadtrees [11], Octrees [47], hierarchical k-means trees [29] and so on, which are mainly for low-dimensional cases and hence improper for ANN search over high-dimensional visual descriptors.

In the query stage, the branch-and-bound methodology [6] is usually applied to searching (approximate) nearest neighbors. This scheme needs to traverse the tree from the root to a leaf by evaluating the query at each internal node, and pruning some subtrees according to the evaluation and the current-identified nearest neighbors. The current state-of-the-art search strategy, priority search [4] or best-first [5], builds a priority queue to produce an order of accessing subtrees so that the data points with large probabilities to be true nearest neighbors are first accessed.

Recently, kd-tree based ANN search methods are widely investigated for multimedia search applications. The scheme about multiple randomized kd-trees is studied in [35]. Partitioning the space, using the trinary combination of the coordinates as the partitioning plane, expects to get better space partitions with still low time cost to locate a leaf node [19].

Hashing. Hashing based ANN search methods also attract a lot of attention. Locality sensitive hashing (LSH) [8], one of the typical representatives, is a method of performing ANN search in high dimensions, dependent on probabilistic dimension reduction of high-dimensional data. The key idea is to hash the points using several hash functions to ensure that for each function the probability of collision is much higher for objects (points) that are close to each other than those far apart. Then, one can determine nearest neighbors by hashing the query and retrieving elements stored in the buckets containing it. LSH has many applications, e.g., for pose matching, contour matching, and mean shift clustering, a literature review could be found in [33]. Recently, a lot of research efforts have been conducted on finding good hashing functions, by using metric-learning-like techniques, such as optimized kernel hashing [16], learned metrics [18], learnt

Algorithm 1 Iterated local search

1. $s_0 \leftarrow$ GenerateInitialSolution
2. $s^* \leftarrow$ LocalSearch(s_0)
3. **repeat**
4. $s' \leftarrow$ Perturbation(s^*, *history*) /*Produce a new configuration from the current optimum s^* and the history.*/
5. $s^{*\prime} \leftarrow$ LocalSearch(s')
6. $s^* \leftarrow$ AcceptanceCriterion(s^*, $s^{*\prime}$, *history*) /*Determine if the new solution is accepted.*/
7. **until** termination condition met

binary reconstruction [21], kernelized LSH [22], and shift kernel hashing [30], semi-supervised hashing [42], weakly-supervised hashing [25], non-metric hashing [26], multi-feature hashing [38], spectral hashing [45], complementary hashing [46]. The learning based strategy actually can also be used in our approach. However, this paper would not make investigation on index construction, and instead focuses mainly on the search strategy. Hashing based algorithms may be good to guarantee good precision and recall performances, but is poor at the query efficiency [27].

There are some other methods for ANN search. LSH essentially is also an embedding method, and other classes of embedding methods include Lipschitz embedding [20] and FastMap [9]. Neighborhood graph methods are another class of index structures. Unlike a tree structure hierarchically organizing subspaces or subsets of data points, it organizes the data with a graph structure to connect data points, for example, Delaunay graph in Sa-tree [28], relative neighborhood graph [40], k-NN (ϵ-NN) graph [32], and degree-reduced neighborhood graph [1]. The focus of this paper does not lie in the neighborhood graph construction, and but focuses on the search procedure. To conduct ANN searches, additional points, called pivots, are required as the starting points to guide the neighborhood graph search, for example, selecting the pivots, by clustering [32] (query independent) or from the first NN candidate of kd-trees [3] (query dependent). These approaches, however, are local search and tend to be stuck at local optima. This paper proposes a query-driven iterated neighborhood graph search approach to address such a problem. As an ongoing work, we are investigating the ANN search over billions of points using a two-stage inverted indexing approach, by combining the proposed approach and the approach presented in [41] and later we will show a demo based on the technology [43] in ACMMM12.

3. OUR APPROACH

Given a set of n reference data points $\mathcal{X} = \{\mathbf{x}_1, \cdots, \mathbf{x}_n\}$ with $\mathbf{x}_i \in \mathbb{R}^k$ being a k-dimensional point, the goal is to build a data structure to index these points so that the nearest neighbors of a query $\mathbf{x}_q$ can be fast found. A neighborhood graph is a directed graph that organizes data points by connecting each data point with its neighboring points. The neighborhood graph is denoted as $G = \{(v_i, Adj[v_i])\}_{i=1}^n$, where v_i corresponds to a point $\mathbf{x}_i$ and $Adj[v_i]$ is a list of nodes that correspond to its neighbors.

3.1 Preliminaries

The following introduces the preliminary techniques local neighborhood graph search [3] that performs ANN search over a neighborhood graph and iterated local search [17] that finds solutions beyond local optima.

Local neighborhood graph search. Local neighborhood graph search for ANNs is a procedure that starts from a set of seeding points as initial NN candidates and propagates the search by continuously accessing their neighbors from previously-discovered NN candidates to discover more NN candidates. The *best-first* strategy [3] is usually adopted for local neighborhood expansion. To this end, a *priority queue* is used to maintain the previously-discovered NN candidates whose neighborhoods are not expanded yet, and initially contains only seeds. The best candidate in the priority queue is extracted out, and the points in its neighborhood are discovered as new NN candidates and then pushed into the priority queue. The resulting search path, discovering NN candidates, may not be monotone, but always attempts to move closer to the query point without repeating points. As a local search that finds better solutions only from the neighborhood of the current solution, the local neighborhood graph search will be stuck at a locally optimal point and has to conduct exhaustive neighborhood expansions to find better solutions. Instead, we present a query-driven iterated neighborhood graph search to efficiently find solutions beyond local optima.

Iterated local search. Various modifications have been done over local search to kick a solution out from a local optimum. A simple modification consists of iterating calls to the local search routine, each time starting from a different initial configuration. This is called repeated local search, and implies that the knowledge obtained during the previous local search phases is not used. In contrast, iterated local search [17] is based on building a sequence of locally optimal solutions by perturbing the current local optimum and applying local search after starting from the modified solution. The standard procedure is outlined in Algorithm 1.

Algorithm 2 Query-driven iterated neighborhood graph search

1. $P_0 \leftarrow$ GenerateInitialSolution(q, T)
2. $R^* \leftarrow$ LocalNGSearch(P_0, G)
3. **repeat**
4. $P' \leftarrow$ Perturbation(R^*, q, T, *history*)
5. $R^{*\prime} \leftarrow$ LocalNGSearch(P', G, *history*)
6. $R^* \leftarrow$ AcceptanceCriterion(R^*, $R^{*\prime}$)
7. **until** termination condition met

3.2 Query-driven iterated search

Our approach improves the local neighborhood graph search from two aspects: iterated search and query-driven. The basic procedure is outlined in Algorithm 2.

- GenerateInitialSolution(q, T) searches over trees T, which are constructed to index the reference data points. The initial solution contains a small amount of initial NN candidates that might not be good enough but have high probabilities to be near true NNs. The trees are kd-trees in our implementation, and the search over trees is the same to the best-first search strategy [19, 27, 35].

- LocalNGSearch(P_0, G) is similar to the local neighborhood graph (NG) search mentioned before, starting from a set of seeds P_0 and searching over G by conducting neighborhood expansions in a best-first manner. The difference lies in that once reaching a locale solution, the NG search will pause and return discovered NNs. We will describe the criterion to inspect the local optimum for our local NG search.

- Perturbation(R^*, q, T, *history*) generates new seeds from trees T according to the search history and previously-identified NNs (R^*), to avoid accessing too many points that are accessed in both searches over trees and the neighborhood graph. The detail is given later.
- LocalNGSearch(P', G, *history*) is slightly different from LocalNGSearch(P_0, G) as the search history, i.e., the NNs discovered up to the current iteration, is considered in neighborhood expansion. During the searches over both trees and the neighborhood graph, a single priority queue is maintained to store NN candidates.

Local optimum inspection. Considering the neighborhood graph $G = \{(v_i, Adj[v_i])\}_{i=1}^n$ and the query point $\mathbf{x}_q$, the distances of this query to vertices can be written as a function over the graph vertices, $f(v_i; \mathbf{x}_q)$. In the continuous case, a function $g(\mathbf{x})$ is said to reach a local minimum at the point $\mathbf{x}^*$, if there exists some $\epsilon > 0$ such that $g(\mathbf{x}^*) \leqslant g(\mathbf{x})$ when $|\mathbf{x} - \mathbf{x}^*| < \epsilon$. We propose an analogical definition of the local optimum (minimum) for local neighborhood graph search.

DEFINITION 1 (LOCAL OPTIMUM FOR LOCAL NG SEARCH). *The distance function $f(v_i; \mathbf{x}_q)$ over the neighborhood graph is said to reach a local minimum at v_i^* if $f(v_i^*; \mathbf{x}_q) \leqslant f(u_i; \mathbf{x}_q)$ for all $u_i \in Adj[v_i^*]$.*

The local minimum can be inspected by checking the graph gradients, $\{f(u_i; \mathbf{x}_q) - f(v_i; \mathbf{x}_q)\}$, at v_i along the edges (u_i, v_i). In this paper, we call a point $\mathbf{x}_i$ corresponding to v_i^* as a promising point if there exists at least one graph gradient $f(u_i; \mathbf{x}_q) - f(v_i^*; \mathbf{x}_q) < 0$ at v_i^*, among u_is that belong to $Adj[v_i^*]$ and have not been accessed. In the implementation, we use an indication variable to record the number of unexpanded promising points among all the previously-checked points. The indication variable reaching zero means that the local neighborhood graph arrives at local solutions.

Perturbation. We generate a small amount of new seeding points according to the query and the search history, called query and history driven perturbation. We still use trees, but perform the search that is slightly different from the conventional search over trees [19, 27, 35] by taking into consideration the search history and using the previously-identified NNs from both trees and neighborhood graph to determine if a subtree should be searched. Seeds generation in perturbation will be conducted by resuming the search in trees that yields the initial solutions. But if using the same procedure with the conventional scheme [19, 27, 35], it will result in that many leaf nodes have already been accessed in the neighborhood graph search, and hence extra much time overhead, locating the leaf nodes in trees, is taken. To reduce the time overhead, but still get useful seeds to help jump out of the local solution, we propose to find only one leaf node as the seed from a subtree, called a compact subtree, which contains a set of points with the average similarity larger than a threshold that is determined by cross validation

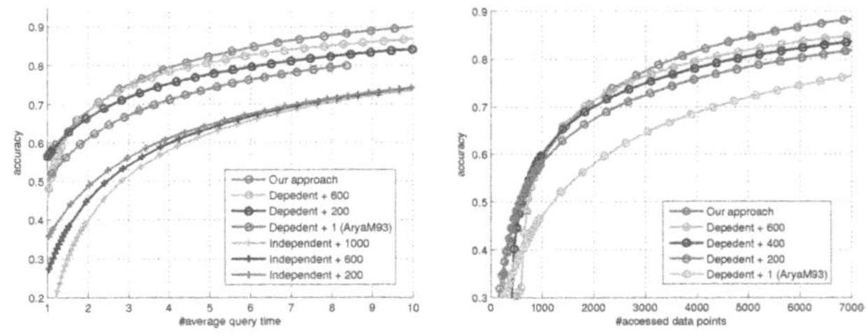

(a) (b)

Figure 2: (a) shows the comparison in terms of average search time vs. search accuracy over query independent, query dependent and query driven iterated (our approach) schemes, and (b) shows the comparison in terms of #accessed data points vs. search accuracy from the query dependent scheme and our approach.

in our implementation. Here, the reason of discovering a single point from a compact tree is that finding the best point through searching the compact tree is more costly than finding the same point by searching the neighborhood graph guided by a point near the best one, e.g., the one from the compact tree here. During the period of building the trees, an extra attribute is associated with each node of the trees, indicating the average similarity of the points within the corresponding subtree and helping determine if a subtree is a compact tree.

Termination. The iteration process will terminate if the number of accessed points reaches the threshold or the true nearest neighbors are found. The former condition is easy to be interpreted. This is equivalent to stopping the search when the search time reaches a predefined threshold. The latter is challenging for the local neighborhood graph search. In [32], the number of better points, similar to the definition of our promising point, is used to determine if the true nearest neighbors have been found. But it could not be theoretically guaranteed to find true NNs, and the experiments show that this stop condition is not reliable. In contrast, the proposed iterated search scheme has a stop condition to guarantee that the true nearest neighbors are found. The condition is similar to the search for exact NNs in trees, and it is that the best lower bound in the priority queue maintained for the search in trees is larger than the worst distance in the previously-identified (K-)NNs.

4. ANALYSIS AND DISCUSSIONS

4.1 Analysis

Empirical analysis. We present the empirical comparison of different search schemes over a neighborhood graph. The schemes include a representative query-independent search scheme [32] that clusters reference data points and regards the cluster centers as the seeding points, a simple query-dependent manner that uses the first NN candidate discovered from kd-trees as the seeding point [3], another query-dependent manner that modifies the scheme [3] and discovers a small amount of NN candidates as the seeding points, and the proposed query driven iterated search scheme.

Fig. 2(a) presents the comparison in terms of average query time vs. search accuracy. "Independent + n" means

Table 1: The comparison of neighborhood graph with partitioning trees and hashing for ANN search.

	search stage			construction stage	
	time overhead	search order	performance	storage cost	time cost
neighborhood graph	low	good	good	medium	high
partitioning trees	high	medium	medium	medium	medium
hashing	low	poor	poor	low	low

the query-independent manner clustering the reference data points into n (200, 600, and 1000) groups [32]. "Dependent + n" means the query-dependent manner finding the first n (1 [3], 200, 600) NN candidates from kd-trees as the seeding points. The comparison shows that query-dependent manners perform better and our approach performs the best. Fig. 2(b) presents the search accuracy when accessing the same number of NN candidates. It shows that our approach accesses a smaller number of NN candidates but achieves the same accuracy.

Theoretical analysis. Our approach is based on a deterministic neighborhood graph, and it is uneasy to give theoretic analysis. We follow [3] to discuss the property over a random neighborhood graph. It has been proved [3] that the query cost is upper bounded.

THEOREM 1 (FROM [3]). *Given any n point set $\mathcal{S} \in \mathbb{R}^k$ and any constant $\epsilon > 0$, one can search over a randomized neighborhood graph from a random seed so that $(1+\epsilon)$-nearest neighbor queries can be answered in $O(\log^3 n)$ expected time.*

Instead of the expected time, we are more interested in the time cost for the good and bad cases.

PROPERTY 1. *In the good case, starting from an ideal seed, the expected query time of the search procedure is $O(\log^2 n)$. In the bad case, the expected query time is $O(\log^3 n)$.*

This property can be proved using the similar arguments in the proof of Theorem 1 [3]. Suppose the former and latter cases in Property 1 appear with the probabilities P and $1-P$, then the expected query time is $O(P\log^2 n + (1-P)\log^3 n)$. (From the perspective of complexity analysis, $O(P\log^2 n + (1-P)\log^3 n) = O(\log^3 n)$, but our analysis differentiates them to analyze more details.) This suggests that the time cost could be reduced with carefully-selected seeds. Motivated by this, our approach aims to find a practical implementation toward a high chance to quickly locate the neighborhood of the optimal solutions (the good case), i.e., increasing P. The time cost getting P can be roughly estimated as $O(r(P)\log n)$ with $r(P)$ representing the number of points accessed in trees.

THEOREM 2. *The expected time cost of the search procedure with P considered by selecting the best seed from a number of seeds is $O(r(P)\log n + P\log^2 n + (1-P)\log^3 n)$.*

A possible way to improve P is a query-driven noniterative one, e.g., generating sufficient seeds at the beginning. This makes it uneasy to get a good balance between the cost improving P and the benefit from greater P as experiments show that $r(P)\log n$ also plays an important role in practice although it can be ignored in theory. Therefore, we have proposed a query-driven iterated way to iteratively generate more seeds to improve P, yielding a better balance.

4.2 Discussion

Neighborhood graph construction cost. The construction itself is a little more costly compared with trees and hashing. There are some approximate methods, e.g., a divide-and-conquer algorithm [7]. However, for most applications, e.g., image search, the neighborhood graph could be built offline, and the construction can also benefit from parallel computing. In our implementation, we build the approximate neighborhood graph using the scheme presented in [44]. The cost is $O(n\log n)$ and acceptable as an offline process. Particularly, the proposed search approach can be applied to boosting the accuracy of the approximate neighborhood graph if more time is available. Moreover, the proposed approach can be directly applied to the incremental neighborhood graph construction when inserting new points into the reference database.

Neighborhood graph storage cost. The neighborhood graph is organized by attaching an adjacent list to each point, which requires additional storage to save adjacent lists including both the indices and distances. The total storage will be $O(n(k+2l))$, with l the length of the adjacent list (i.e., the size of the neighborhood) and k the dimension of the data. In practice, our approach only requires a small neighborhood, and a neighborhood with 20 NNs (in all the experiments) leads to sufficiently good results. Therefore, the increased storage is much smaller than the storage of the data points, in high-dimensional cases (for example, GIST's dimension is 384.). In our experiment, the graph for indexing $1M$ SIFT features takes about $78MB$ storage while the features takes about 120MB, and for 1M GIST features they are about 78MB and 370MB. In contrast, vp-tree and spill-tree would cost $O(n(k+k/b))$ with b being the bucket size associated with the leaf nodes, and $2l$ in our case is usually smaller than k/b. A kd-tree and tp-tree (trinary projection tree [19]) may require relatively smaller storage because only the indexes of one or more splitting coordinates and the partitioning value are attached into each internal node, but the cost of randomized kd-trees for better search performance will increase. With the same storage cost, the ANN search performance of our approach is much better than those of randomized kd-trees and tp-trees.

Advantages over partitioning trees. Compared with partitioning trees, the neighborhood graph search has at least two advantages. On the one hand, the neighborhood structure provides a more efficient way to locate good NN candidates because the candidates can be quickly accessed from the neighborhood by just expanding a neighborhood list, while candidates with partitioning trees are accessed with the necessity of tree branching and tracing. On the other hand, our experiments show that the candidates from the neighborhood are usually better than those from partitioning trees and hence the neighborhood graph yields a better order to access the points. The two advantages have been illustrated in Figs. 1(a) and 1(b).

Advantages over hashing. Hashing based approaches find NN candidates from the bucket that has the same hash code with the query. On the one hand, the bucket may be wrongly located. This drawback could be partially resolved by accessing multiple buckets with the similar hash codes (whose Hamming distance to the hash code of the query is smaller than a constant) or multiple hash coding, but it would increase the number of the data points that need to be accessed and hence leads to much more cost. On the other hand, the search procedure does not discriminate data points in the buckets and has to check each data point without ordering the accessing. This results in a waste of time on data points with low probabilities to be true NNs. The paper [8] suggests to increase gradually the radius R in R-NN search to obtain the approximate NN, which is shown in [27] to be much slower than partitioning trees.

The summary of comparison between neighborhood graph search and partitioning trees, hashing is presented in Tab. 1.

4.3 Implementation details

We present a speedup scheme to eliminate distance computation for the points that definitely cannot be the true NNs. To this end, we record the distances between neighboring points in the NG, which are used to estimate the lower bound of the distance to the query using the triangle inequality. Suppose the distance from the accessed point u to the query q is denoted by $d(u,q)$ and the precomputed distance from the point u to its neighbor point v is denoted by $d(u,v)$, the triangle inequality shows that $d(v,q) \geqslant |d(u,q)-d(u,v)|$. The distance computation $d(v,q)$ could be eliminated, if $d(p^*,q) < |d(u,q)-d(u,v)|$ holds with $d(p^*,q)$ being the worst distance in the previously identified NNs. This elimination could save much time, especially for the high-dimensional case.

Besides, we introduce two practical schemes to balance the local NG search and perturbation for seed generation such that the advantages of local NG search and seed generation are well exploited. We observed that at the early NG search stage it is not easy to reach local solutions. This is because the seeds are still far away from the true NNs and hence the search path has a high chance to get closer to better NNs. As a consequence, there may be a low chance for the NG search to quickly jump toward the true NNs. To deal with this issue, we trigger the perturbation step, if the search has conducted a fixed number of successive neighborhood expansions failing to yield promising points (condition 1).

At the later search stage, instead, it is found that the local search in the neighborhood graph arrives at local solutions frequently and the switch to search in trees is too frequent. The search at this stage mostly aims to conduct a finer search to get the true NNs. But the time overhead of search in trees is larger than in the NG. Therefore, it is desired at this stage not to search trees too frequently. To this end, we introduce a scheme to balance the numbers of points accessed in trees and the NG so that the points from trees do not exceed a fraction of the total accessed points (condition 2). It should be noted that our algorithm does not discriminate whether the search is at the early stage or at the later stage and that the whole search process always checks the two conditions described above

The two parameters, the thresholds of the number of successive failure neighborhood expansions and the ratio between the number of points accessed in trees and total accessed points in the above two schemes, are obtained by cross validation through selecting a small number of points as the validation queries to tune the two parameters. This cross validation scheme is feasible and the cost is very low as it only affects the search procedure without affecting the neighborhood graph construction.

5. EXPERIMENTS

Data sets. We demonstrate the proposed approach to ANN search over visual descriptors, SIFT features for patch matching, and GIST features for similar image search. The SIFT features are collected from the Caltech 101 data set [10] and recognition benchmark images [29]. We extract maximally stable extremal regions (MSERs) for each image, and compute a 128-dimensional SIFT feature for each MSER. For each image set, we randomly sample $1000K$ SIFT features and $100K$ SIFT features, respectively as the reference and query database, and additional $1K$ SIFT features as the validation data to determine the parameters in the search algorithm. We guarantee that the three data sets do not contain the same points.

Besides, we conduct the ANN search experiments on the tiny image set [39] to justify our approach for scalable similar image search. The tiny image data set consists of 80 million images and the sizes of all the images in this database are 32×32. Similar to [22], we use a global GIST descriptor to represent each image, which is a 384-dimensional vector describing the texture within localized grid cells. Its dimension is higher than that of the SIFT feature, and hence the ANN search is more challenging. We generate two data sets for similar image search, each including $1000K$ images as the reference database and $100K$ images as the queries, additional $1K$ images for the validation database.

Evaluation scheme. To evaluate the performance, we adopt the accuracy measurement to check whether the approximate nearest neighbors for each query is exactly the ground truth, the true nearest neighbors. In our experiments, we build the ground truth through the exhaustive linear scan. To evaluate the search performance for approximate K-nearest neighbors, the accuracy is computed by the ratio of the number of data points appearing both in ANN search results and the true nearest neighbors to the number of desired NNs.

We compare the search performances of widely-used ANN search algorithms, with partitioning trees, hashing and existing neighborhood graph search algorithms. Partitioning trees for comparison include tp-trees [19], bd-trees [4], vp-tree [48], spill-trees [23], and flann [27]. We report the result from flann [27] and do not report the results from kd-trees [35] and hierarchical k-means tree (clustering-tree) [29] because flann aims to find the optimal configuration between multiple randomized kd-trees and hierarchical k-means tree and hence expects to be better as described in [27]. In addition, we also report the results from local neighborhood graph search with a single seed (AryaM93) [3], and query-independent ("NG + independent") [32]. In our experiments, kd-trees are adopted as the partitioning trees for our approach. We run the implementations of spectral hashing [45], locality sensitive hashing (LSH) [8], flann, and bd-tree, downloaded from the Web sites, with the parameters determined by their algorithms, to get the search results. We follow the algorithm descriptions in vp-trees, spill-trees and tp-trees, and report results by well implementing the algorithms and tuning the parameters, to get the best results. Consistent with the report in [27], the performance from hashing based approaches is much poorer than tree based methods with even an order of magnitude, and hence we do not plot the curves in the result for clear comparison of our approach with other methods. All the experiments are run on a 2.66GHz desktop PC.

5.1 Comparisons

Quantitative results. The ANN search performance comparison is shown in Fig. 3 on two data sets, similar patch search over SIFT features from the Caltech 101 data set [10] and recognition benchmark images [29]. The horizontal axis corresponds to the average query time (milliseconds), and the vertical axis corresponds to the search accuracy. We can have the following observations from the comparison. The proposed approach consistently gets the best performance. As shown in Figs. 3(a) and 3(b), at the accuracy of 0.9, it gets at least twice speedup compared with all other methods, and even costs only about one-fourth of the time costed by "NG + independent" over the visual descriptors of recognition benchmark images, as shown in Fig. 3(b). The superiority of our approach over other tree-based algorithms is consistent with the analysis in Sec. 4.2.

In addition, we present the comparison for similar image search over the tiny images [39]. The image is represented by a GIST feature, a higher-dimensional feature, which is more challenging. In this case, the superiority of our approach over other methods is even more significant. Figs. 4(a) and 4(c) show the performance comparison for approximate 1-NN search, over two reference databases sampled from tiny images. It can be observed that our approach is much better than partitioning trees and existing local neighborhood graph search methods. Moreover, we present the comparison about searching for top 20 similar images (i.e., approximate 20-NNs), shown in Figs. 4(b) and 4(d), and the improvement is consistently significant.

Through a deep inspection of the comparisons, shown in Fig. 3 (on 128-dimensional descriptors) and Fig. 4 (on 384-dimensional descriptors), it can be observed that the advantage of our approach to ANN search is more significant for high dimensional cases and the superiority at the requirement of higher accuracy in high-dimensional cases is also more significant.

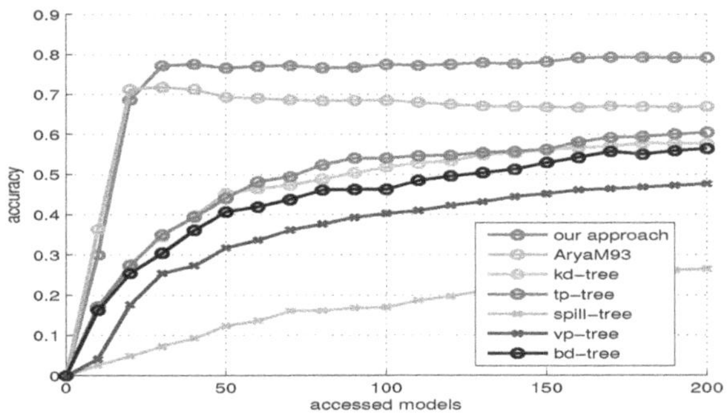

Figure 7: Shape search performance. The horizontal axis corresponds to the number of accessed models, and the vertical axis corresponds to the accuracy.

Qualitative results. We present the qualitative comparisons with representative methods over similar image search, shown in Fig. 5 and Fig. 6, where (a), (b), (c), and (d) show top 10 similar images of our approach, AryaM93 [3], tp-tree [19], and "NG + independent" [32]. In each row, the first image with a blue bounding box is the query, and the ones bounded by red boxes are truly similar images. We can see that the results from our approach are much better than those from other approaches.

5.2 Application with non-metric distances

We present a 3D model retrieval experiment to show the unique advantage of neighborhood search that it works well for the non-metric distance. The input of the 3D model retrieval task is a 2D sketch or a 2D projection, and the goal is to search for 3D models that belong to the same category of the input. To conduct such a task, we organize 3D shapes using their 2D contours. The 2D contours are obtained by rendering perspective 2D contours of each model from 9 views. For each model, we randomly sample one as a query and the remaining eight for the reference database. The 2D contours are further vectorized by fitting line segments to the points with robust moving least-squares [12] and represented by a set of points with 2D coordinates. To match two 2D contours, we estimate an affine transformation between them using RANSAC and use the registration error as the distance, which is described in [34]. In our experiment, we collect all the models in the Princeton Shape Benchmark[1], which contains 1815 models, and then expand the database with models of the same categories from the INRIA GAMMA 3D mesh research database[2], yielding 5000 models, and the storage cost of contour images is about 1.5GB.

We index these 2D contours by connecting each 2D contour with its 20 nearest neighbors using the distance described above to form a matching graph. Particularly we also record the affine transform for each edge so that the matching over the graph from a node v_1 to another one v_2 can be speeded up by combining the recorded transform and the transform from the query to v_1 to get an initial transform estimation to v_2. It takes about four hours to compute the matching graph on a Dell desktop with dual quad-core Intel Xeon E5540 processors, and about 30MB to store. We also represent the 2D contour by a vector, a boundary-descriptor [14]. The vector representations are used to organize the 2D contours by kd-trees and other related index structures.

To compare the search performance, for the proposed approach and local NG search, once a 2D contour is accessed the distance between the associated model and the query is evaluated. For other approaches we search over the index structures to get a set of candidates and then perform a reranking step by matching the query and the models corresponding to the searched 2D contours. Due to the stored transforms over our matching graph, our approach and local NG search are much faster (over 5 times) than other approaches. So we only report the comparison in terms of the accuracy vs. the number of accessed models, shown in Fig. 7. The accuracy is computed by checking if the searched models and the query belong to the same category. As we can see, our approach performs much better than other approaches.

[1]http://shape. cs.princeton.edu/benchmark/
[2]http://www-roc.inria.fr/gamma/ download/

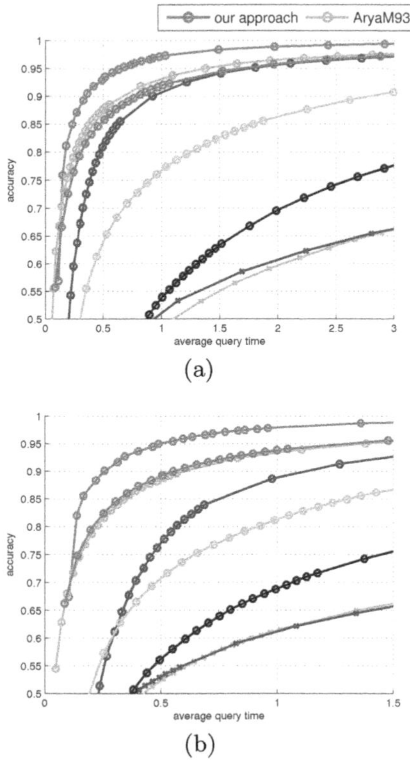

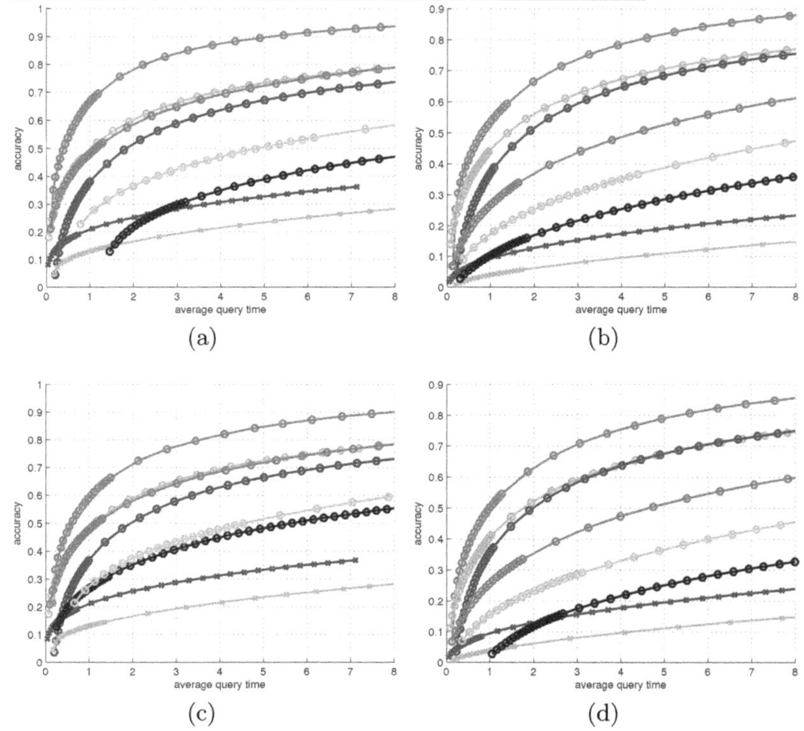

Figure 3: Performance comparison over (a) the Caltech 101 data set [10], (b) recognition benchmark images [29].

Figure 4: Performance comparison of searching for the most similar image in (a) and (c) and top 20 similar images in (b) and (d) over the tiny images [39].

This is because the search with a neighborhood graph is more effectively towards true nearest neighbors and our iteration scheme avoids the local issue that is a problem for the local NG search (AryaM93) [2].

6. CONCLUSIONS

In this paper, we introduce neighborhood graph search for scalable visual descriptor indexing, and propose a query-driven iterated neighborhood graph search to deal with the drawback that the local neighborhood graph search tends to be stuck at a locally optimal point. We handle the key problem, how to perform perturbation to trigger a new local search. The major technologies lie in defining the local solution over a neighborhood graph for ANN search and presenting a query and search history driven perturbation scheme to generate pivots to restart a new local search. Experimental results with metric and non-metric distance show that our approach gets significant improvement over other ANN search algorithms.

7. REFERENCES

[1] K. Aoyama, K. Saito, H. Sawada, and N. Ueda. Fast approximate similarity search based on degree-reduced neighborhood graphs. In *KDD*, pages 1055–1063, 2011.

[2] S. Arya and D. M. Mount. Algorithms for fast vector quantizaton. In *Data Compression Conference*, pages 381–390, 1993.

[3] S. Arya and D. M. Mount. Approximate nearest neighbor queries in fixed dimensions. In *SODA*, pages 271–280, 1993.

[4] S. Arya, D. M. Mount, N. S. Netanyahu, R. Silverman, and A. Y. Wu. An optimal algorithm for approximate nearest neighbor searching fixed dimensions. *J. ACM*, 45(6):891–923, 1998.

[5] J. S. Beis and D. G. Lowe. Shape indexing using approximate nearest-neighbour search in high-dimensional spaces. In *CVPR*, pages 1000–1006, 1997.

[6] J. L. Bentley. Multidimensional binary search trees used for associative searching. *Commun. ACM*, 18(9):509–517, 1975.

[7] J. Chen, H. ren Fang, and Y. Saad. Fast approximate nn graph construction for high dimensional data via recursive lanczos bisection. *Journal of Machine Learning Research*, 10:1989–2012, 2009.

[8] M. Datar, N. Immorlica, P. Indyk, and V. S. Mirrokni. Locality-sensitive hashing scheme based on p-stable distributions. In *Symposium on Computational Geometry*, pages 253–262, 2004.

[9] C. Faloutsos and K.-I. Lin. FastMap: A Fast Algorithm for Indexing, Data-Mining and Visualization of Traditional and Multimedia Datasets. In *SIGMOD Conference*, pages 163–174, 1995.

[10] L. Fei-Fei, R. Fergus, and P. Perona. Learning generative visual models from few training examples: an incremental bayesian approach tested on 101 object categories. In *CVPR 2004 Workshop on Generative-Model Based Vision*, 2004.

[11] R. A. Finkel and J. L. Bentley. Quad trees: A data structure for retrieval on composite keys. *Acta Inf.*, 4:1–9, 1974.

[12] S. Fleishman, D. Cohen-Or, and C. T. Silva. Robust moving least-squares fitting with sharp features. *ACM Trans. Graph.*, 24(3):544–552, 2005.

[13] J. H. Friedman, J. L. Bentley, and R. A. Finkel. An algorithm for finding best matches in logarithmic expected time. *ACM Trans. Math. Softw.*, 3(3):209–226, 1977.

[14] T. A. Funkhouser, P. Min, M. M. Kazhdan, J. Chen, J. A. Halderman, D. P. Dobkin, and D. P. Jacobs. A search engine for 3d models. *ACM Trans. Graph.*, 22(1):83–105, 2003.

[15] K. Hajebi, Y. Abbasi-Yadkori, H. Shahbazi, and H. Zhang. Fast approximate nearest-neighbor search with k-nearest neighbor graph. In *IJCAI*, pages 1312–1317, 2011.

[16] J. He, W. Liu, and S.-F. Chang. Scalable similarity search with optimized kernel hashing. In *KDD*, pages 1129–1138, 2010.

[17] H. H. Hoos and T. Stützle. *Stochastic Local Search Foundations and Applications.* Morgan Kaufmann/Elsevier, 2004.

[18] P. Jain, B. Kulis, and K. Grauman. Fast image search for learned metrics. In *CVPR*, 2008.

[19] Y. Jia, J. Wang, G. Zeng, H. Zha, and X.-S. Hua. Optimizing kd-trees for scalable visual descriptor indexing. In *CVPR*, pages 3392–3399, 2010.

[20] W. Johnson and J. Lindenstrauss. Extensions of Lipschitz mappings into a Hilbert space. *Contemporary Mathematics*, 26:189–206, 1984.

[21] B. Kulis and T. Darrells. Learning to hash with binary reconstructive embeddings. In *NIPS*, pages 577–584, 2009.

[22] B. Kulis and K. Grauman. Kernelized locality-sensitive hashing for scalable image search. In *ICCV*, pages 2130–2137, 2009.

[23] T. Liu, A. W. Moore, A. G. Gray, and K. Yang. An investigation of practical approximate nearest neighbor algorithms. In *NIPS*, 2004.

[24] A. W. Moore. The anchors hierarchy: Using the triangle inequality to survive high dimensional data. In *UAI*, pages 397–405, 2000.

[25] Y. Mu, J. Shen, and S. Yan. Weakly-supervised hashing in kernel space. In *CVPR*, pages 3344–3351, 2010.

[26] Y. Mu and S. Yan. Non-metric locality-sensitive hashing. In *AAAI*, 2010.

[27] M. Muja and D. G. Lowe. Fast approximate nearest neighbors with automatic algorithm configuration. In *VISSAPP (1)*, pages 331–340, 2009.

[28] G. Navarro. Searching in metric spaces by spatial approximation. *VLDB J.*, 11(1):28–46, 2002.

[29] D. Nistér and H. Stewénius. Scalable recognition with a vocabulary tree. In *CVPR (2)*, pages 2161–2168, 2006.

[30] M. Raginsky and S. Lazebnik. Locality-sensitive binary codes from shift-invariant kernels. In *NIPS*, pages 1509–1517, 2009.

[31] H. Samet. *Foundations of multidimensional and metric data structures.* Elsevier, Amsterdam, 2006.

[32] T. B. Sebastian and B. B. Kimia. Metric-based shape retrieval in large databases. In *ICPR (3)*, pages 291–296, 2002.

[33] G. Shakhnarovich, T. Darrell, and P. Indyk. *Nearest-Neighbor Methods in Learning and Vision: Theory and Practice.* The MIT press, 2006.

[34] T. Shao, W. Xu, K. Yin, J. Wang, K. Zhou, and B. Guo. Discriminative sketch-based 3d model retrieval via robust shape matching. *Comput. Graph. Forum*, 30(7):2011–2020, 2011.

[35] C. Silpa-Anan and R. Hartley. Optimised kd-trees for fast image descriptor matching. In *CVPR*, 2008.

[36] J. Sivic and A. Zisserman. Efficient visual search of videos cast as text retrieval. *IEEE Trans. Pattern Anal. Mach. Intell.*, 31(4):591–606, 2009.

[37] N. Snavely, S. M. Seitz, and R. Szeliski. Photo tourism: exploring photo collections in 3D. *ACM Trans. Graph.*, 25(3):835–846, 2006.

[38] J. Song, Y. Yang, Z. Huang, H. T. Shen, and R. Hong. Multiple feature hashing for real-time large scale near-duplicate video retrieval. In *ACM Multimedia*, pages 423–432, 2011.

[39] A. B. Torralba, R. Fergus, and W. T. Freeman. 80 million tiny images: A large data set for nonparametric object and scene recognition. *IEEE Trans. Pattern Anal. Mach. Intell.*, 30(11):1958–1970, 2008.

[40] G. T. Toussaint. The relative neighbourhood graph of a finite planar set. *Pattern Recognition*, 12(4):261–268, 1980.

[41] W. Tu, R. Pan, and J. Wang. Similar image search with a tiny bag-of-delegates representation. In *ACM Multimedia*, 2012.

[42] J. Wang, O. Kumar, and S.-F. Chang. Semi-supervised hashing for scalable image retrieval. In *CVPR*, pages 3424–3431, 2010.

[43] J. Wang, J. Wang, X.-S. Hua, and S. Li. Scalable similar image search by joint indices. In *ACM Multimedia*, 2012.

[44] J. Wang, J. Wang, G. Zeng, Z. Tu, R. Gan, and S. Li. Scalable k-nn graph construction for visual descriptors. In *CVPR*, pages 1106–1113, 2012.

[45] Y. Weiss, A. B. Torralba, and R. Fergus. Spectral hashing. In *NIPS*, pages 1753–1760, 2008.

[46] H. Xu, J. Wang, Z. Li, G. Zeng, S. Li, and N. Yu. Complementary hashing for approximate nearest neighbor search. In *ICCV*, pages 1631–1638, 2011.

[47] K. Yamaguchi, T. L. Kunii, and K. Fujimura. Octree-related data structures and algorithms. *IEEE Computer Graphics and Applications*, 4(1):53–59, 1984.

[48] P. N. Yianilos. Data structures and algorithms for nearest neighbor search in general metric spaces. In *SODA*, pages 311–321, 1993.

[49] S. Zhang, Q. Tian, G. Hua, Q. Huang, and S. Li. Descriptive visual words and visual phrases for image applications. In *ACM Multimedia*, pages 75–84, 2009.

[50] W. Zhou, Y. Lu, H. Li, Y. Song, and Q. Tian. Spatial coding for large scale partial-duplicate web image search. In *ACM Multimedia*, pages 511–520, 2010.

Appendix

The pseudo-code of our approach is outlined as follows.

Algorithm 3 IteratedLocalNGSearch(q, G, T)

```
// R: a max-heap with a fixed size; Q: a priority queue;
// V[G]: the node set of graph G; n: #accessed points;
// m: #promosing points; r: #accessed points from trees T;
for each u ∈ V[G] do
   color[u] ← WHITE;
end for
n ← 0;
m ← 0; r ← 0;
P ← GenerateInitialSolution(q, T)
for each u ∈ P do
   key[u] ← dist(u, q); color[u] ← BLACK;
   Q ← u;
   if MAX(R) > key[u] then
      R ← u;
   end if
   n ← n + 1 ;
   m ← m + 1; r ← r + 1;
end for
t ← 0;
while (Q ≠ ∅ && n < N) do
   u ← EXTRACT-MIN(Q);
   /*Start the local neighborhood graph search.*/
   m ← m − 1; b ← FALSE;
   for each v ∈ Adj[u] do
      if color[v] ≠ BLACK then
         color[v] ← BLACK; key[v] ← dist(v, q);
         Q ← v;
         if MAX(R) > key[v] then
            R ← v;
         end if
         n ← n + 1;
         if IsPromising(v) then
            m ← m + 1; b ← TRUE;
         end if
      end if
   end for
   if b == FALSE then
      t ← t + 1;
   else
      t ← 0;
   end if
   /*m <= 0 means arriving at a local optimum. t >= F and
   r/n < L mean the conditions in the two schemes described
   in Sec. 4.3*/
   if (m <= 0||t >= F)&&(r/n < L) then
      P ← Perturbation(q, T, R);
      for each u ∈ P do
         key[u] ← dist(u, q); color[u] ← BLACK;
         Q ← u;
         if MAX(R) > key[u] then
            R ← u;
         end if
         n ← n + 1; m ← m + 1; r ← r + 1;
      end for
      if t >= F then
         t ← 0;
      end if
   end if
end while
return R;
```

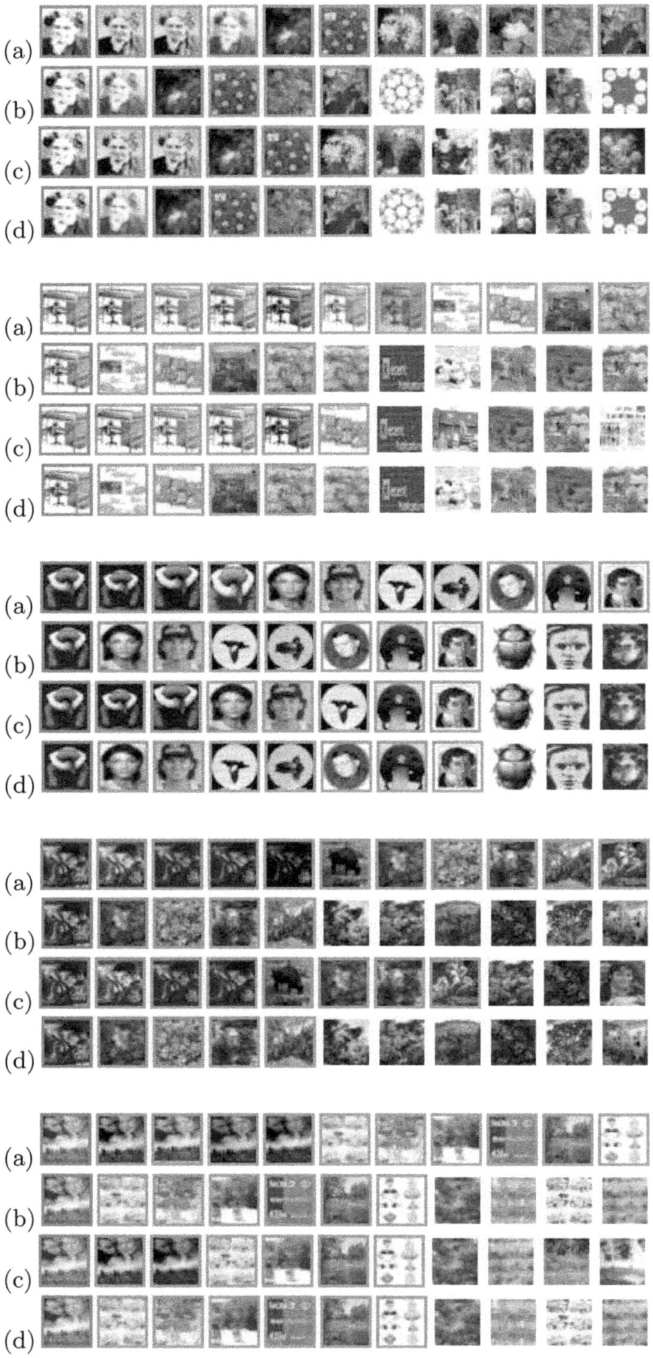

Figure 5: Qualitative comparisons. (a), (b), (c), and (d) show top 10 similar images of our approach, AryaM93 [3], tp-tree [19], and "NG + independent" [32]. In each row, the first image with a blue bounding box is the query, and the ones bounded by red boxes are truly similar images.

Figure 6: Qualitative comparisons. (a), (b), (c), and (d) show top 10 similar images of our approach, AryaM93 [3], tp-tree [19], and "NG + independent" [32]. In each row, the first image with a blue bounding box is the query, and the ones bounded by red boxes are truly similar images.

SymCity: Feature Selection by Symmetry for Large Scale Image Retrieval

Giorgos Tolias, Yannis Kalantidis and Yannis Avrithis
National Technical University of Athens
Iroon Polytexneiou 9, Zografou, Greece
{gtolias,ykalant,iavr}@image.ntua.gr

ABSTRACT

Many problems, including feature selection, vocabulary learning, location and landmark recognition, structure from motion and 3d reconstruction, rely on a learning process that involves wide-baseline matching on *multiple views* of the same object or scene. In practical large scale image retrieval applications however, most images depict unique views where this idea does not apply. We exploit self-similaries, symmetries and repeating patterns to select features within a *single image*. We achieve the same performance compared to the full feature set with only a small fraction of its index size on a dataset of *unique views* of buildings or urban scenes, in the presence of one million distractors of similar nature. Our best solution is linear in the number of correspondences, with practical running times of just a few milliseconds.

Categories and Subject Descriptors

H.3.1 [**Information Storage and Retrieval**]: Content Analysis and Indexing—*Indexing methods*; H.3.3 [**Information Storage and Retrieval**]: Information Search and Retrieval—*Search process, selection process*; I.4.10 [**Image Processing and Computer Vision**]: Image Representation

General Terms

Algorithms and Experimentation

Keywords

feature selection, symmetry detection, self-similarity, indexing, image retrieval

1. INTRODUCTION

The *bag-of-words* (BoW) representation on local features and descriptors, along with geometry verification, has been very successful at particular object retrieval [29][25]. At large scale, the current bottleneck appears to be the *memory footprint* of the index rather precision or speed, and it becomes even more significant in recent attempts to *geometry indexing* [12]. One solution is to abandon BoW in favor of more global representations like *Fisher kernels* [24][13], but these are not compatible with *geometry verification* [25][23], so they cannot reach the same levels of precision yet.

MM'12, October 29–November 2, 2012, Nara, Japan.

Figure 1: Tentative correspondences using all features (top), and selected features (bottom). Feature selection only applied to the image on the right.

So far, *feature selection* is probably the only practical alternative. An increasingly popular idea is to select features from *multiple views*, identified by a baseline retrieval system [32]. Assuming similar images are indeed present in the dataset at hand, this idea has been successful at other tasks as well, including vocabulary learning [10][20], location and landmark recognition [26][9] and 3d reconstruction [1]. In practice however, most images are *unique*, in the sense that they depict a unique view of an object or scene in the dataset and there is nothing to compare to. *Or is there?*

We consider exactly such unique images in this work, using the very same idea: feature selection by *self-similarity*. We develop two *self-matching* alternatives inspired by state-of-the-art spatial matching methods: *fast spatial matching* (FSM) introduced by Philbin *et al.* [25], and *Hough pyramid matching* (HPM), introduced by Tolias and Avrithis [31]. We apply them between each image and either itself or its reflection, where tentative feature correspondences are found in the descriptor space, without quantization. In effect, we detect *repeating patterns* or *local symmetries* and index only the participating features. The underlying motivation is that *features repeating within a single image are quite likely to repeat across different views as well*, hence are good candidates for a more compact image representation that does not sacrifice performance.

Though a limiting choice at first sight, we do achieve a generic method that is successful at least at urban image collections, where symmetries are inherent. But symmetries and self-similarities are not limited to man-made structures like buildings and natural creations like leaves and butterflies: when looking at different scales, *local* symmetries are everywhere. For instance, Bagon *et al.* [3] develop a generic method of *segmentation by composition*, while Shechtman and Irani [28] build a generic *self-similarity descriptor*; both methods operate at pixel level.

In the example of Figure 1, the image on the left (right) is considered a query (database) image, so feature selection is only applied on the right one. There are plenty of local symmetries, giving enough correspondences for matching even after selection, which also appear 'cleaner' in terms of outliers. Less than 20% of index space is needed after selection for this particular image.

On a dataset of one million images, we achieve the same performance with the full feature set, requiring only a small fraction of its memory. Alternatively, we outperform criteria like *feature scale* or *strength*, with the same amount of memory. Since unique images have only been treated as distractors so far, we also build a new *annotated dataset* with a large number of small groups of images depicting urban scenery; one image of each group is in the dataset and rest are only used as queries.

After a study of related work in section 2, we develop our main contribution on unique-view feature selection in section 3. We then present our experiments in section 4 and discuss our result and future directions in section 5.

2. RELATED WORK

Feature selection has recently become a popular way of reducing index space for image retrieval. This is typically an application-dependent task, and two of the earliest approaches have been applied to *location recognition*. Given a dense street-view geo-tagged database, Schindler *et al.* [26] select *informative* features, *i.e.* features occurring mostly in images of some specific location. Similarly, Li and Kosecka [17] obtain an information content probability for each feature with respect to location identification. Both methods rank image features accordingly and keep only a specific subset or percentage of features per image.

Knopp *et al.* [15] densely compute a *local confusion score* for image regions of a geo-tagged database by a sliding window scheme and remove features inside regions with high score. Gammeter *et al.* [9] start from image clusters extracted by geographical proximity and visual similarity, and then use feature matching statistics to estimate a bounding box around the *foreground object* of each image. Although they only index features inside this box, most are still kept. Avrithis *et al.* [2] further build a *scene map* from selected features of aligned views, but the result is a boost in recall rather than a considerable reduction in index size.

All previous models are supervised, making use of location information. Turcot and Lowe [32] on the other hand have introduced an *unsupervised* approach to select *useful* features. The latter are features appearing as inliers during *spatial verification*, when issuing each database image as a query to a baseline retrieval system. Naikal *et al.* [22] avoid spatial matching or structure from motion and, using a training set of images per category, apply sparse PCA on the covariance matrix of the bag-of-words histograms. However, they work with vocabularies of size only up to 10^3, making the solution unsuitable for large scale image retrieval.

Still, all models mentioned so far, including [32], require *multiple views* of the same object or scene. For *unique* images, Turcot and Lowe [32] keep the *largest-scale* features in the index, which is equivalent to reducing image resolution. In section 4 we show that this approach fails in the presence of a large scale distractor dataset. In this work we rather detect *self-similarities*, *repeating patterns* and *symmetries* to select features in a *single image*. To our knowledge, this is the first approach of this kind.

Earlier approaches on *symmetry detection* consider the entire image as a signal and look for one or more axes of symmetry *globally* [30][14]. More recent approaches work on *local features* instead. Tuytelaars *et al.* [33] begin with *invariant neighborhoods* and apply cascaded Hough transform to detect collinear intersections, a solution of high complexity. Cornelius *et al.* [7] also use Hough voting but do not require image descriptors; they detect *local affine frames* (LAFs) from an image and its reflection, match them using their local geometry, and allow each matching LAF pair to vote for a symmetry axis. Similarly, Loy and Eklundh [19] detect symmetric local feature *constellations* via Hough voting, but feature matching is based again on descriptors.

Lazebnik *et al.* [16] *expand* local feature configurations towards geometrically invariant *semi-local* parts of 3d objects. To limit the exponential number of hypotheses, they apply strong geometric and appearance-based consistency constraints on the seed configurations. Still, the complexity remains quadratic in the number of correspondences. We show that *local symmetry detection does not amount to more than any spatial matching scheme*, deriving our two solutions by such methods, one being quadratic [25], and the other *linear* [31] in the number of correspondences.

Structured and *repetitive pattern detection* has recently been applied to image retrieval, but not really for feature selection. Schindler *et al.* [27] detect periodic 2d patterns, matching them to a 3d database of textured *facades*. Doubek *et al.* [8] retrieve buildings by matching only lattice or line repetitive patterns, representing *tiles* by specifically tuned intensity and color descriptors. Both methods lack in generality. Jegou *et al.* [11] rather detect repeated visual elements in a single image to lower the weight of such features in bag-of-words scoring. Although taking into account this *intra-image burstiness*, they still keep all features.

3. FEATURE SELECTION

We introduce here two alternative unsupervised methods for feature selection, both focusing on geometrically consistent feature groups within a single image, roughly representing *repeating patterns* or *local symmetries*. The two methods are developed in sections 3.2 and 3.4. Under both methods, each image is matched to itself as well as its reflection, handling direct and opposite transformations, respectively. The two processes, referred to as *direct* and *flipped* matching, are presented in sections 3.1 and 3.3, respectively. Section 3.1 begins with our general image representation.

The entire method is based on the observation that symmetry or repeating pattern detection in a single image does not differ much from spatial matching between two images. In fact, we only see two issues requiring attention:

1. Spatial matching usually (but not always) assumes *one-to-one correspondence* between features of the two images. This is exactly why constraints like the *ratio test* [18] are usually employed when matching descriptors. This is not the case here because a pattern may be repeating more than twice.

2. Seeking robustness against 'outliers', a *single transformation model* is usually assumed, *e.g.* similarity or homography. This is not the rule, as *e.g.* HPM [31] can find multiple transformations. But for every symmetry or repeating pattern we do need a different transformation: HPM is more appropriate in this sense, but we also extend FSM [25] in this direction.

3.1 Representation

We assume that an image is represented by a set of local features X. Each local feature $x \in X$ is associated with a D-dimensional *descriptor* $d(x) \in \mathbb{R}^D$, encoding *local appearance*, which is then quantized to *visual word* $w(x) \in W$, where W is a given visual *vocabulary*. Assuming features are scale and rotation covariant, it is also associated with position $p(x) \in \mathbb{R}^2$ on the image plane, log-scale $\sigma(x) \in \mathbb{R}$ and orientation $\theta(p) \in (-\pi, \pi]$. All this information is conveniently represented in vector

$$g(x) = [p(x)^{\mathrm{T}} \ \sigma(x) \ \theta(x)]^{\mathrm{T}} \tag{1}$$

in $\mathbb{R}^4$, encoding *local geometry*. Log-scale is employed so that relative scales are expressed as differences rather than ratios. Orientation is alternatively represented by orthogonal matrix $R(x) \in \mathbb{R}^{2\times 2}$ with $\det R(x) = 1$. Finally, position is alternatively represented in *homogeneous coordinates* by vector $\mathbf{p}(x)$ in projective space $\mathbb{P}^2(\mathbb{R})$.

A feature *correspondence* within image X is a pair of features $c \in X^2$. Given correspondence $c = (x, y)$, it is possible to define a similarity transformation that aligns features $x, y \in X$ in the image plane. It turns out [31] that this transformation can also be represented by vector

$$g(x, y) = g(c) = [p(c)^{\mathrm{T}} \ \sigma(c) \ \theta(c)]^{\mathrm{T}} \tag{2}$$

in $\mathbb{R}^4$, where $\sigma(c) = \sigma(y) - \sigma(x)$, $\theta(c) = \theta(y) - \theta(x)$ are the relative scale and orientation respectively, and $p(c) = p(y) - M(c)p(x)$ is the relative position (translation), with $M(c) = \sigma(c)R(c)$ and $R(c) = R(y)R(x)^{-1}$.

It is now is possible to use norm $\|g(x, y)\|$ to measure the *geometric proximity* of features x, y. It is understood here that relative orientation $\theta(y) - \theta(x)$ is first taken to its principal value in $(-\pi, \pi]$. Because feature detectors often respond with multiple overlapping features around highly distinctive regions, we need this proximity measure to exclude nearby features from our search for symmetries. In particular, we say (x, y) is a *valid* pair and write $v(x, y)$ if and only if $\|g(x, y)\| \geq \rho$, with *response threshold* $\rho > 0$. Then, given image X, we define its set of *valid* correspondences

$$C_v(X) = \{(x, y) \in X^2 : v(x, y)\}. \tag{3}$$

This set also excludes *trivial* correspondences (x, x) of a feature x with itself, since $\|g(x, x)\| = 0$.

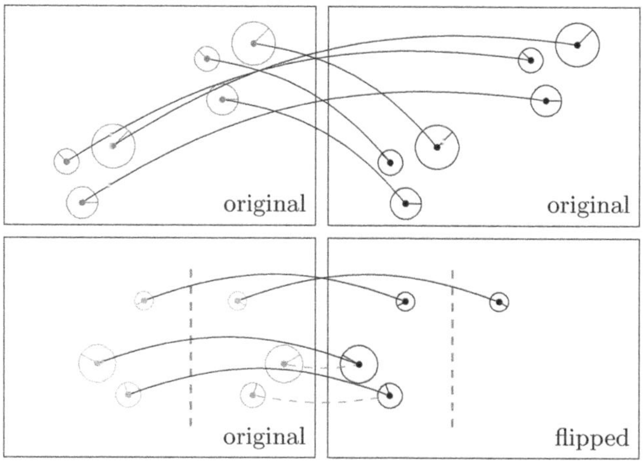

Figure 2: (Top) repeating pattern found by direct matching; magenta: *direct* selection. (Bottom) symmetry found by flipped matching; green: *flipped* selection, cyan: *back-projected* selection. (Left) original image. (Right) image to match; all features in black. Continuous line: tentative correspondences; dashed: back-projection + symmetry axes.

Now, feature correspondences are actually based on appearance. The simplest way is that of the *bag-of-words* model: two features are in correspondence simply when assigned the same *visual word*, which is a vector-quantized version of their descriptor. Depending on the method used for vocabulary construction, quantization may incur significant information loss [5], and since feature selection is an off-line process, we choose to work directly in the descriptor space. In fact, since features are not assigned a visual word before selection, it is also more efficient to seek neighbors among the features of X rather than within an entire vocabulary of typical size 10^6.

In particular, we define the *appearance dissimilarity* $d(x, y)$ of features $x, y \in X$ as their distance $\|d(x) - d(y)\|$ in the descriptor space $\mathbb{R}^D$. We say that features x, y are *similar* if $d(x, y) \leq \delta$, with *similarity threshold* $\delta > 0$. Now, given feature $x \in X$, let its *neighborhood* $N(x)$ be the set of similar features that is restricted to the set $\mathcal{N}_X^k(x)$ of its k-nearest neighbors in X according to dissimilarity d,

$$N(x) = \{y \in X : y \in \mathcal{N}_X^k(x) \wedge d(x, y) \leq \delta\}. \tag{4}$$

We use nearest neighbors to limit the number of correspondences, making the subsequent matching process more efficient; in practice, an *approximate* nearest neighbor scheme is used. Then, the set of *appearance-* or *descriptor-based* correspondences of image X contains all pairs of $x \in X$ with their neighbors,

$$C_d(X) = \{(x, y) \in X^2 : y \in N(x)\}, \tag{5}$$

Observe that $C_d(X)$ is a relation that is not symmetric in general. More important, contrary to typical image matching applications, we do not impose any *mapping constraint* towards *one-to-one* correspondence, like the *ratio test* [18]: we are seeking repeating patterns and a pattern may be repeating more than twice. Definitions (4), (5) allow up to k repetitions.

Finally, the set of *tentative* correspondences of X contains pairs of similar features that are also valid,

$$C_t(X) = C_d(X) \cap C_v(X). \tag{6}$$

All correspondence definitions so far refer to *direct* matching, and will be modified accordingly for flipped matching in section 3.3. Direct matching is illustrated in Figure 2(top), showing a pattern of three features repeating twice while undergoing a translation. Observe that tentative correspondences, being valid, exclude ones between a feature and itself in the two images. The two groups of three correspondences are essentially the same, being of the form (x, y) and (y, x). However, correspondences are not always symmetric. The pattern could repeat three times or more, while all similarity transformations are allowed.

3.2 Spatial self-matching

In order to detect local symmetries or repeating patterns, we need stronger evidence than just a set of independent correspondences, each based on the similarity of a single pair of features. We follow two different approaches, both inspired by existing methods for *spatial matching* between two different images, which however we apply to *self-matching* within a single image. Our first approach seeks *groups* of geometrically verified correspondences, called *inliers*; it is inspired by *fast spatial matching* (FSM) [25].

Given image X, each correspondence $c = (x, y) \in C_t(X)$ gives rise to a similarity transformation represented by vector $g(c)$ defined in (2). This transformation has four degrees of freedom and may as well be represented by a matrix $t(c) \in \mathbb{R}^{3\times3}$, with

$$t(x, y) = t(c) = \begin{bmatrix} M(c) & p(c) \\ \mathbf{0}^{\mathrm{T}} & 1 \end{bmatrix}. \tag{7}$$

This alternative formulation is useful when representing position in homogeneous coordinates. Then, given transformation $h = t(c) = t(x, y)$, the position $\mathbf{p}(z) \in \mathbb{R}^3$ of $z \in X$ is transformed to $h\mathbf{p}(z)$, the latter standing for a matrix-vector product.

FSM is a RANSAC-like process. Given image X and its set of tentative correspondences $C = C_t(X)$, each $c \in C$ defines a transformation *hypothesis* $h = t(c)$ that is verified by looking for *inliers* $I_C(h)$ among all correspondences $(x, y) \in C$, with

$$I_C(h) = \{(x, y) \in C : \|\mathbf{p}(y) - h\mathbf{p}(x)\| < \epsilon\} \tag{8}$$

for $h \in \mathbb{R}^{3\times3}$. The inlier set relies on *inlier threshold* $\epsilon > 0$, given in pixels. Among all hypotheses $t(C) = \{t(c) : c \in C\}$, FSM then seeks the hypothesis $h \in t(C)$ with the highest *inlier support* $|I_C(h)|$. Here is where we differentiate: we seek the best hypothesis *per individual inlier*.

In particular, for each correspondence $c = (x, y) \in C$, we define its set of *associated hypotheses* $H_C(c) = H_C(x, y) \subseteq t(C)$ that align c as an inlier,

$$H_C(x, y) = \{h \in t(C) : \|\mathbf{p}(y) - h\mathbf{p}(x)\| < \epsilon\}. \tag{9}$$

We can now define the *inlier strength* $\alpha(c)$ of correspondence c as the largest inlier support $|I_C(h)|$ over all its associated hypotheses $h \in H_C(c)$,

$$\alpha_C(c) = \max\{|I_C(h)| : h \in H_C(c)\}. \tag{10}$$

The entire self-matching process is summarized in Algorithm 1, which we will refer to as *spatial self-matching*

Algorithm 1: Spatial self-matching (SSM)

1 **procedure** $\alpha \leftarrow \mathrm{SSM}(C, t; \tau_\alpha)$
  input : correspondences C, transformations t
  parameter: inlier threshold τ_α
  output : inlier strengths α
2 **for** $c \in C$ **do** ▷ initialize
3   $inlier(c) \leftarrow$ FALSE ▷ mark as outlier
4   $\alpha(c) \leftarrow 0$ ▷ zero strength
5 **for** $c \in C$ **do** ▷ for all hypotheses
6   **if** $inlier(c)$ **then continue** ▷ skip hypothesis?
7   $h \leftarrow t(c)$ ▷ current hypothesis
8   $I \leftarrow I_C(h)$ ▷ current inliers (8)
9   **if** $|I| < \tau_\alpha$ **then continue** ▷ verified hypothesis?
10   **for** $c' \in I$ **do** ▷ for all inliers
11     $inlier(c') \leftarrow$ TRUE ▷ mark as inlier
12     $\alpha(c') \leftarrow \max(\alpha(c'), |I|)$ ▷ update strength
13 **return** α ▷ inlier strengths

(SSM). The original algorithm [25] is quadratic in the number of correspondences, since all correspondences are considered as inliers to all hypotheses. To speed up the process, we skip hypotheses arising from correspondences that have already been counted as inliers for previous hypotheses (line 6). We have observed that this does not affect feature selection in practice. The process is now quadratic only in the worst case, *i.e.* when no inliers are found at all, but in practice we get significant computational savings.

Once all inlier strengths have been computed, the set of spatially *verified* correspondences $\alpha(C) \subseteq C$ is

$$\alpha(C) = \{c \in C : \alpha_C(c) \geq \tau_\alpha\}, \tag{11}$$

with *selection threshold* $\tau_\alpha > 0$. Finally, given image X with tentative correspondences $C = C_t(X)$, we *select* those features $x \in X$ that are participating in some verified correspondence in $\alpha(C)$,

$$\alpha_d(X) = \pi^1(\alpha(C)) \cup \pi^2(\alpha(C)), \tag{12}$$

where, for $i = 1, 2$, $\pi^i(S)$ is the i-th *projection* of binary relation $S \subseteq X_1 \times X_2$, collecting the i-th element of all its pairs,

$$\pi^i(S) = \{x^i \in X_i : (x^1, x^2) \in S\}. \tag{13}$$

We call $\alpha_d(X)$ the *direct* selection of features in X.

3.3 Flipped matching

So far, we have only considered *direct* similarity transformations, that is, hypotheses h with $\det h > 0$. How about *opposite* transformations with $\det h < 0$, like *reflections*? In fact, once the image is reflected, the patch of each local feature is reflected as well, and its descriptor is no longer the same, unless the patch is symmetric itself. So reflecting the local geometry (1) is not enough: we actually need to reflect the entire image and extract a new set of features and descriptors.

Any opposite transformation will do, and we choose *horizontal flipping*. Let Y be the local feature set extracted from the flipped image. We assume each feature $y \in Y$ has a flipped, *back-projected* counterpart y'. This is the projection of y on the original image with

$$g(y') = [w - p^1(y) \;\; p^2(y) \;\; \sigma(y) \;\; \pi - \theta(y)]^{\mathrm{T}}, \tag{14}$$

Figure 3: Top: sample group of inliers found by SSM on original image, capturing a repeating pattern. Bottom: sample group found by SSM between original and flipped images, capturing a symmetry.

where w is the image width and $p^i(y), i = 1, 2$ are the coordinates of y on the image plane. No descriptor is available for those features in the original image before selection.

Correspondences are formed exactly as in self-matching, but are now defined between features $x \in X, y \in Y$ of the original and flipped image respectively. The sets of *valid*, *appearance-based* and *tentative* correspondences (3), (5), (6) are modified respectively as

$$C_v(X, Y) = \{(x, y) \in X \times Y : v(x, y')\}, \quad (15)$$
$$C_d(X, Y) = \{(x, y) \in X \times Y : y \in N(x)\}, \quad (16)$$
$$C_t(X, Y) = C_d(X, Y) \cap C_v(X, Y). \quad (17)$$

Observe that valid pairs refer to the same image, so we use the back-projected feature y' instead of y in (15).

Given the set $C_f = C_t(X, Y)$ of tentative correspondences between X and Y, the SSM process of section 3.2 remains identical. Let $\alpha(C_f)$ be the resulting set of spatially verified correspondences. The second set of features we select, the *flipped* selection, contains those features of X that participate in a verified correspondence in $\alpha(C_f)$ and are nowhere near any feature in $\alpha_d(X)$ that is already selected,

$$\alpha_f(X) = \pi^1(\alpha(C_f)) \setminus_v \alpha_d(X). \quad (18)$$

By $A \setminus_v B$ we denote those features of A that are *valid with respect to* B,

$$A \setminus_v B = \{a \in A : v(a, b) \text{ for all } b \in B\}. \quad (19)$$

The third set of features, the *back-projected* selection, contains those features of Y that participate in a verified correspondence. We actually use their back-projected counterpart in this case, again ignoring ones that are near selected features in $\alpha_d(X) \cup \alpha_f(X)$,

Figure 4: Initial (left) and selected (right) features by SSM. Original, flipped and back-projected selections shown in red, green and blue respectively.

$$\alpha'_f(X) = [\pi^2(\alpha(C_f))]' \setminus_v (\alpha_d(X) \cup \alpha_f(X)), \quad (20)$$

where $A' = \{y' : y \in A\}$ denotes the back-projection of feature set $A \subseteq Y$. It is now time to extract descriptors from the original image for those selected, back-projected features. Finally, the *complete* set of selected features contains the direct, flipped and back-projected selections,

$$\alpha(X) = \alpha_d(X) \cup \alpha_f(X) \cup \alpha'_f(X). \quad (21)$$

We will just say that $\alpha(X)$ is the set of *selected* features for X. They are the only features to be assigned a visual word and indexed for retrieval.

Flipped matching is illustrated in Figure 2(bottom), showing a pattern of six features that is symmetric with a vertical axis of symmetry. Four of the features (in green) are detected on the original image, giving the *flipped* selection, and four (in black) on the flipped image; the two groups have two features in common, detected in both images. The two features that are only detected on the flipped image give the *back-projected* selection (in cyan) on the original image. Apart from this exception, we are showing for each image only the features that are detected and participating in some correspondence of the chosen pattern or group.

Figure 3 illustrates SSM matching between an image X and itself as well as its flipped counterpart Y, detecting a feature group corresponding to a repeating pattern and a symmetry, respectively, on a real image. There are a lot more detected feature groups not shown here. For the same image, Figure 4 depicts all available original features along with the three different sets of selections made by SSM, in particular the *direct* (α_d), *flipped* (α_f) and *back-projected* (α'_f) selections.

3.4 Relaxed spatial self-matching

Given a set of tentative correspondences C, the spatial self-matching process of section 3.2 is based on FSM [25] and is quadratic in the number of correspondences, $|C|$, in the worst case. On the other hand, *Hough pyramid matching* (HPM) [31] is a recent, *relaxed* spatial matching method, which is linear in $|C|$ and is shown to outperform FSM in spatial re-ranking for image retrieval. HPM is not only faster by not requiring inlier counting, but also free of any threshold defining what an inlier is, like ϵ in (8) or (9). Further, it assigns a *strength* value to each individual correspondence,

Algorithm 2: Hough pyramid self-matching (HPSM)

```
1  procedure β ← HPSM(C, L)
   input  : correspondences C, levels L
   output: strengths β
2  begin
3     B ← PARTITION(L)                ▷ partition space in L levels
4     for c ∈ C do β(c) ← 0            ▷ initialize strengths
5     HPSM-REC(β, C, L − 1, B)         ▷ recurse at top
6     return β/ max(β)                 ▷ normalize

7  procedure HPSM-REC(β, C, ℓ, B)
   in/out : strengths β
   input  : correspondences C, level ℓ, partition map B
8  begin
9     if ℓ < 0 then return
10    for b ∈ B_ℓ do F(b) ← ∅           ▷ initialize histogram
11    for c ∈ C do                     ▷ populate histogram
12       F(q_ℓ(c)) ← F(q_ℓ(c)) ∪ c      ▷ ...by quantizing
13    for b ∈ B_ℓ do
14       F ← F(b)                      ▷ correspondences in b
15       if |F| < 2 then continue      ▷ exclude singles
16       HPSM-REC(β, F, ℓ − 1, B)       ▷ recurse down
17       if ℓ = L − 1 then m ← 2 else m ← 1
18       for c ∈ F do                  ▷ update strengths in b
19          β(c) ← β(c) + 2^{−ℓ} m|F|  ▷ ...as in (22)
```

reflecting whether it is geometrically consistent with others. This is accomplished without ever enumerating all pairs of correspondences.

We consider HPM as the basis for a faster self-matching alternative for feature selection. Instead of an overall matching score between the image and itself (which would be pointless), we rather use the *individual strength* of each correspondence. In this sense, HPM is easier than FSM to apply to self-matching, since individual strengths are inherent in its matching process. However, there are still a couple of deviations from [31].

Given a set of tentative correspondences C, either a subset of X^2 (self-matching) or $X \times Y$ (flipped matching), each correspondence $c = (x, y) \in C$ gives rise to a 4-dof transformation, which we now represent by *transformation parameter* vector $g(c) \in \mathbb{R}^4$ given by (2). Seeing these vectors as points in a 4-dimensional *transformation space*, the problem is now to detect regions of high density in this space, otherwise known as *mode seeking*. Because the dimensionality is low, a *pyramid* matching scheme is an ideal way to linearize the process by avoiding pairwise interactions. We briefly discuss this scheme here.

An L-level *hierarchical partition* of the transformation space is constructed as a sequence of partitions $B_0, \ldots, B_{L-1}$. B_0 is at the finest (bottom) level, while B_{L-1} is at the coarsest (top) level and has a single bin. Each bin in B_ℓ is split into 2^4 bins in $B_{\ell+1}$. A *histogram pyramid* is then constructed by distributing correspondences to bins at all levels of the hierarchy. Given any bin b, let $F(b) = \{c \in C : g(c) \in b\}$ be the set of correspondences with parameter vector falling in b, and $f(b) = |F(b)|$ its count, representing the bin *frequency* in the histogram.

Correspondences falling into the same bin are *grouped*, and we expect to find the most geometrically consistent

Figure 5: Flipped matching with HPSM at $L = 5$ levels. (Top) correspondences in a single bin at level 0, revealing a symmetric feature group. (Bottom) all tentative correspondences, with red (yellow) being the strongest (weakest).

groups in the lower levels of the hierarchy, with larger groups considered to be more consistent. A single correspondence gives no matching evidence and cannot form a group, so the *group size* of a bin is defined as $s(b) = [f(b) - 1]_+ = \max(0, f(b) - 1)$. Let $b_0 \subseteq \ldots \subseteq b_\ell$ be the sequence of bins containing a correspondence c up to level ℓ. The *strength up to level* ℓ of each correspondence $c \in C$, reflecting the above considerations, is given by

$$\beta_\ell(c) = s(b_0) + \sum_{i=1}^{\ell} 2^{-i}\{s(b_i) - s(b_{i-1})\}. \qquad (22)$$

The total strength of c collected up to the top level $L - 1$ is then simply $\beta_{L-1}(c)$, which we convert to a *relative strength*, normalizing by the maximum strength over all correspondences in C:

$$\beta(c) = \beta_{L-1}(c) / \max_{a \in C} \beta_{L-1}(a). \qquad (23)$$

The latter normalization scheme is a deviation from [31], giving the strongest correspondences a chance to participate in feature selection, even if they are not strong enough in absolute value. Another deviation is that we *do not impose an one-to-one mapping*, since this would contradict detection of repeating patterns within a single image, as discussed in section 3.1. The matching process is thus considerably simplified compared to [31], as summarized in Algorithm 2. We will refer to the latter as *Hough pyramid self-matching* (HPSM). Mapping $q_\ell : C \to B_\ell$ appearing in line 12 is used to *quantize* a correspondence to a bin of level ℓ. Histogram representation is sparse and the algorithm remains linear in $|C|$. As in [31], strength update in line 19 is equivalent to the definition given by (22).

Figure 6: Sample images, along with selected features found by HPSM at $L = 5$ levels, colored as in Figure 4.

Now, replacing α by β, we can use HPSM to find the *verified* correspondences $\beta(C) \subseteq C$, modifying (10) as

$$\beta(C) = \{c \in C : \beta(c) \geq \tau_\beta\}, \quad (24)$$

with *selection threshold* $\tau_\beta \in [0, 1]$. Similarly, let $\beta(C_f)$ be the verified correspondences after flipped matching with HPSM. Then the *direct* (β_d), *flipped* (β_f), *back-projected* (β'_f) and *complete* (β) feature selections follow exactly as in sections 3.2, 3.3, simply by substituting β for α in (12), (18), (20), (21) respectively. We will refer to $\beta(X)$ just as the *selected* set of features for image X in this case.

Figure 5 illustrates flipped matching with HPSM, for the same image as in Figures 3,4. In this case, there are no groups of correspondences that are inliers to a single transformation. One may consider the set of correspondences in a single bin instead; the lower the level, the tighter the fit to one transformation. Each tentative correspondence is scored independently according to whether it is geometrically consistent with others. The strongest correspondences are the ones to be selected.

Figure 6 provides further examples of several images, depicting the complete feature selection made by HPSM, including the *direct* (β_d), *flipped* (β_f) and *back-projected* (β'_f) selections. There are plenty of symmetries found despite perspective projection, with most selected features on the main foreground object or surface.

4. EXPERIMENTS

In this section we explore the behavior of SSM and HPSM under different parameter settings and compare their performance and memory usage against the *full feature set* representation on large scale experiments. We also compare the proposed methods against other feature selection approaches for single images based on options available from the feature detector, in particular the feature scale as in [32], and the feature strength.

4.1 Datasets

We use two datasets, namely the new *SymCity* dataset and *World Cities*[1] [31]. *SymCity* is a dataset of 953 annotated images from *Flickr*, split in 299 small groups depicting urban scenes. From each group, a single image is inserted in the database, while all other 654 images are only used as queries. For each query image we then wish to retrieve only a unique database image, and the precision measurement actually depends only on its ranked position. The distractor set of *World Cities* consists of 2M images from different cities; we use the first one million as distractors in our experiments, which we shall refer to as the *distractor* set.

SymCity has been built by a semi-automatic process. We have followed the method of Avrithis *et al.* [2] to first create geo-clusters and then visual clusters of images from 10 cities. Keeping only clusters of up to 4 images, we have selected through visual inspection a set of clusters depicting indeed the same object, building or scene. The 10 cities considered are different from the ones of the distractor set, ensuring that depicted scenes do not appear in both sets. We shall refer to *SymCity* as the *annotated* set; sample images are shown in Figure 7.

4.2 Protocol

We extract SURF [4] features and descriptors for each image and assign them visual words from a generic 100K vocabulary using FLANN [21] and keeping only one nearest neighbor under Euclidean distance. The vocabulary is constructed using approximate k-means (AKM) [25] on an independent set of 15K images depicting urban scenes.

[1] `http://image.ntua.gr/iva/datasets/wc/`

Figure 7: Sample images from the *SymCity* dataset.

In the feature selection process, descriptor matching for tentative correspondences is performed with approximate nearest neighbor search, again using FLANN [21]. Upon failure of symmetry detection, we add more features based on detector information. In particular, SSM fails when it yields no verified hypotheses, while HPSM when it selects less than τ_α features, which is again the minimum number of inliers that would be required to verify a hypothesis. In either case, we select a percentage $\lambda = 15\%$ of the features with the highest detector strength.

For retrieval, we build an independent *inverted file* for each selected feature set. For each query image we then retrieve its visual words from the inverted file and rank them by dot product on ℓ^2-normalized BoW histograms and *tf-idf* weighting [29].

We measure retrieval performance by *mean Average Precision* (mAP) over all queries. In the particular case where there is only a single image to be retrieved for each query, the *average precision* is just the inverse of its rank in the retrieved list of images. We measure *index size* by the number of entries in the inverted index per image, which is the number of unique visual words per image. For each selection method, we define *memory ratio* as the ratio of its index size to that required by the *full feature set*, where all features are kept. The index size of the latter is 635 on average; in particular, an image has 710 features and 635 unique visual words on average before selection.

Running time refers to the entire process of feature selection for one image including both direct and flipped matching for each method, but excluding the time needed to generate feature correspondences and extract features and descriptors in the flipped image, as well as descriptors for back-projected features. We use our own C++ implementations for all methods evaluated and measure times on a 2GHz quad core processor. In all experiments we perform selection only on the 299 images of the *SymCity* dataset ground truth and index *all* features of the distractor images. This is preferred in order to allow a fair comparison to baseline methods, since all methods are now tested using the same amount of distractor features.

4.3 Tuning

We first fix *similarity threshold* (4) $\delta = 0.1$ and SSM *inlier threshold* (8) $\epsilon = 7$ pixels, which we choose after thorough subjective evaluation by visual inspection of correspondences and selected features. The former is specifically chosen for SURF descriptors; the latter is not needed by HPSM. We also fix $L = 5$ levels for HPSM, as in [31].

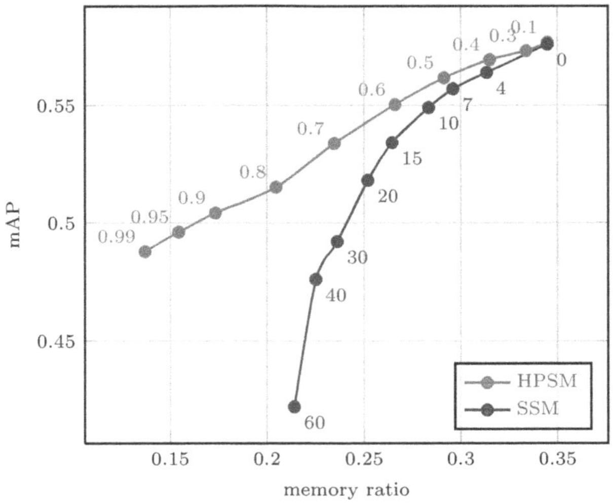

Figure 8: mAP performance of SSM and HPSM for varying selection thresholds τ_α and τ_β respectively versus memory ratio in the presence of 100K distractors, with $k = 3$ nearest neighbors. Selection threshold is shown with text labels near markers.

With these settings, we perform further parameter tuning on the *SymCity* dataset, using a subset of 100K distractors from *World Cities*. In Figure 8 we show mAP and memory ratio measurements for SSM and HPSM with varying *selection thresholds* τ_α (11) and τ_β (24) respectively. Both methods perform equally for high memory ratio, selecting in fact all features participating in tentative correspondences. However, as we become more selective, SSM collapses while HPSM continues to degrade smoothly.

Figure 9 measures average running time for both methods, for varying number k of *nearest neighbors* used for tentative correspondences in (4). The running time for SSM also depends on selection threshold τ_α. A lower threshold will allow more hypotheses to be skipped, degrading performance. The higher the threshold is, the closer the running time is to that of FSM [25]. HPSM is 5 to 15 times faster than SSM on average, so given its higher performance as well, it has a clear advantage. We choose to continue further tuning and large scale experiments with HPSM only.

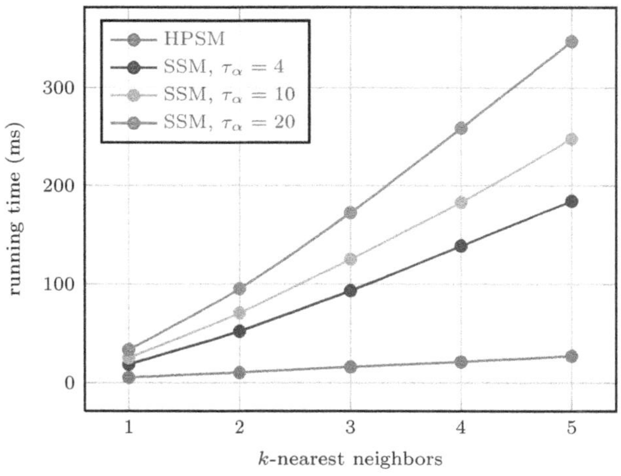

Figure 9: Average running time (ms) for HPSM and SSM versus k-nearest neighbors for tentative correspondences, where τ_α is varying for SSM.

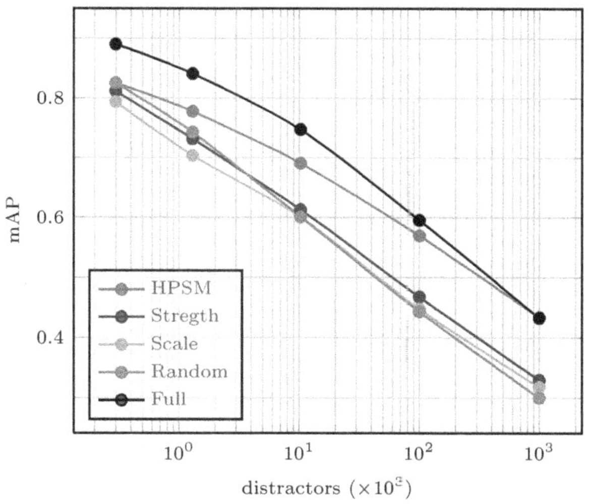

Figure 10: Mean average precision comparison versus number of distractors, with $\tau_\beta = 0.4$ for HPSM and a fixed number of features $n = 300$ for the remaining selection criteria.

k	1	2	**3**	4	5
$\tau_\beta = \mathbf{0.4}$	0.545	0.566	**0.569**	0.566	0.568
$\tau_\beta = 0.6$	0.522	0.538	0.550	0.551	0.547
$\tau_\beta = 0.8$	0.484	0.511	0.515	0.524	0.529

Table 1: HPSM mAP performance versus k-nearest neighbors for varying τ_β in the presence of 100K distractors. Chosen parameters and mAP shown in boldface.

Table 1 compares HPSM performance for varying number k of nearest neighbors. Performance almost stabilizes or even drops with more than 3 neighbors. We therefore choose $k = 3$ nearest neighbors for our remaining experiments. We also choose $\tau_\beta = 0.4$ as default, although there is a further experiment under varying τ_β. The average running time of HPSM for this setting is 16.2ms. Although feature selection is an off-line process, its speed is critical when indexing millions of images. HPSM is particularly efficient, with a running time that is negligible compared *e.g.* to feature detection and visual word assignment.

4.4 Comparisons

Working at larger scale, with up to the full 1M distractor set of *World Cities*, we compare our selection method to the *full feature set*. We also compare to three alternative, simple selection criteria for single images, where in particular a fixed number of features n is selected, having the highest *detector strength*, largest *feature scale* σ as in [32], or *uniformly at random* among the full feature set.

Figure 10 shows mAP performance under varying number of distractor images. While HPSM selection is, not quite unexpectedly, outperformed at small scale, it reaches the full feature set performance at large scale. This may be interpreted as *keeping a limited amount of information, which degrades quality when matching* e.g. *a single image pair, but which withstands severe distractor noise.* An observation of the two curve slopes at 10^6 distractors suggests that HPSM will actually *outperform* the full feature set at even larger scale.

This experiment is carried out with the default selection threshold $\tau_\beta = 0.4$, which yields an average memory ratio of 0.31 on the annotated set, corresponding to 284 selected features per image on average. To allow a fair comparison to the alternative selection criteria, we select a fixed number of $n = 300$ features per image, so that the average memory ratio is roughly the same. HPSM outperforms all three criteria: interestingly, its performance is near that of the three criteria at small scale, but gradually shifts towards that of the full feature set at large scale.

A higher selection threshold τ_β would make the process more selective and decrease memory ratio, at the expense of lower mAP as well. This is a way to *trade off* index size for retrieval quality. Figure 11 shows this trade-off on the full 1M distractor set, revealing that a less selective HPSM can even *outperform* the full feature set on mAP for a memory ratio around 35%. On the other hand, its mAP is in general well above that of the three alternative criteria for the same memory ratio, with an overhead of 13% on average.

5. DISCUSSION

It is quite unexpected that symmetry or self-similarity is a generic feature selection criterion that is able to reach or possibly *outperform the full feature set* at large scale. On the other hand, it is also unexpected that more local criteria like feature scale or strength do not in fact give much benefit over random selection. Besides this being the first work to apply symmetry for feature selection, we have shown that *symmetry detection is not much different in nature from spatial matching*, so given any advance in one problem it is straightforward to apply it to the other. In particular, HPSM is the first method that is *linear in the number of correspondences*, being extremely fast in practice.

Among future directions, *soft assignment* [6] and *geometry verification* [31] are probably the first one may combine

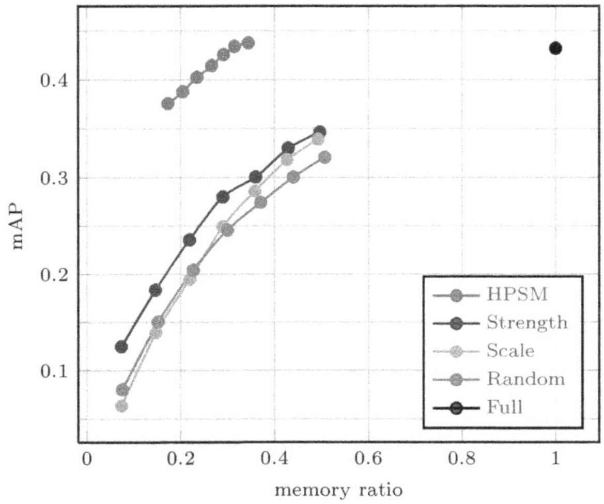

Figure 11: Mean average precision comparison against memory ratio for varying τ_β, n in the presence of 1M distractors.

in the retrieval process. It would be more interesting to extract *feature tracks* from our single image correspondences and employ them to find *visual synonyms* for vocabulary learning, as [20] does from multiple views. All approaches are expected to increase performance without any cost on the index size.

6. REFERENCES

[1] S. Agarwal, N. Snavely, I. Simon, S. M. Seitz, and R. Szeliski. Building Rome in a day. In *ICCV*, 2009.

[2] Y. Avrithis, Y. Kalantidis, G. Tolias, and E. Spyrou. Retrieving landmark and non-landmark images from community photo collections. In *ACM Multimedia*, 2010.

[3] S. Bagon, O. Boiman, and M. Irani. What is a good image segment? A unified approach to segment extraction. In *ECCV*, 2008.

[4] H. Bay, T. Tuytelaars, and L. Van Gool. SURF: Speeded up robust features. In *ECCV*, 2006.

[5] O. Boiman, E. Shechtman, and M. Irani. In defense of nearest-neighbor based image classification. In *CVPR*, 2008.

[6] O. Chum, J. Philbin, J. Sivic, M. Isard, and A. Zisserman. Total recall: Automatic query expansion with a generative feature model for object retrieval. In *ICCV*, 2007.

[7] H. Cornelius, M. Perdoch, J. Matas, and G. Loy. Efficient symmetry detection using local affine frames. In *ECIA*, 2007.

[8] P. Doubek, J. Matas, M. Perdoch, and O. Chum. Image matching and retrieval by repetitive patterns. In *ICPR*, 2010.

[9] S. Gammeter, L. Bossard, T. Quack, and L. V. Gool. I know what you did last summer: Object-level auto-annotation of holiday snaps. In *ICCV*, 2009.

[10] E. Gavves, C. G. M. Snoek, and A. W. M. Smeulders. Visual synonyms for landmark image retrieval. *CVIU*, 2012.

[11] H. Jegou, M. Douze, and C. Schmid. On the burstiness of visual elements. In *CVPR*, 2009.

[12] H. Jegou, M. Douze, and C. Schmid. Improving bag-of-features for large scale image search. *IJCV*, 87(3):316–336, 2010.

[13] H. Jegou, M. Douze, C. Schmid, and P. Perez. Aggregating local descriptors into a compact image representation. In *CVPR*, 2010.

[14] Y. Keller and Y. Shkolnisky. An algebraic approach to symmetry detection. *ICPR*, pages 186–189, 2004.

[15] J. Knopp, J. Sivic, and T. Pajdla. Avoiding confusing features in place recognition. In *ECCV*, 2010.

[16] S. Lazebnik, C. Schmid, and J. Ponce. Semi-local affine parts for object recognition. In *BMVC*, 2004.

[17] F. Li and J. Kosecka. Probabilistic location recognition using reduced feature set. In *ICRA*, 2006.

[18] D. Lowe. Distinctive image features from scale-invariant keypoints. *IJCV*, 60(2):91–110, 2004.

[19] G. Loy and J.-O. Eklundh. Detecting symmetry and symmetric constellations of features. In *ECCV*, 2006.

[20] A. Mikulik, M. Perdoch, O. Chum, and J. Matas. Learning a fine vocabulary. In *ECCV*, 2010.

[21] M. Muja and D. Lowe. Fast approximate nearest neighbors with automatic algorithm configuration. In *ICCV*, 2009.

[22] N. Naikal, A. Yang, and S. Shankar Sastry. Informative feature selection for object recognition via sparse pca. In *ICCV*, 2011.

[23] M. Perdoch, O. Chum, and J. Matas. Efficient representation of local geometry for large scale object retrieval. In *CVPR*, 2009.

[24] F. Perronnin, Y. Liu, J. Sanchez, and H. Poirier. Large-scale image retrieval with compressed Fisher vectors. In *CVPR*, 2010.

[25] J. Philbin, O. Chum, M. Isard, J. Sivic, and A. Zisserman. Object retrieval with large vocabularies and fast spatial matching. In *CVPR*, 2007.

[26] G. Schindler, M. Brown, and R. Szeliski. City-scale location recognition. In *CVPR*, 2007.

[27] G. Schindler, P. Krishnamurthy, R. Lublinerman, Y. Liu, and F. Dellaert. Detecting and matching repeated patterns for automatic geo-tagging in urban environments. In *CVPR*, 2008.

[28] E. Shechtman and M. Irani. Matching local self-similarities across images and videos. In *CVPR*, 2007.

[29] J. Sivic and A. Zisserman. Video Google: A text retrieval approach to object matching in videos. In *ICCV*, pages 1470–1477, 2003.

[30] C. Sun and D. Si. Fast reflectional symmetry detection using orientation histograms. *Real Time Imaging*, 5(1):63–74, 1999.

[31] G. Tolias and Y. Avrithis. Speeded-up, relaxed spatial matching. In *ICCV*, 2011.

[32] P. Turcot and D. Lowe. Better matching with fewer features: the selection of useful features in large database recognition problems. In *ICCV*, 2009.

[33] T. Tuytelaars, A. Turina, and L. Van Gool. Noncombinatorial detection of regular repetitions under perspective skew. *PAMI*, 2003.

Embedding Spatial Context Information into Inverted File for Large-Scale Image Retrieval

Zhen Liu †, Houqiang Li †, Wengang Zhou ‡, Qi Tian ‡
† University of Science and Technology of China, Hefei 230027, P. R. China
‡ University of Texas at San Antonio, Texas, TX 78249
liuzheng@mail.ustc.edu.cn; lihq@ustc.edu.cn; zhwg@mail.ustc.edu.cn; qitian@cs.utsa.edu

ABSTRACT

One most popular approach for large-scale content-based image retrieval is based on the Bag-of-Visual-Words model. Since the spatial context among local features is very important for visual content identification, many approaches index local features' geometric clues, such as location, scale and orientation for post-verification. To obtain consistent accuracy performance, the amount of top ranked images that post-verification approach needs to process is proportional to the image database size. When the database is very large, the verified images will be too many to be processed in real-time response. To address this issue, in this paper, we explore two approaches to embed spatial context information into the inverted file. The first one is to build a spatial relationship dictionary embedded with spatial context among local features, which we call one-one spatial relationship method. The second one is to generate a spatial context binary signature for each feature, which we call one-multiple spatial relationship method. Then we build an inverted file with spatial information between local features. The geometric verification is implicitly achieved while traversing the inverted file. Experimental results on benchmark Holidays dataset demonstrate the efficiency of the proposed algorithm.

Categories and Subject Descriptors

I.2.10 [**Vision and Scene Understanding**]: VISIONS

General Terms

Algorithms, Experimentation, Verification

Keywords

large-scale image retrieval, SIFT, spatial context , spatial relationship dictionary, one-one relationship, one-multiple relationship, feature tuple, spatial context binary signature

1. INTRODUCTION

In recent years, content-based image search has attracted more and more attention in computer vision and multimedia community owing to its great potential in both industry applications and research problems [18] [17] [1] [23] [21] [22]. Most approaches rely on the Bag-of-Visual-Words (BoW) model [18]. Generally, an image is represented by a set of local features. Those local features are extracted by describing local patches around key points. Key points are usually obtained by invariant detectors, such as Difference of Gaussian (DoG) [13], Harris affine detector [15], and MSER [14], etc. Then around a key point, a local patch is described into a local feature, such as SIFT [13]. Local features are usually of high dimension. To achieve a compact representation, a visual dictionary is defined and then local features can be quantized to visual words. The visual dictionary can be constructed off-line by unsupervised clustering algorithm, typically k-means [18], hierarchical k-means (HKM) [16] or approximate k-means (AKM) [17]. Consequently, an image is represented by a set of visual words. Further, scalable indexing techniques are leveraged from information retrieval. Typically, the inverted file structure, which has been successfully applied in textual information retrieval, is leveraged to index large-scale image database.

However, with the ignorance of spatial context among local features, the standard Bag-of-Visual-Words model suffers from limited accuracy [17]. To tackle the problem, many local or global verification methods, such as RANSAC [5] [2], weak geometric consistency [9] [11], geometric coding [25] [26], are proposed to check the geometric consistency among matched local features. RANSAC is one of the most popular methods for global post-verification. Since RANSAC is involved with many times of affine estimation for random sampled matching pairs, it is very time-consuming. By encoding local spatial informatin in stable regions, for example MSER region in [20], "Bundled features" can address the problem to some extent. But, it is still time consuming since the spatial verification between two bundled features is carried out during the retrieval process [21]. In contrast, geometric coding [25] is much efficient, but still unavoidably incurs additional time cost for spatial verification. What's more, such time cost is proportional to the size of image database. Although, on one million image database, the average query time is very short, say less than 100 milliseconds for 400 features in one image, it is still far from acceptable when the database size scales to 100 million or even billion scale. However, if we embed the spatial context information into the indexing structure, no post-verification will be need-

Figure 1: An example of some random selected feature tuples. The green arrow line means the dominate orientation of local feature and the red two pixel width line represents the pair of local features consisting of one feature tuple.

Figure 2: An example of spatial context of 5 random selected features. The green line means the dominate orientation of local feature and the red two pixel width circle represents the range of meaningful feature surrounding of the center feature. What's more, the circle is parted into three parts by the blue two pixel width radius.

ed. Motivated by this, our target is to design an algorithm that can record the spatial context information into the inverted file, because the indexing stage can be done off-line. And in the online retrieval stage, we just need to process the spatial context information of the query image.

In this paper, we explore embedding the spatial information between local features into the inverted file. It has been revealed that two order spatial structure between single features is much more important than other higher order spatial structure [6] [12] [24]. Therefore, we first propose an one-one relationship approach to record feature tuples into the inverted file instead of single feature. The feature tuple consists of a pair of single features and their spatial relationship, as illustrated in **Fig.** 1. In **Fig.** 1, the green arrow line denotes the dominate orientation of local feature and the red two pixel width line represents the pair of features consisting of one feature tuple. As for the high resolution image, a lot of local features can be extracted by the interest feature detector, such as 3000 features per image for Holidays [8]. The available memory limits the number of feature tuples that can be recorded into the inverted file. Thus the amount of spatial structure recorded into the inverted file is limited. To record spatial structure information as much as possible with the limited memory, we propose the one-multiple relationship approach. In the one-multiple relationship approach, for each single feature, its surrounding features are clustered into different groups based on their spatial relationship with it. A toy example is illustrated in **Fig.** 2. The center feature of the red circle is the feature whose spatial context need to be described. And the other features that locate inside the circle are thought to be meaningful neighbors of the center feature. The circle is divided into three parts by the blue radius line which is determined by the dominate orientation of the center feature. Those surrounding features that locate in the same part of the circle belong to the same group. With the help of these grouped surrounding features, we generate a b bits binary signature to describe the center feature's spatial context. Actually, for each feature in the image, we calculate its spatial context binary signature in the same way. In the retrieval stage, we compute the Hamming distance with XOR operation between the spatial context binary signature of two features that are quantized to the same visual word. And with the help of the computed Hamming distance, some false matches are filtered out. Note that our spatial context binary signature is different from the Hamming Embedding approach [9]. Our method is to model spatial structure between single features of an image while Hamming Embedding is a quantization approach.

Thus when traversing the inverted file, we conduct the geometric verification implicitly, which is much more scalable than the post-verification method [5] [17] [25] and make it more suitable for large-scale image search. The main contribution of this paper is summarized as follows:

- We embed the spatial information between local features into the inverted file.
- We build a spatial relationship dictionary to quantize the spatial relationship between local features.
- We produce spatial context binary signature for each local feature to do geometric verification.

The rest of the paper is organized as follows. In **Section** 2, related works are reviewed. In **Section** 3, we introduce our scheme of embedding the spatial information into the inverted index file by building a spatial relationship dictionary. In **Section** 4, we introduce our approach to generate spatial context binary signature for each feature. In **Section** 5, We present experimental results and make some discussions. Finally, we conclude the paper in **Section** 6.

2. RELATED WORK

In the past decade, with the introduction of local features, many image retrieval approaches are proposed based on the popular Bag-of-Visual-Words model. With local features, such as SIFT, quantized to visual words, images are compactly represented by a bag of visual words. Further, by indexing images with the inverted file structure, scalability of image search is achieved.

The spatial context among local features plays an important role in visual content identification. Many approaches [18] [17] [5] [1] [26] [24] [3] explore the spatial context information in images to improve retrieval precision. These approaches can be summarized into pre-verification or post-verification approaches. Some representative approaches of each category are discussed below.

The motivation of pre-verification approaches is to express the spatial context of local features into the image representation. In [19], the statistics in the local neighborhood of invariant features is used as its spatial context to enhance the discriminative power of visual word. The statistics contains the number of neighborhood features, the average characteristic scale difference and the average dominate orientation difference between each local feature and its neighborhood features. The feature matches are weighted by the difference of these statistics. The shortage of this method [19] is that it abandons the information of neighborhood features' descriptors. [1] project local features of an image along different directions to yield ordered spatial-bag-of-features for image search. Then some heuristic operations are exploited to achieve invariance in translation, rotation and scale changes. In [24], geometry-preserving visual phrase is proposed to describe the spatial context of local features, including both co-occurrences and the long-range spatial layouts of visual words. Actually, it transfers the geometric verification from the post-verification stage to the retrieval stage using Hough transform.

The post-verification approaches aim to filter out false matches by imposing spatial consistency. Some approaches are focused on local spatial consistency. The local spatial consistency of some spatial nearest neighbors is used in [18] to suppress false visual word matches. "Bundled features" [20] weights the traditional $tf - idf$ [18] [16] by similarity between feature bundles. The local spatial consistency is measured by projecting feature positions along horizontal and vertical directions in local MSER regions. However bundling feature method is time consuming because the spatial verification between bundles is carried out during the retrieval process. Geometric min-hashing [3] constructs repeatable hash keys with loose local geometric information to obtain more discriminative local description.

To capture spatial relationships of all features in the entire image, global geometric verification approaches such as WGC (weak geometric consistency) [9] [11], RANSAC [17] [5] are often adopted. Weak geometric consistency use a weaker global geometric model. The matches with the dominate relative scale difference and the relative orientation difference are thought to be true matches and other matches are filtered out. What's more, a priori knowledge is added into the weak geometric consistency model to improve the retrieval accuracy one step further based on human shot tendency. RANSAC-based image re-ranking achieves the state-of-art result in terms of retrieval accuracy [17]. But, RANSAC has to randomly sample many subsets of matching pairs and perform affine estimation for each subset to obtain the optimal transformation. Although RANSAC can greatly improve retrieval performance, it is computationally expensive. In practice, it is usually applied to the subset of the top-ranked candidate images to ensure efficiency, which may not benefit the recall performance in large-scale image retrieval systems.

The spatial coding approach [26] and geometric coding approach [25] are another global geometric verification methods proposed to remove false matches based on maps, which are generated by checking the relative locations of local features. They are much more efficient than RANSAC, but still unavoidably incur additional time cost for geometric verification. And such time cost is still proportional to the size of image database.

Based on the analysis above, we propose an algorithm to embed the spatial context information into the inverted file. The time cost to obtain spatial context information is just dependent on the query image. And we do geometric verification while feature matching.

3. ONE-ONE RELATIONSHIP

In this section, we introduce our one-one relationship approach to record the spatial context information of an image into the inverted file. First, we build feature tuples with the spatial relationship dictionary built in **Section** 3.1. Then, we introduce how to index and do retrieval with feature tuples in **Section** 3.2 and **Section** 3.3.

Let us first introduce our notation. We extract the interest points with Hessian-Affine detector [7] and the SIFT descriptor [13] for each image. These interest points are denoted by $\{f_i\}_{i=1}^{N}$, in which N represents the total number of the detected interest points. Each feature f_i includes the descriptor $\boldsymbol{d}_i \in \mathbb{R}^D$, for SIFT descriptor D is 128, the location $\boldsymbol{l}_i \in \mathbb{R}^2$, the characteristic scale s_i and the dominant orientation o_i.

3.1 Build Spatial Relationship Dictionary

With the information provided by interest point detector and descriptor, namely the feature location, the dominant orientation, the characteristic scale, we build a spatial relationship dictionary by image plane division, as shown in **Fig. 3**. For each feature f_i, a reference coordinate system is built, with the location $\boldsymbol{l}_i$ as the origin and the orientation o_i as x axis. The different plane division means different spatial relationship quantization. The spatial relationship between feature f_i and f_j is denoted by R_{ij} and we create a tuple $\{f_i, f_j, R_{ij}\}$ to represent this concept.

We take **Fig.** 3 (a) as an example to illustrate how to build the spatial relationship dictionary and how to quantize the feature pairs with this spatial relationship dictionary. There are two features, A and B on the image plane. For feature A, we build a coordinate system with $\boldsymbol{l}_A$ as its origin and o_A as its x axis. We identify each part of the image plane divided by this coordinate system with an integer number. And feature B is processed in the same way. So there is a tuple in **Fig.** 3 (a), $\{A, B, R_{AB}\}$ or $\{B, A, R_{BA}\}$. The spatial relationship between A and B, namely R_{AB} or R_{BA} , can be easily determined by computing the angle between vector $\overrightarrow{AB}$ and the dominate orientation of A, namely o_A , as shown in **Fig.** 4. So we have the result of $R_{AB} = (1, 2)$ and $R_{BA} = (2, 1)$. Thus for each feature tuple, there are two ways to describe it. Take the feature tuple that consists of A and B as an example, it can be noted as (A, B, R_{AB}) or (B, A, R_{BA}). We just record once for each tuple, so there must be a rule to reveal which version of the feature tuple should be embedded into the inverted file. The problem

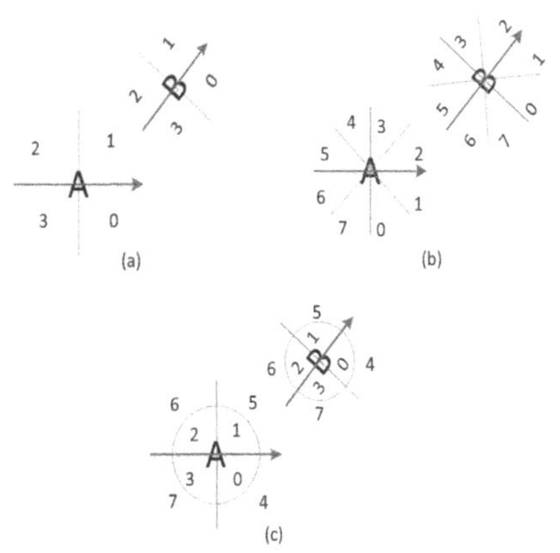

Figure 3: Illustration of relationship quantization between two features, A and B. (a). The plane is divided into four partitions only with the orientation information. (b) The plane is divided into eight partitions only with the orientation information. (c) The plane is divided into eight partitions with the scale information of the feature, in which the radius of the circle is linear to the feature scale.

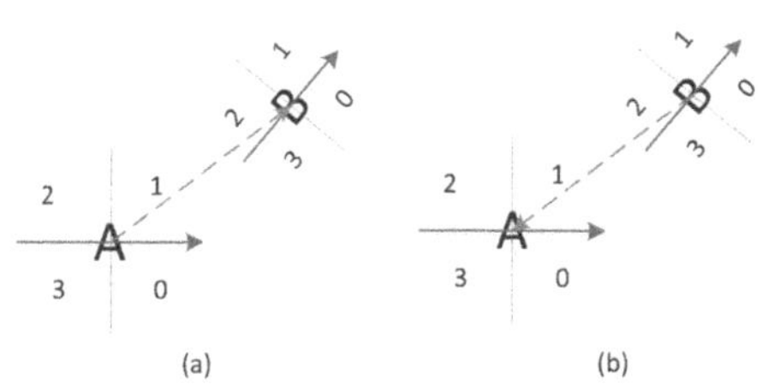

Figure 4: Illustration of how to build a relationship dictionary and how to quantize the relationship between two features with the relationship dictionary.

,which arrow should be kept, can be illustrated by the **Fig.** 4. In our implementation, we just keep the arrow whose head integer tag is bigger than its end integer tag. Thus **Fig.** 4 (a) is kept and we record the feature tuple, consisted of feature A and feature B, as (A, B, R_{AB}).

3.2 Indexing with Spatial Relationship Dictionary

Inspired by the success of text search engines, the inverted file structure has been widely used for large-scale content-based image search. An integer ID is assigned to each feature and those features with the same integer ID are thought as true matches, namely they describe the same local patch. Usually, a visual vocabulary is constructed off-line by unsupervised clustering algorithm, typically k-means, hierarchical k-means (HKM) or approximate k-means (AKM). Each element of the visual vocabulary is called visual word. In the on-line retrieval stage, only those images sharing the same visual word with the query image need to be checked. Thus, the inverted file structure achieves excellent efficiency. Each feature is quantized by the visual vocabulary with approximate nearest neighbor method and the word ID is assigned to the feature as its integer ID.

We also use vocabulary quantization method to assign integer ID to each feature tuple mentioned above, $\{f_i, f_j, R_{ij}\}$. Each feature tuple contains two visual elements, f_i and f_j, and the spatial relationship element, R_{ij}. Spatial relationship element is quantized with the spatial relationship dictionary mentioned in Section 3.1. Visual elements are quantized with visual vocabularies obtained by performing unsupervised clustering algorithm on the random selected local features. To limit the maximum of the integer ID to a modest size, we use two visual vocabularies to quantize two visual elements in each feature tuple. Namely, we built one visual vocabulary by clustering random selected feature samples to quantize f_i and then we built another visual vocabulary to quantize f_j by clustering random selected feature samples again. Note that the two visual vocabularies can be different in size. It is easy to control the maximum of the integer ID assigned to each feature tuple by adjusting the size of two visual vocabularies. The integer ID for each feature tuple can be obtained by

$$\begin{aligned} ID &= Q\{(f_i, f_j, R_{ij})\} \\ &= Q_1(f_i) \cdot vocSize2 \cdot rSize + Q_2(f_j) \cdot rSize + R_{ij} \end{aligned} \tag{1}$$

where ID means the integer ID for the feature tuple $\{f_i, f_j, R_{ij}\}$ and $Q_1(f_i)$, $Q_2(f_j)$ mean the approximate nearest neighbor visual word ID of feature f_i, f_j, respectively, in two visual vocabularies mentioned above and $vocSize2$ means the size of the visual vocabulary that quantizes the second element of the feature tuple and $rSize$ means the size of the spatial relationship dictionary built by the image plane division method. Note that here R_{ij} represents a scalar value. It is the index value in the spatial relationship dictionary mentioned in **Section** 3.1.

3.3 Searching Scheme

Given a query image, the search can be interpreted as a voting scheme. First, for each feature tuple in the query image, an integer ID is assigned to it by formula (1). Second, in the inverted file, we retrieve the list of images that contain this integer ID. For each image in the list, we increment its score by the square of *idf* weight of this integer ID. After processing all feature tuples in the query image, the final score of each image in database gives the dot product of the representation vector of the query image and database image. Then we normalize the score of each image by the number of feature tuples to obtain the cosine similarities for ranking.

4. ONE-MULTIPLE RELATIONSHIP

As there are so many local features extracted, about 3000 local features per image for Holidays image, it limits the number of feature tuples we can record into memory. We propose to generate a binary signature for each single feature to describe its spatial context.

In **Section** 4.1, we explain our algorithm to generate spatial context binary signature for each feature in detail and introduce the index structure and the searching scheme with spatial context binary signature in **Section** 4.2 and **Section** 4.3, respectively.

4.1 Spatial Context Binary Signature

As shown in **Fig.** 5, for each feature, taking feature A as an example, a coordinate system is built with origin at $\boldsymbol{l}_A$

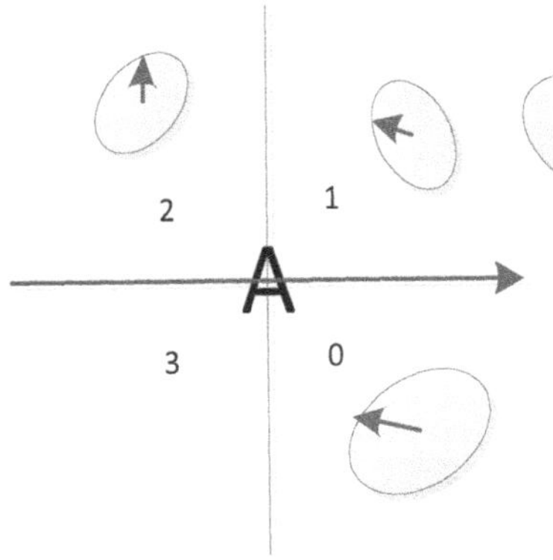

Figure 5: Illustration of feature surroundings.

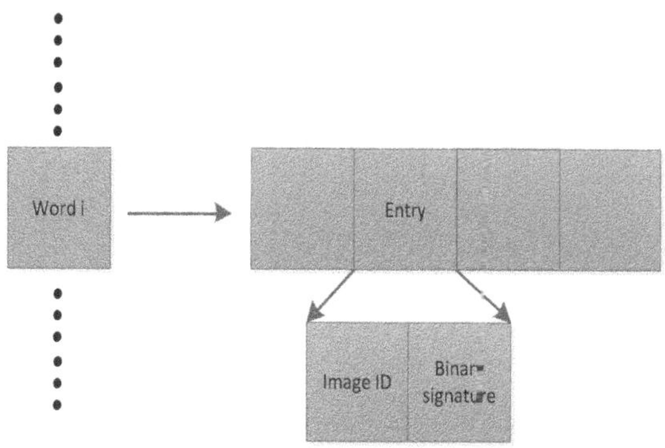

Figure 6: Illustration of indexing structure with spatial context binary signature.

and o_A as its x axis. We divide the image plane into four parts with the built coordinate system in **Fig.** 5. Note that, the image plane can be divided into any parts. And the partition is robust or invariant to rotation changes for that we use each feature's dominant orientation as its x axis. We denote each part by an integer number. Each part has different local features of the image. Given the assumption that true match features have similar surrounding features, we can generate a spatial context descriptor for each feature. The descriptor should be not only describing the distribution of surrounding local features but also the content of these local features. For example, if there is a feature matching with A, in each part its surrounding features should be similar with those surrounding features of A. Therefore, it actually is a problem to measure the similarity of two set of local features. As we try to use some binary bits to represent feature A's spatial context, we first combine the surrounding local features in each part of feature A into a vector descriptor, then hash it into a binary code.

Let us denote feature A by f_A and its surrounding features by $\{f_i\}_{i=1}^{N_A}$, in which N_A represents the number of surrounding features of A. Then, we combine the surrounding local features in each part of feature A into a vector descriptor by computing weighted sum of these surrounding features' SIFT descriptor, as shown in the following formula,

$$DS_A^k = \sum_{f_i \in S_A^k} w_i \cdot d_i \quad k = 1, 2, 3, \ldots \tag{2}$$

where $f_i \in S_A^k$ represents that f_i locates in the kth part of feature A and $\boldsymbol{d}_i$ is the 128 dimension SIFT descriptor of feature f_i and w_i is the weight for feature f_i. In our experiment implementation, we use $w_i = e^{(||\mathbf{l}_i - \mathbf{l}_A||^2/\sigma)}$ to assign weight for feature f_i. Namely, we assign small weight to the features far away from feature A and large weight to those features near feature A. DS_A^k means the combined vector descriptor of kth part of feature A. Then, we cascade DS_A^k together into a long vector, as shown by the following formula,

$$DS_A = [DS_A^1 \quad DS_A^2 \quad DS_A^3 \quad \cdots \quad DS_A^k \quad \cdots]. \tag{3}$$

In the rest of the paper, we refer DS_A as feature surrounding descriptor. To compress feature surrounding descriptor DS_A into a small bits binary signature, for example 64 bits, we generate an orthogonal projection matrix R by keeping the first b rows of an orthogonal matrix obtained by applying QR factorization to a randomly drawn matrix with Gaussian values. The parameter b is the number of bits used to describe the surrounding features. Therefore vector DS_A is reduced to b dimension by multiplying R, as shown in the following formula,

$$DS_{Ab} = DS_A \cdot R \tag{4}$$

Then, we quantize DS_{Ab} into binary format by using a threshold on each dimension of DS_{At} . The threshold is obtained by off-line training in the feature surrounding descriptor subspace of each visual word, to which feature A is quantized. The reason for that is we just do spatial context verification between those features which are quantized to the same visual word. The algorithm to obtain the spatial context binary signature threshold is shown in **Algorithm** 1. Given a feature, we compute its spatial context binary signature by **Algorithm** 2.

Algorithm 1 off-line spatial context binary signature threshold training

1. Random select a large set of feature samples from independent dataset.
2. Produce feature surrounding descriptor with formula (2) and (3). And quantize the feature samples with the visual vocabulary trained by k-means method.
3. Generate an orthogonal projection matrix R by selecting the first b rows of the orthogonal matrix obtained by applying QR decomposition to a randomly drawn matrix with Gaussian value.
4. Reduce the dimension of feature surrounding descriptors computed in step 2 by multiplying the orthogonal projection matrix R to it.
5. For each visual word, compute the mean value on each dimension of the dimension reduced feature surrounding descriptors of the features assigned to this visual word.
6. Set the mean value obtained in step 5 as the spatial context binary signature threshold and save the orthogonal projection matrix R .

4.2 Indexing with Spatial Context Binary Signature

We adopt the inverted file structure widely used by many researchers. Each visual word is followed by an entry list that contains the IDs of images in which the visual word appears. And we add the spatial context binary signature of each feature into it, as illustrated in **Fig.** 6.

4.3 Searching Scheme

The searching scheme is actually quite similar to the method mentioned in **Section** 3.2. We use the spatial context binary signature of each feature, obtained by using **Algorithm** 2, to filter out some false matches that the feature pairs are quantized to the same visual word, but have quite different surrounding features. Therefore the voting scheme in **Section** 3.3 can be modified to the following version.

First, given a query image, the spatial context binary signature is generated by proposed method for each local feature. And each feature is quantized to a visual word. Second, through the inverted file we retrieve the list of images that contain this visual word. We compute the spatial context binary signature distance between query feature and database feature by XOR operation. We just score those database features whose spatial context binary signature distance with the query feature under a certain threshold. The score is the square of *idf* weight of this visual word. After processing all features in the query image, the final score is normalized by the number of local features in each database image. The response list is returned based on the final score of each database image.

Algorithm 2 computing spatial context binary signature for a given feature A

1. Quantize the descriptor of feature A, namely d_A , into a visual word, denoted by $q(A)$.
2. Compute the feature surrounding descriptor of feature A, namely DS_A , by formula (2) and (3)
3. Reduce the dimension of feature surrounding descriptor by formula (4) with orthogonal matrix R generated in step 4 of algorithm 1. Then obtain DS_{Ab} mentioned above.
4. Compare each dimension of DS_{Ab} with the threshold of this dimension of visual word $q(A)$ generated in step 5 of algorithm 1, if the value is bigger than gate produce 1, otherwise produce 0.

5. EXPERIMENTS

We first introduce the baseline method or bag of visual words model used as comparison algorithm in many previous work [17] [20] [1]. Since an image is represented by a set of local features, to obtain a more compact representation, a visual vocabulary is built and the features are quantized to visual words. Hence, an image is transformed to a visual word vector with one component for each visual word in the visual vocabulary. And the similarity between two images is defined as the Euclidean distance of their L_2-normalized visual word vectors. For the inverted file indexing structure of bag of words model, the "Entry" in **Fig.** 6 is each feature's image ID. Usually, the location, the dominate orientation and the characteristic scale are also recorded into

(b)

Figure 7: Illustration of dataset images. (a) Sample images of Holidays (b) Sample images of downloaded Web images

the inverted file for post-verification. Then, we introduce our experimental settings.

We test the proposed algorithm on Holidays dataset, which contains about 1.5K images and 4.5M descriptors. The author of [10] has provided well trained vocabularies with different sizes and the extracted local features of images in Holidays dataset. We first use this dataset to illustrate the impact of different parameters in the proposed algorithm. The author also provided a distractor dataset downloaded from Flickr to perform large-scale image search evaluation. But it is too big to be downloaded. Therefore, to evaluate the performance of the proposed algorithm on large-scale dataset, we build our distractor dataset by crawling one million images from the Web.

We detect the interest points by Hessian-Affine detector and use SIFT descriptor to describe the appearance of local patch centered on the interest points, using the software of [7] with the default parameters. Besides the characteristic scale and the domain orientation, the software [7] also provided the response of the interest points and the affine invariance shape around the interest points.

In the following experiment, mean average precision (mAP) is adopted to evaluate the performance of the proposed two algorithms. Some sample images of Holidays and distractor images downloaded from the Web are shown in **Fig.** 7.

Table 1: The performance with different parameters value of proposed algorithm

vocSize		20K	200K
rSize	(a)	0.585	0.627
	(b)	0.594	0.636
	(c)	0.603	0.643
	(n)	0.486	0.593
baseline		0.451	0.551

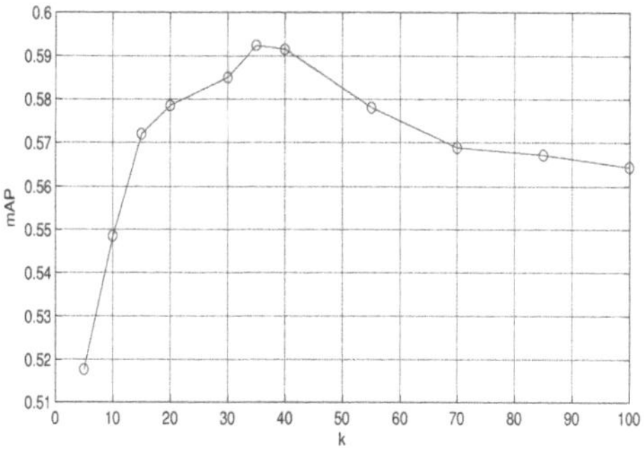

Figure 8: Illustration of factor k when we build feature pairs with spatial k nearest neighbors.

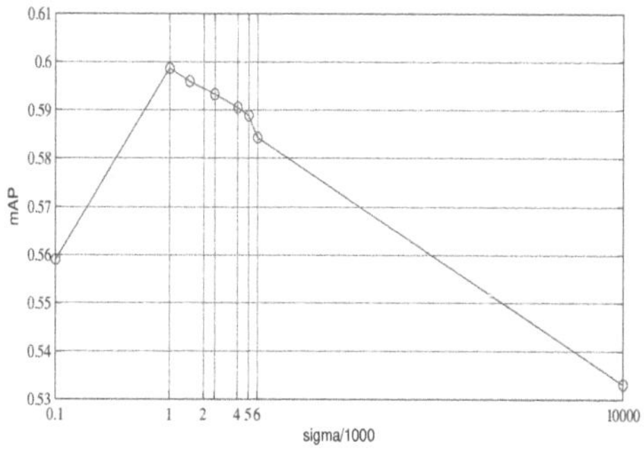

Figure 9: Illustration of impact of σ in the formula (2). When σ is quite large, for example 10000000, it means no weighting scheme in formula (2). The mAP is 0.532 for $\sigma = 10000000$.

5.1 One-one Relationship on Holidays

We test the proposed search algorithm with different size vocabularies provided by Jegou et al. [8]. And we quantize the feature descriptor with approximate nearest neighbor method by the software downloaded from [4]. We choose each feature and their spatial k nearest neighbors to build feature tuples to embed into the inverted file. Firstly, we set k as 30 to test the proposed algorithm's performance with different size vocabularies and different size relationship dictionaries. The results are shown in **Table** 1.

In **Table** 1, (a) (b) (c) represent the relationship dictionaries shown in **Fig.** 3, respectively and (n) means no image plane division, which means the spatial relationship dictionary size equals 1. The bottom line of **Table** 1 is the baseline approach with different size vocabularies, i.e. 20K and 200K. Because we use two independent vocabularies to quantize the first and the second component of each feature tuple, this two components are of equal importance. We test the performance of our proposed algorithm by letting one vocabulary vary while the other one unchanged. We use the vocabularies with sizes of 20K and 200K to quantize the first element of each feature tuple and the vocabulary with size of 200 to quantize the second element of feature tuple in the following experiment. In this experiment, the retrieval time and memory usage are not given because Holidays has only 1.5K images. We will give the retrieval time and analysis memory cost when a large-scale dataset is tested in **Section** 5.3.

Different image plane division means different spatial relationship dictionary. The more parts the plane is divided into, the stronger constraint is imposed on the construction of feature tuples.

From **Table** 1, it can be seen that the baseline approach achieves mAP of 0.451 with a 20K visual vocabulary and mAP of 0.551 with a 200K visual vocabulary. It is almost the same with the result reported in [9]. With no image plane division (in the case of (n)), we get 0.035 mAP improvement. When spatial relationship dictionary is used, we even get 0.152 mAP bonus (in the case of (c) in Table 1). When the vocabulary size increases to 200K, the mAP of both approaches increases, and the one-one relationship approach still has about 0.10 performance improvement.

As we use spatial k nearest neighbor method to build feature tuples, the spatial context range is determined by k in this experiment. The impact of factor k on mAP is illustrated in **Fig.** 8, with 20K and 200 visual vocabularies to quantize the first and the second element of each feature tuple, respectively. It can be observed that when k increases, the mAP first increases to a peak, and then drops gradually. What's more, the best result is gotten when k is 35 for this dataset. This is due to that larger value of k will introduce more feature tuples, namely more spatial context information, which will benefit the visual discrimination. But when k is too large, lots of noisy feature tuples will also be introduced, decreasing the retrieval accuracy performance.

5.2 One-multiple Relationship on Holidays

In this section, we evaluate the performance of our spatial context binary signature method. We will show the impact of the image plane division, the bits number of the spatial context binary signature, soft weighting parameter when combining surrounding features and the Hamming distance threshold when filtering out false matches. In the following experiments, we use the 20K visual vocabulary provided in [8] and adopt approximate nearest neighbor software [4] to quantize feature descriptor.

We use the spatial distance information between features and $w_i = e^{-\|l_i - l_A\|^2/\sigma}$ to assign the weight to feature f_i in formula (2). The impact of parameter σ is shown in **Fig.** 9. Other parameters are set as follows. We divide the image plane into 3 parts and set the spatial binary signature as 64 bits. Hamming distance threshold is set as 20 in retrieval. It can be observed that from **Fig.** 9, when σ increases, the mAP performance first increases and then drops gradually after it reaches the peak. When σ is quite large, for example 10000000, it means almost no weighting scheme in formula (2). The mAP we get is 0.532 for $\sigma = 10000000$. This is reasonable because σ controls the range of the spatial context information that we compress into the spatial context binary signature. When σ is small, we record less spatial cotnext information and when σ is too large, more noisy spatial context information is introduced.

Then, we illustrate the impact of the image plane division. As previous one, we let other parameters unchanged. We set σ in formula (2) as 1000 and also use 64 bits to represent the spatial binary signature and 20 Hamming distance threshold. The result is shown in **Fig.** 10. The image plane is divided into 1, 2, 3, 4 parts respectively. From **Fig.** 10, it is clear that the more parts image plane is partitioned into, the higher mAP performance we can get. Since the more

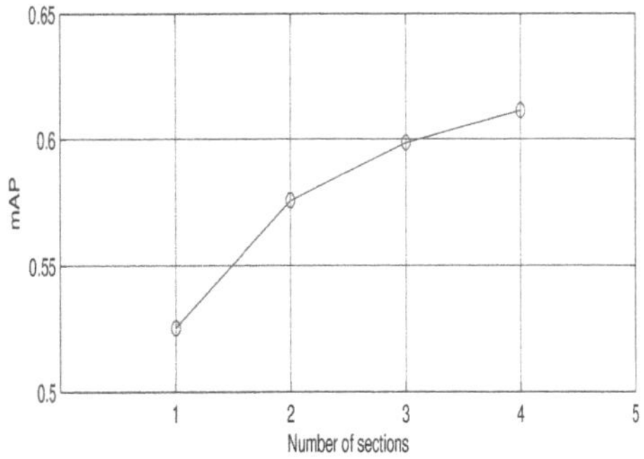

Figure 10: Illustration of impact of section number in formula (2). The image plane is divided into 1,2,3,4 parts, respectively, to test its influence.

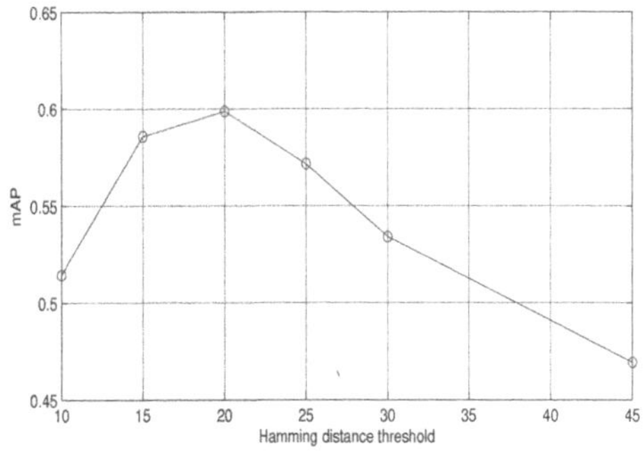

Figure 11: Illustration of impact of Hamming distance threshold when searching with spatial context binary signature.

parts image plane is partitioned into, the longer the feature surrounding descriptor is, namely DS_A in formula (3), we just divide the image plane into 1, 2, 3, 4 parts respectively in **Fig.** 10.

Fig. 12 illustrates the result when we use different bits to represent the spatial context binary signature. We also divide the image plane into 3 parts and set σ as 1000. We find that the best mAP performance can be gotten when Hamming distance threshold is set as around 5/16 of total bits of the spatial context binary signature. Hence, Hamming distance threshold is set as 10, 20, 40 for 32, 64, 128 bits spatial context binary signature, respectively. And as illustrated in **Fig.** 12, the more bits we use to represent the spatial context binary signature, the better mAP performance we can get, because much more spatial context information is recorded into the inverted file.

Fig. 11 illustrates the impact of Hamming distance threshold. We divide the image plane into 3 parts and set σ as 1000 and use 64 bits to represent the spatial context binary signature. For 64 bits spatial context binary signature, the best result, 0.6 mAP performance, is obtained at 20 Hamming distance threshold.

5.3 Evaluation on Large-Scale Dataset

To evaluate the large-scale image retrieval performance, the common practice is to employ a large image database as distrctors included in the ground truth data [17] [20] [10] [16]. We follow the same scheme and download 1M Web im-

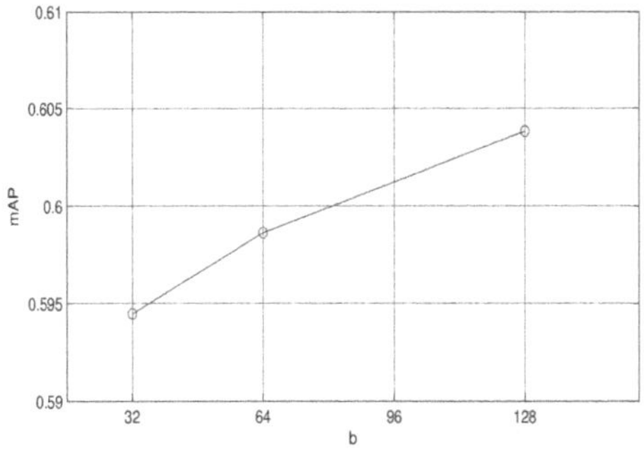

Figure 12: Illustration of bits number kept to represent spatial context binary signature. Hamming distance threshold is 10 for 32 bits and 20 for 64bits and 40 for 128 bits.

ages and some sample images are shown in **Fig.** 7. We put Holidays and the downloaded Web images together to test the performance of the proposed algorithm. The experiment is implemented on the server with 32G memory, 2.4GHz CPU of Intel Xeon.

We use the 20K visual vocabulary provided in [8]. Besides the baseline method, we also implement the geometric coding approach [25] as comparison. For the one-one relationship method, the size of the visual vocabulary to quantize the second element of feature tuple is 200. For the one-multiple relationship approach, the spatial binary signature generated for each feature is set as 64 bits with $\sigma = 1000$ and the Hamming distance threshold 20. The mean average precision (mAP) is adopted to evaluate the performance. The result is shown in **Fig.** 13. To evaluate the performance with respect to the size of dataset, three different dataset sizes, 200K, 500K, 1M are tested in our experiment. And the 1.5K is the size of Holidays without distractors.

For the one-one relationship approach, to reduce the memory cost, in the inverted file, the image ID of the 'Entry' in **Fig.** 6, is set as the increment of current image ID and its previous image ID belonging to the same item of the inverted file, which we call delta-image ID. And we record delta-image ID with 15 bits, and 1 extra bit is used to represent whether the current delta-image ID exceeds the maximum value of 15bits, namely 32767, or not. If it is larger than 32767, we use current 15 bits and the next 15 bits to represent delta-image ID.

From **Fig.** 13, it is obvious that the retrieval performance degrades gradually while increasing the size of database. We get about 0.135 mAP improvement for the one-one relationship method and 0.15 mAP improvement for the one-multiple relationship method when no distractors are added into Holidays. And when 1M images are indexed, for both proposed approaches, we still get about 0.1 mAP improvement comparing with the baseline method. Geometric coding [25] approach does not work well with above setting in Holidays dataset. The reason may be that geometric coding approach is designed for partial duplicate image search and works well on the well structured planar objects, for example trademarks.

As shown in **Table** 2, we present the time cost for each step of our implementation in the on-line retrieval stage. We implement each stage in a parallel way with the PPL library

Table 2: **The time cost of each step at online retrieval stage in our implementation. Note that the image has 3000 feature per image and the database is indexed with 20K visual vocabulary. We implement it with the PPL library of visual studio 2010, except for the retrieval stage of geometric coding approach.**

time (ms)	quantization	pre-processing	retrieval
baseline	183	0	108
one-one	183	62	63
one-multiple	183	47	81
geometric coding	183	0	9.25(s)

Table 3: The memory cost for each feature in our implementation.

memory cost (bytes)	baseline	one-multiple	one-one	geometric coding
per feature	20	(15∼30) × 2	12	14

of visual studio 2010. Local features are quantized with the software download from [4]. In the software, two approaches to find nearest neighbor are implemented, namely *kd*-tree based approximate nearest neighbor method and exact nearest neighbor method. We choose *kd*-tree based approximate nearest neighbor method to perform feature quantization. In our implementation, the feature quantization time with 20K visual vocabulary is about 183 ms for an image with 3000 features. And for the one-one relationship approach, spatial k-NN method, mentioned in the first paragraph of Section 5.1, is adopted to choose feature tuples. Hence the time cost will mainly come from getting k nearest spatial neighbors. As this is performed in two dimension space and can be performed in parallel way, we execute it in about 62 ms. For one-multiple method, the main time cost will be computing the weighted sum feature surrounding descriptor, namely DS_A in formula (2), and multiplying the orthogonal projection matrix to reduce the dimension of feature surrounding descriptor, namely formula (4). To reduce the complexity of computing weighted sum feature surrounding descriptor, those surrounding features far away from the center feature are not included in formula (2). And generating the spatial context binary signature can be implemented in 47ms. As for the retrieval time cost, namely the time cost traversing the inverted file, the minimum time cost is the one-one relationship approach. Because the maximum integer ID in formula (1) is $vocSize1 * vocSize2 * rSize$ that is $vocSize2 * rSize$ times of the baseline method, for which the maximum integer ID is the visual vocabulary size. Therefore, the high dimensional vector representation of an image for the one-one relationship approach is much sparser than the baseline method and the one-multiple approach. With the property of the inverted file, high efficiency for sparsity, the one-one relationship approach gets the best retrieval time efficiency. As for one-multiple approach, some false matches are filtered out with the generated spatial context binary signature , therefore the time cost for update the image matching score is reduced. But XOR operation needs to be done for each feature's spatial context binary signature with database features' spatial context binary signatures. For geometric coding approach, the retrieval stage is per-

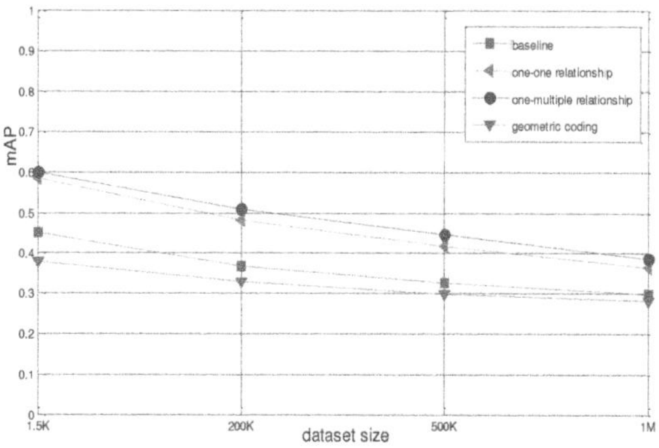

Figure 13: Illustration of proposed algorithm on Holidays dataset with different size of images as distractors to the ground truth.

formed in a single thread way. It needs about 9 s, for which the reason may be that many database images share some visual words with the query image when a 20K vocabulary is used. And we perform post-verification with geometric coding approach to all those images that sharing visual words with the query image.

The memory cost for approaches mentioned in **Fig.** 13 is shown in **Table** 3. For the baseline method, each feature needs an "Entry" in **Fig.** 6 and usually it contains two float type for the location information, one float type for the dominate orientation and one float type for the characteristic scale, besides one unsigned int type for image ID. Thus it needs 20 bytes for each feature. The proposed one-one relationship approach also needs one "Entry" for each feature tuple. We do not record the location, the dominate orientation, the characteristic scale information for each feature tuple, which means just image ID is recorded for each feature tuple. What's more, we use the delta-image ID method to record image ID into the inverted file, namely about two bytes for each feature tuple in average. And if two features in one feature tuple are reciprocal k spatial nearest neighbor to each other, we just record once for this feature tuple, as mentioned in **Section** 3.1. In our implementation, we choose k as 30. Hence, it needs 15 × 2 to 30 × 2 bytes for each local feature in average. As for the one-multiple relationship method, a 64 bits spatial context binary signature is generated for each feature, namely 8 extra bytes for each feature besides image ID. Hence, 12 bytes for each feature are required for one-multiple approach. In geometric coding approach, we use two float type to record the location information and one unsigned char type for the dominate orientation and one unsigned char type for the characteristic scale. Therefore, 14 bytes are used to record each local feature.

5.4 Discussion

The proposed algorithm, either the one-one relationship approach or the one-multiple relationship approach, actually is to record the spatial structure between single features into the inverted file. It is obvious that some spatial structure is much more meaningful than others [6]. If we abandon the meaningless feature structures, we can accelerate the processing speed and the retrieval accuracy one step further, because much noisy feature spatial structures would be avoided.

6. CONCLUSIONS

We explore the implicit geometric verification by embedding the spatial context information into the inverted file, which will save considerable time comparing with other post-verification algorithm. The extra time cost for the proposed algorithm is to obtain feature tuples or the feature spatial context binary signature compared to the baseline method. And it is independent of the returned response image set size, while the extra time cost of post-verification method compared to the baseline approach is dependent on the size of response image set returned by the inverted file. What's more, we can get feature tuples or the feature spatial context binary signature in a parallel way.

The geometric verification can be implicitly achieved while traversing the inverted file. The time cost to build feature tuples or generate the spatial context binary signature is independent of dataset size. So it is much more scalable than other post-verification method and more suitable for large-scale image retrieval. Our experiment on large-scale dataset shows its effectiveness, which we can get 0.1 mAP performance improvement on 1M dataset with comparable time cost to the baseline method.

7. ACKNOWLEDGMENTS

This work was supported in part to Dr. Li by NSFC general project funds "Intelligent Video Processing and Coding Based on Cloud Computing" and in part to Dr. Tian by ARO grant W911NF-12-1-0057, NSF IIS 1052851, Faculty Research Awards by Google, NEC Laboratories of America and FXPAL, UTSA START-R award, respectively.

8. REFERENCES

[1] Y. Cao, C. Wang, Z. Li, L. Zhang, and L. Zhang. Spatial-bag-of-features. In *Computer Vision and Pattern Recognition (CVPR), 2010 IEEE Conference on*, pages 3352–3359. IEEE, 2010.

[2] O. Chum, J. Matas, and S. Obdrzalek. Enhancing ransac by generalized model optimization. In *Proc. of the ACCV*, volume 2, pages 812–817, 2004.

[3] O. Chum, M. Perdoch, and J. Matas. Geometric min-hashing: Finding a (thick) needle in a haystack. In *Computer Vision and Pattern Recognition, 2009. CVPR 2009. IEEE Conference on*, pages 17–24. IEEE, 2009.

[4] FastANN. `http://www.robots.ox.ac.uk/~vgg`.

[5] M. Fischler and R. Bolles. Random sample consensus: a paradigm for model fitting with applications to image analysis and automated cartography. *Communications of the ACM*, 24(6):381–395, 1981.

[6] J. Gao, Y. Hu, J. Liu, and R. Yang. Unsupervised learning of high-order structural semantics from images. In *Computer Vision, 2009 IEEE 12th International Conference on*, pages 2122–2129. IEEE, 2009.

[7] Hessian-Affine Detecor. `http://www.robots.ox.ac.uk/~vgg/`.

[8] Holidays. `http://lear.inrialpes.fr/people/jegou/data.php#holidays`.

[9] H. Jegou, M. Douze, and C. Schmid. Hamming embedding and weak geometric consistency for large scale image search. *Computer Vision–ECCV 2008*, pages 304–317, 2008.

[10] H. Jegou, M. Douze, and C. Schmid. On the burstiness of visual elements. In *Computer Vision and Pattern Recognition, 2009. CVPR 2009. IEEE Conference on*, pages 1169–1176. IEEE, 2009.

[11] H. Jégou, M. Douze, and C. Schmid. Improving bag-of-features for large scale image search. *International Journal of Computer Vision*, 87(3):316–336, 2010.

[12] D. Liu, G. Hua, P. Viola, and T. Chen. Integrated feature selection and higher-order spatial feature extraction for object categorization. In *Computer Vision and Pattern Recognition, 2008. CVPR 2008. IEEE Conference on*, pages 1–8. IEEE, 2008.

[13] D. Lowe. Distinctive image features from scale-invariant keypoints. *International journal of computer vision*, 60(2):91–110, 2004.

[14] J. Matas, O. Chum, M. Urban, and T. Pajdla. Robust wide-baseline stereo from maximally stable extremal regions. *Image and Vision Computing*, 22(10):761–767, 2004.

[15] K. Mikolajczyk and C. Schmid. An affine invariant interest point detector. *Computer VisionąłECCV 2002*, pages 128–142, 2002.

[16] D. Nister and H. Stewenius. Scalable recognition with a vocabulary tree. In *Computer Vision and Pattern Recognition, 2006 IEEE Computer Society Conference on*, volume 2, pages 2161–2168. Ieee, 2006.

[17] J. Philbin, O. Chum, M. Isard, J. Sivic, and A. Zisserman. Object retrieval with large vocabularies and fast spatial matching. In *Computer Vision and Pattern Recognition, 2007. CVPR'07. IEEE Conference on*, pages 1–8. Ieee, 2007.

[18] J. Sivic and A. Zisserman. Video google: A text retrieval approach to object matching in videos. In *Computer Vision, 2003. Proceedings. Ninth IEEE International Conference on*, pages 1470–1477. Ieee, 2003.

[19] X. Wang, M. Yang, T. Cour, S. Zhu, K. Yu, and T. Han. Contextual weighting for vocabulary tree based image retrieval. In *Computer Vision (ICCV), 2011 IEEE International Conference on*, pages 209–216. IEEE, 2011.

[20] Z. Wu, Q. Ke, M. Isard, and J. Sun. Bundling features for large scale partial-duplicate web image search. In *Computer Vision and Pattern Recognition, 2009. CVPR 2009. IEEE Conference on*, pages 25–32. IEEE, 2009.

[21] S. Zhang, Q. Huang, G. Hua, S. Jiang, W. Gao, and Q. Tian. Building contextual visual vocabulary for large-scale image applications. In *Proceedings of the international conference on Multimedia*, pages 501–510. ACM, 2010.

[22] S. Zhang, Q. Tian, G. Hua, Q. Huang, and W. Gao. Generating descriptive visual words and visual phrases for large-scale image applications. *Image Processing, IEEE Transactions on*, (99):1–1, 2011.

[23] S. Zhang, Q. Tian, G. Hua, Q. Huang, and S. Li. Descriptive visual words and visual phrases for image applications. In *Proceedings of the 17th ACM international conference on Multimedia*, pages 75–84. ACM, 2009.

[24] Y. Zhang, Z. Jia, and T. Chen. Image retrieval with geometry-preserving visual phrases. In *Computer Vision and Pattern Recognition (CVPR), 2011 IEEE Conference on*, pages 809–816. IEEE, 2011.

[25] W. Zhou, H. Li, Y. Lu, and Q. Tian. Large scale image search with geometric coding. In *Proceedings of the 19th ACM international conference on Multimedia*, pages 1349–1352. ACM, 2011.

[26] W. Zhou, Y. Lu, H. Li, Y. Song, and Q. Tian. Spatial coding for large scale partial-duplicate web image search. In *Proceedings of the international conference on Multimedia*, pages 511–520. ACM, 2010.

A Smile Can Reveal Your Age: Enabling Facial Dynamics in Age Estimation

Hamdi Dibeklioğlu[‡], Theo Gevers[‡], Albert Ali Salah[§], and Roberto Valenti[‡]
[‡]Intelligent Systems Lab Amsterdam, University of Amsterdam, Amsterdam, The Netherlands
[§]Department of Computer Engineering, Boğaziçi University, Istanbul, Turkey
h.dibeklioglu@uva.nl, th.gevers@uva.nl, salah@boun.edu.tr, r.valenti@uva.nl

ABSTRACT

Estimation of a person's age from the facial image has many applications, ranging from biometrics and access control to cosmetics and entertainment. Many image-based methods have been proposed for this problem. In this paper, we propose a method for the use of dynamic features in age estimation, and show that 1) the temporal dynamics of facial features can be used to improve image-based age estimation; 2) considered alone, static image-based features are more accurate than dynamic features. We have collected and annotated an extensive database of face videos from 400 subjects with an age range between 8 and 76, which allows us to extensively analyze the relevant aspects of the problem. The proposed system, which fuses facial appearance and expression dynamics, performs with a mean absolute error of 4.81 ($\pm$4.87) years. This represents a significant improvement of accuracy in comparison to the sole use of appearance-based features.

Categories and Subject Descriptors

I.2.10 [**Vision and Scene Understanding**]: Video analysis; H.1.2 [**User/Machine Systems**]: Human factors, Human information processing

General Terms

Human Factors, Algorithms, Experimentation

Keywords

Age estimation, Facial dynamics

1. INTRODUCTION

The human face offers a rich and heterogeneous amount of data which have an important role in the communication process between individuals. By analyzing faces, humans can derive different useful attributes such as identity, gender, age, emotion, etc. Nowadays, with the pervasive presence of cameras and processing devices, intelligent systems dedicated to human-computer interaction tasks are also expected to be able to analyze and process the same information. A lot of effort has already been made in the literature on the estimation of each of these human-specific attributes.

In particular, age estimation is a very active topic today due to the growing necessity of including this information in real-world systems. This necessity comes from the fact that age is important to understand requirements or preferences in different aspects of daily life of a person. Systems implementing age specific human computer interaction (ASHCI) can cope with these aspects. Some examples are vending machines capable of denying some products such as alcohol or cigarettes to an underage customer, or advertisements in different automated environments (web pages, displays in stores, etc.) that can be personalized according to the age of the individual interacting with the system.

Age estimation from human faces is a challenging problem with a host of applications in forensics, security, biometrics, electronic customer relationship management, entertainment and cosmetology [1, 8, 22]. The main challenge is the huge heterogeneity in facial feature changes due to aging for different humans. Being able to determine the facial changes associated with age is a hard problem, because they are related not only to gender and to genetic properties, but to a number of external factors such as health, living conditions and weather exposure. Furthermore, gender can also play a role in the aging process, as there are differences in the aging patterns and features in males and females.

Facial expressions might negatively affect the accuracy of automated systems: When a person smiles, for instance, wrinkles are formed and these can be misleading if only the appearance cues are taken into account. Similarly, sagging of the face in a sad expression can resemble the effects of aging. Previous work in the literature tried to cope with this problem, generally by dividing the problem into different sub classes (i.e. one per facial expression), yielding mixed results.

The most important cues that are used in age classification are appearance-based, most notably the wrinkles formed on the face due to deformations in the skin tissue. For this reason, current state of the art systems in the literature mainly focus on static appearance features of the face, as it is the easiest way to obtain accurate results. Hence, the dynamics of facial expressions are largely ignored.

Instead of only considering static appearance features for age estimation, we explore a novel set of features for age estimation in this paper, namely facial feature dynamics. As movement features can be observed during facial expressions, the aim is to use these facial expressions for estimating the age. Since the smile is one of the most frequently used facial expressions, as well as the easiest emotional facial expression to pose voluntarily [5], we focus on smiles and analyze the discrimination power of smile dynamics for age estimation. Our hypothesis is that aging effects the speed with which facial expressions are formed on the face. It is well known that the elastic fibres on the face show fraying and fragmentation at advancing age [23]. By leveraging the movement features of points of interest on the face, we show that we can improve age estimation over systems that use solely appearance-based cues.

2. RELATED WORK

Several works have proposed methods to determine facial pattern changes and evolution associated with the aging process, both from psychological and biological points of view. These studies are mostly aimed at age synthesis, i.e. changing the appearance of a rendered face to show proper effects of aging. Some of these works have been useful in the determination of appropriate facial features for age estimation. For instance, O'Toole *et al.* [19] used 3D models of faces to apply caricaturing processes in order to describe age variations between samples. Wu *et al.* [30] developed a system for simulation of wrinkles and skin aging for facial animation. Suo *et al.* [26] presented a model for face aging processing by analyzing it as a Markov process in a graph, representing different age groups. Tiddeman *et al.* [28] also developed prototype models for aging face images using texture information. In [18], a quantitative approach to face evolution due to aging is presented.

The results of these studies determined that cranio-facial development and skin texture are the most important features for age estimation. In fact, one of the first approaches for age estimation was proposed by Kwon and Lobo [13], where individual faces were classified into three age groups (baby, young and senior). This classification was performed using the theory of cranio-facial development [2] and facial skin wrinkle analysis. Lanitis *et al.* [14] proposed an age estimation method based on regression analysis of the *aging function*. During the training procedure, a quadratic function of facial features is fitted for each individual in the training set as his/her aging function. As for age estimation, they proposed four approaches to determine the suitable aging function for the unseen face image, among which the Weighted Person Specific (WPS) approach achieved the best performance in the experiments. This function, however, relied on profiles of the individual containing external information such as gender, health, living style, etc. In [11] a method for age estimation is presented, where faces are projected into manifolds by using subspace learning and then a regression model is applied to estimate the age. The aging pattern subspace (AGES) method [10] models a sequence of individually aging face images by learning a subspace representation. The age of a test face is determined by the projection in the subspace that can reconstruct the face image the best. This model was later extended by the authors to model the nonlinear nature of human aging by considering learning of nonlinear subspaces, using the model called KAGES (Kernel AGing pattErn Subspace) [9].

Recently, Zhan *et al.* has proposed an extended non-negative matrix factorization method to learn a subspace representation, which could recovers age information while eliminating variations caused by identity, expression, pose, etc. [31]. In [12], Hadid has proposed using volume LBP (VLBP) features to describe spatiotemporal information in videos of talking faces and classify the ages of the subjects into five groups (child, youth, adult, middle-age, and elderly). This is the only study in the literature that uses temporal information for age estimation. However, VLBP features alone are not powerful enoughi and the proposed system could not even reach the accuracy of static image-based age estimation.

Recent work on static image-based age estimation has considered large-scale evaluations, with 175k images [15]. Obviously, there is still room for improvement, and the area is actively researched. Nonetheless, there is a shortcoming in the literature on the evaluated features for age estimation: Facial expression dynamics are not used at all. This may be due to the lack of proper databases to explore the contribution of dynamic features for age estimation. In this paper, we seek to remedy this shortcoming, and focus on the inclusion of expression dynamics to improve age estimation. To the best of our knowledge, this is the first attempt to investigate and integrate the dynamics of facial features (such as speed, acceleration, amplitude, etc.) for the task of age estimation.

3. METHOD

In this section, details of the proposed age estimation system will be given. The proposed system combines the appearance features with the facial expression dynamics. Our method assumes that the input video starts with a moderately frontal face, and has the entire duration of a smile expression. The flow of the system can be summarized as follows. Initially, 11 facial fiducial points are located in the first frame, and tracked during the rest of the video. Then, the tracked points are used to calculate displacement signals of eyelids, cheeks, and lip corners. Temporal phases (onset, apex, and offset) of the smile are estimated using the mean displacement signal of the lip corners. Afterwards, dynamic features for the eyelid, cheek, and lip corner movements are extracted from each phase. Local Binary Patterns (LBP) features are extracted using the first frame of onset phase, where the face is neutral. After a feature selection procedure, the most informative dynamic features are selected and fused with LBP features to train Support Vector Machine (SVM) classifiers/regressors.

3.1 Facial Feature Tracking

To analyze the facial dynamics, 11 facial feature points (eye corners, center of upper eyelids, cheek centers, nose tip, lip corners) are tracked in the videos (see Fig. 1(a)). Each point is initialized in the first frame of the videos for precise tracking and analysis. To track the facial features and pose, we use a piecewise Bézier volume deformation (PBVD) tracker, originally proposed by Tao and Huang [27].

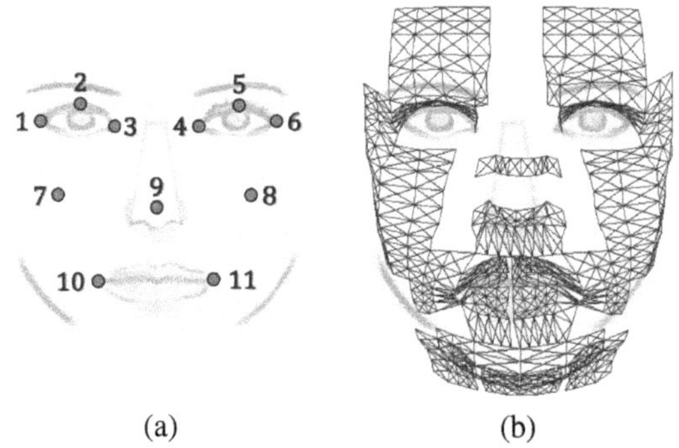

Figure 1: (a) Used facial feature points with their indices and (b) the 3D mesh model

The PBVD tracker employs a model-based approach. A 3D mesh model of the face (see Fig. 1(b)) is constructed by warping the generic model to fit the facial features in the first frame of the image sequence. For comparison reasons, we report results for manual and automatic initialization of these features. The generic face model consists of 16 surface patches. To form a continuous and smooth model, these patches are embedded in Bézier volumes. If $x(u, v, w)$ is a facial mesh point, then the Bézier volumeis defined as:

$$x(u,v,w) = \sum_{i=0}^{n}\sum_{j=0}^{m}\sum_{k=0}^{l} b_{i,j,k} B_i^n(u) B_j^m(v) B_k^l(w), \quad (1)$$

where points $b_{i,j,k}$ and variables $0 < \{u, v, w\} < 1$ control the shape of the volume. $B_i^n(u)$ denotes a Bernstein polynomial:

$$B_i^n(u) = \binom{n}{i} u^i (1-u)^{n-i}. \quad (2)$$

After fitting the face model, facial feature points (as well as head motion) can be tracked in 3D according to the movement and the deformations of the mesh. To measure 2D motion, template matching is used between frames at different resolutions. For more robust tracking, image templates of both the previous frame and the first frame of the sequence are used for matching. The estimated 2D image motion is modeled as a projection of the 3D movement onto the image plane. Then, the 3D movement is calculated using projective motion of several points.

3.2 Features

In the proposed system we extract appearance-based and dynamic features from smile videos. In general, a smile can be identified as the upward movement of the mouth corners, which corresponds to Action Unit 12 (AU12) in the facial action coding system (FACS) [6]. In terms of anatomy, the *zygomatic major* muscle contracts and raises the corners of the lips during a smile [7]. In terms of dynamics, smiles are composed of three non-overlapping phases; the onset, apex, and offset, respectively. Onset is the initial phase of a facial expression and it defines the duration from neutral to expressive state. Apex phase is the stable peak period (may also be very short) of the expression between onset and offset. Likewise, offset is the final phase from expressive to neutral state. According to Ekman there are dozens of smiles which are different in terms of their appearance and meaning. Ekman also identified 18 of them (such as enjoyment, fear, miserable, embarrassment, listener response smiles) by describing the specific visual differences on the face and indicating the accompanying action units [5].

3.2.1 Extraction of Dynamic Features

To analyze and describe the dynamics of a smile, we extract a set of dynamic features from three different face regions such as eyes, cheeks, and mouth [3]. First of all, the tracked 3D coordinates of the facial feature points ℓ_i (see Fig. 1(a)) are used to align the faces in each frame. We estimate the 3D pose of the face, and normalize the face with respect to roll, yaw, and pitch rotations. Since three non-colinear points are enough to construct a plane, we use three stable landmarks (eye centers and nose tip) to define a plane $\mathcal{P}$. Eye centers are defined as middle points between inner and outer eye corners as $c_1 = \frac{\ell_1+\ell_3}{2}$ and $c_2 = \frac{\ell_4+\ell_6}{2}$. Angles between the positive normal vector $\mathcal{N}_\mathcal{P}$ of $\mathcal{P}$ and unit vectors U on X (horizontal), Y (vertical), and Z (perpendicular) axes give the relative head pose as follows:

$$\theta = \arccos \frac{U.\mathcal{N}_\mathcal{P}}{\|U\|\,\|\mathcal{N}_\mathcal{P}\|}, \text{ where } \mathcal{N} = \overrightarrow{\ell_9 c_2} \times \overrightarrow{\ell_9 c_1}. \quad (3)$$

In Equation 3, $\overrightarrow{\ell_9 c_2}$ and $\overrightarrow{\ell_9 c_1}$ denote the vectors from point ℓ_9 to points c_2 and c_1, respectively. $\|U\|$ and $\|\mathcal{N}_\mathcal{P}\|$ are the magnitudes of U and $\mathcal{N}_\mathcal{P}$ vectors. According to the face geometry, Equation 3 can estimate the exact roll (θ_z) and yaw (θ_y) angles of the face with respect to the camera. However, the estimated pitch (θ_x) angle is a subject-dependent measure, since it is relative to the constellation of the eye corners and the nose tip. If we assume that the face is approximately frontal in the first frame, then the actual pitch angles (θ'_x) can be calculated by subtracting the initial value. Once the pose of the head is estimated, tracked points are normalized with respect to rotation, scale, and translation as follows:

$$\ell'_i = \left[\ell_i - \frac{c_1 + c_2}{2}\right] R_x(-\theta'_x) R_y(-\theta_y) R_z(-\theta_z) \frac{100}{\rho(c1, c2)}, \quad (4)$$

where ℓ'_i is the aligned point and R_x, R_y, and R_z denote the 3D rotation matrices for the given angles. $\rho()$ denotes the Euclidean distance between the given points. On the normalized face, the middle point between eye centers is located at the origin and the inter-ocular distance (distance between eye centers) is set to 100 pixels. Since the normalized face is approximately frontal with respect to the camera, we ignore the depth (Z) values of the normalized feature points ℓ'_i, and denote them as l_i.

After the normalization, onset, apex, and offset phases of the smile are detected using the approach proposed by Schmidt *et al.* [24], by calculating the amplitude of the smile as the distance of the right lip corner to the lip center during the smile. Since the faces are normalized, lip center is calculated only once in the first frame. As indicated in [24], the detected smile phases may not necessarily represent the exact definition of smile phases which are defined in [6]. Differently from [24], we estimate the smile amplitude as the mean amplitude of right and left lip corners, normalized by the length of the lip. Let $\mathcal{D}_{\text{lip}}(t)$ be the value of the mean amplitude signal of the lip corners in the frame t. It is estimated as:

$$\mathcal{D}_{\text{lip}}(t) = \frac{\rho(\frac{l_{10}^1+l_{11}^1}{2}, l_{10}^t) + \rho(\frac{l_{10}^1+l_{11}^1}{2}, l_{11}^t)}{2\rho(l_{10}^1, l_{11}^1)}, \quad (5)$$

where l_i^t denotes the 2D location of the ith point in frame t. This estimate is smoothed by 4253H-twice method [29]. Then, the longest continuous increase in $\mathcal{D}_{\text{lip}}$ is defined as the onset phase. Similarly, the offset phase is detected as the longest continuous decrease in $\mathcal{D}_{\text{lip}}$. The phase between the last frame of the onset and the first frame of the offset defines the apex.

To extract dynamic features from the eyelids and the cheeks, additional amplitude signals are computed. We estimate the (normalized) eyelid aperture $\mathcal{D}_{\text{eyelid}}$ and cheek displacement $\mathcal{D}_{\text{cheek}}$ as follows:

$$\mathcal{D}_{\text{eyelid}}(t) = \frac{\kappa(\frac{l_1^t+l_3^t}{2}, l_2^t)\rho(\frac{l_1^t+l_3^t}{2}, l_2^t) + \kappa(\frac{l_4^t+l_6^t}{2}, l_5^t)\rho(\frac{l_4^t+l_6^t}{2}, l_5^t)}{2\rho(l_1^t, l_3^t)}, \quad (6)$$

$$\mathcal{D}_{\text{cheek}}(t) = \frac{\rho(\frac{l_7^1+l_8^1}{2}, l_7^t) + \rho(\frac{l_7^1+l_8^1}{2}, l_8^t)}{2\rho(l_7^1, l_8^1)}, \quad (7)$$

where $\kappa(l_i, l_j)$ denotes the relative vertical location function, which equals to -1 if l_j is located (vertically) below l_i on the face, and 1 otherwise. The distance between the eye center and the point on upper eyelid is calculated for both left and right eyes and the estimated values are divided by the length of the eyes. Afterwards, $\mathcal{D}_{\text{eyelid}}$ is calculated as the mean aperture signal of left and right eyes. $\mathcal{D}_{\text{cheek}}$ is defined as the sequence of the mean distances of left and right cheek points to the middle point between two cheeks. Middle point between cheek landmarks is estimated for once in the first frame (neutral face). $\mathcal{D}_{\text{lip}}$, $\mathcal{D}_{\text{eyelid}}$, and $\mathcal{D}_{\text{cheek}}$ are hereafter referred to as amplitude signals. In addition to the amplitudes, speed $\mathcal{V}$ and acceleration $\mathcal{A}$ signals are extracted by computing the first and the second derivatives of the amplitudes, respectively:

$$\mathcal{V}(t) = \frac{dD}{dt}, \quad (8)$$

$$\mathcal{A}(t) = \frac{d^2\mathcal{D}}{dt^2} = \frac{d\mathcal{V}}{dt}. \tag{9}$$

All the calculated amplitude signals are smoothed by 4253H-twice method [29], and then split into three phases as onset, apex, and offset, which have been previously defined using the amplitude signal $\mathcal{D}_{\text{lip}}$ of the lip corners.

A summary of the proposed dynamic features is given in Table 1. Note that the defined features are extracted separately from each phase of the smile. As a result, we obtain three feature sets for each of the eye, mouth and cheek regions. Each phase is further divided into increasing ($^+$) and decreasing ($^-$) segments, for each feature set. This allows a more detailed analysis of the feature dynamics. In Table 1, signals symbolized with superindex ($^+$) and ($^-$)

Table 1: Definitions of the extracted features

Feature	Definition
Duration:	$\left[\frac{\eta(\mathcal{D}^+)}{\omega}, \frac{\eta(\mathcal{D}^-)}{\omega}, \frac{\eta(\mathcal{D})}{\omega}\right]$
Duration Ratio:	$\left[\frac{\eta(\mathcal{D}^+)}{\eta(\mathcal{D})}, \frac{\eta(\mathcal{D}^-)}{\eta(\mathcal{D})}\right]$
Maximum Amplitude:	$\max(\mathcal{D})$
Mean Amplitude:	$\left[\frac{\sum\mathcal{D}}{\eta(\mathcal{D})}, \frac{\sum\mathcal{D}^+}{\eta(\mathcal{D}^+)}, \frac{\sum\lvert\mathcal{D}^-\rvert}{\eta(\mathcal{D}^-)}\right]$
STD of Amplitude:	$\text{std}(\mathcal{D})$
Total Amplitude:	$\left[\sum\mathcal{D}^+, \sum\lvert\mathcal{D}^-\rvert\right]$
Net Amplitude:	$\sum\mathcal{D}^+ - \sum\lvert\mathcal{D}^-\rvert$
Amplitude Ratio:	$\left[\frac{\sum\mathcal{D}^+}{\sum\mathcal{D}^+ + \sum\lvert\mathcal{D}^-\rvert}, \frac{\sum\lvert\mathcal{D}^-\rvert}{\sum\mathcal{D}^+ + \sum\lvert\mathcal{D}^-\rvert}\right]$
Maximum Speed:	$\left[\max(\mathcal{V}^+), \max(\lvert\mathcal{V}^-\rvert)\right]$
Mean Speed:	$\left[\frac{\sum\mathcal{V}^+}{\eta(\mathcal{V}^+)}, \frac{\sum\lvert\mathcal{V}^-\rvert}{\eta(\mathcal{V}^-)}\right]$
Maximum Acceleration:	$\left[\max(\mathcal{A}^+), \max(\lvert\mathcal{A}^-\rvert)\right]$
Mean Acceleration:	$\left[\frac{\sum\mathcal{A}^+}{\eta(\mathcal{A}^+)}, \frac{\sum\lvert\mathcal{A}^-\rvert}{\eta(\mathcal{A}^-)}\right]$
Net Ampl., Duration Ratio:	$\frac{(\sum\mathcal{D}^+ - \sum\lvert\mathcal{D}^-\rvert)\omega}{\eta(\mathcal{D})}$

denote the segments of the related signal with continuous increase and continuous decrease, respectively. For example, $\mathcal{D}^+$ pools the increasing segments in $\mathcal{D}$. η defines the length (number of frames) of a given signal, and ω is the frame rate of the video. $\mathcal{D}_L$ and $\mathcal{D}_R$ define the amplitudes for the left and right sides of the face, respectively. For each face region, three 24-dimensional feature vectors are generated by concatenating these features.

In some cases, features cannot be calculated. For example, if we extract features from the amplitude signal of the lip corners $\mathcal{D}_{\text{lip}}$ using the onset phase, the decreasing segments will be an empty set ($\eta\left(\mathcal{D}^-\right) = 0$). For such exceptions, all the features describing the related segments are set to zero. This is done to have a generic feature vector format which has the same features for different phases of each face region.

3.2.2 Extraction of Appearance Features

To describe the appearance of faces, we use uniform *Local Binary Patterns* (LBP) on gray scale images. The original LBP operator, which is proposed by Ojala *et al.* [16], takes the intensity value of the center pixel as threshold to convert the neighborhood pixels to a binary code. Computed binary codes describe the ordered pattern of the center pixel. This procedure is repeated for

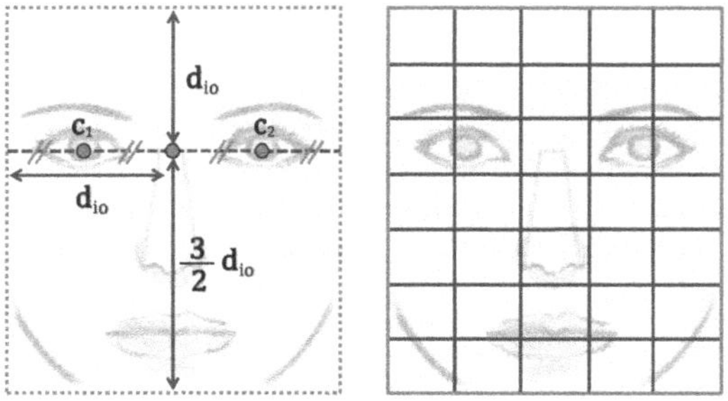

(a) (b)

Figure 2: (a) Scaling/cropping of a face image, and (b) the defined 7×5 blocks to extract appearance features

each pixel on the image and the histogram of the resultant 256 labels can then be used as a texture descriptor. In [17], Ojala *et al.* show that the vast majority of the *Local Binary Patterns* in a local neighborhood contain at most two bitwise transitions from 0 to 1 or 1 to 0, which is called a uniform pattern. Therefore, during the computation of the histograms, the size of the feature vector can be significantly reduced by assigning different bins for each of the 58 uniform patterns and one bin for the rest.

Since the onset of a facial expression starts with a neutral face, the first frame of the previously detected onset phase is selected to extract appearance features. On the selected frame, the roll rotation of the face is estimated and normalized using the eye centers c_1 and c_2. Then, the face is resized and cropped as shown in Fig. 2(a). The inter-ocular distance d_{io} is set to 50 pixels to normalize the scale and cropping. As a result, each normalized face image has a resolution of 125×100 pixels. After the preprocessing step, each face is divided into 7×5 non-overlapping (equally-sized) blocks and uniform LBP descriptors are computed on each block (see Fig. 2(b)). 8 neighborhood pixels (on a circle with a radius of 1 pixel) are used to extract the uniform LBP features. All these features are concatenated to form the appearance feature vector. Resultant appearance feature vector is $7 \times 5 \times 59 = 2065$ dimensional. The dimensionality of the appearance feature vectors is reduced by Principal Component Analysis (PCA) so as to retain 99.99% of the variance.

3.3 Feature Selection and Classification

In our system, we use a two-level classification scheme for age estimation, as shown in Fig. 3. In the first level, one-vs-all Support Vector Machine (SVM) classifiers are used to classify the age of a subject into 7 age groups of 10 years ($8-17, 18-27, \ldots, 68-77$). Then, the age of the subject is fine-tuned using an SVM regressor which is specifically trained for the related age group. For a better estimation, the regressor of each age group is trained with an age interval of -10 to $+10$ years of group boundaries. Then the results are limited with the age range (if the estimated age is less/more than the group boundaries, it is set to minimum/maximum age of the group). The resulting estimation of the age is given as an integer with 1 year resolution.

As described in Section 3.2.1, we extract three 24-dimensional dynamic feature vectors for each face region. To deal with feature redundancy, we use the Min-Redundancy Max-Relevance (mRMR) algorithm to select the discriminative dynamic features [20]. mRMR is an incremental method for minimizing the redundancy while selecting the most relevant information as follows:

$$\max_{f_j \in F - S_{m-1}} \left[I(f_j, c) - \frac{1}{m-1} \sum_{f_i \in S_{m-1}} I(f_j, f_i) \right], \tag{10}$$

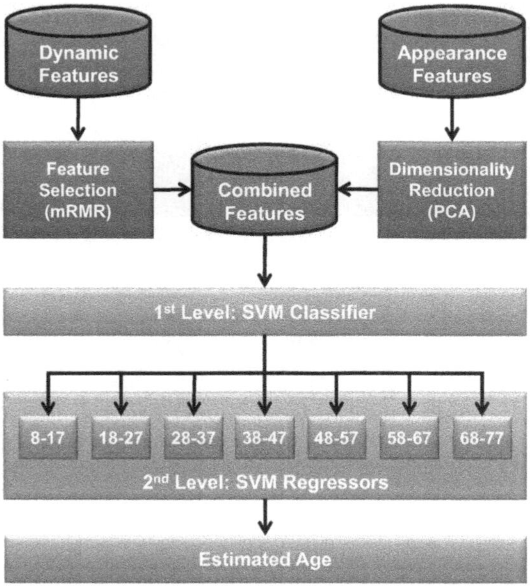

Figure 3: Two-level age estimation architecture using both appearance and dynamic features

where I shows the mutual information function and c indicates the target class. F and S_{m-1} denote the feature set, and the set of $m-1$ features, respectively. Then, all the selected dynamic features are concatenated with the appearance features (which are extracted from the first frame of the smile onset and reduced by PCA) to train the system (see Fig. 3). Minimum classification error on a separate validation set is used to determine the most discriminative dynamic features. Similarly, in order to optimize the SVM configuration, different kernels (linear, polynomial, and radial basis function (RBF)) with different parameters (size of RBF kernel, degree of polynomial kernel) are tested on the validation set and the configuration with the minimum validation error is selected. The test partition of the dataset is not used for parameter optimization.

4. EXPERIMENTAL SETTINGS

4.1 UvA-NEMO Smile Database

The UvA-NEMO Smile Database[1] has been recently collected to analyze the change in dynamics of smiles for different ages [3]. Data collection was carried out in science center NEMO (Amsterdam) as a part of Science Live, the innovative research programme of science center NEMO [25]. NEMO visitors were the volunteers for the data collection. The database and its evaluation protocols are made available to the research community.

This database is composed of videos (in RGB color) recorded with a Panasonic HDC-HS700 3MOS camcorder, placed on a monitor, at approximately 1.5 meters away from the recorded subjects. Videos were recorded with a resolution of 1920×1080 pixels at a rate of 50 frames per second under controlled illumination conditions. Additionally, a color chart is present on the background of the videos for further illumination and color normalization. Sample frames from the database are shown in Fig. 4.

The database has 1240 smile videos (597 spontaneous, 643 posed) from 400 subjects (185 female, 215 male). Ages of subjects vary from 8 to 76 years. 43 subjects do not have spontaneous smiles and 32 subjects have no posed smile samples. Age and gender distributions of the subjects in the database are given in Fig. 5.

For posed smiles, each subject was asked to pose a smile as realistically as possible, sometimes after being shown the proper way in a sample video. Short, funny video segments were used to elicit spontaneous smiles. Approximately five minutes of recordings were made per subject, and genuine smiles were segmented.

For each subject, a balanced number of spontaneous and posed smiles were selected and annotated by seeking consensus of two trained annotators. Each segment starts and ends with neutral or near-neutral expressions.

[1]http://www.uva-nemo.org

4.2 Settings

To evaluate our system and assess the reliability of facial expression dynamics and facial appearance information for age estimation problem, we use the above described smile database of 400 subjects. In our experiments, the two-level classification/regression system is used, and described in section 3.3 The optimum number of selected dynamic features, kernel and parameters of SVM classifiers/regressors are determined on a separate validation partition. To this end, a two level 10-fold cross-validation scheme is used. Each time a test fold is separated, a 9-fold cross-validation is used to train the system, and parameters are optimized without using the test partition. There is no subject overlap between folds. In our experiments, polynomial SVM is found to perform better than linear and RBF alternatives. We initialize the tracking by manually annotated facial landmarks to assess the discrimination power and reliability of individual appearance and dynamic features, and their combination. Additionally, results with automatic initialization are also given for the comparison with other systems, as well as further analysis on different aspects of the age estimation problem.

For automatic facial landmark detection, we use the state-of-the-art system proposed by Dibeklioğlu *et al.* [4]. This method models Gabor wavelet features of a neighborhood of the landmarks using incremental mixtures of factor analyzers and enables a shape prior to ensure the integrity of the landmark constellation. It follows a coarse-to-fine strategy; landmarks are initially detected on a coarse level and then fine-tuned for higher resolution. The mean localization error for the related landmarks (eye corners, center of upper eyelids, cheek centers, nose tip, lip corners; see Fig. 1(a)) is 3.96% (± 3.14) of the inter-ocular distance to the actual location of the landmarks. Correlation coefficients between the extracted amplitude signals with manual and automatic initializations ranged between 0.93 and 1.

5. RESULTS

In this section, we discuss the results of our experiments. First, we will discuss the accuracy of the system when only face dynamics are used, either individually or taken together. Then, we compare these results with the combined use of appearance and dynamics. Finally, we check the effect of gender and expression spontaneity on the accuracy of the system using the combined features.

5.1 Dynamics

Since the proposed dynamic features are extracted from the movements of lip corners, cheeks, and eyelids, we analyze the individual discrimination power of these movements and their combination for age estimation. Furthermore, to assess the reliability of the feature selection step, performance of using automatically selected (most) informative dynamic features and the use of all features without any selection are compared. For the reliability of

(a) (b) (c)

Figure 4: Sample frames from the UvA-NEMO Smile Database: Showing (a) neutral face, (b) posed enjoyment smile, (c) spontaneous enjoyment smile

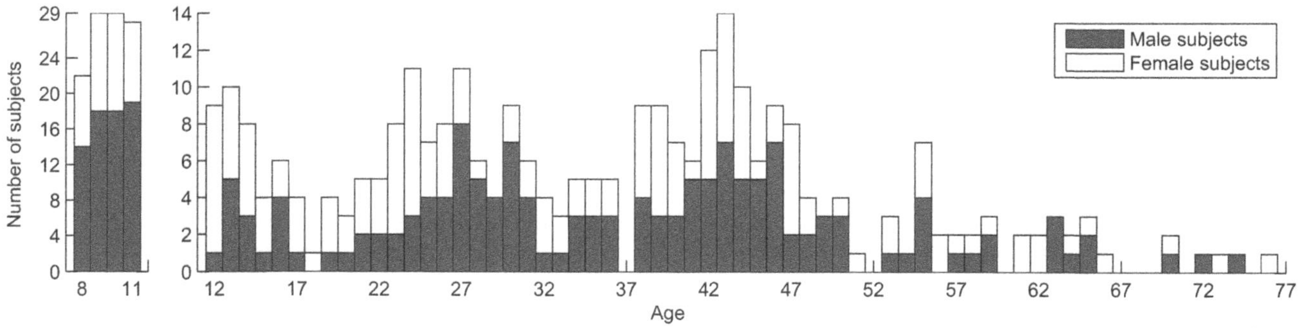

Figure 5: Age and gender distributions of the subjects in the database

results, we use manually initialized tracking in these tests. The resulting *mean absolute error* (MAE) is given in Fig. 6.

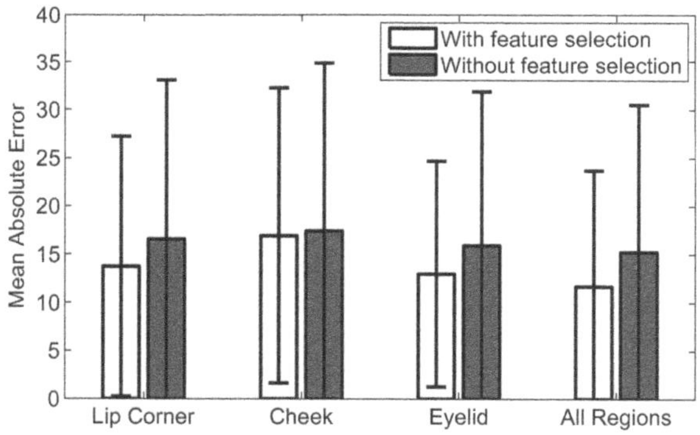

Figure 6: Effect of feature selection on age estimation errors for different facial regions

Our results show that the feature selection increases the accuracy approximately 15% (relative) on average, while reducing the dimensionality of the feature space. Since the efficacy of the feature selection step is confirmed by these results, it is used in the remainder of our experiments. By analyzing the regional results with feature selection, it can be shown that the dynamics of eyelid movements are the most reliable features, with an MAE of 12.98 ($\pm$11.71) years. Lip corner and cheek movement dynamics follow with an MAE of 13.72 ($\pm$13.49) and 16.94 ($\pm$15.30) years, respectively. By combining the dynamic features of different facial regions, the MAE of the age estimation system can be decreased to 11.69 ($\pm$12.02) years.

5.2 Dynamics versus Appearance

In this paper, the aim is to combine facial appearance with expression dynamics for age estimation. However, it is also important to show the discriminative power of facial expression dynamics and appearance, individually. For this purpose, we evaluate the individual and combined use of these features. To assess the effect of tracking initialization on accuracy, we use both manually and automatically annotated facial landmarks to initialize facial tracking in our experiments.

As shown in Table 2, using automatic initialization for tracking increases the MAE by 4.28% and 1.26% for dynamic and appearance features, respectively. Since the reliability of dynamic features is directly related to the accuracy of tracking, automatic initialization affects it more than appearance features. The MAE for combined features is also increased by 2.34% by automatic initial-

Table 2: Mean Absolute Errors for dynamic, appearance, and combined features

Features	Mean Absolute Error	
	Manual Initialization	Automatic Initialization
Dynamics	11.21 (±11.34)	11.69 (±12.02)
Appearance	5.57 (±5.86)	5.64 (±5.90)
Combination	4.71 (±4.75)	4.82 (±4.87)

ization of tracking. However, the use of combined features significantly ($p < 0.001$, Cohen's $d > 0.15$) improve the age estimation accuracy in comparison to the individual use of dynamic and appearance features. Therefore, automatically initialized tracking is used in the remainder of our experiments.

When we analyze the results, it is clear that using only facial dynamics is not enough for an accurate age estimation system. The MAE of using dynamic features is 11.69 (±12.02) years, where the MAE for facial appearance is only 5.64 (±5.90) years. Nevertheless, by combining the dynamic and appearance features, the proposed system is able to achieve the best result with an MAE of 4.82 (±4.87), which is significantly ($p < 0.001$, Cohen's $d > 0.15$) more accurate than using dynamic and appearance features individually.

5.3 Effect of Gender

To assess the effect of gender on the accuracy of the system using the combined features (with automatic initialization of tracking), a gender-specific age estimation system is implemented and compared with the general method. In the gender-specific system, different classifiers/regressors are trained and tested for both males and females, separately. For this method, we assume that the gender labels of all samples are correctly given. The MAEs for both gender-specific and general training are given in Table 3.

Table 3: Comparison of the gender-specific method with the general method for age estimation

Method	Mean Absolute Error		
	Male	Female	Mean
Specific	4.26 (±3.36)	5.01 (±5.73)	4.63 (±4.70)
General	4.59 (±4.80)	5.03 (±4.95)	4.81 (±4.87)

Our results show that the gender-specific training decreases the overall MAE of the system from 4.81 (±4.87) years to 4.63 (±4.70) years. In particular, the gender-specific training decreases the MAE by 7.19% for males, and 0.40% for females, with respect to training on the whole data. These results show the difference of the proposed combined features between males and females. Fig. 7 shows the estimated ages using the general and the gender-specific methods.

5.4 Effect of Expression Spontaneity

In order to assess the effect of expression spontaneity on the accuracy of using combined features, a spontaneity-specific age estimation system is also constructed. Here we compare its accuracy with the general approach (using automatic initialization of tracking). For this purpose, separate classifiers/regressors are trained for spontaneous and posed smiles. It is assumed that the spontaneity of all smiles are correctly classified and the same training procedure is separately applied to each subset.

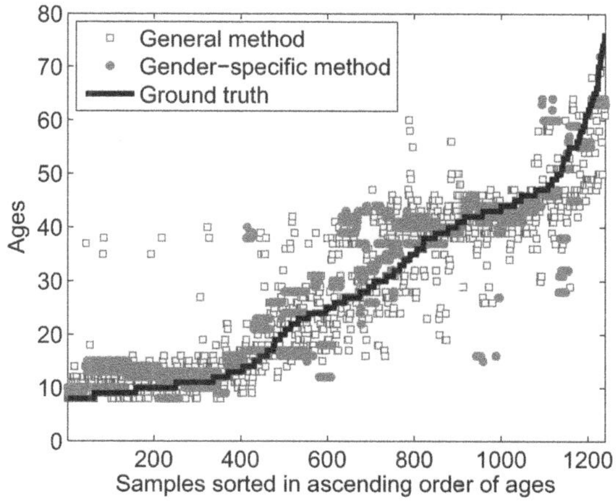

Figure 7: Estimated ages using the general and the gender-specific methods

Table 4: Comparison of the spontaneity-specific method with the general method for age estimation

Method	Mean Absolute Error		
	Spontaneous	Posed	Mean
Specific	4.51 (±5.61)	4.02 (±3.67)	4.26 (±4.71)
General	4.92 (±5.09)	4.70 (±4.66)	4.81 (±4.87)

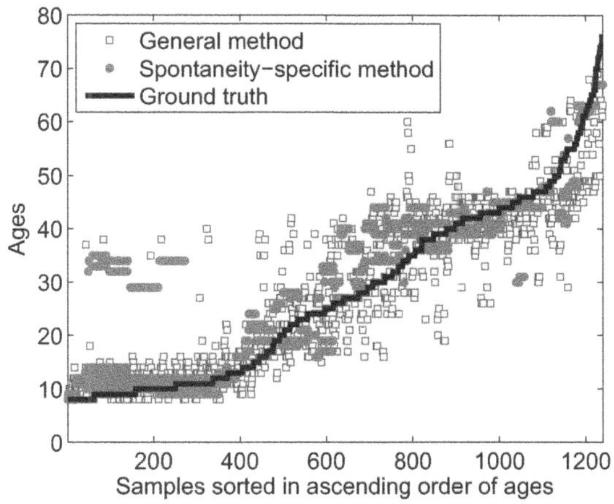

Figure 8: Estimated ages using the general and the spontaneity-specific methods

As shown in Table 4, spontaneity-specific approach performs with an MAE of 4.26 (±4.71), therefore improving the accuracy by 11.43% with respect to the general approach. Spontaneity-specific training decreases the MAE for both posed and spontaneous smiles. Since the automatically detected neutral faces are used to extract the appearance features for both approaches, accuracy improvements by performing spontaneity-specific training indicates the differences between spontaneous and posed smiles in terms of expression dynamics. Plot of the estimated ages using the general and the spontaneity-specific methods are shown in Fig. 8.

5.5 Comparison with other methods

To the best of our knowledge, this is the first study which uses the facial expression dynamics (such as speed, acceleration, amplitude, etc.) for age estimation problem. Except a recent work [12], none of the previous studies in the literature focus on using temporal information for age estimation.

In [12], Hadid proposes to use spatiotemporal information to classify the ages of the subjects into five groups (child: 0 to 9 years old; youth: 10 to 19; adult: 20 to 39; middle-age: 40 to 59 and elderly: above 60). [12] uses volume LBP (VLBP) features with a tree of four SVM classifiers. VLBP features are extracted from different overlapping face blocks. Then the AdaBoost learning algorithm is used to determine the optimal size and locations of the local rectangular prisms, and select the most discriminative VLBP features for classification, automatically. To evaluate the system, 2000 videos of about 300 frames each are randomly segmented from a set of video sequences mainly showing talking faces (collected from the Internet). Additionally an appearance-based (static) system is implemented for comparison. This baseline method classifies each frame in a video, individually, using LBP features with SVM classifiers. Majority voting is used to fuse the classification results of each frame. Hadid reports that the static image (appearance) based approach provides 77.4% correct classification, where the performance of the spatiotemporal approach reaches only 69.2%.

VLBP is a straightforward extension of original LBP operator to describe dynamic textures (image sequences) [32]. VLBP enables the use of temporal space (T), looks the face sequence as a volume, and the neighborhood of each pixel is defined in three dimensional space, where LBP uses only X and Y dimensions of a single image. Then, the histograms of VLBP are used as features. In [32], Zhao *et al.* have proposed to extract LBP histograms from Three Orthogonal Planes (LBP-TOP) XY, XT, and YT, individually, and concatenate them as a single feature vector.

To compare our system with the related approaches, we implement three baseline methods: (1) VBLP-based spatiotemporal approach, (2) spatiotemporal approach using VBLP-TOP features, and (3) appearance-based approach which classifies each frame in a video using LBP features with SVM classifiers, individually, and fuses the classification results by majority voting. Both LBP-TOP- and VBLP-based methods use the same classification/regression architecture with our method. For a fair comparison, all of the compared methods use automatically annotated facial landmarks to initialize the tracking (for face alignment and feature extraction), and 7×5 non-overlapping blocks on the face to compute histograms. To generate histograms, uniform patterns are used for LBP-TOP and LBP. The neighborhood size is set to eight for LBP and LBP-TOP, and two for VBLP. Time interval for volumetric approaches is set to three frames. Zhao *et al.* [32] have shown that these neighborhood and time interval parameters perform well on facial expression classification. The dimensionality of LBP, VLBP, and LBP-TOP features is reduced by Principal Component Analysis (PCA) so as to retain 99.99% of the variance.

The cumulative error distributions of the mean absolute error for different methods are given in Fig. 9 (a). Given error distributions show that the proposed system, which uses both dynamic and appearance features, significantly outperforms all other methods ($p < 0.001$, Cohen's $d > 0.15$). Additionally, Figs. 9 (b-f) show the comparison of the estimated ages using the combined features and the other methods.

As shown in Table 5, the combination of dynamic and appearance features achieves the minimum MAE of 4.81 ($\pm$4.87) years. It is important to indicate that using LBP features extracted on a single, automatically detected neutral image provides more accurate age estimation than using all frames in a video and voting on the results. Spatiotemporal methods can only reach a mean accuracy of 17.03 ($\pm$13.56) and 14.95 ($\pm$11.41) years with VLBP and LBP-TOP features, respectively. By using the proposed dynamic features only, the system is significantly more accurate than when it uses the spatiotemporal features ($p < 0.001$, Cohen's $d > 0.25$). Note that we assume that an age estimate is correct if the error from the ground truth is less than 10 years. In this case, the proposed system which combines appearance and dynamics features improves the correct classification rate by 4.36% (absolute) with respect to the appearance features only.

6. DISCUSSION

In our experiments, we show that dynamics of the eyelid movements perform best for individual regions. Additionally, fusion of eyelid, lip corner, and cheek movement dynamics (with a feature selection step) improves the accuracy of the eyelid dynamics by 9.94%. For dynamic features, using feature selection increases the accuracy approximately by 15% on average, as well as reducing feature dimensionality. This finding indicates that there is a significant amount of noise or confusing information in dynamic features.

Our results show that the individual use of the facial expression dynamics is not enough for an accurate age estimation system. However, accuracy of using solely appearance features of a neutral face (automatically detected as the first frame of the onset phase) is significantly improved ($p < 0.001$, Cohen's $d > 0.15$) by enabling the dynamics of smile expression. Moreover, the proposed combined features outperform all the baseline methods tested in this study. These results confirm the importance of the information hidden in facial expression dynamics.

When we analyze the effect of initialization on facial tracking, it is seen that automatic initialization decreases the reliability of dynamic features approximately three times more than the appearance features, since the reliability of dynamic features are directly related to the accuracy of tracking. However, under both automatic and manual initialization conditions, the use of the combined features significantly ($p < 0.001$, Cohen's $d > 0.15$) improves the age estimation accuracy in comparison to the individual use of dynamic and appearance features.

Using multivariate analysis of variance (MANOVA), we find the most selected dynamic features and significant ($p < 0.001$, $\eta^2 > 0.10$) feature differences between different ages. Our findings indicate that the dynamics of smile onsets are more discriminative than other smile phases for age estimation. During the onset phase of smiles, the maximum speed and the maximum acceleration of both eye closure and lip corner movements significantly change among different ages. Then, we analyzed the significant ($p < 0.001$) differences of these features between spontaneous and posed smiles using the t-test. Our results show that the maximum speed and the acceleration of the lip corner movements are significantly higher for posed smiles during smile onsets ($p < 0.001$, Cohen's $d > 0.40$). Also, the maximum speed and the acceleration of eye closure are significantly higher for spontaneous smiles in smile onsets ($p < 0.001$, Cohen's $d > 0.20$). These findings can explain the higher accuracy of the spontaneity-specific system. Similarly, t-test analysis is repeated for male and female differences. However, no significant difference (in the related dynamic features) is found between male and female subjects. This finding indicates that the

Table 5: Mean Absolute Error for different methods

Method | Age Range	0-9	10-19	20-29	30-39	40-49	50-59	60-69	70-79	Total
Proposed: Dynamics	6.20	8.18	13.55	15.22	10.82	20.62	24.07	29.06	11.69 ($\pm$12.02)
Proposed: Appearance	2.57	3.77	6.53	7.71	5.37	9.91	12.47	13.76	5.64 ($\pm$5.90)
Proposed: Combined	2.73	2.99	5.45	6.83	4.35	8.45	10.87	13.18	4.81 ($\pm$4.87)
Appearance: LBP, Voting	3.27	4.39	7.24	8.10	5.75	11.00	12.83	15.65	6.24 ($\pm$6.44)
Spatiotemporal: VLBP	16.99	15.09	13.28	13.51	16.71	29.83	39.97	53.00	17.03 ($\pm$13.56)
Spatiotemporal: LBP-TOP	15.59	13.48	11.04	11.76	15.16	25.11	33.10	44.94	14.95 ($\pm$11.41)
Number of Samples	158	333	215	171	250	66	30	17	1240

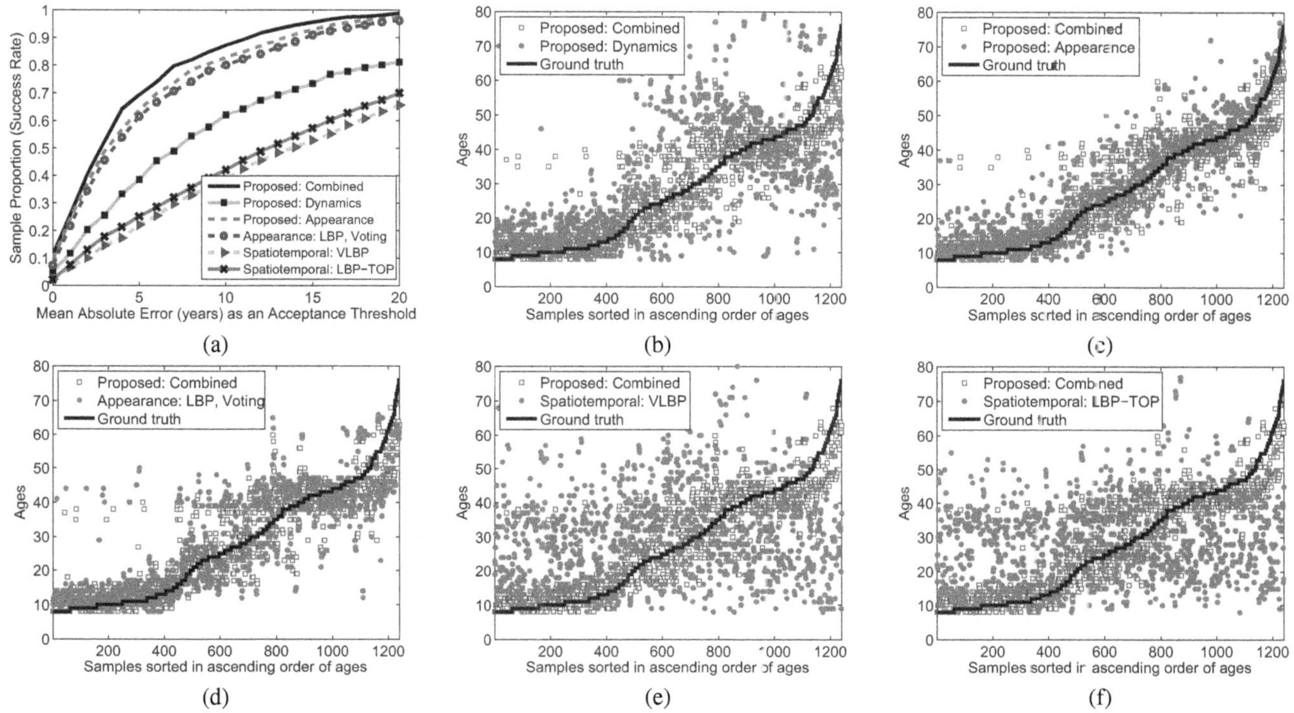

Figure 9: (a) Cumulative error distribution of the mean absolute error for different methods. (b-f) Comparison of the estimated ages using different methods

higher accuracy of gender-specific system is mostly based on LBP-based appearance features.

Experimental results show that spatiotemporal approaches based on VLBP and LBP-TOP are not efficient for age estimation. Even the individual use of our dynamic features outperforms these methods, significantly. Spatiotemporal features describe the change of facial appearance in time, but our proposed method models the appearance on a single neutral image (which is automatically selected as the first frame of the onset phase) and adds the dynamics of the facial expression (such as amplitude, speed, acceleration, etc) on it. As a result, the proposed system (using combined features) is significantly ($p < 0.001$, Cohen's $d > 0.15$) more accurate than all the competitor methods in our experiments.

7. CONCLUSIONS

In this study, we have introduced the usage of dynamic features to improve age estimation. Previously considered methods in the literature evaluate the appearance of the face, as the appearance is the most revealing aspect of aging. However, we have shown that the speed and movement features of facial muscles during smiling can improve the estimation of a person's age. While such dynamic features by themselves are not as accurate as appearance features, their contribution is significant when combined.

We assessed a range of dynamical features in an exploratory fashion, as geriatrics literature on facial aging also mostly focuses on appearance features. Therefore, we were not able to find sufficiently detailed descriptions of age effects on muscle dynamics (except for a study that reports intact muscle dynamics for orbicularis oculi, which contradicts some earlier studies [21]). Among individual regions of the face, our results show that eyelid dynamics are the most revealing in terms of age estimation, followed by lip corners and cheeks. We did not find a significant effect of the proposed features over different genders.

Our results are derived from a recently collected database with 400 subjects aged between 8 to 76 years. This is the most extensive dynamic age evaluation study to this date in the literature. We contrast dynamic information obtained from spontaneous and posed smiles. Posed expressions are somewhat better for age estimation, but not significantly so. We also compare our method to an appearance based baseline, as well as to a recently proposed spatiotemporal approach.

8. ACKNOWLEDGMENTS

This research was part of Science Live, the innovative research programme of science center NEMO that enables scientists to carry out real, publishable, peer-reviewed research using NEMO visitors as volunteers. Additionally, this study is partially supported by Boğaziçi University project BAP-6531.

9. REFERENCES

[1] A. M. Albert, K. Ricanek Jr, and E. Patterson. A review of the literature on the aging adult skull and face: Implications for forensic science research and applications. *Forensic Science International*, 172(1):1–9, 2007.

[2] T. R. Alley. *Social and applied aspects of perceiving faces*. Lawrence Erlbaum Associates, Hillsdale, NJ, 1988.

[3] H. Dibeklioğlu, A. A. Salah, and T. Gevers. Are you really smiling at me? Spontaneous versus posed enjoyment smiles. In *ECCV*, 2012.

[4] H. Dibeklioğlu, A. A. Salah, and T. Gevers. A statistical method for 2-d facial landmarking. *IEEE Trans. on Image Processing*, 21(2):844–858, 2012.

[5] P. Ekman. *Telling lies: Cues to deceit in the marketplace, politics, and marriage*. New York: WW. Norton & Company, 1992.

[6] P. Ekman and W. V. Friesen. *The Facial Action Coding System: A technique for the measurement of facial movement*. Consulting Psychologists Press Inc., San Francisco, CA, 1978.

[7] P. Ekman and W. V. Friesen. Felt, false, and miserable smiles. *Journal of Nonverbal Behavior*, 6:238–252, 1982.

[8] Y. Fu, G. Guo, and T. S. Huang. Age synthesis and estimation via faces: A survey. *IEEE Trans. on PAMI*, 32(11):1955–1976, 2010.

[9] X. Geng, K. Smith-Miles, and Z. Zhou. Facial age estimation by nonlinear aging pattern subspace. In *ACM Multimedia*, pages 721–724, 2008.

[10] X. Geng, Z.-H. Zhou, Y. Zhang, G. Li, and H. Dai. Learning from facial aging patterns for automatic age estimation. In *ACM Multimedia*, pages 307–316, 2006.

[11] G. Guo, Y. Fu, C. R. Dyer, and T. S. Huang. Image-based human age estimation by manifold learning and locally adjusted robust regression. *IEEE Trans. on Image Processing*, 17(7):1178–1188, 2008.

[12] A. Hadid. Analyzing facial behavioral features from videos. In A. A. Salah and B. Lepri, editors, *Int. Workshop on Human Behavior Understanding*, pages 52–61, 2011.

[13] Y. H. Kwon and N. da Vitoria Lobo. Age classification from facial images. *Computer Vision and Image Understanding*, 74(1):1–21, 1999.

[14] A. Lanitis, C. J. Taylor, and T. F. Cootes. Toward automatic simulation of aging effects on face images. *IEEE Trans. on PAMI*, 24(4):442–455, 2002.

[15] B. Ni, S. Yan, et al. Web image and video mining towards universal and robust age estimator. *IEEE Trans. on Multimedia*, 13(6):1217–1229, 2011.

[16] T. Ojala, M. Pietikainen, and D. Harwood. A comparative study of texture measures with classification based on featured distributions. *Pattern Recognition*, 29(1):51–59, 1996.

[17] T. Ojala, M. Pietikainen, and T. Maenpaa. Multiresolution gray-scale and rotation invariant texture classification with local binary patterns. *IEEE Trans. on PAMI*, 24(7):971–987, 2002.

[18] M. Ortega, L. Brodo, M. Bicego, and M. Tistarelli. On the quantitative estimation of short-term aging in human faces. In *ICIAP*, pages 575–584, 2009.

[19] A. J. O'Toole, T. Vetter, H. Volz, and E. Salter. Three-dimensional caricatures of human heads: Distinctiveness and the perception of age. *Perception*, 26:719–732, 1997.

[20] H. Peng, F. Long, and C. Ding. Feature selection based on mutual information criteria of max-dependency, max-relevance, and min-redundancy. *IEEE Trans. on PAMI*, 27(8):1226–1238, 2005.

[21] F. Pottier, N. Z. El-Shazly, and A. E. El-Shazly. Aging of orbicularis oculi. *Archives of Facial Plastic Surgery*, 10(5):346–349, 2008.

[22] N. Ramanathan, R. Chellappa, and S. Biswas. Computational methods for modeling facial aging: A survey. *Journal of Visual Languages & Computing*, 20(3):131–144, 2009.

[23] R. Sanders. Torsional elasticity of human skin in vivo. *Pflügers Archiv European Journal of Physiology*, 342(3):255–260, 1973.

[24] K. L. Schmidt, J. F. Cohn, and Y. Tian. Signal characteristics of spontaneous facial expressions: automatic movement in solitary and social smiles. *Biological Psychology*, 65(1):49–66, 2003.

[25] Science Center NEMO. http://www.e-nemo.nl/.

[26] J. Suo, S. C. Zhu, S. Shan, and X. Chen. A compositional and dynamic model for face aging. *IEEE Trans. on PAMI*, 32(3):385–401, 2010.

[27] H. Tao and T. Huang. Explanation-based facial motion tracking using a piecewise Bezier volume deformation model. In *CVPR*, volume 1, pages 611–617, 1999.

[28] B. Tiddeman, M. Burt, and D. I. Perrett. Prototyping and transforming facial textures for perception research. *IEEE Computer Graphics and Applications*, 21(5):42–50, 2001.

[29] P. F. Velleman. Definition and comparison of robust nonlinear data smoothing algorithms. *Journal of the American Statistical Association*, pages 609–615, 1980.

[30] Y. Wu, N. Thalmann, and D. Thalmann. A dynamic wrinkle model in facial animation and skin aging. *Journal of Visualization and Computer Animation*, 6:195–205, 1995.

[31] C. Zhan, W. Li, and P. Ogunbona. Age estimation based on extended non-negative matrix factorization. In *IEEE Int. Workshop on Multimedia Signal Processing*, 2011.

[32] G. Zhao and M. Pietikainen. Dynamic texture recognition using local binary patterns with an application to facial expressions. *IEEE Trans. on PAMI*, 29(6):915–928, 2007.

Unsupervised Face-Name Association via Commute Distance

Jiajun Bu[1], Bin Xu[1], Chenxia Wu[1], Chun Chen[1], Jianke Zhu[1], Deng Cai[2], Xiaofei He[2]

[1]Zhejiang Provincial Key Laboratory of Service Robot
College of Computer Science, Zhejiang University, Hangzhou, China
{bjj,xbzju,chenxiawu,chenc,jkzhu}@zju.edu.cn

[2]State Key Lab of CAD&CG, College of Computer Science, Zhejiang University, Hangzhou, China
{dengcai,xiaofeihe}@cad.zju.edu.cn

ABSTRACT

Recently, the task of unsupervised face-name association has received a considerable interests in multimedia and information retrieval communities. It is quite different with the generic facial image annotation problem because of its unsupervised and ambiguous assignment properties. Specifically, the task of face-name association should obey the following three constraints: (1) a face can only be assigned to a name appearing in its associated caption or to *null*; (2) a name can be assigned to at most one face; and (3) a face can be assigned to at most one name. Many conventional methods have been proposed to tackle this task while suffering from some common problems, *e.g.*, many of them are computational expensive and hard to make the null assignment decision. In this paper, we design a novel framework named face-name association via commute distance (FACD), which judges face-name and face-null assignments under a unified framework via commute distance (CD) algorithm. Then, to further speed up the on-line processing, we propose a novel anchor-based commute distance (ACD) algorithm whose main idea is using the anchor point representation structure to accelerate the eigen-decomposition of the adjacency matrix of a graph. Systematic experiment results on a large scale and real world image-caption database with a total of 194,046 detected faces and 244,725 names show that our proposed approach outperforms many state-of-the-art methods in performance. Our framework is appropriate for a large scale and real-time system.

Categories and Subject Descriptors

H.3.3 [**Information Search and Retrieval**]: Information filtering; H.3.5 [**Online Information Services**]: Web-based services

General Terms

Algorithms, Performance

MM'12, October 29–November 2, 2012, Nara, Japan.

(a) Britain's Prime Minister **Gordon Brown** and U.S. Democratic presidential candidate **Barack Obama** shake hands before meeting. April 17, 2008.

(b) **Novak Djokovic** ended **Roger Federer**'s winning run at his home-town tournament to lift the *Davidoff* Swiss Indoors title in Basle this afternoon.

Figure 1: Examples of image-caption pairs. Each name in bold is associated with a face in the image while the italic name is not matched.

Keywords

Face-name association, Unsupervised, Commute distance

1. INTRODUCTION

There are a great number of images accompanying by text captions on the Internet. A high percent of these images contain people faces and their captions contain people names. A common observation for these image-caption data is that the name of a face in the image is very likely mentioned by the corresponding caption and vice-versa. This motivates the recent research interest of exploiting the latent associations between faces and names automatically for image-caption pairs. The task is called face-name association [1, 8, 14]. Fig.1 shows two typical examples. The persons in the images are all mentioned by their captions.

Unsupervised face-name association is helpful to generate a huge amount of training annotations at a low cost for many applications, such as face image (instance) retrieval and automatic face annotation. At the same time, it is an important technique for many web systems, such as the social network (*e.g.* Facebook) and the photo sharing service (*e.g.* iPhoto). The unsupervised face-name association problem can be seen as the following challenge: for a given image and its corresponding caption (also called an image-caption item in this paper), determine whether there exist some faces in the image and some names in the caption; if so, point out the latent associations between faces and names, without any explicit manual intervention. With the help of face detector[1] and named entity detector[2] [14], we can directly filter out the image-caption pair without a face in the image or a name in the caption. That is, the remain key task is the automatic face-name matching for a given small list of faces and names, which are extracted automatically from the image-caption pair.

This seems like a traditional classification (or facial image annotation) problem that each of the names in the caption is a class label and we need to assign the labels to the faces. However, the face-name association problem is essentially different with a standard supervised classification problem due to the following important properties:

- Their are no training data: To train a classifier, one needs to collect the training data. In our scenario, we only have a large collection of image-name items, and each item may contain multiple faces and multiple names. There are no exact associations. This problem is essentially an unsupervised learning problem.
- The associations are ambiguous: Not every name mentioned in the caption appears in the image, and, vice-versa, not every face in the image is mentioned by the caption. That is to say, the match result is not necessary to cover all the names and faces in a pair. This is a very common case in real world data, *e.g.*, in Fig.1, the name *Davidoff* is not related to any person appearing in the image. However, for a general classification algorithm, it's possible to match multiple faces to a single name, and it is unknown how to make the face-null association if we don't make any modification.

Many conventional methods have been proposed to tackle the problem of unsupervised face-name association [1,8,14]. These methods suffer from some common problems. For example, many of them are computational expensive, i.e, they are not appropriate for a large scale real-time system. Moreover, some methods are hard to make *null* assignment decisions (a face is not mentioned by the caption). To overcome these drawbacks, in this paper, we design a new framework named FACD (stands for *Face-name Association via Commute Distance*). FACD has two stages: one off-line preprocessing stage and one on-line face naming stage. In the off-line stage, we build an inverted index structure for the large scale name and face database, based on which, in the on-line stage, we efficiently handle the image-caption items one by one. Specifically, we adopt commute distance (CD) on a graph as the metric to match the faces and names, receiving a significant performance improvement over many state-of-the-art methods. Moreover, to further speed up the computation, we propose a novel anchor-based commute distance (ACD) method, which is much faster than CD especially on a large scale database. This nice property makes the proposed ACD more appropriate for a large scale real-time face-name association system. A typical scenario is as follows: one user uploads an image including some people faces as well as some text description including some names to a web system and then, the system automatically match the corresponding names and faces in a short time.

For experiments, we use the large scale database FAN-Large [14], which is the largest and most realistic database supporting the research of face-name association. The whole database contains 125,479 image-caption items with a total of 194,046 detected faces and 244,725 names.

The main contribution of this paper include: (1) we design a new framework FACD, appropriate for a large scale and real-time face-name association system. (2) we propose to solve the face-name association problem via commute distance algorithm, by which both the face-name and face-null assignment problems can be integrated into a unified framework; (3) we propose a novel anchor-based commute distance algorithm to further speed up the computation of commute distance.

The rest of this paper is organized as follows. We briefly discuss some related works in section 2 and some preliminary knowledge in section 3. The framework FACD and the anchor-based commute distance algorithm are described in section 4. We present experimental results and comparisons in section 5. Finally, we provide a conclusion in section 6.

[1]`http://torch3vision.idiap.ch`
[2]`http://opennlp.sourceforge.net`

2. RELATED WORK

In this section we briefly review some closely related works to our paper. They belong to the big topic of automatic face annotation, including the model-based and retrieval-based face annotation and the face-name association.

Generally, the model-based face annotation is formulated as an extended face recognition problem, in which many traditional classifiers are trained from a collection of labeled face instances. Typical examples include face annotation for images [2,27,28,30] and for videos [15,23]. In [30], the authors proposed a transductive kernel fisher discriminant scheme for the task of face annotation. The main idea is to solve the Fisher's discriminant using deformed kernels incorporating the information of both labeled and unlabeled data. Although the annotation accuracy is high in many works, these methods suffer from some problems in common. For example, it is very expensive and time consuming to get a large collection of labeled face instances and the annotation performance decreases when the number of classes (names) increases. Moreover, after gathering some new labeled data, these systems need to re-train the model which is time consuming.

Instead of training classifiers for model-based face annotation approaches, some recent researches focus on exploring retrieval-based face annotation algorithms [18,19,21]. These algorithms utilize the information of a large amount of weakly name-face labeled data collected from public search engines (*e.g.*, Google) to assign the most possible name to a user provided face image. This is a promising way to solve the face annotation task via utilizing the content-based image retrieval technique [3,4,6,9,22,26] in mining massive weakly labeled facial images on the web. However, retrieval-based face annotation algorithms have to face two key challenges: the first is how to retrieve most similar facial images from a large scale facial image database efficiently and the second is how to exploit the noisy and incomplete web images and their weak label information for the face annotation task [19]. The work [21] addressed the first challenge via employing both local and global features as facial image representation. In [19], the authors proposed a weak label regularized local coordinate coding technique, which learned sparse features via local coordinate coding principle as well as the graph-based weak label regularization.

Recently, many researchers focus on the topic of automatic

face annotation for captioned images (the task of face-name association). That means, the faces appearing in an image can only be assigned to a name mentioned by the corresponding caption or to *null*. Most of the existing methods [1,8,14] can be regarded as a type of constrained clustering approach [14], where each cluster of faces is assigned to one name. The algorithm of [1] is a generative model, which treats image captions as bags of names, disregarding any contextual cues. The model associates a Gaussian density in the appearance feature space to each name as well as to the *null* label. In [8], the authors constructs a similarity graph with nodes representing faces and edges weighting by the similarity between two faces. Then, the algorithm searches a number of dense subgraphs with each one corresponding to a person's name. The objective function is formulated as a maximization of the sum of edge weights within each subgraph, and the iterative solution stops at a local optimum.

3. PRELIMINARIES

We introduce some preliminary knowledge including the the random walk [13] technique and two distance measures highly related to the random walk – the hitting time and the commute time [7,10,13,16] in this section. They are helpful for understanding our proposed algorithm in this paper.

3.1 Random Walk

The **random walk** [13] defined on a graph is a sequence of nodes represented by a finite Markov chain. Generally, a graph can be denoted as $G = (V, E, W)$, where V is a set of nodes ($|V| = n$) in which each node represents a data point, $E \subseteq V \times V$ is a set of edges ($|E| = m$) connecting related vertices, and W is an adjacency matrix recording the pairwise weights between nodes. The element $w_{ij} > 0$ if (i, j) is an edge, otherwise, $w_{ij} = 0$. The probability that the random walk on node i at time t jumps to node j at time $t + 1$ is determined by the edge weight on the graph:

$$\text{Pro}(state(t+1) = j)|state(t) = i) = p_{ij} = w_{ij}/d_{ii}, \quad (1)$$

where $d_{ii} = \sum_j w_{ij}$ is the degree of the node i. Thus the transition matrix P is given by $P = D^{-1}W$. Let $\pi(t) = [\pi_1(t)], \pi_2(t), \ldots, \pi_n(t)]^T$ be the state probability distribution at time t, the next distribution is calculated by $\pi(t+1) = P^T\pi(t)$. It is not hard to see that, the stationary distribution of the random walk is proportional to the vertex degree [29], *i.e.*, $\pi = D\mathbf{1}/V_G$, where $V_G = \sum_{i=1}^n d_{ii}$ is the volume of the graph. We get the conclusion from the observation: $P^T\pi = WD^{-1}D\mathbf{1}/V_G = D\mathbf{1}/V_G = \pi$.

3.2 Hitting Time and Commute Time

The **hitting time** $h(i, j)$ is the expected steps that a random walk will expend from node i to node j for the first time [13]. It is defined as:

$$h(i,j) = \begin{cases} 0 & \text{if } i = j \\ 1 + \sum_{k \in \mathcal{N}(i)} p_{ik} h(k,j) & \text{otherwise,} \end{cases} \quad (2)$$

where $\mathcal{N}(i)$ is the set of the nodes each has an edge connected with i and

$$p_{ik} = \begin{cases} w_{ik}/d_i & \text{if } (i,k) \text{ belong to an edge} \\ 0 & \text{otherwise.} \end{cases} \quad (3)$$

is the transition probability from node i to node k.

The **commute time** $c(i, j)$ is the expected steps that a random walk starting from node i will take to arrive at node j and then go back to i again for the first time [13]. It is defined as:

$$c(i,j) = h(i,j) + h(j,i). \quad (4)$$

It is easy to show that the commute time is a metric [7], so it is also called as **Commute Distance**.

4. ALGORITHM FRAMEWORK

In this section, we describe our face-name association framework FACD in detail. FACD has two stages: one off-line preprocessing stage and one on-line face naming stage. In the off-line stage, we build an inverted index structure for the large scale name and face database, based on which, we efficiently handle the image-caption pairs one by one in the on-line stage.

4.1 Problem Formulation

Given a collection of web image-caption pairs with each image having at least one face and each caption has at least one name (We filter out the pairs without a face or a name), find the associations between faces and names for each pair,without any explicit manual help. Moreover, the result should obey the following constraints [14]:

C1: A face can only be assigned to a name appearing in its associated caption, or to *null* if there is no corresponding name in the caption.;

C2: In an image-caption pair, a name can be assigned to at most one face;

C3: In an image-caption pair, a face can be assigned to at most one name.

These constraints are widely considered and used in many existing face-name association systems [1,8,14].

4.2 Off-line Stage

Similar to the term-document inverted index used in Information Retrieval, we construct the name-item inverted index. Here an item is a image-caption pair. Fig.2 is a schematic diagram. We first associate each item to all the names detected in its caption and then, extract the faces in each item to form a name-face index. With this index, we can efficiently retrieve all the related faces given a name (appearing in the same item), which serves the foundation of the efficient processing in the on-line stage.

Unfortunately, the face lists contain many noisy faces – one image may have several faces. To improve the quality of the index, we make effort to re-rank the faces in each list, expecting to put the correct faces on the top positions, and then, try to filter out some mismatched (noisy) faces. Without any manual help, our processing is inspired by some heuristic ideas as follows.

H1: For each list of faces associated with a name (each line in the index), the correct person appears the most times in a high probability.

Since the face images of the same person tend to be similar to each other, in each line in the index, the correct faces (to the name) tend to have higher sum of similarities to all the other faces. Thus, for each line of the index, we compute the

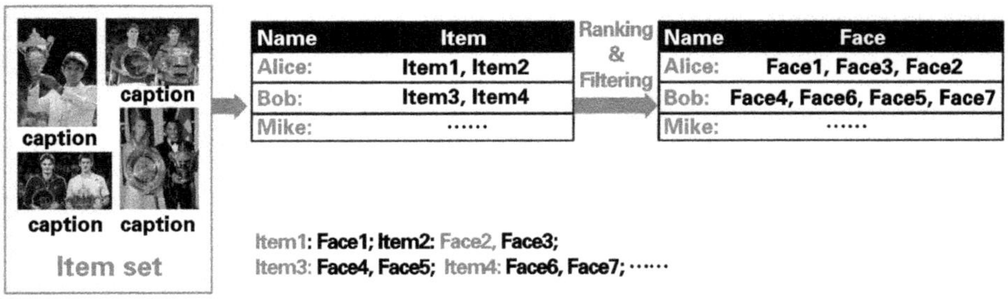

Figure 2: An example of the inverted index established in the off-line stage. An Item represents an image-caption pair. The item set is organized into a name-item inverted index (middle). Then, after ranking and filtering, we have a name-face index (right).

pairwise visual similarities between all the faces. Then we re-rank the face list by the sum of similarities as a metric, which is defined by (the higher the better):

$$S_i = \sum_j s_{ij}, \quad i = 1, \ldots, r \tag{5}$$

where s_{ij} is the similarity of faec i and j in the list and r is the number of faces. The visual similarity is computed by

$$s_{ij} = \exp\left(-d^2(\mathbf{v}_i, \mathbf{v}_j)/\sigma\right), \tag{6}$$

where σ is the heat kernel parameter and $d(\mathbf{v}_i, \mathbf{v}_j)$ is the Euclidean distance of face i and j.

H2: One name can not refer to two or more faces belonging to one image.

We set the rule that buddy faces (appearing in the same image) can not be associated with the same name. So we filter out the the faces (or put them to the tail of the list) which have a buddy face in front of the list. For example, Fig.3 is a toy case of the filtering scheme. The first line of faces are sorted by S_i and the faces connecting with a blue broken line are buddy faces. So we drop the faces f_2,f_4,f_7 and f_8, getting the second line of faces associated with the name.

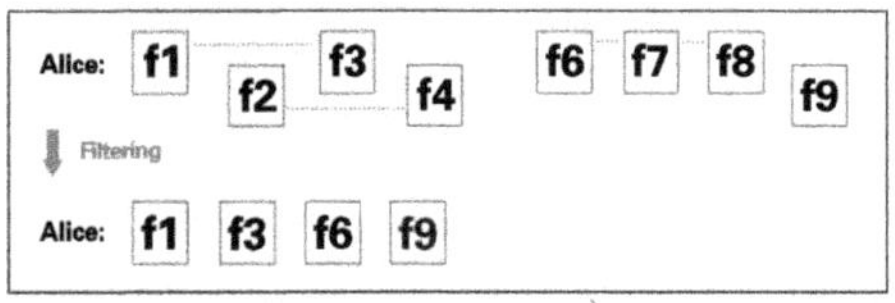

Figure 3: An example of the filtering strategy for a sorted face list. The faces connecting with a blue broken line are buddy faces.

4.3 On-line Stage

The most important property that a face-name association system should have is the low response time for an on-line request. That is to say, the image-caption pairs should be processed one by one (independently) and each processing is very light-weight.

Based on the index architecture established in the off-line stage, one may design a simple strategy called Majority Voting (MV). For a given image-caption pair, the names in the caption are used as queries to get a set of *candidate* faces from the index. Each candidate face is related to a name. Then for each request face, we could search the most visually similar faces from the candidate set, and assign it the name with maximum number of related faces.

Although the majority voting algorithm is very simple to implement, it is not conform with the constraint C2 – two or more faces may be assigned to the same name. At the same time, it is hard to make the *null* assignment (constraint C1) when there are more names than faces.

4.3.1 *Association by Commute Distance*

To conform with all the association constraints described in section 4.1, we need a unified metric to judge which face-name pairs are more likely to be correct pairs, and which faces are not mentioned by the names, and which names are not associated with any face in the image. To achieve these goals, we propose to use a graph structure to model the face-name relationships. In the next, we first give two toy examples to show the intuitive insight and then describe our algorithm in detail.

Fig.4 shows two examples: faces and names are denoted by circles and triangles respectively. Nodes $f_1 - f_4$ are the request faces. Intuitively, in Fig.4(a), we want f_1 associate with n_1, f_2 associate with n_2, and the name n_3 is not used. In Fig.4(b), we want f_3 is associated with n_3, and f_4 is assigned to *null* since it is far away to all the names on the graph. Our judgements are made by the distance estimation on the graph. For an arbitrary and complex graph, we need a unified distance measurement. The commute distance (CD) is a reasonable choice. Recall its definition for two nodes on a graph – it is the expected steps that a random walk will take from the first node to the second and go back again for the first time. It is different with the *shortest path* – even if two nodes have a short path, they still probably have a long commute distance if the subgraph between them is very dense [7]. It is more like a average jump distance estimation on a graph. For this point, the commute distance is conform with our intuitive insight above.

Our algorithm's detailed steps are as follows: An unified *undirected* connected graph is built for an item, whose nodes represent the faces (request faces and candidate faces) and names. The candidate faces are formed by top-p faces from the name-face index for each name of the item. For example, if the target item has a names and b request faces, the graph size (number of nodes) for an item is $(a+b+a*p)$. Parameter p will be discussed in the experiment section.

The candidate faces are bridges of associations between request faces and names. Two types of edges need to be de-

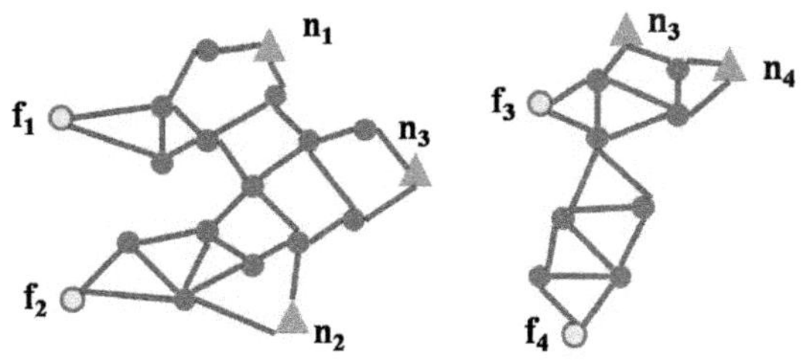

(a) Example1 (b) Example2

Figure 4: Two toy graph examples in which circle nodes representing faces and triangle nodes representing names. $f_1 - f_4$ denote the request faces.

fined: For face-face edges, the weights represent visual similarities of faces measured by Eq.(6); For face-name edges, the weights are 1 or 0 representing whether a candidate face and a name come from the same index list or not. (Note that only the request faces' closest candidates are judged.) So we construct an adjacency matrix W with each element W_{ij} saving the corresponding edge weight.

Instead of running a random walk on the graph and computing the average jump steps for each two nodes, the commute distance can be computed via the Moore-Penrose pseudoinverse of the graph Laplacian matrix . Let $L = D - W$ be the graph Laplacian matrix (D is the degree matrix with $D_{ii} = \sum_j W_{ij}$) and L^+ be the pseudoinverse, then the commute distance $c(i,j)$ is [7, 10]:

$$\begin{aligned} c(i,j) &= V_G(l^+_{ii} + l^+_{jj} - 2l^+_{ij}) \\ &= V_G(\mathbf{e}_i - \mathbf{e}_j)^T L^+(\mathbf{e}_i - \mathbf{e}_j), \end{aligned} \quad (7)$$

where $V_G = \sum_{i=1}^n d_{ii}$ is the graph volume, l^+_{ij} is the (i,j) element of the matrix L^+, and $\mathbf{e}_i$ is a n dimensional column vector with a $\mathbf{1}$ at location i and all $\mathbf{0}$ elsewhere.

Using the equation above, we can directly compute the commute distances between each request face and each name in an image-caption pair. Then, the remain problem is how to associate them automatically and correctly. A big advantage of the commute distance approach is that the distances are all comparable. That is to say, a shorter distance pair is more likely to be a right association. What's more, if we can not find any name has close commute distance to a face, we just assign *null* to the face. Thus we tackle the *null* assignment problem naturally in the same framework. The main steps of the association after we getting the commute distances is described in **Algorithm 1**. $\{P_i = (f^i_a, n^i_b)\}$ is a list of face-name pairs, sorted by the commute distance CD_i corresponding to P_i (ascending). The threshold ϵ is a predefined parameter and we will discuss how to decide this parameter in the experiment.

Using Algorithm 1, we could get all the face-name associations. This is our *Face-name Association by Commute Distance* (FACD) framework. In the next section, we discuss how to accelerate the computation.

4.4 Anchor-based Commute Distance

If there are q nodes (including the candidate faces, request faces and names) in a graph built in the on-line stage, the eigen-decomposition of the graph Laplacian can be written as $L = U\Sigma U^T$, in which $\Sigma = diag(\lambda_1, \lambda_2, \ldots, \lambda_q)$ $(0 = \lambda_1 \leq \lambda_2 \leq \ldots \leq \lambda_q)$, and $U = (\mathbf{u}_1, \mathbf{u}_2, \ldots, \mathbf{u}_q)$ where $\mathbf{u}_i$ is the eigenvector corresponding to the eigenvalue λ_i. The pseudoinverse of L is (assume that the nonzero eigenvalues of L start from λ_2):

$$L^+ = \sum_{i=2}^{q} \frac{1}{\lambda_i} \mathbf{u}_i \mathbf{u}_i^T. \quad (8)$$

Thus, we need to compute the whole eigen-decomposition of L to form the matrix L^+, which has a complexity of $O(q^3)$. This is the main computational cost for each on-line processing via commute distance algorithm. If we could find an efficient way to build L^+, we can accelerate the computation.

The normalized graph Laplacian [17] is (I is an identity matrix) :

$$\begin{aligned} \tilde{L} &= D^{-1/2} L D^{-1/2} \\ &= I - D^{-1/2} W D^{-1/2} \\ &= I - \tilde{W} \end{aligned} \quad (9)$$

which can be used to replace the original graph Laplacian L in Eq.(7). Thus we get a **Normalized Commute Distance**. Let $\tilde{\lambda}_i$ be a eigenvalue of the matrix $\tilde{L}$ $(0 = \tilde{\lambda}_1 \leq \tilde{\lambda}_2 \leq \ldots \leq \tilde{\lambda}_q)$ and vector $\mathbf{v}_i$ be the associated eigenvector of $\tilde{\lambda}_i$, then we have the following derivations:

$$\begin{aligned} & \tilde{L}V = V\Lambda \\ \Rightarrow\ & (I - \tilde{W})V = V\Lambda \\ \Rightarrow\ & \tilde{W}V = V(I - \Lambda), \end{aligned} \quad (10)$$

where $\Lambda = diag(\tilde{\lambda}_1, \tilde{\lambda}_2, \ldots, \tilde{\lambda}_q)$ and $V = (\mathbf{v}_1, \mathbf{v}_2, \ldots, \mathbf{v}_q)$. The equations mean that, the normalized matrix $\tilde{W}$ and $\tilde{L}$ **share** the same eigenvectors and complementary eigenvalues, *i.e.*, the largest eigenvalue of $\tilde{W}$ is the smallest one of $\tilde{L}$. This inspire us to utilize $\tilde{W}$'s eigen-decomposition to construct $\tilde{L}^+$, rather than $\tilde{L}$'s eigen-decomposition.

We propose a novel anchor-based commute distance (ACD) algorithm whose main idea is constructing $\tilde{W}$ with the anchor-based representation $Z \in \mathbb{R}^{d \times q}$ $(d \ll q)$:

$$\tilde{W} = D^{-1/2} Z^T Z D^{-1/2} = H^T H, \quad (11)$$

Algorithm 1: Face-Name Association After Commute Distance Computation

Input : $\{P_i = (f^i_a, n^i_b)\}$, $\{CD_i\}$, $\{f_k\}$, threshold ϵ.
//$\{P_i\}$ is a list of face-name pairs, ascendingly sorted by the commute distance CD_i. $\{f_k\}$ is the set of request faces. ϵ is a predefined threshold.
Output: face-name association list G.
Initialize i = 1
while $CD_i < \epsilon$ **do**
  if f^i_a *is not named* && n^i_b *is not used* **then**
    add P_i to G;
  end
  i = i + 1;
end
//F is the number of faces in an item
for $k = 1$ *to* F **do**
  if f_k *is not named* **then**
    add (f_k, NULL) to G;
  end
end

based on which the eigen-decomposition can be solved in a cost of $O(d^3) + O(qd^2)$, much smaller than the cost of $O(q^3)$. A number of recent works have studied the anchor-based technique (the anchor points are some representative data points), especially for some semi-supervised and graph-based algorithms [5, 11, 12, 20, 22, 24, 25], *e.g.*, in [24], the authors proposed that each data point on manifold can be approximated by a linear combination of its nearby anchor points. Liu et al. [12] designed the adjacency matrix in a probabilistic measure and used it for scalable semi-supervised learning. These works inspire us much.

4.4.1 Graph Construction and Anchor Selection

Now we introduce how to build an anchor graph to model the data. Suppose we have a node set $\mathcal{F} = \{\mathbf{f}_1, \ldots, \mathbf{f}_{q_f}\}$ representing the faces (including request faces and candidate faces), a set $\mathcal{N} = \{\mathbf{n}_1, \ldots, \mathbf{n}_{q_n}\}$ representing the names, and a set $\mathcal{A} = \{\mathbf{a}_1, \ldots, \mathbf{a}_d\}$ denoting the anchor points selected from the face set. Easy to see that $q_f + q_n = q$. We aim to find a weight matrix $Z \in \mathbb{R}^{d \times q}$ that measures the relationships between each node in the graph and each anchor point. Without loss of generality, let

$$Z = [\ Z_f \quad Z_n\ ] \tag{12}$$

where $Z_f \in \mathbb{R}^{d \times q_f}$ is anchor-face weight matrix and $Z_n \in \mathbb{R}^{d \times q_n}$ is anchor-name weight matrix. For anchor-face weights, we use the same measurement in Eq.(6). That is

$$Z_f(\mathbf{a}_i, \mathbf{f}_k) = \exp\left(-d^2(\mathbf{a}_i, \mathbf{f}_k)/\sigma\right), \tag{13}$$

and for anchor-name weights, we simply assign a **1** for each edge connecting an anchor and its correlated name node.

How can we get the anchors? Clustering is a considerable choice. For example, we can use k-means algorithm and then select the points nearest to the centers as anchors. However, k-means is expensive. Random selection is another choice which is extremely efficient, however the quality of anchors might not be good. Taking the advantage our off-line index structure, we propose to use another efficient way: selecting top-d faces from candidate faces for the names appearing in the caption as anchors. The selection is made one-by-one, *i.e.*, we firstly select the top face for one name from its index list and then from the next name's list. The selection won't stop until d non-repeated anchors are collected. If the number of candidate faces is less than d, all of them are selected as anchors.

4.4.2 Adjacency Matrix Construction

The weight matrix $Z \in R^{d \times n}$ can be seen as a d-dimensional anchor-based representation of the data set [5, 12, 22], d is the number of anchor points. That is to say, data points (or nodes) can be represented in the new feature space, no matter what the original features are. With the inner product as the metric to measure the adjacent weights between nodes, we construct the adjacency matrix by

$$\begin{aligned} W &= Z^T Z \\ &= \begin{bmatrix} Z_f^T \\ Z_n^T \end{bmatrix} [Z_f \quad Z_n] \\ &= \begin{bmatrix} Z_f^T Z_f & Z_f^T Z_n \\ Z_n^T Z_f & Z_n^T Z_n \end{bmatrix} \end{aligned} \tag{14}$$

which means that if two data points are correlative (W_{ij} is large), they tend to have similar anchor representations. By sharing the same or similar anchors, data points have similar semantic concepts in a high probability. Thus, this formula is helpful to explore the semantic relationships of the data points on a graph. Moreover, it naturally preserves the nonnegativeness of W, which guarantees the positive semi-definite property of the graph Laplacian.

Note that the bottom right part of W, $Z_n^T Z_n$, should be a diagonal matrix in our consideration, which makes the random walk can't jump from one name node to another name node in one step. That is, one anchor point should not connect to more than one name in the anchor graph.

4.4.3 Efficient Computation

The key point of ACD is efficiently constructing the matrix $\tilde{L}^+$ to speed up commute distance computation. We now offer the derivation with the help of anchor-based representation. For improving the readability, some matrices below are marked with their size. Without loss of generality, we set the number of anchor points be much smaller than the graph size, *i.e.*, $d \ll q$. Let

$$H^T = D^{-1/2} Z^T, \tag{15}$$

and H's SVD decomposition be

$$H_{d\times q} = U_{d\times d} S_{d\times d} V_{q\times d}^T, \tag{16}$$

where S is the singular value matrix with $S = diag(\sigma_1, \ldots, \sigma_d)$, $U_{d\times d} = (u_1, u_2, \ldots, u_d)$ and $V_{q\times d}^T = (v_1, v_2, \ldots, v_d)^T$, then

$$\begin{aligned} \tilde{W}_{q\times q} &= D^{-1/2} Z^T Z D^{-1/2} = H_{d\times q}^T H_{d\times q} \\ &= V_{q\times q} \Sigma_{q\times q} V_{q\times q}^T. \end{aligned} \tag{17}$$

Since $\text{rank}(\tilde{W}) \leq \min(d, q) = d$, the matrix $V_{q\times q}$ and $\Sigma_{q\times q}$ can be represented as

$$V_{q\times q} = [V_{q\times d}\ V_{q\times c}] \textbf{ and } \Sigma_{q\times q} = \begin{bmatrix} \Sigma_{d\times d} & \mathbf{0} \\ \mathbf{0} & \mathbf{0}_{c\times c} \end{bmatrix}, \tag{18}$$

where $c = q - d$ and $\Sigma_{d\times d} = S_{d\times d}^2$. We know that $V_{q\times q}$ is orthogonal and has unit length for each column, so $V_{q\times q} V_{q\times q}^T = I_{q\times q}$ and $V_{q\times q}^{-1} = V_{q\times q}^T$. Then, we get the following important derivations:

$$\begin{aligned} \tilde{L}^+ &= (I - \tilde{W})^+ = V_{q\times q}(I_{q\times q} - \Sigma_{q\times q})^+ V_{q\times q}^T \\ &= [V_{q\times d}\ V_{q\times c}] \begin{bmatrix} (I_{d\times d} - \Sigma_{d\times d})^+ & \mathbf{0} \\ \mathbf{0} & I_{c\times c} \end{bmatrix} \begin{bmatrix} V_{q\times d}^T \\ V_{q\times c}^T \end{bmatrix} \\ &= V_{q\times d}(I_{d\times d} - \Sigma_{d\times d})^+ V_{q\times d}^T + V_{q\times c} V_{q\times c}^T \\ &= V_{q\times d}(I_{d\times d} - \Sigma_{d\times d})^+ V_{q\times d}^T + I_{q\times q} - V_{q\times d} V_{q\times d}^T \\ &= V_{q\times d}[(I_{d\times d} - \Sigma_{d\times d})^+ - I_{d\times d}] V_{q\times d}^T + I_{q\times q} \\ &= V_{q\times d} B_{d\times d} V_{q\times d}^T + I_{q\times q} \\ &= \tilde{V}_{q\times d} \tilde{V}_{q\times d}^T + I_{q\times q}. \end{aligned} \tag{19}$$

Note that $B_{d\times d} = [(I_{d\times d} - \Sigma_{d\times d})^+ - I_{d\times d}]$ is a diagonal matrix and $\tilde{V}_{q\times d} = V_{q\times d} B_{d\times d}^{1/2}$. The derivation implies that the critical problem now is how to compute the matrix $V_{q\times d}$ and $\Sigma_{d\times d}$ efficiently. From Eq.(16), it is not hard to get the following equations:

$$H_{d\times q}H_{d\times q}^T = U_{d\times d}\Sigma_{d\times d}U_{d\times d}^T, \quad (20)$$

and

$$V_{q\times d} = H_{d\times q}^T U_{d\times d} S_{d\times d}^{-1}. \quad (21)$$

Thus we first compute the eigen-decomposition of HH^T, which is in the size of $d \times d$ ($d \ll q$), to get the matrix $U_{d\times d}$ and $\Sigma_{d\times d}$, and then calculate the matrix matrix $V_{q\times d}$ via Eq.(21) (note that $S_{d\times d} = \Sigma_{d\times d}^{1/2}$). Finally, $\tilde{L}^+$ can be constructed by Eq.(19).

What's more, to compute the commute distances between request faces and names, we don't need to really construct the entire matrix $\tilde{L}^+$ by the last line of Eq.(19), with a complexity of $O(dq^2)$. From Eq.(7) and Eq.(19), we have

$$\begin{aligned} c(i,j) &= V_G(\mathbf{e}_i - \mathbf{e}_j)^T\tilde{L}^+(\mathbf{e}_i - \mathbf{e}_j) \\ &= V_G(\sum_{l=1}^{d}(\tilde{v}_{li} - \tilde{v}_{lj})^2 + 2). \end{aligned} \quad (22)$$

where $\tilde{\mathbf{v}}_l$ is the l-th column of $\tilde{V}_{q\times d}$. Thus each commute distance $c(i,j)$ can be calculated in a short time $O(d)$, if we have got the matrix $\tilde{V}_{q\times d}$. As the constant parts of Eq.(22) don't affect the commute distance when it is used as a distance metric, we just simplify the formulation as

$$c(i,j) \doteq \sum_{l=1}^{d}(\tilde{v}_{li} - \tilde{v}_{lj})^2. \quad (23)$$

This is an interesting result. It says, our anchor-based commute distance essentially finds a data representation of the data set, denoted by $\tilde{V}_{q\times d}$, and the distance is just the Euclidean distance on the d-dimensional feature space.

When all the commute distances $c(i,j)$ have been calculated, we use the same association algorithm described in **Algorithm 1** to match face-name or face-null for each image-caption item. This is the end of our proposed algorithm anchor-based commute distance.

4.5 Overview of FACD

Here we make a brief summary of our framework face-name association via commute distance (FACD). We do the following steps:

Off-line Stage:

1a. Establish the name-item inverted index to get the name-face index structure. (Section 4.2)

1b. Re-rank the faces in each name-face list and filter out the buddy faces. (Section 4.2)

On-line Stage:

2a. Build a connected graph for CD algorithm (Section 4.3.1), or an anchor graph for ACD algorithm (Section 4.4.1-4.4.2).

2b. Calculate the distances between request faces and names on the graph by CD (Section 4.3.1), or ACD (Section 4.4.3).

2c. Make the face-name or face-null assignments for each face via Algorithm 1.

4.6 Complexity Analysis

We offer the complexity analysis of our proposed algorithm CD and ACD used in the on-line stage. Specifically, both CD and ACD have two main steps.

CD: (a) building a connected graph (computing W); (b) computing the matrix L^+ via eigen-decomposition of L.

(a) To build the connected graph, we compute visual similarities of all the faces via Eq.(6) as the weights of face-face edges, and assign 0 or 1 for face-name edges. So the construction has a total computational complexity $O(q^2)$, where q is the graph size.

(b) Solving the eigen-decomposition of L requires the complexity of $O(q^3)$.

So the total computational complexity is $O(q^3)$ for CD.

ACD: (a) building an anchor graph (computing Z); (b) solving the eigen-decomposition of $\tilde{W}$ to compute the commute distance.

(a) To build the anchor graph, we compute the similarities of each node to all the d anchors. So the construction has a total computational complexity $O(qd)$, where d is the number of anchors and q is the graph size. Thus, the number of anchors determines the efficiency of the anchor graph construction. In our experiments, $d \ll q$, making the construction very fast.

(b) Solving the eigen-decomposition of $\tilde{W}$ requires to compute the SVD of $H_{d\times q}H_{d\times q}^T$ and form the matrix $V_{q\times d}$, with the complexity of $O(qd^2) + O(d^3)$ and $O(qd^2)$ respectively.

Considering that $d \ll q$, the total complexity of ACD is $O(d^3) + O(qd^2)$, which is much smaller than $O(q^3)$, the complexity of CD. In our experiments, d is usually very small (*e.g.*, $d = 25$), so the algorithm is extremely fast for each on-line processing. In other words, ACD is more appropriate for a real-time system.

5. EXPERIMENTS

In this section, we presents the detailed experimental results and comparisons to evaluate the effectiveness and efficiency of our proposed approach on a large scale and real world image-caption database.

5.1 Database Statistics

A large scale image-caption database *Face And Names Large scale database* (FAN-Large) was published[3]. To our best knowledge, it is the largest and most realistic database supporting the research of face-name association. The data set contains 125,479 image-caption pairs (Items) with a total of 194,046 detected faces and 244,725 names. A nice property of this database is that, all the detected faces are manually assigned a ground truth name or null, which can be used to result evaluation. Detailed information is listed in Table 1.

Besides the entire database, we also conduct our experiments on its four subsets: *Easy*, *Hard*, *Life* and *Buddies*. We follow the same data partitions and experiments setup used in [14]: the face features are extracted using the tool

[3]`http://www.vision.ee.ethz.ch/~calvin/fan-large`

Table 1: **Basic statistics of the FAN-Large database.**

	FAN-Large
# of items	125,479
# of detected faces	194,046
# of detected names	244,725
# of unique names	34,645
# of names appear at least 20 times	1,437

Table 2: Statistics of the whole database and four interesting subsets. The *Hard* subset has the maximum number of average faces and names.

Subset	images	faces/image	names/caption
Easy	39,987	1.55	1.95
Hard	25,607	**1.82**	**4.19**
Life	17,459	1.38	1.78
Buddies	13,651	1.68	3.12
All	125,479	1.55	1.95

Torch3vision[4] and the dimensionality is reduced to 100 using the principal component analysis technique. The visual similarity of any two faces is computed via Eq.(6). Table 2 reports the number of images, average number of detected faces per image and the average number of detected names per caption for each of the subset, as well as the whole database. The four subsets help us to understand more comprehensive about the performance of each algorithm on different data sets. Specifically, in the *Easy* subset each caption has at most 2 names, while in the *Hard* subset each caption has 3 or more names. The *Life* subset has captions written by professional editors and the *Buddies* subset contains items with people frequently appearing together (names that appear at least 50 times together in the whole database).

5.2 Evaluation Metric

We evaluate the face-name association performance via two different methods.

- The first evaluation metric is *Accuracy* [14], which measures the percentage of correct assignments over all detected faces including null assignments (a face is not mentioned by a name);
- The second evaluation metric is *Precision* [14], which is the percentage of correct assignments over all faces assigned to a name (not null).

The null assignment is a special point of the face-name association task distinguishing from the face annotation task. Thus, accuracy is a compositive way to measure both the face-name and face-null assignments, while precision only measures the face-name correctness.

5.3 Comparisons and Experimental Results

We investigate many state-of-the-art unsupervised face-name association algorithms including Constrained GMM (CGMM, [1,8]), Graph-based Clustering (GC, [8]) and Constrained K-means (CKM, [14]). Among these methods, CKM does not conform to the constraint C2 and C3. Moreover, we also conduct the algorithm majority voting described in 4.3 as a simple baseline (BASELINE). Our proposed approach FACD has two versions – association by commute distance and anchor-based commute distance. We use CD and ACD to represent them respectively.

[4]`http://torch3vision.idiap.ch`

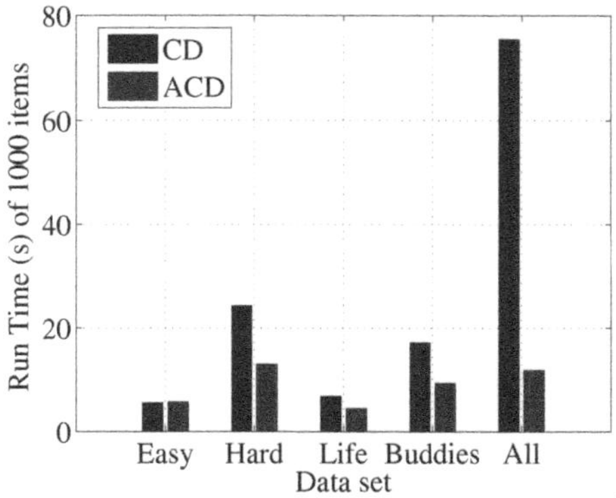

Figure 5: Average on-line running time (seconds) of 1000 items for CD and ACD on each of the four subsets and the whole database.

We evaluate the face-name association for each item of the whole database and its four subsets, and report the average accuracy and precision results in **Table 3** and **Table 4**. Note that, our experimental setup for unsupervised face-name association is exactly the same with that in [14]. From the tables, we find that our algorithms CD and ACD are significantly better than the other comparison methods in some cases. *e.g.*, CD and ACD perform best on the *hard* subset for both accuracy and precision, suggesting that they are particularly well suited for cases in which the captions are noisy (more names than faces). While for the *Buddies* subset, CD and ACD have close performance to the other methods, indicating that they are affected by the high co-occurrence problem. In the buddies item graphs, the buddy people would appear multiple times, making the commute distance less distinguishable for the right associations. In the all, CD and ACD are the best two in the whole database (*all*), which demonstrates the effectiveness of our framework.

Besides the accuracy and precision results, we also record the on-line running time of our method CD and ACD on each of the data set. Note that CD and ACD are the best two methods in performance, so we ignore the running time of the other methods. The time cost is dependent on both the number of items and data complexity (number of faces or names in each item). In Fig.5, the blue/red bar stands for the average running time of 1,000 items for CD/ACD on each data set. We find that, ACD is faster than CD in most cases. Specially, when the data scale is large (*All*), CD requires much more time than ACD. This is because CD's cost is depend on q while ACD is depend on d. The results prove the efficiency of our anchor-based method.

5.4 Parameter Selection

Parameter selection plays a key role to many algorithms. For our methods, there are three main parameters: p and d and ϵ. Parameter p is the number of top faces selected from each name to form the candidate face set in on-line stage. In Fig.6, we record the accuracy results as well as the total running time of CD on *Hard* dataset. When p increases, the total running time grows very fast. So we fix

Table 3: **Accuracy (%) comparisons on the four subsets and the entire database. The best result in each row is indicated by the bold font. If the second best is very close to the first, it is also shown in bold.**

	Comparison methods			Methods proposed in this paper		
Method:	CGMM	GC	CKM	BASELINE	CD	ACD
Easy	55.0	56.6	54.3	45.8	**58.2**	**58.2**
Hard	31.4	28.9	22.5	22.7	**35.7**	**36.0**
Life	50.9	**51.6**	51.5	41.5	48.8	49.4
Buddies	32.9	**34.9**	33.3	29.1	33.5	**34.7**
All	48.1	47.4	42.0	37.0	49.0	**50.9**

Table 4: **Precision (%) comparisons on the four subsets and the entire database. The best result in each row is indicated by the bold font. If the second best is very close to the first, it is also shown in bold.**

	Comparison methods			Methods proposed in this paper		
Method:	CGMM	GC	CKM	BASELINE	CD	ACD
Easy	59.2	58.2	56.0	50.1	**62.9**	**63.0**
Hard	25.6	26.2	22.3	21.0	**29.2**	**29.3**
Life	52.6	53.4	53.1	45.9	**58.9**	**59.2**
Buddies	32.8	34.0	33.3	29.4	35.2	**36.0**
All	46.2	44.4	41.4	35.6	**52.4**	47.6

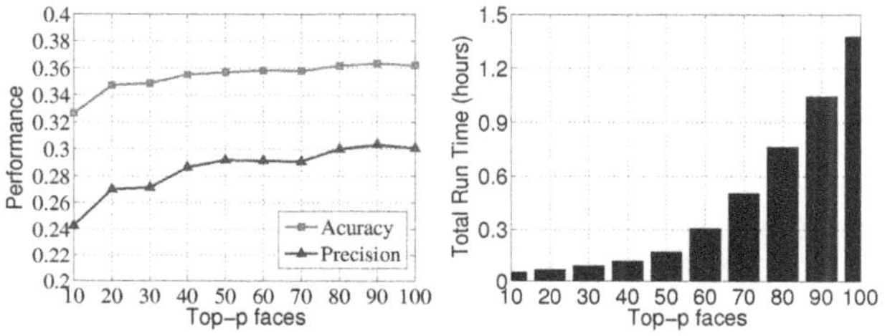

(a) Performance (b) Running Time

Figure 6: Performance and running time vs. parameter p selection for algorithm CD. All the results are evaluated on the *Hard* subset (25,607 itmes).

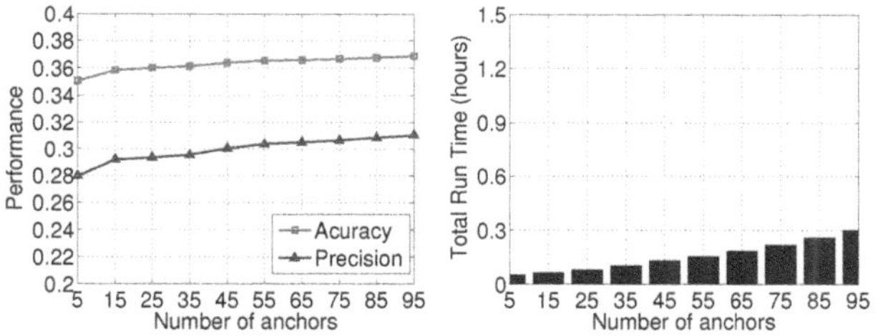

(a) Performance (b) Running Time

Figure 7: Performance and running time vs. number of anchors for algorithm ACD. All the results are evaluated on the *Hard* subset (25,607 itmes).

p to 50 (relative high accuracy and low time cost) for both CD and ACD. Parameter d is the number of anchors used in an anchor graph. In Fig.6, we record the accuracy results as well as the total running time of ACD on *Hard* dataset. When d increases, the accuracy and running time grows very slowly. So we fix d to 25 for ACD.

Threshold ϵ is selected beforehand. In our experiments, we set it to the value at $r\%$ position of all the face-name commute distances (ascending). How to select the parameter r is a problem. We carefully tune it and choose a balance point between good accuracy and precision. Fig.8 is an example: We draw the performance of CD and ACD on the whole set when r varies. The average of accuracy and precision is denoted by a black broken line. Thus, we set $r\% = 0.35$ in this case. Finally, we use 0.4 for *Hard* set, 0.35 for *All* set, and 0.6 for the other three sets. In addition, we set the parameter σ in Eq.(6) to 5.

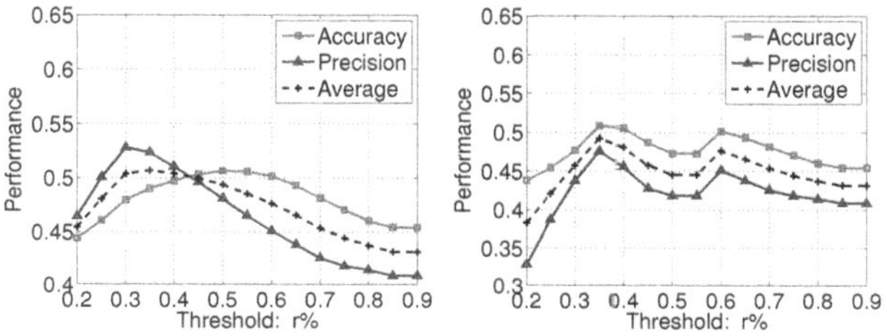

(a) CD (b) ACD

Figure 8: Performance vs. threshold r % on the entire database (*All*). The black broken line is the average of Accuracy and Precision.

6. CONCLUSION AND FUTURE WORK

In this paper, we have proposed a face-name association via commute distance (FACD) framework as a comprehensive framework capable of dealing with the unsupervised face-name association task. FACD has one off-line index stage and one on-line match stage. In the off-line stage, a name-face index structure is established for efficient face retrieval. In the on-line stage, each request image-caption item is processed independently. Specifically, we build a unified graph for each item and measure the face-name relationship via commute distance on the graph. In this way, both the face-name and face-null assignments can be solved in the same framework. Moreover, we propose a novel anchor-based commute distance algorithm to accelerate the distance computation. Experiment results have demostrate the effectiveness and efficiency of our proposed approach.

In our framework, we adopt a simple strategy to determine the threshold ϵ - we use a global threshold. Can we adopt some other method to select it? Is it possible to find a local threshold for each image-caption item? In the future work, we will study these questions. The "right to left" position information is valuable for face naming. However, the data set is collected from the web and the caption style is very free. Only a few images are described in order. What's more, most of the captions don't have the explicit "left to right" or "right to left" words, so we don't know the right order. We will try to use this information in the future work.

7. ACKNOWLEDGEMENT

This work was supported in part by National Natural Science Foundation of China under Grant 91120302 and 61173186, National Basic Research Program of China (973 Program) under Grant 2012CB316404, Fundamental Research Funds for the Central Universities, Program for New Century Excellent Talents in University (NCET-09-0685), Zhejiang Provincial Natural Science Foundation under Grant No Y1101043 and Foundation of Zhejiang Provincial Educational Department under Grant No Y201018240 and Fundamental Research Funds for the Central Universities.

8. REFERENCES

[1] T. Berg, A. Berg, J. Edwards, and D. Forsyth. Who's in the picture? volume 17, pages 137–144, 2005.

[2] T. Berg, A. Berg, J. Edwards, M. Maire, R. White, Y. Teh, E. Learned-Miller, and D. Forsyth. Names and faces in the news. In *Proceedings of the 2004 IEEE Computer Society Conference on Computer Vision and Pattern Recognition*, volume 2, pages II–848, 2004.

[3] D. Cai, X. He, and J. Han. Spectral regression: A unified subspace learning framework for content-based image retrieval. In *Proceedings of the 15th ACM International Conference on Multimedia*, pages 403–412, 2007.

[4] D. Cai, X. He, W.-Y. Ma, J.-R. Wen, and H. Zhang. Organizing WWW images based on the analysis of page layout and web link structure. In *Proceedings of the 2004 IEEE International Conference on Multimedia and Expo*, pages 113–116, 2004.

[5] X. Chen and D. Cai. Large scale spectral clustering with landmark-based representation. In *Proceedings of the Twenty-Fifth AAAI Conference on Artificial Intelligence*, 2011.

[6] R. Datta, D. Joshi, J. Li, and J. Wang. Image retrieval: Ideas, influences, and trends of the new age. *ACM Computing Surveys (CSUR)*, 40(2):5, 2008.

[7] F. Fouss, A. Pirotte, J. Renders, and M. Saerens. Random-walk computation of similarities between nodes of a graph with application to collaborative recommendation. *IEEE Transactions on Knowledge and Data Engineering*, 19(3):355–369, 2007.

[8] M. Guillaumin, T. Mensink, J. Verbeek, and C. Schmid. Automatic face naming with caption-based supervision. In *Proceedings of the 2008 IEEE Computer Society Conference on Computer Vision and Pattern Recognition*, pages 1–8. IEEE, 2008.

[9] X. He, D. Cai, and J. Han. Learning a maximum margin subspace for image retrieval. *IEEE Transactions on Knowledge and Data Engineering*, 20(2):189–201, 2008.

[10] N. Khoa and S. Chawla. Robust outlier detection using commute time and eigenspace embedding. *Advances in Knowledge Discovery and Data Mining*, pages 422–434, 2010.

[11] Y. Lin, R. Jin, D. Cai, and X. He. Random projection with filtering for nearly duplicate search. In *Proceedings of the Twenty-Sixth Conference on Artificial Intelligence*, 2012.

[12] W. Liu, J. He, and S. Chang. Large graph construction for scalable semi-supervised learning. In *Proceedings of the 27th International Conference on Machine Learning*, pages 679–686, 2010.

[13] L. Lovász. Random walks on graphs: A survey. *Combinatorics, Paul Erdos is Eighty*, 2(1):1–46, 1993.

[14] M. Özcan, L. Jie23, V. Ferrari, and B. Caputo. A large-scale database of images and captions for automatic face naming. In *Proceedings of the British Machine Vision Conference*, 2011.

[15] S. Satoh, Y. Nakamura, and T. Kanade. Name-it: Naming and detecting faces in news videos. *IEEE Transactions on Multimedia*, 6(1):22–35, 1999.

[16] D. Spielman and N. Srivastava. Graph sparsification by effective resistances. In *Proceedings of the 40th annual ACM symposium on Theory of computing*, pages 563–568, 2008.

[17] U. Von Luxburg. A tutorial on spectral clustering. *Statistics and Computing*, 17(4):395–416, 2007.

[18] D. Wang, S. Hoi, and Y. He. Mining weakly labeled web facial images for search-based face annotation. In *Proceedings of the 34th international ACM SIGIR conference on Research and development in Information*, pages 535–544, 2011.

[19] D. Wang, S. Hoi, Y. He, and J. Zhu. Retrieval-based face annotation by weak label regularized local coordinate coding. In *Proceedings of the 19th ACM international conference on Multimedia*, pages 353–362, 2011.

[20] C. Wu, J. Zhu, D. Cai, C. Chen, and J. Bu. Semi-supervised nonlinear hashing using bootstrap sequential projection learning. *IEEE Transactions on Knowledge and Data Engineering*, 2012.

[21] Z. Wu, Q. Ke, J. Sun, and H. Shum. Scalable face image retrieval with identity-based quantization and multi-reference re-ranking. In *Proceedings of the 2010 IEEE Computer Society Conference on Computer Vision and Pattern Recognition*, pages 3469–3476, 2010.

[22] B. Xu, J. Bu, C. Chen, D. Cai, X. He, W. Liu, and J. Luo. Efficient manifold ranking for image retrieval. In *Proceedings of the 34th international ACM SIGIR conference on Research and development in Information*, pages 525–534, 2011.

[23] J. Yang and A. Hauptmann. Naming every individual in news video monologues. In *Proceedings of the 12th annual ACM international conference on Multimedia*, pages 580–587, 2004.

[24] K. Yu, T. Zhang, and Y. Gong. Nonlinear learning using local coordinate coding. volume 22, pages 2223–2231, 2009.

[25] K. Zhang, J. Kwok, and B. Parvin. Prototype vector machine for large scale semi-supervised learning. In *Proceedings of the 26th Annual International Conference on Machine Learning*, pages 1233–1240, 2009.

[26] L. Zhang, C. Chen, W. Chen, J. Bu, D. Cai, and X. He. Convex experimental design using manifold structure for image retrieval. In *Proceedings of the 17th ACM international conference on Multimedia*, pages 45–54, 2009.

[27] L. Zhang, L. Chen, M. Li, and H. Zhang. Automated annotation of human faces in family albums. In *Proceedings of the 8th ACM international conference on Multimedia*, pages 355–358, 2003.

[28] L. Zhang, Y. Hu, M. Li, W. Ma, and H. Zhang. Efficient propagation for face annotation in family albums. In *Proceedings of the 12th annual ACM international conference on Multimedia*, pages 716–723, 2004.

[29] D. Zhou, J. Weston, A. Gretton, O. Bousquet, and B. Schölkopf. Ranking on data manifolds. volume 16, pages 169–176, 2004.

[30] J. Zhu, S. Hoi, and M. Lyu. Face annotation using transductive kernel fisher discriminant. *IEEE Transactions on Multimedia*, 10(1):86–96, 2008.

On Shape and the Computability of Emotions

Xin Lu Poonam Suryanarayan Reginald B. Adams, Jr.
Jia Li Michelle G. Newman James Z. Wang*
The Pennsylvania State University, University Park, Pennsylvania
{xinlu, pzs126, regadams, jiali, mgn1, jwang}@psu.edu

ABSTRACT

We investigated how shape features in natural images influence emotions aroused in human beings. Shapes and their characteristics such as roundness, angularity, simplicity, and complexity have been postulated to affect the emotional responses of human beings in the field of visual arts and psychology. However, no prior research has modeled the dimensionality of emotions aroused by roundness and angularity. Our contributions include an in-depth statistical analysis to understand the relationship between shapes and emotions. Through experimental results on the International Affective Picture System (IAPS) dataset we provide evidence for the significance of roundness-angularity and simplicity-complexity on predicting emotional content in images. We combine our shape features with other state-of-the-art features to show a gain in prediction and classification accuracy. We model emotions from a dimensional perspective in order to predict valence and arousal ratings which have advantages over modeling the traditional discrete emotional categories. Finally, we distinguish images with strong emotional content from emotionally neutral images with high accuracy.

Categories and Subject Descriptors

H.3.1 [**Information Storage and Retrieval**]: Content analysis and indexing; I.4.7 [**Image Processing and Computer Vision**]: Feature measurement

General Terms

Algorithms, Experimentation, Human Factors

*J. Li and J. Z. Wang are also affiliated with the National Science Foundation. This material is based upon work supported by the Foundation. Any opinions, findings, and conclusions or recommendations expressed in this material are those of the authors and do not necessarily reflect the views of the Foundation.

MM'12, October 29-November 2, 2012, Nara, Japan.

Keywords

Human Emotion, Psychology, Shape Features

1. INTRODUCTION

The study of human visual preferences and the emotions imparted by various works of art and natural images has long been an active topic of research in the field of visual arts and psychology. A computational perspective to this problem has interested many researchers and resulted in articles on modeling the emotional and aesthetic content in images [10, 11, 13]. However, there is a wide gap between what humans can perceive and feel and what can be explained using current computational image features. Bridging this gap is considered the "holy grail" of computer vision and the multimedia community. There have been many psychological theories suggesting a link between human affective responses and the low-level features in images apart from the semantic content. In this work, we try to extend our understanding of some of the low-level features which have not been explored in the study of visual affect through extensive statistical analyses.

In contrast to prior studies on image aesthetics, which intended to estimate the level of visual appeal [10], we try to leverage some of the psychological studies on characteristics of shapes and their effect on human emotions. These studies indicate that roundness and complexity of shapes are fundamental to understanding emotions.

- **Roundness** - Studies [4, 21] indicate that geometric properties of visual displays convey emotions like anger and happiness. Bar *et al.* [5] confirm the hypothesis that curved contours lead to positive feelings and that sharp transitions in contours trigger a negative bias.
- **Complexity of shapes** - As enumerated in various works of art, humans visually prefer simplicity. Any stimulus pattern is always perceived in the most simplistic structural setting. Though the perception of simplicity is partially subjective to individual experiences, it can also be highly affected by two objective factors, parsimony and orderliness. Parsimony refers to the minimalistic structures that are used in a given representation, whereas orderliness refers to the simplest way of organizing these structures [3].

These findings provide an intuitive understanding of the low-level image features that motivate the affective response, but the small scale of studies from which the inferences have been drawn makes the results less convincing. In order

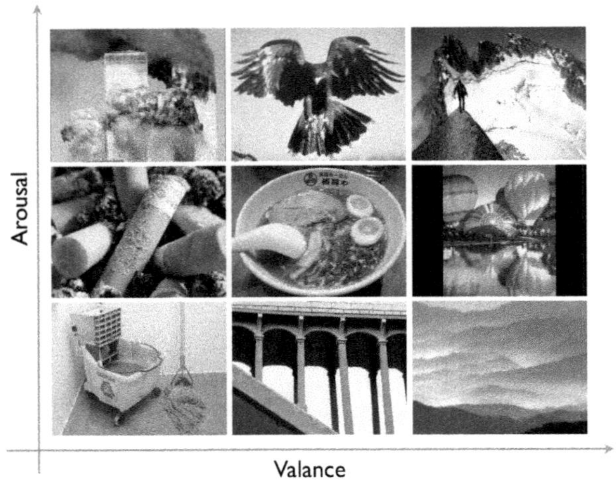

Figure 1: Example images from IAPS (The International Affective Picture System) dataset [15]. Images with positive affect from left to right, and high arousal from bottom to top.

to make a fair comparison of observations, psychologists created the standard International Affective Picture System (IAPS) [15] dataset by obtaining user ratings on three basic dimensions of affect, namely *valence*, *arousal*, and *dominance* (Figure 1). However, the computational work on the IAPS dataset to understand the visual factors that affect emotions has been preliminary. Researchers [9, 11, 18, 23, 25, 26] investigated factors such as color, texture, composition, and simple semantics to understand emotions, but have not quantitatively addressed the effect of perceptual shapes. The study that did explore shapes by Zhang *et al.* [27] predicted emotions evoked by viewing abstract art images through low-level features like color, shape, and texture. However, this work only handles abstract images, and focused on the representation of textures with little accountability of shape.

The current work is an attempt to systematically investigate how perceptual shapes contribute to emotions aroused from images through modeling the visual properties of roundness, angularity and simplicity using shapes. Unlike edges or boundaries, shapes are influenced by the context and the surrounding shapes influence the perception of any individual shape [3]. To model these shapes in the images, the proposed framework statistically analyzes the line segments and curves extracted from strong continuous contours. Investigating the quantitative relationship between perceptual shapes and emotions aroused from images is non-trivial. First, emotions aroused by images are subjective. Thus, individuals may not have the same response to a given image, making the representation of shapes in complex images highly challenging. Second, images are not composed of simple and regular shapes, making it difficult to model the complexity existing in natural images [3].

Leveraging the proposed shape features, the current work attempts to automatically distinguish the images with strong emotional content from emotionally neutral images. In psychology, emotionally neutral images refer to images which evoke very weak or no emotions in humans.

Also, the current study models emotions from a non-categorical or discrete emotional perspective. In previous work, emotions were distinctly classified into categories like anger, fear, disgust, amusement, awe, and contentment,

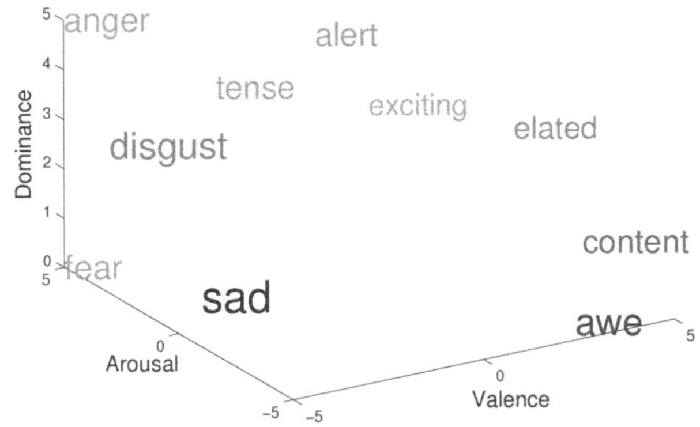

Figure 2: Dimensional representation of emotions and the location of categorical emotions in these dimensions (Valance, Arousal, and Dominance).

among others. This paper is, to our knowledge, the first to predict emotions aroused from images by adopting a dimensional representation (Figure 2). Valence represents the positive or negative aspect of human emotions, where common emotions, like joy and happiness, are positive, whereas anger and fear are negative. Arousal describes the human physiological state of being reactive to stimuli. A higher value of arousal indicates higher excitation. Dominance represents the controlling nature of the emotion. For instance, anger can be more controlling than fear. Researchers [2, 12, 28] have investigated the emotional content of videos through the dimensional approach. Their emphasis was on the accommodation of the change in features over time rather than low-level feature improvement. However, static images, with less information, are often more challenging to interpret. Low-level features need to be punctuated.

This work adopts the dimensional approaches of emotion motivated by recent studies in psychology, which argued for the strengths of dimensional approaches. According to Bradley and Lang [6], categorized emotions do not provide a one-to-one relationship between the content and emotion of an image since participants perceive different emotions in the same image. This highlights the utility of a dimensional approach, which controls for the intercorrelated nature of human emotions aroused by images. From the perspective of neuroscience studies, it has been demonstrated that the dimensional approach is more consistent with how the brain is organized to process emotions at their most basic level [14, 17]. Dimensional approaches also allow the separation of images with strong emotional content from images with weak emotional content.

In summary, our **main contributions** are:

- We systematically investigate the correlation between visual shapes and emotions aroused from images.
- We quantitatively model the concepts of roundness-angularity and simplicity-complexity from the perspective of shapes using a dimensional approach.
- We distinguish images with strong emotional content from those with weak emotional content.

The rest of the paper is organized as follows, Section 2 provides a summary of previous work. Section 3 introduces some definitions and themes which recur throughout the paper. The overall framework followed by details of the perceptual shape descriptors are described in Section 4. Experimental results and in-depth analyses are presented in Section 5. We conclude in Section 6.

2. RELATED WORK

Previous work [11, 26, 18] predicted emotions aroused by images mainly through training classifiers on visual features to distinguish categorical emotions, such as happiness, anger, and sad. Low-level stimuli such as color and composition have been widely used in computational modeling of emotions. Affective concepts were modeled using color palettes, which showed that the bag of colors and Fisher vectors (i.e., higher order statistics about the distribution of local descriptors) were effective [9]. Zhang *et al.* [27] characterized shape through Zernike features, edge statistics features, object statistics, and Gabor filters. Emotion-histogram and bag-of-emotion features were used to classify emotions by Solli *et al.* [24]. These emotion metrics were extracted based on the findings from psycho-physiological experiments indicating that emotions can be represented through homogeneous emotion regions and transitions among them.

The first work that comprehensively modeled categorical emotions, Machajdik and Hanbury [18] used color, texture, composition, content, and semantic level features such as number of faces to model eight discrete emotional categories. Besides the eight basic emotions, to model categorized emotions, adjectives or word pairs were used to represent human emotions. The earliest work based on the Kansei system employs 23 word pairs (e.g., like-dislike, warm-cool, cheerful-gloomy) to establish the emotional space [23]. Along the same lines, researchers enumerated more word pairs to reach a universal, distinctive, and comprehensive representation of emotions in Wang *et al.* [25]. Yet, the aforementioned approaches of emotion representation ignore the interrelationship among types of emotions.

3. CONCEPT INTERPRETATION

This work captures emotions evoked by images by leveraging shape descriptors. Shapes in images are difficult to capture, mainly due to the perceptual and merging boundaries of objects which are often not easy to differentiate using even state-of-the-art segmentation or contour extraction algorithms. In contemporary computer vision literature [7, 20], there are a number of statistical representations of shape through characteristics like the straightness, sinuosity, linearity, circularity, elongation, orientation, symmetry, and the mass of a curve. We chose roundness-angularity and simplicity-complexity characteristics because they have been found previously by psychologists to influence the affect of human beings through controlled human subject studies. Symmetry is also known to effect emotion and aesthetics of images [22]. However, quantifying symmetry in natural images is challenging.

To make it more convenient to introduce the shape features proposed, this section defines the four terms used: line segments, angles, continuous lines, and curves. The framework for extracting perceptual shapes through lines and curves is derived from [8]. The contours are extracted using the algorithm in [1], which used color, texture, and brightness of each image for contour extraction. The extracted contours are of different intensities and indicate the algorithm's confidence on the presence of edges. Considering the temporal resolution of our vision system, we adopted a threshold of 40%. Example results are presented in Figures 3, 4, 5, and 6. Pixels with an intensity higher than 40% are treated equally, which results in the binary contour map presented in the second column. The last three columns show the line segments, continuous lines, and curves.

Line segments - Line segments refer to short straight lines generated by fitting nearby pixels. We generated line segments from each image to capture its structure. From the structure of the image, we propose to interpret the simplicity-complexity. We extracted locally optimized line segments by connecting neighboring pixels from the contours extracted from the image [16].

Angles - Angles in the image are obtained by calculating angles between each of any two intersecting line segments extracted previously. According to Julian Hochberg's theory [3], the number of angles and the number of different angles in an image can be effectively used to describe its simiplicity-complexity. The distribution of angles also indicates the degree of angularity of the image. A high number of acute angles makes an image more angular.

Continuous lines - Continuous lines are generated by connecting intersecting line segments having the same orientations with a small margin of error. Line segments of inconsistent orientations can be categorized as either corner points or points of inflexion. Corner points, shown in Figure 7(a), refer to angles that are lower than 90 degrees. Inflexion points, shown in Figure 7(b), refer to the midpoint of two angles with opposite orientations. Continuous lines and the degree of curving can be used to interpret the complexity of the image.

Curves - Curves are a subset of continuous lines, the collection of which are employed to measure the roundness of an image. To achieve this, we consider each curve as a section of an ellipse, thus we use ellipses to fit continuous lines. Fitted curves are represented by parameters of its corresponding ellipses.

4. CAPTURING EMOTION FROM SHAPE

For decades, numerous theories have been promoted that are focused on the relationship between emotions and the visual characteristics of simplicity, complexity, roundness, and angularity. Despite these theories, researchers have yet to resolve how to model these relationships quantitatively. In this section, we propose to use shape features to capture those visual characteristics. By identifying the link between shape features and emotions, we are able to determine the relationship between the aforementioned visual characteristics and emotions.

We now present the details of the proposed shape features: line segments, angles, continuous lines, and curves. A total of 219 shape features are summarized in Table 1.

4.1 Line segments

Psychologists and artists have claimed that the simplicity-complexity of an image is determined not only by lines or curves, but also by its overall structure and support [3]. Based on this idea, we employed line segments extracted from images to capture their structure. Particularly, we used the orientation, length, and mass of line segments to determine the complexity of the images.

Orientation - To capture an overall orientation, we employed statistical measures of minimum (min), maximum

(a) Original | (b) Contours | (c) Line segments | (d) Continuous lines | (e) Ellipse on curves

Figure 3: Perceptual shapes of images with *high valance*.

(a) Original | (b) Contours | (c) Line segments | (d) Continuous lines | (e) Ellipse on curves

Figure 4: Perceptual shapes of images with *low valance*.

Table 1: Summary of shape features.

Category	Short Name	#
Line Segments	Orientation	60
	Length	11
	Mass of the image	4
Continuous Lines	Degree of curving	14
	Length span	9
	Line count	4
	Mass of continuous lines	4
Angles	Angle count	3
	Angular metrics	35
Curves	Fitness	14
	Circularity	17
	Area	8
	Orientation	14
	Mass of curves	4
	Top round curves	18

(max), 0.75 quantile, 0.25 quantile, the difference between 0.75 quantile and 0.25 quantile, the difference between max and min, sum, total number, median, mean, and standard deviation (we will later refer to these as {statistical measures}), and entropy. We experimented with both 6- and 18-bin histograms. The unique orientations were measured based on the two histograms to capture the simplicity-complexity of the image.

Among all line segments, horizontal lines and vertical lines are known [3] to be static and to represent the feelings of calm and stability within the image. Horizontal lines suggest peace and calm, whereas vertical lines indicate strength. To capture the emotions evoked by these characteristics, we counted the number of horizontal lines and vertical lines through an 18-bin histogram. The orientation θ, of horizontal lines fall within $0° < \theta < 10°$ or $170° < \theta < 180°$, and $80° < \theta < 100°$ for vertical lines.

Length - The length of line segments reflects the simplicity of images. Images with simple structure might use long lines to fit contours, whereas complex contours have shorter lines. We characterized the length distribution by calculating the {statistical measures} of lengths of line segments within the image.

Mass of the image - The centroid of line segments may indicate associated relationships among line segments within the visual design [3]. Hence, we calculate the mean and standard deviation of the x and y coordinates of the line segments to find the mass of each image.

Some of the example images and their features are presented in Figures 8 and 9. Figure 8 presents the ten lowest mean values of the length of line segments. The first row shows the original images, the second row shows the

(a) Original (b) Contours (c) Line segments (d) Continuous lines (e) Ellipse on curves

Figure 5: Perceptual shapes of images with *high arousal*.

(a) Original (b) Contours (c) Line segments (d) Continuous lines (e) Ellipse on curves

Figure 6: Perceptual shapes of images with *low arousal*.

line segments extracted from these images and the third row shows the 18-bin histogram for line segments in the images. The 18 bins refer to the number of line segments with an orientation of $[-90 + 10(i-1), -90 + 10i)$ degrees where $i \in \{1, 2, ..., 18\}$. Similarly, Figure 9 presents the ten highest mean values of the length of line segments.

(a) Corner point (b) Point of inflexion

Figure 7: The corner point and point of inflexion.

These two figures indicate that the length or the orientation cannot be examined separately to determine the simplicity-complexity of the image. Lower mean values of the length of line segments might refer to either simple images such as the first four images in Figure 8 or highly complex images such as the last four images in that figure. The histogram of the orientation of line segments helps us to distinguish the complex images from simple images by examining variation of values in each bin.

4.2 Angles

Angles are important elements in analyzing the simplicity-complexity and the angularity of an image. We capture the visual characteristics from angles through two perspectives.

- **Angle count** - We first calculate the two quantitative features claimed by Julian Hochberg, who has attempted to define simplicity (he used the value-laden term "figural goodness") via information theory: "The smaller the amount of information needed to define a given organization as compared to the other alternatives, the more likely that the figure will be so perceived" [3]. Hence this minimal information structure is captured using the number of angles and the percentage of unique angles in the image.
- **Angular metrics** - We use the {statistical measures} to extract angular metrics. We also calculate the 6- and 18-bin histograms on angles and their entropies.

Some of the example images and features are presented in Figures 10 and 11. Images with lowest and highest number of angles are shown along with their corresponding contours in Figure 10. These examples show promising relationships between angular features and simplicity-complexity of the image. Example results for the histogram of angles in the image are presented in Figure 11. The 18 bins refer to the number of line segments with an orientation in $[10(i-1), 10i)$ degrees where $i \in \{1, 2, ..., 18\}$.

4.3 Continuous lines

We attempt to capture the degree of curvature from continuous lines, which has implications for the simplicity-complexity of images. We also calculated the number of continuous lines, which is the third quantitative feature specified by Julian Hochberg [3]. For continuous lines, open/closeness are factors affecting the simplicity-complexity of an image. In the following, we focus on the

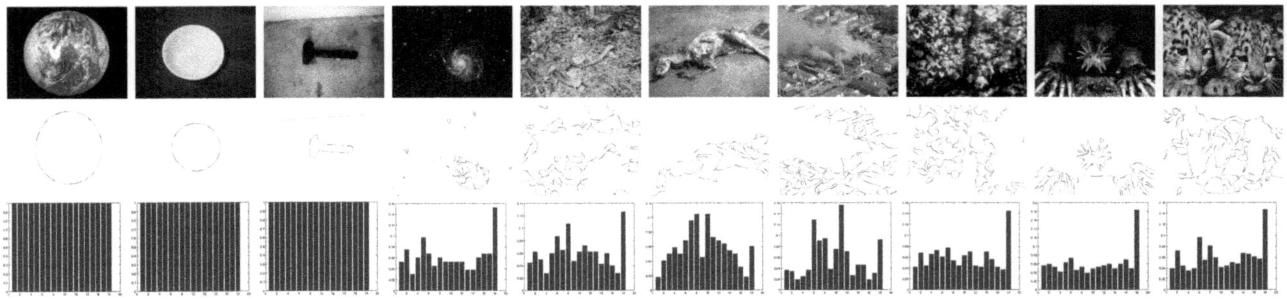

Figure 8: Images with *low* mean value of the length of line segments and their associated orientation histograms. The first row is the original images; the second row shows the line segments; and the third row shows the 18-bin histogram for line segments in the images.

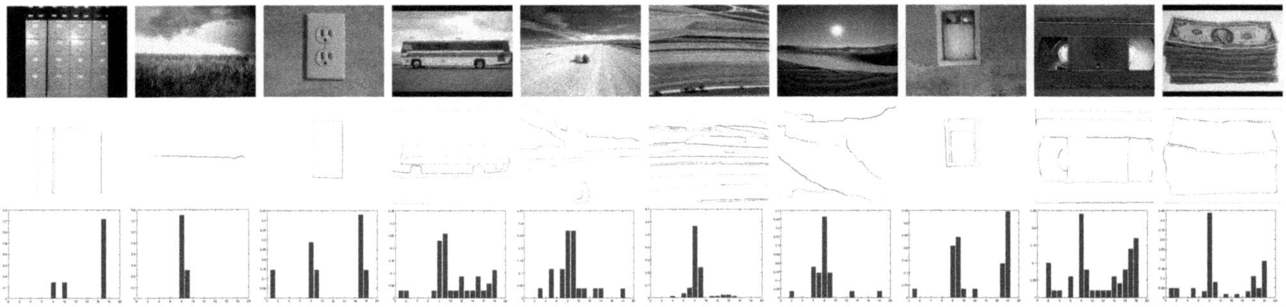

Figure 9: Images with *high* mean value of the length of line segments and their associated orientation histograms. The first row is the original images; the second row shows the line segments; and the third row shows the 18-bin histogram for line segments in the images.

calculation of the degree of curving, the length span value, and the number of open lines and closed lines. The length span refers to the highest Euclidean distance among all pairs of points on the continuous lines.

$$\text{Length Span}(l) = \max_{p_i \in l, p_j \in l} \text{EuclideanDist}(p_i, p_j), \quad (1)$$

where $\{p_1, p_2, ..., p_N\}$ are the points on continuous line l.

- **Degree of curving** - We calculated the degree of curving of each line as

  $$\text{Degree of Curving}(l) = \text{Length Span}(l)/N, \quad (2)$$

  where N is the number of points on continuous line l.

  To capture the statistical characteristics of contiguous lines in the image, we calculated the {statistical measures}. We also generated a 5-bin histogram on the degree of curving of all continuous lines (Figures 12 and 13).
- **Length span** - We used {statistical measures} for the length span of all continuous lines.
- **Line count** - We counted the total number of continuous lines, the total number of open lines, and the total number of closed lines in the image.

4.4 Curves

We used the nature of curves to model the roundness of images. For each curve, we calculated the extent of fit to an ellipse as well as the parameters of the ellipse such as its area, circularity, and mass of curves. The curve features are explained in detail below.

- **Fitness, area, circularity** - The fitness of an ellipse refers to the overlap between the proposed ellipse and the curves in the image. The area of the fitted ellipse is also calculated. The circularity is represented by the ratio of the minor and major axes of the ellipses. The angular orientation of the ellipse is also measured. For each of the measures, we used the {statistical measures} and entropies of the histograms as the features to depict the roundness of the image.
- **Mass of curves** - We used the mean value and standard deviation of $(x,\ y)$ coordinates to describe the mass of curves.
- **Top round curves** - To make full use of the discovered curves and to depict roundness, we included the fitness, area, circularity, and mass of curves for each of the top three curves.

Table 2: Average number of curves in terms of the value of fitness in positive and negative images.

	$(0.8, 1]$	$(0.6, 0.8]$	$(0.4, 0.6]$	$(0.2, 0.4]$
Positive imgs	2.12	9.33	5.7	2.68
Negative imgs	1.42	7.5	5.02	2.73

Table 3: Average number of curves in terms of the value of circularity in positive and negative images.

	$(0.8, 1]$	$(0.6, 0.8]$	$(0.4, 0.6]$	$(0.2, 0.4]$
Positive imgs	0.96	2.56	5.1	11.2
Negative imgs	0.73	2.19	4	9.75

To examine the relationship between curves and positive-negative images, we calculated the average number of curves in terms of values of circularity and fitness on positive images (i.e., the value is higher than 6 in the dimension of valance) and negative images (i.e., the value is lower than 4.5 in the dimension of valance).

The results are shown in Tables 2 and 3. Positive images

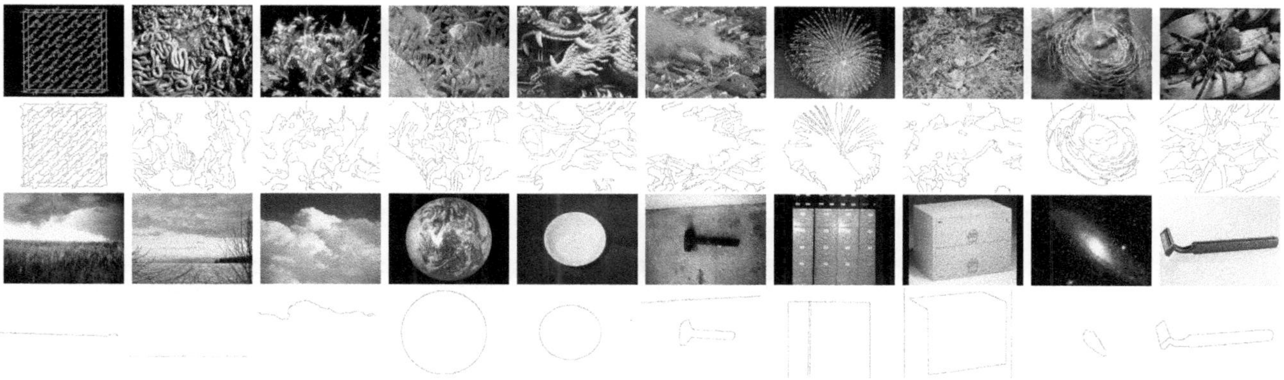

Figure 10: Images with highest and lowest number of angles.

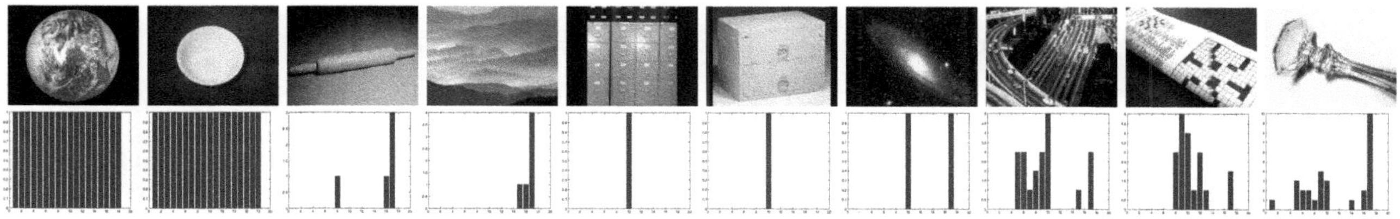

Figure 11: The distribution of angles in images.

have more curves with 60% – 100% fitness to ellipses and higher average curve count.

5. EXPERIMENTS

To demonstrate the relationship between proposed shape features and the felt emotions, the shape features were utilized in three tasks. First, we distinguished images with strong emotional content from emotionally neutral images. Second, we fit valence and arousal dimensions using regression methods. We then performed classification on discrete emotional categories. The proposed features were compared with the features discussed in Machajdik *et al.* [18], and overall accuracy was quantified by combining those features. Forward selection and Principal Component Analysis (PCA) strategies were employed for feature selection and to find the best combination of features.

5.1 Dataset

We used two subsets of the IAPS [15] dataset, which were developed by examining human affective responses to color photographs with varying degrees of emotional content. The IAPS dataset contains 1,182 images, wherein each image is associated with an empirically derived mean and standard deviation of valance, arousal, and dominance ratings.

Subset A of the IAPS dataset includes many images with faces and human bodies. Facial expressions and body language strongly affect emotions aroused by images, slight changes of which might lead to an opposite emotion. The proposed shape features are sensitive to faces hence we removed all images with faces and human bodies from the scope of this study. In experiments, we only considered the remaining 484 images, which we labeled as *Subset A*. To provide a better understanding of the ratings of the dataset, we analyzed the distribution of ratings within valence and arousal, as shown in Figure 14. We also calculated average variations of ratings in each rating unit (i.e., 1-2, 2-3, ..., 7-8). Valence ratings between 3 and 4, and 6 and 7, have the maximum variance for single images. Similarly, arousal ratings between 4 and 5 varied the most.

Subset B are images with category labels (with discrete emotions), generated by Mikels [19]. *Subset B* includes eight categories namely, anger, disgust, fear, sadness, amusement, awe, contentment, and excitement, with 394 images in total. *Subset B* is a commonly used dataset, hence we used it to benchmark our classification accuracy with the results mentioned in Machajdik *et al.* [18].

5.2 Identifying Strong Emotional Content

Images with strong emotional content have very high or very low valance and arousal ratings. Images with values around the mean values of valance and arousal lack emotions and wered used as samples for emotionally neutral images.

Based on dimensions of valance and arousal respectively, we generated two sample sets from *Subset A*. In Set 1, images with valence values higher than 6 or lower than 3.5 were considered images with strong emotional content and the rest to represent emotionally neutral images. This resulted in 247 emotional images and 237 neutral images. Similarly, images with arousal values higher than 5.5 or lower than 3.7 were defined as emotional images, and others as neutral images. With similar thresholds, we obtained 239 emotional images and 245 neutral images in Set 2.

We used the traditional Support Vector Machines (SVM) with radial basis function (RBF) kernel to perform the classification task. We trained SVM models using the proposed shape features, Machajdik's features, and combined (Machajdik's and shape) features. Training and testing were performed by dividing the dataset uniformly into training and testing sets. As we removed all images with faces and human bodies, we did not consider facial and skin features discussed in [18]. We used both forward selection and PCA methods to perform feature selection. In the forward selection method, we used the greedy strategy and accumulated one feature at a time to obtain the subset of features that maximized the classification accuracy. The seed features were also chosen at random over

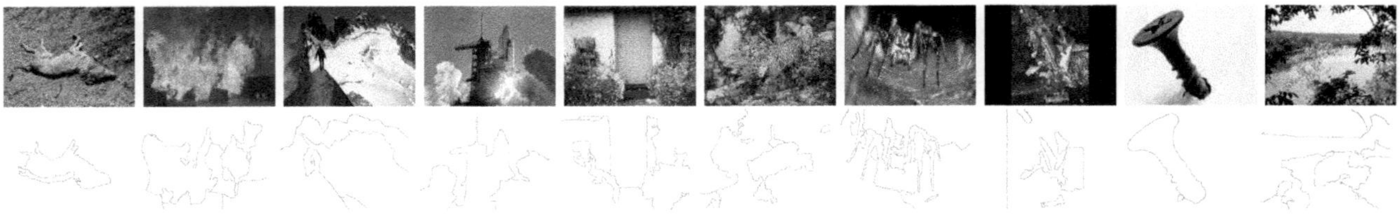

Figure 12: Images with highest degree of curving.

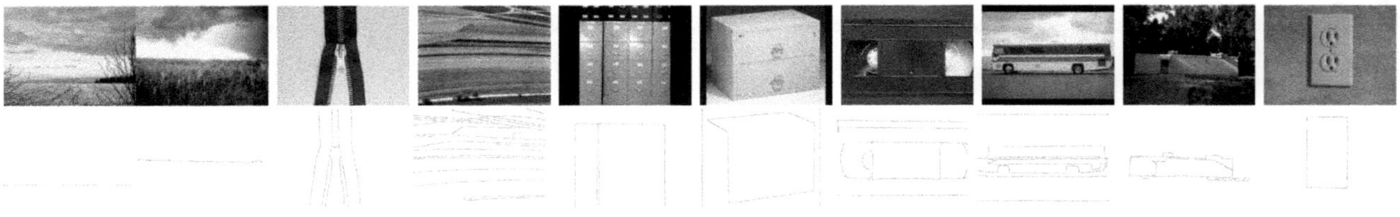

Figure 13: Images with lowest degree of curving.

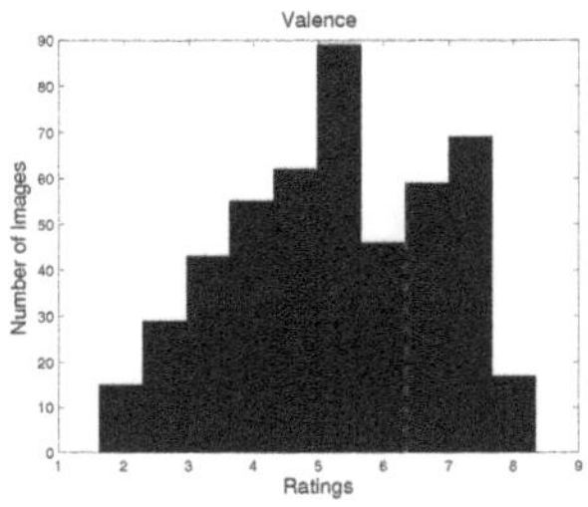

(a) Valence

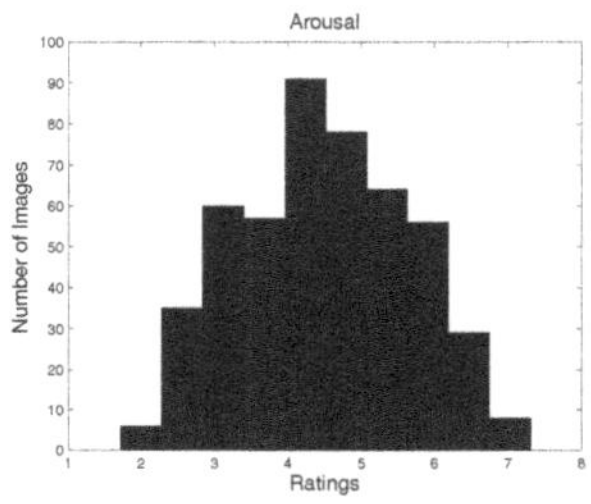

(b) Arousal

Figure 14: Distribution of ratings in IAPS.

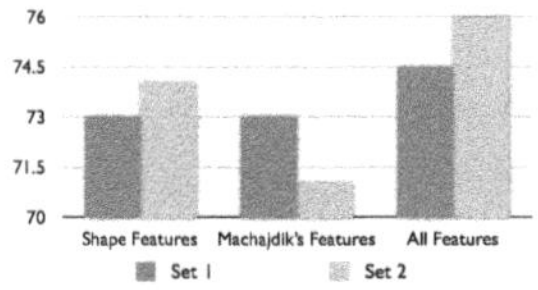

(a) With PCA feature selection

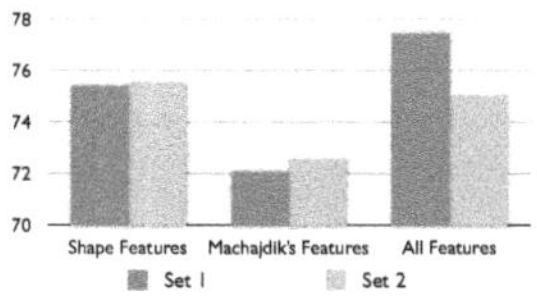

(b) Without PCA

Figure 15: Classification accuracy (%) for emotional images and neutral images (Set 1 and Set 2 are defined in Section 5.2).

multiple iterations to obtain better results. Our analyses showed that the forward selection strategy achieved greater accuracy for Set 2, whereas PCA performed better for Set 1 (Figure 15). The feature comparison showed that the combined (Machajdik's and shape) features achieved the highest classification accuracy, whereas individually the shape features alone were much stronger than the features from [18] (Machajdik's features). This result is intuitive since emotions evoked by images cannot be well represented by shapes alone and can definitely be bolstered by other image features including their color composition and texture. By analyzing valence and arousal ratings of the correctly classified images, we observed that very complex/simple, round and angular images had strong emotional content and high valence values. Simple structured images with very low degrees of curving also tends to portray strong emotional content as well as to have high arousal values.

By analyzing the individual features for classification accuracy we found that line count, fitness, length span, degree of curving, and the number of horizontal lines achieved the best classification accuracy in Set 1. Fitness and line orientation were more dominant in Set 2.

We present a few example images, which were wrongly classified based on the proposed shape features in Figures 16 and 17. The misclassification can be explained as a shortcoming of the shape features in understanding the semantics. Some of the images generated extreme emotions based on image content irrespective of the low-level features. Besides the semantics, our performance was also limited by the performance of the contour extraction algorithm.

5.3 Fitting the Dimensionality of Emotion

Emotions can be represented by word pairs, as previously done in [23]. However, some emotions are difficult to label. Modeling basic emotional dimensions helps in alleviating this problem. We represented emotion as a tuple consisting of valence and arousal values. The values of valence and arousal were in the range of (1, 9). In order to predict the values of valence and arousal we proposed to learn a regression model for either dimension separately.

We used SVM regression with RBF kernel to model the valance and arousal values using shape, Machajdik's features, as well as the combination of features. The mean squared error (MSE) was computed for each of the individual features as well as combined for both valence and arousal values separately. The MSE values are shown in Figure 18(a). These figures show that the valance values were modeled more accurately by Machajdik's features than our shape features. Arousal was well modeled by shape features with a mean squared error of 0.9. However, the combined feature performance did not show any improvements. The results indicated that visual shapes provide a stronger cue in understanding the valence as opposed to the combination of color, texture, and composition in images.

We also computed the correlation between quantified individual shape features and valence-arousal ratings. The higher the correlation, the more relevant the features were. Through this process we found that angular count, fitness, circularity, and orientation of line segments showed higher correlations with valance, whereas angle count, angle metrics, straightness, length span, and orientation of curves had higher correlations with arousal.

5.4 Classifying Categorized Emotions

To evaluate the relationship between shape features and emotions on discrete emotions, we classified images into one of the eight categories, anger, disgust, fear, sadness,

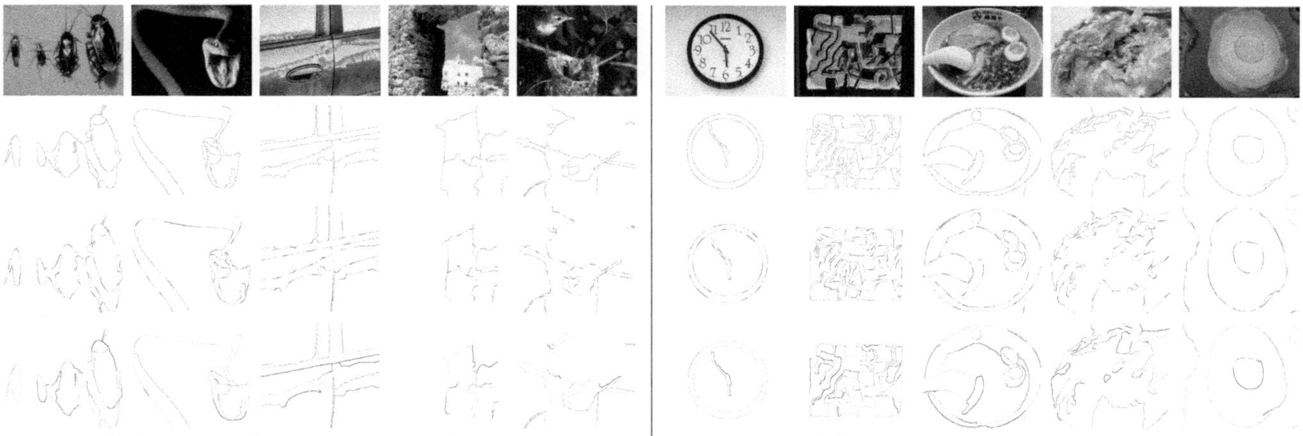

(a) Images with strong emotional content | (b) Emotionally neutral images

Figure 16: Examples of misclassification in Set 1. The four rows are original images, image contours, line segments, and continuous lines.

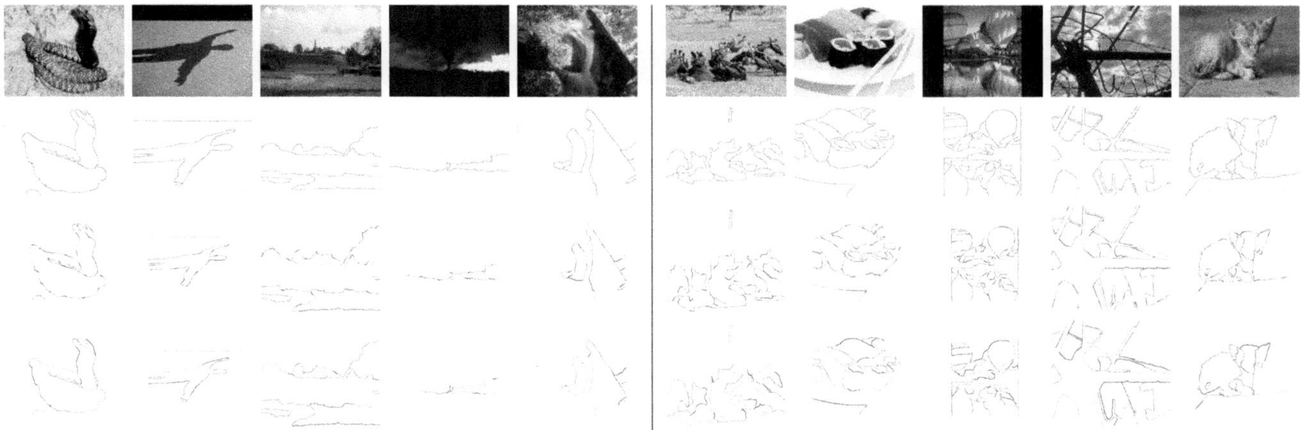

(a) Images with strong emotional content | (b) Emotionally neutral images

Figure 17: Examples of misclassification in Set 2. The four rows are original images, image contours, line segments, and continuous lines.

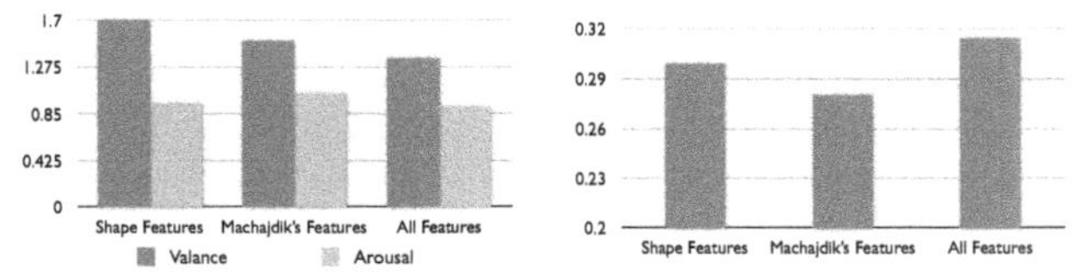

(a) (b)

Figure 18: Experimental results. (a) Mean squared error for the dimensions of valance and arousal. (b) Accuracy for the classification task.

amusement, awe, contentment, and excitement. We followed Machajdik *et al.* [18] and performed one-vs-all classification to compare and benchmark our classification accuracy. The classification results are reported in Figure 18(b). We used SVM to assign the images to one of the eight classes. The highest accuracy was obtained by combining Machajdik's with shape features. We also observed a considerable increase in the classification accuracy by using the shape features alone, which proves that shape features indeed capture emotions in images more effectively.

In this experiment, we also built classifiers for each of the shape features. Each of the shape features listed in Table 4 achieved a classification accuracy of 30% or higher.

Table 4: Significant features to emotions.

Emotion	Features
Angry	Circularity
Disgust	Length of line segments
Fear	Orientation of line segments and angle count
Sadness	Fitness, mass of curves, circularity, and orientation of line segments
Amusement	Mass of curves and orientation of line segments
Awe	Orientation of line segments
Excitement	Orientation of line segments
Contentment	Mass of lines, angle count, and orientation of line segments

6. CONCLUSIONS

We investigated the computability of emotion through shape modeling. To achieve this goal, we first extracted contours from complex images, and then represented contours using lines and curves extracted from images. Statistical analyses were conducted on locally meaningful lines and curves to represent the concept of roundness, angularity, and simplicity, which have been postulated as playing a key role in evoked emotion for years. Leveraging the computational representation of these physical stimulus properties, we evaluated the proposed shape features through three tasks: distinguishing emotional images from neutral images; classifying images according to categorized emotions; and fitting the dimensionality of emotion based on proposed shape features. We have achieved an improvement over the state-of-the-art solution [18]. We also attacked the problem of modeling the presence or absence of strong emotional content in images, which has long been overlooked. Separating images with strong emotional content from emotionally neutral ones can aid in many applications including improving the performance of keyword based image retrieval systems. We empirically verified that our proposed shape features indeed captured emotions in the images. The area of understanding emotions in images is still in its infancy and modeling emotions using low-level features is the first step toward solving this problem. We believe our contribution takes us closer to understanding emotions in images. In the future, we hope to expand our experimental dataset and provide stronger evidence of established relationships between shape features and emotions.

7. REFERENCES

[1] P. Arbelaez, M. Maire, C. Fowlkes, and J. Malik. Contour detection and hierarchical image segmentation. *IEEE Trans. on Pattern Analysis and Machine Intelligence*, 33(5):898–916, 2011.

[2] S. Arifin and P. Y. K. Cheung. A computation method for video segmentation utilizing the pleasure-arousal-dominance emotional information. In *ACM MM*, pages 68–77, 2007.

[3] R. Arnheim. *Art and visual perception: A psychology of the creative eye.* 1974.

[4] J. Aronoff. How we recognize angry and happy emotion in people, places, and things. *Cross-Cultural Research*, 40(1):83–105, 2006.

[5] M. Bar and M. Neta. Humans prefer curved visual objects. *Psychological Science*, 17(8):645–648, 2006.

[6] M. M. Bradley and P. J. Lang. The international affective picture system(IAPS) in the study of emotion and attention. In *Handbook of Emotion Elicitation and Assessment*, pages 29–46, 2007.

[7] S. Brandt, J. Laaksonen, and E. Oja. Statistical shape features in content-based image retrieval. In *ICPR*, pages 1062–1065, 2000.

[8] A. Chia, D. Rajan, M. Leung, and S. Rahardja. Object recognition by discriminative combinations of line segments, ellipses and appearance features. *IEEE Trans. on Pattern Analysis and Machine Intelligence*, 34(9):1758–1772, 2011.

[9] G. Csurka, S. Skaff, L. Marchesotti, and C. Saunders. Building look & feel concept models from color combinations. *The Visual Computer*, 27(12):1039–1053, 2011.

[10] R. Datta, D. Joshi, J. Li, and J. Z. Wang. Studying aesthetics in photographic images using a computational approach. In *ECCV*, pages 288–301, 2006.

[11] R. Datta, J. Li, and J. Z. Wang. Algorithmic inferencing of aesthetics and emotion in natural image: An exposition. In *ICIP*, pages 105–108, 2008.

[12] A. Hanjalic and L. Q. Xu. Affective video content representation and modeling. *IEEE Trans. on Multimedia*, 7(1):143–154, 2005.

[13] D. Joshi, R. Datta, E. Fedorovskaya, Q. T. Luong, J. Z. Wang, J. Li, and J. Luo. Aesthetics and emotions in images. *IEEE Signal Processing Magazine*, 28(5):94–115, 2011.

[14] P. J. Lang, M. M. Bradley, and B. N. Cuthbert. Emotion, motivation, and anxiety: Brain mechanisms and psychophysiology. *Biological Psychiatry*, 44(12):1248–1263, 1998.

[15] P. J. Lang, M. M. Bradley, and B. N. Cuthbert. International affective picture system: Affective ratings of pictures and instruction manual. In *Technical Report A-8, University of Florida, Gainesville, FL*, 2008.

[16] M. K. Leung and Y.-H. Yang. Dynamic two-strip algorithm in curve fitting. *Pattern Recognition*, 23(1-2):69–79, 1990.

[17] K. A. Lindquist, T. D. Wager, H. Kober, E. Bliss-Moreau, and L. F. Barrett. The brain basis of emotion: A meta-analytic review. *Behavioral and Brain Sciences*, 173(4):1–86, 2011.

[18] J. Machajdik and A. Hanbury. Affective image classification using features inspired by psychology and art theory. In *ACM MM*, pages 83–92, 2010.

[19] J. Mikel, B. L. Fredrickson, G. R. Larkin, C. M. Lindberg, S. J. Maglio, and P. A. Reuter-Lorenz. Emotional category data on images from the international affective picture system. *Behavior Research Methods*, 37(4):626–630, 2005.

[20] Y. Mingqiang, K. Kidiyo, and R. Joseph. A survey of shape feature extraction techniques. *Pattern Recognition*, pages 43–90, 2008.

[21] R. Reber, N. Schwarz, and P. Winkielman. Processing fluency and aesthetic pleasure: Is beauty in the perceiver's processing experience? *Personality and Social Psychology Review*, 8(4):364–382, 2004.

[22] H. R. Schiffman. *Sense and Perception: An Integrated Approach.* 1990.

[23] T. Shibata and T. Kato. Kansei image retrieval system for street landscape-discrimination and graphical parameters based on correlation of two image systems. In *International Conference on Systems, Man, and Cybernetics*, pages 274–252, 2006.

[24] M. Solli and R. Lenz. Color based bags-of-emotions. *LNCS*, 5702:573–580, 2009.

[25] H. L. Wang and L. F. Cheong. Affective understanding in film. *IEEE Trans. on Circuits and Systems for Video Technology*, 16(6):689–704, 2006.

[26] V. Yanulevskaya, J. C. Van Gemert, K. Roth, A. K. Herbold, N. Sebe, and J. M. Geusebroek. Emotional valence categorization using holistic image features. In *ICIP*, pages 101–104, 2008.

[27] H. Zhang, E. Augilius, T. Honkela, J. Laaksonen, H. Gamper, and H. Alene. Analyzing emotional semantics of abstract art using low-level image features. In *Advances in Intelligent Data Analysis*, pages 413–423, 2011.

[28] S. L. Zhang, Q. Tian, Q. M. Huang, W. Gao, and S. P. Li. Utilizing affective analysis for efficient movie browsing. In *ICIP*, pages 1853–1856, 2009.

Sense Beauty via Face, Dressing, and/or Voice

Tam V. Nguyen
National University of Singapore
tamnguyen@nus.edu.sg

Si Liu
National Laboratory of Pattern Recognition
sliu@nlpr.ia.ac.cn

Bingbing Ni
Advanced Digital Sciences Center
bingbing.ni@adsc.com.sg

Jun Tan
National University of Defense Technology
tanjun.nudt@gmail.com

Yong Rui
Microsoft Research Asia
yongrui@microsoft.com

Shuicheng Yan
National University of Singapore
eleyans@nus.edu.sg

ABSTRACT

Discovering the secret of beauty has been the pursuit of artists and philosophers for centuries. Nowadays, the computational model for beauty estimation has been actively explored in computer science community, yet with the focus mainly on facial features. In this work, we perform a comprehensive study of female attractiveness conveyed by single/multiple modalities of cues, i.e., face, dressing and/or voice, and aim to uncover how different modalities individually and collectively affect the human sense of beauty. To this end, we collect the first Multi-Modality Beauty (M^2B) dataset in the world for female attractiveness study, which is thoroughly annotated with attractiveness levels converted from manual k-wise ratings and semantic attributes of different modalities. A novel Dual-supervised Feature-Attribute-Task (DFAT) network is proposed to jointly learn the beauty estimation models of single/multiple modalities as well as the attribute estimation models. The DFAT network differentiates itself by its supervision in both attribute and task layers. Several interesting beauty-sense observations over single/multiple modalities are reported, and the extensive experimental evaluations on the collected M^2B dataset well demonstrate the effectiveness of the proposed DFAT network for female attractiveness estimation.

Categories and Subject Descriptors

H.5.1 [**Information Interfaces and Presentation**]: Multimedia Information Systems

General Terms

Algorithms, Experimentation, Human Factors

Keywords

{Face, Dressing, Voice} attractiveness, Attributes, Dual-supervised Feature-Attribute-Task network

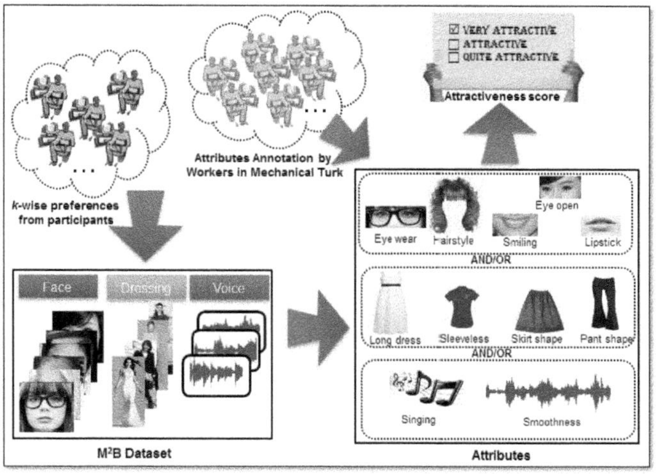

Figure 1: The proposed comprehensive study of sensing human beauty via single/multi-modality cues. The collected dataset contains three modalities, *i.e.*, face, dressing and voice. The attractiveness scores are given by k-wise preferences from participants. All modalities are labeled with extensive attributes by Amazon Mechanical Turk due to its large amount. Both visual and vocal features as well as labeled attributes are collectively utilized to build computational models for estimating female beauty score.

1. INTRODUCTION

Discovering the secret of beauty has been the pursuit of artists and philosophers for centuries [15, 20, 8]. The study on what are the essential elements and how their combinatorial mechanism affects the attractiveness of a person is valuable for many potential applications. For example, when we know the underlying rules how the female's dress and face jointly influence her attractiveness, one system can be developed to recommend how a female can become more attractive by choosing a specific type of lipstick or other make-ups according to her face shape and dress. This research benefits other areas such as fashion, cosmetic, and targeted advertisement. The problem has also attracted many interests from computer science researchers recently. There exist softwares for both automatic human-like facial beauty assessment [19, 25] as well as face beautification [34, 21]. There exist some works from multimedia and social science communities on attractiveness study based on faces [7, 16, 25], bodies [18, 29], and voices [23].

In essence, most of these studies attempt to answer one question: "what elements constitute beauty or attractiveness for human". However, how these individual elements collaborate with each other and jointly affect the human sense of beauty has received little attention. We believe that different modalities can complement and affect each other and there do exist certain underlying interacting mechanism that makes a lady attractive, which is even more important than the elements themselves. There exist obvious examples to support this argument. In real life, a female may not have very attractive face, but she may have a good taste of how to select dresses and makeups to match her face shape, which then makes her also very attractive entirely. Therefore, in this paper, we study how different modalities, *i.e.*, face, dress and voice individually and collectively affect the human sense of beauty (or attractiveness).

To facilitate the human attractiveness study, we first collect the largest multi-culture (Eastern and Western females), Multi-Modality (face, dressing, and voice) Beauty (M^2B) dataset to date. Then, the participants are invited to annotate the k-wise preference for each k randomly selected examples (with modalities of face, and/or dressing, and/or voice). Afterwards, the k-wise preferences are converted into the global attractiveness scores for all the samples. In addition, a set of carefully designed attributes are annotated for each modality of samples by using Mechanical Turk [1], and used as the bridge for boosting attractiveness estimation performance. Finally, we present a novel tri-layer learning framework, called Dual-supervised Feature-Attribute-Task (DFAT) network, to unify the attribute prediction and multi-task attractiveness prediction within a unified formulation. Eventually, the extensive experiments on the collected M^2B dataset demonstrate several interesting cross-modality observations as well as the effectiveness of our proposed DFAT framework.

Figure 1 illustrates the proposed framework for sensing beauty via multi-modality cues. The main contributions of this work can be summarized as follows.

1. To the best of our knowledge, we conduct the first comprehensive study on how multiple interacting modalities (*i.e.*, face, dress and voice) individually and collectively affect the sense of female attractiveness.

2. We propose a user friendly k-wise ranking tool for reliable large-scale attractiveness annotation.

3. We propose a novel dual-supervised framework where attribute models and attractiveness models are learned simultaneously, which is superior over conventional two-stage framework, namely first learning the attribute models followed by learning the models from attributes to attractiveness score.

4. Last but not least, using our computational models, we study the commonalities and differences between the Eastern and Western on how they sense beauty.

The rest of the paper is organized as follows. Section 2 discusses the related work. Then, we describe the process of dataset collection and annotation, and propose the DFAT framework for attractiveness estimation in Section 3 and 4, respectively. Experiments and discussions are presented in Section 5. Section 6 concludes this work.

2. RELATED WORK

In literature, most computer science researches have focused on identifying attractive facial characteristics. Most approaches to this problem can be considered as geometric or landmark feature based methods. Aarabi et al. built a classification system based on 8 landmark ratios and evaluated the method on a dataset of 80 images rated on a scale of $1 - 4$ [7]. Eisenthal et al. used an ensemble of features that include landmark distances and ratios, an indicator of facial symmetry, skin smoothness, hair color, and the coefficients of an eigenface decomposition [16]. Their method was evaluated on two datasets of 92 images each with ratings $1 - 7$. Kagian et al. later improved upon their method using an improved feature selection method [25]. Recently, Guo et al. have explored the related problem of automatic makeup/beautification application, which uses an example to transfer a style of makeup to a new face [21]. Gray et al. presented a method of both quantifying and predicting female facial beauty using a hierarchical feed-forward model without the landmarks [19].

The attractiveness of bodies has also been investigated. Glassenberg et al. discussed the attractive women have a high-degree of facial symmetry, a relatively narrow waist, and V-shaped torso [18]. Studies on attractiveness based on clothing are more centralized in the area of sociology. For example, Lennon's study [29] investigated whether people perceive others differentially as a function of the attractiveness of their clothing with a set of experiments. To the best of our knowledge, there is no existing work specially studying the attractiveness of clothing, which shows the advantage and uniqueness of our work.

Apart from visual attractiveness, Zuckerman et al. investigated the voice attractiveness [40]. They found that attractive voices were louder and more resonant. In addition to this, they found some gender differences, including low-pitch-male voices are perceived as more attractive, while the attractiveness of female voices could not be captured by spectrographic analysis. Susan et al. investigated the relationship between ratings of voice attractiveness and sexually dimorphic differences in shoulder-to-hip ratios and waist-to-hip ratios, as well as different features of sexual behavior [23].

In general, the contemporary datasets used by the previous studies are small-scale and usually restricted to a very small and subset of the population (e.g. uniform ethnicity, age), with less-changed expression, pose and lighting condition. The images are generally studio-quality photos taken by professional photographers. Furthermore, there is no multi-modality datasets for our proposed study on how multiple interacting modalities affect the human sense of beauty. Thus, we construct the new dataset which will be described in the next section.

3. DATASET CONSTRUCTION

3.1 Data Collection

There exist several datasets [19, 7, 25] for attractiveness study but none of them is suitable as they usually contain only one modality of features. Therefore, in order to make a study on our proposed problem, we require a large dataset of faces, dressings and voices along with ground-truth attractiveness scores. However, no such the datasets

Table 1: Exemplar keywords used for downloading online videos from YouTube and their corresponding numbers of high quality video clips downloaded to construct M²B dataset.

Query	#Clip	Query	#Clip
SuperGirl	35	X Factor Auditions	60
Happy Girl	20	Got Talent Auditions	70
Guess-Guess	40	Eurovision	10
Korea Got Talent	5	American Idol	10
Chinese New Year Event	3	Next Top Model	5
Others	22	Total	280

are currently publicly available. Thus, we construct Multi-Modality Beauty (M²B) dataset with face, dressing images and voices. The attractiveness scores are annotated by human subjects. To study how people from different cultures sense beauty, the constructed dataset includes two ethnic groups: Western and Eastern.

The data are collected mainly from the popular video sharing website YouTube [2] similar to [12]. To diversify the dataset, we selected images from videos of various TV reality shows, talk shows, looking-for-idol-like programs with contestants from both Western and Eastern countries. Some of the exemplar programs are SuperGirl, Happy Girl, Guess-Guess, Chinese New Year Event, American Dancing with the stars, Eurovision, Britain Next Top Model, American Idol, X Factor, and Britain Got Talent show with its franchises [1]. Besides, we also collected data from the online academic talks, poems, songs from TED Talk [3], VideoLectures [4], etc. Unlike the previous datasets [31] the face images of which are cropped from low-quality photos taken by cellphone cameras, we only select high quality video clips, e.g. at least 360 pixels wide. The durations of the clips are varied from 28 seconds to 2 hours 48 minutes (averagely 21 minutes per clip). Note that for each clip, there may exist multiple females. The details of actual videos utilized in M²B are reported in Table 1.

For each female instance, we extract several frames from the video. We run Viola-Jones face detector [38] on these frames to extract frontal faces. All the faces are resized to 128×128 pixels. A well-trained human detector [39] is applied on all images, and only the high-confidence detection outputs are kept. Note that for the dressing image, the face size is small, and generally cannot be used for sensing beauty. We extract 5 seconds duration for voice information of each instance. Eventually, we select only one face photo, one full body photo and one voice snippet for one female instance. Totally, our dataset consists of equal 620 vs. 620 instances for Westerners and Easterners, respectively. This database shall be released for the public usage on the research of female beauty.

3.2 Ground-truth Attractiveness Score

3.2.1 Absolute value vs. pair-wise vs. k-wise ratings

There are several kinds of ratings that can be used for annotation for this task. The most popular ones are absolute ratings where a user is presented with a single image and asked to give a score, typically between 1 and 10. Most previous works have used some versions of absolute value ratings, which are usually presented in the form of a Likert scale [30]. This form of rating requires each image to be rated by many users such that a distribution of ratings can be gathered and averaged to estimate the true score. This method is obviously not ideal because different users with different backgrounds have different priors in rating images. Another method used in [33] is to ask a user to sort a collection of images according to some criteria. This method is likely to give reliable ratings, but it is impractical for users to sort a large dataset. The most recent method is to present a user with a pair of images and ask which one is more attractive. This method presents a user with a binary decision, which they have found can be made more quickly than an absolute rating. Greg et al. applied pair-wise comparison for attractiveness study [19]. However, it is usually non-trivial to convert these pair-wise ratings into global scores, which is important for subsequent tasks.

[1]Got Talent franchises are at America, Australia, Albania, Bulgaria, China, Denmark, France, Holland, Korea, Romania, and Serbia.

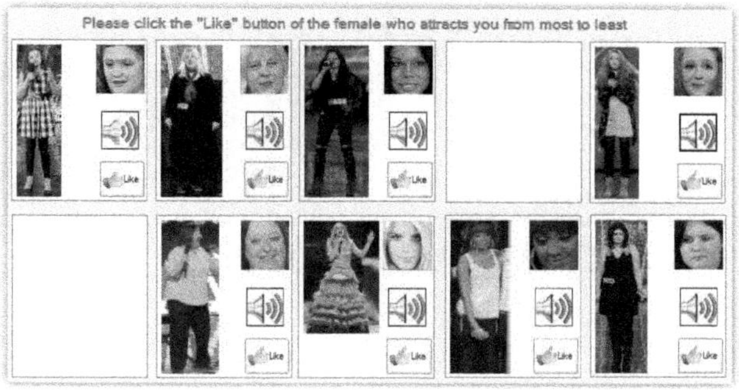

Figure 2: The exemplar user interface of our attractiveness ranking tool on one batch of instances for Western labelling task. The corresponding information of selected top 2 instances disappeared; and the user then proceeds to click "Like" for the next most attractive instance.

In this work, we try to avoid the disadvantages of all above methods and propose a k-wise comparison (with k set as 10). The number of pair-wise preferences obtained from one k-wise rating is $\binom{k}{2}$. For example, when k is 10, the number of pair-wise preferences is 45. Totally, 40 participants (17 females and 23 males who are students and staff members of a university) ranged from 19 to 40 years old (μ=26.4, σ=4.1) participated in the data ranking task. There exists cross-race effect or other-race bias, *i.e.*, the tendency for people of one race to have difficulty in recognizing and processing faces and facial expressions of members of a race or ethnic group other than their own [37, 9]. Therefore, the participants have been split into two groups based on their ethnicities. Westerners labeled for Western group while Easterners labeled for Eastern group. This is the main reason we did not ask workers from Mechanical Turk since the current system cannot well control the ethnicity of the workers. Each participant performs some of the six following tasks: 1) faces (F), 2) voices (V), 3) dressings (D), 4) faces and dressing (FD), 5) faces and voices (FV), and 6) faces, dressings, and voices (FDV). We exclude DV (dressings and voices) task since it is an unnatural and impractical scenario. Each k-wise rating shows 10 random instances to the participant, who ranks each instance from the most attractive to the least attractive. Figure 2 shows the user interface of the k-

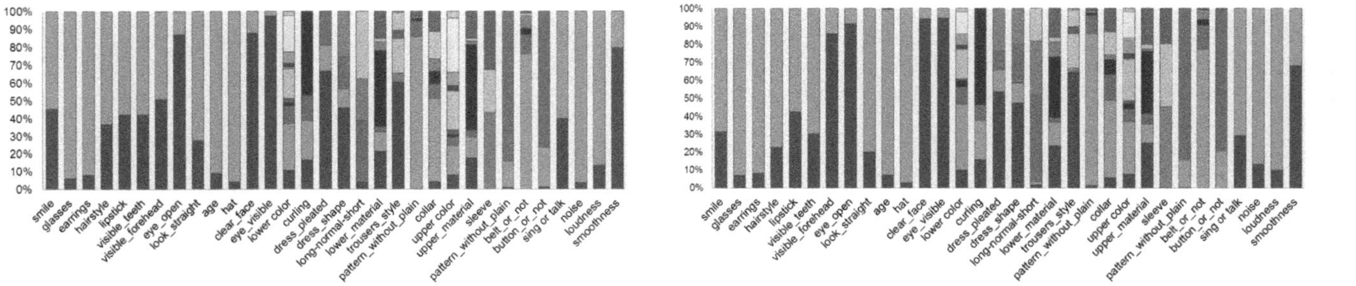

(a) Eastern (b) Western

Figure 3: The distributions of attributes annotated by Mechanical Turk workers. For the two-option attributes, the bottom part corresponds to 'yes', the top part corresponds to 'no'. For the multiple-option attributes, please refer to Figure 4 for their options in order. (Please view in high 400% resolution).

wise rating tool for one k-wise rating. When the user clicks "Like" button, the information of the corresponding instance disappears and the user proceeds to the remaining instances. The rating process continues until every instance is ranked. Each instance in each task has been ranked by at least 15 different participants.

3.2.2 k-wise ratings to global attractiveness score

In our study, we assume that in a large sense people agree on a consistent opinion on facial attractiveness, which is also the assumption of the previous studies [19]. Each individual's opinion can be varied due to factors like culture, race, and education. As aforementioned, k-wise ratings are fast to collect, but in order to use them for subsequent learning tasks, we need to convert the ratings into the global attractiveness scores. To obtain the scores from k-wise, we minimize a cost function defined such that as many of the pairwise preferences as possible are preserved and the scores lie within a specified range, where the pairwise preferences are converted from the k-wise ratings and $\binom{k}{2}$ pair-wise preferences can be obtained from each k-wise rating. Denote Ω as the set of pairwise preferences for k-wise ratings, we formulate the conversion problem as,

$$\min_{s} J(s) = ss^T + \tau \sum_{(p,q)\in\Omega} \xi_{pq}, \\ \text{s.t.} \begin{cases} \xi_{pq} \geq 0, \quad \forall\ (p,q) \in \Omega, \\ s_p - s_q \geq 1 - \xi_{pq},\ \forall\ (p,q) \in \Omega, \end{cases} \tag{1}$$

where $s = [s_1, s_2, ..., s_n]$ is the global attractiveness score row vector for all the n instances of one task, and the constraints correspond to the pairwise preferences. The problem of (1) is right the popular Ranking SVM [24]. Finally, all the scores are re-scaled to be within [1, 10] for each of six tasks.

3.3 Attributes Annotation

Recently, methods that exploit the semantic attributes of objects have attracted significant attention in the computer vision community. The usefulness of attributes has been demonstrated in several different application areas [10, 17, 26, 27]. Visual attributes are important for understanding object appearance and for describing objects to other people. Automatic learning and recognition of attributes can complement category-level recognition and improve the degree for machines to perceive visual objects. Therefore, we also want to explore the usage of attributes in the attractiveness study.

In this context, the attributes defined are not limited to visual attributes. Attributes associated with different modalities such as *eye wear*, *dressing collar*, or *voice smoothness* are also used. In this work, we manually define different

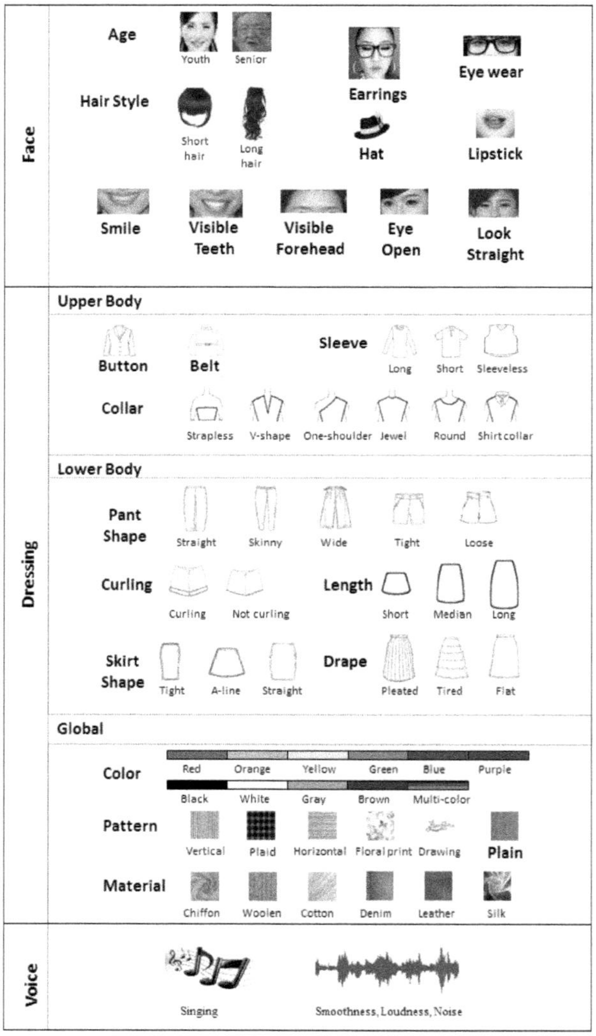

Figure 4: The attributes of different modalities. An example or line drawing is shown to illustrate each attribute value.

types of attributes. The selection of the attributes is determined by the discussions founded on previous related research papers [10, 26] and also related Internet contents, which mean stylists have already implicitly contributed. All the attributes labeled from the dataset are listed in Figure 4. The defined attributes can be summarized into three classes, i.e., face, dressing and voice attributes. Mechanical Turk workers are responsible for labeling the attributes of the newly built dataset [1]. Due to the difficulty in distinguishing the attribute values, different numbers of annotators are assigned to each labeling task. A label was considered as a ground truth if at least more than half of the annotators agreed on the value of the label. To the best of our knowledge, this dataset has the most complete attribute annotations among all contemporary datasets.

4. THE PROPOSED FRAMEWORK

In this section, we first explain the feature extraction applied on the extracted face, body and voice of the collected M^2B dataset. A novel framework, which learns attributes and attractiveness simultaneously, is later introduced.

4.1 Features

4.1.1 *Facial features*

We extract the following popular features, local binary patterns (LBP) [32], Gabor filter responses [14], Color moment for the frontal faces.

LBP is basically a finescale descriptor that captures small texture details. We adopt the same notation $\text{LBP}_{\text{P,R}}$ as in [32], where R is the radius of the circle to be sampled, and P is the number of sampling points. Denote the ring feature for image pixel (x, y) as $B(x, y) =< b_{P-1}, \ldots, b_1, b_0 >$, where $b_i \in \{0, 1\}$. It is common to transform $B(x, y)$ into decimal code via binomial weighting:

$$\text{LBP}_{\text{P,R}}(x, y) = \sum_{i=0}^{P-1} b_i 2^i,$$

which characterizes image textures over the neighborhood of (x, y).

Gabor filter is another appropriate feature for texture representation. Gabor filters encode facial shape and appearance information over a range of spatial scales. The Gabor functions applied for location (x, y) are used as the following form.

$$\text{G}(x, y) = \exp\left(\frac{X^2 + \gamma^2 Y^2}{2\sigma^2}\right) \times \cos\left(\frac{2\pi}{\lambda} X\right),$$

where $X = x\cos\theta + y\sin\theta$ and $Y = -x\sin\theta + y\cos\theta$ are the orientations of the Gabor filters with angle θ which varies between 0 and π. The other parameters, aspect ratio γ, effective width σ, wavelength λ are set as in [35]. In the implementation, we apply 5 scales and 8 orientations to obtain Gabor responses.

Color moment is a low-level color measurement and consists of the first order (mean of color values) and the second order moments (variance of color values) of the input image block. In this work, we divide the input image into 4×4 blocks and then compute the overall color moment. Color information is highly correlated to some attributes such as lipstick or visible forehead.

Since the concatenated features are high-dimensional, we use PCA to reduce the facial dimensionality to 250.

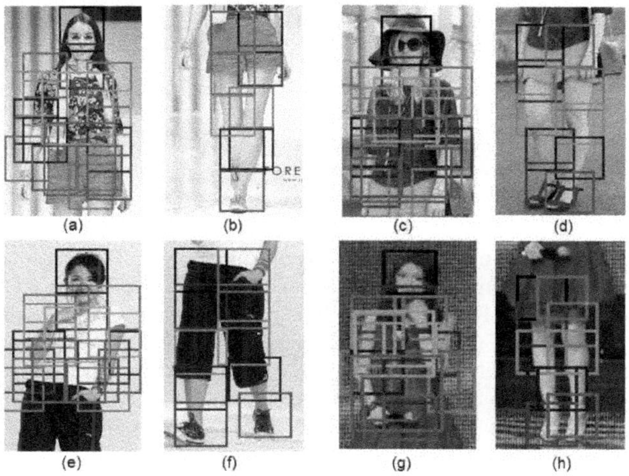

Figure 5: The dressing bounding boxes for dressing feature extraction for Western (a-d) and Eastern (e-h). Each region roughly corresponds to functional parts of the dressing.

4.1.2 *Dressing features*

We consider dressing as the combination of two main parts, upper and lower. Each part consists of the mixture of mini parts, similar to the human body. Following [11, 36], we extract 5 kinds of features from the 20 upper-body parts and 10 lower-body parts. Figure 5 shows the exemplar boxes of dressings. The features used include HOG [13], LBP, Color moment, Color histogram and Skin descriptor. HOG and LBP features are related to dressing texture attributes such as *collar* or *curling*. Meanwhile, Color moment, Color histogram and skin descriptor are useful for depicting color-relevant dressing attributes such as *shirt color* or *pattern*. More specifically, each human part is first partitioned into 16 smaller, spatially evenly distributed regular blocks. 5 features are extracted from each block and features from all blocks are finally concatenated to represent a human part. The block based features can roughly preserve relative spatial information inside each human part. The dimensionality of dressing feature after PCA is 300.

4.1.3 *Vocal features*

We apply the audio feature extraction for the audio snippets in M^2B dataset. The vocal features are extracted by using MIRToolbox [28]. Each voice feature is related to one of the audio dimensions traditionally defined in audio theory. The audio sequence is decomposed into successive frames, which are then converted into the spectral domain, frequency domain and pitch domain. Accordingly, the audio features related to pitch, to spectrum (zerocross, low energy, rolloff, entropy, irregularity, brightness, skewness, flatness, roughness), to tonality (chromagram, key strength and key self-organising map) and to dynamics (root mean square energy) are extracted. Another set of features inherited from automatic speech recognition is used, which is the set of mel-frequency spectral coefficients. Additionally, some features related to rhythm, namely tempo, pulse clarity and fluctuation, are also used. Eventually, these audio features are concatenated and reduced to 50-D by PCA.

4.2 Dual-supervised Feature-Attribute-Task (DFAT) Network

Most previous studies [7, 19, 16] utilize features directly in order to predict the attractiveness score. As earlier mentioned, in this work, we explore the usage of attributes serving as the intermediate layer in order to perform the tasks. The conventional approach to integrate attributes is to perform the following two steps separately: 1) learn the regression model from raw features to attributes and 2) learn another regression model from the output attributes of training data to attractiveness scores. The drawback of this approach is to introduce the unexpected errors into the second regression stage, and it cannot guarantee the outputs from the first model are optimal for the second model. Therefore, we propose to fuse these two steps together and simultaneously optimize them in the sense that two steps mutually affect each other.

We propose the novel Dual-supervised Feature-Attribute-Task (DFAT) network, which jointly learns the beauty estimation models of single/multiple modalities, where the semantic attributes are shared by different tasks, namely the beauty estimation models of different types of features and their combinations. The model contains three layers, i.e., feature, attribute and task layers. The proposed DFAT Network is illustrated in Figure 6. DFAT learns two types of regression models simultaneouly by minimizing two types of prediction errors, one is feature-to-attribute error, and the other is attribute-to-attractiveness error. Note that the main difference between conventional Neural Network [22] and our proposed method is the supervision existing in both attribute and task layers of DFAT. Formally, let us denote X^m as the training data matrix for modality m, where each column is a feature vector and $m \in \{1,2,3\}$, A^m as the regression matrix from raw features to attributes, $Attr^m$ as the groundtruth attributes of modality m, X_t^m as training data for modality m in task t where $t \in \{1,2,3,4,5,6\}$, s_t as the groundtruth attractiveness score row vector for task t, and ω_t^m as the row regression vector for converting attributes of modality m to task t. The learning problem for DFAT network is then formulated as:

Algorithm 1 Procedure to solve Problem (2)

Input: matrices X^m, X_t^m, $Attr^m$, s_t , parameter λ_1, λ_2.
Initialize: A^m by solving $\min \|A^m X^m - Att^m\|^2$, $e_1 = \infty, e_2 = 0$.
while not converged **do**

1. Fix the others and update ω_t^m by:

$$\omega_t^m = (s_t - \sum_{p \in \{1,2,3\} \setminus m} \omega_t^p A^p X_t^p)(A^m X_t^m)^T (A^m X_t^m (A^m X_t^m)^T + \frac{\lambda_2}{\lambda_1} I)^{-1},$$

2. Fix the others and update A^m by gradient descent.

$$A^m = A^m - \gamma \nabla F(A^m),$$

where γ is the step size and $\nabla F(A^m)$ is defined as

$$\nabla F(A^m) = A^m X^m X^{mT} - Att^m X^{mT} + \lambda_2 A^m + \lambda_1 \sum_{t=1}^{6} \omega_t^{mT} (\sum_p \omega_t^p A^p X_t^p - s_t) X_t^{mT}.$$

3. Compute $e_2 = \|F\|_F$.
4. Check the convergence condition: $\|e_1 - e_2\| < \varepsilon$.
5. Update e_1: $e_1 = e_2$.

end while
Output: The optimal solution $\{A^{m*}\}, \{\omega_t^{m*}\}$.

$$\min_{\{A^m\},\{\omega_t^m\}} F = \frac{1}{2} \sum_{m=1}^{3} \|A^m X^m - Attr^m\|^2 + \frac{\lambda_1}{2} \sum_{t=1}^{6} \| \sum_{m=1}^{3} \omega_t^m A^m X_t^m - s_t \|^2 + \frac{\lambda_2}{2} \sum_{m=1}^{3} (\|A^m\|^2 + \sum_{t=1}^{6} \|\omega_t^m\|^2). \quad (2)$$

The first term is the regression from features to attributes, the second term is the regression from attributes to attrac-

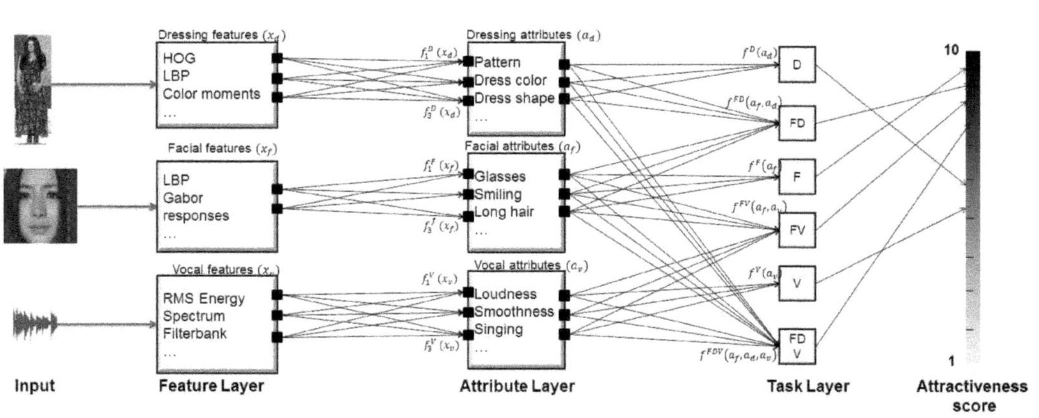

Figure 6: Dual-supervised Feature-Attribute-Task Learning Framework. First, for each modality, i.e, face, dress and voice, different kinds of features are extracted. Then the beauty estimation models of single/multiple modalities are jointly learned. During the learning process, the semantic attributes are shared by different tasks. Different with traditional Neural Network, the proposed DFAT network can seamlessly combine the training attribute labels in the learning process.

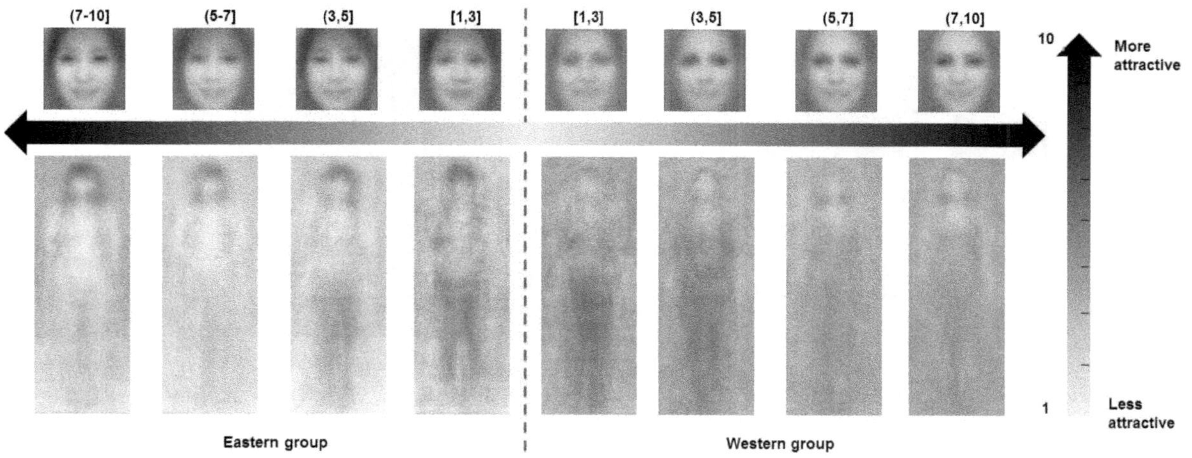

Figure 7: Average faces and dressings of Eastern and Western groups at different attractiveness scores. For better viewing, please see original color pdf file (greatly encouraged for this figure).

tiveness scores, and the last term is the regularization term. Note that for one task t, if the modality m does not exist, we set the corresponding feature matrix X_t^m be all-zero matrix for ease of formulation. The above optimization problem can be solved by any gradient based method and the iterative optimization procedure is listed in Algorithm 1.

5. EXPERIMENTS

In this section, we describe the extensive experiments conducted on the collected M^{2}B dataset for the better understanding of beauty sensing.

5.1 The Attractiveness Scores Distribution

The score of each instance in each task is achieved by solving Equation (1). In order to investigate how the scores distribute in the dataset, we compute the histogram of attractiveness scores across six tasks of both Western and Eastern participants. Recall that Western participants labeled for Western group while Eastern counterparts labeled for Eastern group. We can notice the distributions different between two groups. In Figure 8, the scores of Eastern participants are higher in the range from 4 to 6, while the scores from Western participants dominate the rest of score ranges. This reflects the Golden Mean in traditional Eastern culture [5], where people are more conservative to give the conclusion.

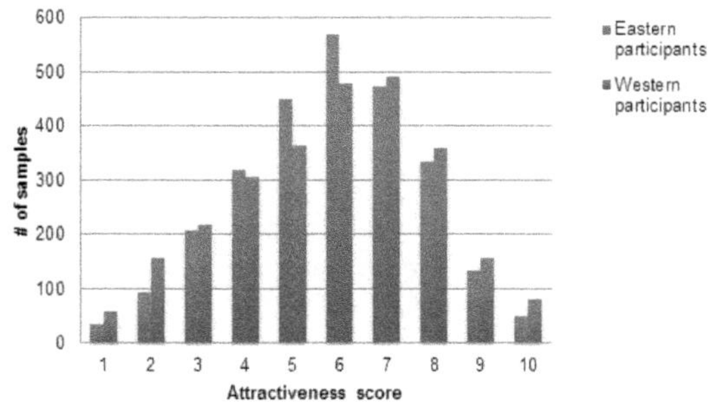

Figure 8: The histograms of attractiveness scores across six tasks of Western and Eastern participants.

5.2 Average Faces and Average Body Shapes

The average faces and dressings show the first glance how people sense the attractiveness. The average faces from the dataset, presented in the top row of Figure 7, have a score within [1, 10]. The average faces present interesting patterns in attractiveness study. One of the early observations in the study of facial beauty was that averaged faces are attractive [8]. There also exist computational tools to generate the average face [6]. Additionally, women with averaged faces have been shown to be considered more attractive. This is possibly due to average features being smoother and, therefore, more comfortable. Average faces are attractive, but not all of them. It is crucial which faces are used to compute an average face. Average face computed from unattractive faces may remain rather unattractive and other ones from attractive faces shall remain attractive. The average faces of *higher scores* look younger and smoother. In contrast, the average faces of *lower scores* look older, and less smooth. Another interesting observation is that Western faces have blonde hair which may blend into the background, while Eastern faces have black hair which has good contrast from the face color.

Similarly, the average dressings are shown in the bottom row of Figure 7 with scores within [1,10]. The less attractive dressings are trouser-like while the more attractive dressings are skirt-like. The background is the same for both groups. The Western group prefers dark color dressing, while the Eastern group favors bright color.

5.3 Cross-modalities Beauty Sense Discrepancy

We compute the distance matrices of both Eastern and Western groups. The distance matrices provide the dissimilarities of attractiveness scores in different tasks. Each element of the matrix represents the distance score between two tasks. This allows more detailed analysis on the differences among tasks. Figure 9 shows the distance matrices that represent the distance scores between the tasks, for Easterns and Westerns, respectively. The distance of task i and task j is computed as follows.

$$d_{i,j} = \frac{1}{n} \sum_{l=1}^{n} |s_l^i - s_l^j| , \qquad (3)$$

where s_l^i is the attractiveness score of instance l in task i, s_l^j is the corresponding score of the same instance l in task j, and n is the number of instances. As can be seen from Figure 9, the results from the Voice-only task are far away from

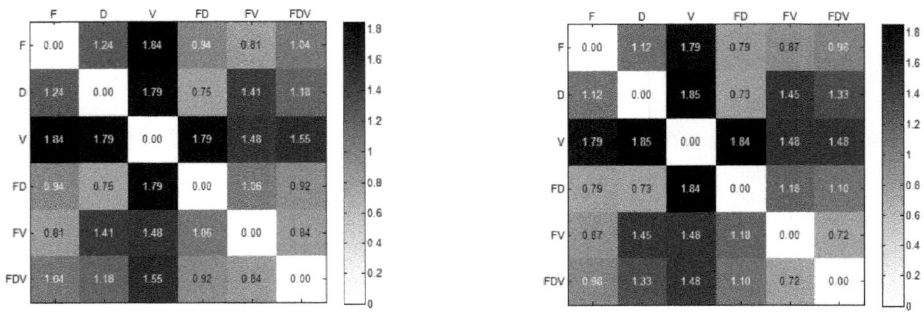

(a) Eastern (b) Western

Figure 9: The distance matrices of Eastern and Western groups. The distances are calculated based on the groudtruth attractiveness scores of different tasks. The small values indicate that two tasks are similar with each other.

all of other tasks' results. In other words, the attractiveness score of one instance in the Voice-only task is greatly different to her score in another task. There also exist the differences between Western and Eastern. Face vs. Voice has the largest dissimilarity of Eastern group. Meanwhile, Dressing vs. Voice has the largest distance in the Western group. Face vs. Face-Dressing has the smallest dissimilarity in Eastern group, while the smallest dissimilarity in Western group is Face-Dressing-Voice vs. Face-Voice. Generally, the scores given in the Face-only task have been changed when other modalities are added.

5.4 Within-culture Attractiveness Prediction

In this subsection, we investigate the attractiveness prediction problem within cultures. For each experiment, we perform a standard 2-fold cross validation test to evaluate the accuracy of our algorithms on the M^{2}B dataset. In 2-fold cross-validation, the original dataset is randomly evenly partitioned into 2 subsets. The cross-validation process is then repeated 10 times, with each of the 2 subsets used as the testing data and the other subset as training data. The 10 results from the folds are averaged to report the final results. We use the Mean Absolute Error (MAE) to evaluate the accuracy of the attractiveness prediction. The MAE is defined as the average of the absolute errors between the predicted attractiveness score and the ground truth.

$$MAE = \sum_{i=1}^{n} |\hat{s_i} - s_i|/n, \tag{4}$$

where s_i is the ground truth attractiveness score for the test instance i, $\hat{s_i}$ is the estimated score, and n is the total number of test instances for one task.

We then compare the performance of DFAT network with four baselines.

1. 1-NN: 1-NN classifier is applied to find the nearest neighbor, and assign the score of the neighbor to the query instance.

2. Ridge Regression: We apply the Ridge Regression to obtain the predicted attractiveness score from the raw features directly.

3. Neural Network: We apply feed-forward neural network to retrieve the attractiveness score from the raw features directly. Note that the difference between NN and DFAT network is the hidden layers. The DFAT network differentiates itself by its supervision in both attribute and task layers.

4. F-A-T: We learn the linear regression between the features and attributes, and then train the second linear regression between the output attributes of training data and the attractiveness scores.

Note that for the first 3 baselines, the attributes are not used. Regarding DFAT, we implement the Algorithm 1 with $\lambda_1 = 0.01$, $\lambda_2 = 10^{-3}$, $\gamma = 10^{-3}$, and $\varepsilon = 10^{-4}$ to learn the transfer matrices. In our experiment, 10 to 20 iterations are required for convergence. As can be seen in Table 2, MAEs of 1-NN are worst in all cases. F-A-T achieves better performance than two baselines, Ridge Regression and Neural Network. The better performance of F-A-T shows the advantage of using attributes in attractiveness study. Meanwhile, our proposed DFAT outperforms all of compared algorithms. Face-only task gets the highest MAE in both two cultures. In the opposite side, Face-Voice task achieves the lowest MAE among tasks across Eastern and Western. In addition, the task of Face-Dressing-Voice also reaches the similar MAE to Face-Voice task. For all baselines, the MAEs tend to have the large value when more modalities are added. In contrast, for DFAT, the results show that more modalities combining with face generally reduce the error when predicting the attractiveness level. In other words, multiple modalities boost the performance of attractiveness prediction.

5.5 Cross-culture Attractiveness Prediction

People from different cultures are often attracted to the same type of faces. This agreement among individuals of different ages and from different cultures suggests attractiveness judgements are not arbitrary but have a "biological basis". Thus, we are interested in exploring the cross-culture attractiveness prediction between Eastern and Western. For this experiment, we train the data on one group and test on the different group by using DFAT.

Table 3 shows the MAEs of the cross-culture experiment on M^{2}B dataset. The MAEs of all tasks increase dramatically compared to the results of training and testing on the same ethnic group. The highest error lies on dressing tasks. The difference can be explained by the significant difference in the average dressings. Recall that Westerners prefer darker color, while Easterners favor brighter color. Also, the MAEs of Face and Face-Dressing task are also high due to the significant difference of faces. Meanwhile, the MAEs

Table 2: MAEs of different algorithms on M^{2}B dataset (the training/testing data within the same culture).

	Eastern						Western					
Algorithm	F	D	V	FD	FV	FDV	F	D	V	FD	FV	FDV
1-NN	2.11	1.50	1.39	1.74	2.16	1.96	1.92	2.02	1.78	1.98	2.25	2.23
Ridge Regression	1.95	1.39	1.15	1.52	1.93	1.79	1.87	1.76	1.37	1.66	2.09	2.13
Neural Network	1.82	1.37	1.12	1.47	1.79	1.82	1.76	1.62	1.38	1.53	1.85	1.87
F-A-T	1.80	1.33	1.12	1.45	1.79	1.67	1.69	1.54	1.34	1.54	1.91	1.93
DFAT	1.77	1.33	1.09	1.42	0.98	1.04	1.66	1.50	1.29	1.50	1.01	1.12

of Face-Voice task achieve is the lowest. This result agrees with the previous finding in [40] that attractive voices have the same effect as attractive faces, meaning that vocal attractiveness parallels visual attractiveness.

Table 3: MAEs of cross-culture attractiveness prediction experiment on M^{2}B dataset.

Task	Train on Eastern - Test on Western	Train on Western - Test on Eastern
F	1.91	2.22
D	2.55	2.71
V	1.55	1.62
FD	2.39	2.42
FV	1.15	1.20
FDV	1.57	1.52

5.6 Task-specific Important Attributes

Firstly we conduct the experiment to measure the accuracy [2] of attribute prediction whose results are shown in Figure 10. Generally, the prediction results are acceptable, except for some attributes such as *lipstick* and *hairstyle*. Then we investigate attributes' importance in different tasks. It is curious to know what the model really learns. We use the absolute values of coefficients obtained from DFAT to represent the importance of attributes to the tasks. All of the values are rescaled within [0, 1] for each task.

Figure 11 depicts all the attributes' responses in both Eastern and Western group. For the face modality, the first impression is that a bright smile is attractive for both groups. Besides, the results show that the ageing has the large impact to the female attractiveness. At a closer look, the attribute *age* is extremely sensitive in Eastern compared with Western. Meanwhile, *glasses* is well-responded in Western. For the dressing modality, the responses of attributes are different in two ethnic groups. The skirt or pant 'length' (i.e. long, normal, short) is very important to determine the attractiveness in Eastern group, but not for Western group. For Western group, *sleeve* is important compared with *dressing patterns*. Surprisingly, *color* has the small impact on the dressing attractiveness. For the voice modality, *smoothness* is the most important attribute to Eastern people. The reason can be explained as the language of Easterners is the isolating language. In the meantime, the loudness of voice plays the main factor to Western people to decide the voice attractiveness. Additionally, there is an 'overridden' phenomena which means one attribute is important but shows less important after new modality is added. For example, in Eastern group, the age's importance decreases when Face is combined with Voice. Another example is that in Western group, *loudness* is important in Voice modality, but its importance lowers when Face, Dressing and Voice are combined together.

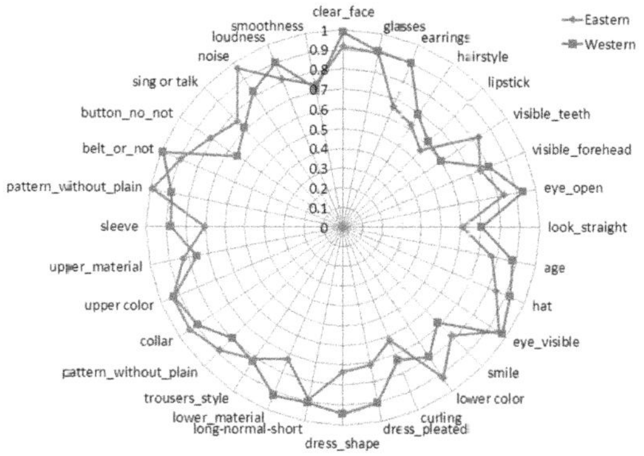

Figure 10: The accuracy of attribute prediction.

6. CONCLUSION AND FUTURE WORK

We have investigated the human sense of beauty via multimodality cues. To the best of our knowledge, we are the first to build female attractiveness dataset of multiple modalities, facial, dressing and voice. Its multi-cultural property may also be helpful for the further researches on cultures. We also proposed a tri-layer learning framework, namely DFAT, to learn attributes and attractiveness simultaneously. Extensive experimental evaluations on the M^{2}B dataset well demonstrate the effectiveness of the proposed DFAT framework for female attractiveness prediction. We believe that the work may help artificial intelligent reaches a new step in order to sense the beauty as human. One of our future directions is to use the latent variable approach for attribute mining. We also plan to investigate more suitable features of different modalities for attractiveness prediction, and build workable real system for practical applications.

7. ACKNOWLEDGEMENT

This work was supported by NExT Research Center funded under the research grant WBS. R-252-300-001-490 by MDA, Singapore. Bingbing Ni is supported by the research grant for the Human Sixth Sense Programme at the Advanced Digital Sciences Center from Singapores Agency for Science, Technology and Research (A*STAR).

8. REFERENCES

[1] Amazon Mechanical Turk. http://www.mturk.com.

[2] YouTube. http://www.youtube.com.

[3] TED Talk. http://www.ted.com.

[4] Video Lectures. http://videolectures.net.

[2]Accuracy is $(TruePositive + TrueNegative)/Total$.

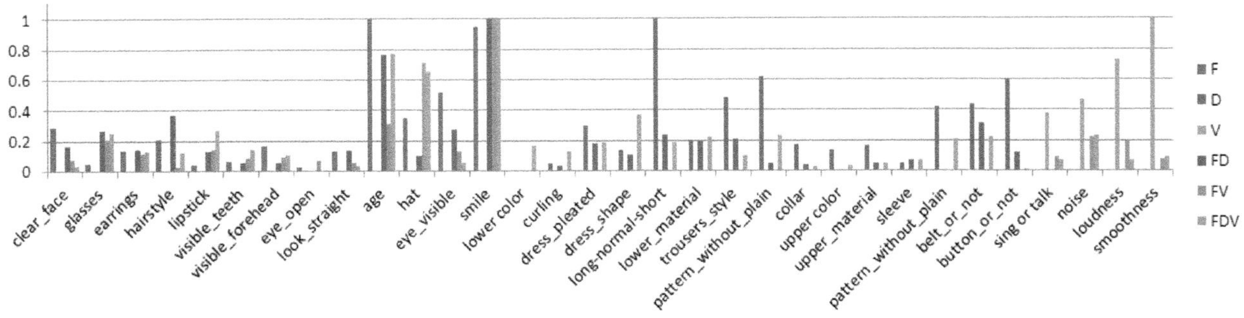

(a) Eastern

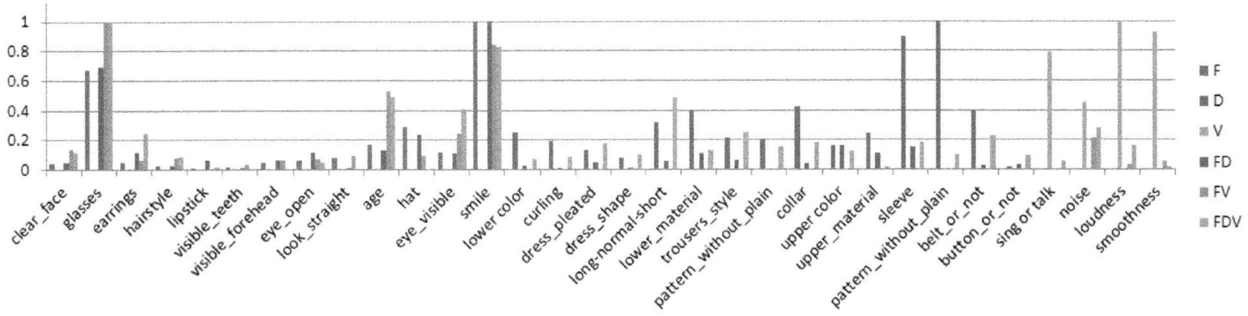

(b) Western

Figure 11: The importance of different attributes with respect to different tasks for (a) Eastern and (b) Western. For better viewing, please see original color pdf file.

[5] Doctrine of the Mean. http://en.wikipedia.org/wiki/Doctrine_of_the_Mean.

[6] Average Face. http://www.faceresearch.org/demos/average.

[7] P. Aarabi, D. Hughes, K. Mohajer, and E. M. The automatic measurement of facial beauty. *ICSMC*, 2001.

[8] T. Alley and M. Cunningham. Averaged faces are attractive, but very attractive faces are not average. *Psychological Science*, 1991.

[9] M. Beaupre. An ingroup advantage for confidence in emotion recognition judgments: The moderating effect of familiarity with the expressions of outgroup members. In *Personality and Social Psychology Bulletin*, 2006.

[10] T. L. Berg, A. C. Berg, and J. Shih. Automatic attribute discovery and characterization from noisy web data. In *ECCV*, 2010.

[11] L. Bourdev, S. Maji, and J. Malik. Describing people: A poselet- based approach to attribute classification. *ICCV*, 2011.

[12] B. Cheng, B. Ni, S. Yan, and Q. Tian. Learning to photograph. In *ACM Multimedia*, 2010.

[13] N. Dalal and B. Triggs. Histograms of oriented gradients for human detection. *CVPR*, 2005.

[14] J. Daugman. Uncertainty relations for resolution in space, spatial frequency, and orientation optimized by two-dimensional visual cortical filters. In *Journal of the Optical Society of America*, 1985.

[15] K. Dion, E. Berscheid, and E. Walster. What is beautiful is good. In *Journal of Applied Social Psychology*, 1972.

[16] Y. Eisenthal, G. Dror, and E. Ruppin. Facial attractiveness: Beauty and the machine. *Neural Computation*, 2006.

[17] A. Farhadi, I. Endres, D. Hoiem, and D. Forsyth. Describing objects by their attributes. In *CVPR*, 2009.

[18] A. Glassenberg, D. Feinberg, B. Jones, A. Little, and L. DeBruine. Sex-dimorphic face shape preference in heterosexual and homosexual men and women. *ASB*, 2009.

[19] D. Gray, K. Yu, W. Xu, and H. Gong. Predicting facial beauty without landmarks. *ECCV*, 2010.

[20] C. Green. All that glitters: A review of psychological research on the aesthetics of the golden section. In *Perception*, 1995.

[21] D. Guo and T. Sim. Digital face makeup by example. *CVPR*, 2009.

[22] S. Haykin. Neural networks. In *Prentice Hall*, 1999.

[23] S. Hughes, F. Dispenza, and G. Gallup. Ratings of voice attractiveness predict sexual behaviour and body configuration. *Evolution and Human Behavior*, 2004.

[24] T. Joachims. Optimizing search engines using clickthrough data. In *KDD*, 2002.

[25] A. Kagian, G. Dror, T. Leyvand, D. Cohen-Or, and E. Ruppin. A humanlike predictor of facial attractiveness. *NIPS*, 2005.

[26] N. Kumar, P. N. Belhumeur, and S. K. Nayar. Facetracer: A search engine for large collections of images with faces. In *ECCV*, 2008.

[27] C. Lampert, H. Nickisch, and S. Harmeling. Learning to detect unseen object classes by between-class attribute transfer. In *CVPR*, 2009.

[28] O. Lartillot and P. Toiviainen. MIR in Matlab: A toolbox for musical feature extraction from audio. In *ISMIR*, 2007.

[29] S. Lennon. Effects of clothing attractiveness on perceptions. In *Home Economics Research Journal*, 1990.

[30] R. Likert. Technique for the measurement of attitudes. *Arch. Psychol*, 1932.

[31] B. Ni, Z. Song, and S. Yan. Web image mining towards universal age estimator. In *ACM Multimedia*, 2009.

[32] T. Ojala, M. Pietikäinen, and T. Mäenpää. Multiresolution gray-scale and rotation invariant texture classification with local binary patterns. *T-PAMI*, 2002.

[33] A. Oliva and A. Torralba. Modeling the shape of the scene: A holistic representation of the spatial envelope. *IJCV*, 2001.

[34] P. Pallett, S. Link, and K. Lee. New golden ratios for facial beauty. In *Vision Research*, 2009.

[35] M. Riesenhuber and T. Poggio. Hierarchical models of object recognition in cortex. In *Nature Neuroscience*, 1999.

[36] Z. Song, M. Wang, X. Hua, and S. Yan. Predicting occupation via human clothing and contexts. *ICCV*, 2011.

[37] J. Tanaka, M. Kiefer, and C. Bukach. A holistic account of the own-race effect in face recognition: evidence from a cross-cultural study. In *Cognition*, 2004.

[38] P. Viola and M. Jones. Robust real-time face detection. *IJCV*, 2004.

[39] Y. Yang and D. Ramanan. Articulated pose estimation with flexible mixtures-of-parts. In *CVPR*, 2011.

[40] M. Zuckerman and K. Miyake. The attractive voice: What makes it so? In *Journal of Nonverbal Behavior*, 1993.

Leveraging Social Network Concepts for Efficient Peer-to-Peer Live Streaming Systems

Haiying Shen, Ze Li and Hailang Wang
Dept. of Electrical and Computer Engineering
Clemson University, Clemson, SC 29634
{shenh, zel, hailanw}@clemson.edu

Jin Li
Microsoft Research
Redmond, WA 98052
jinl@microsoft.com

ABSTRACT

In current peer-to-peer (P2P) live streaming systems, nodes in a channel form a P2P overlay for video sharing. To watch a new channel, a node depends on the centralized server to join in the overlay of the channel. The increase in the number of channels in today's live streaming applications triggers users' desire of watching multiple channels successively or simultaneously. However, the support of such watching modes in current applications is no better than joining in different channel overlays successively or simultaneously, which if widely used, poses heavy burden on the centralized server. In order to achieve higher efficiency and scalability, we propose a Social network-Aided efficient liVe strEaming system (SAVE). SAVE regards users' channel switching or multi-channel watching as interactions between channels. By collecting the information of channel interactions and nodes' interests and watching times, SAVE forms nodes in multiple channels with frequent interactions into an overlay, constructs bridges between overlays of channels with less frequent interactions, and enables nodes to identify friends sharing similar interests and watching times. Thus, a node can connect to a new channel while staying in its current overlay, using bridges or relying on its friends, reducing the need to contact the centralized server. Extensive experimental results from the PeerSim simulator and PlanetLab verify that SAVE outperforms other popular protocols in system efficiency and server load reduction.

Categories and Subject Descriptors

C.2.4 [**Distributed Systems**]: Distributed applications; H.3.5 [**Online Information Services**]: Data sharing

General Terms

Algorithms, Design, Performance

Keywords

P2P live streaming, Social networks, P2P networks

MM'12, October 29–November 2, 2012, Nara, Japan.

1. INTRODUCTION

Peer-to-Peer (P2P) live streaming applications [1, 2, 3] such as PPLive and UUSee are attracting millions of viewers every day. In current P2P live streaming systems, all nodes watching a channel form into a P2P overlay for streaming video sharing between each other. To watch a new channel, a node needs to contact the centralized server for the nodes in the channel in order to join in the channel's overlay. Nowadays, the wide coverage of broadband Internet enables users to enjoy live streaming programs effortlessly, and the increase of channels triggers users' desire of watching multiple channels successively or simultaneously (i.e., multi-channel watching mode). A typical multi-channel interface contains one main view and one or more secondary views (i.e., Picture in Picture (PIP)), so that users can switch freely between main view and PIPs.

However, since most current P2P live streaming systems only allow users to share the stream in one channel, the support of successive and simultaneous watching modes in current applications is no better than joining in different channel overlays successively or simultaneously. Although today's PPStream [3] application can support PIP, it also uses this strategy. A node watching multiple channels stays in multiple P2P overlays, and thus needs to take part in maintaining multiple overlays. As a node opens more channels, its maintenance cost for overlay connections increases dramatically. Also, in order to join in an overlay, a node needs to ask the server which nodes it can connect to. Thus, the successive-channel or multi-channel watching of millions of users poses heavy burden on the centralized server and delayed response leads to inefficiency in P2P live streaming systems [4].

In this paper, we aim to improve the efficiency and scalability of P2P live streaming systems with many users engaging many successive-channel watching or multi-channel watching by releasing the load on the centralized server. We propose a Social network-Aided efficient liVe strEaming system (SAVE). The key of its design is the utilization of social network concepts. By considering channels as nodes in a social network, SAVE regards users' channel switching or multi-channel watching as interactions between channels. By considering users as nodes in a social network, SAVE identifies users with the same interests and watching times as friends with social connections. Note that we leverage social network behavior properties rather than online social networks. Specifically, SAVE incorporates two main schemes: channel clustering and friendlist.

Channel clustering scheme. A node's watching activity is driven by its interests [5, 6]. Thus, nodes with similar interests tend to routinely watch the same channels and may watch them in the same time periods. Also, the channel watching activities of each node is mostly limited to a small number of channels that it is mostly interested in [7, 8, 9]. Therefore, SAVE clusters channels with frequent interactions. It merges channels with high frequent interactions into one overlay and builds bridges between the channels with less frequent interactions. Thus, in successive- or multi-channel watching, nodes can stay in the same overlay or take the inter-channel bridges to join in a new overlay without relying on the server with high probability. We propose a centralized algorithm and a decentralized algorithm for the channel clustering.

Friendlist scheme. Following the small-world property [10, 9, 11] that a node can always find another node within a limited number of hops, a node in a channel can find a node in another channel in a few steps via social connections between friends. Therefore, each node in SAVE maintains a friendlist recording nodes sharing common-interest channels and watching time periods. When a node wants to switch to a channel which is not in its current cluster or when a node returns to the system, it refers to its friendlist to find nodes in the desired channel to join the overlay. We propose an algorithm for identifying friends for the friendlist construction.

From the perspective of the entire system, for the individual nodes' skewed interests, some interests are shared by a large portion of the nodes in the system while others are shared by a small portion of the nodes. The former interests are handled by the channel clustering scheme and the latter interests are handled by the friendlist scheme. The two schemes contribute to three main features of SAVE listed below, and hence enhancing the system efficiency and scalability and the QoS in terms of satisfactory user experience.

- Low overhead. In SAVE, nodes can stay in the same overlay when they switch channels or watch multiple channels in most cases, which greatly reduces the overhead caused by frequent join and leave operations and overlay maintenance.
- Quick response. When switching channels, users experience delay, which is decided by both the buffering speed and the time cost of joining a channel [4]. Switching channels in SAVE in most cases does not cause users to leave current overlay and join in a new overlay, leading to low delay and better user experience.
- Light server load. Light server load can greatly reduce the bandwidth and hardware cost and improve system scalability. In SAVE, nodes can join in a new channel overlay without the participation of the server most of the time, reducing the sever load.

We conducted a survey on user streaming video watching activities. The survey result shows that: (1) users tend to watch different channels successively, (2) the distribution of a user's interests is skewed, and (3) many users share the same interests and watching times. Survey results confirm the social network properties in P2P live streaming systems and demonstrate the feasibility and necessity of SAVE to a certain extent. We conducted simulation in PeerSim [12] and deployed SAVE on PlanetLab [13]. Extensive experimental results prove that SAVE outperforms other popular protocols in terms of system efficiency and server load reduction.

2. RELATED WORK

P2P live streaming channel overlays. P2P live streaming overlays fall into four categories: tree [14, 15, 16, 17, 18, 19], mesh [20, 21, 22, 23, 24, 25, 26, 27], hybrid structure [28, 29, 30, 31, 32, 33] and Distributed Hash Table (DHT) [34]. In tree-based methods, parent nodes push all received chunks to their children. Mesh-based methods [21, 22, 23] connect nodes in a random manner. Each node usually serves a number of nodes while also receives chunks from others. Mesh-based methods are naturally resilient to churn, but they generate higher overhead. Hybrid methods synergistically combine tree-based and mesh-based structures. Wang *et al.* [30, 31] proposed a hybrid structure consisting of two tiers. PRIME [28] is a hybrid system featuring segmented and two-phase chunk delivery. It builds a tree in which nodes' topological distances to the server depend on their hops away from the server. The DHT-based structure [34] builds a hierarchical structure, in which the upper tier consists of stable DHT nodes and the lower tier consists of normal nodes. A video chunk requester relies on DHT functions to find a chunk owner for subsequent chunk retrieval. SAVE can help this approach to join multiple DHT overlays of different channels based on user preference to enhance efficiency.

Multi-channel P2P live streaming techniques. Current works on multi-channel P2P live streaming are mainly focused on bandwidth allocation optimization. In order to optimize the allocation of each node's upload capacity to each channel it is watching, Wu *et al.* [35, 36, 37] used game theory to resolve the conflicts in allocating bandwidth. By noticing that overlays are overlapped in multi-channel applications, DAC [38] divides the nodes in an overlap to several virtual logical nodes, each in a single channel overlay. Then, by mapping the service relationship among the independent overlays, DAC models the bandwidth allocation problem to a solvable global optimization problem. AnySee [22] uses the mesh overlay structure and maps logical overlay to the physical location topology. Path selection is based on physical location topology. Wang *et al.* [39] established linear programming models to answer a question: under what circumstances, should a particular design be used to achieve the desired streaming quality with the lowest implementation complexity?

Social network aided video-on-demand systems. There are few works on video streaming with the aid of social networks. In the video-on-demand system area, Cheng *et al.* [40] investigated the social networks in YouTube videos. They further proposed NetTube [5] that uses the links between related videos to generate a social network of nodes, and then uses a social network assisted prefetching strategy to achieve smooth transition between video playbacks.

3. DESIGN OF THE SAVE SYSTEM

3.1 An Overview of SAVE

Figure 1 shows a high-level view of the structure of SAVE. The server node (denoted by n_s) is the center of the entire network. Initially, all nodes in each channel form an overlay. When a node wants to join an overlay (i.e., to watch a channel), it asks for nodes in the overlay from n_s and then joins in the overlay through the recommended nodes. In SAVE, each channel overlay has a channel head denoted by h_c, which is a stable node with the highest capacity and longest lifetime staying in the channel. We assume that the cluster heads will not be overloaded in this paper, and leave the study of the additional load for functioning as cluster heads as our future work. SAVE has two main schemes: channel clustering and friendlist.

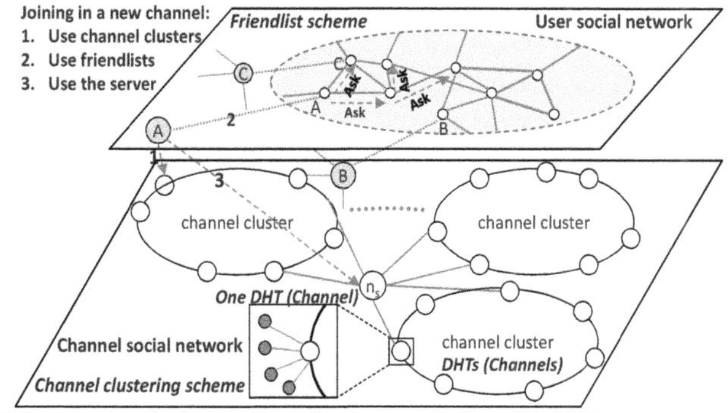

Figure 1: A high-level view of the SAVE structure.

Channel clustering scheme (Section 3.2). This scheme considers the interactions between channels, and connects the frequently-interacted channels (i.e., connects a group of nodes with similar successive- and multi-channel watching activities). As time proceeds, the information of watching activities of the nodes is collected, and the single channels are gradually grouped into channel clusters. Channel overlays in one *channel cluster*, denoted by *cr*, are merged into one overlay or are bridged. By bridged, we mean the head (h_c) of each channel overlay is connected with the heads of other channel overlays in the cluster. Each cluster also has a cluster head, denoted by h_{cr}, connecting with all h_cs in its cluster. The nodes in each channel cluster can, with great probability, quickly switch between or simultaneously watch their favorite channels without the involvement of the central server.

Friendlist scheme (Section 3.3). The friendlist scheme enables a node to maintain a friendlist recording nodes with similar individual channel watching patterns (i.e., interest channels and watching time). When a node wants to join a channel which is not in its current cluster, it can quickly join in the channel relying on the friendlist. Also, when a returning node (non-first-time user) starts to watch a channel, it can rely on its friendlist rather than the server to join the desired overlay.

As a result, when a node connects to a new channel, it first attempts to take advantage of the channel cluster. The node can directly request chunks in its current overlay if the overlay owns the channel. Otherwise, the node tries to take a bridge connecting to the new channel. If it fails, it uses its friendlist. If it cannot find a friend in its desired channel within certain hops, it resorts to the server finally.

3.2 Channel Clustering

We define $s(x, y)$ as a switching activity from channel x to channel y and define $m(x, y)$ as a multi-channel watching activity on both channels x and y. For a node's activity of $s(x, y)$, we define *age* as the time interval between when the switching occurred and the current time, which is used to represent the freshness of the switching activity. We define *duration(x)* as the time interval that the node stays in channel x before the switching of $s(x, y)$, and define *duration(y)* as the time interval that the node stays in channel y before its next switching. Similarly, for a node's activity of $m(x, y)$, we define *age* as the time interval between when the multi-channel watching occurred and the current time. We define *duration(x)* and *duration(y)* as the time interval that the node stays in both channels x and y before the multi-channel watching stops. Parameter $I(x) = 1$ when $duration(x) \geq T_s$; otherwise $I(x) = 0.1$, where T_s is a predefined threshold. In SAVE, each node has a profile that lists the node's interested channels specified by the node. If both x and y are in the node's interested channels, we consider the switching non-accidental, and set the value of parameter $inTags$ to 1. Otherwise, we set $inTags = 0.1$ in order to minimize the influence of accidental switching activities.

The *duration* and $inTags$ reflect, to a certain extent, whether both x and y are the node's favorite channels, and the switching or multi-channel watching is the node's routine activity. We use *channel closeness* of two channels to reflect the frequency of interactions between the channels. If a node's switching or multi-channel watching activity occurred more recently, it spent a certain time period in both channels, and $inTags = 1$, it means the node tends to watch both channels routinely. Such activities of many nodes indicate the higher closeness between the two channels. The channel head of channel y keeps a record of channel watching and switching activities of nodes in channel y, and calculates the *channel closeness* between channel x and y by

$$C(x, y) = \sum_{\Omega} \frac{I(x) \cdot I(y)}{\omega^{age}} \cdot inTags, \qquad (1)$$

where Ω stands for all the activities of $s(x, y)$ and $m(x, y)$, ω is the scaling parameter which exponentially reduces the freshness of switching and watching activities.

In fact, the closeness of two channels can be regarded as an undirected weighted link between the two channels in the social network graph, and the channel clustering is the process of grouping channels with high-weight links. SAVE aims to generate clusters that maximize the number of intra-cluster interactions and minimize the inter-cluster interactions. Driven by this objective, we first develop a centralized method using the server to collect global inter-channel activities for channel clustering. Then, we further develop a decentralized method to cluster channels by utilizing the local inter-channel activity information.

3.2.1 Centralized Channel Clustering

In the centralized clustering method, the centralized server node n_s needs the information of closeness between channels for channel clustering. To fulfill this information collection task, we use a two-tier information aggregation method, in which the activities are reported from nodes to their channel heads which calculate channel closeness and report the information to the server. For the channel clustering, the server relies on the minimum cut tree based algorithm, which generates sub-optimal clustering result but has low computation complexity. First, the server generates an undirected graph $G(V, E)$, where vertices (V) represent channels and edges (E) represent the interactions between channels. The weight of the edge connecting channels x and y is the sum of channel closeness $C(x, y)$ and $C(y, x)$. The server then uses the algorithm to divide the vertices in the entire graph to subsets. Consequently, all channels are clustered into different channel clusters. As shown in Figure 2, a *cut* is a divide of all the nodes V in graph G that separates G into two node subsets A and B. The value of a cut equals the sum of the weights of the edges crossing the cut. The minimum cut tree algorithm creates clusters that have small sum of inter-cluster cuts values and relatively large sum of intra-cluster cut values. Algorithm 1 shows the pseudo-code of the clustering algorithm. First, we insert an artificial sink t into the graph $G(V, E)$ (step 1). The sink is connected with all nodes in the graph with weight α ($0 \leq \alpha \leq 1$) (steps 2-4). α is used to control the number of generated clusters. If $\alpha = 0$, all channels will be in one giant cluster, while $\alpha = 1$ will make all nodes become singletons. Then, we use the maximum flow algorithm [41] which involves a recursive process to construct a minimum cut tree with the minimum sum of the values of cuts (step 5). After that, we remove the sink and graph G is divided into several clusters (steps 6-7). The intra-cluster cut value can be used to measure the tightness of channels in each cluster. If a cluster has tightness higher than a pre-defined threshold, its channels are merged to one overlay. Otherwise, its channels build bridges between each other.

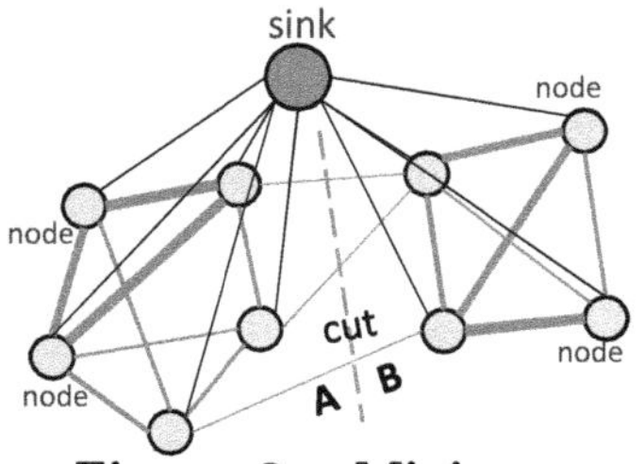

Figure 2: Minimum-cut tree-based clustering algorithm.

Algorithm 1: Centralized channel clustering algorithm executed by n_s.

1 $V' = V \cup t$; *//t is the sink;*
2 *//Connect t to V to generate an expanded graph* $G'(V', E')$;
3 **for** *all nodes* $v \in V$ **do**
4   *Connect v to t with an edge of weight* α;
5 *Calculate the minimum cut tree* T' *of* G';
6 *Remove t from* T';
7 *Divide G to clusters with small sum of inter-cluster cut values and large sum of intra-cluster cut values;*
8 **Return** *all connected sub-graphs as the clusters of G;*

3.2.2 Decentralized Channel Clustering

For ease of presentation, we use *channel cluster* to denote both individual channels and a cluster of multiple channels. Each cluster has a head, which is the most stable node with the highest capacity and longest lifetime staying in the cluster in all channel heads in the cluster. In the decentralized method, each cluster head collects both the intra-cluster and inter-cluster communications in a distributed manner in order to find the clusters with frequent interactions to group with. Consequently, the created clusters converge to a stable status, i.e., they have small sum of inter-cluster closeness and relatively large sum of intra-cluster channel closeness.

The channel head of channel y belonging to channel cluster cr_i collects the information of $I(x)$, $I(y)$, *age* and *inTags* for activities of $s(x, y)$ and $m(x, y)$, and reports the information to its cluster head h_{cr_i}. Then, h_{cr_i} builds a *cluster stability vector* denoted by $\mathcal{V}_d$ with length d, which is the number of channel clusters that its cluster has interacted with. We define an interaction from cluster cr_i to cluster cr_j as a channel switching from a channel in cr_i to a channel in cr_j. Each element in the vector $V(cr_i, cr_j)$ ($1 \leq j \leq d$), called *stability value*, is defined as:

$$V(cr_i, cr_j) = \sum_{\Psi} \frac{I(x) \cdot I(y)}{\omega^{age}} \cdot \nabla \cdot inTags, \quad (2)$$

where ($x \in cr_i, y \in cr_i$ *or* cr_j), Ψ stands for all the activities of $s(x, y)$ and $m(x, y)$ of channel x and channel y; channel x must be a channel in cr_i, while channel y can be a channel in cr_i or cr_j. This means the interactions can be within cr_i or between cr_i and cr_j. When $y \in c_{r_i}$, $\nabla = 1$ and when $y \in c_{r_j}$, $\nabla = -1$. Thus, the interactions between channels in cr_i increase the stability value, and the interactions between cr_i and cr_j decrease the stability value. $V(cr_i, cr_j)$ indicates the stability of cr_i relative to cr_j, and higher $V(cr_i, cr_j)$ means more channel interactions within cr_i than between cr_i and cr_j. This metric is used to form clusters so that the number of intra-cluster interactions is maximized while the number of inter-cluster interactions is minimized.

We use $\mathcal{V}_d^i$ and $\mathcal{V}_d^k$ to denote the $\mathcal{V}_d$ of cr_i and cr_k, respectively. If we group cr_i and cr_k into one cluster (i.e., $cr_{(i,k)} = cr_i \cup cr_k$), the inter-cluster interactions between cr_i and cr_k become intra-cluster interactions. Then, each element in the cluster stability vector of $cr_{(i,k)}$, $V(cr_{(i,k)}, cr_a)$ ($cr_a \in \mathcal{V}_d^i \cup \mathcal{V}_d^k$), equals:

$$V(cr_i, cr_a) + V(cr_k, cr_a) + V(cr_i, cr_k) + V(cr_k, cr_i), \quad (3)$$

where $V(cr_i, cr_a) = 0$ if $cr_a \notin \mathcal{V}_d^i$, and $V(cr_k, cr_a) = 0$ if $cr_a \notin \mathcal{V}_d^k$.

A channel cluster with higher popularity would attract more viewers, which shows the future trend in channel switching. Thus, we further consider the popularity of each channel cluster, measured by the number of users in the cluster, denoted by p, in calculating the cluster stability. If the channels in cr_j are very popular, nodes in cr_i have a higher tendency to watch the channels in cr_j and vice versa. We define *inverse popularity vector* ($\mathcal{P}_d$), which includes $1/p$ of each channel cluster of cr_i's interacted clusters, and calculate the *cluster stability degree* D by

$$D = \mathcal{P}_d \cdot \mathcal{V}_d{}^{\top}. \quad (4)$$

Channel clusters with larger D are more stable, i.e., more interactions occur within the cluster than outside the cluster.

Thus, in the decentralized channel clustering method, each cluster head periodically collects the information of intra-cluster and inter-cluster interactions between its own cluster and other clusters. It also asks for $\mathcal{V}_d$ from the cluster head of every other channel clusters it knows, and calculates the D of the cluster that combines its channel cluster and that cluster. Two clusters are combined if their combination leads to higher D than their individual Ds. Specifically, the head of each channel cluster cr_i conducts Algorithm 2 to identify channel clusters in all clusters Θ known to itself that it can group with so that its D is maximized. h_{cr_i} selects each cluster cr_k (step 3) and generates a virtual cluster $cr_{(i,k)} = cr_i \cup cr_k$ (step 4). Then, h_{cr_i} calculates this virtual cluster's D (step 6-10). If $cr_{(i,k)}$ is more stable than cr_i ($D_{cr_i} < D$), cr_i and cr_k will be combined. Finally, cr_i finds the cluster to group with that can make the cluster more stable, i.e., the number of inter-cluster interactions is minimized and the number of intra-cluster interactions is maximized (step 15).

If channel cluster cr_i selects cr_k to combine with, it sends an invitation to cr_k along with its vector $\mathcal{V}_d^i$. cr_k then decides whether adding cr_i will cause an increase of its D based on its own knowledge and $\mathcal{V}_d^i$. If yes, it accepts the invitation. If $D_{cr_{(i,k)}}$ is greater than a pre-defined threshold, two

Algorithm 2: Decentralized channel clustering procedure executed by cluster head h_{cr_i}.

Calculate $\mathcal{V}_d^i$ *and* D_{cr_i};
for *each channel cluster* $cr_k \in (\Theta - cr_i)$ **do**
  $cr_{(i,k)} = cr_i \cup cr_k$;
  Ask for $\mathcal{V}_d^k$ *from* h_{cr_k};
  for *each current channel cluster* cr_a *in* $\mathcal{V}_d^i \cup \mathcal{V}_d^k$ **do**
    Calculate $V(cr_{(i,k)}, cr_a)$ *in* $\mathcal{V}_d^{(i,k)}$ *(Equ.(3))*;
  Prepare $\mathcal{P}_d$;
  Calculate $D_{cr_{(i,k)}} = \mathcal{P}_d \times \mathcal{V}_d^{(i,k)\top}$;
  if $D_{cr_i} < D_{cr_{(i,k)}}$ **then**
    //$cr_{(i,k)}$ *is more stable than* cr_i;
    Return cr_k; *//return the selected* cr_k

Table 1: The record for a friend in the friendlist.

IP address	Similarity	Profile	Entry creation time

clusters merge to one overlay. Otherwise, they build bridges between each other. In order to make sure that the channels in one cluster have frequent interactions, each cluster head also periodically calculates the degree of its cluster excluding each channel. If excluding one channel leads to higher D, then the cluster head splits the channel from its cluster.

3.2.3 Cluster Combination and Partition

We use "cluster combination and partition" to represent both "bridge construction and removal" and "overlay integration and separation". SAVE has a hierarchical tree structure composed of the server, cluster heads (only in the decentralized clustering method), channel heads and nodes in each level from the top to the bottom. In the centralized clustering method, the server notifies channel heads to combine or partition. In the decentralized clustering method, the cluster heads communicate between each other for the cluster combination and partition. After a bridge is built between several channel clusters, the more stable and higher-capacity cluster head becomes the cluster head of the new cluster. The cluster head notifies the channel heads in other clusters, which update their connections with the new cluster head. The method for the overlay combination is based on the overlay construction method in different overlay structures. The newly selected head maintains a record of the head in each overlay before combination, which is used for possible subsequent overlay partition.

For bridge removal, the notified channel head removes the bridges to other channels in the cluster and becomes the head of the separated channel. The cluster head also notifies the channel heads in other channels in the cluster, which remove corresponding bridges. For overlay partition, the cluster head or server notifies the previous head of the identified cluster to separate its overlay from the cluster, and the remaining nodes in the cluster conduct corresponding updates.

3.3 Friendlist Construction

In SAVE, each node maintains a profile based on its own channel watching activities as shown in Figure 3. The "Interest tag" is a channel category such as comedy, sports and news that a node likes to watch. Today's live streaming applications usually list a number of interest tags for channels. SAVE requests users to fill their interest tags manually when they initially join in the system, and to periodically update their tags along with their increasing watching activities. In the figure, the "Channel" lists the channels that the node frequently watches in an interest tag. "Frequency" and "Watch time" stand for the frequency and time of watching the channels in an interest tag during a certain period. "Active vector" represents the daily watching routine of a node. By dividing the 24 hours of a day to T time slots, we can use a binary string to represent the activity of a node during a day. For example, 00010010 means that each digit stands for 3 hours and the user usually watches video from 10:00am to 1:00pm and 6:00pm to 9:00pm.

Interest tag	Channel	Frequency	Watch time	Active vector
Comedy	CNN, BBC	0.5/day	12 hours	00010010
Sports	ABC....	1.5/day	33 hours	00011010
...		...	...	...

Figure 3: The profile of a node.

To determine the similarity of two nodes' watching patterns, we consider not only their common interests but also their common frequently watched channels and the overlap of their watching time periods. We define the *similarity* of two nodes, n_i and n_j, as the product of the proportion of overlapping interest tags and the active vector,

$$S(n_i, n_j) = \sum_{tag_i \cap tag_j} S_{cl}(n_i, n_j) \times S_{av}(n_i, n_j), \quad (5)$$

where $tag_i \cap tag_j$ is the common tags between n_i and n_j; $S_{cl}(n_i, n_j)$ is the similarity between their two channel lists cl_i and cl_j, defined as $S_{cl}(n_i, n_j) = \frac{|cl_i \cap cl_j|}{|cl_i \cup cl_j|}$; $S_{av}(n_i, n_j)$ is the similarity of active vectors v_i and v_j of node n_i and n_j, define as $S_{av}(n_i, n_j) = \frac{|v_i \cap v_j|}{T}$. The *similarity* of two nodes represents the probability that they watch the same channel at the same time. Unlike other social network based methods [5] that only consider common interests, SAVE considers both interests and watching time for friend clustering, which leverages user routine behavior for efficient video sharing.

Each node in SAVE maintains a friendlist recording a certain number of friends sharing high similarity with itself. The record of a friend consists of the items listed in Table 1. One question is how a node can find friends to build and update its friendlist. Recall that for channel clustering, nodes report their channel switching activities to their channel heads. Then, the channel heads periodically report the information to the server in the centralized channel clustering method, and to their cluster heads which further forward the information to the server in the decentralized channel clustering method. Thus, nodes can piggyback their profiles on the reports. Consequently, the channel heads, and (or) cluster heads and (or) the server have profiles of many nodes. When node n_i communicates with the heads or the server during video watching, it can piggyback its profile on the message. The heads or server then send back a list of friends sharing high similarity with n_i, which updates its friendlist. To keep the friendlist updated, node n_i periodically updates its friendlist by calculating $\frac{S(n_i,n_j)}{Age(n_j)}$, where $Age(n_j)$ is the time interval between the creation/update time of the friend n_j in the friendlist and current time. The profiles with the similarity values less than a pre-defined threshold are discarded.

3.4 Efficient Multi-Channel Video Streaming

When node n_i initially joins in SAVE, it requests n_s to recommend nodes in its desired channel. The node then joins in the channel overlay by connecting to the recommended nodes and retrieve and share chunks with other nodes in the overlay. In a cluster, channels could be merged into one overlay or bridged. Because the channels in a merged overlay are very close to each other (i.e., nodes frequently conduct successive- or multi-channel watchings on these channels), when a node in a merged overlay wants to switch channel or watch multi-channels, it can find its requested chunks from its current overlay using the original chunk search algorithm with high probability. Because the bridged channels are relatively close to each other, a node can easily use the bridges to join in the overlay of its desired channel with high probability. If there is no bridge connecting to the desired channel, the node then uses its friendlist, and finally resorts to the server. The bridges in a channel cluster help a node join a channel frequently watched by itself and other nodes. The friendlist helps a node join a channel frequently watched by itself and its friends. The centralized server handles the case that a node occasionally watches a channel outside of its interests.

To use bridges for switching to channel c_j, node n_i in channel c_i directly sends a request with *chunkName* to its channel head h_{c_i}, which checks whether it connects to h_{c_j}. If yes, it forwards the request to h_{c_j}. Then, h_{c_j} responds to n_i with a few nodes in its channel overlay and also finds the owner of the requested chunk. The chunk owner sends the requested chunk to n_i. n_i connects to the returned nodes, and hence has joined in c_j. If h_{c_i} is not bridged with h_{c_j}, then n_i tries to use its friendlist to find a bootstrap node for joining c_j. n_i sends a request with TTL to all of its friends and TTL denotes the number of hops a request will be forwarded. After receiving the request, a node checks whether it is in the overlay of c_j. If not, it decreases the TTL by one and further forwards the request to its friends. Otherwise, it responds to the requester with a few nodes in its channel overlay. It also finds a chunk provider, which returns the requested chunk to n_i. Then, n_i connects to the returned nodes and has joined in c_j. The node with TTL=0 will notify n_i the failure of search. Then, n_i resorts to the server.

3.5 Structure Maintenance in Node Churn

The node churn is mainly about the node joins and departures from the system, namely the nodes are getting offline or online. SAVE needs to maintain its structure in node churn. To ensure there is always a head node in each channel, when a current channel head is departing, it selects a new head node and transfers all of its information to the new head. Also, it notifies all related nodes including all nodes in its channel and the channel heads of other channels in its cluster about the new channel head. It also notifies the server in the centralized method and notifies its cluster head in the decentralized method. In the decentralized clustering method, before a cluster head leaves, it notifies all channel heads in its cluster and the server about the new cluster head. The notified nodes update their connections accordingly. The new channel head or cluster head is a newly selected node. The joins and departures of normal nodes are handled by the original protocol in the P2P live streaming system. If node n_i has not received a response from its connected node n_j after a certain period of time, it assumes that n_j is dead or has left the system without warning. If n_j is a head, a new head will be elected. SAVE can use multiple channel heads and cluster heads to enhance system reliability, but at the cost of higher maintenance overhead.

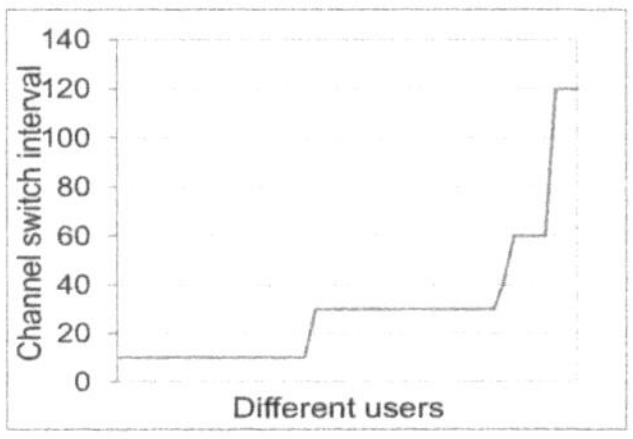

Figure 4: Channel switch interval.

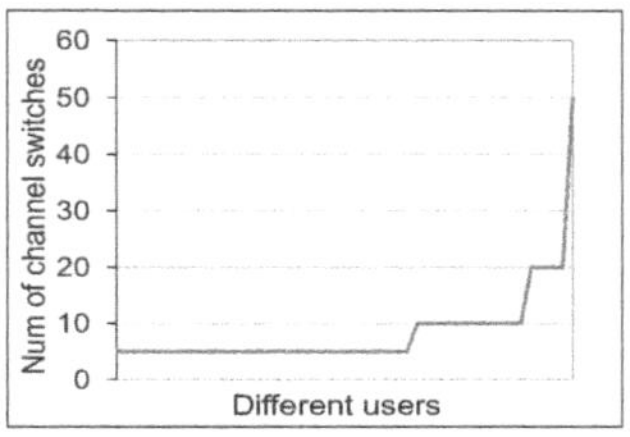

Figure 5: Number of channel switches.

4. SURVEY RESULTS

We conducted an online survey[1] on SurveyMonkey [42] on live streaming video watching activities. Though the survey is not as strong as real trace data, the survey results confirm the social network properties in online live streaming systems to a certain extent. We collected 60 responses in the community of undergraduate and graduate students in Clemson University. We will study more characteristics of successive and simultaneous multiple channel accessing in our future work.

4.1 Channel Switching Activities

One question in the survey is "how long on average do you watch a channel before you switch to another?" Figure 4 shows the channel switch interval in minutes for each user while watching streaming videos. We can see that most users have an interval between 10-30 minutes. 43% users have an interval of 20 minutes, 18% have an interval of more than 40 minutes and 7% have an interval of 120 minutes. The average interval between channel switches for all users is 30 minutes. The result shows a relatively frequent channel switching pattern of most users. We use *session* to represent the process that a user logs in the system, watches the streaming videos and logs out the system. Figure 5 plots the average number of channel switches per session of each user. We see 67% users switch channel 5 times, 22% switch channel 10 times, 9% and 2% switch channel 20 and 50 times, respectively. We then reach the following observation:

Observation(O) 1. *On average, a significant percent of users switch channels relatively frequently. A small percent of users stay in a channel for a relatively long time. Most users switch a certain number of channels per session, and a small percent of users switch channels many times per session.*

The frequent channel switch requests from millions of users would overload the centralized server and increase the latency of responses. This shows the necessity of SAVE. The nodes staying in a channel for a relatively long time can function as cluster heads that build bridges between each other in order to link the channels in a cluster. This reduces the maintenance overhead of bridges.

4.2 Feasibility of Channel Clustering

The result in Figure 5 implies that most users may have a certain number of favorite channels. From Figure 6, we see that the number of interests of each user varies from 1 to 10, with 50% of all users having no more than 3 interests and 96% of all users having no more than 7 interests. Based on Figures 5 and 6, we can reach:

[1]Survey link: http://www.surveymonkey.com/s/CQ2SZ2G

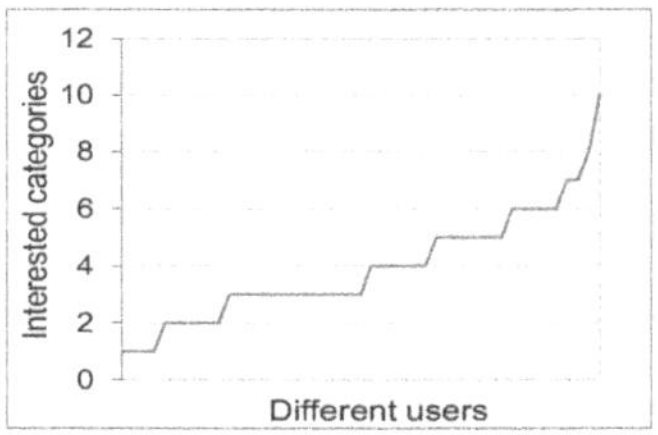

Figure 6: Number of interests.

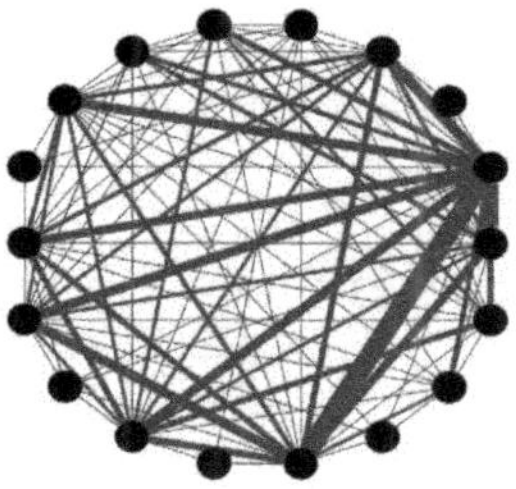

Figure 7: Interest correlation.

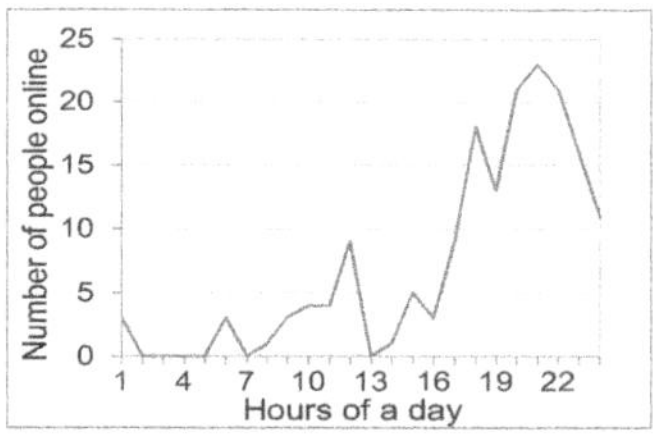

Figure 8: Online periods.

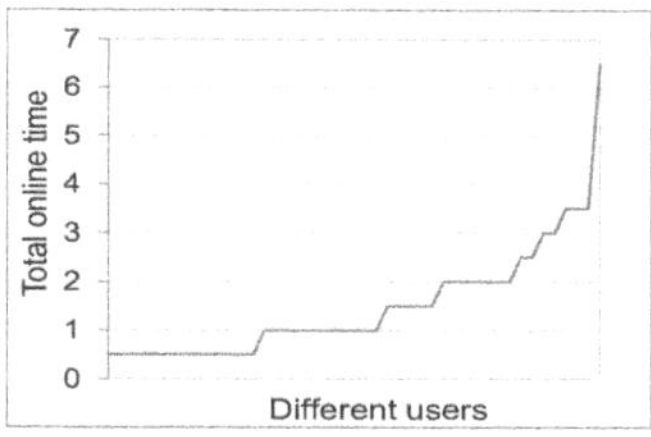

Figure 9: Online time.

O 2. *On average, most users usually watch channels in a few interests. A very small percentage of users switch between many channels.*

SAVE merges or bridges the channels that most users always watch, these users can share chunks in multiple channels or directly jump between the channels without relying on the centralize server. For the very small percent of users that switch between many channels, they can use friendlists for the switching. The server is needed for random channel switches.

We drew a graph for the 18 interests in the questionnaire, shown in Figure 7, in which a vertex represents an interest and a link connecting two interest vertices means one user has both interests. The link between two interest nodes has higher weight when these two interests are shared by more users. We observe that a certain number of interests have high-weight links between each other. This means that a relatively large percent of users share certain interests. In SAVE, clustering the channels in these interests by merging or bridging can facilitate fast switching between these channels. Also, the benefits of clustering would be more than the cost of cluster maintenances since many nodes would benefit from the merged overlay and bridges. We also find that some vertices have links with median weights. The nodes with these interests can use friendlists for switching channels. We arrive at an observation:

O 3. *Many nodes sharing common interests (i.e., watching and switching between the same channels) makes channel clustering and friendlist schemes viable and effective approaches for high video steaming efficiency.*

4.3 Video Watching Behavior Pattern

The user watching behaviors have a large impact on the performance of SAVE in terms of peer online time and channel switching behavior. Figure 8 shows the number of online users at specific hours within the day. We can see that most people watch videos between 18:00-23:00, which we called the "active period" (five hours in total). If we consider a node that has been online for more than half of this period as stable node, then from Figure 9, we can see that about 25% nodes qualify. Actually, according to [31], in video streaming applications, nodes generally have around 1.5 hours online time.

O 4. *Users are online for a relatively long time, with a considerable part of them being stable nodes.*

This observation is consistent with that in [43]. The stable nodes can serve as cluster heads to connect channels in a cluster together by building bridges between each other. Then, the adverse effect of churn on the clusters of SAVE is mitigated.

5. PERFORMANCE EVALUATION

We conducted experiments on the event-driven simulator PeerSim and PlanetLab which is a high-performance computing cluster in Clemson University. Each test lasts for 24 hours. In our simulation, the system consists of 10000 nodes and 100 channels. We set the video bit rate, which is the size of a video segment per second, to 600kbps. The ω in Equ.(2) was set to 1.02. In the PlanetLab experiment, we selected 300 online nodes and chose the computer with IP address 128.112.139.26 in Princeton University as the server. Considering that the PlanetLab test have much fewer nodes than the simulation, we reduced the number of channels to 30 in these two tests.

The TTL for friend lookup through friendlists was set to 2. The number of interests of each node is distributed in [1,7] according to the survey results shown in Figure 6. We regarded one interest as an interested channel. We divided the 30 or 100 channels to 5 groups, and each group has 6 or 20 channels. Each node chose 90% of its interested channels from one group randomly chosen from the 5 groups, and chose the remaining 10% of its interested channels randomly from the channels in other groups. When a node switches channels, it has 90% probability to watch a channel in its interested channels. The warm-up period lasted for 2 hours. The online time for nodes is distributed according to the survey result in Figure 9. The channel switching time is distributed according to the survey result in Figure 4. A node periodically switches channel after its switching interval time has elapsed. In order to keep the same number of nodes in the test while simulating node churn, after a node leaves the system, another node joins in the system. The statistics in [44, 5] is for the distribution of the download bandwidth in the simulation. A node's upload bandwidth is set to 1/3 of its download bandwidth [45].

In all previous P2P live streaming systems, a node needs to contact the central server for changing channels. Since mesh structure is used in most current P2P live streaming systems, we first built SAVE on the mesh structure and compared it with mesh-based system [2] (Mesh), tree-based system [16] (Tree) and DHT-based system (DCO) [34]. For SAVE, we have two variations using the centralized (Section 3.2.1) and decentralized (Section 3.2.2) channel clustering methods, represented by "SAVE-C" and "SAVE-D", respectively. We also built SAVE upon DCO for comparison.

5.1 Switching Delay and Server Load

Figure 10(a) and Figure 11(a) show the switch delays in the simulation and PlanetLab experiments, respectively. We randomly chose 1000 switchings from all switchings. We then ordered the switch delays in an increasing order, calculated the average value of every 100 values, and finally got

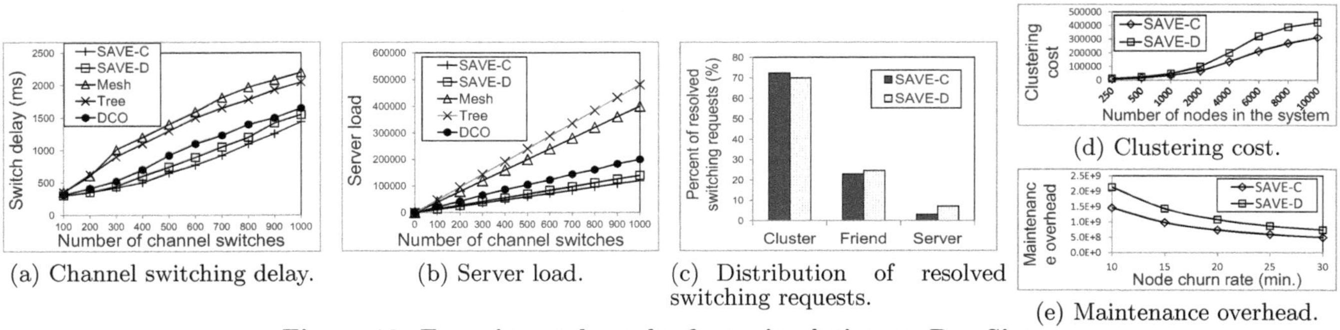

(a) Channel switching delay. (b) Server load. (c) Distribution of resolved switching requests. (d) Clustering cost. (e) Maintenance overhead.

Figure 10: Experimental results from simulation on PeerSim.

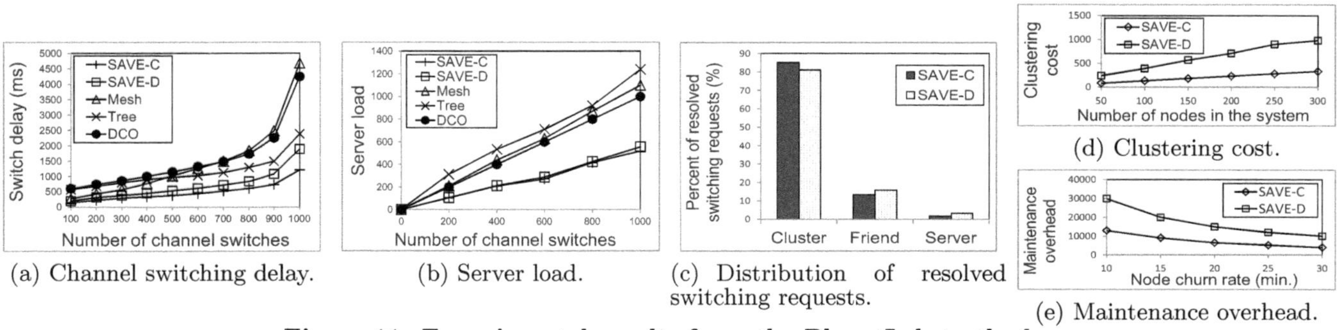

(a) Channel switching delay. (b) Server load. (c) Distribution of resolved switching requests. (d) Clustering cost. (e) Maintenance overhead.

Figure 11: Experimental results from the PlanetLab testbed.

10 average values. We see that both SAVE-C and SAVE-D achieve the fastest switching, which confirms their highly efficient video streaming. In other systems, a node needs to contact the centralized server in order to join in another overlay, generating a longer delay. SAVE-D has a slightly larger startup delay than SAVE-C. This is because SAVE-C has the global information of all channel switching activities of all nodes in the system for more accurate clustering channels, while SAVE-D relies on local cluster information exchanges. We also see that Tree produces slightly shorter delay than Mesh. This is because a node in Mesh needs to pull a chunk from its neighbors, while Tree uses push. DCO generates lower delay than Mesh and Tree in simulation, and generates lower delay than Mesh but higher delay than Tree in the PlanetLab results. DCO uses stable nodes as DHT nodes for locating chunk owners. In the simulation with a stable environment, nodes in DCO can always find chunk owners relying on DHT, leading to lower delay. However, in a less stable environment in the PlanetLab testbed, DHT nodes may fail, leading to chunk owner location failures and longer delay. We also observe that the delay on PlanetLab exhibits exponential growth, which is different from the simulation results. This is because in the simulation test, the bandwidths of nodes are constant while in PlanetLab, nodes' real bandwidth varies and some nodes have very low bandwidth, resulting in long delay in communication.

Figure 10(b) and Figure 11(b) show the server load (total number of requests served by the server) over time in the simulation and PlanetLab experiments, respectively. We observe that SAVE incurs significantly lower server load than other systems. SAVE releases the load on the server by clustering channels with frequent interactions and building friendlists. SAVE-C generates slightly lower server load than SAVE-D due to its more accurate clustering of channels. We see that Mesh generates slightly lower server load than Tree. This is because nodes in Tree needs to contact the server node more frequently because chunks often fail to transmit due to the vulnerability of the tree structure to churn. DCO produces lower server load than Mesh and Tree due to two reasons. First, nodes can easily find chunk owners relying on DHT. Second, nodes can subsequently receive chunks from the located owners.

5.2 Effectiveness of the Social Network in SAVE

Figures 10(c) and 11(c) show the percent of resolved switch requests using clusters, friends and the server in SAVE-C and SAVE-D in the simulation and PlanetLab experiments, respectively. In both systems, a significantly higher percent of switch requests are resolved by clusters. A moderate percent of requests are resolved by friends and a very small percent of requests are resolved by the server. The results demonstrate the effectiveness of the channel clustering and friendlist schemes. We also see that SAVE-C has higher percent in using clusters than SAVE-D because SAVE-C has higher accuracy in clustering channels than SAVE-D with global information.

5.3 Cost of SAVE

Figures 10(d) and 11(d) show the clustering cost of SAVE-C and SAVE-D measured by the total number of messages to cluster channels in the simulation and PlanetLab experiments, respectively. The clustering cost increases as the number of nodes in the system increases. Also, SAVE-D requires more communications than SAVE-C in building the clusters. This is because in SAVE-C, channel heads report to the server about node channel switching activities. In SAVE-D, channel heads report to their cluster heads about node channel switchings, and all cluster heads need to communicate with each other for cluster combining and splitting. However, the communication messages are distributed among many cluster head nodes, which does not increase server load.

Next, we test the maintenance overhead of SAVE in node churn measured by the total number of messages to handle node joins and departures. The lifetime of each node is chosen from $[x - 0.2x, x + 0.2x]$min, where the average lifetime x was varied from 10 to 30 with an increment of 5 in each step. Figures 10(e) and 11(e) show the maintenance

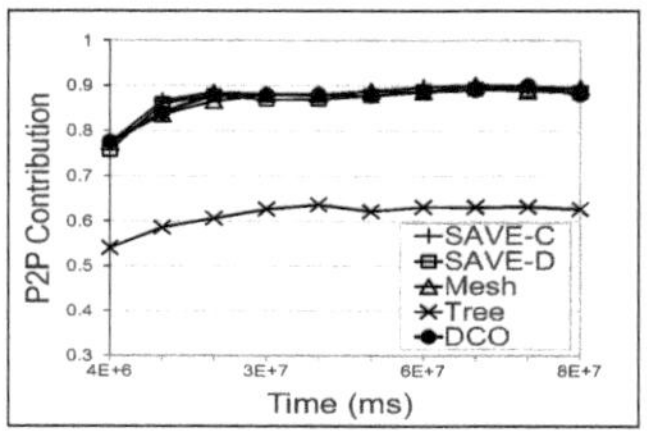

Figure 12: P2P contribution.

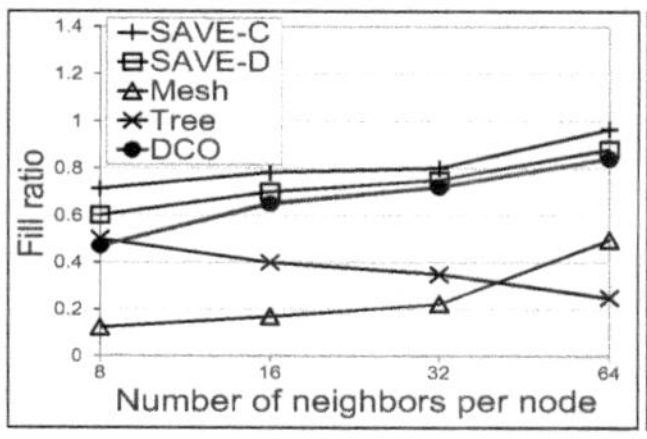

Figure 13: Fill ratio.

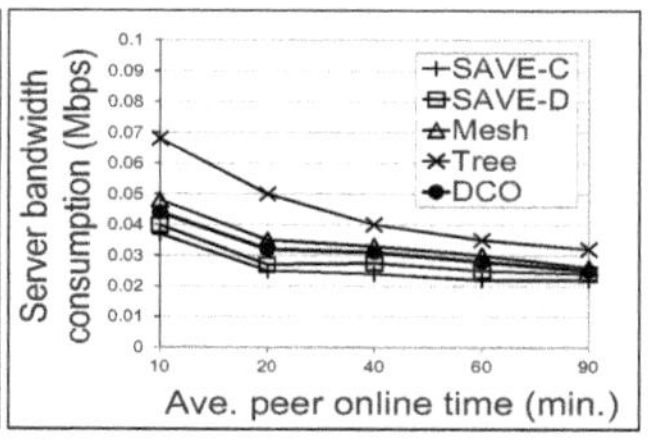

Figure 14: Server bandwidth consumption.

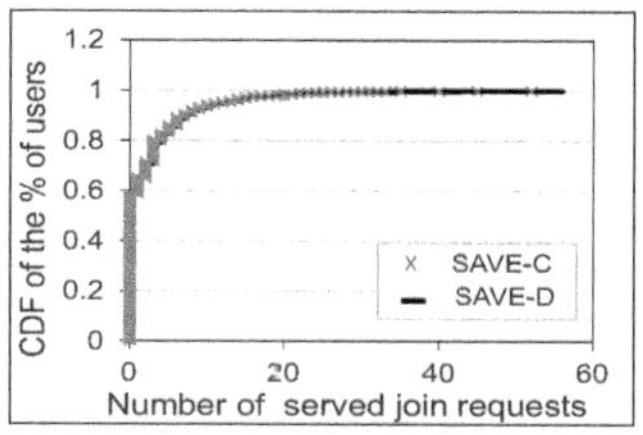

Figure 15: Load balance status.

overhead of SAVE-C and SAVE-D in the simulation and PlanetLab experiments, respectively. As the average lifetime increases, the maintenance overhead decreases. This is because slower node join and departure rate generates less messages for maintaining the SAVE structure. This is because in SAVE-C, channel heads connect with the server, while in SAVE-D, channel heads connect with cluster heads which connect with the server. We can see that SAVE's clustering cost and maintenance overhead is acceptable.

5.4 Overall P2P Performance

Below, we present simulation results for SAVE built on the DHT structure. Figure 12 shows the P2P contribution percentages over time measured by the number of chunk requests that are resolved by peers rather than the server. We see that all the percentages exhibit an increase at the beginning and then become stable. As time goes on, more and more chunks are disseminated to nodes, and chunks can be retrieved from nodes. Tree has a lower P2P contribution because it is more vulnerable to churn.

Fill ratio is defined as the ratio of nodes holding a chunk at a certain time. Figure 13 is the average fill ratio of different systems two seconds after a chunk is distributed by the server. We see that SAVE achieves much higher fill ratio than DCO. Because of SAVE's channel clustering and friendlist schemes, a node can join or switch channels without relying on the server. In DCO, a node needs to contact the centralized server in order to join in another overlay, generating a certain delay in chunk dissemination. SAVE-D has a slightly lower fill ratio than SAVE-C because the decentralized method is not as accurate as the centralized method in channel clustering, increasing the probability that a node's desired channel is not in its current cluster.

We also see that SAVE and DCO generate higher fill ratio than Mesh. In SAVE and DCO, the chunk discovery in each channel is based on DHT, which can guarantee chunk provider discovery. After a provider is located, the client directly asks the provider for subsequent chunks. In Mesh, a node pulls a chunk from their neighbors. As the number of neighbors per node increases, the fill ratio of Mesh increases significantly because more neighbors means chunks can be more quickly delivered to nodes. Tree's fill ratio is better than Mesh's when the number of neighbors is small, but becomes worse as the number increases. This is because each node has a bandwidth constraint. The chunk dissemination speed slows down as the number of children of a node increases.

Figure 14 shows the server bandwidth consumption as a function of the average peer online time. The results follow Tree>Mesh>DCO>SAVE-D>SAVE-C. SAVE based on DHT achieves the least sever bandwidth consumption due to its cluster clustering and friendlist schemes. SAVE-D>SAVE-C is because the centralized clustering method is more accurate. DCO provides high chunk availability with the aid of DHT, generating less sever bandwidth consumption than Mesh. Tree exhibits the highest server side bandwidth consumption because nodes have a higher probability of failing to obtain chunks from its parents under high network churn.

Figure 15 shows the CDF of nodes versus the load (number of channel or switch requests served) of different nodes in SAVE-C and SAVE-D. We see that up to 90% of all nodes have a load less than 20 requests, while more than 20% of all nodes have the opportunity to server other nodes. Hence, SAVE can utilize a significant portion of all nodes in a relatively even manner. Balance load distribution will not overload a node and thus user experience is not greatly degraded.

6. CONCLUSIONS

In this paper, we propose SAVE, a social network-aided efficient P2P live streaming system. SAVE supports successive- and multiple-channel viewing with low switch delay and low server overhead by optimizing the operations of joining and switching channels. SAVE considers the historical channel switching activities as the social relationships among channels and clusters the frequently interacted channels together by merging overlays or building bridges between the overlays. This maximizes the probability that existing users can locate their desired channels within its channel cluster and can take the bridges for channel switches. In addition, each node has a friendlist recording nodes with similar watching patterns, which is used to join a new channel overlay. Our survey on user video streaming watching activities confirms the necessity and feasibility of SAVE. Through the experiments on the PeerSim simulator and PlanetLab testbeds, we prove that SAVE outperforms other representative systems in terms of overhead, video streaming efficiency and server load reduction. Our future work lies in further reducing the cost of SAVE in structure maintenance and node communication. Also, we will design algorithms for cluster separation and cluster head re-election.

Acknowledgements

This research was supported in part by U.S. NSF grants OCI-1064230, CNS-1049947, CNS-1156875, CNS-0917056 and CNS-1057530, CNS-1025652, CNS-0938189, CSR-2008826, CSR-2008827, Microsoft Research Faculty Fellowship 8300751, and Oak Ridge Award 4000111689.

7. REFERENCES

[1] PPLive. http://www.pplive.com.
[2] UUSee. http://www.uusee.com.
[3] PPStream. http://www.ppstream.com.
[4] F. Dobrian, V. Sekar, I. Stoica, and H. Zhang. Understanding the impact of video quality on user engagement. In *Proc. of SIGCOMM*, 2011.

[5] X. Cheng and J. Liu. Nettube: Exploring social networks for peer-to-peer short video sharing. In *Proc. of INFOCOM*, 2009.
[6] M. Mcpherson. Birds of a feather: Homophily in social networks. *Annual Review of Sociology*, 27(1):415–444, 2001.
[7] C. Wilson, B. Boe, A. Sala, K. P.N. Puttaswamy, and B. Y. Zhao. User interactions in social networks and their implications. In *Proc. of EuroSys*, pages 205–218, 2009.
[8] A. Fast, D. Jensen, and B. Levine. Creating social networks to improve peer-to-peer networking. In *Proc. of SIGKDD*, 2005.
[9] A. Iamnitchi, M. Ripeanu, and I. Foster. Small-World File-Sharing Communities. In *Proc. of INFOCOM*, 2004.
[10] J. Kleinberg. The small-world phenomenon: An algorithmic perspective. In *Proc. of STOC*, pages 163–170, 2000.
[11] S. Milgram. The small world problem. *Psychology Today*, 1967.
[12] The PeerSim simulator. http://peersim.sf.net.
[13] PlanetLab. http://www.planet-lab.org/.
[14] Y. Chu, A. Ganjam, T. Ng, S. Rao, K. Sripanidkulchai, J. Zhang, and H. Zhang. Early experience with an internet broadcast system based on overlay multicast. In *Proc. of USENIX*, 2004.
[15] S. Banerjee, B. Bhattacharjee, and C. Kommareddy. Scalable application layer multicast. In *Proc. of SIGCOMM*, Pittsburgh, PA, USA, 2002.
[16] Y. Chu, S. Rao, and H. Zhang. A case for end system multicast. In *Proc. of ACM SIGMETRICS*, 2000.
[17] D. Tran, K. Hua, and T. Do. Zigzag: An efficient peer-to-peer scheme for media streaming. In *Proc. of INFOCOM*, 2003.
[18] V. N. Padmanabhan, H. J. Wang, P. A. Chou, and K. Sripanid-kulchai. Distributed streaming media content using cooperative networking. In *Proc. of ACM NOSSDAV*, 2002.
[19] M. Castro, P. Druschel, A. Kermarrec, A. Nandi, A. Rowstron, and A. Singh. Splitstream: High-bandwidth multicast in cooperative environments. In *Proc. of SOSP*, 2003.
[20] S. Asaduzzaman, Y. Qiao, and G. Bochmann. CliqueStream: an efficient and fault-resilient live streaming network on a clustered peer-to-peer overlay. In *Proc. of P2P*, 2008.
[21] X. Zhang, J. Liu, B. Li, and T. P. Yum. CoolStreaming/DONet: a data-driven overlay network for peer-to-peer live media streaming. In *Proc. of INFOCOM*, 2005.
[22] X. Liao, H. Jin, Y. Liu, L. M. Ni, and D. Deng. AnySee: Peer-to-Peer Live Streaming. In *Proc. of IEEE INFOCOM*, 2006.
[23] V. Pai, K. Kumar, K. Tamilmani, V. Sambamurthy, and A. E. Mohr. Chainsaw: eliminating trees from overlay multicast. In *Proc. of IPTPS*, 2005.
[24] T. Locher, S. Schmid, and R. Wattenhofer. eQuus: a provably robust and locality-aware peer-to-peer system. In *Proc. of P2P*, 2006.
[25] Y. Guo, C. Liang, and Y. Liu. Adaptive queue-based chunk scheduling for P2P live streaming. In *Proc. of IFIP Networking*, 2008.
[26] L. Massoulie, A. Twig, C. Gkantsidis, and P. Rodriguez. Randomized decentralized broadcasting algorithms. In *Proc. of INFOCOM*, 2007.
[27] F. Picconi and L. Massoulie. Is there a future for mesh-based live video streaming? In *Proc. of P2P*, 2008.
[28] N. Magharei and R. Rejaie. PRIME: peer-to-peer receiver-driven mesh-based streaming. In *Proc. of INFOCOM*, 2007.
[29] J. Venkataraman and P. Francis. Chunkyspread: multi-tree unstructured peer-to-peer multicast. In *Proc. of IPTPS*, 2006.
[30] F. Wang, Y. Xiong, and J. Liu. mTreebone: a hybrid tree/mesh overlay for application-layer live video multicast. In *Proc. of ICDCS*, 2007.
[31] F. Wang, J. Liu, and Y. Xiong. Stable Peers: Existence, Importance, and Application in Peer-to-Peer Live Video Streaming. In *Proc. of INFOCOM*, pages 1364–1372, 2008.
[32] J. Mol, A. Bakker, J. Pouwelse, D. Epema, and H. Sips. The design and deployment of a bittorrent live video streaming solution. In *Proc. of ICM*, 2009.
[33] Y. Liu. Delay bounds of chunk-based peer-to-peer video streaming. *TON*, 18(4):1195–1206, 2010.
[34] H. Shen, L. Zhao, Z. Li, and J. Li. A DHT-Aided Chunk-Driven Overlay for Scalable and Efficient Peer-to-Peer Live Streaming. In *Proc. of ICPP*, 2010.
[35] C. Wu and B. Li. Strategies of conflict in coexisting streaming overlays. In *Proc. of INFOCOM*, pages 481–489, 2007.
[36] C. Wu, B. Li, and Z. Li. Dynamic bandwidth auctions in multioverlay p2p streaming with network coding. *IEEE TPDS*, 2008.
[37] C. Wu, B. Li, and S. Zhao. Multi-channel live P2P streaming: Refocusing on servers. In *Proc. of INFOCOM*, 2008.
[38] M., L. Xu, and B. Ramamurthy. Flexible divide-and-conquer protocol for multi-view peer-to-peer live streaming. In *Proc. of P2P*, 2009.
[39] M. Wang, L. Xu, and B. Ramamurthy. Linear Programming Models For Multi-Channel P2P Streaming Systems. In *Proc. of INFOCOM*, 2010.
[40] X. Cheng, C. Dale, and J. Liu. Statistics and social network of youtube videos. In *Proc. of IWQoS*, 2008.
[41] R. Gomory and T. Hu. Multi-Terminal Network Flows. *Journal of the Society for Industrial and Applied Mathematics*, 9(4):551 – 570, 1961.
[42] Surveymonkey: Free online survey software and questionnaire tool. http://www.surveymonkey.com/.
[43] F. Wang, J. Liu, and Y. Xiong. Stable peers: existence, importance, and application in peer-to-peer live video streaming. In *Proc. of IEEE INFOCOM*, 2008.
[44] C. Huang, J. Li, and K. W. Ross. Can internet video-on-demand be profitable? In *Proc. of SIGCOMM*, 2007.
[45] The difference between upload and download speed for broadband DSL. http://www.broadbandinfo.com/cable/speed-test.

Jetway: Minimizing Costs on Inter-Datacenter Video Traffic

Yuan Feng, Baochun Li
Department of Electrical and Computer Engineering
University of Toronto

Bo Li
Department of Computer Science
Hong Kong University of Science and Technology

ABSTRACT

It is typical for video streaming service providers (such as NetFlix) to rely on services from cloud providers (such as Amazon), in order to build a scalable video streaming platform with high availability. The trend is largely driven by the fact that cloud providers deploy a number of datacenters inter-connected by high-capacity links, spanning different geographical regions. Video traffic across datacenters, such as video replication and transit server-to-customer video serving, constitutes a large portion of a cloud provider's inter-datacenter traffic. Charged by ISPs, such inter-datacenter video traffic incurs substantial operational costs to a cloud provider. In this paper, we argue that costs incurred by such inter-datacenter video traffic can be reduced or even minimized by carefully choosing paths, and by assigning flow rates on each inter-datacenter link along every path. We present *Jetway*, a new set of algorithms designed to minimize cloud providers' operational costs on inter-datacenter video traffic, by optimally routing video flows in an online fashion. Algorithms in *Jetway* are designed by following a methodical approach based on an in-depth theoretical analysis. As a highlight of this paper, we have built a real-world system framework to implement and deploy *Jetway* in the Amazon EC2 datacenters. With both simulations and real-world experiments using our implementation, we show that *Jetway* effectively helps transmitting videos across datacenters with reduced costs to cloud providers and satisfactory real-world performance.

Categories and Subject Descriptors

C.2.4 [**Computer-Communication Networks**]: Distributed Systems

Keywords

Inter-Datacenter Traffic, Flow Optimization

1. INTRODUCTION

Due to abundant resource availability and reduced management costs, it is an emerging trend for video streaming service providers, such as Netflix, to resort to the services of cloud providers, such as Amazon Web Services (AWS). As an example, Netflix is using the Amazon Simple Storage Service (S3) for storing all of its video masters, which are further transcoded to a number of video formats, and are then distributed to Content Distribution Networks (CDNs), ready to be served to end users [1,2].

On the other hand, Amazon Web Services as cloud providers have recently introduced *CloudFront*, a CDN service with edge servers around the world, designed to meet the needs of video streaming providers. CloudFront seamlessly integrates with Amazon S3 and the Amazon Elastic Compute Cloud (EC2), so that videos hosted in S3 or EC2 can be streamed using the Real Time Messaging Protocol (RTMP) to end users, from one of the edge servers with geographical proximity and low network latencies [3]. In addition, in order to accommodate high-definition videos, Amazon S3 has substantially raised its limit on object sizes (from 5 GB to 5 TB) in December 2010 [4]. Given such a win-win situation as video streaming providers are going "100% cloud" [1], it will be a near-term certainty that large volumes of video traffic will flow from cloud datacenters (*e.g.,* S3), which host video masters, to CDN edge servers (*e.g.,* CloudFront), which serve end users.

The tenet of providing cloud services is to maximize the sharing of resources, while keeping tenants (*e.g.*, Netflix) satisfied. To provide cloud services with better availability and scalability, it is customary for cloud providers to deploy a number of datacenters across different geographical regions. These datacenters are typically inter-connected with high-capacity links leased from ISPs. With substantial upfront investments to construct these datacenters, it is certainly to the advantage of cloud providers to minimize operational costs. Recent research reveals that traffic costs amount to around 15% of operational costs incurred to a cloud provider, a percentage that is similar to energy costs [5].

As large quantities of high-definition videos are being hosted in these datacenters, a substantial amount of inter-datacenter traffic will be incurred by replicating these videos and by serving these videos to CDN edge servers, in order to provide a highly available and scalable streaming service. Such inter-datacenter video traffic constitutes a large portion of a cloud provider's inter-datacenter traffic. Since most cloud providers today rely on multiple Internet Service Providers (ISPs) to connect their geographically dispersed datacenters [6], operational costs can be effectively reduced, if costs charged by these ISPs on inter-datacenter video traffic can be minimized.

Given dominant percentile-based charging models currently in use by most ISPs [7], *e.g.*, the 95-th percentile charging model, it is feasible to reduce or even minimize cloud providers' costs by designing optimal routing and flow assignment algorithms for inter-datacenter video traffic. In other words, video flows across inter-datacenter links can be — and should be — *split and trans-*

mitted along multiple multi-hop paths, each of which can be optimally and dynamically computed over time. The rationale is that, the cost of transmitting the same amount of videos varies significantly across different inter-datacenter links, due to regional pricing and peering relationships among ISPs [8]. For example, domestic video flows are substantially cheaper than flows to global destinations, and video flows within the backbone network built by cloud providers themselves incur very low costs.

Further, spatial and temporal characteristics of inter-datacenter video traffic also motivates the design of new routing and flow assignment algorithms. *Temporally*, a portion of the video flows across datacenters may be more delay-tolerant than others, if they represent video replication and backups. To reduce costs, we may re-route these delay-tolerant video flows by using intermediate datacenters as relays, flowing over multi-hop paths and splitting into multiple paths [9]. *Spatially*, datacenters located in different time zones experience peak video traffic at different times, providing more opportunities of resource multiplexing.

In this paper, we present *Jetway*, a new set of algorithms designed to minimize operational costs on inter-datacenter video traffic in an efficient and simple way. To guide the design of our algorithms in *Jetway*, we present a methodical and in-depth analytical study on how inter-datacenter video traffic costs are to be minimized by routing video flows via multiple multi-hop paths in an optimized fashion. With *Jetway*, we take advantage of different traffic costs on inter-datacenter links, usually charged by a multitude of ISPs with the percentile-based charging model, taking into account practical constraints of limited link capacities, as well as different *desired transmission rates* of videos, representing their delay tolerance. Our study leads to new combinatorial algorithms that are simple yet efficient enough for cloud providers to implement in practice: video flows are split and routed in an on-the-fly fashion by solving the classic *minimum-cost multicommodity flow* and *maximum concurrent flow* problems. An illustrative example of routing inter-datacenter video flows is shown in Fig. 1, in which the width of each flow denotes the flow rate on a particular link.

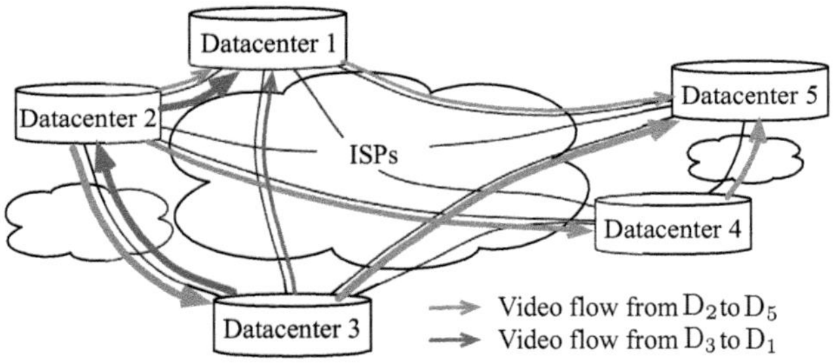

Figure 1: Selecting the best paths for inter-datacenter video traffic in a cloud with 5 datacenters. Based on differing traffic costs on inter-datacenter links and varying transmission rates of videos, the video from Datacenter 2 (D_2) to Datacenter 5 (D_5) is best routed along path $\{D_2 \to D_1 \to D_5\}$, $\{D_2 \to D_3 \to D_5\}$, and $\{D_2 \to D_4 \to D_5\}$, represented by red (light gray) flows; the video from Datacenter 3 (D_3) to Datacenter 1 (D_1) is best routed along path $\{D_3 \to D_2 \to D_1\}$ and $\{D_3 \to D_1\}$, represented by blue (dark gray) flows.

We evaluate the performance of *Jetway* in minimizing costs on inter-datacenter video traffic with our real-world implementation in the Amazon EC2 cloud, as well as extensive simulations. Our *Jetway* implementation has been developed based on a flexible and reusable video streaming framework: a highly-optimized packet forwarder is hosted on each datacenter in the cloud, referred to as a *Jet*. We have developed the *Jet* from scratch using the asynchronous networking interface in the OS kernel, taking advantage of the Asynchronous I/O (`asio`) framework in the Boost C++ library. The *Jet* is optimized to support concurrent video flows, each with its own routing paths and flow assignments. Both our real-world experimental results and simulations have shown that, by routing video flows optimally, *Jetway* is capable of reducing costs on inter-datacenter video traffic.

The remainder of this paper is organized as follows. In Sec. 2, we discuss the challenges of minimizing operational costs on inter-datacenter video traffic to a cloud provider, and formulate the optimal routing and flow assignment problem in an online fashion. In Sec. 3, we propose algorithms in *Jetway* that seek to minimize costs by splitting and routing video flows optimally. In Sec. 4, we present our real-world implementation of *Jetway* in detail, and evaluate its performance with both real-world experiments in the Amazon EC2 cloud and simulations. We discuss related work and conclude the paper in Sec. 5 and Sec. 6, respectively.

2. *JETWAY*: RATIONALE, CHALLENGES, AND PROBLEM FORMUATION

We first present the rationale and challenges that motivate the design of *Jetway*, with an objective of minimizing operational costs on inter-datacenter video traffic.

2.1 Rationale and Challenges

A cloud provider is usually charged by ISPs for its inter-datacenter traffic. The operational costs incurred are typically based on the amount of traffic the cloud provider generates. The percentile-based charging model, which is also called the q-th percentile charging model, is predominantly used by ISPs today. With this charging model, an ISP records the traffic volume a cloud provider generates during each 5-minute interval and sort them in a descending order. At the end of a complete charging period, the q-th percentile of all 5-minute traffic volumes is considered as the charging volume x, which will be used to derive the cost by a piece-wise linear non-decreasing function $c(x)$ [10]. For example, if the 95-th percentile charging model is in use and the charging period is one year, then the charging volume x of the cost function corresponds to the traffic volume sent during the 99864-th sorted interval ($95\% \times 365 \times 24 \times 60/5 = 99864$).

Besides the fact that traffic costs on each inter-datacenter link differ from one another, in that a relay path might incur much lower costs than a direct path, the percentile-based charging model provides further opportunities to reduce operational costs. With a percentile-based charging model, if some video traffic is already generated on one link, idling or transmitting less video traffic in subsequent time intervals within the same charging period will be a waste of capital investment, as these time intervals will be charged based on the already generated traffic volume anyway. As such, a feasible way to reduce costs is to carefully design routing paths and flow assignments for each pair of inter-datacenter video flow — a key idea in the design of *Jetway* — such that the idling and under-utilized time intervals are eliminated as much as possible, and the q-th percentile of video volumes over all time intervals is minimized.

The following example intuitively explains the rationale of optimal routing with the percentile-based charging model. Shown in Fig. 2, 3 videos are to be transferred in an inter-datacenter network with 4 datacenters. Assume that Video 1 and 2 are to be streamed from datacenter D_2 to D_4 with rate 8 and from D_3 to D_1 with rate 6 within the first time interval, respectively; and Video 3 is to be streamed from D_3 to D_4 with rate 5 in the second time interval. For the sake of simplicity, we assume that the 100-th percentile charging model with a linear cost function is in use in this example, which implies that the cost incurred between each datacenter pair is the maximum video volume sent during these time intervals, multiplied by a flat cost per traffic unit shown on the link. The link capacity are assumed to be 5 for all the links.

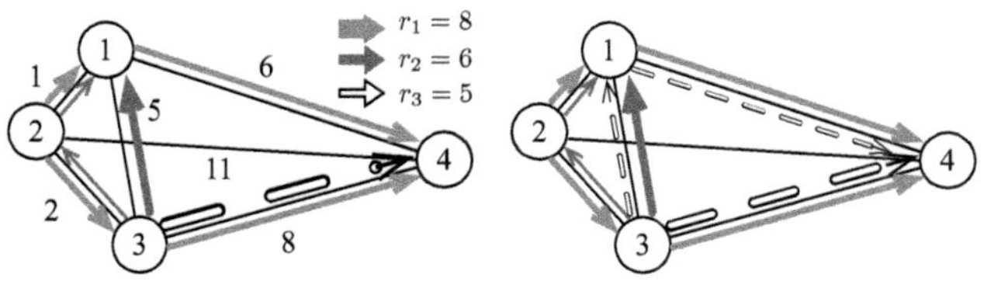

(a) Optimal routing considering link costs only

(b) Optimal routing considering link costs and the charging model

Figure 2: How traffic costs can be reduced with optimal routing: a motivating example.

If the difference of costs per unit of traffic on each inter-datacenter link is considered, cheaper paths are preferred by video flows to reduce traffic costs. Shown in Fig. 2 (a), the optimal routing and flow assignment in this scenario is: Video 1 will take paths $D_2 \to D_1 \to D_4$ and $D_2 \to D_3 \to D_4$, each with a flow of 4 and Video 2 will take paths $D_3 \to D_2 \to D_1$ and $D_3 \to D_1$ with flow 1 and 5, respectively in the first time interval; and Video 3 will take the direct path at the second time interval, leading to a total cost of 104 per time interval.

If we further incorporate the consideration of the 100-percentile charging model in this example, we can see that a part of Video 3 can be routed along the more expensive path $D_3 \to D_1 \to D_4$, taking advantage of the already generated traffic volume on this path in past time intervals, when carrying the flows of Video 1 and 2. Shown in Fig. 2 (b), the optimal routing and flow assignment in this scenario is to route Video 3 through path $D_3 \to D_1 \to D_4$ and $D_3 \to D_4$ in the second time interval, with rates 1 and 4, respectively. By doing so, costs on inter-datacenter video traffic per time interval can be reduced to 96, as Video 3 is carried for free with the percentile-based charging model.

Unfortunately, applying the basic concept of multi-hop routing in each video flow presents formidable challenges when it comes to more general cases, involving multiple video flows with different source-destination datacenters. Due to the consideration of the percentile-based charging model, the dimension of *time* has to be taken into account when computing incurred costs on a link, which increases the complexity of the problem significantly. The cost of inter-datacenter video traffic in one time interval is affected by the traffic volume in time intervals before and after that time interval within the same charging period. If we wish to optimize the cost globally, we will need to estimate future traffic demand within the entire charging period (say, a month or a year), yet inter-datacenter traffic may not be accurately predictable beyond much finer time scales (such as a few seconds) [11]. In order to design algorithms to minimize costs incurred by inter-datacenter video traffic, it is our objective to formulate the problem such that it is practically solvable, yet sufficiently efficient.

2.2 Network Model

Before formulating the problem of minimizing operational costs on inter-datacenter traffic formally, we first introduce our network model in this paper. Important notations used throughout this paper are listed in Table 1.

Table 1: Notations and Definitions

Notation	Definition
$\mathcal{V}$	the set of datacenters operated by a single cloud provider
$\mathcal{E}$	the set of directed links connecting datacenters in $\mathcal{V}$
$\mathcal{K}(t)$	the set of video flows initiated in the time interval t
(s_k, d_k)	source and destination datacenters of video flow k
r_k	the desired transmission rate of video flow k
c_{ij}	the available capacity on link $\{i, j\}$
a_{ij}	the cost per traffic unit on link $\{i, j\}$
f_{ij}^k	the flow assigned on link $\{i, j\}$ for video flow k
$\bar{t}$	the duration of one time interval
I	the number of time intervals in a charging period
$\max_t f_{ij}$	the maximum aggregate flow rate on link $\{i, j\}$ up to interval t
$d_{ij}(t)$	the rate of other inter-datacenter traffic on link $\{i, j\}$ in the time interval t
$\text{cost}_{ij}(t)$	the operational costs on link $\{i, j\}$ up to interval t
$\mathcal{K}_f(t)$	the already paid set of video flows during interval t
$\mathcal{K}_c(t)$	the set of video flows with additional cost during interval t

We consider a cloud with multiple geographically distributed datacenters operated by a single cloud provider. Every datacenter in the cloud is connected to all other datacenters. We use a complete directed graph $\mathcal{G} = (\mathcal{V}, \mathcal{E})$ to represent the inter-datacenter network, where $\mathcal{V}$ indicates the set of datacenters, and $\mathcal{E}$ indicates the set of directed links inter-connecting datacenters. For each link $\{i, j\} \in \mathcal{E}$, we use a non-negative real-value function a_{ij} to denote the cost per traffic unit from datacenter i to j; a positive function $c_{ij}(t)$ to denote the available link capacity at time t, which is the maximum available rate of transmission from datacenter i to j.

Let $\mathcal{K}(t)$ be the set of videos to be transmitted at time t, all of which are represented by source-destination video flows. During its transmission to the destination datacenter, each flow can be split and relayed by other datacenters, *e.g.*, it can be routed over multiple paths and multiple hops within a path. For each video flow $k \in \mathcal{K}(t)$, we use a specification (s_k, d_k, r_k) to describe it. Here, vertices s_k and d_k indicate the source and the destination datacenter from and to which flow k is being routed, and r_k is the desired transmission rate for video flow k. In the interest of minimizing traffic costs incurred on inter-datacenter links, the desired transmission rate for each video flow that is being replicated to other datacenters is obtained by its size divided by its corresponding maximum tolerable transfer time; and is the minimum rate for an enjoyable video playback for transit server-to-customer video flows.

Since the time dimension has to be considered in the percentile-based charging model, we use a time-slotted model to incorporate multiple time intervals in a charging period. Let I be the number of time intervals in a charging period, with t as indices. The duration of one time interval is assumed to be 5 minutes, which is denoted by $\bar{t}$. To focus on the essence of the problem, we assume that the 100-th percentile charging model is in use, *i.e.*, a cloud provider is charged based on the *maximum* of traffic volumes generated over all time intervals in a charging period. Our results can be extended to a cloud environment with any percentile-based charging model, which will be a topic of discussion forthcoming in this paper.

For simplicity, we assume that the cost function $c(x)$ is a linear function $c(x) = a \cdot x$, where x is the traffic volume to be charged. To be exact, if we use $f_{ij}(t)$ to denote the aggregate flow rate on link $\{i, j\}$ in the time interval t, cost on inter-datacenter traffic in one charging period is the dot product:

$$\text{cost} = \sum_{\{i,j\}\in\mathcal{E}} a_{ij}(\max_I f_{ij})\bar{t}I,$$

where $\max_I f_{ij}$ is the maximum aggregate flow rate on link $\{i,j\}$ of all $f_{ij}(t)$, from $1 \le t \le I$. Note that the aggregate flow rate $f_{ij}(t)$ may also contain other inter-datacenter traffic such as backups and propagation of large updates. If we use $d_{ij}(t)$ to denote the rate of this part of flow on link $\{i,j\}$ in the time interval t, then the aggregate flow rate on link $\{i,j\}$ can be represented by

$$f_{ij}(t) = d_{ij}(t) + \sum_{k\in\mathcal{K}(t)} f_{ij}^k(t),$$

where $f_{ij}^k(t)$ indicates the amount of flow assigned on link $\{i,j\}$ for video flow k in the time interval t.

To capture the fact that each video flow k may be initiated at any time in a charging period, and will also be terminated after a period of time, we let $r_k(t)$, the desired transmission rate of video flow k, depend on the time index t, indicating whether or not flow k is in transmission. More precisely:

$$r_k(t) = \begin{cases} r_k & t \in \text{time intervals video flow } k \text{ is in transmission,} \\ 0 & \text{otherwise.} \end{cases}$$

To simplify the model, we assume that video flows are always initiated at the beginning of a time interval, and terminated at the end of a time interval.

2.3 Formulating the Online Problem

In the design of *Jetway*, the problem we are trying to solve is: what is the optimal routing and flow assignment strategy we can apply to inter-datacenter video flows initiated in the current time interval to minimize operational costs, with the assumption that *past* (historical) information is known? In other words, we seek to find optimal routing paths and flow assignments for each video flow initiated in the current time interval t, so that the operational costs to the cloud provider are minimized till the end of time interval t, given all routing paths and flow assignments for video flows initiated from time interval 1 to $t-1$.

If we use $\text{cost}_{ij}(t)$ to denote the operational costs on link $\{i,j\}$ *up to* time interval t, the optimal routing and flow assignment problem in *Jetway* can be formulated as the following optimization problem, with the assumption that all datacenters in the cloud possess information about all video flows:

$$\min_{f_{ij}^k(t)} \quad \sum_{\{i,j\}\in\mathcal{E}} \text{cost}_{ij}(t) \tag{1}$$

$$\text{s.t.} \quad \sum_{k\in\mathcal{K}(t)} f_{ij}^k(t) + d_{ij}(t) \le c_{ij}(t), \forall\{i,j\}\in\mathcal{E} \tag{2}$$

$$\sum_{j\in\mathcal{V}} f_{ij}^k(t) = \sum_{j\in\mathcal{V}} f_{ji}^k(t), \forall k \in \mathcal{K}(t), \forall i \in \mathcal{V}/\{s_k, d_k\}$$

$$\sum_{j\in\mathcal{V}} f_{s_k j}^k(t) - \sum_{j\in\mathcal{V}} f_{j s_k}^k(t) = r_k(t), \forall k \in \mathcal{K}(t) \tag{3}$$

$$f_{ij}^k(t) \ge 0, \forall k \in \mathcal{K}(t), \forall\{i,j\}\in\mathcal{E}, \tag{4}$$

where $\text{cost}_{ij}(t)$ equals the product of the maximum aggregate flow rate on each link over t time intervals and the duration of a time interval with the 100-th percentile charging model, *i.e.*,

$$\text{cost}_{ij}(t) = a_{ij}(\max_t f_{ij})\bar{t}I. \tag{5}$$

The optimization variable of problem (1) is $f_{ij}^k(t)$, which indicates the flow assigned on link $\{i,j\}$ for video flow k in the time interval t. The assumption is that flows assigned on every link for each video flow in the past time intervals, and current flow rates incurred by other applications are known *a priori*, *i.e.*, $f_{ij}^k(1)$ up to $f_{ij}^k(t-1)$ and $d_{ij}(t)$ are known. Inequality (2) stands for the link capacity constraint, which ensures that the total flow assigned on one link will not exceed its current capacity. Inequalities (3) represent the flow conservation constraint. For each video flow, the flows going into any intermediate datacenter should equal to flows going out of that datacenter; while the flows coming from the source datacenter should be exactly the same as its desired transmission rate. Inequality (4) ensures that all flows are non-negative.

With the 100-th percentile charging model, the cost function (5) can be rewritten as:

$$\text{cost}_{ij}(t) = \begin{cases} \text{cost}_{ij}(t-1) & f_{ij}(t) \le \max_{t-1} f_{ij} \\ a_{ij} f_{ij}(t)\bar{t}I & \text{otherwise.} \end{cases}$$

Based on historical information, $\max_{t-1} f_{ij}\bar{t}$, the charging volume up to time interval $t-1$, is known. The cost function on link $\{i,j\}$ up to time interval t is equivalent to:

$$\text{cost}_{ij}(t) = \text{cost}_{ij}(t-1) + a_{ij}(t)\left(f_{ij}(t) - \max_{t-1} f_{ij}\right)\bar{t}I, \tag{6}$$

where $a_{ij}(t)$ is a step-function of $f_{ij}(t)$ that has the form of:

$$a_{ij}(t) = \begin{cases} 0 & f_{ij}(t) \le \max_{t-1} f_{ij} \\ a_{ij} & \text{otherwise.} \end{cases}$$

By substituting Eqn. (6) into the objective function, we get the following optimization problem that is equivalent to problem (1):

$$\min_{f_{ij}^k(t)} \sum_{\{i,j\}\in\mathcal{E}} a_{ij}(t) f_{ij}(t)\bar{t}I. \tag{7}$$

If we focus on decisions in the time interval t, and drop the time indices in the problem expressions, we can see that the optimization problem (7) is in the form of the classic minimum-cost multicommodity flow problem.

However, none of the algorithms solving the minimum-cost multicommodity flow problem can be applied to solve this problem. The reason is that $a_{ij}(t)$ is now a function of $f_{ij}(t)$, which results in a non-linear cost function. Since our objective is to find a simple yet efficient algorithm that can be readily implemented, we would like to study alternative and more tractable formulations of this problem.

3. SPLITTING AND ROUTING FLOWS OPTIMALLY TO MINIMIZE COSTS

From Eqn. (6), we find that the cost on a link up to time interval t equals the sum of the cost on that link up to time interval $t-1$, and the additional cost incurred by the possible overflow in the time interval t. This implies that, if the traffic volume on a link during one time interval is less than the charging volume on that link *up to* the previous time interval, which is the maximum aggregate flow rate on that link over $t-1$ time intervals times the duration of one time interval, no additional costs will be incurred. In other words, the traffic volume in interval t is carried on the link *for free*. However, if the traffic on that link exceeds the previous charging volume, the cloud provider will be charged extra for the overflow.

Fig. 3 illustrates the operational costs on link $\{i,j\}$. Having the charging volume up to time interval $t-1$, the same amount of traffic is already paid for in the time interval t, no matter if it is used up or not. The blue net area in the figure represents the already paid portion of the traffic volume, and the red diagonal area indicates

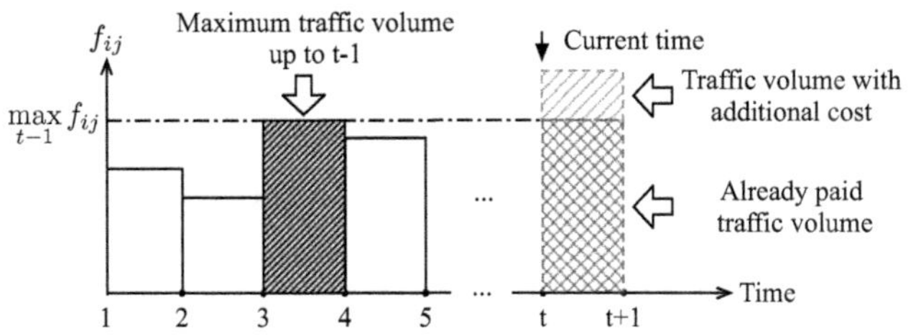

Figure 3: An illustration of the operational costs on link $\{i, j\}$.

the potential traffic volume that will incur additional costs. This implies that, if the video flows on each link are assigned in a fashion that, *the already paid portion of the traffic volume is utilized as much as possible, and the traffic volume with additional costs is minimized*, the operational costs on inter-datacenter traffic up to time interval t will be minimized as a result. Based on this idea, the design of *Jetway* is based on decoupling problem (1) into two sequential optimization problems.

3.1 Fully Utilizing the Already Paid Portion of Traffic Volume

Having $\max_{t-1} f_{ij}\bar{t}$ as the charging traffic volume on link $\{i, j\}$ up to time interval $t-1$, the amount of already paid traffic flow in the time interval t can be obtained as $\sum_{\{i,j\}\in\mathcal{E}} \min(\max_{t-1} f_{ij}, c_{ij}(t) - d_{ij}(t))\bar{t}$, in which the flow on each link is determined by its charging traffic volume up to time interval $t-1$ and its available link capacity in the time interval t. Choosing from video flows initiated in the time interval t, we can obtain a subset $\mathcal{K}_f(t)$, in which the sum of the desired transmission rates are the *maximum* possible amount that is no larger than the already paid traffic volume divided by the duration of a time interval in interval t. $\mathcal{K}_f(t)$ is the already paid set of video flows to be carried during time interval t. In the ideal case, all video flows in $\mathcal{K}_f(t)$ should be carried without incurring additional costs.

As a consequence, for video flows in $\mathcal{K}_f(t)$, our objective is to find their *feasible flow assignments*, under the joint link capacity constraint, the flow conservation constraint, and the non-negative flow assignment constraint. The optimization presentation of this problem is to find the maximum fraction z, such that up to z fraction of each flow's desired transmission rate is assigned on links in the time interval t [12]. Referred to as the *maximum concurrent flow problem*, it has the following form:

$$\max_{f_{ij}^k(t)} \quad z \tag{8}$$

$$\text{s.t.} \quad \sum_{k\in\mathcal{K}_f(t)} f_{ij}^k(t) + d_{ij}(t) \le \min(\max_{t-1} f_{ij}, c_{ij}(t)), \forall\{i,j\}$$

$$\sum_{j\in\mathcal{V}} f_{ij}^k(t) = \sum_{j\in\mathcal{V}} f_{ji}^k(t), \forall k \in \mathcal{K}_f(t), \forall i \in \mathcal{V}/\{s_k, d_k\}$$

$$\sum_{j\in\mathcal{V}} f_{s_k j}^k(t) - \sum_{j\in\mathcal{V}} f_{j s_k}^k(t) = z r_k(t), \forall k \in \mathcal{K}_f(t)$$

$$f_{ij}^k(t) \ge 0, \forall k \in \mathcal{K}_f(t), \forall\{i,j\} \in \mathcal{E}$$

$$0 \le z \le 1.$$

Note that compared to the general maximum concurrent flow problem, optimization problem (8) has its additional constraints resulted from our objective to minimize costs on inter-datacenter video traffic. Instead of being restricted by the available link capacity only, the capacity constraint in problem (8) is further restricted by the already paid portion of video traffic on each link, which ensures that no potential cost is incurred.

There exists a fast combinatorial algorithm to approach the ϵ-optimal solution of this problem. A flow assignment is said to be ϵ-optimal if it overflows the link capacities by at most $1+\epsilon$ factor and has a cost that is within $1+\epsilon$ of the optimum. Since ϵ can be defined as small as possible, the ϵ-optimal solution can approach the optimum value as close as possible. It has been proved that the ϵ-optimal flow can be computed deterministically in $O(\epsilon^{-2} knm \log K \log^3 n)$ time, where K is the number of commodities (video flows), m is the number of links, and n is the number of datacenters in the cloud [13].

The general idea of this algorithm is to find the minimum dual variable λ that indicates the congestion of flows. The procedure is as follows. Routing each video flow separately, an initial flow assignment $\mathbf{f^k}$ that satisfies the desired transmission rate and obeys the link capacity constraint to the extent of λ_k is obtained for all $k \in \mathcal{K}_f(t)$. Define a cost function b_k to each flow assignment $\mathbf{f^k}$ with respect to a non-zero, non-negative length function. Repeatedly examine all flows in $\mathcal{K}_f(t)$ in a round-robin fashion. If a flow is found with a "bad" flow assignment by solving its corresponding minimum-cost flow problem, its flow assignment is updated. Note that the minimum-cost flow problem at each iteration can be solved by successive approximation,which has a running time of $O(\min(nm\log n, n^{5/3}m^{2/3}, n^3)\log(nC))$ [14].

The combinatorial maximum concurrent flow algorithm is described in **Algorithm 1**, where a potential function ϕ is used to guide the algorithm [13].

Algorithm 1 *The combinatorial maximum concurrent flow algorithm.*

Obtain the initial solution $(\mathbf{f^1}, \mathbf{f^2}, ..., \mathbf{f}^{|\mathcal{K}_\mathbf{f}(\mathbf{t})|})$.
Set $\alpha = 3(1+\epsilon)\bar{\lambda}^{-1}\ln m\epsilon^{-1}$; $\sigma = (2\epsilon)/(\alpha\bar{\lambda}^{-1})$.
while $\lambda_f > (1-\frac{\epsilon}{2})\bar{\lambda}$ & $\Delta\phi > \epsilon^2\phi^{(\frac{\epsilon}{k})}$ **do**
  for Each $k \in \mathcal{K}_f(t)$ **do**
    Find the minimum cost flow assignment $\mathbf{f^{k*}}$ over $\mathbf{P^k}$.
    if $b_k - b_k^* \ge \epsilon b_k$ **then**
      Update $\mathbf{f^k} = \mathbf{f^k} + \sigma(\mathbf{f^{k*}} - \mathbf{f^k})$.
    end if
  end for
end while
Return $(\mathbf{f^1}, \mathbf{f^2}, ..., \mathbf{f}^{|\mathcal{K}_\mathbf{f}(\mathbf{t})|})$.

3.2 Minimizing the Additional Cost

The optimal fraction z^* obtained by solving problem (8) indicates that at most z^* fraction of flows from $\mathcal{K}_f(t)$ can be carried using the already paid traffic volume. If $z^* = 1$, all flows in $\mathcal{K}_f(t)$ can be carried without additional cost. If $z^* < 1$, only $z^* F_k$ of each video flow k incurs no extra cost, and the transmission of the remaining part of each flow does incur an additional cost. In this case, we use the same indicator k to denote the leftover part of the original video flow k, which has a transmission rate of $(1-z^*)r_k$.

Let $\mathcal{K}_c(t)$ denote the set of video flows that incur additional costs in the time interval t, including both flows in $\mathcal{K}(t) - \mathcal{K}_f(t)$ and the remaining partial flows in $\mathcal{K}(t)$ after solving optimization problem (8). Since the traffic of carrying video flows in $\mathcal{K}_c(t)$ is bound to incur additional costs, the cost function remains a linear function with a flat per-unit cost. As a result, the optimal flow assignment for these flows can be found by solving a minimum-cost multicommodity flow problem with a linear cost function in the time interval

t, which is exactly in the form of *minimum-cost multicommodity flow problem*.

The conventional way of solving this problem is to express it as a linear program, and then to solve it with a polynomial-time linear program solver [12]. Similar to the maximum concurrent flow problem, there exists a fast combinatorial algorithm to approach the ϵ-optimal solution to this problem, and the running time of this combinatorial algorithm is proved to be $\tilde{O}(\epsilon^{-3}Kmn)$ [15].

The algorithm solves the problem as follows. Represent the flow assignment as $(\mathbf{f^1}, \mathbf{f^2}, ..., \mathbf{f}^{|\mathcal{K}_\mathbf{c}(\mathbf{t})|}) \in (\mathbf{P^1}, \mathbf{P^2}, ..., \mathbf{P}^{|\mathcal{K}_\mathbf{c}(\mathbf{t})|})$, where $\mathbf{f^k}$ is the $|\mathcal{E}| \times 1$ flow assignment vector for flow k, and $\mathbf{f^k} \in \mathbf{P^k}$. The polytope $\mathbf{P^k}$ corresponds to the feasible flow assignments of flow k, *i.e.*, flow assignments that obey the flow conservation constraint and the individual link capacity constraint, disregarding the rest of the video flows. At each iteration, a flow k is randomly chosen for any $k \in \mathcal{K}_c(t)$. Compute the minimum-cost flow assignment $\mathbf{f^{k^*}}$ over $\mathbf{P^k}$, and update its flow assignment $\mathbf{f^k}$ to $(1-\sigma)\mathbf{f^k} + \sigma\mathbf{f^{k^*}}$ if it causes a decrease in the potential function ϕ, which is used to guide the algorithm [15]. Similarly, the minimum-cost flow problem at each iteration can be solved by successive approximation [14]. The combinatorial minimum-cost multicommodity flow algorithm is described in **Algorithm 2**.

Algorithm 2 *The combinatorial minimum-cost multicommodity flow algorithm.*

```
Obtain the initial solution (f^1, f^2, ..., f^{|K_c(t)|}).
Set α = (1/ε) ln(3|E|); σ = Θ(1/α^3).
while φ(f^1, f^2, ..., f^{|K_c(t)|}) > 3|E| do
    Randomly choose k ∈ K_c(t).
    Find the minimum cost flow assignment f^{k*} over P^k.
    if φ(f^1, ..., f^{k*}, ..., f^{|K_c(t)|}) < φ(f^1, ..., f^k, ..., f^{|K_c(t)|}) then
        Update f^k = (1 − σ)f^k + σf^{k*}.
    end if
end while
Return (f^1, f^2, ..., f^{|K_c(t)|}).
```

Our complete routing and flow assignment strategy in *Jetway* in the time interval t is presented in **Algorithm 3**. As indicated by our problem formulation, the routing and flow assignment for video flows in *Jetway* is updated in a periodic fashion, which can be adjusted flexibly by cloud providers.

Implementation Issues. A key assumption in **Algorithm 3** is that every datacenter is required to possess information about all video flows. If we need a distributed heuristic, there are both good and bad news. The good news is that there exist distributed algorithms to approach the ϵ-optimal solution of the maximum concurrent flow problem [16], which we use to maximize the utilization of the already paid portion of the traffic volume. The bad news is that the design of efficient distributed solutions to the minimum-cost multicommodity flow problem — which we use to minimize additional traffic costs — remains an open and elusive problem in theoretical computer science [17]. Fortunately, since all datacenters are operated by the same cloud provider, we believe that, partly due to the small number of datacenters in use, it is technically straightforward to devise a centralized controller to obtain and access information about all the video flows, which makes the algorithm design in *Jetway* much less dependent on the availability of distributed algorithms.

Although the 100-percentile charging model is used as an example in this paper, our algorithm is not only limited to this specific charging model. Instead, it can be applied to any percentile-based

Algorithm 3 *Routing and flow assignment strategy in the time interval t.*

```
Compute the already paid traffic volume in the time interval t.
Obtain the set of video flows K_f(t).
For all flows k ∈ K_f(t), find the optimal flow assignment (f^1, f^2, ..., f^{|K_f(t)|})*_f by solving the maximum concurrent flow problem using Algorithm 1.
Obtain the set of video flows K_c(t).
For all flows k ∈ K_c(t), find the optimal flow assignment (f^1, f^2, ..., f^{|K_c(t)|})*_c by solving the minimum-cost multicommodity flow problem using Algorithm 2.
for Each flow k ∈ K(t) do
    if k ∈ K_f(t) & k ∈ K_c(t) then
        f^{k*} = f^{k*}_f + f^{k*}_c.
    else
        if k ∈ K_f(t) then
            f^{k*} = f^{k*}_f.
        else
            f^{k*} = f^{k*}_c.
        end if
    end if
end for
Return (f^1, f^2, ..., f^{|K(t)|})*.
```

charging model as a feasible approach to reduce traffic cost when no workload prediction is considered. With a general q-th percentile charging model, the charging volume will be the $q*I$-th largest traffic volume over all time intervals in a charging period, which implies that traffic volumes from the $q*I+1$-th to the largest time intervals can be as large as possible since they will not generate additional costs. Again, we seek to find out the optimal routing and flow assignment strategy we can apply at the current time interval, with the objective of minimizing operational costs with a q-th percentile charging model.

To be specific, if we sort the aggregate flow rate on link $\{i,j\}$ from time interval 1 to the last time interval I in a decreasing order, and use $\text{qt}(f_{ij}, q)_I$ to denote the $q*I$-th value in this time series of the aggregate flow rates, the already paid traffic volume in the time interval t can be represented by a general form of $\sum_{\{i,j\}\in\mathcal{E}} \min (\text{qt}(f_{ij}, q)_I, c_{ij}(t) - d_{ij}(t))\bar{t}$. Then **Algorithm 3** can be applied to make the routing and flow assignment strategy with any given q-th percentile charging model.

4. *JETWAY:* PERFORMANCE EVALUATION

We believe that the best way to evaluate *Jetway* is to implement it, and in this section, we evaluate how *Jetway* performs in the Amazon EC2 inter-datacenter network. Our real-world experimental results have validated that, by optimally finding routing paths and assigning flows for videos flows at each time interval, *Jetway* reduces costs on inter-datacenter video traffic by a substantial margin.

4.1 Implementation

Our *Jetway* implementation contains more than 9000 lines of C++ code, and is developed from scratch. To evaluate our proposed algorithms in the Amazon EC2 inter-datacenter network, we need to send actual video traffic between source-destination pairs, over either single-hop or multi-hop paths, with possibilities of splitting flows. For this reason, we have implemented a daemon process that is able to send, receive, and relay video traffic, referred to as a *Jet*. By using asynchronous event-driven networking provided by the Boost `asio` C++ framework, it is designed with performance and

Table 2: Link Capacities and Costs per Traffic Unit in the Amazon EC2 Inter-Datacenter Network

Link Capacity (Mbps)/Cost	North California	Oregon	Virginia	Sao Paulo	Ireland	Singapore	Tokyo
North California	—	520.40/1	252.67/2	116.75/15	98.67/20	103.69/27	173.06/30
Oregon	545.06/1	—	215.84/3	81.18/17	104.22/15	81.99/25	152.75/27
Virginia	240.78/2	210.64/3	—	139.41/10	221.55/10	81.44/15	110.10/17
Sao Paulo	40.98/15	60.84/17	11.85/10	—	22.41/25	9.59/18	62.42/22
Ireland	106.45/20	135.02/15	215.85/10	90.12/25	—	77.89/23	76.10/20
Singapore	124.40/27	110.95/25	84.54/15	57.31/18	80.92/23	—	242.80/5
Tokyo	178.36/30	143.44/27	99.40/17	61.99/22	43.61/20	116.33/5	—

scalability in mind. Since it is supposed to be running in cloud VMs, the *Jet* supports major UNIX variants and Windows. As compared to the traditional thread pool concurrency model, our implementation incurs less memory and CPU overhead, even at high packet processing rates.

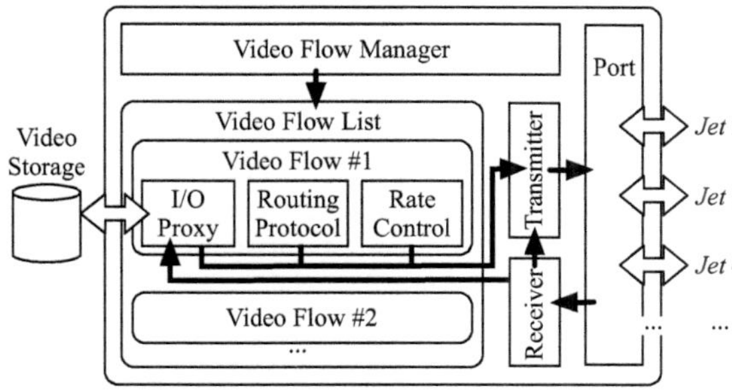

Figure 4: *Jet*: architectural components and design.

Fig. 4 has shown the architecture overview of a *Jet*, comprising of a number of key components.

Video Flow Manager. This component manages all ongoing video flows within each *Jet*, where all video flows are included in the Video Flow List. When the source-destination pair corresponding to a new video flow is initiated, the Video Flow Manager will add the corresponding flow in the video flow list, and create an I/O proxy for transmission between the stored video and the *Jet* at the source datacenter. The *Jet* at the source is responsible for determining the routing paths and their corresponding transmission rates for each video flow, based on our *Jetway* algorithms. All data packets are then passed on to the Transmitter.

Transmitter. For data packets within a video flow, the Transmitter retrieves its route from the Video Flow List, and send them to the corresponding next-hop *Jet*, which is either the destination *Jet* over a direct path, or a relay *Jet* in a multi-hop path with routing information embedded. Further, the flow rate on each path is carefully controlled by the rate control algorithm, so that they conform to the decisions made by the *Jetway* algorithms.

Receiver. As an incoming data packet arrives, the *Receiver* identifies which destination datacenter that packet is addressed to. If it is addressed to the datacenter this *Jet* is located at, the packet will be saved via the I/O proxy. Otherwise, if it belongs to a multi-hop relay path, the packet will be forwarded by the Transmitter to the next-hop jet according to the routing path carried in the header.

Port. This component maintains active connections to all *Jets* for video flows, each of which is located in a different datacenter. The Port is also able to probe link capacities and detect connection failures, such that the routing and flow assignment for each flow can be adjusted adaptively as the network status evolves. The *Jet* is designed to support a large number of concurrent video transmissions. Both higher-level Transmitter and Receiver and the lower-level network Port support multiplexed inter-datacenter connections to reduce additional overhead consumed by each video flow.

4.2 Experiments in the Amazon EC2 Cloud

We have conducted our *Jetway* experiments in the Amazon EC2 Cloud, one of the dominant Infrastructure as a Service (IaaS) cloud providers. Fig. 5 shows the inter-datacenter network topology in the Amazon EC2 cloud that we have used in our experiments. We have launched 7 standard on-demand medium instances with 2 compute unit and 1.7 GB memory in each of the datacenters, installed with our *Jetway* implementation. We log all statistics on every link for each video flow every 30 seconds, including the actual transmission rate, receiving rate, and the end-to-end delay.

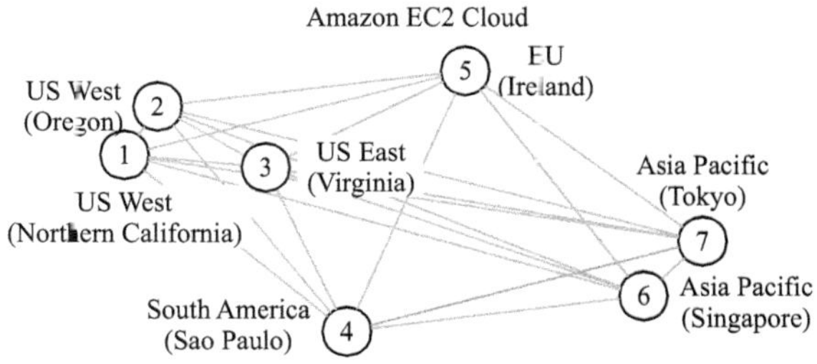

Figure 5: The network topology used in our experiments.

We have first obtained the link capacities in the inter-datacenter network through saturating the outgoing link of each *Jet*. The results are listed in Table 2, showing the average link capacity between each datacenter pair that we observe in 3 minutes. Since costs charged by ISPs on inter-datacenter links in the Amazon cloud are not revealed, we assume a certain cost per Mbps per time interval (5 minutes) on each link, reflecting different costs on transmitting the same amount of video. Costs we used in our experiments are also listed in Table 2.

We conduct our experiments for one hour, which has 12 time intervals in total. We consider the scenario that 10 videos are to be replicated to the datacenter located at Singapore at the beginning of our experiments, with 3 of them being Standard Definition (SD) videos with sizes uniformly random between $[500, 800]$ MB, and 7 of them being High Definition (HD) videos with sizes uniformly random between $[2, 4]$ GB. Source datacenters of these videos are randomly selected from the remaining 6 datacenters in the EC2 cloud. If we assume all video replications have to be finished within 30 minutes, we get the desired transmission rate of each video, ranging from $[2.22, 17.78]$ Mbps. We further assume that there are 3 inter-datacenter video flows satisfying requests from CDN edge servers at the beginning of each time interval, with the source and destination datacenters randomly selected from all 7 datacenters in the cloud. The desired transmission rate for these videos are assumed to be uniformly random between $[2.5, 8]$ Mbps, which are standard rate requirements for today's video streaming services.

For fair comparisons, we have also implemented an alternative routing solution that performs better than the straightforward approach in terms of reducing traffic costs. Referred to as the *time-slotted minimum cost algorithm* (TSMC), it considers different costs per traffic unit on each link only, without considering important aspects of the time dimension. In particular, TSMC solves the multi-commodity minimum cost problem using **Algorithm 2** at each time interval, and obtains the routing paths and flow assignments for the set of videos to be transmitted, based on current available link capacities. To study the effects of a more realistic percentile-based charging model, we have implemented *Jetway* and TSMC, with both the 100-th percentile charging model and the 95-th percentile charging model, and compared their performance with different charging models.

We first present the main performance metric, the total cost per traffic unit over all links in the inter-datacenter network over time. Fig. 6 shows the total cost per traffic unit in the Amazon EC2 inter-datacenter network over one hour by using *Jetway* and TSMC, respectively, with the 100-th percentile charging model. As we can observe, starting from minute 15, *Jetway* is substantially more cost-effective than TSMC. The benefits of *Jetway* is becoming increasingly visible as time elapses, and achieves a cost reduction of 19% after one hour with the 100-th percentile charging model.

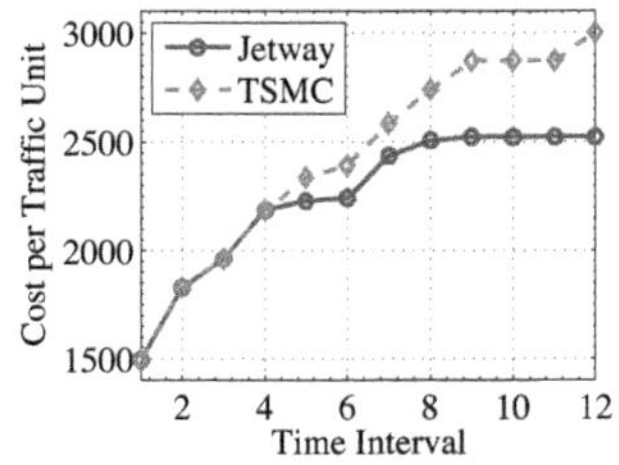

Figure 6: Cost per traffic unit with the 100-th percentile charging model.

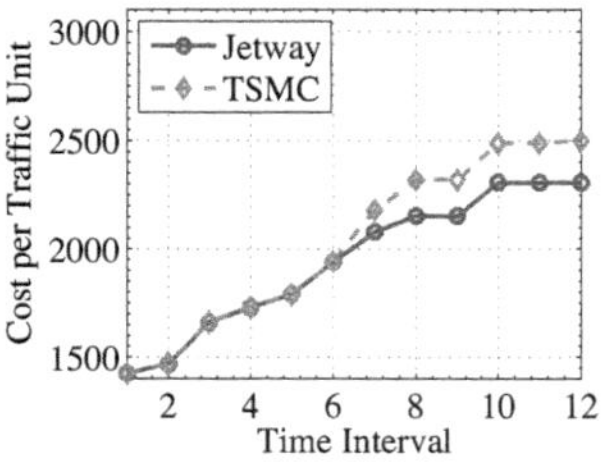

Figure 7: Cost per traffic unit with the 95-th percentile charging model.

Note that both algorithms incurred almost the same cost over the first few time intervals in our experiment. The rationale is that, due to the limited number of video flows over a large number of inter-datacenter links, the already-paid traffic volume can hardly be utilized to the benefit of cost reduction. For each video flow, both algorithms lead to similar optimal routing and flow assignments, by solving the same multi-commodity minimum cost problem. Possibilities of utilizing the already-paid traffic volume increase as time elapses, which results in better performance with *Jetway*. Take the transit server-to-customer video flow (Video 20) from the Ireland datacenter (5) to the Oregon datacenter (2) as an example. Fig. 8 shows the routing and flow assignment for this video flow in *Jetway*. We can see that, initiated at minute 20, the flows of this video takes both cheaper paths $5 \to 3 \to 2$ and $5 \to 3 \to 1 \to 2$, and expensive paths $5 \to 6 \to 3 \to 2$ and $5 \to 6 \to 3 \to 1 \to 2$, taking advantage of links $5 \to 6$ and $6 \to 3$ that are already used for video replication at the first time interval.


```
{
 "Protocol": "TCP",
 "PacketSize": 4096,
 "AverageRate": 3,
 "NodeID": 5,
 "RoutingList": [{ "PathList": ["3,1,2" ], "Weight": 0.334967 },
                 { "PathList": ["3,2"], "Weight": 0.334967 },
                 { "PathList": ["6,3,1,2"], "Weight": 1.8986165 },
                 { "PathList": ["6,3,2"], "Weight": 0.4314495 }
                ],
 "VideoID": 20,
 "StartTime": 1200
}
```


Figure 8: Routing and flow assignment for Video 20 in *Jetway*.

We also present the total cost per traffic unit using both *Jetway* and TSMC with the 95-th percentile charging model in Fig. 7, where we can observe a similar trend. With smaller absolute values in costs, the reduction on the total cost per traffic unit with *Jetway* is up to 8% in this case. Our results have confirmed that *Jetway* can reduce costs on inter-datacenter video traffic substantially, even with the (more realistic) 95-th percentile charging model.

To investigate how our *Jetway* algorithms affect the performance of video streaming services, we record the receiving rates for each video flow every 30 seconds in our experiment. We define the normalized receiving rate to be the actual receiving rate observed at the destination datacenter divided by the desired transmission rate of this video flow. Fig. 9 shows the normalized receiving rates for 5 video flows from the 2nd time interval (minute 5) to the 7th time interval (minute 30). Each of them starts its transmission at the beginning of every time interval, respectively. As we can see, the normalized receiving rates for 3 video flows are 1 most of the time, with minor fluctuations; and the normalized receiving rates for Video 15 and Video 17 exhibit obvious fluctuations, which is resulted by the unstable network status on their common link $3 \to 6$.

We also plot the CDF of the normalized receiving rates for all video flows using *Jetway* in our experiment. Shown in Fig. 10, over 91.5% video flows using *Jetway* exhibit receiving rates that are more than 90% of the desired transmission rates at their destination datacenters. The mean value of the normalized receiving rate is 0.97 by using *Jetway*, which shows that the performance of video streaming regarding the receiving rates is satisfactory by using *Jetway*.

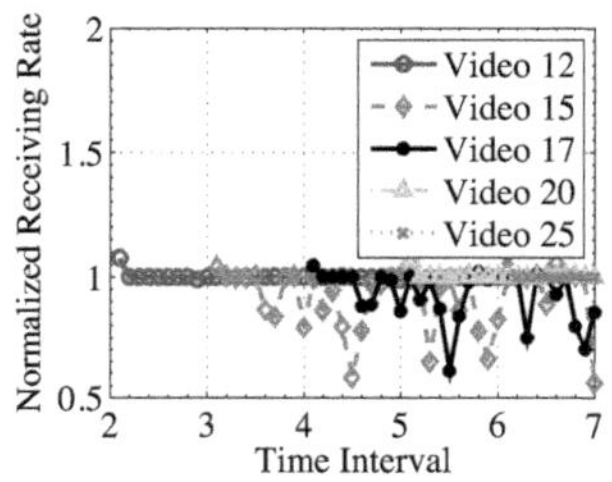

Figure 9: Normalized receiving rates for 5 video flows using *Jetway*.

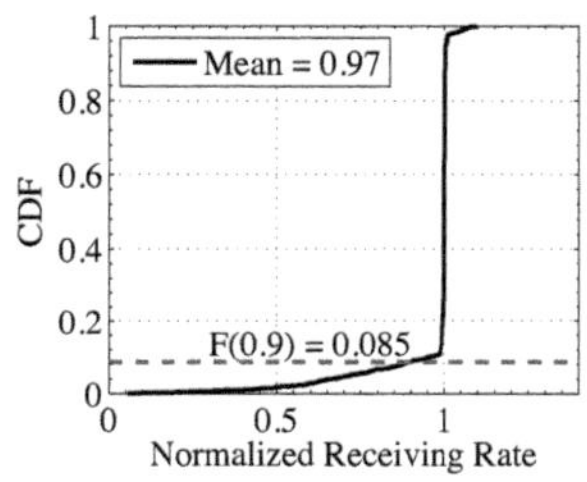

Figure 10: CDF of the normalized receiving rates for all video flows using *Jetway*.

Another important performance metric in video streaming service is the end-to-end delay experienced by each video flow. Since *Jetway* allows multi-path multi-hop transmission, we are interested in investigating whether it will affect the end-to-end delay when transmitting videos. Fig. 11 shows the CDF of the end-to-end delays experienced by all video flows using *Jetway* in our experiment. We can observe that 90% of the video flows experienced end-to-end delays that are smaller than 587.3 ms, and the mean value of end-to-end delays for all videos is 349.09 ms. We believe that these values are reasonable, considering the nature of long-distance inter continental inter-datacenter video transmissions.

To further investigate the effect of *Jetway* on end-to-end delays for video streaming, we take the Singapore datacenter (6) as an example, and compute the average end-to-end delays experienced by video flows from every other datacenter to this one, together with their 95% confidence intervals. For comparisons, we also compute the average end-to-end delays in each direct link, which are obtained by the measured round trip time (RTT) on each link divided by 2, with their corresponding 95% confidence intervals as well. The results are shown in Fig. 12. As we can see, video flows in *Jetway* have experienced almost the same end-to-end delays as compared to those by sending through direct paths. Our results prove that the multi-path multi-hop routing and flow assignment algorithms in *Jetway* will not affect the performance of video streaming services significantly, yet the deployment of *Jetway* leads to substantially reduced operational costs on inter-datacenter video traffic.

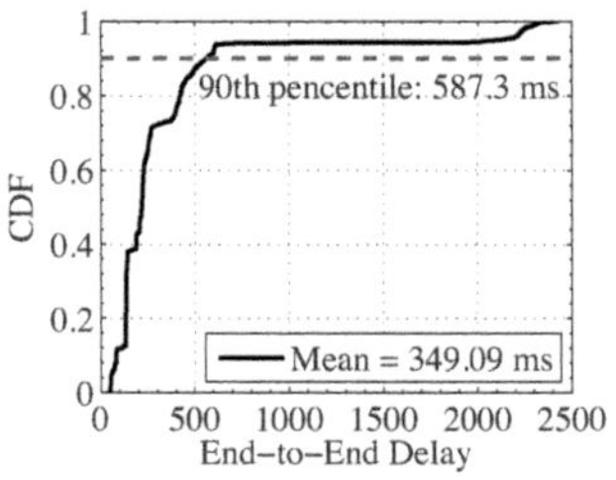

Figure 11: CDF of the end-to-end delays for all video flows using *Jetway*.

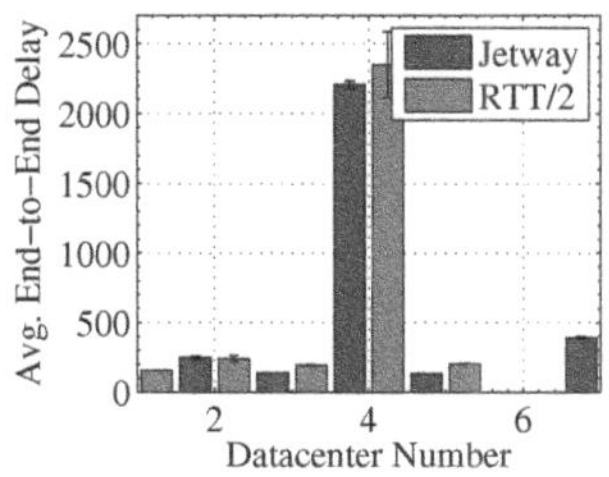

Figure 12: Average end-to-end delays to the Singapore datacenter (6).

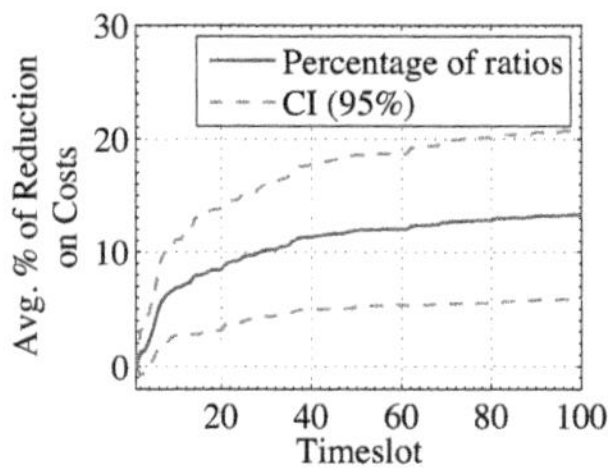

Figure 13: Average percentage of cost reduction with the 100-th percentile charging model.

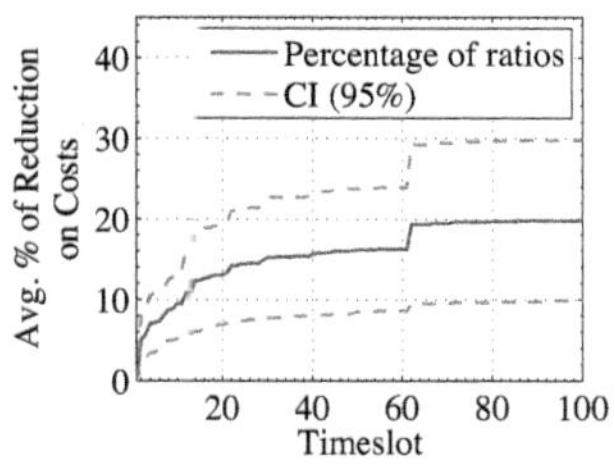

Figure 14: Average percentage of cost reduction with the 95-th percentile charging model.

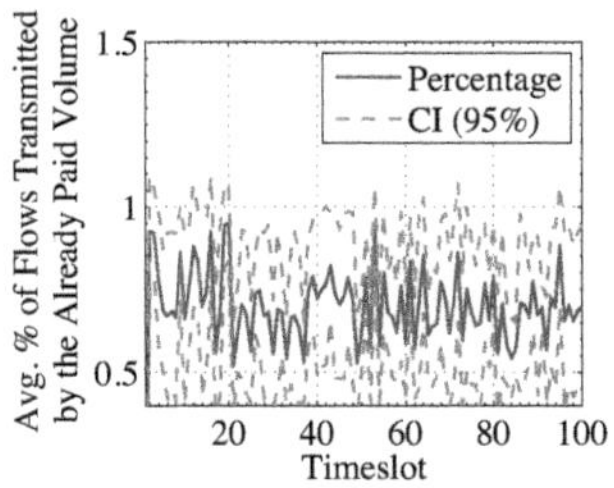

Figure 15: Average percentage of flows carried by utilizing the already paid portion of traffic volume with the 100-th percentile charging model.

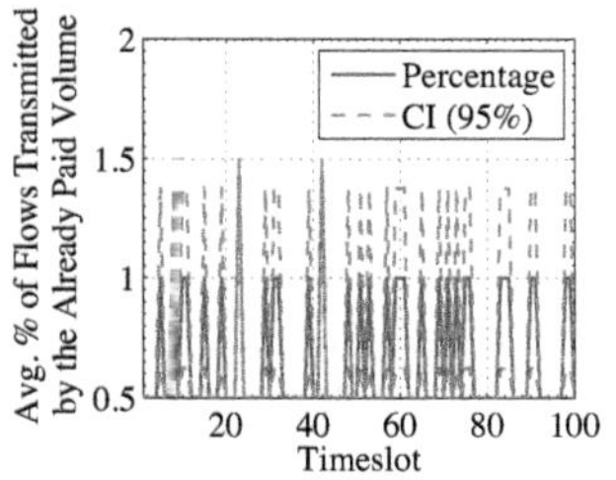

Figure 16: Average percentage of flows carried by utilizing the already paid portion of traffic volume with the 95-th percentile charging model.

4.3 Simulation Results

To investigate the scalability and stability of *Jetway*, we further evaluated it in a time-slotted simulator. The simulated inter-datacenter network has 20 datacenters, forming a complete graph. The capacity on each link is assumed to be 1000 units, and the cost per traffic unit on each link is set to be uniformly random within $[1, 100]$. In each time interval, the number of video flows to be transmitted is uniformly random between $[1, 200]$, each with a desired transmission rate uniformly random between $[1, 10]$ units. The source and destination datacenters of each video flow are also chosen uniformly random from the datacenter set. We conduct our simulations 20 times, each lasts for 100 time slots.

Again, the main performance metric we are interested in is the reduction in the total cost per traffic unit over time by using *Jetway*, as a percentage of the normalized cost reduction ratios compared to TSMC and their 95% confidence intervals. Fig. 13 and Fig. 14 show the average percentage of reduction in the total cost per traffic unit on video traffic with both the 100-th percentile charging model and the 95-th percentile charging model, respectively. Consistent with our experimental results shown in Fig. 6 and Fig. 7, the normalized cost reduction ratio by applying *Jetway* is increasing as time elapses, and reaches up to an average of 13% after 100 time intervals with the 100-th percentile charging scheme. The similar trend is observed with the 95-th percentile charging model, with even more cost reduction of up to 20% in the long term. Our results further confirmed that *Jetway* can successfully reduce costs on inter-datacenter video traffic, even in inter-datacenter networks of larger scales and many video flows.

To further study the effects of the 95-th percentile charging model on *Jetway*, we show the portion of video flows carried by utilizing the already paid portion of traffic volume in *Jetway* with both the 100-th percentile and the 95-th percentile charging models. Shown in Fig. 15 and Fig. 16, around 75% of video flows are carried by utilizing the already paid portion of traffic volume with both charging models. These results have provided further solid evidence that *Jetway* works effectively when it comes to utilizing the *"free of charge"* bandwidth that is available during later time intervals in the same charging period, made possible by any percentile-based charging models typically used by ISPs.

5. RELATED WORK

Geographically dispersed datacenters have attracted recent research attention, as they have brought new opportunities and challenges. Most recent works focus on dynamic load distribution across datacenters, with the objective of minimizing cloud providers' operational costs on energy or minimizing cloud users' performance penalty. Wu *et al.* proposed to migrate social media applications into geo-distributed clouds operated by one or more cloud providers, and designed an online content migration and request distribution algorithm [18]. Liu *et al.* sought to reduce the total energy use of a cloud by geographical load balancing [19]. In terms of improving the operational flexibilities on inter-datacenter communication for cloud providers, GRIPhoN is proposed to offer cost-effective restoration capabilities from the carrier's perspective [20].

Besides analytical results, there are also a few measurement studies regarding the traffic characteristics across multiple datacenters. [21] and [22] shed some light on good designs of caching and load balancing strategies through measuring traffic dynamics in the Google cloud. Chen *et al.* presented a first study of inter-datacenter traffic characteristics via five Yahoo! datacenters [23]. Their measurement results motivate our study of reducing costs on inter-datacenter video traffic.

To our knowledge, there exist two recent papers that considered cloud providers' operational costs on traffic. Zhang *et al.* designed a routing algorithm to optimize the costs on datacenter-to-client traffic [6]. However, with no consideration of the time dimension, their problem is substantially simplified. Laoutaris *et al.* proposed NetStitcher, which takes advantage of the already paid traffic volumes at night to reduce costs on inter-datacenter bulk traffic, such as backups [9]. Our work differs in that, instead of conservatively utilizing leftover bandwidth only for bulk transfers, we argue that such costs can — and should — be minimized by globally optimizing the routing strategies for all inter-datacenter video traffic. In addition, *Jetway* has considered the co-existence of multiple video flows in its problem formulation, which is far more realistic and complicated than the transfer of a single file in NetStitcher.

6. CONCLUDING REMARKS

To stream videos to end users, it is now the norm for video streaming service providers, such as Netflix, to use services of cloud providers, such as Amazon Web Services. To provide a better performance, the cloud provider typically deploys multiple datacenters across different geographical regions, and connect them with an inter-datacenter network. Inter-datacenter traffic is typically charged by ISPs based on a percentile-based charging model, with which cloud providers pay based on the q-th percentile of traffic volumes measured in a short time interval, over a number of such intervals in a charging period. Such a model implies that, if traffic has already been generated during one time interval, up to the same volume of traffic may be carried *free of charge* in subsequent time intervals.

In this paper, we have presented *Jetway*, designed to minimize costs on inter-datacenter video traffic by splitting and routing video flows over multiple multi-hop paths. *Jetway* takes full advantage of our key observation that some of the traffic volumes can be transferred free of charge, while the desired transmission rates of video flows remain satisfied. In order to design *Jetway*, we have formulated the problem of minimizing costs with the intent of maintaining its tractability and the practicality of our solutions. We have evaluated the performance of *Jetway* using our real-world implementation, with actual traffic flowing across seven Amazon EC2 datacenters around the world. We have shown that *Jetway* is capable of reducing traffic costs, while maintaining satisfactory performance with respect to both throughput and end-to-end delay.

7. ACKNOWLEDGMENTS

This research was supported in part by the SAVI Strategic Network (NSERC), and by a grant from NSFC/RGC under the contract N_HKUST610/11, by grants from HKUST under contracts RPC11EG29, SRFI11EG17-C, and SBI09/10.EG01-C, and by a grant from ChinaCache Int. Corp. under the contract CCNT12EG01.

8. REFERENCES

[1] A. Cockcroft, "Netflix in the Cloud," 2011. [Online]. Available: http://velocityconf.com/velocity2011/public/schedule/detail/17785

[2] V. K. Adhikari, Y. Guo, F. Hao, M. Varvello, V. Hilt, M. Steiner, and Z.-L. Zhang, "Unreeling Netflix: Understanding and Improving Multi-CDN Movie Delivery," in *Proc. IEEE INFOCOM*, 2012.

[3] Amazon, "Amazon CloudFront," 2012. [Online]. Available: http://aws.amazon.com/cloudfront/

[4] ——, "Amazon S3: Object Size Limit Now 5 TB," December 2010. [Online]. Available: http://aws.typepad.com/aws/2010/12/amazon-s3-object-size-limit.html

[5] A. Greenberg, J. Hamilton, D. A. Maltz, and P. Patel, "The Cost of a Cloud: Research Problems in Data Center Networks," *SIGCOMM Comput. Commun. Rev.*, vol. 39, no. 1, pp. 68–73, 2009.

[6] Z. Zhang, M. Zhang, A. Greenberg, Y. C. Hu, R. Mahajan, and B. Christian, "Optimizing Cost and Performance in Online Service Provider Networks," in *Proc. 7th Conference on Networked Systems Design and Implementation (NSDI)*, 2010, pp. 1–15.

[7] I. RouteScience Technologies, "Route Optimization for Ebusiness Applications," *White Paper*, 2003.

[8] V. Valancius, C. Lumezanu, N. Feamster, R. Johari, and V. V. Vazirani, "How Many Tiers? Pricing in the Internet Transit Market," in *Proc. ACM SIGCOMM*, 2011, pp. 194–205.

[9] N. Laoutaris, M. Sirivianos, X. Yang, and P. Rodriguez, "Inter-Datecenter Bulk Transfers with NetStitcher," in *Proc. ACM SIGCOMM*, 2011.

[10] D. K. Goldberg, L. Qiu, H. Xie, Y. R. Yang, and Y. Zhang, "Optimizing Cost and Performance for Multihoming," in *Proc. ACM SIGCOMM*, 2004, pp. 79–92.

[11] T. Benson, A. Anand, A. Akella, and M. Zhang, "The Case for Fine-Grained Traffic Engineering in Data Centers," in *Proc. ACM SIGCOMM Workshop: Research on Enterprise Networking (WREN)*, 2010.

[12] T. H. Cormen, C. E. Leiserson, R. L. Rivest, and C. Stein, *Introduction to Algorithms*, 3rd ed. The MIT Press, 2009.

[13] T. Radzik, "Fast Deterministic Approximation for the Multicommodity Flow Problem," in *Proc. 6th Annual ACM Symposium on Discrete Algorithms (SODA)*, 1995, pp. 486–492.

[14] A. Goldberg and R. Tarjan, "Solving Minimum-Cost Flow Problems by Successive Approximation," in *Proc. 9th ACM Symposium on Theory of Computing (SOTC)*, 1987, pp. 7–18.

[15] D. Karger and S. Plotkin, "Adding Multiple Cost Constraints to Combinatorial Optimization Problems, with Applications to Multicommodity Flows," in *Proc. 27th ACM Symposium on Theory of Computing (SOTC)*, 1995, pp. 18–25.

[16] B. Awerbuch and R. Khandekar, "Greedy Distributed Optimization of Multi-Commodity Flows," *Distributed Computing*, vol. 21, pp. 317–329, 2009.

[17] B. Awerbuch, R. Khandekar, and S. Rao, "Distributed Algorithms for Multicommodity Flow Problems via Approximate Steepest Descent Framework," in *Proc. 18th Annual ACM Symposium on Discrete Algorithms (SODA)*, 2007, pp. 949–957.

[18] Y. Wu, C. Wu, B. Li, L. Zhang, Z. Li, and F. C. Lau, "Scalling Social Media Appliations into Geo-Distributed Clouds," in *Proc. IEEE INFOCOM*, 2012.

[19] Z. Liu, M. Lin, A. Wierman, S. H. Low, and L. L. Andrew, "Greening Geographical Load Balancing," *SIGMETRICS Perform. Eval. Rev.*, vol. 39, pp. 193–204, 2011.

[20] A. Mahimkar, A. Chiu, R. Doverspike, M. D. Feuer, P. Magill, E. Mavrogiorgis, J. Pastor, S. L. Woodward, and J. Yates, "Bandwidth on Demand for Inter-Data Center Communication," in *Proc. 10th ACM Workshop on Hot Topics in Networks (HotNets)*, 2011, pp. 1–6.

[21] R. Krishnan, H. V. Madhyastha, S. Srinivasan, S. Jain, A. Krishnamurthy, T. Anderson, and J. Gao, "Moving Beyond End-to-End Path Information to Optimize CDN Performance," in *Proc. 9th Internet Measurement Conference (IMC)*, 2009, pp. 190–201.

[22] V. K. Adhikari, S. Jain, and Z.-L. Zhang, "YouTube Traffic Dynamics and Its Interplay with a Tier-1 ISP: An ISP Perspective," in *Proc. 10th Internet Measurement Conference (IMC)*, 2010, pp. 431–443.

[23] Y. Chen, S. Jain, V. Adhikari, Z.-L. Zhang, and K. Xu, "A First Look at Inter-Data Center Traffic Characteristics via Yahoo! Datasets," in *Proc. IEEE INFOCOM*, 2011, pp. 1620 –1628.

Control of Distributed Servers for Quality-Fair Delivery of Multiple Video Streams

Nesrine Changuel
Alcatel-Lucent - Bell-Labs
France
Nesrine.Changuel@alcatel-lucent.com

Bessem Sayadi
Alcatel-Lucent - Bell-Labs
France
Bessem.Sayadi@alcatel-lucent.com

Michel Kieffer
L2S - CNRS - SUPELEC - Univ Paris-Sud, LTCI - CNRS - Telecom ParisTech, Institut Universitaire de France
Michel.Kieffer@lss.supelec.fr

ABSTRACT

This paper proposes a quality-fair video delivery system able to transmit several encoded video streams to mobile users sharing some wireless resource. Video quality fairness, as well as similar delivery delay is targeted among streams. The proposed control system is implemented within some aggregator located near the bottleneck of the network.

This is done by allocating the transmission rate among streams based on the quality of the already encoded and buffered packets in the aggregator. Encoding rate targets are evaluated by the aggregator and fed back to each remote video server, or directly evaluated by each server in a distributed way. Each encoding rate target is adjusted for each stream independently based on the corresponding buffering delay in the aggregator.

The transmission and encoding rate control problems are addressed with a control-theoretic perspective. The system is described with a multi-input multi-output model and several Proportional Integral (PI) controllers are used to adjust the video quality as well as the buffering delay. The study of the system equilibrium and stability provides guidelines for choosing the parameters of the PI controllers. Experimental results show that better quality fairness is obtained compared to classical transmission rate fair streaming solutions while keeping similar buffering delays.

Categories and Subject Descriptors

C.2 [**Computer communication network**]: Data communications, Network Architecture and Design

General Terms

Algorithms, Experimentation

Keywords

Video, Control design, Distributed systems

1. INTRODUCTION

Traffic corresponding to compressed videos is increasing rapidly, especially to mobile users, which are consuming more and more video-on-demand or mobile TV broadcast services. This trend is likely to continue in the coming years [1]. Streaming or broadcasting videos to several users sharing a bandlimited wireless channel with time-varying characteristics is still a challenging task. The demand for better video quality with limited transmission delays are the main problems to be addressed.

Increasing the rate at which videos are encoded improves their quality, but the price to be paid is an increased congestion at the bottleneck of the network, usually lying at the interface of the wired and wireless part, when considering video delivery to mobile users. To maximize the overall quality of the delivered video streams, it is thus preferable, instead of equally dividing the available resource, *e.g.*, bandwidth or transmission rate, among streams or among users, to have resource allocation and video server control algorithms achieving a fair video quality among streams to deliver streams with comparable (objective or subjective) quality and delivery delay.

This paper proposes a quality-fair video transmission system able to deliver several encoded streams to mobile users over some bottleneck link. Typical application contexts are mobile broadcast or parallel unicast of video contents to users connected to some base station. Video encoding rate adaptation and wireless resource allocation are performed jointly within some Media Aware Network Element (MANE) using feedback control loops. The aim is to provide users with encoded videos of similar quality and with controlled delivery delay, without exchanging information between remotely located video servers.

1.1 Related works

When controlling the multiple video streams, their rate-distortion (R-D) trade-off may be adjusted by selectively discarding frames as in [2, 3] or via an adjustment of the encoding parameters [4, 5]. With scalable video encoders, such as H.264/SVC, the R-D trade-off may be adjusted via packet filtering [6, 7]. In this case, the number of transmitted enhancement layers for each frame is the control parameter.

Video quality fairness among encoded streams may be obtained by sharing quality information, or R-D characteristics via a central controller providing to each server quality or rate targets [8, 9]. This technique enables the encoders to adjust their rate or to drop frames depending on the complexity of the videos and on the available transmission rate.

Control-theoretic approaches to address the video streaming rate control problem have been considered, *e.g.*, in [10, 11, 12, 13], and [14]. In [10], a real-time rate control based on a Proportional Integral Derivative (PID) controller is proposed for a single video stream. The main idea is to determine the encoding rate per frame based on the buffer level to maximize video quality and minimize quality variations over frames. In [11], a flow control mechanism with active queue management and a proportional controller is considered. A flow control is used to reduce the buffer size and avoid buffer overflow and underflow. Stability issues are addressed to show that the flow control mechanism is stable for small buffer sizes and non-negligible round-trip times. In [12], the rate allocation algorithm, performed at the Group of Picture (GoP) level, is in charge of determining the transmission rate from the buffers and a playback adjustment mechanism. A Proportional Integral (PI) controller is adopted at the receiver to maximize the visual quality according to the overall loss and the receiver buffer occupancy.

Later, in [15], a rate control that uses different bit allocation strategies for intra and inter frames is introduced. A PID controller is adopted to minimize the deviation between the target buffer level and the current buffer fullness. However, buffer management is performed at the bit level and delivery delay is not considered. Moreover, [10, 11, 12, 15] address single flow transmission.

For multi-video streaming, in [16], a distributed utility max-min flow control in the presence of round-trip delays is proposed. The distributed link algorithm attains utility max-min bandwidth sharing while controlling link buffer occupancy to a target value at the cost of link under utilization using a PID controller. Stability analysis in case of a single bottleneck and a homogeneous delay is conducted.

In [8], a content-aware distortion-fair video delivery scheme is proposed to deliver video streams based on the characteristics of video frames. It provides a max-min distortion fair resource sharing among streams. The system uses temporal prediction structure of the video sequences with a frame drop distortion metric based on the frame importance to guide resource allocation. This scheme is for stored video, where the side information of the number of bits and importance of the frames is assumed calculated in advance.

A proportional controller is considered in [13] to stabilize the received video quality as well as the bottleneck link queue for both homogeneous and heterogeneous video systems. A PI controller is considered in [14]. Robustness and stability properties are studied. In [13] and [14], a centralized rate control exploits the rate and distortion characteristics of the transmitted video streams to determine the encoding rate for the next frames of each session.

The problem of remotely implemented control law is also considered in [17] leading to the problem of stabilizing an open-loop unstable system with time-varying delay. The problem of remote stabilization via communication networks is considered with an explicit use of the average network dynamics and an estimation of the average delay dynamics in the control law. The control law does not address video transmission issues, so no quality constraint on the transmitted data is considered.

The commercial product described in [18, 19] propose statistical multiplexing systems enabling encoders to adapt their outputs to the available channel rate. Connecting encoders and multiplexers via a switched IP network allows collocated as well as distributed encoders to be part of the multiplexing system. Nevertheless, in these solutions, the rate control process is centralized and quality fairness constraints between programs appear not to be considered among the video quality constraints.

1.2 Main contributions

In this paper, we propose a partially distributed control system to perform jointly (i) encoding rate control of spatially spread video servers without requiring exchange of information between them and (ii) transmission rate control of the encoded streams through some bottelneck link. A MANE, located near the bottelneck link contains dedicated buffers fed by the remote servers. It performs a centralized transmission rate control for each encoded video stream, adjusting the draining rate of each buffer. For that purpose, it uses quality information of the encoded videos to favor programs with lower quality. Dedicated encoding rate controllers observe the buffering delay discrepancy with respect to some reference to adjust the encoding rates. In a *fully centralized* solution, the MANE is then in charge of sending the encoding rate target to each video server. In a *partly distributed* solution, only the individual delay discrepancies are transmitted to the servers, which are then in charge of computing their encoding rate target. The proposed multi-input, multi-output (MIMO) closed-loop feedback control system has to regulate the buffering delay and to provide quality fairness between video streams. For that purpose, the feedback loops involve PI controllers which stability is studied. Quality fairness constraint among streams results in a coupling of the state equation related to each stream. The stability analysis of the coupled state equations is a challenging task which was not performed previously.

Section 2 describes the considered system and the constraints that have to be satisfied. The proposed solution is described in Section 3. A discrete-time state-space representation of the MIMO system is provided, emphasizing the coupling induced by the fairness constraint among video streams. The equilibrium and stability analysis are performed in Section 4. This provides some insight on the way the various PI controllers should be tuned. Then, a typical application context is described in Section 5. Finally, experimental results are detailed in Section 6, showing that the proposed control system allows transmitting several video programs in parallel with comparable video quality and similar buffer delay.

2. SYSTEM DESCRIPTION

Consider a communication system in which N encoded video streams provided by remote servers arrive to some network bottelneck where they have to share a communication channel providing a transmission rate R^c, see Figure 1. Encoded Video Units (VUs) representing a single picture or a Group of Pictures (GoP) are provided by the servers. All VUs are assumed to be of the same duration T and the frame rate $F = 1/T$ is assumed constant over time and identical for all streams. At time index j, all servers encode, transcode, or layer filter (in case of scalable video streams) the j-th VU.

We assume that a Media Aware Network Element (MANE) is located close to the bottelneck of the network, see Figure 1. The aim of the MANE is to allocate the available

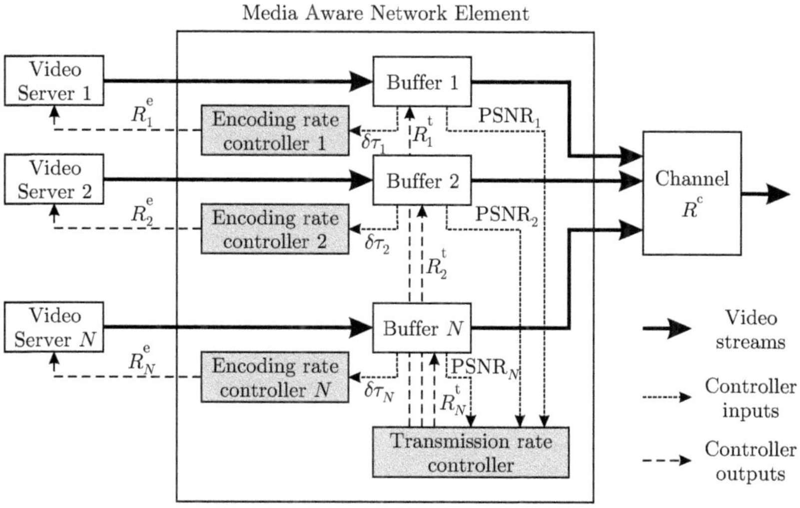

Figure 1: Structure of the proposed quality-fair video delivery system (fully centralized version).

transmission rate R^c among video streams in such a way that they are delivered with similar reconstruction quality (objective or subjective), and with similar delivery delay, to get a quality-fair video delivery system.

For that purpose, encoded and packetized VUs are temporarily stored in dedicated buffers in the MANE. Moreover, two feedback loops are considered to control the encoding and transmission rate of each stream, see Figure 2. In a fully centralized version, each individual encoding rate target is evaluated in the MANE and fed back to each server as shown in Figure 1. In a partly decentralized version, each encoding rate is evaluated by the remote video servers. In both cases, the transmission rates evaluated in a centralized way within the MANE determine the draining of the buffers in the MANE. This control is performed at discrete time instants, with a period T equal to the duration of a VU.

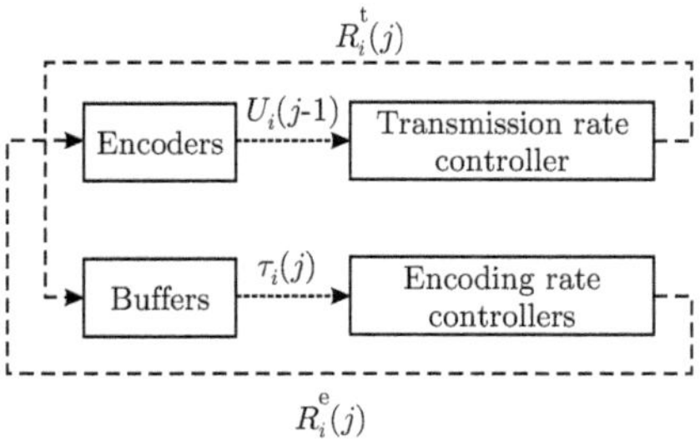

Figure 2: Feedback control loops in the proposed quality-fair video delivery system.

A *utility* U providing information on the video quality (PSNR, SSIM, or any other video quality metrics [20]) of the buffered video packets is assumed to be available to the MANE. The feedback loops have to be designed to minimize the discrepancy between the instantaneous utility of each video stream, and to adjust the buffering delay in the MANE around some reference delay τ_0.

In the proposed solution, the utilities are assumed to be stored in the headers of packets containing the encoded VUs. The MANE evaluates the average utility and allocates more transmission rate to programs with a utility below average. The buffers of these programs are likely to drain faster than those with utility above average. This control, done within the MANE, is thus *centralized.*

The discrepancy of each buffering delay with respect to τ_0 is processed by a dedicated encoding rate (transcoding rate or layer filtering) controller for each video stream. The encoding rate target for the next VU of each video stream is then evaluated to regulate the buffering delay around τ_0 to prevent buffer over or underflow. The encoding rate may be evaluated at the MANE, in which case, the control is fully *centralized.* Here, the video encoders/servers receive only the target bit rate sent by the MANE. Alternatively, the encoding rate may be evaluated in a *decentralized* way at each video encoder/server. For that purpose, the MANE only feeds back to each server the buffering delay discrepancy. The latter solution requires all video encoders/servers to host individually an encoding rate controller, which is mainly possible for managed video servers. Here, the encoding rate target is evaluated within the MANE, but the encoding parameters are evaluated in a *distributed* way by each server [21].

The interaction of both control loops allow to get a quality-fair video delivery. Videos with a quality below average have a buffer in the MANE that is drained faster, and thus is likely to be below τ_0. Their encoding rate target is then increased to increase their quality. In what follows, the stability of both control loops is studied.

3. STATE-SPACE REPRESENTATION

The stability analysis of the control loops requires a state-space representation of the system introduced in Section 2. Several additional hypotheses are needed to get a tractable representation.

3.1 Hypotheses

In what follows, a VU represents a GoP. All encoded VUs processed by the video servers during the $(j-1)$-th time slot $[(j-1)T, jT)$ are assumed to have reached the MANE during the j-th time slot $[jT, (j-1)T)$. This hypothesis allows to take into account some program-dependent and time-varying transmission delays between the servers and the MANE, as long as these delays are less than T. Moreover, due to these delays, for the transmission rate control during the j-th time slot, the MANE is assumed to have only access to the utility $U_i(j-1)$ of the $(j-1)$-th encoded VUs. This utilities are assumed to be stored in encoded packet headers.

Feedback delays between the MANE and the video servers are neglected. This is reasonable when the MANE only feeds back signalization to carry, encoding rate targets or buffering delay discrepancies to the servers. Provided that the network is not too congested, this takes tens of milliseconds, which is negligible compared to the duration of VUs when they represent GoPs. Thus, the encoding rate $R_i^{\mathrm{e}}(j)$ evaluated from the buffering delay discrepancy at the beginning of the j-th time slot for the i-th video stream is assumed available without delay at the i-th remote video server to encode the j-th VU. This assumption is more questionable when performing a control of VUs representing single frames.

3.1.1 Source model

The same parametric rate-utility model is used to describe the evolution of the utility $U_i(j)$ as a function of the rate $R_i^{\mathrm{e}}(j)$ used to encode the j-th VU of the i-th stream

$$U_i(j) = f\left(\mathbf{a}_i\left(j\right), R_i^{\mathrm{e}}(j)\right). \qquad (1)$$

The parameter vectors $\mathbf{a}_i\left(j\right) \in \mathcal{A} \subset \mathbb{R}^{N_a}$ is time varying and program dependent. For all values of $\mathbf{a}$ belonging to the set of admissible parameters $\mathcal{A}$, $f\left(\mathbf{a}, R\right)$ is assumed to be a continuous and strictly increasing function of R, with $f\left(\mathbf{a}, 0\right) = 0$. The time variation of $\mathbf{a}_i\left(j\right)$ is described by

$$\mathbf{a}_i(j+1) = \mathbf{a}_i(j) + \delta\mathbf{a}_i(j), \qquad (2)$$

where $\delta\mathbf{a}_i\left(j\right)$ represents the (uncontrolled) variations of the source characteristics.

The model (1) may represent the variation with then encoding rate of the SNR, the PSNR, the SSIM, or any strictly increasing quality metric. For Gaussian sources, (1) may be easily characterized when the utility is the PSNR in dB, see Example 1, but extends to video streams. For that purpose, the parameter vector $\mathbf{a}_i\left(j\right)$ in (1) has to be estimated at server side, for each VU, using, *e.g.*, encoding trials [22, 23].

EXAMPLE 1. *Assume that samples belonging to the interval* $[0, 255]$ *have been generated by a Gaussian source emitting independent symbols with mean* 128 *and time-varying variance* $\sigma^2(j)$ *with a period* T. *Neglecting the clipping to* $[0, 255]$, *and considering a quadratic distortion measure, the rate-distortion function for this source is*

$$D(j)(R^e(j)T) = \sigma^2(j)2^{-2R^e(j)T} \qquad (3)$$

and assuming that the utility is the PSNR, one gets

$$U(j) = 10\log_{10}\left(\frac{255^2}{\sigma^2(j)}\right) + 6TR^e(j) = a^{(1)}(j) + a^{(2)}\left(j\right)R^e(j), \qquad (4)$$

with $a^{(1)}(j) = 10\log_{10}\left(\frac{255^2}{\sigma^2(j)}\right)$ *and* $a^{(2)}\left(j\right) = 6T$ *dB.s/bit.*

3.1.2 Buffer model

As introduced in Section 2, the MANE contains dedicated buffers for each of the N encoded video streams. The evolution of the level in bits of the i-th buffer between time slot j and $j+1$ is

$$B_i(j+1) = B_i(j) + \left(R_i^{\mathrm{e}}(j-1) - R_i^{\mathrm{t}}(j)\right)T, \qquad (5)$$

where $R_i^{\mathrm{t}}(j)$ is the transmission rate for the i-th stream and $R_i^{\mathrm{e}}(j-1)$ is the encoding rate of the $(j-1)$-th VU. $R_i^{\mathrm{e}}(j-1)$ is considered in (5) due to the time encoded packets require to reach the MANE.

This paper controls the buffering delay instead of the buffering level in bits. In delay-sensitive applications, the buffering delay plays a more important role than the buffer level in bits. Since video programs are not encoded at the same rate, a similar buffer level in bits may correspond to very different buffering delays. Assume that $h_i(j)$ is the number of VUs in the i-th MANE buffer at time j. The buffering delay of the i-th stream at time j is $\tau_i(j) = h_i(j)T$.

Assume that packets containing encoded VUs are segmented to allow a fine granularity of the draining rate. Then $h_i(j)$ is difficult to evaluate within the MANE using only information stored in packet headers. The buffering delay for the i-th buffer is then approximatively evaluated as $\tau_i(j) = B_i(j)/\bar{R}_i^{\mathrm{e}}(j)$, where

$$\bar{R}_i^{\mathrm{e}}(j) = \frac{1}{h_i(j)}\Big(\sum_{\ell=1}^{\lfloor h_i(j)\rfloor} R_i^{\mathrm{e}}(j-\ell) + R_i^{\mathrm{e}}\left(j - \lceil h_i(j)\rceil\right)\left(h_i(j) - \lfloor h_i(j)\rfloor\right)\Big) \qquad (6)$$

is the average encoding rate of the buffered VUs in buffer i at time j and $\lfloor\cdot\rfloor$ and $\lceil\cdot\rceil$ denote rounding towards $-\infty$ and $+\infty$. Since (6) still requires the availability of $h_i(j)$, we choose to estimate it as follows

$$\begin{aligned} \tilde{R_i}^{\mathrm{e}}(1) &= R_i^{\mathrm{e}}(1) \\ \tilde{R_i}^{\mathrm{e}}(j+1) &= \alpha R_i^{\mathrm{e}}(j) + (1-\alpha)\tilde{R_i}^{\mathrm{e}}(j), \; j > 1 \end{aligned} \qquad (7)$$

where $0 < \alpha < 1$ is some tuning parameter. Then, one gets an estimate of the buffering delay $\tau_i(j)$ using (7)

$$\tilde{\tau}_i(j) = B_i(j)/\tilde{R}_i^{\mathrm{e}}(j). \qquad (8)$$

3.2 Rate controllers

A centralized transmission rate controller and N possibly decentralized encoding rate controllers are considered in the video delivery system described in Section 2. PI controllers are used to regulate the transmission rate. At time j, these controllers take as input all utilities $U_i\left(j-1\right)$ of the previously encoded VUs, $i = 1, \ldots, N$, that have reached the buffers in the MANE.

PI controllers are also used to evaluate the encoding rate target of each program in order to regulate the buffering delay around τ_0. Each of these controllers takes as input the estimated buffering delay $\tilde{\tau}_i(j)$ provided by (8) and the reference buffering delay τ_0.

All rates are evaluated with respect to $R_0 = R^{\mathrm{c}}/N$, the average encoding and transmission rate per stream, used if the N streams represent the same encoded video.

3.2.1 Transmission rate control

At time j, the available transmission rate R^{c} is shared between video programs. The delayed utility information available at the MANE at time j for the i-th program is

$$U_i^{\mathrm{d}}(j) = U_i(j-1) \qquad (9)$$

and the discrepancy $\delta U_i^{\mathrm{d}}(j)$ with the average utility is

$$\delta U_i^{\mathrm{d}}(j) = \frac{1}{N}\sum_{\ell=1}^{N}\left(U_\ell^{\mathrm{d}}(j) - U_i^{\mathrm{d}}(j)\right). \qquad (10)$$

The PI transmission rate controller for the i-th program takes $\delta U_i^{\mathrm{d}}(j)$ to evaluate

$$R_i^{\mathrm{t}}(j) = R_0 + \left(K_P^{\mathrm{t}} + K_I^{\mathrm{t}}\right) \delta U_i^{\mathrm{d}}(j) + K_I^{\mathrm{t}} \phi_i(j), \qquad (11)$$

which is the i-th MANE buffer draining rate. In (11), $\phi_i(j)$ is the cumulated utility discrepancy (used for the integral term) evaluated as

$$\phi_i(j+1) = \phi_i(j) + \delta U_i^{\mathrm{d}}(j), \text{ with } \phi_i(0) = 0. \qquad (12)$$

$K_{\mathrm{P}}^{\mathrm{t}}$ and $K_{\mathrm{I}}^{\mathrm{t}}$ are the proportional and integral correction gains. One may easily prove that

$$\sum_{i=1}^{N} R_i^{\mathrm{t}}(j) = R^{\mathrm{c}}. \qquad (13)$$

According to (11), in a first approximation, more (less) rate is allocated to programs with a utility below (above) average.

3.2.2 *Encoding rate control*

At time j, the discrepancy $\delta\tilde{\tau}_i(j)$ between $\tilde{\tau}_i(j)$ and τ_0 is

$$\delta\tilde{\tau}_i(j) = \tilde{\tau}_i(j) - \tau_0 = \left(\tfrac{B_i(j)}{\tilde{R}_i^{\mathrm{e}}(j)} - \tau_0\right). \qquad (14)$$

Buffers with positive $\delta\tau_i(j)$ are filling faster than draining. The encoding/transcoding rate $R_i^{\mathrm{e}}(j)$ has thus to be decreased to limit the increase of the buffering delay. This part of the control process is very similar to back-pressure algorithms [24].

Here, we choose again to evaluate $R_i^{\mathrm{e}}(j)$ as the output of a PI controller fed by $\delta\tilde{\tau}_i(j)$

$$R_i^{\mathrm{e}}(j) = R_0 - \frac{K_P^{\mathrm{e}} + K_I^{\mathrm{e}}}{T}\delta\tilde{\tau}_i(j) - \frac{K_I^{\mathrm{e}}}{T}\Pi_i(j). \qquad (15)$$

where $\Pi_i(j)$ is the cumulated buffer delay discrepancy (used again for the integral term) evaluated as

$$\Pi_i(j+1) = \Pi_i(j) + \delta\tilde{\tau}_i(j), \text{ with } \Pi_i(0) = 0. \qquad (16)$$

$K_{\mathrm{P}}^{\mathrm{e}}$ and $K_{\mathrm{I}}^{\mathrm{e}}$ are the proportional and integral correction gains. According to (15), in a first approximation, the encoding rate increases (decreases) when the buffer is below (above) the reference delay τ_0.

To account for the delayed utility available at the MANE, a state variable representing the delayed encoding rate is introduced

$$R_i^{\mathrm{ed}}(j) = R_i^{\mathrm{e}}(j-1). \qquad (17)$$

The sum of the encoding rates is not necessarily equal to R^{c}. This allows to compensate for the variations of the video characteristics.

Combining (5), (11), and (15), one sees that buffers corresponding to programs producing video with lower utility than the average utility are drained faster. As a consequence, the encoding rate allowed to encode the next VU of such programs is increased.

3.3 State-space representation

To describe the evolution with time of the video delivery system, one has to take into account (1), (2), (7), (11), (12), (15), (16), and (17). One gets the following discrete-time nonlinear state-space representation

$$\begin{cases} \mathbf{a}(j+1) & = \mathbf{a}(j) + \delta\mathbf{a}(j) \\ \mathbf{U}^{\mathrm{d}}(j+1) & = \mathbf{f}\left(\mathbf{a}(j), \mathbf{R}^{\mathrm{ed}}(j+1)\right) \\ \boldsymbol{\phi}(j+1) & = \boldsymbol{\phi}(j) + \frac{1}{N}\sum_{k=1}^{N} U_k^{\mathrm{d}}(j) - \mathbf{U}^{\mathrm{d}}(j) \\ \mathbf{\Pi}(j+1) & = \mathbf{\Pi}(j) + \left(\frac{\mathbf{B}(j)}{\tilde{\mathbf{R}}^{\mathrm{e}}(j)} - \tau_0\right) \\ \tilde{\mathbf{R}}^{\mathrm{e}}(j+1) & = \alpha\left(R_0 - \frac{K_{\mathrm{P}}^{\mathrm{e}}+K_{\mathrm{I}}^{\mathrm{e}}}{T}\left(\frac{\mathbf{B}(j)}{\tilde{\mathbf{R}}^{\mathrm{e}}(j)} - \tau_0\right) - \frac{K_{\mathrm{I}}^{\mathrm{e}}}{T}\mathbf{\Pi}(j)\right) \\ \quad -(1-\alpha)\tilde{\mathbf{R}}^{\mathrm{e}}(j) & \\ \mathbf{R}^{\mathrm{ed}}(j+1) & = R_0 - \frac{K_{\mathrm{P}}^{\mathrm{e}}+K_{\mathrm{I}}^{\mathrm{e}}}{T}\left(\frac{\mathbf{B}(j)}{\tilde{\mathbf{R}}^{\mathrm{e}}(j)} - \tau_0\right) - \frac{K_{\mathrm{I}}^{\mathrm{e}}}{T}\mathbf{\Pi}(j) \\ \mathbf{B}(j+1) & = \mathbf{B}(j) + \mathbf{R}^{\mathrm{ed}}(j)T \\ \quad -\left(R_0\left(K_{\mathrm{P}}^{\mathrm{t}} + K_{\mathrm{I}}^{\mathrm{t}}\right)\left(\frac{1}{N}\sum_{k=1}^{N} U_k^{\mathrm{d}}(j) - \mathbf{U}^{\mathrm{d}}(j)\right) + K_{\mathrm{I}}^{\mathrm{t}}\boldsymbol{\phi}(j)\right)T & \end{cases} \qquad (18)$$

where all boldface letters are vectors, for example $\mathbf{B}(j) = (B_1(j) \ldots B_N(j))^{\mathrm{T}}$ and $\mathbf{a}(j) = \left(\mathbf{a}_1^{\mathrm{T}}(j) \ldots \mathbf{a}_N^{\mathrm{T}}(j)\right)^{\mathrm{T}}$. In (18), the division $\mathbf{B}(j)/\tilde{\mathbf{R}}^{\mathrm{e}}(j)$ is component by component, as well as the difference between a scalar and a vector.

4. EQUILIBRIUM AND STABILITY

The steady-state behavior of the video delivery system described by (18) is studied first. Due to the coupling between controllers induced by the constraint that the discrepancy between the average utility and the utility of each program has to be as small as possible, the stability of the whole system has to be studied. This is performed by linearising (18) around its equilibrium.

4.1 Equilibrium analysis

The system described by (18) reaches an equilibrium when all terms on the left of (18) do not change with time. This leads to the following system of $(6 + N_a)N$ equations with $(6 + N_a)N$ unknowns ($\mathbf{a}^{\mathrm{eq}}$ is assumed to be properly estimated in steady state)

$$\begin{cases} \delta\mathbf{a}^{\mathrm{eq}} & = & \mathbf{0} \\ \mathbf{U}^{\mathrm{eq}} & = & \mathbf{f}\left(\mathbf{a}^{\mathrm{eq}}, \mathbf{R}^{\mathrm{eq}}\right) \\ \mathbf{U}^{\mathrm{eq}} - \frac{1}{N}\sum_{k=1}^{N} U_k^{\mathrm{eq}} & = & \mathbf{0} \\ \mathbf{B}^{\mathrm{eq}} & = & \tau_0 \tilde{\mathbf{R}}^{\mathrm{eq}} \\ \tilde{\mathbf{R}}^{\mathrm{e,eq}} & = & R_0 - \frac{K_{\mathrm{I}}^{\mathrm{e}}}{T}\mathbf{\Pi}^{\mathrm{eq}} \\ \mathbf{R}^{\mathrm{eq}} & = & R_0 - \frac{K_{\mathrm{I}}^{\mathrm{e}}}{T}\mathbf{\Pi}^{\mathrm{eq}} \\ \mathbf{R}^{\mathrm{eq}} & = & K_{\mathrm{I}}^{\mathrm{t}}\boldsymbol{\phi}^{\mathrm{eq}} \end{cases}, \qquad (19)$$

The third equation in (19) imposes that $U_1^{\mathrm{eq}} = \cdots = U_N^{\mathrm{eq}} = U^{\mathrm{eq}}$. All programs have thus the same utility at equilibrium. One has $\tilde{\mathbf{R}}^{\mathrm{e,eq}} = \mathbf{R}^{\mathrm{eq}}$ and $\mathbf{B}^{\mathrm{eq}} = \tau_0\mathbf{R}^{\mathrm{eq}}$, which leads to $B_i^{\mathrm{eq}}/R_i^{\mathrm{eq}} = \tau_i(j) = \tau_0$, $i = 1, \ldots, N$ meaning that at equilibrium, the buffering delay is equal to τ_0 for all streams.

Since f is strictly increasing in R, the rate at equilibrium as a function of U^{eq} is

$$R_i^{\mathrm{eq}} = f_R^{-1}\left(\mathbf{a}^{\mathrm{eq}}, U^{\mathrm{eq}}\right), \; i = 1, \ldots, N \qquad (20)$$

with f_R^{-1} is the inverse of f seen as a function of R only. The value of U^{eq} is determined from the channel rate constraint

$$\sum_{i=1}^{N} R_i^{\mathrm{eq}} = \sum_{i=1}^{N} f_R^{-1}\left(\mathbf{a}_i^{\mathrm{eq}}, U^{\mathrm{eq}}\right) = R^{\mathrm{c}} \qquad (21)$$

Since $f(\mathbf{a}, R)$ is continuous and strictly increasing in R, $f_R^{-1}(\mathbf{a}, U)$ and $\sum_{i=1}^{N} f_R^{-1}(\mathbf{a}_i, U)$ are also continuous and strictly increasing functions of U, with $\sum_{i=1}^{N} f_R^{-1}(\mathbf{a}_i, 0) = 0$. Provided that $\lim_{U\to\infty}\sum_{i=1}^{N} f_R^{-1}(\mathbf{a}_i, U) > R^{c}$, (21) admits a single solution. Then, $\mathbf{\Pi}^{\mathrm{eq}}$ and $\boldsymbol{\phi}^{\mathrm{eq}}$ are deduced from (19) and (20), provided that $K_{\mathrm{I}}^{\mathrm{e}} \neq 0$ and $K_{\mathrm{I}}^{\mathrm{t}} \neq 0$.

The equilibrium is thus unique and the two control loops lead to a satisfaction of the targets introduced in Section 2.

4.2 Stability

The stability analysis of (18) is performed considering its linearization around the equilibrium obtained from (19)

$$\begin{cases} \mathbf{\Delta a}\,(j+1) & = & \mathbf{\Delta a}\,(j) + \delta \mathbf{a}\,(j) \\ \Delta\boldsymbol{\phi}\,(j+1) & = & \Delta\boldsymbol{\phi}\,(j) + \frac{1}{N}\sum_{k=1}^{N}\Delta U_k\,(j) - \Delta\mathbf{U}^{\mathrm{d}}\,(j) \\ \Delta\mathbf{\Pi}\,(j+1) & = & \Delta\mathbf{\Pi}\,(j) - \mathbf{V}\left(\tau_0\Delta\tilde{\mathbf{R}}^{\mathrm{e}}(j) - \Delta\mathbf{B}(j)\right) \\ \Delta\tilde{\mathbf{R}}^{\mathrm{e}}(j+1) & = & (1-\alpha)\Delta\tilde{\mathbf{R}}^{\mathrm{e}}\,(j) \\ +\alpha\left(\frac{K_{\mathrm{P}}^{\mathrm{e}}+K_{\mathrm{I}}^{\mathrm{e}}}{T}\mathbf{V}\left(\tau_0\Delta\tilde{\mathbf{R}}^{\mathrm{e}}(j) - \Delta\mathbf{B}(j)\right) - \frac{K_{\mathrm{I}}^{\mathrm{e}}}{T}\Delta\mathbf{\Pi}\,(j)\right) \\ \mathbf{\Delta R}^{\mathrm{ed}}(j+1) & = & \frac{K_{\mathrm{P}}^{\mathrm{e}}+K_{\mathrm{I}}^{\mathrm{e}}}{T}\mathbf{V}\left(\tau_0\Delta\tilde{\mathbf{R}}^{\mathrm{e}}(j) - \Delta\mathbf{B}(j)\right) - \frac{K_{\mathrm{I}}^{\mathrm{e}}}{T}\Delta\mathbf{\Pi}\,(j) \\ \Delta\mathbf{U}^{\mathrm{d}}\,(j+1) & = & \frac{\partial\mathbf{f}}{\partial\mathbf{a}^T}\left(\mathbf{a}^{\mathrm{eq}},\mathbf{R}^{\mathrm{eq}}\right)\mathbf{\Delta a}\,(j) \\ +\frac{\partial\mathbf{f}}{\partial\mathbf{R}^T}\left(\mathbf{a}^{\mathrm{eq}},\mathbf{R}^{\mathrm{eq}}\right)\left(\frac{K_{\mathrm{P}}^{\mathrm{e}}+K_{\mathrm{I}}^{\mathrm{e}}}{T}\mathbf{V}\left(\tau_0\Delta\tilde{\mathbf{R}}^{\mathrm{e}}(j) - \Delta\mathbf{B}(j)\right) - \frac{K_{\mathrm{I}}^{\mathrm{e}}}{T}\Delta\mathbf{\Pi}\,(j)\right) \\ \mathbf{\Delta B}\,(j+1) & = & \Delta\mathbf{B}\,(j) + \Delta\mathbf{R}^{\mathrm{ed}}(j)T \\ -\left(\left(K_{\mathrm{P}}^{\mathrm{t}}+K_{\mathrm{I}}^{\mathrm{t}}\right)\left(\frac{1}{N}\sum_{k=1}^{N}\Delta U_k^{\mathrm{d}}\,(j) - \Delta\mathbf{U}^{\mathrm{d}}\,(j)\right) + K_{\mathrm{I}}^{\mathrm{t}}\Delta\boldsymbol{\phi}\,(j)\right)T \end{cases} \tag{22}$$

where $\mathbf{V} = \mathrm{diag}\left(1/R_1^{\mathrm{eq}}, \ldots, 1/R_N^{\mathrm{eq}}\right)$ is a diagonal matrix containing the inverse of the encoding rates at equilibrium. The state vector of the linearized system is

$$\mathbf{x}(j) = \left(\Delta\mathbf{a}\,(j), \Delta\boldsymbol{\phi}\,(j), \Delta\mathbf{\Pi}\,(j),\right.$$
$$\left.\Delta\tilde{\mathbf{R}}^{\mathrm{e}}(j), \mathbf{\Delta R}^{\mathrm{ed}}(j), \Delta\mathbf{U}^{\mathrm{d}}\,(j), \mathbf{\Delta B}\,(j)\right)^T. \tag{23}$$

Introduce the $N \times (N \times N^a)$ block diagonal matrix

$$\Xi = \frac{\partial\mathbf{f}}{\partial\mathbf{a}^T}\left(\mathbf{a}^{\mathrm{eq}}, \mathbf{R}^{\mathrm{eq}}\right)$$
$$= \mathrm{diag}\left(\frac{\partial f}{\partial\mathbf{a}_1^T}\left(\mathbf{a}_1^{\mathrm{eq}}, R_1^{\mathrm{eq}}\right), \ldots, \frac{\partial f}{\partial\mathbf{a}_N^T}\left(\mathbf{a}_N^{\mathrm{eq}}, R_N^{\mathrm{eq}}\right)\right),$$

the $N \times N$ diagonal matrix

$$\mathbf{\Gamma} = \frac{\partial\mathbf{f}}{\partial\mathbf{R}^T}\left(\mathbf{a}^{\mathrm{eq}}, \mathbf{R}^{\mathrm{eq}}\right)$$
$$= \mathrm{diag}\left(\frac{\partial f}{\partial R_1}\left(\mathbf{a}_1^{\mathrm{eq}}, R_1^{\mathrm{eq}}\right), \ldots, \frac{\partial f}{\partial R_N}\left(\mathbf{a}_N^{\mathrm{eq}}, R_N^{\mathrm{eq}}\right)\right),$$

and the $N \times N$ circulant matrix

$$\mathbf{L} = \frac{1}{N}\mathrm{toeplitz}\left(N-1, -1, \ldots, -1\right). \tag{24}$$

$\mathbf{I}$ and $\mathbf{0}$ are the identity and null matrix of appropriate size. One then gets from (22) the linear discrete-time state equation

$$\mathbf{x}(j+1) = \mathbf{A}\mathbf{x}(j) + \mathbf{w}(j) \tag{25}$$

where

$$\mathbf{A} = \begin{pmatrix} \mathbf{I} & \mathbf{0} & \mathbf{0} & \mathbf{0} & \mathbf{0} & \mathbf{0} & \mathbf{0} \\ \mathbf{0} & \mathbf{I} & \mathbf{0} & \mathbf{0} & \mathbf{0} & -\mathbf{L} & \mathbf{0} \\ \mathbf{0} & \mathbf{0} & \mathbf{I} & -\tau_0\mathbf{V} & \mathbf{0} & \mathbf{0} & \mathbf{V} \\ \mathbf{0} & \mathbf{0} & -\alpha\frac{K_{\mathrm{I}}^{\mathrm{e}}}{T}\mathbf{I} & (1-\alpha)\mathbf{I} + \alpha\frac{K^{\mathrm{e}}}{T}\tau_0\mathbf{V} & \mathbf{0} & \mathbf{0} & -\alpha\frac{K^{\mathrm{e}}}{T}\mathbf{V} \\ \mathbf{0} & \mathbf{0} & -\frac{K_{\mathrm{I}}^{\mathrm{e}}}{T}\mathbf{I} & \frac{K^{\mathrm{e}}}{T}\tau_0\mathbf{V} & \mathbf{0} & \mathbf{0} & -\frac{K^{\mathrm{e}}}{T}\mathbf{V} \\ \mathbf{\Xi} & \mathbf{0} & -\frac{K_{\mathrm{I}}^{\mathrm{e}}}{T}\mathbf{\Gamma} & \frac{K_{\mathrm{I}}^{\mathrm{e}}}{T}\tau_0\mathbf{\Gamma}\mathbf{V} & \mathbf{0} & \mathbf{0} & -\frac{K_{\mathrm{I}}^{\mathrm{e}}}{T}\Gamma\mathbf{V} \\ \mathbf{0} & -K_{\mathrm{I}}^{\mathrm{t}}T\mathbf{I} & \mathbf{0} & \mathbf{0} & T\mathbf{I} & K^{\mathrm{t}}T\mathbf{L} & \mathbf{I} \end{pmatrix} \tag{26}$$

with $K^{\mathrm{e}} = K_{\mathrm{P}}^{\mathrm{e}} + K_{\mathrm{I}}^{\mathrm{e}}$, $K^{\mathrm{t}} = K_{\mathrm{P}}^{\mathrm{t}} + K_{\mathrm{I}}^{\mathrm{t}}$, and the perturbation

$$\mathbf{w}\,(j) = \left(\ \delta\mathbf{a}\,(j), 0, \ldots 0\ \right)^T. \tag{27}$$

The stability of the system described by (18) is determined by the location of the roots of $\det\left(z\mathbf{I} - \mathbf{A}\right)$ with respect to the unit circle. After some derivations, one obtains

$$\det\left(z\mathbf{I} - \mathbf{A}\right) = \left(\prod_{i=1}^{N}\frac{1}{R_i^{\mathrm{eq}}}\right) z^N\left(z-1\right)^{N(2+N_{\mathrm{a}})}\det\mathbf{F}, \tag{28}$$

with

$$\mathbf{F} = -\,P_6\left(z\right)P_3(z)\left(P_1(z)\mathbf{V}^{-1} - \alpha\tau_0 P_2\left(z\right)\mathbf{I}\right)$$
$$P_1(z)P_2(z)P_4(z)\mathbf{I} + P_1(z)P_2(z)P_5(z)\Gamma\mathbf{L} \tag{29}$$

and

$$\begin{array}{ll} P_1(z) = (z-1)\left(z-1+\alpha\right) & P_2(z) = (z-1)\,\frac{K^{\mathrm{e}}}{T} + \frac{K_{\mathrm{I}}^{\mathrm{e}}}{T} \\ P_3(z) = z\left(z-1\right) & P_4(z) = -\left(z-1\right)T, \\ P_5(z) = -\left(z-1\right)K^{\mathrm{t}}T - K_{\mathrm{I}}^{\mathrm{t}}T & P_6(z) = \left(z-1\right)^2. \end{array}$$

depend on the parameters of the two PI controllers. The $N\left(2+N_{\mathrm{a}}\right)$ zeros at $z=1$ of (28) correspond to the evolution of the source parameters and to the integral terms. The evaluation of $\det\mathbf{F}$ in (28) may only be done numerically. However, (28) may be simplified assuming that all programs have the same characteristics, which leads to $\Gamma = \gamma\mathbf{I}$ and $\mathbf{V} = \frac{1}{R_0}\mathbf{I}$. In this case, $\mathbf{F} = D\left(z\right)\mathbf{I} + K(z)\mathbf{L}$ with

$$D(z) = P_1(z)P_2(z)P_4(z) - P_6(z)P_3(z)\left(R_0 P_1(z) - \alpha\tau_0 P_2(z)\right)$$

and

$$K(z) = \gamma P_1(z)P_2(z)P_5(z)$$

$$\det\mathbf{F} = \det\left(D(z)\mathbf{I} + \frac{1}{N}K(z)\begin{pmatrix} N-1 & -1 & -1 \\ -1 & \ddots & -1 \\ -1 & -1 & N-1 \end{pmatrix}\right) \tag{30}$$
$$= \left(K(z) + D\left(z\right)\right)^N$$

One has thus to study the location of the zeros of $K(z) + D\left(z\right)$, which allow to predict whether a given choice of $K_{\mathrm{P}}^{\mathrm{t}}$, $K_{\mathrm{I}}^{\mathrm{t}}$, $K_{\mathrm{P}}^{\mathrm{e}}$, and $K_{\mathrm{I}}^{\mathrm{e}}$ leads to a stable or to an unstable system, and help to predict the transient evolution of the system.

5. APPLICATION CONTEXT

A typical application scenario for the proposed rate control system is the Mobile TV service delivery using the evolved MBMS standard [25]. Here, we briefly describe the functional architecture of the multiplexing functions. Detailed implementation issues are not addressed.

MBMS is a point-to-multipoint interface specification for 3GPP cellular networks, which is designed to provide efficient delivery of broadcast and multicast services. For broadcast transmission, a single frequency network configuration is introduced in 3GPP LTE specifications which enables a time synchronization between a set of eNBs (base stations) using the same resource block.

The MBMS architecture is composed of three main entities: BM-SC, MBMS-GW and MCE. The Multicast/Broadcast Service Center (BM-SC) is a node that serves as an entry point for the content providers delivering the video sources, used for service announcements, session management. The MANE, considered in the paper in charge of choosing the encoding and the transmission rates, may be located in the BM-SC node. The MBMS-Gateway (GW) is an entity responsible for distributing the traffic across the different eNBs belonging to the same broadcast area. It ensures that the same content is sent from all the eNBs by

Video	Rate(kbit/s)	PSNR (dB)	Activity
Prog 1	1669.9	46.06	low
Prog 2	4929.1	44.23	high
Prog 3	3654.6	44.56	medium
Prog 4	2915.1	44.61	low

Table 1: Average rate and corresponding PSNR of the four considered video streams

using IP Multicast. The Multi-cell/multicast Coordination Entity (MCE) is a logical entity, responsible for allocation of time and frequency resources for multi-cell MBMS transmission. As in [26], we assume that the MBMS-GW periodically notifies the MCE about the resource requirements of video streams so that the resources at eNBs can be re-allocated accordingly. Therefore, the BM-SC should ensure that the encoding rate of the multiplex does not violate the already allocated resources. This is obtained thanks to the proposed rate control scheme.

6. SIMULATION RESULTS

This section considers a typical application context presented in Section 5 concerning mobile TV service delivery over evolved MBMS standard. $N = 4$ video streams, each of 100 s long, extracted from real TV programs: News (Prog 1), Sport (Prog 2), Big Buck Bunny (Prog 3), and Nature Documentary (Prog 4) in 4CIF (704×576) format are encoded with x.264 [27] at a frame rate of $F = 30$ frames/s. GoPs of 15 frames are considered, thus the GoP duration is $T = 0.5$ s. The videos are already encoded using MPEG-4 and then they have been converted to YUV format using *ffmpeg* [28]. The four videos are then processed with the proposed control system. The control is performed at the GoP level. A summary of the video characteristics is provided in Table 1.

Initially, all buffers contain two encoded GoPs corresponding to a buffer delay of 1 s. The reference delay is taken as $\tau_0 = 2$ s. The encoding/transcoding rate (15) is sent to the video encoders which have to choose the encoding parameters for the VU. In this simulation part, the video quality is measured using the PSNR or the SSIM associated to the encoded VUs. This quality metric is transmitted to the MANE in the packet headers. Note that the utility model (1) is only required to characterize the stability of the system and to tune the control parameters. Once the parameters have been chosen, there is no need to know precisely the model (1).

6.1 Constant channel rate and number of users

Here, the four video programs are encoded and transmitted: News (Prog 1), Sport (Prog 2), Cartoon (Prog 3), and Documentary (Prog 4). A constant channel rate $R^c = 3.5$ Mbit/s is considered. The maximum buffer size is $B^{\max} = 4$ Mbits. The proposed *quality fair* (QF) video delivery system is compared to a classical scheme which provide equal transmission rate to the N video streams. This scheme controls the encoding rate as in (15) to limit the buffering delay, this solution is called *transmission rate fair* (TRF) video delivery system.

In order to choose the parameters of all PI controllers and to characterize the stability region, as in[29, 30] a linear PSNR-Rate model is considered so that

$$P_i(j) = U_i(j) = f\left(\mathbf{a}_i(j), R_i^{\mathrm{e}}(j)\right) = a_i^1(j)R_i^{\mathrm{e}}(j) + a_i^2(j) \quad (31)$$

where $P_i(j)$ is the PSNR of program i at time j and the element of the vector $\mathbf{a}_i(j)$ are derived using some encoding trials for the N considered programs. Using f, one can derive the system equilibrium and the stability of the control system. Parameters of the two PI controllers are set in such a way that the roots of $\det(z\mathbf{I} - \mathbf{A}) = 0$ are within the unit circle. Among the values of the parameters leading to a stable system, one may choose the values that provides good performance in terms of both buffering delay and PSNR discrepancy and variance. Good transient behaviors have been obtained with $K_{\mathrm{P}}^{\mathrm{t}} = 4250$, $K_{\mathrm{I}}^{\mathrm{t}} = 425$ $K_{\mathrm{P}}^{\mathrm{e}} = 127500$, and $K_{\mathrm{I}}^{\mathrm{e}} = 3400$, position of the roots of (28) are represented in Figure 3.

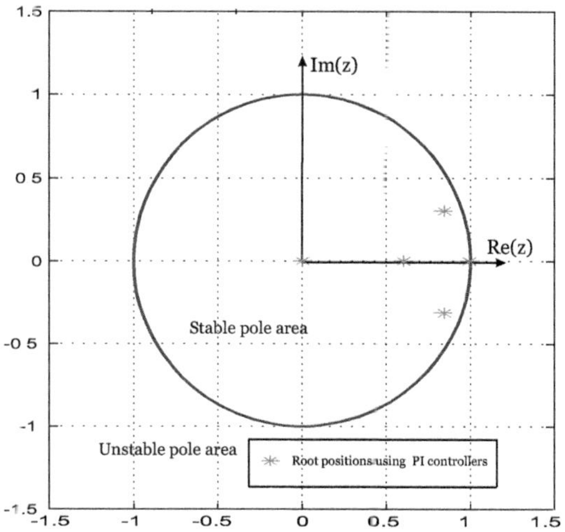

Figure 3: Position of the roots of (28) when $K_{\mathrm{P}}^{\mathrm{t}} = 4250$, $K_{\mathrm{I}}^{\mathrm{t}} = 425$ $K_{\mathrm{P}}^{\mathrm{e}} = 127500$, and $K_{\mathrm{I}}^{\mathrm{e}} = 3400$ (two videos).

The PSNRs $P_i(j)$, the buffering delays $\tau_i(j)$, the encoding rates $R_i^{\mathrm{e}}(j)$, and the transmission rates $R_i^{\mathrm{t}}(j)$ of each video stream are represented in Figure 4 (left) using the proposed QF solution and in Figure 4 (right) using the TRF solution when quality fairness is performed in term of PSNR.

The tuning parameter α used to estimate the buffering delay has been set to $\alpha = 0.7$ corresponding to the least mean squared error between the real buffer delay τ and the estimated buffer delay $\tilde{\tau}$. Table 2 represents $MSE(\tilde{\tau}, \tau)$ as a function of α. The x264 video encoder is used to en-

α	$MSE(\tilde{\tau},\tau)$	α	$MSE(\tilde{\tau},\tau)$
0.5	0.0035	0.6	0.0021
0.65	0.0016	0.7	0.0014
0.75	0.0019	0.8	0.0035

Table 2: MSE of the estimated buffering delay as a function of α.

code on-line the different programs according to the target rate constraint derived by the individual encoding rate controllers. Thus, the rate control function in each video encoder is activated. A two pass control process in the rate control is performed to better fit the target bit rate and reduce the rate discrepancies. However, the obtained rate may be slightly different from that required by the MANE which may introduce some oscillations.

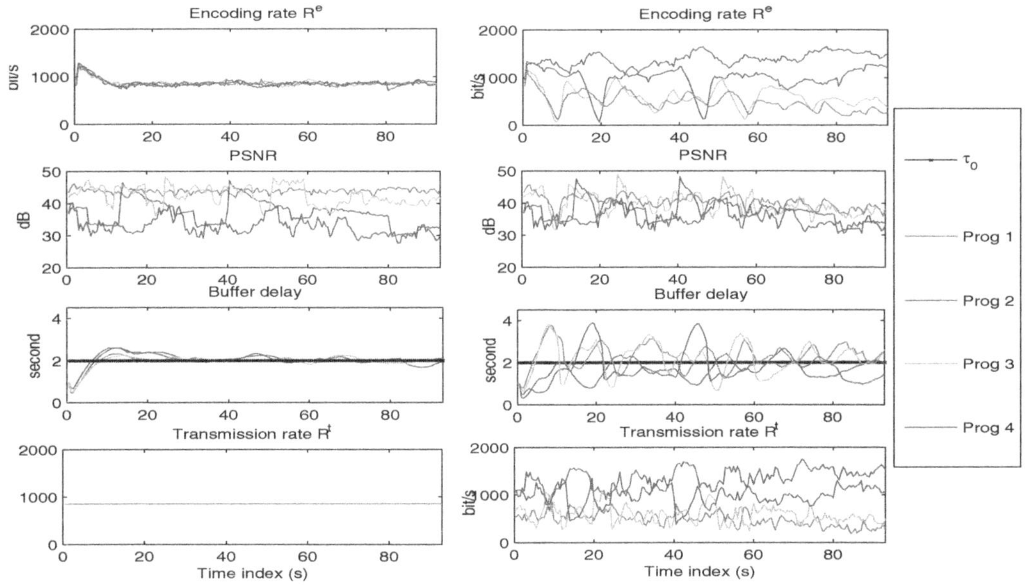

Figure 4: System performance using PI controllers while multiplexing four video programs using the proposed QF solution (left) and the TRF system (right).

The system performance is measured in terms of average discrepancy Δ_τ (in s) of the buffering delay with respect to τ_0, variance of the buffer delay σ_τ^2 (in s^2), PSNR discrepancy Δ_P (in dB), and PSNR variance σ_P^2 (in dB^2), defined by

$$\Delta_\tau = \left| \frac{1}{N} \sum_{n=1}^{N} \left(\frac{1}{M} \sum_{l=1}^{M} (\tau_n(l) - \tau_0) \right) \right|,$$

$$\sigma_\tau^2 = \frac{1}{N} \sum_{n=1}^{N} \left(\frac{1}{M} \sum_{l=1}^{M} (\tau_n(l) - \tau_0)^2 \right),$$

$$\sigma_{PSNR}^2 = \frac{1}{N} \sum_{n=1}^{N} \left(\frac{1}{M} \sum_{l=1}^{M} (P_n(l) - \bar{P}(l))^2 \right),$$

$$\Delta_{PSNR} = \left| \frac{1}{N} \sum_{n=1}^{N} \left(\frac{1}{M} \sum_{l=1}^{M} (P_n(l) - \bar{P}(l)) \right) \right|,$$

where M is the number of GoPs in the video streams.

In Figure 4, one can see that the proposed QF solution provides a significant reduction of the PSNR discrepancy between the four programs compared to the TRF solution. The QF solution reduces the mean PSNR discrepancy to $\Delta_{PSNR} = 2.2$ dB compared to $\Delta_{PSNR} = 4.15$ dB using the TRF solution.

Results are summarized in Table 3 in three cases: *(i)* Only P controllers are used (P, P), *(ii)* P controller is used for the transmission rate control and PI controller for the encoding rate control (P, PI), and *(iii)* PI controllers are used (PI, PI). The PI controller in the encoder rate control loops significantly decreases the discrepancy of the buffering delay Δ_τ compared to a situation where only P controllers are used, without disturbing the behavior of the PSNR regulation. In addition, using PI controllers for the transmission rate control loop reduces the PSNR discrepancy between the programs at the price of some increase of the buffer delay discrepancy and variance.

One can also notice that the average PSNR of Prog 2,

K_P^t, K_I^t	K_P^e, K_I^e	Δ_τ	σ_τ^2	Δ_P	σ_P^2
4250, 0	127500, 0	0.1	0.5	4.15	11.2
4250, 0	127500, 3400	0.008	0.19	4	10.9
4250, 425	127500, 3400	0.01	0.22	2.2	11.18

Table 3: Performance when using (P, P), (P, PI), and (PI, PI) controllers in the proposed QF video delivery system.

characterized by high activity level, is improved from 32 dB to 37 dB which corresponds to a significant improvement of the subjective video quality. This improvement is at the expense of PSNR degradation of Prog 1, characterized by low activity level. The average PSNR of Prog 1 decreases from 47 dB to 42 dB which still correspond to a very good quality. On the other hand, the discrepancy between the buffering delay and τ_0 remains limited for most of the time. The buffering delay variations are due to the interactions of both control loops (encoding rate) and (transmission rate) using two PI controllers. When only the encoding rate is controlled, corresponding to the TRF solution, the buffering delay reaches rapidly τ_0.

6.2 Robustness of the control system

In this section, we analyze the robustness of the proposed control system while considering variations of the channel rate, of the number of video programs, as well as an other utility metric.

6.2.1 Variation of the channel rate and the number of video programs

First, the rate of the channel is varying between $R^c = 3.5$ Mbits/s and $R^c = 4.5$ Mbits/s, see Figure 5 (left). Second, the number of multiplexed video programs is varying with time. This scenario corresponds to a change in the number of users. When a new video program is added to the multiplex, it has no bit rate allocated by the MANE to

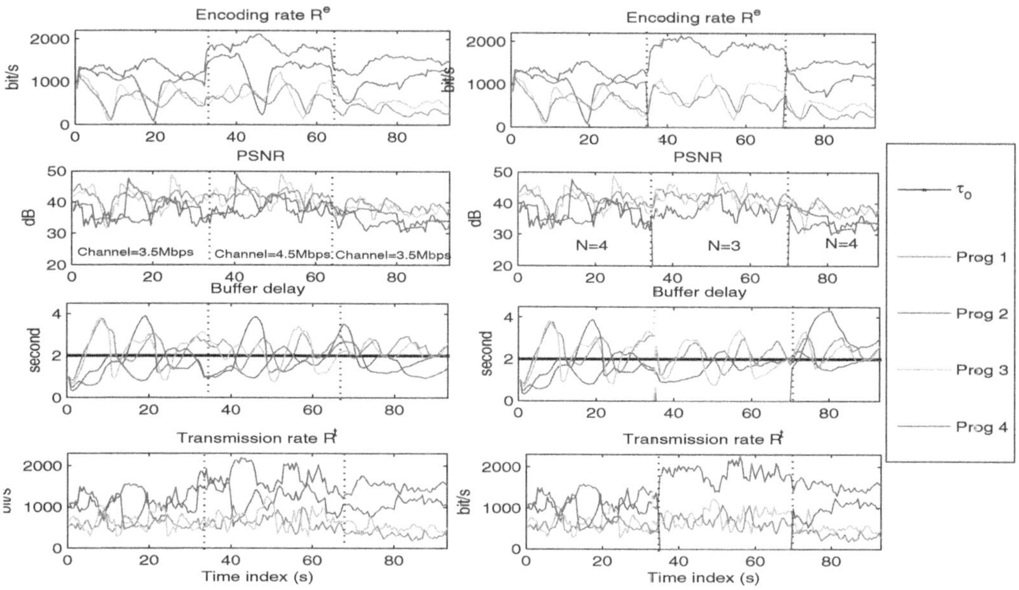

Figure 5: System performance using PI controllers while multiplexing four video programs using the proposed QF solution when considering variations of the channel rate (left) and of the number of programs (right).

it (since at time j the controller derives the encoding rate for time $j+1$). Thus, we choose to set the encoding rate at that time is R^c/N. In Figure 5 (right), Prog 4 is not transmitted between GoP 35 and 65.

When the channel rate increases or when a video program is no more transmitted, the bandwidth allocation adapts rapidly to this change by allocating more rate to programs with low video quality (here Prog 2). When the channel rate decreases or when a new video program is added transmitted, the bandwidth allocation performs well, showing the robustness of the proposed control system to variations of the channel rate and the number of transmitted video programs.

6.2.2 *SSIM fairness*

Here the quality fairness is addressed using the SSIM metric. In order to choose the parameters of all PI controllers and to characterize the stability region, a linear SSIM-Rate model is considered as in [31] so that

$$S_i(j) = U_i(j) = f\left(\mathbf{a}_i(j), R_i^e(j)\right) = a_i^1(j)R_i^e(j) + a_i^2(j) \quad (32)$$

where $S_i(j)$ is the SSIM of program i at time j and the element of the vector $\mathbf{a}_i(j)$ are derived using some encoding trials for the N considered programs. A stable system and good transient behaviors have been obtained with $K_P^t = 4250$, $K_I^t = 425$ $K_P^e = 127500$, and $K_I^e = 3400$.

The SSIMs $S_i(j)$ of each program are represented in Figure 6 using the TRF, then using the proposed QF solution when the channel rate is constant and when it is time varying. Again the proposed QF solution reduces the SSIM discrepancy between the four programs compared to the TRF solution. Using the proposed solution the mean SSIM discrepancy is reduced to $\Delta_{SSIM} = 0.02$ compared to $\Delta_{SSIM} = 0.05$ with the TRF solution.

SSIM or PSNR are generated by the video encoder at each encoding process and transmitted to the MANE for the control process. Thus the control process does not use any trade

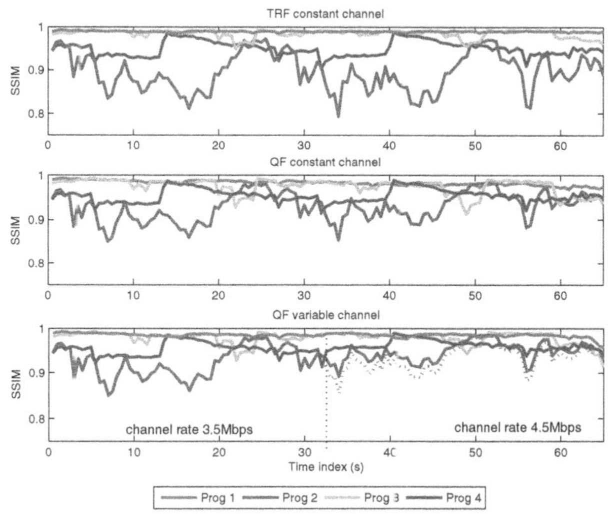

Figure 6: System performance using PI controllers while multiplexing four video programs using the proposed QF solution when fairness in SSIM is considered for both constant and variable channel rates.

off function between the rate and the video quality metric. Other test with subjective video quality fairness can be performed while using QoE-Rate model such as those in [32]. In this case, given the QoE-Rate trade off function, the equilibrium and the stability of the system can be characterized.

7. CONCLUSIONS AND PERSPECTIVES

In this paper, we propose a control system for the encoding and the transmission of multiple video streams targeting similar video quality between streams as well as efficient buffering delay control. The control system is modeled with a discrete-time non-linear state-space representation.

PI controllers for both the transmission rate control and the encoding rate control are considered. Simulation tests show that the quality fairness (measured with PSNR or SSIM) is improved compared to a solution providing a fair transmission rate allocation. Moreover, the jitter of the buffering delay remains reasonable.

This control system can be performed on scalable video sources. The same buffer and rate control system can be used to determine the optimal encoding rate for each video server. Only the rate control algorithm has to be adapted to fit the target bit rate. This can be done by adjusting the number of scalable layers. The main difficulty comes from the fact that not all rate points may be reached in a continuous way (this would require very fine grain scalability).

Control at the frame level should be considered, however this would require to much better model the packet delivery delays between the MANE and the encoders.

Acknowledgments

This work was supported by ANR ARSSO project (grant agreement no 09-VERS-019). Michel Kieffer is partly supported by the Institut Universitaire de France

8. REFERENCES

[1] "Cisco visual networking index: Forecast and methodology, 2008-2013," Tech. Rep., Cisco, 2009.

[2] Z.L. Zhang, S. Nelakuditi, R. Aggarwal, and R.P. Tsang, "Efficient selective frame discard algorithms for stored video delivery across resource constrained networks," *Real-Time Imaging*, vol. 7, no. 3, pp. 255 – 273, 2001.

[3] T-L. Lin, Y. Zhi, S. Kanumuri, P.C. Cosman, and A.R. Reibman, "Perceptual quality based packet dropping for generalized video gop structures," in *Proc. IEEE ICASSP*, 2009, pp. 781 – 784.

[4] S. Ma, W. Gao, and Y. Lu, "Rate-distortion analysis for H.264/AVC video coding and its application to rate control," *IEEE trans. on Circ. Syst. Vid. Techn.*, vol. 15, no. 12, pp. 1533 – 1544, 2005.

[5] Z. He and D. O. Wu, "Linear rate control and optimum statistical multiplexing for H.264 video broadcast," *IEEE trans. on Multimedia*, vol. 10, no. 7, pp. 1237 – 1249, 2008.

[6] S. K. Srinivasan, J. Vahabzadeh-Hagh, and M. Reisslein, "The effects of priority levels and buffering on the statistical multiplexing of single-layer H.264/AVC and SVC encoded video streams," *IEEE trans. on Broadcasting*, vol. 56, no. 3, pp. 281 – 287, 2010.

[7] E. Maani and A.K. Katsaggelos, "Unequal error protection for robust streaming of scalable video over packet lossy networks," *IEEE trans. on Circ. Syst. Vid. Techn.*, vol. 20, no. 3, pp. 407 – 416, 2010.

[8] Y. Li, Z. Li, M. Chiang, and A.R. Calderbank, "Content-aware distortion-fair video streaming in congested networks," *IEEE trans. on Multimedia*, vol. 11, no. 6, pp. 1182 – 1193, 2009.

[9] N. Changuel, B. Sayadi, and M. Kieffer, "Joint encoder and buffer control for statistical multiplexing of multimedia contents," in *Proc. IEEE Globecom*, 2010, pp. 1 – 6.

[10] C.W Wong, O.C. Au, and H.K. Lam, "PID-based real-time rate control," in *Proc. IEEE ICME*, 2004, vol. 1, pp. 221 – 224.

[11] Z. Guo and R. Rojas-Cessa, "Analysis of a flow control system for a combined input-crosspoint buffered packet switch," in *Workshop on High Performance Switching and Routing*, 2005, pp. 336 – 340.

[12] Y-H. Zhang, K.H Li, C.Q. Xu, and L.M. Sun, "Joint rate allocation and buffer management for robust transmission of VBR video," *Acta Automatica Sinica*, vol. 34, no. 3, pp. 1 – 7, 2008.

[13] Y. Huang, S. Mao, and S.F. Midkiff, "A control-theoretic approach to rate control for streaming videos," *IEEE trans. on Multimedia*, vol. 11, no. 6, pp. 1072 – 1081, 2009.

[14] Y. Huang and S. Mao, "Analysis and design of a proportional-integral rate controller for streaming videos," in *Proc. IEEE Globecom*, 2009, pp. 5530 – 5535.

[15] Y. Zhou, Y. Sun, Z. Feng, and S. Sun, "PID-based bit allocation strategy for h.264/avc rate control," *IEEE trans. on Circ. Syst. Vid. Techn.*, vol. 58, no. 3, pp. 184 – 188, 2011.

[16] J.W Cho and S. Chong, "Utility max-min flow control using slope-restricted utility functions," in *Proc. IEEE Globecom*, 2005, vol. 2, pp. 818 – 824.

[17] E. Witrant, C. Canudas-de Wit, D. Georges, and M. Alamir, "Remote stabilization via communication networks with a distributed control law," *IEEE trans. on Autom. Contr.*, vol. 52, no. 8, pp. 1480 – 1485, 2007.

[18] Motorola, "Statistical multiplexing over IP StatmuxIP solution," Tech. Rep., Motorola, 2009, XP002565902.

[19] Harmonic, "IP-based distributed statistical multiplexing solution," Tech. Rep., 2011.

[20] K. Seshadrinathan, R. Soundararajan, A.C. Bovik, and L.K. Cormack, "Study of subjective and objective quality assessment of video," *IEEE trans. on Image Proc.*, vol. 19, no. 6, pp. 1427 – 1441, 2010.

[21] T. Wiegand, H. Schwarz, A. Joch, F. Kossentini, and G.J. Sullivan, "Rate-constrained coder control and comparison of video coding standards," *IEEE trans. on Circ. Syst. Vid. Techn.*, vol. 13, no. 7, pp. 688 – 703, 2003.

[22] S. Ma, W. Gao, and Y. Lu, "Rate-distortion analysis for H.264/AVC video coding and its application to rate control," *IEEE trans. on Circ. Syst. Vid. Techn.*, vol. 15, no. 12, pp. 1533 – 1544, 2005.

[23] H. Wang and S. Kwong, "Rate-distortion optimization of rate control for H.264 with adaptive initial quantization parameter determination," *IEEE trans. on Circ. Syst. Vid. Techn.*, vol. 18, no. 1, pp. 140 – 144, 2008.

[24] K.-B. Kim and H.-J. Kim, "Back-pressure buffering scheme to improve the cell loss property on the output buffered atm switch," in *Proc. IEEE LCN*, 1996, pp. 242 – 248.

[25] ETSI, "Multimedia Broadcast/Multicast service. (MBMS); UTRAN/GERAN requirements," Tech. Rep., 3GPP TR 25.992-140, 2005.

[26] V. Vukadinovic and J. Huschke, "Statistical multiplexing gains of H.264/AVC video in E-MBMS," in *Proc. Int. Symp. on Wirel. Perv. Comp.*, 2008, pp. 468 – 474.

[27] x264 Home Page, "Videolan organization. retrieved 2011-03-11.," 2011.

[28] ffmpeg Documentation, "http://ffmpeg.org/ffmpeg.html," .

[29] J. Yang, Q. Dai, W. Xu, and R. Ding, "A rate control algorithm for MPEG-2 to H.264 real-time transcoding," *Proc. IEEE VCIP*, vol. 5960, pp. 1995 – 2003, 2005.

[30] S. Ma, v Gao, and Y. Lu, "Rate-distortion analysis for H.264/AVC video coding and its application to rate control," *IEEE trans. on Circ. Syst. Vid. Techn.*, vol. 15, no. 12, pp. 1533 – 1544, 2005.

[31] L. Teixeira and L. Corte-Real, "Coding multiple H.264 video streams using SSIM as quality metric," in *Proc. IEEE Int. Workshop on Multimedia Analysis and Processing*, 2008, pp. 741 – 748.

[32] K. Deep Singh, A. Ksentini, and B. Marienval, "Quality of experience measurement tool for SVC video coding," in *ICC*, 2011.

GreenTube: Power Optimization for Mobile Video Streaming via Dynamic Cache Management

Xin Li
Dept. of Computer Science
George Mason University
Fairfax, VA
xlih@gmu.edu

Mian Dong, Zhan Ma, Felix Fernandes
Dallas Technology Lab
Samsung Telecommunications America
Richardson, TX
{mian.dong, zhan.ma, felix.f}@samsung.com

ABSTRACT

Mobile video streaming has become one of the most popular applications in the trend of smartphone booming and the prevalence of 3G/4G networks, i.e., HSPA, HSPA+, and LTE. However, the prohibitively high power consumption by 3G/4G radios in smartphones reduces battery life significantly and thus severely hurts user experience. To tackle this challenge, we designed *GreenTube*, a system that optimizes power consumption for mobile video streaming by judiciously scheduling downloading activities to minimize unnecessary active periods of 3G/4G radio. GreenTube achieves this by dynamically managing the downloading cache based on user viewing history and network condition. We implemented GreenTube on Android-based smartphones. Experimental results show that GreenTube achieves large power reductions of more than 70% (on the 3G/4G radio) and 40% (for the whole system). We believe GreenTube is a desirable upgrade to the Android system, especially in the light of increasing LTE popularity.

Categories and Subject Descriptors

C.4 [**Performance of Systems**]: Measurement techniques, Design studies, Performance attributes; C.2.1 [**Network Architecture and Design**]: wireless communication

Keywords

Power Optimization, Mobile Video Streaming

1. INTRODUCTION

Power optimization for smartphones continues to be a relevant problem. The problem is becoming pronounced, especially with the rapid growth of mobile data usage for a large variety of multimedia applications, including games, music, videos, etc. The 3G/4G networks, such as HSPA, HSPA+, and LTE, offer their users much faster mobile data access speeds and enable data-intensive applications such as HD video streaming. However, the wireless communications also impose a significant power cost on smartphones [1].

Our goal is *to make mobile video streaming more power efficient over 3G/4G networks*. Not only is video streaming among the most popular smartphone apps (applications) according to recent studies [2] [19], but also its data-intensive nature indeed leads to extremely high power consumption. For example, the average power consumption by Galaxy Nexus is 2.3 W to play a 720p video from HTTP streaming via Verizon LTE network according to our measurement. As a result, a battery of full capacity (1850 mAh) can only support three hours of video streaming. Such prohibitively high power consumption severely hurts user experience.

We choose 3G/4G radio as our major target for power optimization because 3G/4G radio contributes a significant portion of system power consumption. In comparison to the previous example, the average power consumption by Galaxy Nexus is only 1.1 W to play the same video from SD card. In other words, more than 50% of the system power is consumed by the LTE radio. Thus, optimizing power consumption of 3G/4G radio is essential for maximizing the smartphone battery life and improving user experience. To the best of our knowledge, this paper is the first to discuss power optimization for mobile video streaming via 3G/4G networks. As the first study, we must answer the following research questions.

First, why does the 3G/4G radio consume so much power in video streaming? Through control experiments and video streaming trace analysis, we show that a significant amount of power is consumed due to the conflict between the video streaming support in state-of-the-art smartphone systems and the power control mechanism in 3G/4G networks. That is, the time interval between successive downloading sessions is too short for the radio to enter power saving mode, or idle state, defined in 3G/4G networks. As a result, the 3G/4G radio has to remain active throughout the video streaming session even if there is no downloading session going on.

Second, will the problem be solved by using a large downloading cache? A natural solution to solve the above problem is to download the whole video into a large cache and turn off the radio when the downloading session ends. This approach will work if the user chooses to watch through the whole video. However, according to our study, 80% of YouTube sessions in smartphones are less than half of the corresponding video durations. As a result, downloading the whole video will lead to waste in both data usage and power.

Finally, will the problem be solved by traffic reshaping?

MM'12, October 29–November 2, 2012, Nara, Japan.

Many WiFi power optimization works [11] [4] propose to reshape the wireless traffic and create sufficient long periods for WiFi radios to enter power saving mode. Directly using this approach, however, does not work for 3G/4G networks because the 3G/4G radios, unlike their WiFi counterparts, simply can not enter power saving mode immediately after traffic ends as defined in 3G/4G standards. Instead, they need to wait for a fairly long period, e.g., 10 seconds in Verizon LTE network, before entering power saving mode. The length of such period is comparable to that of each downloading session. Therefore, it requires judicious scheduling of each downloading session to effectively reduce power consumption of 3G/4G radios.

In this paper, we present *GreenTube*, a system that optimizes power consumption for mobile video streaming by judiciously scheduling downloading activities to minimize unnecessary active period of 3G/4G radios. GreenTube achieves this via dynamically managing the downloading cache based on user viewing history and network condition. We implemented GreenTube on Android-based smartphones and experimental results show large power reductions of more than 70% (on the 3G/4G radio) and 40% (for the whole system).

In designing and realizing GreenTube, we make the following contributions:

- **Characterize the problem of conflict between the power state transition defined in 3G/4G networks and the video streaming support in state-of-the-art smartphone systems.** Through three motivational studies we show the significant energy impact of such a conflict and summarize the design requirements of a system that can address this issue (Section 3).
- **Design a light-weight system, GreenTube, to reduce power consumption.** The design of GreenTube extensively leverages the findings from the motivational studies in order to meet the design requirements (Section 4).
- **Implement and evaluate GreenTube on Android-based smartphones.** Promising power improvements provide confidence that GreenTube is an important step towards energy-efficient mobile video streaming via 3G/4G networks (Section 5).

The rest of this paper is organized as follows. Section 2 provides necessary background information. Section 3 motivates the GreenTube design through three studies, followed by the system design in Section 4. Section 5 presents system implementation and evaluation. Section 6 surveys related work. Section 7 discusses the limitations and future work. Section 8 concludes this paper.

2. BACKGROUND

We start with a brief overview of mobile video streaming, then introduce power states defined in 3G/4G network, and finally discuss the video streaming support in state-of-the-art smartphone systems.

2.1 Mobile Video Streaming Overview

A video streaming system can be implemented in many ways. It can be built using a conventional Content Delivery Network (CDN) architecture such as YouTube, Hulu, etc, or purely peer-to-peer (P2P) such as PPLive, PPStream, or even hybrid CDN-P2P [21]. HTTP, RTSP, P2P protocols are implemented to realize the successful streaming system. Among them, our focus is the popular and dominant HTTP video streaming. For instance, YouTube, Hulu, etc, use the HTTP streaming protocol for content delivery. One promising feature of the HTTP protocol is the support for resuming the broken or interrupted downloads. This enables our system design to close TCP connection and thus improve power consumption.

Video delivered over the Internet can be encapsulated using many container formats such as AVI, FLV, MP4, MKV, etc. FLV was dominant in the past. Recently, however, streaming video contents are increasingly contained in MP4 format, rather than FLV, especially for HD contents. To support our study, we used a crawler to download 3 Terabytes of the most popular YouTube videos over a 45-day span. From this massive dataset, videos with 720p and 1080p resolutions are all encapsulated in the MP4 container. Like other modern container formats, MP4 allows streaming over the Internet. We use MP4 videos exclusively in this paper.

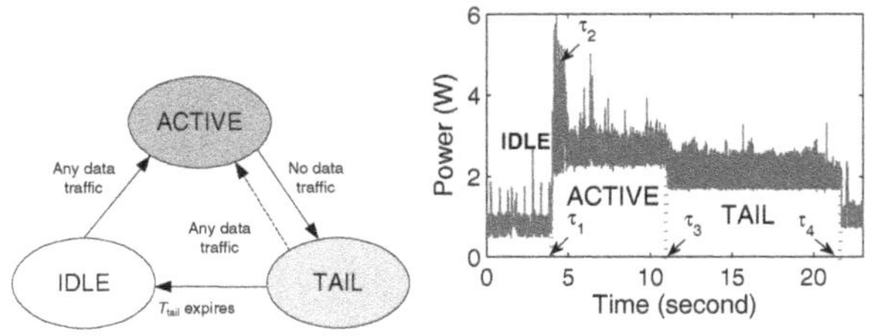

(a) (b)

Figure 1: 3G/4G RRC and power states, (a) simplified RRC state transition; (b) power trace

2.2 Power States in 3G/4G Network

We next cover the necessary background on state machine behavior and corresponding power characteristics of the 3G/4G network.

Both 3G and 4G networks share the similar generalized radio resource control (RRC) states, IDLE, ACTIVE and TAIL as shown in Figure 1(a). For a typical data exchange, assuming the device starts at IDLE state, current state is promoted to the ACTIVE state for data transmission with a certain delay (i.e., noted as promotion delay [9, 18]). After data transmission, it is usually demoted from the ACTIVE state requiring higher radio resource and radio power consumption to the TAIL state with lower radio resource and power consumption, until the tail timer (noted as T_{tail}) expires and finally puts the device into the IDLE state.

Given the state machine for 3G/4G networks, the power trace on smartphones can be easily explained. As shown in Figure 1(b) for video streaming over Verizon LTE network, we observe that the network activities accurately match the different states with associated power levels. Smartphones consume almost zero power in IDLE state. Power consumption rises when the smartphone is promoted from the IDLE state to ACTIVE after sending a packet at time τ_1. After a certain promotion delay, the device starts active data transfer at time τ_2, until it enters the TAIL state with lower power at τ_3. After the tail timer expires at τ_4, the smart-

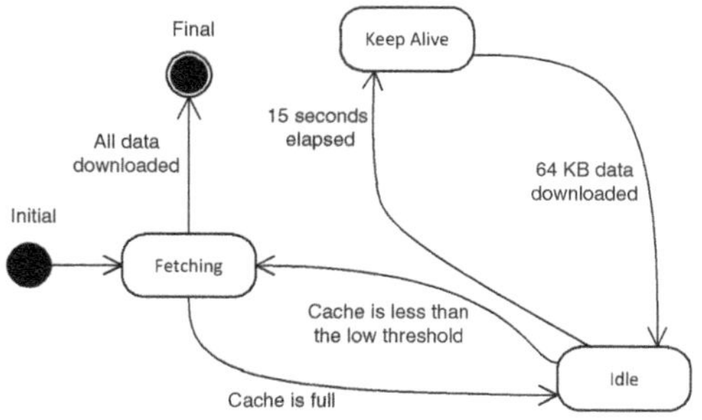

Figure 2: Android HTTP data source provider state machine

phone enters IDLE and the allocated radio resource is released. Note that our findings are consistent with the work presented in [9].

2.3 HTTP Streaming Support in Smartphones

We next introduce HTTP streaming support in Android, one of the most popular smartphone OSes.

In the Android Multimedia Framework, the major components involved in video playback include data source providers (like disk file, HTTP streaming, etc), video container demuxers, audio/video codecs and a media player. The HTTP streaming downloading behaviour is largely determined by the data source provider which interacts with the HTTP server and feeds the data to the media player. The HTTP streaming data source provider is stateful and there are three states: *Fetching*, *Idle* and *Keep Alive*. In the data source provider, the video data downloaded from the HTTP server is held in a large memory cache, or downloading cache. The size of the cache is bounded by a high threshold. There is also a low threshold, the lower bound of the cache, which is used to improve the playback smoothness. By default, the high threshold and low threshold are is set to 20 MB 4 MB respectively.

During an HTTP video streaming session, the data is downloaded periodically. We now explain this process in detail using the state machine in Figure 2. Initially, when the user starts a video streaming session, the data source provider enters into the *Fetching* state and continuously downloads the video data from the HTTP server. When the cache size reaches the high threshold, it transits to the *Idle* state. By default, while in the *Idle* state, a keep-alive mechanism is automatically triggered every 15 seconds to transition into the *Keep Alive* state. On entering into the *Keep Alive* state, 64 KB video data is downloaded and then the state transits back into the *Idle* state. Once the cached video content size falls below the designated low threshold, the state moves to *Fetching* and another continuous downloading begins.

The different states of the HTTP data source provider can be mapped to the different states of the 3G/4G networks. In other words, the different states correspond to different power consumption states. As a result, the power consumption during video playback is largely determined by this periodic downloading behaviour. This relationship is further studied and explored in the following sections.

One exception worth mentioning is that although the YouTube app directly utilizes the Android Multimedia Framework for video playback, it uses an undocumented feature which disables the keep-alive mechanism and closes the TCP connection every time the cache is filled up. This effectively eliminates all data traffic between the HTTP server and the smartphone in the *Idle* state.

Table 1: Smartphone Specifications

Model	Galaxy S	Galaxy S II	Galaxy Nexus
Processor	Hummingbird	Snapdragon	OMAP4
Memory	512MB	1GB	1GB
Network	ATT HSPA	Tmobile HSPA+	Verizon LTE
Android	2.3.6	2.3.6	4.0.3

3. MOTIVATION

We next report three studies that directly motivate the design of GreenTube: mobile video streaming power characterization, YouTube usage by smartphone users, and LTE network speed measurement.

3.1 Power Characterization

3.1.1 Methodology

Video Content: As briefly mentioned earlier, we developed a YouTube crawler that automatically downloads 720p video files from different categories on the YouTube website. Using this crawler, we collected more than 22, 000 720p video files from YouTube over 45 days. The average size of the video files is 94 MB, the average duration is 358 seconds and the average bitrate is 2200 Kbps. We randomly chose 500 out of the 22, 000 video files for the video streaming power characterization.

Choice of Smartphones: For power characterization, we chose the Galaxy S, Galaxy S II, and Galaxy Nexus smartphones. Table 1 lists their detailed specifications.

Video Streaming Setup: We stored all the downloaded video files on an internet-accessible HTTP server. We developed a simple Android video player based on the Android Multimedia Framework. This video player reads a list of test videos stored on the HTTP server and automatically plays the video files with a 10-second interval between two consecutive playbacks.

Power Measurement: We measure the power consumed by the smartphones using the Monsoon Power Monitor [3]. The smartphones are powered by the power monitor so they never run out of the battery during the experiments. The power monitor supplies current to the phone and is able to sample the current drawn by the device at a frequency of 5000 Hz. The power consumption data recorded by the power monitor software is time-stamped. The simple android video player also logs when a video playback begins and finishes. With the 10-second interval between playbacks, the offline analysis tool can extract the power consumption data for each video playback from the power trace recorded by the power monitor.

3.1.2 Results

For each smartphone, we measure the average power consumption for playing a video from SD card and from HTTP streaming. Figure 4 shows the average power consumption of the two cases for three smartphones. As shown in the figure, average power consumption by the three smartphones in video streaming is 1.4 W, 1.2 W, and 2.3 W, respectively. Considering the battery capacity of each smartphone, we estimate the battery life of the three smartphones for mobile

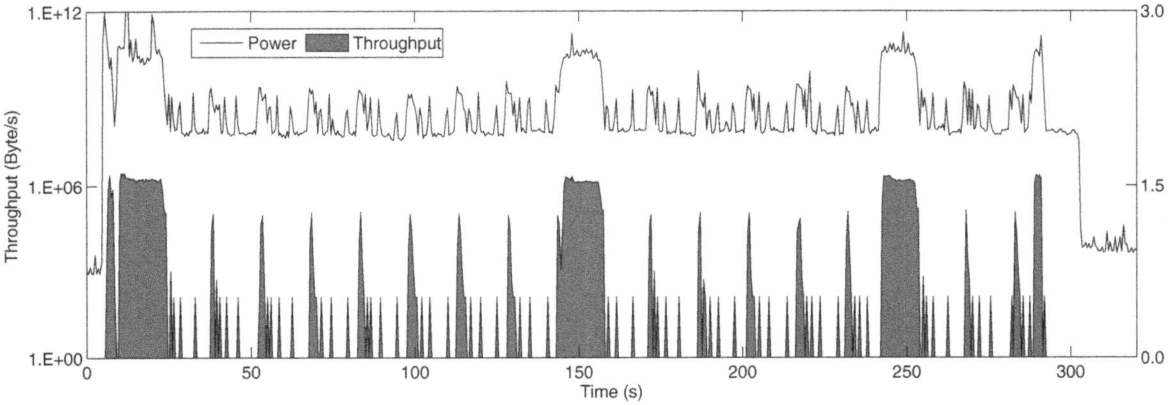

Figure 3: Power trace of 720p HTTP video streaming using Verizon LTE network

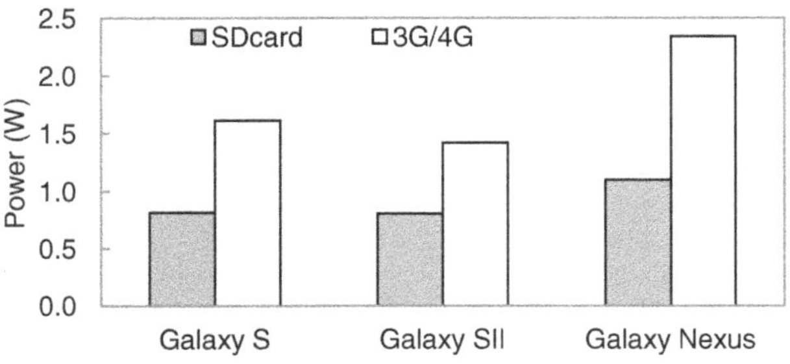

Figure 4: Power consumption characterization

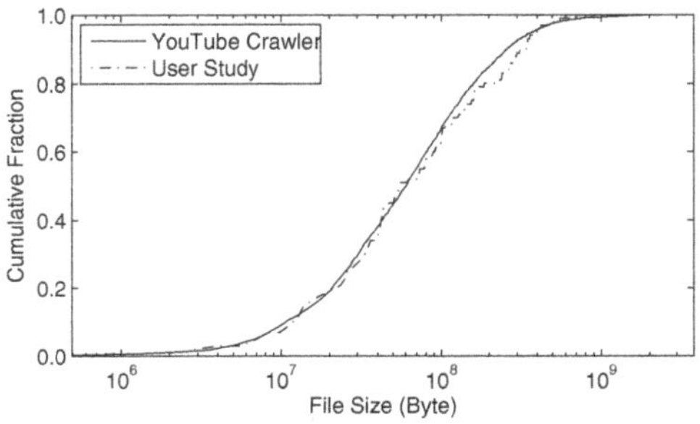

Figure 5: File size distribution of YouTube videos in our experiment

video streaming is 5, 6, and 3 hours, respectively. Moreover, Figure 4 also shows power consumption of video streaming via 3G/4G networks is about 2X of that of playback from SD card. In other words, the 3G/4G radios account for about 50% of the total system power consumption. To summarize, mobile video streaming via 3G/4G network is prohibitively power hungry, and 3G/4G radios are the most significant power consumer in smartphones for video streaming.

A natural question is why 3G/4G radio consumes so much power. We shall now answer this question using the power trace. Figure 3 depicts the transient power consumed by a smartphone (Galaxy Nexus) that is receiving a 2 Mbps video stream from a HTTP server via Verizon LTE network. The figure also shows the corresponding time-stamped data traffic between the HTTP server and the smartphone.

As shown in Figure 3, there are three different data traffic patterns. Each of the four large continuous chunks represents a high-speed downloading session in the *Fetching* state to fill the cache; each of the 15 second interval peaks corresponds to a 64 KB downloading in the Keep-Alive state; and the tiny peaks are caused by TCP zero window probes sent by the HTTP server and the corresponding TCP ACKs as responses from the smartphone. The sequence of data traffic patterns strictly conforms to the state machine described in section 2.3.

Interestingly, the power consumption data shows an almost identical pattern. The highest power consumption happens during the four continuous high-speed downloading, each of the 64 KB downloading slots causes a much lower power consumption peak and the tiny peaks in the data traffic generate several much narrower power consumption peaks. Obviously, there is a 10 second TAIL power state after the last chunk of continuous high-speed downloading which completes the streaming task. After the 10 second TAIL state, the LTE modem enters the IDLE state and the power consumption drops to a dramatically lower level. Given that the interval between 64 KB downloadings is 15 seconds (which is longer than the 10 second TAIL state), it is natural to wonder why the LTE modem never enters the IDLE state before the last continuous downloading. The reason is that the TCP zero window probes and the corresponding TCP ACKs are small packets that effectively bring the LTE modem from the TAIL state back to the ACTIVE state and thus prohibit the LTE modem from staying in the TAIL state long enough.

Thus, excessive power consumption will occur when more than two downloading sessions are needed, i.e., the file size of the video is more than 20 MB. Figure 5 shows the file size distribution of the videos downloaded by our crawler. More than 80% of the 720p videos are larger than 20 MB and thus suffer from excessive power consumption.

3.2 YouTube Usage by Smartphone Users

3.2.1 Methodology

Apparatus: We implemented a logger to record the user inputs in the YouTube app on Android smartphones. Unfortunately, we are unable to modify the YouTube app directly due to its close-source nature. Instead, we implement the logger in the underlying media player of the Android Multimedia Framework. The logger is able to record both video file information and user inputs during a video play-

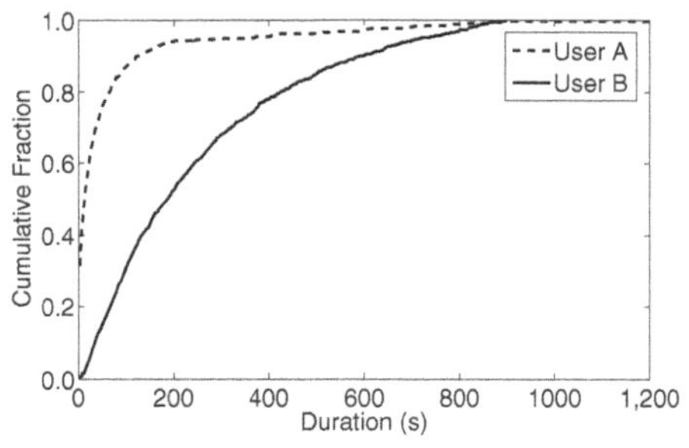

Figure 6: Distribution of user viewing time

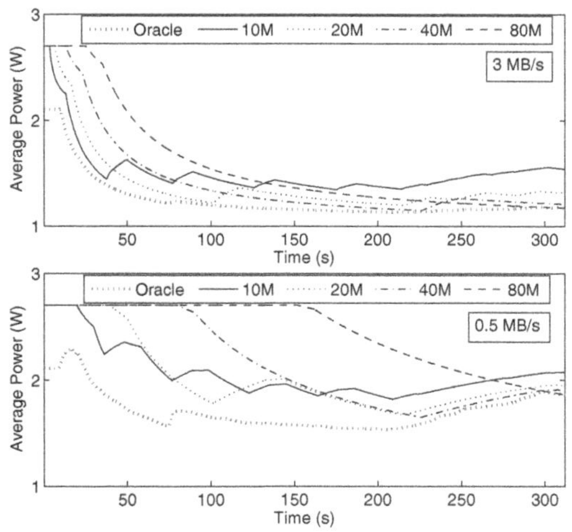

Figure 7: Average power consumption with different cache sizes and different network speeds

back when an app, including YouTube, calls for the service provided the Multimedia Framework. We are particularly interested in the following information: 1) The UID of the app which uses the media player service; 2) The size and the duration of the video file; 3) The time at which the user starts, pauses, resumes, seeks or stops the video playback. Since Android assigns a unique UID for each app, we could filter the log and collect the traces for the YouTube app afterwards.

Subjects: We recruited 10 unpaid participants from Samsung Telecommunications America. Their ages range from 25 to 36. Out of the 10 participants, 4 are female. Every participant is a self-described, heavy, mobile YouTube user who watches at least 10 YouTube videos on his/her smartphone per day, according to our survey.

Procedures: We provided each participant a Galaxy Nexus, with the logger pre-installed, as his/her personal phone for two months. We paid their phone bills for the two months and asked them to use the Verizon LTE network whenever available. Finally, we collected the phones and analyzed the logs after the two month study.

3.2.2 Results

First, most video sessions are short. We define a video session from a start operation to a stop operation. We also treat a forward seek operation as starting a new video session if the seek destination is out of range of the caching content and thus requires a new downloading session.In particular, 80% of YouTube sessions in smartphones are less than half of the corresponding video durations. As a result, downloading the whole video into a large cache and turning off the radio will not solve the problem because of the waste in both data transfer and power. Instead, we should still use multiple download sessions in a video streaming session.

Second, user viewing patterns are different. Figure 6 shows two typical users. For User A, around 80% of the session time is less than 70 seconds. While for User B, over 50% of the session time is larger than 200 seconds. Therefore, we should apply different downloading schedules to different users.

These observations naturally inspired us to explore the power consumption with different cache sizes. We studied this by running simulations with a 75 MB, 312 second long 720p video file. The power consumption is calculated using the Verizon LTE modem power profile measured in section 3.1. We chose four different high threshold values: 10 MB, 20 MB, 40 MB and 80 MB. We also ran an Oracle scheme which knows exactly how much data the user consumes and thus downloads all the data in only one shot.

The top figure of Figure 7 shows the simulation result under 3 MB/s network speed. The bottom one is simulated under 0.5 MB/s network speed and the difference between the two simulations is explained in Section 3.3.2. In this section we focus on the top figure.

The Oracle always has the lowest average power consumption no matter when the user stops the video playback. When the viewing time is short, for example, less than 60 seconds, the average power consumption of a small cache size is better than that of a larger one and the difference is usually non-trivial. With longer viewing time, a choice of large cache size is preferred since it has better average power consumption. Another trend is that as the viewing time grows, the average power consumption difference becomes much smaller, especially for the cache sizes 40 MB and 80 MB.

After observing the different user viewing behaviors, we now propose a better way to manage the cache size in order to reduce power consumption: for users with short viewing durations (User A in Fig. 6), a small cache size is preferred while for users with long viewing durations (User B in Fig. 6), a large cache size is a better choice.

3.3 LTE Network Speed

3.3.1 Methodology

We developed a speed-test app running on the Galaxy Nexus. The app downloads a 100 MB file from a HTTP server every 60 minutes. During the downloading, the app measures the average speed of each 5-second period and logs the speed to a disk file.

3.3.2 Results

We ran the speed-test app for a week and analyzed its log file. Figure 8 shows the result for a typical day. As shown in the figure, the average network speed measured at each hour varies dramatically throughout the day. We observe higher speed during night when the number of active users are much less. Most importantly, the network speed varies sharply even within a short period. For example, at 8PM, the highest speed and lowest speed is 4 MB/s and 1 MB/s, or 4X difference.

To study the impact of network speed variation on power

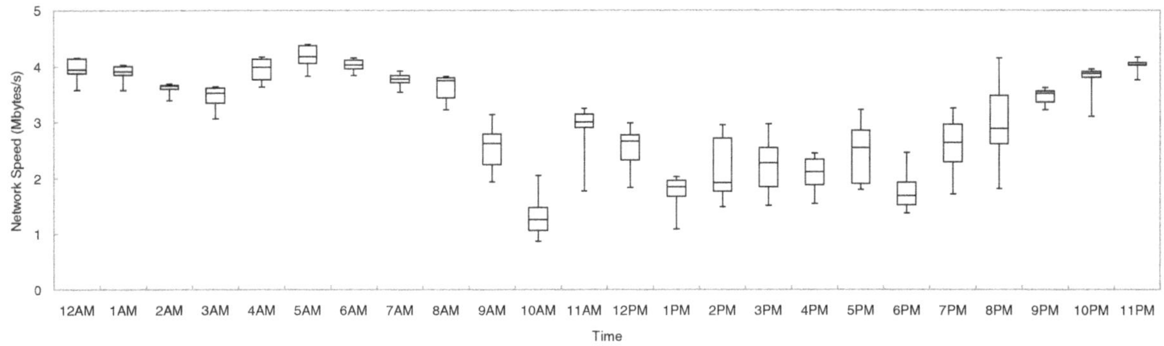

Figure 8: Verizon LTE network speed

consumption, we performed a simulation similar to that described in section 3.2, but with different network speed settings. As shown in Figure 7, the network speeds for the top figure and the bottom figure are 3 MB/s and 0.5 MB/s respectively. The average power consumption with 0.5 MB/s is higher for all cache sizes. The power consumption difference between different cache sizes are much larger and the curves converge much slower the curves with the higher network speed. In observance of such obvious impact of network speed on power consumption, we must adapt the cache size to real time network speed.

4. GREENTUBE DESIGN

We now describe the design of GreenTube as motivated by the results from the preceding studies.

4.1 Key Design Decisions

The results from the preceding motivational studies lead us to make the following design decisions for GreenTube.

Close the TCP connection when the cache is full. To reduce excessive power consumption as illustrated in Section 2.1, GreenTube disconnects from the HTTP server after each downloading session when the cache is full. Note that there are many other options to disconnect from the HTTP server. For example, we could have turned off the 3G/4G radio and released the IP address. However, we chose to close the TCP connection for two reasons. First, both alternatives need to wait for the base station to re-allocate an IP address when a new downloading session needs to start. This re-allocation process can take as long as 5 seconds in Verizon LTE network according to our measurements. In contrast, to re-establish a new TCP connection with the HTTP server requires less than 0.2 seconds. This 25x delay reduction significantly decreases the risk of streaming interruption and excessive power wastage. Second, unlike turning off the radio or releasing the IP address, closing the TCP connection will not affect background services that may require network connection, such as email checking and data synchronization. Actually, such TCP disconnection feature has also been adopted by the YouTube app that is shipped with the Android system, as described in Section 2.3. GreenTube improves over the YouTube app in the following aspects.

Record user-specific viewing history. GreenTube keeps a record of the user viewing time for each streaming session and utilizes this historical record to generate a probability distribution for the user viewing time. Such a probability distribution, as demonstrated in Section 2.2, has a significant impact on average power consumption of the streaming session. At the beginning of each downloading session, GreenTube uses the probability distribution to estimate the expected viewing time for the user and chooses the optimal cache size that leads to minimal expected power consumption. Note that GreenTube treats forward seek operation as starting a new video session if the seek destination is out of range of the caching content and thus requires a new downloading session.

Adapt cache size to network speed. GreenTube samples network speed in each downloading session. As discussed in Section 2.3, network speed has a huge impact on power consumption and varies dramatically over a short period. As a result, the optimal cache size should adapt to the network in real time. In each downloading session, GreenTube estimates the network speed for every second using the downloaded data size from the previous second. Based on this estimation, GreenTube adjusts the cache size accordingly.

Set maximal cache size based on user's choice. GreenTube chooses cache size from a fixed set. The maximal cache size is equal to the worst-case amount of excessive downloaded data in a streaming session and thus should be determined by the user based on his/her tolerance for data wastage. Besides the user's choice, GreenTube also sets a cache-size upper limit because the marginal power saving will diminish as cache-size increases. To quantitatively decide such a limit, we measured the average power consumption by Galaxy Nexus for video streaming via Verizon LTE network using different cache sizes. Given a cache size, we used it for all the test videos and then compiled Figure 9 to show the average power consumption corresponding to each cache size. As illustrated in the figure, the marginal power saving is negligible when cache size is larger than 80 MB. Therefore, GreenTube sets the maximum cache size to be the lower of 80 MB and the user's choice.

To summarize, GreenTube fetches a video file from the HTTP server in multiple downloading sessions and disconnects from the server after each downloading session ends. The starting and ending time of each downloading session (except for the starting time of the first session and ending time of the last session) is determined by cache size. GreenTube judiciously schedules downloading sessions by adaptively adjusting the cache size according to user viewing history and real-time network speed. We call this adaptive adjustment process *Dynamic Cache Management.*

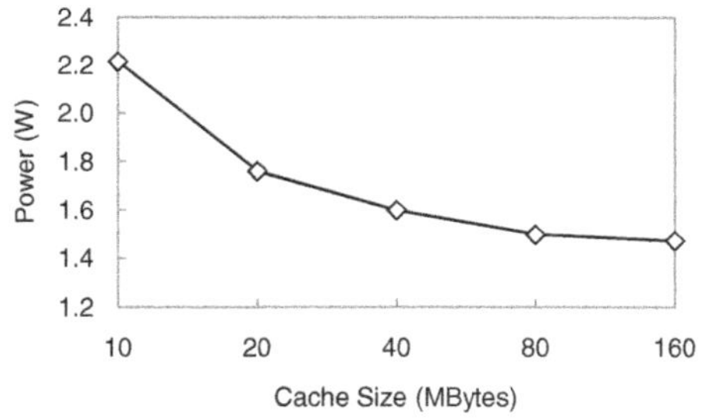

Figure 9: Power consumption by Galaxy Nexus for video streaming via Verizon LTE network using different cache sizes

4.2 Dynamic Cache Management

We next present the *Dynamic Cache Management* (DCM) algorithm. The basic idea is to adaptively adjust the high threshold value of the cache based on the sampled network speed and the expected viewing time calculated from the probability distribution for the user's viewing time. After each second has elapsed, the algorithm computes the high threshold value that correponds to minimal energy consumption assuming that the user will stop viewing at the expected viewing time.

Algorithm 1 shows pseudocode for the DCM algorithm. th_h and th_l are the high threshold value and low threshold value respectively. Initially the high threshold value is set to 10 MB while the low threshold value always remains fixed at 4 MB. D is the video duration while A is the size. This information is extracted from the MP4 header after the header has downloaded completely. $S_{history}$ is the discrete probability distribution calculated from the user viewing history and it is normalized. Every time the user watches a new video, the data is added to $S_{history}$. B is the set of candidate high threshold values. P_{active}, P_{tail}, P_{idle} and T_{tail} are power profile related power consumption parameters derived from our measurement. Specifically for the Verizon Galaxy Nexus, P_{active} is the average power consumption when the LTE modem is in the ACTIVE state, P_{tail} is the average power consumption in the TAIL state, P_{idle} is the average power consumption in the IDLE state and T_{tail} is the maximum time the LTE modem stays in the TAIL state before it transits into the IDLE state.

The DCM algorithm is event-driven. It adjusts th_h every second during a continuous, active downloading. There is no need to adjust th_h in the *Idle* state because it will have absolutely no impact on the downloading behaviour. The adjustment is done in two steps: 1) Calculate the expected viewing time using function EXPECTED-VIEWING-TIME; 2) Using the expected viewing time, estimate the energy consumption for each high threshold candidate and thus determine the optimal th_h.

We obtain the energy-consumption estimate by simulating the periodic behaviour observed in our video playback power measurement. Given the current time t_{cur}, the expected viewing time t_{exp}, the current network speed s, the size of the video A, the size of the consumed video content a_{cur}, the duration of the video D and the various power-profile parameters (P_{active}, P_{tail}, P_{idle}, and T_{tail}), the function OPTIMAL-CACHE-SIZE first estimates the time spent in the ACTIVE, TAIL and IDLE states respectively in the time period from t_{cur} to t_{exp}. It then uses this time estimate to derive the energy consumption.

Algorithm 1 The DCM Algorithm

Wait for *event*
if *event* is downloading started **then**
  Set *timer* to expire in 1 second
else if *event* is timer expired **then**
  t_{exp} = EXPECTED-VIEWING-TIME(t_{cur})
  x_{opt} = OPTIMAL-CACHE-SIZE(t_{exp}, t_{cur})
  $th_h = x_{opt}$
  Set *timer* to expire in 1 second
else if *event* is downloading stopped **then**
  Cancel the *timer*
end if

function EXPECTED-VIEWING-TIME(t_{cur})
  $\widehat{S} = \{p_i | p_i \in S_{history}, i \cdot \frac{D}{|S_{history}|} \geq t_{cur}\}$
  $S'_{history} = normalize(\widehat{S})$
  $n = |S'_{history}|$
  $t_{exp} = \sum_{i=1}^{n} p_i \cdot (t_{cur} + (i-1) \cdot \frac{D}{n}),\ p_i \in S'_{history}$
  return t_{exp}
end function

function OPTIMAL-CACHE-SIZE(t_{exp}, t_{cur})
  s = current downloading speed
  Set bitrate $r = \frac{A - a_{cur}}{D - t_{cur}}$
  $e_{opt} = +\infty$
  $x_{opt} = 0$
  for each b in B **do**
    $t = t_{cur}$
    $t_{active} = 0$
    $t_{idle} = 0$
    while $t < t_{exp}$ **do**
      $t_d = min(t_{exp} - t, \frac{b - th_l}{s})$
      $t_d = min(\frac{A - a_{cur} - th_l}{s}, t_d)$
      $a_{cur} = a_{cur} + s \cdot t_d$
      $t_{active} = t_{active} + t_d$
      if $a_{cur} + th_l \geq A$ **then**
        $t_v = \frac{s \cdot t_d + th_l}{r}$
      else
        $t_v = \frac{s \cdot t_d}{r}$
      end if
      $t_v = min(t_v, t_{exp} - t)$
      $t_{idle} = t_{idle} + min(t_v - t_d, T_{tail})$
      $t = t + t_v$
    end while
    $t_{idle} = (t_{exp} - t_{cur}) - t_{active} - t_{tail}$
    $e = P_{active} \times t_{active} + P_{tail} \times t_{tail} + P_{idle} \times t_{idle}$
    if $e < e_{opt}$ **then**
      $e_{opt} = e$
      $x_{opt} = b$
    end if
  end for
  return x_{opt}
end function

5. EVALUATION

In this section, we present the implementation of GreenTube and evaluate its performance.

5.1 Implementation

To evaluate the performance of GreenTube, we implemented a C++ prototype based on the Android Multimedia Framework. We created a new data-source provider that wraps the default HTTP streaming data-source provider and incorporates our dynamic cache management algorithm.

Configuration settings allow Android apps to decide at runtime whether to use our dynamic cache management. By doing so, the impact to the existing code is minimum and the modification is transparent to the Android apps. The implementation changes 6 source files around 700 lines of code. According to our measurements, the computational cost of our implementation is negligible. On average, our DCM algorithm consumes less than 100 microseconds on the Galaxy Nexus.

5.2 Evaluation Methodology

As mentioned in section 3.2, we conducted a user study with the popular YouTube app and obtained 4000 video playback traces over a period of 2 months with 10 users. By analyzing the traces, we obtained the URLs of all the videos and downloaded them from YouTube. We stored these videos on an Internet-accessible HTTP server. The videos and the corresponding traces were used to evaluate GreenTube.

We implemented a simple media player which 1) uses the dynamic cache management enabled data source provider, and 2) is able to read the user study trace, set the video source to the user watched video stored on our HTTP server and mimic the recorded user viewing behavior. To run the experiment automatically without user intervention, the media player also reads a play list containing ordered sequence of video files for testing. To automatically synchronize the video playback and the power trace, we again leverage the logger facility in the Android Multimedia Framework to log the time when each video playback starts and stops. Also, there is a 10-second interval between two consecutive video playbacks, to enable our offline analysis tool to easily extract the power traces for individual video playbacks.

The videos watched by each user were randomly divided into 8 groups. In round-robin fashion, each one of the 8 groups of videos is chosen as the test set and the traces of the remaining 7 groups were used only for prediction. By iteratively choosing each of the 8 groups as the testing group, all videos watched by the users were covered.

We compare the following four schemes:

- **Android:** The default Android scheme which is discussed in section 2.3. It usually produced the highest power consumption.
- **YouTube:** The scheme used by the YouTube app, which closes the TCP connection every time the cache is full. This greatly increases the time the LTE modem stays in the IDLE state so the power consumption can be substantially improved.
- **DCM:** Our DCM scheme, which is based on the YouTube scheme but changes the cache size dynamically according to both user behavior and network speed.
- **Oracle:** The Oracle scheme, which always knows when the user stops the video playback and downloads the exact amount of data. Such scheme, although impossible to implement practically, is included as the optimal bound, i.e., the lowest power consumption that can be achieved.

5.3 Performance Results

We now present evaluation results from measurements and simulations.

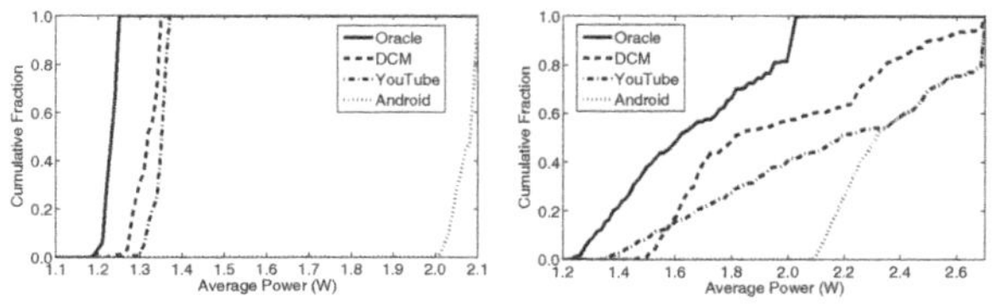

Figure 10: Power consumption distribution with Verizon LTE network for different users

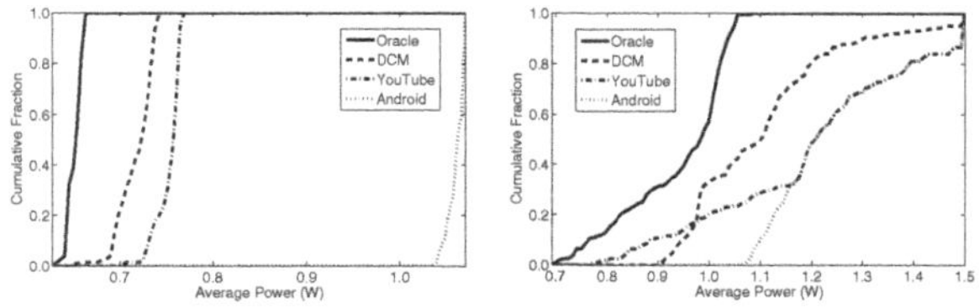

Figure 11: Power consumption distribution with ATT HSPA network for different users

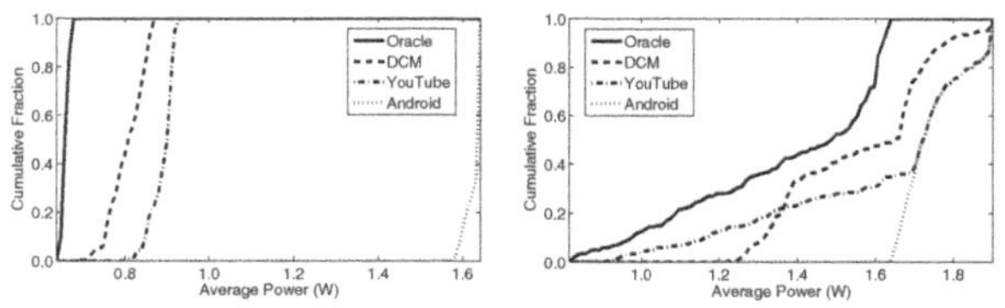

Figure 12: Power consumption distribution with T-Mobile HSPA+ network for different users

5.3.1 Overall Power Reduction

Figure 10, 11 and 12 show the power consumption distribution of the four schemes on Verizon LTE network, ATT HSPA network and T-Mobile HSPA+ network respectively.

Figures on the left in each of the three pairs of figures depict users (for example, User B) who tend to finish viewing the videos. Figures on the right depict users (for example, User A) who usually watch only the very beginning portion of the video.

For all networks, when the user tends to finish the video, our DCM scheme clearly consumes much less power than the YouTube and the Android schemes. The Android scheme has the worst power consumption and the the performance gap is huge. Although both the DCM and the YouTube schemes use the "disconnect when cache is full" feature, our DCM scheme clearly outperforms the YouTube scheme because of the accurate viewing-time prediction and the dynamic selection of a larger cache.

For users who stop viewing a video very early, our DCM scheme is much better than the Android scheme. Comparing against the YouTube scheme, the DCM scheme performs slightly worse in a few cases while in other cases, the advantage is much more obvious than for the other type of users. Our analysis of the traces shows that when the predicted viewing time is larger than the actual viewing time, our DCM scheme tends to choose a cache size larger than 20 MB which is used in the YouTube scheme. Thus our DCM scheme downloads more data and consumes more energy than the YouTube scheme. For other cases, our DCM scheme tends to choose a smaller cache size and the power saving is substantial.

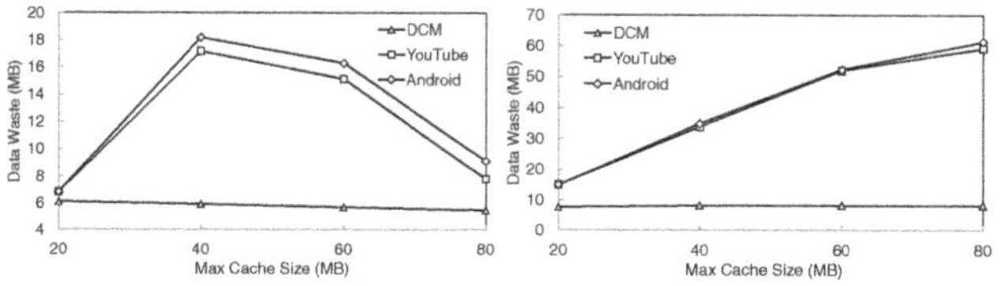

(a) (b)

Figure 13: Data wastage with different maximum cache sizes for different users

5.3.2 *Impact on Data Wastage*

To evaluate each scheme's impact on data wastage, we collected the size of wasted data, i.e., the video data which is downloaded but not viewed by the user. We excluded the Oracle from this analysis because it never wastes data. We ran a series of simulations for the other three schemes with the following cache sizes: 20 MB, 40 MB, 60 MB and 80 MB. For the DCM scheme, these values are the maximum cache sizes.

The simulation results in Figure 13 show the data wastage for users who tend to finish viewing videos. For the YouTube and the Android schemes, the trend is almost the same. When the cache size increases, the data wastage for the two schemes first increases and then decreases. This trend is caused by the mismatch of the data downloaded in the periodic fashion and the data actually consumed by the user. The YouTube and the Android schemes waste the same amount of data at the cache size 20 MB and the Android scheme wastes slightly more data with larger cache sizes. This small difference is caused by the 64-KB data chunk downloading between two consecutive *Fetching* state instances. This also applies to Figure 13(b). Our DCM scheme performs very well regardless of the maximum cache size and the data wastage is almost constant. The reduction in data wastage can be as high as 60%.

Figure 13(b) shows the data wastage for users who stop viewing a video very early. Again, our DCM scheme performs very well and the data wastage is almost constant. Since the user only watches the video for several tens of seconds and our DCM scheme can capture and predict this behaviour, cache sizes smaller than 20 MB are preferred. As a result, the maximum cache size larger than 20 MB has almost no impact on the data wastage. For the YouTube and the Android schemes, the data wastage increases drastically when the cache size increases. Since the user only watches the video for a short duration and the network speed is much higher than the video bitrate, even a cache size of 20 MB is larger than the average size of the viewed video content, the data wastage under these two schemes increases monotonically.

6. RELATED WORK

Wireless interface power optimization: Many pioneering works have been performed to study the air-interface power consumption and optimization. For instance, uPM [11] allows WiFi state adjustment at micro seconds level, Catnap [4] schedules the TCP transfers based on the granularity of the application data units to put WiFi interface into longer sleep. Mohapatra *et al.* [15] proposed an integrated power management approach. Among them, network traffic regulation is closely related to our work. It proposes to use additional buffer at Access Point (AP), then stream data can be transmitted to the client using burst rate. After the burst, the WiFi interface can be switched into a sleep state. In our work, we studied the energy consumption for WiFi, 3G and 4G LTE in video streaming scenario. Our proposal can be combined with these proposed optimization scheme to further reduce the interface energy.

Video streaming: Efficient video streaming over a network has been studied extensively for many years. For example, peer-to-peer (P2P) streaming has been proposed and deployed successfully [22, 10]. More studies have been carried out to improve the existing P2P system, such as using machine learning [16], using hybrid P2P structure [21], and using layered video [14]. Note that almost all these works try to improve the network utility or throughput for video streaming. However, none of them considers the energy-constrained mobile streaming scenario, which is the other important topic addressed extensively in the literature. For instance, Xiao *et al* [20] performed power-consumption measurement for YouTube video streaming on Nokia S60 platform over WCDMA and WLAN networks. However, their power-consumption measurements will be quite different from those in our work because of significant recent SmartPhone hardware advances. Later Mohamed *et al* [8] proposed to transmit the video using bursts on DVB-H system such that mobile devices can receive a burst of traffic and then turn off their radio frequency circuits till the next burst in order to save energy. However, it is inefficient to turn off the radio circuits for 3G and 4G/LTE since it requires much more power for re-connection. He *et al.* [7] proposed a parametric power-rate-distortion model for H.263 based video encoding, and wireless streaming. This work can be combined with our solution. Moreover, both CoolSpots [17] and BlueStreaming [13] use BlueTooth to offload delay sensitive control traffic (which is about twice as much as streaming data traffic based on Internet measurement [12]) while keeping WiFi for data traffic streaming in P2P video streaming scenario. BlueTooth interface is always active, however the power consumption overhead can be over-compensated by putting WiFi interface into power saving mode (since WiFi does not need to transmit control traffic actively). In general, our work is complementary to CoolSpots and BlueStreaming.

7. DISCUSSION

We next discuss the limitation of our work and future direction.

7.1 Display Power in Video Streaming

The focus of this paper is to optimize the energy efficiency of 3G/4G radios that contribute to over 50% of system power consumption of a smartphone. However, other hardware components are also worth investigating. Many researchers have identified the display, especially OLED display, as a major power consumer [6] [5]. Fortunately, we found that the OLED display power consumption in video streaming is not as significant as in other applications, such as web browsing [5]. We arrived this conclusion after performing the following experiments. First, we analyzed the RGB value distribution from the video files downloaded from YouTube. Then, we estimated the average power consumption by OLED display to play these videos using the OLED power model described in [5]. Our result shows that the OLED display power consumption on Galaxy S, Galaxy S II, and Galaxy Nexus is 190 mW, 200 mW, and 150 mW, respectively. Such low power consumption is due to the relatively low RGB values in real-world videos.

7.2 Network Support

As discussed in this paper, the fundamental reason why 3G/4G radio consumes so much power is the presence of relatively long TAIL state. Therefore, an alternative and effective solution to reduce 3G/4G radio power is to make the smartphone notify the base station and initialize the power state demotion after completion of each downloading session. By doing this, the smartphone can immediately set the interface into IDLE state instead of waiting for the expiration of the tail timer. As aforementioned, such a TAIL state consumes a large portion of the power as well. By eliminating the tailstate power, the 3G/4G radio can be very power efficient. This type of feedback channel enabling between mobile client and base station is worthy of further study and standardization along with the process of 3GPP LTE and LTE-Advanced protocols.

8. CONCLUSION

The power consumption of a 3G/4G radio is a significant drain on the battery of a smartphone and thus severely hurts the user experience of mobile video streaming. We show that such high power consumption is due to the conflict between HTTP streaming support in state-of-the-art smartphone systems and power state transition defined in 3G/4G networks. To resolve this conflict, we present the design and realization of GreenTube, a light-weight software solution that is readily deployable on off-the-shelf Android-based smartphones. GreenTube employs a novel, dynamic cache management algorithm that judiciously schedules downloading sessions to reduce average power consumption for mobile video streaming. Our results show that GreenTube achieves up to 70% and 40% power reduction for 3G/4G radio and the whole smartphone system, respectively. Besides power reduction, GreenTube also reduces data wastage by 60%. Because of its superior performance, we believe GreenTube is worth considering as a revision to the current Android system.

9. REFERENCES

[1] http://www.techweekeurope.co.uk/news/lte-power-consumption-triggers-battery-worry-61769/.

[2] http://www.allot.com/MobileTrends_Report_H2_2011.html?campid=701D0000000l2aR/.

[3] http://www.msoon.com/LabEquipment/PowerMonitor/.

[4] Dogar, F. R., Steenkiste, P., and Papagiannaki, K. Catnap: exploiting high bandwidth wireless interfaces to save energy for mobile devices. In *Proc. of the 8th international conference on Mobile systems, applications, and services* (2010), pp. 107–122.

[5] Dong, M., and Zhong, L. Chameleon: a color-adaptive web browser for mobile oled displays. In *Proc. of the 9th international conference on Mobile systems, applications, and services* (2011), pp. 85–98.

[6] Falaki, H., Mahajan, R., Kandula, S., Lymberopoulos, D., Govindan, R., and Estrin, D. Diversity in smartphone usage. In *Proc. of the 8th international conference on Mobile systems, applications, and services* (2010), pp. 179–194.

[7] He, Z., Liang, Y., Chen, L., Ahmad, I., and Wu, D. Power-rate-distortion analysis for wireless video communication under energy constraints. *IEEE Trans. on Circ. and Sys. for Video Tech. 15*, 5 (May 2005), 645 – 658.

[8] Hefeeda, M., and Hsu, C.-H. On burst transmission scheduling in mobile tv broadcast networks. *IEEE/ACM Trans. Netw. 18*, 2 (Apr. 2010), 610–623.

[9] Huang, J., Qian, F., Gerber, A., Mao, Z. M., Sen, S., and Spatscheck, O. A close examination of performance and power characteristics of 4G LTE networks. to appear ACM MobiSys '12.

[10] Huang, Y., Fu, T. Z., Chiu, D.-M., Lui, J. C., and Huang, C. Challenges, design and analysis of a large-scale p2p-vod system. In *Proc. of the ACM SIGCOMM 2008 conference on Data communication* (2008), pp. 375–388.

[11] Liu, J., and Zhong, L. Micro power management of active 802.11 interfaces. In *MobiSys* (2008), pp. 146–159.

[12] Liu, Y., Guo, L., Li, F., and Chen, S. An empirical evaluation of battery power consumption for streaming data transmission to mobile devices. In *Proc. of the 19th ACM international conference on Multimedia* (2011), pp. 473–482.

[13] Liu, Y., Li, F., Guo, L., Guo, Y., and Chen, S. Bluestreaming: towards power-efficient internet p2p streaming to mobile devices. In *Proc. of the 19th ACM international conference on Multimedia* (2011), pp. 193–202.

[14] Liu, Z., Shen, Y., Ross, K. W., Panwar, S. S., and Wang, Y. Layerp2p: using layered video chunks in p2p live streaming. *IEEE Trans. Multi. 11*, 7 (Nov. 2009), 1340–1352.

[15] Mohapatra, S., Cornea, R., Dutt, N., Nicolau, A., and Venkatasubramanian, N. Integrated power management for video streaming to mobile handheld devices. In *Proc. of the 11th ACM international conference on Multimedia* (2003), pp. 582–591.

[16] Niu, D., Li, B., and Zhao, S. Self-diagnostic peer-assisted video streaming through a learning framework. In *Proc. of the ACM international conference on Multimedia* (2010), pp. 73–82.

[17] Pering, T., Agarwal, Y., Gupta, R., and Want, R. Coolspots: reducing the power consumption of wireless mobile devices with multiple radio interfaces. In *Proceedings of the 4th international conference on Mobile systems, applications and services* (2006), pp. 220–232.

[18] Qian, F., Wang, Z., Gerber, A., Mao, Z., Sen, S., and Spatscheck, O. Profiling resource usage for mobile applications: a cross-layer approach. In *Proc. of the 9th international conference on Mobile systems, applications, and services* (2011), pp. 321–334.

[19] Shepard, C., Rahmati, A., Tossell, C., Zhong, L., and Kortum, P. Livelab: measuring wireless networks and smartphone users in the field. *SIGMETRICS Perform. Eval. Rev. 38*, 3 (Jan 2011), 15–20.

[20] Xiao, Y., Kalyanaraman, R. S., and Yla-Jaaski, A. Energy consumption of mobile youtube: Quantitative measurement and analysis. In *Proc. of the 2nd International Conference on Next Generation Mobile Applications, Services, and Technologies* (2008), pp. 61–69.

[21] Yin, H., Liu, X., Zhan, T., Sekar, V., Qiu, F., Lin, C., Zhang, H., and Li, B. Design and deployment of a hybrid CDN-P2P system for live video streaming: experiences with livesky. In *Proc. of the 17th ACM international conference on Multimedia* (2009), pp. 25–34.

[22] Zhang, X., Liu, J., Li, B., and Yum, T.-S. P. Coolstreaming/donet: a data-driven overlay network for peer-to-peer live media streaming. In *Proc. of IEEE INFOCOM* (2005), pp. 2102–2111.

A Multimedia Analytics Framework for Browsing Image Collections in Digital Forensics

Marcel Worring
Informatics Institute
University of Amsterdam
P.O. Box 94323
1098 XH Amsterdam
The Netherlands
m.worring@uva.nl

Andreas Engl
Informatics Institute
University of Amsterdam
P.O. Box 94323
1098 XH Amsterdam
The Netherlands
lynn@cephea.de

Camelia Smeria
Informatics Institute
University of Amsterdam
P.O. Box 94323
1098 XH Amsterdam
The Netherlands
camyyssa@gmail.com

ABSTRACT

Searching through large collections of images to find patterns of use or to find sets of relevant items is difficult, especially when the information to consider is not only the content of the images itself, but also the associated metadata. Multimedia analytics is a new approach to such problems. We consider the case of forensic experts facing image collections of growing size during digital forensic investigations. We answer the forensic challenge by developing specialised novel interactive visualisations which employ content-based image clusters in both the analysis as well as in all visualizations. Their synergy makes the task of manually browsing these collections more effective and efficient. Evaluation of such multimedia analytics is a notoriously hard problem as there are so many factors influencing the result. As a controlled evaluation, we developed a user simulation framework to create image collections with time and directory information as metadata. We apply it in a number of scenarios to illustrate its use. The simulation tool is available to other researchers via our website.

Categories and Subject Descriptors

H.3 [**Information storage and retrieval**]: Information Search and Retrieval

Keywords

Image Search, Information Visualization, Visual Analytics

1. INTRODUCTION

Searching for images in large collections is difficult as the information of interest might be captured in any of the various modalities associated with the image. The determining clues for the search might be in the content of the image, but might also be in its metadata. Furthermore, the best way to search is highly dependent on the task, ranging from seeking an abundance of results to little nuggets of information. To cater for all these tasks a flexible and interactive integral view of the different information channels is needed. In this paper we focus on the specific case of image collections and their metadata in the context of digital forensics, but many of the ideas transfer easily to other application fields in which along with images multiple channels of information play a role.

In digital forensics an investigator is often tasked to analyse a data source containing more than a million images and their metadata. In order to filter out files, the cryptographic hashes of all files are compared with large databases of known incriminating material as well as common benign files. The most famous reference set is the National Software Reference Library (NSRL) which contains hashes for over 31 million files [24]. With such an approach we can make a significant reduction in the number of images to consider for example used in XIRAF [1]. The more cautious offenders can easily circumvent such an attack as changing a single bit will radically alter the hash of a file. The police is therefore now moving to near copy detection to solve this [18]. This reduces the workload, but doesn't solve the real problem namely that the interest lies in finding evidence in unknwown material. Apart from the content of the images there is a lot of information present in the metadata. It is e.g. rarely the case that a person got into possession of illicit image material randomly. Downloading and filesharing habits are often governed by usage patterns with varying complexity and we can use the MAC times (last modified, last accessed and created) to understand patterns of use. Similarly, the file path can be used to extract hierarchical information that can shed light on naming patterns and other organisational schemes. To perform digital forensics on such a collection, Richard et al. argue that this "not only requires better acquisition tools, but also better analysis tools", as "investigators must be relieved of manual, time-consuming tasks" [24]. We focus on automated methods to make the search in image collections easier by considering both the content and the metadata.

Along the dimension of varying degrees of automation there are essentially four different categories that arise.

Most traditional designs in forensics do not go beyond presenting images as a sequential list of files that have to be inspected one by one, thus "manual browsing" is still the dominant category.

To support browsing, methods in the second category focus on the metadata alone. CyberForensics Timelab [21] is an example of a system which is focused on time as metadata. Standard file explorers and text search systems can find relevant filenames.

The third category methods aim to arrange the images in a meaningful way. By doing so, images of a target class are closer together, thus finding at least one image of that class will make the process of finding related images easier. At the same time, images that are very different from the target class will have a low probability of relevant images in its vicinity, thus the surrounding region can be browsed with less attention and - consequently - faster. Quadrianto does so using a grid based approach [22] whereas Nguyen uses a similarity preserving projection ([19]) coupled with an approach to minimise the overlap between images.

The fourth and last category is Content-Based Image Retrieval and there is a wide variety of different approaches and features (see Datta et al. [8] for a recent survey). In theory this allows the highest possible degree of automation: given a perfect classifier for our target class we would not have to look at a single image anymore. In practice, however, humans still outperform machines in a classification task in terms of accuracy, and frequent misclassifications are not uncommon.

It should be clear that using traditional techniques on the problem of browsing large image collections is insufficient. Manual browsing is clearly too time-consuming, but each of the three automated categories by themselves do not provide a solution either. Visualisation-based browsing and content-based retrieval discard important meta-information, while retrieval purely based on meta-data doesn't consider the actual contents of images. Even in state-of-the-art research, full automation has not been achieved with any of the approaches. Interactive browsing techniques such as [31] are promising avenues to improve the seach performance, but they focus on the underlying algorithm only and ignore the visualization.

All of the three semi-automated techniques have their merits, but the references study them in isolation. The overarching aim of this paper is to combine the strength of each method in order to overcome the individual weaknesses. This means we need to communicate the result of content-based retrieval methods to a human operator who uses a visualisation-based browsing interface to make sense of them. Further, all of the meta-information available in the dataset has to be reflected by the design of the visualisations and accessible to the operator. Then, and only then, will we be able to take full advantage of the available data as well as computational and human resources. Research argues that a suitable framework for such an undertaking is Visual Analytics [15].

Visual Analytics is a relatively young field, and even the term has only been in use since "Illuminating the Path" [27] was published in 2005 [3]. Keim et al. [15] define it as "combining automated analysis techniques with interactive visualisations for an effective understanding, reasoning and decision making on the basis of very large and complex datasets". From this definition it becomes clear that Visual Analytics puts a stronger emphasis on the human component than its sibling disciplines. It strives to combine the strengths of human and that of electronic data processing - a semi-automated analytical process. Even more recently visual analytics has been combined with multimedia analysis, coined as multimedia analytics [6][9]. This paper is the first to develop a framework in which multimedia analysis and visualizations work in conjunction to support the browsing of large visual collections in digital forensics.

Section 2 will highlight similar or related systems, both in terms of the underlying problem as well as systems that use approaches that might potentially be relevant for the task at hand. Section 4 presents our visualisation system for browsing image collections which integrates a set of advanced visualizations with content based analysis into a multimedia analytics solution. To evaluate the system we have developed tools to simulate users which are made available to the community. These are defined in Section 5. Section 6 walks through a series of scenarios that serve as use-cases to test the system. Finally section 7 summarises the results.

2. RELATED WORK

From the thus far mentioned prior art one can identify three different approaches to visually analysing large image collections. Although time-based visualisations have a long and successful history in research, the application of time as a primary or auxiliary dimension for purposes of digital forensics is surprisingly shallow. The arguably most prevalent category of techniques in the context of using visualisations to browse image collections is visualising the images on a 2D plane, usually underlying a layouting algorithm that maximises visibility and/or groups similar images closer together. The third category of systems arranges images in a network or tree in order to make relationships (e.g. similarity) between the images verbose. This section shows novel, related achievements in research in each of these three areas.

2.1 Time-based Visualisation Systems

In [14] it is argued that time is an especially relevant dimension in almost all visualisations since we are actively living in space and time. As such, all information has at least some relation to time which is especially true for digital files: all major disk formatting tables include time stamp information. Unsurprisingly, visualisations that are centred on the time dimension are a pervasive topic in research.

The influential Continuum [2] added a lot of new insights to timeline visualisations. By using histograms as an overview Continuum scales to an arbitrary number of items since time intervals for each histogram bin can be chosen independently from the data. The detail view is comprised of bars where related information is aggregated into a single item. In its essence, each bar in Continuum represents a cluster of information. Cluster Calendar View [29] makes the use of clusters even more explicit. Using a simple bottom-up clustering algorithm, it uses two visualisations, a calendar and a timeline. The calendar shows dominant clusters for any given day by colour-coding them. The timeline displays the averaged data for all clusters across a periodic time interval. This effectively condenses the data in order to emphasise trends and outliers, e.g. revealing differences between workdays and weekends.

In forensic investigations [7] time has rarely been used as a primary dimension in forensic visualisation systems. We highlight two systems. Zeitline [4], allows hierarchical organisation of events by grouping discrete events into what they call "super events", such as the installation of a program which is comprised of many read and write events of various files. These events are simply displayed in a hierarchical tree view, thus the visualisation capabilities are very limited. The CyberForensic TimeLab [21] is motivated by the lack of overview in Zeitline. TimeLab's viewer is comprised of a vertically stacked list of histograms, where each row corresponds to a specific source. The x-axis represents time, thus histogram bars show activity within a certain time interval. When a selection is made, a detail view shows a textual list of events.

2.2 2D Information Landscapes

Nguyen et al. [19] demonstrate a system for image annotation that uses a combination of projection techniques to map a large number of images into two-dimensional space. A point cloud is used as an overview over the entire image collection, whereas a number of representative images are shown in the central view. Each of these represent one cluster and are sampled using k-means, picking the images closest to the cluster centroids as representatives. Once the user selects an image he/she descends into the corresponding cluster and is able to annotate it.

Zooming as an interaction technique has also been explored by Girgensohn et al.'s MediaGLOW, [11] a visualisation system that aims to support users in organising their personal photo collection. Much like Nguyen et al.'s system [19] it projects cluster representatives (clusters are called "stacks") onto an information landscape by minimising the energy of a fully-connected, spring-based graph, with edges corresponding to the similarity between stacks of images. Analogous to the idea of zoom modifiers in Zoomable Object-oriented information Landscapes [13], MediaGLOW's zoom keeps the size of images constant while performing a geometric zoom, with the result that images that partially overlap gradually become visible. The combination with a timeline histogram provides both an overview in time and in space as well as a selection mechanism on either dimension.

TimeScape [23] uses an information landscape in combination with a time-based organisational approach. This spatio-temporal personal information management system enables users to exclusively use their desktop to spatially lay out their documents. Effectively this replaces hierarchical organisation with a temporal one. TimeSpace [17] extends this idea by partitioning the desktop into "multiple activity-oriented virtual workspaces".

Unlike time-based visualisations, there is very little consent on both the organisation as well as the interaction techniques for images in information landscapes. These systems are very usage specific, and their purposes range from full personal information management down to very specific tasks such as image annotation or browsing photo collections. As a consequence the layout of the images is often context specific or even entirely positioned by the user, but in most cases there is an underlying graph algorithm that uses some measure of similarity in order to cluster related images.

2.3 Graph-based Image Visualisation Systems

The distinction between images as leaves of a tree or nodes in a network, to that of projection into an information landscape is sometimes a shallow one as many of these projections use the very same graph-based layouting algorithms to position the images in space. Explicitly drawing the connections between individual items enables the user to reason about the relationship between items and to reflect on the resulting layouts rather than being forced to take it for granted. Trees and networks also allow a set of operations that would otherwise be impossible, such as "cutting" a connection in order to filter a branch or sub-network.

Chen et al. [5] developed an image retrieval technique based on Pathfinder networks that were originally devised to analyse proximity data in psychology. Using a similarity score based on colour, shape and texture features, Pathfinder networks are constructed in order to group images with similar appearance. Although the reference introduces a nice visualization, it doesn't allow for interaction.

Vizster [12], derives its network structure from a social network, yet still qualifies in this context as images are chosen to represent profiles. Vizster employs a force-directed layouting strategy which automatically groups users into communities, or, in more general terms, nodes into clusters.

PEx-Image [10] is a tool that creates a static projection of a collection of images. What is novel here is that the underlying structure is a rooted tree, not a network, more specifically a phylogenetic tree originally used for visualising evolutionary relationships and thus more commonly seen in bio-informatics. Using the neighbour-joining algorithm with a radial layout and subsequently applying a custom force-based algorithm to minimise the tree's energy, PEx-image accomplishes very compact, clustered graphs.

3. TIME, EVENTS, AND CLUSTERS

While most concepts will be defined when introduced, the notion of events will appear throughout the paper in various different contexts. As events are time based let us first define a timestamp:

- *Timestamp:* a specific moment in time, here we consider it to consist of the Microsoft Windows modified, accessed, created metadata.
- *Event:* a temporal abstraction of an image collection i.e. an aggregation of several images along a common, time-based criterion.

As an example, an event can be "a batch operation (e.g. a download of several images) that was started on March 23rd at 8:00 am". It could also be the subsequent operation where the user moved the same images to a different folder. Chow et al. [7] created a large list of such events that in an investigation are identifiable by looking at the associated timestamps of the images only.

Clusters are a similar notion as events, but not based on time, but aggregation based on visual content:

- *Cluster:* a group of visually similar images.

4. CLUSTER-BASED VISUALISATION

We will first define how to represent clusters across the visualisation and then consider the interaction design of the visualisation system by looking at each visualisation in turn.

4.1 Cluster Representation

Different visualisations often require different ways of depicting primitives. In a timeline where time is mapped to the Y axis and the primitives encode duration, they need to be stretched horizontally to indicate the start and end.

In the graph visualisation, we can arbitrarily assign a representation for the node, but using the same bars as in the timeline hardly makes sense as the X axis encodes spatial information. Yet the primitives in either visualisation are not only of the same type, they are two different views on the same data.

Ideally we want to be able to link the spatial (similarity) information to the temporal given those two visualisations. If we can design the primitive representation in such a way that every single primitive in the visualisation is discernible along at least one of the visual channels, the user can simply single out any primitive by searching for the same properties of the channel in the other visualisation. As long as the representation is identical we don't even have to know the exact channel that distinguishes an item, our bias in the primary visual cortex is adjusted automatically along all of the channels.

First, however, we need to solve the problem of primitives having different representations in the timeline and graph visualisation. This turns out to be reasonably straightforward: since primitive representations in the graph are arbitrary - vertices have no visual encoding themselves - we can simply choose them to have icon representations, where each image cluster is assigned a unique icon. Regardless of what we pick for the timeline primitives (e.g. lines or bars) we can associate them by visually linking them with the same icons.

To choose the icons, Colin Ware [30] gives an excellent overview on how Visual Search is optimised along the channel of colour and elementary shape. He suggests that the two primary considerations for picking colours are visual distinctness and learnability. The opponent-process theory gives us a set of strong hues that are visually very distinct. We can follow these up by colours with relatively consistent names, such as Orange, Purple, Grey or Pink. We can sacrifice some of the discernibility along the colour channel by shifting the colours towards a more aesthetic colour scheme. We can recover and even improve much of the learnability aspect by introducing objects that are close to the original shapes by having some real-world meaning, while improving the overall design at the same time. Once the location of an object has been learnt, spatial memory ensures that it can easily be found again. Figure 1, 2 and 3 show how the cluster icons are used in each of the visualizations with the aim to visually link them.

4.2 Timeline Visualisation

Primitives are structured and arranged. In addition to bars that encode the temporal dimension on the horizontal axis, each cluster or event contains a histogram. A histogram bin shows the activity for a fixed time segment. The icon that represents the cluster is superimposed on the bar to aid Visual Search of a cluster in related visualisations.

The timeline aims at revealing trends that are either self-evident by looking at the temporal information itself, such as an increased amount of activity during a certain period of time, or are revealed in conjunction with other dimensions, such as a directory that has seen many changes recently. The first activity is supported on a largely behavioural level. We have learnt to read Gantt-like diagrams and histograms so well that there is little reflection needed in order to spot trends, outlier, activity spikes or other emerging patterns. To see relations with other channels, we need a wider arsenal of interactive tools to facilitate reflection.

Filter-Select-Highlight

The Visual Analytics Mantra [16] compels us to "show the important", and the timeline is designed to support that proposition by encoding events and activity in a straightforward way. But it has to be backed up with zooming and filtering capabilities to support the full Visual Analytics process. Besides highlighting and selecting clusters with the mouse by means of hovering and clicking respectively, the timeline additionally enables temporal highlighting and selections. Histogram bins can be hovered to highlight contained images. Alternatively, a time period can be selected by clicking anywhere to set a start point, dragging and finally releasing the mouse button to complete the selection (see figure 1).

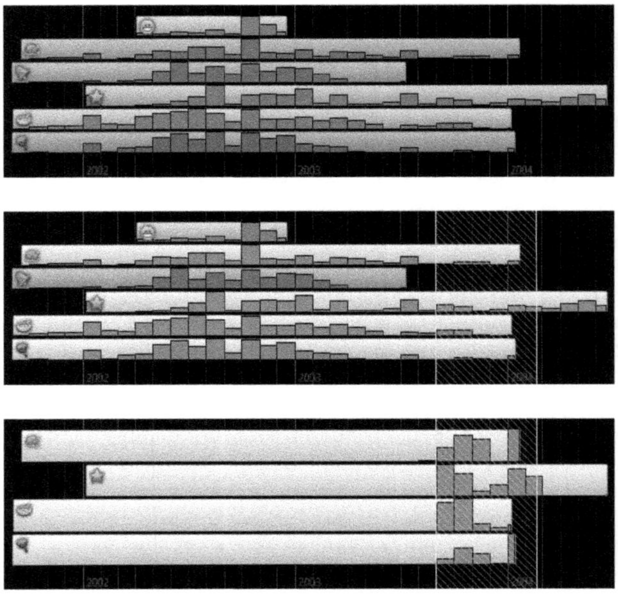

Figure 1: The timeline before (top) and after (middle) selecting a time period. Turning the selection into a filter (bottom) re-evaluates the histograms and strips empty clusters.

At any point, a selection (which can be composed of criteria along multiple dimensions) can be turned into a filter. If a filter contains a criterion other than a set of clusters, the histogram is updated to reflect the distribution of the remaining images in the data set (see figure 1).

It was Shneiderman [25] who noted that "[users] have highly varied needs for filtering". We use his principle of "dynamic queries", or "direct-manipulation queries". Graphically manipulating objects on the screen, e.g. by dragging a rectangle in the timeline, is linked to a certain filter criterion. Using "rapid, incremental and reversible actions" along with immediate feedback, users can build up complex filtering conditions composed of temporal and spatial conditions without ever having to explicitly formulate a query. Note that selection and filtering conditions do not have to be formulated in one visualisation alone - they can be freely combined across the system.

4.3 Graph Visualisation

The graph visualisation shows a network of image clusters, the topology of which is constructed using Pathfinder networks [5], whereas the layout is calculated using a force-based algorithm. Each node in the network represents an image cluster. The edges between clusters encode their similarity.

The aim of the graph is to provide an overview over a part of the spatial dimension of our image collection. This is accomplished on several levels. After the initial layout is calculated it is purposely held fixed throughout the remaining interaction steps (unless the user explicitly wishes to re-arrange the nodes). On a pre-attentive level this helps the user to form a spatial memory of the image clusters.

On the reflective level it allows reasoning about the clustering, and thus implicitly about the image collection. This level differs depending on what clustering the user chooses. For similarity-based clusters it will reveal how diverse the image collection is. If the collection consists only of holiday photos, most of which are taken outdoors, it will result in a more densely collected network, for example. A time-centred clustering, on the other hand, might put holiday trips undertaken at different times in different clusters, possibly connecting those that show similar sceneries or were edited or browsed in close temporal proximity. Figure 2 shows an example of a Pathfinder network.

Filter-Select-Highlight

A cluster is highlighted when hovering it with the mouse. By clicking it, it becomes selected. Both highlighted and selected clusters are marked with a distinct, coloured frame. By using a modifier key, clusters can be added or removed from the current selection. Furthermore, multiple clusters can be selected by click-dragging with the mouse, which creates a selection rectangle.

Clusters are visible as long as there is still an unfiltered image in the data source, but they will disappear once all images have been filtered. Any selection can be turned into a filter as well, either filtering out selected or unselected clusters.

Detail-on-demand: Peeking

With clustering methods using a variety of different criteria, reasoning about the image collection becomes increasingly complicated. Even though the detail visualisation allows us to browse the contents of a cluster, depending on the intra-cluster ordering of images it can still be a time-consuming process to obtain a sense of what a certain cluster encompasses. For that reason the graph implements an additional operation called "peeking", or "peek zoom".

Peeking is initiated by highlighting a cluster and then using the mousewheel to zoom into it. A pseudo-geometric zoom animation is displayed which will reveal a limited number of cluster representatives; images that best summarise the cluster. The distance between these clusters is used to construct an ad-hoc network of the representatives. The choice of representatives and their distances is specific to the clustering algorithm.

The zooming uses a variety of techniques. Fixed-shape zooming is used to retain the size of the clusters. Once zoomed in, the focused cluster is semantically enhanced by showing its representatives, an operation known as "semantic zooming". Clusters connected by at least one edge are

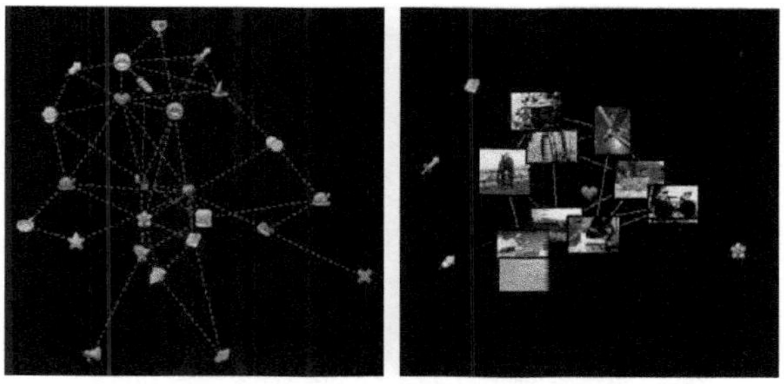

Figure 2: A pathfinder network based on visual similarity (left) and illustration of a zoom-in on a cluster showing representative images (right).

projected onto a circle around the zoomed cluster, and thus the distance is no longer correct, but the angle is retained. This provides a sense of context to the zoomed view. The illusion of a geometric zoom is accomplished by moving unconnected clusters out of the view. The movement vector is calculated by taking the vector from the centre of the visualisation to each cluster, normalising it and multiplying it by a constant. Refer to figure 2 for "peeking" as it is used in practice.

4.4 Hierarchy Visualisation

The purpose of the hierarchy visualisation is to connect the clusters and individual images back to their physical location on the disk, and thus complements the spatial dimension. The major difference to the spatial information provided in the graph visualisation is that the file structure has a natural hierarchy. The heatmap uses greyvalues, as these are the best in conveying different values, is used to provide a visual representation of the connection between the different directories and the derived clusters. This is illustrated in figure 3.

Filter-Select-Highlight

Even without any interaction, the hierarchy visualisation offers an easy to understand overview of all the folders on the hard drive that contain images, and how they are nested. It is the integration into the system, however, that truly makes this visualisation a good fit.

Highlighting works in various ways. Upon hovering an image with the cursor anywhere in the visualisation, the background of the corresponding folder is coloured. If a cluster is highlighted instead, the colour spreads across all the directories that contain images that are contained in this cluster. An exact number is shown next to each folder to indicate the number of hits. Additionally, the intensities of the background colouring is scaled by the number of hits over the maximum number of hits (meaning the folder that has the highest number, not the sum of all of them; see figure 3). This redundant encoding helps the user to quickly determine the dominant folders for a given cluster.

Directories within the visualisation itself can be highlighted as well. This will cause all other visualisations to both highlight the images that are contained in this folder, as well as the clusters that contain one or more of these images.

The hierarchy visualisation - just like the timeline and the graph visualisations - can be used as an entry point for the detail visualisation by selecting a directory. Cluster

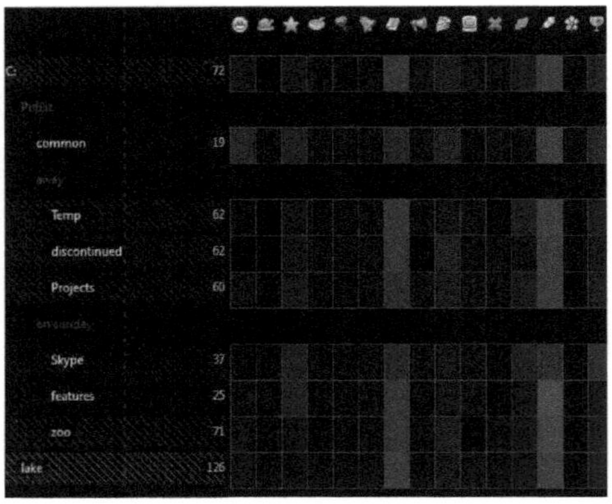

Figure 3: A heatmap showing the distribution of images in directories over the different clusters to aid the process of finding the directories with most candidate matches or suspicious distribution.

selections are shown analogous to cluster highlights, except encoded in a different colour.

Once all images of a certain directory are filtered out, the corresponding entry in the directory tree disappears as well.

4.5 Detail Visualisation

The detail visualisation is responsible for allowing the user to browse the actual images exhaustively. For reasons of simplicity and familiarity the detail visualisation is a simple grid of images (see figure 4).

Figure 4: A selection of three clusters shown in the detail visualisation. Icons on top of the images identify the cluster each image is part of.

To ensure a connection between the detail view and the clusters as well as providing some limited sense of overview without having to resort to other visualisations, the detail visualisation introduces an enhanced version of a regular scrollbar. Just like a traditional scrollbar it shows the fraction and position of the actual visible region in relation to the entire set of selected images. It improves this concept by additionally plotting the different clusters as coloured regions - the order of the images as shown in the grid is partitioned into clusters - which can be clicked in order to jump between clusters. The icon representation of each cluster is embedded into the region as well. Refer to figure 4 for an example of the scrollbar.

5. A SIMULATION ENVIRONMENT

Evaluating complex user interfaces is a notoriously difficult problem. In complex multimedia analytics scenarios, the functionality of the interface is typically very rich and it is difficult and not even desirable to steer and formalize the users' quest for information. Therefore, it is unfeasible to test various usage scenarios with formal user studies which are typically meant to test small variations of the same interface. Benchmarks are another option and TRECvid has played an important role in developing interactive retrieval methods [26]. But there we have also seen that comparing the merits of different methods is difficult, even while the solutions are very much driven by the given benchmark task. North even advocates that for visualization driven systems benchmarks should be abandoned completely and that the focus should shift to the insight gained by using the interface [20] by freely employing its functionality in complex tasks. This is indeed the ultimate aim of any multimedia analytics interface, but before that the developers themselves should be able to flexibly test different scenarios, different visualizations and algorithms and see whether the expected patterns indeed are visible and whether they have the potential to support the search process.

5.1 Actions and events

For the digital forensics case, a diverse range of disk images with large image collections would be required as well as semantic information on the images (such as concepts present in the image). Unfortunately the research data available for digital forensics comes nowhere close to meeting any of these requirements, making the evaluation of the interface unfeasible using existing disk images. We have therefore developed a user simulation framework to create and manipulate usage patterns building upon the rules defined in [7]. The simulation provides us with a meta-data structure (consisting of the Microsoft Windows modified, accessed and created timestamps and the file paths) for the images and therefore it is only concerned with user patterns that directly influence time, paths and actions or events [1].

The actions (e.g. moving files from one location to another, scanning the files) are referred to as high level actions and represent the usage model that generates a certain pattern (based on the different rules defined in [7]). They generally refer to batch operations (i.e. operations applied to more than one file) or operations applied to multiple files in quick succession. Low-level actions represent actions on single files. Patterns are timestamp relationships on one or multiple files that can be observed on the final disk image. The distinction between high level and low level operations is important as the simulation builds timestamp information using basic actions (according to high level actions), while a forensic investigation starts from the timestamp information and (attempts to) derive high level actions or in general terms events based on it.

5.2 User Profiles

The sequence of actions is steered by a user profile, representing all characteristics that differentiate the model behind a system, or disk image, from another where the term refers both to user specific and system specific characteristics. The

[1]The Python based simulation environment we developed is available for download via www.science.uva.nl/~worring/forensics-simulation

model refers to trends in the usage of a system e.g. a user that downloads frequently files from the Internet, as well as system specific details e.g. the download speed. One user model, as it is probabilistic, generates a different output disk image every time it is used. Users are characterized along the following dimensions:

Spatial user patterns: The level of semantic organization on the system based on the directory tree:

- **The organized user**: has a directory for most of the important concepts he is interested in and puts images in their proper directory when entered into the system.
- **The unorganized user**: utilizes one general directory to put everything in, or the directory structure of the images is random, with no direct relation to semantics.

Temporal user pattern: The extent to which semantics and time are correlated and secondly the regularity of use:

- **The single-task user**: works with images containing different contents at different moments in time without mixing them. Generally significant periods of time pass when switching between different concepts. Batch operations are applied to files belonging to the same semantic concept.
- **The multi-task user**: The multi-task user handles images with different semantic contents at the same moment in time, including during the same system operation.

The second categorization leads to:

- **The sporadic user**: The sporadic user initiates events in bursts, with significant time intervals in between.
- **The regular user**: The regular user manipulates images at relatively regular intervals in time e.g. every day or once every 6 days.

The Time Section

For user actions time is modeled as a series of Gaussian distributions to choose the days containing actions as well as the time during the day the actions are performed. System actions, are statically defined as a list of timesteps.

Timestamp variation for multiple files included in a batch operation (for each action) is modeled as well using a Gaussian distribution. The mean of the action is already known (the timestamp for the action chosen) and therefore only the variation specific to each action needs to be defined.

User action timestamps are generated in several steps: choosing the days containing actions, choosing the time of the day that (batches of) actions are performed at, and choosing individual timestamps for each of the files that will be part of the action - denoted as scrambling (needed for batch operations).

Actions are chosen according to a Markov model, independent of path or timestamp for the action. The states of the Markov Model are represented by the low-level actions (operations on individual files) corresponding to the high-level actions in the simulation. The propabilities generating various sequences are defined in a user profile which are characteristic for the specific types of users identified. An example Markov model and user profile is shown in figure 6.3.

The Path Section

This section is in charge of building the directory tree to be used for the file operations. Each file instance consists of a file name and path (on the simulated system) and the three timestamps (modified, accessed and created) and is responsible for updating them on the occurrence of a low-level action.

The decision of what directory and what files are chosen is done based on the action and, optionally, the semantics set for the action. Semantics are modeled as a Markov Model. Whether file semantics play a role in choosing the files depends on sthe user profile.

The tree is built starting from each partition (as the root node) and building the directory structure level by level. At each level we decide whether to build the level or stop according to the height probability. Building the level consists of choosing a number of directories again according to a Gaussian distribution.

Choosing files for the actions

The directory for the action is chosen according to a Gaussian distribution from the directories previously selected. The number of files that the action will be applied on is determined according to a Gaussian distribution specific to each action (in accordance with the number of files in the directory).

6. EXPERIMENTS

The dataset on which we perform experiments is the Visual Object Classes Challenge 2010 [2] with around 10.000 images. As a surrogate class for illegal material, we consider the horse category containing around 350 images as our target. As features, we use a method from van de Sande [28]. We compute a visual codebook, consisting of 64 elements based on a Harris-Laplace point detector and C-SIFT descriptors. For a more detailed explanation of the algorithms the reader is directed to the reference. As similarity function we use the Euclidean distance between the vectors. The images are clustered into a fixed number of clusters (15 in the following experiments) using a standard k-means algorithm. For each cluster a set of representative images is computed.

We consider two different use-cases to exemplify the usage of our visualisation system. Even though the organisational scheme of the user that has created this image collection is unknown in a real investigation and determined by examining results of different clustering schemes, we shall assume it is prior knowledge for the purpose of these experiments.

6.1 The Organised User

For our first experiment we consider the rather simple case of an organised user. This type of user neatly puts images of the same category into the same directory, an overview of the steps in the investigation are presented in figure 5.

6.2 Single-task User

Let us move to a more challenging scenario. In this case the user is rather disorganised - or at least the user's sense of organisation does not match the clustering, which is a very likely scenario in practice. More importantly, the user's organisational scheme doesn't categorise the target images

[2]http://pascallin.ecs.soton.ac.uk/challenges/VOC/voc2010/

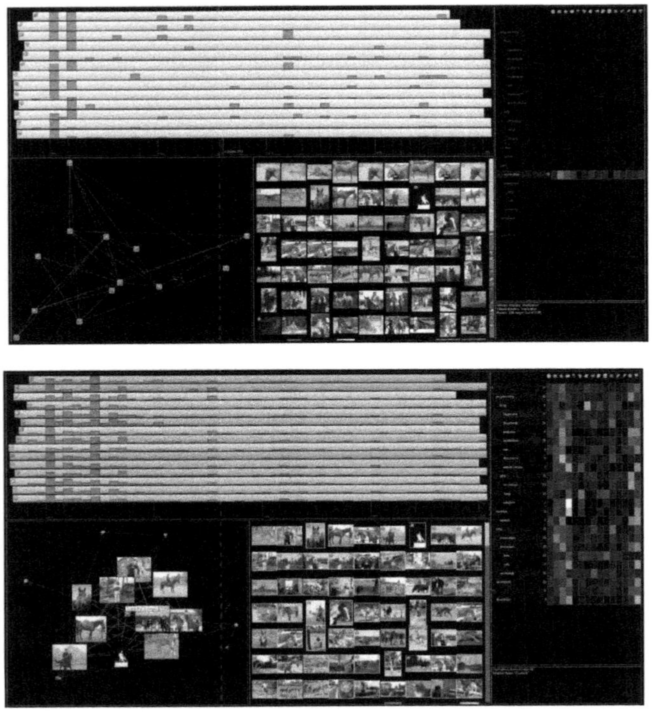

Figure 5: Screenshots from the investigation. (Top) As we are expecting an organized user we start by checking all directories one-by-one viewing one page of results in the detail view. When we hit the "moderation" directory we observe several target images. The heatmap reveals that "cluster 14" is represented most in this directory. Zooming into the cluster indeed reveals several target images among the representatives as well as in the detail view and also reveals several target images in various other directories.

as it was the case previously. Ideally k-means would put all target images into a single cluster, but practically that is a very unlikely outcome. However, unless the clustering fails completely, the resulting clusters will have varying densities of target images. We can now verify that the user is in fact disorganised in the sense that k-means doesn't match his organisational scheme. Hovering any cluster shows that the cluster images are seemingly randomly spread across all directories (see figure 6) so we should resort to time as a starting point.

An investigator can now proceed to find more images that might have been modified at a different time by successively repeating this strategy. At the end of each cycle, all images that have been seen so far (the image was visible in the detail visualisation) can be filtered out, supporting a systematic approach to an exhaustive search.

6.3 Exploration Strategies

As a final experiment we consider a more general strategy to use the visualisation system and compare its performance across several user types. Typically the challenge lies in finding a suitable entry point into the visualisation. The overview provided by the timeline, the graph and the hierarchy visualisation may give the investigator an idea about the type of user he is dealing with. We will propose a strategy that is independent of this, however, and can be used as a fallback.

First we need to find some initial images belonging to the target class. This is accomplished in three ways: either peeking into clusters in the graph visualisation, clicking through the clusters systematically in the timeline or graph and examining them in the detail visualisation, or checking in turn each directory in which this cluster is dominant. If none of these yield a single image of the target class, the preprocessing step (clustering) step needs to be revisited.

Once one or more target images have been found perform the following steps:

1. Roughly memorise the timestamp of the image. This is accomplished by hovering the image and reading the highlight label in the timeline visualisation.
2. Continue browsing the cluster/directory for more images using the detail visualisation.
3. If we find enough target images
   (a) filter using the timeline if the timestamps are similar

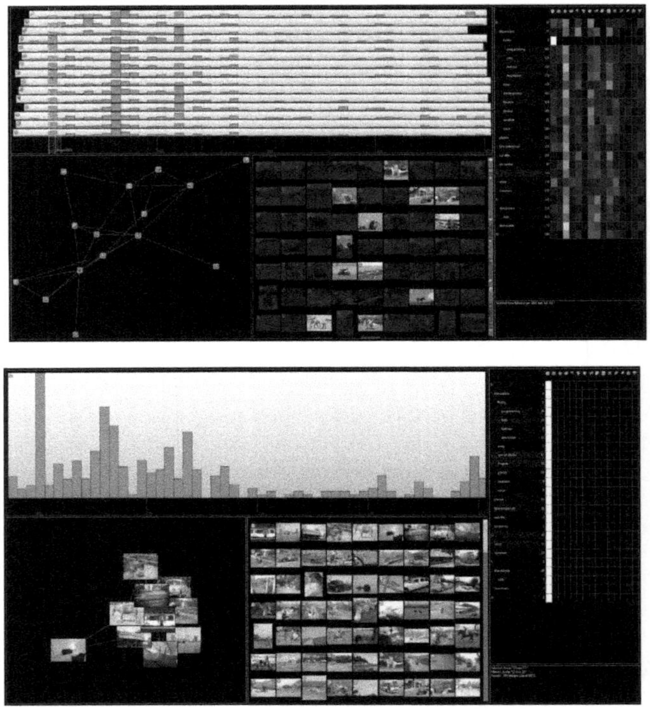

Figure 6: The second scenario. (Top) Inspecting images by looking at small intervals of the timeline reveals that that there are several target images with a timestamp around januari 2002. Looking at the cluster icons reveals that those are mostly coming from one cluster. Inspecting this cluster yields several additional target images at other moments in time (bottom). By focussing on one cluster the distribution of images over time becomes more apparent.

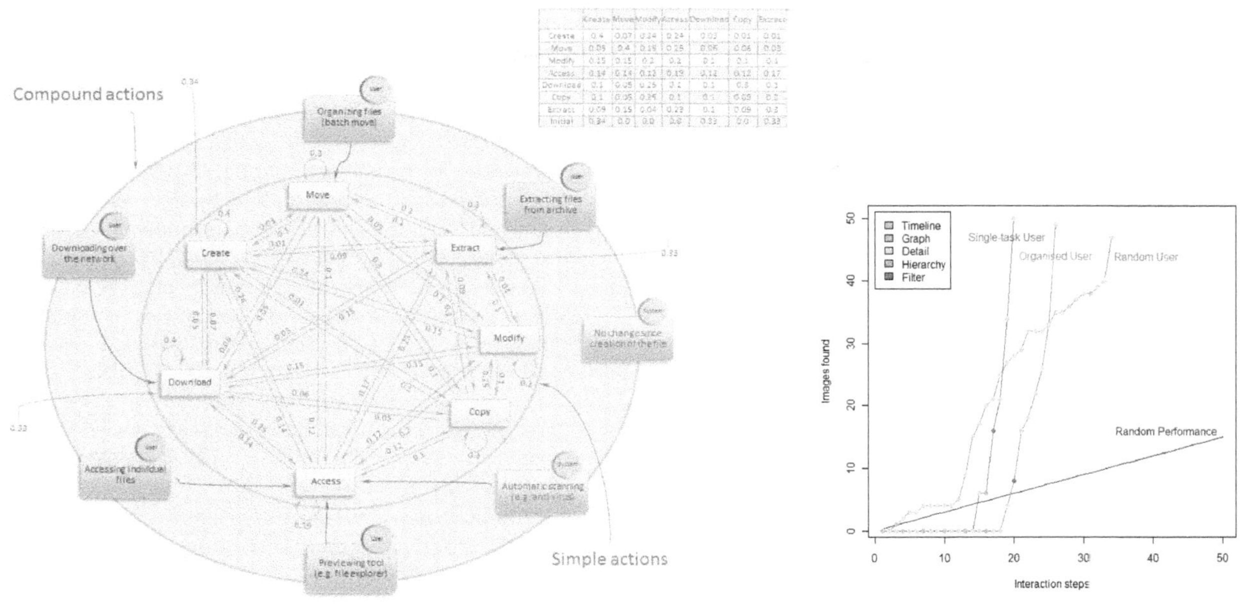

Figure 7: Left: Markov model determining the sequence of actions on the system. The numbers on the arrows represent arbitrary probabilities of transitioning between two states. The three arrows starting in the exterior of the model represent the prior probabilities for the Markov model. Right: Performance of a custom exploration strategy on various instantiations of the model using the visualisation system against unaided random browsing (grey line). At each interaction step, a circle colour-codes the visualisation that was used for the specific interaction step.

(b) filter using the hierarchy visualisation if images fall in the same directory

(c) continue browsing the cluster otherwise

4. If the cluster/directory does not yield any more images within a reasonable amount of interaction steps, choose another and go to step 1 of this procedure.

Using this guideline we revisited the user types from the previous two scenarios, as well as a "random" user, who is following no particular scheme and is thus considerably more difficult. Time is used for comparing performance and is discretised into interaction steps. Examining a four-by-four grid of images counts as a single step, as does changing clusters, directories, making a selection or filtering. Peek-zooming in and out counts as a single step as well. Highlighting images is not considered for reasons of simplicity.

The experiments stop once at least 40 images belonging to the target class have been found. The results are summarised in figure 6.3.

Despite the lucky start for the random user where a good cluster was found almost instantly, initial performance of the visualisation system is typically worse since many interaction steps are used to find the clusters with a high density of target images. Once found, performance is better than random by a wide margin. Although the user profiles tested in this paper are fairly limited and more specialised real-world cases will certainly require adaptation, we are confident that the outlined exploration strategy provides a solid basis for using the visualisation system in other scenarios as well.

7. CONCLUSION

The emerging field of Multimedia Analytics where content analysis and visualization seamlessly merge into a framework to support the task of the user in an optimal way has high potential. Especially in the context of digital forensics where large collections of images need to be examined only a combined approach can truly support the investigative process. A characteristic of these complex tasks is that the content of the images is only one clue, whereas the metadata provides other interesting entries into the dataset.

In this paper, we presented a framework for browsing images and their metadata (in this case time and directory information) in which multimedia analysis is performed to derive content based clusters as basis for exploration. A timeline, graph, and directory visualization provide different ways to find patterns in the data. The highly interactive visualizations are visually connected through carefully chosen, easy to remember, icons and through the various interactions.

As multimedia analytics solutions are difficult to evaluate, we have developed a probabilistic tool to create disk images, in particular creating different timestamps and directory structures and content using Markov models to capture different user profiles. The tool is made available to other researchers so they can pursue different solutions to the same type of tasks. In this paper a limited set of simulated disk images and scenarios are illustrated. They show the possibilities of the developed framework. By looking at various simulated disk images and by considering the generic type of patterns they create in the various visualizations provides us insight in how to extend the framework into a solution where the system is proactively highlighting patterns of interest.

8. REFERENCES

[1] W. Alink, RAF Bhoedjang, PA Boncz, and AP De Vries. XIRAF-XML-based indexing and querying for digital forensics. *Digital Investigation*, 3:50–58, 2006.

[2] P. André, M.L. Wilson, A. Russell, D.A. Smith, and A. Owens. Continuum: designing timelines for hierarchies, relationships and scale. In *Proceedings of the 20th annual ACM symposium on User interface software and technology*, pages 101–110. ACM, 2007.

[3] G. Andrienko et.al. Space, time and visual analytics. *International Journal of Geographical Information Science*, 24(10):1577–1600, 2010.

[4] F. Buchholz and C. Falk. Design and implementation of Zeitline: a forensic timeline editor. In *Digital Forensics Research Workshop*. Citeseer, 2005.

[5] C. Chen, G. Gagaudakis, and P. Rosin. Similarity-based image browsing. In *Proceedings of the 16th IFIP World Computer Congress. International Conference on Intelligent Information Processing*. Citeseer, 2000.

[6] N.A. Chinchor, J.J. Thomas, P.C. Wong, M.G. Christel, and W. Ribarsky. Multimedia analysis + visual analytics = multimedia analytics. *Computer Graphics and Applications, IEEE*, 30(5):52 –60, sept.-oct. 2010.

[7] KP Chow, F.Y.W. Law, M.Y.K. Kwan, and P.K.Y. Lai. The Rules of Time on NTFS File System. In *Systematic Approaches to Digital Forensic Engineering, 2007. SADFE 2007. Second International Workshop on*, pages 71–85. IEEE, 2007.

[8] R. Datta, D. Joshi, J. Li, and J.Z. Wang. Image retrieval: Ideas, influences, and trends of the new age. *ACM Computing Surveys (CSUR)*, 40(2):1–60, 2008.

[9] O. de Rooij, M. Worring, and J. J. van Wijk. Mediatable: Interactive categorization of multimedia collections. *IEEE Computer Graphics and Applications*, 30(5).

[10] D.M. Eler, M.Y. Nakazaki, F.V. Paulovich, D.P. Santos, G.F. Andery, M.C.F. Oliveira, J. Batista Neto, and R. Minghim. Visual analysis of image collections. *The Visual Computer*, 25(10):923–937, 2009.

[11] A. Girgensohn, F. Shipman, L. Wilcox, T. Turner, and M. Cooper. MediaGLOW: organizing photos in a graph-based workspace. In *Proceedings of the 13th international conference on Intelligent user interfaces*, pages 419–424. ACM, 2009.

[12] J. Heer and D. Boyd. Vizster: Visualizing Online Social Networks. In *Proceedings of the Proceedings of the 2005 IEEE Symposium on Information Visualization*, page 5. IEEE Computer Society, 2005.

[13] H.C. Jetter, W.A. König, J. Gerken, and H. Reiterer. ZOIL-a cross-platform user interface paradigm for personal information management. In *In" Personal Information Management: PIM 2008", CHI 2008 Workshop*, 2008.

[14] V. Kaptelinin and M. Czerwinski. *Beyond the Desktop Metaphor: Designing Integrated Digital Work Environments*. MIT Press, Cambridge, Mass., 2007.

[15] D. Keim, J. Kohlhammer, G. Ellis, and F. Mansmann, editors. *Mastering the Information Age Solving Problems with Visual Analytics*, chapter Data Mining, pages 39–56. Eurographics Association, 2010.

[16] D. Keim, F. Mansmann, J. Schneidewind, and H. Ziegler. Challenges in visual data analysis. In *Information Visualization, 2006. IV 2006. Tenth International Conference on*, pages 9–16. IEEE, 2006.

[17] A. Krishnan and S. Jones. TimeSpace: activity-based temporal visualisation of personal information spaces. *Personal and Ubiquitous Computing*, 9(1):46–65, 2005.

[18] H. Lejsek et.al. Videntifier forensic: large-scale video identification in practice. In *Proceedings of the 2nd ACM workshop on Multimedia in forensics, security and intelligence*, MiFor '10, pages 1–6, 2010.

[19] GP Nguyen and M. Worring. Interactive access to large image collections using similarity-based visualization. *Journal of Visual Languages & Computing*, 19(2):203–224, 2008.

[20] C. North. Toward measuring visualization insight. *Computer Graphics and Applications, IEEE*, 26(3):6 –9, may-june 2006.

[21] J. Olsson and M. Boldt. Computer forensic timeline visualization tool. *Digital Investigation*, 6:78–87, 2009.

[22] N. Quadrianto, K. Kersting, T. Tuytelaars, and W.L. Buntine. Beyond 2d-grids: a dependence maximization view on image browsing. In *ACM International Conference on Multimedia Information Retrieval*, 2010.

[23] J. Rekimoto. TimeScape: a time machine for the desktop environment. In *CHI'99 extended abstracts on Human factors in computing systems*, pages 180–181. ACM, 1999.

[24] G.G. Richard III and V. Roussev. Next-generation digital forensics. *Communications of the ACM*, 49(2):76–80, 2006.

[25] B. Shneiderman. The eyes have it: A task by data type taxonomy for information visualizations. In *Proceedings of the 1996 IEEE Symposium on Visual Languages*, pages 336–, Washington, DC, USA, 1996. IEEE Computer Society.

[26] A.F. Smeaton, P. Over P, and W. Kraaij. Evaluation campaigns and TRECvid. In *Proceedings of Multimedia Information Retrieval*, 2006.

[27] J.J. Thomas, K.A. Cook, Institute of Electrical, and Electronics Engineers. *Illuminating the path: The research and development agenda for visual analytics*. IEEE Computer Society, 2005.

[28] K.E.A. Van De Sande, T. Gevers, and C.G.M. Snoek. Evaluating color descriptors for object and scene recognition. *Pattern Analysis and Machine Intelligence, IEEE Transactions on*, 32(9):1582–1596, 2010.

[29] J.J. Van Wijk and E.R. Van Selow. Cluster and calendar based visualization of time series data. In *Information Visualization, 1999.(Info Vis' 99) Proceedings. 1999 IEEE Symposium on*, pages 4–9. IEEE, 1999.

[30] C. Ware. *Visual thinking for design*. Morgan Kaufmann Pub, 2008.

[31] X-Y. Wei X-Y. and Z-Q. Yang. Coached active learning for interactive video search. In *Proceedings of ACM Multimedia*, 2011.

Submodular Video Hashing: A Unified Framework Towards Video Pooling and Indexing

Liangliang Cao
Multimedia Group
IBM Watson Research Center
liangliang.cao@us.ibm.com

Zhenguo Li, Yadong Mu, Shih-Fu Chang
Dept. of Electrical Engineering
Columbia University
zgli,muyadong,sfchang@ee.columbia.edu

ABSTRACT

This paper develops a novel framework for efficient large-scale video retrieval. We aim to find video according to higher level similarities, which is beyond the scope of traditional near duplicate search. Following the popular hashing technique we employ compact binary codes to facilitate nearest neighbor search. Unlike the previous methods which capitalize on only one type of hash code for retrieval, this paper combines heterogeneous hash codes to effectively describe the diverse and multi-scale visual contents in videos. Our method integrates feature pooling and hashing in a single framework. In the pooling stage, we cast video frames into a set of pre-specified components, which capture a variety of semantics of video contents. In the hashing stage, we represent each video component as a compact hash code, and combine multiple hash codes into hash tables for effective search. To speed up the retrieval while retaining most informative codes, we propose a graph-based influence maximization method to bridge the pooling and hashing stages. We show that the influence maximization problem is submodular, which allows a greedy optimization method to achieve a nearly optimal solution. Our method works very efficiently, retrieving thousands of video clips from TRECVID dataset in about 0.001 second. For a larger scale synthetic dataset with 1M samples, it uses less than 1 second in response to 100 queries. Our method is extensively evaluated in both unsupervised and supervised scenarios, and the results on TRECVID Multimedia Event Detection and Columbia Consumer Video datasets demonstrate the success of our proposed technique.

Categories and Subject Descriptors

H.3.3 [**Information Search and Retrieval**]: Retrieval models

General Terms

Algorithms, Experimentation

Keywords

video hashing, indexing, feature pooling, multiple feature hashing, submodular

1. INTRODUCTION

The power of word-based document indexing has been demonstrated by the success of modern text-based search engines like Yahoo, Google and Bing. Nowadays billions of users can easily enter search terms to query enormous repositories of text documents in a flexible way. In contrast, video retrieval is still in its early stage: most video search systems still rely on textual titles or comments rather than visual features. One reason is that it is still very expensive to compute distance metrics between video queries and tremendous video corpus on the Web. Consequently, personalized video search where users can impose individual preference of visual features is still far from being a reality. On the one hand, more video contents are being generated. On the other hand, it appears to be more difficult for effectively retrieve relevant contents.

The difficulty in large scale video indexing stems from the complex nature of video contents. Unlike text retrieval where a document can be retrieved by words in constant time using inverted index structure, a video is composed of multiple frames with dynamic backgrounds and evolving people activities. The semantic gap between low-level features and high-level concepts makes it difficult to model rich video semantics. Additionally, data structures based on inverted index files are not readily applicable for content-based retrieval of videos which are represented by high-dimensional visual features.

To capture the diversity of video contents, a straightforward approach is to employ multiple video features to describe different aspects of visual contents. However, there are two challenges of using multiple features. First, most multiple feature learning algorithms rely on supervised learning. While more features may capture sufficient video contents, non-discriminative or noisy features may degrade the performance substantially. Second, employing multiple features increases the computational complexity and makes large-scale visual retrieval slower. There is a trade-off between the quality of the retrieval and the corresponding efficiency. If the feature dimensionality is too high, nearest neighbor search will be expensive and undiscriminative due to the curse of high dimensionality [9].

In this paper, we propose a new framework, called *submodular video hashing*, for efficient video retrieval with large-scale feature selection. The approach achieves fast retrieval speed and scales well to very large video data sets. The contributions of this new framework lie in three aspects:

- It captures the diversified contents of video frames using novel visual pooling methods in the temporal domain. By pooling the frames with similar visual features, it can distinguish different scenes in a video and group them into different video components. The temporal pooling method is especially useful in modeling long sequences or videos with multiple scenes.
- It develops a new selection strategy from multiple scene components and multiple features. To handle the trade-off between efficiency and accuracy, we prove that our feature selection formulation is submodular, and thus can be solved nearly optimally by greedy optimization.
- Finally, it uses multiple hash tables to combine the results from selected features and video components. Our hash tables work similarly to inverted indexes in text retrieval and support video retrieval with very low computational complexity.

Note that the objective of submodular video hashing is different from near-duplicate search and image hashing. Near-duplicate video search is a classical problem in multimedia field, which aims to find similar frames among videos, and is very useful in protecting copyright and intelligence property. In contrast, our submodular video hashing, can be used to find videos according to higher level similarities, such as video styles or topics. Image hashing has been a popular topic in recent years, but it does not consider the temporal pooling problem as in this paper. There is also another subtle but practically very important difference between our method and prior image hashing techniques. A number of prior efforts on image hashing [33] [34] require computation of the Hamming distances between the query and images in the datasets, which implies huge computational cost for large-scale video datasets. Following the paradigm in Indyk *et al.*'s seminal work [8], this paper utilizes hashing table as inverted indexes to enable very efficient retrieval and develops a novel submodular framework for combining multiple hash tables.

The rest of this paper is organized as follows: Section 2 first reviews related work on image pooling and submodular optimization. Section 3 generalizes previous studies by extending pooling from image domain to video domain. The proposed pooling technique comprises multiple components that can provide a comprehensive description of video contents. Based on these video components, Section 4 develops a novel submodular video hashing strategy. Section 5 reports experimental results using submodular video hashing techniques that show excellent performance. Finally we conclude this paper in Section 6 and report on future directions.

2. RELATED WORK

Our work is partly motivated by the recent progress in image hashing. Shaknarovich and Darrell [31] proposed BoostSSC to compute a weighted Hamming distance. However, the weighted Hamming distance makes it difficult to find the neighbors efficient in their approach. Torralba et al. used small hash codes to represent 80 million tiny images [33]. Weiss et al. developed spectral hashing [34] to improve the hashing quality using spectral graph theory. Liu et al. employed anchor nodes to speed up the hashing process on large-scale graphs [26]. Hashing with supervised information is also considered in recent studies [23], [25]. Zhang et al. [38] proposed to integrate information from several different sources by adjusting the weights on each individual source for maximizing the coding performance, and enabling fast conversion from query examples to their binary hash codes. However, all the above approaches adopt just a single hash code to represent an instance, which cannot capture the diversified content of video clips.

In contrast to previous studies in image hashing, this paper proposes to represent a video using multiple components produced by temporal video pooling. The pooling operation has been widely used in image recognition. Boureau et al. argued in [2] that many recent progresses in image recognition can be viewed as a combination of alternating series of coding and spatial pooling steps. Average pooling [20] tries to compute the mean of the feature vectors within a spatial neighborhood. Bag-of-words model can be viewed as a special case of average pooling. Max pooling is found to be useful for sparse coding features [37]. This idea is recently generalized in [1], by enlarging the spatial bins in feature space clustering. Video pooling is different from image pooling in the sense that the regularity in temporal domain is not as significant as that in the spatial domain. A video event can either happen at the beginning part of the video or the second half of the video, or it can last throughout the whole sequence.

It is worth noting that this paper is also different from classical near-duplicate video search problem that are chiefly motivated by the problem of copyright detection. Many of the proposed solutions decompose videos into multiple key-frames and look for similar key-frames across pairs of videos [16], [35], [15], [12], [32]. Some recent work considers pair-wise distances of key-frames [24], which can further improve the detection accuracy but suffers from heavy computational burden. This prior work does not generalize for content-based video retrieval because: (1) General video retrieval requires support for content-based search based on high-level semantics rather than visual duplication. (2) Traditional near-duplicate search requires a distance measure between key-frames, and the performance is determined by the quality of low-level features of key-frames in unsupervised learning scenario. In contrast, a single low-level feature may not work well for general video retrieval, which often requires supervised learning. (3) Video retrieval systems are desired to support personalized retrieval, where user profile or retrieval history improves retrieval performance. This cannot be accomplished by classical near-duplicate retrieval.

This paper employs hash tables as the basic data structure and develops a novel method to construct multiple hash tables. The contribution in this paper is in developing a unified submodular framework that integrates video pooling and hashing, and provides an efficient strategy exploring the rich contents in video retrieval. In recent years, submodular optimization has emerged as a powerful optimization tool in a variety of machine learning problems including active learning, structure learning, clustering, and ranking. A submodular function is essentially characterized by a diminishing return property which states that, the marginal gain of adding a new element to a subset B is higher than that of adding it to any larger subset A, where $B \subset A$. Formally, let P be the power set of a set $\mathbb{V}$. A set function $h : P \to \mathbb{R}$

is said to be submodular [18] if

$$h(\mathbb{A}\cup\{v\})-h(\mathbb{A}) \leq h(\mathbb{B}\cup\{v\})-h(\mathbb{B}) \quad \forall \mathbb{B} \subset \mathbb{A} \subset \mathbb{V}, v \in \mathbb{V}\backslash\mathbb{A}. \tag{1}$$

The very desirable consequence of submodularity is that provably (near-)optimal solutions can be found via efficient greedy optimization [18]. Some typical submodular functions explored in machine learning include set cover, influence in social network [21], electricity network [18], anisotropic diffusion [17], and sparse representation [6]. In this paper, we will prove that our hash code selection is also a submodular problem and can be solved by an efficient greedy approach.

3. VIDEO POOLING

The basic idea of our video hashing algorithm is to exploit the rich semantics of videos and construct binary codes corresponding to different characteristics of video contents. Our methods contrast with previous image based hashing methods by considering video feature pooling in frame-level.

Suppose there is a video with T frames, where each frame is represented by a feature vector x_t. We generate temporal pooling component k as

$$z^k = \sum_{t=1}^{T} p_t^k x_t. \tag{2}$$

Here p_t^k stands for the probability $Pr(k|x_t)$ that captures the amount of contribution of frame t in forming the scene component k. We approximate the probability using soft vector quantization on GIST features.

From (2), we can see that to obtain different scene component $z^k = \sum_{t=1}^{T} p_t^k x_t$, in fact is equivalent to decompose each frame feature x_t into different scenes

$$x_t \rightarrow [p_t^1 x_t, p_t^2 x_t, \cdots], \tag{3}$$

From eqs (2) and (3) one can see that our new model is a feature pooling method [1]. The unique characteristic of our method is that our pooling weights p_t^k are on video frames instead of spatial domain. Here we force the pooling weights p_t^k to follow the constraint $\sum_k p_t^k = 1$. We will explain how to compute p_t^k in the following.

Following the previous studies [29] [30] [36], we use GIST features to represent the scenes of video frames and then to compute p_t^k. Note that the pooling weights are computed based on Euclidean distance, which is not reliable for sparse histogram features like SIFT. On the other hand, GIST is easy to compute and gives a reliable measure on how different two frames look holistically [29]. With all the training data, we compute the GIST features for all frames and cluster them into C centers using the K-means algorithm. The C center is represented as $g_c^1, g_c^2, \cdots, g_c^C$. To compute the pooling weight p_t^k for frame t in a training or test video clip, we extract it GIST feature vector g_t . The pooling weight is derived by comparing $\{g_c^k\}$ and g_t.

One simple way to compute pooling weights is by vector quantization (VQ), which forces all but the nearest one p_t^k to be zero. However, VQ is well-known to be sensitive to noises. In this paper, we consider a soft voting pooling weights as

$$p_t^k = \frac{1/(d_t^k)^3}{\sum_{l=1}^{C} 1/(d_t^l)^3}, \tag{4}$$

Algorithm 1 Video Pooling Algorithm.

Input: A video with the set of frame feature vectors $\{x_t\}$, $1 \leq t \leq T$. A codebook with C centers of GIST feature g_c^k, $1 \leq k \leq C$.

Extract GIST descriptor g_t for every frame t.
Compute the pooling weight p_t^k using eq. (4).
Compute scene component z^k using eq. (2).
Normalize z^k and encode each component with a hash code.

where d_t^k is the Euclidean distance between centers g_c^k and frame feature g_t. It is not difficult to see that our pooling weights satisfy the constraint $\sum_k p_t^k = 1$. Also our pooling weights rely on GIST feature, regardless of the event label y. This means we will use the same pooling strategy independent with events. We call the method in eq. 4 as concurrent VQ. Compared with traditional VQ, our new pooling method penalizes the impact of large outliers, and assigns more weights to the centers closer to g_t.

Note that this paper chooses an unsupervised way to model pooling weights. The reasons why unsupervised learning is preferred are as follows: First, unsupervised learning can save the extra labeling efforts; On the other hand, in our model, the goal is not to recognize the exact scene category but to do pooling according to scene context, and thus supervised learning is not necessary. Algorithm 1 summarizes the workflow of our video pooling algorithm.

Our recent experiments show [4] that Support Vector Machine (SVM) classifiers with video pooling components can significantly improve the recognition accuracy for complex video events. However, this paper is different from [4] in the fact that it considers the video hashing problem (as elaborated in the next section) instead of SVM classification. After temporal pooling components $\{z^k\}$ are computed, we further learn a compact hash code (less than 32 bits) for each pooling component. We generate a number of hash codes using different temporal pooling. We use both random projection [8] and spectral hashing [34] in this paper, but note that our system is also flexible to be combined with other hashing functions.

4. SUBMODULAR VIDEO HASHING

4.1 Model

Suppose we have n_f features indexed by $f = 1, \ldots, n_f$, where each (f) is captured by multiple (C) components $(v_f^1, \cdots, v_f^C)$ and each component (v_f^j) is expressed by a compact binary hash code[1]. Our first observation is that not every code is equally informative and there can be significant redundancy among the codes. On the other hand, it is critical to use compact representation for large-scale video retrieval. Inspired by these observations, we aim to select a *small* number of "informative" codes which can well "represent" the entire set of codes. We found these concepts can be effectively modeled using a graph over the codes whose edge weights capture the degree of overlapping or similarity between pairwise codes. In this section, we assume that the mechanism to compute pairwise code similarity is known (which will be addressed in the next subsection).

[1]Our model applies to any other feature representation.

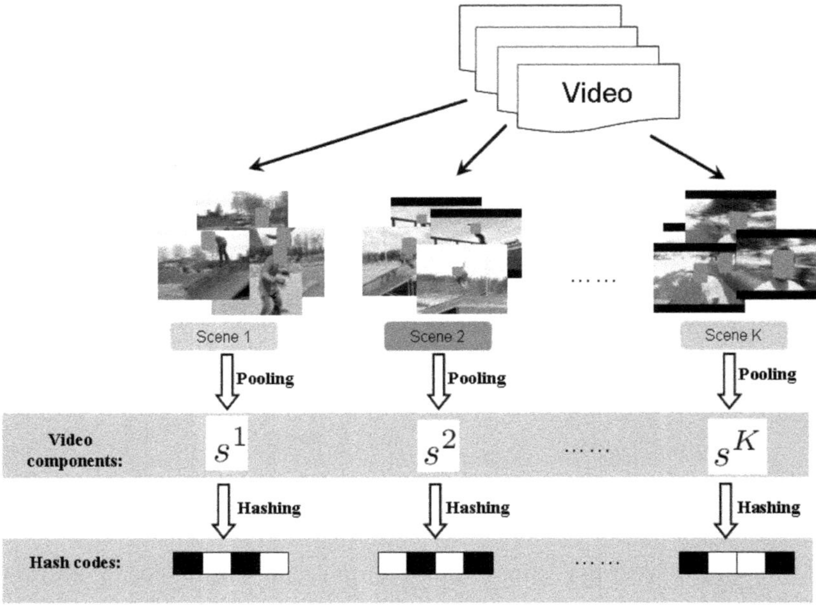

Figure 1: Temporal pooling for video hashing.

Let $\mathcal{G} = \{\mathbb{V}, W\}$ be a graph with node set $\mathbb{V}$ consisting of the hash codes considered, i.e., $\mathbb{V} = \{v_f^k | k = 1, \ldots, C; f = 1, \ldots, n_f\}$, and similarity matrix $W = [w_{ij}]$ where w_{ij} captures the similarity between codes i and j. Our goal is to select m representative nodes from the graph, where m can be manually specified or determined automatically. We cast this node selection problem as an influence maximization problem where the influence of the selected m nodes can be *maximally* propagated to the rest of the nodes in the graph.

Denote $\mathbb{A}$ as the set of selected nodes whose influences are assigned and fixed to 1's. We use a score $u_{\mathbb{A}}(i) \in [0, 1]$ to quantify the influence node i received from $\mathbb{A}$. For technical reason that will be clear soon, we introduce a sink node s to the graph that is connected to each node with a small constant weight. The sink node s is very "cool" in that it is never influenced by others or tries to influence others. So its influence is fixed to 0. For simplicity and a little abuse of notations, we still denote the graph as $\mathcal{G} = \{\mathbb{V}, W\}$ but keep in mind that $s \in \mathbb{V}$ and W is expanded accordingly. We also denote $\hat{\mathbb{A}} = \mathbb{A} \cup s$ and $\mathbb{N}$ the set of remaining nodes, i.e., $\hat{\mathbb{A}} \cap \mathbb{N} = \emptyset$ and $\hat{\mathbb{A}} \cup \mathbb{N} = \mathbb{V}$. Formally, we propose the following influence maximization framework:

$$\max_{\mathbb{A} \subset \mathbb{V}} \Omega(\mathbb{A}) := \sum_{i \in \mathbb{N}} u_{\mathbb{A}}(i). \tag{5}$$

To instantiate the above framework, a concrete model for influence propagation is needed. Since label propagation on graph is a well studied problem in machine learning [39], we adapt it for influence, though other propagation techniques can be employed [3] [13]. Specifically, we use the concept of Harmonic fields from Zhu et al. [40] which has been shown to be a highly effective label propagation model.

Denote $u_{\mathbb{A}}(i) = 1$ if $i \in \mathbb{A}$ and $u_{\mathbb{A}}(s) = 0$. Our influence model enjoys a "harmonic" interaction among the nodes as follows:

$$u_{\mathbb{A}}(i) = \frac{1}{d_i} \sum_{j \in \mathcal{N}(i)} w_{ij} u_{\mathbb{A}}(j), \; i \in \mathbb{N} \tag{6}$$

where $\mathcal{N}(i)$ denotes the set of neighbors of node i and $d_i = \sum_{j \in \mathcal{N}(i)} w_{ij}$ is the degree of node i. In other words, *the influence on node i is the weighted sum of the influences on its neighbors.*

Recall that our objective is to select m nodes $\mathbb{A}$ to maximize the overall influence $\Omega(\mathbb{A})$, which appears to be a difficult discrete optimization problem. However, we will show below that set function $\Omega(\mathbb{A})$ is *submodular* (see eq. (1)), whose optimization can be done in a greedy manner which is guaranteed to converge to a solution that is nearly optimal [28]. Our strategy is partially inspired by previous work in semi-supervised learning [40] and image co-segmentation [17]. Our work differs in a new formulation for hash function selection as well as a novel and easier way for showing the submodularity of the influence maximization problem.

We introduce some notations first. Denote

$$W = \begin{bmatrix} W_{\hat{\mathbb{A}}\hat{\mathbb{A}}} & W_{\hat{\mathbb{A}}\mathbb{N}} \\ W_{\mathbb{N}\hat{\mathbb{A}}} & W_{\mathbb{N}\mathbb{N}} \end{bmatrix}.$$

Let $\mathbf{u}_{\hat{\mathbb{A}}}$ and $\mathbf{u}_{\mathbb{N}}$ be the two vectors corresponding to the influences on $\hat{\mathbb{A}}$ and $\mathbb{N}$, respectively. Then (6) becomes

$$D_{\mathbb{N}\mathbb{N}} \mathbf{u}_{\mathbb{N}} = W_{\mathbb{N}\hat{\mathbb{A}}} \mathbf{u}_{\hat{\mathbb{A}}} + W_{\mathbb{N}\mathbb{N}} \mathbf{u}_{\mathbb{N}}, \tag{7}$$

where $D_{\mathbb{N}\mathbb{N}}$ is the diagonal matrix corresponding to degrees of nodes in $\mathbb{N}$.

Below we will show that $\Omega(\mathbb{A}) = \sum_{i \in \mathbb{N}} u_{\mathbb{A}}(i)$ is submodular. Since any non-negative linear combination of submodular functions is also submodular, it suffices to show $u_{\mathbb{A}}(i)$ is submodular w.r.t. $\mathbb{A}$ for any $i \in \mathbb{N}$.

PROPOSITION 1. *The matrix $L_{\mathbb{N}\mathbb{N}} := D_{\mathbb{N}\mathbb{N}} - W_{\mathbb{N}\mathbb{N}}$ is positive definite and $L_{\mathbb{N}\mathbb{N}}^{-1}$ is non-negative.*

PROOF. Denote $D_{\mathbb{N}} = \text{diag}(W_{\mathbb{N}\mathbb{N}}\mathbf{1})$ where $\mathbf{1}$ is a vector of one of appropriate size. Then $\hat{D} = D_{\mathbb{N}\mathbb{N}} - D_{\mathbb{N}}$ is a diagonal matrix whose every diagonal element is no less than a. Here a denotes the weight between the sink node and each of the other nodes. So $L_{\mathbb{N}\mathbb{N}} = \hat{D} + L_{\mathbb{N}}$ where $L_{\mathbb{N}} := D_{\mathbb{N}} - W_{\mathbb{N}\mathbb{N}}$ is known to be positive semi-definite [5]. Thus $L_{\mathbb{NN}}$ is positive definite.

Note that to show $L_{\mathbb{NN}}^{-1}$ is non-negative is equivalent to showing $L := D_{\mathbb{NN}}^{1/2} L_{\mathbb{NN}}^{-1} D_{\mathbb{NN}}^{1/2}$ is non-negative. However, $L = (I-C)^{-1}$ where $C = D_{\mathbb{NN}}^{-1/2} W_{\mathbb{NN}} D_{\mathbb{NN}}^{-1/2}$ is a non-negative matrix whose eigenvalues are of magnitude less than 1[2]. Thus $L = \sum_{\ell=0}^{\infty} C^{\ell}$ is non-negative since each component in the summation is non-negative. □

PROPOSITION 2. *$u_{\mathbb{A}}(i) = 0$ if $\mathbb{A} = \emptyset$.*

PROOF. Since $\mathbb{A} = \emptyset$, we have $\hat{\mathbb{A}} = \mathbb{A} \cup s = \{s\}$. So $\mathbf{u}_{\hat{\mathbb{A}}} = 0$. By (7), $L_{\mathbb{NN}}\mathbf{u}_{\mathbb{N}} = \mathbf{0}$ which yields $\mathbf{u}_{\mathbb{N}} = \mathbf{0}$ since $L_{\mathbb{NN}}$ is invertible (Proposition 1). □

PROPOSITION 3. *$u_{\mathbb{A}}(i)$ is non-decreasing.*

PROOF. To show $u_{\mathbb{A}}(i)$ is non-decreasing is to show $u_{\mathbb{A}}(i) \le u_{\mathbb{A}\cup e}(i)$ where $e \in \mathbb{N}$. Denote $\hat{N} = \mathbb{N} \setminus \{e\}$, and write $\mathbf{u} = [\mathbf{u}_{\hat{\mathbb{A}}}^{\top}, u_e, \mathbf{u}_{\hat{\mathbb{N}}}^{\top}]^{\top}$ and

$$W = \begin{bmatrix} W_{\hat{\mathbb{A}}\hat{\mathbb{A}}} & W_{\hat{\mathbb{A}}e} & W_{\hat{\mathbb{A}}\hat{\mathbb{N}}} \\ W_{e\hat{\mathbb{A}}} & W_{ee} & W_{e\hat{\mathbb{N}}} \\ W_{\hat{\mathbb{N}}\hat{\mathbb{A}}} & W_{\hat{\mathbb{N}}e} & W_{\hat{\mathbb{N}}\hat{\mathbb{N}}} \end{bmatrix}$$

When only A is selected, we have

$$D_{\hat{\mathbb{N}}\hat{\mathbb{N}}}\mathbf{u}_{\hat{\mathbb{N}}} = W_{\hat{\mathbb{N}}\hat{\mathbb{A}}}\mathbf{u}_{\hat{\mathbb{A}}} + W_{\hat{\mathbb{N}}e}u_e + W_{\hat{\mathbb{N}}\hat{\mathbb{N}}}\mathbf{u}_{\hat{\mathbb{N}}}.$$

When both $\mathbb{A}$ and e are selected, we have

$$D_{\hat{\mathbb{N}}\hat{\mathbb{N}}}\mathbf{u}'_{\hat{\mathbb{N}}} = W_{\hat{\mathbb{N}}\hat{\mathbb{A}}}\mathbf{u}_{\hat{\mathbb{A}}} + W_{\hat{\mathbb{N}}e}1_e + W_{\hat{\mathbb{N}}\hat{\mathbb{N}}}\mathbf{u}'_{\hat{\mathbb{N}}}.$$

Thus

$$(D_{\hat{\mathbb{N}}\hat{\mathbb{N}}} - W_{\hat{\mathbb{N}}\hat{\mathbb{N}}})(\mathbf{u}'_{\hat{\mathbb{N}}\hat{\mathbb{N}}} - \mathbf{u}_{\hat{\mathbb{N}}}) = W_{\hat{\mathbb{N}}e}(1_e - u_e),$$

yielding

$$(\mathbf{u}'_{\hat{\mathbb{N}}\hat{\mathbb{N}}} - \mathbf{u}_{\hat{\mathbb{N}}}) = (D_{\hat{\mathbb{N}}\hat{\mathbb{N}}} - W_{\hat{\mathbb{N}}\hat{\mathbb{N}}})^{-1} W_{\hat{\mathbb{N}}e}(1_e - u_e), \quad (8)$$

which is non-negative since $(D_{\hat{\mathbb{N}}\hat{\mathbb{N}}} - W_{\hat{\mathbb{N}}\hat{\mathbb{N}}})^{-1}$ is non-negative (Proposition 1) and $u_e \le 1$ [40]. □

PROPOSITION 4. *$u_{\mathbb{A}}(i)$ is submodular.*

PROOF. To show $u_{\mathbb{A}}(i)$ is submodular is to show that for any $\hat{\mathbb{B}} \subseteq \mathbb{B} \subseteq \mathbb{V}$, the following inequality holds

$$u_{\hat{\mathbb{B}}\cup\{e\}}(i) - u_{\hat{\mathbb{B}}}(i) \ge u_{\mathbb{B}\cup\{e\}}(i) - u_{\mathbb{B}}(i). \quad (9)$$

By (8), $\delta_{\hat{\mathbb{N}}} := \mathbf{u}'_{\hat{\mathbb{N}}} - \mathbf{u}_{\hat{\mathbb{N}}}$ decreases (component-wisely) as u_e is larger (i.e., more nodes are selected), which confirms (9). □

PROPOSITION 5. *$\Omega(\mathbb{A}) = \sum_{i\in\mathbb{N}} u_{\mathbb{A}}(i)$ is submodular.*

PROOF. This is true because any non-negative linear combination of submodular functions is also submodular [18]. □

Based on the above development, we are in a position to employ Nemhauser et al.'s celebrated result on the maximization of submodular functions [28], which is stated as follows:

PROPOSITION 6. *If h is submodular, nondecreasing, and $h(\emptyset) = 0$, then the greedy algorithm finds a set $\mathbb{A}$ such that $h(\mathbb{A}) \ge (1 - \frac{1}{c}) \max_{|\mathbb{B}|\le m} h(\mathbb{B})$ where $c \sim 2.718$ is the natural logarithm base.*

[2]This can be seen by noting C is similar to $\hat{C} := D_{\mathbb{NN}}^{-1/2} C D_{\mathbb{NN}}^{1/2} = D_{\mathbb{NN}}^{-1} W_{\mathbb{NN}}$ while the sum of each row in $\hat{C}$ is less than 1 [11].

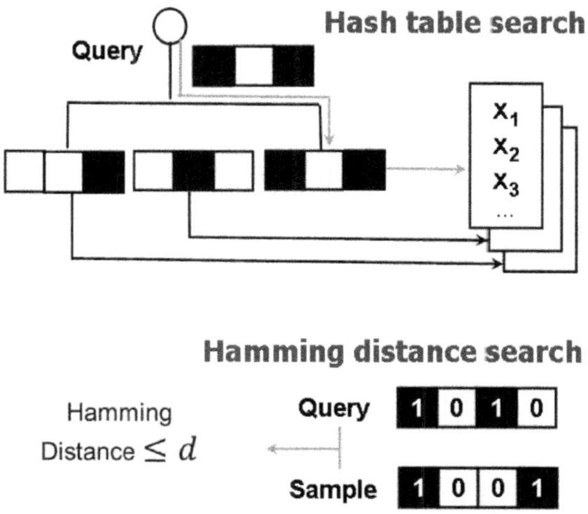

Figure 2: Comparing the difference between the searching methods using hash table and Hamming distance.

Since our objective $\Omega(\mathbb{A})$ for the hash function selection problem is submodular, we can obtain a nearly optimal combination of hash codes by a greedy algorithm. We start from an empty set $\mathbb{A}_0 := \emptyset$ and iteratively adds a code y to $\mathbb{A}_i$ that maximizes the increase of influence of Ω. Specifically, we select the node y_{i+1} in step $i+1$ using the following criterion

$$y_{i+1} = \arg\max_{y\in\mathbb{N}_i} \Omega(\mathbb{A}_i \cup \{y\}) - \Omega(\mathbb{A}_i) \quad (10)$$

where $\mathbb{A}_i$ denotes the set of nodes selected in the previous i steps and $\mathbb{N}_i$ denotes the remaining nodes (the sink node s is excluded).

4.2 Implementation

In this subsection, we discuss several important issues in implementing the submodular video hashing: how to build hash tables and how to measure the similarity between two hash codes.

Hash Tables: A lot of previous studies [34] [31] employ the Hamming distance of binary codes to approximate the neighborhood structure in Euclidean space. However, there are two shortcomings of computing Hamming distance. First, when the dataset is large, computing the pairwise Hamming distance is still expensive and requires a lot of storage. Moreover, when the length of hashing codes grows high, the Hamming approximation will become less precise and the Hamming ball algorithm will be ineffective [10]. These problems will become more serious when multiple hash codes are involved for video indexing. In this paper, we do not compute the hamming distance between query and samples in the datasets. On the contrary, we use hash tables to find nearest neighbors. Hash tables, which are in principle similar with inverted index [41], build a series of bucket containing the indices of the documents with the same hash code. Given a query, we can find the bucket corresponding hash codes in near constant time, and return all the documents in the bucket as the retrieval results. Figure 2 compares the different searching methods using hash table and hamming distance. It is easy to see that searching based on

Hamming distance means computing the pairwise distance between queries and samples in the database, and hence the computational complexity increases with the growing number of samples and length of the hash codes. On the other hand, searching with hash tables does not compute the pairwise distance and is scalable to large-scale data, which is especially useful for video retrieval. The cost of our efficient search lies in the efforts of building hash tables and overlooking those hash codes which are different from the query. However, such cost is acceptable for our retrieval systems. The hash tables can be built once and used for ever, and we employ multiple hash codes to catch the similarity in different feature descriptions.

Hash Functions: The structure of hash table is flexible enough to accommodate various hash codes. There have been a lot of studies of designing hash function and generating hash codes. This paper tries two types of popular hash functions: random projection [8] and spectral hashing [34]. The random projection method generates some random vectors, and computes the inner project of a random vector and the feature vectors which are thresholding to binary variables. To remove the affects of unorganized data, we choose the threshold as randomly sampling from the data. The other method, spectral hashing, develops the hashing function by minimizing the weighted sum of Hamming distance on graph Laplacian. Weiss et al. showed that spectral hashing can be obtained by evaluating small eigenvalues in PCA direction [34]. In the original spectral hashing algorithm, the authors compute the Hamming distance between query and other hash codes. In this paper, we employ hash tables for the retrieval task without computing the Hamming distance.

Similarity between Hash Functions: How to measure the similarity between hash codes is a crucial question. We first consider the scenario of unsupervised learning. Suppose there are two hash function h_i and h_j. Given a query q, we can retrieve its similar videos $\mathbb{R}_i(q)$ and $\mathbb{R}_j(q)$ which share the same hash code using i and j, respectively. We can explore whether the two hash functions are similar by examining how much overlapping $\mathbb{R}_i(q)$ and $\mathbb{R}_j(q)$ enjoy. If $\mathbb{R}_i(q)$ and $\mathbb{R}_j(q)$ are similar, we can expect the two hash functions are similar. Otherwise we expect the hash functions are different from each other. To measure the overlapping of retrieval results we employ the Jaccard index

$$\gamma_{ij}(q) = \frac{|\mathbb{R}_i(q) \cap \mathbb{R}_j(q)|}{|\mathbb{R}_i(q) \cup \mathbb{R}_j(q)|}.$$

By averaging the Jaccard index scores over a number of queries, we get the similarity between two codes as

$$w_{ij} = E_q\left[\gamma_{ij}(q)\right], \tag{11}$$

where E_q denotes the expectation over all queries.

In addition to unsupervised modeling, it is often interesting to consider the semi-supervised scenario where part of the videos are labeled. Suppose $\mathbb{T}_i(q)$ and $\mathbb{T}_j(q)$ are two sets with labeled samples, we consider the Jaccard index of labeled samples

$$\delta_{ij}(q) = \frac{|\mathbb{T}_i(q) \cap \mathbb{T}_j(q)|}{|\mathbb{T}_i(q) \cup \mathbb{T}_j(q)|}, \tag{12}$$

and the similarity is measured by

$$w_{ij} = E_q\left[\alpha\gamma_{ij}(q) + (1-\alpha)\delta_{ij}(q)\right]. \tag{13}$$

Algorithm 2 Submodular Video Hashing

Stage I: Video Pooling
Set the set of hash code $\mathbb{V} = \emptyset$.
for every feature f **do**
  create C video pooling component using feature f.
  for every component $k = 1$ to C **do**
    generate a hashing function using component f^k.
    build a hashing table where each bucket store video names corresponding to the same hash code.
    add the hash code to the set $\mathbb{V} = \mathbb{V} \cup \{f^k\}$.
  end for
end for
Stage II: Submodular Code Selection
Build a graph with $|\mathbb{V}|$ nodes corresponding to all possible hash codes.
Measure the similarity between each pair of the codes.
Select m hash codes in a greedy way using eq. (10). The set of selected hash codes is denoted as $\mathbb{A}$.
Stage III: Video Retrieval
for every query q **do**
  Initialize the retrieve set as $\mathbb{R} = \emptyset$.
  for code m in $\mathbb{A}$ **do**
    $\mathbb{R} = \mathbb{R} \cup \{$samples in the same bucket of q using code $m\}$.
  end for
end for
Output: Return $\mathbb{R}$ as the retrieved videos.

Note here α is the weighting factor to balance the labeled and unlabeled information.

So far we have discussed the important issues in implementing the submodular video hashing. The overall video indexing algorithm is described in Algorithm 2.

4.3 Analysis

Diversified Ranking of Hash Functions: The goal of our hash function selection is to select representative hash codes to reduce redundancy while maintaining their diversity. Intuitively, in order to maximize the code influence, the selected codes should be densely connected to other codes with good similarity. Simultaneously, the selected codes should be sufficiently distant from each other to have a broad and balanced coverage of the search. Once a node is selected, the marginal gains of including its neighbors largely drop because they have been well represented by the selected node. To illustrate this, we employ a toy example to illustrate our code selection method. As shown in Figure 3, there are five hash codes, and each code corresponds to a set of retrieval result for a given query. For the ease of clearness, in this toy example we measure hash code similarity based on only a single query. In practice we randomly select 100 queries and compute the average of the Jaccard scores. We compute similarity between these codes using Jaccard index score, and apply our submodular code selection method on this toy data. The results show that our greedy method first selects hash code 1 and then code 4. We also plot the corresponding nodes with their similarity relationship for intuitive observation.

Computational Complexity: By combining multiple hash tables, our system can retrieve large-scale video dataset very efficiently. Suppose there are N videos and $|\mathbb{A}|$ hash codes, each hash code corresponds to b bits hash function. Given a query, the computational complexity of our sys-

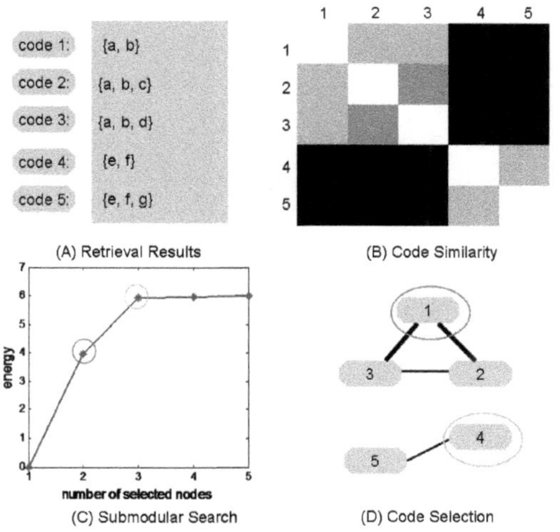

Figure 3: Toy data: representative hash function selection and diversified ranking.

tem is $O(|\mathbb{A}|)$, while the complexity of Hamming distance search is $O(bN|\mathbb{A}|)$. To validate the analysis, we generate a synthetic dataset with 1,000,000 randomly generated binary hash codes, and another 100 codes as queries. We compare different code length: 8 bits, 16 bits and 32 bits. For each code length, we compare the speeds using Hamming distance search and hash tables. Note that the hamming distance is computed efficiently using fast bit XOR operation with the help of look up table so that it has been used in quite a number of studies [33] [32]. However, as Figure 4 shows, computing Hamming distances even with the fast X-OR operation is still much less efficient than our hash table method.

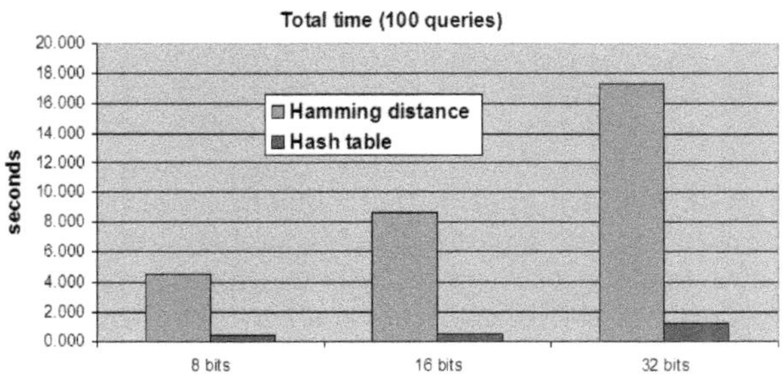

Figure 4: Comparing the speed of Hamming distance search and hash table search.

5. EXPERIMENTS

In recent years, there has been a proliferation of Web-shared videos, with about 48 hours of video uploaded on Youtube every minute, and over 700 billion videos watched in 2010. The large amount of online videos calls for efficient ways to organize and retrieve methods for online video sharing communities. However, those online videos are difficult to model since most of them are free of editing, accompanied with non-professional recording and variety of illumination, camera motion, and cluttered background.

In our experiments, we select two datasets most similar to real world online videos:

- TRECVID Multimedia Event Detection (MED 2011) dataset is the largest annotated dataset specifically designed to model complex video events. There are about 1570 hours of clips in the Event-Kit and Development collections. The video duration is similar to YouTube videos, and the average duration is about 2 to 3 minutes. The evaluation of MED is separated in two test sets: the mid size dryrun evaluation and the large final evaluation set. We report results on both dry run and final evaluation sets respectively.

- Columbia Consumer Video (CCV) dataset [14] contains 9,317 YouTube videos over 20 semantic categories. Jiang et al. [14] used Amazon MTurk platform to perform manual annotation. The database was collected with extra care to ensure relevance to consumers' interest and originality of video content without post-editing. Such videos typically have very little textual annotation and thus can benefit from the development of automatic content analysis techniques.

Experiments on both datasets are conducted on a computer with quad-core 2.33 Intel Xeon CPU and 16G RAM. All the experiments use only one thread and have the potential of further speeding up using multiple threads.

A practical question in submodular video hashing is to select the number of video components and the number of features. We use C to represent the number of components as well as the number of scenes. In traditional scene recognition, Fei-Fei and Perona [7] employed 13 scenes in their experiment, which is later enlarged to 15 scenes by Lazebnik *et al.* [19]. Following their research, we choose the number of video component as $C = 16$, although our method can deal with any number of components.

Another important question is to model the correlation between hash codes. In Section 4.2 we describe retrieval similarity measures in both unsupervised and supervised learning. We apply the unsupervised measure for the MED dataset and the semi-supervised measure for CCV dataset. Since each video in the CCV dataset is assigned a label from 20 semantic categories, we evaluate retrieval performance for all categories. Note that since many of the videos in MED dataset have no labels, further effort is needed to assess the retrieval performance.

5.1 Results on MED datasets

The dataset of MED 2011 is composed of dryrun evaluation stage and final evaluation stage. In the dryrun evaluation, 5 events are considered: *attempting a board trick, feeding an animal, landing a fish, wedding ceremony, working on a woodworking project.* The final evaluation stage, on the other hand, considers 10 new events: *birthday party, changing a vehicle tire, flash mob gathering, getting a vehicle unstuck, grooming an animal, making a sandwich, parade, parkour, repairing an appliance,* and *working on a sewing project.* In addition to these 15 events, there are a lot of videos which are not associated with any event. The public dataset contains labels for more than 13K video clips.

Since the dryrun evaluation is of a relatively small scale, we utilize several low-level features to test their effectiveness. We explore the following features: edge histogram (edge-

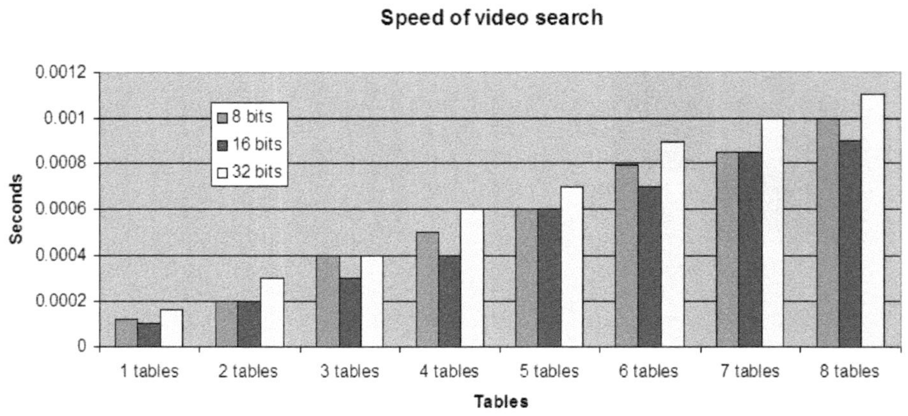

Figure 5: Speed of video retrieval on MED final evaluation dataset.

hist), linear binary pattern (LBP), color histogram (colorhist) and SIFT histogram (SIFT). We extract video frame feature and compute 16 video components for every feature. Our method represents every video component with a hashing function and select a number of hash tables using the submodular search approach in Section 4. We use two types of hashing functions: random projection (RP) and spectral hashing (SH).

To measure the performance of our hashing method, we use every video in the five event categories as query and check how many videos in the retrieved results with the same event category as the recall for the query. Since more hash tables call for more retrieve results, we compare the number of recall subject to different number of hash tables. We retrieve the videos for every query and compute the average of the recalls.

To validate the success of our submodular hashing, we compare its performance of classical hashing methods. Following the previous work [35], we compute a video signature by accumulating all the key-frames in the video using different features (edgehist, LBP, colorhist, dense SIFT). To make a fair comparison, we employ random projections to construct the same number of hash tables, and compare the recalled samples with our submodular hashing techniques. The results in Figure 6 show that our submodular hashing method is significantly better, This confirms the crucial benefit of employing multiple scene components for video representation and the submodular selection strategy for hash table construction The results also show that the performance of low-level features such as LBP and color histogram are inferior than SIFT histogram, which motivate us to focus on powerful features like SIFT and its variants in the final run.

After we finish the dryrun evaluation, we also apply the proposed method on the final evaluation dataset. Since the final submission is larger, it contains more diversified contents and poses harder challenging for video hashing. We select several powerful features: dense SIFT, sparse SIFT, and a new semantic concept feature named 780 dimensional model vectors. Our semantic model vector is an intermediate level semantic representation, by evaluating 780 concept classifiers for each frames. The 780 classifiers are trained separately using thousands of labeled web photos. A number of recent research studies [27] [22] show that similar semantic features are complementary to low-level features and can be useful in many retrieval and annotation tasks. As shown in Figure 7, semantic feature vectors work better than SIFT features for video retrieval, however, our submodular hash methods still clearly boost the performance over these features. The results also show that random projection works better than spectral hashing, which is probably because the objective function of spectral hashing applies to the hamming distances between all the samples, of which a large proportion has been ignored in our hash table structure. Despite that, the contributions of the video component and submodular selection are still consistent in both cases.

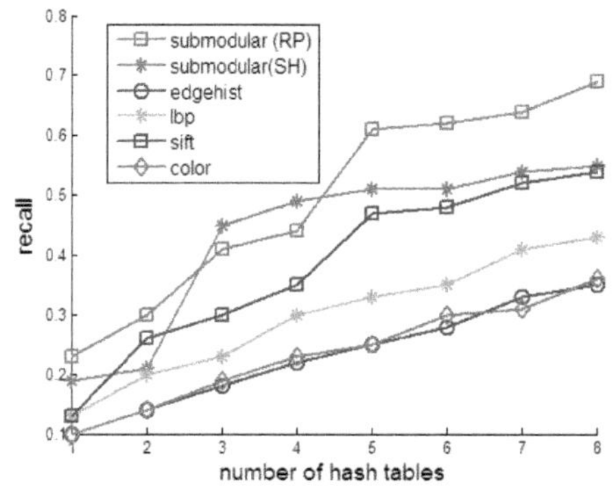

Figure 6: Comparing the performance on MED Dryrun dataset.

In practice, a big advantage of our submodular video hashing lies in the speed even in large-scale dataset. Figure 5 compares the speed of our hash table based method and hamming distance based searching methods on MED final evaluation dataset. These experiments are evaluated on a windows 64bit workstation with 2.33G CPU. The results show that although the search speed decreases with more hash tables, we can still finish the retrieval in about 0.001 seconds for each query even with 8 hash tables.

5.2 Results on CCV dataset

The CCV dataset hosts 9.2K video clips, where a video corresponds one of the 20 events: *basketball*, *baseball*, *soccer*, *ice skating*, *skiing*, *swimming*, *biking*, *cate*, *dog*, *bird*,

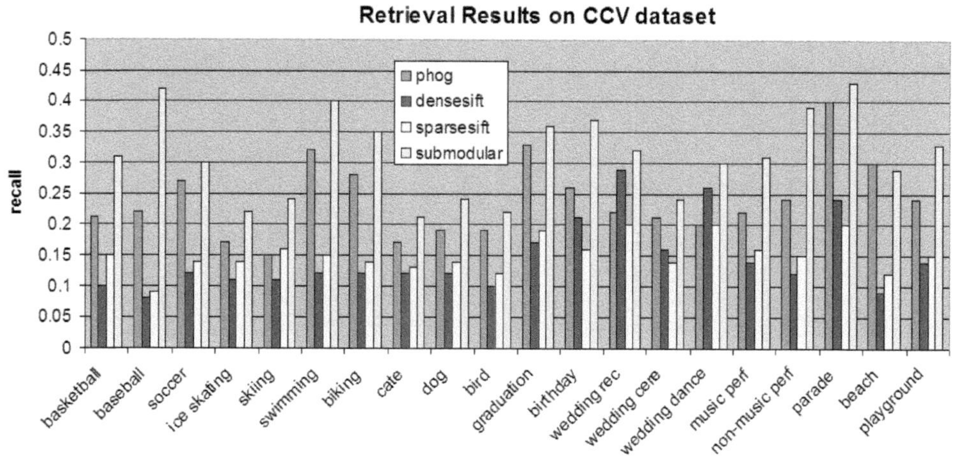

Figure 8: Video retrieval performance on CCV dataset.

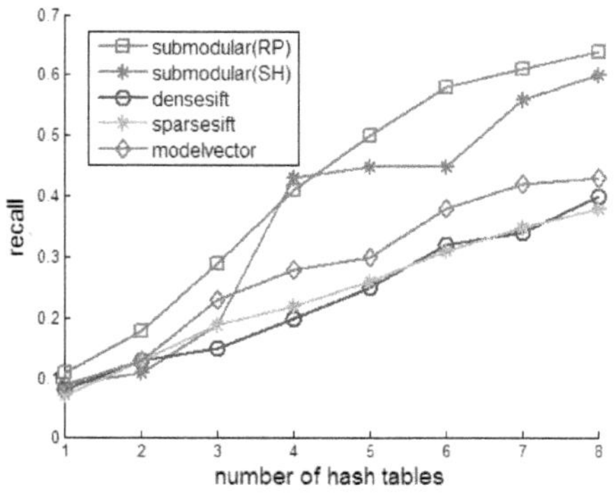

Figure 7: Comparing the performance on MED Final dataset.

graduation, birthday, wedding reception, wedding ceremony, wedding dance, music performance, non-music performance, parade, beach, playground. Every category contains 200-800 positive videos. Since there are rich amount of positive samples, we can employ eq. (13) to measure the code similarity for each category with the parameter $\alpha = 0.8$. In this dataset, we employ three features including sparse sift, dense sift, and pyramid histogram of oriented gradients (PHOG). Since the similarity of different hash codes depends on the category label, we also compare the retrieval performance for each category. To make a fair comparison, we report the results with four hash tables. The average recall is used to measure retrieval accuracy as we did on the MED dataset. As shown in Figure 8, our submodularity based video hashing is consistently better than hashing accumulated video features.

6. CONCLUSIONS

This paper develops a novel framework for large-scale video retrieval. We view a video as a collections of scene components and represent them with multiple hash codes. We cast the code selection problem as an influence maximization problem where the influence of the selected nodes can be maximally propagated to the rest of the nodes in the graph. We prove that the code selection is submodular and can be solved by a greedy method with guaranteed lowerbound. Benefiting from the three key components (video pooling, submodular selection, and multiple hash tables), our video hashing framework works efficiently for large-scale video retrieval and obtains superior performance on TRECVID MED and Columbia CCV datasets.

We plan to extend our work in the following directions:

- Heterogenous feature fusion for video retrieval. One advantage of our submodular video hashing method is that it can easily accommodate various features. We plan to generalize this approach to multi-modal features, including not only visual but also audio features and tag features.
- Personalized video retrieval. It is also attractive to leverage users' interests at individual levels. Our method provides a flexible way to capture interesting scenes or contents according to user interests and has the potential to be combined with more complex user profile information for improved retrieval.

Acknowledgement

This research is supported by Intelligence Advanced Research Projects Activity (IARPA) via Department of Interior National Busyness Center contract number D11PC20070. The U.S. government is authorized to reproduce and distribute reprints for Governmental purposes notwithstanding any copyright thereon. Disclaimer: The views and conclusions contained herein are those of the authors and should not be interpreted as necessarily representing the official policies or endorsements, either expressed or implied, of IARPA, DoI/NBC, or the U.S. Government.

7. REFERENCES

[1] Y. Boureau, N. Le Roux, F. Bach, J. Ponce, and Y. LeCun. Ask the locals: multi-way local pooling for image recognition. In *ICCV*, 2011.

[2] Y.-L. Boureau, F. Bach, Y. LeCun, and J. Ponce. Learning mid-level features for recognition. In *CVPR*, 2010.

[3] S. Brin and L. Page. The anatomy of a large-scale hypertextual web search engine. *Computer networks and ISDN systems*, 30(1-7):107–117, 1998.
[4] L. Cao, Y. Mu, S.-F. Chang, A. Natsev, G. Hua, and J. R. Smith. Scene aligned pooling for complex video recognition. In *ECCV*, 2012.
[5] F. Chung. *Spectral graph theory*. Number 92. Amer Mathematical Society, 1997.
[6] A. Das and D. Kempe. Submodular meets spectral: Greedy algorithms for subset selection, sparse approximation and dictionary selection. *ICML*, 2011.
[7] L. Fei-Fei and P. Perona. A bayesian hierarchy model for learning natural scene categories. In *CVPR*, 2005.
[8] A. Gionis, P. Indyk, and R. Motwani. Similarity search in high dimensions via hashing. In *VLDB*, pages 518–529, 1999.
[9] J. He, S. Kumar, and S.-F. Chang. On the difficulty of nearest neighbor search. In *ICML*, 2012.
[10] J. He, W. Liu, and S. Chang. Scalable similarity search with optimized kernel hashing. In *SIGKDD*, pages 1129–1138, 2010.
[11] R. Horn and C. Johnson. *Matrix analysis*. Cambridge Univ Pr, 1990.
[12] Z. Huang, H. Shen, J. Shao, X. Zhou, and B. Cui. Bounded coordinate system indexing for real-time video clip search. *ACM Transactions on Information Systems*, 27(3):17, 2009.
[13] G. Jeh and J. Widom. Simrank: a measure of structural-context similarity. In *ACM SIGKDD*, pages 538–543, 2002.
[14] Y.-G. Jiang, G. Ye, S.-F. Chang, D. Ellis, and A. C. Loui. Consumer video understanding: A benchmark database and an evaluation of human and machine performance. In *ICMR*, 2011.
[15] A. Karpenko and P. Aarabi. Tiny videos: A large dataset for nonparametric video retrieval and frame classification. *TPAMI*, 33(3):618–630, 2011.
[16] Y. Ke, R. Sukthankar, and L. Huston. An efficient parts-based near-duplicate and sub-image retrieval system. In *ACM Multimedia*, pages 869–876, 2004.
[17] G. Kim, E. Xing, L. Fei-Fei, and T. Kanade. Distributed cosegmentation via submodular optimization on anisotropic diffusion. In *ICCV*, pages 169–176, 2011.
[18] A. Krause and C. Guestrin. Beyond convexity: Submodularity in machine learning. *ICML Tutorials*, 2008.
[19] S. Lazebnik, C. Schmid, and J. Ponce. Beyond bags of features: Spatial pyramid matching for recognizing natural scene categories. In *CVPR*, volume 2, pages 2169–2178, 2006.
[20] Y. LeCun, L. Bottou, Y. Bengio, and P. Haffner. Gradient-based learning applied to document recognition. *Proceedings of the IEEE*, 86(11):2278–2324, 1998.
[21] J. Leskovec, A. Krause, C. Guestrin, C. Faloutsos, J. VanBriesen, and N. Glance. Cost-effective outbreak detection in networks. *KDD*, 2007.
[22] L.-J. Li, H. Su, E. P. Xing, and L. Fei-Fei. Object bank: A high-level image representation for scene classification and semantic feature sparsification. In *NIPS*, 2010.
[23] Z. Li, H. Ning, L. Cao, T. Zhang, Y. Gong, and T. Huang. Learning to search efficiently in high dimensions. *NIPS*, 24, 2011.
[24] J. Liu, Z. Huang, H. Shen, and B. Cui. Correlation-based retrieval for heavily changed near-duplicate videos. *ACM Transactions on Information Systems*, 29(4):21, 2011.
[25] W. Liu, J. Wang, R. Ji, Y.-G. Jiang, and S.-F. Chang. Supervised hashing with kernels. CVPR, 2012.
[26] W. Liu, J. Wang, S. Kumar, and S.-F. Chang. Hashing with graphs. ICML, 2011.
[27] M. Merler, L. X. Bert Huang, G. Hua, and A. Natsev. Semantic model vectors for complex video event recognition. *IEEE Transactions on Multimedia*, 2011.
[28] G. L. Nemhauser, L. A. Wolsey, and M. L. Fisher. An analysis of approximations for maximizing submodular set functions. *Mathematical Programming*, 14:265–294, 1978.
[29] A. Oliva and A. Torralba. Modeling the shape of the scene: a holistic representation of the spatial envelope. *IJCV*, 2001.
[30] B. Russell, A. Torralba, C. Liu, R. Fergus, and W. T. Freeman. Object recognition by scene alignment. In *NIPS*, 2007.
[31] G. Shakhnarovich, P. Viola, and T. Darrell. Fast pose estimation with parameter-sensitive hashing. In *ICCV*, pages 750–757, 2003.
[32] J. Song, Y. Yang, Z. Huang, H. Shen, and R. Hong. Multiple feature hashing for real-time large scale near-duplicate video retrieval. In *ACM Multimedia*, pages 423–432, 2011.
[33] A. Torralba, R. Fergus, and Y. Weiss. Small codes and large image databases for recognition. In *CVPR*, 2008.
[34] Y. Weiss, A. Torralba, and R. Fergus. Spectral hashing. NIPS, 2008.
[35] X. Wu, A. Hauptmann, and C. Ngo. Practical elimination of near-duplicates from web video search. In *ACM Multimedia*, pages 218–227, 2007.
[36] J. Xiao, J. Haysy, K. A. Ehinger, A. Oliva, and A. Torralba. Sun database: Large-scale scene recognition from abbey to zoo. In *CVPR*, 2010.
[37] J. Yang, K. Yu, Y. Gong, and T. Huang. Linear pyramid matching using sparse coding for image classification. In *CVPR*, 2009.
[38] D. Zhang, F. Wang, and L. Si. Composite hashing with multiple information sources. In *SIGIR*, pages 225–234, 2011.
[39] X. Zhu. Semi-supervised learning literature survey. 2005.
[40] X. Zhu, Z. Ghahramani, and J. Lafferty. Semi-supervised learning using gaussian fields and harmonic functions. In *ICML*, 2003.
[41] J. Zobel, A. Moffat, and K. Ramamohanarao. Inverted files versus signature files for text indexing. *ACM Transactions on Database Systems*, 23(4):453–490, 1998.

Exploratory Search of Long Surveillance Videos

Greg Castañón and Venkatesh Saligrama
Boston University
Boston, MA, USA
gdc1@bu.edu, srv@bu.edu

André Louis Caron and Pierre-Marc Jodoin
Université de Sherbrooke
Sherbrooke, Quebec, Canada
andre.louis.caron@usherbrooke.ca, pierre-marc.jodoin@usherbrooke.ca

ABSTRACT

We present a fast and flexible content-based retrieval method for surveillance video. Designing a video search robust to uncertain activity duration, high variability in object shapes and scene content is challenging. We propose a two-step approach to video search. First, local features are inserted into an inverted index using locality-sensitive hashing (LSH). Second, we utilize a novel dynamic programming (DP) approach to robustify against temporal distortion, limited obscuration and imperfect queries. DP exploits causality to assemble the local features stored in the index into a video segment which matches the query video. Pre-processing of archival video is performed in real-time, and retrieval speed scales as a function of the number of matches rather than video length. We derive bounds on the rate of false positives, demonstrate the effectiveness of the approach for counting, motion pattern recognition and abandoned object applications using seven challenging video datasets and compare with existing work.[1]

Categories and Subject Descriptors

I.4.8 [**Computing Methodologies**]: Image Processing and Computer Vision—*Scene Analysis*; I.5.4 [**Computing Methodologies**]: Pattern Recognition—*Applications*

General Terms

Algorithms

Keywords

Exploratory search, Video search, Dynamic programming, Surveillance

1. INTRODUCTION

Surveillance video camera networks are increasingly ubiquitous, providing pervasive information gathering capabilities. In many applications, surveillance video archives are used for forensic purposes to gather evidence after the fact. This calls for content-based retrieval of video data matching user defined queries with robustness to clutter and distortion.

Exploratory search [22] is a specialization of information-seeking developed to address such situations. It describes the activity of attempting to obtain information through a combination of querying and collection browsing. Development of exploratory search systems requires addressing two critical aspects: video browsing and content-based retrieval. The focus of this paper is the latter. We present a method for fast content-based retrieval adapted to characteristics of surveillance videos. The most challenging of these are:

1.) Data lifetime: since video is constantly streamed, there is a perpetual renewal of video data. This calls for a model that can be updated incrementally as video data is made available. The model must also scale well with the temporal mass of the video.

2.) Unpredictable queries: the nature of queries depends on the field of view of the camera, the scene itself and the type of events being observed. The system should support queries of different nature that can retrieve both recurrent events such as people entering a store and infrequent events such as abandoned objects and cars performing U-turns.

3.) Unpredictable event duration: events are unstructured. They start anytime, vary in length, and overlap with other events. The system is nonetheless expected to return complete events regardless of their duration and whether or not other events occur simultaneously.

4.) Clutter and occlusions: Tracking and tagging objects in urban videos is challenging due to occlusions and clutter; especially when real-time performance is required.

1.1 Related Work

Previous approaches to image and video-based retrieval are based on summarization and scene understanding. Summarization methods are loosely related to search. They attempt to reduce the video to its relevant sections, typically dividing the video into "shots" [17, 15] by locating and annotating key frames corresponding to scene transitions or an absence of motion. Unfortunately, such scene transitions are infrequent in surveillance video, rendering most summarization approaches unsuitable for exploratory search in complex scenes, the focus of this paper.

Scene-understanding methods have been suggested for exploratory search [10, 19, 25]. These methods in general focus on classifying observed activities in terms of activities learned from a training video. For instance, activities observed in public areas often follow some basic rules (such as traffic lights, highways, building entries, etc), which are learned during the training phase. Common topic modeling techniques include

[1]This research was supported by ONR grant N000141010477, NGA grant HM1582-09-1-0037, NSF grant CCF-0905541, and DHS grant 2008-ST-061- ED0001

MM'12, October 29–November 2, 2012, Nara, Japan.

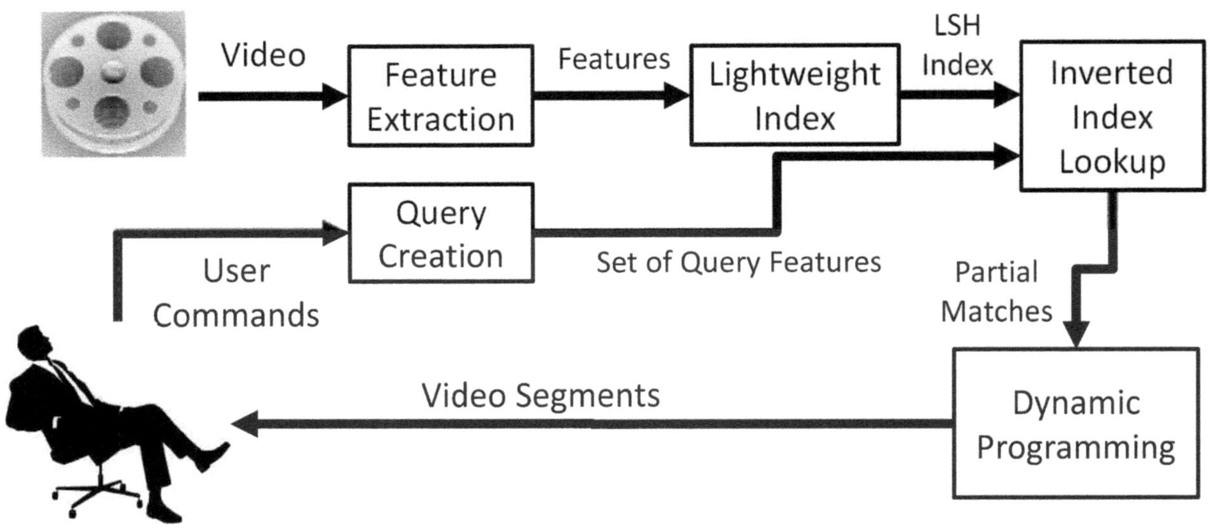

Figure 1: From streaming video, local features for each document are computed and inserted into a fuzzy, lightweight index. A user inputs a query, and partial matches (features which are close to parts of the query) are inserted into a dynamic programming (DP) algorithm. The algorithm extracts the set of video segments which best matches the query.

HMMs [13, 10], Bayesian networks [23], context free grammars [20], and other graphical models [11, 14, 21]. We point out that techniques that require global behavior understanding often rely on tracking [13, 11] while those devoted to isolated action recognition rely on low-level features [7, 26]. The classification stage can then be used to retrieve pre-defined patterns of activity [10]).

Scene understanding techniques which focus on global explanations operate at a competitive disadvantage in search: the preponderance of clutter (requirement four) in surveillance video makes the training step of scene understanding prohibitively difficult. Second, since these techniques often focus on understanding recurrent activities, they are unsuited for retrieving infrequent events - this can be a problem, given that queries are unpredictable (requirement two). Finally, the training step in scene understanding can be prohibitively expensive, violating requirement three, large data lifetimes.

Unlike summarization approaches, we extract a full set of features; this is mandatory, as we have no a-priori knowledge of what query will be asked. Unlike scene understanding techniques, we have no training step; this would be incompatible with the data lifetimes and magnitudes of the corpus. Instead, we develop an approach based on exploiting temporal orders on simple features, which allows us to find arbitrary queries quickly while maintaining low false alarm rates. We demonstrate a substantial improvement over scene-understanding methods such as [23, 10] on a number of datasets in Section 5.

2. OVERVIEW

To address the challenges of exploratory search, we utilize a two-step process that first reduces the problem to the relevant data, and then reasons intelligently over that data. This process is shown in Fig. 1. As data streams in, video is pre-processed to extract relevant features - activity, object size, color, persistence and motion. These low-level features are hashed into a fuzzy, light-weight lookup table by means of LSH [8]. LSH accounts for spatial variability and reduces the search space for a user's query to the set of relevant partial (local) matches.

The second step is a search engine optimization which reasons over the partial matches to produce *full matches*; segments of video which fit the entire query pattern, as opposed to part of it. This optimization operates from the advantageous standpoint of having only to reason over the partial matches, which are the relevant subset of the video. In surveillance video, where a long time can pass without relevant action, this dramatically reduces the workload of the optimization algorithm.

We then present two solutions for finding full matches. The first is a greedy approach which flattens the query in time. The second, a novel dynamic programming (DP) approach, exploits the causal ordering of component actions that makeup a query. DP reasons over the set of partial matches and finds the best full match. We also rigorously establish theoretical guarantees (Theorem 4.1). We show that the number of false positives in a surveillance environment - as actions become more complex – the probability of random actions mimicking them goes to zero.

3. LIGHTWEIGHT INDEX

Surveillance video frequently contains long periods of inactivity and irrelevance. In this section we describe an approach for creating a lightweight index with local features in order to reduce complexity for the search engine.

3.1 Feature extraction

3.1.1 Structure

For the purpose of feature extraction, a video is considered to be a spatio-temporal volume of size $H \times W \times F$ where $H \times W$ is the image size in pixels and F the total number of frames in the video. The video is divided along the temporal axis into contiguous *documents* each containing A frames. As shown in Fig. 2, each frame is divided into tiles of size $B \times B$. An *atom* is formed by grouping the same tile over A frames. These values vary depending on the size of the video - for our videos, we chose B equal to 8 or 16 pixels, and A equal to 15 or 30 frames, depending on frame rate. As the video streams in, features are extracted from each frame. Whenever a document is created, each atom n is assigned a set of features (see Sec. 3.1.2) describing the dynamic content over that region.

We construct a pyramidal structure to robustify our algorithm to

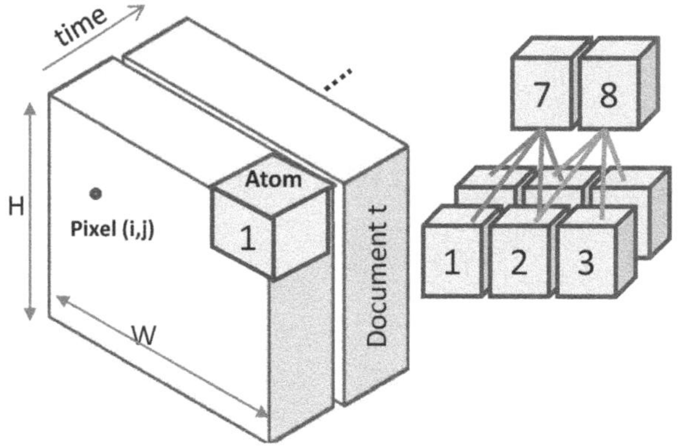

Figure 2: (Left) Given an $W \times H \times F$ video, *documents* are non-overlapping video clips each containing A frames. Each of the frames are divided into *tiles* of size $B \times B$. Tiles form an *atom* when aggregated together over A frames. (Right) Atoms are grouped into two-level trees - every adjacent set of four atoms is aggregated into a parent, forming a set of partially overlapping trees.

location and size variability in detected features. Each element of the pyramid has four children. This structure is made of k-level trees, each containing $M = \sum_{l=1}^{k} l^2$ nodes (Fig. 2). In this approach, a document containing $U \times V$ atoms will be assigned $(U-k+1) \times (V-k+1)$ partially overlapping trees to be indexed. For instance, in Figure 2, we draw a depth two tree on a document which is 2×3 atoms, resulting in two overlapping trees, each containing $M = 5$ nodes.

Each node of a tree is assigned a feature vector obtained by aggregating the feature vector of its children. Let n be a non-leaf node and a, b, c, d its four children. The aggregation process can be formalized as

$$\vec{x}_f^{(i)} = \psi_f\left(\vec{x}_f^{(a)}, \vec{x}_f^{(b)}, \vec{x}_f^{(c)}, \vec{x}_f^{(d)}\right),$$

where ψ_f is an aggregation operator for feature f. Sec. 3.1.2 presents more details on the aggregation operator. Given that several features are extracted for each atom, aggregating a group of $k \times k$ atoms results in a set of feature trees $\{\text{tree}_f\}$, one for each feature f. Given that a k-level tree contains M nodes, each tree_f contains a list of M feature instances, namely $\text{tree}_f = \left\{\vec{x}_f^{(i)}\right\}$ where i stands for the ith node in the tree.

3.1.2 Features

As reported in the literature [12, 18, 24], atom features can be of any kind such as color, object shape, object motion, tracks, etc. We chose to use local processing due to the computational efficiency which makes it better suited to the constant data renewal constraint and real-time feature extraction. Because our focus is surveillance video, we assume a stable camera. To be effective on a moving or zooming camera, motion and zoom compensation would have to be applied in advance of feature extraction. Feature extraction computes a single value for each atom, which is aggregated into feature trees. Our method uses the following five features:

(1) Activity x_a: Activity is detected using a basic background subtraction method [5]. The initial background is estimated using a median of the first 500 frames. Then, the background is updated using the running average method. At the leaf level, x_a contains the proportion of active pixels within the atom. Aggregation for non-leaf nodes in feature trees, ψ_a, is the mean of the four children.
(2) Object Size x_s: Objects are detected using connected components analysis of the binary activity mask obtained from background subtraction [5]. Object size is the total number of active pixels covered by the connected component. The aggregation operator ψ_s for non-leaf nodes in feature trees is the median of non-zero children. Whenever all four children have a zero object size, the aggregation operator returns zero.
(3) Color $\vec{x}_c$: Color is obtained by computing the quantized histogram over every active pixel in the atom. RGB pixels are then converted to the HSL color space. Hue, saturation and luminance are quantized into 8, 4 and 4 bins respectively. The aggregation operator ψ_c for non-leaf nodes in feature trees is the bin-wise sum of histograms. In order to keep relative track of proportions during aggregation, histograms are not normalized at this stage.
(4) Persistence x_p: Persistence is a detector for newly static objects. It is computed by accumulating the binary activity mask obtained from background subtraction over time. Objects that become idle for a long periods of time thus get a large persistence measure. The aggregation operator ψ_p for non-leaf nodes in feature trees is the maximum of the four children.
(5) Motion $\vec{x}_m$: Motion vectors are extracted using Horn and Schunck's optical flow method [6]. Motion is quantized into 8 directions and an extra "idle" bin is used for flow vectors with low magnitude. $\vec{x}_m$ thus contains a 9-bin motion histogram. The aggregation operator ψ_m for non-leaf nodes in feature trees is a bin-wise sum of histograms. In order to keep relative track of proportions during aggregation, histograms are not normalized at this stage.

As mentioned previously, these motion features are extracted while the video streams in. Whenever a document is created, its atoms are assigned 5 descriptors, namely $\{x_a, x_s, \vec{x}_c, x_p, \vec{x}_m\}$. These descriptors are then assembled to form the 5 feature trees $\{\text{tree}_a\}, \{\text{tree}_s\}, \{\text{tree}_c\}, \{\text{tree}_p\}, \{\text{tree}_m\}$. These feature trees are the basis for the indexing scheme presented in section 3.2. After feature trees are indexed, all extracted feature content is discarded, ensuring a lightweight representation. It is worth noting that these features are intentionally simple. This speeds up feature extraction and indexing while being robust to small distortions because of the coarse nature of the features. While motion can be sensitive to poorly-compensated camera motion or zoom, and color can be sensitive to illumination changes, the other features have been shown to relatively robust to these effects [5]. In addition, we leverage on the dynamic programming in section 4.2.2 to limit false activity detection.

3.2 Indexing & Hashing

When a document is created, features are aggregated into $(U - k+1) \times (V-k+1)$ k-level trees. Each tree is made of 5 feature trees, namely $\{\text{tree}_a\}, \{\text{tree}_s\}, \{\text{tree}_c\}, \{\text{tree}_p\}, \{\text{tree}_m\}$. To index a given feature tree tree_f efficiently, our method uses an inverted index for content retrieval. Inverted index schemes, which map content to a location in a database, are popular in content-based retrieval because they allow extremely fast lookup in very large document databases. For video, the goal is to store the document number t and the spatial position (u, v) in the database based on the content of tree_f. This is done with a mapping function which converts "tree_f" to an entry in the database where (t, u, v) is stored. Two trees with similar contents, therefore, should be mapped to proximate locations in the index; by retrieving all entries which are near a query tree, we can recover the locations in the video of all features trees that are similar.

This mapping and retrieval can be made for which update and lookup exhibit flat performance ($O(1)$ complexity). Because similar content at different times is mapped to the same bin, the time required to find the indices of matching trees does not scale with the length of the video. Obviously, the total retrieval time must scale linearly with the number of matching trees, but this means that the run-time of the retrieval process scales only with the amount of data which is relevant. In videos where the query represents an infrequently-performed action, this optimization yields an immense improvement in runtime.

Hashing: A hash-based inverted index uses a function to map content to an entry in the index. This is done with a hashing function h such that $h : \text{tree}_f \rightarrow j$, where j is a hash table bucket number. Usually, hash functions attempt to distribute content uniformly over the hash space by minimizing the probability of collisions between two non-equal entries:

$$\vec{x} \neq \vec{y} \implies P\{h(\vec{x}) = h(\vec{y})\} \approx 0.$$

However, in a motion feature space, descriptors for two similar events are never exactly equal. Moreover, it is unlikely that a user query can be translated to feature vectors with sufficient accuracy for such a strict hash function.

As a solution, we resort to a locality-sensitive hashing (LSH) [8] technique. LSH is a technique for approximation of nearest-neighbor search. In contrast to most hashing techniques, LSH attempts to cluster similar vectors by maximizing the probability of collisions for descriptors within a certain distance of each other:

$$\vec{x} \approx \vec{y} \implies P\{h(\vec{x}) = h(\vec{y})\} \gg 0.$$

If feature trees are close in Euclidian distance (the element-wise square of the distances between node values in the two trees is small), then the probability of them having the same hash code is high. Because our feature trees contain M real-valued variables, LSH functions can be drawn from the p-stable family:

$$h_{\vec{a},b,r}(\text{tree}_f) = \left\lfloor \frac{\vec{a} \cdot \text{tree}_f + b}{r} \right\rfloor,$$

where $\vec{a}$ is a M-dimensional vector with random components drawn from a stable distribution, b is a random scalar drawn from a stable distribution and r is an application-dependent parameter. Intuitively, $\vec{a}$ represents a random projection, an alignment offset b and a radius r controlling the probability of collision inside the radius.

Indices are built and searched independently for each feature. Thus, the database is made of five indices I_f, one for each feature f. Each index I_f is composed of a set of n hash tables $\{T_{f,i}\}$, $\forall i = 1, \ldots, n$. Each hash table is associated its own hash function $H_{f,i}$ drawn from the p-stable family $h_{\vec{a},b,r}$. The parameter r can be adjusted to relax or sharpen matches. In our implementation, r is fixed for a given feature. The random parameters $\vec{a}$ and b ensure projections from the different hash functions complement each other.

Given a feature tree tree_f with hash code $H_{f,i}(\text{tree}_f) = j$, $T_{f,i}[j, u, v]$ denotes the set of document numbers $\{t\}$ such that feature trees at (t, u, v) have similar content. Lookup in the index I_f consists of taking the union of document numbers returned by lookup in all tables $\{T_{f,i}\}$:

$$I(\text{tree}_f, u, v) = \cup_{i=1}^{n} T_{f,i}\left[H_{f,i}(\text{tree}_f), u, v\right].$$

Fig. 3 illustrates several feature trees partitioned into groups, where trees in the same group have been given the same hashing key. For a given video, we plotted the content of four of the most occupied buckets for the motion feature tree_m. As one can see, the trees associated to similar motion patterns in various parts of the scene have been coherently hashed into similar buckets.

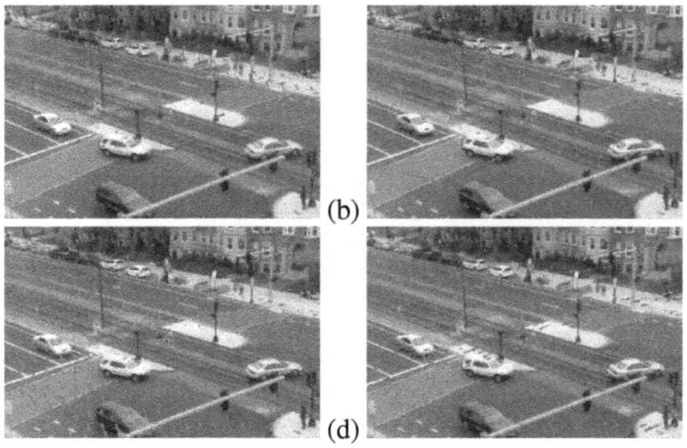

Figure 3: Contents of four buckets of a hash table for the *motion* feature. Arrows size is proportional to the number of hits at the specified location across the entire video. The hash buckets are associated to activity (a) side walk (b) upper side of the street (c) lower side of the street (d) crosswalk.

3.2.1 Data structure

As described previously, the inverted index stores in the same bucket the spatio-temporal position $\{(t, u, v)\}$ of all trees whose content is similar. As shown in Fig. 4, each bucket is a $(U - k + 1) \times (V - k + 1)$ matrix (see Sec. 3.1.1) whose cells contain a list of document numbers $\{t\}$. In that way, having an (u, v) matrix lookup located right after the hashing lookup ensures a retrieval time of $O(1)$.

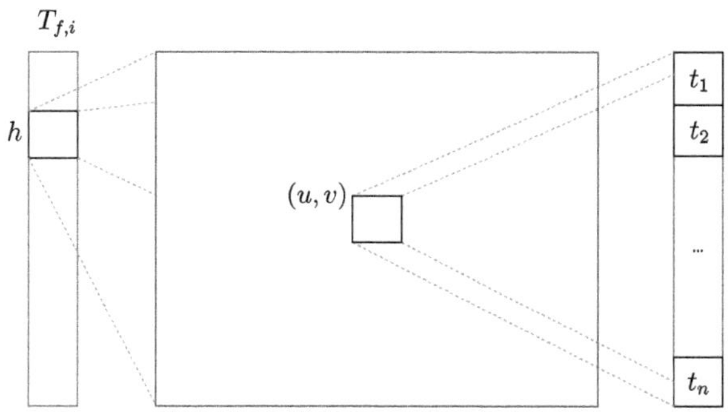

Figure 4: Hash table structure. For a given tree tree_f with $H_{f,i}(\text{tree}_f) = j$, lookup $T_{f,i}[j, u, v]$ is performed in two steps: (1) fetch the bucket at position j and (2) fetch the list of document numbers at position (u, v) in the bucket.

Lightweight Storage: In contrast to approaches relying on a distance metric, such as K-nearest neighbor search, the hash-based index representation does not require storage of feature descriptors. $T_{f,i}$ contains only document numbers $\{t\}$, which are stored in 4-byte variables. Our features, being local and primitive, are dependent on foreground content. As such, both our indexing times and storage scale linearly with the amount of foreground content in the video. This is a useful feature for surveillance video, which can have persistently inactive spaces or times throughout a video. For example, the size of the index for a 5 hour video with an activity rate of 2.5% is only 150kb while the input color video requires almost 7Gb (compressed).

Building Lookup Table: As video streams in, the index for each feature is updated by a simple and fast procedure. After extraction of feature f for document t is completed, the extracted features are grouped into trees, as described in Sec. 3.1. Then, I_f is updated with the mapping $\text{tree}_f \rightarrow (t, u, v)$ for each tree position (u, v)

covering an area with significant activity. This is repeated for each feature f.

4. SEARCH ENGINE

We showed in Sec. 3 how to extract low-level features from a video sequence, bundle them into trees and index them for $O(1)$ content-based retrieval. Here we explain how to use feature index for high-level search.

4.1 Queries

In video search without exemplars, it's essential to provide a straightforward way for a user to input a query. For our purposes, a query is defined as an ordered set of *action components* (for simple queries, a single component frequently suffices), each of which is a set of feature trees. To create a query, the user types in the number of action components, and is then presented with a GUI, shown in Figure 5 containing the first frame of the video to search for each of the action components. The user then selects the type of feature he wishes to search for, and draws the region of interest (ROI) that he wishes to find it in. These regions and the features (directions of motion, in this case) are shown in Fig.8 as green areas and red arrows, respectively.

As an example, to describe a u-turn, the user might describe three action components: one detecting motion approaching an intersection, one detecting motion turning around, and one detecting motion leaving the intersection. Likewise, a man hopping a subway might be represented by somebody approaching the subway, jumping up, and then continuing past the subway.

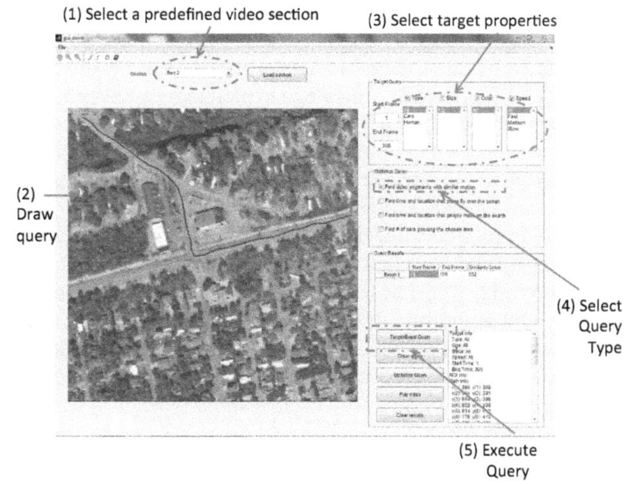

Figure 5: The query creation GUI provides a straightforward way to construct queries. The user draws each action component (shown in blue), and can additionally specify features.

Because our features (activity, size, color, persistence, and motion) are semantically meaningful, this method of input is a relatively accessible way to define a query. After the features and the ROI are selected, a feature tree $tree_f$ is created to represent that action component. Note that this formulation provides the user with a way to produce a complex query vocabulary. A single component could describe a search for "small red stationary objects" or 'large objects moving to the right". While our claims to simplicity are theoretical, they are also supported by anecdotal evidence. People unfamiliar with the system are able to create their own queries in under a minute after a brief explanation of the tools.

After the action component has been input, the set of feature trees is extracted from it using the formulation in Section 3.1. These feature trees is used to query the inverted index of Section 3.2 to produce a set of documents and locations called *partial matches* $M(q)$ that contained similar trees to query q. In the case where the query contains multiple feature trees, the set of matching locations is the intersection of the matches for individual trees. Fig.8 presents 10 different queries with their ROI.

4.2 Full matches

Search in a surveillance video requires more than partial matches. Activities in a video are inherently complex and show significant variability in time duration. For instance, a fast car taking a U-turn will span across fewer documents and generate different motion features than a slow moving car. Also, due to the limited size of a document (typically between 30 to 100 frames), partial matches may only correspond to a portion of the requested event. For example, partial matches in a document t may only correspond to the beginning of a U-turn. The results expected by a user are so-called *full maches*, i.e. video segments $[t, t+\Delta]$ containing one or more documents ($\Delta > 0$). For example, the video segment $R = \{t, t+1, t+2\}$ corresponds to a full U-turn match when documents $t, t+1, t+2$ contain the beginning, the middle and the end of the U-turn. Given a query q and a set of partial matches $M(q)$, a full match starting at time τ is defined as

$$R_{q,\tau}(\Delta) = \{(u,v) | (t,u,v) \in M(q),\ \forall t \in [\tau, \tau+\Delta]\}. \quad (1)$$

Thus, $R_{q,\tau}(\Delta)$ contains the set of distinct coordinates of trees partially matching q in the video segment $[\tau, \tau+\Delta]$.

We propose two algorithms to identify these full matches from the set of partial matches. The first is a greedy optimization procedure based on the total number of partial matches in a document that does not exploit the temporal ordering of a query. The second approach (Sec. 4.2.2), uses dynamic programming to exploit temporal structure of the of a query's action components.

4.2.1 Full matches using a greedy algorithm

The main difficulty in identifying full matches comes with the inherent variability between the query and the target. This includes time-scaling, false detections and other local spatio-temporal deformations. Consequently, we are faced with the problem of finding which documents to fuse into a full match given a set of partial matches. We formulate it in terms of the following optimization problem:

$$\Delta^* = \arg\max_{\Delta>0} v_{q,\tau}(\Delta). \quad (2)$$

where q is the query, τ is a starting point and Δ the length of the retrieved video segment. The value function $v_{q,\tau}(\Delta)$ maps the set of partial matches in the interval $[\tau, \tau+\Delta]$ to some large number when the partial matches fit q well and to a small value when they do not. To determine the optimal length of a video segment starting at time τ we maximize the above expression over Δ.

While many value functions are viable, depending upon user preference, a simple and effective $v_{q,\tau}(\Delta)$ is:

$$v_{q,\tau}(\Delta) = |R_{q,\tau}(\Delta)| - \lambda\tau, \quad (3)$$

where $R_{q,\tau}(\Delta)$ is defined by Eq. (1) and $|R_{q,\tau}(\Delta)|$ is the total number of distinct matching locations found in the interval $[\tau, \tau+\Delta]$. The value function is time-discounted since $R_{q,\tau}(\Delta)$ is increasing in Δ (by definition, $R_{q,\tau}(\Delta) \subseteq R_{q,\tau}(\Delta+1)$). The parameter λ is a time-scale parameter and loosely controls size of retrieved video segment.

We can determine Δ by a simple and fast greedy algorithm. The algorithm finds a set of non-overlapping video segments and a natural ranking based the value function provided above. As will be shown in Sec. 5, Eq. (3) produces compact video segments while keeping low false positives and negatives rates.

It may seem strange that such a simple value function provides accurate results over a wide range of queries and videos. Intuitively, this is because the more complex a query is, the less likely it is to be generated by unassociated actions. We state this formally in theorem 4.1.

Theorem 4.1 *Suppose that we have a random video: we sample independently across time and at each instant uniformly from the set of all trees with replacement. Suppose the query q consists of $|q|$ distinct trees and the random video has $R_{q,\tau}(\Delta)$ matches. For $\Delta = \gamma|q|$ the probability that $\log(v_{q,\tau}(\Delta)) \geq \alpha|q|$ for some $\alpha \in (0, 1)$ is smaller than $O(1/|q|^2)$.*

This result suggests that the false alarm probability resulting from an algorithm that is based on thresholding $v_{q,\tau}(\Delta)$ is small. This result is relevant because we expect $\log(v_{q,\tau}(\Delta))$ for video segments that match the query to have a value larger than $\alpha|q|$ for some α when $\Delta = \Omega(|q|)$.

PROOF. For simplicity we only consider each document to contain a single random tree drawn from among $|\mathcal{H}|$ trees. The general result for a fixed number of trees follows in an identical manner. We compute the value of random video of length τ, i.e.,

$$P\left\{v_{q,0}(\Delta) \geq \exp(\alpha|q|)\right\} = P\left\{|R_{q,0}(\Delta)| \geq \alpha|q| + \gamma\right\},$$

where we substituted $\frac{\Delta}{\lambda} = \gamma$ and taken logarithms on both sides to obtain the second equation. Let, Δ_j be the number of documents before we see a new document among the set q after just having seen the $j-1$th new document. This corresponds to the inter-arrival time between the $(j-1)$th and jth document. Given our single tree random model we note that $R_{q,0}(\Delta)$ is a counting process in Δ and so we have the following equivalence,

$$R_{q,0}(\Delta) \geq \ell \iff \sum_{j=1}^{\ell} \Delta_j \leq \Delta.$$

Thus we are now left to determine the $P\left\{\sum_{j=1}^{\ell} \Delta_j \leq \Delta\right\}$ where $\ell = \alpha|q| + \gamma$. Next, $\Delta_1, \Delta_2, \ldots$ are independent geometric random variables. The jth random variable Δ_j has a geometric distribution with parameter $p_i = \frac{|q|-j}{|\mathcal{H}|}$. Using these facts we can determine the mean value and variance of the sum using linearity of expectations. Specifically, it turns out that

$$E\left(\sum_{j=1}^{\ell} \Delta_j\right) = \sum_{j=1}^{\ell} \frac{1}{p_i};\ Var\left(\sum_{j=1}^{\ell} \Delta_j\right) = \sum_{j=1}^{\ell} \frac{1-p_i}{p_i^2}.$$

Upon computation the mean turns out to be $O(|\mathcal{H}|)$, while the variance turns out to be $O(|\mathcal{H}|^2/|q|^2)$. We now apply Chebyshev inequality to conclude $P\left\{v_{q,0}(\Delta) \geq \exp(\alpha|q|)\right\} \leq O(1/|q|^2)$, which establishes the result. □

4.2.2 Full matches with Dynamic Programming(DP)

We can improve upon the performance of the greedy algorithm in Sec. 4.2.1 by exploiting the order of the action components. For example, in the example of a man hopping a subway turnstile, he has to approach the turnstile from the wrong direction, hop over it, and continue. For a car taking a u-turn, it has to approach the intersection, turn across it, and depart the way it came. While these component actions have many valid configurations when examined independently, there is only one order in which they represent the desired full action. This is illustrated in Fig. 6.

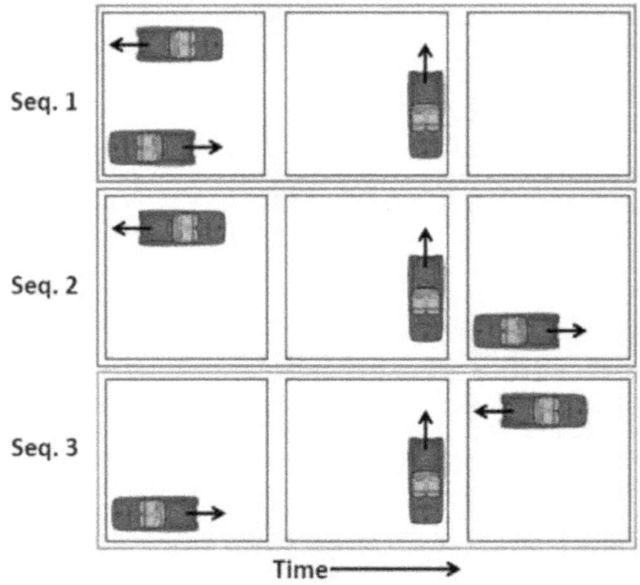

Figure 6: Three sequences of actions. All have equivalent values of $R_{Q,\tau}(\Delta)$; only the third row is valid U-turn.

In the greedy optimization of Section 4.2.1, we ignore the time-ordering that a set of queries contains. The value function $R_{q,\tau}(\Delta)$ does not differentiate between the sequences of actions *(Forward, Left, Back)* and the sequence of actions *(Back, Forward, Left)*. Intuitively, this should hurt performance - false matches are more likely to appear than were we to exploit this causality.

After a user uses the GUI described in Section 4.1 to create a query containing a set of N action components, we search through the inverted index to retrieve N sets of matching locations within the video, one for each action component.

After this pre-processing step, we adapt the Smith-Waterman dynamic programming algorithm [16] , originally developed for gene sequencing, to determine the best set of partial matches in the query. Our algorithm, described in Algorithm 1, operates over the set of matches $m_{\tau,\alpha}$ which contains matches in document α to action component τ to recover a query that has been distorted. For the purposes of our videos, we consider three types of distortion, namely insertion, deletion and continuation.

(1) Insertion covers documents where we believe the query is happening but there are no partial matches. This can happen if unrelated documents are inserted, if there is a pause in the execution of the activity, or if the activity is obscured.

(2) Deletion covers documents where sections of the query are missing. If a deletion has occurred, one (or more) of the action components in the query will not be present in the video. Deletions can happen because of obscuration, or simply because somebody does not perform one component of the full action.

(3) Continuation covers documents where we continue to see an action component which we have already seen. This is important because of time distortion; a single action component does not necessarily occur in multiple consecutive documents before the next action component is reached.

As described in Algorithm 1, to search for a query with $|q|$ action components in a video with N documents, our dynamic programming approach creates an $N \times |q|$ matrix, V, which is

Algorithm 1 Dynamic programming (DP) algorithm

procedure SEARCH(m, W, T)
  $V \leftarrow 0; paths \leftarrow \emptyset; \tau \leftarrow 1; \alpha \leftarrow 1$
  while $\tau \leq$ number of documents **do**
    while $\alpha \leq$ number of action components **do**

$$V_{\tau,\alpha} \leftarrow \max \begin{cases} 0 \\ (V_{\tau-1,\alpha-1} + W_{match}) * m_{\tau,\alpha} \\ (V_{\tau-1,\alpha} + W_{cont}) * m_{\tau,\alpha} \\ (V_{\tau-1,\alpha} + W_{delete}) * (1 - m_{\tau,\alpha}) \\ (V_{\tau,\alpha-1} + W_{insert}) * (1 - m_{\tau,\alpha}) \end{cases}$$

      Let (a, b) be the index which was used to generate the maximum value
      if $V_{(\tau,\alpha)} > 0$ **then**
        $paths_{\tau,\alpha} \leftarrow paths_{a,b} \cup (\tau, \alpha)$
      else
        $paths_{\tau,\alpha} \leftarrow paths_{a,b}$
      end if
      $\alpha \leftarrow \alpha + 1$
    end while
    $\tau \leftarrow \tau + 1$
  end while
  $Matches \leftarrow \emptyset$
  while $max(V) > T$ **do**
    Let (a, b) be the index of V containing the maximum value
    $Matches \leftarrow Matches \cup paths_{a,b}$
    for $\tau, \alpha \in paths_{a,b}$ **do**
      $V_{\tau,\alpha} = 0$
    end for
  end while
  Return $Matches$, the set of paths above threshold T
end procedure

filled out from the top left to the bottom right. A path through the matrix is defined as a set of adjacent (by an 8-neighborhood) matrix element, where each element of the path represents a hypothetical assignment of an action component taking place in a document. A path containing element $V_{a,b}$ would indicate that that path believed that action component b occured in document a.

As the matrix is filled out, each element chooses to append itself to the best possible preceding path - which, by definition, ends immediately above it, immediately to the left of it, or both. It stores the resulting value, and a pointer to the preceding element, in the value matrix V. When the matrix is fully filled out, the optimal path can be found by starting at the maximal value in the matrix and tracing backwards. In order to find multiple matches, we repeatedly find the maximal value in V, the optimal path associated with it, set the values along that path to zero, and repeat until the maximum value in V is below a threshold T. An example of this matrix, with paths overlaid, is shown in figure 7.

For a given penalty on each type of distortion W_I, W_D, W_C (corresponding to insertion, deletion, and continuation) and a given bonus for each match, W_M, the DP algorithm (Algorithm 1) is guaranteed to find the set of partial matches which maximizes the sum of the penalties and bonuses over an interval of time. For our queries, we were relatively certain that elements of the query would not be obscured, but we were uncertain about our detection rate on features and how long an event would take. Thus, we set $W_I = -2$, $W_D = -10$, $W_C = 1$, and $W_M = 8$. These values preclude optimal solutions which involve deletions, look for longer sequences that match, and are relatively robust to missed detection.

We note that because it reasons over specific partial matches,

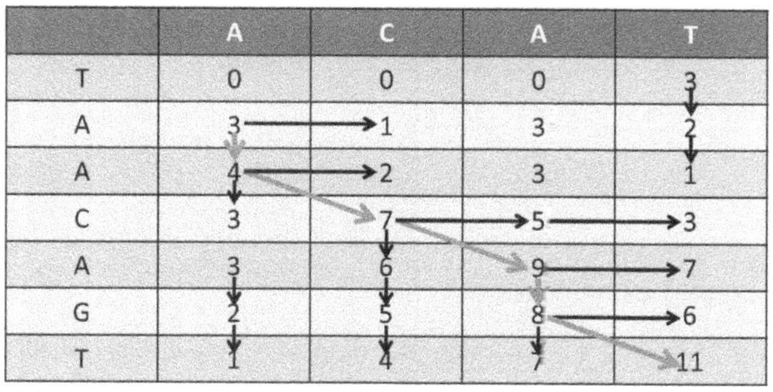

Figure 7: An example of the V matrix. The query is actions A, C, A, T, and the seven documents in the video corpus each contains a single action, T, A, A, C, A, G, T. The values for W_I, W_D, W_C and W_M are $-1, -2, 1$ and 3 respectively. The optimal path, A,A,C,A,G,T, involves an insertion, a continuation and a deletion. It is found by tracing backwards from the maximal element, valued at 11.

our dynamic programming approach also finds the locations in the video segments where the event occurs, but this is not exploited in the results of this paper.

5. EXPERIMENTAL RESULTS

5.1 Datasets

In order to evaluate performance of the two-step problem formulation, and the DP approach in particular, we initially tested our two-step approach on seven surveillance videos (see table 1 and Fig. 8). These videos were selected to test the application of this basic approach to multiple domains, as well as to provide a basis for comparison to other algorithms. The *Winter driveway*, *U-Turn* and *Abandoned object* sequences were shot by us, *PETS* and *Parked-vehicle* and *MIT-traffic* come from known databases [3, 1], *MIT-traffic* was made available to us by Wang *et al.* [2]; *Subway* from Adam *et al.* [4].

As listed in Table 1, we tested different queries to recover moving objects based on their color, size, direction, activity and persistence. We queried for rare and sometimes anomalous events (cat in the snow, illegal U-turns, abandoned objects and people passing turnstile in reverse) as well as usual events (pedestrian counting, car turning at a street light, and car parking). Some videos featured events at a distance *MIT-traffic*, while others featured people moving close to the camera *Subway*. We searched for objects, animals, people, and vehicles. Given these queries, we watched the videos and created a ground-truth list for each task.

5.2 HDP Comparison

For the purposes of comparison, we employed high-level search functions based on scene understanding techniques using Hierarchical Dirichelet Processes (HDP) [23, 10]. We chose this, because unlike [11, 9], it does not require tracking, which can be difficult to do in complex scenes and is computationally prohibitive. At each iteration, the HDP-based learning algorithm assigns each document to one or more high-level activities. This classification is used as input to the next training iteration. Xiang *et al.* [23] propose a search algorithm that uses learned topics as high-level semantic queries. The search algorithm is based on the classification outputs from the final HDP training iteration. We compare our method to this HDP-based search algorithm.

Figure 8: Screen shots of the ten tasks. These images show the search queries (with green ROI) and a retrieve frame (with a red rectangle). The red dots correspond to the tree whose profile fit the query.

Task	Video	Search query	Features	Video size	Index size
1	Winter driveway	black cat appearance	color and size	6.55 GB	147 KB
2	Subway	people passing turnstiles	motion	2.75 GB	2.3 MB
3	Subway	people hopping turnstiles	motion	2.75 GB	2.3 MB
4	MIT Traffic	cars turning left	motion	10.3 GB	42 MB
5	MIT Traffic	cars turning right	motion	10.3 GB	42 MB
6	U-turn	cars making U-turn	motion	1.97 GB	13.7 MB
7	U-turn	cars turning left, no U	direction	1.97 GB	13.7 MB
8	Abandoned object	abandoned objects	size and persistence	682 MB	2.6 MB
9	Abandoned object	abandoned objects	size, persistence and color	682 MB	2.6 MB
10	PETS	abandoned objects	size and persistence	1.01 GB	5.63 KB
11	Parked-vehicle	parked vehicles	size and persistence		

Table 1: Tasks' number, videos, search query, associate features, video size and index size. Tasks 1, 8, 9, 10, and 11 use compound search operators. The index size can be several orders of magnitude smaller than raw video. Our use of primitive local features implies that index times and index size are both proportional to the number of foreground objects in the video. Consequently, index size tends to be a good surrogate for indexing times.

Queries are specified as the ideal classification distribution and the search algorithm compares each document's distribution over the learned topics against this ideal distribution. Comparison is performed using the relative entropy (Kullback-Leibler divergence) between the two distributions. The Kullback-Leibler divergence gives a measure of distance between the query q and the distribution p_j for document j over the K topics:

$$D(q, p_j) = \sum_{k=1}^{K} q(k) \log \frac{q(k)}{p_j(k)}.$$

The query q is created by looking at the ideal documents and assigning to q a uniform distribution over the topics present in them. The search procedure evaluates $D(q, p_j)$ for each document j and ranks the documents in order of increasing divergence.

5.3 Eleven Tasks

Once we had defined the queries, we watched all of the videos and created a ground-truth list for each task. Ground truth was obtained manually by noting the range of frames containing each of the expected results. Comparison is obtained by computing the intersection of the ranges of frames returned by the search procedure to the range of frames in the ground truth. Events are counted manually by viewing the output results. An event is marked as detected if it appears in the output video and at least 1 partial match hits objects appearing in the event. The greedy-optimization results are displayed in Fig. 8 and summarized in table 2. The comparable results for HDP are summarized below in table 2.

The "Ground truth" column of table 2 indicates the true number of events which exist in the dataset. The "Greedy

Task	Video	Duration (minutes)	Ground Truth (events)	Greedy True (events found)	HDP [10] True (events found)	Greedy False (events found)	HDP [10] False (events found)	Runtime (seconds)
1	Winter driveway	253	3	2	–	1	–	7.5
2	Subway	79	117	116	114	1	121	0.3
3	Subway	79	13	11	1	2	33	3.0
4	MIT Traffic	92	66	61	6	5	58	0.4
5	MIT Traffic	92	148	135	54	13	118	0.5
6	U-turn	3.4	8	8	6	0	23	1.2
7	U-turn	3.4	6	5	4	1	14	0.6
8	Abandoned object	13.8	2	2	–	0	–	4.8
9	Abandoned object	13.8	2	2	–	0	–	13.3
10	PETS	7.1	4	4	–	0	–	20.2
11	Parked-vehicle	32	14	14	–	0	–	12.3

Table 2: Results for the elevens tasks using greedy optimization and HDP labels. Crossed-out rows correspond to queries for which there was no corresponding topic in the HDP search.

True" column indicates the number of correct detections (true positives) for the Greedy algorithm and "HDP True" the number of correct detections (true positives) for the HDP-based search [21]. Likewise, the "Greedy False" and "HDP False" indicate the number of false alarms that were found for those eleven tasks.

Table 2 demonstrates the robustness of the two-step method in a wide-array of search applications, outperforming the HDP baseline significantly in detection and false alarm rate. The figures in the table are given for results of total length approximately equal to that of the ground truth. As can be seen from the figures in the table, the absolute detection rate is strong.

In table 2, we learn that HDP-search deals well with search of recurring large-scale activities and poorly otherwise. While several queries could not be executed because of a lack of topics that could be used to model the query, the results nonetheless demonstrate some of the shortcomings of the algorithm. The HDP search scales linearly with the number of documents, an undesirable quality with large datasets. Further, the cost of the training phase is prohibitive (approximately 2 days for the "subway" sequence) and must be paid again every time thatmore video data is included.

5.4 Dynamic Programming

Of the eleven tasks described in table 1, only tasks two to seven had temporal structure which could be exploited through dynamic programming. As it turned out, the features used in these tasks were purely motion. In order to demonstrate the potential gain from exploiting this structure, we chose tasks three, four and six and performed dynamic programming using the full query, as well as greedy and HDP search algorithms. The ROC curves for those three scenarios are provided in Fig 9, contrasting dynamic programming with HDP and Greedy Optimization.

Fig. 9 demonstrates the type of improvement that can be attained by the two-step approach to search. The ROC curves for LSH-based greedy optimization dominate the HDP curves, and there is clear improvement from employing time-ordering with DP. These improvements come as no surprise - HDP is doing a global search, attempting to create a topic for each action. LSH does a compelling local search which is fast and produces low false alarm rate. This is largely due to the global nature of HDP - the topics it discovers are more likely to be common events, so infrequent events such as u-turns and turnstile-hopping pose a problem. Note that the gap between local and global searches narrow on the MIT-traffic dataset, where the event being found (left turns at a light) is a relatively common occurrence with enough repetition to fill a topic model.

5.5 Discussion

This approach represents a fundamentally different way of approaching the video search problem. Rather than relying on an abundance of training data or finely-tuned features to differentiate actions of interest from noise, we rely on simple features and causality. In addition to the clear benefits in terms of a run-time which scales sub-linearly with the length of the video corpus, the simple features and hashing approach render the approach robust to user error as well as poor-quality video. The results of section 5.4 demonstrate clearly that causality and temporal structure can be powerful tools to reduce false alarms. Another added benefit is how the algorithm scales with query complexity. Whereas algorithms such as topic modeling or a feature-based matching suffer as queries becomes more complex due to efforts to characterize the query, the two-step approach becomes more successful - the more action components in a query, the more likely it is to differentiate itself from noise. There is, of course, non-temporal structure that we have yet to exploit. Spatial positioning of queries, such as "The second action component must occur to the northeast of the first", or "The second action component must be near the first" is a simple attribute which may further differentiate queries of interest from background noise. This is not to say that the approach is not without its limitations. It requires that the activity being described contain discrete states, each of which is describable by a simple feature vocabulary. Complex actions like sign language or actions which are to fast or too small to be identified at the atom level will be difficult to search for.

6. CONCLUSION

We presented a method that summarizes the dynamic content of a surveillance video in a way that is compatible with arbitrary user-defined queries. We divide the video into documents each containing a series of atoms. These atoms are grouped together into trees all containing a feature list. These features describing the size, the color, the direction and the persistence of the moving objects. The coordinates of these trees are then stored into a hash-table based feature index. Hash functions group trees whose content is similar. In this way, search becomes a simple lookup as user-specified queries are converted into a table index. Our method has many advantages. First, because of the indexing strategy, our search engine has a complexity of $O(1)$ for finding partial matches. Second, the index requires only minimal storage. Third, our method requires only local processing, making it suitable for facing constant data renewal. This makes it simple to implement and easy to adjust. Fourth, our method summarizes the entire

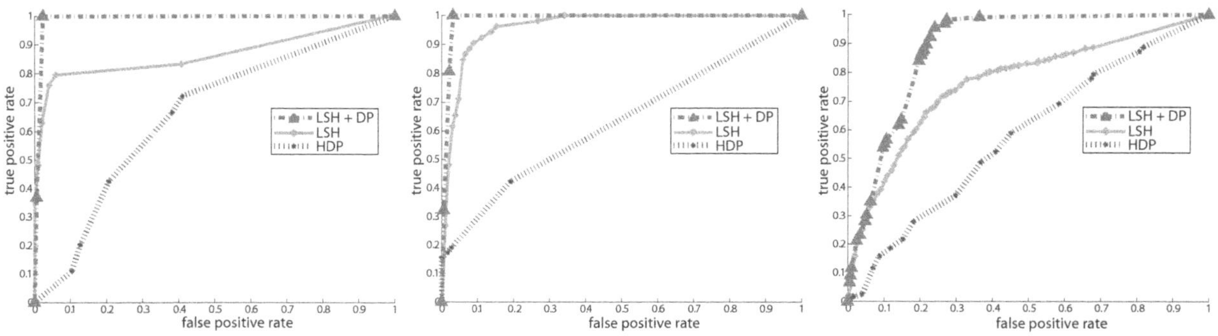

Figure 9: ROC curves for the U-turn, subway and traffic datasets. Both our greedy search and DP significantly outperform scene-understanding methods such as HDP methods [23, 10].

video, not just the predominant modes of activity: it can retrieve any combination of rare, abnormal and recurrent activities.

7. REFERENCES

[1] i-lids. computervision.wikia.com/wiki/I-LIDS.

[2] Mit traffic. people.csail.mit.edu/xgwang/HBM.html.

[3] Pets 2006. http://ftp.pets.rdg.ac.uk/.

[4] A. Adam, E. Rivlin, I. Shimshoni, and D. Reinitz. Robust real-time unusual event detection using multiple fixed-location monitors. *IEEE Trans. Pattern Anal. Machine Intell.*, 30(3):555–560, 2008.

[5] Y. Benezeth, P.-M. Jodoin, B. Emile, H. Laurent, and C. Rosenberger. Comparative study of background subtraction algorithms. *J. of Elec. Imaging*, 19(3):1–12, 2010.

[6] B.Horn and B. Schunck. Determining optical flow. *Artif. Intell.*, 17(1-3):185–203, 1981.

[7] Q. Dong, Y. Wu, and Z. Hu. Pointwise motion image (PMI): A novel motion representation and its applications to abnormality detection and behavior recognition. *IEEE Trans. Circuits Syst. Video Technol.*, 19(3):407–416, 2009.

[8] A. Gionis, P. Indyk, and R. Motwani. Similarity search in high dimensions via hashing. In *Proc. Int. Conf. on Very Large Data Bases*, pages 518–529, 1999.

[9] W. Hu, X. Xiao, Z. Fu, D. Xie, T. Tan, and S. Maybank. A system for learning statistical motion patterns. *IEEE Trans. Pattern Anal. Machine Intell.*, 28(9):1450–1464, 2006.

[10] D. Kuettel, M. Breitenstein, L. Gool, and V. Ferrari. What's going on? discovering spatio-temporal dependencies in dynamic scenes. In *Proc. IEEE Conf. Computer Vision Pattern Recognition*, pages 1951–1958, 2010.

[11] G. Medioni, I. Cohen, F. Bremond, S. Hongeng, and R. Nevatia. Event detection and analysis from video streams. *IEEE Trans. Pattern Anal. Machine Intell.*, 23(8):873–889, 2001.

[12] J. Meessen, M. Coulanges, X. Desurmont, and J.-F. Delaigle. Content-based retrieval of video surveillance scenes. In *MRCS*, pages 785–792, 2006.

[13] I. Pruteanu-Malinici and L. Carin. Infinite hidden markov models for unusual-event detection in video. *IEEE Trans. Image Process.*, 17(5):811–821, 2008.

[14] C. Simon, J. Meessen, and C. DeVleeschouwer. Visual event recognition using decision trees. *Multimedia Tools and Applications*, 2009.

[15] J. Sivic and A. Zisserman. Video Google: A text retrieval approach to object matching in videos. In *Proc. IEEE Int. Conf. Computer Vision*, volume 2, pages 1470–1477, 2003.

[16] T. Smith and M. Waterman. Identification of common molecular subsequences. *J. of Molecular Biology*, 147, 1981.

[17] X. Song and G. Fan. Joint key-frame extraction and object segmentation for content-based video analysis. *IEEE Trans. Circuits Syst. Video Technol.*, 16(7):904–914, 2006.

[18] E. Stringa and C. Regazzoni. Content-based retrieval and real time detection from video sequences acquired by surveillance systems. In *Proc. IEEE Int. Conf. Image Processing*, pages 138–142, 1998.

[19] Y.-L. Tian, A. Hampapur, L. Brown, R. Feris, M. Lu, A. Senior, C.-F. Shu, and Y. Zhai. Event detection, query, and retrieval for video surveillance. In Z. Ma, editor, *Artificial Intelligence for Maximizing Content Based Image Retrieval*. Information Science Reference; 1 edition, 2008.

[20] H. Veeraraghavan, N. Papanikolopoulos, and P. Schrater. Learning dynamic event descriptions in image sequences. In *Proc. IEEE Conf. Computer Vision Pattern Recognition*, pages 1–6, 2007.

[21] X. Wang, X. Ma, and E.Grimson. Unsupervised activity perception in crowded and complicated scenes using hierarchical bayesian models. *IEEE Trans. Pattern Anal. Machine Intell.*, 31(3):539–555, 2009.

[22] R. W. White and R. A. Roth. *Exploratory Search: Beyond the Query-Response Paradigm*. Morgan-Claypool, VT, U.S.A., 2009.

[23] T. Xiang and S. Gong. Video behavior profiling for anomaly detection. *IEEE Trans. Pattern Anal. Machine Intell.*, 30(5):893–908, 2008.

[24] Y. Yang, B. Lovell, and F. Dadgostar. Content-based video retrieval (cbvr) system for cctv surveillance videos. In *Proc of Dig. Img. Comp. Tech. and App.*, pages 183–187, 2009.

[25] C. Yeo, P. Ahammad, K. Ramchandran, and S. Sastr. High speed action recognition and localization in compressed domain videos. *IEEE Trans. Circuits Syst. Video Technol.*, 18(8):1006 – 1015, 2008.

[26] A. Yilmaz and M. Shah. A differential geometric approach to representing the human actions. *Comput. Vis. Image Und.*, 109(3):335–351, 2008.

When Video Search Goes Wrong: Predicting Query Failure Using Search Engine Logs and Visual Search Results *

Christoph Kofler †, Linjun Yang ‡, Martha Larson †, Tao Mei ‡, Alan Hanjalic †, Shipeng Li ‡

† Multimedia Information Retrieval Lab, Delft University of Technology, Delft, The Netherlands

‡ Microsoft Research Asia, Beijing, P. R. China

{c.kofler, m.a.larson, a.hanjalic}@tudelft.nl, {linjuny, tmei, spli}@microsoft.com

ABSTRACT

The recent increase in the volume and variety of video content available online presents growing challenges for video search. Users face increased difficulty in formulating effective queries and search engines must deploy highly effective algorithms to provide relevant results. Although lately much effort has been invested in optimizing video search engine results, relatively little attention has been given to predicting for which queries results optimization is most useful, i.e., predicting which queries will fail. Being able to predict when a video search query would fail is likely to make the video search result optimization more efficient and effective, improve the search experience for the user by providing support in the query formulation process and in this way boost the development of video search engines in general. While insight about a query's performance in general could be obtained using the well-known concept of query performance prediction (QPP), we propose a novel approach for predicting a failure of a video search query in the specific context of a search session. Our *context-aware query failure* prediction approach uses a combination of *user indicators* and *engine indicators* to predict whether a particular query is likely to fail in the context of a particular search session. User indicators are derived from the search log and capture the patterns of query (re)formulation behavior and the click-through data of a user during a typical video search session. Engine indicators are derived from the video search results list and capture the visual variance of search results that would be offered to the user for the given query. We validate our approach experimentally on a test set containing 1+ million video search queries and show its effectiveness compared to a set of conventional QPP baselines. Our approach achieves a 13% relative improvement over the baseline.

Categories and Subject Descriptors

H.3.3 [**Information Storage and Retrieval**]: Information Search and Retrieval—*Search process, Information filtering, Query formulation*; H.3.1 [**Information Storage and Retrieval**]: Content Analysis and Indexing;

General Terms

Algorithms, Experimentation, Human Factors, Performance

Keywords

Video search, query failure, transaction log analysis, query performance prediction, visual relatedness

* This work was performed when Christoph Kofler was visiting Microsoft Research Asia as a research intern.

MM'12, October 29–November 2, 2012, Nara, Japan.

Figure 1: A visualization of an excerpt from an ongoing search session from the transaction log. The query *'new york'* was not successful, gets reformulated to *'new york alicia keys'* leading to a query success.

1. INTRODUCTION

As the volume and diversity of video data on the Internet increases, the interaction between users and search engines becomes increasingly complex. Users, on the one hand, can be expected to have a less complete overview of the full scope of the content available, resulting in increased difficulty in formulating successful video search queries. Video search engines, on the other hand, can be expected to have more difficulty pinpointing content that matches user information needs. Recently, a number of approaches have been developed that improve the performance of video search engines operating on web-scale data. Key examples of these techniques include concept-based video search [26], re-ranking of video search results [9, 30] and query suggestion [31]. Such approaches could be more effectively deployed if it were possible to predict at which points in the sequence of user interactions with a video search engine (i.e., the video search session) the user is likely to be confronted with non-relevant search results.

In this paper, we introduce an approach for the prediction of *context-aware query failure* in video search. We consider a query, issued by a user in the context of a video search session as failed if it produces a results list containing no search results the user considers relevant enough to click. We adopt methodology from transaction log analysis including assumptions about the relationship between clicks and relevance from the field of text retrieval

[3, 15]. Hereby we solely take the 'effective' part of a results list for relevance into account, i.e., results so low in the list that they are never reached are not regarded [3]. We approach query failure prediction as a multimodal binary classification problem and introduce a technique that combines two information sources: *user indicators* (derived from search engine logs recording user interaction) and *engine indicators* (derived from the results list that the search engine delivers in response to the user query).

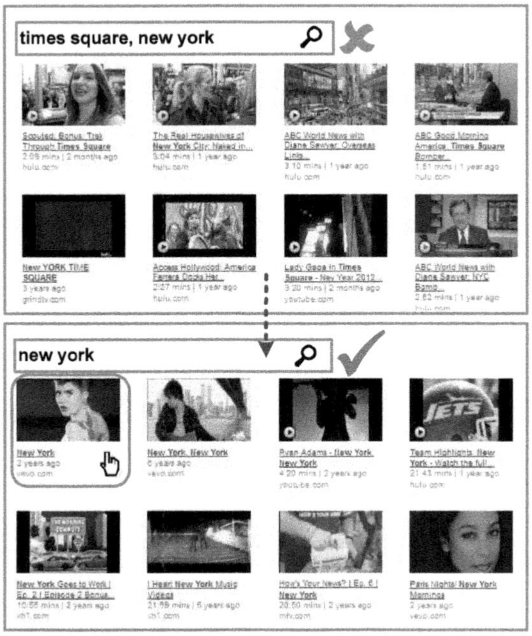

Figure 2: A visualization of an excerpt from an ongoing search session from the transaction log. The query *'times square, new york'* was not successful, gets reformulated to *'new york'* leading to a query success.

The context-aware query failure prediction problem is a challenging one. Figure 1 illustrates this problem with an excerpt from an ongoing search session consisting of a failed query followed by a query expansion that leads to a successful query. The user is trying to find a video of the song 'Empire State of Mind' and the first query depicted is *'new york'*, a more common designation for 'The Empire State'. The resulting query is too broad, returning a results list in which the user does not click. The user then adds the name of the soloist 'Alicia Keys' to the query, which leads to a results list containing a video the user does click. The challenge of query failure prediction lies in the enormous range of variability in user query patterns and engine responses, and the link to success is not straightforward. The contrast between Figure 2 and Figure 1 provides a simple illustration of the unexpectedness of user query patterns. In Figure 2, the first query *'times square, new york'* does not lead to a result that the user finds to be worth a click, but a reduction of the query to *'new york'* does. Possibly the user is looking for information about New York City entertainment, concentrated at, but not limited to, the Times Square area. Clearly, the success of the query '*new york*' is strongly dependent on the local context of the search session, which supports the need for context-aware query failure prediction. The fact that either query expansion or reduction can lead to query success illustrates the difficulty of query failure prediction and motivates us to propose a query failure approach that goes beyond simplistic characteristics of query sequences within a search session when designing our approach.

A critical insight is that the problem of context-aware query failure prediction cannot be reduced to the problem of predicting the failure of specific queries independently of their context in the search session (e.g., the query string *'new york'*). Figure 3 depicts statistics for different queries calculated over ~108K queries drawn from users' interactions with several video search engines. The relative frequency of queries with different success rates is shown in terms of bars color coded according to the video search engine where they were submitted. The success rate of a query is defined as the relative proportion of cases in which a user submits that query to the search engine and subsequently clicks on a result in the returned results list. A query with a success rate of 0% never results in a user click and a query with a success rate of 100% always results in a user click. The majority of the queries across all engines can be seen in Figure 3 to fall midway between the two extremes. The distribution provides evidence that a single query can correspond to different underlying information needs, corresponding to different user decisions to click on a result. This evidence provides support for our position that context-aware query prediction is the most productive form of query failure prediction. This form of prediction does not treat all instances of a query equally, but rather takes the context of the query within the search session into account when predicting search failure.

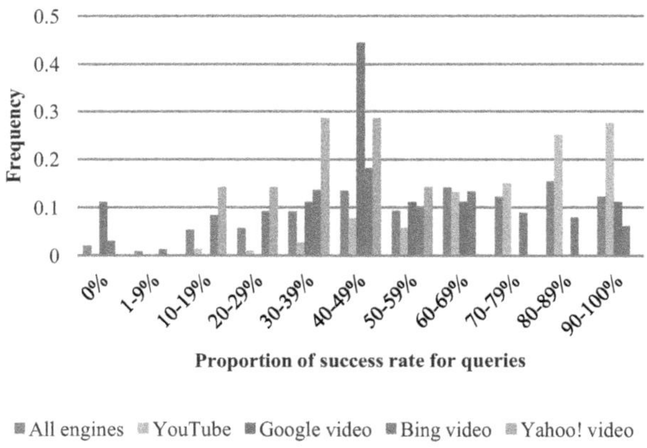

Figure 3: Distribution of success rates for queries submitted to four major video search engines.

The starting point of our proposed approach are *query performance prediction* (QPP) techniques that have been developed in the area of conventional text-based information retrieval [2, 7, 11, 32]. These techniques treat the query independently of its context. Our approach builds on QPP and extends it with two innovations. First, we extend conventional, context-independent QPP with user indicators that are derived from session information drawn from a video search engine log. These features allow us to take the context of a query into account when predicting failure. Second, we demonstrate the potential of adapting context-independent QPP specifically to video search by extending a conventional text-based predictor with visual features drawn from the video search results list (specifically, from thumbnails accompanying individual video results). To the best of our knowledge, this work is the first to treat the prediction of query failure for video search engines. Here, we restrict ourselves to tackling the failure prediction problem, but note that the ultimate value of our approach will be its usefulness to steer the application of already existing search engine performance enhancing techniques, thereby maximizing their benefit. The suitability of our query failure prediction approach to steering other methods will be critically dependent on its ability to operate online during a user search session. For this reason, we direct our attention at information derived from the ongoing search session, i.e., we exclude the possibility of learning user profiles or global search patterns in order to predict failure. By limiting ourselves to sessions we ensure that our approach can be tested or applied without access to the large amounts of transaction log data that are used to carry out the investigations reported here.

The main contributions of this paper are twofold:

- We carry out a qualitative analysis of search engine logs to build an understanding of why video search engine queries fail.
- Building on observations made during the analysis, we propose and validate a framework for query failure prediction.

Validation is carried out in the form of an extensive series of experiments designed to answer the following research questions: RQ1: Do context-aware user indicators derived from transaction logs improve the performance of query prediction over conventional context-independent QPP? RQ2: Which user indicators extracted from transaction logs are particularly helpful? RQ3: What is the potential of visual features to improve conventional text-based QPP in the case of video search? RQ4: Can QPP integrating visual features be combined with context-aware user indicators to further improve search results? The experimental evaluation is completed with a detailed analysis of results that demonstrates its particular usefulness for long-tail queries.

The remainder of the paper is organized as follows. After positioning our proposed approach with respect to the related work in Section 2, we carry out a qualitative analysis of search engine logs in Section 3 and explain our approach in detail in Section 4. Section 5 reports the experimental validation of our approach. We discuss our results in Section 6 and conclude the paper with an outlook on future work in Section 7.

2. RELATED WORK

2.1 Search Failure

Our definition of query failure adopts widely-applied assumptions from the field of text retrieval. Joachims [15] showed that a click on a search result indicates a relevance judgment: a user scans the top search results returned by a search engine for a particular query from the top to the bottom and must have noticed result 1 before clicking result 2, making a decision not to click result 1. Fox et al. [3] collected and compared both implicit and explicit relevance judgments of search results and showed that implicit judgments, including clicked search results, are indicative for actual relevance. Using these observations, for our investigations we consider a query instance *successful* if it leads to a search results click and, consequentially, *failed* if it does not lead to a click in the generated video search results list. The same assumption concerning the connection of clicks and relevance has been applied in [8, 10].

Work investigating search failure has been limited, both in the text-based information retrieval community as well as in the multimedia retrieval community. The existing work can be categorized according to the exact definition of failure that is adopted: a failed query can either be a query that performs poorly with respect to a retrieval metric that measures results relevance or be a query that returns no results (i.e., a zero-hit query). Our work falls into the former category, in contrast to important recent work, which falls into the latter category. Important recent work from the field of information retrieval are Mastora et al. [21], who showed that failed queries represent 36% of overall submitted queries, and Kim and Can [16], who investigated failure as a factor characterizing queries in different search tasks. In the field of multimedia retrieval, Pu [22] compared characteristics of successful and failed image queries and Kofler et al. [17] investigated video search failure search using expressions of failed user needs posted on a social forum.

2.2 Query Performance Prediction

Query performance prediction (QPP) originated in the area of conventional text information retrieval and aims to predict whether a particular query will have a high or low retrieval performance. In our work, we make use of the most widely-used and highly successful post-retrieval QPP predictor, the clarity score [2], which captures the topical focus of the results list returned by the search engine in response to the query. We adopt this post-retrieval QPP predictor to inspire our engine indicators, applying the assumption that a low clarity score reflects a high likelihood of failure. Conventional text retrieval also uses pre-retrieval QPP predictors [7, 11, 32], although they are generally overall less successful than post-retrieval predictors. Pre-retrieval predictors do not take the actual results list produced by a search engine into account but rather analyze different aspects of the query, such as specificity, ambiguity, and term relatedness of queries. We adopt both a post-retrieval predictor [2], as well as specific pre-retrieval predictors [7, 11, 32] as baselines to test our proposed approach.

2.3 Transaction Log Analysis

Transaction log analysis (TLA) was established in the field of text information retrieval. In our work, we use transaction logs both as a source of ground truth concerning which queries have failed and also as a source of information on user interactions, which we use to create user indicators. The literature has shown user interactions derived from transaction logs to be a reliable source of information that can be used to make predictions on aspects of user search sessions. Key examples from the area of text retrieval include White et al. [28], who predicted a user's short-term interests based on context derived from the current query and pre-query session activity, and Kotov et al. [18], who predicted which queries and tasks are related to each other across sessions using features of individual queries and long-term user search behavior. Xiang et al. [29] used information from query generalization, reformulation and specialization to improve ranking. Our work makes use of similar indicators, but as part of a much broader inventory of user indicators. The ultimate benefit of our work is also improved ranking, but because we target query failure and not exclusively ranking, we leave the possibility open for other applications (such as improved query suggestion). Guo et al. [4] can be considered to be the work most similar to our own since they use the query, search results and user interaction to predict query performance. They found that the way in which users interact with search results provides a strong indication of the quality of those results. However, this work differs from our approach in that query performance is predicted independently of the other queries constituting the context of the query within the search session. Comparable little work has been carried out applying TLA for multimedia search. Jansen et al. [14] and Tjondronegoro et al. [27] show the form of multimedia queries differs from text queries. These differences provide motivation for our own work, which is dedicated specifically to video search.

3. LOG ANALYSIS OF FAILED QUERIES

In this section, we report on a qualitative analysis of query failure in video search engine logs, which identified useful categories of context-aware user indicators (i.e., features which capture the context of a query within a search session) in our query failure prediction approach.

3.1 Transaction Log

The investigations reported in this paper make use of a large-scale anonymized transaction log of the Bing video search engine collected via the Internet Explorer 8 Internet browser used by millions of users world-wide. The transaction log contains, in addition to information on search engine-based interactions, all interactions of a user with the Internet browser and provides a realistic picture of the video search behavior of Internet users. Entries of the transaction log contain a timestamp for each interaction with the Internet browser, the anonymized URL of each request, and the URL of the preceding request. Since there is one log entry for each transaction, not every transaction has a query. If there is a query present, the transaction contains both the query string and the search engine vertical on which the query was executed (e.g., Web, image, video).

The investigations and experiments described in this paper are based on sessions logged from June 1, 2011 until June 7, 2011. Typical of transaction logs [12, 27], our logs contain corrupted data entries like missing fields or information, resulting from errors in the logging procedure and were subjected to a standard cleaning process [12]. To remove variability introduced due to regional or linguistic differences, we take into account exclusively user interactions of US-based English speakers. Sessions start with the first interaction of the user with the Internet browser, terminate if there is an inactivity of the user exceeding 30 minutes and have at least one search engine interaction. Session data did not contain information about different Internet browser tabs or windows used by users while surfing; therefore, we ordered user actions within each session chronologically.

For the purposes of this paper, we focus on sessions containing at least one query submitted to the video vertical of the search engine. This results in 174,955 sessions having 1,218,936 total and 445,859 unique queries. The average session duration was 11 minutes and 18 seconds containing an average of 13 actions per session. The video search engine does not adapt to any context of the user. We can therefore assume that users, independently of how they interact with the video search engine or where they are located, will receive similar search results for the same query. Further details, including the separation of the development and test sets, are explained in Section 5.1 'Experimental Framework'.

3.2 Observations

We performed an exploratory investigation to extract observations decisive for failure, where we zero in on user indicators from the transaction log. We sampled the 100 most-submitted queries having both, successful and failed query instances in our development set and manually investigated the search session in which they were submitted. The result of our transaction log analysis was a number of observations concerning sources of query failure.

The first observation concerns other interactions within the search session that may not have proven satisfactory to a user. In our observations we discover cases in which clicked videos are watched for a relatively short amount of time, resulting in either a query reformulation or further investigation of the original search results list. Similar observations have been made in [3]. Continuous switching behavior between query formulation and watching results for a short amount of time has implications for how long the search session lasts and how many interactions the user has with the search engine and where in the local context of the search session a query was submitted [5]. We define this observation as:

Previous dissatisfaction: If the user is dissatisfied with results thus far in the session, the current query is more likely to fail.

The second observation concerns query reformulation behavior. A user might reformulate a query after it has failed to return acceptable results: the query was either too specific or too general. According to [13, 29] query reformulation follows four strategies: formulating a *new query*, and *generalizing*, *specializing*, or *reformulating* a query. With the exception of 'new query,' all other strategies involve the same query topic with variations depending on whether the user wants to get more general (e.g., *'spongebob lost episode'* → *'spongebob'*), specific (e.g., *'spongebob'* → *'spongebob dance'*), or other results (e.g., *'spongebob lost episode'* → *'spongebob house party'*). It is not necessarily decisive that the more specific a query gets, the higher the probability that the query instance will be successful: the video search engine might return no useful results for a too specific query, leading the user to submit generalizations of the same query. Figure 4 contains an example that ultimately leads to a successful query. Similar observations have proven useful in related investigations [4, 18].

how to make a napoleon total war comentary	×
how to make a commentary video for total war game	×
how to make a commentary video for napoleon total war	×
how to upload a video from a game	×
how to upload a video from a videogame	✓

Figure 4: Excerpt of a search session showing iterations of query reformulation.

Lack of clicking behavior during reformulation was also revealed as important by our investigation. We summarize our findings on interactions with an observation on query iterations:

Query iterations: The more query reformulations (without search result clicks), precede a query in a search session, the more likely the query will not fail.

How clear a user expresses his search goal is crucial for query failure. A search goal is the high-level goal a user wants to achieve using video search and results in a set of user actions [23]. We observe that users with different types of search goals engage in different interactions (i.e., users who freely browse vs. others pursuing a specific goal). Figure 5 contains an example from the log of a sequence of queries that are not clearly related and all fail.

body snatcha ent	×
hood to hood atlanta	×
Facebook	×
Utube	×

Figure 5: Excerpt of a search session showing a sequence of video search queries that are not clearly related.

We observe that browsing users tend to switch to other verticals of the search engine and vary in how often a particular search result was clicked. We summarize these findings with the following observation:

Goal-lessness: If the user is browsing randomly without a specific search goal, the more likely that the current query does fail.

In contrast to browsing behavior, our analysis revealed that in some cases, users will enter successively more focused queries, suggesting that these users are not browsing, but rather pursuing a specific goal. Figure 6, illustrates a series of queries from the log that is increasingly specific and ultimately leads to success.

sons of anarchy	×
sons of anarchy season premier	×
sons of anarchy season 4 premier	✓

Figure 6: Visualization of a search session showing the development of a search goal and its query expressions.

We conjecture that how directed the goal formulation of a user is, is represented by topical focus or topical overlap expressed in consecutive queries. We define this observation as:

Goal-directedness: If the current query expresses a more specific search goal formulation than the previous queries, the current query is less likely to fail.

Our final observation concerns how familiar a user is with interacting with a search engine. This observation concerns whether the search session reveals evidence that the user understands the possibilities offered by the search engine, including the search engine verticals. We define this observation as:

User familiarity: Within the bounds of a given search session, the greater the familiarity with the video search engine demonstrated by the user, the more likely that the current query does not fail.

4. APPROACH

4.1 Overview

Figure 7 contains an overview of our approach. We define a set of features (Sections 4.2 and 4.3) corresponding to each of the observations obtained from the transaction log analysis of failed queries. In an offline step, we extract these features from the local search session and use them to train classifiers (Section 4.4), which predict whether the current query a user is submitting to a video search engine will fail or be successful.

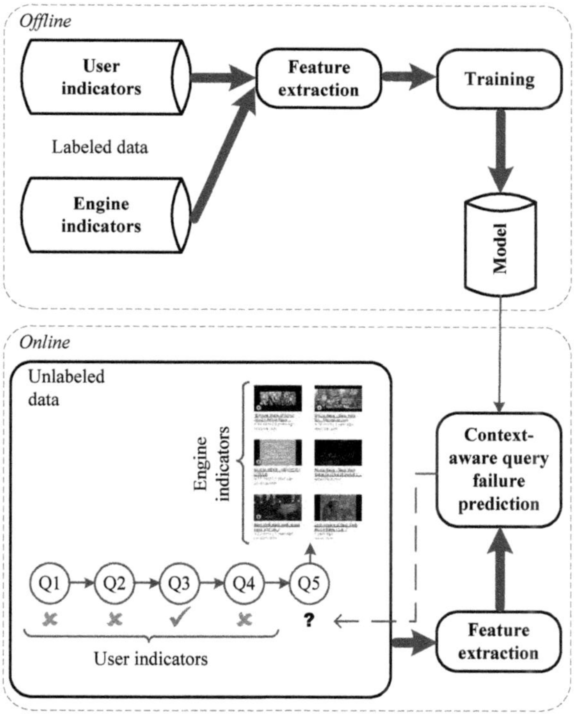

Figure 7: Overview of our context-aware query failure prediction approach for video search including model training in an offline step and the actual prediction in an online step.

In an online step, we again extract features based on user indicators (in the example above: query instances Q1-Q4 and corresponding click-through- and session-data) and engine indicators (in the example above: visual search results of the current query instance Q5) from a user's search session and perform the context-aware query failure prediction step for the current query instance (in the example above: Q5).

4.2 User indicator features

Since our context-aware query failure prediction approach aims to predict the outcome of the current query instance the user submits to the video search engine, we extract features from the local search session relative to this query. Previous queries are considered queries submitted chronologically before the current query. We differentiate between two types of pre-query session histories: the *session query history* is the set of all queries submitted in a search session before the current query; the *query-specific reformulation history* (*QRH*) is the local set of queries submitted in a search session *before* the current query. It is a sequence of topically related queries within a session and a subset of the session query history.

Table 1 gives an overview and description of features derived from user indicators and grouped by observation. We extract features related to the different sources of information associated with the transaction logs, which can be characterized by the following three groups (i) general Internet browser session and search session statistics, (ii) query (re)formulation behavior and clarity of search goal expressiveness, and (iii) click-through data in the video search results lists generated by the queries in the search session. Note that we do not claim that the features are independent of each other. We investigate a variety of features corresponding to each observation and later use feature selection to choose the most useful subsets for classification.

For most features, the information provided in Table 1 is sufficient to explain their generation. However, a few cases require additional details, which are explained here. We use features calculated on the QRH and also on the whole session in order to supply the classifier with information at different local resolutions. A QRH boundary is set by classifying subsequent queries into query-reformulation classes and then defining a boundary whenever the class type changes. The class types that we use are: reformulations, generalizations, and specializations and they are calculated using the algorithm proposed in [13]. The algorithm takes query statistics such as overlapping terms and query length into account. The feature *Count{Reformulated, Generalized, Specialized}Queries[QRH]* uses counts of query-reformulation types generated by the algorithm.

Query clarity [2] is a conventional post-retrieval query performance predictor based on the assumption that a query for which the search engine performs well will enjoy topical coherence among the top items (referred to as documents due to the origin of the clarity score in text retrieval) returned in the results list. The predictor estimates a language model from search results for each query and a language model of the overall document collection as shown in Eq. 1 (R is the set of retrieved documents, D is a document, w is a term in the overall vocabulary V, and Q is a query).

$$P_{QM}(w) = \sum_{D \in R} P(w|D)P(D|Q) \qquad (1)$$

The similarity between these language models, usually defined as the *Kullback-Leibler* (KL) divergence, categorizes the clarity of the query (Eq. 2).

$$QC = D_{KL}(P_{QM} \| P_{CM}) = \sum_{w \in V} P_{QM}(w) \log \frac{P_{QM}(w)}{P_{CM}(w)} \qquad (2)$$

We take the difference between the clarity scores as an indicator (*QueryClarityDifferenceToAllQueries[QRH]*) for parts of the observation about goal-directedness.

Table 1: Overview of the user indicator features based on our observations from the log analysis.

Feature name	Feature description
	Previous dissatisfaction
CountRequests	Number of requests in the session query history excluding the current query.
SessionDuration	Duration of session until current query in seconds.
TimeToPreviousQuery	Time difference in seconds between current query and previous query.
RankSubmitQuery[QRH]	Current number of total submitted queries in the session query history/query-specific reformulation history.
RatioResultsClicked{Videos, Web, Other}	Average number of {video, web, non-web- and non-video-vertical} results clicked per unique {video, web, non-web- and non-video-vertical} query.
CountVideosWatchedDuration[QRH]	Number of videos watched for a duration less than k seconds (k set here to 15) in the session query history/query-specific reformulation history.
	Query iterations
Count{Reformulated, Generalized, Specialized}Queries[QRH]	Number of {reformulated, generalized, specialized} queries in the session query history/query-specific reformulation history.
RatioUnclickedQueriesVideos[QRH]	Average number of unclicked video search results per unique video query in the session query history/query-specific reformulation history.
	Goal-lessness
CountVideoQueries{Total, Unique}	{Total, Unique} number of video-vertical queries submitted in the query session history.
CountMutualExclusiveQueryTopics	Number of mutually exclusive query topics in the query session history.
CountWebQueries{Total, Unique}	{Total, Unique} number of web-vertical queries submitted in the query session history.
CountOtherQueries{Total, Unique}	{Total, Unique} number of non-web- and non-video-vertical queries submitted in the query session history.
RatioVideo{Unclicked, OneClicked, MoreClicked}Queries	Average number of {unclicked, once-clicked, more-than-once-clicked} video search results per unique video query.
	Goal-directedness
QueryClarityDifferenceToAllQueries[QRH]	Difference between query clarity score of the query, calculated using the top n most relevant video vertical search results to all queries in the session query history/query-specific reformulation history.
QueryTermsOverlap{BothQueries, PreviousQuery, CurrentQuery}Expanded	Number of terms which occur {in both the current query and the previous query, only in the previous query, only in the current query} using query expansion based on co-occurring terms of top n most relevant video vertical search results.
	User familiarity
CountVerticalSwitches	Number of vertical switches before current query.
CountUniqueDomainsVisited	Number of unique domains visited in the overall session history.
CountSearchEngineSwitches	Number of search engines used before current query.
QueryAlreadySubmitted	Flag indicating whether the current query was already submitted.
RatioWeb{Unclicked, OneClicked, MoreClicked}Queries	Average number of {unclicked, once-clicked, more-than-once-clicked} web search results per unique video query.

Indicative for a query and its development with increasing session duration is how well topics overlap expressed in consecutive queries. We expand queries by using the top n videos returned on the video vertical of the search engine. If, within these video search results, a term had a higher-than-average co-occurrence with a query term, it was used to expand the query. For calculating the query clarity score and performing query expansion we use the title information of the top $n = 25$ video search results returned by the search engine.

4.3 Engine indicator features

Our engine indicators are features that extend insights from conventional text QPP to video search results by exploiting visual information of thumbnails associated with each search result. We assume that the consistency of the visual content of top search results will reflect the topical focus of the results list. High consistency should then indicate that the search engine has achieved good performance on the query that generated the results list.

Visual thumbnails can be represented and the visual content consistency can be evaluated at different levels of abstraction, such as the pixel-, visual object-, semantic concept-, scene composition- or scene interpretation-level. Insights acquired in [24] regarding the potential of the visual channel to help retrieve videos using topical queries showed that representation of the visual channel at higher abstraction levels, and in this particular case using distributions of outcomes of a selected number of semantic concept detectors aggregated from long videos, are helpful for this purpose.

While we conjecture that a similar approach could be developed for evaluating the results lists consisting of static visual thumbnails, in this work we do not search for the appropriate representation of the thumbnails, but limit our goal solely to showing, in a light-weight fashion, the potential of the visual information contained in the thumbnails to be helpful for the purpose of such evaluation. We conjecture, namely, that if engine indicators solely based on low-level features (i.e., pixel-level representation) are capable of contributing to query failure prediction, then thumbnail representations at higher abstraction levels will likely make an even larger contribution. We therefore represent video search results visually by extracting standard low-level visual features from thumbnails.

Each visual thumbnail has representations based on local and global visual features. We use a Pyramid Histogram Of visual Words (PHOW) [1] representation for appearance and extract SIFT descriptors from each image on a dense grid. We quantize the descriptors using a vocabulary of 1,000 clusters and compose them in a pyramid histogram. For shape information of the entire image we use a Pyramid Histogram Of Gradients (PHOG) [1] representation. We use a Pyramid Self-Similarity (PSS) [25] representation for capturing the layout of shape context and, similarly to PHOW, quantized descriptors into 1,000 clusters. In general, pyramid histogram construction is done using three levels. Global features were extracted using the open source implementation Lucene Image Retrieval (LIRe) [20]. We extracted the following features: color histograms; MPEG-7 descriptors scalable color, color layout and edge histogram; Tamura texture features coarseness, contrast and directionality; Gabor; color and edge directivity descriptor; fuzzy color and texture histogram; and auto color correlation feature. Visual features are extracted from thumbnails at indexing time and the variance among these thumbnails is calculated in real-time at query time.

The consistency among the top `n` visual search results is calculated in terms of the variance *VD* among the visual thumbnails, represented by visual descriptors. Visual variance within a results list has also been used in [19] to weigh feature vector components and can be formulated as

$$VD = \frac{1}{|RL_n|} \sum_{i=1}^{|RL_n|} \left(\overrightarrow{V_{v_i}} - \vec{M}\right)^2 \quad (3)$$

where RL_n is the set of top `n` video search results and where `n = 25` in our case. Further, $\overrightarrow{V_{v_i}}$ is the i-th visual thumbnail and $\vec{M}$ is the mean of the thumbnails' descriptor components.

4.4 Model Training and Prediction

In the offline step, we apply supervised learning to train generic classifiers on our development set using the extracted features. Ground truth for query instance failure was generated using click information from the transaction log on search sessions. We formulate the context-aware query failure prediction task as binary classification: query instances falling in the class query instance failure `+qif` (query instance success `-qif`) are considered failed (successful).

We trained one binary classifier for each feature set representing a particular observation from user and engine indicators and combine all features of user and engine indicators in generic classifiers trained on all features. For combination of features we use both early and late fusion. For early fusion, all involved features are combined in one single feature vector used for training. For late fusion, different classifiers are first trained and their prediction results are combined in one final feature vector, which is again used for training a final classifier.

We adopted well-known classifiers for our task. Random Forest classifiers are sets of decision trees that return the most likely class label based on the results of the individual internal decision trees. They run efficiently on large datasets and estimate what features and feature sets are crucial in the classification process. We further investigated the usage of rule-based classifiers, pure decision trees, and Naïve Bayes classifiers. Their performance was comparable with the one achieved by the Random Forest classifier, therefore we do not report specific experimental results using these additional classifiers. We use the classifier implementations from the Weka data mining framework [6]. For feature selection we use the *CfsSubsetEval* implementation combined with *Best First search.*

Although we make use of supervised learning, similar to [30], our approach is not restricted and applicable to predict query failure for unseen queries: in an online search session, we extract features from the user indicators and engine indicators and use our trained models in order to make a prediction.

5. EXPERIMENTS

5.1 Experimental Framework

Dataset: From the set of total queries we randomly sampled 108,692 queries for our development set (56,396 unique queries) and 1,110,244 queries for our test set (429,482 unique queries), resulting in a session-based separation of 24,734 and 150,221 sessions for the development and test set, respectively. The development set and test set contain mutually exclusive search sessions. 392,809 unique queries exclusively occur in the test set. Additionally to the user actions available in this transaction log, we collected information from the search results produced by the search engine for each query in our development and test set. We collected textual information—the titles—and visual information—the visual thumbnails—of the 25 most-relevant search results returned by the video search engine. We assume that the first results page of search results contains around 25 documents which are most decisive for the user's satisfaction with the query [3].

Baselines: In order to show that our prediction results using user indicators and engine indicators are non-trivial, we compare them against a set of baselines represented by existing query performance prediction methods: post-retrieval methods are represented by query clarity (QC) [2], and pre-retrieval methods are represented by normalized similarity score between query and collection (NSCQ) [32], query scope (QS) [7], normalized co-degree score (NCDS) [11], and query length (QL) [7]. These baseline scores are calculated using the title information of the top `n = 25` video search results returned by the video search engine. We further calculate the dominant class (DC) baseline—the larger class of `-qif` and `+qif` on our ground truth and assume the worst case that all query instances belong to this class. For the total number of 1,110,244 query instances in our test set, 667,600 are labeled as `-qif` in the ground truth and 442,644 as `+qif`.

Evaluation: The classification results are generated using *10-fold cross-validation* on our test set. Results are reported in terms of Weighted F-measure (WF), defined as F-measure—the harmonic mean of precision and recall—weighted by class size of classes `-qif` and `+qif`. F-measure (F) performance for individual classes `-qif` and `+qif` are also provided in order to see the differences between prediction performance for the two classes. Statistical significant tests were performed using the Wilcoxon signed-rank test ($p<0.05$).

5.2 Baseline Performance

All baseline performances are reported in Table 2.

Table 2: Performance overview of QPP baselines.

Baseline	WF	F (`-qif`)	F (`+qif`)
DC	0.4516	0.751	0.253
QL	0.5453	0.727	0.271
NCDS	0.5669	0.751	0.289
QS	0.6523	0.731	0.533
NSCQ	0.6810	0.744	0.586
QC	**0.6862**	**0.748**	**0.593**

Both, NSCQ and QC baselines achieve a good balance between correctly classified instances of `-qif` and `+qif`, however QC outperforms NCSQ. The relatively strong performance of the conventional QPP baseline demonstrates the potential and the strength of the text-retrieval methods to transfer to video retrieval problems. For the remainder of the experiments we compare performance against the best-performing conventional QPP baseline achieved by the query clarity score

5.3 Prediction Using User Indicators

Here we report results of our methods based on user indicators from the search log. A performance overview is presented in Table 3. We (i) perform feature selection using feature sets derived from our observations of the transaction log, and (ii) combine these feature sets in an early and late fashion. We perform classification derived from features from individual observations and report performance for each observation.

Table 3: Performance overview of user indicator methods.

Features	WF	F (-qif)	F (+qif)
Previous dissatisfaction	0.7647	0.821	0.680
Qu. iterations (all)	0.7153	0.771	0.631
Qu. iterations (QRH)	0.7257	0.783	0.639
Goal-lessness	0.7322	0.783	0.655
Goal-directedness	0.7161	0.778	0.623
User familiarity	**0.7694**	**0.826**	**0.684**
Early fusion	0.7620	0.821	0.673
Late fusion	0.7678	0.820	0.688

Our user indicator-based query failure prediction methods statistically significantly outperform the conventional QPP baseline (QC in Table 2) and achieve an 8% improvement in absolute performance solely by taking local search context into account. The best-performing method is the classifier built on features derived from 'User familiarity'. Another strong performer is 'Previous dissatisfaction', reflecting previous failures in the session. For the observation 'Query iterations', using local features from the query-specific reformulation region of the search session increases the performance compared to using the entire query history results, suggesting the value of using narrow local context. The relatively poor performance achieved by observation 'Goal-directedness' suggests that search goal clarity evolving over a search session is not consistent. Early and late fusions perform well but do not succeed in outperforming individual well-performing observations. Looking at F-measure values of individual classes shows that classifying `+qif` using the proposed classifiers is more conservative than classifying `-qif` instances. Observations clearly achieve a much better result for `-qif` than for `+qif`. The characteristics of successful queries are presumably more stable, most likely reflecting the relatively greater stability of the characteristics of the successful query.

These results allow us to give a positive answer to our first and second research questions RQ1 and RQ2. Context-aware user indicators do outperform conventional context-independent QPP and certain individual observations emerge as more helpful. Because we are interested in investigating a general combined classifier that is robust to the incidental failure of any one particular feature, we continue our experiments on the whole set of features, rather than singling out the top performing individual features.

5.4 Prediction Using Engine Indicators

Here we report results of our methods based on engine indicators from the relatedness of the video items in the search results list. For our experiments, we use the variance among the visual search results (Eq. 3) inspired by the same principle as clarity score. A performance overview is presented in Table 4. We experiment with (i) global and (ii) local visual descriptors of the visual thumbnails in the search results list and (iii) further combine these descriptors using early and late fusion. We performed exploratory experiments with feature selection, which did not show appreciable differences.

Table 4: Performance overview of engine indicator methods.

Features	WF	F (-qif)	F (+qif)
Global visual feat.	0.7348	0.787	0.657
Local visual feat.	0.7349	0.787	0.656
Early fusion	0.7350	0.787	0.657
Late fusion	**0.7356**	**0.788**	**0.656**

All classifiers built using engine indicators statistically significantly outperform the best-performing QPP method (QC in Table 2). Combining existing QPP methods with the variance of the video items in the search results list expressed in terms of visual variance adds 4% improvement in absolute performance. The best performance is achieved using the late fusion approach of classifiers based on visual variance among the search results list represented by global and local visual features extracted from the visual thumbnails.

Since adding information of visual results list relatedness in terms of variance among search results for video search increases classifier performance, we can give a positive answer to our third research question RQ3: visual features have the potential to improve conventional text-based QPP in the scenario of video search. The improvement for query failure predication is quite modest, however, consistent with our expectations for our relatively simple visual representations. However, the demonstration that even a simple representation is able to outperform conventional text-only QPP approaches is a clear sign that the visual component of video search results should not be ignored, but rather potentially makes an important contribution to query failure prediction.

5.5 Prediction Using Combined Indicators

Here we report results on the integration of user indicators and engine indicators achieved by combining all features from both indicators using early and late fusion. A performance overview is presented in Table 5.

Table 5: Performance overview of combined methods.

Features	WF	F (-qif)	F (+qif)
Early fusion	**0.7744**	**0.830**	**0.690**
Late fusion	0.7692	0.819	0.694

The results achieved by our combined methods statistically significantly outperform the best QPP baseline (QC in Table 2). The best performance is achieved using early fusion which achieves almost 9% absolute (13% relative) performance improvement over the baseline. Combining both indicators is helpful for context-aware query failure prediction since the combination exceeds the top performance of user indicators and engine indicators used separately (cf. Table 3 and Table 4).

These results allow us to answer RQ4 positively: there is indeed a potential for engine indicators encoding the visual variance to further improve query failure prediction beyond the performance achievable with only transaction log-derived user indicators.

6. DISCUSSION

To attain a better understanding of our approach and gain additional insights we investigate the prediction results in more detail. Our first investigation focuses on the performance of individual queries and their local search session context in order to understand the usefulness of user indicator features. For each query in our test set, we calculated the performance improvement achieved by our late fusion approach over our best-performing QPP baseline. Three classes of queries emerged as being particularly dramatically improved by user indicator features. We specify the observation corresponding to most important features used by the random forest classifier for each class.

- Queries such as *'youtube'* that returned results that could technically be considered relevant, but did not satisfy the user. We conjecture that users do not click in these results lists because they were actually looking for personalized recommendations and not general results. (Important features from observations 'Goal-lessness' and 'Goal-directedness'.)
- Queries such as *'free movies'* that do not return interesting results due to lack of availability of content. (Important features from observations 'Previous dissat.' and 'Query iterations'.)

- Queries that were submitted to the video vertical of the search engine, but were probably intended for another vertical (*'yahoo mail login'*) and/or were misspelled or otherwise malformed (*'rkellyvideo', 'facebok'*). (Important features from observations 'User familiarity' and 'Previous dissatisfaction'.)

We turned to investigate queries for which user indicator features fail to outperform the baseline and discovered in many cases that these were 'cold-start' queries, i.e., queries which were submitted in the beginning of a user's search session. Their failure is understandable since the session must accumulate sufficient information about query (re)formulation behavior and click-through data to make an appropriate decision. In general, features based on the query-specific reformulation history perform better than features extracted from the whole session query history, implying that the locality of the search session context makes an important contribution for our approach and that only very little information is needed to address the cold start issue.

Our second investigation focuses on the use of representations of visual variance. Visual variance among video search results can, to a certain extent, positively influence poor predictions based on user indicators alone. Figure 8 gives examples of the two queries for which the combination of user indicators and engine indicators outperforms the prediction of our best-performing baseline and helps making correct predictions.

(a) Query *'justin bieber'* (`-qif`) correctly predicted

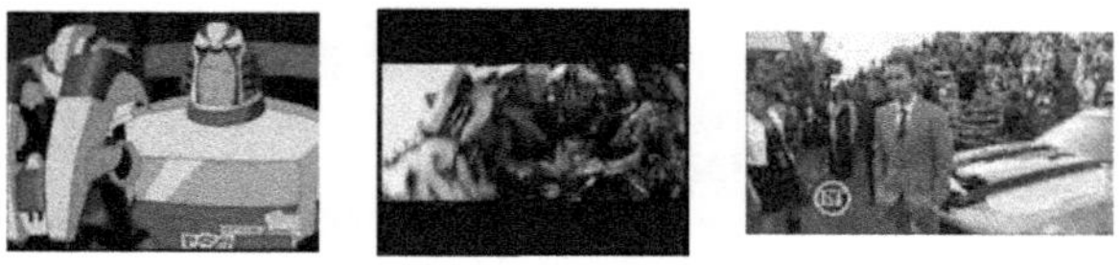

(b) Query *'transformers autobot'* (`+qif`) correctly predicted

Figure 8: Two example queries for which the combination of user indicators and engine indicators positively influence query failure prediction.

For (a), all visual thumbnails show similar content (Justin Bieber in different situations), while for (b) completely different visual thumbnails are presented to the user (scenes from both the comic and the movie of 'Transformers' and a thumbnail from an interview). Based on the idea of visual variance among thumbnails in the search results list, the thumbnails help making a correct prediction. We emphasize that the effect is not dramatic, but that our experimental results clearly serve to demonstrate its potential.

Our final investigation involves the performance of our context-aware query failure prediction approach for video search carried out on long-tail queries, i.e., queries that are very rarely submitted to the video search engine. The long tail is important, as witnessed by the fact that in our test set 36% of all video queries were submitted only one time. We visualize the performance improvement between our best-performing approach using both user indicators and engine indicators and the best-performing conventional QPP baseline and average this improvement over sets of queries submitted with the same frequency (i.e., equally often) to the video search engine. Figure 9 contains this averaged improvement ordered by decreasing query frequency (queries submitted ~8,000 times down to queries submitted 1 time).

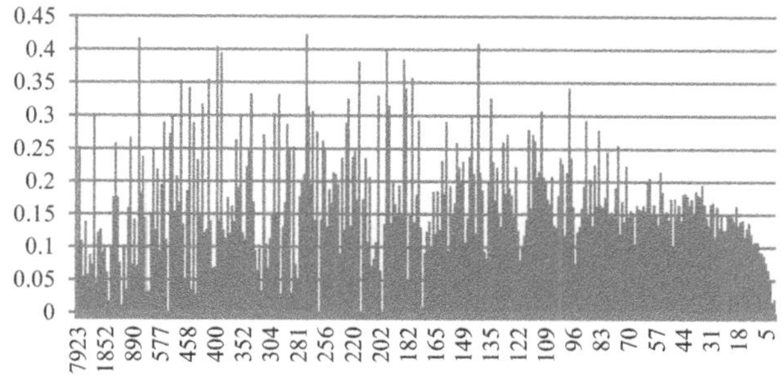

Figure 9: Performance increase between our best-performing method and best-performing baseline, averaged and ordered (from left to right) by decreasing query frequency.

We observe that improvement of the combined approach over the QPP baseline occurs throughout the full range of query frequencies. This distribution demonstrates that the contribution of the search session context features is independent of the frequency of query submission. In other words, the approach performs well not only for general and often submitted queries (e.g., *'youtube music videos', 'clarice taylor', 'seinfeld'*), but also for long-tail queries (e.g., *'number one hit with sade', 'micheal jackon', 'boku no atama'*). Figure 9 also reveals that the improvement over the conventional QPP baseline is more consistent for the long tail, implying that our approach delivers particularly reliable improvement in cases where conventional QPP reaches its limitations, presumably due to too few search results or unexpected diversity. This observation demonstrates the performance our context-aware query failure prediction approach achieves in a specific situation in which the conventional context-independent approach is inadequate.

7. CONCLUSION AND OUTLOOK

We have presented a novel context-aware approach able to predict query failure in video search using user indicators and engine indicators. We performed an exploratory investigation in order to derive observations indicative for context-aware query failure prediction and designed a scalable approach using features derived from these observations. Our results, obtained via experiments performed on a large test set of 1+ million video queries, yield a series of important insights. First, they show that applying conventional QPP methods using textual information from search results lists provided by a video search engine yields reasonable results. We are able to confirm that the basic principle of QPP is transferable from conventional text retrieval to multimedia search and use the best-performing conventional text QPP as baseline against which to compare our proposed method. Second, our results show that conventional QPP is too rigid and that user indicator features derived from the local context of the search session is useful and improves the prediction of query failure. Third, the basic success of QPP motivates us to further adopt a QPP-related consistency criterion to visually capture the quality of the video search results list using the thumbnails associated with each result. This relatively simple engine indicator using low-level thumbnail presentations exploits visual variance of results lists and is capable of delivering a modest, however promising improvement that confirms the potential of visual features. Finally, our results show that the good performance already achieved using prediction approaches based on user indicators can further be improved by combining them with engine indicators.

Our future work will address several aspects. First, we will work on the improvement of engine indicators using visual information from the video search results list. As suggested in Section 4.3, a higher-level representation of thumbnails, such as using the scene composition level of abstraction rather than operating solely on the pixel level is likely to further improve our initial findings. Following the same reasoning, including additional sources of visual information such as motion thumbnails, which are played back once the user hovers over a static thumbnail of a search result, can be assumed to further make a positive contribution to engine indicators. Second, we would like to integrate query performance prediction into video search engines, since the experiments reported here reveal that the performance of our query failure prediction approach is already strong enough to be useful in applications. A promising place to start would be the optimization of ranking, since, as mentioned above, initial work from the text retrieval field has demonstrated that a restricted set of search-session-derived indicators can be successfully exploited to optimize ranking [29]. Ultimately, however, we anticipate that the ability to predict when a video search query would fail will serve to enhance the performance of an entire range of video search engine optimization techniques. For example, a video search engine can attempt to back-off to concept-based video retrieval for queries for which other forms of video retrieval are predicted to fail. Alternatively, query suggestion could be adapted based on the goal of bringing users more quickly to highly successful queries. Further, since search engines are steadily improving their performance and functionality—e.g., the implementation of motion thumbnails, which allows users to briefly preview video without actually clicking it—we aim to work on adaptive query failure prediction for video search which can easily accommodate improvements of search engines and provide consistently good prediction results.

8. ACKNOWLEDGMENTS

This publication was supported by the Dutch national program COMMIT. The authors would like to thank Bing Lang for providing the transaction logs and Yang Yang and Guangxin Ren for their constructive suggestions and support.

9. REFERENCES

[1] Bosch, A., Zisserman, A. and Muoz, X. Image Classification using Random Forests and Ferns. 2007.

[2] Cronen-Townsend, S., Zhou, Y. and Croft, W. B. Predicting query performance. In SIGIR (2002). ACM, 299-306.

[3] Fox, S., Karnawat, K., Mydland, M., Dumais, S. and White, T. Evaluating implicit measures to improve web search. ACM Trans. Inf. Syst., 23, 2, 2005, 147-168.

[4] Guo, Q., White, R. W., Dumais, S. T., Wang, J. and Anderson, B. Predicting query performance using query, result, and user interaction features. In Adaptivity, Personalization and Fusion of Heterogeneous Information (2010), 198-201.

[5] Guo, Q., White, R. W., Zhang, Y., Anderson, B. and Dumais, S. T. Why searchers switch: understanding and predicting engine switching rationales. In SIGIR (2011). ACM, 335-344.

[6] Hall, M., Frank, E., Holmes, G., Pfahringer, B., Reutemann, P. and Witten, I. H. The WEKA data mining software: an update. SIGKDD Explor. Newsl., 11, 1, 2009, 10-18.

[7] He, B. and Ounis, I. Inferring Query Performance Using Pre-retrieval Predictors. 2004.

[8] Hollink, V. and Vries, A. d. Towards an automated query modification assistant. ACM, 2011.

[9] Hsu, W. H., Kennedy, L. S. and Chang, S.-F. Reranking Methods for Visual Search. IEEE MultiMedia, 14, 3, 2007, 14-22.

[10] Huang, J. and Efthimiadis, E. N. Analyzing and evaluating query reformulation strategies in web search logs. In CIKM (2009). ACM, 77-86.

[11] Imran, H. and Sharan, A. Co-occurrence based predictors for estimating query difficulty. In International Conference on Data Mining Workshops (2010). IEEE Computer Society, 867-874.

[12] Jansen, B. J. Search log analysis: What it is, what's been done, how to do it. Library & Information Science Research, 28, 3, 2006, 407-432.

[13] Jansen, B. J., Booth, D. L. and Spink, A. Patterns of query reformulation during Web searching. J. Am. Soc. Inf. Sci. Technol., 60, 7, 2009, 1358-1371.

[14] Jansen, B. J., Spink, A. and Pedersen, J. The effect of specialized multimedia collections on web searching. J. Web Eng., 3, 3, 2004, 182-199.

[15] Joachims, T. Optimizing search engines using clickthrough data. In SIGKDD (2002). ACM, 133-142.

[16] Kim, J. and Can, A. Characterizing Queries in Different Search Tasks. In Hawaii International Conference on System Sciences (2012). IEEE Computer Society, 1697-1706.

[17] Kofler, C., Larson, M. and Hanjalic, A. To seek, perchance to fail: expressions of user needs in internet video search. In ECIR (2011). Springer-Verlag, 611-616.

[18] Kotov, A., Bennett, P. N., White, R. W., Dumais, S. T. and Teevan, J. Modeling and analysis of cross-session search tasks. In SIGIR (2011). ACM, 5-14.

[19] Leuken, R. H. v., Garcia, L., Olivares, X. and Zwol, R. v. Visual diversification of image search results. In WWW (2009). ACM, 341-350.

[20] Lux, M. and Chatzichristofis, S. A. Lire: lucene image retrieval: an extensible java CBIR library. In MM (2008). ACM, 1085-1088.

[21] Mastora, A., Kapidakis, S. and Monopoli, M. Failed Queries: a Morpho-Syntactic Analysis Based on Transaction Log Files. In (2011)

[22] Pu, H.-T. An analysis of failed queries for web image retrieval. J. Inf. Sci., 34, 3, 2008, 275-289.

[23] Rose, D. E. and Levinson, D. Understanding user goals in web search. In WWW (2004). ACM, 13-19.

[24] Rudinac, S., Larson, M. and Hanjalic, A. Exploiting noisy visual concept detection to improve spoken content based video retrieval. In MM (2010). ACM, 727-730.

[25] Shechtman, E. and Irani, M. Matching Local Self-Similarities across Images and Videos. 2007.

[26] Snoek, C. G. M. and Worring, M. Concept-Based Video Retrieval. Found. Trends Inf. Retr., 2, 4, 2009, 215-322.

[27] Tjondronegoro, D., Spink, A. and Jansen, B. J. A study and comparison of multimedia Web searching: 1997-2006. J. Am. Soc. Inf. Sci. Technol., 60, 9, 2009, 1756-1768.

[28] White, R. W., Bennett, P. N. and Dumais, S. T. Predicting short-term interests using activity-based search context. In CIKM (2010). ACM, 1009-1018.

[29] Xiang, B., Jiang, D., Pei, J., Sun, X., Chen, E. and Li, H. Context-aware ranking in web search. In SIGIR (2010). ACM, 451-458.

[30] Yang, L. and Hanjalic, A. Supervised reranking for web image search. In MM (2010). ACM, 183-192.

[31] Zha, Z.-J., Yang, L., Mei, T., Wang, M., Wang, Z., Chua, T.-S. and Hua, X.-S. Visual query suggestion: Towards capturing user intent in internet image search. ACM Trans. Multimedia Comput. Commun. Appl., 6, 3, 2010, 1-19.

[32] Zhao, Y., Scholer, F. and Tsegay, Y. Effective pre-retrieval query performance prediction using similarity and variability evidence. In ECIR (2008). Springer-Verlag, 52-64.

Don't Ask Me What I'm Like, Just Watch and Listen

Ruchir Srivastava
ECE, National University of Singapore
ruchir@nus.edu.sg

Jiashi Feng
ECE, National University of Singapore
a0066331@nus.edu.sg

Sujoy Roy
Institute for Infocomm Research, Singapore
sujoy@i2r.a-star.edu.sg

Shuicheng Yan
ECE, National University of Singapore
eleyans@nus.edu.sg

Terence Sim
SOC, National University of Singapore
tsim@comp.nus.edu.sg

ABSTRACT

Traditional (based on psychology) approaches for personality assessment of an individual require him/her to fill up a questionnaire. This paper presents a novel way of *utilizing multimodal cues to automatically fill up the questionnaire*. The contributions of this work are three-fold. (1) Novel **psychology-based audio/visual/lexical features are proposed** and shown to be effective in predicting answers to a personality questionnaire, Big-Five Inventory-10 (BFI-10). (2) Extracted features are used to learn linear and kernel versions of a **novel regression model**, 'SLoT', to automatically predict BFI-10 answers. The model is based on **S**parse and **Lo**w-rank **T**ransformation (SLoT). (3) Predicted answers are used to compute personality scores using standard BFI-10 scoring scheme. We evaluated our approach on a dataset of 3907 clips (for 50 characters from movies of diverse genres) manually labeled with BFI-10 answers and personality scores as ground-truth. Experiments indicate that the proposed 'SLoT' model effectively automates the answering process by emulating human understanding. We also conclude that predicting personality scores through predicting answers first is better than directly predicting scores based on audio/visual features (as studied in state-of-the art methods).

Categories and Subject Descriptors

I.4 [**Image Processing and Computer Vision**]: Applications; J [**Computer Applications**]: Social and Behavioral Sciences

Keywords

Emotion Recognition, Multimodal Features, Personality Assessment, Movie Analysis

1. INTRODUCTION

Personality tests have become ubiquitous tools for analyzing personality traits. They are designed to test candidates' suitability for a job, test for specific character traits, find personal preferences for facilitating personalized services, etc. Research in psychology significantly correlate personality traits and service preferences. For example, a person seeking sensation would prefer rock, and heavy metal rather than religious music [13]. An extrovert person prefers cheerful music with vocals. Consequently, knowledge about user's personality can significantly benefit a music recommendation system [11].

MM'12, October 29–November 2, 2012, Nara, Japan.

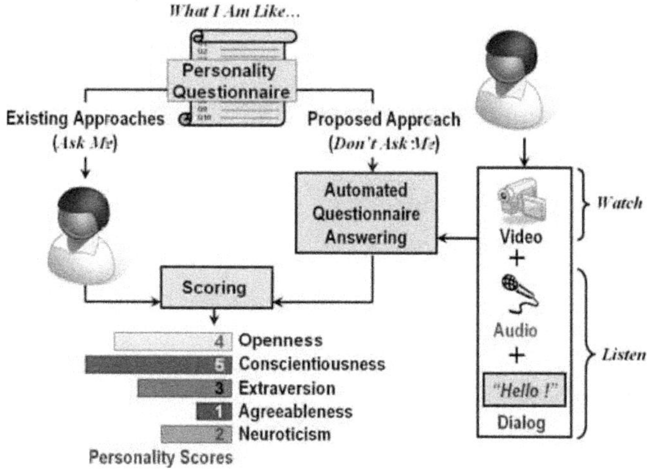

Figure 1: Proposed framework for automating the process of answering personality questionnaire by utilizing multimodal information. Predicted answers are utilized to obtain personality scores along the Big-Five dimensions, i.e. Openness, Conscientiousness, Extraversion, Agreeableness and Neuroticism.

Existing personality assessment methods are mostly based on self-reporting where the individual being assessed (referred hereafter as *target*) fills up a questionnaire. A set of scores, which constitute a measure of the target's personality traits, is computed based on one's responses. However, it has been observed that personality varies over time [25]. Also conducting personality tests at frequent intervals may cause psychological disorders in the target [27].

To remove intervention of the target in personality assessment, one alternative is to automate the answering of personality questionnaires. In this paper, an approach (Figure 1 a.) is proposed in this direction to automate answering one of the most popular personality questionnaires among professionals, the Big Five Inventory (BFI) originally containing 44 questions. A shorter version of the BFI comprising of 10 questions (BFI-10) is used as a first step towards evaluating our approach, which is found to be reliable [23] even though it cannot substitute the full version of the BFI. BFI is based on the Five Factor Model (FFM) [16] which defines the per-

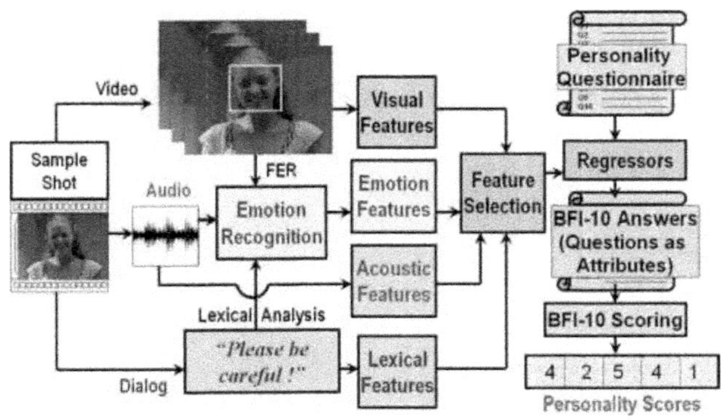

Figure 2: Algorithm of the framework proposed to automatically answer personality questionnaire (Big-Five Inventory-10, in this case). Evaluation is performed on movie characters. Answers to the questionnaire are mapped to the personality scores along the Big-five dimensions (Table 1).

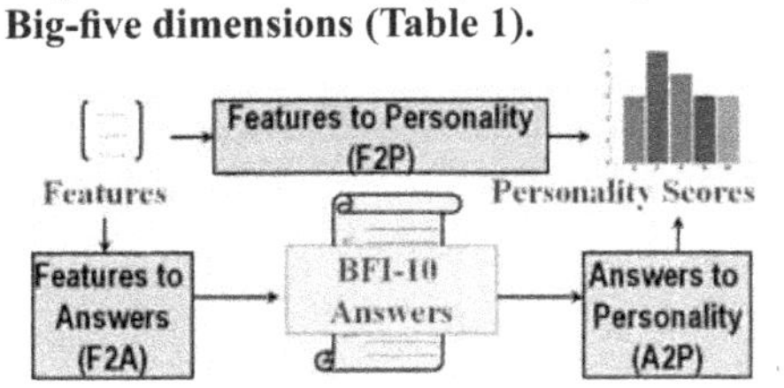

Figure 3: Two approaches for predicting scores for the Big-Five personality traits.

sonality along five dimensions, i.e. *Openness*, *Conscientiousness*, *Extraversion*, *Agreeableness* and *Neuroticism* (Section 3). Henceforth, usage of the term 'BFI' refers to BFI-10.

The proposed approach is evaluated by answering BFI for characters in movies (Figure 2). In the first step, cues from video, audio and dialog are combined for recognizing emotions of the character and subsequently extracting relevant 'emotion features'. Emotion features along with other features (Table 3), inspired by psychological studies, are used to learn linear regression models which relate the features to BFI answers. The linear regression models are regularized by simultaneous sparse and low rank priors, thus providing insights into features relevant for answering each question. Then the selected features are further used to construct kernels for learning kernel-based regression models which predict answers more accurately. In addition, final personality scores, in the range of 1 to 5, are computed from the predicted answers using the BFI scoring scheme (Section 5.2), which is widely adopted by psychologists.

2. RELATED WORKS

Apart from the approach taken in this work, there are works which predict personality traits directly from the multimodal features without taking the route of answering the personality questionnaire. Among such approaches, one of the early works was pioneered by Argamon et al. [2] who used lexical cues from informally written texts to detect Neuroticism and Extraversion in authors. Oberlander and Nowson [18] tried to improve the approach of Argamon et al. by extending to more personality dimensions. Zen et al. [29] estimated levels of Extraversion and Neuroticism of a person using cues from proxemics and visual attention. Going beyond identifying only few of the five personality traits mentioned in the Five Factor Model (FFM), Mairesse et al. [14] analyzed all five personality traits using acoustic features including pitch statistics, intensity statistics, voiced time and speech rate (words per second), in conjunction with lexical features. Mohammadi et al. [17] identified all five personality traits using prosodic features including average, minimum, maximum and relative entropy of pitch, formant frequencies, energy and speaking rate. They obtain satisfactory performance only for Extraversion and Conscientiousness.

The works presented above attempt to directly predict the personality scores from the audio, visual and/or lexical features. However, predicting a semantically high level concept such as personality can be facilitated by recognizing personality attributes which are less subtle as compared to the Big-Five traits. For example, a characteristic *attribute* of Neuroticism is getting nervous easily. It is easier to judge whether a person gets easily nervous than to judge the level of Neuroticism in him/her. Tendency of becoming easily nervous is ascertained using the personality questionnaire.

The proposed work takes this route of answering questions first (F2A + A2P, Figure 3) instead of directly predicting personality traits from the features (F2P). These questions address specific personality attributes which are easier to define than the Big-Five personality traits. Note that this approach is analogous to the *attribute-based classification* introduced for object detection [10]. Under this classification scheme, objects are described using human-defined attributes and these attributes are used for detection instead of training images.

Contributions: The contributions of this work are three-fold. **(1)** We investigate clues provided by psychologists to answer BFI-10. Based on these clues, we propose a collection of novel features extractable from audio/visual/lexical stream of individuals (Section 4). A subset of this pool of features will be relevant for answering each question in BFI-10. **(2)** To learn this subset, a novel regression model, 'SLoT' is proposed. The model is based on **S**parse and **Lo**w-rank **T**ransformation (SLoT) and it predicts BFI-10 answers using the learnt subset of features. Both linear and kernel versions of the model are presented (Section 5.1). **(3)** The idea of automating answering of personality questionnaires (F2A in Figure 3) is novel. Moreover, F2A combined with A2P is found to perform better than the existing F2P approach (Section 6.4).

3. FIVE FACTOR MODEL

The Five Factor Model (FFM) [16] describes human personality along five dimensions (also known as the Big-Five dimensions (or factors) of personality), i.e., *Openness*, *Conscientiousness*, *Extraversion*, *Agreeableness* and *Neuroticism* (Table 1). FFM is chosen for this work since it is gaining popularity among the psychologists as compared to other models of personality [9]. Scores along these dimensions are computed for a person from his/her answers to a questionnaire (personality test).

One such personality test is the Big Five Inventory (BFI) with 44 questions. The shorter version of BFI (BFI-10) contains only 10 questions (Table 4) but is still reliable [23]. Due to its simplicity, BFI-10 has been used in this work to evaluate the proposed approach of automating the process of answering the personality questionnaire. Henceforth the term 'BFI' refers to BFI-10. Manually answering each question of BFI requires selecting one choice (value) from *Disagree Strongly (1), Disagree a little (2), Neither agree nor disagree (3), Agree a little (4), Agree Strongly (5)*. A pair of questions together are used to score each FFM factor (Section 5.2).

4. FEATURE EXTRACTION

Given a movie, before feature extraction, faces of each character are clustered using the method proposed in [7]. After this step, a face track is available for each recognized face, over each shot. Scene change detection is performed by using similarity between

Table 1: The Big-Five dimensions along which personality is scored and the associated traits. Examples of each trait are presented.

Dimension	Associated traits of someone scoring high in the factor	Example: Image frame	Example: Dialog	Remarks
Openness	Appreciation for arts, Imagination, Curiosity, Valuing intellectual matters		That's very sweet	The actress is appreciative.
Conscientiousness	Sense of Responsibility, Order, Dutifulness, Achievement striving, Self-discipline, Deliberation		But I got to get going, because, frankly, I have an ark to build. Busy, busy, busy, busy. Nice meeting you.	The actor is dutiful.
Extraversion	Warmth, Gregariousness, Assertiveness, Activity, Excitement seeking, Positive emotions		...but I really think I can do this!	The actor on the right (speaker) is excited.
Agreeableness	Trust, Straightforwardness, Altruism, Compliance, Modesty, Tender-mindedness		..but with all due respect, miss...	The actor is modest.
Neuroticism	Anxiety, Self-pity, Depression, Being self-conscious, Anger Impulsiveness, Fluctuating moods		You've made a mockery of our entire mission	The actor is angry.

Table 2: Notations used in defining the features

nd	Number of dialogs spoken by the character
D	Dialog
$p(w)$	Polarity of word w (Section 4.1)
E	Emotion set {An, Di, Fe, Ha, Sa, Su, Ne}
t_1	Begin time for dialog
t_2	End time for dialog
z	Acoustic pitch
en	Spectral energy
f_1, f_2	First and second formant frequencies
e	A certain emotion in the emotion set E

Table 3: Explanations of the features extracted from each clip (Notations defined in Table 2)

Feature (Explanation)	Computation
s (Character speaker indicator)	= 0 (non-speech) = 1(speech)
$ep(e)$ (Emotion probability)	Emotion Feature Estimation (Section 4.2)
n_w (Number of words in a dialog)	From dialog
t (Time spent per dialog)	$t = (t_2 - t_1)/n_w$
$p(D)$ (Dialog polarity)	$= \frac{1}{n_w} \sum_{w \in D_c} p(w)$
n (Number of persons)	Maximum no. of faces in the scene containing the clip
$h_{mean}, h_{min}, h_{max}, h_{re}$ Mean, minimum, maximum and relative entropy of h over the clip, where $h \in \{z, en, f_1, f_2\}$	Acoustic analysis (Section 4.1)

color histogram of successive frames [30]. Some manual intervention was needed to correct the errors in recognizing the characters and scene segmentation. Dialog for a shot is found by matching the begin and end times of the shot with the timings of the dialogs from the subtitles. Leading characters are chosen as mentioned in Section 6.1. Multimodal features (Table 3) are extracted from each clip of a character (Section 4.1). Relevant features are selected for answering each question (Section 5.1). Notations used in defining features are described in Table 2.

4.1 Definition of the Features

Each of the used features is chosen based on its utility in answering BFI questionnaire, as identified by psychological studies. The features extracted from each clip (Table 3) are explained below along with the reasons for their choices. The number in bracket tells the number of features associated with each item. Details about the methodology and experiments are presented in Sections 5 and 6, respectively.

1. s: Whether the character speaks ($s = 1$) or not ($s = 0$). More reserved persons are expected to be quiet. Speaker detection is performed by identifying the character with the most prominent lip movements [7].

2. $ep(e)$ (Feature no. 1 to 7): Probability that the character expresses the emotion 'e' ($e \in$ {*Anger (An), Disgust (Di), Fear (Fe), Happiness (Ha), Sadness (Sa), Surprise (Su), Neutral (Ne)*}). Expressed emotions are found to be correlated with personality traits. For example, outgoing and sociable persons are expected to be happier. [19]. Tendency to become easily nervous is reflected in the extent to which a person is fearful [15]. A person getting nervous easily is also prone to depression and becomes sad [22]. Someone doing a thorough job can restrain his anger and consequently doesn't seem to be angry most often [8].

3. t (Feature no. 8): Time taken to speak a dialog.

4. n_w (Feature no. 9): Number of words in a dialog. Number of words combined with the time taken to speak a dialog is indicative of the speech rate which is low for a person with artistic interests [1].

5. $p(D)$ (Dialog Polarity) (Feature no. 10): Indicates whether the dialog has positive ($p(D) > 0$) or negative ($p(D) < 0$) connotation as determined using Dictionary of Affect in Language (DAL) [26]. E.g. the word 'excellent' has positive connotation while 'poor' has negative connotation. Polarity of the dialog is calculated by averaging the polarity of all the words in the dialog which are present in DAL. Persons expressing more positive emotions are expected to be more trustworthy as compared to those expressing mostly negative emotions.

6. n (Feature no. 11): Number of persons in the scene containing the clip under consideration. A sociable person is expected to be with more people as compared to a reserved person. All persons in a scene may be visible only in few frames of the scene. Therefore the number of persons in a scene is computed as the maximum number of faces detected over all the frames in the scene.

7. $h_{mean}, h_{min}, h_{max}, h_{re}$ (Features no. 12 to 27): Mean, minimum, maximum and relative entropy of the parameter h in a clip, $h \in \{z, en, f_1, f_2\}$. Variable '$z$' has been used to represent acoustic pitch in order to avoid confusion with probability represented by 'p'. en, f_1 and f_2 represent spectral energy, first and second formant frequencies for the audio signal related to the clip. Spectral energy is a measure of energy at different frequencies and is high at dominant frequencies. First Formant frequency is the amplitude peak in the frequency spectrum of the audio signal corresponding to the lowest frequency. The amplitude peak with the next higher frequency is the second formant frequency. Relative entropy of a random variable h with possible values $x_1, x_2, x_3 ..., x_n$, is a measure of the uncertainty of a random variable and is defined as [17]:

$$h_{re} = \frac{1}{\log(|h|)} \left(- \sum_{i=1}^{n} P(x_i) \log(P(x_i)) \right). \quad (1)$$

Here $|h|$ denotes the cardinality of h. Note that the item 7 above indicate the voice properties which are found to be useful in answering the questions [17]. For example, a fault finder is more likely to shout at others. Also a person who can handle stress well is usually expected to speak softly.

4.2 Emotion Feature Estimation

Probability of the presence of each of the seven emotions in a clip is predicted by combining predictions from facial expression recognition, acoustic analysis and lexical analysis using Support Vector Machines (SVM) in a late fusion scheme. The details are explained below.

Facial Expression Recognition (FER) For each clip, faces detected in each frame are resized to 50×50 pixels and Gabor features were extracted [3]. Principal Component Analysis (PCA) is applied on the resultant feature matrix to reduce its dimension from $50 \times 50 \times 8 \times 9 \times N (= 180,000 \times N)$ to $100 \times N$, where N is the number of frames. Reduced feature matrix is fed to SVM to predict the posterior probability of each of the seven emotions. Posterior probability for the whole clip is obtained as the mean of posterior probabilities of all the frames in that clip.

Acoustic Analysis From the audio track in a clip, prosodic features, namely mean values of spectral energy, first and second formant frequencies, Mel Frequency Cepstral coefficients (MFCC) features, Linear Predictive Coding coefficients and pitch are extracted. Other features extracted are standard deviation of amplitude and maximum, minimum and standard deviation of pitch. An SVM classifier trained using features extracted from the training data predicts the probability of the audio track of a test clip belonging to each of the seven emotions.

Note that some of the acoustic features namely mean values of spectral energy, first two formant frequencies and pitch are also used for F2A (Section 4.1). This is because apart from emotions, these features also indicate personality traits such as shouting which may not be always captured in the expressed emotion.

Lexical Analysis of Dialogs Each clip is accompanied by one or more dialogs. In the case of multiple speakers, we only consider the dialog(s) spoken by the character whose personality is being assessed. Emotions conveyed through the dialog are recognized based on emotions associated with 'emotional words' in the dialog. Examples of emotional words are 'scary', 'jubilant' etc. which convey emotions. Lexical analysis proposed in [6] is applied to obtain the probability of an emotional word belonging to each emotion class.

Multimodal Fusion In this work, we employ decision level multimodal fusion. For decision level fusion, SVM has been found to perform much better as compared to other methods and thus we use SVM for our multimodal fusion task. To fuse the three modalities, namely, Visual, Acoustic and Lexical, the probability scores from these three modalities for a particular clip are concatenated to form a feature vector which is passed to SVM and the outputs are the probabilities of the seven emotions being present in the clip. Details about the experimental settings are given in Section 6.2.

4.3 Forming Feature Matrices for Regression

Multi-modal features are extracted from clips containing speech (*i.e.*, $s = 1$). Extracted features from training clips are stacked to form a matrix F_{tr} which is used for learning the linear regression model. If N_s and N_f are the total number of training clips and the number of features respectively, then F_{tr} is an $N_s \times N_f$ matrix. The matrix F_{tes} of test clips is formed in the similar way by using features extracted from testing clips.

5. PERSONALITY ASSESSMENT FRAMEWORK

This section describes the personality assessment framework. Instead of using F2P approach (Figure 3), the proposed approach consists of two stages (Figure 3): **(1) F2A:** Constructing a transformation from features to the BFI answers that takes into account its underlying sparse and low-rank structure. **(2) A2P:** Computing personality scores (for the Big-Five personality dimensions) from the predicted answers using the standard BFI scoring scheme [23].

This two-stage approach is motivated by the fact that the relationship between the features and abstract personality traits is generally difficult to describe through a simple linear model, as previously explained in Section 2. Thus, we attempt to learn a model for predicting answers to BFI-10 questionnaire from features which is like a mid-level step in understanding the semantic hierarchy from features to personality traits.

5.1 F2A by Sparse and Low-rank Transformation (SLoT)

Formulation: The linear transformation from features to BFI-10 answers contains both sparse and low-rank structure (explained later in this section). Therefore, in learning such a transformation, we enforce these structures via specific matrix norms in addition to minimizing the regression error.

Let Z be a $10 \times N_{tr}$ matrix containing the ground truth of the 10 answers for all the training clips, F_{tr} be the training matrix defined in Section 4.3 and W be a $10 \times N_f$ matrix containing the param-

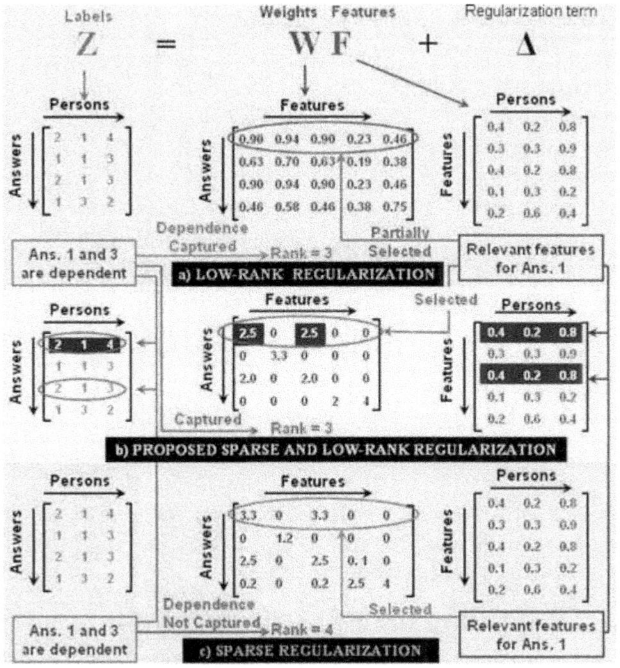

Figure 4: Effect of enforcing (b) both low-rank and sparse regularization (LS) compared to enforcing either (a) Low-rank regularization (LR) or (c) Sparse regularization (SR) for F2A. W learnt by LS is both sparse and not full rank. Lines and text in green (red) refer to desirable (not desirable) properties.

eters of the regression model. The objective is to estimate W, the transformation matrix, with sparse and low-rank structure from the training samples (F_{tr}, Z), which can be formulated as,

$$\min_{W} \left\{ \frac{1}{2}\|Z - WF_{tr}\|_F^2 + \lambda_1\|W\|_* + \lambda_2\|W\|_1 \right\}. \quad (2)$$

Here $\|\cdot\|_F$ represents matrix Frobenius norm, $\|\cdot\|_*$ denotes the matrix nuclear norm which is a well-known convex surrogate for the matrix rank, and $\|\cdot\|_1$ is the matrix ℓ_1 norm which is known to be convex surrogate for the matrix ℓ_0 norm.

Reasons for Enforcing Sparse and Low-Rank Structure: In F2A, the answers may be closely related. For example, a person who is outgoing and sociable (Question 6) would want to be thorough in his activities (Question 8) as this may attract others. These correlations would make the answers lie in a lower dimensional subspace. This means, if the rows in Z are correlated, then the corresponding rows in W should reflect that correlation. This makes W low-rank. The term $\|W\|_*$ in Equation 2 is a regularization to enforce W to be low rank. Moreover, intuitively, each answer is influenced by only a subset of all the features. This means, many of the entries in W should be close to zero resulting in W to be sparse. The term $\|W\|_1$ in Equation 2 enforces W to be sparse. In this way we enforce the linear regression model to be sparse and low-rank simultaneously [31]. λ_1 and λ_2 are regularization parameters meant to achieve a trade off between regression error and the desired sparse and low-rank structure.

Figure 4 depicts an illustrative example of the need for enforcing (b) both low-rank and sparse regularization (LS) compared to either (a) Low-rank regularization (LR) or (c) Sparse regularization (SR) for F2A. Only 4 answers, 3 persons and 5 features are considered. Note that answers 1 and 3 are dependent (similar for the same person). To capture this in W, rows 1 and 3 should be correlated, which means W should be low-rank. Further, the answers should be influenced by only a subset of the features in F which means many of the elements in W should be close to zero (sparse). Figure 4(a) presents W learnt using LR. Note that although W is not full-rank (row 1 and 3 are correlated), it is not sparse (no zero elements). Figure 4(c) presents W learnt using SR. Note that although W is sparse (zero elements), it is full rank (row 1 and 3 are not correlated). Figure 4(b) presents W learnt using LS. Note that W is both sparse (zero elements) and not full rank (row 1 and 3 are correlated), thus satisfying the requirement for sparse and low-rank structure.

Solving Equation 2 The objective function in Equation (2) can be verified to be convex and solved effectively. However, due to the non-smoothness of the regularization terms, the above problem can not be directly solved using traditional first-order or second-order optimization methods. In this work, we adopt the Augmented Lagrange Multiplier (ALM) method due to its efficiency and fast convergence rate [12].

Before applying ALM, we reformulate the primal problem by introducing two additional variables W_1 and W_2 as follows such that in each iteration we can have closed-form solution.

$$\min_{W,W_1,W_2} \left\{ \frac{1}{2}\|Z - WF_{tr}\|_F^2 + \lambda_1\|W_1\|_* + \lambda_2\|W_2\|_1 \right\}$$
$$\text{subject to}: \; W = W_1, W = W_2. \quad (3)$$

It can be seen that the above problem is equivalent to the original problem in Equation (2). And its corresponding augmented Lagrange function is defined as:

$$\mathcal{L} = \left\{ \frac{1}{2}\|Z - WF_{tr}\|_F^2 + \lambda_1\|W_1\|_* + \lambda_2\|W_2\|_1 + \langle Y_1, W - W_1\rangle + \langle Y_2, W - W_2\rangle + \frac{\mu}{2}\|W - W_1\|_F^2 + \frac{\mu}{2}\|W - W_2\|_F^2 \right\}. \quad (4)$$

Here, μ is a positive constant to control the approximation precision and grows in the optimization iterations. The variables Y_1 and Y_2 are Lagrange multipliers for the penalty terms. By introducing the two additional variables W_1 and W_2, the problem in Equation (4) can be optimized alternatively w.r.t. W, W_1 and W_2 by fixing the other two variables.

For the convenience of describing the details of the optimization process, we first introduce the following soft-thresholding (shrinkage) operator:

$$\mathcal{S}_\varepsilon[x] = \begin{cases} x - \varepsilon, & \text{if } x > \varepsilon, \\ x + \varepsilon, & \text{if } x < -\varepsilon, \\ 0, & \text{otherwise,} \end{cases} \quad (5)$$

where ε is the threshold magnitude.

We optimize the problem in an alternative manner. Firstly, we fix the variables W and W_2, then the objective function w.r.t. W_1 is

$$\min_{W_1} \left\{ \lambda_1\|W_1\|_* + \langle Y_1, W - W_1\rangle + \frac{\mu}{2}\|W - W_1\|_F^2 \right\}.$$

Since it is standard that [12],

$$U\mathcal{S}_\varepsilon[S]V^T = \underset{X}{\operatorname{argmin}} \left(\varepsilon\|X\|_* + \frac{1}{2}\|X - W\|_F^2 \right),$$

we can obtain the closed form solution for W_1:

$$W_1 = U\mathcal{S}_{\lambda_1\mu^{-1}}[S]V^T, \quad (6)$$

where $(U, S, V) = \text{svd}(W + \mu^{-1}Y_1)$ is obtained from the singular value decomposition.

When fixing W and W_1, the objective function for W_2 becomes,

$$\min_{W_2} \left\{\lambda_2\|W_2\|_1 + \langle Y_2, W - W_2\rangle + \frac{\mu}{2}\|W - W_2\|_F^2\right\}.$$

Since we know [12],

$$\mathcal{S}_\varepsilon[W] = \operatorname*{argmin}_X \left(\varepsilon\|X\|_1 + \frac{1}{2}\|X - W\|_F^2\right),$$

the closed form solution to W_2 can be obtained:

$$W_2 = \mathcal{S}_{\lambda_2\mu^{-1}}[W + \mu^{-1}Y_2]. \tag{7}$$

For W, the objective function is a standard quadratic function and the closed form solution of W is:

$$W = \left(ZF_{tr}^T + \mu(W_1 + W_2) - Y_1 - Y_2\right)\left(F_{tr}F_{tr}^T + \mu I\right)^{-1}. \tag{8}$$

The details of the optimization algorithm for estimating W are shown in Algorithm 1. The estimated model W is a $10 \times N_f$ matrix with each row corresponding to a question and each column corresponding to a feature. Predictions on test data are obtained as $Z_{tes} = WF_{tes}$ and are rounded to the nearest whole number. For Kernel Regression, the top 5 weight magnitudes for each question (row of W) are selected and the corresponding features are assumed relevant for answering that question. The selected features are further used to construct kernel for learning kernel-based regressor by slightly changing the formulations presented here.

Extension to Kernel Regression: The method presented above performs linear regression since W relates the feature matrix to the BFI answers. In order to extend it to Kernel regression, we need to Kernelize the feature matrix. As mentioned above, for predicting different answers, we select different relevant features and use the selected ones to construct the kernel matrix. Let $K^{(a)}$ be the desired kernel matrix for the a-th answer prediction whose elements $k_{ij}^{(a)}$ is calculated as:

$$k_{ij}^{(a)} = \exp\left(-\frac{1}{\sigma^2}(\|\mathbf{f}^{(a)}{}_i - \mathbf{f}^{(a)}{}_j\|^2)\right) \tag{9}$$

Here $\mathbf{f}^{(a)}{}_i$ refers to the selected features of the ith sample. The problem in Equation (2) is now re-formulated as:

$$\min_W \left\{\sum_{a=1}^{10} \frac{1}{2}\|Z_a - W_a K_{tr}^{(a)}\|_F^2 + \lambda_1\|W_a\|_* + \lambda_2\|W_a\|_1\right\}. \tag{10}$$

where Z_a and W_a denote the a-th row of the corresponding matrices. Note that in the kernelized case, sparse regularization is still imposed to encourage the regression model to select a small fraction of the training samples (serve as support samples as in SVM) for the answers prediction. Since for different answers prediction, their regression models W_a's are independent and we can optimize them separately. And each sub-problem is similar to the optimization of Equation (2) and we can apply Algorithm 1 directly.

A Note on Convergence The solution derived from the applied ALM method is guaranteed to converge to the optimal solution by following theorem [12].

THEOREM 1 (ADAPTED FROM [12]). *Any accumulation point W^* of W_k^* is an optimal solution to the primal problem* (3) *and the convergence rate is at least $O(\mu_k^{-1})$ in the sense that*

$$\left|\frac{1}{2}\|Z - W^*F\|_F^2 + \lambda_1\|W_k^*\|_* + \lambda_2\|W_k^*\|_1 - f^*\right| = O(\mu_k^{-1}),$$

where f^* is the optimal value of problem (3).

Algorithm 1 ALM algorithm for objective (3).

Input: $Z \in \mathbb{R}^{10\times N_{tr}}$, $F \in \mathbb{R}^{N_f \times N_{tr}}$, λ_1, λ_2, iter$_{\max}$ and ϵ.
Output: $W \in \mathbb{R}^{10\times N_f}$.
Initialization: $W^{(0)} = W_1^{(0)} = W_2^{(0)} = Y_1^{(0)} = Y_2^{(0)} = 0$, $\mu_0 > 0, \rho > 1, k = 0$.
repeat
  Calculate $W_1^{(k+1)^*} \leftarrow W_1$ according to Equation (6);
  Calculate $W_2^{(k+1)^*} \leftarrow W_2$ according to Equation (7);
  Calculate $W^{(k+1)^*} \leftarrow W$ according to Equation (8);
  $Y_1^{(k+1)} = Y_1^{(k)} + \mu_k\left(W^{(k+1)^*} - W_1^{(k+1)^*}\right)$;
  $Y_2^{(k+1)} = Y_2^{(k)} + \mu_k\left(W^{(k+1)^*} - W_2^{(k+1)^*}\right)$;
  $\mu_{k+1} = \rho\mu_k, k \leftarrow k + 1$.
until $t >$ iter$_{\max}$ or $|f(W^{(k+1)}) - f(W^{(k)})| < \epsilon$

From the above theorem, we can see that as the value of μ_k grows, the optimization algorithm will converge faster and it provides a Q-linear convergence rate [5].

5.2 A2P using the BFI scoring scheme

Answers obtained for each of the ten questions are mapped onto personality scores along five dimensions using the standard methodology used for scoring BFI-10 [23]. The scoring scheme is mentioned below.

The questions associated with each of the five factors are mentioned in Table 4b. Where suffix 'R' to a question number indicates that the answer for this question will be reverse scored. The values of answers are in the range of 1 to 5. In order to reverse score an answer the value is subtracted from 6. For example, if questions 1 and 6 have values of 2 and 3 respectively, in order to calculate extraversion score, value for question one will be subtracted from 6 and it becomes 4 while value for question 6 remains 3. Next, for each of the Big Five factors, the values of questions associated with that factor are averaged. In our example, the final score for extraversion will be average of 4 and 3 i.e. 3.5.

6. EXPERIMENTS AND DISCUSSIONS

6.1 Dataset

Unlike emotions or mood, personality is a long-lived trait [21] of a person, which makes personality assessment an interesting topic. But this also means automatic personality assessment would require observing the target over a long period of time in different surroundings and contexts. Hence getting real-life data for our experiments would require monitoring individuals in real-life over long periods of time. Although not impossible, this would require huge amount of effort and overcoming of many practical concerns like privacy etc.

To get around these social and technical issues and still attempt to investigate the problem at hand we have chosen to track characters in movie's as our targets and create a data set consisting of clips of individual characters in the movies. Although, movies cannot fully substitute for real life behaviour, actions and emotions of movie characters are close to real life [28]. Having a diverse collection of genres could reduce the possibility of bias. We also note that emotions expressed by characters in movies are mostly spontaneous, subtle and real. Following is a distribution of the emotions of characters in our data set as labelled by labellers (ground-truth discussed in detail later) corresponding to the 7 emotion classes discussed in Section 4.1 - {10.6,0.3,5.6,17.4,3.8,56.3}. Note that

Table 4: a. Big Five Inventory-10 (BFI-10) used to assess personality along with F2A results. Shaded columns correspond to the proposed methods. Comparison is made with classic SVM (l-SVM), sparse SVM (s-SVM), Ridge Regression (RR) and kernel-SVM (k-SVM). b. Questions in BFI-10 used for computing scores for each factor. c. Accuracies in recognizing each emotion (in %). Average Recognition Rate (ARR) = 79.21%. Note that ARR won't be equal to the mean of individual accuracies due to different number of samples for each emotion. An: Anger, Di: Disgust, Fe: Fear, Ha: Happiness, Sa: Sadness, Su: Surprise, Ne: Neutral, Acc: Accuracy.

Instruction: How well do the following statements describe the character's personality?						
You see the character as someone who ...	Accuracy (%)					
	Linear				Kernel	
	l-SVM	s-SVM	RR	l-SLoT	k-SVM	k-SLoT
1... is reserved	87.0	86.6	84.0	86.2	87.4	87.4
2... is generally trusting	75.0	72.1	71.9	73.8	73.8	75.1
3... tends to be lazy	85.2	94.4	91.9	93.0	94.1	94.5
4... is relaxed and handles stress well	64.7	60.3	59.9	63.2	64.6	65.1
5... has few artistic interests	94.3	93.4	91.3	93.0	88.6	94.4
6... is outgoing, sociable	75.2	73.9	73.4	75.0	74.6	75.8
7... tends to find fault with others	71.5	71.2	69.0	71.9	72.9	73.3
8... does a thorough job	84.7	82.7	81.2	84.2	84.8	84.8
9... gets nervous easily	73.9	81.1	78.5	80.4	78.1	81.2
10... has an active imagination	85.0	88.1	85.7	87.2	87.0	88.2
Mean accuracy	79.7	80.4	78.7	80.8	80.6	**82.0**

a.

Factor	Qs
O	5R, 10
C	3R, 8
E	1R, 6
A	2, 7R
N	4R, 9

b.

Emotion	Acc.
An	86.8
Di	80.2
Fe	73.3
Ha	78.2
Sa	77.7
Su	79.0
Ne	78.6

c.

Figure 5: Images showing relevant features predicted using l-SLoT, Sparse SVM (s-SVM) and psychological findings. A white cell at position (i, j) means that the jth feature is predicted to be relevant for predicting the ith answer. The F1 scores for feature selection using l-SLoT and s-SVM are 0.81 and 0.70 respectively. A higher F1 score for l-SLoT indicates that it is better than s-SVM for feature selection.

(a) l-SLoT (b) Psychology (c) Sparse SVM

56% of the characters were indicated to have neutral emotion. This is possible only when the characters indeed did not display any emotions or the emotions expressed were too subtle to detect. The second possibility is highly likely as we are dealing with actors. In real life, peoples emotions are very subtle and display of exaggerated emotions are few. This also justifies why several recent works [4] have tried to analyse movie data, considering them near to real-life.

However we do admit that movie data have their advantages which can be considered as shortcomings in imitating a real situation. They are well recorded, viz. in general, faces are frontal or near frontal (compared to CCTV footages of individuals), audio quality is clearer and sometimes carries the mood of the situation and dialogues are machine understandable.

Our dataset consists of 3907 clips corresponding to 50 characters from movies of diverse genres namely Comedy (917 clips), Adventure (981 clips), Drama (952 clips), Fantasy (626 clips) and Action (431 clips) [1]. While a movie contains many more clips of actors, we selected shots of characters with minimum 30 dialogues to ensure that we consider only characters who can be observed for a longer time. Each clip is of around 4-7 seconds duration at 30 frames per seconds. The video resolution varies from 640×272 to 720×360. Dialogs along with the timings are given in subtitles. Overall, our dataset covers more scenarios of life as compared to existing context specific datasets [29, 17, 20].

Ground truth: Clips are labeled by 5 domain experts (graduate students in psychology) who have good knowledge about emotions and the Big-Five Factor theory. The reliability of agreement between labelers is measured by Fleiss Kappa (fk) measure. Each clip contains labels for (1) emotion of the main character in the clip (fk=0.2603), (2) answers to the BFI-10 questions for each clip indicated by an integer in the range [1,5] corresponding to the 5 intensity levels discussed in Section 3 (fk=0.2410) and (3) personality score for each clip based on the Big-Five dimensions discussed in Section 3 (fk=0.2010). The fk values show a higher inter labeler agreement for emotions as compared to BFI answers and personality scores. This is because it may be easier to recognize emotions rather than personality traits. For all the three labels, the fk values do not show a very high agreement. This is because it is hard to understand the semantics of emotions and personality traits. Moreover fk values depend on the number of labelers and using more labelers can increase the agreement between them. Majority voting was used to decide the final label. Note that personality scores can also be obtained from the the labeled BFI-10 answers using the BFI-scoring scheme (Section 5.2).

The dataset is divided into training and testing clips. Training clips are used to train SVM models for (1) facial expression recognition, (2) acoustic analysis, (3) multimodal fusion (Section 4.2) and (4) regressors based on l-SLoT and k-SLoT.

Training and Testing Data: 25% of the clips are used for training and remaining clips are used for testing. The training clips are uniformly sampled from each movie genre. 4-fold cross-validation is performed to ensure that each clip is tested once.

[1]The clips are from these movies: *Comedy: Evan Almighty, Adventure: Meet Dave, Titanic, Drama: The Prestige, Fantasy: Bedtime stories* and *Action: You don't mess with the Zohan.*

6.2 F2A Experimental Results

This subsection presents experimental results for F2A prediction. A major intermediate step in F2A is emotion recognition whose accuracy is given in Table 4c. Average Recognition Rate (79.2%) is low possibly because movie data is close to reality and has difficulties such as low illumination or resolution, background noise in audio etc.

Table 4 presents 4-fold cross-validation performance for both linear and kernel based methods. The performances of the proposed l-SLoT and k-SLoT methods have been compared with other possible methods for F2A.

Linear methods: For l-SLoT, $\lambda_1 = 4$ and $\lambda_2 = 5$ based on cross validation on the training data. For ALM optimization, the parameters are selected as $\mu = 10^{-4}, \epsilon = 10^{-8}, iter_{max} = 10^3$ and $\rho = 1.1$.

Performance of l-SLoT is compared with Ridge Regression (RR) which uses the standard l_2 norm regularization. This comparison demonstrated the efficacy of using Sparse and Low-Rank regularization. Results are better results in the case of l-SLoT as compared to RR in Table 4.

Instead of regression, F2A can also be treated as a 5-class classification problem, each class corresponding to one of the 5 values for the answers (Section 3). The classification problem is solved using different versions of SVM namely Linear SVM (l-SVM) and Sparse SVM (s-SVM) and compared with l-SLoT.

Kernel based methods: For k-SLoT, λ_1 and λ_2 are set as 3 and 4 respectively and a Radial Basis Function (RBF) kernel with $\sigma = 4$ is used, these values being selected based on cross validation on training data.

From the results (Table 4), it is observed that k-SLoT performs the best. Prediction accuracy using k-SLoT exceeds 70% (well above the accuracy by chance, 20%) for all answers except answer no. 4, related to the character being relaxed and handling stress well.

Answer no. 4 is observed to have the worst predicted accuracy for all the selected methods. Note that for predicting this answer, the highest weighted feature was feature number 6 i.e. emotion probability for Surprise. Moreover, feature selection results in Figure 5a. show that feature number 6 (column 6 in the image) is selected only for answer 4. It is possible that emotion probability of Surprise may not be a reliable feature for our problem so it was not selected for other answers. However, it has been wrongly selected for this answer (Answer no. 4). It is possible that extending the pool of features can introduce more reliable features and reduce such errors.

Feature-Selection: Since, feature selection is not inherent in classic (linear) SVM (l-SVM) or kernel SVM (k-SVM), irrelevant features need to be removed before feeding to the SVM classifier. Effectiveness of feature selection using l-SLoT is demonstrated in this subsection and compared with feature selection using s-SVM.

For F2A, both l-SLoT and s-SVM output a weight to each feature. The first k highest weighted features are selected such that sum of their weights (absolute value) achieve 50% of the sum of all the weights (Figure 5). Each of the two feature selection techniques is compared while considering the feature choice inspired by psychology as the ground truth (Figure 5).

The F1-score for feature selection using l-SLoT and s-SVM are found to be 0.81 and 0.70 respectively. F1-score is an accuracy measure which should be high for a greater accuracy. l-SLoT outperforms s-SVM in feature selection as reflected by its higher F1-score. Out of all the selected features, only top 5 are used for experiments using SVM since it was observed that for some of the features only 5 weights were significant.

Table 5: Results of predicting scores for the Big-Five personality traits for both F2A+A2P and F2P approaches. The column corresponding to the proposed method is shaded. O: Openness, C: Conscientiousness, E: Extraversion, A: Agreeableness, N: Neuroticism.

Trait	Accuracies				
	F2A+A2P			F2P	
	k-SLoT	s-SVM	k-SVM	[17]	DS
O.	84.8	84.1	83.7	21.7	15.2
C.	81.1	79.4	80.7	5.3	12.5
E.	69.4	67.7	63.0	20.5	28.5
A.	60.3	57.5	58.9	12.3	12.8
N.	58.0	54.6	56.0	9.8	42.5
Avg.	**70.7**	68.7	68.5	13.9	22.3

6.3 F2A+A2P Experimental Results

After obtaining the answers to BFI, personality scores are computed based on the algorithm presented in Section 5.2. Table 5 tabulates the results for F2A + A2P approaches wherein k-SLoT is compared with the following baseline approaches:

Using Sparse SVM (s-SVM) : Answers are predicted using s-SVM (Section 6.2) and then the personality scores are predicted using the BFI scoring scheme.

Using Kernel SVM (k-SVM) : Answers are predicted using k-SVM with RBF kernel (Section 6.2) and then the personality scores are predicted using the BFI scoring scheme.

The results in Table 5 show that k-SLoT performs the best in predicting all of the Big-Five personality traits. [17] report a much higher accuracy on their dataset (66.4% Avg. accuracy in predicting the Big-Five personality traits) on a 2 class (High and Low) problem. Note that we are solving a 5 class problem (predictions are whole numbers from 1 to 5).

There exists correlation between the accuracies of predicted answers and the personality traits. Neuroticism has the worst prediction accuracy which can be attributed to the low prediction rate of answer 4, which Neuroticism is associated with. Similarly, Agreeableness is associated with answers 2 and 7 which also have lower prediction accuracy. Consequently, prediction of Agreeableness is affected.

Confusion matrices for personality prediction using KR2 are presented for each of the Big-Five dimensions in Table 6. The confusion matrices show that confusion is mainly in between scores close to each other. For example, for openness, the score of 1 is confused mainly with 2 (confusion is 33% of times). This indicates an acceptable prediction since 1 refers to disagree strongly and 2 refers to disagree a little. Disagreement is present in both the scores although degree of disagreement may differ.

Table 9 shows examples of prediction on a few sample clips. In most of the cases, 4 out of 5 personality scores were predicted correctly.

6.4 F2P Experimental Results

The following methods are evaluated which use the F2P approach (Figure 3) for predicting scores for the Big-Five personality traits:

Direct Scoring (DS): In the case of direct prediction from features, the input is the feature matrix F_{tr} (Section 4.3) and the ground truth labels are the personality scores for all characters used for training sparse SVM for the five dimensions. The ground truth labels are obtained as mentioned in Section 6.1. The learned sparse SVM then predicts the personality scores for the test characters.

Mohammadi et al. ([17], see Section 2) RBF kernel SVM is used for predicting personality scores as integers in [1,5].

Table 6: Confusion matrices for A2P using k-SLoT.

Openness

	1	2	3	4	5
1	66.67	33.33	0.00	0.00	0.00
2	9.80	75.16	7.84	3.27	3.92
3	0.83	6.27	85.10	7.18	0.62
4	1.00	7.00	6.67	79.00	6.33
5	0.00	3.33	6.67	6.67	83.33

Conscientiousness

	1	2	3	4	5
1	66.67	16.67	16.67	0.00	0.00
2	10.29	72.06	12.65	2.94	2.06
3	1.02	10.15	81.30	6.64	0.89
4	3.92	4.90	6.54	83.99	0.65
5	3.03	3.03	3.03	6.06	84.85

Extraversion

	1	2	3	4	5
1	60.00	20.00	6.67	13.33	0.00
2	16.18	60.50	13.24	6.62	3.47
3	2.55	12.34	71.09	10.48	3.54
4	3.16	6.93	11.60	63.70	14.61
5	1.36	23.13	21.09	15.65	38.78

Agreeableness

	1	2	3	4	5
1	59.91	21.62	11.04	6.98	0.45
2	17.41	55.56	18.51	4.87	3.65
3	17.29	15.36	61.79	4.61	0.95
4	3.15	9.97	20.73	58.27	7.87
5	7.41	3.70	7.41	18.52	62.96

Neuroticism

	1	2	3	4	5
1	63.64	21.21	15.15	0.00	0.00
2	20.01	60.60	10.60	6.95	1.84
3	12.36	24.36	58.19	3.89	1.21
4	3.10	11.21	29.99	54.33	1.37
5	10.95	5.71	26.67	14.76	41.90

Table 7: Effectiveness of individual/multiple modalities in predicting BFI-10 answers using k-SLoT. V: Visual, L: Lexical, A: Acoustic.

Ques. No.	Accuracy (%)						
	V	L	A	V+L	V+A	L+A	V+L+A
1	80.7	69.1	80.7	80.2	84.0	81.5	87.4
2	70.9	62.6	69.9	73.2	75.2	73.1	75.1
3	87.3	77.6	88.6	89.9	92.3	90.1	94.5
4	61.5	55.1	58.3	62.9	60.3	63.5	65.1
5	87.0	75.9	88.2	89.0	91.9	89.5	94.4
6	72.8	62.3	71.9	75.6	75.9	73.9	75.8
7	69.1	55.9	69.0	72.8	74.3	72.2	73.3
8	80.0	68.7	80.2	83.8	84.7	82.6	84.8
9	77.0	66.4	76.7	80.3	82.0	79.6	81.2
10	83.7	73.8	83.3	87.3	88.3	86.4	88.2
Avg.	77.0	66.7	76.7	79.5	80.9	79.2	82.0

From the experimental results presented in Table 5, it is observed that F2P is less effective that F2A + A2P even using the same set of features (DS).

6.5 Comparing Individual Modalities

This subsection presents results of experiments performed to assess the effectiveness of each modality for F2A and A2P .

F2A (Table 7) : Results show that visual clues have the best prediction accuracy. Acoustic clues also perform almost similar to visual clues and lexical clues perform the worst. Consequently the combination of visual and acoustic clues is found to be better than any other combination, taking two modalities at a time. However, fusing all the three clues performs better than using only two clues. This justifies fusion of the three clues.

In terms of accuracy in answering individual questions, the trend is the same for all the three clues. Question 3 is answered with the best accuracy and question 4 with the worst accuracy, for all the combinations tried out.

A2P (Table 8): Prediction accuracy using Visual and Acoustic clues individually is almost the same. Lexical clues again perform the worse. In predicting personality scores, when only lexical clues are used, Agreeableness is predicted with the worst accuracy although not very low as compared to that of Neuroticism. Whereas for all other combinations Neuroticism has worst prediction accuracy.

Note that the combination of modalities used is the same for the experiments presented in this subsection and for emotion recognition. The accuracy of F2A and A2P is expected to be even better for data captured in more controlled environment. This is because movies may have difficulties such as non-frontal faces, poor illumination, low face resolution, auditory noise and so on.

7. CONCLUSION AND FUTURE WORK

In this work we have proposed audio/visual features for answering BFI-10 questionnaire based on psychological studies which to

Table 8: Effectiveness of individual modalities in predicting the scores along the Big-Five personality dimensions using k-SLoT. V: Visual, L: Lexical, A: Acoustic.

Trait	Accuracies						
	V	L	A	V+L	V+A	L+A	V+L+A
O.	76.8	70.9	77.5	83.4	84.4	80.3	84.8
C.	74.3	68.0	73.9	80.0	80.7	77.0	81.1
E.	60.9	54.0	62.0	65.3	67.5	63.8	69.4
A.	53.7	47.1	53.1	56.5	59.2	58.0	60.3
N.	51.4	48.0	49.2	56.5	53.7	56.3	58.0
Avg.	63.4	57.6	63.1	68.3	69.1	67.1	70.7

our knowledge is novel. The proposed method can be extended to the full version of BFI with a different scoring scheme. Hence, a future effort would be to learn a model for predicting personality scores using BFI model irrespective of the size of questionnaire. This would make the F2A+A2P method fully data driven. For other questionnaires such as NEO-PIR [16] a different set of audio/visual features and scoring schemes will have to be identified.

In this work we have shown that the F2A+A2P approach is superior than the F2P approach for automatic personality assessment. Our proposed 'SLoT' model effectively selects the right combination of audio/visual features necessary for answering personality based questionnaires. This clearly demonstrates the efficacy of combining psychology and computational approaches in solving real-life problems like personality assessment.

Ideally the proposed approach should be evaluated on real-life datasets. However, obtaining audio-visual information of real-life situations over a significant amount of time is challenging and will be considered for future work.

Application: One possible application of knowing personality traits is automatic music recommendation. Rentfrow and Gosling et. al. [24] propose four musical preference groups (*reflective and complex*: blues, jazz, classical, and folk; *intense and rebellious*: rock, alternative, and heavy metal music; *upbeat and conventional*: country, religious, and pop music; *energetic and rhythmic*: rap/hip-hop, soul/funk and electronic/dance music) and empirically show that these preferences are related to individual differences in personality, ability and self-perception. Their study finds links between music preferences and personality (based on BFI-model). Automatic assessment of personality traits will facilitate such applications. With the explosion of audio-visual sensors all around us, even in personal devices that one carries everywhere, it should become easier to assess personality traits.

8. ACKNOWLEDGEMENTS

This research is partially supported by the Singapore National Research Foundation under its International Research Centre @ Singapore Funding Initiative and administered by the IDM Programme Office.

Table 9: **Examples of predicted personality scores for a few sample scenes. Sample frame, dialog and the predicted and actual personality scores are shown. Personality scores are in the order O: Openness, C: Conscientiousness, E: Extraversion, A: Agreeableness and N: Neuroticism. Length of a bar is proportional to the corresponding score. G.T.: Ground Truth for the scores, Pred: Predicted scores**

Sample frame and dialog	Scores
 You are so annoying. Wait, I don't have to leave. This is my part of the ship. You leave.	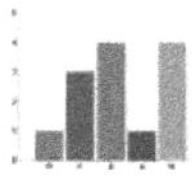 G.T. :[1 3 4 1 4] 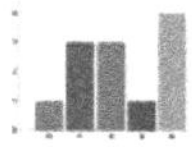 Pred.: [1 3 3 1 4]
 I have a good idea. Let's combine the action and the romance and make a romaction story.	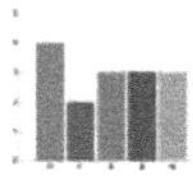 G.T. :[4 2 3 3 3] 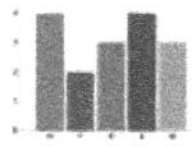 Pred.: [4 2 3 4 3]
 Dave, that was amazing! You are a Wiener-eating champ.	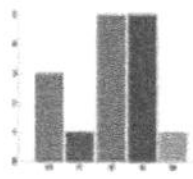 G.T. :[3 1 5 5 1] 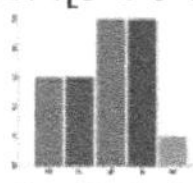 Pred.: [3 3 5 5 1]

9. REFERENCES

[1] W. Apple, L. Streeter, and R. Krauss. Effects of pitch and speech rate on personal attributions. *J. Pers. Soc. Psychol.*, 37(5):715–727, 1979.

[2] S. Argamon, S. Dhawle, M. Koppel, and J. Pennebaker. Lexical predictors of personality type. In *Proc. 2005 Joint Annual Meeting of the Interface and the Classification Society of North America*, 2005.

[3] M. Bartlett, G. Littlewort, M. Frank, C. Lainscsek, I. Fasel, and J. Movellan. Fully automatic facial action recognition in spontaneous behavior. In *FG*, 2006.

[4] S. Benini, L. Canini, and R. Leonardi. A connotative space for supporting movie affective recommendation. *IEEE T. Multimedia*, 13(6):1356–1370, 2011.

[5] S. Boyd and L. Vandenberghe. *Convex optimization.* Cambridge Univ Pr, 2004.

[6] R. Calix, S. Mallepudi, B. Chen, and G. Knapp. Emotion Recognition in Text for 3-D Facial Expression Rendering. *IEEE T. Multimedia*, 12(6):544–551, 2010.

[7] M. Everingham, J. Sivic, and A. Zisserman. "Hello! My name is... Buffy" – automatic naming of characters in TV video. In *BMVC*, 2006.

[8] L. Jensen-Campbell, J. Knack, A. Waldrip, and S. Campbell. Do big five personality traits associated with self-control influence the regulation of anger and aggression? *J. Res. Pers.*, 41(2):403–424, 2007.

[9] O. John, L. Naumann, and C. Soto. Paradigm shift to the integrative Big Five trait taxonomy: History, measurement, and conceptual issues. *In O.P. John, R.W. Robins and L.A. Pervin (Eds.) Handbook of Personality: theory and research*, pages 114–158, 2008.

[10] C. Lampert, H. Nickisch, and S. Harmeling. Learning to detect unseen object classes by between-class attribute transfer. In *CVPR 2009.*

[11] A. Lampropoulos, P. Lampropoulou, and G. Tsihrintzis. A cascade-hybrid music recommender system for mobile services based on musical genre classification and personality diagnosis. *Multimed. Tools Appl.*, pages 1–18, 2011.

[12] Z. Lin, M. Chen, L. Wu, and Y. Ma. The augmented lagrange multiplier method for exact recovery of corrupted low-rank matrices. *Arxiv preprint arXiv:1009.5055*, 2010.

[13] P. Litle and M. Zuckerman. Sensation seeking and music preferences. *Pers. Indiv. Differ.*, 7(4):575–578, 1986.

[14] F. Mairesse, M. Walker, M. Mehl, and R. Moore. Using linguistic cues for the automatic recognition of personality in conversation and text. *J. Artif. Intell. Res.*, 30(1):457–500, 2007.

[15] R. Mattick and J. Clarke. Development and validation of measures of social phobia scrutiny fear and social interaction anxiety. *Behav. Res. Ther.*, 36(4):455–470, 1998.

[16] R. McCrae and O. John. An introduction to the five-factor model and its applications. *J. Pers.*, 60(2):175–215, 1992.

[17] G. Mohammadi, A. Vinciarelli, and M. Mortillaro. The voice of personality: mapping nonverbal vocal behavior into trait attributions. In *Proc. 2nd international workshop on Social signal processing*, 2010.

[18] J. Oberlander and S. Nowson. Whose thumb is it anyway?: classifying author personality from weblog text. In *Proc. COLING/ACL on Main conference poster sessions*, 2006.

[19] W. Pavot, E. Diener, and F. Fujita. Extraversion and happiness. *Pers. Indiv. Differ.*, 11(12):1299–1306, 1990.

[20] F. Pianesi, N. Mana, A. Cappelletti, B. Lepri, and M. Zancanaro. Multimodal recognition of personality traits in social interactions. In *ICMI*, 2008.

[21] R. Picard. *Affective computing*. The MIT press, 2000.

[22] M. Power and M. Tarsia. Basic and complex emotions in depression and anxiety. *Clin. Psychol. Psychot.*, 14(1):19–31, 2007.

[23] B. Rammstedt and O. John. Measuring personality in one minute or less: A 10-item short version of the Big Five Inventory in English and German. *J. Res. Pers.*, 41(1):203–212, 2007.

[24] P. Rentfrow and S. Gosling. The do re mi's of everyday life: The structure and personality correlates of music preferences. *J. Pers. Soc. Psychol.*, 84(6):1236–1256, 2003.

[25] S. Srivastava, O. John, S. Gosling, and J. Potter. Development of personality in early and middle adulthood: Set like plaster or persistent change? *J. Pers. Soc. Psychol.*, 84(5):1041–1053.

[26] C. Whissell. The dictionary of affect in language. *Emotion: Theory, research, and experience*, 4:113–131, 1989.

[27] C. Windle. Further studies of test-retest effect on personality questionnaires. *Educ. Psychol. Meas.*, 15(3):246–253, 1955.

[28] P. Wojcik. *Movie acting, the film reader*. Psychology Press, 2004.

[29] G. Zen, B. Lepri, E. Ricci, and O. Lanz. Space speaks: towards socially and personality aware visual surveillance. In *Proc. 1st ACM international workshop on Multimodal pervasive video analysis*, 2010.

[30] Y. Zhai and M. Shah. Video scene segmentation using markov chain monte carlo. *IEEE T. Multimedia*, 8(4):686–697, 2006.

[31] G. Zhu, S. Yan, and Y. Ma. Image tag refinement towards low-rank, content-tag prior and error sparsity. In *ACM Multimedia*, 2010.

Controlling Urban Lighting by Human Motion Patterns Results from a Full Scale Experiment

Esben S. Poulsen
Department of Architecture, Design, and Media Technology
Aalborg University
Denmark
espo@create.aau.dk

Hans J. Andersen
Department of Architecture, Design, and Media Technology
Aalborg University
Denmark
hja@create.aau.dk

Ole B. Jensen
Department of Architecture, Design, and Media Technology
Aalborg University
Denmark
obj@create.aau.dk

Rikke Gade
Department of Architecture, Design, and Media Technology
Aalborg University
Denmark
rg@create.aau.dk

Tobias Thyrrestrup
Department of Architecture, Design, and Media Technology
Aalborg University
Denmark
toth@create.aau.dk

Thomas B. Moeslund
Department of Architecture, Design, and Media Technology
Aalborg University
Denmark
tbm@create.aau.dk

ABSTRACT

This paper presents a full-scale experiment investigating the use of human motion intensities as input for interactive illumination of a town square in the city of Aalborg in Denmark. As illuminators sixteen 3.5 meter high RGB LED lamps were used. The activity on the square was monitored by three thermal cameras and analysed by computer vision software from which motion intensity maps and peoples trajectories were estimated and used as input to control the interactive illumination. The paper introduces a 2-layered interactive light strategy addressing ambient and effect illumination criteria totally four light scenarios were designed and tested. The result shows that in general people immersed in the street lighting did not notice that the light changed according to their presence or actions, but people watching from the edge of the square noticed the interaction between the illumination and the immersed persons. The experiment also demonstrated that interactive can give significant power savings. In the current experiment there was a difference of 92% between the most and less energy consuming light scenario.

Categories and Subject Descriptors

J.5 [**Arts and Humanities**]: Architecture; K.4.0 [**Computers and Society**]: General

General Terms

Human Factors, Experimentation, Design.

Keywords

Urban Light Design, Urban Lighting, Responsive Light Design, Interactive Illumination.

1. INTRODUCTION

For the first time in human history, more than half of the human population inhabits urban environments, and this now presents itself as second nature to humans. The urban context is of a very complex nature and is composed by a multitude of different networks, infrastructures and volumes. The city has become the dominant scenery for everyday life. As such it presents still greater design challenges for an improved urban spatial performance, which can adapt to changes and present inspiring, efficient and stimulating public spaces.

One must acknowledge that urban spaces are sites of movement and interaction that contain unused potential [15, 16]. If we can monitor and potentially understand how the urban space is used in terms of movement and occupancy patterns, we can generate site-specific maps that can be used to control elements in the environment such as the illumination,.

People will in this way interact direct or indirect with elements in the environments, thus establish an exchange also described as feedback in the world of computation. The study of feedback in computer systems, describing the relationship between sensor and acting environments, can be tracked back to Norbert Wieners [29] notion of cybernetics; a marriage of control theory, information science, and biology that seeks to explain the common principles of control and communication in both animals and machines [29]. Since then much work has been done in the field of computer human interaction. Research fields such as robotics [1], responsive environments [19], situated technologies [24] all contributes to a particular focus within the field of sensing and responding to change.

Inspired by the cybernetic notions from Gorden Pask [22] Usman Haque presents experiments that utilize sensor technologies and lighting as part of a larger collective constructed environment where people and objects collaboratively create social domains as in the case of Sky Ear and Open Burble [11]. In the two cases environmental feedback between weather systems (electromagnetic waves and local winds) and social actors are essential in the temporary composition of the color and the intensity of the light. Hence the balloons mediate a direct relation between subjects and weather phenomena, it establish a platform for conversations, between the humans, calling a balloon, causing waves of light to appear between the sky ear and the observers. On the level of the subject, internal conversations presents questions related to the level of engagement;

(a) Overview of the Kennedy square without the lamps, seen from the position of the thermal cameras.

(b) Kennedy square with the lamps at daytime. The main train station in the background.

Figure 1: Kennedy square in the city of Aalborg in Denmark.

Figure 2: Overview of the Kennedy square with the 16 lamps, seen from the position of the thermal cameras.

to what level does I feel like participating? As performer, actor or just a passive observer enjoying the show? More external stimuli are constantly affecting our choices and engagement in the event, (weather, social norms, economy etc.) these internal and external conversations is a keystone in the understanding of systems and knowledge produced within them [21]. Another example is MY Studios Low Rez reactive sound poles [18], which is a spatial sequencer, allowing the by-passer to compose different sound-scapes. This installation has proven to be a mediator for vivid interactions between performers and observers of the event [25].

Within the contemporary art field Philipe Beesley [2] pushes the exploration of responsive environment inspired by reaction patterns in nature, exemplified in the art installations Endothelium and Hydrozoic. In these Beesley explore how he, inspired by nature, can design artificial life forms that produce life like behaviors and appearances, this artistic approach motivate a series of internal conversations; What is this? Is it a life? I am just a significant small part of the interaction pattern, but still I affect the ecology like behavior etc. Thus the installations are not build to be interactive toys but rather responsive environments, where relations and interdependencies are to be explored. In the project Dune [4] the artist Daan Roosegaarde brings a 60 meter long permanent reactive light and sound installation into the landscape along the Mass river in Rotterdam. The installation consists of thousands illuminating light straws that react in different behaviors. Similar to Beeslys the behavior of the lighting is inspired by natural mechanisms, hence it can be scared, excited, curios. Within the last decade these and many other art installations represent cases in the emergence of a new artistic expression in media, interactive and installation art that has proven a creative aesthetic, social and architectural potential for a design discipline concerned with feedback between humans and environments.

Within the industry of lighting, firms like Echelolon [5] and Philips [13] has entered the development of technologies for large-scale control systems of outdoor lighting. They contribute to the development of tools and techniques for new types of light designs, which open the window into the design of behaviors of the light. Within the larger urban perspective notions of the smart grid [6] also support this trend of a more efficient and intelligent energy use. This responsive paradigm is deeply related to the discipline of design.

This study will focus on the development, implementation and investigation of interactive urban lightings. It is motivated by the fact that in the coming years urban illumination will change from light sources based on mercury or similar technologies into Light Emitting Diodes (LED) or other less energy demanding light sources. Especially LED light sources is from a control point of view interesting as they will open for new ways to control the illumination, allowing designers and engineers to develope interactive light settings that for example dim or change color in real-time.

To fully release this potential it will be necessary to automatically monitor the activity in the urban environments. This task is very difficult and can be solved at various levels of detail. In the fully monitored situation a persons status of mind could be estimated, as being glad, sad, busy, relax etc. This is, however, at the moment not feasible with the current sensing technologies and models for human behavior at hand, which will require front views and high resolution images of the face [20, 17]. However, computer vision technologies has developed so it is now possible to track peoples trajectory in urban environments and in this context especially newer thermal imaging cameras has shown promising results [26]. In this study we will utilize recent results within thermal

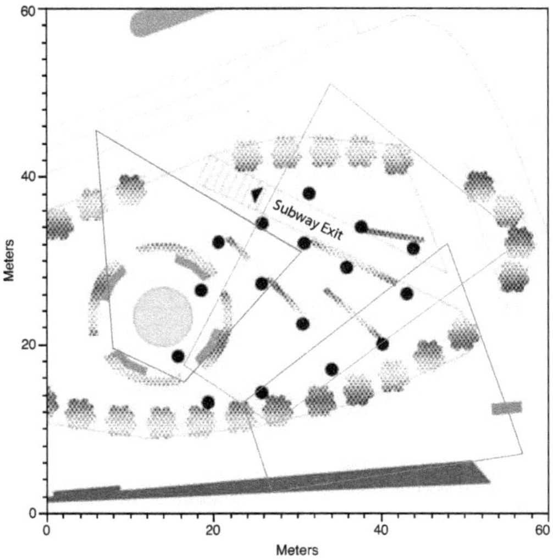

Figure 3: Overview map of Kennedy square with the areas covered by the three cameras.

computer vision combined with new LED lights for development of an interactive illumination setting where the ambition is to make the illumination provide safety, being energy effective, aesthetic appealing and potentially give the people another experience of the urban space.

During January these technologies were used in a full-scale experiment on a town square in the city of Aalborg in Denmark. Figure 1(a) shows an overview of the square seen from the position of the thermal cameras and figure 1(b) shows the interactive lamps at daytime. In figure 2 the light setup is shown at nighttime. The activity on the square was monitored using three thermal cameras mounted on a building facing the square. The trajectories of the pedestrians where estimated using computer vision analysis and used as input to control the light behavior in four different responsive light scenarios.

The finding of the study was that in general people immersed in the interactive light setting did not notice that the illumination was changing according to their motion despite the fact that in one of the scenarios the illumination was dimmed significantly in comparison to the normal illumination of the square. On the other hand people watching the square from the outside clearly noticed the interactive light setting and hence got a new experience and impression of the square.

The paper is organised as follows, first the experimental site and setup is presented followed by and introducing to the applied computer vision analysis and the interactive illumination design. The observations of the four different light scenarios are then presented and discussed and finally the findings are concluded.

2. MATERIAL AND METHODS

The experiment took place at Kennedy square in the city of Aalborg in Denmark. The square is located between the main train and bus station and the city center and serves primarily as a transit space between these two locations, see figure 1(a) To monitor the square three thermal cameras type Axis Q-1921-E, with a 19mm lens were mounted in the height of 15 meters at one of the buildings facing the square. The cameras covered the area from where an exit of a subway from the main train station is located to where people leave the square on their way to the city center, as illustrated in 3. Along this pathway the 16 RGB LED lamps were placed, figure 1.

The street lamp is composed of a 70 cm tall Riegens Ray light fixture, figure 4(a), a 3.5 meter tall light post and a 60x60 cm concrete tile as foundation. An LED module containing 18 1W LEDs, six in each color (RGB) was mounted in the bottom of the light fixture. The individual LEDs are mounted on the module in a two rings configuration, where the inner ring holds the 6 red LEDs and the outer ring holds 6 green LEDs interleaved with 6 blue LEDs, figure 4(b). The LED module is connected to a DMX module installed inside the lamp post. This module enables a 0-255 step brightness control of each led color as well as an unique address of each lamp.

(a) Profile of the lamp housing. (b) LED module.

Figure 4: The LED lamp head.

2.1 Qualitative assessment methodology

To evaluate the performance of the computer vision analysis and the control of the illumination a mobile phone application was used to display the activity at the square and the light setting of the lamps, figure 5. The application also gave the possibility to control the lamps. Using the application it was possible in real-time to evaluate if the computer vision analysis worked as expected and that the light scenarios gave the right response according to the position and velocity of people passing through the light setup.

2.2 Observations

During the experiment observations of body language, gestures and behavior of the occupants on the square were made. The observation methodology was based on ethnographic studies and fieldwork techniques as they are articulated by the sociologists such as Erving Goffman and Edward T. Hall [9, 10, 16] and utilized by architects such as Jan Gehl, William Whyte [28, 7]. By observing the interactions from the edge of the street we were able to describe "space routines" in the transit space [7] and evaluate if people where immersed in or affected by the different light scenarios.

2.3 Computer vision analysis

Detecting and tracking people is a large research area in computer vision, most approaches using normal visual cameras. But due to falling prices on thermal cameras new approaches using these sensors have been developed lately. Thermal cameras measure the amount of thermal radiation that lies in the long-wavelength infrared spectrum (8-15 μm). All objects with a temperature higher than the absolute zero emit thermal radiation. The intensity and dominating wavelength depends on the temperature.

Since thermal cameras do not measure visible light, they have a clear advantage over visual cameras in night conditions. Also with visual cameras it is illegal to film public places in Denmark, but since people can not be identified from thermal images, this is not an issue with thermal cameras. This is the primary reason to utilize thermal cameras in this work. Figure 6(a) shows an example of the input image from one of the camera views.

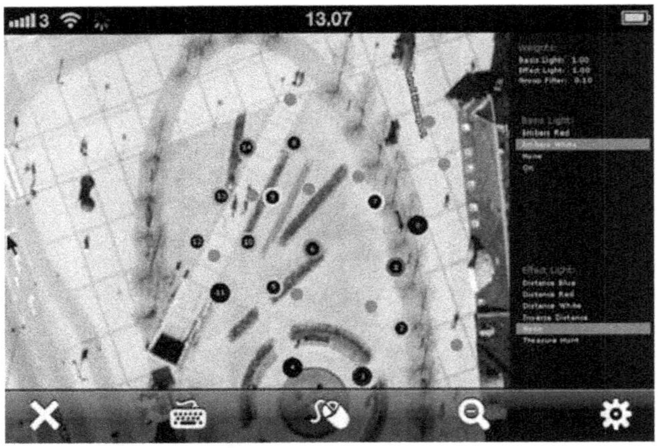

Figure 5: Snapshot of the iPhone application by which it was possible in real-time to see the result of the computer vision tracking and the resulting control of lamps. It was also possible to manually control the lamps by the application.

(a) Thermal image.

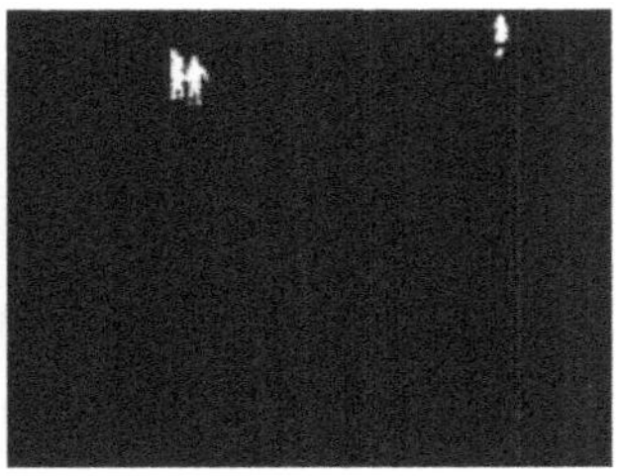

(b) Binary image.

Figure 6: Example of the thermal input image and resulting binary image from one camera view.

As input to the illumination system real-time information about the position and velocity of people at the square should be found. The experiment is conducted in outdoor environment running continuously for a week. The temperature naturally changes, which gives a slowly changing background. Therefore it is chosen to perform a running average background subtraction as the first step in detecting people [23]. The background will be updated with selectivity, meaning that only if the pixel is segmented as background it will contribute to the new background:

$$B_{t+1}(x,y) = \begin{cases} \alpha F_t(x,y) + (1-\alpha)B_t(x,y) & \text{if } F_t(x,y) \text{ background} \\ B_t(x,y) & \text{if } F_t(x,y) \text{ foreground} \end{cases} \quad (1)$$

where B_t is the current background, F_t the current input image, α the learning rate and B_{t+1} the new background image.

As the experiments take place at an urban space with limited car access, it is assumed that all activity detected is human activity of interest. The difference image produced by background subtraction is binarised with a threshold value of 10. The resulting BLOB's with area of minimum 10 pixels are considered objects of interest.

The detected objects must be mapped to real world coordinates at the square in order to correspond to the lamps positions. The mapping is calculated using a homography matrix [3]. This matrix can be calculated using at least four corresponding points in image and world coordinates. Since the camera views are not aligned, a mapping must be calculated for each individual view. Figure 7 illustrates the mapping from image to world plane.

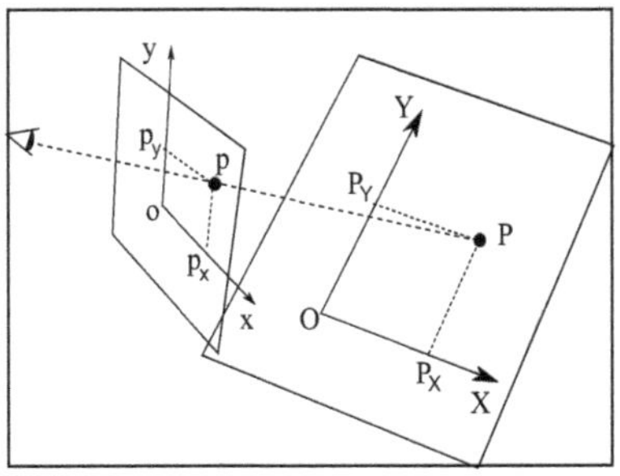

Figure 7: Example of the thermal input image from one camera view.

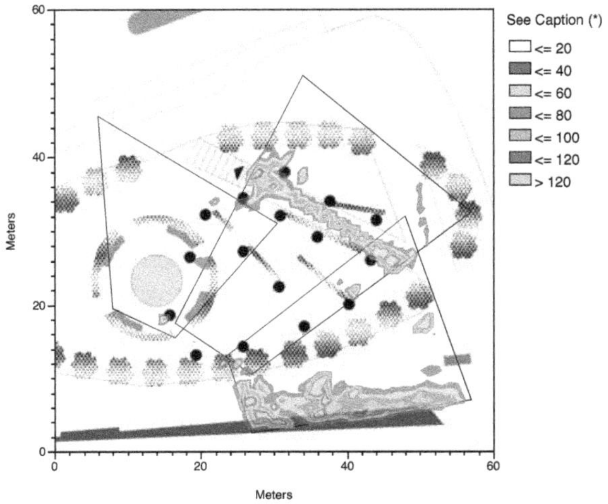

Figure 9: Occupancy map of the square counting number of observed persons in 1x1 meter cells sampled per 10 second.

For this purpose of illumination control from tracking data, groups of people should be considered as one object. The individual objects detected are grouped using single linkage clustering [12] with a distance threshold of 3 meters. This grouping also ensures that an imprecise segmentation, resulting in one person split in more BLOB's, or more persons found in one BLOB, does not change the result, as they will be treated as one group anyway.

In order to determine stable positions and velocity of the groups, a Kalman filter is applied to track the groups [27]. Splits and merging of groups are handled based on the distance between predictions of group tracks.

From the analysis it is now possible to estimate trajectories of persons on the square. Figure 8 shows the results of such trajectories in (a) for one minute, (b) two minutes, and in (c) the velocities vectors for persons walking on the square for a period of one hour. This information may also be illustrated by how the square is occupied, that is not taking the motion of the persons into account. Such an occupancy map with a resolution of 1x1 meter for 24 hour is illustrated in figure 9 sampled for every 10th second.

In this way it is possible to both get information about the instant motion of people on the square and accumulated motion over time. The first information may be used for instant control of the illumination whereas the later representation can be used for placement of lamps, that is the physical design of the illumination setup for a given urban environment, and to design basic illumination according to how the area is being used.

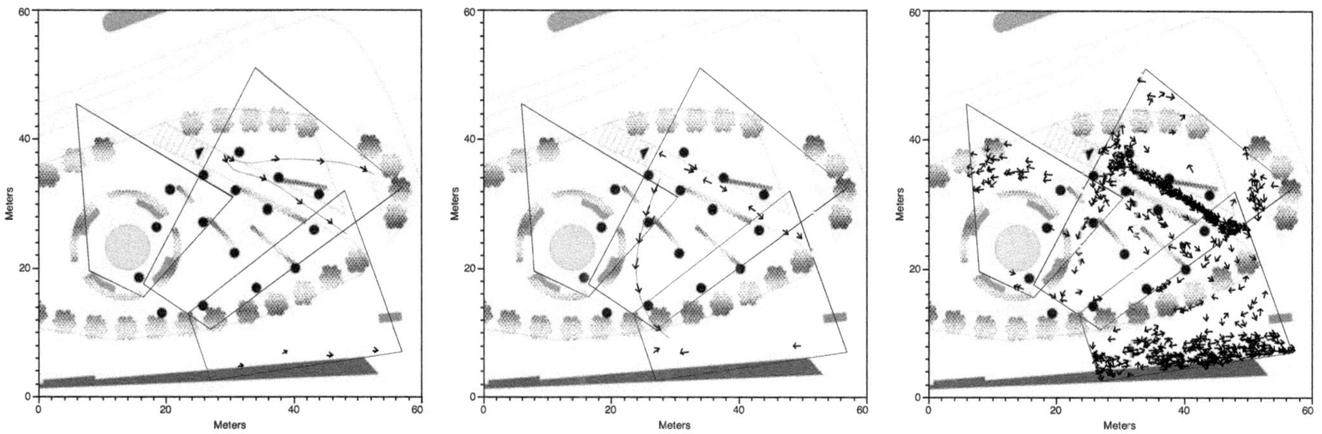

(a) One minute trajectories for two persons splitting up and leaving the subway.

(b) Two minute trajectories, with one person showing a distinct path towards the Bank located on the square.

(c) One hour velocity map of the activity that clearly demonstrates the used of the square. Especially, the use of the pathway from the subway to and from the main train station and the city center.

Figure 8: Estimated velocities vectors for people on the square.

2.4 Interactive illumination design

To approach a responsive light design of an urban square calls for a creative process similar to that needed in the development of architectural space. In addition, we need to develop tools to provide creative techniques where interactive scenarios can be sketched and evaluated in a creative and intuitive design process. To approach the design challenge, a physical 1:50 model of the square was developed. Simple white LEDs were used to represent the lamps, and, by using video input recorded on-site by the thermal cameras, we could test how different illumination designs would unfold on the square. In this way, we could simulate the light design using real-life video feeds and evaluate response times, rhythms and the placement of the lamps. When designing interactive illumination for a square, there are multiple factors affecting the formalized lighting, and the illumination becomes a result of many variables including security, social space, functionality, aesthetics, and energy. When these are merged together in a layered model, one can develop more or less interactive or playful light strategies, which still fulfill functional and aesthetic requirements.

2.5 Interactive lighting strategy

To ensure a persistent minimum illumination of the square when there were no occupants, we divided the illumination design into an ambient contribution and an effect contribution, which are later summarized into the final illumination.

2.5.1 *Ambient Illumination*

The ambient illumination is used to ensure that the square is illuminated when there are no occupants. We followed the hypothesis that a minimum of light is necessary to ensure that people feel that it is secure to enter the square. In the experiment, we worked with two ambient light scenarios:

1. A global minimum; all lamps are dimmed down equally to 10% of the full intensity.
2. Ember; the light slowly fades up and down between 0 to 20% in a random pattern.

2.5.2 *Effect illumination*

Effect illumination is the response that occur if an event takes place at the square. The event is detected by the computer vision analysis that in turn controls what light response to give according to the activity on the square. One can design a range of different complicated, banal or playful scenarios depending on the level of occupancy, velocity, climate, time of day etc. In this initial experiment, we tested the following two effects:

1. Light circle; as an illuminated aura around the occupants the localized light would secure an illuminated circle on min. 10 meter in diameter. This would allow the occupant to perceive variations in pavement and the face of people passing by, which in turn facilitate a secure navigation and travel over the square.
2. Light wave; As a playful illumination scenario we designed a treasure hunt scenario where two of the lights on the square indicate (blue light) the position of a trigger causing a wave of white light to travel over the square. After 10 seconds, a new blue light will emerge in another location. The hypothesis was to make a playful illumination that engaged people in playful and creative situations.

2.5.3 *Final illumination*

Summarizing the intensities from the ambient and effect illumination gives the light emitted from each lamp. If the sum of the two exceeds its maximum, the effect is truncated to 100%. The ambient illumination is active when no one is occupying the actual space. This, however, does not mean that the square is not experienced. Typically, it will be observed from a distance, a balcony, a living room, cafe etc. The illumination can then, with very low power consumption, make light patterns that are embracing, inspiring, scary, natural or just neutral depending on the design intentions. However, when people enter the space effect lighting strategies will secure a suitable illumination that potentially address security, aesthetics and social requirements.

3. EXPERIMENT

The experiment was conducted in the last week of January 2012 from late afternoon and into the early evening. At this time the sun set at 17.00 and thus collection of data and observations took place from 17.00 and until 20.00. The weather during this period was very cold by Danish standards, ranging from -5 to -10 degrees Celsius and very windy. Data was collected by observations and by logging of the results of the computer vision analysis. Between 100 to 150 persons passed the square each day in the observations period. The observations of them was done from the train and bus station and a bar facing the square. Each day 10 to 15 persons were interviewed.

4. RESULTS

During the experiment the experience and effect of the four different light scenarios were investigated. The normal illumination of the square was turned off during the experimental period. See appendix A for video examples.

4.1 Scenario 1, "Ambient Illumination"

Figure 10: Illumination scenario 1 "Ambient Illumination"

The first scenario is a homogeneous illumination of the square. The 16 lamps had a static intensity of 80% white light and no effect was added. This light scenario was similar to, what could have been a traditional static illumination of the square, and was motivated by a need to compare the change of flow and social behavior on the square in different light scenarios.

It seemed that people did not see the changed illumination and acted like nothing was changed from the everyday life. When people were asked about the illumination only a few recognized the changed lighting, even though the lighting before were very limited.

4.2 Scenario 2, "Glowing Light"

The intention of the slowly fading white illumination was to make a lighting that would illuminate the square in an aperiodic way, leaving the square half lit but always in a process of fading down or up, this would give a feeling of overview of the square and support the feeling of security (figure 11). As a playful chance encounter a light wave effect was introduced.

A few people, realized the changing lighting and stopped to look at it, some looked like they thought the light fixtures were broken or out of order, one even asked if there was a loose connection and laughed. The majority of the by-passers did not seem to notice the change in the light intensity when they triggered the light wave; it was like the contrast between the slowly fading lamps in the ember scenario and the slowly moving wave was too small. Observed from a distance the slowly fading lamps had a calming, inspiring and lively expression, one should look very carefully to notice the wave.

Figure 11: Illumination scenario 2 "Glowing Light"

Figure 12: Illumination scenario 3 "White Aura". Notice how the light is following the person on the pathway.

4.3 Scenario 3, "White Aura"

Because of the relative big illuminated area around the people (10 meters) they did not seem to realize the darker square surrounding them. Observed from a distance one could se how people on the edge of the square were making pointing gestures towards the "performing" people moving over the square. The simple effect and the large contrast to the surrounding darkness made the pedestrian a natural focal point on the square.

4.4 Scenario 4, "Red Treasure Hunt"

The hypothesis of this scenario was to establish an unusual illumination, an illumination that made people stop up and confront the lighting in a playful manner. Figure 13 shows a sequence of images visualizing the effect scenario. 1 - A person is approaching the blue "trigger" light. 2 - The person triggered the effect which sends out a wave of light from the triggered lamp outwards. 3,4 - The light wave travels through the square. 5 - The light wave has ended and the trigger point is disabled for 10 seconds before it lights up a lamp again and a new person can trigger yet another light wave.

The few people who realized the changing illumination, did engage in the investigation of the lighting. When they realized that the illumination changed based on their presence, they began calling the lamp "it", which shows that they are giving the lamp a personality.

4.5 Energy consumption

In figure 14, the energy consumption for the different light scenarios is illustrated. The Ambient Illumination scenario as reference gave an energy consumption of approximately 230 Watt for the sixteen lamps. The other three scenarios are fluctuating in energy consumption due to the deliberate effects and the reactive effects according to the activity at the square. Clearly, the energy consumption of these scenarios are depending on the light design, and especially the choice of ambient light has a significant contribution of the mean value that the scenario fluctuate around. The

Figure 13: Illumination scenario 4 "Red Treasure Hunt" seen from the perspective of a person walking towards the subway entrance.

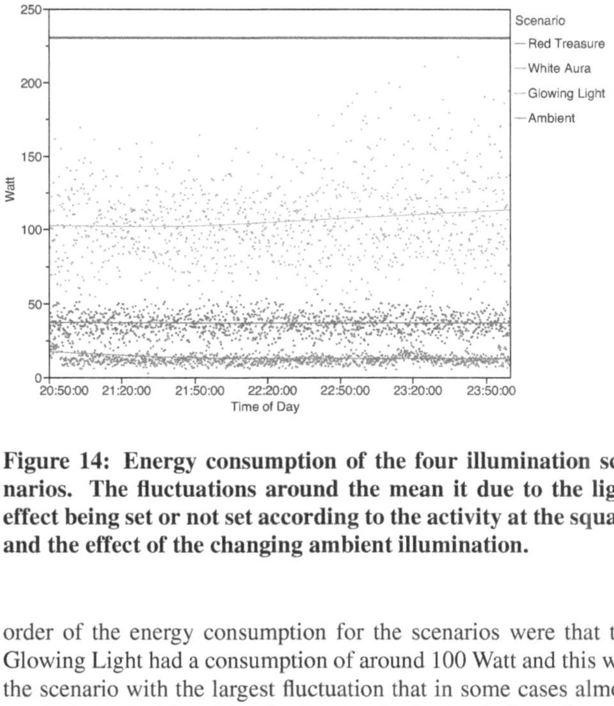

Figure 14: Energy consumption of the four illumination scenarios. The fluctuations around the mean it due to the light effect being set or not set according to the activity at the square and the effect of the changing ambient illumination.

order of the energy consumption for the scenarios were that the Glowing Light had a consumption of around 100 Watt and this was the scenario with the largest fluctuation that in some cases almost reached the Ambient Illumination level. In the design a lamp is chosen at random and then the light level is set to 10% of the maximum level from which it is then decreased. The Red Treasure Hunt had the second lowest energy consumption and was the scenario that fluctuated most due to the activity at the square whereas the White Aura had the overall lowest energy consumption about 20 Watt in average or 11.5% of the Ambient Illumination scenario. This is also the scenario that mainly depends on the activity at the square.

5. DISCUSSION AND FUTURE WORK

The flow maps of the 4 different light scenarios present no change in movement patterns; there is high intensity of movement on the paths in south and towards the subway, which correlate with the observations, done from the balcony. Hence, we can conclude that the reactive light patterns do not affect the overall movement and use of the square. People did not engage in, what we designed as "playful" and did not engage in the exploration of the reactive light system. This can be due to a less successful design, the fact that people mind their own business, because of the cold evening hours of the Danish winter climate or because of the evening time, that produced a dominate goal oriented behavior. The effect illuminations were directly triggered by the action of individuals, in the initial hypothesis we assumed that these effects would change the behavior of people and affect their way of seeing each other. In the observations of the life on the street, we did observe that people crossing the square, did not realize the changing lighting, but people observing from a distance could see how people "painted" light paths on the square or triggered a wave The observer could be a person in a bus, on a balcony, in the waiting room for the cinema etc. For them the square became a stage setting where actors, whiteout being aware of it affected the lighting and was observed more carefully. This observation supports the concept of passive surveillance as presented by Jane Jacobs [14].

These observations leave the light designers with a new challenge: How can we design adaptive systems that change behavior due to changing situations and needs? In times of low occupancy a simple and functional reactive light strategy might be sufficient whereas in a warmer climate interactive playful scenarios might be applicable. Furthermore, at public events the street lighting might be used as an extension of the stage lighting. Extending the notion of centralized light control in to the world of smart phones, one can imagine a light system that knows your personal preferences for lighting and prepare the city or park with your favorite settings, as such it becomes an extension of your expression of mood, identity or just favorite color. These possibilities are subjects for future experiments. Furthermore the experiment underline the hypothesis that reactive and sensor based lighting systems will save energy and the amount of energy saved depends on the designed light scenarios. In the experiment we present an energy saving of 92%. However to access this resource new robust technologies need to be developed.

This contribution encourages a stronger link between studies in the contemporary interactive art scene and the behavior design of public lighting. The authors have not been able to find systematic research in the field of experienced social and aesthetic qualities of responsive light design in the "smart city" context. When we still have the centralized control unit for sketching light scenarios, a wide range of design drivers has the capacity to control the illumination and there are three main challenges in the future work: 1) to further develop design scenarios, and develop the ethnographical and qualitative evaluation techniques of such, 2) to face the technical challenge and build simple reactive and robust stand alone solutions, which perform sensing and acting behaviors, and 3) we suggest further development and explorations of the flow maps, which can inform us about usage of space instantly and over time and thermal comfort.

To approach these design challenges will call for interdisciplinary research, where engineers and architects will work together for development of new robust tools and novel design methods, to be tested in the 'laboratory of the street'. Favoring a design side of mediated lighting can cause inefficient light tools and favoring a technical side would risk to create normative and boring environments. Embarking in this interdisciplinary journey, we will search for skills to develop new tools and techniques to modulate a new creative environment.

6. CONCLUSION

Street lighting is build to illuminate the square extending the potential use of public space into the dark hours. Until now we have focused on the energy performance of the light bulb street lamp. Because of the recent development in the field of sensor and LED technologies we are now able to modulate the light to any given control paradigm. This study shows new possibilities and reflections for applying simple reactive light strategies, together with pragmatic reactive lighting models in the design of interactive urban lighting scenarios. It does this through four experiments using thermal cameras and computer analysis that allow designers to detect occupancy and flow patterns on the street. The data is utilized both as input to a real-time light control system and as a mapping of long-term occupancy and flow, allowing researchers and urban planners to access data on the use of urban spaces. In this paper, the evaluation of three interactive light strategies; Glowing Aura, Glowing Light & Red Treasure Hunt, reveal the possibility for reactive lighting to be applied in public spaces and present a significant energy saving up to 90% without people changing behavior.

This result shows that very dramatic changes are needed if light designers are to engage a person in transit. However people making light patterns as actors on a stage, underline the points of Presentation of Self in Everyday Life by Erving Goffman [8]. The majority of the visitors did not realize the changing of the light, the first time of their visit, but after observing other people perform from a distance their occupancy and flow patterns became a natural part of the architectural expression of the square.

7. ACKNOWLEDGMENTS

This work was funded by Aalborg University and Center of Danish Lighting in collaboration with private collaborators Team Tronic, Riegnes, Alfred Priess, Thanks to Nykredit and The municipality of Aalborg for practical support. The experiments were carried out at Research Cluster for Mobility and Tracking Technologies (MOTT), Aalborg University.

8. REFERENCES

[1] R. C. Arkin. *Behaviour-based Robotics*. MIT Press, London, 1998.

[2] P. Beesley. *Kinetic Architectures and Geotextile Installations*. Riverside Archtiectural Press, Toronto, 1 edition, 2010.

[3] A. Criminisi. Computing the plane to plane homography. 1997.

[4] T. R. de, A. Chong, and D. Roosegaarde. *Daan Roosegaarde: Interactive Landscapes*. NAI Publishers, Rotterdam, 1 edition, 2011.

[5] Echelon. Monitoring outdoor lighting:market, challenges, solutions, and next steps., 2007.

[6] European Communities. European smartgrid technology platform, vision and strategy for europes electricity networks of the future, 2006.

[7] J. Gehl. *Cities for People*. Island Press, Washington DC, 2010.

[8] E. Goffman. *presentation of self in everyday life Garden City*. Doubleday, New York, 1959.

[9] E. Goffman. *Behavior in public places : notes on the social organization of gatherings*. Grenwood Press, Westport, 1980.

[10] E. T. Hall. *The silent language*. Anchor Press/Doubleday, New York, 1973.

[11] U. Haque. 4dsocial: inter active design environments. *Distinguishing concepts*, 77(4):24–31, 2007.

[12] J. A. Hartigan. *Clustering Algorithms*. Wiley, 1975.

[13] IBM. Smarterplanet, 2012.

[14] J. Jacobs. *The death and life of great American cities*. Random House, New York, 1961.

[15] O. B. Jensen. Flows of meaning, cultures of movements - urban mobility as meaningful everyday life practice. *Mobilities*, 4(4):139–158, March 2009.

[16] O. B. Jensen. Negotiation in motion: Unpacking a geography of mobility. *Space and Culture*, 13(4):389–402, 2010.

[17] T. Kanade, J. Cohn, and Y. Tian. Comprehensive database for facial expression analysis. In *Automatic Face and Gesture Recognition, 2000. Proceedings. Fourth IEEE International Conference on*, pages 46 –53, 2000.

[18] C. Linn. MY studio hweler+yoon architecture's lo rez hi fi gives a D.C. building a much-needed sense of place. *Architectural Record*, 195(11):190–192, 2007.

[19] N. Negroponte. *Architecture Machine*. MIT Press, Cambridge, 1970.

[20] Z. Niu and X. Qiu. Facial expression recognition based on weighted principal component analysis and support vector machines. In *Advanced Computer Theory and Engineering (ICACTE), 2010 3rd International Conference on*, volume 3, pages V3–174 –V3–178, aug. 2010.

[21] P. Pangaro. Thoughtstricker 1986. *Kybernetes*, 30(5/6):790, 1986.

[22] G. Pask. *An approach to cybernetics*. Harper, New York, 1962; 1961. With a pref. by Warren S. McCulloch.; Includes bibliography.

[23] M. Piccardi. Background subtraction techniques: a review. In *Systems, Man and Cybernetics, 2004 IEEE International Conference on*, volume 4, pages 3099 – 3104 vol.4, oct. 2004.

[24] M. Shepard, T. Scholz, and O. Khan. Urban computing and its discontents. 1, 2010.

[25] B. S. Thomsen. *Perfomative Environments*. PhD thesis, Doctoral Shcool of Planning and Development, Aalborg University, 2009.

[26] W. Wang, J. Zhang, and C. Shen. Improved human detection and classification in thermal images. In *Image Processing*

(ICIP), 2010 17th IEEE International Conference on, pages 2313 –2316, sept. 2010.
[27] G. Welch and G. Bishop. An introduction to the kalman filter. *Design*, 7(1):1–16, 2001.
[28] W. H. Whyte. *Rediscovering the Centre*. University of Pennsylvania, Philadelphia, 1988.
[29] N. Wiener. *Cybernetics*. Wiley, New York, 1948.

APPENDIX

A. VIDEO

For video examples of the scenarios explored in the experiment please go to the following urls:

Glowing Light

http://vimeo.com/40589332

White Aura

http://vimeo.com/40653666

Red Treasure Hunt

http://vimeo.com/40589333

In the Eye of the Beholder: Employing Statistical Analysis and Eye Tracking for Analyzing Abstract Paintings

Victoria Yanulevskaya[1], Jasper Uijlings[1], Elia Bruni[2], Andreza Sartori[1,3], Elisa Zamboni[2], Francesca Bacci[4], David Melcher[2], Nicu Sebe[1]

[1] DISI, University of Trento, Italy;
{yanulevskaya, jrr, andreza.sartori, sebe}@disi.unitn.it

[2] CiMEC, University of Trento, Italy;
{elia.bruni, david.melcher}@unitn.it, elisa.zamboni@student.unitn.it

[3] Telecom Italia - SKIL, Trento Italy

[4] Museum of Art of Trento and Rovereto, Rovereto, Italy;
f.bacci@mart.tn.it

ABSTRACT

Most artworks are explicitly created to evoke a strong emotional response. During the centuries there were several art movements which employed different techniques to achieve emotional expressions conveyed by artworks. Yet people were always consistently able to read the emotional messages even from the most abstract paintings. Can a machine learn what makes an artwork emotional? In this work, we consider a set of 500 abstract paintings from Museum of Modern and Contemporary Art of Trento and Rovereto (MART), where each painting was scored as carrying a positive or negative response on a Likert scale of 1-7. We employ a state-of-the-art recognition system to learn which statistical patterns are associated with positive and negative emotions. Additionally, we dissect the classification machinery to determine which parts of an image evokes what emotions. This opens new opportunities to research *why* a specific painting is perceived as emotional. We also demonstrate how quantification of evidence for positive and negative emotions can be used to predict the way in which people observe paintings.

Categories and Subject Descriptors

J.5 [**Computer Applications**]: Arts and Humanities - fine arts; I.2 [**Artificial Intelligence**]: Vision and Scene Understanding; H.3.1 [**Information Search and Retrieval**]: Content Analysis and Indexing

General Terms

Algorithms, Experimentation, Theory

MM'12, October 29–November 2, 2012, Nara, Japan.

Keywords

Visual Art, Abstract Paintings, Emotion Recognition, Eye tracking

1. INTRODUCTION

Most art is created to evoke emotions. These emotions are not only contained within the narrative of the art piece, as for example in religious art, but also in the very techniques used to create it. In many abstract paintings the idea is to evoke emotions purely through the (non-figurative) elements that make a painting: colours, lines, shapes, and textures. For example, Kandinsky described the effect of colours on the spirit of the observer "not a 'subjective' effect, but an objective one, determined by the characteristics of the colors and their interactions" [32]. The fact that for many paintings observers report similar emotions, shows that indeed there is consistency in the way people interpret colours and patterns when looking at these paintings. An interesting question is then which part of a painting evokes what kind of emotion. In this paper we aim to answer this question using state-of-the-art computer vision techniques.

Recent research shows that computer vision has become mature enough to predict the aesthetics [16], interestingness [8], and emotions [14, 34] of images, paintings, and even web pages [33]. Surprisingly, both [16] and [8] showed that the popular Bag-of-Visual-Words framework performed better in aesthetics prediction than the theory inspired features such as the golden rule. Hence, while improving prediction performance, the lack of success for the theory inspired features made the reasons *why* a specific image was deemed positive or beautiful less clear, especially as the exact workings of Bag-of-Visual-Words are little understood.

In this paper we aim for a better understanding of why a painting evokes a certain emotion by determining where the classification evidence resides. In particular, we train a Bag-of-Visual-Words model to predict if a painting evokes positive or negative emotions. We use a collection of abstract paintings which evoke emotions purely through geometry and colour, exactly the properties that are well captured by Bag-of-Words. Afterwards, we use the method in [29] to dissect the classification machinery to determine which parts of an image evokes what emotions.

The quantification of evidence for positive and negative emotions opens up a new toolbox for both researchers and artists alike. It allows art researchers to provide more quantitative data and hence objective grounds for forming and verifying their art theories. For artists it can help them better understand why their paintings evoke certain emotions and how they can make emotional content even stronger. As an application in this paper we test the positive attentional bias, which states that people prefer to look at the positive parts of an image, regardless if the overall image tends towards negativity or positivity.

To summarize, our main contributions are: (1) we use computer vision to help quantify which part of the image evokes what emotion; (2) we present an in-depth analysis to investigate if there is a positive attentional bias when looking at abstract paintings; and finally (4) we propose a new method of analysis useful for both art researchers and artists alike.

The rest of the paper is structured as follows. Section 2 presents the related work covering the art theory aspect as well as the existing emotion recognition approaches using computer vision techniques. Section 3 presents the details of our proposed approach. In Section 4, we demonstrate how scene analysis and machine learning techniques can be used not only to differentiate between emotionally positive and negative abstract paintings, but also to identify emotional parts of the paintings. In Section 5, we present an eye tracking study to prove that in general, people prefer to focus on the positive parts of the paintings. Section 6 presents the final discussions and conclusions.

2. RELATED WORK

2.1 Art Theory

Arnheim defines art as "the product of organisms and therefore probably neither more nor less complex than these organisms themselves" [1]. The discipline of art history encompasses the study of development of art works, in a specific period of time, and the explanation of how to interpret these based on historical context and styles. The evolution of art works has seen many painting styles that have become the main pillars of the art philosophy over time [9]. Furthermore, artists have employed the use of several features and techniques to evoke specific emotions in the viewer through their art. Many works try to comprehend the perception, evaluation and the consequent emotion that is evoked in the viewer by a piece of art. Hagtvedt *et al.* [7] developed a model based on the cognitive and emotional elements that are stimulated by a piece of art. In addition, they employed a structured equation model that integrates these elements in the evaluation process. They concluded that perception and emotion of a visual art piece depend on factors such as curiosity and aesthetic appeal, complexity, typicality or familiarity [7]. Pelowski and Akiba [18] developed a five-stage model of art perception that relates art-viewing to the viewer's personality. Recently, McManus *et al.* [17] used the Arnheim's Gestalt theory of visual balance in order to examine the visual composition of art photographs and abstract images. Similar works which deal with perception include [4, 10] and emotional responses to art [22]. In this paper we propose a novel method for analysing emotions in art: we train a computer vision system to predict emotions in paintings, and then dissect its decision such that we can see exactly what parts of the image are responsible for this emotion. This provides a new angle to test and verify art theories.

2.2 Emotion Recognition

Humans can autonomously perceive and evaluate emotional signals of visual surroundings. However, it is a difficult task for machines to recognize emotions automatically. Recent works that observed emotional responses invoked by pictures deal with interdisciplinary fields such as art, aesthetics and psychology [9]. These aspects are important in order to comprehend the interaction between features of the scene and the viewer, as well as the physical, social and historical contexts where the visual experience occurs.

Several recent works have focused on emotion recognition in art. Yanulevskaya *et al.* [34] proposed an emotion categorization system which is based on the assessment of local image statistics followed by supervised learning of emotion categories using Support Vector Machines. Their system was trained on the International Affective Picture System, which is a standard emotion evoking image set in psychology [11], and was then applied to a collection of masterpieces. The work by Machajdik and Hanbury [14] combined low-level features with concepts from psychology and art theory for categorization of emotion in affective images and art works. Surprisingly, they obtained better accuracy in categorization of affective images which are semantically rich in comparison with abstract paintings which are non-figurative and thus semantics free. These works demonstrate that it is possible to use computer vision techniques for emotion recognition. In our analysis, we concentrate on the basis of why such categorization happens.

The comprehension of how people observe paintings is essential for the realization of the features contained within an image that evoke emotions in the viewer's mind. Analysing eye movements and fixations has been used as an important tool to understand the human perception and the features contained in an artwork that are closely related to a specific emotion [19]. Moreover, emotional stimuli are shown to attract attention. Recently, Subramanian *et al.* [24, 25] demonstrated how eye movements can be used in order to understand social and affective scenes. In this paper we investigate the link between emotional content and the way people look at abstract paintings. Particularly, we hypothesize that people prefer to focus on the positive parts of the paintings.

3. PROPOSED METHOD

To learn the difference between positive and negative paintings, we use a state-of-the-art Bag-of-Visual-Words classification framework which largely follows [28].

3.1 General Bag-of-Visual-Words Framework

For paintings representation we use a standard bag-of-visual-words framework, inspired by NLP [23]. This approach relies on the notion of a common vocabulary of "visual words" that can serve as discrete representations for a collection of images. The standard pipeline to form a so-called "visual vocabulary" consists of (1) collecting a large sample of features from a representative corpus of images, and (2) quantizing the feature space according to their statistics. Typically, k-means clustering is used for the quantization. In that case, the visual "words" are the k cluster centers. Once the vocabulary is established, the corpus of sampled features can be discarded. Then the features of a new image can be translated into words by determining which visual word they are nearest to in the feature space (i.e., based on the Euclidean distance between the cluster centers and each descriptor feature) [6]. Finally, each image is represented as a histogram of its visual words.

3.2 Descriptors

To take into account two most important characteristics of abstract art works, in our analysis we represent paintings with colour based LAB visual words and texture based SIFT visual words.

3.2.1 LAB

The LAB color space plots image data in 3 dimensions along 3 independent (orthogonal) axes, L for brightness and a and b for the color-opponent dimensions, based on non-linearly compressed CIE XYZ color space coordinates. One problem with the CIE XYZ color system, is that colorimetric distances between the individual colors do not correspond to perceived color differences. In LAB, luminance corresponds closely to brightness as recorded by the brain-eye system; chrominance (red-green and yellow-blue) axes mimic the oppositional color sensations the retina reports to the brain [26]. To map LAB descriptors to visual words, we quantize the color space into 343 different colours by uniformly dividing each colour channel into 7 different levels.

3.2.2 SIFT

The SIFT descriptor proposed by Lowe [13] describes the local shape of a region using edge orientation histograms. It is derivative-based and contains local spatial information. Particularly, SIFT descriptors capture contours, edges, and textures within images. They demonstrate invariance to image scale transformations, and also provide a robust matching across affine distortion, noise and change in illumination.

In this paper, we take local patches of 16- by-16 pixels which are sampled at every single pixel. From these patches we extract grey-scale SIFT descriptors and two colour variants, RGB-SIFT and RGI-SIFT as recommended by van de Sande *et al.* [30]. To create a visual vocabulary we quantize 250,000 randomly selected SIFT descriptors into 4096 clusters using a hierarchical version of k-means clustering [31].

3.3 Classification

The extracted representations for abstract paintings are used to train a classifier to distinguish between the positive and negative emotions. We use a Support Vector Machine classifier with a Histogram Intersection kernel [15] for supervised learning of emotions. We run two separate frameworks, one based on LAB descriptors, and another one based on SIFT descriptors. To combine both frameworks, we use late fusion, i.e. we average the scores of the two frameworks.

3.4 Backprojection

Backprojection (BP) is a technique which allows to determine the relative contribution which comes from each pixel in the image to the classification task. In our case, thanks to BP we are able to detect those visual words which convey the most positive or negative information according to our classifier. In other words, this technique permits us to label a certain region as being "positive" or "negative", as we might expect human subjects to do. To implement BP, we follow [29]. Consider the classification function for the Histogram Intersection kernel, defined as

$$h(\mathbf{x}) = b + \sum_{j=1}^{m} \alpha_j t_j \left(\sum_{i=1}^{n} \min(x_i, z_{ij}) \right), \qquad (1)$$

where $\mathbf{x} = \{x_1, \ldots, x_n\}$ is the vector to be classified, $\mathbf{z}_j = \{z_{1j}, \ldots, z_{nj}\}$ is the j-th support vector, α_j is its corresponding positive weight, $t_j \in \{-1, 1\}$ is its corresponding label, m is the number of support vectors, and $\sum_{i=1}^{n} \min(x_i, z_i)$ is the Histogram Intersection kernel function. In this function the outer sum is over the m support vectors. However, for determining which visual word contributes how much to the classification, we need the outer sum to be over the n visual words. This is possible because the Histogram Intersection kernel is an *additive* kernel [15] where the inner sum can be brought outside, leading to:

$$\begin{aligned} h(\mathbf{x}) &= b + \sum_{i=1}^{n} \sum_{j=1}^{m} \alpha_j t_j \min(x_i, z_{ij}) && (2) \\ &= b + \sum_{i=1}^{n} w_i. && (3) \end{aligned}$$

The evidence per visual word channel is represented therefore by the weights w_i, which are equally distributed over the number of words of that type in the painting. By keeping the locations of each visual word, we can then backproject this evidence into the painting.

4. EMOTION RECOGNITION FOR ABSTRACT PAINTINGS

In this section we demonstrate how scene analysis and machine learning techniques can be used not only to differentiate between emotionally positive and negative abstract paintings, but also to identify emotional parts of the paintings.

4.1 MART Dataset

4.1.1 The painting collection

We selected 500 images of abstract paintings from the art collection of the MART museum in Rovereto, Italy (the digitalized images of the artworks are contained in the electronic archive of MART). The artworks were realized between 1913 and 2008 by Italian as well as European and American artists. The collection presents some characteristics that are interesting from the point of view of art history. In particular, there are four authors whose work is well represented in the group of paintings which were used in this experiment: Carlo Belli, Aldo Schmid, Luigi Senesi, and Luigi Veronesi. These artists are particularly interesting because their work is not the result of an improvisation but it is part of a deep theoretical reflection on the elements that make a painting (colors, lines, shapes, textures). They all wrote their theoretical reflections declaring the principles that inspired and shaped their artworks.

4.1.2 Participants

We recruited a total of 100 people (74 females, 26 males; ages 18-65. $M = 39.87$). Most participants were teachers in primary schools, operators at MART, visitors of the museum, and students. They reported to visit from a minimum of 1 to a maximum of 100 museums per year ($M = 5.5$). All subjects participated in our experiment voluntarily without getting any reward.

4.1.3 Scoring procedure

In this paper, we are interested in analysing whether positive or negative feelings are conveyed by abstract paintings. Therefore, we follow the standard procedure [5, 20] and consider positive-negative valenced emotional judgements. In our experiment, we asked the participants to look at the MART paintings and report their emotions elicited by them. Particularly, the participants got the following instructions: "You are asked to judge all the paintings that will be presented. Let your instinct guide you and follow your first impression of the painting." The judgements were given according to a Likert scale of 1-to-7-points, where number 1 meant a highly negative emotion and 7 meant a highly positive emotion. The scale was presented on a separated sheet of paper, although paintings were accessed through a code to prevent subjects from getting influenced by the artwork's title or its author. While the participants did not have a fixed time window, they were explicitly instructed to score the paintings as fast as possible in order to encourage the rise of very instinctive emotions, and to prevent that previous knowledge about the artworks could come into play. On average, people spent about 9 seconds per painting to make their judgement.

During the experiment, the images of the paintings were randomly divided into five groups, 100 works each, and only one group was presented to a single subject. Therefore, each subject rated 100 paintings and each artwork received 20 judgments from 20 different subjects. We presented the paintings on a gray background, because gray is usually considered to be a neutral color, with no impact to the other colors (and withcoming emotions). After every ten images, a gray slide was presented in order to give participants the opportunity to rest.

To check for preferential biases, we analyse the data according to the gender of the participants (74 females versus 26 males), the age of the participants (48 people under 40 years old versus 52 people over 40 year old), and the art background. The participants that visited more than 5 museums per year are considered to be knowledgable in art (31 people), whereas the rest are not (69 people). We did not observe significant difference in judgement within all these three groups (p values of a double t-test ≥ 0.4596).

Figure 1 illustrates the distribution of paintings from the most negative (average score of 1.95) to the most positive (average score of 6.2). The images, emotional scores and recorded eye-movements described in Section 5 have been made available online[1].

4.2 Classification Results

To construct a ground truth, for each painting the average of all available scores is computed. We define paintings with average scores lower or equal to 4 as negative, and paintings with average scores higher than 4 as positive. As a result, 183 paintings were assigned to the negative class, and 317 to the positive class. We tested our model on a two-fold cross-validation repeated ten times. The training/testing sets are from a random 50% and 50% split of the MART dataset. The average accuracy is reported in Table 1.

Table 1: Classification accuracy.

	LAB	SIFT	LAB+SIFT
Accuracy	0.76	0.73	0.78

To analyse the contribution of each type of visual words we evaluate separately the accuracy of the system based on LAB visual words and on SIFT visual words. Then we combine both systems by averaging their classification scores. Overall, the proposed method performs significantly better than chance level which reaches accuracy of 0.63 in our experimental settings. We observe that LAB visual words are more effective for emotional classification of abstract paintings compared to SIFT visual words, the accuracy is 0.76 versus 0.73 respectively. The combination of LAB and SIFT visual words raises the accuracy to 0.78. This indicates that both colour-based LAB visual words and texture-based SIFT visual words are important for emotion recognition.

4.3 Backprojections

In this section we visualize how the classifier "sees" paintings while deciding whether they are positive or negative. We use the method described in Section 3.4 and backproject the relative contribution which comes from each pixel in the painting. The results for 4 paintings which are classified as highly positive and 4 paintings which are classified highly negative are shown in Figures 2 and 3 respectively. The contributions of LAB visual words are displayed in the second rows. The background colours typically yield neutral information which is coherent with their purpose to be a background for more emotional parts of the painting. Dark colours have mostly negative response, while red, yellow, and blue often evoke positive emotions.

The third rows in Figures 2 and 3 demonstrate the emotional evidence from SIFT visual words. Positive emotions often come from straight lines and smooth curves. In contrast, chaotic textured regions often evoke negative emotions even if their colour is on the positive side. The last rows show the combined evidence from LAB and SIFT visual words. Here evidence coming from colour and texture of the painting is effectively mixed together.

5. EYE MOVEMENTS AND EMOTIONAL CONTENT

In the previous section we showed that we can classify MART paintings as being positive and negative and determine which parts of the image evoke what emotion. As a practical application, in this section we use this to investigate the link between emotional content and the way people look at abstract paintings. We hypothesize that, in general, people prefer to focus on the positive parts of the paintings.

To check our hypothesis, we recorded eye movements of 9 observers while they viewed art works from the MART dataset. In order to ensure variability of emotional con-

[1] http://disi.unitn.it/~yanulevskaya/mart.html

Figure 1: Paintings from the MART collection ordered by human scores.

tent, for this experiment we selected paintings which contain positive, negative, and neutral parts at the same time. Specifically, for each painting we required that at least 25% of its pixels yield positive contribution to the classification. Similarly, at least 25% of pixels of the same painting are required to yield negative contribution to the classification. In this way 110 paintings were chosen, where 71 paintings are scored as positive by humans and 39 are scored as negative.

5.1 Eye Movement Recording

Eye movements were recorded using an EyeLink 1000 Tower Mount which samples pupil positions at 1000 Hz. Subjects were seated in a darkened room at 85 cm from a computer monitor and used a chin-rest so that their head position was stable. To calibrate the eye positions and to validate the calibration, subjects were asked to focus on 12 fixation spots on the screen, which appeared one by one in random order. The mean spatial accuracy of the eye tracker calibration was 0.36°, with a standard deviation of 0.07°, where one visual angle 1° equals to 30 pixels in our experimental settings.

During the experiment, stimuli were presented on a 23 inch screen (ASUS VG236H, 1920x1080 resolution) for 7 seconds. After each presentation of the stimulus, a gray background was shown for 0.5 second to prevent after-image effects. The order in which stimuli were displayed was randomized for every observer. Fixation locations and durations were calculated online by the eye tracker. The MATLAB psychophysics toolbox was used for stimulus presentation [2].

Nine participants took part in the experiment, each had normal or corrected to normal vision. No participant had formal art training and all were naive to the purpose of the experiment. Their instructions were to freely look at the paintings as they would do it in a museum.

5.2 Data Analysis

According to Locher *et al.* [12], viewers of art (no matter if representational or abstract) occupy the first two seconds to do a sweep of the image, analyzing its "gist". Only after this first explorative stage, viewers tend to focus on finer details. Moreover, it has been shown that during this period, bottom-up saliency plays an important role in the allocation of eye movements [3, 27, 35, 36]. In this paper we are interested in the influence on gaze patterns of such a high level information as emotional content. Therefore, in our analysis we consider eye movements which occur between the second and seventh seconds.

To quantify the relationship between emotional content detected by the classifier as traced with backprojection technique and human's gaze pattern, we compared emotional evidence which comes from fixated and non-fixated loca-

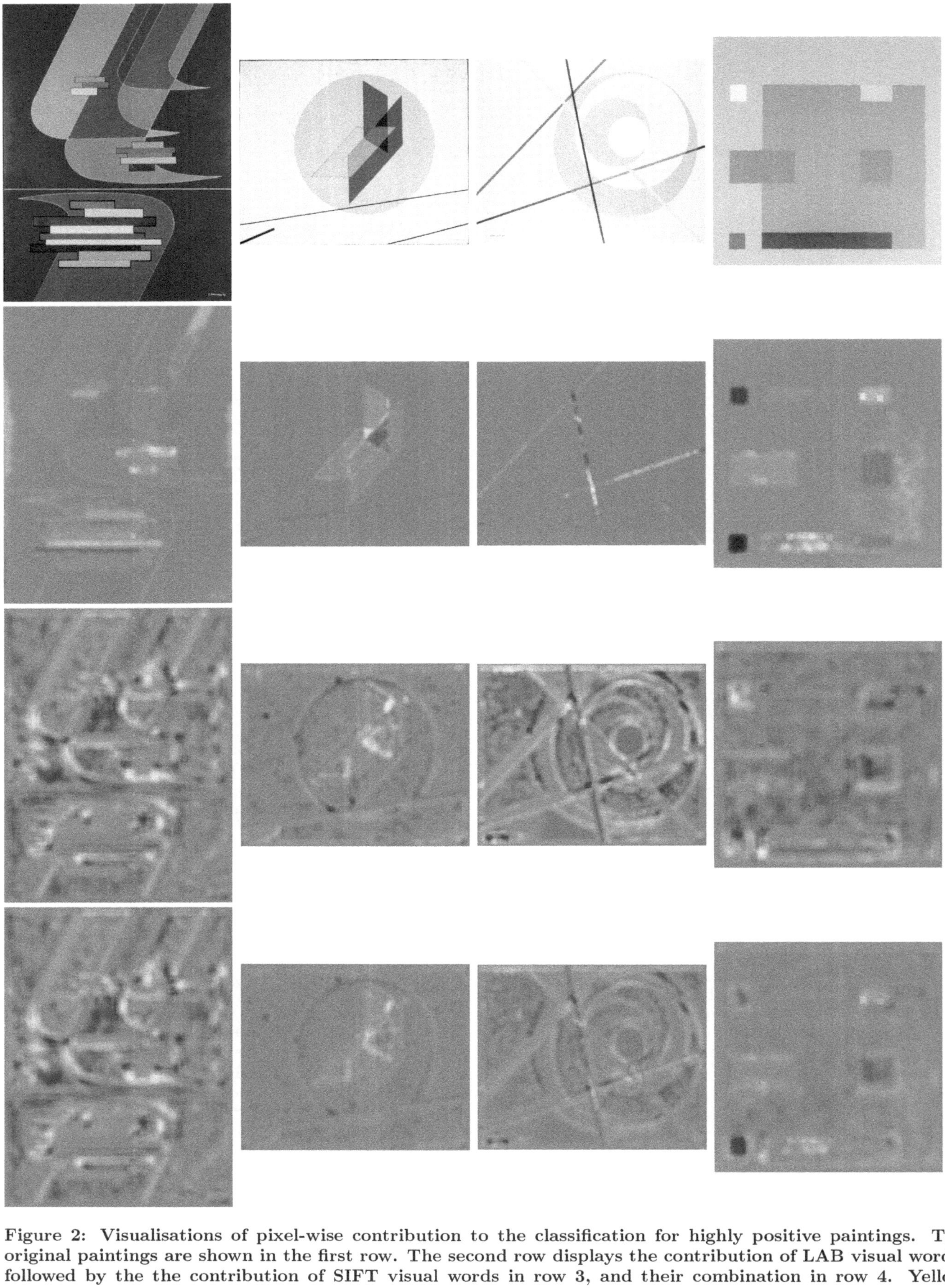

Figure 2: Visualisations of pixel-wise contribution to the classification for highly positive paintings. The original paintings are shown in the first row. The second row displays the contribution of LAB visual words, followed by the the contribution of SIFT visual words in row 3, and their combination in row 4. Yellow colour corresponds to the positive emotional evidence and blue colour corresponds to the negative emotional evidence. (Courtesy of MART photographic archive, Rovereto)

Figure 3: Visualisations of pixel-wise contribution to the classification for highly negative paintings. The original paintings are shown in the first row. The second row displays the contribution of LAB visual words, followed by the the contribution of SIFT visual words in row 3, and their combination in row 4. Yellow colour corresponds to the positive emotional evidence and blue colour corresponds to the negative emotional evidence. (Courtesy of MART photographic archive, Rovereto)

tions. Particularly, we averaged pixel-wise contributions to the classifier from the region around the fixated locations and compared it with the averaged pixel-wise contributions from the region around non-fixated locations. The regions around the fixations are taken to be fovea sized (1°, i.e. 30x30 pixels), as this is the area which is sampled in high resolution by the human eye. Now if people prefer to focus on those parts of the painting which contain positive information, then emotional statistics of fixated regions should be higher than the ones of non-fixated regions.

To determine the non-fixated locations for a painting, we followed [21, 27] and sampled from the fixated locations recorded while viewing another paintings. In this process, we required the same amount of fixated and non-fixated locations per painting, where non-fixated locations should be at least 1° (30 pixels) apart from the fixated locations. This guarantees similar distributions of fixated and non-fixated regions [27].

Table 2: Distribution of paintings according to "emotions" of the attentional bias.

LAB+SIFT	#	PAB	NAB	Neutral
All paintings	110 (100%)	82 (74%)	26 (24%)	2 (2%)
Pos paintings	71 (100%)	59 (83%)	11 (16%)	1 (1%)
Neg paintings	39 (100%)	23 (59%)	15 (38%)	1 (3%)

We call Positive Attentional Bias (**PAB**) the situation when average contribution to the classifier from the fixated regions is *higher* than average contribution to the classifier from the non-fixated regions. We call Negative Attentional Bias (**NAB**) the opposite condition. When emotional statistics of fixated and non-fixated regions do not differ significantly according to the 2 sample t test, the attentional bias is neutral to positive and negative emotions. To test if people prefer to focus on emotionally positive visual information, we calculate how many abstract paintings evoke PAB. To backproject emotional evidences, we use our best performing classifier according to Table 1 which combines LAB and SIFT descriptors. Table 2 contains averaged results over 50 independent samplings of non-fixated locations. Only for 2 paintings attentional bias demonstrates neutral behaviour, whereas 74% of considered paintings show the positive attentional bias. As it can be expected, PAB holds for most of the emotionally positive paintings (83%). Interestingly, even while observing negative paintings, in 59% of cases people still prefer to look at positive parts. Therefore, we conclude that at least for this dataset, the positive attentional bias holds. Figure 4 illustrates several examples of paintings together with the recorded fixated locations.

Figure 4: Paintings with superimposed fixated locations: the first row displays positive paintings with PAB, the second row displays negative paintings with PAB, the second row displays positive paintings with NAB, and the last row displays negative paintings with NAB. (Courtesy of MART photographic archive, Rovereto)

6. CONCLUSION

In this paper we sought for a better understanding of which part of an image evoked what kind of emotions through advanced computer vision techniques. We trained a Bag-of-Visual-Words system to distinguish between positive and negative abstract paintings. Afterwards we backprojected the classification contributions back to the painting to have an accurate visualization of which part of the painting conveyed positive emotions and negative emotions. At first, qualitative analysis showed that the results follow long-known observations in art: bright colours evoke positive emotions, dark colours tend to evoke negative emotions. Smooth lines are generally positive. Chaotic texture is generally negative.

The ability of localising the evidence for emotions opens up a new toolbox for researchers and artists for the verification and formulation of art theories. Theoretically, the technique is not limited to emotions but can be applied to better study aspects such as aesthetics and interestingness as well. We are planning to do so in future work.

As a practical application, we used the localisation of the emotion evidence in combination with recorded eye movements to test where people prefer to focus while observing abstract art works. We hypothesized that positive parts attract most of the attention. Indeed, our results demonstrated that positive attentional bias holds for 74% of considered paintings, and even in paintings with a negative emotional content people prefer to look at their positive parts.

7. ACKNOWLEDGMENTS

Victoria Yanulevskaya, Jasper Uijlings, and Nicu Sebe were partially supported by the FIRB S-PATTERNS project. Francesca Bacci was supported by a CARITRO (Fondazione Cassa di Risparmio di Trento e Rovereto) grant. The authors would like to thank MART photographic archive for allowing the use of the images for this study.

8. REFERENCES

[1] R. Arnheim. *Art and Visual Perception: A Psychology of the Creative Eye*. University of California Press, Nov. 2004.

[2] D. H. Brainard. The psychophysics toolbox. *Spatial Vision*, 10(4), 1997.

[3] N. Bruce and J. Tsotsos. Saliency, attention, and visual search: An information theoretic approach. *Journal of Vision*, 9(3), 2009.

[4] G. C. Cupchik, O. Vartanian, A. Crawley, and D. J. Mikulis. Viewing artworks: Contributions of cognitive control and perceptual facilitation to aesthetic experience. *Brain and Cognition*, 70:84–91, 2009.

[5] M. Dellagiacoma, P. Zontone, G. Boato, and L. Albertazzi. Emotion based classification of natural images. In *Int. workshop on Detecting and Exploiting Cultural Diversity on the Social Web*, pages 17–22, 2011.

[6] K. Grauman and B. Leibe. *Visual Object Recognition*. Synthesis Lectures on Artificial Intelligence and Machine Learning. Morgan & Claypool Publishers, 2011.

[7] H. Hagtvedt, R. Hagtvedt, and V. Patrick. The perception and evaluation of visual art. *Empirical Studies of the Arts*, 26(2):197–218, 2008.

[8] P. Isola, J. Xiao, A. Torralba, and A. Oliva. What makes an image memorable? In *IEEE Conference on Computer Vision and Pattern Recognition*, 2011.

[9] D. Joshi, R. Datta, E. A. Fedorovskaya, Q.-T. Luong, J. Z. Wang, J. Li, and J. Luo. Aesthetics and emotions in images. *IEEE Signal Process. Mag.*, 28(5):94–115, 2011.

[10] D. Joshi, R. Datta, E. A. Fedorovskaya, Q.-T. Luong, J. Z. Wang, J. Li, and J. Luo. Aesthetic judgement of orientation in modern art. *i-Perception*, 3:18–24, 2012.

[11] P. J. Lang, M. M. Bradley, and B. N. Cuthbert. International affective picture system (iaps): Technical manual and affective ratings. 1999.

[12] P. Locher, E. A. Krupinski, C. Mello-Thoms, and C. F. Nodine. Visual interest in pictorial art during an aesthetic experience. *Spatial Vision*, 21(1-2):55–77, 2007.

[13] D. G. Lowe. Distinctive Image Features from Scale-Invariant Keypoints. *Int. J. Comput. Vision*, 60:91–110, 2004.

[14] J. Machajdik and A. Hanbury. Affective image classification using features inspired by psychology and art theory. In *ACM Multimedia*, pages 83–92, 2010.

[15] S. Maji, A. C. Berg, and J. Malik. Classification using intersection kernel support vector machines is efficient. In *IEEE Conference on Computer Vision and Pattern Recognition*, 2008.

[16] L. Marchesotti, F. Perronnin, D. Larlus, and G. Csurka. Assessing the aesthetic quality of photographs using generic image descriptors. In *International Conference on Computer Vision*, 2011.

[17] I. C. McManus, K. Stöver, and D. Kim. Arnheim's gestalt theory of visual balance: Examining the compositional structure of art photographs and abstract images. *i-Perception*, 2:615–647, 2011.

[18] M. Pelowski and F. Akiba. A model of art perception, evaluation and emotion in transformative aesthetic experience. *New Ideas in Psychology*, 29:80–97, 2011.

[19] E. Pihko, A. Virtanen, V. Saarinen, S. Pannasch, L. Hirvenkari, T. Tossavainen, A. Haapala, and R. Hari. Experiencing art: The influence of expertise and painting abstraction level. *Front Hum Neurosci*, 5, 2011.

[20] E. Pihko, A. Virtanen, V. M. Saarinen, S. Pannasch, L. Hirvenkari, T. Tossavainen, A. Haapala, and R. Hari. Experiencing art: the influence of expertise and painting abstraction level. *Frontiers in human neuroscience*, 5, 2011.

[21] P. Reinagel and A. Zador. Natural scene statistics at the centre of gaze. *Network: Computation in Neural Systems*, 10(4), 1999.

[22] P. J. Silvia. Emotional responses to art : From collation and arousal to cognition and emotion. *Review of general psychology*, 9(4):342–357, 2005.

[23] J. Sivic and A. Zisserman. Video Google: A text retrieval approach to object matching in videos. In *Proceedings of the International Conference on Computer Vision*, pages 1470–1477, Oct. 2003.

[24] R. Subramanian, H. Katti, N. Sebe, M. Kankanhalli, and T. S. Chua. An eye-fixation database for saliency detection in images. *European Conference on Computer Vision*, 2010.

[25] R. Subramanian, V. Yanulevskaya, and N. Sebe. Can computers learn from humans to see better? Inferring scene semantics from viewers' eye movements. In *ACM Multimedia*, pages 33–42, 2011.

[26] R. Szeliski. Computer vision: Algorithms and applications. 2010.

[27] B. W. Tatler, R. J. Baddeley, and I. D. Gilchrist. Visual correlates of fixation selection: Effects of scale and time. *Vision Research*, 45(5), 2005.

[28] J. R. R. Uijlings, A. W. M. Smeulders, and R. J. H. Scha. Real-time Visual Concept Classification. *IEEE Transactions on Multimedia*, 12, 2010.

[29] J. R. R. Uijlings, A. W. M. Smeulders, and R. J. H. Scha. The Visual Extent of an Object. *International Journal of Computer Vision*, 2012.

[30] K. E. A. van de Sande, T. Gevers, and C. G. M. Snoek. Evaluating color descriptors for object and scene recognition. *IEEE Transactions on Pattern Analysis and Machine Intelligence*, 32(9), 2010.

[31] A. Vedaldi and B. Fulkerson. VLFeat – an open and portable library of computer vision algorithms. In *ACM Multimedia*, 2010.

[32] L. Veronesi. *Luigi Veronesi. Con una antologia di scritti.* Torino, 1968.

[33] O. Wu, Y. Chen, B. Li, and W. Hu. Evaluating the visual quality of web pages using a computational aesthetic approach. In *Association of Computing Machinery conference on Web search and data mining*, pages 337–346, 2011.

[34] V. Yanulevskaya, J. V. Gemert, K. Roth, A. Herbold, N. Sebe, and J. Geusebroek. Emotional valence categorization using holistic image features. In *IEEE International Conference on Image Processing*, pages 101–104, 2008.

[35] V. Yanulevskaya, J. B. Marsman, F. Cornelissen, and J. M. Geusebroek. An image statistics based model for fixation prediction. *Cognitive Computation*, 3(1), 2011.

[36] Q. Zhao and C. Koch. Learning a saliency map using fixated locations in natural scenes. *Journal of vision*, 11(3), 2011.

Online Crowdsourcing Subjective Image Quality Assessment *

Qianqian Xu
Graduate University, Chinese Academy of Sciences, Beijing 100049, China
qqxu@jdl.ac.cn

Qingming Huang
Graduate University, Chinese Academy of Sciences, Beijing 100049, China
qmhuang@jdl.ac.cn

Yuan Yao⋆
School of Mathematical Sciences, LMAM and LMP, Peking University, Beijing 100871, China
yuany@math.pku.edu.cn

ABSTRACT

Recently, HodgeRank on random graphs has been proposed as an effective framework for multimedia quality assessment problem based on paired comparison method. With the random design on large graphs, it is particularly suitable for large scale crowdsourcing experiments on Internet. However, to make it more practical toward this purpose, it is necessary to develop online algorithms to deal with sequential or streaming data. In this paper, we propose an online rating scheme based on HodgeRank on random graphs, to assess image quality when assessors and image pairs enter the system in a sequential way in a crowdsourceable scenario. The scheme is shown in both theory and experiments to be effective by exhibiting similar performance to batch learning under the Erdös-Rényi random graph model for sampling. It enables us to derive global rating and monitor intrinsic inconsistency in the real time. We demonstrate the effectiveness of the proposed framework on LIVE and IVC databases.

Categories and Subject Descriptors

H.5.1 [**Information Interfaces and Presentation**]: Multimedia Information Systems—*Evaluation/methodology*; C.4 [**Performance of Systems**]: Design studies; H.1.2 [**Models and Principles**]: User/Machine Systems—*Human factors*

General Terms

Performance, Experimentation, Human Factors

Keywords

Subjective Image Quality Assessment, Online, Crowdsourcing, Paired Comparison, HodgeRank, Random Graphs, Triangular Curl, Topology Evolution, Persistent Homology

*Area chair: Heng Tao Shen.
⋆Corresponding author.

1. INTRODUCTION

Image Quality Assessment (IQA) fundamentally relies on subjective experiments to capture the *true* perception of human observers. Therefore, subjective tests are often used to provide the ground-truth and verification for objective models in IQA. In a typical Mean Opinion Score (MOS) test [1], individuals are asked to give a rating from Bad to Excellent (e.g. Bad-1, Poor-2, Fair-3, Good-4, and Excellent-5) to grade the quality of an image. However, such a test may suffer from various problems such as ambiguity in definition of scales, dissimilar interpretations of the scale among users, etc. [7]. Therefore, paired comparison method is recently gaining rising attention, in which raters are asked to compare two images simultaneously and vote which one has the better quality; this is an easier and less demanding task for raters, whence more reliable in practice.

However, paired comparison approach leaves a heavier burden on participants with a larger number $\binom{n}{2}$ of comparisons. To address this issue, there has been a large volume of statistical literature on deterministic incomplete block design [11]. However, these designs are not suitable for crowdsourcing on Internet where the raters are distributive over network with varied backgrounds and it is hard to control with traditional experimental designs. To meet this challenge, the work in [15] proposes a randomized paired comparison method which randomly selects small subsets of pairs for each assessor to view; the work shows that randomization is effective in reducing costs of a complete design without jeopardizing the intended purpose. However, it leaves some open problems arising from randomization: (1) how to systematically deal with the resulting imbalanced and incomplete data; (2) how many samples are needed to achieve certain approximation of the complete design.

To address these two questions, a new framework called HodgeRank on Random Graphs (***HRRG***) is introduced to analyze the imbalanced and incomplete data in random design experiments [40, 39]. In this framework, paired comparison data are mapped to edge flows on a paired comparison graph which is often a random multigraph in random design, and then Hodge decomposition on graphs [19] leads to an orthogonal decomposition of such edge flows into global rating as gradient flow, local inconsistency as triangular curl flow, and global inconsistency as harmonic flow. Random graphs are shown as good models to design random sampling schemes in particular for crowdsourcing experiments. For example, Erdös-Rényi random graphs select pairs of videos or images uniformly from all possible candidates, while random k-regular graphs keep a balanced sampling for each video/image which receives the same number of comparisons against others and thus important for sparse graph designs [39]. Consistent with recent developments in random graph theory, when sampling complexity is large enough one can remove the global inconsistency. Experiments show that such a scheme in random designs provides good approximations of global ratings derived from complete experimental designs. In the successful developments above for subjective multimedia assessment, it leaves open to explore the online algorithms to deal with streaming data in crowdsourcing experiments on Internet.

Crowdsourceable quality assessment on Internet collects paired comparison data in a distributive and streaming way from a large population over Internet participants [7]. The streaming data calls for online algorithms as a sequential decision process via incremental data updates to improve its prediction accuracy. Although the image quality itself is constant, in subjective IQA, preferences may vary over raters and image pairs with different criteria based on different salient features of images in attention, noise from environment, and levels of attention, etc. Thus it is a fundamental question in subjective IQA to aggregate preferences of multiple assessors into a consistent global score, reflecting the statistical consensus on image quality over population. In this paper, we fill in this gap by presenting an online rating algorithm for HodgeRank on random graphs. Our algorithm is based on the classic Robbins-Monro procedure [28] which has been widely exploited in online learning, e.g. [32, 41].

Online algorithms could offer significant computational advantages over batch algorithms and the benefits of online learning become more evident when dealing with streaming or large-scale data. Besides, to tackle the scenario that in crowdsourcing assessors and image pairs come in an unspecified way, Erdös-Rényi random graph is systematically exploited in the paper which is equivalent to the standard assumption in statistical learning that the sample sequence is independent and identically distributed (I.I.D.). Furthermore, we note that online algorithms can be applied to more general settings with edge independent sampling such as Mutli-attribute random graphs, dependent sampling such as Markov sampling, and tracking time-varying environment.

We demonstrate the effectiveness and generality of the proposed framework on LIVE [3] and IVC [2] databases, which include 15 different reference images and 15 distorted versions of each reference. Totally 186 observers have carried out the experiment via Internet, providing us 23,097 paired comparisons. Experimental results show that the proposed online rating algorithm is promising and a robust assessment method suitable for crowdsourceable subjective IQA.

Our contribution in this work is the following:

1. To the best of our knowledge, it is the first time to propose an online rating framework for exploratory quality assessment. The framework provides the possibility of making assessment procedure significantly faster without deteriorating the accuracy, while maintaining the freedom of assessors.

2. The online rating algorithm is based on Robbins-Monro procedure or stochastic gradient descent for HodgeRank on random graphs. For an independent sampling process, the online rating reaches minimax convergence rates whence asymptotically as efficient as a batch algorithm. Moreover, online tracking of ranking inconsistency is possible in this framework.

3. Crowdsourcing image assessment experiments are conducted based on Erdös-Rényi random graph designs, which further confirms the theoretical analysis by showing that the proposed online rating algorithm achieves similar convergences to batch algorithms.

The remainder of this paper is organized as follows. Section 2 contains a review of related works. Then we describe the proposed framework in Section 3, and establish the online HodgeRank models based on batch HodgeRank. The detailed experiments are demonstrated in Section 4. Section 5 presents the conclusive remarks along with discussion for future work.

2. RELATED WORK

2.1 Subjective Quality Assessment

There have been studies on the design of subjective tests to evaluate image/video quality in paired comparison method. One such example is [7], which proposes a crowdsourceable framework based on paired comparison. However, one major shortcoming of [7] lies in that it makes a strong assumption that all paired comparison data collected are complete which is impossible for a large number of videos. For example, the way to evaluate Transitivity Satisfaction Rate (TSR) depends on such complete design assumption. To address this issue, the work in [15] suggests a randomised pair comparison method in which a random subset of all pairs are chosen for different participants to reduce the number of comparisons. However, this work does not address how to deal with the imbalanced and incomplete data arisen in random sampling, and also leaves the issue open on how many samples one needs.

To solve these problems, [40, 39] present a framework based on HodgeRank [19] on random graphs, which deal with incomplete and imbalanced data distributed on random graphs and further derive the constraints on sampling complexity in crowdsourcing experiment that the random selection must adhere to.

2.2 Online Learning

Online learning is a well established subfield of machine learning concerned with estimation problems with limited access to the entire data. It is a sequential decision process $(f_t)_{t\in N}$ in the hypothesis space, where each f_t is decided by the current observation $z_t = (x_t, y_t)$ and f_{t-1} which only depends on previous examples, i.e. $f_t = T_t(f_{t-1}, z_t)$. As a contrast, batch learning refers to a decision utilizing the whole set of examples available at time t [33, 10]. Examples of online learning algorithms include Perceptrons [29] and Adaline [35], etc.

The performance of the online learning algorithms is often measured by a loss function, which is often assumed to be convex such that convex optimization technique can be used to solve the problem. Typical examples of loss functions include hinge loss and square loss. The hinge loss is used in Support Vector Machines (SVM) [9] for classifications and the square loss leads to Least Mean Square method, such as Adaline and its variations [36].

Because of the lower computational cost of online learning compared with batch leaning, it has been shown to benefit a number of computer vision applications such as object recognition [12, 18], object detection [25, 38] and tracking [26, 17, 22]. The benefits of online learning become more evident when dealing with streaming or very large-scale data.

In this paper, we propose an online learning scheme based on stochastic gradient decent method in the setting of crowdsourceable subjective IQA.

2.3 Random Graphs

Random graph is a graph generated by some random process [5, 8]. It starts with a set of n vertices and adds edges between them at random. With such models we aim at crowdsourcing experimental designs where assessors may select image pairs at random. Different random graph models produce different probability distributions on graphs. The most commonly studied one is the Erdös-Rényi random graph [16] which is a stochastic process that starts with n vertices and no edges, and at each step adds one new edge uniformly. Besides, there are some other kinds of random models, such as random regular graph [37], preferential attachment random graph [4], small world random graph [34], and geometric random graph [24], which may also play important roles under certain circumstances.

However, as Erdös-Rényi random graph can be viewed as a random sampling process of image pairs or edges independently and identically distributed (I.I.D.), and thus is well suited to our online crowdsourcing test system. In this paper, we particularly focus on this kind of random graph, Erdös-Rényi random graph, leaving other models for future studies.

3. ONLINE HODGERANK

In this section, we propose a new online design to conduct paired comparison for subjective IQA and Erdös-Rényi random graph model is chosen to tackle the scenario that in crowdsourcing raters and pairs come in an unspecified way. Specifically, we first describe Hodge theory on general graphs, and then explain how to develop the online rating algorithms. An upper bound for convergence of such online rating algorithms is given to justify the settings that minimax parametric rate is met. Finally, we discuss how to online track triangular curls and topological changement.

3.1 Batch HodgeRank on Graphs

HodgeRank [19] is a general framework to decompose paired comparison data on graphs, possibly imbalanced (where different image pairs may receive different number of comparisons) and incomplete (where every participant may only give partial comparisons), into three orthogonal components:

$$\textit{aggregate paired ranking} =$$

$$\textit{global ranking} \bigoplus \textit{local inconsistency} \bigoplus \textit{global inconsistency}$$

To be precise, consider paired ranking data on a graph $G = (V, E)$, $Y_\alpha : E \to R$ such that $Y_{ij}^\alpha = -Y_{ji}^\alpha$ where α is the participant index. Without loss of generality, one assumes that $Y_{ij}^\alpha > 0$ if α prefers i to j and $Y_{ij}^\alpha \le 0$ otherwise, with the magnitude representing the degree of preference. In a dichotomous choice, Y_{ij}^α can be taken as $\{\pm 1\}$.

In subjective multimedia assessment, it is natural to assume

$$Y_{ij}^\alpha = s_i^* - s_j^* + \varepsilon_{ij}^\alpha \tag{1}$$

where $s^* : V \to \mathbb{R}$ is some true scaling score on V and ε_{ij}^α are independent noise of mean zero and fixed variance.

Under such assumptions, Gauss-Markov theorem tells us that the unbiased estimator is given by the following least square problem

$$\min_{s \in \mathrm{R}^{|V|}} \sum_{i,j,\alpha} \omega_{ij}^\alpha (s_i - s_j - Y_{ij}^\alpha)^2, \tag{2}$$

where ω_{ij}^α denotes the number of paired comparisons on $\{i, j\}$ made by rater α. It can be rewritten as the following weighted least square form

$$\min_{s \in \mathrm{R}^{|V|}} \sum_{i,j} \omega_{ij} (s_i - s_j - \hat{Y}_{ij})^2, \tag{3}$$

where $\hat{Y}_{ij} = (\sum_\alpha \omega_{ij}^\alpha Y_{ij}^\alpha)/(\sum_\alpha \omega_{ij}^\alpha)$ and $\omega_{ij} = \sum_\alpha \omega_{ij}^\alpha$.

To characterize the solution and residue of (3), we first define the triangle set of G as all the 3-cliques in G:

$$T = \left\{ \{i, j, k\} \epsilon \binom{V}{3} \,|\, \{i, j\}, \{j, k\}, \{k, i\} \epsilon E \right\}. \tag{4}$$

Then every $\hat{Y}$ admits an orthogonal decomposition adapted to G

$$\hat{Y} = \hat{Y}^g + \hat{Y}^h + \hat{Y}^c, \tag{5}$$

where

$$\hat{Y}_{ij}^g = \hat{s}_i - \hat{s}_j, \quad \text{for some } \hat{s} \in \mathrm{R}^V, \tag{6}$$

$$\hat{Y}_{ij}^h + \hat{Y}_{jk}^h + \hat{Y}_{ki}^h = 0, \text{ for each } \{i, j, k\} \in T, \tag{7}$$

$$\sum_{j \sim i} \omega_{ij} \hat{Y}_{ij}^h = 0, \text{ for each } i \in V. \tag{8}$$

where $\hat{Y}^g$ satisfies (6) and $\hat{Y}^h$ satisfies two conditions (7) and (8). The residue $\hat{Y}^c$ actually satisfies (8) but not (7). Residues $\hat{Y}^h$ and $\hat{Y}^c$ account for inconsistencies of the global ranking obtained which show the validity of the ranking and can be further studied in terms of its geometric scale, namely whether inconsistency in the ranking data arises locally or globally. Local inconsistency can be fully characterized by triangular cycles (e.g. $i \succ j \succ k \succ i$), while global inconsistency involves loops consisting nodes more than three (e.g. $i \succ j \succ k \succ \ldots \succ i$), which may arise due to data incompleteness and once presented with a large component indicates some serious conflicts in ranking data.

Global rating score can be the minimal norm least square solution $\hat{s}$ of the following normal equation

$$\Delta_0 \, \hat{s} = \delta_0^* \hat{Y} \tag{9}$$

where $\delta_0 : \mathrm{R}^V \to \mathrm{R}^E$ is a finite difference operator (matrix) on G defined by $\delta_0((i,j), i) = -1$, $\delta_0((i,j), j) = 1$, and otherwise zero, $\delta_0^* = \delta_0^T W$ ($W = \mathrm{diag}(\omega_{ij})$), $\Delta_0 = \delta_0^* \cdot \delta_0$ is the unnormalized graph Laplacian defined by $(\Delta_0)_{ii} = \sum_{j \sim i} \omega_{ij}$ and $(\Delta_0)_{ij} = -\omega_{ij}$, and $(\cdot)^\dagger$ is the Moore-Penrose (pseudo) inverse.

An interesting variation of this l_2-norm scheme (3) is an analogous l_1-projection onto the space of gradient flows,

$$\min_{s \in \mathrm{R}^{|V|}} \sum_{i,j} \omega_{ij} |s_i - s_j - \hat{Y}_{ij}|. \tag{10}$$

This optimization problem is applied to the case that the noise is sparse but can be large, often regarded as outliers. It is more robust to outliers when compared with the l_2-norm, and thus can be regarded as robust ranking. For more details, readers may refer to [19, 23].

As the input of this HodgeRank framework is a paired comparison multigraph (the whole set of paired comparison data in one batch) provided by participants, we may call this type of work as batch HodgeRank. For details of the theoretical development, readers may refer to [19]. The work in [40] adopts such batch HodgeRank to obtain quality scores of videos. However, for crowdsourcing test on Internet, participants and image pairs enter the system one by one in a dynamic and random way. Therefore, batch HodgeRank is not an efficient tool for crowdsourcing. To meet this challenge, we propose an online HodgeRank as Robins-Monro procedure or stochastic approximation of (9).

3.2 Online Rating Algorithms

The online rating algorithm considered in this paper is constructed from Robbins-Monro procedure [28] to solve linear operator equation $\bar{A}x = \bar{b}$,

$$x_{t+1} = x_t - \gamma_t(A_t x_t - b_t),\ E(A_t) = \bar{A},\ E(b_t) = b. \quad (11)$$

Now consider the normal equation (9) for the least square problem (2), $\Delta_0 s = \delta_0^* \hat{Y}$. In this case, at time t when a new rating $Y_t(i_t, j_t) = -Y_t(j_t, i_t)$ entered on pair (i_t, j_t), we have

- A_t is a $|V|\times|V|$ matrix defined by $A_t(i_t,i_t) = A_t(j_t,j_t) = -A_t(i_t,j_t) = -A_t(j_t,i_t) = 1$ and otherwise zero;
- b_t is a $|V|$-dimensional vector defined by $b_t(i_t) = -b_t(j_t) = Y_t(i_t,j_t)$ and otherwise zero.

Let $s_t = x_t$. The Robbins-Monro procedure becomes

$$\begin{aligned} s_{t+1}(i_t) &= s_t(i_t) - \gamma_t[s_t(i_t) - s_t(j_t) - Y_t(i_t,j_t)] \\ s_{t+1}(j_t) &= s_t(j_t) + \gamma_t[s_t(i_t) - s_t(j_t) - Y_t(i_t,j_t)] \quad (12) \end{aligned}$$

where the initial choice is $s_0 = 0$ or any vector such that $\sum_i s_0(i) = 0$, and the step size γ_t is a nonnegative sequence whose choice is often taken in the following form

$$\gamma_t = \frac{a}{(t+t_0)^\theta}, \quad \theta \in [0,1].$$

The choice of step size will be discussed in more detail in the next subsection with a convergence analysis which shows minimax rates with independent and identically distributed sampling. Algorithm 1 below shows the procedure of this online rating method.

For the sake of comparison, we also present a stochastic subgradient method for online rating with l_1-norm in (10), which is given by:

$$\begin{aligned} s_{t+1}(i_t) &= s_t(i_t) - \gamma_t \operatorname{sign}(s_t(i_t) - s_t(j_t) - Y_t(i_t,j_t)) \\ s_{t+1}(j_t) &= s_t(j_t) + \gamma_t \operatorname{sign}(s_t(i_t) - s_t(j_t) - Y_t(i_t,j_t)) \end{aligned} \quad (13)$$

with similar choices on initial score and steps.

Note that updates here only occur locally on the nodes associated with edge $\{i_{t+1}, j_{t+1}\}$, which is suitable for asynchronized parallel implementation.

Note that for l_1-based online algorithm it suffices to change $g_{ij} = \operatorname{sign}(s_t(i_t) - s_t(j_t) - Y_t(i_t,j_t))$.

Algorithm 1: Online Rating Procedure.

```
Initialization:
s_0 = 0 or any vector such that Σ_i s_0(i) = 0;   // Initialize the quality scores of each images.
With a new rating Y_t(i_t, j_t);   // A new paired comparison (i_t, j_t) occurs at time t.
Compute g_ij = s_t(i_t) − s_t(j_t) − Y_t(i_t, j_t);
Then
s_{t+1}(i_t) = s_t(i_t) − γ_t * g_ij;
s_{t+1}(j_t) = s_t(j_t) + γ_t * g_ij.   // Quality scores at time t+1.
```

3.3 Convergence Analysis

There have been studies on convergence analysis of subgradient methods, e.g. [31]. Typical convergence results require the conditions that step sizes $\sum_t \gamma_t^2 < \infty$ while $\sum_t \gamma_t = \infty$, and boundedness of subgradients, which are in particular $s(i) - s(j) - Y(i,j)$ and $\operatorname{sign}(s(i) - s(j) - Y(i,j))$ here. When general convex loss functions are assumed, the analysis is typically formulated as regret bounds [27].

In particular, when the square loss is adopted, one may achieve the following probabilistic upper bound, whose proof is given by [21] for general edge independent random graphs, which in fact reaches the minimax optimal rates for parametric regression up to a logarithmic factor.

In the following theorem, assume that $Y_t(i_t, j_t)$ is an independent and identically distributed (I.I.D.) sequence. For example, each rater follows a sampling on Erdös-Rényi random graph. Another example is Multiplicative-Attribute Graph Models [20] once node attributes are given which is however not pursued in this paper. The convergence analysis can be based on general Robbins-Monro procedure (11) with independent sampling sequence.

Define a random matrix

$$\Pi_k^t = \begin{cases} (I - \gamma_t A_t)\dots(I - \gamma_k A_k), & k \le t; \\ I, & k > t. \end{cases} \quad (14)$$

If we replace A_i by $\bar{A}$, we obtain a deterministic positive definite matrix, say $\bar{\Pi}_k^t$.

The following lemma leads to a martingale decomposition for error $x_t - x^*$, given in [32, 41], which is crucial to lead to the error bounds.

Lemma. For all $t \in \mathbb{N}$,

$$x_t = \Pi_1^{t-1} x_0 + \sum_{k=1}^{t-1} \gamma_k \Pi_{k+1}^{t-1} b_t \quad (15)$$

and

$$x_t - x^* = \bar{\Pi}_1^{t-1}(x_0 - x^*) - \sum_{k=1}^{t-1} \xi_k, \quad (16)$$

where

$$\xi_k = \begin{cases} \gamma_k \bar{\Pi}_{k+1}^{t-1}((A_k - \bar{A})x_k - (b_k - \bar{b})), & 1 \le k < t; \\ 0, & k \ge t. \end{cases}$$

is a martingale difference sequence such that $E[\xi_t : \mathcal{F}_{t-1}] = 0$ for a filtration $\mathcal{F}_{t-1}$ up to time $t-1$.

The first part in error, $\bar{\Pi}_1^{t-1}(x_0 - x^*)$, is called the *initial error* and the martingale difference tail, $\sum \xi_k$, is called the *sample error*. Initial error can be bounded deterministically, while the sample error can be bounded via a Pinelis-Bernstein probabilistic inequality. Combining these bounds will lead to the following theorem, whose derivation follows closely [41].

Theorem 3.3. *Let E consists of the edge set of the expected graph, and $0 = \lambda_0 < \lambda_1 \leq \ldots \leq \lambda_{n-1}$ are eigenvalues of expected graph Laplacian $\Delta_0 = E(A_t)$. Assume that $A = 2 \vee \lambda_{n-1}$ and $|Y_t(i,j)| \leq B$. Then there exists a choice of step size $\gamma_t = a/(t+t_0)$ (e.g. $a = 1/\lambda_1$ and $t_0 \geq B/\lambda_1$) such that the following holds for all $t \in \mathbb{N}$ with probability at least $1-\delta$ ($\delta > 0$),*

$$\|s_t - s^*\|_2 \leq \frac{7\sqrt{A}B|E|}{\lambda_1^{3/2}} t^{-1/2} \log(t+t_0) \cdot \log\frac{2}{\delta}$$

where s_t is defined by (12).

The theorem says that the online rating algorithm converges to the underlying true score s^* under independent sampling process. The convergence rate is minimax optimal at $O(t^{-1/2})$. The choice of step size $\gamma_t \sim t^{-1}$ is crucial, with large enough t_0. Although the choice of a and t_0 does not affect the asymptotic rate in theory, in practice they influence the speed of convergence when t is small. We shall see this in experimental section. Moreover, in our applications, we find the performance distinctions are ignorable between two types of online algorithms, least square (12) and least absolute value (13), whence we do not pursue a thorough convergence analysis here for l_1-based online rating (13).

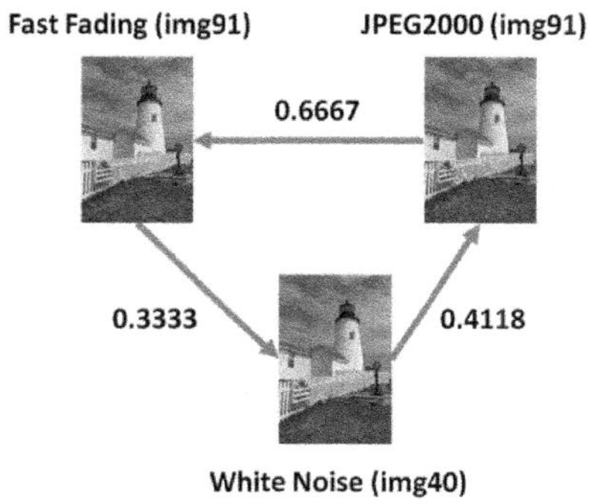

Figure 1: Large curl due to multicriteria in paired comparisons among users. The image is undistinguishable due to its small size, so image IDs in LIVE database are printed here.

3.4 Online Tracking of Triangular Curls

Hodge decomposition (5) has a component $\hat{Y}^c$ which satisfies $\hat{Y}^c_{ij} + \hat{Y}^c_{jk} + \hat{Y}^c_{ki} \neq 0$ for each triangle $(i,j,k) \in T$. This encodes the information about triangular or local inconsistency. For a graph $G = (V,E)$ whose 3-clique complex $\chi_G = (V,E,T)$ does not contain a "loop" (i.e. the first Betti number $\beta_1 = 0$), global inconsistency vanishes and such triangular inconsistency explains all sorts of inconsistency. It happens when Erdös-Rényi random graphs and k-regular random graphs are sufficiently dense [40, 39]. Due to such an importance, it is desired to track triangular curls:

$$curl_{ijk} = \hat{Y}^c_{ij} + \hat{Y}^c_{jk} + \hat{Y}^c_{ki} = \hat{Y}_{ij} + \hat{Y}_{jk} + \hat{Y}_{ki}.$$

which is nothing but triangular trace of $\hat{Y}$ [19]. Curl is easy for online and parallel realizations. In [40], another relative curl is introduced as extensions of combinatorial intransitive triangles,

$$rel\text{-}curl_{ijk} = \frac{|\hat{Y}_{ij} + \hat{Y}_{jk} + \hat{Y}_{ki}|}{|\hat{Y}_{ij}| + |\hat{Y}_{jk}| + |\hat{Y}_{ki}|} \in [0,1].$$

Relative curl on a triangle $(i,j,k) \in T$ is one if and only if (i,j,k) is intransitive.

The existence of large curls or intransitive triangles may be either due to noise or suggesting the existence of multicriteria in paired comparisons. If the latter case happens on a triangule (i,j,k), on each edge say $(i,j) \in E$, it will have a $\hat{Y}_{ij}$ consistently away from zero, and incur a large curl. In Figure 1, we exhibit one example of such intransitive triangle existing in the data we collected so far, which indicates a stable cyclic preference on a natural scene picture in LIVE dataset such that JPEG2000 (img91) is better than Fast Fading (img91), Fast Fading (img91) is better than White Noise (img40), and White Noise (img40) is better than JPEG2000 (img91). This is due to the fact when different pairs of images are presented to raters, different salient features are adopted by raters implicitly. Triangular curls due to noise will vanish when the sample size goes to infinity while curls due to multicriteria will persist with the increase of sample complexity. Therefore, online tracking of curls will be useful to identify such a kind of inconsistency.

Algorithm 2 outlined below shows how to track the triangular curl in an online way.

Algorithm 2: Online Tracking of Curls.

With a new rating $Y^{(t)}_{ij}$;

$n^{(t+1)}_{ij} = n^{(t)}_{ij} + 1$; // $n^{(t)}_{ij}$ is the number of paired comparisons up to time t.

$\hat{Y}^{(t+1)}_{ij} = (1 - 1/n^{(t+1)}_{ij})\hat{Y}^{(t)}_{ij} + Y^{(t)}_{ij}/n^{(t+1)}_{ij}$; // $\hat{Y}^{(t)}_{ij}$ follows the same definition in Section 3.1.

for *each k s.t. (i,j,k) is a triangle* **do**

  $curl^{(t+1)}_{ijk} = \hat{Y}^{(t+1)}_{ij} + \hat{Y}^{(t+1)}_{jk} + \hat{Y}^{(t+1)}_{ki}$

  $rel\text{-}curl^{(t+1)}_{ijk} = \frac{|curl^{(t+1)}_{ijk}|}{|\hat{Y}^{(t+1)}_{ij}| + |\hat{Y}^{(t+1)}_{jk}| + |\hat{Y}^{(t+1)}_{ki}|}$

end

3.5 Online Tracking of Topology Evolution

The work in [40] shows that when the resultant graph provided by assessors is connected, we can derive global scores for all the images in comparison from batch HodgeRank. Besides, when its clique complex is loop-free, there is no global inconsistency whence tracking local inconsistency (triangular curls) presented above will be enough. Motivated by these two observations, [40] adopts persistent homology [14, 42, 6, 13] to check if a given graph instance satisfies the two conditions.

In fact, persistent homology is an online algorithm to check topology evolution when nodes, edges and triangles enter in a sequential way. Here we just discuss in brief the application of persistent homology to monitor the number of connected components (β_0) and loops (β_1) in our online settings. In random graph designs for image comparisons, we can assume that the images (nodes) are created at the same time, after that pairs of images (edges) are presented to assessors independently one by one. A triangle $\{i,j,k\}$ is created immediately when all the three associated edges

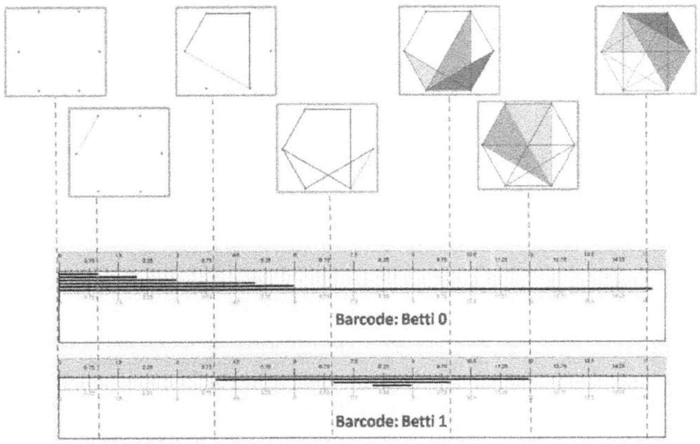

Figure 2: An example of persistence Barcodes of Betti numbers .

appeared. In practice with sampling of multigraph data, one may consider certain thresholds on edges and triangles for their presence, which can be dealt with in a similar way. With such a streaming data, persistent homology may return the number of β_0 and β_1 at each time when a new node/edge/triangle is born.

Figure 2 illustrates an example of this birth process and its associated Betti numbers (β_0 and β_1) that are computed and plotted by JPlex [30]. At the first frame (say $t = 0$), 6 images as nodes are collected, which corresponds to $\beta_0 = 6$ at $t = 0$ in Barcode: Betti 0. On the second frame ($t = 1$), an edge connecting a pair of nodes is created which drops the number of connected components from 6 to 5, i.e. $\beta_0 = 5$ at $t = 1$ in Barcode: Betti 0. The same procedure follows and particularly at the fifth frame $t = 4$, it creates a loop and there are 3 connected components in the graph, which can be read from $\beta_0 = 3$ at $t = 4$ and $\beta_1 = 1$ at $t = 4$, respectively. Note that after the thirteenth frame $t = 12$, there is only one connected component $\beta_0 = 1$ left and no loop exists $\beta_1 = 0$ as indicated by the Barcodes.

4. EXPERIMENTS

In this section, we systematically evaluate the performance of the proposed online HodgeRank algorithm against batch HodgeRank. First, the datasets used for the experiments are briefly explained. Then we present the experimental design of obtaining online paired comparison data, followed by the results with online and batch methods. Finally, we show how to track the curls and topological evolution online with persistent homology.

4.1 Datasets

Two publicly available datasets, LIVE [3] and IVC [2], are used in this work. The LIVE dataset contains 29 reference images and 779 distorted images. The distorted images are obtained using five different distortion processes–JPEG2000, JPEG, White Noise, Gaussian Blur, and Fast Fading Rayleigh. Considering the resolution limit of most test computers, we only choose 6 different reference images (480×720) and 15 distorted versions of each reference, for a total of 96 images. The second dataset, IVC, which is also

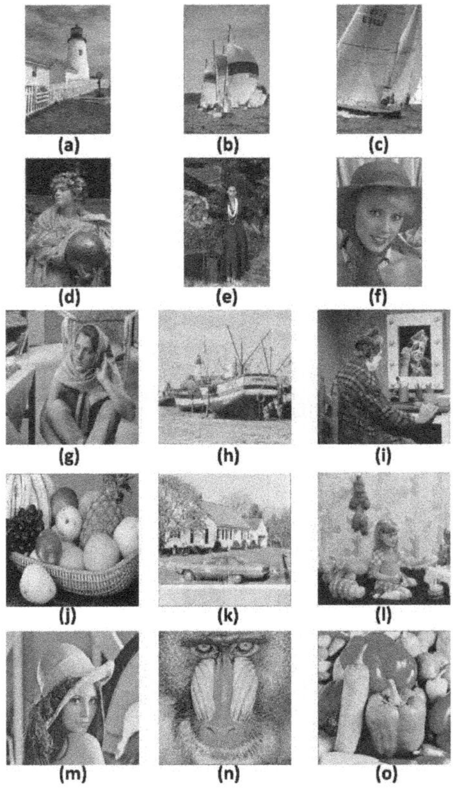

Figure 3: Images in LIVE and IVC databases (The first six are images from LIVE and the remaining images are from IVC).

a broadly adopted dataset in the community of IQA, includes 10 reference images and 185 distorted images derived from four distortion types–JPEG2000, JPEG, LAR Coding, and Blurring. Following the collection strategy in LIVE, we further select 9 different reference images (512×512) and 15 distorted images of each reference. Eventually, we obtain a medium-sized image set that contains a total of 240 images from 15 references, as illustrated in Figure 3. Note that we do not use the subjective scores in LIVE and IVC, but only borrow the image sources they provide. Different from them, we propose to assess image quality with paired comparison method. There are two aspects about the size of dataset: (1) number of distortion types; (2) number of reference images. The first is the number of nodes in our paired comparison graphs, which is n=16 here. Even on such a scale, it is almost impossible for a single person to perform all $\binom{n}{2}$ paired comparisons. So it suffices to illustrate the performance of online algorithm against batch algorithm. The second does not affect the computational complexity of algorithms, whence a random choice 15 from LIVE and IVC database is to show performance consistency over these examples.

4.2 Online Paired Data Collection

We now present our experiment design for collecting the set of online paired data. Different from traditional complete design in paired comparison, a session in our test can have an arbitrary duration (down to a single pair) and par-

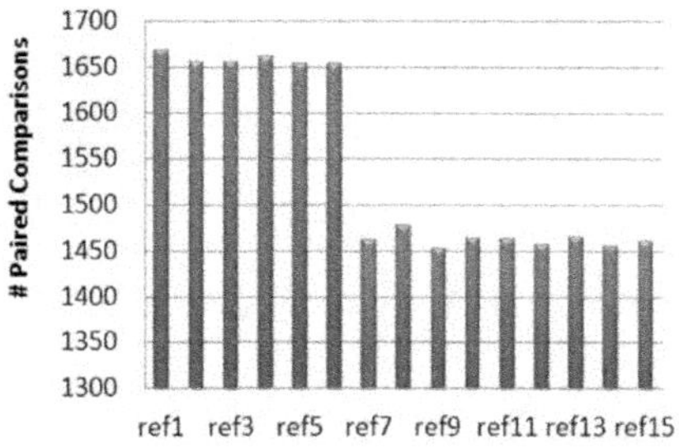

Figure 4: Number of paired comparisons each reference received in LIVE and IVC databases.

ticipants are free to decide when to quit. In other words, the number of pairs (*#pairs*) shown to participants can be adjusted according to their time constraint and preference. That is, when a participant's time is adequate, *#pairs* can be a bigger value. But if he/she is under the pressure of time or prefers not to spend more time with the experiment , *#pairs* will be smaller.

Before starting the experiment, each participant is briefed about the goal of the experiment and given a short training session to familiarize themselves with the testing procedure. In the testing process, images are displayed side by side at their native resolutions to prevent any distortions due to scaling operations performed by software or hardware. Besides, to make it impossible for participants to cheat our system by inputting "smart" answers, the order of each pair and the order within each pair are totally random for each participant. Each assessor is allowed to take as much time as needed to enter their choice. However, the assessors could not change their choice once entered or view the image again. Once the choice is entered, the next image pair is displayed.

Moreover, we hope to avoid the situation with successive pairs of test images from the same reference, to avoid contextual and memory effects in their judgments of quality. For this purpose, after the playlist for one participant is constructed, our program would go over the entire playlist to determine if adjacent pairs correspond to the same reference. If such a case is detected, one of the pairs would be swapped with another randomly chosen pair in the playlist which does not suffer from the same problem.

Finally, 186 observers of different cultural level (students, tutors, and researchers), each of whom performs a varied number of comparisons via Internet, provide 23,097 paired comparisons in total. The number of responses each reference image receives is different, as illustrated in Figure 4. It should be noted that, for ref1-6 from LIVE database, we start our test from October 10th, 2011. Later, 9 references images (ref7-15) from IVC database are added to our test system from November 2nd, 2011. Our collecting task is still on-going now for further larger-scale studies.

4.3 Comparison with "Batch" HodgeRank

The experimental evaluation involves evaluating the online HodgeRank algorithms (12) on various data sets against the performance of batch HodgeRank. We also compare these algorithms against the l_1-norm online algorithm in (13) on the same data sets.

The metric that we used in the evaluation of the performance of various algorithms is the Mismatch Ratio (***MR***),

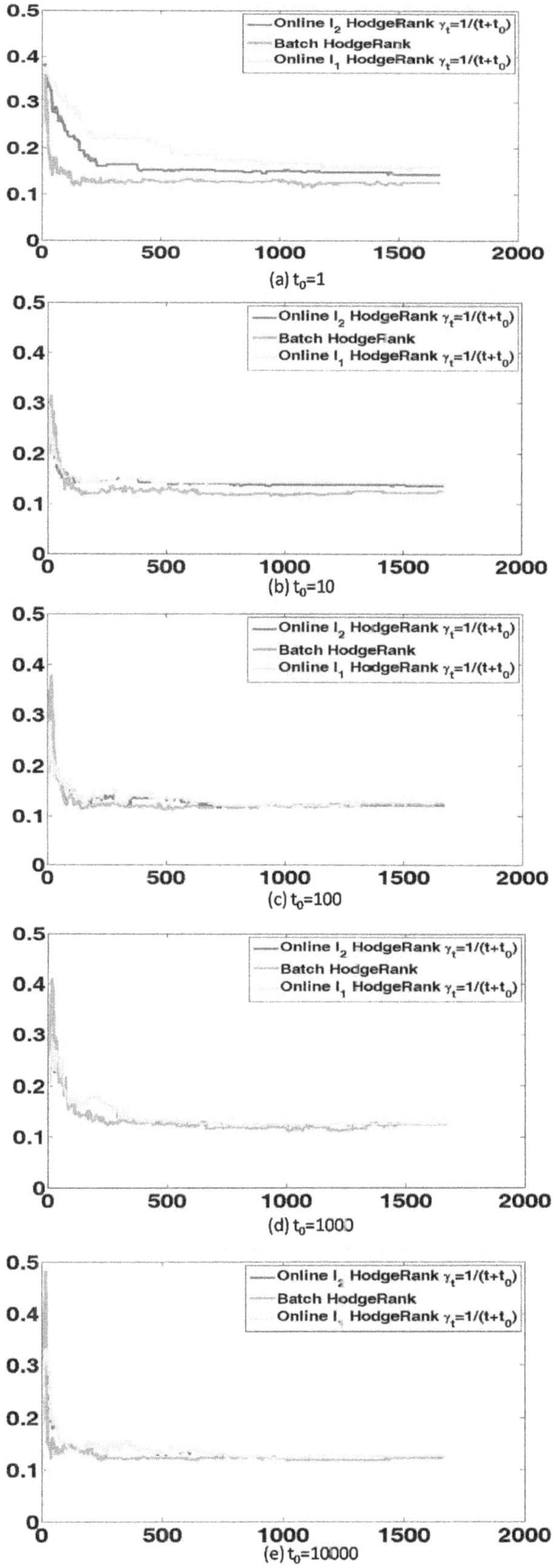

Figure 5: The impact of the t_0 parameter on the performances. *MR* (y-axis) versus the number of samples (x-axis) on reference1.

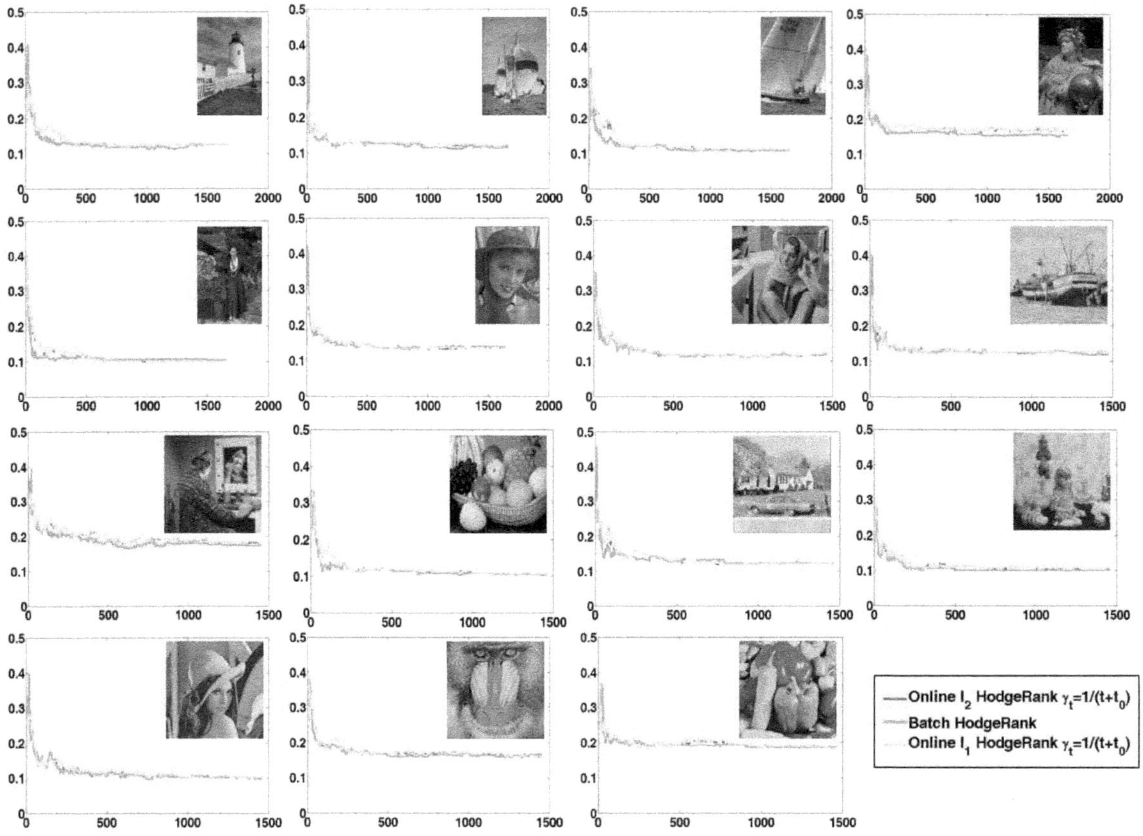

Figure 6: Experimental results of online HodgeRank vs. batch HodgeRank. *MR* (y-axis) versus the number of samples (x-axis) on 15 reference datasets.

i.e., at time t, the percentage of mismatch pairs of a global rating s_t made on all previous examples,

$$\epsilon_t = \frac{1}{2t}\sum_{\tau=1}^{t} |\text{sign}(s_t(i_\tau)-s_t(j_\tau))-Y_\tau(i_\tau,j_\tau)|, \quad Y_\tau(i,j)\in\{\pm 1\}$$

Since in this paper we use the simplest binary choice for $Y_t(i,j)$, one natural performance measure for different algorithms is simply to count the ratio of mismatched paired comparisons up to time t. Minimization of such an objective function is known to be NP-hard. However, in our experiments we find the batch HodgeRank, online l_2 HodgeRank and online l_1 HodgeRank exhibit similar effects on minimizing such an objective function, whose distinctions thus can be ignored in practice like this.

Although in theory, the choice of t_0 won't affect asymptotic convergence rates (Theorem 3.3); one has to be careful on choosing it in practice. First, we study the impact of the t_0 parameter in (12) and (13) on the performances of online rating algorithms. For simplicity, we randomly take reference1 as an illustrative example while other reference images exhibit similar results. Figure 5 shows the influences of t_0 on mismatch ratios, in a comparison with batch HodgeRank. It can be seen from this figure that with the increase of collected data, the ***MR*** curve generally decreases. When t_0 is chosen to be small, l_2 online rating (12) shows better performance than l_1 online (13). However, when t_0 increases (e.g. from 1 to 10000), such a performance difference diminishes and both methods approach performance of batch HodgeRank. We note that when t_0 is chosen to be too large, initial tracking performance will drop which shows a lag behind of batch learning curve. Although this does not hurt the long term behavior eventually, those who care the initial iterations should be careful on this. In the following experiments, we will choose $t_0 = 1000$ as a balance of these effects for further studies.

Figure 6 shows the performance comparisons of online HodgeRank against batch HodgeRank with $t_0 = 1000$ for other 14 reference datasets. It is interesting to see that on all of these large scale data collections, both of these two online algorithms are able to maintain competitive performances with the batch case. From these results, we may conclude that large amplitude outliers are not a significant issue in our crowdsourcing data collection as $|Y_t(i,j)|$ is bounded by 1. Besides, Table 1 shows the computation complexity achieved by l_2 online HodgeRank, l_1 online HodgeRank and batch HodgeRank. It is easy to see that on our dataset, online HodgeRank can achieve up to nearly 370 times faster than batch HodgeRank, with similar prediction errors.

4.4 Online Tracking of Topology and Curls

In our online settings, due to the multiple comparisons between a pair of images, a natural question is raised that how many samples are needed to satisfy the connected & loop-free conditions? As each reference is similar in sampling scheme, we compute the online mean Betti numbers

Table 1: **Computation complexity (s) comparison of online and batch HodgeRank.**

	ref1	ref2	ref3	ref4	ref5	ref6	ref7	ref8	ref9	ref10	ref11	ref12	ref13	ref14	ref15	mean
l_2	0.166	0.158	0.159	0.162	0.164	0.163	0.125	0.128	0.131	0.125	0.130	0.128	0.133	0.135	0.133	0.143
l_1	0.159	0.162	0.165	0.166	0.162	0.163	0.132	0.127	0.125	0.124	0.125	0.123	0.124	0.129	0.132	0.141
Batch	59.28	60.78	58.25	58.65	60.09	58.22	53.15	49.58	47.45	47.81	47.84	48.01	50.29	47.40	47.43	52.95

over 15 references, as illustrated in Figure 7 (a). As we can see, after about 70 samples on this multigraph, with high probability the resultant graph is connected & loop-free. In other words, it is easy to meet these two requirements and thus can avoid the possible issue of harmonic inconsistency in global ranking.

In addition, we can further set a threshold for each edge which can be treated as a confidence level. That is to say, only edges on which the number of paired comparisons are larger than this threshold will be added in our resultant graph. The bigger the threshold is set, the more robust the topological structure of the graph is. Figure 7 (b) shows the online tracking of the first two Betti numbers by persistent homology when threshold is set to be 3. One can see more examples (250) are needed to reach the connected and loop-free condition.

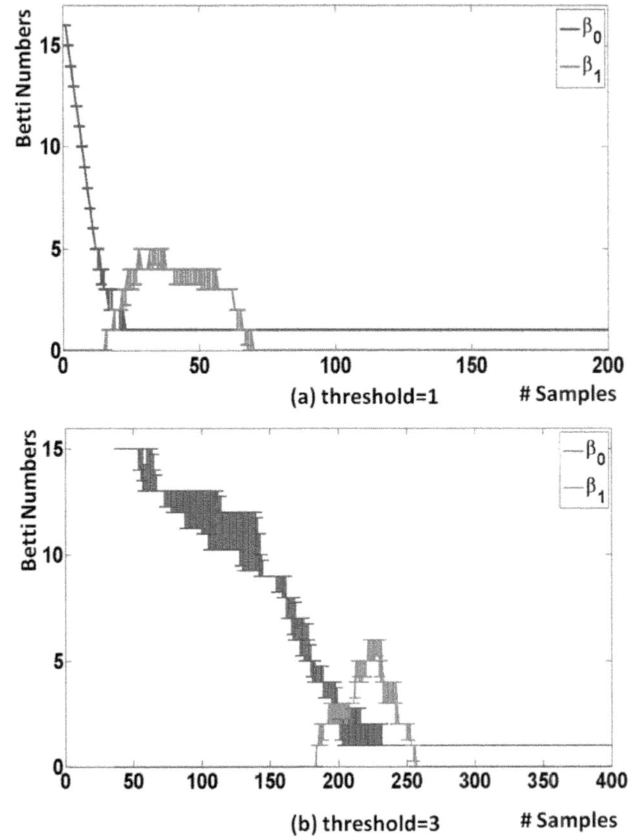

Figure 7: Number of samples versus number of online Betti numbers. For each sample number level, the median number of Betti numbers over 15 references with [0.25, 0.75] confidence interval are plotted in the figure.

Triangular curls and relative curls defined in the last section are helpful to identify possible inconsistency or the existence of multicriteria adopted by raters in different paired comparisons. By online tracking of relative curls in Figure 8, we find the intransitive triangle shown in Figure 1 that JPEG2000 (img91) is better than Fast Fading (img91), Fast Fading (img91) is better than White Noise (img40), and White Noise (img40) is better than JPEG2000 (img91). The phenomenon suggests that one should explore the hidden multicriteria behind the paired comparisons among these images which will be left for future studies.

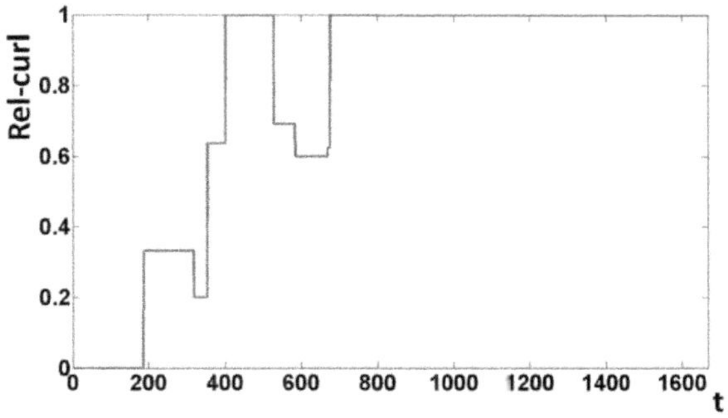

Figure 8: Online tracking of relative curl on triangle (JPEG2000 (img91), Fast Fading (img91), White Noise (img40)). One can see the intransitive triangle constantly appears over time which suggests possible different criteria adopted by users in paired comparisons made among them.

5. CONCLUSIONS

In this paper, online algorithms are proposed for crowdsourcing subjective image quality assessment where the data are collected in a streaming way. The algorithms are based on Robbins-Monro procedure or stochastic approximation to solve a HodgeRank problem on random graphs. Two variations are studied against the batch HodgeRank: one based on classical l_2-minimization or least square problem to deal with independent noise of zero mean and bounded variance, and the other based on l_1-minimization problem to deal with outliers. Experiments with the images available in LIVE and IVC databases are conducted, including 15 different reference images and 15 distorted versions of each reference in total. It is shown that in our applications, the l_2-based online HodgeRank can achieve as nearly good performance as batch HodgeRank, in both theory and experiments. Moreover, l_1-based online rating exhibits similar performance to l_2 online algorithm and thus batch HodgeRank in our experiments which indicates the binary choice in crowdsourcing data collection won't suffer much the outlier issue. Furthermore, we investigate the online tracking of triangular curls and topology evolution of the paired ranking complex. In particular, we show that online tracking of triangular curls provides us important information about inconsistency, which may suggest the existence of multicriteria in rater's judgement of different object pairs.

Our studies show that online HodgeRank provides us an efficient approach to study large scale crowdsourcing subjective IQA on Internet. It enables us to derive global rating as well as monitor the inconsistency occurring in the data in the real time.

Additionally, we would like to point out here that the theory developed in this paper takes the standard I.I.D. sampling assumption as the main stream of statistical machine learning. It is a largely unexplored field for online learning with dependent sampling, such as Markov sampling and active sampling, which will be our future directions.

6. ACKNOWLEDGMENTS

This work was supported in part by National Basic Research Program of China (973 Program): 2012CB316400, 2012CB825501, 2011CB809105, in part by National Natural Science Foundation of China: 61025011, 61071157, and 60833006.

7. REFERENCES

[1] *ITU-R Recommendation P.800. Methods for subjective determination of transmission quality*, 1996.

[2] Subjective quality assessment irccyn/ivc database. `http://www2.irccyn.ec-nantes.fr/ivcdb/`, 2005.

[3] LIVE image and video quality assessment database. `http://live.ece.utexas.edu/research/quality/`, 2008.

[4] A.-L. Barabasi and R. Albert. Emergence of scaling in random networks. *Science*, 286(5439):509–512, 1999.

[5] B. Bollobas. *Random Graphs*. Cambridge University Press, 2001.

[6] G. Carlsson. Topology and data. *Bulletin of the American Mathematical Society*, 46(2):255–308, 2009.

[7] K.-T. Chen, C.-C. Wu, Y.-C. Chang, and C.-L. Lei. A crowdsourceable QoE evaluation framework for multimedia content. pages 491–500. ACM Multimedia, 2009.

[8] F. Chung and L. Lu. *Complex Graphs and Networks*. CBMS Regional Conference Series in Mathematics, American Mathematical Society, 2006.

[9] N. Cristianini and J. Shawe-Taylor. *An Introduction to Support Vector Machines and Other Kernel-based Learning Methods*. Cambridge Unversity Press, 2000.

[10] F. Cucker and S. Smale. On the mathematical foundations of learning. *Bull. of the Amer. Math. Soc.*, 29(1):1–49, 2002.

[11] H. David. *The method of paired comparisons*. 2nd Ed., Griffin's Statistical Monographs and Courses, 41. Oxford University Press, New York, NY, 1988.

[12] Y. S. E. Granger and P. Lavoie. A pattern reordering approach based on ambiguity detection for online category learning. *PAMI*, 25:525–529, 2003.

[13] H. Edelsbrunner and J. Harer. Computational topology : an introduction. 2010.

[14] H. Edelsbrunner, D. Letscher, and A. Zomorodian. Topological persistence and simplification. *Discrete and Computational Geometry*, 28(4):511–533, 2002.

[15] A. Eichhorn, P. Ni, and R. Eg. Randomised pair comparison: an economic and robust method for audiovisual quality assessment. pages 63–68. NOSSDAV, 2010.

[16] P. Erdos and A. Renyi. On random graphs i. *Publ. Math. Debrecen*, 6:290–297, 1959.

[17] H. Grabner and H. Bischof. On-line boosting and vision. CVPR, 2006.

[18] G. H. H. Bekel, I. Bax and H. Ritter. Adaptive computer vision: Online learning for object recognition. DAGM, 2004.

[19] X. Jiang, L.-H. Lim, Y. Yao, and Y. Ye. Statistical ranking and combinatorial Hodge theory. *Mathematical Programming*, 2010.

[20] M. Kim and J. Leskovec. Multiplicative attribute graph model of real-world networks. *Internet Mathematics*, 8(1-2):113–160, 2012.

[21] L.-H. Lim and Y. Yao. Online ranking on random graphs. *preprint*, 2012.

[22] S. A. O. Javed and M. Shah. Online detection and classification of moving objects using progressively improving detectors. CVPR, 2005.

[23] B. Osting, J. Darbon, and S. Osher. Statistical ranking using the l_1-norm on graphs. *AIMS'*, 2012.

[24] M. Penrose. *Random Geometric Graphs (Oxford Studies in Probability)*. Oxford University Press, 2003.

[25] M. T. Pham and T. J. Cham. Online asymetric boosted classifiers for object detection. CVPR, 2007.

[26] Y. L. R. T. Collins and M. Leordeanu. Online selection of discriminative tracking features. *PAMI*, 27:1631–1643, 2005.

[27] A. Rakhlin. *Statistical Learning Theory and Sequential Prediction*. Lecture Notes in University of Pennsyvania, 2012.

[28] H. Robbins and S. Monro. A stochastic approximation method. *The Annals of Mathematical Statistics*, 22(3):400–407, 1951.

[29] F. Rosenblatt. The perceptron: A probabilistic model for information storage and organization in the brain. *Psychological Review*, 65(6):386–408, 1958.

[30] H. Sexton and M. Johansson. JPlex: a java software package for computing the persistent homology of filtered simplicial complexes. `http://comptop.stanford.edu/programs/jplex/`, 2009.

[31] N. Shor. *Minimization Methods for Non-Differenliable Functions*. Springer-Verlag, 1985.

[32] S. Smale and Y. Yao. Online learning algorithms. *Foundation of Computational Mathematics*, 6(2):145–170, 2006.

[33] V. N. Vapnik. *Statistical Learning Theory*. Wiley-Interscience, 1998.

[34] D. Watts and S. Strogatz. Collective dynamics of 'small-world' networks. *Nature*, (393):440–442, 1998.

[35] B. Widrow and M. Hoff. Adaptive switching circuits. *IRE WESCON Convention Record*, (4):96–104, 1960.

[36] B. Widrow and M. A. Lehr. 30 years of adaptive neural networks: Perceptron, madaline, and backpropagation. pages 1415–1442. Proceedings of the IEEE, 1990.

[37] N. Wormald. Models of random regular graphs. pages 239–298. In Surveys in Combinatorics, 1999.

[38] B. Wu and R. Nevatia. Improving part based object detection by unsupervised, online boosting. CVPR, 2007.

[39] Q. Xu, Q. Huang, T. Jiang, B. Yan, W. Lin, and Y. Yao. HodgeRank on random graphs for subjective video quality assessment. *IEEE Transactions on Multimedia*, 14(3):844–857, 2012.

[40] Q. Xu, T. Jiang, Y. Yao, Q. Huang, B. Yan, and W. Lin. Random partial paired comparison for subjective video quality assessment via HodgeRank. pages 393–402. ACM Multimedia, 2011.

[41] Y. Yao. On complexity issue of online learning algorithms. *IEEE Transactions on Information Theory*, 56(12):6470–6481, 2010.

[42] A. Zomorodian and G. Carlsson. Computing persistent homology. *Discrete and Computational Geometry*, 33(2):249–274, 2005.

Image Colorization Using Similar Images

Raj Kumar Gupta[1*] Alex Yong-Sang Chia[2*] Deepu Rajan[1] Ee Sin Ng[2] and Huang Zhiyong[2]

[1]School of Computer Engineering, Nanyang Technological University
50, Nanyang Avenue, Singapore – 639798

[2]Institute for Infocomm Research (I[2]R)
1 Fusionopolis Way, #21-01 Connexis, Singapore – 138632
{rajk0005, asdrajan}@ntu.edu.sg, {ysachia, nges, zyhuang}@i2r.a-star.edu.sg

ABSTRACT

We present a new example-based method to colorize a gray image. As input, the user needs only to supply a reference color image which is semantically similar to the target image. We extract features from these images at the resolution of superpixels, and exploit these features to guide the colorization process. Our use of a superpixel representation speeds up the colorization process. More importantly, it also empowers the colorizations to exhibit a much higher extent of spatial consistency in the colorization as compared to that using independent pixels. We adopt a fast cascade feature matching scheme to automatically find correspondences between superpixels of the reference and target images. Each correspondence is assigned a confidence based on the feature matching costs computed at different steps in the cascade, and high confidence correspondences are used to assign an initial set of chromatic values to the target superpixels. To further enforce the spatial coherence of these initial color assignments, we develop an image space voting framework which draws evidence from neighboring superpixels to identify and to correct invalid color assignments. Experimental results and user study on a broad range of images demonstrate that our method with a fixed set of parameters yields better colorization results as compared to existing methods.

Categories and Subject Descriptors

I.4.9 [**Image Processing and Computer Vision**]: Applications;

General Terms

Algorithms

*denotes equal contributions.

Keywords

Automatic colorization, cascade feature matching

1. INTRODUCTION

The goal of image colorization is to add colors to a gray image such that the colorized image is perceptually meaningful and visually appealing. A key challenge of this problem is that it is under constrained since there are potentially many colors that can be assigned to the gray pixels of an input image (e.g. leaves may be colored in green, yellow and brown). Hence, there is no one correct solution to the colorization problem and human intervention often plays an important role in the colorization process.

In general, colorization methods can be broadly divided into two main classes: interactive colorization methods and automatic colorization methods. Interactive colorization techniques [9, 7, 18, 15, 13] require a user to manually mark color scribbles on the target image. Colors from these scribbles are then smoothly propagated across the entire image based on an optimization framework. A key weakness of such methods is that they demand extensive efforts from a user. Additionally, for such methods, colorization quality is strongly dependent on the user supplied color scribbles, and it is often difficult for a novice user to provide sufficiently good color scribbles to achieve desirable colorization results. Automatic colorization methods [17, 6, 2, 12] take a different approach to image colorization. Specifically, rather than obtaining chromatic values from the user, these methods take a reference color image as input, and transfer colors from the reference image to the target image. While these methods can reduce the extent of user effort, in many cases, these methods often require careful tuning of a large number of parameters to yield satisfactory results.

In this paper, we propose a new automatic colorization method which exploits multiple image features to transfer the color information from reference color image to input gray image. Specifically, other than intensity and standard deviation features which are used by other colorization methods e.g. [17, 8], we incorporate the highly discriminative SURF and Gabor features in our method. The power of discriminative image features to reliably find correspondence between images has been demonstrated by Liu *et al.* [11] where they exploit SIFT features to find correspondences between images for scene alignment. The use of information rich Gabor and SURF features empowers our method to reliably find correspondences between the reference and target images for color transfer. Here, we choose Gabor feature for its effective representation of texture and popularity in the computer vision domain, while SURF feature is chosen for its excellent discriminative ability and compactness. We find correspondences at the resolutions of superpixels. This affords our method to exhibit a stronger level of spatial coherency than that possible with independent pixels. To support fast color transfer, we use a fast cascade feature matching scheme to quickly find correspondences between reference and target superpixels. At the first cascade step, we identify for each target superpixel a set of reference superpixels which are most similar to the target based on a particular feature type. This set of reference superpixels are screened at subsequent steps of the cascade using different feature types to sieve out matching reference superpixels. An initial set of color values is then assigned to target superpixels based on its matching reference superpixels. We note that these matchings are found based solely on image features and thus could be unreliable at image regions where features cannot be reliably extracted [16] (e.g. at regions corresponding to object boundaries). To improve the colorization results, we further enforce spatial consistency in the colorization by exploiting an image space voting framework which draws evidence from neighboring superpixels to quickly identify and correct invalid matchings. This leads to improved colorization results.

We evaluate our method on a diverse range of images comprising portrait, painting, landscape as well as on images containing deformable and rigid foreground objects. Experimental results demonstrate that our method, while straightforward, is sufficiently powerful to yield perceptually meaningful and visually appealing colorizations on these complex images. Additionally, comparison against existing state-of-the-art methods also demonstrates our method to be more effective at colorization, even with a fixed set of parameters.

2. RELATED WORK

Adding realistic colors to a gray image can improve the photorealism of the image, and has attracted much attention in the research community. Levin *et al.* [9] proposed a simple yet effective colorization algorithm that requires a user to provide color scribbles at various image regions. These color scribbles are then propagated automatically to the entire image by a least-squares optimization method. Huang *et al.* [7] improved on this method to reduce color blending at image edges. Yatziv and Sapiro [18] used multiple scribbles to colorize a pixel, where the combination weights are computed by a distance measure between the pixel and the scribble. While these methods have been shown to achieve good colorization results, a main shortcoming of these previous approaches is that they require a large number of color scribbles on the gray image as input. To reduce the number of color scribbles, Qu *et al.* [15] and Luan *et al.* [13] propagated scribbles that are marked on an image patch to other patches that have similar texture features. While their methods reduce the number of required scribbles, like all other interactive colorization methods, they demand substantial artistic skills of the user to mark appropriate colors on image patches to yield desirable colorizations.

Rather than obtaining colors directly from a user, Welsh *et al.* [17] obtained colors from a user-supplied reference color image. They extracted small image patches at each pixel of the target image and matched these patches to those of the reference image. These matches are then used to directly transfer colors from the reference image to the target image. Their method requires the user to manually mark corresponding regions between the reference and target to yield satisfactory color transfer, and is considerably less intuitive than our method which only needs a user-supplied reference image. Additionally, their method completely ignores spatial information of the pixels and hence their colorizations often yield very weak spatial consistency.

To address the spatial coherency problem, Irony *et al.* [8] proposed a method which used a segmented reference color image as an additional input. Here, they exploit color and texture information from segmented regions of the reference image to automatically segment the target gray image into a set of locally homogeneous image patches. Colors from the segmented regions of the reference image are then transferred to the image patches of the target image as color scribbles. Colors are propagated across the entire image by [9]. Their method demands segmentation masks as input, and is unsuitable for colorizing complex images e.g. foreground objects with fine scale structures. Charpiat *et al.* [2] assign colors to a gray image by minimizing an energy function using the graph cut approach. While their algorithm does not requires any user intervention during the colorization process, colorization results by their method are heavily influenced by the choice of many parameters.

Liu *et al.* [12] proposed an example-based colorization technique which is robust to illumination variations in the target and reference images. Their method downloads multiple reference images from the internet based on user-supplied keywords, and computes precise per-pixel registration between the reference and target images for color transfer. A key weakness of their method is that it is limited to colorizing foreground objects for which an exact replica of the target gray foreground object can be found. Consequently, their method is limited to rigid objects (e.g. landmarks) and is unsuitable for colorizing images which contain deformable objects such as those shown in this paper.

Recently, Chia *et al.* [3] developed a method which also exploits internet images for colorization. Relevant internet images are found with a novel image filtering framework, and colors are transferred from the reference to target with the belief-propagation framework. Very good colorization results are achieved by their method, though their method requires manual segmentation of major foreground objects of the target gray image.

In all previous works that we have discussed above in this section, Irony *et al.* [8] method is more similar to the proposed algorithm which also uses nearest-neighbor search and image space voting. However, our algorithm differs from their work in the following aspects:

- Irony's method requires manually segmented reference color image as an additional input. This segmented image is used to construct a feature space and a corresponding classifier, and hence affects the colorization result significantly. To minimize user intervention, the use of automatic image segmentation, which often generates small image segments in case of dense textured image regions, leads to poor colorization.

- To enforce the spatial consistency, Irony performs image space voting in feature space followed by a global

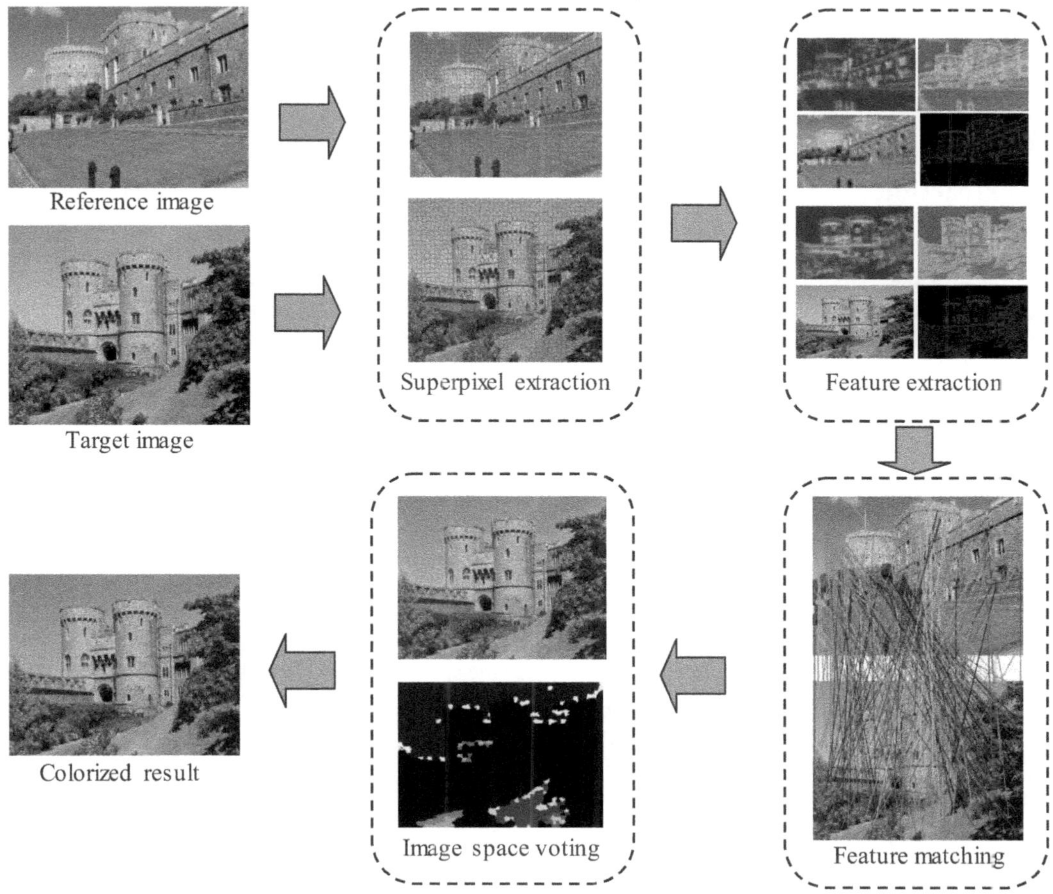

Figure 1: Overview of our colorization method. We work at the level of superpixels to extract different types of image features from the reference and target images, and find correspondences between features by a fast cascade feature matching scheme. These correspondences provide cues to the initial set of color assignments, which is refined by an image voting step to yield the final colorized result.

optimization. Their voting scheme identifies similar image regions in gray image with the same texture features as specified by the input reference color image segmentation mask. In our algorithm, the use of superpixels helps us to achieve spatial consistency in small image regions. After computing the initial color values for each of these superpixels, we group these superpixels and perform the image space voting in color space to update their previously assigned color values. Our primary focus is to enforce uniform color values to all connected pixels that are the part of same image segment. It enables us to achieve higher spatial consistency and better colorization results.

- Irony used the Discrete Cosine Transform (DCT) coefficients of a fix block size as a texture descriptor. While DCT coefficients are not sensitive to translations and rotations, they are more sensitive to scale changes. Here, we use a rich set of image features, including features computed at different scales, to find appropriate matches in reference image to transfer the color information.

3. COLORIZATION METHOD

The proposed algorithm colorizes gray input images by a user-supplied reference color image. We do not restrict the reference image to contain identical object instances as the input image. Instead, our only constraint is that the reference images should be semantically similar to the input image i.e. the reference image needs only to contain similar scene object types as the input image (e.g. castle). An overview of our method is given in Figure 1. As shown, our method comprises four key stages: (a) superpixel extraction (b) feature extraction, (c) feature matching, and (d) image space voting. We describe each of these steps below.

3.1 Superpixel extraction

We extract features from the color reference and target gray images at the resolution of superpixels, and transfer colors between superpixels to yield image colorization. An advantage of using a superpixel based representation is that it speeds up the colorization method. More importantly, it also affords our method with an ability to maintain stronger spatial coherency in the colorization as compared to that using individual pixels. To compute the superpixels, we use a geometric-flow based algorithm proposed by [10]. The algorithm computes the compact superpixels with uniform size and shape and preserves original image edges.

For all experiments presented in this paper, the input *time step* value and the *maximum number of iterations* are taken as 0.5 and 500, respectively. These values are the default parameter values provided by the authors along with their source code[1]. Depending on the image size, the input *number of superpixels* are chosen to keep an average superpixel size of around 40 pixels.

3.2 Feature extraction

For each superpixel in input gray image and reference color image, we compute 172−dimensional (2+2+40+128) feature vector based on their intensity, standard deviation, gabor features and SURF descriptors. To compute this feature vector for a superpixel, we compute a 172−dimensional feature vector at each image pixel and then compute the mean value of all feature vectors that belong to the pixels within a superpixel to represent that superpixel. We compute this feature vector as follows:

Intensity features A two-dimensional feature vector is computed for each superpixel based on the intensity values. The first dimension is the average intensity values of all pixels within the superpixel S,

$$f_1(i) = \frac{1}{n} \sum_{(x,y)\in i} I_{(x,y)} \tag{1}$$

where $I_{(x,y)}$ is the intensity of pixel (x, y) and n is the total number of pixels within the superpixel S_i. The second dimension is computed as the average intensity values of the neighboring superpixels of S_i,

$$f_2(i) = \frac{1}{N} \sum_{j\in\eta} f_1(j), \tag{2}$$

where η represents the neighboring superpixels of S_i and N is the number of neighboring superpixels.

Standard deviation features Similar to intensity, we also compute a two-dimensional feature based on the standard deviation values in small pixels neighborhoods around each image pixel. For all experiments in this paper, we used a 5×5 square window to compute the standard deviation value at each image pixel. The standard deviation feature for the superpixel is then computed in the same way as that computed for the intensity feature.

Gabor features We apply Gabor filters [14] to an image with eight orientations varying in increments of $\pi/8$ from 0 to $7\pi/8$, and with five exponential scales $\exp(i \times \pi)$, $i = 0, 1, 2, 3, 4$ to compute a 40-dimensional feature at each pixel. The Gabor feature for the superpixel is then computed as the average Gabor feature of all pixels within the superpixel.

Speeded Up Robust features Similar to the Gabor features, we also extract a 128-dimensional extended SURF descriptors [1] at each image pixel. Extended SURF descriptors for each superpixel in then computed in the same way as the computation of the Gabor features.

3.3 Cascade feature matching scheme for initial color assignment

We exploit the features which are extracted in the previous section to find correspondences between the reference and target superpixels, and harness these correspondences to assign a set of initial colors to the target superpixels. Here, for each target superpixel, one can search among *all* reference superpixels across *all* feature types to find the reference superpixel which is most similar to the target. This however demands large processing time. For greater efficiency, we instead employ a fast cascade feature matching scheme which continually prunes the search space at each step of the cascade and concentrates the search only on reference superpixels which are sufficiently similar to the target. To ensure that the search space are pruned reliably, we exploit the more discriminative Gabor and SURF features at the initial cascade steps to sieve out a set of matching reference superpixels for a target superpixel, before relying on the intensity and standard deviation features to find its final matching reference superpixel. In our work, we found feature matches to be largely unaffected by using SURF before/after Gabor and intensity before/after standard deviation.

Let $\{r_i\}$ denote the set of reference superpixels which are extracted from the reference image I_r. Consider a target superpixel t_i. Starting at the first cascade step, we find a set of α reference superpixels from $\{r_i\}$ which are most similar to t_i based on the Gabor features. Let this set of α reference superpixels be denoted as Φ_i. We compute distance between two features of the same type by the Euclidean distance measure. Following that, at the second level, we find $\frac{\alpha}{2}$ reference superpixels from Φ_i which is most similar to the currently considered target superpixel t_i based on the SURF features. Intensity and standard deviation features are then used in the third and fourth levels respectively to find the set of reference superpixels which are most similar to t_i. Let Υ_i denote the set of reference superpixels found by the cascade filtering process to be most similar to t_i at the final step of the cascade. The reference superpixel r_a within Υ_i which correspond to t_i is then identified as one with the least matching cost across different feature types to t_i,

$$a = \arg\min_b \; F(r_b, t_i), \quad r_b \in \Upsilon_i, \tag{3}$$

and

$$\begin{aligned} F(r_b, t_i) &= w_1 C_1(r_b, t_i) + w_2 C_2(r_b, t_i) \\ &+ w_3 C_3(r_b, t_i) + w_4 C_4(r_b, t_i). \end{aligned} \tag{4}$$

We denote C_1, C_2, C_3 and C_4 as the Euclidean distance between the Gabor, SURF, intensity and standard deviations features, and w as their accompanying weights. For all experiments in this paper, we fixed w_1, w_2, w_3 and w_4 to be 0.2, 0.5, 0.2 and 0.1 respectively.

We use the CIELab color space to transfer the color from reference superpixel to target superpixel. While transferring the color, we only transfer the chromatic color values a and b of the reference superpixel as micro-scribbles to the center of its matching target superpixel. These color scribbles are spread across all the pixels with an optimization-based color interpolation algorithm [9]. The algorithm is based on the principle that neighboring pixels with similar luminance should also have similar colors. The algorithm attempts to minimize the difference $J(C)$ between the color assigned to a pixel p and the weighted average of the colors assigned to its neighbors,

$$J(C) = \sum_{p\in l} \left(C(p) - \sum_{q\in N(p)} w_{pq}\, C(q) \right)^2, \tag{5}$$

where the weights w_{pq} are determined by the similarity of

[1]http://www.cs.toronto.edu/ babalex/research.html

(a) (b) (c) (d) (e) (f)

Figure 2: Colorization results obtained at different steps of cascade feature matching. We assign chromatic values *ab* of the reference superpixels as micro-scribbles to the center of its matching target superpixels, and propagate the colors across the entire image by [9]. Target gray and reference color images are shown in (a) and (b) respectively. Colorizations obtained at the first (Gabor only), second (Gabor + SURF only), third (Gabor + SURF + intensity only) and fourth (Gabor + SURF + intensity + standard deviation) steps of cascade are shown respectively in (c) to (f). Circled regions in (f) depict visually invalid color assignments at the final step of the cascade, which are automatically identified and corrected by image space voting as detailed in Section 3.4. Best viewed on screen.

(a) (b) (c) (d)

Figure 3: Colorization results obtained by a single feature type of (a) Gabor, (b) SURF, (c) intensity and (d) standard deviation. Poor colorizations are obtained using a feature type independently, since no one feature type can model difference image regions sufficiently well.

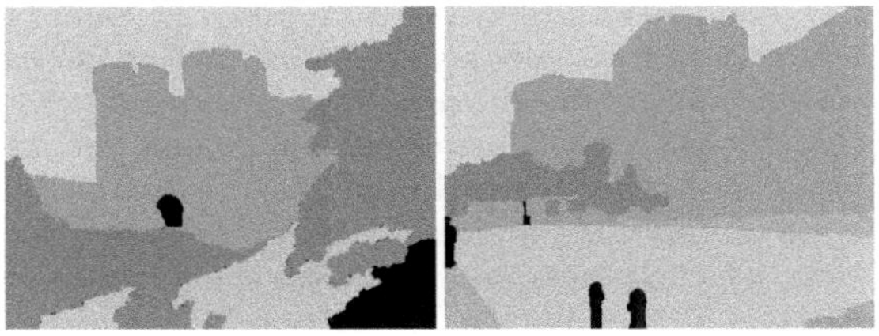

(a) (b)

Figure 4: Manually labeled regions on (a) reference and (b) target images. Regions with similar labels are depicted by similar colors.

their luminance (Y),

$$w_{pq} \propto e^{-(Y(p)-Y(q))^2/2\sigma_p^2}. \quad (6)$$

Figure 2 shows intermediate colorization results obtained at each cascade step. For comparison, we show in Figure 3 colorization results that are obtained by using each feature type independently. It can be seen that colorizations are poor with a single feature type (Figure 3). This is due to the inability of a single feature type to correctly find correspondences across different regions of an image. On the other hand, by collectively exploiting different feature types, we show the synergy of different feature types can markedly improve colorization quality (Figure 2 (f)). To illustrate the improvement following each cascade step, we manually label image regions (i.e. sky, castle etc.) in both the target gray and reference images of Figures 2 (a) and (b) as shown in Figures 4 (a) and (b) respectively. These labels are used

(a) (b)

Figure 5: Extracted superpixels and image segments are shown overlaid on target image in (a) and (b) respectively. Image segments which participate in the image space voting are highlighted within yellow border in (b).

to quantify the extent of matching errors at each cascade step, where the matching error is computed based on the target gray image superpixels that have the same labels as its matching reference image superpixels

Without using the cascade feature matching scheme, the matching errors obtained with Gabor, SURF, intensity and standard deviation features independently are 48.7%, 37.9%, 33.1% and 46.1%, respectively. The matching errors reduce significantly with the proposed cascade feature matching scheme. Specifically, the matching errors at the first, second, third and fourth cascade steps are 48.7% (Gabor), 34.8% (Gabor + SURF), 27.1% (Gabor + SURF + Intensity) and 16.5% (Gabor + SURF + Intensity + Standard deviation), respectively. This error can be further reduced using image space voting, as discussed in the following section.

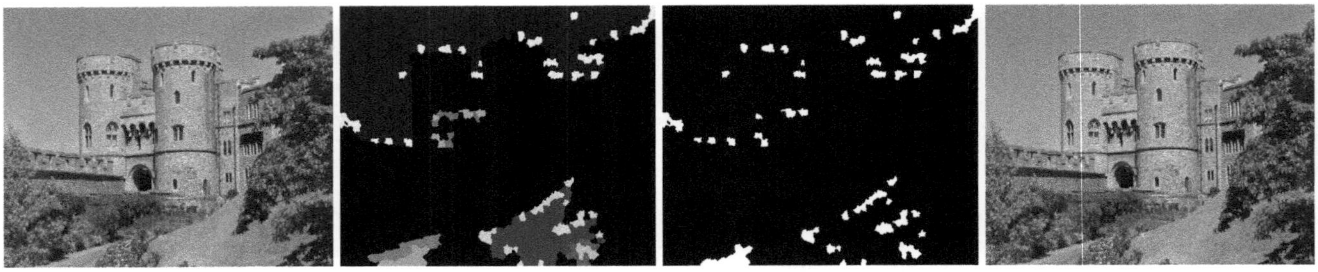

Figure 6: Comparison of colorization results following the color reassignment step. (a) Colorization from the feature matching step. (b) Confidence of correct color assignment, where brighter superpixels indicate weaker confidence for its color assignment. (c) Superpixels (indicated in white) whose colors are reassigned. (d) Final colorization following color reassignment.

3.4 Image space voting for color reassignment

The correspondences found by the above matching step assign colors to superpixels based solely on image features. While our use of multiple feature types improves color assignments significantly as compared to that using a single feature type, there could be some visually invalid assignments due to incorrect correspondences found (circled regions in Figure 2(f)). To improve the color assignments, we enforce spatial consistency in the colorization by explicitly voting for the color assignments in the image space. Here, our basic intuition is that color assignment for a superpixel is likely to be correct if its neighboring superpixels which have similar image properties are also assigned similar colors. Consequently, we can exploit neighboring superpixels to identify and to correct invalid color assignments.

Let I be a target image, and $\{s_i\}$ be the set of image segments. To extract these image segments, we use the mean-shift algorithm proposed by Comaniciu *et al.* [4]. We use their source code[2] with the default input parameters *SpatialBandwidth* and *RangeBandwidth* as 2 and 3, respectively. After computing the image segments, we keep only such image segments for voting that contain at least three superpixels in it as shown in Figure 5, where the selected segments have been highlighted using yellow border. Intuitively, each image segment s_i is a grouping of connected superpixels which have similar image properties. For each image segment s_i, we cluster its corresponding superpixels based on their initial a and b chromatic color values (which are obtained from Section 3.3) with k-means clustering. Densely populated clusters provide strong evidence for the correct color assignments of its member superpixels, while superpixels from sparsely populated clusters indicate that such superpixels have little support for its color assignments. In this regard, the clustering procedure identifies invalid color assignments by pooling evidence from its neighboring superpixels together, where the confidence of a color assignment for a target superpixel is computed as the number of member superpixels belonging to the same cluster as the target superpixel. Here, we identify sparsely populated clusters as those which have less than $\frac{1}{2k}$ the number of superpixels in segment s_i. We reassign colors to superpixels from sparsely populated clusters by the average color values of the superpixels from the most populated cluster. For all experiments in this paper, we set k to be 2.

[2]http://coewww.rutgers.edu/riul/research/code/EDISON/

We show colorization obtained directly with the cascade feature matching scheme on an example image in Figure 6(a). The confidence of its color assignments that are obtained with the feature matching step is visualized in Figure 6(b), where brighter patches indicate weaker confidence for correct assignment. It is seen that most superpixels identified to have low confidences for their correct color assignments are located at image regions where there are sharp changes in image properties (e.g. along castle-sky and field-leaves boundaries). This is not surprising since patch based features (as used here) are often affected by changes in intensity and textures, and hence features extracted from such superpixels are often less reliably matched as those located on a more homogeneous image patches. We depict superpixels whose colors are reassigned as the white patches in Figure 6(c), and the resulting colorized results in Figure 6(d). It can be seen that visually invalid colors, such as those from the grass and sky segments, have been reassigned to yield a perceptually more appealing colorization where the matching errors are further reduced from 16.5% to 9.24%. These errors are concentrated in image segments with very few superpixels, which reduces the robustness of the image voting step. This is further discussed in Section 4.2.

4. EXPERIMENTS

We present colorization results on a diverse range of images, and compare them to those obtained with existing state-of-the-art colorization methods. For all experiments, the following same fixed parameters are used for our method. We normalize the reference and target images to have a diagonal length of 500 pixels, and extract around 3000 superpixels [10] from an image using the input parameters mentioned in Section 3.1. The cascade feature matching step finds correspondences between reference and target superpixels with α equal to 600, and weights w_1, w_2, w_3 and w_4 equal to 0.2, 0.5, 0.2 and 0.1 respectively. Colors reassignment are obtained with k fixed as 2. For the comparison methods, we used the default parameters which are supplied by the authors.

Figure 7 shows colorization results of our method, with comparisons to existing state-of-the-art methods [17, 8, 2] which have similar extent of user interaction as our method. The algorithm [8] requires the segmentation mask of the reference color image as an additional input. We compute this mask by using automatic image segmentation with same input parameters as we used in Section 3.4. It is seen that our

Figure 7: Comparison with existing state-of-the-art colorization methods which have similar extent of user interaction as our method. Last column shows reference color images that are used by all algorithms for colorizing the input images. The input segmentation masks used by Irony *et al.* [8] are computed with the method discussed in Section 3.4.

(a) (b) (c) (d) (e) (f)

Figure 8: Comparison against Liu *et al.* [12] and Chia *et al.* [3] which have additional constraints. (a) and (b) show the input gray image and reference color image used for color transfer. (c) shows our colorization result. (d) shows the colorization results obtained with Liu *et al.* [12] which requires reference image to have the exact object instances as the gray image. (e) shows colorization results obtained by Chia *et al.* [3] which requires segmentation masks. For comparison, results obtained with Irony *et al.* [8], which is most similar to our method, are included in (f).

(a) (b) (c) (d)

Figure 10: Colorization using multiple exemplars by our method. (a) Input gray image. (b,c) Reference color images. (d) Colorization obtained using both reference images.

method yields perceptually more appealing colorization results than other methods. Our method is seen to work well on these complex images which exhibit variations in intensity and texture, even with the same fixed set of parameters.

Figure 8 compares our method against other colorization methods which have additional input constraints. From the figure, we can see that the algorithms [12] (which requires exact object instances to be present in both reference and gray images) and [3] (which requires segmentation masks of foreground objects) are able to transfer the exact color values at few pixel locations due to their use of spatial positions during the color transfer. The use of spatial position restricts the flexibility of these algorithms and works well only if the reference images used to transfer the color have been taken from the same viewing angle. Although, the proposed algorithm does not use such constraint, it is still able to achieve comparable colorization result and clearly outperforms Irony's method [8], which is most similar to the proposed algorithm.

In Figure 9, we demonstrate colorization with user-supplied keywords (rather than with user-supplied color images). Here, given a target gray image and a keyword, we automatically find semantically relevant reference color images for colorization. Specifically, based on the user-supplied keyword, we download 2000 images from photo sharing websites such as Flickr and Google Image Search. We evaluate the colorfulness of the downloaded images by using the method proposed by Hasler *et al.* [5], and discard those images whose

Figure 11: Examples of images displayed for quantitative evaluation during the user study. The second image is artificially colored with our colorization method, while the others are original color images.

colorfulness scores are below the recommended thresholds suggested in [5]. From among the remaining images, we used near duplicate key frame search method [19] to identify the internet image which is the most similar to the input gray image. Figure 9 shows colorization results obtained by user-supplied keywords, where the keywords are shown at the top of each reference color image. It is seen that colorization results are weak with coarse keyword (first colorized results with the 'lighthouse' keyword). This is not surprising since the retained internet image does not provide sufficient semantically similar image and color information to correctly colorize the input image. On the other hand, when more specific keywords are used (remaining results), colorization results improved markedly. Note that the first two rows of Figure 9 depict colorizations on the same grayscale image using different reference images.

Extension of our method to colorize gray image using multiple exemplars are depicted in Figure 10. Here, we extract superpixels from multiple exemplars and match the target superpixels with them in the cascade feature matching step. Figure 10(a) shows a grayscale image, while reference images used for its colorization are shown in Figures 10(b) and (c). We show the colorization result in Figure 10(d).

4.1 User study

We performed a user study to quantitatively compare our colorization method with the state-of-the-art methods. Here, we use the exact framework and the same set of test images as those used by Chia *et al.* [3] for the evaluation. We engage 30 volunteers and present to them a set of images. Some of these images are artificially colorized, while the rest are real color images. We show each subject a set of four different images at a time (such as in Figure 11) for a total of 30

Figure 9: Colorization with user-supplied keywords. The first column shows the input gray images. The second and third columns show the colorization results obtained by our method and Charpiat *et al.* [2], respectively. Last column shows the reference color images, along with the keywords (shown at the top of each image) which used to download the reference images from the internet.

sets, and ask the subjects to identify all artificially colorized images in each set. Each subject was given five seconds to view an image set. Prior to the experiment, the subjects were told that at most two images from each set were artificially colorized. Using our method, the subjects classified colorized images obtained by our method as real 64.9% of the time. This compares favorably to 48.90% obtained by [17], 53.2% by [8], and 32.30% by [2]. While it attains slightly weaker colorization results as compared to Chia *et al.* [3] (which obtains 66.59%), we note that [3] directly exploits spatial information in their colorization and hence require users to manually segment major foreground objects from the input image. In contrast, our method only require users to present a semantically similar color image as input, which is substantially more intuitive.

Figure 12: Limitations of automatic image colorization. (a)-(c) show the input gray image, automatic segmented input image and the colorization result, respectively. Circled regions in (c) depict some artifacts generated due to small image segments.

4.2 Limitations

There are a few limitations in our method. First, our use of superpixel representation, while supporting more spatial coherency in colorization, can be inaccurate at object boundaries or thin image structures. This could potentially lead to bleeding artifacts at object boundaries. Second, image segments generated in Section 3.4 are often very small in dense textured regions. This reduces the robustness of the image voting step since these segments have fewer superpixels within them than larger segments. Consequently, voting for the colors within these segments by its superpixels become less reliable. This is shown in Figure 12, where Figures 12(a) and (b) show an input gray image and segmented mask used for image space voting respectively, and colorization artifacts due to small segments are shown within circled regions in Figure 12(c). Finally, our method relies on the availability of color exemplar which is semantically similar to the gray image. Consequently, our method may fail when suitable color exemplars are unavailable.

5. CONCLUSIONS

In this paper, we present a new method for colorizing gray images using semantically similar reference images. Our method works at the resolution of superpixels, in which we extract a variety of features from the reference and target images. Correspondences between superpixels are found by a fast cascade feature matching scheme which examines different feature types at each cascade step. Leveraging on spatial information, we identify and correct invalid correspondences through an automatic image space voting paradigm. This, coupled with our superpixel representation, empowers our method to attain a strong extent of spatial consistency in the colorization. Experimental results on a wide array of images demonstrate our method achieves perceptually appealing colorizations, even with a fixed set of parameter settings. Additionally, comparisons against existing state-of-the-art methods also demonstrate our method to be more effective at colorization.

As future work, we would like to employ more features for finding correspondences between reference and target images. In particular, our current framework employs patch based features only, and we will explore how these features can be combined with contour fragment features. Additionally, we would also want to explore more advanced techniques to fuse various feature types to improve their overall discriminative potential. Finally, we have shown the potential of our method to colorize an image using internet images downloaded with user-supplied keywords. In the future, we also plan to study how we can identify semantically more relevant internet images, perhaps by incorporating object recognition abilities into the image filtering framework.

6. REFERENCES

[1] H. Bay, A. Ess, T. Tuytelaars, and L. V. Gool. Surf: Speeded up robust features. *Computer Vision and Image Understanding (CVIU)*, 110(3):346–359, 2008.

[2] G. Charpiat, M. Hofmann, and B. Scholkopf. Automatic image colorization via multimodal predictions. In *Proc. European Conference on Computer Vision*, 2008.

[3] A. Y.-S. Chia, S. Zhuo, R. K. Gupta, Y.-W. Tai, S.-Y. Cho, P. Tan, and S. Lin. Semantic colorization with internet images. *ACM Transactions on Graphics*, 30(6), 2011.

[4] D. Comaniciu and P. Meer. Mean shift: A robust approach toward feature space analysis. *IEEE Transactions on Pattern Analysis and Machine Intelligence*, 24(05):603–619, 2002.

[5] D. Hasler and S. Séžűstrunk. Measuring colourfulness in natural images. *SPIE Electronic Imaging*, 5007:87–95, 2003.

[6] A. Hertzmann, C. E. Jacobs, N. Oliver, B. Curless, and D. H. Salesin. Image analogies. *Proc. SIGGRAPH*, pages 327–340, 2001.

[7] Y.-C. Huang, Y.-S. Tung, J.-C. Chen, S.-W. Wang, and J.-L. Wu. An adaptive edge detection based colorization algorithm and its applications. In *ACM Multimedia*, pages 351–354, 2005.

[8] R. Irony, D. Cohen-Or, and D. Lischinski. Colorization by example. In *Proc. Eurographics Symposium on Rendering*, 2005.

[9] A. Levin, D. Lischinski, and Y. Weiss. Colorization using optimization. *ACM Transactions on Graphics*, 23(3):689–694, 2004.

[10] A. Levinshtein, A. Stere, K. N. Kutulakos, D. J. Fleet, S. J. Dickinson, and K. Siddiqi. Turbopixels: Fast superpixels using geometric flows. *IEEE Transactions on Pattern Analysis and Machine Intelligence*, 31(12):2290–2297, 2009.

[11] C. Liu, J. Yuen, and A. Torralba. Sift flow: dense correspondence across different scenes and its applications. *IEEE Transactions on Pattern Analysis and Machine Intelligence*, 33(5), 2011.

[12] X. Liu, L. Wan, Y. Qu, T.-T. Wong, S. Lin, C.-S. Leung, and P.-A. Heng. Intrinsic colorization. *ACM Transactions on Graphics*, 27(5):152:1–152:9, 2008.

[13] Q. Luan, F. Wen, D. Cohen-Or, L. Liang, Y.-Q. Xu, and H.-Y. Shum. Natural image colorization. In *Proc. Eurographics Symposium on Rendering*, 2007.

[14] B. S. Manjunath and W. Y. Ma. Texture features for browsing and retrieval of image data. *IEEE Transactions on Pattern Analysis and Machine Intelligence*, 18(8):837–842, 1996.

[15] Y. Qu, T.-T. Wong, and P.-A. Heng. Manga colorization. *ACM Transactions on Graphics*, 25(3):1214–1220, 2006.

[16] J. Shotton, A. Blake, and R. Cipolla. Multiscale categorical object recognition using contour fragments. *IEEE Transactions on Pattern Analysis and Machine Intelligence*, 30(7):1270–1281, 2008.

[17] T. Welsh, M. Ashikhmin, and K. Mueller. Transferring color to greyscale images. *ACM Transactions on Graphics*, 21(3):277–280, 2002.

[18] L. Yatziv and G. Sapiro. Fast image and video colorization using chrominance blending. *IEEE Transactions on Image Processing*, 15(5):1120–1129, 2006.

[19] J. Zhu, S. C. H. Hoi, M. R. Lyu, and S. Yan. Near-duplicate keyframe retrieval by semi-supervised learning and nonrigid image matching. *ACM Transactions on Multimedia Computing, Communications, and Applications*, 7(1), 2011.

Semi-Automated Magazine Layout Using Content-based Image Features

Mikko Kuhna
Aalto University
Dept. of Media Technology
Otaniementie 17
Espoo, Finland
mikko.kuhna@aalto.fi

Ida-Maria Kivelä
Aalto University
Dept. of Media Technology
Otaniementie 17
Espoo, Finland
ida-maria.kivela@aalto.fi

Pirkko Oittinen
Aalto University
Dept. of Media Technology
Otaniementie 17
Espoo, Finland
pirkko.oittinen@aalto.fi

ABSTRACT

We present a system for automating magazine layout process and data on its performance in a user evaluation test. The purpose of the study is to find the feasibility of the key system variables on the end-user. This semi-automatic system is based on content-based image feature algorithms to automate the layout process. The image related automation includes image cropping, overlaying text on top of images, image color palette creation, and image alignment. The algorithms rely on principles of photography and are used here together in the context of graphic design. For example the rule-of-space and leading line concepts can be extended to layout contexts for improved alignment of text and images. The computation is based on automatic analysis, such as face detection, color saliency, and textureness. We used the automation to create a functional prototype, an iPad magazine, using an open HTML5 eBook framework, which relies on CSS3 media queries for the layout adaptation. User experiments (40 participants) were conducted where the system was compared against two commercial iPad magazine systems in terms of overall usability with emphasis on visual aspects. Questionnaires and free commenting was used in a task-based usage scenario. The experiments were video recorded and the user comments were transcribed and coded into attributes. Usability results mixed with qualitative observation are reported. Results show that usability, readability and visuality are important to the users. Our system was considered more usable than the other two systems with some of the defining aspects being simplicity in terms of usability, subjective readability and visual clarity.

Categories and Subject Descriptors

H.5.1 [**Multimedia Information Systems**]: Evaluation / methodology; I.4.7 [**Feature Measurement**]: Features—*color, face detection, perspective lines, saliency*; I.7.2 [**Document Preparation**]: Desktop publishing, Photocomposition / typesetting; I.7.4 [**Electronic Publishing**]

General Terms

Algorithms Design, Experimentation

Keywords

Page layout, image feature, responsive design, layout adaptation, user evaluation

1. INTRODUCTION

Magazine publishing is at a turning point. Print publishing is still the norm, but publishers have started to adopt digital tablets as a new platform. Other publication types have been supporting digital platforms for a long time. The relatively slow publication intervals of magazines defy the business logic of the web. The transformation of magazines has been slowed down, among other things, by high demands for usability, readability and visual appeal. So they cannot really be compared to Web publishing, which is fast-paced and typically free of charge. There are paid digital publication types in the form of eBooks, and personal readers like Amazon Kindle have become popular. However, the problem is that those platforms do not support the visual appearance of magazines. A magazine loses its selling point if it loses its high-quality visual appeal.

Tablets provide a digital platform that makes the high-quality visual appearance of a magazine possible. The form factor of most tablets is also very similar to current print formats. Computer operating systems enforce multitasking with multiple windows and menu bars etc., whereas a tablet is more of a single-task device. Tablet operating systems force the active application to use almost 100 % of the display. Touch-based interaction also resembles the natural browsing experience of a magazine.

Current tablet magazines (typically made with e.g. Woodwing Tablet Publishing or Adobe Digital Publishing) are for the most part PDF-style print replicas, or manually laid-out print variants with some added interactive elements. Tablet magazines are rendered as layered images in a desktop publishing software. As a result, text is rendered as bitmap images and is not selectable by the user. Another shortcoming is that a magazine can take up to hundreds of megabytes per issue while supporting often only one orientation mode.

In this work the layout automation is based on content-based image features, and the content is displayed using HTML5, CSS3 and JavaScript, utilizing a design concept called responsive design. Responsive design [23] essentially means that a web site is crafted to use W3C CSS3 media queries[1] in order to adapt the layout to the viewing environment. A similar approach is used in adaptive grid-based layout overall, where responsive design only states that CSS3 media queries are the technique used.

System development and evaluation were accomplished as an industrial collaboration with a magazine publisher (Sanoma Magazines Finland[2]) and a technology supplier. The long-term focus is to automate tasks in the magazine publishing workflow to make cross-media publishing efficient. In this study we only test different orientation modes, but adaptation to completely different device form factors is currently studied. Our system is designed to be implemented in editorial systems or any authoring tools. The focus here is magazine publishing, but the system design can be modified for any types of publications where images are used as layout elements.

In this first stage of our system development we evaluate the performance of the content-based image feature algorithms and our first functional magazine prototype. Currently we are developing a magazine content model for handling content and related metadata. In the last stage we will develop the authoring tool and test it in an editorial office with professionals (project page[3]).

2. BACKGROUND

2.1 Adaptive layout

A grid-based layout is used in the print layout of newspapers and magazines. Many solutions have been presented to allow adaptation of layout to different screen sizes, such as the adaptive grid-based document layout [15] and its extension to dynamically aggregated documents [27]. These types of systems generally use grid-based layout templates and some flexibility in the templates is solved using layout constraints. The constraints are used for example so that the title element is constrained to begin at the top of the page and the font type is increased as long as the title element fits the page width. Images are treated as one element type in the layout, albeit with dimensions and perhaps some placement constraints.

Another approach is to process images to fit the layout constraints. Methods such as image retargeting [28] and seam carving [2] can be used for scaling images without losing the important objects in the image. Methods have also been presented for retargeting other visual media types such as web pages [17] and other documents [5]. For image-heavy publications, such as photo books, there are also automation solutions that utilize image features [26].

Most systems have focused on paginating the content and also separating the content and the presentation. XML or HTML is generally used to specify the content and CSS is used for presentation. HTML is often seen as too limiting for paginated content [27] although with the new features in CSS3, pagination has become more accessible [25].

Our approach uses a responsive web design framework for the layout templates for different screen sizes. The framework is also based on a grid-based approach. The images are automatically cropped to fit the layout constraints based on

[1]http://www.w3.org/TR/css3-mediaqueries/
[2]http://www.sanomamagazines.fi
[3]http://mikkokuhna.com/researcher/magazinelayout/

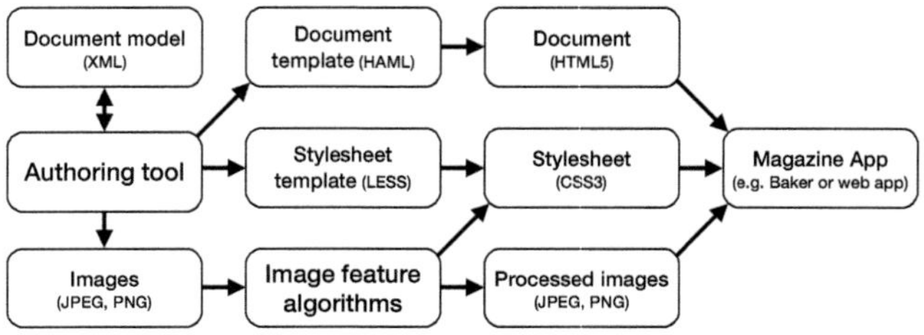

Figure 1: System overview diagram.

image importance. Unlike previous systems, our system is designed especially for magazine style image heavy content and does not rely on pagination.

2.2 Image features

Photographic principles [13] such as the rule-of-thirds have been used in many studies. Other photographic concepts include for instance the use of shallow depth-of-field or color contrast to separate the main subject from the background. These principles are used for example in photo quality assessment [16, 29], computational aesthetics [10], photo and video quality assessment [22], photography systems [4, 9], photobook systems [26] and web image search [12].

In this study, photographic principles are utilized in the graphic design context by employing content-based image features. The purpose is to automate image related layout tasks. For example the rule-of-space (head room or lead room) concept is used to apply a sense of movement in the photograph. A photo is framed so that there is more empty space towards the side of the photo where the main object is facing. This is often also true in layout. An image is placed so that there is more empty room towards the side of the page where the main object in the image is facing. A concept called leading lines is used similarly for photos with a clear perspective.

3. LAYOUT SYSTEM

3.1 Overview

A semi-automatic system for creating layouts for magazine articles (incl. text, images, captions, headings etc.) was created. Its novelty lies in utilizing content-based image feature algorithms for the layout of high-quality visual content (here, magazine articles) with the aid of responsive web design techniques to adapt content to different devices and orientations. The layout templates are based on Laker[4] templates that use open web frameworks (e.g. LESS[5] and jQuery[6]). Our focus is on tablets, but adaptation to smaller mobile and desktop browsing conditions may also be done.

An overview of the system is illustrated in Figure 1. The content is inserted into the system with an authoring tool. Document template (i.e. article type) and stylesheet templates are selected by the user. Images added into the authoring tool are processed using the developed image feature algorithms. In the end the document, the stylesheet and the processed images are composed into a web page and presented in the magazine app. The image feature algorithms

[4]http://lakercompendium.com
[5]http://lessframework.com
[6]http://jquery.com

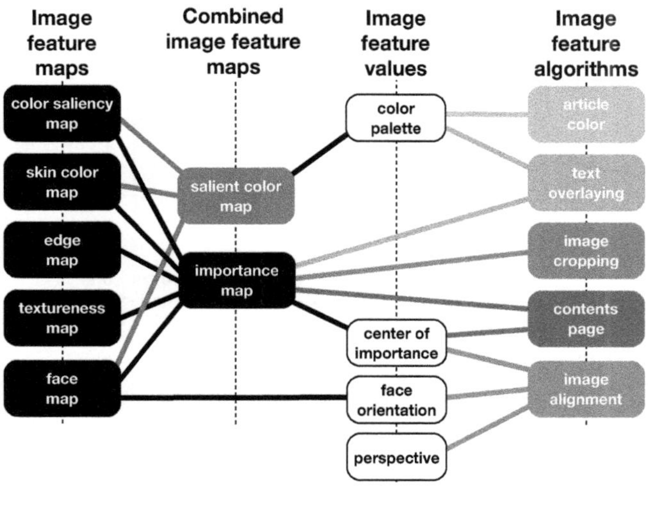

Figure 2: Image feature algorithms and corresponding computational approaches.

form the automatic part of the system. For non-image layout operations the system relies on the defined templates.

3.2 Image feature algorithms

Content-based image feature algorithms are used to automate the layout creation. The focus is on automating image-related tasks in the creation of an adaptive layout. Figure 2 illustrates the image feature algorithms and the computational features used. The features are results of image analysis and are grouped here in maps, combined maps and values. The algorithms were implemented in the MATLAB environment. The automated image process for one example image is illustrated in Figure 3 (next page).

Table 1 gives a summary of the feature maps and their values. A more detailed discussion of the algorithms is beyond the scope of this paper. This is because many of the computations are content-specific and have so far only be tested for images of a few magazines. These principles should be generalizable for most kinds of editorial publications and our future work includes tuning the algorithms for different publications and adding more automated tasks for specific image types (e.g. food photography and interior design).

3.2.1 Article color

Colors are important for both visual experience and brand management [8]. In magazines it is typical to select for each article an identifying color, which is then used in different elements, such as titles and pull quotes. Our approach creates an image-based color palette considering all the images in the article. Based on this palette a single article color is chosen.

The computation of an article color is illustrated in Figure 4. Color palettes of are created for all images belonging to an article. The best article color candidate is selected for each image based on its recurrence in other color palettes and color difference to the representative colors of the publication. One future approach could be to include some kind of text-based semantic content analysis [14].

3.2.2 Text overlaying

Interaction of text and other elements is a common chal-

Table 1: Feature maps and values.

Feature maps	
Color saliency	Color difference relative to the average color of an image. [1]
Skin color	Color difference to a selected skin color value.
Edge	Average of the horizontal and vertical Sobel filtered R, G and B color channels.
Textureness	Cross-bilateral filtered L* channel. Basically it is the remainder of an edge-preserving filter. [3]
Face	OpenCV face detection algorithm. [30]
Combined feature maps	
Salient color	Weighted sum of the color saliency, skin color and face maps.
Importance	Weighted sum of the color saliency, skin color, edge, textureness and face maps.
Feature values	
Color palette	Derived from the salient color map by first thresholding the map into salient and non-salient regions. The a*- and b*-channels of the salient and non-salient regions are then clustered separately with k-means clustering. The seven-color palette is the average RGB color of the first four clusters of the salient region and the first three clusters of the non-salient region.
Center of importance	Center mass coordinate of the importance map.
Face orientation	Derived from non-frontal face detection and whether there are more faces detected with left- or right-oriented pose.
Perspective	Based on Hough transform, which looks for continuing lines. The horizontal coordinate of the perspective point is analyzed. [11]

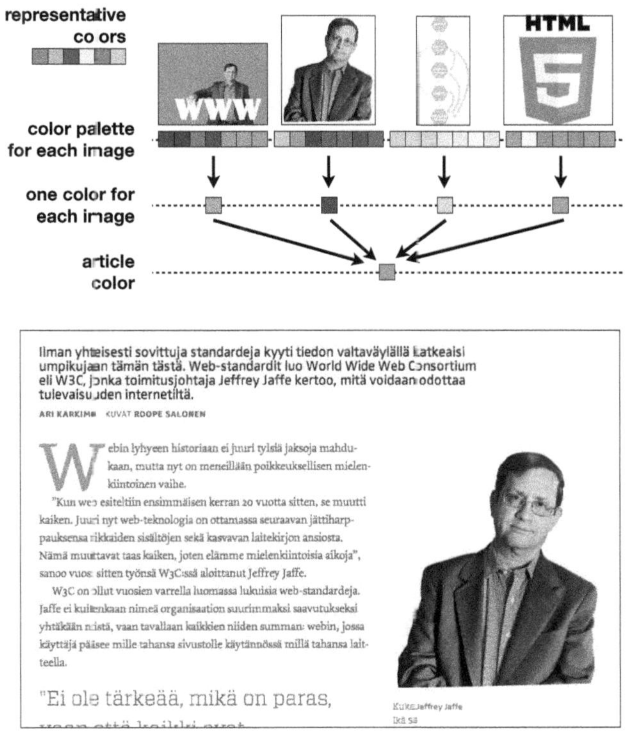

Figure 4: Article color is selected based on the color palettes of all images in an article. The bottom image is an example of how the article color is used in typographic layout elements.

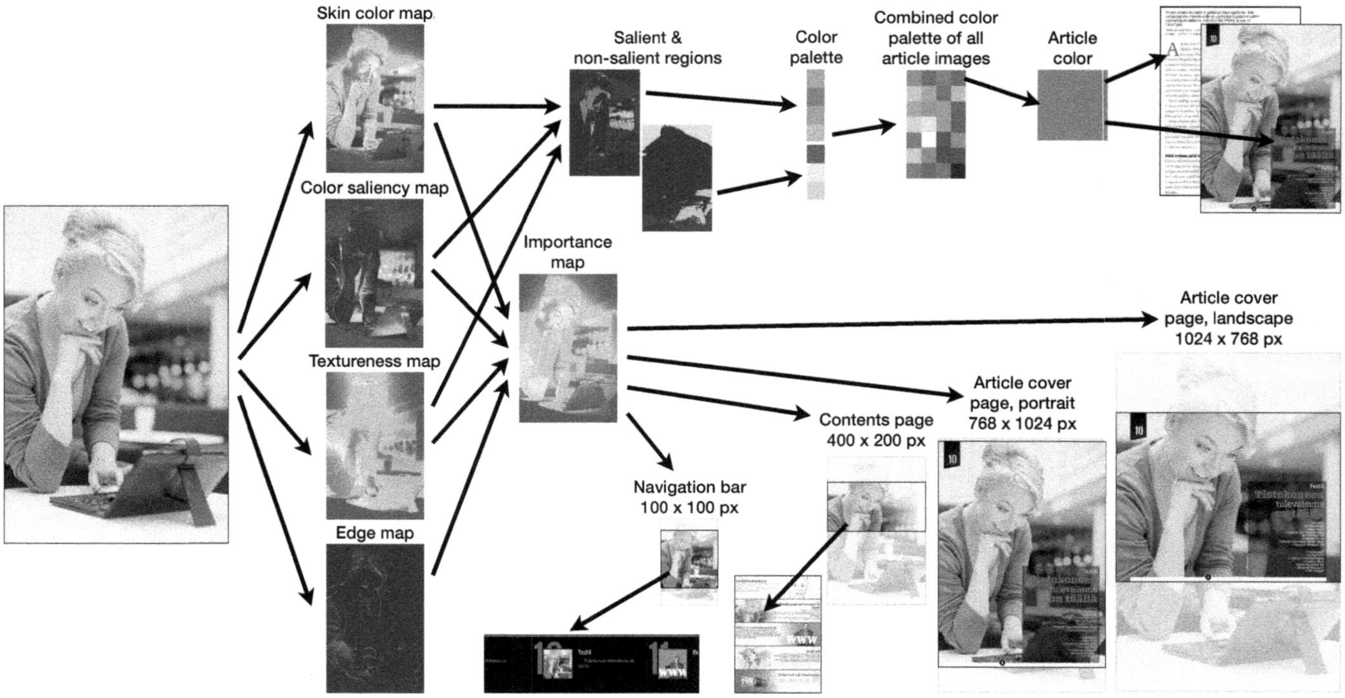

Figure 3: An example of the automated process for the main image of an image heavy article. In this example the face detection algorithm did not find a face and therefore the skin color map has a greater weight. Skin color, color saliency, textureness and edge maps are combined to form an importance map, which is used to create the cover image for both orientation modes and thumbnails for the contents page and navigation bar. Skin color, color saliency and textureness maps are also used for determining salient regions, which are used in the color palette processing.

lenge in layout creation [18]. Articles need to combine text and graphics in ways that connect them but do not harm the readability. The importance of images needs to be analyzed and text placed over the least important areas of the selected background image. Our approach is to use text overlaying in the generation of the cover page of image heavy articles (Figure 3).

The positioning of the title block is automatically computed from the importance map as the area with the lowest importance. The article color, black or white, is used as the title color. The color with the highest color difference to the area in the underlying image is selected. If there is too much texture variation in the area in the underlying image, a white, black, translucent white or translucent black box is added to the background to increase color contrast.

3.2.3 *Image cropping*

It is challenging to create adaptive layouts without cropping images. Full-page images are common in magazines, producing a need to crop portrait images for a landscape layout and vice versa. Our approach uses the importance map to crop the image to make a thumbnail image for the contents page and navigation bar as well as full-page images for both orientation modes for the article cover page (Figure 3).

The image cropping is based on maximizing the corresponding area of the importance map. A summed area table is used in the computation. The importance map is a weighted sum of color saliency, skin color, edge, textureness and face maps. The face map is weighted the highest, because faces, if present, generally are the main objects in images. If faces are not found, the skin color map is given greater weight in case there are undetected human objects in the image. The color saliency map is designed to find non-human main objects whereas edge and texture maps are designed to find the main objects in shallow depth-of-field images.

3.2.4 *Contents page*

Some magazine layout tasks can be completely automated with proper content metadata. Creating the magazine contents page is an example of such a task. Our approach is to create a landscape orientation preview image of the main image of each article using the same image cropping method (Figure 3). The article main image is determined in the authoring tool. The contents page then consists of an article list with a preview image and some text elements of each article. The image and text alignment is also automatically done based on the center of importance of the cropped image.

3.2.5 *Image alignment*

Optimal image placement as a whole is a very high-level concept and difficult to compute. Nevertheless, some simple rules can be applied to select, for example, whether an image should be aligned left or right in relation to the text. Our approach is based on the rule-of-space and leading line concepts. Rule-of-space is used to apply a sense of movement, for example by adding whitespace towards where a person is looking or moving. The concept of leading line has the

Figure 5: An example analysis of an image with continuing perspective lines. Red and green lines indicating most relevant detected lines and green lines indicating lines that connect in a same perspective point. The perspective point in this image is located right from the center and the image should therefore be left-aligned.

same goal, but here perspective lines are used to guide the focus of the viewer.

Image alignment computation is based on the center of importance, face orientation and perspective feature values. Face orientation, given the greatest weight, tells whether more faces are facing left or right. The center of importance works similarly for non-face objects. The perspective feature value is used for the leading line concept. A value for left alignment is given if the face orientation is faced to the right, if the center of importance is located left from the center and if the perspective point is located right from the center. The reverse is true for right alignment. An example of the leading line and the perspective analysis is shown in Figure 5.

4. TEST SETUP

A test magazine was created with the designed layout system using a published print magazine (Tietokone[7]) as the material for full experimentation of the performance of the system. It was selected because at that time it was one of the few Finnish language magazines with a commercial tablet version available for comparison. Images in the magazine are typical magazine feature images and technical product images.

As the commercial solution was available for the Apple iPad platform, it was chosen as the evaluation platform. The magazine was created with the Baker eBook Framework[8] for iPad, but the content is extendable to any platform with HTML5 support.

The magazine is fully operational in modern browsers, but the eBook framework enables some interactive and performance features. A native application can be created using the platform. The magazines pages can be defined using the HPub specification[9].

The interactive features in the framework were related to

[7]http://www.tietokone.fi/lehti

[8]http://bakerframework.com/

[9]http://github.com/Simbul/baker/wiki/hpub-specification

Table 2: Magazine solution comparison.

<table>
<tr><th></th><th>Manual</th><th>Automatic</th><th>Responsive</th></tr>
<tr><td colspan="4">Layout</td></tr>
<tr><td>Layout style</td><td>Magazine style</td><td>Newspaper style</td><td>Magazine style</td></tr>
<tr><td>Pagination</td><td>Paged</td><td>Paged</td><td>Continuous</td></tr>
<tr><td>Orientation modes</td><td>Vertical</td><td>Both</td><td>Both</td></tr>
<tr><td>Columns</td><td>Mainly two-column</td><td>Mainly two-column</td><td>Mainly one-column</td></tr>
<tr><td>Fullscreen images with overlaid text</td><td>Yes</td><td>No</td><td>Yes</td></tr>
<tr><td>Use of colors</td><td>Article color</td><td>Section color</td><td>Article color</td></tr>
<tr><td colspan="4">Authoring</td></tr>
<tr><td>Image processing</td><td rowspan="5">Manual</td><td>Downscaling</td><td rowspan="5">Automatic, content-dependent</td></tr>
<tr><td>Article color</td><td>Automatic</td></tr>
<tr><td>Overlaid text placement</td><td>Unsupported</td></tr>
<tr><td>Image placement</td><td>Automatic</td></tr>
<tr><td>Contents page</td><td>Automatic, priority-based</td></tr>
<tr><td colspan="4">Navigation</td></tr>
<tr><td>Between articles</td><td>Horizontal swipe</td><td>Horizontal swipe</td><td>Horizontal swipe</td></tr>
<tr><td>Within articles</td><td>Vertical swipe</td><td>Vertical swipe</td><td>Vertical swipe</td></tr>
<tr><td>Navigation bar</td><td>Yes</td><td>Yes, section-based</td><td>Yes</td></tr>
<tr><td>Navigation levels</td><td>Articles</td><td>Sections and articles</td><td>Articles</td></tr>
<tr><td colspan="4">Contents page</td></tr>
<tr><td>Style</td><td>List</td><td>Collection</td><td>List</td></tr>
<tr><td>Information</td><td>Only title</td><td>Text and images</td><td>Text and images</td></tr>
<tr><td colspan="4">Interactive features</td></tr>
<tr><td>Customizable font size</td><td>No</td><td>Yes</td><td rowspan="4">No, not implemented in this version</td></tr>
<tr><td>Image gallery</td><td>Yes</td><td>Yes</td></tr>
<tr><td>Interactive images</td><td>Yes</td><td>No</td></tr>
<tr><td>Scrolling frames</td><td>Yes</td><td>No</td></tr>
</table>

navigation. Horizontal swipe was used to navigate between the articles. An interactive navigation bar was included and accessible to the user by double tapping the display. Otherwise the magazine was intentionally left without other interactive features to get more feedback related to the visual aspects.

Our responsive magazine prototype was compared against two other commercially available magazine solutions. Table 2 summarizes the main differences between the systems. The first solution is a retail version of the magazine sold in the Apple App Store. It was made by a graphic design company contracted by the publisher and manually laid-out in a desktop publishing software with Woodwing publishing tools[10]. The automatic system is a commercial

[10]http://woodwing.com/

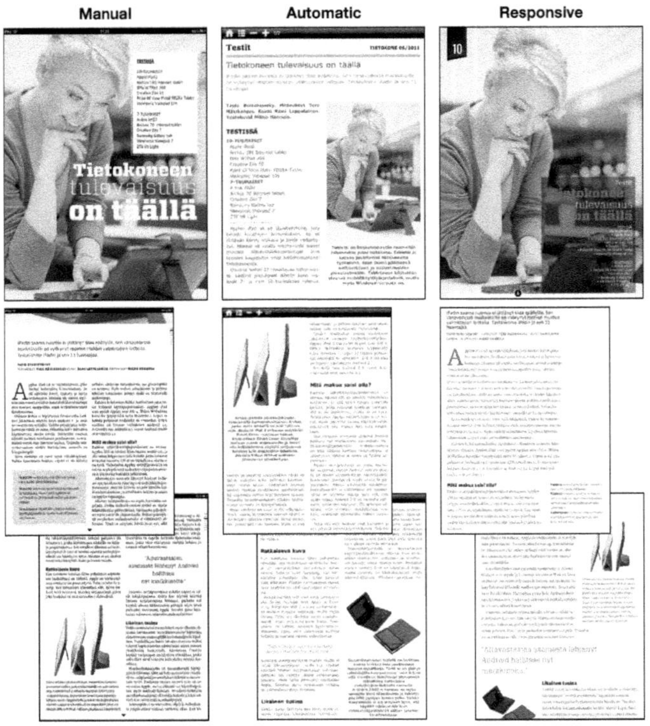

Figure 6: Layout comparison of the magazine solutions with an image heavy article example.

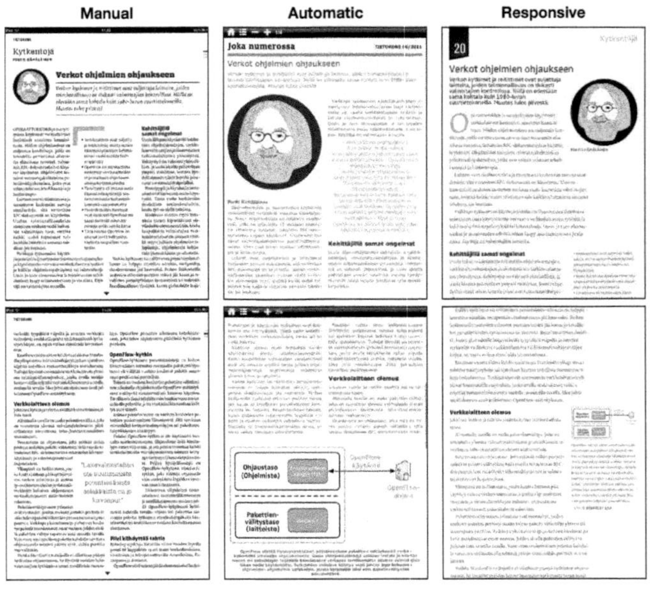

Figure 7: Layout comparison of the magazine solutions with a text heavy article example.

cross-platform application (Anygraaf AnyReader[11]) that adapts the layout to any screen resolution. It was originally made for newspaper content, but modified for this experiment to have better support for magazine content. It was designed to be connected to an editorial system and the adaptation was carried out only based on the display pixel dimensions.

The developed prototype magazine differs from typical currently existing digital magazines in many ways. In our prototype the pages are not paginated, which naturally affects the layout process. However, usually the article cover is the most demanding in terms of layout and it can be designed as a page with responsive design. Non-paginated and mostly one-column articles have a simple structure, known to produce a better reading experience in digital environments [6, 21]. We included different types of magazine layout solutions in our test so that the qualitative evaluations would reflect broad design choices and could be analyzed to produce guidelines for developing digital magazines.

4.1 Layout style

The layout style differs in many ways between the solutions (Figure 6 and Figure 7). The automatic solution uses a grid-based layout that resembles a newspaper layout, whereas the manual and responsive solutions aim to mimic the print magazine layout. The manual and automatic solutions paginate the articles, whereas the responsive solution relies on a web-style continuous layout. The manual solution supports only the portrait orientation mode, whereas the other solutions adapt the layout to both modes.

The responsive solution uses mainly a one-column layout for article text, whereas the manual and automatic solutions use mainly two columns. The automatic solution lacks the magazine style fullscreen images with overlapping text. All the solutions have colors in the layout. The manual solution uses one or multiple colors for each article, the responsive solution uses one color for each article, whereas the automatic solution uses one color for each section.

4.2 Authoring

The layout for the manual system is made with a desktop publishing software and the layout is non-adaptable. Therefore all the authoring tasks are manual. The automatic solution is developed together with an editorial system and it automatically creates the layout for different display dimensions. Images are downscaled to fit the layout constraints and a default color is assigned for different sections. The system does not support overlaid text, and image placement is automatic, whereas the contents page is automatically created using the article priority metadata.

4.3 Navigation

The navigation approaches are very similar between the solutions. Navigation between articles is carried out with horizontal swiping and navigation within articles is carried out with vertical swiping. However, there are differences in navigation between the solutions especially due to the differences in pagination and navigation levels.

All the solutions have somewhat different navigation bars. The navigation bar is opened in the manual solution by tapping the bottom part of the display and in the responsive solution by double tapping any part of the display. In the automatic solution the navigation bar is shown each time the user navigates to a new page as well as by tapping the display.

The automatic solution differs the most from the other solutions in terms of navigation as it has two navigation levels. The first level consists of section pages, where articles

[11]http://www.anygraaf.fi/

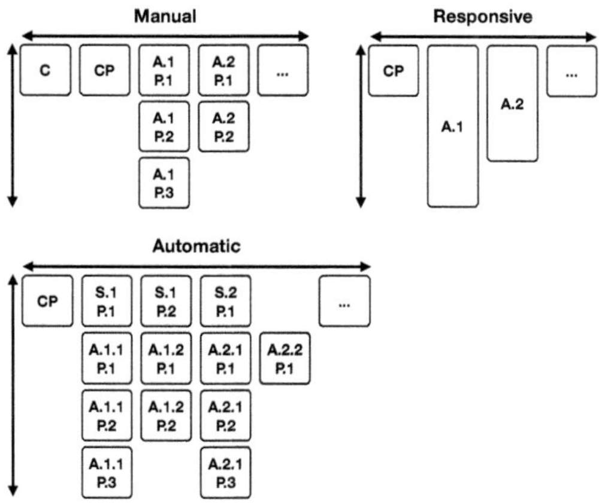

Figure 8: Navigation in the magazine solutions. C = Cover, CP = Contents page, A = Article, P = Page and S = Section.

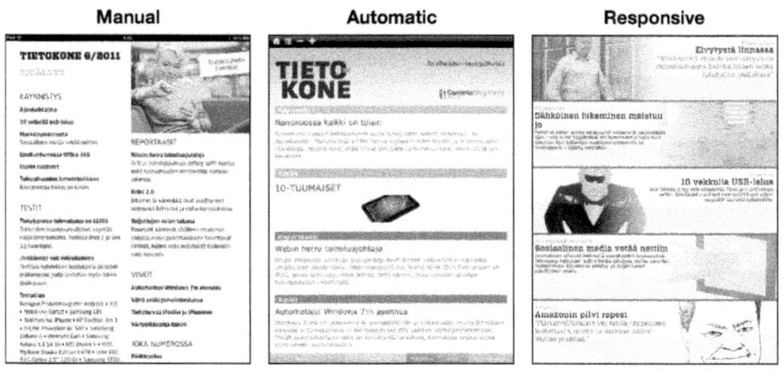

Figure 9: Layout comparison of the magazine solutions with a contents page example.

are laid out in a newspaper style layout. The section pages show only a sample of the article (a title, some text and sometimes an image). A greater area is given to higher priority articles. By tapping an article, the user navigates to the corresponding article in the article level and by swiping upwards in the article level, the user navigates back to the corresponding section page. Figure 8 illustrates the differences in navigation between the solutions.

4.4 Contents page

All the solutions have a contents page as the first page of the magazine (the retail solution has a cover page before the contents page). The contents pages are shown in Figure 9. The manual solution only lists the article titles in sections, whereas the responsive solution lists the articles in reading order by showing an image and text of the article. The automatic solution has a section-based contents page with images and text, but it only shows a few highest priority articles and uses the section pages as more detailed contents pages.

4.5 Interactive features

The manual and automatic solutions have some interactive features that were not implemented in this version of the responsive solution. The automatic solution includes a feature to alter the text size. Both the manual and automatic solutions have an image gallery. In addition to the gallery, the manual solution has different types of interactive images, which are activated by tapping the image (to enlarge, show a caption or detailed information, etc.). The manual system also has scrolling frames inside the paginated pages. Those are used both for text blocks and images.

5. USER EVALUATION

We performed evaluations of the magazine solutions that included usability, covering also readability, and visual aspects. Our 40 participants were undergraduate and postgraduate students in various engineering disciplines ranging from computer science to electrical engineering and chemical engineering. Their mean age was 25 years ($SD = 2$). The majority (64%) had used a tablet computer but mainly for other purposes than reading magazines (28%). Only a few (10%) owned a tablet.

Each participant interacted with articles from a single magazine issue using two of the three magazine solutions (manual or automatic solution and our responsive solution) in a task-based usage scenario. Using one solution after the other (the order was counterbalanced across four participant groups), the participants were instructed to first browse at least 10 of the 22 articles and then read one article more thoroughly.

After the interaction period of roughly 10 minutes of navigating and reading the magazine on the first solution, the participants answered the system usability scale (SUS) questionnaire [7]. It was filled only for the first solution interacted with, to avoid priming effects. The SUS questionnaire was scored according to the two-factor structure [20].

Next, the participant moved onto the second solution and browsed at least 10 articles for 5 minutes in total. The experimenter then prompted the participant to pick four views where they had something to comment about the layout in comparison to the previous solution. These views were recorded as screenshots and will enable the use of computational layout metrics in the future.

A layout-related questionnaire with a 7-point Likert scale was filled for each screenshot. The questions were based on the tools developed for assessing visual aesthetics [24, 19], but extended here with questions covering the use of images, font type and readability. There were two types of questions in the layout questionnaire. The first type of questions included *"fully agree"* (positive) or *"fully disagree"* (negative) types of statements and the second type of questions included *"too little"* (negative), *"neutral"* (zero) or *"too much"* (positive) types of statements. The questionnaire statements are shown together with the average scores in Table 3 (next page).

The experiments were video recorded and participants were also asked to comment on each screenshot and the solution overall. The user comments were transcribed and coded to attributes using the ATLAS.ti software[12]. The attributes were selected based on the verbal user comments, where the context implied if the attribute was considered positive or negative.

The comments were coded so that if many participants used the same wording (e.g. clarity) or described a given detail of the solution in different words (e.g. navigation bar), it was used as an attribute. In all 33 different attributes were used in 837 instances, 423 of those being negative and

[12]http://www.atlasti.com

Table 3: Average layout questionnaire scores. $CI_{95\%}$ in parenthesis.

Statements	Manual	Automatic	Responsive	Manual vs. Automatic	Manual vs. Responsive	Automatic vs. Responsive
"fully disagree" (−3) or *"fully agree"* (+3)						
I like the current section	-0.10 (0.57)	0.45 (0.44)	0.43 (0.40)			
Appearance is interesting	0.58 (0.55)	0.68 (0.53)	0.98 (0.39)			
Appearance is clear	0.00 (0.65)	0.73 (0.62)	1.30 (0.40)		$p < .01$	
Colors are pleasing	0.53 (0.53)	0.43 (0.47)	1.30 (0.36)		$p < .05$	$p < .01$
Readability is good	0.20 (0.54)	0.30 (0.54)	1.05 (0.41)		$p < .05$	$p < .05$
Font type is good	0.05 (0.50)	0.03 (0.57)	0.65 (0.41)		$p < .10$	$p < .10$
"too little" (−3), *"neutral"* (±0) or *"too much"* (+3)						
Number of images	-0.02 (0.28)	0.05 (0.31)	0.05 (0.19)			
Amount of text	0.33 (0.29)	-0.30 (0.33)	0.08 (0.19)	$p < .01$		$p < .05$
Size of images	0.05 (0.31)	0.23 (0.23)	-0.06 (0.23)			$p < .10$
Amount of whitespace	-0.55 (0.29)	0.33 (0.29)	-0.05 (0.21)	$p < .01$	$p < .01$	$p < .05$

414 positive attributes. Of those, 402 were given to the responsive solution (it was commented by 20 participants), 210 for the automatic solution (10 participants) and 225 for the manual solution (10 participants).

6. RESULTS

6.1 Questionnaires

The SUS questionnaire resulted in no statistical differences between the different solutions. Clearly, device-related aspects were more important than the differences between solutions. Participants who regularly read newspapers or magazines gave lower SUS scores ($df = 14$, $F = 2.18$ and $p < .05$) and participants who did not own Apple devices gave higher scores ($df = 14$, $F = 2.23$ and $p < .05$).

As for the layout questionnaire (Table 3), for the *"fully disagree"* or *"fully agree"* types of statements statistically significant differences are observed in clarity of the layout, use of color, readability and font type. Our responsive solution received the highest scores for those statements. The statements related to overall appearance and interestingness resulted in no statistical significant differences between the three magazine manifestations.

For the *"too little"*, *"neutral"* or *"too much"* types of statements, statistically significant differences are observed in the amount of text, size of images and the amount of whitespace. The responsive solution received the most neutral scores for those statements. There are no statistically significant differences for the statement related to the number of images.

6.2 Free comments

Overall, the attributes were divided almost evenly between positive (49.5%) and negative (50.5%). Of all the attributes given to the manual solution, 29.5% were positive, whereas 33% were positive for the automatic and 69% for the responsive solution. The attributes were categorized resulting in 11 different usability attributes, 6 readability attributes and 16 visuality attributes. The number of different types of attributes given to each solution is summarized in Table 4.

The most commonly mentioned attributes are shown in Figure 10 (next page). Clarity was the single most mentioned attribute. It was mostly used to describe the simplicity of a solution in a positive sense and complexity in a negative sense. Some of the attributes like pagination, navigation, interaction, sections and image gallery show how the participants described different features of the solutions.

Table 4: The number of negative (−) and positive (+) attributes mentioned for each magazine solution.

	Manual		Automatic		Responsive		Total	
	−	+	−	+	−	+	−	+
Usability	84	24	64	19	33	122	181	165
Readability	34	6	33	10	33	61	100	77
Visuality	30	32	53	46	59	94	142	172
Total	148	62	150	75	125	277	423	414

Continuous versus paged layout was one the differences between the solutions. Both the manual and automatic solutions relied on paged layout and received mostly negative pagination comments, whereas the responsive solution received only positive comments. The automatic solution used more complex navigation. It received noticeably more negative navigation comments than the other two solutions.

Interaction was the most used negative attribute for the manual solution. The manual solution had many interaction-related features that the other solutions did not have. Overall usability was the most used negative attribute for the automatic solution. Image gallery functionality was not implemented in this version of the responsive solution and it resulted image gallery being the most used negative attribute for the responsive solution.

Section pages was a feature that only the automatic solution had, and the solution received many comments related to it. The sections attribute for the automatic solution is distributed almost evenly between negative and positive.

7. DISCUSSION

In this first stage of system development, we evaluated our functional prototype against commercial iPad magazines. Overall, the magazines covered many design choices (Table 2). As the magazines differ in many aspects (e.g. layout, navigation and interaction), the experimental setup was very challenging. The evaluation was user-centered, and

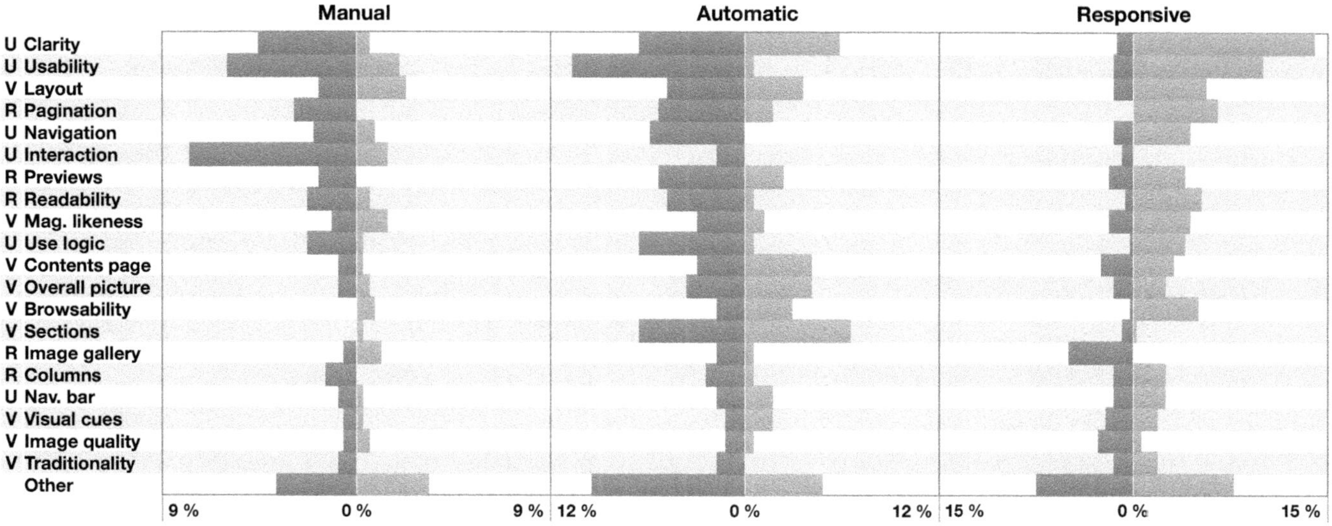

Figure 10: The most used attributes for the manual, automatic and responsive solutions sorted by the total number of comments. Red bar = negative comments and Green bar = positive comments. U = Usability, R = Readability and V = Visuality.

thus well suited to reveal functional design solutions. A combination of usability and exploratory methods helped to uncover guidelines for making good digital magazines. There were shortcomings and advantages in all magazines. Had we just compared layout differences, other aspects related to design choices would not have been found.

Overall, the responsive magazine solution was evaluated better than the other magazine solutions in terms of usability and layout, although there were no statistical differences in the SUS scores. The layout questionnaire scores show that our responsive solution received better scores in terms of clarity, use of colors, readability and font type. Also, the amount of text and the amount of whitespace were considered better than in the other solutions. The SUS questionnaire did not reveal statistically significant differences between the systems, which might originate from these solutions being different in many ways and individual preferences leveling things out in such a general questionnaire.

The positive and negative attributes resulted in clear differences between the solutions ($chi^2 = 117.6$, $df = 2$ and $p =< .01$). By comparing the different solutions (Table 2) and the attributes received by each solution (Figure 10), many aspects can be concluded. First, the manual solution received mostly negative usability comments, especially related to interaction features, which shows that the use of these types of features should be carefully considered.

For the automatic solution overall usability and navigation were the most used negative comments, whereas the use of section pages produced mixed opinions. Therefore in the development of that solution, more effort should be put into the implementation of the user interface, but the use of section pages should not be abandoned.

In all, our responsive prototype received noticeably more positive comments than the other solutions. Clarity, used to describe the simplicity of the solution, was the most used attribute. Pagination was also one defining factor of our prototype compared to the other solutions. Our prototype received only positive comments about the continuous page layout, while the other solutions received mostly negative comments related to the paged layout. It was commented as being much easier to read, and subjective readability was noticeably better with our prototype.

The most used comments for our responsive prototype were related to usability (41%), as there were still many usability flaws, some were related to readability (21%), and relatively many were related to visual aspects (38%). The most fragmented group of variables was visual aspects. This is probably because it is hard to describe visual shortcomings in words.

8. CONCLUSION

In this paper we aimed to show that digital magazines are a viable solution and that image analysis based automation produces high quality results. Here we discuss the functional prototype of the digital magazine and image processing, a major part of the planned layout engine.

Layout adaptation with content-based image features was shown to be feasible as it had a positive impact even under the cluttered experimental conditions. As the algorithmic methods are content-dependent, further development is needed and is already underway to be applicable to different types of editorial images.

Responsive design techniques enable sufficient versatility to create magazine articles that meet the necessary high visual demands. In this experiment we focused only on the iPad form factor, but modern web techniques and responsive design should be an obvious choice in creating adaptive cross-media publications. The newest CSS specification also includes many layout-related improvements (e.g. CSS Regions, Exclusions and Templates), which will hopefully soon be supported by browsers.

Image-related automation would be a big change for any editorial publishing. Nevertheless, it is a viable solution for making the cross-media publishing process more efficient and also produces content-based layout variation.

9. ACKNOWLEDGMENTS

This research was funded by the Finnish Funding Agency for Technology and Innovation TEKES via the Next Media program by the Strategic Centre for Science, Technology and Innovation TIVIT. We would like to thank all those who participated in the experiments as well as the partnering companies (Sanoma Magazines Finland and Anygraaf) for providing the material.

10. REFERENCES

[1] R. Achanta, S. Hemami, F. Estrada, and S. Süsstrunk. Frequency-Tuned Salient Region Detection. In *IEEE Conference on Computer Vision and Pattern Recognition*, pages 1597–1604, 2009.

[2] S. Avidan and A. Shamir. Seam Carving for Content-Aware Image Resizing. *ACM Transactions on Graphics*, 26(3):10, 2007.

[3] S. Bae, S. Paris, and F. Durand. Two-Scale Tone Management for Photographic Look. *ACM Transactions on Graphics*, 25(3):637, 2006.

[4] S. Banerjee and B. Evans. In-Camera Automation of Photographic Composition Rules. *IEEE Transactions on Image Processing*, 16(7):1807–1820, 2007.

[5] K. Berkner and B. Erol. Adaptation of Document Images to Display Constraints. In *Proceedings of SPIE*, volume 6806, page 68061C, 2008.

[6] C. Braganza, K. Marriott, P. Moulder, M. Wybrow, and T. Dwyer. Scrolling Behaviour with Single- and Multi-column Layout. In *International World Wide Web Conference*, pages 831–840, 2009.

[7] J. Brooke. SUS: A Quick and Dirty Usability Scale. In P. W. Jordan, B. A. Weerdmeester, B. Thomas, and I. L. McClelland, editors, *Usability Evaluation in Industry*, chapter SUS, pages 189–194. Taylor and Francis, 1996.

[8] W.-l. Chang and H.-l. Lin. The Impact of Color Traits on Corporate Branding. *Journal of Business*, 4(15):3344–3355, 2010.

[9] B. Cheng, B. Ni, S. Yan, and Q. Tian. Learning to Photograph. In *Proceedings of the ACM International Conference on Multimedia - MM '10*, pages 291–300, 2010.

[10] R. Datta, D. Joshi, J. Li, and J. Z. Wang. Studying Aesthetics in Photographic Images Using a Computational Approach. In *European Conference on Computer Vision*, pages 288–301, 2006.

[11] L. Fernandes and M. Oliveira. Real-Time Line Detection Through an Improved Hough Transform Voting Scheme. *Pattern Recognition*, 41(1):299–314, 2008.

[12] B. Geng, L. Yang, C. Xu, X.-S. Hua, and S. Li. The Role of Attractiveness in Web Image Search. In *Proceedings of the ACM International Conference on Multimedia - MM '11*, pages 63–72, 2011.

[13] T. Grill and M. Scanlon. *Photographic Composition.* Fountain Press, 1984.

[14] C. Havasi, R. Speer, and J. Holmgren. Automated Color Selection Using Semantic Knowledge. In *AAAI Fall Symposium*, pages 40–45, 2010.

[15] C. Jacobs, W. Li, E. Schrier, D. Bargeron, and D. Salesin. Adaptive grid-based document layout. *ACM Transactions on Graphics*, 22(3):838–847, 2003.

[16] Y. Ke, X. Tang, and F. Jing. The Design of High-Level Features for Photo Quality Assessment. In *IEEE Computer Society Conference on Computer Vision and Pattern Recognition*, pages 419–426, 2006.

[17] R. Kumar, J. Kim, and S. R. Klemmer. Automatic Retargeting of Web Page Content. In *Human Factors in Computing Systems - CHI EA*, pages 4237–4242, 2009.

[18] C.-Y. Lai, P.-H. Chen, S.-W. Shih, Y. Liu, and J.-S. Hong. Computational Models and Experimental Investigations of Effects of Balance and Symmetry on the Aesthetics of Text-Overlaid Images. *Journal of Human Computer Studies*, 68(1-2):41–56, 2010.

[19] T. Lavie and N. Tractinsky. Assessing Dimensions of Perceived Visual Aesthetics of Web Sites. *International Journal of Human-Computer Studies*, 60(3):269–298, 2004.

[20] J. R. Lewis and J. Sauro. The Factor Structure of the System Usability Scale. In *Proceedings of the International Conference on Human Centered Design*, pages 94–103, 2009.

[21] M. D. S. Lonsdale, M. C. Dyson, and L. Reynolds. Reading in Examination-Type Situations: The Effects of Text Layout on Performance. *Journal of Research in Reading*, 29(4):433–453, 2006.

[22] Y. Luo and X. Tang. Photo and Video Quality Evaluation: Focusing on the Subject. In *European Conference on Computer Vision*, pages 386–399, 2008.

[23] E. Marcotte. *Responsive Web Design.* A Book Apart, 2011.

[24] M. Moshagen and M. T. Thielsch. Facets of Visual Aesthetics. *International Journal of Human-Computer Studies*, 68(10):689–709, 2010.

[25] M. Nebeling, F. Matulic, L. Streit, and M. C. Norrie. Adaptive Layout Template for Effective Web Content Presentation in Large-Screen Contexts. In *Proceedings of the 11th ACM Symposium on Document Engineering - DocEng '11*, page 219, 2011.

[26] P. Sandhaus, M. Rabbath, and S. Boll. Employing Aesthetic Principles for Automatic Photo Book Layout. In *International Conference on Advances in Multimedia Modeling*, pages 84–95, 2010.

[27] E. Schrier, M. Dontcheva, C. Jacobs, G. Wade, and D. Salesin. Adaptive Layout for Dynamically Aggregated Documents. In *Proceedings of the ACM International Conference on Intelligent User Interfaces*, pages 99–108, 2008.

[28] V. Setlur, S. Takagi, R. Raskar, M. Gleicher, and B. Gooch. Automatic Image Retargeting. In *International Conference on Mobile and Ubiquitous Multimedia*, pages 59–68, 2005.

[29] X. Sun, H. Yao, R. Ji, and S. Liu. Photo Assessment Based on Computational Visual Attention Model. In *Proceedings of the ACM International Conference on Multimedia - MM '09*, pages 541–544, 2009.

[30] P. Viola and M. Jones. Robust Real-time Object Detection. *International Journal of Computer Vision*, 57(2):137–154, 2001.

Understanding Screen Contents for Building a High Performance, Real Time Screen Sharing System

Surendar Chandra, Jacob T. Biehl, John Boreczky, Scott Carter, Lawrence A. Rowe
FX Palo Alto Laboratory Inc., 3174 Porter Drive, Palo Alto, CA 94304
surendar@acm.org, {biehl,johnb,carter,rowe}@fxpal.com

ABSTRACT

Faithful sharing of screen contents is an important collaboration feature. Prior systems were designed to operate over constrained networks. They performed poorly even without such bottlenecks. To build a high performance screen sharing system, we empirically analyzed screen contents for a variety of scenarios. We showed that screen updates were sporadic with long periods of inactivity. When active, screens were updated at far higher rates than was supported by earlier systems. The mismatch was pronounced for interactive scenarios. Even during active screen updates, the number of updated pixels were frequently small. We showed that crucial information can be lost if individual updates were merged. When the available system resources could not support high capture rates, we showed ways in which updates can be *effectively* collapsed. We showed that Zlib lossless compression performed poorly for screen updates. By analyzing the screen pixels, we developed a practical transformation that significantly improved compression rates. Our system captured 240 updates per second while only using 4.6 Mbps for interactive scenarios. Still, while playing movies in fullscreen mode, our approach could not achieve higher capture rates than prior systems; the CPU remains the bottleneck. A system that incorporates our findings is deployed within the lab.

Categories and Subject Descriptors

J.m [**Computer Applications**]: Miscellaneous

General Terms

Experimentation, Measurement, Performance

Keywords

ScreenCast, DisplayCast, Screen Capture, Screen Sharing

1. INTRODUCTION

Screen sharing is integral to collaboration scenarios such as auditorium projection, remote learning and debugging, multi-user screen sharing and interaction as well as in screencast archival. Consider an usage scenario: Emily presents her simulation plots from cloud servers on a high resolution auditorium projector. Amy watches this presentation on her laptop using the intranet wireless while Bob joins in using in-flight WiFi. Bob then displays another article on the projector that portends the impact of Emily's work. Impressed by these results, Amy sends these screens to other colleagues.

Even though the participants want to share without any restriction on their shared contents, resource availability places some restrictions. Emily might use a dedicated Gbps wired link between the cloud servers that generate her plots and the projector PC. However, Bob laptop's small display and slow in-flight network limits his ability to watch these plots in high fidelity. We desire a system that can faithfully capture the screens while operating in a resource rich environment and yet be adaptable to modest scenarios.

The screen capture mechanism also plays a crucial role. Emily could share her data for plotting on the projector PC and on Bob's laptop. Similarly, Bob sends his PowerPoint report to the projector PC. These data objects are likely compact and network efficient. However, the recipient is required to have the appropriate software setup; Amy needs a PowerPoint player to read the report shared by Bob. Also, privacy concerns might limit sharing the entire data; Bob only wants to send select portions to the projector PC.

Instead, we focus on sharing screen pixmaps. A pixmap represents the screen image as an array of pixel color values. Pixmaps are generated after any application specific rendering. Graphics rendering frameworks also create pixmaps for display. Most operating systems provide a mechanism to capture and display pixmaps. Hence, sharing pixmaps is portable and popular; systems such as Virtual Network Computing (VNC) [21], Microsoft Remote Desktop (RDP) [5], Google Chrome Remote Desktop and Cisco WebEx (`http://www.webex.com/`) also capture pixmaps.

We target resource rich intranet scenarios. Modern laptops use fast, multicore processors. IEEE 802.11n WLAN supports bandwidths of 600 Mbps while the upcoming IEEE 802.11ac promises bandwidths of over 1 Gbps. Earlier systems were designed to operate in resource constrained environments. They were unable to scale to support scenarios that did not experience such bottlenecks. Using wired networks, Wallace et al. [26] only measured a pixmap delivery rate of 4.5 frames per second for VNC.

To understand the requirements for a high performance screen sharing system, we investigated the nature of screen updates; both in terms of the rate at which they are generated as well as the kinds of pixels that comprise them. The update dynamics is application dependent. Hence, we analyzed the screen dynamics while using various applications ranging from playing movies to computer generated animations, presentations, web browsing and interactive editors. We wanted a portable approach. Hence we performed experiments under Windows 7 and Mac OS X Snow Leopard. We used two different laptops to assess the impact of hardware capability.

Screen contents were dynamic and behaved differently than fixed frame rate videos. Pixmap generation rates were sporadic with long inactivity durations. Computer generated animations and interaction artifacts created new pixmaps at rates that were only limited by the laptop processing capability. On modern laptops, pixmaps need to be captured at rates far higher than 100 updates per second (ups) to minimize the pixels lost during capture. Future processor improvements will necessitate even higher update rates. We observed significant differences between applications. Sometimes, the same application (e.g., Adobe Flash game) behaved differently between Windows 7 and Mac OS X. Different applications behaved differently while operating on the same object. For the same H.264 compressed movie, Windows Media player doubled the rendering rate as compared to the Quicktime player. Inexplicably, the captured pixmaps also exhibited less inter-update similarity than with the Quicktime player. Windows 7 created more small pixmaps and a faster processor increased the number of small updates.

We showed the inadequacy of Zlib compression for screen updates. We quantified the redundancy in screen pixmaps and devised schemes to achieve higher compression efficiency by transforming the inter-update pixel temporal redundancy into intra-update spatial redundancy. We improved the compression factor of 5.1:1 achieved by Zlib to 143:1; a 28 fold improvement in compression efficiency.

We built DisplayCast [13], a high performance screen sharing system using our observations. Our system captures and compresses over 240 ups for interactive scenarios. We devised ways of effectively responding to scenarios in which the update rates overwhelm the available resources. We empirically show that in Windows 7, a delay of 16 msec to wait to capture the end of an update flurry was reasonable. Our system natively operates in Windows 7 and in Mac OS X and is deployed in a production setting.

Next, §2 describes prior work. §3 describes the experiment setup. §4 analyzes pixel generation rate for various usage scenarios. §5 analyzes the spatial overlap between updates and devices schemes for *effectively* responding to resource constraints. §6 analyzes the pixels and devices a transformation to Zlib that improves screen pixmap compression efficiency. We briefly describe the DisplayCast system that uses our findings in §7 and conclude in §8.

2. RELATED WORK

Prior systems used several ways for screen capture. Some approaches partitioned applications with the local component sending the encoded objects for remote rendering. For example, Apple Airplay [6] sends audio and video for playback to an Apple TV while Microsoft Windows Media player [10] sends media to the RDP player. Similarly, the Access Grid Distributed PowerPoint tool [25] remotely shares PowerPoint presentations. Since these systems use the original objects, they achieve high network efficiency without requiring additional CPU resources. On the other hand, they require tight integration between the endpoints. Remote components must precisely render the redirected objects. They must also enforce all access control restrictions. Thus, Microsoft's own Mac OS X RDP player does not support player redirection. This lack of generality limits this form of screen sharing.

Another approach captures the rendering commands sent by applications to frameworks such as Apple Cocoa, Microsoft DirectX and OpenGL. For example, GLX [3] extensions to the X windows protocol provides remote rendering capability for OpenGL applications. WireGL [17] renders OpenGL commands across a cluster of servers in a display wall scenario. Estes et al. [15] describe a display abstraction that allows applications to expose some application semantics to remote displays. Note that applications can choose among a variety of frameworks. They can also use more than one framework; limiting the generality of this approach.

Capture appliances such as NCast (`ncast.com`) digitize and encode a VGA stream sent from the laptop to the projector. Using a proprietary point-to-point wireless network, WHDI [7] supports 1080p uncompressed video. The Intel WiDi [4], Apple Airplay mirroring [6] and Sony wireless screen mirroring encode screen updates into a wireless H.264 stream using special encoding hardware. These systems treat the screen contents as a movie and transmit them at fixed update rates. We empirically show that the rate of update creation on typical laptops is far higher than is supported by these systems. The playback devices are also not ubiquitous.

Screen capture as a sequence of pixelmaps is also popular. VNC [21] shares screen pixmap updates using the remote framebuffer (RFB) distribution protocol [20]. Wallace et al. [26], Boyaci et al. [11] and Satoshi [22] extend VNC to share pixmap updates from specific application windows. RFB is a client driven lazy request-response protocol that sends the captured pixmaps uncompressed or compressed using lossless Zlib [19] or lossy JPEG [12]. Clients adapt to network conditions by requesting new updates on receipt of responses for prior requests. The server is not required to respond to a client request within a specific time limit (if at all). Thus, pixmap updates can be missed because the client was too slow in requesting the next update or because the server was unwilling to respond faster. Prior work did not quantify the nature of pixmaps or the interactions between the RFB protocol and the screen capture. We empirically show the inadequacy of the pixmap delivery rate of 4.5 that was measured for traditional VNC servers [26].

Sun et al. [24] note high update rates for interactive thin-client applications. We empirically measure the update rates for various application scenarios. They improve compression efficiency by caching several prior pixmaps on the client and server. We only maintain current and prior screen contents on the server.

Schmidt et al. [23] describe the SLIM extension to VNC where remote application activity triggers update push from the server. In §5, we show that pixmaps need to be sent at high rates (that are unsupported by VNC) to avoid losing pixels to spatial overlap.

Intel Active Management Technology (AMT) implements a BIOS VNC server that does not rely on the operating system. Since the framebuffer does not retain information about whether any contents were updated, AMT periodically polls the entire framebuffer.

Google Chrome Remote Desktop encodes the screen as a VP8 video. The frame rate depends on VP8 performance on a particular device. H.264 compression is efficient. However, our state-of-the-art laptop achieved less than 10 fps while using hardware accelerated H.264 encoding. OnLive (`onlive.com`) hosts video games and applications on its cloud servers. The output screen is then divided into 16 segments, each of which is compressed separately using a special H.264 encoder to achieve low latency compression.

MS RDP is a proprietary screen sharing system. RDP reconfigures the desktop to ease the screen capture. It supports redirecting audio, GPU, file system, printer, pointer, port, aero glass and Windows Media player using tight integration between the service, operating system and applications. Not all RDP features are available in all OS versions. Our pixmap capture approach is portable and is applicable to the pixmap capture component of RDP.

Screencast is the act of capturing and distributing a podcast video of the display screen contents, especially during lecture presentations. For example, the TechSmith Camtasia tool allows for easy presentation screen capture and distribution through the `http://screencast.com` portal. They create a fixed frame rate video without considering the effect of pixel loss due to spatial overlap.

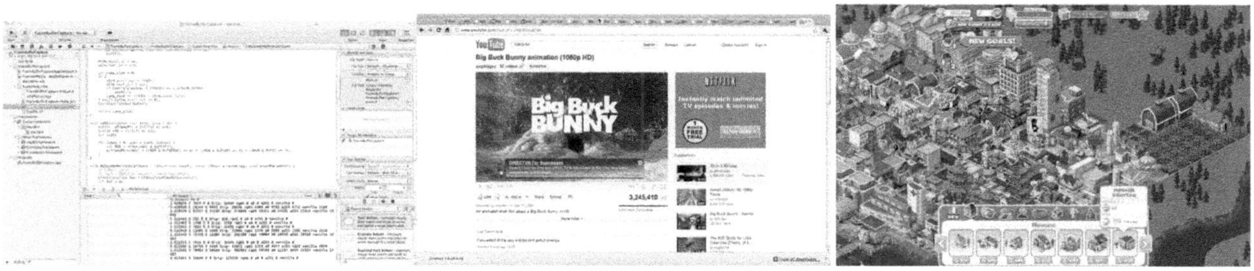

(a) Xcode (b) YouTube (c) Cityville

Figure 1: Screen capture from three usage scenarios

3. EXPERIMENT SETUP

3.1 Pixmap update collection framework

We used two 15" Macbook Pro laptops: one with a 2.66 GHz Intel Core 2 Duo CPU, 4 GB of 1067 MHz DDR3 memory, NVidia GeForce 9400M and 9600M GPUs with 256 MB of VRAM and a 1440x900 pixel display and another with a 2 GHz quad core Intel i7 CPU, 8 GB of 1067 MHz DDR3 memory, Radeon HD 6490M GPU with 256 MB of GDDR5 memory and Intel HD Graphics 3000 GPU with 384 MB shared memory and a 1680x1050 pixel display. We refer to these laptops as *C2D* and *i7*, respectively.

Each laptop was dual booted to either Windows 7 SP1 or Mac OS X SL (10.6.8) using Apple BootCamp. On Mac OS X, we used the *CGRegisterScreenRefreshCallback()* call to receive asynchronous notifications regarding screen updates, and *CGDisplayCreateImageForRect()* call to retrieve the pixel data. On Windows 7, we used the DemoForge mirror driver [2] to collect pixmap updates. This driver implements the Windows mirroring function [9]. The driver intercepts and stores the boundaries of the 20,000 most recent updates. Our analyzer polled the driver (every msec) to collect these stored updates. It then memory mapped the mirror driver's framebuffer copy to access the pixels that correspond to each pixmap update. Thus, the updates are pushed to our analyzer by Mac OS X while we use a polling model for Windows 7. We refer to each OS setup for the *C2D* and *i7* laptops as *C2D-Win7*, *C2D-Mac*, *i7-Win7* and *i7-Mac*, respectively. Note that applications running on Mac OS X and Windows 7 are optimized for direct display to the local monitor. Their behavior is likely to be different from applications that are optimized for network based X windows display system.

3.2 Activities analyzed

We capture screen pixmaps for the following operations.

- **HD trailer**: We played a full screen Avatar movie trailer using Quicktime X player on Mac OS X and Windows Media player on Windows 7. The H.264 trailer was 4:07 minutes long and was encoded at 1920x1080 pixels, 23.98 fps for a target bitrate of 9 Mbps. We refer to this scenario as *Avatar*.
- **Presentation**: We created a 1024x768 pixel resolution presentation using the Apple Keynote software and converted it to PowerPoint format. We played these presentations using Keynote on Mac OS X and PowerPoint on Windows 7. We transitioned each slide after about 15 seconds. We refer to these scenarios as *Keynote* and *PowerPoint*, respectively.
- **Integrated Development Environment (IDE)**: We analyzed the pixmaps created while developing our software instrumentation tools. We used Apple Xcode 4.0 on Mac and Visual Studio 2010 in Windows. These tools divide the screen into rectangular regions and use them for code editing, file browsing, function help and debugger outputs (Figure 1(a)). We referred to them as *Xcode* and *VS 2010*, respectively.
- **YouTube**: We watched the 1080p HD *"Big Buck Bunny"* animation clip (`http://youtu.be/XSGBVzeBUbk`), both in the default browser spatial resolution as well as in full screen mode using the Chrome browser. With the default spatial resolution, YouTube displays flash advertisements as well as comments and suggested videos around the video clip (Figure 1(b)). While using full screen, advertisements were overlaid on top of the clip. These scenarios are referred to as *YouTube* and *YouTube-FS*, respectively.
- **CNN.com**: We browsed *cnn.com* using Chrome (referred as *CNN-Chrome*). We read a whole article before skimming over others. CNN extensively uses advertisement banners.
- **Cityville game**: Finally, we played the Adobe Flash based Zynga Cityville game (at Level 66), in the native and full screen resolution (referred as *Cityville* and *Cityville-FS*, respectively). Cityville is a casual social city-building simulation game (Figure 1(c)). AppData estimated 100 million active players in January 2011. The game shows animations of people loitering; the rate of such movement depends on the rendering capabilities available to the browser.

4. RATE OF PIXEL GENERATION

Building a high performance real time screen sharing system requires an understanding of the rate of pixel generation, the spatial overlap between updates (§5) and the nature of the pixels (§6).

First we analyse the rate of pixel generation, the number of pixels in each pixmap and the rate at which each pixmap is created. This analysis helps choose between a design optimized to capture 24 full screen updates (to play a movie) vs another that captures 240 pixmaps, each of which has $\frac{1}{10}^{th}$ the number of pixels per second.

For the various applications, we tabulate the mean and standard deviation of the total number of pixels and updates per second in Table 1. The total number of pixels varied between 0.6 and 34.0 on *C2D* and between 1.5 and 49.9 on *i7*. Average update rate varied between 9.6 and 50.1 for *C2D* and between 9.5 and 80.7 for *i7*. The standard deviation of the update rates was high: e.g., *PowerPoint* had a mean update rate of 40.1 and standard deviation of 64.0.

C2D and *i7* should generate 38.9 and 52.9 Mpixels while refreshing the screen at 30 fps, respectively. Thus, the number of pixels were less than would be generated for treating the screen as a fixed frame rate (30 fps) movie: the rate of pixmap generation was higher. The mismatch was pronounced for interactive scenarios such as *Xcode/VS 2010*, *Keynote/PowerPoint* and *CNN* which exhibited high update rates with a small number of updated pixels (<10K pixels). E.g., *PowerPoint* in Windows 7 generated 61.9 updates per second (σ: 113.5) and only 1.7 Mpixels per second.

scenario	Million pixels per second								Updates per second							
	C2D				i7				C2D				i7			
	Mac		Win7		Mac		Win7		Mac		Win7		Mac		Win7	
	μ	σ	μ	σ	μ	σ	μ	σ	μ	σ	μ	σ	μ	σ	μ	σ
Avatar	27.4	3.8	26.8	5.5	37.6	4.8	36.6	7.0	24.4	5.1	49.5	13.7	25.1	8.8	51.2	18.2
Cityville	10.1	3.6	10.0	1.5	12.2	4.2	18.2	2.6	30.8	11.8	41.9	23.8	52.3	18.8	63.2	39.6
Cityville-FS	25.3	8.1	20.4	4.4	42.3	10.3	47.8	7.1	22.4	16.1	47.1	41.5	30.1	21.8	47.9	36.0
CNN-Chrome	3.9	5.5	2.5	3.3	9.0	10.9	2.5	4.0	19.9	22.9	50.1	41.6	80.7	62.3	40.9	39.1
Keynote	5.5	1.9			6.2	3.2			9.6	13.6			9.5	13.4		
PowerPoint			2.6	2.3			1.5	1.9			29.7	34.0			40.1	64.0
Xcode	2.0	2.8			1.6	2.1			13.1	14.6			16.3	16.4		
VS 2010			0.6	2.2			1.7	5.9			37.8	39.4			61.9	113.5
YouTube	6.2	0.6	5.5	0.5	6.1	0.7	5.5	0.8	29.3	8.8	31.9	10.8	28.5	13.6	33.8	15.6
YouTube-FS	34.0	5.7	33.6	5.0	46.0	8.9	49.9	7.4	27.5	5.7	28.9	15.6	28.0	6.7	31.4	14.6

Table 1: Pixel generation characteristics

The 24 fps *Avatar* trailer created around 24 and 50 ups while using Mac OS X and Windows 7, respectively. The number of pixels updated was around 27 and 37 Mpixels for Mac OS X and Windows 7 with little variation in the number of pixels between the two laptops. The Windows Media player was aggressively displaying partial frames as they were decoded. *YouTube* (video played by Adobe Flash, both within the browser and in full screen mode) did not exhibit much variation between the different operating systems or laptops. *Cityville* scenario required high update rates and high number of updated pixels especially with Windows 7 requiring more updates for the same number of updated pixels.

Next, we drill down on the number of pixels in each update as well as the duration between updates.

4.1 Number of pixels in each update

For the various usage scenarios, we plot the cumulative distribution of the number of pixels in each update in Figure 2. For *Avatar*, about 5% of the pixmaps contained less than 10,000 pixels. The remaining 95% of the pixmaps occupied 90% of the screen with Mac OS X and 45% of the screen with Windows 7. This movie clip was played by the Quicktime player on Mac OS X and by Windows Media player on Windows 7. In §4.2, we show that the rate of pixmap creation was different between these scenarios. For *YouTube-FS*, less than 4% of pixmaps on Mac OS X and 12% of the pixmaps on Windows 7 were less than 10,000 pixels. The remaining pixmaps updated the entire screen. When letterboxed, unlike Flash player, Quicktime and Windows Media player only updated the active region. We describe its implications in §4.2.

Even though *Cityville-FS* used the Flash player plugin on both operating systems, it produced different screen pixmap behavior. On Windows 7, 50% and 65% of the updates were small while on Mac OS X, only 20% and 10% of the updates were small with *C2D* and *i7* laptops, respectively. The flash plugin likely implements the graphics primitives differently between the two OSs.

For *Keynote*, 55% and 65% of the updates were small on the *C2D* and *i7* laptops, respectively. While using *PowerPoint*, 75% and 95% of the pixmaps were small using *C2D* and *i7* laptops, respectively. Similar results were observed for other scenarios as well. In general, a faster processor allows for faster animation experience which manifests itself in many small updates. In §6.2, we investigate the inter-update redundancy among these updates.

4.2 Duration between updates

Next we plot (Figure 3) a distribution of the duration between pixmaps for the various usage scenarios. For Mac OS X, the discrete nature of the durations (about 18 msec apart) is an artifact of the OS policies for scheduling callbacks.

For *Avatar*, 49% of the pixmaps were sent 50 msec apart while the remaining pixmaps were sent around 32 msecs apart with Mac OS X. The movie was encoded at 24 fps, which corresponds to a duration of 42 msec between frames; the screen pixmaps do not correspond to constant frame creation rates. While using Windows 7, the screen pixmaps were equally distributed between 0 and 42 msecs apart. As we noted in Table 1, on average, this corresponds to twice the frame rate as the encoded rate; Windows Media player appears to progressively decode the movie. With Mac OS X and *YouTube-FS*, 20%, 40% and 40% of the pixmaps were captured at 18, 32 and 50 msec apart, With Windows 7, 50% were received about 42 msec apart while the remaining pixmaps were received between 0 and 42 msec apart. Deducing whether the user is watching a movie by computing the pixmap update geometry and the rate in which they are updated (similar to [11, 18]) would fail.

For interactive scenarios, Windows 7 creates updates at a furious pace. With *VS-2010*, 20% and 40% of the updates were created immediately after each other with the remaining 60% and 50% of the updates were sent within 10 msec of each other for *C2D* and *i7* laptops, respectively. The numbers were similar for *PowerPoint* in which 60% of the updates were sent immediately and 95% of the updates sent within 16 msec of each other. The remaining updates were sent several seconds apart. For *Xcode*, between 40% and 50% of the pixmaps were captured immediately after each other. These values were similar for *Keynote* scenario as well.

To summarize, many applications generated large spikes of screen updates during user interaction. Movies updated the screen at a rate that was largely driven by the media object. However, some movie players showed partially decoded frames. Animations are GPU accelerated which adds to their visual appeal. However, they generated pixmaps at a rate that was only limited by the available computational resources. Improvements in processing power exacerbate this trend. In all scenarios, the number of updated pixels was smaller than for treating the screen as a fixed frame rate movie. Prior systems that used heuristics such as the update dimensions and rate to deduce information about the screen contents (e.g., movie playback) were shown to be fragile.

5. SCREEN SHARING CONSTRAINTS

§4 showed the update rates for various usage scenarios. Storage and network capacity limitations require compressing the screen pixmaps (uncompressed, *i7* requires 1.7 Gbps at 30 fps). However, the available computational capacity might not allow for com-

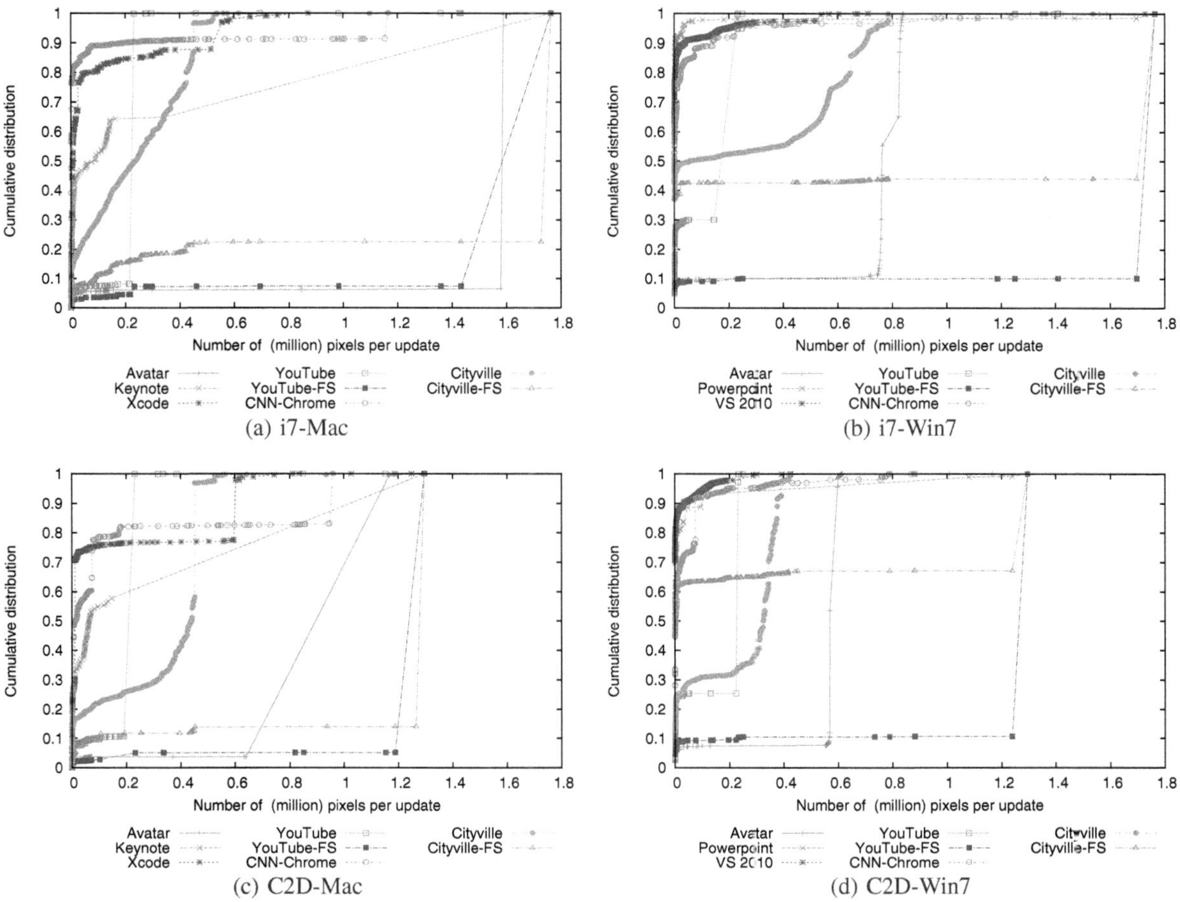

Figure 2: Distribution of number of pixels in each update

pression at high capture rates, especially since this computational need competes with processes that are simultaneously rendering to the screen. Even when they are compressed, the network capacity might be insufficient; e.g., Bob's in-flight WiFi severely constrains his ability to receive many updates from Emily's cloud servers.

X windows applications reduce the network load by rendering offline and then infrequently updating the screen. However, applications designed for desktop platforms (Mac OS X and Windows 7) choose faster update rates (§4). Future trends portend to hardware accelerated screen elements that generate even more updates.

Ideally, sharing systems will capture, compress and deliver the updates at the rate in which they are generated. When resource constraints make this infeasible, they can buffer all updates and eventually transmit them (even if the pixels are super-ceded). This buffering causes CPU, memory and network data spikes during active durations. We investigate ways to address this mis-match.

5.1 Coalescing updates

One approach coalesces and creates a new screen update that encompasses all unsent updates. Unlike disjoint updates, spatially overlapping pixels are lost. The effect of this loss depends on the application scenario. During Quicktime movie playback, a delay in capturing a frame results in a lower frame rate video viewing experience. As noted in §4, Windows Media player aggressively displays partially decoded segments of a movie frame. Any delay causes a low frame rate video viewing experience in which each captured frame might consist of elements from multiple movie frames. In a network constrained remote login scenario, we frequently observed this effect while using VNC/RDP with Windows Media playback from a Mac OS X (the MS RDP player for Mac does not support media player redirection which masks this effect). The pixels lost through spatial overlap also affects systems such as [16] that analyze the screen using optical character recognition techniques. Delaying and removing pixels causes these systems to miss pixels that could be crucial for the recognition task.

We investigate spatial overlap using a fixed period in which all updates are coalesced (similar to Camtasia and Quicktime). We plot the percentage of unseen pixels for capture frequencies of 10, 15, 20, 24, 30, 60 and 100 ups while using Mac OS X and Windows 7 on *i7* in Figure 4. For brevity, we highlight two representative scenarios: interactive (*VS-2010* and *Xcode*) and video (*YouTube-FS*). Applications using *C2D* created fewer updates and hence experienced slightly lower number of lost pixels (not illustrated).

For *YouTube-FS*, slow capture rates of 20 ups, 15 ups and 10 ups lost about 30%, 45% and 65% of the pixels, respectively. Capture frequencies of 60 ups lost 5% of the pixels. Even though the *Avatar* trailer was encoded at 24 fps, our analysis in §4.2 showed that the updates were not always received at uniform intervals on Mac OS X. Thus, from watching the *Avatar* trailer on Mac OS X, capturing the update at 24 ups, sometimes, two updates are received within the fixed capture duration leading to a loss of 50% of the pixels. A higher frequency (e.g., 30 ups) reduces the percentage of unseen pixels. On Windows 7, the media player doubles the rendering rate

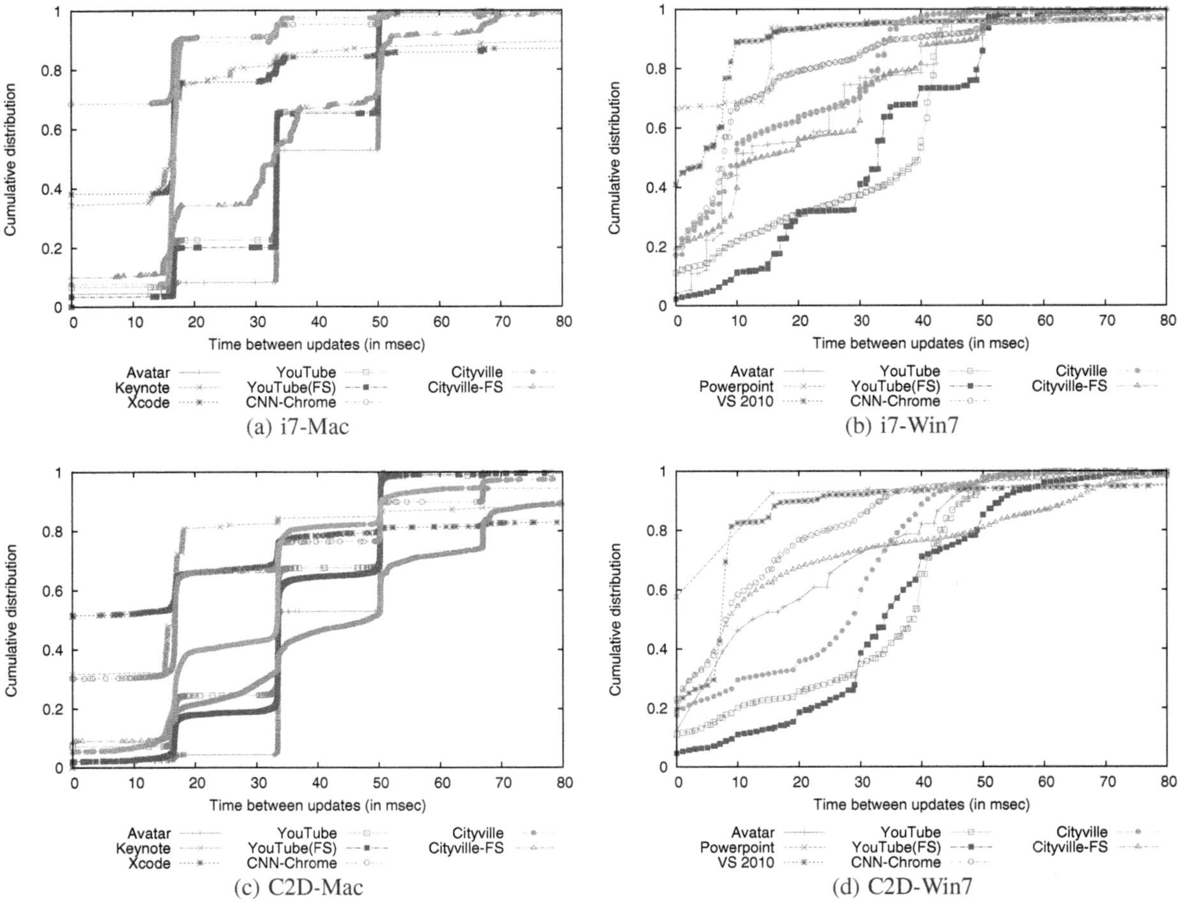

Figure 3: Distribution of duration between each update

to 50 ups. Capture frequencies of 20 ups, 15 ups, and 10 ups lose about 18%, 38% and 59% pixels, respectively.

Scenarios in which screen updates were driven by user interaction (*Xcode*, *VS 2010*, *Keynote*, *PowerPoint* and *CNN-Chrome*), there were durations in which lower capture rates were acceptable. For example, presenters advance to the next slide and then discuss the slide contents for several minutes with no further screen updates. However, when the user interacted with the system, there was a flurry of activity. For example, the *Xcode* scenario lost 20% of the pixels even at a capture rate of 30 ups; we require a rate of over 60 ups to capture all the pixels. For a *Keynote* presentation, the updates were few and far between. However, *Keynote* extensively uses GPU accelerated transitions. During a slide transition, a large number of updates were created in a short duration; over 40% of which can be lost for capture rates of 30 updates per second. Even at 60 ups, 20% of the pixels were lost.

We observed little loss when choosing a capture rate of 100 ups.

5.2 Selectively choosing updates

Another approach could prioritize pixmaps and dynamically drop low priority ones. Consider a sequence of updates u_1, u_2, u_3, u_4, u_{10} and u_{20} using the notation that u_n was captured at time n. When the resource availability could only sustain three updates, we might choose u_4, u_{10} and u_{20} instead of u_1, u_2, u_{20}. In the former case, we waited for the flurry of updates (u_1, u_2, u_3 and u_4) to subside and then chose u_4 while the latter case aggressively sends all updates until resource limitation forces it to drop pixmaps. The challenge is to perform these choices without application support, especially when multiple application elements with differing requirements might be overlaid on the same screen. Note that scenarios such as *Cityville* continuously create fast updates; we require a policy that waits for a certain duration before sending the next update. Using our results in Figure 3, we investigate the duration that we should wait before choosing an update for sharing.

§4.2 showed that Mac OS X delivered callbacks at intervals of 18 msec with many updates delivered immediately after each other. Thus, waiting an additional msec after the callback achieves our goal of picking the last update in an animation sequence. If the pixmaps can be compressed and sent during the 18 msec interval between callbacks, Mac OS X can sustain 60 ups.

Besides pixmaps which were delivered immediately after each other, duration between updates varied uniformly for up to 50 msec in Windows 7. Interactive scenarios delivered a majority of their screen updates in a short duration. E.g., with *i7*, 90% and 95% of the updates for *VS 2010* and *PowerPoint* were delivered within ten and 16 msec, respectively. For *C2D*, 90% of the pixmaps were delivered within 16 msec. Hence, 16 msec is a reasonable duration to wait to capture the end of an update flurry in Windows 7.

6. COMPRESSION IMPROVEMENT

Next, we investigate spatial and temporal similarity that is inherent in the screen pixmaps. Compression algorithms achieve high compression factors by exploiting both these forms of redundancy.

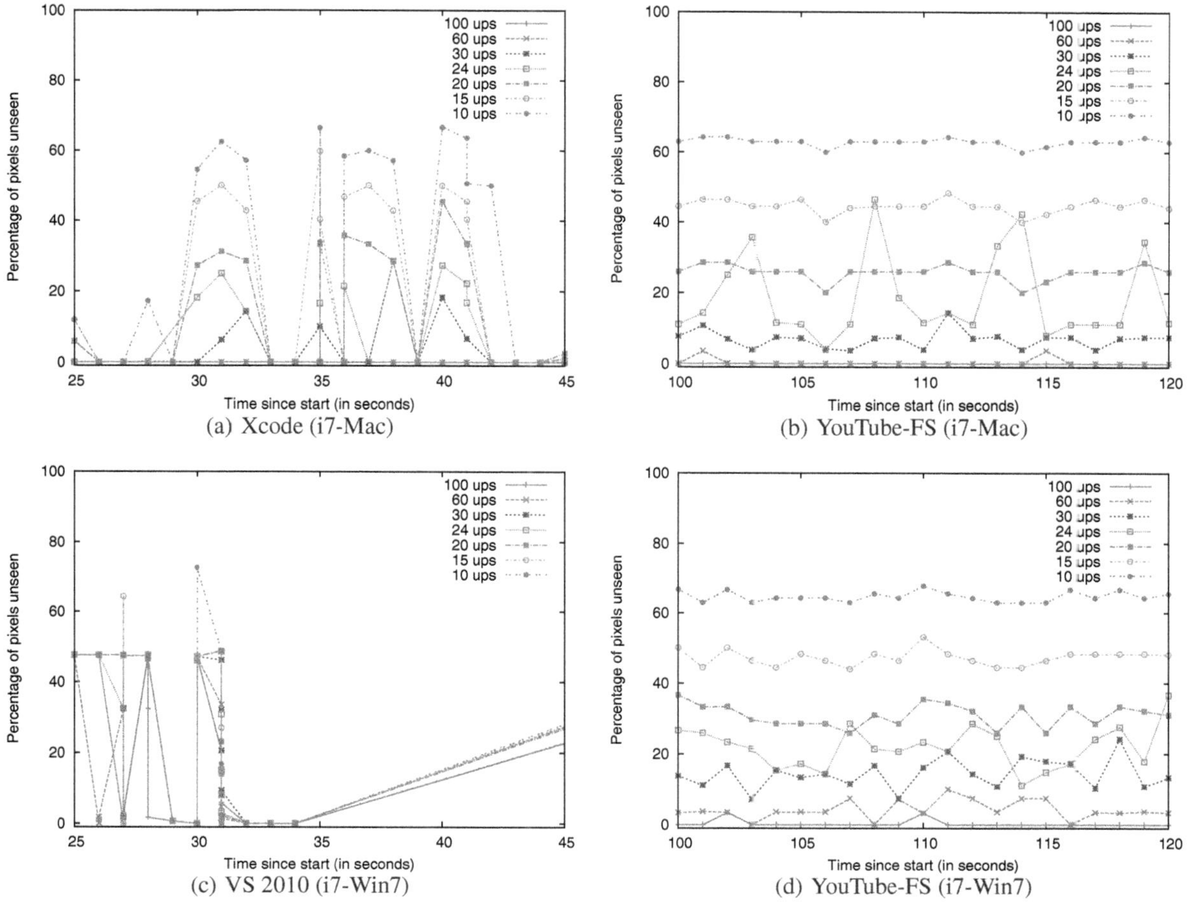

(a) Xcode (i7-Mac)

(b) YouTube-FS (i7-Mac)

(c) VS 2010 (i7-Win7)

(d) YouTube-FS (i7-Win7)

Figure 4: Pixels occluded by coalescing updates

scenario	Mac OS X	Windows 7
Avatar	21.0:1	8.7:1
Cityville	5.3:1	5.1:1
Cityville-FS	3.2:1	2.8:1
CNN-Chrome	5.9:1	12.5:1
Keynote/PowerPoint	25.6:1	9.6:1
Xcode/VS 2010	23.2:1	21.4:1
YouTube	4.8:1	2.4:1
YouTube-FS	10.5:1	5.9:1

Table 2: Average Zlib compression factor

scenario	C2D		i7	
	comp	fps	comp	fps
Avatar	190.6:1	11.9	349.1:1	11.8
Cityville	252.0:1	11.1	171.5:1	14.0
Cityville-FS	102.9:1	11.1	84.9:1	12.6
CNN-Chrome	2283.0:1	7.1	2139.3:1	7.9
Keynote	5956.5:1	5.1	7797.7:1	5.1
Xcode	282.5:1	11.7	2432.3:1	7.3
YouTube	239.5:1	15.0	262.3:1	14.9
YouTube-FS	284.9:1	14.8	499.3:1	14.7

Table 3: H.264 screen capture with Quicktime

Note that screen pixmaps are heterogeneous; mechanisms [27] that were developed for computer generated images need not always achieve good compression factors.

6.1 Inter-update temporal similarity

First, we investigate the similarity between an pixmap and the corresponding displayed pixels. We can avoid sharing fully redundant updates. Partial redundancy requires further processing to avoid sending those redundant pixels. Note that the screen capture mechanism should minimize its share of CPU usage; precluding motion vectors and other mechanisms that locate translated pixels.

6.1.1 Pixmap similarity metric

We measure the inter-update redundancy using a pixmap similarity metric. For each pixmap, we calculate the percentage of pixels that were the same as the corresponding displayed pixel. Thus, a pixel similarity metric of 50 could mean that every other pixel remained the same or the entire top half of the pixmap was similar. These two pixmaps could exhibit different compression performance. We plot the cumulative distribution of the similarity metric for the various usage scenarios in Figure 5.

For the *Avatar* trailer, 9% and 2% of the pixmaps had a similarity metric of 100 while using Windows 7 and Mac OS X, respectively. Even though Windows Media player doubled the pixmap rate (§4.2), the pixmaps covered disjoint regions and did not translate into a similarity metric of 50. Also, a larger share of pixmap updates had less pixel similarity while using Windows 7 than with

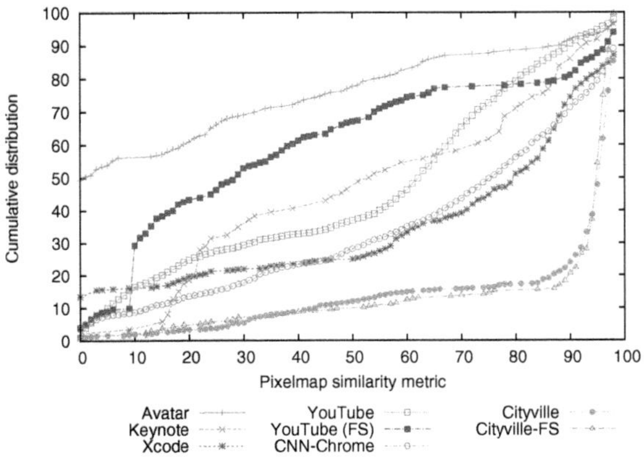

(a) i7-Mac

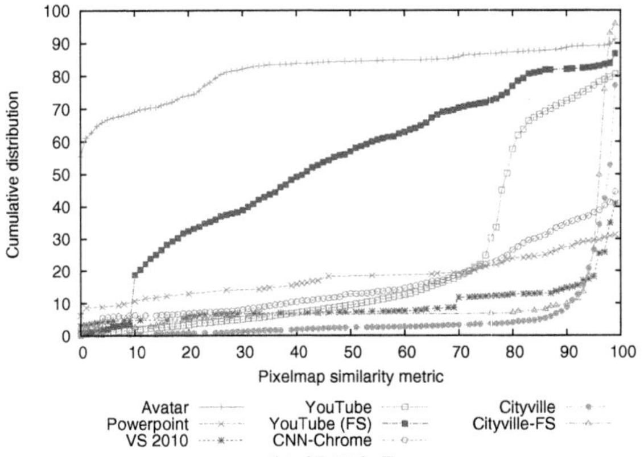

(b) i7-Win7

Figure 5: Pixel similarity from prior update

scenario	i7-Mac				i7-Win7			
	alpha-0	*alpha-255*	*RGB(5:6:5)*	*bitmap*	*alpha-0*	*alpha-255*	*RGB(5:6:5)*	*bitmap*
Avatar	39.3:1	39.0:1	46.9:1	89.3:1	14.1:1	12.1:1	14.1:1	35.1:1:1
Cityville	67.0:1	66.2:1	9.1:1	99.0:1	53.6:1	44.0:1	8.2:1	143.7:1
Cityville-FS	34.2:1	34.0:1	5.3:1	40.0:1	28.7:1	25.2:1	6.0:1	53.5:1
CNN-Chrome	49.5:1	48.5:1	11.7:1	80.1:1	49.2:1	39.3:1	18.0:1	134.0:1
Keynote/PowerPoint	35.8:1	36.0:1	50.6:1	42.9:1	23.8:1	20.5:1	13.3:1	43.9:1
Xcode/VS 2010	82.4:1	81.5:1	33.1:1	142.1:1	42.7:1	36.0:1	28.6:1	82.4:1
YouTube	16.6:1	16.5:1	10.9:1	28.1:1	7.8:1	6.9:1	4.5:1	12.7:1
YouTube-FS	44.6:1	44.6:1	20.8:1	104.0:1	12.9:1	10.8:1	10.3:1	29.2:1

Table 4: Compression factors for various pixmap transformations (followed by Zlib)

Mac OS X. For example, 66% of Mac OS X updates and 79% of Windows 7 pixmaps had a pixel similarity metric of 25 or lower.

For all other scenarios, Windows 7 showed a higher similarity metric than Mac OS X. For example, with Windows 7, between 80% (*PowerPoint*) and 97% (*Cityville*) of the pixmaps had a similarity metric higher than 70. With Mac OS X, these values corresponded to between 50% (*CNN-Chrome*) and 85% (*Cityville-FS*). Windows 7 appears to create more updates, each of which were temporally similar to prior updates at the same screen location.

6.2 Intra-update spatial redundancy

Next, we empirically investigate intra-update spatial redundancy and its impact on compressing the update pixmaps using Zlib [14]. Zlib is a popular lossless compression mechanism that uses a variation of LZ77 [29] algorithm. It is widely available in a range of computing platforms and is an inherent component of Java and .NET. VNC uses Zlib for compressing screen updates.

We tabulate the average compression factor using Zlib for the various application scenarios in Table 2. Higher compression factors are preferred. The compression factor depends on the application scenario with better performance on Mac OS X (because of different compression quality vs CPU usage tradeoff, we use .NET 4.0 - *DeflateStream()*). *Avatar* achieves a compression factor of about 21:1 on Mac OS X and only 8.7:1 in Windows 7. *YouTube* and *YouTube-FS* achieve twice the improvement on Mac OS X. Scenarios which require user interaction (e.g., *PowerPoint*, *Keynote*, *Xcode* and *VS 2010*) achieve compression factors of about 20:1. The improvements are more modest for other scenarios.

For comparison, we repeated the various scenarios and performed an H.264 compressed screen capture using the Quicktime X player on Mac OS X. We analyzed these compressed movies and tabulate the compression factors as well as the frame rates achieved in Table 3. Each GOP on these H.264 encoded movies consist of a sequence of IPBPBPBP frames. The compression factors were computed as a factor of the compressed frame size (I, P or B frames) to the full movie spatial dimension (ie, 1440x900 24 bit pixels for the *C2D* laptop and 1680x1080 for the *i7* laptop). Rather than naively compressing the entire screen, it is likely that the Quicktime compressor only considered changed pixel regions. Otherwise, the frame rate would be constant irrespective of the usage scenario; we observed a frame rate range between 5 and 20. Quicktime achieves compression factors between 84:1 and 6000:1. The Quicktime X player is highly optimized to use the laptop GPUs. The captured movies are also heavily compressed (lossy) using H.264 parameters.

Next, we investigate ways to improve the compression efficiency for high capture rates using lossless Zlib.

6.3 Transformation for better compression

§6.2 showed the poor compressibility of screen pixmaps. Zlib compression only uses intra-update redundancy. We improve compression ratios by incorporating inter-update similarity (§6.1). We also exploit the way pixels are represented in pixmaps. Screen pixmaps are represented in a 32 bit RGBA format with opaque alpha value (0xFF). We make the temporally redundant pixel transparent by setting the alpha value to 0x00. We can then change the RGB values of these transparent pixels to any arbitrary value that will improve the pixmap compression factor; we chose either 0x00 or 0xFF for *alpha-0* and *alpha-255*, respectively. For example, a high pixel similarity metric pixmap, will contain a large sequence of 0x00FFFFFF with *alpha-255* and 0x00000000 with *alpha-0*. The receivers recover the original pixel values by alpha compositing the transformed pixmap.

	C2D						i7					
	Mac			Win7			Mac			Win7		
	μ	max	σ	μ	max	σ	μ	max	σ	μ	max	σ
Avatar	43.9	80.2	15.4	69.0	126.1	24.2	49.7	97.8	19.2	94.2	191.4	36.6
Cityville	5.6	24.4	4.6	41.5	52.7	10.5	6.5	27.9	6.2	65.7	78.5	13.7
Cityville-FS	5.1	27.5	4.6	44.1	54.1	9.3	9.0	36.1	4.0	65.6	95.2	12.0
CNN-Chrome	3.1	25.5	5.0	2.6	46.6	6.5	4.6	44.2	7.3	2.8	61.2	8.8
Keynote	0.1	5.4	0.5				0.2	15.7	1.3			
PowerPoint				0.4	8.3	1.4				0.2	4.6	0.7
Xcode	0.6	6.1	1.3				0.5	12.4	1.2			
VS 2010										1.0	12.1	2.1
YouTube	24.4	48.0	10.4	84.9	123.4	18.2	27.8	55.6	12.0	100.6	150.2	25.4
YouTube-FS	41.7	78.9	14.0	69.3	112.8	16.2	48.9	92.6	14.6	116.9	191.8	32.5

Table 5: Bandwidth consumed for *bitmap* encoding

	C2D						i7					
	Mac			Win7			Mac			Win7		
	μ	max	σ	μ	max	σ	μ	max	σ	μ	max	σ
Avatar	4.0	59.0	6.5	8.9	91.0	9.6	4.1	73.0	8.1	10.2	122.0	13.7
Cityville	19.9	174.0	18.3	30.2	119.0	20.0	35.3	100.0	15.1	58.2	157.0	26.5
Cityville-FS	12.8	112.0	9.3	10.6	73.0	10.5	16.3	143.0	20.9	14.4	172.0	27.4
CNN-Chrome	20.8	134.0	26.6	11.8	188.0	26.7	47.2	175.0	54.5	21.3	117.0	18.8
Keynote	1.0	76.0	5.8				1.0	53.0	4.9			
PowerPoint				2.7	115.0	13.8				3.6	240.0	21.4
Xcode	12.8	85.0	15.7				16.1	75.0	18.8			
VS 2010										49.2	207.0	38.6
YouTube	41.1	82.0	11.8	52.1	163.0	8.7	40.5	108.0	11.7	31.9	156.0	16.9
YouTube-FS	4.9	87.0	8.5	4.8	219.0	16.1	4.8	112.0	11.2	5.7	114.0	11.6

Table 6: Frame rates achieved for *bitmap* encoding

We also investigated two other transformations. For *bitmap*, we separated pixmaps into a similarity byte-map and pixel data. We use 0x00 and 0xFF to represent similar and dissimilar pixels in the byte-map, respectively. The pixel data is a sparse array that stores the 24 bit RGB values of dissimilar pixels. We also considered a lossy colormap transformation to *RGB(5:6:5)* format.

The transformed pixmaps were then Zlib compressed. For the various pixmap transformations, we tabulated the average compression factor for *i7-Mac* and *i7-Win7* scenarios in Table 4. The transformations improved the compression factors achieved with Zlib (Table 2) in all scenarios. For Mac OS X and Windows 7, we see the best improvement in all scenarios for the *bitmap* transformation. *alpha-0* provides the next best improvement except *Avatar* where RGB(5:6:5) doubles the compression factor over Zlib.

For *Avatar* in Windows 7, the transformation only improved the compression factor of 8.67:1 achieved by Zlib to 14.13:1, 12.06:1 and 35.08:1 for *alpha-0*, *alpha-255*, and *bitmap* transformations. This improvement was similar for the *YouTube-FS* scenario, where Zlib achieved a compression factor of 5.95:1, while the transformations improved them to 12.85:1, 10.79:1 and 29.22:1 for *alpha-0*, *alpha-255*, and *bitmap* transformations, respectively.

Even though the computer generated animation of *Cityville-FS* was unsuitable for Zlib (compression factor around 3:1), pixmap transformations showed an order of magnitude improvement (40:1 for Mac OS X and 53:1 for Windows 7). These improvements still dwarf the compression factors achievable with lossy H.24 compression (Table 3). On the other hand, we can achieve higher update rates (discussed in more detail in §6.3.1).

We also showed that the transformations were more effective for highly similar pixmaps (not illustrated for lack of space).

6.3.1 *bitmap transformation performance*

Bitmap uses the inter-update redundancy found in most scenarios to improve Zlib performance. Next, we tabulate the mean, standard deviation and maximum bandwidth consumed as well as the pixmap update rates achieved using a *bitmap* based screen sharing system in Mac OS X and Windows 7 in Tables 5 and 6, respectively.

On average, the *Avatar* clip consumed about 47 and 80 Mbps while achieving 4 and 10 ups on Mac OS X and Windows 7, respectively. Since Windows Media player doubled the update rate, this corresponds to a video playback rate of 5 fps. These values were worse than the 9 Mbps and 24 fps achieved by Quicktime screen capture. Similarly, *YouTube-FS* consumed about 45 and 100 Mbps to achieve a update rate of 4.9 and 5.2 for using Mac OS X and Windows 7, respectively. The .NET 4.0 *DeflateStream()* sacrifices compression efficiency for computation overhead. Regardless, the CPU was the bottleneck in both scenarios. We are investigating ways to automatically detect movie playback and then encode movie pixmaps using hardware assisted H.264 encoding (AV Foundation in Mac OS X and Intel Media SDK for Windows 7).

For *Cityville-FS*, we required 7 and 55 Mbps while achieving on average 15 and 12.5 ups on Mac OS X and Windows 7 respectively. However, the system achieved maximum pixmap rates of 172 ups while consuming 95 Mbps. Similarly, *PowerPoint* and *Keynote* sometimes generated up to 240 and 76 ups. We captured up to 86 updates for *Xcode* and 207 updates for *VS 2010*. The maximum bandwidth consumed for all scenarios was within the capacity of IEEE 802.11n wireless network. The upcoming IEEE 802.11ac also promises significant network capacity improvements.

Even though *bitmap* does not achieve the compression factors achievable with H.264, it compresses them at a higher rate than is even achievable with hardware assisted H.264 encoding. On a wireless LAN network, this tradeoff of higher update rate while using more network bandwidth was acceptable.

7. IMPLEMENTATION EXPERIENCE

Based on the observations described in this paper, we have built and deployed a DisplayCast system [13] for screen capture and distribution. Native implementations in Mac OS X and Windows 7 provide utilities to capture the screen, play them back in real time as well as archive them to a H.264 movie. The various components locate each other using Zeroconf [28]. We provide a HTTP/REST API to control the system. Our system is open sourced.

8. DISCUSSION

We empirically analyzed the performance of pixmap screen capture and showed that the capture rates need to be as high as hundred ups for interactive scenarios. Moore's law advancement in processor capability as well as recent trends of using hardware assisted screen artifacts further exacerbates these rates. We offer practical guidelines for adapting to lower capture rates under resource constrained environments. We devised a simple mechanism to transform inter-update temporal redundancy into intra-update spatial redundancy in order to achieve good compression factors and high capture rates. We incorporate our findings into a practical and open sourced system that works in Mac OS X and in Windows 7 [13].

Newer operating systems such as Mac OS X Mountain Lion [1] and Windows 8 [8] are introducing tablet inspired features such as swiping, pinching, zooming and other operations that are invoked using multi-touch gestures. These operations make extensive use of hardware acceleration capabilities that are built into modern computers. Though these features improve the user experience, they generate enormous amounts of screen updates. For example, a full screen swipe that is tied to the rate in which the user flips the trackpad generates a full screen update that shifts the entire screen by one pixel. High resolution retina displays can also increase the number of pixels in each update. There is a need to implement higher capture rates to avoid losing pixels on these newer systems.

9. REFERENCES

[1] Apple - OS X mountain lion. `http://www.apple.com/osx/`.

[2] Demoforge mirage driver (dfmirage video hook driver). `http://www.demoforge.com/dfmirage.htm`.

[3] GLUT and OpenGL utility libraries. `http://www.opengl.org/resources/libraries/glx/`.

[4] Laptop to TV with Intel® wireless display (WiDi). `http://www.intel.com/content/www/us/en/architecture-and-technology/intel-wireless-display.html`.

[5] Remote desktop connection. `http://windows.microsoft.com/en-US/windows7/products/features/remote-desktop-connection`.

[6] Stream movies and music wirelessly with airplay. `http://www.apple.com/ipad/features/airplay/`.

[7] WHDI - wireless home digital interface. `www.whdi.org`.

[8] Windows 8 release preview. `http://windows.microsoft.com/en-US/windows-8/release-preview`.

[9] Windows mirror drivers. `http://msdn.microsoft.com/library/ff568315.aspx`.

[10] Multimedia redirection improvements in Windows 7 and WS2008 R2. `http://goo.gl/W7Uv4`, July 2009.

[11] Boyaci, O., and Schulzrinne, H. Bass application sharing system. In *IEEE International Symposium on Multimedia* (Berkeley, CA, USA, 2008), ISM '08, pp. 432–439.

[12] CCITT Recommendation T.81. *Digital Compression and Coding of Continous-Tone Still Images - Requirements and guidelines*. International Telecommunication Union(ITU), Geneva, Sept. 1992.

[13] Chandra, S., and Rowe, L. A. DisplayCast: a high performance screen sharing system for intranets. In *ACM Multimedia 2012* (Nara, Japan, Oct. 2012). `https://github.com/DisplayCast`.

[14] Deutsch, P. Deflate compressed data format specification version 1.3. RFC 1951, May 1996.

[15] Estes, C. D., and Mayer-Patel, K. The n-dimensional display interface: a more elastic narrow waist for the display pipeline. In *MMSys '12* (Chapel Hill, NC, USA, Feb. 2012), pp. 119–129.

[16] Hilbert, D. M., Turner, T., Denoue, L., and Sankarpandian, K. Autonomous presentation capture in corporate and educational settings. In *IADIS e-Learning'08* (Amsterdam, The Netherlands, July 2008), pp. 239–246.

[17] Humphreys, G., Eldridge, M., Buck, I., Stoll, G., Everett, M., and Hanrahan, P. WireGL: a scalable graphics system for clusters. In *SIGGRAPH '01* (Los Angeles, CA, USA, 2001), pp. 129–140.

[18] Kim, H., Jeong, J., Hwang, J., Lee, J., and Maeng, S. Scheduler support for video-oriented multimedia on client-side virtualization. In *MMSys '12* (Chapel Hill, NC, USA, 2012), pp. 65–76.

[19] loup Gailly, J., and Adler, M. zlib: A massively spiffy yet delicately unobtrusive compression library. `zlib.net`.

[20] Richardson, T., and Levine, J. The remote framebuffer protocol. RFC 6143, Mar. 2011.

[21] Richardson, T., Stafford-Fraser, Q., Wood, K. R., and Hopper, A. Virtual network computing. *IEEE Internet Computing 2* (Jan. 1998), 33–38.

[22] Satoshi, U. MetaVNC - a window aware VNC. `http://metavnc.sourceforge.net/`.

[23] Schmidt, B. K., Lam, M. S., and Northcutt, J. D. The interactive performance of slim: a stateless, thin-client architecture. In *SOSP '99* (Charleston, SC, USA, 1999), pp. 32–47.

[24] Sun, Y., and Tay, T.-T. Analysis and reduction of data spikes in thin client computing. *J. Parallel Distrib. Comput. 68*, 11 (Nov. 2008), 1463–1472.

[25] von Hoffman, J. T. *Guide to Distributed PowerPoint*. Boston University, 2001.

[26] Wallace, G., and Li, K. Virtually shared displays and user input devices. In *USENIX Annual Technical Conference '07* (Santa Clara, CA, USA, June 2007), pp. 375–380.

[27] Yun, H. C., Guenter, B. K., and Mersereau, R. M. Lossless compression of computer generated animation frames. *ACM Trans. Graph. 16* (October 1997), 359–396.

[28] Zero configuration networking (zeroconf). `http://www.zeroconf.org/`.

[29] Ziv, J., and Lempel, A. A universal algorithm for sequential data compression. *IEEE Transactions on Information Theory 23*, 3 (May 1977), 337–343.

El-pincel - A Painter Cloud Service for Greener Web Pages

Bhojan Anand, Lee Kee Chong, Ee-Chien Chang, Mun Choon Chan
Akkihebbal L. Ananda, Wei Tsang Ooi
School of Computing, National University of Singapore
{banand,cleekee,changec,chanmc,ananda,ooiwt}@comp.nus.edu.sg

ABSTRACT

Due to their thin size, vivid colors, high contrast and power efficiency, OLED (Organic Light-Emitting Diode) display and its variants such as AMOLED (Active Matrix OLED) displays are increasingly replacing traditional LCD (Liquid Crystal Display) screens in smart phones. However, the power efficiency of OLED screens greatly depends on the luminance and colors of the displayed contents on the screen. Web browsing is one of the most widely used applications in mobile devices [8]. In this paper, we present our cloud service, which intelligently re-paints the web pages in real-time with power efficient colors and HVS (Human Visual System) based tone mapping techniques, without adversely affecting the identity (brand color) of the web pages as well as the user's browsing experience. El-pincel helps to save up to 60% of OLED energy with color combinations that ensure good legibility and pleasing affective response to human eyes.

Categories and Subject Descriptors

H.5.2 [**Information Interfaces & Presentation**]: User Interfaces; I.4.3 [**Image Processing & Computer Vision**]: Enhancement

General Terms

Algorithms, Design, Human Factors, Experimentation

Keywords

OLED display, low power, color transformation, tone mapping, cloud service, color harmony, browsing

1. INTRODUCTION

The current generation of mobile smartphones are frequently used as mobile PC replacements that can edit documents, browse the web, check emails, and play games. To enable the usage of these rich applications, smartphones are now equipped with reasonably fast CPUs, large memory, bigger displays and fast network connections. However, these capabilities come at the cost of battery lifetime as battery technologies are not growing in par with the rest of the hardware. In modern smartphones, the three main sources of power consumption are, 1) the CPU, 2) the display, and 3) the network interfaces, among which the display alone consumes more than 45% of the overall system energy [2].

Figure 1: Webpages designed using Brand Colors in their Logos

Power efficiency of OLED displays greatly depends on two parameters - the color and the luminance of the content being displayed. The higher the luminance of the content, the more power it consumes. In most OLED displays, blue color consumes more power than green or red color. In this work we present a cloud service (*El-pincel*) for web pages which exploits the properties of OLED display and characteristics of HVS, to repaint the web pages to power efficient versions for OLED based mobile devices. El-pincel is an extended version of our previous abstract paper and demonstration [1]. The cloud service handles text, background colors and images which are the most common objects in a web page. Our solution is based on the following key observations.

1. Power consumption of OLED displays depends on the luminance and color of the content [2].

2. For texts in web pages, readability and brand colors are more important than color fidelity. Most organisations have a standard color scheme for their web pages, logos, banners, etc. In this paper we call it as *brand colors*. For example, DBS bank [9] and Verizon [28] web pages primarily use a shade of Red and Black color (Figure 1). These are the main colors in their corporate logos. Our approach is based on brand color. The web pages are re-painted with respect to the brand colors of the original pages. This is in contrast to the previous works [12], where the entire web page is darkened and mapped to shades of green color. Such approaches make web pages look dark and greenish. This may bring dissatisfaction to the owners or designers of the web sites. Moreover, it won't be interesting to view all web pages in same color for the users. In addition, these approaches are browser dependent and work only for a particular browser.

3. Some browsers allow the users to define their own CSS (Cascading Style Sheet) to repaint the color of text and back-

ground layouts in a web page with a different color. However, most modern web pages utilise more than one color to display text and background. Our observations show that most of the popular webpages use two or more background colors and three or more foreground colors. By applying the user defined CSS, all the different colors will be transformed into a single color, losing the web pages' design aesthetics and color harmony.

4. For images (and videos), color fidelity is important. Hence, we cannot abruptly change the colors of these contents. We exploit HVS properties to dynamically change the colors and luminance of the images for power efficiency while preserving their visual quality. HVS properties:- 1) HVS has different sensitivity to different colors. The human eyes are more sensitive towards green than blue, therefore green appears much brighter when both colors are having the same absolute brightness [3]. The majority of the photoreceptor cones present in human eyes are sensitive to green and red, and only a few are sensitive to blue. Hence, a given pixel color can be mapped to a power efficient color that produces same level of perceived brightness. 2) HVS is more sensitive to local contrast over global contrast [21, 20]. 3) HVS has a nonlinear perceptual response to luminance [13]. For example, a source having a luminance only 18% of a reference luminance appears about half as bright [24]. The lightness perception to human eyes is roughly logarithmic. When an image is sufficiently bright, reducing some amount of brightness to the image will result in less noticeable difference as compared to reducing the same amount of brightness to a darker image.

5. The computational cost of image tone mapping in mobile clients is expensive and often results in low or negative power saving and higher latency [12]. Hence, in El-pincel, color transformations are completely done in the cloud and cached for reuse. With the exponential growth rate of smartphones, the demand for computation, storage at the server side and possibility for reuse will continueously increase.

With these insights, we devised an integrated solution which handles texts and images (adaptable to videos). We have developed novel schemes and algorithms based on the observations described above. We evaluated our approach using a combination of analytical and user testing. Our results show that we are able to save up to 60% of the display power with no perceptible loss to text readability and color harmonicity of a web page, and save up to 50% of the display power for images in a web page if the user is willing to tolerate a small amount of loss in image quality. In overall, the main contributions of this paper are as follows:

1. We present a *brand color* based novel approach for intelligently changing colors of the textual contents in a web page to power efficient colors without compromising readability.

2. We present *HVS* based novel approach for transforming images to their power efficient versions.

3. We present a *configurable cloud service* that can be configured dynamically by the user based on client's energy efficiency requirements.

4. We show that power savings can be achieved for almost all web pages. We also show that the loss of quality due to image and video transformations is kept minimum using industry standard *objective* quality metrics and *subjective* user study.

2. BACKGROUND - OLED

Organic light-emitting diode (OLED) is an emerging display technology that uses a thin film of organic compounds which emit light in response to electric current. The power consumption of OLED displays depends on the luminance and color of the content being displayed. We describe the dependencies below at higher level for easier understanding.

The organic components for each sub-pixel (red, green, blue) on the display are individually powered up to illuminate the pixels. Hence, power consumption of OLED displays depends on the luminance of the displayed content.

The OLED material used to produce blue light degrades significantly more rapidly than the materials that produce other colors. This results in a faster decrease of blue light output relative to the other colors. Manufacturers address this issue by optimising the size of the red, green and blue sub-pixels to reduce the current density through the sub-pixels, in order to equalise lifetime at full luminance [26]. This leads to an uneven power consumption by objects with different colors (while their luminance is constant). In this case, an image with a dominant blue shade consumes more power than an image with a dominant red or green shade.

3. RELATED WORK

Chuang et al. [14] proposes a color mapping algorithm that swaps current colors with an iso-lightness color set within a certain restrictions, so that the overall lightness of the final display is still the same with the original display. The original colors are significantly changed in the process and not suitable to be applied to photos and videos, in which color accuracy is important.

Dong et al. [11] describes two approaches of reducing power consumption of OLED displays through structured color transformation of standard background and foreground GUI objects, or unstructured transformation of individual pixel colors of arbitrary GUI elements. The approaches dramatically alters the original color of the displayed objects, again making it unsuitable for contents which are sensitive to color fidelity changes, such as images and videos. In their next paper [12], foreground images are simply darkened without considering HVS characteristics. Moreover, pixel-by-pixel processing is compute-intensive task.

Chulwoo et al. [18] describes a power-constrained contrast enhancement algorithm for OLED displays using log-modified histogram equalisation (LMHE) scheme, which reduces over stretching artifacts of conventional histogram equalisation technique. The algorithm is constrained by OLED power model. Their approach is more focused on contrast enhancement than power saving.

There are various works on backlight scaling for conserving display energy [17] [22] [4] [6] [5]. In all these works the content is dynamically brightened and the backlight is dimmed. A more efficient way of backlight scaling using HVS aware tone mapping is proposed by Iranli et al. [13]. However, these methods cannot be applied to OLED display which do not utilise a backlight.

4. SYSTEM DESIGN

4.1 Design Objectives

The major design objectives of our cloud service are listed below.

- Maps set of colors in a page to energy efficient colors according to user/client requirements (remaining battery level, quality requirements).
- Apply color transformation to the source file instead of the finally rendered pixels for more efficient power saving.
- Ensures readability of text, brand color identity, color fidelity of foreground images.

- Makes the solution Browser Independent. It should work seamlessly with all types of browsers.
- Introduces no additional CPU/GPU load in mobile devices, which may reduce the efficiency in power saving.

4.2 The System Components

The components of El-pincel are shown in Figure 2.

4.2.1 *Client Analyzer (CA)*

The Client Analyzer (CA) is the primary contact point for clients. CA gets information about a client such as device model, screen size, remaining battery power, user specified requirements (e.g. power efficiency or quality level) from the *Proxy Configurator (PC)* of the client and the HTTP requests from the browsers of the client.

Proxy Configurator (PC). Proxy configurator is a small piece of software at the client side that performs the following two tasks. 1) It configures the mobile device to use the *El-pincel* service while browsing web pages using any browser by changing the global proxy settings. 2) It collects *device specific information* (device model, remaining battery level) from the device and *user requirements (UR)* (power efficiency required, enable/disable image transformation) through user interface and transfers the data to CA. These two tasks are performed only once when the PC application is started by the user.

Communication between CA and PC. To transform the *device specific information* and *UR*, the CA do not make an explicit contact with the PC. Instead, the PC simply adds all these data in a format predefined by the CA to each web browser's proxy authentication option field. We exploit the proxy authentication service introduced in the HTTP/1.1 protocol [16] to transfer these data from mobile client to CA. When a browser makes a request to a webpage, these non-HTTP specific details are automatically added to the HTTP header by the by the browser.

The CA checks the HTTP header of each client's request packet for the *Proxy-Authorization* header field. If it does not exist, the CA sends back a *407 (Proxy Authentication Required)* response (shown in Figure 3), containing a *Proxy-Authenticate* header field, requesting for client's credentials. The client will then respond by resending the original packet with a *Proxy-Authorization* header field, containing the credentials in the form of *username:password*, encoded as Base64 string. (Note:- For the subsequent requests, the browsers will automatically add the *Proxy-Authorization* header field).

The client's *device specific information* and *user requirements* are sent through the *username* part of the credentials. The CA will decode the Base64 encoded credentials upon receiving the resent packet, and extract out these data from the *Proxy-Authorization* HTTP header of the HTTP request packet.

By exploiting proxy authentication service, we identify the client's requirement without having to implement a client-side proxy to intercept client's packets and insert custom fields to communicate with the server-side proxy. In our approach, the *Proxy Configurator (PC)* can be any Android application capable of setting proxy configurations with proxy authentication. In the current implementation, the CA expects only Device Model (DM) and UR. The UR comprises of power efficiency (percentage of power saving required) and a flag for image tone mapping.

Handling requests for HTTP pages. If a request comes from non-OLED device or unknown OLED device, the CA simply forwards the request to the source web server and simply acts as a forwarding proxy. Unknown OLED devices are those devices for which the El-pincel service do not have the *power model* in its database. If the request comes from a known OLED device, CA forwards the

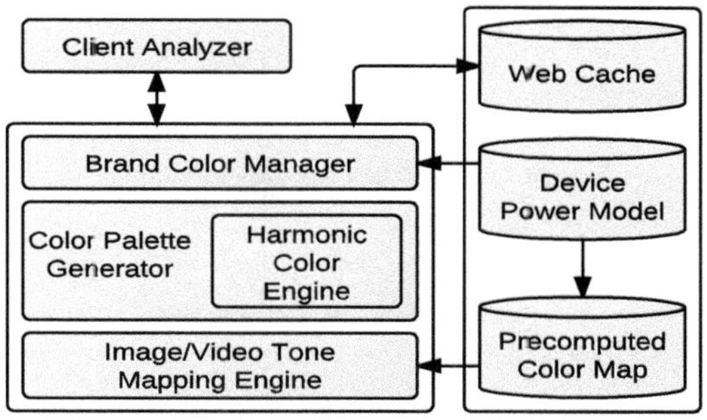

Figure 2: El-pincel Cloud System Architecture

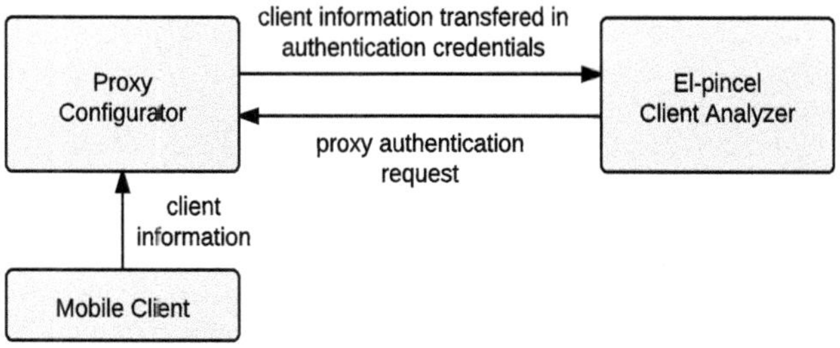

Figure 3: Client Information Transfer

URL, UR and DM to *brand color manager* (described below) for further processing.

4.2.2 *Brand Color Manager (BCM)*

Brand Color Manager gets the key image associated with the page request. The key image can be a favicon, a logo or any image with a filename *keyimage.png or keyimage.gif* located in the root of the web server. Almost all websites use *favicons* today. Favicons are usually placed in predefined URL '/favicon', which is relative to the server root. Favicons of many websites are made up of brand colors. Most of the time the favicon is simply a miniature of the company logo image. For example, Intel and our university websites use their logos as favicons (Figure 4). Hence, it is one of the useful tool to easily obtain the brand color. If favicon is not present, BCM looks for other key images. The key image is used to generate one or more base colors for the page using the *base color generation algorithm* given below. If a key image is not found, then it will default to *black* color which uses the lowest possible power.

Algorithm: Base Color Generation
Input:website URL (URL), User Requirements (UR),
Device Model (DM)

- if (cache entry exists for URL & UR & DM) then {
return the style sheet;
}
- if (cache entry does NOT exists for URL) then {
** Obtain the key image (e.g. favicon image, logo) of website;*
** Create a RGB histogram of the key image;*
** Quantise to 4096 web safe colors (256×256×256) colors;*
** Rank the colors according to their presence in key image and select the top 'n' colors; (Figure 5)*
}
- Select the specific RGB-Power model (Figure 6) for the device.
- Return 'm' power efficient colors from the 'n' colors, with power consumption of each color determined from equation (1);

Power consumption of a pixel displaying color depends on the power model of the OLED display module specific to each device, and is calculated using the equation below:

$$E(C) = E_R\, r' + E_G\, g' + E_B\, b' \tag{1}$$

Figure 4: Logos are used as Favicons

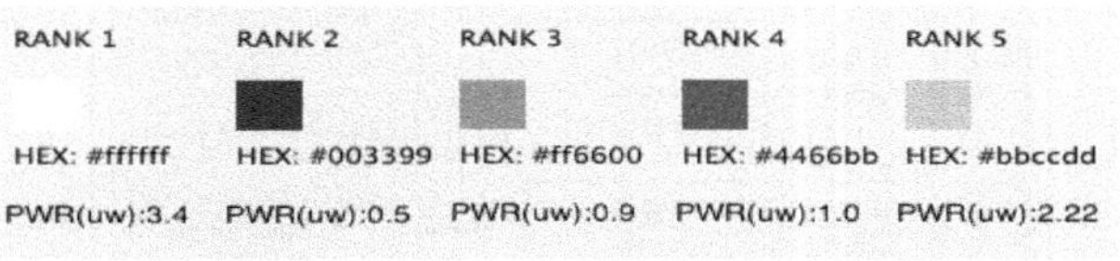

Figure 5: Color Extraction and Ranking from NUS favicon

where r', g', b' are the gamma-corrected linear RGB values of color C. E_R, E_G, and E_B are constants that varies with different OLED displays [10], and are determined from the device-specific power model in Figure 6.

Figure 5 shows the top *n* colors picked from favicon of our university website. The colors are ranked according to their presence in the logo. Total number of pixels in the image representing a color determines the presence of the color in the image. A color with higher presence gets higher rank. The power required in $\mu Watt$ to display one pixel in the selected color with respect to the power model in Figure 6 is also shown in the image.

4.2.3 Color Palette Generator

The Color Palette Generator selects a color from 'm' base colors based on the requirements from client (e.g. level of power saving required). Then, using the color wheel [7] depicted in Figure 7 it selects set of *monochromatic* (from types I,V,T) and *complementary* colors (from types I, Y, X) for the color palette. From these colors a set of monochromatic and complementary colors which are harmonic to each other are selected by the **Harmonic Color Engine**. From the selected set, the monochromatic colors are used as background colors and the complementary colors are used as foreground colors to ensure sufficient *chromatic contrast*. These colors are used to generate new CSS after assuring W3C recommended [25] amount of *achromatic contrast* (or brightness difference) between them for good legibility. W3C recommends minimum 125 units of brightness difference between two colors for good color visibility. Color brightness is determined by:

$$Br = 0.299\, r' + 0.587\, g' + 0.114\, b' \qquad (2)$$

where, Br is brightness and r', g' and b' are gamma corrected values of the red, green and blue sub pixels.

Note: W3C takes this equation from a formula for converting RGB values to YIQ values. This brightness value gives a perceived brightness for a color.

4.2.4 Image Tone Mapping Engine

The image tone mapping engine converts all images to power

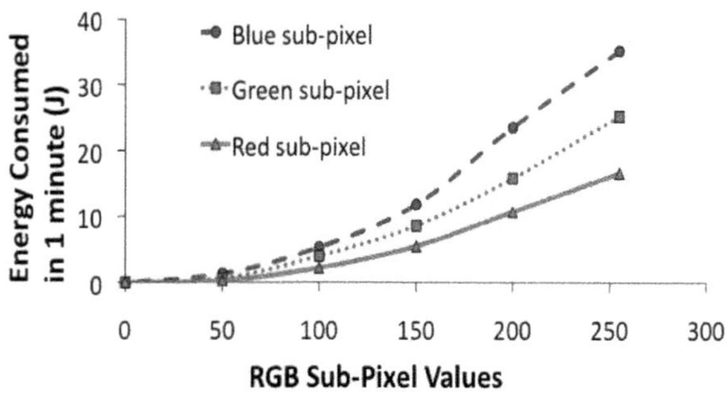

Figure 6: RGB Pixels Power Model(Google Nexus One OLED display)

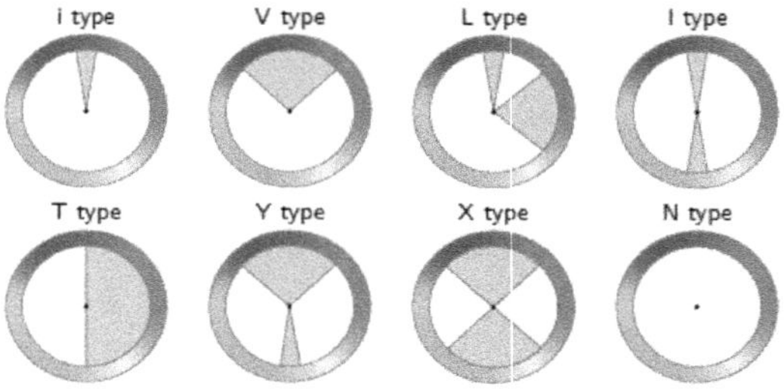

Figure 7: Color (Hue) Wheel Types

efficient version based on the client requirements. We devised a HVS based approach to convert the images without distorting the visual quality. The details are described in Section 4.3.

4.2.5 Web Cache

Most of the current research works on mobile energy management are focused on saving energy in the mobile client alone for longer battery lifetime. Saving energy on one computer causes another to consume more energy, increasing overall carbon emissions [19]. El-pincel stores the processed CSS stylesheets and images of popular (top *n*) sites in cache for future retrieval by the same user or new users. This key component saves power at the server side, reducing overall energy consumption of the whole system instead of simply mitigating the required energy consumption to the server side. We cache different versions of modified pages for each device model and each power efficiency requirement. To minimise the cache size, the power efficiency requirements are discretised into 16 levels in multiples of 5%. That is, 5%, 10%, 15% .... 80% power saving levels. For instance, if *n* is 20, the cache will have data for *10 x 16 x number of device models* which is a manageable size for cloud storage. The cache is updated with HTTP *Conditional-GET* whenever a request comes for a page.

4.3 Basic Approaches for Image Tone Mapping

There are a few basic approaches to generate energy efficient images:

Approach 1 - Simple Darkening: Darken the image to appropriate levels. By decreasing the RGB sub-pixel values of each pixel uniformly by a constant value, the brightness, *Br* can be reduced (3). Such naive approaches result in degradation of the content (image or video frame) quality. If the image is already dark, a large number of pixels will saturate resulting in a flat image with loss of contrast compared to the original image (Figure 8).

$$Br_{reduced} = Br_{original} - x \qquad (3)$$

Approach 2 - Relative Darkening Alternatively, the brightness of each pixel can be reduced by a certain percentage to avoid saturation (4). For example, 10% brightness reduction on a sub-pixel with a value of 200 will reduce the value to 180, whereas if the sub-pixel value is 10, it will be reduced to 9. However, this results in the compression of the color histogram, which results in greater contrast loss (Figure 8).

$$Br_{reduced} = Br_{original} \times y\% \qquad (4)$$

4.4 HVS based Tone Mapping for Images

4.4.1 Overview

As discussed in section 3, simple color mapping approach is not applicable for images where it is important to preserve color hue. Also, reducing brightness of an image results in contrast loss, although HVS is more sensitive to local contrast than global contrast.

Original image   Simple darkening   Relative darkening

Figure 8: Effects of basic approaches on Image Contrast

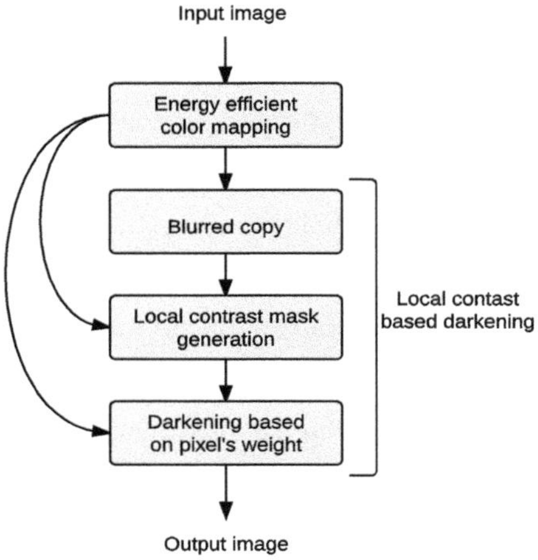

Figure 9: Image Transformation Flowchart

We have devised an algorithm (Figure 9) that transforms an image so that the power saving can be approximated to the required level. This is achieved by distributing the exact required power saving to each pixel of the image.

Instead of simple color mapping, we apply *energy efficient color mapping* that is constrained by luminance, hue and saturation of the original colors. Luminance between original and mapped color is maintained in this step. To retain the local contrast, we generate a local contrast mask that applies less weight on area with higher local contrast, which is approximated by detecting edges in an image. Using *local contrast based darkening* technique, area with higher weight values (lower local contrast) will experience higher drop in luminance to achieve power saving.

4.4.2 Energy Efficient Color Mapping

Given a power model for an OLED display, a one to one mapping from the original color to energy efficient color is generated. This is an offline process in which the mapping is computed once for each power model and stored in the El-pincel database. The mapping for each color is decided by solving an optimisation problem as follows.

For each color C_0, we want to map it to a $C' = (r', g', b')$ with minimum power consumption subjected to some constraints on the differences between C' and C_0. Specifically, given $C_0 = (r_0, g_0, b_0)$ we want to

$$\begin{aligned} \text{minimise} \quad & E(C') \\ \text{subject to} \quad & L(C') \geq L(C_0) \\ & |H(C') - H(C_0)| \leq a \\ & (1-b)\cdot S(C_0) \leq S(C') \leq (1+b)\cdot S(C_0) \end{aligned}$$

where a, b are configurable parameters that controls the strictness

Figure 10: Local Contrast Mask

of the constraints. In our implementation, $a = 9$ and $b = 0.25$ provides the optimal balance between power saving and image distortion.

The function to minimise is the power consumption (in microwatts) of the pixel displaying the color, determined from equation (1).

Luminance, L(C) is the perceived brightness of color C derived from equation (2).

$H(C)$ and $S(C)$ is based on the hue and saturation component of the HSV color space.

Hue, $H(C)$, measures the similarity of color C to well described color such as red, green and blue.

$$H(C) = \operatorname{atan2}(\sqrt{3}\cdot(g-b), 2\cdot(r-g-b)) \tag{5}$$

Saturation, $S(C)$, describes the colorfulness of color C from grayscale to pure color.

$$S(C) = \frac{\max(r,g,b) - \min(r,g,b)}{\max(r,g,b)} \tag{6}$$

4.4.3 Local Contrast Based Darkening

The energy efficient color mapped (EECM) image is passed through a Gaussian blur filter with a suitable blur radius. Each pixel value of the blurred copy is then subtracted from the corresponding pixel value of the EECM image to generate the local contrast mask (Figure 10). The local contrast mask acts as a weight map for pixel darkening with each value in the weight map corresponds to a weight, $W(x)$ to determine the intensity of darkening for pixel x.

The weight is further adjusted for each pixel x based on current power consumption of the pixel. The more power the pixel consumes, the higher is the adjusted weight.

$$W'(x) = W(x) \cdot \frac{P(x)}{\sum_{n=0}^{N} P_{max}(x)} \tag{7}$$

$P_{max}(x)$ is the maximum power consumption of a pixel in the current power model.

Target power saving of each pixel, S_x is then distributed based on each pixel's adjusted weight $W'(x)$.

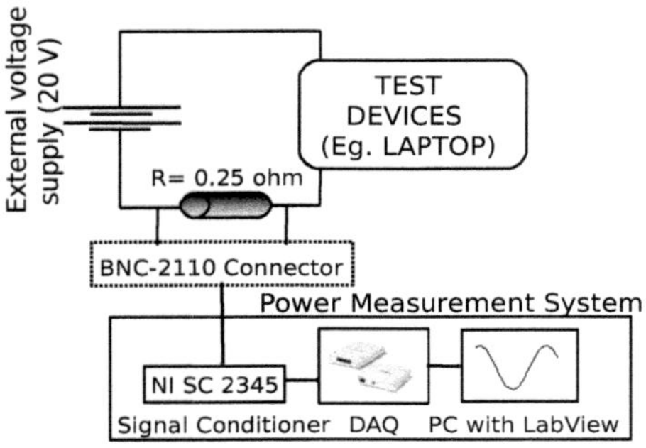

Figure 11: Power Measurement Setup

$$S_x = P_T \cdot \frac{W'(x)}{\sum_{n=0}^{N} W'(n)} \tag{8}$$

where P_T is the total desired power saving.

Finally, the original *RGB* values for each pixel x will be reduced according to assigned target power saving, S_x to get final $R'G'B'$ values:

$$R' = R \cdot d, \quad G' = G \cdot d, \quad B' = B \cdot d \tag{9}$$

with d determines the percentage drop in RGB value for pixel x corresponding to S_x target power saving.

5. EVALUATION & RESULTS

In this section, we present our evaluation methodology and the results. Our goal was to find the amount of power saved by our system and its impact on the quality of the content.

To calculate the amount of power saved, we measured the power consumed by the original and modified content. These results are presented in Section 5.2. We present the objective evaluation using the metrics - Chromatic Contrast (CC) and Achromatic Contrast (ACC) for texts to show that our system follows W3C recommendations and hence it is legible. We use industry standard metrics - Global Contrast Loss (GCL) and Structural Similarity Index (SSIM) for images to show that our approach retains the quality of the content to be close to the original content. We have also conducted two user studies to compare the original and modified contents. The results are presented in Section 5.2.

5.1 Evaluation Methodology

5.1.1 Power Measurements

We performed our power measurements on a Google Nexus One phone using Power Tutor software [27], and arrived at the power model shown in Figure 6. The graph gives the power consumption of a pixel for red, green and blue components. We have used these values to compute precisely the power consumption of original and modified contents. Hence, the results here are based on the OLED screen in Google Nexus One smart phone. However, for most of the phones the blue pixels consume approximately two times the power of red and blue pixel. Hence, it can be easily genralised for most other OLED smartphones.

To measure the current consumption of the cloud service, we run El-pincel in a *Lenovo W500 laptop* and measured the current consumption by removing the battery and then intercepting the power intake. The current consumed (in Amps) was measured using a Data Acquisition (DAQ) device as shown in Figure 11, for a period of over one minute with the voltage set at 20V.

5.1.2 Communication Cost

Due to additional processing and communication, El-pincel introduces the following communication costs: 1) additional communication latency for routing packets through El-pencil, 2) processing latency for color transformation and 3) additional bandwidth. We have written a small script in Java to measure the time between requesting for an object and receiving it at the client side. We measured the processing latency by recording the time taken for image and CSS color transformation. El-pincel do not introduce any additional communication at the client side. With El-pincel, the number of messages sent and received by a client do not change except for *Proxy-Authorization* information exchange which is performed once when the client connects to the El-pincel service. However, it is important that the cloud service hosting El-pincel must be scalable and be provided with sufficient bandwidth to support all client requests.

5.1.3 Quality Measurements - Objective Metrics

Chromatic Contrast (CC) (Difference in Hue) and Achromatic Contrast (ACC) (or Color Brightness Difference) are used for texts to ensure legibility. Traditional metrics for image quality measurement such as Mean Square Error (MSE) and Peak Signal to Noise Ratio (PSNR) tend to ignore the attributes of HVS perception. As described above, HVS has different levels of sensitivity to different colors and different luminance levels. Hence, we used Global Contrast Loss (GCL) and Structural Similarity Index (SSIM) for images. We define *global contrast* as the standard deviation among all the pixel values in the image. A low contrast results in the image appearing "washed out" as all the pixels look similar. For example, if the image is more or less flat (pixel values are close to each other), saturating x% of pixels makes the image complete black. We define GCL as the difference (loss) in global contrast between the modified and original content.

To account for HVS, we used SSIM, a more complex metric which accounts for human perception, and is gaining increasing popularity among the image processing community.

The principle philosophy underlying the SSIM approach is that HVS is highly adapted to extract structural information from visual scenes. In particular, images are highly structured and these structures are important cues about perceived image quality. To account for this property, SSIM breaks an image into patches and compares the quality of each patch with other patches using three attributes of quality; namely luminance, contrast and structural similarity.

Let x be the pixel array of the patch from the original image and y be the pixel array of the patch from the modified image. The SSIM Index between these two patches, SSIM(x,y) is defined in Equation 10. The index ranges from -1 to +1, with -1 representing high distortion and +1 representing low distortion (high quality). The SSIM index will be +1 when a patch is compared with itself.

$$SSIM(x,y) = \frac{(2\mu_x\mu_y + c_1)(2\sigma_{xy} + c_2)}{(\mu_x^2 + \mu_y^2 + c_1)(\sigma_x^2 + \sigma_y^2 + c_2)} \tag{10}$$

where,

- μ_x, μ_y the average of x, y;
- σ_x^2, σ_y^2 the variance of x, y;
- σ_{xy} the covariance of x and y;
- $c_1 = (k_1L)^2$, $c_2 = (k_2L)^2$ two variables to stabilise the division with weak denominator;
- L the dynamic range of the pixel-values (typically, this is $2^{no.of bits\ per\ pixel} - 1$);
- $k_1 = 0.01$ and $k_2 = 0.03$ by default. These values are obtained through experiments [29].

In this paper, we are interested in comparing two complete images. Hence we use the *Mean SSIM* (MSSIM) value, shown in

Equation 11, that averages the SSIM values of all the patch comparisons. More detailed explanation of the SSIM, including its complex mathematical derivation and improvements over the existing approaches is available elsewhere [29].

$$MSSIM(x,y) = \frac{1}{N}\sum_{j=1}^{N} SSIM(x_j, y_j) \tag{11}$$

where N is the number of patches or windows.

5.1.4 *Quality Measurements - Subjective User Study*

As our content transformation techniques are HVS based, the study on the perceived quality with actual human subjects is essential to validate the approach. We did two user studies with 65 student users with different backgrounds. As our service is developed for mobile devices, we let the users view the original and modified contents over the WWW (accessible by any internet connected devices including smartphones) in various lighting conditions (e.g. office, outdoor, day/night) to validate the practical usability of our service. The user demography is shown in Table 1.

Total Number	65 (in age group 19-35)
Gender	Male (55), Female(10)
Photography Experience	Beginner (30), Amateur (27), Semi-professional (6), Professional (2)
Photo Editing Tool	Photoshop (37), Paintshop Pro (2), others (40). [some use morethan 1]
Web Development Experience	Beginner (29), Amateur (24), Semi-professional (11), Professional (1)
Web surfing per day using smartphones/tabs	Never (15), 1-5 Hrs (43), 5-10 Hrs(5), morethan 10 hrs(2)

Table 1: Demographics Statistics for the User Study

Our first user study compares the original and the modified versions of web pages for various energy efficiency settings. The users were asked to rank the readability of the text with 3-point Likert Scale, where 1 indicates *hard to read*, 2 indicates *readable with some efforts* and 3 indicates *clearly readable*. The users also ranked harmonicity of the colors of the page contents with 3-point Likert Scale, where 1 indicates *not harmonious*, 2 indicates *somewhat harmonious* and 3 indicates *harmonious*. Each user was presented with 20 web pages from a pool of original, 20%, 40%, 60% and 80% power saving versions of the web pages.

Our second user study compares our image manipulation technique with the basic approaches. We gave a pair of images from a pool of original, 20%, 40%, 60% and 80% power saving versions of images generated using simple darkening, relative darkening and our HVS based approach. We presented 40 image pairs in random order to the users. The users were asked to select the most visually appealing image in each pair.

5.2 Evaluation Results

The results of accessing web pages on a Google Nexus One smart phone with and without the cloud service are given in Figure 12. The results are shown for saving around 20%, 40% and 60% power. The power saving level is a user selectable parameter in the cloud service. The chromatic contrast of the texts in original pages are 700-800 and that of the modified pages are 650-700. The achromatic contrast (brightness contrast) are 200-250 and 175-220 for original and modified pages respectively. W3C recommended values for minimum chromatic and a chromatic contrast are 500 and 125 respectively [25]. The transformed pages maintain this

Figure 12: Web Page Transformation with El-pincel

requirement while saving required amount of display power. In addition, the colors of a transformed page are harmonious to each other irrespective of the amount of power saved. The pixel by pixel darkening and greening approaches for GUI objects and Texts in previous works [12] do not guarantee harmonicity and contrast (chromatic and achromatic) requirements for comfortable reading. Moreover, as shown in Figure 13 they do not retain brand identity. ESPN brand colors are red, white and black.

We have used a mixed set of popular and unpopular websites for the user study. They are *wordpress.com*, *apple.com*, *netlingo.com*, *foohack.com*, *anuflora.com* and *clickbank.com*. We have selected the pages with less Flash contents as the service is yet to evolve to handle Flash. After removing six invalid users (selected same option for all) with biased entries, the final results are presented in Figure 14. The score is the sum of the Likert scale options (3, 2 or 1) selected by users, where 3 is the best quality. The pages are displayed in random. For up to 60% energy saving, the transformation provides good legibility and harmonicity score close to or higher than the original version while up to 80% is acceptable for most users.

5.2.1 *Evaluation results of HVS based Image Manipulation*

We have selected a random set of six images from Kodak test image database [15] for evaluation. For objective analysis we have

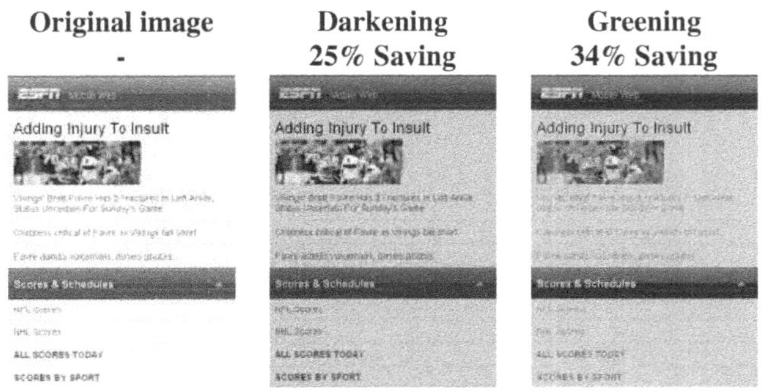

Figure 13: Previous Works - GUI and Texts [12]

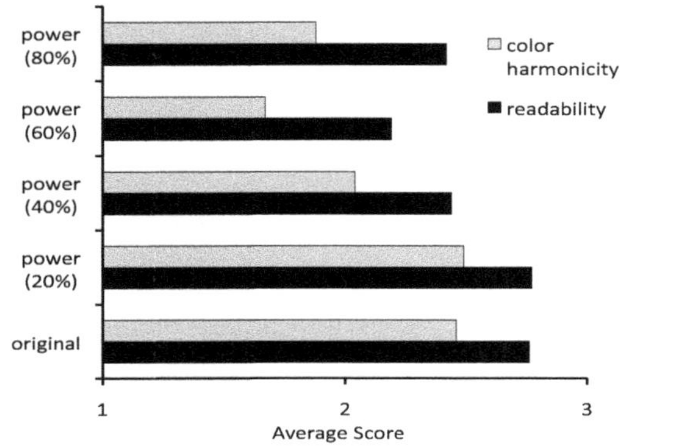

Scores for Readability: 1 - *hard to read*, 2 - *readable with some efforts* and 3 - *clearly readable*.
Scores for Harmonicity: 1 - *not harmonious*, 2 - i *somewhat harmonious* and 3 - *harmonious*.
power(xx%) - is the amount of power saved by the transformed page.

Figure 14: Web Page Transformation - User Study

applied all these approaches on the original images while keeping constant power saving. Power and quality measurement for all the three images (out of six due to space constraint) and their power optimised versions are shown in Figure 15. All approaches are calibrated to consume roughly same amount of power. As expected the simple darkening approach provides lower GCL. However, it experiences lower PSNR and MSSIM. The relative darkening approach gives better MSSIM while its GCL is high making the images flat. Our approach performs better in both the parameters and ensures better visual quality.

The user study shows mixed results. The results after removing biased entries are shown in Figure 16. Normalised performance count is a ratio between total number of times the image appeared in the pair for selection and number of times it is selected as the best. For high power saving, HVS outperforms other and for low power saving, simple darkening approach performs better. This may be due to its capability to retain global contrast when minimal changes are made. Hence, we planed to deploy a power level adaptive approach for our cloud service.

5.2.2 Communication and Processing Cost

The costs were measured while the service is running as a personal cloud service in a *DELL Power Edge T610 Tower Server* with a hexa-core processor, 24GB RAM and 1 TB HDD. We have disabled the cache to get the actual end-to-end latency. El-pincel introduces an additional latency of 250 ms on average between requesting and receiving an image object from a client over a 3G-WCDMA 7.2 Mbps network. For CSS files (for text color transformation), it introduces an average additional latency of 175 ms. For other files, it is about 90 ms. The latency for images and CSS files also

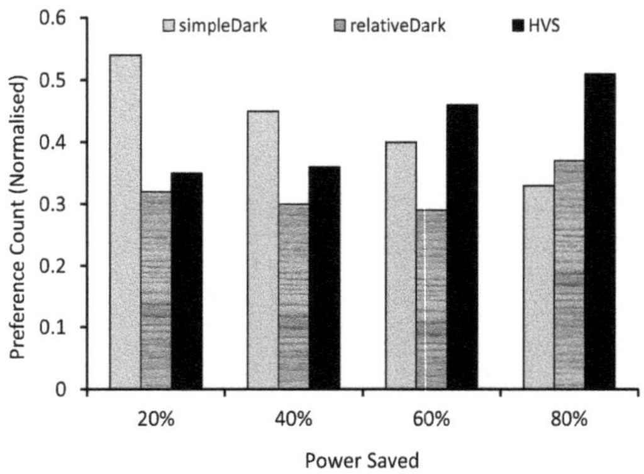

Figure 16: Image Transformation - User Study

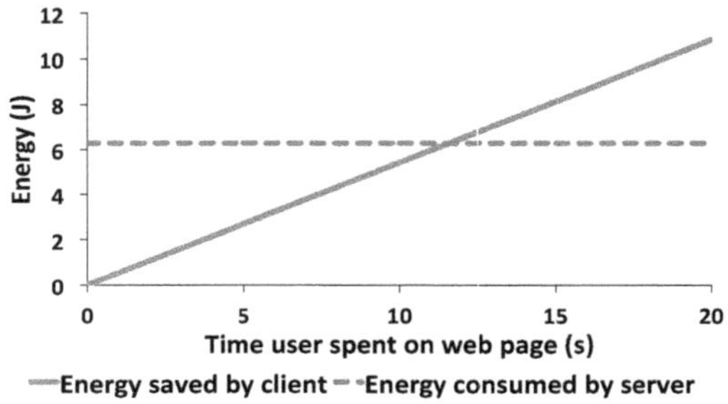

Figure 17: Break-even point between Client Energy Saving and Server Energy Consumption

includes the processing latency (for color transformation) at the El-pincel server, which is less than 100 ms for images and CSS files. However, when objects are retrieved in parallel, the net delay per object is much lower. These latencies can be further reduced with better implementation (optimising the code) of our approach.

5.2.3 Energy Cost

Overall energy efficiency increases when the duration a user spends in reading a power efficient page increases, as there will be a break-even point where the energy saved on client side offsets the energy spent on the cloud for processing and transforming the web pages. This is illustrated in Figure 17. We measured the energy consumption of displaying the home page of *amazon.com* at 50% display power saving on both client and server. Energy consumption on server side is constant because the server is not doing any work once the page is processed and transferred to client. The idle energy consumption of server is not considered as it is negligible as the cloud service scales in size.

From our experiment, the break-even point occurs after 11.5 seconds are spent by user on the web page. Beyond this time, there is a positive net saving of energy. The break-even point differs for different web pages and different amount of required power saving, but our experiment shows that it is reasonably within the time period a person would normally spent on a web page.

5.2.4 Overall Result: System Works Very Well

We now combine the results of both text and image transformations. The trade-offs involved in saving OLED display power are when high energy saving is required, it is clear that the key image based text/background color transformation approach should be combined with HVS based image transformation approach to save 60% (and above) power while providing best possible quality. With this combination, the users experienced an additional latency of 2-5 seconds in getting the contents through the cloud for up to 65 users accessing the service concurrently. For saving power up

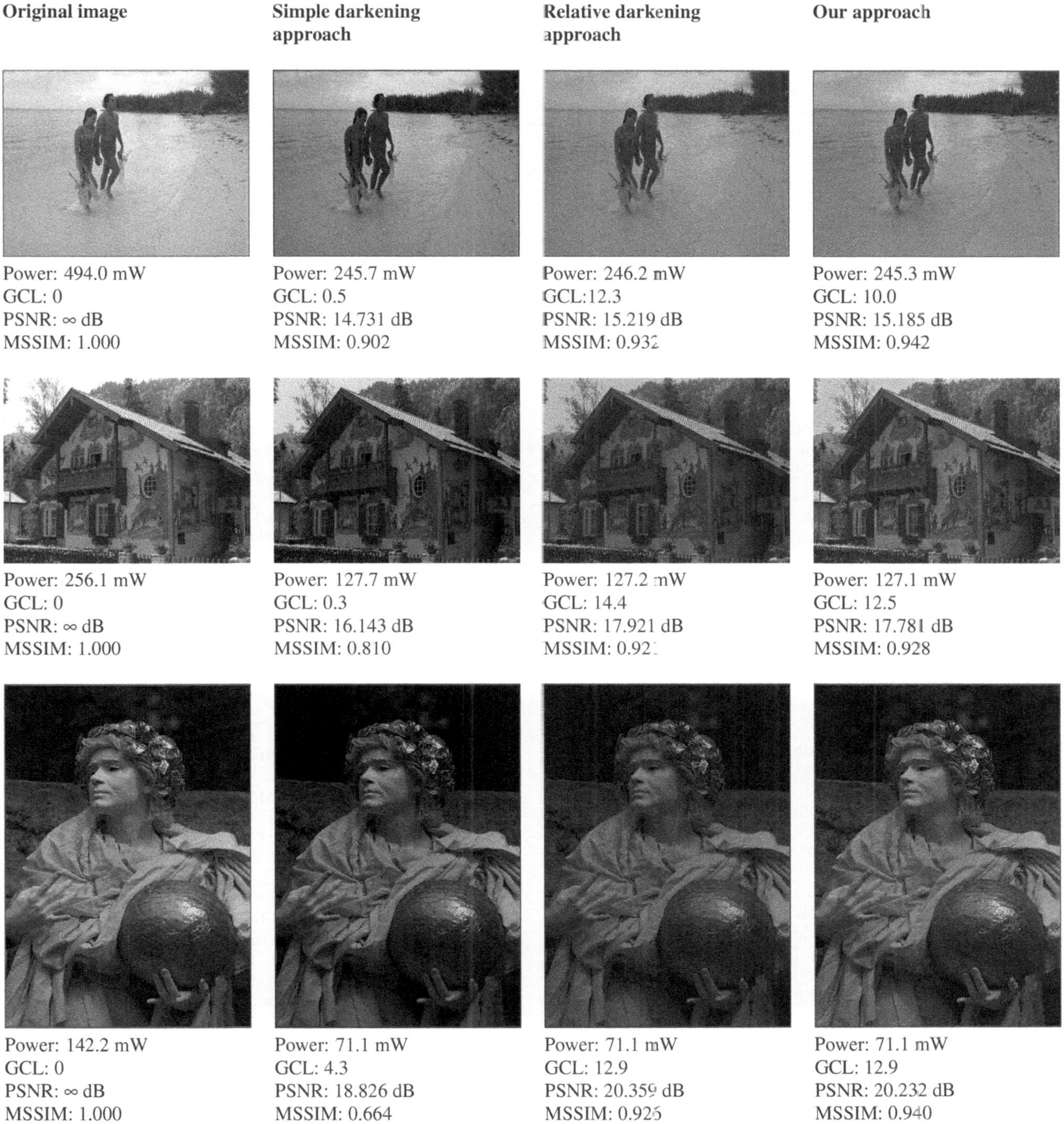

Figure 15: Power Consumption and Quality Measurements

to 50% it is recommended to use simple darkening approach with text transformation. With this combination, the user experienced less than 2 seconds additional latency, as the processing latency for simple darkening is very low. To support large number of users, existing powerful clouds with cluster of servers can be used.

6. DISCUSSION & FUTURE WORK

We presented the web content transformation techniques and the possibility of running it as a cloud service. However, we did not focus on the resource requirements at the cloud. We assumed infinite amount of resources (perfect scalability) in the cloud and did not study the performance issues such as, cache efficiency (cache hit rates) and cloud load balancing. We defer this to future work.

We plan to study the effect of our algorithms on other contents such as flash contents, videos and animations in the future. For live video streaming, performance is critical. As the average changes between the successive frames in a typical video are minimum, we can store the computed contrast mask values of current frame and apply the same values to the successive frames which are similar to the current frame. Such data are easily obtainable in widely used video streaming formats such as MPEG-2. MPEG-2 stores video frames in GOP (group of pictures) structure, where each GOP contains an I frame and a set of P and/or B frames [23].

7. CONCLUSION

We have presented our cloud service which repaints the web texts with power efficient colors while ensuring the legibility and brand color identity. Our service intelligently exploits the properties of HVS to transform images and videos into power efficient versions while ensuring the color fidelity. We have evaluated our approach with both objective and subjective metrics. With our service the mobile phone users can save up to 60% of energy with acceptable quality levels while browsing web pages. As display is the dominant power consuming component, this translates to about 28% of overall system power saving.

The authors would like to thank the anonymous reviewers and our Shepherd, Professor Heng Tao Shen for their comments and help in improving this paper.

8. REFERENCES

[1] Anand, B., Kannan, P. G., Ananda, A. L., and Chan, M. C. El-pincel - a painter cloud service for greener web pages. *ACM Mobisys 2011*, july 2011.

[2] Anand, B., Thirugnanam, K., Sebastian, J., Kannan, P. G., Ananda, A. L., Chan, M. C., and Balan, R. K. Adaptive display power management for mobile games. *ACM Mobisys*, 2011.

[3] Bigelow, R. Perception: Color and luminosity - part 3, the eye and the brain. `http://ronbigelow.com/articles/color-perception-3/perception-3.htm`.

[4] Chang, N., Choi, I., and Shim, H. Dls: dynamic backlight luminance scaling of liquid crystal display. *Very Large Scale Integration (VLSI) Systems, IEEE Transactions on*, 12(8):837 - 846, aug 2004.

[5] Cheng, L., Mohapatra, S., El Zarki, M., Dutt, N., and Venkatasubramanian, N. Quality-based backlight optimization for video playback on handheld devices. *Adv. MultiMedia*, 2007:4–4, January 2007.

[6] Cheng, W.-C., Hou, Y., and Pedram, M. Power minimization in a backlit tft-lcd display by concurrent brightness and contrast scaling. *Design, Automation and Test in Europe Conference and Exhibition, 2004. Proceedings*, volume 1, pages 252 - 257 Vol.1, feb 2004.

[7] Cohen-Or, D., Sorkine, O., Gal, R., Leyvand, T., and Xu, Y.-Q. Color harmonization. *ACM Trans. Graph.*, 25:624–630, July 2006.

[8] ComScore, Inc. The comscore 2010 mobile year in review. Technical documentation, Reston, VA, Feb. 2011.

[9] DBS. Dbs bank global home page. `http://www.dbs.com/home/Pages/default.aspx`, Jan. retrieved 2012.

[10] Dong, M., Choi, Y.-S. K., and Zhong, L. Power modeling of graphical user interfaces on oled displays. *Proceedings of the 46th Annual Design Automation Conference*, DAC '09, pages 652–657, New York, NY, USA, 2009. ACM.

[11] Dong, M., Choi, Y.-S. K., and Zhong, L. Power-saving color transformation of mobile graphical user interfaces on oled-based displays. *Proceedings of the 14th ACM/IEEE international symposium on Low power electronics and design*, ISLPED '09, pages 339–342, New York, NY, USA, 2009. ACM.

[12] Dong, M. and Zhong, L. Chameleon: a color-adaptive web browser for mobile oled displays. *Proceedings of the 9th international conference on Mobile systems, applications, and services*, MobiSys '11, pages 85–98, New York, NY, USA, 2011. ACM.

[13] Iranli, A. and Pedram, M. Dtm: dynamic tone mapping for backlight scaling. *Design Automation Conference (DAC)*, Anaheim, California, June 2005.

[14] J. Chuang, D. W. and MÃűller, T. Energy aware color set. *In Proceedings of the Eurographics Conference*, 2009.

[15] Kodak. Kodak lossless true color image suite. `http://r0k.us/graphics/kodak/`.

[16] Krishnamurthy, B., Mogul, J. C., and Kristol, D. M. Key differences between http/1.0 and http/1.1. *Proceedings of the WWW-8 Conference*, May 1999.

[17] Lai, Y.-K., Lai, Y.-F., and Chen, P.-Y. Content-based lcd backlight power reduction with image contrast enhancement using histogram analysis. *Display Technology, Journal of*, 7(10):550 –555, oct. 2011.

[18] Lee, C., Lee, C., and Kim, C.-S. Power-constrained contrast enhancement for oled displays based on histogram equalization. *Image Processing (ICIP), 2010 17th IEEE International Conference on*, pages 1689 –1692, sept. 2010.

[19] Lu, Y.-H., Qiu, Q., Butt, A., and Cameron, K. End-to-end energy management. *Computer*, 44(11):75 –77, nov. 2011.

[20] Majumder, A. and Irani, S. Contrast enhancement of images using human contrast sensitivity. *Proceedings of the 3rd symposium on Applied perception in graphics and visualization*, APGV '06, pages 69–76, New York, NY, USA, 2006. ACM.

[21] Majumder, A. and Irani, S. Perception-based contrast enhancement of images. *ACM Trans. Appl. Percept.*, 4, November 2007.

[22] Pasricha, S., Luthra, M., Mohapatra, S., Dutt, N., and Venkatasubramanian, N. Dynamic backlight adaptation for low-power handheld devices. *Design & Test of Computers*, 21(5):398–405, Sept.-Oct. 2004.

[23] Pinnacle Systems. Mpeg-2 white paper. Technical documentation, Mountain View, CA, Feb. 2000.

[24] Poynton, C. Gamma faq - frequently asked questions about gamma. `http://www.poynton.com/notes/colour_and_gamma/GammaFAQ.html`.

[25] Ridpath, C. and Chisholm, W. Techniques for accessibility evaluation and repair tools. `http://www.w3.org/TR/AERT#color-contrast`, Nov. retrieved 2011.

[26] Rollings, M. Nexus One - AMOLED Screen under the microscope. `http://www.stealthcopter.com/blog/2010/06/nexus-ones-amoled-screen-under-the-microscope/`.

[27] University of Michigan. *A Power Monitor for Android-Based Mobile Platforms*. `http://powertutor.org/`, 2010.

[28] Verizon. Verizon home page. `http://www.verizon.com`, Jan. retrieved 2012.

[29] Wang, Z., Bovik, A. C., Sheikh, H. R., and Simoncelli, E. P. Image quality assessment: From error visibility to structural similarity. *Transactions on Image Processing*, 13(4):600–612, Apr. 2004.

Low Bitrate Source-filter Model Based Compression of Vibrotactile Texture Signals in Haptic Teleoperation

Rahul Chaudhari
Institute for Media Technology
Technische Universität München
Munich, Germany
rahul.chaudhari@tum.de

Burak Çizmeci
Institute for Media Technology
Technische Universität München
Munich, Germany
burak.cizmeci@tum.de

Katherine J. Kuchenbecker
GRASP Laboratory
MEAM Department
University of Pennsylvania
Philadelphia, USA
kuchenbe@seas.upenn.edu

Seungmoon Choi
Haptics & Virtual Reality Laboratory
POSTECH
Pohang, Korea
choism@postech.ac.kr

Eckehard Steinbach
Institute for Media Technology
Technische Universität München
Munich, Germany
eckehard.steinbach@tum.de

ABSTRACT

Vibrotactile signals convey the touch-based characteristics of object surfaces felt through a tool. They particularly enhance the quality of human-machine interactions by providing realistic haptic perception of textures. In this paper, inspired by the similarities observed between vibrotactile texture signals and speech signals, we present a novel vibrotactile texture codec for bilateral teleoperation, based on well-known speech coding techniques. The proposed low bitrate, high quality codec preserves not only the spectral signature vital to the general feel of the texture, but also important temporal features of the texture signal. We report a compression ratio of 8:1 (12.5%) with a *constant* output bitrate of 4 kbps, and we validate the perceptual transparency of the codec via rigorous subjective tests and analyses.

Categories and Subject Descriptors

E.4 [**Coding and information theory**]: Data compaction and compression; H.5.2 [**User Interfaces**]: Haptic I/O; I.2.9 [**Robotics**]: Sensors, Manipulators, Operator interfaces

Keywords

haptic textures, data compression, teleoperation

1. INTRODUCTION

In the past decade, the emerging field of haptics has introduced a new dimension – physical interactivity – into multimodal interactions. Mediated by specialized haptic interfaces, the possibility to physically affect real/virtual surroundings while perceiving convincing touch feedback has stimulated haptics research worldwide. Multimedia research has recognized the potential of haptics, among other things, for immersive multimedia applications [19] in healthcare [30], education [6], e-commerce and entertainment [3].

Haptic teleoperation [7] (see Figure 1) is a technology that facilitates physical operation in a remote environment, while providing the subjective feeling of being *present* and *immersed* in it. Herein, the human operator controls the activities of a remote robot, while multimodal (audio-visual-haptic) information sensed at the remote site is fed back to her/him. Typically, the audio-visual-haptic modalities are multiplexed together before transmission from the remote teleoperator side to the operator side. During transmission over packet-switched networks like the Internet, (lossy) media coding schemes enable efficient usage of available network resources. These schemes ensure the lowest possible bitrate consumption per modality, while keeping the associated coding distortion in the signal stream as low as possible (ideally below human perceptual thresholds). Thus the immersive capabilities of the system are maximized given the available transmission capacity.

Traditionally, the haptic sense is divided into two submodalities: kinesthetic and tactile. Initially, technical haptic systems concentrated primarily on kinesthetics, which involves large amplitude low-frequency force feedback (imagine pressing against an object). However, they were found lacking in realism due to the absence of high-frequency transients (occurring, e.g., when tapping on hard surfaces) [14] and small-scale surface details occurring during exploration of textured surfaces [23]. Such information can be well represented and delivered by means of vibrotactile stimuli. [13, 14, 23] demonstrate that sensing high-frequency acceleration signals arising out of interactions with the (remote) environment and incorporating them as tactile feedback to the human leads to a significant improvement in the perceived realism of haptic interaction. Improved immersion and/or performance gains have been obtained due to such tactile feed-

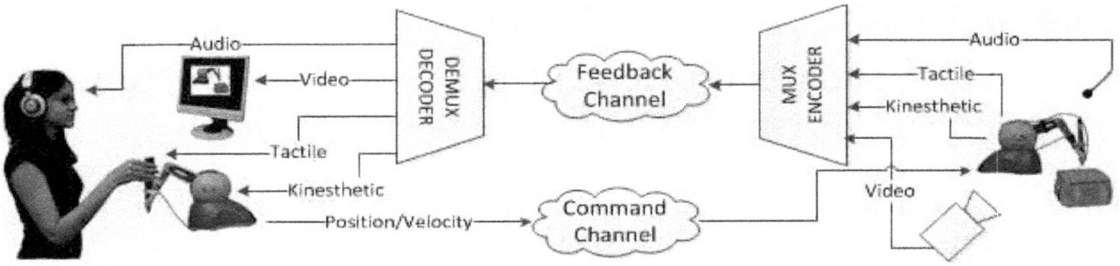

Figure 1: Block schematic of a typical multimodal teleoperation system (based on [7]). Audio-visual-haptic signals from the teleoperator side are individually encoded and multiplexed together before transmission to the operator side. At the operator side, after demultiplexing, respective decoders reconstruct the corresponding signals for presentation to the operator.

back in inspection, exploration and manipulation tasks in general [13] and in specific applications like telesurgery [22].

Transmission of digitized haptic data for realtime teleoperation and its storage for later playback necessitate data compression. This necessity is further accentuated by the trend towards including multiple channel haptic feedback for bimanual [22] and multi-finger interaction [8], increasing the data volume by multiples. Moreover in teleoperation, as mentioned before, haptic signals will typically be multiplexed with the associated (1 Mbps – 40 Mbps) video and (22 kbps – 200 kbps) audio signals which are themselves bitrate-hungry. Such multiplexing further motivates the development of techniques for haptic data compression. While kinesthetic coding schemes have been developed and optimized in the past decade [10, 12], little research has been reported in this regard for the tactile modality. With this work, we endeavor to rectify this situation.

Inspired by the similarities that we have observed between texture signals and speech signals, we adapt speech coding techniques for developing a perceptually transparent low bitrate texture codec. In particular, we establish that Algebraic Code-Excited Linear Prediction coding (ACE-LPC) [11] is well suited for texture compression (more details in Section 2). Thus, by emulating principles from speech coding, we take a top-down approach to texture coding, rather than working ground-up. The haptic texture signals that we treat in this work are produced during interactions between a probe and surface asperities. The dynamics of such interactions have been modeled successfully by LPC filters in [15]. This past work provides a strong rationale for basing our coding approach on LP models of texture production. Moreover, Analysis-by-Synthesis coders like LPC are known to exhibit low bitrates with high subjective quality. On the other hand, waveform coding methods like ADPCM are known to have higher bitrates to preserve waveform fidelity and thus high quality. Additionally, the delay performance of the LPC-based G.729 speech codec [11] we adapt (15ms) is much better than generic audio coders like AAC (20-405ms) and mp3 (>100ms), which is important for realtime teleoperation. Furthermore, the wideband nature of AAC/mp3 might make them unsuitable for coding textures, which have significantly lower perception bandwidth (1 kHz).

1.1 Related work

Our approach is based on the following general model-based compression principle: represent texture signals using a texture production model and then transmit encoded model parameters instead of the signal itself. Model parameters typically require a more modest bit budget as compared to the original data, leading to effective data compression.

Significant research has been devoted toward modeling tactile texture signals. One of the earliest efforts by Okamura *et al.* [26] represents vibrotactile signals arising from coarse regularly patterned textures (see Figure 4(a)) by decaying sinusoids. Furthermore, they establish that stochastic texture signals (see Figure 4(b)) are best encoded by frequency domain parameters like the mean and maximum power frequencies. In [15], Kuchenbecker *et al.* expound on the concept of *haptography*, a haptic analog to photography. Haptography, as conceived by the authors, involves all aspects relevant to capturing the *realistic* feel of a textured surface and reproducing it in haptic interactions later. In the process, they propose a novel texture modeling approach based on linear prediction. In [9], Guruswamy *et al.* propose an approach for recording real-world vibrotactile texture signals and segmenting them using signal processing techniques. Each segment is then associated with a physical surface feature. These segments are fitted with IIR-filters, and the corresponding filter parameters are stored. A virtual visual-haptic model of the real surface is then constructed, and haptic rendering is performed based on the previously extracted surface features. All of the above works are, however, geared toward offline processing of texture signals. Moreover, they are neither motivated by nor optimized for compression. In this paper, we present a low bitrate and perceptually robust realtime vibrotactile texture compression approach for haptic teleoperation based on insights derived from these modeling approaches.

Okamoto and Yamada presented a frequency-domain texture compression algorithm loosely based on the knowledge of human vibrotactile perception in [25]. In their approach, textured surfaces are firstly scanned with an ultra high-resolution laser scanner. These surfaces are then reconstructed as a waveform representing surface height as a function of lateral distance on the object surface. Under the assumption of a constant scan velocity, this waveform is transformed to the temporal frequency domain using the Discrete Cosine Transform (DCT). For compression, the DCT coefficients are thresholded based on perceptual detection thresholds and then quantized with step sizes derived from the knowledge of frequency-domain amplitude-Just Noticeable Differences (JND) for vibrotactile stimuli [5]. Finally, the thresholded-quantized frequency-domain representation is transformed back to a height waveform, that is used for position-based texture rendering. This inverse transformation again assumes the same constant scan velocity as before.

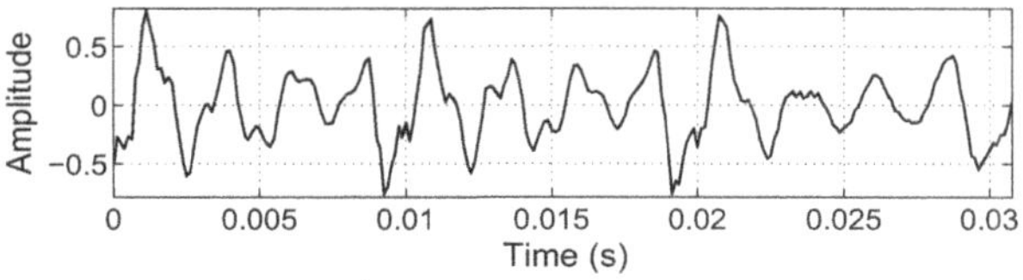

(a) Voiced speech

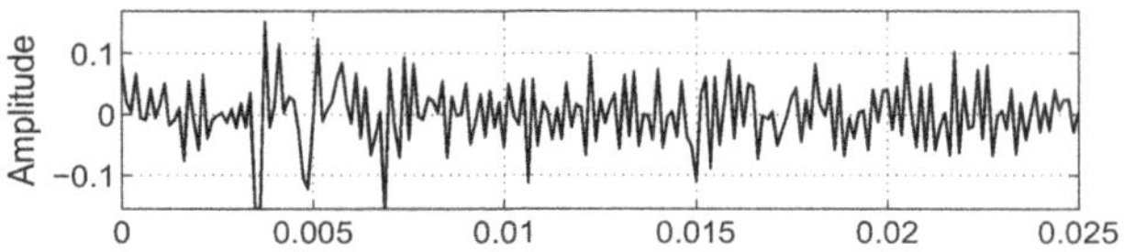

(b) Unvoiced speech

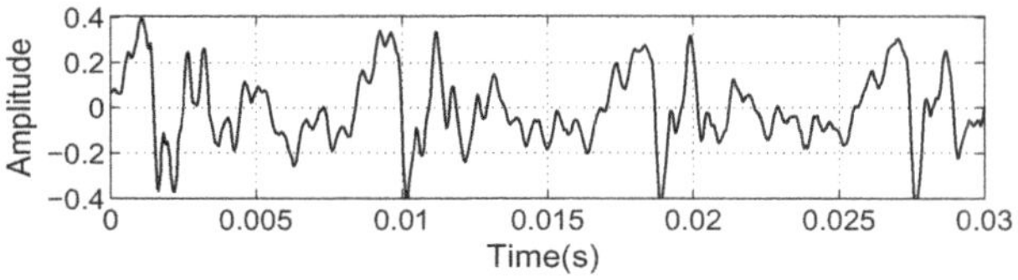

(c) Voiced fricative

Figure 2: Typical speech signal classes. Quasi-periodicity of voiced speech is visible in (a). (b) shows random noise-like appearance of unvoiced speech. (c) shows a mixture of (a) and (b).

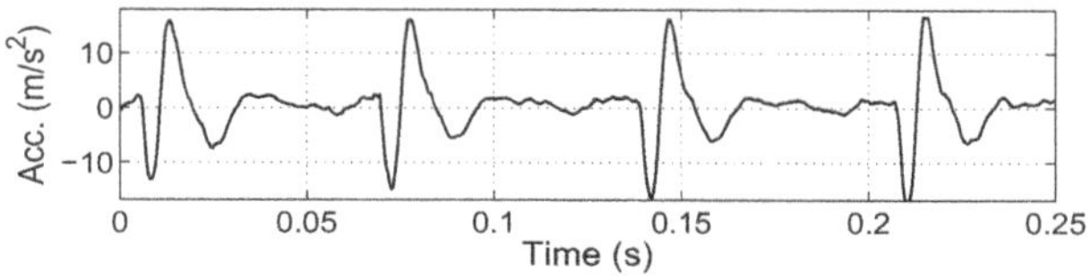

(a) Coarse (here, regularly patterned) texture

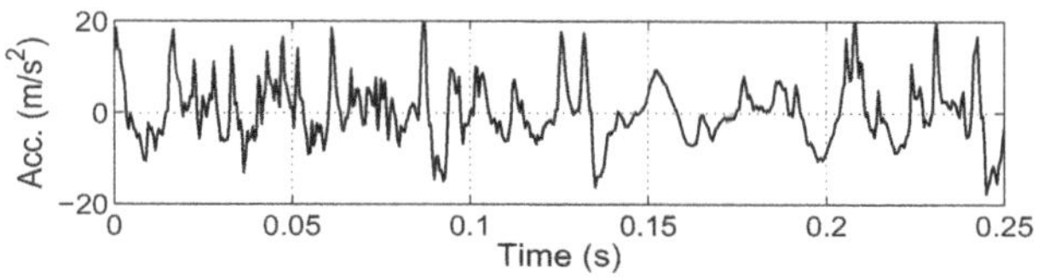

(b) Fine random texture

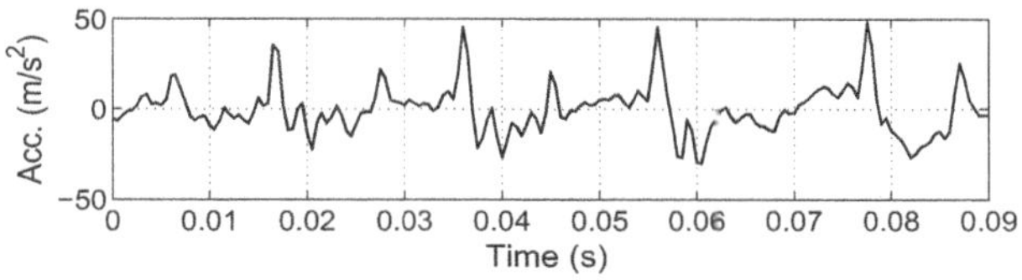

(c) Mixed texture

Figure 4: Typical texture signal classes. Coarse (here, regularly patterned or quasi-periodic) texture is shown in (a). (b) shows the noise-like appearance of fine random textures. (c) shows a mixture of – coarse surface features with fine intermediate features ("Acc." denotes "Acceleration").

The above algorithm was evaluated for perceptual quality in subjective tests where subjects traversed the displacement profile with a haptic device [25]. These tests showed that the proposed algorithm is perceptually transparent (i.e., quantization noise goes unnoticed) up to a quantization as coarse as 12-levels. The algorithm leads to an impressive 75% compression of the texture data. Unfortunately, there are a couple of limitations to the applicability of this approach in real-time haptic teleoperation. To begin with, similar to the texture modeling approaches mentioned before, the algorithm is offline in nature – meaning that the system needs the entire surface profile in advance. A more severe limitation is the assumption of a constant (and predetermined) texture scan velocity, necessary to transform the spatial-domain data to the temporal-frequency domain. Both these limitations can, in principle, be overcome by proposing a window-based realtime adaptation of the algorithm. However, we refrain from pursuing this idea since it will be analytically proven in Section 2.3 that for comparable subjective quality, the compression performance of the algorithm proposed in this paper is better than that of the above algorithm. It should be noted here that compression is achieved by the above algorithm by discarding information based on a model of the human vibrotactile perception (the *sink* for texture signals). On the contrary, the approach we propose in this paper is based on a model for texture signal production (the *source*).

Another point of distinction between [25] and this work is the way surface texture is represented. In particular, textures are represented by position signals in [25]. On

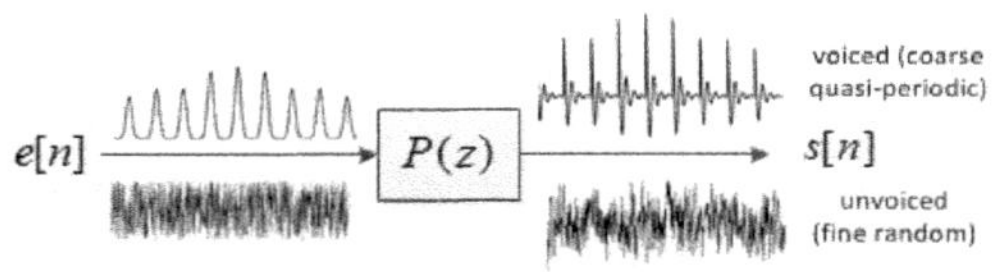

Figure 3: Excitation of a linear synthesis filter $P(z)$ with periodic pulses and with noise-like excitation to produce voiced and unvoiced speech.

the other hand, they are represented by acceleration signals sensed by Microelectromechanical Systems (MEMS)-based acceleration sensors in [9, 15, 26]. We employ MEMS sensors for our work, since they are inexpensive compared to position-sensing systems with comparable resolutions, and lightweight making them easy to mount on the teleoperator end-effector. Position sensors built into a typical haptic device have insufficient bandwidth for sensing texture signals.

Some relevant work in the area of multi-toned texture signal perception exists [2, 20, 21]. However, to the best of our knowledge, a full model of wide-band vibrotactile perception (including, e.g., masking phenomena) usable for our purpose is not yet available at the time of this writing. Moreover, studies employ a wide variety of methods for tactile stimulation, making results less portable to other tactile systems. Given these restrictions, we integrate the perceptual factor into our coding mechanism by maintaining a high Signal-to-Noise ratio (SNR) in the coding process. This approach is thus not strictly based on existing perceptual evidence, and therefore we evaluate it for perceptual performance (transparency) using rigorous subjective testing.

1.2 Paper overview

This paper is organized as follows. Section 2 draws an analogy between speech and texture production models, and details our speech coding-inspired haptic texture codec algorithm. It also analyses the codec performance objectively in terms of bitrate and introduced (algorithmic and processing) delays. Section 3 details subjective tests conducted for the purpose of establishing perceptual transparency of the codec. Section 4 discusses the results of these subjective tests. Finally, Section 5 summarizes the contributions of this research and outlines directions for future research.

2. LOW BITRATE VIBROTACTILE TEXTURE SIGNAL COMPRESSION

2.1 Speech-texture analogy

A well known model for speech production represents the human vocal tract by an all-pole speech synthesis filter [28]. This speech synthesis filter is excited by an air flow originating from the lungs and shaped by the opening/closing of the vocal cords, followed by any intermediate constrictions on its way to the vocal tract. Depending upon the nature of this excitation (quasi-periodic pulses or random noise or a mixture of both), a variety of sounds are produced (voiced sounds or unvoiced sounds or voiced fricatives, respectively) (see Figures 2 and 3).

In haptic teleoperation, the operator explores an object's texture by stroking it with the slave robot's end-effector. Wide-band acceleration signals result from such strokes and are picked up in our work by an accelerometer mounted on the end-effector. The acceleration signals (see Figure 4) encode the dynamics of the interaction between the end-effector and large and small asperities on the object surface. These signals can be modeled as a sum of damped sinusoids [9] and, similar to speech signals, can be represented well by all-pole filters [15].

We treat coarse textures as being analogous to voiced sounds (compare Figure 4(a) to Figure 2(a)), fine textures to unvoiced sounds (compare Figure 4(b) to Figure 2(b)) and a mixture of coarse and fine textures to voiced fricatives (compare Figure 4(c) to Figure 2(c)). This qualitative similarity serves as a cue in this work for applying speech coding techniques to texture compression. The results of the subjective tests we report justify this approach.

2.2 ACELP-based texture coding algorithm

Motivated by the similarities between speech and texture signals, we evaluate the adaptability of speech coding techniques for texture coding. The most widely used speech coding techniques are based on linear predictive (LP) modeling of signal segments (or frames), followed by the transmission of the corresponding model parameters [4]. We found that this technique, along with an algebraic code approximation of the associated LP filter excitation, adapts well to texture coding. In the following, we outline the salient steps in a typical linear prediction-based speech coding algorithm [4, 28]. Wherever necessary, we point out any modifications required for its application to haptic textures.

Linear predictive analysis (LPA)

The sampled speech (texture) signal is subdivided into frames that are processed in succession. As mentioned before, the frame content is modeled by an LP-filter. The LP parameters and the corresponding filter excitation are encoded and sent to the receiver side for decoding and display.

In the LPA algorithm, future samples are predicted on the basis of a linear weighting of N past samples:

$$\hat{x}[n] = \sum_{i=1}^{N} a_i \cdot x[n-i] \tag{1}$$

where $\boldsymbol{a} = [a_i]_{i=1:N}$ are the LPA coefficients and N is the order of the LPC filter.

The mean square prediction error is given as:

$$E = \sum_{n=1}^{L} (e[n])^2 \tag{2}$$

where L is the number of samples in the analysis buffer and $e[n] = x[n] - \hat{x}[n]$. E is minimized by setting the partial derivatives $\left(\frac{\partial E}{\partial a_i}\right)_{i=1:N}$ to 0, leading to a linear system of equations:

$$\boldsymbol{R}_{N\times N} \cdot \boldsymbol{a}_{N\times 1} = \boldsymbol{r}_{N\times 1} \tag{3}$$

where $\boldsymbol{R}$ is the autocorrelation matrix of $x[n]$ and $\boldsymbol{r} = [R(1)...R(N)]$ (first row of $\boldsymbol{R}$). A well-known efficient recursive method, the Levinson-Durbin algorithm [28] is used to solve for $\boldsymbol{a}$. If $\boldsymbol{A}(z) = \left(\sum_{i=1}^{N} a_i \cdot z^{-i}\right)$, the corresponding LP analysis filter can be written as $H(z) = (1 - A(z))$ and the synthesis filter as $P(z) = 1/H(z)$ (see Figure 5).

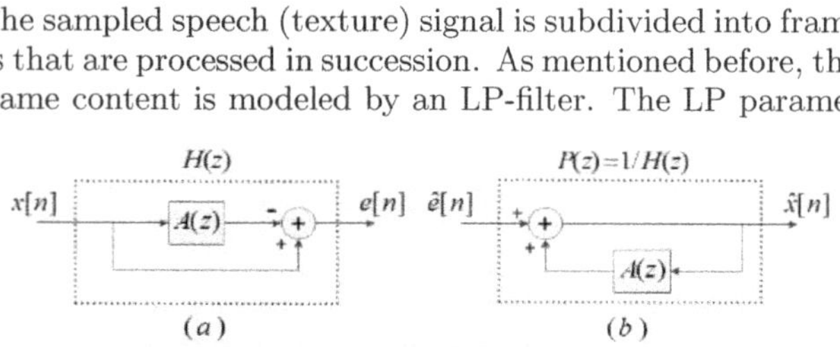

Figure 5: $H(z)$ - LP analysis filter, $P(z)$ - LP synthesis filter, $x[n]$ - input signal to be predicted, $e[n]$ - residual output of the LP analysis filter. $\hat{e}[n]$ - an approximation made to $e[n]$ by the encoder. $\hat{x}[n]$ - reconstructed output, i.e., an approximation to $x[n]$ at the decoder output (adapted from [15]).

Perceptual weighting

This coding algorithm is lossy since it *approximates* the spectral response with its poles and the synthesis filter excitation with an algebraic code. Moreover, these codec parameters are vector quantized before transmission. Thus, the coding process introduces distortion into the encoded signal. In order to ensure perceptual transparency of the codec, this coding distortion should be kept as low as possible (ideally below perceptual thresholds). In other words, the difference between the codec input and output signals should be as low as possible (ideally imperceptible). This necessitates the inclusion of a psychophysical model for speech (texture) perception in the coding process.

As mentioned in Section 1, despite the existence of some studies on suprathreshold wideband vibrotactile perception, results usable for our algorithm could not be found. Hence, we employ a simplified assumption in this regard, namely – maintaining a high SNR across the entire frequency spectrum will lead to a perceptually transparent codec. How good this assumption holds will become clear from subjective tests.

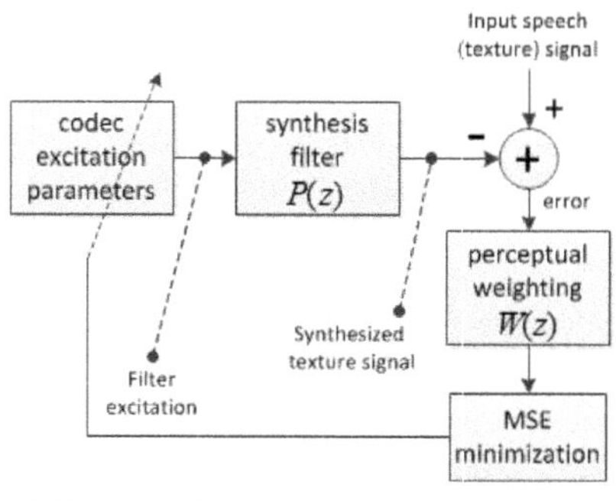

Figure 6: The excitation parameters are optimized to obtain minimum perceptual MSE.

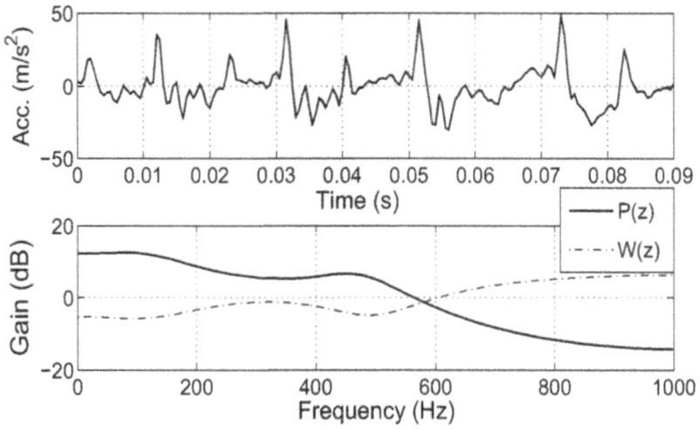

Figure 7: Top: a segment of texture data. Bottom: the corresponding perceptual weighting filter $W(z)$ for this segment and the LP synthesis filter $P(z)$.

In order to maintain a high SNR, a perceptual weighting filter $W(z)$ is identified that weights the mean square error (MSE) between the original speech (texture) signal and the speech (texture) signal reconstructed by the codec. The excitation parameters for the LP filters are searched for by minimizing this weighted MSE (see Figure 6).

We deduce the transfer function for the perceptual weighting filter as a function of the LP synthesis filter response as:

$$W(z) = \frac{P(z/\alpha_2)}{P(z/\alpha_1)} \tag{4}$$

where $0 < \alpha_{1,2} < 1$. Thus, the poles of $W(z)$ lie at the same angles as the poles of $P(z)$, but at radii α_2 times those of $P(z)$'s poles. On the other hand, the zeros of $W(z)$ lie at the same angles as the poles of $P(z)$, but at radii α_1 times those of $P(z)$'s poles. If $\alpha_1 > \alpha_2$, the frequency response of $W(z)$ is like a *controlled* inverse filter of $H(z)$ [28] (see Figure 7 for an illustration). Speech coding techniques typically choose $\alpha_1 = 0.9$ and $0.4 \leq \alpha_2 \leq 0.7$ [28]. This nature of the frequency response of $W(z)$ assures that the coding process admits very low noise energy in comparison with the signal energy throughout the frequency spectrum.

The general feel of haptic textures is governed by their spectral signature [15]. In an LP-based algorithm, this feel is represented by the spectral response of the LP synthesis filter. In principle, it can be recreated by simply exciting the synthesis filter with white noise. However, in many cases (e.g., in teleoperation), transient temporal events occurring due to surface features and scan velocity changes are equally important. Therefore, it is necessary to transmit not only the LP parameters determined above, but also an encoded version of the excitation that goes with it and decides the temporal response of the LP synthesis filter.

Long-term LP synthesis filter excitation

The long-term excitation represents the (quasi-)periodicity in the speech (texture) signal waveform. It is encoded by two parameters – the period T (we call it "pitch delay" in the following to be consistent with speech literature) and the pitch gain β. A preliminary range for T is first determined from calculations of the autocorrelation function for the entire frame. This is referred to as "open-loop" search for T. A value for β and a final refined value for T are then estimated in the so-called "closed-loop" search by minimizing the perceptually weighted MSE, as will be described in the section titled "Excitation parameter search" below.

Short-term LP synthesis filter excitation

The short-term excitation governs the short-term (within a period) output of the LP synthesis filter. It is represented by two parameters – an index i and a gain G. 'i' indexes into a fixed (one that never changes) codebook based on an algebraic codebook structure. This codebook contains a set of generic 20-long vectors. Each of these vectors contains four non-zero pulses, with the rest of the samples set to zero. Each pulse can have an amplitude of either +1 or -1. The pulses can assume only specific positions in the vector. The fixed codebook is very efficiently searchable on account of its algebraic nature. Similar to the long-term excitation, both these parameters are estimated in a "closed-loop" search by minimizing the perceptually weighted MSE (see below).

Excitation parameter search

We now describe the procedure for determining the aforementioned parameters in more detail. Please refer to the encoder structure in Figure 8 for this discussion. Branches 1, 2 and 3 successively remove their contributions from the original input speech (texture) signal, producing a new target signal for the branch below.

The contribution of Branch 1 is the zero-input-response (ZIR) of the LPC synthesis filter, i.e., filter response on account of its past memory, facilitating a smooth transition from one frame to the next.

The contribution of Branch 2 is the long-term zero-state-response (ZSR, i.e., the filter response with the filter memory set to zero) that accounts for the periodicity in the speech (texture) signal. Branch 2 removes its contribution actively by searching for the best (corresponding to minimum MSE) long-term excitation parameters. This is done as follows. Once the open-loop search gives an initial range for T, an adaptive codebook populates itself with sections of past (long-term + short-term) excitation corresponding to each T value. This codebook is called "adaptive" since it is constantly updated depending upon past excitation and T values. As mentioned before, a closed-loop search yields best estimates of T and β, leading to minimum MSE. The contribution of the adaptive codebook corresponding to these final estimates is removed from the target signal generated by Branch 1, producing new target signal for Branch 3.

The contribution of Branch 3 is the short-term zero-state-response. It accounts for the novelty in the current signal frame that could not be "explained away" by the upper branches. Branch 3 also removes its contribution actively

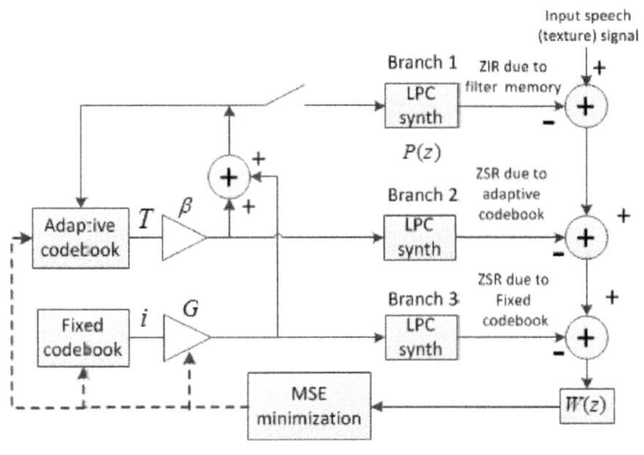

Figure 8: Search procedure for excitation parameters at the encoder side. ZIR: zero-input-response, ZSR: zero-state-response (adapted from [4]).

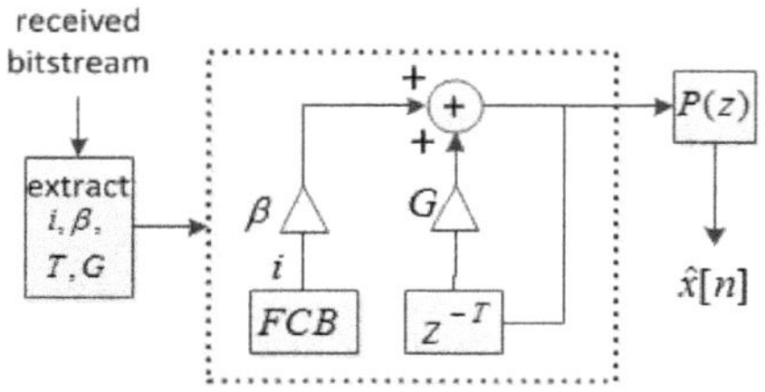

Figure 9: Decoder operation (FCB: fixed codebook).

by searching for the best short-term excitation parameters, leading to a minimum perceptual MSE.

After the three branches are executed in that order and all excitation parameters are found, the switch shown closes momentarily to update the filter memory and the adaptive codebook (described below) for processing the next frame.

Decoder operation

At the decoder side (see Figure 9), the LP filter and excitation parameters are recovered from the received bit stream. The excitation is then constructed by adding the adaptive and fixed-codebook vectors scaled by their respective gains. It is then passed through the LP synthesis filter to reconstruct the texture signal for presentation to the operator.

Implementation

Our implementation of the above algorithm for texture compression is based on the efficient C-library for the G.729 ACELP-based speech codec, available from the International Telecommunication Union [11]. Modifications to this library for adapting it to haptic texture signals are described here. The choice of certain parameters below is a trade-off between performance and ease of reuse of the G.729 library.

It is generally accepted that the human vibrotactile perception mediated by the Pacinian neural channel is sensitive to vibrations upto a bandwidth of 1 kHz [1]. Hence, we sample the texture signal at the teleoperator side at a Nyquist rate of 2 kHz. In order to remove DC-bias, the sampled signal is then digitally high-pass filtered with a 4th order Butterworth filter with a cutoff frequency of 40 Hz.

Texture signals are short-term stationary for natural texture scan motions (slow changes in scan velocity and operator applied force) and when the surface features do not change drastically. For natural scans, it was found that an LPA analysis buffer length of 0.06 s is a good choice for time/frequency-domain tracking performance. The sampled texture signal is therefore subdivided into frames of length $L = 120$ samples that are processed in succession. Furthermore, an LPC order $N = 10$ which captures 5 spectral peaks, was found to be a good trade-off between compression performance and compatibility with the G.729 codec.

To summarize, we adapt the G.729 codec [11] to work with an input bitrate of 32 kbps (against the original 128 kbps for speech) and a frame-length of 120 (against the original 240 for speech). All other parts of the G.729 codec have been retained without modification. The overall bit budget of 80 bits/frame is distributed among the various codec components as shown in Table 1.

Parameter	Bits per frame
LPA coefficients	18
Delay T	14
Fixed-codebook index i	26
Fixed-codebook signs	8
Codebook gains	14
Total	80

Table 1: Bit budget allocation [11].

2.3 Compression performance

The uncompressed bitrate for texture signals:

$$\begin{aligned} \text{bitrate}_{\text{uc}} &= \text{sampling rate} \times \text{number of bits/sample} \\ &= 2000\,\text{samples/sec.} \times 16\,\text{bits/sample} \\ &= 32\,kbps \qquad (5) \end{aligned}$$

The compression algorithm described above encodes every frame of 40 samples with 80 bits. Accordingly, the compressed bitrate can be calculated as follows:

$$\text{frames/sec.} = \frac{2000\,\text{samples/sec.}}{40\,\text{samples/frame}} = 50 \qquad (6)$$

$$\begin{aligned} \text{bitrate}_{\text{c}} &= 50\,\text{frames/sec.} \times 80\,\text{bits/frame} \\ &= 4\,kbps \qquad (7) \end{aligned}$$

This amounts to a compression ratio of 8:1. To match this performance, for every frame of 40 samples, the codec described in [25] should generate 80 bits. That is, the corresponding 40 DCT coefficients should be quantized with a 2-bit (4-level) linear quantizer. However, [25] reports a compression ratio of approximately 4:1 with a 12-level quantizer (fewer than 12 levels trigger significant perceptual differences between the original and quantized textures). This comparison proves that in terms of bitrate reduction, the ACELP-based codec described above performs better by at least a factor of 2. Given the novelty of this research area, no work other than [25] could be found for comparison. It remains to be seen from our subjective test results whether the proposed codec is also perceptually transparent.

2.4 Delay performance

An algorithmic delay of 20 ms is introduced into the signal stream due to frame buffering (40 samples per frame at a sampling rate of 2 kHz). Additionally, a look-ahead delay of 10 ms occurs due to buffering of 20 future samples. On a very common PC configuration (Intel(R) Xeon(R) CPU EE5506, quad-core @2.13 GHz and 4 GB RAM), the average encoding time was measured to be around 230 μs, and the average decoding time around 18 μs. Thus, the encoder/decoder are very efficient in terms of timing and introduce a negligible delay in comparison with the buffering delay of 30 ms.

During manipulation, the presence of delay in the haptic signal stream is detected by humans at approximately 40 ms[24]. Furthermore, subjective degradation in the perception of textures is shown to creep in at about 60 ms of delay. Thus, for our codec, a further channel transmission delay of around 10 ms is tolerable before the human delay-detection threshold is reached, while a further channel transmission delay of around 30 ms is tolerable before subjective degradation in texture perception results.

Figures 10 and 11 show the time- and frequency-domain performance, respectively, of the ACELP-based codec.

3. SUBJECTIVE QUALITY EVALUATION

Let us firstly outline the requirements of subjective evaluation for assessing the perceptual performance of the ACELP-based codec. We would like to prove that our compression

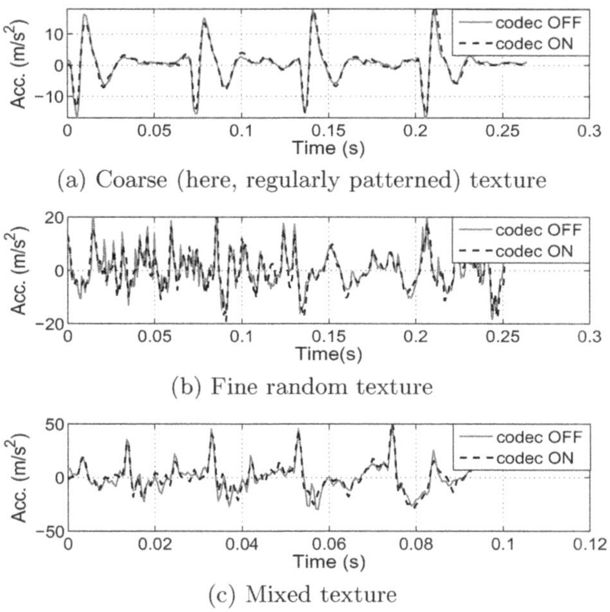

(a) Coarse (here, regularly patterned) texture

(b) Fine random texture

(c) Mixed texture

Figure 10: Time-domain view of the codec operation. Codec input (codec OFF) and output (codec ON) are shown. It can be seen that the codec has a very good temporal tracking performance.

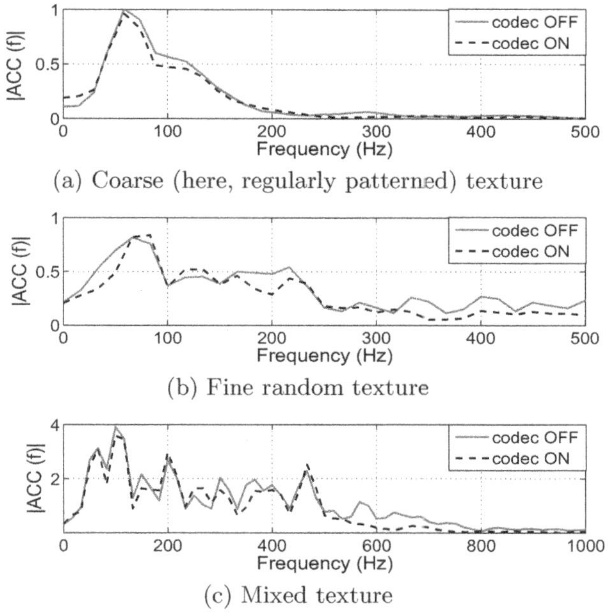

(a) Coarse (here, regularly patterned) texture

(b) Fine random texture

(c) Mixed texture

Figure 11: Frequency-domain view of the codec operation for a texture frame (120 samples, i.e., 0.06 seconds long). It can be seen that the spectral signature is faithfully captured.

algorithm is perceptually *transparent*. This means that, *ceteris paribus*, subjects are unable to discriminate between the tactile stimuli perceived:

1. when the codec is inactive, i.e., switched OFF. Let us denote this stimulus set as $C1_i$ (where i is an index into this set): sensed tactile signals presented directly to the subject without any intermediate processing – in other words, the codec input, and,
2. when the codec is active, i.e., switched ON. Let us denote this stimulus set as $C2_j$ (where j is an index into this set): compressed-decompressed tactile signals - in other words, the codec output.

Thus, a binary decision needs to be made if pairs of stimuli, each containing one stimulus from every set above, feel the *same* or *different*. In the real world, such choices are made by subjects in the presence of uncertainty. For instance, non-idealities like internal noise in the human sensory process might lead to different percepts for the same physical stimulus in two different trials separated by time and/or space. Additionally, at a cognitive level, a bias in the subject's decision process may push her/his response in a certain direction.

To achieve robustness toward uncertainties and account for response bias, we take a Signal Detection Theory (SDT) [18] approach for perceptual performance evaluation. In particular, we employ the two-alternative forced-choice (2AFC) experimental paradigm for our purpose. Herein, subjects experience a pair of stimuli and must make a choice between two alternatives – do the two stimuli feel the "same" or "different". This is followed by an SDT analysis of the results.

Another consideration unique to haptics should be mentioned here. Contrary to audio and video where information flows unidirectionally from a technical system to the human, we can actively affect the feedback we perceive in case of the haptic modality. This complicates the perceptual comparison of two stimuli in realtime teleoperation. This is because it cannot be made certain that the human elicits two *temporally* comparable stimuli – one from each set $C1$ and $C2$ – in two separate trials. To work around this problem, we break down the subjective evaluation into two experiments:

- Experiment 1 (2AFC): subjects judge *recorded* pairs of stimuli haptically (haptic playback), with no visual feedback. Thus in this experiment, manipulability of the haptic interface is sacrificed in the interest of a fair temporal comparison between two stimuli.
- Experiment 2: subjects perform realtime teleoperation with visual-haptic feedback. For a given texture, they compare the general feel of the surface for two modes of operation – when the codec is switched OFF versus when it is switched ON. Note that we are primarily interested in judgments based on haptic perception. We therefore exclude audio feedback since audio signals are highly correlated with texture signals and tend to interfere with haptic perception (see [29] and the references therein). The consistency (or the lack thereof) of the tactile feedback with the visual of the remote environment may also potentially act as a cue to differentiate between the two modes of operation.

3.1 Experimental setup

Our experiments are based on a teleoperation setup similar to the one presented by McMahan *et al.* in [23]. As shown in Figure 12, the master and slave robots are both PHANToM Omni haptic devices (Sensable Technologies).

The slave Omni end-effector is instrumented with a three-axis LIS344ALH accelerometer from ST Microelectronics. This MEMS-based analog accelerometer has a range of ± 6 g

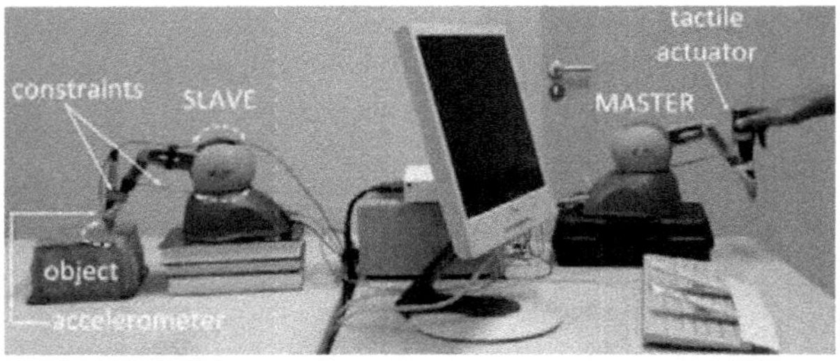

Figure 12: Teleoperation setup used for this work.

($\pm$ 58 m/s^2), and its output is filtered with an on-board analog low-pass filter (cutoff frequency 956 Hz). Since the actuator has only one degree of freedom, the three-axis accelerometer output needs to be reduced to a single dimension. A solution to this issue would be to sum the three acceleration components together sample-by-sample. However, this approach leads to a loss of vital texture information due to destructive interferences whenever the acceleration components are negatively correlated. To avoid such occurrences, we employ the DFT321 algorithm proposed by Landin *et al.* in [16] for dimensional reduction. The DFT321 algorithm combines the three-axis data in the frequency-domain in a perceptually optimal manner, while preserving both important spectral and temporal properties of the texture signals.

The master Omni's custom handle contains an NCM02-05-005-4JB linear voice coil actuator from H2W Technologies, Inc. The actuator coil can move up and down on linear bearings, and it is centered in its 7.6 mm workspace by a pair of pre-loaded compression springs. Passing current through the coil creates equal and opposite electromagnetic interaction forces on the handle and the coil, which induces high frequency accelerations on the user's hand. The handle itself is 3D-printed in ABS plastic, and the voice coil actuator is driven by a high bandwidth linear current amplifier.

A quad-core 2.13 GHz PC with Windows XP and Sensable OpenHaptics 3.0 library is used to control the teleoperation system. It operates a servo loop at approximately 1 kHz, sensing the 3D position of each Omni and specifying its 3D force output at each time step.

An NI PCI 6221 data acquisition card is used to sample the accelerometer output at 2 kHz with a 16-bit ADC. It also drives the actuator via a 16-bit DAC output at a 2 kHz update rate. To limit the motions used by subjects and to simplify the setup, the elbow and gimbal joints of both Omnis are immobilized using physical constraints. The shoulder joint's two rotational degrees of freedom allow the handle to move on a spherical surface. As a result, the slave end-effector traverses the remote object surface along an arc.

Subjects

The same nine subjects participated in both experiments, 1 female and 8 males, ranging in age from 23-30 years. Such a subject sample is typical to psychophysical tests conducted in the field of haptics, e.g., [27]. None of them reported having any ailments that would hamper their sensorimotor performance. Two of them were researchers in haptics, using commercial kinesthetic devices like the PHANToM Omni on a regular basis. However, none of them had prior experience with tactile feedback systems. In a preliminary session, all the subjects were made familiar with the experimental setting and the operation of the hardware.

3.2 Experiment 1 (offline)

In this experiment, only the master side of the teleoperation system shown in Figure 12 was used to present prerecorded texture stimuli to the subjects. They were asked to give binary "same/different" judgments for each pair of texture stimuli presented. This choice of the experimental paradigm was driven by the fact that binary decisions are the easiest for subjects to make and tend to yield results that are cleaner than those from other methods like magnitude estimation. We believe proving the perceptual indiscriminability of uncompressed and compressed textures (analogous to watermarked textures in [27]) is sufficient for the scope of this paper.

Subjects could switch between the two stimuli in a pair as many times as they wanted before reaching a decision and moving on to the next pair. A cardboard barrier shielded the haptic device and the subject's hand from her/his vision during the actual experiment to prevent visual observation of the moving coil. Moreover, auditory cues from the voice coil were masked out by playing pink noise through headphones. Thus, isolation of haptic perception was ensured in the experiment.

There were a total of 80 pairs of stimuli to be judged. These were divided as follows (32 + 32 + 16):

1. Ground truth: "different": $\{C1_i \Leftrightarrow C2_j | i = j \in \{1, 2, ...32\}\}$ (corresponding codec input and output signals),
2. Ground truth: "same": $\{C1_i \Leftrightarrow C1_i | i \in \{33, 34, ...64\}\}$ (same stimulus repeated twice for each of the 32 pairs),
3. Ground truth: "different": 16 randomly selected pairs from $\{C1_i \Leftrightarrow C1_k | i \neq k \in \{33, 34, ...64\}\}$

The 80 pairs were randomly ordered and the order changed randomly from subject to subject. Each stimulus was an approximately 1 *s* long texture signal segment recorded while scanning four different textures (ABS plastic, shoe sole, rock, and vinyl, see Figure 13). The recording and segmentation was done by the experimenter in advance before the experiment. The segments were carefully selected to cover representatives of a wide variety of stimuli from every category of texture stimuli – coarse, fine random and mixed.

Isolation of the subject's tactile modality ensured that "same/different" judgments were made purely on the basis of tactile perception. Since manipulability of the haptic device was removed, temporal fairness was maintained in the comparisons, and every subject judged the same stimulus pairs with exactly the same time-frequency profiles. Moreover, subjects were not required to remember long durations of stimuli when making comparisons. Psychophysical studies have shown that a relative motion between the human hand and the textured surface is vital to texture perception [17]. In this sense, this experimental setup is comparable to realtime teleoperation, only that the texture moves relative to the user, rather than the other way round.

3.3 Experiment 2 (online / realtime teleoperation)

In this experiment, subjects teleoperated the slave omni through the master (see Figure 12). They had a direct visual of the remote teleoperator side. Visual observation of the voice coil movements by the subject was prevented by a

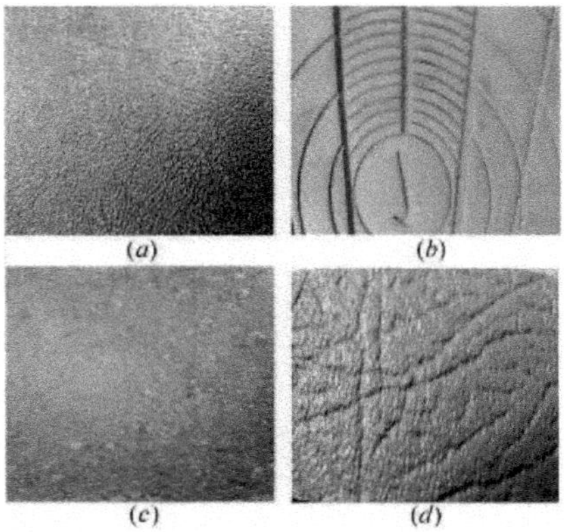

Figure 13: Textures used: (a) rough ABS plastic (fine random), (b) shoe sole (coarse regularly patterned), (c) rock (mixed), and (d) vinyl (mixed).

cardboard shield. Headphones playing pink noise masked out any auditory cues from the tactile actuator.

One by one, the subjects scanned each of the four textures, while turning the intermediate codec between the teleoperator and operator sides ON and OFF using a keyboard. They could explore the four textures as long as they wanted. They were then asked to judge if the textures felt the "same" or "different" in the two modes of operation.

At an average, the experiments required a total of 45 min. to complete, excluding training sessions at the beginning.

4. SUBJECTIVE RESULTS

For all stimuli, the number of "hits" (h) and "false alarms" (f) are counted as follows for every subject:

$$h = \sum(\text{decision "same"} \mid \text{ground truth "same"})$$
$$f = \sum(\text{decision "same"} \mid \text{ground truth "different"})$$

Accordingly, the "hit rate" (H) and the "false-alarm rate" (F) are given as $H = h/32$ and $F = f/32$.

For our analyses, we use a stimulus sensitivity parameter from SDT called d' [18]. d' represents the ability of a subject to discriminate between stimuli belonging to two different classes. Low values of d' indicate that the stimuli are not easily discriminable, whereas high values indicate higher discriminability. SDT commonly assumes a Gaussian noise model of the human sensory process. Accordingly, the sensitivity parameter can be computed as $d' = z(H) - z(F)$, and the response bias $c = \frac{-[z(H) + z(F)]}{2}$, where $z()$ denotes the inverse Gaussian cumulative distribution function.

The results of the analysis of data from experiment 1 are shown in Figures 14 and 15. It is generally accepted that if $|d'| < 1.0$, the difference between the stimuli is below human perceptual thresholds. From Figure 14, it can be seen that across all subjects, $|d'| < 0.5$ consistently. In informal accounts from the subjects, it was noted that all of them found the stimuli to be "very difficult to distinguish" in general.

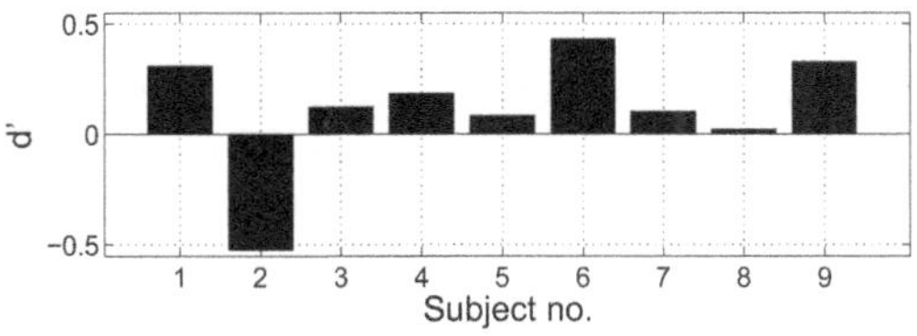

Figure 14: Experiment 1 results: d'.

Figure 15 shows that across subjects, the response bias is consistently negative. This means that the subjects were more inclined to decide that the stimuli were "same" rather than "different". Moreover, from informal pilot tests before the conduction of the experiments, no perceptible distortion was observed in the codec. The response bias result can thus be combinedly assigned to experimental design (choice of stimulus pairs: 32 pairs - codec input-output and 32 pairs - "same") and to good perceptual performance of the codec.

Finally in the realtime teleoperation experiment, all subjects except one found no perceivable differences in the feel of the textures between the two modes of operation (with and without codec). This further corroborates the conclusions drawn from the results of the first experiment.

5. CONCLUSION

In this paper, we propose a source-filter (LPA) model-based approach for vibrotactile texture compression in haptic teleoperation and adapt well known speech coding techniques for this purpose. The texture codec presented has a very low bitrate (4 kbps, with a compression ratio of 8:1) and a good delay performance (with room for 30 ms of channel transmission delay, before delay-induced perceptual degradations result). A constant output bitrate ensures a deterministic packet-rate, considerably simplifying audio-video-haptic multiplexer design. Frame-by-frame processing ensures that free realtime natural scanning of textured surfaces is possible. We establish the perceptual transparency of the compression algorithm with rigorous subjective tests.

A number of refinements to this work are planned for the future. A wideband vibrotactile perception model should be identified and incorporated into the codec. A thorough analysis of the effects of the codec parameters (e.g., LP filter order, frame length, error-weighting) and their optimization has not been considered in this work. This is a key topic for future research. Finally, this paper establishes a baseline for texture compression without any perceptual degradation. In the future, starting from this baseline, we plan to introduce bitrate vs. quality tunability in the codec by varying quantization coarseness. A rate-distortion curve with an optimal operating point at which subjects just perceive signal degradation will then be found.

6. ACKNOWLEDGMENTS

The authors deeply appreciate William McMahan's support during Rahul Chaudhari's visit to the Penn Haptics Group. This work has been supported in part by the German Research Foundation (DFG) under the project STE 1093/4-1, in part by the European Research Council under the European Union's Seventh Framework Programme (FP7/2007-2013)/ERC Grant agreement no. 258941, and in part by the U.S. National Science Foundation under Grant

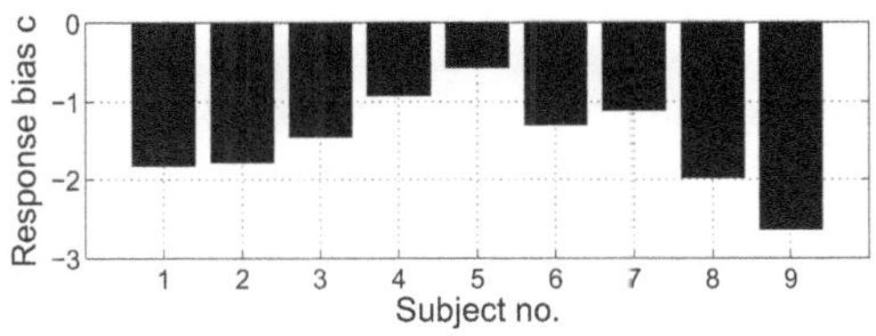

Figure 15: Experiment 1 results: Response bias.

No. 0845670. Special thanks to the IEEE Technical Committee on Haptics for partially supporting the first author's research visit to the Penn Haptics Group. The first author gratefully acknowledges the support of the TUM Graduate School's Faculty Graduate Center (Electrical Engineering and Information Technology) at the TU München.

7. REFERENCES

[1] S. Bensmaïa and M. Hollins. The vibrations of texture. *Somatosensory Motor Research*, 20(1):33–43, 2003.

[2] S. Bensmaïa, M. Hollins, and J. Yau. Vibrotactile intensity and frequency information in the pacinian system: a psychophysical model. *Perception & Psychophysics*, 67(5):828–41, Jul. 2005.

[3] J. Cha, Y.-S. Ho, Y. Kim, J. Ryu, and I. Oakley. A framework for haptic broadcasting. *IEEE MultiMedia*, 16(3):16–27, 2009.

[4] J. Chen and J. Thyssen. *Analysis-by-Synthesis speech coding.* In J. Benesty, M. M. Sondhi, Y. Huang (Eds.), Springer Handbook of Speech Processing, Springer Berlin-Heidelberg, 2008.

[5] J. Craig. Difference threshold for intensity of tactile stimuli. *Attention, Perception & Psychophysics*, 11:150–152, 1972.

[6] M. A. Eid, M. Mansour, A. H. El Saddik, and R. Iglesias. A haptic multimedia handwriting learning system. In *Proc. int. workshop EMME'07*, pages 103–108, New York, NY, USA, 2007. ACM.

[7] W. R. Ferrell and T. B. Sheridan. Supervisory control of remote manipulation. *IEEE Spectrum*, 4(10):81–88, Oct. 1967.

[8] J. Fishel, V. Santos, and G. Loeb. A robust micro-vibration sensor for biomimetic fingertips. In *Biomedical Robotics and Biomechatronics, 2008. BioRob 2008. 2nd IEEE RAS EMBS International Conference on*, pages 659–663, Oct. 2008.

[9] V. Guruswamy, J. Lang, and W.-S. Lee. IIR filter models of haptic vibration textures. *IEEE Trans. on Instru. and Measurement*, 60(1):93–103, Jan. 2011.

[10] P. Hinterseer, S. Hirche, S. Chaudhuri, E. Steinbach, and M. Buss. Perception-based data reduction and transmission of haptic data in telepresence and teleaction systems. *IEEE Trans. on Signal Processing*, 56(2):588–597, Feb. 2008.

[11] ITU-T. G.729 : Coding of speech at 8 kbit/s using conjugate-structure algebraic-code-excited linear prediction (CS-ACELP). Technical report, International Telecommunications Union-SS, Jan. 2007.

[12] J. Kammerl, R. Chaudhari, and E. Steinbach. Exploiting directional dependencies of force perception for lossy haptic data reduction. In *IEEE Int. Symp. on Haptic Audio Visual Environments and Games (HAVE 2010)*, Phoenix, Arizona, USA, Oct. 2010.

[13] D. A. Kontarinis and R. D. Howe. Tactile display of vibratory information in teleoperation and virtual environments. *Presence*, 4:387–402, 1996.

[14] K. J. Kuchenbecker, J. P. Fiene, and G. Niemeyer. Improving contact realism through event-based haptic feedback. *IEEE Trans. on Visualization and Computer Graphics*, 12(2):219–230, Mar./Apr, 2006.

[15] K. J. Kuchenbecker, J. M. Romano, and W. McMahan. Haptography: Capturing and recreating the rich feel of real surfaces. In *Int. Symp. on Robotics Research (invited paper)*, Aug. 2009.

[16] N. Landin, J. M. Romano, W. McMahan, and K. J. Kuchenbecker. Dimensional reduction of high-frequency accelerations for haptic rendering. EuroHaptics 2010, pages 79–86. Springer-Verlag, 2010.

[17] S. Lederman. The perception of surface roughness by active and passive touch. *Bulletin of the Psychonomic Society*, 18:253–255, 1981.

[18] N. Macmillan and C. Creelman. *Detection theory: A user's guide (2nd Ed.).* Mahwah, NJ: Erlbaum, 2005.

[19] N. Magnenat-Thalmann and U. Bonanni. Haptics in virtual reality and multimedia. *Multimedia, IEEE*, 13(3):6–11, July-Sept. 2006.

[20] J. Makous, R. Friedman, and C. J. Vierck. A critical band filter in touch. *The Journal of Neuroscience*, 15(4):2808–18, Apr. 1995.

[21] L. Marks. Sensory processes. *The Journal of Neuroscience*, 3(2):188–203, Jun. 1979.

[22] W. McMahan, J. Gewirtz, D. Standish, P. Martin, J. A. Kunkel, M. Lilavois, A. Wedmid, D. I. Lee, and K. J. Kuchenbecker. Tool contact acceleration feedback for telerobotic surgery. *IEEE Trans. on Haptics*, 4(3):210–220, Jul. 2011.

[23] W. McMahan, J. M. Romano, A. M. A. Rahuman, and K. J. Kuchenbecker. High frequency acceleration feedback significantly increases the realism of haptically rendered textured surfaces. In *Proc. IEEE Haptics Symp.*, pages 141–148, Mar. 2010.

[24] S. Okamoto, M. Konyo, S. Saga, and S. Tadokoro. Identification of cutaneous detection thresholds against time-delay stimuli for tactile displays. In *IEEE Int. Conf. on Robotics and Automation*, pages 220–225, May 2008.

[25] S. Okamoto and Y. Yamada. Perceptual properties of vibrotactile material texture: Effects of amplitude changes and stimuli beneath detection thresholds. In *IEEE/SICE Int. Symp. on System Integration*, pages 384 –389, Dec. 2010.

[26] A. Okamura, J. Dennerlein, and R. Howe. Vibration feedback models for virtual environments. In *IEEE Int. Conf. on Robotics and Automation*, volume 1, pages 674–679, May 1998.

[27] D. Prattichizzo, M. Barni, G. Menegaz, A. Formaglio, H. Tan, and S. Choi. Perceptual issues in haptic digital watermarking. *Multimedia, IEEE*, 14(3):84–91, July-Sept. 2007.

[28] L. Rabiner and R. Schafer. *Introduction to Digital Speech Processing.* Foundations and Trends in Signal Processing. Now Publishers, 2007.

[29] Y. Suzuki, J. Gyoba, and S. Sakamoto. Selective effects of auditory stimuli on tactile roughness perception. *Brain Research*, 1242(0):87–94, 2008.

[30] O. Wongwirat and S. Ohara. Haptic media synchronization for remote surgery through simulation. *IEEE MultiMedia*, 13(3):62–69, July 2006.

Vibrotactile Feedback of Motor Performance Errors for Enhancing Motor Learning

Troy McDaniel, Morris Goldberg, Shantanu Bala, Bijan Fakhri, Sethuraman Panchanathan
Center for Cognitive Ubiquitous Computing
School of Computing, Informatics, and Decision Systems Engineering
Arizona State University
Tempe, Arizona, USA 85281
{troy.mcdaniel, shantanu.bala, bfakhri, panch}@asu.edu, mgoldberg@ieee.org

ABSTRACT
Feedback related to motor performance is integral to improving the control, timing and coordination of movements. However, motor learning traditionally occurs within a group setting, limiting the quality of instruction and feedback. Even during one-on-one instruction, there are impediments to feedback such as physical separation between trainer and trainee, common in many sports such as snowboarding and swimming. We propose an inexpensive solution for real-time vibrotactile positioning and speed feedback that can complement traditional motor learning, and is compatible with existing vibrotactile motor instructions. We present a psychophysical study that examined participants' initial reactions to feedback stimuli pertaining to position and speed adjustments. Results support the proposed design in terms of both usability and naturalness, and provide insight into participants' conceptualization of feedback signals and feedback for rotational movements.

Categories and Subject Descriptors
H.5.2 [User Interfaces]: Haptic I/O.

Keywords
Vibrotactile feedback, instructions, motor learning.

1. INTRODUCTION
Movement is an integral component of perception and action. Through body movement, we not only act upon our environment to alter it, but sense and perceive our surroundings—the percepts of which ultimately influence action. Sensation is mediated through the extensive modalities of our sensory systems. For example, mechanoreceptors of the skin, muscles and joints facilitate rich haptic feature extraction during active exploration of objects and surfaces. We employ manual manipulations to optimize feature extraction through so-called exploratory procedures [1]. Visual sensation and perception requires eye movements (eye saccades) to change the direction of our eye gaze and quick, involuntary, detail-extracting movements between salient visual features while observing a scene.

We strive to learn new motor skills, and perfect existing capabilities, to enrich our health and well-being through physical activity, recreation, career/job needs, and/or activities of daily living. Given the importance of movement and motor skills, the pedagogy of motor skill acquisition warrants attention.

Traditionally, motor skills are taught within large group classes through observation and mimicry of a trainer's movements complemented with verbal description [2] and visual, auditory and/or physical (contactual) feedback. Effective motor learning requires feedback of motor performance errors. Two types of feedback are available [3]: *intrinsic feedback* naturally occurs as part of actuating and perceiving our own movements; and *extrinsic* (or *augmented*) feedback is provided externally by a trainer or device to complement intrinsic feedback—critical while learning complex, unfamiliar movements. Augmented feedback may describe performance at two levels of abstraction [3]: *knowledge of results* is feedback related to performance goals and achievement of desired movements; and *knowledge of performance* is feedback related to low-level performance attributes such as positioning and speed.

One-on-one (dyadic) instruction provides an ideal setting for motor learning by facilitating high fidelity visual and auditory communication channels with frequent trainer feedback and improved trainee motivation. Given the cost of one-on-one instruction, however, group instruction is more common. But this setting presents several limitations. The difficulty of mimicry, which involves mapping movements onto the trainee's own frame of reference, is amplified when movements must be viewed across a room or from the back of a class. Visual and auditory communication channels become noisy from other students and distractions in the environment. The frequency of feedback is significantly reduced given the divided attention of the trainer as he or she must attend to the entire class. But even one-on-one training has shortcomings. In many sports, for example, there is a large physical separation between the trainer and trainee during motor performances—such as in snowboarding [4]. During this time, trainers cannot provide real-time feedback. For many applications, real-time feedback from the trainer interrupts motor performances, such as while playing a musical instrument, rather than complementing intrinsic feedback in real-time.

Since the 1990's, virtual and augmented reality multimedia systems have been proposed to complement or replace traditional motor learning with real-time visual, acoustic, or kinesthetic motor instruction and/or performance feedback. Virtual reality approaches (e.g., [5]) map a user's physical movements, extracted through visual capture, to a virtual avatar for comparison with a trainer's virtual avatar viewed through a head mounted display.

Acoustic approaches (e.g., [6]) vary dimensions of sound, such as rhythm and tempo, to provide real-time feedback indicative of sensed motor performance characteristics including overall correctness, timing and/or intensity. Kinesthetic approaches (e.g., [7]) provide instruction and feedback through haptic guidance or resistance. However, these approaches tend to be bulky, expensive, lack portability, and/or obstruct modalities (vision, hearing) already occupied as part of the motor learning task.

An alternative channel for communicating performance errors is vibrotactile stimulation of the skin. This form of communication provides a solution that is inexpensive, wearable, portable, unobtrusive and discreet. Section 2 presents related work and proposed approaches for vibrotactile instruction or feedback. In section 3, we present a novel vibrotactile feedback system which addresses the limitations of current approaches. Section 4 gives the details of the implementation. In section 5, two psychophysical studies are presented that assess the naturalness and usability of our proposed approach. Finally, in section 6, possible directions for future work are outlined.

2. RELATED WORK

Lieberman and Breazeal's Tactile Interaction for Kinesthetic Learning (TIKL) system [8] complemented traditional motor learning and physical therapy with vibrotactile feedback delivered to the arm. Trainees watched a video of a movement being performed, and then attempted to mimic the movement. The location of the vibrotactile stimulation on the arm indicated the joint position in error (with respect to a fundamental movement), and the intensity of the vibration was proportional to the degree of error. Errors are corrected by moving in the opposite direction of the vibration; that is, the stimulation "pushes" the limb it stimulates. Saltation patterns, rather than localized stimulation, were used as feedback for forearm rotations. Saltation [9] is a perceptual illusion that gives the impression of phantom vibrotactile bursts traveling across the skin between actual stimulated sites.

Spelmezan et al. [4] proposed *tactile motion instructions* for snowboarding. Saltation patterns traveling the length of the legs or torso, or around the torso, could be actuated by a coach as an instruction or feedback to flex/stretch the legs; shift weight left/right or front/back; or rotate the upper body, respectively. The directionality of the saltation patterns were interpreted as "pushing" or "pulling"; Spelmezan et al. referred to this conceptual mapping as the *push* or *pull metaphor*.

McDaniel et al. [10] proposed vibrotactile motor instructions for targeting fundamental movements of the arm for use in any motor learning application. Saltation patterns were used given their intuitiveness for conveying directionality. Two conceptual mappings were explored: *push/pull metaphor* and the *follow-me concept*, each with different motor configurations.

The StrokeSleeve [11], intended for rehabilitation, is a wearable sleeve augmented with vibrotactile actuators for real-time joint angle error feedback, and magnetic trackers for motion capture. A band of vibration motors near the wrist joint was used for elbow flexion/extension and shoulder rotation feedback; and a band near the elbow joint was used for shoulder flexion/extension and shoulder abduction/adduction feedback. Vibrations were interpreted as "attracting" ("pulling") a limb.

Wall, III and Kentala [12] developed a waist-worn device for vibrotactile feedback of body tilt to help vestibulopathic patients control their balance and reduce sway. Vibration motors were arranged on the stomach (just above the waist) and back (just above the waist) each in two columns of three vibration motors each to convey forward tilt and backward tilt, respectively. As tilt increases, vibration motors farther from the waist (i.e., higher up the columns) were actuated. An inertial measure unit was used for tilt measurements.

Existing approaches for vibrotactile instruction and feedback have several limitations. The aforementioned approaches are largely designed to deliver either instruction or feedback, but not both. Some instruction-based approaches, such as [4][10], may be used to provide feedback (e.g., if the wrong movement is performed, the correct movement may be presented), but only at a high-level without capabilities for motion guidance. Currently, vibrotactile feedback systems, such as [8][11], deliver instructions through video media, which increases costs, reduces portability and limits applicability to those applications where the visual modality is available for communication. Therefore, a novel vibrotactile instruction/feedback design is needed to improve versatility, ensuring applicability to a multitude of motor learning applications and scenarios including those where the visual and/or auditory modality are unavailable or overloaded.

Thus far, vibrotactile feedback approaches have focused on performance errors related to joint angles, largely ignoring joint angle rate. Joint angle rate (or speed) is an important characteristic of movement related to timing, intensity, control and coordination. No vibrotactile feedback designs, with the exception of the TactaPack, present speed error information for speed adjustments. The TactaPack [13], developed by Lindeman et al., provides vibrotactile feedback ("nudges") during physical therapy activities to alert the user when a target acceleration is exceeded or not yet reach. No vibrotactile design details are given, and the proposed approach is more of a conceptualization or proof-of-concept with no usability study conducted to evaluate naturalness and usability of the signals. Lastly, in addition to tilt angle, Wall, III and Kentala [12] explored the presentation of tilt rate, but to adjust tilt rather than tilt speed.

Finally, although proposed vibrotactile feedback systems have been evaluated through studies involving complex movements consisting of multiple fundamental movements [8][11], no psychophysical analysis of *individual signals* has been conducted to assess distinctness and naturalness through initial reactions and response time. Such data is the foundation for developing more complex motor learning systems across different applications domains.

To fill these gaps, we propose a wearable device for vibrotactile feedback that provides the following contributions over existing approaches: (1) Two modes of feedback: positioning (joint angle) error and speed (joint angle rate) error for position and speed adjustments, respectively; (2) A vibrotactile feedback design that is compatible with and facilitates vibrotactile motor instructions for improved applicability and usability by avoiding potentially unavailable or overloaded modalities (namely, vision or hearing); and (3) A psychophysical evaluation to gauge initial reactions and response times of these stimulations to better understand the intuitiveness and usability of feedback information delivered to the skin. Moreover, the proposed system is designed for portability and affordability ($500 or less) through use of inertial measurement units for motion capture and wearable electronics powered by rechargeable batteries. Fundamental movements are targeted, rather than application-specific movements, to keep the system versatile in that it may be used across many motor learning application domains such as sports training, music and rehabilitation. Integrating vibrotactile instructions and feedback will support training regimens created by coaches, therapists and other movement instructors. Vibrotactile feedback can provide discreet, real-time error information during a motor performance (e.g., playing a sport) that may lessen distraction compared to other modalities such as vision or hearing. Lastly, the portability offered by the proposed approach is critical in many applications such as sports and tele-rehabilitation.

3. APPROACH

Two types of feedback related to performance errors are explored: (1) positioning errors with respect to joint angle or degree of rotation; and (2) speed errors with respect to joint angle rate or rotation rate. For versatility, we target fundamental movements as almost any complex movement may by decomposed into a sequence of fundamental movements. The human body's most basic movements consist of five fundamental movements [14]: flexion, extension, abduction, adduction and rotation. Assume the body to be in the anatomical position with arms extended by the side and palms facing forward. For movements occurring within the sagittal plane (which divides the body through its midline), flexion/extension decreases/increases the joint angle. For movements occurring within the frontal plane (which divides body into front and back), abduction/adduction is movement away/toward the sagittal plane. For movement occurring within the horizontal plane (which divides the body into a top and bottom), supination/pronation is rotation away/toward the sagittal plane. These five fundamental movements are found across the body, articulated by rotary joints and uniaxial, biaxial and triaxial hinge joints. To simplify both the proposed implementation and user study, we limit the focus to fundamental movements of the right arm below the shoulder.

To ensure that the proposed vibrotactile feedback design is compatible with vibrotactile instructions, we chose an existing, versatile, well-documented vibrotactile instruction set to base our design upon: vibrotactile motor instructions [10]. As previously described, these instructions use saltation patterns, and although different conceptual mappings were explored [10], those found most natural by participants were chosen:

- Elbow joint flexion and extension are cued with vibrotactile stimulations traveling up or down, respectively, the length of the arm, centered at the elbow joint (ventral side). This conceptual mapping is referred to as the *push/pull metaphor* since the directionality of the vibration simulates "pushing" or "pulling" of the forearm.
- Forearm supination and pronation are cued with vibrotactile stimulations traveling clockwise or counter clockwise, respectively, through a cross-section of the forearm (roughly centered between the wrist and elbow joint). Rotations use the conceptual mapping, *follow-me*, since it is intuitive to rotate along the direction of stimulation.
- Wrist flexion and extension are cued with vibrotactile stimulations running medially along the wrist from the dorsal to ventral side, or ventral to dorsal side, respectively. The *follow-me* concept is used given the naturalness of following the vibrations "up" or "down". To accommodate motion sensors, these vibration motors were moved onto the hand, just anterior to the wrist joint.
- Wrist abduction and adduction are cued with vibrotactile stimulations running medial to lateral, or lateral to medial, respectively, across the back of the hand. The *follow-me concept* is used given the naturalness of following the vibrations "left" or "right". These vibration motors were moved distally onto the fingers to accommodate motion sensors.

The proposed feedback designs, described next, utilized the aforementioned motor configurations for seamless integration between instruction and feedback. The relative angles between limbs are extracted in real-time through use of on-body inertial measurement units, described in Section 4.

3.1 Feedback for Positioning Errors

The feedback signal for positioning errors is inspired by the gentle nudges delivered by a physical therapist for guiding movements; it is in the form of quick, gentle vibrotactile bursts of duration 120 ms (separated by gaps of 120 ms). Pilot tests revealed this "tapping" signal to feel natural for guiding a limb to a correct position. A steady, constant vibration was also evaluated, and found to be just as natural. The choice between these feedback signal designs will ultimately depend on the application and preference of the user. When a user reaches a target angle, the vibration stops (plus or minus an acceptable amount of error—referred to here as *padding*). Pilot tests revealed that insufficient padding frustrated users. Therefore, a padding of at least +/- 5 degrees (or more) is recommended for usability; but the amount of padding will ultimately depend on the application. Lastly, the steady vibration, as opposed to the tapping vibration, may be more applicable for those applications requiring accurate positioning with small errors given timing delays (120 ms or less) introduced by the pauses between taps.

The motor configuration and positioning feedback signal design for each fundamental movement is depicted in figure 1. The design utilizes the motor configurations of the instructions previously described to facilitate the seamless delivery of feedback following the presentation of an instruction. For scalability, the system provides the option of using feedback separate from instructions, which might be more applicable to expert users who are perfecting known movements; as opposed to novice users who benefit from knowing what movements to perform, perhaps as part of a trainer's recommended practice regimen, followed by feedback to improve the movements. The general operation of positioning feedback mode, irrespective of joint, is now described; followed by joint-specific vibrotactile stimulation.

Upon receiving a vibrotactile instruction, e.g., flex or extend at the elbow joint, the user performs the requested movement, attempting to reach a target angle (potentially unknown on the first attempt). When the user stops moving, if his or her joint angle is not within the padding of the target angle, vibrotactile feedback will guide the limb to the correct angle (if the user instead reached the correct angle, no feedback would be felt). Vibrotactile stimulation ceases when the correct angle is reached.

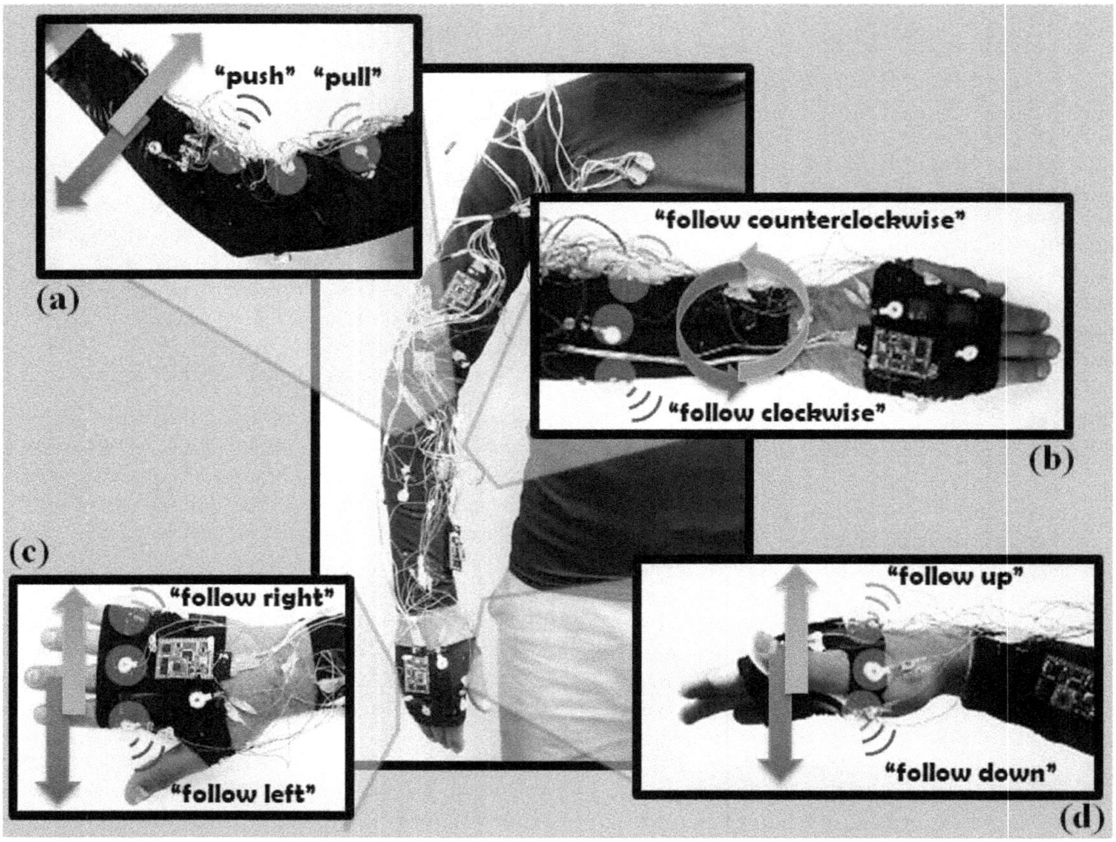

Figure 1. Motor configurations (highlighted in yellow) for delivery of both instructions and positioning feedback for each fundamental movement of the right arm: (a) flexion/extension at elbow joint; (b) supination/pronation of forearm; (c) abduction/adduction at wrist joint; and (d) flexion/extension at wrist joint. The postures shown are those used during the user study (section 5). Abduction/adduction is specific to the posture shown. The "pulses" indicate the motors used as part of feedback, and the arrows indicate the intended direction of movement based on the feedback signal.

To ensure the user has found the correct position, the system requires the user to hold the position for a short duration (less than a second) before providing a stimulation (a vibration running up the length of the arm) to indicate correctness.

Positioning feedback for elbow flexion/extension (figure 1a) taps the ventral side of the forearm to "push" the forearm to extend the limb at the elbow joint; and taps the ventral side of the upper arm (above the area of the bicep) to "pull" the forearm to flex the limb at the elbow joint. The angle of elbow flexion/extension is determined by the relative angle between the forearm and upper arm. Positioning feedback for rotation (figure 1b) taps the lateral side of the forearm to cue a clockwise rotation (supination); or taps the medial side of the forearm to cue a counterclockwise rotation (pronation). The degree of rotation is determined by the orientation of the hand relative to the upper arm. Positioning feedback for wrist abduction/adduction (figure 1c) taps the lateral side of the hand on the little finger to cue abduction; and taps the medial side of the hand on the index finger to cue adduction. The angle of wrist abduction/adduction is determined by the relative angle between the hand and forearm. Positioning feedback for wrist flexion/extension (figure 1d) taps the volar side of the hand to cue a flexion at the wrist joint; and taps the dorsal side of the hand to cue an extension at the wrist joint. The angle of wrist flexion/extension is determined by the relative angle between the hand and forearm.

The aforementioned design was extensively evaluated through pilot testing. Participants found both the vibration signal and interactivity of the system natural for correcting positioning errors. Regarding interactivity, participants appreciated the mirrored feedback resulting from overshooting and undershooting a target angle. This allowed users to get a "feel" for the correct position on the first attempt, after which they could accurately move to the correct angle on subsequent tries, usually without needing guidance even when small padding was used. The system delivers feedback for only one fundamental movement at a time since, especially for novices, too much feedback can overwhelm and distract students—feedback related to a specific error, preferably the movement most in error, is more useful for effective motor learning [3].

3.2 Feedback for Speed Errors

The feedback signal for speed errors indicates the direction to adjust speed (slow down or speed up) through tempo variations of a vibrotactile rhythm. The rhythm is presented to the elbow for a common body site across all arm movements, and to ensure distinctness from vibrotactile instructions and other feedback signals. Two presentation modes were evaluated through pilot testing: real-time speed feedback and near real-time speed feedback.

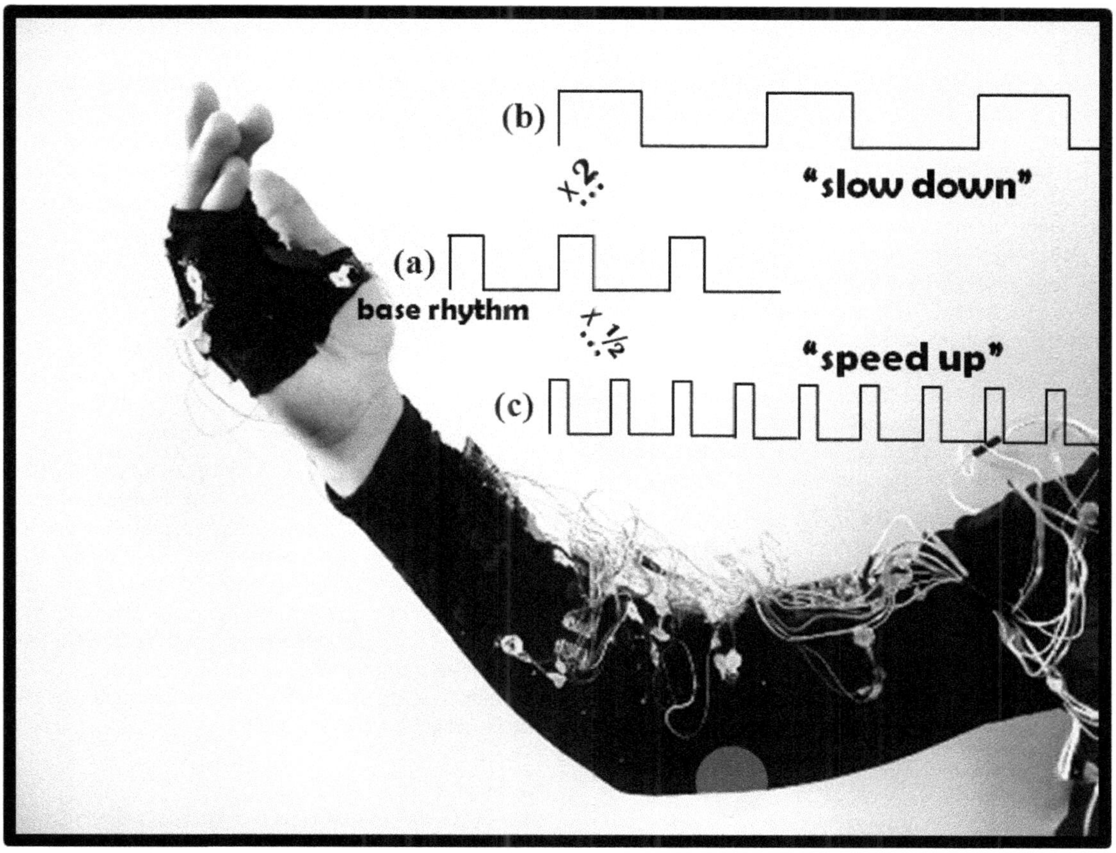

Figure 2. Visualization of vibrotactile rhythms for correcting speed errors. Rhythms are presented near the elbow (highlighted). The rhythms for slowing down or speeding up both begin with a base rhythm (a), followed by either a tempo decrease (b) or tempo increase (c), respectively. The base rhythm consists of three pulses, each of 200 ms duration, separated by 500 ms, for a total duration of 2.1 seconds at 1.428 pulses/s. The tempo decrease consists of three pulses, each of 400 ms duration, separated by 1000 ms, for a total duration of 4.2 seconds at 0.714 pulses/s. The tempo increase consists of nine pulses, each of 100 ms duration, separated by 250 ms, for a total duration of 3.15 seconds at 2.857 pulses/s.

For real-time speed feedback, a slow rhythm tempo indicates "slow down" and a fast rhythm tempo indicates "speed up", presented in real-time during a movement, and dependent upon the user's current speed. The rhythm ceases when the target speed is reached (within a pre-defined padding) and maintained. This mode of speed feedback was not successful during pilot testing. The tempo fluctuated too rapidly due to acceleration at the start of a movement, deceleration toward the end of a movement, and not enough time to respond to the feedback given the short range of motion involved in most fundamental arm movements.

Further pilot testing revealed a near real-time feedback scheme to be a more useful and natural form of speed feedback where speed adjustment is presented after a movement based on the median speed to remove acceleration/deceleration effects. After a user feels a vibrotactile motor instruction, he or she performs the requested fundamental movement with a constant speed. After stopping, if the speed is not within the padding of a target speed, or a pre-defined speed range (e.g., "slow", "medium", etc.), the speed adjustment is presented to the user's elbow (figure 2). A base rhythm (figure 2a) is presented, followed by a tempo change: a tempo decrease indicates "slow down" (figure 2b), whereas a tempo increase indicates "speed up" (figure 2c). Pilot test participants found the tempo variations intuitive, and easy to learn and recognize. After the rhythm is presented, users move with an updated speed, and the system once again compares the user's speed with the target speed. This procedure repeats until the target speed is reached, which then initiates a vibration running up the length of the arm to indicate correctness. As before, pilot test participants appreciated the interactivity of the system. They also appreciated that the rhythm was always presented to the same body site rather than localized for each joint.

4. IMPLEMENTATION

Inertial measurement units (IMUs) were used for motion capture to enhance portability and affordability compared to other motion capture solutions such as magnetic tracking or marker-based visual capture. Although more accurate (but more expensive) sensing platforms exist, the accuracy of IMUs is sufficient for motion sensing where individual IMU measurements for roll, pitch and yaw were found to be accurate up to several degrees relative to Earth when drift errors are handled appropriately. An IMU uses an accelerometer and gyroscope to sense acceleration and angular velocity, respectively—the data of which is sufficient for computing the relative orientation between IMUs. We used the ArduIMU+ V2 (Flat), which has a triple-axis accelerometer, triple-axis gyroscope and onboard processor. A triple-axis magnetometer was later added to account for drift errors. The

Attitude Heading Reference System (AHRS) firmware was used for calculating roll (around the sensor's x-axis), pitch (around the sensor's y-axis) and yaw (around the sensor's z-axis). Each IMU was calibrated once, and the calibration file was loaded automatically for subsequent start-ups. The roll, pitch and yaw samples of each IMU are sent to a LilyPad microcontroller (ATmega328). The microcontroller also controls vibration motors (pancake motors, 150 Hz). All electronics are attached to a Men's compression shirt; vibration motors and IMUs are attached to the sleeve (figure 1), whereas the microcontroller and power supply are attached to the back of the shirt. The construction of a custom actuator/sensor sleeve (as described) was decided over leveraging an existing technology, such as smartphones, due to size and weight restrictions. While smartphones have impressive computational power, vibrotactile feedback capabilities and a multitude of motion sensors, they are and will remain too bulky to attach to most parts of the body; e.g., the back of the hand. Furthermore, we attach many actuators embedded in a bodysuit.

The back of the hand, the medial side of the forearm, and the area above the bicep of the upper arm, were each augmented with an IMU via Velcro (figure 1)—which we refer to as *IMU_H*, *IMU_F* and *IMU_B*, respectively. We refer to the *forward-vector*, *side-vector* and *up-vector* as those vectors aligned with the sensor's local coordinate system (x, y and z), which rotates through space as the orientation of the sensor changes. To calculate joint angles, we compared the orientation between IMUs within a specific plane. The angle between *IMU_F*'s *forward-vector* and *IMU_B*'s *forward-vector* gives the angle between the forearm and upper arm related to elbow flexion/extension. The angle between *IMU_H*'s *up-vector* and *IMU_F*'s *forward-vector* gives the angle between the hand and forearm related to wrist flexion/extension. The angle between *IMU_H*'s *side-vector* and *IMU_F*'s *forward-vector* gives the angle between the hand and forearm related to wrist abduction/adduction. The angle between *IMU_H*'s *side-vector* and *IMU_B*'s *side-vector* gives the degree of rotation between the forearm and upper arm related to forearm supination/pronation.

The *forward-vector*, *side-vector* or *up-vector* of an IMU was found by rotating the respective unit vector (along x, y or z) using the following rotation matrices:

$$R_x = \begin{bmatrix} 1 & 0 & 0 \\ 0 & \cos(roll) & -\sin(roll) \\ 0 & \sin(roll) & \cos(roll) \end{bmatrix},$$

$$R_y = \begin{bmatrix} \cos(pitch) & 0 & \sin(pitch) \\ 0 & 1 & 0 \\ -\sin(pitch) & 0 & \cos(pitch) \end{bmatrix},$$

$$R_z = \begin{bmatrix} \cos(yaw) & -\sin(yaw) & 0 \\ \sin(yaw) & \cos(yaw) & 0 \\ 0 & 0 & 1 \end{bmatrix},$$

where *roll*, *pitch* and *yaw* are the sensor's current orientation estimates in radians. The angle theta between any of the aforementioned vectors was calculated by rearranging the dot product:

$$\theta = \cos^{-1}\left(\frac{\boldsymbol{a} \cdot \boldsymbol{b}}{\|\boldsymbol{a}\|\|\boldsymbol{b}\|}\right)$$

where ***a*** and ***b*** are vectors.

Each IMU is sampled at 8 samples/s. This sampling rate was largely determined by the overhead of the LilyPad's firmware—particularly, the processing requirements to actuate vibration motors and sense the IMUs simultaneously during feedback mode. However, this sampling rate was found to be sufficient for the slow to moderate speed movements involved; fast movements were not tested as these saturated the gyroscopes of the IMUs.

Feedback for either positioning errors or speed errors begins after a user has started and stopped a movement. We refer to this movement as the initial movement. A threshold speed is used to discard false movements such as jitter. A movement is considered the initial movement if it has a speed of 15°/s or greater, and maintains this speed for at least 3 samples—after which, falling below 15°/s will initiate feedback. Pilot testing revealed the aforementioned threshold speed to work well in terms of ignoring subtle, unintentional movements and jitter.

A graphical interface was developed to provide control over system operation. Through the user interface, users can send vibrotactile motor instructions; record movements without feedback; record movements with positioning feedback by entering a fundamental movement and target angle (with padding); record movements with speed feedback by entering a fundamental movement and target speed (with padding). The user interface also has parsing capabilities in that users can segment raw motion data files into fundamental movements based on speed thresholds (such as 15°/s).

5. USER STUDY

Aim: A user study was conducted to assess the distinctness, naturalness and usability of the proposed feedback designs, respectively position and speed adjustments, through two experiments. Each subject participated in both experiments (within-subject design), and the order of experiments was counterbalanced to remove order effects. The study was approved by Arizona State University's Institutional Review Board.

Subjects: Sixteen subjects (8 males, 8 females) completed the study. Ages ranged between 18 and 32 (*M:* 24, *SD:* 8). No subjects had any known motor or tactile impairments.

Apparatus: The firmware and software of the system was altered to accommodate the study. In particular, feedback was not linked to motor performance—that is, requiring a user to reach a desired target angle or speed; but rather, feedback signals were randomly presented, and initial responses were recorded, for psychophysical assessment of initial reactions to the stimuli. The raw movement recordings were automatically annotated with the start and end angle and timestamp of the initial movement, and the time in the recording when feedback began. Samples were recorded every 120 ms. A motion segmentation algorithm accommodated slow speeds captured during feedback. A speed threshold of 5°/s was used to segment responses to positioning feedback as well as speed feedback instructing to slow down since participants often responded with very slow speeds. A speed threshold of 15°/s was used to segment responses to speed feedback instructing to speed up since faster speed responses were made. All slow movements were manually verified as valid movements as opposed to jitter based on their timing and range of motion.

Procedure: Each participant was randomly assigned in advance the order in which the experiments were applied. After donning the wearable system, participants were introduced to layman terminology for describing the movements involved: *elbow-*

up/elbow-down (elbow flexion/extension, arm held out in front of body with palm facing up); *wrist-up/wrist-down* (wrist extension/ flexion, arm held out in front of body with palm down), *wrist-right/wrist-left* (wrist abduction/adduction, arm held out in front of body with palm down), *rotate-clockwise/rotate-counterclockwise* (forearm supination/ pronation, arm held out in front of body). During this time, the experimenter demonstrated these movements. Participants were asked to stand facing the experimenter during the study, but were allowed to sit during breaks which could be taken as often as needed.

In both experiments, participants underwent a familiarization, training and testing phase each involving recording sessions where movements are recorded during feedback presentation. A recording session is referred to as a *trial*. As the focus of this evaluation is on feedback rather than instruction, before each trial, the participant is instructed by the experimenter (rather than the system) to perform a specific *initial* movement before feedback is felt. For example, during testing, participants are instructed to perform an *elbow-up*, *elbow-down*, etc. before feedback is felt. During familiarization and training, the direction of the initial movement is not controlled—for example, the experimenter would inform the participant to perform an elbow movement, either up or down. The initial movement direction was counterbalanced across testing trials to reduce effects of movement direction immediately before feedback is felt. Since the IMUs' gyroscopes saturate at high speeds, participants were asked to perform smooth, constant speeds at slow (15°/s) to moderate (100°/s) speeds during the study. These speeds were demonstrated to subjects by the experimenter. The following description of the different phases of the study is the same for both experiments.

During familiarization, participants were introduced to the purpose and operation of the system, and presented with all eight feedback signals. We refer to the presentation of all eight feedback signals as a *set*. Repetitions were allowed, and participants were told in advance the adjustments that the feedback signals would request.

During training, a sequence of sets was presented to participants. Within each set, the order of feedback signals is randomized. The experimenter corrected wrong guesses (adjustments), and confirmed those that were correct. To move onto testing, participants had to achieve a recognition accuracy of 80% or better (7 out of 8 feedback signals). Since analysis is done offline through a parsing algorithm, the experimenter provided feedback manually through visual observation (training phase only). Responses were documented as *correct*, *incorrect* or *corrected*, where the latter response involves an incorrect initial reaction followed by an adjustment to correct the response. Corrected responses are found only for positioning feedback since speed feedback is near real-time. Those corrected responses with excessive durations (> 500 ms) were not counted in favor of the 80% threshold. Observational accuracy was later confirmed through performance comparison with parser.

During testing, each of the eight feedback signals were presented four times (initial movement directions were counterbalanced) with their order randomized for 32 trials in total. The experimenter did not provide feedback during testing. After the completed user study, participants were asked to fill out a questionnaire pertaining to the usability of the system, and the distinctness, naturalness and usability of the feedback signals.

Regardless of phase, each trial involved the following system operation (positioning feedback is described first, following by speed feedback): A trial begins with the participant feeling a one second vibration, "start signal", at the dorsal side of the elbow joint. Participants are asked to move only after the start signal ends as this is when the system begins recording. As previously described, the system detects a movement when 15°/s is surpassed and briefly maintained. (During familiarization, participants are asked to move faster when speeds are too slow for system detection.) Since participants will need to adjust their position once the initial movement is completed, they are asked to stop in the center of their full range of motion of the involved joint. Once the initial movement is completed, the system immediately delivers feedback to adjust position (left or right, up or down, clockwise or counterclockwise, depending on the fundamental movement). The participant follows the feedback to adjust his or her current position until the experimenter stops the recording. For this study, feedback is not linked to motor performance (no target angle or target speed is needed for each trial).

The operation of the system during near real-time speed feedback is slightly different from that of real-time positioning feedback: As before, a trial begins with the participant feeling a start signal—this time, at the back of the hand to avoid confusion with the rhythms presented to the elbow joint. Participants were once again asked to move only after the "start signal" ends, and a speed threshold of 15°/s is also used for this experiment. After stopping (participants were instructed to move through their full range of motion), participants immediately feel a feedback signal at their elbow requesting a speed adjustment (slow down or speed up). While the rhythm is being presented, the system does not record movement. During this time, the participant moves back to his or her starting position, and waits briefly for the second "start signal"; after which, the participant moves through his or her full range motion with the updated speed based on the feedback. Recording commences immediately following the second start signal. As before, feedback signals are randomly presented by the experimenter as opposed to being linked to actual motor performance (for the purposes of this psychophysical analysis).

Results: The mean number of training sets for each experiment was 1.25, *SD:* 0.57 (positioning feedback) and 1.12, *SD:* 0.34 (speed feedback). For positioning and speed feedback, 160 and 144 training trials were captured, respectively. The data files from 7 and 12 trials, respectively, were corrupted due to sensor saturation and were omitted from the analysis. Coherence between experimenter feedback during training and the segmentation algorithm was later verified; no inconsistencies were found for positioning feedback, and only four inconsistencies (out of 144 trials) were found for speed feedback during training.

For responses to positioning feedback, we differentiate between what we term *recognition accuracy* and *response accuracy*. We define recognition accuracy as the number of both correct and *corrected* responses out of the total number of trials, where a corrected response is initially incorrect, but eventually corrected. Response accuracy does not count corrected responses as correct, and therefore considers only the initial reaction to the stimuli. The mean recognition and response accuracy for positioning feedback, averaged across participants and signals, was respectively, 94.2%, *SD:* 6.2% and 91.2%, *SD:* 7.1%. Mean recognition and response accuracies for individual signals are shown in figure 3(a). Only 14 testing trails involved corrected responses; and of these, nine

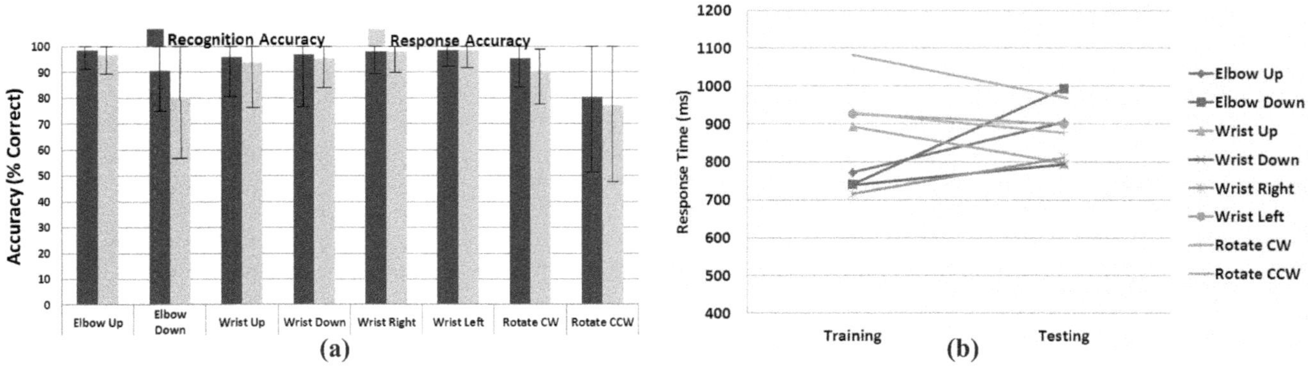

Figure 3. Positioning feedback results: (a) Mean recognition accuracy and response accuracy per signal. Error bars are standard deviations. (b) Mean response time per signal between training and testing.

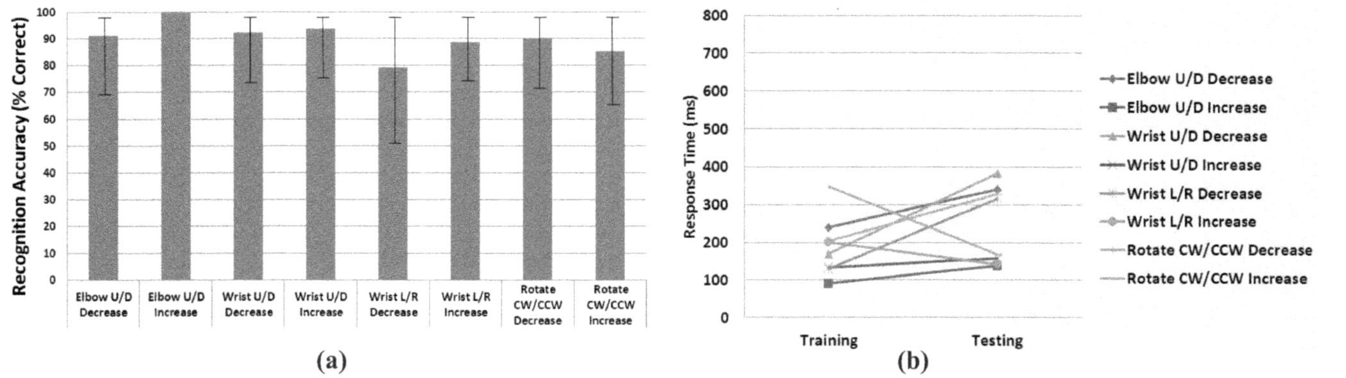

Figure 4. Speed feedback results: (a) Mean recognition accuracy per signal. Error bars are standard deviations. (b) Mean response time per signal between training and testing.

responses were corrected in less than a second, three in just over a second; and two in about two seconds. Of the 512 recorded testing trials, 18 were corrupted due to saturation; these were omitted from analysis. For speed feedback, we do not differentiate between recognition and response accuracy since the user performs one speed adjustment movement, which is recorded as correct or incorrect. The mean recognition accuracy for speed feedback, averaged across participants and signals, was 90%, *SD:* 9.7%. Mean recognition accuracies for individual signals are shown in figure 4(a). As before, some recorded testing trials were corrupted due to saturation; 20 trials out of 512 were corrupted, and hence, omitted from analysis.

Response time to stimuli was extracted from the files of recorded trial data. For positioning feedback, response time is defined as the time between onset of the feedback signal, and movement in response to this signal. For speed feedback, response time is defined as the time between the end of the second start signal, and movement in response to this event. The mean response time for positioning feedback, averaged across participants and signals, was 847 ms, *SD:* 202 ms, and 881 ms, *SD:* 205 ms, for training and testing respectively. The mean response time for speed feedback, averaged across participants and signals, was 198 ms, *SD:* 214 ms, and 247 ms, *SD:* 182 ms, for training and testing respectively. Mean response time for individual signals during training and testing are shown in figure 3(b) and 4(b) for positioning feedback and speed feedback, respectively. Lastly, mean responses to general usability questions are shown in table 1; and mean responses to questions related to the learnability, distinctness and naturalness of positioning and speed feedback signals are shown in table 2 and 3, respectively.

Discussion: The learning rate of both experiments, estimated in terms of the mean number of training sets, is impressive, showing that the feedback signals were easy to learn. This correlates with subjective results where participants gave high marks to learnability: table 2, *Q2*, and table 3, *Q2*, for positioning and speed feedback, respectively. Given these short training times, the mean recognition and response accuracies for positioning feedback, figure 3(a), are impressive. However, a significant difference was found between recognition accuracies, $\chi^2(7) = 20$, $p < 0.05$, and response accuracies, $\chi^2(7) = 18.2$, $p < 0.05$, indicating that some feedback signals were more difficult to recognize than others. Indeed, the recognition and response accuracies for 'Elbow Down', 'Rotate CW' and 'Rotate CCW' are noticeably lower, although still satisfactory, compared to other signals. These results correlate with subjective feedback in terms of both ease of recognition (table 2, *Q1*) and naturalness (table 2, *Q3*). Half of participants commented that is was difficult to adjust to the "pushing" involved in 'Elbow Down' as all other movements used the *follow-me concept*. Under the *push/pull metaphor*, participants were trained to interpret a vibration on the ventral side of the forearm as "pushing". However, if participants were expecting a *follow-me* signal, then this same stimulation would be interpreted as "pulling". Indeed, 9 of the 14 corrected movements were corrections for misinterpreting 'Elbow Down' as 'Elbow Up'. The signal for 'Elbow Up' was confused less often given that a *follow-me signal* would occur on the dorsal side of the forearm rather than above the area of the bicep. This confusion seems to indicate difficulty with switching between conceptual mappings, at least with the limited training underwent by participants during this study. Therefore, to reduce training and improve usability, it is recommended that a consistent conceptual mapping is used across all positioning feedback signals. Six participants commented that positioning feedback for rotational movements was harder to recognize and less natural compared to other signals. The challenge of recognizing and responding to vibrotactile feedback for rotational adjustments has been noted in the literature [8]. We observed that the positions of vibration motors change during rotations as the arm rotates *within* the sleeve. This might have created some confusion for participants, although recognition accuracy was still satisfactory. However, it is recommended that the signal for rotational adjustments be moved off the forearm, and onto either the hand or upper arm.

The mean recognition accuracies for speed feedback, figure 4(a), are remarkable given the short training times. However, a significant difference was found between recognition accuracies, $\chi^2(7) = 17.1, p < 0.05$, indicating that some feedback signals were more difficult to recognize than others. From figure 4(a), we can observe that the recognition accuracies for 'Wrist L/R Decrease', 'Wrist L/R Increase', and 'Rotate CW/CCW Increase' are noticeably lower, although still satisfactory, compared to other signals. But subjective results don't reveal any difficulties with recognition (table 3, *Q1*), and participants found all speed feedback signals very natural (table 3, *Q3*). We speculate that this discrepancy arises not from detectability, but rather, participants' ability to perform the requested speed adjustments. Speed adjustments for wrist abduction/adduction and rotational movements might have been more difficult compared to other movements given their shorter range of motion. Indeed, we observed greater physical effort during these movements to achieve the requested speed adjustments; and several participants commented that the shorter range of motion made speed adjustments slightly more difficult.

The mean response time to positioning feedback is less than a second for training or testing, figure 3(b), with the exception of 'Rotate CCW'. The difference in mean response time between training and testing was not significant, $t(15)=0.689$, $p=0.5$, two-tailed (data normalized using $\log_{10}$), suggesting that either participants quickly adjusted to the feedback signals or longer practice times are needed to see larger gains in improvement. A significant difference was found between mean response times of signals, $\chi^2(7) = 15.3, p < 0.05$, indicating that reaction was slower for some signals compared to others. Indeed, figure 3(b) suggests higher response times for 'Elbow Down' and 'Rotate CCW', which correlates with recognition difficulties. The mean response time to speed feedback signals is less than 400 ms for training or testing, figure 4(b). The improved response times of speed feedback compared to positioning feedback is due to the near real-time operation of the system: in the case of speed feedback, participants had a small delay to prepare for the second start signal before making their speed adjustments. Similar to positioning feedback, the difference in mean response time between training and testing was not significant, $t(15) = -1.045$, $p = 0.312$, two-tailed (data normalized using $\log_{10}$). No significant

Table 1. Mean responses to system usability questions. Ratings are based on Likert scale: 1 (low) to 5 (high).

Questions	Mean	SD
1) How easy was it to put on the suit?	3.68	0.87
2) How easy was it to take off the suit?	3.43	1.15
3) How easy was it to perform the movements?	4.43	0.62
4) How comfortable was the suit?	3.87	0.95
5) How lightweight was the suit?	4.75	0.57
6) How silent were the suit's vibration motors?	3.37	0.95

Table 2. Mean responses to questions related to positioning feedback. Ratings based on Likert scale: 1 (low) to 5 (high).

Questions	Mean	SD
1) How easy was it to recognize the following feedback signals for changing position:		
• a) Elbow 'up' adjustment:	4.37	0.88
• b) Elbow 'down' adjustment:	4.00	1.09
• c) Wrist 'up' adjustment:	4.87	0.34
• d) Wrist 'down' adjustment:	4.68	0.47
• e) Wrist 'right' adjustment:	4.56	0.62
• f) Wrist 'left' adjustment:	4.62	0.50
• g) Rotate 'right' (CW) adjustment:	3.68	1.19
• h) Rotate 'left' (CCW) adjustment:	3.75	1.18
2) How easy was it to learn the following feedback signals for changing position:		
• a) Elbow 'up' adjustment:	4.50	0.73
• b) Elbow 'down' adjustment:	4.12	1.02
• c) Wrist 'up' adjustment:	4.93	0.25
• d) Wrist 'down' adjustment:	4.93	0.25
• e) Wrist 'right' adjustment:	4.87	0.34
• f) Wrist 'left' adjustment:	4.87	0.34
• g) Rotate 'right' (CW) adjustment:	3.87	1.14
• h) Rotate 'left' (CCW) adjustment:	3.93	1.12
3) How natural (intuitive) were the following feedback signals for changing position:		
• a) Elbow 'up' adjustment:	4.37	0.80
• b) Elbow 'down' adjustment:	3.81	1.10
• c) Wrist 'up' adjustment:	4.68	0.70
• d) Wrist 'down' adjustment:	4.68	0.70
• e) Wrist 'right' adjustment:	4.68	0.70
• f) Wrist 'left' adjustment:	4.68	0.70
• g) Rotate 'right' (CW) adjustment:	3.62	1.14
• h) Rotate 'left' (CCW) adjustment:	3.68	1.13

Table 3. Mean responses to questions related to speed feedback. Ratings based on Likert scale: 1 (low) to 5 (high).

Questions	Mean	SD
1) How easy was it to recognize the following feedback signals for changing speed:		
• a) Decrease speed for elbow... ('up'/'down'):	4.56	0.81
• b) Increase speed for elbow... ('up'/'down'):	4.81	0.54
• c) Decrease speed for wrist... ('up'/'down'):	4.62	0.80
• d) Increase speed for wrist... ('up'/'down'):	4.87	0.34
• e) Decrease speed for wrist... ('left'/'right'):	4.62	0.80
• f) Increase speed for wrist... ('left'/'right'):	4.87	0.34
• g) Decrease speed for forearm rotation ('left'/'right'):	4.62	0.80
• h) Increase speed for forearm rotation ('left'/'right'):	4.87	0.34
2) How easy was it to learn the following feedback signals for changing speed:		
• a) Decrease speed for elbow... ('up'/'down'):	4.68	0.70
• b) Increase speed for elbow... ('up'/'down'):	4.87	0.34
• c) Decrease speed for wrist... ('up'/'down'):	4.56	0.81
• d) Increase speed for wrist... ('up'/'down'):	4.75	0.57
• e) Decrease speed for wrist... ('left'/'right'):	4.50	0.96
• f) Increase speed for wrist... ('left'/'right'):	4.68	0.79
• g) Decrease speed for forearm rotation ('left'/'right'):	4.68	0.70
• h) Increase speed for forearm rotation ('left'/'right'):	4.87	0.34
3) How natural (intuitive) were the following feedback signals for changing speed:		
• a) Decrease speed for elbow... ('up'/'down'):	4.75	0.77
• b) Increase speed for elbow... ('up'/'down'):	4.81	0.54
• c) Decrease speed for wrist... ('up'/'down'):	4.75	0.77
• d) Increase speed for wrist... ('up'/'down'):	4.87	0.34
• e) Decrease speed for wrist... ('left'/'right'):	4.75	0.77
• f) Increase speed for wrist... ('left'/'right'):	4.87	0.34
• g) Decrease speed for forearm rotation ('left'/'right'):	4.75	0.57
• h) Increase speed for forearm rotation ('left'/'right'):	4.81	0.40

difference was found between mean response times of signals, $\chi^2(7) = 8.42$, $p = 0.297$, indicating that participants did not hesitate to make speed adjustments. This correlates with the positive ratings received for ease of recognition and naturalness. Lastly, the positive usability ratings of table 1 show that the system was easy to don/doff, comfortable and discreet; and very easy to move in and lightweight. Through open-ended response questions, participants commented that they liked the purpose and overall concept of the system; and overall, found the feedback signals easy to recognize and natural.

6. CONCLUSION AND FUTURE WORK

A novel vibrotactile positioning and speed feedback extension to an existing vibrotactile instruction set was proposed and evaluated. This makes several contributions: (1) The proposed approach bridges the divide between vibrotactile instructions and feedback, enabling the introduction of enhanced motor learning systems that scale well between novice and expert users who have different needs in terms of instruction and feedback delivery; (2) A novel feedback design for speed corrections, which participants found intuitive, and particularly appreciated the coherence of the signal between movements; and (3) A psychophysical evaluation of the proposed feedback signals to better understand the distinctness and naturalness of feedback signals by examining initial reactions and response times. Although this work did not explore vibrotactile instruction and feedback compatibility, their integration will be investigated as part of future work. The decision to focus evaluation solely on the proposed designs for vibrotactile feedback was motivated by the need for a thorough psychophysical evaluation before exploring human perception and usability of instructions with feedback.

As part of future work, we plan to further explore the perceptual and cognitive difficulties involved in switching between conceptual mappings, and evaluate different positioning feedback designs for rotational movements. A more long term goal is a longitudinal system evaluation within a real-world application such as physical therapy. Our first target application will be occupational therapy in which patients could benefit from a "take-home therapist" to practice and relearn movements away from the clinic. Vibrotactile instructions will provide a practice regimen, created by the therapist, targeting specific fundamental movements in need of continued practice at home and/or clinic. Motor rehabilitation often involves exercises to extend a patient's range of motion to what was normal. Vibrotactile feedback may be used to indicate when a specific range of motion (joint angle) has not been reached by the patient, helping to motivate the patient and indicate progress. The system will also alert the user when he or she is in danger of re-injury, such as when movements might be too fast. Toward the goal of a "take-home therapist", the main processing element (a laptop) will be replaced by a lightweight smartphone that can fit in a pocket.

7. ACKNOWLEDGMENTS

Work supported by the Arizona State University Graduate and Professional Student Association's JumpStart Grant Program.

8. REFERENCES

[1] Lederman, S. J., and Klatzky, R. L. 1987. Hand movements: A window into haptic object recognition. *Cognitive Psychology*, 19, 342-368.

[2] Kennedy, C. A., and Yoke, M. M. 2009. *Methods of Group Exercise Instruction*. Human Kinetics, Champaign, IL.

[3] Schmidt, R. A., and Wrisberg, C. A. 2000. *Motor Learning and Performance: A Problem-Based Learning Approach*. 2nd edition. Human Kinetics, Champaign, IL.

[4] Spelmezan, D., Jacobs, M., Hilgers, A., and Borchers, J. 2009. Tactile motion instructions for physical activities. *In Proc. of the 27th International Conference on Human Factors in Computing Systems*, 2243-52.

[5] Yang, U., and Kim, G. J. 2002. Implementation and evaluation of 'Just Follow Me': An immersive, VR-based motion-training system. *Presence: Teleoperators and Virtual Environments*, 11, 3 (June 2002), 304-23.

[6] Drobny, D., Weiss, M., and Borchers, J. 2009. Saltate!: a sensor-based system to support dance beginners. *In Proc. of the 27th International Conference Extended Abstracts on Human Factors in Computing Systems*, 3943–48.

[7] Grindlay, G. 2008. Haptic guidance benefits musical motor learning. *In Proc. of the Symposium on Haptic Interfaces for Virtual Environment and Teleoperator systems*, 397-404.

[8] Lieberman, J., and Breazeal, C. 2007. TIKL: Development of a wearable vibrotactile feedback suit for improved human motor learning. *IEEE Transactions on Robotics*, 23(5), 919-926.

[9] Geldard, F. A., and Sherrick, C. E. 1972. The cutaneous 'rabbit': a perceptual illusion. *Science*, 178, 4057 (October 1972), 178 -79.

[10] McDaniel, T., Goldberg, M., Villanueva, D., Viswanathan, L.N., Panchanathan, S. 2011. Motor learning using a kinematic-vibrotactile mapping targeting fundamental movements. *In Proc. of the ACM International Conference on Multimedia*, 543-552.

[11] Bark, K., Khanna, P., Irwin, R., Kapur, P., Jax, S. A., Buxbaum, L. J., and Kuchenbecker, K. J. 2011. Lessons in using vibrotactile feedback to guide fast arm motions. *In Proc. of the IEEE World Haptics Conference*, 355-360.

[12] Wall, III, C., and Kentala, E. 2010. Effect of displacement, velocity, and combined vibrotactile tilt feedback on postural control of vestibulopathic subjects. *Journal of Vestibular Research*, 20, 61-69.

[13] Lindeman, R. W., Yanagida, Y., Hosaka, K., Abe, S. 2006. The TactaPack: a wireless sensor/actuator package for physical therapy applications. *In Proc. of the 14th Symposium on Haptic Interfaces for Virtual Environment and Teleoperator Systems*, 337-41.

[14] Behnke, R. S. 2006. *Kinetic Anatomy*. Human Kinetics, Champaign, IL.

MOGAT: Mobile Games with Auditory Training for Children with Cochlear Implants

Yinsheng Zhou[1], Khe Chai Sim[1], Patsy Tan[2], Ye Wang[1]
[1]School of Computing, National University of Singapore, 117417, Singapore
[2]Singapore General Hospital, 169608, Singapore
{yzhou86, simkc, wangye}@comp.nus.edu.sg, patsy.tan.l.p@sgh.com.sg

ABSTRACT

Cochlear implants have improved the lives of tens of thousands of the hearing impaired by providing sufficient auditory perception for speech, but these devices are far from satisfactory for music perception. Many cochlear implant recipients, especially pre-lingually deafened children, have difficulty recognizing and producing specific pitches. To improve musical auditory habilitation for children post cochlear implantation, we developed MOGAT: MObile Games with Auditory Training. The system includes three musical games built with off-the-shelf mobile devices to train their pitch perception and intonation skills respectively, and a cloud-based web service which allows music therapists to monitor and design individual training for children. The design of the games and web service was informed by a pilot survey (N=60 children). To ensure widespread use with low-cost mobile devices, we minimized the computation load while retaining highly accurate audio analysis. A 6-week user study (N=15 children) showed that the music habilitation with MOGAT was intuitive, enjoyable and motivating. It has improved most children's pitch discrimination and production, and several children's improvement was statistically significant ($p < 0.05$).

Categories and Subject Descriptors

H.5.2 [**User Interfaces**]: User-centered design; H.5.5 [**Sound and Music Computing**]: Signal analysis, synthesis, and processing; K.4.2 [**Social Issues**]: Assistive technologies for persons with disabilities

General Terms

Design, Experimentation, Human Factors.

Keywords

Music, mobile, game, auditory habilitation, cochlear implant, children.

1. INTRODUCTION

Music plays an important role in people's lives. The vast majority of people perceive music with their unaided ears, but millions of people have partially or profoundly impaired hearing. How can they experience music? One approach is through amplifying vibrations with mechanical devices; Beethoven was an early adopter of such technology [19]. Another approach is to sense the tactile vibrations; the highly acclaimed percussionist Evelyn Glennie "feels" music with different parts of her body [26]. It must be noted that these musicians experienced sounds before the onset of deafness. As a result, they could imagine music in their minds [28] without hearing it. However, some children are deaf before forming memories of music or even language. For those pre-lingually deafened children, the only avenue to develop their hearing sense is via cochlear implants (CI). By surgically implanting electronic devices in their cochleas, children[1] with CI are able to hear sound and music [21].

CIs are quite successful in supporting spoken communication, but they are still less than ideal for encoding and transmitting musical sounds [30]. The rich spectrum of musical sounds are not well preserved by feature extraction devices; intelligible speech only requires a very narrow frequency bandwidth. CI recipients generally have poorer perception and identification of melodic patterns [22] and musical timbre [18] than normal hearing people.

Auditory habilitation is an important part of the implant process to boost recipients' adaption for the devices post cochlear implantation. It must encompass many features including not only speech but also music perception and production [13]. As such, musical auditory habilitation is usually set up as an adjuvant habilitation process to their standard habilitation programs [35]. Musical habilitation has shown improvement in recipients' melody recognition [24], timbre identification [23], and can enhance recipients' self-esteem and increase their motivation for practicing [13]. The main obstruction is a lack of appropriate teaching resources, professional training and administrative support [27].

In order to focus on their musical habilitation, it was imperative to involve children with CI in the design loop from the beginning. Therefore, a pilot study is conducted to understand their deficiency in terms of pitch and rhythm perception/pitch production in contrast to normal hearing peers. Based on those findings, we designed and developed

[1]Estimates show that as of December 2010, approximately 219,000 people worldwide have received implants [12], of which at least 60,000 are children recipients [11] whose number is increasing dramatically every year

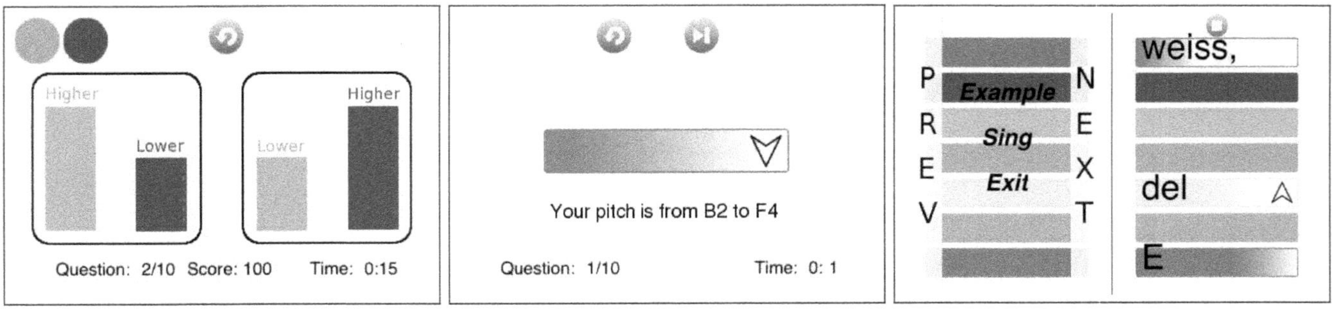

(a) *Higher Lower* (b) *Vocal Matcher* (c) *Ladder Singer*

Figure 1: The game interfaces in MOGAT

MObile Games with Auditory Training (MOGAT) using off-the-shelf mobile devices. MOGAT aims to provide a fun, intuitive, and cost-effective way to enhance musical habilitation for children with CI.

Since MOGAT was designed for pre-lingually deafened children with cochlear implants, their unique characteristics must be considered when selecting objectives, content, and particular stimuli. Pre-lingually deafened children with CI are not exposed to sound until their implantation, while post-lingually deafened adults with CI have in their mind the experience of sound established prior to their deafness. As such, the training methods for children with CI should be specifically designed, which will be different from the existing music training program for adults [25]. Delay in their language development may affect their cognitive and behavioral development [33, 32], which will further inform the choice of vocabulary and material for those students.

MOGAT contains three structured music games focusing on pitch-based habilitation. *Higher Lower* (Figure 1a) trains pitch interval perception ability; *Vocal Matcher* (Figure 1b) focuses on single pitch production with appropriate voice control; *Ladder Singer* (Figure 1c) combines pitch, breath, and lyrics in an intuitive user interface to guide users in singing songs. Using highly accurate singing analysis algorithm, it transcribes users' pitch and provides real-time feedback to help them to sing correctly. With optimized computation load, MOGAT can be built into low-cost mobile devices to provide a cost-effective way for children's habilitation. Audio is recorded on mobile devices and uploaded to a server. With all the data synchronized, stored, and managed in our server, MOGAT realizes a cloud computing service to enable music teachers and therapists to support a large number of children's habilitation. The MOGAT web application allows teachers to visualize the progress of individual students over days, weeks, and months. Furthermore, teachers are able to pinpoint students' singing problems and send comments or encouragements to their students.

This paper's main contributions can be summarized as:

- MOGAT is the first integrated solution to support musical (rather than general audio) habilitation for children with cochlear implants.
- An analysis of users' pitch/rhythm perception and intonation accuracy that guides the design, which is catered specifically to their musical needs and cognitive abilities.
- We conducted systematic and in-depth user evaluation to test the effectiveness of MOGAT in enhancing musical habilitation for children with CI.

2. RELATED WORK

2.1 Auditory Habilitation and Its Applications

For children with CI, auditory habilitation is critical to their hearing and speech development [38]. Due to the spectrally degraded signal pattern provided by the implant and the large interpersonal variability [37], passive adaptation via long-term use of the devices may not be adequate. Nevertheless, active learning via auditory habilitation has been shown to be effective in the speech recognition and production of the hearing impaired [15, 16, 36]. Meanwhile, auditory training with music stimuli can help to improve music recognition and production for cochlear implant users [24, 13, 22]. However, because of time and cost considerations, it is almost impossible for hearing healthcare professionals and therapists to provide extensive and intensive auditory therapy to CI recipients [21].

Recently, computer-assisted speech training (CAST) system has been developed to augment auditory habilitation approaches by providing greater flexibility with minimal costs and supervision. Research shows that moderate amounts of auditory training performed at home with the computer-based speech training (CAST) software resulted in significant improvements in the speech recognition for both adult CI recipients [21, 20] and children with CI [38]. A typical example is Sound Express Auditory Training (SEAT) system [8], a self-directed auditory training program on personal computers. Although it has some useful features (e.g., interactive interface and feedback) to help CI users to practice their perception of spoken sounds, it is not optimized for musical habilitation and lacks teacher guidance.

Unlike speech perception, music perception relies more strongly on pitch perception and thus contains information very differently from verbal communication. Due to the device limitation, implant listeners are reported to have great difficulty with complex pitch perception in comparison with speech perception [30]. Unfortunately, relatively few studies have explored the effects of auditory training on CI users' music perception or production. The only system for this purpose was designed for post-lingually deafened adults [25, 24]. However, music perception by pre-lingually deafened children with CI is very different from post-lingually deafened adult CI users [22] who already have the experience of acoustic sound before their deafness. Pre-lingually deafened children begin to form their concept of sound until implantation, and all their central speech and music patterns are developed in the context of electric hearing. Therefore, it is imperative and important to develop a musical auditory system specifically for children with CI.

2.2 Music Education Applications

The objectives of the existing music training applications are not compatible with our purpose. Most vocal training applications (e.g., [10, 9, 29]) were designed to develop specific professional listening and performing techniques for users who already have decent hearing acuity (e.g., recognition of chords, harmonics, and development of unique vocal style or instrument skills). Therefore, the components of these applications are not able to assist children with CI for their habilitation which has a different focus (e.g., pitch and rhythm perception and fundamental singing ability). Although Karaoke games [5, 4, 3] seem to have some values in learning singing songs using real-time visual feedback and machine scoring, our study show that it is harder for them to understand and use this kind of Karaoke games than our designed singing game. Family Ensemble [31] and MySong [34] use automatic accompaniment generation technique to enhance users' motivation in piano playing and vocal singing. MOGCLASS [40, 39] provides a collaborative music system to enhance students' music experience during music classes. However, all these projects are designed for normal people, so they will not be so useful for our special user group.

3. AUDIO ANALYSIS

3.1 Automatic Note Annotation

3.1.1 *Note Segmentation*

Since users will be singing the hard consonant "La" (see Section 4.1.1), notes onsets are easily identified in a spectrogram (Figure 2). Our input audio is a monophonic signal at 24 kHz. We take the short-term fourier transform (STFT) with a hamming window, using a window size of 512 and a FFT length of 512. The detection function is constructed using the half-wave rectified spectral flux,

$$SF(k) = \sum_{i=0}^{n-1} H(s(k,i) - s(k-1,i)) \quad (1)$$

where $s(k,i)$ is the magnitude of the ith frequency bin in the kth frame, and $H(x) = (x + |x|)/2$ is a half-wave rectifier assigning zeros for its negative arguments. The rectification emphasizes onsets rather than offsets. The spectral flux was first normalized to $[0,1]$ by subtracting the minimum and dividing the maximum absolute difference. Then, a low-pass filter was applied to remove jitter and noise. Finally, a high-pass FIR filter adaptive threshold was subtracted from the normalized spectral flux to create a "pruned" flux.

$$SF_{pruned}(k) = \alpha + \frac{\beta}{H}\sum_{i=k-H/2}^{k+H/2} SF(i) \quad (2)$$

We empirically determine the moving window size $H = 10$, and $\alpha = 0.03, \beta = 1.2$. After post-processing and thresholding the detection function, peak-picking is used to identify the local maxima in the adjusted spectral flux above the defined threshold.

3.1.2 *Pitch Estimation*

We used the YIN pitch estimation algorithm [17]. In order to find the periodicity (indicated by $\tilde{\tau}$, i.e., the number of samples in the period) of a discrete time-domain signal s,

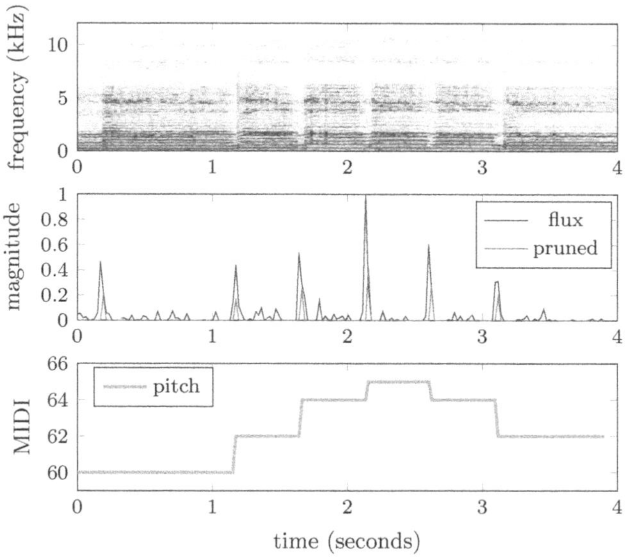

Figure 2: Note segmentation result on a singer's recording. The top plot is a spectrogram; the lower plot is the normalized and adjusted spectral flux.

we begin by calculating the squared difference function $d(\tau)$ for a desired range of lag values:

$$d(\tau) = \sum_{n=0}^{N-1} (s(n) - s(n+\tau))^2 \quad (3)$$

We then use a cumulative mean normalized difference function to determine the aperiodicity of the audio frame:

$$d'(\tau) = \begin{cases} 1, & \tau = 0 \\ d(\tau)/[(1/\tau)\sum_{j=1}^{\tau} d(j)], & \text{otherwise} \end{cases} \quad (4)$$

Next, we search for the smallest value of τ that gives a minimum of $d'(\tau)$ smaller than a given absolute threshold $\kappa = 0.10$. If no such value is found, we instead search for the global minimum of $d'(\tau)$. Once we find the lag value $\hat{\tau}$ from last step, we interpolate $d'(\tau)$ at $\hat{\tau}$ and its immediate neighbors with a second order polynomial. The length of the period $\tilde{\tau}$ corresponds to the minimum of the polynomial in the range of $(\hat{\tau}-1, \hat{\tau}+1)$, and the pitch is estimated as the sampling rate divided by $\tilde{\tau}$. Since consonant and silence frames have relatively high aperiodicity, we omit values of $d'(\tau) > 0.15$ (value set experimentally). We then convert the pitch (in Hz) to a MIDI pitch value.

Within each note segment, we adopt the median as the pitch value for all frames. After note segmentation and pitch estimation, the output of automatic note annotation is the note sequence $\mathbf{O} = o_1, o_2, ..., o_t$, which will be the input for the singing evaluator in the following section.

3.2 Singing Evaluator

In this study, "intonation accuracy" refers to the similarity between subject's pitch contour and the reference one. In order to find the optimal matching path between pitch contours $\mathbf{A} = \{a_1, a_2, ..., a_N\}$ (the reference from sheet music) and $\mathbf{B} = \{b_1, b_2, ..., b_M\}$ (the detected values from Section 3.1), we adopt the classic note-level Dynamic Time Warping (DTW) method. A singer may shift the pitch up or down ("transposition" in musical terms) by a constant in-

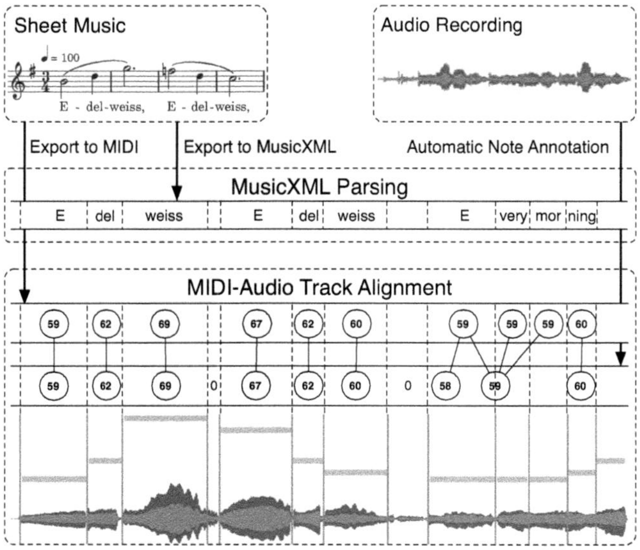

Figure 3: Alignment of recorded audio with the reference MIDI and MusicXML files. There are three rows of information for alignment from top to bottom: lyrics, MIDI pitch sequence, and audio track annotation. A "pitch" of 0 indicates breath noise or silence.

terval to fit his/her vocal range. To detect transposition, we enumerate 12 semitones in a octave and shift the subject's pitch contour from one octave down to one octave up to find the minimum matching cost. The absolute differences between two pitch contours then are averaged across all the notes in reference sequence $\mathbf{A}$ (5).

$$C_{DTW}(\mathbf{A},\mathbf{B}) = \frac{1}{N}\min_{i\in[-12,12]\cap\mathbb{Z}}\{Dist(\{a_1,a_2,...,a_N\},\{b_1+i,b_2+i,...,b_M+i\})\} \quad (5)$$

where

$$Dist(\{a_1,a_2,...,a_N\},\{b_1,b_2,...,b_M\}) = D_{N,M} \quad (6)$$

$$D_{i,j} = d(a_i,b_j) + \min(D_{i-1,j-1}, D_{i-1,j-2}, D_{i-2,j-1}) \quad (7)$$

$$d(a_i,b_j) = |a_i - b_j| \quad (8)$$

where $d(a_i,b_j)$ is the absolute difference between note a_i and b_j. $D_{i,j}$ is the minimum cumulative absolute difference up to a_i and b_j. $Dist(\mathbf{A},\mathbf{B})$ is the absolute difference between two pitch contours $\mathbf{A}$ and $\mathbf{B}$, note by note.

3.3 Audio Alignment to MIDI and Lyrics

The meta-data in the game of *Ladder Singer* consists of the pitches, onsets, lyrics, and sample audio. The sample audio was recorded from one of our female teachers' singing, while other data was extracted directly from the sheet music. For score editing, we used Noteflight [7] to associate each note with its corresponding syllable in a word in lyrics. After editing, the notes and lyrics were exported into MIDI and MusicXML files respectively. To control the animation synchronously with audio playback, we need to align the MIDI with the audio track.

Alignment is performed with the algorithm in Section 3.1 to detect breath and silence events before aligning notes with the score (Figure 3). The alignment is done by finding the minimum cumulative cost in DTW (see Section 3.2). There are sometimes ambiguous note boundaries among some consecutive notes with the same pitch which are occasionally detected as one long note. In order to separate them for further manual adjustment, we automatically separate the long note into a number of matched notes in proportion to their lengths in the MIDI file. After alignment, we modify the "Note On" and the "Note Off" events for each note in MIDI files to its matched note onset and offset in the audio track. Experiments show that over 90% notes are aligned to the accurate positions and the rest are positioned at the approximate positions which are then adjusted manually. As a result, our alignment method significantly reduces the time and effort required for annotation.

Table 1: Subjects in pilot survey

Grade	Age	CI students	NH students
Primary 2	7 - 9	9	9
Primary 1	6 - 8	8	8
Kindergarten	5 - 7	13	13

4. MOGAT DESIGN

In order to understand the disadvantages of children with CI and to further analyze their musical needs, we performed a pilot study to compare the music abilities of children with CI and normal hearing (NH) children. This led to several design principles which informed the design of three games and our web service for teachers.

4.1 Pilot study

All children in the study (see Table 1) were from Canossian School and its affiliated school for the hearing impaired. The study was approved by the school principal and carried out during their normal school time.

4.1.1 Procedure

We adopted their regular music assessment exercises as our assessment protocol, which were built into our iPad application beforehand to easily and quickly collect their answers and recordings. The app contains three modules for testing users' abilities in pitch perception (10 questions), rhythm perception (10 questions), and intonation accuracy (11 questions). In three modules, piano sound is used for audio playback. This is because the music educators use piano to teach music for children with CI, and thus they are more familiar with this instrument than other instruments.

In the pitch perception module, subjects first hear two notes played by a piano sound and then they are asked to identify if they are the same or different by choosing one of two buttons displayed on the touch screen. The maximum interval between two notes is a fifth.

In the rhythm perception module, subjects first hear a two-bar rhythmic phrase synthesized by a piano sound and then they need to tap on the touch screen to reproduce all the note onsets. The app records the time stamps of user tappings and saves them into a log file.

The singing module is relatively more complicated than the other two. During the example demonstration, the app plays a synthesized two-bar melodic phrase using a piano sound. Immediately after the melody finishes playing, the app displays countdown ("3, 2, 1, Go") label on the screen, and subjects are then to sing "La" for each note without hearing the synthesized piano sound. Recording stops automatically once the animation finishes. Subjects are always

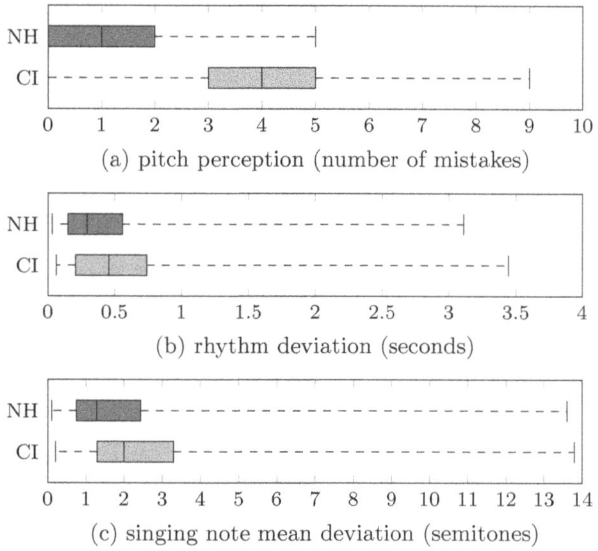

Figure 4: Three metrics used for evaluating music perception and singing ability in the two subject groups. Each box plot shows the lower limit, lower quartile, median, upper quartile, and the upper limit of the data. Lower numbers indicate fewer mistakes.

shown the visual animation of the note sequence in a piano roll format during demonstration and recording, where the visual note sequence moves from right to the left piano keyboard, indicating the active note currently being played.

4.1.2 Analysis

Our hypotheses were that the results of pitch perception, rhythm perception and intonation accuracy would be worse for children with CI than NH children. We used unpaired t-test to test the difference of means between the control and the test groups. We took the statistical significance p-value equal to 0.01. Results are presented in Figure 4.

Pitch perception: This test presented children with a choice of two pitch intervals; children with CI chose the incorrect option a significantly higher number of times than NH children with $t(56) = 5.935, p = 7 \times 10^{-8}$. Since this test is asking for a choice of between two options, random guessing should result in a score of 5/10.

Rhythm perception: We define our rhythm perception metric as the mean absolute deviation between user taps and reference sequence after aligning the first detected onset to the first reference onset. CI and NH children did not differ significantly in this measure with $t(161) = 2.392, p = 0.018$. On the basis of this experiment we reject the null hypothesis and conclude that the rhythm perception of children with CI has not shown to be worse than children with normal hearing, which agrees with previous research [30, 18].

Intonation accuracy: We used the mean note deviation calculated by the singing evaluator in Section 3.2 to represent intonation accuracy. Children with CI demonstrated significantly larger mean note deviation than NH children with $t(661) = 4.039, p = 6.1 \times 10^{-5}$. Our data also revealed large individual variability in both NH children and children with CI.

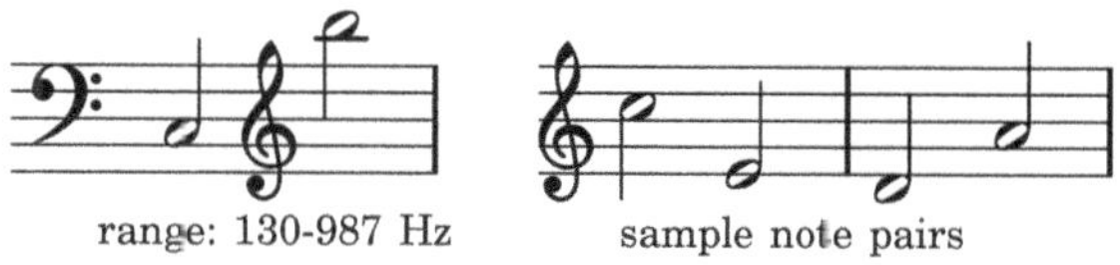

Figure 5: Range of *Higher Lower*, and minimum difference between the pairs of notes used for CI children.

4.2 Design Goals

Based on our pilot study, we established four goals:

- Improve students' pitch perception skills by determining the relative pitch difference.
- Improve students' pitch production skills with appropriate use of voice and breath support in singing.
- The interfaces should be easy and intuitive to use, and the games should be fun and interesting to play.
- Supply a remote centralized administration allowing teachers to easily monitor and personalize habilitation.

The emphasis on pitch perception and production arises from the deficiencies found in the pilot study. Our music therapist required that the system support breath control in singing by testing children's ability to sustain the correct pitch for a certain duration.

On the basis of our pilot study and design goals, we created three games for students and a web service for teachers.

4.3 Game Design

Children with CI are a special user group, in terms of not only their hearing disabilities but also their cognitive ability. In order to achieve an intuitive design, we organized a multi-discipline research team and adopted the relevant design methodology in HCI (e.g., participatory design, iterative design, and user-centered design). We actively involved all stakeholders in the design process including music teachers, music therapists, CI children, and the school principal.

4.3.1 Higher Lower (pitch perception)

The game begins by playing two notes with a piano sound because of their familiarity with this instrument. The student then indicates whether the first note is higher than the second, or vice versa (Figure 1a). The total range of the pitches is shown in Figure 5, while the minimum difference between two pitches can be altered according to the players' ability. Players can replay the sound by pressing a button on the interface.

In our user study, we followed the advice of the children's music educator and chose 7 semitones as the minimum difference between two notes. To a skilled musician this may appear to be a rather easy game, but test results show that some children with CI find this quite challenging.

4.3.2 Vocal Matcher (singing individual pitches)

In this game, players listen to a note, and then they sing the pitch and sustain it for 1 second until the note bar is filled up (Figure 1b). In order for a player to practice the pitches matching his/her vocal pitch range, the game will search for the player's pitch range in the beginning of the game. When the pitch range is found, the program will log the data into the device, and will randomly select notes from this range for playing in the future. We provide automatic note checking for players' pitch in comparison with the reference.

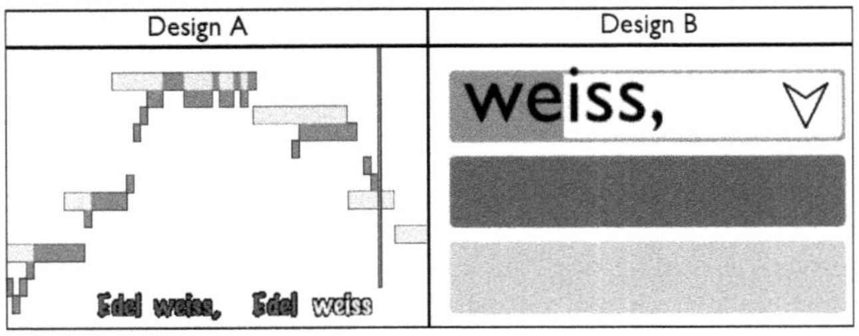

Figure 6: The comparison of two game designs. In Design A, the reference MIDI is in green; the users' pitch contour is in red. In Design B, the downward/upward arrow on the right means that users' pitch is higher/lower than the reference and they should lower/increase their pitch.

When players are singing the correct pitch, its note bar will gradually fill up until they sustain that pitch for the note duration; when players are singing the wrong pitch, on the right of the note bar appears an arrow to indicate whether players should increase or decrease their pitch. Players can replay or skip the sound if they deem it too difficult to sing.

Following the advice of the children's music teacher, any pitch within 3 semitones of the correct one will be accepted.

4.3.3 Ladder Singer (singing a melody)

To design this game, we began by studying the common features of existing Karaoke games and found that most of them display one row of pitch contour and another row of lyrics in parallel, with animation highlighting the relevant portion in time with the playback of audio track. In order to investigate the usability of this kind of games in our scenario, we implemented a Karaoke game incorporating the basic mechanism of Karaoke games on mobile devices shown in Design A of Figure 6. However, feedback from special educators and users suggested the following 2 problems:

1. Pitch correction: Design A uses a vertical bar to indicate the current singing progress, under which players' pitch is displayed. However, it does not check the correctness of players' pitch, and thus players have to rely on the relative positions of their past pitch contour compared with the reference to do pitch adjustment. This adds additional cognitive burden on players during the game play.

2. Lyrics reading: Due to problem 1, lyrics are difficult to read as players' vision is already overloaded with information from reading pitch feedback, especially when lyrics are displayed as merely one sentence at the bottom of the screen while the pitch contour occupies the most screen space.

These are not serious problems for adults and children with normal hearing, singing well-known songs for entertainment, as they likely have the lyrics memorized and have good pitch detection and singing ability. However, our target group is younger children with CI, so a different design is necessary.

Design B in Figure 6 shows the interface design of *Ladder Singer*. We used a "color ladder", a simple metaphor used in their math textbooks, where each note is one "stair" in the ladder and notes are sorted ascendingly from bottom to top on the screen, which is a consistent high-low concept adopted in *Higher Lower*. In order to guide players to sing each note, we first empty its corresponding note bar. To solve problem 1, automatic note checking as in *Vocal Matcher* is provided to help players to adjust their pitch. To solve problem 2, we display each corresponding word inside the note bar. In this way, all the necessary information including note, duration, lyrics, and hints for correction are seamlessly integrated into the narrow space of a note bar. Furthermore, we break down the whole song into phrases so that students can learn the song phrase by phrase. As a result, it is easier for players to concentrate on both lyrics and note information simultaneously. Figure 7 shows the internal game state of *Ladder Singer*. There are two stages in the game: listening and singing. Players begin the game by selecting a musical phrase to listen to with note animation. During singing, the game checks the correctness of players singing pitch and provides the relevant feedback. Meanwhile, it will automatically proceed to the next note when players finish the current one, and return to the listening stage when they finish the phrase. We will validate the usability of Design B compared with Design A in Section 6.3.

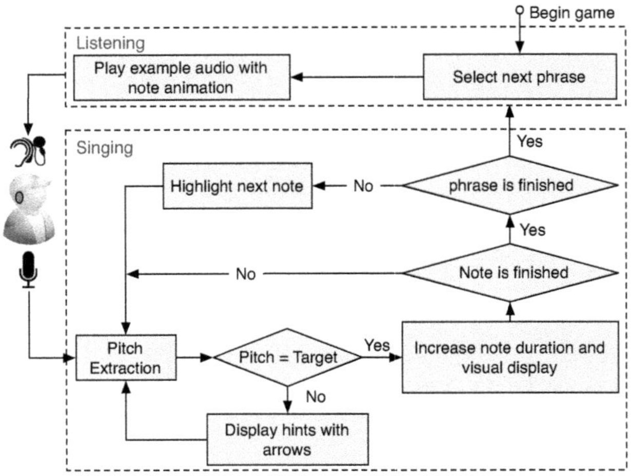

Figure 7: Internal game-state of *Ladder Singer*

4.4 Cloud Computing Service

In order to facilitate special music teachers' communication with children with CI, we built a cloud computing service for this community with the following main features:

A. Individual progress tracking: Teachers can view a graphical visualization of a student's scores over a daily, weekly, or monthly period. Furthermore, they can listen to students' singing recorded in games to pinpoint students' problems.

B. Enabling reciprocal interaction: Teachers can examine students' singing, give overall rating, and post comments. The rating displayed is the collective average of all teachers' ratings. The elements of social media interaction in the website grant more flexibility and accessibility to students and teachers for communicating with each other.

C. Events planning: Teachers can plan students' habilitation in an event calendar by which they can decide time, location, game, and difficulty for a student to play according to his/her performance.

D. Leader board: Students and teachers can check the score leader board within one day, a week, and a month, which can introduce a moderate amount of competition to increase motivation to practice.

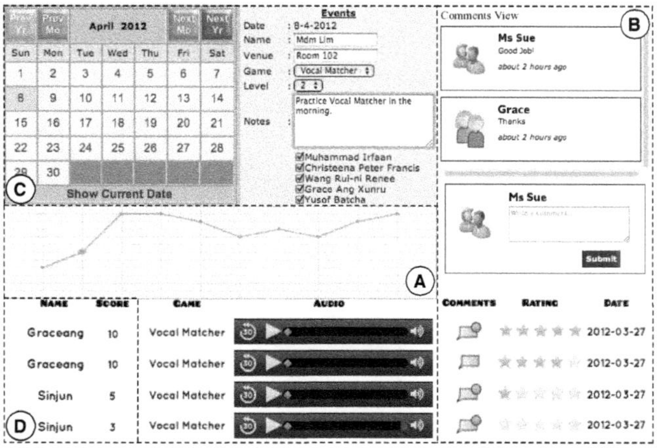

Figure 8: A montage of teacher view

5. IMPLEMENTATION

5.1 Games

The games were developed using Objective-C in iOS SDK. We adopted the cocos2d [2] framework for the graphics and animation rendering. The score layout layer, which parses midi and lyrics files for scheduling the note animation and displaying lyrics respectively, was implemented using the C++ library libjdkmidi [6]. In order to permit widespread deployment, we targeted older 2nd-generation iPod Touches to reduce the devices' cost for children's parents. As a result, we must seriously consider the less advanced computational power of these devices during the development. We compared the computational cost and latency of two audio frameworks, Audio Unit (AU) and Audio Queue Services (AQS) in the CoreAudio framework.

To investigate the performance and latency of AQS and AU in our application, we implemented both in our application and performed the same tasks (i.e., pitch estimation and audio recording) in their callback functions. The sample rate was 24000 Hz and we used three buffers of 1024 samples ($\approx$ 43ms). We measured the average CPU usage of the application and average latency of callback functions using Activity Monitor of instruments in Xcode 4, and present the results in Table 2. We found that the CPU usage and latency were much better with AQS. It should be noted that AU allows highest level of control and simultaneous audio I/O with low latency, and other high-level audio frameworks including AQS are built upon it. However, the render callback in AU lives on a real-time priority thread on which subsequent render calls arrive asynchronously [1], which has a very strict performance requirement.

If the callback performs a time-consuming task such as autocorrelation-based YIN algorithm ($O(n^2)$), it will lose its advantage of low latency and high performance and even get gaps in the sound. Rather, AQS use the buffer queue whose callback function gets called whenever its audio buffers come in. It allows computing with less strict time constraints so that we can synchronously perform an accurate but time-consuming algorithm as well as writing audio buffers to the file system.

With iOS vDSP framework, the spectral domain YIN algorithm [14] ($O(n \log(n))$) can fully optimize the computational cost for both AU and AQS (see Table 2). In order

Table 2: Performance comparison of *Vocal Matcher* between AQS and AU in our app on an iPod Touch (2nd-generation).

	YIN		YIN FFT	
	AQS	AU	AQS	AU
CPU Usage (%)	28.49	53.47	27.57	37.06
Latency (ms)	0.021	0.624	N/A	0.022

to handle both audio recording and real-time audio processing simultaneously, AQS is used finally in conjunction with Audio File Services which is for writing audio buffers into recording files.

In the callback function of AQS, we defined a fixed threshold to exclude frames of silence or irrelevant background noise and to preserve those representing potential singing voice. The volume was calculated by getting the decibel value from the root mean square of the audio signal within the frame. We empirically chose 30 dB as the threshold. We implemented spectral domain YIN algorithm with vDSP framework to do pitch detection for any frames which were not deemed to be silence.

5.2 Cloud Service

The server backend of the web service used PHP server to handle the HTTP requests and MySQL for the database. For the web front-end, we use HTML5, JavaScript, CSS3, and jQuery, a commonly used JavaScript framework. Furthermore, the web service adopts the RESTful architecture. The metadata (including scores, user ids, and recordings in games) are automatically sent to the web server via JSON, which are then parsed and stored into our database. This allows minimal end user actions, which makes the data transmission process seamless and offers a better user experience.

6. USER STUDY

15 students with CI were selected at random from a Canossian School (ages 6 to 10) for the hearing impaired. Their average hearing age after implantation is 4 years and 10 months. The evaluation approved by the school principal was carried out in their daily school time.

MOGAT was installed on 15 2nd-generation iPod Touches which do not have built-in microphones. We plugged an audio adapter containing a microphone into each iPod Touch to enable its audio input. We connected students' cochlear devices directly with audio adapters via their own personal audio cables, which provided better sound quality than the speakers on iPod Touches.

The first three games were evaluated in the order of *Higher Lower*, *Vocal Matcher* and *Ladder Singer*. Students were asked to play each game once everyday for two weeks under their teachers' supervision.

6.1 User Performance Evaluation

We tracked the students' skill in the games.

Higher Lower (*HL*): To match the initial pilot study, we tracked the number of incorrect answers to measure their pitch perception skills.

Vocal Matcher (*VM*): Since students should sing a specific pitch for 1 second before the game progresses to the next exercise, we consider the total time a student spends on each exercise to indicate how quickly they can reach the correct pitch. A student's intonation skill is therefore in-

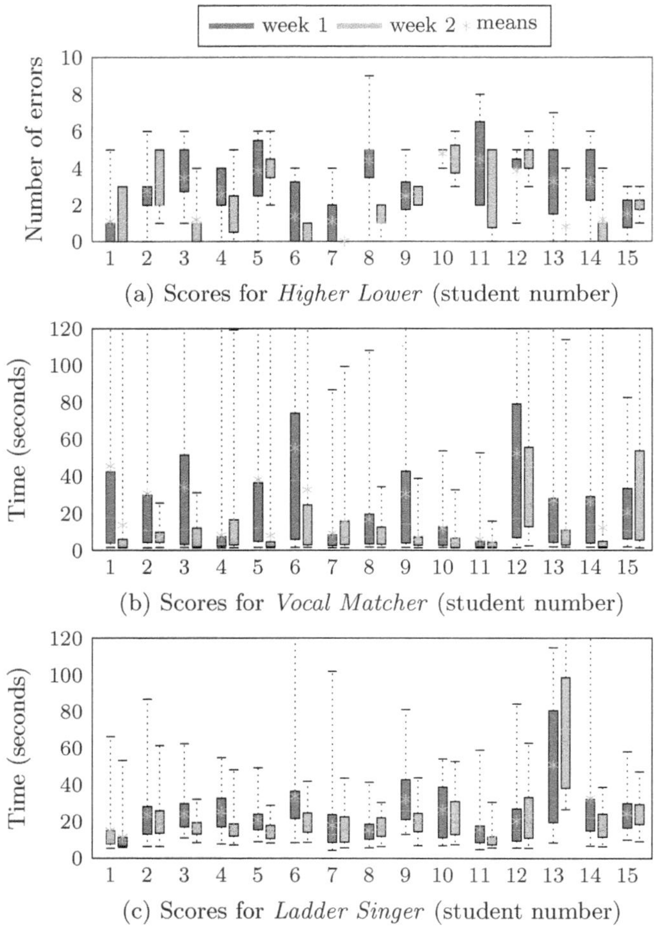

(a) Scores for *Higher Lower* (student number)

(b) Scores for *Vocal Matcher* (student number)

(c) Scores for *Ladder Singer* (student number)

Figure 9: Evolution of students' scores during the user study: Students' scores in the first week are compared to their scores in the second week in three games. Lower numbers indicate fewer mistakes, i.e., better proficiency.

versely proportional to the time. We excluded those recordings with extremely long duration ($\geq$ 120 seconds) when students were not familiar with the interface.

Ladder Singer (*LS*): A music phrase is a combination of multiple individual notes. We consider the total time a student spends on completing all the notes within the phrase to measure their pitch production skills in singing the song of Edelweiss.

Figure 9 shows individual students' score in the first and the second weeks, while Table 3 shows the one-way ANOVA test comparing scores from two weeks for those students whose scores improved between the two weeks. The mean error in *HL* decreased significantly from 2.82 to 1.98 ($F = 9.892, p = 0.002$). The mean time for completing single pitch in *VM* decreased significantly from 25.99s to 13.86s ($F = 36.49, p < 0.001$). The mean time for completing single phrase in *LS* decreased significantly from 24.33s to 18.97s ($F = 21.23, p < 0.001$). Furthermore, none of these students, who did worse in the 2nd week (N/A in Table 3), showed statistically significant degradation in score. The improvement among subjects was also highly variable. In *HL*, there were totally 9 students who have improved their score within two weeks, and 3 out of these 9 students (S3, S7, and S8) had statistically significant performance improvement ($p < 0.05$). In *VM*, there were totally 12 students who improved their skills in two weeks, and 7 out of 12 children (S2, S3, S5, S8, S9, S10, and S13) children had statistically significant improvement ($p < 0.05$). In *LS*, there were totally 12 students who had improvement, and 6 out of 12 children (S3, S5, S6, S9, S11, and S14) had statistically significant improvement ($p < 0.05$). In sum, 5 out of 15 children (S3, S6, S10, S11, and S14) had improvement in all three categories and 1 child (S3) had significant improvement among all categories.

Table 3: The one-way ANOVA test results (F-statistic and p-value) on comparing each student's scores in the first week and his/hers in the second week ($^*p < 0.05$, $^{**}p < 0.01$). N/A means no improvement in their second-week scores compared to their first-week scores.

	Higher Lower		*Vocal Matcher*		*Ladder Singer*	
	The factor of weeks					
	F	p	F	p	F	p
S1	N/A		2.479	0.126	1.185	0.287
S2	N/A		**12.561**	**0.001****	0.056	0.814
S3	**18.778**	**0.012***	**15.161**	**10^{-4}****	**10.862**	**0.002****
S4	0.641	0.454	N/A		0.416	0.53
S5	N/A		**10.757**	**0.002***	**4.651**	**0.038***
S6	3.447	0.137	2.378	0.134	**8.402**	**0.007****
S7	**10**	**0.025***	N/A		0.578	0.451
S8	**46**	**0.002***	**5.497**	**0.023***	N/A	
S9	N/A		**23.506**	**10^{-5}****	**13.037**	**0.001****
S10	0.273	0.638	**7.368**	**0.01***	0.385	0.55
S11	0.388	0.578	1.942	0.171	**5.664**	**0.024***
S12	N/A		0.198	0.659	N/A	
S13	3.103	0.153	**6.566**	**0.014***	N/A	
S14	4.966	0.09	1.789	0.189	**4.785**	**0.037***
S15	N/A		N/A		0.004	0.947

6.2 User Experience

Our user experience evaluation is based on the following three criteria: *naturalness*, *enjoyment*, and *motivation*. At the end of the first week, the students were asked to rate questions using a five-point likert scale.

- *I feel the game is easy to play.*
- *I enjoyed playing this game.*
- *I would play this game for fun if I had it.*

Figure 10 shows the results averaged over all the students. In terms of naturalness, *HL* is the most intuitive one to play with. *VM* is a simplified version of *LS*, and it has the practice and carryover effect on *LS*. Therefore, although *LS* is relatively hard to play with, the naturalness score of

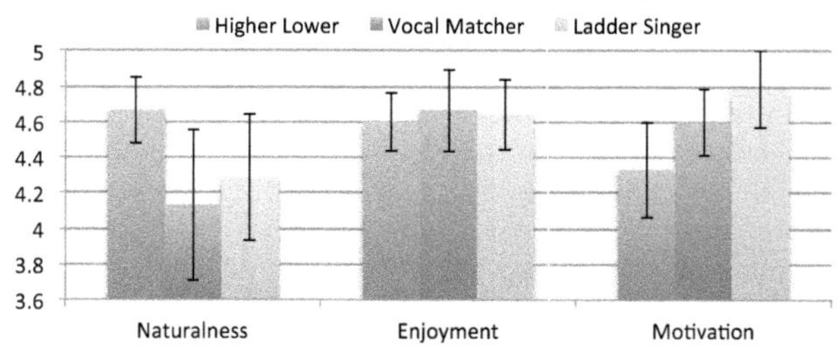

Figure 10: Results of user experience

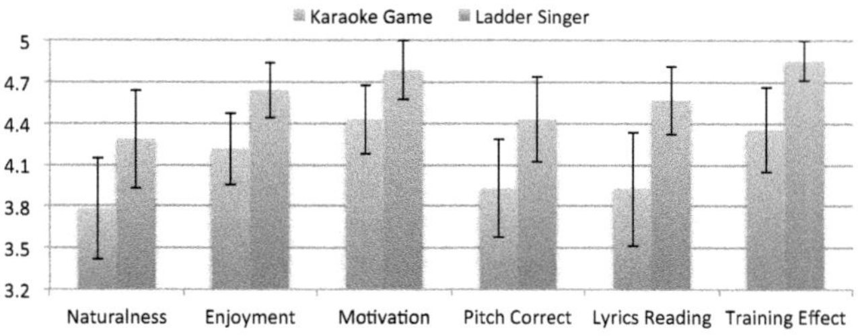

Figure 11: Karaoke Game v.s. *Ladder Singer*

LS was slightly higher than *VM*. Furthermore, the students enjoyed playing three games to a similar extent. Last but not least, the students expressed strong motivation to play all three games for fun in the future (ratings are all over 4.3), especially *LS* (rating is 4.8).

6.3 Ladder Singer v.s. Karaoke Game

We organized a comparison study between Karaoke Game (Design A) and *LS* (Design B) mentioned in Section 6 before the evaluation of *VM*. During the process, we randomly chose the order of two games to counterbalance the practice and carryover effects. After each game, users were asked to rate the games using three additional factors (*pitch correction, lyrics reading, training effect*) in addition to the criteria of user experience.

- *I can correct my pitch based on the game feedback.*
- *I can follow the lyrics during singing.*
- *The game can help me with learning this song.*

Figure 11 shows the results averaged across 15 users. We can see that *LS* was ranked higher than Karaoke Game in all aspects. During the experiment, we observed that most of their pitch contours displayed in Karaoke Game were quite flat, which illustrates that they could not easily correct their pitch according to the reference. Nevertheless, it is impossible in *LS*, where they can proceed to the next note if and only if users perform correctly.

6.4 Web Service Evaluation

Our purpose is to evaluate whether our cloud-based web service can enhance special teachers in supporting students' musical habilitation. We recruited two special musical educators in this study. First, they received a sheet of instructions demonstrating the interface and features of the website. Teachers were then asked to use it by themselves without facilitators' intervention. Finally, teachers answered a questionnaire related to the usability of the web service.

Overall, the participants responded that MOGAT web service was fairly easy to use, all giving it a 4 on a scale of 1 (extremely difficult to use) to 5 (extremely easy to use). Participants also expressed satisfaction and willingness to use the website to support children's habilitation. However, they requested that we improve the documentation for more advanced features such as setting up an event. They asked us to describe the ratings detailedly in the website so that different teachers can keep a consistent rating criteria.

7. DISCUSSION

While most children benefited from MOGAT-enhanced auditory training, there was large individual variability in the amount of improvement among subjects. Many factors may affect the outcomes. For example, training materials (i.e., sound stimuli), training difficulties, and training duration. Although these independent variables were controlled in our user study, it is most desirable for us to deeply understand how they affect individual's performance. It could help us to design the most suitable individualized training protocols. We will investigate this problem in the future.

We would like to mention that teaching hearing-impaired children singing allows them to not only just sing better but also do what normal children can do, which can enhance their confidence and self-esteem. Moreover, singing can help them to learn language and improve their speech intelligibility. Thus we focus on this special user group and it is almost impossible for hearing-impaired children to achieve the same skills by merely playing any other video games.

It is important to emphasize that throughout the project we aim to train users' relative pitch production ability rather than their absolute pitch ability because different singer has his/her own vocal pitch range. The singing evaluator was thus developed to transpose the pitch to fit their vocal range.

The limitation of the work is that the audio-MIDI alignment algorithm is not ideal and requires manual adjustment. Nevertheless, the statistical model can be used to solve this problem. First, the DTW-based algorithm can help to build the training dataset, saving the work in human annotation. We can then train a Hidden Markov Model (HMM) on the dataset to do the alignment. It will become our future work.

8. CONCLUSION

We have presented the design, development, and deployment of MOGAT, the first integrated training system to assist pre-lingually deafened children with music habilitation. After investigating their problems in pitch-based metrics in comparison with normal hearing children from our pilot study, we developed three music games with off-the-shelf mobile devices which are designed specifically for their musical needs and cognitive abilities. In order to maximize the limited teaching resources, we developed a cloud-based web application to connect special music teachers with children with CI to provide them with administrative and teaching support. A comprehensive user study has demonstrated the effectiveness and efficiency of MOGAT in enhancing children' musical habilitation as well as teachers' teaching and management tasks, and its large potential in enhancing pitch perception and production of children with CI.

ACKNOWLEDGEMENTS

We are grateful to Ms. Terry Theseira and her colleagues and students from Canossian School for assistance and participation in the user studies. We would like to thank Graham Percival for his kindly support in paper proofreading, and thank Kenny Tan and Yong Shen Wong for their system implementation and design. We appreciate all our reviewers for their excellent comments and feedback.

9. REFERENCES

[1] Audio unit hosting guide for ios. `http://developer.apple.com/library/ios/`.

[2] Cocos2d. `http://www.cocos2d-iphone.org/` .

[3] Glee karaoke. `http://itunes.apple.com/sg/app/glee-karaoke/id360736774?mt=8`.

[4] Karaoke revolution. `http://www.konami.com/games/karaoke-revolution/`.

[5] Karaokeparty. http://www.karaokeparty.com/.

[6] libjdkmidi. http://opensource.jdkoftinoff.com/jdks/docs/libjdkmidi/.

[7] Noteflight. http://www.noteflight.com.

[8] Sound express auditory training, tigerspeech technology. http://www.tigerspeech.com/tst_soundex.html.

[9] Theta music trainer. http://trainer.thetamusic.com/.

[10] Voice tutor. http://voicetutorapp.com/.

[11] Cochlear implants for children, July 2008. http://www.cochlear.com/au/hearing-loss-teatments/cochlear-implants-children.

[12] National institute on deafness and other communication disorders, cochlear implants, March 2011. http://www.nidcd.nih.gov/health/hearing/pages/coch.aspx.

[13] S. Abdi, M. Khalessi, M. Khorsandi, and B. Gholami. Introducing music as a means of habilitation for children with cochlear implants. *International Journal of Pediatric Otorhinolaryngology*, 59:105–113, 2001.

[14] P. Brossier. *Automatic Annotation of Musical Audio for Interactive Applications*. PhD thesis, Queen Mary University of London, UK, August 2006.

[15] P. A. Busby, S. A. Roberts, Y. C. Tong, and G. M. Clark. Results of speech perception and speech production training for three prelingually deaf patients using a multiple-electrode cochlear implant. *Br J Audiol*, 25(5):291–302, 1991.

[16] P. W. Dawson and G. M. Clark. Changes in synthetic and natural vowel perception after specific training for congenitally deafened patients using a multichannel cochlear implant. *Ear and Hearing*, 18:488–501, 1997.

[17] A. De Cheveigne and H. Kawahara. Yin, a fundamental frequency estimator for speech and music. *Journal of the Acoustical Society of America*, 2002.

[18] W. R. Drennan and J. T. Rubinstein. Music perception in cochlear implant users and its relationship with psychophysical capabilities. *J. of Rehabilitation Research & Development*, 45(5):779–790, 2008.

[19] G. T. Ealy. Of ear trumpets and a resonance plate: Early hearing aids and beethoven's hearing perception. *19th-Century Music*, 17(3):pp. 262–273, 1994.

[20] Q.-J. Fu, J. Galvin, X. Wang, and G. Nogaki. Moderate auditory training can improve speech performance of adult cochlear implant patients. *Acoustical Society of America*, 6(3):106–111, 2005.

[21] Q.-J. Fu and J. J. Galvin. Computer-assisted speech training for cochlear implant patients: Feasibility, outcomes, and future directions. *Seminar in Hearing*, 28:142–150, 2007.

[22] J. J. Galvin, Q.-J. Fu, and R. V. Shannon. Melodic contour identification and music perception by cochlear implant users. *The Neuroscience and Music III - Disorders and Plasticity*, 1169:518–533, 2009.

[23] K. Gfeller, S. Witt, M. Adamek, M. Mehr, J. Rogers, J. Stordahl, and S. Ringgenberg. Effects of training on timbre recognition and appraisal by postlingually deafened cochlear implant recipients. *Journal of the American Academy of Audiology*, 13(3):132–145, 2002.

[24] K. Gfeller, S. Witt, J. Stordahl, M. Mehr, and G. Woodworth. The effects of training on melody recognition and appraisal by adult cochlear implant recipients. *Journal of the Academy of Rehabilitative Audiology*, 33:115–138, 2000.

[25] K. Gfeller, S. A. Witt, K.-H. Kim, M. Adamek, and D. Coffman. Preliminary report of a computerized music training program for adult cochlear implant recipients. *Journal of the Academy of Rehabilitative Audiology*, 32:11–27, 1999.

[26] E. Glennie. Hearing essay, 1993. http://www.evelyn.co.uk/Resources/Essays/Hearing%20Essay.pdf.

[27] V. S. Hagedorn. Musical learning for hearing impaired children. *Research perspective in music education*, (3):13–17, 1992.

[28] P. Harrison. The effects of deafness on musical composition. *Journal of the Royal Society of Medicine*, 81:598–601, 1988.

[29] O. Mayor, J. Bonada, and A. Loscos. The singing tutor: Expression categorization and segmentation of the singing voice. In *Proceedings of the AES 121st Convention*, 2006.

[30] H. J. McDermott. Music perception with cochlear implants: A review. *Trends In Amplification*, 8:49–82, 2004.

[31] C. Oshima, K. Nishimoto, and M. Suzuki. Family ensemble: a collaborative musical edutainment system for children and parents. In *ACM Multimedia*, 2004.

[32] C. C. Peterson. Theory-of-mind development in oral deaf children with cochlear implants or conventional hearing aids. *J Child Psychol Psychiatry*, 45(6):1096–1106, 2004.

[33] A. L. Quittner, P. Leibach, and K. Marciel. The impact of cochlear implants on young deaf children: new methods to assess cognitive and behavioral development. *Arch Otolaryngol Head Neck Surg*, 2004.

[34] I. Simon, D. Morris, and S. Basu. Mysong: automatic accompaniment generation for vocal melodies. In *ACM CHI'08*.

[35] D. L. Sorkin and N. Caleffe-Schenck. Cochlear implant rehabilitation. Online, June 2008. http://www.cochlear.com/files/assets/ci_rehab_not_just_for_kids.pdf.

[36] R. Sweetow and C. V. Palmer. Efficacy of individual auditory training in adults: A systematic review of the evidence. *Journal of the American Academy of Audiology*, 16(7):494–504, June 2005.

[37] E. A. Tobey, A. E. Geers, C. Brenner, D. Altuna, and G. Gabbert. Factors associated with development of speech production skills in children implanted by age five. *Ear and Hearing*, 24:36S–45S, February 2003.

[38] J.-L. Wu, H.-M. Yang, Y.-H. Lin, and Q.-J. Fu. Effects of computer-assisted speech training on mandarin-speaking hearing-impaired children. *Audiology and Neurotology*, 12:307–312, 2007.

[39] Y. Zhou, G. Percival, X. Wang, Y. Wang, and S. Zhao. Mogclass: a collaborative system of mobile devices for classroom music education. In *ACM Multimedia '10*.

[40] Y. Zhou, G. Percival, X. Wang, Y. Wang, and S. Zhao. Mogclass: evaluation of a collaborative system of mobile devices for classroom music education of young children. In *ACM CHI'11*.

Visual Knowledge Transfer among Multiple Cameras for People Counting with Occlusion Handling

Ming-Fang Weng
Institute of Information Science,
Academia Sinica, Taipei 115, Taiwan
mfueng@iis.sinica.edu.tw

Yen-Yu Lin
Research Center for Information Technology
Innovation, Academia Sinica, Taipei 115, Taiwan
yylin@citi.sinica.edu.tw

Nick C. Tang
Institute of Information Science,
Academia Sinica, Taipei 115, Taiwan
nickctang@gmail.com

Hong-Yuan Mark Liao
Institute of Information Science,
Academia Sinica, Taipei 115, Taiwan
liao@iis.sinica.edu.tw

ABSTRACT

We present a framework to count the number of people in an environment where multiple cameras with different angles of view are available. We consider the visual cues captured by each camera as a knowledge source, and carry out cross-camera knowledge transfer to alleviate the difficulties of people counting, such as partial occlusions, low-quality images, clutter backgrounds, and so on. Specifically, this work distinguishes itself with the following contributions. First, we overcome the variations of multiple heterogeneous cameras with different perspective settings by matching the same groups of pedestrians taken by these cameras, and present an algorithm for accomplishing cross-camera correspondence. Second, the proposed counting model is composed of a pair of collaborative regressors. While one regressor measures people counts by the features extracted from intra-camera visual evidences, the other recovers the yielded residual by taking the conflicts among inter-camera predictions into account. The two regressors are elegantly coupled, and jointly lead to an accurate counting system. Additionally, we provide a set of manually annotated pedestrian labels on the PETS 2010 videos for performance evaluation. Our approach is comprehensively tested in various settings and compared with competitive baselines. The significant improvement in performance manifests the effectiveness of the proposed approach.

Categories and Subject Descriptors

H.3.1 [**Information Storage and Retrieval**]: Content Analysis and Indexing—*indexing method*; I.2.10 [**Artificial Intelligence**]: Vision and Scene Understanding—*video analysis*.

General Terms

Algorithms, Theory, Experimentation.

Keywords

People counting, Transfer learning, Correspondence estimation.

1 Introduction

The goal of *people counting*, such as [9, 24, 27, 29, 31, 36], is to estimate the number of people or the density of crowds in a monitored environment. It is receiving recent attention in many fields, e.g., multimedia, computer vision, and video surveillance, since it plays a critical role in a broad range of applications. First of all, pedestrian counts serve as one of the most important indices for video data, and hence counting the number of people has become a key component in video understanding, retrieval, and surveillance. Further, both the long-term and short-term statistics of people counts of an environment provide useful information for strategy planning or event detection. For instance, one could measure the degree of crowdedness for traffic flow planning, analyze the benefit of the advertisement for potential revenue estimation, or identify abnormal gatherings for crime prevention. In addition, researches on people counting can be applied to adaptive device control for energy-saving purposes. For example, the number of people in a transit station is helpful in deciding how low the A/C (air conditioning) temperature should go or how many escalators should be operated.

Despite the great applicability of people counting, most of vision-based counting systems are still hindered by the following challenges. First, mutual occlusion among people yields the severe change of pedestrian appearances or the loss of extracted features. It often leads to the underestimate of the number of people. This situation becomes worse in crowded environments. Second, the problems caused by low-resolution or blur images, especially for the pedestrians far from the camera, often degrade the stability of a counting system. Further, the large variations in pedestrian appearances, and lighting conditions, or clutter backgrounds make people counting quite difficult.

In this work, we address the aforementioned issues by establishing a *multiple camera people counting* (MCPC) system, where multiple cameras are installed to monitor an identical region but with different angles of view. Videos taken by these cameras contain complementary information. It follows that fusing visual cues in these videos generally facilitate the accomplishment of a more robust and accurate counting system. An illustration of our idea is given in Figure 1, where two different views of an environment are available, while two examples of complementary visual cues catched by the two camera views are shown. In the first example, View 2 consists of useful information to compensate for the underestimate caused by occlusions in View 1. In the other, View 1 provides high-resolution visual cues to enhance the performance of estimation for View 2. So far, two questions arise: 1) How to

Figure 1: Illustration of our multiple camera people counting (MCPC) system in which visual knowledge are transferred across cameras to establish a more accurate and robust counting system.

work with multiple cameras so that all the captured visual cues can be shared across different camera views? 2) For each view, how to couple both the *intra-camera* and *inter-camera* visual knowledge to result in a more robust and accurate counting system?

To work with the multiple cameras with diverse perspective settings, we propose a correspondence estimation algorithm that maps each segmented group of moving people in one view to its corresponding group in another view. We call these matched groups *components*, upon each of which knowledge can be transferred across cameras. The identity numbers in Figure 1 index the matched components. In this situation, both the intra-camera (captured by itself) and inter-camera (transferred from others) visual cues are available in each view, and we present a two-pass regression framework to carry out the multiple camera people counting system. Specifically, the first-pass regressor measures the people count by using the visual features extracted from the intra-camera knowledge. The second-pass regressor estimates the residual yielded in the first pass by taking the conflicts among inter-camera knowledge into account. Since the second-pass regression is built on knowledge conflicts, we cast the training of the second-pass regressor as a transfer learning problem [33], in which useful knowledge transfer is encouraged while error propagation is prevented.

This work distinguishes itself with the following contributions. First, we propose to incorporate multiple heterogeneous cameras with different perspective settings via matching the components, and present an algorithm for cross-camera correspondence estimation with high precision. Second, a pair of collaborative regressors is introduced to accomplish cross-camera knowledge transfer. The two regressors are elegantly coupled so that both intra-camera and inter-camera visual knowledge are taken into account simultaneously, and lead to a more robust counting system. Third, we create a set of manually annotated pedestrian labels on the PETS 2010 videos which are publicly accessible in the research community.

2 Related Work

In this section, we review a few research topics and techniques relevant to the establishment of the proposed framework, including people counting, correspondence estimation among multiple cameras, and transfer learning.

2.1 People Counting

The literature of people counting is quite comprehensive [19,44]. We focus on only the computer-vision-based methods, since they are closely related to our work. For the ease of discussion, these methods are divided into the two categories, *counting-by-detection* and *counting-by-regression*.

Counting-by-detection. Methods of this category determine the number of people present in an image by explicitly locating the position of each individual pedestrian and then counting the total number of detected ones. The work by Lin et al. [28] is a good example of this category, in which they proposed to learn head-like contours and exhaustively search for human heads. In addition to the visual features that are embedded in static images, motion features that can be extracted from sequences of video frames, e.g., dynamic textures and motion patterns, have been shown to be useful to detect individual moving entities [1,8,34].

These methods work well in controlled environments, but they probably result in suboptimal performance in a more general setting because most of them cannot clearly define the appearance or the shape of pedestrians in advance. The trend of this kind of systems is to employ a pedestrian detector to find people [21,26]. While pedestrian detectors have been demonstrated to be robust to variations caused by different illumination, poses, and image sizes [12,13,32], the performance of detection results can be farther improved by modeling the geometric structures among body parts [41]. However, training such detectors in general requires a great number of manually collected data. Moreover, since the training samples are usually of a high resolution and no occlusions are involved, the performance of these detectors severely degrades when they are applied to find pedestrians with partial occlusions or of low resolutions. Additionally, the computational time at detection stage is typically too high to support yielding real-time responses.

Counting-by-regression. Methods of this class is relatively more efficient. They estimate the size of a group via extracting low-level features to represent the corresponding region which is typically assumed to be yielded by background subtraction or motion segmentation approaches [23,24,27]. Since these methods do not solve the localization problem, they are suitable for estimating the density of a crowd with a certain level of crowdedness rather than precisely evaluating the exact number of people appearing in a scene. Followed by the methods which linearly map a set of perspectively normalized features to the number of people, nonlinear regression models such as neural networks, Gaussian process, and Poisson process, recently are adopted to enhance the performance of people counting [9,10,36].

Despite the use of discriminative visual features and powerful machine learning techniques, people counting systems of both the two categories suffer from the problems caused by occlusions, low-quality images, and large variations of pedestrian appearances. It is worth mentioning that the most similar work to ours is that of Ma et al. [31], in which visual cues from two cameras are fused to

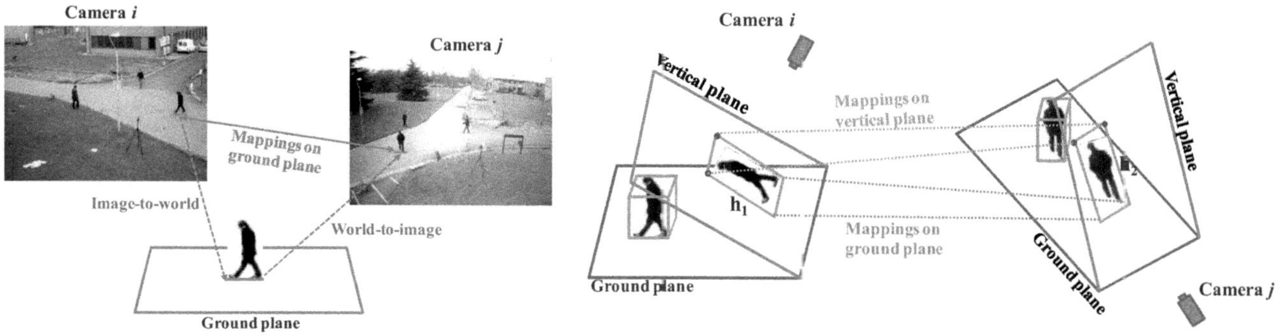

(a) Cross-camera ground plane matching (b) Ground plane matching vs. Vertical plane matching

Figure 2: The proposed approach to cross-camera blob localization and matching.

deal with the problem resulting from occlusions. They combine human detection results from two cameras with the verification of the *homography constraint*. However, their system depends on the reliable results of the two single-view detection. As mentioned above, methods developed upon pedestrian detectors do not work well with partial or heavy occlusions. Thus the abilities of occlusions handling in their approach may be restricted in crowded environments. Unlike [31], we investigate the evidences revealed in the prediction confliction among multiple cameras, and cast the estimation of occlusions as an instance of transfer learning. Our system can deal with the problem of underestimate even if heavy occlusions appear in all the camera views.

2.2 Correspondence among Multiple Cameras

One critical task of synchronizing multiple cameras and realizing visual knowledge transfer is to establish the correspondence among these cameras. Conventional methods of camera correspondence estimation can be roughly divided into the following two categories.

Homographic-based Methods. In [22], Khan and Shah integrate multi-view information by introducing a *planar homographic constraint*. They first estimate plane homographies by matching the SIFT [30] features, and then discover the correspondence among multiple cameras. Eshel and Moses [15] propose to detect head blob of each person via the *multiple height planar homographies*, and alleviate the problem of performance degradation in tracking occluded objects. Arsie et al. [2] suggest to track people based on a homographic transformation between the target blob boundaries. However, methods mentioned above are sensitive to the large variation of appearances of objects, perspective settings of cameras, and video qualities by heterogeneous camcorders. This is because that homographic-based approaches rely on consistent matching. However, it is generally not available in real environments.

Calibration-based Methods. The goal of camera calibration is to estimate the model of a camera, including not only the extrinsic parameters, e.g., position and orientation relative to the real world coordinate system, but also the intrinsic parameters of the camera, e.g., image central, focal length, and distortion coefficients. Xiong and Quek [42] present an approach, in which a box with the specific pattern of dots and markers is employed, to calibrate both the intrinsic and extrinsic parameters of camera networks. Aslan et al. [3] develop a set of features based on the positions of all the detected pedestrians' heads, and automatically calibrate the extrinsic parameters of multiple cameras via these features. Tsai [38] present a two-stage approach to computing the position, orientation, and the intrinsic parameters of a camera. This approach is adopted in a wide range of applications, since it is capable of dealing with both the *coplanar* and *non-coplanar* points. Having a precise planar transformation among multiple cameras would facilitate counting people in the crowded environments. Generally speaking, calibration-based methods tend to provide more precise camera transformations than the ones by homographic-based methods, and hence are more suitable in our cases.

2.3 Transfer Learning

Transfer learning [33] refers to an information delivering process that aims to improve the target task by leveraging abundant knowledge available in the source tasks. The exploration of auxiliary knowledge drawn from different tasks has received a rapidly growing interest in the field of machine learning. The methods exploiting additional knowledge sources to benefit the accomplishment of the underlying task can be generally divided into four categories [33]: transfer by *model parameters* [14, 43], by *data instances* [7], by *feature representation* [6], and by *contextual information* [20, 40]. However, these methods are established upon the assumption that data of the source and target tasks have the same domains for knowledge transfer. In this work, we consider the visual cue captured by each camera as a knowledge source, and aim to establish a robust counting system via sharing knowledge across cameras.

3 Cross-camera Blob Matching

We propose to make use of visual information from different camera views to alleviate the problems, such as partial occlusions or imperfect foreground segmentations, in people counting. To work with heterogeneous cameras together with various perspective settings, one of the most important tasks is to *match* the corresponding *blobs* among these cameras, so that visual knowledge can be transferred across cameras and support the establishment of an accurate counting system.

3.1 Blob Extraction

We represent a video frame by a set of *blobs*, each of which is a group of spatially connected foreground (moving) pixels. We consider blob as a natural unit for people counting, since each pedestrian typically appears within one blob, while a pedestrian can be occluded by other pedestrians residing in the same blob. Thus not only the scale and appearance normalization but also the occlusion evaluation can be performed blob-wisely. To extract foreground blobs, we first apply the background subtraction algorithm [5] to every video frame to segment out the foreground areas. Then, spatially connected foreground pixels are clustered to yield the blobs. Each extracted blob in Figure 1 is highlighted by a specific color.

3.2 Blob Localization and Matching

Once the blobs from all the camera views are extracted, our goal is to localize and match the corresponding blobs across cameras.

(a) Bottom boundaries of blobs (b) Their mappings

Figure 3: Blob mapping on the ground plane.

Figure 4: Blob mapping on both the ground and vertical planes.

To this end, we propose a blob matching algorithm, including the *ground plane mapping* and the *vertical plane mapping*. We illustrate the localization algorithm in Figure 2.

First, we develop a reverse variant of Tsai's camera calibration model [38], which computes the transformation from the *image coordinate system* to the *world coordinate system* on the *ground plane*, to generate the *world-to-image* coordinate transformation. Then, we detect the *bottom boundary* of each blob. To this end, the *convex hull* of each blob is generated, such that the bottom boundary of the blob can be determined by the bottom contour. Some examples of the detected bottom boundaries are shown in Figure 3(a). Each of them is drawn with one particular color. Based upon the assumption that the bottom boundary of a blob touches the ground plane, its correspondence across cameras hence can be fulfilled via Tsai's camera calibration model and its reverse variant. This procedure is summarized in Figure 2(a), in which every pixel residing on the bottom boundary in camera i is first transformed to the world coordinate system, and then transformed to the image plane of camera j. By the procedure, one can establish the mappings of the bottom boundaries of blobs between any the video frames taken by two distinct cameras. Figure 3(b) shows the mapping results where each correspondence is plotted with one distinct color. Symmetrically, we can also match blobs extracted in camera j to those in camera i. We use the set of these resulting mappings as an initial guess of the correspondence of each blob in two cameras. However, due to the imperfect blob segmentation, the bottom boundary of a blob does not always touch the ground plane in our empirical tests. Therefore, we need to validate the correctness of the estimated correspondence by using the mappings on the *vertical plane* of each blob.

For computing mappings on the vertical plane of each blob, we need to estimate the image height of a pedestrian at every position in the camera view. Based on the work by Hoiem et al. [18], we assume that the image height of a pedestrian (denoted as h) is linearly dependent on his/her bottom location (denoted as v) in the vertical position of the image, i.e.,

$$h(v) = \alpha \cdot v + \alpha_0, \tag{1}$$

where α and α_0 are the two parameters of the camera model. Thus, we adopt the procedure, described in Algorithm 1, to compute the perspective parameters of each camera via employing a off-the-shelf pedestrian detector [32]. On the one hand, the detected pedestrians can be used to estimate the camera model. On the other hand, the estimated model can filter out false detections. The two steps are done alternately until convergence.

After having the mapping of bottom boundary of each blob, we can further compute the head positions of the blob according to the estimated camera perspective model. It follows that based on both the mappings of the bottom boundary and the head position of each blob, we can calculate the *planar homographies*, project every pixel in the blob from camera i to camera j on the vertical plane, and vice versa. The relation between the ground plane matching and the vertical plane matching is given in Figure 2(b). An example of estimated mappings of blobs on the vertical planes is shown in Figure 4, where all the pixels of each blob is involved in the projection.

Algorithm 1 Automatic Perspective Parameter Estimation Algorithm. $(\alpha, \alpha_0) = \mathbf{Algo}(\mathcal{D}, \tau, \mathrm{T})$. Given a set of detected windows, $\mathcal{D}$, and two parameters, τ and T, which are respectively a tolerance and the maximum number of iterations, return the camera's perspective parameters, (α, α_0).

let d_i be a detected pedestrian in $\mathcal{D}$ and v_i and h_i respectively represent the bottom position and the image height of d_i
initialize $\mathcal{D}^1 = \mathcal{D}$
for $t = 1$ **to** T **do**
  estimate parameters α and α_0 using $\mathcal{D}^t$ by minimizing $J^t(\alpha, \alpha_0) = \sum_{i=1}^{|\mathcal{D}|} (\alpha \cdot v_i + \alpha_0 - h_i)^2$
  build $\mathcal{D}^{t+1} = \{d_i | (\alpha \cdot v_i + \alpha_0 - h_i) \leq \tau,\ d_i \in \mathcal{D}^t\}$
  if $\mathcal{D}^{t+1}$ and $\mathcal{D}^t$ are the same **then**
    return perspective camera parameters, α and α_0
  end if
end for

3.3 Matched Component Extraction

After the correspondences of blobs between two cameras are established, we can group blobs into *components*, in each of which the same entities present in both the two camera views. Let's illustrate the grouping process by the example given in Figure 5. Suppose that $\{b_1^{(i)}, b_2^{(i)}, \ldots, b_6^{(i)}\}$ and $\{b_1^{(j)}, b_2^{(j)}, \ldots, b_4^{(j)}\}$ are the extracted blobs in camera i and j, respectively. A *bipartite graph* of ten nodes is then constructed. An edge between two nodes in the opposite sides is added if the two corresponding blobs are matched in any direction. Via computing the *connected components* in the graph, components $\{c_1^{(i)}, c_2^{(i)}, c_3^{(i)}\}$ and $\{c_1^{(j)}, c_2^{(j)}, c_3^{(j)}\}$ are obtained for camera i and j, respectively. Note that since each corresponding component refers to the same group of pedestrians in both the two cameras, it implies that visual cues of the component captured by the two cameras can be shared directly. That is, we in this work propose to match the components, upon each of which visual knowledge can be transferred across cameras.

4 Two-pass Regression

This section describes how the proposed MCPC system improves the accuracy of people counting by incorporating visual cues extracted from a specified camera with the knowledge shared by other collaborative cameras. Suppose that we have a set of M cameras, $\mathbf{P} = \{P_m\}_{m=1}^{\mathrm{M}}$, which monitor an environment. Let $\mathbf{V} = \{V_m\}_{m=1}^{\mathrm{M}}$ be the videos taken by these cameras respectively. Without loss of generality, we assume each video consists of T

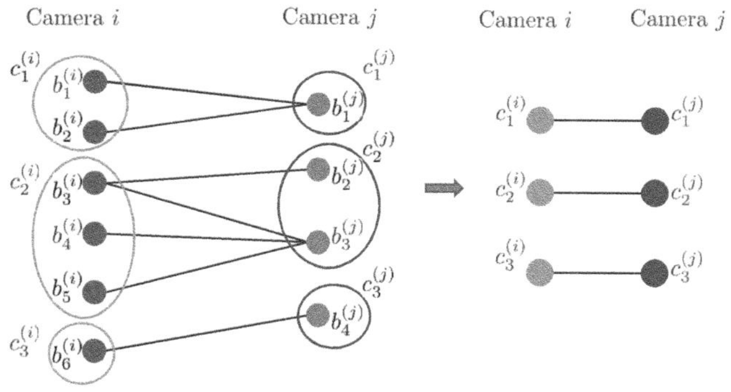

Figure 5: Matching components across cameras.

frames and all the frames are *synchronized* across different cameras. In the following, we use $I_t^{(m)}$ to denote the tth frame of V_m. Our goal here is to yield a matrix $\boldsymbol{A} \in \mathbb{R}^{\mathrm{M}\times\mathrm{T}}$ whose element $a_{m,t}$ is the prediction of the number of people present in frame $I_t^{(m)}$.

Our approach is an instance of the *counting-by-regression* systems that map a set of unintelligible features to the prediction of the people count, but distinguishes itself by jointly considering both intra-camera and inter-camera knowledge. Specifically, the proposed two-pass regression framework is motivated by the observation that the number of people in an image can be approximated by two different parts—the *regular* part and the *residual* part, as illustrated in Figure 6. The estimations of the two parts are carried out by two regressors respectively. The estimation of the regular part is an inference on the number of people within an image blob according to its own low-level features, just like what a common counting-by-regression approach does. Due to many unavoidable effects such as the failure in foreground segmentation (like shadows), partial occlusions, and the likes, the inference based on low-level features is typically imperfect, and a residual is hence yielded. In our approach, we borrow the knowledge captured by the collaborative cameras to measure the residual, and cast it as an instance of the transfer learning problem.

In this work, both the tasks of the regular estimation and the residual estimation are accomplished by the multi-kernel extension of support vector regression [39]. In the following, a brief introduce to multi-kernel support vector regression is first given. The designs of the two regressors are then depicted respectively.

4.1 Multi-kernel Support Vector Regression

In view of the large variations in crowd appearance, it is usually difficult to find a single feature to well characterize blobs. Therefore, we turn to seek a set of weights to linearly and optimally combine the given features in a unified domain. To this end, we leverage *multiple kernel learning* (MKL) [4,17,25,35,37] to fuse a set of base kernel matrices or functions, each of which is created based on a specific kind of features, and to derive the regressor simultaneously.

Given D different feature descriptors, the kernel bank $\{K_d\}_{d=1}^{\mathrm{D}}$ can be constructed for data by the corresponding kernel functions $\{k_d(\cdot,\cdot)\}_{d=1}^{\mathrm{D}}$. Fusing data characteristics captured by multiple feature descriptors now can be achieved via kernel matrix combination, i.e.,

$$K = \sum_{d=1}^{\mathrm{D}} \beta_d K_d, \text{ s. t. } \beta_d \geq 0, \tag{2}$$

where β_d is the ensemble coefficient of base kernel K_d (or the weight for the dth kind of feature descriptors). Consequently, the multi-kernel support vector regressor f from a set of labeled training data $\{(\mathrm{x}_n, y_n \in \mathbb{R})\}_{n=1}^{\mathrm{N}}$ can typically be expressed by

$$\begin{aligned} f(\mathrm{x}) &= \sum_{n=1}^{\mathrm{N}} \alpha_n y_n k(\mathrm{x}_n, \mathrm{x}) + b \\ &= \sum_{n=1}^{\mathrm{N}} \alpha_n y_n \sum_{d=1}^{\mathrm{D}} \beta_d k_d(\mathrm{x}_n, \mathrm{x}) + b. \end{aligned} \tag{3}$$

The task of MKL is to determine the optimal values of the sample coefficients $\{\alpha_n\}_{n=1}^{\mathrm{N}}$, the kernel weights $\{\beta_d\}_{d=1}^{\mathrm{D}}$, and the offset b. Actually, various objective functions, e.g., the *structural risk function* with ℓ_1- or ℓ_2-norm regularization, together with different optimization techniques, e.g., *semi-definite programming* (SDP) or *semi-infinite linear programs* (SILPs) are developed to accomplish the task. In this work, we adopt *SimpleMKL* [35] to learn the regressors due to its efficiency and effectiveness.

4.2 First-pass Regular Regression

The first-pass regressor works, including training and predicting, on extracted blobs. We describe the representation of blobs and the learning of the regressor as follows.

4.2.1 *Blob Representation*

Since knowledge for people counting is only shared among frames taken at the same time, for simplicity we consider only frames at time t. Thus, for frame $I_t^{(m)}$ taken by camera P_m, the index t can be dropped without ambiguity. As mentioned previously, each frame can be expressed as a set of blobs, i.e., $I^{(m)} = \{(\mathrm{x}_b^{(m)}, y_b^{(m)})\}_{b=1}^{\mathrm{n}_b}$, where $\mathrm{x}_b^{(m)}$ is the feature representation of the bth blob while $y_b^{(m)}$ is the number of people in the blob. In the training phase, $y_b^{(m)}$ is given while in the testing phase, it is exactly what we attempt to estimate. With this representation, the number of people in $I^{(m)}$ can be calculated by summing over the ones estimated in the blobs, i.e., $a_m = \sum_{b=1}^{\mathrm{n}_b} y_b^{(m)}$.

4.2.2 *Learning with Intra-camera Visual Features*

We have implemented three representative features to characterize the properties of blobs, including

Area. This attribute represents the total number of foreground pixels occupied by the blob, roughly reflecting the volume size of moving objects in the scene.

Canny edge pixels. We calculate the total number of edge pixels, located by Canny edge detector, included in the blob to capture the structural properties of crowdedness.

Oriented gradients. The feature consists of two independent values representing the gradient magnitudes of vertical and horizontal orientations, respectively.

As these features capture diverse characteristics, we treat each one as a unique descriptor. Thus, each blob is represented by four different descriptors, each of which correspond to a specific kernel. To reduce the influence of perspective effects, all adopted features are normalized by applying geometric distortion correction coefficients [9] to approximate the real scale in the scene.

We adopt the multi-kernel support vector regression to implement the regular estimation in the first stage of our MCPC system. We learn the $\mathcal{F}^{(m)}$ by using a number of manually labeled blobs and the resulting four kernels. In the stage, training data are collected within a single camera, without referencing any information out of the camera. Besides, we also derive four additional support vector regressors $\{\mathcal{F}_d^{(m)}\}_{d=1}^{\mathrm{D}}$, where $\mathcal{F}_d^{(m)}$ is learned with the same training blobs, but only the dth kernel is considered. The value of

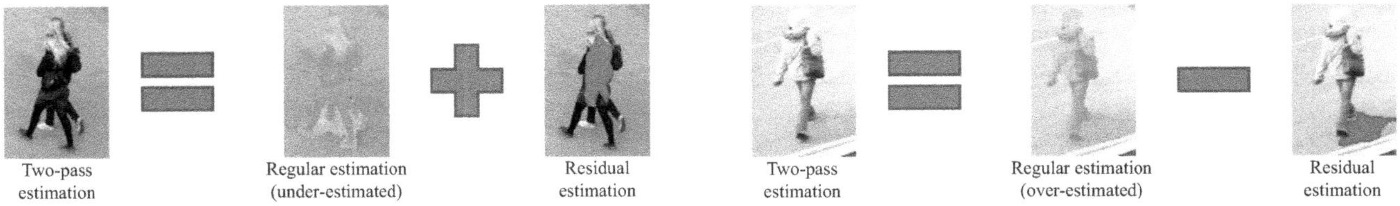

(a) Illustration of occlusion handling

(b) Illustration of shadow handling

Figure 6: Our two-pass regression framework consists of a regular estimation and a residual estimation. While the former infers the number of people of a blob based using intra-camera low-level features, the later estimates the residual by exploiting inter-camera information. Fusing both together compensates for the difference between the ground truth and the estimated value, thus yielding higher accuracy than either.

D is four here. All the procedures described above are repeated for each camera P_m.

4.3 Second-pass Residual Regression

The goal of this stage is to estimate and recover the yielded residual in the first pass by borrowing the visual knowledge captured by other collaborative cameras. The second-pass regressor works upon the *matched components*, upon which the additional inter-camera knowledge are transferred.

4.3.1 Component Representation

A video frame can also be represented by a set of components once we conduct the blob matching algorithm on all synchronized frames. Since we know that the corresponding components on different views refer to a group of the same entities, the number of people in each of them should be identical. The conflict of predictions among multiple views reveals that residual occurs. Based on this fact, knowledge like intra-camera estimation results shared among matched components can be directly adopted without requiring any further transformation or adaption. Suppose that frame $I^{(m)}$ consists of $\tilde{n}_c$ components. Its *component representation* can be expressed as $\{(z_c^{(m)}, \tilde{y}_c^{(m)})\}_{c=1}^{\tilde{n}_c}$, where $\tilde{y}_c^{(m)}$ is the residual of component c yielded in the first pass, and $z_c^{(m)}$ is the feature representation. Similar to the first pass, $\tilde{y}_c^{(m)}$ is given in training, and is what we need to measure in prediction. For the ease of discussion, the definitions of $\tilde{y}_c^{(m)}$ and $z_c^{(m)}$ are given in the following section.

4.3.2 Learning with Inter-camera Visual Knowledge

Since a component is composed of a set of blobs, its residual in the training phase can be precisely computed. Let's illustrate this with an example component $z^{(m)}$, taken by camera P_m, that consists of blobs $\{(x_b^{(m)}, y_b^{(m)})\}_{b=1}^{N}$. The residual of $z^{(m)}$ in the first stage can be defined as

$$\tilde{y}^{(m)} = \sum_{b=1}^{N} y_b^{(m)} - \sum_{b=1}^{N} \mathcal{F}^{(m)}(x_b^{(m)}). \tag{4}$$

We now design the feature representation of component $z^{(m)}$ by considering inter-camera knowledge. To begin with, the people counts of $z^{(m)}$ predicted by support vector regressors $\{\mathcal{F}_d^{(m)}\}_{d=1}^{D}$ are evaluated, i.e., ,

$$\mathbf{v}(z^{(m)}) = [\mathcal{F}_1^{(m)}(z^{(m)}) \cdots \mathcal{F}_D^{(m)}(z^{(m)})]^\top \in \mathbb{R}^D, \tag{5}$$

$$\text{where } \mathcal{F}_d^{(m)}(z^{(m)}) = \sum_{b=1}^{N} \mathcal{F}_d^{(m)}(x_b^{(m)}). \tag{6}$$

For the matched components taken by other cameras, we similarly have $\{\mathbf{v}(z^{(m)})\}_{m=1}^{M}$. Since component $z^{(m)}$ refers to a group of the same entities taken by these cameras, the people counts estimated $\{\mathbf{v}(z^{(m)})\}_{m=1}^{M}$ can be compared directly. Further, the yielded conflict provides strong evidences to infer the residual. We hence develop the following four kinds of descriptors for component $z^{(m)}$, i.e.,

Cross-camera Conflict. This descriptor directly captures the conflict between camera P_m and other cameras w.r.t. each of the adopted visual feature, i.e.,

$$z^{(m)}.cc = \frac{\sum_{m'=1, m' \neq m}^{M} \mathbf{v}(z^{(m')})}{M-1} - \mathbf{v}(z^{(m)}). \tag{7}$$

Negative Trimmed. We are motivated by the observation that due to the camera angle relative to the motion direction of pedestrians or the distance to the monitored environment, people counts predicted from some camera tend to be underestimated. In the situation, only the positive part in Equation (7) are useful in residual estimation. This descriptor is hence defined as

$$z^{(m)}.nt = \max(z^{(m)}.cc, \mathbf{0}). \tag{8}$$

Positive Trimmed. Symmetrical to $z^{(m)}.nt$, we also have descriptor

$$z^{(m)}.pt = -\min(z^{(m)}.cc, \mathbf{0}). \tag{9}$$

Intra-camera Conflict. Motivated by the fact that the sensitivities of visual features to occlusions are different, the prediction conflict among these features is also to recover the residual caused by occlusions [29]. This descriptor is designed as

$$z^{(m)}.ic = [\mathcal{F}_i^{(m)}(z^{(m)}) - \mathcal{F}_j^{(m)}(z^{(m)})], \text{ for } 1 \leq i < j \leq D. \tag{10}$$

In the training phase, we match the blobs across cameras, and obtain a set of components. By measuring the residual in Equation (4) and extracting the four features in Equation (7) ~ Equation (10) for each matched component, a support vector regressor, $\mathcal{S}^{(m)}$, with four kernels as input can be derived.

4.4 On People Counting

After the training procedure, the final regressors of the two passes $\{(\mathcal{F}^{(m)}, \mathcal{S}^{(m)})\}_{m=1}^{M}$ are available. In the testing phase, suppose that we are given frame taken by camera P_m, and it is of blob representation $\{x_b^{(m)}\}_{b=1}^{n_b}$ and component representation $\{z_c^{(m)}\}_{c=1}^{\tilde{n}_c}$. Our approach estimates the number of people in this frame by

$$y_m = \sum_{b=1}^{n_b} \mathcal{F}^{(m)}\left(x_b^{(m)}\right) + \sum_{c=1}^{\tilde{n}_c} \mathcal{S}^{(m)}\left(z_c^{(m)}\right). \tag{11}$$

We complete this section by concluding that the proposed MCPC system integrates not only the intra-camera visual features but also the inter-camera visual knowledge, and alleviates the problems caused by occlusions, low-quality images, or imperfect background segmentations. In the experiments, we show that it significantly outperforms single-view systems and the systems that simply average the outcomes of multiple views. Besides, it supports real-time people counting.

5 Experiments and Results

In this section we present the estimation performance of the proposed system and compare this with other competitive approaches. We first describe the experimental settings and then discuss the results of various methods.

5.1 Experimental Settings

To evaluate the performance of the proposed MCPC system, we conduct experiments on the PETS 2010 Benchmark Data [16]. This data set consists of a collection of videos captured by several stationary camcorders. These camcorders are located at distinct positions and set up to monitor the same scene. We select three representative video clips of two views, denoted as SPARSE, MEDIUM, and HEAVY, respectively. While SPARSE and MEDIUM are two videos with sparse individuals and small groups of pedestrians (i.e., less or moderate occlusions), HEAVY generally contains highly crowded groups (i.e., heavy occlusions). Since these selected videos span a wide spectrum of occlusion levels, collecting them together forms a good test bed to measure the effectiveness of occlusion handling for people counting. The details of the experimental data are given in Table 1.

Because supervised learning approaches require labeled examples, however, to the best of our knowledge, few proper benchmarks along with groundtruth annotations are publicly available in the computer vision or multimedia community. Therefore, we have put manual effort into annotating videos and obtained a large set of pedestrian labels on the PETS 2010 videos. To fuel people counting research, particularly using multiple cameras, these data are released and can be downloaded from our project website[1].

For performing quantitative evaluations for people counting, we divide each video clip into a non-overlapping training and testing set. We use the preceding half of frames of each video as training data and report the performance by testing on the remaining frames. In experiments, we adopt mean absolute error (MAE) as the criterion to measure the performance. Furthermore, average MAE, the average of multiple MAE over all evaluation videos, is used to reflect the overall performance of people counting methods.

To examine the stability of people counting approaches, we conduct experiments with four different settings, including using one video only (HEAVY), combinations of two videos (SPARSE +HEAVY and MEDIUM+HEAVY), and using all three videos (SPARSE +MEDIUM+HEAVY) as training data. Therefore, we can evaluate the performance sensitivity to the changes of the diversity of training data. Since a few parameters of support vector regression and multiple kernel learning have significant influence on performance of established systems, we thus build our MCPC system with the optimal parameters, selected from a reasonable parameter space via five-fold cross validation. The automatically tuned parameters include the epsilon in loss function and the penalty cost to errors in LIBSVM [11], and the regularization term in SimpleMKL [35].

5.2 Results

We first evaluate the accuracy of our blob correspondence estimation algorithm by manually and visually checking the consistency of the matched components between two views. For the ease of validation, we assign the same color and the same number to both of the matched components in two views, as shown in Figure 8. Then, we calculate the percentage of correct matches over the whole matches. From Table 1, we observe that the proposed algorithm is able to obtain sufficiently accurate results, ranging from 96.4% to 98.5% of component matching precision, over three videos with different crowdedness levels.

To understand what the MCPC system advances single-camera people counting systems, we use the estimation results yielded in the first stage as our baseline (BS-MKL). We have also implemented a Gaussian process method and a neural network method, similar to the state of the art approaches proposed by Chan et al. [9] and Ryan et al. [36], respectively, to count the number of people. By using the same low-level (local) features, we thus establish another two sets of estimation results, i.e., BS-GP and BS-NN. Note that these three approaches merely use intra-camera visual cues and do not involve any knowledge transfer among cameras. In our current survey, the only MCPC system related to ours is a fusion approach that combines human detection results from multiple cameras [31]. As mentioned in section 2, however, this method is not suitable to handle the scenes with dense crowds like the PETS 2010 datasets used in our experiments. To make meaningful comparisons, therefore, we develop two variants of the approach to fuse complementary information. We introduce two fusion manners, frame-based fusion (FRAME-AVG) and component-based fusion (COMPO-AVG), which averagely combine the estimation results of synchronized frames and matched components, respectively. Finally, we refer to our MCPC system as OURS.

Table 2 displays the overall estimation errors (MAE) on SPARSE, MEDIUM, and HEAVY when using our MCPC system (OURS) and comparisons with the BS-MKL, BS-GP, BS-NN, FRAME-AVG, and COMPO-AVG methods. When taking into account only intra-camera visual features, the BS-MKL outperforms the BS-GP approach in most settings based on average MAE. The only two exceptions are on View 1 when using only HEAVY as training data and on View 2 when using all SPARSE, MEDIUM, and HEAVY as training data. This shows the effectiveness of applying multiple kernel learning techniques to people counting when we have a number of features. Furthermore, we observe that the performance gains of the multiple-camera systems using either of average fusion approaches is modest since this kind of approaches definitely performs an interpolation of the estimations given by different views. Although this fashion may yield higher accuracy, in most cases errors are propagated, thus degrading performance. In contrast, our MCPC system is able to handle this difficulty and achieves significant improvement. Overall, OURS reduces the estimation errors of the first pass (BS-MKL) ranging from 15.8% $\left(\frac{1.49-1.77}{1.77}\right)$ to 78.6% $\left(\frac{1.21-5.66}{5.66}\right)$, and the ones of frame-based fusion (FRAME-AVG) ranging from 13.8% $\left(\frac{3.07-3.56}{3.56}\right)$ to 74.8% $\left(\frac{1.00-3.97}{3.97}\right)$, in terms of relative improvement.

Figure 7 shows the number of people frame-by-frame on the three testing videos, including manually annotated groundtruth and estimations yielded by BS-MKL, BS-GP, BS-NN, FRAME-AVG, COMPO-AVG, and OURS, respectively, in two experimental settings. From these figures, we note that the proposed MCPC generally gains significant performance on HEAVY, while the improvement on SPARSE is not obvious in a few settings. There are two possible reasons. First, occlusions are seldom observed in the SPARSE video. Therefore, people counting with a single camera may be sufficient. Second, the appearance variation of small groups of pedestrians is usually modest, whereas highly occluded crowds could represent a large variation. Thus, complementary information and inter-camera knowledge are more useful to handle highly crowded scenes (heavy occlusions) than to handle sparse scenes. To better explain our observation, we show several examples of video frames with the estimations on extracted components in Figure 8. In these examples, one can observe that diverse properties are captured by different cameras.

[1] http://research.twnct.net/MCPC_MM2012/

Table 1: Description of the PETS 2010 datasets used in our experiments.

video clips	SPARSE		MEDIUM		HEAVY	
	View 1	View 2	View 1	View 2	View 1	View 2
Total number of frames	360		190		40	
Minimal number of pedestrians in a frame	4	4	4	4	40	40
Maximal number of pedestrians in a frame	8	8	17	19	41	41
Mean of the number of pedestrians	6.8	6.8	10.7	11.9	40.5	41.0
Standard deviation of the number of pedestrians	0.9	1.1	3.8	4.9	0.5	0.2
Total number of segmented blobs	1854	1554	744	670	195	197
Precision of blob matching (%)	98.5		96.4		98.0	

Table 2: Summary of estimation errors of people counting on three videos with different occlusion levels, when applying the proposed MCPC system (OURS) and comparisons with the first-pass estimation results (BS-MKL), Chan et al.'s approach (BS-GP) [9], Ryan et al.'s approach (BS-NN) [36], and two average fusion methods (FRAME-AVG and COMPO-AVG). Note that the BS-MKL, BS-GP, and BS-NN are three methods which do not involve knowledge transfer, while others exploit complementary information perceived in multiple camera systems. Additionally, these quantitative results are reported in either MAE or average MAE.

training data	testing data	View 1						View 2					
		BS-MKL	BS-GP	BS-NN	FRAME-AVG	COMPO-AVG	OURS	BS-MKL	BS-GP	BS-NN	FRAME-AVG	COMPO-AVG	OURS
HEAVY	SPARSE	5.94	5.71	3.10	4.86	4.77	**1.80**	15.64	18.09	13.42	4.84	5.00	**4.72**
	MEDIUM	5.98	3.40	3.74	3.79	3.30	**2.26**	10.11	11.51	7.42	2.52	3.00	**2.42**
	HEAVY	**1.24**	2.11	1.28	3.33	3.33	1.72	6.50	5.77	5.64	3.33	3.33	**2.06**
	OVERALL	4.39	3.74	2.71	3.99	3.80	**1.93**	10.75	11.79	8.82	3.56	3.77	**3.07**
SPARSE+HEAVY	SPARSE	1.75	3.78	1.74	**1.15**	1.51	1.24	0.97	1.94	0.91	**0.72**	0.82	0.88
	MEDIUM	1.80	1.85	1.73	1.75	1.81	**1.60**	1.63	1.84	1.76	1.59	**1.46**	2.41
	HEAVY	1.84	2.12	1.82	5.02	5.02	**1.08**	8.25	7.36	6.89	5.02	5.02	**2.19**
	OVERALL	1.80	2.59	1.76	2.64	2.78	**1.31**	3.62	3.71	3.19	2.44	2.43	**1.83**
MEDIUM+HEAVY	SPARSE	2.04	5.83	2.13	4.05	4.64	**1.38**	6.13	7.15	6.96	4.03	3.45	**0.73**
	MEDIUM	1.68	3.16	1.73	3.53	2.84	**1.04**	3.99	4.95	4.10	1.55	1.94	**1.02**
	HEAVY	1.82	1.44	1.45	4.33	4.33	**0.58**	6.86	6.88	6.34	4.33	4.33	**1.89**
	OVERALL	1.85	3.48	1.77	3.97	3.93	**1.00**	5.66	6.33	5.80	3.30	3.24	**1.21**
SPARSE+MEDIUM+HEAVY	SPARSE	1.64	3.85	1.75	**1.31**	1.73	1.95	1.58	1.96	1.38	1.11	**0.68**	1.32
	MEDIUM	1.57	1.71	1.57	2.75	2.17	**1.37**	3.24	2.34	2.09	1.20	1.35	**1.02**
	HEAVY	2.10	1.65	1.79	5.71	5.71	**1.16**	9.33	7.82	7.98	5.71	5.71	**1.20**
	OVERALL	1.77	2.40	1.70	3.26	3.20	**1.49**	4.71	4.04	3.82	2.67	2.58	**1.18**

Our approach effectively makes use of these properties and leads to salient improvement.

6 Conclusions

In this paper, we have introduced a multiple camera people counting system based on the spirit of transfer learning to improve the weakness of using a single camera. This work has three main contributions. The first is an exploration of inter-camera knowledge. We developed a two-pass regression framework which has been shown effective in adapting heterogeneous information for people counting. Second, a novel blob matching algorithm was proposed to obtain a set of consistent entities among cameras, thus leading to the success of knowledge sharing. Finally, we released sets of manually annotated pedestrian labels based on the PETS 2010 Benchmark Data, which are considered as a valuable resource for multiple camera people counting research.

Acknowledgments

This work was partially supported by the National Science Council of Taiwan, R.O.C., under grants NSC100-2221-E-001-013-MY3, NSC100-2631-H-001-020, and NSC100-2218-E-001-004.

7 References

[1] N. Ahuja and S. Todorovic. Extracting texels in 2.1D natural textures. In *Proc. of IEEE ICCV*, 2007.

[2] D. Arsié, B. Schuller, and G. Rigoll. Multiple camera person tracking in multiple layers combining 2D and 3D information. In *Proc. of M2SFA2*, 2008.

[3] C. Aslan, K. Bernardin, and R. Stiefelhagen. Automatic calibration of camera networks based on local motion features. In *Proc. of M2SFA2*, 2008.

[4] F. Bach, G. Lanckriet, and M. Jordan. Multiple kernel learning, conic duality, and the SMO algorithm. In *Proc. of ICML*, 2004.

[5] O. Barnich and M. V. Droogenbroeck. ViBe: A universal background subtraction algorithm for video sequences. *IEEE Trans. Image Process.*, 20(6):1709–1724, 2011.

[6] E. Bart and S. Ullman. Cross-generalization: Learning novel classes from a single example by feature replacement. In *Proc. of IEEE CVPR*, 2005.

[7] S. Bickel, M. Bruckner, and T. Scheffer. Discriminative learning for differing training and test distributions. In *Proc. of ICML*, 2007.

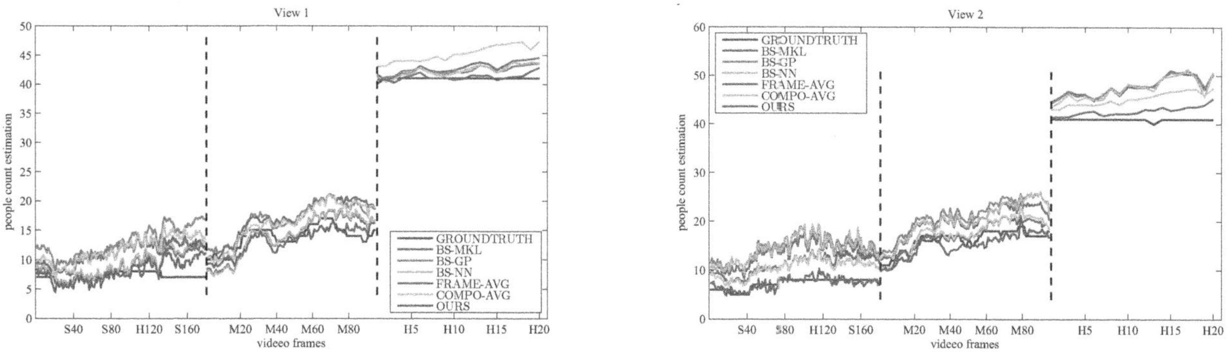

(a) Using MEDIUM and HEAVY as training data

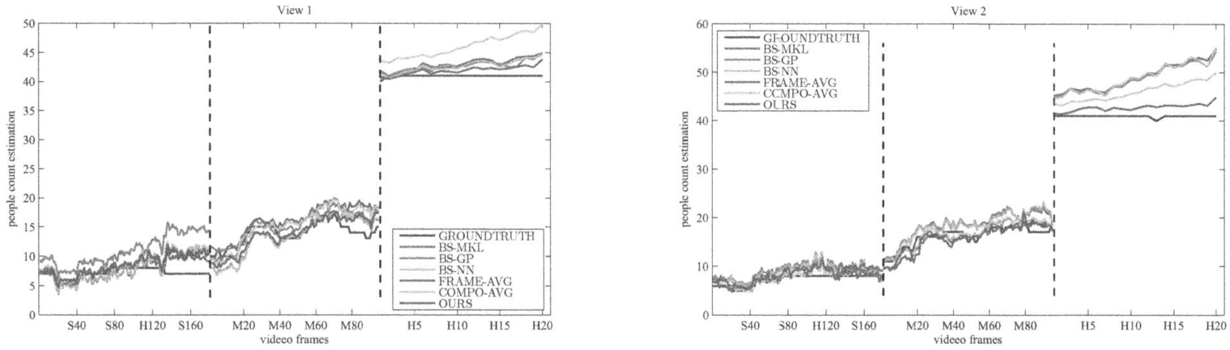

(b) Using all SPARSE, MEDIUM and HEAVY as training data

Figure 7: The number of people of individual frames on the testing data reported with groundtruth, first-pass estimation (BS-MKL), Chan et al.'s approach (BS-GP) [9], Ryan et al.'s approach (BS-NN) [36], two average fusion methods (FRAME-AVG and COMPO-AVG), and our MCPC system (OURS). Note that the BS-MKL, the BS-GP, and the BS-NN are three methods which use only intra-camera visual features while others utilize additional knowledge among collaborative cameras.

[8] G. Brostow and R. Cipolla. Unsupervised bayesian detection of independent motion in crowds. In *Proc. of IEEE CVPR*, 2006.

[9] A. Chan, Z. Liang, and N. Vasconcelos. Privacy preserving crowd monitoring: Counting people without people models or tracking. In *Proc. of IEEE CVPR*, 2008.

[10] A. Chan and N. Vasconcelos. Bayesian Poisson regression for crowd counting. In *Proc. of IEEE ICCV*, 2009.

[11] C.-C. Chang and C.-J. Lin. LIBSVM: A library for support vector machines. *ACM Trans. Intell. Syst. Technol.*, 2:1–27, 2011.

[12] N. Dalal and B. Triggs. Histogram of oriented gradient for human detection. In *Proc. of IEEE CVPR*, 2005.

[13] P. Dollar, C. Wojek, B. Schiele, and P. Perona. Pedestrian detection: A benchmark. In *Proc. of IEEE CVPR*, 2009.

[14] L. Duan, I. Tsang, D. Xu, and S. Maybank. Domain transfer SVM for video concept detection. In *Proc. of IEEE CVPR*, 2009.

[15] R. Eshel and Y. Moses. Homography based multiple camera detection and tracking of people in a dense crowd. In *Proc. of IEEE CVPR*, 2008.

[16] J. Ferryman and A. Ellis. PETS2010: Dataset and challenge. In *Proc. of IEEE AVSS*, 2010.

[17] M. Gönen and E. Alpaydin. Multiple kernel learning algorithms. *J. Mach. Learn. Res.*, 12:2211–2268, 2011.

[18] D. Hoiem, A. Efros, and M. Hebert. Putting objects in perspective. In *Proc. of IEEE CVPR*, 2006.

[19] J. Jacques Junior, S. Musse, and C. Jung. Crowd analysis using computer vision techniques. *IEEE Signal Process. Mag.*, 27:66–77, 2010.

[20] Y.-G. Jiang, J. Wang, S.-F. Chang, and C.-W. Ngo. Domain adaptive semantic diffusion for large scale context-based video annotation. In *Proc. of IEEE ICCV*, 2009.

[21] M. Jones and D. Snow. Pedestrian detection using boosted features over many frames. In *Proc. of ICPR*, 2008.

[22] S. M. Khan and M. Shah. Tracking multiple occluding people by localizing on multiple scene planes. *IEEE Trans. Pattern Anal. Mach. Intell.*, 31(3):505–519, 2009.

[23] P. Kilambi, E. Ribnick, A. J. Joshi, O. Masoud, and N. Papanikolopoulos. Estimating pedestrian counts in groups. *Comput. Vis. Image Underst.*, 110(1):43–59, 2008.

[24] D. Kong, D. Gray, and H. Tao. Counting pedestrians in crowds using viewpoint invariant training. In *Proc. of BMVC*, 2005.

[25] G. Lanckriet, N. Cristianini, P. Bartlett, L. Ghaoui, and M. Jordan. Learning the kernel matrix with semidefinite programming. *J. Mach. Learn. Res.*, 5:27–72, 2004.

[26] B. Leibe, E. Seemann, and B. Schiele. Pedestrian detection in crowded scenes. In *Proc. of IEEE CVPR*, 2005.

[27] V. Lempitsky and A. Zisserman. Learning to count objects in images. In *NIPS*, 2010.

[28] S.-F. Lin, J.-Y. Chen, and H.-X. Chao. Estimation of number of people in crowded scenes using perspective transformation. *IEEE Trans. Syst., Man, Cybern. A*, 31:645–654, 2001.

[29] T.-Y. Lin, Y.-Y. Lin, M.-F. Weng, Y.-C. Wang, Y.-F. Hsu, and

View 1						View 2					
ID	GT	MKL	GP	AVG	OURS	ID	GT	MKL	GP	AVG	OURS
1	41	44.7	44.9	48.0	42.2	1	41	51.4	50.4	48.0	42.5

(a) An example frame of HEAVY. The results are yielded by those models learned from the combination of SPARSE and HEAVY.

View 1						View 2					
ID	GT	MKL	GP	AVG	OURS	ID	GT	MKL	GP	AVG	OURS
1	7	9.2	10.8	12.3	6.8	1	7	15.4	16.4	12.3	8.2
2	1	1.0	1.6	1.4	1.0	2	1	1.9	2.0	1.4	1.3

(b) An example frame of SPARSE. The results are yielded by those models learned from the combination of MEDIUM and HEAVY.

View 1						View 2					
ID	GT	MKL	GP	AVG	OURS	ID	GT	MKL	GP	AVG	OURS
1	9	10.2	9.8	12.7	10.9	1	12	15.7	16.2	12.7	11.9
2	4	5.2	5.8	5.6	4.9	2	4	5.4	5.1	5.6	5.1
—	—	—	—	—	—	3	1	1.1	1.3	1.1	1.1

(c) An example frame of MEDIUM. The results are yielded by those models learned from all three SPARSE, MEDIUM, and HEAVY.

View 1						View 2					
ID	GT	MKL	GP	AVG	OURS	ID	GT	MKL	GP	AVG	OURS
1	1	0.7	1.0	0.8	1.0	1	1	0.9	1.0	0.8	1.1
2	1	1.1	1.5	1.2	1.4	2	1	1.3	1.4	1.2	1.4
3	3	2.3	3.7	2.8	3.4	3	3	3.3	3.5	2.8	3.7
4	1	0.9	1.4	0.9	0.9	—	—	—	—	—	—
5	1	0.7	1.3	0.7	0.7	—	—	—	—	—	—

(d) An example frame of SPARSE. The results are yielded by those models learned from HEAVY.

Figure 8: Several sample frames selected from the videos used in our experiments. The quantitative results reported on components demonstrate the effectiveness of our MCPC system.

H.-Y. M. Liao. Cross camera people counting with perspective estimation and occlusion handling. In *Proc. of IEEE WIFS*, 2011.

[30] D. Lowe. Distinctive image features from scale-invariant keypoints. *Int. J. Comput. Vision*, 60(2):91–110, 2004.

[31] H. Ma, C. Zeng, and C. X. Ling. A reliable people counting system via multiple cameras. *ACM Trans. Intell. Syst. Technol.*, 3(2):1–22, 2012.

[32] S. Maji, A. C. Berg, and J. Malik. Classification using intersection kernel support vector machines is efficient. In *Proc. of IEEE CVPR*, 2008.

[33] S. Pan and Q. Yang. A survey on transfer learning. *IEEE Trans. Knowl. Data Eng.*, 22(10):1345–1359, 2010.

[34] V. Rabaud and S. Belongie. Counting crowd moving objects. In *Proc. of IEEE CVPR*, 2006.

[35] A. Rakotomamonjy, F. R. Bach, S. Canu, and Y. Grandvalet. SimpleMKL. *J. Mach. Learn. Res.*, 9:2491–2521, 2008.

[36] D. Ryan, S. Denman, C. Fookes, and S. Sridharan. Crowd counting using multiple local features. In *Proc. of DICTA*, 2009.

[37] S. Sonnenburg, G. Rätsch, C. Schäfer, and B. Schölkopf. Large scale multiple kernel learning. *J. Mach. Learn. Res.*, 7:1531–1565, 2006.

[38] R. Tsai. A versatile camera calibration technique for high-accuracy 3D machine vision metrology using off-the-shelf TV cameras and lenses. *IEEE J. Robot. Autom.*, 3(4):323–344, 1987.

[39] V. Vapnik. *Statistical Learning Theory*. Wiley, 1998.

[40] M.-F. Weng and Y.-Y. Chuang. Cross-domain multi-cue fusion for concept-based video indexing. *IEEE Trans. Pattern Anal. Mach. Intell.*, 99(PrePrints), 2011.

[41] B. Wu and R. Nevatia. Detection and segmentation of multiple, partially occluded objects by grouping, merging, assigning part detection responses. *Int. J. Comput. Vision*, 82(2):185–204, 2009.

[42] Y. Xiong and F. Quek. Meeting room configuration and multiple camera calibration in meeting analysis. In *Proc. of ICMI*, 2005.

[43] J. Yang, R. Yan, and A. G. Hauptmann. Cross-domain video concept detection using adaptive SVMs. In *Proc. of ACM MM*, 2007.

[44] B. Zhan, D. Monekosso, P. Remagnino, S. Velastin, and L.-Q. Xu. Crowd analysis: A survey. *Mach. Vision Appl.*, 19:345–357, 2008.

Leveraging High-level and Low-level Features for Multimedia Event Detection

Lu Jiang, Alexander G. Hauptmann, Guang Xiang
School of Computer Science
Carnegie Mellon University
Pittsburgh, PA 15213
{lujiang,alex,guangx}@cs.cmu.edu

ABSTRACT

This paper addresses the challenge of Multimedia Event Detection by proposing a novel method for high-level and low-level features fusion based on collective classification. Generally, the method consists of three steps: training a classifier from low-level features; encoding high-level features into graphs; and diffusing the scores on the established graph to obtain the final prediction. The final prediction is derived from multiple graphs each of which corresponds to a high-level feature. The paper investigates two graph construction methods using logarithmic and exponential loss functions, respectively and two collective classification algorithms, i.e. Gibbs sampling and Markov random walk. The theoretical analysis demonstrates that the proposed method converges and is computationally scalable and the empirical analysis on TRECVID 2011 Multimedia Event Detection dataset validates its outstanding performance compared to state-of-the-art methods, with an added benefit of interpretability.

Categories and Subject Descriptors

H.4 [**Information Systems Applications**]: Miscellaneous

General Terms

Algorithms, Experimentation, Performance

Keywords

Collective classification, feature fusion, multi-modal integration

1. INTRODUCTION

In the past decade, the Internet has witnessed an explosion of multimedia content. Comparable to the days in the late 1990s, when people usually got lost in the rising sea of web pages, now they are overwhelmed by the vast amounts of multimedia content on the web. To advance the development of new technologies for content understanding, the NIST TRECVID effort initiated a new task called Multimedia Event Detection(MED) in 2010. The task is more challenging than the previous ones such as object recognition and action detection, since an event is often more difficult to be characterized and thus to be detected. An event is "an activity-centered happening that involves people engaged in process-driven actions with other people and/or objects at a specific place and time". For example, the event "attempting a board trick" includes video clips such as skating, skiing, surfing and even finger skating. Because of the inherent difficulties of this task, all research tries to exploit multiple types of features to achieve better performance. Generally these feature can be divided into two categories, namely high-level and low-level features. Low-level features such as SIFT and STIP[1], capture the local appearance and texture statistics of objects in the video represented by a collection of interest points. On the other hand, high-level features are represented by a real number estimating the probability of observing a concept in the video. Detection based on high-level features is more consistent with human's understanding and reasoning about the task, where an event is characterized by the presence/absence of certain concepts rather than interest points. E.g. a video is probably about "birthday party" if visual concepts such as "birthday cake", "faces" and the audio concept "cheering" are present. Therefore, high-level features or attributes are favored in the event and scene detection in many studies[2, 3].

The process of combining multiple modalities is called fusion, which can be achieved either by combing the feature vectors into a single long vector based on which a model is trained, namely early fusion[4], or by learning different models for different modalities and aggregating the outputs by different models, usually called late fusion[5]. Many studies [3, 6, 7] have shown that fusing features often leads to better performance as features are usually complementary. Current fusion approaches offer a simple yet effective way for combination of multiple modalities. However, the major problem, especially for the early fusion, is the lack of interpretability of the reason for the score change during the fusion. Therefore it is difficult for a human to understand and trust the fusion result. To tackle this problem, in this paper, we propose a method called Feature Fusion by Collective Classification(FFCC). Our work is motivated by the successful work in classification on social networks [8] and collaboration networks[9]. The intuition behind the method is straightforward and can be summarized into the following process: first we train a classifier we call a local classifier with low-level features to capture the general idea of the events in the video

MM 12, October 29–November 2, 2012, Nara, Japan.

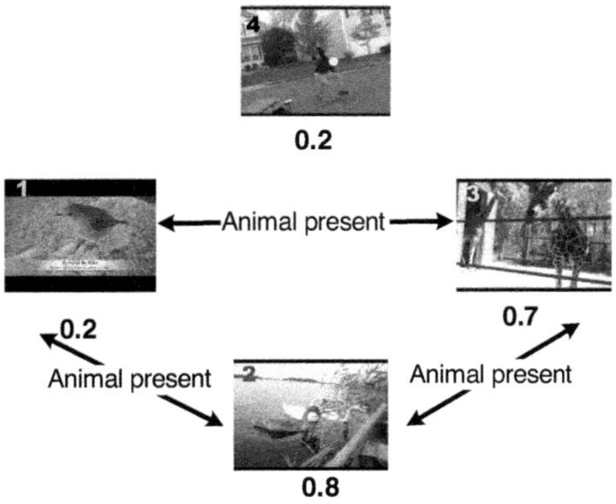

Figure 1: An illustrative graph on high-level feature "animal". The video ID is presented at the left-top of each video and the number below indicates the score generated by the local classifier.

clips; then we construct a set of graphs, one graph for each high-level feature, in which two video clips are linked if the high-level feature concept is either present or absent in both clips, see Fig. 1. Finally, the event scores obtained from the local classifier are diffused through the graphs to obtain the final prediction. The probability diffusion is achieved with a collective classification algorithm [10], such that the final score of all video clips are inferred simultaneously, by updating a video's score according to the scores of its neighbors. Unlike other problems on social network, which only involve a single graph, in this paper, we consider a video clip connected through multiple graphs, each of which corresponds to a high-level concept. The reason for adopting the multiple graphs representation is its interpretability. Leveraging the graph structure, FFCC can correct the false positive connected with true negatives, or false negative connected with true positives. For example, suppose we are detecting the event "feeding an animal" using the graph in Fig. 1, the score of video 1 will be boosted during collective classification because it receives support from scores of video clip 2 and 3. The score of video 4, on the other hand, stays unchanged as it is isolated from the concept graphs of the other videos.

Compared to early and late fusion methods, FFCC has the following three benefits: first, it is a probabilistic approach thus has a solid theoretical background; secondly, the fusion result is interpretable. Since each edge in the graphs carries semantic meaning, the score changes during the collective classification can be understood and validated or verified through inspection. In addition, FFCC represents a good means to incorporate prior knowledge into the graph, which is especially useful for ad-hoc event detection where the training samples are extremely scarce.

In summary, the contributions of this paper are twofold:

- We introduce a novel feature fusion method based on collective classification on multiple graphs. The empirical analysis demonstrates that the proposed method improves not only the performance but also the interpretability over the state-of-the-art fusion methods.
- We propose to use Markov Random Walk as an alternative collective classification algorithm and prove its convergence in our framework.

The rest of this paper is organized as follows: Section 2 gives a brief introduction of related work. Section 3 presents FFCC in details. The experimental results are discussed in Section 4 and conclusions are presented in the final section.

2. RELATED WORK

The idea of feature fusion has been broadly applied in various tasks in multimedia retrieval and classification. Snoek et al. propose the concept of early and late fusion and empirically evaluate their performance on the TRECVID video retrieval benchmark [3]. A successful application of early fusion is the spatial pyramid matching[11, 12], in which each image is divided into tiles and features extracted from different tiles are concatenated to form the final feature vector. By fusing the features from different tiles, it encodes the spatial information about the image. In terms of the late fusion, Kludas et al. claims that maximal performance will be obtained while fusing independent modalities[6]. However, independent modalities are rare in practice and thus many researchers concentrate on studying the statistical dependency between modalities. Wu et al. propose a method based on Principle Component Analysis (PCA) and Independent Component Analysis (ICA) to exploit the dependency between different modalities[13]. However, since the method is based on PCA, it assumes 1) that features with large variances are important and 2) that the principal components are orthogonal. As these assumption is too restrictive to hold in many data sets, Rasiwasia el al.[14] propose to eliminate the dependency by Canonical Correlation Analysis (CCA) i.e. projecting the original feature spaces into a so-called semantic space that maximizes the correlation between different modalities. As CCA only requires a linear relationship between the variable in different modalities, the assumptions of Wu's method are relaxed. Compared to Wu's idea, our paper can be regarded as an attempt to study the non-linear correlation in modality fusion.

Collective classification have been drawing increasing attention in the machine learning community because of its outstanding classification performance on network data such as the Web[15], social networks [8] and collaboration networks[10, 9]. Its distinguishing property, compared with supervised and unsupervised learning, is that the independent and identical distribution assumption can be ignored. The most dominant collective classification methods are Loopy Belief Propagation and Gibbs Sampling. In this paper, we investigate Markov random walk as an alternative collective classification algorithm.

3. MODALITIES FUSION

In this section, we present the FFCC algorithm. Specifically, Section 3.1 introduces some intuitions and the high-level algorithm. The two key issues of graph construction and collective classification are discussed in Section 3.2 and Section 3.3. Finally, the computational complexity is analyzed in the last section.

3.1 Overall Algorithm

First of all, we formulate our intuition as a binary classification problem. Suppose we are given a set of training samples consists of $X_{tr} = \{x_i\}_{i=1}^N$, $Z_{tr} = \{z_i\}_{i=1}^N$ ($x_i \in \mathbb{R}^{M_L}$, $z_i \in \mathbb{R}^{M_H}$) and their labels $Y_{tr} = \{y_i\}_{i=1}^N$ ($y_i \in \mathcal{Y} = \{-1, +1\}$) where x_i,z_i represents the low-level and high-level feature vector for the ith sample in the training set, respectively. Similarly, test samples for high-level and low-level features are represented by $X_{ts} = \{x_i\}_{i=1}$ and $Z_{ts} = \{z_i\}_{i=1}$. Our goal is to learn a final hypothesis h_f for all test samples. For the convenience, we will use the subscript to index sample and superscript to index the feature dimension. E.g. x_i^j denotes the value of jth dimension of the ith sample.

We define a graph $G = (V, E)$, where the vertex set encompasses all samples in both training and test set, accordingly $V = V_{tr} \cup V_{ts}$. Each edge e_{ij}, which connects vertex v_i and v_j, is associated with a weight w_{ij} measuring the intensity of the connection. In this paper we only consider undirected graphs i.e. for each edge $w_{ij} = w_{ji}$.

A local hypothesis h_l denotes the real valuated function learned from low-level features which estimates the posterior probability of the label conditioned on low-level features. We call it local because it inherits the i.i.d. assumption that the data is independent and identically distributed. Most classification algorithms that follow this assumption, e.g. logistic regression and SVM, can be plugged in to learn a local hypothesis. However, for a non-probabilistic model such as SVM, a calibration may be useful to convert the scores into a posterior probability. In contrast to the local hypothesis, a relational hypothesis h_r is a posterior probability learned by collective classification algorithms, in which i.i.d. is no longer expected to hold and the probability of a sample's label is affected by those of its neighbors in graph G.

Algorithm 1: Overview of the Feature Fusion by Collective Classification

1 train a local hypothesis h_l using low-level training samples (X_{tr}, Y_{tr});
2 **foreach** $\mathbf{z}^i$ **do**
  construct a graph G_i;
  train a relational hypothesis h_{r_i};
end
3 return the optimal final hypothesis found in the training set;

Given the above notations, the proposed method can be summarized in the following three steps listed in Algorithm 1. First the algorithm obtains a local hypothesis h_l from a local classifier; then it constructs a graph for each high-level feature $\mathbf{z}^i$, on which a relational hypothesis h_{r_i} is trained using a collective classification algorithm; finally, it searches the best hypothesis over the training set and returns it as the final hypothesis h_f. For instance, we may train a SVM classifier on low-level features in Step 1; then in Step 2 a set of graphs are constructed by high-level features and the SVM prediction scores are updated by the collective classification algorithm on the established graphs. Finally, the optimal scores are selected from the updated ones as the final hypothesis.

If we assume the graphs are mutually independent, the final hypothesis can be calculated from (see Appendix for the derivation):

$$\log h_f = \sum_{z^i \in S} \log h_{r_i} - (|S| - 1) \log h_l \tag{1}$$

where S is a subset of high-level features. If the graphs are dependent, the average of the relational hypothesis can be applied to estimate the final hypothesis. Sometimes when the number of training samples is insufficient, we may need to smooth the final hypothesis with the local hypothesis:

$$\tilde{h}_f = \frac{1 - \alpha}{h_l^{|S|-1}} \prod_{z^i \in S} h_{r_i} + \alpha h_l \tag{2}$$

The first part of the right hand side can be regard as the weighted average of all relational hypothesis. Eq. 2 models the final hypothesis h_f as a linear interpolation of the relational hypothesis with the local hypothesis with the coefficient α. Smoothing is often applied in the case where training samples are insufficient to obtain an accurate hypothesis. Notice that in both Eq. 1 and Eq. 2 only a subset of features that are relevant to the label contribute to the final hypothesis. Searching the global optimal features subset is an NP-hard problem, consequently in Step 3 we apply a forward wrapper with hill-climbing search to get the subset of features resulting in a locally optimal final hypothesis. In the following two subsections, we will elaborate the non-trivial methods in Step 2 by answering two questions: how to construct a graph from training data and how to train a relational hypothesis?

3.2 Graph Construction

The goal of graph construction is to construct "homophilous" graphs using high-level features, in which the samples with same labels tends to be linked with higher weights than those with different labels. In this paper, we concentrate on graph construction using individual high-level feature, i.e. the connection between two samples solely depends on a single high-level feature, say the kth feature $\mathbf{z}^k$. Two video clips are connected if in which the corresponding high-level concept is present (or similarly defined as absent) in both clips. For each vertex $v_i, v_j \in \mathbf{V}$ the edge weight is calculated from the following equation.

$$w_{ij} = \begin{cases} |z_i^k - z_j^k| & (z_i^k - \delta)(z_j^k - \delta) > 0 \\ 0 & \text{otherwise} \end{cases} \tag{3}$$

where δ is a threshold determined by the training set (Z_{tr}, Y_{tr}). A plausible way of learning a reasonable δ is through mutual information:

$$\delta = \arg\max_{\delta} H(Y_{tr}) - H(Y_{tr} | Z_{tr}^k; \delta) \tag{4}$$

where $H(Y_{tr})$ and $H(Y_{tr}|Z_{tr}^k; \delta)$ are entropy and conditional entropy of the label. The optimal δ is obtained when the correlation between the feature and the label is maximized. In other words, the amount of information on label is maximized using the high-level feature with the optimal δ.

Mutual information offers an intuitive yet aggressive way for the graph construction. We call it aggressive because it preferentially exploits more potential edges between vertices. In contrast, we may conceive a cautious way which selects the parameter δ that minimizes the following loss function:

$$\delta = \arg\min_{\delta} {}_{z_i \in \mathbf{Z_{tr}}} e^{\epsilon(z_i^k;\delta)} - \sum_{i=1}^{N} I((z_i^k - \delta) y_i > 0) \tag{5}$$

where $\epsilon(z_i^k; \delta) = \sum_{i=1}^N I((z_i^k - \delta) y_i < 0)$ and $I(\cdot)$ is the indicator function equaling 1 when $(z_i^k - \delta) y_i < 0$, 0 otherwise. In the above loss function, $\epsilon(z_i^k; \delta)$ counts the number of incorrectly connected vertices in the graph and penalizes them by the exponential loss. The loss attains minima if

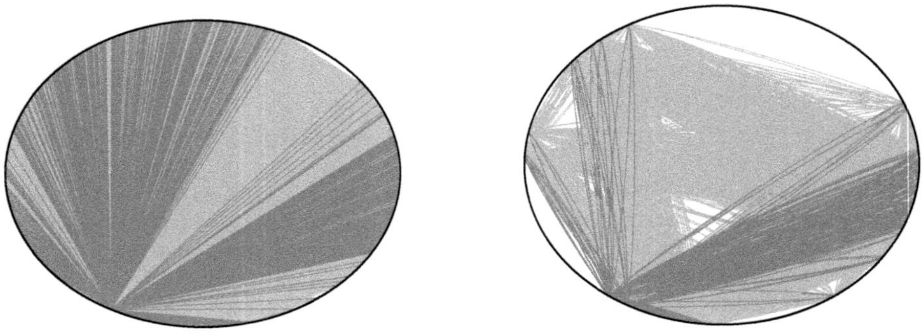

(a) log-loss (b) exp-loss

Figure 2: The graph generated by log and exp loss function on feature "walk/running" in Event "Parkour"

the high-level feature perfectly separates the training vertices into two components with all positive samples residing in one set and all negative samples in the other, otherwise the loss increases exponentially with $\epsilon(z_i^k;\delta)$ grows. Based on this thought, we call Eq. 4 logarithmic loss function since $\forall i, H(Y_{tr})$ is fixed and maximizing Eq. 4 is equivalent to minimizing $H(Y_{tr}|Z_{tr}^k)$ which is a logarithmal like function. The difference between the two loss functions lies in that exponential loss function proves to be a "cautious" method for the graph construction as it imposes a significant penalty when the number of incorrect vertices becomes larger. On the other hand, a logarithmic loss function tolerates a large number of incorrect vertices and thus retrieves more (probably incorrect) edges into the graph.

	Parkour		Wedding Ceremony	
Rank	log-loss	exp-loss	log-loss	exp-loss
1	windows	walk/running	dresses	adult
2	walk/running	building	asian people	person
3	body parts	suburban	adult	body parts
4	road	outdoor	talking	male person
5	streets	face	adult female	standing

Table 1: Top 5 features selected by log and exp loss function on the events "parkour" and "wedding ceremony".

As it turns out both methods are good at exploiting high-level features which are highly related to an event. For example, Tab. 1 lists the top 5 high-level features selected by the two methods in terms of their loss (in decreasing order) on our experimental high-level feature set. It can be seen that both methods capture essential high-level features distinguishing the event from others. However, there is a huge disparity between their generated graphs, see Fig. 2, where the correct edge which connects two positive or two negative samples is marked in grey whereas the incorrect edge in red. The graph generated by the log-loss function is much more dense and includes more incorrect edges. For instance, the density of the graph illustrated in Fig. 2(a) is approximately 31 times that of Fig. 2(b), whereas the number of incorrect edges in Fig. 2(a) is about twice of that in Fig. 2(b).

Being "cautious" increases precision by preventing the error spreading throughout the graph but it decreases recall because some potential edges may be missing. We always face such a tradeoff between precision and recall in practice and the answer may vary given different datasets and evaluation criteria. However, it should be noted that the collective classification works on graphs where the error between vertices can also be propagated to the neighbors of nodes and finally to all vertices within the connected component. Sometimes a tiny error cascades onward until is renders the whole estimation inaccurate. Therefore, in a general sense, being too "aggressive" may not be a prudent policy.

3.3 Collective Inference

The goal of collective learning is to estimate a posterior probability distribution on class labels conditional on the established graph G and local hypothesis h_l. The learning algorithm directly models the marginal distribution rather than the joint distribution on the label, since the discriminative approach generally requires less training data. Suppose $\mathcal{N}_i$ represents a set of immediate neighbors of the vertex v_i. Following the first-order Markov assumption, given h_l, the label probability of vertex v_i only involves its neighbors $\mathcal{N}_i$, which can be formulated by [10]:

$$P(y_i|G,h_l) = P(y_i|\mathcal{N}_i,h_l) = \frac{1}{Z}\prod_{v_j\in\mathcal{N}_i} P(y_j|\mathcal{N}_j,h_l)^{w_{ij}} \quad (6)$$

where Z is a normalizer and h_l can be regarded as a prior embedded in the marginal distribution. In practice, log probability is applied to avoid the underflow and for the rest of the paper, we assume the log probability is used.

According to Eq. 6, the label probability of a vertex is determined by the weighted combination of those of its neighbors. Because of the recursive definition, the probability of each vertex must be inferred simultaneously. In the rest of this subsection, we will discuss two famous algorithms and how they solve the inferencing problem.

Gibbs sampling [16] becomes increasingly popular recently as it is broadly regarded as the most accurate approximate inference algorithm [9]. The basic idea of Gibbs sampling is to iteratively sample the label probability over their neighbors, see Algorithm 2. Specifically, first, we initialize the posterior probability with the prior distribution h_l. For convenience, $y_i^{(j)}$ denotes $P(y_i|G,h_l)^{(j)}$ and let the superscript

[1]Relaxing the assumption is beyond the topic of this paper. Interested audiences are encouraged to refer [10] for a discussion.

Algorithm 2: FFCC using Gibbs sampling

input : a graph G, a local hypothesis h_l
output: a posterior distribution $P(y|G, h_l)$

1 **foreach** $v_i \in V$ **do** $y_i^{(0)} = h_l(v_i)$;
2 **for** $j = 1$ **to** 200 **do** //brun-in
3 Generate a ordering O over V and $Q \leftarrow \varnothing$;
5 **while** *O is not empty* **do**
6 $y_i^{(j)} = \sum_{v_k \in (\mathcal{N}_i \cap Q)} w_{ik} y_k^{(j)} + \sum_{v_k \in (\mathcal{N}_i \cap O)} w_{ik} y_k^{(j-1)}$;
7 $O = O \backslash v_i$; $Q = Q \cup v_i$;
8 **end**
9 normalize l ;
10 **end**
11 initialize a label vector $l^T = (y_1^{(200)}, \ldots y_N^{(200)})^T$;
12 **for** $j = 201$ **to** 2200 **do** //sampling
13 Generate a ordering O over V and let $Q \leftarrow \varnothing$;
14 **while** *O is not empty* **do**
15 $y_i^{(j)} = \sum_{v_k \in (\mathcal{N}_i \cap Q)} w_{ik} y_k^{(j)} + \sum_{v_k \in (\mathcal{N}_i \cap O)} w_{ik} y_k^{(j-1)}$;
16 $l_i = l_i + y_i^{(j)}$;
17 **if** j mod $T = 0$ **then**
18 **foreach** $v_k \in V$ **do** $l_k = \frac{l_k}{T+1}$;
19 **end**
20 $O = O \backslash v_i$; $Q = Q \cup v_i$;
21 **end**
22 normalize l ;
23 **end**
24 **return** l

indicates the iteration number in Gibbs sampling. Step 2 through 9 is a period called "burn-in", in which some iterations are ignored in order to eliminate some inaccurate estimations occurring at the beginning of the sampling. In Step 3, we create a random ordering over all vertices in G and a set Q to store all vertices that currently have been sampled. In Step 6, the label probability y_i is updated using the log form of Eq. 6. Those $y_k^{(j)}$ are applied on the right side of the equation if they have been sampled at iteration j, otherwise $y_k^{(j-1)}$ are applied instead. After the vertex v_i is sampled, sets O, Q are updated accordingly in Step 7. Step 11 through 20 is the period where we actually sample a posterior distribution from the given graph and prior. It consists of the same steps as those in burn-in period excepts that a row vector l is introduced to maintain the sampling statistics and is updated very T iterations (see Step 17). After statistics are collected through sufficient iterations, the algorithm outputs the normalized posterior probability represented by l. In practice, it is difficult to decide on a sufficient number of iterations for both burn-in and sampling period as the convergence tests are neither robust nor well understood [16]. In this paper, we follow the commonly predefined settings in [10, 9] and run 200 and 2000 iterations for burn-in and sampling period, respectively.

Although Gibbs sampling proves to be an effective collective classification approach over many datasets, there is no guarantee that Gibbs sampling will converge within an acceptable number of iterations. In this paper, we instead propose to use Markov random walk which is also a famous model but has not been studied as a collective classification algorithm. The basic idea can be interpreted as the following process: the posterior probability y_i of a vertex v_i is updated by a random walker, who jumps to any of v_i's neighbors with probability d and jumps back to the local hypothesis $h_l(v_i)$ with probability $1-d$. d is a constant number, called the damping factor, measuring the frequency of the jump back. The above process is a Markov chain because of the first-order Markov assumption. To model the above process, we modify Eq. 6 by introducing an additional term quantifying the probability updates of the jump back, which gives us:

$$\log P(y_i|\mathcal{N}_i, h_l) = \frac{1}{Z'}((1-d)h_l(v_i) + d \sum_{v_j \in \mathcal{N}_i} \frac{w_{ij} P(y_j|\mathcal{N}_j, h_l)}{\sum_{v_k \in \mathcal{N}_j} w_{jk}}) \tag{7}$$

where Z' is a normalizer and $h_l(v_i)$ represents the local hypothesis for vertex v_i. Note as d decreasing, Eq. 7 imposes more weights on the prior h_l and when $d = 0$, it degenerates to the local hypothesis, in which only low-level features are considered. In contrast, when $d = 1$ it ignores the prior and the process may be unstable and thus may not converge. The denominator of the second part counts the degree (precisely out-degree) of vertex v_j in the weighted graph G and for the isolated vertices we add a self-loop to avoid the denominator becoming 0. Compared with Eq. 6, the probability passing from vertex v_j to v_i is determined not only by $P(y_j|\mathcal{N}_j, h_l)$ and w_{ij} but also by v_j's out-degree and the more neighbors a node has, the less probability each of its neighbors will receive. In other words, the probability passing from a vertex is locally normalized by its out-degree.

Following the markov process, we define the Markov transition matrix $\mathbf{M}$ as:

$$\mathbf{M}_{ij} = (1-d)h_l(v_i) + \frac{d \times w_{ij}}{\sum_{v_k \in \mathcal{N}_j} w_{jk}}, \tag{8}$$

based on which the collective classification by Markov random walk can be brought forward, see Algorithm 3. Similar to Gibbs sampling, it initializes the posterior probability with the prior h_l. The posterior probability is then updated by Eq. 7 in Step 5 until it eventually converges. Following the graph construction method discussed in Section 3.2, the convergence is guaranteed(see the proof in Appendix). Furthermore based on our empirical observations, the algorithm converges very fast, typically in fewer than 20 iterations.

Algorithm 3: FFCC using Random Walk

input : a graph G, a local hypothesis h_l
output: a posterior distribution $P(y|G, h_l)$

1 **foreach** $v_i \in V$ **do** $y_i^{(0)} = h_l(v_i)$;
2 $j = 0$;
3 **do**
4 $j = j + 1$;
5 $\mathbf{y}^{(j)} = \mathbf{M}\mathbf{y}^{(j-1)}$
6 **while** $||\mathbf{y}^{(j)} - \mathbf{y}^{(j-1)}||_2 < \eta$;
7 normalize $\mathbf{y}$;
8 **return y**

Compared with the Markov Random walk algorithm, the performance of Gibbs sampling may vary as its convergence is not guaranteed. We study the comparison on a tractable example that allows for clearer diagnosis, illustrated in Fig. 3. Suppose we have 4 positive samples: v_1,v_2,v_3 and v_5 and a negative sample v_4. The local hypothesis h_l is depicted

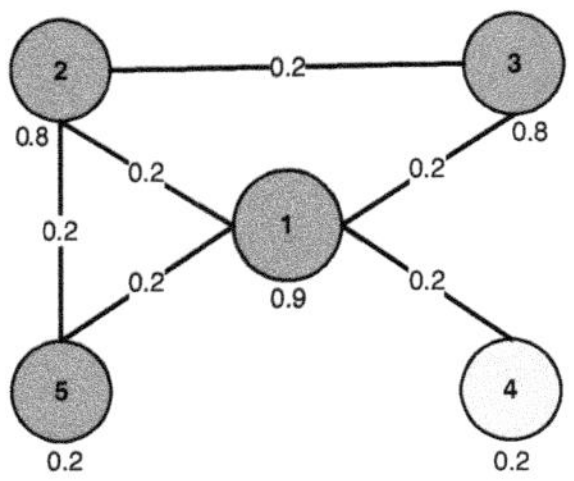

Gibbs Sampling

	r1	r2	r3
1	0.968	0.729	1.000
2	0.748	0.735	0.633
3	0.504	0.419	0.339
4	0.291	0.364	0.493
5	0.393	0.654	0.399

Random Walk

	r1	r2	r3
1	0.957	0.957	0.957
2	0.736	0.736	0.736
3	0.532	0.532	0.532
4	0.232	0.232	0.232
5	0.442	0.442	0.442

Figure 3: Comparison between Gibbs sampling and Random Walk on a tractable example. Shaded vertices are positive samples. The number on edge indicates the weight and the number below each vertex is the probability outputted by local hypothesis. The two tables on the right are the updated probability under different runs

under each vertex. Since high-level features are imperfect, the graph usually includes incorrect edges, e.g. (v_1, v_4). We use Non-interpolated Mean Average Precision (MAP) as the evaluation criteria. The MAP for the local hypothesis is 0.95. We run Gibbs Sampling and Random Walk ($d = 0.85$) three times and list the result in the two tables in Fig. 3. Since the convergence in Random Walk is guaranteed, all three runs converge to the same distribution, where the MAP is improved to 1.0 since the probability of v_5 is increased by receiving the probability passed from v_2 and v_3. On the other hand, Gibbs sampling yields 3 different results. Though the first run (column r1) resembles the Random Walk's estimation, the other two runs are quite different. Moreover, the third run's MAP is 0.888 even worse than the local hypothesis. Therefore it is worth noting that Gibbs Sampling may yield different results even with the same configuration. Random Walk is therefore a recommendable alternative because of its convergence property.

3.4 Complexity Analysis

This subsection discusses the computational complexity analysis for the proposed method, which may shed a light on the method's scalability as datasets grow in size. Recall that the dimension of high-level feature vector is M_h, low-level features M_l, and the number of total samples in the training set equals to N. Regarding the graph construction, since the two methods discussed in Sec. 3.2 are essentially the same method with different loss functions, they share the same upper bound $O(M_h(N + N^2)) = O(M_h N^2)$. The time complexity for Gibbs sampling is $O(M_h(B + S)N^2)$, where B and S are two constants representing the number of iterations for burn-in and sampling period, respectively. Random walk is $O(RM_h N^2)$, where R is the constant number representing the average iterations to converge. Based on the assumption that $B + S = 2200$ and $R \leq 20$, random walk is expected to be much more efficient than Gibbs Sampling. The time complexity of training a local hypothesis depends on the model and usually is done once beforehand, therefore we skip this part in the analysis. Regarding the feature wrapper in Step 3 Algorithm 1, since we adopt a forward wrapper using a hill climbing search, the complexity becomes $O(M_h^2 N)$. Note that here we precompute and maintain the local and relational hypothesis so that they can be directly applied in the wrapper. As a result, the time complexity of the proposed method is $O(M_h N^2 + M_h^2 N)$ for both Gibbs sampling and Markov random Walk.

4. EXPERIMENTS

In this section, we conduct a series of experiments validating the claim that the proposed method not only improves the performance but also the interpretability over the state-of-the-art method. Specifically, we first compare the proposed method with the baseline method in Section 4.2, then we study the impact of parameters on system performance. Finally, the performance of different graph construction and collective classification algorithms are compared in the last subsection.

4.1 Setup

Using the MED11 dataset, we conducted the experiment on the labeled samples development set in TRECVID 2011 contest, which consists of 15 predefined events and 2049 video clips. The details about the dataset are presented in Figure 4. The datset is adopted mainly for two reasons: there are not many public datasets aviablable on event detection and TRECVID MED11 is one of the most representative and challenging public datset. MED11 embraces various types of video clips for each event, e.g. skating, skiing, surfing and even finger skating in the event "attempting a board trick".

Color SIFT (CSIFT) is adopted as the low-level feature. Soft histogram assignment[17] is applied while constructing the code book, with the number of centroids equaling to 4096. Then spatial Bag of Words (BoWs) with a Pyramid Match Kernel[11, 12] is also used to further improve the classification result. The local hypothesis is trained using SVM with Chi-square kernel and multi-class classification is achieved using one-versus-all SVM. The semantic indexing object bank from the TRECVID 2011 contest, which consists of 346 visual concepts, is incorporated as the high-level feature[19]. Each visual concept is encoded as a real value ranging from 0 to 1. The final hypothesis is derived from the average of relational hypothesis and smoothed by the local hypothesis. Regarding the collective classification algorithm, we set the damping factor d (see Algorithm 3) to 0.85 and T (see Algorithm 2) to 10. The default loss function is the exp-loss function and the collective classification algorithm is the Markov random walk.

We compare the proposed method with four baseline methods using 5-fold cross-validation. In the first three baseline methods we train an SVM with Chi-square kernel where the difference in methods lies in how they combine the high-level and low-level features. We call the first method Early Fusion by Feature Concatenation(EF-FC), which simply concatenates the low-level features and high-level features in a new high dimensional feature space with which Chi-square kernel is then calculated; the second method Early Fusion by Kernel Fusion (EF-FC) averages their kernel matrixes and then training a model using the new kernel matrix; the third one is called Late Fusion (LF), which averages the classification results of high-level and low-level features; The last method follows the idea in [14], where we first project the two original feature spaces into two latent spaces with the maximum correlation by Canonical Correlation Analysis (CCA)[18] and then we late fuse the outputs of the SVM classifiers that are trained on the latent spaces. We call it

CCA and according to [6] it achieves the best result given a linear correlation between high-level and low-level features.

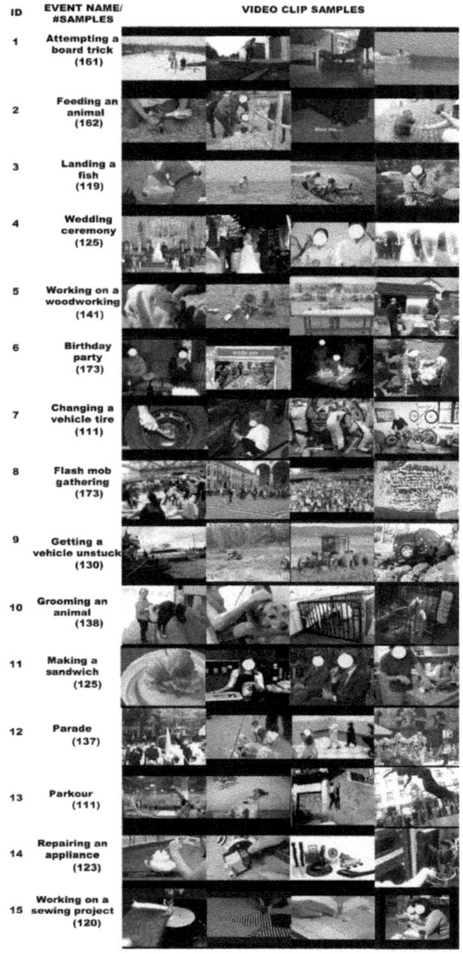

Figure 4: Overview of MED 11 dataset

The standard metric used in TRECVID MED Contest Normalized Detection Cost (NDC) function [19] is adopted as the evaluation metric. NDC is a weighted linear combination of the system event specific missed detection and false alarm probabilities. For each event E we have:

$$NDC(E) = \frac{0.999 \times P_{FA}(E) + 0.08 \times P_{MD}(E)}{0.08} \quad (9)$$

where $P_{MD}(E)$ equals the number of miss detection divides the number of positive clips for event E and $P_{FA}(E)$ equals the number of false alarms over the number of negative clips. Minimum NDC (Min NDC) is introduced to ignore the decision threshold, which measures the best prediction of a method. Min NDC equals to 0 for the perfect model where $P_{FA}(E) = P_{MD}(E) = 0$ and to 1 for the mute model that classifies every sample as the negative sample.

4.2 Comparison with Baseline Methods

To evaluate the performance of the proposed method, we compare it with the baseline method and list the result in Tab. 2. As can be seen, the performance is boosted by fusing the low-level features and high-level features in all methods except for CCA. On average, the proposed method outperforms other fusion methods and achieves the best score in 12 out of 15 events. According to the t-test, it is significantly better than other baseline methods at the 0.005 level(P-value ≤ 0.0006). The average performance of EF-FC, EF-KF and LF are virtually the same whereas CCA has the poorest performance which suggests a non-linear correlation between the feature spaces in this problem. Regarding the runtime, on a single core Intel Core i7 CPU@2.8GHz with 4GB memory, the experiment of Alg. 1 takes around 18 hours for Markov ràndom walk and 66 hours for Gibbs sampling using R (http://www.R-project.org).

As mentioned above, one of the merit that the proposed method enjoys is the interpretability. We analyze the fusion result by inspecting the high-level features used in each event. Generally, for the events the reason FFCC is better due to it selects the distinguishing high-level features reasonably summarizing the current event and separating it from the others. E.g. for the event "feeding an animal" (ID=2), it selects the features such as "cows", "cetacean", "male person", "forest", "birds" and etc.; for the event "wedding ceremony" (ID=4), such as "room", "adult", "child", "legs" and etc. We also found that some features that seems meaningless for some event turns out useful in improving the performance e.g. concept "airplane" in the event "wedding ceremony". It may be due to either these feature's corresponding patterns rarely present in the event or the unknown pattern that the high-level feature's classifier captures is actually useful. On the other hand, for some events the proposed method is worse because it fails to find the robust features relevant to the event. We conclude two reasons account for the failure. First the object bank we used is biased for different types of events. It embraces many features for some events, e.g. "feeding an animal" (ID=2) and "landing a fish" (ID=3) whereas only a few for the others e.g. "working on a woodworking" (ID=5). Second high-level features are not equally accurate. Therefore some inaccurate features result in poor performance even if they are relevant to the event.

ID	LL	HL	EF-FC	EF-KF	LF	CCA	FFCC
1	0.576	0.490	0.492	0.508	0.497	0.633	**0.454**
2	0.872	0.786	0.810	0.828	0.792	0.875	**0.743**
3	0.588	0.526	0.476	0.498	0.502	0.629	**0.408**
4	0.430	0.360	0.353	0.331	0.339	0.422	**0.250**
5	0.722	0.719	0.682	0.658	**0.652**	0.803	0.688
6	0.673	0.553	0.575	0.568	0.539	0.562	**0.481**
7	0.790	0.700	0.635	0.657	0.683	0.749	**0.542**
8	0.455	0.396	0.378	**0.343**	0.391	0.457	0.355
9	0.547	0.389	0.376	0.407	0.415	0.562	**0.347**
10	0.807	0.701	0.680	0.707	0.675	0.562	**0.611**
11	0.682	0.787	0.772	0.746	0.697	0.803	**0.566**
12	0.624	0.488	0.483	0.524	**0.472**	0.655	0.493
13	0.598	0.450	0.438	0.443	0.458	0.542	**0.429**
14	0.544	0.556	0.459	0.443	0.495	0.544	**0.408**
15	0.724	0.653	0.646	0.683	0.690	0.721	**0.543**
AVG	0.642	0.570	0.550	0.556	0.553	0.647	**0.488**

Table 2: Performance comparison with baseline methods in terms of Min NDC. LL for low-level features, HL high-level features, EF-FC early fusion by feature concatenation, EF-KF early fusion by kernel fusion, LF late fusion and FFCC for the proposed method. The best method for each event is in bold.

FFCC also allows for interpreting fusion results for individual video clips. Fig. 5 illustrates an example where we select the two video clips with the greatest change during the collective classification in the event "wedding ceremony".

Since the result interpretation is beyond the topic of this paper, here we adopt a simple way to calculate the contribution for each high-level feature. Given a high-level feature, we use its proportion in the difference between the final hypothesis and local hypothesis to represents its contribution. In the first video clip (HVC390469) the score is 0.359 according to the CSIFT feature whereas because of the presence of visual concept "kitchen" and "anchorperson" which rarely present in the event "weeding ceremony"; the score is decreased by 0.076 and 0.062. In the second video clip (HVC631950), because of the presence of visual concepts "legs", "adult" and "child" that are commonly seen in the event; the score is increased by 0.049, 0.094 and 0.034. It is worth mentioning that as the features are imperfect, some interpretation may disagrees with human's prior knowledge. Nevertheless the experiment demonstrates FFCC's capability in interpreting the final result, which allows for appreciating not only which features update the score, but also how much the change is.

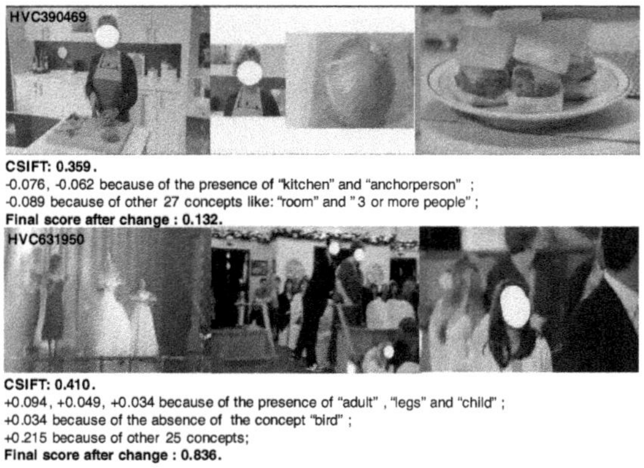

Figure 5: Interpreting the change for individual video clips

4.3 Parameter Changes

The number of high-level features incorporated in the final hypothesis is determined by the feature wrapper in Algorithm 1. However, an interesting question is that how does the number of features affect the final result? We conducted experiments to investigate how the performance changes when the number of high-level feature grows[2]. Fig. 6 illustrates the result on two representative events, in which x-axis represents the number of features incorporated and y-axis presents the corresponding Min NDC. At the origin no high-level feature is used, y value simply denotes the performance of low-level features. As it can be seen, at first the curve starts to fall sharply when the number of features grows and surpasses the baseline curves quickly. However, given a certain number of features have been incorporated, adding more features renders the curve rising. The underlying reason may be that due to the lack of sufficient information, less features often fails to estimate a good model so adding more features improves the performance. Nevertheless after sufficient relevant features are incorporated, adding more features may cause the overfitting thus the performance starts to drop. The subset of high-level features leads to the best Min NDC is called the optimal subset of features. Though the size of the optimal subset for all events is less than 125, the number for different events varies with the mean 68.7 and standard derivation 30.4. E.g. in Fig. 6(a) the size is 120 whereas in Fig. 6(b) the size equals to 32. Because the size of optimal subset is much less than the size of high-level features, which is 346, a considerable amount of resource could be saved when the method is applied to a large dataset.

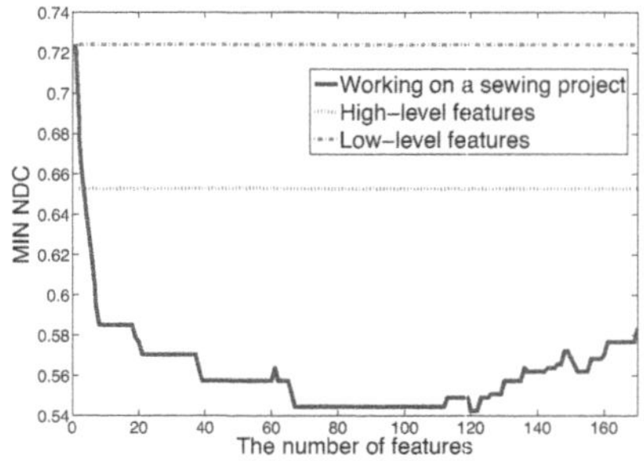

(a) working on a sewing project

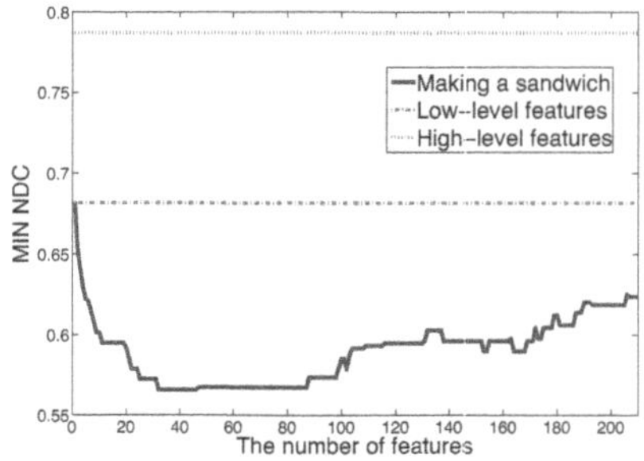

(b) Making a sandwich

Figure 6: Performance change with the number of high-level features increased on two events.

Another observation we found is that unlike the other classification problem on social network, smoothing turns out to be very useful in our problem, see Eq. 2. The reason stems from the fact that number of training samples in our problem is insufficient to obtain an accurate final hypothesis, e.g. the feature dimensionality is 32768 but the number of positive training samples is less than 200. Recall the parameter α is leant in the training set and apply in the test set. We conducted the following experiments to study the impact of changes of α on the final performance. We analyze the event "wedding ceremony" (event ID 4) and "working on a woodworking" (event ID 5) where the proposed method has the greatest and least improvement over the baseline method. Fig. 7 presents the results in 5-fold in both events. The x-axis denotes the value of α and y-axis Min NDC value. The purple circle red triangle represents the Min NDC in training set and test set, respectively; the solid ones denotes the optimal α. Generally, the training and testing set follow the similar distribution and the smoothed hypothesis outperforms both the local and relational hypothesis while α scaling between 0.2 to 0.6.

[2]We did not reduce the feature dimension in the baseline methods as decreasing the number of high-level features in them leads to worse results.

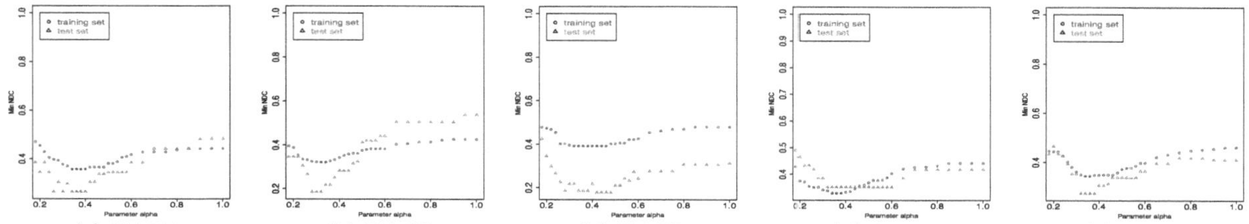

(a) E4-F1 (b) E4-F2 (c) E4-F3 (d) E4-F4 (e) E4-F5

(f) E5-F1 (g) E5-F2 (h) E5-F3 (i) E5-F4 (j) E5-F5

Figure 7: The impact of parameter α in the 5 folds of the event "wedding ceremony"(E4) and "working on a woodworking"(E5)

4.4 Comparison among proposed methods

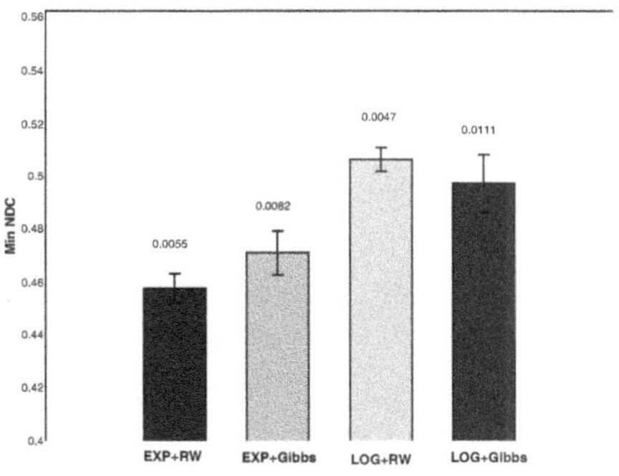

Figure 8: Comparison with different loss functions and collective classification algorithms. RW denotes for Random Walk , Gibbs for Gibbs Sampling, EXP for exponential loss function and LOG for logarithmic function. The number above each bar indicates the standard derivation.

In Section 3, we investigate two approaches to construct graphs by different loss functions and two collective classification algorithms namely Gibbs sampling and Markov random walk to inference posterior distributions. To evaluate the performance of different methods, we run each experiment 5 times with different cross validation partitions and report the mean and variance of the average minimum NDC, illustrated in Fig. 8 in which y-axis denotes for the average minimum NDC over 15 events. First of all, as can be seen, random walk with exponential loss function is the best configuration. In addition it enjoy a relative small variance. Generally, the variance of random walk is smaller than that of Gibbs Sampling because of its convergence property. Besides, the exponential loss function seems to be better than the logarithmic function, which suggests introducing too much error in graphs is harmful for the system.

5. CONCLUSIONS

In this paper, we approached Multimedia Event Detection with a novel method that fuses high-level and low-level features based on collective classification. Our method consists of three steps: training a classifier from low-level features; encoding high-level features into graphs; and diffusing the scores on the established graph to obtain the final prediction. We investigated two graph construction methods using logarithmic and exponential loss functions, respectively and two collective classification algorithms namely Gibbs sampling and Markov random walk. The theoretical analysis showed that the proposed Markov Random Walk converges and is computationally scalable, and thus superior to Gibbs sampling. The empirical analysis on the TRECVID 2011 Multimedia Event Detection dataset validates the method with very good performance compared to state-of-the-art methods, with an added benefit of interpretability. Besides, the comparison among the proposed method suggests that Markov random walk on graphs constructed by exponential loss function is the best configuration in our framework with respect to the minimum NDC.

6. ACKNOWLEDGMENTS

This work has been supported by the Intelligence Advanced Research Projects Activity (IARPA) via Department of Interior National Business Center contract number D11-PC20066. The U.S. Government is authorized to reproduce and distribute reprints for Governmental purposes notwithstanding any copyright annotation thereon. The views and conclusions contained herein are those of the authors and should not be interpreted as necessarily representing the official policies or endorsements, either expressed or implied, of IARPA, DOI/NBC, or the U.S. Government.

7. REFERENCES

[1] I. Laptev, T. Lindeberg. Space-time interest points. In *ICCV*, pages 432–439, Nice, France, 2003.

[2] Li-Jia Li, Hao Su, Eric Xing, Fei-Fei Li. Object bank: a high-level image representation for scene

classification and semantic feature sparsification. In *NIPS*, pages 1378–1386, Vancouver, Canada, 2010.

[3] C. Snoek, M. Worring, A. W. M. Smeulders. Early versus late fusion in semantic video analysis. In *ACM Multimedia*, pages 399–402, Singapore, 2005.

[4] T. Pham, N. Maillot, J. Lim, J. Chevallet. Latent semantic fusion model for image retrieval and annotation. In *CIKM*, pages 439–444, Lisbon, Portugal, 2007.

[5] H. Escalante, C. Hernández, L. Sucar, M. Montes. Late fusion of heterogeneous methods for multimedia image retrieval. In *ACM MIR*, pages 172–179, Vancouver, Canada, 2008.

[6] J. Kludas, E. Bruno, S. Marchand-Maillet. Information fusion in multimedia information retrieval. In *Adaptive Multimedia Retrieval*, pages 147–159, Paris, France, 2007.

[7] L. Bao et al. Informedia@TRECVID 2011. In *Trecvid Video Retrieval Evaluation Workshop, NIST*, Gaitherburg, USA, 2011.

[8] H. Eldardiry, J. Neville. Across-Model collective ensemble classification. In *AAAI*, to appear, San Francisco, USA, 2011.

[9] P. Sen, G. Namata, M. Bilgic, L. Getoor, B. Gallagher, and T. Eliassi-Rad. Collective classification in network data. *AI Magazine*, 29(3):93–106, 2008.

[10] S. Macskassy, and F. Provost. Classification in networked data: A toolkit and a univariate case study. *JMLR*, 8:935–983, 2007.

[11] S. Lazebnik, C. Schmid, and J. Ponce. Beyond bags of features: Spatial pyramid matching for recognizing natural scene categories. In *CVPR*, pages 2169–2178, New York, USA, 2006.

[12] A. Bosch, A. Zisserman, and X. Munoz. Representing shape with a spatial pyramid kernel. In *CIVR*, pages 401–408, Amsterdam, Netherlands, 2007.

[13] Y. Wu, E. Y. Chang, K. C. Chang, J. R. Smith. Optimal multimodal fusion for multimedia data analysis. In *ACM Multimedia*, pages 572–579, New York, USA, 2004.

[14] N. Rasiwasia, JC. Pereira, E. Coviello, G. Doyle, G. Lanckriet, R. Levy, N. Vasconcelos. A new approach to cross-modal multimedia retrieval. In *ACM Multimedia*, pages 251–260, Firenze, Italy, 2010.

[15] L. K. McDowell, K.M. Gupta, D.W. Aha. Cautious inference in collective classification. In *AAAI*, pages 596–601, Vancouver, Canada, 2007.

[16] W. R. Gilks,S. Richardson and D. J. Spiegelhalter. Markov chain Monte Carlo in Practice. *Chapman Hall/CRC Interdisciplinary Statistics*, 1996.

[17] J. Gemert, J. Geusebroek, C. Veenman, A. Smeulders. Kernel codebooks for scene categorization. In *ECCV*, pages 696–709, Marseille, France, 2008.

[18] H. Hotelling. Relations between two sets of variates. *Biometrika*, 28:321–377, 1936.

[19] P. Over, G. Awad, J. Fiscus, B. Antonishek, and M. Michel. Trecvid 2010 - an overview of the goals, tasks, data, evaluation mechanisms and metrics. In *Trecvid Video Retrieval Evaluation Workshop, NIST*, Gaitherburg, USA, 2010.

[20] Doeblin, W. Exposé sur la théorie des chaînes simples constantes de Markoff à un nombre fini d'états. *Rev. Math. Union Interbalkanique*, 2:77–105, 1938.

APPENDIX

THEOREM 1. *Let h_l be the local hypothesis, $h_{r_i} = P(y|G_i, h_l)$ be the ith relational hypothesis and $h_f = P(y|G_1, ...G_n, h_l)$ be the final hypothesis. Assume $G_1, ...G_n$ are independent of each other then*

$$\log h_f = \sum_{i=1}^{n} \log h_{r_i} - (n-1) \log h_l$$

PROOF. For graphs $\{G_1, ...G_n\}$, according to Bayes rule we have:

$$P(y|G_1, ...G_n, h_l) = \frac{P(G_1, ...G_n|y, h_l)P(y|h_l)}{P(G_1, ...G_n|h_l)}.$$

Since $G_1, ...G_n$ are independent we have:

$$\begin{aligned} P(y|G_1, ...G_n, h_l) &= \frac{P(y|h_l)\prod_{i=1}^{n} P(G_i|y, h_l)}{\prod_{i=1}^{n} P(G_i)} \\ &= \frac{P(y|h_l)\prod_{i=1}^{n} P(G_i|y, h_l)}{\prod_{i=1}^{n} P(G_i)} \frac{P(y|h_l)^{n-1}}{P(y|h_l)^{n-1}} \\ &= \frac{1}{P(y|h_l)^{n-1}} \prod_{i=1}^{n} P(y|G_i, h_l) \end{aligned}$$

Taking the log on both side of the above equation:

$$\log P(y|G_1, ...G_n, h_l) = \sum_{i=1}^{n} \log P(y|G_i, h_l) - (n-1) \log P(y|h_l).$$

Since $P(y|h_l) = h_l$, substituting h_f and h_{r_i} for $P(y|G_1, ...G_n, h_l)$ and $P(y|G_i, h_l)$ gives the logarithmic form of the final hypothesis. □

THEOREM 2. *Algorithm 3 converges to a stationary distribution in finite time on the graph generated by Eq. 3.*

PROOF. Let $\pi_t(i) = P(y_i|G, h_l)$ denotes the label distribution over all $v_i \in V$ at time t and $\pi_0 = h_l$. The goal is to prove $\pi_t = \mathbf{M}\pi_{t-1} = \pi_{t-1}$ for some finite time t.

For each connect component C_j in the Graph G:

- if C_j contains a single vertex $v_i \in C_j$: for $t \geq 2$, we have $\pi_t(i) = \pi_{t-1}(i)$.
- if C_j contains more than one vertices: according to Eq. 3, $\forall v_i, v_j \in C_j$, there is an edge between from v_i to v_j. In other words, the subgraph C_j is strongly connected and any two vertices are mutually reachable. Therefore $\mathbf{M}$ is irreducible.

  Besides, for any pair of vertices in C_j as they are mutually reachable they must have the same period. Consequently all in C_j states have the same period. Furthermore, according to Eq. 7, each vertex has a self-loop edge therefore each vertex has the period 1 and thus $\mathbf{M}$ is aperiodic.

  As $\mathbf{M}$ is irreducible and aperiodic, then $\forall v_i \in C_j, \exists t$, s.t. $\pi_t(i) = \pi_{t-1}(i)$, i.e. the algorithm converges to a unique stationary distribution for all vertices in C_j[20].

Consequently, suppose the convergence time for connect component C_j is t_j. Let $t = \max_{C_j \subseteq G}(t_j)$, then $\forall v_i \in G$, $\pi_t(i) = \pi_{t-1}(i)$. In other words the label distribution converges to a stationary distribution $\pi_t(i)$ after t iterations. □

Interactive Data-Driven Discovery of Temporal Behavior Models From Events In Media Streams

Chreston Miller
Center for HCI, Virginia Tech
2202 Kraft Drive, Blacksburg,Va. 24060, USA
chmille3@vt.edu

Francis Quek
Center for HCI, Virginia Tech
2202 Kraft Drive, Blacksburg,Va. 24060, USA
quek@vt.edu

ABSTRACT

This paper investigates a technique for the discovery of temporal behavior models within multimedia event data. Advancements in both technology and the marketplace present us the opportunity for research in analysis of situated human behavior using video and other sensor data (media streams). By situated analysis, we mean the study of behavior *in time* as opposed to looking at behavior in the form of aggregated data divorced from how they occur in context. Human and social scientists seek to model behavior captured in media, and these data may be represented in a multi-dimensional event data space derived from media streams. The knowledge of these scientists (experts) is a valuable resource which can be leveraged to search this space. We propose a solution that incorporates the expert in an iteratively, interactive data-driven discovery process to evolve a desired behavior model. We test our solution's accuracy on a multimodal meeting corpus with a progressive three tiered approach.

Categories and Subject Descriptors

I.2.4 [**Artificial Intelligence**]: Knowledge Representation Formalisms and Methods—*relation systems, temporal logic*

General Terms

Design, Algorithms

Keywords

Structure Model Learning, Human-Machine Cooperation, Temporal Behavior Models, Model Evolution, Event Data

1. INTRODUCTION

In this paper, we address how human and social scientists may derive models of human behavior that are captured in media streams as these behaviors are situated in time. Such situated analysis considers the study of behavior *in time* as opposed to looking at behavior in the form of aggregated data divorced from how they occur in context. This requires the traversal of two 'semantic gaps' from media stream to meaning-units of behavior [14, 19, 44]. First, relate the entities detected (e.g., image histograms, audio frequency processing, color blobs, face recognition, and person tracking) to events relevant to a particular analysis (e.g., person A has started looking in the direction of person B). Second, relate the detected events to the high level behaviors of interest to human and social scientists studying such behaviors. Our focus in this paper is the second of these.

Human and social scientists approach data from a theoretical viewpoint, forming hypotheses of what behaviors they see or expect to see in the data. Analyzing a large amount of event data derived from media streams, however, is a tedious endeavor, and it is desirable to apply machine learning approaches to assist in this process. Machine learning, on the other hand often takes a *tabula rasa* approach that is not able to take advantage of the knowledge of human experts. Many machine learning approaches produce their own models requiring only that experts provide labeled data. Furthermore, many behavioral models are structural in nature requiring construction of relationships between events and component behaviors. Automated learning, on the other hand, is often framed as the learning of weights and parameters, as opposed to the structure of the model itself.

Our approach is to reason with temporal events (e.g., [A approaches B, start]) out of which a temporal model graph is constructed. A model of a greeting between two individuals may begin with a simple structural relationship (e.g., [A approaches B, start] <followed by within 1 sec> [B extends hand, start]) where one could potentially 'evolve' the model by successively adding/removing relationships with other events in the graph, and/or pruning graph connections until a desired formulation is reached. However, evolving this graph without guidance is a very large search space even for a small graph.

Our solution is to use real occurrences in data to help constrain the generation of alternatives and produce a convergence to a desired model. We engage the expert in an interactive data-driven discovery process to evolve a behavior model to a desired formulation. The expert brings to the table ideas and hypotheses with which she creates an initial exploration model (seed) to start narrowing the possibilities. The challenge is to find likely, relevant extensions to the model that somehow recur in the data-set, and to allow the expert to steer the evolution process iteratively. Given a seeded model, the system identifies situated instances that occur in the data. Potentially relevant extensions to the

MM'12, October 29–November 2, 2012, Nara, Japan.
Copyright 2012 ACM 978-1-4503-1089-5/12/10 ...$15.00.

model, based on the situated instances, are presented to the expert. Upon choosing an extension, the model is updated. The system then identifies situated instances of the newly updated model. This process continues iteratively with the end result being a model representing a behavior as it exists in the data, and yet reflecting the expert's knowledge.

Our target domain is understanding the behavior interactions amongst humans. However, our approach is applicable to any temporal modeling involving graphs of discrete events, such as seismic event data, Internet network traffic, and production process modeling.

In §2 we describe the data domain that motivates our research, the kinds of events we process, and connections to other multimedia data. We then describe related work in §3. §4 provides a detailed description of our model evolution process. Afterwards, in §5 we describe our experiments, results, and provide discussion. We then close with conclusions and future work in §6.

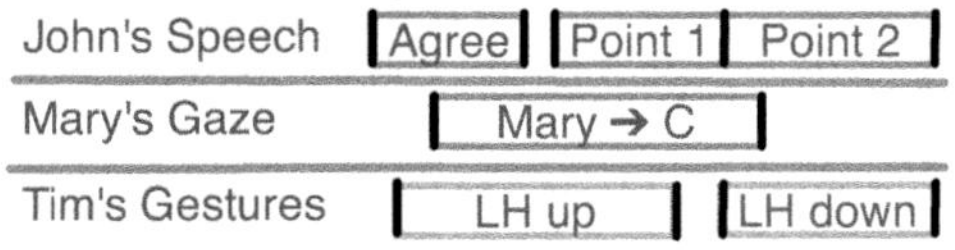

Figure 1: Example of multi-channel event data (*S-I's* highlighted as vertical bold lines)

2. DATA DOMAIN

The motivating domain of our research is a subset of multimedia analysis known as behavior analysis. We first explain our notion of an event. An event, or interval, is an occurrence in time that has a beginning, an end, a description, and an associated actor/source of the event (subset of event aspects in [48]). The atomic units (beginning and end) of an event are semi-intervals (*S-I's*) as described in [12]. A series of events in succession are an event sequence (Figure 1). These sequences may include overlaps between events, but all the events in a sequence have ordered relations (e.g. '<' or '=') with respect to each other.

Behavior analysis includes the analysis and understanding of interactions among humans. More specifically, our focus is on a meeting room setting in which a small group of individuals is gathered to discuss topics of interest or solve a proposed problem. The meeting is normally recorded using multi-channel video and audio and sometimes with other sensor data such as motion capture [6, 8, 39, 46]). The analysis of the signals recorded is known as multimodal analysis which integrates multiple data channels (e.g., gaze, gesture, and speech) where incorporation of such information provides more accurate analysis results [39]. The events within these data channels (i.e., events that describe the gaze, gesture, and speech of the participants) are produced through segmenting and annotating the media signals. This process is performed through manual and automated means as discussed in [8, 28]. It is these annotations (segmented events) that our approach is applied to. At a more abstract level, these events represent segmented temporal events from multimedia signals and in turn application of our approach to analyze a wider range of multimedia data is feasible

Since human behavior is variant, the idea that represents an interaction, e.g., a greeting, may be formulated many different ways in the data making modeling difficult. How does one identify situated instances of behavior when the way they exist in the data may be unknown? Also, every observed behavior has the potential to be relevant to an expert depending on her analysis goals. Hence, there is no concept of "noise" but rather one of relevance. For example, consider the situation where three students are working together on a math problem when a door slams nearby and draws their attention. One expert may analyze the co-construction of space based on the students' aligned gaze while another may analyze interrupting events. The door slam is "noise" to the first expert but not the second. These aspects of behavior analysis pose challenges to modeling.

3. RELATED WORK

Our proposed approach is to evolve a model from a seed model graph. This is related to the general domain of Evolutionary Computing (EC) where our model evolution strategy is most closely tied to Genetic Programming (GP)[23]. GP is applied to change and update the structure of models iteratively to arrive at a solution. Bastian in [2] employed GP for creating fuzzy logic models which generates models that represent relationships between nominal data and uses pre-defined relational models. Gray et al. [13] comment on how expert knowledge is useful in molding solutions during a trial and error approach and how such input is necessary in initializing the models and appropriate functions for GP. The idea of operating on a model's structure has also been explored in other domains. The predominant application has been to numerical contexts where numerical model modification has been used, as in [10, 21, 26].

Our data is inherently multimodal. A prominent area of research for multimodal interaction data processing is human behavior analysis. Two different classes of approaches, unimodal (e.g., speech-only [5, 16]) and multimodal (e.g., speech, gesture, and gaze [8, 28, 30, 39]), have been employed to categorize and analyze interactions among humans. These approaches capture different signal sources and present the data to experts to analyze through automatic and manual means. This analysis domain exemplifies the synergy of human and machine.

The coupling of human and machine is realized in varying degrees. On one side is full automation for learning models where the most common approach is explicating a training data-set and constructing a representative model based on the data. The results are then presented to the user. Learning, in this class of approaches, is often construed as learning the weights or parameters of the model, rather than changing the model's underlying structure. Some approaches approximate structural modification by over-specifying the model, and allowing some weights to go to zero (or infinity) through the learning process, but such approaches cannot make additions to the original model. Classic examples are Hidden Markov Models and Neural Nets [41].

The other side is incorporation of human input such as Relevance Feedback [40] where a model is refined by adjusting weights according to user choices. These weights are hidden to the user making it difficult to understand the model structure. Other research, such as [11, 42, 47], have incorporated expert knowledge as a guiding force in discovery. Notably [47] investigates different visualization techniques for supporting exploratory search of temporal event sequences.

Ordered relations inherent in temporal event data are an active area of research. Allen in [1] formulated thirteen relationship principles that express all the possible orderings between two event intervals. These orderings describe how events relate. Research, such as [15, 20, 33, 43], has focused on processing numerical or descriptive univariate, multivariate, or symbolic temporal data with the goal of discovering events and temporal relationships from temporal data. Others have explored the discovery of temporal knowledge and associated patterns, such as [17, 24, 34].

The stream data of multimedia data-sets is a mixture of ordinal and nominal data. As per the temporal data models reported in [34], gesture traces are a collection of univariate numerical time series (ordinal) while speech and gaze target fixations are multivariate symbolic interval series in which their meaning is categorically descriptive (nominal). Explorations into the relational structures of nominal (event) data can be seen in [9, 25, 49]. More specifically, [32] explored how to structure event data based on semi-interval processing using n-gram techniques from speech processing. Other research [12, 35] has explored the concept of breaking temporal events into core units of beginnings and endings through *S-I* temporal ordered processing. Previously mentioned research ([1, 20, 33, 43]) has investigated patterns and relations among interval data irrespective of the data being ordinal or nominal.

4. MODEL EVOLUTION

The idea of model evolution is motivated by GP, an EC approach that operates on a model's structure to reach a maximum fit for a problem [23]. In GP, there is a population of individuals consisting of potential solutions to a problem. Each individual's fitness is based on how well they solve the problem. This "wellness" is usually determined by some numerical error function. Individuals are chosen based on their fitness to undergo different genetic operations and produce the next generation. The less fit "die" off leading to successive generations converging to an optimal solution. Genetic operations usually consist of reproduction, crossover, recombination, and mutation. However, due to the nature of our problem, we approach a genetic operation as an incremental change to the model structure.

4.1 Evolving a Model

We view the creation of a model as "evolving" its structure towards a goal. We start with an initial model and modify it incrementally to arrive at a desired structure. We perform evolution at the *S-I* level, which we call a *1-step* change. This represents the smallest modification possible given our event representation. Each *S-I* can be viewed as an element in a sequence. A pathway, or link, between *S-I's* represents the occurrence of order such as a branch in a temporal graph. Figure 2A represents an example sequence of four *S-I's* where the arrows show possible pathways. The pathway chosen depends on the order of the *S-I's* observed in the data. A *1-step* change could be: $(C1)$ add a *S-I*, $(C2)$ replace a *S-I*, $(C3)$ remove a *S-I*, $(C4)$ add a link, or $(C5)$ remove a link. However, we only want the changes that will better advance the model. A brute force calculation of all possible variations could be performed with the "best" chosen, but, the possible variations of *1-step* changes are exponential with respect to the size of the model as is explained in the following discussion.

Let G be a graph model of *S-I's*. For each *S-I* $X \in G$, a new *S-I* Y can be placed in three general positions with respect to X: *before*, *after*, or *concurrent-with* (Figure 2B). These are a subset of Allen's principles [1]. These general positions stem from the left-to-right ordered properties of G

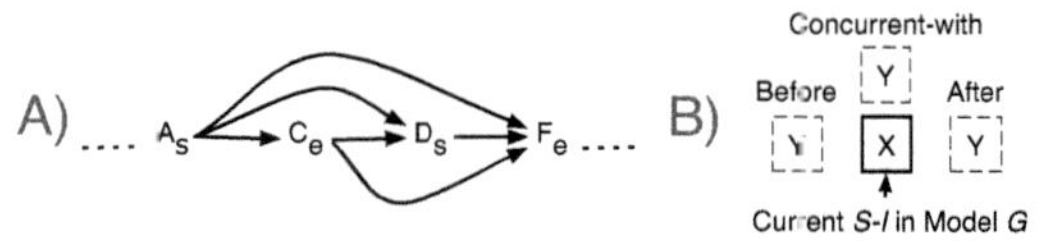

Figure 2: A) Example sequence of *S-I's*. Arrows are connecting links. B) General positions for a new *S-I* Y with respect to a current *S-I* X in model G.

where relative position infers specific order. Since G has this ordered property, all *S-I's* in G can be spatially organized. Each *S-I* can be placed at its respective unique ordered position *S-I*$_t$, $t \geq 0$, with *S-I's* sharing a t placed concurrently. Given the above, the following theorem can be stated.

THEOREM 1. *Let G be a graph model of ordered* S-I's *and $|G|$ be the number of* S-I's *in G. Each* S-I *in G has a* S-I$_t$, *$0 \leq t < T$ where T is the last left-to-right ordered unique position for any* S-I. *Then $0 < T \leq |G|$ since some* S-I's *in G will occur concurrently. Then for a new* S-I Y, *the number of possible positions x in G for Y is $2T + 1$.*

The proof for this theorem is in Appendix A.

A new *S-I* can be potentially linked to all other *S-I's* in G assuming no restrictions from matching *S-I's*. For every new *S-I* Y, there are $\binom{n}{k}$ possible links, where $n = |G|$ and $1 \leq k \leq n$. Then, for every Y, the number of possible link combinations is $\sum_{k=1}^{n} \binom{n}{k}$. Since there are a maximum of $2T + 1$ possible placement positions for Y, there are

$$(2T + 1) \sum_{k=1}^{n} \binom{n}{k} \tag{1}$$

possible unique *1-step* addition changes for G. Since some additions for Y may not be feasible due to relative order restrictions, equation 1 is an upper bound.

Using equation 1 and $T = |G|$, a model with $T = 10$ has 21,843 possible unique *1-step* changes and 2.5480×10^{32} for $T = 100$. These calculations only include the *1-step* changes that add a *S-I* and potential links (C1 and C2) and do not include the other possible modifications (C3-C5).

It is difficult to fully automate informed selection for *1-step* changes absent of human knowledge. The relational order of the data automatically prunes possible link connections. Adding expert guidance provides further pruning. However, even with expert guidance, there are still many potential modifications to choose from.

Comparison Metrics: The appropriate *1-step* change at any point depends idiosyncratically on the behavior being modeled. The comparison metrics we used extend from [32] where n-gram processing is adapted from speech processing. N-grams are a probabilistic method based on conditional probability where history and context are used to provide an informed probability of what might occur next in a given sequence [4]. Figure 3A shows how n-grams are used in speech processing where bigrams and trigrams ($N = 2$ and $N = 3$, respectively) are used to provide conditional probability of what word will come next given what has been previously seen. Figure 3B shows a simple example of how n-gram processing can be applied to a sequence of *S-I's*.

N-grams provide a probability metric to compare temporally near *S-I's* to a model instance's *S-I's*. These temporally near *S-I's* are *related* to the instance. These *related S-I's* can be labeled under three relational categories: *previous* [32], *current* [31] and *next* [32]. Each *S-I* of the model has *related S-I's* potentially falling into these three categories. These relational categories stem from the general positions

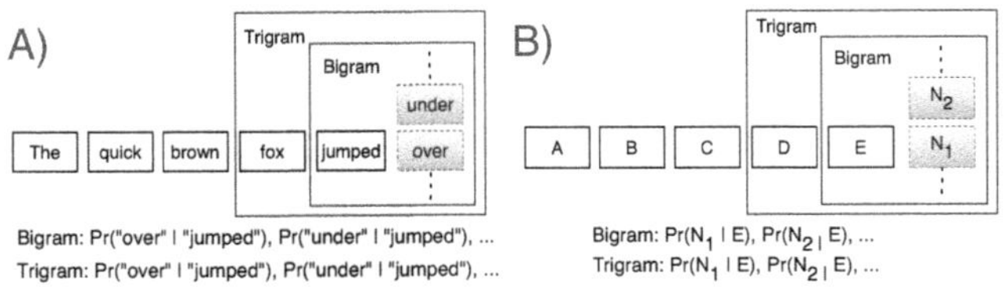

Figure 3: A) Example of n-gram use in speech processing. B) Simple example of applying n-gram processing to a sequence of *S-I's*.

described in Figure 2B. The *related S-I's* to a particular instance are *suggestions* to consider for extension. Selecting a *suggestion* for an extension represents a *1-step* change. We extend the relational categories by defining an ε time window for determining and constraining each category similar to the **window-size** of [20]. For *current* this is $[-\varepsilon,+\varepsilon]$, and for *previous/next* this is $[-\hat{\varepsilon},-\varepsilon)$ and $(+\varepsilon, +\hat{\varepsilon}]$, respectively.

Result Rankings: The convention in most speech processing research is to use n-grams of order $N = 2$ and $N = 3$ [4, 18, 27]. Sun and Applebaum [45] used $2 \le N \le 6$. We combine the results of several n-gram processing passes of varying N values: 2, 3, and the whole model. Our rationale is that N values of 2 and 3 provide local and internal results with respect to the *S-I's* within the model. Meanwhile the whole model provides results pertinent to the current chosen sequence of *S-I's* overall. Due to multi-pass processing, *suggestions* will occur in duplicate. However, the results from one processing pass will differ in meaning with respect to another. Each pass uses a different N, leading to varying degrees of *confidence* in the pass results. The greater the N, the more *confidence* there is in the results, because the greater the N, the more history and context is used in the calculation. For example, in Figure 3B, the bigram results will have a confidence ranking of 1, the trigram 2, and the whole model 5. Hence, the *suggestion* results are reported with an associated n-gram probability and a *confidence* level.

4.2 GP Variation

We developed a variation to the standard GP formulation because a direct mapping to GP was impractical for our problem domain as our data is not entirely numerical and interactions with the expert requires a more easily understandable model structure. In our solution, an individual in the population is viewed as a model instance in the data-set (the population). The fitness for an individual is the subjective *1-step* change chosen by the expert. An operation is a *1-step* change based on the context of instance(s). A *1-step* change focuses the evolution to individuals that better match the interest of the expert. A generation is produced after each *1-step* change, signifying one evolution iteration.

An added facet of our approach is the analysis focus can be performed from two different views. The first focuses on one instance (an individual in the population) of a model and views the instance situated in context. This is a situated view. The second views all potential evolvable directions in an aggregated view. All results from each instance are shown to the user. The utility of both have been studied in [31].

The pseudocode of our approach can be seen in Algorithm 1. Given the user specified initial model M and N events in a data-set, all x possible instances of M and all b bigrams and t trigrams are identified in the data-set. N-gram processing is then applied resulting in *previous/current/next suggestions* for each $S\text{-}I \in M$, bigrams and trigrams with associated probabilities. From these *suggestions*, the user can make

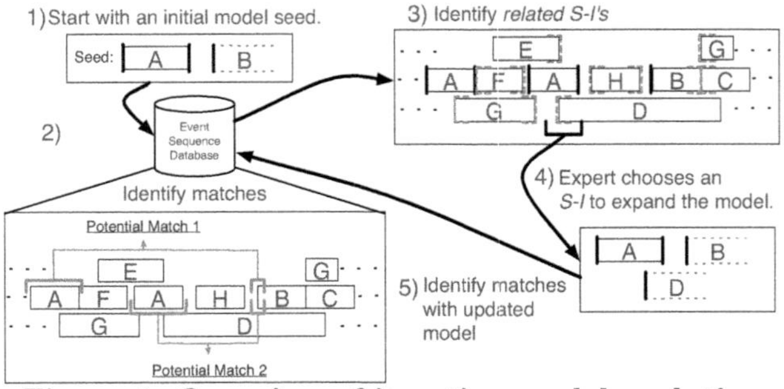

Figure 4: Overview of iterative model evolution.

a choice of which *1-step* change to accept. When one is accepted, new *suggestions* based on the updated model are presented signifying the end of one evolution iteration. As new *suggestions* are accepted, choices for new modifications dynamically change based on the evolving model.

Algorithm 1 Pseudocode for Model Evolution Algorithm

Start with initial model $M_i, i = 0$, data-set of N events
repeat
  Identify instances of M_i, bigrams, and trigrams
  for all Instances **do**
    Extract the *prev/current/next suggestions*
  end for
  Gather *suggestions* and calculate probabilities
  Display for user, user chooses a *suggestion*
  M_i is updated to $M_{i+1}, i = i + 1$
until the user is satisfied with the model

The time complexity of our algorithm is linear with respect to the input (e.g., number of events in the data-set). The identification of all instances of M and each bigram and trigram, x, b, and t, respectively, each require a pass through all the events. For *suggestions*, each instance has a list of p *previous*, c *current*, and n *next suggestions* for the first and last semi-interval (6 in total). The algorithm requires a visit to each item in the lists. The size of each list depends on the time window and the data-set density. For determining time complexity, we assume they are the same size for all instances. Hence, the size of each list is $\alpha_x = 2(p_x + n_x + c_x)$, $\alpha_b = 2(p_b + n_b + c_b)$, and $\alpha_t = 2(p_t + n_t + c_t)$, for M, bigrams and trigrams, respectively. Therefore, for each M, bigram and trigram, there is one iteration through the data-set (N) plus an α for each instance, leading to:

$$(N + x\alpha_x) + (N + b\alpha_b) + (N + t\alpha_t)$$

For probability calculations, the complexity follows from [4] where the members of each *suggestion* list of each instance are visited to count a total and sum the unique events in the lists. Then one calculation is performed for each unique event found with the worst case being all events are unique (same number of calculations as prior step). Hence, for each α and its respective number of instances, e.g., x, the calculation is $2x\alpha_x$. Adding to the prior equation:

$$(N + x\alpha_x) + (N + b\alpha_b) + (N + t\alpha_t) + 2(x\alpha_x + b\alpha_b + t\alpha_t)$$

Which simplifies to:

$$3N + 3x\alpha_x + 3b\alpha_b + 3t\alpha_t$$

The time complexity will not be linear if any of the α's and/or x, b, or t's are N, which either means the entire data-set is included in one of the *suggestion* lists or the data-set consists of the same model repeated. Either is an unlikely scenario for the applicable domain.

An example of the operation of this algorithm is in Figure 4. The expert starts with an initial model seed (1) which is

Table 1: Data-sets' Contents.

Data-set	S-I's	Unique S-I's	Speech Length			Gaze Length			Gesture Length			# Gaze	# Speech	# Gesture
			Ave	Min	Max	Ave	Min	Max	Ave	Min	Max			
Generated	22812	240	1.26	0.1	5	1.28	0.1	5	1.28	0.1	5	7560	7678	7574
									Nodding, Phrase					Nodding, Phrase
AFIT 1	7802	342	1.59	0.1	64.46	2.16	0.1	158.86	0.99, 0.84	0.23, 0.3	10.71, 11.68	4704	1414	1018, 666
AFIT 2	13362	226	2.28	0.03	124.6	1.09	0.1	58.22	0.89, 1.0	0.27, 0.27	13.78, 9.21	11456	1126	610, 170

used to identify matches within the event sequence database (2). From the matches, *related S-I's* are identified given the defined timing windows (3). The expert then chooses a *related S-I* to expand the model (4) signifying one evolution iteration. Then matches of the updated model are identified in the database marking the next iteration (5).

5. EXPERIMENTS

Here we present the results of experiments focused on three aspects: 1) The accuracy of identifying relevant patterns conducted using several data-sets in a controlled environment, 2) How our approach compares to a traditional pattern mining algorithm, and 3) The ability to identify relevant patterns amongst extracted events from a media source.

5.1 Methodology

The nature of our problem domain makes experimentation a challenge. Quantitative metrics are difficult to devise for evaluation of model discovery dependent on an expert's interest. In order to verify the accuracy of our approach to identify models, data-sets with known ground truth (i.e., known relevant patterns) are required. Such patterns must also have significant interest to an expert. Hence, to provide a controlled environment where our results can be measured, we insert models into data-sets at known locations and apply our approach to see if they can be identified. We choose 5 categories of behavior models in a meeting room setting deemed important by experts [8, 28]. Our test of accuracy is three tiered; each builds upon the prior.

Tier 1: The first tier consists of generating a data-set based on the parameters of a real data-set similar to bootstrap aggregating (bagging) [3]. We then insert models based on the 5 behavior categories. Each model is based on relational structures observed by experts. For each model, we insert 10 instances into its own copy of the generated data-set, i.e., there is no interference between the models. Then, for each model, we seed our approach with a relevant starting point of the model, identify its locations, then evolve the model to the desired structure and see how many inserted instances are identified. Since the data-set is generated, there is some concern that the model instances inserted already exist due to random generation. However, the probability that the generated data-set has many model instances present is very low (See Appendix B). This tier allows us to see how our approach operates in a dense data-space as the generated data-set is denser than the real ones it is modeled after.

Tier 2: The second tier comprises two real data-sets and follows the same procedure of the first tier where the only difference is these data-sets are real. This tier allows us to see how our approach operates within a real data-space. The first and second tier will demonstrate the accuracy of our approach to identify relevant patterns.

Tier 3: The third tier uses the same two real-world data-sets and does not insert any model instances. Instead, we search for known, relevant patterns that are reported by experts who have analyzed the data-sets. In some cases, we do know the exact location of a model instance, however, in most cases we only know the general structure of a behavior as described by the experts in their reported analysis. Since most results cannot be verified as in the prior two tiers, this tier allows us to demonstrate the flexibility of our approach to identify model structures without exact knowledge of how the models are realized in the data.

Baseline: As a baseline, we apply a Frequent Episode Mining (FEM) algorithm [36] to discover the models in all tiers. FEM is a well tested and widely used approach to finding an event sequence (pattern) within temporal event data. Our interest is in comparing against a mining approach based on frequency. Hence, we choose to compare against an FEM algorithm that specifically performs frequency of patterns. We tuned the FEM algorithm to use a 3 second window and identify patterns with a frequency of at least 7 or 8 (depending on the data-set). We tested with a *S-I* and interval version of each data-set.

5.2 Implementation

Our approach is implemented in C++ using QT 4.7 [37] for the user interface and a SQLite database to store the data-sets. The current interface of our system is not shown as it is not the focus of this paper. We set the timing window parameters to: $\varepsilon = 0.033$, $\hat{\varepsilon} = 1.0$ and $\dot{\varepsilon} = 1.0$. The value of ε represents the time of 1 frame in video (33 ms at 30 fps). This is the smallest granularity of the camera allowing a 1 frame buffer on either side. The timeframe of behavior models is normally temporally tight (on the order of milliseconds or seconds), hence, setting $\hat{\varepsilon}$ and $\dot{\varepsilon}$ to 1 second. When matching *S-I's* of a model to instances in the data-set, we use a 3 second window between each model *S-I*. This allows identification of instances that are just outside our 1 second window or identify instances that are temporally longer.

5.3 Data-sets

Here we describe the data-sets used for our experiments. Our experiments were conducted using the VACE/AFIT multimodal meeting room corpus [8, 28].

VACE/AFIT: This data-set consists of several meeting sessions of Airforce Officers from the Airforce Insitute of Technology (AFIT) partaking in war-gaming scenarios. We focus on two sessions (*AFIT 1* and *AFIT 2*). Each session is a scenario in which five officers (C, D, E, F, and G) are given a problem to discuss and resolve. The room where the sessions took place was instrumented for multi-channel audio and video, and motion capture of the officers (see [8] for instrumentation details). The officers in *AFIT 1* are discussing potential candidates for a scholarship. The scenario is that C, D, F, and G are department heads meeting with the institute commandant E to select three scholarship award recipients. The officers in *AFIT 2* are discussing options for exploiting an enemy missile that has been discovered. Each session is approximately 45 minutes with manual and automated annotations for speech, gaze fixations, F-formations, and several gestural forms (including gesture phrases) for each officer. F-Formations, or focus formations, were first identified by Adam Kendon to be units of topical cohesion marked by gaze cohesion of participants to common objects or spaces [22]. Gesture phrases are atomic gestural motions marking a single motion trajectory that typically coincide with atomic speech phrases [29]. These annotations are events based on low-level feature extraction and manual inspection of the synched audio,

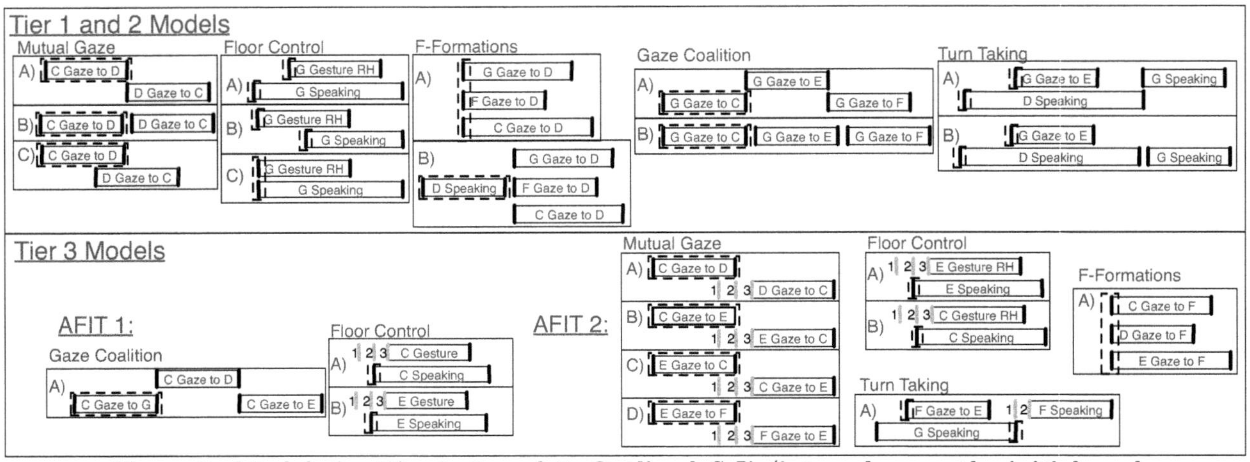

Figure 5: Models for Tier 1, 2, and 3. Outlined *S-I's*/intervals were the initial seed.

video, and motion capture data and describe the officers' interactions. (further details in [8]). All annotations were either created or validated by human annotators (behavioral psychologists) with cross validation. The speech was automatically segmented and time-aligned with manual inspection to correct errors. No uncertainties associated with the annotations were recorded. McNeill in [28] did report gaze coding issues with officers wearing glasses, however, there was only a problem with 8% of gaze judgements for such officers and less than 3% for the best officer. The sum of the annotations is a data-set consisting of multiple channels (21 for *AFIT 1*, 19 for *AFIT 2*) of overlapping event data. The sequences of behavior described by the annotations are rich and descriptive. Each data-set is summarized in Table 1.

Generated: We generated a data-set based on the parameters of the VACE data. For five fictitious people, we randomly generate 45 minutes of annotations for parallel channels of speech, gaze fixations, and gesture phrases. For each person and each channel, we generate a timeline of events with varying lengths and gaps between them totaling 15 parallel channels. This is fewer channels but much denser as can be seen in Table 1 with significantly more *S-I*s.

5.4 Models

Here we describe the behavior categories used to create the models inserted. One observation to take note of when looking at the structures of the different behavior categories is that it is not just the structure that provides meaning to the models but the meaning of the events in the specific temporal order. The specific models used for all tiers can be seen in Figure 5. The outlined *S-I's* and intervals were the initial model seeds. Also, the actors chosen for the models inserted into *AFIT 1* and *2* were intentionally chosen to not coincide with those involved in the models reported by the experts in [7, 28]. This was done to prevent interference from the actual models observed by the experts.

Mutual Gaze (MG): In the AFIT sessions, different participants controlled the floor at different times (i.e., leading the discussion for the moment). When the control passed from one participant to the next, there was a mutual gaze exchange between the current holder of the floor to the next.

Gaze Coalition (GC): It was discovered in *AFIT 1* that the social interaction amongst the participants had as much to do with the outcome of the meeting as the specific merits of the scholarship candidates being discussed. The participants dynamically formed coalitions to support each-other's candidates through a process of mutual gaze fixations and back-channel expressions of support during discussions [30].

A coalition to support a proposed idea is initialized when the proposer seeks to make eye-contact with other participants while he is presenting the idea. Participants who supported the idea would return the eye-contact, while those who disagreed would avert gaze. When a return gaze was attained, the presenter's gaze moved to another member.

Floor Control (FC): During a session, a participant would gain floor control through a hand movement (gesture) and start speaking. This was deemed 'floor capturing' in [7].

Turn Taking (TT): As detailed above, each session had a meeting manager who normally was the dominant participant and facilitated the meeting. When a participant sought to take a turn speaking, the participant might look at the meeting manager while the current floor controller spoke. Once the current floor controller finished speaking, the participant seeking a turn would then begin speaking.

F-formation (Ff): F-formations were observed throughout the sessions. The defining behavior for the F-formations observed were concurrent focus on the same person (or object) or an action causing such synchronized focus.

Tier 3 Models: In *AFIT 1* a GC model was known to exist from unpublished analysis, and FC models were reported in [7]. In *AFIT 2*, MG, FC, TT, and a Ff model were reported in [7, 28]. For the FC and MG models, the exact actors are unknown. Therefore, given the participation statistics of each actor in [7, 28] we choose the actors with the most and least frequent activity (e.g., most gaze events or least frequent gaze target). Note that some models for Tier 3 in Figure 5 have numbered, grey *S-I's*. These represent the pieces of the model our evolution strategy aimed to identify. Since we did not know how the structure existed in the data, we tried these relational possibilities. They also represent the key part of the model to discover from the initial seed, hence, the complete structure was not sought after their discovery. The results discussed later use these numbers to identify which structure(s) were found. Also, the seed for TT differs in this tier because of how the model exists in the data (this was discovered during our discovery/evolution process). At first, our timing window did not allow discovery of the model with the original seed. We then modified the seed to the relevant part of TT: transition from one participant to another (correlation between F's gaze start, G's ending speech, and F starting to speak).

5.5 Results

The performance of our approach was tested in several ways. First, we observe a convergence behavior of our al-

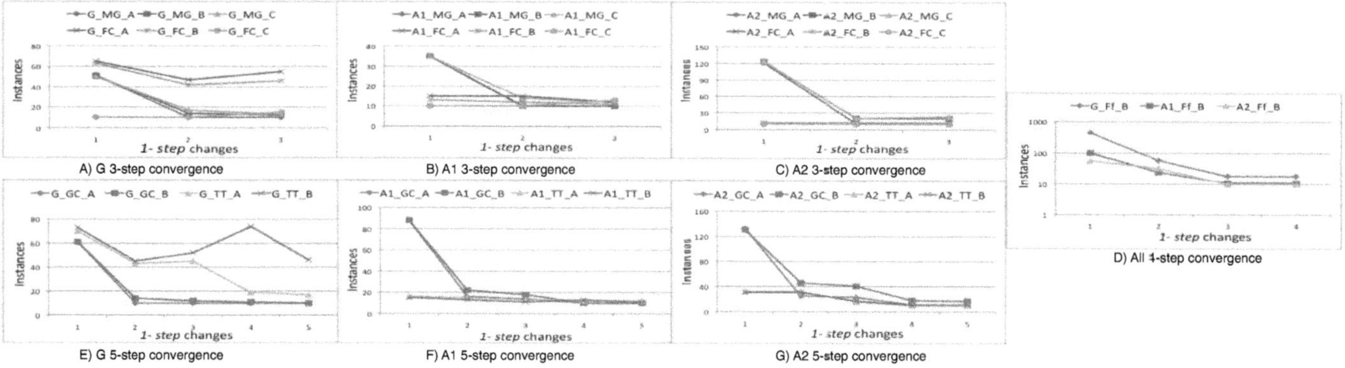

A) G 3-step convergence B) A1 3-step convergence C) A2 3-step convergence D) All 4-step convergence E) G 5-step convergence F) A1 5-step convergence G) A2 5-step convergence

Figure 6: Tier 1 and 2 convergence for model evolution (note scale differences).

gorithm during the evolution process. Then we perform a power/penalty analysis. For Tiers 1 and 2, each algorithm was run on 36 models (72 total) and for Tier 3, our algorithm ran on 52 models and FEM for 10; in total 134 models were explored. For simplicity, we use the naming schema X_Y_Z to reference each model where X is the data-set, Y is the model abbreviation, and Z is the model variation. For example, *A1_MG_A* is mutual gaze model A from *AFIT 1*.

Convergence: During our experiments, we observed a convergence behavior of our algorithm. Overall, each *1-step* change decreased the number of identified situated instances (Figure 6). The convergence of each model is grouped by the number of *1-step* changes needed and the data-set. Convergence in most cases was obtained, even if the resulting instances identified were more than the 10 inserted. Outliers were seen in Figure 6A (*G_FC_ A* and *G_FC_B*) and 6E (*G_TT_B*). This is due to the large number of speech events in the generated data-set and a logic error later found in our algorithm which is currently being addressed. The ordered relations with the speech *S-I's* in these models are flexible (*previous* and *next*) leading to many matches. The more constraining ordered relation *current* aided with convergence. This is why *G_TT_A* and *G_FC_C* had better convergence. Even though some models did not converge to the desired 10, a nicely pruned sub-set resulted. Also, there was no need for a convergence graph for *Ff_A* as the initial seed was the desired structure, converging instantly, exemplifying how an informed starting point can significantly aid in relevant instance identification.

Power/Penalty Analysis: For describing the results, we use power/penalty analysis of [38] which reports a power and penalty percentage. If there are x known instances of a phenomenon in a data-set, y instances identified by a method or algorithm, and z number of instances common amongst the known and identified, $z \leq x$, then the power percentage is $z/x * 100$. For example, if $x = 10$, $y = 18$ and $z = 7$, then the power is $7/10 * 100 = 70\%$, i.e., the method's power is 70% in identifying the relevant instances. The other 11 identified instances are part of the penalty. These are the extra instances the expert must go through and, in turn, are an extra cost. The penalty $= (y-z)/y * 100$, in our example, penalty $= (18-7)/18 * 100 = 61.11\%$.

The overall results can be seen in Table 2. Our approach was able to identify all inserted models (Tier 1-3), giving it 100% power. For FEM, in Tier 1 and 2, all but 6 models (Figure 8) had a 100% power rating. The most feasible explanation for the two with the lowest power (*A2_Ff_A* and *G_FC_C*) is these models included *S-I's* that were "equal" and the models that were identified by FEM were matches that coincidently included pieces of the inserted models (i.e., the start *S-I* of a few of the inserted models). Another observation for *A2_Ff_A* is FEM found 18 instances but none of them were the models inserted. What was found were other occurrences of the three events in the model within 3 seconds of each other. Since the FEM algorithm only considers start *S-I's* of an interval, this explains the trouble with model *A2_TT_B*. In some cases, the start *S-I's* of the model were temporally too far away. For the other three, the reason is likely the high number of gaze and speech events in the generated data-set and the high number of gaze events in *AFIT 2*. The high concentration of such events were observed to cause some challenges for both algorithms.

Table 2: Overall results.

	Tier 1	Tier 2	Tier 3
Misses			
Ours	0	0	0
FEM	30	65	63
Mean Power			
Ours	100	100	100
FEM	75	72.92	71.48
Mean Penalty			
Ours	33.09	11.41	N/A
FEM	62.26	37.72	41.74

The penalty percentage results can be seen in Figure 7. Model names (x-axis) with an '*' in 7 are models identified using *S-I's* in the FEM algorithm. The rest were identified with an interval representation (reason discussed in §5.6). Penalty of 100% meant none of the inserted model occurrences were identified or the algorithm failed (result of its limitations). Each graph compares the penalties of each data-set. For the generated data-set, our approach's penalty was lower than FEM's for 9 of the 12 models. For *AFIT 1*, our approach had comparable penalty to FEM, however, FEM had 100% penalty for 3 models and our max penalty was 23.08% (mean: 8.36%). For *AFIT 2*, our approach had a lower penalty for 8 of the 12 models. Overall, our approach had zero penalty for 15 models while FEM had zero for 5.

For Tier 3, there were only three known locations of ground truth models which our approach found. For the other models, the instance count ranged from 1 to 33. We could only compute the power/penalty of FEM as compared to our approach's results, hence, Table 2, Tier 3 is FEM's results as compared to ours. However, given our approach's results for Tier 1 and 2, we are confident in its Tier 3 results. Since FEM's purpose is mining frequency, we did not attempt to identify instance occurrences less than 8. Doing so caused an explosion of results. In Figure 7D, we see the power/penalty analysis of FEM compared to our Tier 3 results. As can be seen, FEM had a fairly high penalty with an adequate power.

5.6 Discussion

Overall, we observed our approach performed very well compared to the FEM algorithm. We were able to provide a solution with high power and substantially less penalty

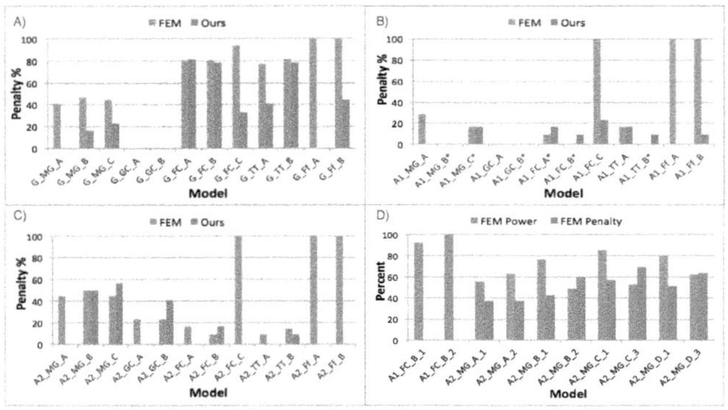

Figure 7: A) Tier 1 Penalty. B) Tier 2 A1 Penalty. C)Tier 2 A2 Penalty. D) FEM Tier 3 Power and Penalty as compared to our Tier 3 results.

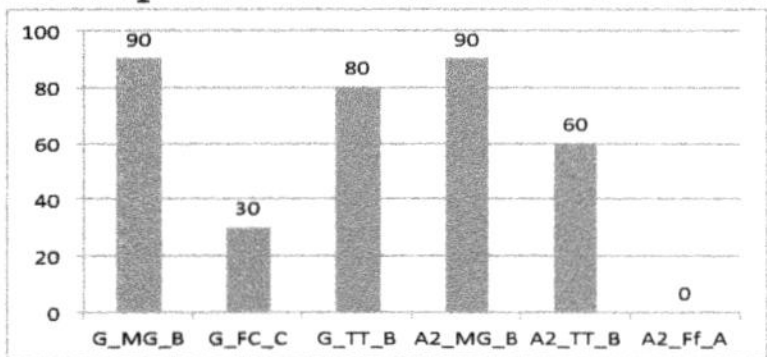

Figure 8: FEM models with Power % less than 100.

than the frequency approach of FEM. There were some cases where FEM performed better, however, the successful use of *S-I* granularity allowed our approach to identify all models. The models FEM did not identify can be explained by limitations discovered during experimentation. It was unable to identify any *S-I's* occurring at the same time or intervals sharing a start time. The FEM algorithm did not appear to be built for this situation. When creating the models to insert into the data-sets, if two *S-I's* were "equal", we set their times to be the same. However, in real model instances, this may not occur due to granularity limitations of the recording equipment. But, it may at the discretion of whomever is creating the data-set. Also, most of the FEM results were from the interval version of the data-sets since when using *S-I's*, too many results were returned (on the order of 40-100K) which overloaded the output functionality of the FEM program or the program ran out of memory on machines with 8 and 10GB of RAM. Overall, significant effort was required to tune the FEM algorithm for our purpose.

In order to identify the relevant models within the FEM results, an expert would have to search through them. Arguably, an expert could seek out relevant models within the FEM results, however, doing so is non-trivial as she would need to define a starting point of interest and sift through the results (which is the motivation of this paper). Hence, an expert would need an approach similar to ours anyway.

As for identifying more instances than inserted (penalty %), the cause was a combination of several aspects of the data and tuning of the algorithms. Several of the data-sets had a large percentage of specific event types (e.g., gaze or speech). Matches for the algorithms also were on a 3 second window between each *S-I* or start time of an interval. Hence, the mixture of a high number of certain event types and the time window allowed for many matches. The number of events cannot be controlled (unless some filtering is introduced), however, the time window can be tuned for the specific data-set and characteristics of the models sought. Our approach aided in limiting *suggestions* at each evolution iteration by reporting them within a 1 second window beyond the equality window. However, during instance identification between *1-step* changes, a 3 second window is used allowing flexibility of matching but possibly causing many results. We also observed (notably for Tier 3 *A2_Ff_A*) the necessity to have dynamically controlled timing windows as the model sought was slightly out of range.

We observed for our approach that several aspects of the model structure aided in identification of the relevant models. The *current* relation caused better convergence during the evolution process. This makes sense as it is the relation that is the tightest, hence, including this relation in the initial seed (if feasible) facilitates model identification. Also, the initial seed may actually lead the expert to the model instances desired as observed in *Ff_A*'s case.

During the evolution process, the probabilities for the *S-I's* sought were generally high, however, they were not so in some cases. What an event represented (conceptually) aided in choosing. This was true even when the probability was high exemplifying that the importance lies in the expert's interest and that we provide an informed view of the data. In some cases, completing an interval (both start and end *S-I's*) increased or decreased the number of instances found. Hence, the usage of partial knowledge through *S-I's* can be advantageous depending on the behavior model sought. Sometimes, an expert is only interested in when a behavior (event) starts or ends in relation to another behavior. This was observed for Tier 3 *A2_TT_A*.

We chose not to perform a run-time comparison since each approach comprises two different timings. For our approach, the first is the processing time for instance identification and *suggestion* processing. The second is how long the user spends choosing a *1-step* change, sparking the next processing step. This time is relative. For FEM, the first is a processing time for identifying frequent patterns (automatic). The second is the user looking through the list of patterns manually, hoping to find what is wanted (assuming this is known). Although, the initial processing time would seem to be relevant for comparison, our method processes a sub-set of the data-set with each evolution step instead of FEM's one-time processing of the whole data-set making meaningful comparison difficult. In light of these differences, such timing information may not be beneficial or informative.

The data we operate on have varying aspects, such as uncertainty or granularity of the annotations. Such aspects are at the discretion of the creator of the data. For uncertainty, or "fuzziness", this may be a uncertainty score (e.g., $0 \leq e \leq 1$) associated with each annotation. For granularity, this is the level of detail captured by the annotations. This does not affect the processing but the level of meaning possible from the annotations. For example, the resolution of an image determines the detail level extractable from the image. A 640x480 image and a 2560x1440 image each provides a certain level of detail in which the latter can potentially provide more information. The resolution of the annotations dictates the resolution of the resulting model(s). Overall, what is provided dictates what can be done and represented.

6. CONCLUSION AND FUTURE WORK

In this paper we presented a model evolution technique for identifying relevant temporal behavior models within temporal event data. We demonstrated the accurate identification of relevant patterns while comparing against a well established temporal mining algorithm (FEM). We found our approach was well suited for the data domain and, through power/penalty analysis, we saw our approach performed overall better than FEM. We demonstrated that our approach is well suited for relevant model instance identification necessary in situated behavior analysis and in doing so, displayed its ability to identify relevant patterns amongst extracted events from a media source. However, our approach can be applied to a wider scope of temporal event data extracted from media in which challenging questions about the media contents may be answered. One such domain we will be applying our approach to is a news broadcast corpus consisting of several news networks over multiple years. We will be able to analyze topic and transition structure amongst the networks, how different news shows transition between topics, and the structure of anchor/reporter interactions for different topics. The creation of this corpus is in progress.

For future development, we identified implementation improvements which should decrease erroneous model instance matches allowing more robust convergence. Supporting other aspects of the data, such as uncertainty, is being investigated. We are currently developing a set of temporal relationship principles for defining interactions amongst *S-I's* for behavior models. This paper used a subset with extensions under development.

7. ACKNOWLEDGMENTS

We would like to thank Debprakash Patnaik for his help in using FEM and Christa Miller for invaluable input as an outside observer and editor. This research was partially funded by FODAVA grant CCF-0937133 and NSF IIS-1053039.

8. REFERENCES

[1] J. F. Allen. Maintaining knowledge about temporal intervals. *Commun. ACM*, 26(11):832–843, 1983.

[2] A. Bastian. Identifying fuzzy models utilizing genetic programming. *Fuzzy Sets and Systems*, 113(3):333 – 350, 2000.

[3] L. Breiman. Bagging predictors. *Machine Learning*, 24:123–140, 1996. 10.1007/BF00058655.

[4] P. Brown et al. Class-based n-gram models of natural language. *Comp. Linguist.*, 18(4):467–479, 1992.

[5] R. Calix and G. Knapp. Affect corpus 2.0: an extension of a corpus for actor level emotion magnitude detection. In *MMsys '11*, pages 129–132.

[6] J. Carletta et al. The ami meeting corpus: A pre-announcement. In *MLMI*, volume 3869 of *LNCS*, pages 28–39. Springer Berlin / Heidelberg, 2006.

[7] L. Chen et al. A multimodal analysis of floor control in meetings. In *MLMI'06*, pages 36–49.

[8] L. Chen et al. Vace multimodal meeting corpus. *MLMI '06*, pages 40–51.

[9] V. Cheng et al. Dissimilarity learning for nominal data. *Pattern Recognition*, 37(7):1471 – 1477, 2004.

[10] C.-P. Chou and P. M. Bentler. Model modification in structural equation modeling by imposing constraints. *Comput. Stat. Data Anal.*, 41(2):271–287, 2002.

[11] R. Cowie et al. 'feeltrace': An instrument for recording perceived emotion in real time. In *SpeechEmotion-2000*, pages 19–24, 2000.

[12] C. Freksa. Temporal reasoning based on semi-intervals. *Artificial Intelligence*, 54(1-2):199 – 227, 1992.

[13] G. J. Gray et al. Nonlinear model structure identification using genetic programming. *Control Engineering Practice*, 6(11):1341 – 1352, 1998.

[14] V. Gudivada and V. Raghavan. Content based image retrieval systems. *Computer*, 28(9):18 –22, sep 1995.

[15] G. Guimarães and A. Ultsch. A method for temporal knowledge conversion. *AIDA*, pages 369–380, 1999.

[16] M. Hearst. Texttiling: A quantitative approach to discourse segmentation. Technical report, University of California, Berkeley, 1993.

[17] F. Höppner. *Knowledge Discovery from Sequential Data.* PhD thesis, Technischen Universität Braunschweig Genehmigte, 2003.

[18] Z. Huang, V. Eidelman, and M. Harper. Improving a simple bigram hmm part-of-speech tagger by latent annotation and self-training. In *NAACL '09*, pages 213–216, Morristown, NJ, USA, 2009. ACL.

[19] Y.-G. Jiang, C.-W. Ngo, and S.-F. Chang. Semantic context transfer across heterogeneous sources for domain adaptive video search. In *MM '09*, pages 155–164.

[20] P. Kam and A. Fu. Discovering temporal patterns for interval-based events. *Data Warehousing and Knowledge Discovery*, pages 317–326, 2000.

[21] D. Kaplan. Evaluating and modifying covariance structure models: A review and recommendation. In *Multivariate Behavioral Research*, volume 25, pages 137–155. Psychology Press, 1990.

[22] A. Kendon. *Conducting Interaction: Patterns of Behavior in Focused Encounters.* Cambridge: Cambridge University Press, 1990.

[23] J. R. Koza. *Genetic programming: on the programming of computers by means of natural selection.* MIT Press, Cambridge, MA, USA, 1992.

[24] S. Laxman and P. Sastry. A survey of temporal data mining *Sadhana*, 31(2):173–198, 04 2006.

[25] C. Li and G. Biswas. Unsupervised learning with mixed numeric and nominal data. *IEEE Trans. on Knowl. and Data Eng.*, 14(4):673–690, 2002.

[26] V. Y. Lunin and A. G. Urzhumtsev. Improvement of protein phases by coarse model modification. *Acta Crystallographica Section A*, 40(3):269–277, May 1984.

[27] S. Martin, J. Liermann, and H. Ney. Algorithms for bigram and trigram word clustering. *Sp. Comm.*, 1998.

[28] D. McNeill. Gesture, gaze, and ground. In *MLMI'06*, volume 3869 of *LNCS*, pages 1–14.

[29] D. McNeill. *Hand and Mind: What gestures reveal about thought.* Chicago: U. of Chicago Press, 1992.

[30] D. McNeill et al. Mind-merging. In *Expressing oneself / expressing one's self: Communication, language, cognition, and identity*, 2007.

[31] C. Miller and F. Quek. Toward multimodal situated analysis. In *ICMI '11.*

[32] C. Miller, F. Quek, and N. Ramakrishnan. Structuring ordered nominal data for event sequence discovery. In *ACM MM '10.*

[33] F. Mörchen. Algorithms for time series knowledge mining. In *KDD '06*, pages 668–673.

[34] F. Mörchen. Unsupervised pattern mining from symbolic temporal data. *SIGKDD Explor. Newsl.*, 9(1):41–55, 2007.

[35] F. Mörchen and D. Fradkin. Robust mining of time intervals with semi-interval partial order patterns. In *SIAM Conference on Data Mining (SDM)*, 2010.
[36] D. Patnaik, P. S. Sastry, and K. P. Unnikrishnan. Inferring neuronal network connectivity from spike data: A temporal data mining approach. *Scientific Programming*, 16(1):49–77, January 2007.
[37] Qt. *http://qt.nokia.com/*, Last Checked: Mar., 2012.
[38] F. Quek. The catchment feature model: a device for multimodal fusion and a bridge between signal and sense. *EURASIP J. Appl. Signal Process.*, 2004:1619–1636, Jan. 2004.
[39] F. Quek, T. Rose, and D. McNeill. Multimodal meeting analysis. In *IA*, 2005.
[40] Y. Rui et al. Relevance feedback: a power tool for interactive content-based image retrieval. *TCSVT*, 8(5):644–655, Sep 1998.
[41] S. Russell and P. Norvig. *Artificial Intelligence A Modern Approach.* Prentice Hall, 2003.
[42] K. Schoeffmann, M. Taschwer, and L. Boeszoermenyi. The video explorer: a tool for navigation and searching within a single video based on fast content analysis. In *MMsys '10*, pages 247–258.
[43] E. Schwalb and L. Vila. Temporal constraints: A survey. *Constraints*, 3(2/3):129–149, 1998.
[44] A. Smeulders et al. Content-based image retrieval at the end of the early years. *IEEE Trans. Pattern Anal. and Mach. Intel.*, 22(12):1349 –1380, 2000.
[45] X. Sun and T. H. Applebaum. Intonational phrase break prediction using decision tree and n-gram model. In *Proc. of Eurospeech2001*, pages 3–7, 2001.
[46] M. Voit and R. Stiefelhagen. 3d user-perspective, voxel-based estimation of visual focus of attention in dynamic meeting scenarios. In *ICMI-MLMI '10*, pages 51:1–51:8.
[47] T. D. Wang et al. Exploratory search over temporal event sequences: Novel requirements, operations, and a process model. *3rd Workshop on Human-Computer Information Retrieval*, 2009.
[48] U. Westermann and R. Jain. Toward a common event model for multimedia applications. *IEEE MultiMedia*, 14:19–29, January 2007.
[49] L. Zadeh. Fuzzy logic = computing with words. *IEEE TFS*, 4(2):103–111, May 1996.

APPENDIX

A. THEOREM 1 PROOF

Theorem 1 can be proven through induction:

PROOF. Let our base cases be $\hat{T} = |\hat{G}| = 1$ where $2\hat{T}+1 = 3$, and $\bar{T} = |\bar{G}| = 2$ where $2\bar{T}+1 = 5$. Then $2\bar{T}+1 = (2\hat{T}+1)+2$.

For the induction step, assume true for $T = |G| = n$ and $T-1 = |G-1| = n-1$. Show true for $T+1$. We know

$$2T+1 = (2(T-1)+1)+2$$

Then,

$$\begin{aligned} 2T+1 &= (2(T-1)+1)+2 \\ 2T+1 &= 2T-2+1+2 \\ 2T+1+2 &= 2T+1+2 \\ 2(T+1)+1 &= (2T+1)+2 \\ 2(T+1)+1 &= (2((T+1)-1)+1)+2 \end{aligned}$$

which is the same as $2T+1 = (2(T-1)+1)+2$ but for $T+1$ and $T \Rightarrow$ true for $T+1$

Hence, $\forall\ T \leq |G|$, $2T+1 = (2(T-1)+1)+2$, then the number of possible positions x for Y is $2T+1$. Assuming all the *S-I's* in G do not match Y as a beginning or end and since there are only three relative places to place Y for each $S\text{-}I_t$, $0 \leq t < T$, $2T+1$ is an upper bound. If Y's matching *S-I* is already in the model, then $x < 2T+1$ since an ending *S-I* cannot go before its matching beginning *S-I*. □

B. MODEL OCCURRENCE LIKELIHOOD

There is a low probability that a model will be randomly generated within the data-set. Most behavior models in behavior analysis are temporally tight. Hence, we simplify proving this claim through focusing on small temporal windows within the data-set (i.e., small window along the timeline of the events in the data-set).

Given $\hat{T}$ number of unique time slots for a *S-I* to be placed in a timeline, let w be a fixed sized temporal window being $|w|$ time slots wide and x be the set of unique *S-I's* that may occur at each time slot (at least one per time slot), cardinality of $|x|$. Then, for a model m of size $|m|$, an estimated probability for m to be present is:

$$\frac{(\hat{T}-|w|+1)(\frac{1}{|x|^{|m|}})\binom{|w|}{|m|}}{|w|-|m|+1}$$

PROOF. For each window, the number of ways to choose $|m|$ amongst w's time slots is $\binom{|w|}{|m|}$. We are looking for a specific sequence chosen from x. Note that an *S-I* in x can only be chosen once per time slot due to the nature of the data despite multiple overlapping channels (e.g., cannot have two occurrences of person A's gaze to person B at the same time). Hence, each *S-I* in x has a $\frac{1}{|x|}$ probability of occurring at each time slot.

Since there are $|m|$ *S-I's* in the model, then there is a $\frac{1}{|x|^{|m|}}$ probability of choosing the model *S-I's* and $\binom{|w|}{|m|}$ ways the model can appear in the window. Therefore, Pr(model in w) $= \frac{1}{x^{|m|}}\binom{|w|}{|m|}$. However, this is for one window and we need to account for all windows, including overlap between them. Taking a sliding window approach, start with w_0 (first window in the timeline), then slide w_0 to the right one time slot producing w_1. Continuing this process produces $\hat{T}-|w|+1$ windows. Hence,

$$Pr(m \text{ in timeline}) = (\hat{T}-|w|+1)(\frac{1}{|x|^{|m|}})\binom{|w|}{|m|}$$

Since we are using a sliding window, there is a chance for double counting an instance of m. Hence, after w_0, we are only interested in models that end in the last time slot of w_i, $0 < i < \hat{T}-|w|+1$. The probability of a model's ending *S-I* occurring in the last time slot is $\frac{1}{|w|-|m|+1}$. Therefore, the probability of a model m being generated is approximately:

$$Pr(m \text{ in timeline}) \approx \frac{(\hat{T}-|w|+1)(\frac{1}{|x|^{|m|}})\binom{|w|}{|m|}}{|w|-|m|+1}$$

This is an approximate probability as the complexity of the generated data-set leads to many variables to consider. An exhaustive proof is unnecessary as it can be seen from the approximation that the likelihood of a specific model being generated is very low. For example, our generated data-set has $\hat{T} = 21,855$ and $|x| = 240$. Give the smallest model inserted where $|m| = 4$, and $|w| = 10$, the $Pr(m$ in timeline$) \approx$ 0.000197618, hence for all 10 is 0.00197618. □

Knowledge Adaptation for Ad Hoc Multimedia Event Detection with Few Exemplars *

Zhigang Ma
DISI, University of Trento, Italy
ma@disi.unitn.it

Yi Yang
SCS, Carnegie Mellon University, USA
yiyang@cs.cmu.edu

Yang Cai
SCS, Carnegie Mellon University, USA
caiyang@cs.cmu.edu

Nicu Sebe
DISI, University of Trento, Italy
sebe@disi.unitn.it

Alexander G. Hauptmann
SCS, Carnegie Mellon University, USA
alex@cs.cmu.edu

ABSTRACT

Multimedia event detection (MED) has a significant impact on many applications. Though video concept annotation has received much research effort, video event detection remains largely unaddressed. Current research mainly focuses on sports and news event detection or abnormality detection in surveillance videos. Our research on this topic is capable of detecting more complicated and generic events. Moreover, the curse of reality, *i.e.*, precisely labeled multimedia content is scarce, necessitates the study on how to attain respectable detection performance using only limited positive examples. Research addressing these two aforementioned issues is still in its infancy. In light of this, we explore Ad Hoc MED, which aims to detect complicated and generic events by using few positive examples. To the best of our knowledge, our work makes the first attempt on this topic. As the information from these few positive examples is limited, we propose to infer knowledge from other multimedia resources to facilitate event detection. Experiments are performed on real-world multimedia archives consisting of several challenging events. The results show that our approach outperforms several other detection algorithms. Most notably, our algorithm outperforms SVM by 43% and 14% comparatively in Average Precision when using Gaussian and χ^2 kernel respectively.

Categories and Subject Descriptors

H.3.1 [**Information Search and Retrieval**]: Content Analysis and Indexing; I.2.10 [**Vision and Scene Understanding**]: Video analysis

General Terms

Algorithms, Experimentation, Performance

Keywords

Multimedia Event Detection (MED), Ad Hoc MED, Knowledge Adaptation, Structural Adaptive Regression (SAR)

*Area chair: Gang Hua

MM'12, October 29–November 2, 2012, Nara, Japan.

1. INTRODUCTION

With ever expanding multimedia collections, multimedia content analysis is becoming a fundamental research issue for many applications such as indexing and retrieval, *etc.* Multimedia content analysis aims to learn the semantics of multimedia data. To do so, it has to bridge the semantic gap between the low-level features and the high-level semantic content description [11, 33]. Different approaches have been proposed to bridge the semantic gap in the literature, either at concept level or event level.

We first highlight the difference between a concept and an event. A "concept" means an abstract or general idea inferred from specific instances, *e.g. fish, sky*. In multimedia research, a major thrust for multimedia content analysis is to learn the semantic concepts of the multimedia data and to use these concepts for multimedia indexing and retrieval. Multimedia concept analysis has been widely studied for images and videos [17, 25, 24, 15]. However, as shared personal video collections, news videos and documentary videos have explosively proliferated these years, video event analysis gradually is attracting more research interest. An "event" refers to an observable occurrence that interests users, *e.g. making a cake, landing a fish*. Compared with concept analysis, where concepts are usually describable by a single shot, event understanding is a more challenging task due to its dynamic attribute and semantic richness. For example, the event *making a cake* consists of a combination of several concepts such as *cake, people, kitchen* together with the action *making* within a longer video sequence.

Annotation and detection are two different topics of both concept and event analysis. Multimedia annotation, also known as recognition, aims to associate multimedia data with one or multiple semantic labels (tags). For an image/video to be annotated, it is assigned to a specific concept or event that is already known. Many approaches have been proposed to improve the annotation accuracy for both images and videos [17, 30, 26]. The detection task, however, is different from annotation in that it aims to detect the existence of concepts or events through pre-trained detectors. Compared with annotation, detection is more challenging. In detection, there may only be a few positive examples while the negative examples come from an infinite semantic space. We have no clue about all the concepts or events these negative examples include. This provides limited information for obtaining a robust detector.

The TREC Video Retrieval Evaluation (TRECVID) community [3] has notably contributed to the research of video concept or event detection by providing a common testbed for evaluating different detection approaches [20]. In the field of multimedia, many other works have also focused on *concept detection*, e.g., [25, 32, 14]. However, the research on video *event detec-*

tion is still in its infancy. Most existing research on event detection is limited to the events in sports [22, 31, 24] and news video archives [29], or those with repetitive patterns like *running* [28] or unusual events in surveillance videos [4]. In 2010, the TRECVID community launched the task of "Event detection in Internet multimedia (MED)" which aims to encourage new technologies for detecting more complicated events, *e.g.*, *landing a fish*. The definition of the MED task from National Institute of Standards and Technology (NIST) is: detect the occurrence of an event within a video clip based on an Event Kit, which contains some text description about the concept and some example videos. Though few systems have been designed for the MED task [6, 7], they only focus on predefined events. In 2012, NIST proposed an even more challenging problem of MED. The problem is how to attain respectable detection accuracy when the system is not optimized for a limited set of known events and with very few positive examples (*a.k.a.* Ad Hoc MED[1]) since precisely labeled training data are difficult to obtain in the real world. In this paper, we focus on designing a novel algorithm for Ad Hoc MED which deals with the limited number of positive training examples. To the best of our knowledge, this work is the first research on Ad Hoc MED.

Ad Hoc MED faces two major challenges, *i.e.*, complicated events and few positive examples. SVM has been shown to be the most effective tool for predefined MED [6, 7, 13]. However, it is not suitable for Ad Hoc MED when there are only a few positive examples. Since there are some available video archives with annotated concept labels, we can leverage them to facilitate Ad Hoc MED. The difficulty is that those concepts are different from the event to be detected. Hence, a method is in demand to bridge the gap between the concepts and the event, thus being able to utilize the concepts-based videos. Inspired by [32, 12, 8], we propose to adapt the knowledge from concept level to assist in Ad Hoc MED. Specifically, we use the available video corpora with annotated concepts as our auxiliary resource and Ad Hoc MED is performed on the target videos. The concepts are relevant to the event to be detected.

The main contributions of our work are as follows:

(1) We perform the first exploration of Ad Hoc MED research by proposing a novel approach built atop knowledge adaptation.

(2) Unlike many knowledge adaptation methods, our approach does not require that auxiliary videos have the same events as the target videos. We exploit videos with several semantic *concepts* to facilitate the Ad Hoc *Event* Detection on the target videos; the event differs from the concepts and video collections are different from each other.

(3) Compared to other detectors, leveraging knowledge from an auxiliary video archive enables us to obtain improved detection rates in the target video archive with only few positive examples.

2. RELATED WORK

In this section, we briefly review the related works on video semantic analysis and knowledge adaptation.

2.1 Video Semantic Analysis

In the past, although multimedia event analysis has been less focused, video concept annotation has been widely studied. For instance, in [26] Tseng *et al.* have proposed using integrated mining of visual features, speech features, and frequent semantic patterns of videos for annotation. Besides, Snoek *et al.* have studied the challenging problem of automatically indexing 101 semantic concepts [25]. Their work also provides the research community with a manually annotated lexicon containing 101 semantic concepts. In [14], a general post-filtering framework using association and temporal analysis has been proposed for concept classification.

Event detection is a more challenging problem, which has not been sufficiently studied. Most of the existing research efforts are limited to the detection of sports events, news events, unusual surveillance events or those with repetitive patterns. For example, Xu *et al.* propose using web-casting text and broadcast video to detect events from the live sports game [31]. In [29], a model based on a multi-resolution, multi-source and multi-modal bootstrapping framework has been developed for events detection in news videos. Adam *et al.* present an algorithm using multiple local monitors which collect low-level statistics to detect certain types of unusual events in surveillance videos [4]. Sports events, news events and unusual events are usually predefined so that we can identify some event-specific rules or templates to facilitate detection of the particular event. For example, to detect the event *goal* in sports videos, we can utilize people's cheers as a strong evidence. However, in Ad Hoc MED events are more generic and we do not know what the events are before conducting the detection task. Thus, the aforementioned methods may not work well for Ad Hoc MED. Wang *et al.* have proposed a new motion feature by using motion relativity and visual relatedness for event detection [28]. Their approach primarily applies to events that have repetitive motion attributes and are usually describable by a single shot, *e.g. walking* and *dancing*. In contrast, Ad Hoc MED focuses on events that have varying motion attributes within a longer video sequence. For instance, *making a cake* includes different motions such as getting the flour, adding water and baking within a longer video sequence. Moreover, there are few positive examples for training. Thus, the approach in [28] is unsuitable for Ad Hoc MED.

More recently, some researchers began to study the predefined MED [6, 7, 13]. Compared to sports events, news events, unusual surveillance events or those with repetitive patterns, the events in predefined MED are more complicated and difficult to detect. In predefined MED, SVM is widely used and shows good performance. As opposed to predefined MED, we focus on an even more difficult problem Ad Hoc MED, which detects generic events. However, SVM is not suitable for Ad Hoc MED due to the "curse of reality", *i.e.*, few precisely labeled positive examples are provided. Therefore, effective algorithms are in demand for Ad Hoc MED to promote video semantic analysis to a more mature level.

2.2 Knowledge Adaptation for Multimedia Analysis

Knowledge adaptation, also known as transfer learning, aims to propagate the knowledge from an auxiliary domain to a target domain [32, 12, 8, 10]. A number of algorithms have been proposed but most of them require that the auxiliary domain and the target domain have the same classes. However, Ad Hoc MED deals with very complicated events which are not predefined and come from unlimited semantic space. Hence, most existing methods are not applicable. For example, Yang *et al.* have proposed to use Adaptive SVMs for cross-domain video concept detection [32]. The method obtained encouraging results but has some shortcomings. The proposed approach requires that the auxiliary videos and the target videos have the same video concepts. However, in Ad Hoc MED the event to be detected is unknown before we perform the detection task. Collecting many auxiliary videos with the same event description as the target videos is impossible. Jiang *et al.* [12] have used the image context of Flickr to select concept detectors. These pre-selected detectors are then refined by the semantic context transfer from the target domain. In this way, more precise concept detectors are obtained for video search. The proposed method

[1]http://www.nist.gov/itl/iad/mig/med12.cfm

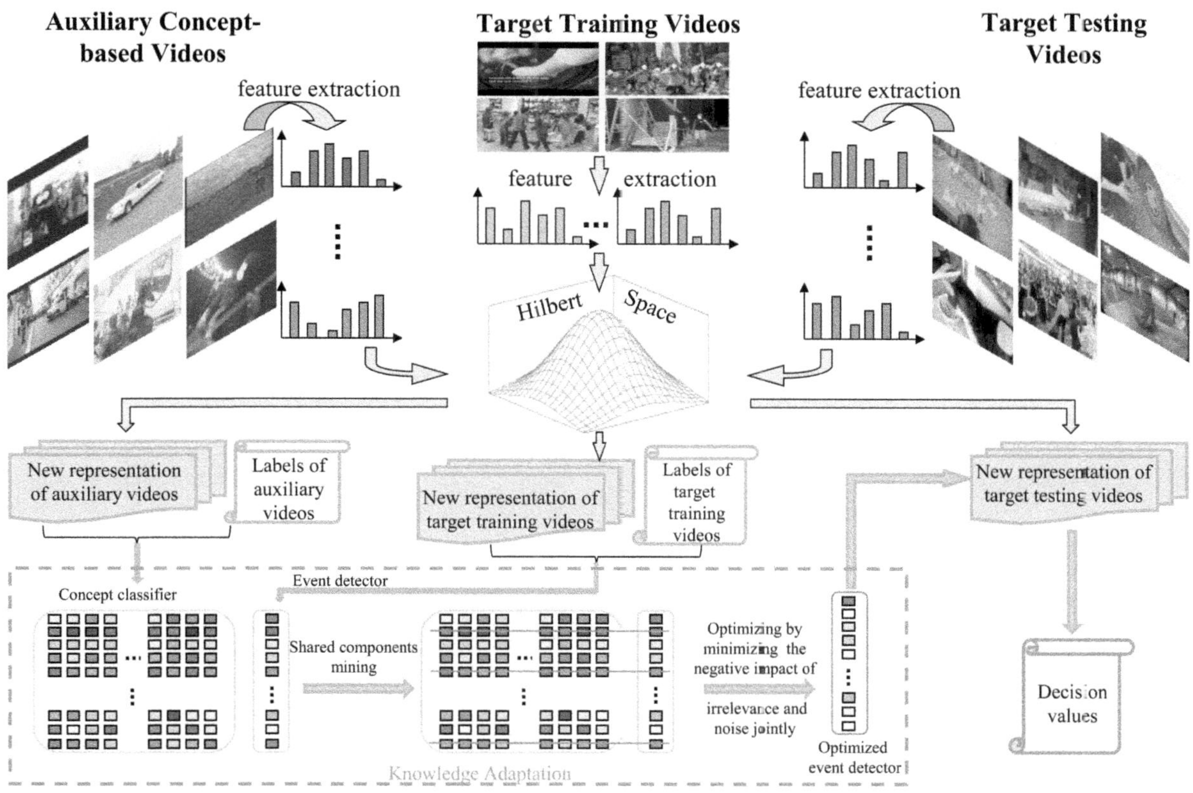

Figure 1: The illustration of our framework. We first map the low-level features of the auxiliary and target videos into a Hilbert Space. The video concept classifier and the video event detector presumably have common components which contain irrelevance and noise. We propose to remove such negative information by optimizing the concept classifier and the event detector jointly.

is interesting but the selected concept detectors cannot be handily used for event detection without other sophisticated algorithms. Besides, as in Ad Hoc MED we only have very few positive examples, using these examples to refine the concept detectors is not reliable. Another algorithm proposed by Duan *et al.* [8] realizes event recognition of consumer videos by leveraging web videos. Their method does not require that the auxiliary domain and the target domain have the same events. However, the approach is very time consuming so it is not suitable for real-world applications.

To progress beyond these aforementioned works, we propose a new knowledge adaptation method for Ad Hoc MED. It explores the shared knowledge between the concepts-based auxiliary videos and the event-based target videos. The shared knowledge can be used to refine the detector of the target videos for Ad Hoc MED. Different from the state of the art, our algorithm does not require that the auxiliary videos have the same event as the target videos. It is also computationally efficient.

3. VIDEO REPRESENTATION

Now we illustrate our framework for Ad Hoc MED. Figure 1 shows the framework of our approach. The video archive where the Ad Hoc MED is to be conducted is our target domain. The low-level features of both auxiliary and target videos are mapped into a Hilbert Space where the shared knowledge between them is to be explored. The video concept classifier and the video event detector presumably have common components which contain irrelevance and noise. We propose to remove such components by optimizing the concept classifier and the event detector jointly, thereby resulting in a more discriminative event detector when we have very few positive examples.

We first introduce the video representation in this section. It has been demonstrated that using multiple features for multimedia representation always yields better performance [34, 13]. We use the SIFT feature [16] and CSIFT feature [27] for video representation. Considering computational efficiency, we use a shot boundary detection algorithm to extract key frames. The shot boundary detection algorithm works as follows: First, it calculates the color histogram of every 5 frames; Second, it subtracts the histogram with that of the previous frame; Third, the frame will be a shot boundary if the subtracted value is larger than an empirically set threshold. Once we get the shot, the frame in the middle of the shot is used to represent that shot. Then we use the Harris-Laplace interest point detector to detect interest points. The SIFT/CSIFT descriptor is subsequently used and we obtain a 4096 dimension Bag-of-Words feature, for which we sum over all the interest points in a video, which is then normalized. The SIFT and CSIFT features are further combined so we use an 8192 dimension feature to represent each video.

Suppose there are n_t training videos for event detector training. The training videos consist of both positive and negative examples. Denote $X_t = [x_t^1, x_t^2, ..., x_t^{n_t}] \in \mathbb{R}^{d \times n_t}$ as the BoW feature of these training videos. d is the feature dimension ($d = 8192$ in this paper). As it has been reported that kernelization is an effective way to deal with BoW features for video analysis [6], after extracting BoW features from the videos, we leverage kernel tricks to transform x_t^i to $\tilde{x}_t^i$. Specifically, we perform full rank principal component analysis in another Hilbert Space H, which is related to the input space by a nonlinear map $\Phi : \mathbb{R}^d \rightarrow H$. The covariance matrix in H is given by $C_H = \frac{1}{n_t}\sum_{i=1}^{n_t}\Phi(x_t^i)\Phi(x_t^i)^T$ [23], where x_t^i is the ith training MED video sequence. We aim to find eigenvalues $\lambda \geq 0$ and eigenvectors V satisfying $\lambda V = CV$. Although H could have an arbitrarily large, possibly infinite dimensionality, the inner product of any two data $\Phi(x_i)$ and $\Phi(x_j)$ can be explicitly expressed by a kernel matrix K, *i.e.*, $K_{ij} = (\Phi(x_i)\cdot\Phi(x_j))$. It turns out that we need to solve the eigenvalue problem $n_t\lambda\alpha = K\alpha$, where $\alpha = [\alpha_1, ..., \alpha_{n_t}]^T$ are coefficients such that $V = \sum_{i=1}^{n_t}\alpha_i\Phi(x_t^i)$ [23]. Let $\alpha^1, ..., \alpha^r$ be the normalized eigenvectors corresponding to all the non-zero eigenvalues $0 < \lambda_1 \leq ... \leq \lambda_r$. For a testing video sequence x_{te} and an auxiliary video sequence x_a, the projection into the eigenvectors $V^p (1 \leq p \leq r)$ in H can be computed according to $\sum_{i=1}^{n_t}\alpha_i^p(\Phi(x_t^i)\cdot\Phi(x_{te}))$ and $\sum_{i=1}^{n_t}\alpha_i^p(\Phi(x_t^i)\cdot\Phi(x_a))$.

4. CONCEPTS ADAPTATION ASSISTED EVENT DETECTION

Next, we explain how the knowledge adaptation is accomplished for Ad Hoc MED. Our approach is grounded on two components: one is the knowledge from the available target training examples and the other one is the knowledge propagated from the auxiliary concepts-based videos.

We first demonstrate how to exploit the knowledge from the target training examples. Denote the target training videos in H by $\tilde{X}_t = [\tilde{x}_t^1, \tilde{x}_t^2, ..., \tilde{x}_t^{n_t}] \in \mathbb{R}^{d_h \times n_t}$. $y_t = [y_t^1, y_t^2, ..., y_t^{n_t}]^T \in \{0,1\}^{n_t \times 1}$ are the labels for the target training videos. $y_t^i = 1$ if the ith video x_t^i is a positive example whereas $y_t^i = 0$ otherwise. The low-level representations and high-level semantics of videos can be associated by a decision function f which, for an input video sequence x, predicts an output y. In this paper, we define f_t as:

$$f_t(\tilde{X}_t^i) = \tilde{X}_t^T W_t + 1_t b_t, \tag{1}$$

where $W_t \in \mathbb{R}^{d_h \times 1}$ is an event detector which correlates $\tilde{X}_t$ with their labels y_t. $b_t \in \mathbb{R}^1$ is a bias term and $1_t \in \mathbb{R}^{n_t \times 1}$ denotes a column vector with all ones. f_t is decided by minimizing the following objective based on the training examples X_t and their labels y_t:

$$\min_{f_t} loss(f_t(X_t), y_t) + \mu\Omega(f_t). \tag{2}$$

$loss(\cdot)$ is a loss function and $\alpha\Omega(f_t)$ is the regularization function on f_t with μ as its parameter. Different loss functions such as the hinge loss and the least square loss can be used. In this paper, we use the $\ell_{2,1}$-norm based loss function because it is robust to outliers [18]. Thus, Eq. (2) is reformulated as:

$$\min_{W_t, b_t} \left\| \tilde{X}_t^T W_t + 1_t b_t - y_t \right\|_{2,1} + \mu\Omega(W_t). \tag{3}$$

Now we show how to adapt the knowledge from auxiliary videos which are associated with different concepts to assist in Ad Hoc MED. Denote the auxiliary videos in H by $\tilde{X}_a = [\tilde{x}_a^1, \tilde{x}_a^2, ..., \tilde{x}_a^{n_a}] \in \mathbb{R}^{d_h \times n_a}$. $Y_a = [y_a^1, y_a^2, ..., y_a^{n_a}]^T \in \{0,1\}^{n_a \times c_a}$ is their label matrix where c_a indicates that there are c_a different concepts. Y_a^{ij} denotes the jth datum of y_a^i and $Y_a^{ij} = 1$ if x_a^i belongs to the jth concept, while $Y_a^{ij} = 0$ otherwise. The fundamental step is to mine the correlation between the low-level representations and high-level semantics of the auxiliary concepts-based videos. Similarly to Eq. (3), we realize that by the following objective:

$$\min_{W_a, b_a} \left\| \tilde{X}_a^T W_a + 1_a b_a - Y_a \right\|_{2,1} + \gamma\Omega(W_a) \tag{4}$$

where a concept classifier $W_a \in \mathbb{R}^{d_h \times c_a}$ is used to correlate $\tilde{X}_a$ with their labels Y_a. $b_a \in \mathbb{R}^{1 \times c_a}$ is a bias term and $1_a \in \mathbb{R}^{n_a \times 1}$ is a column vector with all ones.

Next, we illustrate how to adapt knowledge from the auxiliary concepts-based videos for a more discriminating event detector. The concepts-based videos presumably share some common components with the target event-based videos. For instance, the concepts *fish*, *water*, *people* are relevant with the event *landing a fish*. It is reasonable to leverage such relevance to improve the target event detection when we have only few positive examples. As the classifier W_a and the detector W_t correlate the low-level representations with the high-level concepts and event for each domain respectively, we explore the shared knowledge between the two to optimize the learning of W_t. The video representation in H is potentially noisy. In Ad Hoc MED, only few training examples are provided. The limited information is usually not sufficient to effectively deal with the underlying noise. On the other hand, the concepts of $\tilde{X}_a$ and the event of $\tilde{X}_t$ are related and grounded on similar low-level representations. The irrelevant or noisy components in W_a and W_t should be similar, which can be uncovered by learning W_a and W_t jointly. Thus, we exploit the concept classifier W_a to help remove the noise in W_t for a more discriminative event detector.

Denote $W_a = [w_a^1, ..., w_a^{d^h}]^T$, $W_t = [w_t^1, ..., w_t^{d^h}]^T$. Then we combine them and define a joint analyzer $W = [w^1, ..., w^{d^h}]$ where w^i is the horizontal concatenation of w_a^i and w_t^i, *i.e.*, $w^i = [w_a^i, w_t^i]$. In this sense, w_i reflects the joint information from the auxiliary videos and the target training videos. Through proper optimization of w_i, we can remove the shared irrelevant or noisy components. Previous work has shown that sparse models are useful for feature selection by eliminating redundancy and noise [5, 19, 18]. The sparse models are used to make some of the feature coefficients shrink to zeros to achieve feature selection. These works, though focusing on different problems, provide us with the inspiration that the "shrinking to zero" idea can be applied to uncover the common structures shared by the concept classifier and the event detector. In this way, we can similarly remove the shared irrelevance and noise, thus obtaining a more discriminative event detector. Specifically, we propose to minimize $\|W\|_{2,p} = \left(\sum_{i=1}^{d_h}(\sum_{j=1}^{c_a+1}|W_{ij}|)^{\frac{p}{2}}\right)^{\frac{1}{p}}$ to achieve that goal. $\|\cdot\|_{2,p}$ denotes the $\ell_{2,p}$-norm (0 < p < 2). By minimizing $\|W\|_{2,p}$, we can reduce the negative impact of the irrelevant or noisy w_i's. p is used to control the degree of shared structures. The lower p is, the more correlated are the concept classifier and the event detector. Consequently, we can obtain an optimal event detector W_t.

To this end, we propose the following objective function to adapt the knowledge from auxiliary videos for Ad Hoc MED:

$$\begin{aligned}\min_{W_a, W_t, b_a, b_t} & \|\tilde{X}_a^T W_a + 1_a b_a - Y_a\|_{2,1} + \|\tilde{X}_t^T W_t + 1_t b_t - y_t\|_{2,1} \\ & + \alpha\left(\sum_{i=1}^{d_h}(\sum_{j=1}^{c_a+1}|W_{ij}|)^{\frac{p}{2}}\right)^{\frac{1}{p}} + \beta(\|W_a\|_F^2 + \|W_t\|_F^2)\end{aligned} \tag{5}$$

where $\beta(\|W_a\|_F^2 + \|W_t\|_F^2)$ is added to control the capacity of the classifier and the detector.

Once W_t is obtained, we apply it to the testing videos in H for event detection. Our method builds upon the knowledge adaptation from concepts-based videos to event-based videos by leveraging the shared structures between them. We therefore name it Structural Adaptive Regression (SAR).

5. OPTIMIZING THE EVENT DETECTOR

In this section, we present our solution for obtaining the target event detector. Our problem in Eq. (5) involves the $\ell_{2,1}$-norm and the $\ell_{2,p}$-norm which are both non-smooth and cannot be solved in a closed form. We propose to solve it as follows. For the detailed solution, please see Appendix.

Denote $\tilde{X}_a^T W_a - Y_a = [u^1, ..., u^{n_a}]^T$, $\tilde{X}_t^T W_t - y_t = [v^1, ..., v^{n_t}]^T$. Next, we define three diagonal matrices D_a, D_t and D with their diagonal elements $D_a^{ii} = \frac{1}{2\|u^i\|_2}$, $D_t^{ii} = \frac{1}{2\|v^i\|_2}$, $D^{ii} = \frac{1}{\frac{2}{p}\|w^i\|_2^{2-p}}$ respectively. In this way, we can get the concept classifier W_a as:

$$W_a = (\tilde{X}_a H_a D_a H_a \tilde{X}_a^T + \alpha D + \beta I_d)^{-1} \tilde{X}_a H_a D_a H_a Y_a \tag{6}$$

$H_a = I_a - \frac{1}{n_a} 1_a 1_a^T$. $I_a \in \mathbb{R}^{n_a \times n_a}$ and $I_d \in \mathbb{R}^{d_h \times d_h}$ are two identity matrices. The event detector W_t is obtained as:

$$W_t = (\tilde{X}_t H_t D_t H_t \tilde{X}_t^T + \alpha D + \beta I_d)^{-1} \tilde{X}_t H_t D_t H_t y_t. \tag{7}$$

where $H_t = I_t - \frac{1}{n_t} 1_t 1_t^T$ and $I_t \in \mathbb{R}^{n_t \times n_t}$ is an identity matrix.

Next, we propose Algorithm 1 to solve the objective function in Eq. (5). It can be proved that the objective function in Eq. (5) is convex and the objective function value monotonically decreases in each iteration until convergence using Algorithm 1. Due to the space limit, we omit the proof. For training, the computational complexity of Algorithm 1 is $O(d_h^3)$. Note that $d_h \leq n_t$ because usually there are few training examples in Ad Hoc MED. Thus, the training process is not very computationally expensive. During testing, computing kernels between the testing data and the training data is the most expensive process. Suppose there are n_{te} testing videos, we need to compute $n_t n_{te}$ kernels. Each datum is d_h dimensional so the complexity is $O(d_h n_t n_{te})$.

Algorithm 1: Optimizing the event detector.

Input:

The auxiliary data $\tilde{X}_a \in \mathbb{R}^{d_h \times n_a}, Y_a \in \mathbb{R}^{n_a \times c_a}$;

The target training data $\tilde{X}_t \in \mathbb{R}^{d_h \times n_t}, y_t \in \mathbb{R}^{n_t \times 1}$;

Parameters α and β.

Output:

Optimized $W_t \in \mathbb{R}^{d_h \times 1}$ and $b_t \in \mathbb{R}^1$.

1: Set $t = 0$, initialize $W_a \in \mathbb{R}^{d_h \times c_a}$ and $W_t \in \mathbb{R}^{d_h \times 1}$ randomly;

2: **repeat**

Compute $\tilde{X}_a^T W_a - Y_a = [u^1, ..., u^{n_a}]^T$,
$\tilde{X}_t^T W_t - y_t = [v^1, ..., v^{n_t}]^T$, and $W = [w^1, ..., w^d]^T$;

Compute the diagonal matrix D_a^t, D_t^t and D^t according to $D_a^{ii} = \frac{1}{2\|u^i\|_2}$, $D_t^{ii} = \frac{1}{2\|v^i\|_2}$, and $D^{ii} = \frac{1}{\frac{2}{p}\|w^i\|_2^{2-p}}$ respectively;

Update W_a^{t+1} as:
$W_a^{t+1} = (\tilde{X}_a H_a D_a \tilde{X}_a^T + \alpha D + \beta I_d)^{-1} \tilde{X}_a H_a D_a H_a Y_a^T$;

Update b_a^{t+1} as: $b_a^{t+1} = \frac{1}{n_a} 1_a^T Y_a - \frac{1}{n_a} 1_a^T \tilde{X}_a^T W_a^{t+1}$;

Update W_t^{t+1} as:
$W_t^{t+1} = (\tilde{X}_t H_t D_t \tilde{X}_t^T + \alpha D + \beta I_d)^{-1} \tilde{X}_t H_t D_t H_t y_t^T$;

Update b_t^{t+1} as: $b_t^{t+1} = \frac{1}{n_t} 1_t^T y_t - \frac{1}{n_t} 1_t^T \tilde{X}_t^T W_t^{t+1}$;

$t = t + 1$.

until *Convergence*;

3: Return W_t and b_t.

---

6. EXPERIMENTS

In this section, we present the experiments which aim to evaluate the performance of our Structural Adaptive Regression (SAR) for Ad Hoc MED.

6.1 Datasets

NIST has provided so far the largest video corpora for MED. Our experiments on Ad Hoc MED are conducted on the TRECVID MED 2010 (MED10) and TRECVID MED 2011 (MED11) development set. MED10[2] includes 3 events defined by NIST, which are *Making a cake*, *Batting a run*, and *Assembling a shelter*. MED11[3] includes 15 events, *i.e.*, *Attempting a board trick*, *Feeding an animal*, *Landing a fish*, *Wedding ceremony*, *Working on a woodworking project*, *Birthday party*, *Changing a vehicle tire*, *Flash mob gathering*, *Getting a vehicle unstuck*, *Grooming an animal*, *Making a sandwich*, *Parade*, *Parkour*, *Repairing an appliance* and *Working on a sewing project*. The two datasets are combined together (MED10-11 for short) in our experiments so we have a dataset of 9822 video clips consisting of 361,623 key frames.

We use the development set from TRECVID 2011 semantic indexing task (SIN11) as the auxiliary videos. The SIN11 covers 346 concepts but some of them have few positive examples. Additionally, "events" usually refer to "semantically meaningful human activities, taking place within a selected environment and containing a number of necessary objects [9]." Hence, we removed the concepts with few positive examples and selected 65 concepts that are related to human, environment and objects. We thus use a subset with 2529 video frames.

6.2 Setup

The videos are represented by the SIFT and CSIFT features. We ran our program on the Carnegie Mellon University Parallel Data Lab cluster, which contains 300 cores, to extract features and perform the bag-of-words mapping.

According to the MED task definition from NIST, each event is detected independently. Therefore, there are 18 individual detection tasks. NIST has defined that the number of positive training examples is 10 for Ad Hoc MED [2]. However, there is no standard training and testing set partition provided by NIST. Hence, we randomly split the MED10-11 dataset into two subsets, one as the training set and the other one as the testing set. We follow the Ad Hoc MED definition by NIST and randomly select 10 positive examples for each event. Another 300 negative examples are selected and combined with the positive examples as the training data. The remaining 9512 videos are our testing data. The experiments are independently repeated 5 times with randomly selected positive and negative examples. The average results are reported.

We use three evaluation metrics. The first one, Minimum NDC (MinNDC), is officially used by NIST in TRECVID MED 2011 evaluation [1]. Lower MinNDC indicates better detection performance. The second one is the Probability of Miss-Detection based on the Detection Threshold 12.5. This evaluation metric is used by NIST in TRECVID MED 2012 [2] to evaluate MED performance. We denote it Pmd@TER=12.5 for short. Likewise, lower Pmd@TER=12.5 indicates better performance. For more details about the above two evaluation metrics, please see the TRECVID 2011 and 2012 evaluation plans [1, 2]. The third one is Average Precision (AP). Higher AP indicates better performance.

6.3 Ad Hoc MED Results

In this section, we show the Ad Hoc MED results. As SVM is the most widely used and robust event detector for MED [13, 6, 11, 28], we first compare our method SAR with SVM. We use two kernels, *i.e.*, Gaussian kernel and χ^2 kernel for both SAR and SVM. To be clear, we use G-SAR, G-SVM, χ^2-SAR and χ^2-SVM to refer

[2]http://nist.gov/itl/iad/mig/med10.cfm
[3]http://www.nist.gov/itl/iad/mig/med11.cfm

Table 1: Average detection accuracy of SAR and SVM using Gaussian kernel. LOWER MinNDC and Pmd@TER=12.5 indicate BETTER performance. HIGHER AP indicates BETTER performance. Better results are highlighted in bold.

Evaluation Metric	G-SVM	G-SAR
MinNDC	0.954	**0.910**
Pmd@TER=12.5	0.751	**0.674**
AP	0.072	**0.103**

Table 2: Average detection accuracy of SAR and SVM using χ^2 kernel. LOWER MinNDC and Pmd@TER=12.5 indicate BETTER performance. HIGHER AP indicates BETTER performance. Better results are highlighted in bold.

Evaluation Metric	χ^2-SVM	χ^2-SAR
MinNDC	0.904	**0.881**
Pmd@TER=12.5	0.665	**0.626**
AP	0.115	**0.131**

to different implementations. For SAR, we tune the two parameters α and β both from $\{10^{-3}, 10^{-2}, ..., 10^2, 10^3\}$, and the parameter p from $\{0.5, 1, 1.5\}$. For SVM, we use LIBSVM and tune the parameters C and γ similarly from $\{10^{-3}, 10^{-2}, ..., 10^2, 10^3\}$. We report the best results for each algorithm.

Figure 2 shows the comparison between the four approaches. Note that LOWER MinNDC and Pmd@TER=12.5 indicate BETTER performance; HIGHER AP indicates BETTER performance. We observe that: 1) In general, χ^2-SAR and χ^2-SVM are better than G-SAR and G-SVM respectively, demonstrating that χ^2 kernel is better than Gaussian kernel for video analysis. 2) χ^2-SAR proposed in this paper is consistently the most competitive algorithm. Specifically, χ^2-SAR attains the best detection performance for 14, 14 and 13 events in MinNDC, Pmd@TER=12.5 and AP respectively; χ^2-SAR gets the advantageous performance for the remaining events. 3) For average performance over the 18 events, G-SAR, χ^2-SAR outperform G-SVM, χ^2-SVM respectively using all the three evaluation metrics. The detailed numbers of the average results are listed in Table 1 and Table 2. 4) We also notice that the performance of G-SAR does not change significantly compared with χ^2-SAR. However, for most events, the performance of G-SVM drops drastically compared with χ^2-SVM, which indicates that SVM is sensitive to kernel change. In fact, the advantage of G-SAR over G-SVM is remarkably large for many events. For few events, *e.g.*, *Working on a woodworking project* and *Grooming an animal*, χ^2-SAR is worse than χ^2-SVM. Nonetheless, G-SAR outperforms G-SVM dramatically.

Next, we add two state of the art detectors for comparison:

(1) TaylorBoost [21]: a state of the art algorithm extended from AdaBoost.

(2) Adaptive Multiple Kernel Learning (A-MKL) [8]: a recent knowledge adaptation algorithm built upon SVM.

For these algorithms, we use the code shared by the authors. A-MKL is a knowledge adaptation based algorithm, which similarly utilizes the SIN11 dataset as auxiliary data.

Since χ^2-SAR and χ^2-SVM show better performance in the last experiment, we only list their results to compare with the other three approaches. Note that we use SAR and SVM for short here.

Figure 3 shows the detection results of different approaches. Note that lower MinNDC and Pmd@TER=12.5 indicate better performance; higher AP indicates better performance. We can see that our method SAR is still the most competitive algorithm. Specifically, SAR is the best for 14, 13 and 10 events in MinNDC, Pmd@TER=12.5 and AP respectively. For the remaining events, SAR obtains the advantageous performance. For average performance, SAR is the best algorithm using all the three evaluation metrics. We also observe that A-MKL generally attains the second best performance. However, we would point out that A-MKL is not suitable for large scale multimedia analysis due to its low computational efficiency. The calculation of 80 different kernel matrices consumes up to 30GB memory and the detection for one event is much more computationally expensive than our algorithm.

6.4 Using Fewer Concepts

To study whether the number of concepts affects the Ad Hoc MED performance, we conduct an experiment by choosing fewer concepts out of the 65 concepts from the auxiliary videos. We manually selected 30 concepts which are supposed to be most related to generic events. The videos related to these 30 concepts are used as auxiliary data. Figure 4 displays the corresponding results. We only show the results in Average Precision due to the space limit. It can be seen that the performance does not vary much when using only 30 auxiliary concepts. This observation indicates that it is not very critical to decide how many concepts should be selected as auxiliary knowledge with our method.

6.5 Do Negative Examples Help?

We further conduct an experiment to evaluate whether negative examples contribute much to the detection accuracy by reducing the number of negative examples to 100. Figure 5 shows the performance comparison between using 100 negative examples and using 300 negative examples. Similarly, Average Precision is chosen as the evaluation metric. It can be seen that using 300 negative examples is clearly better than merely using 100 negative examples, which indicates that negative examples do help improve the detection accuracy. Since negative examples are quite easy to obtain in the real world, it is reasonable and beneficial to leverage such cheap resources for boosted detection accuracy.

7. CONCLUSION

In this paper, we have introduced the first research exploration of Ad Hoc MED. This is an important research issue as it focuses on more generic, complicated and meaningful events that reflect our daily activities. In addition, the situation we are faced in the real world requires that only few positive examples are used. To achieve good performance, we have proposed to borrow strength from available concepts-based videos for Ad Hoc MED. In our joint optimization framework, we first mine the shared irrelevance and noise between the auxiliary videos and the target videos. Then a sophisticated method is exerted to alleviate the negative impact of the irrelevance and noise to obtain a more robust event detector. We also proposed an efficient iterative algorithm to solve our objective function. Extensive experiments using real-world multimedia archives were conducted with results showing that our method generally outperforms all compared state of the art detection algorithms. This promising performance indicates that it is beneficial to leverage auxiliary knowledge for Ad Hoc MED when we do not have sufficient positive examples. However, knowledge adaptation is based on the assumption that there are shared structures between the source and the target. If the two have very different structures, we may get negative transfer which degrades the detection performance on the target. Therefore, it would be interesting and important to study how to judge the structural commonness to better utilize knowledge adaption in the future.

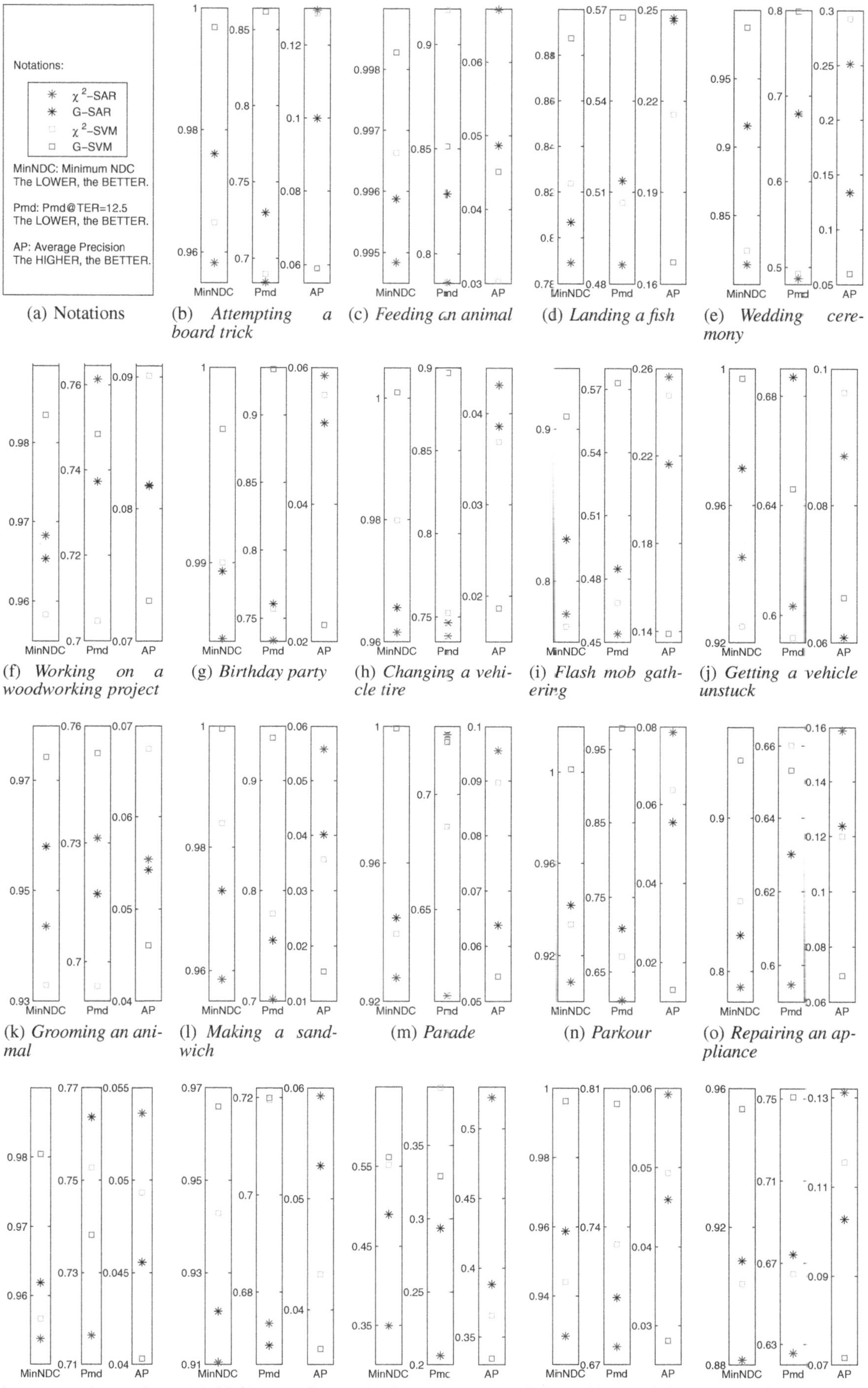

(a) Notations (b) *Attempting a board trick* (c) *Feeding an animal* (d) *Landing a fish* (e) *Wedding ceremony*

(f) *Working on a woodworking project* (g) *Birthday party* (h) *Changing a vehicle tire* (i) *Flash mob gathering* (j) *Getting a vehicle unstuck*

(k) *Grooming an animal* (l) *Making a sandwich* (m) *Parade* (n) *Parkour* (o) *Repairing an appliance*

(p) *Working on a sewing project* (q) *Making a cake* (r) *Batting a run* (s) *Assembling a shelter* (t) *Average*

Figure 2: Performance Comparison between SAR and SVM using different kernels. Note that LOWER MinNDC and Pmd@TER=12.5 indicate BETTER performance; HIGHER AP indicates BETTER performance.

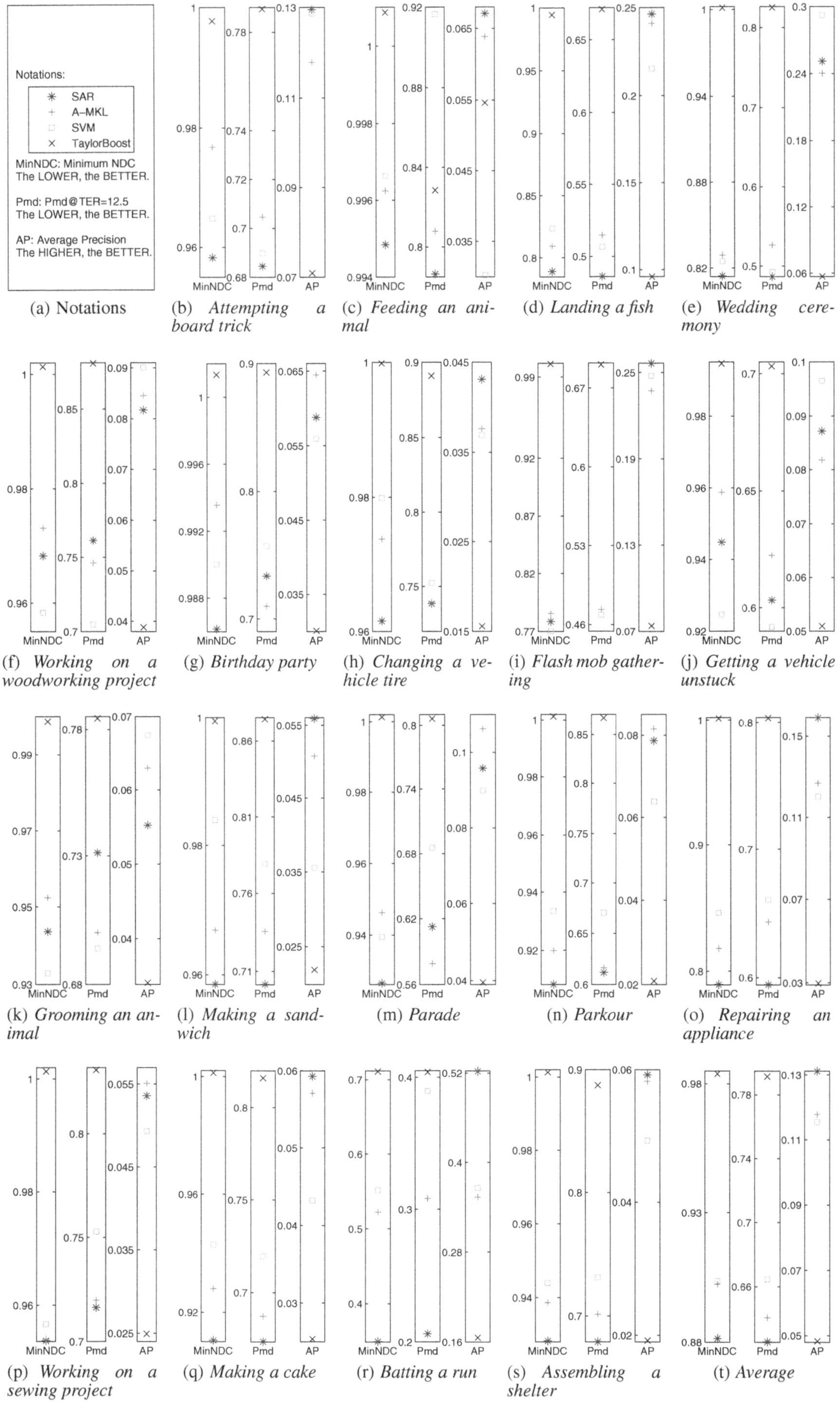

(a) Notations (b) *Attempting a board trick* (c) *Feeding an animal* (d) *Landing a fish* (e) *Wedding ceremony*

(f) *Working on a woodworking project* (g) *Birthday party* (h) *Changing a vehicle tire* (i) *Flash mob gathering* (j) *Getting a vehicle unstuck*

(k) *Grooming an animal* (l) *Making a sandwich* (m) *Parade* (n) *Parkour* (o) *Repairing an appliance*

(p) *Working on a sewing project* (q) *Making a cake* (r) *Batting a run* (s) *Assembling a shelter* (t) *Average*

Figure 3: Performance Comparison on Ad Hoc MED. Note that LOWER MinNDC and Pmd@TER=12.5 indicate BETTER performance; HIGHER AP indicates BETTER performance.

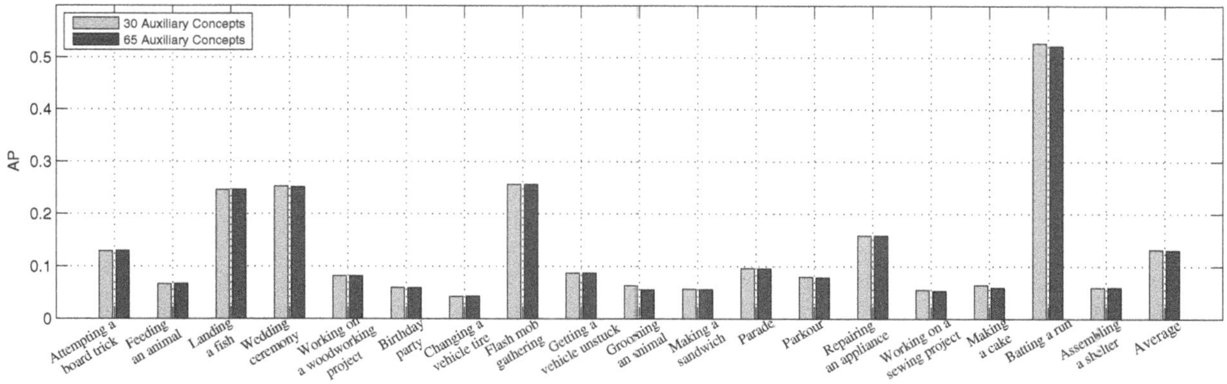

Figure 4: Performance comparison between using 30 auxiliary concepts and using 65 auxiliary concepts.

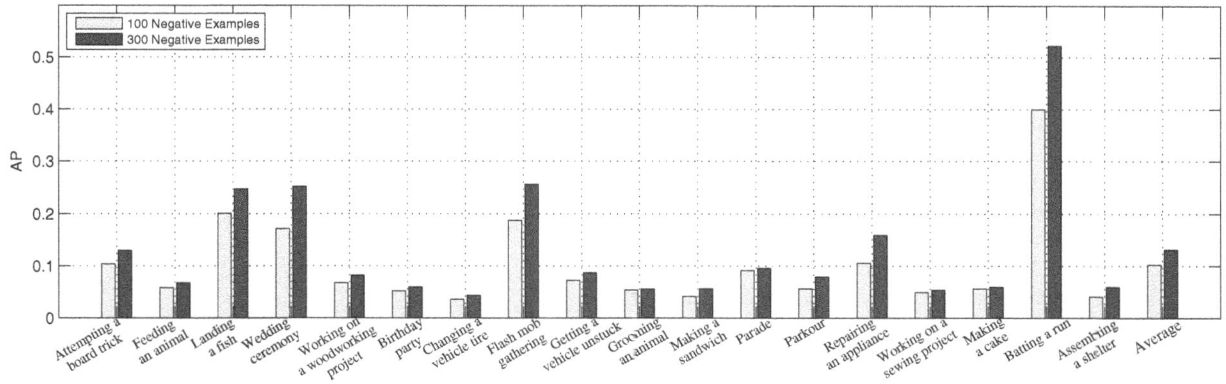

Figure 5: Performance comparison between using 100 negative examples and using 300 negative examples.

8. ACKNOWLEDGMENTS

This paper was partially supported by the Glocal FP7 IP project, the S-PATTERNS FIRB project and the Intelligence Advanced Research Projects Activity (IARPA) via Department of Interior National Business Center contract number D11PC20068. The U.S. Government is authorized to reproduce and distribute reprints for Governmental purposes notwithstanding any copyright annotation thereon. Disclaimer: The views and conclusions contained herein are those of the authors and should not be interpreted as necessarily representing the official policies or endorsements, either expressed or implied, of IARPA, DoI/NBC, or the U.S. Government.

9. REFERENCES

[1] http://www.nist.gov/itl/iad/mig/upload/med11-evalplan-v03-20110801a.pdf.

[2] http://www.nist.gov/itl/iad/mig/upload/med12-evalplan-v01.pdf.

[3] Trec video retrieval evaluation. National Institute of Standards and Technology. *http://www-nlpir.nist.gov/projects/trecvid/.*

[4] A. Adam, E. Rivlin, I. Shimshoni, and D. Reinitz. Robust real-time unusual event detection using multiple fixed-location monitors. *IEEE Trans. Pattern Anal. Mach. Intell.*, 30(3):555–560, 2008.

[5] A. Argyriou, T. Evgeniou, and M. Pontil. Multi-task feature learning. In *NIPS*, pages 41–48, 2006.

[6] L. Bao, L. Zhang, S.-I. Yu, Z. zhong Lan, L. Jiang, A. Overwijk, Q. Jin, S. Takahashi, B. Langner, Y. Li, M. Garbus, S. Burger, F. Metze, and A. Hauptmann. Informedia @ TRECVID2011. In *NIST TRECVID Workshop*, 2011.

[7] L. Cao, S.-F. Chang, N. Codella, C. Cotton, D. Ellis, L. Gong, M. Hill, G. Hua, J. Kender, M. Merler, Y. Mu, A. Natsev, and J. R. Smith. IBM Research and Columbia University TRECVID-2011 Multimedia Event Detection (MED) System. In *NIST TRECVID Workshop*, 2011.

[8] L. Duan, D. Xu, I. W.-H. Tsang, and J. Luo. Visual event recognition in videos by learning from web data. In *CVPR*, 2010.

[9] L. Fei-Fei and L.-J. Li. What, Where and Who? Telling the Story of an Image by Activity Classification, Scene Recognition and Object Categorization. *Studies in Computational Intelligence- Computer Vision*, pages 157–171, 2010.

[10] Y. Han, F. Wu, Y. Zhuang, and X. He. Multi-label transfer learning with sparse representation. *IEEE Trans. Circuits Syst. Video Techn.*, 20(8):1110–1121, 2010.

[11] A. G. Hauptmann, R. Yan, W.-H. Lin, M. G. Christel, and H. D. Wactlar. Can high-level concepts fill the semantic gap in video retrieval? a case study with broadcast news. *IEEE Transactions on Multimedia*, 9(5):958–966, 2007.

[12] Y.-G. Jiang, C.-W. Ngo, and S.-F. Chang. Semantic context transfer across heterogeneous sources for domain adaptive video search. In *ACM Multimedia*, pages 155–164, 2009.

[13] Z.-Z. Lan, L. Bao, S.-I. Yu, W. Liu, and A. G. Hauptmann. Double fusion for multimedia event detection. In *MMM*, pages 173–185, 2012.

[14] K.-H. Liu, M.-F. Weng, C.-Y. Tseng, Y.-Y. Chuang, and M.-S. Chen. Association and temporal rule mining for

post-filtering of semantic concept detection in video. *IEEE Transactions on Multimedia*, 10(2):240–251, 2008.

[15] Y. Liu, F. Wu, Y. Zhuang, and J. Xiao. Active post-refined multimodality video semantic concept detection with tensor representation. In *ACM Multimedia*, pages 91–100, 2008.

[16] D. G. Lowe. Distinctive image features from scale-invariant keypoints. *International Journal of Computer Vision*, 60(2):91–110, 2004.

[17] J. Luo, J. Yu, D. Joshi, and W. Hao. Event recognition: viewing the world with a third eye. In *ACM Multimedia*, pages 1071–1080, 2008.

[18] Z. Ma, F. Nie, Y. Yang, J. Uijlings, and N. Sebe. Web image annotation via subspace-sparsity collaborated feature selection. *IEEE Transactions on Multimedia*, 2012.

[19] Z. Ma, Y. Yang, F. Nie, J. R. R. Uijlings, and N. Sebe. Exploiting the entire feature space with sparsity for automatic image annotation. In *ACM Multimedia*, pages 283–292, 2011.

[20] M. R. Naphade and J. R. Smith. On the detection of semantic concepts at trecvid. In *ACM Multimedia*, pages 660–667, 2004.

[21] M. J. Saberian, H. Masnadi-Shirazi, and N. Vasconcelos. Taylorboost: First and second-order boosting algorithms with explicit margin control. In *CVPR*, 2011.

[22] D. A. Sadlier and N. E. O'Connor. Event detection in field sports video using audio-visual features and a support vector machine. *IEEE Trans. Circuits Syst. Video Techn.*, 15(10):1225–1233, 2005.

[23] B. Schölkopf, A. J. Smola, and K.-R. Müller. Nonlinear component analysis as a kernel eigenvalue problem. *Neural Computation*, 10(5):1299–1319, 1998.

[24] M.-L. Shyu, Z. Xie, M. Chen, and S.-C. Chen. Video semantic event/concept detection using a subspace-based multimedia data mining framework. *IEEE Transactions on Multimedia*, 10(2):252–259, 2008.

[25] C. Snoek, M. Worring, J. van Gemert, J.-M. Geusebroek, and A. W. M. Smeulders. The challenge problem for automated detection of 101 semantic concepts in multimedia. In *ACM Multimedia*, pages 421–430, 2006.

[26] V. S. Tseng, J.-H. Su, J.-H. Huang, and C.-J. Chen. Integrated mining of visual features, speech features, and frequent patterns for semantic video annotation. *IEEE Transactions on Multimedia*, 10(2):260–267, 2008.

[27] K. E. A. van de Sande, T. Gevers, and C. G. M. Snoek. Evaluating color descriptors for object and scene recognition. *IEEE Trans. Pattern Anal. Mach. Intell.*, 32(9):1582–1596, 2010.

[28] F. Wang, Y.-G. Jiang, and C.-W. Ngo. Video event detection using motion relativity and visual relatedness. In *ACM Multimedia*, pages 239–248, 2008.

[29] G. Wang, T.-S. Chua, and M. Zhao. Exploring knowledge of sub-domain in a multi-resolution bootstrapping framework for concept detection in news video. In *ACM Multimedia*, pages 249–258, 2008.

[30] M. Wang, X.-S. Hua, X. Yuan, Y. Song, and L.-R. Dai. Optimizing multi-graph learning: towards a unified video annotation scheme. In *ACM Multimedia*, pages 862–871, 2007.

[31] C. Xu, J. Wang, K. Wan, Y. Li, and L. Duan. Live sports event detection based on broadcast video and web-casting text. In *ACM Multimedia*, pages 221–230, 2006.

[32] J. Yang, R. Yan, and A. G. Hauptmann. Cross-domain video concept detection using adaptive SVMs. In *ACM Multimedia*, pages 188–197, 2007.

[33] Y. Yang, F. Nie, D. Xu, J. Luo, Y. Zhuang, and Y. Pan. A multimedia retrieval framework based on semi-supervised ranking and relevance feedback. *IEEE Trans. Pattern Anal. Mach. Intell.*, 34(4):723–742, 2012.

[34] Y. Yang, Y. Zhuang, F. Wu, and Y. Pan. Harmonizing hierarchical manifolds for multimedia document semantics understanding and cross-media retrieval. *IEEE Transactions on Multimedia*, 10(3):437–446, 2008.

APPENDIX

The objective in Eq. (5) is equivalent to:

$$\begin{aligned}&\min_{W_a,W_t,b_a,b_t} Tr\left((\tilde{X}_a^T W_a + 1_a b_a - Y_a)^T D_a (\tilde{X}_a^T W_a + 1_a b_a - Y_a)\right)\\&+Tr\left((\tilde{X}_t^T W_t + 1_t b_t - y_t)^T D_t (\tilde{X}_t^T W_t + 1_t b_t - y_t)\right)\\&+\alpha Tr(W^T D W) + \beta(\|W_a\|_F^2 + \|W_t\|_F^2)\end{aligned} \tag{8}$$

where $Tr(\cdot)$ denotes the trace operator. By setting the derivative of Eq. (8) *w.r.t.* b_a to zero, we get:

$$\begin{aligned}&2 1_a^T D_a \tilde{X}_a^T W_a + 2 1_a^T D_a 1_a b_a - 2 1_a^T D_a Y_a = 0\\&\Rightarrow b_a = \frac{1}{n_a} 1_a^T Y_a - \frac{1}{n_a} 1_a^T \tilde{X}_a^T W_a.\end{aligned} \tag{9}$$

Similarly, we obtain b_t as:

$$b_t = \frac{1}{n_t} 1_t^T y_t - \frac{1}{n_t} 1_t^T \tilde{X}_t^T W_t. \tag{10}$$

Substituting Eq. (9) and Eq. (10) into Eq. (8), it becomes:

$$\begin{aligned}&\min_{W_a,W_t} Tr\Big([\tilde{X}_a^T W_a + 1_a(\frac{1}{n_a} 1_a^T Y_a - \frac{1}{n_a} 1_a^T \tilde{X}_a^T W_a) - Y_a]^T D_a\\&[\tilde{X}_a^T W_a + 1_a(\frac{1}{n_a} 1_a^T Y_a - \frac{1}{n_a} 1_a^T \tilde{X}_a^T W_a) - Y_a]\Big)\\&+Tr\Big([\tilde{X}_t^T W_t + 1_t(\frac{1}{n_t} 1_t^T y_t - \frac{1}{n_t} 1_t^T \tilde{X}_t^T W_t) - y_t]^T D_t\\&[\tilde{X}_t^T W_t + 1_t(\frac{1}{n_t} 1_t^T y_t - \frac{1}{n_t} 1_t^T \tilde{X}_t^T W_t) - y_t]\Big)\\&+\alpha Tr(W^T D W) + \beta(\|W_a\|_F^2 + \|W_t\|_F^2)\end{aligned} \tag{11}$$

Let $H_a = I_a - \frac{1}{n_a} 1_a 1_a^T$ and $H_t = I_t - \frac{1}{n_t} 1_t 1_t^T$ where $I_a \in \mathbb{R}^{n_a \times n_a}$ and $I_t \in \mathbb{R}^{n_t \times n_t}$ are two identity matrices. We then rewrite Eq. (11) as:

$$\begin{aligned}&\min_{W_a,W_t} Tr\left((H_a \tilde{X}_a^T W_a - H_a Y_a)^T D_a (H_a \tilde{X}_a^T W_a - H_a Y_a)\right)\\&+Tr\left((H_t \tilde{X}_t^T W_t - H_t y_t)^T D_t (H_t \tilde{X}_t^T W_t - H_t y_t)\right)\\&+\alpha Tr(W^T D W) + \beta(\|W_a\|_F^2 + \|W_t\|_F^2)\end{aligned} \tag{12}$$

Setting the derivative of Eq. (12) *w.r.t.* W_a to zero, it becomes:

$$\begin{aligned}&2\tilde{X}_a H_a D_a H_a \tilde{X}_a^T W_a + 2\alpha D W_a + 2\beta W_a - 2\tilde{X}_a H_a D_a H_a Y_a = 0\\&\Rightarrow W_a = (\tilde{X}_a H_a D_a H_a \tilde{X}_a^T + \alpha D + \beta I_d)^{-1} \tilde{X}_a H_a D_a H_a Y_a\end{aligned} \tag{13}$$

where $I_d \in \mathbb{R}^{d_h \times d_h}$ is an identity matrix. In the same manner, we obtain the event detector W_t as:

$$W_t = (\tilde{X}_t H_t D_t H_t \tilde{X}_t^T + \alpha D + \beta I_d)^{-1} \tilde{X}_t H_t D_t H_t y_t. \tag{14}$$

Multi-View Learning from Imperfect Tagging

Zhongang Qi, Ming Yang, and Zhongfei (Mark) Zhang
Dept. of ISEE, Zhejiang University, China
{zhongangqi, cauchym, zhongfei}@zju.edu.cn

Zhengyou Zhang
Microsoft Research
One Microsoft Way, Redmond, WA, USA
zhang@microsoft.com

ABSTRACT

In many real-world applications, tagging is imperfect: incomplete, inconsistent, and error-prone. Solutions to this problem will generate societal and technical impacts. In this paper, we investigate this arguably new problem: learning from imperfect tagging. We propose a general and effective learning scheme called the Multi-view Imperfect Tagging Learning (MITL) to this problem. The main idea of MITL lies in extracting the information of the imperfectly tagged training dataset from multiple views to differentiate the data points in the role of classification. Further, a novel discriminative classification method is proposed under the framework of MITL, which explicitly makes use of the given multiple labels simultaneously as an additional feature to deliver a more effective classification performance than the existing literature where one label is considered at a time as the classification target while the rest of the given labels are completely ignored at the same time. The proposed methods can not only complete the incomplete tagging but also denoise the noisy tagging through an inductive learning. We apply the general solution to the problem with a more specific context — imperfect image annotation, and evaluate the proposed methods on a standard dataset from the related literature. Experiments show that they are superior to the peer methods on solving the problem of learning from imperfect tagging in cross-media.

Categories and Subject Descriptors

H.3.3 [**Information Storage and Retrieval**]: Information Search and Retrieval—*Retrieval models*; H.2.8 [**Database Management**]: Database Applications—*Data mining, Image databases*

General Terms

Algorithms, experimentation

Keywords

Imperfect tagging; multi-label space; image annotation completion, correction and prediction

MM'12, October 29–November 2, 2012, Nara, Japan.

(a) (b)

Figure 1: (a) An example of an incompletely tagged image. (b) An example of a noisily tagged image.

1. INTRODUCTION

Tagging, as one of the content forms contained in multimedia, demonstrates a strong power in helping develop effective solutions to many important real-world problems, especially in the cross-media field. For example, with an appropriate tagging to images as part of the annotation, one can develop powerful image annotation and/or image retrieval techniques [15]; with an appropriate tagging to movies as part of the reviews, one can develop powerful movie recommendation systems [25]; and with an appropriate tagging to Web-pages as part of the comments, one can develop more powerful search engines [10].

However, with the typically explosive amount of data to be tagged, one can hardly do tagging manually. Consequently, social tagging has become an effective alternative to many such problems [11], also partly due to the ubiquitous access to the Internet. For social tagging, the tagging results can never be expected to be perfect. The imperfect tagging may result in either of or both of the following two possible tagging scenarios: (1) incomplete tagging, and (2) noisy tagging. Incomplete tagging means that the given tags to a document still fail to give a complete description of the content of the document up to all the details. Figure 1(a) shows such an example for the tags as the annotation to an image. The given annotations of this image are *buildings*, *cityscape*, *sky*, and *street*. However, it is clear from this image that the given annotation tagging is far away from being actually complete. There are many other things missed to be tagged, such as person, tree, water, fountain, and street lamp. Noisy tagging means that the given tags to a document contain errors; in other words, some of the tags are incorrect in describing the content of the document or even completely irrelevant to the document. Figure 1(b) shows such an example of noisy tagging. One of the given tags for the image of Figure 1(b) is *fish*, while it is obvious that the animal in the image of Figure 1(b) is bird instead of fish, and the label *fish* is given incorrectly.

In general an N-class classification problem can always be decomposed into N binary classification problems in one-vs-all (OVA) mode. Figure 2 shows examples of perfect tagging and imperfect tagging in such an OVA binary classification problem. Figure 2(a) is an example of perfect tagging where all the data points are

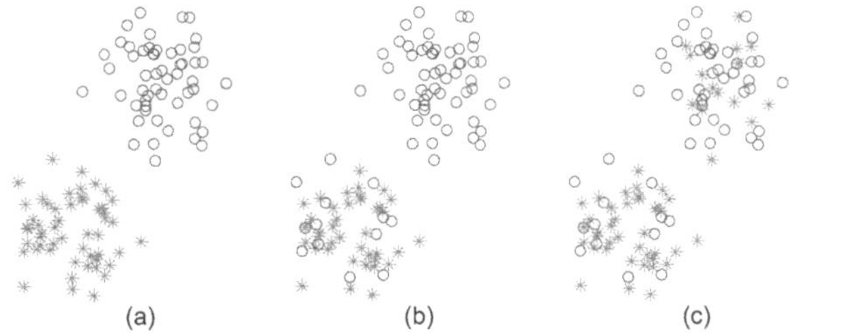

Figure 2: (a) Perfect tagging (The asterisks are tagged as positive ones; the circles are tagged as negative ones). (b) Incomplete tagging (The asterisks are tagged as positive ones; the circles are untagged ones). (c) Noisy tagging (The asterisks are tagged as positive ones; the circles are tagged as negative ones).

correctly tagged. Figure 2(b) visualizes the OVA binary classification with incomplete tags where the asterisks are the given correctly tagged but incomplete data from the positive class, and the circles are the untagged data points possibly from both classes. Figure 2(c) is an example of the OVA binary classification with noise where both the asterisks and the circles contain the data from the positive and the negative classes, and consequently, are cross-tagged in error in the two classes. In fact, incomplete tagging can be considered as a special case of noisy tagging where all the given positive samples are correct.

It is easy to understand that the more tags the data are given, the more information the tag space contains. However, most of the discriminative methods for the multi-label classification problem only consider the multi-label space as the classification target, and fail to make use of the information contained in the multi-label space effectively. Especially in the OVA mode, these classification methods only consider one tag at a time as the classification target while at the same time completely ignore the rest of the tags. In this paper, we explicitly consider all the given tags simultaneous as an additional feature which further helps improve the classification performance. Figure 3 shows exemplar images with multiple tags. The images in the first row in Figure 3, which are all tagged as *fish*, always have the accompanied tags of *water*, *coral*, and *ocean*, while the images in the second row in Figure 3, which are all tagged as *bird*, always have the accompanied tags of *sky*, *cloud*, *grass*, and *tree*. Obviously, these accompanied tags can be utilized as an additional feature to help better distinguish images tagged as *fish* from images tagged as *bird*.

This paper addresses the arguably new problem of learning from imperfect tagging not only to complete the incomplete tagging but also to denoise the noisy tagging through an inductive learning. Even though there is recent literature to address the incomplete tagging and noisy classification separately, combining them as a single, overall problem and thus developing a synergistic solution to address them together in a single framework to this problem are still significant and challenging. On the other hand, an effective solution to this problem shall benefit not only the research community but also the society in substantially improving the quality of the techniques and technologies that rely on social tagging, generating great societal and technical impacts. Further, this paper proposes a new way to make use of the given multiple tags simultaneously as an additional feature to deliver a more effective classification in solving a general multi-label classification problem.

While it is a challenge for a classifier to learn from imperfect tagging, if a multi-view based technique is ready to apply to this problem, an effective classification framework can be constructed to take advantage of the imperfect tagging. The multiple views to be used in the proposed classification framework are similar to the various records obtained by different historians independently on the

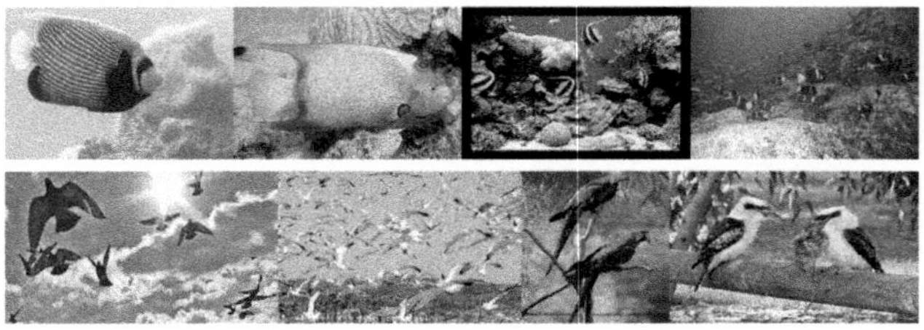

Figure 3: Exemplar images with multiple tags.

same historical event. Though there exist overlaps in these records, the most valuable benefit lies in the non-overlap parts, which help contribute systematically to recovering the whole event or even correcting the sporadic subjectivity existing in the individual records obtained by different historians. Likewise, the classification can be completed or corrected under the multiple classifiers' results systematically in the multi-view based classification framework.

In this paper, we develop a general and synergistic solution which we call Multi-view Imperfect Tagging Learning (MITL) to the problem of learning from imperfect tagging. The main idea of this work lies in extracting the information of the imperfectly tagged training dataset from multiple views to differentiate the data points in the role of classification. Further, a novel discriminative classification method (MSS-2K) which takes advantage of the information contained in the multi-label space is proposed under the framework of MITL. We apply the general solution to the problem with a more specific context — imperfect image annotation, and demonstrate through extensive evaluations using real data that the proposed methods perform well in comparison with the peer methods as an effective and promising solution to the problem of learning from imperfect tagging in cross-media.

2. RELATED WORK

We begin by reviewing the literature in the incomplete tagging and noisy classification areas, and then review the related work on multi-view learning. Finally, we introduce the literature in the field of image annotation and retrieval for we apply MITL to the problem of learning from imperfect tagging with a more specific context — imperfect image annotation.

Most of the existing classification methods, based on either supervised learning or semi-supervised learning, assume that the tagged training data are perfect, which means that there are no incomplete tags or noisy tags contained in the training set. There has been work of incomplete tagging learning and noisy data learning separately in the literature. Partially supervised learning [14] studies the problem where the training set contains a small set of positive examples and a large set of unlabeled examples within both positive and negative instances, as shown in Figure 2(b). In [8, 14, 17], instances which are with the highest confidence to be negative are extracted as the labeled negative examples used to train the classifier based on supervised or semi-supervised learning. Compared with the partially supervised learning of the binary classification problem, Sun et al. [24] propose the Weak Label Learning method which considers the correlation between the labels to solve the weak label problem as a type of multi-label learning. Qi et al. [22] consider the partially annotated image learning as a multi-label problem and solve it by a statistical model.

The noise among the data is categorized into two types: attribute noise and class noise. In this paper, we focus on eliminating the bad effect raised by the class noise. There are a number of denoising methods for classification; they can be further classified into two categories: filtered preprocessing of the data and robust design of the algorithms. In the former category, filtered preprocessing is developed to remove the noise from the training set as much as possible [27, 32]. For the latter category, robust algorithms are designed to reduce the impact of the noise in the classification [16, 19, 26]. Lin and Wang [16] propose the fuzzy SVM to classify the noisy data by assigning a fuzzy membership to the cost of a target function. Liu and Zheng [19] propose the soft SVM, which is capable of dealing with binary as well as real-valued class memberships.

Data represented by multiple views exist in many real-world applications. It has been shown extensively in the literature that leveraging the redundancy among the multiple views can improve the learning performance [6, 13, 23]. Farquhar et al. [6] incorporate the correlation between two views into a single classifier called SVM-2K. Rosenberg et al. [23] plug the multi-view kernel into the standard kernel methods that are based on data-dependent regularization in reproducing kernel Hilbert spaces. However, all the above multi-view approaches use datasets of perfectly tagged instances as the training set, and ignore the noisy and incomplete tags of the training instances in the real-world scenarios.

The image annotation and retrieval problem has been cast as a multi-label learning problem in the literature with various approaches proposed [5]. One category of these approaches is to introduce a set of bridge variables to learn the joint distribution between the image features and the semantic labels by generative models. Barnard et al. [1] propose the mixture of multi-modal Latent Dirichlet Allocation model using the latent variables as the bridge. Blei and Jordan [2] propose the correspondence Latent Dirichlet Allocation model under which each label shares a latent variable with a randomly selected image feature descriptor in one image. In [7, 12], the annotated images in the training set are used as the connection variables to compute the joint probability between the labels and the image regions.

Different from the above approaches, another paradigm for image annotation is to reduce the problem to a set of binary classification problems solved by discriminative methods where each semantic label is considered as an independent class. Boutell et al. [3] introduce several transformation methods that map the multi-label learning problem into the single-label classification problem. A more complicated situation beyond the multi-label learning problem is when an image is represented as a bag of instances, and belongs to a bag of classes. Hence, the original annotation problem becomes a multi-instance and multi-label learning problem. Zhou and Zhang [30] solve this multi-instance and multi-label learning problem by mapping it into a single-instance and multi-label learning problem. The representative technique for this category of approaches is the classification technique such as the Support Vector Machine (SVM), which demonstrates a strong discrimination power [9, 21, 29]. Yang et al. [29] propose an asymmetrical support vector for region-based image annotation. Qi and Han [21] propose an automatic image annotation system, which integrates the multiple instance learning (MIL)-based and global-feature-based SVMs for annotation. However, most of these discriminative methods for image annotation only consider the multi-label space as the classification target, and fail to make use of the given multiple labels simultaneously as an additional feature.

There has been work on image tag refinement in the literature. Wang et al. [28] address the tag optimization problem given the tagging labels of images obtained by a classifier; Zhu et al. [31] propose a classification method to address the noisy tagging problem; neither of the methods explicitly tackles the incomplete tagging problem. Liu et al. [18] propose a solution that denoises the noisy tagging and enriches the incomplete tagging, while their enrichment can only add synonyms and hypernyms, and needs the availability and assistance from WordNet. In addition, the classification solutions in [18] and [31] are not inductive in learning.

Compared with the existing work which is either only able to handle the incomplete tagging learning problem and the noisy data learning problem separately, or is transductive learning only, our work tackles the imperfectly tagged data synergistically not only to make the incomplete tagging to be more complete, but also to make the noisy tagging to be more noise-free through an inductive learning. By reducing the image annotation problem to a set of binary classification problems, the proposed methods are successfully applied to solving the problem of learning from imperfectly annotated images. Further, our work explicitly considers all the given labels simultaneously as an additional feature. Hence, the information contained in the multi-label space can be taken as an advantage to improve the performance of the classification.

3. MODEL FORMULATION

We assume the existence of different views to a dataset, which is typically true in many real-world problems such as image annotation where we have different views to an image dataset from image texture, color, shape, correlated text information, etc. We claim that leveraging the redundancy among the multiple views can improve the performance when learning from the dataset with imperfect tags. It is easy to understand that an instance which is classified into the same category from most of the multiple views is a valuable representation of this category in the role of classification. On the other hand, an instance which is classified into different categories from most of the multiple views is a useless representation of any category in the role of classification. Due to the existence of imperfect tags, different weights should be given to different training instances from the combination of multiple views to reflect their confidence of classification. Without loss of generality, we focus on two views, and develop an iterative learning approach to update the imperfect tagging with a better tagging by leveraging the complementary information from the two views. Further, a novel discriminative classifier based on two views is proposed, which takes advantage of the information contained in the multi-label space to improve the performance when learning from imperfect tagging.

3.1 Data Representations and Symbols

We denote a training dataset as $\mathcal{I}$. Two views of the dataset $\mathcal{I}$ are denoted as $\mathcal{F}^{(a)}$ and $\mathcal{F}^{(b)}$, respectively. Ideally, the two views are conditionally independent. Each instance $I_i \in \mathcal{I}$ is tagged with various tags. The whole tag vocabulary for $\mathcal{I}$ forms the S-dimensional multi-label space $\mathcal{T}$. When one tag T_r $(1 \leq r \leq S)$ is chosen as the classification target, the other tags can form the additional feature space of tags, denoted as $\mathcal{L}$. Obviously, $dim(\mathcal{L})$ is $S-1$. For each $I_i \in \mathcal{I}$, there exist feature descriptors $\mathbf{x}_i^{(a)}$ and $\mathbf{x}_i^{(b)}$ in $\mathcal{F}^{(a)}$ and $\mathcal{F}^{(b)}$, respectively. Let an S-dimensional vector $\mathbf{d}_i = (d_{i,1}, d_{i,2}, \ldots, d_{i,S})'$ be the tag representation for I_i, where $d_{i,r} \in \{0,1\}, 1 \leq r \leq S$ represents the occurrence of the rth tag T_r for I_i. For each tag T_r, $1 \leq r \leq S$, an imperfectly tagged training set of D_r data points is denoted as $\mathscr{D}_r = \{I_i\}_{i=1}^{D_r} = \{\mathbf{x}_i^{(a)}, \mathbf{x}_i^{(b)}, \mathbf{d}_i\}_{i=1}^{D_r}$. For each I_i in $\mathscr{D}_r$, we denote $y_{i,r}$ as the weight of I_i, $f_{i,r}^{(a)}$ and $f_{i,r}^{(b)}$ as the returned values of the classifiers for I_i in $\mathcal{F}^{(a)}$ and $\mathcal{F}^{(b)}$, respectively. Further, $p_{i,r}^{(a)}$ and $p_{i,r}^{(b)}$ are the calibrated posterior probabilities for I_i in $\mathcal{F}^{(a)}$ and $\mathcal{F}^{(b)}$, respectively (see Section 3.4).

3.2 The Overall Framework of MITL

We now apply a learning scheme to the imperfectly tagged training dataset by iteratively updating the weight $y_{i,r}$ of each data point

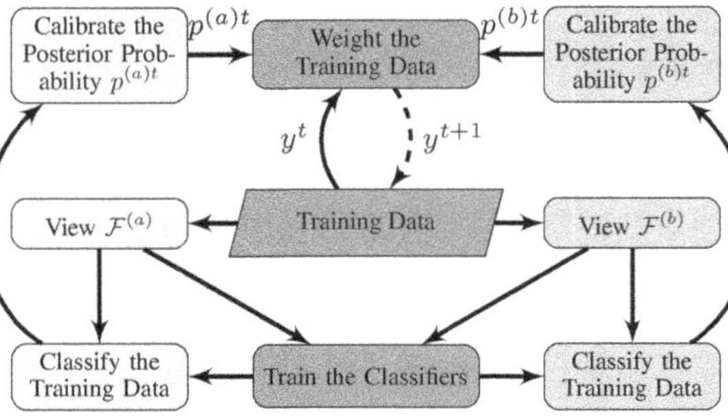

Figure 4: The flow chart of the MITL approach.

I_i in the training set $\mathscr{D}_r$ from views $\mathcal{F}^{(a)}$ and $\mathcal{F}^{(b)}$. The flow chart of MITL is shown in Figure 4. First, we extract feature vectors $\mathbf{x}_i^{(a)}$ and $\mathbf{x}_i^{(b)}$ in views $\mathcal{F}^{(a)}$ and $\mathcal{F}^{(b)}$, respectively. Second, the feature vectors and the weights of the training data are used to train classifiers. Third, the training data are re-classified using the trained classifiers, and the returned $f_{i,r}^{(a)}$ and $f_{i,r}^{(b)}$ are transformed to the posterior probability $p_{i,r}^{(a)}$ and $p_{i,r}^{(b)}$ in $\mathcal{F}^{(a)}$ and $\mathcal{F}^{(b)}$, respectively. Finally, we update the weights of the training data which are the prior of the next iteration. Through updating the weight $y_{i,r}$ from the combination of the two views, the model progressively identifies the missing tags and the incorrect tags, and ultimately makes the classification in each view more precise and complete. Although different views are used jointly during the training process, each view can be utilized independently when predicting tags of any new, untagged instance after the training.

In principle, any classification method which uses the weights of the training data as the prior can be used in the framework of MITL. In this paper, we have developed the Multi-label Soft Support Vector Machine in two views (called MSS-2K) as the core classifier to facilitate incorporating the information contained in the multi-label space, and use the Sigmoid model to calibrate the posterior probability of the classifier. The methods to weight the training data in Figure 4 are different between dealing with the incorrect tags and dealing with the missing tags. The algorithm of the MITL approach is described in Algorithm 1. We discuss the details of the different components of the MITL approach in the following subsections. For the reference purpose, we call the MITL with MSS-2K as the core classifier as MITL in the rest of the paper.

Algorithm 1: MITL algorithm

Initialize $y_{i,r}^0$
  foreach $T_r,\ 1 \le r \le S$ **do**
    foreach $I_i \in \mathscr{D}_r$ **do**
      $y_{i,r}^0 = 2 \cdot d_{i,r} - 1;$
Let $t = 0$;
while $t <$ *the maximum number of iterations* **do**
  foreach $T_r,\ 1 \le r \le S$ **do**
    Select two-thirds instances of $\mathscr{D}_r$ **randomly**
      to form the set $\mathscr{K}_r^t$, $\mathscr{S}_r^t = \mathscr{D}_r - \mathscr{K}_r^t$;
    Train MSS-2K using $y_{i,r}^t$, $\mathbf{x}_i^{(a)}$, $\mathbf{x}_i^{(b)}$, and $\mathbf{d}_i$ of each
      instance $I_i \in \mathscr{K}_r^t$;
    foreach $I_i \in \mathscr{D}_r$ **do**
      Compute the returned values $f_{i,r}^{(z)t}$ of MSS-2K
        in $\mathcal{F}^{(z)}$, $z = a, b$;
    Train the Sigmoid models using $f_{i,r}^{(z)t}$ and $y_{i,r}^t$ of
      each instance $I_i \in \mathscr{S}_r^t$ in $\mathcal{F}^{(z)}$, $z = a, b$;
    foreach $I_i \in \mathscr{D}_r$ **do**
      Calibrate $p_{i,r}^{(z)t+1}$ through the Sigmoid models
        in $\mathcal{F}^{(z)}$, $z = a, b$;
      Update $y_{i,r}^{t+1}$ using $p_{i,r}^{(a)t+1}$, $p_{i,r}^{(b)t+1}$, and $y_{i,r}^t$;
  Let $t = t + 1$;

3.3 Classification: MSS-2K

In the two views learning, we assume that the data in the target dataset are of the following formulation: $I_i = \{\mathbf{x}_i^{(a)}, \mathbf{x}_i^{(b)}, l_i\}_{i=1}^n$, where $\mathbf{x}_i^{(a)}$ ($\mathbf{x}_i^{(b)}$) is a feature vector of I_i in view $\mathcal{F}^{(a)}$ ($\mathcal{F}^{(b)}$), and $l_i \in \{-1, +1\}$ is a class label of I_i. The classic SVM-based classification is achieved through minimizing the distance between support planes constrained by the plane equations of the support vectors. In the two views learning, additional constraints are introduced to maximize the similarity between the classification results of the same instances in the two views. These two views constraints are presented as follows:

$$\forall_{i=1}^n : \quad |\mathbf{w}^{(a)T}\mathbf{x}_i^{(a)} + \hat{b}^{(a)} - \mathbf{w}^{(b)T}\mathbf{x}_i^{(b)} - \hat{b}^{(b)}| \le \eta_i, \ \ \eta_i \ge 0 \quad (1)$$

where $\mathbf{w}^{(a)}$, $\hat{b}^{(a)}$ ($\mathbf{w}^{(b)}$, $\hat{b}^{(b)}$) are the weight and bias of the SVM in $\mathcal{F}^{(a)}$ ($\mathcal{F}^{(b)}$), respectively.

The SVM-based methods solve the binary classification problem by finding the division plane to separate the instances of the two classes. In the OVA mode, these methods only utilize one tag of the data at a time, and ignore the other tags the data contain at the same time. It is easy to understand that the more the number of the tags, the more the information contained in the tag space. Hence, the multi-label space can not only be considered as the classification target, but also be considered as an additional feature to improve the performance of the classification. However, most of the SVM-based methods fail to utilize the given multiple tags simultaneously.

In the OVA mode, when one tag T_r is chosen as the classification target, the other tags can form the additional feature space of the tags $\mathcal{L}$. It is a reasonable assumption that the similarity of the classification is inversely proportional to the distance of the instances in $\mathcal{L}$. Closer instances in $\mathcal{L}$ have a higher similarity in the classification. We denote the feature vector of I_i in $\mathcal{L}$ as L_i, where $L_i = (d_{i,1}, \ldots, d_{i,r-1}, d_{i,r+1}, \ldots, d_{i,S})'$. The neighborhood of L_i in $\mathcal{L}$ (including L_i itself) is denoted as $\mathscr{N}(L_i)$. The information of the multi-label space can then be added into the two views learning by introducing the following constraints:

$$\forall_{i=1}^n \ \textit{and} \ \forall j \in \mathscr{N}_i :$$
$$|\mathbf{w}^{(a)T}\mathbf{x}_i^{(a)} + \hat{b}^{(a)} - \mathbf{w}^{(b)T}\mathbf{x}_j^{(b)} - \hat{b}^{(b)}| \le \eta_{ij}^{(ab)}, \ \ \eta_{ij}^{(ab)} \ge 0 \quad (2)$$
$$|\mathbf{w}^{(b)T}\mathbf{x}_i^{(b)} + \hat{b}^{(b)} - \mathbf{w}^{(a)T}\mathbf{x}_j^{(a)} - \hat{b}^{(a)}| \le \eta_{ij}^{(ba)}, \ \ \eta_{ij}^{(ba)} \ge 0 \quad (3)$$

where $\mathscr{N}_i \triangleq \{j | L_j \in \mathscr{N}(L_i)\}$. Combining these two views constraints (2) and (3) with the typical SVM constraints and allowing different regularization constants, we obtain the following optimization:

$$\min_{\mathbf{w}^{(a)}, \mathbf{w}^{(b)}} \frac{1}{2}\|\mathbf{w}^{(a)}\|^2 + \frac{1}{2}\|\mathbf{w}^{(b)}\|^2 + C^{(a)}\sum_{i=1}^n \xi_i^{(a)} + C^{(b)}\sum_{i=1}^n \xi_i^{(b)}$$
$$+ \sum_{i=1}^n \sum_{j \in \mathscr{N}_i} C_{ij}(\eta_{ij}^{(ab)} + \eta_{ij}^{(ba)})$$
$$C_{ij} = \begin{cases} C & i = j \\ C^* / e^{dis(L_i, L_j)} & i \ne j \quad (C^* < C) \end{cases} \quad (4)$$
$$s.t. \quad \forall_{i=1}^n : \ l_i(\mathbf{w}^{(a)T}\mathbf{x}_i^{(a)} + \hat{b}^{(a)}) \ge 1 - \xi_i^{(a)}, \ \ \xi_i^{(a)} \ge 0$$
$$l_i(\mathbf{w}^{(b)T}\mathbf{x}_i^{(b)} + \hat{b}^{(b)}) \ge 1 - \xi_i^{(b)}, \ \ \xi_i^{(b)} \ge 0$$
$$\forall_{i=1}^n \ \textit{and} \ \forall j \in \mathscr{N}_i :$$
$$|\mathbf{w}^{(a)T}\mathbf{x}_i^{(a)} + \hat{b}^{(a)} - \mathbf{w}^{(b)T}\mathbf{x}_j^{(b)} - \hat{b}^{(b)}| \le \eta_{ij}^{(ab)}, \ \ \eta_{ij}^{(ab)} \ge 0$$
$$|\mathbf{w}^{(b)T}\mathbf{x}_i^{(b)} + \hat{b}^{(b)} - \mathbf{w}^{(a)T}\mathbf{x}_j^{(a)} - \hat{b}^{(a)}| \le \eta_{ij}^{(ba)}, \ \ \eta_{ij}^{(ba)} \ge 0$$

where $dis(L_i, L_j)$ represents the distance between L_i and L_j in $\mathcal{L}$.

In order to reduce the optimization complexity, we need to approximate the optimization by reducing the constraint (3). We show that constraint (3) can be approximately obtained from constraint (2), and vice versa. For $\forall_{i=1}^{n}, \forall j \in \mathcal{N}_i$, we obtain the following constraint from constraint (2):

$$\begin{cases} |w^{(b)T}x_i^{(b)} + \hat{b}^{(b)} - w^{(a)T}x_j^{(a)} - \hat{b}^{(a)}| \le \eta_{ji}^{(ab)} & \text{if } i \in \mathcal{N}_j \\ |w^{(b)T}x_i^{(b)} + \hat{b}^{(b)} - w^{(a)T}x_j^{(a)} - \hat{b}^{(a)}| \le \tilde{\eta}_{ij} & \text{if } i \notin \mathcal{N}_j \end{cases} \quad (5)$$

where $\tilde{\eta}_{ij} = \eta_{ij}^{(ab)} + \eta_{ii}^{(ab)} + \eta_{jj}^{(ab)}$. When $i \in \mathcal{N}_j$, $\eta_{ij}^{(ba)} = \eta_{ji}^{(ab)}$, and (5) coincides with constraint (3) strictly; when $i \notin \mathcal{N}_j$, for $\eta_{ii}^{(ab)}(\eta_{jj}^{(ab)}) < \eta_{ij}^{(ab)}$, (5) coincides with (3) approximately with a little larger constraint variable. Hence, we only select constraint (2) as the multi-label constraint in order to decrease the dimensionality of the parameters, as well as the computational complexity.

Further, in order to use the various weights of the training data in the role of classification, the range of the class label l_i is relaxed from $\{-1, +1\}$ to an interval $[-1, 1]$, which means that l_i can take any real value in $[-1, 1]$ other than only two values in $\{-1, 1\}$. Consequently, MSS-2K is appropriate to be used in MITL by utilizing y_i, the weight of each instance I_i in the training set, as the class label. In MSS-2K, y_i is decomposed into two parts: the sign and the absolute value, i.e., $y_i = \text{sgn}(y_i) \cdot |y_i|$, where $\text{sgn}(y_i)$ is the indicator of the classification, and $|y_i|$ reflects the confidence of the classification. Since $\text{sgn}(y_i) \in \{-1, +1\}$, the constraint in MSS-2K is analogous to the typical SVM constraints:

$$\text{sgn}(y_i) \cdot (\mathbf{w}^T \mathbf{x}_i + \hat{b}) \ge |y_i| - \xi_i, \ \ \xi_i \ge 0. \quad (6)$$

Hence, the optimization is reduced to

$$\begin{aligned} \min_{\mathbf{w}^{(a)}, \mathbf{w}^{(b)}} \ & \frac{1}{2}\|\mathbf{w}^{(a)}\|^2 + \frac{1}{2}\|\mathbf{w}^{(b)}\|^2 + C^{(a)}\sum_{i=1}^{n}|y_i|\xi_i^{(a)} \\ & + C^{(b)}\sum_{i=1}^{n}|y_i|\xi_i^{(b)} + \sum_{i=1}^{n}|y_i|\sum_{j\in\mathcal{N}_i} C_{ij}\eta_{ij}^{(ab)} \\ C_{ij} = & \begin{cases} C & i = j \\ C^*/e^{dis(L_i,\, L_j)} & i \ne j \quad (C^* < C) \end{cases} \\ s.t.\ \forall_{i=1}^{n}: \ & y_i(\mathbf{w}^{(a)T}\mathbf{x}_i^{(a)} + \hat{b}^{(a)}) \ge |y_i|^2 - |y_i|\xi_i^{(a)}, \ \xi_i^{(a)} \ge 0 \\ & y_i(\mathbf{w}^{(b)T}\mathbf{x}_i^{(b)} + \hat{b}^{(b)}) \ge |y_i|^2 - |y_i|\xi_i^{(b)}, \ \xi_i^{(b)} \ge 0 \\ \forall_{i=1}^{n} & \ and\ \forall j \in \mathcal{N}_i: \\ |\mathbf{w}^{(a)T}&\mathbf{x}_i^{(a)} + \hat{b}^{(a)} - \mathbf{w}^{(b)T}\mathbf{x}_j^{(b)} - \hat{b}^{(b)}| \le \eta_{ij}^{(ab)}, \ \eta_{ij}^{(ab)} \ge 0 \end{aligned} \quad (7)$$

With the Lagrange multipliers, we have the target function

$$\begin{aligned} \mathbf{L} = & \frac{1}{2}\|\mathbf{w}^{(a)}\|^2 + \frac{1}{2}\|\mathbf{w}^{(b)}\|^2 + C^{(a)}\sum_{i=1}^{n}|y_i|\xi_i^{(a)} \\ & + C^{(b)}\sum_{i=1}^{n}|y_i|\xi_i^{(b)} + \sum_{i=1}^{n}|y_i|\sum_{j\in\mathcal{N}_i} C_{ij}\eta_{ij}^{(ab)} \\ & - \sum_{i=1}^{n}\alpha_i^{(a)}\left[y_i(\mathbf{w}^{(a)T}\mathbf{x}_i^{(a)} + \hat{b}^{(a)}) - |y_i|^2 + |y_i|\xi_i^{(a)}\right] \\ & - \sum_{i=1}^{n}\alpha_i^{(b)}\left[y_i(\mathbf{w}^{(b)T}\mathbf{x}_i^{(b)} + \hat{b}^{(b)}) - |y_i|^2 + |y_i|\xi_i^{(b)}\right] \\ & - \sum_{i=1}^{n}(\mu_i^{(a)}\xi_i^{(a)} + \mu_i^{(b)}\xi_i^{(b)}) - \sum_{i=1}^{n}\sum_{j\in\mathcal{N}_i}\Big[\mu_{ij}^{(ab)}\eta_{ij}^{(ab)} \\ & + \beta_{ij}^{(ab)+}(\eta_{ij}^{(ab)} - \mathbf{w}^{(a)T}\mathbf{x}_i^{(a)} - \hat{b}^{(a)} + \mathbf{w}^{(b)T}\mathbf{x}_j^{(b)} + \hat{b}^{(b)}) \\ & + \beta_{ij}^{(ab)-}(\eta_{ij}^{(ab)} + \mathbf{w}^{(a)T}\mathbf{x}_i^{(a)} + \hat{b}^{(a)} - \mathbf{w}^{(b)T}\mathbf{x}_j^{(b)} - \hat{b}^{(b)})\Big] \end{aligned} \quad (8)$$

where $\alpha_i^{(a)}$, $\alpha_i^{(b)}$, $\beta_{ij}^{(ab)+}$, $\beta_{ij}^{(ab)-}$, $\mu_i^{(a)}$, $\mu_i^{(b)}$ and $\mu_{ij}^{(ab)}$ are the Lagrange multipliers. We claim that if the KKT condition of (8) shown in (9) is satisfied, the solution to (7) is the same as that to its dual problem.

$$\begin{cases} \nabla\mathbf{L} = 0 \\ \forall_{i=1}^{n}: \ \alpha_i^{(z)}\left[y_i(\mathbf{w}^{(z)T}\mathbf{x}_i^{(z)} + \hat{b}^{(z)}) - |y_i|^2 + |y_i|\xi_i^{(z)}\right] = 0, \\ \quad \mu_i^{(z)}\xi_i^{(z)} = 0, \quad z = a,\ b \\ \forall_{i=1}^{n}\ and\ \forall j \in \mathcal{N}_i: \ \mu_{ij}^{(ab)}\eta_{ij}^{(ab)} = 0, \\ \quad \beta_{ij}^{(ab)+}(\eta_{ij}^{(ab)} - \mathbf{w}^{(a)T}\mathbf{x}_i^{(a)} - \hat{b}^{(a)} + \mathbf{w}^{(b)T}\mathbf{x}_j^{(b)} + \hat{b}^{(b)}) = 0, \\ \quad \beta_{ij}^{(ab)-}(\eta_{ij}^{(ab)} + \mathbf{w}^{(a)T}\mathbf{x}_i^{(a)} + \hat{b}^{(a)} - \mathbf{w}^{(b)T}\mathbf{x}_j^{(b)} - \hat{b}^{(b)}) = 0. \end{cases} \quad (9)$$

Let $\nu_{ij}^{(ab)} = \beta_{ij}^{(ab)+} - \beta_{ij}^{(ab)-}$. From $\nabla\mathbf{L} = 0$, we have

$$\begin{aligned} & \mathbf{w}^{(a)} = \sum_{i=1}^{n}\alpha_i^{(a)}y_i\mathbf{x}_i^{(a)} - \sum_{i=1}^{n}\sum_{j\in\mathcal{N}_i}\nu_{ij}^{(ab)}\mathbf{x}_i^{(a)} \\ & \mathbf{w}^{(b)} = \sum_{i=1}^{n}\alpha_i^{(b)}y_i\mathbf{x}_i^{(b)} + \sum_{i=1}^{n}\sum_{j\in\mathcal{N}_i}\nu_{ij}^{(ab)}\mathbf{x}_j^{(b)} \\ & \sum_{i=1}^{n}(\alpha_i^{(a)}y_i - \sum_{j\in\mathcal{N}_i}\nu_{ij}^{(ab)}) = \sum_{i=1}^{n}(\alpha_i^{(b)}y_i + \sum_{j\in\mathcal{N}_i}\nu_{ij}^{(ab)}) = 0 \\ & \forall_{i=1}^{n}: \ C^{(a)}\,y_i| - \alpha_i^{(a)}|y_i| - \mu_i^{(a)} = C^{(b)}|y_i| - \alpha_i^{(b)}|y_i| - \mu_i^{(b)} = 0 \\ & \forall_{i=1}^{n}\ and\ \forall j \in \mathcal{N}_i: \ \beta_{ij}^{(ab)+} + \beta_{ij}^{(ab)-} + \mu_{ij}^{(ab)} - |y_i|C_{ij} = 0 \end{aligned} \quad (10)$$

Substituting the results from (9) and (10) to (8), we obtain the dual problem of (7) as follows:

$$\begin{aligned} \max \ & -\frac{1}{2}\sum_{i,k=1}^{n}\Big[(\alpha_i^{(a)}y_i\mathbf{x}_i^{(a)} - \sum_{j\in\mathcal{N}_i}\nu_{ij}^{(ab)}\mathbf{x}_i^{(c)}) \\ & \cdot(\alpha_k^{(a)}y_k\mathbf{x}_k^{(a)} - \sum_{h\in\mathcal{N}_k}\nu_{kh}^{(ab)}\mathbf{x}_k^{(a)}) \\ & + (\alpha_i^{(b)}y_i\mathbf{x}_i^{(b)} + \sum_{j\in\mathcal{N}_i}\nu_{ij}^{(ab)}\mathbf{x}_j^{(b)}) \\ & \cdot(\alpha_k^{(b)}y_k\mathbf{x}_k^{(b)} + \sum_{h\in\mathcal{N}_k}\nu_{kh}^{(ab)}\mathbf{x}_h^{(b)})\Big] + \sum_{i=1}^{n}(\alpha_i^{(a)} + \alpha_i^{(b)})|y_i|^2 \\ s.t. \ & \sum_{i=1}^{n}(\alpha_i^{(a)}y_i - \sum_{j\in\mathcal{N}_i}\nu_{ij}^{(ab)}) = 0 \\ & \sum_{i=1}^{n}(\alpha_i^{(b)}y_i + \sum_{j\in\mathcal{N}_i}\nu_{ij}^{(ab)}) = 0 \\ & \forall_{i=1}^{n}: \ 0 \le \alpha_i^{(a)} \le C^{(a)}, \quad 0 \le \alpha_i^{(b)} \le C^{(b)} \\ & \forall_{i=1}^{n}\ and\ \forall j \in \mathcal{N}_i: \ \beta_{ij}^{(ab)+/-} \ge 0, \ \ \beta_{ij}^{(ab)+} + \beta_{ij}^{(ab)-} \le |y_i|C_{ij} \end{aligned} \quad (11)$$

3.4 Calibrating the Posterior Probability

After the process of training MSS-2K for each T_r $(1 \le r \le S)$, the parameters of the classifiers, $\mathbf{w}_r^{(z)}$ and $b_r^{(z)}$ $(z = a,\ b)$, have been optimized and the returned values of the classifiers $f_{i,r}^{(z)} = \mathbf{w}_r^{(z)T}\mathbf{x}_i^{(z)} + \hat{b}_r^{(z)}$ in view $\mathcal{F}^{(z)}$ $(z = a, b)$ can be computed. The value of $f_{i,r}^{(z)}$ should be confined to $[0, 1]$ to cast a posterior probability of the class labels using the Sigmoid model [20] as

$$p_{i,r}^{(z)} = (e^{Af_{i,r}^{(z)}+B})/(1 + e^{Af_{i,r}^{(z)}+B}) \quad z = a,\ b \quad (12)$$

Hence, the posterior log-likelihood of the class labels in the training dataset of size n is

$$\mathbf{H}_r^{(z)} = \log \prod_{i=1}^{n} P[\mathrm{sgn}(y_{i,r}) = 1 | f_{i,r}^{(z)}]^{t_{i,r}} P[\mathrm{sgn}(y_{i,r}) = -1 | f_{i,r}^{(z)}]^{1-t_{i,r}}$$

$$= \sum_{i=1}^{n} t_{i,r} \log p_{i,r}^{(z)} + (1 - t_{i,r}) \log(1 - p_{i,r}^{(z)}), \quad z = a, b \qquad (13)$$

where $t_{i,r} = \frac{1}{2}(1 + \mathrm{sgn}(y_{i,r}))$ is an index variable. The regression coefficients A and B for each T_r $(1 \leq r \leq S)$ in view $\mathcal{F}^{(z)}$ $(z = a, b)$ can be obtained numerically by maximizing the posterior log-likelihood.

As shown in Algorithm 1, we randomly select two-thirds data points from $\mathscr{D}_r$ to form the set $\mathscr{K}_r^t$ in each iteration t, which is used to train MSS-2K for each tag T_r $(1 \leq r \leq S)$. The remaining data points in $\mathscr{D}_r - \mathscr{K}_r^t$ are used to train the sigmoid model, and all the data points in $\mathscr{D}_r$ are re-weighted as the prior to the next iteration. This iterative process avoids the over-fitting problem [20].

3.5 Weighting the Training Data

The methods to weight the training data in Figure 4, i.e., Step 20 in Algorithm 1, are different between dealing with the incorrect tags and handling the missing tags. The details of the methods are shown in Algorithm 2 and Algorithm 3, respectively.

3.5.1 *Correcting the incorrect tags*

As shown in Figure 2(c), both the asterisks and the circles contain the data from the positive and the negative classes. First, we give different weights to different data points in the training set by integrating the results of the two views and shifting the weights to the range $[-1, 1]$ in Step 2 of Algorithm 2. It is assumed that the number of the correctly tagged data points is always larger than that of the incorrectly tagged data points in each class in the training set. Hence, we reinforce the classification confidence of the instance and set $|y_{i,r}| = 1$ if the updated values of $y_{i,r}$ are both larger than e or both smaller than $-e$ in the consecutive two iterations. Here e is a threshold which is set appropriately in $(\frac{1}{2}, 1)$ to select the instances with the highest confidence to be positive or negative.

Algorithm 2: Weight the Training Data for Incorrect Tags

```
1 foreach I_i ∈ D_r do
2     Compute q_{i,r}^{t+1} = p_{i,r}^{(a)t+1} + p_{i,r}^{(b)t+1} - 1;
3     if sgn(q_{i,r}^{t+1}) = sgn(y_{i,r}^t) and |q_{i,r}^{t+1}| > e and |y_{i,r}^t| > e then
4         sgn(y_{i,r}^{t+1}) = sgn(q_{i,r}^{t+1}), |y_{i,r}^{t+1}| = 1;
5     else
6         y_{i,r}^{t+1} = q_{i,r}^{t+1};
```

3.5.2 *Completing the missing tags*

In the binary classification of the OVA mode, the incompletely tagged training set only contains correctly tagged positive instances and untagged instances. As Figure 2(b) shows, the asterisks are all the correctly tagged data points from the positive class, and we do not know which class each of the circles belongs to. In the initialization, we randomly select the untagged data points to be tagged as negative instances with the same number of the positive instances to train the classifiers, i.e., for each $I_i \in \mathscr{D}_r$, if I_i is untagged but selected as an initially negative instance, $y_{i,r}^0 = -1$. In the subsequent iterations, different weights are given to all the data points in $\mathscr{D}_r$, while the initially positive instances, i.e. $\mathrm{sgn}(y_{i,r}^0) = 1$, should be kept positive in all the iterations. Hence, in Step 8 of Algorithm 3, we shift the initially positive instances, which are set to negative values in the updating process, from the updating range to the range $[0, c]$ linearly, where c is set appropriately in $(0, \frac{1}{2})$ for these instances are not typical as the representations of the positive category in the training process.

Algorithm 3: Weight the Training Data for Missing Tags

```
1 foreach I_i ∈ D_r do
2     Compute q_{i,r}^{t+1} = p_{i,r}^{(a)t+1} + p_{i,r}^{(b)t+1} - 1;
3 Find Max_r = max_i q_{i,r}^{t+1} and Min_r = min_i q_{i,r}^{t+1},
      when sgn(q_{i,r}^{t+1}) = -1 and sgn(y_{i,r}^0) = 1;
4 foreach I_i ∈ D_r do
5     if sgn(q_{i,r}^{t+1}) = sgn(y_{i,r}^t) and |q_{i,r}^{t+1}| > e and |y_{i,r}^t| > e then
6         sgn(y_{i,r}^{t+1}) = sgn(q_{i,r}^{t+1}), |y_{i,r}^{t+1}| = 1;
7     else if sgn(q_{i,r}^{t+1}) = -1 and sgn(y_{i,r}^0) = 1 then
8         y_{i,r}^{t+1} = c · (q_{i,r}^{t+1} - Min_r)/(Max_r - Min_r),
          where 0 < c < 1/2;
9     else
10        y_{i,r}^{t+1} = q_{i,r}^{t+1};
```

4. EXPERIMENTS

4.1 Data and Parameter Setting

We apply our methods, including MSS-2K and MITL, to the problem of learning from imperfect tagging with a more specific context — imperfect image annotation. Since the current literature considers the learning from imperfect tagging problem as incomplete tagging learning and noisy data learning two separate problems, two groups of comparative experiments on these two tasks are conducted to evaluate the performances of our methods. On the former task, we compare MSS-2K and MITL with SVM, iter-SVM [17], co-training (with SVMs as classifiers), and SVM-2K [6] using the incompletely tagged images as the training set. On the latter task, we compare MSS-2K and MITL with SVM, fuzzy SVM [16], co-training, and SVM-2K using the noisily tagged images as the training set.

The NUS-WIDE [4] image database is used in the experiments. It includes 269,648 web images and 81 concepts which we treat as the ground truth tags. Since the database has a very uneven distribution for the number of images corresponding to each concept, we choose the top 75 concepts whose numbers of positive examples are larger than 350 from the database to form the multi-label space $\mathcal{T}$. Hence, the dimensionality of the additional feature space of tags ($\mathcal{L}$) for each $\mathcal{T}_r$ is 74. For each concept, we randomly choose 150 positive examples and 150 negative examples to form the perfectly tagged training set. In the testing set, the numbers of the positive and negative examples are both 100. The left 100 positive examples and 100 randomly selected negative examples form the extra untagged data used only for co-training. For the task of completing missing tags, we formulate the untagged data of the incompletely tagged training set through combining all the negative instances of the perfectly tagged training set with $v\%$ randomly selected positive instances of the perfectly tagged training set. The whole incompletely tagged training set, as shown in Figure 2(b), comprises the newly created untagged instances and the residual $1 - v\%$ positive instances. For the task of correcting incorrect tags, $s\%$ noise is added into both of the positive and negative

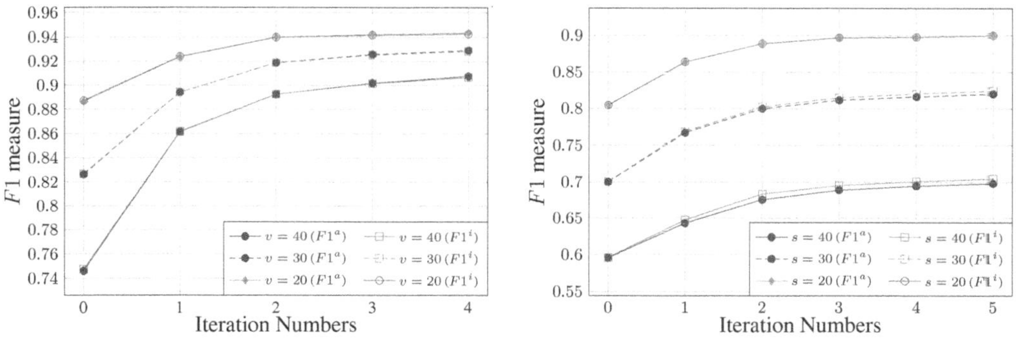

(a) Incomplete tagging learning (b) Noisy data learning

Figure 5: The F1 measure for the imperfectly tagged training set using MITL when $\mathbf{u} = 4$ and $\mathbf{R} = 1.2$.

examples of the perfectly tagged training set for each concept to form the noisily tagged training set. In the experiments, the 500-D bag of words feature based on SIFT descriptions is used as the feature of view $\mathcal{F}^{(a)}$, and the 1000-D bag of text words feature which describes the text information correlated to the images provided by the database is used as the feature of view $\mathcal{F}^{(b)}$. For the task of completing the missing tags, SVM, co-training, SVM-2K, and MSS-2K use the same initialization as MITL does described in Section 3.5.2 to obtain the initially negative training data from the incompletely tagged training set.

The size u of the neighborhood $\mathcal{N}(L_i)$ for each L_i is defined as the count of the nearest neighbors of L_i in $\mathcal{L}$. When $u = 1$ and each $|y_i| = 1$, MSS-2K is reduced to SVM-2K. We define R as the ratio between different kinds of regularization constants. For MSS-2K, $R = \sum_{i=1}^{n} \sum_{j \in \mathcal{N}_i} C_{ij} / \left(\frac{n}{2} \cdot (C^a + C^b)\right)$. The returned value of the classifiers in two views combined is denoted as $f_{i,r}^{(ab)}$, $f_{i,r}^{(ab)} = 0.5 \cdot (f_{i,r}^{(a)} + f_{i,r}^{(b)})$.

4.2 Results and Discussions

For each tag T_r, let CT_r be the number of correctly predicted examples, GT_r be the number of the examples which actually have the tag as the ground truth, and PT_r be the number of all the predicted examples with the tag. Then the precision Pre_r, recall Rec_r, and $F1_r$ measure are defined as

$$Pre_r = \frac{CT_r}{PT_r};\; Rec_r = \frac{CT_r}{GT_r};\; F1_r = \frac{2Pre_r Rec_r}{Pre_r + Rec_r} = \frac{2CT_r}{PT_r + GT_r}$$

We evaluate the performances of the methods using the standard performance measures of Macro-$F1$ and Micro-$F1$. Macro-$F1$ averages the $F1$ measures on the predictions of different tags; Micro-$F1$ computes the $F1$ measure on the predictions of different labels as a whole.

$$F1^a = \frac{1}{S}\sum_{r=1}^{S} F1_r; \quad F1^i = \frac{2\sum_{r=1}^{S} CT_r}{\sum_{r=1}^{S} PT_r + \sum_{r=1}^{S} GT_r}$$

We describe the $F1$ measure for the incompletely tagged training set and for the noisily tagged training set using MITL as a function of the iteration in Figure 5(a) and Figure 5(b), respectively. We observe from Figure 5 that the $F1$ measures increase 6% to 16% for the incompletely tagged training set, and 9% to 12% for the noisily tagged training set after the iteration progresses, which shows that MITL is effective in completing the missing tags and in correcting the incorrect tags for the training set. Due to the elimination of the incompleteness and noise in the training set, the training accuracies increase. The curves in Figure 5(a) level up more than those in Figure 5(b), because the initially positive examples are kept positive during the whole iterations on the task of completing the missing tags. We choose the maximum numbers of iterations for MITL based on the $F1$ measure of the training set. The curves for the $F1$ measure of MITL in Figure 5(a) and Figure 5(b) all exhibit their major elevation between the first two iterations, then level off during the subsequent iterations and quickly converge, indicating that MITL converges fast.

In Table 1, we summarize the $F1$ measure for the testing set with the imperfectly tagged training set in View $\mathcal{F}^{(a)}$, in View $\mathcal{F}^{(b)}$, and in two views combined, respectively. On incomplete tagging learning, we compare our methods with SVM, iter-SVM, co-training, and SVM-2K when v is selected as 40, 30, 20, and 10, respectively. On noisy data learning, we compare our methods with SVM, fuzzy SVM, co-training, and SVM-2K when s is selected as 40, 30, 20, and 10, respectively.

Compared with our proposed method MITL, SVM with the imperfectly tagged training set considers the training set as the perfectly tagged set and mistakenly takes the missing or incorrect tags as perfect tags. MSS-2K also considers the training set as the perfectly tagged set, while it utilizes the information contained in the multi-label space which helps eliminate the incompleteness and noise in the imperfectly tagged training set. Although iter-SVM and fuzzy SVM consider the training set as incompletely tagged or noisily tagged dataset, respectively, they cannot use the information contained in multiple views synergistically, and cannot consider all the given multiple tags simultaneously as an additional feature as MSS-2K and MITL do. SVM-2K utilizes the information contained in multiple views synergistically, but it mistakenly takes the missing or incorrect tags as perfect tags in the imperfectly tagged training set. Consequently, from Table 1, we see that MITL performs better than SVM, iter-SVM, SVM-2K, and MSS-2K with the incompletely tagged training set, and performs better than SVM, fuzzy SVM, SVM-2K, and MSS-2K with the noisily tagged training set all in view $\mathcal{F}^{(a)}$, in view $\mathcal{F}^{(b)}$, and in two views combined when v and s are selected as 40, 30, 20, and 10, respectively. The performance of MSS-2K is inferior to the performance of MITL but superior to the performances of the other methods. The performance of MITL is much better than those of co-training both with incompletely tagged and noisily tagged training sets when v and s are chosen as 40, 30, and 20, respectively. When the ratios of the incomplete tags and the noisy tags are small, i.e., $v = 10$ and $s = 10$, MITL performs slightly better than co-training because of the usage of the extra untagged training set in co-training, which is not available to MITL. Co-training considers the imperfectly tagged training data as perfectly tagged data and holds both the

Table 1: The F1 measure for the testing set.

(a) The $F1^a \backslash F1^i$ for the testing set on incomplete tagging learning in View $\mathcal{F}^{(a)}$ and View $\mathcal{F}^{(b)}$, respectively.

	$F1^a \backslash F1^i$ *in View* $\mathcal{F}^{(a)}$				$F1^a \backslash F1^i$ *in View* $\mathcal{F}^{(b)}$			
	$v = 40$	$v = 30$	$v = 20$	$v = 10$	$v = 40$	$v = 30$	$v = 20$	$v = 10$
SVM	0.6441\0.6492	0.6816\0.6844	0.6971\0.6988	0.7142\7164	0.7836\0.7855	0.8080\0.8089	0.8255\0.8263	0.8420\0.8438
Iter-SVM	0.6617\0.6675	0.6903\0.6931	0.7033\0.7051	0.7156\0.7179	0.8100\0.8077	0.8149\0.8160	0.8301\0.8292	0.8440\0.8440
Co-training	0.6577\0.6625	0.6877\0.6901	0.7060\0.7076	0.7212\0.7233	0.7887\0.7905	0.8140\0.8147	0.8322\0.8328	0.8505\0.8521
SVM-2K	0.6539\0.6605	0.6904\0.6930	0.6978\0.6993	0.7139\0.7159	0.7889\0.7895	0.8117\0.8124	0.8292\0.8304	0.8483\0.8494
MSS-2K	0.6811\0.6859	0.7092\0.7118	0.7194\0.7208	0.7259\0.7274	0.8101\0.8119	0.8271\0.8276	0.8370\0.8383	0.8505\0.8519
MITL	**0.7043\0.7088**	**0.7227\0.7243**	**0.7264\0.7266**	**0.7280\0.7290**	**0.8346\0.8360**	**0.8443\0.8445**	**0.8476\0.8467**	**0.8554\0.8563**

(b) The $F1^a \backslash F1^i$ for the testing set on noisy data learning in View $\mathcal{F}^{(a)}$ and View $\mathcal{F}^{(b)}$, respectively.

	$F1^a \backslash F1^i$ *in View* $\mathcal{F}^{(a)}$				$F1^a \backslash F1^i$ *in View* $\mathcal{F}^{(b)}$			
	$s = 40$	$s = 30$	$s = 20$	$s = 10$	$s = 40$	$s = 30$	$s = 20$	$s = 10$
SVM	0.5698\0.5761	0.6279\0.6330	0.6830\0.6852	0.7084\0.7093	0.6065\0.6133	0.7062\0.7099	0.7796\0.7815	0.8314\0.8307
Fuzzy SVM	0.5891\0.5954	0.6430\0.6481	0.6922\0.6944	0.7137\0.7146	0.6288\0.6314	0.7233\0.7261	0.7901\0.7903	0.8352\0.8342
Co-training	0.5768\0.5819	0.6353\0.6401	0.6895\0.6915	0.7148\0.7157	0.6127\0.6176	0.7129\0.7163	0.7857\0.7874	0.8361\0.8352
SVM-2K	0.5708\0.5776	0.6315\0.6375	0.6990\0.7018	0.7087\0.7098	0.6080\0.6116	0.7020\0.7056	0.7702\0.7721	0.8362\0.8362
MSS-2K	0.6036\0.6130	0.6648\0.6737	0.7071\0.7097	0.7210\0.7213	0.6365\0.6433	0.7451\0.7489	0.8076\0.8090	0.8414\0.8410
MITL	**0.6265\0.6349**	**0.6819\0.6896**	**0.7181\0.7208**	**0.7268\0.7272**	**0.6808\0.6863**	**0.7865\0.7888**	**0.8328\0.8338**	**0.8529\0.8521**

(c) The $F1^a \backslash F1^i$ for the testing set in two views combined on incomplete tagging learning and on noisy data learning, respectively.

	$F1^a \backslash F1^i$ *in two views combined on incomplete tagging learning*					$F1^a \backslash F1^i$ *in two views combined on noisy data learning*			
	$v = 40$	$v = 30$	$v = 20$	$v = 10$		$s = 40$	$s = 30$	$s = 20$	$s = 10$
SVM	0.7850\0.7887	0.8207\0.8221	0.8381\0.8397	0.8532\0.8549	SVM	0.6140\0.6210	0.7137\0.7184	0.7956\0.7984	0.8452\0.8443
Iter-SVM	0.8177\0.8161	0.8285\0.8304	0.8433\0.8430	0.8543\0.8552	Fuzzy SVM	0.6393\0.6423	0.7337\0.7384	0.8101\0.8101	0.8498\0.8489
Co-training	0.7927\0.7959	0.8236\0.8248	0.8470\0.8484	0.8636\0.8651	Co-training	0.6190\0.6258	0.7229\0.7271	0.8030\0.8046	0.8563\0.8554
SVM-2K	0.7962\0.7996	0.8271\0.8281	0.8443\0.8455	0.8597\0.8610	SVM-2K	0.6138\0.6188	0.7183\0.7230	0.7965\0.7983	0.8516\0.8510
MSS-2K	0.8175\0.8209	0.8444\0.8454	0.8527\0.8543	0.8623\0.8639	MSS-2K	0.6387\0.6466	0.7614\0.7665	0.8249\0.8265	0.8584\0.8580
MITL	**0.8419\0.8447**	**0.8589\0.8595**	**0.8606\0.8619**	**0.8670\0.8681**	MITL	**0.6841\0.6907**	**0.7986\0.8030**	**0.8475\0.8492**	**0.8672\0.8662**

initially positive and initially negative instances unchanged. In the training process, co-training extracts the instances with the highest confidence to be positive or negative from the extra untagged set added into the training set iteratively and progressively from multiple views. The higher the ratios of the imperfect tags in the training set, the more noisy the instances extracted from the extra untagged set to be added into the training set by co-training. Consequently, co-training performs much worse than MITL when more imperfect tags are contained in the training set. In general, MITL and MSS-2K perform well with the imperfectly tagged training set not only on the task of completing the missing tags, but also on the task of correcting the incorrect tags. Combining the two views delivers a better performance than using any of the two views independently, while we also observe from Table 1 that after the training process, the classifiers in each of the two views $\mathcal{F}^{(a)}$ and $\mathcal{F}^{(b)}$ can work independently without the information of the other view, and perform more precisely when predicting tags of any new, untagged image. Further, from Table 1 we also observe that our proposed methods perform much better than the other methods when the incompleteness ratio $v\%$ increases and the noise ratio $s\%$ increases, respectively.

We describe the $F1$ measure for the testing set as a function of u when using MSS-2K and MITL on incomplete tagging learning and on noisy data learning in Figure 6(a) and Figure 6(b), respectively. We observe from Figure 6 that the $F1$ measures for the testing set all increase when the size of the neighborhood for each $\mathcal{N}(L_i)$ increases, which shows that it is helpful to use the nearest neighbors of each L_i in $\mathcal{L}$ to further improve the classification performance, and that it is able to deliver a more effective classification performance when considering all the given tags simultaneous as an additional feature in the proposed methods. The curves for the F1 measures of MSS-2K and MITL in Figure 6 all exhibit their major elevation from $u = 1$ to $u = 4$, then level off or even decline a little when u continues to increase, indicating that there is no need to choose a much larger u which would increase the computational complexity. As we describe before, when $u = 1$ and each $|y_i| = 1$, MSS-2K is reduced to SVM-2K. Figure 6 shows that the performances of MSS-2K and MITL are much better than that of SVM-2K.

Figure 7(a) and Figure 7(b) show the $F1$ measure for the testing set as a function of R when using MSS-2K and MITL on incomplete tagging learning and on noisy data learning, respectively. As we defined before, R represents the ratio between different kinds of regularization constants. When R increases, the proportion of the two views constraints in the optimization also increases, while the proportion of the typical SVM constraints in the optimization decreases. We observe from Figure 7 that when R increases, the curves for the $F1$ measures of MSS-2K and MITL ascend, which shows that the two views constraints are more valuable than the typical SVM constraints in MSS-2K and MITL, and that it is helpful to take advantage of the information contained in the multi-label space to further improve the classification performance. Further, in Figure 7, the performance of MITL is better than that of MSS-2K regardless of what value R is, indicating the effectiveness of the general framework of MITL.

Figure 8 shows the $F1$ measure of each tag for the testing set using MITL on incomplete tagging learning when $v = 30$, and Figure 9 shows the $F1$ measure of each tag for the testing set using MITL on noisy data learning when $s = 20$.

As a further case study to demonstrate the superiority of the MITL performance, Figure 1(a) is one of the imperfectly tagged training images in the training data of NUS-WIDE database with the given ground truth tags to this image as *buildings*, *cityscape*, *sky*, and *street*, and Figure 1(b) is another imperfectly tagged training images in the training data of NUS-WIDE database with the given ground truth tags to this image as *animal* and *fish*. After the learning with MITL, Figure 1(a) is also tagged with the missing tags *person*, *tree*, and *water*, which actually are the objects in the

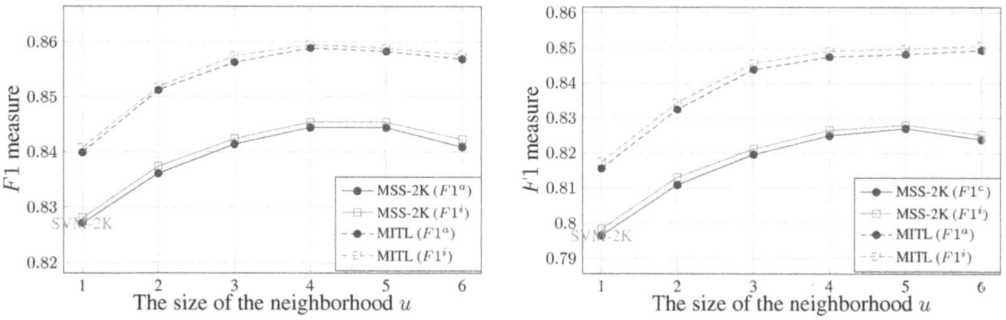

(a) Incomplete tagging learning when $v = 30$. (b) Noisy data learning when $s = 20$.

Figure 6: The F1 measure for the testing set in two views combined using MSS-2K and MITL when R = 1.2.

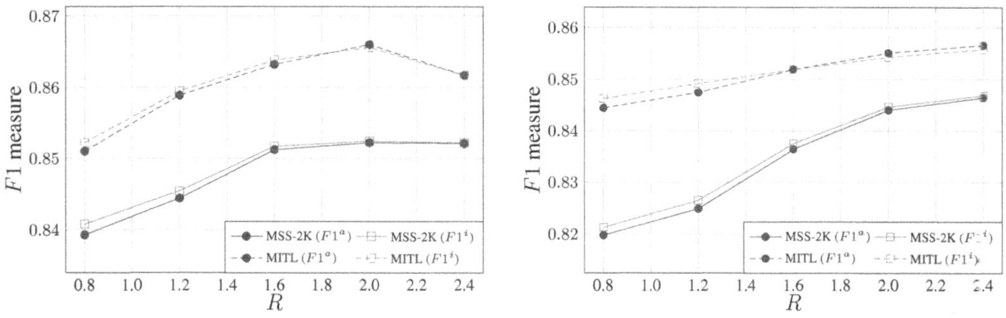

(a) Incomplete tagging learning when $v = 30$. (b) Noisy data learning when $s = 20$.

Figure 7: The F1 measure for the testing set in two views combined using MSS-2K and MITL when u = 4.

image but are not originally given in the ground truth. With MITL, the animal in Figure 1(b) is tagged as *bird* instead of *fish*, which is identified as a noisy tag originally given in the ground truth incorrectly. Further, Figure 1(b) is also tagged with the missing tag *plants*, which actually is the object in the image but is not originally given in the ground truth. This shows that MITL is an effective discriminative method not only to complete the missing tags for the incompletely tagged training set, but also to correct the incorrect tags originally given in the noisily tagged training set.

5. CONCLUSION

This paper studies the arguably new and important problem of learning from imperfect tagging. We argue that this problem exists in many real-world applications and that the solutions to this problem shall generate great societal and technical impacts. We then develop a general and effective solution which we call Multi-view Imperfect Tagging Learning (MITL) to this problem. The novelty of the proposed approach is that it can not only use the incompletely tagged training data to complete the missing tags, but also use the noisily tagged training data to correct the incorrect tags through an inductive learning. Multiple views are used in the training process while each view can be utilized independently when predicting tags of any new, untagged data, and the performances of the classifiers in the multiple views are significantly improved after the training. Further, a novel discriminative classification method called MSS-2K is proposed under the framework of MITL, which explicitly makes use of the given multiple labels simultaneously as an additional feature to deliver a more effective classification performance than the existing literature where one label is considered at a time as the classification target while the rest of the given labels are completely ignored at the same time. We apply our methods MITL and MSS-2K to the problem with a more specific context — imperfect image annotation, and evaluate them on a standard dataset from the related literature in comparison with peer methods from the recent literature. Experimental results demonstrate the effectiveness and promise of our methods as solutions to the problem of learning from imperfect tagging.

6. ACKNOWLEDGMENTS

This work is supported in part by National Basic Research Program of China (2012CB316400), and ZJU–Alibaba Joint Lab. Zhongfei Zhang is also supported in part by US NSF (IIS-0812114, CCF-1017828).

7. REFERENCES

[1] K. Barnard, P. Duygulu, D. Forsyth, N. de Freitas, D. M. Blei, and M. I. Jordan. Matching words and pictures. *Journal of Machine Learning Research*, 3:1107–1135, 2003.

[2] D. M. Blei and M. I. Jordan. Modeling annotated data. In *Proceedings of the 26th International ACM SIGIR Conference*, 2003.

[3] M. R. Boutell, J. Luo, X. Shen, and C. M. Brown. Learning multi-label scene classification. *Pattern Recognition*, 37(9):1757–1771, 2004.

[4] T. S. Chua, J. Tang, R. Hong, H. Li, Z. Luo, and Y. Zheng. Nus-wide: a real-world web image database from national university of singapore. In *Proceedings of the ACM International Conference on Image and Video Retrieval*, pages 1–9, 2009.

[5] R. Datta, D. Joshi, J. Li, and J. Z. Wang. Image retrieval: Ideas, influences, and trends of the new age. *ACM Computing Surveys*, 40:1–60, 2008.

[6] J. Farquhar, D. Hardoon, H. Meng, J. Shawe-Taylor, and S. Szedmak. Two view learning: SVM-2K, theory and

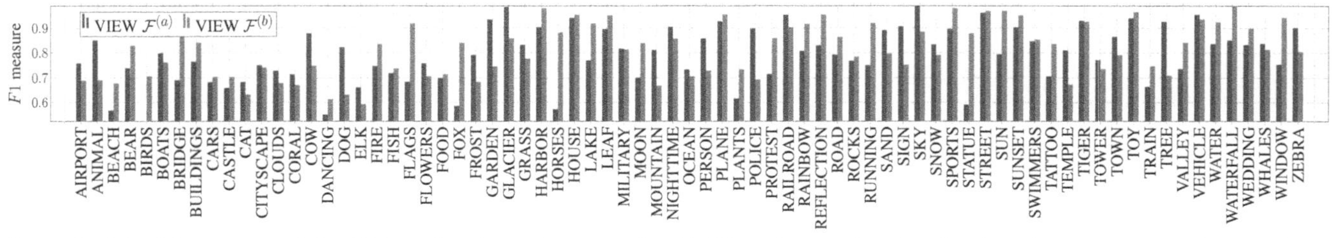

Figure 8: The F1 measure of the 75 tags for the testing set using MITL on incomplete tagging learning when $v = 30$, $u = 4$, and $R = 1.2$.

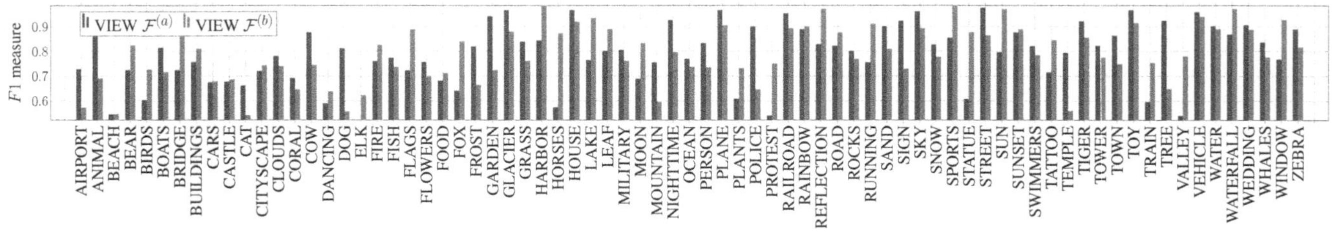

Figure 9: The F1 measure of the 75 tags for the testing set using MITL on noisy data learning when $s = 20$, $u = 4$, and $R = 1.2$.

practice. In *Advances in Neural Information Processing Systems*. MIT Press, 2006.

[7] S. Feng, R. Manmatha, and V. Lavrenko. Multiple bernoulli relevance models for image and video annotation. In *Proceedings of CVPR*, pages 1002–1009, 2004.

[8] G. P. C. Fung, J. X. Yu, H. Lu, and P. S. Yu. Text classification without negative examples revisit. *IEEE Transactions on Knowledge and Data Engineering*, 18:6–20, 2006.

[9] K.-S. Goh, E. Chang, and K.-T. Cheng. SVM binary classifier ensembles for image classification. In *Proceedings of the tenth international conference on Information and knowledge management*, pages 395–402, 2001.

[10] J. Grappone and G. Couzin. *Search Engine Optimization: An Hour a Day*. Wiley Publishing, Indianapolis, 2006.

[11] P. Heymann, D. Ramage, and H. G. Molina. Social tag prediction. In *Proceedings of the 31st International ACM SIGIR Conference*, pages 531–538, 2008.

[12] V. Lavrenko, R. Manmatha, and J. Jeon. A model for learning the semantics of pictures. In *Proceedings of Neural Information Processing Systems*, 2003.

[13] G. Li, S. C. H. Hoi, and K. Chang. Two-view transductive support vector machines. In *SDM*, pages 235–244, 2010.

[14] X. Li and B. Liu. Learning to classify text using positive and unlabeled data. In *Proceedings of the 18th international joint conference on Artificial intelligence*, pages 587–592, 2003.

[15] Y. Li, D. J. Crandall, and D. P. Huttenlocher. Landmark classification in large-scale image collections. In *Proceedings of International Conference on Computer Vision*, pages 1957 - 1964, 2009.

[16] C. F. Lin and S. de Wang. Training algorithms for fuzzy support vector machines with noisy data. *Pattern Recognition Letters*, 25:1647–1656, 2004.

[17] B. Liu, Y. Dai, X. Li, W. S. Lee, and P. S. Yu. Building text classifiers using positive and unlabeled examples. In *Proceedings of ICDM*, pages 179–186, 2003.

[18] D. Liu, X.-S. Hua, M. Wang, and H.-J. Zhang. Image retagging. In *Proceedings of ACM MM*, pages 491–500, 2010.

[19] Y. Liu and Y. F. Zheng. Soft SVM and its application in video-object extraction. *IEEE Transactions on Signal Processing*, 55(7-1):3272–3282, 2007.

[20] J. C. Platt. Probabilistic outputs for support vector machines and comparisons to regularized likelihood methods. In *Advances in Large Margin Classifiers*. MIT Press, 1999.

[21] X. Qi and Y. Han. Incorporating multiple SVMs for automatic image annotation. *Pattern Recognition*, 40:728–741, 2007.

[22] Z. Qi, M. Yang, Z. Zhang, and Z. Zhang. Mining partially annotated images. In *Proceedings of the 17th International ACM SIGKDD Conference*, pages 1199–1207, 2011.

[23] D. S. Rosenberg, V. Sindhwani, P. L. Bartlett, and P. Niyogi. A kernel for semi-supervised learning with multi-view point cloud regularization. In *IEEE Signal Processing Magazine*, 2009.

[24] Y.-Y. Sun, Y. Zhang, and Z.-H. Zhou. Multi-label learning with weak label. In *Proceedings of AAAI Conference*, pages 593–598, 2010.

[25] M. Szomszor, C. Cattuto, H. Alani, K. O'Hara, A. Baldassarri, V. Loreto, and V. D. Servedio. Folksonomies, the semantic web, and movie recommendation. In *4th European Semantic Web Conference: Bridging the Gap between Semantic Web and Web 2.0*, 2007.

[26] J. Tang, R. Hong, S. Yan, T.-S. Chua, G.-J. Qi, and R. Jain. Image annotation by knn-sparse graph-based label propagation over noisily tagged web images. *ACM Transactions on Intelligent Systems and Technology*, 2:14:1–14:15, 2011.

[27] J. Van Hulse and T. M. Khoshgoftaar. Class noise detection using frequent itemsets. *Intelligent Data Analysis*, 10:487–507, 2006.

[28] C. Wang, F. Jing, L. Zhang, and H.-J. Zhang. Content-based image annotation refinement. In *Proceedings of CVPR*, pages 1–8, 2007.

[29] C. Yang, M. Dong, and J. Hua. Region-based image annotation using asymmetrical support vector machine-based multi-instance learning. In *Proceedings of CVPR*, 2006.

[30] Z.-H. Zhou and M.-L. Zhang. Multi-instance multilabel learning with application to scene classification. In *Proceedings of NIPS*, pages 1609–1616, 2007.

[31] G. Zhu, S. Yan, and Y. Ma. Image tag refinement towards low-rank, content-tag prior and error sparsity. In *Proceedings of ACM MM*, pages 461–470, 2010.

[32] X. Zhu, X. Wu, and Q. Chen. Eliminating class noise in large datasets. In *Proceeding of International Conference on Machine Learning*, pages 920–927, 2003.

Joint Statistical Analysis of Images and Keywords with Applications in Semantic Image Enhancement

Albrecht Lindner
School of Computer and Communication Sciences
EPFL, Switzerland
Albrecht.Lindner@epfl.ch

Appu Shaji
School of Computer and Communication Sciences
EPFL, Switzerland
Appu.Shaji@epfl.ch

Nicolas Bonnier
Océ Print Logic Technologies
Créteil, France
Nicolas.Bonnier@gmail.com

Sabine Süsstrunk
School of Computer and Communication Sciences
EPFL, Switzerland
Sabine.Susstrunk@epfl.ch

ABSTRACT

With the advent of social image-sharing communities, millions of images with associated semantic tags are now available online for free and allow us to exploit this abundant data in new ways. We present a fast non-parametric statistical framework designed to analyze a large data corpus of images and semantic tag pairs and find correspondences between image characteristics and semantic concepts. We learn the relevance of different image characteristics for thousands of keywords from one million annotated images. We demonstrate the framework's effectiveness with three different examples of semantic image enhancement: we adapt the gray-level tone-mapping, emphasize semantically relevant colors, and perform a defocus magnification for an image based on its semantic context. The performance of our algorithms is validated with psychophysical experiments.

Categories and Subject Descriptors

L.01 [**Media Content Analysis and Processing**]: semantic concept detection

Keywords

semantic image processing, statistical analysis, image understanding, crowd sourcing, large-scale experimentation

1. INTRODUCTION

The abundance of data in online image-sharing communities gives new perspectives and possibilities to the multimedia research community. Photos and associated semantic tags can be analyzed on a large scale in order to gain mathematical models that relate human language (annotated keywords) to computer language (numeric pixel values). We present a statistical framework that estimates this correspondences between image keywords and characteristics, and design it to be fast even on large-scale databases. Such correspondence can be exploited for imaging applications that need to interpret semantic input, as is the case in semantic image enhancement for which we present three algorithms. First, we adjust an image's gray-level tone-mapping for a semantic concept. Second, we emphasize related colors in order to strengthen a semantic concept. And third, we magnify the defocus of an image to account for its semantic content.

Figure 1 shows an example for each of the three implemented algorithms. Figure 1(a) shows the adaptation of an image to the semantic concepts *dark* and *sand*, respectively. Figure 1(b) shows how an image's colors can be re-rendered in order to emphasize its semantics – *strawberry*. Finally, Figure 1(c) demonstrates a defocus magnification to account for the semantic concept *macro*.

Our statistical framework (Sec. 3) is non-parametric and learns associations between any image characteristic and semantic tag as it is not necessary to assume an underlying distribution. This makes it fast in comparison to other learning techniques that depend on parameter-tuning (e.g., SVM or boosting). Hence, we are able to use a database of one million annotated images [7] and learn associations for thousands of keywords. In addition to that, a parameter- and tuning-free method opens the door to applications where it is difficult to numerically measure the quality of the result: for example the perceptual appeal of a semantically enhanced image in our case.

The philosophy behind our approach to semantic image enhancement is that it is not possible to optimize the visual appearance of an image based only on the pixel values. For an optimal result, it is indispensable to know its semantic context. This is demonstrated in Figure 1(a), which shows a beach scene (top) that can be enhanced in order to emphasize that it was almost dark (bottom left) or to show the sandy beach (bottom right). Conventional image-statistics based enhancement algorithms such as contrast stretching are not able to do this because they do not take into account the semantic context.

The three presented algorithms for semantic image en-

MM'12, October 29–November 2, 2012, Nara, Japan.

(a) gray-level re-rendering, *dark* and *sand* (b) color re-rendering, *strawberry* (c) frequency re-rendering, *macro*

Figure 1: Examples for the three semantic image enhancement algorithms presented in this paper. All algorithms take as inputs a single image and an associated semantic expression, which is indicated in the sub-caption in *italic*. Left: The gray levels of the input image at the top are tone mapped to adjust for the semantic concepts *dark* and *sand*. Middle: The input image's colors are re-rendered in order to emphasize the concept *strawberry*. Right: Defocus magnification to adapt to the semantic concept *macro*. The input image (top) is reproduced from Zhuo and Sim [30].

hancement (Sec. 4) are based on two components: 1) the semantic context as defined by a keyword 2) the image content as defined by the pixel values. The significance values from the statistical test allow to determine whether a specific processing of an image under a given semantic context is meaningful and, if yes, how the processing has to be done in order to achieve an optimal result. This is combined with information from the pixel values in order to tailor the semantic processing to a specific image. The combination of semantic and pixel-based information for image enhancement is another novelty presented here.

We evaluate the semantic gray-level enhancement with two psychophysical experiments. The first shows that our enhanced image is preferred over the original image. The second compares our algorithm against other algorithms that are not semantically adaptive. Our method performs on average 2.5 times better than the second best.

2. RELATED WORK

Our paper addresses image semantics and image enhancement. Here we present related publications that inspired this work.

Torralba and Freeman published a "tiny image database" [24] with 80 million 32×32 images associated with 75,062 non-abstract nouns from the WordNet lexical database [13]. It enables large-scale image classification, but is limited to non-abstract nouns. ImageNet [4] is a similar project aimed at populating each synset of WordNet with 1000 images on average. ImageNet is used by Deselaers and Ferrari [5] to show that images with semantically similar annotations have more visual attributes in common than images with dissimilar annotations. This work proves that an image's semantics can be associated with its low-level image descriptor, which we also exploit here. Ordonez et al. present an approach to leverage one million tagged photographs in order to automatically create a verbal image description for a new input image [17]. This can be seen as the inverse of our application, because we aim at changing image characteristics given a tagged keyword.

The MIR Flickr database [7] contains one million high-quality photographs that are selected based on Flicker's "interestingness" score. The images are provided with the Flickr community's annotations, which sets this database apart from the previously mentioned. The annotations are of lower quality because they come from a large uncontrolled group of people (social tagging [22]), but they are abundant. Both the high quality of the photographs and the social tagging made us choose this database.

Associating image features with semantic tags has been investigated for several applications. In most cases, for example in image retrieval [23, 28], the goal is to link image features with a set of semantic classes. However, our method does the inverse and associates semantic labels with images. Generating training data for the former is cumbersome as it involves hand labeling of image regions, whereas we profit from user annotated images that are readily available from various crowd-sourcing data repositories. This allows us to scale to millions of images and to an unlimited vocabulary.

Our application scenario is image enhancement, which is a widely explored field. Image enhancement algorithms can be classified into different groups. One group of algorithms relies on a set of rules (defined by a human expert) that an enhanced image should satisfy. An input image is then modified so that it better respects these rules. These methods can work on a single image without any other input. A simple example is the rule that in an image's histogram, the bin counts should be more or less equal. This so-called histogram equalization process improves an image's contrast and has been known for a few decades [8]. Another example is unsharp masking, where the input image is convolved with a high-pass filter and added back to the original image in order to make it look sharper [19].

More recent and sophisticated examples are methods to increase region saliency from Fredembach [6] or to adjust color harmony in an image from Cohen-Or et al. [3] or Sauvaget and Boyer [21]. Wang et al. [26] and Murray et al. [15] present methods to adjust an image's color composition with predefined color themes, such as "nostalgic" or "spicy". However, their approaches are limited as the color themes are manually defined. On the contrary, our approach can interpret any semantic expression at the input and deduce an appropriate image processing from it.

Another group of image enhancement algorithms are example-based. In this case, the algorithm adjusts the characteristics of an input image with those of one or more example images: depending on the example images, different enhancements can be achieved. Reinhard et al. [20] propose a system that transfers the colors from an example image to an input image. Kang et al. [10] develop a method where a user creates personal example images in a previous step. The parameters from the example set are then used to personalize the enhancement of a new input image. Wang et al. [27] present a framework to map colors and gradients. They use an example set of registered image pairs of scenes taken with a low-end and a high-end camera. The mappings from the low to the high-end images are then applied to an input image. Our approach can be seen as example-based, but instead of creating our own image examples, we use keywords whose dominant image descriptors are derived from a large number of freely available images.

Another approach to automatic image enhancement is to classify an image (or regions of it) into a fixed set of image categories before applying a class-dependent image enhancement. Such systems have been proposed by Moser and Schroeder [14] and Ciocca et al. [2]. They use common classes, such as "sky", "skin", or "vegetation". Both approaches are adapted to image semantics. However, only seven and three semantic concepts are distinguished, respectively, whereas our framework can deal with an arbitrary number of keywords.

A somewhat different group of image enhancement algorithms create artistic effects. An example of this is defocus magnification, where the goal is to additionally blur out-of-focus regions so that the object in focus is more accentuated [1, 30]. These algorithms first compute a defocus map [16] and then intentionally blur the image according to the estimated defocus level.

The main difference between our semantic image processing and all the above mentioned methods is that the semantic concept provides a second independent input to our workflow in addition to the image features. Other approaches only classify an image into a limited number of pre-selected semantic classes [2, 14] and then process according to that classification. Thus, these methods do not allow rendering the same input image for two different semantic concepts, as our approach is able to do (see Fig.1(a)).

3. STATISTICAL FRAMEWORK

In this section we present the framework that relates keywords with image characteristics. To do this, we learn correspondences between image characteristics and keywords by using the MIR Flickr database with 1 million annotated high-quality images [7].

3.1 Measuring Correspondence

Our database consists of image/annotation pairs $(I_i, A_i) \in I_{db}$. An annotation is an ordered set of one or more keywords $A_i = \{w_1, w_2, \ldots\}$. Given a keyword w, the database can be split into two subsets $I_w = \{I_i | w \in A_i\}$ and $I_{\overline{w}} = \{I_i | w \notin A_i\}$ that contain all images annotated with keyword w and all remaining images, respectively. It is $I_w \cap I_{\overline{w}} = \emptyset$ and $I_w \cup I_{\overline{w}} = I_{db}$.

For an image I, a characteristic $C \in \mathbb{R}$ can be computed from it. This can be anything we want to characterize in an image. Examples are the percentage of pixels that have a certain gray level or the output of Gabor filters. The set $\mathcal{C}^j_w = \{C^j_i | I_i \in I_w\}$ unites the characteristic j of all images annotated with keyword w. The set $\mathcal{C}^j_{\overline{w}}$ unites analogously the characteristic j from images in $I_{\overline{w}}$.

In order to assess how a keyword influences a characteristic j, the values in the sets $\mathcal{C}^j_w$ and $\mathcal{C}^j_{\overline{w}}$ have to be compared against each other. The task is to determine how the values of the two sets differ.

In the general case, the values do not follow a known distribution. Hence, we use methods from non-parametric statistics. A commonly used test is the Mann-Whitney-Wilcoxon (**MWW**) ranksum test [29, 12], which assesses whether two observations have equally large values, i.e., by how much their means differ.

For given characteristics (j)[1], let the computed scalar values from the positive set be $\mathcal{C}_w = \{C_1, C_3, C_4, \ldots\}$ and that from the negative set $\mathcal{C}_{\overline{w}} = \{C_2, C_5, C_6, \ldots\}$ for a given keyword w. We first sort the concatenated set $\mathcal{C}_w \cup \mathcal{C}_{\overline{w}}$. The ranksum is defined as the sum of positional indexes that the elements of $\mathcal{C}_w$ occupy in the sorted list of $\mathcal{C}_w \cup \mathcal{C}_{\overline{w}}$. Wilcoxon denoted this statistic with T

For example, consider the two sets $\mathcal{C}_w = \{17.5, -2\}$ and $\mathcal{C}_{\overline{w}} = \{23, -11.7, 3.1, 0.9, 42\}$. The ordered sequence of all C_i's is: $\overset{1}{-11.7}$, $\overset{2}{-2}$, $\overset{3}{0.9}$, $\overset{4}{3.1}$, $\overset{5}{17.5}$, $\overset{6}{23}$, $\overset{7}{42}$ (rank indexes stacked on top for convenience), and thus the ranksum $T = 2 + 5 = 7$. The expected mean and variance are [29, 12]:

$$\mu_T = \frac{N_w(N_w + N_{\overline{w}} + 1)}{2} \tag{1a}$$

$$\sigma_T^2 = \frac{N_w N_{\overline{w}}(N_w + N_{\overline{w}} + 1)}{12} \tag{1b}$$

where $N_w = |\mathcal{C}_w|$ and $N_{\overline{w}} = |\mathcal{C}_{\overline{w}}|$ are the cardinalities of either set, respectively.

There are other tests such as the Kolmogorov-Smirnov test or the χ^2 test that additionally assess whether two distributions have different shapes [25]. As in our application, image enhancement, the absolute values are more important than the shape of their distribution, we us the **MWW**-test. We have found it to be more robust for our experiments.

Finally, we compute the standardized z value:

$$z = \frac{T - \mu_T}{\sigma_T} \tag{2}$$

We give more details on statistical tests and our choice to favor the **MWW**-test on the project webpage[2].

3.2 Interpretation of the z value

The z value is a useful measure to assess the relationship between keywords and low-level image features. The higher its magnitude, the more the corresponding characteristic is important for the keyword, and vice versa.

To give a better intuition for the z value, we consider an example where the tested image characteristic is a 16 bin gray-level histogram. For each of the equidistant bins, we calculate z^j_{night} from the two sets $\mathcal{C}^j_{night}$ and $\mathcal{C}^j_{\overline{night}}$, where $j = 1 \ldots 16$.

Figure 2 shows the distributions of all pairs, along with their corresponding z^j_{night} values. It is clearly visible that

[1]superscript ^{j} omitted in this paragraph for clarity.
[2]`http://ivrg.epfl.ch/SemanticEnhancement.html`

images annotated with *night* have more dark pixels ($z > 0$ for low gray levels) and less bright pixels ($z < 0$ for high gray levels). The z values smoothly vary between -130 and 124. The difference between $\mathcal{C}^j_{night}$ and $\mathcal{C}^j_{\overline{night}}$ is less significant for z values close to zero, which is the case for $j = 5$ (a medium gray level). Overall though, an image's "*night*ness" is strongly related to its gray-level distribution.

Figure 3 shows the same plots but for the keyword *statue*. The two distributions are much more similar, the z values are closer to zero. This tells us that an image's gray-level distribution and its "*statue*ness" are not related.

We can thus introduce a simple ranking criterion for a given descriptor and keyword, which is the difference between the maximum and the minimum z-value as indicated in Figure 2. According to the examples depicted in Figures 2 and 3, we obtain $\Delta z^{\text{gray-level hist}}_{night} = 124.3 - (-130.0) = 254.3$ and $\Delta z^{\text{gray-level hist}}_{statue} = 6.5 - (-1.2) = 7.7$.

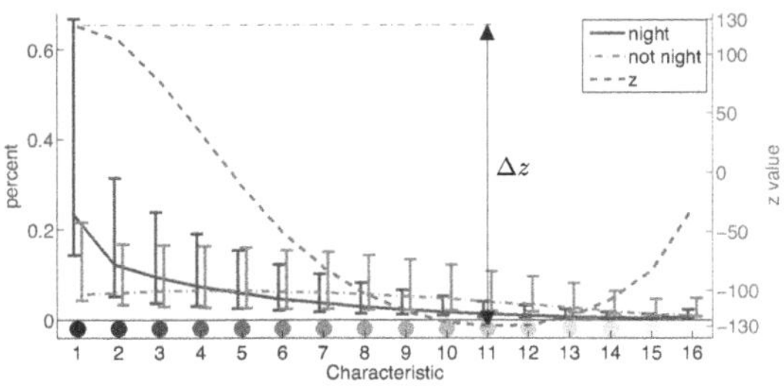

Figure 2: Left axis: The 16 characteristics of the sets $\mathcal{C}^j_{night}$ and $\mathcal{C}^j_{\overline{night}}$ measuring the percentage of image pixels falling into each bin. Each characteristic is represented with its median and its 25% and 75% quantiles. The markers at the bottom indicate the mean gray level of each characteristic. For visualization purposes the two curves have a small horizontal offset. Right axis: The corresponding z values indicate that images annotated with *night* contain more dark ($z > 0$) and less bright ($z < 0$) pixels than the other images not annotated with *night*.

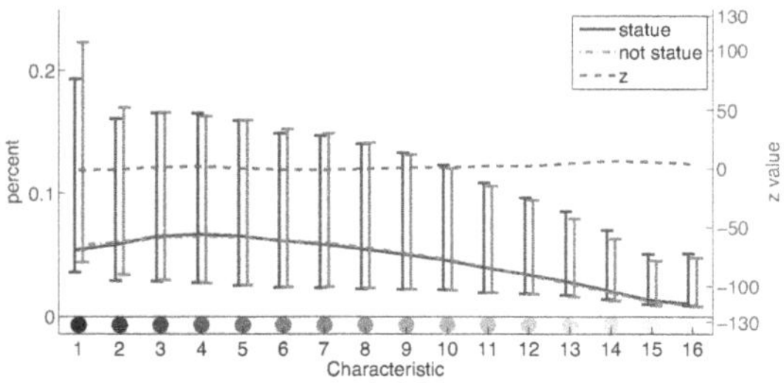

Figure 3: Same plot as in Figure 2 but for keyword *statue*. The distributions are more similar and the z values are closer to zero.

3.3 Comparing z values from Different Keywords and Characteristics

The z values can be computed for many keywords and characteristics. We use all keywords that occur in at least 500 images of the MIR Flickr database, 2858 in total. Additionally to the gray levels, we compute other image characteristics: lightness, chroma, hue angle (all three in CIELAB space [9]), linear binary patterns [11], responses of high-pass and Gabor filters (image details), and frequency distributions in the Fourier domain. They are either summarized in a 16-bin histogram or in a 64-dimensional layout descriptor[3].

3.3.1 Dependency on N_w

The z value depends on the number of images per keyword N_w as can be seen in Equations 1 and 2. This is an inherent property of any statistical test: more samples increase credibility and thus result in a higher significance value.

If the significance values from keywords with different numbers of samples have to be compared it is necessary to introduce a reference sample size N^*_w. All the variables from the statistical test can then be converted to this reference sample size as follows:

$$T^* = \frac{N^*_w}{N_w} \cdot T \tag{3a}$$

$$\mu^*_T = \frac{N^*_w}{N_w} \cdot \mu_T \tag{3b}$$

$$\sigma^{*2}_T = \frac{N^*_w N^*_{\overline{w}}}{N_w N_{\overline{w}}} \cdot \sigma^2_T \tag{3c}$$

$$z^* = \sqrt{\frac{N^*_w N^*_{\overline{w}}}{N_w N_{\overline{w}}}} \cdot z \tag{3d}$$

The better comparability can be demonstrated with the keywords *bw*, *blackandwhite* and *blackwhite*. The standard significance values are $\Delta z^{\text{chroma}}_{bw} = 502.1$, $\Delta z^{\text{chroma}}_{\text{blackandwhite}} = 379.0$ and $\Delta z^{\text{chroma}}_{blackwhite} = 230.1$, respectively. The unequal values are a consequence of the different sample sizes $N_{bw} = 30294$, $N_{blackandwhite} = 17092$ and $N_{blackwhite} = 6157$. The compensated values are $\Delta z^{\text{chroma}*}_{bw} = 63.5$, $\Delta z^{\text{chroma}}_{blackandwhite}{}^* = 64.3$ and $\Delta z^{\text{chroma}}_{blackwhite}{}^* = 65.4$, respectively. All three values are relatively equal, which is in accordance with the fact that they express the same semantic concept.

3.3.2 Examples and Implementation on a Large Scale

Figure 4 shows $\Delta z_w{}^*$ values for different combinations of characteristics and 50 selected keywords w The scores are intuitively clear; *night* relates strongly to the gray-level histogram as the respective images tend to be very dark. *Blue* and *flower* have strong correspondence with hue and chroma characteristics. Spatial layouts are significant for the keywords *sunrise* and *sunset* as they have a distinct spatial distribution of colors. The keywords *macro*, *flower* and *bokeh* strongly relate to high frequency content as these images often have a blurred background. However, there are also keywords that do not show strong correspondence with the tested characteristics, e.g. *happy* or *day*. Thus, our framework allows us to explicitly test if a given keyword has a predominant corresponding image characteristic or not.

This is important for image applications in general, as the absence of a significant characteristic implies that a given algorithm will not affect these images. With regards to our application, image enhancement, the algorithm will not try to automatically improve images where the keyword indicates that a certain characteristic is not important.

[3]We superpose a regular 8×8 grid over the image independent of its size or aspect ratio. Then we compute for each grid cell the average value of the respective characteristic, leading to a 64-dimensional layout descriptor.

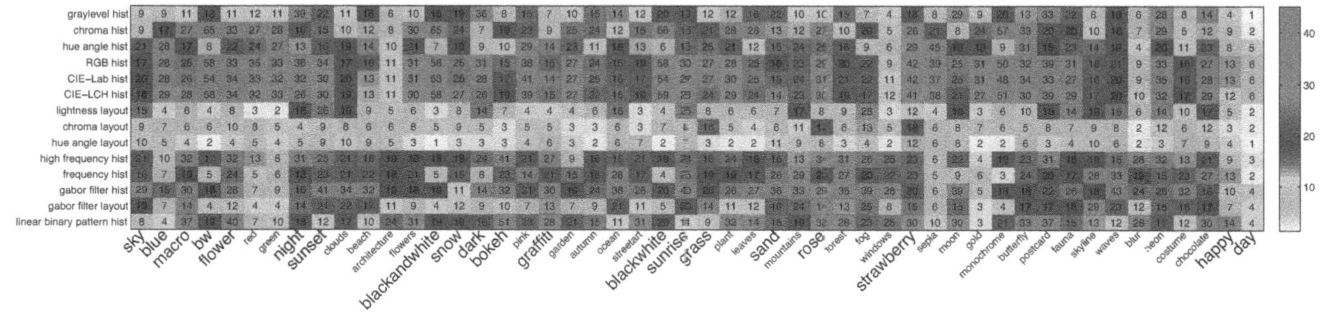

Figure 4: Δz^* values for 50 keywords and 14 characteristics. Note how the different keywords correspond to different characteristics. For instance, *bw* strongly equates with the chroma histogram (absence of high chromatic colors), *sunset* has a distinct spatial lightness layout (bright center and dark surrounding), and *graffiti* strongly relates to an image's high frequency content and linear binary patterns. *Day* and *happy* have very weak correspondence to any of the tested characteristics. Keywords that are referred to in the article have a larger font size. Access a complete listing of all 2858 keywords: http://ivrg.epfl.ch/SemanticEnhancement.html

If the one million example images are always the same, their characteristics can be computed and sorted offline. Then, to compute the ranksum statistic for a keyword, we need only to sum the corresponding elements' ranks in the pre-sorted list. Computing this indexed sum takes 35.9ms for 16 z values (e.g. gray-level histogram) on a MacBook Pro (2.5GHz Core 2 Duo). The code is written in Matlab and the core functions are implemented as mex-files. The main bottleneck of our current implementation is the query for a given keyword, as we parse text files with regular expressions in Matlab. This takes 50s per keyword, but we are confident that a standard MySQL implementation will reduce this time significantly.

4. SEMANTIC IMAGE ENHANCEMENT

The general framework presented in the previous section can be used for any application where image characteristics have to be linked to image semantics. In this publication, we focus on semantic image enhancement, which aims at re-rendering an image to adapt to a given semantic context. We define re-rendering as taking as input an image that has been processed in-camera or even enhanced afterwards and that we process to better visually match a semantic concept.

The proposed image enhancement is based on two components: 1) the image content as defined by the pixel values 2) the image semantics as described by a keyword. The first component uses standard image processing techniques. The novelty is the combination with the second component to make the processing semantically adaptive. We use the significance values in order to assess whether changing a characteristic is meaningful and if yes, how it has to be changed for an optimal adaption to the semantic context.

The significance values offer great potential to automatize semantic image processing, because they indicate whether a keyword and a characteristic are correlated. Keywords with lower significance values can be automatically discarded (e.g. *happy* or *day* as shown in Fig. 4) as they are not meaningful in terms of image processing. Also, we can automatically detect when images are "wrongly" annotated, i.e. no region in the image has significant characteristics corresponding to a particular keyword.

In the following, we present three semantic image enhancement algorithms beginning with a re-rendering for gray levels in Section 4.1. The efficiency and superiority over other commonly used methods is demonstrated with psychophysical experiments and described in Section 4.1.3. We further propose a method to re-render the colors in an image as shown in Section 4.2. Finally, we demonstrate in Section 4.3 the usage of the statistical framework for a very different type of enhancement: altering an image's frequencies in order to create artistic blurring effects that match the image's semantics.

4.1 Semantic Gray-Level Re-Rendering

For the first re-rendering application, a gray-level tone-mapping curve is computed that accounts for the image's semantic context. It is a global operation that maps an input pixel's gray level to a new gray level in the output image and thus alters the image's gray-level distribution.

4.1.1 Assessing a Characteristic's Required Change

To re-render an image for a specific semantic concept, its characteristic needs to be changed according to the two previously mentioned components: semantic context and image content. Hence we define two conditions that need to be fulfilled in order to alter the gray-level distribution: 1. the characteristic is significant for the semantic concept (i.e., high Δz as shown in Fig. 2); 2. the characteristic in the present image is too low or too high for the given concept. An image will not be altered if the characteristic is not influenced by the keyword or if the image is already a good example for it.

The first component is the significance of the semantic concept and is assessed via the z value from Equation 2. If the z value is positive (negative), the value of the corresponding characteristic has to be increased (decreased). We assume a linear relationship between the z values and the strength of the image processing; meaning that if the z value's absolute value is k times higher, the processing is k times stronger.

The second component is image dependent. We assess how well the given image already fulfills the desired characteristics for its semantic concept. We compare the image's characteristics to the characteristics of all images with the same keyword. Therefore, we compute the difference to a quantile:

$$\delta^j_{I,w} = \begin{cases} \max\left[0, Q_{1-p}\left(\mathcal{C}^j_w\right) - C^j_I\right] & \text{if } z^j_w \geq 0 \\ \max\left[0, C^j_I - Q_p\left(\mathcal{C}^j_w\right)\right] & \text{if } z^j_w < 0 \end{cases} \quad (4)$$

where $\delta^j_{I,w}$ signifies the difference measure for input image I with keyword w under characteristic j, C^j_I is image I's characteristic j, $Q_p(\cdot)$ measures a set's p-quantile and $\mathcal{C}^j_w$ are all characteristics j of images annotated with w.

If we use the 50% quantile $Q_{0.5}$ to compute the difference in equation 4, the second condition is already fulfilled ($\delta = 0$) if the input image's characteristic is average for its semantic concept. If, however, we want to emphasize the significant characteristics more, a lower quantile has to be chosen. We found that a 25%-quantile is a good tradeoff between a desired enhancement and an extreme overshooting, which would happen for quantiles in the order of 5%.

Similarly to the dependency on the z values, we implement a linear relationship between the δ values and the strength of the enhancement. Thus, the image processing has to be proportional to the product of z and δ values.

Figure 5 shows an example for the semantic concepts *dark* and *snow*. The example input image is the one from Figure 6 that is annotated with both keywords. The top part shows the median and quantiles of the distributions of $\mathcal{C}^j_{dark}$ and $\mathcal{C}^j_{snow}$ and the input image's characteristics. The middle part shows the δ value calculated from Equation 4. The bottom part shows the product of z (significance related) and δ (image related) values. The values indicate that, for the concept *snow*, the image needs fewer dark and more bright pixels, whereas for concept *dark* it needs more dark pixels.

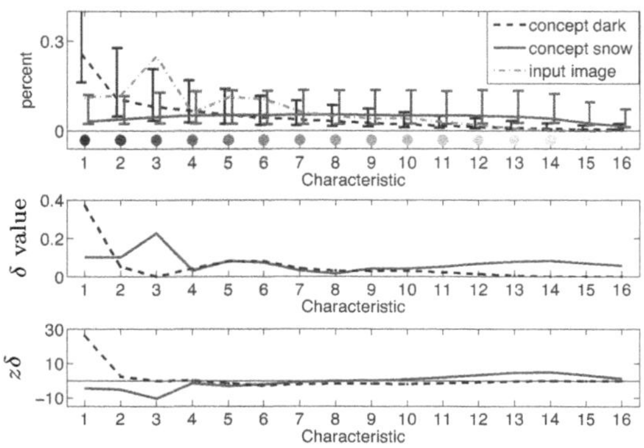

Figure 5: Top: Median and quantiles of the distributions for concepts *dark* and *snow* together with the used input image's characteristics (Fig. 1 right image). Middle: δ values according to Equation 4. Bottom: Product of z and δ values. For keyword *snow*, the image needs fewer dark pixels ($z\delta < 0$) and more bright pixels ($z\delta > 0$); the opposite is true for keyword *dark*.

4.1.2 Building a Tone-Mapping Function

We use the z value from Equation 2 and the δ value from Equation 4 to determine a tone-mapping of an image's gray levels. According to our previous assumptions, the product $z\delta$ is proportional to the change a processing introduces to an image.

In the case of a tone-mapping function, the strength is given by its slope. If at gray-level g, the slope is $m(g)$, the pixels in the interval around g are redistributed to a gray-level interval of $m(g)$ times the size. This holds for $m > 1$ (decreasing density) as for $m < 1$ (increasing density). A slope equal to one is the identity transform. As the $z\delta$ value indicates how strongly a characteristic has to be altered, the slope is:

$$m = \begin{cases} 1/(1 + Sz\delta) & \text{if } z\delta \geq 0 \\ 1 + S|z\delta| & \text{if } z\delta < 0 \end{cases} \tag{5}$$

where S is a proportionality constant that controls the overall strength of the tone-mapping.

Extreme slope values are not desirable. A very steep mapping increases quantization artefacts and noise in homogeneous areas, and a very flat mapping reduces local contrast. Thus, the slope is cropped to a range $[1/m_{max}\ m_{max}]$. This is an inherent problem for any tone-mapping applications [18] and not specific to this approach. We used $m_{max} = 5$, which is a good compromise between limiting extreme tone-mappings and allowing visible changes.

The slope values from Equation 5 are linearly interpolated for 256 values in the interval [0 255] by using the representative mean gray level of each characteristic. Because these values specify the slope, they are the derivative of the tone-mapping function. An integration thus yields the desired function.

Due to the continuity of the slope values, the mapping function is continuous and differentiable. This guarantees a certain smoothness constraint that is beneficial for non-invasive processing. In a final step, we scale the mapping function to the interval [0 255] in order to maintain the image's black and white points.

The graph in Figure 6 shows tone-mapping functions for different proportionality constants S for keyword *snow*. The smaller the S is, the closer the mapping function is to the identity transform, which is depicted by the thin black line. Higher S values lead to a more extreme mapping. The three images show the input and the output for $S = 0.5$ and $S = 2$.

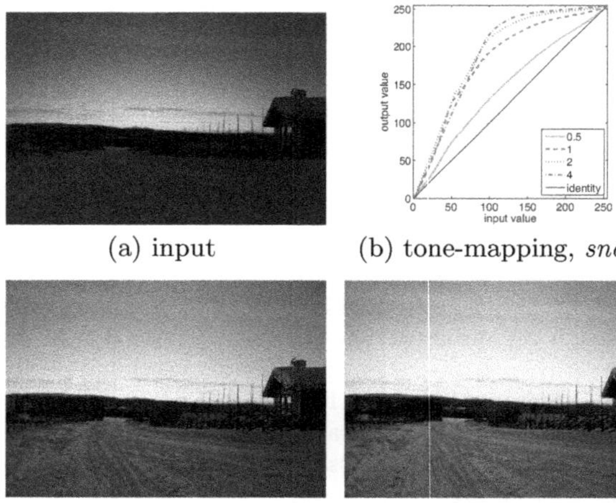

(a) input (b) tone-mapping, *snow*

(c) $S = 0.5$ (d) $S = 2$

Figure 6: Top: Input image and tone-mapping function to increase the semantic concept *snow* derived from the $z\delta$ values in Figure 5 ($S \in \{0.5\ 1\ 2\ 4\}$). Bottom: Two output images for $S = 0.5$ and $S = 2$, respectively.

4.1.3 Psychophysical Experiments

We evaluate the semantic gray-level enhancement with two psychophysical experiments. The first experiment shows that the semantically enhanced version is better than the original image and in the second experiment we demonstrate that our algorithm outperforms other gray-level enhancement algorithms.

For the first experiment, we choose eight keywords with relatively high z values because low z values intentionally generate tone-mapping curves close to identity (see Eq. 5). The keywords w and their corresponding Δz_w values are *white* (88), *dark* (130), *sand* (72), *snow* (108), *contrast* (39), *silhouette* (79), *portrait* (80), and *light* (131), respectively.

For each keyword we selected 30 images from Flickr that have been annotated with the respective keyword, and we semantically re-rendered them with four different parameters $S \in \{0.5, 1, 2, 4\}$. Thus, we tested 960 images in total.

We set up a large-scale experiment using Amazon Mechanical Turk, where we showed the original and the enhanced image next to each other together with the corresponding keyword in the title. We asked 30 observers to select the image that best matches the keyword and payed them 1 cent per comparison.

Figure 7(a) shows the results of the psychophysical experiment. The S parameter is plotted on the horizontal axis and the approval rate for the enhanced image on the vertical axis. The approval values for all parameters S and all, except one, keywords are above 50%. Overall, the enhanced images are preferred and images in the *white* category have the highest rate (93%). This is not surprising as it is directly related to the gray-level characteristics.

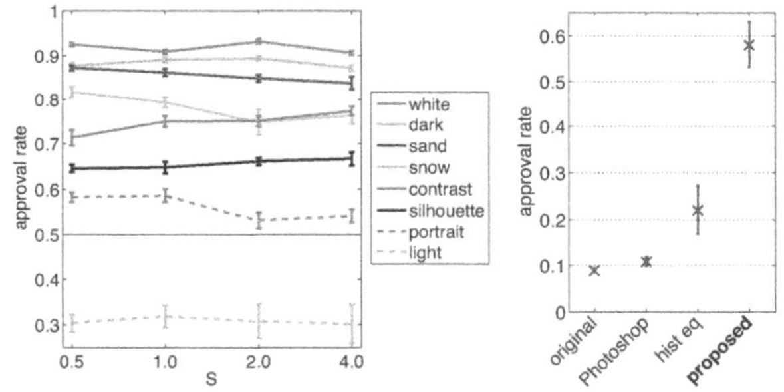

(a) 1st experiment (b) 2nd experiment

Figure 7: Results from two psychophysical experiments. Left: Approval rates from 30 observers for different S values. Images of all except one semantic concepts are enhanced with success rates of up to 93%. The approval rate for *light* jumped to 62% in another experiment where we invited only artists. Right: Approval rate from 40 observers comparing the proposed method against other contrast enhancement methods (histogram equalization and Photoshop's auto contrast function). The proposed method scores more than 2.5 times better than the 2nd best. The error bars in both figures show the variances across different images.

The approval rate for images with *light* is surprisingly low and the variances are relatively large, which is due to the fact that there are two interpretations for this semantic term: 1) the image is bright in general 2) the image shows a light source that is visually important due to the dark surrounding. We reason that photographers and artists have rather the second point of view and carried out another experiment. We invited 20 photographers to judge the 30 images with keyword *light* ($S = 1$) and the resulting approval rate significantly jumped to 62% in favor of our algorithm.

The second psychophysical experiment compares our semantic image enhancement against other image only based contrast enhancements. We used four versions of each image, which were the original and three enhanced versions from Photoshop's auto contrast, Matlab's histogram equalization and our semantic framework for $S = 1$, respectively. In order to show the benefit of our semantically adaptive image enhancement we selected all images of the previous experiment that were annotated with more than two of the eight keywords. In total there are 29 such cases as the examples for *sand* and *dark* in Figure 1. The images were judged by 40 non-expert observers.

Figure 7(b) visualizes the results: 58.1% voted for our version, 22.2% for the histogram equalization, 10.8% for Photoshop's auto contrast and 8.9% for the photographer's original. The variances across the different images is shown in the form of vertical error bars. We see that our semantic enhancement has significantly higher approval rates and scores on average more than 2.5 times better than the 2nd best method. This is due to the fact that our semantic enhancement is the only method able to adapt to an image's semantic context.

4.2 Semantic Color Transfer

On the same lines as the gray-level tone-mapping, we can implement a semantic color transfer. As before, this requires two components that adapt to the image keyword and to the image pixels, respectively. The goal is to emphasize the colors in an image that are related to a given semantic concept.

However, it is important not to apply a global color shift to the entire image as this would look unnatural in certain image regions, such as a human face or a blue sky. Therefore, the image dependent component (δ in the gray-level case) has to be spatially varying in the color case.

This requirement is accounted for with a spatial weight map ω that encodes how much each pixel belongs to the semantic concept (see Fig. 8(b)). The map is simply the z value for each pixel color col(p) at position p in the image under the given semantic concept w. To assure smooth transitions, the map is blurred with a Gaussian blurring kernel with a sigma σ of 1% of the image diagonal. Further, the 5% and 95% quantiles ($Q_{0.95}$ and $Q_{0.05}$) are linearly mapped to 0 and 1, respectively, to remove noise.

$$\tilde{\omega} = g_\sigma * z_w(\text{col}(p)), \quad \forall p \in \text{image plane} \tag{6}$$

$$\omega = \min\left(1, \frac{\max(0, \tilde{\omega} - Q_{0.05})}{Q_{0.95} - Q_{0.05}}\right) \tag{7}$$

The semantic component is again based on z values, but this time with an $8 \times 8 \times 8$ histogram in sRGB color space. The tone-mapping curve is derived as before with Equation 5 and for each color channel separately. The only difference is that the δ value is omitted as this is accounted for by the weight map (Fig. 8(b)). The three tone-mapping curves derived for the semantic concept of *autumn* are reproduced in Figure 8(c).

We apply the derived tone-mapping on each color channel of the input image I_{in} resulting in a globally processed image I_{tmp}. As explained before, the final output has to show processed pixels only in those regions that belong to the semantic concept. The output image I_{out} is thus a linear combination of the input image and the intermediary globally processed image I_{tmp}, and the weights are taken from the weight map ω:

$$I_{\text{out}} = (1 - \omega) \cdot I_{\text{in}} + \omega \cdot I_{\text{tmp}} \qquad (8)$$

The resulting output image I_{out} is reproduced in Figure 8(d). Note that the image does not have a global color cast, but the semantic concept is emphasized only in image regions that are already part of it in the input image. Figure 9 shows another example, but for the semantic concept of *grass*.

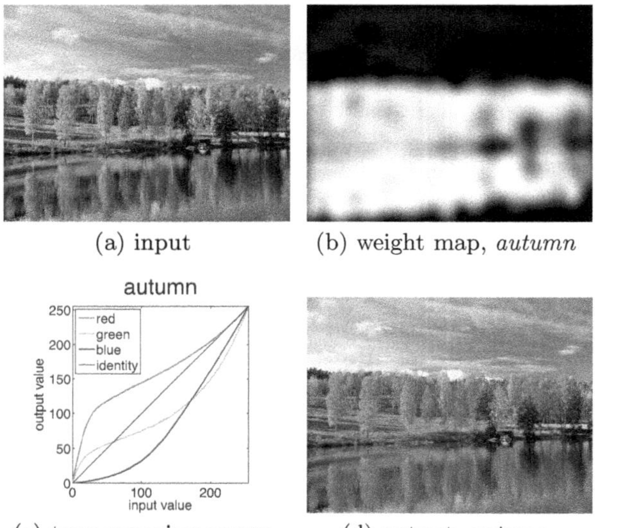

(a) input (b) weight map, *autumn*

(c) tone-mapping curves (d) output, *autumn*

Figure 8: Top: input image and associated weight map for the semantic concept of *autumn*. The bright regions in the map indicate regions that belong to the concept in the input image. Bottom row: Tone-mapping curves for the three color channels and the final output image. The semantic concept is emphasized only in those regions that already belong to it in the input image; other regions remain unprocessed.

Figure 9: Other example of the semantic color transfer for keyword *grass*.

Additionally, our algorithm for the semantic color transfer is able to handle different semantic concepts for the tone-mapping curves and the weight map, respectively. Hence, it can be used to exchange two semantic concepts in an image. Figures 10(a) and 10(b) show an image of a rose and the associate weight map for the concept of *rose*. However, the tone-mapping we apply stems from the keyword *blue*, as shown in Figure 10(c). Figure 10(d) shows the output image in which the roses are colored in blue. This is similar to other color transfer methods [26, 15]. Note, however, that our method handles an arbitrary semantic expression.

(a) input (b) weight map, *rose*

(c) tone-mapping curves (d) output, *rose->blue*

Figure 10: color transfer using two different semantic concepts. Top: input image and weight map for the semantic concept of *rose*. Bottom: tone-mapping curves for semantic concept *blue* and final output image. The roses are colored in blue.

Figure 11 shows a failure case for the semantic concept of *sky*. The algorithm re-colored the cloud in the upper right corner in blue, which looks unnatural. The reason for the failure is an erroneous weight map as shown in Figure 11(c). Our detection method to find regions that correspond to a semantic concept is based on colors only. In this case the very dark clouds are classified as part of *sky* because it correlates also with dark grays in the MIR Flickr database. A more robust image region detection should improve results, but this is out of the scope of this publication.

4.3 Semantic Defocus Magnification

Defocus magnification is important in cases where a photographer intends an artistic blur of the background in order to accentuate the object in focus. In order to demonstrate the versatility of the presented statistical framework, we show how the significance values can be used in this context.

To account for the semantics, we compute z values describing the spatial frequency content in the Fourier domain. We do not distinguish between different orientations and thus obtain a radially averaged one-dimensional descriptor with 16 bins. The first bin describes the DC component and the lowest frequencies and the following bins describe increasing frequencies, respectively. The example plot in Figure 12(a) shows that the keyword *macro* relates to an absence of high frequencies, as indicated by the negative z values.

As we do not want to alter the brightness of the image, we shift the curve up with an additive constant so that the first z value (representing the DC component) is equal to

(a) input

(b) output, *sky*

(c) weight map, *sky*

Figure 11: Failure case for the semantic concept of *sky*. The cloud in the top right corner has been mistaken for *sky* and re-colored in blue. The reason is an erroneous weight map based on color information. Other computer vision techniques can improve detection results, but this is out of the scope of this publication.

zero. These shifted values are denoted z_{origin} as their graph starts at the origin. We then compute the necessary change in the frequency domain similar to Equation 5:

$$F = \begin{cases} 1/\left(1 + S \cdot |z_{\text{origin}}|\right) & \text{if } z_{\text{origin}} < 0 \\ 1 + S \cdot z_{\text{origin}} & \text{if } z_{\text{origin}} \geq 0 \end{cases} \tag{9}$$

where S is a proportionality constant that controls the overall strength, and F is the filter in the Fourier domain. In order to multiply it with the Fourier transform of an image we generate a radially symmetric version with a simple linear interpolation as shown in Figure 12(b) for $S = 1$.

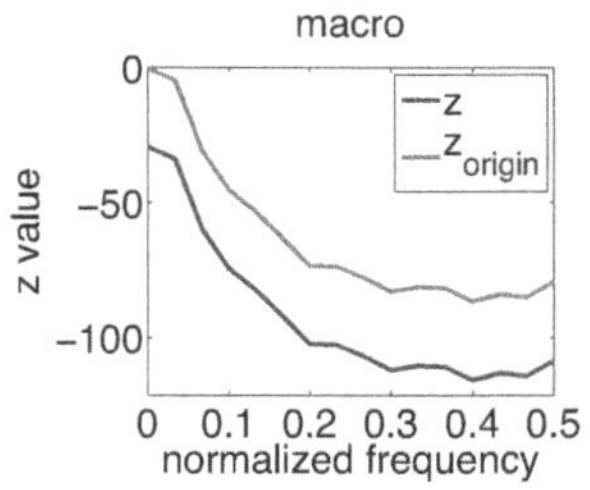

(a) significance values

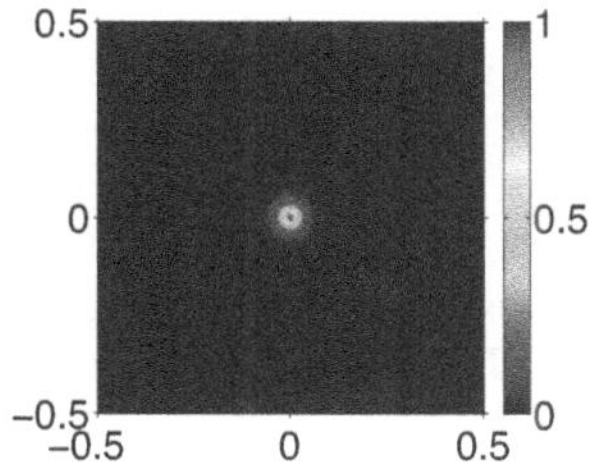

(b) F

Figure 12: Left: z and z_{origin} values for semantic concept *macro*. The negative values indicate an absence of high frequencies. Right: Corresponding multiplier in the Fourier domain computed with Eq. 9 and $S = 1$; it has a strong low-pass behavior.

Similar to our two previous image enhancement examples, we not only implement a semantic component, but also an adaption to the input image itself. In this case, we need a map indicating regions with only low frequency content as it is done in defocus estimation [30]. Figures 13(a) and 13(b) show an image and its corresponding defocus map reproduced from Zhuo and Sim [30].

We compute an intermediary image I_{tmp} using the input image I_{in} and the filter F:

$$I_{\text{tmp}} = \mathscr{F}^{-1}\Big(\mathscr{F}(I_{\text{in}}) \cdot F\Big) \tag{10}$$

where $\mathscr{F}(\cdot)$ and $\mathscr{F}^{-1}(\cdot)$ denote the Fourier transform and its inverse, respectively.

We again use a linear weighting of the images I_{in} and I_{tmp} (Eq. 8), where the weights are taken from the defocus map. The final output is shown in Figure 13(c). Note that the background is more blurred than in the input image, whereas the boy remains in focus.

(a) input

(b) weight map, *macro*

(c) output, *macro*

Figure 13: Example for the semantic concept *macro*. Top row: input and associated weight map. Images reproduced from Zhuo and Sim [30]. Bottom: Output image; note that the background is more blurred whereas the boy remains in focus.

5. CONCLUSIONS

We have presented a framework that learns associations between image characteristics and image keywords from a large database of annotated images [7]. The associations are quantified as a significance value from a simple non-parametric significance test. The framework needs no parameter tuning or optimization of a cost function, which makes it easy to scale to millions of images and thousands of semantic concepts.

The associations are then used for three semantic image enhancement methods where the goal is to re-render an image based on its semantic context. All methods are based on two components: 1) semantic context as described by the keywords 2) numeric content as described by pixel values. The novelty is the first component that enables an adaptation to an arbitrary semantic context; conventional enhancement methods lack this dimension.

We demonstrate three enhancement algorithms that all adapt to a given semantic context (a keyword): 1) gray-level tone-mapping to semantically adjust an image's gray-level distribution 2) semantic color transfer to emphasize a given context 3) semantic defocus magnification creating artistic blur effects expressed by an associated keyword. Example images for the three semantic enhancements are reproduced in Figure 1 and throughout Section 4.

We demonstrate with psychophysical experiments that our semantic gray-level enhancement outperforms other enhancement methods that are based on pixel values only. Moreover, our method interprets semantic expressions from an uncontrolled vocabulary as opposed to other methods that restrict the user to a small number of predefined choices [26, 15].

Due to the simplicity and computational speed of the framework – even at large scales – we see potential to use it in other image-related areas that include semantics, such as annotation, labeling, or retrieval. For this reason we make the code publicly available for research purposes under `http://ivrg.epfl.ch/SemanticEnhancement.html`.

For future work we propose to use computer vision techniques in order to estimate more robust weight maps (see Figure 11). Also, assuming a linear relationship between the significance values and the processing strength proved to be good (Sec. 4.1.3), but other non-linear dependencies can be investigated to further improve the performance. It is also interesting to investigate other types of image enhancement algorithms that exploit different characteristics and validate them with more psychophysical experiments.

6. REFERENCES

[1] S. Bae and F. Durand. Defocus magnification. *Eurographics*, 26(3):571–579, 2007.

[2] G. Ciocca, C. Cusano, F. Gasparini, and R. Schettini. Content aware image enhancement. In *Artificial Intelligence and Human-Oriented Computing*, volume 4733/2007, pages 686–697, Rome, September 2007.

[3] D. Cohen-Or, O. Sorkine, R. Gal, T. Leyvand, and Y.-Q. Xu. Color harmonization. *ACM Trans. Graphics*, 25(3):624–630, 2006.

[4] J. Deng, W. Dong, R. Socher, L.-J. Li, K. Li, and L. Fei-Fei. Imagenet: a large-scale hierarchical image database. In *CVPR*, pages 248–255, Miami, 2009.

[5] T. Deselaers and V. Ferrari. Visual and semantic similarity in imagenet. In *CVPR*, pages 1777–1784, 2011.

[6] C. Fredembach. Saliency as compact regions for local image enhancement. In *CIC*, pages 14–18, 2011.

[7] M. J. Huiskes and M. S. Lew. The MIR flickr retrieval evaluation. In *ACM MIR*, 2008.

[8] R. Hummel. Image Enhancement by Histogram Transformation. *CGIP*, 6(2):184–195, 1977.

[9] ISO 11664-4:2008(E)/CIE S 014-4/E:2007. *CIE Colorimetry - Part 4: 1976 L*a*b* Colour Space*, 2007.

[10] S. B. Kang, A. Kapoor, and D. Lischinski. Personalization of image enhancement. In *CVPR*, pages 1799–1806, 2010.

[11] T. Mäenpää. *The Local Binary Pattern Approach To Texture Analysis – Extensions and Applications*. PhD thesis, University of Oulu, 2003.

[12] H. B. Mann and D. R. Whitney. On a test of whether one of two random variables is stochastically larger than the other. *The Annals of Mathematical Statistics*, 18(1):50–60, 1947.

[13] G. A. Miller. Wordnet: a lexical database for english. *Communications of the ACM*, 38(11):39–41, 1995.

[14] S. Moser and M. Schroeder. Usage of DSC meta tags in a general automatic image enhancement system. In *EI*, volume 4669, pages 259–267, San Jose, CA, USA, January 2002.

[15] N. Murray, S. Skaff, and L. Marchesotti. Towards automatic concept transfer. In *ACM SIGGRAPH/Eurographics*, pages 167–176. ACM Press, 2011.

[16] V. Namboodiri. Recovery of relative depth from a single observation using an uncalibrated (real-aperture) camera. In *CVPR*, pages 1–6, 2008.

[17] V. Ordonez, G. Kulkarni, and T. L. Berg. Im2text: describing images using 1 million captioned photographs. In *NIPS*, 2011.

[18] S. M. Pizer, E. P. Amburn, J. D. Austin, R. Cromartie, A. Geselowitz, T. Greer, B. ter Haar Romeny, J. B. Zimmerman, and K. Zuiderveld. Adaptive histogram equalization and its variations. *JCVGIP*, 39:355–368, 1987.

[19] A. Polesel, G. Ramponi, and V. J. Mathews. Image enhancement via adaptive unsharp masking. *TIP*, 9(3):505–510, March 2000.

[20] E. Reinhard, M. Ashikhmin, B. Gooch, and P. Shirley. Color transfer between images. *IEEE Computer Graphics and Applications*, 21(5):2–9, 2001.

[21] C. Sauvaget and V. Boyer. Harmonic colorization using proportion contrast. In *AFRIGRAPH*, pages 63–69, 2010.

[22] N. Sawant, J. Li, and J. Z. Wang. Automatic image semantic interpretation using social action and tagging data. In *Multimedia Tools and Applications*, volume 51, pages 213–246, 2011.

[23] I. K. Sethi, I. Coman, and D. Stan. Mining association rules between low-level image features and high-level concepts. In *Data Mining and Knowledge Discovery III*, volume 4384, pages 279–290, 2001.

[24] A. Torralba, R. Fergus, and W. T. Freeman. 80 million tiny images: a large dataset for non-parametric object and scene recognition. *Trans. PAMI*, 30(11):1958–1970, 2008.

[25] R. Walpole, R. Myers, and S. Myers. *Probability and Statistics*, volume 6. Prentice Hall International, 1998.

[26] B. Wang, Y. Yu, T.-T. Wong, C. Chen, and Y.-Q. Xu. Data-driven image color theme enhancement. In *SIGGRAPH Asia*, volume 29, 2010.

[27] B. Wang, Y. Yu, and Y.-Q. Xu. Example-based image color and tone style enhancement. In *SIGGRAPH Asia*, volume 30, 2011.

[28] X.-J. Wang, W.-Y. Ma, and X. Li. Exploring statistical correlations for image retrieval. *Multimedia Systems*, 11(4):340–351, 2006.

[29] F. Wilcoxon. Individual comparisons by ranking methods. *Biometrics Bulletin*, 1(6):80–83, 1945.

[30] S. Zhuo and T. Sim. Defocus map estimation from a single image. *Pattern Recognition*, 44(9):1852–1858, 2011.

Image Annotation by Semantic Sparse Recoding of Visual Content

Zhiwu Lu and Yuxin Peng*
Institute of Computer Science and Technology, Peking University, Beijing 100871, China
{luzhiwu, pengyuxin}@pku.edu.cn

ABSTRACT

This paper presents a new semantic sparse recoding method to generate more descriptive and robust representation of visual content for image annotation. Although the visual bag-of-words (BOW) representation has been reported to achieve promising results in image annotation, its visual codebook is completely learnt from low-level visual features using quantization techniques and thus the so-called semantic gap remains unbridgeable. To handle such challenging issue, we utilize both the annotations of training images and the predicted annotations of test images to improve the original visual BOW representation. This is further formulated as a sparse coding problem so that the noise issue induced by the inaccurate quantization of visual features can also be handled to some extent. By developing an efficient sparse coding algorithm, we successfully generate a new visual BOW representation for image annotation. Since such sparse coding has actually incorporated the high-level semantic information into the original visual codebook, we thus consider it as semantic sparse recoding of the visual content. Although the predicted annotations of test images are also used as inputs by the traditional image annotation refinement, we focus on the visual BOW representation refinement for image annotation in this paper. The experimental results on two benchmark datasets show the superior performance of our semantic sparse recoding method in image annotation.

Categories and Subject Descriptors

H.3.3 [**Information Storage and Retrieval**]: Information Search and Retrieval—*retrieval models*

General Terms

Algorithms, Experimentation, Performance

*Corresponding author.

Keywords

Image annotation, visual BOW representation, semantic gap, semantic sparse recoding

1. INTRODUCTION

Since image annotation plays an important role in image retrieval, it has been extensively studied in the literature [5, 15, 21]. The main goal of image annotation is to model the relationships between a set of textual keywords and the visual content of images so that we can easily perform image retrieval by text queries that most users are likely to choose instead of image retrieval by image examples. Besides modeling the relationships between textual keywords and visual content, it is also crucial for image annotation to generate a descriptive representation of the visual content. In this paper, we focus on such challenging task of visual representation generation. To bridge the gap between low-level visual features and high-level semantics, many efforts have been made to generate an intermediate representation [7, 24, 28] based on local interest points (or regions) for image annotation. In particular, one influential work is the visual bag-of-words (BOW) representation, which quantizes the local visual features to form a codebook and thus summarizes each image as a histogram of visual words. This visual BOW representation has been reported to achieve promising results in image annotation [9, 11, 27].

However, the traditional visual BOW representation has two inherent drawbacks. Firstly, its visual codebook is completely learnt from low-level visual features by quantization and thus the so-called semantic gap remains unbridgeable. Although the supervisory information with respect to local interest points has been exploited for visual codebook optimization in [19, 27], this type of high-level semantics is commonly very expensive to obtain in practice. Secondly, due to the inaccurate quantization of visual features in the traditional visual BOW representation, the noise issue becomes rather severe and thus leads to obvious performance degradation. In the literature, various unsupervised methods [12, 17] have been developed to handle such noise issue associated with the traditional visual BOW representation. The main problem of these unsupervised methods is that they do not consider any semantic information. In summary, to the best of our knowledge, very little attempt has been made to simultaneously overcome the two drawbacks of the traditional visual BOW representation.

In this paper, we focus on semantic sparse recoding of visual content so that more descriptive and robust visual representation can be generated for image annotation. In the

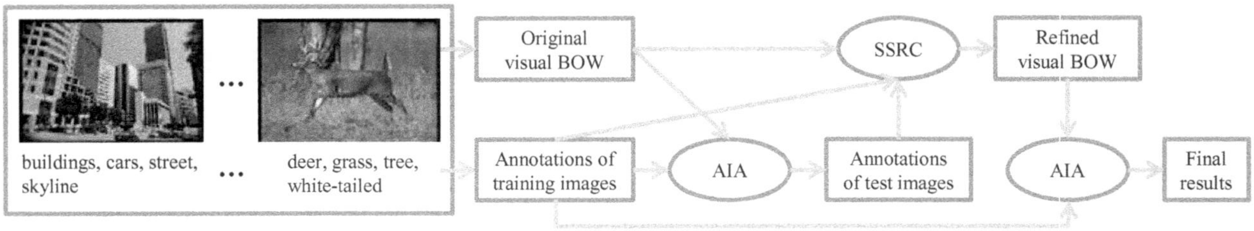

Figure 1: The flowchart of automatic image annotation (AIA) by our semantic sparse recoding (SSRC) of visual content. Here, the first round of AIA is used to generate the textual BOW representation over all the images for our SSRC algorithm.

following, the annotations of training images and the predicted annotations of test images are used as the high-level semantic information for such visual BOW representation refinement. Moreover, to handle the noise issue induced by the inaccurate quantization of visual features, we formulate the challenging problem of visual BOW representation refinement as a sparse coding problem [1, 4, 25], which can be solved efficiently using a dimension reduction technique. Since such sparse coding mainly aims to incorporate the semantic information into the original visual codebook, it can actually be considered as semantic sparse recoding of the visual content for image annotation. Although the predicted annotations of test images are also used as inputs by the traditional image annotation refinement [15, 16, 23], we focus on visual BOW representation refinement for image annotation in this paper. This also distinguishes our present work from tag filtering [21] over noisily tagged web images.

It is worth noting that our semantic sparse recoding of visual content is different form other sparse coding methods used for image annotation. In [24], sparse coding was adopted to model an image as linear combination of other images, and the obtained reconstruction relationships were further exploited for feature extraction and label propagation. Unlike our semantic sparse recoding directly for visual BOW representation refinement, the problem of feature extraction or label propagation was actually not formulated as a sparse coding problem in [24]. In [26, 29], group sparse coding was directly used for feature selection from multiple groups of visual features. However, these two methods had ignored the high-level semantic information during feature selection, different from our semantic sparse recoding that exploits the annotations of images for visual BOW representation refinement. In [11], sparse coding was directly utilized to model the relationships between textual keywords and visual words, regardless of the semantic refinement of visual words for image annotation. Similarly, the semantic refinement of visual words was also ignored in [9] which modeled image classification and annotation as group sparse coding over textual keywords and visual BOW representation.

To verify the effectiveness of our semantic sparse recoding of visual content, we apply the obtained new visual BOW representation to the task of image annotation, which takes exactly the same settings as the process of predicting the initial annotations of test images for our semantic sparse recoding. The flowchart of automatic image annotation (AIA) by our semantic sparse recoding (SSRC) of visual content is illustrated in Figure 1, where two rounds of AIA are considered. The later experimental results have demonstrated that the refined new visual BOW representation obtained by our SSRC method is significantly more descriptive and robust than the original visual BOW representation in image annotation. Although only tested in the task of image annotation, our SSRC method can be readily applied to other more challenging tasks (e.g. tag filtering) where the noisy tags of images are provided initially. Finally, we summarize our main contributions as follows:

- This is the first attempt to develop semantic sparse recoding of visual content to generate more descriptive and robust visual representation for image annotation.
- Different from other visual codebook optimization methods, our semantic sparse recoding method can simultaneously overcome the two drawbacks (i.e. semantic gap and inaccurate quantization) of the traditional visual BOW representation to some extent.
- Our method is shown to achieve *significant gains* in image annotation, which becomes *more impressive* given that we do not make use of extra semantic information (like [15, 22, 23]) or multiple visual features (like [10, 18, 26, 29]). When the spatial context of visual words and the global color histogram are also considered, we *obtain the best results so far* in the image annotation literature, to the best of our knowledge.
- Our method can be readily applied to many other challenging tasks in computer vision and image analysis. More notably, it has an important and wide use in graph-based learning (see Section 2.3).

The remainder of this paper is organized as follows. In Section 2, we present our semantic sparse recoding method for visual BOW representation refinement. In Section 3, we apply the refined new visual BOW representation to image annotation. In Section 4, we provide the experimental results on two benchmark datasets to verify the effectiveness of our semantic sparse recoding in image annotation. Finally, Section 5 gives the conclusions.

2. SEMANTIC SPARSE RECODING OF VISUAL CONTEXT

In this section, we formulate the challenging problem of visual BOW representation refinement as semantic sparse recoding of visual content, followed by an insightful explanation of the L_1-norm smoothness used in our semantic sparse recoding. Moreover, motivated by the fast iterative shrinkage-thresholding method [1], we develop an efficient algorithm for our semantic sparse recoding.

2.1 Motivation

Although visual BOW representation has been reported to achieve promising results in image annotation [9, 11, 27], it has two distinct drawbacks. Firstly, since the visual codebook is completely learnt from low-level visual feature vectors (i.e. local descriptors) using quantization techniques, the high-level semantic information is actually ignored in the traditional visual BOW representation, which means that the semantic gap remains unbridgeable. Secondly, due to the inherent limitation of quantization, the visual codebook may be far from accurate and thus the labels of local descriptors may be rather noisy. In the literature, various supervised [19, 27] and unsupervised [12, 17] methods have been developed for visual codebook optimization. However, most of them can not simultaneously overcome the two drawbacks of the traditional visual BOW representation.

To address the above problems, we focus on semantic sparse recoding of visual content to generate more descriptive and robust visual representation for image annotation. In this paper, the annotations of training images and the predicted annotations of test images (obtained by the first round of image annotation shown in Figure 1) are used as the high-level semantic information for our semantic sparse recoding. Similar to the formation of the visual BOW representation, we generate a new textual BOW representation with the annotations of all images, i.e., the high-level semantic information has been encoded into the textual BOW representation. Hence, the main goal of our work is just to refine the visual BOW representation based on the textual BOW representation. Considering the distinct advantage (i.e. noise robustness) of sparse coding as reported in [25], we further formulate such challenging visual BOW representation refinement as a sparse coding problem so that the noise issue associated with the visual BOW representation can also be handled to some extent. Since such sparse coding has actually incorporated the high-level semantic information into the original visual codebook, we thus consider it as semantic sparse recoding of the visual content for image annotation. We will elaborate it as follows.

2.2 Notations and Problem Formulation

For a standard image annotation task, we initially have: a visual BOW representation $Y \in R^{n\times M}$ over all the images (n is the total number of images and M is the number of visual words), and a training set of images annotated with C textual keywords. Such initial annotations can be collected into a single matrix $Z = \{z_{ij}\}_{n\times C}$, where $z_{ij} = 1$ if image i is annotated with keyword j and $z_{ij} = 0$ otherwise. It is worth noting that the test images have also been considered in this definition since we always have $z_{ij} = 0$ for each test image. Based on the visual BOW representation Y and the initial annotation matrix Z, we predict the annotations of the test images by performing the first round of image annotation illustrated in Figure 1. When the annotations of training and test images are considered together, we generate a textual BOW representation, from which a linear kernel matrix $W \in R^{n\times n}$ can be derived. Here, we only define linear kernel over the textual BOW representation.

In this paper, we make attempt to formulate semantic sparse recoding of visual content from a graph-based learning viewpoint. Hence, we first give the graph definition before problem formulation. More concretely, by regarding W as a weight matrix, we define an undirected weighted graph $\mathcal{G} = (\mathcal{V}, W)$ with its vertex set $\mathcal{V}$ being the set of all images. The normalized Laplacian matrix of $\mathcal{G}$ is given by

$$\mathcal{L} = I - D^{-1/2}WD^{-1/2}, \quad (1)$$

where I is an $n\times n$ identity matrix and D is an $n\times n$ diagonal matrix with its i-th diagonal element being the sum of the i-th row of W. We further derive a new matrix B from $\mathcal{L}$:

$$B = \Sigma^{\frac{1}{2}}V^T, \quad (2)$$

where V is an $n \times n$ orthonormal matrix with each column being an eigenvector of $\mathcal{L}$, and Σ is an $n \times n$ diagonal matrix with its diagonal element Σ_{ii} being an eigenvalue of $\mathcal{L}$ (sorted as $0 \leq \Sigma_{11} \leq ... \leq \Sigma_{nn}$). Since the eigenvalue decomposition of $\mathcal{L}$ is denoted as $\mathcal{L} = V\Sigma V^T$, we can represent $\mathcal{L}$ in a symmetrical decomposition form:

$$\mathcal{L} = (\Sigma^{\frac{1}{2}}V^T)^T\Sigma^{\frac{1}{2}}V^T = B^TB. \quad (3)$$

Based on the visual BOW representation Y and the new matrix B derived from the annotations of all images, we formulate semantic sparse recoding of visual content as the following L_1-norm optimization problem:

$$\min_{F,\hat{Y}} \frac{1}{2}||F - \hat{Y}||_F^2 + \lambda||BF||_1 + \gamma||\hat{Y} - Y||_1, \quad (4)$$

where $F \in R^{n\times M}$ denotes the refined visual BOW representation, $\hat{Y} \in R^{n\times M}$ denotes the ideal visual BOW representation, and λ (or γ) denote the positive regularization parameter. The first and third terms of the above objective function are the L_2-norm and L_1-norm fitting constraints, respectively. The second term is the graph smoothness constraint, which means that a good refined visual BOW representation should not change too much between similar images. In the next subsection, we will make it clear that this L_1-norm graph smoothness is closely related to the well-known Laplacian regularization [30, 31] which has been widely used for graph-based learning in the literature.

It should be noted that, besides the refined visual BOW representation F, we also introduce the ideal visual BOW representation $\hat{Y}$ into the above visual BOW representation refinement problem. Our main motivation is to impose direct noise reduction on Y by extra consideration of the L_1-norm fitting constraint $||\hat{Y} - Y||_1$. Although this L_1-norm fitting constraint is only defined over $\hat{Y}$, the effect of noise reduction can be transferred to F by solving equation (4) with $\hat{Y}$ being an intermediate representation. In summary, we have induced not only the smoothness sparsity $||BF||_1$ in the compressed domain (sparse coding is closely related to compressed sensing) but also the noise sparsity $||\hat{Y} - Y||_1$ in the original space into our semantic sparse recoding.

Although we have successfully given the problem formulation for visual BOW representation refinement from a graph-based learning viewpoint, there remain two key problems to be concerned: *how to explain the L_1-norm smoothness more insightfully*, and *how to solve the L_1-norm optimization problem (4) efficiently*. In the next two subsections, we will address these two problems, respectively.

2.3 L_1-Norm Smoothness

In spectral graph theory, the traditional smoothness measure used as Laplacian regularization is defined as $\Omega(F) = \text{tr}(F^T\mathcal{L}F)$, where $\text{tr}(\cdot)$ denotes the trace of a matrix. Different from $\Omega(F)$, the L_1-norm smoothness measure is defined as $\tilde{\Omega}(F) = ||BF||_1$. As for this new L_1-norm smoothness measure, we have the following proposition, which will be further used as *the basis of dimension reduction* to develop an efficient algorithm in Section 2.4.

PROPOSITION 1. *(i) If $\tilde{\Omega}(F) \leq 1$, $\Omega(F) \leq \tilde{\Omega}(F)$; (ii) For an eigenvector $V_{.i}$ of $\mathcal{L}$, $\tilde{\Omega}(V_{.i}) = \Sigma_{ii}^{\frac{1}{2}}$; (iii) If $F = VU$ and $U = \{u_{ij}\}_{n\times M}$, $\tilde{\Omega}(F) = \sum_{j=1}^{M}\sum_{i=1}^{n}|u_{ij}|\Sigma_{ii}^{\frac{1}{2}}$.*

Proof: (i) If $\tilde{\Omega}(F) = ||BF||_1 \leq 1$, we have

$$\begin{aligned}
\Omega(F) &= \mathrm{tr}(F^T\mathcal{L}F) = \sum_{j=1}^{M} F_{.j}^T\mathcal{L}F_{.j} = \sum_j F_{.j}^T B^T BF_{.j} \\
&= \sum_j ||BF_{.j}||_2^2 = \sum_j\sum_i (B_{i.}F_{.j})^2 \\
&\leq (\sum_j\sum_i |B_{i.}F_{.j}|)^2 = ||BF||_1^2 = (\tilde{\Omega}(F))^2 \\
&\leq \tilde{\Omega}(F),
\end{aligned}$$

where $B_{i.}$ denotes the i-th row of B and $F_{.j}$ denotes the j-th column of F.
(ii) Since V is orthonormal, we have

$$\begin{aligned}
\tilde{\Omega}(V_{.i}) &= ||BV_{.i}||_1 = ||\Sigma^{\frac{1}{2}}V^TV_{.i}||_1 \\
&= ||\Sigma^{\frac{1}{2}}[V_{.1}^TV_{.i}, ..., V_{.i-1}^TV_{.i}, \\
&\qquad V_{.i}^TV_{.i}, V_{.i+1}^TV_{.i}, ..., V_{.n}^TV_{.i}]^T||_1 \\
&= ||[0, ..., 0, \Sigma_{ii}^{\frac{1}{2}}, 0, ..., 0]^T||_1 = \Sigma_{ii}^{\frac{1}{2}}.
\end{aligned}$$

(iii) Similarly, if $F = VU$, we have

$$\begin{aligned}
\tilde{\Omega}(F) &= ||(\Sigma^{\frac{1}{2}}V^T)(VU)||_1 = \sum_{j=1}^{M}||\sum_{i=1}^{n} u_{ij}\Sigma^{\frac{1}{2}}V^TV_{.i}||_1 \\
&= \sum_j||\sum_i u_{ij}[0, ..., 0, \Sigma_{ii}^{\frac{1}{2}}, 0, ..., 0]^T||_1 \\
&= \sum_j\sum_i |u_{ij}|\Sigma_{ii}^{\frac{1}{2}}.
\end{aligned}$$

Proposition 1(i) shows that our L_1-norm smoothness can ensure the traditional smoothness if we can reduce the former below 1. Proposition 1(ii) shows that eigenvectors with smaller eigenvalues are smoother in terms of our L_1-norm smoothness measure. Since any matrix $F \in R^{n\times M}$ can be denoted as $F = VU = [\sum_{i=1}^{n} u_{i1}V_{.i}, ..., \sum_{i=1}^{n} u_{iM}V_{.i}]$, we can conclude from Proposition 1(iii) that each column of a smooth matrix is actually a linear combination of the eigenvectors with small eigenvalues. These nice properties will be used to develop an efficient algorithm in Section 2.4.

We can clearly see that our new L_1-norm smoothness measure used in equation (4) is an L_1-norm formulation of Laplacian regularization. However, it has two distinct advantages over the traditional smoothness measure. Firstly, it can induce another type of sparsity into visual BOW representation refinement, besides the fitting error sparsity $||\hat{Y} - Y||_1$. Due to these two types of sparsity, the noise issue associated with the visual BOW representation can be handled effectively, as shown in later experiments. Secondly, our L_1-norm formulation of Laplacian regularization can help to explain the visual BOW representation refinement in the framework of sparse coding. That is, according to Proposition 1(iii), the visual BOW representation refinement can be formulated as a linear reconstruction problem by setting $F = VU$. More importantly, this linear reconstruction problem can be solved efficiently (see Section 2.4) by sparse coding over only a small subset of eigenvectors (i.e. only partial columns of V are used), which is especially suitable for large image datasets. In contrast, as for other L_1-norm generalizations [3, 20] of Laplacian regularization which approximately take the form of $\sum_j\sum_{ii'} w_{ij}|f_{ij} - f_{i'j}|$, they are not explicitly defined based upon the eigenvectors of $\mathcal{L}$ and the dimension reduction technique is hard to be used for $F = \{f_{ij}\}_{n\times M}$. Hence, the sparse coding algorithms developed in [3, 20] incur very large time cost.

Although originally designed for visual BOW representation refinement, our new L_1-norm Laplacian regularization can be readily applied to other challenging graph-based learning problems (especially when noise reduction is needed in complicated cases), considering the wide use of Laplacian regularization [30, 31] in the literature. This important extension will be discussed in our future work.

2.4 Efficient SSRC Algorithm

Although we can find a unique global solution for the visual BOW representation refinement problem (4) by convex optimization, it is not an easy task to develop an efficient algorithm for such convex optimization. Fortunately, the L_1-norm optimization problem (4) can be approximately solved in two alternate optimization steps:

$$\begin{aligned}
F^* &= \arg\min_F \frac{1}{2}||F - \hat{Y}^*||_F^2 + \lambda||BF||_1, \\
\hat{Y}^* &= \arg\min_{\hat{Y}} \frac{1}{2}||\hat{Y} - F^*||_F^2 + \gamma||\hat{Y} - Y||_1.
\end{aligned}$$

Here, we set $\hat{Y}^* = Y$ initially. As a basic L_1-norm optimization problem, the second subproblem has an explicit solution based on the soft-thresholding function:

$$\hat{Y}^* = \mathrm{soft}(F^* - Y, \gamma) + Y, \tag{5}$$

where $\mathrm{soft}(y, \gamma) = \mathrm{sign}(y)\max\{|y| - \gamma, 0\}$. In the following, we focus on developing an efficient sparse coding algorithm to solve the first L_1-norm optimization subproblem.

As we have mentioned in Section 2.3, the dimension of our semantic sparse coding of visual content can be reduced dramatically by working only with a small subset of eigenvectors of $\mathcal{L}$. That is, similar to [2, 8], we significantly reduce the dimension of F by requiring it to take the form of $F = V_mU$ where U is an $m \times M$ matrix that collects the reconstruction coefficients and V_m is an $n \times m$ matrix whose columns are the m eigenvectors with smallest eigenvalues (i.e. the first m columns of V). According to Proposition 1(iii), such dimension reduction can ensure that F is as smooth as possible in terms of our L_1-norm smoothness. The first L_1-norm optimization subproblem of our visual BOW representation refinement can now be formulated as follows:

$$\begin{aligned}
&\arg\min_U \frac{1}{2}||V_mU - \hat{Y}^*||_F^2 + \lambda||BV_mU||_1 \\
&= \arg\min_U \sum_{j=1}^{M} \frac{1}{2}||V_mU_{.j} - \hat{Y}_{.j}^*||_2^2 + \lambda||BV_mU_{.j}||_1, \quad (6)
\end{aligned}$$

where $\hat{Y}_{.j}^*$ and $U_{.j}$ denote the j-th column of $\hat{Y}^*$ and U, respectively. The above problem can be further decomposed into the following M independent subproblems:

$$\arg\min_{U_{.j}} \frac{1}{2}||V_m U_{.j} - \hat{Y}^*_{.j}||_2^2 + \lambda||BV_m U_{.j}||_1$$
$$= \arg\min_{U_{.j}} \frac{1}{2}||V_m U_{.j} - \hat{Y}^*_{.j}||_2^2 + \lambda||\sum_{i=1}^{m} \Sigma^{\frac{1}{2}} V^T V_{.i} u_{ij}||_1$$
$$= \arg\min_{U_{.j}} \frac{1}{2}||V_m U_{.j} - \hat{Y}^*_{.j}||_2^2 + \lambda \sum_{i=1}^{m} \Sigma_{ii}^{\frac{1}{2}} |u_{ij}|. \quad (7)$$

The first term of the above objective function denotes the linear reconstruction error which just takes the same form as that used in sparse coding, while the second term denotes the weighted L_1-norm sparsity regularization over the reconstruction coefficients. That is, the first subproblem of our visual BOW representation refinement has been successfully transformed into a generalized sparse coding problem.

The formulation $F_{.j} = V_m U_{.j}$ used in equation (7) has two distinct advantages. Firstly, we can derive a linear reconstruction problem from the original visual BOW representation refinement problem, and correspondingly we can *explain it in the framework of sparse coding*. This also provides further insight into Laplacian regularization. In fact, the term of $\sum_{i=1}^{m} \Sigma_{ii}^{\frac{1}{2}} |u_{ij}|$ corresponds to both Laplacian regularization and sparsity regularization. By unifying these two types of regularization, we thus successfully develop novel semantic sparse recoding of visual content for image annotation. Secondly, since the sparse coding is performed with respect to $U_{.j} \in R^m$ ($m \ll n$), we can readily develop efficient algorithms for our semantic sparse recoding. That is, although many sparse coding algorithms scale polynomially with m, they have linear time complexity with respect to the data size n. More importantly, we *have eliminated the need to compute the full matrix* B in equation (4), which is especially suitable for image annotation on large image datasets. In fact, we only need to compute the m smallest eigenvectors of $\mathcal{L}$. To speed up this step, we choose to construct k-NN graphs for our semantic sparse recoding. Given a k-NN graph ($k \ll n$), the time complexity of finding m smallest eigenvectors of the sparse matrix $\mathcal{L}$ is $O(m^3 + m^2 n + kmn)$, which is scalable with respect to the data size n.

In theory, any efficient sparse coding algorithm can be adopted to solve the L_1-norm optimization problem (7). In this paper, we only consider the fast iterative shrinkage-thresholding algorithm (FISTA) [1], since its implementation mainly involves lightweight operations such as vector operations and matrix-vector multiplications. To adjust the original FISTA for our semantic sparse recoding, we only need to modify the soft-thresholding function as:

$$\text{soft}(u_{ij}, \frac{\lambda\Sigma_{ii}^{\frac{1}{2}}}{||V_m||_s^2}) = \text{sign}(u_{ij}) \max\{|u_{ij}| - \frac{\lambda\Sigma_{ii}^{\frac{1}{2}}}{||V_m||_s^2}, 0\},$$

where $||V_m||_s$ represents the spectral norm of the matrix V_m. For large problems, it is often computationally expensive to directly compute the Lipschitz constant $||V_m||_s^2$. In practice, it can be efficiently estimated by a backtracking line-search strategy [1]. In summary, we have successfully developed an efficient algorithm to solve the first subproblem of our visual BOW representation refinement.

Considering the two alternate optimization steps together, our efficient algorithm for semantic sparse recoding (SSRC) of visual content is outlined as follows:

(1) Construct a k-NN graph with its weight matrix W being defined over the textual BOW representation.

(2) Compute the normalized Laplacian matrix $\mathcal{L} = I - D^{-\frac{1}{2}} W D^{-\frac{1}{2}}$ according to equation (1).

(3) Find the m smallest eigenvectors of the normalized Laplacian matrix $\mathcal{L}$ and store them in V_m.

(4) Initialize the deal visual BOW representation as $\hat{Y}^* = Y$ (Y is the original visual BOW representation).

(5) Find the best solution U^* of the L_1-norm optimization problem (6) by running the modified FISTA with respect to each visual word.

(6) Update the deal visual BOW representation $\hat{Y}^*$ with the refined visual BOW representation $F^* = V_m U^*$ as: $\hat{Y}^* = \text{soft}(F^* - Y, \gamma) + Y$.

(7) Iterate Steps 5 and 6 until the stopping condition is satisfied, and output the final refined visual BOW representation F^*.

In our later experiments, we find that our SSRC algorithm generally converges in very limited number of iteration steps (< 5). Moreover, according to our aforementioned analysis, both Steps 3 and 5 are scalable with respect to the data size n. Hence, our SSRC algorithm for visual BOW representation refinement can be applied to large image datasets.

2.5 Discussion

In this subsection, we briefly discuss what is the relation between our semantic sparse coding and the well-known graph-based semi-supervised learning. In fact, when we utilize the traditional Laplacian regularization instead of our L_1-norm version and also discard the L_1-norm fitting constraint $||\hat{Y} - Y||_1$, the semantic sparse coding problem (4) is reduced to the traditional graph-based semi-supervised learning problem [30]. This means that our semantic sparse coding can be regarded as a variant of graph-based semi-supervised learning. To illustratively verify the effectiveness of our L_1-norm Laplacian regularization (used by our semantic sparse coding) in noise reduction, we show a toy example in Figure 2, where only the two-class semi-supervised learning problem is concerned. From Figure 2(a), we can observe that two data points are incorrectly labeled initially. Such noisy labels are further shown to be effectively removed (see Figure 2(c)) by semi-supervised learning with our L_1-norm Laplacian regularization (i.e. the traditional Laplacian regularization used in [30] is replaced by our L_1-norm version), which is otherwise not true for semi-supervised learning [30] with the traditional Laplacian regularization. That is, we can indeed benefit from the sparsity induced by our L_1-norm Laplacian regularization and thus suppress the negative effect of the noisy labels. This ability of noise reduction is crucial for the success of our semantic sparse coding of the visual content in the task of image annotation.

More notably, the toy example given by Figure 2 also shows that semi-supervised learning (either with our L_1-norm Laplacian regularization or with the traditional version) has the outstanding ability of label propagation. Hence, as a variant of semi-supervised learning, our semantic sparse coding is inherently able to handle the incompletely labeling issue (due to inaccurate quantization) associated with

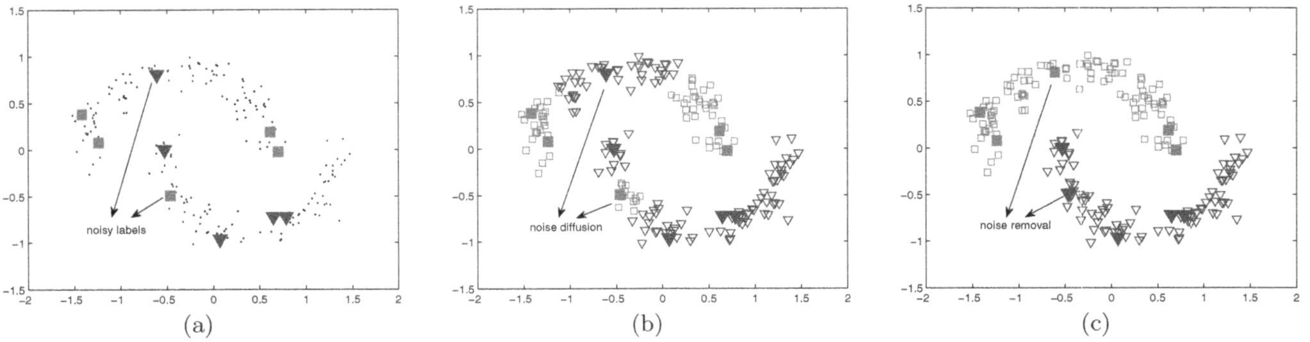

Figure 2: Illustration of the difference between the traditional Laplacian regularization and our new L_1-norm Laplacian regularization for semi-supervised learning with noisy labels: (a) the two-moons toy dataset with each class having one incorrectly (out of five) labeled data point initially; (b) the classification results by semi-supervised learning with the traditional Laplacian regularization; (c) the classification results by semi-supervised learning with our new L_1-norm Laplacian regularization.

the visual BOW representation. That is, the initial noisy visual words can be cleaned by our semantic sparse coding (i.e. noise reduction) and simultaneously propagated to semantically similar images along the manifolds determined by the textual BOW representation (i.e. label propagation), which results in more descriptive and robust visual BOW representation as shown in our later experiments.

3. IMAGE ANNOTATION WITH REFINED VISUAL BOW REPRESENTATION

To evaluate the performance of our SSRC algorithm, we directly apply the refined visual BOW representation to image annotation, as shown in Figure 1. Such second round of image annotation takes exactly the same settings as the first round whose main goal is to generate the textual BOW representation for our SSRC algorithm. Although any image annotation method can be used here, we only consider the correlated label propagation method [13, 16] and take the same implementation setup as our previous work [16]. Moreover, we define histogram-intersection kernel (HIK) over the visual BOW representation for correlated label propagation in both rounds of image annotation. The full algorithm for image annotation is summarized as follows:

(1) Generate the initial visual BOW representation by k-means clustering on dense SIFT descriptors.

(2) Perform the first round of image annotation using the initial visual BOW representation to generate the textual BOW representation for our SSRC algorithm.

(3) Refine the initial visual BOW representation by our SSRC algorithm with the textual BOW representation.

(4) Perform the second round of image annotation using the refined visual BOW representation.

Although sparse coding has drawn recent attention in the context of image annotation [24, 26, 29, 11, 9], our semantic sparse recoding of visual content is different form other sparse coding methods used for image annotation. In [24], sparse coding was adopted to model an image as linear combination of other images, and the obtained reconstruction relationships were further exploited for feature extraction and label propagation. Unlike our semantic sparse recoding directly for visual BOW representation refinement, the problem of feature extraction or label propagation was actually not formulated as a sparse coding problem in [24]. In [26, 29], group sparse coding was directly used for feature selection from multiple groups of visual features, but the semantic information has been ignored by such feature selection, different from our semantic sparse recoding that exploits the annotations of images for visual BOW representation refinement. In [11, 9], sparse coding was directly utilized to model the relationships between textual keywords and visual BOW representation, regardless of the semantic refinement of visual words for image annotation.

It is worth noting that the visual and semantic information used by our semantic sparse recoding is just the same as the standard image annotation task. That is, we do not exploit extra semantic information (e.g. semantic context of textual keywords derived from WordNet, an image search engine, or a photo-sharing website) for our semantic sparse recoding, which is not the case for [15, 22, 23]. However, even with such simple experimental setting, our semantic sparse recoding (see our later experimental results) has been shown to achieve significant gains in image annotation. This becomes much more impressive, considering that we do not make use of multiple visual features like many previous image annotation methods [10, 18, 26, 29].

4. EXPERIMENTAL RESULTS

In this section, our SSRC algorithm is evaluated in the task of image annotation on the Corel 5K [5] and IAPR TC12 [6] benchmark datasets. We focus on comparing the following three methods: (1) image annotation with the refined BOW representation by our SSRC algorithm; (2) image annotation with the refined BOW representation by using the traditional Laplacian regularization in equation (4) instead; (3) image annotation with the initial BOW representation. We define histogram-intersection kernels (HIK) over all the visual BOW representations. Moreover, when the traditional Laplacian regularization is used in equation (4) instead of our L_1-norm version, the optimization problem can be considered as a semi-supervised learning problem and thus be efficiently solved by label propagation (LP) [30]. Hence, the three methods for comparison are denoted as SSRC+HIK, LP+HIK, and HIK, respectively.

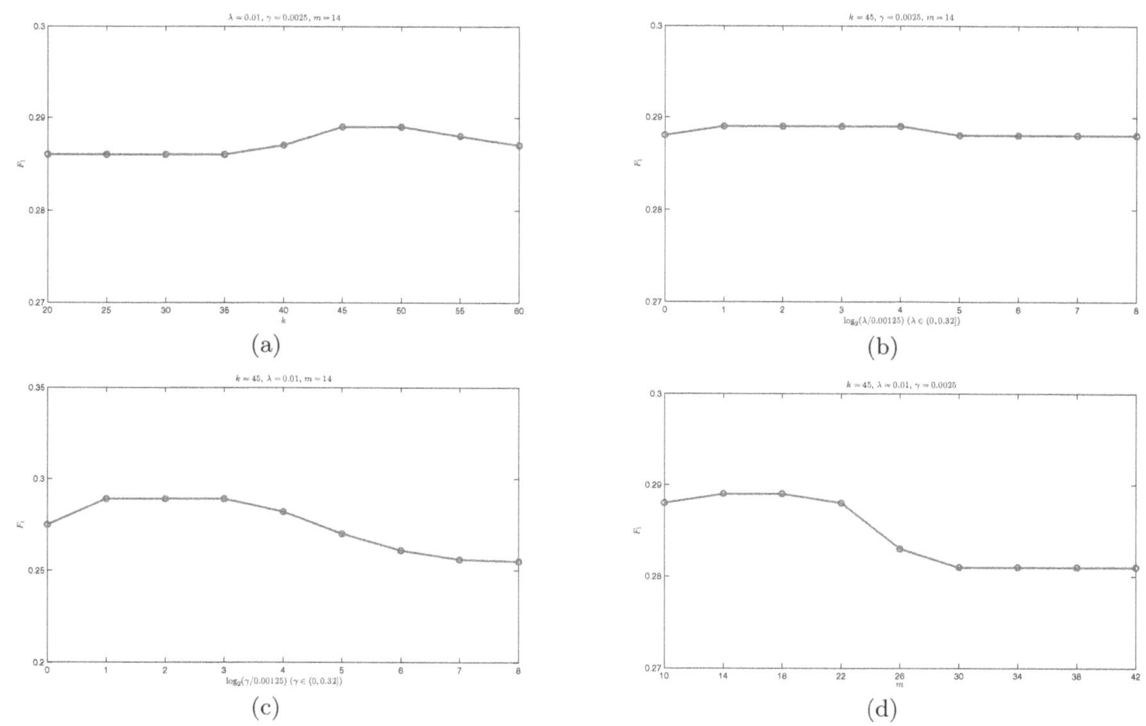

Figure 3: The annotation results by fivefold cross-validation on the training set of the Corel 5K benchmark dataset for our SSRC algorithm.

4.1 Experimental Setup

We conduct the experiments on two different benchmark datasets. The first dataset is the Corel 5K benchmark [5] that consists of 5,000 images annotated with 371 keywords. Each image is annotated by an average of 3.5 keywords. This dataset is split into 4,500 training images and 500 test images, which has been widely used for annotation evaluation in previous work [7, 15, 24]. The second dataset is the IAPR TC12 benchmark [6] that contains 20,000 images annotated with 291 keywords. Each image is annotated by an average of 4.7 keywords. This dataset is split into 18,000 training images and 2,000 test images. The task of image annotation is rather challenging on such a large dataset.

For these two benchmark datasets, we take the same strategy to generate the visual BOW representations. More concretely, we extract the SIFT descriptors of 16×16 pixel blocks computed over a regular grid with spacing of 8 pixels. The extracted SIFT descriptors are further quantized into $M = 1,500$ visual words by k-means clustering. Here, we aim to make the visual BOW representation more noisy by considering a relatively larger visual vocabulary.

The image annotation performance is evaluated by comparing the results from different algorithms with ground-truth annotations. Similar to previous work, for each test image, we use the top 5 annotations with the largest predicted scores as the final annotations. Furthermore, the obtained annotations of the test images are evaluated through the process of retrieving these test images with single keyword. For each keyword, the number of correctly annotated images is denoted as N_c, the number of retrieved images is denoted as N_r, and the number of truly related images in test set is denoted as N_t. The recall, precision, and F_1 measures are defined as follows: recall $= N_c/N_t$, precision $= N_c/N_r$, $F_1 = 2\,\text{recall} \cdot \text{precision}/(\text{recall} + \text{precision})$. These measures for annotation evaluation are finally averaged over all the keywords that occur in the test set.

However, the above three measures ignore the rank order. To address this problem, we also evaluate the semantic retrieval performance. Given a semantic query, one would want to return all the images which are automatically annotated with that keyword, ranked according to the predicted scores of these images. Such semantic retrieval can be evaluated by mean average precision (MAP) which has been widely used in the image retrieval literature.

For fair comparison, we construct the same k-NN graph based on the HIK matrix for different image annotation methods. The parameters of our SSRC algorithm can be selected by fivefold cross-validation on the training set. For example, according to Figure 3, we set the parameters of our SSRC algorithm on the Corel dataset as: $k = 45$, $\lambda = 0.01$, $\gamma = 0.0025$, and $m = 14$. Moreover, we take the same parameter selection strategy for other related methods.

4.2 Results of Automatic Annotation

The results of automatic annotation on the Corel 5K and IAPR TC12 benchmark datasets are listed in Table 1 and Table 2, respectively. The immediate observation is that our SSRC+HIK method for automatic annotation can achieve significant gains (29% for Corel and 17% for IAPR) over HIK in terms of the F_1 measure. This may be due to the fact that our SSRC method not only exploits the high-level semantic information for visual BOW representation refinement but also induces the nice property of sparsity for noise reduction in the initial visual BOW representation. That is, through handling the semantic gap and noise issues simultaneously, our SSRC method can generate more descriptive and robust visual representation for image annotation. As compared to LP+HIK that utilizes the traditional Laplacian

Corel images			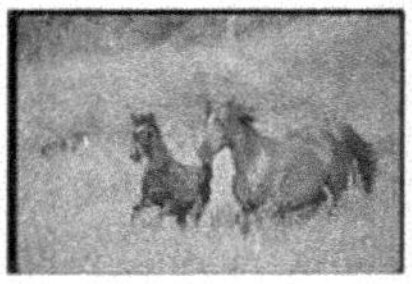	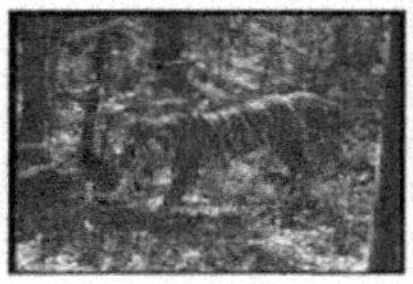	
Ground truth	coral, fish, ocean, reefs	wall, cars, tracks, formula	field, horses, mare, foals	forest, cat, tiger, Bengal	rocks, iguana, lizard, marine
Predicted keywords	coral, fish, ocean, *sea*, reefs	wall, cars, tracks, formula, *turn*	field, horses, *grass*, mare, foals	forest, cat, tiger, Bengal, *tree*	rocks, iguana, lizard, *water*, marine
IAPR images					
Ground truth	fountain, tree	face, middle, rock, statue	jungle, middle, waterfall	sea, wave	horizon, orange, sky, sun
Predicted keywords	fountain, *garden*, *sky*, *tile*, tree	face, middle, rock, *cliff*, statue	jungle, middle, *cloud*, *summit*, waterfall	sea, *beach*, *boat*, *sky*, wave	horizon, *landscape*, orange, sky, sun

Figure 4: Comparison of the predicted keywords obtained by our SSRC algorithm with ground-truth annotations on the Corel 5K (top lines) and IAPR TC12 (bottom lines) benchmark datasets. The differences in predicted keywords (from ground-truth annotations) are marked in italic font.

Table 1: The annotation results on the Corel 5K benchmark dataset (MVF: multiple visual features)

Methods	MVF	recall	precision	F_1
SSRC+HIK	no	0.371	0.315	0.341
LP+HIK	no	0.326	0.263	0.291
HIK	no	0.289	0.242	0.264
[7]	no	0.250	0.240	0.245
[15]	yes	0.291	0.253	0.271
[24]	no	0.320	0.250	0.281
[18]	yes	0.320	0.270	0.293
[22]	no	0.390	0.250	0.310
[29]	yes	0.330	0.300	0.314
[16]	no	0.349	0.287	0.315
[28]	yes	0.360	0.310	0.333
[10]	yes	0.423	0.327	0.369

Table 2: The annotation results on the IAPR TC12 benchmark dataset (MVF: multiple visual features)

Methods	MVF	recall	precision	F_1
SSRC+HIK	no	0.322	0.413	0.362
LP+HIK	no	0.305	0.361	0.331
HIK	no	0.285	0.336	0.308
[7]	no	0.230	0.240	0.235
[16]	no	0.236	0.258	0.247
[18]	yes	0.290	0.280	0.285
[29]	yes	0.290	0.320	0.304
[10]	yes	0.352	0.460	0.399

regularization in equation (4) instead of our L_1-norm version, our SSRC+HIK can still achieve obvious gains (17% for Corel and 9% for IAPR) in terms of the F_1 measure, although they both take visual BOW representation refinement into account. This means that our SSRC can indeed benefit from the sparsity induced by our L1-norm Laplacian regularization and thus suppress the negative effect of the noisy labels in the initial visual BOW representation.

Moreover, we also make comparison with the state-of-the-art results in the image annotation literature. Here, it should be noted that the baseline methods in Table 1 and Table 2 are all implemented on benchmark datasets with standard training/test split, just the same as our method. The main difference between our method and these baseline methods lies in that our method exploits much less semantic or visual information for image annotation (see more explanation in Section 3). However, we still find that our method outperforms most of these baseline methods, due to semantic sparse coding of the visual content. The unique exception is [10] which utilizes more than 10 types of visual features (local and global) for image annotation and thus obtains the best results until now (to the best of our knowledge). Considering that we only use one type of visual features here, it is really impressive that our method can achieve the second best results with such simple experimental setting.

Figure 4 presents several examples of the annotations predicted by our method, which contain at least one mismatched keyword compared with the ground-truth annotations. The results given by Figure 4 show that, when our method annotates an image with a keyword not contained in the ground-truth keyword set, this keyword frequently explains the image well. This means that our method can annotate an image with more semantically related keywords through semantic sparse coding of the visual content.

Besides the above advantages in image annotation, our SSRC method has another advantage, i.e., it can run very efficiently even on large datasets. For example, the running time of visual BOW refinement taken by SSRC and LP on IAPR is 2.8 and 9.0 minutes, respectively. Here, we run the algorithms (Matlab code) on a server with 3GHz CPU and 32GB RAM. Interestingly, we also find that the time taken by visual BOW refinement using our SSRC is comparable to that by image annotation using correlated label propagation (e.g. 2.8 minutes vs. 2.2 minutes for IAPR).

Figure 5: Semantic retrieval results by our SSRC algorithm on the IAPR TC12 benchmark dataset. Each row shows the top five matches to a semantic query. From top to bottom: "boat", "brush", "shade", and "slope". We can clearly observe the visual appearance diversity of the returned images.

Table 3: The semantic retrieval results measured by MAP on the Corel 5K and IAPR TC12 benchmark datasets (MVF: multiple visual features)

Methods	MVF	Corel	IAPR
SSRC+HIK	no	0.388	0.347
LP+HIK	no	0.349	0.312
HIK	no	0.316	0.296
[7]	no	0.300	–
[24]	no	0.420	–
[10]	yes	0.418	0.399

4.3 Results of Semantic Retrieval

The results of semantic retrieval on the Corel 5K and IAPR TC12 benchmark datasets are listed in Table 3, where MAP is used as the evaluation measure. In general, we can make the same observations as we have done in the automatic annotation task. It should be noted that the annotation results reported in last subsection ignore the rank order of results, while the MAP measure used here particularly involves the rank order of the semantic retrieval results. The superior performance of our method in the semantic retrieval task shows that it not only can annotate images with more correct keywords, but also can annotate different images using the same keyword with relatively proper weights. This means that, given a semantic query, the returned images may have obvious visual appearance diversity. Such visual appearance diversity can also be clearly observed from Figure 5 which shows several semantic retrieval examples by our method on the IAPR TC12 benchmark dataset.

4.4 Discussion

In this paper, we focus on semantic sparse recoding of the visual context for image annotation and then only make use of one type of visual features (dense SIFT). In fact, the refined visual BOW representation obtained by our SSRC method can be readily combined with other types of visual features by feature fusion. For example, when the spatial context of local SIFT descriptors (like [14]) and the global color histogram are fused with our refined visual BOW representation, we obtain MAP=**0.439** and **0.403** for Corel and IAPR, respectively. To our best knowledge, these are the best results reported in the image annotation literature.

5. CONCLUSIONS

We have investigated the challenging problem of visual BOW representation refinement in the context of image annotation. To deal with the semantic gap and noise issues associated with the traditional visual BOW representation, we have incorporated the annotations of images into visual BOW representation refinement and thus formulated it as semantic sparse recoding of the visual content. By developing an efficient algorithm, we have successfully generated more descriptive and robust visual BOW representation. To our best knowledge, we have made the first attempt to develop semantic sparse recoding of the visual content for image annotation. The experimental results show the significant gains achieved by our semantic sparse recoding method, which becomes more impressive given that we do not use extra semantic information or multiple visual features. When the spatial context of visual words and the global color histogram are also considered, we *obtain the best results so far* in the image annotation literature. In the future work, our semantic sparse recoding method will be applied to many other challenging tasks in computer vision and image analysis. Moreover, considering the wide use of Laplacian regularization, our new L_1-norm Laplacian regularization can be extended to different graph-based learning problems.

6. ACKNOWLEDGMENTS

This work was supported by National Natural Science Foundation of China under Grant 61073084, Beijing Natural Science Foundation of China under Grant 4122035, National Hi-Tech Research and Development Program (863 Program) of China under Grant 2012AA012503, and National Key Technology Research and Development Program of China under Grants 2012BAH07B01 and 2012BAH18B03.

7. REFERENCES

[1] A. Beck and M. Teboulle. A fast iterative shrinkage-thresholding algorithm for linear inverse problems. *SIAM Journal on Imaging Sciences*, 2(1):183–202, 2009.

[2] O. Chapelle, B. Scholköpf, and A. Zien, editors. *Semi-Supervised Learning*. MIT Press, 2006.

[3] X. Chen, Q. Lin, S. Kim, J. G. Carbonell, and E. P. Xing. Smoothing proximal gradient method for general structured sparse learning. In *UAI*, pages 105–114, 2011.

[4] D. Donoho. For most large underdetermined systems of linear equations the minimal ℓ^1-norm solution is also the sparsest solution. *Communications on Pure and Applied Mathematics*, 59(7):797–829, 2004.

[5] P. Duygulu, K. Barnard, N. de Freitas, and D. Forsyth. Object recognition as machine translation: Learning a lexicon for a fixed image vocabulary. In *ECCV*, pages 97–112, 2002.

[6] H. Escalante, C. Hernández, J. Gonzalez, A. López-López, M. Montes, E. Morales, L. Sucar, L. Villasenor, and M. Grubinger. The segmented and annotated IAPR TC-12 benchmark. *Computer Vision and Image Understanding*, 114(4):419–428, 2010.

[7] S. Feng, R. Manmatha, and V. Lavrenko. Multiple Bernoulli relevance models for image and video annotation. In *CVPR*, volume 2, pages 1002–1009, 2004.

[8] R. Fergus, Y. Weiss, and A. Torralba. Semi-supervised learning in gigantic image collections. In *NIPS 22*, pages 522–530, 2010.

[9] S. Gao, L.-T. Chia, and I.-H. Tsang. Multi-layer group sparse coding - for concurrent image classification and annotation. In *CVPR*, pages 2809 –2816, 2011.

[10] M. Guillaumin, T. Mensink, J. Verbeek, and C. Schmid. TagProp: Discriminative metric learning in nearest neighbor models for image auto-annotation. In *ICCV*, pages 309–316, 2009.

[11] S. He and J. Jia. Image annotation by sparse logistic regression. In *PCM*, pages 22–30, 2010.

[12] R. Ji, X. Xie, H. Yao, and W.-Y. Ma. Vocabulary hierarchy optimization for effective and transferable retrieval. In *CVPR*, pages 1161–1168, 2009.

[13] F. Kang, R. Jin, and R. Sukthankar. Correlated label propagation with application to multi-label learning. In *CVPR*, volume 2, pages 1719–1726, 2006.

[14] S. Lazebnik, C. Schmid, and J. Ponce. Beyond bags of features: Spatial pyramid matching for recognizing natural scene categories. In *CVPR*, pages 2169–2178, 2006.

[15] J. Liu, M. Li, Q. Liu, H. Lu, and S. Ma. Image annotation via graph learning. *Pattern Recognition*, 42(2):218–228, 2009.

[16] Z. Lu, H. Ip, and Y. Peng. Contextual kernel and spectral methods for learning the semantics of images. *IEEE Trans. Image Processing*, 20(6):1739–1750, 2011.

[17] Z. Lu, Y. Peng, and H. Ip. Spectral learning of latent semantics for action recognition. In *ICCV*, pages 1503–1510, 2011.

[18] A. Makadia, V. Pavlovic, and S. Kumar. A new baseline for image annotation. In *ECCV*, pages 316–329, 2008.

[19] P. Mallapragada, R. Jin, and A. Jain. Online visual vocabulary pruning using pairwise constraints. In *CVPR*, pages 3073–3080, 2010.

[20] S. Petry, C. Flexeder, and G. Tutz. Pairwise fused Lasso. *Dept. of Statistics: Technical Reports, Nr. 102*, 2011.

[21] J. Tang, R. Hong, S. Yan, T.-S. Chua, G.-J. Qi, and R. Jain. Image annotation by kNN-sparse graph-based label propagation over noisily tagged web images. *ACM Trans. Intelligent Systems and Technology*, 2(2):14:1–14:15, 2011.

[22] A. Ulges, M. Worring, and T. Breuel. Learning visual contexts for image annotation from Flickr groups. *IEEE Trans. Multimedia*, 13(2):330–341, 2011.

[23] C. Wang, F. Jing, L. Zhang, and H.-J. Zhang. Image annotation refinement using random walk with restarts. In *ACM MM*, pages 647–650, 2006.

[24] C. Wang, S. Yan, L. Zhang, and H.-J. Zhang. Multi-label sparse coding for automatic image annotation. In *CVPR*, pages 1643–1650, 2009.

[25] J. Wright, A. Yang, A. Ganesh, S. Sastry, and Y. Ma. Robust face recognition via sparse representation. *IEEE Trans. PAMI*, 31(2):210–227, 2009.

[26] F. Wu, Y. Han, Q. Tian, and Y. Zhuang. Multi-label boosting for image annotation by structural grouping sparsity. In *ACM MM*, pages 15–24, 2010.

[27] L. Wu, S. Hoi, and N. Yu. Semantics-preserving bag-of-words models and applications. *IEEE Trans. Image Processing*, 19(7):1908–1920, 2010.

[28] Y. Xiang, X. Zhou, T.-S. Chua, and C.-W. Ngo. A revisit of generative model for automatic image annotation using Markov random fields. In *CVPR*, pages 1153–1160, 2009.

[29] S. Zhang, J. Huang, Y. Huang, Y. Yu, H. Li, and D. Metaxas. Automatic image annotation using group sparsity. In *CVPR*, pages 3312 –3319, 2010.

[30] D. Zhou, O. Bousquet, T. Lal, J. Weston, and B. Schölkopf. Learning with local and global consistency. In *NIPS 16*, pages 321–328, 2004.

[31] X. Zhu, Z. Ghahramani, and J. Lafferty. Semi-supervised learning using Gaussian fields and harmonic functions. In *ICML*, pages 912–919, 2003.

Annotating Web Images using NOVA: NOn-conVex group spArsity

Fei Wu
College of Computer Science, Zhejiang University
Hangzhou, Zhejiang, China
wufei@cs.zju.edu.cn

Ying Yuan
College of Computer Science, Zhejiang University
Hangzhou, Zhejiang, China
tracy1108@cs.zju.edu.cn

Yong Rui
Microsoft Research Asia
No. 5, Dan Ling Street,
Haidian District Beijing, China
yongrui@microsoft.com

Shuicheng Yan
Department of Electrical and Computer Engineering
NUS, Singapore
eleyans@nus.edu.sg

Yueting Zhuang
College of Computer Science, Zhejiang University
Hangzhou, Zhejiang, China
yzhuang@cs.zju.edu.cn

ABSTRACT

As image feature vector is large, selecting the right features plays a fundamental role in Web image annotation. Most existing approaches are either based on individual feature selection, which leads to local optima, or using a *convex* penalty, which leads to inconsistency. To address these difficulties, in this paper we propose a new sparsity-based approach NOVA (NOn-conVex group spArsity). To the best of our knowledge, NOVA is the first to introduce non-convex penalty for group selection in high-dimensional heterogeneous features space. Because it is a group-sparsity approach, it approximately reaches global optima. Because it uses non-convex penalty, it achieves the consistency. We demonstrate the superior performance of NOVA via three means. First, we present theoretical proof that NOVA is consistent, satisfying un-biasness, sparsity and continuity. Second, we show NOVA converges to the true underlying model by using a ground-truth-available generative-model simulation. Third, we report extensive experimental results on three diverse and widely-used data sets Kodak, MSRA-MM 2.0, and NUS-WIDE. We also compare NOVA against the state-of-the-art approaches, and report superior experimental results.

Categories and Subject Descriptors

H.3 [**Information Storage and Retrieval**]: Information Search and Retrieval; I.4.7 [**Image Processing and Computer Vision**]: Feature Measurement—*feature representation*

General Terms

Algorithms, Experimentation

Keywords

NOn-conVex group spArsity, Consistent, Group Feature Selection, Image Annotation

1. INTRODUCTION

The number of Web images already reached the order of 100 Billion. Out of these images, however, only a limited percent are annotated. Developing an effective way to accurately annotate the Web images automatically are therefore of great importance. While an image is worth a thousand words, it is also true that we can extract a large number, sometimes even more than a thousand, of visual features from an image. These features may include global features, e.g., color, texture and shape, and local features, e.g., SIFT, Shape Context and GLOH (Gradient Location and Orientation Histogram) [25]. The size of the concatenated feature vector can be large, but only a subset of features carry the biggest discriminating power. As a result, selecting the right features plays a fundamental role in image annotation with high-dimensional features.

Motivated by the recent advance in compressed sensing, *sparsity*-based feature selection approaches are developed in both machine learning and multimedia communities [27]. The basic idea of sparsity-based feature selection is to employ regularizers to induce sparsity during discriminative feature selection. Depending on if the feature selection is based on individual or group features and if the regularizers are convex or non-convex, the existing approaches can be categorized into four quadrants, as shown in Table 1, e.g., *convex individual-sparsity, convex group-sparsity, nonconvex individual-sparsity, nonconvex group-sparsity.*

- The *lasso* (least absolute shrinkage and selection operator) [24] and nonnegative garrote [4] fall into the first quadrant (i.e., *convex individual-sparsity*), which deals with individual feature selection using a convex relaxation such as the ℓ_1-norm.
- The group *lasso* [30], sparse group *lasso* [15], composite absolute penalty (a generalization of the group *lasso*)[33], exclusive group lasso [34], and overlapped group *lasso* [18] are in the second quadrant (i.e., *convex group-sparsity*) which model the features as groups, but still use a convex relaxation.

- Residing in the fourth quadrant (i.e., *nonconvex individual-sparsity*) are the smoothly clipped absolute deviation (SCAD) [12], adaptive *lasso* [35], log-sum penalty [6], pseudo l_q-norm with $q < 1$ [16], and the minimax concave (MC) penalties [32]. While they utilize a non-convex penalty to obtain prediction consistency, it only works on top of individual features.
- Note that approaches in quadrant 3 (i.e., *nonconvex group-sparsity*) are still missing.

While good progress has been made over the years in various domains and applications, the above mentioned existing approaches in quadrants 1, 2 and 4 suffer from one or both of the following difficulties.

- Note that the original high-dimensional heterogeneous features are inherently partitioned into different groups, e.g., color vs. SIFT, and different groups of features describe different aspects of visual characteristics. That is, the Web image annotation problem is inherently the problem of selecting grouped variables (features) for accurate prediction in regression, a classic statistical problem as described in [30]. Different groups of features have different intrinsic discriminative power to characterize the high-level semantics for different images [7][9][28][17]. Approaches in quadrants 1 (*convex individual-sparsity*)and 4 (*nonconvex individual-sparsity*) are designed for selecting individual features, not for group features as in Web image annotation. They make selection based on the strength of individual features instead of the strength of groups of features, which result in selecting unnecessary features. Furthermore, they lead to local optimal instead of the global one – depending on how the features orthonormalized, they converge to different solutions [30].
- Because approaches based on convex regularizers, i.e., the approaches in quadrants 1 (*convex individual-sparsity*) and 2 (*convex group-sparsity*), are computationally efficient, and are very popular [24][4][30][15][18]. However, they do not lead to *consistent* prediction. That is, the correct sparse subset of the relevant features cannot be identified asymptotically with large probability [21][26].

  As pointed out in [12][36], the *lasso* as well as other *lasso*-type methods are sub-optimal in model selection due to their *convex* relaxation, which is prone to inducing inconsistent estimates for the data with high-dimensional features. Because *lasso* both shrinks and selects, it often relaxes the penalty on the relevant features. Furthermore, in Wei *et al.*'s work [26], they derived a similar theoretical proof that group *lasso* in general is not selection consistent.

  Given the data x with p input features, $\mathbf{x} = (x_1, \ldots, x_p)^T \in \mathbb{R}^p$, the interesting question is whether there is a *true* model that can select all the necessary features from x to denote its corresponding semantic. Assume a *true* (an *oracle*) model can be found to select out the features from x and the coefficients of the selected features are denoted as $A = \{m : \beta^*_m \neq 0\}$ and $|A| = p_0 < p$. If $\hat{\beta}(\delta)$ is the estimated coefficients produced by a fitting procedure δ, the question is whether the selection result by δ is the same as that of the result by the *true* model. According to [12][35], δ is called an *oracle* model to produce a consistent selection result if $\hat{\beta}(\delta)$ has the following oracle properties: δ can identify the correct subset, $\{m : \hat{\beta}_j \neq 0\} = A$; and δ has the optimal estimate rate. This oracle properties imply that the penalty function must be singular at the origin and *non-convex* over $(0, \infty)$.

To address the above two key difficulties, in this paper we propose a brand new approach, filling the empty space in the third quadrant (*nonconvex group-sparsity*). We call it NOVA (NOn-conVex group spArsity). Figure 1 illustrates the algorithm flow of our proposed NOVA, including feature extraction, feature selection and image annotation. In Figure 1, we can see NOVA can select out the important groups of features for image annotation. The strength of the proposed NOVA endows the feature space with additional group structure into a non-convex regularizer for consistent group selection due to its *oracle* properties. To the best of our knowledge, NOVA is the first to introduce non-convex penalty for group selection in high-dimensional heterogeneous features space.

The rest of the paper is organized as follows. In Section 3, we present detailed algorithm of NOVA, including problem formulation and step-by-step derivation. In Section 4, we give theoretical proof that NOVA is consistent, satisfying un-biasness, sparsity and continuity. Complementing to the theoretical proof, we also report extensive experimental results in Section 5 via three diverse and widely-used data sets.

2. NON-CONVEX GROUP SPARSITY FOR FEATURE SELECTION

2.1 Notation

Suppose we are given a set of training data with n images and C labels $\{(\mathbf{x}_i, \mathbf{y}_i) \in \mathbb{R}^p \times \{-1, 1\}^C : i = 1, \ldots, n\}$, where $\mathbf{x}_i = (x_{i1}, \ldots, x_{ip})^T \in \mathbb{R}^p$ represents a p-dimensional feature vector for the ith image, and $\mathbf{y}_i = (y_{i1}, \ldots, y_{iC})^T \in \{-1, 1\}^C$ is a C-dimensional label vector. Here, we assume $y_{ij} = 1$ if the ith image has the jth label and $y_{ij} = -1$ otherwise. Since different types of features can be extracted from images, we further assume that the p features are divided into G disjoint groups. Therefore, the feature vector of the ith image $\mathbf{x}_i$ can be rewritten as $\mathbf{x}_i = (x_{i,1}; \ldots; x_{i,G})$ where $x_{i,g} \in \mathbb{R}^{d_g} (g = 1, \ldots, G)$ is the gth feature vector of this image, and $\sum_{g=1}^{G} d_g = p$.

Let $X = (\mathbf{x}_1, \ldots, \mathbf{x}_n)^T$ be the $n \times p$ training data matrix, and $Y = (\mathbf{y}_1, \ldots, \mathbf{y}_n)^T$ the corresponding $n \times C$ label indicator matrix. In the following, we assume that the feature matrix X is centered.

2.2 Problem Formulation

For each label $c \in \{1, \ldots, C\}$, we aim to estimate the vector of regression coefficients $\beta^c = (\beta^c_1; \ldots; \beta^c_G)$ where $\beta^c_g \in \mathbb{R}^{d_g} (g = 1, 2, ..., G)$ by minimizing the following objective function with a linear regression model:

$$l(\beta^c) = \frac{1}{2n} \sum_{i=1}^{n} (y_{ic} - \sum_{g=1}^{G} x_{i,g}^T \beta^c_g)^2 + \sum_{g=1}^{G} p_\lambda(||\beta^c_g||_2) \quad (1)$$

Table 1: Four paradigms of sparsity-based feature selection methods (i.e., *convex individual-sparsity*, *convex group-sparsity*, *nonconvex individual-sparsity*, *nonconvex group-sparsity*)

	group	individual
convex	group *lasso*[30] sparse group *lasso* [15] overlapping group lasso [18] exclusive group lasso [34] structural grouping sparsity[28]	*lasso*[24] nonnegative garrote [4]
nonconvex	NOVA	SCAD [12] adaptive *lasso* [35] log-sum penalty [6] pseudo l_q-norm with $q < 1$ [16] the minimax concave (MC) penalties [32]

where $p_\lambda(.)$ is the penalty function characterized by a tuning parameter λ.

In this section, after the introduction of one of *nonconvex individual-sparsity*, e.g., smoothly clipped absolute deviation (SCAD) [12], we will describe how to introduce the group structure into SCAD and define our proposed nonconvex group-sparsity peanly, e.g., NOn-conVex group spArsity (NOVA).

SCAD was proposed in [12] to circumvent the weakness of penalties with a convex relaxation and had interesting theoretical properties to induce a consistent selection result. SCAD is defined as follows

$$p_\lambda(|\beta_j|) = \begin{cases} \lambda|\beta_j|, & \text{if } |\beta_j| \leq \lambda; \\ -\dfrac{(|\beta_j|^2 - 2a\lambda|\beta_j| + \lambda^2)}{2(a-1)}, & \text{if } \lambda < |\beta_j| \leq a\lambda; \\ \dfrac{(a+1)\lambda^2}{2}, & \text{if } |\beta_j| > a\lambda; \end{cases}$$

where $a > 2$ and $\lambda > 0$ are tuning parameters.

The SCAD penalty corresponds to a quadratic spline function with two knots at λ and $a\lambda$, leaves large values of β_j not excessively penalized and makes the solution continuous [12]. Fan and Li [12] showed that the penalized likelihood estimators perform as well as the *oracle* procedure in terms of selecting the consistent features, when the regularization parameter is appropriately chosen. The significance of the *oracle* procedure is that the proposed procedures outperform the maximum likelihood estimator and perform as well as we expect. They also showed that the Bayesian risks are not very sensitive to the values of a and suggested to use $a = 3.7$, which was also used in this paper.

Traditional *nonconvex individual-sparsity* SCAD does not encode group structure during feature selection. In the real world, given one image, we can obtain p-dimensional heterogeneous features and these p-dimensional features are naturally partitioned into G disjoint groups. Similar to *convex group-sparsity* penalty group *lasso* [30], we tend to introduce the group structure into SCAD for consistent selection of group features. Here we use an $\ell_{2,1}$-norm $||\beta_g^c||_2$ to substitute the ℓ_1-norm $|\beta_j|$. The $\ell_{2,1}$-norm encourages sparsity at the group level. In other words, if the coefficients in β_g^c are non-zero, the gth group of features are all selected out to make the cth label discernible. On the contrary, some groups of features may be dropped out if the coefficients in β_g^c are equal to zeros. Thus we can extend *nonconvex individual-sparsity* SCAD to *nonconvex group-sparsity* NOVA as follows

$$p_\lambda(||\beta_g^c||_2) = \begin{cases} \lambda||\beta_g^c||_2, & \text{if } ||\beta_g^c||_2 \leq \lambda; \\ -\dfrac{(||\beta_g^c||_2^2 - 2a\lambda||\beta_g^c||_2 + \lambda^2)}{2(a-1)}, & \text{if } \lambda < ||\beta_g^c||_2 \leq a\lambda; \\ \dfrac{(a+1)\lambda^2}{2}, & \text{if } ||\beta_g^c||_2 > a\lambda; \end{cases}$$

for $g = 1, \ldots, G$ and $c = 1, \ldots, C$.

Some other *convex group-sparsity* methods such as group *lasso* [30] or group LARS [11] end up shrinking the coefficients more for the *good* variables to induce sparsity. If these selected *good* variables are strongly correlated, this effect is exacerbated, and may mistakenly include other variables to this model. On the contrary, the proposed *nonconvex group-sparsity* method NOVA can overcome these drawbacks and give rise to the consistent group selection compared with group *lasso* or group LARS.

2.3 Algorithm and Group Selection

The *nonconvex group-sparsity* penalty NOVA is singular at the origin and does not have continuous second order derivatives. In order to solve the non-convex penalized regression problem, we use the following local quadratic approximation (LQA):

$$p'_\lambda(|\beta_j|) = p'_\lambda(|\beta_j|)sgn(\beta_j) \approx \{p'_\lambda(|\beta_j|)/|\beta_j^{(0)}|\}\beta_j$$

where $\beta_j^{(0)}$ is an initial value of β_j and $\beta_j^{(0)} \neq 0$. That is to say,

$$p_\lambda(|\beta_j|) \approx p_\lambda(|\beta_j^{(0)}|) + 1/2\{p'_\lambda(|\beta_j^{(0)}|)/|\beta_j^{(0)}|\}(\beta_j^2 - \beta_j^{(0)2}) \quad \text{for } \beta_j \approx \beta_j^0. \tag{2}$$

To avoid numerical instability, Fan and Li [12] suggested that if $|\beta_j|$ in (2) is very close to 0, say $|\beta_j| < \epsilon_0$ (a prespecified value), then set $\beta_j = 0$ and delete the jth component of X in the iteration. A drawback of this approximation is the backward stepwise variable selection: if a covariate is deleted at any step in the LQA algorithm, it will necessarily be excluded from the final selected model. Furthermore, one has to choose ϵ_0, which practically becomes an additional tuning parameter. The value of ϵ_0 potentially affects the sparsity degree of the solution as well as the speed of convergence.

In our algorithm, a similar quadratic approximation is used by substituting $|\beta_j|$ with $||\beta_g||_2$, $g = 1, \ldots, G$. The

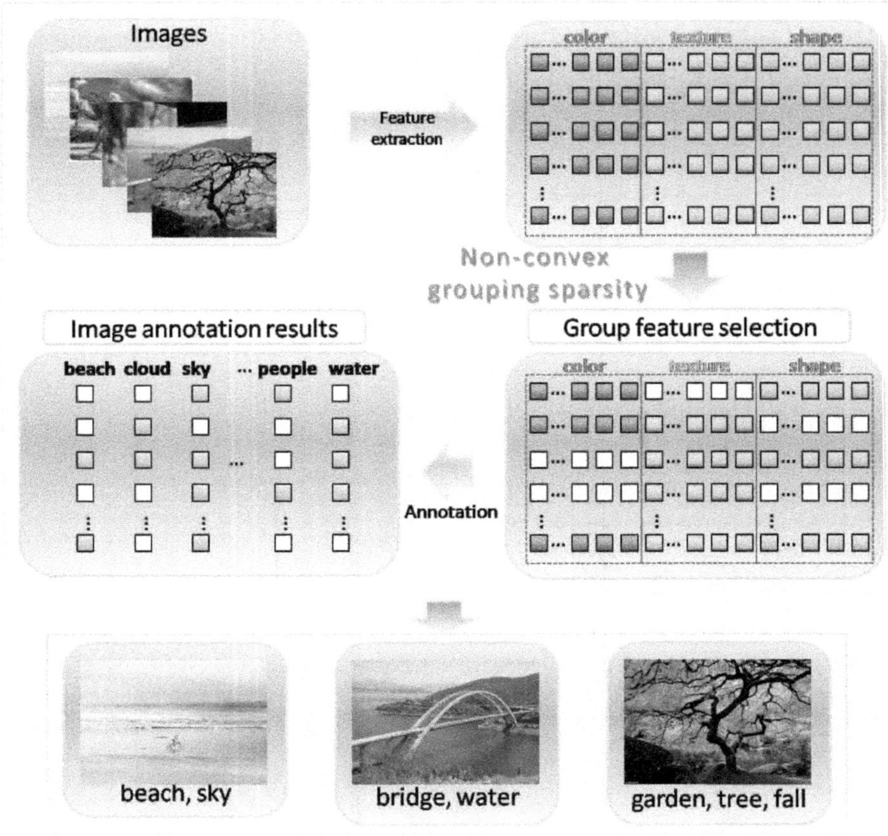

Figure 1: System overview of our proposed NOVA framework for multi-label image annotation. The NOVA can select the groups of features and train the image annotation model simultaneously.

non-convex penalty $p_\lambda(||\beta_g||_2)$ can be approximated as

$$p_\lambda(||\beta_g||_2) \approx p_\lambda(||\beta_g^{(0)}||_2) + 1/2\{p'_\lambda(||\beta_g^{(0)}||_2)/||\beta_g^{(0)}||_2\} (\beta_g^T\beta_g - (\beta_g^{(0)})^T\beta_g^{(0)}), \text{ for } \beta_g \approx \beta_g^0,$$

and the Newton-Raphson algorithm can be conducted.

Under this approximation, the equation (1) is transformed as

$$\min_{\beta^c} \frac{1}{2n}(Y - X\beta^c)^T(Y - X\beta^c) + \frac{1}{2}(\beta^c)^T\Sigma\beta^c \quad (3)$$

where

$$\Sigma = diag\{p'_\lambda(||\beta_1^{c(0)}||_2)/||\beta_1^{c(0)}||_2 e_{d_1}^T, \ldots, p'_\lambda(||\beta_G^{c(0)}||_2)/||\beta_G^{c(0)}||_2 e_{d_G}^T\} \quad (4)$$

is a $p \times p$ matrix. Each item $p'_\lambda(||\beta_g^{c(0)}||_2)/||\beta_g^{c(0)}||_2$ of Σ is repeated d_g times where d_g is the dimension of the gth feature as aforementioned.

The penalized equation (3) is a quadratic problem and can be solved by

$$(X^TX + \Sigma)\beta^c = \frac{1}{n}X^TY \quad (5)$$

We summarize the proposed algorithm in Algorithm 1. As in the maximum likelihood estimation (MLE) setting, with the good initial value $\beta^{c(0)}$, the one-step procedure can be as efficient as the fully iterative procedure, namely, the penalized maximum likelihood estimator, when the Newton-Raphson algorithm is used [2]. Therefore, in the initialization step, we utilize a ridge regression to get an approximate initial estimation of β^c. In step 4, if some $||\beta_g^c||_2$ is very close to zero, that is to say, smaller than a certain threshold ϵ_1, we set $\beta_g^c = 0$ and treat the gth group of features irrelevant with the cth label. In our algorithm, we set ϵ_1 to 10^{-3}.

Algorithm 1: Group Selection with NOn-conVex group spArsity (NOVA)

---

1 **For** each label c ($c = 1, 2, ..., C$) **do**
2 Initialize $\beta^{c(0)}$;
3 **For** $k = 1, \ldots$
  Obtain $\Sigma^{(k)}$ by (4) and solve $\beta^{c(k)}$ by (5) until convergence;
 end
4 **For** $g = 1, \ldots, G$ **if** $||\beta_g^c||_2 < \epsilon_1$
  Set $\beta_g^c = 0$.
 end

2.4 Multi-label Boosting for Annotation

The introduction of correlations between multiple tags can improve the performance of multi-label annotation. As one of approaches to learn the correlations between two vari-

Algorithm 2: Multi-label Boosting by Structured Sparse Canonical Correlation Analysis ($S^2C\&W$)

1 Perform structured sparse canonical correlation analysis on selected features X and labels Y;
2 Output u_{x_i} and v_{y_i} $(i = 1, 2, \ldots, C)$;
3 Compute ρ_i and s_i by (6) and (7);
4 Form matrix $S = diag(s_1, \ldots, s_C)$;
5 Form matrix $V = (v_{y1}, \ldots, v_{yC})^T$;
6 Compute matrix $B = V^{-1}SV$;
7 Compute the estimated indicators $\tilde{Y} = \hat{Y}B$.

ables, the curds and whey (C&W) [5] has been conducted for multi-label annotation[29] [28]. C&W builds up the connection between multiple response regression and canonical correlation analysis, and can be used to boost the performance of multi-label prediction given by the prediction results from the individual regression of each label.

Let $\beta = (\beta^1, \ldots, \beta^C) \in \mathbb{R}^{p \times C}$ be the coefficient vector output by Algorithm 1, and we can get the predicted vector $\hat{Y} = X\beta$. According to [5][23], a more accurate prediction $\tilde{Y}$ can be inferred by a linear combination $\tilde{Y} = \hat{Y}B$ after the introduction of the significant correlations between labels.

We can derive the estimates of the matrix $B \in \mathbb{R}^{C \times C}$ that take the form $B = V^{-1}SV$ where V is the $C \times C$ matrix whose rows are the label canonical coordinates output by canonical correlation analysis (CCA) and $S = diag(s_1, \ldots, s_C)$ is a diagonal *shrinking* matrix which can be estimated by a generalized cross-validation (GCV) approach.

The solution by [5] of s_i is

$$s_i = \frac{\rho_i^2}{\rho_i^2 + \gamma(1 - \rho_i^2)} \tag{6}$$

with

$$\rho_i = \frac{u_{x_i}^T X^T Y v_{y_i}}{\sqrt{(u_{x_i}^T X^T X u_{x_i})(v_{y_i}^T Y^T Y v_{y_i})}} \tag{7}$$

and $\gamma = p/n$. The matrix V can be expressed as $V = (v_{y1}, \ldots, v_{yC})^T$. Different from traditional curds and whey (C&W) method, the label canonical coordinates u_{x_i} and v_{y_i} are obtained by the the structured sparse canonical correlation analysis [8] in this paper, referred as $S^2C\&W$, since we can incorporate the rich prior structural information among label space. We summarize the multi-label annotation by $S^2C\&W$ in Algorithm 2.

3. JUSTIFICATION ON CONSISTENCY

The consistent selection of groups of features is a major concern in this paper. This section provides both theoretical and experimental evidence that our NOVA does produce a consistent group selection without compromising classification accuracy or computational efficiency.

3.1 The Oracle Properties of NOVA

A good penalty that induces consistent feature selection should result in an estimator with an *oracle* property: unbiasedness, sparsity and continuity [12]. That is to say, the penalty function is bounded by a constant to produce nearly unbiased estimates for large coefficients, be singular at the origin which is also said to be a thresholding rule of the resulting estimator to produce sparse solutions, and be continuity by certain conditions, which is also said to be stable of the model.

Now we consider the first order derivative of $p_\lambda(||\beta_g^c||_2)$ with respect to β_g^c, which is

$$p'_\lambda(||\beta_g^c||_2) = \lambda\{I(||\beta_g^c||_2 \le \lambda) + \frac{(a\lambda - ||\beta_g^c||_2)_+}{(a-1)\lambda} I(||\beta_g^c||_2 > \lambda)\}.$$

The *oracle* property of NOn-conVex group spArsity (NOVA) can be proved as

1. The sufficient condition for unbiasedness is that when $||\beta_g^c||_2$ is sufficiently large, $p'_\lambda(||\beta_g^c||_2) = 0$, which is obvious satisfied.
2. The sufficient condition for the thresholding rule is that the minimum of the function $||\beta_g^c||_2 + p'_\lambda(||\beta_g^c||_2)$ is positive, which is satisfied with the assumption $a > 2$.
3. The sufficient and necessary condition for continuity is that the minimum of the function $||\beta_g^c||_2 + p'_\lambda(||\beta_g^c||_2)$ attained at 0. Obvious this condition can be satisfied when $||\beta_g^c||_2 = 0$.

The proposed NOVA in equation (1) solves a quadratic optimization problem (equation (3)), which can be solved by equation (5) with a global solution. As illustrated in references [30] and [36], the individual feature selection is often trapped into a local optimal solution rather than the global optimal one.

3.2 Complexity of NOVA

The computational complexity is crucial for the successful application of an algorithm. The complexity of group lasso is $O(p + kln(G))$ where p is the dimension of data, G is the number of groups, and k is the sparsity number which means the features selected out by the algorithm. From the description of Algorithm 1, we can see the main time-consuming operations are the initialization step and the solving process of equation (4) and (5) whose computational complexity is $O(np^2)$ where n is the sample size of data. So the complexity of NOVA is roughly $O(np^2)$ which is the same as SCAD.

3.3 Consistent Group Selection on Synthetic Data

In this section, we numerically compare our proposed *non-convex group-sparsity* NOVA with its counterpart *convex group-sparsity* group *lasso* [30] [1] in terms of consistent group selection on the synthetic data.

We sampled $X \in \mathbb{R}^{n \times p}$ from a normal distribution with zero mean vector and a covariance matrix of size $n = 200, p = 8$ for $G = 4$ groups of size $d_i = 2, i = 1, \ldots, G$. Then we sampled Y from $Y = X\beta + \epsilon$ with the noise ϵ which is generated from $N(0, 1)$ and the regression coefficients $\beta = (\beta_1, \ldots, \beta_G)$. For the indices of the 3rd and 4th groups, we set the corresponding entries of β_3 and β_4 to be zero and the other entries are sampled from i.i.d. $N(0, 1)$.

In Figure 2, we plot the regularization paths corresponding to the aforementioned synthetic data computed by NOVA and group *lasso* [30]. The left subfigure shows the values of the estimated coefficients $\hat{\beta}_i, i = 1, \ldots, G$ with the changing parameter λ in equation (1). The right subfigure shows the values computed by group *lasso* [1]. The dotted straight lines are the paths of prior defined regression coefficients

β, and the other four lines are the paths of predicted coefficients. Figure 2 illustrates that the non-convex NOVA regularizer is more consistent for the selection of group of features than the convex regularizer group *lasso*.

3.4 The Selection of Image Attributes

In recent years, Human-nameable visual *attributes* are taken as middle-level features to improve the performance of image classification [14][19]. To validate the effectiveness of NOVA for image attributes selection, we conduct experiments on the well-devised Animals with Attributes (AwA) data set [19] which consists of 30475 images of 50 animals classes with 85 numeric values of visual attributes for each image. The visual attributes in AwA are manually labeled. Different from the synthetic data, if the labeled attributes are taken as predictors (features), we can psychologically and physiologically judge whether the selected features are consistent (true) or inconsistent based on the ground truth in AwA.

In order to select the attributes of different classes, we define the input matrix $X \in \mathbb{R}^{n \times a}$ and $Y \in \mathbb{R}^{n \times C}$ where n is the number of samples, $a = 85$ is the number of attributes and $C = 50$ is the number of classes. We numerically compare NOVA with Linear SVM and group *lasso* [24] for the performance of feature (attribute) selection. Since there is no explicit group information in the attributes of AwA, as a special case of group *lasso* and NOVA, we consider the 85 different attributes as 85 groups which means the group size $d_g = 1$ for all $g = 1, \ldots, G$.

In this section, we utilize the precision criterion to measure the performance:

$$precision = \frac{TP}{TP + FP}$$

where TP means the true positives, and FP means the false positive.

We randomly select 1000 images for training, and the remaining for testing. This process is repeated ten times to generate ten random training/test partitions, and we report the average results with their variances in Table 2.

Figure 3 shows the selection results with the values of exemplary attributes assigned to the corresponding classes. Taking the manually labeled attributes as the ground truth, it can be shown that the selected attributes by NOVA are superior to the selected ones by group *lasso*.

4. MULTI-LABEL IMAGE ANNOTATION

This section is devoted to systematically evaluating the effectiveness of our proposed NOVA for automatic multi-label image annotation on real world data. Before presenting the experiment results, we introduce the data sets as well as the criteria used for evaluation.

4.1 Experiment Data Sets

To evaluate the performance of the proposed NOVA for image annotation, we conduct experiments on two open benchmark image data sets, i.e., MSRA-MM 2.0 [20] and NUS-WIDE [10], as well as a personal image collection, i.e., Kodak [22].

The MSRA-MM 2.0 data set aims to encourage research in multimedia information retrieval and related areas. The images and videos in the data set are collected from internet search engines. The NUS-WIDE data set is a real-world web image data set from Flickr created by National University of Singapore. We remove the images with zero label or one label for our multi-label experiments. Images in these data sets are associated with more than one labels and the labels are used as ground truth for image annotation.

For each image in the data sets, we extract its heterogeneous features and concatenate those heterogeneous features as a vector. Each kind of homogeneous features is taken as a group. We describe the three evaluated data sets with the number of groups in features which are provided by the data set as follows:

- Kodak [22] with 3590 images and 22 labels: 657-D features are divided into 7 groups. Namely, 144-D color correlogram, 16-D co-occurrence texture features, 73-D edge direction histogram, 7-D face features, 64-D color histogram, 225-D block-wise color moments, and 128-D wavelet texture features.
- MSRA-MM 2.0 [20] with 42266 images and 100 labels: 899-D features are divided into 7 groups. Namely, 144-D color correlogram, 75-D edge direction histogram, 7-D face features, 64-D color histogram, 225-D block-wise color moments, 256-D RGB and 128-D wavelet texture features.
- NUS-WIDE [10] with 209347 images and 81 labels: 1134-D features are divided into 6 groups. Namely, 144-D color correlogram, 73-D edge direction histogram, 500-D bag of words, 64-D color histogram, 225-D block-wise color moments and 128-D wavelet texture features.

4.2 Evaluation Criteria

The area under the ROC curve, called AUC, is used to measure the performance of image annotation [13]. ROC curve is used to characterize compromise relations between TP and FP. A ROC curve is a two-dimensional depiction of classifier performance which cannot be compared with each other directly for their overlap. To compare classifiers we may want to reduce ROC performance to a single scalar value representing expected performance. A common method is to calculate the area under the ROC curve, abbreviated AUC [3]. In this work, we use MacroAUC, MicroAUC scores and precision to measure the annotation performance across multiple labels.

4.3 Experiment Setup

For each data set, we randomly select $25 \times C$ images for training where C is the number of labels, and the remaining for testing. During the sampling process, each label is guaranteed to appear in at least one image. This process is repeated ten times to generate ten random training/test partitions, and we report the average results along with their variances.

For each label c, we first perform NOVA to select groups of features on the training data in order to obtain the best discriminant groups of features for label c , and then we can obtain the predicted vector $\hat{Y}$ by the new feature vector with some kinds of groups of features are dropped out and others are kept for distinguishing different objects. Taking the correlations and interdependent among labels into account, we utilize the S^2C&W method to improve the annotation accuracy by $\tilde{Y} = \hat{Y}B$.

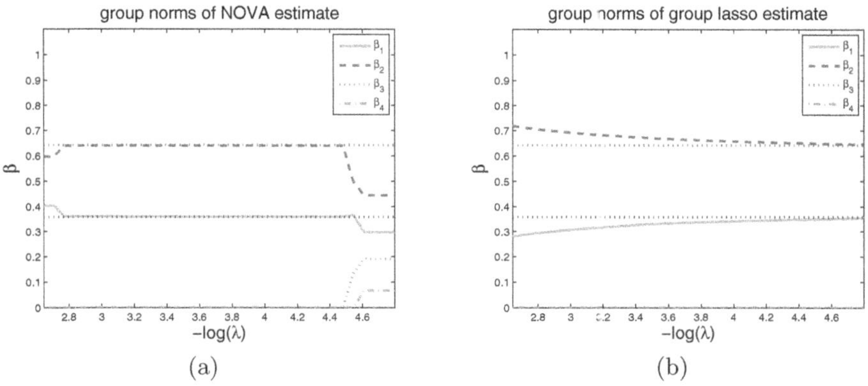

Figure 2: The regularization paths of NOVA and group *lasso*. Note that the $||\beta_3||$, $||\beta_4||$ are equal to zero, and they are overlapped on the 0-line.

Table 2: Performance of image attributes selection in terms of precision

	SVM	group *lasso*	NOVA
Precision	0.9289 ± 0.0054	0.9568 ± 0.0042	**0.9784 ± 0.0156**

4.4 Parameters Tuning

There are two parameters which need to be tuned for each label. The first one is λ in (1), and the second one is α in the ridge regression method for initializing $\beta^{c(0)}$. The parameters are tuned by 5-folded cross-validation based on MacroAUC for each data set.

We depict three examples of parameter tuning by the 5-fold cross validation with respect to MacroAUC in Figure 4. From this figure, we can see that the proposed algorithm is insensitive to the parameters.

4.5 Performance Comparison

As discussed before, in general, there are four paradigms of sparsity-based feature selection, namely, *convex individual-sparsity*, *convex group-sparsity*, *nonconvex individual-sparsity*, *nonconvex group-sparsity*. In order to testify the consistent selection of groups of features plays an fundamental role for image annotation, we compare our proposed NOVA with its counterpart algorithms. Without a special explanation, the annotation performance of all of compared sparsity-based are boosted by structured sparse canonical correlation analysis (S^2C&W)[8]. Under such a setting, the annotation performance is solely influenced by the different schemas of sparsity-based feature selection.

The compared sparsity-based feature selection algorithms with our proposed NOVA are listed as following:

- **convex individual-sparsity: *lasso***: Least Absolute Shrinkage and Selection Operator (*lasso*) [24] selects the important features individually and disregards the group structure in features.
- **convex group-sparsity: group *lasso***: group *lasso* [30] encodes the group structure in features to encourage the selection of groups of features.
- **nonconvex individual-sparsity: SCAD**: Smoothly Clipped Absolute Deviation (SCAD) [12] is a nonconvex penalty for individual feature selection.

All the methods are repeated ten times for ten random training/test partitions, and we report the average results and their standard deviation. Table 3 shows the performances in terms of MacroAUC, MicroAUC and precision on three data sets. The results shown in boldface are best results.

From the results in Table 3, we can make the following observations:

- The proposed NOVA achieves the best performance of image annotation in almost all of metrics for all the three data sets thanks to its group-based sparsity and non-convex penalty.
- For MSRA-MM 2.0 data set, group *lasso* performs better than NOVA in the precision measure. But for multi-label image annotation, MacroAUC and MicroAUC are more accurate indicators of true performance For those two measures, NOVA continues outperforming group *lasso*.
- The approaches in the first quadrant, e.g., *lasso*, have the worst performance This is easy to understand their feature selection is performed on top of individual features, which leads to local optima, and their penalty is convex, which lead to inconsistency.
- The approaches in the second and fourth quadrants have better performance than Lasso, but worse than NOVA, as they only solved one of the two difficulties.

To visually illustrate the superior performance of NOVA, Figure 5 shows example annotation results from the MSRA-MM 2.0 data set by NOVA and group *lasso*. The annotations with underlines denote the wrong ones. We can see that group *lasso* made several mistakes, e.g., building, water, and candle. Furthermore, while not completely wrong, group *lasso* missed a few annotations from the ground truth, e.g., building and animal. A key reason for the wrong and missed annotations was because group *lasso*'s convex penalty is inconsistent as discussed in earlier sections.

Image samples with class labels

Attributes	Ground truth	group *lasso*	NOVA
black:	yes	yes	yes
white:	yes	yes	yes
furry:	yes	no	yes
longleg:	no	no	no
claws:	yes	yes	yes
slow:	yes	no	yes
strong	yes	yes	yes
...			
brown:	yes	yes	yes
furry:	yes	yes	yes
big:	yes	no	yes
lean:	yes	yes	yes
hooves:	yes	yes	yes
tail:	yes	yes	yes
horns	no	yes	no
...			
brown:	yes	yes	yes
gray:	yes	yes	yes
furry:	yes	yes	yes
fast:	no	no	no
insects	no	no	no
meat:	yes	yes	yes
smart:	yes	no	yes
...			

Figure 3: Some exemplar results of attributes selection with the classes and the corresponding attributes. On the right side of the images shows the classes and the corresponding groundtruth of attributes and that selected by group *lasso* and NOVA respectively.

5. CONCLUSIONS

To address the difficulties from individual feature selection and convex penalty, this paper proposed a new sparsity-based approach termed NOVA (NOn-conVex group spArsity). We have demonstrated the superior performance of NOVA via three means in the paper. First, we derived the theoretical proof that NOVA is consistent, satisfying un-biasness, sparsity and continuity. Second, we showed that NOVA converges to the true underlying model by using a groundtruth-available generative-model simulation. The comparisons between NOVA and the state-of-the-art approaches in the other three quadrants showed that NOVA achieved the best performance.

However, high-dimensional heterogeneous features extracted from the image are often embedded in a nonlinear and inseparable subspace. Some kernel-based methods such as [31] have been proposed to discern the embedded subspace but do not lead to *consistent* prediction. Therefore, non-convex kernel methods is worthy of consideration and research.

6. ACKNOWLEDGEMENTS

This work was supported in part by National Basic Research Program of China (2012CB316400), NSFC (60833006, 61070068), National Key Technology R&D Program (2011BAD24B03), National HeGaoJi Key Project (2010ZX01042-002-003).

7. REFERENCES

[1] F. Bach. Consistency of the group lasso and multiple kernel learning. *The Journal of Machine Learning Research*, 9:1179–1225, 2008.

[2] P. Bickel. One-step huber estimates in the linear model. *Journal of the American Statistical Association*, pages 428–434, 1975.

[3] A. Bradley. The use of the area under the roc curve in the evaluation of machine learning algorithms. *Pattern recognition*, 30(7):1145–1159, 1997.

[4] L. Breiman. Better subset regression using the nonnegative garrote. *Technometrics*, pages 373–384, 1995.

[5] L. Breiman and J. Friedman. Predicting multivariate responses in multiple linear regression. *Journal of the Royal Statistical Society: Series B (Statistical Methodology)*, 59(1):3–54, 1997.

[6] E. Candes, M. Wakin, and S. Boyd. Enhancing sparsity by reweighted l_1 minimization. *Journal of Fourier Analysis and Applications*, 14(5):877–905, 2008.

[7] L. Cao, J. Luo, F. Liang, and T. Huang. Heterogeneous feature machines for visual recognition. *Proceedings of the IEEE Internation Conference on Computer Vision*, 2009.

[8] X. Chen, H. Liu, and J. Carbonell. Structured sparse canonical correlation analysis. 2012.

[9] X. Chen, X. Yuan, S. Yan, J. Tang, Y. Rui, and T. Chua. Towards multi-semantic image annotation with graph regularized exclusive group lasso. In

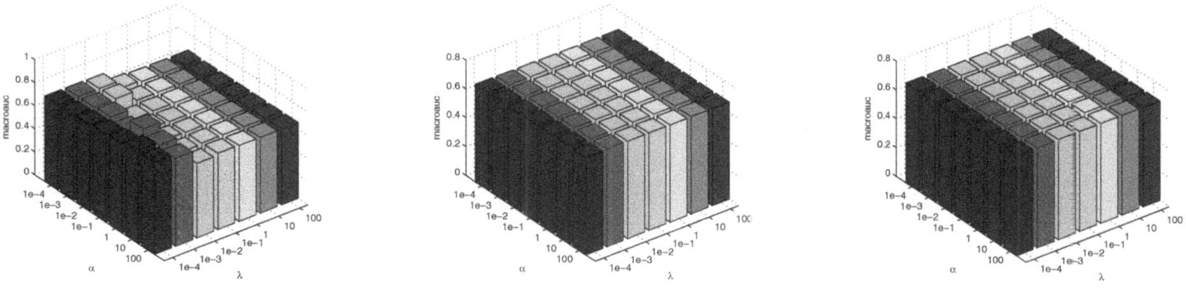

(a) Kodak (b) MSRA-MM 2.0 (c) NUS-WIDE

Figure 4: The change of MacroAUC scores as the regularization parameters α and λ vary in the range [10^{-4}, 10^{-3}, 10^{-2}, 10^{-1}, 1, 10, 100] for the Kodak (left panel), MSRA-MM (middle panel), and NUS-WIDE (right panel) data sets.

Groundtruth:	boat, sky ,water	building, cloud, sky	beach, people, sky
group *lasso*:	building, sky, water	cloud, sky	people, sky, water
NOVA:	boat, sky, water	building, cloud, sky	beach, sky

Groundtruth:	cloud, sky, sun	animal, zebra	birthday, cake
group *lasso*:	cloud, sky, water	zebra	birthday, cake, candle
NOVA:	cloud, sky, sun	animal, zebra	birthday, cake

Figure 5: Image annotation results on test images from the MSRA-MM 2.0 dataset. The first row shows the corresponding groundtruths, the seconde row shows annotation results by *convex group-sparsity* based method group *lasso* and the third row shows the results from our *nonconvex group-based sparsity* NOVA method.

Proceedings of the 19th ACM international conference on Multimedia, pages 263–272, 2011.

[10] T. Chua, J. Tang, R. Hong, H. Li, Z. Luo, and Y. Zheng. Nus-wide: A real-world web image database from national university of singapore. In *Proceeding of the ACM International Conference on Image and Video Retrieval*, pages 1–9, 2009.

[11] B. Efron, T. Hastie, I. Johnstone, and R. Tibshirani. Least angle regression. *The Annals of statistics*, 32(2):407–499, 2004.

[12] J. Fan and R. Li. Variable selection via nonconcave penalized likelihood and its oracle properties. *Journal of the American Statistical Association*, 96(456):1348–1360, 2001.

[13] T. Fawcett. An introduction to roc analysis. *Pattern recognition letters*, 27(8):861–874, 2006.

[14] V. Ferrari and A. Zisserman. Learning visual attributes. *Proceedings of Advances in Neural Information Processing Systems*, 2008.

[15] J. Friedman, T. Hastie, and R. Tibshirani. A note on the group lasso and a sparse group lasso. *Arxiv preprint arXiv:1001.0736*, 2010.

[16] W. Fu. Penalized regressions: the bridge versus the lasso. *Journal of computational and graphical statistics*, pages 397–416, 1998.

[17] Y. Han, F. Wu, Q. Tian, and Y. Zhuang. Image annotation by input-output structural grouping sparsity. *IEEE Transactions on Image Processing*, 21(6):3066–3079, 2012.

[18] L. Jacob, G. Obozinski, and J. Vert. Group lasso with overlap and graph lasso. In *Proceedings of the 26th Annual International Conference on Machine Learning*, pages 433–440, 2009.

[19] C. Lampert, H. Nickisch, and S. Harmeling. Learning to detect unseen object classes by between-class

Table 3: Performance comparison in terms of MacroAUC, MicroAUC and Precision. The average of metrics over ten random training/test partitions are reported. The results shown in boldface are best results.

A. Multi-label annotation comparison on Kodak data set.

		MacroAUC	MicroAUC	Precision
convex individual-sparsity	*lasso* [24]	0.7919 ± 0.0110	0.8023 ± 0.0211	0.8751 ± 0.0201
convex group-sparsity	group *lasso* [30]	0.8029 ± 0.0201	0.8103 ± 0.0018	0.8813 ± 0.0128
nonconvex individual-sparsity	SCAD [12]	0.8231 ± 0.0089	0.8210 ± 0.0012	0.8953 ± 0.0087
nonconvex group-sparsity	NOVA	**0.8365 ± 0.0278**	**0.8800 ± 0.0162**	**0.9131 ± 0.0317**

B. Multi-label annotation comparison on MSRA-MM 2.0 data set.

		MacroAUC	MicroAUC	Precision
convex individual-sparsity	*lasso*[24]	0.6266 ± 0.0083	0.7826 ± 0.0121	0.8300 ± 0.0124
convex group-sparsity	group *lasso* [30]	0.6412 ± 0.0012	0.7906 ± 0.0010	**0.9315 ± 0.0202**
nonconvex individual-sparsity	SCAD [12]	0.6438 ± 0.0018	0.8037 ± 0.0162	0.8245 ± 0.0065
nonconvex group-sparsity	NOVA	**0.6714 ± 0.0071**	**0.8255 ± 0.0035**	0.8466 ± 0.0400

C. Multi-label annotation comparison on NUS-WIDE data set.

		MacroAUC	MicroAUC	Precision
convex individual-sparsity	*lasso* [24]	0.6540 ± 0.0112	0.7654 ± 0.0106	0.7532 ± 0.0182
convex group-sparsity	group *lasso* [30]	0.6612 ± 0.0040	0.7806 ± 0.1002	0.7612 ± 0.1024
nonconvex individual-sparsity	SCAD [12]	0.6931 ± 0.0016	0.7821 ± 0.0102	0.7631 ± 0.0338
nonconvex group-sparsity	NOVA	**0.7029 ± 0.0045**	**0.7830 ± 0.0115**	**0.7934 ± 0.0400**

attribute transfer. In *Proceedings of Computer Vision and Pattern Recognition*, pages 951–958, 2009.

[20] H. Li, M. Wang, and X. Hua. MSRA-MM 2.0: A Large-Scale Web Multimedia Dataset. In *2009 IEEE International Conference on Data Mining Workshops*, pages 164–169, 2009.

[21] H. Liu and J. Zhang. Estimation consistency of the group lasso and its applications. In *Proceedings of the Twelfth International Conference on Artificial Intelligence and Statistics*, 2009.

[22] A. Loui, J. Luo, S. Chang, D. Ellis, W. Jiang, L. Kennedy, K. Lee, and A. Yanagawa. Kodak's consumer video benchmark data set: concept definition and annotation. In *Proceedings of the international workshop on Workshop on multimedia information retrieval*, pages 245–254. ACM, 2007.

[23] P. Rai and H. Daumé III. Multi-label Prediction via Sparse Infinite CCA. *Proceedings of the Conference on Neural Information Processing Systems*, 2009.

[24] R. Tibshirani. Regression shrinkage and selection via the lasso. *Journal of the Royal Statistical Society. Series B (Methodological)*, pages 267–288, 1996.

[25] T. Tuytelaars and K. Mikolajczyk. Local invariant feature detectors: a survey. *Foundations and Trends® in Computer Graphics and Vision*, 3(3):177–280, 2008.

[26] F. Wei and J. Huang. Consistent group selection in high-dimensional linear regression. *Bernoulli: official journal of the Bernoulli Society for Mathematical Statistics and Probability*, 16(4):1369–1384, 2010.

[27] F. Wu, Y. Han, X. Liu, J. Shao, Y. Zhuang, and Z. Zhang. The heterogeneous feature selection with structural sparsity for multimedia annotation and hashing: a survey. *International Journal of Multimedia Information Retrieval*, 1(1):3–15, 2012.

[28] F. Wu, Y. Han, Q. Tian, and Y. Zhuang. Multi-label boosting for image annotation by structural grouping sparsity. In *Proceedings of the international conference on Multimedia*, pages 15–24, 2010.

[29] F. Wu, Y. Yuan, and Y. Zhuang. Heterogeneous feature selection by group lasso with logistic regression. In *Proceedings of the international conference on Multimedia*, pages 983–986, 2010.

[30] M. Yuan and Y. Lin. Model selection and estimation in regression with grouped variables. *Journal of the Royal Statistical Society: Series B (Statistical Methodology)*, 68(1):49–67, 2006.

[31] Y. Yuan, F. Wu, Y. Zhuang, and J. Shao. Image annotation by composite kernel learning with group structure. In *Proceedings of the 19th ACM international conference on Multimedia*, pages 1497–1500, 2011.

[32] C. Zhang. Nearly unbiased variable selection under minimax concave penalty. *The Annals of Statistics*, 38(2):894–942, 2010.

[33] P. Zhao, G. Rocha, and B. Yu. Grouped and hierarchical model selection through composite absolute penalties. *Department of Statistics, UC Berkeley, Tech. Rep*, 703, 2006.

[34] Y. Zhou, R. Jin, and S. Hoi. Exclusive lasso for multi-task feature selection. *JMLR W&C Proceedings (AISTATS2010)*, pages 988–995, 2010.

[35] H. Zou. The adaptive lasso and its oracle properties. *Journal of the American Statistical Association*, 101(476):1418–1429, 2006.

[36] H. Zou and R. Li. One-step sparse estimates in nonconcave penalized likelihood models. *Annals of Statistics*, 36(4):1509–1566, 2008.

Query-Adaptive Shape Topic Mining for Hand-Drawn Sketch Recognition

Zhenbang Sun[1] *, Changhu Wang[2], Liqing Zhang[1], Lei Zhang[2]
[1]Brain-like Computing Lab, Shanghai Jiao Tong University, Shanghai 200240, P.R.China
[2]Microsoft Research Asia, No. 5 Danling Street, Beijing 100080, P.R.China
sunzhenbang@hotmail.com, chw@microsoft.com
zhang-lq@cs.sjtu.edu.cn, leizhang@microsoft.com

ABSTRACT

In this work, we study the problem of hand-drawn sketch recognition. Due to large intra-class variations presented in hand-drawn sketches, most of existing work was limited to a particular domain or limited pre-defined classes. Different from existing work, we target at developing a general sketch recognition system, to recognize any semantically meaningful object that a child can recognize. To increase the recognition coverage, a web-scale clipart image collection is leveraged as the knowledge base of the recognition system. To alleviate the problems of *intra-class shape variation* and *inter-class shape ambiguity* in this unconstrained situation, a query-adaptive shape topic model is proposed to mine object topics and shape topics related to the sketch, in which, multiple layers of information such as sketch, object, shape, image, and semantic labels are modeled in a generative process. Besides sketch recognition, the proposed topic model can also be used for related applications such as sketch tagging, image tagging, and sketch-based image search. Extensive experiments on different applications show the effectiveness of the proposed topic model and the recognition system.

Categories and Subject Descriptors

H.3.1 [**Information Storage and Retrieval**]: Content Analysis and Indexing

General Terms

Algorithms, Experimentation

Keywords

Sketch Recognition, Query-adaptive Shape Topic Model, Sketch-based Image Search

*Zhenbang Sun performed this work while being an intern at Microsoft Research Asia.

MM'12, October 29–November 2, 2012, Nara, Japan.

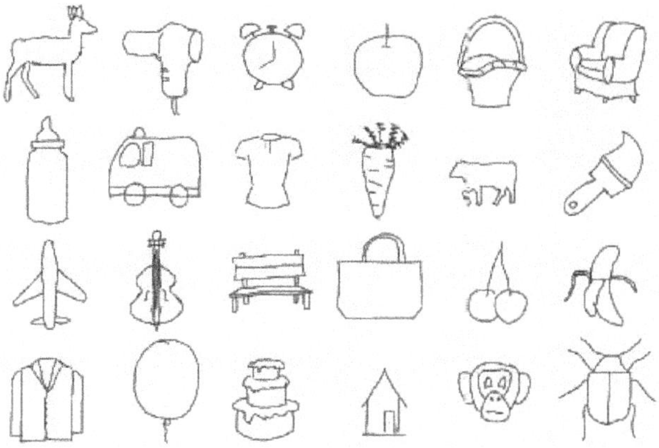

Figure 1: Examples of hand-drawn sketches. The sketch recognition system targets at recognizing a reasonable hand-drawn sketch.

1. INTRODUCTION

Nowadays, sketching has become one of the most natural ways for human-computer interaction, especially as the increasing popularity of devices with touch screens. Thus, how a computer can recognize a human's hand-drawn sketch, as a basic problem of artificial intelligence, has attracted more and more attentions. An effective sketch recognition system can help a computer know more about human intentions, and thus will be of great value to a variety of applications, such as human-computer interaction, game design, sketch-based search, and children education.

Sketch recognition has been studied since 1990s in computer vision and graphics. Most of existing approaches for sketch recognition [1, 11, 12, 13, 18, 23, 26, 27] mainly focus on recognizing basic shapes in specific domains such as UML diagrams and mechanical engineering. The dependency on domain-specific knowledge makes it difficult to adapt these algorithms to solve problems in other domains, let alone recognize an arbitrary hand-drawn sketch.

Related work such as shape recognition and classification [2, 19, 20, 21] mainly targets at designing effective shape descriptors and matching models to handle global and/or local non-rigid shape deformations. Thus, although kept from the uncertainty bought by hand-drawn sketches, this kind of work is still limited in small-scale datasets, due to the complexity of matching models and the lack of an efficient index solution.

Figure 2: Examples of intra-class variation. The shapes of the same objects are still of large diversity.

Figure 3: Examples of inter-class ambiguity. Different objects might present quite similar shapes.

In this work, we study the problem of hand-drawn sketch recognition. There is no particular constraint, and any semantically meaningful object a child can recognize might be a drawing target, as shown in Fig. 1. This differentiates the problem we are targeting at from existing work, and thus some new challenges arise, i.e. object coverage[1], intra-class shape variation, inter-class shape ambiguity, and sketch uncertainty.

Object coverage: Since there are potentially unlimited objects with typical shapes in the world, a practical sketch recognition system should have the ability to recognize as many objects as possible.

Intra-class shape variation: As shown in Fig. 2, even for one object, there might be many shapes. Traditional domain-specific shape modeling methods might not work here, since the shape models of potentially unlimited objects will be of large diversity.

Inter-class shape ambiguity: In such an unconstraint situation in terms of potentially unlimited objects and shapes, there might exist many ambiguous shapes which could represent different objects, as shown in Fig. 3. This makes the recognition process more challenging, and motivate us to find other information besides shape features.

Sketch uncertainty: Hand-drawn sketches always exhibit variations and ambiguities, as shown in Fig. 4. The recognition process should not only well reflect the shape of the sketch query, but also be robust enough to an imprecise sketch.

[1]With a slight abuse of terminology, in this work we use "object" to represent a class of objects with a same semantic meaning.

Figure 4: Examples of sketch uncertainty. The hand-drawn sketches from different persons might be quite diverse even when drawing the same object.

To increase the *object and shape coverage*, a large-scale database is highly desired to be the knowledge base of the recognition system. Thus, we collected one million clipart images from the web as the knowledge base, for the contours in clipart images have a similar style to hand-drawn sketches. Most of these images have noisy textual information such as titles and the surrounding text. Since it is impractical to model all objects and shapes in this huge knowledge base, an effective sketch-based image search technology [7] is leveraged to find visually similar images to the sketch, and then a query-adaptive image collection is obtained. Thus, the problem is reduced to how to recognize the sketch based on a collection of images with noisy words.

Due to *sketch uncertainty*, their might be different objects with variant shapes in the collection, which causes the problems of *intra-class shape variation* and *inter-class shape ambiguity*. These problems, together with the noisy descriptions of the images, make it less effective to mine keywords directly from the textual information of the collection. Thus, to alleviate these problems, we leverage both the shape and textual features to recognize the sketch.

Therefore, the task of sketch recognition is to discover *object topics* and *shape topics* from the query-adaptive image collection, both of which are actually coupled together due to the problems of *shape variation* and *ambiguity*. For example, as shown in Fig. 2 and Fig. 3, the shapes of the same object may be very different, while those of different objects may be visually similar. Therefore, for the task of sketch recognition, an effective algorithm is required to simultaneously model object topics and shape topics, with ability of handling both visual and textual features. Here an *object topic* represents a kind of object that occurs in the collection, and a *shape topic* represents a certain shape of objects.

In this work, we propose a probabilistic topic model for hand-drawn sketch recognition, i.e. Query-adaptive Shape Topic (QST) model, to simulate the generative process of an image and its textual information. In QST, two layers of latent topics, i.e. object topics and shape topics, are presented to alleviate the *shape variation* and *ambiguity* problems. More specifically, an image is supposed to contain one object topic, and this object topic generates a typical shape topic and related semantic tags. Moreover, the sketch query is not only used to find the query-adaptive image collection, but also supervises the generative process of the shape features from shape topics in QST.

The QST model is appropriate for solving the sketch recognition problem because of the following aspects. First, the concurrent generating of textual features and shape features makes it possible to differentiate objects with similar shapes, and thus alleviate the shape ambiguity problem. Second, the representation of two-layer latent topics helps overcome the shape variation problem, since it can group together multiple shapes of one object. Moreover, this hierarchical structure is robust to hand-drawn variances, and related objects and shapes could be discovered for an imprecise sketch, as shown in Fig. 5.

As far as we know, this is the first work to target at recognizing an arbitrary but semantically meaningful hand-drawn sketch. Besides sketch recognition, the proposed system can also be used for related applications, such as sketch tagging, image tagging, and sketch-based image search. Extensive experiments on different applications show the effectiveness of the proposed QST model and sketch recognition system.

2. RELATED WORK

In this section, we present the related work in sketch recognition, shape classification, and topic models.

Sketch recognition. Sketch recognition has been studied for decades in computer vision and graphics. Early research mainly focused on domain-specific sketch recognition, such as recognizing basic shapes in UML diagrams [12], mechanical engineering [27], and webpage design [18]. In order to alleviate the substantial efforts in developing sketch interfaces in new domains, in 2003, a sketch description language LADDER [14] was introduced, based on which a domain-independent sketch recognition system was built. However, to recognize sketches in a new domain, users still need to write a sketch grammar describing the domain-specific information. Based on LADDER, sketch recognition systems such as PaleoSketch [23] were developed, most of which need strong domain knowledge, focusing on recognizing limited basic shapes, such as line, polyline, circle, ellipse, and arc. In 2008, an open-domain sketch recognition system CogSketch [11] was built, which, however, is a sketch managing tool focusing on reasoning over recognition. Note that previous systems only recognized on the order of at most 20 different shapes. In 2010, Hammond et al. [13] tried to recognize hundreds of shapes. However, the target was to recognize course-of-action diagrams instead of arbitrary natural objects. Thus, in spite of continuous efforts, most of existing recognition systems focus on specific domains with limited shapes.

Shape classification. The studies in shape recognition and classification mainly target at designing effective shape descriptors and matching models to handle global and/or local non-rigid shape deformations. Roughly speaking, shape descriptors differ according to whether they are applied to contours or regions. Contour-based shape descriptors include wavelets [22], Fourier descriptors [30], contour descriptors [20], etc. Region-based shape descriptors include [17, 25, 28], etc. Shape matching is usually influenced by the adopted descriptors. Typical algorithms include contour matching [2] to solve the optimal assignment problem to discover the mapping of two set of points, and descriptor matching [21] to measure the similarity of two set of local descriptors. Most existing studies target at limited classes and each shape has explicit labels, which are not easy to adapted for solving our problem.

Topic models. In recent years, probabilistic topic models, such as PLSA[16], LDA[5], have been widely used in semantic data mining owing to their capability of discovering meaningful latent topics. To leverage the class information of data, supervised topic models such as s-LDA[4] were proposed. Topic models were also successfully applied to problems with multi-type features such as image classification/annotation [3], in which both visual features and semantic tags exist. Moreover, some more complex models were further designed to solve specific problems. For example, for the task of web image categorization, [10] proposed a topic model which was derived from PLSA[16], by additionally considering the locations of visual words. In [24], the author-topic model, which was extended from LDA [5], was proposed to discover topics in academic articles. In the domain of multimedia document mining, [15] modeled the process of generating travelogues. However, in spite of the success in many applications, existing work is either too simple to handle the problems we meet in sketch recognition, or leverages too much domain knowledge from specific problems and thus is difficult to adapt to solve our problem. For example, PLSA and LDA were designed for one type of features, whereas our data contains both shapes and words. Corr-LDA and s-LDA cannot be easily adapted to handle so many layers including sketch, object, shape, image, and semantic words.

3. QUERY-ADAPTIVE SHAPE TOPIC MODEL

In this section, we present the proposed Query-adaptive Shape Topic (QST) model for sketch recognition. Besides the generative process of the model and its parameter estimation, we also show how to utilize the model for sketch recognition and tagging, followed by some illustrations to the effectiveness of the latent topics.

3.1 Query-Adaptive Image Collection

We collected one million clipart images from the web as a knowledge base to recognize a hand-drawn sketch. Most of these images are created by humans and might cover most of drawings of familiar objects.

For a hand-drawn sketch, we leverage the technology of Edgel Index [7, 29] and build a sketch-based clipart image search engine to search similar images to the sketch. After filtering out complex images, most clipart images in our database only contain one single object. Thus, in the clipart engine, both of the sketch query and contours of database images are normalized to a uniform location and size before searching and indexing, which makes this engine invariant to sketch/shape translation and scaling. The effectiveness of this engine has been validated in different retrieval tasks [7, 8, 29]. For details please refer to [7, 8, 29].

Based on this engine, for each hand-drawn sketch, the visually similar images to the sketch, their surrounding texts, and their matching scores, will be used as the input for the QST model to recognize the sketch query.

3.2 Problem Formulation

The sketch recognition problem is formulated as how to discover semantic topics possibly representing the sketch from the query-adaptive image collection.

We first analyze and discover the generative process for the observed information and latent topics. Since there are only simple clipart images in the collection, it is natural to assume there is only one object topic in each image. To overcome the challenge of *shape ambiguity*, besides the visual

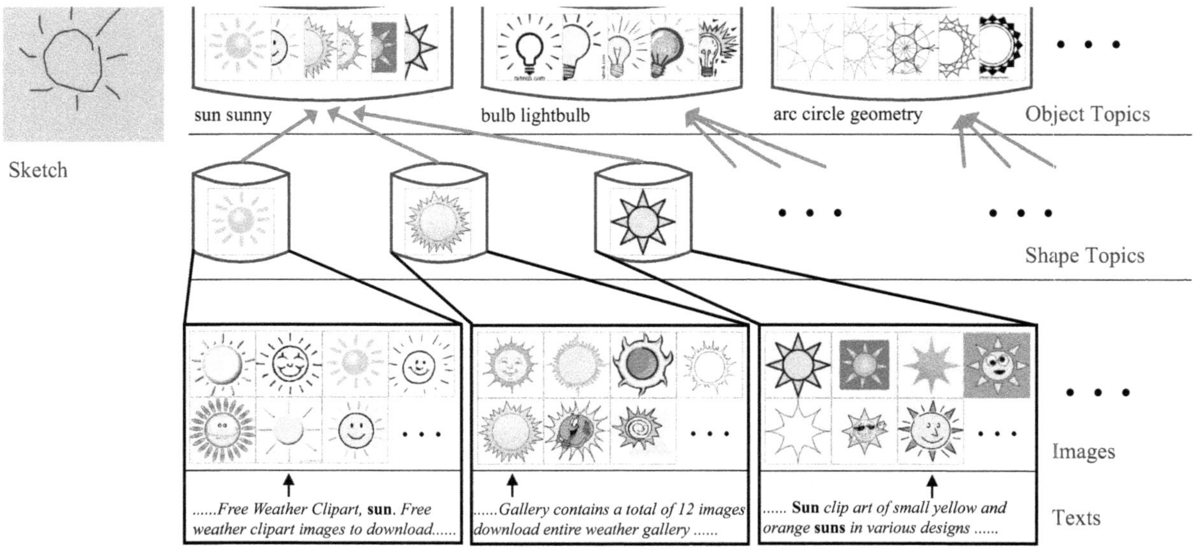

Figure 5: The hierarchical structure of the two-layer latent topics. Assume the image I has shape feature r_I. The shape topic s of image I is determined by the highest probability $p(r_I|s)$, and the object topic z which the shape topic s belongs to is determined by the highest probability $p(s|z)$.

feature, the textual information of images is also leveraged in the model. Therefore, for each image, its object topic further generates both visual information like shapes and semantic information like the surrounding text of the image.

Since one object might correspond to different shapes, it is natural to add another layer of topics, i.e. shape topics, to represent variant types of shapes related to the sketch. This can further alleviate the problems of *shape variation* and *shape ambiguity*. The shape feature is then generated according to the shape topic.

Instead of a purely unsupervised topic mining problem, in this work it is necessary to discover object topics that are more relevant to the sketch query. Different from sLDA [4], in which the supervised information (a response variable) is generated by the latent topics, in QST we use the sketch query to influence the possibility of generating a shape feature from a shape topic. This guarantees that the discovered shape topics are more relevant to the sketch query, and so are the object topics.

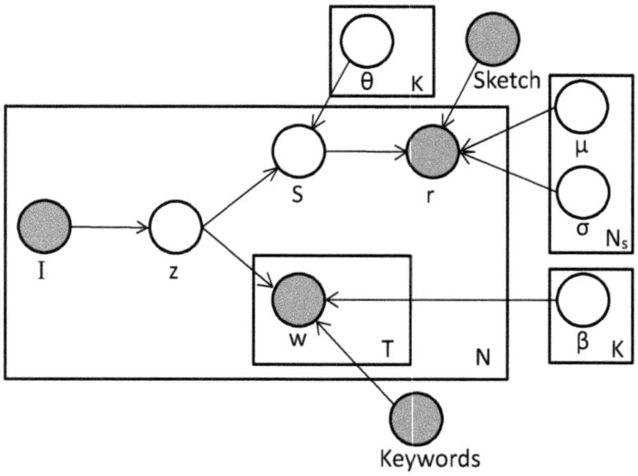

Figure 6: Graphical representation of the proposed QST model.

3.3 Generative Process

The graphical representation of the QST model is shown in Fig. 6. It should be noted that, to make the model more general, we also enable users to optionally add keywords when they draw sketches. Thus, two factors, i.e. the sketch and the keywords, will supervise the generative process, in which the keywords could be an empty set $\emptyset$.

We first introduce some notations and definitions. Assume there are N images $\{I_1, I_2, ..., I_N\}$ in the collection, and the words in the dictionary are $\{w_1, w_2, ..., w_M\}$. The shape feature of I_n is represented by r_n and the noisy labels of image I_n are represented by $\{w_1, w_2, ..., w_T\}$. $\delta(w_m, I_n) = 1$ if $w_m \in \{w_1, w_2, ..., w_T\}$; and 0, otherwise.

Let z denote a latent variable to represent an object topic, with discrete values $z = 1, ..., K$, and s denote a latent variable to represent a shape topic, with discrete values $s = 1, ..., N_s$. We abbreviate "sketch" and "keywords" to "ske" and "key" for long equations. Given N, M, K and N_s, the generative process of QST model is given as follow:

1. For each image I_n, sample the object topic: $z \sim p(z|I_n)$
2. For each object topic z:
(a) sample T words $\{w_1, w_2, ..., w_T\}$, in which for each word w_m we have:
$w_m \sim p(w_m|z, \beta, keywords) = \beta_{z,w_m}^{\delta(w_m, keywords)}$
(b) sample the shape topic:
$s \sim p(s|z, \theta) = \theta_{z,s}$
3. For each shape topic s, sample the shape feature:

$$\begin{aligned} r_n &\sim p(r_n|s, \mu, \sigma, \beta, sketch) \\ &= \frac{1}{\sqrt{2\pi\sigma_s^2}} \exp(-\frac{dist(r_n, \mu_s)^2}{2\sigma_s^2} dist(r_n|sketch)), \end{aligned}$$

in which $dist(r_n, \mu_s)$ is defined as the distance between r_n and μ_s, and $dist(r_n|sketch)$ is the distance between r_n and the sketch. Both of $dist(r_n, \mu_s)$ and $dist(r_n|sketch)$ are obtained according to [7]. In particular, we define $\delta(w, \emptyset) = 1$.

Given the parameters θ, μ, σ, and β, we can get the following joint probability of a set of N object topics z, a set of N shape class s, and a set of N shape feature $\mathbf{r}$ and words $\mathbf{w}$:

$$\begin{aligned} &p(\mathbf{I}, \mathbf{w}, \mathbf{r}, z, s|\theta, \mu, \sigma, \beta, sketch, keywords) \\ &= \prod_{n=1}^{N}\{p(I_n)p(z|I_n)p(r_n|s, \mu, \sigma, \beta, sketch)p(s|z, \theta) \\ &\qquad \prod_{m=1}^{M}(p(w_m|z, \beta, keywords))^{\delta(I_n, w_m)}\}. \end{aligned}$$

3.4 Parameter Estimation

We estimate the parameters by maximizing the log-likelihood function using the EM algorithm. The log-likelihood L could be written by:

$$L = F + \sum_{n=1}^{N} KL(q(z, s)||p(z, s|I_n, \mathbf{w}, r_n, \theta, \mu, \sigma, \beta, ske, key)),$$

in which the lower bound F of the log-likelihood is:

$$F = \sum_{n=1}^{N}\sum_{z}\sum_{s} q(z, s)\log\frac{p(I_n, \mathbf{w}, r_n, z, s|\theta, \mu, \sigma, \beta, ske, key)}{q(z, s)}.$$

We use the EM algorithm to iteratively maximize the lower bound F and minimize the KL divergence. Thus, the E-step is to calculate:

$$q(z, s|I = I_n) = \frac{p(z, s, I = I_n, \mathbf{w}, r_n|\theta, \mu, \sigma, \beta, ske, key)}{p(I = I_n, \mathbf{w}, r_n|\theta, \mu, \sigma, \beta, ske, key)}.$$

With some deductions which will be omitted due to space limitation, we can get the estimate of latent variables:

$$\begin{aligned} q(z, s|I = I_n) &\propto p(I = I_n)p(z|I = I_n) \\ &\times p(s|z, \theta)p(r_n|s, \mu, \sigma, \beta, sketch) \\ \prod_{m=1}^{M} &(p(w_m|z, \beta, keywords))^{\delta(I_n, w_m)}. \end{aligned}$$

Since we can obtain the joint distribution of s and z in condition of observed variables and parameters, we do not need variational approach to separate the joint probability of s and z.

By maximizing the lower bound F, in the M-step we can get:

$$\begin{aligned} p(z|I_n) &\propto \sum_{s} q(z, s|I_n), \\ \theta_{z,s} = p(s|z, \theta) &\propto \sum_{n=1}^{N} q(z, s|I_n), \\ \beta_{z,m} = p(w_m|z, \beta) &\propto \sum_{n=1}^{N}\sum_{s} \delta(I_n, w_m)q(z, s|I_n). \end{aligned}$$

Since it is not easy to find a vectorized expression of the shape feature [7], the expectation of Gaussian is represented by the centremost sample of the distribution:

$$\mu_s = \arg\max_{\mu} \sum_{n=1}^{N}\sum_{z} q(z, s|I_n)dist(r_n|ske)(-\frac{dist(r_n, \mu)^2}{2\sigma_s^2}).$$

The estimated variance is

$$\sigma_s = \sqrt{\frac{\sum_{n=1}^{N}\sum_{z=1}^{K} q(z, s|I_n)dist(r_n|sketch)dist(r_n, \mu_s)^2}{\sum_{n=1}^{N}\sum_{z=1}^{K} q(z, s|I_n)dist(r_n|sketch)}}.$$

We iteratively conduct E-step and M-step, until the parameters become convergent.

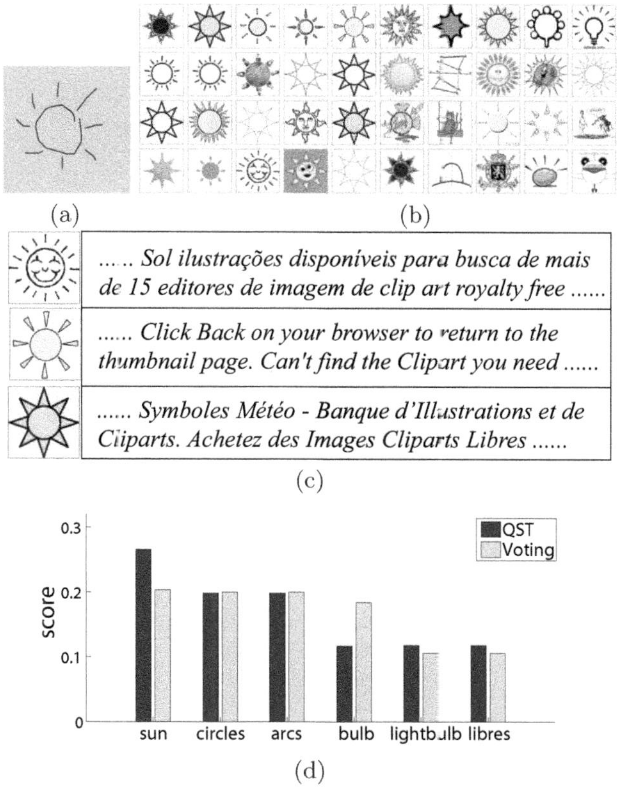

Figure 7: Illustration of the effectiveness of latent topics. (a) A hand-drawn sketch of the 'sun'. (b) Top results of a sketch-based image search engine. (c) Object-irrelevant labels of some images. (d) Comparison of the scores, i.e. $p(w|sketch)$, of the recommended tags by QST and a voting-based approach.

3.5 Utilizing the Model

Based on the probability of latent topics and the word distribution under each object topic, the probability of each word given the sketch can be used for sketch recognition and tagging:

$$p(w = w_m|sketch) = \sum_{n=1}^{N} p(I_n)\sum_{z} p(w = w_m|z, \beta)p(z|I_n).$$

The recommended tags are ranked according to their probabilities, and the top ones will be considered as the recognition/tagging results.

3.6 Effectiveness of Latent Topics

In this section, we illustrate the effectiveness of the QST model in object and shape topic mining.

3.6.1 Object Topic Mining

The QST model has the ability to discover the relationship between visual features and textual features, and thus fully utilizes the images without object-relevant labels.

For example, if we draw a sketch of the sun, in the query-adaptive image collection, there might be some images without any object-relevant labels, as shown in Fig. 7. In this case, a voting-based method (see Section 4.2), which only takes account of the word frequencies in this collection re-

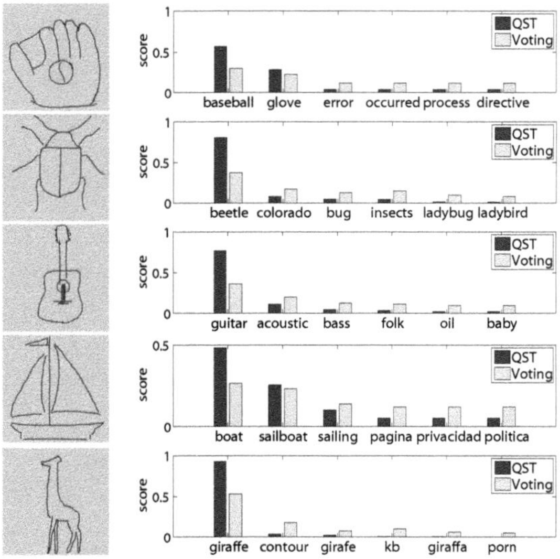

Figure 8: Example recognition results. For each sketch, the top six tags recommended by the two approaches together with their scores are shown.

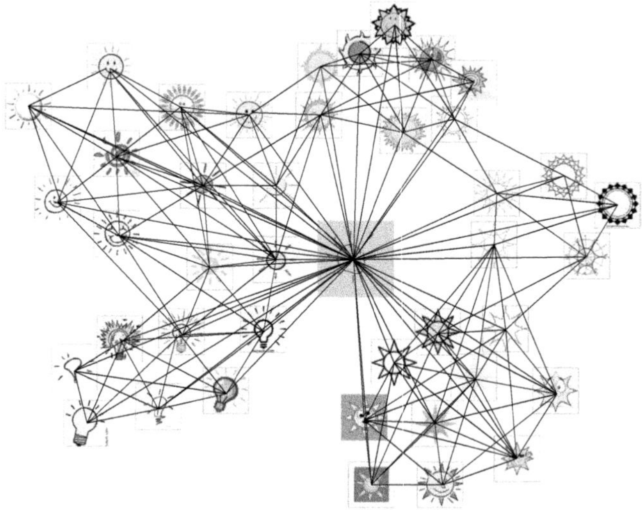

Figure 9: The images projected to a 2D space. The distance between two images represents the dissimilarity of their shape features. If the dissimilarity between two shapes is larger than a certain threshold, the line between these two images is not shown.

gardless of visual features, could not tell from the top three tags, i.e. sun, circle, and arc, as shown in Fig. 7 (d). However, in the QST model, for a 'sun' image without a useful label, the model can still recognize the image as the 'sun', for the probability $p(z = sun|I)$ will be relatively high. Thus, the final probability $p(w = \text{`}sun\text{'}|sketch)$ will be large enough to distinguish from other tags.

To further see the advantages of QST, we show more comparisons in Fig. 8. We can see that, in some cases, although these two algorithms might recommend the same tags which will result in the same recognition results, the QST model has better ability to distinguish the right tags from noisy ones.

3.6.2 *Shape Topic Mining*

To illustrate the effectiveness of QST in shape topic mining, we project the images related to a drawing of the sun to a 2D space, preserving the relative shape dissimilarity between images, as shown in Fig. 9. We can see that, the shapes of the 'sun' locate at different clusters, and some of the 'sun' images are even closer to other objects.

We can consider the process of modeling data as a grouping process. If we use only one layer of object topics, the images of one object might not be merged together to one group but several groups, due to the variance of their shape features.

When we use the two-layer latent topics in QST to model the images, as shown in Fig. 5, they will be organized in a hierarchical way, in which different objects will be clustered into different groups, and each object group corresponds to multiple shape topics.

4. EXPERIMENTS

In this section, we evaluate the proposed QST model for sketch recognition.

Two data sets, i.e. the MPEG-7 20-category shape data set and the manually collected 500-category sketch data set (called Sketch-500 in this work), are used as testing sets to test the sketch recognition system.

4.1 Global Parameters of QST Model

In this part, we introduce the preprocess of the topic model to estimate some global parameters, i.e. the number of images in the collection N, the candidate word list $\{w_1, w_2, ..., w_M\}$, the number of object topics K, and the number of shape topics N_s. Both N and M are empirically set to be 30. The most frequent words in the collection are used as the candidate word list. Given the shape similarities between images[2], we use the graph-cut algorithm [9] to group the images, and use N_s to denote the number of groups. The number of object topics K is obtained in a similar way, excepted that the surrounding text in the vector space is used to replace the shape feature.

4.2 Voting-based Approach

As far as we know, this is the first work for general hand-drawn sketch recognition. Thus, we implemented a voting-based approach as the baseline for comparison. After getting the query-adaptive image collection for the sketch query, it is natural to select the most frequent word(s) as the recognition result(s)[3]. Considering both the image similarity to the sketch and the word frequency, the score of a word w, $Score(w|sketch)$, is calculated as follows:

$$Score(w|sketch) = \sum_{n=1}^{N} \#(w, I_n) \times Score(I_n|sketch),$$

where $\#(w, I_n)$ is the occurrence number of w in the surrounding text of image I_n, and $Score(I_n|sketch)$ represents the similarity between I_n and the sketch query as in [7].

[2]We use the two-way chamfer matching [7] to calculate the similarity between two images, which will not be introduced in this work due to space limitation.

[3]The stopwords were filtered out in advance.

Figure 10: Shape examples in MPEG-7. The names of shape classes from left to right are apple, bat, beetle, bell, bone (first line), bird, device8, device4, comma, device2, and brick (second line).

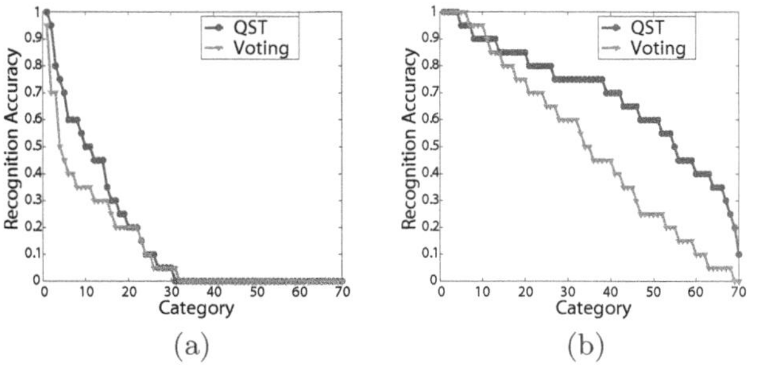

Figure 11: Shape recognition results on MPEG-7. The categories are ranked based on the performance. (a) Recognition results using unlimited tags. (b) Recognition results after filtering out the tags which do not belong to the names of the 70 classes.

Then, the word with the highest score is used as the recognition result for the sketch.

4.3 Shape Recognition on MPEG-7

MPEG-7 data set [6] defines 70 shape classes, where each shape class contains 20 different shape contours in the form of binary images. In total, this data set contains 1400 shape contours. A subset of the shape classes are illustrated in Fig. 10.

Different from existing shape classification work such as [19, 28], which were well trained in the 1,400 shapes, in this experiment, we try to use our system to recognize the shapes in MPEG-7 without any class-specific training. That is, the database, the vocabulary, and the evaluation are not constrained to the 1,400 shapes and 70 labels, which makes the recognition problem much more challenging.

For each category, we measure the proportion of shapes correctly recognized by the recommended tag with highest $Score(w = w_m|sketch)$, in which correct recognition means that the tag is the same as the class label or its synonymy. Recognition results for each category are shown in Fig. 11 (a), in which the categories are ranked based on the performance. We can see that, the performance of QST model is much better than that of the voting-based method.

Moreover, as shown in Fig. 11 (a), for some shape classes, such as heart, cellular phone, and truck, the performances are quite good; while for some other classes, such as glas, device0, and comma, the performances are really bad, most of which are zero. The reasons are three folds. First, the task of shape classification is quite different from sketch recognition. That is, the shapes in one category might represent different objects, and in this case the category name is not meaningful at all. Examples are the categories of device0 to device8. Second, some shapes are not very common in clipart images, such as the shape "comma" as shown in Fig. 10, and thus cannot be recognized by our system. Third, most importantly, the unlimited tags and training data make the problem quite difficult. For some shapes, some noisy tags might be ranked higher than the groundtruth tag, and thus the recognition performance is not good. If we remove all recommended tags which do not belong to the 70 labels, the performance will become much better, as shown in Fig. 11 (b). We can also imagine that there will be another performance increase if we also constrain the database from one million to the 1,400 shapes as in [19, 28], which is however not the target of this system. The performance difference of Fig. 11 (a) and (b) also shows the difference of the sketch recognition task and existing shape classification work to some extent.

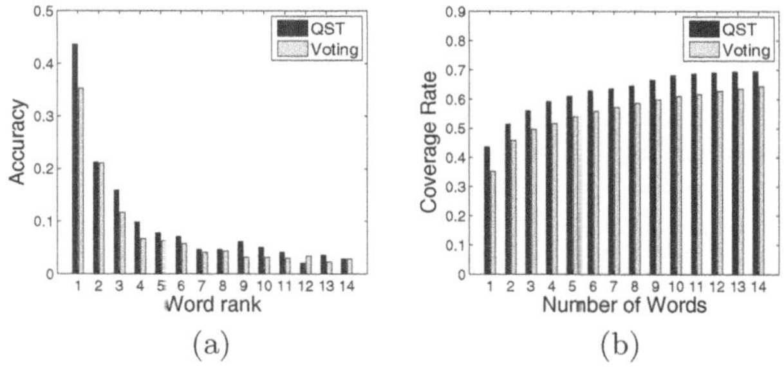

Figure 12: Recognition performance on Sketch-500. (a) Percentages of sketches correctly recognized by the kth recommended word. (b) Percentages of sketches correctly recognized by at least one word among the top k words.

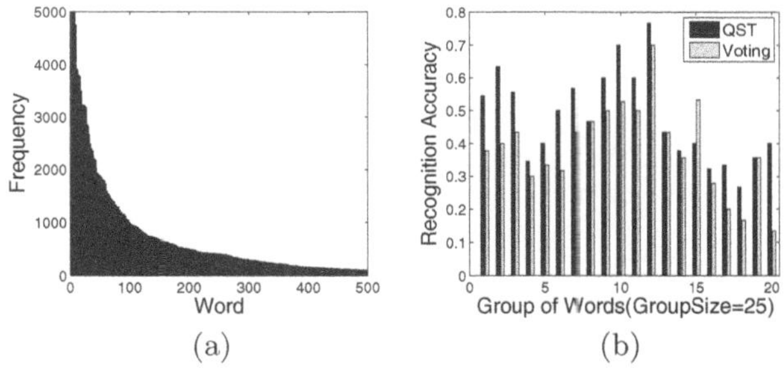

Figure 13: Relationship between the recognition performance and keyword frequency in the database. (a) Frequency of the 500 nouns in Sketch-500. (b) Average recognition results for each 25 sketches ordered by the frequency of the nouns.

4.4 Sketch Recognition on Sketch-500

Since there is not an open data set for the task of recognizing an arbitrary but semantically meaningful hand-drawn sketch, we manually build the Sketch-500 data set to test the performance of the proposed recognition system. The Sketch-500 data set is built based on a list of 1000 non-abstract nouns[4], which is a free word list collected for elementary students and contains most of commonly used nouns. For each word, we asked a graduate student to manually draw a sketch based on the top results returned from a commercial keyword-based clipart image search engine. We ignored the words which are hard to draw a sketch to represent, such as "back", "earthquake", and "dust", and finally collected 500 sketches together with groundtruth names. Example sketches are shown in Fig. 1.

The performance of sketch recognition is reported in Fig. 12 from two aspects. (a) shows the accuracy, i.e. the percentage of sketches correctly recognized by the kth word recommended by the system, and (b) is the coverage rate, i.e. the percentage of sketches correctly recognized by at least one word among the top k words. We can see that, only based on the top-one tag recommended by the system, the recognition rate is about 45%, which is a quite impressive performance, considering that the system is an open system without any preference to the testing data. We can also see that, compared with the voting-based algorithm, the QST model performs higher recognition accuracy. For example, the accuracy on the top-one tag is almost 10 percent higher than that of the voting-based algorithm.

To discover the relationship between the system's recognition ability to an object and the amount of data of the object in the system, we grouped the sketches into different groups according to the occurrence numbers of their names in the database, and calculated the average recognition performance for each group, as shown in Fig. 13. We can see that, the recognition system is somewhat robust to the frequency of occurrences of an object in the database.

Since there might be large intra-class variations in human drawings, to test this point, we randomly and independently moved all the strokes of a sketch to different directions. The moving distance is a parameter multiplied by the longer side of the sketch, and this parameter is called "variance" in this work. Fig. 14 shows the recognition results under different variances. We can see that, for a relatively large variance, e.g. the fish with variance 20%, the recognition results are still acceptable.

Besides recognizing sketches, our system can also suggest semantically related keywords to a sketch. A graduate student was asked to manually label whether a recommended tag is related to the groundtruth keyword. For example, the keyword "fruit" is a good tag for groundtruth keyword "apple", which however was considered as a wrong recognition result in previous experiments. The performance of the sketch tagging task is shown in Fig. 15. We can see that, there is about a 20% performance increase if we relax the recognition criteria from exactly matching the objet name or its synonymy to matching a semantically related keyword.

4.5 Other Applications

The learnt probabilities between variables of the QST model can be used in various applications, such as sketch-based image search and image tagging. In this section, we will illustrate the effectiveness of QST in the above two applications.

4.5.1 *Enhance Sketch-based Image Search*

[4]http://www.free-teacher-worksheets.com/support-files/list-of-nouns.pdf

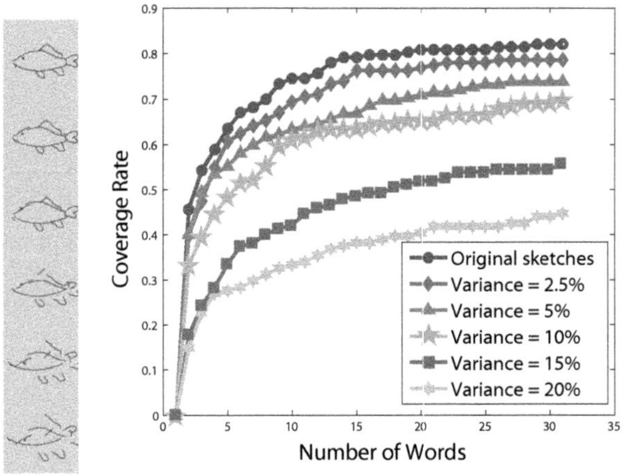

Figure 14: Recognition results under different variances. Left: an example with variances of 0%, 2.5%, 5%, 10%, 15%, 20%. Right: the coverage rates under different variances.

An important application of QST is to enhance the sketch-based image search. Based on the sketch recognition system, there are two ways to refine the search results.

The first way is to use the probabilities of the trained QST model, which is called "QST refined" here. The distance between the sketch and a database image could be measured in the topic space:

$$Dist(I_n, sketch) = KL(p(z|I = I_n)||p(z|sketch)),$$

in which

$$p(z = k|sketch) = \sum_{n=1}^{N} p(z = k|I_n)p(I_n).$$

The probabilities $p(z|I = I_n)$, $p(z = k|I_n)$, and $p(I_n)$ can be obtained from the QST model. Then, the search results are refined by sorting the images in the ascending order of $Dist(I_n, sketch)$.

The second method is to combine the recognition result with the sketch itself to query the clipart engine, which is named as "Sketch+Recognition".

In this experiment, we randomly selected 20 sketches from Sketch-500 data set as the queries, and evaluated the precision of top N search results returned from the clipart image search engine using different algorithms. For all methods in our comparison, the criteria of relevance is not only structurally (in terms of shape) but also semantically (in terms of concept) matched with the sketch query. The comparison results are shown in Fig. 17, from which we can see the effectiveness of the two methods in enhancing sketch-based image search. Some examples are shown in Fig. 18. We can see that some irrelevant results will be filtered out after understanding the sketch.

Besides, the recognition results based on the clipart image collection can also be used to improve the natural image search. As indicated by [7], sketch-based natural image search is more challenging than clipart search, since the cluttered background in natural images makes it not easy to extract the salient objects. Thus, the assumption that there is only one object in an image cannot be adopted, which causes that the search is translation and scaling sensitive

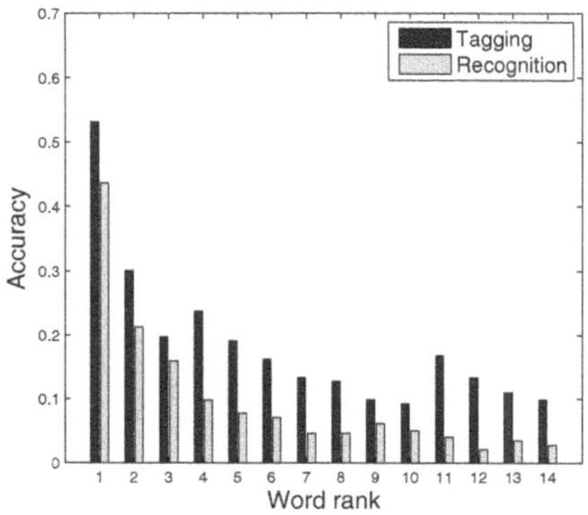

Figure 15: The performance of sketch tagging.

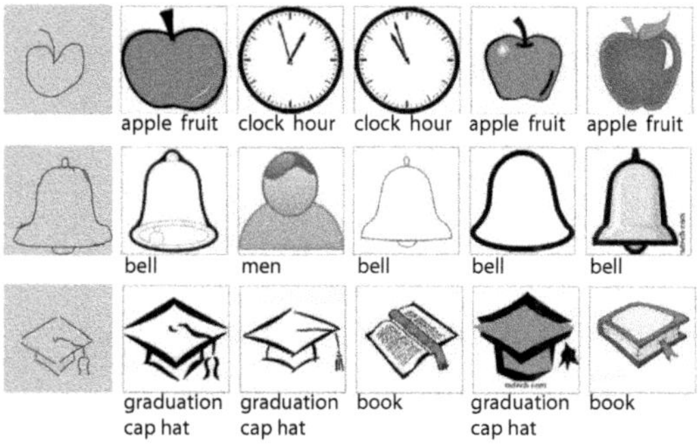

Figure 16: Examples of image tagging.

(to some extent). Hence, in many cases, even if the sketch query has a good shape, the search results might still be unacceptable. Fig. 18 also shows some examples of the search results on a 2-million natural image database. We can see that, by leveraging the recognition results to the sketch, the search results were greatly improved compared with the EI-S method [7] (denoted by 'original search'). It should be noted that, the "QST refined" method cannot be used for natural image search, since the QST was learnt based on the clipart collection.

4.5.2 *Image Tagging*

As aforementioned, the collection of images we are using are not well labeled. Although each image has corresponding surrounding text, there may be many irrelevant and incorrect tags, as shown in Fig. 7 (c). Therefore, the QST model can be used to recommend tags to the images for further indexing and searching. The probability of a word given an image is used here:

$$p(w = w_m | I = I_n) = \sum_z p(w = w_m | z, \beta) p(z | I = I_n),$$

in which the probabilities on the right side are obtained by the QST model. The words with highest probabilities which are above a certain threshold will be used to tag the image. Some examples of image tagging are shown in Fig. 16.

5. CONCLUSIONS

In this work, we studied the problem of hand-drawn sketch recognition, and developed a practical system to recognize an arbitrary but semantically meaningful sketch. Based on the analysis to the difficulties in this unconstrained situation, the Query-adaptive Shape Topic (QST) model was

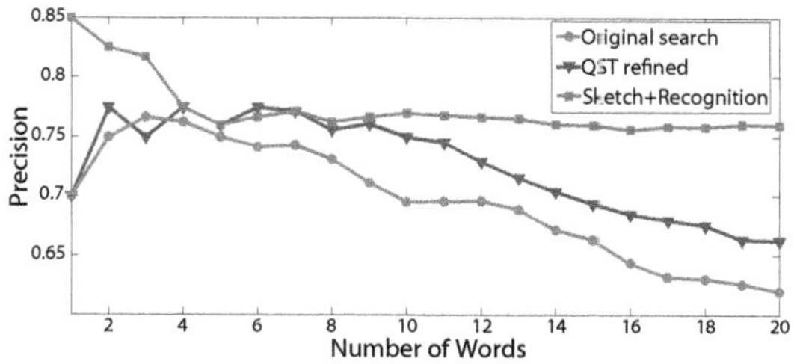

Figure 17: Performance comparison for sketch-based image search.

proposed to model the recognition process and discover related object and shape topics. The learnt probabilistic relations in QST model could support various applications, such as *sketch recognition and tagging*, *image tagging*, and *sketch-based image search*. Extensive experiments have shown the effectiveness of the proposed model and recognition system.

6. ACKNOWLEDGEMENTS

The work of Zhenbang Sun and Liqing Zhang was partially supported by the National Natural Science Foundation of China (Grant No. 90920014, 91120305) and NSFC-JSPS international exchange program (Grant No. 61111140019).

7. REFERENCES

[1] C. Alvarado and R. Davis. Sketchread: a multi-domain sketch recognition engine. In *SIGGRAPH*, 2007.

[2] S. Belongie, J. Malik, and J. Puzicha. Shape matching and object recognition using shape contexts. *PAMI*, 2002.

[3] D. Blei and M. Jordan. Modeling annotated data. In *SIGIR*, 2003.

[4] D. Blei and J. McAuliffe. Supervised topic models. *Arxiv preprint arXiv:1003.0783*, 2010.

[5] D. Blei, A. Ng, and M. Jordan. Latent dirichlet allocation. *JMLR*, 2003.

[6] M. Bober. Mpeg-7 visual shape descriptors. *CSVT*, 2001.

[7] Y. Cao, C. Wang, L. Zhang, and L. Zhang. Edgel index for large-scale sketch-based image search. In *CVPR*, 2011.

[8] Y. Cao, H. Wang, C. Wang, Z. Li, L. Zhang, and L. Zhang. Mindfinder: Interactive sketch-based image search on millions of images. In *ACM Multimedia*, 2010.

[9] P. Felzenszwalb and D. Huttenlocher. Efficient graph-based image segmentation. *IJCV*, 2004.

[10] R. Fergus, L. Fei-Fei, P. Perona, and A. Zisserman. Learning object categories from google's image search. In *ICCV*, 2005.

[11] K. Forbus, J. Usher, and A. Lovett. Cogsketch: Open-domain sketch understanding for cognitive science research and for education. In *EUROGRAPHICS*, 2008.

[12] T. Hammond. Tahuti: A geometrical sketch recognition system for uml class diagrams. In *SIGGRAPH*, 2006.

[13] T. Hammond. et al. a sketch recognition interface that recognizes hundreds of shapes in course-of-action diagrams. In *CHI*, 2010.

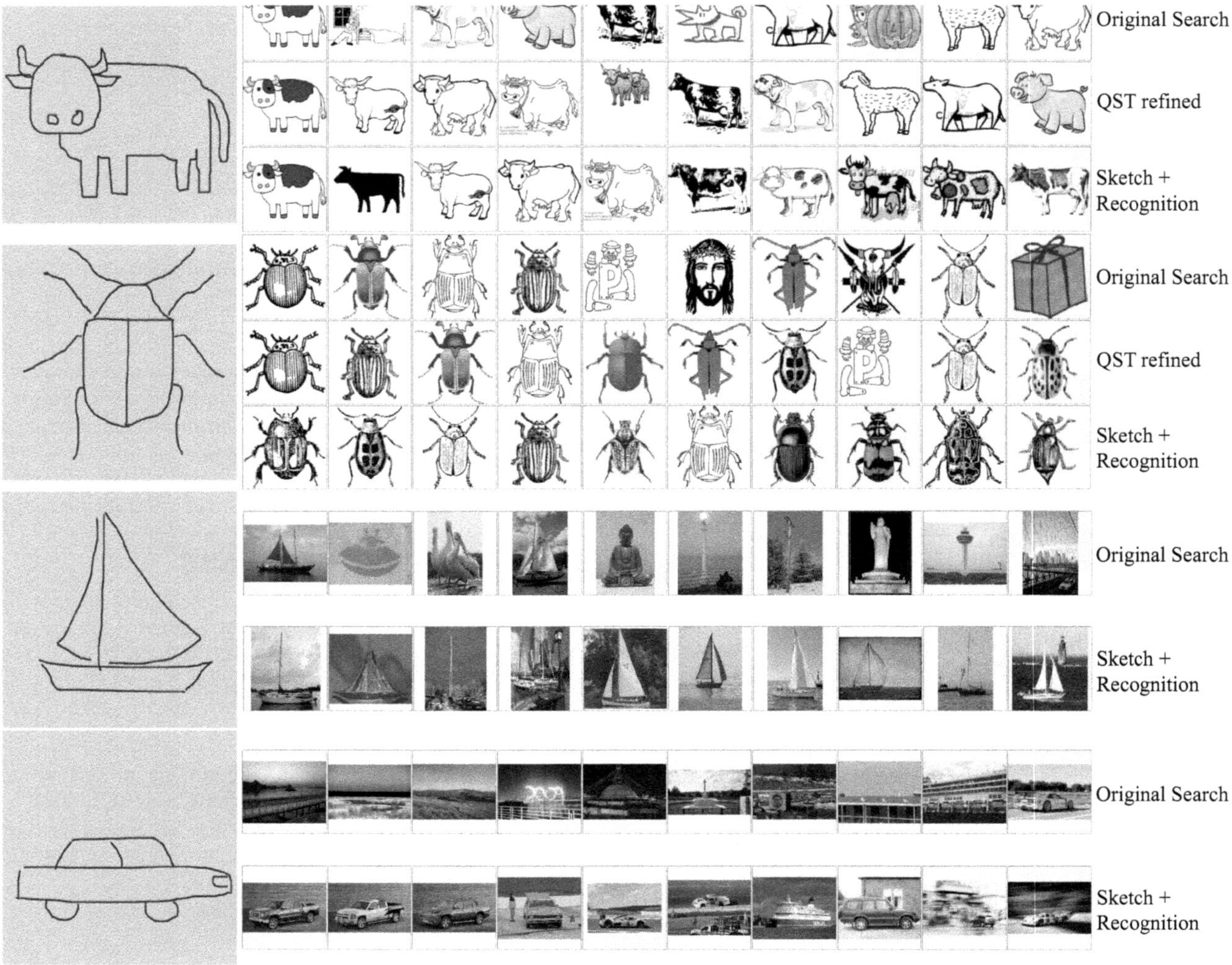

Figure 18: Example of enhanced sketch-based image search. Top two rows: top results of clipart image search. Bottom two rows: top results of natural image search.

[14] T. Hammond and R. Davis. Ladder, a sketching language for user interface developers. *Computers & Graphics*, 2005.

[15] Q. Hao, R. Cai, C. Wang, R. Xiao, J. Yang, Y. Pang, and L. Zhang. Equip tourists with knowledge mined from travelogues. In *WWW*, 2010.

[16] T. Hofmann. Probabilistic latent semantic indexing. In *SIGIR*, 1999.

[17] Y. Lee and K. Grauman. Shape discovery from unlabeled image collections. In *CVPR*, 2009.

[18] J. Lin, M. Newman, J. Hong, and J. Landay. Denim: finding a tighter fit between tools and practice for web site design. In *SIGCHI*, 2000.

[19] H. Ling and D. Jacobs. Shape classification using the inner-distance. *PAMI*, 2007.

[20] K. Mikolajczyk, A. Zisserman, C. Schmid, et al. Shape recognition with edge-based features. 2003.

[21] G. Mori, S. Belongie, and J. Malik. Efficient shape matching using shape contexts. *PAMI*, 2005.

[22] E. Paquet, M. Rioux, A. Murching, T. Naveen, and A. Tabatabai. Description of shape information for 2-d and 3-d objects. *Signal Processing: Image Communication*, 2000.

[23] B. Paulson and T. Hammond. Paleosketch: accurate primitive sketch recognition and beautification. In *IUI*, 2008.

[24] M. Rosen-Zvi, T. Griffiths, M. Steyvers, and P. Smyth. The author-topic model for authors and documents. In *UAI*, 2004.

[25] T. Sebastian, P. Klein, and B. Kimia. Recognition of shapes by editing their shock graphs. *PAMI*, 2004.

[26] T. Sezgin and R. Davis. Hmm-based efficient sketch recognition. In *IUI*, 2005.

[27] T. Stahovich. Sketchit: a sketch interpretation tool for conceptual mechanism design. In *MIT AI Lab. TR*, 1996.

[28] A. Temlyakov and B. Munsell. Two perceptually motivated strategies for shape classification. In *CVPR*, 2010.

[29] C. Wang, J. Zhang, B. Yang, and L. Zhang. Sketch2cartoon: composing cartoon images by sketching. In *ACM Multimedia*, 2011.

[30] D. Zhang and G. Lu. A comparative study of fourier descriptors for shape representation and retrieval. In *ACCV*, 2002.

Correlated Attribute Transfer with Multi-task Graph-Guided Fusion

Yahong Han
School of Computer Science and Technology
Tianjin University, China
yahong@tju.edu.cn

Fei Wu
College of Computer Science
Zhejiang University, China
wufei@zju.edu.cn

Xinyan Lu
College of Computer Science
Zhejiang University, China
luxinyan1988@gmail.com

Qi Tian
Department of Computer Science
University of Texas at San Antonio
qitian@cs.utsa.edu

Yueting Zhuang
College of Computer Science
Zhejiang University, China
yzhuang@zju.edu.cn

Jiebo Luo
Department of Computer Science
University of Rochester
jluo@cs.rochester.edu

ABSTRACT

Due to the *describable* or *human-nameable* nature of visual attributes, the attribute-based methods have been receiving much attentions in recent years in many applications. The advantages of the utilization of visual attributes are that they can be composed to create descriptions at various levels of specificity or they can be learned once and then applied to recognize new objects or categories. Therefore, attribute prediction becomes an essential problem to boost image understanding. This paper proposes an approach for correlated attribute transfer from a well-defined *source* image set to an uncontrolled *target* image set for attribute prediction. We call it correlated attribute transfer with multi-task graph-guided fusion (CAT-MtG^{2}F). The novelty of CAT-MtG^{2}F is to encourage highly correlated attributes to share a common set of relevant low-level features and transfer the learned common structure from the source image set to the target image set. The experiments show that the proposed CAT-MtG^{2}F achieves better performance in attribute prediction.

Categories and Subject Descriptors

H.3 [INFORMATION STORAGE AND RETRIEVAL]: Content Analysis and Indexing

General Terms

Algorithms, Experimentation

Keywords

Feature Selection, Multi-task Graph-Guided Fusion, Attribute Prediction, Transfer Learning

1. INTRODUCTION

In recent years, the recognition of object-level categories in images has become a major focus of computer vision and multimedia retrieval. Different from the tag-based image understanding [13] and retrieval [33], however, an object also has many other intrinsic human-nameable qualities (*visual attributes*) apart from its corresponding category (semantic tag) and they can be computed to boost image understanding [9]. For example, a zebra can be stripped and a wolf is furry.

As a middle-level cue that bridges low-level image features and high-level object classes, visual attributes have been shown to be beneficial for improving the performance of image understanding [12, 18, 23]. For examples, attribute-based classification is proposed in [18] to facilitate zero-shot learning or serendipitous transfer learning [39] by sharing information via an attribute layer. Different from the prediction of the presence of an attribute in a single image, relative attributes are computed to indicate the strength of an attribute in an image with respect to other images in [23]. It is quite obvious that appropriate learning and inferring visual *attributes* of objects in images provide a compelling way to improve image understanding.

Using the same intuitions in [4, 35] that different features describe different aspects of visual characteristics, Hwang *et al.* [15] assumed that all attributes can rely on some shared structure in their corresponding original low-level visual feature space, and proposed a convex multi-task learning approach with an ℓ_1/ℓ_2-norm to learn a shared low dimensional representation of attributes. The goal is to favor common sparsity patterns in attributes.

However, according to the work in [15], not all attributes will benefit feature sharing, and therefore traditional multi-task learning methods [1, 38, 24] will be detrimental for attribute prediction. These approaches are intended for learning multiple related tasks jointly. The goal is to induce a common-across-tasks sparse representation by analyzing data from all of the tasks at the same time, instead of considering each task individually.

This point in [15] is also supported by the images in the real-worlds. Using the *Animals with Attributes* image dataset (AwA) [18] as an example, AwA contains 30,475 images, 50

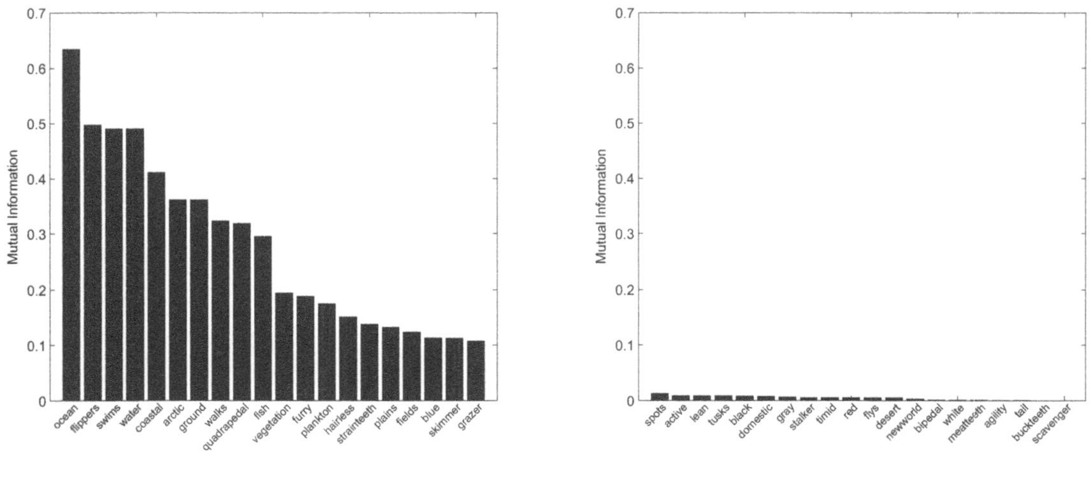

Figure 1: Mutual information of the "ocean" attribute with other attributes in *Animals with Attributes* (AwA) image dataset. Left: 20 attributes in AwA with highest mutual information with attribute "ocean". Right: by contrast, 20 attributes in AwA with lowest mutual information with attribute "ocean".

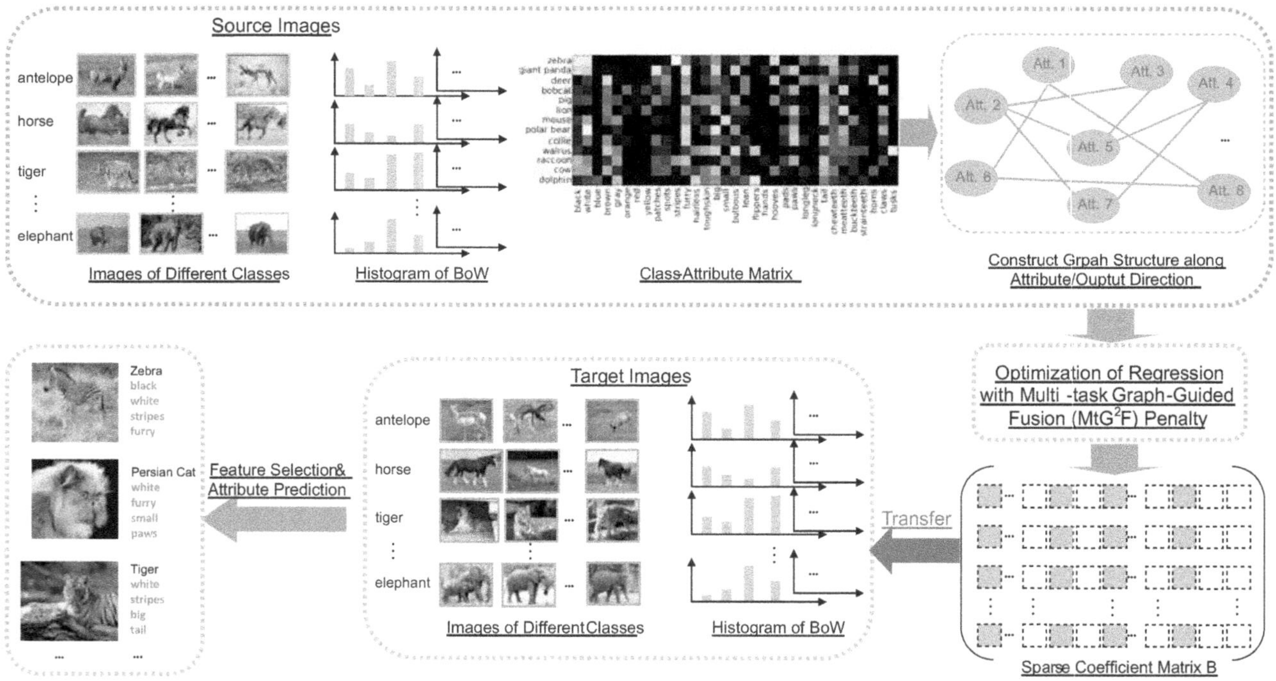

Figure 2: The Flowchart of Correlated Attribute Transfer with Multi-task Graph-Guided Fusion (CAT-MtG^{2}F) penalty. We extracted SIFT features for the source and target images and represent each image by the histogram of Bag of visual Words (BoW). Given the class-attribute matrix, we construct a graph structure along the attribute (output) direction. Then we optimize a regression process regularized with Multi-task Graph-Guided Fusion (CAT-MtG^{2}F) and ℓ_1-norm penalty. The output sparse coefficient matrix can be used to transfer the correlated information among attributes in the source images and conduct feature selection. Finally, we predict attributes for the target images from the selected visual features by using the trained classifiers.

animal classes, and 85 attributes. Each image is labeled by the animal class and related attributes. Figure 1 illustrates the mutual information of the "*ocean*" attribute with other left attributes in AwA. As we can see, the "*ocean*" attribute has different correlations with other attributes, for example, a strong correlation with the "*water*" attribute and a weak correlation with the "*dessert*" attribute. That is to say, given the images in the real-world, some attributes are often more closely related and more likely to share common relevant low-level features than other attributes. Therefore, the introduction of a more appropriate structured regularizer into multi-task learning can discover the shared visual features of related attributes, which poses a great challenge for image understanding.

As a result, unlike the utilization of a mixed-norm regularization such as ℓ_1/ℓ_2- and ℓ_l/ℓ_∞-norms in previous multi-task learning that assumes all tasks (outputs) to be equally related to inputs (features), we investigate a feature selection approach to encourage highly correlated attributes to share a common set of relevant visual features. As sparse coefficient matrix is particular suitable for feature selection [36][35][34], we propose a sparsity-based feature selection method.

Furthermore, since visual attributes are human-specified descriptions of the objects in images, the collection of well-labeled training set for attribute prediction is a tedious work. Assuming that we are given a well-defined *source* image set, in which each image has appropriately labeled attributes and categories, we tend to utilize the cues in the *source* image set to predict the attributes of images in the *target* set.

In order to achieve this goal, this paper is focused on attribute learning by a graph regularizer with structured sparsity in the *source* image set and transferring the learned knowledge to a *target* image set for attribute prediction. We call this correlated attribute transfer with multi-task graph-guided fusion (CAT-MtG^{2}F). The flowchart of CAT-MtG^{2}F is shown in Figure 2. CAT-MtG^{2}F includes three key steps: (1) learning the model of feature selection with correlated attribute transfer (conducted in *Source Images*); (2) feature selection for each attribute (conducted in *Target Images*); (3) predicting attributes from the selected visual features using the trained classifiers.

The strength of our proposed CAT-MtG^{2}F lies in that the correlation information in the output variables (attributes) are naturally exploited. We formulate CAT-MtG^{2}F to be a multi-task learning process so as to discover the shared structures of low-level features for related attributes. CAT-MtG^{2}F uses a graph structure as the guide to find the set of relevant input features that can jointly affect highly correlated outputs. Figure 2 gives out the implementation details of the CAT-MtG^{2}F.

The remainder of this paper is organized as follows. We first introduce the related work in Section 2, and provide the details of CAT-MtG^{2}F in Section 3. In Section 4, we present the construction of an attribute graph. The experimental analysis and conclusions are given in Section 5 and Section 6, respectively.

2. RELATED WORKS

2.1 Attribute Learning for Image Understanding

Due to the *describable* or *human-nameable* nature of visual attributes, attribute-based methods have shown promising potential in object recognition and have recently been receiving much attention. Its success in recognition is largely accredited to the introduction of "attribute", a middle-level cue with meaningful semantical representation. For example, some research works have shown their impact for strengthening face verification [17], object recognition [8], generating natural language descriptions from unfamiliar images [16], facilitation of "zero-shot" transfer learning [18], and prediction of the relative strength of an attribute with respect to other novel images [23].

For the success of aforementioned attribute learning approaches, training of attribute classifiers or regressors from low-level features plays an important role. In these cases, regularization is essential because the inputs (low-level image features) are very high-dimensional with complex variations, and training data are always limited.

In this paper, we are interested in attribute learning by a graph regularizer with structured sparsity in the source image set and transfer the learned knowledge to the *target* image set for attribute prediction. A common goal of transfer learning methods is to discover the common embedded representations from source data and introduce such representation to similar but different target data [26]. In this domain adaptation setting, transfer learning is used to leverage the data available in the source domain to improve the accuracy of the model when testing on target domain examples. The rationale behind transfer learning is to bring the empirical source distribution closer to the target domain, and thus increase the accuracy of the classifier when evaluated on the target domain data. For examples, [18] proposed direct attribute prediction (DAP) and indirect attribute prediction (IAP) for attribute-based classification by transferring information between disjoint training and test classes.

2.2 Structured Sparsity and Fused-lasso based Methods

In the real-world, we can extract high dimensional low-level features from a given image and only limited features distinguish each attribute in the image from others. The problem is that the same visual features might be trivial in one context but crucially significant in another, i.e., some of visual features are most visually important for many related attributes and low-level features are attribute-dependent (or scene-dependent) [28, 15].

As a result, *sparsity* is a reasonable assumption since only a small fraction of visual features are associated with their corresponding attributes. As one of *sparsity*-based feature selection approaches, ℓ_1-norm (namely *lasso*, least absolution shrinkage and selection operator) tends to set up an interpretable model for feature selection [30]. However, *lasso* is prone to selecting features individually and cannot be applied to encode certain structured prior into the process of high-dimensional feature selection.

In order to discover the shared structure of visual features for correlated attributes, it is natural to treat each attribute as a task and perform multi-task learning (MTL) over all of attributes (tasks). The idea of MTL is that, when the tasks to be learned are similar enough or are related in some sense, it may be advantageous to take into account these relations between tasks. In general, MTL can be formulated as a regularization framework [7]. For example, an ℓ_1/ℓ_2-norm is proposed in [1, 20] to learn a common subset of features across all tasks, while the ℓ_l/ℓ_∞-norm is used to promote feature sharing across tasks and discover solutions where only a few features are non-zero in any of the tasks (i.e. jointly sparse solutions) [25].

Graph has been successfully utilized to model the context correlations of images [29, 13] and videos [32]. For example, different relationships among video units are well represented and unified by multiple graphs [32]. To explicitly incorporate the graph-structured context constraint into the sparse learning framework, some previous structured sparse learning methods could partially accomplish this task. The fused lasso [31] penalizes both the ℓ_1-norm of the coefficients and their successive differences. The grouping pursuit [27] utilizes a penalty involving pairwise comparisons for each pair of coefficients. That is, the grouping pursuit assumes each pair of variables are all correlated. It is worth noting that, the penalties by fused lasso and grouping pursuit introduce two special graph structures, i.e., a chain of successive nodes and a full-connected graph of all the nodes, respectively. To be more general than the fused lasso and grouping pursuit, we need a structured sparse penalty defined on the general graph structure so as to incorporate the graph-structured context constraint into the sparse reconstruction framework.

According to [15], during the learning of shared features of attributes, some of the attributes are often more closely related and more likely to share common relevant visual features than other attributes. Thus, it is desirable to take into account the complex correlation structure in the outputs for a more effective multi-task learning. Chen *et al.* [6] proposed a structured regularized regression approach called graph-guided fused lasso (GFlasso) for sparse multi-task learning problems to encourage tasks correlated in the graph to have a similar sparsity pattern. GFlasso employs a "fusion penalty" [31] that fuses regression coefficients across correlated outputs by using the weighted connectivity of the output graph as a guide.

2.3 Transfer Learning and Feature Representation Transfer

Transfer learning aims to help improve the learning of the target predictive function in a target domain using the knowledge in a source domain [22]. In multimedia and computer vision research, many works utilized knowledge transfer to improve the performance [14, 26, 37]. In [26], sparse prototype representations were learned from source images, which are used to get better performance in target images. Similarly, in [14], a multi-label encoded sparse linear embedding space was learned from source domain. Mapping target images into the learned new representations, better performance of image annotation can be obtained. According to the survey in [22], transferred approaches in [14] and [26] can be categorized into the "feature-representation-transfer", which is similar in spirit as the proposed framework of CAT-MtG^{2}F. In transferred framework of CAT-MtG^{2}F, see Fig. 2, the correlated information among attributes in source images is encoded into a learned sparse coefficient matrix, in which each column represents correlated visual features for each attribute and thus can be used to perform feature selection for target images. Thus, the correlated information among attributes is transferred and the goal is to get a better representation for target images. Though knowledge transfer is also used to perform cross-view action recognition in [19], the transferred knowledge of [19] is between two views of video cameras, which is different from the proposed framework of CAT-MtG^{2}F.

3. FEATURE SELECTION WITH CORRELATED ATTRIBUTE TRANSFER

3.1 Notation

Assume that we have a training set of N labeled images from J semantic categories. Matrix $\mathbf{X} \in \mathbb{R}^{N\times P}$ represents the image data matrix, P is the dimensionality of image features. Matrix $\mathbf{Y} \in \{0,1\}^{N\times J}$ represents the label indicator matrix of image data, $\mathbf{Y}_{(i,j)} = 1$ if the ith image belongs to the jth categories and $\mathbf{Y}_{(i,j)} = 0$ otherwise. Let $\mathbf{A} \in \{0,1\}^{J\times L}$ denote the class-attribute matrix, in which $\mathbf{A}_{(j,l)} = 1$ if the jth class has the lth attribute and $\mathbf{A}_{(j,l)} = 0$ otherwise. Given matrices $\mathbf{Y}$ and $\mathbf{A}$, we can construct matrix $\mathbf{T} \in \{0,1\}^{N\times L}$ to represent the attribute indicator matrix of image data, $\mathbf{T}_{(i,l)} = 1$ if the ith image has the lth attributes and $\mathbf{T}_{(i,l)} = 0$ otherwise. Matrix $\mathbf{B} \in \mathbb{R}^{P\times L}$ represents the coefficient matrix, and $\mathbf{B}_{(:,l)}$ $(l = 1,\ldots,L)$ is the coefficient vector for the lth attribute. We let $||\mathbf{M}||_F$ denote the matrix Frobenius norm, $||\mathbf{M}||_1$ denote the matrix entry-wise ℓ_1-norm, $\mathbf{x}^T$ and $\mathbf{M}^T$ represent the transpose of vector $\mathbf{x}$ and matrix $\mathbf{M}$, respectively.

Without loss of generality, $\mathcal{S} = \{\mathbf{X}^{\mathcal{S}}, \mathbf{Y}^{\mathcal{S}}, \mathbf{A}^{\mathcal{S}}\}$ denotes the visual features, label indicator and class-attribute from source image dataset $\mathcal{S}$ and are available during training. $\mathcal{T} = \{\mathbf{X}^{\mathcal{T}}, \mathbf{Y}^{\mathcal{T}}, \mathbf{A}^{\mathcal{T}}\}$ denotes the visual features, label indicator and class-attribute from target image dataset $\mathcal{T}$ and only $\mathbf{X}^{\mathcal{T}}$ is available during testing. The goal of this paper is to boost the performance of predicting the attribute indicator matrix $\mathbf{T}^{\mathcal{T}}$ of target images by borrowing strength from the source image dataset $\mathcal{S}$.

Algorithm 1 Feature Selection with Correlated Attribute Transfer (FSCAT)

Input: source image dataset $\mathcal{S} = \{\mathbf{X}^{\mathcal{S}}, \mathbf{Y}^{\mathcal{S}}, \mathbf{A}^{\mathcal{S}}\}$; target images $\mathcal{T} = \{\mathbf{X}^{\mathcal{T}}\}$; k is the number in the k nearest neighbor graph construction; f is the number of features to be selected.

Output: index ind_l of the top f selected features, $l = 1,\ldots,L$

1: Construct graph G on columns of matrix $\mathbf{A}$ using the mutual k nearest neighbor (kNN) strategy;
2: Solve Eq. (1) and output the coefficient matrix $\hat{\mathbf{B}}$;
3: For $l = 1,\ldots,L$
4: Rank elements in vector $\mathbf{B}_{(:,l)}$ according to the value of $|\mathbf{B}_{(p,l)}|$ $(p = 1,\ldots,P)$ in descending order;
5: Output the index ind_l of the top f selected features;
6: End For

3.2 Learning Correlated Attributes from Source Images

Suppose we have a well-devised source image dataset $\mathcal{S} = \{\mathbf{X}^{\mathcal{S}}, \mathbf{Y}^{\mathcal{S}}, \mathbf{A}^{\mathcal{S}}\}$, our goal is to predict $\mathbf{T}^{\mathcal{T}}$ of the target images $\mathcal{T} = \{\mathbf{X}^{\mathcal{T}}\}$. As introduced above, we can construct matrix $\mathbf{T}^{\mathcal{S}} \in \{0,1\}^{N\times L}$ from $\mathbf{Y}^{\mathcal{S}}$ and $\mathbf{A}^{\mathcal{S}}$ to represent the attribute indicator matrix of source image data. Since one class may correlate multiple attributes, correlations among attributes are encoded in matrix $\mathbf{T}^{\mathcal{S}}$. In order to utilize the correlated information in the source images, we formulate a multi-task learning process and learn the the coefficient matrix $\mathbf{B}$ for transferred feature selection in the target images.

We propose to optimize the following multi-task regression problem:

$$\min_{\mathbf{B}\in\mathbb{R}^{P\times L}} ||\mathbf{T}^{\mathcal{S}} - \mathbf{X}^{\mathcal{S}}\mathbf{B}||_F^2 + \gamma\Omega_G(\mathbf{B}) + \lambda||\mathbf{B}||_1, \quad (1)$$

where $\Omega_G(\mathbf{B})$ is a structured sparsity-inducing norm penalty with a structure G defined over the output direction of $\mathbf{B}$. That is to say, G is defined over L attributes to represent specific correlation structure. $||\mathbf{B}||_1$ is the entry-wise matrix ℓ_1-norm of B (i.e.,$||\mathbf{B}||_1 = \sum^P\sum^L|\mathbf{B}(:,:)|$). γ and λ are regularization parameters respectively that control the complexity of the model. A larger value of γ leads to a greater fusion effect. Assuming that a graph structure over the L attributes is given as G with a set of nodes $V = \{1,\ldots,L\}$ each corresponding to an attribute and a set of edges E. Thus the Multi-task Graph-Guided Fusion (MtG^{2}F) penalty for a structured multi-task regression is given as:

$$\Omega_G(\mathbf{B}) = \sum_{e=(m,l)\in E, m<l} w_{ml}\sum_{p=1}^{P}|\mathbf{B}_{(p,m)} - \mathbf{B}_{(p,l)}|, \quad (2)$$

where $\mathbf{B}_{(p,m)}$ and $\mathbf{B}_{(p,l)}$ are coefficients in $\mathbf{B}$ corresponding to the coefficients of the mth and lth attributes for the pth feature, respectively. The weight w_{ml} measures the fusion penalty for each edge $e = (m,l)$ such that $\mathbf{B}_{(p,m)}$ and $\mathbf{B}_{(p,l)}$ for highly correlated attributes with larger w_{ml} receive a greater fusion effect. Therefore, the multi-task graph-guided fusion (MtG^{2}F) penalty in Eq. (1) encourages highly correlated attributes corresponding to a densely connected subnetwork in G to be jointly encoded in the multi-task regression process. Furthermore, the matrix entry-wise ℓ_1-norm $||\mathbf{B}||_1$ in Eq. (1) encourage sparsity in matrix $\mathbf{B}$, making it particularly suitable for feature selection. If we construct the graph structure G appropriately, e.g., encoding correlation information among the attributes into the graph structure, we can expect a better coefficient matrix $\mathbf{B}$, which can be used to transfer the information of correlated attributes and perform feature selection.

3.3 Selecting Transferred Features in Target Images

Let the estimated coefficient matrix $\hat{\mathbf{B}}$ be the output of solving Eq. (1), many coefficients in $\hat{\mathbf{B}}$ are expected to shrink to zeros (both in rows and columns) owing to the penalty of the matrix entry-wise ℓ_1-norm $||\mathbf{B}||_1$ in Eq. (1). In other words, for predicting the mth attribute, the learned discriminative regression coefficient vector $\mathbf{B}_{(:,m)}$ only utilizes the features when the corresponding elements in vector $\mathbf{B}_{(:,m)}$ are not zero. Alternatively, we can rank each feature of the ith target images $\mathbf{X}^{\mathcal{T}}_{(i,p)}|_{p=1}^{P}$ according to the value of $|\mathbf{B}_{(p,m)}|$ in descending order and select top ranked features. In the following, we summarize the algorithm of Feature Selection with Correlated Attribute Transfer in Algorithm 1

3.4 Solutions and Algorithm

In this section, we firstly introduce the solutions of structured multi-task regression optimization for attribute transfer in Eq. (1), then we will summarize the algorithm of attribute prediction for target images.

3.4.1 Optimization of Structured Multi-task Regression for Attribute Transfer

Although the optimization problem in Eq. (1) is convex, the main difficulty for the optimization of Eq. (1) arises from the non-separability of $\mathbf{B}$ in the non-smooth penalty function $\Omega_G(\mathbf{B})$. In this paper, we solve Eq. (1) by a general smoothing proximal gradient (SPG) method [6]. The SPG first finds a separable and smooth approximation of $\Omega_G(\mathbf{B})$, and then solves this transformed simple ℓ_1-norm penalized sparse learning problem by the Fast Iterative Shrinkage-Thresholding Algorithm (FISTA) [2]. According to SPG [6], key steps of the approximation process are as follows.

(1) The Multi-task Graph-Guided Fusion (MtG^{2}F) penalty $\Omega_G(\mathbf{B})$ is reformulated into a linear transformation of $\mathbf{B}$ via the dual norm as follows:

$$\Omega_G(\mathbf{B}) = \max_{\mathbf{A}\in\mathcal{Q}} < C\mathbf{B}^T, \mathbf{A} >, \quad (3)$$

where $< U, V >\equiv \mathrm{Tr}(U^TV)$ denotes a matrix inter product. $\boldsymbol{\alpha} \in \mathcal{Q} = \{\boldsymbol{\alpha}|||\boldsymbol{\alpha}||_\infty \leq 1, \boldsymbol{\alpha} \in \mathbb{R}^{|E|}\}$ is a column vector in the auxiliary matrix $\mathbf{A}$ and is associated with $||C\mathbf{B}^T||_1$. Matrix $C \in \mathbb{R}^{|E|\times L}$ is the edge-vertex incident matrix with the form of

$$C_{e=(m,l),l'} = \begin{cases} w_{ml}, & \text{if } l' = m, \\ -w_{ml}, & \text{if } l' = l, \\ 0, & \text{otherwise}, \end{cases} \quad (4)$$

where $l' = 1,\ldots,L$ index the output (i.e., the attribute) direction of matrix $\mathbf{B}$.

(2) Introduce the smoothing approximation function $f_\mu(\mathbf{B})$ as follows:

$$f_\mu(\mathbf{B}) = \max_{\mathbf{A}\in\mathcal{Q}} < C\mathbf{B}^T, \mathbf{A} > -\mu d(\mathbf{A}), \quad (5)$$

where $\mu \geq 0$ is the smoothness parameter and $d(\mathbf{A}) \equiv \frac{1}{2}||\mathbf{A}||_F^2$.

Substitute $\Omega_G(\mathbf{B})$ in Eq (1) with $f_\mu(\mathbf{B})$, our goal is to solve the following optimization problem:

$$\min_{\mathbf{B}\in\mathbb{R}^{P\times L}} ||\mathbf{T}^{\mathcal{S}} - \mathbf{X}^{\mathcal{S}}\mathbf{B}||_F^2 + \gamma f_\mu(\mathbf{B}) + \lambda||\mathbf{B}||_1, \quad (6)$$

Because the first two terms of Eq. (6) are convex and smooth, Eq. (6) can be efficiently solved by the FISTA algorithm [2]. It has been proved in [6] that, SPG can achieve $O(\frac{1}{\epsilon})$ convergence rate for a desired accuracy ϵ.

3.4.2 Attribute Prediction for Target Images

In this section, we will introduce the algorithm of attribute prediction for target images. Specifically, the algorithm includes three key steps: (1) learning the model of feature selection with correlated attribute transfer (conducted in *Source Images*); (2) feature selection for each attribute (conducted in *Target Images*); (3) predict attributes from the selected visual features by the trained classifiers, e.g., the kNN classifier. We summarize the algorithm of attribute prediction for target images in Algorithm 2.

Thus, we propose the Correlated Attribute Transfer with Multi-task Graph-Guided Fusion (CAT-MtG^{2}F) in Algorithm 1 and 2. Since we have the groundtruth of class-attribute matrix $\mathbf{A}$, see Section 3.1, we can straightforwardly conduct class detection for testing images in target dataset after we successfully predict the attributes of the images

Algorithm 2 Attribute Prediction for Target Images

Input: source image dataset $\mathcal{S} = \{\mathbf{X}^{\mathcal{S}}, \mathbf{Y}^{\mathcal{S}}, \mathbf{A}^{\mathcal{S}}\}$; target images $\mathcal{T} = \{\mathbf{X}^{\mathcal{T}}\}$; k' is the number in the k'NN classifier.
Output: attribute indicator matrix $\mathbf{T}^{\mathcal{T}}$ for testing images of target data

1: Output the index ind_l $(l = 1, \ldots, L)$ of visual feature selection for each attribute by FSCAT in Algorithm 1;
2: For $l = 1, \ldots, L$
3: Perform feature selection of target images by

$$\mathbf{X}^{\mathcal{T}}_{selected} = \mathbf{X}^{\mathcal{T}}(:, ind_l);$$

4: Predict attribute by training and testing on $\mathbf{X}^{\mathcal{T}}_{selected}$ using k'NN classifier;
5: End For
6: Output the attribute indicator matrix $\mathbf{T}^{\mathcal{T}}$ for testing images in the target dataset.

by Algorithm 2. Therefore, the proposed framework of feature selection with correlated attribute transfer for image understanding dedicates to predict both attribute and corresponding semantic category for target images.

4. ATTRIBUTE GRAPH CONSTRUCTION

One semantic category may correlate multiple attributes, e.g., attributes "black", "white", and "stripes" are taken as the high-level description of image semantic category "zebra". On the other hand, several correlated attributes are usually used simultaneously to describe the multiple semantic categories, e.g., attributes "water" and "eat fish" appear to describe image class "otter" and "polar bear". Taking the class-attribute matrix $\mathbf{A} \in \{0,1\}^{J \times L}$ in the AwA dataset [18] (as shown in Figure 2) for example, let each column vector represent one attribute and then the attributes with similar binary patterns in the corresponding column vectors will be correlated with each other.

We use the mutual k nearest neighbor (kNN) strategy to discover the relationship between attributes. Specifically, two attributes (represented by column vectors $\mathbf{A}_{(:,m)}$ and $\mathbf{A}_{(:,l)}$ in $\mathbf{A}$) are linked with an edge $e = (m, l) \in E$ if $\mathbf{A}_{(:,m)}$ is among the k nearest neighbors of $\mathbf{A}_{(:,l)}$ and vice versa. In this setting, graph G is undirected and the adjacent relations between two regions are symmetric.

Euclidean distance is used to calculate the graph weight w_{ml} as follows:

$$w_{ml} = \begin{cases} e^{-\frac{\|\mathbf{A}_{(:,m)} - \mathbf{A}_{(:,l)}\|_2^2}{2\sigma^2}}, & \text{if } m \in N_k(l) \text{ or } l \in N_k(m), \\ 0, & \text{otherwise,} \end{cases} \quad (7)$$

where $N_k(m)$ and $N_k(l)$ denote the vertex index set for the k nearest neighbors of the mth and lth vertex, respectively.

5. EXPERIMENTS

In this section, we evaluate the effectiveness of our proposed CAT-MtG^{2}F algorithm for the task of attribute learning for target images. To show the competitive performance of transferred feature selection for attribute learning, we compare our algorithm with other state-of-the-art feature selection methods. The experimental results show that our algorithm achieves a better performance of attribute prediction owing to the strength transferred from the source

(a) Images selected from AwA (source) image dataset

(b) Images selected from AIN (target) dataset

Figure 3: Sample images selected from the source and target image datasets. Images in the top rows are from the category "dolphin". Images in the bottom rows are from the category "fox".

images. Furthermore, the sparse coefficient matrix $\hat{\mathbf{B}}$ (see Eq. (1)) are obtained by introducing the graph structure among attributes into the process of multi-task regression. In this experiment, we will also demonstrate that the learned matrix $\hat{\mathbf{B}}$ successfully discovers some latent correlations between attributes and visual features (the SIFT BoW used in this experiment).

5.1 Dataset and Feature Extraction

5.1.1 Source Images and Target Images

Two image datasets are respectively used as source images and target images in this experiment. A well-devised "Animals with Attributes" (AwA) dataset [18] is used as source images, which contains 30,475 animal images that are categorized into 50 classes. To boost the research of attribute based classification [18] and image understanding with attribute [18, 8, 23], Lampert *et al.* align the 50 animals classes with the classical class-attribute matrix [21], thus providing 85 numeric attribute values for each class, which can be taken as the groundtruth of class-attribute correlations. Images in each class of AwA are crawled and selected from the Web. So AwA can be considered as a well-devised source image datase.

For target images, we submitted the 50 animal (class) names in AwA as 50 query keywords to ImageNet and downloaded images for each class. As a result, we collected altogether 48,199 images to form the target image dataset and these images are categorized into the same animal classes as in AwA. Thus, the collected images are appropriate to

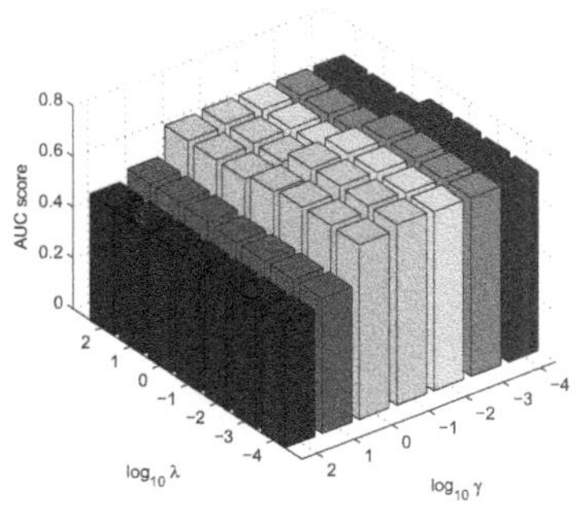

Figure 4: Parameter tuning results of γ and λ. The ranges of γ and λ are {0.0001, 0.001, 0.01, 0.1, 1, 10, 100}

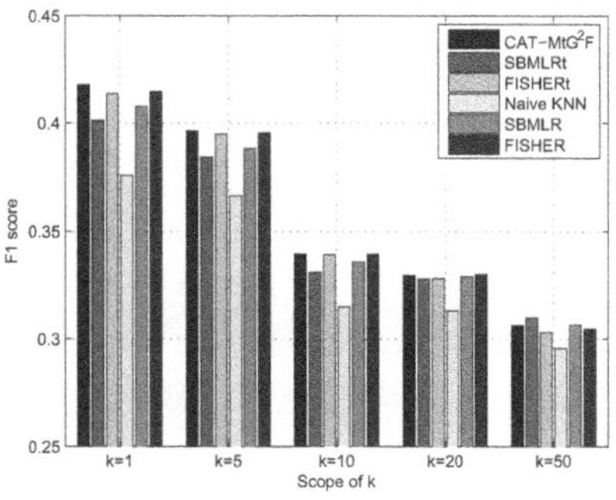

Figure 5: Performance comparison when k is set to different values. The results were obtained when 10% of target images are used as training images.

be considered as the target images and used to evaluate the performance of the proposed CAT-MtG^{2}F algorithm. In the following, we denote this dataset as "Animals from ImageNet" (AIN). To demonstrate the differences between the source images and target images, we show some sample images in Figure 3(a) and Figure 3(b).

Moreover, to further demonstrate the ability of attribute prediction of CAT-MtG^{2}F, we also transfer knowledge learned from AwA to images in the dataset of "Animal on the Web" (AoW) [3]. Thus, two target image datasets AIN and AoW are respectively used in this experiment to be the test bed for evaluation of the correlated attribute transfer from source images in AwA.

5.1.2 Visual Features

As shown in Figure 3, though coming from the same semantic category, images may have very variant visual features, e.g., variant colors, variant shapes, variant textures etc. Inspired by the research in object recognition and detection [11], the keypoint based local features are more robust. In this experiment, we first extract SIFT points for each images in AwA, AIN, and AoW. The randomly selected set of SIFT points are clustered and produced the 1,000 centers as the visual dictionary. Then each image is quantized into a 1,000 dimensional histogram of bag-of-visual-words (BoW).

5.1.3 Partition of Training/Testing Images

For all the 48,199 images in AIN dataset, we randomly sample 10,000 images to form the target images for algorithm evaluation. For the partition of training/testing images in the selected target image dataset, we randomly sample 1,000 to 3,000 samples to form the training data and the remaining data are used as the corresponding testing images. For each partition, all above sampling processes are repeated ten times to generate 10 random training/test partitions. The average performance and standard deviation are reported.

5.2 Evaluation Metrics

The F_1 score is used to measure the performance of attribute prediction, which is defined as the harmonic mean of precision and recall:

$$F_1 = 2 \cdot \frac{precision \cdot recall}{precision + recall}$$

Since there are multiple attributes in our experiment, we use the macroaveraging scheme and average the F_1 scores over multiple attributes.

In the process of parameter (γ and λ in Eq. (1)) tuning in source image dataset, prediction performance of the learned matrix $\mathbf{B}$ need to be evaluated. Since $\mathbf{B}$ is trained and learned from a structured multi-task regression process, the values of predicted responses are continuous but binary. Thus, in the process of parameter tuning, we use the Aera Under the Roc Curve (AUC) [10] as the evaluation metic.

5.3 Parameter Tuning

Effects of graph-guided fusion and sparsity by ℓ_1-norm penalty is mainly determined by parameters γ and λ in Eq. (1). In this experiment, we use a 5-fold cross validation on the source image dataset to tune the value of parameters γ and λ. We choose those parameters which perform best at the source test dataset and then the values are then fixed throughout the experiments.

The ranges of γ and λ are {0.0001, 0.001, 0.01, 0.1, 1, 10, 100}. The parameter tuning results are shown in Figure 4. We can observe that the highest performance (AUC=0.711) of two parameters is achieved at some intermediate values. Thus we set $\gamma = 0.01$ and $\lambda = 0.1$ and under this parameter setting the ratio of sparsity of matrix $\mathbf{B}$ is 83%.

5.4 Experimental Results

5.4.1 Comparison Methods

Having learned the coefficient matrix $\mathbf{B}$ from source images in AwA dataset by Algorithm 1, we conduct attribute prediction by Algorithm 2 on the target image dataset by feature selection with correlated attribute transfer from source images to target images.

We compare our method CAT-MtG^{2}F with Fisher Score and Sparse Bayesian Multinomial Logistic Regression (denoted by SBMLR in the following) [5]. SBMLR is a sparse multinomial logistic regression method, in which the sparsity arises from the use of a Laplacian prior. Fisher Score is a statistical score which can output feature rankings and is dependent on the choice of the classifier. One can use Fisher's criterion to calculate the Fisher Score of each feature. The larger the Fisher Score is, the more likely this feature is discriminative. Therefore, we perform the feature selection by ranking the scores.

We have two versions of settings for the SBMLR and

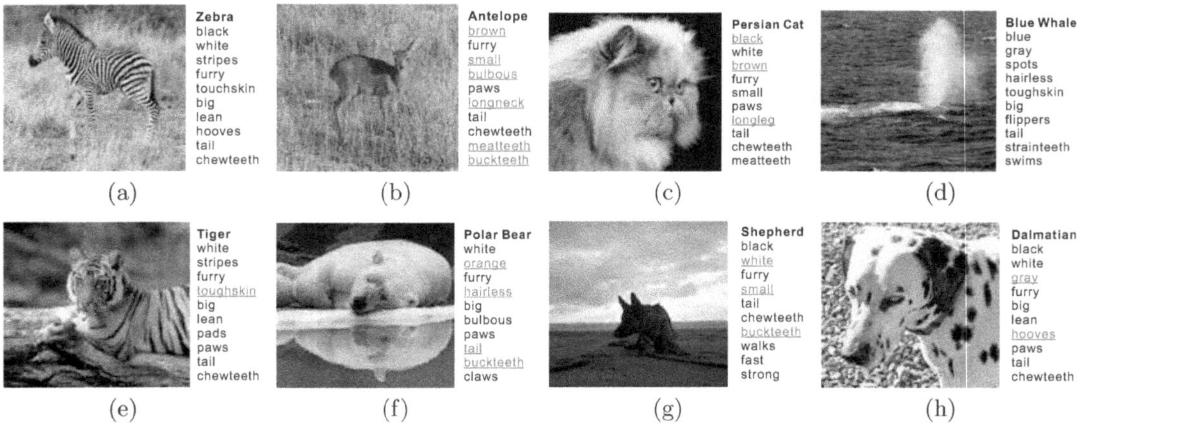

Figure 6: Attribute predictions on the target set (underlined red texts denote the false positive predictions)

Fisher Score algorithms: transferred and without transferr. For the transferred SBMLR and transferred Fisher Score (denoted by SBMLRt and FISHERt for short), algorithms SBMLR and Fisher Score are performed after we conduct feature selection by Step 3 in Algorithm 2, i.e., $\mathbf{X}^T_{selected} = \mathbf{X}^T(:, ind_l);$. For SMLR and Fisher Score without transfer (denoted by SBMLR and FISHER for short), the algorithms are performed on the original visual features. For all methods, we use kNN classifier to train and predict each binary attribute. To further show the effect of correlated attribute transfer, we also compare CAT-MtG^{2}F with performing kNN on the original visual features of the target images, which is denoted by "Naive kNN" in the following.

5.4.2 Attribute Prediction Results

We first investigate the performance of comparing CAT-MtG^{2}F with state-of-the-art methods for k in kNN classifier is set to be different values. In Figure 5, we plot the attribute prediction results from different methods when $k \in \{1, 5, 10, 20, 50\}$. As can be seen, as the value of k increases, the performance of all the methods decreases. Though the performance of CAT-MtG^{2}F is worse than Fisher Score and SBMLR when $k = 50$, the performance of CAT-MtG^{2}F is better than other methods when $k = 1, 5, 10, 20$. Especially, the improvement of CAT-MtG^{2}F is prominent when $k = 1$.

To investigate the performance of attribute prediction with a different number of selected features and different number of training data for training the kNN classifier, we compare and list the results in Table 1 and Table 2. From the results we can observe that: (1) generally, CAT-MtG^{2}F produces better performance of attribute prediction owing to the feature selection with correlated attribute transfer; (2) though not so significant improvement comparing with SBMLR and Fisher Score, the improvement of CAT-MtG^{2}F comparing with Naive kNN is over 5%. Thus the results demonstrate that the effectiveness of the proposed transferred feature selection framework.

In Figure 6, we show some examples of attribute prediction on the AIN dataset. We can see the prediction on "Zebra" matches the truth perfectly. On the other hand, the attribute prediction performances on different animals may differ. To further show the effectiveness of transferred attribute prediction, in Figure 7, we show some examples of attribute prediction for "unseen" animals of AoW dataset.

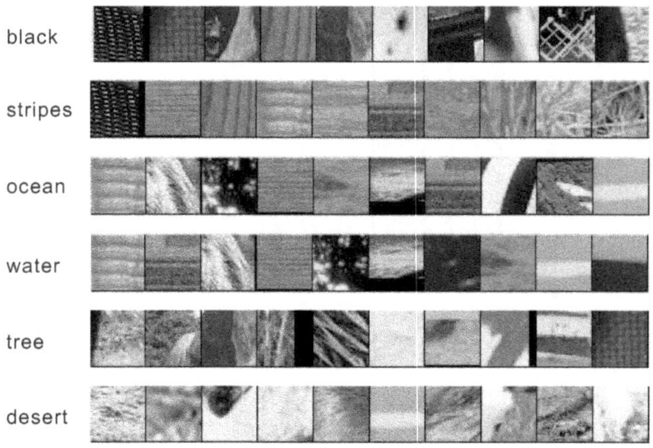

Figure 8: Attribute - Visual words correlation example. Of the 6 example attributes, "ocean" and "water" share high mutual information, while "tree" and "desert" low mutual information. With our method, attribute "ocean" and "water" share the same correlated visual words.

5.4.3 Demonstration of Visual Words and Attributes

Now we look into the matrix **B** obtained by solving the regression problem in Eq. (1) . Each column of **B** represents correlated feature for each attribute, in which higher amplitude means stronger correlation between attribute and corresponding feature while zero means no correlation. We depict the top 10 highest-ranked visual features (visual words in our experiment) of 6 example attributes in Figure 8.

In human cognition, "ocean" and "water" should be correlated (we have seen that from Figure 1) and they should share similar visual feature. The examples in Figure 8 demonstrates this: "ocean" and "water" have 8 out of the 10 highest-ranked visual words in common. In contrast, "desert" should be an "cognitive" antonym of "tree" and they share no common features: the "tree" attribute's most correlated visual words represents some kind of "energy" while the "desert" attribute represents desolation.

6. CONCLUSIONS

In this work, we have shown how to predict attributes

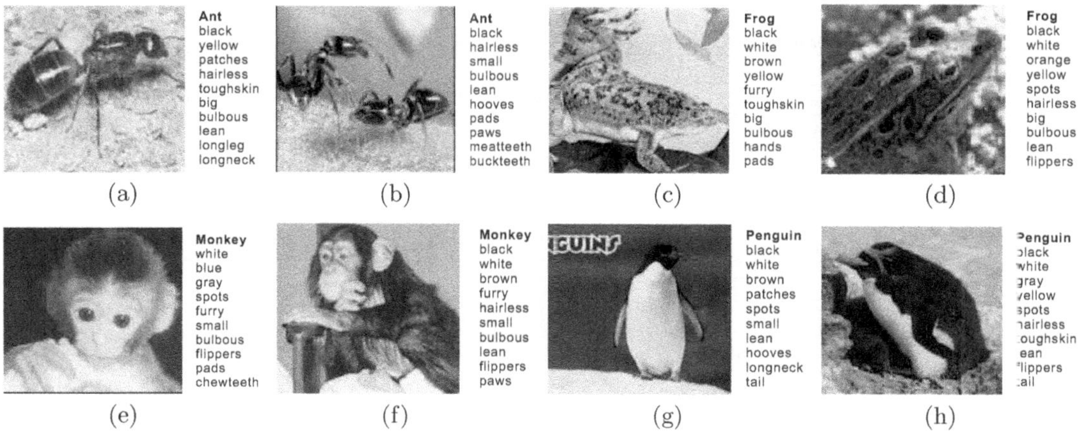

Figure 7: Attribute predictions on AoW dataset

Table 1: Performance comparison with 50 selected features and 10%, 20%, 30% train data separately.

Method / % train data	10%	20%	30%
CAT-MtG^{2}F	**0.4179±0.0043**	**0.4258±0.0025**	**0.4281±0.0017**
SBMLRt	0.4012±0.0028	0.4013±0.0038	0.4024±0.0033
FISHERt	0.4136±0.0042	0.4217±0.0024	0.4254±0.0033
Naive kNN	0.3759±0.0236	0.4033±0.0113	0.4092±0.0092
SBMLR	0.4077±0.0208	0.4154±0.0101	0.4148±0.0050
FISHER	0.4146±0.0033	0.4221±0.0033	0.4239±0.0039

of image objects through the correlated-attribute transfer to boost the image understanding . The multi-task graph-guided fusion penalty utilized in CAT-MtG^{2}F encourages the attributes within a densely connected subgraph to share common low-level features. We demonstrated the effectiveness of the proposed CAT-MtG^{2}F method and showed that our proposed CAT-MtG^{2}F method is comparable to or better than the state-of-the-art methods. Investigation of the correlation between attributes and selected visual words also demonstrated the effectiveness of the proposed transferred feature selection method.

7. ACKNOWLEDGMENTS

This work was supported in part by National Basic Research Program of China (2010CB327904), National HeGaoJi Key Project (2010ZX01042-002-003), NSFC (No. 90920303, 61070068) and the Fundamental Research Funds for the Central Universities. The work of Qi Tian was supported in part by ARO grant W911NF-12-1-0057, NSF IIS 1052851, Faculty Research Awards by Google, NEC Laboratories of America and FXPAL, UTSA START-R award, respectively.

8. REFERENCES

[1] A. Argyriou, T. Evgeniou, and M. Pontil. Convex multi-task feature learning. *Machine Learning*, 73(3):243–272, 2008.

[2] A. Beck and M. Teboulle. A fast iterative shrinkage-thresholding algorithm for linear inverse problems. *SIAM Journal on Imaging Sciences*, 2(1):183–202, 2009.

[3] T. Berg and D. Forsyth. Animals on the web. In *Proceedings of CVPR 2006*, volume 2, pages 1463–1470. IEEE, 2006.

[4] L. Cao, J. Luo, F. Liang, and T. Huang. Heterogeneous feature machines for visual recognition. In *Proceedings of ICCV 2009*, pages 1095–1102. IEEE, 2009.

[5] G. Cawley, N. Talbot, and M. Girolami. Sparse multinomial logistic regression via bayesian l1 regularisation. *Advances in neural information processing systems (NIPS)*, 19:209, 2007.

[6] X. Chen, Q. Lin, S. Kim, J. Carbonell, and E. Xing. Smoothing proximal gradient method for general structured sparse learning. In *Uncertainty in Artificial Intelligence (UAI)*, 2011.

[7] T. Evgeniou and M. Pontil. Regularized multi–task learning. In *Proceedings of the tenth ACM SIGKDD*, pages 109–117. ACM, 2004.

[8] A. Farhadi, I. Endres, and D. Hoiem. Attribute-centric recognition for cross-category generalization. In *Proceedings of CVPR 2010*, pages 2352–2359. IEEE, 2010.

[9] A. Farhadi, I. Endres, D. Hoiem, and D. Forsyth. Describing objects by their attributes. In *Proceedings of CVPR 2009*, pages 1778–1785. IEEE, 2009.

[10] T. Fawcett. An introduction to roc analysis. *Pattern recognition letters*, 27(8):861–874, 2006.

[11] L. Fei-Fei, R. Fergus, and P. Perona. Learning generative visual models from few training examples: An incremental bayesian approach tested on 101 object categories. *Computer Vision and Image Understanding*, 106(1):59–70, 2007.

[12] V. Ferrari and A. Zisserman. Learning visual attributes. In *Proceedings of Advances in Neural Information Processing Systems (NIPS 2007)*, 2008.

[13] Y. Han, F. Wu, Q. Tian, and Y. Zhuang.

Table 2: Performance comparison with 100 selected features and 10%, 20%, 30% train data separately.

Method / % train data	10%	20%	30%
CAT-MtG^{2}F	**0.4155±0.0063**	**0.4261±0.0045**	**0.4288±0.0027**
SBMLRt	0.4012±0.0028	0.4013±0.0038	0.4024±0.0033
FISHERt	0.4114±0.0059	0.4234±0.0037	0.4271±0.0056
Naive *k*NN	0.3759±0.0236	0.4033±0.0113	0.4092±0.0092
SBMLR	0.4075±0.0208	0.4154±0.0101	0.4148±0.0050
FISHER	0.4136±0.0047	0.4253±0.0048	0.4274±0.0036

Graph-guided sparse reconstruction for region tagging. In *Proceedings of CVPR 2012*. IEEE, 2012.

[14] Y. Han, F. Wu, Y. Zhuang, and X. He. Multi-label transfer learning with sparse representation. *Circuits and Systems for Video Technology, IEEE Transactions on*, 20(8):1110–1121, 2010.

[15] S. Hwang, F. Sha, and K. Grauman. Sharing features between objects and their attributes. In *Proceedings of CVPR 2011*, pages 1761–1768. IEEE, 2011.

[16] G. Kulkarni, V. Premraj, S. Dhar, S. Li, Y. Choi, A. Berg, and T. Berg. Baby talk: Understanding and generating simple image descriptions. In *Proceedings of CVPR 2011*, pages 1601–1608. IEEE, 2011.

[17] N. Kumar, A. Berg, P. Belhumeur, and S. Nayar. Describable visual attributes for face verification and image search. *Pattern Analysis and Machine Intelligence, IEEE Transactions on*, (99):1–1, 2011.

[18] C. Lampert, H. Nickisch, and S. Harmeling. Learning to detect unseen object classes by between-class attribute transfer. In *Proceedings of CVPR 2009*, pages 951–958. IEEE, 2009.

[19] J. Liu, M. Shah, B. Kuipers, and S. Savarese. Cross-view action recognition via view knowledge transfer. In *Proceedings of CVPR 2011*, pages 3209–3216. IEEE, 2011.

[20] G. Obozinski, B. Taskar, and M. I. Jordan. Multi-task feature selection. *Technical Report of UC Berkeley*, 2006.

[21] D. Osherson, J. Stern, O. Wilkie, M. Stob, and E. Smith. Default probability. *Cognitive Science*, 15(2):251–269, 1991.

[22] S. Pan and Q. Yang. A survey on transfer learning. *Knowledge and Data Engineering, IEEE Transactions on*, 22(10):1345–1359, 2010.

[23] D. Parikh and K. Grauman. Relative attributes. In *Proceedings of ICCV 2011*. IEEE, 2011.

[24] N. Quadrianto, A. Smola, T. Caetano, S. Vishwanathan, and J. Petterson. Multitask learning without label correspondences. In *Proceedings of Advances in Neural Information Processing Systems (NIPS 2011)*, 2011.

[25] A. Quattoni, X. Carreras, M. Collins, and T. Darrell. An efficient projection for $l_{1,\infty}$ regularization. In *Proceedings of ICML 2009*, pages 857–864. ACM, 2009.

[26] A. Quattoni, M. Collins, and T. Darrell. Transfer learning for image classification with sparse prototype representations. In *Proceedings of CVPR 2008*, pages 1–8. IEEE, 2008.

[27] X. Shen and H. Huang. Grouping pursuit through a regularization solution surface. *Journal of the American Statistical Association*, 105(490):727–739, 2010.

[28] A. Shrivastava, T. Malisiewicz, A. Gupta, and A. Efros. Data-driven visual similarity for cross-domain image matching. *ACM Transaction of Graphics (TOG)(Proceedings of ACM SIGGRAPH ASIA)*, 30(6), 2011.

[29] J. Tang, R. Hong, S. Yan, T. Chua, G. Qi, and R. Jain. Image annotation by k nn-sparse graph-based label propagation over noisily tagged web images. *ACM Transactions on Intelligent Systems and Technology (TIST)*, 2(2):14, 2011.

[30] R. Tibshirani. Regression shrinkage and selection via the lasso. *Journal of the Royal Statistical Society. Series B (Methodological)*, pages 267–288, 1996.

[31] R. Tibshirani, M. Saunders, S. Rosset, J. Zhu, and K. Knight. Sparsity and smoothness via the fused lasso. *Journal of the Royal Statistical Society: Series B (Statistical Methodology)*, 67(1):91–108, 2005.

[32] M. Wang, X. Hua, R. Hong, J. Tang, G. Qi, and Y. Song. Unified video annotation via multigraph learning. *Circuits and Systems for Video Technology, IEEE Transactions on*, 19(5):733–746, 2009.

[33] M. Wang, K. Yang, X. Hua, and H. Zhang. Towards a relevant and diverse search of social images. *Multimedia, IEEE Transactions on*, 12(8):829–842, 2010.

[34] F. Wu, Y. Han, X. Liu, J. Shao, Y. Zhuang, and Z. Zhang. The heterogeneous feature selection with structural sparsity for multimedia annotation and hashing: a survey. *International Journal of Multimedia Information Retrieval*, pages 1–13, 2012.

[35] F. Wu, Y. Han, Q. Tian, and Y. Zhuang. Multi-label boosting for image annotation by structural grouping sparsity. In *Proceedings of ACM Multimedia 2010*, pages 15–24. ACM, 2010.

[36] Y. Yang, H. Shen, Z. Ma, Z. Huang, and X. Zhou. $\ell_{2,1}$-norm regularized discriminative feature selection for unsupervised learning. In *Proceedings of IJCAI 2011)*, pages 1589–1594, 2011.

[37] Y. Yang, Y. Yang, Z. Huang, and H. Shen. Transfer tagging from image to video. In *Proceedings of ACM Multimedia 2011*, pages 1137–1140. ACM, 2011.

[38] K. Yu, V. Tresp, and A. Schwaighofer. Learning gaussian processes from multiple tasks. In *Proceedings of ICML 2005*, pages 1012–1019. ACM, 2005.

[39] D. Zhang, Y. Liu, and L. Si. Serendipitous learning: learning beyond the predefined label space. In *Proceedings of the 17th ACM SIGKDD*, pages 1343–1351. ACM, 2011.

Spatial Pooling of Heterogeneous Features for Image Applications

Lingxi Xie*
Tsinghua University
Beijing 100084, China
198808xc@gmail.com

Qi Tian
Univ. of Texas at San Antonio
Texas, TX 78249
qitian@cs.utsa.edu

Bo Zhang
Tsinghua University
Beijing 100084, China
dcszb@mail.tsinghua.edu.cn

ABSTRACT

The Bag-of-Features (BoF) model has played an important role for image representation in many multimedia applications. It has been extensively applied to many tasks including image classification, image retrieval, scene understanding, and so on. Despite the advantages of this model such as simplicity, efficiency and generality, there are also notable drawbacks for this model, including poor power of semantic expression of local descriptors, and lack of robust structures upon single visual words. To overcome these problems, various techniques have been proposed, such as multiple descriptors, spatial context modeling and interest region detection. Though they have been proven to improve the BoF model to some extent, there still lacks a coherent scheme to integrate each individual module.

To address the problems above, we propose a novel framework with spatial pooling of heterogeneous features. Our framework differs from the traditional Bag-of-Features model on three aspects. First, we propose a new scheme for combining texture and edge based local features together at the descriptor extraction level. Next, we build geometric visual phrases to model spatial context upon heterogeneous features for mid-level representation of images. Finally, based on a smoothed edgemap, a simple and effective spatial weighting scheme is performed on our mid-level image representation. We test our integrated framework on several benchmark datasets for image classification and retrieval applications. The extensive results show the superior performance of our algorithm over state-of-the-art methods.

Categories and Subject Descriptors

H.3.1 [**Information Storage and Retrieval**]: Content Analysis and Indexing

*Lingxi Xie and Bo Zhang are from the State Key Laboratory of Intelligent Technology and Systems, Tsinghua National Laboratory for Information Science and Technology (TNList), and Department of Computer Science and Technology, Tsinghua University.

MM'12, October 29–November 2, 2012, Nara, Japan.

General Terms

Algorithms, Experimentation

Keywords

BoF Framework, Image Representation, Complementary Descriptors, Geometric Visual Phrases, Phrase Pooling, Spatial Weighting, Multimedia Applications

1. INTRODUCTION

Today, there are many multimedia applications based on image understanding and processing, such as image retrieval, image classification, scene understanding, and so on. Although different tasks vary in their goals, they share a key idea seeking for discriminative representations of images.

Traditional Bag-of-Features (BoF) framework has been widely used for various image applications mentioned above. It aims at providing better representations for images. For this purpose, local descriptors such as SIFT [16] are extracted from images, and a codebook is built upon all descriptors, depressing noises and forming a semantic visual vocabulary for the dataset. Finally, descriptors are quantized onto the codebook, and visual words are pooled for a statistical representation of the original image.

Despite the great success of BoF framework, there still exist many drawbacks in it. These drawbacks come mainly from the well-known semantic gap [17] between low-level local descriptors and high-level image semantics. Many researchers such as Yuan *et.al* [24] have noticed that SIFT descriptor suffers from both synonymy and polysemy. To overcome, the following schemes are widely adopted.

- **Different descriptions of local patches.** For single descriptors might fail to capture the rich information within local patches, it is reasonable to extract multiple descriptors for compensation. Various descriptors represent local patches from different aspects, providing more descriptive and discriminative information. By simply concatenating appearance and shape features together, [2] outperforms state-of-the-art models using single descriptors by a margin.

- **Mid-level representation connecting low-level and high-level concepts.** In BoF framework, an image is represented as a large set of visual words. However, there is a big semantic gap between low-level features and high-level concepts [17]. Therefore, many researchers have proposed some mid-level representations, such as macro-descriptors [3] or visual

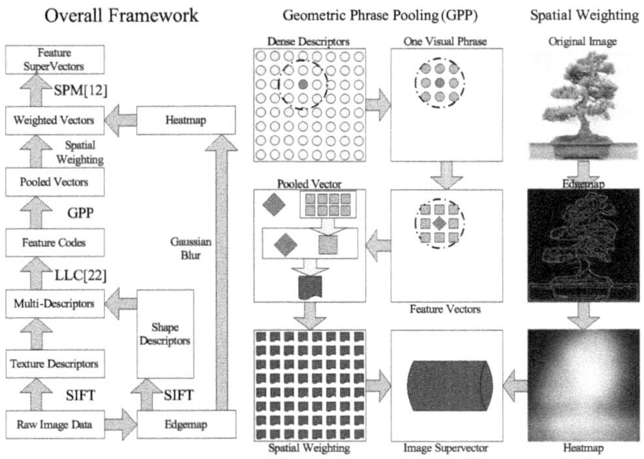

Figure 1: Flowcharts and of the framework and key modules. Left: the modified BoF framework. Right: Geometric Phrase Pooling and spatial weighting.

phrases [24], for better image understanding. Both of them bridge the semantic gap to some extent.

- **Spatial weighting of images.** Not all regions on a natural image are really useful for representation. Background clutters might bring in noises, which are harmful to training robust models. Therefore, detection of Regions of Interest (ROI) is usually proposed. Using a simple rectangular bounding box, [2] gives better representation on the less aligned datasets.

Based on these observations, we propose several novel algorithms from new aspects. With the help of edge detectors, we obtain an edgemap for each original image. Upon this, we claim a threefold contribution. First, we simultaneously extract SIFT and Edge-SIFT descriptors and combine them in the generation of BoF model. Earlier fusion of descriptors makes it easier to mine complementary information from both descriptors. Second, we propose geometric visual phrases upon traditional visual words, and take them as mid-level image representation as well as apply a novel pooling algorithm to them. Third, we use naive Gaussian blur to obtain a weighting heatmap for spatial weighting on the image plane. Integrating all the techniques produces a much more powerful framework, which outperforms state-of-the-art systems by a margin on various applications.

The proposed algorithm is illustrated in Figure 1. Compared with the traditional BoF framework, some differences should be marked. First, we generate edgemaps from original images using the Compass Operator [19], an improved version of Canny Operator [4], laying an important foundation of our algorithm. On original images as well as edgemaps, we extract two kinds of descriptors, *i.e.*, SIFT and Edge-SIFT, and mix them as a large set of local features. After codebook is constructed and descriptors are quantized onto the visual vocabulary, we build geometric visual phrases as the mid-level representation of our model. Before the traditional max-pooling step, we insert two new steps, *i.e.*, phrase pooling and spatial weighting, for better description of geometric visual phrases. Finally, we apply SPM [12] for spatial context modeling, and obtain the representation vectors of images.

The remainder of this paper is organized as follows. In Section 2, we introduce the traditional Bag-of-Features framework for image applications. Section 3 presents our algorithm extracting and fusing complementary descriptors, as well as provides a detailed analysis of the strategy. In Section 4, we introduce a new pooling algorithm named Geometric Phrase Pooling. It is very effective to find structural information beyond visual words. Section 5 introduces a simple spatial weighting scheme for interesting region detection. Various image applications of our framework are shown in Section 6. We draw our conclusions in Section 7.

2. THE BAG-OF-FEATURES FRAMEWORK

The Bag-of-Features (BoF) framework is one of the most widely used models for image representation. In this section, we give a brief introduction, and build a mathematical notation system for this framework.

2.1 Local Descriptor Extraction

In computer, an original **image I** is a $W \times H$ matrix:

$$\mathbf{I} = (a_{ij})_{W \times H} \quad (1)$$

where a_{ij} is the **pixel** on position (i, j). For grayscale images, a_{ij} is a single floating number ranged in $[0, 1]$, while it is a 3-dimensional vector for RGB-space color images.

Due to the poor semantic meaning of raw image pixels, we extract **local descriptors** from small patches on the image plane. There are many works on describing local patches. Among those, SIFT [16] and HOG [6] are probably the most widely used ones. They are both gradient based descriptors extracted on **Interest Points** of images. Detecting Interest Points is also a challenging problem. Since many detectors such as DoG [16] or MSER [18] sometimes fail to find semantic and discriminative patches. we use an alternative method by performing dense sampling of local patches, leading to the **Dense-SIFT** or **Dense-HOG** algorithm [1].

After descriptor extraction, the image **I** could be represented as a set of local descriptors, $\mathcal{M}$:

$$\mathcal{M} = \{(\mathbf{d}_1, \mathbf{l}_1), (\mathbf{d}_2, \mathbf{l}_2), \ldots, (\mathbf{d}_M, \mathbf{l}_M)\} \quad (2)$$

where $\mathbf{d}_m$ and $\mathbf{l}_m$ denote the D-dimensional description vector and the geometric location of the m-th descriptor, respectively. M is the total number of dense descriptors, which could be hundreds or even thousands under dense sampling.

Note that SIFT or HOG descriptors only provide texture features of images. By extracting various kinds of descriptors, it is possible to cover other important features such as shape, color, and so on. Many systems on this topic, such as [2], have been proposed, showing a much better performance over those using single descriptors.

2.2 Quantization for Descriptors

After descriptors have been extracted, they are often quantized to be compact. For this purpose, we train a **codebook B** using descriptors from the whole dataset. It is a $B \times D$ matrix, or B vectors with dimension D, each of which, *i.e.*, $\mathbf{c}_b$, is called a **codeword**. Most often, the codebook is constructed with K-Means clustering algorithm. Recent years, there are also some works targeting at improving the performance of K-Means [14] [20], and building discriminative codebooks for large-scale image applications [26].

Next, descriptors are projected onto the codebook for a histogram representation. This process is called **coding**, for we are actually encoding each descriptor into a sparse vector. Hard quantization strategy presents a descriptor using single codeword, leading to a large quantization error. In recent years, soft quantization methods have been proposed as alternatives to the hard one. By projecting a descriptor onto the subspace spanned by a small group of codewords, it produces smaller quantization error, and performs more effective. Sparse Coding [13] [23] and Locality-constrained Linear Coding [22] techniques are such cases. Given a codebook with B codewords, the quantization vector or **feature vector** for a descriptor $\mathbf{d}_m$ would be a B-dimensional vector $\mathbf{v}_m$. We name $\mathbf{v}_m$ the corresponding **visual word** of **descriptor** $\mathbf{d}_m$. In our terminology, there is a clear difference between the concepts of descriptors and visual words.

2.3 Feature Pooling

After all the descriptors are quantized as visual words, we shall aggregate them for image representation. We call this step **feature pooling**, for we are putting visual words into a pool for statistics. For this purpose, two major pooling strategies are often used. The **max-pooling** strategy calculates the maximal responses on each codeword:

$$\mathbf{w} = \max_{1 \leq m \leq M} \mathbf{v}_m \tag{3}$$

where the notation $\max_m$ denotes the element-wise maximization, M denotes the number of local patches of the image, and $\mathbf{v}_m$ is the m-th visual word. Differently, the **average-pooling** strategy calculates the average responses:

$$\mathbf{w} = \frac{1}{M} \sum_{m=1}^{M} \mathbf{w}_m \tag{4}$$

Here $\mathbf{w}$, a D-dimensional vector, is named **representation vector** or **feature vector** of the image.

Some researchers [3] have discussed the choice of max-pooling versus average-pooling. Max-pooling gives more discriminative representation under soft quantization strategies, while average-pooling fits hard quantization better. Recently, various methods have been proposed to improve the traditional pooling methods, such as the complex optimization in the Geometric ℓ_p-norm Pooling [9] algorithm.

2.4 Spatial Context Modeling

Spatial context could greatly help us understand the semantics of images [29]. Therefore, various models are used for constructing spatial structures. Among those, Spatial Pyramid Matching [12] is a successful trial. After coding, images are divided into hierarchical subregions for individual pooling, and the pooled vectors are concatenated to form a **supervector**. For datasets with good alignment such as Caltech101 [8], SPM improves classification accuracy by an impressive margin of 10%. However, it shows little improvements or even worse performances on less aligned datasets.

Another line for spatial context modeling is to use visual phrases [15] [27] [28]. Compared with visual words, visual phrases are more semantic and robust [25], therefore produce more discriminative vectors for image representation. Also, spatial coding of visual phrases are widely used in large-scale web image search and retrieval systems [29].

2.5 The Baseline Systems

We compare our model with two baselines. The first is LLC [22], a standard implementation of traditional BoF framework with single SIFT descriptors. The other one is the system by Bosch *et.al.* [2]. In [2], various techniques are exploited, including multiple descriptors, detection of regions of interest, and so on. Both baselines represent state-of-the-art performances for image representation.

3. COMPLEMENTARY DESCRIPTORS

In this section, we propose a novel system for image representation using two kinds of descriptors. First, we introduce an edge based descriptor named Edge-SIFT. Though they come from heterogeneous domains of original images and edgemaps, SIFT and Edge-SIFT descriptors share the same physical meaning in their corresponding dimension, therefore we could mix them to train a BoF model. We test our model and perform detailed analysis on the effect of multiple descriptors. Also, we make a short comment on the early fusion strategy to reveal its advantages.

3.1 SIFT and Edge-SIFT Descriptors

For an image $\mathbf{I}$, we first extract dense SIFT [16] descriptors from the image. Denote the set of SIFT descriptors as $\mathcal{M}_\mathrm{S}$:

$$\mathcal{M}_\mathrm{S} = \{(\mathbf{d}_{\mathrm{S}1}, \mathbf{l}_{\mathrm{S}1}), (\mathbf{d}_{\mathrm{S}2}, \mathbf{l}_{\mathrm{S}2}), \ldots, (\mathbf{d}_{\mathrm{S}M_\mathrm{S}}, \mathbf{l}_{\mathrm{S}M_\mathrm{S}})\} \tag{5}$$

where the subscript S stands for SIFT, and M_S is the number of SIFT patches on the image plane.

As we know, SIFT descriptors are effective on describing texture features. To compensate, we can also extract shape descriptors. Following [2], we apply an edge detector on image $\mathbf{I}$, producing another $W \times H$ grayscale image $\mathbf{I}_\mathrm{E}$:

$$\mathbf{I}_\mathrm{E} = \{e_{ij}\}_{W \times H} \tag{6}$$

where e_{ij}, a floating value ranged within $[0, 1]$, is the significance quantity for pixel (i, j) locating on an edge. We call $\mathbf{I}_\mathrm{E}$ the corresponding **edgemap** for original image $\mathbf{I}$.

We use Compass Operator [19] for edge detection. One of the detected edgemaps is shown in Figure 2, while more of them could be found in Figure 4 and 13. On edgemaps, texture details are filtered and the shape of the objects becomes more clear. Therefore, it is reasonable to extract SIFT descriptors on edgemaps for shape description. We call them Edge-SIFT descriptors, to differ from original SIFT ones. Denote the set of Edge-SIFT descriptors as $\mathcal{M}_\mathrm{E}$:

$$\mathcal{M}_\mathrm{E} = \{(\mathbf{d}_{\mathrm{E}1}, \mathbf{l}_{\mathrm{E}1}), (\mathbf{d}_{\mathrm{E}2}, \mathbf{l}_{\mathrm{E}2}), \ldots, (\mathbf{d}_{\mathrm{E}M_\mathrm{E}}, \mathbf{l}_{\mathrm{E}M_\mathrm{E}})\} \tag{7}$$

where the subscript E stands for Edge-SIFT, and M_E is the number of descriptors, which could be different with M_S.

3.2 Fusing Descriptors

After different descriptors are extracted, we simple mix them on the same image plane:

$$\mathcal{M} = \mathcal{M}_\mathrm{S} \cup \mathcal{M}_\mathrm{E} \tag{8}$$

Here, $\mathcal{M}$ is the new set of descriptors for image representation. Figure 2 illustrates the fusion operation.

We shall emphasize that both SIFT and Edge-SIFT descriptors are 128-dimensional histograms of gradients, therefore share the same physical meaning though extracted from different sources of images. Note that it is important to guarantee the same physical meaning on the corresponding dimensions, for we shall compare and combine the descriptors dimension-wise at the clustering and quantization steps.

Finally, we shall make a short comment to compare our work with [2]. In [2], descriptors are also extracted from

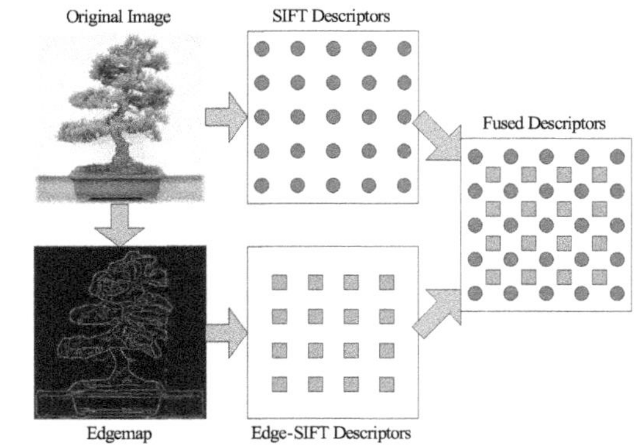

Figure 2: Fusing two categories of dense descriptors on the image plane.

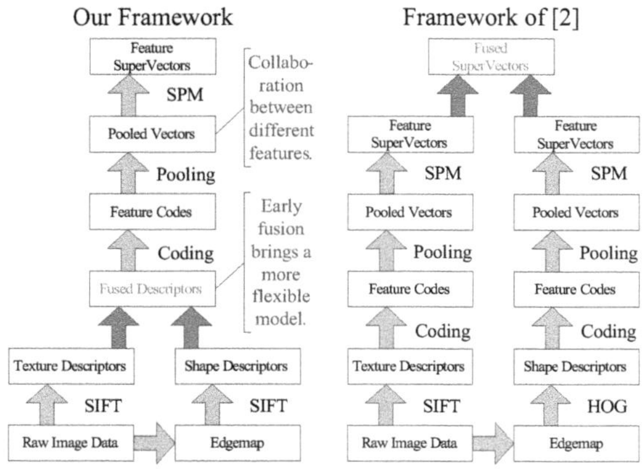

Figure 3: Difference between our model and [2] (best viewed in color PDF). Red arrows and texts highlight the fusion step in both frameworks.

original images and edgemaps respectively. However, two categories of descriptors are individually processed through BoF framework, until fusion is performed on the BoF representation of images to form a concatenated supervector. As we could see in Section 4.5, late fusion limits the flexibility of the model, and makes it impossible to construct spatial structures consisting of both kinds of descriptors. On the contrary, we finish the fusion step much earlier, obtaining a new set containing both categories of descriptors. We illustrate the difference between the models in Figure 3, and will further discuss the advantages of our model in Section 4.5.

3.3 Experiments and Discussions

Now, we test our model on the Caltech101 dataset. To make comparison, we inherit the remaining parts of our framework from LLC [22]. Table 1 shows our results on different combinations of descriptors as well as on single ones. When we fuse different kinds of descriptors, *i.e.*, SIFT and Edge-SIFT, our system gives the best performance, while we observe dramatic accuracy drops when the same kind of descriptors, *i.e.*, both SIFT, are merged. Therefore, the compensation between two kinds of descriptors is very clear.

To give a better intuition to this finding, we return to systems using single descriptors. We choose parameters from the best after-fusion performance in Table 1, *i.e.*, the step

Table 1: Results on combined descriptors as well as on single ones. The numbers in brackets are respectively step and patch sizes for SIFT extraction.

Desc 1	Desc 2	Only 1	Only 2	Both
SIFT(7,7)	SIFT(6,12)	74.41%	72.69%	75.14%
SIFT(7,7)	Edge(6,12)	74.41%	73.08%	78.75%
SIFT(7,7)	SIFT(7,12)	74.41%	73.77%	75.75%
SIFT(7,7)	Edge(7,12)	74.41%	72.89%	**78.94%**
SIFT(7,7)	SIFT(8,12)	74.41%	73.60%	75.32%
SIFT(7,7)	Edge(8,12)	74.41%	72.93%	78.92%

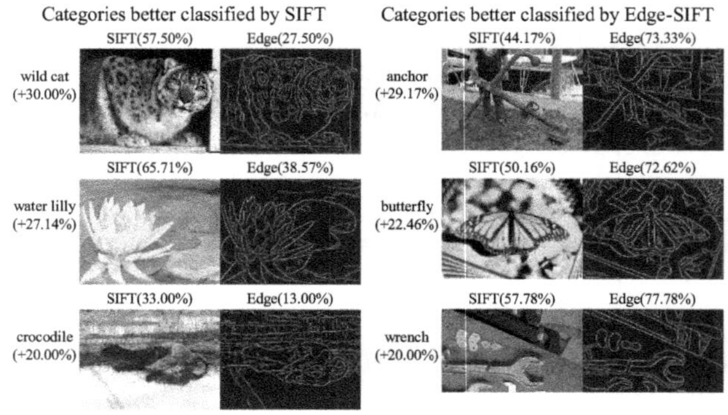

Figure 4: Comparison of different descriptors. Classification accuracies with single descriptors are listed above sample images.

sizes of SIFT and Edge-SIFT are both 7 pixels, while the sizes of local patches are chosen to be 7 and 12 pixels, respectively. To compare different descriptors, we separately evaluate the classification accuracies by category, and list those categories with largest accuracy gaps in Figure 4.

It is clear that different types of objects are better described using different types of descriptors. For objects with less deformation such as manmade tools, the better strategy is to filter their texture details and pay more attention on the edgemaps. Therefore, Edge-SIFT descriptors give a better description on these objects. However, there are also a number of objects in which texture features are more discriminative, while shape description is less robust. Animals and plants are such cases, where it is better to preserve texture details in original images and use SIFT descriptors.

Since different kinds of descriptors are complementary for discriminating objects, it is reasonable to preserve both of them for a more robust image representation. Figure 5 shows an example of four categories. It is hard to classify them using any single kind of descriptors, for the between-category similarity in texture or shape features. Only using both categories of descriptors makes it possible for our model to distinguish them well.

4. GEOMETRIC PHRASE POOLING

Till now, we have described a framework for image representation using two kinds of descriptors. However, it is worth noting that different descriptors are individually coded and pooled in the algorithm. The lack of cooperation between them limits the discriminativity of our model. In this

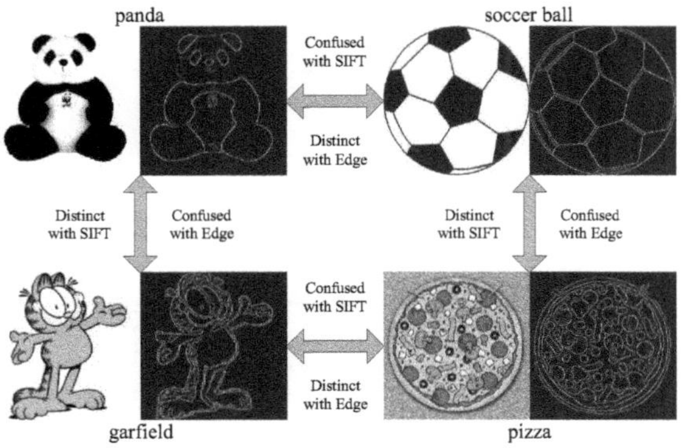

Figure 5: Combining different kinds of descriptors helps to discriminate confusing categories.

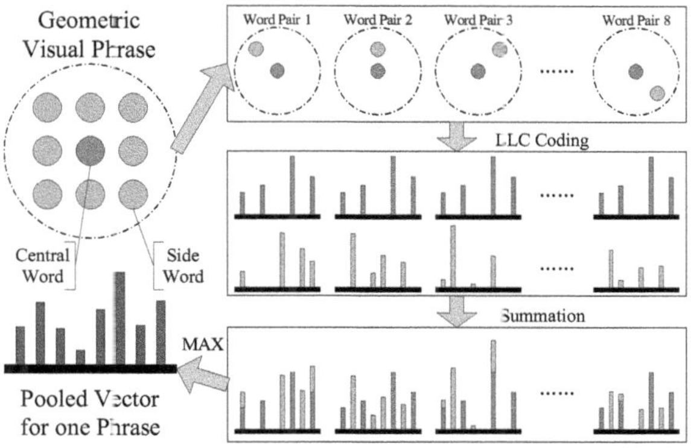

Figure 6: Illustration of Geometric Phrase Pooling. We group the central word and each side word as a pair and add their feature vectors together. At last, maximization is performed on the whole phrase.

section, we shall introduce a novel structure named geometric visual phrase. It shall provide us a mid-level representation containing both texture and shape features. We illustrate our algorithm in the right column of Figure 1.

4.1 The GPP Algorithm

Let's start from Equation (8), and rewrite it as:

$$\mathcal{M} = \{(\mathbf{d}_1, \mathbf{l}_1), (\mathbf{d}_2, \mathbf{l}_2), \ldots, (\mathbf{d}_M, \mathbf{l}_M)\} \quad (9)$$

To begin with, we give a new definition of geometric visual phrases. Following [24], we regard a visual phrase as a combination of visual words. By intuition, phrases often consist of words close to each other on the image plane. As local patches on images are not ordered so well as textual words, we ignore the order and take a phrase as a disordered set of visual words. Following this basic rule, we propose a simple algorithm. Define a positive integer K, $K \ll M$. For the m-th descriptor, we search for its K nearest neighbors on the image plane and form a word group:

$$\mathcal{G}_m = \{(\mathbf{d}_{m,0}, \mathbf{l}_{m,0}), \ldots, (\mathbf{d}_{m,K}, \mathbf{l}_{m,K})\}, \qquad m = 1, 2, \ldots, M \quad (10)$$

$\mathcal{G}_m$ is the m-th **geometric visual phrase**. The **central word** of $\mathcal{G}_m$ is defined as the zeroth descriptor $(\mathbf{d}_{m,0}, \mathbf{l}_{m,0})$, which is simply $(\mathbf{d}_m, \mathbf{l}_m)$ itself. The **location** of phrase $\mathcal{G}_m$ is defined by $\mathbf{l}_{m,0}$. Other K descriptors are called **side words**. K is the **order** of $\mathcal{G}_m$, which contains $K+1$ words.

Suppose that we have trained a codebook $\mathbf{B}$ with B codewords. For a phrase $\mathcal{G}_m$, we respectively perform LLC [22] coding for each of its words. LLC is a sparse coding scheme. Given $\mathbf{B}$ and number of bases r (most often $r \ll B$), it produces feature vectors with at most r nonzero elements among totally B dimensions. For $\mathcal{G}_m$, there will be $K+1$ sparse feature vectors, one for each visual word. Denote $\mathbf{v}_{m,k}$ as the feature vector of k-th word in $\mathcal{G}_m$.

Now, **Geometric Phrase Pooling** (GPP) is performed on the $K+1$ feature vectors:

$$\mathbf{w}_m = \max_{1 \leq k \leq K} \{\mathbf{v}_{m,0} + \mathbf{v}_{m,k}\} \quad (11)$$

$$= \mathbf{v}_{m,0} + \max_{1 \leq k \leq K} \mathbf{v}_{m,k} \quad (12)$$

where the notation $\max_k$ denotes element-wise maximization on K vectors with B dimensions.

Equation (11) is the core equation of GPP, while (12) is an equivalent version for easier implementation. We illustrate the simple working mechanism of (11) in Figure 6.

After GPP, we obtain a B-dimensional vector $\mathbf{w}_m$ as the feature vector for the m-th visual phrase $\mathcal{G}_m$. Finally, a max-pooling step is performed over all the phrases:

$$\mathbf{w} = \max_{1 \leq m \leq M} \mathbf{w}_m \quad (13)$$

and $\mathbf{w}$ is obtained as the feature vector of the image.

4.2 Deep Insights for GPP

The formulation of GPP is very easy to understand. However, the intuition behind the simple algorithm is not that straightforward. Here, we clarify the advantages within the formulation to give a better understanding of GPP.

First, we shall provide an intuitive explanation. Go back to Equations (11) and (13). Simple derivation gives:

$$\mathbf{w} = \max_{1 \leq m \leq M} \mathbf{w}_m \quad (14)$$

$$= \max_{1 \leq m \leq M} \left\{ \max_{1 \leq k \leq K} \{\mathbf{v}_{m,0} + \mathbf{v}_{m,k}\} \right\} \quad (15)$$

$$= \max_{1 \leq m_1 < m_2 \leq M, m_1 \diamond m_2} \{\mathbf{v}_{m_1} + \mathbf{v}_{m_2}\} \quad (16)$$

where $m_1 \diamond m_2$ means that visual words m_1 and m_2 are adjacent ones, *i.e.*, when one of them is taken as central word, the other is one of the side words Hence, $\mathbf{w}$ is the maximization over summations of all adjacent word pairs. Define $\mathbf{v}_{m_1} + \mathbf{v}_{m_2}$ as the contribution to GPP from word pair (m_1, m_2).

Now, recall the formulation of max-pooling algorithm and rewrite it into an equivalent version:

$$\mathbf{w} = \max_{1 \leq m \leq M} \mathbf{v}_m \quad (17)$$

$$= \max_{1 \leq m \leq M} \left\{ \max_{1 \leq k \leq K} \{\max\{\mathbf{v}_{m,0}, \mathbf{v}_{m,k}\}\} \right\} \quad (18)$$

$$= \max_{1 \leq m_1 < m_2 \leq M, m_1 \diamond m_2} \{\max\{\mathbf{v}_{m_1}, \mathbf{v}_{m_2}\}\} \quad (19)$$

Naturally, $\max\{\mathbf{v}_{m_1}, \mathbf{v}_{m_2}\}$ is defined as the contribution to max-pooling from word pair (m_1, m_2).

For an adjacent word pair (m_1, m_2), consider its contributions to GPP and max-pooling. For simplicity, we denote feature vectors for them as $\mathbf{v}_1$ and $\mathbf{v}_2$, respectively. If $\mathbf{v}_1$

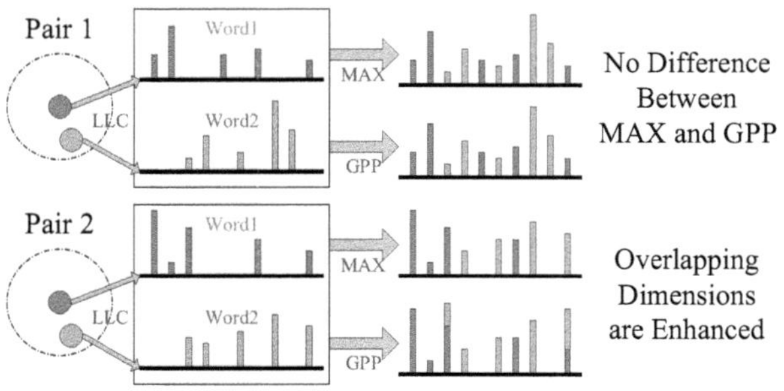

Figure 7: Intuition of GPP (best viewed in color PDF). Cases of non-overlapping word pair and partial overlapping word pair are shown respectively.

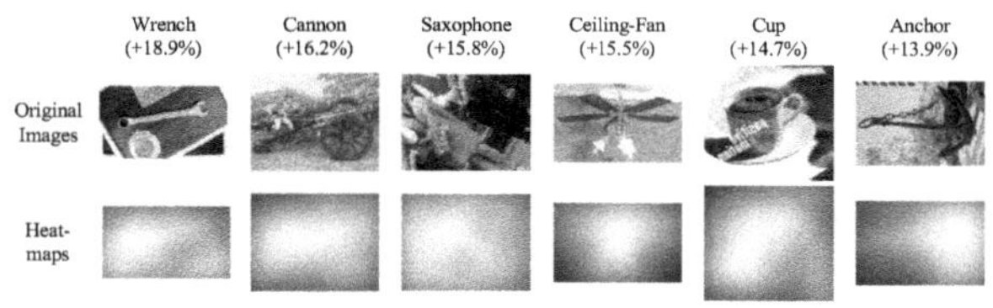

Figure 8: Heatmaps generated from the percentages of useful pairs of visual words on the image plane. Numbers in brackets are accuracy gains for those categories, from LLC to GPP.

and $\mathbf{v}_2$ have no nonzero dimensions in common, we have $\max\{\mathbf{v}_1, \mathbf{v}_2\} = \mathbf{v}_1 + \mathbf{v}_2$. In this case, the word pair contributes equally to max-pooling and GPP. However, if there are common nonzero dimensions in $\mathbf{v}_1$ and $\mathbf{v}_2$, things will be different: this word pair would better contribute to GPP by enhancing the overlapping dimensions. We illustrate our intuition in Figure 7.

From the analysis above, we have learned that only word pairs with nonzero dimensions in common would make contribution to GPP. In our framework, we perform descriptor quantization using LLC [22], a locality sensitive coding scheme. Descriptors are projected onto overlapping dimensions only if they are similar in feature space. Therefore, GPP latently selects those word pairs both similar and adjacent, and enhance their nonzero responses in common.

There is an acknowledged observation that on natural images, local patches with the same semantics are more likely to be correlated, *i.e.*, visually similar. Therefore for a geometric visual phrase consisting of one central word and K side words, the correlation between central word and side words will be high (visually similar) if this geometric visual phrase is located on a semantic patch. This high correlation turns to be the common nonzero dimensions of the visual words. Therefore, GPP enhances the responses of such highly correlated patches, or word pairs, in a latent way.

To verify our inference, we need some additional statistics. For each visual phrase, we count the percentage of side words with common nonzero dimensions with the central word. This could be taken as a histogram on the image plane. Smoothing it gives us a heatmap illustrating the visual correlations on the corresponding patches. Figure 8 shows some randomly selected examples from the Caltech101 dataset. We could see that significantly enhanced

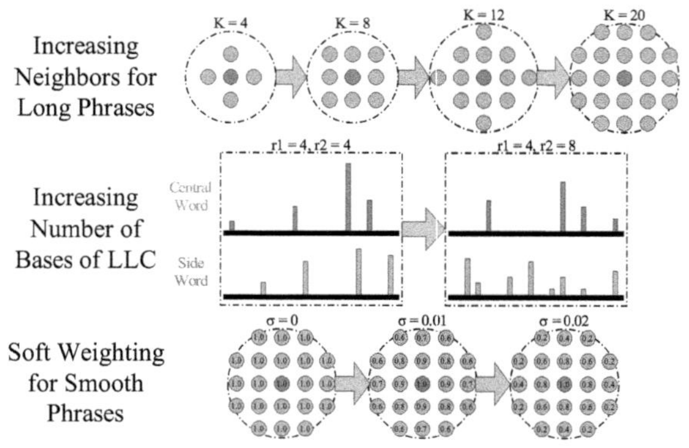

Figure 9: Illustration of different improvements for GPP (best viewed in color PDF). Above: increasing K for long phrases. Middle: Enlarging number of bases in LLC for more overlapping. Below: Soft weighting on geometric visual phrases, where floating numbers are the soft weights on visual words.

visual responses are mainly distributed on the semantic regions. By paying more attention on these regions, GPP produces better representations than LLC.

In summary, we could conclude that GPP is indeed a superior pooling method with a clear motivation and convincing improvements.

4.3 Enhancing GPP

In this section, we will discuss three ideas to improve the effectiveness of GPP. All of them are illustrated in Figure 9.

4.3.1 Increasing Neighbors for Long Phrases

In Section 4.2, we observe that word pairs with similar appearance and geometric location would contribute to GPP. To search for more such pairs, it is straightforward to increase the order of phrases, *i.e.*, K. However, increasing K would also bring in more irrelevant side words. We don't set K automatically, but choose the best performance ($K = 20$) after testing a wide range of K (from 5 to 40).

4.3.2 Numbers of Bases of Visual Phrases

As LLC [22] is a sparse coding algorithm, the number of bases r is much smaller than the visual codebook size B. In this case, histogram representations of adjacent visual words could hardly overlap, therefore percentage of word pairs that contribute to GPP is small. Increasing r produces more useful word pairs, but also damages the locality of LLC. The selection of r is a tradeoff between description and robustness.

The central word is the most significant component in a visual phrase, therefore its robustness is more important than side ones'. For this, we use a larger r for side words and yet a small r for central one. To clarify, we denote r_1 and r_2 as numbers of bases for central words and side words respectively. In our experiments, $r_1 = 5$ and $r_2 = 30$.

4.3.3 Soft Weighting for Smooth Phrases

By intuition, if the distance between visual words is large, the relationship between them is loose. Therefore, we apply an exponential decay on side words, assigning lower weights onto distant ones. For a side word $(\mathbf{d}_{m,k}, \mathbf{l}_{m,k})$ with feature

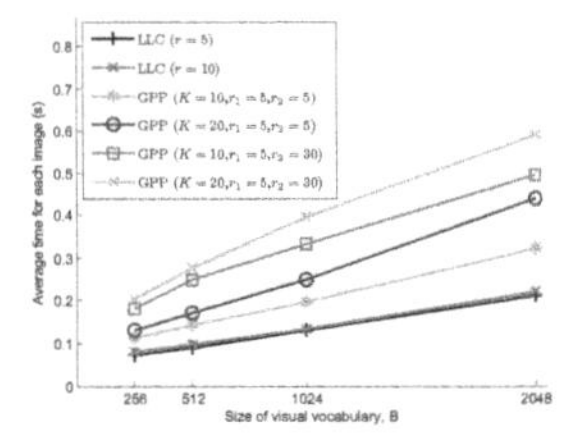

Figure 10: Average time required for each image. Data are tested on 4×2.0GHz CPUs.

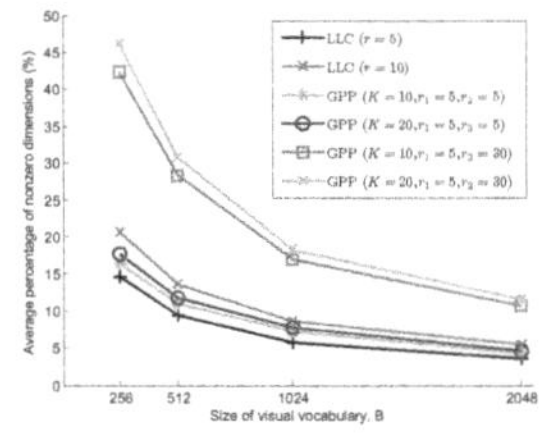

Figure 11: Average percentage of nonzero dimensions in pooled vectors.

vector $\mathbf{v}_{m,k}$, we penalize it with weight s_k defined as:

$$s_k = \exp\{-\sigma_w \times \|\mathbf{l}_0 - \mathbf{l}_k\|_2\} \quad (20)$$

where σ_w is the smoothing parameter on visual words, and $\|\cdot\|_2$ is the Euclidean distance. Now, we obtain a smoother version of GPP formulation (12):

$$\mathbf{w}_m = \mathbf{v}_{m,0} + \max_{1 \leq k \leq K} s_k \times \mathbf{v}_{m,k} \quad (21)$$

In all the experiments, we take $\sigma_w = 0.01$.

4.4 Time Complexity and Sparsity

Here, we test the time complexity and the sparsity of GPP to show its simplicity and efficiency. To make comparison, we use the implementation of LLC with code downloaded from the website provided by [22]. GPP with different parameters is added into the BoF framework as an intermediate step. We denote the original framework as LLC and our framework as GPP, construct different sizes of codebooks, and respectively record the average coding and pooling time for each image, as well as the average percentage of nonzero dimensions in the feature vector $\mathbf{w}$.

Results are plotted in Figure 10 and 11. Owe to the simplicity, our framework is very efficient to carry out. Geometric Phrase Pooling requires no more than 0.4s on a single image, which is much better than those complicated pooling algorithms such as GLP [9]. On the other hand, Figure 11 reveals that GPP generates much denser feature vectors for image representation, especially in the scenarios with longer phrases and more coding bases. A comment needs to be made here. People have been debating the use of dense versus sparse features for a long time. Yang *et. al* [23] have claimed the effectiveness of sparse feature vectors. Our experiments give a neutral argument about this topic: denser features do not mean to provide worse results, but we need proper structures to organize them. GPP actually provides a compromise between sparse and dense representations of images.

4.5 Early Fusion vs. Late Fusion

Finally, we return to the discussion of early fusion versus late fusion in Section 3. On the Caltech101 dataset, we test different combinations of fusion strategies and pooling methods. Results are listed in Table 2. From the table, we could clearly observe the advantage of early fusion over late fusion. When the geometric visual phrases are not built, they show comparable performances. However, GPP helps to construct robust mid-level structures upon fused descriptors, resulting in a notable improvement on the early fusion system. In Figure 12, we illustrate the architectures of visual phrases over single and complementary descriptors. Containing both texture and shape features, mid-level structures upon fused descriptors are more robust and semantic meaningful.

Table 2: Caltech101 classification results on frameworks with different fusion and pooling strategies.

	Late Fusion [2]	Early Fusion (Ours)
LLC [22]	79.12%	78.94%
GPP (Ours)	79.48%	81.36%

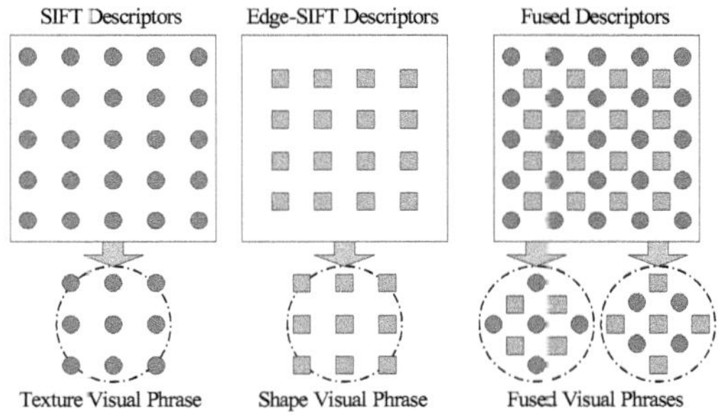

Figure 12: Applying GPP on fused descriptors helps to generate complementary visual phrases.

5. SPATIAL WEIGHTING

For less aligned datasets, we need to detect Regions of Interest (ROI) on the original images. This is equivalent to a spatial weighting, or heatmap learning process. In this section, we provide a simple spatial weighting strategy using a gradient based edge detector, for the observation that higher contrast regions provide stronger stimuli to our vision [11].

Following (6), an edgemap $\mathbf{I}_\mathrm{E}$ is a $W \times H$ matrix with elements representing the intensities of edge responses. Based on it, we calculate a $W \times H$ **weighting matrix** $\mathbf{W}$:

$$\mathbf{W} = \{w_{ij}\}_{W \times H} \quad (22)$$

Here, w_{ij} is the spatial weight at position (i, j), which is accumulated from decayed edge responses:

$$w_{ij} = \sum_{i',j'} e_{i'j'} \times \exp\{-\sigma_e \|(i,j) - (i',j')\|_2\} \quad (23)$$

Here, coordinate (i', j') are traversed on the whole image, σ_e is the smoothing parameter on edge responses, and $\|\cdot\|_2$ is the Euclidean distance. As σ_e goes up, there shall be smaller weights accumulated on pixels far from edges. In our experiments, σ_e is fixed to 0.05.

With spatial weights, formulation (13) becomes:

$$\mathbf{w} = \max_{1 \leq m \leq M} \{w_m \times \mathbf{w}_m\} \quad (24)$$

where w_m is the weight at $\mathbf{l}_m$, the central pixel of $\mathcal{G}_m$.

To evaluate the proposed spatial weighting scheme, we test it on the Caltech101 dataset. Again we calculate the classification accuracies by category and list the most improved ones in Figure 13. For better visualization, we plot the corresponding weighting matrices $\mathbf{W}$ as heatmaps for

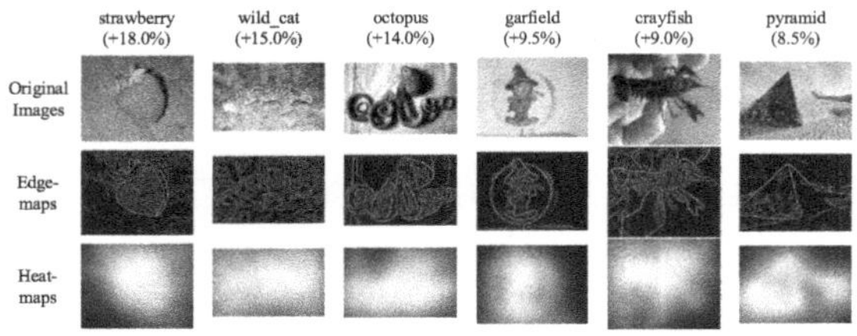

Figure 13: Edgemaps and weighting heatmaps of images from those categories with most accuracy gains (numbers in brackets) after spatial weighting.

comparison. Since higher weights often appear in the foreground, the feature vector obtained with (24) is more robust.

Finally let us note that (23) is very computing expensive, for it requires a complete enumeration on each pairs of pixels. On a 300×300 image, it might take more than 30 seconds on a single-core CPU. Here, we exploit an approximation by skipping the calculation of the pairs with Euclidean distances larger than 50 pixels. Taking our best smoothing parameter, *i.e.*, $\sigma_e = 0.05$, the maximal ignored coefficient could be $\exp\{-0.05 \times 50\} \approx 0.08$, which is relatively small. The approximation algorithm only requires less than 0.5 second on a single image. It is efficient in practise considering the calculation is required only once.

6. CASE STUDIES

In this section, we provide the experimental results on several widely used datasets with various tasks, *i.e.*, image classification, retrieval and scene understanding. To show the efficiency of our algorithm, we use the same settings as state-of-the-art algorithms, and the best settings learned from previous sections for GPP and spatial weighting.

- **Edge detection.** We use the Compass Operator [19] for edge detection. The radius parameter σ is fixed as 4 as proposed in the same literature.
- **Image descriptors.** We use the VLFeat [21] library to extract SIFT descriptors. The step size and the scale of patches are discussed separately for each dataset.
- **Codebook construction.** We use a traditional K-Means algorithm for clustering. The size of codebook is 2048 for Caltech101 and 15-scene dataset and 4096 for other two. The number of descriptors collected for clustering does not exceed 2 million.
- **Coding and pooling method.** We apply the original source code provided by authors of LLC [22] for coding. Upon that, we apply GPP with the best parameters: $K = 20$, $\sigma_w = 0.01$, $r_1 = 5$ and $r_2 = 30$.
- **Spatial weighting.** We take $\sigma_e = 0.05$ for edge based spatial weighting scheme.
- **SPM settings and normalization.** We apply a 3-layer SPM for enhancing the spatial context of features. After that, a ℓ_2-norm normalization is performed to produce comparable feature vectors.
- **SVM for tagging.** A linear SVM by Chang *et.al* [5] is used for training and testing. For retrieval tasks, we rank the images according to the confidence probabilities reported by SVM.
- **Accuracy evaluation.** For Pascal VOC 2007 Challenge, we use the standard benchmark method. On other datasets, we randomly selected fixed number of images for training, and test the model on others to evaluate the average classification accuracy over all categories. We repeat random selection for 10 times and report the average performance.

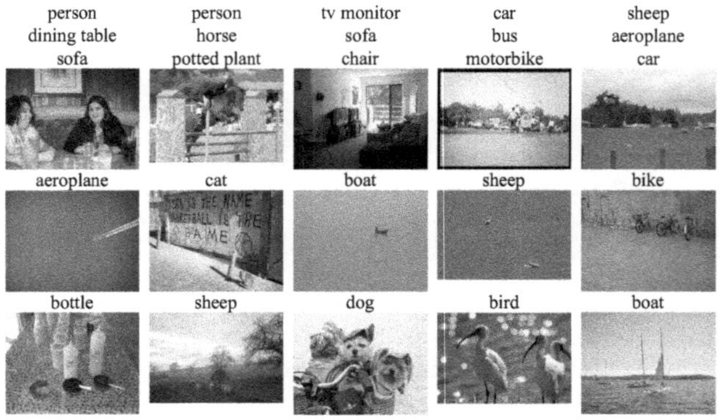

Figure 14: Sample images from Pascal VOC 2007 dataset. Upper: images with objects of multiple categories. Middle: images with small objects. Bottom: images with many objects of same category.

Figure 15: Sample images from Caltech101 dataset. Upper: categories on which our framework reports 100% accuracies (30 trains). Bottom: categories on which our framework most outperforms LLC [22].

6.1 Pascal VOC 2007 Dataset

There are 9963 images containing 20 categories of objects in the Pascal VOC 2007 dataset [7], a competition dataset for image retrieval. From sample images listed in Figure 14, we could find it a challenging dataset, for the significant varying of the appearances, scales, numbers and locations of the objects. A standard benchmark is provided by Pascal Challenge, calculating the Average Precision (AP) measure.

The step size and scale of patches for SIFT descriptors are 6 and 4, while 7 and 12 for Edge-SIFT descriptors. We report a 53.89% precision, winning LLC [22] (49.13%) remarkably by 4.74%.

6.2 Caltech101 Dataset

The Caltech101 dataset [8] contains 9144 images of 102 categories, including a background category. There exists significant deformation among different objects from the same category. Sample images are listed in Figure 15.

Table 3: Classification results on Caltech101.

# training	5	10	15	20	30
Lazebnik [12]	-	-	56.4	-	64.6
Yang [23]	-	-	67.0	-	73.2
Wang [22]	51.15	59.77	65.43	67.74	73.44
Boureau [3]	-	-	-	-	75.7
Bosch [2]	-	-	-	-	81.3
Ours	**61.90**	**71.75**	**76.03**	**78.53**	**82.45**
	±0.54	±0.60	±0.63	±0.39	±0.59

Figure 16: Sample images from Caltech256 dataset. Upper: categories on which accuracies are 90% or higher (30 trains). Middle: images with small objects. Bottom: images with many objects.

In this dataset, we use 7×7 SIFT patches and 12×12 Edge-SIFT patches, and the step sizes are both fixed to 7. We have used 5, 10, 15, 20, 30 images per category for training, and others for testing. Results are concluded in Table 3. In all cases, GPP outperformed LLC by more than 9%, or even more than 10% in scenarios of fewer training samples.

6.3 Caltech256 Dataset

The Caltech256 dataset [10] contains 30607 images of 257 categories, including a clutter category. It is much more challenging than Caltech101, for the objects in it not only suffer from significant size changes and deformation, but are also located on different positions on images. Figure 16 shows some sample images for this dataset.

In this dataset, 5×5 SIFT patches and 8×8 Edge-SIFT patches are extracted with a fixed step size of 5. We have used 5, 15, 30, 45, 60 images per category for training, and others for testing. Results are listed in Table 6.3.

6.4 15-scene Dataset

The 15-scene dataset [12] contains 15 scenes and 4485 images. It might be the most widely used dataset for scene understanding tasks, in which we need to discriminate various categories of scenes listed in Figure 17.

Table 4: Classification results on Caltech256.

# training	5	15	30	45	60
Griffin [10]	-	28.3	34.1	-	-
Wang [22]	-	34.36	41.19	45.31	47.68
Bosch [2]	-	-	44.0	-	-
Ours	**26.12**	**36.35**	**45.07**	**48.02**	**50.33**
	±0.21	±0.31	±0.24	±0.25	±0.18

Figure 17: Sample images from 15-scene dataset

Table 5: Results on 15-scenes dataset.

# training	10	20	30	50	100
Lazebnik [12]	-	-	-	-	81.4
Wang [22]	66.97	72.44	75.78	78.84	82.34
Ours	**70.67**	**76.12**	**78.74**	**81.72**	**85.13**
	±0.46	±0.73	±0.88	±0.48	±0.72

5×5 patches with step size 5 are extracted for SIFT, and 8×8 patches with step size 8 are used for Edge-SIFT extraction. 10, 20, 30, 50, 100 images per category are used for training. Results are shown in Table 5.

7. CONCLUSIONS AND FUTURE WORK

In this paper, we propose a novel framework for image representation, and apply it for various image applications. We claim three major contributions. First, we extract SIFT and Edge-SIFT descriptors from original images and the corresponding edgemaps respectively, and then mix them together to train a joint BoF model. Experiments have revealed good compensation property of SIFT and Edge-SIFT descriptors. On the other hand, fusing them at very early stage gives us more room for spatial modeling. Second, we propose a novel pooling strategy named Geometric Phrase Pooling. By constructing geometric visual phrases upon complementary visual words, it is possible to model spatial structures containing both texture and shape features, providing more robust mid-level representation. Third, based on edge detection, we propose a simple and effective spatial weighting scheme to detect Regions of Interest. Integrating all the above coherently, we obtain a very powerful model that outperforms state-of-the-art algorithms on image classifications, retrieval and understanding applications.

However, there are still some open problems in our framework. As we have seen, objects are better described by different heterogeneous features such as texture and shape. If we could integrate heterogeneous features in a coherent way, it is possible to obtain a more discriminative description of different objects. When we are constructing spatial structures, we simply group adjacent visual words together, ignoring the size and orientation of local descriptors, which could be useful for sophisticated spatial modeling. Also, the information contained in edgemaps is not completely exploited, and our spatial weighting scheme based on region of interest is still naive. For these problems, we might seek help from Computational Geometric algorithms for better understanding of the detected edgemaps. We will investigate these problems in our future work.

8. ACKNOWLEDGMENTS

This work was supported by the National Basic Research Program (973 Program) of China under Grant 2012CB316301, and Basic Research Foundation of Tsinghua National Laboratory for Information Science and Technology (TNList). This work was also supported in part to Dr. Qi Tian by ARO grant W911NF-12-1-0057, NSF IIS 1052851, Faculty Research Awards by Google, NEC Laboratories of America and FXPAL, UTSA START-R award, respectively.

9. REFERENCES

[1] A. Bosch, A. Zisserman, and X. Munoz. Scene Classification via pLSA. *International Conference on Computer Vision*, pages 517 – 530, 2006.

[2] A. Bosch, A. Zisserman, and X. Muoz. Image Classification using Random Forests and Ferns. *International Conference on Computer Vision*, pages 1 – 8, 2007.

[3] Y. Boureau, F. Bach, Y. LeCun, J. Ponce, et al. Learning Mid-Level Features for Recognition. *Computer Vision and Pattern Recognition*, pages 2559 – 2566, 2010.

[4] J. Canny. A Computational Approach to Edge Detection. *Pattern Analysis and Machine Intelligence*, (6):679 – 698, 1986.

[5] C. Chang and C. Lin. LibSVM: A Library for Support Vector Machines. *ACM Transactions on Intelligent Systems and Technology (TIST)*, 2(3):27, 2011.

[6] N. Dalal and B. Triggs. Histograms of Oriented Gradients for Human Detection. *Computer Vision and Pattern Recognition*, 1:886 – 893, 2005.

[7] M. Everingham, L. Van Gool, C. K. I. Williams, J. Winn, and A. Zisserman. The PASCAL Visual Object Classes Challenge 2007 (VOC2007) Results. 2007.

[8] L. Fei-Fei, R. Fergus, and P. Perona. Learning Generative Visual Models from Few Training Examples: An Incremental Bayesian Approach Tested on 101 Object Categories. *Computer Vision and Image Understanding*, 106(1):59 – 70, 2007.

[9] J. Feng, B. Ni, Q. Tian, and S. Yan. Geometric Lp-norm Feature Pooling for Image Classification. *Computer Vision and Pattern Recognition*, pages 2609 – 2704, 2011.

[10] G. Griffin, A. Holub, and P. Perona. Caltech-256 Object Category Dataset. 2007.

[11] L. Itti, C. Koch, and E. Niebur. A Model of Saliency-Based Visual Attention for Rapid Scene Analysis. *Pattern Analysis and Machine Intelligence*, 20(11):1254 – 1259, 1998.

[12] S. Lazebnik, C. Schmid, and J. Ponce. Beyond Bags of Features: Spatial Pyramid Matching for Recognizing Natural Scene Categories. *Computer Vision and Pattern Recognition*, 2:2169 – 2178, 2006.

[13] H. Lee, A. Battle, R. Raina, and A. Ng. Efficient Sparse Coding Algorithms. *Neural Information Processing Systems*, 19:801, 2007.

[14] D. Li, L. Yang, X. Hua, and H. Zhang. Large-Scale Robust Visual Codebook Construction. In *ACM Multimedia*, pages 1183–1186, 2010.

[15] D. Liu, G. Hua, P. Viola, and T. Chen. Integrated Feature Selection and Higher-Order Spatial Feature Extraction for Object Categorization. In *Computer Vision and Pattern Recognition*, pages 1–8, 2008.

[16] D. G. Lowe. Distinctive Image Features from Scale-Invariant Keypoints. *Internatial Journal of Computer Vision*, 60(2):91 – 110, 2004.

[17] Y. Lu, L. Zhang, J. Liu, and Q. Tian. Constructing Lexica of High-level Concepts with Small Semantic Gap. *IEEE Transactions on Multimedia*, 12(4), 2010.

[18] J. Matas, O. Chum, M. Urban, and T. Pajdla. Robust Wide-Baseline Stereo from Maximally Stable Extremal Regions. *Image and Vision Computing*, 22(10):761 – 767, 2004.

[19] M. Ruzon and C. Tomasi. Color Edge Detection with the Compass Operator. *Computer Vision and Pattern Recognition*, 2, 1999.

[20] Q. Tian, S. Zhang, W. Zhou, R. Ji, B. Ni, and N. Sebe. Building Descriptive and Discriminative Visual Codebook for Large-scale Image Applications. *Multimedia Tools and Applications*, 51(2):441 – 477, 2011.

[21] A. Vedaldi and B. Fulkerson. VLFeat: An Open and Portable Library of Computer Vision Algorithms. *ACM Multimedia*, pages 1469 – 1472, 2010.

[22] J. Wang, J. Yang, K. Yu, F. Lv, T. Huang, and Y. Gong. Locality-Constrained Linear Coding for Image Classification. *Computer Vision and Pattern Recognition*, pages 3360 – 3367, 2010.

[23] J. Yang, K. Yu, Y. Gong, and T. Huang. Linear Spatial Pyramid Matching using Sparse Coding for Image Classification. *Computer Vision and Pattern Recognition*, pages 1794 – 1801, 2009.

[24] J. Yuan, Y. Wu, and M. Yang. Discovery of Collocation Patterns: from Visual Words to Visual Phrases. *Computer Vision and Pattern Recognition*, pages 1 – 8, 2007.

[25] J. Yuan, M. Yang, and Y. Wu. Mining Discriminative Co-occurrence Patterns for Visual Recognition. *Computer Vision and Pattern Recognition*, pages 2777 – 2784, 2011.

[26] S. Zhang, Q. Huang, G. Hua, S. Jiang, W. Gao, and Q. Tian. Building Contextual Visual Vocabulary for Large-Scale Image Applications. In *ACM Multimedia*, pages 501 – 510, 2010.

[27] S. Zhang, Q. Tian, G. Hua, Q. Huang, and S. Li. Descriptive Visual Words and Visual Phrases for Image Applications. In *ACM Multimedia*, pages 75–84, 2009.

[28] Y. Zhang, Z. Jia, and T. Chen. Image Retrieval with Geometry-Preserving Visual Phrases. In *Computer Vision and Pattern Recognition*, pages 809–816, 2011.

[29] W. Zhou, Y. Lu, H. Li, Y. Song, and Q. Tian. Spatial Coding for Large Scale Partial-Duplicate Web Image Search. In *ACM Multimedia*, pages 511 – 520, 2010.

Efficient Image Annotation for Automatic Sentence Generation

Yoshitaka Ushiku
Grad. School of Information Science and Technology
The University of Tokyo
Tokyo, Japan
ushiku@isi.imi.i.u-tokyo.ac.jp

Tatsuya Harada
Grad. School of Information Science and Technology
The University of Tokyo / JST PRESTO
Tokyo, Japan
harada@isi.imi.i.u-tokyo.ac.jp

Yasuo Kuniyoshi
Grad. School of Information Science and Technology
The University of Tokyo
Tokyo, Japan
kuniyosh@isi.imi.i.u-tokyo.ac.jp

ABSTRACT

Sentence generation from images is an ultimate goal of image recognition. In this paper, we attack a novel problem, the "multi-keyphrase problem", to address this goal. We hypothesize that image contents can be described with multi-keyphrases, and that a natural sentence can be generated by connecting multi-keyphrases with an experimental grammar model. Existing methods require semantic knowledge such as labels of an object, action, or scene. Using these methods, we must strive to prepare a highly organized dataset. Therefore, we propose a novel online learning method for multi-keyphrase estimation. The proposed framework, although simple and scalable, can generate sentences from images with no semantic knowledge. Moreover, the proposed method for multi-keyphrase estimation is applicable to image annotation, and it achieves state-of-the-art performance. Our experiment using only images and texts demonstrates that the proposed framework is useful for sentence generation from images.

Categories and Subject Descriptors

I.2.10 [**Artificial Intelligence**]: Vision and Scene Understanding

General Terms

Algorithms, Theory, Experimentation

Keywords

Online learning, Passive-Aggressive, Multi-stack decoding

1. INTRODUCTION

With advances in information technology, the explosively increasing multimedia environment has created demand for methods by which computers can interpret multimedia contents on behalf of humans. By virtue of such methods, we can use multimedia efficiently. We can seek desired data from vast amounts of multimedia, and we can have computers infer their contents without viewing them.

During this decade, image understanding has been widely studied: image classification [28, 5, 14] to assign each image one label, and image annotation [30, 33] to assign each image some labels. These labels represent the objects' names, actions, holistic scenes, etc.

Recently, as a much more comprehensive method of image understanding, sentence generation from images has been studied. A natural sentence tells us not only each object, action, and scene but also their mutual relations. For example, we can understand not only the existence of "dog", "man", and "bite", but also whether "a man bites a dog" or "a dog bites a man". This inference of their association facilitates more accurate and flexible image understanding.

Almost all existing methods [1, 7, 8, 12, 13, 22, 35, 36] assume well-controlled semantic knowledge, objects, actions, scenes, and so on. However, using these methods, we must manage the label set for each attribute and manually associate the labels to each image. Consequently, the dataset tends to be small, and tends to lack coverage to generate sentences from various images.

In general terms, collecting a large amount of data from the web is a common means to understand various images. What we can collect automatically are images associated not with semantically clear labels but with surrounding sentences and uncontrolled words. Indeed, [22] collects a million pairs of an image and a sentential caption from the web for sentence generation from images.

Our objective is to generate a sentence such as "A man bites a white dog in his arms." even from an unusual image like an example in the left of Fig.1 because, on Web, there are many unusual images which we tend to feel amusing. Estimating the goal sentence from image features directly is unrealistic because learning among various images and huge quantities of word combinations is necessary. Although not a complete sentence, however, we can estimate some descriptive phrases[1] (keyphrases) such as "man–bites", "white–dog", and "his–arms" and combine them into a sentence with an experimental grammar knowledge: we know that "in" tends

[1]As described in this paper, a phrase means just a sequence of words. It has no other grammatical meaning.

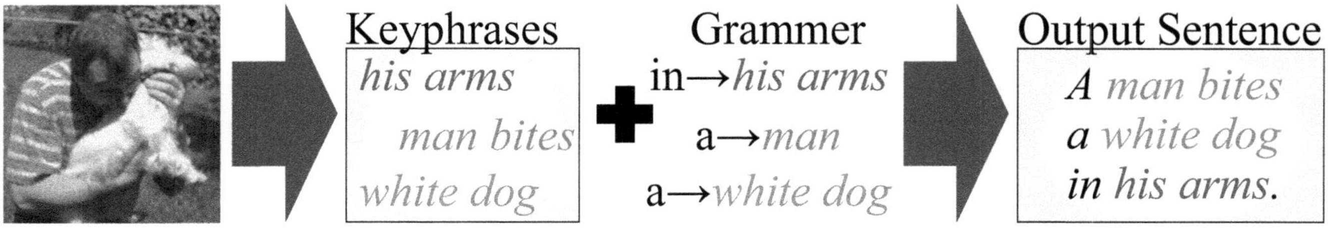

Figure 1: Pipeline of the proposed framework. We first estimate some *keyphrases* from an input image. Then a sentential caption is generated by spinning them with an experimental grammar model.

to come immediately before "his arms", an indefinite article would tend to come immediately before "white dog" and "man", and so on. Therefore we infer the following, and propose a novel but simple framework to generate sentences through *multi-keyphrase* estimation.

HYPOTHESIS 1. *Almost all contents of an image are identifiable with a few descriptive phrases (keyphrases). A sentential caption can be generated by connecting these with an experimental grammar model.*

In this paper, we present a novel problem, called *Multi-keyphrase Problem* for sentence generation from images. We seek to learn the relation between *keyphrases* and images from pairs of an image and a sentence, and to obtain a grammar model from the all pairs. Consequently, a proposed framework is extendable for sentence generation from large-scale images because a sentence can be generated with no semantic knowledge such as the object, action, or scene.

Given an input image I, n_p keyphrases are estimated. We define i-th keyphrase K_i as,

$$K_i = \{w_1^{K_i}, \dots, w_{n_w}^{K_i}\}, (i = 1, \dots, n_p), \qquad (1)$$

where w represents a word. As the first step for multi-keyphrase problem, we regard different word sequences as independent labels. Consequently, as a subproblem, a multi-keyphrase problem comes down to image annotation.

In existing works for image annotation, non-parametric approaches are mainstream. With such approaches, an input image is annotated with the labels of images which are located near the input image according to a certain metric. Although multi-keyphrase estimation using such an approach is conceivable, the complexity for calculating the distances between the input image and all N training samples is $O(N)$. This means that the execution time increases with the number of training samples.. Moreover, the state-of-the-art methods require the complexity to be within $O(N) \sim O(N^2)$ for metric learning. Therefore, scalability remains an open question for non-parametric approaches.

To annotate images efficiently, smaller time complexity and higher accuracy are required. Therefore, learning one model for each keyphrase seems to be a good approach. Because we need only match a feature of an input image to all models, the time for keyphrase estimation is $O(1)$ (independent of N). Although some existing works propose such model-based methods [15], their accuracy is inferior to those of non-parametric approaches.

As described in this paper, we interpret a model-based approach as inferior to a non-parametric approach because the learning methods for models are unsuitable for multi-label problems. Existing works mostly use binary classification such as SVM with a one-vs.-the-rest manner. The classifier for a label is obtained by regarding images associated with the label as positive samples and the rest images as negative samples. Furthermore, labels are output according to the scores from the binary classifiers. Nevertheless, no guarantee exists that the output of SVMs for different classifiers will have appropriate scales. Sadghi [26] also proposes image recognition using "Visual Phrases" based on object detection. However, there are following problems: (i) binary classification is performed for each phrase, and (ii) detection-based phrase estimation requires manually managed datasets including bounding boxes.

Therefore, we propose a learning method for a multi-keyphrase problem in which each image is associated with more than one label. The proposed method is formulated by improving online multiclass learning so that more than one label for a training sample can be used efficiently. This method, which is applicable not only to multi-keyphrase estimation but also to image annotation, achieves state-of-the-art performance on some benchmark datasets.

The contributions of this paper are as follows.

- Presentation of a *Multi-keyphrase Problem* for sentence generation from images.
- Proposal of a multi-label learning method for annotation, a subproblem of *Multi-keyphrase Problem.*
- Validation of the proposed method for multi-label learning using datasets for image annotation. We achieved state-of-the-art performance on these datasets.
- Validation of the proposed approach by which sentences are generated by connecting keyphrases with an experimental grammar model using a dataset only with images and sentences.

The remainder of this paper is organized as follows: Sec. 2 describes related works. Sec. 3 presents the proposed framework and a practical method for estimating multi-keyphrase and connecting the estimated keyphrases. Sec. 4 shows that our method obtains state-of-the-art accuracy on the datasets for image annotation. Then, in Sec. 5, we confirm the utility of the proposed framework through experiments using a dataset including images and sentences only. Finally, Sec. 6 concludes our manuscript and presents future works.

2. RELATED WORKS

This section introduces existing works for sentence generation from images at first. Secondly, we describe related works for image annotation, a subproblem of the presented multi-keyphrase problem.

2.1 Sentence Generation from Images

Sentence generation from image contents was started by [36] published in 2010. An input image was segmented for each object, and each segment was homologized to a verbal expression. Finally, an output sentence was generated using these expressions while maintaining correct grammar. Since this approach requires numerous special datasets for each process, extension to a dataset of various images is difficult.

Some methods in the literature reuse the whole sentence associated with the training image that is sought from an input image. In [7], all images are labeled with a triplet: ⟨ object, action, scene ⟩. An image with the same labels estimated from an input image is retrieved. In another method [22], images are labeled according to their objects, stuff, people, and scenes from different datasets. Similarity to estimated labels from an input image and matching of local descriptors are used to search for similar images from one million images. To use a whole sentence directly, vastly numerous images related to all combinations of image contents must be used. Moreover, similar images must be retrieved exactly from such a supergiant dataset.

Therefore, some works generate a new sentence. In [12], images are explained sententially with respect to the objects' name, number, and their spatial relations by learning objects, stuff, and attributes from different datasets. [35] extended the concepts described earlier in [7] to generate a new sentence learning not only ⟨ object, action, and scene ⟩ but also preposition. Although new sentences can be generated, many datasets must be used for each attribute.

Another method [1] uses the geo tag of an input image to retrieve related articles and summarize them as a sentential caption. This approach is useful for some contents such as landmarks. Previous works described by Feng [8] and by Ushiku [31] are most related to our work. Feng [8] used an annotation method to generate a sentence from images. Ushiku [31] also applies a method for image annotation, called Canonical Contextual Distance (CCD) [19]. With CCD, distances in image feature space are improved according to labels. [31] modified CCD to use not labels but sentences associated with images. Then images that are similar to an input image are sought and a sentence is generated from the sentences associated with those images.

The weaknesses of these methods are as follows. First, as one example, [8] requires manual selection of labels, subject, actions, and adjectives. Furthermore, although an output sentence is generated by connecting phrases, [8] regards phrases as grammatical. Because parsing and word tagging are necessary for grammatical phrase extraction, (i) additional training datasets for parsing and tagging are also required and (ii) mistakes of these process ill-affect generated sentences. Secondly, the approach described in [31], from another perspective, estimates phrases to generate a sentence from similar images' sentences. However, (i) time spent on neighbor search increases linearly with the number of training samples, and (ii) absence of grammar model might make the generated sentences unnatural.

In this paper, we regard arbitrary word sequences as phrases and generate natural sentences using an experimental grammar model. Additionally, we investigate an efficient multi-keyphrase estimation method. The proposed method for multi-keyphrase estimation takes constant time for the data amount and tolerate noise like some phrases which are irrelevant to the contents of images.

2.2 Image Annotation

As described in Sec. 1, our method for multi-keyphrase estimation is related to image annotation, a problem to estimate multiple labels for one image. A non-parametric approach, with which training labels of neighbor samples are used for annotation, is undertaken in [11]

Recently, almost all existing works have adopted a wide range of image features. Joint Equal Contribution (JEC) [17] uses color histograms and wavelets, and computes the distances from an input image and all training samples with a proper metric[2]. All distances are normalized and are simply summed up to search for neighbor samples. Although simple, [17] achieved state-of-the-art performance in 2008 when the method was proposed. TagProp [10] uses 15 features such as Gist [21], Bag-of-Features representation of SIFT [16], and color histograms. TagProp learns the proper weight of each distance to obtain the best performance whereas JEC simply adds those distances. Moreover, TagProp learns the weight for each label in neighbor samples because minor labels that are rarely associated with images are not often used for annotation TagProp applies the logistic discriminant model to learn the weight of labels. Therefore, TagProp, proposed in 2009, has achieved state-of-the-art performance on several benchmark datasets to date. In 2011, [29] proposed 43 features from foreground and background inferred according to saliency, for integration with TagProp. In some cases, [29] yields slightly superior performance to that of TagProp. In [19], Canonical Contextual Distance (CCD) is proposed. With CCD, low-dimensional space is computed using probabilistic canonical correlation analysis with image features and label features so that correlations between image features and label features might be largest. Thus distances between image features are improved thanks to similarities between labels; the performance of CCD is comparable to that of TagProp [18].

However, the more important problem with a non-parametric approach is the computational cost. As described in Sec. 1, calculating all distances between an input image and all training samples is necessary for annotation. Therefore, the time used for annotation increases linearly with the data amount. Regarding the computational cost for the learning metric, JEC is constant to the data amount because it needs only feature extraction. TagProp and CCD require all distances between training samples for metric learning. Although they make efforts so that learning can be performed only with distances among all samples and a part of all samples, the number of a part of all samples will increase when the whole dataset increases. Consequently, they lack scalability as the training time increases to become more than linear to the data amount.

To realize scalability, usage of a linear classifier appears to be a promising method. When each image has only a single label, the problem of estimating the label is designated as image classification. In this area, as pipeline alternatives to Bag-of-Features of SIFT and Kernel SVM, richer image representation than Bag-or-Features and linear SVM is actively pursued [25, 32]. With these image representations, feature extraction and learning for classification can be done linearly to the data amount. Moreover, the time for label estimation is constant to the data amount.

[2]For example, χ^2 distance is ideal for histograms, L_1 distance is ideal for the wavelets.

However, existing work uses SVM for annotation is inferior to JEC proposed in the same year. We claim that binary classification with SVM is inappropriate for multi-class settings such as annotation. As described in Sec. 1, in the one-versus-the-rest manner, all samples are divided into positive or negative for each class. However, it renders positive and negative samples as highly imbalanced, and no guarantee exists that the output of SVMs for different classifiers will have appropriate scales.

Recent studies for large scale image classification adopt online learning for linear classification. In [28, 14], high-dimensional features in [25, 32] are used for learning 1000 classes from over a million images. Batch learning by loading all training samples is impossible. Therefore, online SVM learning with Stochastic Gradient Descent[2] (SGD-SVM) is applied. In an online learning scheme, each training sample is classified repeatedly with the classifiers at the time. Then some are updated if a mistake occurs. For reading one training sample at a time, online learning is suitable for a large dataset. Moreover, [2] reports that it is the same in classification performance, although it is faster than the batch SVM. However, SVM has problems presented above.

In this paper, therefore, other online algorithms of multi-classification—Passive-Aggressive (PA) [3], and Normal distribution HERDing (NHERD) [4]—are investigated. Indeed, Weston [34] proposes an online learning method for image annotation. The authors devote their attentions to develop an algorithm fits on a laptop. Though various approximations are included, their method outperforms approximated nearest neighbor and binary PA. Moreover, we propose a novel learning method for training samples with multiple labels by generalizing PA. The method is called Passive-Aggressive with Averaged Pairwise Loss (PAAPL).

3. SENTENCE GENERATION WITH MULTI-KEYPHRASE ESTIMATION

In this section, we first describe the means to extract keyphrases to be learned. Secondly we describe the methods used to estimate keyphrases. Finally, we explain the method used for spinning keyphrases into one sentence.

3.1 Multi-keyphrase Extraction

Learning with noisy keyphrases unrelated to images harms the accuracy of multi-keyphrase estimation. Therefore, we investigate a filter to extract keyphrases from each sentence of an image. We want to select phrases (i), which are related to the image contents and (ii), which appear to some extent in many sentences. Consequently, we investigate two filters.

Local TF-IDF filter. We regard the typicality of each phrase as a clue to how the phrase relates to the image's contents. For example, some phrases such as "is a" and "this is" appear frequently though the phrases and are apparently irrelevant to the contents. Conversely, "living room" and "black dog" are expected to be typical phrases. Therefore, we regard phrases which appear many times in the sentence (high Term Frequency) and which rarely appear in other sentences (Inverse Document Frequency) as typical. Therefore, top-n_k TF-IDF [27] valued phrases are extracted.

Global DF filter. With local TF-IDF filter, overly rare phrases are unsuitable for model learning because small samples for a phrase might engender low accuracy. Here we make much of the sample size for each keyphrase to learn it stably. We extract phrases only according to bounds of n_d, the number of samples where each phrase appears.

3.2 Baselines of Multi-keyphrase Learning

Whichever filter we employ, some noisy phrases exist in extracted keyphrases. To learn the models for each keyphrase from various images, requirements are not only compatibility of scalability for the data amount and accuracy for keyphrase estimation, but also tolerability of noise.

Given the t-th training sample $\boldsymbol{x}_t \in \mathbb{R}^d$ associated with a label set Y_t, a subset of $\mathcal{Y} = \{1, \ldots, n_y\}$, it is classified with the present weight vector $\boldsymbol{\mu}_t^{y_i}$ $(i = 1, \ldots, n_y)^3$ as,

$$\hat{y}_t = \arg\max_{y_i} \boldsymbol{\mu}_t^{y_i} \cdot \boldsymbol{x}_t. \quad (2)$$

If necessary, multiple labels are estimated in score order.

Multi-labeling for one sample is applicable by defining $n_y > 1$. Here, hinge-loss ℓ is given as,

$$\ell(\boldsymbol{\mu}_t^{r_t}, \boldsymbol{\mu}_t^{s_t}; (\boldsymbol{x}_t, Y_t)) = \begin{cases} 0 & \boldsymbol{\mu}_t^{r_t} \cdot \boldsymbol{x}_t - \boldsymbol{\mu}_t^{s_t} \cdot \boldsymbol{x}_t \geq 1 \\ 1 - (\boldsymbol{\mu}_t^{r_t} \cdot \boldsymbol{x}_t - \boldsymbol{\mu}_t^{s_t} \cdot \boldsymbol{x}_t) & \text{otherwise} \end{cases}. \quad (3)$$

where $r_t = \arg\min_{r \in Y_t} \boldsymbol{\mu}_t^r \cdot \boldsymbol{x}_t$ and $s_t = \arg\max_{s \notin Y_t} \boldsymbol{\mu}_t^s \cdot \boldsymbol{x}_t$.

3.2.1 PA

PA is an online learning method for binary and multiclass classification, regression, uniclass estimation and structure estimation. The biggest benefit of PA is that the update coefficient is analytically calculated according to the loss. In contrast, SGD based methods and traditional perceptron require designing the coefficient.

Here we seek to decrease the hinge-loss of multi-classification and not to change the weight radically. Consequently, we obtain the following formulation.

$$\boldsymbol{\mu}_{t+1}^{r_t}, \boldsymbol{\mu}_{t+1}^{s_t} = \arg\min_{\boldsymbol{\mu}^{r_t}, \boldsymbol{\mu}^{r_t}} ||\boldsymbol{\mu}^{r_t} - \boldsymbol{\mu}_t^{r_t}||^2 + ||\boldsymbol{\mu}^{s_t} - \boldsymbol{\mu}_t^{s_t}||^2 + C\xi, \quad (4)$$

$$\text{s.t. } \ell(\boldsymbol{\mu}^{r_t}, \boldsymbol{\mu}^{s_t}; (\boldsymbol{x}_t, Y_t)) \leq \xi \text{ and } \xi \geq 0. \quad (5)$$

Therein, ξ denotes a slack variable representing the bound of the loss. C signifies a parameter to reduce the negative influence of noisy labels. It can be derived using Lagrange's method of undetermined multipliers. Therefore we obtain,

$$\boldsymbol{\mu}_{t+1}^{r_t} = \boldsymbol{\mu}_t^{r_t} + \tau_t \cdot \boldsymbol{x}_t, \; \boldsymbol{\mu}_{t+1}^{s_t} = \boldsymbol{\mu}_t^{s_t} - \tau_t \cdot \boldsymbol{x}_t, \quad (6)$$

$$\tau_t = \min\{C, \ell(\boldsymbol{\mu}_t^{r_t}, \boldsymbol{\mu}_t^{s_t}; (\boldsymbol{x}_t, Y_t))/(2||\boldsymbol{x}_t||^2)\}. \quad (7)$$

This PA is called PA-I in [3]. NHERD has a generalized form of PA-II. PA and SGD-SVM have a closed form. Indeed, PA for binary classification and SGD-SVM without L_2 regularization have the same update rule. Differences between SGD-SVM and PA-I here are (1) binary or multi-class, (2) regularization form, and (3) the number of parameter to be tuned. Consequently, not only SGD-SVM but also PA can be regarded as online learning for SVM.

3.2.2 NHERD

The main difference between NHERD and PA is that NHERD has not only a weight $\boldsymbol{\mu}$ but also the confidence

[3]Here, the bias b is included in $\boldsymbol{\mu}_t$ as $\boldsymbol{\mu}_t^\top \leftarrow [\boldsymbol{\mu}_t^\top, b]$ by redefining $\boldsymbol{x}_t^\top \leftarrow [\boldsymbol{x}_t^\top, 1]$

weight Σ, a diagonal $d \times d$ matrix. If a classifier learns about a certain dimension of feature vectors many times, then the classifier must be more confident about the dimension. In other words, the classifier is expected to update less-confident-dimensions as larger. Therefore, NHERD considers $\boldsymbol{\mu}$ as a normal distribution $\mathcal{N}(\boldsymbol{\mu}, \Sigma)$, and literally "herds" normal distributions with linear transform $\boldsymbol{\mu}_{t+1} = A_t\boldsymbol{\mu}_t + \boldsymbol{b}_t$.

3.3 Proposed Multi-keyphrase Learning

Both PA and NHERD are online learning methods for classification, but it presents no problem if a sample is associated with multiple labels. Indeed, the Passive–Aggressive Model for Image Retrieval (PAMIR) [9] is proposed by application of PA to image retrieval.

However, they treat only one relevant label and one irrelevant label. Apparently, models of some labels are not well updated and that convergence becomes delayed.

Therefore, we propose a novel online learning algorithm for which multiple labels are attached to one sample. As discussed in Sec. 2, general online learning methods consist of two steps: classification of the t-th sample, and update of the t-th models. Given the d-dimensional weight vectors $\boldsymbol{\mu}$ for all n_y labels, the complexity for classification of a sample is $O(dn_y)$, while the complexity for update of a model is $O(d)$. If we update all models with given labels Y_t, its complexity becomes $O(d|Y_t|)$. In image annotation and especially sentence generation, we can assume $n_y \gg |Y_t|$. Therefore, since classification is the rate-controlling step, total computation time remains much the same whether we update one model or $|Y_t|$ models. Fig.2 shows the conceptual difference between hinge-loss and the loss used in proposed method. Thus the proposed PAAPL achieves efficiency by averaging all pairwise loss between relevant and irrelevant labels.

1. Given a t-th image, define label set $\bar{Y}_t$ of n_y labels by selecting highly scored and irrelevant labels.
2. Randomly select one relevant label r_t from Y_t and one irrelevant label s_t from $\bar{Y}_t$.
3. Based on a hinge-loss between r_t and s_t, $1-(\boldsymbol{\mu}_t^{r_t} \cdot \boldsymbol{x}_t - \boldsymbol{\mu}_t^{s_t} \cdot \boldsymbol{x}_t)$, update models according to PA.

Additionally, we investigate a way to reduce the complexity $O(dn_y)$ for the classification step. In [34], the approximation of a loss function by the random selection of labels is an important step for online learning when using less powerful computers. Although random selection may miss incorrectly-classified labels at a higher rate, it was experimentally verified that correct models can be obtained eventually. Therefore, we also adopted random selection.

1. Randomly select one relevant label r_t from Y_t.
2. Define irrelevant label s_t with random selection from $\bar{Y}_t$ and compute the hinge-loss $1-(\boldsymbol{\mu}_t^{r_t} \cdot \boldsymbol{x}_t - \boldsymbol{\mu}_t^{s_t} \cdot \boldsymbol{x}_t)$. Continue selecting s_t until the loss becomes positive.
3. If the hinge-loss becomes positive, update models for r_t and s_t according to PA; otherwise move on to next training sample.

3.4 From Multi-keyphrases to a Sentence

Generated sentences for an input image I_t are expected to include many keyphrases and must be grammatically correct. We can solve a sentence-generation problem by minimizing the sum of costs: phrase cost $\phi_p(w_1, \ldots, w_n)$, and length cost $\phi_l(l)$. The optimization problem is,

$$\{w_1, \ldots, w_l\} = \underset{w_1,\ldots,w_l}{\arg\min}\, \phi_l(l) + \lambda_p \sum \phi_p(w_1, \ldots, w_n), \quad (8)$$

where λ_p is weight parameter for phrase cost. This problem can be regarded as an integer programming, but the length cost complicates this problem. Therefore, we investigated the effects of relaxation using multi-stack beam search modified in [31]. Beam searching saves some high rank candidate sentences in one stack. The stacks are divided according to the length of the generated sentence. The highest-ranked sentence wedged between two edge-of-sentences (EOS), which is a special word representing the edge of a sentence, is chosen as the output. If there are too few contents compared to the target length, keyphrases are quickly expended, leading a large increase in grammar cost and ultimately shortening the generated sentences. Thus, short sentences are generated for images with little content.

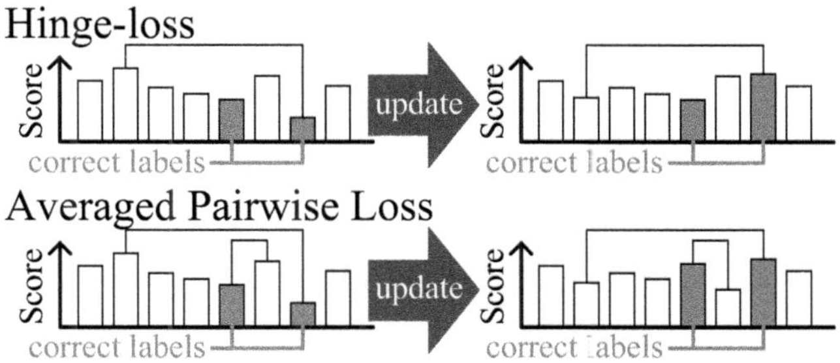

Figure 2: Comparison between hinge-loss and averaged pairwise loss.

The rest of this section describes the details of the costs terms/functions.

3.4.1 Phrase Cost

The phrase cost is calculated with two probability functions. Given a phrase $\{w_1, \ldots, w_n\}$, the phrase is evaluated with the keyphrase probability $P_k(w_1, \ldots, w_n|I_t)$ if the phrase is one of the estimated keyphrases $\mathcal{K}$ for the input image I_t. Otherwise, the phrase is evaluated with the grammar probability $P_g(w_{n_g}|w_1, \ldots, w_{n_g-1})$.

$$\phi_p(w_1, \ldots, w_n) = \begin{cases} -\log P_k(w_1, \ldots, w_n|I_t) & \{w_1, \ldots, w_l\} \in \mathcal{K} \\ -\log P_g(w_n|w_1, \ldots, w_{n-1}) & \text{otherwise} \end{cases}. \quad (9)$$

For grammar probability, we investigate a well-known ngram model which uses statistical frequency $P_g(w_n; w_1, \ldots, w_{n-1})$ to estimate a word w_n after a word sequence $\{w_1, \ldots, w_{n-1}\}$. The ngram model is a common method for natural language processing (e.g., statistical machine translation).

Alternatively, the combination of two probabilities like $\phi_p = -\log P_k - \lambda_g \log_g P_g$ with a weight parameter λ_g is plausible. In this paper, however, we simply encourage the maximal use of keyphrases by defining $P_k(w_1, \ldots, w_n|I_t) = 1$ in order to investigate the influence of the keyphrase estimation on the accuracy of generated sentences.

3.4.2 Length Cost

Using only phrase cost tends to generate sentences that are too short because the cost sum increases with sentence length increases. Thus we introduce the following length cost with the target length $l_0 = 10 + 2$ EOS as,

$$\phi_l(l) = -\log P_l(l), \tag{10}$$

where $P_l \propto \mathcal{N}(l_0, \sigma_0)$, and σ_0 represents strictness of length.

4. EVALUATION OF MULTI-KEYPHRASE ESTIMATION

In this section, we evaluate the proposed method for multi-keyphrase estimation. Particularly, we investigate performances of image annotation using three benchmark datasets.

4.1 Experiment Setting

We use the following three de-facto standard datasets. As described in [10], Corel5k is relatively easy to learn. What we have to did is compare the performance on more than one datasets.

Corel 5k. Corel 5k consists of about 4500 training samples and 500 test samples. Each training sample is associated with 3.4 labels, on average, from 260 labels.

ESP Game. ESP Game has about 60,000 images that are manually annotated through a game. Existing works for annotation [17, 10] select about 20,000 images. Each image is associated with 4.7 labels, on average, from 268 labels.

IAPR-TC12. IAPR-TC12 is released for image retrieval between several languages. Existing works for annotation [17, 10] select about 20,000 images. Each training sample is associated with 5.7 labels, on average, from 291 labels.

As an image feature, we use Fisher Vector (FV) [25] from SIFT [16]. We extracted SIFT descriptor from a regular grid with step size 6 pixels at multiple scales: 16×16, 25×25, 36×36, 49×49, and 64×64. Then we reduce the dimensions to 64 using PCA, and obtain a Gaussian Mixture Model (GMM) with 256 components. Then FV is calculated respectively over 1×1, 2×2, and 3×1 cells.

As ESP Game and IAPR-TC12 has many data, we reduce the memory usage with Product Quantization (PQ) according to [28]. We divide FV into each of eight dimension vectors, and generate 256 clusters using k-means method. All FVs of training samples are quantized with those clusters, and approximated with the centroids of each cluster when learning with the training sample.

For a fair comparison of annotation method, we also use 15 features provided in the paper of TagProp [10]. To combine different features, we independently learn the models for each feature at first, and estimate labels for test samples with the sum of the scores from models of each feature. We sum every score in annotation performance order and continue summing while the integrated performance increases.

We evaluate the performance for annotation with the following three indicators. Given a sample, we define the number a as correctly estimated labels, b as correct labels, and c as estimated labels.

Precision (*P*). The ratio of correctly estimated labels to estimated labels, i.e., $P = a/c$.

Recall (*R*). The ratio of correctly estimated labels to correct labels i.e., $R = b/c$.

F-measure (*F*). Because there is a tradeoff between Precision and Recall, we use the harmonic average, i.e.,

$$F = \frac{2 \times P \times R}{P + R} = \frac{2ab}{(a+b)c} \tag{11}$$

Table 1: Comparison of performance in terms of *P*, *R*, and *F* on Corel 5K.

	P	***R***	***F***
JEC [17]	27	32	29
Matrix Factorization [15]	29	29	29
TagProp [10]	33	42	37
CCD [18]	36	41	38
TagProp43 [29]	35	41	37
PAAPL on 15 features	**40**	**57**	**47**
PAAPL on FV	**44**	**62**	**51**

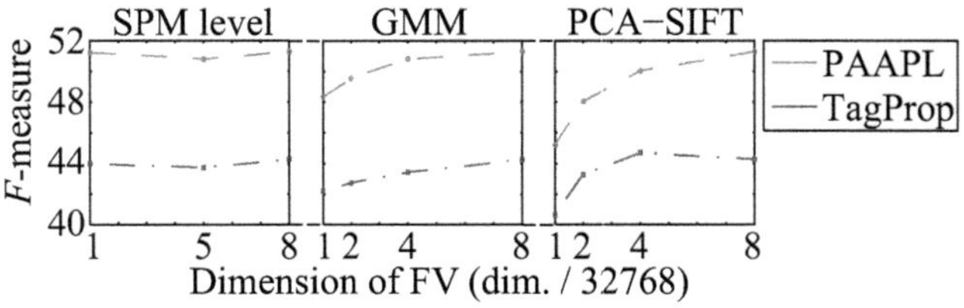

Figure 3: Comparison between PAAPL and TagProp with lower dimensional FVs.

Following existing works, we fix $c = 5$. Additionally, we multiply all indicators by 100, i.e., $0 \leq P, R, F \leq 100$.

4.2 Experiment Result on Benchmark Datasets

We present the result of annotation with Corel 5k in Table 1. TagProp43 [29] represents the integration of 43 features proposed in [29] and metric learning with TagProp. PAAPL on 15 features uses 15 features provided in the paper of TagProp [10][4]. As shown in Table 1, we outperform existing works. Even if TagProp's 15 features are used, the performance of PAAPL is superior to that of TagProp.

Moreover, the combination of proposed PAAPL and FV achieves the best F-measure of 51. However, the combination of FV and TagProp is not reported. Moreover, high-dimensional features are incompatible with neighbor search. Therefore, we reduce the dimensions of FV with following way and compare the performance of PAAPL and TagProp.

SPM level. Reduce the SPM cells from $1\times1+2\times2+3\times1$ (262144 dim.) to $1 \times 1 + 2 \times 2$ (163840 dim.), and to 1×1 (32768 dim.).

GMM component. Reduce the components of GMM from 256 (262144 dim.) to 128 (131072 dim.), to 64 (65536 dim.), and to 32 (32768 dim.).

PCA-SIFT dimension. Reduce the dimensions with PCA from 64 (262144 dim.) to 32 (131072 dim.), to 16 (65536 dim.), and to 8 (32768 dim.).

A comparison of results is shown in Fig.3. First, the combination of FV and TagProp is also superior to existing results on Corel 5k. Secondly, SPM does not affect the performance on Corel 5k because FV for whole image itself has sufficient isolation for this dataset. Thirdly, FV with 32 dim. PCA-SIFT is better than full FV for TagProp. Finally, with all FVs, PAAPL outperformed TagProp.

Next we compare the respective convergence speeds of

[4]Features and codes of TagProp are provided on http://lear.inrialpes.fr/pubs/2009/GMVS09/.

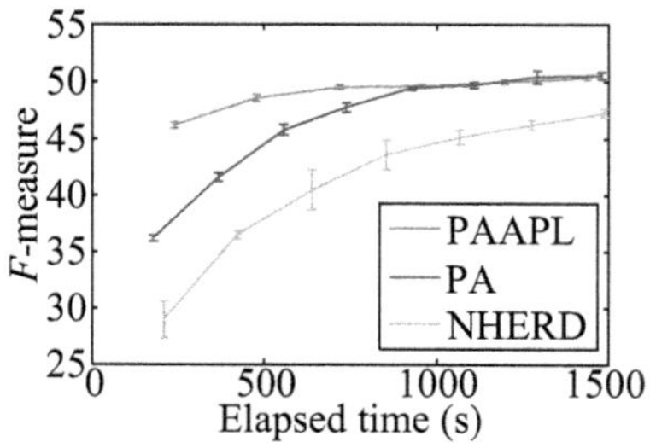

Figure 4: Convergence comparison conducted among online learning methods.

Table 2: Comparison of performance in terms of *P*, *R*, and *F* on ESP Game and IAPR-TC12.

	ESP Game			IAPR-TC12		
	P	*R*	*F*	*P*	*R*	*F*
JEC [17]	22	25	23	28	29	28
TagProp [10]	39	27	32	46	35	40
CCD [18]	36	24	29	44	29	35
TagProp43 [29]	43	23	30	-	-	-
PAAPL on 15 features	32	**35**	**33**	40	**38**	39
PAAPL on FV	36	**40**	**38**	38	**36**	37

Table 3: Statistics of all phrases and filtered phrases with local TF-IDF. The upper side of each cell represents the number of training samples include at least one keyphrase. The lower side represents the number of keyphrases.

Local TF-IDF					All
top-1	top-3	top-5	top-7	top-9	∞
900	900	900	900	900	900
764.6	1983.6	3117.0	4504.2	6111.0	15443.2

Table 4: Statistics of filtered phrases with global DF. The upper side of each cell represents the number of training samples include at least one keyphrase. The lower side represents the number of keyphrases.

Bound		Upper 300	Upper 200	Upper 100
Lower	5	900.0	900.0	900.0
		1226.6	1221.8	1207.8
	10	900.0	900.0	899.6
		500.6	495.8	481.8
	50	889.0	863.6	694.6
		43.4	38.6	24.6

PAAPL, PA, and NHERD. Note that all methods are implemented using MATLAB. Fig.4 shows the performances at every iteration. The proposed PAAPL obtains good performance with a few iterations. Such a trend will become pronounced in multi-keyphrase estimation using many more labels. Indeed, such a result is obtained in Sec. 5.

We present comparison results of ESP Game and IAPR-TC12 in Table 2. PAAPL is comparable to existing methods on IAPR-TC12 and outperforms them on ESP Game. Note that the computational time for learning is proportional to the data amount and that for annotation is constant in relation to the data amount. Because the proposed method achieves a better score than TagProp, the scalability of which is a problem, PAAPL is shown to be competitive.

5. EXPERIMENT AND DISCUSSION OF SENTENCE GENERATION

In this section, PASCAL Sentence [7] is used for experimentation. It has 20 categories, each with 50 images. Each image has about five captions of around 10 words each. We split the dataset into training data and test data according to [31]: 45 pairs of an image and a text per category are chosen as training samples. All splits are defined randomly five times. Then the scores are averaged.

We regard [31], which also uses only PASCAL Sentence, as a baseline. Therefore, we extract the same features and perform the same dimension reduction as a preprocess. As an image feature for the shape information, we extracted a SIFT descriptor from a regular grid with step size 6 pixels at 16×16 scale. Then LLC with 1024 codewords is calculated respectively over 1×1, 2×2, and 4×4 cells. For the texture information, we extract HLAC [23], Gist [21], and LBP [20].

Additionally, as [31] does, we extract word TF-IDF vectors as text features and reduce the dimension of image feature with Canonical Contextual Distance (CCD) [19]. Because CCD is a name for a metric, we refer to compressed features as Canonical Contextual Coordinate (C^3). Because keyphrases are estimated through neighbor search in this space in [31], we refer [31] as C^3+knn.

We extract two-word sequences as keyphrases and learn the model by PA, NHERD, and PAAPL with 10 iterations on C^3. Then keyphrases are connected with the grammar model consisting of bigram and trigram. We adopt the standard back-off smoothing because the training samples are too few to accurately estimate ngram. We define $\lambda_p = 0.05$, and estimate five keyphrases. Alternatively, we extract FV with the same protocol in Sec. 4 and generate sentences through multi-keyphrase learning.

Keyphrases are extracted according to the filter described in Sec. 3. The statistics of the number of keyphrases and usable training samples are presented in Table 3 and Table 4: for statistics with no filter and local TF-IDF filter, and for the statistics with global DF filter, respectively. The number of top phrases to be used, n_k, is defined 1, 3, 5, 7, or 9. The bounds of n_d, the number of samples where each phrase appears are defined so that the number of samples for each phrase might be ensured and so that over-frequent (and meaningless) phrases such as "is-a" might be eliminated.

5.1 Examples of Generated Sentences

Fig.6 presents some examples of generated sentences. As shown, sentences can be generated by using as many keyphrases as the method can. We can learn keyphrases about spatial relations (e.g., "in front") because we extract features using Spatial Pyramid and grid cells and preserve spatial information. Moreover, words which do not appear in the keyphrases can be used in interpolated from keyphrases found using the ngram model.

Table 5: **Accuracy of multi-keyphrase estimation and of generated sentence for each method.**

	P	R	F	BLEU	NIST
C^3+knn (baseline)	2.6	0.6	1.0	3.59±0.82	2.03±0.04
C^3+knn+Ngram	2.6	0.6	1.0	3.68±0.67	2.01±0.03
C^3+PA+Ngram	6.4	1.5	2.5	4.90±1.50	2.31±0.20
C^3+NHERD+Ngram	6.4	1.5	2.4	4.99±1.07	2.20±0.21
C^3+PAAPL+Ngram (proposed)	**20.2**	**4.9**	**7.8**	**6.15±2.07**	**2.34±0.11**
FV+PAAPL+Ngram (proposed)	**26.9**	**6.4**	**10.4**	**7.52±1.89**	**2.65±0.18**

5.2 Automatic Evaluation

Automatic evaluation for generated sentence is important and difficult. Some studies [7, 35, 36] evaluated the sentences using humans instead of automatic evaluation. However, it is extremely difficult to compare the performance without automatic evaluation. Automatic evaluation is difficult mainly because of the large variety of representations for one image. Even if each image has one correct sentential caption, as do other benchmark datasets for other image recognition, processing word order variation and synonyms appropriately is difficult.

Some works [22, 1, 12, 13] use automatic evaluations for statistical machine translation. In addition, for statistical machine translation, evaluation adopting word order variation and synonyms is ideal. Evaluation methods such as BLEU [24] and NIST [6] subsume that various reference translations are associated with one test datum. The translation output is evaluated in terms of the degree to which word sequences are common in output and references. Consequently, because word order variation and synonyms are partly adapted, correlation between automatic evaluations and human evaluations exists. [12] shows low correlation between BLEU and human evaluation, but this is true because references of the types in PASCAL Sentence and their Baby Talk differ greatly: PASCAL Sentence describes the main content of each image, whereas Baby Talk describes all objects' names, numbers, and their local relations.

Therefore, we use BLEU and NIST for evaluation[5] with the default order of ngrams for BLEU (up to 4-gram) and NIST (up to 5-gram). Using multiple evaluations, the performance comparison is more reliable.

5.3 Discussion

The performance of multi-keyphrase estimation and accuracy of generated sentence of all compared methods including the base line is shown in Table 5. For a fair comparison to baseline, we show the results when using all phrases as keyphrases. PA and NHERD is superior to knn in terms of multi-keyphrase estimation, however, PAAPL clearly outperforms other methods because the convergence of PA and NHERD with normal hinge-loss becomes much delayed in the situation where one image has multiple phrases. For the accuracy of generated sentences, PAAPL achieves the best score. Merely applying a grammar model to baseline [31] does not affect the accuracy. Although PA and NHERD outperform knn in terms of keyphrase estimation, the accuracy of the generated sentence does not increase greatly.

Fig.5 shows the result of PAAPL with FV and each keyphrase filter. As it is shown, global DF filter with $300 \geq n_d \geq 10$ yields the best performance. Though the accuracy increases with larger n_k of local TF-IDF filter, Table 3 and Table 4 show that the number of keyphrases from local TF-IDF filter with $n_k = 9$ is much larger than that from global DF filter with $300 \geq n_d \geq 10$. It can be said that a phrase should be regarded as a keyphrase when the sample numbers which contain the phrase are greater than the lower bound.

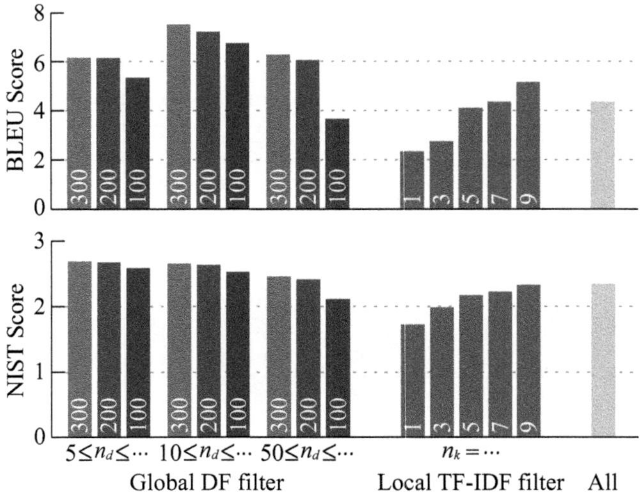

Figure 5: Accuracy of generated sentences with each filter for keyphrase extraction.

Although the proposed method achieves the best result, the performance still must be improved mainly because the keyphrases are large w.r.t. the number of training samples. In [13], manually generated sentences for images get BLEU of almost 50. Low accuracy of multi-keyphrase estimation harms the final performance of generated sentences.

The simplest way to cope with the shortage of training samples is collecting a larger dataset. Because the proposed method is applicable for a large dataset, the accuracy of generated sentence will be improved when numerous data consisting of pairs of an image and a sentence are collected.

Another way to improve the accuracy is interpretation of a multi-keyphrase problem by introducing "structure learning" which adjusts the weights for keyphrase according to differences in temporal outputs and references. In this paper, we raise and tackle this problem by resolution into image annotation for the first step. Consequently, for example, "dog-bites" and "dog-sits" are regarded as independent labels. However, these phrases are common in the sense of

[5]In particular, we use the evaluation tool provided by NIST (http://www.itl.nist.gov/iad/mig/tools/).

treating "dog". Updating not only models of keyphrases directly attached to the training sample but also models of keyphrases which partially conform to attached keyphrases improves the accuracy. Moreover, many images are associated not even with sentences but with some words on Web. We can reduce the ratio to estimate irrelevant keyphrases incorrectly by using such labels.

6. CONCLUSION AND FUTURE WORK

In this paper, we propose a novel approach to generate sentences from images. We present *Multi-keyphrase Problem* to estimate keyphrases and to generate a sentence by connecting the keyphrases using a grammar model. Our method requires only pairs of an image and an associated sentence. Manual preparation of semantic knowledge such as subjects, actions, scenes is not necessary.

Because we consider different word sequences as independent phrases, the multi-keyphrase problem is reduced to image annotation. Therefore, we propose a novel online learning called PAAPL for training samples with multiple labels.

Experimental results demonstrate that sentences can be generated with the proposed framework. The accuracy of generated sentences is better than that of the existing work. Moreover, the proposed PAAPL method is superior in terms of scalability and performance on image annotation. However, its accuracy is still low, mainly because *keyphrase* estimation requires more training samples, as discussed in Sec. 5. Our feature work is development of a learning method to update models of phrases that do not appear in the training sample but which have a common subsequence to other phrases which appear in the training sample.

7. REFERENCES

[1] A. Aker and R. Gaizauskas. Generating image descriptions using dependency relational patterns. In *ACL*, 2010.

[2] L. Bottou. Large-Scale Machine Learning with Stochastic Gradient Descent. In *COMPSTAT*, 2010.

[3] K. Crammer, O. Dekel, J. Keshet, S. Shalev-Shwartz, and Y. Singer. Online Passive-Aggressive Algorithms. *JMLR*, 7:551–585, 2006.

[4] K. Crammer and D. D. Lee. Learning via Gaussian Herding. In *NIPS*, 2010.

[5] J. Deng, W. Dong, R. Socher, L.-J. Li, K. Li, and L. Fei-Fei. ImageNet: A Large-Scale Hierarchical Image Database. In *CVPR*, 2009.

[6] G. Doddington. Automatic Evaluation of Machine Translation Quality Using N-gram Co-Occurrence Statistics. In *HLT*, 2002.

[7] A. Farhadi, M. Hejrati, M. A. Sadeghi, P. Young, C. Rashtchian, J. Hockenmaier, and D. Forsyth. Every Picture Tells a Story: Generating Sentences from Images. In *ECCV*, 2010.

[8] Y. Feng and M. Lapata. How Many Words is a Picture Worth? Automatic Caption Generation for News Images. In *ACL*, 2010.

[9] D. Grangier, F. Monay, and S. Bengio. A Discriminative Approach for the Retrieval of Images from Text Queries. In *ECML*, 2006.

[10] M. Guillaumin, T. Mensink, J. Verbeek, and C. Schmid. TagProp: Discriminative Metric Learning in Nearest Neighbor Models for Image Auto-Annotation. In *ICCV*, 2009.

[11] J. Jeon, V. Lavrenko, and R. Manmatha. Automatic Image Annotation and Retrieval using Cross-Media Relevance Models Categories and Subject Descriptors. In *ACM SIGIR*, 2003.

[12] G. Kulkarni, V. Premraj, S. Dhar, S. Li, Y. Choi, A. C. Berg, and T. L. Berg. Baby Talk: Understanding and Generating Image Descriptions. In *CVPR*, 2011.

[13] S. Li, G. Kulkarni, T. L. Berg, A. C. Berg, and Y. Choi. Composing Simple Image Descriptions using Web-scale N-grams. In *CoNLL*, 2011.

[14] Y. Lin, F. Lv, S. Zhu, M. Yang, T. Cour, K. Yu, L. Cao, and T. Huang. Large-scale Image Classification: Fast Feature Extraction and SVM Training. In *CVPR*, 2011.

[15] N. Loeff and A. Farhadi. Scene Discovery by Matrix Factorization. In *ECCV*, 2008.

[16] D. G. Lowe. Distinctive Image Features from Scale-Invariant Keypoints. *IJCV*, 60(2):91–110, 2004.

[17] A. Makadia, V. Pavlovic, and S. Kumar. A New Baselines for Image Annotation. In *ECCV*, 2008.

[18] H. Nakayama. *Linear Distance Metric Learning for Large-scale Generic Image Recognition*. PhD thesis, The University of Tokyo, 2011.

[19] H. Nakayama, T. Harada, and Y. Kuniyoshi. Evaluation of dimensionality reduction methods for image auto-annotation. In *BMVC*, 2010.

[20] T. Ojala, M. Pietikäinen, and D. Harwood. A comparative study of texture measures with classification based on feature distributions. *Pattern Recognition*, 29(1):51–59, 1996.

[21] A. Oliva and A. Torralba. Modeling the shape of the scene: A holistic representation of the spatial envelope. *IJCV*, 42(3):145–175, 2001.

[22] V. Ordonez, G. Kulkarni, and T. L. Berg. Im2Text: Describing Images Using 1 Million Captioned Photographs. In *NIPS*, 2011.

[23] N. Otsu and T. Kurita. A new scheme for practical flexible and intelligent vision systems. In *IAPR Workshop on Computer Vision*, 1988.

[24] K. Papineni, S. Roukos, T. Ward, and W.-J. Zhu. BLEU: a Method for Automatic Evaluation of Machine Translation. In *ACL*, 2002.

[25] F. Perronnin, J. Sánchez, and T. Mensink. Improving the Fisher Kernel for Large-Scale Image Classification. In *ECCV*, 2010.

[26] M. A. Sadeghi and A. Farhadi. Recognition Using Visual Phrases. In *CVPR*, 2011.

[27] G. Salton and C. S. Yang. On the specification of term values in automatic indexing. *Journal of documentation*, 29(4):351–372, 1973.

[28] J. Sánchez and F. Perronnin. High-Dimensional Signature Compression for Large-Scale Image Classification. In *CVPR*, 2011.

[29] S. Sarin, M. Fahrmair, M. Wagner, and W. Kameyama. Holistic Feature Extraction for Automatic Image Annotation. In *MUE*, 2011.

[30] A. Torralba, R. Fergus, and W. T. Freeman. 80 million tiny images: a large dataset for non-parametric object and scene recognition. *IEEE TPAMI*, 30(11):1958–70, 2008.

[31] Y. Ushiku, T. Harada, and Y. Kuniyoshi. Automatic Sentence Generation from Images. In *ACM MM*, 2011.

[32] J. Wang, J. Yang, K. Yu, F. Lv, T. Huang, and Y. Gong. Locality-constrained Linear Coding for Image Classification. In *CVPR*, 2010.

[33] X.-J. Wang, L. Zhang, M. Liu, Y. Li, and W.-Y. Ma. ARISTA - Image Search to Annotation on Billions of Web Photos. In *CVPR*, 2010.

[34] J. Weston, S. Bengio, and N. Usunier. WSABIE: Scaling Up To Large Vocabulary Image Annotation. In *IJCAI*, 2011.

[35] Y. Yang, C. L. Teo, H. Daumé III, and Y. Aloimonos. Corpus-Guided Sentence Generation of Natural Images. In *EMNLP*, 2011.

[36] B. Z. Yao, X. Yang, L. Lin, M. W. Lee, and S.-C. Zhu. I2T: Image Parsing to Text Description. *Proceedings of the IEEE*, 98(8):1485–1508, 2010.

	Input Image	Keyphrases	Sentence	Input Image	Keyphrases	Sentence
Successfully Generated		field EOS front of in front a black tracks EOS	A black and white cow in front of a man.		group of a group EOS two at a front of	Front of a group of people sitting at a table.
		and a sitting on a woman in front front of	Front of a woman in front of people sitting on.		a brown water EOS field EOS brown horse a horse	Sandy field with a brwon horse stainding in a horse.
Keyphrases are Appropriate		and a room with a black computer EOS a computer	Room with a computer and a black and white photo.		front of in front street EOS the street a city	Front of a city skyline in front of the street.
		front of in front is parked bus is a large	E1 bus is parked in front of a large black.		and a room with EOS an dining room front of	A furnished dining room with gardens in front of a.
		a table table EOS at a a group a man	Table with a group of a man in a table.		room with living room and a a small table EOS	Room with a small black and a black and whtie.
Humorous Mistakes		close up close-up of a close a brown the camera	A brown horse with a close up of the camera.		grass EOS a field a white field EOS the grass	A white cat laying on a field in the grass.
		at a a group group of a man and a	At a man and a group of peopele sitting around.		sitting on at a a computer and a a table	At a blackbird sitting on a table and a computer

Figure 6: Examples of estimated keyphrases and generated sentences. The first row shows successful examples. The second row have partly correct examples thanks to appropriate keyphrases. The last row includes humorous mistakes.

Dinner of Luciérnaga- An Interactive Play with iPhone App in Theater

Yu-Chuan Tseng
Shih Hsin University
Department of Public Relations and Advertising
#1 Lane17 Sec.1, Mu-Cha Rd, Taipei, Taiwan (R.O.C.)
886-939-120838
t.yuchuan@gmail.com

Kuan-Ying Wu
National Chiao Tung University,
Graduate Institute of Architecture
1001 University Road, Hsinchu, Taiwan 300, ROC
886-3-5712121
rainage@arch.nctu.edu.tw

Yi-Ching Huang
National Taiwan University
Graduate Institute of Networking and Multimedia
No.1, Sec. 4,Roosevelt Road,Taipei,Taiwan(R.O.C.)
886-2-33663366
d00944010@csie.ntu.edu.tw

Chi-Ping Chin
MUTIENLIAO Interactive dct TW
Room 11, 19F, No.186, Sec. 1, Wenxin Rd., Nantun Dist., Taichung City 408, Taiwan (R.O.C.)
886-919-049871
marychin@mutienliao.com

ABSTRACT
Interactive digital art in the field of performance is emerging as an increasingly important form of artistic expression in Taiwan. *Dinner of Luciérnaga* is an interdisciplinary project produced by more than ten talented members which include the director, dancer, choreographer, artist, interactive designer, sound designer, iPhone app engineer, image processing designer, stage designer and light designer. The goal of this project is to create new modes of interactive participation between the performers and audience through the use of an innovative iPhone application that links dancer to audience and audience to dancer. The application not only plays a key role in connecting the audience and dancer, but also uses an interesting sound generation application that enhances the spectators' experience. It creates and shares special interactive experiences. *Dinner of Luciérnaga* is a story about the relationship of light and human in the digital era. It is a stunning performance in visuals and interactive process with focus on new interface that are put into use in authentic environments for validation by audience.

In this paper, we will discuss our artistic motivation, the development of the digitally interactive performances, and our process for creating the digitally interactive performance entitled *Dinner of Luciérnaga.*

Categories and Subject Descriptors
C.2.1 [COMPUTER-COMMUNICATION NETWORKS]: Network Architecture and Design-*Wireless communication*; D.1.7 [Programming Techniques]: Visual Programming; H.5.2 [INFORMATION INTERFACES AND PRESENTATION]: User Interfaces-*Graphical user interfaces*; J.5 [Computer Applications]: ARTS AND HUMANITIES-*Arts, fine and performing, Performing arts.*

General Terms
Experimentation

Keywords
Mobile art, Digital performance, interaction, iPhone App, Image Processing

1. INTRODUCTION
Dinner of Luciérnaga provides artists with an opportunity for pursuing bold new experiences that is enhanced by innovative iPhone application technology. Experimenting with a new form of mapping projection in combination with the use of the iPhone app allows for a more interactive experience for this performance. The audience will encounter and participate in the creation of spontaneous, visual and auditory art as individual spectators connect with the performance via the iPhone application. The performance piece entitled Dinner of *Luciérnaga* is well suited for this endeavor. In this performance, we create a story about "light," which is the source of all life in both nature and even artificially created environments. We need "light" to live.

The Dancers in this story elucidate a concept of solitude, which resembles the virtual world, and connect images of illusion with meditation.

2. ARTISTIC MOTIVATION

2.1 "Light" in life
"Light" is just there. Humans rely on the sun everyday. Without sunlight, life cannot exist. Those who live in the digital era rely on "light" just like our ancestors.

Human eyes are organs that detect light and convert it into electro-chemical impulses within the neurons. The simplest photoreceptors in conscious vision connect light to movement, just like a camera also captures images in terms of light. On a monitor, the electrical signals determine the images. These signals comprise of photons that exist amongst us on the Internet. Validating their own existence, they feed on "light" and are displayed on screens as a single pixel. Hence, "Light" is the medium for the reproduction of beautiful images via projectors, flat panel televisions, and LED displays. The stunning visuals and beauty of "light" are presented in many and various guises.

The detection and the capture of light by the human eye or camera lens, depends on physics and human physiological processes to differentiate colors. Physically, color is light at a particular frequency. When light refracts off the surface of a red apple, the "red" frequency is reflected while the other frequencies are absorbed. This causes the apple to appear red. The decoding of different colors by humans is then explained through physiology. When light is reflected off an object and enters the retina, nerves relay this information to our brain for processing. Our minds then interpret the information into images that are based on our experience and training.

2.2 Living by the "Light"

During the 80s, Fritz-Albert Popp, a professor of biophysics at the University of Marburg at the time, proposed that photons are the energy of life. He believed that when we eat plant foods, the light waves, or photons, in the plants are taken in and stored by your body. When we consume broccoli, for example, and digest it, it is metabolized into carbon dioxide (CO_2) and water, plus the light stored from the sun and photosynthesis. We extract the CO_2 and eliminate the water, but the light, an EM wave, must be stored. When taken in by the body, the energy of these photons dissipates and becomes distributed over the entire spectrum of EM frequencies, from the lowest to the highest. This energy is the driving force for all the molecules in our body. [1]

According to Popp, DNA stores "light waves" and uses them for energy. The waves are the driving force for every molecule in our body and a type of life energy. In this context, a "light wave" is more than just a carrier of an electromagnetic wave. Through data transmission, the wave fuels a system filled with its harnessed energy. It also becomes parts of our body.

2.3 "Light" in Digital Art

New media artists choose to work directly with light--which is also utilized as a reveal- along with the physical manifestations of light such as images or video projections. In a 1998 art piece entitled *Rapt*, we see how Justine Cooper scanned her body into a Magnetic Resonance Imaging (MRI) machine and later used the scans together with medical software to animate them into a haunting black and white video that takes us into the interior vistas of soft tissue. (Figure 1) Another example has to do with *Light in Forest - Heart's Core* by He-Lin Luo and I-Chun Chen. The art piece is an artificial entity of light that emits brighter light when awakened by a participant's touch. When participants are not within the space of the piece and not touching it, the tentacles of the Light in Forest breathe lightly and rhythmically, revealing a semi-dormant state. When the participants enter and start the "Light in Forest" dance, their bodies respond to each of its dancing tentacles. In this circulatory system of a "semi-dormant method of breathing" and "exercise model for an awakened state," the message of human existence is converted into visual symbols and control parameters of light. (Figure 2)[2] In Marie-Jeanne Musiol's *the Radiant Forest: Energy Herbarium*, electro photographic imaging and Kirlian photography expose the magnetic fields surrounding different life forms and present an alternative view of our world. When observing the continuously changing light signals surrounding the living organisms, one no longer sees life in a static form. Rather, life is perceived as an open system or dynamic entity that interacts with energy fields. [3] (Figure 3)

Figure 1. Justine Cooper, 1998, Rapt. RAPT II (1998), incorporates 76 slices/MRI scans to create Cooper's 10 meter long databody. See http://justinecooper.com/

Figure 2. He-Lin Luo and I-Chun Chen, 2011, Light in Forest - Heart's Core

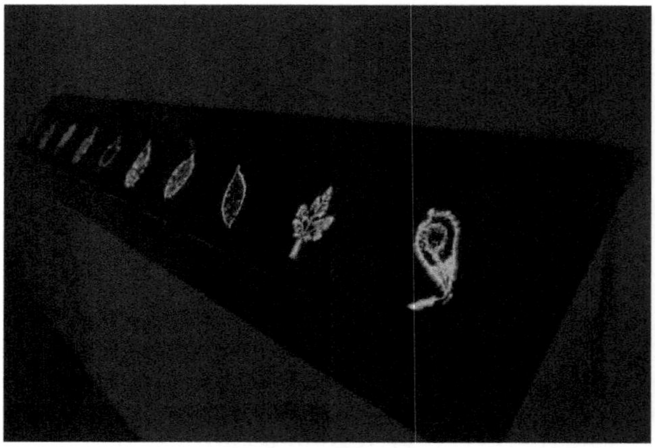

Figure 3. Marie-Jeanne Musiol, 2011, the Radiant Forest: Energy Herbarium," Electromagnetic Photography, Lightboxes and Video.

3. PERFORMANCES WITH MOBILE PHONE

3.1 Mobile Art

As mobile phones become cheaper, smaller, and more powerful, mobiles have become an increasingly important form of media and tool to facilitate art. From the earliest days of mobile art, James Buckhouse's *Tap* in collaboration with Holly Brubach, was commissioned by Dia Center for the Arts in 2002. He created virtual dancers that could be trained and exchanged in users' palms. [4] The utilization of mobile phones in public spaces is an emerging form of artistic expression nowadays. Mark Shepard's *Tactical Sound Garden* draws on the urban, community gardening culture to posit a participatory environment for new spatial practices and social interactions within technologically mediated environments. [5] [6]

3.2 Mobile phones as an interface in Theater

The use of digital technology has become more frequent within theater. The application of new media to performance is extremely diverse. Important digital performance subjects include virtual reality, liquid architecture, telematics, and surveillance. [7] Despite the ubiquitous use of digital technology in theatre, mobile phones are rarely used in performance. An inspiring example of the use of mobile technology in theatre is *Dialtones*(A Telesymphony, 2001), a project by artist Golan Levin. The production used ring tones to create a concert performance whose sounds were wholly produced through the carefully choreographed ringing of the audience's own mobile phones. The concert was presented at the Ars Electronica Festival in September 2001, and at the Swiss National Exposition in May and June of 2002. [8]

4. THE DESIGN THINKING OF INTERACTIVE TOOL AND PROCESS

4.1 An Interactive digital performance

How does one present the characteristics of real time interactive digital performance? How can the audience play a role in the performance? How can the audience become an essential element in a performance? The reason why we raise these three questions is because these questions illustrate an important point. Though there are many real time interactive performances that connect both audience and performers via images and a medley of apparatuses in other countries, interaction between the audience and performers is rare in Taiwan. However, the answers to these three questions aren't difficult to answer thereby implying that there is great room to create interactive performances here in Taiwan. Audience participation in theatre has a long history that begins with the 'Happenings in the 1960.' [9] In 1965, Robert Rauschenberg presented *Open Score* in the event named "9 Evenings: Theatre and Engineering." At this spectacle, two tennis players were given racquets with fitted, contact microphones. When the racquets hit the ball, the racquets picked up the reverberations produced by the sound of the balls. The sound triggered an automatic mechanism that shut off the 36 lights on the Armory ceiling one by one. Nearly 500 people then assembled on the stage where they were filmed by infrared cameras that had been set up on the balcony. Each participant was required to move around in accordance with ten memorized instructions provided by Rauschenberg. (Figure 4) [10]

Cultivating the spirit of our aforementioned predecessors, we embarked on a mission to create a new type of "interactive performance." In the beginning, we considered making a control instrument for each member of the audience. However, budgetary demands and insufficient capability of the control instrument rendered this solution impractical. According to the script, the apparatus necessary for the performance would need to be capable

Figure 4. Robert Rauschenberg presented "Open Score"

of taking photos, playing sound and animations, and connecting a wireless network that would then link to a server that would control images on stage. Also, it would be beneficial if the audience could bring a device into the theatre that they were familiar with and didn't require preparation on our part. To fulfill these necessities, we had to find a device that included said features. On the basis of the above criteria, we chose the iPhone as the interactive apparatus.

To use the iPhone as our interactive tool, we designed an application that could capture a picture, generate sound and receive commands. We define the function of captured pictures as the meaning of light capturing implement and optical storage. The sound generation function turns the iPhone into an instrument. The function of receiving commands helps execute broadcasting and animation broadcasting functions. With those functions, audiences can follow the instructions to execute artistic preferences and to receive data.

5. DINNER OF LUCIÉRNAGA

5.1 Light as metaphor

We use the term "Luciérnaga" as a metaphor to indicate how humans interact with light. Luciérnaga is symbolic in many ways. In Spanish, Luciérnaga means firefly. It also refers to the notions of you and I, information and instruction, as well as demand and hope. The "Luciérnaga" is a firefly, is light, is we. Therefore, the *Dinner of Luciérnaga* is a story of how light is a resource of energy resembling the role of food. The light is the key elements to construct a kitchen. It could be the cooking material and could be the dinner ingredient. At the end of the performance, the light in itself is a dinner.

In this performance, there are a series of light dots that represent the audience's response to the performers actions. The dancers respond to these dots by spontaneously, but smoothly incorporating this new set of stimuli in the performance. Inherent in this production is the interaction and inevitable tension between performers and audience. However, such a relationship spurs creativity and mutual understanding.

In order to facilitate this sort of interaction we had to create an interface named-"Luciérnaga" so the invited audience could enjoy this production. This simple iPhone application enables music generation, unique sounds due to an accelerometer, and the ability to capture light and images via camera. So that the audience can fully participate with the performers, spectators must download the app from the iTunes App store prior to entering the theatre.

5.2 The scenario of play

The play includes five parts and is 50 minutes in length. The first part challenges the mobile phone connected and controlled platform. It is the initial basis of whole play. The second part shows the relationship between human and light. The third and fourth parts present one's solitude. The final part shows the collapse of the virtual world with paper scraps.

1. When members of the audience enter the theater, they will get a unique identifier printed on a piece of paper. Also, they are asked to access our wireless local network and save their unique identifier in the "Luciérnaga" app. When the signal is connected, the audience becomes one of the light dots presented on stage. The audience members can control their own lights by waving the iPhone. Also, when the iPhone is waved, a unique sound is generated according to the direction and force of the shaking. In the app, there is one light ball that will change its size by analyzing the brightness of the photo that people took. The audience can send the message-- including the size of light ball-- to the stage by touching down on the iPhone screen. (Figure 5, 6)

Figure 5. The audiences are interacting with their iPhone.

Figure 6. The light dots represent the audience.

2. After the interactive opening, the light dots are random and out of control as the dancer walks into the center of stage. The dancer starts to play with the light in the mode of push, adhesion and integration by using different body movements. The relation between dancer and light are conflicted. He plays with the light, but at the same time tries to escape from the light. (Figure 7, 8)

Figure 7. Dancer played with light, but also tried to escape from light.

Figure 8. The dancer was Inundated **by light.**

3. However, the light is proves to be inescapable. It becomes the elements to build up a kitchen. The dancer constructs the kitchen with the light and creates a blueprint kitchen. (Figure 9)

Figure 9. The dancer constructs a kitchen with the light and creates a blueprint kitchen

4. In the kitchen, the dancer cooks his own dinner while waiting for another to join him for dinner. Alas, no one came. (Figure 10) During the dancer's process of cooking, the audience would send commands to trigger the music clips stored in the audience's iPhone and dynamically control the parameters to create a special surround sound effect. The animation of creatures-- such as a cat or butterfly-- would

spontaneously appear and disappear on the stage and then appear in the audience's iPhone through wireless network. In this final scene, the dancers seem to walk into the audience's iPhone in terms of a virtual animation, and turned to be fragmentation.

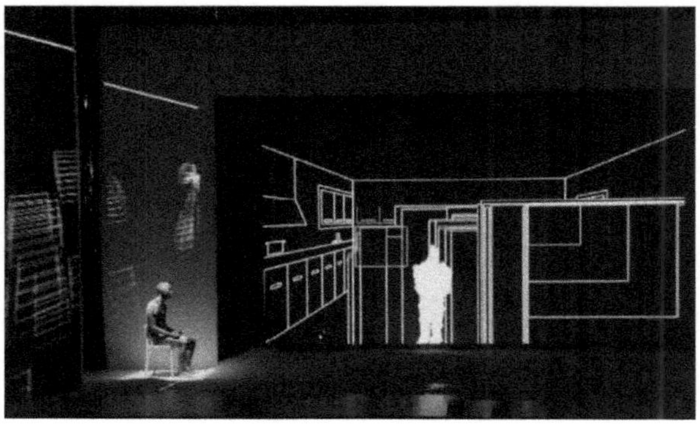

Figure 10. Dancer cooks it owns dinner waiting for someone to have dinner with him. Alas, no one came.

5. Finally, the dancer is still having dinner alone, while the virtual world has collapsed. The virtual world continues to fall apart, while in reality objects of paper scraps are pouring down symbolizing the effects of the virtual world. (Figure 11) It symbolized that in deeper of our hearts, we always influenced and swing back and forth between the real and virtual worlds.

Figure 11. The world is falling apart.

5.3 Interactive performance experience with the iPhone

Generally, the audience watches a performance and receives messages passively from the digital image of performance. In this project, the audience sends messages to the digital image control apparatus in the performance and can therefore interact with the dancer using their mobile phones. To do this, we developed an iPhone app named Luciérnaga that is available in the iTunes App Store. As we know, iPhone is with camera function. In some sense, it can use to capture light and storage light. In our performance, we adopt this concept and people can use this function to play the light ball showed on iPhone. In the theater, the audience can use their iPhone to take part in the performance. They can control the objects on the stage and generate special sounds to create a soundscape for the live performance. Therefore, the Luciérnaga app is a medium between audience and performance.

6. SYSTEM FRAMEWORK

6.1 Stage Design and Equipment Supply

Generally speaking, the projection is only used on the screen of the stage or the bottom of the stage. In order to increase the projection area on the stage, we use picture-frame stage design. (Figure 12) Each layer of the frame is marked to three different depths on the stage space. First, we used a paper model to explore the relationship among image, stage, and dancer.

Figure 12. This paper model simulates the stage design.

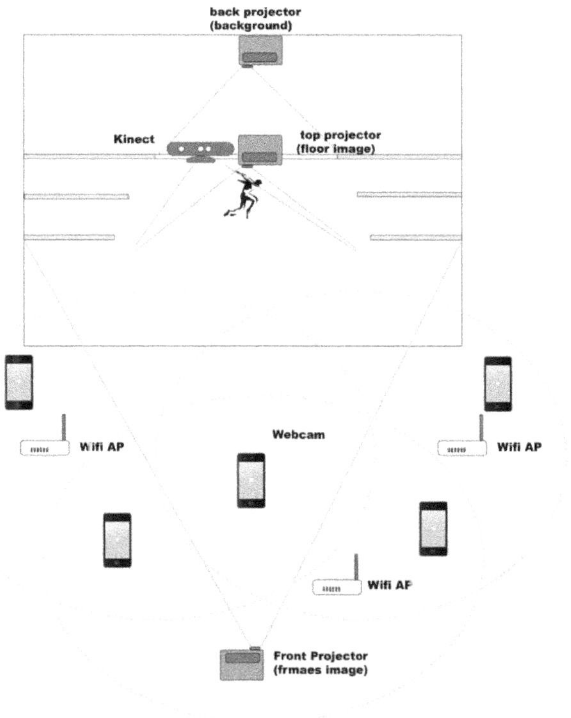

Figure 13. The hardware installations for image display set on the stage and auditorium in theater.

Overall, there are three projection areas on the stage. They are the floor, background screen, and frames. In order to avoid the shadow of the dancer on the background screen, we set the back projector on the stage. Three projectors are connected to three computers separately, but in a synchronized operation through internal LAN. (Figure 13) Each computer sends and receives simultaneously. Therefore, even if the background screen and frames use different projectors, the animation of the image is linked.

6.2 Luciérnaga App for iPhone

The Luciérnaga App is an iPhone application developed by openFramewoks and utilizes PureData for audio synthesis. It is a sound production application that allows spectators to use the camera and motion sensor in iPhone to generate a special sound. We analyze the captured pictures to change the size of the light ball based on the brightness and adjust the sound frequency based on the size of light ball. (Figure 14) The app can generate a unique sound depending on the different gestures and accelerometer values. The sound generation algorithm is shown in Table 1.

There are two hidden functions activated by using a trigger from Luciérnaga Server. One is sound creation and the other is animation. For sound creation, we have one professional sound artist who is responsible for controlling the soundtrack in the live performance. Through our system, the artist can use a DJ controller to send some commands that activate all iPhones in the audience. The designed sound clips were already part of the app and the artist can easily decide which sound clip and at what volume he wants a clip to play at any given moment. For animation, the audience can interact with the performance unexpectedly. There is one scene that shows animations such as a running cat or a flying butterfly appearing in the projection screen on stage. When the animation disappears on the big screen, the system will send messages to the users' iPhones to trigger the corresponding animation via our server in a wireless local network.

In the theater, we arrange eight zones for the iPhone users. Based on their unique identifier, we can know accurately determine their positions since the connection is built up. With our wireless local network, we can send different commands to activate different sound effects or trigger different animations on the users' iPhone that correspond to the scene (Figure 15) In the performance, the artist can control all connected iPhones to create different sounds at different volumes or orders in different zones. The sounds from the different zones are then synthesized into a melody. This process brings a unique sound experience for the audience and the overall performance.

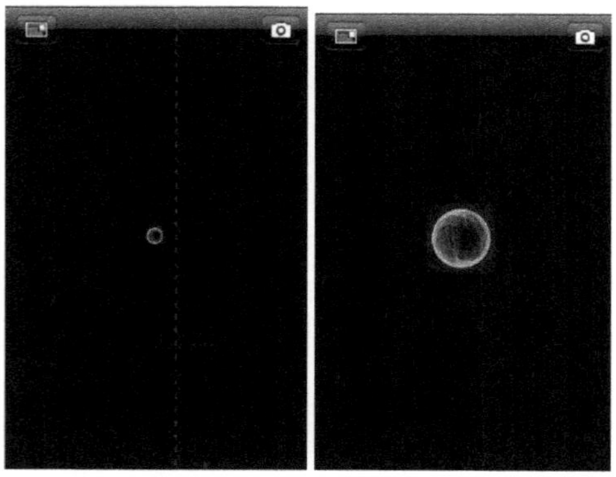

Figure 14. Capturing pictures to change the size of light ball.

Figure 15. Animation will be triggered during the performance.

INPUT: accelerometer data x, y, z and ball_size from user
volume and Q from server
OUTPUT: special sound

Q is a parameter sent from server
x , y , z and ball_size are sent from user by iPhone
α and β parameters.
f(x), g(y) and h(z) are linear functions.
τ_1 is a constant value for delay time.
θ_1 and θ_2 are parameters used in filter.

Function *SoundGenerator* (x, y, z, ball_size, volume, Q)
Begin
sound = *BandpassFilter*(sound, Q)
modulator_delay = $\alpha \times (1 + \sin(y))$
sound_delay = *Delay*(sound, modulator_delay)
gain = $\beta \times (\mid f(x) \mid + \mid g(y) \mid)$
modulated_faded = *LogarithmicGain*(sound_delay, gain)
effect = $h(z) \times$ *Delay*(modulated_faded, τ_1)

mix = modulated_faded + effect
mix_1 = *LowpassFilter*(mix , θ_1)
mix_2 = *HighpassFilter*(mix_1 , θ_2)
mix_compressed = *Compressor*(mix2, δ)
new_sound=*LogarithmicGain*(mix_compressed,volume)
return new_sound
End

Table 1. SoundGenerator Algorithm in iPhone

6.3 iPhone Wireless network control

We set up a local wireless network with three wireless access points and arrange them in accordance to the 8 different zones in the theater. In order to make sure the stability of the signals are strong enough and the bandwidth sufficient enough to connect with 96 iPhones, we set three AP with Wi-Fi signals in the auditorium arranged in a triangle. Open sound control protocols are used to communicate with each other. This type of system framework can synchronize the visual generation, sounds, and iPhone control. Therefore, there are two key components in our framework. One is the Luciérnaga Server and the other is the Luciérnaga app.

The Luciérnaga Server is a control server written by Processing. It can monitor the statuses of the iPhone and send commands to online iPhones to activate different events during the different scenes in the performance. Luciérnaga Server has a control panel that displays the online status of users launching the Luciérnaga app. Figure 16 is the screenshot of the control panel of Luciérnaga Server. The top left of the panel shows the current status of performance. The bottom left of the panel shows the iPhone online/offline status corresponding to the user's seat position in the theater. The Black color means that the user is online and the white color means the user is offline. Each position has a unique identifier and the user can connect to the server via the app. The seat position indicators will change from white to black when the seat owner successfully connects to server. The seat number correlates to different zones. There are five buttons on the top right panel to send some commands to the Luciérnaga app via OSC protocol in a local wireless network. Through the server, we can utilize the physical sound controller to change the volume of each iPhone. We can also adjust the volume for iPhones in different zones.

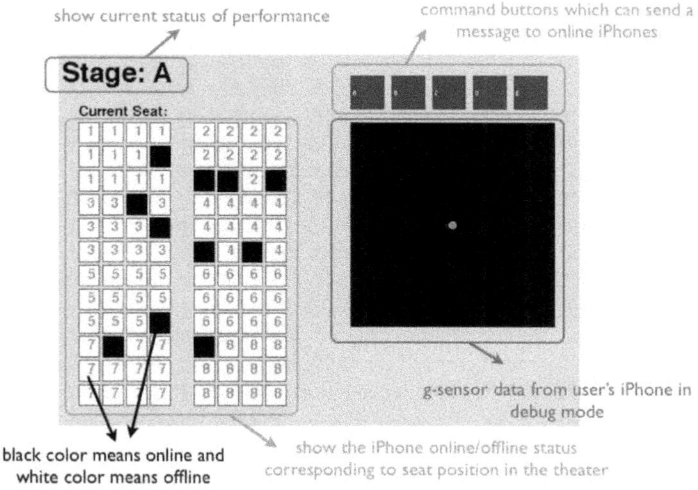

Figure 16. The control panel of Luciérnaga Server

6.4 Real-time image processing

Based on the stage design, we use a number of design principles. Firstly, each layer of the frame will be treated as an independent display. (Figure 17) Secondly, the image on the stage is specially designed according to the depth of the space and the scenario of the play. (Figure 18) Thirdly the three-frames are regarded as one.

Figure 17. The visual elements are generated and stacked within the first frame.

Figure 18. The projection of the kitchen is mapping the depth of the space to each picture-frame.

We generate real-time animation by using an open source programming language called Processing. In the scene with the light ball game played with the iPhone, we use Processing to create over 96 balls in advance. Before the iPhone is connected on the Wireless Network Server, the movement of the balls is randomly control by Processing. Control will be transferred when the Wireless Network Server broadcasts the on-line ID of iPhones to Processing through OSC protocol. The audience can control where their ball passes through in the different projection areas. Each Processing program between computers that connect with the projector is also connected through the OSC protocol. (Figure 19)

We used 3D Project Mapping for visual animation design in order to enhance the immersion of the picture-frame stage. The physical engine of the Processing libraries creates boxes, eclipses, triangles stacked in a particular projection space. The 3D kitchen, in line with the frame structure, is constructed on the stage and rotates to follow dancer's movements. The dancer can open the fridge in the left side of the second layer of the frames and turn on the tap in the left side of the background screen.

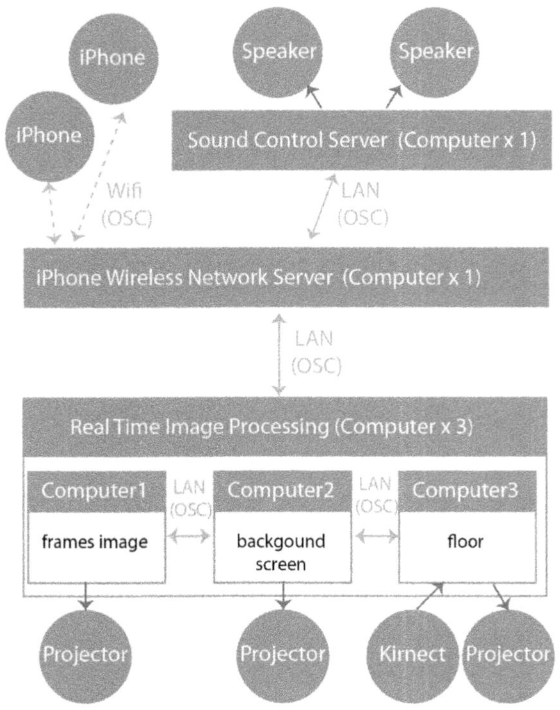

Figure 19. The software connection delivers the signals among each kind of hardware.

6.5 Motion Capture on the Dance and Choreography

The whole performance of *Dinner of Luciérnaga* is done through only one dancer on the stage. In order to create better translation of actions into an image, a Kinect sits upon the dancer to detect movement and to get positional information. All the image effects are real time determined by the dancer movements. The Kinect Program design has two modes. One is to detect the dancer's displacement then convert it into the acceleration, the x-axis, and the y-axis in Processing. Another is to capture the depth data of Kinect that reflects the dance movements such as floor work or jump. These data values for the variables can be used to generate the image color, shape, quantity and size in Processing.

The interaction between dancer and the projection image occurs mainly in the construction of the virtual kitchen scene. In the beginning, the dancer is in a position to "collect" the light ball generated by the audience's iPhone. The light ball will move around the dancers. A special action is then set up – one leg elevation and then fall – in this part of dance to centralize the light ball. In this process, the light ball gradually becomes sticky then finally transforms into a group of lights. In the next part of dance, the dancer needs to create the kitchen components with the light group. Therefore, this choreography is a combination of the seven methods of measurement that include angle, length, number, depth, frequency, brightness, and weight. The element of motion capturing is important to consider when each measurement of action is designed. For example, the angle variables in the programming are controlled by the three-points that are detected from dancer's hands and body. When the variables change, the image on the stage will change immediately.

7. THE CHALLENGE AND USER EXPERIENCE

7.1 The challenge

The project had three challenges. The first challenge is to get the Luciérnaga App on the app store in time. We distributed the Luciérnaga App only one day ahead of when the show began. The second challenge is that we only had four days to work in the theater which included setting up the stage, positioning the projectors and Wifi control system, system testing and rehearsal. Before work in the theater began, we didn't have a chance to integrate whole parts of the performance, since we didn't have the rehearsal space. In the morning of final day, we were still testing the system, programming the images and adjusting the light design.

The third challenge was in helping the audience to understand the interactive process. Since there were 8 different zones, the audiences needed to find seats according to the login identity number and log on to the Luciérnaga Server. The audience also needed to turn on the phone and turn the volume up during the performance. The audience also had to learn to use the app. We recruited volunteers to help and instructed the spectators as they arrived.

7.2 Response from the audience

Overall, the audience enjoyed the production. After entering the theatre and connecting to the server, the spectators enjoyed seeing the light dot on stage. Members of the audience began sway their iPhone to create sound. When the iPhones were swayed in different angles and speed, different sounds were produced, and the light dot began rolling. Also, they were surprised to see a cat or butterfly show up on the screen of iPhone later in the performance. However, members of the audience were confused and uncomfortable when the iPhones were turned on and the volume turned up at certain scenes even though the spectators were told this info. The second issue is that not all members of the audience had an iPhone. We were told that we should create a Luciérnaga app for a android phone. However, one spectator said that she very much enjoyed the show even though she didn't have iPhone. She was surprised when she saw the images and heard the sounds coming from the other iPhones. All the spectators enjoyed the show. The scenes of the projected images were significant and the stage design was simple, but beautiful. The dancer as choreographer, developed a performance that resonates with the emotional anxiety of humans nowadays.

8. CONCLUSION

In terms of the iPhone application, the audience uses it to capture the light and get interaction in this performance. It symbolizes that this procedure have the audience into part of the light, and invite them to capture, explore, and believe the existence of the light. In doing so, we in turn, validate our own existence and that of our world. The main theme of the performance – Luciérnaga is to investigate the nature of the light, and study how people build the immersive relationship with the light.

In the working process, we are in a search for new communication styles and new forms of theatrical expression. When you enter the theatre hall with an iPhone, you become a part of the performance. You are not just a viewer, but become one of the performers, creators, and actors. The interactive process through the iPhone is an experiment. With personal interface, we wish to create a brave, new theatrical experience.

9. ACKNOWLEDGMENTS

Dinner of Luciérnaga premiered in Quanta Hall, Taoyuan , Taiwan, Sept. 22, 2011. It was awarded funding from the Council for Cultural Affairs' 2011 fund for performance arts that utilize technology. It was created through the collaboration of Yu-Chuan TSENG (Project Director, TW), Chien-Wei WU (Dancer and Choreographer, TW), Liang-Yen LIU (Director, TW), Kuan-Ying WU and Chi-Ping CHIN(Interactive images and programming, TW), Yi-Ching Huang (iPhone application design, TW), Santiago Latorre (Composition and sound design, SP), Chia-Hui Chen (Stage desgin), Chi-Hsiung Hus (Lighting Designer, TW), and Wei-Ting Chen (Director of Interactive Engineering, TW).

REFERENCES

[1] Mctaggart, Lynne (2006). *The Field : the quest for the secret force of the universe*, Chinese edition. Taipei: Business Weekly Publications, Inc.

[2] Ivanova, Antoanetta (2011). Let there be Light. *Photon+, The International Techno Art Exhibition of New Taipei City*, 2011. New Taipei City: Cultural Affairs Department

[3] Tseng, Yu-Chuan (2011). Photons⁺- A Messaging System that Relies on Light for its Existence. *Photon+, The International Techno Art Exhibition of New Taipei City, 2011*. New Taipei City: Cultural Affairs Department

[4] Dia Art Foundation (2002), http://awp.diaart.org/buckhouse/intro.html

[5] http://www.tacticalsoundgarden.net/

[6] Scheible, Jürgen (2010). *Empowering Mobile Art PracticeA Recontextualization of Mobile and Ubiquitous Computing*. Finland: WS Bookwell Ltd.

[7] Dixon, Steve (2007). *Digital Performance: A History of New Media in Theater, Dance, Performance Art, and Installation.* MS:the MIT press. P1-79

[8] http://www.flong.com/projects/telesymphony/

[9] Dixon, Steve (2007). *Digital Performance: A History of New Media in Theater, Dance, Performance Art, and Installation.* MS:the MIT press. P581-582

[10] Robert Rauschenberg, Open Score (performance)(2006). http://www.fondation-langlois.org/html/e/page.php?NumPage=642

[11] Virilio, Paul. *The Aesthetics of Disappearance*. (English edition) Semiotext(e). 1991. 52

Accelerating SURF Detector on Mobile Devices

Xin Yang and Kwang-Ting (Tim) Cheng
Dept. of Electrical and Computer Engineering, University of California, Santa Barbara, CA, 93106, USA
xinyang@umail.ucsb.edu, timcheng@ece.ucsb.edu

ABSTRACT

Running a SURF (Speeded Up Robust Features) detector on mobile devices remains too slow to support emerging applications such as mobile augmented reality. Porting it without adapting the algorithm to account for mobile platform limitations could result in significant runtime degradation. In this paper, we identify two mismatches between the SURF algorithm and the mobile hardware that cause substantial slow-down of the point detection process: 1) *mismatch between the data access pattern and the small cache size, and 2) mismatch between the huge amount of branches and high pipeline hazard penalty.*

To address the mismatches, we propose two techniques: *tiled SURF* and *gradient moment based orientation assignment.* Tiled SURF improves data locality and greatly reduces memory traffic. A method for determining the optimal tile sizes, named *content-aware tiling*, is designed to minimize runtime and maximize detection accuracy. To avoid the penalties caused by pipeline hazards, we replace the original orientation operator with branching-free gradient moment computations.

The proposed techniques are tested on three mobile platforms. Comparing to the original SURF, the accelerated SURF achieves a 6x~8x speedup without sacrificing recognition accuracy. Meanwhile, it achieves 59%~80% reductions in the runtime ratio of the detector running on mobile platforms compared with on x86-based PCs.

Categories and Subject Descriptors:
I.4.7 [Image Processing and Computer Vision]: Feature Measurement – *feature representation.*

Keywords

SURF, point detection, acceleration, mobile phones, data access patterns, cache miss, branch prediction, pipeline hazards penalty

1. INTRODUCTION

With the pervasive presence of low-cost, high quality cameras on mobile devices such as smartphones, we are witnessing an explosive growth of embedded computer vision applications like mobile augmented reality, mobile object recognition and image search. Interest point detection is a common task for these applications. Over the past decades, several detectors [1, 2, 3, 4, 5, 16] have been developed. The SURF detector [1], which stands for Speeded Up Robust Features, is arguably one of the best detectors for achieving both high efficiency and robustness.

MM'12, October 29–November 2, 2012, Nara, Japan.

Table 1. Comparison of ORB and SURF Detector on mobile device (Motorola Xoom1) and PC (Thinkpad T420)

Time / Detector	Phone (ms)	PC (ms)	Speedup
ORB	170	40	**4x**
SURF	2156	143	**15x**

However, even with enormous advancements in the application processor (AP), the computing power and memory bandwidth of mobile devices are still limited. These limitations are exacerbated when running a SURF detector on a mobile platform, leading to much higher performance overhead than other lighter-weight detectors. As shown in Table 1, running an ORB (Oriented Fast and Rotated BRIEF) detector [3], a state-of-the-art detector designed primarily for efficiency, takes 170ms on a Motorola Xoom1 and 40ms on an i5-based laptop, yielding a 4x speed gap. However, running a SURF detector on them takes 2156ms and 143ms respectively, indicating a 15x speed gap.

Although some light-weight detectors [3, 4, 5] are more efficient than SURF, none of them can match SURF's robustness [22]. They generally cannot achieve satisfactory performance for those mobile applications which demand high accuracy or require handling content with large photometric/geometric changes. There are also several techniques for improving SURF's efficiency by exploiting coherency between consecutive frames [8], employing graphics processing units (GPU) for parallel computing [10] or optimizing various aspects of the implementation [9]. However, none of them analyzes the causes for a SURF detector's poor efficiency on a mobile platform.

We argue that the efficiency capability of a SURF detector on mobile platforms is considerably undervalued. In this paper, we identify and analyze two mismatches between the computations used in the existing SURF algorithm and common mobile hardware platforms, which are the sources of significant performance degradation:

1) *Mismatch between data access pattern and small cache size of a mobile platform.* A SURF detector relies on an integral image and accesses it using a sliding window of successively larger size for different scales. But a 2D array is stored in a row-based fashion in memory (cache and DRAM), not in a window-based fashion; pixels in a single sliding window reside in multiple memory rows (see Figure 1 (a)). The data cache size of a mobile AP, typically 32KB for today's devices, is too small to cache all memory rows for pixels involved in one sliding window, leading to cache misses and cache line replacements and, in turn, incurring expensive memory access.

2) *Mismatch between a huge amount of data-dependent branches in the algorithm and high pipeline hazard penalty of the mobile platform.* To identify a dominant orientation, a SURF detector analyzes gradient distribution around an interest point via a gradient histogram. During this analysis, every pixel around an interest point is mapped to corresponding histogram bins via a set of branch operations. The total number of pixels involved in this

analysis is huge. Thus, the entire process involves an enormous amount of data-dependent branch operations which are not easily predicted. However, the branch predictor and the speculation of out-of-order execution of an ARM (Advanced RISC Machines) based mobile AP are usually not as advanced as that of a laptop or desktop processor. Consequently, it incurs high pipeline hazard penalties, yielding significant performance degradation.

In this paper we propose two techniques, namely *tiled SURF* and *gradient moment based orientation assignment*, to effectively address the above mismatches. Tiled SURF divides an image into tiles (see Figure 1 (b)) and performs point detection for each tile individually to exploit local spatial coherences and reduce memory traffic. Selecting proper tile size is essential to the success of the tiled SURF technique. In this paper we propose a content-aware tile size selection method, based on which a set of heterogeneous tile sizes can be automatically selected to minimize memory traffic and maximize recognition accuracy. To avoid pipeline hazards penalties, we replace the original gradient histogram method with a new branching-free orientation operator based on gradient moments. The two proposed techniques can be seamlessly integrated into a single SURF point detection framework and respectively speed up the two steps (i.e. point detection and orientation estimation) of the process.

The proposed techniques are evaluated using three mobile platforms. Experimental results demonstrate an overall 6x~8x speedup comparing to the latest OpenCV SURF implementation [14] and 59%~80% reductions in the runtime ratio of the detector running on mobile platforms compared with those on an Intel i5-based *PC*. For mobile recognition tasks with 228 objects, the accelerated SURF achieves similar detection rate and precision compared to the original SURF and 58% improvement relative to an ORB detector.

The following paper is organized as follows: Sec. 2 gives an overview of the related work. Sec. 3 discusses the two causes for the inferior performance of SURF on mobile platforms, and Sec. 4 provides details of two proposed solutions. In Sec.5, we provide empirical results on three mobile platforms for speed and robustness evaluation. Sec. 6 concludes the paper.

2. RELATED WORK

There are several light-weight point detectors designed primarily for high efficiency on mobile devices. Among them, the FAST (Features from Accelerated Segment Test) detector [4, 5] and its variants have been proven quite successful for many real-time mobile applications such as mobile pose tracking [6] and mobile panoramic mapping [7]. FAST is efficient and can find interest points with a reasonable accuracy, but it is neither scale-invariant nor rotation-invariant. To address these limitations, ORB [3] augments FAST with an image pyramid scheme for scale and an orientation operator based on intensity moments. Although FAST and ORB are faster than SURF, both of them are less robust with respect to photometric and geometric changes. In practice, FAST, ORB and SURF provide alternative detector choices to meet specific requirements for various mobile applications.

There have been several successful attempts to speed up SURF. Ta *et al.* [8] proposed a *SURFTrac* algorithm which exploits coherency in video frames to quickly detect interest points at constrained locations. They achieved a 5x speedup compared to the original SURF, but their approach can only be used for applications with continuous image frames. Chen *et al.* [9] proposed a series of implementation optimizations and achieved a 30% speedup over the baseline implementation. In particular, their optimizations include adjusting the sampling rate to reduce computations for local maximum extraction, using approximation for the *arctan* function and reducing floating point computations in the orientation computation phase. Terriberry *et al.* [10] described an efficient SURF implementation on GPUs using OpenCL. However, to date, mobile GPUs only support OpenGL ES and thus porting an implementation from desktop-based GPUs to mobile GPUs remains a tedious task. As mentioned before, none of these techniques identifies the bottlenecks and causes for the slow-down of running a SURF detector on mobile platforms. In this paper, we focus on understanding these reasons and addressing them.

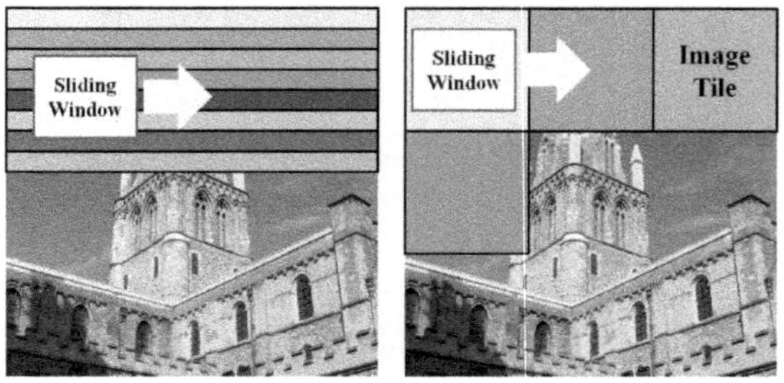

Figure 1. Illustration of data locality and access pattern in (a) the original SURF detector, and (b) the tiled SURF. Each color represents data stored in a unique DRAM row. In the original SURF, a sliding window needs to access multiple DRAM rows, leading to frequent cache misses, while in tiled SURF, all required data within a sliding window can be

Several attempts have been made to improve the performance of mobile computer vision through optimization of mobile hardware. The authors in [12] provided a mobile computer vision benchmarking suite, called MEVBench, to understand mobile vision processing characteristics at the architectural level. Silpa *et al.* [13] attempted to improve the performance by patch memory optimization when using texture memory in mobile GPUs. Clemons *et al.* [11] proposed an embedded heterogeneous multicore design named EFFEX for feature extraction. EFFEX incorporates a new patch memory architecture which stores data in region-order, rather than scan-line order, leading to high spatial locality in data access. Their goal of improving data locality is similar to our tiled SURF. However, they leverage new hardware design, while we rely on software adaptation and optimization.

3. SURF ON MOBILE DEVICES

In this section, we analyze the two causes for the substantial slow-down of running a SURF detector on mobile platforms.

3.1 Mismatch of Data Access Pattern and Small Cache Size of Mobile Platforms

In this subsection, we first review the relevant terms and features of cache miss and reuse. Then we briefly describe the SURF detection process and its data access pattern. After that we discuss why this data access pattern could cause high cache miss on mobile platforms.

3.1.1 Background

A cache miss refers to a failed attempt to read or write a piece of data in the cache, resulting in a main memory access with much longer latency. It can be divided into three categories:

- *Compulsory miss* – Occurs when a cache line is referred for the first time. These misses are inevitable.
- *Capacity miss* – Occurs due to the finite size of the cache. When a program's working set size is larger than the cache size and a cache line containing data that will be reused is replaced before it is reused, a capacity miss occurs when the displaced data is referenced again.
- *Interference miss* – Occurs due to a conflict of cache mapping, i.e. a cache line that contains reusable data is replaced by another cache line that is mapped to the same location. Interference misses on arrays can be divided into two categories: 1) *self-interference misses* that are caused by an element in the same array. 2) *cross-interference misses* that are caused by an element in a different array.

Reuse can be divided into two categories:

- *Spatial reuse* – accesses to the same cache line by references to neighboring data elements.
- *Temporal reuse* – accesses to the same data element multiple times.

3.1.2 Review of SURF Point Detection

A SURF detector selects interest points based on the determinant of Hessian matrix $H(X,\sigma)$:

$$H(X,\sigma)=\begin{bmatrix} L_{xx}(X,\sigma) & L_{xy}(X,\sigma) \\ L_{xy}(X,\sigma) & L_{yy}(X,\sigma) \end{bmatrix}$$

where $X=(x,y)$ is a pixel location in an Image I, σ is a scale factor, $L_{xx}(X,\sigma)$ is the convolution of the Gaussian second-order derivative at location X and similarly for $L_{xy}(X,\sigma)$ and $L_{yy}(X,\sigma)$.

To speed up the process, a SURF detector approximates the Gaussian second-order derivatives with a combination of box filter responses, computed using the integral image technique. The approximated derivatives are denoted as D_{xx}, D_{xy} and D_{yy} and accordingly the approximate Hessian determinant is:

$$\det(H_{approx})=D_{xx}D_{yy}-(0.9D_{xy})^2$$

A SURF detector computes Hessian determinant values for every image pixel i over scales using box filters of successively larger size, yielding a determinant pyramid for the entire image. Then it applies a 3x3x3 local maximum extraction over the determinant pyramid to select interest points' locations and corresponding salient scales. *Pseudo Code 1* shows the process of Hessian determinant pyramid construction. In each iteration of the outer loop S, one layer of Hessian determinant pyramid is constructed based on a reuse of integral image array $I_{integral\_img}$. In the inner loop P, elements of $I_{integral\_img}$ are accessed using a sliding window for computing D_{xx}, D_{xy} and D_{yy} of every image pixel sequentially.

Pseudo Code 1: Determinant Pyramid Construction

Input:	*scales*: total number of scales
	img_pixels: total number of image pixels
Output:	det_{pyr}: Hessian determinant pyramid
Variants:	$I_{integral\_img}$: integral image array
	D_{xx}, D_{yy}, D_{xy}: approximate Gaussian second-order derivatives in *x*, *y* and *x*-*y* directions

```
procedure ConstructDeterminantPyr
  construct integral image I_integral_img
  for S = 1: scales
    for P = 1: img_pixels
      access 8 elements of I_integral_img → compute D_xx
      access 8 elements of I_integral_img → compute D_yy
      access 12 elements of I_integral_img → compute D_xy
      compute det → write back to det_pry[S][P]
    end
  end
```

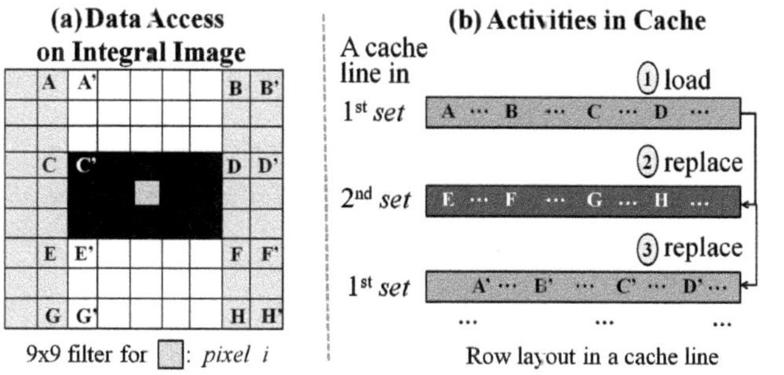

Figure 2. Illustration of (a) one exemplar data access pattern on an integral image, and (b) corresponding activities in cache. In (a) the grey, white and black colors indicate that corresponding values are multiplied by 0, 1 and -2 respectively. Each color in (b) represents a unique set of consecutive rows that can concurrently reside in a cache.

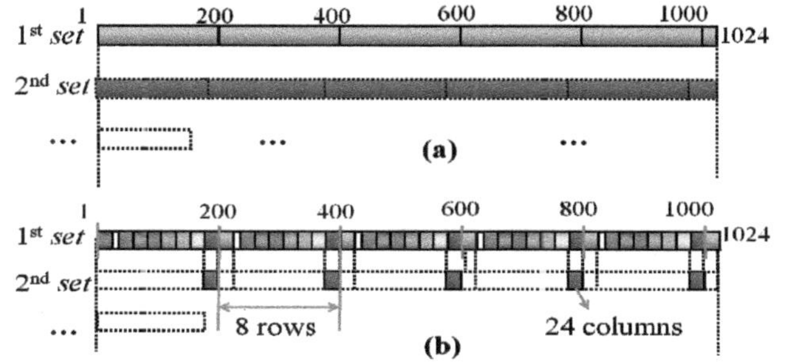

Figure 3. Row layout in a 1024-element cache for (a) 200x200 $I_{integral\_img}$ and (b) tiled $I_{integral\_img}$, tile size is (8*5+1) rows * 24 columns

3.1.3 Data Access Pattern of SURF Leads to Many Self-Interference Misses

The data access pattern of SURF is determined by the box filter's type and size. For example, a 9x9 box filter for D_{yy} accesses 8 *elements* in a 9x9 rectangle in each iteration, e.g. *element-sets={A,B,C,D,E,F,G,H}* in Figure 2 (a). In the next iteration P, the box filter is shifted one pixel to the right and accesses the 8 elements located to the right of *element-set*, e.g. *element-set' = {A',B',C',D',E',F',G',H'}* in Figure 2 (a).

We use a simple example to illustrate cache activities, shown in Figure 2 (b), caused by this data access pattern. Consider the layout of a 200x200 array $I_{integral\_img}$ in a direct mapped cache that can hold 1024 elements of $I_{integral\_img}$ (see Figure 3 (a)). Without loss of generality, we assume the first element of $I_{integral\_img}$ falls in the first position of the cache and *element-set = {A,B,C,D,E,F,G,H}* is used for the first 9x9 D_{yy} box filter. The 2D $I_{integral\_img}$ array is stored in a row-based order in the cache and *sets* are defined as groups of consecutive rows that can concurrently reside in the cache. In the example of Figure 3 the first *set* consists of rows 1 thought 5 and the first 24 elements of row 6.

As SURF detection starts, the first *set* is loaded into the cache, as shown in Figure 2(b)-①, enabling references to *{A, B, C, D}*, which are located in the 1st and 4th rows. Then to access *{E, F, G, H}* which are in the 7th and 9th rows, the second *set* needs to be fetched from memory and replaces the first *set* (see Figure 2(b)-②). When shifting the box filter one pixel to the right, adjacent elements of {*A*, *B*, *C*, *D*} need to be accessed again (see Figure 2(b)-③). But at this moment, the first *set* has been replaced, and a self-interference miss occurs. In the worst case, every access to the first four elements of a box filter replaces cache lines that contain the latter four elements. Then accessing elements adjacent to the first four elements would cause another self-interference miss. As a result, sequentially computing 9x9 D_{yy} box filter responses based on a 200x200 integral image leads to as many as 80,000 cache misses and cache line replacements. Similarly, computing D_{xx} and D_{xy} would also cause a similar amount of self-interference misses. The self-interference miss would become more significant for both larger box filters and larger images. For instance, computing a 15x15 box filter response on a 200x200 image or a 9x9 filter response on a 400x400 image, each *set* can only contain two elements of a box filter, resulting in twice as many cache misses.

Today's mobile devices, for example Motorola's Xoom1 tablet, typically feature a 32KB L1 data cache, a 512KB L2 data cache and a 1280x800 display. An integral image size of 1281x801 (one pixel larger in width and height to store the sums of all pixels left and above a 1280x800 image) includes 1,026,081 elements. Since each element of an integral image is a 4-Byte integer, 32KB L1 cache and 512KB L2 data cache can only hold up to 8,000 and 128,000 elements, i.e. 16 rows and 99 rows of the array, respectively. As a result, box filters larger than 16x16 and 99x99 would lead to L1 and L2 cache misses in the worst case. In practice, operating systems and other programs inevitably occupy some of the cache, thus there is even smaller available cache size for user applications. As a result even smaller box filters than the above-mentioned would incur cache misses.

3.2 Mismatch of Branches and High Pipeline Hazards Penalty of Mobile Platforms

In this subsection, we first briefly review the orientation computation used in a SURF detector. Then we discuss why this computation incurs a large penalty in mobile platforms.

3.2.1 Review of SURF Orientation Assignment

SURF relies on gradient histograms to identify dominant orientations. First, the entire orientation space is quantized into N histogram bins, each of which represents a sliding orientation window covering an angle of $\pi/3$. Then we compute gradient responses of every pixel in a circular neighborhood of an interest point. Based on the gradient orientation of a pixel, we map it to the corresponding histogram bins and add its gradient response to these bins. Finally, the bin with the largest responses is utilized to calculate the dominant orientations of interest points. *Pseudo Code 2* illustrates an OpenCV2.3.1 implementation of this process.

3.2.2 Pipeline Hazard Penalty

A large number of pixels are involved in the orientation analysis. Assuming that an interest point involves ~100 pixels in its neighborhood, then for ~2000 interest points, there would be ~200k pixels involved in total. According to *Pseudo Code 2*, each pixel is mapped to the corresponding histogram bins via a series of branch operations, i.e. "If-then-else" expression. Accordingly, the entire process involves a huge number of branches.

Pseudo Code 2: Orientation by Histogram of Gradient

```
Input:    interest-pts: interest points
          step: orientation increase step
Output:   dominate-oris: dominant orientations
Variants: hist_gradient: gradient histogram
          pixels_neigh: neighboring pixels of interest point
          responses: gradient response array of pixels_neigh
          oris: gradient orientation array of pixels_neigh

procedure: ComputeDominateOris
  for Pt = interest-pts
     compute responses
     compute oris
     for Ori = 0: step: 360
        for P = pixels_neigh
           if (-PI/6 < (oris[P]-Ori) <= PI/6)
              hist_gradient [Ori/step] += responses[P]
           endif
        end
     end
     dominate-oris [Pt] = argmax( hist_gradient )
  end
```

Branches cause control hazards (also called branch hazards) in a hardware pipeline, i.e. when a branch instruction is fetched, the next instruction location is not known until the branch instruction finishes execution. Mis-predicting locations of the subsequent instructions would require flushing the entire pipeline and thus incur a penalty. Modern mobile processors usually use a deep pipeline to increase the CPI, which increase the penalty of each mis-prediction. Moreover, for mobile processors, the branch predictor hardware and other hazard solutions (e.g. out-of-order execution), while improving for each new generation, are still not as sophisticated as desktop and laptop processors (e.g. Intel cores i5 and i7). A conventional SURF implementation involves a huge number of branching operations which cause a substantial penalty due to pipeline hazards and degrade its performance on a mobile platform.

To evaluate the impact of control hazard penalty on the runtime, we implemented another version, i.e. *hist-lookup table*, using a lookup table which stores the correlations between each orientation and the corresponding histogram bins. Without changing the functionality and other computations, the new implementation replaces branches with a lookup table thus avoids control hazards. We compare the time cost of the two implementations on three mobile platforms, Motorola Droid, HTC Thunderbolt, and Motorola Xoom1 tablet.

The results are summarized in Table 2, from which two observations can be made. First, comparing the time cost of *hist-branch* vs. *hist-lookup table* on three mobile platforms and an i5-based laptop, *hist-lookup table* can greatly reduce the runtime by 52% on a Droid, 60% on a Thunderbolt, and 32% on a Xoom1. But it only achieves a 9.6% runtime reduction on a T420 laptop. This result confirms that branch hazard penalty has a much greater runtime impact on a mobile platform than on a PC.

Table 2. Runtime of Orientation Computation based on Gradient Histogram on Mobile Devices and Thinkpad T420

Time Cost (ms)	Droid	Thunder-bolt	Xoom1	ThinkPad T420
hist-branch	2954	1295	717	75
hist-lookup table	1401	518	485	83

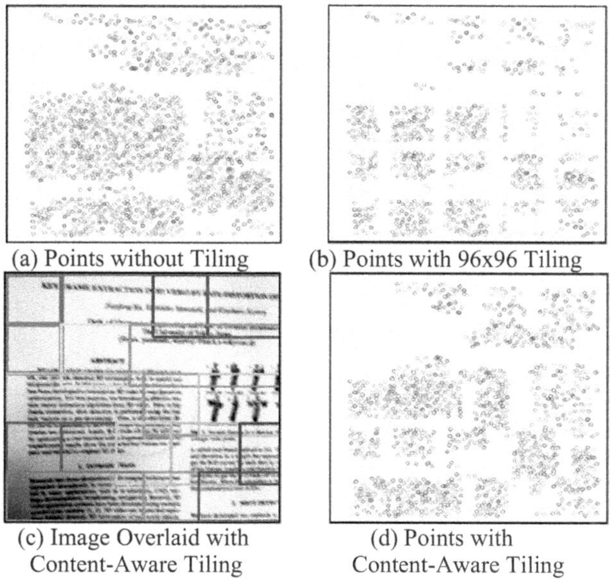

Figure 4. Illustration of interested points detected on an image (a) without tiling, (b) with 96x96 tiling, (c) original image overlaid with content-aware tiling, (d) interest points detected on it with content-aware tiling

Therefore, avoiding such penalties is critical for a mobile implementation. Second, we observe that the *hist-lookup table* version achieves larger runtime reduction on the Droid and Thunderbolt than Xoom1. This is because the mobile processors in three devices have different degrees of pipeline hazard penalty. Droid uses a Cortex-A8 processor and Thunderbolt uses a Scorpion, both of which have a 13-cycle branch mis-predict penalty, while Xoom1 features a Cortex-A9 processor that shortens the pipeline to 8 cycles.

While this simple adjustment in implementation to a large degree alleviates the problem, the performance of *hist-lookup table* is still too slow for some mobile applications such as augmented reality. In the following section, we present a new method to further improve SURF's speed. It should also be pointed out that although we use SURF to illustrate the problem, the mismatch also exists in several other computer vision algorithms so the proposed solution is applicable to a broader spectrum of mobile applications.

4. PROPOSED TECHNIQUES

In this section, we introduce two techniques, namely *content-aware tiling based SURF* and *gradient moment based orientation assignment*, to address the mismatches discussed in Section 3.

4.1 Content-Aware Tiling based SURF

Tiling has been extensively studied and applied to graphics rending [17] and complier optimization [18]. In graphics, tiled rendering divides an image into regular grids in the image space to exploit local spatial coherences and reduces the hardware resources required in graphic rendering. In compiler optimization, tiling (also known as blocking) is performed on nested loops to move accesses to reused data closer together in the iteration space to eliminate capacity misses.

Our problem is similar to a loop optimization problem. However, advanced compliers cannot solve our problem because compiler optimization requires loops being tillable, i.e. no cross data references between tiles. For our problem, box filters inevitably access neighboring pixels which may be located in a different tile. Although the loop-permutation and skewing techniques can remove cross-references to some extent, varying cross-reference patterns arising from up-scaling box filters make it impossible for compliers to find a solution for our target problem.

4.1.1 Tiled SURF

Tiled SURF is conceptually similar to tiled rendering and is remarkably simple. We divide an input image into non-overlapping regular grids (i.e. image tiles), and an integral image for each image tile (i.e. integral image tile), is generated. After that, we construct the Hessian determinant pyramid based on each integral image tile and perform point detection and scale selection for every image tile individually.

Tiling reduces the volume of integral image data accessed between reuses of an element, so that the data can remain in the cache for re-access. Figure 3 (b) illustrates the raw layout of a tiled integral image array in a 1024 element cache. In this example, the chosen column size of a tile is 24, so that 8 rows of 24-element columns can fit into a cache space which would otherwise accommodate only one row of a 200-element column. Including the first 24 elements of the 6th row, 41 rows of 24-element columns can fit in the cache without any interference. Therefore, any box filter smaller than 24x41 would not incur any self-interference misses in the 1024-element cache.

4.1.2 Content-Aware Tile Size Selection

The objective of tile size selection is to choose the optimal tile size to minimize memory traffic. The results are platform-dependent and image-size-dependent. We could utilize existing tile size selection algorithms [18] based on a given cache size and cache line size. The problem, however, is that the cache size allocated for user applications is usually smaller than the total cache size and is unknown to application developers. Therefore, using the entire cache size for calculation of the optimal tile size would not be accurate. Empirical selection by running exhaustive experiments on all reasonable tile sizes would be too laborious.

Another problem is that tiling the image would result in loss of interest points at tile borders. This is because a box filter cannot process pixels at borders if at these locations the box filter exceeds the boundary of tiles. Figure 4 (a) and (b) display interest points detected without tiling vs. with 96x96 tiling. Obvious point discontinuities at tile borders can be observed for 96x96 tiling. Overlapping adjacent tiles can compensate interest point loss, but it incurs redundant computational costs due to processing pixels at borders twice.

Intuitively, a larger tile size should incur fewer lost interest points and a smaller accuracy drop than a smaller tile size. But according to a recognition experiment using a set of tile sizes we observe

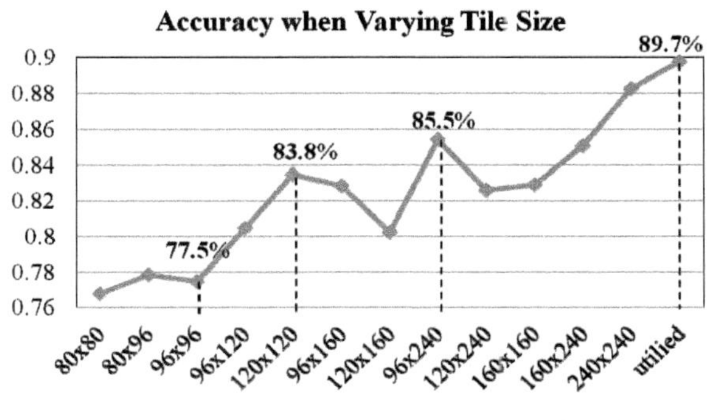

Figure 5. Recognition accuracy when varying tile size

that a larger tile size not always guarantee superior recognition accuracy to a smaller tile size. Figure 5 shows the recognition accuracy of tiled SURF using different tile sizes over 109 images size of 480x480. The tile sizes 120x120 and 96x240 achieve local optima for recognition accuracy. Increasing the tile size from 120x120 to 120x160 or from 96x240 to 160x240, adversely decreases the accuracy. This is because an improper tile size may separate coherent contents (e.g. a continuous text paragraph) into several parts, resulting in informative content residing at tile borders, and the loss of such interest points causes reduction of recognition accuracy. To address this problem, we design a content-aware tile size selection method which uses the following two principles: 1) fitting the reused SURF data into the cache as much as possible, thereby reducing memory access, and 2) minimizing information loss by taking content continuity into consideration.

We use entropy based on intensity probability to represent the amount of information within an image region, where i is an intensity value ranging from 0 to 255 and $P(i)$ is the probability of intensity i within an image region:

$$entropy = -\sum_{0 \le i \le 255} P(i)\log(P(i)) \; . \qquad (1)$$

We define an image region is the *maximum continuous region* (*MCR* for short) if enlarging each sub-region within it can increase the entropy of the sub-region; while further increasing the size of the *MCR* would not further increase the entropy. We select a set of *MCRs* which cover the entire image and each *MCR* in the set is selected as an image tile for the following SURF detection process.

The selection *of MCRs* starts from the top left corner of an image. To reduce the search space, we limit potential tile sizes to a set of pre-determined choices and set the initial size as 96x96. We first compute the entropy for the initial tile. If its entropy is too small, implying little information in the current tile, we skip point detection for this tile. Otherwise, we enlarge the tile to the next larger size and compute the entropy of new tile. The process iterates until the entropy stops increasing as tile size increases or it reaches the largest candidate tile size. The size at which the iteration stops is selected as an *MCR*. Then we move to the next non-overlapping tile and repeat the process. *Pseudo Code 3* shows the selection process of *MCRs*. Figure 4 (c) and (d) displays an exemplar image with content-aware tiling and corresponding detected points on the image. This example exhibits that our method can automatically place larger tiles in long blocks of text, reducing the information loss in these regions. In addition, our method can remove unnecessary processing for non-informative regions (e.g. blank regions), as indicated by the red bold rectangles in Figure 4 (c).

It is worth mentioning that content-aware tiling may also result in a loss of large-scale features, i.e. features whose scale size are larger than the tile size. But according to our experiments on 228 images (details of the dataset please see Section 5.3.2) using the default SURF setting, there are only 0.8% of the features with scale size larger than the smallest tile size 96x96. In addition, among all the large-scale features, only a portion of them can be correctly matched in object recognition tasks. Therefore, the impact of such loss on the final performance is negligible. Object recognition results in Sec. 5.3 will further confirm this argument.

Pseudo Code 3: Content-Aware Tile Size Selection

```
Input:     TSCs : tile size candidates
Output:    MCRs: maximum continuous regions
Variants:  tile-size, tile-size_next: tile size before and
                    after increase of this iteration
           entropy, entropy_next: entropy of a tile
                    before and after increase

procedure SelectMCRs
  Initialize TSCs = {96x96, 96x120,...}
  for each tile
      tile-size = 96x96
      entropy = Entropy( tile-size)
      if (entropy < ε )
          continue
      for T = 2:end
          tile-size_next = TSCs [T]
          entropy_next = Entropy( tile-size_next )
          if ( entropy_next > entropy)
              tile-size = tile-size_next
              entropy = entropy_next
          else
              break
          endif
      end
  end
```

4.2 Orientation by Gradient Moments

In Section 3.2.2, the implementation using a lookup table demonstrates 30%~60% time cost reduction for computing dominant orientations. But updating gradient histograms still takes a significant amount of time. In addition, the lookup table increases memory cost. In this section, we propose an alternative orientation operator based on the gradient moments to further accelerate the SURF detector.

The gradient moment [20] of a patch is defined as:

$$mG_{pq} = \sum_{x,y} x^p y^q G(x,y) \; . \qquad (2)$$

where $G(x,y)$ is the gradient responses of location (x,y). With the gradient moments of a patch, we define the *gradient centroid* of the patch as:

$$C_{gradient} = \left(\frac{mG_{10}}{mG_{00}}, \frac{mG_{01}}{mG_{00}} \right) \; . \qquad (3)$$

The *gradient centroid* is analogous to the density centroid of an object, but it is obtained based on the gradient distribution rather than the material density. Much like the density centroid of a non-uniform object is usually offset from its geometric center; the *gradient centroid* of a corner is offset from its center. According to this, we can construct a vector $\overrightarrow{OC}_{gradient}$ from the corner's center O to the *gradient centroid* $C_{gradient}$. $\overrightarrow{OC}_{gradient}$ is determined by the intrinsic characteristic of a corner, thus it is rotation invariant and can be used to compute an orientation. Accordingly, the orientation of the patch is:

$$\theta = \tan^{-1}(m_{01}, m_{10}) = \tan^{-1}\left(\frac{\sum_{x,y} yG(x,y)}{\sum_{x,y} xG(x,y)} \right) \; . \qquad (4)$$

The gradient moment based approach does not involve any branches, nor extra memory overhead arising from a lookup table. Therefore, it completely averts branch hazard penalties and extra memory accesses which are inevitable in the gradient histogram analysis process. In addition, it avoids the time cost of updating the gradient histogram for every pixel. Although the gradient moment based approach incurs two additional multiplication instructions to compute the gradient moments, i.e. multiplying gradients with x and y coordinates, multiplication is reasonably fast for execution, especially with the DSP accelerators commonly available in mobile APs.

Another option for efficiently computing dominant orientations is based on intensity moments, as used in [3]. Computing first order intensity moment only needs one instruction, i.e. multiplying x or y with image intensity $I(x,y)$:

$$m_{pq} = \sum_{x,y} x^p y^q I(x,y) \,. \tag{5}$$

At first glance, this intensity based approach is faster than using gradient moments: computing the gradient responses in x or y direction requires 6 operations based on an integral image. However, the intensity moment based approach utilizes an image pyramid, i.e. a series of down sampled images, for interest points at different scales. While the SURF detector replaces the expensive image pyramid construction phase by processing the original image using up-scaling box filters, no image pyramid is generated in SURF detection. As a result, the intensity moments based approach cannot be employed in the SURF detector.

5. EXPERIMENTS AND RESULTS

In this section, we first describe key features of the mobile platforms used in our experiments in Section 5.1. Then we examine the speedup achieved by each proposed technique in Section 5.2. In Section 5.3, we apply the proposed techniques to mobile recognition tasks. We compare the accelerated SURF with the state-of-the-art ORB detector in terms of recognition accuracy and efficiency.

5.1 Experiment Platforms

We conducted experiments on three mobile platforms: a Motorola Droid, an HTC Thunderbolt, and a Motorola Xoom1 tablet.

The Motorola Droid smartphone runs Android 2.2 Froyo. Launched in Q4 of 2009, Droid' application processor (AP) is TI OMAP 3430 SoC which contains 32KB/32KB L1 instruction/data caches, a 256KB L2 cache and an ARM Cortex-A8 processor running at 600MHz. The Cortex-A8 has a dual-issue in-order 13-stage pipeline and program flow prediction hardware, also known as branch predictor. With program flow prediction enabled, a mis-predicted branch incurs a penalty of 13 cycles.

The HTC Thunderbolt is the first 4G LTE smartphone, which runs Android 2.3.4 Gingerbread. It was launched in Q1 of 2011. Thunderbolt's AP is the second generation 1GHz Scorpion processor from Qualcomm's own design, and has a 13-stage load/store pipeline and two integer pipelines. One of the integer pipelines has 10 stages and can perform simple arithmetic operations while the other has 12 stages and can perform both simple and more complex arithmetic operations. While the cache size of the Scorpion has not been made public, its L1 and L2 caches should be around 32KB and 512KB respectively.

The Motorola Xoom1 is an Android-based tablet, which runs Android 3.0 Honeycomb. It was first introduced at CES in Q1 of 2011. Xoom1's AP is Nvidia's Tegra 2 SoC which features a dual-core ARM Cortex-A9 processor. Each A9 core has its own private 32KB L1 instruction and data caches. The L2 cache is up to 1MB in size, shared by all cores in the AP. The Cortex-A9 has an 8-stage pipeline and follows a dual-issue out-of-order architecture, instead of A8's in-order architecture. While there are multiple cores in the A9, we used only one core in our experiments.

Here, we focus on Android-based platforms. While trying our ideas on iOS-based devices could be interesting, neither approach proposed in this paper utilizes OS-specific functions for the speedup (e.g. setting higher priority for the program in scheduling or calling DMA for fast memory access). Therefore, the trend observed in the results should be OS-independent. In addition, based on the experiments on three different versions of Android OS (see Sec. 5.2) we observe that, the resulting trend is similar and there is no indication that a different OS would make a difference.

To compare the runtime on mobile platforms vs. x86-based PCs, we also run experiments on a Lenovo Thinkpad T420 laptop which is powered by an Intel core i5-2410M running at 2.3GHz.

5.2 Speed Evaluation

5.2.1 Implementation Details

All of our experiments are based on the OpenCV2.3.1 implementation [14] originally released for Windows PCs. Other libraries such as OpenSURF can also be used for the evaluation. But since we compare SURF and ORB, using OpenCV for both detectors provides a more fair comparison: both of them would have similar overhead if any due to other modules of OpenCV. To make a fair comparison between mobile platforms and x86-based PCs, we re-compiled the OpenCV library for all platforms using the same source code.

We tested the runtime of the two proposed techniques using 109 document images of size 480x480. We used the default scale space parameter settings: the initial box filter size is 9x9 and there are 3 octaves, each of which contains 4 layers. Based on these settings, the largest box filter size is 156x156 and on average 2000 points are detected by the original SURF detector.

We used two versions of SURF detector, U-SURF and O-SURF [1]. U-SURF stands for upright SURF, i.e. the dominant orientation is not computed. Since most cache misses occur in the point detection phase, while few happen in the orientation computation phase, we evaluated the tiled SURF based on U-SURF. O-SURF stands for oriented SURF, i.e. dominant orientation is computed. We evaluated the gradient moment orientation operation based on O-SURF.

Computing gradient responses is the basis of SURF point detection and orientation estimation. OpenCV2.3.1 implements this computation in a static function called *icvCalcHaarPattern*, incurring huge call stack overhead. To avoid such overhead and other compiler-related issues, we replaced the function call by manually inlining *icvCalcHaarPattern*. In the following part, we denote the original OpenCV2.3.1 implementation as version 1(v1 for short) and the revised version as version 2 (v2 for short).

5.2.2 Evaluation of Tiled SURF

We evaluated tiled SURF using two experiments. In the first experiment, we examine the relationship between the tile size and the runtime on our three mobile platforms. Two metrics are used in this evaluation: 1) *time cost* and 2) *time cost per operation*. We report *time cost per operation* because the number of box filtering operations varies with respect to tile sizes, i.e. a smaller tile size requires fewer operations. Time cost per operation more accurately reflects the overhead resulting from memory traffic.

Six tile-size configurations are considered: 96x96, 120x120, 160x160, 160x240, 240x240 and 480x480. Figure 6 summarizes the results, from which two observations can be made: 1) The

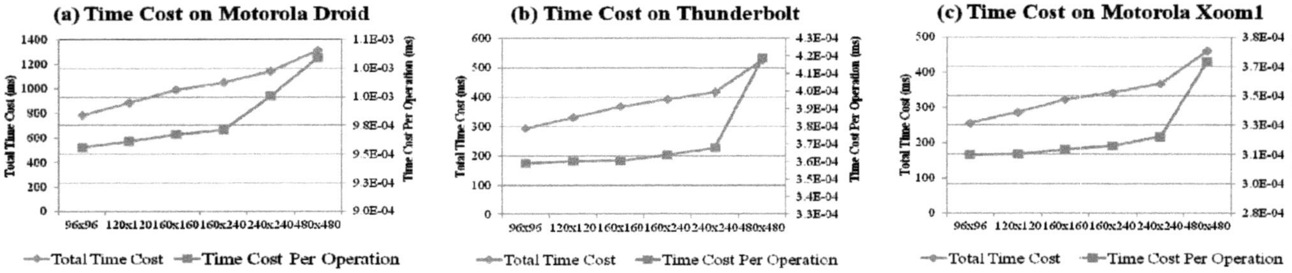

Figure 6. Time cost and time cost per operation of tiled SURF (a) on Droid with Cortex-A8, (b) on Thunderbolt with Scorpion, and (c) on Xoom1 with Cortex-A9

time cost decreases monotonically as the tile size decreases for all three mobile platforms. These results confirm that using smaller tiles can help reduce the time cost. 2) For the curve of time cost per operation, there is a turning point. Increasing the tile size before reaching this point, cost per operation increases slowly; while after this point it increases sharply. The cause of this phenomenon is that when space needed for storing the working set of a tile exceeds the cache size, the number of cache misses increases dramatically, leading to a sudden time cost increase resulting from memory access. We also notice that the turning point varies for different platforms. For a Droid, the turning point is around 160x240, while for a Thunderbolt and a Xoom1, it occurs at 240x240. These results are consistent with the cache sizes of their APs. The Scorpion and the Cortex-A9 have a larger L2 cache than the Cortex-A8, and thus can hold larger data arrays than the latter.

The next experiments focus on examining the speedup achieved by the tiled U-SURF with Content-Aware Tiling (CAT) and how effective it is in narrowing the speed gap between a mobile platform and a x86-based PC. We compare the *time cost* and the *Phone-to-PC ratio* between the original U-SURF and tiled SURF with CAT. The *Phone-to-PC ratio* is the runtime of a program running on a mobile platform divided by that on an x86-based PC, which reflects the speed gap between them.

$$Phone\text{-}to\text{-}PC\ ratio = \frac{\text{runtime on mobile platform}}{\text{runtime on x86-based PC}}$$

The first two rows of Tables 3 and 4 compare the *time cost* and *Phone-to-PC ratio* of U-SURF without and with CAT. The remaining rows of Tables 3 and 4 will be discussed in the next subsection. As expected, U-SURF with CAT can greatly reduce both *time cost* and *Phone-to-PC ratio,* compared to the original U-SURF. At the same time, it reduces the *Phone-to-PC ratio* by 12.5% - 42.9% on the three devices. The reduction in *Phone-to-PC ratio* further indicates that the *mismatch of data access pattern and a small cache size* leads to more severe runtime degradation on mobile platforms than x86-based PCs, so alleviating this problem is critical for performance optimization when porting algorithms to mobile platforms.

5.2.3 Evaluation of Gradient Moment based Method

In this section, we first examine the *Phone-to-PC ratio* and *time cost* for computing orientation alone. Then we integrate the gradient moment based method into SURF and compare the performance of the accelerated SURF with the original SURF, its variant implementations and ORB.

Results of the first experiment are illustrated in Figures 7(a) and (b). First, we compare the *Phone-to-PC ratio* of *hist-branch* and *hist-lookup table* in Figure 7(a) to evaluate branch hazard penalty on runtime for mobile platforms. The results show that *hist-lookup table* greatly reduces the *Phone-to-PC ratio*, demonstrating that the SURF detector running on a mobile platform suffers much greater branch hazard penalty than on an Intel i5-based laptop. Secondly, we investigate the relationship between *Phone-to-PC ratio* reduction and pipeline depth of mobile processors. Since the Cortex-A8 and the Scorpion have a 13-stage pipeline, while the Cortex-A9 has a shorter pipeline of 8 stages, running a SURF detector on the Cortex-A9 has a smaller pipeline hazard penalty and thus avoiding such penalty achieves smaller improvement to *Phone-to-PC ratio.* Thirdly, we inspect the runtime improvement achieved by the *gradient moment.* We compare the absolute time costs of *gradient moment, hist-branch* and *hist-lookup table* in Figure 7 (b). The results confirm that *gradient moment* takes the least amount of time among the three. Specifically, it achieves a 14x-28x speedup compared to *hist-branch,* and a 6x-19x speedup compared to *hist-lookup table* on these three mobile devices.

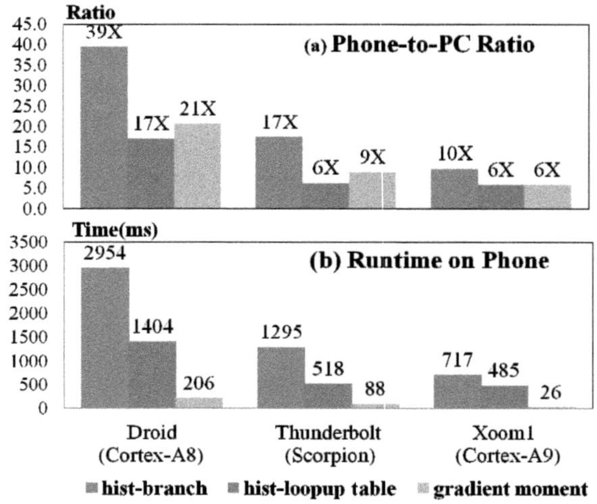

Figure 7. Comparison of (a) Phone-to-PC ratio and (b) runtime on mobile platforms

In the second experiment, we incorporate the gradient moment operator into O-SURF and examine the overall improvement in runtime and *Phone-to-PC ratio* compared to the three versions of the original O-SURF. Runtime and *Phone-to-PC ratio* are shown in the 3th~6th rows of Tables 3 and 4 respectively. Compared to the original SURF implementation using gradient histograms (i.e. O-SURF v1), the gradient moment based method reduces the overall runtime by 80% on a Droid, 75% on a Thunderbolt and 76% on a Xoom1. At the same time, it improves the *Phone-to-PC ratio* by 65%, 53% and 53% over O-SURF v1, respectively. Finally we apply the two proposed techniques to the O-SURF and compare it with ORB. The results are listed in the last two rows of Tables 3 and 4. Based on the results in 7th and 8th rows of Table 3, with the application of these two proposed techniques, the runtime ratio of running a SURF detector to running an ORB detector on a mobile platform is reduced to 1.6x-1.9x, from 12x-13x if the techniques are not applied. Moreover, the *Phone-to-PC ratio* of the accelerated SURF is reduced to 3x-13x which is similar to that of an ORB detector.

5.3 Mobile Object Recognition

Mobile object recognition is a fundamental task for many embedded computer vision applications, including mobile augmented reality, mobile image search, etc., thus it would be the most effective task to evaluate the performance of the accelerated SURF. In this section, we present results on mobile object recognition to evaluate the robustness of the accelerated SURF.

5.3.1 Implementation Details

We implemented a conventional object recognition pipeline similar to [3]: we first detect interest points and extract descriptors for a query image and then match them to images in a database. We consider the first returned database image with sufficient number of matched points as the result for a query image.

We combine the accelerated SURF detector with two widely used descriptors, the SURF descriptor [1] and the BRIEF descriptor [19], respectively. Each SURF descriptor is a 64-dimensional integer vector; we utilize a k-d tree to fast match the SURF descriptors. The BRIEF descriptor is a 256-bit binary string; correspondingly, we leverage Locality Sensitive Hashing (LSH) for fast matching of the BRIEF descriptors. We use the OpenCV2.3.1 implementation for the descriptors and the indexing structures and set identical parameters for all experiments.

5.3.2 Database and Testing Images

Database [21]: our database consists of two types of images – 109 document images generated from the *ICME06* proceedings and 119 natural scene images containing buildings and people selected from Oxford Building 5K, yielding 228 images in total.

Testing images [21]: we manually captured two pictures for each database image - one of which has ~45° rotation relative to the database image and is used for testing orientation operators while the other one is upright and used for testing the tiled U-SURF. In mobile applications, images are often blurred due to the motion. In order to examine the robustness of point detectors with respect to such distortions, we implemented motion blur distortions using ImageMagick [15] and applied them to all testing images. Exemplar testing images are shown in Figure 8.

5.3.3 Results

We first focus on investigating the robustness by comparing between: 1) the original SURF vs. the tiled SURF; 2) the original SURF and the tiled SURF vs. the lighter-weight detector ORB. In this experiment we use testing images without rotations. For each detector, we combine it with the SURF descriptor and the BRIEF descriptor, yielding 6 different combinations in total.

Figure 9 displays the detection rate and precision of the 6 detector-descriptor combinations. Two conclusions can be drawn from the results. 1) Original SURF vs. Tiled SURF: tiling does not degrade on the robustness of a SURF detector, as evidenced by the fact that tiled SURF with CAT achieves similar detection rate and precision as the original SURF. Comparing the curves between "U-SURF untiled+SURF" and "U-SURF CAT+SURF", and between "U-SURF untiled+BRIEF" and "U-SURF CAT+BRIEF", the gap between each of these two pairs of curves is very small. 2) SURF (either original or tiled) vs. ORB: both original SURF and tiled SURF are more robust than ORB with respect to motion blur distortions. As shown in Figure 9, the detection rate and precision of the ORB detector combined with the SURF or BRIEF descriptors decrease sharply with increasing motion blurs, while these two numbers remain almost identical for "U-SURF Untiled+SURF" and "U-SURF CAT+SURF". In comparison. the detection rate and precision of "U-SURF Untilied+BRIEF" and "U-SURF CAT+BRIEF" also drops as motion blur increases, but the slope is still smaller than that of ORB. We think the lack of distinguishing ability for the BRIEF descriptor might account for the drops of these two configurations.

In the second recognition experiment, we compare the performance of the orientation operator using gradient histograms and using gradient moments. In this experiment, we use testing

Table 3. Time Cost Comparison on Three Mobile Platforms

Time (ms)	Droid	Thunder bolt	Xoom1
U-SURF v2	1310	525	461
U-SURF CAT	930	356	243
O-SURF v1	7700	2495	2156
O-SURF v2	4264	1820	1178
O-SURF Table	2714	1043	946
O-SURF GMoment	1516	613	519
O-SURF CAT+GMoment	1053	404	269
O-ORB [3]	615	209	170

Table 4. Speed Ratio Comparison on Three Mobile Platforms

Phone-to-PC Ratio (x)	Droid	Thunder bolt	Xoom1
U-SURF v2	20	8	7
U-SURF CAT	14	7	4
O-SURF v1	54	17	15
O-SURF v2	30	13	8
O-SURF Table	18	7	6
O-SURF GMoment	19	8	7
O-SURF CAT+GMoment	13	7	3
O-ORB [3]	15	5	4

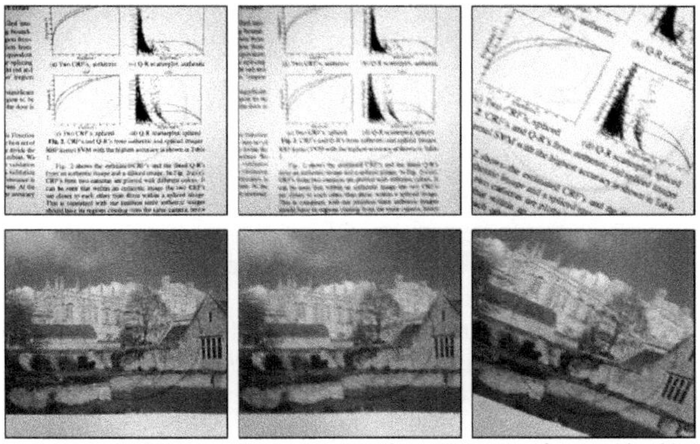

(a) captured Image (b) motion blur(sigma=8) (c) rotation + motion blur

Figure 8. Exemplar testing images (a) without motion blur, (b) with motion blur, (c) with rotation and motion blur

Table 5. Performance on 228 Testing Images with Rotations

Detector (O-SURF)	Detection Rate	Precision
Untiled + GradHist	0.963	0.963
Untiled + GradMoment	0.961	0.963
CAT + GradMoment	0.961	0.963

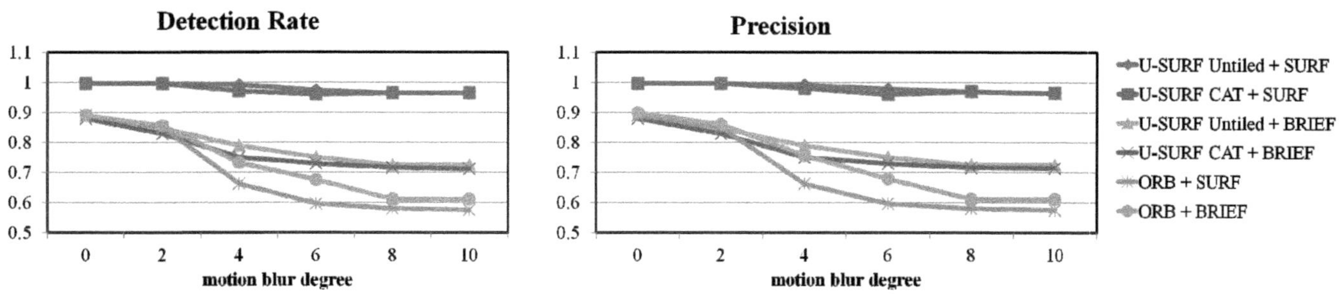

Figure 9. Detection rate and precision on testing images with motion blur distortion of different degrees. We change the blur degree (standard deviation) from 0 to 10 to simulate blur caused by different motion speed.

images with rotations and motion blurs. Table 5 shows the results for testing images whose sigma of motion blur is equal to 8. For other motion blur parameters, the trend is very similar. The first two rows compare the detection rate and precision achieved by the two orientation operators. Both methods achieve very similar performance, demonstrating that the proposed method does not reduce its robustness for producing repeatable dominant orientations. The last row shows the performance achieved by using the two proposed techniques together. The result is consistent with the observations in Figure 9 – the detection rate and precision obtained by using content-aware tiling are very close to those achieved by not using it.

6. CONCLUSION AND FUTURE WORK

In this paper, we analyze the SURF algorithm and identify two mismatches between its required computations and mobile platforms, which result in significant runtime degradation. To address the mismatches, two techniques – content-aware tiling and a gradient moment based orientation operator, are proposed to speed up SURF detection. We successfully demonstrate the high efficiency, high recognition accuracy, and a low *Phone-to-PC runtime ratio* of our accelerated SURF compared to the original SURF detector and the ORB detector.

Despite demonstrating the performance using a single-core mobile AP, the proposed techniques are directly applicable to multi-core APs as well. Future work includes examining the acceleration ability of the proposed methods in parallel computing. It is also worth mentioning that although we focus on SURF detection in this paper, the two identified mismatches may exist in other computer vision algorithms as well. For instance, face detection algorithms which also rely on varying-sized box filers (or Harr features) would suffer from a large number of cache misses due to poor data locality, or decision tree-based algorithms may have high branch mis-prediction penalty arising from many conditional branches while traversing a tree structure. Therefore, adapting existing vision algorithms, which were not designed for embedded systems, to alleviate the problems caused by these mismatches would be the right approach for performance optimization of porting such tasks to mobile platforms.

7. REFERENCES

[1] Bay, H., Ess, A., Tuytelaars, T. and Gool, L.V.. SURF: Speeded-up Robust Features. *In Proc. of ECCV'06.*

[2] Bay, H., Ess, A., Tuytelaars, T. and Gool, L.V.. Speeded-up Robust Features (SURF). *In CVIU,* 110(3), June, 2008.

[3] Rublee, E., Rabaud, V., Konolige, K., and Bradski, G.. ORB: an Efficient Alternative to SIFT or SURF. *In Proc. of ICCV'11.*

[4] Rosten, E. and Drummond, T.. Machine Learning for High Speed Corner Detection. *In Proc. of ECCV'06.*

[5] Rosten, E., Porter, R., and Drummond, T.. Faster and Better: A machine learning approach to corner detection. *In IEEE Trans. PAMI*, 32:105–119, 2010.

[6] Wagner, D., Reitmayr, G., Mulloni, A., Drummond, T. and Schmalstieg, D.. Pose tracking from natural features on mobile phones. *In Proc. of ISMAR'08.*

[7] Wagner, D., Mulloni, A., Langlotz, T., and Schmalstieg, D.. Real-time Panoramic Mapping and tracking on Mobile Phones. *In Proc of VR'10.*

[8] Ta, D.N., Chen, W.C., Gelfand, N., and Pulli, K.. SURFTrac: Efficient Tracking and Continuous Object Recognition using Local Feature Descriptors. *In Proc. of CVPR'09.*

[9] Chen, W.C., Xiong, Y. G., Gao, J., Gelfand, N. and Grzeszczuk, R.. Efficient Extraction of Robust Image Features on Mobile Devices. *In Proc. of ISMAR'07.*

[10] Terriberry, T. B., French, L. M., and Helmsen, J.. GPU Accelerating Speeded-Up Robust Features. *In Proc. of 3DPVT'08.*

[11] Clemons, J., Jones, A., Perricone, R., Savarese, S., and Austin, T.. EFFEX: An Embedded Processor for Computer Vision Based feature Extraction. *In Proc. of DAC'11.*

[12] Clemons, J., Zhu, H.S., Savarese, S., and Austin, T.. MEVBench: A Mobile Computer Vision Benchmarking Suite. *In Proc. of ISWC'11.*

[13] Silpa, B.V.N. and Patney, A. and Krishna, T. and Panda, P.R. and Visweswaran, G.S.. Texture Filter Memory; A Power-Efficient and Scalable Texture Memory Architecture for Mobile Graphics Processors. *In Proc. of ICCAD'08.*

[14] OpenCV2.3.1, http://sourceforge.net/projects/opencvlibrary/

[15] ImageMagick, http://www.imagemagick.org/script/index.php

[16] Lowe, D. G.. Distinctive image features from scale-invariant keypoints. *In IJCV*, 60(2):91–110, 2004.

[17] Foley, J. D., Dam, A. V., Feiner, S. K., and Hughes ,J. F.. *Computer Graphics, Principles and Practice, Second Edition.* Addison-Wesley, Reading, Massachusetts, 1990.

[18] Coleman, S. and McKinley, K. S.. Tile size selection using cache organization and data layout. *In Proc. of SIGPLAN'95.*

[19] Calonder, M., Lepetit, V., Strecha, C., and Fua, P.. BRIEF: Binary Robust Independent Elementary Features. In *Proc. of ECCV'10.*

[20] Rosin, P. L.. Measuring Corner Properties. *In CVIU*, 73(2):291 – 307, 1999.

[21] Yang, X., Liu, Q., Liao, C.Y., and Cheng, K.T.. Large-Scale EMM Identification Based on Geometry-Constrained Visual Word Correspondence Voting. *In Proc. of ICMR' 11.*

[22] Gauglitz, S., Hollerer, T., and Turk, M.. Evaluation of Interest Point Detectors and Feature Descriptors for Visual Tracking. *In IJCV*, 94(3):335-360, 2011.

IMShare: Instantly Sharing Your Mobile Landmark Images by Search-based Reconstruction

Lican Dai
Univ. of Science and Technology of China
licand@mail.ustc.edu.cn

Huanjing Yue
Tianjin University
dayueer@tju.edu.cn

Xiaoyan Sun, Feng Wu
Microsoft Research Asia
{xysun, fengwu}@microsoft.com

ABSTRACT
Instantly sharing captured landmark images is becoming fashionable, much like when you write a blog or chat with friends by mobile phone. However, real-time transmission of high-resolution images poses a significant challenge to contemporary mobile networks. Either long delays in transmission or largely reduced image resolution can lead to bad user experience. In this paper, we propose a novel mobile-cloud scheme *IMShare* to enable instant sharing of high-resolution images. On the mobile side, high-resolution images are described by their thumbnails and SIFT (Scale-Invariant Feature Transform) descriptors. After compression, data sent by mobile phones can be reduced to an average of 2.6 kilobytes (KB) per mega pixel. On the cloud side, high-resolution images are reproduced from a large-scale image database by retrieving partial duplicate images by SIFT descriptors and stitching corresponding image patches together under the guidance of the thumbnails. *IMShare* is the first scheme to demonstrate that not only visually pleasant images can be reconstructed using this mobile-cloud method but also the reconstruction can be done in seconds using parallel computing. Our user study of a half million images in a database shows that the proposed *IMShare* significantly outperforms the current method on subjective quality.

Categories and Subject Descriptors
I.2.10 [Vision and Scene Understanding]: VISION

General Terms
Algorithms, Experimentation

Keywords
Image sharing, Partial duplicate image retrieval, SIFT descriptor, Image reconstruction.

1. INTRODUCTION
We have witnessed rapid development of mobile phones in the past decades. It has been extended from a cell phone to an integrated and ubiquitous platform for communication, social networking, entertainment, and information acquisition. Cameras in mobile phones have been upgraded to 5 mega pixels as a standard configuration. People are getting used to taking pictures with mobile phones anytime and instantly sharing their experiences with family, friends and even unknown fans. We refer to this kind of application as instant mobile image sharing.

However, real-time transmission of megapixel images poses a big challenge to modern mobile networks. Although mobile networks have been developed up to the fourth generation (4G), most regions even in large cities are covered by 2G and 3G networks. It often takes minutes to send one high-resolution JPEG image over a given mobile network. Furthermore, the process consumes a lot of power, the most important resource in operating a mobile phone. One popular solution is for high-resolution images to be greatly down-sampled before sharing, making them look small and unimpressive in a high-definition (HD) monitor. Either long delay in transmission or largely reduced image resolution can result in a bad user experience.

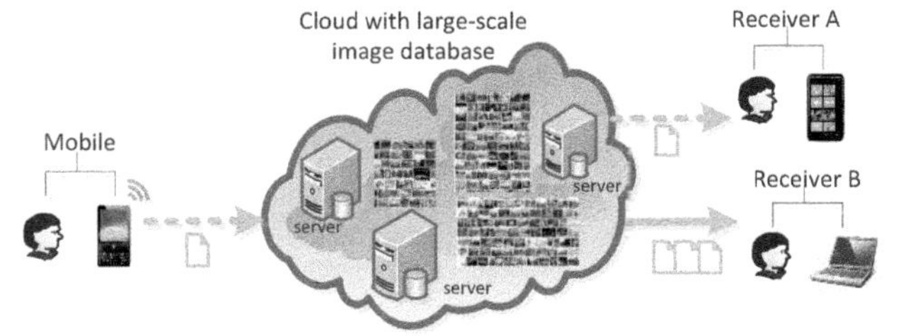

Figure 1: The proposed *IMShare* for instant mobile image sharing.

To break through the above limitations in mobile phones, we propose a novel mobile-cloud scheme called *IMShare* to enable new user experiences on instant mobile sharing, as shown in Figure 1. On the mobile side, high-resolution images are first described by thumbnails and SIFT descriptors. By utilizing the thumbnail for the compression of SIFT descriptors, the description size of every image can be reduced to about 10 kilobytes and can be easily transmitted even over a 2G network. On the cloud side, there is a large-scale image database. High-resolution images are reconstructed from the database via their descriptions. Finally, the reconstructed images are transmitted to receivers with broadband network in JPEG format, whereas the thumbnails are transmitted to mobile receivers.

Implementing the proposed *IMShare* faces several challenges. First, can megapixel images be described only by several kilobytes when high visual quality is expected by receivers? State-of-the-art image compression techniques are not currently capable of achieving this. Second, even if some highly correlated images can be found in the database, do reconstructed images always have appealing quality? Do the reconstructed images look like the original ones? Third, reconstructing images from a large-scale database is a data intensive and computing intensive process. Can it be done in a short time? Fourth, what will happen if there are no correlated images found in the database? All of these questions will be answered in this paper.

We summarize the contributions of *IMShare* three-fold. (1) Some hardware limitations of mobile phone that are due to mobility can be greatly relieved and even removed through the powerful cloud. *IMShare* presents a promising application for mobile-cloud computing. (2) Reconstructing images of visually pleasant quality is feasible when a proper description is selected and a large-scale image database is available. (3) Although image reconstruction is often considered intensive computing, it can be done in a short time with current computing resources.

The rest of this paper is organized as follows. Section 2 gives a brief overview of related work. Section 3 presents the proposed image description and its compression. Section 4 discusses how to reconstruct images from the large-scale database. Section 5 focuses on the parallel implementation. Experimental results and a user study are presented in Section 6. Finally, Section 7 concludes this paper and discusses our future work.

2. RELATED WORK

This section starts from current image sharing schemes. Although we have not found similar schemes reported previously, the components of the proposed *IMShare* are related to multiple fields in multimedia.

2.1 Image Sharing

Image sharing is one of the most popular applications on the Internet. Flickr's success is ample evidence [1], where hundreds of billions of images are shared and millions of images are uploaded every day. Current research in this field assumes that users are sharing images to Web albums. This application does not require a real-time experience. The main problem to solve is how to automatically tag and manage shared images. Therefore, Marlow et al. propose a taxonomy system to tag shared images [2]. Sarvas et al. propose MobShare that enables controlled and organized sharing of mobile images [3]. Davis et al. propose MMM2 to combine camera phones with automatic uploading to a web-based archiving and sharing application [4].

IMShare targets emerging live experience sharing. For example, when you go sightseeing, you take some landmark images by mobile phone and share them with friends immediately. Your friends can comment on said images very soon after. Similar things often happen when you use a mobile phone to write a blog or chat in Facebook. *IMShare* enables users to share their experiences in real-time using high-resolution images.

2.2 Description Compression

In *IMShare*, high-resolution images are described by thumbnails and SIFT descriptors. They have to be compressed before transmission. It is easy to compress thumbnails by JPEG or H.264 intra frame coding [5]. Both of them have been extensively supported in mobile devices.

Compression of SIFT descriptors has recently become required by mobile applications. The dimension of every feature descriptor is 128 [6]. Dimension reduction is proposed by using PCA [7] and linear discriminant analysis [8]. Yeo et al. propose using coarsely quantized random projections of feature descriptors to build binary hashes [9]. Several other approaches try to directly reduce generated dimension. SURF (Speed Up Robust Feature) descriptors reduce the dimension to 64 [10]. Compressed histogram of gradient (CHoG) descriptors, proposed by Chandrasekhar et al. in [11], are designed for compression. It not only changes the generation of descriptors but also compresses them by tree coding and entropy coding.

Approaches for image compression are also adopted. Chandrasekhar et al. propose transform coding of feature descriptors [12]. Later on, Makar et al. propose compressing image patches at different scales and then extract SIFT descriptors from decompressed patches [13]. It shows that the compression of image patches sometimes has a better performance than direct compression of SIFT descriptors. However, if there are many descriptors to compress for an image, these patches will overlap each other, thus leading to low compression performance.

In *IMShare*, SIFT descriptors are compressed in a different way. The basic idea is to fully exploit the thumbnail. Only the locations, scales and orientations of SIFT descriptors are extracted and compressed on the mobile side. By using this data, 128-dimension feature vectors are recovered from the decompressed thumbnail in the cloud. It significantly reduces both the size of SIFT descriptors and computation in mobile devices.

2.3 Image Reconstruction

Several papers have proposed reconstructing images from a large-scale database in recent years. Eitz et al. propose to take a sketch drawn by a user as input [14]. Chen et al. improve the scheme by taking both sketch and text labels as input [15]. Recently, Johnson et al. propose taking a computer-generated (CG) image as an input [16]. They are more applicable for reconstructing images with simple structures. The most related work in this line is to reconstruct an image with SIFT descriptors from an image database [17]. The purpose of [17] is to show that an image can be reconstructed just from its SIFT descriptors even if there is no similar image in the database, creating a potential security issue. However, the reconstructed images are very low quality because they only use local descriptors. It is difficult to verify searched image patches. They have to be stitched together with smooth constraints.

In *IMShare*, reconstructed images visually look much better than the results reported in [17] because there is a thumbnail available. Mismatched image patches can be removed completely or partially with the thumbnail. Matched image patches are stitched according to their reliabilities to the thumbnail. In addition, reconstructing images is a time-consuming process. Previous schemes have never claimed that it can be done rapidly. In *IMShare*, we propose a simple 1D geometric model for spatial verification in partial duplicate image retrieval, adopt a greedy graph-based segmentation instead of graph cuts and adopt a new set of convolution pyramids for approximating Poisson blending. Furthermore, the reconstruction is implemented parallel to a multi-core server so that it can be done in seconds.

3. MOBILE COMPUTING

Images captured by current mobile phones often have 5M or more pixels. For a given image I, it is first down-sampled to a thumbnail I_d in *IMShare*. The ratio is 2^N: 1 in each dimension, where N is often set as 4. The thumbnail is compressed by JPEG and sent to the cloud. SIFT descriptors are extracted from image I via difference-of-Gaussian detection. A SIFT descriptor is denoted as $S = \{x_f, s, \theta, V\}$. x_f, where subscript f indicates a feature point, tells the location of S in the original image. Scale s indicates local region size covered by the SIFT descriptor. Orientation θ is the dominant direction of the local gradient histogram. Feature vector V is a 128-dimension vector that characterizes local region by gradient histogram at different directions.

SIFT descriptors with small scales have little effect on image reconstruction. Thus only SIFT descriptors with scale $s \geq N - 1$ are selected. To further reduce data for transmission and computation on mobile devices, even for these SIFT descriptors, only locations, scales and orientations are extracted and sent to the cloud after compression, whereas 128-dimension feature vectors are recovered from the thumbnail in the cloud according to received locations, scales and orientations. The number of SIFT descriptors for a megapixel image is more than one thousand on average. As shown in Figure 2, it is enough to cover most image regions.

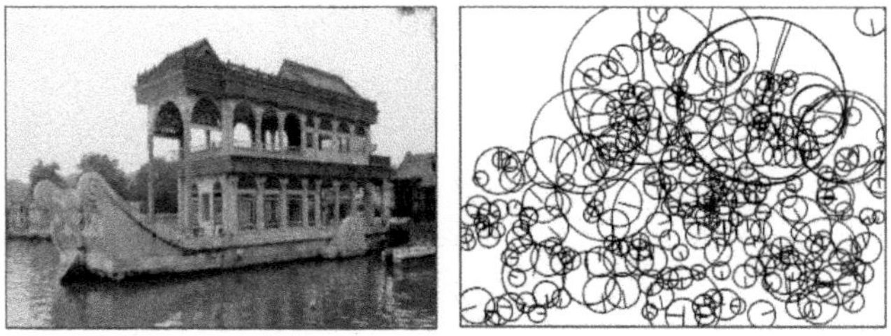

Figure 2: An example of an input image and the coverage of extracted SIFT descriptors with scale $s \geq N-1$.

Locations are quantized into integers in original resolution. Given $\mathcal{L} = \{x_f(1), \ldots, x_f(M)\}$ as the set of locations of all SIFT descriptors, where M is the total number, we first generate a binary matrix B_l. Its size is the same as that of I and its element is defined as

$$b_l(x) = \begin{cases} 1, if\ x \in \mathcal{L} \\ 0, if\ x \notin \mathcal{L} \end{cases} \quad (1)$$

x is the location of a pixel in I. This matrix is compressed using binary arithmetic coding. For any $b_l(x) = 1$, an integer is compressed to indicate the number of SIFT descriptors at x. It is most likely one but up to four are allowed. It is compressed by small-alphabet arithmetic coding. The location compression is similar to that for a block of DCT coefficients in H.264 [5].

s decides local region sizes to calculate θ and V. Taking the structure of s into account, the integer part (ranging from $N-1$ to $N+6$) is first coded by 3 bits. The fractional part is quantized into 16 levels at precision of 1/16 that is represented by 4 bits. θ decides rotation invariance of SIFT descriptors. It is quantized into 128 levels at precision of $360°/128 \approx 3°$ and represented by 7 bits. Therefore, for a SIFT descriptor, s and θ together take up 14 bits.

4. CLOUD COMPUTING

SIFT descriptors with scale $s \geq N-2$ of all images in the database are first extracted. 100 million SIFT feature descriptors are randomly selected and trained into a vocabulary of 1 million visual words by approximate K-means [18]. Visual words are organized into k-d trees for the nearest neighbor searching during quantization. After that, a visual word v is assigned to every SIFT feature vector V of all images according to the nearest Euclidian distance. Furthermore, visual words of every image have been organized into tens to hundreds of groups that will be discussed in Section 4.1. All of these have been prepared in advance.

A server in the cloud decodes the thumbnail $\tilde{I}$ and up-samples it to the original resolution $\tilde{I}_u$. The up-sampled thumbnail $\tilde{I}_u$ incrementally convolves with Gaussians to produce images in a scale space similar to [6]. After decoding locations, scales and orientations, all SIFT descriptors with scale $s \geq N-1$ are recovered by calculating feature vectors in the Gaussian scale space. These SIFT descriptors will be used as query in the cloud. Visual words are assigned to all feature vectors and organized into groups too.

4.1 Partial Duplicate Image Retrieval

In *IMShare*, duplicate image regions are expected in every region in I. It is similar to the problem of partial duplicate image retrieval. The approaches proposed previously to solve this problem are to bundle visual words together. Wu et al. propose bundling visual words in a maximally stable region as a group [19]. Furthermore, visual words in a group are ordered by 1D linear model. In retrieval, visual words have to be matched in the proper order. It is a weak geometric verification. Zhou et al. propose a 2D geometric verification in Cartesian coordinate system [20], which is implemented by novel spatial coding. But it is not easy to handle rotated regions.

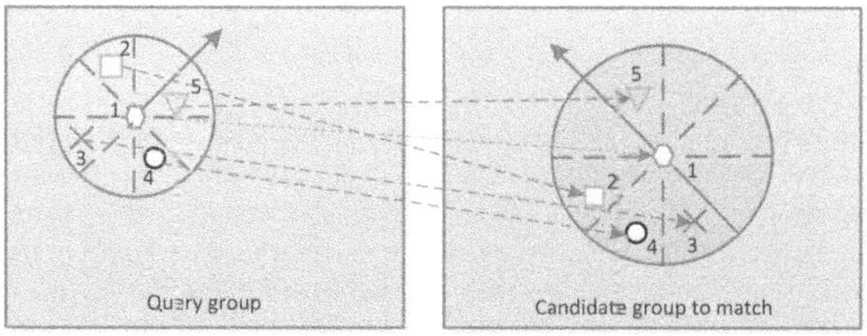

Figure 3: Matching two groups of visual words. "1" denotes the central SIFT descriptor. {"2",…,"5"} denote member SIFT descriptors. The polar axis, which aligns with the orientation of the central SIFT descriptor, is denoted by the line with an arrow.

In this paper, we directly bundle overlapped SIFT descriptors in the same image as a group. As shown in Figure 3, "1" in origin is the central SIFT descriptor. Its region completely covers the regions of member SIFT descriptors {"2", …, "5"}. If the number of member SIFT descriptors is more than 3, they are bundled as a group. This bundling does not need additional detection of stable regions. Furthermore, 1D geometric modeling in a polar coordinate system is proposed here. As shown in Figure 3, the polar axis aligns with the orientation of the central SIFT descriptor. The polar plane is partitioned into R sectors ordered counter clockwise. A sector index r is assigned to each member SIFT descriptor in the group. This geometric verification is simple and allows for rotation invariance.

Therefore, the SIFT descriptors in the cloud are extended as $S = \{x_f, s, \theta, v, r, V\}$ by adding visual word v and sector index r. As shown in Figure 3, assume two groups of visual words to match. $G_p = \{S_p(i)\}$ in the left side is a query group and $G_q = \{S_q(j)\}$ in the right side is a candidate group from one image in the cloud. The matching is scored as follows

$$E_m(G_p, G_q) = E_v(G_p, G_q) - E_r(G_p, G_q). \quad (2)$$

$E_v(G_p, G_q)$ is the number of matched visual words between two groups. According to the proposed 1D geometric model in polar coordinate system, matched visual words should have the same sector index. $E_r(G_p, G_q)$ is the number of matched visual words but with different sector indices. It should be subtracted from $E_v(G_p, G_q)$.

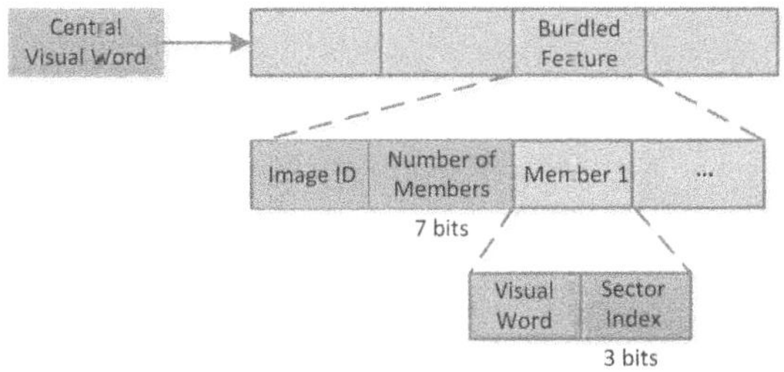

Figure 4: The inverted-file index used in this paper.

The inverted-file index [21] is adopted in this paper to find groups of visual words that match. Its structure is illustrated in Figure 4. Each visual word has an entry in the index that contains the list of images in which the visual word appears. Because a group of visual words are used in this paper, besides Image ID, there are a number of members. It is a non-zero integer if the visual word is the center of a group. The following are member visual words and sector indices. The number of member visual words in a group is limited to 128. The number of sectors is at most 8 and usually set as 4.

For the example shown in Figure 3, central visual word "1" in the query group is first used to find groups with the same central visual word in the inverted-file index. Every candidate group is scored by (2). In Figure 3, there are four pairs of member visual words matched. Thus $E_v(G_p, G_q)$ is 5 after counting the central visual word. But visual words "4" have sector index 6 and 3 in the two groups, respectively. They are inconsistent and $E_r(G_p, G_q)$ is equal to 1. Finally, the matching score $E_m(G_p, G_q)$ of two groups is 4. This score is assigned to the image that contains the candidate group. After all query groups are matched, several images with high sum scores are retrieved as partial duplicate images.

4.2 Patch Retrieval and Registration

Patch retrieval is performed only on the selected partial duplicate images. Since the number of images is limited, every query SIFT feature descriptor is directly matched with those on the partial duplicate images. It can fully utilize the discriminative power of SIFT descriptors. For a query descriptor $\tilde{S}$, if the Euclidean distance of the closest neighbor is smaller than 2/3 distance of the second-closest neighbor, the closest neighbor is a correct matched SIFT descriptor S.

For a pair of matched descriptors $\tilde{S}$ and S, according to their locations, scales and orientations, two image patches $P_{\tilde{S}}$ and P_S are found in the up-sampled thumbnail $\tilde{I}_u$ and the image that contains S. An example is illustrated in Figure 5 (a) and (b), respectively. It is difficult to estimate the transformation between them by matching corresponding pixels because $P_{\tilde{S}}$ is too blurred. Fortunately, the locations of query SIFT descriptors are extracted from original image and are reliable. Therefore, the feature-based registration is adopted in this paper.

It is easy to find SIFT descriptors located in the patches $P_{\tilde{S}}$ and P_S. The correspondences are established by matching every SIFT feature descriptor in $P_{\tilde{S}}$ with those in P_S. As marked by "+" in Figure 5 (a) and (b), the locations of matched pairs of SIFT descriptors are used to estimate the transformation H between $P_{\tilde{S}}$ and P_S by the RANSAC algorithm [22]. The perspective model is adopted in this paper. Therefore, four pairs of locations are randomly selected to calculate H. The rest of the pairs of locations are used to verify H. If a pair of locations fits with H, it is counted as an inlier; otherwise it is an outlier. Finally, we can get H with the maximum number of inliers.

If the scales of SIFT descriptors are small, the retrieved patches are small too. The pairs of matched descriptors may be less than four. In this case, we directly write the transformation H from locations, scales and orientations of $\tilde{S}$ and S. H between $P_{\tilde{S}}$ and P_S is assumed as a combination of translation, rotation and scaling

$$H = \begin{bmatrix} \frac{\tilde{s}}{s} R & T \end{bmatrix}, \tag{3}$$

$$R = \begin{bmatrix} cos(\tilde{\theta} - \theta) & -sin(\tilde{\theta} - \theta) \\ sin(\tilde{\theta} - \theta) & cos(\tilde{\theta} - \theta) \end{bmatrix}, \quad T = \begin{bmatrix} \tilde{x}_f - x_f \\ \tilde{y}_f - y_f \end{bmatrix}.$$

Figure 5 (c) is the result $\hat{P}_S$ of image patch P_S in Figure 5 (b) after the transformation H estimated by pairs of matched SIFT descriptors. We can observe that image patch $\hat{P}_S$ in Figure 5 (c) has a good alignment with the image patch $P_{\tilde{S}}$ in Figure 5 (a) but contains rich, detailed content.

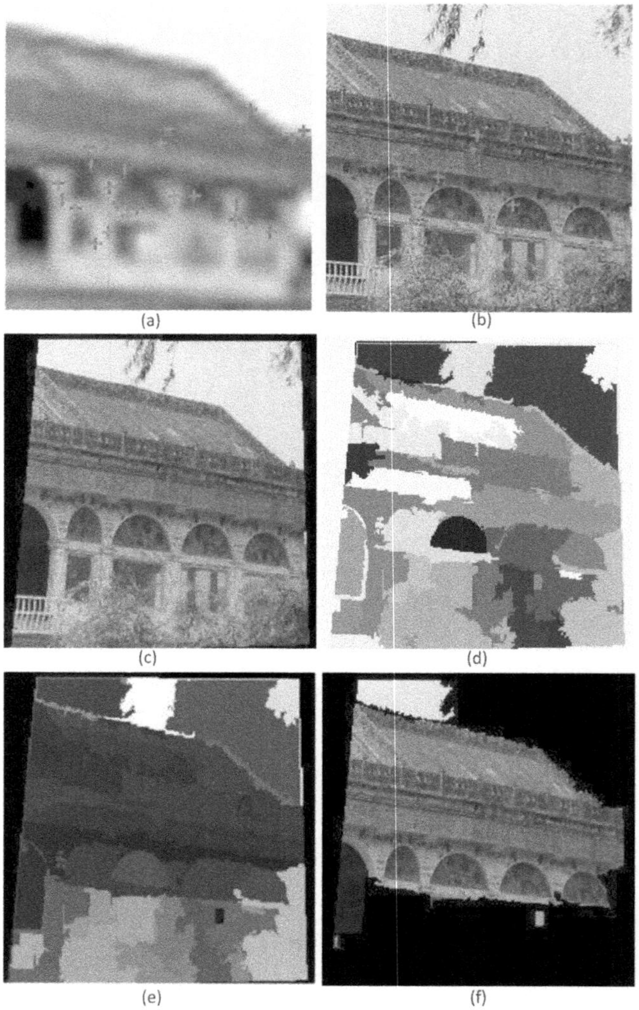

Figure 5: Image patch process: (a) Image patch extracted from the up-sampled thumbnail with SIFT locations; (b) Image patch extracted from a partial duplicate image with SIFT locations; (c) Image patch after transformation; (d) The result after graph-based segmentation; (e) The MSE verification by the up-sampled thumbnail; (f) The final patch to stitch.

4.3 Inconsistent Region Removal

After transformation, an aligned high-resolution patch is ready to stitch. However, as shown in Figure 5 (c), we often observe that these image patches contain partial contents that do not exist in the image to reconstruct. One solution is to segment and remove them before stitching. The effective approach is the interactive segmentation based on graph cuts [23], where a user has to indicate some pixels which are inside the object to segment and some pixels outside. Although the user interactions are minimal, it is not allowed in *IMShare*.

Therefore, the graph-based image segmentation [24] is adopted in this paper. The image patch $\hat{P}_S$ is modeled as an undirected graph $G = (V, E)$, where a vertex $v_i \in V$ corresponds to a pixel and an edge $(v_i, v_j) \in E$ connects a pair of neighboring vertices $v_i, v_j \in V$. Each edge is associated with a non-negative weight $w(v_i, v_j)$ to measure the dissimilarity between two vertices. For two neighboring regions $C1, C2 \subseteq V$, the largest weights within these two regions are denoted as $w_{C1}$and w_{C2}, respectively. The minimum weight of the boundary between $C1$ and $C2$ is denoted as $w_{C1,C2}$.The segmentation between $C1$ and $C2$ is made as

$$\mathcal{F}(C1,C2) = \begin{cases} True & if\ w_{C1,C2} > \min(w_{C1} + \tau_{C1}, w_{C2} + \tau_{C2}) \\ False & otherwise \end{cases}. \tag{4}$$

τ_{C1} and τ_{C2} are inversely proportional to the number pixels in $C1$ and $C2$. They control the over-segmentation. The segmentation result is depicted in Figure 5 (d), where different luminance indicates a different region. Although it replaces the max-flow min-cut optimization in graph cuts with a greedy approach, the result is good enough for our purpose. Furthermore, this approach runs in time nearly linear in the number of edges and is fast in practice.

After segmentation, every region is verified by the up-sampled thumbnail $\tilde{I}_u$. The mean square error (MSE) of every region is calculated with regard to the corresponding region in $\tilde{I}_u$. As shown in Figure 5(e), luminance in a region indicates its MSE value. If the MSE value of a region is larger than a threshold, the region is removed from the patch. Figure 5 (f) is the result after region removal. We can observe that the regions with leaves have large MSE values and thus are removed. The remained region has a good match with the thumbnail, whereas the removed region can be recovered from other retrieved patches.

4.4 Patch Stitching

The patches are stitched according to their MSE values with regard to the thumbnail in the increasing order. For $\hat{P}_S$, after removing inconsistent regions, we get the patch $\tilde{P}_S$ to stitch. Since $\tilde{P}_S$ may come from an image with different illumination, directly stitching it to the up-sampled image $\tilde{I}_u$ will result in block artifacts on illumination, as shown in Figure 6 (a).

Instead of directly stitching $\tilde{P}_S$, the gradient field $\boldsymbol{g}$ of $\tilde{P}_S$ is often applied to interpolate the corresponding image patch f in $\tilde{I}_u$. It can be formulated as the following minimization problem

$$\min_f \iint_\Omega |\nabla f - \boldsymbol{g}|^2, \text{ with } \tilde{I}_u|_{\partial\Omega} = f|_{\partial\Omega}. \tag{5}$$

Here Ω is the region of $\tilde{P}_S$ to stitch. $\partial\Omega$ is the boundary of $\tilde{P}_S$ in $\tilde{I}_u$. ∇ is the gradient operator. The solution to (5) is the unique solution of the Poisson equation with Dirichlet boundary conditions [25]

$$\Delta f = div\ \boldsymbol{g} \text{ over } \Omega, \text{ with } \tilde{I}_u|_{\partial\Omega} = f|_{\partial\Omega}. \tag{6}$$

Δ is the Laplacian operator. $div\ \boldsymbol{g}$ is the divergence of $\boldsymbol{g}$. However, solving Poisson equation (6) is an intensive computing process. According to [25], solving the Poisson equation is equivalent to solving the following Laplace equation

$$\Delta \tilde{f} = 0 \text{ over } \Omega \text{ with } (\tilde{I}_u - \tilde{P}_s)|_{\partial\Omega} = \tilde{f}|_{\partial\Omega}. \tag{7}$$

In this case, the image patch to stitch is $f = \tilde{P}_s + \tilde{f}$.

Instead of solving either the Poisson equation (6) or the Laplace equation (7), we adopt the membrane interpolation used in [26]. $\tilde{f}$ is approximated by smoothly spreading the discrepancies along the boundary to the entire region Ω. The interpolation value $\tilde{f}$ can be written as

$$\tilde{f} = (G * \tilde{r})/(G * \tilde{R}), \tag{8}$$

$$\text{where } \tilde{r}(\boldsymbol{x}_i) = \begin{cases} \tilde{I}_u(\boldsymbol{x}_i) - \tilde{P}_S(\boldsymbol{x}_i), & \forall \boldsymbol{x}_i \ni \partial\Omega \\ 0, & otherwise \end{cases}.$$

$*$ is the convolution. $\tilde{R}(\boldsymbol{x}_i)$ is 1 if $\tilde{r}(\boldsymbol{x}_i)$ is non-zero; otherwise 0. $G(\boldsymbol{x}_i, \boldsymbol{x}_j)$ is the translation-invariant Green's functions in two dimensions as

$$G(\boldsymbol{x}_i, \boldsymbol{x}_j) = G(\|\boldsymbol{x}_i - \boldsymbol{x}_j\|) = 2\pi \log \frac{1}{\|x_i - x_j\|}. \tag{9}$$

$\boldsymbol{x}_i$ and $\boldsymbol{x}_j$ are two points in two dimensions. The function value is only dependent on the distance between $\boldsymbol{x}_i$ and $\boldsymbol{x}_j$. Furthermore, the convolution (8) can be calculated rapidly with three short-support filters in a multi-scale scheme similar to wavelet transform [26]. The computation has linear time $O(n)$ to the number of pixels. The image in Figure 6 (b) is the result after correcting it with (8).

(a) (b)

Figure 6: The reconstructed images without and with illumination correction.

5. PARALLEL IMPLEMENTATION

The parallel architecture for the proposed image reconstruction is shown in Figure 7. The upper part of Figure 7 is kernel instances to be assigned to different processes and the bottom part is input and output data requested by the corresponding process. The reconstruction is organized into a pipeline from left to right. The processes at patch level, including patch retrieval, patch registration and patch segmentation, are highly parallel. The computation of patches is independent on each other and can be assigned to as many cores as possible. Although the stitching is also operated patch by patch, it cannot be performed parallel because the stitching result of one patch has an effect to that of following patches.

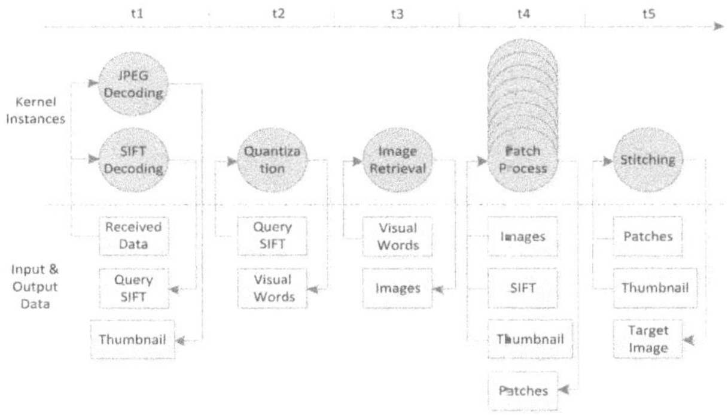

Figure 7: The parallel architecture for the proposed image reconstruction.

The proposed reconstruction in cloud can support the scalability of system. Assume that ten million images are collected in a restricted domain. They are distributed to servers in cloud and each stores a half million images. When a request is received, all servers start to perform image search. Our results in Table 3 show that it averagely needs about 0.12s. After exchanging the retrieved results among servers, several images are selected and sent to a server for reconstruction. The module of patch process has the maximum processing time of about 2 seconds. One server can process 43,200 requests per day. For 1M requests per day, 24 servers are enough that are not difficult to offer in cloud.

6. EXPERIMENTAL RESULTS

The proposed *IMShare* targets on instant landmark image sharing in mobile devices. One of the typical applications is visiting a famous landmark, taking some images and sharing them with your friends immediately. Therefore, as listed in Table 1, ten famous places, which are located in China, Egypt and Japan, are selected to collect images for our experiments.

Table 1: Key words selected to collect images in our experiments

Country	Key Words
China	Summer Palace, Great Wall, Forbidden City
Egypt	Aswan Temple, Luxor Temple, Sphinx
Japan	Kinkakuji Temple, Kiyomizu Temple, Nijo Castle, Ryoanji Temple

In *IMShare*, images in the database must be high resolution and high quality. They are crawled by the key words listed in Table 1 from Flickr [1]. Only images with a size larger than 1024x768 are kept, resulting in a database with 535,518 images. Total file sizes in JPEG is 245GB. The testing images are crawled from Google by using the same key words. However, most images found in Google are too small. As shown in Figure 8, we select the following 12 images for testing according to two rules: the image resolution must be high and there are no same images found in the database.

Figure 8: Testing images denoted by letters "a", "b", ..., "l".

6.1 Description Size

On the mobile side, every testing image is first down-sampled by 256:1. The down-sampling ratio is much larger than that in conventional super-resolution. The down-sampled image is then compressed by JPEG with a setting quality at 95. Only the locations, scales and orientations of SIFT descriptors with $s \geq 3$ are calculated. They are compressed by the approach described in Section 3. All images with original resolution, number of SIFT descriptors, compressed SIFT data size and thumbnail size in JPEG are listed in Table 2.

The average resolution of 12 testing images is 3.13M pixels. After 256:1 down-sampling, the average file size of thumbnails in JPEG is 6.05 KB per image. The number of SIFT descriptors extracted from every image is 734 in average. After compression, the data size of SIFT locations, scales and orientations is 2356 bytes in average. In other words, each SIFT descriptor only costs 25.68 bits. The average description size is 8.22 KB per image. It is equivalent to 2.63 KB per mega pixels. Therefore, it is easy to transmit the proposed description even for 2G network.

Table 2: Image resolution and description size

Images	Resolution (Pixels)	No. SIFT	SIFT (Byte)	JPEG (KB)	Total (KB)
A	768x1024	251	827	2.12	2.93
B	1600x1200	291	996	4.6	5.6
C	1280x960	205	702	2.86	3.56
D	1024x768	168	567	2.53	3.08
E	2560x1920	1044	3598	9.49	13
F	2560x1920	1495	4965	11.2	16.05
g	2560x1920	1181	3981	9.65	13.63
h	2560x1704	1057	3557	9.41	12.88
i	2560x1704	1027	3474	7.42	10.81
j	2560x1704	666	2382	4.58	6.91
k	1024x682	182	603	2.39	2.98
l	2560x1700	752	2625	6.43	7.16
Average	3.13M	734	2356	6.05	8.22

PCA-SIFT [7] and CHoG [11] directly compress feature vectors. PCA-SIFT needs 160 bits per SIFT feature vector and CHOG needs 60 bits. For 734 SIFT descriptors, the compressed data size will be 14.68 KB and 5.51 KB for PCA-SIFT and CHoG, respectively. The former is already larger than the data size of the proposed scheme. But they only provide SIFT feature vectors and do not contain the thumbnail and SIFT locations, scales and orientations. Unlike the image search, all of them are important for image reconstruction as we have discussed in Section 4. Without these data, the reconstructed images are very poor that will be shown in Section 6.4.

6.2 Reconstruction Time and Quality

In the cloud, we deployed a Dell R910 server with four Intel E7-4870 CPUs. Each CPU has 10 cores running at 2.4GHz. There are a total of 40 cores in the server. The memory is 128G and the storage is 12 SAS hard disks each with a capacity of 1T. SIFT descriptors with scale $s \geqslant 2$ of all images in the database are extracted. There are a total of 950,652,052 SIFT descriptors extracted. 100 million SIFT feature descriptors are randomly selected and trained into a vocabulary of 1 million visual words by approximate K-means. Furthermore, the visual words of every image have been organized into groups according to the approach described in Section 4.1. An inverted-file index is built in advance.

Table 3: Computation time (in millisecond) of different modules in the proposed image reconstruction

Images	Image Search	Patch Search	Transformation & Segmentation	Stitching
a	103	326	1236	130
b	80	389	1106	119
c	83	249	1126	146
d	63	230	409	132
e	264	1388	896	858
f	200	1596	4609	865
g	314	1609	4672	1732
h	236	1482	1389	1295
i	245	1701	1202	1092
j	138	1389	1030	932
k	48	380	1149	325
l	355	1558	2589	1022
Average	117.4	1024.8	1784.4	720.7

The computation time of every module in the reconstruction process is first evaluated. The reconstruction process is organized to partial duplicate image search, patch search, processing and stitching. The time of every module is listed in Table 3. We can observe that the time for reconstructing an image is 3.65 seconds on average. The average time for partial duplicate image search is 0.12 seconds. The time for stitching is also below 1 second with the convolution pyramid approach. The patch search, transformation and segmentation still take the most time although they are carried out by tens of cores in parallel. In particular, the image "d" with resolution 1024x768 can be reconstructed in 0.83 seconds.

Limited by the pages in this paper, four reconstructed images are shown in Figure 9. The first row is the original images and the second row is the reconstructed images. These images have to be resized to display in this paper. Thus we select an interesting region in every image, as indicated by red rectangles in the first row, to show in normal size. The third row is the selected regions in original images. The forth row is the corresponding regions in the up-sampled thumbnails. We can observe that most of details are lost there and they are blurred too much. The regions reconstructed by the proposed approach are shown in the fifth row. The quality is significantly improved compared with the results in the fourth row. They look like those in the original images.

The reconstructed images also often contain several artifacts. As indicated by a red ellipse in the last image of the fifth row, one of the typical artifacts is geometric deformation especially when different parts of an object have different depths. It is difficult to calculate the transformation model correctly. If partial image contents cannot be found in the database, the corresponding regions in the reconstructed image will be blurred. The contents that do not exist in the input image cannot be completely removed by our thumbnail verification and segmentation. Although there are some artifacts, the overall visual quality of the reconstructed images is still impressive due to their high resolution, which is verified by the user study in Section 6.3.

Figure 9: The reconstructed images "b", "e", "j" and "l". The first row is the original images and the second row is our reconstructed results. To see details clearly, the selected interest regions, indicated by red rectangles, are shown in normal size from the third row to the fifth row. They correspond to original images, thumbnails and reconstructed images. The red ellipse shows the reconstructed artifacts in the proposed scheme.

Figure 10: Reconstructed results of image "f" with three different sets of retrieved images. The first column is the reconstructed images and the second one is the local region indicated by the red rectangle. The last column is the four retrieved images.

In Figure 10, we investigate how retrieved partial duplicate images affect reconstructed images. In the first row, four images on the right side are the partial duplicate images with the highest ranking. The reconstructed image and the selected interest region in this row look good. In the second row, four partial duplicate images do not have the top part of the interest region. So the reconstructed image is blurred in the region and the other regions still look good. In the third row, four partial duplicate images are not retrieved correctly and the reconstructed image is similar to the up-sampled thumbnail because there is not related content available. One important feature we can observe from Figure 10 is that our approach can control the reconstructed quality well through thumbnail verification.

6.3 User Study

We select the current solution as an anchor, where shared images are first down-sampled to a given resolution. This down-sampling solution reduces transmission delay but greatly degrades visual quality. After noting the details of the shared images in SINA micro blog, we find that the width of the shared images is set as 440 pixels. Therefore, in the down-sampling solution, the width of the testing images is also down-sampled to 440 pixels and the height is decided by the aspect ratio. The down-sampled images are compressed by JPEG and transmitted to the receiver. The received images are resized and displayed in a Dell 30 inch monitor, which has a resolution of 2560x1600.

In [28], 20 kbps and 60 kbps uplink speeds are used in mobile searching. Considering that some sightseeing locations are in the countryside or rural areas, where network speed is low. We select 20 kbps as the uplink speed in our user study. For the proposed *IMShare*, the delay for users mainly comes at the transmission time and the reconstruction time in the cloud. Given the uplink speed, we can calculate the transmission time according to the description size listed in Table 2. The reconstruction time has been listed in Table 3. In order to allow users to easily compare these two schemes, we adjust JPEG quality in the down-sampling solution so that the delay of these two schemes is the same for users. The average JPEG size of 12 images is 20.42KB after down-sampling.

In this study, users only need to evaluate the visual quality of reconstructed images by the two schemes. 10 volunteers are asked to serve as users. Most of them have experiences with blogs. They do not know how the displayed images are generated. Furthermore, the images are displayed randomly. Each user is asked to score the displayed image from 1 to 5, indicating very annoying, annoying, slightly annoying, perceptible and imperceptible, respectively. The results are shown in Figure 11. The horizontal coordinate is 12 testing images and vertical coordinates is user score.

The scores of the proposed *IMShare* are shown in blue and the scores of the down-sampling solution are shown in red. We can observe from Figure 11 that the proposed *IMShare* usually has a higher score than the down-sampled solution, where every testing image can correctly retrieve partial duplicate images from the database. The average user score of 12 testing images is 4.0 for our scheme, while the score is 2.46 for the down-sampling solution.

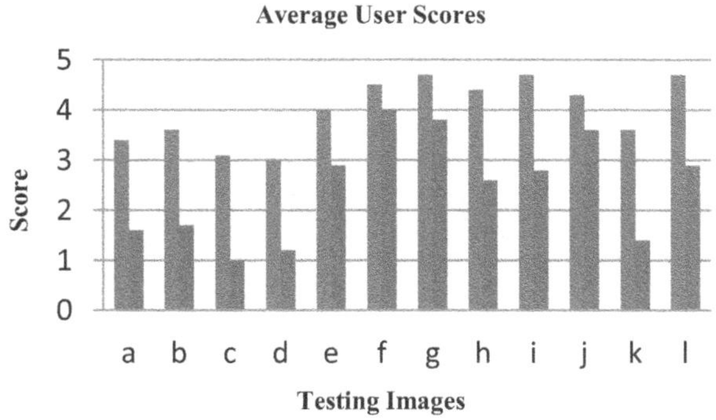

Figure 11: The average user scores of 12 testing images.

6.4 Reconstruction Comparisons

Finally, we compare *IMShare* with the scheme proposed in [17], which only uses SIFT feature descriptors and does not have the thumbnail. In [17], INRIA Holiday database is used [27]. It has 1491 high-resolution images and further has multiple images in the same scene but with different viewpoints and focus lengths. Since we do not have the implementation in [17], *IMShare* also uses the Holiday database here. The comparisons are shown in Figure 12, where our results are in left side and the results from [17] are in right side.

Figure 12: The comparison between *IMShare* and the scheme proposed in [17].

It is clear that our results are much better than those in [17]. The reason is that we have both thumbnails and SIFT descriptors. For the image in the first row, 2369 SIFT descriptors are extracted. After compression, the size including the JPEG thumbnail is 27.37 KB. For the image in the second row, 768 SIFT descriptors are extracted and the total size is 10.73 KB. For the scheme in [17], if the same numbers of SIFT descriptors are extracted and the PCA-based SIFT compression is adopted, where one SIFT vector will cost 160 bits [7], the description sizes will be 47.38KB and 15.36KB, respectively. Although *IMShare* needs a thumbnail, the total description size is still small because 128-dimension feature vector can be recovered from the thumbnail.

6.5 Limitations

Highly correlated images in the database play an important role in *IMShare*. As we have shown in Figure 10, given a lack of correlated images, *IMShare* can provide users with better quality up-sampled thumbnails partially or even completely. Furthermore, in the scenario that we are considering in this paper, there are often persons positioned in front of famous landmarks. Although the background part can be reconstructed from the correlated images, it is hard to accurately reconstruct a face from other images. One solution for this issue is to segment the foreground using some user interactions and then compress the foreground with traditional image compression. Images in some complicated scenes (e.g., billboards, windmills, etc.) may be also difficult to reconstruct.

Besides the issues in reconstruction, *IMShare* may also bring copyright and privacy concerns. One advantage is that content owners can share their images without uploading the high-resolution versions. Although *IMShare* can enhance user experience, the reconstructed images at this moment still have a clear gap from the original images. Considering from another viewpoint, with more and more images collected in the database, it is easy to reproduce some images protected by others. In addition, because there are always some artifacts in reconstructed images, they should be fine just for browsing, it is impossible to replace image compression in archive. Probably, they will not meet the approval of professional photographers.

7. CONCLUSIONS AND DISCUSSIONS

This paper proposes a novel mobile-cloud solution for instant mobile landmark image sharing. On the mobile side, we propose to describe high-resolution images by thumbnails and SIFT descriptors. The description size can be reduced to 2.63 kilobytes per mega pixels. On the cloud side, the high-resolution images are reconstructed from a large-scale database via the descriptions. To make sure the reconstructed images are of visually pleasant quality, we propose an approach to bundle visual words for partial duplicate image retrieval, adopt RANSAC for image patch alignment, adopt graph-based segmentation to remove mismatched regions and adopt the convolution pyramids for fast patch stitching. With the proposed parallel implementation, the image reconstruction can be done in 3.65 seconds on average. The user study with roughly half a million images in the database shows that the proposed *IMShare* significantly outperforms the current solution in terms of user experiences on visual quality.

The large-scale image database plays the most important role in *IMShare*. Images in the database must be high resolution and high quality. It is unknown how many images are needed for *IMShare* in the real world. But it is feasible for several limited scenes. For example, Google owns a large number of street view images. When you randomly take a picture in street, most likely the background can be found in their database. Therefore, we plan to extend the selected places to 100 and collect 100 million images. When the scale of the images is significantly enlarged, the partial duplicate image retrieval will become more challenging. A promising solution is to use multiple clues as proposed in [29]. Last but not least, this paper only considers image reconstruction. The really challenging work will be video reconstruction. The compact video description has been proposed in [30]. However, it is not clear yet how to reconstruct visually pleasant video from a large-scale database.

8. ACKNOWLEDGMENTS

The authors would like to thank Dr. Kaiming He and Ms. Jiangyu Liu for valuable insight on image reconstruction, Dr. Tao Mei for good suggestions how to present our work in this ACM multimedia paper, and the anonymous reviewers and shepherds, Dr. Gerald Friedland and Dr. Doree Duncan, for their valuable comments and suggestions to improve the quality of this paper.

9. REFERENCES

[1] Flickr, http://www.flickr.com.

[2] C. Marlow, M. Naaman, D. Boyd, M. Davis, "HT06, tagging paper, taxonomy, Flickr, academic article, to read," *ACM Conference on Hypertext and Hypermedia*, pp. 31-40, 2006.

[3] R. Sarvas, M. Viikari, J. Pesonen, H. Nevanlinna, "Mob-Share: controlled and immediate sharing of mobile images," *ACM Conference on Multimedia*, pp. 724-731, 2004.

[4] M. Davis, N. House, J. Towle, S. King, S. Ahern, C. Burgener, D. Perkel, M. Finn, V. Viswanathan, M. Rothenberg, "MMM2: Mobile Media Metadata for Media Sharing," *CHI extended abstracts on Human factors in computing systems*, pp. 1335-1338, 2005.

[5] T. Wiegand, G. J. Sullivan, G. Bjontegaard, A. Luthra, "Overview of the H.264/AVC video coding standard," *IEEE Trans. on Circuits and Systems for Video Technology*, vol. 13, pp. 560-576, 2003.

[6] D. G. Lowe, "Distinctive image features from scale-invariant keypoints," *International Journal of Computer Vision*, vol. 60, pp.91-110, 2004.

[7] Y. Ke, R. Sukthankar, "PCA-SIFT: a more distinctive representation for local image descriptors," *IEEE Conference on Computer Vision and Pattern Recognition*, vol. 2, pp. 506-513, 2004.

[8] G. Hua, M. Brown, S. Winder, "Discriminant embedding for local image descriptors," *IEEE Conference on Computer Vision*, pp. 1-8, 2007.

[9] C. H. Yeo, P. Ahammad, K. Ramchandran, "Rate efficient visual correspondences using random projections," *IEEE Conference on Image Processing*, pp. 217-220, 2008.

[10] H. Bay, T. Tuytelaars, L. V. Gool, "SURF: Speeded up robust features," *European Conference on Computer Vision*, pp. 404-417, 2006.

[11] V. Chandrasekhar, G. Takacs, D. Chen, S. S. Tsai, R. Grzeszczuk, B. Girod, "CHoG: compressed historgram of gradients a low bit-rate feature descritpor," *IEEE Conference on Computer Vision and Pattern Recognition*, pp. 2504-2511, 2009.

[12] V. Chandrasekhar, G. Takacs, D. Chen, S. S. Tsai, J. Singh, B. Girod, "Transform coding of image feature descriptors," *SPIE Conference on Visual Comm. and Image Processing*, vol. 7257, 2009.

[13] M. Makar, C. L. Chang, D. Chen, S. S. Tsai, B. Girod, "Compression of image patches for local feature extraction," *IEEE Conference on Acoustics, Speech and Signal Processing*, pp. 821-824, 2009.

[14] M. Eitz, K. Hildebrand, T. Boubekeur, M. Alexa, "PhotoSketck: a sketch based image query and composition," *ACM Conference on Graphics*, 2009.

[15] T. Chen, M. M. Cheng, P. Tan, A. Shamir, S. M. Hu, "PhotoSketch: Internet image montage," *ACM Conference on SIGGRAPH ASIA*, 2009.

[16] M. K. Johnson, K. Dale, S. Avidan, H. Pfister, W. T. Freeman, "CG2Real: Improving the realism of computer generated images using a large collection of photographs," *IEEE Trans. on Visualization and Computer Graphics*, vol. 17, pp. 1273-1285, 2011.

[17] P. Weinzaepfel, H. Jegou, P. Perez, "Reconstructing an image from its local descriptors," *IEEE Conference on Computer Vision and Pattern Recognition*, pp. 337-344, 2011.

[18] J. Philbin, O. Chum, M. Isard, J. Sivic, A. Zisserman, "Object retrieval with large vocabularies and fast spatial matching," *IEEE Conference on Computer Vision and Pattern Recognition*, pp. 1-8, 2007.

[19] Z. Wu, Q. F. Ke, M. Isard, J. Sun, "Bundling features for large scale partial-duplicate web image search," Proc. of *IEEE Conference on Computer Vision and Pattern Recognition*, pp. 25-32, 2009.

[20] W. G. Zhou, Y. J. Lu, H. Q. Li, Y. B. Song, Q. Tian, "Spatial coding for large scale partial-duplicate web image search," *ACM Conference on Multimedia*, pp. 511-520, 2010.

[21] J. Sivic, A. Zisserman, "Video Google: a text retrieval approach to object matching in videos," *IEEE Conference on Computer Vision*, vol. 2, pp. 1470-1477, 2003.

[22] M. A. Fischler, R. C. Bolles, "Random sample consensus," *Communication ACM*, vol. 24, pp. 381-395, 1981.

[23] Y. Boykov, M. P. Jolly, "Interactive graph cuts for optimal boundary and region segmentation of objects in n-d images," *IEEE Conference on Computer Vision*, pp. 105-112, 2001.

[24] P. F. Felzenszwalb, D. P. Huttenlocher, "Efficient graph-based image segmentation," *International Journal of Computer Vision*, vol. 59, pp. 167-181, 2004.

[25] P. Perez, M. Gangnet, A. Blake, "Poisson image editing," *ACM Conference on SIGGRAPH*, pp. 313-318, 2003

[26] Z. Farbman, R. Fattal, D. Lischinski, "Convolution pyramids," *ACM Conference on SIGGRAPH ASIA*, 2011.

[27] H. Jegou, M. Douze, C. Schmid, "Hamming embedding and weak geometric consistency for large scale image search," *European Conference on Computer Vision*, 2008.

[28] V. Chandrasekhar, G. Takacs, D. M. Chen, S. S. Tsai, R. Grzeszczuk, Y. Reznik, B. Girod, "Compressed histogram of gradients: a low bitrate descriptor," *International Journal of Computer Vision*, vol. 96, pp. 384-399, 2012.

[29] R. Ji, L.-Y. Duan, J. Chen, H. Yao, Y. Rui, S.-F. Chang, W. Gao, "Towards low bit rate mobile visual search with multiple-channel coding," *ACM Conference on Multimedia*, pp. 573–582, 2011.

[30] L. X. Tang, T. Mei, X.-S. Hua, "Near-lossless video summarization," *ACM Conference on Multimedia*, pp. 351-360, 2009.

Discovering Areas of Interest with Geo-tagged Images and Check-ins

†Jiajun Liu †Zi Huang #Lei Chen †Heng Tao Shen *Zhixian Yan

†The University of Queensland
{jiajun,huang,shenht}@itee.uq.edu.au
#Hong Kong University of Science and Technology
leichen@cse.ust.hk
*Ecole Polytechnique Federale de Lausanne
zhixian.yan@epfl.ch

ABSTRACT

Geo-tagged image is an ideal source for the discovery of popular travel places. However, the aspects of popular venues for daily-life purposes like dining and shopping are often missing in the mined locations from geo-tagged images. Fortunately check-in websites provide us a unique opportunity of analyzing people's preferences in their daily lives to complement the knowledge mined from geo-tagged images. This paper presents a novel approach for the discovery of Areas of Interest (AoI). By analyzing both geo-tagged images and check-ins, the approach exploits travelers' flavors as well as the preferences of daily-life activities of local residents to find AoI in a city. The proposed approach consists of two major steps. Firstly, we devise a density-based clustering method to discover AoI, mainly based on the image densities but also reinforced by the secondary densities from the images' neighboring venues. Then we propose a novel joint authority analysis framework to rank AoI. The framework simultaneously considers both the location-location transitions, and the user-location relations. An interactive presentation interface for visualizing AoI is also presented. The approach is tested with very large datasets for Shanghai city. They consist of 49,460 geo-tagged images from Panoramio.com, and 1,361,547 check-ins from the check-in website Qieke.com. By evaluating the ranking accuracy and quality of AoI, we demonstrate great improvements of our method over compared methods.

Categories and Subject Descriptors

H.3.1 [**Information Storage and Retrieval**]: Content Analysis and Indexing methods

General Terms

Algorithms, Performance, Experimentation

Keywords

Geo-tagged image, check-in data, areas of interest

1. INTRODUCTION

This is the century when world becomes flat. The role that traveling plays in people's lives has gained itself an unprecedented level of importance. One solid proof of this change is the dramatically increasing number of the trails of such traveling activities. Old school travel logs are no longer the only form of such trails. Instead, powered by the advances in mobile devices, modern technologies have given us rich options of producing such trails. In contrast to the vague nature of text-based logs, modern forms of travel trails are much more effective on the preservation of location and time, and even scenes during traveling.

Geo-tagged image exists as one form of such trails. In addition to the beautiful scenes we see during traveling, it also keeps records of the location where the image is taken. As geo-tagged image has become popular, e.g., over 42 million geo-tagged images have been uploaded to Panoramio.com in 2011, the vital information it contains provides researchers with excellent opportunities of discovering people's traveling patterns as well as significant scenic places in the real world. Many applications are therefore developed [5, 8, 7, 14, 10]. These applications exploit the fact that geo-tagged images often indicate the popularity of an area among the travelers implicitly. However, when used alone, such data have a subtle inadequacy in the coverage of local venues. The fact that local people are less motivated to take images at the venues they visit on a regular basis has made those venues nearly invisible from geo-tagged images. But in reality these venues can be very helpful for the travelers to choose which areas to visit when they travel to a city. Naturally, a traveler wants to visit a certain area of a city, expecting to see tourist attractions like beaches or parks. Such needs are well covered by geo-tagged images. Yet his or her needs of experiencing local people's life style by exploring local people's favorite restaurants, shopping centers, or theaters cannot be fulfilled. Fortunately, a particularly popular service nowadays, a.k.a the check-in service, provides us unique and sufficient information to cover such requirements.

A check-in is a user's status message in a social network with the purpose of letting friends know his or her current location (normally a venue with a name). By connecting the GPS coordinates with the venues' names, the service enables

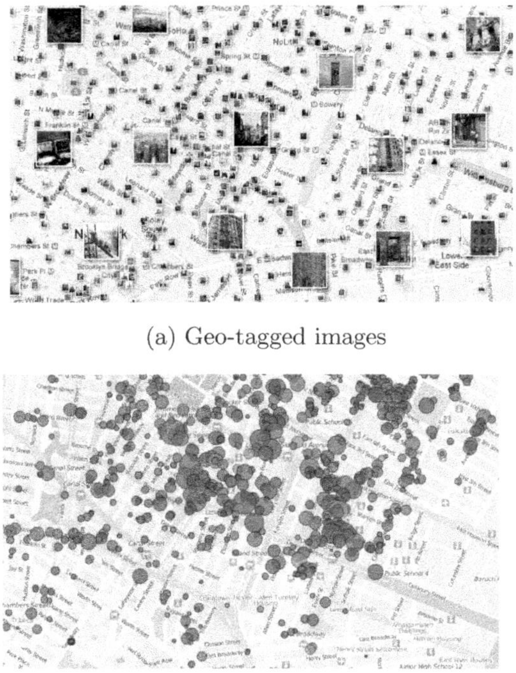

(a) Geo-tagged images

(b) Check-ins

Figure 1: Images and Check-ins from New York

the user to conveniently publish his or her visit to the venue. As such services popularize (e.g., Foursquare, a very popular website known for the check-in service, has received 380 million check-ins in the single year of 2010), check-ins emerge as a new form of people's living trails from their daily lives. Unlike geo-tagged images, check-ins often reflect local people's preferences in every kinds of venues. If a restaurant is mentioned by a significant amount of check-ins, local people may have positive opinions on this restaurant. This assumption is also valid for shopping centers and other venues that local people visit in their daily lives, making check-ins an ideal source for obtaining local people's knowledge and preferences. In Figure 1, we display the mesh-ups for geo-tagged images and check-ins for the same area in New York. Clearly the interests from the user groups of the two services are quite different but mutually complementary.

Consequently, in this paper, we propose a novel concept called *Area of Interest* (AoI), meaning an area in a city with numerous tourist attractions and popular venues amongst the locals. When people visit this AOI, not only they can see the most wonderful scenes a city can provide, but also they can experience the popular restaurants, malls, and cinemas like local residents do. A series of methods and refinements are proposed to discover and rank such AoI. To summarize, we make the following major contributions:

- We analyze geo-tagged images and check-ins so that we can confirm their semantic and statistic significance. A comparison of geo-tagged images, check-ins and raw GPS records is also presented.
- We describe the concept of AoI, and use both geo-tagged images and check-ins to assist the finding of AoI. We devise a method called secondary-density reinforced clustering to discover AoI, followed by a novel joint authority analysis framework which simultaneously considers both the location-location transitions and the user-location relations to rank AoI as well as the important scenes and venues in them.
- We verify the advantages of our approach with extensive experimental results on real-life datasets.

The rest of the paper is organized as follows. Section 2 provides an overview of the related literature. Then we analyze the significance and characteristics of geo-tagged image and check-ins in Section 3. The overview of the proposed approach is presented in Section 4. An enhanced density-based clustering method is proposed in Section 5 to discover AoI. Following is a novel ranking method called joint authority analysis, with the support of a cross-data transition inference stage, to solve the problem of AoI ranking in Section 6. The effect of the proposed methods is verified in Section 7, followed by the conclusion in Section 8.

2. RELATED WORK

Currently, geo-tagged images are widely used in landmark recognition, trip visualization and recommendation [14, 10, 8, 7, 5, 12]. An excellent survey on the applications and approaches of geo-tagged media is given in [15]. For instance, a tourism recommendation framework is presented in [5]. In this framework, popular sceneries are extracted by clustering geo-tagged images based on their locations. Images' tags are also indexed so that the user can either input a location or an image as the query. Based on the similarity to the query, the representative images are returned to the user. Another interesting work, the TravelScope [10], enables the user to take virtual tours in certain region. Besides geo-tagged images, it also uses user generated travel logs to discover points of interest. In [7], tourist maps with the icons for landmarks are generated from geo-tagged images. The work also uses geo-tags and user tags of images to cluster images, while content similarity is not considered. [12] proposes a k-means based method to classify the images for the landmark search results. It uses k-means to cluster the image set by their visual content and locations, then ranks the clusters and their representative images. [8] demonstrates a system to render multimedia travel stories in response to spatial queries. Most of the work have shown similar limitations. Images like those on Panoramio mostly reflect people's choice for sight seeing. However, a traveler's interest should involve many other aspects than sight seeing. Those aspects, including dining, shopping, and so on, are not well covered by geo-tagged images. Similar geo-tagged images, researchers are investigating application of geo-tagged video search and advertising in [16, 2, 3]. However, there are very limited data sources on geo-tagged videos. A graph-based video clustering method is proposed to perform content-based clustering in [11]. In Section 6.6 we will discuss how to adapt it to further identify significant scenes inside an AoI.

Besides geo-tagged images and videos, GPS trajectories are another form of human trails during traveling (here GPS trajectories mean the locations sampled by a certain time interval on dedicated GPS devices, like GPS navigators). GPS trajectories represent a vivid picture of people's decisions and preferences in a more continuous way than geo-tagged images. They also preserve the transitions of people among the locations. [19] pioneered in exploiting such properties to discover popular locations and travel sequences with HITS-based link analysis techniques. [18] then further developed such an approach for recommending locations and friends based on one's GPS history. Meanwhile, GPS trajectories are also used to mine and rank semantic locations [6], and to recommend trips [17]. GPS trajectories are generally very detailed and concise. However, there are also concerns for the use of GPS trajectories for these tasks. Limited by the sample size, the data collected by dedicated GPS devices heavily depend on destinations people choose to travel to and the way people choose to do travel. For instance, in a shopping complex with all venues built in together and with car access limited, dedicated GPS devices are not able to provide information concise enough for the tracking of people's trails inside the complex. On the other hand, if people choose to take buses or walks to their destinations, dedicated GPS devices are often absent in such trips. Privacy is also a concern. Such background behaviors of continuously monitoring a user's trails, which may contain locations the user does not want to disclose, is highly arguable. Finally, the excessive sampled data also bring difficulties in mining the true points of interest. For example, a district with awful traffic conditions generates dense trails in dedicated GPS devices, but is obviously a place of least interests for any user on travel. By using check-ins instead, these issues can be overcome.

Check-ins are actively shared by the users, which implies the following properties. Check-ins are less private and the information within is shared by user's will. They are more semantically meaningful and accurate than GPS trajectories as they represent real-world venues. In check-ins, locations are already associated with names and travelers, making it more effective in the mining of locations of interest. Also importantly, the spatial and temporal information and dependencies are well kept in check-ins, making it still convenient to ming transitions from check-ins. In this paper, we present the first study on integrating geo-tagged images and check-ins to effectively discover areas of interests and further rank locations.

3. FORMAT AND SIGNIFICANCE OF DATA

One of the major contributions we make is to consider geo-tagged images in joint with check-ins. Note that check-ins have some unique characteristics when compared with geo-tagged images and raw GPS records. The location carried by a geo-tagged image does not indicate a specific venue, so as to a GPS record. A typical geo-tagged image is embedded with a title, while a GPS record is not natively associated with any semantic information. That means check-ins have richer and more accurate semantic information than the other two data types. On the other hand, check-ins represent more of the daily-life activities, while geo-tagged images often show more tourist attractions. Raw GPS records could contain both, but in a vague and inaccurate fashion. Two datasets are collected for our work:

1. **Check-in1M** consists of a total number of 1,361,547 check-in entries, all of which are created from the city of Shanghai. Check-ins are in the format of a series of vectors, each of which is denoted as:

   $c =< venue\_name\ , venue\_id, longitude, latitude, user\_id, timestamp >$.

2. **GeoImg50K** is composed of 49,460 geo-tagged images crawled from Panoramio.com. All images are taken in Shanghai as well. The image meta data are also represented by vectors, each of which is denoted as:

   $p =< title, longitude,\ latitude, user\_id, timestamp >$.

The two groups of users in the above two dataset are independent. The venue names and the image titles provide us with an excellent opportunity to exploit the semantic meanings of locations. The user information enables a more dynamic and reasonable evaluation for the significance of locations.

No. entries	1,361,547
No. users	79,650
No. venues	182,551
Avg. no. entries/user	17.1
Avg. no. entries/venue	7.46
Avg. no. entries from top 10% users	145
Avg. no. entries at top 10% venues	50
Percentage of entries from top 10% users	87%
Percentage of entries at top 10% venues	67%

Table 1: Facts of Check-in1M

No. images	49,460
No. users	7,827
Avg. no. images/user	6.31
Avg. no. images from top 10% users	44.56
Percentage of images from top 10% users	70.31%

Table 2: Facts of GeoImg50K

Next let us examine the statistical significance for both datasets. Table 1 lists some facts about the dataset Check-in1M, revealing how differently people interact with this check-in service, as well as how the venues are treated quite contrastingly by people. These check-in entries are contributed by 79,650 unique users, and 182,551 unique venues are covered. Naturally, among the vast user community, most of them remain rather inactive, as the average number of entries per user is only 17.1. If we examine the average number of entries regarding venues (7.46), it is even more scattered as there are many more venues than users. However there are obvious winners in terms of activity and popularity among the users and venues. That is, the top 10% active users have contributed 87% of the total check-in entries, and the top 10% visited venues have received 67% of the total check-in entries. While for the dataset GeoImg50K, Table 2 shows that 7,827 unique users have an average number of 6.31 images created. Again, the top 10% active user have shared 70.31% of all the images uploaded, with each top user uploads 44.56 images in average. The distributions of entries and images among users and venues are well demonstrated in Figure 2. Unsurprisingly, the power law persists. In all of the three sub-figures, the top 20%(approximately) users and venues show unchallengeable dominance, while the users at the long tail remain very inactive and the venues in the same position keep rarely mentioned by the community. The analysis helps us understand the data and devise an appropriate approach to discover the preferences carried in the data entries.

4. APPROACH OVERVIEW

Throughout the paper, the term *location* is referred to either *scenic location*, or *venue*.

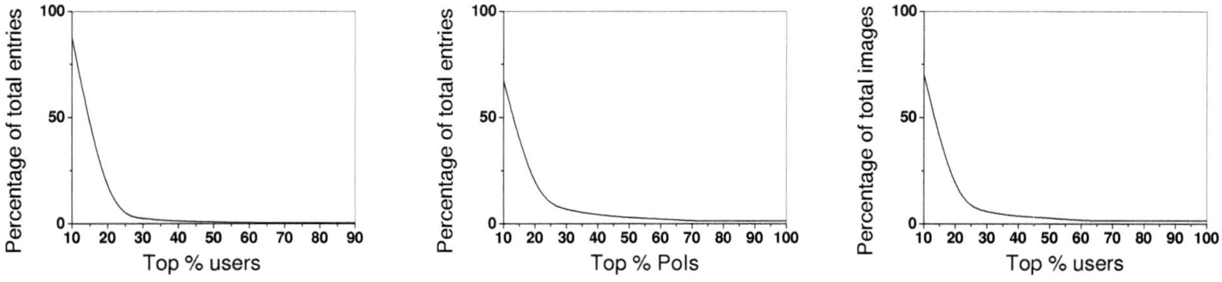

(a) Check-ins among users (b) Check-ins among venues (c) Images among users

Figure 2: Data Statistics

- *Scenic location*: a scenic location, carried in a geo-tagged image, is simply a pair of GPS coordinates, i.e., $< longitude, latitude >$. For example, <31.247378, 121.475067> is a scenic location, indicating the location where the image is associated. In this work, we assume that images are associated with locations where there are certain scenic views. Each geo-tagged image is embedded with a scenic location.

- *Venue*: a venue, carried in an check-in entry, is a specific venue name with a pair of its GPS coordinates, i.e., $< venue\_name, longitude, latitude >$. For example, <'Coffee Club', 31.247378, 121.475067> is a venue. Each check-in entry is attached with a venue.

We define the *Area of Interest (AoI)* as a heterogeneous structure that consists of one set of scenic locations from geo-tagged images and one set of venues from check-ins. Semantically, an AoI covers an area of a city in real life. The area is of remarkable interest to both the travelers and local residents. We assume that geo-tagged images represent more on the travelers' interests, while check-ins represent more on the local residents' interests. The interests are primarily reflected by the densities of images and check-ins in the area.

Our approach focuses on catering the typical requirements occurring in traveling scenarios. When traveling to other cities, if without sufficient knowledge about the city, a traveler often needs to find out which areas of the city may be interesting. Moreover, in that particular area, the traveler also likes to know which scenic locations or venues should be visited. To help a travel find an interesting area of a city, and help him/her find splendid scenic views and enjoy local experiences within the area, is the typical use case of our application. There are two major tasks in our approach:

1. *Discovering AoI*: As we target at helping travelers, their interest is our foremost consideration. To reflect their interest, we primarily use geo-tagged images to form the AoI structures. Given the geo-tagged image dataset, we extract the scenic locations from the images, and perform density-based clustering on the scenic locations to generate the clusters, which are called AoI in our application. To further include local residents' preferences, we modify the basic density-based clustering and reinforced it with a secondary density that is obtained from the scenic locations' neighboring venues, so that the venues are also considered in the AoI generation. This task returns a set of identified AoIs.

2. *Ranking AoI*: With a group of AoI, we identify the top scenic locations and top venues with authority analysis, so that the AoI are ranked accordingly. In this task, we join the two datasets, GeoImg50K and Checkin1M, into a unified space with cross-data transition inference. In the unified space, all the venues and scenic locations from both datasets are treated equivalently as locations, and the users and transitions from both datasets are combined. We then use the user-location relations and location-location transitions in a novel framework called *joint authority analysis*, in which the locations are assessed and assigned with authority scores. Based on these authority scores and the discovered AoI structures, all the AoIs are ranked.

5. DISCOVERING AOI

Inspired by DBSCAN [9] and OPTICS [1], we adopt an improve density-based clustering algorithm to take both geo-tagged images and check-in data into account for the discovery of AoI. First let us illustrate the basic density-based clustering algorithm. Unless otherwise informed, the term *distance* or the function $d(*)$ in our work refers to the Euclidean distance.

5.1 Density-based Clustering

The basic idea of density-based clustering is to obtain the spatial densities of points in the space and determine the clustering structures from the spatial distances and densities. The density of a particular point is computed from its distance to its k-neighboring points within a given range. This is called the core-distance. To evaluate if two points belong to the same cluster, we need to verify if they have each other within their ranges to the kth nearest neighbors. If positive, they are very likely to be in the same cluster if there are no better choices in which they can be assigned to more dense clusters. The basic density-based clustering uses the reachability-distance to represent how close a point is to a certain cluster, and the points are outputted in a unique order in which cluster members have similar reachability-distances and are put together. Finally, the clusters are extracted by a specific type of dendrogram called reachability-plot with an ϵ threshold.

In our case, the input of the clustering is a set of scenic locations. Through the algorithm, the densities of the scenic locations represent how significant the scenic location is to the travelers. The clusters generated are considered as the initial AoIs. As we aim to provide AoIs within a particular city, there is also a distance constraint for the maximal distance among the scenic locations within the same AoI. Based on the average scenic locations density of our datasets, we set ϵ to 250m and $k = 30$, representing that only the 30 neighbors within 250m need to be considered when a cluster expands. More details about the basic density-based clustering can be found in [1].

In the basic AoI discovery method, after performing the density-based clustering on the scenic locations, the venues are attached to their nearest AoI. However, it is clear that the density-based clustering does not initially consider any information from venues. Next we propose to use the venue density to enhance the basic clustering to make the method cover both aspects simultaneously.

5.2 Secondary Density Reinforcing

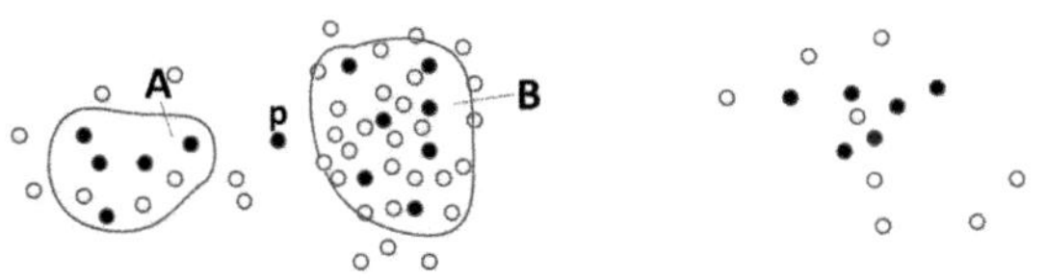

(a) Case 1 (b) Case 2

Figure 3: Effect of Secondary Density Reinforcing

Secondary density reinforcing can be understood as reconfiguring the order in which scenic locations are processed, and adding a venue density constraint when a scenic location is assigned to a cluster in the basic algorithm. As a result, the AoIs are slightly tweaked according to the scenic locations' surrounding venues. The AoI discovery algorithm will still prioritize the scenic location densities but will also consider the densities of venues.

In the basic density-based clustering, the scenic locations are processed without a specified order. Instead the procedure goes through the scenic locations as the clusters are expanded. Such a behavior could cause that the ideal results expected can not be obtained. For instance, Figure 3a demonstrates two clusters A and B, and a scenic location p between A and B (black points are scenic locations and white points are venues). Assume that p is not a core point (the cluster can not further expand from p) and it can be included to either A or B, depending on which cluster is processed first. Now if the clustering algorithm processes A first, p is a member of A after the clustering ends. However, we expect p to be part of B, because despite having similarly scenic location densities, B also has more dense venues, which is an important aspect we expect the modified clustering algorithm to emphasize.

On the other hand, in Figure 3b it shows a potential AoI in the boundary of a city where venues are rare and sparse. We want the modified algorithm to be still capable of detecting this cluster without much impact from the venue aspect. The most appropriate method is to use a secondary density to reinforce the order in which the images are processed in the density-based clustering, and to constrain the choice of which cluster to assign to for a middle scenic location like p in Figure 3a. For this purpose, we define the Neighboring Venue Density:

Definition 1 (Neighborhood Venue Density). *Given a scenic location p_i, its neighborhood venue density, denoted as $d_{k,k'}(p_i)$, is computed as:*

$$d_{k,k'}(p_i) = \overline{d_{k'}(p_j)}, \quad (1)$$

where p_j is one of p_i's k nearest scenic locations, $d_{k'}(p_j)$ is the average distance of p_j to its k' nearest venues, and $\bar{\cdot}$ represents the average.

Neighborhood Venue Density is a measure of how easily a traveler can access neighboring venues around a neighborhood of scenic locations. For each scenic location p_i, its k nearest scenic locations are first identified. For each of its neighbor p_j all its k' nearest venues are then determined and the average distance of p_j to its k' nearest venues is finally used to compute the neighborhood venue density of p_i by the average function again.

In the secondary density reinforcing, first we reorder the scenic locations by their neighborhood venue densities. Then we also add a constraint on the policy for choosing clusters. Originally, when a scenic location in the seed queue has a new reachability-distance that is smaller than its old reachability-distance, that seed is moved towards the head of the queue, meaning that it is very likely to be assigned to another cluster instead of the old one. In secondary density reinforcing, when a seed has a new reachability-distance, only when the difference between the old and new reachability-distances is greater than the loss of the secondary densities, can a seed be moved up. That means even the new cluster has a slightly higher primary density, but if it has a much lower secondary density, the scenic location is still assigned to the original cluster. On the other hand, the k' nearest venues of a scenic location are bound to it. That means when a scenic location is assigned to a cluster, its neighboring venues are also assigned to the cluster if the venue is not yet assigned. Note that a venue can only be assigned once.

These changes ensure that scenic locations with more dense neighboring venues are processed first, and the clustering prioritizes the clusters with higher neighborhood venue densities. Consequently in cases like Figure 3a, the scenic location p will be assigned to cluster B. While in cases like Figure 3b, the cluster structures will receive no abruption from the modification. Here k is set the same as in the basic density-based clustering, i.e., k=30, and k' is set to 250 according to the average venue density in our check-in dataset. Though visual analysis is vital for landmark identification, in our applications it is not considered as the spatial information embedded in the images is far more important. Next we discuss how to rank AoI.

6. RANKING AOI

An AoI is a structure composed of locations (scenic locations and venues), so its significance is largely determined by the locations within. Thus we rank the locations to get the significance of AoI.

In our datasets, locations are explicitly obtained from geotagged images and check-ins, and the transitions of users amongst locations can also be mined. Authority analysis is the natural solution for this ranking problem. First we describe how to extract and infer the transitions from the datasets, and then we propose the joint authority analysis framework to assess the locations. Finally, how to rank AoI is explained.

6.1 Transition History Extraction

We first introduce the concept of transition history.

Definition 2 (Transition History). *A transition $l_a \rightarrow l_b$ indicates one travel activity from one location l_a to* *another l_b. It is generated from a pair of geo-tagged images (or venues) with two locations l_a and l_b, if and only if the following conditions are met:*

1. *The pair of images (or check-ins) are generated by the same user.*
2. *The pair of images (or check-ins) are are two adjacent entries in term of their timestamps among all the entries from that user.*
3. *The pair of images (or check-ins) are generated in the same day, and they are generated at different locations.*

A transition history $t_{l_a \to l_b}$ is the number of transitions occurred from l_a to l_b.

Extracting transition histories from geo-tagged images or check-ins is fairly simple by programmatic manipulation. However, as the two datasets do not share the same user set, more effort is required to extract the transition histories from a combined location set from both datasets, so that all the data is used in a mutually-complementary and unified fashion.

6.2 Cross-data Transition Inference

We will show how to extract the inferred transition histories from both datasets together. The intuition is to use the transition histories in GeoImg50K and Check-in1M to infer the transitions among locations from different datasets. If a user travels from one scenic location to another in the same day, he or she probably has also visited the venues between the two scenic locations. Vice versa, if a local resident travels from one venue to another in the same day, the scenic locations which are located in between are very likely to be seen as well. Based on these assumptions, we define Inferred Transition History.

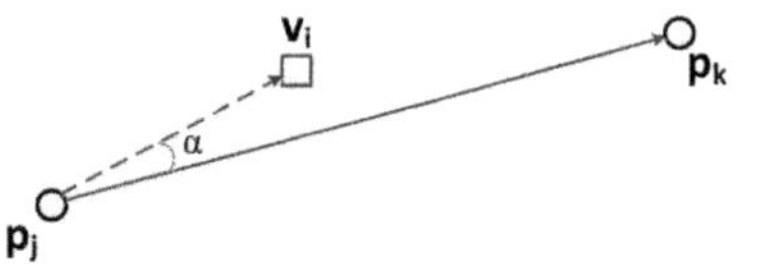

Figure 4: Cross-data Transition Inference

Definition 3 (Inferred Transition History). *We denote v_* as venues and p_* as scenic locations. Given a transition from p_j to p_k (Figure 4), the transition from p_j to v_i is an inferred transition if $d(v_i, p_j) \leq d(p_j, p_k)$, and the angle α between the two transitions is not greater than a threshold θ. The inferred transition history from p_j to v_i is estimated as:*

$$t_{p_j \to v_i} = \cos\alpha \frac{d(p_j, p_k) - \min\left(d(v_i, p_j), d(v_i, p_k)\right)}{d(p_j, p_k)} t_{p_j \to p_k} \frac{\bar{t}_{v_* \to v_i}}{\bar{t}_{p_j \to p_*}}. \quad (2)$$

where $\bar{t}_{v_* \to v_i}$ means the average transition history from other venues to v_i, and $\bar{t}_{p_j \to p_*}$ means the average transition history from p_j to other scenic locations.

The inferred transition history from venues to scenic locations can be defined similarly.

The inferred transition history is composed of three components. Take Equation 2 for instance, the first component $\cos\alpha \frac{d(p_j,p_k)-\min\left(d(v_i,p_j),d(v_i,p_k)\right)}{d(p_j,p_k)}$ models the probability of the user detours from the transition $p_j \to p_k$ and stops by at v_i. The more similar the directions are and the smaller the distance is to either p_j or p_k, the bigger the probability. The second component $t_{p_j \to p_k}$ indicates how significant the transition history is, and the third component normalizes this significance to make the values of the inferred transition history numerically compatible with other transition histories. The distance and angle constraints $d(v_i, p_j) \leq d(p_j, p_k)$ and $\alpha \leq \theta$ ensure that only minor detours are considered. In our setting, θ is set to 15°. The inferred transition history is considered to belong to the users who contribute the transition, i.e., the owners of $t_{p_j \to p_k}$ in Equation 2. We denote $\mathcal{T}$ as the complete transition histories, including inferred ones.

6.3 Basic Authority Analysis

With the complete transition histories, we describe a HITS-based link analysis framework to rank AoI. We can model locations and their relations in a graph. Formally, $\mathcal{G} = \{\mathcal{L} = \{l_1, ..., l_n\}, \mathcal{T} = \{t_{12}, ..., t_{ij}\}\}$, where each node l_i in the graph is either a scenic location or a venue, and the directional edge t_{ij} represents the transition from the node l_i to l_j with the weight as the transition history from l_i to l_j.

As the first step, we introduce the basic authority analysis, in which the hub scores and authority scores are used to describe the nodes' significance outwards and inwards. In matrix form, we denote the hub scores and authority scores for all the locations as $h = (h_1, ..., h_n)^T$ and $a = (a_1, ..., a_n)^T$, we summarize the iterations of authority analysis as repeated applications of the following two mutually reinforcing operations, $AUTH(*) = T^T$ and $HUB(*) = T$, as:

$$a = AUTH(h) = T^T h, \quad (3)$$
$$h = HUB(a) = Ta, \quad (4)$$
$$a^{i+1} = AUTH(HUB(a^i)) = T^T T a^i, \quad (5)$$
$$h^{i+1} = HUB(AUTH(h^i)) = T T^T h^i. \quad (6)$$

where i is the number of iteration. Here the adjacency matrix T is defined as the matrix form of the directional edges $\mathcal{T}$ between each pair of nodes in $\mathcal{L}$.

6.4 Joint Authority Analysis

One major weakness of the basic authority analysis is that it does not consider the users' experiences, ergo each transition is treated equally. In real life however, we observe that each transition should have difference significance, according to the user's experience and degree of being active. We assume that if a user is more experienced, his or her preference is more significant. To reflect this, we propose a joint authority analysis framework to model such a perspective.

In this framework, we unify the two mutually reinforcing models in a single authority analysis framework. The first one models the transition histories among locations to assess the location authorities, and the second models the user-location relations to assess the user authorities. Hence two hub scores are considered, i.e., the hub score $h_l = (h_{l_1}, ..., h_{l_n})^T$ from the location-location transitions and the hub score $h_u = (h_{u_1}, ..., h_{u_m})^T$ from the user-location relations, with the joint authority score $a = (a_1, ..., a_n)^T$ for the locations. Here n is the number of unique locations and m is the number of unique users. Also, in this framework, despite the T_l adjacency matrix derived from the transition histories $\mathcal{T}$, we also construct another user-location matrix

T_u of $m \times n$. The value of $t_{u_{ij}}$ means the ith user has contributed $t_{u_{ij}}$ visits to the jth location. In matrix form, we propose the novel authority analysis framework as:

$$h_l = HUB_l(a) = T_l a, \quad (7)$$
$$h_u = HUB_u(a) = T_u a, \quad (8)$$
$$a = AUTH(h_l, h_u) = T_l^T h_l \diamond T_u^T h_u. \quad (9)$$

The $\diamond$ means element-wise product. Note the h_u component accumulates the authority scores from the locations that a user has visited, then the $T_u^T h_u$ component in the $AUTH$ operation re-generates the authority scores for each location from the user hub scores and their visiting histories. Two mutually-reinforcing operations are modeled here. First, if a location has more outbound transitions to significant locations, it is a quality hub; if a location has more inbound transitions from significant locations, it is a quality authority. Second, if a user has more outbound transitions to significant locations, the user is a quality hub; if the locations has more inbound transitions from significant users, it is a quality authority. The initialization of the joint link analysis guarantees that there is no zero value assigned to either the authority score or hub score, so that their scores are updateable. The iterative solution of Equation 9 is summarized as:

$$a^{i+1} = AUTH(HUB_l(a^i), HUB_u(a^i))$$
$$= T_l^T T_l a^t \diamond T_u^T T_u a^t. \quad (10)$$

Similarly we have $h_l^{i+1} = T_l a^i$, and $h_u^{i+1} = T_u a^i$. The equation is solved with the power iteration method. After each iteration, the hub scores and authority scores are all normalized, i.e. $a_j^i = \frac{a_j^i}{\sqrt{\sum a_*^{i2}}}$, to ensure convergence. In our experiments, the framework converges within four iterations.

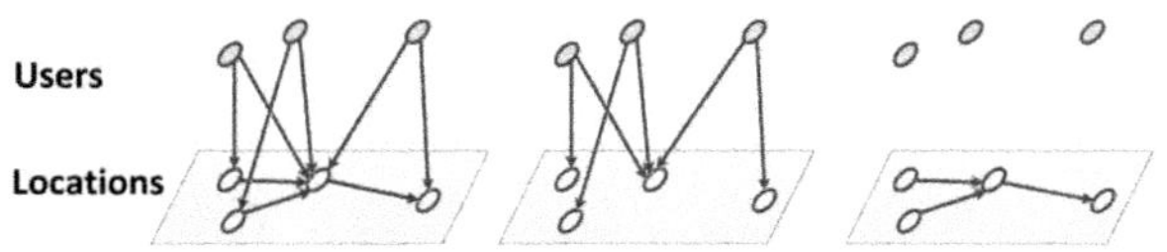

Figure 5: The Joint Authority Analysis

From left to right, the sub-figures in Figure 5 depict the different models of the joint authority analysis, and the framework described in [19], as well as the basic authority analysis. Clearly, in basic authority analysis, only the transitions among locations are explored. The framework described in [19] considers only the user-location relations, but not the location-location transitions. Instead, our framework covers both the user experience from the user-location relations as well as the location popularity from the transition histories. Another comparable approach is proposed in [6], where a random walk based unified framework is defined to analyze the significance of locations. The concept of the two-layered unified analysis as well as reinforcing location significance with user experience is similar to our work but there exist two major differences. First, [6] uses an intermediate step to connect the user-location relation and the location-location relation with the Markov chain, while we propose to unify them into the same HITS-based model. Second, in our work we need to effectively use two difference types of data, therefore the proposed cross-data transition inference is an extra effort for such new challenges.

6.5 Observation and Refinement

With the result of the joint authority analysis, we obtain the ranking of locations mainly based on their authority scores. However, there are still cases in which tweaks are needed for our framework to reduce the impact of the noises.

6.5.1 Text-based Location Elimination

It is observed that some locations obtain remarkable authority scores, but in fact they are unlikely to interest a normal traveler. For instance, a metro station or a hospital near a commercial center is often to be ranked with a high authority score. However, such locations do not appear as so interesting as their scores indicate because our targeted user is a traveler who wants to tour the city.

In this scenario, the text information embedded in the images and check-ins is of great importance, as they effectively indicate the type of locations. For instance, if a location has *restaurant* in its name, most likely it is a restaurant. There are many types of venues that are obviously of little interest to a traveler, e.g., hospitals, schools, etc. However, they are also likely to be assigned with high authority scores as lots of local people visit these locations frequently. It is surprising that how people are so willing to record every aspect of their lives by check-ins. For example, in our check-in dataset, 2751 users have repeated checked-in at their offices where they work for more than 10 times, 1046 users have check-in activities in their commuting bus or metro trips; more than 20000 check-ins are contributed at bus lines or metro lines, and more than 10000 check-ins are uploaded from hospitals. Such user practices disrupt the assumption that if a location is more frequently visited from other locations, it is likely to be more interesting to the travelers. To make the ranking more meaningful to the target travelers, we borrow the concept of stemming and stop words, to eliminate the locations that belong to these less interesting types. Our stop word list consists of 29 concepts that represent 29 types of locations, such as hospital, airport, post office, gas station, school, etc. If a location belongs to one of the 29 types, it is basically removed from the ranking list (by assigning an infinitely small authority score). The procedure is executed after the joint authority analysis.

6.5.2 Temporal Significance Modifier

Another interesting phenomenon is also observed. If a check-in's timestamp falls into the working hours in the working days, the venue it is attached to is very likely to be a place with strong business purpose. Otherwise, in off-work hours and weekends, the venues mentioned in check-ins are mostly casual places like parks, gyms, cinemas, shopping centers, restaurants, etc. Hence, we treat check-ins differently when the joint authority analysis is performed, based on the timestamps of check-ins. Specifically, we penalize the working-hour check-ins with an authority score modifier when the adjacency matrix T_l is built. When a user checks-in at a certain venue for more than or equal to three times a week during working hours, we apply this modifier on the corresponding transition histories. The value of the modifier is decided by a smooth function that equals 1 at the edges of the working hours and descends towards the center with the minimal value of 0.2.

6.6 AoI Ranking

After the joint authority analysis, AoI ranking still requires more effort to be accomplished. We know that a venue has its accurate semantically meaning, while a scenic location may not be necessarily semantically accurate. Such a difference suggests they should be treated differently. Although they are assessed together in the joint authority analysis framework, in the AoI ranking stage they are considered separately. Venues are ranked directly by their authority scores, while geo-tagged images are further analyzed to form meaningful scenes.

A scene comprises of a group of visually similar images. Given an AoI, we adopt the graph-based near-duplicate clustering method in [11] to find all the significant scenes from the images in the AoI. The clustering is content-based, and after the clusters are extracted, one text tag is extracted by performing text clustering with their titles. Each cluster is called a scene, consisting of a set of similar images in the AoI, and the text tag indicates their location's semantic meaning. The scenes are then ranked by the average authority scores of the scenic locations within the scenes. The venues are directly ranked by their authority scores from the joint authority analysis. Finally, an AoI is ranked based on the sum of the average scene ranking score and the average venue ranking score in the AoI.

7. EXPERIMENTS

The major contributions of our work including the joint link analysis for AoI ranking as well as the secondary-density reinforcing for AoI discovery. They exploit the different yet mutually-complementary knowledge about people's preferences from geo-tagged images and check-ins. Therefore in the experiments we focus on the verification of these two proposed methods. We examine the following aspects in our experiments. First, *venue ranking accuracy*, *scene ranking accuracy*, and *AoI ranking accuracy* are examined to verify the effectiveness of the joint authority analysis. Then *AoI Quality* is used to test the effectiveness of the secondary-density reinforced clustering. *Venue ranking accuracy* is the average MAP of the venues from all the AoI. *Scene ranking accuracy* is the average MAP of the scenes from all the AoI. *AoI ranking accuracy* is the MAP of the AoI. *AoI Quality* is an accumulative ranking score for the venues and scenes from an AoI. As only the top venues and scene are finally presented to the users, these top venues and scenes determine how much the AoI can interest the users. We use the ranking scores of venues and scenes from the ground-truth to compute the AoI quality so that the effect of our clustering method is isolated from the authority analysis. Next let us describe the baseline methods.

7.1 Baseline Methods

In the rest of the experiments, we call the proposed AoI ranking approach as Joint Authority Analysis with cross-data transition Inference(JAAI). We compare other 5 baseline methods with JAAI. The other methods are:

- Joint Authority Analysis (JAA): the joint authority analysis without cross-data transition inference.
- UL Authority Analysis (ULAA): the authority analysis method described in [19].
- Baseline Authority Analysis (BAA): the HITS-based authority analysis method described in [13].
- Rank-by-Visits (RV): the accumulative counts of visits to the AoI to rank AoI.
- Rank-by-Users (RU): the accumulative counts of unique users who have visited the AoI to rank AoI.

In JAA, ULAA, BAA, RV and RU, venues and scenes are ranked separately to isolate the effect of cross-data transition inference. The refinements described in Section 6.5 are applied to both JAAI and JAA. Similarly, we call the AoI discovery approach as the Secondary-density Reinforced Clustering (SRC). We also use the following baseline methods to compare with the SRC method:

- Density-based Clustering (DC): the basic density-based clustering without secondary density reinforcing.
- KMeans: the classic KMeans clustering.

For DC and K-means, geo-tagged images are used to generate the initial clustering results, forming the initial AoI. The venues are then attached to the AoI with closest distance from the venue to the AoI center.

7.2 Ground-truth Generation

Similar to the problems of web page ranking [4] or GPS-trajectory-based location mining [20, 19, 6], our problem does not have absolute ground-truth. Next we show how we obtain the ground-truth from the shared knowledge online and from human efforts offline.

We obtain ground-truth for the venues ranking from a real-life review website dianping.com[1]. For a venue, we use the sum of its normalized number of reviews and its normalized average review score from expert reviews on this website as our ranking score in the ground-truth. The venues are then ranked by these ranking scores as our ground-truth.

The ground-truth generation for the scene ranking involves human effort. Specifically, scenes inside each AoI, along with their images and neighboring venues, are displayed to the annotator. The annotator then marks each of them a scene quality score between 1 to 5. The quality scene quality score indicates how significant or interesting it is to the annotator. For each scene, the average quality score from all the annotators are used as its ranking score in the ground-truth. 13 annotators are involved in the annotation, including 8 male and 5 female, with sufficient common knowledge about Shanghai city and the famous scenes in it. The criteria of different quality scores are listed in Table 3.

Scene Quality	Criteria
5	I would definitely visit the scene.
4	I would visit the scene if possible.
3	It does not matter if I visit it or not.
2	I would not visit the scene if possible.
1	I definitely would not visit the scene.

Table 3: Levels of Scene Ranking Scores

7.3 Effect of Joint Authority Analysis

Figure 6(a) depicts the different venue ranking accuracies that are obtained with JAAI and its comparative methods. JAAI outperforms other methods convincingly with the average venue ranking accuracy of 0.72, indicating excellent

[1]www.dianping.com, the largest venue review website in China, similar to Yelp.com

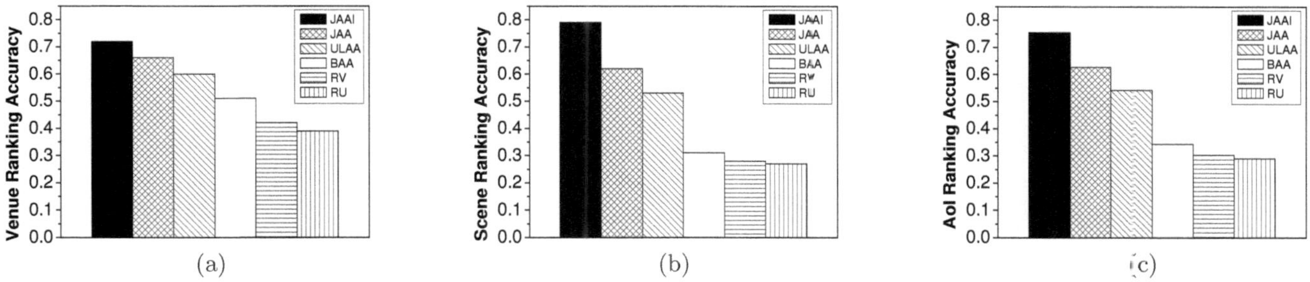

Figure 6: Effect of JAAI

distinguishing power on the venue popularity. The user-location relation and the location-location transitions are both being considered in the analysis, this is the major reason why it obtains superior results. JAA gains the closest performance of nearly 0.66, as the result of the joint authority analysis being used. The marginal difference suggests that the cross-data inference makes positive effect on the ranking accuracy. But due to the limited size of the image data, the effect is also limited. ULAA yields the third best result, followed by BAA. As naive methods, RV and RU both have average accuracies around 0.4. Because these simple methods are easily interfered by the noises, like uninteresting but crowded locations, and also ignore the user-location and location-location relations, their performance is expected to be unsatisfactory.

The results for the scene ranking are illustrated in Figure 6(b). The overall performance of the methods are similar to those of the venue ranking. However, there are also several noticeable differences. Comparing to the venue ranking results, where JAA obtains very close result to JAAI, in scene ranking JAA's result is far worse than JAAI's. ULAA's performance is also much closer to JAA. This is because that JAA heavily relies on the transition histories, but geo-tagged images contribute insufficient transitions to support this aspect. JAAI has the cross-data transition inference to compensate such weakness, while JAA does not. This explains the huge difference between JAAI and JAA. For ULAA, it only considers the relations between the users and locations, so it is not as heavily impacted as JAA is. Its performance stays similar to that in the venue ranking. Generally, because the scenes and venues are ranked separately, and check-ins are not considered, the performance is proven to be less satisfactory for JAA, ULAA, BAA, RV and RU. The overall AoI ranking accuracy presented in Figure 6(c) supports such an observation.

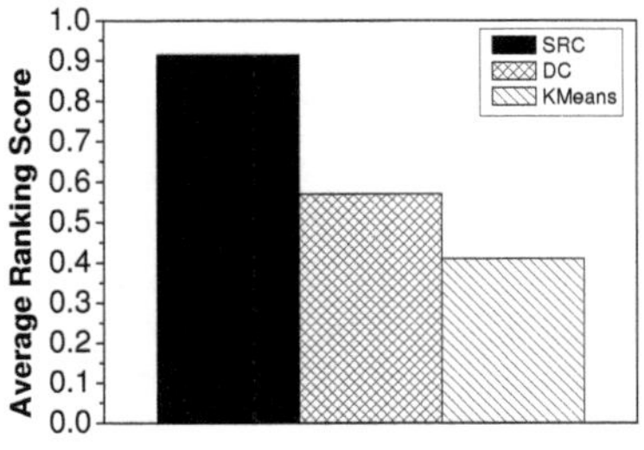

Figure 7: Effect of SRC

7.4 Effect of Secondary Density Reinforcing

The comparison of SRC and other baseline methods is demonstrated in Figure 7. SRC outperforms the baseline methods by great margins. DC has better result than KMeans because of its ability of finding clustering with irregular shapes, which is sometimes important in AoI discovery. For example, DC may be able to find a pedestrian-only commercial street. KMeans does not find such an AoI accurately. The average ranking scores of the AoI generated by DC and KMeans are obviously lower than SRC, indicating that SRC is able to generate AoI of superior quality.

7.5 AoI Presentation

We also design an interactive interface that displays top AoI in a city, and a sub-interface in which the affiliated scenes and venues are displayed for further inspection. Figure 8 is a snapshot of the AoI presentation interface. In the interface, each AoI is represented by a circle, where the letter in the circle indicates its ranking (starting with 'A'). When an AoI is chosen, the circle is highlighted, and a window pops up to show the magnified map and the details of the AoI, just as the figure shows at the upper-right corner. The circles in the AoI window are the scenes, in which all the thumbnail images are display. Top venues inside the AoI are presented by red balloons at the venues' actual locations. When a particular thumbnail image is clicked, the original image is displayed in the upper-left corner. When a balloon is clicked, a text message is displayed with the venue's name. For limited space, no more than 20 AoI are presented for a city, and only the top 10 scenes and top 50 venues are presented for each AoI.

8. CONCLUSION

Location-based media services have attracted phenomenal attention from researchers lately. Many applications and approaches are built on-top of geo-tagged images. However, check-in as a new form of location-based data is relatively less studied. In this work, by fusing geo-tagged images as well as check-ins for the same city, we propose a novel approach for AoI discovery and ranking, to discover areas in a city in which popular scenic locations and popular venues are located for the travelers. We analyze their mutually-complementary nature and discuss their statistical significance. A modified density-based clustering method is devised to discover AoI. Then a novel authority analysis framework is proposed to analyze the significance of the locations embedded in images and check-ins. In the framework we utilize the intuitions that if a location is more frequently transitioned from other locations, the location is more sig-

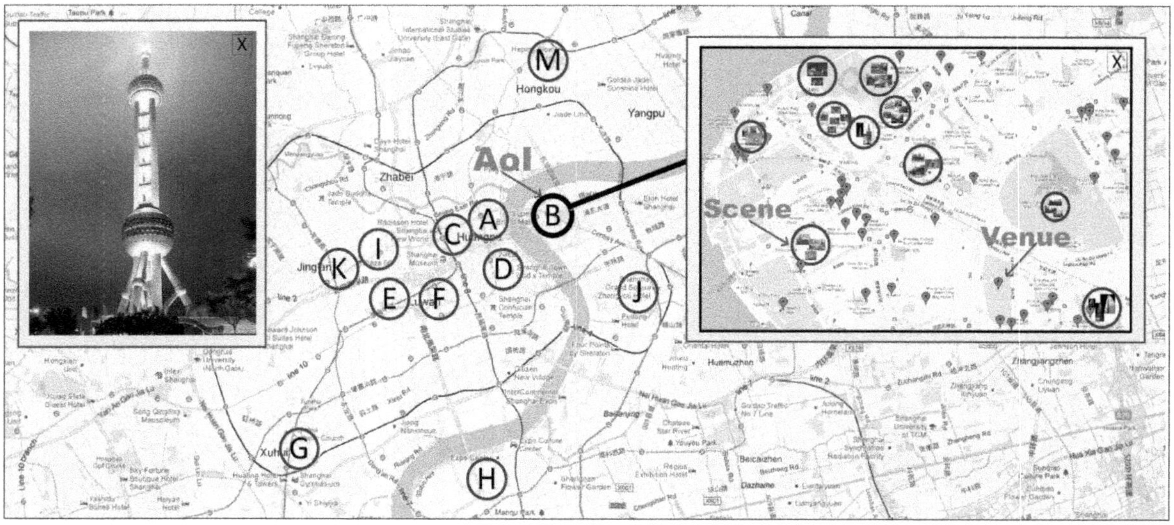

Figure 8: The AoI Presentation Interface

nificant; if a user has more experiences on traveling, his or her travel activities should have better indication on the significance of the destination. We unify these two aspects into a single framework to evaluate the significance of the locations. To further improve the framework for the targeted users, namely the travelers, we applied refinement technics based on the temporal patterns in check-ins, and the text titles of both dataset, to ensure our framework better matches the user needs semantically. In the experiments, we employ online knowledge base and human effort to obtain groundtruth and verify the novelty of our approach. In future work we will study the possibility of combining the AoI discovery and ranking into a single framework, and will consider using more visual information.

9. REFERENCES

[1] M. Ankerst, M. M. Breunig, H.-P. Kriegel, and J. Sander. Optics: Ordering points to identify the clustering structure. In *SIGMOD*, pages 49–60, 1999.

[2] S. A. Ay, L. Zhang, S. H. Kim, M. He, and R. Zimmermann. Grvs: a georeferenced video search engine. In *ACM Multimedia*, pages 977–978, 2009.

[3] S. A. Ay, R. Zimmermann, and S. H. Kim. Relevance ranking in georeferenced video search. *Multimedia Syst.*, 16(2):105–125, 2010.

[4] S. Brin and L. Page. The anatomy of a large-scale hypertextual web search engine. *Computer Networks*, 30(1-7):107–117, 1998.

[5] L. Cao, J. Luo, A. C. Gallagher, X. Jin, J. Han, and T. S. Huang. A worldwide tourism recommendation system based on geotaggedweb photos. In *ICASSP*, pages 2274–2277, 2010.

[6] X. Cao, G. Cong, and C. S. Jensen. Mining significant semantic locations from gps data. *PVLDB*, 3(1):1009–1020, 2010.

[7] W.-C. Chen, A. Battestini, N. Gelfand, and V. Setlur. Visual summaries of popular landmarks from community photo collections. In *ACM Multimedia*, pages 789–792, 2009.

[8] G. C. de Silva and K. Aizawa. Retrieving multimedia travel stories using location data and spatial queries. In *ACM Multimedia*, pages 785–788, 2009.

[9] M. Ester, H.-P. Kriegel, J. Sander, and X. Xu. A density-based algorithm for discovering clusters in large spatial databases with noise. In *KDD*, pages 226–231, 1996.

[10] Q. Hao, R. Cai, J.-M. Yang, R. Xiao, L. Liu, S. Wang, and L. Zhang. Travelscope: standing on the shoulders of dedicated travelers. In *ACM Multimedia*, pages 1021–1022, 2009.

[11] Z. Huang, B. Hu, H. Cheng, H. T. Shen, H. Liu, and X. Zhou. Mining near-duplicate graph for cluster-based reranking of web video search results. *ACM Trans. Inf. Syst.*, 28(4):22, 2010.

[12] L. S. Kennedy and M. Naaman. Generating diverse and representative image search results for landmarks. In *WWW*, pages 297–306, 2008.

[13] J. M. Kleinberg. Authoritative sources in a hyperlinked environment. *J. ACM*, 46(5):604–632, 1999.

[14] Y. Li, D. J. Crandall, and D. P. Huttenlocher. Landmark classification in large-scale image collections. In *ICCV*, pages 1957–1964, 2009.

[15] J. Luo, D. Joshi, J. Yu, and A. C. Gallagher. Geotagging in multimedia and computer vision - a survey. *Multimedia Tools Appl.*, 51(1):187–211, 2011.

[16] Y. Wang, T. Mei, J. Wang, H. Li, and S. Li. Jigsaw: interactive mobile visual search with multimodal queries. In *ACM Multimedia*, pages 73–82, 2011.

[17] Y. Zheng and X. Xie. Learning travel recommendations from user-generated gps traces. *ACM TIST*, 2(1):2, 2011.

[18] Y. Zheng, L. Zhang, Z. Ma, X. Xie, and W.-Y. Ma. Recommending friends and locations based on individual location history. *TWEB*, 5(1):5, 2011.

[19] Y. Zheng, L. Zhang, X. Xie, and W.-Y. Ma. Mining interesting locations and travel sequences from gps trajectories. In *WWW*, pages 791–800, 2009.

[20] C. Zhou, N. Bhatnagar, S. Shekhar, and L. G. Terveen. Mining personally important places from gps tracks. In *ICDE Workshops*, pages 517–526, 2007.

Scalable Mining of Small Visual Objects

Pierre Letessier
INA & INRIA Sophia-Antipolis
4 av de l'Europe
94360 Bry sur Marne, France
pletessier@ina.fr

Olivier Buisson
INA
4 av de l'Europe
94360 Bry sur Marne, France
obuisson@ina.fr

Alexis Joly
INRIA Sophia-Antipolis
161 rue Ada
34095 Montpellier, France
alexis.joly@inria.fr

ABSTRACT

This paper presents a scalable method for automatically discovering frequent visual objects in large multimedia collections even if their size is very small. It first formally revisits the problem of mining or discovering such objects, and then generalizes two kinds of existing methods for probing candidate object seeds: weighted adaptive sampling and hashing-based methods. The idea is that the collision frequencies obtained with hashing-based methods can actually be converted into a prior probability density function given as input to a weighted adaptive sampling algorithm. This allows for an evaluation of any hashing scheme effectiveness in a more generalized way, and a comparison with other priors, e.g. guided by visual saliency concerns. We then introduce a new hashing strategy, working first at the visual level, and then at the geometric level. This strategy allows us to integrate weak geometric constraints into the hashing phase itself and not only neighborhood constraints as in previous works. Experiments conducted on a new dataset introduced in this paper will show that using this new hashing-based prior allows a drastic reduction of the number of tentative probes required to discover small objects instantiated several times in a large dataset.

Categories and Subject Descriptors

H.3.3 [**Information Search and Retrieval**]: Search process

Keywords

Computer Vision, Mining, Discovery, Scalable, Small Objects, Weak geometry, Hashing, LSH, RMMH

1. INTRODUCTION

Automatically linking multimedia documents that contain one or several instances of the same visual object is gaining more and more interest. Visual features and rigid objects matching techniques are actually mature enough to produce accurate visual links, trustable from a user's point of view. Automatically discovering such objects and links in a given multimedia collection or across different media has many applications including: salient media events detection, content-based filtering recommendation, web browsing, etc.

Whereas efficient methods now exist that aim to searching for rigid objects in large collections, discovering them from scratch is still challenging in terms of scalability, particularly when the targeted objects are rather small compared to the whole visual content. It is for instance noticeable that most previous works on object discovery were evaluated on the popular Oxford buildings dataset, where the targeted objects (buildings) occupy a very large fraction of the images themselves.

One of the claims of this paper is that the complexity of mining repeated visual objects is closely related to the relative size of the targeted objects and to their frequency of occurrence. Therefore, the complexity of classical mining algorithms for discovering repeated item sets is known to be highly related to their frequency. To illustrate the variety of problems, let us compare the objects considered in the Oxford buildings dataset to those considered in the BelgaLogos dataset, another popular evaluation dataset focused on trademark logos. Figure 1 shows the repartition of the instance sizes for these two datasets. The measure used here to analyze the sizes of instances is the number of SIFT features falling into the bounding boxes of the objects in the ground truth. We found 29,968,910 features in Oxford buildings, with 6,056,353 belonging to objects in the ground truth, and 38,093,296 descriptors in BelgaLogos, with 184,698 belonging to the annotated logos. We observe that the coverage of objects in Oxford buildings is around 20% while it is only 0.5% in BelgaLogos.

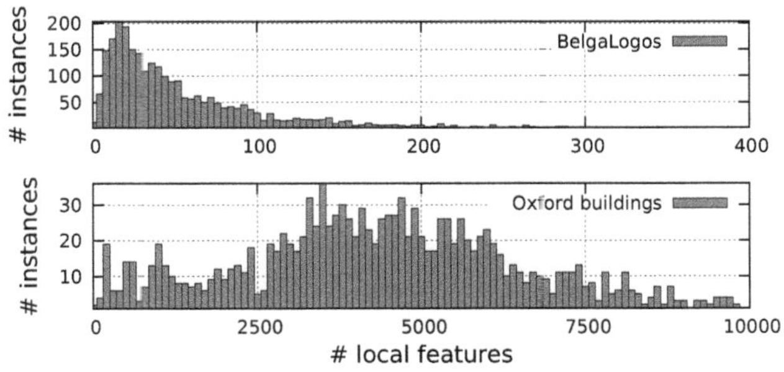

Figure 1: Comparison of instances size in BelgaLogos and Oxford buildings

2. RELATED WORKS

The scalable mining of visual content database is recently emerging [2, 15, 11, 18, 17, 19]. Most of these methods are dedicated and tested to the discovery of large objects (more than 20% of the images) in image collections [2, 15, 17, 19]. There are very few papers about small visual objects discovery and mining. In [2] is presented a qualitative evaluation of small visual objects mining in large scale dataset. Consistent Visual Words Mining with Adaptive Sampling [11] is a rare work where the technology is dedicated to discover and mine small visual objects and where a quantitative evaluation is presented.

This method [11] can be summarized by four main successive steps:

Image description: The images are described by Sift features [13], one of the most widely used.

Features Indexing A Posteriori Multi-Probe Locality Sensitive Hashing (APMP-LSH) method proposed by Joly et al. [7] that allows sublinear search time with reduced memory space costs. This method approximates the nearest neighbor search of similar Sift features.

Seeds Generation: Seeds are Region Of Interest where there are potential instances of repeated objects. To generate the seeds, they propose a generic framework based on an adaptive weighted sampling scheme. This sampling process starts with some prior distribution and iteratively converges to unvisited ROI. Different natures of prior distribution allow them to define different types of ROI. For examples, they propose a prior distribution based on a face detector in order to discover ROI containing faces. They also proposed another prior to avoid textured areas (to suppress false alarms). In [11], the priors only exploit intra-image saliency information.

Seeds Verification and Retrieval: In [11], to suppress the ROI containing false alarms where there are no object instances, they directly propose to launch a process of local region search. In fact, the selected seeds or ROI are queries of this process. The local region search is based on the framework proposed in [8] to retrieve small objects: APMP-LSH method [7] for Sift similarity search, match verification (RANSAC [5]) to suppress false matches and an A Contrario Query Expansion (QE) [8] to improve the recall of small object instances. An equivalent strategy of match verification and QE is also used to discover small objects in [2].

The framework, proposed in [11], is then flexible and generic, because it could be possible to define new types of priors to discover different objects or to change the discovering strategy. The main computational cost of this framework is the last step: Seeds Verification and Retrieval. These costs could be reduced if the adaptive sampling would more quickly focus on the ROI where the instances of repeated objects are. It could be faster if the priors used by the adaptive sampling were more efficient to discover small visual objects.

In this paper, we propose a formulation to accurately analyze these costs and a new type of priors to drastically decrease the computational costs. We then integrate these priors into the framework proposed by [11]. As discussed below, our priors are based on Weak Geometry (WG) and hashing methods.

The evaluation dataset BelgaLogos used in [11], and proposed in [8], is designed to evaluate methods to retrieve small visual objects' instances. This dataset's ground truth is not fully adapted to evaluate a mining process. Apart from the queries' ground truth, in this image dataset, there are a lot of visual objects' instances which are not annotated (buildings, faces, ...). These instances could be considered as false alarms by the evaluation process. To our knowledge, there doesn't exist specific dataset which is designed to evaluate small visual object discovery and mining methods! We therefore propose an adapted dataset and ground truth to evaluate theses two tasks.

3. PROBLEM FORMULATION

3.1 Notations

Let us first introduce some notations. We consider a dataset $\mathbf{I}$ of N_I images described by a set $\mathbf{X}$ of N local feature vectors $\mathbf{x}_i$, each being extracted at position $\mathbf{p}_i = (I_i, \chi_i, \psi_i)$ where I_i is the identifier of the image and (χ_i, ψ_i) the coordinates of the local feature in the image.

Now, we consider a set $\mathbf{O}$ of objects O^m, each being represented by S_m instances O_s^m. An instance O_s^m is associated with a unique area A_s^m (in a single image) and contains a set of local features:

$$\mathbf{X}_s^m = \{\mathbf{x}_i \mid \mathbf{p}_i \in A_s^m\}_{1 \le i \le N}$$

We will now introduce some basic definitions that will help us to formalize our object's discovery and mining problems, and model our approach.

Definition - Global cover

The global cover $c_{\mathbf{X}}(O^m)$ of an object O^m is defined by:

$$c_{\mathbf{X}}(O^m) = \frac{1}{N} \sum_{s=1}^{S_m} |\mathbf{X}_s^m| \tag{1}$$

It measures the fraction of features in the dataset covered by all instances of a given object.

Definition - Average cover

The average cover $c(O^m)$ of an object O^m is defined by:

$$c(O^m) = \frac{1}{S_m} \sum_{s=1}^{S_m} \frac{1}{N_{I_s}} |\mathbf{X}_s^m| \tag{2}$$

with N_{I_s} the number of features in the image including O_s^m.

It measures the average fraction that an instance of the object occupies in an image.

Definition - Frequency

The *frequency* $f(O^m)$ of an object O^m is defined by:

$$f(O^m) = \frac{S_m}{N_I} \tag{3}$$

Definition - $\{c, f\}$-frequent object

An object O^m is said $\{c, f\}$-*frequent* if:

$$\begin{cases} c(O^m) = c \\ f(O^m) = f \end{cases}$$

We also notice here that if the number of features per image is rather stable then we can consider that $c_{\mathbf{X}} \approx c.f$

3.2 Problems

We define the two following problems as the main objectives to be solved by objects mining and discovery methods.

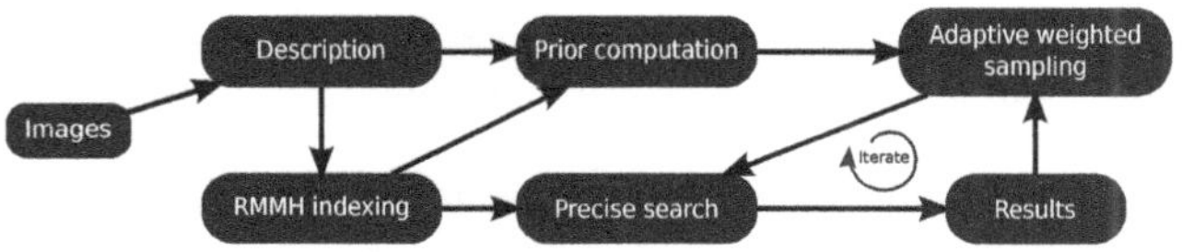

Figure 2: Object mining framework

Objects Discovery: find at least one instance O_q^m of all $\{c, f\}$-*frequent* objects O^m such that:

$$\begin{cases} c \geq c_0 \\ f \geq f_0 \end{cases}$$

Objects Mining: find all instances O_s^m of all $\{c, f\}$-*frequent* objects O^m such that:

$$\begin{cases} c \geq c_0 \\ f \geq f_0 \end{cases}$$

The underlying idea is that the complexity of these two problems depends mainly on the parameters c and f, so we suggest including them in the query formulation of the problem as done in classical data mining approaches (e.g. for mining frequent item sets).

4. OBJECT MINING FRAMEWORK AND MODELING

We use the same object mining framework as the one proposed in [11]. The main principle of this approach is to use a *weighted* and *adaptive* sampling strategy to select the most relevant query regions to be issued afterwards to a precise object search algorithm (e.g. based on large scale matching and RANSAC registration). To avoid querying all possible regions of interest while keeping a good coverage of the contents, *Sampling* is indeed a simple yet efficient statistical paradigm allowing to yield some knowledge about a population without surveying it entirely. Adaptive weighted sampling is a more advanced paradigm allowing to iteratively update the sampling distribution according to the results obtained during previous iterations. This allows the mining process to progressively focus on unvisited image regions and consequently reduce the number of required probes for achieving a good completeness of the mining.

Our global object mining framework is presented in Figure 2. It is composed of three main steps:

SIFT features extraction: All images in $\mathbf{I}$ are described with SIFT features [13], resulting in a set $\mathbf{X}$ of N 128-dimensional feature vectors $\mathbf{x}_i$. Each extracted feature $\mathbf{x}_i$ is associated to a position $\mathbf{p}_i = (I_i, \chi_i, \psi_i)$, a principal orientation θ_i and a local scale σ_i.

Prior distribution computation: The aim of this step is to compute a prior probability mass function p_0 on $\mathbf{X}$, where $p_0(\mathbf{x}_i)$ is the probability of a given $\mathbf{x}_i$ to be sampled at the first iteration of the adaptive weighted sampling step. Since building p_0 is the core contribution of our work, we will come back to this issue in section 5.

Adaptive Weighted Sampling and Precise Search: This step works in the same way as in [11], so we will let the reader refers to this work for more details. The algorithm iteratively samples a candidate feature $\mathbf{x}_t$ $(0 \leq t < T)$ according to the probability mass function p_t on $\mathbf{X}$. A query window centered around $\mathbf{x}_t$ is then issued to a *precise search* algorithm allowing it to find other instances of the object captured by the query window (if any exist in the dataset). The probability mass of the features belonging to the retrieved instances are then decreased, resulting in a new probability mass function p_{t+1} to be used in the next sampling iteration.

As the prior distribution p_0 is the initial condition of the Adaptive Weighted Sampling algorithm, the way it is built has a strong impact on the whole performances of the mining process, i.e. on the number T of iterations required to discover instances of (c, f)-frequent objects. As we will see in the rest of the paper, building an accurate prior distribution can divide by up to 32 the number of required probes compared to a uniform sampling.
Admittedly, the speed and the effectiveness of the *precise search* algorithm also have an influence on the performance of the method, but in a more limited way. The overall complexity of the approach actually remains $O(T)$ whatever the speed of the search algorithm used, e.g. [15, 6, 1, 8, 9] (because one single search remains an expensive process). Regarding the effectiveness of the precise search algorithm, things are more complex. The quality of the mining after T iterations actually depends on the recall and precision of the search strategy, in a way that is difficult to model accurately. Starting with a perfect search algorithm however gives us some insights about what happens overall.
Let us actually consider a dataset with one single $\{c, f\}$-*frequent* object O^m. Now let $\mathbf{x}_t$ be the candidate query feature selected at random from $\mathbf{X}$ according to the probability mass function p_t. While $\mathbf{x}_t$ does not belong to an instance O_s^m of O^m, p_t remains equal to p_0 if we consider a precise search algorithm with a perfect precision. On the other side, if $\mathbf{x}_t$ belongs to an instance O_s^m of O^m, the full mining problem is completed (when considering a precise search algorithm with perfect recall). So that the number of required iterations T follows a negative binomial distribution $BR(1, 1-c_0(O^m))$ where the failure probability $c_0(O^m)$ is the probability that a sampled feature belongs to an instance O_s^m of O^m, i.e.

$$c_0(O^m) = \sum_{\mathbf{x}_i \in \{O_s^m\}} p_0(\mathbf{x}_i)$$

The expected number of probes $\hat{T}$ is therefore equal to

$$\hat{T} = \frac{1 - c_0(O^m)}{c_0(O^m)} = \frac{1}{c_0(O^m)} - 1 \tag{4}$$

and the complexity of the algorithm is $O(\frac{1}{c_0(O^m)})$. We generally refer to $c_0(O^m)$ as the prior statistical cover of the object O^m since it measures the fraction of the prior distribution captured by the object. This shows that the complexity of the algorithm is strongly related to the prior distribution p_0. If we consider for instance a perfect prior distribution, so that $p_0(\mathbf{x}_i) = 0$, $\forall \mathbf{x}_i \notin \{X_s^m\}$ and $p_0(\mathbf{x}_i) = 1/N$, $\forall \mathbf{x}_i \in \{X_s^m\}$, then we have $c_0(O^m) = 1$ and the complexity of the algorithm is $O(1)$.
On the other side, if we consider an uniform prior distribution so that $p_0(\mathbf{x}_i) = 1/N$, $\forall \mathbf{x}_i \in \mathbf{X}$ then the complexity is $O(c_{\mathbf{X}}(O^m))$ where $c_{\mathbf{X}}(O^m)$ is the global cover of the object as defined in section 3.1. And since $c_{\mathbf{X}}(O^m) \approx c(O^m).f(O^m)$ the complexity of mining a (c, f)-frequent object with an uniform sampling is roughly $O(\frac{1}{cf})$. This illustrates well

why mining small objects (with small values of c) might be a much more difficult task than objects occupying a large fraction of the image ($c \approx 1$).

If we now consider a real precise search algorithm rather than a perfect one, so that it returns only a fraction r of the instances of an object O^m when a query feature $\mathbf{x}_t$ belonging to one of the instance is sampled. Then, good recall will be achieved only if a sufficient number μ of instances of the same object are selected by the sampling. Under the hypothesis that the retrieved instances are independent from one query to another, the probability that an instance is missed after μ queries is equal to $(1-r)^\mu$. If we want this probability to be lower than a probability ϵ, then we get $\mu > \log(\epsilon)/\log(1-r)$. In that case, the number of required iterations T would follow a negative binomial distribution $BR(\mu, 1-c_0(O^m))$ instead of $BR(1, 1-c_0(O^m))$. And the expected number of probes would be

$$\hat{T} = \frac{\log(\epsilon)}{\log(1-r)}\left(\frac{1}{c_0(O^m)} - 1\right) \quad (5)$$

The complexity of the whole mining process is therefore still $O(\frac{1}{c_0(O^m)})$ for fixed values of r and ϵ. For relatively good recall values r and moderate variations between existing search methods, we can argue that the prior distribution p_0 has a much larger impact on the complexity than the effectiveness of the precise search algorithm used on top of the adaptive sampling algorithm.

5. HASHING-BASED PRIOR DISTRIBUTION COMPUTATION

As stated before, our objective is to compute a prior probability mass function p_0 on $\mathbf{X}$, so that $p_0(\mathbf{x}_i)$ reflects as much as possible the likelihood that a given local feature $\mathbf{x}_i$ belongs to a (c,f)-frequent object. In other words, we attempt to maximize $c_0(O^m)$ for all (c,f)-frequent objects in the dataset. Rather than using visual saliency measures computed at the image level as in [11], we propose building much more effective prior distributions based on the construction of visual and WG hash tables on the whole dataset. The cost to compute such prior is actually higher than simple image-based priors but the complexity reduction of the sampling-and-search phase still makes it widely profitable. As done in conventional weighted random sampling methods [14], our hashing-based probability mass function p_0 is computed in practice by normalizing a scoring function z_0 on $\mathbf{X}$. The computation of all individual scores $z_0(\mathbf{x}_i)$ mainly relies on collisions frequency in hash tables making our algorithm scalable and easily distributable if needed. It includes the three following steps:

1. Construction of a hashing-based visual index (cf. 5.1)
2. Visual filtering and WG hashing (cf. 5.2)
3. Prior distribution computation (cf. 5.3)

5.1 Visual hashing

There are two main strategies for efficient visual similarity search of local features: visual vocabulary associated with inverted-list [15, 1] and the hashing [8, 9]. These two types of methods have a common aim: to reduce the computational cost of the similarity search by compressing the local features.

Most visual similarity search methods are based on visual vocabulary. Visual vocabulary allows us to describe images from a set of quantified local features. The vocabulary is usually generated by a K-means algorithm [16, 3, 15, 1] applied on the local features set of the considered corpus. In [15], the retrieval efficiency is accurately studied in functions of the vocabulary size K and the database size N (local feature number). It demonstrates that $K \approx \beta.N$ with $\beta \in [0.05, 0.10]$ to have efficient visual retrieval. Moreover, the best visual retrieval results are obtained if the visual vocabulary is learned with the current database to index. In the case of very large databases ($N > 10^8$), [15] propose distributed Approximate K-Means (AKM) which has a complexity of $O(I.N.log(K))$, with I the iteration number. For example in [15], it took 5 hours for $N = 17.0 \times 10^6, K = 10^6, I = 30$ with 32 CPU cores. Based on AKM complexity and these CPU performances, we can coarsely estimate the computational time for $N = 500 \times 10^6$, $K = 35 \times 10^6$, $\beta = 0.07$ and $I = 30$: 185 hours. This computational time is too prohibitive for a large scale process, because at this stage, the discovery and mining process has not yet started.

Due to these computational costs, we have chosen to use hashing based methods to index the visual feature. The hashing based methods have demonstrated equivalent performances to retrieval visual objects in [8, 11]. Moreover, we demonstrate in the evaluation chapter that the computational time to hash a dataset of $N = 500 \times 10^6$ Sift is lower than 4 hours with 12 CPU Core. This visual indexing is very efficient and adapted for a large scale process.

Rather than using classical LSH functions, our method is based on a more efficient method: Random Maximum Margin Hashing (RMMH, [9]), an original hash function family introduced recently. The main originality of RMMH is to **train** purely **random splits** of the data, regardless of the closeness of the training samples (i.e. without any supervision). Concretely, the method works by learning a set of *randomly trained classifiers* from a small fraction of the dataset. For each hash function, M training points are selected at random from $\mathbf{X}$ and are then **randomly labeled** (half of the points with -1 and the other half with 1). If we denote as x_j^+ the resulting $\frac{M}{2}$ positive training samples and as $\mathbf{x}_j^-$ the $\frac{M}{2}$ negative training samples, each hash function is then computed by training a binary classifier $h(\mathbf{x})$ such that:

$$h(\mathbf{x}) = argmax_{h_\theta} \sum_{j=1}^{\frac{M}{2}} h_\theta(\mathbf{x}_j^+) - h_\theta(\mathbf{x}_j^-) \quad (6)$$

Using a linear Support Vector Machine (SVM) as a binary classifier, we get:

$$h_(\mathbf{x}) = sgn\left(\sum_{i=1}^{m} \alpha_i^* \mathbf{x}_i^* . \mathbf{x} + b_m\right) \quad (7)$$

where $\mathbf{x}_i^*$ are the m support vectors selected by the SVM ($\mathbf{x}_i^* \in \{\mathbf{x}_j^+, \mathbf{x}_j^-\}$) and it estimates α_i^* and b_m. In [9], they demonstrate that $M = 40$ is adapted for different types of features and different size of feature databases. In the following chapter, we finally denote as $\mathbf{h}_l(\mathbf{x})$ the k-length hash code produced by the concatenation of k individual binary hash functions for the l-th hash function.

5.2 Visual filtering and WG hashing

Once the visual index has been created, our algorithm computes individual scores $z_0(\mathbf{x}_i)$ by independently processing all images $I_j \in \mathbf{I}$ one by one (either iteratively or across multiple threads or machines). Let us denote I_Q the image processed at the Q-th iteration and $\mathbf{X}_Q$ the set of local features belonging to it.

5.2.1 Visual collisions filtering

To reduce the amount of collisions in the visual index for all $\mathbf{x}_q \in \mathbf{X}_Q$, we apply three complementary filtering strategies:

Intra-image collision frequency: as claimed in [2], visual features that are unique in the image are more likely to produce relevant candidate matches in the whole dataset. This paradigm actually allows the reduction of a large fraction of false positives produced by textures and other repeated visual structures. Rather than keeping only unique features, we propose a smoother strategy that bounds the collision frequency in the image to a maximum value ζ. So that a reduced set $\mathbf{X'}_Q$ of candidate features is obtained from $\mathbf{X}_Q$ through:

$$\mathbf{X'}_Q = \{\mathbf{x_q} \in \mathbf{X}_Q \mid f_Q(\mathbf{x_q}) < \zeta\} \tag{8}$$

where the intra-image collision frequency f_Q is estimated by its mean across the L visual hash tables:

$$f_Q(\mathbf{x_q}) = \frac{1}{L}\sum_{l=1}^{L} \#\{\mathbf{x} \in \mathbf{X}_Q \mid \mathbf{h}_l(\mathbf{x}) = \mathbf{h}_l(\mathbf{x}_q)\} \tag{9}$$

Empirically, ζ was set to a default value $\zeta = 3$.

Inter-tables collision frequency: As suggested by the Frequency-based LSH method [12], we then filter the set of features colliding with $\mathbf{X'}_Q$ in the whole index, according to their collision frequency across the L hash tables of the visual index. The resulting set of candidate matches can be expressed as:

$$\mathbf{Y}_Q = \{(\mathbf{x}_q, \mathbf{x}_i) \in (\mathbf{X}'_Q, \mathbf{X}) \mid f_L(\mathbf{x}_q, \mathbf{x}_i) > \tau\} \tag{10}$$

where $f_L(\mathbf{x}_q, \mathbf{x}_i)$ is the number of times $\mathbf{x}_q$ and $\mathbf{x}_i$ are hashed in the same bucket across the L hash tables. As suggested in [12], the threshold τ can be computed numerically as a function of L and α, where α is a lower bound on the collision frequency in one single hash function. This frequency-based thresholding is approximating a range query in the original feature space when LSH is used. With RMMH family, it is more likely to approximate a density-based threshold.

KNN filtering: To reduce the impact of ambiguous visual features that are present many times in the dataset (typically texts), we further reduce the number of candidate matches by a KNN filtering computed with a Hamming distance on the concatenated hash codes. So that the final candidate set of matches for image I_q is given by:

$$\mathbf{Z}_Q = \{(\mathbf{x}_q, \mathbf{x}_m) \in \mathbf{Y}_Q \mid d_H(\mathbf{h}(\mathbf{x}_q), \mathbf{h}(\mathbf{x}_m)) \leq r_H(\mathbf{x}_q, K)\} \tag{11}$$

where $r_H(\mathbf{x}_q, K)$ is the Hamming distance of the K-th nearest neighbor hash code of $\mathbf{h}(\mathbf{x}_q)$. K was empirically fixed to 200 in the experiments.

5.2.2 WG hashing

Now that we have a set $\mathbf{Z}_Q$ of visual matches for the Q-th image I_Q, we propose computing our weighting scores $z_o(\mathbf{x}_q)$ through a WG hashing approach. It is in essence similar to the WG consistency method proposed by Jegou et al. [6] that estimates the geometric consistency of a candidate's visual match based on the spatial metadata associated to each SIFT feature (scale and orientation). Our method differs in three main points. First we suggest using a sparse multi-dimensional voting space rather than voting on each mono-dimensional attribute separately. This will consistently increase the discrimination of the consistency score. Secondly, we propose to use the positions of the features additionally to the scale and orientation parameters. This allows adding a neighboring constraint to the consistency score and consequently favors small objects in detriment to large frequent objects such as backgrounds or near duplicates. Thirdly, our vote process works at the dataset scale; whereas the WG original version [6] is based on image pairs.

More concretely, for each candidate visual match $(\mathbf{x}_q, \mathbf{x}_m) \in \mathbf{Z}_Q$ we compute the following WG attributes vector:

$$\mathbf{\Delta}_{q,m} = (\Delta\theta_{q,m}, \Delta\sigma_{q,m}, \chi_q, \psi_q) \tag{12}$$

where (χ_q, ψ_q) is the position of $\mathbf{x}_q$ in image I_Q, $\Delta\sigma_{q,m} = \sigma_m - \sigma_q$ is the weak scaling factor estimation, and $\Delta\theta_{q,m}$ is the weak rotation angle estimation computed as:

$$\Delta\theta_{q,m} = \frac{\arctan(\sin(\theta_m - \theta_q), \cos(\theta_m - \theta_q))}{\pi} \tag{13}$$

To create a sparse multi-dimensional voting space from the initial WG space in which lies the vectors $\mathbf{\Delta}_{q,m}$, we propose building a LSH family adapted from the classical Euclidean LSH family [4]. Notice that the WG space is first standardized so that all attributes range in $[-1, 1]$. Standardized vectors $\mathbf{\Delta}_{q,m}$ are then hashed with L' distinct LSH functions, each composed of k' random projections of the form:

$$h'(\mathbf{\Delta}) = \left\lfloor \frac{\mathbf{a}.\mathbf{\Delta} + b}{w} \right\rfloor \tag{14}$$

The slight modification that we introduce over this classical LSH family is to have an adaptive value of w for each random projection. An L_2-sensitive hashing is actually not especially adapted for creating our voting space. We rather would like to guaranty a good and normalized dynamic on each of the projection axis. So that we introduce the following constraints:

$$\min_{\Delta \in [-1;1]^d} \frac{\mathbf{a}.\mathbf{\Delta} + b}{w} = -2^\gamma, \qquad \max_{\Delta \in [-1;1]^d} \frac{\mathbf{a}.\mathbf{\Delta} + b}{w} = +2^\gamma \tag{15}$$

Leading to $w = \frac{\|a\|_1}{2^\gamma}$ where γ is the number of bits used to quantify each projection axis. Finally we get

$$h'(\mathbf{\Delta}) = \left\lfloor 2^\gamma \frac{\mathbf{a}.\mathbf{\Delta} + b}{\|a\|_1} \right\rfloor \tag{16}$$

and we denote as $\mathbf{h}'_l(\mathbf{\Delta})$ the k'-length hash code produced by the concatenation of k' individual hash functions for the l-th hash function.

The WG voting process now simply works by maintaining one associative container H_l^Q for each of the L' hash functions (we use a C++ *map* container in practice). Having such sparse storage for the accumulators is essential regarding the memory space required by the full mining algorithm. The *key value* used to insert the visual matches in the containers is defined as the pair

$$\mathbf{h}''_l(\mathbf{\Delta}_{q,m}) = (\mathbf{h}'_l(\mathbf{\Delta}_{q,m}), I_{c,m}) \tag{17}$$

where $\mathbf{h}_l'(\mathbf{\Delta}_{q,m})$ is the WG hash code (i.e. the estimation of the geometric transform) and $I_{q,m}$ is the identifier of the image containing the matched feature $\mathbf{x}_m$. On the other side, the *mapped value* of the associative containers is used to count the number of occurrences in the bucket identified by $\mathbf{h}_l''(\mathbf{\Delta}_{q,m})$. Note that the L' accumulators H_l^Q are empty at the beginning of the Q-th iteration of the full algorithm. All accumulators are then incremented in parallel when looping on the visual matches $(\mathbf{x}_q, \mathbf{x}_m) \in \mathbf{Z}_Q$ one by one. Each WG key value $\mathbf{h}_l''(\mathbf{\Delta}_{q,m})$ is mapped onto the accumulators H_l^Q and the associated *mapped values* are incremented according to

$$H_l^Q(\mathbf{h}_l''(\mathbf{\Delta}_{q,m})) += f_L(\mathbf{x}_q, \mathbf{x}_m) \tag{18}$$

where we recall that $f_L(\mathbf{x}_q, \mathbf{x}_m)$ is the number of collisions in the visual index (cf. Equation 10).
After all visual matches $(\mathbf{x}_q, \mathbf{x}_m) \in \mathbf{Z}_Q$ have been inserted in the accumulators, WG consistency scores $z_0(\mathbf{x}_q)$ are computed by counting the number of collisions across the L' accumulators

$$z_0(\mathbf{x}_q) = \sum_{l=1}^{L'} \sum_{(\mathbf{x}_q,\mathbf{x}_m)\in\mathbf{Z}_Q} H_l^Q(\mathbf{h}_l''(\mathbf{\Delta}_{q,m})) \tag{19}$$

So that $z_0(\mathbf{x}_q)$ measures the number of visual matches in $\mathbf{Z}_Q$ that are geometrically consistent with the direct visual matches $(\mathbf{x}_q, \mathbf{x}_m)$. The higher $z_0(\mathbf{x}_q)$, the more likely $\mathbf{x}_q$ belongs to a frequent object.

5.3 Prior distribution computation

After all images $I_Q \in \mathbf{I}$ have been processed, the conversion of WG scores z_0 to our final probability mass function p_0 is done according to

$$p_0 = \frac{z_0}{z_{\max}} \cdot \frac{1}{p_z(z_0)} \tag{20}$$

where

$$z_{max} = \max_{\mathbf{x}_i \in \mathbf{X}} z_0(\mathbf{x}_i)$$

and $p_z(z)$ represents the probability that the WG score z_0 reaches the value z in the whole dataset:

$$p_z(z) = \frac{\#\{\mathbf{x}_i \in \mathbf{X} \mid z_0(\mathbf{x}_i) = z\}}{N} \tag{21}$$

This equally distributes the probability masses on the range of values z_0 reaches. Simply normalizing z_0 across all features would indeed have put too much probability mass on very low scores that correspond to the majority of features (that do not belong to any frequent object). This is illustrated by Figure 3 that shows the histogram of z_0 score values (i.e. $N.p_z(z_0)$) on the FlickrBelgaLogos dataset used in our experiment. Note that the number of occurrences is in log-scale.

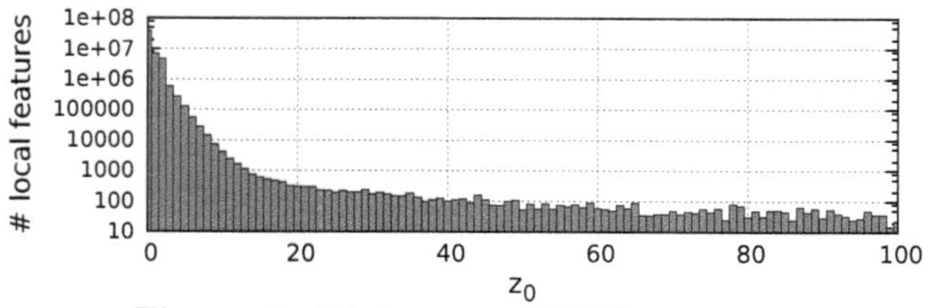

Figure 3: Histogram of WG scores z_0

6. EVALUATION DATASETS

6.1 FlickrBelgaLogos

Evaluating the accuracy of object discovery and mining algorithms is more challenging than evaluating object retrieval with a pre-fixed set of queries. We actually need a complete ground truth with all (c, f)-frequent objects of the dataset and with the precise location of all their instances. No previous evaluation dataset meeting these objectives exists, so that a contribution of this paper was to build one. We first extended the image-level ground truth of BelgaLogos dataset [8] by annotating manually the bounding boxes of all instances of the 37 targeted logos (correcting few errors along the way). The 9842 annotated instances were then visually classified as *kept* or *rejected* by 3 users, depending on whether or not they were all able to recognize the instance with confidence after it had been cropped from its image. After this step, only 2695 instances were classified as *kept*. The resulting dataset, called *BelgaLogos II* is publicly available on the Web[1].

This extended annotation is however not sufficient to evaluate the precision of object mining algorithms. Besides the 37 logos, other objects are actually instantiated several times in the dataset as well (including other logos, buildings, faces, near duplicates, etc.), so that they would be considered as false positives when detected. We therefore decided to create a new synthetic dataset by cutting and pasting the cropped logos of *BelgaLogos II* into a dataset of 10K distractor images crawled from Flickr. To reduce the probability of finding (c, f)-frequent objects in the distractors, all images come from distinct users and distinct geographic areas (1 degree of longitude and latitude). The BelgaLogos instances were then pasted without any modifications (rotation or scaling, ...) at random positions in the distractors. The resulting dataset, called *FlickrBelgaLogos* is also publicly available on the Web[2].

6.2 FrenchTVFrames

To evaluate the scalability of our method, we also performed some experiments on a larger dataset composed of 1,809,080 video frames extracted from 2,051 hours of 7 French television channels (TF1, France 2, Euronews, BMFTV, France 24, i>TELE, LCI), ranging from June 10 2011 to March 28 2012. Only one hour per day was kept for each channel, corresponding to the hour with the most TV news contents. We described this dataset with 549,484,617 SIFT features.

7. EXPERIMENTS

7.1 Experimental setup

Computers used in the following experiments are equipped with 2 hexa-core processors (Intel X5660). All processing times are measured by absolute time. In order to evaluate the prior performance, we define two measures: the *prior recall* and *prior precision*. The prior recall, for a given threshold η_0, is the percentage of instances in the ground truth

[1]http://www-sop.inria.fr/members/Alexis.Joly/BelgaLogos/BelgaLogos.html
[2]http://www-sop.inria.fr/members/Alexis.Joly/BelgaLogos/FlickrBelgaLogos.html

having at least one local feature $\mathbf{x}$ with a probability mass greater than η_0, i.e $p_0(\mathbf{x}) > \eta_0$. The prior precision is the percentage of all local features having a prior value greater than η_0 that belong to an instance in the ground truth. Note that these two evaluation criteria are fully independent from the precise search algorithm used on top of our method and are very useful to compare different prior distributions.
However, they do not measure the performances of the whole mining and discovery processes. To this end, we propose to analyze the object recall (for the discovery problem) and the instance recall (for the mining problem) with regard to the number T of precise search probes. We remind that the complexity of our algorithm is mainly $O(T)$. Note that these two recall measures depend on the performances of the precise search algorithm but that the relative performances are mainly determined by the prior sampling distributions to be compared. The precise search parameters used in the following experiments are proposed in [7, 8, 9] : RMMH: dot-product kernel, $M = 40$ and 128 bits for Hamming Embedding; APMP-LSH: KNN size is 300 and retrieval recall is 0.80; Match verification: A Contrario threshold is 0.95.

7.2 Prior distributions evaluation and parameters study

7.2.1 WG contribution

All the following experiments have been made on the FlickrBelgaLogos dataset.

WG attributes.

This first evaluation aims at measuring the contribution of the different attributes of the WG vector $\mathbf{\Delta}$. We can see in Figure 4 that using WG features is clearly improving the recall/precision. The curve $0, 0, 0, 0$ measures the performances without using any WG (visual hashing and vote only). The others curves have been computed with a subset of the proposed WG features. They show that each attribute (position, scale and orientation) provides a consistent contribution and that the best recall/precision trade-off is finally obtained with the complete set of attributes.

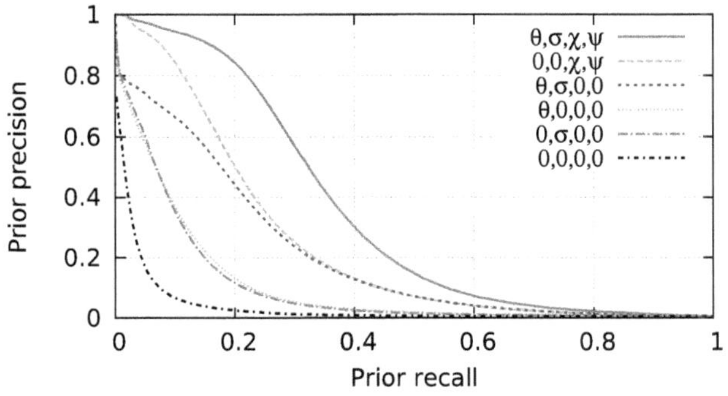

Figure 4: Contribution of WG attributes $\theta, \sigma, \chi, \psi$ on prior recall and precision

WG hash codes length.

In this experiment, we are studying the effect of the number of hash functions k' used to compute the WG hash codes and the number of bits γ used for the scalar quantization of each projection. To improve the readability of the graph displayed in Figure 5, we manually grouped the curves into four clusters (identified by four colors), according to their performance range. The best qualities are obtained with $\gamma \in [3, 5]$ and $k' \in [3\ 10]$. We remark that using a high value for γ is a rather a bad idea, since it decreases the probability of having a significant number of collisions. On the contrary, a low value for γ can be counterbalanced by a higher number k' of hash functions, to increase the histogram discrimination. In the following experiments, we use the parameters of the black curve ($k' = 6$ and $\gamma = 4$).

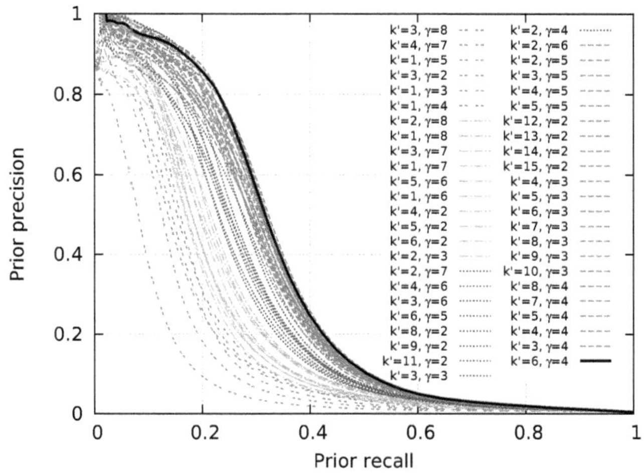

Figure 5: WG hash codes length

Number of WG histograms.

The evaluation presented in Figure 6 is comparing the quality achieved with different value of L', i.e. the number of sparse LSH-based histograms. We also give the performances of a standard multi-dimensional grid, using the same number of bits overall. We can see that LSH-based histograms are clearly better than the fix grid. Regarding the value of L', it is not profitable to use more than one single LSH-based histogram, contrary to high-dimensional feature space (the low dimension of our WG feature space is equal to 4 attributes).

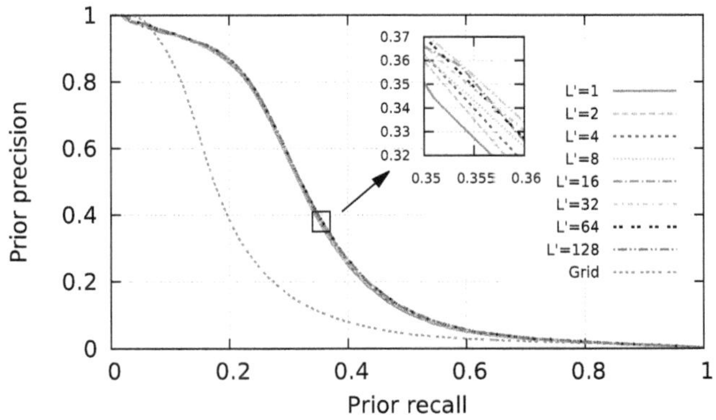

Figure 6: Number of WG histograms

7.2.2 *Visual hashing tuning*

The two main parameters of the visual hashing are L, the number of RMMH tables and α the threshold on the collision probability. For the larger value of $L = 64$ we first estimated an empiric optimum for α that was found to be equal to $\hat{\alpha} = 0.904$. This actually corresponds to keep only very similar visual features. As a comparison, the average collision probability for an arbitrary pair in the exact 1-nn graph is similarly equal to 0.902. That means that a high precision on the kept visual matches is more profitable than high recall. In the following experiments, we used $\hat{\alpha} = 0.9$, that we think is a quite generic value, even for other visual features if they are hashed by RMMH.

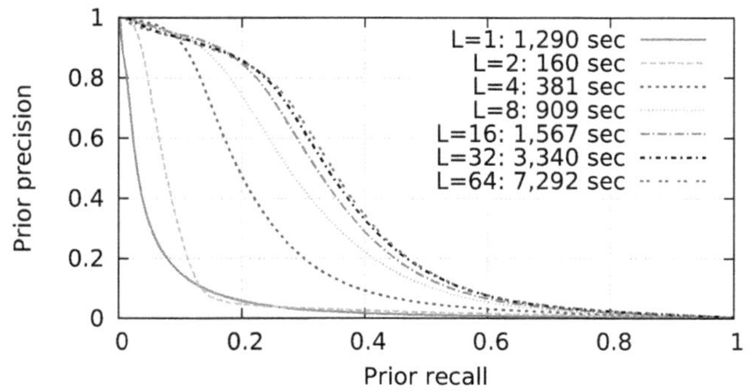

Figure 7: Number of visual hash tables

Regarding Figure 7, using more than 16 visual hash tables is not profitable.

Note that the time needed to compute the prior distribution with a single visual hash table is much more expensive than with two tables, because of the impossibility to filter on the inter-tables collision frequency f_L when $L = 1$.

7.3 Full mining and discovery process evaluation

We now evaluate our complete objects mining algorithm based on the weighted adaptive sampling strategy initialized with our WG prior distribution p_O. To this end, we measure on FlickrBelgaLogos the instance and object recall with regard to the number T of precise search probes.

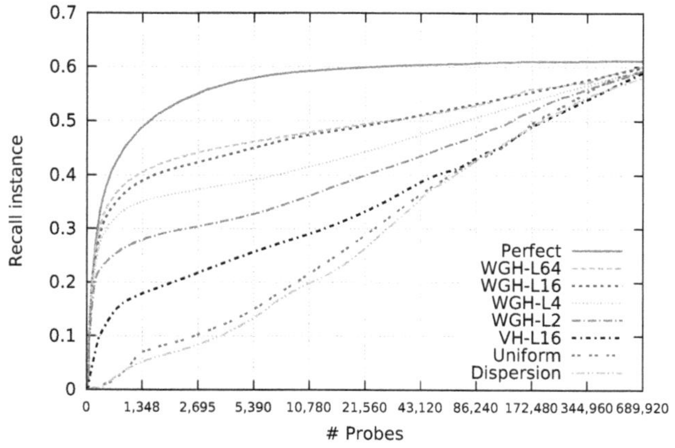

Figure 8: Instance recall vs. number of probes

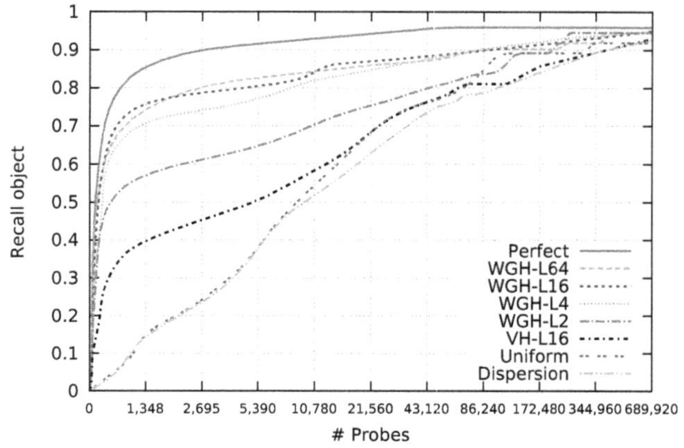

Figure 9: Object recall vs. number of probes

We compare our proposed prior distribution to a uniform distribution ($p_O(\mathbf{x}_i) = 1/N$, $\forall \mathbf{x}_i \in \mathbf{X}$), a perfect prior distribution ($p_O(\mathbf{x}_i) = 0$, $\forall \mathbf{x}_i \notin \{X_s^m\}$ and $p_O(\mathbf{x}_i) = 1/N$, $\forall \mathbf{x}_i \in \{X_s^m\}$), and to the feature-space dispersion prior proposed in [11]:

$$p_O(\mathbf{x}_i) = \frac{1}{d}\sum_{j=1}^{d} \mathrm{Var}_{R_i}\mathbf{x}[\mathbf{j}]$$

with $\mathbf{x} \in R_i$ and R_i is the set of spatial neighbors of $\mathbf{x}_i$, and d the dimension of $\mathbf{x}_i$.

Figures 8 and 9 shows that our new prior distribution (with typically $L = 16$ RMMH tables) is much closer to the perfect distribution than to the uniform one. This proves that the WG scores $z_O(\mathbf{x}_i)$ quantify well the likelihood that a feature $\mathbf{x}_i$ belongs to a small frequent object of the ground truth. Interestingly all evaluated distributions converge to 91% of discovered objects and 61% of discovered instances, which is actually the maximum reachable with the precise search engine used in this experiment (with a very high number of probes > 600K).

With low numbers of probes, our method discovers much more objects than using other distributions. We see that after 1,348 precise search probes (i.e. half of the number of instances), our best runs have retrieved half of all retrievable instances and objects.

The table 1 gives an overview of the time/quality trade-off of our method compared to the uniform sampling distribution (U) of [11]. We observe that with all costs included, our method allows speed-up factors going from 2 to 18. A visual example of a tentative probe and its precise search results is presented in the Figure 10.

7.4 Real-world experiment: application to transmedia events discovery

We finally ran our method on the very large FrenchTV dataset (with settings $L = 8$, $\alpha = 0.9$). The visual hashing step was achieved in 4 hours. The computation of the prior distribution (with WG) ran in 17 hours and used a maximum of 70GB of RAM. The precise search took 18 hours to run 50,000 probes making in total 39 hours for discovering objects in more than 1.8M images. Mining such big data gives rise to a well known issue: most of TV frames are composed of opening or closing credits, commercials, etc. To reduce this noise and focus on more informative media

Table 1: **Time and speed-up of our method over uniform sampling. VH refers to Visual hashing (without using WG), and WGH to WG hashing. L16 means $L = 16$. Hashing time is the time needed to hash the local features. Note that we need at least 128 bits per feature for the precise search. Prior time is the computation time of the prior distribution. Then for a given recall, we show the total time (hashing + prior + precise search). Speed-up factor (in red) is given, compared to the uniform distribution [11] total time.**

	U [11]	VH-L16	WGH-L2	WGH-L4	WGH-L16	WGH-L64
Hashing time	627s	1,567s	634s	641s	1,567s	7,292s
Prior time	0s	1,128s	163s	320s	1,280s	5,120s
Full time	**U [11]**	**VH-L16**	**WGH-L2**	**WGH-L4**	**WGH-L16**	**WGH-L64**
Rec. ins. = 0.20	8,858s	4,482s / x2.0	919s / x9.6	1,045s / x8.5	2,925s / x3.0	12,491s / x0.7
Rec. ins. = 0.30	23,588s	14,753s / x1.6	2,874s / x8.2	1,282s / x18.4	3,073s / x7.7	12,597s / x1.9
Rec. ins. = 0.40	55,825s	47,731s / x1.2	19,676s / x2.8	7,471s / x7.5	4,113s / x13.6	13,225s / x4.2
Rec. ins. = 0.50	159,973s	158,105s / x1.0	120,289s / x1.3	60,146s / x2.7	30,751s / x5.2	37,066s / x4.3
Full time	**U [11]**	**VH-L16**	**WGH-L2**	**WGH-L4**	**WGH-L16**	**WGH-L64**
Rec. obj. = 0.30	4,078s	3,054s / x1.3	901s / x4.5	1,039s / x3.9	2,916s / x1.4	12,467s / x0.3
Rec. obj. = 0.50	7,854s	7,111s / x1.1	1,136s / x6.9	1,163s / x6.8	2,982s / x2.6	12,520s / x0.6
Rec. obj. = 0.70	20,661s	23,081s / x0.9	9,898s / x2.1	1,830s / x11.3	3,248s / x6.4	12,916s / x1.6
Rec. obj. = 0.90	281,205s	199,128s / x1.4	184,419s / x1.5	55,234s / x5.1	96,441s / x2.9	78,261s / x3.6

Figure 10: The first probe issued from the WGH-L64 prior distribution (left image), and its precise search results, in the FlickrBelgaLogos dataset.

event, we reranked all the detections by favoring: (i) visual objects appearing across a large number of TV channels (ii) visual objects appearing only during a short period of time. More precisely, each discovered visual object was affected the following score C:

$$C = \frac{\#\{\mathcal{C}\}.\hat{f}}{f_d} \tag{22}$$

where $\#\{\mathcal{C}\}$ is the number of channels, $\hat{f}$ is the estimation of the object frequency f (number of detections) and f_d is the temporal frequency (number of days). According to this criterion, Figure 2 displays the top-1 discovered object for 3 different categories of object size. They all illustrate one of the most salient media events in the concerned period.

8. CONCLUSION

Several contributions were introduced in this paper: we first revisit the problem of discovering and mining small visual objects with a new formalism and a modeling of the complexity of existing approaches based on sampling. We then proposed a new hashing-based method for computing the likelihood that a given local feature belongs to a small frequent object. Its main originality relies on using Sparse multi-dimensional Histograms of WG attributes that efficiently group geometrically consistent visual matches in the whole dataset. We finally introduced a new evaluation dataset and testbed that allow us to complete the first accurate evaluation of small visual objects discovery algorithms. Results did show that our WG hashing scheme provides a good approximation of a perfect distribution, i.e. where only features belonging to an object of the ground truth would be considered as candidates for a precise search. In future work, we foresee evaluating our method by using pairs of local features in the visual hashing step, like done in [2] or [10]. We also plan to extend our WG hashing based on sparse histograms to more attributes including new geometric parameters (such as translation [20]) or contextual information.

9. ACKNOWLEDGMENTS

This work was partially funded by the French ANR project OTMedia[3] (No. 2010CORD015) and the EU project GLOCAL[4] (Grant Agreement No. 248984).

[3] http://www.otmedia.fr
[4] http://www.glocal-project.eu

Table 2: **Top 1 detected objects by size category (small, medium, large) in 2051 hours of French TV**

G20 Summit *Nov 2011* Small object $< 33\%$ of image area $\#\{\mathcal{C}\} = 6$, $\hat{f} = 15$, $f_d = 2$ $\Big\}$ $C = 45$			
Kim Jong-il death *Dec 2011* Medium object $< 66\%$ of image area $\#\{\mathcal{C}\} = 6$, $\hat{f} = 8$, $f_d = 1$ $\Big\}$ $C = 48$			
The Artist *Feb 2012* Large object $> 66\%$ of image area $\#\{\mathcal{C}\} = 7$, $\hat{f} = 39$, $f_d = 8$ $\Big\}$ $C = 34$			

10. REFERENCES

[1] O. Chum, A. Mikulik, M. Perdoch, and J. Matas. Total recall ii: Query expansion revisited. In *CVPR*, pages 889–896, Colorado Springs, USA, 2011. IEEE.

[2] O. Chum, M. Perdoch, and J. Matas. Geometric min-hashing: Finding a (thick) needle in a haystack. In *CVPR*, pages 17–24. IEEE, June 2009.

[3] O. Chum, J. Philbin, J. Sivic, M. Isard, and A. Zisserman. Total recall: Automatic query expansion with a generative feature model for object retrieval. In *ICCV*. IEEE, October 2007.

[4] M. Datar and P. Indyk. Locality-sensitive hashing scheme based on p-stable distributions. In *SCG*, pages 253–262. ACM Press, 2004.

[5] M. A. Fischler and R. C. Bolles. Random sample consensus: A paradigm for model fitting with applications to image analysis and automated cartography. *Commun. ACM*, 24(6):381–395, 1981.

[6] H. Jégou, M. Douze, and C. Schmid. Hamming Embedding and Weak Geometry Consistency for Large Scale Image Search. Research Report RR-6709, INRIA, 2008.

[7] A. Joly and O. Buisson. A Posteriori Multi-Probe Locality Sensitive Hashing. In *ACM Multimedia*, pages 209–218, Vancouver, Canada, oct 2008.

[8] A. Joly and O. Buisson. Logo retrieval with a contrario visual query expansion. In *ACM Multimedia*, pages 581–584, Beijing, China, october 2009.

[9] A. Joly and O. Buisson. Random Maximum Margin Hashing. In *CVPR*, Colorado Springs, 2011. IEEE.

[10] Y. Kalantidis, L. Pueyo, M. Trevisiol, R. van Zwol, and Y. Avrithis. Scalable triangulation-based logo recognition. In *ICMR*, pages 20:1–20:7, Trento, Italy, 2011. ACM.

[11] P. Letessier, O. Buisson, and A. Joly. Consistent visual words mining with adaptive sampling. In *ICMR*, pages 49:1–49:8. ACM, april 2011.

[12] K. Ling and G. Wu. Frequency based locality sensitive hashing. In *ICMT*, pages 4929 –4932, july 2011.

[13] D. Lowe. Object recognition from local scale-invariant features. In *ICCV*, page 1150, Kerkyra, 1999. IEEE.

[14] F. Olken. *Random Sampling from Databases*. PhD thesis, University of California, 1993.

[15] J. Philbin. *Scalable Object Retrieval in Very Large Image Collections*. PhD thesis, Univ. of Oxford, 2010.

[16] J. Philbin, O. Chum, M. Isard, J. Sivic, and A. Zisserman. Lost in quantization: Improving particular object retrieval in large scale image databases. In *CVPR*, pages 1–8, Anchorage, USA, june 2008. IEEE.

[17] G. F. Pineda, H. Koga, and T. Watanabe. Object discovery by clustering correlated visual word sets. In *ICPR*, pages 750–753, Washington, USA, 2010. IEEE.

[18] T. Tuytelaars, C. H. Lampert, M. B. Blaschko, and W. Buntine. Unsupervised object discovery: A comparison. *IJCV*, 88:284–302, June 2010.

[19] T. Weyand and B. Leibe. Discovering favorite views of popular places with iconoid shift. In *ICCV*, pages 1132–1139. IEEE, Nov. 2011.

[20] W. Zhao, X. Wu, and C.-W. Ngo. On the annotation of web videos by efficient near-duplicate search. *IEEE Transactions on Multimedia*, 12(5):448–461, 2010.

Snap-and-Ask: Answering Multimodal Question by Naming Visual Instance *

Wei Zhang, Lei Pang, Chong-Wah Ngo
Department of Computer Science, City University of Hong Kong, Kowloon, Hong Kong
{wzhang34, leipang3}@student.cityu.edu.hk, cscwngo@cityu.edu.hk

ABSTRACT

In real-life, it is easier to provide a visual cue when asking a question about a possibly unfamiliar topic, for example, asking the question, "Where was this crop circle found?". Providing an image of the instance is far more convenient than texting a verbose description of the visual properties, especially when the name of the query instance is not known. Nevertheless, having to identify the visual instance before processing the question and eventually returning the answer makes multimodal question-answering technically challenging. This paper addresses the problem of visual-to-text naming through the paradigm of answering-by-search in a two-stage computational framework, which is composed out of instance search (IS) and similar question ranking (QR). In IS, names of the instances are inferred from similar visual examples searched through a million-scale image dataset. For recalling instances of non-planar and non-rigid shapes, spatial configurations that emphasize topology consistency while allowing for local variations in matches have been incorporated. In QR, the candidate names of the instance are statistically identified from search results and directly utilized to retrieve similar questions from community-contributed QA (cQA) archives. By parsing questions into syntactic trees, a fuzzy matching between the inquirer's question and cQA questions is performed to locate answers and recommend related questions to the inquirer. The proposed framework is evaluated on a wide range of visual instances (e.g., fashion, art, food, pet, logo, and landmark) over various QA categories (e.g., factoid, definition, how-to, and opinion).

Categories and Subject Descriptors

H.4.m [**Information Systems Applications**]: Miscellaneous

*Area chair: Frank Nack

MM'12, October 29–November 2, 2012, Nara, Japan.

Question: What causes the foul smell of this flower?
Answer: In the dense jungles of Sumatra a small inflorescence that relies on aroma to ....
Suggestions:
1. How to get rid of the Rafflesia?
2. What temperature does the Rafflesia live in?

Figure 1: A text-based question referring to a picture. The target "Rafflesia" is first named through instance search. The answer is then retrieved from the cQA website, together with some suggested questions.

General Terms

Algorithms, Performance, Experimentation

Keywords

Multimedia question answering, visual instance search, similar question search

1. INTRODUCTION

While intensive research efforts have been devoted to multimedia search [12], multimedia question-answering (MQA) in broad domains is still a relatively new and largely untapped research area. With the convergence of mobile and social media computing, MQA is predicted to play a more prominent role that is complementary to general search for two main reasons. First, mobile devices are emerging as the major instrument used to access the Internet. Due to small form factors and limited battery power/bandwidth, browsing a long list of search results, especially multimedia items, is not as convenient as on desktop machines. Instead, the majority of mobile users expect a short list of answers that directly address their concern. With rich sensors embedded in mobile devices, it has also become natural for mobile users to ask a question through speech, or by texting a short sentence with an image example as a reference. Second, the proliferation of social media suggests that MQA could be tackled by leveraging the massive amount of multimedia data accumulated online for answering questions. Furthermore, for certain categories of questions (e.g., how-to), it is more intuitive to answer the questions with multimedia content than with pure text description [14].

This paper addresses a practical scenario in MQA: a user snaps a picture and asks a question referring to the picture. Figure 1 shows an example of a text-based question referring to a picture with the instance "Rafflesia". Multimodal questions are different from text-based QAs where, rather than

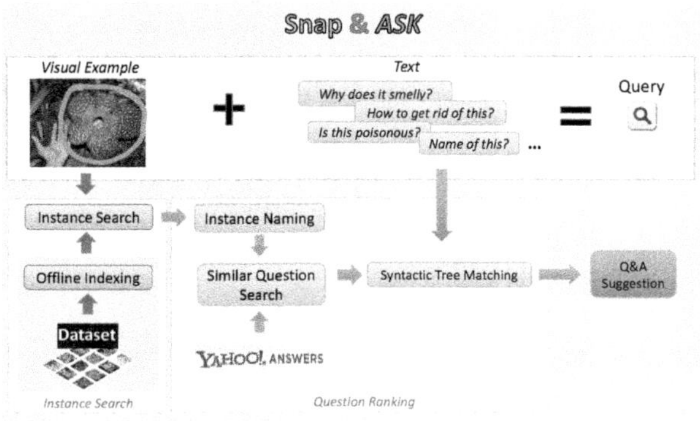

Figure 2: Framework for Snap-and-Ask.

providing a long textual description for the visual instance in a question, visual examples, which are more direct and intuitive, are given, possibly with the target instance masked by the inquirer. The returned result is a short ranked list of QA pairs crawled from community-contributed QA (cQA) archives that best match the inquirer's request. The ranked list not only serves as the right answer, but also recommends some related questions, similar in spirit to query suggestion [10] in commercial search engines.

Figure 2 shows an overview of the proposed framework for MQA, which is composed out of two major components: instance search (IS) and question ranking (QR). Given a multimodal question, the provided image example is first treated as visual query and searched against a million-scale Web image dataset. This search scenario is different from typical image or near-duplicate search in the following two aspects: the retrieved target items could appear in different background contexts – a task that is different from near-duplicate search [25, 27]; and the target could be an object of non-planar surface or non-rigid shape (e.g., flag, food, animal) – a task that commercial mobile search engines [3], such as Google Goggles[1], cannot deal with. Our proposed technique considers the use of spatial topology for enhancing the robustness and scalability of the matching. The candidate names of an instance are then extracted from the metadata of the retrieved items through syntactic and semantic analysis of natural language. Each candidate name is then treated as a query to the cQA website "Yahoo! Answers"[2] for retrieving similar questions. Due to the fact that questions given by various users could be phrased in wildly different ways, the pool of questions obtained from multiple queries are subsequently parsed into syntactic trees, and matched against the inquirer's question. To this end, a small subset of QA pairs is selected, ranked, and finally presented to the user.

The main contribution of this paper is the proposal of a novel framework for addressing a practical scenario of MQA, where a mobile user snaps a picture and texts a short question while on the move. In contrast to other existing works, which assume text-based questions [1, 16, 26], and operate in a specific domain (e.g., news [28], product [29], cooking [13]), the framework, grounded on the answering-by-search paradigm, deals with questions in broad domains, covering different types of instances and question categories. Additionally, the framework also tackles problems in large-scale search of visual instances, and the matching of community-based questions by automatically naming the visual instance of the inquirer's question. The former remains an open problem in the literature, while the latter has not been previously attempted in the domain of multimedia QA. The remaining of the paper is organized as follows. Section 2 describes related works in MQA, as well as the state-of-the-art techniques in instance, near-duplicate, and mobile search. Section 3 presents the proposed technique for visual instance search, by considering the spatial configuration. Section 4 describes our algorithm for naming visual instances, while Section 5 details the parsing, matching, and ranking of similar questions. Section 6 presents experimental results, and finally Section 7 concludes the paper.

[1]http://www.google.com/mobile/goggles/
[2]http://answers.yahoo.com/

2. RELATED WORK

The proposed work is rooted in various content based retrieval techniques, ranging from query-by-example [12], multimodal query processing (e.g., search with text plus visual examples in TRECVID [22]), and data-driven search [24]. However, these techniques mostly deal with non-question-oriented queries, and are thus different from our work. In the following, we mainly summarize the related works in two areas: multimedia answering and visual instance search.

Most existing works in *multimedia answering* are extended from text-based QA systems, which aim to find multimedia content (e.g., images and videos) as answers to text questions in a specific domain. In the news domain, VideoQA [28] is an early system, which supports factoid QAs by leveraging visual content, ASR (Automatic Speech Recognition) transcripts, and online information for locating news video segments as answers. In the documentary domain, a passage retrieval algorithm, which is based on video caption recognition and ranking, was proposed in [26] to return passages associated with short video clips as answers. In the domain of educational video, QA was investigated by [1] based on lexical pattern matching on ASR transcripts and PowerPoint slides. Basically these systems rely heavily on rich and relatively clean textual information extracted from ASR transcripts and video captions. Applying these techniques directly to UGC (user generated content) from the Internet is difficult, due to the poor accuracy of speech and caption recognition. Recently, in the domain of consumer electronics, a community-based QA system supporting how-to QAs was developed for retrieving Web videos as answers [14]. The system adopts a two-step approach: first it develops concept classifiers for visual recognition, and second it detects concepts from user questions by searching for similar questions on a cQA website. The two sets of concepts are then compared for ranking video answers. While interesting, this work is not easily extended to other domains for the requirement to train a large number of domain-specific visual classifiers, which remains practically difficult based on current technology. More recently, the problem of media selection for generating answers was also addressed by [16], where given a text-based QA pair, the media type (text, image, or video) that will best answer the question is predicted. Different from the proposed work, all the aforementioned papers consider text-based questions only. The most similar work compared to our work is Photo-based QA [29], which also considers multimodal questions (text and photo). The system first performs visual matching of the query photo

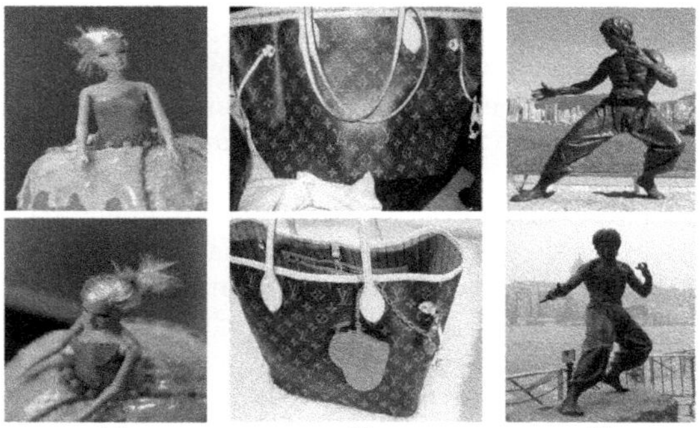

Figure 3: Challenging examples for instance search.

with images from a database, and then answers are extracted from a QA repository named START[3] by text-based template matching. Although similar in spirit, Photo-based QA only considers factoid QAs, and the use of template matching also limits the types of questions that can be answered. Furthermore, issues of instance search, such as scalability when using a large image dataset, and matching robustness against non-planar and non-rigid objects, are not addressed.

Visual instance search (IS) aims to find multimedia examples that contain the same target, but not necessarily with the same background context as the query. A recent pilot study in TRECVID [22] indicated that the search task could be challenging when the target instance exhibits variations in size, viewpoint, and resolution under different backgrounds. The utilization of spatial layout and context for efficient indexing and searching remains unexplorered [11]. A close relative of IS is near-duplicate (ND) search [25, 27], where the matching is performed at the full image level. ND has received numerous research attention recently, and the existing techniques can be grouped into several categories. First, feature point matching with bag-of-visual-words, supported by inverted file indexing, is performed, followed by strong geometric verification for the top few retrieved items [19]. Second, auxiliary information, such as the position, scale, orientation, and signature of words, is also indexed for fast filtering of false matches by weak geometric verification [8]. Third, spatial information, such as spatially close feature points, are indexed for constraint matching [27, 32]. Some of these techniques have been successfully adopted for mobile media search in different vertical domains, such as CD, book cover, and location search [4], but not on instances with non-planar surfaces and non-rigid shapes.

3. VISUAL INSTANCE SEARCH

There are two peculiarities, when an inquirer provides an image as reference for a text question. First, the query picture will be snapped with care, and hence with acceptable visual quality. It is reasonable to assume that an inquirer may retake the same instance multiple times, such that pictures with artifacts (e.g., motion blur and occlusion) will not be issued. Second, with the support of multi-touch technologies on mobile devices, inquirers can easily draw a mask on a query image to distinguish the instance-of-interest from background context.

While queries could be assumed to be generated in a relatively clean setting, the challenge of instance search, however, originates from the wide range of instances that can possibly be taken as queries. With reference to Figure 3, the difficulties can be briefly summarized as: *visual variation*, *spatial constraint*, and *context utilization*. As shown in Figure 3(a), the instance candidates to be retrieved from a reference dataset could appear in wildly different forms, especially for 3D objects, under different lighting conditions and capturing viewpoints. Furthermore, certain instance types, such as fashion and art, can be rich of repeated patterns as in Figure 3(b), in addition to being non-rigid 3D instances. Matching instances with a linear transformation model, as adopted in near-duplicate search [19], is no longer suitable. Finally, instances snapped outdoors, for example, the "Bruce Lee Statue" in Figure 3(c), might benefit from using the background context for searching. However, this assumption can not be generalized to other instances such as fashion and logos. This section addresses the former two difficulties, while leaving the last problem as our future work.

3.1 Retrieval Model

Our model is grounded on the recent advances in bag-of-visual-words representation (BoW) [21]. Initially a large vocabulary tree of one million leaf visual words is constructed from the public image dataset MIRFLICKR [6]. The implementation is based on [17], where local features (SIFT) are clustered by k-means hierarchically in a top-down manner, and a branching factor of 100 is used to split each non-leaf node. During the offline indexing, SIFT descriptors extracted from Web images are parsed down the tree until they reach the leaf nodes that best match the descriptors. Through this step, descriptors are quantized to the nearest visual word, and indexed into an inverted file structure for fast online retrieval. Auxiliary information, including the signatures and the spatial locations, are also indexed for word filtering and geometric verification. The signatures, represented as a binary vector of 32 bits, are generated by Hamming embedding (HE) [8]. During online retrieval, a similar procedure is carried out for processing the instance-of-interest marked by the inquirer. To alleviate the adverse effect due to the quantization error, a descriptor is assigned to multiple visual words by soft-weighting [20]. By traversing the index file with HE filtering, images sharing common visual words with the query are rapidly retrieved from the reference dataset. Finally, spatial topology consistency is taken into account for better image ranking.

3.2 Spatial Configuration

As background context is not utilized, the information content of a query is thereby reduced. Modeling the spatial configuration of visual instance for geometric verification becomes crucial for an effective search. The existing models, which rely on a set of linear transformations, impose either too weak or too strong constraints for instance matching. For example, WGC (weak geometric consistency) [8], which efficiently votes for the dominant differences of scale and orientation among matched visual words, only weakly enforces spatial consistency, and does not guarantee the local regularity (e.g., relative position) of correspondences. On the other hand, spatial verification [19], which warps the matched visual words between images to discover the dominant linear transformation, imposes strict constraint, and only works well for near-duplicate scenes, and planar or rigid objects.

[3]http://start.csail.mit.edu/

Figure 4: Construction of triangulation meshes based on the matching visual words between two images. The matched words are indicated with the same color.

3.2.1 Matching by sketching meshes

We model the spatial information by seeking a compromised model, based on Delaunay Triangulation (DT) [2, 9], which is neither too weak to identify the spatial inconsistency nor too strong to rule out the positive spatial configurations. DT is a technique used in computer graphics for building meshes out of a point set, such that no point is inside the circumcircle of any triangles. For instance search, given the matched words between a query instance $\mathcal{Q}$ and a reference image $\mathcal{R}$, DT sketches the spatial structures of $\mathcal{Q}$ and $\mathcal{R}$ respectively based on the matches. Figure 4 shows an example of triangulation meshes constructed from matched visual words of $\mathcal{Q}$ and $\mathcal{R}$. With $\Delta\mathcal{Q}$ denoting the mesh of $\mathcal{Q}$, the geometric consistency of $\mathcal{R}$ and $\mathcal{Q}$, named *bonus factor*, is measured as:

$$\mathbf{BF}(\mathcal{Q},\mathcal{R}) = \log(N+1) \times \exp\{\text{Sim}_{DT}(\Delta\mathcal{Q},\Delta\mathcal{R})\}, \quad (1)$$

where N is the total number of matched features by traversing the inverted file. Sim_{DT} measures the percentage of common edges[4] between $\mathcal{Q}$ and $\mathcal{R}$:

$$\text{Sim}_{DT}(\Delta\mathcal{Q},\Delta\mathcal{R}) = \frac{\mathbf{E}_{\Delta\mathcal{Q}} \cap \mathbf{E}_{\Delta\mathcal{R}}}{\mathbf{E}_{\Delta\mathcal{Q}}}, \quad (2)$$

where $\mathbf{E}_{\Delta\mathcal{Q}}$ denotes the edge set of $\Delta\mathcal{Q}$. In Equation (1), note that Sim_{DT} is weighted by a factor of $\log(N+1)$, so that an image, sharing more matched visual words with $\mathcal{Q}$, receives a higher **BF** value. For constructing meshes, the one-to-one mapping constraint needs to be enforced. This is done by allowing a point from $\mathcal{Q}$ to match another point on $\mathcal{R}$ with the smallest Hamming distance. The enforcement effectively prevents an excessive number of redundant matches, a problem known as the "burstiness" effect [7], which could corrupt similarity scores when there are repeated patterns in images.

While simple, DT has the following merits: (1) the relative spatial position of words is considered, (2) no assumption of any transformation model is made, (3) a certain degree of freedom for variations of word positions is allowed. Compared to WGC [8], criterion (1) considers the topology of words, and thereby is more effective in measuring geometric consistency. Compared with strict spatial verification [31], criterion (2) does not impose any prior knowledge on types of instances and transformations, and thus the checking of geometric coherency is looser. However, by allowing variations of local changes as stated by criterion (3) without the assumption of a transformation model, DT is a flexible model, which is more adaptable to non-rigid and non-planar instances under different capturing conditions. A fundamental difference between DT and other spatial verification methods is that no pruning of false matches or model estimation is involved. Instead, DT enumerates the potential true matches with the local topology consistency based on criteria (1) and (3), while tolerating false matches by not imposing any prior constraints based on criterion (2). Since DT acts positively in finding true matches rathar than negatively penalizing false matches, we name our measurement in Equation (1) the "bonus factor".

[4]Two edges are regarded as common if their vertices share the same visual words.

3.2.2 Computational Complexity

Two major steps of DT are the construction of triangulation meshes and the searching of common edges for Equation (2). The first step can be efficiently conducted by the divide-and-conquer method with a complexity of $O(n \log n)$, where n is the number of matched words between $\mathcal{Q}$ and $\mathcal{R}$. The second step can be done by a simple linear scan of edges with $O(|e|)$, where $|e| = O(n)$ is the number of edges. Basically, the computation is dominated by $O(n \log n)$. Based on our retrieval model, due to the use of the large vocabulary tree with one million words, n is usually a small number. In the case where the value of n is large, in our implementation, random sampling is performed, such that only a small subset of matches is evaluated by Equation (1). As DT is a "bonus model" which enumerates potential true matches, performance will not degrade severely with the down-sampling process.

4. NAME THE INSTANCE

Intuitively, given the search result, the name of an instance could be mined from the metadata based on statistical analysis, such as the term frequency (TF). Nevertheless, TF is measured at the word level, while a name is more appropriate to be represented at the phrase level. Furthermore, user-provided description could be inconsistent. For example, the recipe "beef broccoli" may be phrased as "broccoli beef" or "beef with broccoli". Directly applying TF could result in misleading statistics. This section presents the mining of instance names by phrase frequency, with the consideration of the potential noise in metadata. In addition, semantic similarity is also taken into account for reranking candidate names by random walk.

4.1 Noun Phrase Extraction

In general, an instance name could be a single word, an idiom, a restricted collocation, or a free combination of words. We regard a name as a noun phrase, and apply the Berkeley Parser[5] for producing the syntactic tree for each sentence in the metadata. The parser basically decomposes a sentence into units like subject, verb, and noun phrase, and then represents the relationship among units as a syntactic tree based on grammar formalism. In our case, we directly extract the subtrees, which correspond to the NP (noun phrase) units, from the tree as name candidates. However, a special case is when the metadata contains only one word in the title or the description. To boost recall, we also include these words as candidates. Note that we do not consider user tags here because some Web images (e.g., from Google image search) do not contain any tags.

[5]http://code.google.com/p/berkeleyparser/

4.2 Phrase Frequency

As a phrase could be more than one word, measuring the phrase frequency is not as straightforward as the word frequency. Given a phrase $\mathcal{P}_1$ composed out of one or multiple words, we measure the degree in which a second phrase $\mathcal{P}_2$ could be matched to $\mathcal{P}_1$ and thus contributes a score (≤ 1) to the phrase frequency (PF) of $\mathcal{P}_1$. This could be measured by counting the proportion of common words between $\mathcal{P}_1$ and $\mathcal{P}_2$. For example, if $\mathcal{P}_1$ is "Kony 2012" while $\mathcal{P}_2$ is "Kony", then $\mathcal{P}_2$ will contribute 0.5 to PF of $\mathcal{P}_1$. However, the degree of contribution should consider the source (i.e., the metadata and the image) $\mathcal{P}_2$ is extracted from. We consider two clues to model the noise level of the metadata. Generally speaking, the title of the metadata provides more reliable information than the description. Specifically, if the instance is the main subject of an image, the chance that the name of the instance appears in the title is also higher. Whereas for a description, the extracted name phrases are relatively diverse and likely to be contextually ralated rather than by content to the main subject (e.g., the name of a photographer, or the date of a publication). Second, the inherent noise level is also heuristically proportional to the document length, where the probability of a phrase corresponding to a correct name is higher if extracted from a brief description. For image-level noise, the score by instance search basically hints at the quality of a phrase extracted from an image. To this end, with $\mathbf{N}$ denoting the set of phrases extracted from the images retrieved by instance search, the frequency of a phrase $\mathcal{P}_i \in \mathbf{N}$ is defined as:

$$\text{PF}(\mathcal{P}_i) = \sum_{\mathcal{P}_j \in \mathbf{N}, j \neq i} \frac{\alpha \times Sim^I(\mathcal{K}_j) \times Sim^S(\mathcal{P}_i, \mathcal{P}_j)}{\log D(\mathcal{P}_j)}, \quad (3)$$

where Sim^I returns the relevant score measured by instance search for the image, $\mathcal{K}_j$, where $\mathcal{P}_j$ is extracted from. The parameter α is empirically set to 1.0 if $\mathcal{P}_j$ is from the title of metadata and 0.3 otherwise. The function $D(\cdot)$ calculates the length of a document, used to penalize the phrases extracted from a lengthy description. The function Sim^S, measuring the syntactic relationship between two phrases, is defined as:

$$Sim^S(\mathcal{P}_i, \mathcal{P}_j) = \frac{|\mathcal{P}_i \cap \mathcal{P}_j|}{|\mathcal{P}_i \cup \mathcal{P}_j|}, \quad (4)$$

where $|\mathcal{P}_i|$ is the number of words in $\mathcal{P}_i$. Equation (4) basically measures the proportion of common words between two phrases by discounting ordering information. For example, the phrases "Kony 2012" and "2012 Kony" will be treated as the same phrase.

4.3 Re-ranking by Semantics

While Equation (3) suggests ranking noun phrases as name candidates by means of frequency, the relationship among phrases is not exploited. The set of noun phrases can be modeled as a graph, such that phrases can interact through information propagation by algorithms such as random walk [18]. The end result could lead to more realistic ranking: the significance of phrases can get boosted if actively communicating with peers, and otherwise diminished due to the isolation with other phrases. The major obstacle for constructing such a graph is the measurement of phrase relatedness, where existing similarity measures, such as the WordNet ontology, cannot be directly applied.

We propose an approach based on the work in [15] for measuring phrase similarity. Given two phrases, a vocabulary $\mathcal{V}$ is constructed, consisting of the number of distinctive words from them. A matrix $\mathcal{M}$ of size $|\mathcal{V}| \times |\mathcal{V}|$ is then formed, with each entry of $\mathcal{M}$ corresponding to the semantic similarity between two words in $\mathcal{V}$. By employing the technique described in [5], the similarity is measured based on the hypernym (is-a), meronymy (part-of), antonymy, and entailment relationships of the WordNet ontology. With $\mathcal{M}$, a phrase $\mathcal{P}$ is represented as a lexical semantic vector $\mathcal{L}$ of size $|\mathcal{V}|$, with each element $l_i = \max_{w_j \in \mathcal{P}} \mathcal{M}(i,j)$. The similarity between two phrases $\mathcal{P}_i$ and $\mathcal{P}_j$ is calculated as the cosine similarity between their vectors $\mathcal{L}_i$ and $\mathcal{L}_j$.

With the semantic similarity, we represent the phrase relationship as a graph, with phrases as nodes attributed by their frequencies, and pairwise semantic similarities between phrases as edges. By adopting random walk on the graph, the information is iteratively propagated among phrases till convergence, which results in a new ranked list of candidate names to be utilized for question matching.

5. QUESTION MATCHING AND RANKING

The cQA websites provide a good source of questions and answers manually crafted by human subjects. This section presents the techniques for finding similar questions (and hence answers) from online QA repositories. The general idea is by separately issuing the higher ranked candidate instance names as query to QA repositories, and then retrieving different sets of similar questions. This forms a pool of questions for further filtering and ranking by natural language processing, and eventually an inquirer is presented with the top ranked questions, which ideally contain the best answer and some suggested questions.

Ranking similar questions, however, is not trivial. For example, the questions "How to cook this dish?" and "Any tips for preparing this dish?" are similar, but share very few common keywords. We adopt the syntactic tree matching technique [23] to measure the question similarity. The technique divides the parse tree of a question into tree fragments, where each fragment captures the syntactic information of the question at a different granularity level based on grammar rules. The matching between two questions is carried out by recursively comparing the structures of tree fragments, while assigning higher weights to the matched fragments with larger sizes and deeper tree levels. In addition to the syntactic based matching, the words (leaf nodes of parse trees) of questions are also fuzzily matched based on WordNet's semantic similarity measure. This basically upgrades the similarity score for questions with different words but similar intention. We adopt this technique because no training is required, and furthermore, the similarity metric is tolerant to some grammatical errors, which are common on QA websites. In our implementation, when matching questions crawled from QA repositories, not only the question title but also the "content" of the question, which is provided by a user to detail the question, are compared. This will greatly improve the recall. For example, the question "What type of message is Kony 2012 trying to send?" could be matched to an inquirer's question "What does this poster mean?" if the content part has a description about the "Kony 2012" poster.

For multimodal QA, there are two strategies for matching an inquirer's question, where the instance name is phrased

Table 1: **Dataset summary for multimodal questions.**

QA categories	*Instance types*									*Total*
	fashion	food	pet	flower	art	product	logo	landmark	vehicle	
Factoid	19	8	9	12	13	9	7	10	9	96
Definition	10	5	5	4	6	1	5	8	3	47
How-to	14	20	9	8	6	23	4	1	5	90
Opinion	17	6	7	6	17	8	4	8	2	75
Total	60	39	30	30	42	41	20	27	19	308

as "this", with similar questions. The first strategy is to augment each parse tree with the candidate name before question matching by simply replacing a pronoun (e.g., "this") with the name. However, this strategy could be risky in producing misleading ranking of questions, when the candidate is not the actual name. For robustness, we only consider the top-1 ranked candidate name for this strategy. In other words, only the most confident candidate is employed for retrieving similar questions and augmenting the parse tree. The second strategy is a direct comparison between the original question and the retrieved similar questions without augmenting a candidate name. In this case, the pronoun "this" in a question will be treated as a noun phrase by the parser, and matched syntactically with similar questions. For this strategy, the top-k candidate names could be employed, so as to boost the recall of finding similar questions.

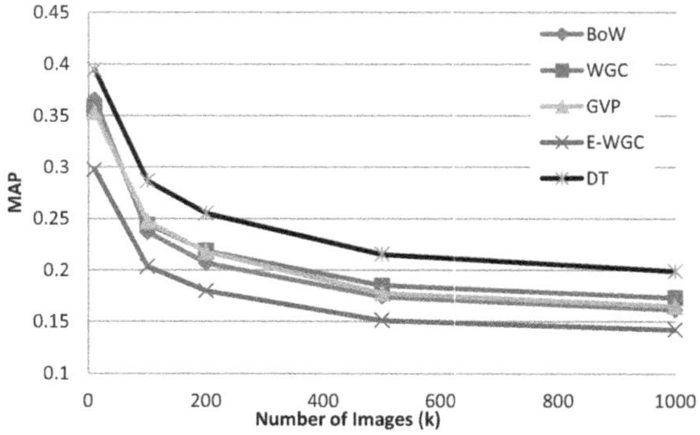

Figure 5: Instance search: Performance comparison of various approaches by varying the dataset size.

6. EXPERIMENT

6.1 Dataset Construction and Evaluation

Constructing a realistic MQA dataset is challenging, due to the lack of a publicly available dataset that consists of questions asked in the multimodal setting. Furthermore, the existing cQA archives are all text-based, which makes the dataset construction even harder. In Yahoo! Answers, for instance, users ask questions in text, and then have an option to provide further details (or question contents) by textually elaborating the questions or attaching hyperlinks to visual examples. To construct a test set for MQA, we first issued the names of instances as query keywords to Yahoo! Answers for retrieving the candidate questions. The returned results were usually mixed with irrelevant and redundant questions. We browsed through the results, and manually selected the sample questions that refer to the query instances. On the other hand, the same set of queries was also issued to Flickr and Google image search for crawling images as visual queries. Finally, the text-based questions were manually "transformed" into multimodal questions, by replacing the names of visual instances with the word "this", which refers to the image examples crawled from search engines.

To guarantee that a wide range of visual instances is considered in the test set, we issued a total number of 52 queries involving various instance types (e.g., fashion, art, pet, and etc.) to Yahoo! Answers, Flickr, and Google image search. Eventually, a test set of 308 questions was constructed, and there were six questions collected for each instance on average. Additionally, there were 438 images crawled as visual instances. For each of the queries, we randomly picked one image as the visual example for a question and as the query image for visual instance search. The remaining examples were then treated as the ground truth for the queries. The constructed questions were further grouped into four categories: factoid, definition, how-to, and opinion QAs. Table 1 summarizes the types of instances and questions in our dataset. Table 2, on the following page, lists a few sample questions in our dataset. To evaluate the scalability of the proposed approach for instance search, we also constructed a dataset including one million recent-uploaded pictures crawled from Flickr as distracting images, in addition to the 386 images as the ground-truth of the 52 instance queries.

For performance evaluation, we used the following metrics: *MAP* (mean average precision) for instance search; *MRR@K* (mean reciprocal rank at rank K) for instance naming and question answering; and *P@K* (precision at rank K) for question ranking. *MRR* measures the reciprocal rank of the first correctly returned item. The measure provides insights into the ability to return a correct instance name (or QA pair) at the top of the rankings. The metric P measures the proportion of related questions in a ranked list. Similar to *MAP*, *MRR* and P are averaged over all queries. The values of all metrics are in the range of [0,1], with 1 being the perfect, and 0 the worst performance.

6.2 Instance Search

We compared our approach, named DT, with the baseline BoW, GVP (geometric preserving visual phrases) [30], WGC (weak geometric consistency) [8], and E-WGC (enhanced WGC) [31]. For fair comparison, all the tested approaches were implemented upon the retrieval model described in Section 3.1, including the use of the large vocabulary tree, Hamming embedding, and multiple assignments. The major difference among them is the use of the spatial information. BoW does not impose any spatial constraints, while GVP is a voting approach that uses offset (or translation) information for rapid geometric checking. WGC, in contrast, utilizes the dominant scale and orientation voting for fast but weak

Table 2: **Sample questions (*Ask*) referring to visual examples (*Snap*).**

Instance type	*Ask*	*Snap and Name*
Fashion	1.What to wear with this boots?	
Food	2.How to make this?	
Pet	3.What's the breed of this dog?	
Flower	4.Why does this flower smell badly?	
Art	5.What does this mean?	
Product	6.How can I connect this to computer without ethernet?	
Logo	7.What is the meaning of this logo?	
Landmark	8.Who is this guy?	
Vehicle	9.Has anybody painted their car like this one? How?	

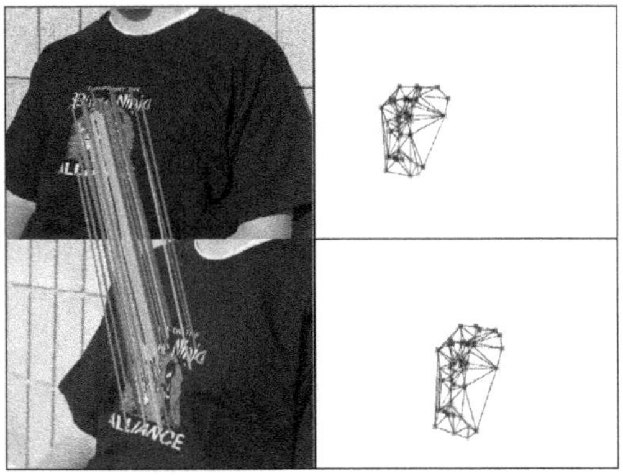

Figure 6: Meshes for non-planar instances: locally folded "Pirate Ninja Alliance" t-shirts.

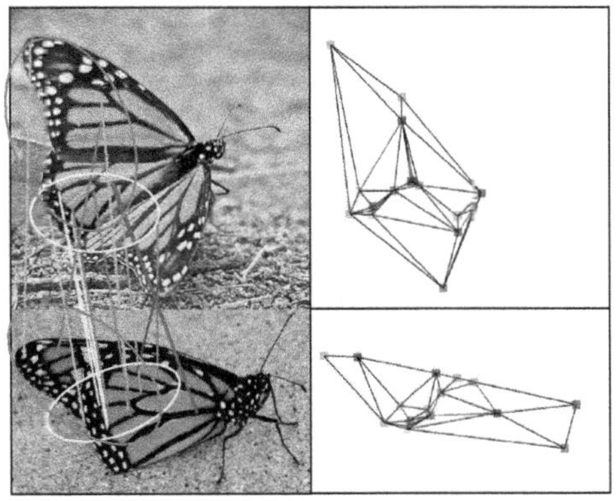

Figure 7: Meshes for non-rigid instances: "Monarch buttery" with flapping wings.

geometric verification. E-WGC incorporates the advantages of GVP and WGC by voting the translation after scale and orientation compensation.

Figure 5 shows the performance comparison in terms of *MAP* for the 52 queries, when the size of the dataset gradually increases from 0.01 million to 1.0 million Web images. Overall, DT consistently outperforms all other testing methods across different scales, and more importantly, the margin of improvement gets larger as the scale approaches one million. This result indicates the robustness and scalability of DT. We attribute the encouraging result to the merit of DT in effective topology consistency measurement, which tolerates local variations in matching, resulting in better ranking of candidate instances, especially for non-planar and non-rigid instances.

Referring to Figure 5, the performance is somewhat related to the degree of the transformation constraint imposed by each approach. Enforcing weaker constraints, such as GVP (2 degrees-of-freedom in spatial locations), exhibits slightly higher *MAP* than WGC (2 degrees-of-freedom in rotation and scale). E-WGC, which allows 4 degrees-of-freedom in depicting translation after scale and orientation compensation, results in the worst performance. Basically these approaches are sensitive to local perturbation of word matching on non-planar surfaces and non-rigid objects. E-WGC, which imposes stronger spatial constraints, tends to prune more true matches for these cases. With the use of the large vocabulary and Hamming Embedding, which already provide fine quantization for BoW matching, these approaches either exhibit a slight improvement (GVP and WGC) or a worse performance (E-WGC) than BoW. DT, in contrast, is not sensitive to local variations on word matching, as long as the perturbation does not alter the spatial topology or relative positions of the matched words. For instance, it is possible for DT to match the full regions of a locally folded t-shirt (Figure 6), but not the other approaches, which heavily prune potential true matches at the folded part. As a consequence, DT offers a higher capability (for non-rigid and non-planar instances) and tolerance (with the increase in the dataset size) in ranking, thus significantly improves the BoW baseline.

Figure 7 shows an example of matching the "Monarch butterfly" on two images. Owning to the non-rigid motion, the assumption of linear transformation is violated. E-WGC is only able to locate five out of ten true matches for similarity ranking. DT, which enforces the consistency of the spatial topology rather than a strict transformation, is able to accumulate evidence of matches from both wings (regions with yellow and red circles), and obtains a high similarity score of 0.67. In our dataset, there are plenty of man-made instances containing repeated patterns, such as the LV handbag and Arduino board. The matches by BoW are perturbed by these repeated patterns, and it is basically not wise to impose a strong spatial constraint to rule out these large numbers of perturbed but useful match patterns. DT measures topology consistency by enumerating the relative positions of words and usually ends up with a higher similarity than other approaches. In brief, DT benefits from being tolerant to local variations in BoW matches, while being sensitive to changes in topology, making it a more suitable model for instance search than other techniques.

Figure 8 further details the *MAP* for different categories of

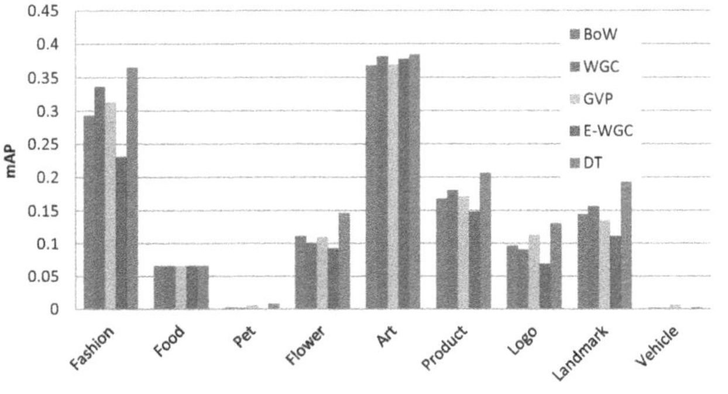

Figure 8: The performance of different approaches on various instance types.

visual instances. DT consistently shows better performances in eight out of nine categories. The instances in the "food" category mostly produce noisy BoW matches due to variations in visual appearance. All approaches can only retrieve the duplicates of a given query, resulting in equal MAP performances. For the category "pet", most failure cases are due to the excessive numbers of noisy BoW matches (e.g., the dot textures of "Dalmatian dog"). For the "vehicle" category, on the other hand, there are very few feature points extracted from the query instances (air force one, bumblebee, barrage balloon), which are texturally sparse, resulting in a poor performance. For the "landmark" category, the queries include some difficult examples, such as "Wall Street Bull" and "Bruce Lee Statue". However, DT is still able to retrieve more instances from the large dataset than other approaches. The matching for this category could become easier, if background context is also considered.

6.3 Instance Naming and Question-Answering

For ***"instance naming"***, we contrasted the performance of candidate ranking with semantic-based re-ranking (Section 4.3) turned off (PF) or on (PF+). In addition, both PF and PF+ are compared against the baseline term frequency (TF), which measures frequency by the exact matching of phrases. For fair comparison, TF is also weighted by the score from instance search, i.e., Sim^I in Equation (3). Table 3 shows the $MRR@10$ performance based on the result of instance search on the one million image dataset. On average, PF+ achieves a performance close to 0.5, indicating that, for most queries, the instance names can be correctly located within the top-2 positions of a ranked list. As shown in Table 3, the correct names are ranked in top-1 position for 22 out of 52 queries by PF+.

By analyzing the result, we find that, in the metadata, users tend to use dominant words or abbreviations, instead of the full instance name. For example, using "cake" instead of "Barbie cake", and "CK billboard" instead of "Calvin Klein billboard". This is especially true for phrases extracted from the description of metadata. As a consequence, TF tends to rank dominant words and abbreviations higher than the full name. PF, in contrast, by considering the syntactic relationship as in Equation (4), "cake" can also contribute to the frequency of "Barbie cake". Furthermore, by considering the potential noise from the metadata as in Equation (3), a full instance name extracted from the title can have a better chance to be upgraded to a higher rank. By further considering semantic similarity between phrases, PF+ contributes to a further improvement. For example, the rank for the instance name "leopard boot" is significantly boosted because of related words such as "leather".

Table 3: Instance naming: Comparison of MRR@10 by ranking with PF (phrase frequency), PF+ (PF plus semantics), and TF (term frequency) on the one million dataset. The () in the last row indicates the number of correct names ranked at top-1 position.

Instance	PF+	PF	TF
Fashion	0.62	0.53	0.48
Food	0.33	0.33	0.18
Pet	0.20	0.20	0.30
Flower	0.63	0.61	0.53
Art	0.43	0.36	0.57
Product	0.55	0.46	0.31
Logo	0.63	0.63	0.58
Landmark	0.67	0.50	0.33
Vehicle	0.00	0.00	0.00
Average	0.48	0.42	0.38
(top-1 #)	(22)	(17)	(15)

In general, the performance of instance naming is related to instance search. For example, the "vehicle" category yields a poor performance due to the failure in instance search. However, the relationship is not necessarily linear, and the performance is also dependent on the quality of metadata. For example, the performance of "flower" is similar to that of "fashion", though the MAP for the former is about 0.15, and the latter is more than 0.35. A special case is the "pet" category, where the performance is reasonably well, despite the low MAP in instance search. The performance is contributed by true positives from the one million distracting images, which are not labeled and considered as false responses in visual instance search.

For ***"question-answering"***, we compared strategy-1 and strategy-2 described in Section 5. The former uses the top-1 name candidate to retrieve similar questions, and then augments the parse tree for question ranking. The latter employs the top-10 candidate names for retrieval, but does not perform the name augmentation. Table 4, on the following page, summarizes the results. In terms of $MRR@10$, both strategies show similar performance. Basically, when a retrieved question stands out to be closely similar to an inquirer's question, both strategies are able to rank the question high. Strategy-1 shows slightly worse results, when the top-1 candidate is related but not exactly the instance name. In terms of $P@10$, strategy-1 shows an apparent advantage over strategy-2, by augmenting the instance name directly with "this" in the parse tree. This is because, without name augmentation, the syntactic tree matching technique mainly matches similar questions based on grammar structures. For example, the question "What is the easiest way to make this?" ("this" refers to "Barbie cake") will match to "What is the best recipe to make a tiered cake?". When the instance name is missing in the parse tree, the nouns and verbs (e.g., the words "way" and "make") are assigned with higher weights during matching. By strategy-1, the instance name is directly considered for matching, and the question "What are some tips for making a Barbie cake?" is ranked higher.

In Table 4, the category "Definition" performs much worse

Table 4: **Performance for question-answering.** MRR **measures the first correct question found in the ranked list.** P **measures the proportion of correct and related questions. For the notation** $X(Y)$, X **is the result by considering the top-1 candidate name, while** Y **is by considering the top-10 candidates.**

Category	*MRR@10*	*P@10*
Factoid	0.20 (0.17)	0.30 (0.21)
Definition	0.08 (0.09)	0.30 (0.20)
How-to	0.24 (0.27)	0.38 (0.31)
Opinion	0.28 (0.27)	0.35 (0.39)
Average	0.210 (0.214)	0.334 (0.279)

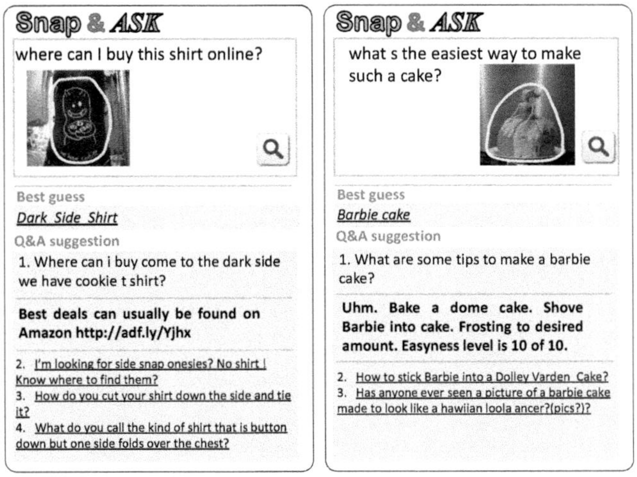

Figure 9: Examples of question-answering using our developed system. For the purpose of illustration, only the best and related questions are highlighted.

than others, mainly due to the fact that more than half of the questions fail to identify the exact instance names. However, as related, though not exact, names are found, there are still about 3 out of 10 questions related to the original questions. Figure 9 shows a few snapshots of QA examples in our testing.

6.4 Speed Efficiency

The experiments were conducted on two 8-core 2.67GHz computers with 20GB RAM each. Table 5 details the average running time for answering a multimodal question. Instance search basically completes a query within 1.5 seconds with a multi-threading implementation. The memory consumption is about 30G, mainly for keeping the Hamming signature, spatial location, dominant scale and orientation of each feature in the inverted file. Although the speed is slower than WGC, which takes about 0.9 second, the longer running time is compensated by the significantly better performance in the searching result. By processing the first 100-ranked images, instance naming takes about 11 seconds for ranking, where the time is largely spent on querying WordNet for semantic similarities. The major portion of the processing time (about 64%) is consumed by question searching and matching, when the top-1 candidate name is considered (strategy-1). Overall, the current implementation takes less than one minute to answer a question.

Table 5: Speed efficiency of our proposed framework for answering one multimodal question.

Key step	*Speed*
Instance search	1.5 sec
Name candidate ranking	11 sec
Online question search and tree parsing	5 sec
Syntactic tree matching for question ranking	18 sec
Total	35.5 sec

6.5 User Study

To evaluate the system utility, we also conducted a user study to compare Snap-and-Ask against Yahoo! Answers. A total number of 14 evaluators (8 males and 6 females) from different education backgrounds, including computer science (7), biology (2), and business (5), were invited for the subjective evaluation. The average age of the evaluators is 27, and the ages range from 24 to 31. All the evaluators are familiar with Yahoo! Answers. During the evaluation, each subject was prompted with eight different questions, of which four of them should be posted to Snap-and-Ask and the other four to Yahoo! Answers. Each question includes a text description in Chinese language referring to a picture. A subject was asked to interpret the question in English, and then pose the question to one of the systems. For Yahoo! Answers, a subject needed to textually describe the visual object for question asking. To minimize the carryover effect, questions and systems were assigned randomly. Specifically, each subject was requested to use Snap-and-Ask to answer the first four questions, followed by Yahoo! Answers for the next four questions, or vice versa.

We evaluated the systems using five criteria. At the end of each answer circle, a subject was asked to rate the system with three criteria: 1) *Accuracy*: the quality of the returned answer; 2) *Image cropping*: the use of a bounding box for question asking; 3) *Time*: the approximate time spent from formulating a question to obtaining the answer. For criterion-1, as a means to encourage full engagement in the evaluation, a subject was asked to write down the answer for each question. Note that criteria-2 is only applicable to Snap-and-Ask. For criteria-3, the evaluators were requested to note down the time they started working on a question and the time before rating the system. After completing the eight questions, a subject was also asked to compare the two systems in terms of 4) *Engagement*: how effective and efficient a system performs in returning informative answers and related questions; 5) *Acceptance*: the preference of one system over the other, based on the overall user experience. Except *Time* and *Acceptance*, all the criteria are rated on a scale of 1 to 5, with 5 being the best and 1 being the worst.

Table 6, on the following page, lists the result of the user study. Overall, Snap-and-Ask is clearly the favorite for all five criteria. Almost all subjects preferred our system when asking questions involving visual instances. From the verbal feedback, we noticed that the evaluators have a tendency to give low ratings to Yahoo! Answers, whenever they cannot name an instance and encountered difficulties in describing the visual properties. In addition, the rating of Snap-and-Ask is dependent on whether the name of the instance could be identified by the system, which in turn decides the quality of an answer. Overall, using our system, a subject spent a relatively shorter time in formulating a question, and gen-

Table 6: Comparative user study between Snap-and-Ask and Yahoo! Answers. The first three criteria show the average rating and standard deviation. The last two criteria show the preference of a system over the other, and the average time for getting an answer, respectively.

	Snap-and-Ask	*Yahoo! Answers*
Accuracy	3.6 ± 1.8	1.9 ± 1.6
Engagement	3.7 ± 1.8	1.8 ± 1.5
Image Crop	3.5 ± 0.5	*NA*
Acceptance	92.9%	7.1%
Time	2 min 20 sec	4 min 34 sec

erally regarded image cropping as a user-friendly option, especially when there are multiple objects, or when the target instance occupies a small fraction of the picture.

7. CONCLUSIONS

We have presented our framework for answering multimodal questions, along with the proposal of techniques for scalable instance search, robust naming of instance, and rigorous ranking of similar questions. The key findings include the needs for the appropriate use of spatial constraint for instance search, and syntactic as well as semantic based ranking of names and questions, for boosting the chance of finding the right answer from a number of huge but imperfect and noisy sources. For instance search, our approach, which emphasizes coherency in spatial topology while allowing local perturbation of word matching, offers apparent advantages over other methods, in terms of the scalability and robustness for non-planar and non-rigid instances occurring frequently in real-world. Experimental results demonstrate that, by searching from a million-scale image dataset and using the top-1 name candidate, an answer can be returned to an inquirer within one minute, with a good chance of finding the desired answer and three related questions out of ten suggestions.

The current system can still be improved on several aspects. Future extensions include the adaptive use of context in instance search for benefiting certain instance types (e.g., landmark), and distributed matching of similar questions by syntactic tree matching, which is currently the slowest component in our framework.

8. ACKNOWLEDGMENTS

The work described in this paper was fully supported by a grant from the Research Grants Council of the Hong Kong Special Administrative Region, China (CityU 118812).

9. REFERENCES

[1] J. Cao and J. F. Nunamaker. Question answering on lecture videos: a multifaceted approach. In *ACM/IEEE Conf. on Digital Libraries*, 2004.

[2] B. N. Delaunay. Sur la sphère vide. *Bulletin of Academy of Sciences of the USSR*, (6):793–800, 1934.

[3] B. Erol, J. Luo, S.-F. Chang, M. Etoh, H.-W. Hon, Q. Lin, and V. Setlur. Mobile media search: Has media search finally found its perfect platform? Part II. In *ACM Multimedia*, pages 911–912, 2009.

[4] M. Gilbert, A. Acero, J. Cohen, H. Bourlard, S.-F. Chang, and M. Etoh. Mobile search in mobile devices. *IEEE Multimedia Magazine*, 2010.

[5] T. Hughes and D. Ramage. Lexical semantic relatedness with random graph walks. In *EMNLP-CoNLL 2007*, pages 581–589. ACL, 2007.

[6] M. J. Huiskes and M. S. Lew. The MIR flickr retrieval evaluation. In *ACM MIR*, 2008.

[7] H. Jégou, M. Douze, and C. Schmid. On the burstiness of visual elements. In *CVPR*, 2009.

[8] H. Jégou, M. Douze, and C. Schmid. Improving bag-of-features for large scale image search. *IJCV*, 87(3):192–212, May 2010.

[9] Y. Kalantidis, L. Pueyo, M. Trevisiol, R. van Zwol, and Y. Avrithis. Scalable triangulation-based logo recognition. In *ICMR*, April 2011.

[10] M. Kamvar and S. Baluja. Query suggestions for mobile search: understanding usage patterns. In *SIGCHI*, pages 1013–1016, 2008.

[11] D. Le, C. Zhu, S. Poullot, and S. Satoh. National institute of informatics, Japan at TRECVID 2011. *TRECVID*, 2011.

[12] M. S. Lew, N. Sebe, C. Djeraba, and R. Jain. Content-based multimedia information retrieval: State of the art and challenges. *ACM Trans. Multimedia Comput. Commun. Appl.*, 2(1):1–19, Feb. 2006.

[13] G. Li, R. Hong, Y.-T. Zheng, S. Yan, and T.-S. Chua. Learning cooking techniques from youtube. In *Multimedia Modeling*, pages 713–718, 2010.

[14] G. Li, Z.-Y. Ming, R. Hong, T.-S. Chua, H. Li, and S. TangChua. Question answering over community-contributed web videos. *IEEE Multimedia*, 17:46–57, 2010.

[15] Y. Li, D. McLean, Z. Bandar, J. O'Shea, and K. A. Crockett. Sentence similarity based on semantic nets and corpus statistics. *IEEE Trans. Knowl. Data Eng.*, 18(8):1138–1150, 2006.

[16] L. Nie, M. Wang, Z. Zha, G. Li, and T.-S. Chua. Multimedia answering: enriching text QA with media information. In *ACM SIGIR*, pages 695–704, 2011.

[17] D. Nister and H. Stewenius. Scalable recognition with a vocabulary tree. In *CVPR*, pages 2161–2168, 2006.

[18] L. Page, S. Brin, R. Motwani, and T. Winograd. The pagerank citation ranking: Bringing order to the web. In *World Wide Web Conference*, pages 161–172, 1998.

[19] J. Philbin, O. Chum, M. Isard, J. Sivic, and A. Zisserman. Object retrieval with large vocabularies and fast spatial matching. In *CVPR*, 2007.

[20] J. Philbin, M. Isard, J. Sivic, and A. Zisserman. Lost in quantization: Improving particular object retrieval in large scale image databases. In *CVPR*, 2008.

[21] J. Sivic and A. Zisserman. Video Google: A text retrieval approach to object matching in videos. In *ICCV*, volume 2, pages 1470–1477, Oct. 2003.

[22] A. F. Smeaton, P. Over, and W. Kraaij. Evaluation campaigns and trecvid. In *ACM MIR*, 2006.

[23] K. Wang, Z. Ming, and T.-S. Chua. A syntactic tree matching approach to finding similar questions in community-based qa services. In *SIGIR*, pages 187–194, 2009.

[24] X.-J. Wang, L. Zhang, X. Li, and W.-Y. Ma. Annotating images by mining image search results. *IEEE Trans. Pattern Anal. Mach. Intell.*, 30(11):1919–1932, Nov. 2008.

[25] X. Wu, A. G. Hauptmann, and C.-W. Ngo. Practical elimination of near-duplicates from web video search. In *ACM Multimedia*, pages 218–227, 2007.

[26] Y.-C. Wu and J.-C. Yang. A robust passage retrieval algorithm for video question answering. *IEEE Trans. on Circuits and Systems for Video Technology*, 18(10):1411 -1421, 2008.

[27] Z. Wu, Q. Ke, M. Isard, and J. Sun. Bundling features for large scale partial-duplicate web image search. In *CVPR*, pages 25–32, Aug. 2009.

[28] H. Yang, L. Chaisorn, Y. Zhao, S. yong Neo, and T. seng Chua. VideoQA: Question answering on news video. In *ACM MM*, pages 632–641, 2003.

[29] T. Yeh, J. J. Lee, and T. Darrell. Photo-based question answering. In *ACM MM*, 2008.

[30] Y. Zhang, Z. Jia, and T. Chen. Image retrieval with geometry preserving visual phrases. In *CVPR*, 2011.

[31] W. Zhao, X. Wu, and C. W. Ngo. On the annotation of web videos by efficient near-duplicate search. *IEEE Trans. on Multimedia*, 12(5):448–461, 2010.

[32] W. Zhou, Y. Lu, H. Li, Y. Song, and Q. Tian. Spatial coding for large scale partial-duplicate web image search. In *ACM Multimedia*, 2010.

"Hi, Magic Closet, Tell Me What to Wear!"

Si Liu[1,2], Jiashi Feng[1], Zheng Song[1], Tianzhu Zhang[3]
Hanqing Lu[2], Changsheng Xu[2], Shuicheng Yan[1]
[1] ECE Department, National University of Singapore
[2] NLPR, Institute of Automation, Chinese Academy of Science
[3] ADSC, Advanced Digital Sciences Center
{dcslius,a0066331,zheng.s,eleyans}@nus.edu.sg,{tzzhang,luhq,csxu}@nlpr.ia.ac.cn

ABSTRACT

In this paper, we aim at a practical system, magic closet, for automatic occasion-oriented clothing recommendation. Given a user-input occasion, *e.g.*, wedding, shopping or dating, magic closet intelligently suggests the most suitable clothing from the user's own clothing photo album, or automatically pairs the user-specified reference clothing (upper-body or lower-body) with the most suitable one from online shops.

Two key criteria are explicitly considered for the magic closet system. One criterion is to *wear properly*, *e.g.*, compared to suit pants, it is more decent to wear a cocktail dress for a banquet occasion. The other criterion is to *wear aesthetically*, *e.g.*, a red T-shirt matches better white pants than green pants. To narrow the semantic gap between the low-level features of clothing and the high-level occasion categories, we adopt middle-level clothing attributes (*e.g.*, clothing category, color, pattern) as a bridge. More specifically, the clothing attributes are treated as latent variables in our proposed latent Support Vector Machine (SVM) based recommendation model. The *wearing properly* criterion is described in the model through a feature-occasion potential and an attribute-occasion potential, while the *wearing aesthetically* criterion is expressed by an attribute-attribute potential. To learn a generalize-well model and comprehensively evaluate it, we collect a large clothing What-to-Wear (WoW) dataset, and thoroughly annotate the whole dataset with 7 multi-value clothing attributes and 10 occasion categories via Amazon Mechanic Turk. Extensive experiments on the WoW dataset demonstrate the effectiveness of the magic closet system for both occasion-oriented clothing recommendation and pairing.

Categories and Subject Descriptors

H.3.3 [**Information Search and Retrieval**]: Retrieval models; I.2.6 [**Learning**]: Knowledge acquisition

General Terms

Algorithms, Experimentation, Performance

MM'12, October 29–November 2, 2012, Nara, Japan.

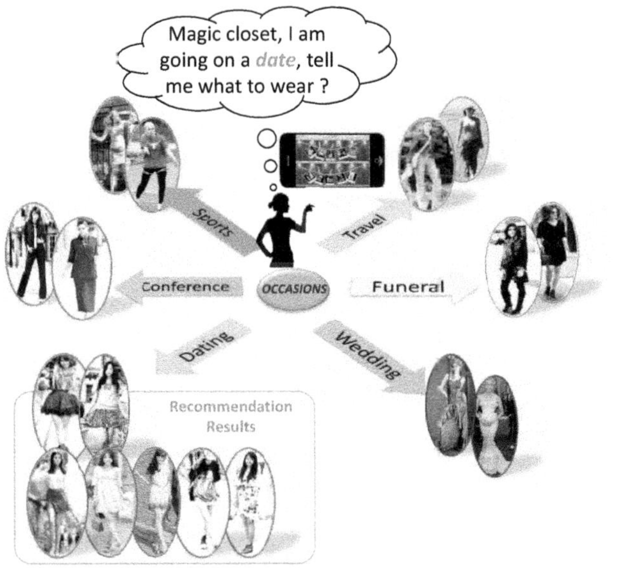

Figure 1: Scenario illustration of magic closet. A user specifies an occasion, and the most suitable clothing are recommended from the user's mobile photo album. For going on a date, the recommended clothing are sweet, have bright color and skirts are preferred. For better view, please refer to the original color pdf file.

Keywords

Clothing recommendation, Clothing pairing, Latent SVM

1. INTRODUCTION

Studies on clothing are receiving increasing interest these days mainly due to the huge market related with clothing. In China, the potential market is expected to break 20 billion US dollars[1]. Such huge market prospect greatly motivates clothing relevant research. However, related research literature is still quite limited and most of them only focus on clothing segmentation [14] and recognition [13].

In this paper, we explore a brand-new topic of occasion-oriented clothing recommendation. When people select clothing, occasion is the most important factor to consider[2]. Selecting suitable clothing for a certain occasion can reflect a person's courtesy, especially in some special occasions. For example, for an official interview, wearing a mini skirt is

[1] http://www.bizjournals.com/prnewswire/press_releases/2012/04/02/SP80325
[2] http://www.azcentral.com/style/fashion/articles/2008/10/02/20081002whattowear.html

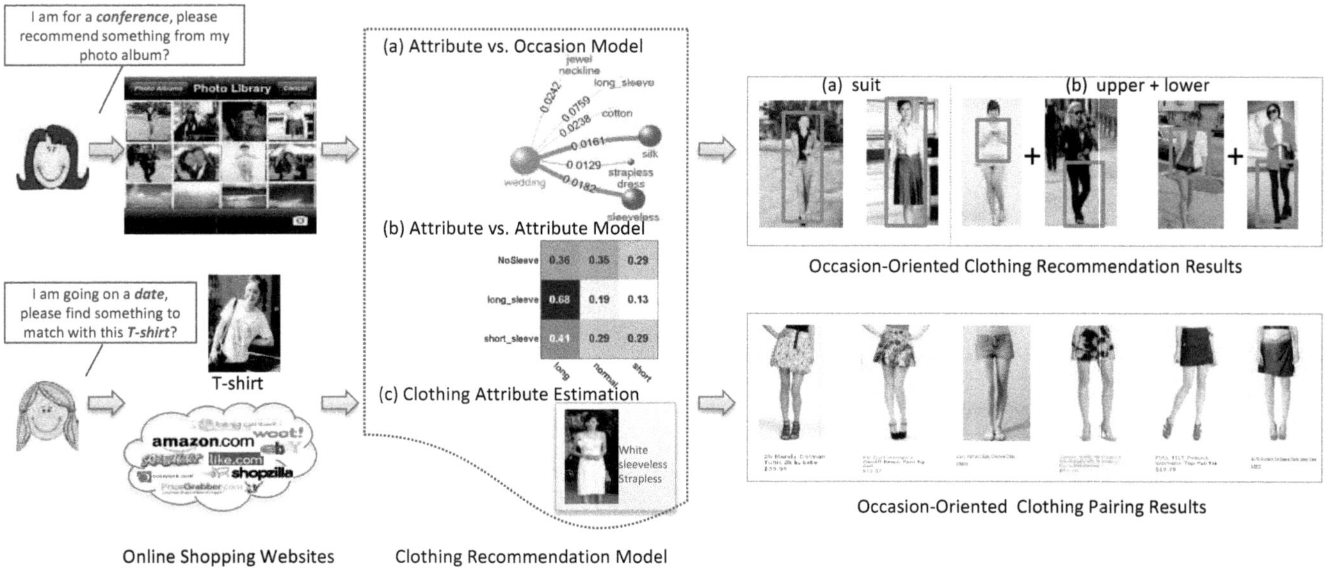

Figure 2: Two typical clothing recommendation scenarios for magic closet. (Top panel) Clothing suggestion: given an occasion, the most suitable clothing combinations from one's photo album are suggested. The suggested clothing can be one piece of suits, or two pieces of clothing. (Bottom panel) Clothing pairing: given an occasion and a reference clothing, the clothing most suitable for the occasion and most matched with the reference clothing is recommended from online shopping websites.

impolite; and it is even offensive to wear red coat when attending funeral. As shown in Figure 1, different occasions generally possess their own distinctive dressing styles. In this work, we aim to explore such clothing-occasion and clothing-clothing matching rules. And based on those mined rules we construct automatic clothing recommendation system, called magic closet, which can recommend the most suitable clothing for a user specified occasion.

Magic closet mainly targets at two clothing recommendation scenarios. The first scenario is *clothing suggestion*. As shown in the top panel of Figure 2, a user specifies an occasion and the most suitable suits or two separate clothing items (such as one T-shirt and one pair of trousers) are suggested from the user's own photo album. In terms of this function, magic closet can be implemented as a mobile application. The second scenario is *clothing pairing*. As shown in the bottom panel of Figure 2, a user inputs an occasion and one reference clothing item (such as a T-shirt the user wants to pair), the most matched clothing from the online shopping website is returned (such as a skirt). The returned clothing should aesthetically pair with the reference clothing well and also together be suitable for the specified occasion. From this perspective, magic closet system can serve as a plug-in application in any online shopping websites for shopping recommendation.

We mainly consider two key principles when designing magic closet. One is *wearing properly*. Wearing properly means putting on some decent, suitable clothing, which conforms to the *dress codes*[3] and common sense. The other is *wearing aesthetically*. There are some atheistic rules which need to be followed when one pairs the upper-body coat and lower-body trousers. For example, it looks weird to wear a red coat and a green pants together.

In the model learning process, to narrow the semantic gap between the low-level visual features of clothing and the high-level occasion categories information, we propose to utilize middle-level clothing attributes. Attributes have shown to be quite useful in many computer vision tasks [3, 2, 10, 16]. Here we define 7 multi-value clothing attributes, including the category attribute (*e.g.*, "jeans", "skirts") and detail attributes, describing certain properties of clothing (*e.g.*, color, pattern).

We propose to learn the clothing recommendation model through a unified latent Support Vector Machine (SVM) framework. The model integrates four potentials: 1) visual features vs. attribute, 2) visual features vs. occasion, 3) attributes vs. occasion, and 4) attribute vs. attribute. Here the first three concern about clothing-occasion matching and the last one describes the clothing-clothing matching. Embedding these matching rules into the latent SVM model explicitly ensures that the recommended clothing satisfies the requirement of *wearing properly* and *wearing aesthetically* simultaneously.

Few existing works target at the clothing recommendation task. Some online websites [4] and pioneering works [20] can support the service of recommending the most suitable clothing for an occasion. However, their works are mainly based on the commonsense reasoning technology. As for the pairing, Daniel Cohen-Or *et al.* [7] studied the problem on how different colors can be paired together to produce a harmonious feeling. Similar idea was also explored in [6]. However, few works investigate the problem of clothing pairing. Iwata *et al.* [15] construct a fashion coordinates system, but the important occasion factors are not considered. To our best knowledge, magic closet is the first one to investigate the task of occasion-oriented clothing recommendation and clothing pairing, which mines the matching rules among more semantic attributes from real images automatically.

Main contributions of this work can be summarized as:

[3]Dress codes are written and unwritten rules with regards to clothing.

[4]http://www.dresscodeguide.com/

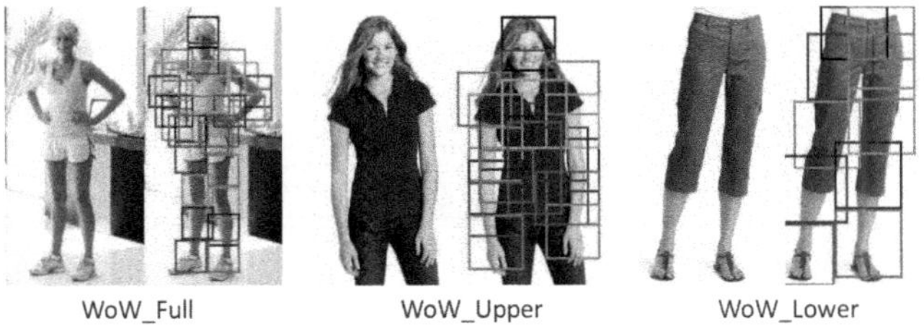

Figure 3: Detected upper/lower-body parts from WoW_Full, WoW_Upper and WoW_Lower subsets.

- It is the first time to explore two interesting practical problems: 1) how to automatically suggest the most suitable clothing for an occasions from one's photo album, and 2) how to retrieve clothing from online shopping websites to pair with a user specified clothing and also suitable for a specified occasion.
- We construct a large dataset, called What-to-Wear (WoW), containing 24,417 clothing. The collected WoW dataset contains complete attribute and occasion annotations. It is the largest fully annotated clothing dataset to date.
- We adopt a latent SVM based framework to learn the occasion-oriented clothing recommendation model and simultaneously mine the clothing matching rules, which has shown to be quite effective through comprehensive evaluations.

2. THE WOW DATASET

There are several existing clothing datasets, but none of them are suitable for evaluating the occasion-oriented clothing recommendation tasks. For example, in the dataset collected by Yang *et al.* [13], human in the images are not clear enough for detailed clothing attribute estimation. Another dataset constructed by Bourde *et al.* [5] only contains 5 attributes related with clothing. Here, we construct a new dataset specific for the occasion-oriented clothing recommendation, named as "What-to-Wear" (WoW) dataset.

2.1 Clothing Image Collection

The WoW dataset is collected from both online shopping websites and popular photo sharing websites (*e.g.*, Flickr.com), by using queries such as "street shot", "shopping girls", etc, similar with previous online dataset collection methods [18]. And those images in the photo sharing websites which are favored by lots of users are downloaded to guarantee their aestheticness. The well-trained human upper-body and lower-body detectors [25] are both applied on all these images and only the high-confidence detection outputs are retained. Thus, the possible false alarms from background are removed. Several exemplar human body detection results are shown in Figure 3.

The collected WoW dataset is split into three subsets based on the detection results. The first subset WoW_Full includes 9,469 images containing visible full-body. The second subset, denoted as WoW_Upper, contains 8,421 images with only upper-body, such as T-shirts, Fashion hoodies. And the 6,527 images containing lower-body clothing, such as Jeans and Skirts, are put into WoW_Lower.

According to different source of data, WoW_Upper is further split into two subsets, one is WoW_Upper_DP where all the images are Daily Photos (DP), which are crawled from popular photo sharing websites, while the other one is WoW_Upper_OS, the photos of which are crawled from Online Shopping (OS) websites. Similarly, both WoW_Lower and WoW_Full subsets are further split into DP and OS subsets in the same way.

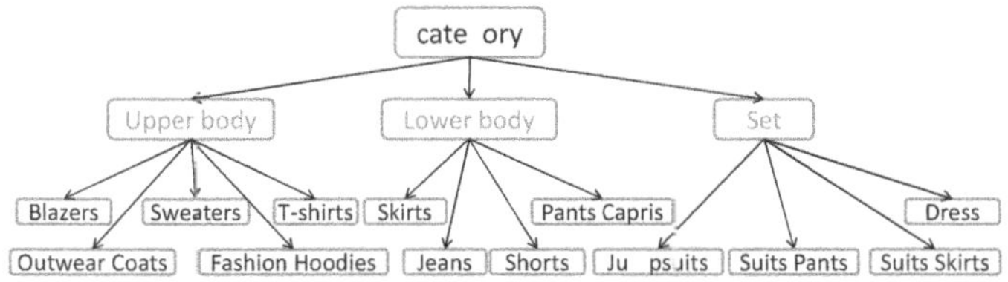

Figure 4: Clothing category attributes. All the attributes are organized in a tree structure and only the leaf nodes are considered in this work.

	Attribute Na e	Attibute Values			Attribute Na e	Attibute Values	
GLOBAL	**Color**	Red Black Green Blue	Oran e White Brown Purple	Yellow Gray Multi-color	**Material**	Cotton Silk Deni	Chiffon Woolen Leather
	Pattern	Vertical Drawin	Plaid Plain	Horizontal Floral print			
UPPER	**Colla**	Strapless Jewel	V-shape Round	One-shoulder Shirt collar	**Sleeve**	Lon Sleeveless	Shot
LOWER	**Length**	Lon	Median	Short			

Figure 5: Detail attributes definition.

2.2 Attribute and Occasion Annotation

As aforementioned, two types of attributes are used in this paper. The first type is the category attribute, which is treated as one multi-value attribute. And its values are shown in Figure 4. The category values are defined manually based on a comprehensive study of many online shopping websites, and organized in a tree structure. Only the leaf nodes in the tree correspond to category values, and in total we have 13 categories. The second type of attributes are detail attributes, which are manually selected according to previous research [19]. These attributes describe different properties of the clothing and can be further summarized into three classes, *i.e.*, global, upper-body and lower-body attributes as shown in Figure 5. In this work, we consider 10 common occasions, which are summarized from fashion websites and shown in Figure 6.

We use Amazon Mechanical Turk [5] to annotate clothing attributes and occasion categories of the whole WoW dataset. Five annotators are assigned for each annotation task. A label is considered as groundtruth if at least more than half of the annotators agree on it. Note that each clothing may belong to different occasions, so we use multiple options for occasion annotation. Table 1 shows the distribution of each attribute. Some exemplar images of different occasions are shown Figure 6. The distribution on different occasions are shown in Figure 7.

3. HUMAN BODY PARSING AND FEATURE EXTRACTION

3.1 Human Body Parsing

Previous research on human attribute analysis tends to first align human parts [5, 21] due to the large pose varia-

[5]https://www.mturk.com/mturk/

Figure 6: Exemplar images in the What-to-Wear (WoW) dataset. For each occasion, four exemplar images are shown.

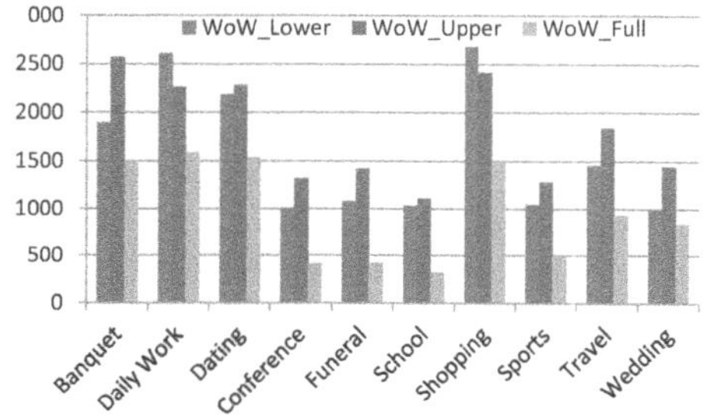

Figure 7: The image number distribution of different occasions in the WoW dataset.

tions and background noises in daily photos. The part-based detection [25, 4] is proven to be able to assist in matching human parts and thus facilitate the appearance modeling for attribute classification. In this paper, we follow this line and design a part-based detection scheme for the clothing recommendation task. We use the annotated key points in human photos provided in [4] and train one human upper-body detector and one human lower-body detector [25]. Figure 3 shows several human detection results, which also demonstrate the necessity of human parts alignment.

3.2 Feature Extraction

Following [21, 5] , we extract 5 types of features from the 20 upper-body parts and 10 lower-body parts. The features include Histograms of Oriented Gradient (HOG) [8], Local Binary Pattern (LBP) [1], color moment, color histogram and skin descriptor [5]. More specifically, each human part is first partitioned into several smaller, spatially evenly distributed regular blocks. Features extracted from all the blocks are finally concatenated into a 28,770 dimensional feature vector to represent a human part. The block

Table 1: Number of labels for each upper/lower-body attribute. Here "all" counts all the labeled clothing.

	color	pattern	material	collar	sleeve	all
UPPER	11971	14192	10082	14743	17615	17890

	color	pattern	material	length	all
LOWER	12410	14329	9108	14826	15996

based features can roughly preserve relative position information inside each human part.

4. CLOTHING RECOMMENDATION VIA LATENT SVM BASED MODEL

As aforementioned, we aim at an occasion-oriented clothing recommendation system, magic closet. It takes photos of user's own clothing and a specified occasion as the inputs and automatically suggests the most suitable clothing for the occasion from the provided photos or retrieves the clothing from online shops which pair with a reference clothing well. In particular, magic closet is based on a latent SVM model, which is learned from the visual features of the given clothing photos with full annotations on occasions and attributes. The model describes the matching rules among visual features, clothing attributes (treated as latent variables) and occasions. Based on this model, we can obtain occasion-oriented rank of the clothing photos and aesthetic scores of the candidate clothing pairs. In this way, magic closet provides suitable clothing recommendations. In this section, we first formally describe the clothing recommendation model constructed based on latent SVM. Then we introduce the model learning and inference process for clothing recommendation. We use the same latent SVM as the work in [24], but here we would like to emphasize that each potential function in the adopted latent SVM is defined specifically for the clothing recommendation task.

4.1 The Latent SVM Based Model

Given a set of clothing photos with full annotations of occasions and attributes, we aim to construct a recommendation model to capture the underlying rules for the clothing and occasion matching. In this work, instead of directly predicting the occasion based on the low-level visual features from the whole body, we use several aforementioned clothing attributes to represent the middle-level information. Meanwhile, we also aim to explore the matching rules of upper and lower-body clothing in the recommendation model.

A training clothing image is denoted as a tuple $(\mathbf{x}, \mathbf{a}_u, \mathbf{a}_l, \mathbf{o})$. Here $\mathbf{x}$ is the visual features from the whole body clothing, which is formed by directly concatenating the upper-body clothing feature $\mathbf{x}_u$ and lower-body clothing feature $\mathbf{x}_l$, namely $\mathbf{x} = [\mathbf{x}_u; \mathbf{x}_l]$. The occasion categories of the clothing are represented by $\mathbf{o} \subset \mathcal{O}$, where $\mathcal{O}$ denotes the finite occasion category set. Note that each clothing may have multiple occasion category labels. The attributes of the upper-body clothing are denoted by a vector $\mathbf{a}_u = [a_1^u, \ldots, a_{K_u}^u]^T$, where K_u is the number of attributes considered for the upper-body clothing. Each attribute describes certain characteristic of the upper-body clothing, *e.g.*, color, collar. Similarly, the attributes of the lower-body clothing are denoted as a vector $\mathbf{a}_l = [a_1^l, \ldots, a_{K_l}^l]^T$. All the attributes considered in this work are listed in Figure 4 and Figure 5. We denote the attribute set for the upper-body and lower-body as $\mathcal{A}^u$ and $\mathcal{A}^l$ respectively. Note that each attribute is multi-valued and we represent each attribute by a multi-dimensional binary value vector in the model learning process. For example, the attribute "color" has 11 different values, *e.g.*, red, orange, etc. Then we represent the "color" attribute by an 11-dimensional vector with each element corresponding to one specific type of color.

Given N training examples $\{(\mathbf{x}^{(n)}, \mathbf{a}_u^{(n)}, \mathbf{a}_l^{(n)}, \mathbf{o}^{(n)})\}_{n=1}^N$, our goal is to learn a model that can be used to recommend the most suitable clothing for a given occasion label $o \in \mathcal{O}$, which considers clothing-occasion and clothing-clothing matching simultaneously. Formally speaking, we are interested in learning a scoring function $f_\mathbf{w} : \mathcal{X} \times \mathcal{O} \rightarrow \mathbb{R}$, over an image $\mathbf{x}$ and a user specified occasion label o, where $\mathbf{w}$ are the parameters of $f_\mathbf{w}$. Here $\mathcal{X}$ denotes the clothing image space. During testing, $f_\mathbf{w}$ can be used to suggest the most suitable clothing $\mathbf{x}^*$ from $\mathcal{X}^t$ (candidate clothing repository) for the given occasion o as $\mathbf{x}^* = \arg\max_{\mathbf{x} \in \mathcal{X}^t} f_\mathbf{w}(\mathbf{x}, o)$. While for the clothing pairing recommendation, given specified lower-body clothing $\mathbf{x}_l$, $f_\mathbf{w}$ can select the most suitable upper-body clothing $\mathbf{x}_u^*$ as $\mathbf{x}_u^* = \arg\max_{\mathbf{x}_u \in \mathcal{X}_u^t} f_\mathbf{w}([\mathbf{x}_u; \mathbf{x}_l], o)$, where $\mathcal{X}_u^t$ denotes candidate upper-body clothing repository. For the lower-body clothing pairing, it works similarly.

In this work, we propose to introduce the middle-level clothing attributes to more accurately explore and describe the clothing matching rules. Here, the attributes are treated as latent variables. And inspired by the latent Support Vector Machine (SVM) [11], we assume $f_\mathbf{w}(\mathbf{x}, o)$ takes the following form: $f_\mathbf{w}(\mathbf{x}, o) = \max_{\mathbf{a}_u, \mathbf{a}_l} \mathbf{w}^T \Phi(\mathbf{x}, \mathbf{a}_u, \mathbf{a}_l, o)$, where $\Phi(\mathbf{x}, \mathbf{a}_u, \mathbf{a}_l, o)$ is a feature vector depending on the images $\mathbf{x}$, the attributes $\mathbf{a}_u$,$\mathbf{a}_l$ and occasion label o. And $\mathbf{w}$ is the model parameter.

To explore the matching rules of upper and lower-body clothing, we need to consider certain dependencies between attributes of upper-body and those of lower-body (a_j^u, a_k^l) in the model $f_\mathbf{w}(\mathbf{x}, o)$. For example, the attributes a_j^u and a_k^l may correspond to the "color" attribute of upper and lower-body clothing, and might take the value of "red" and "green" respectively. Then their values are highly exclusive, since generally the "red" does not match "green" and they should not be recommended as a suitable pair. Here we assume that only the values of the same attribute are correlated (*e.g.*, upper "red" and lower "green"). This assumption is reasonable since which color of the upper-body clothing is generally independent of the material of the lower-body clothing. We use a directed graph $G = (\mathcal{V}, \mathcal{E})$, which we call the attribute relation graph, to represent these dependency relations of the attribute pairs of upper-body and lower-body clothing. A vertex $j \in \mathcal{V}$ in the graph G corresponds to one attribute with certain value, and an edge $(j, k) \in \mathcal{E}$ indicates that attributes a_j^u and a_k^l have certain dependency (highly correlated or exclusive).

We define the recommendation function as follows:

$$
\begin{aligned}
& \mathbf{w}^T \Phi(\mathbf{x}, \mathbf{a}_u, \mathbf{a}_l, o) \\
= \; & \mathbf{w}_o^T \phi(\mathbf{x}, o) + \sum_{j \in \mathcal{A}^u \cup \mathcal{A}^l} \mathbf{w}_{a_j}^T \varphi(\mathbf{x}, a_j) \qquad (1) \\
& + \sum_{j \in \mathcal{A}^u \cup \mathcal{A}^l} \mathbf{w}_{o,a_j}^T \omega(a_j, o) + \sum_{(j,k) \in \mathcal{E}} \mathbf{w}_{j,k}^T \psi(a_j^u, a_k^l).
\end{aligned}
$$

In this model, the parameter vector $\mathbf{w}$ is the concatenation of the parameters in all the factors. The model presented in Eqn. (1) simultaneously considers the dependencies among visual features, attributes and occasions. In particular, its first term predicts occasion from visual features; the second term describes the relationship between visual features and attributes; the third term captures the relationship between attributes and occasion; and the last term expresses the dependencies between the attributes of upper and lower-body clothing. Instead of predicting the occasion from visual features or attributes directly, we mine much richer matching rules among them explicitly. The impacts of different relationships on the matching score in Eqn. (1) are automatically determined in the learning process, therefore, the four relationships are not treated equally. The details of functions $\phi(\cdot)$, $\varphi(\cdot)$, $\omega(\cdot)$ and $\psi(\cdot)$ and the parameters $\mathbf{w}_o$, $\mathbf{w}_{a_j}$, $\mathbf{w}_{o,a_j}$ and $\mathbf{w}_{j,k}$ are described in Section 4.2.

In the model learning process, we learn the model parameter $\mathbf{w}$ of the discriminative function $f_\mathbf{w}(\cdot)$ that tends to assign the highest score to the most suitable clothing for a given occasion o and considers the upper and lower-body clothing matching simultaneously. Though the groundtruth attributes of the training samples are provided, we treat them as latent variables in the model learning process. The reasons are two-fold: 1) the groundtruth attributes of the testing samples are not provided; 2) according to [23], treating the attributes of training samples as latent variables can yield more discriminate scoring function and thus better performance. Note that the information of training samples attributes are well utilized in designing potential functions.

In this work, we adopt the latent SVM formulation to learn the model as follows [11]:

$$
\begin{aligned}
& \min_{\mathbf{w}, \xi} \beta \|\mathbf{w}\|^2 + \sum_{n=1}^{N} \xi^{(n)} \\
\text{s.t.} \quad & \max_{\mathbf{a}_u, \mathbf{a}_l} \mathbf{w}^T \Phi(\mathbf{x}^{(n)}, \mathbf{a}_u, \mathbf{a}_l, \mathbf{o}^{(n)}) - \max_{\mathbf{a}_u, \mathbf{a}_l} \mathbf{w}^T \Phi(\mathbf{x}^{(n)}, \mathbf{a}_u, \mathbf{a}_l, o) \\
& \geq \Delta(o, \mathbf{o}^{(n)}) - \xi^{(n)}, \forall n, \forall o \in \mathcal{O}, \qquad (2)
\end{aligned}
$$

where β is the trade-off parameter controlling the amount of regularization, and $\xi^{(n)}$ is the slack variable for the n-th training sample to handle the soft margin. Such an objective function requires that the score of clothing for a suitable occasion should be much higher than for a non-suitable occasion. $\Delta(o, \mathbf{o}^{(n)})$ is a loss function defined as:

$$
\Delta_{0/1}(\mathbf{o}^{(n)}, o) = \begin{cases} 1 & \text{if } o \notin \mathbf{o}^{(n)} \\ 0 & \text{otherwise} \end{cases}
$$

In Eqn. (2) we aim to learn a discriminative occasion-wise scoring function on each pair of clothing (more specifically, on their features and inferred attributes) such that the scoring function can rank clothing correctly by maximizing the score difference between suitable ones and unsuitable ones for the interest occasion.

4.2 Potential Function Design for Clothing Recommendation

Here, we describe the details of the potential functions used in Eqn. (1) for clothing recommendation.

4.2.1 Feature vs. Occasion Potential $\mathbf{w}_o^T \phi(\mathbf{x}, o)$

This potential is a standard linear model for occasion prediction, which is only based on low-level visual features and does not consider clothing attributes. Here $\phi(\mathbf{x}, o)$ represents a certain mapping of the feature vector $\mathbf{x}$ extracted from the clothing and the mapping result depends on the occasion label o. In this work, rather than keeping $\phi(\mathbf{x}, o)$ as a high dimensional vector as in traditional implementation [22], we follow the strategy in [24] and simply represent $\phi(\mathbf{x}, o)$ as the score of the pre-trained multi-class linear SVM. In the SVM training process, we ignore the attributes annotated in the training samples and train a multi-class occasion classifier from $\{\mathbf{x}^{(n)}, o^{(n)}\}_{n=1}^{N}$. Then we define the mapping function $\phi(\cdot)$ such that the mapped feature $\phi(\mathbf{x}, o) \in \mathbb{R}^{|\mathcal{O}|}$ has only one non-zero element whose value is equal to the SVM score of the occasion specified by o. And the dimension of the mapped feature $\phi(\mathbf{x}, o)$ is the same as the number of occasions. In this model, the parameter $\mathbf{w}_o$ re-weights the output scores from pre-trained multi-class SVM to guarantee more accurate occasion predictions.

4.2.2 Feature vs. Attribute Potential $\mathbf{w}_{a_j}^T \varphi(\mathbf{x}, a_j)$

This potential is a standard linear model trained to predict the value of the j-th attribute given a visual feature vector $\mathbf{x}$. Similar to the potential function in feature vs. occasion model, here the potential function $\varphi(\mathbf{x}, a_j)$ also represents the confidence score from a standard multi-class linear SVM. Since there are several attributes used to describe the clothing and each attribute admits multiple values (see Figure 4 and Figure 5), we need to train multiple multi-class SVM classifiers. Each multi-class SVM corresponds to a specific attribute (*e.g.*, the j-th attribute) and is learned from $\{(\mathbf{x}^{(n)}, a_j^{(n)})\}_{n=1}^{N}$ with only considering the j-th attribute annotation. For each attribute, the dimension of the output feature from potential function $\varphi(\mathbf{x}, a_j)$ is equal to the number of different values for the attribute. For example, suppose the j-th attribute is "color", and there are 11 different values for the "color" attribute, then the dimension of the mapped feature $\varphi(\mathbf{x}, a_j)$ is 11. And only the a_j-th element of the vector $\varphi(\mathbf{x}, a_j)$ takes non-zero value, which is equal to the score assigned from multi-class SVM.

4.2.3 Attribute vs. Occasion Potential $\mathbf{w}_{o,a_j}^T \omega(a_j, o)$

This potential represents a standard linear model for occasion recognition based on only attributes. It integrates the matching rules between the attributes and occasions in its parameter $\mathbf{w}_{o,a_j}$. The value of $\omega(a_j, o)$ is equal to the co-occurrence statistics between the j-th attribute and the occasion o, which is estimated from the training samples $\{a_j^{(n)}, o^{(n)}\}_{n=1}^{N}$. The parameter $\mathbf{w}_{o,a_j}$ is also a re-weighting vector for predicting the possibility of the j-th attribute having value a_j to appear in the occasion o.

4.2.4 Attribute vs. Attribute Potential $\mathbf{w}_{j,k}^T \psi(a_j^u, a_k^l)$

This potential is used to describe the matching rules between the attributes a_j^u and a_k^l, from upper-body clothing and lower-body clothing respectively. Here $\psi(a_j^u, a_k^l)$ is a sparse vector with dimension $|\mathcal{A}_j^u| \times |\mathcal{A}_k^l|$, where $|\mathcal{A}_j^u|$ denotes the number of different values for the j-th upper-body clothing attribute and $|\mathcal{A}_k^l|$ denotes for the lower-body clothing. The value of the element in the vector $\psi(a_j^u, a_k^l)$ indexed by (a_j^u, a_k^l) is equal to the co-occurrence statistics of a_j^u and a_k^l, which approximates the probability of the clothing pairing that the j-th attribute of upper-body clothing takes value a_j^u while the k-th attribute of lower-body clothing takes value a_k^l. Note that for this model, we only consider the co-occurrence of the attributes linked in the attribute relation graph as discussed in Section 4.1.

The parameter $\mathbf{w}_{j,k}$ is a template to capture the matching degree of the considered attributes. For example, for the attribute "color", if the upper-body is red, then $\mathbf{w}_{j,k}$ may encourage the lower-body to be black by assigning their co-occurrence a higher weight while prevents it from being green by lowering their co-occurrence weight. After the model learning, the parameter $\mathbf{w}_{j,k}$ can be seen as incorporating the mined matching rules between the upper-body and lower-body clothing.

4.3 Optimization and Inference for Clothing Recommendation

4.3.1 Optimization for Model Learning

In this work, we adopt a non-convex cutting plane method proposed by [9] to solve the optimization problem in Eqn. (2) due to its ease of use. First, it is easy to show that Eqn. (2) is equivalent to $\min_{\mathbf{w}} L(\mathbf{w}) = \beta\|\mathbf{w}\|^2 + \sum_{n=1}^{N} R^n(\mathbf{w})$ where $R^n(\mathbf{w})$ is a hinge loss function defined as:

$$\begin{aligned} R^n(\mathbf{w}) &= \max_{o} \left(\Delta(o, o^{(n)}) + \max_{\mathbf{a}_u, \mathbf{a}_l} \mathbf{w}^T \Phi(\mathbf{x}^{(n)}, \mathbf{a}_u, \mathbf{a}_l, o) \right) \\ &\quad - \max_{\mathbf{a}_u, \mathbf{a}_l} \mathbf{w}^T \Phi(\mathbf{x}^{(n)}, \mathbf{a}_u, \mathbf{a}_l, o^{(n)}). \end{aligned} \quad (3)$$

The non-convex cutting plane method in [9] aims to iteratively build an increasingly accurate piecewise quadratic approximation of $L(\mathbf{w})$ based on its sub-gradient $\partial_{\mathbf{w}} L(\mathbf{w})$. Let us define:

$$\begin{aligned} \{\mathbf{a}_u^{(n)^*}, \mathbf{a}_l^{(n)^*}\} &= \arg\max_{\mathbf{a}_u, \mathbf{a}_l} \mathbf{w}^T \Phi(\mathbf{x}^{(n)}, \mathbf{a}_u, \mathbf{a}_l, o), \forall n, \forall o \in \mathcal{O}, \\ \{\mathbf{a}_u^{(n)}, \mathbf{a}_l^{(n)}\} &= \arg\max_{\mathbf{a}_u, \mathbf{a}_l} \mathbf{w}^T \Phi(\mathbf{x}^{(n)}, \mathbf{a}_u, \mathbf{a}_l, o^{(n)}), \forall n \end{aligned}$$

and

$$o^{(n)^*} = \arg\max_{o} \left(\Delta(o, o^{(n)}) + \mathbf{w}^T \Phi(\mathbf{x}^{(n)}, \mathbf{a}_u^{(n)}, \mathbf{a}_l^{(n)}, o) \right).$$

It is easy to show a sub-gradient $\partial_{\mathbf{w}} L(\mathbf{w})$ can be calculated as follows:

$$\begin{aligned} \partial_{\mathbf{w}} L(\mathbf{w}) &= 2\beta \cdot \mathbf{w} + \sum_{n=1}^{N} \Phi\left(\mathbf{x}^{(n)}, \mathbf{a}_u^{(n)^*}, \mathbf{a}_l^{(n)^*}, o^{(n)^*}\right). \\ &\quad - \sum_{n=1}^{N} \Phi\left(\mathbf{x}^{(n)}, \mathbf{a}_u^{(n)}, \mathbf{a}_l^{(n)}, o^{(n)}\right). \end{aligned} \quad (4)$$

Given the sub-gradient $\partial_{\mathbf{w}} L(\mathbf{w})$ computed by Eqn. (4), we can minimize $L(\mathbf{w})$ using the cutting plane method in [9].

4.3.2 Inference for Clothing Recommendation

After learning the model, we can use it to score any image-occasion pair $(\mathbf{x}, o)$. The score is inferred as $f_{\mathbf{w}}(\mathbf{x}, o) = \max_{\mathbf{a}_u, \mathbf{a}_l} \mathbf{w}^T \Phi(\mathbf{x}, \mathbf{a}_u, \mathbf{a}_l, o)$. Thus after specifying the occasion o, we can obtain a rank of the clothing from the user's clothing photo album. In particular, given the parameter model $\mathbf{w}$, we need to solve the following inference problem during recommendation:

$$\{\mathbf{a}_u^*, \mathbf{a}_l^*\} = \arg\max_{\mathbf{a}_u, \mathbf{a}_l} \mathbf{w}^T \Phi(\mathbf{x}, \mathbf{a}_u, \mathbf{a}_l, o),$$

which can be solved by linear programming since the attributes form a tree structure [23]. And then the clothing obtaining the highest score will be suggested, namely

$$\mathbf{x}^* = \arg\max_{\mathbf{x}} \left\{ \max_{\mathbf{a}_u, \mathbf{a}_l} \mathbf{w}^T \Phi(\mathbf{x}, \mathbf{a}_u, \mathbf{a}_l, o) \right\}. \quad (5)$$

Usa e	I a e Source		Subset Na e
Train	WoW_Full_OS	WoW_Full_DP_1	
Exp1:Repository		WoW_Full_DP_2	WoW_Full
Exp2: Query	WoW_Upper_DP	WoW_Upper_OS	WoW_Upper
Exp2: Repository	WoW_Lower_OS	WoW_Lower_DP	WoW_Lower

Figure 8: Split of the dataset for different experiments. Arrows indicate query vs. repository relationship.

Figure 9: The estimated latent variables (clothing attributes) of the testing sample clothing. Incorrect estimations are highlighted.

Similarly, for the clothing pairing recommendation, given a specified upper-body clothing $\mathbf{x}_u$ and the occasion o, the most suitable lower-body clothing $\mathbf{x}_l^*$ is paired as:

$$\mathbf{x}_l^* = \arg\max_{\mathbf{x}_l} \left\{ \max_{\mathbf{a}_u, \mathbf{a}_l} \mathbf{w}^T \Phi\left([\mathbf{x}_u; \mathbf{x}_l], \mathbf{a}_u, \mathbf{a}_l, o\right) \right\}. \quad (6)$$

The upper-body clothing recommendation for a given lower-body clothing is conducted in the similar way.

5. EXPERIMENTS

5.1 Model Analysis

The WoW dataset is split as shown in Figure 8 for model learning and evaluation. Here we use the WoW_Full_OS and WoW_Full_DP_1 subsets to train the model and the WoW_Full_DP_2 subset for testing.

Attribute prediction: We first evaluate the performance of the latent SVM model in attribute prediction. The prediction is performed through jointly maximizing the feature vs. attribute and attribute vs. attribute potentials in Eqn. (1). Here since we do not concern the occasion, the attribute vs. occasion potential is discarded. Figure 9 shows several exemplar results of attribute prediction. From the figure, it can be seen that the latent SVM model accurately predicts most of the attributes, such as the collar, pattern and sleeve. Though some predictions are not correct, for these cases the predicted attribute values are quite similar to their groundtruth. For example, the material attribute of the third clothing in the first row is predicted as "silk". This is acceptable as its visual feature is quite similar to silk. And the category attribute of this clothing is inferred as "T-shirt" (upper-body) and "skirts" (lower-body). If we treat the upper and lower-body of this clothing separately, the predicted attribute value can be considered as correct. The precision of each attribute is shown in Figure 10.

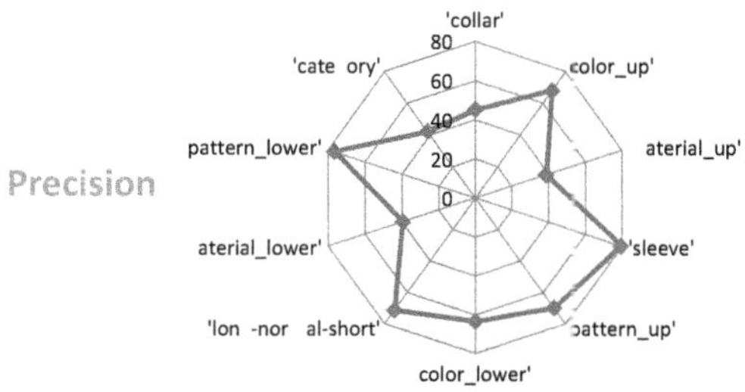

Figure 10: The precision of each attribute (%).

Visualization of the mined attribute-attribute matching rules: Here we show the mined matching rules among attributes in Figure 11 by visualizing the attribute vs. attribute potential parameter $\mathbf{w}_{j,k}$ in Eqn. (1). The model parameter vector is reshaped as a matrix. From the figure, we can see that the mined rules generally conform with common sense. For example, the upper "outerwear coats" matches well with lower "jeans", while does not match "shorts"; the upper clothing pattern "letter" matches lower clothing 'plain" well and does not match "letter" and "plaid".

Visualization of occasion-attribute matching rules: Similarly, in Figure 12, we visualize the attribute vs. occasion potential in the learned model to show the matching rules between occasion (wedding, funeral) and attributes (category, materials, sleeve length, color, etc.). It can be seen that many meaningful rules (consistent with common sense) are accurately captured by the model. For example, the "wedding" occasion matches "dress" best; "funeral" matches "black_upper" and "black_lower" well. These results demonstrate the effectiveness of the proposed model in matching rules mining.

5.2 Occasion-Oriented Clothing Suggestion

In this subsection, we present the experimental evaluation of the magic closet system for occasion-oriented clothing suggestion. In this scenario, given an occasion specified by a user, the task is to find the clothing which is most suitable for the occasion from the user's clothing photo album.

5.2.1 Experimental Setting

Though in practical system, all the clothing photos are from the same user, here in order to comprehensively evaluate the magic closet system for suggesting clothing with different attributes, we simulate the suggestion scenario on WoW_Full_DP dataset, which contains 6,661 images from multiple users. We evenly split the WoW_Full_DP subset into two groups as shown in Figure 8. The first half WoW_Full_DP_1 together with WoW_Full_OS (contain 2,808 images) are used for training the latent SVM based model embedded in magic closet. And the second half WoW_Full_DP_2 is used as repository for testing. Given an occasion, the clothing from the WoW_Full_DP_2 which maximizes the score function in Eqn. (5) is suggested by magic closet.

We compare the proposed magic closet with two linear SVM based models. The first baseline is a feature-occasion multi-class linear SVM which predicts occasion from visual features directly without considering attributes. After train-

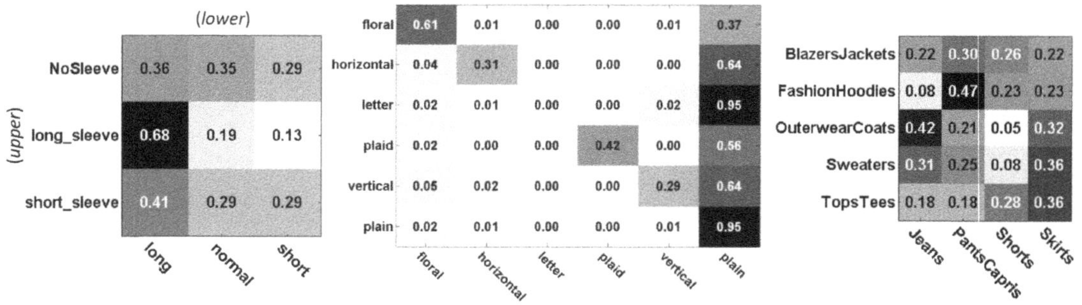

Figure 11: The mined attribute-attribute matching rules. The darker color means stronger correlation.

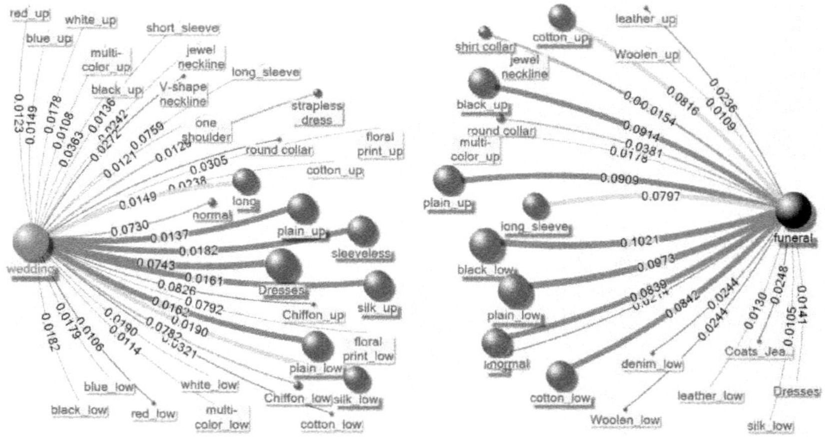

Figure 12: The mined occasion-attribute matching rules. The left is for the wedding occasion and the right is for the funeral occasion. Balls are for occasion or attributes. The size of balls and links between balls indicates the strength of their correlation.

ing based on $\{\mathbf{x}^{(n)}, \mathbf{o}^{(n)}\}_{n=1}^{N}$, given an occasion, all the clothing in the repository are ranked according to the output confidence score of the feature-occasion SVM. The second baseline feature-attribute-occasion SVM is composed of two-layer linear SVM. The first-layer SVM linearly maps visual features to attribute values, which is trained based on $\{\mathbf{x}^{(n)}, \mathbf{a}_u^{(n)}, \mathbf{a}_l^{(n)}\}_{n=1}^{N}$. Then the visual features are converted into attribute confidence score vectors via such first-layer SVM. The second-layer SVM is trained on these attribute confidence vectors to predict their occasion labels. Similar to feature-occasion SVM, all clothing in the repository are ranked based on the output of the two-layer feature-attribute-occasion SVM.

We evaluate their performance via Normalized Discounted Cumulative Gain (NDCG) [12, 17] which is commonly used to evaluate ranking systems. NDCG is defined as follows,

$$NDCG@k = \frac{1}{Z}\sum_{j=1}^{k}\frac{2^{\text{rel}(j)}-1}{\log(1+j)}, \tag{7}$$

where rel$(\cdot)$ is a binary value indicating whether the sample is relevant (with value 1) or irrelevant (with value 0), and Z is a constant to normalize the calculated score.

5.2.2 *Results and Discussion*

Quantitative evaluation results of the clothing suggestion are shown in Figure 13. From the results, we can make following observations. 1) The feature-occasion SVM consistently outperforms the feature-attribute-occasion SVM. This is because that the visual features we adopt possess relatively strong discriminative power and its high dimensionality benefits linear classifiers in classification. Compared with this, it is harder to construct linear relationship between low-dimensional attribute confidence vector and occasions. 2) The proposed latent SVM model outperforms the two baseline models significantly. This result well demonstrates the effectiveness of the proposed model in mining matching rules among features, attributes, occasions and utilizing their correlation in occasion-oriented clothing suggestion.

Some exemplar clothing suggestion results from magic closet are shown in Figure 14. In this figure, for each occasion, clothing in the repository are ranked by their scores from the latent SVM model and the top 6 suggestions are presented. From the figure, we can observe that most of the suggestions match the corresponding occasions quite well. For the conference occasion, the magic closet suggests formal clothing (most of them are the "suit pants" with "shirt collar"). For the "sports" occasion, all the top suggestions from magic closet are made from "cotton" and comfortable. Though some suggestions are not perfect, but most of their attributes conform with the underlying matching rules. For example, in the "funeral" occasion, the two incorrect suggestions are also "black" and "long", which are distinctive characteristics of the clothing for funeral.

5.3 Occasion-Oriented Clothing Pairing

Here, we evaluate the effectiveness of magic closet in another scenario: given an occasion and one's daily clothing as reference, the task is to find the most suitable clothing from online shopping dataset which pairs well with the reference clothing and simultaneously is suitable for the occasion.

5.3.1 *Experimental Setting*

To simulate this scenario, all queries (*i.e.*, reference clothing) are selected from the WoW_Upper_DP (5,921 images) and WoW_Lower_DP (2,736 images) subsets as in Figure 8.

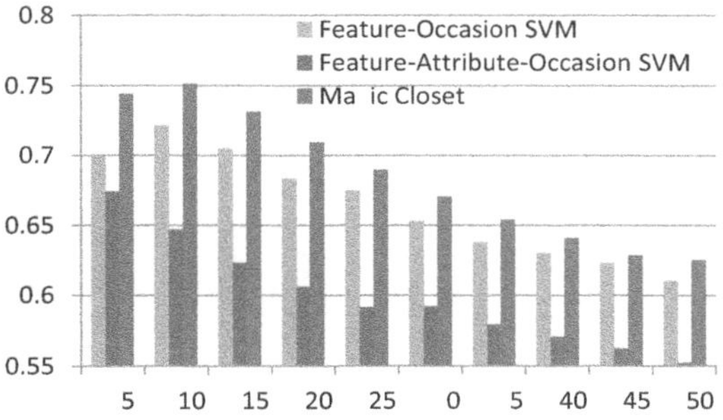

Figure 13: Comparison of magic closet with two baselines on the clothing suggestion task (NDCG vs. # returned samples).

Figure 14: Examples of the clothing recommendations. The clothing with highest scores for each occasions are shown in descending order. Incorrect recommendations are highlighted by red rectangles.

For each occasion, 20 clothing (10 upper-body and 10 lower-body) are randomly chosen as the queries. Summing up across 8 occasions[6], the total number of queries is 160.

The repository consists of clothing from online shopping dataset, including two subsets WoW_Upper_OS (2,500 images) and WoW_Lower_OS (3,791 images). We observe that many clothing are quite similar in the dataset. Therefore, we first cluster the clothing images from the two subsets based on their labeled attributes into 160 clusters, respectively. And only the most representative ones near the cluster centers are collected into the repository. This strategy ensures that the repository has wide coverage of the whole dataset. Reducing the size of repository also reduces the complexity of collecting ranking groundtruth, and is a good trade-off between an accurate evaluation and small labeling effort.

In clothing pairing, for each query of upper/lower-body clothing, we provide the rank of the candidate lower/upper-body clothing in the online shop dataset. The rank is calculated based on the pair's aesthetic score and suitableness for the specified occasion, as evaluated in Eqn. (6). To obtain the ranking ground truth of the returned clothing, we do not require labelers (40 people aging from 19 to 40) to score each candidate pair. We follow Grey et al. [13] and adopt the group-wise labeling strategy: given an occasion, we randomly show 8 clothing as a group to the labelers. So, labelers only need to rank the clothing within each group and the final rank is obtained using the method as in [13]. Such strategy can alleviate the burden of labelers significantly. Each pair is labeled at least 10 times and thus the potential inaccurate rank can be eliminated via averaging.

In the clothing pairing evaluation, we use the same two baseline models as in Section 5.2. For the proposed latent SVM based model (adopted by the magic closet), the clothing maximizing the pairing score as in Eqn. (6) is returned. And the ranking of the clothing is based on their scores. And NDCG in Eqn. (7) is also used to evaluate the performance of the magic closet and the baselines for clothing pairing. Note that here ref(·) is the score from the labelers.

5.3.2 *Results and Discussion*

Figure 15 shows the NDCG value w.r.t. the increasing number of returned samples of the baseline models and magic closet system. From the figure, we can have the following observations. 1) For the two baseline methods, the feature-attribute-occasion SVM significantly performs better than the feature-occasion SVM. This is because that the feature-occasion SVM is a linear model. The calculated pairing score equals to $\mathbf{w}^T[\mathbf{x}_u;\mathbf{x}_l] = \mathbf{w}_u^T\mathbf{x}_u + \mathbf{w}_l^T\mathbf{x}_l$. The maximization of this score w.r.t. $\mathbf{x}_l$ is independent of $\mathbf{x}_u$. Therefore, in a specified occasion, for different queries, the returned results are identical. However, due to the good performance of feature-occasion SVM in occasion prediction, it can still return suitable clothing for the occasion. Thus its performance is still acceptable. While for the feature-attribute-occasion SVM, since the features are mapped to the attribute space at first, this issue is alleviated. Moreover, the attribute-based features are more robust to cross-domain variation (DP vs. OS). 2) The proposed magic closet outperforms the two baseline models. This result is as expected since magic closet can better capture matching rules among attributes and thus recommend more aesthetic clothing pairs, which has been verified partially in Section 5.2.

For more intuitive illustration, we give more exemplar paired clothing returned by magic closet for different queries in Figure 16. We can see that most of the returned clothing match the query and the specified occasion quite well. For the "sports" occasion, the query is "short pants", and the top 5 returned clothing all have "short sleeves" and are made of "cotton". For the second query in "sports", though the second returned result is scored lower by the labelers, it actually can be considered as pairing the query well considering its "long sleeves". For the "conference" occasions, the first query has "long sleeve" and "black" color, and the returned results also have "dark color" and are all "long pants". The paired clothing appear quite formal and are suitable for conference. While for the second query, the color is much "brighter" and long pants with brighter color are returned. We can further observe that most results are consistent with the groundtruth. These results clearly demonstrate the advantages of the magic closet in the clothing pairing scenario.

6. CONCLUSIONS

In this work, we developed a practical occasion oriented clothing recommendation and pairing system, named magic closet. Given a user specified occasion, the magic closet sys-

[6]The "wedding" and "banquet" occasions are not considered since the most suitable clothing are dress and pairing is not necessary.

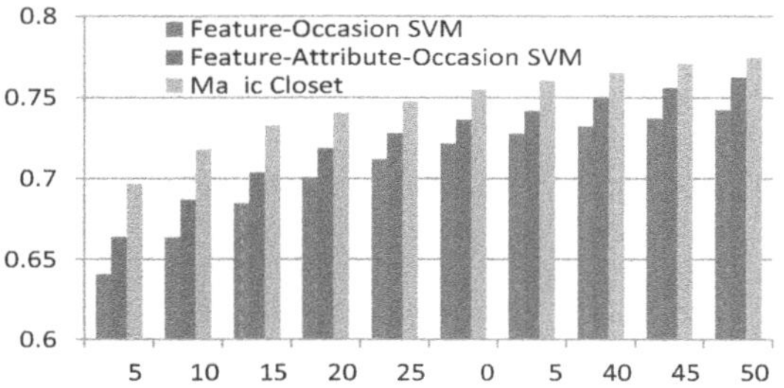

(a) Pairing with upper-body clothing

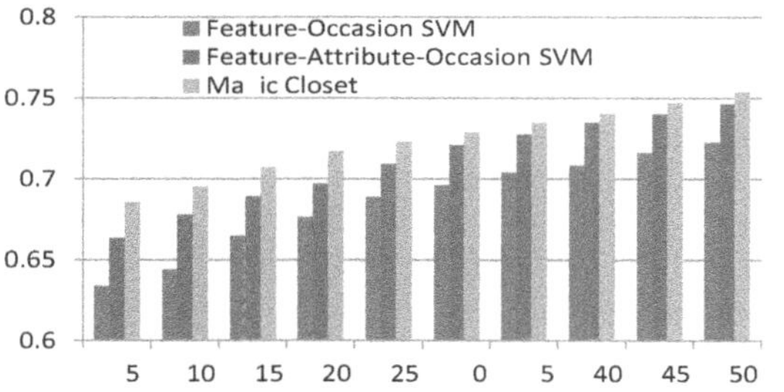

(b) Pairing with lower-body clothing

Figure 15: Comparison of magic closet with baselines for clothing pairing (NDCG vs. # returned samples).

tem is able to automatically recommend the most suitable clothing by considering the *wearing properly* and *wearing aesthetically* principles. We adopted a latent SVM based recommendation model to incorporate the matching rules among visual feature, attribute and occasion within a unified framework. To learn and evaluate the model, we collected a large clothing dataset with full attribute and occasion annotations. Extensive experiments were conducted on the collected dataset for the occasion-oriented clothing recommendation and clothing pairing tasks, and showed the effectiveness of the proposed model in capturing the underlying rules and recommending suitable clothing.

Note that the performance of the proposed model heavily depends on the human detection accuracy. Limited by the current performance of human detector in handling pose variance, some clothing in the user's clothing photo album may be misdetected. This issue can be further alleviated along with the development of state-of-the-art detection methods. In this work, we mainly focus on mining general rules and therefore we collect clothing from various users. In fact, the proposed framework can be personalized for specific users through taking their clothing images as training data and mining rules from them, or giving heavier weights on the training data from users'own clothing collection. In the future, we will investigate such personalization thoroughly.

Acknowledgment

This work was supported by 973 Program No. 2010CB327905, the National Science Foundation under Grant No. 60833006 & 60905008 and NExT Research Center funded under the research grant WBS. R-252-300-001-490 by MDA, Singapore.

7. REFERENCES

[1] T. Ahonen, A. Hadid, and M. Pietikainen. Face description with local binary patterns: Application to face recognition. *TPAMI*, 2006.

[2] T. Berg, A. Berg, and J. Shih. Automatic attribute discovery and characterization from noisy web data. In *ECCV*, 2010.

[3] M.K. Berkowitz and G.H. Haines Jr. Relative attributes. In *ICCV*, 2011.

[4] L. Bourdev, S. Maji, T. Brox, and J. Malik. Detecting people using mutually consistent poselet activations. In *ECCV*, 2010.

Figure 16: Some exemplars of the paired clothing, given an occasion and one reference clothing. The most favored clothing for each occasion are shown in descending order. Their groundtruth scores are shown nearby.

[5] L. Bourdev, S. Maji, and J. Malik. Describing people: A poselet-based approach to attribute classification. In *ICCV*, 2011.

[6] C. Cheng, M. Chung, M. Yu, M. Ouhyoung, H. Chu, and Y. Chuang. Chromirror: a real-time interactive mirror for chromatic and color-harmonic dressing. In *CHI*, 2008.

[7] D. Cohen-Or, O. Sorkine, R. Gal, T. Leyvand, and Y. Xu. Color harmonization. In *SIGGRAPH*, 2006.

[8] N. Dalal and B. Triggs. Histograms of oriented gradients for human detection. In *CVPR*, 2005.

[9] T. Do and T. Artières. Large margin training for hidden markov models with partially observed states. In *ICML*, 2009.

[10] A. Farhadi, I. Endres, D. Hoiem, and D. Forsyth. Describing objects by their attributes. In *CVPR*, 2009.

[11] P. Felzenszwalb, D. McAllester, and D. Ramanan. A discriminatively trained, multiscale, deformable part model. In *CVPR*, 2008.

[12] R. Feris and L. Davis. Image ranking and retrieval based on multi-attribute queries. In *CVPR*, 2011.

[13] D. Gray, K. Yu, W. Xu, and Y. Gong. Predicting facial beauty without landmarks. In *ECCV*, 2010.

[14] B. Hasan and D. Hogg. Segmentation using deformable spatial priors with application to clothing. In *BMVC*, 2010.

[15] T. Iwata, S. Wanatabe, and H. Sawada. Fashion coordinates recommender system using photographs from fashion magazines. In *IJCAI*, 2011.

[16] C. Lampert, H. Nickisch, and S. Harmeling. Learning to detect unseen object classes by between-class attribute transfer. In *CVPR*, 2009.

[17] Z. Li, M. Wang, J. Liu, C. Xu, and H. Lu. News contextualization with geographic and visual information. In *MM*, 2011.

[18] B. Ni, Z. Song, and S. Yan. Web image mining towards universal age estimator. In *ACM MM*, 2009.

[19] Liu S., Song Z., Liu G.C., Xu C.S., Lu H.Q., and Yan S.C. Street-to-shop: Cross-scenario clothing retrieval via parts alignment and auxiliary set. In *CVPR*, 2012.

[20] E. Shen, H. Lieberman, and F. Lam. What am i gonna wear?: scenario-oriented recommendation. In *IUI*, 2007.

[21] Z. Song, M. Wang, X. Hua, and S. Yan. Predicting occupation via human clothing and contexts. In *ICCV*, 2011.

[22] I. Tsochantaridis, T. Joachims, T. Hofmann, and Y. Altun. Large margin methods for structured and interdependent output variables. *JMLR*, 2006.

[23] Y. Wang and G. Mori. Max-margin hidden conditional random fields for human action recognition. In *CVPR*, 2009.

[24] Y. Wang and G. Mori. A discriminative latent model of object classes and attributes. In *ECCV*, 2010.

[25] Y. Yang and D. Ramanan. Articulated pose estimation with flexible mixtures-of-parts. In *CVPR*, 2011.

Constraint-Optimized Keypoint Inhibition/Insertion Attack: Security Threat to Scale-Space Image Feature Extraction

Chun-Shien Lu*
Institute of Information Science
Academia Sinica, Taipei, Taiwan
lcs@iis.sinica.edu.tw

Chao-Yung Hsu
Institute of Information Science
Academia Sinica, Taipei, Taiwan
cyhsu@iis.sinica.edu.tw

ABSTRACT

Scale-space image feature extraction (SSIFE) has been widely adopted in broad areas due to its powerful resilience to attacks. However, the security threat to SSIFE-based applications, which will be addressed in this paper, is relatively unexplored. The security threat to SSIFT (called ST-SSIFE), composed of a constrained-optimization keypoint inhibition attack (KIHA) and a keypoint insertion attack (KISA), is specifically designed in this paper for scale-space feature extraction methods, such as SIFT and SURF.

In ST-SSIFE, KIHA aims at making a fool of feature extraction protocols in that the detection rules are purposely violated so as to suppress the existence of a local maximum around a local region. We show that KIHA can be accomplished quickly via Lagrange multiplier but the resultant new keypoint generation (NKG) problem can be solved via Karush Kuhn Tucker (KKT) conditions. In order to leverage among keypoint removal with minimum distortion, suppression of NKG, and complexity, we further present a hybrid scheme of integrating Lagrange multiplier and KKT conditions. On the other hand, KISA is designed via an efficient coarse-to-fine descriptor matching strategy to yield fake feature points so as to create false positives. Experiments, conducted on keypoint removal rate evaluation and an image copy detection method operating on a web-scale image database as a case study, demonstrate the feasibility of our method.

Categories and Subject Descriptors

H.3.3 [**Information Storage and Retrieval**]: Information Search and Retrieval; H.4 [**Information Systems Applications**]: Miscellaneous

General Terms

Security, Algorithm, Design

*Corresponding author

MM'12, October 29–November 2, 2012, Nara, Japan.

Keywords

Attack, Feature extraction, Optimization, Scale-space, Security, SIFT

1. INTRODUCTION

1.1 Background

Feature point detection has been an indispensable step in various topics of multimedia, pattern recognition, and computer vision. In particular, feature points in an image have been recognized as an important but invariant attribute that can be utilized for the design of robust watermarking, content authentication, and media hashing methodologies as the means to various applications of multimedia security.

For image copy detection, feature-based image hashing methods [6, 16, 20] exploiting the robustness of feature points were proposed. In copyright protection via robust image watermarking, feature-based watermarking has been extensively studied [7, 21] (also see references therein). Among the existing feature point extraction techniques, Harris detector, scale-space filtering, and Mexican-Hat wavelet filtering have been widely used. Nevertheless, they indeed rely on the belief that the feature points representing visual characteristics of an image cannot be easily removed without significantly affecting the visual quality.

Recently, scale-invariant feature transform (SIFT) [17] has attracted considerable attention in diverse topics, including near-duplicate image detection and retrieval [5, 6, 8, 11], image copy detection [16], face recognition [14], fingerprint verification [22], mobile location search [24], and image similarity assessment [10], due to its powerful attack resilient keypoint detection mechanism. As a countermeasure to the aforementioned SIFT-based solutions, an intuitive method is to remove original feature points or insert fake feature points in an image while maintaining certain visual quality. In 2009, we addressed the security breach of SIFT in [9] and another related work was proposed by Kijak *et al.* [12].

To illustrate the security breach of image matching due to keypoint removal, Fig. 1 shows an example of SIFT-based keypoint matching before and after keypoint removal. Fig. 1(a) shows a Stirmark [23] cropped Peppers image. Fig. 1(b) shows the matching result between the original Peppers image and the cropped one, where there are a total of 90 matched keypoint pairs shown by the lines connecting pairs of keypoints. Moreover, Fig. 1(c) shows a cropped image with some keypoints removed, while the matching result obtained between Fig. 1(c) and the original Peppers image is shown in Fig. 1(d). We can observe that the number of matching pairs in Fig. 1(d) is greatly reduced by the keypoint removal attack (only 10 matching pairs can be found). Another kind of attack is shown in Fig. 1(e), where partial features of Peppers are copied and pasted to Lenna. Fig. 1(f) shows the keypoint matching result between the image Peppers and Fig. 1(e), where there are only 10 keypoint matching pairs, which might be enough for some applications to fool a system. We can observe that Fig. 1 clearly illustrates the security breach of keypoint extraction-based applications. The above observations motivate us to investigate the potential security threat to keypoint extraction techniques, including SIFT [17] and SURF [22].

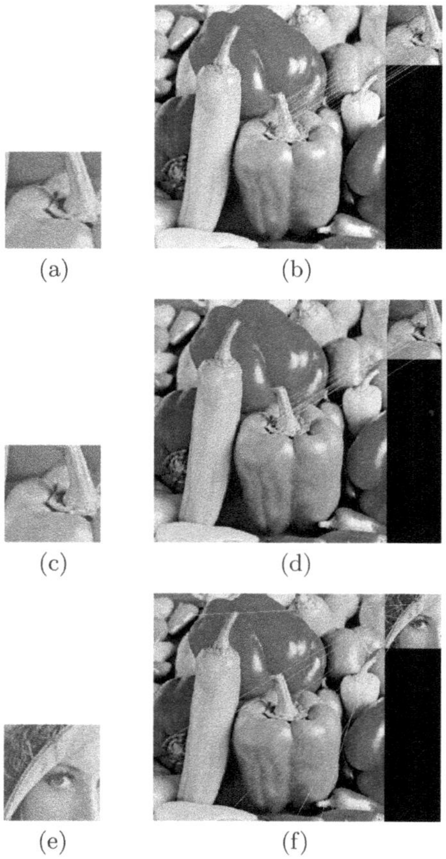

Figure 1: SIFT-based keypoint matching: (a) Stirmark cropped Peppers image; (b) SIFT keypoint matching between (a) and the original Peppers image; (c) keypoint removed version of (a); (d) keypoint matching between (c) and its original; (e) Stirmark cropped Lenna image with fake keypoints inserted; and (f) keypoint matching between (e) and Peppers.

1.2 Related Work

In [9], we first noted the security breach of SIFT with an eye on the wide use of SIFT in the literature. This study investigates the potential weakness of SIFT, meaning that the SIFT features can be deleted or destroyed while maintaining acceptable visual quality. We then propose an improved scheme to enhance the security of SIFT by introducing a key-based transform process to images. However, our attack is not perfect in that the authors [3] have figured out that our keypoint removal attack cannot completely remove all keypoints of an image due to a new keypoint possibly being generated near an original keypoint, which is selected to be removed by our scheme. In particular, if the new point is close enough to its original one, the keypoint removal attack may fail for some applications. So, we call this kind of problem a "New Keypoint Generation" problem (NKG).

In [2, 12], the authors further claim that it is possible to conceal images from the SIFT-based recognition process by designing very SIFT-specific attacks. The proposed attacks that were successful in deluding the system can simultaneously remove keypoints and forge new keypoints in the images to be concealed. Although their attacks are efficient, the quality of an attacked image is also significantly reduced. Recently, Do *et al.* [4] presented another viewpoint of deluding content-based image retrieval (CBIR) systems based on SIFT. They attack/change the orientations of keypoints in order to change the descriptors and impact SIFT matching.

1.3 Overview and Contributions of This Paper

In this paper, we study the issue of security threats to scale-space image feature extraction (ST-SSIFE) mechanisms, like SIFT [17] and SURF [1]. The proposed security threat is composed of a constrained-optimization keypoint inhibition attack (KIHA) and a keypoint insertion attack (KISA) based on coarse-to-fine descriptor matching exploiting the orientation histogram of keypoints. The goal is to improve our previous work [9] and address the question raised by the authors in [3]. This study can lead to a better understanding of the security issues of scale-space feature extraction.

Specifically, in ST-SSIFE, KIHA aims at making a fool of feature extraction protocols in that the detection rules are purposely violated in order to suppress the existence of local maximum around a local region. We show that KIHA, achieving the tradeoff between keypoint removal and image distortion minimization, can be accomplished quickly via Lagrange multiplier. However, new keypoint generation sometimes unavoidably accompanies keypoint removal. The resultant so-called new keypoint generation (NKG) problem will be optimally solved in terms of Karush Kuhn Tucker conditions in this paper. Moreover, in order to leverage among keypoint removal with minimum distortion, suppression of NKG, and computational complexity, we further present a hybrid scheme of integrating Lagrange multiplier and Karush Kuhn Tucker (KKT) conditions.

In addition to keypoint removal, keypoint insertion is harmful to scale-space image feature extraction in a manner similar to keypoint removal. We propose an efficient coarse-to-fine descriptor matching strategy exploiting the orientation histogram of keypoints to yield fake feature points so as to create the false positive problem.

Basically, our proposed attacks, KIHA and KISA, are not blind in that they exploit the knowledge of the building blocks in the feature point extraction algorithms in order to suppress or make up the feature points. In fact, our attacks aim at identifying the security weakness of the systems that employ scale-space keypoint detection mechanisms and should not be interpreted as the conventional attacks (signal processing or geometric attacks) that are blind in destroying the keypoints. The former is a security issue but the latter is relevant to robustness.

1.4 Organization of This Paper

The remainder of this paper is organized as follows. Sec. 2 briefly reviews two representative scale-space feature extraction methods, including SIFT and SURF, with the inherent security breach being pointed out. In Sec. 3, some attacks on scale-space feature extraction mechanisms are discussed first to identify their security weaknesses. Then, a typical concept of concealing the keypoints from being detected is formulated. In Sec. 4, the proposed constrained optimization-based keypoint inhibition attacks are described. Moreover, Sec. 5 describes a keypoint insertion attack designed to trigger false positives. In Sec. 6, experimental results are provided to demonstrate the feasibility of our methods. Sec. 7 concludes the paper.

2. SCALE-SPACE FEATURE EXTRACTION AND INHERENT SECURITY BREACH

We first review the scale-space representation of an image in Sec. 2.1. Then, we discuss in Sec. 2.2 and Sec. 2.3 two scale-space feature extraction methods, SIFT [17] and SURF [1], that are widely used in the literature[1]. In Sec. 2.4, the security breach problems are identified.

2.1 Scale-Space Image Representation

Scale-space theory represents an image as a one-parameter family of smoothed images to keep image structures at different scales. This framework allows visual operations to be made scale invariant, which is necessary for dealing with the size variations that may occur in image data. In this framework, a parameter s is referred to as the scale parameter. A widely used type of scale-space is the Gaussian scale-space, which exhibits broad applicability as well as the attractive property of being able to be derived from a small set of scale-space axioms. For each octave of scale-space, the initial image $I_s(m,n)$ is repeatedly convolved with Gaussians to produce a set of scale-space images. More specifically, given an image $I(x,y)$, the initial image at each octave in the scale-space of $I(x,y)$ can be derived as:

$$I_s(m,n) = I(s\cdot m, s\cdot n); 1 \le m \le \frac{X}{s}, 1 \le n \le \frac{Y}{s}, \quad (1)$$

where X and Y are the horizontal and vertical sizes, respectively, of the image I. A Gaussian filter is defined as:

$$f_s(p,q,\sigma) = \frac{1}{\sqrt{2\pi}s\sigma} e^{-\frac{(p^2+q^2)}{2(s\sigma)^2}}, \quad (2)$$

where σ is the standard deviation. Then, the Gaussian scale-space representation of image I is a family of derived signals $L(m,n,s\sigma)$ defined by the convolution of $I_s(m,n)$ with the s-th scale Gaussian kernel $f_s(p,q,\sigma)$ as:

$$L(m,n,s\sigma) = \sum_{p=1}^{P}\sum_{q=1}^{Q} I_s(m-p,n-q) f_s(p,q,\sigma), \quad (3)$$

where P and Q are the horizontal and vertical sizes, respectively, of the filter $f_s(p,q,\sigma)$.

[1]It is, however, noted that our method can be generally applied to any feature point detector that is operated in the scale-space domain.

2.2 Scale-Invariant Feature Transform (SIFT)

In the SIFT framework [17], the feature points (or keypoints) are detected via differences of the Gaussian-blurred images. For this, the image is convolved with Gaussian filters at different scales, and the differences of Gaussian-blurred images are taken. Specifically, a Difference-of-Gaussian (DoG) image obtained at the joint scale s_{ij} of s_i and s_j is given by:

$$D(m,n,s_{ij}\sigma) = L(m,n,s_i\sigma) - L(m,n,s_j\sigma). \quad (4)$$

Hence, a DoG image obtained from two scales $s_i\sigma$ and $s_j\sigma$ is just the difference of the Gaussian-blurred images at scales $s_i\sigma$ and $s_j\sigma$. For scale-space extreme detection in the SIFT algorithm, the image is first convolved with Gaussian-blurs at different scales. The convolved images are grouped by octave. Then, the Difference-of-Gaussian images are taken from adjacent Gaussian-blurred images per octave. Once DoG images have been obtained, keypoints are identified as local minima/maxima of the DoG images across scales. This is done by comparing each pixel in the DoG images to its 26 neighboring pixels within a $3\times 3\times 3$ cube centroid at that pixel. If the pixel has an extreme value among its neighbors, it is selected as a candidate keypoint.

2.3 Speeded Up Robust Features (SURF)

Different from SIFT, SURF [1] detects keypoints based on the Hessian matrix because of its good performance in terms of computation time and accuracy. Rather than using the same measure strategy as the DoG filter of SIFT for keypoint detection, SURF relies on the determinant of the Hessian matrix. Given an image $I_s(m,n)$, the Hessian matrix $H(m,n,s\sigma)$ at the position (m,n) and scale $s\sigma$ is defined as:

$$H(m,n,s\sigma) = \begin{pmatrix} L_{mm}(m,n,s\sigma) & L_{mn}(m,n,s\sigma) \\ L_{nm}(m,n,s\sigma) & L_{nn}(m,n,s\sigma) \end{pmatrix},$$

where $L_{mm}(m,n,s\sigma)$ is the convolution of the Gaussian second-order derivative $\frac{\partial^2}{\partial^2 m^2} f_s(m,n,\sigma)$ with the image $I_s(m,n)$, and $L_{nm}(m,n,s\sigma)$, $L_{mn}(m,n,s\sigma)$, and $L_{nn}(m,n,s\sigma)$ being defined accordingly. In order to localize keypoints of an image in the scale-space, nonmaximum suppression conducted in a $3\times 3\times 3$ cube is applied, similar to the one used in SIFT.

2.4 Security Threat to Scale-Space Feature Extraction

The keypoint detection mechanisms of SIFT and SURF both aim to select the local extrema of filtered images across scales. Since they have been widely applied in broad areas [5, 8, 11, 14, 22, 24, 25], inhibiting the detection of genuine keypoints or triggering the detection of fake keypoints naturally commits a breach of intended security and purposes. As an example, for SIFT-based copy detection, the copies of database data are detected from the Internet via comparing the descriptors of both the query and database data. From the viewpoint of the illegal copy user, (s)he is encouraged to modify the SIFT features/descriptors for the sake of not being detected, while maintaining certain quality of modified media data. A major security threat to SIFT originates from the fact that the keypoints can always be exactly extracted by anyone due to the lack of barriers in breaching SIFT. Thus, an illegal copy user is able to break the keypoint matching protocol easily in order that the generated copy cannot be detected.

As described, the security threat to scale-space feature extraction considered here contains (i) keypoint removal or inhibiting the detection of genuine keypoints and (ii) fake keypoint insertion. Genuine keypoint removal is easy to achieve because it is said that a keypoint is not detected if it is not an extremum around a local region. On the contrary, the successful insertion of a fake keypoint requires more effort, which includes (i) the inserted fake keypoint having to be a local extremum and (ii) the fake keypoint having to satisfy a successful match, which means that the corresponding feature descriptor also has to be forged.

3. ATTACKS ON SCALE-SPACE FEATURE EXTRACTION: KEYPOINT REMOVAL

Content-based image feature point extraction techniques have been widely adopted in the literature due to the robustness of keypoints against image manipulations. As an example, the image manipulations in the field of multimedia security include some common image processing attacks and geometric attacks (such as Stirmark [23]). Despite the recognized robustness of some keypoint extraction techniques, we propose an efficient image keypoint removal attack in this section to highlight the security breach to scale-space keypoint extraction mechanisms. Figs. 1(c) and (d) illustrate an example. We describe the principle and problem formulation of the proposed attack. We show that the proposed attack readily gets rid of the belief that the keypoints are stable enough and the removal of keypoints will severely degrade the image quality.

3.1 Principle

We adopt the scale-space feature extraction methods described in Sec. 2 as the platform to study the proposed security threat as genuine keypoint removal and fake keypoint insertion. Note that the principle of keypoint removal here is to make a fool of feature extraction protocols [1, 17] in that the detection rules are purposely violated so that no local maximum can be found in a local region. Thus, the keypoints seem to be hidden by the attack. The idea behind our keypoint removal attack is based on the observation that an original keypoint will not be detected by scale-space keypoint detection if another extremum is maliciously generated nearby. The fake extremum can be generated with only limited distortions being imposed on the image. In other words, there are two equal extrema around a local region such that the duplicate extremum is enforced to be at one of the eight neighbors in the scale-space to evade keypoint detection.

3.2 Duplicate Local Extrema for Restraining Keypoint Detection in the Scale-Space Domain: Problem Formulation

In both the scale-space keypoint detection methods referred to as SIFT and SURF here, a pixel is decided as a keypoint if and only if it is a local maximum in a scale-space cube. As defined in Eq. (3), the convolution result of each entry in a $3 \times 3 \times 3$ scale-space cube centered at $(m_0, n_0, s\sigma)$ can be derived as:

$$\begin{aligned} & L(m_0+k, n_0+l, (s+w)\sigma) \\ = & \sum_{p=1}^{P}\sum_{q=1}^{Q} I_s(m_0-p+k, n_0-q+l) f_{s+w}(p-k, q-l, \sigma), \end{aligned} \tag{5}$$

where k, l, and $w \in [-1, 0, 1]$, and P and Q are the horizontal and vertical sizes, respectively, of the filter $f_{s+w}(p-k, q-l, \sigma)$.

To find the local maximum in a cube, the 27 filtering responses $L(m_0+k, n_0+l, (s+w)\sigma)$'s are sorted in a descending order and expressed as corresponding r_i's ($1 \leq i \leq 27$) for notation simplicity, *i.e.*, $r_1 > r_2 > \cdots > r_{27}$. For each r_i, the associated Gaussian kernel, as indicated in Eq. (5), is simplified as f_i. Let the local extremum and its associated Gaussian filter be denoted as r_1 and f_1, respectively. As described previously, the goal here is to maliciously add distortions into the area of pixels $I_s(m_0-p, n_0-q)$'s affected by filtering to generate another extremum near the origin $I_s(m_0, n_0)$. Intuitively, to reduce the imposed distortions averagely, the first two largest modified extrema can be derived as:

$$\begin{aligned} r_1' &= \Sigma_{p,q} I_s'(m_0-p, n_0-q) f_1(p,q) \\ &= \Sigma_{p,q} I_s'(m_0-p, n_0-q) f_2(p,q) = r_2' = \frac{r_1+r_2}{2}, \end{aligned} \tag{6}$$

where r_1' and r_2' are modified version of r_1 and r_2 in the scale-space, respectively; I_s' is the modified image of I_s; f_1 and f_2 denote the corresponding filters of the first and second largest extrema r_1 and r_2, respectively. To determine the distortion added into the image, a local distortion patch $d_s(m_0-p, n_0-q)$ is defined to satisfy:

$$I_s'(m_0-p, n_0-q) = I_s(m_0-p, n_0-q) + d_s(m_0-p, n_0-q), \tag{7}$$

for all p and q. Plugging $I_s'(m_0-p, n_0-q)$ into Eq. (6), we have the formulation of duplicate local extrema generation as:

$$\begin{cases} \Sigma_{p,q} d_s(m_0-p, n_0-q) f_1(p,q) = \frac{r_2-r_1}{2} \\ \Sigma_{p,q} d_s(m_0-p, n_0-q) f_2(p,q) = \frac{r_1-r_2}{2}. \end{cases} \tag{8}$$

Actually, the solution to Eq. (8) is to solve the $P \times Q$ unknown variables in the distortion patch $d_s(m_0-p, n_0-q)$. Any solution that simultaneously satisfies Eq. (8) can make that the original keypoint is not detected by SIFT or SURF.

The current formulation of the proposed attack, however, is still preliminary and incurs some problems.

- First, the target of the proposed attack is to modify pixel values in the scale-space domain. The derived distortion patch must be rescaled back to the spatial domain so that the patch can be added into the original image in the spatial domain. The rescaling will unavoidably introduce the so-called "scaling error" into the distortion patch, which may cause the values of the first two largest modified extrema (r_1' and r_2') to be changed such that the proposed attack will not function as designed.
- Second, the formulation in Eq. (8) is not optimal for distortion minimization, leading to undesired distortion imposed on the attacked image.
- Finally, the new keypoint generation problem pointed out by the authors in [3] still exists in the current formulation of our keypoint removal attack.

To solve these problems, we propose constraint-optimized genuine keypoint removal and fake keypoint insertion attacks as the security threat to scale-space feature detection schemes in the next two sections.

4. CONSTRAINT-OPTIMIZED SECURITY THREAT TO SCALE-SPACE FEATURE EXTRACTION: KEYPOINT REMOVAL

To deal with the problems described in Sec. 3.2, two convex optimization solutions to the keypoint removal attack will be described in this section. In Sec. 4.1, we exploit the Lagrange multiplier to quickly satisfy Eq. (8). Nevertheless, the NKG problem exists in the Lagrange multiplier-based keypoint removal attack. By imposing more constraints, we investigate Karush Kuhn Tucker conditions (also known as the Kuhn-Tucker or KKT conditions) in Sec. 4.2 to solve the NKG problem while minimizing the induced distortions. However, due to the high computational complexity of KKT-based optimization, in Sec. 4.3, we propose a hybrid scheme of combining Lagrange multiplier and KKT conditions optimization to simultaneously reduce the complexity of keypoint removal and avoid the NKG problem.

4.1 Keypoint Removal via Lagrange Multiplier in Spatial Domain

As described previously, the genuine keypoint removal attack is proposed to conceal the keypoints by modifying the pixels in the scale-space domain, as indicated in Eq. (8). The derived distortions $d_s(m_0-p, n_0-q)$'s must be rescaled back to the spatial domain and added into the original image. In order to avoid the scaling error due to rescaling, we propose to directly conduct the attack in the spatial domain.

For this, we first have to find the filter coefficients in the spatial domain according to the filter f_i, $1 \leq i \leq 27$, in the DoG domain. Suppose there exists a filter F_i in the spatial domain that can calculate r_i directly by convoluting the filter with a local path $I(x_0-u, y_0-v)$ of original image, that is:

$$r_i = \Sigma_{u,v} I(x_0-u, y_0-v)F_i(u,v), 1 \leq u \leq U, 1 \leq v \leq V, \quad (9)$$

where U and V denote the horizontal and vertical sizes, respectively, of the spatial domain filter F_i. Based on the relation between $I(x,y)$ and $I_s(m,n)$, which is

$$\sum_{x\in\{x|\lfloor\frac{x-1}{s}\rfloor+1=m\}, y\in\{y|\lfloor\frac{y-1}{s}\rfloor+1=n\}} I(x,y) = I_s(m,n), \quad (10)$$

the spatial domain filter corresponding to scale-space filter can be derived as:

$$F_i(u,v) = f_i(\lfloor\frac{u-1}{s}\rfloor+1, \lfloor\frac{v-1}{s}\rfloor+1). \quad (11)$$

Once Eq. (11) is derived, Eq. (8) can be rewritten in the spatial domain as:

$$\begin{cases} \Sigma_{u,v} d(x_0-u, y_0-v)F_1(u,v) = \frac{r_2-r_1}{2} \\ \Sigma_{u,v} d(x_0-u, y_0-v)F_2(u,v) = \frac{r_1-r_2}{2} \end{cases}, \quad (12)$$

where $d(x_0-u, y_0-v)$ denotes the distortion required to attack the local extreme at position (x_0-u, y_0-v) in the spatial domain.

Taking the goals of distortion minimization and duplicate extrema into consideration, we model the image keypoint inhibition attack conducted in the spatial domain as a constrained minimization problem as:

$$(P)\begin{cases} \text{minimize } D(z_0) = \sum_t d^2(z_0-t) \text{ subject to} \\ \Sigma_t d(z_0-t)F_1(t) = \frac{r_2-r_1}{2}, \text{ and} \\ \Sigma_t d(z_0-t)F_2(t) = \frac{r_1-r_2}{2}, \ 1 \leq t \leq T \end{cases}, \quad (13)$$

where $T = U \times V$, and z_0 and t, respectively, denote the pixel position (x_0, y_0) and the filter coefficient position (u,v) for notation simplification. In Eq. (13), the objective function $D(z_0)$ to be minimized is L2-norm, which is proven to be convex. Moreover, the two constrained functions are also convex. Thus, Eq. (13) can be solved using nonlinear programming. In mathematical optimization, Lagrange multipliers provide a strategy for finding the maxima and minima of a function subject to constraints. Let the two variables λ_1 and λ_2 be Lagrange multipliers. Eq. (13) can be rewritten as a Lagrange multiplier optimization function as:

$$\begin{aligned}\Lambda(d(z_0-t), \lambda_1, \lambda_2) &= \sum_t d^2(z_0-t) \\ &+\lambda_1[\Sigma_t d(z_0-t)F_1(t) - \tfrac{r_2-r_1}{2}] \\ &+\lambda_2[\Sigma_t d(z_0-t)F_2(t) - \tfrac{r_1-r_2}{2}].\end{aligned} \quad (14)$$

If $d(z_0-t')$ is a minimum for the constraint optimization problem, then there exists a point $(d(z_0-t'), \lambda_1, \lambda_2)$ that is a stationary point for the Lagrange function (stationary points are those points where the partial derivatives of Λ are zero). In order to solve the constraint optimization problem, we set the derivative $d\Lambda = 0$, which yields the system of equations as:

$$\begin{aligned}\frac{\partial\Lambda}{\partial d(z_0-t)} &= 2d(z_0-t) + \lambda_1 F_1(t) + \lambda_2 F_2(t) = 0, \\ \frac{\partial\Lambda}{\partial\lambda_1} &= \Sigma_t d(z_0-t)F_1(t) - \tfrac{r_2-r_1}{2} = 0, \\ \frac{\partial\Lambda}{\partial\lambda_2} &= \Sigma_t d(z_0-t)F_1(t) - \tfrac{r_2-r_1}{2} = 0,\end{aligned} \quad (15)$$

where $t = 1, 2, \cdots, T$. In Eq. (15), we have $(T+2)$ unknown variables and $(T+2)$ equations. We can solve Eq. (15) and find the points that satisfy Eq. (15). These points are known as the solution with the minimum distortion.

4.2 Keypoint Removal via Karush Kuhn Tucker (KKT) Conditions in Spatial Domain

In [2], the authors proposed erasing a local extreme via adding a patch ϵ to the original image $I(x,y)$ to produce a modified image $I'(x,y) = I(x,y) + \epsilon$ in the spatial domain, which is equivalent to $D'(m,n,s\sigma) = D(m,n,s\sigma) + \delta$. In order to reduce the perceptual degradation, the added patch should have the minimal Euclidean norm. This resorts to an optimization procedure under the constraint:

$$\epsilon = \arg \min_{\epsilon: D'(m,n,s\sigma)=D(m,n,s\sigma)+\delta} \|\epsilon\|^2.$$

A simple Lagrangian solver yields [2]:

$$\epsilon = \frac{\delta}{\|\Delta G\|^2}\tau_{(x,y)}(\Delta G),$$

where ΔG denotes the difference of Gaussian kernel at scale δ and $\tau_{(x,y)}$ is the 2D translation operator of a shift (x,y). However, the method [2] also modifies the values around the neighborhood unavoidably, thus, incurs the NKG problem. To deal with the problem, the authors [12] introduce the constraint of forcing the patch to not modify $D(m,n,s\sigma)$'s in the neighborhood previously defined, and solve the resulting problem by the Karush Kuhn Tucker theorem [13, 15]. As claimed by the authors, the added constraints lead to production of more visible artifacts at larger scales.

Although the proposed optimization scheme in Sec. 4.1 solves the distortion minimization problem via the constraints that are different from [2], the NKG problem as we have described previously, still cannot be solved. To overcome the NKG problem, the key we found is that the modified DoG pixel values around the original keypoint must be all less than the two largest extrema. This constraint can guarantee the situation where no new keypoint can be accidently generated. Different from Do *et al.*'s solution [2], we do not force the proposed method to not modify the DoG pixels around the original keypoint. Instead, the attacked DoG pixels are limited to be less than the mean (*i.e.*, $\frac{r_1+r_2}{2}$) of the first two largest DoG pixels (see Eq. (6)). Let $r'_1 > r'_2 > \cdots > r'_{27}$ be a descending order of filtering responses obtained via spatial domain DoG filters. Similar to the filtering response obtained in the DoG domain defined in Eq. (6), we have the corresponding filtering responses obtained in the spatial domain within a cube as:

$$r'_i = \sum_t I'(z_0 - t)F_i(t),\ i \in [1, 27], \tag{16}$$

where $r'_1 = r'_2 = \frac{r_1+r_2}{2}$ are the same as the constraints described in Sec. 4.1. Except for the two largest ones, the remaining DoG pixels are considered as additional constrains to control the modified spatial domain pixels as:

$$r'_i = \sum_t I'(z_0 - t)F_i(t) \leq \frac{r_1 + r_2}{2} = r'_1 = r'_2,\ i \in [3, 27]. \tag{17}$$

Subtract the original DoG pixel r_i from both sides of Eq. (17) to simplify the inequality, and we can have:

$$r'_i - r_i = \sum_t d(z_0 - t)F_i(t) \leq \frac{r_1 + r_2}{2} - r_i, \tag{18}$$

where $I'(z_0 - t) - I(z_0 - t) = d(z_0 - t)$ defined in the spatial domain with respect to the one defined in Eq. (7) in the scale-space domain is exploited. By considering the inequalities in Eq. (18) as constraints, the NKG problem can be solved by a new minimization problem with inequality constraints. In mathematics, the Karush-Kuhn-Tucker (KKT) conditions [13, 15] are necessary for a solution in nonlinear programming to be optimal, provided that some regularity conditions are satisfied. Therefore, based on KKT, the following nonlinear optimization problem is formulated:

$$(P)\begin{cases} \text{minimize } D(z_0) = \sum_t d^2(z_0 - t) \text{ s.t.} \\ C_i(z_0) = \Sigma_t d(z_0 - t)F_i(t) = \frac{r_1+r_2}{2} - r_i,\ 1 \leq i \leq 2 \\ K_i(z_0) = \Sigma_t d(z_0 - t)F_i(t) \leq \frac{r_1+r_2}{2} - r_i,\ 3 \leq i \leq 27 \end{cases}, \tag{19}$$

where $D(z_0)$ is the function to be minimized, $K_i(z_0)$'s are the functions of the inequality constraints, $C_i(z_0)$'s are the functions of the equality constraints, and the numbers of inequality and equality constraints are 25 and 2, respectively.

Allowing inequality constraints, the KKT approach to nonlinear programming generalizes the method of Lagrange multipliers, which only permits equality constraints. Since the objective function, *i.e.*, the function to be minimized, and the constraint functions are continuously differentiable, the optimized solution of Eq. (19) can be derived by:

$$\begin{aligned} &\Lambda(D(z_0), \alpha_1, \alpha_2, \beta_3, \cdots, \beta_{27}) \\ = \;& D(z_0) + \sum_{i=1}^{2} \alpha_i \nabla C_i(z_0) + \sum_{i=3}^{27} \beta_i \nabla K_j(z_0) = 0. \end{aligned} \tag{20}$$

In Eq. (20), we have $(T+27)$ unknown variables and $(T+27)$ equations. We can solve Eq. (20) and find the points $d^*(z_0 - t)$'s that satisfy the system of equations if and only if the gradients of the active inequality constraints and the gradients of the equality constraints are linearly independent at $d^*(z_0 - t)$'s. This is a so-called linear independence constraint qualification (LICQ) condition in the context of KKT. By adding the distortions $d^*(z_0 - t)$'s into the original image, the scale-space keypoints can be hidden while maintaining visual quality of the attacked image with minimized distortions. Moreover, no new keypoint can be generated after such an constraint-optimized keypoint inhibition attack is performed.

4.3 Keypoint Removal via A Hybrid of Lagrange Multiplier and KKT Conditions in Spatial Domain

While the KKT conditions can solve the NKG problem introduced by the keypoint inhibition attack, the algorithm is more complex than Lagrange multiplier based optimization. In addition, by considering the fact that not every keypoint removal described in Sec. 4.1 will introduce a new keypoint, the more complicated optimization mechanism, KKT, is not required to be applied everywhere. To leverage computational complexity and keypoint removal efficiency, a solution that combines the Lagrange multiplier and KKT conditions is proposed. The pseudo code of the hybrid optimization algorithm is depicted in Algorithm 1.

Now, we explain each step in detail. In Step 1, the number of keypoints and their locations are obtained from a given original image I via some keypoint detection algorithms, like SIFT and SURF. In Step 2, the corresponding filter coefficients in the spatial domain are calculated from the filter coefficients in the scale-space domain (Sec. 4.1). After the filter coefficients are calculated, the Lagrange multiplier in Step 3 is adopted to find the distortion vector for each keypoint quickly at (x_k, y_k) iteratively. In Step 4, each distortion vector is verified with the constraints introduced in KKT to find if the NKG problem exists after the keypoint inhibition attack is applied (*i.e.*, verify whether the distortion vector satisfies the whole inequalities). If the "while" condition in Step 4 is satisfied, KKT-based constraint-optimized keypoint inhibition attack is performed to update the distortion vector. In Step 5, the distortion at the k-th iteration is added into the original image I. This procedure (from Step 3 to Step 5) repeats until the distortions of all keypoints are verified. Finally, the attacked image I' is produced.

5. ATTACKS ON SCALE-SPACE FEATURE EXTRACTION: FAKE KEYPOINT INSERTION

We discuss in Sec. 5.1 the penalty of removing all keypoints. However, if a portion of genuine keypoints are reserved, then the inefficiency of keypoint removal appears. To address this issue, we then present the fake keypoint insertion attack, which triggers the false positive problem and can repair the inefficiency of being unable to remove all keypoints, in Sec. 5.2.

5.1 Limit of Removing All Keypoints

Even though each keypoint can be removed theoretically by the proposed keypoint inhibition attack, some keypoints cannot be removed if the visual quality of an attacked image is considered. The unacceptable distortion comes from $|\frac{r_1-r_2}{2}|$, as defined in Eq. (8), which is introduced to make the two largest filtering responses equal. In particular, the

Algorithm 1 A Hybrid Constraint-Optimized Keypoint Inhibition Attack (KIHA).

Input: original image I.
Step 1:
Perform keypoint detection for I;
Set the filter bank f_i's in the scale-space domain, where $1 \leq i \leq 27$, as described in Sec. 3.2;
Set N=number of keypoints in I;
Set (x_k, y_k)'s=positions of keypoints, $1 \leq k \leq N$;
Step 2:
Calculate each corresponding spatial domain filter F_i from f_i; //Sec. 4.1 and Eq. (11)
$k = 0$.
Step 3:
if $k \leq N$ **then**
  $k = k + 1$
  //Let d denote the distortion required to remove a keypoint.
  $d = LagrangeMultiplier(I, F_i's, x_k, y_k)$ //Eq. (13)∼Eq. (15)
  Step 4:
  //Let r_1 and r_2 denote the first two largest filtering responses, as described in Sec. 3.2
  while $\Sigma_{u,v} d(x_k - u, y_k - v)F_i(u, v) > \frac{r_1+r_2}{2} - r_i, \exists i\ (i \neq 1, 2)$ **do**
    //refer to Eq. (18) and Eq. (19)
    $d = KKT(I, F_i's, x_k, y_k)$ //Sec. 4.2
  end while
  Step 5:
  $I' = I + d$
end if
Output: keypoint inhibition attacked image I'

removal of keypoints at the coarse scales (or low frequencies) easily will create large distortions or obvious perceptual degradations. To avoid generating unacceptable visual distortions, a portion of keypoints at coarser scales will be retained. Among the applications of adopting feature point extraction, some of them, such as image copy detection and image retrieval, consider that two images are matched via only few matched descriptor pairs. Unfortunately, the survival of a few keypoints (say 10%) may still be sufficient for some applications. Under this circumstance, a single keypoint inhibition attack may not entirely achieve the goal of security breach. In view of this, a fake keypoint insertion attack (KISA) is presented in the next subsection to assist in lowering the matching score.

5.2 Fake Keypoint Insertion

5.2.1 Rationale

Triggering a false positive is a general way to reduce the reliability of a system. Figs. 1(e) and (f) illustrate an example. To achieve this goal in an image copy detection system, an original image can be hidden with some fake keypoints to build an attacked image, which, when used as a query, can retrieve some other images irrelevant to the original one as the top query results while the original one may be away from the retrieval list. The strategy we use for inserting new keypoints with the minimum distortions is almost the same as the one for inhibiting keypoint detection. The major difference between keypoint insertion and keypoint inhibition is the constraint set listed in Eq. (18). For keypoint insertion, our goal is to create a new but fake keypoint that is located at the centroid of a local region. For this, the centroid of a DoG cube must be a local extrema and Eq. (18) is modified as:

$$K_i(z_0) = \sum_t d(z_0 - t)F_i(t) \leq r_1 - r_i,\ i \in [2, 27], \qquad (21)$$

where $K_i(z_0)$, similar to the one defined in Eq. (19), denotes the inequality constraint.

In addition to creating the fake keypoint, it is important for it to function as the genuine one. This means that the inserted fake keypoint has to satisfy two conditions: (i) it can be detected as a keypoint (Eq. (21) has to be satisfied) and (ii) the descriptor corresponding to the fake keypoint should mimic the genuine one to actually finish a successful match. Therefore, to insert a given keypoint and its corresponding descriptor into a target image, we first find a similar descriptor in the scale-space of the target image by exhaustive search. When a similar descriptor is found, we insert a fake keypoint to the location of found descriptor. However, one disadvantage of the exhaustive similar descriptor search is that it is "blind" in that, when the search space is large enough, the search performance will become poor. To improve the search efficiency, we propose a new coarse-to-fine descriptor matching strategy.

5.2.2 Descriptor Matching via Coarse-to-Fine Search

To obtain a SIFT descriptor, the gradient information around a key-point is used in Lowe's scheme [17]. Gradients within a circular region (defined as a local patch $I_s(m-p, n-q)$ here centered at (m, n) with the support defined over the corresponding filter) are used to compute an orientation histogram with 36 bins denoted as $h(\alpha)$ $(1 \leq \alpha \leq 36)$, and the maximum bin denoted as $h(\alpha_{Max})$ $(1 \leq \alpha_{Max} \leq 36)$ is used as the characteristic orientation such that the descriptor can be represented relative to this orientation thereby achieving rotation invariance.

After the orientation histogram is obtained, the surrounding region of a keypoint is divided into 4×4 sub-patches. From each sub-patch, an orientation histogram with 8 bins is computed and concatenated to form a single feature vector for descriptor matching. To speed up the similar descriptor searching, the orientation histogram is treated as a coarse feature for descriptor matching since the orientation histogram has been readily obtained from the off-the-shelf SIFT descriptor. Therefore, we do not need to pay additional cost to derive the features used for descriptor matching of sub-patches beyond the descriptors of SIFT keypoints.

Actually, to insert a given/fake keypoint from a source image (say, the Pepper image in Fig. 1(f)) with its orientation histogram denoted as h_f into a target image I (say, the Lenna image in Fig. 1(e)), a set $h_{(m,n,s\sigma)}$ of orientation histograms is calculated from scale-space patches $I_s(m-p, n-q)$ for all p and q for histogram matching (coarse matching). Before matching, each orientation histogram is normalized as: $Nh(\alpha) = \frac{h(\alpha)}{\sum_{i=1}^{36} h(i)}$, $1 \leq \alpha \leq 36$. Then, the normalized histograms count the cumulative number of observations in all of the bins from the maximum bin $Nh(\alpha_{Max})$ circularly to the specified bin $Nh(\beta + \alpha_{Max})$.

That is, the cumulative histogram is defined as:

$$Ch(\beta) = \sum_{\alpha=\alpha_{Max}}^{\beta+\alpha_{Max} \bmod 36} Nh(\alpha),\ 1 \leq \beta \leq 36, \tag{22}$$

where β is the index of cumulative histogram Ch. Finally, the similarity between Ch_f, which corresponds to h_f, and $Ch_{(m,n,s\sigma)}$, which is the cumulative version corresponding to $h_{(m,n,s\sigma)}$ of a local patch $I_s(m-p, n-q)$, is defined as the Euclidean distance between them. That is:

$$Sim(Ch_f, Ch_{(m,n,s\sigma)}) = \|Ch_f - Ch_{(m,n,s\sigma)}\|. \tag{23}$$

When $Sim(Ch_f, Ch_{(m,n,s\sigma)})$ between a fake keypoint's histogram and a local patch histogram is smaller than a threshold, the SIFT descriptors of the fake keypoint and the local patch are computed and compared for further fine descriptor matching. If the two descriptors are matched, we insert a fake keypoint into the local patch $I_s(m-p, n-q)$.

6. EXPERIMENTAL RESULTS

Two kinds of experiments were conducted to evaluate the performance of the proposed constraint-optimized scale-space keypoint inhibition attack (KIHA) and fake keypoint insertion attack (KISA). In Sec. 6.1, the keypoint removal rate is adopted as a criterion to evaluate our method. Do *et al.*'s method [2], which figures out the weakness of our previous work [9], was used for comparison here. In Sec. 6.2, we describe a case study on an image copy detection system with a web-scale image database. The aim is to verify whether the proposed keypoint insertion and removal attacks can be an efficient security breach to the real system. More specifically, we combine the proposed keypoint inhibition attack and/or fake keypoint insertion attack with some kinds of geometric attacks (*e.g.*, Stirmark [23]) to build a more efficient attack. In Sec. 6.3, some remarks are given.

6.1 Keypoint Removal Rate

In order to evaluate the proposed keypoint inhibition attack (Algorithm 1), keypoint removal rate (KRR), which is defined as the ratio of the number of removed keypoints over the total number of keypoints, was adopted as the criterion. In KRR, the number of removed keypoints is calculated by subtracting the number of matched keypoints obtained after attacks from the number of original keypoints. In addition, in order not to inhibit keypoint detection arbitrarily, we examine the relationship between image quality (in terms of Peak Signal-to-Noise Ratio (PSNR)) and KRR.

In the experiment, eight 512×512 standard test images, Barbara (I_1), Baboon (I_2), Bridge (I_3), F16 (I_4), Goldhill (I_5), Lena (I_6), Pepper (I_7), and Sailboat (I_8) images were used. For performance comparison with Do *et al.*'s method [2], their method was first adopted to attack these 8 images. In this test, each image was manipulated to yield attacked images with four different PSNRs, which means that there are four different KRRs produced for each image. Then, we purposely controlled the qualities of our attacked images to be nearly equal to those of Do *et al.*'s attacked images for pair comparison. The keypoint removal rates obtained from both methods are shown in Table 1. It can be observed that our constraint-optimized scale-space keypoint inhibition attack can more efficiently remove the keypoints than Do *et al.*'s method.

Table 1: Comparison of Our Method with Do *et al.*'s [2] in terms of KRR vs. PSNR, where $0 \leq KRR \leq 1$.

Image	I_1	I_2	I_3	I_4
PSNR (dB)	48.5	45.3	46.1	49.1
KRR of Do *et al.*'s [2]	0.371	0.312	0.331	0.364
KRR of Our method	0.467	0.382	0.372	0.452
PSNR (dB)	39.6	36.7	36.9	39.7
KRR of Do *et al.*'s [2]	0.491	0.425	0.443	0.471
KRR of Our method	0.552	0.527	0.519	0.569
PSNR (dB)	35.1	31.9	32.5	34.6
KRR of Do *et al.*'s [2]	0.512	0.473	0.462	0.493
KRR of Our method	0.671	0.551	0.573	0.642
PSNR (dB)	30.3	27.7	27.8	29.6
KRR of Do *et al.*'s [2]	0.622	0.505	0.544	0.592
KRR of Our method	0.827	0.670	0.703	0.784
Image	I_5	I_6	I_7	I_8
PSNR (dB)	46.7	48.1	47.6	46.7
KRR of Do *et al.*'s [2]	0.339	0.389	0.377	0.364
KRR of Our method	0.403	0.451	0.422	0.415
PSNR (dB)	37.7	39.1	39.4	38.6
KRR of Do *et al.*'s [2]	0.443	0.477	0.463	0.452
KRR of Our method	0.533	0.582	0.591	0.552
PSNR (dB)	32.0	35.3	34.9	34.1
KRR of Do *et al.*'s [2]	0.473	0.533	0.522	0.533
KRR of Our method	0.582	0.663	0.642	0.654
PSNR (dB)	28.1	29.2	29.1	28.5
KRR of Do *et al.*'s [2]	0.523	0.606	0.592	0.584
KRR of Our method	0.692	0.797	0.771	0.812

6.2 Security Threat to Image Copy Detection System: A Case Study

Our proposed keypoint removal/insertion attacks were evaluated using a web-scale image database, which is composed of 1,000,000 Flickr images (MIRFLICKR-1M) that are very diverse in content. We examine the security threat to the image copy detection system in [8]. Three different attacks were adopted to evaluate the retrieval rate of image copy detection. Again, 8 standard images used in the previous subsection were also adopted here. Three query sets were generated and used for evaluation. First, each test image was manipulated by 40 attacks defined in the Stirmark benchmarks [23] (*e.g.*, signal processing and geometric attacks) to generate, in total, 320 images, which were used as the queries to the image copy detection system [8]. The first set was labeled as Stirmark Attacked (SA) queries. Second, the SA queries were further manipulated by the keypoint inhibition attack (KIHA), described in Sec. 4, to generate the second set of queries, which was labeled as (SA+KIHA). Finally, the set of (SA+KIHA) queries were manipulated using the keypoint insertion attack (KISA), described in Sec. 5, to generate the third set of queries, which was labeled as (SA+KIHA+KISA). An example of attacked images from the three sets of queries is shown in Fig. 2 for visual inspection. Although some salt-and-pepper noises can still be perceived in Figs. 2(c) and (d), the image quality is still perceptually kept better than most of the Stirmark attacks [21, 23] widely employed in multimedia security applications.

The three sets of attacked images, composed of 960 query images, were used as the queries to the web-scale database image copy detection system [8]. When the image having rank 1 in the list of retrieval results is the original corresponding to the query, then the system succeeds; otherwise it fails. The ratio of the number of successful retrieval to total number of queries is defined as the retrieval rate, which is used as the metric for performance evaluation of our attacks. From the viewpoint of our security threat to an image copy detection, the lower, the better. The retrieval rates of the three sets of queries with respect to the 8 images were shown in Table 2. We have the following observations. (i) A single (Stirmark [23]) attack may not be able to remove the keypoints so as to make an image copy detection system fail. (ii) When the proposed keypoint inhibition attack (KIHA) is further imposed and incorporated with SA, the retrieval rate is apparently reduced. (iii) If the proposed keypoint insertion attack (KISA) is adopted, the overall retrieval rate is remarkably reduced. The experimental results reveal that both the proposed KIHA and KISA are efficient as the security threats to multimedia security applications that depend on scale-space feature extraction.

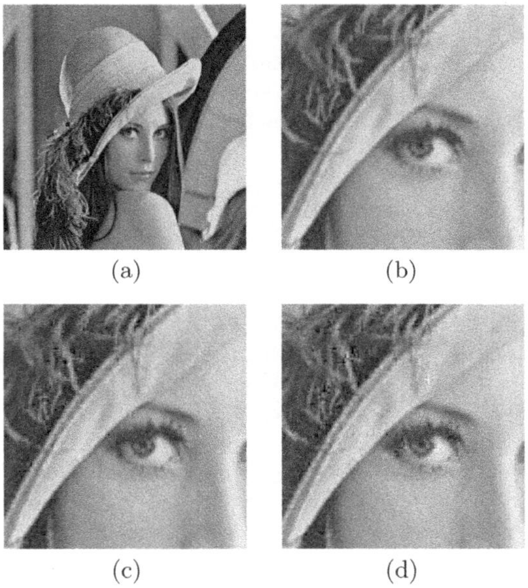

Figure 2: Attacked images: (a) Original Lenna; (b) Stirmark attack (SA); (c) SA+KIHA (PSNR: 33.24dB)(d) SA+KIHA+KISA (PSNR: 30.67dB).

Table 2: Security threat to a web-scale image copy detection system [8] in terms of retrieval rate.

Image	SA	SA+KIHA	SA+KIHA+KISA
I_1	0.7	0.5	0.225
I_2	0.525	0.35	0.225
I_3	0.575	0.375	0.2
I_4	0.65	0.5	0.25
I_5	0.6	0.425	0.25
I_6	0.675	0.525	0.3
I_7	0.725	0.525	0.275
I_8	0.625	0.375	0.225

We further conducted an experiment similar to Table 2 but with a larger set of query images. We randomly selected 100 test images from Flickr images (MIRFLICKR-1M) and each image again was manipulated by 40 Stirmark attacks to generate in total 4000 Stirmark attacked images. Similar to the experiments conducted previously three query sets of SA, SA+KIHA, and SA+KIHA+KISA were used as the queries to the image copy detection system in [8]. Due to the use of large query images (12,000), the average copy detection results, instead of the one tabulated in Table 2, are reported here. The average retrieval rate for the first query set SA is 0.67. When the second query set SA+KIHA was used, the average retrieval rate, however, is reduced to 0.40. Finally, the average retrieval rate is reduced to 0.18 if the third query set SA+KIHA+KISA was used. We can observe that the results for a larger set of query images are still comparable to those in Table 2.

6.3 Remarks

6.3.1 ST-SSIFE vs. Data Hiding

The proposed security threat to scale-space image feature extraction (ST-SSIFE) methods aims at removing or inserting keypoints of images at the expense of degrading image quality. In fact, Eq. (6) and Eq. (21) can also be interpreted as a kind of data hiding mechanism [18] but with different purposes. In our earlier work [18], we employed the same idea of changing the scale-space features for embedding information in an image. It is known in the context of data hiding that modifying low-frequency features will violate the human visual model and bring obvious perceptual distortions. That is why we keep a portion of the keypoints intact. Moreover, we also investigated in [19] a scale-space image signature method for image authentication purposes. Our results again show that lower-frequency features preserve image content well and are difficult to be manipulated without causing perceptual distortions.

Therefore, it is better to understand that removing all keypoints is not permitted practically and in certain cases a single keypoint inhibition attack (like the one proposed in this paper) cannot guarantee to entirely defeat scale-space feature extraction techniques.

6.3.2 Lesson Learnt from ST-SSIFE

Another case study about security threat to feature-based image watermarking is briefly summarized as follows. As our previous work [21] indicated, the stability of feature point extraction mainly affects the overall performance of a feature-based watermarking method. More specifically, feature shift (less than 4 pixels) essentially degrades watermark detection performance. When some prior knowledge, like the one presented in this paper, is employed to remove the original or insert the fake keypoints, the created instability for detected features greatly impacts on the watermarking performance. Our results show that the keypoint inhibition attack acts like a non-blind attack and is found to degrade watermark detection very efficiently (better than [21]).

Based on the above results, we learn that watermarking performance can be possibly improved if keypoints are enhanced before watermark embedding is conducted. Keypoint enhancement means that a keypoint is not just a local extremum but can be properly modified to strengthen its existence by the similar constraint-optimization formulation investigated in this paper. We plan to further study this interesting but unexplored issue in the future.

7. CONCLUSIONS

We first noted the security threat to scale-space feature extraction-based multimedia security applications in [9]. In order to remedy its insufficiency, we study constrained optimization based keypoint inhibition/insertion attacks as the guaranteed security threat to those applications and systems that exploit scale-space feature extraction. In order to properly leverage the computation complexity and keypoint removal efficiency, we further develop a hybrid method of incorporating both Lagrange multiplier-based and KKT-based optimized attacks. We also study a keypoint insertion attack exploiting the similar principle of keypoint inhibition attack in order to create the false positive problem.

Two issues are worthy of further studying. First, the creation of two equal local extrema, as shown in Eq. (6), may be included into our framework of constraint-optimized security threat for possible distortion reduction. Second, the mechanism for insertion of fake keypoints, as described in Sec. 5, should further take consistent keypoint matching into consideration because a (forged) matching may be simply an outlier.

8. ACKNOWLEDGMENTS

This work was supported by National Science Council, Taiwan, under grants NSC 100-2631-H-001-013 and NSC 101-2631-H-001-007.

9. REFERENCES

[1] H. Bay, A. Ess, T. Tuytelaars, and L.-V. Gool, "SURF: Speeded Up Robust Features," *Computer Vision and Image Understanding (CVIU)*, Vol. 110, No. 3, pp. 346-359, 2008.

[2] T. T. Do, E. Kijak, T. Furon, and L. Amsaleg, "Deluding image recognition in SIFT-based CBIR systems," *ACM workshop on Multimedia in Forensics, Security and Intelligence at ACM MM*, pp. 7-12, 2010.

[3] T. T. Do, E. Kijak, T. Furon, and L. Amsaleg, "Understanding the security and robustness of SIFT," *ACM MM*, pp. 1195-1198, 2010.

[4] T. T. Do, E. Kijak, L. Amsaleg, and T. Furon, "Enlarging Hacker's Toolbox: Deluding Image recognition by Attacking Keypoint Orientations," *IEEE ICASSP*, 2012.

[5] J. J. Foo, J. Zobel, R. Sinha, and S. Tahaghoghi, "Detection of Near-duplicate Images for Web Search," *6th ACM Int. Conf. on Image and Video Retrieval (CIVR)*, pp. 557-564, 2007.

[6] J. J. Foo and R. Sinha, "Pruning SIFT for Scalable Near-Duplicate Image Matching," *Proc. the Eighteenth Conf. on Australasian Database*, pp. 63-71, 2007.

[7] X. Gao, C. Deng, X. Li, and D. Tao, "Geometric Distortion Insensitive Image Watermarking in Affine Covariant Regions," *IEEE Trans. on Systems, Man, and Cybernetics, Part C: Applications and Reviews*, Vol. 40, No. 3, pp. 278-286, 2010.

[8] K. Grauman and T. Darrell, "Efficient Image Matching with Distributions of Local Invariant Features," *IEEE CVPR*, Vol. 2, pp. 627-634, 2005.

[9] C.-Y. Hsu, C.-S. Lu, and S.-C. Pei, "Secure and robust SIFT," *ACM MM*, pp. 637-640, Beijing, China, Oct. 19-24, 2009.

[10] L.-W. Kang, C.-Y. Hsu, H.-W. Chen, C.-S. Lu, C.-Y. Lin, and S.-C. Pei, "Feature-based Sparse Representation for Image Similarity Assessment," *IEEE Trans. on Multimedia*, Vol. 13, No. 5, pp. 1019-1030, 2011.

[11] Y. Ke, R. Sukthankar, and L. Huston, "Efficient Near-duplicate and Sub-image Retrieval," *ACM MM*, pp. 869-876, 2004.

[12] E. Kijak, T. Furon, and L. Amsaleg, "Challenging the Security of CBIR System," Research Report RR-7153, INRIA, 2009.

[13] W. Karush, "Minima of Functions of Several Variables with Inequalities as Side Constraints," *M.Sc. Thesis*, Dept. of Mathematics, Univ. of Chicago, 1939.

[14] J. Krizaj, V. Struc, and N. Pavesic, "Adaptation of SIFT Features for Robust Face Recognition," *Proc. Int. Conf. on Image Analysis and Recognition*, LNCS 6111, pp. 394-404, 2010.

[15] H. W. Kuhn and A. W. Tucker, "Nonlinear programming," *Proceedings of 2nd Berkeley Symposium*, Berkeley: University of California Press, pp. 481-492, 1951.

[16] H. Ling, H. Cheng, Q. Ma, F. Zou, and W.-Q. Yan, "Efficient Image Copy Detection Using Multiscale Fingerprints,", *IEEE Multimedia Magazine*, Vol. 19, No. 1, pp. 60-69, 2012.

[17] D. Lowe, "Distinctive image features from scale invariant keypoints," *International Journal of Computer Vision*, Vol. 60, pp. 91-110, 2004.

[18] C.-S. Lu, "Wireless Multimedia Error Resilience via A Data Hiding Technique," *IEEE MMSP*, 2002.

[19] C.-S. Lu and H.-Y. Mark Liao, "Structural Digital Signature for Image Authentication: An Incidental Distortion Resistant Scheme," *IEEE Trans. on Multimedia*, Vol. 5, No. 2, pp. 161-173, 2003.

[20] C.-S. Lu and C.-Y. Hsu, "Geometric Distortion-Resilient Image Hashing Scheme and Its Applications on Copy Detection and Authentication," *ACM Multimedia Systems Journal*, special issue on Multimedia and Security, Vol. 11, No. 2, pp. 159-173, 2005.

[21] C.-S. Lu, S.-W. Sun, C.-Y. Hsu, and P.-C. Chang, "Media Hash-dependent Image Watermarking Resilient Against Both Geometric Attacks and Estimation Attacks Based on False Positive-Oriented Detection," *IEEE Trans. on Multimedia*, Vol. 8, No. 4, pp. 668-685, 2006.

[22] U. Park, S. Pankanti, and A. K. Jain, "Fingerprint Verification Using SIFT Features," *Proc. SPIE Defense and Security Symposium*, Vol. 6944, 2008.

[23] F. Petitcolas, R. J. Anderson, and M. G. Kuhn, "Attacks on Copyright Marking Systems," *Int. Workshop on Information Hiding*, LNCS 1575, pp. 219-239, 1998.

[24] Z. Ye, X. Chen, and Z. Li, "Video Based Mobile Location Search with Large Set of SIFT Points in Cloud," *MCMC Workshop at ACM Multimedia Conference*, pp. 25-30, 2010.

[25] J. Zhu, S. Hoi, M. R. Lyu, and S. Yan, "Near-Duplicate Keyframe Retrieval by Nonrigid Image Matching," *ACM MM*, pp. 41-50, 2008.

Mining In-Class Social Networks for Large-Scale Pedagogical Analysis

Xiao-Yong Wei
Machine Intelligence Laboratory
College of Computer Science
Sichuan University
610065, Chengdu, China
cswei@scu.edu.cn

Zhen-Qun Yang
Machine Intelligence Laboratory
College of Computer Science
Sichuan University
610065, Chengdu, China
jessicayang@scu.edu.cn

ABSTRACT

Modeling the in-class student social networks is a highly desired goal in educational literature. However, due to the difficulty to collect social data, most of the conventional studies can only be conducted in a qualitative way on a small-scale of dataset obtained through questionnaires or interviews. We propose to solve the problems of data collection, social network construction and analysis with multimedia technology, in the way that we can automatically recognize the positions and identities of the students in classroom and construct the in-class social networks accordingly. With the social networks and the statistics on a large-scale dataset, we have demonstrated that the pedagogical analysis for investigating the co-learning patterns among the students can be conducted in a quantitative way, which provides the statistical clues about why prior studies reach conflicting conclusions on the relation between the students' positions in social networks and their academic performances. The experimental results have validated the effectiveness of the proposed approaches in both technical and pedagogical senses.

Categories and Subject Descriptors

J.4 [**Computer Applications**]: Social and Behavioral Sciences

General Terms

Algorithms, Experimentation, Human Factors, Verification

Keywords

In-Class Social Networks, Pedagogical Analysis

1. INTRODUCTION

In educational literature, social interactions among learners is of great importance, for its effectiveness to promote the learning process by facilitating learner-to-learner co-construction of knowledge and the sharing of information and resources [1–5]. Therefore, a large amount of effort has been carried out to identify and investigate the social networks in which the learners are involved, in the hope of designing proper pedagogical strategies accordingly. However, even the proposal of the idea may date back to 1930s [1,6], most of the investigations are still limited in a small scale which usually include less than 100 students (e.g., 25 students in [5], 11 students in [7]), due to the fact that the traditional way for collecting social data through questionnaires and interviews is time-consuming and expensive. The rapid development of online technologies seems to be a new opportunity to address this problem for its promise to collect the immense social data in an automatic manner. In this regard, online social network analysis has led to tremendous emerging researches in various disciplines such as sociology, pedagogy, psychology, and computer science.

In contrast with the overwhelming interest among practitioners, as commented by Boyd & Ellison [8], the majority of existing studies on online social networks still remain both conceptual and empirical, with a few of them having explored the link between social networks and education. Furthermore, researches along this line mainly focus on the "out-of-school" or "after-school" social practices of students within the "virtual" networking environment (e.g., [7,9,10]), where they may not behave naturally [8,9]. By contrast, the study on the students' social learning patterns in their "real-life" at school has not been sufficiently conducted, although it is highly desired even before the birth of the term "social network" (by Jacob Moreno's work in 1930s). This is again due to the difficulty for obtaining social data from the real-life educational environment. Moreover, most existing educational researches have been conducted using "qualitative" analysis which samples a small-scale of students from the whole population for case studies [11]. It is thus easy to cause conflicting conclusions when the sampling are not representative in a statistical sense, e.g., Divjak *et al.* have reported in [12] that there is no relation between a student's position in student social network and her/his academic performance, while most of other researchers believe the existence of the relation [3,4].

In this paper, we conduct a pilot study aiming to equip conventional pedagogical analysis with multimedia technology, for *automatic* and *large-scale* in-class social data collection and analysis. We first propose a novel image-based method to identify the in-class social networks which encapsulates both the student-to-student and student-to-teacher interaction-ships, on the basis of which we investigate their relations to the students' academic performances. The method can be easily applied to real-life classroom environment.

The framework of our method for in-class social network mining is shown in Figure 1, which consists of three parts:

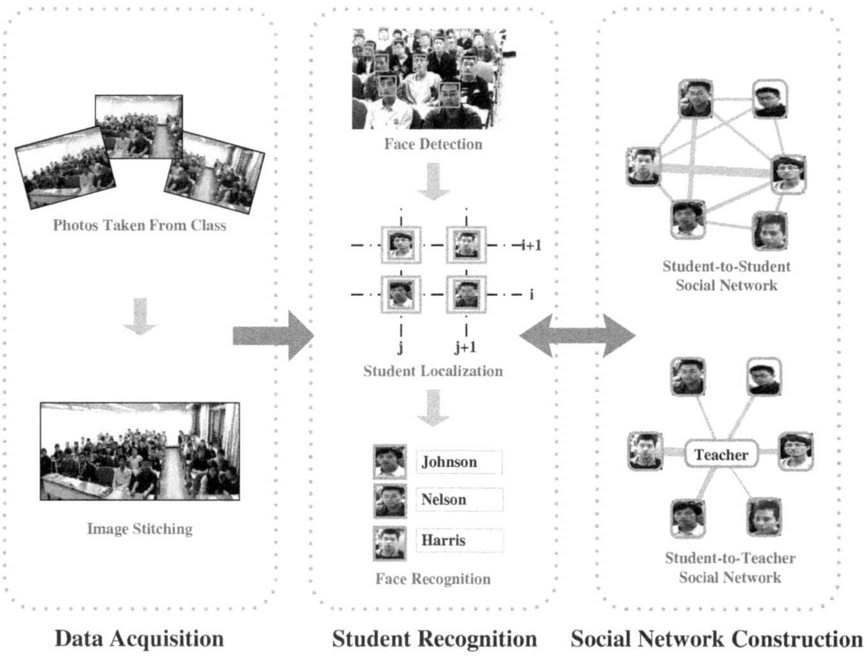

Figure 1: Framework of In-Class Social Network Mining[1].

data acquisition, student recognition, and social network construction. In data acquisition, a teacher takes a set of photos of the students in the class and the photos are combined into a single image using image stitching algorithm [13]. The faces in the image are then detected with their positions (i.e., row and column numbers in the classroom) identified by the student localization algorithm, on the basis of which face recognition is employed to identify the names of the students. In each course under investigation, we leave 9-13 weeks for the students to form teams for the course project, so as to encourage them to choose to sit and discuss with potential teammates. Therefore, at the end of the semester, the statistics on how each student sits together with her/his peers for co-learning and her/his preference of the sitting position can be obtained, for constructing the student-to-student and student-to-teacher social networks respectively. In the framework, the student recognition and the social network construction are two interdependent parts, in the way that the social network construction needs the information about the students' identities and their sitting positions, and the performance of face recognition can be improved if the social interaction-ship among students are known a priori. Therefore, we dynamically update the social networks after each class and the result will be used to help face recognition in the classes followed. There are several technical challenges which have been addressed in this framework, including

- *Face Recognition in Extreme Conditions*: Face recognition has been intensively studied for over four decades since 1970s [14] and still remains an active research topic nowadays. However, its performance is often limited when applied to real applications, due to the variations of illuminations, poses, facial expressions, motions, occlusions, and so on [15–17]. In additional to all these issues, as shown in Figure 2, we meet an even worse situation when applying face recognition to the photos captured in classroom, in the way that the faces are with various sizes and resolutions, sometimes being distorted seriously, and possibly with the majority of facial areas missing. According to our study, this makes most of the state-of-the-art face recognition approaches work awkwardly, because nearly all of them are developed on datasets that are acquired in well-controlled environments [16, 18]. We argue that conventional approaches mainly focus on the facial area of a person, ignoring the fact that the target's social context (e.g., the potential teammates he/she often sits with) is of great help to the identification process. To address this problem, we propose a *social inference scheme* which recognizes a student with the respect to the identifications of her/his socially related peers (learnt from the in-class social network), with the hope that, when the student's appearance in current photo is not visually distinguishable, her/his identity can still be inferred when her/his potential teammates are recognized at the neighboring seats;

- *Large-Scale Labeling Efforts*: Like all supervised learning approaches, before applying face recognition, we need to annotate a large scale of samples for training, which, in general, is costly. We bypass the difficulty by encouraging the students to label their faces by themselves. In particular, an "attendance checking" function for fun is embedded into all course homepages, which allows teachers to upload the photos and automatically stich the photos into a single one, on which the students (after login for downloading course materials) can tick their faces to confirm their attendances (if there are no machine-predicted labels available for their faces) or just to correct (if the predictions are wrong). The attendance records not only leave a good reference to the pedagogical analysis, but also accomplish the labeling at the same time. Fur-

[1]All portraits in this paper are used with the consents from the students.

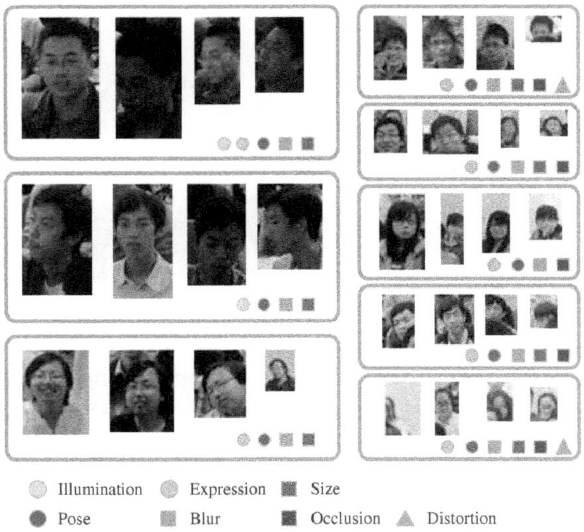

Figure 2: Challenges for face detection/recognition in an uncontrolled environment.

thermore, the function itself is used for case-study in several courses related to Image Processing, Pattern Recognition, Data Mining, or Multimedia Computing. It has significantly boosted the students' interest;

- *Sitting Position Identification*: Detecting where a student sits in the classroom from the 2D image is not a trivial task, as the sitting heights of the students are diverse and it is impossible to obtain in advance. Moreover, the stitched images are with highly inconsistent view points and are often seriously distorted. We propose to use linear regression to model the seat arrangements in the classroom so as to estimate the positions of students and construct the in-class social networks. The details will be given in Section 3.2.

The contributions of this paper can be summarized as: the integration of multimedia technology into pedagogical analysis, the proposal of a practical approach for large-scale in-class social network construction, and the introduction of the social inference scheme into face recognition for working in extreme conditions.

2. RELATED WORK

The topic of this paper is related to several disciplines which may include social science, educational research, data mining, computer vision and computer graphics. Due to the highly interdisciplinary nature and the space limitation, we can only provide a brief review with the effort to cover the related studies to the largest extent.

It has been widely believed that social learning or community-centered learning within social networks has positive influence on a student's academic success [1–5]. Although the belief may have a much longer history than that of its formal proposal in 1930s [1, 6], however, due to the lack of large-scale data for social network modeling and quantitative validation, it has remained conceptual until the emergence of online social network sites (SNSs, e.g., Facebook, MySpace). SNSs provide not only a way to attract the students' participation, but also a tool to collect social data during the online communications (e.g., interaction-ship to their peers, material/information exchanged) , which in turn initiates a large amount of emerging researches for sociology, pedagogy, psychology, and computer science [8]. With the help of SNSs, educational researchers have conducted intensive studies to explore the relation between the students' academic performances and the social communities they are involved, with many positive results reported (e.g., researches by Ellison *et al.* [19] conducted on Facebook and Kraut *et al.* on general Internet communities [20]). However, despite the disagreements which also appear all the time, as stated by Boyd & Ellison [8], most of these studies are still conceptual and empirical in nature. Furthermore, many researchers (e.g., Walter *et al.* [21] and Boyd & Ellison [8]) have realized that the social interaction-ship revealed from the virtual network environment is significantly different from that of face-to-face communications in the students' real life. Therefore, most of SNSs proponents can only claim a "complementary" role for their findings to the traditional pedagogical analysis.

In contrast to the studies for the "out-of-school" SNSs, modeling the students' social interactions in "in-class" environment is always highly desired [22, 23], as it is one of the essentials of our pedagogical system. Due to the difficulty of collecting social data again, there are a few studies that have investigated the relation between the students' academic performance and their "in-school" social interactions. Examples along this direction include [12] which has investigated the relation in two social networks (of "teamwork" and "material exchanging"), and [5] which conducts a similar investigation within a social network constructed from social connections (e.g., friendship, collaboration-ship) reported by students. In these studies, social network analysis [24] is employed to measure the different types of networking positions, such as *betweenness*, *closeness*, and *degree* (which we will introduce in Section 4), for discovering the social ties or social capital (the leadership or controllership) in the communities. However, the data collecting process in these studies are still following the conventional fashion of questionnaires and interviews, resulting in none of them having directly constructed an "in-class" social network. Moveover, these investigations are still in a small-scale (e.g., 27-52 students in [12], 25 students in [5]), making the results not convincing enough in a statistical sense.

While the studies mentioned above are mainly focusing on the student-to-student social connections, the student-to-teacher interaction-ship have also attracted a lot of research attentions (e.g., [22, 25–28]), given the fact that most of our pedagogical systems are teacher-centered. These studies are mainly conducted by investigating the influence of seat arrangement in a teacher-centered classroom on the students' performances, in the sense that students sitting at different positions can have different chances to receive instructions from or to interact with the teacher, which determines their achievement at the end of the semester. The data of these studies are usually collected by fixing the students' sitting positions so as to investigate the effect of the arrangement on the students' academic performances [27, 28]. Even with evidential correlation between seat arraignment and academic performance reported, these studies are all conducted in a qualitative way, which cannot quantitatively answer questions like: how far (the exact distance) the student sitting from the teacher would be an advantage/disadvantage? Furthermore, the method for collecting data is questionable, because forcing a student to sit in a fixed position can distort her/his natural behaviors during learning.

In this paper, we propose to address the social data collecting problem with multimedia technology, with the hope that the social data can be collected in an automatic manner, and the in-class networks can be captured in a natural way (the students are allowed to choose where to sit freely). The method will not bias the students' social preferences and is applicable to large-scale investigation at the same time. Technically speaking, our methods for student localization and recognition are related to techniques of image stitching/alignment [13] and face recognition [15–17] respectively.

Image stitching is developed to compose images with varying degrees of overlap into a single one for providing a wider view of the target. To this end, nearly all approaches utilize the assumption that one image is the result of a linear transformation from another image within the Homogeneous Coordinate System, which can be modeled by a transformation matrix. Therefore, once the matrix is learnt, we can transform one image back to the same plane where another image lies in (this has been sophisticatedly developed in Computer Graphics) so as to compose the two image into a single one. The transformation matrix is learnt by finding correspondence between points in the overlapping areas of two images. Various features have been proposed for detecting the correspondence (matching points) [13], among which the Scale Invariant Feature Transform (SIFT) by Lowe's [29] is considered one of the state-of-the-art. We adopt the same feature in this study. Due to space limitation, the reader is referred to [29] for more details.

Face recognition is one of the most intensively studied technologies in computer vision, with new approaches emerging every year and encouraging results reported. According to recent survives [15–17], however, most existing studies are conducted on data captured in controlled environment. It makes the successes of those approaches limited to real applications, where the variations of illuminations, poses, facial expressions, motions, occlusions and so on always raise big challenges for both face detection and recognition. As most of those challenges are still considered as open questions, generally, there is no conclusion on which approach(es) can perform the best. Nevertheless, there are some approaches are more popularly employed than others. For example, the Viola-Jones detector [30] is considered the start-of-the-art for face detection in a survey [17] mainly written for Viola-Jones detector and its variations. For face recognition, the methods using Eignfaces [31], Fisherfaces [32] and Sparse Coding [33] are popularly adopted as baselines. In this paper, our aim is not to solve the open questions of face recognition in a general sense, but instead to bypass those difficulties in a classroom sitting with the help of the contextual information obtained from the in-class social networks. Since in our framework the student recognition and the construction of the in-class social networks are two interdependent processes, we will introduce the recognition first and then turn to social network construction.

3. STUDENT RECOGNITION

To stitch multiple photos, we adopt the method proposed in [10], which automatically find the matching points between two photos using SIFT features, and compose them into a single image accordingly. The resulting image will be used for face detection, student localization and recognition.

3.1 Face Detection

We detect the faces in the stitched image mainly using the Viola-Jones detector [30] which is considered the state-of-the-art in a recent survey [17] and has been implemented in OpenCV. However, due to the difficulties introduced in Section 1 and the fact that the OpenCV implementation is mainly trained on frontal faces, it can only detect 78% of the faces in our experiment. To deal with this problem, we implement the simple skin-color based detector [34] and pool the results from both detectors. The teachers will help to filter out the non-facial areas (less than 3% of those in the pool) with tiny effort before the student localization and recognition being carried out.

Figure 3: Student localization by linear regression and image alignment ($\frac{a|b}{c|d}$): (a) faces in the stitched image for the first class (the source image) are manually associated to row and column numbers, on the basis of which a line indicator (yellow line) is trained for each row or column using linear regression; (b) the matching points between a newly taken image (the target image) and the source image are detected (as connected with green lines); (c) the source image is aligned to the target with all line indicators being transformed; (d) RANSAC algorithm is applied on each transformed line indicator to obtain its new model in the target.

3.2 Student Localization

Prior to face recognition, we detect where (i.e., row and column numbers) each student sits in the classroom. There are mainly two difficulties, namely the diversity of the students' sitting heights and the inconsistency of view-points across the stitched images. To tackle the first issue, we manually annotate the row and column numbers of each student in the image taken in the first class (call source image hereafter), and use linear regression for the centers of faces appearing at the same row (column). As shown in the upper-left of Figure 3, the result is a line (the yellow ones) for each row (column) indicating the places where the face centers will likely to appear, so that, under the assumption that all the lines can be correctly detected in a newly taken image (call target image hereafter), we can assign a face to the nearest line(s) to identify its row (column) number(s). To detect the lines in the target image, we use the method [29] again (which we employ for image stitching) to find matching points between the source and target images (see the green lines from the upper-left to upper-right in Figure 3), and to calculate the coordinate transformation matrix, on the basis of which we transform the source image into the coordinate plane of the target (as shown in the bottom-left of Figure 3). This process is called image alignment in literature [13], which also transforms each row (column) indicator (i.e., line) into the target coordinate plane, so that we can

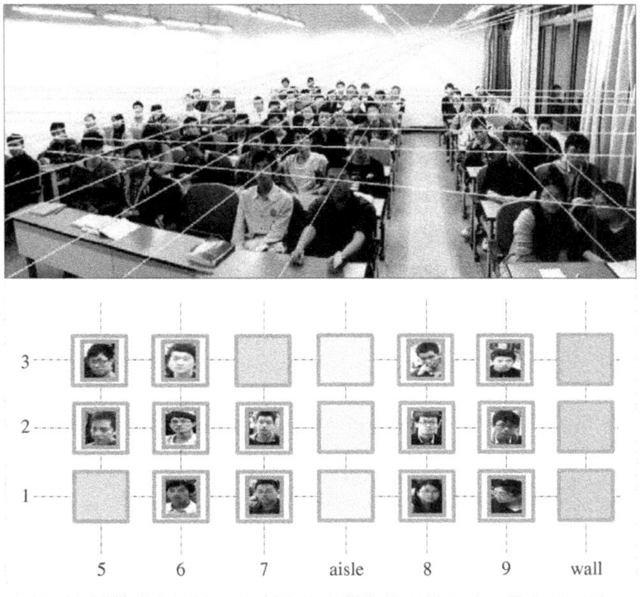

Figure 4: Result of student localization and a partial view of the face graph $\mathcal{G}$.

use Random Sample Consensus (RANSAC) [35] to find the regression model for each of the transformed row (column) indicator and then apply to the target image. To avoid being biased by noises or outliers when using all points for regression, RANSAC automatically searches a set of points which can represent the distribution of the majority of the data, so that, in our case, using RANSAC for regression can filter out the points lying in the distorted parts of each transformed row (column) indicator (see the bottom-left of Figure 3). The result of RANSAC is shown in the bottom-right of Figure 3. Since the image alignment is a comparably matured technique, we skip the details here for space limitation. The reader is referred to [29] for more details. Note that the alignment has solved the inconsistency issue of view-points at the same time. As shown in Figure 4, the result of student localization can be represented as a face graph $\mathcal{G}$ for further analysis, where three types of extra nodes, i.e., the "empty seats", "aisle" and "wall", are automatically added for providing more precise neighboring information. To traverse the face graph conveniently, we define a function $\mathcal{N}(\boldsymbol{x})$ on $\mathcal{G}$, which returns a set of faces that are the neighbors for any given $\boldsymbol{x}$ within an 8-neighbor system.

3.3 Face Recognition within A Social Context

Our scheme for recognizing the identities of students include two stages: a *local classification* stage which recognizes each student individually by only considering her/his visual features, and a *social inference* stage which infers the identity of a student regarding to those of her/his neighbors in current classroom, with the hope that further considering the social context of a student can help improve the performance of weak classifiers in the local stage. This can be formulated as an iterative process as

$$\boldsymbol{p}^{(i+1)}(\boldsymbol{x}) = \lambda\, Social^{(i)}(\boldsymbol{x}) + (1-\lambda)\, Local(\boldsymbol{x}) \qquad (1)$$

where the superscript $(i+1)$ indicates the iteration number, $\boldsymbol{x}$ represents an observation of a face, $\boldsymbol{p}^{(i+1)}(\boldsymbol{x})$ is a vector encapsulating a posterior probability distribution $p(l_k|\boldsymbol{x})$ at the $(i+1)$-th iteration over a set of identity labels (e.g., names, student IDs) $\mathcal{L} = \{l_k\}_{k=0}^{|\mathcal{L}|}$, $Local(.)$ and $Social(.)$ are functions for local classification and social inference respectively, and $\lambda \in [0,1]$ is a factor to control speed of converging and to balance the influence of the two functions at the same time. The process will converge when $\|\boldsymbol{p}^{(i+1)}(\boldsymbol{x}) - \boldsymbol{p}^{(i)}(\boldsymbol{x})\| \rightarrow 0$. There are two strategies which have been considered to utilize the social context of $\boldsymbol{x}$ for improving student recognition. First, the process iteratively fuses the result of social inference into that of the local classification, so that the classification results of the weak local classifiers can be improved through collaborative learning with the neighboring classifiers. Second, the process will be performed on the face graph $\mathcal{G}$ (see Figure 4) which defines the neighboring interaction-ship. This enables the effort of collaboration to be propagated to the whole classroom, with the hope that, once the process converges, the identity labels assigned to faces are the most consistent one to both the neighboring interaction-ship in the face graph and the social context encapsulated in the social network. In the rest of this section, we describe our methods for implementing the local classification and social inference functions.

3.3.1 Local Classification Function $Local(.)$

The local classification can be implemented by employing any state-of-the-art face recognition approach developed in Computer Vision. In our case, we choose the one proposed by Wright *et al.* [33], which picks several sample images from each student to compose a dictionary, and represents each instance $\boldsymbol{x}$ as a linear combination of the samples in the dictionary by associating each sample with a coefficient through Sparse Coding. This results in a set of coefficients with a minimized number of non-zero entities assigned to the samples that are most similar to $\boldsymbol{x}$. Therefore, we can calculate the posterior probability that $\boldsymbol{x}$ is from a given student by accumulating the coefficients of her/his sample images. By repeating this for all the students, the output of $Local(.)$ is a vector $\boldsymbol{q}(\boldsymbol{x})$ which encapsulates another posterior probability distribution $q(l_k|\boldsymbol{x})$ over $\mathcal{L}$.

3.3.2 Social Inference Function $Social(.)$

To utilize the in-class social context for student recognition, a basic belief is that a student would likely to appear if her/his potential teammates appear at the neighboring seats. Let us temporarily assume this co-occurrence can be learnt form the in-class student-to-student social network (the details of the network construction will be given later in Section 4). The interaction-ship of any label pair (l_k, l_n) can thus be represented as a conditional probability $\pi(l_k|l_n)$ indicating how likely l_k will be observed when l_n appear at its neighboring seats. The pair-wise interaction-ship can be encapsulated into a matrix $\mathbf{R}_{|\mathcal{L}|\times|\mathcal{L}|}$ where each entity equals to $\mathbf{R}_{k,n} = \pi(l_k|l_n)$. The social inference function is then implemented as

$$Social^{(i)}(\boldsymbol{x}) = \frac{1}{|\mathcal{N}(\boldsymbol{x})|} \sum_{\boldsymbol{y}\in\mathcal{N}(\boldsymbol{x})} \mathbf{R}\cdot \boldsymbol{p}^{(i)}(\boldsymbol{y}) \qquad (2)$$

where $\mathcal{N}(\boldsymbol{x})$ is the neighboring function we define in Section 3.2. Eq. (2) is intuitively a function which summarizes the recognition results of $\boldsymbol{x}$'s neighbor nodes on $\mathcal{G}$. Later in Eq. (1), the summarized result will be iteratively prorogated to $\boldsymbol{x}$ after fusing with the output of $Local(.)$.

It is worth mentioning that this iterative recognition scheme might be closely related to the Random Walk Model, and also possible to be extended to Markov Random Field or Conditional Random Field. To keep this pilot study as simple/straightforward as possible, we leave these for future investigation.

Once the iteration is converged, we can obtain a vector $\hat{\boldsymbol{p}}(\boldsymbol{x})$ for each face, indicating its identity potentials over the label set $\mathcal{L}$. Now we need to make a decision by assigning $\boldsymbol{x}$ to a determined identity label, which can be represented as an unit vector $\boldsymbol{e}$ over the label set $\mathcal{L}$. The components of $\boldsymbol{e}$ are all zeros excepting the k-th one, indicating the assignment of $\boldsymbol{x}$ to the k-th label in $\mathcal{L}$. The rationality of the assignment can then be measured by the inner product $< \hat{\boldsymbol{p}}(\boldsymbol{x}), \boldsymbol{e} >$, on the basis of which we can use Dynamic Programming to maximize the sum of rationalities of all faces, and therefore complete the recognition process.

4. SOCIAL NETWORK CONSTRUCTION AND PEDAGOGICAL ANALYSIS

In this section, we construct two in-class social networks, namely the student-to-student and student-to-teacher networks respectively, on the basis of which we perform pedagogical analysis following some of the educational literature (e.g., [5,12,22,25–28], where the analysis are conventionally conducted by questionnaires/interviews).

4.1 Student-to-Student Social Network

With the positions and identities recognized in last section, the construction of student-to-student network can be performed by using students as vertexes and connecting two vertexes according to the frequency (or co-occurrence) of the corresponding students sitting in neighboring seats (i.e., the joint probability $\pi(l_k, l_n)$). We also record the frequency of the attendance for each vertex as it can be used as the prior probability for each label (i.e., $\pi(l_k)$). This will make the calculations of $\pi(l_k|l_n)$ and $\pi(l_n|l_k)$ in Section 3.3 be easily carried out using Bayes' formula. Note that, for the first class, when the position indicators and the face detectors have not been trained yet, these probabilities are calculated from the results of manual annotation (i.e., positions identified by teachers and labels provided by the students during attendance checking).

Following the main stream of pedagogical studies using social network analysis (SNA) [24], to measure the "sense of community" of each student, we calculate the *betweenness*, *closeness* and *degree* (which are commonly adopted measures in educational research, e.g., [5, 12]) for each vertex in the student-to-student social network. Linear regression analysis can then be applied on these measures to investigate their relation to students' performance (the final grades).

Let us denote $\mathcal{V}$ the set of vertexes in the network. The *betweenness* (usually called *betweenness centrality* in literature) is defined as

$$Betweenness(v) = \sum_{s \neq v \neq t,\ s,v,t \in \mathcal{V}} \frac{g_{st}(v)}{g_{st}} \tag{3}$$

where g_{st} is the number of shortest paths from $s \in \mathcal{V}$ to $t \in \mathcal{V}$, and $g_{st}(v)$ is the number of shortest paths from s to t that $v \in \mathcal{V}$ lies in. In SNA theory, the *betweenness* measures a student's connectivity by further considering the "neighbors" she/he is indirectly connected with, which gives a higher value to those bridging social groups. A "between" student is the cutpoint in the shortest path connecting two other students, and thus might control the flow of information/resource exchange. The larger *betweenness* a student has, the higher centrality she/he is in the community.

The *closeness* is measured by

$$Closeness(v) = \left[\sum_{v \neq t,\ v,t \in \mathcal{V}} d(v,t) \right]^{-1} \tag{4}$$

where $d(v,t) = d(t,v)$ is the shortest distance (called *geodesic distance* in SNA) between two vertexes $v \in \mathcal{V}$ and $t \in \mathcal{V}$. The *closeness* is intuitively the inverse of the sum of geodesic distances from a students to her/his peers, which reflects the ability of a student to access information through other community members.

The $Degree(v)$ of a student is defined as the number of students with whom v is directly connected. It is a local measure of centrality of a student within the small social group she/he is directly involved.

4.2 Student-to-Teacher Social Network

As introduced in Section 2, in educational literature, the student-to-teacher interaction-ship is usually inferred from the students' preference of sitting positions. The corresponding network is thus a star shaped graph with the teacher at the center, connected by the students through edges weighted by their in-class distances to the teacher (as shown in Figure 1). With the student localization method proposed in Section 3, we can calculate the distances more accurately, rather than a qualitative measure by "far" or "close" (indicated by which row a student sits) in conventional studies [22, 25–28]. Furthermore, once the distances are determined, we can employ linear regression analysis again to investigate the "quantitative" relation between the students' sitting preference and their academic performances, which is not easy to be obtained in conventional studies.

Suppose a student is sitting at the i-th row and j-column in the classroom. With two additional "virtual rows" added in front of the first row and every aisle being considered as a "virtual column", the student's distance to teacher can be estimated by her/his geometric distance to the center of the podium (where most teachers usually stand at) as

$$Distance(i,j) = \sqrt{i^2 + (j - \frac{c}{2})^2} \tag{5}$$

where c is the total numbers of columns, and the podium is assumed to be placed at the 0-th row and the $(\frac{c}{2})$-th column.

5. EXPERIMENT-I: DOSE THE APPROACH TECHNICALLY WORK?

In this section, we validate the practicability of the proposed framework with a technical perspective, while the pedagogical effectiveness will be evaluated in next section. All the experiments are conducted on a dataset collected from 6 courses (related to Image Processing, Pattern Recognition, Data Mining, or Multimedia Computing) at two universities across two semesters, which include 379 students aging from 20 to 24 with 5,040 faces captured at 132 classes. Discussions between students are highly encouraged in class so as to observe the co-learning patterns. The ground-truth is composed of labels provided (when no machine labels

Figure 5: **Results of student localization in a sparse, normal and dense classroom respectively.**

are predicted) or corrected (when machine predictions are wrong) by the students themselves through the "attendance checking" website. The dataset can be downloaded at our demonstration page[2].

5.1 Student Localization

With method introduced in Section 3.2, we are able to detect the positions of students accurately. Figure 5 shows three examples form the sparse, normal, and dense class respectively. It is easy to see that the localization method works well for the students located at the central-front areas, even when the density is considerably high. In general, columns are easier to be correctly detected than rows. To further evaluate the accuracy, we manually check the localization results for 11 classes of the most dense course, where 631 positions in total need to be recognized. The precision is as high as 83.77%, and 94.17% of the errors are caused by mis-assignments of the student with only one row shift to front or back. Due to the 8-neighbor system adopted in face recognition (cf. Section 3.3), the influence of the one-row mis-assignment errors is not significant for the processes after localization.

5.2 Face Recognition with Social Inference

To evaluate our social network (SN) based face recognition scheme, we use three popularly employed baselines: sparse coding method (*Sparse*) [33], *Eigenfaces* [31], and *Fisherfaces* [32]. All baselines are integrated into the proposed scheme to create three network-based versions as *Sparse+SN*, *Eigenfaces+SN*, and *Fisherfaces+SN* (with the the λ in Eq. (1) empirically set to 0.85). Since in our study, the students will provide the labels for theirs faces after each class, the number of training examples for each student is then in-

[2]http://www.cs.cityu.edu.hk/~xiaoyong/in.class.sn/

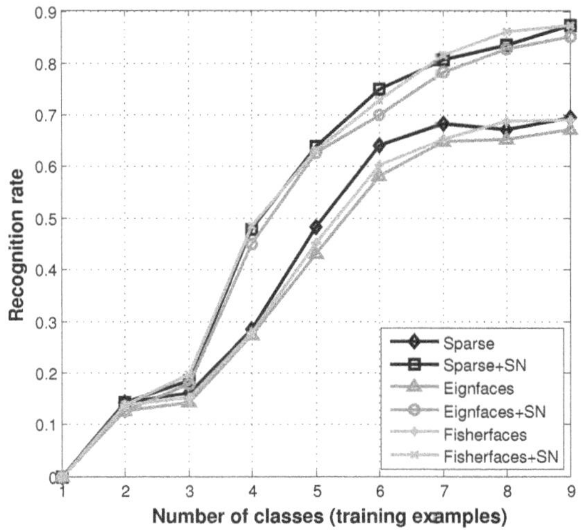

Figure 6: Comparison of recognition rates.

creasing periodically, and the corresponding classifier will be retrained with the same manner.

The result of performances comparison is shown in Figure 6, where the recognition rate is defined as the rate of students being correctly recognized across all classes at the point of time. The maximal number of classes in Figure 6 is 9 because the minimal number of classes for a course is 10 in our dataset. It is easy to see that, with the help of the in-class social network, the recognition rates of the baselines are significantly improved by 28.28%±18.56, 32.79%±16.33, and 34.74% ± 18.75, for *Sparse*, *Eignfaces* and *Fisherfaces*, respectively. The accuracies of the network-based versions are all approaching 65% after the 4-th class (i.e., there are generally 4 training examples for each student), which technically means that more than 3/5 of the students no longer need to label their faces. It has largely reduced the annotation effort.

For the three baselines, *Sparse*, *Eignfaces* and *Fisherfaces* have all demonstrated moderate performances with the final recognition rates less than 70%, which are much lower than those reported in literature (e.g., generally over 80% for all of them in [33]). It might confirm the hypothesis in several recent surveys [15–17] that most of the conventional approaches may work awkwardly in an uncontrolled environment. Nevertheless, *Sparse* still appears to work slightly better than the other two, which may attribute to its "example-based" nature. In a scenario where the training faces are scarce and are with high diversity, "summarizing" the examples with holistic features may even cause confusion, which sequentially affects the performances of *Eignfaces* and *Fisherfaces*. By contrast, without the modeling process, example-based methods like *Sparse* may work better in this case, with the hope that a new instance can be matched to some of the training examples with high probability when the corresponding student occasionally sit at the similar position in the classroom where she/he sits previously, so that her/his pose to the camera, even might be a difficult case for conventional face recognition, is similar to those of the training examples. However, the slight favorite of *Sparse* disappears when all the baselines are upgraded to their network-based versions. This again confirms that the employment of social inference is the biggest contributor to the recognition rate improvement.

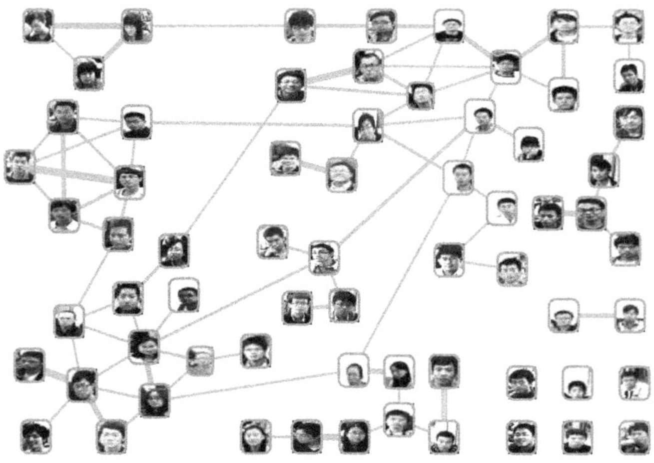

Figure 7: Student-to-student social network constructed from the course with the highest density. The edges with weights smaller than 0.3 are removed for better visualization.

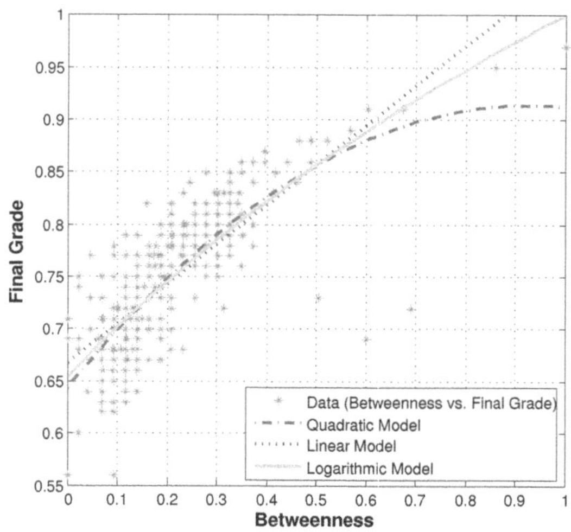

Figure 8: Regression analysis on the relation between the students' *betweenness* and final grades.

5.3 Social Network Construction

With the students' positions localized and their faces recognized, the construction of the in-class social networks are straightforward by following the methods introduced in Section 4. Figure 7 shows the student-to-student social network for the most dense course including 66 students, where the students who are closely related in the network are those frequently sitting near to each other, while the students apart from the center of the community are those who choose their seat randomly. The student-to-teacher social network has also been successfully constructed, which is simply a star shaped graph as shown in Figure 1. We skip its presentation here for space limitation. The whole graph can be found on our demonstration page[2].

To validate the ability of the social network to model the students' relationship in real-life, a quick email survey has been conducted involving all the students by asking them to a) rate the top-5 classmates she/he most communicates with; b) give classmates (up to 5) she/he builds friendship with. Till the time of writing, 324 students have responded. Using the data as ground-truth, we observe that the student-to-student social network can predict the in-class interaction-ship with mean average precision (MAP) as high as 96.67% and the real-life friendship with 87.23%.

6. EXPERIMENT-II: DOSE THE PEDAGOGICAL ANALYSIS MAKE SENSE?

In this section, we investigate the students' positions in the two in-class social networks in related to their academic performances. All measures (i.e., *betweenness*, *closeness*, *degree*, *distances*, and final grades) are normalized into the range of $[0, 1]$. Regression analysis is adopted to study the relations.

6.1 Student-to-Student Interaction-ship

Figure 8 shows the students' final grades over their *betweenness* to investigate whether the *betweenness* can be a predictor for the academic performance (as in [5,12]). While a positive correlation between the two variables can be seen apparently, we conduct a linear regression following the work in [5]. The model fits the data well, further confirming the positive correlation between the performance and the *betweenness*. Note that in [5], the authors have observed a negative correlation between these two variables. This is not conflicting to our result, in the way that the student social network in [5] is constructed from the communication logs (of an online forum) where the students having high *betweenness* might be those who have spent comparably more time online and who are enthusiastic about replying the posts of others. Our result further suggests the difference between the students' behaviors in their "virtual" and "real" lives. Compared with the result reported in [12] where the network is learnt from the questionnaires in which the students rate their interaction-ship to others, our result is consistent to the first conclusion the authors have made that the successful students are those with high *betweenness* because they are willing to communicate with others and benefit from the co-learning. However, the authors have also concluded that the students with high *betweenness* are not necessarily those successful in school, because one exception has been observed in their study. On the basis of the fact that the conclusions in [12] are made on only 4 students with high *betweenness*, we argue that the one exception is possibly one of those outliers (can also be found in bottom-right of Figure 8) which makes the conclusion statistically unfair. Nevertheless, we treat our result not conclusive. It needs investigations in larger scale and interdisciplinary collaborations. In addition, we have also conducted the regressions with logarithmic and quadratic models, as shown in Figure 8, in which the logarithmic model demonstrates the best ability to fit the data than the other two.

For the *closesness* and *degree*, the regression results shown in Figures 9 and 10 have demonstrated similar relations. This suggests that a student is tend to success in school if she/he has an averagely shorter path to access the knowledge of others, or if she/he has more "friends" to provide immediate information for learning. The results is consistent to those reported in [12] and [5]. Moreover, the linear, logarithmic and quadratic have demonstrated similar abilities for regression analysis in both Figures 9 and 10.

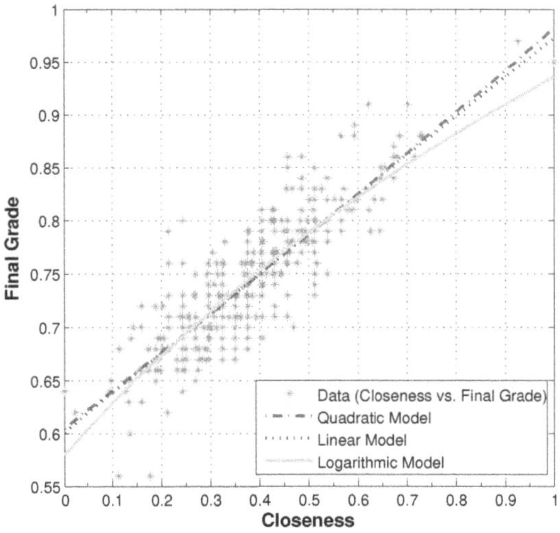

Figure 9: Regression analysis on the relation between the students' *closeness* and final grades..

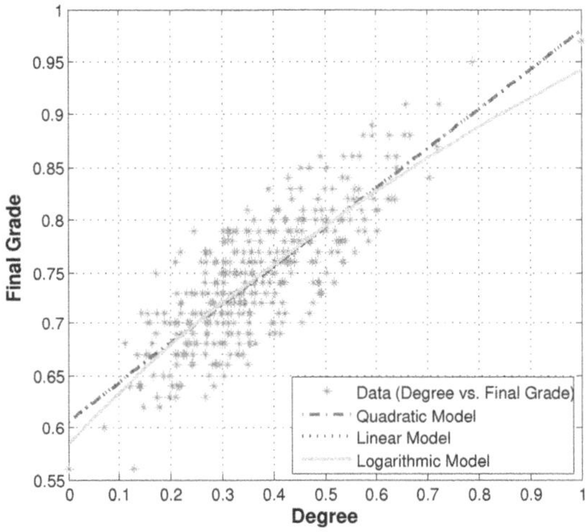

Figure 10: Regression analysis on the relation between the students' *degrees* and final grades.

6.2 Student-to-Teacher Interaction-ship

Figure 11 depicts the relation between the students' final grades and their average distances to the teachers. Compared to the relations observed in the student-to-student social network, the data are more sparsely distributed, which makes none of the linear, quadratic, and logarithmic regression model it well. At the first glance, this seems contradictory to the conventional belief among educational researchers that successful students sit at the central-front of the classroom. However, after investigating 10 students (randomly picked) who achieve high grades but do not always sit at the central-front, we find 80% of them prefer to communicate with the teachers by asking questions after the classes. According to the study by Waller [1], those student can represent the self-starters who do not depend too much on teachers for learning, so that they may not always choose the central-front to sit. In this case, we perform a RANSAC algorithm [35] to search the best model which explains the majority of the data. The resulting model named "Majority Model" in Figure 11 indicates that in a general sense, the closer the students sit to the teachers, the better

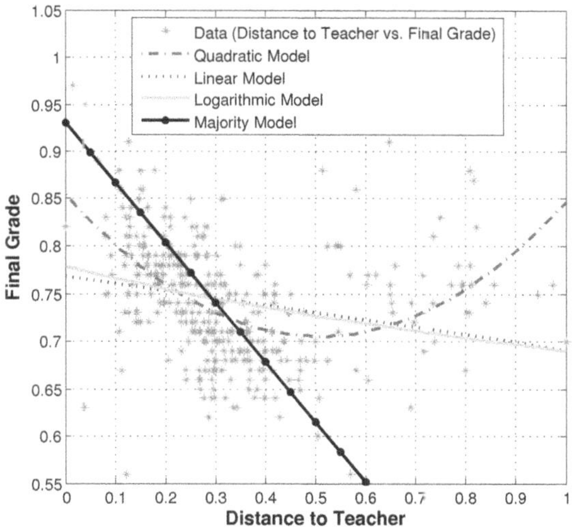

Figure 11: Regression analysis on the relation between the students' *distance-to-teacher* and their final grades.

achievement they obtain in school. In fact, Figure 11 provides a statistical explanation to the dispute about whether the seat preference determines the academic success, in the way that using qualitative approaches on only several samples, it is easy for conventional studies to reach the conclusions that there is no correlation between the seat preference and the academic performance (like in [23] and our first attempt) when one models the whole population with linear model, and that the two are closely related (like in conventional belief and those reported in [22,25–28]) when samples are mainly picked from the main body of the population. In other words, in conventional studies, it is thus easy to be confused when the statistical evidences on a large-scale population are not available.

6.3 Test of Generalizability

We have conducted two leave-one-out cross validation experiments to validate the generalizability of the results in Sections 6.1 and 6.2. Given one class for testing and the rest of classes for training, we check a) if the distribution learnt from the training is statistically form the same distribution of the class for testing using two-sample Hotelling T-Square test; b) if the regression model learnt from the training can explain that of the class for testing. The answers for a) are all YES at significance level 0.01, with the answers for b) are all YES as well indicated by the goodness-of-fit measured by R^2 all above 86.34%.

7. CONCLUSION

We have conducted a pilot study for equipping conventional pedagogical analysis with multimedia technology. With the image-based approach proposed in this paper, we are able to collect the large-scale in-class social data in an automatic manner, and conduct the pedagogical analysis in a quantitative way. The experimental results have validated both the technical and pedagogical effectiveness of the approach. In addition, we have demonstrated that, with the support of the large-scale statistics, it is possible to find why some educational researchers reach conflicting conclusions on the relation between the students' positions in social networks and their academic performances. Furthermore, compared with the student-to-teacher interaction-ship, the student-to-student interaction-ship seems a more reliable predictor for the students' academic performances. However, since the focus of this paper is mainly on the practicability of utilizing multimedia technology for educational studies, the results of the pedagogical analysis reported in between are thus not conclusive. It needs more interdisciplinary collaborations to explain. Moreover, we believe that, with more sophisticated data mining techniques, there are more valuable information which can be explored from the in-class social networks constructed in this paper.

8. ACKNOWLEDGMENTS

The work described in this paper was supported by a grant from the National Natural Science Foundation of China (No. 61001148) and the Open Projects Program of National Laboratory of Pattern Recognition, China.

9. REFERENCES

[1] Willard W. Waller. *The sociology of teaching*. New York: Willey, 1932.

[2] Kaveri Subrahmanyam and Patricia Greenfield. Online communication and adolescent relationships. *The Future of Children*, 18(1):119–140, 2008.

[3] David W. Johnson. Student-student interaction: The neglected variable in education. *Educational Researcher*, 10(1):5–10, 1981.

[4] James C. McCroskey and Rod W. McVetta. Classroom seating arrangements: Instructional communication theory versus student preferences. In *Annual Meeting of the International Communication Association*.

[5] Shane Dawson. A study of the relationship between student social networks and sense of community. *Educational Technology & Society*, 11(3):224–238, 2008.

[6] John Dewey. *Experience and education*. Macmillan, 1938/1997.

[7] Christine Greenhow and Beth Robelia. Old communication, new literacies: Social network sites as social learning resources. *Journal of Computer-Mediated Communication*, 14(4):1130–1161, 2009.

[8] D. M. Boyd and N. B. Ellison. Social network sites: Definition, history, and scholarship. *Journal of Computer-Mediated Communication*, 13(1):119–140, 2007.

[9] Grace Salas and Julie S Alexander. Technology for institutional enrollment, communication, and student success. *Directions for Student Services*, 2008(124):103–116, 2008.

[10] Brigid Barron. Interest and self-sustained learning as catalysts of development: A learning ecology perspective. *Human Development*, 49(4):193–224, 2006.

[11] A. Martínez, Y. Dimitriadis, B. Rubia, E. Gómez, and P. de la Fuente. Combining qualitative evaluation and social network analysis for the study of classroom social interactions. *Computers & Education*, 41(4):353–368, 2003.

[12] Blaženka Divjak and Petra Peharda. Relation between student academic performance and their position in a social network. In *Central European conference on information and intelligent systems*, pages 65–71, 2010.

[13] Richard Szeliski. Image alignment and stitching: A tutorial. Technical report, Microsoft Research, 2004.

[14] M. D. Kelly. Visual identification of people by computer. Technical report, AI-130, Stanford AI Project, 1970.

[15] W. Zhao, R. Chellappa, P. J. Phillips, and A. Rosenfeld. Face recognition: A literature survey. *ACM Computing Surveys*, 35(4):399–458, 2003.

[16] Xiaoyang Tan, Songcan Chen, Zhi-Hua Zhou, and Fuyan Zhang. Face recognition from a single image per person: A survey. *Pattern Recognition*, 39(9):1725–1745, Sep. 2006.

[17] Cha Zhang and Zhengyou Zhang. A survey of recent advances in face detection. Technical report, MSR-TR-2010-66, Microsoft Research, 2010.

[18] Xiaozheng Zhang and Yongsheng Gao. Face recognition across pose: A review. *Pattern Recognition*, 42(11):2876–2896, 2009.

[19] N. B. Ellison and *et al.* The benefits of facebook "friends": Social capital and college students' use of online social network sites. *Journal of Computer-Mediated Communication*, 12(4):1143–1168, 2007.

[20] Robert Kraut and *et al.* Internet paradox revisited. *Journal of Social Issues*, 58(1):49–74, 2002.

[21] J. B. Walther and M. R. Parks. Cues filtered out, cues filtered in: Computer mediated communication and relationships. *The Handbook of Interpersonal Communication*, pages 529–563, 2002.

[22] İkram Çinar. Classroom geography: Who sit where in the traditional classrooms? *Journal of International Social Research*, 3(10):200–212, 2010.

[23] Christopher M Johnson. A survey of current research on online communities of practice. *Internet and Higher Education*, 4(1):45–60, 2001.

[24] S. Wasserman and K. Faust. *Social Network Analysis: Methods and applications*. New York: Cambridge University Press, 1994.

[25] Ed Baines, Peter Blatchford, and Peter Kutnick. Changes in grouping practices over primary and secondary school. *International Journal of Educational Research*, 39(1-2):9–34, 2003.

[26] Mary Ellen Benedict and John Hoag. Seating location in large lectures: Are seating preferances or location related to course performance. *Journal of Economic Education*, 35(3):215–231, 2004.

[27] Katherine K. Perkins and Carl E. Wieman. The surprising impact of seat location on student performance. *The Physics Teacher*, 43(1):30–33, 2005.

[28] Steven Kalinowski and Mark L. Taper. The effect of seat location on exam grades and student perceptions in an introductory biology class. *Journal of College Science Teaching*, 36(4):54–57, 2007.

[29] M. Brown and D. G. Lowe. Recognising panoramas. In *The Ninth IEEE International Conference on Computer Vision*, pages 1218–1225, 2003.

[30] P. Viola and M. Jones. Rapid object detection using a boosted cascade of simple features. In *IEEE Computer Society Conference on Computer Vision and Pattern Recognition*, pages 511–518, 2001.

[31] M. Turk and Alex Pentland. Eigenfaces for recognition. *Journal of Cognitive Neuroscience*, 3(1):71–86, 1991.

[32] Peter N. Belhumeur and *et al.* Eigenfaces vs. fisherfaces: Recognition using class specific linear projection. *IEEE Transactions on Pattern Analysis and Machine Intelligence*, 19(7):711–720, 1997.

[33] J. Wright, A.Y. Yang, A. Ganesh, S.S. Sastry, and Yi Ma. Robust face recognition via sparse representation. *IEEE Transactions on Pattern Analysis and Machine Intelligence*, 31(2):210–22, 2009.

[34] Peter Peer, Jure Kovac, and Franc Solina. Human skin colour clustering for face detection. In *EUROCON 2003 - International Conference on Computer as a Tool*, pages 144–148, 2003.

[35] Martin A. Fischler and Robert C. Bolles. Random sample consensus: a paradigm for model fitting with applications to image analysis and automated cartography. *Communications of the ACM*, 24(6):381–395, 1981.

SocialTransfer: Cross-Domain Transfer Learning from Social Streams for Media Applications*

Suman D. Roy †, Tao Mei ‡, Wenjun Zeng †, Shipeng Li ‡
† University of Missouri, Columbia, USA
‡ Microsoft Research Asia, Beijing, P. R. China
sdr5x8@mail.missouri.edu; {tmei, spli}@microsoft.com; zengw@missouri.edu

ABSTRACT

The usage and applications of social media have become pervasive. This has enabled an innovative paradigm to solve multimedia problems (e.g., recommendation and popularity prediction), which are otherwise hard to address purely by traditional approaches. In this paper, we investigate how to build a mutual connection among the disparate social media on the Internet, using which cross-domain media recommendation can be realized. We accomplish this goal through *SocialTransfer*—a novel cross-domain real-time transfer learning framework. While existing transfer learning methods do not address how to utilize the real time social streams, our proposed *SocialTransfer* is able to effectively learn from social streams to help multimedia applications, assuming an intermediate topic space can be built across domains. It is characterized by two key components: 1) a topic space learned in real time from social streams via Online Streaming Latent Dirichlet Allocation (OSLDA), and 2) a real-time cross-domain graph spectra analysis based transfer learning method that seamlessly incorporates learned topic models from social streams into the transfer learning framework. We present as use cases of *SocialTransfer* two video recommendation applications that otherwise can hardly be achieved by conventional media analysis techniques: 1) socialized query suggestion for video search, and 2) socialized video recommendation that features socially trending topical videos. We conduct experiments on a real-world large-scale dataset, including 10.2 million tweets and 5.7 million YouTube videos and show that *SocialTransfer* outperforms traditional learners significantly, and plays a natural and interoperable connection across video and social domains, leading to a wide variety of cross-domain applications.

Categories and Subject Descriptors

H.3.5 [**Information Storage and Retrieval**]: Online Information Services—*Web-based services*

General Terms

Algorithms, Experimentation, Human Factors.

* This work was performed at Microsoft Research Asia.

MM'12, October 29–November 2, 2012, Nara, Japan.

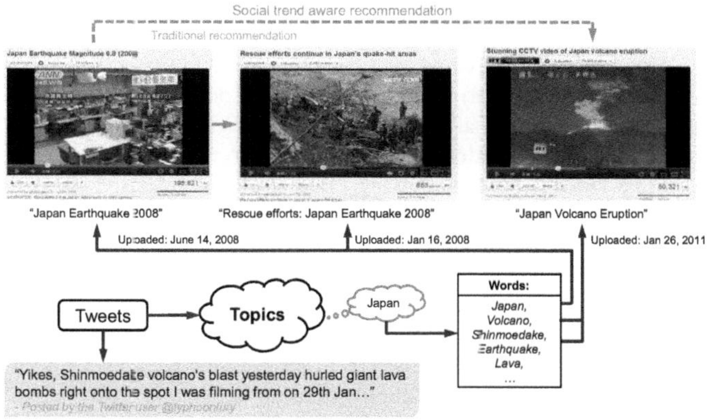

Figure 1: Example of using social topics in building social trend aware multimedia applications. In this example, we show that related video (i.e. video-video) recommendation can be enriched by using topics learned from the domain of social streams. This cross-domain transfer of knowledge is accomplished through a mutual topic space (e.g., the space includes the topics like "Japan" containing words like "volcano," "earthquake," and so on).

Keywords

Cross-domain media retrieval, recommendation, transfer learning, social media.

1. INTRODUCTION

Social media has become a disruptive platform for addressing many multimedia problems that could not be elegantly solved previously. For example, real-time social data is being utilized in semantic video indexing, image/video context annotation [17] and visualizing political activity and flu outbreaks [13]. Social streams like Twitter are a good indicator of crowd sourcing activity of a social community. The information in social streams is real time, thus it can be used to learn about real life events quickly. Major world events in recent times, such as the Egyptian Revolution, the London riots and the Japan Earthquake have been extensively captured using social streams such as Twitter and Facebook updates, as shown in Fig. 1.

One aspect of social micro-blogs like Twitter is its short text format, which is fast, real-time, and allows events to be instantly reported and broadcasted online [17]. Consider this in the light of a traditional media application like video recommendation, e.g., a user is watching an old video on "Egypt" (uploaded in 2008) on the eve of the "Egyptian revolutions" (Jan 29th 2011). Also, consider a journalist who just uploaded a live video of the revolution in YouTube [10]. Most existing video recommendation systems have no way to *relate* these two videos, i.e., the seed video the user is watching and the related newly uploaded video [10, 26], in spite of their striking similarity in topics. It has been previously noted that use of social data could boost recommender systems [18]. Socialized recommendation using social streams has the potential to model factual world events in real time by topic extraction and subsequently perform interesting tasks such as video associations among the old and fresh videos belonging to similar topics. Learning fresh video associations is important to improve the performance of multimedia applications, such as video recommendation in terms of topical relevance and popularity. As shown in Fig. 1, fresh socially relevant videos (e.g., Japan's Shinmoedake Volcano Eruption in 2012) can be associated to older videos (e.g., Japan Earthquake in 2008) to facilitate social trend aware recommendations. Social trend aware recommendation includes videos belonging to related trending topics for recommendation.

However, social streams (like Twitter) and traditional media (like video publishing sites) exist across disparate domains on the Internet. Thus, the potential of these two resources is limited within the domain where it resides. For example, video recommendation [3, 16] and video popularity ranking [5] is often judged based only on view counts [10] or user activity (co-clicks) [26], but not on how socially trending the video topic is in real life. Thus, incorporating social knowledge into traditional media applications requires cross-domain information transfer, which contains the *wisdom of the crowds*. It is therefore important to develop a cross-domain knowledge transfer mechanism from the crowd-sourced social domain to traditional media (video) domain.

There are significant challenges in using social streams to perform cross-domain recommendations. The main concern is to transfer knowledge across domain and align features that are common to both domains (e.g., video tags and social stream topic words as shown in Fig. 1). Specifically, there are distinct challenges in cross domain socialized recommendations:

- A unified framework to combine the social and multimedia feature information which has different domain-specific properties.
- A transfer learning algorithm that can seamlessly propagate the knowledge (i.e., social topics) mined from the crowd-sourced social streams to the video domain.
- The scaling up and adaptation of the transfer learning algorithm to the ever bursty real-time nature of the social streams.
- Dealing with the noisy, incomplete, ambiguous, and short form nature of social stream data. Each tweet is limited to 140 characters and often improperly structured in grammar/syntax. Traditional language model (e.g., Bag-of-Words) would fail to scale up with such kind of data.

In this paper, we present *SocialTransfer*—a scalable technique for real-time transfer learning between the domains of social streams and traditional media (like video). *SocialTransfer* utilizes topics extracted from social streams to build an intermediate topic space in between the social and video domains. The topic space is an abstract space containing several clusters of words belonging to various topics that reflect world events in real time, including current and past trends. We use the Online Stream LDA model (OSLDA) to learn topics from social streams [1]. *SocialTransfer* uses a graph based framework to model the transfer learning problem (what feature information is transferable and how) between the social and the video domains. Spectral analysis of this graph fetches the eigenvectors, using which we can represent both the social and the video feature information as a combined feature representation [15]. Since the stream is temporal nature, *SocialTransfer* also allows progressively updating the topic space and seamlessly incorporating newer

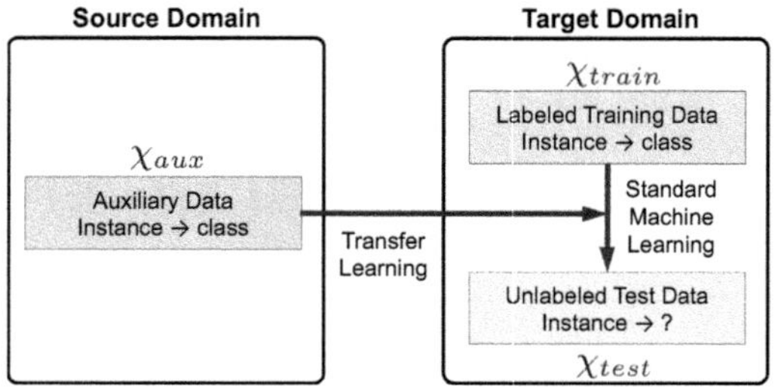

Figure 2: A basic framework for transfer learning. Cross-domain transfer learning assumes the class labels of instances of the source and target domain have the same overall category.

trends into the transfer learning framework for socially aware media recommendations. Fig. 1 shows an example of this kind. The framework we develop can be reused for several multimedia applications where social influence is capable of improving performance. Our results show that *SocialTransfer* considerably outperforms traditional learners without transfer learning.

The main contributions of this work are as follows:

- We propose the concept of bridging social media from disparate sources by building a common latent topic space, which represents one of the first attempts toward answering sociological problems using cross-domain social media.
- We propose *SocialTransfer*, a novel transfer learning framework based on efficient graph spectra analysis by seamlessly integrating the topic space learned from social stream in real time.
- We present several interesting media applications based on *SocialTransfer*, which could otherwise hardly be realized in conventional approaches, and evaluate through large-scale real-world social media data.

The rest of this paper is organized as follows. Section 2 reviews related work. Section 3 introduces our proposed *SocialTransfer* and explains techniques employed to ensure scalable transfer learning from social streams. Section 4 describes two novel applications based on *SocialTransfer*. Section 5 describes the experimental data (videos and tweets). Section 6 presents experiments and evaluations, followed by conclusions in Section 7.

2. RELATED WORK

We discuss related work in the fields of transfer learning, mining social streams, and video recommendation.

Transfer Learning. Common machine learning techniques traditionally address isolated tasks. In contrast, transfer learning aims to transfer knowledge learned in one source domain and use it to improve learning in a related target domain. Fig. 2 shows the basic concept of transfer learning. The source domain data Z_{src} contains the auxiliary data, while target domain Z_{tar} contains the training and test data. A comprehensive survey of transfer learning techniques is provided in [21]. A unified framework for transfer learning in scenarios ranging from cross-domain, cross-category and self-taught learning is described in [8]. Transfer learning has been previously used in various cases including classification, image clustering, collaborative filtering, and sensor based location prediction [8, 21, 28].

Our *SocialTransfer* framework is inspired by the work in [8]. However, we distinguish ourselves from [8] in scaling transfer learning to specifically incorporate social stream data as source domain and show how topic learning can be smoothly combined with transfer learning in real-time. To the best of our knowledge, a framework that can handle social stream topics distinctively as source domain for cross-domain transfer learning has not been proposed before. This is challenging due to the unique characteristics of social stream data [17].

Domain-independent feature representation in transfer learning can also have significant effects on performance (e.g., to avoid negative transfer) [8]. Spectral techniques have been used to address the problem of combined feature representation [2]. However, such spectral techniques (e.g., eigenvector extraction [19]) should scale to dynamic social stream traffic, which is addressed in this paper. Although [24] attempts to use transfer learning for social recommendation, their model is not real time and limited to non-streaming data only. Instead, we show how to model transfer learning from streaming social data in real time, which is a significantly challenging problem not yet resolved.

Mining Social Streams. Social data from Twitter streams can be mined to build a relevant topic space using topic modeling [17, 22]. Such topic space can act as a bridge between the social and the traditional media domain, supporting multimedia applications like social video recommendation and social video popularity. Topic modeling aims to extract topics from large corpus of unlabeled documents by using generative models like Latent Dirichlet Allocation (LDA) [12]. There have been previous efforts to incorporate social data for recommendation [18, 24], but they do not use social streams specifically [22]. Social streams are more challenging to extract topics from; due to their dynamic, noisy, short and real-time nature [17]. Thus, large scale matrix decomposition is infeasible for social streams [18].

Previous research on mining social stream data assumes that the entire tweet stream is available to the algorithm at the beginning of the run. This assumption is only applicable in ideal case; it does not hold in real life situations. In our paper, we simulate the tweet stream in pseudo real-time, where the *SocialTransfer* algorithm has not seen the entire tweet stream in advance. Instead, the complete timeline is divided into time slots, and a certain number of tweets occupy each time slot as they are generated in real life, similar to the technique in [1]. Tweet chunks are fed to the *SocialTransfer* algorithm in time-sequential batches based on the time slots in which they are generated (pseudo real-time). We show later how *SocialTransfer* is a unique method to combine scalable social stream topic modeling and transfer learning; providing a natural interface for topic modeling to fit into the process of transfer learning and seamlessly integrate topic model and transfer learning.

Video Recommendation. Videos can be recommended based on several parameters, like multimodal fusion and relevance feedback [20, 25], user activity [10, 16], meta-data [6] and the social web [13]. In related video recommendation, the aim of the recommender is to recommend related videos with respect to a seed video that the user is currently watching. The list of related videos given a particular seed video can be considered to be a graph where the seed video is the root node and has an edge to every related video which are child nodes. Such a recommendation network of videos is called a Related Video Graph (RVG) [10], which is described in [26, 3] for the YouTube recommendation system. A detailed statistical analysis of the social network of YouTube videos is provided in [7]. Categorization of videos has also been a hot topic for research. There have been efforts to categorize videos based on related tags [23] and comments [11].

The fact that RVG-based recommendation has significant effect on video popularity (based on view counts etc.) is discussed in [5]. Efforts on video recommendation using certain traditional techniques without co-clicks fail to do any better. For example, recommendation using video modal features as described in [20, 25] might not be worthwhile since the calibration effort is too expensive [17]. However, recent research has shown that analyzing video meta-data such as tags, title, and comments can considerably help understand categorical association of videos [6, 11, 23].

Table 1: Notations of auxiliary, training, and test data for *SocialTransfer*

Dataset	Notation	Domain	Domain Type	Instances	Labels
Training	χ_{train}	Z_{tar}	Online video	$\{x_{tr}^{(m)}\}$	$\mathbb{C} = \{c^i\}$
Testing	χ_{test}	Z_{tar}	Online video	$\{x_{ts}^{(n)}\}$	N/A
Auxiliary	χ_{aux}	Z_{src}	Social stream	$\{x_{ax}^{(k)}\}$	$\mathbb{C} = \{c^i\}$

3. SOCIALTRANSFER

In this section, we will first present the problem statement and overview of *SocialTransfer*. Then, we will introduce online topic modeling, spectral graph learning, and algorithm of *SocialTransfer*.

3.1 Problem Statement

In *SocialTransfer*, we have two datasets in the target domain; the target training data $\chi_{train} = \{x_{tr}^m\}_{m=1}^M$ with labels and the target test data $\chi_{test} = \{x_{ts}^n\}_{n=1}^N$ without labels. The training data contains M instances whereas the test data contains N instances. Unlike traditional machine learning, we also have an auxiliary data set $\chi_{aux} = \{x_{ax}^k\}_{k=1}^D$. consisting of D tweets instances. We assume that the target data and the auxiliary data share the same categories (e.g., both a tweet and a video can be regarding music), but exist in different domains (e.g., tweet is social text-based micro-blogging while RVGs consist of videos).

Consider a set of B videos in the target domain. For a video v_i $(1 \leqslant i \leqslant B)$, we can represent the set of tags of v_i as $\{tags(v_i)\}$. Each tag in the set $\{tags(v_i)\}$ is a word, represented as $w_j^i, 1 \leqslant j \leqslant |tags(v_i)|$. Now consider a stream of D tweets picked from the source domain to be used for modeling the social topic space. For a tweet t_k $(1 \leqslant k \leqslant D)$, let $tpw(t_k)$ represent the topical words in the topic of t_k (we consider only the principal topic, i.e. topic for which the conditional probability of topic given tweet is maximum). Then each instance/label of the twitter stream data can be represented as $t_k \rightarrow tpw(t_k)$. These instances can be combined into the auxiliary data set $\chi_{aux} = \{x_{ax}^k\}_{k=1}^D$.

As shown in Table 1, all the instances $x \in \chi_{train} \cup \chi_{test} \cup \chi_{aux}$ are represented by the features in the feature space $\mathcal{F} = \{f_S^{(i)}\}_{i=1}^S$. Our goal is to learn an accurate classifier $f'(\cdot)$ from χ_{train} and χ_{aux} that can predict the testing data with minimum classification error. We call this classifier $f'(\chi_{test})$. Thus, the goal of transfer learning is to minimize the prediction error on χ_{test} by leveraging the auxiliary data from χ_{aux}.

3.2 Approach Overview

Our goal is to combine the training, test and auxiliary data into a single transfer framework for prediction. There are two problems we particularly need to solve in this framework: (1) we must learn the interconnected pattern of shared features between the source and the target data, and (2) since the topics modeled from social stream (auxiliary data) changes with the real world trends, we need a transfer framework that can allow *progressive inclusion of topics in pseudo real-time*.

Let us focus on the first problem and understand how to learn the interconnected structure of shared features across the domains. The single transfer framework we use for this purpose is represented as a graph called the transfer graph G (see Fig. 5), which contains the videos, tweets, feature words and category information. To learn

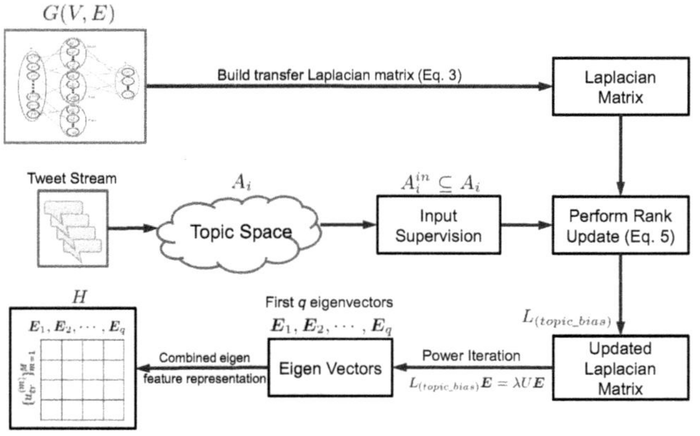

Figure 3: The flow diagram addresses the overall approach in solving the two key problems of *SocialTransfer*: (1) learning the shared feature representation across domains in terms of eigenvectors using Spectral Learning (Power Iteration), and (2) reflecting the progressive inclusion of topics by updating the transfer Laplacian matrix.

the interconnected pattern of shared features between the source and the target data, we perform spectral analysis [2] of the transfer graph. As shown in Fig. 3, spectral learning uses a technique called Power Iteration [14] to extract the eigenvectors from the Laplacian representation of the transfer graph. Spectral analysis of the transfer graph gives us the combined feature representation of the auxiliary and the training data using eigenvectors. This eigen feature representation reflects the intrinsic structure in terms of the principal components of the combined source and training data. Traditional learners, e.g., Support Vector Machines (SVM) [4], can then use the combined features for prediction rather than using only the training features.

Now, we focus on the second problem of how to progressively include social topics. Since the tweet stream is incrementally witnessed by the algorithm, the transfer graph needs to be updated in order to progressively include the twitter topics in pseudo-real time. Said alternately, in order to include topics as they are generated in real time, we must update the transfer graph and recalculate the graph spectra. This is achieved by treating the topics as input supervision before spectral learning (as shown in Fig. 3). In particular, to incorporate the new topical information to the existing transfer graph, we utilize selected topics from the topic space (described in Section 3.3) created from the tweets. We can treat the topical words of tweets and the corresponding topics as labeled instances, and then incorporate the new tweet information as a semi-supervised rank update on the existing Laplacian matrix (details in Section 3.5) as shown in the flow diagram Fig. 3 [1]. In other words, selected topics act as input supervision for the Laplacian matrix which allows for smooth incorporation of social topics into the transfer learning framework.

3.3 Learning Topics from Social Streams via OSLDA

We use the Online Streaming LDA (OSLDA) model for real-time topic learning from Twitter stream [1]. Each topic is comprised of a group of related words called *topical* words. Topic learning treats each tweet as a document and builds a generative model to connect the tweet to one or more topics. Thus, the topic of a tweet contains words (topical words) that are related to the tweet words but might not be explicitly present in the tweet itself. More precisely, the topic modeling generates two distributions, a tweet-topic distribution and a topic-word distribution.

[1] A rank update refers to cases where a matrix is updated using outer product (as opposed to dot product).

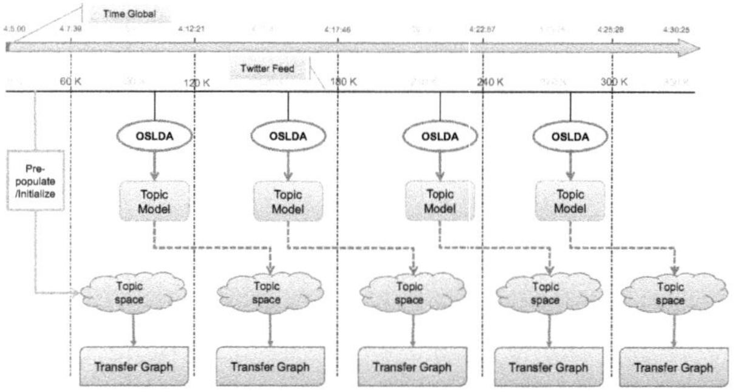

Figure 4: Updating transfer graph with topics modeled using OSLDA. The topic space is updated with new topics learned from previous tweet chunk, which is subsequently used to update the transfer graph.

Table 2: Example Topical Words and Related Topics

Topical Words	Assigned Topic	YouTube Category
dance, adventure, photography, visit	events	Travel & Events
anime, hero, online, celebrity, diva	films	Films & Animation
iphone, games, showcase	electronics	Sci. & Tech
war, economy, army, revolution, blog, egypt	politics	News & Politics
trailer, show, live, watch	entertainment	Entertainment
wow, rap, jam, gaga	music	Travel & Music

As we have mentioned, extracting topics from social streams is non-trivial, due to the unique characteristics of social stream data [17]. Previous work has however shown that significantly popular topics (e.g. trending topics) can be extracted from social streams with reasonable accuracy [1]. Since every topical word in the topic space has an assigned topic label as shown in Table 2, the entire topic space can be treated as some sort of social bias for any semi-supervised learning task that requires social influence. Again, devising a natural way to incorporate this social bias into transfer learning is not trivial, which is one of the important issues addressed in this paper.

Note that each assigned topic consists of a cluster of topical words. Similarly, each topic can be considered a cluster in the topic space. We can limit ourselves to incorporating only selected topics from the topic space as input supervision (an additional set of labeled instances) for the transfer learning task. This choice will depend on factors such as whether we want to model only fresh (trending) topics or only video category specific topics. Thus for K topics in the global topic space, we can choose a particular set of topical words $A_i^{in} \subseteq A_i$, for $i = 1, 2, \ldots, K$ to act as the bias or input supervision to update the transfer graph before spectral learning. This sort of input topic supervision is fed into the transfer graph progressively, as is depicted in Fig. 4, where topics modeled in real-time from the social stream using OSLDA is used to update the transfer graph by means of a ranked update (Eq. 5) on the transfer Laplacian matrix representation of the transfer graph. This allows progressive and seamless inclusion of topics into the transfer graph as shown in Fig. 4, facilitating the social influence in transfer learning.

3.4 Transfer Graph

A general graph based framework for cross-domain transfer learning was proposed in [8], which includes the target and the auxiliary data with some common relations and attributes between them. We

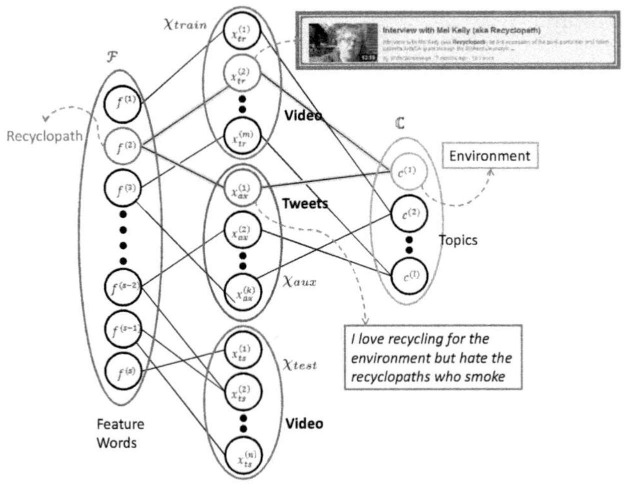

Figure 5: Transfer graph for *SocialTransfer* with connections among auxiliary and target data including features and class labels.

adapt that framework in our scenario. However, the graph in [8] cannot update itself to incorporate streaming tweets topic information in scalable fashion. Instead, the transfer graph in *SocialTransfer* is capable of updating itself with new tweets stream topics in real-time. The transfer graph's main purpose is to capture the cross-domain attributes of social streams and videos for using in the transfer learning task and model the relation between the auxiliary data from Twitter and the target video data. This 'transfer graph' (Fig. 5) contains the instances, features and class labels of the target data and the observed auxiliary data as vertices. The edges are set up based on the relations between the auxiliary and the target data nodes. The transfer graph presents a unified graph structure to represent the task of transfer learning from social domain to video domain.

Before diving into the details of the transfer graph, it is important we mention that the novelty of our approach lies in how we incorporate the learned social topics into this transfer graph. As described later in Section 3.5.1, we incorporate the learned topic model into the transfer graph by means of a ranked update on the Laplacian matrix representation of the transfer graph. SocialTransfer is a unique method to combine topic modeling and transfer learning; providing a natural interface for topic modeling to seamlessly fit into the process of transfer learning.

We can see the example in the transfer graph in Fig. 5. The feature word `'recyclopath'` occurs in the training video instance `'Interview with Mel Kelly'` `'(aka Recyclopath)'` shown in the top right. Since the video lacks any tags related to `'Environment'`, a traditional learner will find it difficult to extract the topic of this video to be related to `'Environment'`. However, the auxiliary data has a tweet instance belonging to the `'Environment'` topic having the word `'recyclopath'`. Thus, the transfer learner can label this video as 'Environment'-related and associate this video to another 'Environment'-related video. This is an example of discovery of video associations by understanding video topics with the help of social topics.

As shown in Fig. 5, the transfer graph $G(V, E)$ consists of vertices representing instances, features or class labels, and edges E denoting co-occurrences between end nodes in the target and the auxiliary data i.e.:

$$V = \chi_{train} \cup \chi_{test} \cup \chi_{aux} \cup \mathcal{F} \cup \mathbb{C} \quad (1)$$

The weight of each edge where one of the end nodes belongs to $\mathbb{C}$ indicates the number of such co-occurrences. Let $\omega_{(x,f)}$ represent the importance of the feature $f \in \mathcal{F}$ that appears in instance $x \in \chi_{train} \cup \chi_{test} \cup \chi_{aux}$. Then, the weight of an edge where one of the end nodes belongs to $\mathcal{F}$ is indicated by $\omega_{(x,f)}$. The importance of a feature word $\omega_{(x,f)}$ can be calculated using the topic-word probability distribution matrix obtained from OSLDA. The total number of features and class label nodes remain fixed in the transfer graph. Let $T(x)$ represent the true label of the instance. If e_{ij} denotes the weight of an edge between two nodes ϑ_i and ϑ_j in the transfer graph, then edge weights can be assigned as:

$$e_{ij} = \begin{cases} \omega_{\vartheta_i,\vartheta_j} & \vartheta_i \in \chi_{train} \cup \chi_{test} \cup \chi_{aux} \wedge \vartheta_j \in \mathcal{F} \\ \omega_{\vartheta_j,\vartheta_i} & \vartheta_i \in \mathcal{F} \wedge \vartheta_j \in \chi_{train} \cup \chi_{test} \cup \chi_{aux} \\ 1 & \vartheta_i \in \chi_{train} \wedge \vartheta_j \in \mathbb{C} \wedge T(\vartheta_i) = \vartheta_j \\ 1 & \vartheta_i \in \chi_{aux} \wedge \vartheta_j \in \mathbb{C} \wedge T(\vartheta_i) = \vartheta_j \\ 1 & \vartheta_i \in \mathbb{C} \wedge \vartheta_j \in \chi_{train} \wedge T(\vartheta_j) = \vartheta_i \\ 1 & \vartheta_i \in \mathbb{C} \wedge \vartheta_j \in \chi_{aux} \wedge T(\vartheta_j) = \vartheta_i \end{cases} \quad (2)$$

For all other cases except the ones mentioned in Eq. (2), we set $e_{ij} = 0$. The edge weights thus represent the occurrence/importance of a category or feature present in the auxiliary/target data, which will be eventually utilized as a distance metric during spectral clustering. Some nodes in the graph may be isolated with no edge connections. The matrix updating process (Section 3.5.1) adds new edges to the isolated nodes. The transfer graph G is usually sparse, symmetric, real and positive semi-definite, which allows the possibility of calculating its spectra efficiently [2]. The graph spectrum in terms of eigenvectors is the impression of the structure of relations among the source and target data. This structural relation between the cross domain data is the essence of transfer learning [8]. Thus, it is necessary to represent the source and target data as a transfer graph and then analyze their structural relation by learning the graph spectrum.

3.5 Learning Transfer Graph Spectra

The highlight of *SocialTransfer* is how it learns transfer graph spectra and incorporates new social topics into the transfer graph in real-time. This task is non-trivial, since if not properly done, it may incur substantial costs in terms of scalability (e.g., in eigen-feature extraction) and interoperability (in integration of topics) between topic modeling and transfer learning. In this section, we demonstrate how we achieve both these goals efficiently.

Once the transfer graph $G = (V, E)$ is built, we can use graph spectra analysis to form an eigen feature representation, which combines the principal component features from the training and the auxiliary data. In order to extract the top-q eigenvectors of the transfer graph $G = (V, E)$, we first need to convert the graph into a Laplacian matrix. Let $deg(\vartheta_i)$ denote the degree of the i-th vertex in G. Then the transfer graph Laplacian $L_{input} := (l'_{i,j})_{|V| \times |V|}$, can be obtained as:

$$l'_{i,j} := \begin{cases} deg(\vartheta_i) & if\ i = j \\ -1 & if\ i \neq j \wedge e_{ij} = 1 \\ 0 & otherwise \end{cases} \quad (3)$$

If the Laplacian eigen values are represented as $\lambda_0 = 1 \geqslant \lambda_1 \geqslant \cdots \geqslant \lambda_q$, then the eigen gap can be defined as: $eigengap = \frac{\lambda_q}{\lambda_{q-1}}$.

Since the Twitter stream is extremely dynamic, topics and trends change overtime. This requires a feature extraction scheme that can reflect and scale with the social stream. Previous approaches for spectral feature representation in transfer learning have suggested the use of the normalized cut (Ncut) technique for eigenvector extraction [8]. However, our experiments (Fig. 12 in Section 6.3) showed that the normalized cut technique is incapable of scaling with the twitter stream.

Therefore, we use a Power Iteration technique for computing the q largest eigenvectors of L_{input} [14]. The method begins with a random $|V| \times q$ eigenvector matrix and iteratively performs matrix multiplication and ortho-normalization until convergence [2]. The speed of convergence of this method depends on the eigen gap, i.e. the difference between successive eigen values. In fact, Bach *et.al.* mention that the number of steps required for the orthogonal convergence in the Power Iteration method is $O(\frac{1}{1-eigengap})$ [2].

Since topics are updated in the topic space with time, we need to devise a way to progressively incorporate these new topics into the transfer graph. These topics could be incorporated by picturing them to be a time-dependent labeled bias (like a semi-supervised bias) which is an additional set of labeled instances acting as input supervision. One option for incorporating the semi-supervised topic bias as input supervision into the Laplacian representation of the transfer graph (L_{input}) is by producing a ranked update on L_{input} (see Eq. 5). The update in effect recalculates the weights of edge/path between the features and the corresponding labels within the transfer graph, thus updating the characteristic of the Laplacian (Eq. 2 and 3). Essentially, the ranked update on the Laplacian using the topic bias adds positive weights between feature words that share the same topic and adds negative weights between feature words that belong to different topics. Thus, the target and the auxiliary data instances act as sort of virtual nodes enabling this re-weighing of the feature edges.

An additional reason for using the ranked update technique is that previous work has also rigorously demonstrated that when Laplacians such as L_{input} is positive semi-definite [19], a ranked update can improve eigenvector extraction speed by spreading the eigen gap. In the next, we will show the use of ranked updates to incorporate semi-supervised topic bias and update the transfer Laplacian.

3.5.1 Incorporating Social Topics

We know from topic modeling that the words in tweets can be clustered into topics. Let us consider there are K such topic clusters. The semi-supervised topic bias is implemented by assuming we know the correct topic labels for a subset of the feature words. Said in terms of the transfer graph, the supervised bias is an additional input of the correct cluster labels for a subset of the feature vertices. This input is learned by topic modeling using OSLDA, which was described in Section 3.3.

The semi-supervised bias consists of a set of topical words for each topic $A_i^{in} \subseteq A_i$ $(i = 1, 2, \ldots, K)$ that act as input supervision. Let us consider the simple case of two topic clusters A_1^{in} and A_2^{in}, such that $A^{in} = A_1^{in} \cup A_2^{in}$ denotes the set of labeled bias instances. Moveover, consider $d_i = \sum_j e_{ij}$ and $vol(A_k) = \sum_{i \in A_k} d_i$, then we can define a regularization vector δ_1 as:

$$\delta_1(i) = \begin{cases} \sqrt{\frac{d_i}{vol(A^{in})}} f(i), & i \in A^{in} \\ 0, & i \notin A^{in} \end{cases} \tag{4}$$

where $f(i) = \sqrt{\frac{vol(A_2^{in})}{vol(A_1^{in})}}$ if $i \in A_1^{in}$, and $f(i) = -\sqrt{\frac{vol(A_1^{in})}{vol(A_2^{in})}}$ if $i \in A_2^{in}$. The above Eq. 4 is to introduce a quadratic penalty if there is a violation in the topic bias label constraints. Said otherwise, this will cause vertices of features that belong to the same topic to cluster together while vertices of different topics will be assigned to separate clusters (due to the penalty). A rank-1 update on the original Laplacian can be made by

$$L_{topic\_bias} = L_{input} + \gamma \cdot \delta_1 \delta_1^T. \tag{5}$$

Algorithm 1 *SocialTransfer*: Transfer Learning from Social Stream

Input: A target classification task which includes the target training data χ_{train}, the source auxiliary data χ_{aux}, and the target test data χ_{test}.

Output: Classification result on χ_{test}

1: Construct the initial transfer graph $G(V, E)$ based on the social transfer clustering task (c.f. Section 3.2).
2: Calculate transfer Laplacian matrix: L_{input} from G by Eq. (3).
3: **for** each chunk of tweets entering the system **do**
4: Calculate the regularization vector δ_1 using the input supervision of social topics A^{in} by Eq. (4).
5: Perform semi-supervised topic bias update on transfer Laplacian: $L_{topic\_bias} = L_{input} + \gamma \cdot \delta_1 \delta_1^T$ by Eq. (5).
6: Use Power Iteration to calculate the first q eigenvectors of L_{topic_bias}: $\boldsymbol{E}_1, \boldsymbol{E}_2, \cdots, \boldsymbol{E}_q$ which satisfy the generalized eigenproblem: $L_{topic\_bias}\boldsymbol{E} = \lambda U \boldsymbol{E}$. The resulting eigenvectors will be used as initial eigenvectors for the next updated Laplacian matrix.
7: **end for**
8: Construct matrix H with $\boldsymbol{E}_1, \boldsymbol{E}_2, \cdots, \boldsymbol{E}_q$ as columns.
9: **for** each $\chi_{tr}^m \in \chi_{train}$ **do**
10: Let u_{tr}^m be the corresponding row in H w.r.t x_{tr}^m.
11: **end for**
12: Use a traditional classification algorithm (we use SVM) to train the classifier $f'(\chi_{test})$ based on $\mathfrak{U}_{tr} = \{u_{tr}^m\}_{m=1}^M$ instead of the original training set $\chi_{train} = \{x_{tr}^m\}_{m=1}^M$ and then classify $\chi_{test} = \{x_{ts}^n\}_{n=1}^N$ in the eigen feature space.

Similarly, if there are K topics, we can modify the original matrix L_{input} with a rank-k update [19] instead of a rank-1 update. This supervised ranked update firstly allows us to seamlessly incorporate streaming data progressively. Secondly, it aims at tuning certain algebraic properties of the input Laplacian matrix which are related to the convergence rate of the Power Iteration method, eventually speeding the eigen decomposition [19].

In summary, the input supervision using topics learned from the social stream allows us to implement rank-k updates on the transfer-Laplacian matrix as a similarity learning mechanism, where vertex similarities are adjusted on the basis of the topic bias. Note that the number of nodes in the graph is not changed during updating (dimension $|V|$ is fixed); instead the updates only introduce new edges or re-weights existing edges in the graph as it iteratively reuses the eigenvectors from previous update. Due to lack of space, we refrain from describing in detail how the rank-k update improves the speed of eigenvector extraction. Essentially, the ranked update increases the eigen gap, which accelerates the convergence of the Power Iteration method. For a detailed explanation of how a supervised bias using rank-k update accelerates the eigenvector extraction process, please refer to [19].

3.6 Algorithm for SocialTransfer

Once the first q eigenvectors $\boldsymbol{E}_1, \boldsymbol{E}_2, \ldots, \boldsymbol{E}_q$ have been found by iteratively using the Power Iteration method with the topic-based input supervision, we can form a combined feature representation that depends on both the training and the auxiliary data. Traditional learners like SVMs can use the combined features that include the transfer task to train a classifier $f'(\chi_{test})$. Algorithm 1 shows the proposed *SocialTransfer* for classification in the target domain based on auxiliary social streams.

4. SOCIAL APPLICATIONS

We present two applications which are difficult to realize purely by traditional multimedia techniques (i.e., without incorporating knowledge from social data). These applications, though seemingly unrelated, can both be boosted by learning from the social domain using the intermediate topic space. *SocialTransfer* can be potentially applied to a wide variety of new social applications by effectively transferring the knowledge from social to multimedia domain.

4.1 Socialized Query Suggestion for Video Search

We first describe an application using the topic modeling via OSLDA within the *SocialTransfer* framework. Our intuition is that lack of a collaborative cross-domain recommendation environment compels users into unguided video search (pure querying rather than smart recommendation). One effect of such activity is that users will use the words of trending issues and topics (topical words) when performing video search queries on the Internet. Learning topical words in real time from social streams could be leveraged to suggest queries for video search. We believe this is an important application of real time topical analysis from social streams. In Section 6.1, we show experimental results which suggest: (1) user search queries in video search engines do contain words which we recovered as topical words from social streams using OSLDA. (2) There is a noticeable time lag between (a) OSLDA topic trend detection from social stream and (b) the increasing volume of search queries on that trend in an external (non-social stream) video search portal. This correspondence can be leveraged to augment user experience by socialized query suggestion for video search.

Socialized query suggestion for video search using the OSLDA model in *SocialTransfer* aims to recommend good query words in response to users query keywords. This will help searchers to better seek the more topic-relevant videos they are looking for, since the suggested topical words are connected to videos in the transfer graph. Said alternately, socialized query suggestion aims to localize the topic of the video the user is querying for by suggesting additional topical words. This is more effective in relevant video retrieval than just matching query keywords to video tags. Therefore, the prior knowledge of which query words the user will use for video search will not only enable the system to suggest better topical words for the user, but also improve the system capability in predicting which keywords the user will use for search and which videos the user will potentially watch in the future.

4.2 Socialized Video Recommendation

Modern video publishing sites like YouTube use related video recommendation techniques [7] based on RVGs to recommend a video to the user. The recommended video is related to the seed video which the user is currently watching by co-clicks or co-views, i.e. some signed-in user has clicked on both the seed and the related video [10] in sequence. In contrary, Socialized Video Recommendation recommends videos which bear similar topics to a seed video the user is watching. Thus, Socialized Video Recommendation is independent of the click through nature among videos, and has several advantages over traditional related video recommendation [7, 26], such as: (1) it considers video content/context (as in topics) while recommending videos, (2) its performance does not decrease as click data gets sparse, (3) it can recommend fresher videos that do not have significant user activity but are extremely relevant to the seed video and (4) it does not require signed-in user activity to learn and build RVGs.

For related video recommendation, the system must be able to predict which videos are 'related' to a seed video and are good candidates for recommendation. The first step in solving this is to detect the topic of the seed video. Thus, the job of the classifier is to classify the topic of a test seed video. Once we detect the topic of the test seed video, we can assume all the videos belonging to that topic are candidates for related video recommendation of the seed. We then recommend only those videos from the candidate pool whose tags match the seed. A socialized video recommender can be developed by creating a learner that uses auxiliary tweet data by means of transfer learning. Given a set of RVG videos in the target domain, a traditional Non-Transfer learner like SVM [4] will aim to predict the related videos of a given seed video in the test data set by building a classifier only from the training data. Instead, *SocialTransfer* builds a classifier using both training video data and auxiliary tweet data.

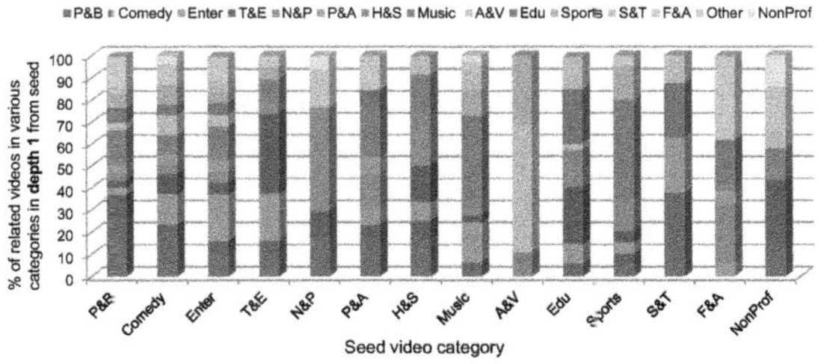

(a) depth = 1

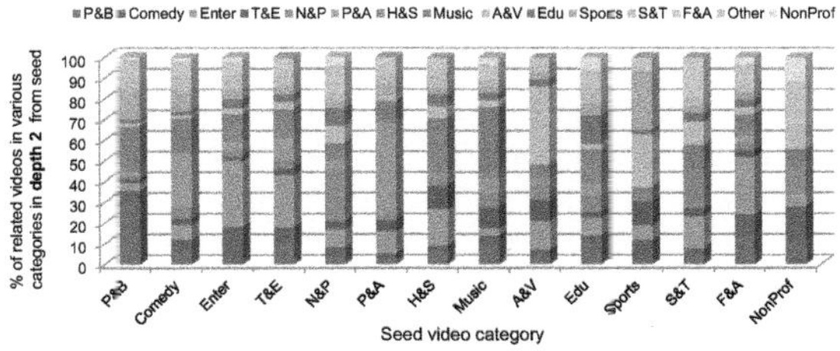

(b) depth = 2

Figure 6: Distribution of video categories of recommended videos by RVG at the depth 1 and 2 from the seed video, showing the diverse nature of video recommendation in YouTube.

5. DATA DESCRIPTION

Our study is based on a 5.7 million videos crawled from YouTube and 10.2 million tweets obtained from the NIST Twitter dataset [9]. The source domain is Twitter and the target domain is YouTube. The notations for data from each domain are included in Table 1.

5.1 YouTube Videos—Target Domain

We use a preliminary list of YouTube related video ids collected for experiments in [7]. Video meta-data includes values for entities such as video id, title, tags, view count, age (in days since uploading), category, related video ids (which comprises related videos at depth 1 of RVG) etc. As mentioned earlier, the videos related to a given seed video is captured using a directed graph, which is known as Related Video Graph (RVG) [10, 3]. Thus, if a video y is in the related video list of a seed video x, then there is a directed edge/path $x \rightarrow y$ in the RVG [10]. Moreover, for an edge $x \rightarrow y$ in the RVG, its tags can be represented as the instance: $\{tags(x)\} \rightarrow \{tags(y)\} - \{tags(x)\}$, where $\{tags(x)\}$ represents the set of tags of video x and '−' means set difference. All such instance/label combinations of the B videos have to be randomly divided into two sets for training and testing, called χ_{train} and χ_{test} respectively; where $|\chi_{train}| = M$ and $|\chi_{test}| = N$ represented as $\chi_{train} = \{x_{tr}^{m}\}_{m=1}^{M}$, $\chi_{test} = \{x_{ts}^{n}\}_{n=1}^{N}$ where $M + N = B$ and $\frac{M}{N} \approx 1.5$.

We have collected related video information up to five depths from an initial seed video ranging across the 14 main YouTube categories: Comedy, Entertainment ('Enter'), Education ('Edu'),

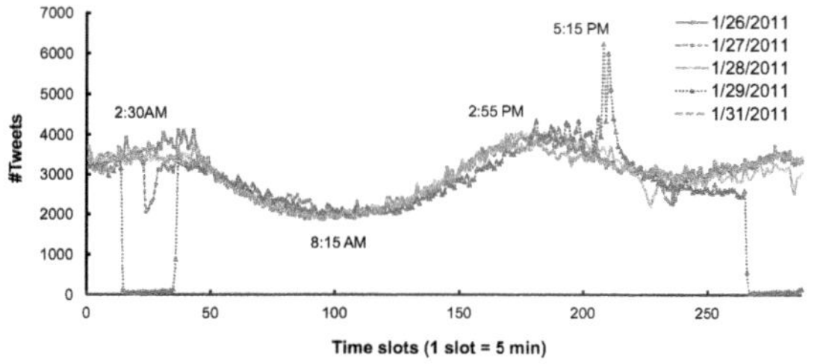

Figure 7: Daily tweet stream during 26th—31st Jan. 2011.

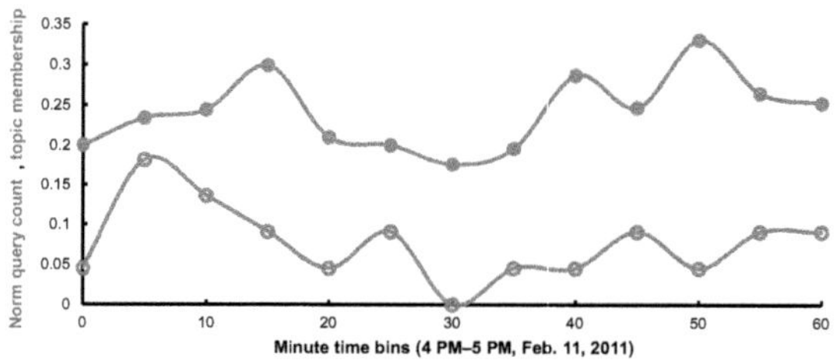

Figure 8: OSLDA trend detection on Twitter (top blue) vs. topical word search trend in a commercial video search engine (bottom brown).

Music, Film & Animation('F&A'), Non-Profits & Activism ('Non-Prof'), Science & Technology ('S&T'), Travel & Events ('T&E'), Pets & Animals (P&A), HowTo & Style ('H&S'), Autos & Vehicles ('A&V'), News & Politics ('N&P'), Sports, and People & Blogs ('P&B'). Some videos are categorized unavailable, and in such cases we use the category of its parent video. Apart from these main categories, [11] has suggested around 75 sub-categories to the main YouTube categories. We include all of these as the pool of categories from which class labels can be drawn. Therefore, we tune the OSLDA to detect tweets where the tweet words fall into the tag space belonging to any of these category videos.

Since RVGs are essentially related recommendation networks, distribution of categories over videos changes as we move one depth to the next. This introduces some degree of intended diversity in the next video recommended [10], since it might be of a different category compared to the seed but somehow related. Although [10] mentions the existence of this diversity in YouTube recommendations, it does not provide quantitative results to capture the diversity. Instead, we have thoroughly analyzed the dataset and used a histogram to study the diversity issue in YouTube video recommendations. Fig. 6 shows the category distribution of related videos at depth 1 and 2 from the seed video. In other words, the X-axis represents the category of the seed video while the Y-axis represents the category distribution of the recommended video in succesive levels. On average, we found that the next recommended video has 25% chance of being in the same category as the seed video.

5.2 Twitter Streams—Source Domain

The Twitter dataset consists of 10.2 million tweets generated in the US and collected between Jan. 26th 2011 and Feb. 11th 2011. We simulate the twitter data as a stream, with each batch of tweets representing approximately five min. The resulting rate at which tweets streams over the last week of Jan, 2011 is shown in Fig. 7, where the 5 min batch time slots account for a total of 288 slots spanning 24 hours in the horizontal axis. We show the temporal stream volume (in No. of tweets generated) distribution only across seven days in order to avoid cluttering in Fig. 7.

From Fig. 7 we can conclude that under normal circumstances, the tweet rate distribution has a general pattern over 24 hours: there is a minima around 8:15 AM, followed by a gradual rise until 3 PM in the afternoon, where a local maxima is achieved. Interestingly, another spike is usually noticed in tweets around 2:30 AM in the morning. The drops to almost zero on Jan. 29th can be accounted for by Twitter downtimes and the Blackberry outage in USA. The high spike around 5:15 PM on Jan. 29th is caused due to a high volume of tweets during the onset of the Egyptian revolutions.

6. EXPERIMENTS

We focus our experiments for the first two applications mentioned in Section 4, namely socialized query suggestion for video search using OSLDA and socialized video recommendation.

6.1 Evaluations on Socialized Query Suggestion for Video Search

Experiments were conducted using video query logs from a commercial video search engine and 10.2 million tweets. The goal is to find a temporal pattern or common terms between tweet topic words and video search keywords from video logs. Fig. 8 shows the distribution of search queries with time in video query logs for the topic *'Egypt'* with real-time trend variation on Twitter as detected by OSLDA.

We notice that there is few min's time lag between a trend topic appearing on Twitter, and the same topical words being searched on the commercial video search engine. This means as trends rise and fall in Twitter, the volume of queries on the same topic rises and falls for video search. To further support our claim that people search for Twitter trends outside Twitter, Fig. 9 shows the query keywords used in a commercial video search engine on Feb 11, 2011. If we eliminate daily searches such as 'cats,' 'movies,' and 'funny commercials' which are common (green dotted circles), then it is hard to miss that topical words (red solid circles) take up a significant portion of the remaining video search keywords. In the video search engine logs and for all queries on Feb 11th that are not daily search terms (like 'cats'), 63% of query words were detected by OSLDA.

In fact, this technique of socialized query suggestion can be extended beyond video search. We used Google Insights to understand search patterns for web and image search on Feb 11, 2011. It was not surprising that *'Egypt'* was the hottest search topic that day. In fact, Google Web Insights provided us with the top 10 web search keywords related to *'Egypt'*; 7 of which had already been detected by OSLDA earlier. For Google Image search, 6 of the top 10 search keywords were detected by OSLDA. This is convincing evidence that the OSLDA detects relevant socially active topics within the *SocialTransfer* framework.

6.2 Evaluations of Socialized Video Recommendation

For socialized video recommendation, we test *SocialTransfer* against a traditional learner like SVM [4], where *SocialTransfer* uses auxiliary social data in combination with training data, whereas a traditional learner uses only the training data for prediction (called Non-Transfer) and serves as our benchmark. Here, the classification task is simple: given a seed test video, classify whether another video is a related video of the seed or not. This in aggregation is same as the case: given a seed test video, predict the list of related videos for the seed test video.

For the experiments, we set $\gamma = 1.25$, limit the power method to extracting top-25 eigenvectors and include 60% of the topic space for input supervision. The reasoning of these choices is explained over the following sections. We have three datasets for transfer learning—the target training data, the target test data and the source

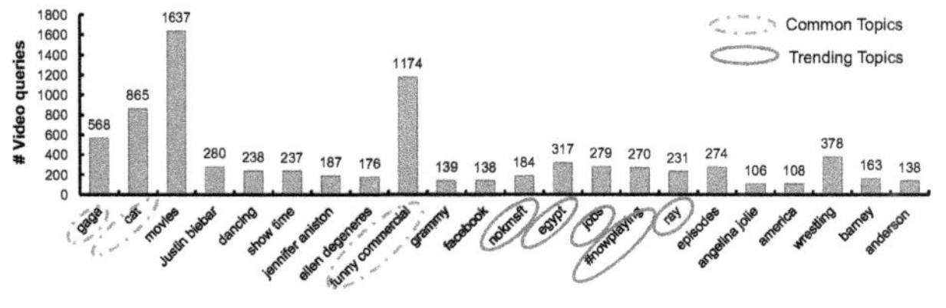

Figure 9: A significant majority of video search keywords come from trending topical words (red circles).

Table 3: Number of video instances in popular categories.

Category	#Training video	#Testing video
Comedy	254,254	169,502
Film & Animation	249,697	166,464
Entertainment	740,225	493,484
Sports	221,411	147,607
People & Blogs	252,617	168,412
Music	720,554	480,362

auxiliary data. The target dataset consists of 5.7 million videos in total along with their RVGs (contains a list of related videos for each seed video). However, some videos do not have categories or are removed from YouTube, and therefore we experiment on a reduced set of 4.8 million videos. Our training data consists of 60% videos randomly picked from the 4.8 million YouTube videos. The rest 40% videos ($\sim$ 2 million) are used for testing. As auxiliary data, we use the 10.2 million tweets from the Twitter stream. We ensure to extract topics from tweets based on approximately 90 categories (16 main + 75 other) so that the source and target domains share same categories. Additionally, we also evaluate category-specific predictions based on six popular categories (Comedy, Film & Entertainment, Sports, People & Blogs, Music). Table 3 shows the number of video instances used for evaluation in some of the popular categories.

In Table 4, we report the average error in prediction for the Non-Transfer cases (SVM on training only) vs. *SocialTransfer*. Non-Transfer refers to application of the traditional SVM learner to the original target dataset with no social influence (only training features are used); *SocialTransfer* means to apply SVM on the combined feature representation learned using transfer learning from social data (training + auxiliary).

The performance in Table 4 is measured in error rate by averaging 10 random repeats on each dataset by the two evaluation methods. For each repeat, we randomly select 5,000 instances per category as target training data. We report the prediction error rate in each of the main categories, along with the overall error for the entire data set. We also report the standard deviation of the repeats in Table 4. The two methods are well-tuned using 10-fold cross validation. The overall gain using *SocialTransfer* is around 35.1% compared to non-transfer settings. Please note that the overall error rate is averaged over all the main categories and not just the six categories shown in Table 4. Performance improvement using transfer learning is most in category 'People & Blogs.' In all the major categories, *SocialTransfer* performs better than a traditional non-transfer learner. We further test the prediction error in the *SocialTransfer* framework based on several factors including scalability and learning capability per day of stream inflow.

Accuracy variation with tweet stream inflow. We test the rate at which the prediction error decreases with incoming stream of tweets (Fig. 10) every day across 12 days of the social data (Jan 26th—Feb 7th). It is clear from Fig. 10 that the influence of Twitter is significant (rapid decrease in error in first three days), and the chatter over a week consists of substantial number of words in every video category. However, some topical words co-occur in different topics, for example the word 'live' might refer to music or entertainment. On course of the 12 days, we see a 41.4% net reduction of error. Interestingly, within the first three days (26th—29th Jan.), the error is reduced by almost 20%, while the rest of the nine days involve an almost equal amount of error reduction.

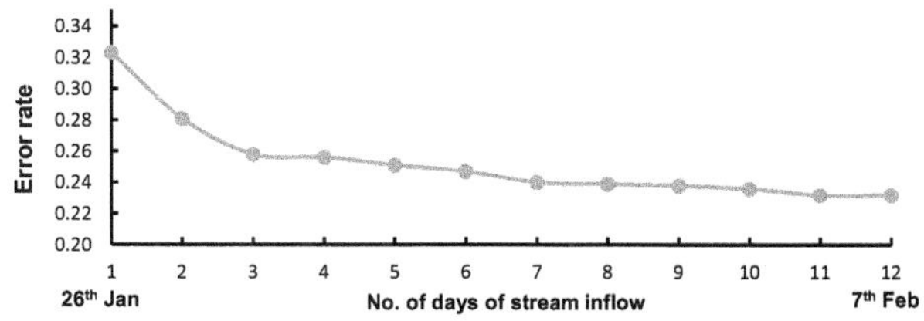

Figure 10: Drop in prediction error rate with daily stream inflow from Twitter.

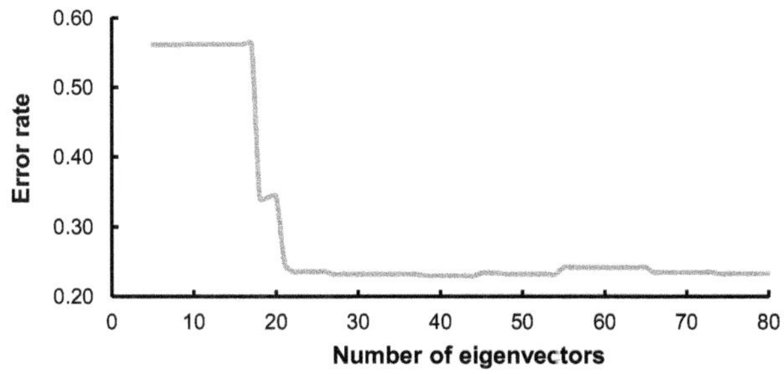

Figure 11: The influence of the number of eigenvectors extracted on the error rate.

Eigenvectors. Previously we mentioned that for the experiments, we fix the number of eigenvectors to be extracted from the transfer Laplacian to 25. The reason for this choice is due to results of Fig. 11, which shows the variation of the error rate with the number of eigenvectors extracted. We see that when the number of eigenvectors extracted is greater than 23, the error rate is almost constant. However, there is a trade-off between the time required for extraction vs. error rate of prediction for a certain number of eigenvectors to be extracted. Thus, since the variation of reduction in error rate is not significant beyond $22-25$ eigenvectors, we can safely assume that the extraction of more than 25 eigenvectors is not necessary.

Scalability. The speed at which the incoming stream of tweets is explored for topics by OSLDA together with the time required for eigen feature extraction from the transfer graph using spectral learning is important for maintaining scalability with the real-time social stream. In our system, the topic modeling is done in parallel with the eigenvector extraction to save time. Thus, our main aim should be to limit the time required to complete either of these tasks within the incoming tweet flow time.

Fig. 12 shows the comparison of runtimes for various settings of OSLDA, eigenvector extraction using power iteration (PI) and eigenvector extraction using Normalized cut (Ncut) with the time taken on average for an incoming chunk of tweets to stream in. For OSLDA, '$20k$' (in legend) refers to 20 topics extracted and '$50i$' refers to 50 iterations of the generative process. Experiments were run on a IBM server with 2.67 GHz processor and 8 GB RAM.

From Fig. 12, we can safely conclude that the model scales to incoming bursts of tweets, since the matrix decomposition with Power Iteration and the topic modeling using OSLDA require less time than the speed of incoming tweets. Note that Ncut does not scale as it takes longer time to extract eigenvectors than the speed of the incoming burst of tweets. Moreover, for more than 40,000 tweets, Ncut causes our system to run out of memory.

Table 4: Experimental results in error rate for predicting relevant videos for Socialized Video Recommendation. The results are the averages of 10 random repeats along with their standard deviations. Both methods are tuned with 10-fold cross validation.

Approach	Overall	Comedy	Film & Animation	Entertainment	Sports	People & Blogs	Music
Non-Transfer	0.357 ± 0.049	0.429 ± 0.059	0.334 ± 0.063	0.386 ± 0.023	0.394 ± 0.072	0.247 ± 0.066	0.356 ± 0.036
SocialTransfer	0.232 ± 0.043	0.397 ± 0.065	0.242 ± 0.051	0.219 ± 0.015	0.282 ± 0.082	0.112 ± 0.032	0.230 ± 0.029

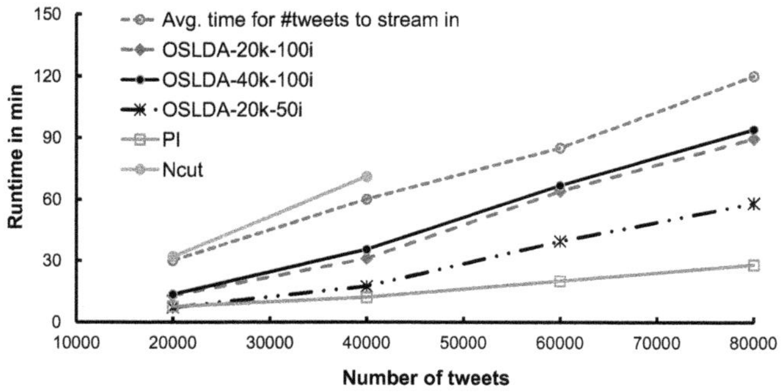

Figure 12: Runtime comparison for topic modeling and eigen decomposition with incoming tweet stream in *SocialTransfer*.

7. CONCLUSION

This paper presents *SocialTransfer*, a novel cross-domain real time transfer learning approach based on social streams. *SocialTransfer* can be applied to various multimedia applications which are boosted by the knowledge acquired from cross-domain data. We demonstrate the use of the *SocialTransfer* in realizing two unique applications, namely socialized video recommendation and socialized query suggestion for video search. Evaluation of video popularity prediction using *SocialTransfer* is left for future work. To aid the transfer process across domains in scaling with dynamic social streams, we propose a tweet topic based semi-supervised bias/ input supervision on the transfer graph that can help seamlessly incorporate new trend topics and accelerate the extraction of combined social and video features using eigen decomposition. To the best of our knowledge, such a framework that unites transfer learning and topic modeling in a scalable fashion for social stream data has not been proposed before. Experimental results show that *SocialTransfer* can outperform traditional learners by almost 35.1% reduction of error rate in predicting related videos during recommendation. The main contribution of this work is the scalable model for cross-domain real time transfer learning from social streams and using social topics in building novel multimedia applications that can hardly be realized by traditional multimedia techniques alone.

8. REFERENCES

[1] S. D. Roy, T. Mei, W. Zeng and S. Li. Empowering Cross-Domain Internet Media With Real-Time Topic Learning From Social Streams. In *Proc. of ICME*, 2012.

[2] F. R. Bach and M. I. Jordan. Learning spectral clustering, with application to speech separation. *Journal of Machine Learning Research*, 7:1963–2001, 2006.

[3] S. Baluja, R. Seth, D. Sivakumar, Y. Jing, J. Yagnik, S. Kumar, D. Ravichandran, and M. Aly. Video suggestion and discovery for youtube: taking random walks through the view graph. In *Proc. of WWW*, 2008.

[4] B. E. Boser, I. Guyon, and V. Vapnik. A training algorithm for optimal margin classifiers. In *Proc. of Workshop on Computational Learning Theory*, 1992.

[5] G. Chatzopoulou, C. Sheng, and M. Faloutsos. A first step towards understanding popularity in youtube. In *Proc. of INFOCOM Workshop*, 2010.

[6] Z. Chen, J. Cao, Y. Song, J. Guo, Y. Zhang, and J. Li. Context-oriented web video tag recommendation. In *Wide Web Conference*, pages 1079–1080, 2010.

[7] X. Cheng, C. Dale, and J. Liu. Statistics and social network of youtube videos. In *Proc. of Inter. Workshop on Quality of Service*, pages 229–238, 2008.

[8] W. Dai, O. Jin, G.-R. Xue, Q. Yang, and Y. Yu. Eigentransfer: a unified framework for transfer learning. In *Proc. of ICML*, page 25, 2009.

[9] http://trec.nist.gov/data/tweets/.

[10] J. Davidson, B. Liebald, J. Liu, P. Nandy, T. V. Vleet, U. Gargi, S. Gupta, Y. He, M. Lambert, B. Livingston, and D. Sampath. The youtube video recommendation system. In *Proc. of International Conference on Recommender Systems*, pages 293–296, 2010.

[11] K. Filippova and K. B. Hall. Improved video categorization from text metadata and user comments. In *Proc. of SIGIR*, 2011.

[12] M. D. Hoffman, D. M. Blei, and F. R. Bach. Online learning for latent dirichlet allocation. In *Proc. of Neural Information Processing Systems*, pages 856–864, 2010.

[13] X. Jin, A. C. Gallagher, L. Cao, J. Luo, and J. Han. The wisdom of social multimedia: using flickr for prediction and forecast. In *Proc. of ACM Multimedia*, pages 1235–1244, 2010.

[14] F. Lin and W. W. Cohen. Power iteration clustering. In *Proc. of ICML*, pages 655–662, 2010.

[15] X. Ling, W. Dai, G.-R. Xue, Q. Yang, and Y. Yu. Spectral domain-transfer learning. In *ACM Conference on Knowledge Discovery and Data Mining*, pages 488–496, 2008.

[16] H. Luo, J. Fan, D. A. Keim, and S. Satoh. Personalized news video recommendation. In *Proc. of MMM*, pages 459–471, 2009.

[17] M. Namaan. Social multimedia: highlighting opportunities for search and mining of multimedia data in social media applications. *Multimedia Tools and Applications*, 56(1):9, 2012.

[18] H. Ma, T. C. Zhou, M. R. Lyu, and I. King. Improving recommender systems by incorporating social contextual information. *ACM Transactions on Information Systems*, 29(2):9, 2011.

[19] D. Mavroeidis. Mind the eigen-gap, or how to accelerate semi-supervised spectral learning algorithms. In *Proc. of IJCAI*, pages 2692–2697, 2011.

[20] T. Mei, B. Yang, X.-S. Hua, and S. Li. Contextual Video Recommendation by Multimodal Relevance and User Feedback. *ACM Trans. on Information Systems*, 29(2):10, 2011.

[21] S. J. Pan and Q. Yang. A survey on transfer learning. *IEEE Trans. on Knowledge and Data Engineering*, 22:1345–1359, 2010.

[22] D. Ramage, S. T. Dumais, and D. J. Liebling. Characterizing microblogs with topic models. In *Proc. of AAAI Conf. on Weblogs and Social Media*, 2010.

[23] G. Toderici, H. Aradhye, M. Pasca, L. Sbaiz, and J. Yagnik. Finding meaning on youtube: Tag recommendation and category discovery. In *Proc. of CVPR*, pages 3447–3454, 2010.

[24] Q. Xu, E. Xiang, and Q. Yang. Social-behavior transfer learning for recommendation systems. *Proc. of Workshop on Social Web Mining*.

[25] B. Yang, T. Mei, X.-S. Hua, L. Yang, S.-Q. Yang, and M. Li. Online video recommendation based on multimodal fusion and relevance feedback. In *Proc. of CIVR*, pages 73–80, 2007.

[26] R. Zhou, S. Khemmarat, and L. Gao. The impact of youtube recommendation system on video views. In *Proc. of International Conference on Internet Measurement*, pages 404–410, 2010.

[27] L. Wu, L. Yang, N. Yu, and X.-S. Hua. Learning to tag. In *Proc. of WWW*, pages 361–370, 2009.

[28] P. Zhao, S. C. H. Hoi. OTL: A Framework of Online Transfer Learning. In *Proc. of ICML*, pages 1231–1238, 2010.

Hybrid Social Media Network

Dong Liu
Dept. of Electrical Engineering
Columbia University
New York, NY 10027, USA
dongliu@ee.columbia.edu

Guangnan Ye
Dept. of Electrical Engineering
Columbia University
New York, NY 10027, USA
yegn@ee.columbia.edu

Ching-Ting Chen
Dept. of Electrical Engineering
Columbia University
New York, NY 10027, USA
cc3016@columbia.edu

Shuicheng Yan
Dept. of ECE
National Univ. of Singapore
Singapore, 117576, Singapore
eleyans@nus.edu.sg

Shih-Fu Chang
Dept. of Electrical Engineering
Columbia University
New York, NY 10027, USA
sfchang@ee.columbia.edu

ABSTRACT

Analysis and recommendation of multimedia information can be greatly improved if we know the interactions between the content, user, and concept, which can be easily observed from the social media networks. However, there are many heterogeneous entities and relations in such networks, making it difficult to fully represent and exploit the diverse array of information. In this paper, we develop a *hybrid social media network*, through which the heterogeneous entities and relations are seamlessly integrated and a joint inference procedure across the heterogeneous entities and relations can be developed. The network can be used to generate personalized information recommendation in response to specific targets of interests, e.g., personalized multimedia albums, target advertisement and friend/topic recommendation. In the proposed network, each node denotes an entity and the multiple edges between nodes characterize the diverse relations between the entities (e.g., friends, similar contents, related concepts, favorites, tags, etc). Given a query from a user indicating his/her information needs, a propagation over the hybrid social media network is employed to infer the utility scores of all the entities in the network while learning the edge selection function to activate only a sparse subset of relevant edges, such that the query information can be best propagated along the activated paths. Driven by the intuition that much redundancy exists among the diverse relations, we have developed a robust optimization framework based on several sparsity principles. We show significant performance gains of the proposed method over the state of the art in multimedia retrieval and recommendation using data crawled from social media sites. To the best of our knowledge, this is the first model supporting not only aggregation but also judicious selection of heterogeneous relations in the social media networks.

Categories and Subject Descriptors

H.3.1 [**Information Storage and Retrieval**]: Content Analysis and Indexing

General Terms

Algorithms, Experimentation, Performance

Keywords

Hybrid Social Media Network, Edge Selective Information Propagation, Multimedia Retrieval and Recommendation.

1. INTRODUCTION

The modern information era is marked by the explosively growing networks of people, information and the rich interactions between them as demonstrated in the prevalent use of many well known social media networks, such as Flickr, Youtube and Facebook. Rather than simply searching for and passively consuming media content, users in such networks actively create and exchange rich multimedia content (including videos, images, music, blogs and so on) for social interactions [2], which brings greatly expanded experiences for end users.

Notably, the social media networks are characterized by the heterogeneous entities and relations. Take Facebook as an example, where the user, concept and multimedia object coexist in the network with various types of relations. Users may share multiple relations such as friendship, group membership, message communication and so on. Multimedia objects may also have multiple relations, each of which reflects the similarity in certain features or attributes (e.g., color, shape, attributes, or metadata). In addition, each user can post comments or rating for a multimedia object, bookmark it as favorite, or even assign notes to certain regions in the object, which forms multiple relations between the user and the multimedia object. The richness of entities and relations provides a comprehensive description of the contextual information, facilitating the design of novel multimedia applications with new user experiences.

However, the richness and diversity of the entities and relations mentioned above bring new challenges in leveraging such information for multimedia analysis. First, there are heterogeneous entities and relations in the social media network, in which some relations are multi-faceted (e.g., relations between two images could be measured based on

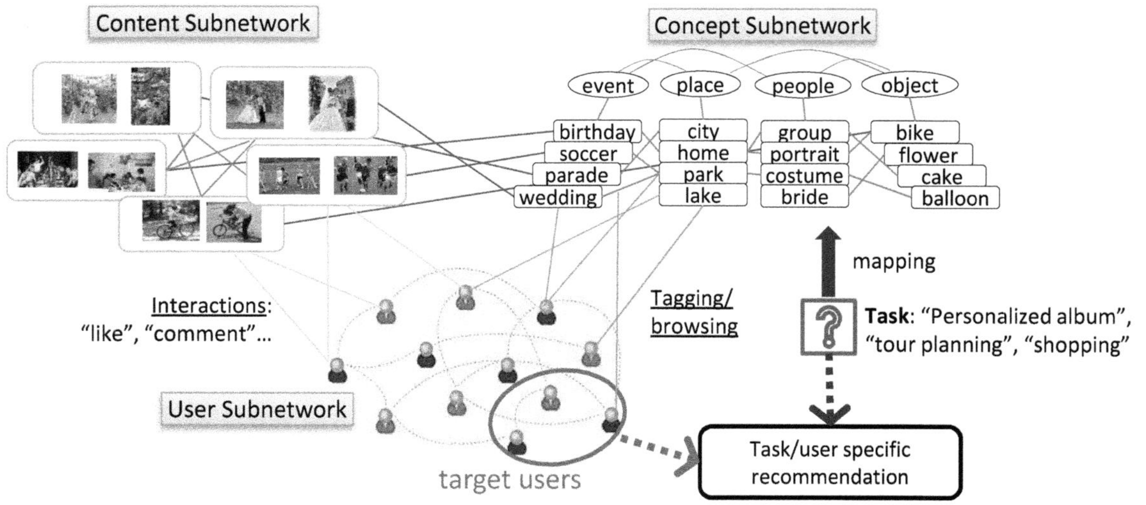

Figure 1: Different from the conventional network models that treat nodes in a homogeneous way, the proposed hybrid social media network preserves the heterogeneous types of entities and relations from subnetworks of user, content, and concept. Given a query from a user or task, the inference process dynamically selects the most informative links and relation types based on a sparsity constrained optimization model, and propagates the information along the activated paths only. The results can be used to recommend information in a personalized way for applications like personalized album generation, friend topic recommendation, and target ads.

similarities of different raw features as well as mid-level attributes) while some relations are beyond pairwise (e.g. a user annotates a photo with a tag, which forms a three-way relation among the three entities), making it difficult to develop a unified model to capture such heterogeneous data types and relations. Second, to exploit the rich entities and relations, straightforward application of traditional methods (like information propagation [23] and spectral clustering [13, 6]) designed for homogeneous networks is no longer adequate. We need to investigate novel solutions that can not only fuse complex relations but also prudently select most useful information to improve the overall performance in information propagation.

In this work, we propose a novel *hybrid social media network* model, through which entities of heterogeneous types and their relations can be seamlessly integrated and new inference techniques can be developed. The hybrid social media network is illustrated in Figure 1. Specifically, the hybrid network spans several homogeneous subnetworks (made of content, people and concept) and the rich multi-faceted and possibly high-order connections both within and between subnetworks. It differs from the conventional networks by incorporating the much richer types of entities and relations. For example, users may form relations based on friendship, author-subscriber, or group membership as discussed earlier. In the concept subnetwork, there may be rich statistical and ontological relationships. Between the subnetworks, users may view, like, dislike, or recommend content, while individual photos, videos, albums, or channels may be assigned various concepts (about scenes, objects, events, or aesthetics). In addition, users can assign concepts to the specific content, forming high-order relations among the three subnetworks. The proposed representation over the hybrid networks provides great flexibility for encoding various types of complex relations at different levels.

The proposed hybrid network can be used as an effective system for information propagation and recommendation. The specific targets of interest (about user, concept, or content) can be first formulated as a query vector with the vector elements corresponding to the target nodes set to 1 and the rest 0. For example, a task of "recommend media content about architecture and fashion of New York for user A" can be formulated as a query vector specifying the corresponding entities as the targets. The goal is to propagate the information contained in the query vector to other nodes in the network, through the large diverse pool of relation links. After the propagation process is complete, each node in the network will be associated with a predicted utility score, which can then be used to rank and recommend the most relevant information in response to the initial targets.

We investigate how to determine the best mechanism for propagating information over the network and propose a solution based on edge-selective optimizations, which activates only a sparse subset of relations for information propagation. Specifically, we define the propagation process as a Markov random walk in which the transition probability between each node pair can be calculated by the weighted combination of only the selected relations along the edges. The consistency between the predicted utility scores and the initial scores of the query provides a natural supervision step. To achieve effective edge selection, we use the $\ell_{2,1}$-norm induced group sparsity to determine a subset of relation types while using ℓ_1-norm induced sparsity to reduce the total number of edges selected and eliminate the potential redundancy that may exist among the diverse relations. We formulate the approach as a sparsity regularized objective and derive an optimization process that can simultaneously estimate the node utility scores and the edge selective indicators.

The use of the sparsity principles can be justified in several ways. First, given the large array of relations captured in the network, it is natural to expect information redundancy. For example, the similarities between images may be redundantly manifested in several features like edges, local features, and textures. Likewise, contact relations between users may strongly bias the existence of favorite relations or the use of similar tags in content annotation. Second, judicious selections of a small subset of relations may greatly reduce the computational complexity of the information propagation process. We will confirm the validity of the above rationales using empirical experiment results to be presented in Section 6.3.

We will demonstrate experimentally the proposed hybrid network can achieve significant performance gains when evaluated over various use scenarios such as personalized content recommendation, topic/friend discovery, and target ad, etc. We will also show clear evidences confirming the capabilities of the model for dynamically selecting the most useful relations in answering each query.

2. RELATED WORK

Some recent work [7, 21] focused on aggregating the rich variety of information in the social network, through which the performance of information retrieval can be improved. However, these works typically aggregate information using a simple weighted average and then directly utilize the aggregation results for final analysis. Such an averaging operation blindly converts the hybrid relations into a homogeneous type and cannot adapt the edge combination weights for each query dynamically. In contrast, we emphasize the core challenge addressed in our work is how to harness the heterogeneous nodes and relations in solving the associated optimization problem. Our main contribution is the explicit modeling and optimal selection of diverse edges in the hybrid network based on a sound sparsity principle. The edge selection technique is key, which simultaneously exploits a large pool of heterogeneous edges (instead of blindly aggregating all the edges as in the prior work) and explicitly determines a subset of edges for each query dynamically (the selected edges will be assigned with different weights reflecting the importance of each edge for each specific query). Solving the dynamic edge selection problem is crucial in successful modeling of hybrid networks, but has not been addressed in the literature so far.

Graph-based ranking has shown effective performance in propagating information in sparsely connected networks. One representative work along this direction is the manifold ranking method proposed by Zhou *et al.* [23], which ranks the samples based on the intrinsic manifold structure among the samples. Given a query vector that indicates the relevant nodes in the graph (treated as initial positive labels), the objective is to estimate a function that predicts the relevance score of each node in the rest of the graph. The optimization process finds the optimal solution that fits the initial query and is smooth over the graph. He *et al.* [9] employed such ranking method for content-based image retrieval and obtained good performance. The other popular method is the graph based random walk, where the stationary probability of the random walk process is used as the ranking scores of the nodes. Such ranking method has been widely used in video search reranking [11], social media tag ranking [15], etc. However, all these methods are limited to homogeneous networks with nodes of the same type, which are inadequate for modeling the heterogeneous entities and relations.

Some recent work also used graphs to model the multiple types of entities and relations. The recent works in [1, 24] proposed to build multiple graphs, each of which models a distinct feature type, but the approach was to aggregate the diverse types of relations into a single composite type, which is fundamentally different from our proposed hybrid network model using an explicit joint learning procedure over heterogeneous entities and edges. Notably, the recently proposed hypergraph [3] is also a generalization of the traditional graph, where a hyperedge can connect any number of nodes and thus models the high-order relations among the entities. In [4], the authors employed the hypergraph to combine the social media information and music content, and achieved good performance on mucic recommendation. The work in [8] employed the hypergraph to model the multi-typed objects including documents, tags and users, based on which a personalized tag recommendation task is cast into a graph based ranking problem. Despite the capability in modeling heterogeneous entities and relations, such graph-based models aim at describing the high-order relationship among a collection of entities, but cannot model the multi-faceted yet diverse relations among entities. Specifically, none of the prior work addressed the issue of "selecting" the subset of most informative relations. Instead, all of them went on to develop "fusion" or "aggregation" of a potentially over-populated pool of relations – likely suffering from the problem of information overload.

The heterogeneous information network [10, 12] in the data mining community also attempts to model the relations between heterogeneous entities. However, the modeling is performed by connecting any two entities with a single kind of relation, which actually falls in the single edge graph and thus differs from our proposal here. In particular, the authors in [16] introduced a homogeneous multi-edge graph model to describe multiple parallel relations between the multi-label images, where an edge connects two similar local regions in different images. However, it can only handle the homogeneous entities (local regions) and relations (pairwise regional similarities), and hence cannot be applied into the heterogeneous scenarios.

3. USE SCENARIOS OF THE HYBRID SOCIAL MEDIA NETWORK

Our hybrid network can be used as an effective system for information propagation and recommendation. We present a few sample use cases below to exemplify the recommendation process. Additional cases can also be easily constructed.

Personalized recommendation of contents, friends, and topics: Given a specific user and his/her interest (e.g., "NYC" + "The statue of liberty") as the target query (i.e., setting the nodes corresponding to the users and the concepts to 1 in the initial query vector), the hybrid network is used to propagate the information throughout the network and predict the utility scores for all other nodes. After the propagation, the highest ranked images can be used to generate a personalized multimedia album relevant to the specific interest. The nodes corresponding to users receiving the highest utility scores can be used as the candidates for recommending friends who may share similar interests. Additionally, other concepts (like "art" and "jewelry") may be discovered as recommended topics of interest to the user.

Target media ads: We can also set a certain set of media objects or topical concepts as the initial query and propagate such information through the network. The final predicted utility scores associated with the user nodes in the network can be used to identify the best group of users

Table 1: Statistics of the entities and relations.

Entities	Notation	Avg. #
Tags	$\mathcal{C}$	100
Users	$\mathcal{U}$	778
Photos	$\mathcal{O}$	7,046
Relation Types	**Order**	**Avg. #**
user-image favorite	second	467
user-user favorite	second	1,322
user-user contact	second	2,146
user-image comment	second	4,203
concept-concept co-occurrence	second	5,231
user-image ownership	second	7,046
image-image SIFT similarity	second	21,138
image-image mid-level similarity	second	21,138
user-concept ownership	second	23,115
concept-image tagging	second	23,115
user-image-tag tagging	third	23,026

that may be interested in receiving such media objects or topics. Media objects and their associated products (e.g., music, art, or food) can be pushed to such identified user groups. Note the explicit use of heterogeneous relations (e.g., image content similarity, ontological concept relations) provides unique benefits that will allow recommendation results to go beyond what has been done in the collaborative filtering community which often focuses on user preference rating data only.

4. CONSTRUCTION OF HYBRID SOCIAL MEDIA NETWORK

In this section, we will construct a sample hybrid social media network by crawling the real-world social images from Flickr. We first introduce the details on the crawling process and then explain how to extract the observable relations to construct the hybrid social media network.

4.1 Social Media Dataset

To construct a sample hybrid social media network for modeling the heterogeneous entities and relations, we collected social media data from the popular social media website Flickr. Specifically, we crawled 10 photo groups including "Beijing", "New York", "Taipei", "IKEA", "Universal Studio", "Fashion", "Korean Food", "Sneaker", "Painted", and "Wildlife", each of which is a self-organized photo sharing community with common interests. We chose these groups to cover a diverse set of user groups, ranging from cities, tourist sites, products, and life styles. We downloaded all the photos, users and tags in each group. To ensure that each tag corresponds to a meaningful semantic concept, a filtering process was performed to remove the meaningless tags. We ranked the tags based on their occurring frequencies, and selected the top 100 tags as the concept set of each group (excluding the stop words and other meaningless words)[1]. The final set of users, photos, and concepts are used as the entity nodes of the constructed network. For the heterogeneous relations between the entities, we crawled the observable relations between the different entities in Flickr and obtained 8 types of relations, which include *user-user contact relation*, *user-user favorite relation*, *user-image ownership relation*, *user-image comment relation*, *user-image favorite relation*, *user-concept ownership relation*, *concept-image tagging relation* and *user-image-tag tagging relation*. Besides these relations from Flickr, we also constructed the *concept-concept co-occurrence relation* and two kinds of *image-image similarity relations* to exemplify the relations between the corresponding entities, resulting in 11 types of relations in total. Table 1 shows the statistics of the entities and relations averaged across the 10 groups.

[1]Though advanced techniques can be used to extract higher-level semantic concepts from tags, in this paper it is not our focus and the terms "tag" and "concept" are used equally.

4.2 Hybrid Network Construction

For each photo group, a hybrid social media network can be built. Denote by $\mathcal{O} = \{o_1, \ldots, o_{|\mathcal{O}|}\}$, $\mathcal{C} = \{c_1, \ldots, c_{|\mathcal{C}|}\}$ and $\mathcal{U} = \{u_1, \ldots, u_{|\mathcal{U}|}\}$ the entities of multimedia objects, concepts and users in a group respectively, where $|\cdot|$ denotes the cardinality of a set. We treat each entity as one node and establish the relational edges (both pair-wise and high-order) and their associated weights as follows:

User-user contact: For users u_i and u_j, we establish an edge if one user is listed in the contact list of the other, and the weight w_{ij} is set as 1.

User-user favorite: An edge is built to connect u_i and u_j if one user favorites the images owned by the other user. The edge weight is estimated as $w_{ij} = t_{ij}/\max(t_{ij})$, where t_{ij} is total number of favorite images between the two users, and $\max(t_{ij})$ denotes the maximum number of image favorites between any two users.

User-image ownership favorite comment: For the first two relations, if a user owns or favorites one image, there will be an edge with weight set as 1. For the comment relation, an edge is built to connect a user and an image, and the weight is determined as the number of comments the user has provided for the image divided by the maximum comment number between any pair of user and image.

User-concept ownership: If concept c_j has appeared in the photos of u_i, an edge will be built between u_i and c_j and the weight is set as 1.

Concept-image tagging: We establish an edge if one image is annotated with one tag and the corresponding edge weight is set as 1.

User-image-concept tagging: If a user has tagged one image with one concept, there will be a hyperedge connecting these three entities and the weight is 1.

Concept-concept co-occurrence: Given tag c_i and c_j, we estimate their statistical relation as $w_{ij} = f(c_i, c_j)/|\mathcal{O}|$, where $f(c_i, c_j)$ denotes the number of images in the group that are simultaneously tagged by c_i and c_j while $|\mathcal{O}|$ denotes the total number of images in the network. Currently, we use co-occurrence relations among concepts to facilitate the hybrid network study. Our framework allows incorporation of other relations like lexical and ontological ones.

Image-image similarity: We use two kinds of features to estimate the image similarity, resulting in two types of relations. One feature is the SIFT Bag-of-Words (BoW) feature [14], and for each image we extract 128-dimensional SIFT feature from the keypoints detected by two kinds of detectors: Difference of Gaussian and Hessian Affine [18]. Then, k-means method is applied to group the SIFT features into 5,000 clusters. Finally, each image is represented by a 5,000-dimensional BoW feature. The second feature is the mid-level Classeme feature [22], which is a 2,659-dimensional feature vector corresponding to the classifier output scores for 2,659 semantic concepts. In this work, we choose the nearest neighbor graph to construct the image-image similarity subnetwork. For each image o_i, we find its K nearest neighbors and establish an edge between o_i and its neighbors. The similarity between images is defined as

$$w_{ij} = \begin{cases} \exp(-\frac{d(o_i,o_j)}{\sigma}), & \text{if } j \in \mathcal{N}_K(i) \text{ or } i \in \mathcal{N}_K(j), \\ 0, & \text{otherwise,} \end{cases} \quad (1)$$

where $\mathcal{N}_K(j)$ denotes the index set of the K nearest neighbors of sample o_j (we set $K = 3$), $d(o_i, o_j)$ denotes the distance between two samples (We use χ^2 distance for SIFT BoW and use Euclidean distance for Classeme), σ is the radius parameter of the Gaussian function, which is set as the mean value of all pairwise distances between the samples.

5. INFORMATION PROPAGATION OVER HYBRID SOCIAL MEDIA NETWORK

In this section, we present the proposed information propagation method over the hybrid network. We first present the formulation based on the multi-level sparsity and then introduce an efficient procedure for the optimization.

5.1 Problem Formulation

Denote by r the total number of relation types amongst the multimedia objects, concepts and users. Let $G = (V, E)$ denote a hybrid social media network with the set of nodes V and the set of edges E. The node set is a finite set $V = \{v_1, \ldots, v_n\} = \{o_1, \ldots, o_{|\mathcal{O}|}, c_1, \ldots, c_{|\mathcal{C}|}, u_1, \ldots, u_{|\mathcal{U}|}\}$ with $n = |\mathcal{O}| + |\mathcal{C}| + |\mathcal{U}|$. The edge set is a family of multi-edge set $E = \{\mathcal{E}_{ij} \bigcup \mathcal{H}_{ij}\}$ amongst V where $\mathcal{E}_{ij} = \{e_{ij}^1, \ldots, e_{ij}^{n_{ij}}\}$ denotes the multiple edges between node v_i and v_j with the number of edges $n_{ij} = |\mathcal{E}_{ij}|$ and each e_{ij}^k characterizes one type of relations between the two nodes. Furthermore, $\mathcal{H}_{ij} = \{h_{ij}^1, \ldots, h_{ij}^{m_{ij}}\}$ is the set of hyperedges that are associated with v_i and v_j, where each h_{ij}^k denotes one type of high-order relation composed of v_i, v_j and other nodes in V, m_{ij} is the total number of hyperedges that contain v_i and v_j. To ease the representation, we harmonize the edges and hyperedges associated with v_i and v_j as $\mathcal{S}_{ij} = \{s_{ij}^1, \ldots, s_{ij}^{n_{ij}}, s_{ij}^{n_{ij}+1}, \ldots, s_{ij}^{n_{ij}+m_{ij}}\}$, where each s_{ij}^k denotes an edge ($k = 1, \ldots, n_{ij}$) or a hyperedge ($k = n_{ij}+1, \ldots, n_{ij}+m_{ij}$). Furthermore, we use w_{ij}^k to denote the edge affinity weight associated with edge s_{ij}^k.

Given the initial query nodes, the task is to propagate the initial information contained in the query through the network to predict the utility scores for each node in the entire network. Let $\mathbf{f} = [f_1, \ldots, f_n]^\top$ denote the predicted utility score vector for all the nodes. We define a query vector $\mathbf{y} = [y_1, \ldots, y_n]^\top$ in which $y_i = 1$ if $v_i \in V$ is in the query and $y_i = 0$ otherwise. For example, for the aforementioned query "recommend content about architecture and fashion of New York to user A", y_i for the nodes "architecture", "fashion", "New York", and "user A" will be set to 1.

The information propagation over the hybrid social media network is to infer the utility score of each node based on the hybrid network as well as the label information conveyed by the query. However, we are facing challenges particularly in view of the large number of relation links of heterogeneous types. It is intuitive to assume that when propagating information for each query, many of the relations are redundant and only a small subset of relation types should be used. Therefore, the edges should be selected so that only the most appropriate ones are retained as the suitable path for information propagation. To realize the edge selective information propagation, we resort to sparsity induced regularizer to couple the edge selection and information propagation together. Given an edge/hyperedge s_{ij}^k and its associated affinity weight w_{ij}^k, we establish an edge strength function $\phi(w_{ij}^k) = \alpha_{ij}^k w_{ij}^k$ to indicate the importance of the edge in the propagation, where $\alpha_{ij}^k \geq 0$ is a selective parameter controlling whether the edge is selected. An edge is strong if its affinity value is high and it is selected. The selective parameter plays a key role in our framework – only edges assigned non-zero values are selected for information propagation. Note w_{ij}'s capture the raw relations computed offline from the data, while α_{ij}'s are learned for each query dynamically online. It is important to note that we only associate a single selective parameter for a multi-way hyperedge, which means that all the node pairs involved in a hyperedge will share the same edge selective parameter. In this way, the high-order hyper-relation can be well preserved in our model.

To handle each type of relations differently, we also group the selective parameters for edges belonging to the same type (e.g., all edges corresponding to color similarities, user-friendship, user-content favorites, etc) together and denote each type as $\boldsymbol{\alpha}_g$, with g indicating the type. Denote by $\boldsymbol{\alpha}$ the vector comprising of all selective parameters. Then we formulate the edge selective optimization problem as minimizing the following objective function:

$$\Omega(\mathbf{f}, \{\phi(w_{ij}^k)\}) + \frac{\lambda}{2}\|\mathbf{f} - \mathbf{y}\|_2^2 + \gamma(\sum_{g=1}^{r} \|\boldsymbol{\alpha}_g\|_2 + \|\boldsymbol{\alpha}\|_1), \quad (2)$$

where $\lambda, \gamma > 0$ are two trade-off parameters among the three competing terms. The first term Ω is a regularization term responsible for the information propagation. The second term is the label fitness constraint enforcing that a good propagation should not deviate too much from the initial label assignment of the query nodes. The third term is sparse penalty on the edges that explicitly achieves the sparse edge subset selection at both the group and individual edges. The ℓ_{21}-norm in the last term ensures the sparse selection principle is applied to the group level, namely, only a small number of relation types will be selected and the ℓ_1-norm is used to ensure only a small set of individual edges are selected. This is quite intuitive: for instance, for friend recommendation, it is likely that the image similarity edges will not contribute much and the optimization process may result in the complete deselection of all relation edges of this type. In the case when all types of relations are useful, selection of edges at the individual levels is still useful for minimizing the redundancy. Note that the relation selection process is optimized for each query dynamically instead of using a fixed set of selection rules for different queries.

In this work, we establish the connection between the edge strength function $\phi(w_{ij}^k)$ and the node utility score f_i within the term Ω based on a Markov random walk process. Denote by Q_{ij} the transition probability from node v_i to node v_j, which can be calculated by,

$$Q_{ij} = \begin{cases} \frac{\exp(\sum_k \alpha_{ij}^k w_{ij}^k)}{\sum_j \exp(\sum_k \alpha_{ij}^k w_{ij}^k)}, & \text{if } \mathcal{S}_{ij} \in E, \\ 0, & \text{otherwise.} \end{cases} \quad (3)$$

According to Markov random walk process, the stationary distribution vector $\mathbf{f}$ is the solution of the following eigenvector equation:

$$\mathbf{f} = \mathbf{Q}^\top \mathbf{f}. \quad (4)$$

Note that the above equation unifies the utility scores of both labeled and unlabeled nodes in the network, which achieves the information propagation along the network structure. Recall that an edge is strong if its affinity value is high and it is selected after the propagation process. A strong edge can help propagate scores from one node to its neighboring nodes through the random walk framework in Eq. (4). This is enforced by minimizing $\|\mathbf{f} - \mathbf{Q}^\top \mathbf{f}\|_2^2$ – two nodes connected by selected strong edges will have similar scores after the propagation. In this way, Eq. (4) establishes the connection between node utility scores and the edge selective parameters via the transition matrix $\mathbf{Q}$, which estimates the node scores based on the edge strengths and thus offers the capability for selecting the most appropriate edges during propagation. Note other functional forms, such as graph Laplacian, may be considered as alternatives to the random walk formulation above. Here, we adopt this approach due to its amenity to the optimization process to be presented below. Finally, the objective function can be written as:

$$\begin{aligned} F(\mathbf{f}, \boldsymbol{\alpha}) &= \frac{1}{2}\|\mathbf{f} - \mathbf{Q}^\top \mathbf{f}\|_2^2 \\ &+ \frac{\lambda}{2}\|\mathbf{f} - \mathbf{y}\|_2^2 + \gamma(\sum_{g=1}^{r} \|\boldsymbol{\alpha}_g\|_2 + \|\boldsymbol{\alpha}\|_1). \quad (5) \end{aligned}$$

By minimizing the objective function, the node utility scores and the edge selective parameters can be derived as:

$$\begin{aligned} \min_{\mathbf{f}, \boldsymbol{\alpha}} \quad & F(\mathbf{f}, \boldsymbol{\alpha}), \\ \text{s.t.} \quad & \mathbf{f} \geq 0, \ \boldsymbol{\alpha} \geq 0. \quad (6) \end{aligned}$$

The above objective function is non-convex, and thus can only achieve a local optimum. In the next subsection, we will use a gradient based optimizer to solve it.

5.2 Optimization Procedure

In Eq. (5), the gradient of $\mathbf{f}$ can be directly calculated. However, the gradient of $\boldsymbol{\alpha}$ cannot be calculated due to the non-smoothness of the ℓ_{21}-norm and ℓ_1-norm regularizer. In this subsection, we will show that, using the dual norm, these sparsity terms can be approached by a smoothing approximation such that the gradient can be calculated. Then we will employ the gradient based method for optimization.

5.2.1 Smoothing Approximation

Since the dual norm of ℓ_2-norm is still ℓ_2-norm, we can write $\sum_{g=1}^{r} \|\boldsymbol{\alpha}_g\|_2$ in Eq. (5) as:

$$\sum_{g=1}^{r} \|\boldsymbol{\alpha}_g\|_2 = \sum_{g=1}^{r} \max_{\|\boldsymbol{\beta}_g\|_2 \leq 1} \langle \boldsymbol{\beta}_g, \boldsymbol{\alpha}_g \rangle = \max_{\boldsymbol{\beta} \in \mathcal{B}} \boldsymbol{\beta}^\top C \boldsymbol{\alpha}, \quad (7)$$

where $\boldsymbol{\beta}_g$ is a vector of auxiliary variables associated with $\boldsymbol{\alpha}_g$, and $\langle \cdot, \cdot \rangle$ denotes the inner product operator. Let $\boldsymbol{\beta} = [\boldsymbol{\beta}_1^\top, \ldots, \boldsymbol{\beta}_r^\top]^\top$ and its domain is $\mathcal{B} = \{\boldsymbol{\beta} \| \|\boldsymbol{\beta}_g\|_2 \leq 1, g = 1, \ldots, r\}$. Denote by n_g the number of edges in the gth relation $\mathcal{G}_g$, and let $J = \sum_{g=1}^{r} n_g$ the total number of edges in the hybrid social media graph. Then $C \in \mathbb{R}^{\sum_{g=1}^{r} n_g \times J}$ is a matrix whose rows are indexed by all pairs of $(i, g) \in \{(i, g) | i \in \mathcal{G}_g, i \in \{1, \ldots, J\}\}$, and the columns are indexed by $j \in \{1, \ldots, J\}$. Each element of C is defined as:

$$C_{(i,g),j} = \begin{cases} 1, & \text{if } i = j, \\ 0, & \text{otherwise.} \end{cases} \quad (8)$$

Based on Nesterov's smoothing approximation method [20], we construct a smooth approximate of $\sum_{g=1}^{r} \|\boldsymbol{\alpha}_g\|_2$ as:

$$h_\mu(\boldsymbol{\alpha}) = \max_{\boldsymbol{\beta} \in \mathcal{B}} \langle \boldsymbol{\beta}, C\boldsymbol{\alpha} \rangle - \frac{\mu}{2}\|\boldsymbol{\beta}\|_2^2, \quad (9)$$

where μ is a positive smoothness parameter to control the accuracy of the approximate. For a fixed $\boldsymbol{\alpha}$, the optimal solution of Eq. (9) can be defined as:

$$\boldsymbol{\beta}_g(\boldsymbol{\alpha}_g) = S_2(\frac{\boldsymbol{\alpha}_g}{\mu}), \quad (10)$$

where S_2 is the projection operator which projects any vector $\mathbf{x}$ to the ℓ_2-ball:

$$S_2(\mathbf{x}) = \begin{cases} \frac{\mathbf{x}}{\|\mathbf{x}\|_2}, & \|\mathbf{x}\|_2 > 1, \\ \mathbf{x}, & \|\mathbf{x}\|_2 \leq 1. \end{cases} \quad (11)$$

On the other hand, the dual of ℓ_1-norm is ℓ_∞-norm, the $\|\boldsymbol{\alpha}\|_1$ can be approximated by the following smooth function:

$$l_\mu(\boldsymbol{\alpha}) = \max_{\|\mathbf{u}\|_\infty \leq 1} \langle \mathbf{u}, \boldsymbol{\alpha} \rangle - \frac{\mu}{2}\|\mathbf{u}\|_2^2, \quad (12)$$

where the optimal auxiliary variable $\mathbf{u}(\boldsymbol{\alpha})$ can be defined as:

$$\mathbf{u}(\boldsymbol{\alpha}) = S_\infty(\frac{\boldsymbol{\alpha}}{\mu}), \quad (13)$$

where S_∞ is the projection operator which projects a value to the ℓ_∞-ball:

$$S_\infty(x) = \begin{cases} x, & -1 \leq x \leq 1, \\ 1, & x > 1, \\ -1, & x < -1. \end{cases} \quad (14)$$

Based on the above two approximations, we arrive at the following smoothed objective function:

$$F_\mu(\mathbf{f}, \boldsymbol{\alpha}) = \frac{1}{2}\|\mathbf{f} - \mathbf{Q}^\top \mathbf{f}\|_2^2 + \frac{\lambda}{2}\|\mathbf{f} - \mathbf{y}\|_2^2 + \gamma \quad {}_\mu(\boldsymbol{\alpha}), \quad (15)$$

where $\quad {}_\mu(\boldsymbol{\alpha})$ is given by

$$\quad {}_\mu(\boldsymbol{\alpha}) = h_\mu(\boldsymbol{\alpha}) + l_\mu(\boldsymbol{\alpha}). \quad (16)$$

Apparently, the original sparsity term in Eq. (5) can be written as $\quad {}_0(\boldsymbol{\alpha})$ with $\mu = 0$. We have the following theorem on the accuracy of the approximation:

THEOREM 1. *The maximum gap between* $\quad {}_0(\boldsymbol{\alpha})$ *and* $\quad {}_\mu(\boldsymbol{\alpha})$ *is* $\mu(r + J)/2$, *i.e.,*

$$\quad {}_\mu(\boldsymbol{\alpha}) \leq \quad {}_0(\boldsymbol{\alpha}) \leq \quad {}_\mu(\boldsymbol{\alpha}) + \mu(r + J)/2. \quad (17)$$

It shows that a smaller μ will result in a more precise approximation, which makes the solution of Eq. (15) sufficiently close to the optimal solution of Eq. (5). In our implementation, we set μ to be 10^{-4}. The following theorem shows that $\quad {}_\mu(\boldsymbol{\alpha})$ is smooth w.r.t $\boldsymbol{\alpha}$ with a simple form of gradient.

THEOREM 2. *For any* $\mu > 0$, *the approximation function* $\quad {}_\mu(\boldsymbol{\alpha})$ *is convex and continuously differentiable function of* $\boldsymbol{\alpha}$ *and its gradient is*

$$\nabla \quad {}_\mu(\boldsymbol{\alpha}) = C^\top \boldsymbol{\beta}(\boldsymbol{\alpha}) + \mathbf{u}(\boldsymbol{\alpha}). \quad (18)$$

The proofs of the above two theorems are straightforward by following the proofs in [5].

Algorithm 1 Gradient descent optimization for information propagation over hybrid social media network

1: **In t:** $\{w_{ij}^k\}$, $\in \{0,1\}^n$, ${}^0 \in \mathbb{R}^n$, $\boldsymbol{\alpha} \in \mathbf{R}^J$, λ and γ.
2: **Initialization:** Set t 0, initialize ^{t} 1 and $\boldsymbol{\alpha}^t$ 1.
3: **re eat**
4: Fix $\boldsymbol{\alpha}^t$, and then employ PR conjugate gradient algorithm to estimate ${}^{t+1}$ based on $\partial_{\mathbf{f}} F_\mu({}^t, \boldsymbol{\alpha}^t)$.
5: Force the negative entries in ${}^{t+1}$ to 0.
6: Fix ${}^{t+1}$, and employ PR conjugate gradient algorithm to estimate $\boldsymbol{\alpha}^{t+1}$ based on $\partial_{\boldsymbol{\alpha}} F_\mu({}^{t+1}, \boldsymbol{\alpha}^t)$.
7: Force the negative entries in $\boldsymbol{\alpha}^{t+1}$ to 0.
8: t t 1.
9: **ntil** convergence.
10: **O t t:** The optimized * and $\boldsymbol{\alpha}^*$.

5.2.2 *Smoothing Gradient Descent*

It is apparent that the smooth objective function $F_\mu(\mathbf{f}, \boldsymbol{\alpha})$ is differentiable w.r.t $\{f_i\}$ and $\{\alpha_{ij}^q\}$ as follows:

$$\begin{aligned} \partial_{f_i} F_\mu &= (f_i - \sum_k f_k Q_{ki}) + \sum_{j \in \mathcal{N}_i} (f_j - \sum_k f_k Q_{kj})(-Q_{ij}) \\ &+ \lambda(f_i - y_i), \qquad (19) \\ \partial_{\alpha_{ij}^q} F_\mu &= (f_i - \sum_k f_k Q_{ki})(-f_j \frac{\partial Q_{ji}}{\partial \alpha_{ij}^q}) \\ &+ (f_j - \sum_k f_k Q_{kj})(-f_i \frac{\partial Q_{ij}}{\partial \alpha_{ij}^q}) + \gamma \nabla \ {}_\mu(\alpha_{ij}^q), \qquad (20) \end{aligned}$$

where $\mathcal{N}_i$ in Eq. (19) denotes the indices of the nodes in the hybrid network connecting to node v_i. The derivation of $\partial Q_{ji}/\partial \alpha_{ij}^q$ and $\partial Q_{ij}/\partial \alpha_{ij}^q$ in Eq. (20) can be calculated by,

$$\begin{aligned} \frac{\partial Q_{ji}}{\partial \alpha_{ij}^q} &= \frac{w_{ij}^q \exp(\sum_k \alpha_{ij}^k w_{ij}^k)}{\sum_p \exp(\sum_k \alpha_{jp}^k w_{jp}^k)} - \frac{w_{ij}^q \left(\exp(\sum_k \alpha_{ij}^k w_{ij}^k)\right)^2}{\left(\sum_p \exp(\sum_k \alpha_{jp}^k w_{jp}^k)\right)^2}, \\ \frac{\partial Q_{ij}}{\partial \alpha_{ij}^q} &= \frac{w_{ij}^q \exp(\sum_k \alpha_{ij}^k w_{ij}^k)}{\sum_p \exp(\sum_k \alpha_{ip}^k w_{ip}^k)} - \frac{w_{ij}^q \left(\exp(\sum_k \alpha_{ij}^k w_{ij}^k)\right)^2}{\left(\sum_p \exp(\sum_k \alpha_{ip}^k w_{ip}^k)\right)^2}. \end{aligned}$$

Based on the gradients, we can iteratively update $\mathbf{f}$ and $\boldsymbol{\alpha}$ by gradient descent method. Our implementation uses the Polack-Ribière (PR) conjugate gradient method [19], which is efficient for solving large-scale problems due to its simplicity and low storage. Given a function and its partial derivatives, the solver iteratively improves the estimates of the variables, converging to a local optimum. After obtaining the converged solution for $\mathbf{f}$ or $\boldsymbol{\alpha}$ in each iteration, we further enforce the negative entities in these vectors to be 0 such that the nonnegative constraints can be maintained. The entire optimization procedure is shown in Algorithm 1.

5.2.3 *Algorithmic Analysis*

Note that each gradient descent iteration in Algorithm 1 will monotonically decrease the objective function, and hence the algorithm will approach a local optimum. Figure 2 shows the convergence process of the iterative optimization which is captured in our later experiment. As seen, the objective function converges after 6 iterations, and thus the convergence speed is fast.

The time complexity of Algorithm 1 is $\mathcal{O}\big(l(n+J)\big)$, where l, n and J are respectively iteration number, node number and edge number. It is linear in the number of entities and relations. In the image ranking experiment of a

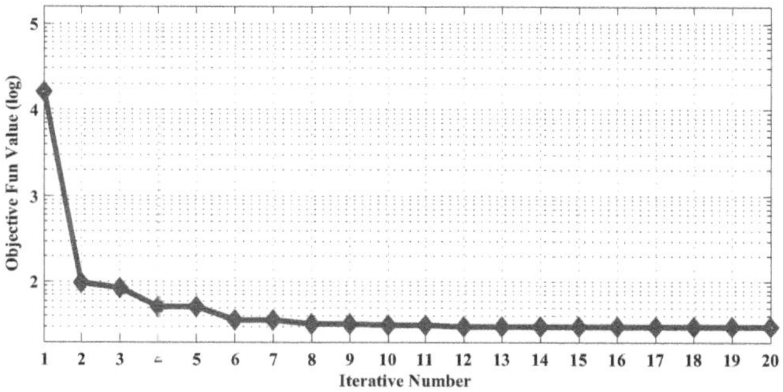

Figure 2: The convergence curve of Algorithm 1 on the IKEA group when performing image ranking for a Task-II query (see Section 6).

Task-II query on IKEA group (see Section 6) implemented on the MATLAB platform on an Intel XeonX5660 workstation with 3.2 GHz CPU and 18 GB memory, Algorithm 1 can be finished within 1.2 minutes. Of course, since the objective function is not convex, some care must be taken to avoid the local minima. However, we empirically find that the convergence behavior is pretty stable (see Figure 2) and is not sensitive to the initialization. To verify this, we test different initialization options including all-one vector and random vector for initializing $\mathbf{f}$ and $\boldsymbol{\alpha}$ when performing Task-II experiment. We found small differences in the accuracy, but the all-one initialization converges about 3 times faster. This provides some empirical justifications that using all-one vector as the initialization is a good choice for the optimization, through other initial values can also be used if prior knowledge about the score distribution is available.

6. EXPERIMENTS

In this section, we evaluate the effectiveness of the proposed information propagation algorithm over the hybrid network. We first present the experimental setup and then introduce the performance comparison and analysis.

6.1 Experiment Setup

As discussed in Section 4, we construct a hybrid network for each photo-sharing social group. The following three tasks will be used for performance evaluation. (1) **Task-I**: Given a user in the network as query, rank all entities in the network and then show the top ranked concepts/images/users as the customized recommendation. (2) **Task-II**: Given a user plus few concepts as query, rank all entities in the network and then use the top ranked concepts/images/users for recommendation. (3) **Task-III**: Given an image plus its associated concepts, rank the users to find the potential users who may have interests in receiving such media objects and topics.

For each of the above tasks, we compare the performances of the following four methods. (1) Edge Averaging based Information Propagation (EAIP). In this method, we average the multiple edge weights between each node pair to obtain a fused weight. This is actually the most common method for early fusion of heterogeneous graphs. Some works like [7, 21] extended the fusion to simple weighted averaging. However, it's unclear how optimal fusion weights can be determined and thus its impact on performance is uncertain. After the edge fusion, we employ the graph ranking method in [23] to obtain the ranking scores. The method in [23] also includes optimization terms based on graph smoothness and label

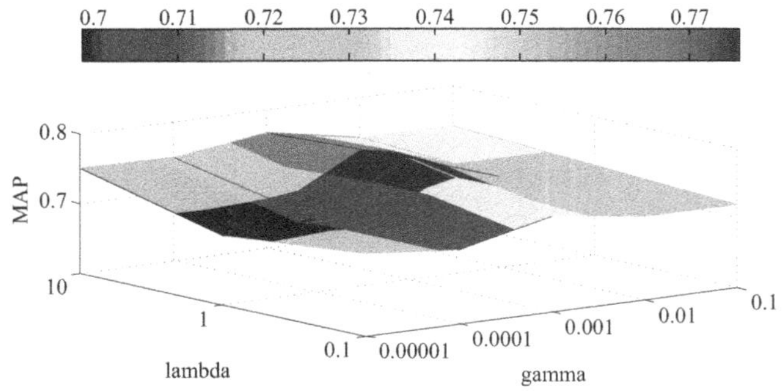

Figure 3: MAP of our method as a function of the combination of parameter λ and γ. This figure is generated when performing image ranking for a Task-II query on the IKEA group (see Section 6).

fitness. But it did not involve edge selection and sparsity penalties. (2) Edge Selective Information Propagation (ESIP). We only use ℓ_1-norm regularizer to guide the individual edge selection while removing the $\ell_{2,1}$-norm regularizer from the objective function. (3) Relation Selective Information Propagation (RSIP), where we only keep the $\ell_{2,1}$-norm regularizer while removing the ℓ_1-norm regularizer. This essentially selects the relations at the macro level – relations of the same type will tend to be selected or deselected altogether instead of individually. (4) Our proposed Edge and Relation Selective Information Propagation (ERSIP).

To evaluate the performances of different methods mentioned above, we define the ground truths for each task as follows. (1) For Task-I where the query is a user, the relevant images are all the images that the user owns, likes or comments on; the relevant concepts are all the concepts of the relevant images, and the relevant users are the users who have contact, comment or favorite relations with respect to the query user (as explained in Section 4.2). (2) For Task-II where the query is a user plus a few concepts, the relevant images are those which are not only relevant to the user but also are annotated with the query concepts. (3) For Task-III where the query is an image plus its associated concepts, the relevant users are defined as those who have comment, own or favorite relations with respect to the query image.

To avoid the data scarcity of the evaluation, for Task-I and Task-II, we only select the users who have own 70 or more images as the query user. For Task-II, we employ the most frequent 3 tags appearing in the images of the query user as the query concepts which will be combined with the user as a combined query. Finally, for Task-III, we select the images which have 5 or more relevant users (as defined in the previous paragraph) as the query image and then employ its concepts as the query concepts. This results in totals of 197, 197, and 221 distinct queries for task I, II, and III respectively. In each query task, we randomly select 50% of edges which have connections with the relevant entities as the test set for performance evaluation. To achieve this, we remove these edges in the hybrid network, making them invisible in the information propagation. Given a ranking method, we expect the entities connected by these removed relations are still ranked at relatively higher positions.

In this work, we employ the Average Precision (AP) as the evaluation metric. Notably, each query of Task-I and Task-II is composed of three subtasks including image ranking, user ranking and concept ranking. For each subtask, we calculate AP for each query and then calculate the Mean Average Precision (MAP) across all the queries for each social group. Finally, we average all MAP's across the 10 social groups and employ the Average MAP as the final evaluation metric of the subtask. For parameter setting, we use the cross validation to determine the appropriate parameter values for each method. Specifically, we vary the values of λ and γ on the grid of $\{10^{-1}, 10^{0}, 10^{1}\}$ and $\{10^{-5}, 10^{-4}, \ldots, 10^{-1}\}$ respectively, and then run 2-fold cross validation (parameter setting on the training set and performance evaluation on the held-out test set separately). The same parameter setting procedure is used for all other methods compared. Figure 3 shows the performance sensitivity under various parameter combinations for our method. It showed a relatively stable performance, within a variation range of 10%.

6.2 Performance Comparison

In this subsection, we compare the performance of different information propagation methods over the hybrid social media network. Figure 4(a)–4(c) show the performance (average MAP computed at the full length) for all the methods in comparison over three tasks respectively. From the results, we have the following observations: (1) The proposed ERSIP method consistently beats all the other baseline methods for every task by a large margin, which demonstrates its effectiveness in propagating information across heterogeneous entities and relations. Moreover, it shows significant performance improvements on all social groups (except one) of different interest, ranging from geolocations, tourist sites, products, or life styles. It confirms the general benefits of the purposed hybrid social media network. (2) The edge selective methods including ERSIP, ESIP and RSIP outperform the EAIP on most of the tasks. This is due to the fact that the former methods are able to remove some noisy or redundant relations and edges by enforcing sparsity on the edge selection indicators while the latter simply fuses all the information in an aggregated manner without comparing their individual contributions. (3) The final proposed ERSIP method performs significantly better than the ESIP and RSIP methods. This implies that simultaneously selecting the relation types and the individual edges at multiple levels does improve the robustness of information propagation. Moreover, although ESIP enforces to select the fewest number of edges during the propagation, its performance is not promising. The reason may be that it ignores the correlation of the edges in the same relation type, and hence cannot sufficiently discover the most informative edges for information propagation. Similarly, RSIP is only able to distinguish the significance of each relation type, but may fail to discover the most useful edges for the query task. In Figure 4(c), we show the performance comparisons for each of the 10 social groups. Figure 5(a)–5(c) show the average MAP of our method at different return depth. As seen, the average MAPs are pretty high when the depth varies from 10 to 100 where all results are higher than 0.7. This clearly demonstrates that our method is able to rank the most relevant entities at top positions in the ranking list. Figure 6 shows the image ranking result of a Task-II query.

6.3 Effect of Edge Selection

The proposed information propagation method over the hybrid network is able to dynamically pick the best subset of edges for customized recommendation in response to the specific needs of different users, tasks and queries. Although

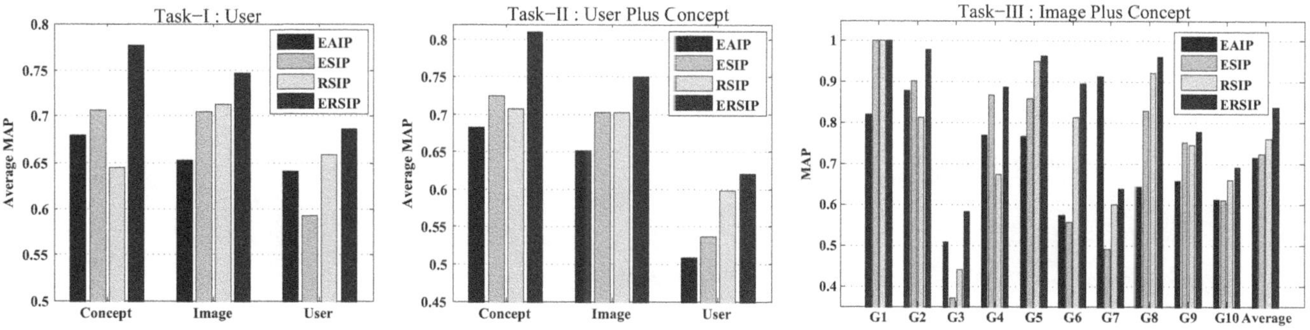

(a) Task-I (b) Task-II (c) Task-III

Figure 4: Performance of different methods over the three tasks. (a) and (b) show the average MAP comparison on the three subtasks of Task I, II respectively. (c) shows the MAP comparison for each social group, where the 10 groups from left to right in the horizontal axis are respectively (1)"Beijing", (2)"Fashion", (3)"IKEA", (4)"Korean food", (5)"New York", (6)"Painted", (7)"Sneaker", (8)"Taipei", (9)"Universal studio" and (10)"Wildlife", and the final one is the average MAP. This figure is best viewed in color.

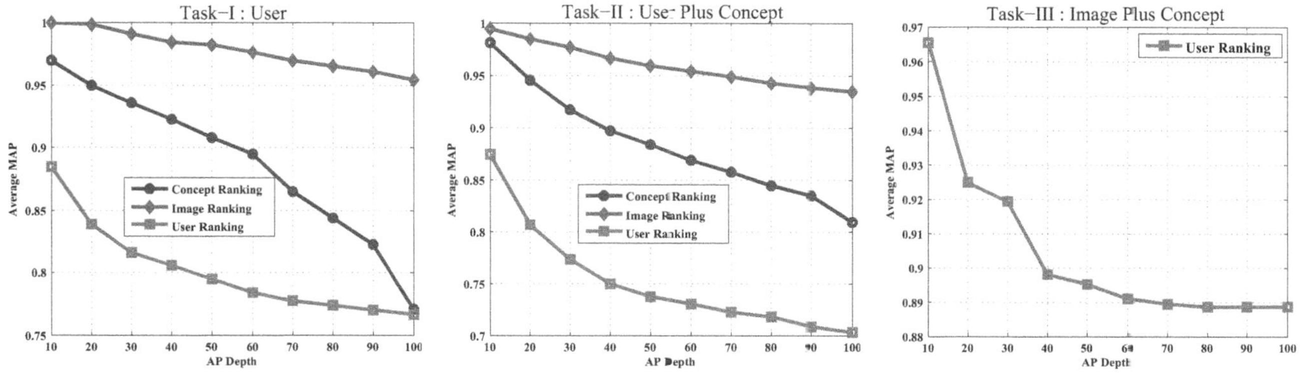

(a) Task-I (b) Task-II (c) Task-III

Figure 5: Average MAP of our method at variant return depths over the three tasks.

the experiment results in Section 6.2 have verified the benefits of edge selection, we perform analysis to gain further insights on how relations are selected for different queries. To this end, for each query, we calculate the average edge strength in each relation type (i.e., the sum of all $w_{ij}^k\alpha_{ij}^k$ in a relation type divided by the number of edges in this relation) and then average across all queries as an estimate of the contributions of each specific relation type. We calculate such information in the three tasks individually and plot the results in Figure 7(a)–7(c). As shown in Figure 7(a), if the query is user, the relations associated with the user will have more influence while other relations that are not associated with user tend to be less important. For example, the average edge strengths from the two types of image-image similarity relations are very tiny for user related queries, indicating that edges in these two relations are not informative for the query. Similarly, from Figure 7(b) and Figure 7(c) we can see that, if the query is composed of concept or image, the relations associated with these entities tend to be more important compared with those relations that do not contain the query entity. From these results obtained from different query tasks, we can see that the edge selection strategy is able to identify the relations that are closely related to the query, which further verifies the power of the edge selection.

7. CONCLUSIONS

We introduced a novel hybrid social media network, upon which the the heterogeneous types of entities, relations and the interactions among users, multimedia objects and concepts can be seamlessly integrated within a unified framework. To fully explore the diverse types of entities and relations in the hybrid network, we developed an edge selective information propagation method which can adaptively select a sparse subset of the most informative relations from the massively connected network so that the information can be best propagated through the activated paths in the network. Given a target user and a specific task, our system maps the task to relevant concepts and formulates the query. Then the query information is propagated throughout the selected edges so that the utility scores of other nodes can be predicted. The predictions can be used to recommend information in a task-specific personalized way for various applications like personalized album generation, friend/topic recommendation, target ad, etc. Although we evaluated the proposed model on a prototype based on Flickr, the proposed methods are general. They can be applied to enhance search and recommendation functions of other complex systems involving hybrid data types and relations.

For future work, we will investigate the application of the hybrid social media network in the task-specific social media community discovery which automatically groups related entities into a number of community clusters based on the diverse types of relations. Besides, we will also study efficient methods for scaling the proposed optimization framework to a large network.

Figure 6: Top 30 ranked images in response to a query composed of a specific user and three concepts. Images with green borders have half of their relations removed in the network. They are still successfully retrieved due to the effective information propagation through optimally selected paths in the hybrid social media network. This figure is best viewed in color.

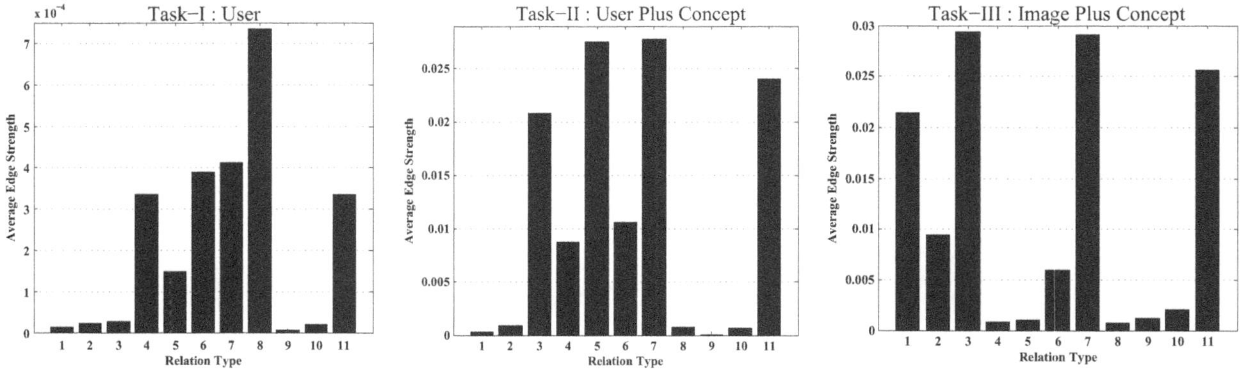

(a) Task-I (b) Task-II (c) Task-III

Figure 7: Average edge strength in each type of relations over the three different tasks, where the 11 relations from left to right in the horizontal axis are respectively (1) *image-image SIFT similarity*, (2) *image-image mid-level similarity*, (3) *concept-image tagging relation*, (4) *user-concept ownership relation*, (5) *user-image comment relation*, (6) *user-image favorite relation*, (7) *user-image ownership relation*, (8) *user-user contact relation*, (9) *user-user favorite relation*, (10) *concept-concept co-occurrence relation*, (11) *user-image-concept tagging relation*.

8. ACKNOWLEDGEMENT

This work is supported in part by Office of Naval Research (ONR) grant #N00014-10-1-0242, and NExT Research Center funded by MDA Singapore grant #WBS R-252-300-001-490.

9. REFERENCES

[1] A. Argyriou, M. Herbster, and M. Pontil. ombining graph laplacians for semi supervised learning. In *NIPS*, 200 .

[2] M. Ames and . aaman. hy we tag: motivations for annotation in mobile and online media. In *CHI*, 200 .

[3] S. Agarwal, K. Branson, and S. Belongie. Higher order learning with graphs. In *ICML*, 2006.

[4] J. Bu, S. Tan, . hen, . ang, H. u, L. hang, and . He. Music recommendation by uni ed hypergraph : ombining social media information and music content. In *MM*, 2010.

[ ] . hen, . Lin, S. Kim, J. arbonell and . ing. Smoothing proximal gradient method for general structured sparse learning. In *UAI*, 2011.

[6] I. Dhillon. o clustering documents and words using biparitite graph partitioning. In *KDD*, 2001.

[ ] I. Guy, etc. Harvesting with S AR: the value of aggregating social network information. In *CHI*, 200 .

[ ] . Guan, J. Bu, . Mei, . hen, and . ang. Personalized tag recommendation using graph based ranking on multi type interrelated objects. In *SIGIR*, 200 .

[ ] J. He, M. Li, H. hang, H. Tong, and . hang. Manifold ranking based image retrieval. In *MM*, 2004.

[10] J. Han, . Sun, . an, and P. u. Mining heterogeneous information networks. In *KDD*, 2010.

[11] . Hsu, L. Kennedy, and S. hang. Video search reranking through random walk over document level context graph. In *MM*, 200 .

[12] M. Ji, J. Han, and M. Danilevsky. Ranking based classi cation of heterogeneous information networks. In *KDD*, 2011.

[13] A. Langville and . Meyer. A survey of eignvector methods for web information retrieval. *SIAM Review*, 200 .

[14] D. Lowe. Distinctive image features from scale invariant keypoints. *IJCV*, 2004.

[1] D. Liu, . Hua, L. ang, M. ang, and H. hang. Tag ranking. In *WWW*, 200 .

[16] D. Liu, S. an, . Rui, and H. hang. Uni ed tag analysis with multi edge graph. In *MM*, 2010.

[1] J. Liu, . Lai, . Hua, . Huang, and S. Li. Video search re ranking via multi graph propagation. In *MM*, 200 .

[1] K. Mikolajczyk and . Schmid. Scale and affine invariant interest point detectors. *IJCV*, 2004.

[1] J. ocedal, etc. umerical optimization. *Springer*, 1 .

[20] . esterov. Smooth minimization of non smooth functions. *Mathematical Programming*, 200 .

[21] I. Ronen, etc. Social networks and discovery in the enterprise (Sa D). In *SIGIR*, 200 .

[22] L. Torresani, M. Szummer, and A. Fitzgibbon. fficient object category recognition using classemes. In *ECCV*, 2010.

[23] D. hou, etc. Ranking on data manifolds. In *NIPS*, 2003.

[24] D. hou, etc. Learning multiple graphs for document recommendations. In *WWW*, 200 .

Discovering Informative Social Subgraphs and Predicting Pairwise Relationships from Group Photos

Yan-Ying Chen*†, Winston H. Hsu*, Hong-Yuan Mark Liao†
*National Taiwan University, Taipei, Taiwan
†Academia Sinica, Taipei, Taiwan
yanying@cmlab.csie.ntu.edu.tw, winston@csie.ntu.edu.tw, liao@iis.sinica.edu.tw

ABSTRACT

An increasing number of users are contributing the sheer amount of group photos (e.g., for family, classmates, colleagues, etc.) on social media for the purpose of photo sharing and social communication. There arise strong needs for automatically understanding the group types (e.g., family vs. classmates) for recommendation services (e.g., recommending a family-friendly restaurant) and even predicting the pairwise relationships (e.g., mother-child) between the people in the photo for mining implicit social connections. Interestingly, we observe that the group photos are composed of atomic subgroups corresponding to certain social relationships. For this work, we propose a novel framework to (1) connect faces of different attributes and positions as a face graph and (2) discover informative subgraphs to represent social subgroups in group photos. A group photo can be further represented by a bag-of-face-subgraphs (BoFG) – the occurring frequency of social subgroups, which is informative to categorize specific group types or events. We demonstrate the effectiveness of BoFG in recognizing family photos and achieve 30.5% relative improvement over the state-of-the-art low-level features. Moreover, we propose to predict the pairwise relationships (e.g., husband-wife) in a face graph by the co-occurrence information (e.g., co-occurring with a child) in the mined subgraphs. The experiments demonstrate that the informative social subgroups significantly outperform prior work (36% relatively) which considers merely facial attributes for determining pairwise relationships.

Categories and Subject Descriptors

I.4 [**Image Processing and Computer Vision**]: Feature Measurement

General Terms

Algorithms, Experimentation, Human Factors

Keywords

Face graph, face subgraph mining, social relationship

MM'12, October 29–November 2, 2012, Nara, Japan.

Figure 1: It is difficult to determine the pairwise relationships, e.g., couple or friends in (a) and siblings or classmates in (b), if the observations are limited to the pairs only. Interestingly, the ambiguity greatly decreases when all the faces are considered simultaneously as shown in (c). The contribution comes from the contextual cues from all the other faces. The social links resemble a graph parameterized by facial attributes and topological information. Therefore, we propose a novel graph representation to model the potential social subgroups among a group of people and to predict pairwise relationships by leveraging atomic subgroups in the group photos. (Photo courtesy of Spencer Finnley [1].)

1. INTRODUCTION

With the prevalence of capturing devices and photo sharing services, the volume of community-contributed photos has increased exponentially. Isola et al. [11] pointed out that the photos containing people are the most memorable, especially those containing families or friends. The desire of social communication motivates users to share group photos on the social media to keep close relationships with others. In our study from more than 17 million photos collected from Flickr using the "family" keyword, we found that around 60% of them contain at least one face. [1]

Such freely available media provide a cost-effective way to obtain demographic information – the statistics for the user preferences in certain events or locations such as restaurants, hotels, landmarks, etc., which is essential for marketing, ad-

[1] All of the images presented in this paper attribute to various Flickr users under Creative Commons license, and the images for experiments are downloaded from the public dataset [9].

vertising, and recommendation systems. Such rich information collected from the huge user-contributed photos reveals diverse activities and preferences and can be treated as multimedia life "logs." To deal with the big data, many studies focus on exploiting facial content analysis such as facial attribute detection (e.g., gender, age, race, etc.) to support large-scale demographic research. For example, Cheng et al. [4] adopted the associated contexts (e.g., time, location) and the people attributes mined from community-contributed photos to facilitate profiling consumer activities for mobile recommendations.

In fact, consumer activities and user intentions are not limited in individuals. Group recommendation, which recommends to a group of people instead of individuals, is vital for daily life. In Li et al.'s work [16], they analyzed the transaction logs and discovered that different types of consumer groups (e.g. family, friends, couple) have quite different preferences when searching for travel accommodations. For example, family groups prefer the hotels in downtown areas while friend groups are more concerned about transportation convenience. The discoveries evidence the importance in profiling consumer groups. However, transaction logs are not easily accessible due to complicated privacy and commercial issues. As a substitute for transaction logs, group activities can be observed from the growing and freely available sources – social media. As aforementioned, the large-scale user-contributed media possess a huge number of group photos and the associated metadata. Besides, mining from the rich media not only improves the accessibility but also escapes from the huge language gaps and culture differences (cf. Fig. 8 (a)).

It has been evidenced that the social interactions and relationships can be observed from the social contexts in a photo [21, 9, 25]; for example, a mother stands close to her child(ren) and they naturally form a subgroup in the group photo. For group analysis, it has been shown that the cohesive subgroups represent an important construct to study a group and individuals [7]. For example, the basic properties of a social group (e.g., a family as Fig. 1 (c)), are organized by the **social subgroups** (e.g., a couple as (a) and siblings as (b)). In other words, the social subgroups provide meaningful features to infer the overall look of a group.

In addition, social subgroups also play a critical role in understanding individuals, because individuals are influenced the most by the members of their tight subgroup than others [8]. For example, if we have identified a social subgroup as a "couple" relation (as Fig. 1 (a)) and have also known the identity of a member (e.g., the wife's name), the identity of the other (e.g., the husband) can be intuitively inferred. Because social subgroups act as the crucial link to holistic group and individuals, we argue to automatically discover informative social subgroups embedded in community-contributed group photos. The mined subgroups would strongly benefit (1) classifying the holistic group types and (2) predicting the pairwise relationships in a (dense) group photo [2].

Intuitively, the correlation of a social group and its social subgroups resembles that of a graph and its subgraphs. Using a graph to link faces in a group photo preserves the social connections among the whole group (e.g., Fig. 1 (c)) and does not limit the social contexts to one or two individuals (e.g., Fig. 1 (a)(b)). Therefore, we represent the faces in a photo by their gender and age attributes [3], and further consider the spatial proximity among them to form a **face graph**. Also, we enumerate the subgraphs of a face graph to automatically discover the potential subgroups in a group photo. Applying on a large number of consumer photos, we can extract the informative subgroups in the communities, i.e., a vocabulary of face subgraphs. The mined subgraphs are informative to represent a group photo by **a bag of face subgraphs (BoFG)**, which records the occurrence pattern of meaningful social subgroups appearing in certain group types or events. Taking family-type image classification as an example, we demonstrate that learning by BoFG achieved 30.5% relative improvement comparing to the state-of-the-art low-level features for image classification. The proposed framework can excel on photos of more group types (e.g., nuclear family, friends of different ages, etc.) and further enables investigating comprehensive demographics in group photos.

Moreover, the mined subgraphs bring the co-occurrence information from the other faces, which benefit predicting pairwise relationships in a face graph. For example, the pairwise relationship "husband-wife" usually co-occurs with a child in the same subgraph. We demonstrate that using the co-occurrence in subgraphs as features can successfully predict four typical pairwise relationships in a family photo. Because labeling names in a photo is very tedious, predicting pairwise relationships is precious to help the association of faces and names for automatic name annotation. In summary, the primary contributions of this work include:

- Proposing a novel graph representation to model a group of people in a photo.
- Devising a methodology to automatically discover informative subgraphs, which resemble the meaningful social subgroups in communities.
- Introducing a novel feature, BoFG, for representing a group of people and demonstrating its effectiveness in recognizing family-type photos.
- Investigating the various factors, i.e., subgraph selection, learning with kernels and sensitivity to normalization, which affect the performance of BoFG.
- Arguing to predict pairwise relationships by the co-occurrence information in the mined subgraphs.

2. RELATED WORKS

Facial attribute detection is an important technique in facial photo analysis. Dozens of works demonstrate that the detected attributes are quite helpful for image retrieval [15], personalized recommendation [4], and face verification [14]. Facial attributes have been broadly exploited as additional knowledge to categorize or recognize the person of interest. Since consumer photos usually contain more than one person, the coming challenge is how to represent a group of persons. In those cases, simply aggregating or averaging attributes from individuals may lead to information loss.

[2]Note that, in this work, we target at group photos with more people since they contain richer social relationships and are more challenging for the existing technologies.

[3]Though we only involve gender and age attributes in this work, there is a potential to extend to dozens of attributes with reasonable detection accuracies (>80%) [14].

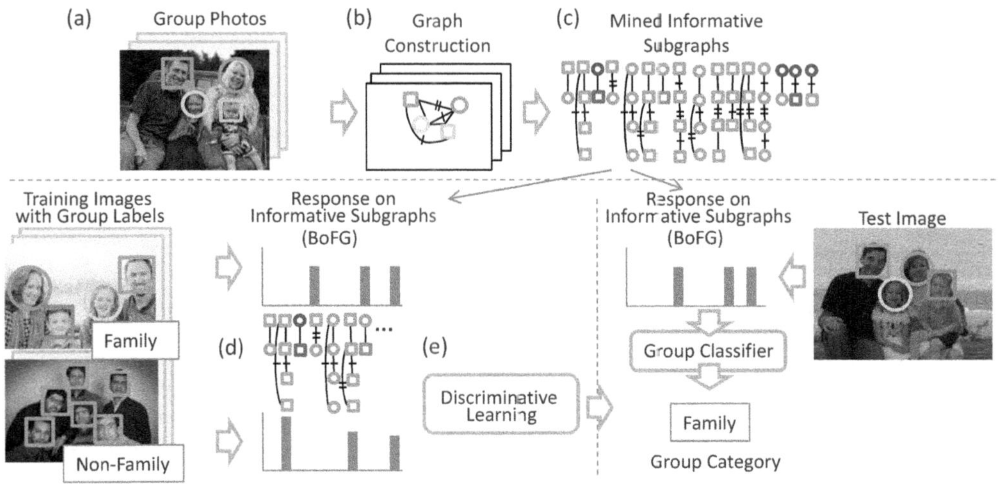

Figure 2: Framework – The inputs (a) of our approach are consumer photos containing faces with automatically estimated gender and age attributes (extendable to other attributes as well). The faces in a photo are modeled as a face graph (b) by the proposed graph construction method. From the face graphs, we can automatically discover the informative subgraphs (c) which resemble the social subgroups commonly appearing in communities. We propose to represent a photo by a bag-of-face-subgraphs (BoFG) (d). BoFG preserves the occurrence patterns of social subgroups among a group of faces and acts as effective features for classifying family-type photos by supervised learning (e). (Best seen in color.)

The phenomenon is getting obvious when the group becomes larger and more diverse in attributes.

The early studies tend to predefine several typical pairwise relationships (e.g., mother-child, sibling) between people to compensate the lack. Singla et al. [21] used rule-based approach to identify pairwise relationships in photos by a predefined knowledge base. Afterwards, Gallagher [9] gathered real statistics of facial attributes, positions, face size to correlate the social contexts with certain pairwise relationships in consumer photos. Wang et al.[25] further proposed to involve pairwise relationships as cues for learning the correspondence between facial appearances and their names. Pairwise relationships were also adopted as an index for personal photo management [31, 26] and aesthetic assessment [17] when it comes to group photos. The aforementioned works have evidenced that pairwise relationships concern the arrangement of face positions in a photo; however, they only focused on a small set of pairwise relations and limited the social contexts to one or two individuals.

In fact, the social contexts between two persons are only partial factors in inferring their relationship. In a number of cases, the pairwise relationship is ambiguous when only two persons are exposed. For example, it is very difficult to identify whether the two persons in Fig. 1 (a) are a couple or just friends. Similarly, we have not enough cues to identify the relationship between the two kids in Fig. 1 (b). Interestingly, the ambiguity extremely drops when we observe the holistic faces in the photo (Fig. 1 (c)). Merely relying on the social contexts from a pair of faces neglects the connections with other faces in the social group. On the other hand, if we consider all the faces and the possible social links among the faces as a graph, each of them can propagate its contextual cues to the others. Seeing the potential cues, we propose to exploit the holistic relations in a photo by a face graph. Graph representation has been adopted for modeling co-occurrences and geometrical relations among a set of visual words in image categorization [20]. Due to the large variations in scene and object images, the graph representations are much complicated and very possible to be interfered by cluttered backgrounds. As for face graph, it is relatively easy to filter out unintended points of interest by face detection [24].

Resembling to mining the subcomponents in chemical compound [6], we enumerate all the substructures in consumer photos by subgraph mining [27] to preserve pattern regarding both the facial attributes and the topological proximity. Furthermore, subgraph selection is introduced to reduce the representative dimensionality [19], and thus ensures the scalability for the proposed framework. In the rest of this paper, we will depict how to transform a group photo (Fig. 2 (a)) to a face graph (Fig. 2 (b)) in Sec. 3 and how to discover informative face subgraphs (Fig. 2 (c)) as a vocabulary over a set of face graphs. We will further represent every photo as a bag of face subgraphs (Fig. 2 (d)) for profiling group types or events in Sec. 4 and predict pairwise relationships (Fig. 6) in Sec. 5. Finally, we demonstrate the effectiveness of BoFG for recognizing family-type photos (as Fig. 2 (e)) and the superior performance in predicting pairwise relationships in Sec. 6.

3. BUILDING A VOCABULARY OF FACIAL SUBGRAPHS

A rich amount of social subgroups are embedded in a group photo and also shown effective for understanding group activities and pairwise relationships [7, 8]. We argue to automatically discover the meaningful subgroups from community-contributed photos. In our approach, a social subgroup resembles a subgraph in a face graph constructed from a group photo. We first establish a face graph to model a group of faces as shown in Fig. 3 (c). Then, we enumerate the potential subgraphs (as Fig. 3 (e)) in a face graph. Applying graph construction and enumeration to all the collected photos, we discover and select a small set of informative subgraphs, which are analogous to the subgroups commonly

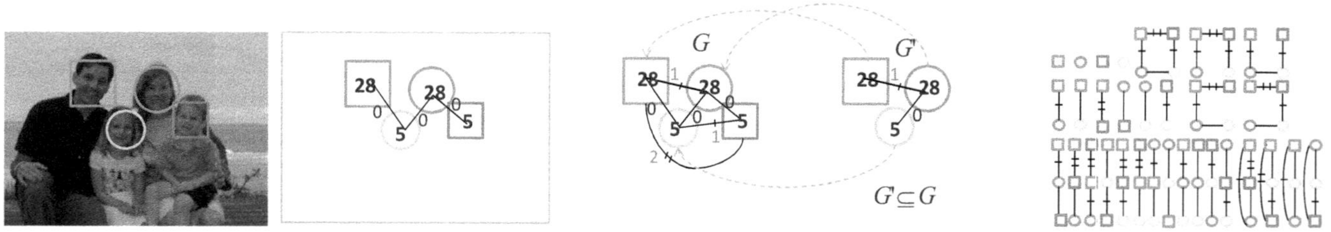

(a) Group Photo (b) Minimum Spanning Tree (c) A Face Graph (d) A Subgraph (e) Enumeration of All Subgraphs

Figure 3: Once the faces in a photo are detected as (a), we depict the basic skeleton of a group as a minimum spanning tree (MST) (b) weighted by pixel distance of any two faces. The face vertices are then fully connected as (c), where an edge of two vertices are labeled by the order distance (numbers on the edges) – the length of the shortest path from one vertex to the other in the MST, which represents the social order to other members. To discover potential subgraphs (e.g., (d)) of the face graph, we enumerate all the subgraphs as (e) by subgraph mining. Each of the subgraphs resembles a certain social subgroup. (Best seen in color. Photo courtesy of Steve Polyak [1].)

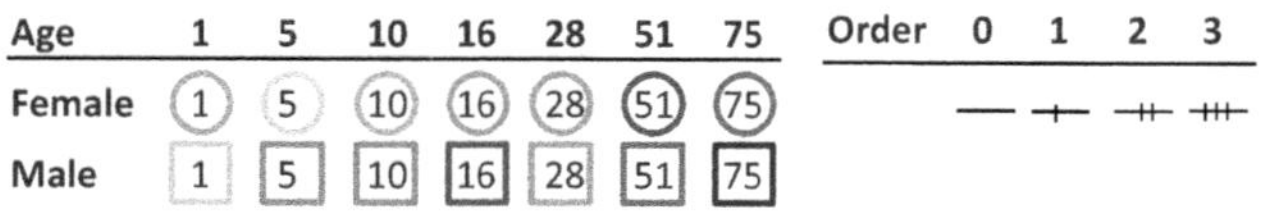

(a) Vertex Labels (b) Edge Labels

Figure 4: For describing a face vertex, the ages are quantized into seven clusters coupled with gender attribute, thus resulting in fourteen vertex labels as (a). The label of an edge between two face vertices is the order distance between them. (b) denotes the edge labels with order distance equal to 0, 1, 2, 3.

appearing in consumer photos, as a vocabulary for semantic representations.

3.1 Graph Construction

We establish a face graph by all the faces in a photo (as Fig 3 (a)), where each face is regarded as a vertex. All of the vertices are categorized by their (automatically detected) facial attributes. For example, the pink circle means a female who is around 28 years old and the blue square means a 5-year-old boy. The ages are quantized into seven clusters [4] coupled with the gender attribute, thus resulting in fourteen vertex labels (cf. Fig. 4 (a)). The spatial distance between any two faces is used as the edge label to represent the closeness of two persons.

The spatial distance between two people is strongly correlated with their interactions and relationship [10]. Therefore, pixel distance is adopted as an informative cues to measure the interpersonal relation in a photo [25, 31, 26]. Unfortunately, pixel distance is sensitive to environment factors like obstacles, atypical poses and culture differences [2]. Another critical problem is how to normalize the pixel distance under various image resolutions and discretize continuous distance into separate degrees of closeness. These concerns make pixel distance lose its superiority (also confirmed in our experiments in Sec. 6.4). Actually, for a group of people, "**order distance**" can be another index to evaluate the closeness between any two people. *Order distance between two faces means how the group people intervene the space between them.* The concept originates from that people who do not want to interact would seldom arrange themselves with the other side-by-side [23]. That is, order distance also approximates the tendency to interact in a social group.

The following challenge is how to estimate the order distance of any two faces. Measuring pixel distance will not suffice because people arrange themselves in a free organization rather than in a strict line. We have to shape the basic skeleton of a group at first. Here, we propose to use a minimum spanning tree (MST) to find the basic structure as shown in Fig 3 (b). We first leverage the pixel distance of two face vertices as the weights to find a unique MST. This way, we preserve the influence of pixel distance in estimating order distance. Once the MST of a group is obtained, the order distance of two faces can be estimated by the shortest path starting from one vertex to the other on the MST. As shown in Fig. 3 (b), the order is counted from 0, which means no face intervenes in between, and steps up progressively as the number of intermediate faces increases. For example, the order distance between the green and blue squares is 2.

In the face graph construction (Fig 3 (c)), all the faces are fully connected using the order distances as edge labels. For example, the edge labels for the edge with order distance equal to 0, 1, 2, 3 would be denoted as the symbols in Fig. 4 (b). Due to the space limitation, we only show four edge labels in the notation. In real implementation, the number of edge labels depends on the number and the structure of people in a photo. A larger group may require more edge labels to denote the growing order distance. Due to the nature of group photos, the range of order distance is bounded [5]. After graph construction, a group photo would be translated into a face graph (as Fig. 3 (c)) represented by a 4-tuple $G = (V, E, L, l)$. V is a set of vertices. $E \subseteq V \times V$ is a set of edges. L is a set of labels. l is a mapping for assigning labels to V and E, where $l : V \cup E \rightarrow L$.

3.2 Enumeration of Subgraphs

In real life, a group of people comprises many smaller subgroups, which are important characteristics of the group

[4]The age categories are decided by the social status of a person, including infant, kid, school-age child, teenager, youth, middle-aged adult and elder, totally seven clusters as shown in Fig. 4. Note that the framework can be extended to other attributes such as race, etc.

[5]In our investigation, the informative subgraphs discovered from consumer photos seldom contain the edges with order distance larger than 4. Therefore, removing the edges with order distance > 4 only has little effects on mining results.

itself [7]. The subgroups resemble the subgraphs in the face graphs constructed from the numerous consumer photos. For example, Fig. 3 (a) is a family, and the faces of the family form a face graph G in Fig. 3 (c). A subgraph $G' = (V', E', L', l')$ of G should satisfy the criteria, $V' \subseteq V$, $E' \subseteq E$, $L' \subseteq L$ and $l' = l$. By definition, G' in Fig. 3 (d) is a subgraph of G. Semantically speaking, G' is a subgroup of parents-child and G is the whole family. In this way, we further enumerate all the subgraphs of a face graph G. After subgraph enumeration, a face graph would be decomposed into a set of subgraphs as shown in Fig. 3 (e). An enumerated subgraph indicates a social subgroup, which is not limited in two or three people. The subgraph G' in a face graph G contains $|V'|$ people, where $0 < |V'| \leq |V|$.

To gather various types of social subgroups, we propose to extract the informative social subgraphs from consumer photos. We categorize the subgraphs which preserve the same structure and correspondences in terms of facial attributes (the labels of vertices) and order distance (the labels of edges). To examine the mapping between two subgraphs, we exploit graph isomorphism which allows us to identify identical subgraph representations among face graphs (photos). In graph theory, an **isomorphism** of graphs G and H is a bijection f between the vertex sets of G and H, where $f : V(G) \rightarrow V(H)$. That means any two vertices v_α and v_β of G are adjacent in G if and only if $f(v_\alpha)$ and $f(v_\beta)$ are adjacent in H. We write $G \cong H$. For example, the subgraph G_1 in Fig. 5 (a) and the subgraph G_2 in Fig. 5 (b) are isomorphic ($G_1 \cong G_2$) and are categorized as the same type of subgraph in a vocabulary. The subgraphs G_3 and G_4 in Fig. 5 (b) are isomorphic as well ($G_3 \cong G_4$). Similar to calculating text terms in a document, we can count subgraphs of the same type in an image. To accelerate the mining process, we adopt the subgraph mining algorithm [27] which combines enumerating and checking into one procedure. The algorithm transfers graphs to tree-based codes and apply depth first search to speed up the mining process. Finally, the face graphs of a set of consumer photos M would generate a subgraph-image matrix T of $|M| \times |S|$, where S is a subgraph vocabulary mined from M, $\forall s_i, s_j \subseteq S, \nexists s_i \cong s_j$. The m-th row in T contains the frequency of occurrence of subgraph appearing in the m-th image. The i-th column in T comprises the frequency of occurrence of i-th subgraph appearing in each image.

Actually, enumerating subgraphs is time-consuming when the number of vertices in a graph is huge. The computation load is relatively light in our approach since the number of people in a group photo is not as many as the vertices in complicated networks. Besides, the process would be done in the training phase and the mined subgraphs are general for different learning tasks. However, the subgraph matching in the test phase is inevitable. The effort increases along with the size of subgraph vocabulary (S). To ensure scalability, we further introduce the subgraph selection and representation in the next section.

4. BAG-OF-FACE-SUBGRAPHS

The subgraph vocabulary enables interpreting a group photo by a bag-of-subgraphs; for example, the m-th photo in M can be represented by the m-th row in subgraph-image matrix T. Extending the proposed bag-of-face-subgraphs (BoFG) as features for classification tasks would confront two challenges: (1) how to reduce costly graph matching in the test phase, (2) how to translate bag-of-facial-subgraphs into an effective feature representation.

4.1 Subgraph Selection

We conduct feature (subgraph) selection for reducing the substantially large subgraph vocabulary generated in Sec. 3.2. The huge amount of subgraphs would be a big problem for scalability in learning models. Besides, it may incur intensive computation for graph matching in the classification (test) phase, and thus makes it infeasible to analyze the large-scale social media. Seeing the requirements, we investigate two approaches for subgraph selection, (1) document frequency and (2) sequential covering, to reduce the size of subgraph vocabulary.

4.1.1 Document Frequency (DF)

Document frequency (df), is a manner of feature selection commonly used in text categorization [30] and visual-words based image classification [28]. df_i is the number of photos that contain the i-th facial subgraph. According to df, the subgraphs are selected by how common they are in the whole training data set without considering the class labels. The approach does not require class labels, and therefore saves the effort to re-select subgraphs for different classification tasks.

4.1.2 Sequential Covering (SC)

In addition to document frequency, we introduce a feature selection approach, sequential covering [19], by taking into account the class labels. Sequential covering algorithm proceeds by iteratively selecting the most discriminative subgraph from the candidates, by measuring its individual classification capability as provided the class labels. Here we treat a subgraph s as a feature (and classifier quality measure $C(s)$) and iteratively select a subgraph s^* which has maximum discriminative capability (classification accuracy) in the remaining training images compared with the other candidate subgraphs in S.

$$\begin{aligned} & s^* \leftarrow \max_s \frac{\sum_m^{|M|} C_m(s)}{|M|}, \\ & S \leftarrow S \backslash s^*, \\ & W \leftarrow W \cup s^*, \end{aligned} \tag{1}$$

where W is the selected subgraphs, $C_m(s)$ is the result of the m-th training image classified by s. $C_m(s) = 1$, if the m-th image is correctly classified, otherwise $C_m(s) = 0$. The process would repeat iteratively until the designated number of subgraphs is selected. To speed up the selection process, we first take document frequency in the training images as the initial ranking. The subgraphs are initially ordered by the confidence scores (i.e., DFs) [18]. The prefiltering step greatly reduces the number of checking processes on the training images.

4.2 Feature Representation of Group Photos

Image categorization and retrieval are research problems of great interest; therefore, dozens of image features are proposed for solving different challenges. For example, Histograms of Oriented Gradient (HoG) descriptor [5] shows its superiority to extract subtle edge features for human detection. Pyramid HoG (PHoG) [3] further preserves the traits

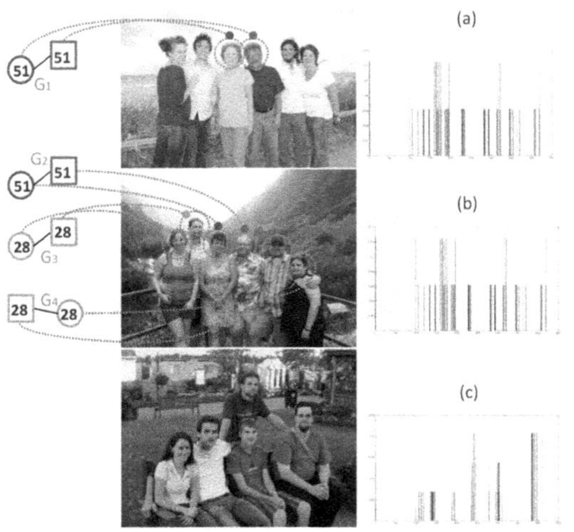

Figure 5: Representativeness of BoFG for different social groups (e.g., family vs. non-family). The first and second photos are with the same group type (e.g., family), thus generating very similar BoFG features ((a) and (b)). The third group photo contains much different social subgroups, therefore, the feature vector (c) generated from the photo is quite different.

of spatial layout in the image representation. The aforementioned works have demonstrated that local shape patterns and spatial information are effective for scene classification. As for understanding human activities or group types of a photo, the occurrences of social subgroups should be more critical than the visual shape patterns. Our experiments also confirmed that in Sec. 7.

Our approach, BoFG, stands as better representation when considering the facial attributes, the social links, and the spatial proximity for a group of people. Motivated by visual words [22] that extract the local patterns of a image, face subgraphs represent local relation approximated by the people attributes. The feature representation of bag-of-face-subgraphs is analogous to that of the bag-of-visual-words [28] and is applicable for group photo classification. The bag-of-face-subgraphs of a group photo are represented by a feature vector f_j,

$$f_j = (t_1, ..., t_i, ...t_{|W|})^T, \tag{2}$$

$$t_i = \frac{n_{ij}}{n_j}, \tag{3}$$

where W is the selected subgraphs in Eq. 1. n_{ij} is the frequency of occurrence of the i-th subgraph appearing in image j. n_j is the number of subgraphs in the image j.

The feature vector f_j contains the histogram information of each subgraph, and is normalized by the total number of subgraphs in image j. Subgraph frequency t_i resembles term frequency (tf) in text domains and likewise each face subgraph is a term and each image is a document. The feature representation is visualized in Fig. 5 (a)(b)(c). The first and second photos are of the same group type (i.e., family) and possess similar social subgroups, thus generating very similar feature vectors ((a) and (b)). On the other hand, the third group photo contains much different social subgroups. Therefore, the feature vector (c) is quite different from (a) and (b). Accordingly, BoFG can capture the informative cues of social subgroups in a group of faces.

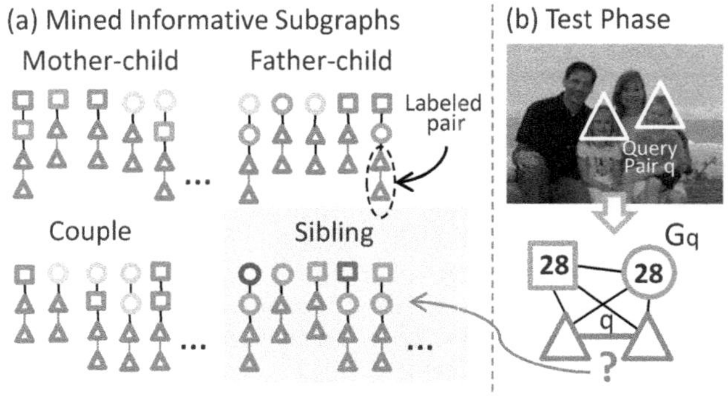

Figure 6: (a) shows the mined informative subgraphs (from supervised learning) containing different pairwise relationships including mother-child, father-child, couple and sibling (denoted by gray triangles and their connected line). For "sibling" relation, the informative subgraphs often contain a woman or a man, which are possibly their mother or father. When a query pair of faces (b) arrives, we predict its relationship by checking the presence of the informative subgraphs belonged to each pairwise relationship. (Best seen in color.)

5. PREDICTING PAIRWISE RELATIONSHIPS

Through the studies, users are reluctant to annotate photos and even the faces in photos. The phenomenon makes automatically predicting pairwise relationship (e.g., mother-child, father-child) by image content more important. Besides annotation by face recognition, which is still very challenging for (wild) consumer photos, once the pairwise relationships are identified, the unknown identities are potential to be automatically inferred by partial name labels and their existing social relationships. Traditionally, predicting pairwise relationships relied on the social contexts between the two people, such as relative distance, face size, gender and age attributes [21, 25]. As mentioned in Fig. 1 (a)(b), the social contexts between two people are really limited, and thus lead to poor performance in recognition. However, more contextual cues can be inferred when all the faces are considered in a holistic way as shown in (c). Therefore, we hypothesize that inferring the pairwise relationships by the proposed face graph is promising.

The face graph of a group photo may contain many faces which might inevitably confuse co-occurrence measurement. On the other hand, informative subgraphs are potential to filter out unintended information, and also preserve the co-occurring relationships. Therefore, we exploit the subgraphs co-occurring with the designated pairwise relationship as the features. In the training phase, we manually label pairwise relationships on a face graph according to their social relationships in the photo. By subgraph mining (as the process in Sec. 3.2) from the labeled face graphs, we discover the informative subgraphs containing the edges labeled with the designated relationship. As shown in Fig. 6 (a), the mined informative subgraphs are different for different designated pairwise relationships (denoted by gray triangles and their connected lines). Taking "sibling" as an example, the informative subgraphs often contain a woman (circle) or a man (rectangle), which are possibly their mother or father.

When predicting a pair q (as shown in 6 (b)), we first construct the face graph G_q as the process in Sec. 3.1. In

G_q, we use graph matching to check the presence of informative subgraph s_i, mined from the training images. Finally, the pairwise relationship r^* is predicted by Naive Bayesian classifier by taking the image frequency $P(s_i|r_l)$ of the informative subgraph s_i in the image collections containing r_l pairwise relationship:

$$r^* = argmax_{r_l} \prod_i P(s_i|r_l), \quad (4)$$

Because the subgraphs in G_q is relatively few, appropriately smoothing $P(s_i|r_l)$ is required. In the experiments, we will demonstrate its superiority against prior work in predicting four typical pairwise relationships.

6. EXPERIMENTS

In this section, we will (1) evaluate the effectiveness of BoFG for classifying family-type photos and then (2) evaluate the capability of informative subgraphs for predicting pairwise relationships (in Sec. 6.6). The techniques of face detection and facial attribute detection have been developed for years either in academic studies or commercial products. The previous work [14] has shown that the classification accuracy of facial attributes can achieve more than 80% on average. However, to prevent the evaluation from the error caused by face attributes, we experiment on the public data set [9], which provides group photos and the associated attributes of the faces. The data set is collected from social media (Flickr) with specific keywords, and categorized to family images, group images and wedding images. We leverage the keywords as the soft ground truth to obtain family-type images. Totally, 1,167 family images and 1,263 non-family images are retained for experiments which are conducted with 5-fold cross-validation. Note that, we evaluate the proposed approach by the photos containing at least three faces because those groups are more complex and very challenging for analysis and prediction. For groups containing less than three people, the prediction can be intuitively conducted by their attributes and distance directly [25]. Moreover, the proposed approach involves facial attributes rather than face identities; therefore, the discovered informative subgraphs are general and cross-family. In other words, our method operates on a per photo basis rather than a per family basis. We further investigate vital factors such as (1) different learning approaches, (2) the mined informative subgraphs , (3) sensitivity to normalization and (4) subgraph selection to evaluate classifying family photo by BoFG.

6.1 Classification

The analysis from text categorization [12] has concluded that Support Vector Machines (SVMs) is excellent in classification for BoW-like representations. The proposed bag-of-facial-subgraphs is in the similar paradigm, therefore we adopt SVMs as the learning method for family photo classification. To maximize the performance, we evaluate three common SVM kernels for group classification.

$$Linear : K(x,y) = x^T y,$$

$$RBF : K(x,y) = e^{-\gamma\|x-y\|^2},$$

$$RBF-\chi^2 : K(x,y) = e^{-\sum \gamma \frac{(x_k-y_k)^2}{\frac{1}{2}(x_k+y_k)}},$$

where x, y are BoFG feature vectors and $\gamma > 0$. RBF kernel

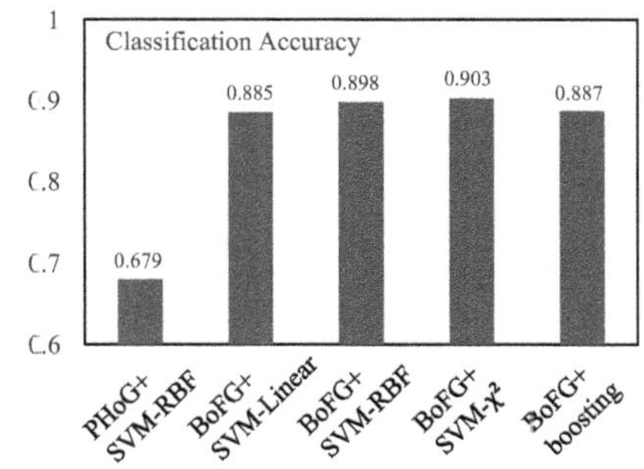

Figure 7: Performance comparisons for social group type classification (family vs. non-family) by different features. Chi-square kernel shows its superiority over both linear and RBF kernels as it has been found excellent in histogram representations (e.g., BoW [28], BoFG). Note that, the accuracy for using low-level feature PHoG is only 67.94 %.

can map the training data to high dimensional space non-linearly, therefore can handle the case when the mapping between class label and feature vector is nonlinear. RBF-χ^2 kernel is another type of non-linear kernel, which are commonly used in image classification.

Although SVMs is a very powerful algorithm for learning high-dimensional features, it is deficient in feature selection and can only work on fixed (provided) features (subgraphs). Due to the high computation cost from subgraph enumeration, Kudo et al. [13] proposed a boosting-based algorithm to couple the subgraph mining and classification, which avoids wasting time to enumerate non-discriminative subgraphs. In the experiments, the aforementioned kernel-based and boosting-based approaches are both applied to compare the effects from different learning methods on the proposed feature representation.

6.2 Effects from Learning Approaches

As shown in Fig. 7, linear kernel results in the worse accuracy by BoFG features, partially due to the number of training data is relatively few comparing with the adopted high-dimensional features. On the other hand, RBF kernel can non-linearly map training data to the high-dimensional space, therefore leads to better classification results. In our experiments Chi-square kernel shows its superiority to both linear and RBF kernels, because the proposed features are basically organized by histograms of informative subgraphs. Actually there is no big difference in accuracy generated by linear and non-linear kernels, because the proposed feature representations are sparse and discriminative. Therefore, similar to the cases in document vector or visual word vector, they are more linearly separable [29]. The classification accuracy of the boosting-based approach also achieve 88.67%, which is on par with SVMs with linear kernel. We also train a family photo classifier by SVMs using low-level (and competitive) PHoG feature. The classification accuracy only achieved 67.94%, mainly due to the lack of (semantic) social cues addressed by BoFG.

6.3 Mined Informative Subgraphs for Family

In Fig. 8, we display the mined informative subgraphs for the two different classes organized by the number of vertices ($|V'|$) in them. Block (a) is the most informative subgraphs in family photos and block (b) holds the counterparts. Ob-

Figure 8: Block (a) is the most informative subgraphs (G') in family photos and block (b) holds the counterparts. Both of them are grouped by the number of vertices ($|V'|$). Obviously, the informative subgraphs in family photos contain faces with larger age gaps (e.g., a-2, a-3, a-4). Besides, the order distance between two faces are much smaller; that is, the families tend to stand closer to each other. Also, the couple-like subgroups frequently co-occur with kids in family photos (e.g., a-2). On the other hand, the informative subgraphs in non-family groups are mostly comprised of young people with smaller age gaps. People of the same gender stand together more frequently than that in family photos. They might like to arrange themselves in a row (e.g., b-3, b-4); therefore, the order distance is relatively larger. (Best seen in color.)

viously, the informative subgraphs in family photos contain faces with larger age gaps (e.g., Fig. 8 a-2, a-3, a-4). Besides, the order distance between two faces are much smaller (most are equal to 0). That is, the families tend to stand closer to each other. Also, the couple-like subgroups frequently co-occur with kids in family photos (e.g., a-2). The seniors tend to stand in the center of a family group (e.g., a-4) such that have smaller order distance and usually link to the others. On the other hand, the informative subgraphs in non-family groups are mostly comprised of young people with smaller age gaps (due to the collected dataset photos). People of the same gender stand together (e.g., b-4) more frequently than that in family photos. They might like to arrange themselves in a row; therefore, the order distance is relatively larger (e.g., b-3, b-4).

The classification results in Fig. 9 confirm the same discoveries in the mined subgraphs. The positions of people in family photos are much concentrated, comparing to the structure of the non-family group (e.g., friends or colleagues). Furthermore, the people in family photos usually form a smaller subgroup implicitly, such as a couple or a parent-child relations, therefore result in many subgraphs with members of opposite sexes. We also show some failure cases not consistent with the learned rules. Fig. 10 (a)(b) are two photos misclassified as families. Those photos also match the subgraphs existing in most family photos, which contain closer subgroups or more subgroups with people of different genders. On the other hand, Fig. 10 (c)(d) show two false negatives misclassified as non-families, where they have relatively smaller age and gender differences in most subgroups. Besides, their positions are less centralized.

We also found that, in some photos, family groups are mixed with non-family groups (e.g., Fig. 10 (b)) thus resulting in uncertainty. Actually, a group of mixed types is commonly seen in certain events such as graduation ceremony or wedding party. Analyzing photos by social subgroups can further clarify the organizations of a group. In such cases, the detailed subgroup information would be useful for softly categorizing a group in a photo.

6.4 Sensitivity in Pixel vs. Order Distance

BoFG adopts order distance as the edge labels and are free of different photo variations (e.g., size, face number, etc.). As for pixel distance, the sensitivity to normalization scale is relatively high. In the experiments, we reveal that pixel distance normalized by different scales results in unstable classification performance. We quantized the pixel distance into different scale ranged from 5 to 15 degrees. The normalized distance degrees are then used as the edge labels. Fig. 11 shows the classification accuracy using BoFG constructed by pixel distance and constructed by order distance. All of them are learned by the boosting-based approach. As

Figure 9: Example photos for social group classification. The positions of people in family photos are much concentrated, comparing to the structure of the non-family groups (e.g., friends or colleagues). Furthermore, the people in family photos usually contain smaller subgroups, such as a couple or a parent-child relationship.

Figure 10: Failure cases for social group classification. (a)(b) are the examples misclassified as families, where the photos contain more closer subgroups with people of opposite sexes. (c)(d) are two cases misclassified as non-families, where they have smaller age and gender differences in most subgroups.

it shows, the results of pixel distance fluctuate by varying normalization scales and somehow are affected by the test photos. The proposed order distance can escape from the instability and perform robustly across consumer photos.

6.5 Effects of Subgraph Selection

The large number of features (subgraphs) would inevitably incur heavy computation cost in learning models and on-line classification. This problem is especially critical for social media, where the data are growing exponentially. To reduce the size of subgraph vocabulary, we further select the informative subgraphs by document frequency and sequential covering (Sec. 4.1). As Fig. 12 shows, both subgraph selection methods can effectively retain only 10% subgraphs but still ensure the same classification accuracy (89.75% with 4,315 subgraphs), therefore make the proposed framework more scalable. The performance of sequential covering (Fig. 12, DF+SC) is slightly better than document frequency (Fig. 12, DF). The difference may come from the utilities of the given class labels, which are provided in sequential covering only. Interestingly, increasing the number of subgraphs is not always a gain for learning. As the experiment shows, the classification accuracy notably degrades

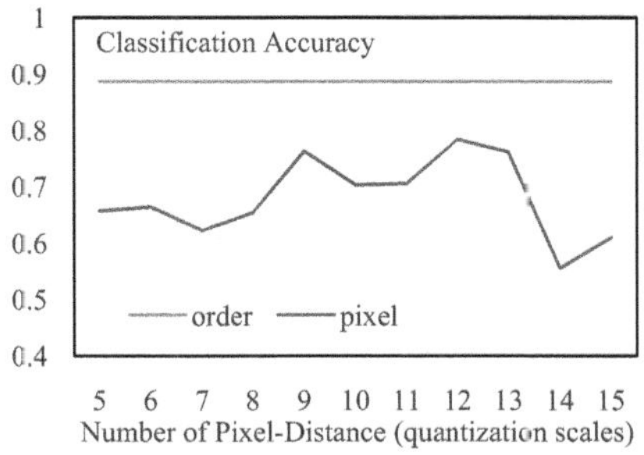

Figure 11: The pixel distance adopted in prior work suffers from the high variations in photo sizes, face scales, number of people, etc. The proposed order distance is more robust to the variances.

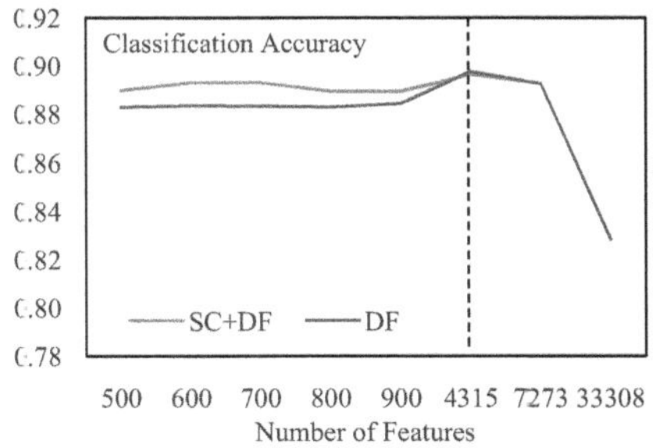

Figure 12: Both the subgraph selection methods, document frequency (DF) and sequential covering (SC), can effectively retain only 10% subgraphs but still ensure the classification accuracy and therefore make the proposed framework more scalable. Notably, besides efficiency, subgraph selection is vital since avoiding the overfitting problem commonly observed in learning from high-dimensional features.

while the number of features is larger than 30,000. The drops should be attributed to the overfitting problem in learning from high dimensional features.

6.6 Performance of Predicting Pairwise Relationships

We use the family photos in [9] for experiments and predict the four pairwise relationships, including couple, mother-child, father-child, sibling. Totally 1,332 pairwise relationships are labeled in 772 photos (at least 250 labels for each pairwise relationship). We use one half of the labeled data for training and one half for testing. To verify the supports from the informative subgraphs, we remove the attributes of the two people involved in a pairwise relationship. That is, the social contexts between the two people are blind both in the training and testing phases. The confusion matrix in Fig. 13 shows that solely relying on the information from the subgroups on the face graph can successfully infer the pairwise social relationships and achieve very impressive accuracy. The results also support that the additional information augmented by face graph can compensate errors in estimating social contexts between the pair of faces. We also derive superior performance (36% relative improvement on the average) as comparing with the confusion matrix of classification in [25] which are experimented on the same database [9]. For example, the recognition of "sibling" relationship in [25] is less accurate and is probably due to

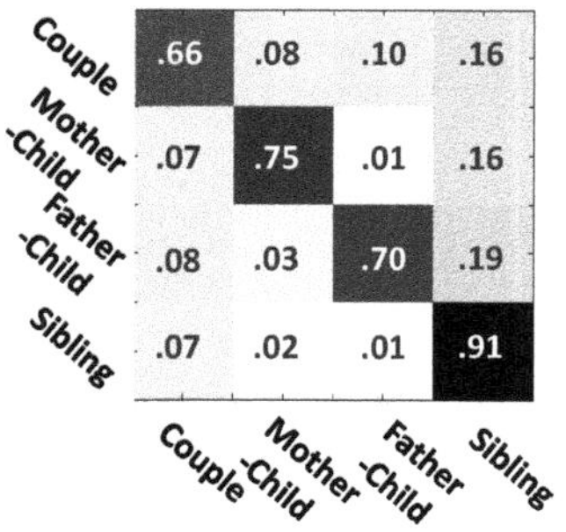

Figure 13: The confusion matrix for predicting pairwise relationships. The results outperform those reported in [24] since the informative subgroups provide supplemental supports for determining the pairwise relationship. For example, the most gain is in "sibling" since the co-occurring parent-like subgroups bring more supports.

the social contexts (relative distance, gender, etc.) between sibling is very ambiguous; as for our work, the co-occurred subgraphs, which frequently have the links to their parents, can provide further supports in recognizing pairwise relationships.

7. CONCLUSION

We saw the sheer amount of consumer photos, which mostly contain groups of people. In this paper, we propose a novel graph feature, bag-of-face-subgraphs for describing the social subgroups in a group photo. The informative subgraphs are automatically discovered from community-contributed photos, which reflect the social subgroups commonly appearing in the communities. BoFG preserves the occurrence pattern of social subgroups that are effective for analyzing human-related activities and group types. We demonstrate the capability to classify family-type photos and achieved great improvement (30.5% relatively) against prior works using state-of-the-art low-level visual features. The proposed framework considers subgraph selection for ensuring the scalability as well. Furthermore, the co-occurrence cues in the informative subgraphs can also help predicting pairwise relationships, which benefit inferring unknown identities in group photos and show salient improvement over the prior work (36% relatively). In the near future, we will investigate more social contexts (e.g., face angles) and people attributes (e.g., race) to enrich the potential social interactions in the emerging group photos. Moreover, we will extend the social groups discovered from the user-contributed photos to inferring implicit interactions in social networks.

8. REFERENCES

[1] available at http://www.flickr.com/photos/spencerfinnley/5377578656/, http://www.flickr.com/photos/spolyak/1031569673/.

[2] M. Argyle and J. Dean. Eye-contact, distance and affliation. In *Sociometry*, 1965.

[3] A. Bosch et al. Representing shape with a spatial pyramid kernel. In *CIVR*, 2007.

[4] A.-J. Cheng et al. Personalized travel recommendation by mining people attributes from community-contributed photos. In *ACM Multimedia*, 2011.

[5] N. Dalal and B. Trigg. Histograms of oriented gradients for human detection. In *CVPR*, 2005.

[6] M. Deshpande et al. Frequent sub-structure-based approaches for classifying chemical compounds. In *TKDE*, 2005.

[7] K. A. Frank. Identifying cohesive subgroups. In *Social Networks*, 1995.

[8] K. A. Frank and J. Y. Yasumoto. Linking action to social structure within a system: Social capital within and between subgroups. In *American Journal of Sociology*, 1998.

[9] A. C. Gallagher and T. Chen. Understanding images of groups of people. In *CVPR*, 2009.

[10] E. T. Hall. The hidden dimension. In *Culture*, 1966.

[11] P. Isola et al. What makes an image memorable? In *CVPR*, 2011.

[12] T. Joachims. Text categorization with support vector machines: Learning with many relevant features. In *ECML*, 1998.

[13] T. Kudo et al. An application of boosting to graph classification. In *NIPS*, 2004.

[14] N. Kumar et al. Attribute and simile classifiers for face verification. In *ICCV*, 2009.

[15] Y.-H. Lei et al. Where is who: Large-scale photo retrieval by facial attributes and canvas layout. In *ACM SIGIR*, 2012.

[16] B. Li et al. Towards a theory model for product search. In *WWW*, 2011.

[17] C. Li et al. Aesthetic quality assessment of consumer photos with faces. In *ICIP*, 2010.

[18] B. Liu et al. Integrating classification and association rule mining. In *KDD*, 1998.

[19] T. M. Mitchell. In *Machine Learning*, 1998.

[20] S. Nowozin and K. Tsuda. Weighted substructure mining for image analysis. In *CVPR*, 2007.

[21] P. Singla et al. Discovery of social relationships in consumer photo collections using markov logic. In *CVPRW*, 2008.

[22] J. Sivic and A. Zisserman. Video google: A text retrieval approach to object matching in videos. In *ICCV*, 2003.

[23] R. Sommer. Further studies of small group ecology. In *Sociometry*, 1965.

[24] P. Viola and M. Jones. Rapid object detection using a boosted cascade of simple features. In *CVPR*, 2001.

[25] G. Wang et al. Seeing people in social context: Recognizing people and social relationships. In *ECCV*, 2010.

[26] P. Wu et al. Close & closer: Discover social relationship from photo collections. In *ICME*, 2009.

[27] X. Yan and J. Han. gspan: Graph-based substructure pattern mining. In *ICDM*, 2002.

[28] J. Yang et al. Evaluating bag-of-visual-words representations in scene classification. In *MIR*, 2007.

[29] J. Yang et al. Linear spatial pyramid matching using sparse coding for image classification. In *CVPR*, 2009.

[30] Y. Yang and J. O. Pedersen. A comparative study on feature selection in text categorization. In *ICML*, 1997.

[31] T. Zhang et al. Consumer image retrieval by estimating relation tree from family photo collection. In *CIVR*, 2010.

Author Index

www.ingramcontent.com/pod-product-compliance
Ingram Content Group UK Ltd.
Pitfield, Milton Keynes, MK11 3LW, UK
UKHW051455290926
15471UKWH00008B/1213

9 781450 320085